12th Edition

Business Law Today

Comprehensive Edition
Text & Cases

BUSINESS LAW TODAY SERIES

Roger LeRoy Miller
Institute for University Studies
Arlington, Texas

CENGAGE

Australia • Brazil • Mexico • Singapore • United Kingdom • United States

Business Law Today, Comprehensive Edition
Text & Cases
12th Edition
Roger LeRoy Miller

Senior Vice President, Higher Ed Product, Content, and Market Development: Erin Joyner

Product Director: Bryan Gambrel

Senior Product Manager: Vicky True-Baker

Senior Content Manager: Martha Conway

Cengage Subject Matter Expert: Lisa Elliott

Learning Designer: Sarah Huber

Digital Delivery Lead: Jennifer Chinn

Product Assistant: Christian Wood

Marketing Manager: Andrew Miller

Intellectual Property Analyst: Jennifer Bowes

Intellectual Property Project Manager: Jillian Shafer

Production Service: SPi Global

Designer: Chris Doughman

Cover and Internal Designer: Ke Design/Ted Knapke

Cover Image: Ditty_about_summer/ ShutterStock.com

Design Images: Front & back matter header: Ditty_about_summer / Shutterstock.com; Unit-opener statue of Lady Justice: Michal Kalasek/Shutterstock.com; Case: silvae/ Shutterstock.com; Classic Case: Orhan Cam/ Shutterstock.com; Spotlight Case: Kozlik/ Shutterstock.com; Linking Business Law: Hekla/ Shutterstock.com; Unit-ending Task-Based Simulation: Kamil Fazrin Rauf/Shutterstock.com; Adapting the Law to the Online Environment: Artem Samokhvalov/Shutterstock.com; Landmark in the Law: Yuriy Kulik/Shutterstock. com; Business Law Analysis: winui/Shutterstock. com; Business Web Log: Creative Images/ Shutterstock.com; Beyond Our Borders: iDEAR Replay/Shutterstock.com; Ethical Issue puzzle piece: Gary Lanfer/Shutterstock.com; Managerial Strategy: Rawpixel.com/Shutterstock.com

For product information and technology assistance, contact us at **Cengage Customer & Sales Support, 1-800-354-9706** or **support.cengage.com.**

For permission to use material from this text or product, submit all requests online at **www.cengage.com/permissions**.

Library of Congress Control Number: 2018953610

Soft-cover Edition:
ISBN: 978-0-357-03818-5

Loose-leaf Edition:
ISBN: 978-0-357-03030-1

Cengage
20 Channel Center Street
Boston, MA 02210
USA

Cengage is a leading provider of customized learning solutions with employees residing in nearly 40 different countries and sales in more than 125 countries around the world. Find your local representative at **www.cengage.com**.

Cengage products are represented in Canada by Nelson Education, Ltd.

To learn more about Cengage platforms and services, register or access your online learning solution, or purchase materials for your course, visit **www.cengage.com**.

Printed at CLDPC, USA, 01-20

Contents in Brief

Contents

Chapter 20

Title and Risk of Loss   448

Chapter 21

Performance and Breach of Sales and Lease Contracts   464

Chapter 22

Negotiable Instruments   496

Chapter 23

International and Space Law   532

Chapter 24

Banking in the Digital Age   554

Unit 4   Agency and Employment Law   637

Unit 6 Government Regulation 871

Chapter 37

Administrative Law 872

Unit 7   Property and Its Protection 971

Preface

The study of business law and the legal environment has universal applicability. A student entering any field of business must have at least a passing understanding of business law in order to function in the real world. *Business Law Today: Comprehensive Edition,* provides the information in an interesting and contemporary way. The Twelfth Edition continues its established tradition of being the most up-to-date text on the market.

Instructors have come to rely on the coverage, accuracy, and applicability of *Business Law Today: Comprehensive Edition.* This best-selling text engages your students, solidifies their understanding of legal concepts, and provides the best teaching tools available. I have spent a great deal of effort making this edition more contemporary, exciting, and visually appealing than ever before. Special pedagogical devices within the text focus on legal, ethical, global, and corporate issues, while addressing core curriculum requirements.

The Twelfth Edition incorporates the latest legal developments and United States Supreme Court decisions. It also includes more than fifty new features and sixty new cases, hundreds of new examples and case examples, new exhibits, learning objectives, margin definitions, and case problems.

New and Updated Features

The Twelfth Edition of *Business Law Today: Comprehensive Edition* is filled with exciting new and updated features designed to cover current legal topics of high interest.

1. **Entirely new *Business Web Log* features** underscore the importance of the text material to real-world businesses. Each of these features discusses a major U.S. company that is engaged in a dispute involving a topic covered in the chapter. Some examples include:

    - *Samsung and Forced Arbitration* (Chapter 4)
    - *Amazon Faces Fake Products* (Chapter 7)
    - *Facebook and Google in a World of Antitrust Law* (Chapter 38)

2. **Entirely new *Business Law Analysis* features** appear in numerous chapters of the text. These features are useful tools to help students master the legal analysis skills that they will need to answer questions and case problems in the book, on exams, and in business situations. Subjects include:

    - *Deciding If a Court Would Impose a Quasi Contract* (Chapter 10)
    - *Enforceability of Liquidated Damages Provisions* (Chapter 17)
    - *When Will a Court Order the Dissolution of an LLC?* (Chapter 32)

3. **Entirely new hypotheticals** in many chapter introductions provide a real-world link that generates student interest and highlights specific legal concepts that will be discussed in the chapter. These hypotheticals—often based on real cases or business situations—help to introduce and illustrate legal issues facing managers, companies, and even industries.

4. ***Adapting the Law to the Online Environment*** features examine cutting-edge cyberlaw topics, such as:

    - *Does Everyone Have a Constitutional Right to Use Social Media?* (Chapter 2)
    - *Using Twitter to Cause Seizures—A Crime?* (Chapter 9)
    - *Programs That Predict Employee Misconduct* (Chapter 33)

5. ***Ethical Issue*** features focus on the ethical aspects of a topic being discussed in order to emphasize that ethics is an integral part of a business law course. Examples include:

   - *How Enforceable Are Click-on Agreements to Donate Funds to Charity?* (Chapter 11)
   - *Is It Ethical (and Legal) to Brew "Imported" Beer Brands Domestically?* (Chapter 23)
   - *Is It Fair to Classify Uber and Lyft Drivers as Independent Contractors?* (Chapter 27)

6. ***Beyond Our Borders*** features illustrate how other nations deal with specific legal issues to give students a sense of the global legal environment. Topics include:

   - *Does Cloud Computing Have a Nationality?* (Chapter 33)
   - *Can a River Be a Legal Person?* (Chapter 39)

7. ***Managerial Strategy*** features emphasize the management aspects of business law and the legal environment, such as:

   - *Marriage Equality and the Constitution* (Chapter 2)
   - *The Criminalization of American Business* (Chapter 9)
   - *The SEC's New Pay-Ratio Disclosure Rule* (Chapter 36)

8. ***Landmark in the Law*** features discuss a landmark case, statute, or development that has significantly affected business law. Examples include:

   - *Palsgraf v. Long Island Railroad Co.* (Chapter 5)
   - *The Bankruptcy Abuse Prevention and Consumer Protection Act* (Chapter 26)
   - *Changes to Regulation A: "Reg A+"* (Chapter 36)

9. ***Linking Business Law to [one of the six functional fields of business]*** features appear in select chapters to underscore how the law relates to other fields of business. For instance, Chapter 7 has a feature titled *Linking Business Law to Marketing: Trademarks and Service Marks,* and Chapter 37 has a feature called *Linking Business Law to Corporate Management: Dealing with Administrative Law.*

New Emphasis on Making Ethical Business Decisions—The IDDR Approach

The ability of businesspersons to reason through ethical issues is now more important than ever. For the Twelfth Edition of *Business Law Today: Comprehensive Edition,* I have created a completely new framework for helping students (and businesspersons) make ethical decisions—**the IDDR approach**, which is introduced in Chapter 3. This systematic approach provides students with a clear step-by-step process to analyze the legal and ethical implications of decisions that arise in everyday business operations. The IDDR approach uses four logical steps:

- **Step 1: Inquiry**
- **Step 2: Discussion**
- **Step 3: Decision**
- **Step 4: Review**

Students can easily remember the first letter of each step by using the phrase "I Desire to Do Right." A **completely revised Chapter 3 (Ethics in Business)** details the goals of each IDDR step and then provides a sample scenario to show students how to apply this new approach to ethical decision making. In addition to introducing the IDDR approach, I have made Chapter 3 more current and more practical and reduced the amount of theoretical ethical principles it presents. The text now focuses on real-life application of ethical principles.

After Chapter 3, to reinforce the application of the IDDR approach, students are asked to use its steps when answering each chapter's *A Question of Ethics* problem. Each of these problems has been updated and is based on a 2017 case. In addition, the Twelfth Edition retains the *Ethical Issue* feature in most chapters, many of which have been refreshed with timely topics involving the ever-evolving technologies and trends in business.

New Cases and Case Problems

The Twelfth Edition of *Business Law Today: Comprehensive Edition* has new cases and case problems from 2018 and 2017 in every chapter. The new cases have been carefully selected to illustrate important points of law and to be of high interest to students and instructors. I have made it a point to find recent cases that enhance learning and are straightforward enough for business law students to understand.

Certain cases and case problems have been carefully chosen as good teaching cases and are designated as *Spotlight Cases* and *Spotlight Case Problems*. Some examples include *Spotlight on Apple, Spotlight on Beer Labels, Spotlight on Nike,* and *Spotlight on the Seattle Mariners*. Instructors will find these *Spotlight* decisions useful to illustrate the legal concepts under discussion, and students will enjoy studying the cases because they involve interesting and memorable facts. Other cases have been chosen as *Classic Cases* because they establish a legal precedent in a particular area of law.

Each case concludes with a section, called *Critical Thinking*, that includes at least one question. Each question is labeled *Ethical, Economic, Legal Environment, Political, Social,* or *What If the Facts Were Different?* In addition, *Classic Cases* include an *Impact of This Case on Today's Law* section that clarifies how the case has affected the legal environment. Suggested answers to all case-ending questions can be found in the *Solutions Manual* for this text.

Many New Highlighted and Numbered Case Examples

Many instructors use cases and examples to illustrate how the law applies to business. This edition of *Business Law Today: Comprehensive Edition* offers hundreds of highlighted and consecutively numbered *Examples* and *Case Examples*. *Examples* illustrate how the law applies in a specific situation, and *Case Examples* present the facts and issues of an actual case and then describe the court's decision and rationale.

New to this edition are *Spotlight Case Examples,* which deal with especially high-interest cases, and *Classic Case Examples,* which discuss older, landmark decisions. The numbered *Examples* and *Case Examples* features are integrated throughout the text to help students better understand how courts apply legal principles in the real world.

Critical Thinking and Legal Reasoning Elements

For this edition of *Business Law Today: Comprehensive Edition* I have included a discussion of legal reasoning in Chapter 1. The all-new *Business Law Analysis* features that can be found throughout the text emphasize legal reasoning skills as well. Critical thinking questions conclude most of the features and cases in this text. Also, at the end of each chapter, a *Debate This* question requires students to think critically about the rationale underlying the law on a particular topic.

The chapter-ending materials also include a separate section of questions that focus on critical thinking and writing. This section always includes a *Time-Limited Group Assignment* and may also include a *Critical Legal Thinking* question requiring students to think critically about some aspect of the law discussed in the chapter or a *Business Law Writing* question requiring students to compose a written response.

Answers to all *critical thinking* questions, as well as to the ***Business Scenarios and Case Problems*** at the end of every chapter, are presented in the Twelfth Edition's *Solutions Manual*. In addition, the answers to one case problem in each chapter, called the ***Business Case Problem with Sample Answer,*** appear in *Appendix E.*

Other Pedagogical Devices within Each Chapter

- ***Learning Objectives*** (questions listed at the beginning of each chapter and repeated in the margins of the text provide a framework of main chapter concepts for the student).
- **Margin definitions** of each boldfaced ***Key Term***.
- **Quotations** and ***Know This*** (margin features).
- **Exhibits** (in most chapters).
- **Photographs** (with critical-thinking questions) **and cartoons**.

Chapter-Ending Pedagogy

- ***Practice and Review*** (in every chapter).
- ***Debate This*** (a statement or question at the end of *Practice and Review*).
- ***Key Terms*** (with appropriate page references to their margin definitions).
- ***Chapter Summary*** (in table format).
- ***Issue Spotters*** (in every chapter with answers in *Appendix D*).
- ***Business Scenarios and Case Problems*** (including in every chapter, a *Business Case Problem with Sample Answer* that is answered in *Appendix E*; in selected chapters, a *Spotlight Case Problem*; and in every chapter, a new *A Question of Ethics* problem—based on a 2017 case—that applies this Twelfth Edition's ***IDDR approach*** to business ethics).
- ***Critical Thinking and Writing Assignments*** (including a *Time-Limited Group Assignment* in every chapter, and a *Business Law Writing* or a *Critical Legal Thinking* question in selected chapters).

Unit-Ending Pedagogy

Each of the seven units in the Twelfth Edition of *Business Law Today: Comprehensive Edition* concludes with a ***Task-Based Simulation.*** This feature presents a hypothetical business situation and then asks a series of questions about how the law applies to various actions taken by the firm. To answer the questions, the student must apply the laws discussed throughout the unit. (Answers are provided in the *Solutions Manual*.)

Supplements

Business Law Today: Comprehensive Edition provides a substantial supplements package designed to make the tasks of teaching and learning more enjoyable and efficient. The following supplements are available for instructors.

MindTap Business Law for *Business Law Today: Comprehensive Edition*, Twelfth Edition

MindTap™ is a fully online, highly personalized learning experience built on authoritative Cengage Learning content. By combining readings, multimedia, activities, and assessments into a singular Learning Path, *MindTap Business Law* guides students through their course with ease and engagement. Instructors personalize the Learning Path by customizing

Cengage Learning resources and adding their own content via apps that integrate into the *MindTap* framework seamlessly with Learning Management Systems.

The *MindTap Business Law* product provides a four-step Learning Path, Case Repository, Adaptive Test Prep, and an Interactive eBook designed to meet instructors' needs while also allowing instructors to measure skills and outcomes with ease. Each and every item is assignable and gradable. This gives instructors knowledge of class standings and students' mastery of concepts that may be difficult. Additionally, students gain knowledge about where they stand—both individually and compared to the highest performers in class.

Cengage Testing Powered by Cognero

Cengage Testing Powered by Cognero is a flexible online system that allows instructors to do the following:

- Author, edit, and manage *Test Bank* content from multiple Cengage Learning solutions.
- Create multiple test versions in an instant.
- Deliver tests from their Learning Management System (LMS), classroom, or wherever they want.

Start Right Away! *Cengage Testing Powered by Cognero* works on any operating system or browser.

- Use your standard browser; no special installs or downloads are needed.
- Create tests from school, home, the coffee shop—anywhere with Internet access.

What Instructors Will Find

- *Simplicity at every step.* A desktop-inspired interface features drop-down menus and familiar, intuitive tools that take instructors through content creation and management with ease.
- *Full-featured test generator.* Create ideal assessments with a choice of fifteen question types—including true/false, multiple choice, opinion scale/Likert, and essay. Multi-language support, an equation editor, and unlimited metadata help ensure instructor tests are complete and compliant.
- *Cross-compatible capability.* Import and export content into other systems.

Instructor's Companion Website

The *Instructor's Companion Website* contains the following supplements:

- *Instructor's Manual.* Includes sections entitled "*Additional Cases Addressing This Issue*" at the end of selected case synopses.
- *Solutions Manual.* Provides answers to all questions presented in the text, including the *Learning Objectives*, the questions in each case and feature, the *Issue Spotters*, the *Business Scenarios and Case Problems*, *Critical Thinking and Writing Assignments*, and the unit-ending *Task-Based Simulation* features.
- *Test Bank.* A comprehensive test bank contains multiple choice, true/false, and short essay questions.
- *Case-Problem Cases.*
- *Case Printouts.*
- *PowerPoint Slides.*
- *Lecture Outlines.*
- *MindTap Integrated Syllabus.*
- *MindTap Answer Key.*

Acknowledgments

Since I began this project many years ago, numerous business law professors and users of *Business Law Today: Comprehensive Edition* have been kind enough to help me revise the book, including the following:

John J. Balek
Morton College, Illinois

John Jay Ballantine
University of Colorado, Boulder

Lorraine K. Bannai
Western Washington University

Marlene E. Barken
Ithaca College, New York

Laura Barnard
Lakeland Community College, Ohio

Denise A. Bartles, J.D.
Missouri Western State University

Daryl Barton
Eastern Michigan University

Merlin Bauer
Mid State Technical College, Wisconsin

Donna E. Becker
Frederick Community College, Maryland

Richard J. Bennet
Three Rivers Community College,
Connecticut

Dr. Anne Berre
Schreiner University, Texas

Robert C. Bird
University of Connecticut

Bonnie S. Bolinger
Ivy Tech Community College, Wabash Valley
Region, Indiana

Brad Botz
Garden City Community College, Kansas

Teresa Brady
Holy Family College, Pennsylvania

Dean Bredeson
University of Texas at Austin

Lee B. Burgunder
California Polytechnic University,
San Luis Obispo

Thomas D. Cavenagh
North Central College, Illinois

Bradley D. Childs
Belmont University, Tennessee

Corey Ciocchetti
University of Denver, Colorado

Peter Clapp
St. Mary's College, California

Dale Clark
Corning Community College, New York

Tammy W. Cowart
University of Texas, Tyler

Stanley J. Dabrowski
Hudson County Community College,
New Jersey

Sandra J. Defebaugh
Eastern Michigan University

Patricia L. DeFrain
Glendale College, California

Julia G. Derrick
Brevard Community College, Florida

Joe D. Dillsaver
Northeastern State University, Oklahoma

Claude W. Dotson
Northwest College, Wyoming

Larry R. Edwards
Tarrant County Junior College,
South Campus, Texas

Jacolin Eichelberger
Hillsborough Community College, Florida

George E. Eigsti
Kansas City, Kansas, Community College

Florence E. Elliott-Howard
Stephen F. Austin State University, Texas

Tony Enerva
Lakeland Community College, Ohio

Benjamin C. Fassberg
Prince George's Community College, Maryland

Joseph L. Flack
Washtenaw Community College, Michigan

Jerry Furniss
University of Montana

Joan Gabel
Florida State University

Elizabeth J. Guerriero
Northeast Louisiana University

Phil Harmeson
University of South Dakota

Nancy L. Hart
Midland College, Texas

Mo Hassan
Cabrillo College, California

Andy E. Hendrick
Coastal Carolina University, South Carolina

Janine S. Hiller
Virginia Polytechnic Institute & State University

Karen A. Holmes
Hudson Valley Community College, New York

Fred Ittner
College of Alameda, California

Susan S. Jarvis
University of Texas, Pan American

Jack E. Karns
East Carolina University, North Carolina

Sarah Weiner Keidan
Oakland Community College, Michigan

Richard N. Kleeberg
Solano Community College, California

Bradley T. Lutz
Hillsborough Community College, Florida

Diane MacDonald
Pacific Lutheran University, Washington

Darlene Mallick
Anne Arundel Community College, Maryland

John D. Mallonee
Manatee Community College, Florida

Joseph D. Marcus
Prince George's Community College, Maryland

Woodrow J. Maxwell
Hudson Valley Community College, New York

Diane May
Winona State University, Minnesota

Beverly McCormick
Morehead State University, Kentucky

William J. McDevitt
Saint Joseph's University, Pennsylvania

John W. McGee
Aims Community College, Colorado

James K. Miersma
Milwaukee Area Technical Institute, Wisconsin

Susan J. Mitchell
Des Moines Area Community College, Iowa

Jim Lee Morgan
West Los Angeles College, California

Jack K. Morton
University of Montana

Annie Laurie I. Myers
Northampton Community College, Pennsylvania

Solange North
Fox Valley Technical Institute, Wisconsin

Jamie L. O'Brien
South Dakota State University

Ruth R. O'Keefe
Jacksonville University, Florida

Robert H. Orr
Florida Community College at Jacksonville

George Otto
Truman College, Illinois

Thomas L. Palmer
Northern Arizona University

David W. Pan
University of Tulsa, Oklahoma

Victor C. Parker, Jr.
North Georgia College and State University

Donald L. Petote
Genesee Community College, New York

Francis D. Polk
Ocean County College, New Jersey

Gregory Rabb
Jamestown Community College, New York

Brad Reid
Abilene Christian University, Texas

Anne Montgomery Ricketts
University of Findlay, Ohio

Donald A. Roark
University of West Florida

Hugh Rode
Utah Valley State College

Gerald M. Rogers
Front Range Community College, Colorado

Dr. William J. Russell
Northwest Nazarene University, Idaho

William M. Rutledge
Macomb Community College, Michigan

Martha Wright Sartoris
North Hennepin Community College, Minnesota

Anne W. Schacherl
Madison Area Technical College, Wisconsin

Edward F. Shafer
Rochester Community College, Minnesota

Lance Shoemaker, J.D.,
M.C.P., M.A.
West Valley College, California

Lou Ann Simpson
Drake University, Iowa

Denise Smith
Missouri Western State College

Hugh M. Spall
Central Washington University

Catherine A. Stevens
College of Southern Maryland

Maurice Tonissi
Quinsigamond Community College,
Massachusetts

James D. Van Tassel
Mission College, California

Russell A. Waldon
College of the Canyons, California

Frederick J. Walsh
Franklin Pierce College, New Hampshire

James E. Walsh, Jr.
Tidewater Community College, Virginia

Randy Waterman
Richland College, Texas

Jerry Wegman
University of Idaho

Edward L. Welsh, Jr.
Phoenix College, Arizona

Clark W. Wheeler
Santa Fe Community College, Florida

Lori Whisenant
University of Houston, Texas

Kay O. Wilburn
The University of Alabama at Birmingham

John G. Williams, J.D.
Northwestern State University, Louisiana

James L. Wittenbach
University of Notre Dame, Indiana

Eric D. Yordy
Northern Arizona University

Joseph Zavaglia, Jr.
Brookdale Community College,
New Jersey

In addition, I give my thanks to the staff at Cengage Learning, especially Vicky True-Baker, senior product manager; Bryan Gambrel, product director; Martha Conway, senior content manager; Sarah Huber, learning designer; Jennifer Chinn, digital delivery lead; Lisa Elliott, subject matter expert; and Christian Wood, product assistant. I also thank Andy Miller in marketing; Jillian Shafer, permissions project manager; and Jennifer Bowes, permissions analyst. Additionally, I would like to thank project managers Ann Borman and Phil Scott at SPi Global, our compositor, for accurately generating pages for the text and making it possible for me to meet my ambitious schedule for the print and digital products.

I give special thanks to Katherine Marie Silsbee for managing the project and providing exceptional research and editorial skills. I also thank William Eric Hollowell, co-author of the *Solutions Manual* and *Test Bank*, for his excellent research efforts. I am grateful for the copyediting services of Jeanne Yost and proofreading services of Beverly Peavler. I also thank Vickie Reierson, Roxanna Lee, and Suzanne Jasin for their many efforts on this project and for helping to ensure an error-free text.

Roger LeRoy Miller

Dedication

To Darlene Young,

The memories will always be there.
The good thoughts from the past, too.
We are all richer because of them.

R.L.M.

Michal Kalasek/Shutterstock.com

Unit 1
The Legal Environment of Business

1

1 | Law and Legal Reasoning

Learning Objectives

The four Learning Objectives *below are designed to help improve your understanding. After reading this chapter, you should be able to answer the following questions:*

1. What are four primary sources of law in the United States?

2. What is a precedent? When might a court depart from precedent?

3. What is the difference between remedies at law and remedies in equity?

4. What are some important differences between civil law and criminal law?

Law A body of enforceable rules governing relationships among individuals and between individuals and their society.

"Laws should be like clothes. They should be made to fit the people they are meant to serve."

Clarence Darrow
1857–1938
(American lawyer)

In the chapter-opening quotation, Clarence Darrow asserts that law should be created to serve the public. Because you are part of that public, the law is important to you. In particular, those entering the world of business will find themselves subject to numerous laws and government regulations. A basic knowledge of these laws and regulations is beneficial—if not essential—to anyone contemplating a successful career in today's business environment.

Although the law has various definitions, all of them are based on the general observation that **law** consists of *enforceable rules governing relationships among individuals and between individuals and their society.* In some societies, these enforceable rules consist of unwritten principles of behavior. In other societies, they are set forth in ancient or contemporary law codes. In the United States, our rules consist of written laws and court decisions created by modern legislative and judicial bodies. Regardless of how such rules are created, they all have one feature in common: *they establish rights, duties, and privileges that are consistent with the values and beliefs of a society or its ruling group.*

In this introductory chapter, we look at how business law and the legal environment affect business decisions. For instance, suppose that Hellix Communications, Inc., wants to buy a competing cellular company. It also wants to offer unlimited data plans once it has acquired this competitor. Management fears that if the company does not expand, one of its bigger rivals will put it out of business. But Hellix Communications cannot simply buy its rivals. Nor can it just offer a low-cost cell-phone plan to its customers. It has to follow the laws pertaining to its proposed actions. Some of these laws (or regulations) depend on interpretations by those running various regulatory federal agencies. The rules that control Hellix Communications' actions reflect past and current thinking about how large telecommunications companies should and should not act.

Our goal in this text is not only to teach you about specific laws, but also to teach you how to think about the law and legal environment, and to develop your critical-thinking and legal reasoning skills. The laws may change, but the ability to analyze and evaluate the legal (and ethical) ramifications of situations as they arise is an invaluable and lasting skill.

1–1 Business Activities and the Legal Environment

Laws and government regulations affect almost all business activities—from hiring and firing decisions to workplace safety, the manufacturing and marketing of products, business financing, and more. To make good business decisions, businesspersons need to understand the laws and regulations governing these activities.

Realize also that in today's business world, simply being aware of what conduct can lead to legal **liability** is not enough. Businesspersons must develop critical-thinking and legal reasoning skills so that they can evaluate how various laws might apply to a given situation and determine the best course of action. Businesspersons are also pressured to make ethical decisions. Thus, the study of business law necessarily involves an ethical dimension.

Liability The state of being legally responsible (liable) for something, such as a debt or obligation.

1–1a Many Different Laws May Affect a Single Business Transaction

As you will note, each chapter in this text covers a specific area of the law and shows how the legal rules in that area affect business activities. Although compartmentalizing the law in this fashion facilitates learning, it does not indicate the extent to which many different laws may apply to just one transaction. Exhibit 1–1 illustrates the various areas of the law that may influence business decision making.

Example 1.1 When Mark Zuckerberg, as a Harvard student, first launched Facebook, others claimed that Zuckerberg had stolen their ideas for a social-networking site. They filed a lawsuit against him alleging theft of intellectual property, fraudulent misrepresentation, and violations of partnership law and securities law. Facebook ultimately paid $65 million to settle those claims out of court.

Since then, Facebook has been sued repeatedly for violating users' privacy (and federal laws) by tracking their website usage and by scanning private messages for purposes of data mining and user profiling. Facebook's business decisions have also come under scrutiny by federal regulators, such as the Federal Trade Commission (FTC), and by international authorities, such as the European Union. The company settled a complaint filed by the FTC alleging that Facebook had failed to keep "friends" lists and other user information private. ■

Justin Sullivan/Getty Images

Mark Zuckerberg, founder of Facebook, has faced numerous legal challenges. These include privacy issues and the alleged theft of intellectual property. Can large Internet firms completely avoid such legal problems?

1–1b Linking Business Law to the Six Functional Fields of Business

In all likelihood, you are taking a business law or legal environment course because you intend to enter the business world, though some of you may plan to become attorneys. Many of you are taking other business school courses and may therefore be familiar with the functional fields of business listed below:

1. Corporate management.

2. Production and transportation.

Exhibit 1–1 Areas of the Law That May Affect Business Decision Making

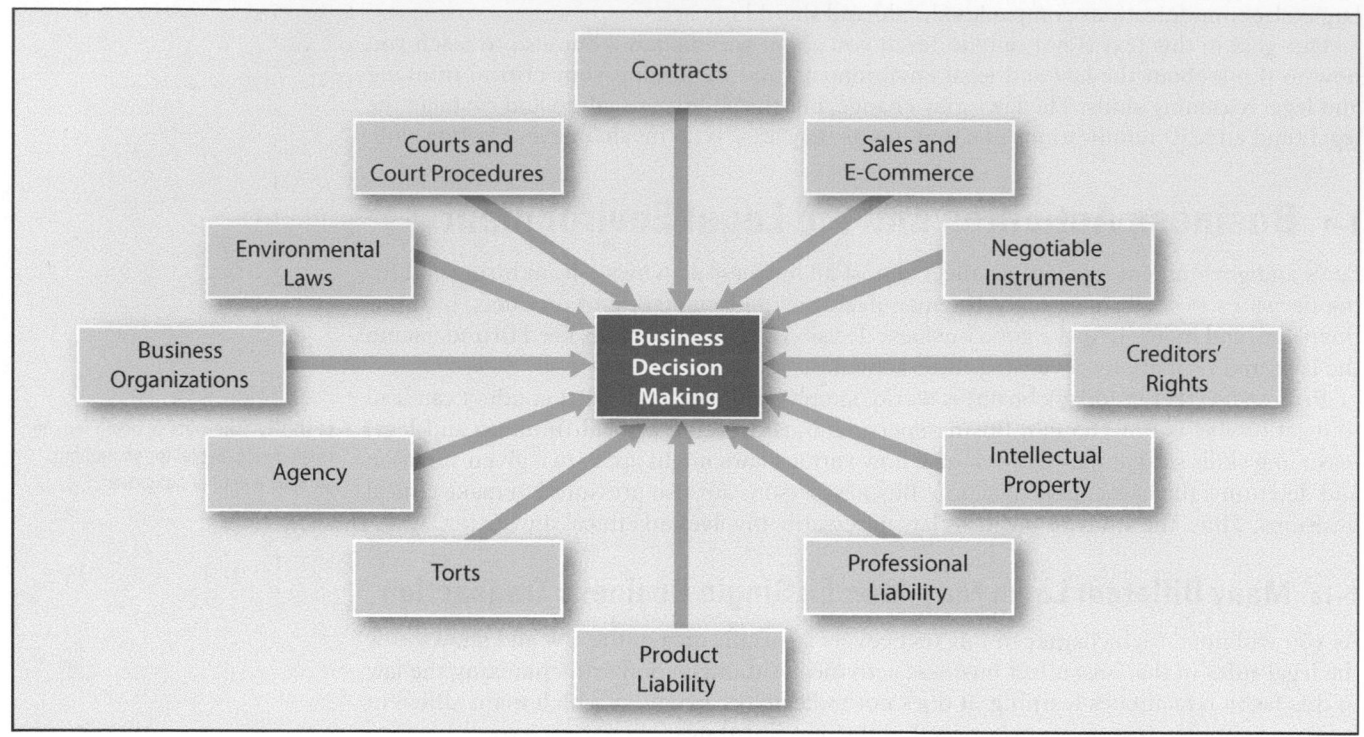

3. Marketing.

4. Research and development.

5. Accounting and finance.

6. Human resource management.

One of our goals in this text is to show how legal concepts can be useful for managers and businesspersons, whether their activities focus on management, marketing, accounting, or some other field. To that end, numerous chapters, including this chapter, contain a special feature called "*Linking Business Law to* [one of the six functional fields of business]."

1–2 Sources of American Law

Primary Source of Law A document that establishes the law on a particular issue, such as a constitution, a statute, an administrative rule, or a court decision.

There are numerous sources of American law. **Primary sources of law**, or sources that establish the law, include the following:

- The U.S. Constitution and the constitutions of the various states.
- Statutory law—including laws passed by Congress, state legislatures, and local governing bodies.
- Regulations created by administrative agencies, such as the federal Food and Drug Administration.
- Case law (court decisions).

Learning Objective 1

What are four primary sources of law in the United States?

We describe each of these important primary sources of law in the following pages. (See the appendix at the end of this chapter for a discussion of how to find statutes, regulations, and case law.)

Secondary sources of law are books and articles that summarize and clarify the primary sources of law. Legal encyclopedias, compilations (such as *Restatements of the Law*, which summarize court decisions on a particular topic), official comments to statutes, treatises, articles in law reviews published by law schools, and articles in other legal journals are examples of secondary sources of law. Courts often refer to secondary sources of law for guidance in interpreting and applying the primary sources of law discussed here.

Secondary Source of Law A publication that summarizes or interprets the law, such as a legal encyclopedia, a legal treatise, or an article in a law review.

1–2a Constitutional Law

The federal government and the states have written constitutions that set forth the general organization, powers, and limits of their respective governments. **Constitutional law,** which deals with the fundamental principles by which the government exercises its authority, is the law as expressed in these constitutions.

The U.S. Constitution is the basis of all law in the United States. It provides a framework for statutes and regulations, and thus is the supreme law of the land. A law in violation of the U.S. Constitution, if challenged, will be declared unconstitutional and will not be enforced, no matter what its source.

The Tenth Amendment to the U.S. Constitution reserves to the states all powers not granted to the federal government. Each state in the union has its own constitution. Unless it conflicts with the U.S. Constitution or a federal law, a state constitution is supreme within that state's borders.

Constitutional Law The body of law derived from the U.S. Constitution and the constitutions of the various states.

1–2b Statutory Law

Laws enacted by legislative bodies at any level of government, such as the statutes passed by Congress or by state legislatures, make up the body of law generally referred to as **statutory law.** When a legislature passes a statute, that statute ultimately is included in the federal code of laws or the relevant state code of laws.

Whenever a particular statute is mentioned in this text, we usually provide a footnote showing its **citation** (a reference to a publication in which a legal authority—such as a statute or a court decision—or other source can be found). In the appendix following this chapter, we explain how you can use these citations to find statutory law.

Statutory Law The body of law enacted by legislative bodies (as opposed to constitutional law, administrative law, or case law).

Citation A reference to a publication in which a legal authority—such as a statute or a court decision—or other source can be found.

Local Ordinances Statutory law also includes local **ordinances**—regulations passed by municipal or county governing units to deal with matters not covered by federal or state law. Ordinances commonly have to do with city or county land use (zoning ordinances), building and safety codes, and other matters affecting only the local governing unit.

Ordinance A regulation enacted by a city or county legislative body that becomes part of that state's statutory law.

Applicability of Statutes A federal statute, of course, applies to all states. A state statute, in contrast, applies only within the state's borders. State laws thus may vary from state to state. No federal statute may violate the U.S. Constitution, and no state statute or local ordinance may violate the U.S. Constitution or the relevant state constitution.

Example 1.2 The tension between federal, state, and local laws is evident in the national debate over so-called sanctuary cities— cities that limit their cooperation with federal immigration authorities. Normally, law enforcement officials are supposed to alert federal immigration authorities when they come into

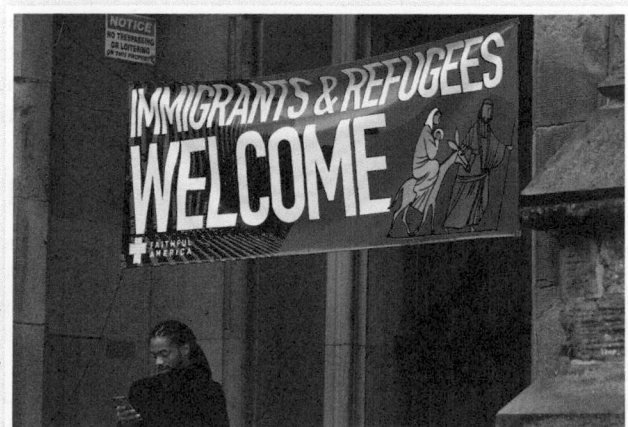

How have local "sanctuary cities" frustrated federal immigration procedures?

contact with undocumented immigrants. Then, immigration officials request the state and local authorities to detain the individual for possible deportation.

But a number of cities across the United States have adopted either local ordinances or explicit policies that do not follow this procedure. Police in these cities often do not ask or report the immigration status of individuals with whom they come into contact. Other places refuse to detain undocumented immigrants who are accused of low-level offenses.

Uniform Laws During the 1800s, the differences among state laws frequently created difficulties for businesspersons conducting trade and commerce among the states. To counter these problems, a group of legal scholars and lawyers formed the National Conference of Commissioners on Uniform State Laws (NCCUSL, online at **www.uniformlaws.org**) in 1892 to draft **uniform laws** ("model statutes") for the states to consider adopting. The NCCUSL still exists today and continues to issue uniform laws.

Uniform Law A model law developed by the National Conference of Commissioners on Uniform State Laws for the states to consider enacting into statute.

Each state has the option of adopting or rejecting a uniform law. *Only if a state legislature adopts a uniform law does that law become part of the statutory law of that state.* Furthermore, a state legislature may choose to adopt only part of a uniform law or to rewrite the sections that are adopted. Hence, even though many states may have adopted a uniform law, those laws may not be entirely "uniform."

The Uniform Commercial Code (UCC) One of the most important uniform acts is the Uniform Commercial Code (UCC), which was created through the joint efforts of the NCCUSL and the American Law Institute.[1] The UCC was first issued in 1952 and has been adopted in all fifty states,[2] the District of Columbia, and the Virgin Islands.

The UCC facilitates commerce among the states by providing a uniform, yet flexible, set of rules governing commercial transactions. Because of its importance in the area of commercial law, we cite the UCC frequently in this text. From time to time, the NCCUSL revises the articles contained in the UCC and submits the revised versions to the states for adoption.

> "Laws and institutions, like clocks, must occasionally be cleaned, wound up, and set to true time."
>
> **Henry Ward Beecher**
> 1813–1887
> (American clergyman and abolitionist)

1–2c Administrative Law

Another important source of American law is administrative law, which consists of the rules, orders, and decisions of administrative agencies. An administrative agency is a federal, state, or local government agency established to perform a specific function. Rules issued by various administrative agencies now affect almost every aspect of a business's operations, including the firm's capital structure and financing, its hiring and firing procedures, its relations with employees and unions, and the way it manufactures and markets its products. We will discuss administrative law in greater detail in a later chapter.

1–2d Case Law and Common Law Doctrines

The rules of law announced in court decisions constitute another basic source of American law. These rules of law include *interpretations* of constitutional provisions, of statutes enacted by legislatures, and of regulations created by administrative agencies.

Case Law The rules of law announced in court decisions. Case law interprets statutes, regulations, and constitutional provisions, and governs all areas not covered by statutory or administrative law.

Today, this body of judge-made law is referred to as **case law.** Case law—the doctrines and principles announced in cases—governs all areas not covered by statutory law or administrative law and is part of our common law tradition. We look at the origins and characteristics of the common law tradition in some detail in the pages that follow.

---

1. This institute was formed in the 1920s and consists of practicing attorneys, legal scholars, and judges.
2. Louisiana has adopted only Articles 1, 3, 4, 5, 7, 8, and 9.

1–3 The Common Law

Because of our colonial heritage, much American law is based on the English legal system. Knowledge of this system is crucial to understanding our legal system today because judges in the United States still apply common law principles when deciding cases.

1–3a Early English Courts

After the Normans conquered England in 1066, William the Conqueror and his successors began the process of unifying the country under their rule. One of the means they used to do this was the establishment of the king's courts, or *curiae regis*. Before the Norman Conquest, disputes had been settled according to the local legal customs and traditions in various regions of the country. The king's courts sought to establish a uniform set of rules for the country as a whole. What evolved in these courts was the beginning of the **common law**—a body of general rules that applied throughout the entire English realm. Eventually, the common law tradition became part of the heritage of all nations that were once British colonies, including the United States.

Courts developed the common law rules from the principles underlying judges' decisions in actual legal controversies. Judges attempted to be consistent, and whenever possible, they based their decisions on the principles suggested by earlier cases. They sought to decide similar cases in a similar way and considered new cases with care because they knew that their decisions would make new law. Each interpretation became part of the law on the subject and served as a legal **precedent**—that is, a court decision that furnished an example or authority for deciding subsequent cases involving identical or similar legal principles or facts.

In the early years of the common law, there was no single place or publication where court opinions, or written decisions, could be found. Beginning in the late thirteenth and early fourteenth centuries, however, portions of significant decisions from each year were gathered together and recorded in *Year Books*. The *Year Books* were useful references for lawyers and judges. In the sixteenth century, the *Year Books* were discontinued, and other reports of cases became available. (See the appendix to this chapter for a discussion of how cases are reported, or published, in the United States today.)

1–3b *Stare Decisis*

The practice of deciding new cases with reference to former decisions, or precedents, eventually became a cornerstone of the English and U.S. judicial systems. The practice forms a doctrine called *stare decisis*[3] (a Latin phrase meaning "to stand on decided cases").

Under the doctrine of *stare decisis*, judges are obligated to follow the precedents established within their jurisdictions. (The term *jurisdiction* refers to a geographic area in which a court or courts have the power to apply the law.) Once a court has set forth a principle of law as being applicable to a certain set of facts, that court must apply the principle in future cases involving similar facts. Courts of lower rank (within the same jurisdiction) must do likewise. Thus, *stare decisis* has two aspects:

1. A court should not overturn its own precedents unless there is a strong reason to do so.
2. Decisions made by a higher court are binding on lower courts.

Controlling Precedents Precedents that must be followed within a jurisdiction are known as controlling precedents. Controlling precedents are binding authorities. A **binding authority** is any source of law that a court must follow when deciding a case. Binding authorities include constitutions, statutes, and regulations that govern the issue being decided, as well as court decisions that are controlling precedents within the jurisdiction. United States Supreme Court case decisions, no matter how old, remain controlling until they are overruled by a subsequent decision of the Supreme Court, by a constitutional amendment, or by congressional legislation.

---

3. Pronounced *stahr*-ee dih-*si*-sis.

Common Law The body of law developed from custom or judicial decisions in English and U.S. courts, not attributable to a legislature.

Learning Objective 2

What is a precedent? When might a court depart from precedent?

Precedent A court decision that furnishes an example or authority for deciding subsequent cases involving identical or similar facts.

Stare Decisis A common law doctrine under which judges are obligated to follow the precedents established in prior decisions.

Binding Authority Any source of law that a court *must* follow when deciding a case.

Know This

Courts normally must follow the rules set forth by higher courts in deciding cases with similar fact patterns.

***Stare Decisis* and Legal Stability** The doctrine of *stare decisis* helps the courts to be more efficient because if other courts have carefully reasoned through a similar case, their legal reasoning and opinions can serve as guides. *Stare decisis* also makes the law more stable and predictable. If the law on a given subject is well settled, someone bringing a case to court can usually rely on the court to make a decision based on what the law has been.

Departures from Precedent Although courts are obligated to follow precedents, sometimes a court will depart from the rule of precedent. If a court decides that a precedent is simply incorrect or that technological or social changes have rendered the precedent inapplicable, the court may rule contrary to the precedent. Cases that overturn precedent often receive a great deal of publicity.

▥ **Classic Case Example 1.3** In *Brown v. Board of Education of Topeka*,[4] the United States Supreme Court expressly overturned precedent. The Court concluded that separate educational facilities for whites and blacks, which had previously been upheld as constitutional,[5] were inherently unequal. The Supreme Court's departure from precedent in the *Brown* decision received a tremendous amount of publicity as people began to realize the ramifications of this change in the law. ▮

When There Is No Precedent Occasionally, courts must decide cases for which no precedents exist, called *cases of first impression*. For instance, as you will read throughout this text, the Internet and certain other technologies have presented many new and challenging issues for the courts to decide.

Example 1.4 Google Glass is a Bluetooth-enabled, hands-free, wearable computer. A person using Google Glass can take photos and videos, surf the Internet, and do other things through voice commands. When it was first sold, many people expressed concerns about this wearable technology because it makes it much easier to secretly film or photograph others. Numerous bars and restaurants banned the use of Google Glass to protect their patrons' privacy. Police officers were concerned about driver safety. A California woman was ticketed for wearing Google Glass while driving. But the court dismissed this case of first impression because it was not clear whether the device had been in operation at the time of the offense. ▮

When deciding cases of first impression, courts often look at **persuasive authorities** (legal authorities that a court may consult for guidance but that are not binding on the court). A court may consider precedents from other jurisdictions, for instance, although those precedents are not binding. A court may also consider legal principles and policies underlying previous court decisions or existing statutes. Additionally, a court might look at fairness, social values and customs, and public policy (governmental policy based on widely held societal values). Federal courts can also look at unpublished opinions (those not intended for publication in a printed legal reporter) as sources of persuasive authority.[6]

***Stare Decisis* and Legal Reasoning** In deciding what law applies to a given dispute and then applying that law to the facts or circumstances of the case, judges rely on the process of **legal reasoning**. Through the use of legal reasoning, judges harmonize their decisions with those that have been made before, as the doctrine of *stare decisis* requires.

Students of business law and the legal environment also engage in critical thinking and legal reasoning. For instance, you may be asked to provide answers for some of the case problems that appear at the end of every chapter in this text. Each problem describes the

Ira Berger/Alamy

Under what circumstances could a user of Google Glass be violating the right to privacy of others?

Persuasive Authority Any legal authority or source of law that a court may look to for guidance but need not follow when making its decision.

Legal Reasoning The process of reasoning by which a judge harmonizes his or her opinion with the judicial decisions in previous cases.

---

4. 347 U.S. 483, 74 S.Ct. 686, 98 L.Ed. 873 (1954).
5. See *Plessy v. Ferguson*, 163 U.S. 537, 16 S.Ct. 1138, 41 L.Ed. 256 (1896).
6. Rule 32.1 of the Federal Rules of Appellate Procedure.

facts of a particular dispute and the legal question at issue. If you are assigned a case problem, you will be asked to determine how a court would answer that question, and why. In other words, you will need to give legal reasons for whatever conclusion you reach.

Basic Steps in Legal Reasoning. At times, the legal arguments set forth in court opinions are relatively simple and brief. At other times, the arguments are complex and lengthy. Regardless of the length of a legal argument, however, the basic steps of the legal reasoning process remain the same. These steps, which you can also follow when analyzing cases and case problems, form what is commonly referred to as the *IRAC method* of legal reasoning. IRAC is an acronym formed from the first letters of the words *Issue, Rule, Application*, and *Conclusion*. To apply the IRAC method, ask the following questions:

1. **Issue—*What are the key facts and issues?*** This may sound obvious, but before you can analyze or apply the relevant law to a specific set of facts, you must clearly understand those facts. In other words, you should read through the case problem carefully—more than once, if necessary. Make sure that you understand the identities of the **plaintiff** (the one who initiates the lawsuit) and the **defendant** (the one being sued) in the case, and the progression of events that led to the lawsuit.

   Suppose that a plaintiff, Anna Tovar, comes before the court claiming *assault* (words or acts that wrongfully and intentionally make another person apprehensive of harmful or offensive contact). Tovar claims that the defendant, Bryce Maddis, threatened her while she was sleeping. Although the plaintiff was unaware that she was being threatened, her roommate, Jan Simon, heard the defendant make the threat. So, in this scenario, the identities of the parties are obvious. Tovar is the plaintiff, and Maddis is the defendant.

   The legal issue in this case is whether the defendant's action constitutes the tort of assault even though the plaintiff was unaware of that threat at the time it occurred. (A tort is a wrongful act brought under civil rather than criminal law.)

2. **Rule—*What rule of law applies to the case?*** A rule of law may be a rule stated by the courts in previous decisions, by a state or federal statute, or by a state or federal administrative agency regulation. Often, more than one rule of law will be applicable to a case.

   In our hypothetical case, Tovar **alleges** (claims) that Maddis committed a tort. Therefore, the applicable law is the common law of torts—specifically, tort law governing assault. Case precedents involving similar facts and issues thus would be relevant.

3. **Application—*How does the rule of law apply to the particular facts and circumstances of this case?*** This step is often the most difficult because each case presents a unique set of facts, circumstances, and parties. Although cases may be similar, no two cases are ever identical in all respects.

   Normally, judges (and lawyers and law students) try to find **cases on point**—previously decided cases that are as similar as possible to the one under consideration. In this situation, there might be case precedents showing that if a victim is unaware of the threat of harmful or offensive contact, then no assault occurred. These would be cases on point that tend to prove that the defendant did not commit assault and should win the case.

   There might, however, also be cases showing that a sexual assault, at least, can occur even if the victim is asleep. These would be cases on point in the plaintiff's favor. You will need to carefully analyze if there are any missing facts in Tovar's claim. For instance, you might want to know the specific threat that Maddis made (and Tovar's roommate overheard). Did he threaten to rape, kill, or beat her? Did he know that she was asleep when he made the threat? Did he know that her roommate heard the threat and would relay it to her when she awoke? Sometimes, you will want to obtain additional facts before analyzing which case precedents should apply and control the outcome of the case.

4. **Conclusion—*What conclusion should be drawn?*** This step normally presents few problems. Usually, the conclusion is evident if the previous three steps have been followed carefully. In our sample problem, for instance, you may determine that Maddis did not commit a tort because Tovar could not prove all of the required elements of assault.

Plaintiff One who initiates a lawsuit.

Defendant One against whom a lawsuit is brought or the accused person in a criminal proceeding.

Allege To state, recite, assert, or charge.

Case on Point A previous case involving factual circumstances and issues that are similar to those in the case before the court.

There Is No One "Right" Answer. Many people believe that there is one "right" answer to every legal question. In many legal controversies, however, there is no single correct result. Good arguments can usually be made to support either side of a legal controversy. Quite often, a case does not involve a "good" person suing a "bad" person. In many cases, both parties have acted in good faith in some measure or in bad faith to some degree. Additionally, each judge has her or his own personal beliefs and philosophy. To some extent, these personal factors shape the legal reasoning process.

1–3c Equitable Remedies and Courts of Equity

Remedy The relief given to an innocent party to enforce a right or compensate for the violation of a right.

A **remedy** is the means given to a party to enforce a right or to compensate for the violation of a right. **Example 1.5** Elena is injured because of Rowan's wrongdoing. If Elena files a lawsuit and is successful, a court can order Rowan to compensate Elena for the harm by paying her a certain amount. The compensation is Elena's remedy. ■

The kinds of remedies available in the early king's courts of England were severely restricted. If one person wronged another, the king's courts could award either money or property, including land, as compensation. These courts became known as *courts of law*, and the remedies were called *remedies at law*. Even though this system introduced uniformity in the settling of disputes, when a person wanted a remedy other than property or economic compensation, the courts of law could do nothing, so "no remedy, no right."

Learning Objective 3

What is the difference between remedies at law and remedies in equity?

Remedies in Equity *Equity* is a branch of law—founded on notions of justice and fair dealing—that seeks to supply a remedy when no adequate remedy at law is available. When individuals could not obtain an adequate remedy in a court of law, they petitioned the king for relief. Most of these petitions were referred to the *chancellor*, an adviser to the king who had the power to grant new and unique remedies. Eventually, formal chancery courts, or *courts of equity*, were established. The remedies granted by the chancery courts were called *remedies in equity*.

Plaintiffs (those bringing lawsuits) had to specify whether they were bringing an "action at law" or an "action in equity," and they chose their courts accordingly. A plaintiff might ask a court of equity to order the defendant to perform within the terms of a contract. A court of law could not issue such an order because its remedies were limited to the payment of money or property as compensation for damages.

A court of equity, however, could issue a decree for *specific performance*—an order to perform what was promised. A court of equity could also issue an *injunction*, directing a party to do or refrain from doing a particular act. In certain cases, a court of equity could allow for the *rescission* (cancellation) of the contract, thereby returning the parties to the positions that they held prior to the contract's formation. Equitable remedies will be discussed in greater detail in the chapters covering contracts.

Know This

Even though courts of law and equity have merged, the principles of equity still apply, and courts will not grant an equitable remedy unless the remedy at law is inadequate.

The Merging of Law and Equity Today, in most states, the courts of law and equity have merged, and thus the distinction between the two courts has largely disappeared. A plaintiff may now request both legal and equitable remedies in the same action, and the trial court judge may grant either form—or both forms—of relief.

The distinction between legal and equitable remedies remains significant, however, because a court normally will grant an equitable remedy only when the remedy at law (property or monetary damages) is inadequate. To request the proper remedy, a business-person (or her or his attorney) must know what remedies are available for the specific kinds of harms suffered. Exhibit 1–2 summarizes the procedural differences (applicable in most states) between an action at law and an action in equity.

Exhibit 1–2 Procedural Differences between an Action at Law and an Action in Equity

PROCEDURE	ACTION AT LAW	ACTION IN EQUITY
Initiation of lawsuit	By filing a complaint	By filing a petition
Decision	By jury or judge	By judge (no jury)
Result	Judgment	Decree
Remedy	Monetary damages or property	Injunction, specific performance, or rescission

Equitable Maxims Over time, the courts have developed a number of **equitable maxims** that provide guidance in deciding whether plaintiffs should be granted equitable relief. Because of their importance, both historically and in our judicial system today, these maxims are set forth in this chapter's *Landmark in the Law* feature.

Equitable Maxims General propositions or principles of law that have to do with fairness (equity).

Jurisprudence The science or philosophy of law.

1–3d Schools of Legal Thought

How judges apply the law to specific cases, including disputes relating to the business world, depends on their philosophical approaches to law, among other things. The study of law, often referred to as **jurisprudence,** includes learning about different schools of legal thought and discovering how each school's approach to law can affect judicial decision making.

The Natural Law School According to the **natural law** theory, a higher, or universal, law exists that applies to all human beings. Each written law should reflect the principles inherent in natural law. If it does not, then it loses its legitimacy and need not be obeyed.

The natural law tradition is one of the oldest and most significant schools of jurisprudence. It dates back to the days of the Greek philosopher Aristotle (384–322 B.C.E.), who distinguished between natural law and the laws governing a particular nation. According to Aristotle, natural law applies universally to all humankind.

The notion that people have "natural rights" stems from the natural law tradition. Those who claim that certain nations, such as China and North Korea, are depriving many of their citizens of their human rights are implicitly appealing to a higher law that has universal applicability.

The question of the universality of basic human rights also comes into play in the context of international business operations. For instance, U.S. companies that have operations abroad often hire foreign workers as employees. Should the same laws that protect U.S. employees apply to these foreign employees? This question is rooted implicitly in a concept of universal rights that has its origins in the natural law tradition.

Legal Positivism *Positive,* or national, *law* is the written law of a given society at a particular point in time. In contrast to natural law, it applies only to the citizens of that nation or society. Those who adhere to **legal positivism** believe that there can be no higher law than a nation's positive law.

According to the positivist school, there is no such thing as "natural rights." Rather, human rights exist solely because of laws. If the laws are not enforced, anarchy will result.

What is the basic premise of Aristotle's natural law theory?

Natural Law The oldest school of legal thought, based on the belief that the legal system should reflect universal ("higher") moral and ethical principles that are inherent in human nature.

Legal Positivism A school of legal thought centered on the assumption that there is no law higher than the laws created by a national government. Laws must be obeyed, even if they are unjust, to prevent anarchy.

Thus, whether a law is morally "bad" or "good" is irrelevant. The law is the law and must be obeyed until it is changed—in an orderly manner through a legitimate lawmaking process.

A judge who takes this view will probably be more inclined to defer to an existing law than would a judge who adheres to the natural law tradition.

Historical School A school of legal thought that looks to the past to determine what the principles of contemporary law should be.

The Historical School The **historical school** of legal thought emphasizes the evolutionary process of law by concentrating on the origin and history of the legal system. This school looks to the past to discover what the principles of contemporary law should be. The legal doctrines that have withstood the passage of time—those that have worked in the past—are deemed best suited for shaping present laws. Hence, law derives its legitimacy and authority from adhering to the standards that historical development has shown to be workable.

Followers of the historical school are more likely than those of other schools to adhere strictly to decisions made in past cases.

Equitable Maxims

In medieval England, courts of equity were expected to use discretion in supplementing the common law. Even today, when the same court can award both legal and equitable remedies, it must exercise discretion.

Students of business law and the legal environment should know that courts often invoke equitable maxims when making their decisions. Here are some of the most significant equitable maxims:

1. *Whoever seeks equity must do equity.* (Anyone who wishes to be treated fairly must treat others fairly.)
2. *Where there is equal equity, the law must prevail.* (The law will determine the outcome of a controversy in which the merits of both sides are equal.)
3. *One seeking the aid of an equity court must come to the court with clean hands.* (Plaintiffs must have acted fairly and honestly.)
4. *Equity will not suffer a wrong to be without a remedy.* (Equitable relief will be awarded when there is a right to relief and there is no adequate remedy at law.)

5. *Equity regards substance rather than form.* (Equity is more concerned with fairness and justice than with legal technicalities.)
6. *Equity aids the vigilant, not those who rest on their rights.* (Equity will not help those who neglect their rights for an unreasonable period of time.)

The last maxim has come to be known as the *equitable doctrine of laches.* The doctrine arose to encourage people to bring lawsuits while the evidence was fresh. If they failed to do so, they would not be allowed to bring a lawsuit. What constitutes a reasonable time, of course, varies according to the circumstances of the case.

Time periods for different types of cases are now usually fixed by *statutes of limitations*—that is, statutes that set the maximum time period during which a certain action can be brought. After the time allowed under a statute of limitations has expired, no action can be brought, no matter how strong the case was originally.

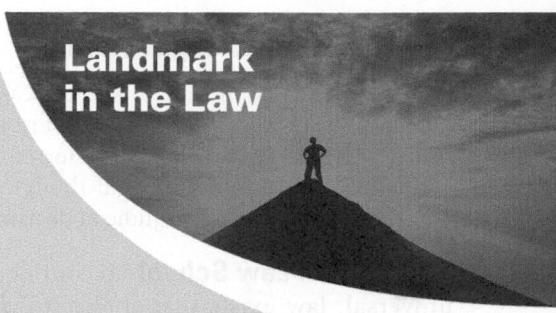

Landmark in the Law

Application to Today's World *The equitable maxims listed here underlie many of the legal rules and principles that are commonly applied by the courts today—and that you will read about in this book.*

For instance, in the contracts materials, you will read about the doctrine of promissory estoppel. Under this doctrine, a person who has reasonably and substantially relied on the promise of another may be able to obtain some measure of recovery, even though no enforceable contract exists. The court will estop (bar) the one making the promise from asserting the lack of a valid contract as a defense. The rationale underlying the doctrine of promissory estoppel is similar to that expressed in the fourth and fifth maxims just listed.

Legal Realism In the 1920s and 1930s, a number of jurists and scholars, known as *legal realists*, rebelled against the historical approach to law. **Legal realism** is based on the idea that law is just one of many institutions in society and that it is shaped by social forces and needs. This school reasons that because the law is a human enterprise, judges should look beyond the law and take social and economic realities into account when deciding cases.

Legal realists also believe that the law can never be applied with total uniformity. Given that judges are human beings with unique experiences, personalities, value systems, and intellects, different judges will obviously bring different reasoning processes to the same case. Female judges, for instance, might be more inclined than male judges to consider whether a decision might have a negative impact on the employment of women or minorities.

Legal Realism A school of legal thought that holds that the law is only one factor to be considered when deciding cases, and that social and economic circumstances should also be taken into account.

1–4 Classifications of Law

The law may be broken down according to several classification systems. One classification system divides law into **substantive law** (all laws that define, describe, regulate, and create legal rights and obligations) and **procedural law** (all laws that establish the methods of enforcing the rights established by substantive law).

Example 1.6 A state law that provides employees with the right to workers' compensation benefits for any on-the-job injuries they sustain is a substantive law because it creates legal rights. Procedural laws, in contrast, establish the method by which an employee must notify the employer about an on-the-job injury, prove the injury, and periodically submit additional proof to continue receiving workers' compensation benefits. ▮ Note that a law may contain both substantive and procedural provisions.

Other classification systems divide law into federal law and state law, and private law (dealing with relationships between persons) and public law (addressing the relationship between persons and their governments). Frequently, people use the term **cyberlaw** to refer to the emerging body of law that governs transactions conducted via the Internet, but cyberlaw is not really a classification of law. Rather, it is an informal term used to refer to both new laws and modifications of traditional legal principles that relate to the online environment.

Substantive Law Law that defines, describes, regulates, and creates legal rights and obligations.

Procedural Law Law that establishes the methods of enforcing the rights established by substantive law.

Cyberlaw An informal term used to refer to all laws governing electronic communications and transactions, particularly those conducted via the Internet.

1–4a Civil Law and Criminal Law

Civil law spells out the rights and duties that exist between persons and between persons and their governments, as well as the relief available when a person's rights are violated. Typically, in a civil case, a private party sues another private party who has failed to comply with a duty. Much of the law that we discuss in this text—including contract law and tort law—is civil law.

Note that *civil law* is not the same as a *civil law system*. As you will read shortly, a **civil law system** is a legal system based on a written code of laws. (See this chapter's *Beyond Our Borders* feature for a discussion of the different legal systems used in other nations.)

Criminal law has to do with wrongs committed against society for which society demands redress. Criminal acts are proscribed by local, state, or federal government statutes. Thus, criminal defendants are prosecuted by public officials, such as a district attorney (D.A.), on behalf of the state, not by their victims or other private parties.

Whereas in a civil case the object is to obtain a remedy (such as monetary damages) to compensate the injured party, in a criminal case the object is to punish the wrongdoer in an attempt to deter others from similar actions. Penalties for violations of criminal statutes consist of fines and/or imprisonment—and, in some cases, death.

Learning Objective 4

What are some important differences between civil law and criminal law?

Civil Law The branch of law dealing with the definition and enforcement of all private or public rights, as opposed to criminal matters.

Civil Law System A system of law derived from Roman law that is based on codified laws (rather than on case precedents).

Criminal Law The branch of law that defines and punishes wrongful actions committed against the public.

National Law Systems

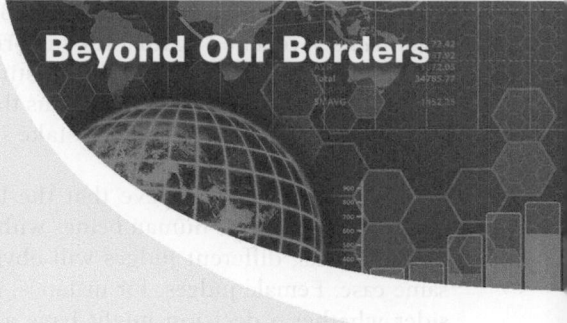

Despite their varying cultures and customs, almost all countries have laws governing torts, contracts, employment, and other areas. Two types of legal systems predominate around the globe today. One is the common law system of England and the United States, which we discussed earlier. The other system is based on Roman civil law, or "code law," which relies on the legal principles enacted into law by a legislature or governing body.

Civil Law Systems

Although national law systems share many commonalities, they also have distinct differences. In a *civil law system*, the primary source of law is a statutory code, and case precedents are not judicially binding, as they normally are in a common law system. Although judges in a civil law system commonly refer to previous decisions as sources of legal guidance, those decisions are not binding precedents (*stare decisis* does not apply).

Common Law and Civil Law Systems Today

Exhibit 1–3 lists some countries that follow either the common law system or the civil law system. Generally, countries that were once colonies of Great Britain have retained their English common law heritage. The civil law system, which is used in most continental European nations, has been retained in the countries that were once colonies of those nations. In the United States, the state of Louisiana, because of its historical ties to France, has in part a civil law system, as do Haiti, Québec, and Scotland.

Islamic Legal Systems

A third, less prevalent legal system is common in Islamic countries, where the law is often influenced by *sharia*, the religious law of Islam. Islam is both a religion and a way of life. *Sharia* is a comprehensive code of principles that governs the public and private lives of Islamic persons and directs many aspects of their day-to-day lives, including politics, economics, banking, business law, contract law, and social issues.

Although *sharia* affects the legal codes of many Muslim countries, the extent of its impact and its interpretation vary widely. In some Middle Eastern nations, aspects of *sharia* have been codified in modern legal codes and are enforced by national judicial systems.

Critical Thinking

Does the civil law system offer any advantages over the common law system, or vice versa? Explain.

Exhibit 1–3 The Legal Systems of Selected Nations

CIVIL LAW		COMMON LAW	
Argentina	Indonesia	Australia	Nigeria
Austria	Iran	Bangladesh	Singapore
Brazil	Italy	Canada	United Kingdom
Chile	Japan	Ghana	United States
China	Mexico	India	Zambia
Egypt	Poland	Israel	
Finland	South Korea	Jamaica	
France	Sweden	Kenya	
Germany	Tunisia	Malaysia	
Greece	Venezuela	New Zealand	

1–4b National and International Law

U.S. businesspersons increasingly engage in transactions that extend beyond our national borders. For this reason, those who pursue a career in business today should have an understanding of the global legal environment.

The law of a particular nation, such as Japan or Germany, is **national law.** National law, of course, varies from country to country because each country's law reflects the interests, customs, activities, and values that are unique to that nation's culture. Even though the laws and legal systems of various countries differ substantially, broad similarities do exist.

In contrast, international law applies to more than one nation. **International law** can be defined as a body of written and unwritten laws observed by independent nations and governing the acts of individuals as well as governments. It is a mixture of rules and constraints derived from a variety of sources, including the laws of individual nations, customs developed among nations, and international treaties and organizations.

The key difference between national law and international law is that government authorities can enforce national law. If a nation violates an international law, however, enforcement is up to other countries or international organizations, which may or may not choose to act. If persuasive tactics fail, the only option is to take coercive actions against the violating nation. Coercive actions range from the severance of diplomatic relations and boycotts to sanctions and, as a last resort, war.

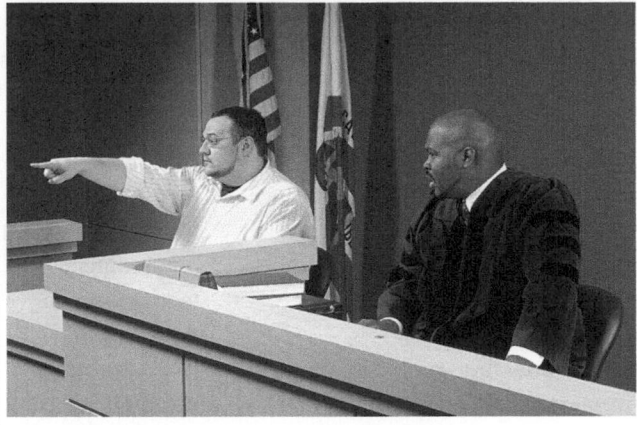

A witness points out someone in the courtroom to the judge.

National Law Law that pertains to a particular nation (as opposed to international law).

International Law Law that governs relations among nations.

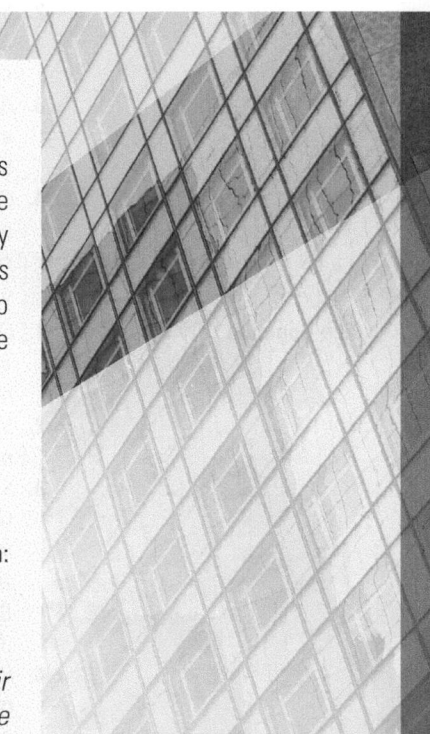

Practice and Review

Suppose that the California legislature passes a law that severely restricts carbon dioxide emissions of automobiles in that state. A group of automobile manufacturers files a suit against the state of California to prevent enforcement of the law. The automakers claim that a federal law already sets fuel economy standards nationwide and that these standards are essentially the same as carbon dioxide emission standards. According to the automobile manufacturers, it is unfair to allow California to impose more stringent regulations than those set by the federal law. Using the information presented in the chapter, answer the following questions.

1. Who are the parties (the plaintiffs and the defendant) in this lawsuit?

2. Are the plaintiffs seeking a legal remedy or an equitable remedy? Why?

3. What is the primary source of the law that is at issue here?

4. Read through the appendix that follows this chapter, and then answer the following question: Where would you look to find the relevant California and federal laws?

Debate This

Under the doctrine of stare decisis, courts are obligated to follow the precedents established in their jurisdiction unless there is a compelling reason not to do so. Should U.S. courts continue to adhere to this common law principle, given that our government now regulates so many areas by statute?

Key Terms

allege 9	equitable maxims 11	persuasive authority 8
binding authority 7	historical school 12	plaintiff 9
case law 6	international law 15	plurality opinion 25
case on point 9	jurisprudence 11	precedent 7
citation 5	law 2	primary source of law 4
civil law 13	legal positivism 11	procedural law 13
civil law system 13	legal realism 13	remedy 10
common law 7	legal reasoning 8	secondary source of law 5
concurring opinion 25	liability 3	*stare decisis* 7
constitutional law 5	majority opinion 25	statutory law 5
criminal law 13	national law 15	substantive law 13
cyberlaw 13	natural law 11	uniform law 6
defendant 9	ordinance 5	
dissenting opinion 25	*per curiam* opinion 25	

Chapter Summary: Law and Legal Reasoning

Sources of American Law	1. *Constitutional law*—The law as expressed in the U.S. Constitution and the various state constitutions. The U.S. Constitution is the supreme law of the land. State constitutions are supreme within state borders to the extent that they do not violate the U.S. Constitution or a federal law.
	2. *Statutory law*—Laws or ordinances created by federal, state, and local legislatures. None of these laws can violate the U.S. Constitution, and no state statute or local ordinance can violate the relevant state constitution. Uniform laws, when adopted by a state legislature, become statutory law in that state.
	3. *Administrative law*—The rules, orders, and decisions of federal or state government administrative agencies. Federal administrative agencies are created by enabling legislation enacted by the U.S. Congress. Agency functions include rulemaking, investigation and enforcement, and adjudication.
	4. *Case law and common law doctrines*—Judge-made law, including interpretations of constitutional provisions, of statutes enacted by legislatures, and of regulations created by administrative agencies. Case law governs all areas not covered by statutory law or administrative law, and is part of our common law tradition.
The Common Law	1. *Common law*—Law that originated in medieval England with the creation of the king's courts, or *curiae regis*, and the development of a body of rules that were common to (or applied in) all regions of the country.
	2. *Stare decisis*—A doctrine under which judges "stand on decided cases"—or follow the rule of precedent—in deciding cases. *Stare decisis* is the cornerstone of the common law tradition.
	3. *Stare decisis and legal reasoning*—Judges use legal reasoning to harmonize their decisions with those that have been made before, as required by the doctrine of *stare decisis*. The basic steps of legal reasoning form what is often referred to as the *IRAC method* of legal reasoning. IRAC stands for *Issue, Rule, Application,* and *Conclusion*. First, clearly grasp the relevant facts and identify the issue. Second, determine the rule of law that applies to the case. Third, analyze (using *cases on point*) how the rule of law applies to the particular facts of the dispute, and fourth, arrive at a conclusion.
	4. *Remedies*—A remedy is the means by which a court enforces a right or compensates for a violation of a right. Courts typically grant legal remedies (monetary damages or property) but may also grant equitable remedies (specific performance, injunction, or rescission) when the legal remedy is inadequate or unavailable.

5. *Schools of legal thought*—Judges' decision making is influenced by their philosophy of law. The following are four important schools of legal thought, or legal philosophies:
   a. Natural law—One of the oldest and most significant schools of legal thought. Those who believe in natural law hold that there is a universal law applicable to all human beings and that this law is of a higher order than positive, or conventional, law.
   b. Legal positivism—A school of legal thought centered on the assumption that there is no law higher than the laws created by the government. Laws must be obeyed, even if they are unjust, to prevent anarchy.
   c. Historical school—A school of legal thought that stresses the evolutionary nature of law and looks to doctrines that have withstood the passage of time for guidance in shaping present laws.
   d. Legal realism—A school of legal thought that generally advocates a less abstract and more realistic approach to the law. This approach takes into account customary practices and the social and economic circumstances in which transactions take place.

Classifications of Law	The law may be broken down according to several classification systems, such as substantive or procedural law, federal or state law, and private or public law. Two broad classifications are civil and criminal law, and national and international law. Cyberlaw is not really a classification of law but a term that refers to the growing body of case and statutory law that applies to Internet transactions.

Issue Spotters

1. The First Amendment to the U.S. Constitution provides protection for the free exercise of religion. A state legislature enacts a law that outlaws all religions that do not derive from the Judeo-Christian tradition. Is this law valid within that state? Why or why not? (See *Sources of American Law.*)

2. Under what circumstances might a judge rely on case law to determine the intent and purpose of a statute? (See *Sources of American Law.*)

—**Check your answers to the *Issue Spotters* against the answers provided in Appendix D at the end of this text.**

Business Scenarios and Case Problems

1–1. Binding versus Persuasive Authority. A county court in Illinois is deciding a case involving an issue that has never been addressed before in that state's courts. The Iowa Supreme Court, however, recently decided a case involving a very similar fact pattern. Is the Illinois court obligated to follow the Iowa Supreme Court's decision on the issue? If the United States Supreme Court had decided a similar case, would that decision be binding on the Illinois court? Explain. (See *The Common Law.*)

1–2. Sources of Law. This chapter discussed a number of sources of American law. Which source of law takes priority in the following situations, and why? (See *Sources of American Law.*)
1. A federal statute conflicts with the U.S. Constitution.
2. A federal statute conflicts with a state constitutional provision.
3. A state statute conflicts with the common law of that state.
4. A state constitutional amendment conflicts with the U.S. Constitution.

1–3. Remedies. Arthur Rabe is suing Xavier Sanchez for breaching a contract in which Sanchez promised to sell Rabe a Van Gogh painting for $150,000. (See *The Common Law.*)
1. In this lawsuit, who is the plaintiff, and who is the defendant?
2. If Rabe wants Sanchez to perform the contract as promised, what remedy should Rabe seek?
3. Suppose that Rabe wants to cancel the contract because Sanchez fraudulently misrepresented the painting as an original Van Gogh when in fact it is a copy. In this situation, what remedy should Rabe seek?
4. Will the remedy Rabe seeks in either situation be a remedy at law or a remedy in equity?

1–4. Philosophy of Law. After World War II ended in 1945, an international tribunal of judges convened at Nuremberg, Germany. The judges convicted several Nazi war criminals of "crimes against humanity." Assuming that the Nazis who were convicted had not disobeyed any law of their country and had merely been following their government's (Hitler's) orders, what law had they violated? Explain. (See *The Common Law.*)

1–5. Spotlight on AOL—Common Law. AOL, LLC, mistakenly made public the personal information of 650,000 of its members. The members filed a suit, alleging violations of California law. AOL asked the court to dismiss the suit on the basis of a "forum-selection" clause in its member agreement that designates Virginia courts as the place where member disputes will be tried. Under a decision of the United States Supreme Court, a forum-selection clause is unenforceable "if enforcement would contravene a strong public policy of the forum in which suit is brought." California has declared in other cases that the AOL clause contravenes a strong public policy. If the court applies the doctrine of *stare decisis*, will it dismiss the suit? Explain. [*Doe 1 v. AOL, LLC*, 552 F.3d 1077 (9th Cir. 2009)] (See *The Common Law*.)

1–6. Business Case Problem with Sample Answer—Reading Citations. Assume that you want to read the entire court opinion in the case of *Worldwide TechServices, LLC v. Commissioner of Revenue*, 479 Mass. 20, 91 N.E.3d 650 (2018).

Refer to the appendix to this chapter, and then explain specifically where you would find the court's opinion. (See *Finding Case Law*.)

—**For a sample answer to Problem 1–6, go to Appendix E at the end of this text.**

Critical Thinking and Writing Assignments

1–8. Business Law Writing. John's company is involved in a lawsuit with a customer, Beth. John argues that for fifty years higher courts in that state have decided cases involving circumstances similar to his case in a way that indicates he can expect a ruling in his company's favor. Write at least one paragraph discussing whether this is a valid argument. Write another paragraph discussing whether the judge in this case must rule as those other judges did, and why. (See *The Common Law*.)

1–9. Time-Limited Group Assignment—Court Opinions. Read through the subsection entitled "Decisions and Opinions" in the appendix following this chapter. (See *Reading and Understanding Case Law*.)

1–7. A Question of Ethics—The Doctrine of Precedent. *Sandra White operated a travel agency. To obtain lower airline fares for her nonmilitary clients, she booked military-rate travel by forwarding fake military identification cards to the airlines. The government charged White with identity theft, which requires the "use" of another's identification. The trial court had two cases that represented precedents.*

In the first case, David Miller obtained a loan to buy land by representing that certain investors had approved the loan when, in fact, they had not. Miller's conviction for identity theft was overturned because he had merely said that the investors had done something when they had not. According to the court, this was not the "use" of another's identification.

In the second case, Kathy Medlock, an ambulance service operator, had transported patients for whom there was no medical necessity to do so. To obtain payment, Medlock had forged a physician's signature. The court concluded that this was "use" of another person's identity. [*United States v. White*, 846 F.3d 170 (6th Cir. 2017)] (*See* Sources of American Law.)

1. Which precedent—the *Miller* case or the *Medlock* case—is similar to White's situation, and why?
2. In the two cases cited by the court, were there any ethical differences in the actions of the parties? Explain your answer.

1. One group will explain the difference between a concurring opinion and a majority opinion.
2. Another group will outline the difference between a concurring opinion and a dissenting opinion.
3. The third group will explain why judges and justices write concurring and dissenting opinions, given that these opinions will not affect the outcome of the case at hand, which has already been decided by majority vote.

Appendix to Chapter 1

Finding and Analyzing the Law

This text includes numerous references, or *citations*, to primary sources of law—federal and state statutes, the U.S. Constitution and state constitutions, regulations issued by administrative agencies, and court cases. A citation identifies the publication in which a legal authority—such as a statute or court decision—can be found. In this appendix, we explain how you can use citations to find primary sources of law. Note that in addition to being published in sets of books, as described next, most federal and state laws and case decisions are available online.

Finding Statutory and Administrative Law

When Congress passes laws, they are collected in a publication titled *United States Statutes at Large*. When state legislatures pass laws, they are collected in similar state publications. Most frequently, however, laws are referred to in their codified form—that is, the form in which they appear in the federal and state codes. In these codes, laws are compiled by subject.

United States Code

The *United States Code* (U.S.C.) arranges all existing federal laws of a public and permanent nature by subject. Each of the fifty-two subjects into which the U.S.C. arranges the laws is given a title and a title number. For example, laws relating to commerce and trade are collected in "Title 15, Commerce and Trade." Titles are subdivided by sections.

A citation to the U.S.C. includes title and section numbers. Thus, a reference to "15 U.S.C. Section 1" means that the statute can be found in Section 1 of Title 15. ("Section" may be designated by the symbol §, and "Sections" by §§.) In addition to the print publication of the U.S.C., the federal government also provides a searchable online database of the *United States Code* at **www.gpo.gov** (click on "Libraries" and then "Core Documents of Our Democracy" to find the *United States Code*).

Commercial publications of these laws are available and are widely used. For example, Thomson Reuters publishes the *United States Code Annotated* (U.S.C.A.). The U.S.C.A. contains the complete text of laws included in the U.S.C., notes of court decisions that interpret and apply specific sections of the statutes, and the text of presidential proclamations and executive orders. The U.S.C.A. also includes research aids, such as cross-references to related statutes, historical notes, and other references. A citation to the U.S.C.A. is similar to a citation to the U.S.C.: "15 U.S.C.A. Section 1."

State Codes

State codes follow the U.S.C. pattern of arranging laws by subject. The state codes may be called codes, revisions, compilations, consolidations, general statutes, or statutes, depending on the state.

In some codes, subjects are designated by number. In others, they are designated by name. For example, "13 Pennsylvania Consolidated Statutes Section 1101" means that the statute can be found in Title 13, Section 1101, of the Pennsylvania code. "California Commercial Code Section 1101" means the statute can be found in Section 1101 under the subject heading "Commercial Code" of the California code. Abbreviations may be used. For example, "13 Pennsylvania Consolidated Statutes Section 1101" may be abbreviated "13 Pa. C.S. § 1101," and "California Commercial Code Section 1101" may be abbreviated "Cal. Com. Code § 1101."

Administrative Rules

Rules and regulations adopted by federal administrative agencies are initially published in the *Federal Register*, a daily publication of the U.S. government. Later, they are incorporated into the *Code of Federal Regulations* (C.F.R.).

Like the U.S.C., the C.F.R. is divided into titles. Rules within each title are assigned section numbers. A full citation to the C.F.R. includes title and section numbers. For example, a reference to "17 C.F.R. Section 230.504" means that the rule can be found in Section 230.504 of Title 17.

Finding Case Law

Before discussing the case reporting system, we need to look briefly at the court system. There are two types of courts in the United States: federal courts and state courts.

Both the federal and the state court systems consist of several levels, or tiers, of courts. *Trial courts*, in which evidence is presented and testimony is given, are on the bottom tier (which also includes lower courts handling specialized issues). Decisions from a trial court can be appealed to a higher court, which commonly is an intermediate *court of appeals*, or an *appellate court*. Decisions from these intermediate courts of appeals may be appealed to an even higher court, such as a state supreme court or the United States Supreme Court.

State Court Decisions

Most state trial court decisions are not published (except in New York and a few other states, which publish selected trial court opinions). Decisions from state trial courts are typically filed in the office of the clerk of the court, where the decisions are available for public inspection. (Increasingly, they can be found online as well.)

Written decisions of the appellate, or reviewing, courts, however, are published and distributed (in print and online). Many of the state court cases presented in this book are from state appellate courts. The reported appellate decisions are published in volumes called *reports* or *reporters*, which are numbered consecutively. State appellate court decisions are found in the state reporters of that particular state. Official reports are published by the state, whereas unofficial reports are published by nongovernment entities.

Regional Reporters State court opinions appear in regional units of the National Reporter System, published by Thomson Reuters. Most lawyers and libraries have these reporters because they report cases more quickly and are distributed more widely than the state-published reports. In fact, many states have eliminated their own reporters in favor of the National Reporter System.

The National Reporter System divides the states into the following geographic areas: Atlantic (A., A.2d, or A.3d), *North Eastern* (N.E., N.E.2d, or N.E.3d), *North Western* (N.W. or N.W.2d), *Pacific* (P., P.2d, or P.3d), *South Eastern* (S.E. or S.E.2d), *South Western* (S.W., S.W.2d, or S.W.3d), and *Southern* (So., So.2d, or So.3d). (The *2d* and *3d* in the abbreviations refer to *Second Series* and *Third Series*, respectively.) The states included in each of these regional divisions are indicated in Exhibit 1A–1, which illustrates the National Reporter System.

Exhibit 1A–1　The National Reporter System—Regional/Federal

Regional Reporters	Coverage Beginning	Coverage
Atlantic Reporter (A., A.2d, or A.3d)	1885	Connecticut, Delaware, District of Columbia, Maine, Maryland, New Hampshire, New Jersey, Pennsylvania, Rhode Island, and Vermont.
North Eastern Reporter (N.E., N.E.2d, or N.E.3d)	1885	Illinois, Indiana, Massachusetts, New York, and Ohio.
North Western Reporter (N.W. or N.W.2d)	1879	Iowa, Michigan, Minnesota, Nebraska, North Dakota, South Dakota, and Wisconsin.
Pacific Reporter (P., P.2d, or P.3d)	1883	Alaska, Arizona, California, Colorado, Hawaii, Idaho, Kansas, Montana, Nevada, New Mexico, Oklahoma, Oregon, Utah, Washington, and Wyoming.
South Eastern Reporter (S.E. or S.E.2d)	1887	Georgia, North Carolina, South Carolina, Virginia, and West Virginia.
South Western Reporter (S.W., S.W.2d, or S.W.3d)	1886	Arkansas, Kentucky, Missouri, Tennessee, and Texas.
Southern Reporter (So., So.2d, or So.3d)	1887	Alabama, Florida, Louisiana, and Mississippi.

Federal Reporters		
Federal Reporter (F., F.2d, or F.3d)	1880	U.S. Circuit Courts from 1880 to 1912; U.S. Commerce Court from 1911 to 1913; U.S. District Courts from 1880 to 1932; U.S. Court of Claims (now called U.S. Court of Federal Claims) from 1929 to 1932 and since 1960; U.S. Courts of Appeals since 1891; U.S. Court of Customs and Patent Appeals since 1929; U.S. Emergency Court of Appeals since 1943.
Federal Supplement (F.Supp., F.Supp.2d, or F.Supp.3d)	1932	U.S. Court of Claims from 1932 to 1960; U.S. District Courts since 1932; U.S. Customs Court since 1956.
Federal Rules Decisions (F.R.D.)	1939	U.S. District Courts involving the Federal Rules of Civil Procedure since 1939 and Federal Rules of Criminal Procedure since 1946.
Supreme Court Reporter (S.Ct.)	1882	United States Supreme Court since the October term of 1882.
Bankruptcy Reporter (Bankr.)	1980	Bankruptcy decisions of U.S. Bankruptcy Courts, U.S. District Courts, U.S. Courts of Appeals, and the United States Supreme Court.
Military Justice Reporter (M.J.)	1978	U.S. Court of Military Appeals and Courts of Military Review for the Army, Navy, Air Force, and Coast Guard.

NATIONAL REPORTER SYSTEM MAP

Case Citations   After appellate decisions have been published, they are normally referred to (cited) by the name of the case and the volume, name, and page number of the reporter(s) in which the opinion can be found. The citation first lists information from the state's official reporter (if different from the National Reporter System), then the *National Reporter*, and then any other selected reporter. (Citing a reporter by volume number, name, and page number, in that order, is common to all citations.) When more than one reporter is cited for the same case, each reference is called a *parallel citation*.

Note that some states have adopted a "public domain citation system" that uses a somewhat different format for the citation. For example, in Ohio, an Ohio court decision might be designated "2018 -Ohio- 79," meaning that the decision was the 79th decision issued by the Ohio Supreme Court in 2018. Parallel citations to the *Ohio Appellate Court Reporter* and the *North Eastern Reporter* are included after the public domain citation.

Consider the following citation: *Connecticut Coalition for Justice in Education Funding, Inc. v. Rell*, 327 Conn. 650, 176 A.3d 28 (2018). We see that the opinion in this case can be found in Volume 327 of the official *Connecticut Reports*, on page 650. The parallel citation is to Volume 176 of the *Atlantic Reporter, Third Series*, page 28.

When we present opinions in this text (starting in Chapter 2), in addition to the reporter, we give the name of the court hearing the case and the year of the court's decision. Sample citations to state court decisions are listed and explained in Exhibit 1A–2.

Federal Court Decisions

Federal district (trial) court decisions are published unofficially in the *Federal Supplement* (F.Supp., F.Supp.2d, or F.Supp.3d), and opinions from the circuit courts of appeals (federal reviewing courts) are reported unofficially in the *Federal Reporter* (F., F.2d, or F.3d). Cases concerning federal bankruptcy law are published unofficially in the *Bankruptcy Reporter* (Bankr. or B.R.).

The official edition of United States Supreme Court decisions is the *United States Reports* (U.S.), which is published by the federal government. Unofficial editions of Supreme Court cases include the *Supreme Court Reporter* (S.Ct.) and the *Lawyers' Edition of the Supreme Court Reports* (L.Ed. or L.Ed.2d). Sample citations for federal court decisions are also listed and explained in Exhibit 1A–2.

Unpublished Opinions

Many court opinions that are not yet published or that are not intended for publication can be accessed through Westlaw® (abbreviated in citations as "WL"), an online legal database. When no citation to a published reporter is available for cases cited in this text, we give the WL citation (such as 2018 WL 266332, which means it was case number 266332 decided in the year 2018). In addition, federal appellate court decisions that are designated as unpublished may appear in the *Federal Appendix* (Fed.Appx.) of the National Reporter System.

Sometimes, both in this text and in other legal sources, you will see blanks left in a citation. This occurs when the decision will be published, but the particular volume number or page number is not yet available.

Old Cases

On a few occasions, this text cites opinions from old, *classic cases* dating to the nineteenth century or earlier. Some of these cases are from the English courts. The citations to these cases may not conform to the descriptions given above.

Reading and Understanding Case Law

The cases in this text have been condensed from the full text of the courts' opinions and paraphrased by the authors. For those wishing to review court cases for future research projects or to gain additional legal information, the following sections will provide useful insights into how to read and understand case law.

Exhibit 1A–2 How to Read Citations

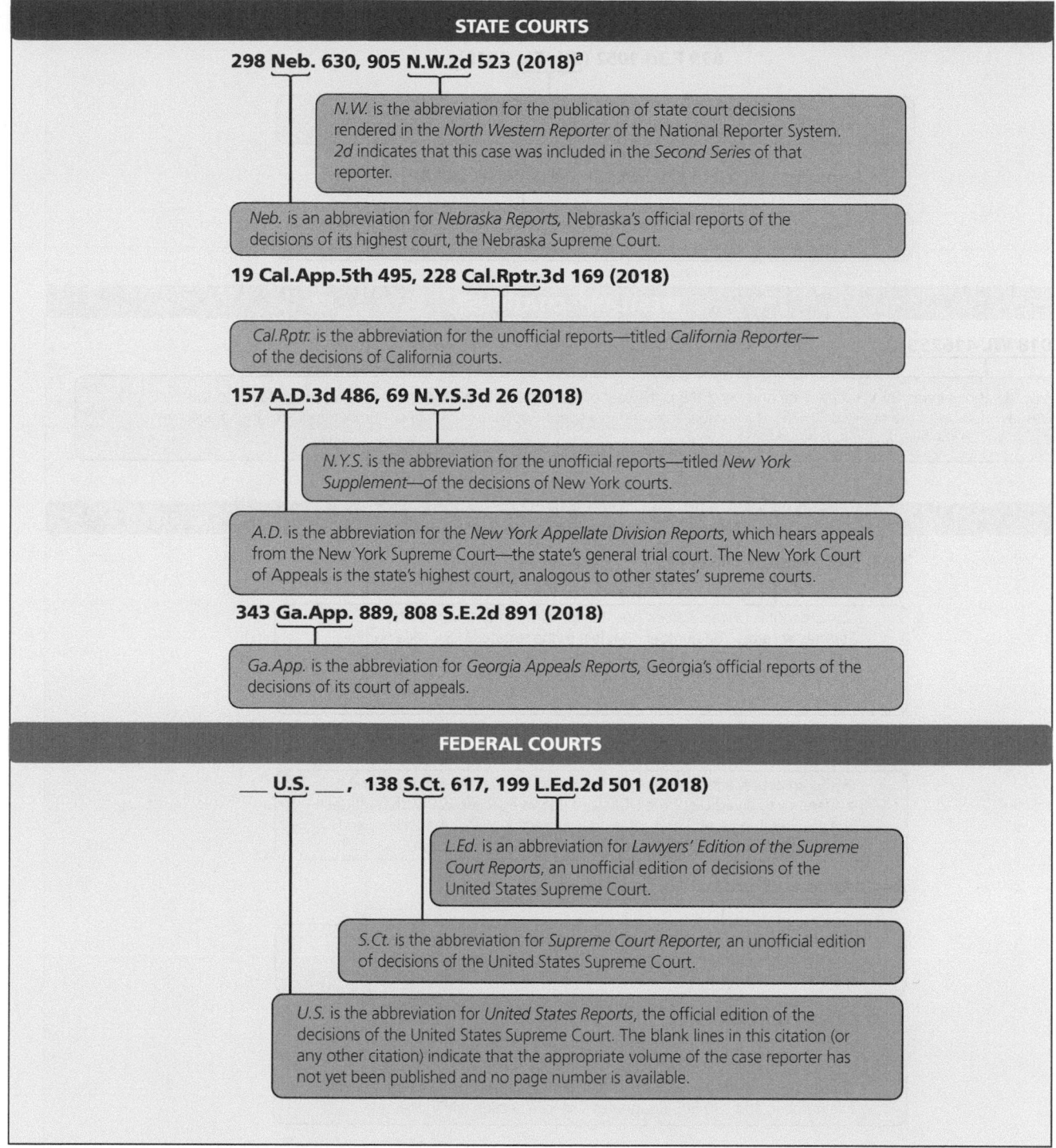

STATE COURTS

298 Neb. 630, 905 N.W.2d 523 (2018)[a]

> *N.W.* is the abbreviation for the publication of state court decisions rendered in the *North Western Reporter* of the National Reporter System. *2d* indicates that this case was included in the *Second Series* of that reporter.

> *Neb.* is an abbreviation for *Nebraska Reports,* Nebraska's official reports of the decisions of its highest court, the Nebraska Supreme Court.

19 Cal.App.5th 495, 228 Cal.Rptr.3d 169 (2018)

> *Cal.Rptr.* is the abbreviation for the unofficial reports—titled *California Reporter*—of the decisions of California courts.

157 A.D.3d 486, 69 N.Y.S.3d 26 (2018)

> *N.Y.S.* is the abbreviation for the unofficial reports—titled *New York Supplement*—of the decisions of New York courts.

> *A.D.* is the abbreviation for the *New York Appellate Division Reports*, which hears appeals from the New York Supreme Court—the state's general trial court. The New York Court of Appeals is the state's highest court, analogous to other states' supreme courts.

343 Ga.App. 889, 808 S.E.2d 891 (2018)

> *Ga.App.* is the abbreviation for *Georgia Appeals Reports,* Georgia's official reports of the decisions of its court of appeals.

FEDERAL COURTS

___ U.S. ___ , 138 S.Ct. 617, 199 L.Ed.2d 501 (2018)

> *L.Ed.* is an abbreviation for *Lawyers' Edition of the Supreme Court Reports*, an unofficial edition of decisions of the United States Supreme Court.

> *S.Ct.* is the abbreviation for *Supreme Court Reporter,* an unofficial edition of decisions of the United States Supreme Court.

> *U.S.* is the abbreviation for *United States Reports,* the official edition of the decisions of the United States Supreme Court. The blank lines in this citation (or any other citation) indicate that the appropriate volume of the case reporter has not yet been published and no page number is available.

a. The case names have been deleted from these citations to emphasize the publications. It should be kept in mind, however, that the name of a case is as important as the specific page numbers in the volumes in which it is found. If a citation is incorrect, the correct citation may be found in a publication's index of case names. In addition to providing a check on errors in citations, the date of a case is important because the value of a recent case as an authority is likely to be greater than that of older cases from the same court.

Exhibit 1A–2 How to Read Citations—Continued

FEDERAL COURTS (Continued)

879 F.3d 1052 (9th Cir. 2018)

> *9th Cir.* is an abbreviation denoting that this case was decided in the U.S. Court of Appeals for the Ninth Circuit.

___ F.Supp.3d ___, 2018 WL 388590 (W.D.Wash. 2018)

> *W.D.Wash.* is an abbreviation indicating that the U.S. District Court for the Western District of Washington decided this case.

WESTLAW® CITATIONS[b]

2018 WL 416255

> *WL* is an abbreviation for Westlaw. The number 2018 is the year of the document that can be found with this citation in the Westlaw database. The number 416255 is a number assigned to a specific document. A higher number indicates that a document was added to the Westlaw database later in the year.

STATUTORY AND OTHER CITATIONS

18 U.S.C. Section 1961(1)(A)

> *U.S.C.* denotes *United States Code*, the codification of *United States Statutes at Large*. The number 18 refers to the statute's U.S.C. title number and 1961 to its section number within that title. The number 1 in parentheses refers to a subsection within the section, and the letter A in parentheses to a subsection within the subsection.

UCC 2–206(1)(b)

> *UCC* is an abbreviation for *Uniform Commercial Code*. The first number 2 is a reference to an article of the UCC, and 206 to a section within that article. The number 1 in parentheses refers to a subsection within the section, and the letter b in parentheses to a subsection within the subsection.

***Restatement (Third) of Torts,* Section 6**

> *Restatement (Third) of Torts* refers to the third edition of the American Law Institute's *Restatement of the Law of Torts*. The number 6 refers to a specific section.

17 C.F.R. Section 230.505

> *C.F.R.* is an abbreviation for *Code of Federal Regulations*, a compilation of federal administrative regulations. The number 17 designates the regulation's title number, and 230.505 designates a specific section within that title.

b. Many court decisions that are not yet published or that are not intended for publication can be accessed through Westlaw, an online legal database.

Case Titles and Terminology

The title of a case, such as *Adams v. Jones*, indicates the names of the parties to the lawsuit. The v. in the case title stands for versus, which means "against." In the trial court, Adams was the plaintiff—the person who filed the suit. Jones was the defendant.

If the case is appealed, however, the appellate court will sometimes place the name of the party appealing the decision first, so the case may be called *Jones v. Adams*. Because some reviewing courts retain the trial court order of names, it is often impossible to distinguish the plaintiff from the defendant in the title of a reported appellate court decision. You must carefully read the facts of each case to identify the parties.

The following terms and phrases are frequently encountered in court opinions and legal publications. Because it is important to understand what these terms and phrases mean, we define and discuss them here.

Parties to Lawsuits The party initiating a lawsuit is referred to as the *plaintiff* or *petitioner*, depending on the nature of the action, and the party against whom a lawsuit is brought is the *defendant* or *respondent*. Lawsuits frequently involve more than one plaintiff and/or defendant.

When a case is appealed from the original court or jurisdiction to another court or jurisdiction, the party appealing the case is called the *appellant*. The *appellee* is the party against whom the appeal is taken. (In some appellate courts, the party appealing a case is referred to as the *petitioner*, and the party against whom the suit is brought or appealed is called the *respondent*.)

Judges and Justices The terms *judge* and *justice* are usually synonymous and are used to refer to the judges in various courts. All members of the United States Supreme Court, for instance, are referred to as justices. Justice is the formal title usually given to judges of appellate courts, although this is not always the case. In New York, a justice is a judge of the trial court (which is called the Supreme Court), and a member of the Court of Appeals (the state's highest court) is called a judge. The term *justice* is commonly abbreviated to J., and justices to JJ. A Supreme Court case might refer to Justice Sotomayor as Sotomayor, J., or to Chief Justice Roberts as Roberts, C.J.

Decisions and Opinions Most decisions reached by reviewing, or appellate, courts are explained in written *opinions*. The opinion contains the court's reasons for its decision, the rules of law that apply, and the judgment. You may encounter several types of opinions as you read appellate cases, including the following:

- When all the judges (or justices) agree, a *unanimous opinion* is written for the entire court.

- When there is not unanimous agreement, a **majority opinion** is generally written. It outlines the views of the majority of the judges deciding the case.

- A judge who agrees (concurs) with the majority opinion as to the result but not as to the legal reasoning often writes a **concurring opinion**. In it, the judge sets out the reasoning that he or she considers correct.

- A **dissenting opinion** presents the views of one or more judges who disagree with the majority view.

- Sometimes, no single position is fully supported by a majority of the judges deciding a case. In this situation, we may have a **plurality opinion**. This is the opinion that has the support of the largest number of judges, but the group in agreement is less than a majority.

- Finally, a court occasionally issues a ***per curiam* opinion** (*per curiam* is Latin for "of the court"), which does not indicate which judge wrote the opinion.

Majority Opinion A court opinion that represents the views of the majority (more than half) of the judges or justices deciding the case.

Concurring Opinion A court opinion by one or more judges or justices who agree with the majority but want to make or emphasize a point that was not made or emphasized in the majority's opinion.

Dissenting Opinion A court opinion that presents the views of one or more judges or justices who disagree with the majority's decision.

Plurality Opinion A court opinion that is joined by the largest number of the judges or justices hearing the case, but less than half of the total number.

***Per Curiam* Opinion** A court opinion that does not indicate which judge or justice authored the opinion.

A Sample Court Case

To illustrate the various elements contained in a court opinion, we present an annotated court opinion in Exhibit 1A–3. The opinion is from an actual case that the United States Court of Appeals for the Tenth Circuit decided in 2018.

Exhibit 1A–3 A Sample Court Case

This section contains the citation—the name of the case, the name of the court that heard the case, the reporters in which the court's opinion can be found, and the year of the decision.	**YEASIN v. DURHAM** United States Court of Appeals, Tenth Circuit, 719 Fed.Appx. 844 (2018).
This line provides the name of the judge (or justice) who authored the court's opinion.	Gregory A. *PHILLIPS*, Circuit Judge. * * * *
The court divides the opinion into sections, each headed by an explanatory heading. The first section summarizes the facts of the case.	**BACKGROUND** * * * *

[Navid] Yeasin and A.W. [were students at the University of Kansas when they] dated from the fall of 2012 through June 2013. On June 28, 2013, Yeasin physically restrained A.W. in his car, took her phone from her, threatened to commit suicide if she broke up with him, threatened to spread rumors about her, and threatened to make the University of Kansas's "campus environment so hostile, that she would not attend any university in the state of Kansas."

Battery is an unexcused and harmful or offensive physical contact intentionally performed.

For this conduct, Kansas charged Yeasin with * * * **battery** * * * . A.W. * * * obtained a **protection order** against Yeasin.

A *protection order* is an order issued by a court that protects a person by requiring another person to do, or not to do, something. The order can protect someone from being physically or sexually threatened or harassed.

* * * A.W. filed a complaint against Yeasin with the university's Office of Institutional Opportunity and Access (IOA). * * * The IOA * * * issued * * * a

A *no-contact order* prohibits a person from being in contact with another person.

no-contact order * * * [that] "prohibited [Yeasin] from initiating, or contributing through third-parties, to any physical, verbal, electronic, or written communication with A.W., her family, her friends or her associates."

[Despite the order,] Yeasin posted more than a dozen tweets about A.W., including disparaging comments about her body.

A *hearing* is a proceeding before a decision-making body. Testimony and other evidence can be presented to help determine the issue.

[The university held a **hearing** to **adjudicate** A.W.'s complaint against Yeasin. Both

To *adjudicate* is to hear evidence and arguments in order to determine and resolve a dispute.

parties testified. The hearing panel submitted the **record** to Dr. Tammara Durham, the university's vice provost for student affairs, for a decision regarding whether and how to

A *record* is a written account of proceedings.

sanction Yeasin's conduct.]

Exhibit 1A–3 A Sample Court Case, Continued

Sexual harassment can consist of language or conduct that is so offensive it creates a hostile environment.

First Amendment rights include the freedom of speech, which is the right to express oneself without government interference. This right is guaranteed under the First Amendment to the U.S. Constitution.

Moved to dismiss means that a party filed a motion (applied to the court to obtain an order) to dismiss a claim on the ground that it had no basis in law.

To *appeal* is to request an appellate court to review the decision of a lower court.

The second major section of the opinion responds to the party's appeal.

An *enclave* is a distinct group within a larger community.

To *circumscribe* is to restrict.

* * * Durham found that Yeasin's June 28, 2013 conduct and his tweets were "so severe, pervasive and objectively offensive that it interfered with A.W.'s academic performance and equal opportunity to participate in or benefit from University programs or activities." She found that his tweets violated the [university's] **sexual-harassment** policy because they were "unwelcome comments about A.W.'s body." And she found that his conduct "threatened the physical health, safety and welfare of A.W., making the conduct a violation of * * * the [university's Student] Code."

* * * Durham * * * expelled Yeasin from the university and banned him from campus.

* * * *

Yeasin contested his expulsion in a Kansas state court. The court set aside Yeasin's expulsion, reasoning that * * * "KU and Dr. Durham erroneously interpreted the Student Code of Conduct by applying it to off-campus conduct."

* * * *

Yeasin then brought this suit in federal court, claiming that Dr. Durham had violated his **First Amendment rights** by expelling him for * * * off-campus speech. * * * Dr. Durham **moved to dismiss** * * * Yeasin's claim * * * . The * * * court granted the motion after concluding that Dr. Durham hadn't violated Yeasin's clearly established rights.

[Yeasin **appealed** to the U.S. Court of Appeals for the Tenth Circuit.]

DISCUSSION

* * * *

Yeasin's case presents interesting questions regarding the tension between some students' free-speech rights and other students' * * * rights to receive an education absent * * * sexual harassment.

Colleges and universities are not **enclaves** immune from the sweep of the First Amendment. * * * The [courts] permit schools to **circumscribe** students' free-speech rights in certain contexts [particularly in secondary public schools].

* * * *

(Continues)

Exhibit 1A–3 A Sample Court Case, Continued

Yeasin argues that [three United States Supreme Court cases—*Papish v. Board of Curators of the University of Missouri*, *Healy v. James*, and *Widmar v. Vincent*] clearly **establish** * * *

> Here, *establish* means to settle firmly.

that universities may not restrict university-student speech in the same way secondary public school officials may restrict secondary-school student speech. * * * Yeasin argues these cases clearly establish his right to tweet about A.W. without the university being able to place restrictions on, or discipline him for, * * * his tweets.

> Judges are obligated to follow the precedents established in prior court decisions. A *precedent* is a decision that stands as authority for deciding a subsequent case involving identical or similar facts. Otherwise, the decision may be persuasive, but it is not controlling.

But **none of the * * * cases present circumstances similar to his own**. *Papish*, *Healy*, and *Widmar* don't concern university-student conduct that interferes with the rights of other students or risks disrupting campus order.

* * * *

* * * In those cases no student had been charged with a crime against another student and followed that up with sexually-harassing comments affecting her ability to feel safe while attending classes. Dr. Durham had a **reasonable belief** based on the June 28, 2013 incident

> A *reasonable belief* exists when there is a reasonable basis to believe that a crime or other violation is being or has been committed.

and on Yeasin's tweets that his continued enrollment at the university threatened to disrupt A.W.'s education and interfere with her rights.

At the intersection of university speech and social media, First Amendment **doctrine** is

> A *doctrine* is a rule, principle, or tenet of the law.

unsettled. Compare *Keefe v. Adams* [in which a federal appellate court concluded] that a college's removal of a student from school based on off-campus statements on his social media page didn't violate his First Amendment free-speech rights, with *J.S. v. Blue Mountain School District* [in which a different federal appellate court held] that a school district violated the First Amendment rights of a plaintiff when it suspended her for creating a private social media profile mocking the school principal.

In conclusion, Yeasin can't establish that Dr. Durham violated clearly established law when she expelled him, in part, for his * * * off-campus tweets.

> In the third major section of the opinion, the court states its decision.

* * * *

CONCLUSION

> To *affirm* a lower court's ruling is to validate the decision and give it legal force.

For the reasons stated, we **AFFIRM** the [lower] court's grant of Dr. Durham's motion to dismiss.

Cases Presented in This Text Note that the cases in this text have already been analyzed and partially briefed by the author. The essential aspects of each case are presented in a convenient format consisting of three basic sections: *Background and Facts, In the Words of the Court* (excerpts from the court's opinion), and *Decision and Remedy*.

In addition to this basic format, each case is followed by one or two *Critical Thinking questions* regarding some issue raised by the case. We offer these questions as tools to help you develop your critical-thinking and legal reasoning skills. Finally, a section entitled *Impact of This Case on Today's Law* concludes the *Classic Cases* that appear in selected chapters to indicate the significance of the case for today's legal landscape.

Editorial Practice You will note that triple asterisks (* * *) and quadruple asterisks (* * * *) frequently appear in the excerpted court opinions. The triple asterisks indicate that we have deleted a few words or sentences from the opinion for the sake of readability or brevity. Quadruple asterisks mean that an entire paragraph (or more) has been omitted. Additionally, when the opinion cites another case or legal source, the citation to the case or source has been omitted, again for the sake of readability and brevity. These editorial practices are continued in the other court opinions presented in this book. Lastly, whenever we present a court opinion that includes a term or phrase that may not be readily understandable, a bracketed definition or paraphrase has been added.

How to Brief Cases

Knowing how to read and understand court opinions and the legal reasoning used by the courts is an essential step in performing legal research. A further step is "briefing," or summarizing, the case. Briefing cases facilitates the development of critical-thinking skills that are crucial for businesspersons when evaluating relevant business law.

Legal researchers routinely brief cases by reducing the texts of the opinions to their essential elements. Generally, when you brief a case, you first summarize the background and facts of the case, as the authors have done for most of the cases presented in this text. You then indicate the issue (or issues) before the court. An important element in the case brief is, of course, the court's decision on the issue and the legal reasoning used by the court in reaching that decision.

There is a fairly standard procedure that you follow when you "brief" any court case. You must first read the case opinion carefully. When you feel that you understand the case, you can prepare a brief of it. Although the format of the brief may vary, typically it will present the essentials of the case under headings such as the following:

1. **Citation.** Give the full citation for the case, including the name of the case, the court that decided it, and the year it was decided.

2. **Facts.** Briefly indicate (a) the reasons for the lawsuit, (b) the identity and arguments of the plaintiff(s) and defendant(s), respectively, and (c) the lower court's decision—if the decision is from a reviewing court.

3. **Issue.** Concisely phrase, in the form of a question, the essential issue before the court. (If more than one issue is involved, you may have two—or even more—questions.)

4. **Decision.** Indicate here—with a "yes" or "no," if possible—the court's answer to the question (or questions) in the *Issue* section.

5. **Reason.** Summarize as briefly as possible the reasons given by the court for its decision (or decisions) and the case or statutory law relied on by the court in arriving at its decision.

See this chapter's *Business Law Analysis* feature for a sample case brief and a discussion of how the brief relates to the IRAC method of legal reasoning.

Case Briefing and IRAC Legal Reasoning

Here is a sample case brief of the opinion shown in Exhibit 1A–3.

1. **Citation.** *Yeasin v. Durham*, United States Court of Appeals for the Tenth Circuit, 719 Fed.Appx. 844 (2018).

2. **Facts.** Navid Yeasin and A.W. were students at the University of Kansas (KU). They dated for about nine months. When A.W. tried to end the relationship, Yeasin restrained her in his car, took her phone, and threatened to make the "campus environment so hostile that she would not attend any university in the state of Kansas." He repeatedly tweeted disparaging comments about her. Tammara Durham, the university's vice provost for student affairs, found that Yeasin's conduct and tweets violated the school's student code of conduct and sexual-harassment policy. She expelled him. Yeasin filed a suit in a Kansas state court against Durham, and the university reinstated him. He then filed a suit in a federal district court against Durham, claiming that she had violated his First Amendment rights by expelling him for the content of his off-campus speech. The court dismissed the claim. Yeasin appealed to the U.S. Court of Appeals for the Tenth Circuit.

3. **Issue.** Could KU and Dr. Durham expel Yeasin for his tweets?

4. **Decision.** Yes. The U.S. Court of Appeals for the Tenth Circuit affirmed the lower court's dismissal of Yeasin's suit. "Yeasin can't establish that Dr. Durham violated clearly established law when she expelled him."

5. **Reason.** Taken together, court decisions show that "at the intersection of university speech and social media,

First Amendment doctrine is unsettled." In some cases, the courts permit schools to circumscribe students' free-speech rights in certain contexts. Yeasin argued, however, that three cases decided by the United States Supreme Court clearly established his right to tweet about A.W. without the university being able to place restrictions on, or discipline him for, his tweets. In response, the court here pointed out that those cases did not involve circumstances similar to Yeasin's situation. In those cases, no student had been charged with a crime against another student and then made sexually harassing comments affecting her ability to feel safe while attending classes. And, the court concluded, in this case Dr. Durham could reasonably believe, based on Yeasin's conduct and his tweets, that his presence at the university would disrupt A.W.'s education and interfere with her rights.

Analysis: Notice how the sections in a case brief include the information necessary to perform IRAC legal reasoning. (Recall from the chapter that IRAC stands for *Issue, Rule of Law, Application*, and *Conclusion*.) Step 1 in IRAC reasoning is *Issue*. You need to understand the relevant facts, identify the plaintiff and defendant, and determine the specific issue presented by the case. You will find this information in the first two sections of your brief. The *Facts* section identifies the plaintiff and the defendant. Yeasin is the plaintiff. Dr. Tammara Durham is the defendant. The *Facts* also describes the events leading up to this suit and the allegations made by the plaintiff in the suit. Because this case is a decision of one of the U.S. courts of

appeals, the lower court's ruling, the party appealing, and the appellant's contention on appeal are included here.

It is important to carefully frame the issue so that you can look for the appropriate *Rule of law* that will guide a decision. In this case, the court considers whether the University of Kansas, where Yeasin was a student, and Dr. Durham, the university's vice provost for student affairs, violated clearly established law when they expelled him.

Result and Reasoning: The *Reason* section includes references to the relevant laws and legal principles that the court applied in coming to the conclusion arrived at in the case. The *Rule of Law* in this case included court decisions on whether, and in what circumstances, schools can circumscribe students' free-speech rights. The *Reason* section also explains the court's *Application* of the law to the facts in this case. Because Yeasin was charged with a crime for sexually harassing tweets that caused another student to fear for her safety, the court reasoned that the university had legitimate reasons for disciplining him. Dr. Durham could reasonably believe that Yeasin's presence at the university would disrupt A.W.'s education and interfere with her rights. The court arrived at the *Conclusion* that this was one of those contexts in which a court will permit a school to circumscribe students' free-speech rights.

Constitutional Law

"The United States Constitution has proved itself the most marvelously elastic compilation of rules of government ever written."

Franklin D. Roosevelt
1882–1945
(Thirty-second president of the United States, 1933–1945)

The U.S. Constitution is brief. It contains only about seven thousand words—less than one-third as many as the average state constitution. Its brevity explains, in part, why the Constitution has proved to be so "marvelously elastic," as Franklin Roosevelt described it in the chapter-opening quotation. It might also explain why the U.S. Constitution has survived for more than two hundred years—longer than any other written constitution in the world.

Laws that govern business have their origin in the lawmaking authority granted by the Constitution. Neither Congress nor any state can enact a law that conflicts with the Constitution.

Disputes over constitutional rights frequently come before the courts. Consider Norman's, Inc., a family-owned pharmacy in Olympia, Washington. The owners of Norman's have religious objections to the use of Plan B emergency contraception ("the morning-after pill"). Nevertheless, Washington state requires every pharmacy to stock an assortment of drugs approved by the Food and Drug Administration (FDA). In addition, Washington state has enacted new administrative rules that effectively prevent pharmacies from refusing to provide FDA-approved devices or drugs (such as Plan B contraception) to patients for religious reasons.

Norman's owners believe that these state administrative rules violate their constitutional rights to freedom of religion and equal protection, and file a suit against Washington State Department of Health. Do these rules violate the free exercise clause? Do they violate the equal protection clause? In this chapter, we examine these and other constitutional issues that businesses and courts must deal with in today's world.

Learning Objectives

The four Learning Objectives below are designed to help improve your understanding. After reading this chapter, you should be able to answer the following questions:

1. What constitutional clause gives the federal government the power to regulate commercial activities among the states?

2. What is the Bill of Rights? What freedoms does the First Amendment guarantee?

3. Where in the Constitution can the due process clause be found?

4. Which constitutional amendments have been interpreted as implying a right to privacy?

2–1 The Constitutional Powers of Government

Following the Revolutionary War, the United States created a *confederal* form of government in which the states had the authority to govern themselves and the national government could exercise only limited powers. When problems arose because the nation was facing an economic crisis and state laws interfered with the free flow of commerce, a national convention was called. The delegates drafted the U.S. Constitution. This document, after its ratification by the states in 1789, became the basis for an entirely new form of government.

2–1a A Federal Form of Government

The new government created by the Constitution reflected a series of compromises made by the convention delegates on various issues. Some delegates wanted sovereign power to remain with the states, whereas others wanted the national government alone to exercise sovereign power. The end result was a compromise—a **federal form of government** in which the national government and the states *share* sovereign power.

Federal Powers The Constitution sets forth specific powers that can be exercised by the national government. It also provides that the national government has the implied power to undertake actions necessary to carry out its expressly designated powers. All other powers are "reserved" to the states.

Federal Form of Government A system of government in which the states form a union and the sovereign power is divided between the central government and the member states.

Sovereignty The power of a state to do what is necessary to govern itself. Individual state sovereignty is determined by the U.S. Constitution.

Police Powers Powers possessed by the states as part of their inherent sovereignty. These powers may be exercised to protect or promote the public order, health, safety, morals, and general welfare.

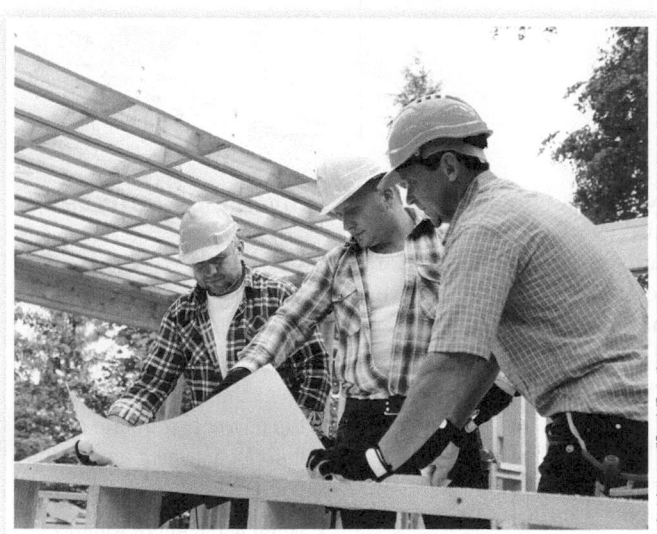

Because the Constitution reserves to the states all powers not delegated to the national government, the states can and do regulate many types of commercial activities within their borders. So, too, do municipalities. One of these powers is the imposition of building codes. What is the general term that applies to such powers?

elenaleonova/iStock/Getty Images

Regulatory Powers of the States As part of their inherent **sovereignty** (power to govern themselves), state governments have the authority to regulate certain affairs within their borders. This authority stems, in part, from the Tenth Amendment, which reserves all powers not delegated to the national government to the states or to the people.

State regulatory powers are often referred to as **police powers.** The term encompasses more than just the enforcement of criminal laws. Police powers also give a state government broad rights to regulate private activities to protect or promote the public order, health, safety, morals, and general welfare. Fire and building codes, antidiscrimination laws, parking regulations, zoning restrictions, licensing requirements, and thousands of other state statutes have been enacted pursuant to states' police powers. Local governments, such as cities, also exercise police powers.

2–1b Relations among the States

The U.S. Constitution also includes provisions concerning relations among the states in our federal system. Particularly important are the *privileges and immunities clause* and the *full faith and credit clause*.

Privileges and Immunities Clause Article IV, Section 2, of the U.S. Constitution requires states not to discriminate against one another's citizens. A resident of one state, when in another state, cannot be denied the privileges and immunities of that state.

The Privileges and Immunities Clause Article IV, Section 2, of the Constitution provides that the "Citizens of each State shall be entitled to all Privileges and Immunities of Citizens in the several States." This clause is often referred to as the interstate **privileges and immunities clause.** It prevents a state from imposing unreasonable burdens on citizens of another state—particularly with regard to means of livelihood or doing business.

When a citizen of one state engages in basic and essential activities in another state (the "foreign state"), the foreign state must have a *substantial reason* for treating the nonresident differently than its own residents. Basic activities include transferring property, seeking employment, and accessing the court system. The foreign state must also establish that its reason for the discrimination is *substantially related* to the state's ultimate purpose in adopting the legislation or regulating the activity.

The Full Faith and Credit Clause Article IV, Section 1, of the U.S. Constitution provides that "Full Faith and Credit shall be given in each State to the public Acts, Records, and judicial Proceedings of every other State." This clause, which is referred to as the **full faith and credit clause,** applies only to civil matters. It ensures that rights established under deeds, wills, contracts, and similar instruments in one state will be honored by other states. It also ensures that any judicial decision with respect to such property rights will be honored and enforced in all states.

The legal issues raised by same-sex marriage involve, among other things, the full faith and credit clause, because that clause requires each state to honor marriage decrees issued by another state. See this chapter's *Managerial Strategy* feature for a discussion of marriage equality laws.

Full Faith and Credit Clause
A provision in Article IV, Section 1, of the U.S. Constitution that ensures that rights established under deeds, wills, contracts, and similar instruments in one state will be honored by other states and that judicial decisions will be honored and enforced in all states.

Marriage Equality and the Constitution

Managerial Strategy

The debate over same-sex marriage has been raging across the country for years. The legal issues raised by marriage equality involve privacy rights and equal protection. Although marriage equality may not appear at first glance to be business related, it is an important legal issue for managers. Companies like Barilla USA, Chick-fil-A, Exxon Mobil, and Target Corporation have lost significant business for purportedly supporting antigay organizations and legislation.

The Definition of Marriage

Before 1996, federal law did not define marriage, and the U.S. government recognized any marriage that was recognized by a state. Then Congress passed the Defense of Marriage Act (DOMA), which explicitly defined *marriage* as the union of one man and one woman. DOMA was later challenged, and a number of federal courts found it to be unconstitutional in the context of bankruptcy, public employee benefits, and estate taxes. In 2013, the United States Supreme Court struck down part of DOMA as unconstitutional.[a] Today, once again, no federal law defines marriage.

Bans on Same-Sex Marriage Eliminated by the Supreme Court

Over time, federal courts became increasingly likely to invalidate state bans on same-sex marriage. In 2013, a federal district court held that Utah's same-sex marriage ban was unconstitutional.[b] In 2014, federal district courts in Arkansas, Mississippi, and Oklahoma struck down state same-sex marriage bans.[c] Moreover, public sentiment on the issue had shifted, and more states recognized the rights of same-sex couples. By 2015, thirty-seven states, as well as the District of Columbia, had legalized same-sex marriage.

Ultimately, the United States Supreme Court determined that the remaining state-level prohibitions on same-sex marriage were unconstitutional. In a landmark decision, the Court ruled that the Fourteenth Amendment requires individual states to (1) issue marriage licenses to same-sex couples and (2) recognize

same-sex marriages performed in other states.[d]

The landmark Supreme Court decision requiring all states to recognize same-sex marriage means that businesses must make adjustments. Company policies need to be revised to specify how same-sex partners will be treated in terms of family and medical leave, health-insurance coverage, pensions, and other benefits.

Business Questions

1. *Can a business manager's religious beliefs legally factor into the business's hiring and treatment of same-sex partners? Why or why not?*

2. *Must business owners in all states provide the same benefits to employees in a same-sex union as they do to heterosexual couples?*

a. *United States v. Windsor,* 570 U.S. 744, 133 S.Ct. 2675, 186 L.Ed.2d 808 (2013).

b. *Kitchen v. Herbert,* 961 F.Supp.2d 1181 (D.Utah 2013).
c. *Campaign for Southern Equality v. Bryant,* 64 F.Supp.3d 906 (S.D.Miss. 2014); *Jernigan v. Crane,* 64 F.Supp.3d 1260 (E.D.Ark. 2014); and *Bishop v. U.S. ex rel. Holder,* 962 F.Supp.2d 1252 (N.D.Okla. 2014).

d. *Obergefell v. Hodges,* ___ U.S. ___, 135 S.Ct. 2584, 192 L.Ed.2d 609 (2015). See also, *Pavan v. Smith,* ___ U.S. ___, 137 S.Ct. 2075, 198 L.Ed.2d 636 (2017).

How did the U.S. Constitution's full faith and credit clause affect the issue of equality for same-sex marriages?

The full faith and credit clause has contributed to the unity of American citizens because it protects their legal rights as they move about from state to state. It also protects the rights of those to whom they owe obligations, such as persons who have been awarded monetary damages by courts. The ability to enforce such rights is extremely important for the conduct of business in a country with a very mobile citizenry.

2–1c The Separation of Powers

To make it difficult for the national government to use its power arbitrarily, the Constitution divided the national government's powers among the three branches of government. The legislative branch makes the laws, the executive branch enforces the laws, and the judicial branch interprets the laws. Each branch performs a separate function, and no branch may exercise the authority of another branch.

Checks and Balances The system under which the powers of the national government are divided among three separate branches—the executive, legislative, and judicial branches— each of which exercises a check on the actions of the others.

Additionally, a system of **checks and balances** allows each branch to limit the actions of the other two branches, thus preventing any one branch from exercising too much power. The following are examples of these checks and balances:

1. The legislative branch (Congress) can enact a law, but the executive branch (the president) has the constitutional authority to veto that law.

2. The executive branch is responsible for foreign affairs, but treaties with foreign governments require the advice and consent of the Senate.

3. Congress determines the jurisdiction of the federal courts, and the president appoints federal judges, with the advice and consent of the Senate. The judicial branch has the power to hold actions of the other two branches unconstitutional.

2–1d The Commerce Clause

To prevent states from establishing laws and regulations that would interfere with trade and commerce among the states, the Constitution explicitly gave the national government the power to regulate interstate commerce. Article I, Section 8, of the U.S. Constitution expressly permits Congress "[t]o regulate Commerce with foreign Nations, and among the several States, and with the Indian Tribes." This clause, referred to as the **commerce clause,** has had a greater impact on business than any other provision in the Constitution.

Commerce Clause The provision in Article I, Section 8, of the U.S. Constitution that gives Congress the power to regulate interstate commerce.

Initially, the commerce power was interpreted as being limited to *interstate* commerce (commerce among the states) and not applicable to *intrastate* commerce (commerce within a state). In 1824, however, the United States Supreme Court decided the case of *Gibbons v. Ogden* (see this chapter's *Landmark in the Law* feature). The Court ruled that commerce within a state could also be regulated by the national government as long as the commerce *substantially affected* commerce involving more than one state.

Learning Objective 1

What constitutional clause gives the federal government the power to regulate commercial activities among the states?

The Expansion of National Powers under the Commerce Clause As the nation grew and faced new kinds of problems, the commerce clause became a vehicle for the additional expansion of the national government's regulatory powers. Even activities that seemed purely local came under the regulatory reach of the national government if those activities were deemed to substantially affect interstate commerce. In 1942, the Supreme

SolStock/iStock/Getty Images

Gibbons v. Ogden (1824)

The commerce clause of the U.S. Constitution gives Congress the power "[t]o regulate Commerce with foreign Nations, and among the several States, and with the Indian Tribes." Before the commerce clause came into existence, states tended to restrict commerce within and beyond their borders, which made trade more costly and inefficient. The goal of the clause was to unify the states' commerce policies and improve the efficiency of exchanges.

The problem was that although the commerce clause gave Congress some authority to regulate trade among the states, the extent of that power was unclear. What exactly does "to regulate commerce" mean? What does "commerce" entail? These questions came before the United States Supreme Court in 1824 in the case of *Gibbons v. Ogden*.[a]

Background In 1803, Robert Fulton, the inventor of the steamboat, and Robert Livingston, who was the ambassador to France, secured a monopoly from the New York legislature on steam navigation on the waters in the state of New York. Their monopoly extended to interstate waters—waterways between New York and another state. Fulton and Livingston licensed Aaron Ogden, a former governor of New Jersey and a U.S. senator, to operate steam-powered ferryboats between New York and New Jersey.

Thomas Gibbons already operated a ferry service between New Jersey and New York, which had been licensed by Congress under a 1793 act regulating trade along the coast. Although the federal government had licensed Gibbons to operate boats in interstate waters, he did not have the state of New York's permission to compete with Ogden in that area. Ogden sued Gibbons. The New York state courts granted Ogden's request for an injunction—an order prohibiting Gibbons from operating in New York waters. Gibbons appealed the decision to the United States Supreme Court.

Marshall's Decision The issue before the Court was whether the law regulated commerce that was "among the several states." The chief justice on the Supreme Court was John Marshall, an advocate of a strong national government. Marshall defined the word *commerce* as used in the commerce clause to mean all commercial intercourse—that is, all business dealings that affect more than one state. This broader definition included navigation.

In addition to expanding the definition of commerce, Marshall also validated and increased the power of the national legislature to regulate commerce. Said Marshall, "What is this power? It is the power . . . to prescribe the rule by which commerce is to be governed."

Marshall held that the power to regulate interstate commerce is an exclusive power of the national government. This power includes the power to regulate any intrastate commerce that substantially affects interstate commerce. Accordingly, the Court decided in favor of Gibbons.

Application to Today's World
Marshall's broad definition of the commerce power established the foundation for the expansion of national powers in the years to come. Today, the national government continues to rely on the commerce clause for its constitutional authority to regulate business activities.

Marshall's conclusion that the power to regulate interstate commerce was an exclusive power of the national government has also had significant consequences. By implication, this means that a state cannot regulate activities that extend beyond its borders, such as out-of-state online gambling operations that affect the welfare of in-state citizens. It also means that state regulations over in-state activities normally will be invalidated if the regulations substantially burden interstate commerce.

a. 22 U.S. (9 Wheat.) 1, 6 L.Ed. 23 (1824).

Court held that wheat production by an individual farmer intended wholly for consumption on his own farm was subject to federal regulation.[1]

The following *Classic Case* involved a challenge to the scope of the national government's constitutional authority to regulate local activities.

---

1. *Wickard v. Filburn*, 317 U.S. 111, 63 S.Ct. 82, 87 L.Ed. 122 (1942).

Classic Case 2.1

Heart of Atlanta Motel v. United States

Supreme Court of the United States, 379 U.S. 241, 85 S.Ct. 348, 13 L.Ed.2d 258 (1964).

Background and Facts In the 1950s, the United States Supreme Court ruled that racial segregation imposed by the states in school systems and other public facilities violated the Constitution. Privately owned facilities were not affected until Congress passed the Civil Rights Act of 1964, which prohibited racial discrimination in "establishments affecting interstate commerce."

President Lyndon Johnson signs the 1964 Civil Rights Act.

LBJ Library photo by Cecil Stoughton

The owner of the Heart of Atlanta Motel, in violation of the Civil Rights Act of 1964, refused to rent rooms to African Americans. The motel owner brought an action in a federal district court to have the Civil Rights Act declared unconstitutional on the ground that Congress had exceeded its constitutional authority to regulate commerce by enacting the statute.

The owner argued that his motel was not engaged in interstate commerce but was "of a purely local character." The motel, however, was accessible to state and interstate highways. The owner advertised nationally, maintained billboards throughout the state, and accepted convention trade from outside the state (75 percent of the guests were residents of other states).

The district court ruled that the act did not violate the Constitution and enjoined (prohibited) the owner from discriminating on the basis of race. The owner appealed. The case ultimately went to the United States Supreme Court.

In the Words of the Court
Mr. Justice *CLARKE* delivered the opinion of the Court.

* * * *

While the Act as adopted carried no congressional findings, the record of its passage through each house is replete with evidence of the burdens that discrimination by race or color places upon interstate commerce * * * . This testimony included the fact that our people have become increasingly mobile with millions of all races traveling from State to State; that Negroes in particular have been the subject of discrimination in transient accommodations, having to travel great distances to secure the same; that often they have been unable to obtain accommodations and have had to call upon friends to put them up overnight. * * * These exclusionary practices were found to be nationwide, the Under Secretary of Commerce testifying that there is "no question that this discrimination in the North still exists to a large degree" and in the West and Midwest as well * * * .

This testimony indicated a qualitative as well as quantitative effect on interstate travel by Negroes. The former was the obvious impairment of the Negro traveler's pleasure and convenience that resulted when he continually was uncertain of finding lodging. As for the latter, there was evidence that this uncertainty stemming from racial discrimination had the effect of discouraging travel on the part of a substantial portion of the Negro community * * * . We shall not burden this opinion with further details since the voluminous testimony presents overwhelming evidence that discrimination by hotels and motels impedes interstate travel.

* * * *

It is said that the operation of the motel here is of a purely local character. But, assuming this to be true, "if it is interstate commerce that feels the pinch, it does not matter how local the operation that applies the squeeze." * * * *Thus the power of Congress to promote interstate commerce also includes the power to regulate the local incidents thereof, including local activities in both the States of origin and destination, which might have a substantial and harmful effect upon that commerce.* [Emphasis added.]

Decision and Remedy The United States Supreme Court upheld the constitutionality of the Civil Rights Act of 1964. The power of Congress to regulate interstate commerce permitted the enactment of legislation that could halt local discriminatory practices.

Critical Thinking

• **What If the Facts Were Different?** *If this case had involved a small, private retail business that did not advertise nationally, would the result have been the same? Why or why not?*

• **Impact of This Case on Today's Law** *If the United States Supreme Court had invalidated the Civil Rights Act of 1964, the legal landscape of the United States would be much different today. The act prohibits discrimination based on race, color, national origin, religion, or gender in all "public accommodations," including hotels and restaurants. The act also prohibits discrimination in employment based on these criteria. Although state laws now prohibit many of these forms of discrimination as well, the protections available vary from state to state—and it is not certain whether such laws would have been passed had the outcome in this case been different.*

The Commerce Clause Today   Today, at least theoretically, the power over commerce authorizes the national government to regulate almost every commercial enterprise in the United States. The breadth of the commerce clause permits the national government to legislate in areas in which Congress has not explicitly been granted power. Only occasionally has the Supreme Court curbed the national government's regulatory authority under the commerce clause.

The Supreme Court has, for instance, allowed the federal government to regulate noncommercial activities relating to medical marijuana that take place wholly within a state's borders. **⁕ Spotlight Case Example 2.1**   More than half the states, including California, have adopted laws that legalize marijuana for medical purposes (and a handful of states now permit the recreational use of marijuana). Marijuana possession, however, is illegal under the federal Controlled Substances Act (CSA).[2]

After the federal government seized the marijuana that two seriously ill California women were using on the advice of their physicians, the women filed a lawsuit. They argued that it was unconstitutional for the federal statute to prohibit them from using marijuana for medical purposes that were legal within the state.

The Supreme Court, though, held that Congress has the authority to prohibit the *intrastate* possession and noncommercial cultivation of marijuana as part of a larger regulatory scheme (the CSA).[3] In other words, the federal government may still prosecute individuals for possession of marijuana regardless of whether they reside in a state that allows the use of marijuana.

The "Dormant" Commerce Clause   The United States Supreme Court has interpreted the commerce clause to mean that the national government has the *exclusive* authority to regulate commerce that substantially affects trade and commerce among the states. This express grant of authority to the national government, which is often referred to as the "positive" aspect of the commerce clause, implies a negative aspect—that the states do *not* have the authority to regulate interstate commerce. This negative aspect of the commerce clause is often referred to as the "dormant" (implied) commerce clause.

The dormant commerce clause comes into play when state regulations affect interstate commerce. In this situation, the courts normally weigh the state's interest in regulating a certain matter against the burden that the state's regulation places on interstate commerce. Because courts balance the interests involved, predicting the outcome in a particular case can be extremely difficult.

Case Example 2.2   Maryland imposed personal income taxes on its residents at the state level and the county level. Maryland residents who paid income tax in another state were allowed a credit against the *state* portion of their Maryland taxes, but not the *county* portion. Several Maryland residents who had earned profits in and paid taxes to other states but had not received a credit against their county tax liability sued. They claimed that Maryland's system discriminated against interstate commerce because those who earned income in other states paid more taxes than residents whose only income came from within Maryland. When the case reached the United States Supreme Court in 2015, the Court held that Maryland's personal income tax scheme violated the dormant commerce clause.[4]

2–1e The Supremacy Clause

Article VI of the Constitution provides that the Constitution, laws, and treaties of the United States are "the supreme Law of the Land." This article, commonly referred to as the **supremacy clause,** is important in the ordering of state and federal relationships.

Supremacy Clause The provision in Article VI of the U.S. Constitution that the Constitution, laws, and treaties of the United States are "the supreme Law of the Land."

2. 21 U.S.C. Sections 801 *et seq.*

3. *Gonzales v. Raich,* 545 U.S. 1, 125 S.Ct. 2195, 162 L.Ed.2d 1 (2005).

4. *Comptroller of Treasury of Maryland v. Wynne,* ___ U.S. ___, 135 S.Ct. 1787, 191 L.Ed.2d 813 (2015). Also see *State of South Dakota v. Wayfair, Inc.,* 2017 S.D. 56, 901 N.W.2d 754 (2017), *cert.* granted, 138 S.Ct. 735 (2018).

Preemption Under the supremacy clause, when there is a direct conflict between a federal law and a state law, the state law is rendered invalid. Because some powers are *concurrent* (shared by the federal government and the states), however, it is necessary to determine which law governs in a particular circumstance.

Preemption A doctrine under which certain federal laws preempt, or take precedence over, conflicting state or local laws.

Preemption occurs when Congress chooses to act exclusively in a concurrent area. In this circumstance, a valid federal statute or regulation will take precedence over a conflicting state or local law or regulation on the same general subject.

Congressional Intent Often, it is not clear whether Congress, in passing a law, intended to preempt an entire subject area against state regulation. In these situations, the courts determine whether Congress intended to exercise exclusive power.

Generally, congressional intent to preempt will be found if a federal law regulating an activity is so pervasive, comprehensive, or detailed that the states have little or no room to regulate in that area. Also, when a federal statute creates an agency—such as the National Labor Relations Board—to enforce the law, the agency's decisions in matters that come within its jurisdiction will likely preempt state laws.

Classic Case Example 2.3 A man who alleged that he had been injured by a faulty medical device (a balloon catheter that had been inserted into his artery following a heart attack) sued the manufacturer. The case ultimately came before the United States Supreme Court. The Court noted that the relevant federal law (the Medical Device Amendments) included a preemption provision.

Furthermore, the device had passed the U.S. Food and Drug Administration's rigorous premarket approval process. Therefore, the Court ruled that the federal regulation of medical devices preempted the man's state law claims for negligence, strict liability, and implied warranty.[5]

BioMedical/Shutterstock.com

How can preemption affect lawsuits against manufacturers of medical devices—such as a balloon catheter used in heart procedures—when those suits are based on state laws?

2–2 Business and the Bill of Rights

Bill of Rights The first ten amendments to the U.S. Constitution.

The importance of having a written declaration of the rights of individuals eventually caused the first Congress of the United States to enact twelve amendments to the Constitution and submit them to the states for approval. The first ten of these amendments, commonly known as the **Bill of Rights,** were adopted in 1791.

The Bill of Rights embodies a series of protections for the individual against various types of conduct by the federal government.[6] Some constitutional protections apply to business entities as well. For example, corporations exist as separate legal entities, or legal persons, and enjoy many of the same rights and privileges as natural persons do.

Summarized next are the protections guaranteed by the first ten amendments:

1. The First Amendment guarantees the freedoms of religion, speech, and the press and the rights to assemble peaceably and to petition the government.

2. The Second Amendment guarantees the right to keep and bear arms.

3. The Third Amendment prohibits, in peacetime, the lodging of soldiers in any house without the owner's consent.

---

5. *Riegel v. Medtronic, Inc.,* 552 U.S. 312, 128 S.Ct. 999, 169 L.Ed.2d 892 (2008); see also *Mink v. Smith & Nephew, Inc.,* 860 F.3d 1319 (11th Cir. 2017).
6. One of the proposed amendments was ratified more than two hundred years later (in 1992) and became the Twenty-seventh Amendment to the Constitution.

4. The Fourth Amendment prohibits unreasonable searches and seizures of persons or property.

5. The Fifth Amendment guarantees the rights to *indictment* (formal accusation) by a grand jury, to due process of law, and to fair payment when private property is taken for public use. The Fifth Amendment also prohibits compulsory self-incrimination and double jeopardy (prosecution for the same crime twice).

6. The Sixth Amendment guarantees the accused in a criminal case the right to a speedy and public trial by an impartial jury and with counsel. The accused has the right to cross-examine witnesses against him or her and to solicit testimony from witnesses in his or her favor.

7. The Seventh Amendment guarantees the right to a trial by jury in a civil (noncriminal) case involving at least twenty dollars.[7]

8. The Eighth Amendment prohibits excessive bail and fines, as well as cruel and unusual punishment.

9. The Ninth Amendment establishes that the people have rights in addition to those specified in the Constitution.

10. The Tenth Amendment establishes that those powers neither delegated to the federal government nor denied to the states are reserved for the states.

Mike Twohy/Conde Nast

We will look more closely at several of these amendments in a later chapter. In this chapter, we examine two important guarantees of the First Amendment—freedom of speech and freedom of religion. First, though, we look at how the Bill of Rights puts certain limits on government.

2–2a Limits on Federal and State Governmental Actions

As originally intended, the Bill of Rights limited only the powers of the national government. Over time, however, the United States Supreme Court "incorporated" most of these rights into the protections against state actions afforded by the Fourteenth Amendment to the Constitution.

The Fourteenth Amendment Passed in 1868 after the Civil War, the Fourteenth Amendment provides, in part, that "[n]o State shall . . . deprive any person of life, liberty, or property, without due process of law."

Starting in 1925, the Supreme Court began to define various rights and liberties guaranteed in the national Constitution as constituting "due process of law," which was required of state governments under the Fourteenth Amendment. Today, most of the rights and liberties set forth in the Bill of Rights apply to state governments as well as to the national government.

Judicial Interpretation The rights secured by the Bill of Rights are not absolute. Many of the rights guaranteed by the first ten amendments are described in very general terms. For instance, the Second Amendment states that people have a right to keep and bear arms, but it does not explain the extent of this right. As the Supreme Court once stated, the right does not extend so far that people can "keep and carry any weapon whatsoever in any manner whatsoever and for whatever purpose."[8] Legislatures can prohibit the carrying of concealed weapons or certain types of weapons, such as machine guns.

Ultimately, the Supreme Court, as the final interpreter of the Constitution, gives meaning to constitutional rights and determines their boundaries. (For a discussion of how the Supreme Court may consider other nations' laws when determining the appropriate balance of individual rights, see this chapter's *Beyond Our Borders* feature.)

Know This
Although most of the rights in the Bill of Rights apply to actions of the states, some of them apply only to actions of the federal government.

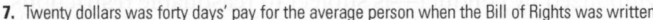

7. Twenty dollars was forty days' pay for the average person when the Bill of Rights was written.
8. *District of Columbia v. Heller*, 554 U.S. 570, 128 S.Ct. 2783, 171 L.Ed.2d 637 (2008).

The Impact of Foreign Law on the United States Supreme Court

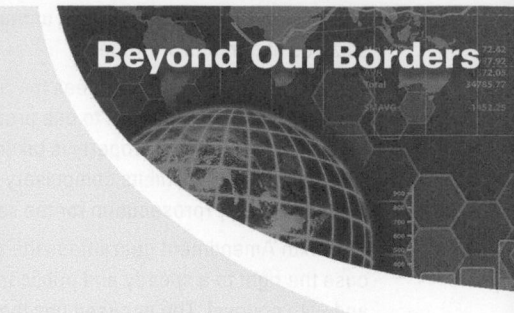

The United States Supreme Court interprets the rights provided in the U.S. Constitution. Changing public views on controversial topics, such as privacy in an era of terrorist threats or the rights of gay men and lesbians, may affect the way the Supreme Court decides a case. But should the Court also consider other nations' laws and world opinion when balancing individual rights in the United States?

Justices on the Supreme Court have increasingly considered foreign law when deciding issues of national importance. This trend started in 2003 when, for the first time ever, foreign law was cited in a majority opinion of the Supreme Court. The case was a controversial one in which the Court struck down laws that prohibited oral and anal sex between consenting adults of the same gender. In the majority opinion, Justice Anthony Kennedy mentioned that the European Court of Human Rights and other foreign courts have consistently acknowledged that homosexuals have a right "to engage in intimate, consensual conduct."[a]

The practice of looking at foreign law has many critics, including some conservative members of the Supreme Court, who believe that foreign views are irrelevant to rulings on U.S. law. Other Supreme Court justices, however, including Justice Stephen Breyer and Justice Ruth Bader Ginsburg, have publicly stated that in our increasingly global community we should not ignore the opinions of courts in the rest of the world.

Critical Thinking

Should U.S. courts, and particularly the United States Supreme Court, look to other nations' laws for guidance when deciding important issues—including those involving rights granted by the Constitution? If so, what impact might this have on their decisions? Explain.

a. *Lawrence v. Texas*, 539 U.S. 558, 123 S.Ct. 2472, 156 L.Ed.2d 508 (2003).

Symbolic Speech Nonverbal expressions of beliefs. Symbolic speech, which includes gestures, movements, and articles of clothing, is given substantial protection by the courts.

2–2b The First Amendment—Freedom of Speech

A democratic form of government cannot survive unless people can freely voice their political opinions and criticize government actions or policies. Freedom of speech, particularly political speech, is thus a prized right, and traditionally the courts have protected this right to the fullest extent possible.

Symbolic speech—gestures, movements, articles of clothing, and other forms of expressive conduct—is also given substantial protection by the courts. The burning of the American flag to protest government policies, for instance, is a constitutionally protected form of expression. Similarly, wearing a T-shirt with a photo of a presidential candidate or taking a knee during the national anthem at a sporting event would be a constitutionally protected form of expression.

The test is whether a reasonable person would interpret the conduct as conveying some sort of message. **Example 2.4** As a form of expression, Eric has gang signs tattooed on his torso, arms, neck, and legs. If a reasonable person would interpret this conduct as conveying a message, then it might be a protected form of symbolic speech. ■

Reasonable Restrictions Expression—oral, written, or symbolized by conduct—is subject to reasonable restrictions. A balance must be struck between a government's obligation to protect its citizens and those citizens' exercise of their

Can a tattoo be considered symbolic speech? Why or why not?

Robert Nickelsberg/Getty Images News/Getty Images

rights. Reasonableness is analyzed on a case-by-case basis. (See this chapter's *Adapting the Law to the Online Environment* feature for a discussion of how the United States Supreme Court balanced the government's obligation against the rights of a convicted sex offender.)

Content-Neutral Laws. Laws that regulate the time, manner, and place, but not the content, of speech receive less scrutiny by the courts than do laws that restrict the content of expression. If a restriction imposed by the government is content neutral, then a court may allow it. To be content neutral, the restriction must be aimed at combating some secondary societal problem, such as crime, and not be aimed at suppressing the expressive conduct or its message.

Courts have often protected nude dancing as a form of symbolic expression. Nevertheless, the courts typically allow content-neutral laws that ban *all* public nudity. **Case Example 2.5** Rita Ora was charged with dancing nude at an annual "anti-Christmas" protest in Harvard Square in Cambridge, Massachusetts. Ora argued that the statute was overly broad and unconstitutional, and a trial court agreed. On appeal, a state appellate court reversed. The court found that the statute was constitutional because it banned public displays of open and gross lewdness in situations in which there was an unsuspecting or unwilling audience.[9]

Laws That Restrict the Content of Speech. If a law regulates the content of the expression, it must serve a compelling state interest and must be narrowly written to achieve that interest. Under the **compelling government interest** test, the government's interest is balanced

> **Compelling Government Interest** A test of constitutionality that requires the government to have convincing reasons for passing any law that restricts fundamental rights, such as free speech, or distinguishes between people based on a suspect trait.

---

9. *Commonwealth of Massachusetts v. Ora*, 451 Mass. 125, 883 N.E.2d 1217 (2008).

Does Everyone Have a Constitutional Right to Use Social Media?

Adapting the Law to the Online Environment

Social media have become the predominant means by which many Americans communicate, obtain news updates, and discover what is "trending." At least one state, though, legislated a ban on the use of social media by convicted sex offenders. One sex offender chose to challenge the law.

North Carolina and the Use of Social Media

North Carolina's legislature passed the "Protect Children from Sexual Predators Act" in 2008. The goal, of course, was to prevent predators from finding potential victims on the Internet. Part of that act was codified as North Carolina General Statute 14-202.5. About one thousand sex offenders have been prosecuted for violating it.

A Long Road through the Courts

When convicted sex offender Lester Packingham, Jr., wrote a Facebook post about a traffic ticket, a police officer saw the post and reported it, and Packingham was convicted of violating a criminal statute. He fought his conviction, and on appeal it was overturned.[a] The state, though, continued to fight the appellate decision. The North Carolina Supreme Court ruled in favor of the state.

Packingham then appealed to the United States Supreme Court, where he prevailed.[b] The Court pointed out that prohibiting sex offenders from accessing all social media violates their First Amendment rights to free speech. Further, this prohibition "bars access to what for many are the principle sources of knowing current events, checking ads for employment,

speaking and listening in a modern public square, and otherwise exploring the vast realms of human thought and knowledge."

Critical Thinking

The Court said in its opinion that "specific criminal acts are not protected speech even if speech is the means for their commission." What use of social media and the Internet might therefore still be unlawful (and not protected free speech) for registered sex offenders?

---

a. *North Carolina v. Packingham*, 229 N.C.App. 293, 748 S.E.2d 146 (2013).
b. *Packingham v. North Carolina*, ___ U.S. ___, 137 S.Ct. 1730, 198 L.Ed.2d 273 (2017).

against the individual's constitutional right to be free of government interference. For the statute to be valid, there must be a compelling governmental interest that can be furthered only by the law in question.

The United States Supreme Court has held that schools may restrict students' speech at school events. ⬥ **Spotlight Case Example 2.6** Some high school students held up a banner saying "Bong Hits 4 Jesus" at an off-campus but school-sanctioned event. The majority of the Court ruled that school officials did not violate the students' free speech rights when they confiscated the banner and suspended the students for ten days. Because the banner could reasonably be interpreted as promoting drugs, the Court concluded that the school's actions were justified. Several justices disagreed, however, noting that the majority's holding creates a special exception that will allow schools to censor any student speech that mentions drugs.[10] ▪

In the following case, the issue before the court was whether a restriction on the making of audio and video recordings of an agricultural production facility could meet the narrow tailoring requirement.

---

10. *Morse v. Frederick*, 551 U.S. 393, 127 S.Ct. 2618, 168 L.Ed.2d 290 (2007).

■ **Case 2.2**

Animal Legal Defense Fund v. Wasden

United States Court of Appeals, Ninth Circuit, 878 F.3d 1184 (2018).

Background and Facts An animal rights activist, who worked at an Idaho dairy farm, secretly filmed ongoing animal abuse. After being posted online, the film attracted national attention. The dairy owner fired the abusive employees, established a code of conduct, and undertook an animal welfare audit of the farm. Meanwhile, the Idaho state legislature enacted the Interference with Agricultural Production statute targeted at undercover investigation of agricultural operations. The statute's "Recordings Clause" criminalized making audio and video recordings of an agricultural production facility without the owner's consent.

The Animal Legal Defense Fund filed a suit in a federal district court against Lawrence Wasden, the Idaho attorney general, alleging that the statute's Recordings Clause violated the First Amendment of the U.S. Constitution. The court issued an injunction against its enforcement. The state appealed this order to the U.S. Court of Appeals for the Ninth Circuit.

In the Words of the Court
McKEOWN, Circuit Judge:
* * * *

* * * The Recordings Clause regulates speech protected by the First Amendment and is a classic example of a content-based restriction that cannot survive strict scrutiny.

We easily dispose of Idaho's claim that the act of creating an audiovisual recording is not speech protected by the First Amendment. This argument is akin to saying that even though a book is protected by the First Amendment, the process of writing the book is not. *Audiovisual recordings are protected by the First Amendment as recognized organs of public opinion and as a significant medium for the communication of ideas.* [Emphasis added.]
* * * *

The Recordings Clause prohibits the recording of a defined topic—"the conduct of an agricultural production facility's operations." * * * A regulation is content-based when it draws a distinction on its face regarding the message the speaker conveys or when the purpose and justification for the law are content based. The Recordings Clause checks both boxes. * * * A videographer could record an after-hours birthday party among co-workers, a farmer's antique car collection, or a historic maple tree but not the animal abuse, feedlot operation, or slaughterhouse conditions.
* * * *

As a content-based regulation, the Recordings Clause is constitutional only if it * * * is necessary to serve a compelling state interest and is narrowly drawn to achieve that end. * * *

Idaho asserts that the Recordings Clause protects both property and privacy interests. *Even assuming a compelling government interest, Idaho has not satisfied the narrow tailoring requirement because the statute is both under-inclusive and over-inclusive.* [Emphasis added.]

[For example,] prohibiting only "audio or video recordings," but saying nothing about photographs, is suspiciously under-inclusive. Why the making of audio and video recordings of operations would implicate property or privacy harms, but photographs of the same content would not, is a mystery.

* * * *

The Recordings Clause is also over-inclusive and suppresses more speech than necessary to further Idaho's stated goals of protecting property and privacy. Because there are various other laws at Idaho's disposal that would allow it to achieve its stated interests while burdening little or no speech, the law is not narrowly tailored. For example, agricultural production facility owners can vindicate their rights through tort laws against theft of trade secrets, * * * invasion of privacy, [and] defamation.

Decision and Remedy The U.S. Court of Appeals for the Ninth Circuit affirmed the lower court's order preventing the enforcement of the statute. A law that concerns rights under the First Amendment must be narrowly tailored to accomplish its objective. The federal appellate court concluded that Idaho's Recordings Clause could not "survive First Amendment scrutiny" and was unconstitutional.

Critical Thinking

• **Legal Environment** *How does the making of "audio and video recordings of an agricultural production facility" fall under the protection of the First Amendment?*

• **What If the Facts Were Different?** *Suppose that instead of banning recordings of an agricultural production facility's operations, the state had criminalized misrepresentations by journalists to gain access to such a facility. Would the result have been different? Explain.*

Ethical Issue

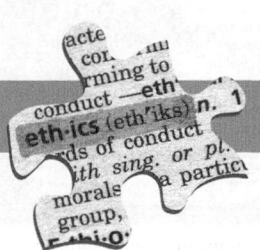

Can a high school suspend teenagers from extracurricular activities because they posted suggestive photos of themselves online at social networking sites? T.V. and M.K. were students at a public high school. During summer sleepovers, the girls took photos of each other pretending to suck penis-shaped, rainbow-colored lollipops and holding them in various suggestive positions. They later posted the photos on Facebook, MySpace, and Photo Bucket to be seen by persons granted "friend" status or given a password. When a parent complained to the school about the provocative online display, school officials suspended both girls from the high school volleyball team. M.K. was also suspended from the cheerleading squad and the show choir. Through their parents, the girls filed a lawsuit claiming that the school had violated their First Amendment rights.

A federal judge in Indiana ruled that a high school did not have the right to punish students for posting suggestive photos of themselves on the Internet. Expressive conduct is entitled to First Amendment protection if it is intended to convey a particular message and is likely to be understood by those viewing it as expressing a message. Here, both girls testified that they were just trying to be funny when they took the photos and posted them online for their friends to see. The court reasoned that the conduct depicted in the photos was intended to be humorous and would be understood as such by their teenage audience. Therefore, the photos were entitled to First Amendment protection as symbolic speech.[11]

---

11. *T.V. ex rel. B.V. v. Smith-Green Community School Corp.*, 807 F.Supp.2d 767 (N.D.Ind. 2011).

Corporate Political Speech Political speech by corporations also falls within the protection of the First Amendment. Many years ago, the United States Supreme Court reviewed a Massachusetts statute that prohibited corporations from making political contributions or expenditures that individuals were permitted to make. The Court ruled that the Massachusetts law was unconstitutional because it violated the right of corporations to freedom of speech.[12] The Court has also held that a law prohibiting a corporation from using bill inserts to express its views on controversial issues violated the First Amendment.[13]

Corporate political speech continues to be given significant protection under the First Amendment. **Classic Case Example 2.7** In *Citizens United v. Federal Election Commission*,[14] the Supreme Court overturned a twenty-year-old precedent on campaign financing. The case involved Citizens United, a nonprofit corporation.

Citizens United had produced a film called *Hillary: The Movie* that was critical of Hillary Clinton, who was seeking the Democratic presidential nomination. Campaign-finance law prohibited Citizens United from broadcasting the movie, however. The Court ruled that the restrictions were unconstitutional and that the First Amendment prevents limits from being placed on independent political expenditures by corporations. ■

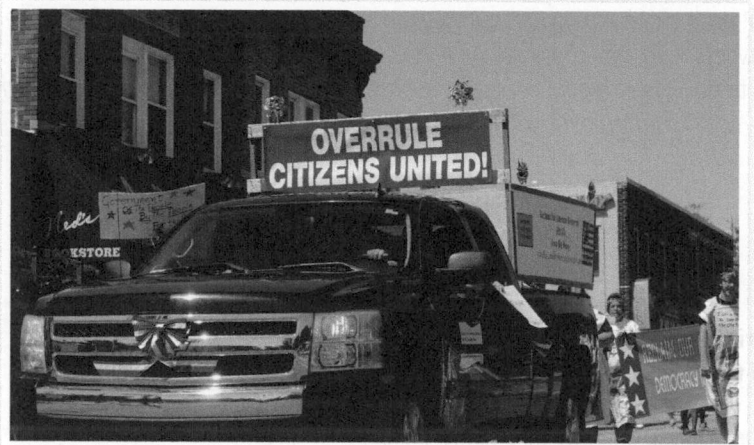

The U.S. Supreme Court decision *Citizens United* allows corporations to spend to elect or defeat candidates for president and Congress. Why did this decision upset some people?

Commercial Speech The courts also give substantial protection to *commercial speech*, which consists of communications—primarily advertising and marketing—made by business firms that involve only their commercial interests. The protection given to commercial speech under the First Amendment is not as extensive as that afforded to noncommercial speech, however. A state may restrict certain kinds of advertising, for instance, in the interest of protecting consumers from being misled.

States also have a legitimate interest in the beautification of roadsides, and this interest allows states to place restraints on billboard advertising. **Example 2.8** Café Erotica, a nude dancing establishment, sues the state after being denied a permit to erect a billboard along an interstate highway in Florida. Because of the state's legitimate interest in highway beautification and safety, a court will likely rule that it is not an unconstitutional restraint on commercial speech. ■

Generally, a restriction on commercial speech will be considered valid as long as it (1) seeks to implement a substantial government interest, (2) directly advances that interest, and (3) goes no further than necessary to accomplish its objective. A substantial government interest exists when the government has an important stake in the matter at hand. For instance, the substantial-interest requirement limits the power of the government to regulate commercial speech.

At issue in the following *Spotlight Case* was whether a government agency had unconstitutionally restricted commercial speech when it prohibited the use of a certain illustration on beer labels.

12. *First National Bank of Boston v. Bellotti*, 435 U.S. 765, 98 S.Ct. 1407, 55 L.Ed.2d 707 (1978).
13. *Consolidated Edison Co. v. Public Service Commission*, 447 U.S. 530, 100 S.Ct. 2326, 65 L.Ed.2d 319 (1980).
14. *Citizens United v. Federal Election Commission*, 558 U.S. 310, 130 S.Ct. 876, 175 L.Ed.2d 753 (2010).

Spotlight on Beer Labels: Case 2.3

Bad Frog Brewery, Inc. v. New York State Liquor Authority

United States Court of Appeals, Second Circuit, 134 F.3d 87 (1998).

Background and Facts Bad Frog Brewery, Inc., makes and sells alcoholic beverages. Some of the beverages feature labels with a drawing of a frog making the gesture generally known as "giving the finger." Renaissance Beer Company was Bad Frog's authorized New York distributor. Renaissance applied to the New York State Liquor Authority (NYSLA) for brand label approval, as required by state law before the beer could be sold in New York. The NYSLA denied the application, in part, because "the label could appear in grocery and convenience stores, with obvious exposure on the shelf to children of tender age."

Can a label be too offensive?

Eric Isselee/ShutterStock.com

Bad Frog filed a suit in a federal district court against the NYSLA, asking for, among other things, an injunction against the denial of the application. The court granted summary judgment in favor of the NYSLA. Bad Frog appealed to the U.S. Court of Appeals for the Second Circuit.

In the Words of the Court
Jon O. *NEWMAN,* Circuit Judge.

* * * *

* * * To support its asserted power to ban Bad Frog's labels [NYSLA advances] * * * the State's interest in "protecting children from vulgar and profane advertising" * * *.

[This interest is] substantial * * *. States have a compelling interest in protecting the physical and psychological well-being of minors * * *. [Emphasis added.]

* * * *

* * * NYSLA endeavors to advance the state interest in preventing exposure of children to vulgar displays by taking only the limited step of barring such displays from the labels of alcoholic beverages. *In view of the wide currency of vulgar displays throughout contemporary society, including comic books targeted directly at children, barring such displays from labels for alcoholic beverages cannot realistically be expected to reduce children's exposure to such displays to any significant degree.* [Emphasis added.]

* * * If New York decides to make a substantial effort to insulate children from vulgar displays in some significant sphere of

activity, at least with respect to materials likely to be seen by children, NYSLA's label prohibition might well be found to make a justifiable contribution to the material advancement of such an effort, but its currently isolated response to the perceived problem, applicable only to labels on a product that children cannot purchase, does not suffice. * * * A state must demonstrate that its commercial speech limitation is part of a substantial effort to advance a valid state interest, not merely the removal of a few grains of offensive sand from a beach of vulgarity.

* * * *

* * * Even if we were to assume that the state materially advances its asserted interest by shielding children from viewing the Bad Frog labels, it is plainly excessive to prohibit the labels from all use, including placement on bottles displayed in bars and taverns where parental supervision of children is to be expected. Moreover, to whatever extent NYSLA is concerned that children will be harmfully exposed to the Bad Frog labels when wandering without parental supervision around grocery and convenience stores where beer is sold, that concern could be less intrusively dealt with by placing restrictions on the permissible locations where the appellant's products may be displayed within such stores.

Decision and Remedy The U.S. Court of Appeals for the Second Circuit reversed the judgment of the district court and remanded the case for the entry of a judgment in favor of Bad Frog. The NYSLA's ban on the use of the labels lacked a "reasonable fit" with the state's interest in shielding minors from vulgarity, and the NYSLA did not adequately consider alternatives to the ban.

Critical Thinking

• **Legal Environment** *Whose interests are advanced by the banning of certain types of advertising?*

• **What If the Facts Were Different?** *If Bad Frog had sought to use the label to market toys instead of beer, would the court's ruling likely have been the same? Explain your answer.*

Unprotected Speech The United States Supreme Court has made it clear that certain types of speech will not be given any protection under the First Amendment. Speech that harms the good reputation of another, or defamatory speech, will not be protected. Also, speech that violates criminal laws (such as obscene speech) is not constitutionally protected.

Threatening Speech. Note that in the case of threatening speech, the speaker must have posed a "true threat." In other words, the speaker must have meant to communicate a serious intent to commit an unlawful, violent act against a particular person or group. **Case Example 2.9** After Anthony Elonis's wife, Tara, left him and took their two children, Elonis was upset and experienced problems at work. A coworker filed five sexual harassment reports against him. When Elonis posted a photograph of himself in a Halloween costume holding a toy knife to the coworker's neck, he was fired from his job. He then began posting violent statements on his Facebook page, mostly focusing on his former wife. After posting statements about killing his former wife, Elonis eventually was arrested and prosecuted for the posts.

Elonis was convicted by a jury of violating a statute and ordered to serve time in prison. He appealed to the United States Supreme Court, which held that it is not enough that a reasonable person might view the defendant's Facebook posts as threats. Elonis must have intended to issue threats or known that his statements would be viewed as threats to be convicted of a crime. The Court reversed Elonis's conviction and remanded the case back to the lower court to determine if there was sufficient evidence of intent.[15] ▪

Obscene Speech. The First Amendment, as interpreted by the Supreme Court, also does not protect obscene speech. Numerous state and federal statutes make it a crime to disseminate and possess obscene materials, including child pornography. Objectively defining obscene speech has proved difficult, however. It is even more difficult to prohibit the dissemination of obscenity and pornography online.

Most of Congress's attempts to pass legislation protecting minors from pornographic materials on the Internet have been struck down on First Amendment grounds when challenged in court. One exception is a law that requires public schools and libraries to install **filtering software** on computers to keep children from accessing adult content.[16] Such software is designed to prevent persons from viewing certain websites based on their Internet addresses or **meta tags,** or key words. This act does not unconstitutionally burden free speech because it is flexible and libraries can disable the filters for any patrons who ask.

Another exception is a law that makes it a crime to intentionally distribute *virtual child pornography*—which uses computer-generated images, not actual people—without indicating that it is computer-generated.[17] In a case challenging the law's constitutionality, the Supreme Court held that the statute is valid because it does not prohibit a substantial amount of protected speech.[18] Nevertheless, because of the difficulties of policing the Internet, as well as the constitutional complexities of prohibiting online obscenity through legislation, it remains a problem worldwide.

Filtering Software A computer program that is designed to block access to certain websites, based on their content. The software blocks the retrieval of a site whose URL or key words are on a list within the program.

Meta Tag A key word in a document that can serve as an index reference to the document. On the Web, search engines return results based, in part, on the tags in Web documents.

2–2c The First Amendment—Freedom of Religion

The First Amendment states that the government may neither establish any religion nor prohibit the free exercise of religious practices. The first part of this constitutional provision is referred to as the *establishment clause*, and the second part is known as the *free exercise clause*. Government action, both federal and state, must be consistent with this constitutional mandate.

---

15. *Elonis v. United States,* ___ U.S. ___, 135 S.Ct. 2001, 192 L.Ed.2d 1 (2015).
16. Children's Internet Protection Act (CIPA), 17 U.S.C. Sections 1701–1741.
17. The Prosecutorial Remedies and Other Tools to End the Exploitation of Children Today Act (Protect Act), 18 U.S.C. Section 2252A(a)(5)(B).
18. *United States v. Williams,* 553 U.S. 285, 128 S.Ct. 1830, 170 L.Ed.2d 650 (2008).

The Establishment Clause

The **establishment clause** prohibits the government from establishing a state-sponsored religion, as well as from passing laws that promote (aid or endorse) religion or show a preference for one religion over another. Although the establishment clause involves the separation of church and state, it does not require a complete separation.

Applicable Standard. Establishment clause cases often involve such issues as the legality of allowing or requiring school prayers, using state-issued vouchers to pay tuition at religious schools, and teaching creation theories versus evolution in public schools. Federal or state laws that do not promote or place a significant burden on religion are constitutional even if they have some impact on religion. For a government law or policy to be constitutional, it must not have the primary effect of promoting or inhibiting religion.

Religious Displays. Religious displays on public property have often been challenged as violating the establishment clause. The United States Supreme Court has ruled on a number of such cases, often focusing on the proximity of the religious display to nonreligious symbols or on the balance of symbols from different religions. The Supreme Court eventually decided that public displays having historical, as well as religious, significance do not necessarily violate the establishment clause.

Case Example 2.10 Mount Soledad is a prominent hill near San Diego. There has been a forty-foot cross on top of Mount Soledad since 1913. In the 1990s, a war memorial was constructed next to the cross that included six walls listing the names of veterans. The site was privately owned until 2006, when Congress authorized the property's transfer to the federal government "to preserve a historically significant war memorial."

Steve Trunk and the Jewish War Veterans filed lawsuits claiming that the cross display violated the establishment clause because it endorsed the Christian religion. A federal appellate court agreed, finding that the primary effect of the memorial as a whole sent a strong message of endorsement and exclusion (of non-Christian veterans). The court noted that although not all cross displays at war memorials violate the establishment clause, the cross in this case physically dominated the site. Additionally, the cross was originally dedicated to religious purposes, had a long history of religious use, and was the only portion visible to drivers on the freeway below.[19] To gain a better understanding of how courts analyze whether public displays violate the establishment clause, see this chapter's *Business Law Analysis* feature.

The Free Exercise Clause

The **free exercise clause** guarantees that people can hold any religious beliefs they want or can have no religious beliefs. The constitutional guarantee of personal religious freedom restricts only the actions of the government, however, and not those of individuals or private businesses.

Restrictions Must Be Necessary. The government must have a compelling state interest for restricting the free exercise of religion, and the restriction must be the only way to further that interest. **Case Example 2.11** Gregory Holt, an inmate in an Arkansas state prison, was a devout Muslim who wished to grow a beard in accord with his religious beliefs. The state corrections department prohibited inmates from growing beards. Holt asked for an exemption to grow a half-inch beard on religious grounds, and prison officials denied his request. Holt filed a suit in a federal court against Ray Hobbs, the director of the department, and others. A federal statute prohibits the government from taking any action that substantially burdens the religious exercise of a prisoner unless it is the least restrictive means of furthering a compelling governmental interest.

Establishment Clause The provision in the First Amendment that prohibits the government from establishing any state-sponsored religion or enacting any law that promotes religion or favors one religion over another.

Know This
The free exercise clause applies only to the actions of the state and federal governments, not to private employers. Private employers may nonetheless be required to accommodate their employees' religious beliefs.

Free Exercise Clause The provision in the First Amendment that prohibits the government from interfering with people's religious practices or forms of worship.

---

19. *Trunk v. City of San Diego*, 629 F.3d 1099 (9th Cir. 2011).

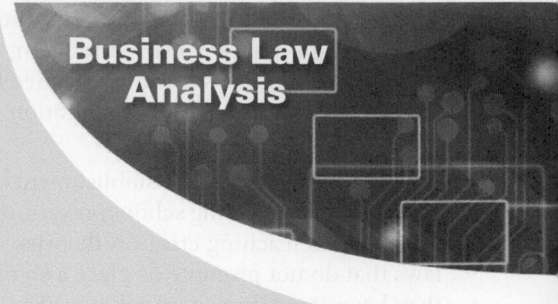

Determining When Public Religious Displays Violate the Establishment Clause

Judge James DeWeese hung a poster in his courtroom showing the Ten Commandments. The poster also included a number of editorial statements made by DeWeese, such as "God is the final authority, and we acknowledge His unchanging standards of behavior."

The American Civil Liberties Union (ACLU) filed a suit, alleging that the poster violated the establishment clause. DeWeese responded that his purpose was not to promote religion but to educate others about two conflicting legal philosophies—moral relativism and moral absolutism. DeWeese expressed his view that "our legal system is based on moral absolutes from divine law handed down by God through the Ten Commandments."

Does displaying this poster in a courtroom violate the establishment clause?

Analysis: The establishment clause prohibits the government from passing laws or taking actions that promote religion or show a preference for one religion over another. In assessing a government action (in this case, displaying a religious poster in a courtroom), the courts look at the predominant purpose for the action and ask whether the action has the effect of endorsing religion. Although DeWeese claimed to have a nonreligious (educational) purpose for displaying the poster of the Ten Commandments, his own statements showed a religious purpose. DeWeese was trying to teach others to believe as he believes, that

our legal system is based on moral truths handed down by God.

Result and Reasoning: DeWeese's statements reflected his views about "warring" legal philosophies and his belief that "our legal system is based on moral absolutes from divine law handed down by God through the Ten Commandments." Based on his statements, DeWeese's poster had the religious purpose of endorsing Judeo-Christian religious views, which violated the establishment clause.

The defendants argued that beards compromise prison safety—a compelling government interest—because contraband can be hidden in them and because an inmate can quickly shave his beard to disguise his identity. The case ultimately reached the United States Supreme Court, which noted that "an item of contraband would have to be very small indeed to be concealed by a 1/2-inch beard." Furthermore, the Court reasoned, the department could simply search the beard, the way it already searched prisoners' hair and clothing. Therefore, the department's policy, which prevented Holt from growing a half-inch beard, violated his right to exercise his religious beliefs.[20]

Restrictions Must Not Be a Substantial Burden. To comply with the free exercise clause, a government action must not be a substantial burden on religious practices. A burden is substantial if it pressures an individual to modify his or her behavior and to violate his or her beliefs.

Case Example 2.12 Michael Thompson, a Muslim, was an inmate at a prison in Wisconsin. A central practice of the Islamic faith is a sunrise-to-sunset fast during the month of Ramadan. The prison accommodates this practice by providing "meal bags" at sunset to each Muslim prisoner listed as eligible. Ten days into Ramadan, Randall Lashock, a prison guard, withheld Thompson's meal bags for two days. Thompson felt pressure to break his fast by going to the prison cafeteria, but under prison policy he would thereby forfeit meal bags for the rest of the fast. He did not know when—or even if—he would again be added to the Ramadan list and be given a meal bag. Meanwhile, hunger caused him to miss prayers and anxiety

---

20. *Holt v. Hobbs*, ___ U.S. ___, 135 S.Ct. 853, 190 L.Ed.2d 747 (2015).

undercut his experience of Ramadan. Thompson sued several prison guards for violating his right to exercise his religion freely. A federal appellate court ultimately ruled in his favor. "Forcing an inmate to choose between daily nutrition and religious practice is a substantial burden" on the inmate's free exercise right.[21]

Public Welfare Exception. When religious *practices* work against public policy and the public welfare, the government can act. For instance, the government can require that a child receive certain types of vaccinations or receive medical treatment when the child's life is in danger—regardless of the child's or parent's religious beliefs.

In other words, when public safety is an issue, an individual's religious beliefs often must give way to the government's interests in protecting the public. **Example 2.13** In public, a woman of the Muslim faith may choose to wear a scarf, known as a *hijab*, over her head. Nevertheless, due to public safety concerns, many courts today do not allow the wearing of any headgear (hats or scarves) in courtrooms.

Can prison policy prevent a devout Muslim from keeping a short beard?

2–3 Due Process and Equal Protection

Two other constitutional guarantees of great significance to Americans are mandated by the due process clauses of the Fifth and Fourteenth Amendments and the equal protection clause of the Fourteenth Amendment.

2–3a Due Process

Both the Fifth and the Fourteenth Amendments provide that no person shall be deprived "of life, liberty, or property, without due process of law." The **due process clause** of each of these constitutional amendments has two aspects—procedural and substantive. Note that the due process clause applies to "legal persons," such as corporations, as well as to individuals.

Procedural Due Process Procedural due process requires that any government decision to take life, liberty, or property must be made fairly. This means that the government must give a person proper notice and an opportunity to be heard. The government must also use fair procedures in determining whether a person will be subjected to punishment or have some burden imposed on him or her.

Fair procedure has been interpreted as requiring that the person have at least an opportunity to object to a proposed action before a fair, neutral decision maker (who need not be a judge). **Example 2.14** Doyle Burns, a nursing student in Kansas, poses for a photograph standing next to a placenta used as a lab specimen. Although she quickly deletes the photo from her library, it ends up on Facebook. When the director of nursing sees the photo, Burns is expelled. She sues for reinstatement and wins. The school violated Burns's due process rights by expelling her from the nursing program for taking a photo without giving her an opportunity to present her side to school authorities.

Substantive Due Process Substantive due process focuses on the content of the legislation rather than the fairness of the procedures. Substantive due process limits what the

Learning Objective 3

Where in the Constitution can the due process clause be found?

Due Process Clause The provisions in the Fifth and Fourteenth Amendments that guarantee that no person shall be deprived of life, liberty, or property without due process of law. State constitutions often include similar clauses.

---

21. *Thompson v. Holm*, 809 F.3d 376 (7th Cir. 2016).

Equal Protection Clause
The provision in the Fourteenth
Amendment that requires state
governments to treat similarly
situated individuals in a similar
manner.

government may do in its legislative and executive capacities. Legislation must be fair and reasonable in content and must further a legitimate governmental objective.

If a law or other governmental action limits a fundamental right, the courts will hold that it violates substantive due process unless it promotes a compelling state interest. Fundamental rights include interstate travel, privacy, voting, marriage and family, and all First Amendment rights. Thus, for instance, a state must have a substantial reason for taking any action that infringes on a person's free speech rights.

In situations not involving fundamental rights, a law or action does not violate substantive due process if it rationally relates to any legitimate governmental end. It is almost impossible for a law or action to fail the "rationality" test. Under this test, almost any government regulation of business will be upheld as reasonable.

2–3b Equal Protection

Under the Fourteenth Amendment, a state may not "deny to any person within its jurisdiction the equal protection of the laws." The United States Supreme Court has used the due process clause of the Fifth Amendment to make the **equal protection clause** applicable to the federal government as well. Equal protection means that the government must treat similarly situated individuals in a similar manner.

Equal protection, like substantive due process, relates to the substance of the law or other governmental action. When a law or action limits the liberty of all persons to do something, it may violate substantive due process. When a law or action limits the liberty of some persons but not others, it may violate the equal protection clause. **Example 2.15** If a law prohibits all advertising on the sides of trucks, it raises a substantive due process question. If the law makes an exception to allow truck owners to advertise their own businesses, it raises an equal protection issue. ■

In an equal protection inquiry, when a law or action distinguishes between or among individuals, the basis for the distinction—that is, the classification—is examined. Depending on the classification, the courts apply different levels of scrutiny, or "tests," to determine whether the law or action violates the equal protection clause. The courts use one of three standards: strict scrutiny, intermediate scrutiny, or the "rational basis" test.

Strict Scrutiny If a law or action prohibits or inhibits some persons from exercising a fundamental right, the law or action will be subject to "strict scrutiny" by the courts. A classification based on a *suspect trait*—such as race, national origin, or citizenship status—will also be subject to strict scrutiny. Under this standard, the classification must be necessary to promote a *compelling government interest*.

Compelling state interests include remedying past unconstitutional or illegal discrimination, but do not include correcting the general effects of "society's discrimination." **Example 2.16** For a city to give preference to minority applicants in awarding construction contracts, it normally must identify past unconstitutional or illegal discrimination against minority construction firms. Because the policy is based on suspect traits (race and national origin), it will violate the equal protection clause *unless* it is necessary to promote a compelling state interest. ■ Generally, few laws or actions survive strict-scrutiny analysis by the courts.

Intermediate Scrutiny Another standard, that of "intermediate scrutiny," is applied in cases involving discrimination based on gender or legitimacy. Laws using these classifications must be substantially related to *important*

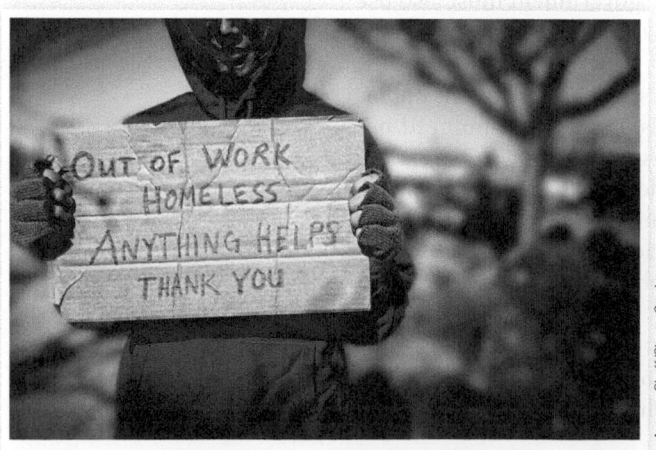

Does the equal protection clause protect the homeless? If so, how?

Annette Shaff/ShutterStock.com

government objectives. **Example 2.17** An important government objective is preventing illegitimate teenage pregnancies. Males and females are not similarly situated in this regard because only females can become pregnant. Therefore, a law that punishes men but not women for statutory rape will be upheld even though it treats men and women unequally.

The state also has an important objective in establishing time limits (called *statutes of limitation*) for how long after an event a particular type of action can be brought. Nevertheless, the limitation period must be substantially related to the important objective of preventing fraudulent or outdated claims. **Example 2.18** A state law requires illegitimate children (born out of wedlock) to bring paternity suits within six years of their births in order to seek support from their fathers. A court will strike down this law if legitimate children are allowed to seek support from their parents at any time. This is because distinguishing between support claims on the basis of legitimacy is not related to the important government objective of preventing fraudulent or outdated claims.

The "Rational Basis" Test In matters of economic and social welfare, a classification will be considered valid if there is any conceivable "rational basis" on which the classification might relate to a *legitimate government interest.* It is almost impossible for a law or action to fail the rational basis test.

Case Example 2.19 A Kentucky statute prohibits businesses that sell substantial amounts of staple groceries or gasoline from selling wine and liquor. Maxwell's Pic-Pac (a grocer) filed suit against the state, alleging that the statute was unconstitutional under the equal protection clause. The court applied the rational basis test and ruled that the statute was rationally related to a legitimate government interest in reducing access to products with high alcohol content.

The court cited the problems caused by alcohol, including drunk driving, and noted that the state's interest in limiting access to such products extends to the general public. Grocery stores and gas stations pose a greater risk of exposing members of the public to alcohol than do other retailers. For these and other reasons, the state can restrict these places from selling wine and liquor.[22]

2–4 Privacy Rights

The U.S. Constitution does not explicitly mention a general right to privacy. In a 1928 Supreme Court case, *Olmstead v. United States*,[23] Justice Louis Brandeis stated in his dissent that the right to privacy is "the most comprehensive of rights and the right most valued by civilized men." The majority of the justices at that time, however, did not agree with Brandeis.

It was not until the 1960s that a majority on the Supreme Court endorsed the view that the Constitution protects individual privacy rights. In a landmark 1965 case, *Griswold v. Connecticut*,[24] the Supreme Court invalidated a Connecticut law that effectively prohibited the use of contraceptives on the ground that it violated the right to privacy. The Supreme Court held that a constitutional right to privacy was implied by the First, Third, Fourth, Fifth, and Ninth Amendments.

Today, privacy rights receive protection under various federal statutes as well as the U.S. Constitution. State constitutions and statutes also secure individuals' privacy rights, often to a significant degree. In addition, privacy rights are protected to an extent under tort law, consumer law, and employment law.

Learning Objective 4
Which constitutional amendments have been interpreted as implying a right to privacy?

---

22. *Maxwell's Pic-Pac, Inc. v. Dehner,* 739 F.3d 936 (6th Cir. 2014).
23. 277 U.S. 438, 48 S.Ct. 564, 72 L.Ed. 944 (1928).
24. 381 U.S. 479, 85 S.Ct. 1678, 14 L.Ed.2d 510 (1965).

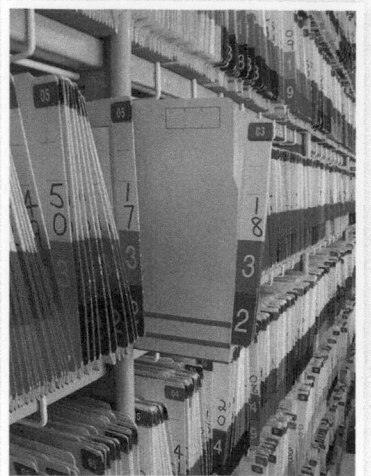

Most medical records are being put online. What law protects patients' right to privacy with respect to their online medical files?

2–4a Federal Privacy Legislation

Congress has enacted a number of statutes that protect the privacy of individuals in various areas of concern. Most of these statutes deal with personal information collected by governments or private businesses.

In the 1960s, Americans were sufficiently alarmed by the accumulation of personal information in government files that they pressured Congress to pass laws permitting individuals to access their files. Congress responded by passing the Freedom of Information Act, which allows any person to request copies of any information on her or him contained in federal government files. Congress later enacted the Privacy Act, which also gives persons the right to access such information.

In the 1990s, responding to the growing need to protect the privacy of individuals' health records—particularly computerized records—Congress passed the Health Insurance Portability and Accountability Act (HIPAA).[25] This act defines and limits the circumstances in which an individual's "protected health information" may be used or disclosed by health-care providers, health-care plans, and others. These and other major federal laws protecting privacy rights are listed and briefly described in Exhibit 2–1.

2–4b The USA Patriot Act

The USA Patriot Act was passed by Congress in the wake of the terrorist attacks of September 11, 2001, and then reauthorized twice.[26] The Patriot Act has given government officials increased authority to monitor Internet activities (such as e-mail and website visits) and to gain access to personal financial information and student information. Law enforcement officials can track the telephone and e-mail communications of one party to find out the identity of the other party or parties. Privacy advocates argue that this law adversely affects the constitutional rights of all Americans, and it has been widely criticized in the media.

---

25. HIPAA was enacted as Pub. L. No. 104-191 (1996) and is codified in 29 U.S.C.A. Sections 1181 *et seq.*

26. The Uniting and Strengthening America by Providing Appropriate Tools Required to Intercept and Obstruct Terrorism Act of 2001, also known as the USA Patriot Act, was enacted as Pub. L. No. 107-56 (2001), and last reauthorized by Pub. L. No. 112-114 (2011).

Exhibit 2–1 Federal Legislation Relating to Privacy

TITLE OF ACT	PROVISIONS CONCERNING PRIVACY
Freedom of Information Act (1966)	Provides that individuals have a right to access information about them collected in government files.
Family Educational Rights and Privacy Act (1974)	Limits access to computer-stored records of education-related evaluations and grades in private and public colleges and universities.
Privacy Act (1974)	Protects the privacy of individuals about whom the federal government has information. Regulates agencies' use and disclosure of data, and gives individuals access to and a means to correct inaccuracies.
Electronic Communications Privacy Act (1986)	Prohibits the interception of information communicated by electronic means.
Driver's Privacy Protection Act (1994)	Prevents states from disclosing or selling a driver's personal information without the driver's consent.
Health Insurance Portability and Accountability Act (1996)	Requires health-care providers and health-care plans to inform patients of their privacy rights and of how their personal medical information may be used. States that medical records may not be used for purposes unrelated to health care or disclosed without permission.
Financial Services Modernization Act (Gramm-Leach-Bliley Act) (1999)	Prohibits the disclosure of nonpublic personal information about a consumer to an unaffiliated third party unless strict disclosure and opt-out requirements are met.

To gain access to these communications, the government must certify that the information likely to be obtained is relevant to an ongoing criminal investigation, but it does not need to provide proof of any wrongdoing. **Example 2.20** General David Petraeus, who ran the wars in Iraq and Afghanistan, resigned as director of the Central Intelligence Agency in 2012 after his extramarital affair with Paula Broadwell, his biographer, became public. Apparently, after Petraeus broke off the affair with Broadwell, she sent harassing e-mails to another woman, who reported the harassment. The FBI investigated, accessed Petraeus's e-mail accounts, and discovered that he had communicated with Broadwell via messages left in a draft folder on his e-mail account. Although there was no evidence that Petraeus had done anything illegal, he was urged to resign and did so.

> "There was, of course, no way of knowing whether you were being watched at any given moment."
>
> **George Orwell**
> 1903–1950
> (English author, from his famous novel 1984)

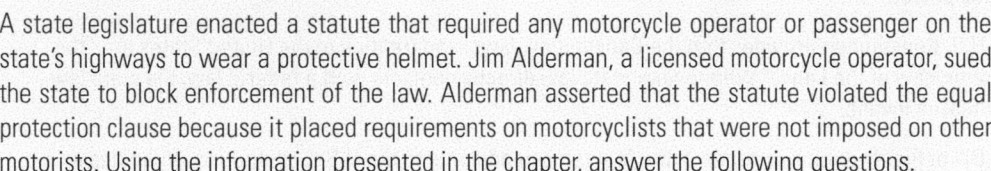

Practice and Review

A state legislature enacted a statute that required any motorcycle operator or passenger on the state's highways to wear a protective helmet. Jim Alderman, a licensed motorcycle operator, sued the state to block enforcement of the law. Alderman asserted that the statute violated the equal protection clause because it placed requirements on motorcyclists that were not imposed on other motorists. Using the information presented in the chapter, answer the following questions.

1. Why does this statute raise equal protection issues instead of substantive due process concerns?

2. What are the three levels of scrutiny that the courts use in determining whether a law violates the equal protection clause?

3. Which level of scrutiny or test would apply to this situation? Why?

4. Under this standard or test, is the helmet statute constitutional? Why or why not?

Debate This

Legislation aimed at protecting people from themselves concerns the individual as well as the public in general. Protective helmet laws are just one example of such legislation. Should individuals be allowed to engage in unsafe activities if they choose to do so?

Key Terms

Bill of Rights 38
checks and balances 34
commerce clause 34
compelling government interest 41
due process clause 49
equal protection clause 50

establishment clause 47
federal form of government 32
filtering software 46
free exercise clause 47
full faith and credit clause 33
meta tags 46

police powers 32
preemption 38
privileges and immunities clause 32
sovereignty 32
supremacy clause 37
symbolic speech 40

Chapter Summary: Constitutional Law

The Constitutional Powers of Government	The U.S. Constitution established a federal form of government, in which government powers are shared by the national government and the state governments. At the national level, government powers are divided among the legislative, executive, and judicial branches. The Tenth Amendment reserves to the states all powers not expressly delegated to the national government. Under their police powers, state governments may regulate private activities in order to protect or promote the public order, health, safety, morals, and general welfare.
The Commerce Clause	1. *The expansion of national powers*—The commerce clause expressly permits Congress to regulate commerce. Over time, courts expansively interpreted this clause, thereby enabling the national government to wield extensive powers over the economic life of the nation. 2. *The commerce clause today*—Today, the commerce clause authorizes the national government, at least theoretically, to regulate almost every commercial enterprise in the United States. 3. *The "dormant" commerce clause*—If state regulations substantially interfere with interstate commerce, they will be held to violate the "dormant" commerce clause of the U.S. Constitution. The positive aspect of the commerce clause, which gives the national government the exclusive authority to regulate interstate commerce, implies a "dormant" aspect—that the states do not have this power.
The Supremacy Clause	The U.S. Constitution provides that the Constitution, laws, and treaties of the United States are "the supreme Law of the Land." Whenever a state law directly conflicts with a federal law, the state law is rendered invalid.
Business and the Bill of Rights	The Bill of Rights, which consists of the first ten amendments to the U.S. Constitution, embodies a series of protections for individuals—and, in some instances, business entities—against various types of interference by the federal government. Today, most of the protections apply against state governments as well. Freedoms guaranteed by the First Amendment that affect businesses include the following: 1. *Freedom of speech*—Speech, including symbolic speech, is given the fullest possible protection by the courts. Corporate political speech and commercial speech also receive substantial protection under the First Amendment. Certain types of speech, such as defamatory speech and obscene speech, are not protected under the First Amendment. Government attempts to regulate unprotected forms of speech in the online environment have, to date, met with numerous challenges. 2. *Freedom of religion*—Under the First Amendment, the government may neither establish any religion (the establishment clause) nor prohibit the free exercise of religion (the free exercise clause).
Due Process and Equal Protection	1. *Due process*—Both the Fifth and the Fourteenth Amendments provide that no person shall be deprived of "life, liberty, or property, without due process of law." Procedural due process requires that any government decision to take life, liberty, or property must be made fairly, using fair procedures. Substantive due process focuses on the content of legislation. Generally, a law that limits a fundamental right violates substantive due process unless the law promotes a compelling state interest, such as public safety. 2. *Equal protection*—Under the Fourteenth Amendment, a law or action that limits the liberty of some persons but not others may violate the equal protection clause. Such a law may be upheld, however, if there is a rational basis for the discriminatory treatment of a given group or if the law substantially relates to an important government objective.
Privacy Rights	The Constitution does not contain a specific guarantee of a right to privacy, but such a right has been derived from guarantees found in several constitutional amendments. A number of federal statutes protect privacy rights. Privacy rights are also protected by many state constitutions and statutes, as well as under tort law, consumer law, and employment law.

Issue Spotters

1. South Dakota wants its citizens to conserve energy. To help reduce consumer consumption of electricity, the state passes a law that bans all advertising by power utilities within the state. What argument could the power utilities use as a defense to the enforcement of this state law? (See *Business and the Bill of Rights*.)

2. Suppose that a state imposes a higher tax on out-of-state companies doing business in the state than it imposes on in-state companies. Is this a violation of the equal protection clause if the only reason for the tax is to protect the local firms from out-of-state competition? Explain. (See *Due Process and Equal Protection*.)

    —**Check your answers to the *Issue Spotters* against the answers provided in Appendix D at the end of this text.**

Business Scenarios and Case Problems

2–1. The Free Exercise Clause. Thomas worked in the non-military operations of a large firm that produced both military and nonmilitary goods. When the company discontinued the production of nonmilitary goods, Thomas was transferred to the plant producing military equipment. Thomas left his job, claiming that it violated his religious principles to participate in the manufacture of goods to be used in destroying life. In effect, he argued, the transfer to the military equipment plant forced him to quit his job. He was denied unemployment compensation by the state because he had not been effectively "discharged" by the employer but had voluntarily terminated his employment. Did the state's denial of unemployment benefits to Thomas violate the free exercise clause of the First Amendment? Explain. (See *Business and the Bill of Rights*.)

2–2. Spotlight on Plagiarism—Due Process. The Russ College of Engineering and Technology of Ohio University announced in a press conference that it had found "rampant and flagrant plagiarism" in the theses of mechanical engineering graduate students. Faculty singled out for "ignoring their ethical responsibilities" included Jay Gunasekera, chair of the department. Gunasekera was prohibited from advising students. He filed a suit against Dennis Irwin, the dean of Russ College, for violating his due process rights. What does due process require in these circumstances? Why? [*Gunasekera v. Irwin*, 551 F.3d 461 (6th Cir. 2009)] (See *Due Process and Equal Protection*.)

2–3. Business Case Problem with Sample Answer— Freedom of Speech. Mark Wooden sent an e-mail to an alderwoman for the city of St. Louis. Attached was a nineteen-minute audio that compared her to the biblical character, Jezebel—she was a "bitch in the Sixth Ward," spending too much time with the rich and powerful and too little time with the poor. In a menacing, maniacal tone, Wooden said that he was "dusting off a sawed-off shotgun," called himself a "domestic terrorist," and referred to the assassination of President John F. Kennedy, the murder of a federal judge, and the shooting of Congresswoman Gabrielle Giffords. Feeling threatened, the alderwoman called the police.

Wooden was convicted of harassment under a state criminal statute. Was this conviction unconstitutional under the First Amendment? Discuss. [*State v. Wooden*, 388 S.W.3d 522 (Mo. 2013)] (See *Business and the Bill of Rights*.)

—**For a sample answer to Problem 2–3, go to Appendix E at the end of this text.**

2–4. Equal Protection. Abbott Laboratories licensed SmithKline Beecham Corp. to market an Abbott human immunodeficiency virus (HIV) drug in conjunction with one of SmithKline's drugs. Abbott then increased the price of its drug fourfold, forcing SmithKline to increase its prices and thereby driving business to Abbott's own combination drug. SmithKline filed a suit in a federal district court against Abbott. During jury selection, Abbott struck the only self-identified gay person among the potential jurors. (The pricing of HIV drugs is of considerable concern in the gay community.) Could the equal protection clause be applied to prohibit discrimination based on sexual orientation in jury selection? Discuss. [*SmithKline Beecham Corp. v. Abbott Laboratories*, 740 F.3d 471 (9th Cir. 2014)] (See *Due Process and Equal Protection*.)

2–5. Procedural Due Process. Robert Brown applied for admission to the University of Kansas School of Law. Brown answered "no" to questions on the application asking if he had a criminal history and acknowledged that a false answer constituted "cause for . . . dismissal." In fact, Brown had criminal convictions for domestic battery and driving under the influence. He was accepted for admission to the school. When school officials discovered his history, however, he was notified of their intent to dismiss him and given an opportunity to respond in writing. He demanded a hearing. The officials refused to grant Brown a hearing and then expelled him. Did the school's actions deny Brown due process? Discuss. [*Brown v. University of Kansas*, 599 Fed.Appx. 833 (10th Cir. 2015)] (See *Due Process and Equal Protection*.)

2–6. The Commerce Clause. Regency Transportation, Inc., operates a freight business throughout the eastern United States. Regency maintains its corporate headquarters, four warehouses, and a maintenance facility and terminal location for repairing and storing vehicles in Massachusetts. All of the vehicles in Regency's fleet were bought in other states. Massachusetts imposes a use tax on all taxpayers subject to its jurisdiction, including those that do business in interstate commerce, as Regency does. When Massachusetts imposed the tax on the purchase price of each tractor and trailer in Regency's fleet, the trucking firm challenged the assessment as discriminatory under the commerce clause. What is the chief consideration under the commerce clause when a state law affects interstate commerce? Is Massachusetts's use tax valid? Explain. [*Regency Transportation, Inc. v. Commissioner of Revenue*, 473 Mass. 459, 42 N.E.3d 1133 (2016)] (See *The Constitutional Powers of Government.*)

2–7. Freedom of Speech. Wandering Dago, Inc. (WD) operates a food truck in Albany, New York. WD brands itself and the food it sells with language generally viewed as ethnic slurs. Owners Andrea Loguidice and Brandon Snooks, however, view the branding as giving a "nod to their Italian heritage" and "weakening the derogatory force of the slur." Twice, WD applied to participate as a vendor in a summer lunch program in a state-owned plaza. Both times, the New York State Office of General Services (OGS) denied the application because of WD's branding. WD filed a suit in a federal district court against RoAnn Destito, the commissioner of OGS, contending that the agency had violated WD's right to free speech. What principles apply to the government's regulation of the content of speech? How do those principles apply in WD's case? Explain. [*Wandering Dago, Inc. v. Destito*, 879 F.3d 20 (2d Cir. 2018)] (See *Business and the Bill of Rights.*)

2–8. A Question of Ethics—Free Speech. Michael Mayfield, the president of Mendo Mill and Lumber Co., in California, received a "notice of a legal claim" from Edward Starski. The "claim" alleged that a stack of lumber fell on a customer as a result of a Mendo employee's "incompetence." The "notice" presented a settlement offer on the customer's behalf in exchange for a release of liability for Mendo. In a follow-up phone conversation with Mayfield, Starski said that he was an attorney—which, in fact, he was not. Starski was arrested and charged with violating a state criminal statute that prohibited the unauthorized practice of law. [*People v. Starski*, 7 Cal.App.5th 215, 212 Cal.Rptr.3d 622 (1 Dist. Div. 2 2017)] (See Business and the Bill of Rights.*)*

1. Starski argued that "creating an illusion" that he was an attorney was protected by the First Amendment. Is Starski correct? Explain.

2. Identify, discuss, and resolve the conflict between the right to free speech and the government's regulation of the practice of law.

Critical Thinking and Writing Assignments

2–9. Business Law Writing. Puerto Rico enacted a law that required specific labels on cement sold in Puerto Rico and imposed fines for any violations of these requirements. The law prohibited the sale or distribution of cement manufactured outside Puerto Rico that does not carry a required label warning and barred that cement from being used in government-financed construction projects.

Antilles Cement Corp., a Puerto Rican firm that imports foreign cement, filed a complaint in federal court. Antilles claimed that this law violated the dormant commerce clause. (The dormant commerce clause doctrine applies not only to commerce among the states and U.S. territories, but also to international commerce.) Write three paragraphs discussing whether the Puerto Rican law violates the dormant commerce clause. Explain your reasons why or why not. (See *The Constitutional Powers of Government.*)

2–10. Time-Limited Group Assignment—Free Speech and Equal Protection. For many years, New York City has had to deal with the vandalism and defacement of public property caused by unauthorized graffiti. In an effort to stop the damage, the city banned the sale of aerosol spray-paint cans and broad-tipped indelible markers to persons under twenty-one years of age. The new rules also prohibited people from possessing these items on property other than their own. Within a year, five people under age twenty-one were cited for violations of these regulations, and nearly nine hundred individuals were arrested for actually making graffiti.

Lindsey Vincenty and other artists wished to create graffiti on legal surfaces, such as canvas, wood, and clothing. Unable to buy supplies in the city or to carry them in the city if they were bought elsewhere, Vincenty and others filed a lawsuit on behalf of themselves and other young artists against Michael Bloomberg, the city's mayor, and others. The plaintiffs claimed that, among other things, the new rules violated their right to freedom of speech. (See *The Constitutional Powers of Government.*)

1. One group will argue in favor of the plaintiffs and provide several reasons why the court should hold that the city's new rules violate the plaintiffs' freedom of speech.

2. Another group will develop a counterargument that outlines the reasons why the new rules do not violate free speech rights.

3. A third group will argue that the city's ban violates the equal protection clause because it applies only to persons under age twenty-one.

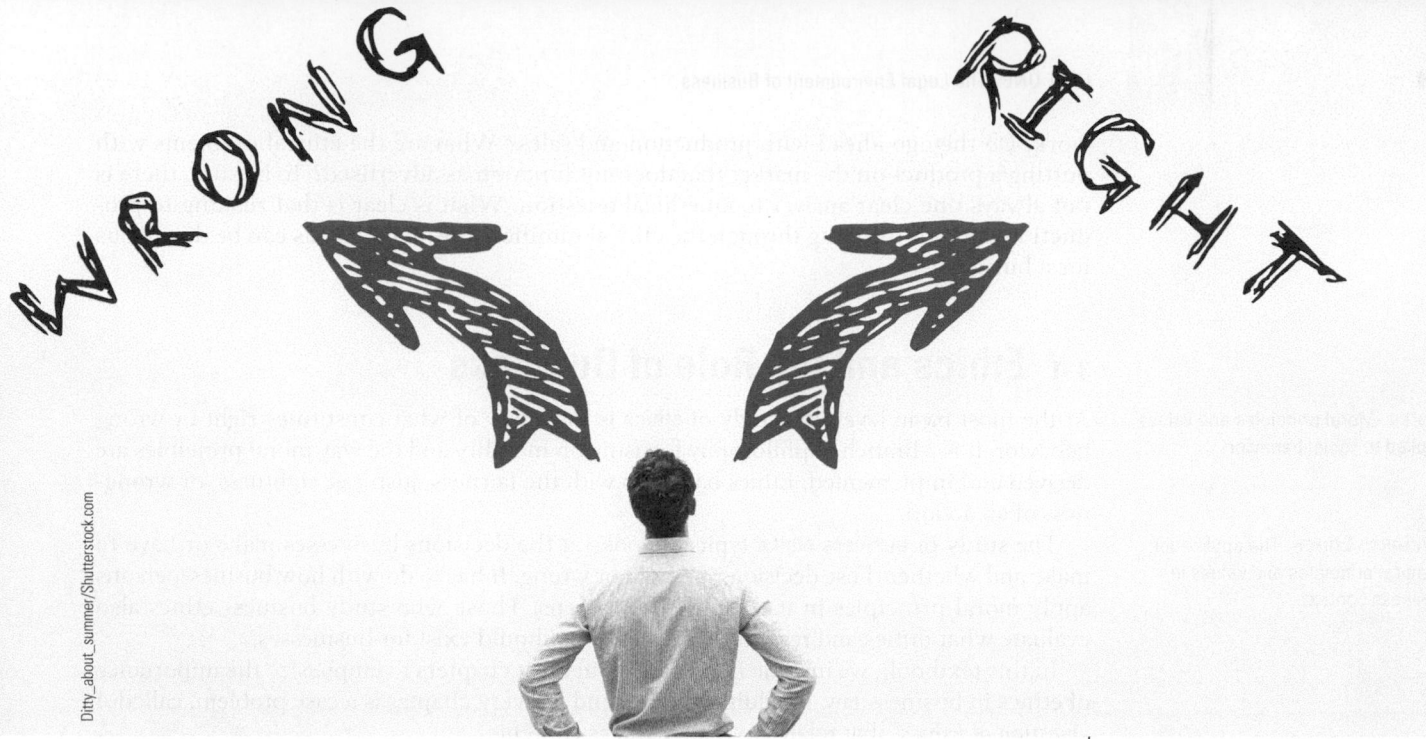

Ethics in Business

3

"New occasions
teach new duties."

James Russell Lowell
1819–1891
(American editor, poet, and
diplomat)

One of the most complex issues that businesspersons and corporations face is ethics. Ethics is not as clearly defined as the law, and yet it can substantially impact a firm's finances and reputation, especially when the firm is involved in a well-publicized scandal. Some scandals arise from conduct that is legal but ethically questionable. At other times, the conduct is both illegal and unethical. Business law and legal environment students must be able to think critically about both legal and ethical issues. As noted in the chapter-opening quotation, "New occasions teach new duties."

Suppose that Finn Clayborn dropped out of Harvard University to start a company in Silicon Valley that developed and sold finger-prick blood-test kits. Clayborn raised millions from investors by claiming that his new technology would revolutionize blood testing by providing a full range of laboratory tests from a few drops of blood. The kits were marketed as a better alternative to traditional, more expensive lab tests ordered by physicians. They were sold at drugstores for a few dollars each and touted as a way for consumers to test their blood type and monitor their cholesterol, iron, and many other conditions. Within six years, Clayborn and his company were making millions. But complaints started rolling in that the test kits didn't work and the results were not accurate (because more blood was needed). Numerous consumers, drugstores, and government agencies sued the company for fraudulent and misleading marketing practices. Clayborn's profitable start-up now faces an uncertain future.

The goal of business ethics is not to stifle innovation. There is nothing unethical about a company selling an idea or technology that is still being developed. In fact, that's exactly what many successful start-ups do—take a promising idea and develop it into a reality. But businesspersons also need to consider what will happen if new technologies do not

Learning Objectives

The five Learning Objectives *below are designed to help improve your understanding. After reading this chapter, you should be able to answer the following questions:*

1. What are two different views of the role of business in society?

2. How do duty-based ethical standards differ from outcome-based ethical standards?

3. What is short-term profit maximization, and why does it lead to ethical problems?

4. What are the four steps in the IDDR approach to ethical decision making?

5. What ethical issues might arise in the context of global business transactions?

work. Do they go ahead with production and sales? What are the ethical problems with putting a product on the market that does not function as advertised? To be sure, there is not always one clear answer to an ethical question. What is clear is that rushing to production and not thinking through the ethical ramifications of decisions can be disastrous for a business.

3–1 Ethics and the Role of Business

Ethics Moral principles and values applied to social behavior.

At the most basic level, the study of **ethics** is the study of what constitutes right or wrong behavior. It is a branch of philosophy focusing on morality and the way moral principles are derived and implemented. Ethics has to do with the fairness, justness, rightness, or wrongness of an action.

Business Ethics The application of moral principles and values in a business context.

The study of **business ethics** typically looks at the decisions businesses make or have to make and whether those decisions are right or wrong. It has to do with how businesspersons apply moral principles in making their decisions. Those who study business ethics also evaluate what duties and responsibilities exist or should exist for businesses.

In this textbook, we include *Ethical Issues* in most chapters to emphasize the importance of ethics in business law. In addition, at the end of every chapter is a case problem, called *A Question of Ethics*, that relates to that chapter's contents.

3–1a The Relationship of Law and Ethics

The government has institutionalized some ethical rights and duties through the passage of laws and regulations. Many laws are designed to prevent fraudulent (misleading, deceptive) conduct in various contexts, including contracts, health care, financial reporting, mortgages, and sales. **Example 3.1** The Fraud Reduction and Data Analytics Act was passed by Congress in 2016 to identify and assess fraud risks in federal government agencies. The purpose of the law is to prevent, detect, and respond to fraud (including improper payments) in federal programs. ■ (This chapter's *Business Web Log* feature outlines a well-publicized fraud scandal.)

Sometimes, major legislation is passed after well-publicized ethical transgressions by industries or companies result in harm to the public. **Example 3.2** After alleged ethical lapses on Wall Street contributed to a financial crisis, Congress passed the Dodd-Frank Wall Street Reform and Consumer Protection Act.[1] Dodd-Frank made sweeping changes to the United States' financial regulatory environment in an attempt to promote financial stability and protect consumers from abusive financial services practices.

Similarly, Congress enacted the Sarbanes-Oxley Act[2] (SOX) after Enron, a major energy company, engaged in risky financial maneuvers that resulted in the loss of billions of dollars to shareholders. SOX was designed to help reduce corporate fraud and unethical management decisions by setting up accountability measures for publicly traded

"Have you noticed ethics creeping into some of these deals lately?"

Henry Martin/The New Yorker Collection/Cartoon Bank.Com

---

1. Pub. L. No. 111–203, 124 Stat. 1376, July 21, 2010, 12 U.S.C. Sections 5301 *et seq.*
2. 15 U.S.C. Sections 7201 *et seq.*

Bogus Bank and Credit Card Accounts at Wells Fargo Bank

Business Web Log

Wells Fargo Bank discovered in 2016 that its employees had opened 2 million fake bank and credit card accounts for current customers without their authorization. The scam occurred over a period of five years. The bogus accounts generated extra fees for the bank and helped employees artificially inflate their sales (of new accounts) figures to meet company goals and earn bonuses.

Wells Fargo fired 5,300 employees who were involved, paid $185 million in fines to the government, and refunded $5 million to customers. No executives were terminated initially, but the bank later fired four mid-level executives, and took stock awards and bonuses away from four other executives. Wells Fargo's accreditation rating with the Better Business Bureau dropped, and a number

of state and local governments (as well as consumers) pulled their business from the bank. After an internal investigation, Wells Fargo announced in 2017 that it would take back an additional $75 million in compensation from two top executives.

Angry customers filed lawsuits against Wells Fargo alleging fraud, invasion of privacy, negligence, and breach of contract. They claim that Wells Fargo managers acted unethically and pushed employees into committing fraud by requiring them to meet unreasonably high sales quotas and create eight new customer accounts per day. Federal and state governments and agencies continued to investigate the wrongdoing. In 2018, federal government regulators decided on an additional punishment: Until Wells Fargo makes significant improvements, the bank will

be restricted from growing any larger than it was (in total asset size) at the end of 2017.

Key Point

The employees' conduct was both unethical and illegal, but Wells Fargo's managers may not have acted illegally (assuming that they had no knowledge of the fraud). Nonetheless, management may have acted unethically by fostering a culture that encouraged questionable, and even illegal, sales practices. Not all unethical conduct is illegal.

companies. Company heads must verify that they have read quarterly and annual reports and vouch for their accuracy. SOX also requires companies to set up confidential systems so that employees and others can "raise red flags" about suspected illegal or unethical auditing and accounting practices.[3] Laws cannot, however, codify all ethical requirements.

Gray Areas in the Law For a number of reasons, laws may sometimes be difficult to interpret and apply. When legislatures draft laws, they typically use broad language so that the provisions will apply in a variety of circumstances. It can be hard to determine how such broad provisions apply to specific situations. In addition, laws intended to address one situation may apply to other situations as well. And the legislative body that passes a law may not give clear guidance on the purpose of the law or the definition of terms in the law.

What ethical lessons can be drawn from the scandal involving Wells Fargo Bank's fraudulent company practices?

---

3. In one such system, employees can click on an on-screen icon that anonymously links them with NAVEX Global to report suspicious accounting practices, sexual harassment, and other possibly unethical behavior.

Know This

When it is not entirely clear how a law applies, a company's best defense to allegations of misconduct is to show that the firm acted honestly and responsibly under the circumstances.

Moral Minimum The minimum level of ethical behavior expected by society, which is usually defined as compliance with the law.

Other issues arise because laws are created through the political process. They therefore often involve compromises among competing interests and industries. As a result, a law's provisions may be ambiguous, may be weaker than intended by the original drafters, or may lack a means of enforcement. In short, the law is not always clear, and these "gray areas" in the law make it difficult to predict with certainty how a court will apply a given law to a particular action.

The Moral Minimum Compliance with the law is sometimes called the **moral minimum**. If people and entities merely comply with the law, they are acting at the lowest ethical level that society will tolerate.

Failure to meet the moral minimum can have significant consequences, especially in the context of litigation. A businessperson who fails to respond to a lawsuit filed against him or her can be held liable. **Case Example 3.3** Rick Scott deposited $2 million into an escrow account maintained by a company owned by Salvatore Carpanzano. Immediately after the deposit was made, the funds were withdrawn in violation of the escrow agreement. When Scott was unable to recover his money, he filed a suit against Salvatore Carpanzano and others, including Salvatore's daughter, Carmela. In the complaint, Scott made no allegations of acts or knowledge on Carmela's part. (The complaint claimed only that she had received a $46,600 Land Rover Range Rover purchased with the funds.)

Salvatore failed to cooperate with discovery and did not respond to attempts to contact him by certified mail, regular mail, and e-mail. He also refused to make an appearance in court and did not finalize a settlement negotiated between the parties' attorneys. Carmela denied that she was involved in her father's business or the Scott transaction. The court found that the defendants had intentionally failed to respond to the litigation and issued a judgment for more than $6 million in Scott's favor. On appeal, a federal appellate court affirmed the district court's judgment against Salvatore but reversed the judgment against Carmela. The court reasoned that there was no evidence that Carmela was willfully involved in her father's wrongdoing.[4]

Although the moral minimum is important, the study of ethics goes well beyond these legal requirements to evaluate what is right for society. *Businesspersons must remember that an action that is legal is not necessarily ethical.* For instance, a company can legally refuse to negotiate liability claims for injuries allegedly caused by a faulty product. But if the company's refusal is meant to increase the injured party's legal costs and force the party to drop a legitimate claim, the company is not acting ethically.

Private Company Codes of Ethics Most companies attempt to link ethics and law through the creation of internal codes of ethics. (We present the code of ethics of Costco Wholesale Corporation as an example in the appendix following this chapter.) Company codes are not laws. Instead, they are rules that the company sets forth and that it can enforce (by terminating an employee who does not follow them, for instance). Codes of conduct typically outline the company's policies on particular issues and indicate how employees are expected to act.

Example 3.4 Google's code of conduct starts with the motto "Don't be evil." The code then makes general statements about how Google promotes integrity, mutual respect, and the highest standard of ethical business conduct. Google's code also provides specific rules on a number of issues, such as privacy, drugs and alcohol, conflicts of interest, co-worker relationships, and confidentiality—it even includes a dog policy. The company takes a stand against employment discrimination that goes further than the law requires. It prohibits discrimination based on sexual orientation, gender identity or expression, and veteran status.

Industry Ethical Codes Numerous industries have also developed codes of ethics. The American Institute of Certified Public Accountants (AICPA) has a comprehensive Code of Professional Conduct for the ethical practicing of accounting. The American Bar Association

---

4. *Scott v. Carpanzano,* 556 Fed.Appx. 288 (5th Cir. 2014).

(ABA) has model rules of professional conduct for attorneys, and the American Nurses Association (ANA) has a code of ethics that applies to nurses. These codes can give guidance to decision makers facing ethical questions. Violation of a code may result in the discipline of an employee or sanctions against a company from the industry organization. Remember, though, that these internal codes are not laws, so their effectiveness is determined by the commitment of the industry or company leadership to enforcing the codes.

3–1b The Role of Business in Society

Over the last two hundred years, public perception has moved toward expecting corporations to participate in society as corporate citizens. Originally, though, the only perceived duty of a corporation was to maximize profits and generate revenues for its owners. Although many people today may view this idea as greedy or ruthless, the rationale for the profit-maximization theory is still valid.

Business as a Pure Profit Maximizer In theory, if all firms strictly adhere to the goal of maximizing profits, resources flow to where they are most highly valued by society. Corporations can focus on their strengths. Other entities that are better suited to deal with social problems and perform charitable acts can specialize in those activities. The government, through taxes and other financial allocations, can shift resources to those other entities to perform public services. Thus, profit maximization can lead to the most efficient allocation of scarce resources.

Even when profit maximization is the goal, companies benefit by ethical behavior. For instance, customer satisfaction with a company is key to its profitability. Repeat customers are good for business. When customers are happy, word gets around, and it generates more business for the firm. Unsatisfied customers go elsewhere for the goods or services that the firm provides. When a business behaves badly, customers quickly report this online by posting bad reviews on such sites as Angie's List, Yelp, and TripAdvisor. Bad reviews obviously hurt a business's profits, while good reviews lead to higher profits.

Business as a Corporate Citizen Over the years, many people became dissatisfied with profit-maximization theory. Investors and others began to look beyond profits and dividends and to consider the **triple bottom line**—a corporation's profits, its impact on people, and its impact on the planet. Magazines and websites began to rank companies based on their environmental impacts and their ethical decisions. Corporations came to be viewed as "citizens" that were expected to participate in bettering communities and society.

A Four-Part Analysis Whether one believes in profit-maximization theory or corporate citizenship, ethics is important in business decision making. When making decisions, a business should evaluate each of the following:

1. The legal implications of each decision.
2. The public relations impact.
3. The safety risks for consumers and employees.
4. The financial implications.

This four-part analysis will assist the firm in making decisions that not only maximize profits but also reflect good corporate citizenship.

3–1c Ethical Issues in Business

Ethical issues can arise in numerous aspects of doing business. A fundamental ethical issue for business is developing integrity and trust. Businesspersons should exhibit integrity in their dealings with other people in the company, other businesses, clients, and the community. Be honest and treat people fairly. Earn their trust.

Learning Objective 1
What are two different views of the role of business in society?

Triple Bottom Line A measure that includes a corporation's profits, its impact on people, and its impact on the planet.

"It's easy to make a buck. It's a lot tougher to make a difference."

Tom Brokaw
1940–present
(American television journalist)

Businesses should also ensure that the workplace respects diversity and enforces equal opportunity employment and civil rights laws. In addition, businesses must comply with a host of federal and state laws and regulations, including those pertaining to the environment, financial reporting, and safety standards. Compliance with these rules can involve ethical issues. See this chapter's *Adapting the Law to the Online Environment* feature for a discussion of an ethical issue that has arisen from employees' work-related use of digital technology after work hours.

Should Employees Have a "Right of Disconnecting"?

Adapting the Law to the Online Environment

Almost all jobs today involve digital technology, whether it be e-mails, Internet access, or smartphone use. Most employees, when interviewed, say that digital technology increases their productivity and flexibility. The downside is what some call an "electronic leash"— employees are constantly connected and therefore end up working when they are not "at work." Over one-third of full-time workers, for example, say that they frequently check e-mails outside normal working hours.

Do Workers Have the Right to Disconnect?

Because the boundaries between being "at work" and being "at leisure" can be so hazy, some labor unions in other countries have attempted to pass rules that allow employees to disconnect from e-mail and other work-related digital communication during nonworking hours. For example, a French labor union representing high-tech workers signed an agreement with a large business association recognizing a "right of disconnecting."

In Germany, Volkswagen and BMW no longer forward e-mail to staff from company servers after the end of the working day. Other German firms have declared that workers are not expected to check e-mail on weekends and holidays. The government is considering legislating such restrictions nationwide.

The Thorny Issue of Overtime and the Fair Labor Standards Act

In the United States, payment for overtime work is strictly regulated under the Fair Labor Standards Act (FLSA). According to the Supreme Court, in this context, *work* is "physical or mental exertion (whether burdensome or not) controlled or required by the employer and pursued necessarily for the benefit of the employer and his business."[a] This definition was extended to off-duty work if such work is an "integral and indispensible part of [employees'] activities."[b] For example, a court recently ruled that Hormel Foods Corporation had to pay its factory workers for the time it took them to change into and out of the required white clothes before and after their shifts.[c]

Today's modern digital connectivity raises issues about the definition of *work*. Employees at several major companies, including Black & Decker, T-Mobile, and Verizon, have sued for unpaid overtime related to smartphone use. In another case, a police sergeant has sued the city of Chicago, claiming that he should have been paid overtime for hours spent using his personal digital assistant (PDA). The police department had issued PDAs to officers and required them to respond to work-related communications even while off duty. The court agreed that some of the officers' off-duty PDA activities were compensable. Nevertheless, it ruled in favor of the city because the officers had failed to follow proper procedures for filing overtime claims.[d]

Not All Employees Demand the "Right to Disconnect"

In a recent Gallup poll, 79 percent of full-time employees had either strongly positive or somewhat positive views of using computers, e-mail, tablets, and smartphones to work remotely outside of normal business hours. According to the same poll, 17 percent of them report "better overall lives" because of constant online connectivity with their work. Working remotely after business hours apparently does not necessarily result in additional work-related stress.

Critical Thinking

From an ethical point of view, is there any difference between calling subordinates during off hours for work-related questions and sending them e-mails or text messages?

a. *Tennessee Coal, Iron & R. Co. v. Muscoda Local No. 123,* 321 U.S. 590, 64 S.Ct. 698, 8 L.Ed. 949 (1944). Although Congress later passed a statute that superseded the holding in this case, the statute gave the courts broad authority to interpret the FLSA's definition of *work.* 29 U.S.C. Section 251(a). See *Integrity Staffing Solutions, Inc. v. Busk,* ___ U.S. ___, 135 S.Ct. 513, 190 L.Ed.2d 410 (2014).

b. *Steiner v. Mitchell,* 350 U.S. 247, 76 S.Ct. 330, 100 L.Ed. 267 (1956).

c. *United Food & Commercial Workers Union, Local 1473 v. Hormel Food Corp.,* 367 Wis.2d 131, 876 N.W.2d 99 (2016).

d. *Allen v. City of Chicago,* 2015 WL 8493996 (N.D.Ill. 2015).

The most difficult aspect of ethics that businesses face is in decision making, which is the focus of this text. Businesspersons must learn to recognize ethical issues, get the pertinent facts, evaluate the alternatives, and then make a decision. Decision makers should also test and reflect on the outcome of their decisions.

3–1d The Importance of Ethical Leadership

In ethics, as in other areas, employees take their cues from management. Talking about ethical business decision making is meaningless if management does not set standards. Furthermore, managers must apply the same standards to themselves as they do to the company's employees. This duty starts with top management.

Attitude of Top Management One of the most important ways to create and maintain an ethical workplace is for top management to demonstrate its commitment to ethical decision making. A manager who is not totally committed to an ethical workplace will rarely succeed in creating one. More than anything else, top management's behavior sets the ethical tone of a firm.

Managers have found that discharging even one employee for ethical reasons has a tremendous impact as a deterrent to unethical behavior in the workplace. This is true even if the company has a written code of ethics. If management does not enforce the company code, the code is essentially nonexistent.

The administration of a university may have had this concept in mind in the following case when it applied the school's professionalism standard to a student who had engaged in serious misconduct.

Know This

One of the best ways to encourage good business ethics at a workplace is to take immediate corrective action in response to any unethical conduct.

■ **Case 3.1**

Al-Dabagh v. Case Western Reserve University

United States Court of Appeals, Sixth Circuit, 777 F.3d 355 (2015).

Background and Facts The curriculum at Case Western Reserve University School of Medicine identifies nine "core competencies." At the top of the list is professionalism, which includes "ethical, honest, responsible and reliable behavior." The university's Committee on Students determines whether a student has met the professionalism requirements.

Amir Al-Dabagh enrolled at the school and did well academically. But he sexually harassed fellow students, often asked an instructor not to mark him late for class, received complaints from hospital staff about his demeanor, and was convicted of driving while intoxicated. The Committee on Students unanimously refused to certify him for graduation and dismissed him from the university.

He filed a suit in a federal district court against Case Western, alleging a breach of good faith and fair dealing. The court ordered the school to issue a diploma. Case Western appealed.

Under what circumstances can a medical school withhold a diploma from one of its students?

In the Words of the Court
SUTTON, Circuit Judge.
＊ ＊ ＊ ＊
＊ ＊ ＊ Case Western's student handbook ＊ ＊ ＊ makes clear that the only thing standing between Al-Dabagh and a diploma is the Committee on Students's finding that he lacks professionalism. Unhappily for Al-Dabagh, that is an academic judgment. And *we can no more substitute our personal views for the Committee's when it comes to an academic judgment than the Committee can substitute its views for ours when it comes to a judicial decision.* [Emphasis added.]
＊ ＊ ＊ ＊
＊ ＊ ＊ *The Committee's professionalism determination is an academic judgment. That conclusion all but resolves this case. We may overturn the Committee only if it substantially departed from accepted academic norms when it refused to approve Al-Dabagh for graduation. And given Al-Dabagh's track*

(Continues)

record—one member of the Committee does not recall encountering another student with Al-Dabagh's "repeated professionalism issues" in his quarter century of experience—we cannot see how it did. [Emphasis added.]

To the contrary, Al-Dabagh insists: The Committee's decision was a "punitive disciplinary measure" that had nothing to do with academics. * * * His argument fails to wrestle with the prominent place of professionalism in the university's academic curriculum— which itself is an academic decision courts may not lightly disturb.

Even if professionalism is an academic criterion, Al-Dabagh persists that the university defined it too broadly. As he sees it, the only professional lapses that matter are the ones linked to academic performance. That is not how we see it or for that matter how the medical school sees it. That many professionalism-related cases involve classroom incidents does not establish that only classroom incidents are relevant to the professionalism inquiry * * * . Our own standards indicate that professionalism does not end at the courtroom door. Why should hospitals operate any differently?

As for the danger that an expansive view of professionalism might forgive, or provide a cloak for, arbitrary or discriminatory behavior, we see no such problem here. Nothing in the record suggests that the university had impermissible motives or acted in bad faith in this instance. And nothing in our deferential standard prevents us from invalidating genuinely objectionable actions when they occur.

The U.S. Court of Appeals for the Sixth Circuit reversed the lower court's order to issue a diploma to Al-Dabagh. The federal appellate court found nothing to indicate that Case Western had "impermissible motives," acted in bad faith, or dealt unfairly with Al-Dabagh.

Decision and Remedy The federal appellate court reversed the lower court's order to issue a diploma to Al-Dabagh. The court found nothing to indicate that Case Western had "impermissible motives," acted in bad faith, or dealt unfairly with Al-Dabagh.

Critical Thinking

• **What If the Facts Were Different?** *Suppose that Case Western had tolerated Al-Dabagh's conduct and awarded him a diploma. What impact might that have had on other students at the school? Why?*

Unrealistic Goals for Employees Certain types of behavior on the part of managers and owners contribute to unethical behavior among employees. Managers who set unrealistic production or sales goals increase the probability that employees will act unethically. If a sales quota can be met only through high-pressure, unethical sales tactics, employees will try to act "in the best interest of the company" and behave unethically. A manager who looks the other way when she or he knows about an employee's unethical behavior also sets an example—one indicating that ethical transgressions will be accepted.

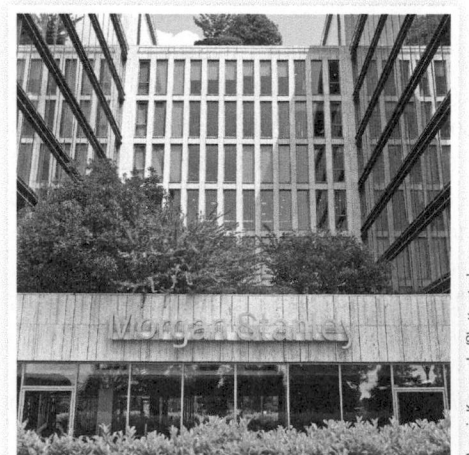

Why is a sales contest not a good idea for many companies?

Note that even when large companies have policies against sales incentives, individual branches may still promote them. **Case Example 3.5** The financial firm Morgan Stanley Smith Barney, LLC, has an internal policy barring sales contests. Nevertheless, Morgan Stanley branches in Massachusetts and Rhode Island held a sales contest in which brokers were given cash incentives of up to $5,000 for selling securities-based loans, or SBLs (loans that allow clients to borrow against their investments). Thirty financial advisers participated in the sales contest for almost a year until Morgan Stanley's compliance office noticed and halted the practice. One regional branch reportedly tripled its loans as a result of the contest. In 2016, the state of Massachusetts sued Morgan Stanley, claiming that the practice violated state securities rules.[5]

Fostering of Unethical Conduct Business owners and managers sometimes take more active roles in fostering unethical and illegal conduct, with negative

---

5. *In re Morgan Stanley Smith Barney, LLC,* Docket No. E-2016-0055. *www.sec.state.ma.us.* 3 Oct. 2016. Web.

consequences for their businesses. **Case Example 3.6** Dr. Rajendra Gandhi and his wife were devout Hindus who wanted to redecorate their entire home with high-quality custom designer furniture and draperies. They hired Sonal Furniture and Custom Draperies, LLC, because Sonal's owner, Shyam Garg, represented himself to be culturally and religiously like-minded. Garg told the Gandhis that he would use only the highest-quality materials in their home, and Dr. Gandhi gave Garg a $20,000 deposit. Garg later showed up at the couple's home unannounced with four trucks full of furniture. The Gandhis paid Garg $190,000 (for a total of $210,000).

Within weeks, the Gandhis began noticing that the items provided were of inferior quality. Nearly every piece was damaged in some way. Eventually, Dr. Gandhi demanded a full refund from Garg. Garg threatened to pursue criminal action against Dr. Gandhi, among other things. The Gandhis sued Sonal Furniture and Garg. An expert testified that the furniture was "not actually intended for functional use, almost like movie set furniture," and "would be very difficult to repair." The court ruled in favor of the Gandhis and awarded a full refund of the price, plus $100,000 in damages. The court found that Garg had misrepresented the quality of the furniture and had preyed on the Ghandis' cultural and religious heritage, using outrageous threats, coercion, and extortion. The judgment was affirmed on appeal.[6]

3–2 Ethical Principles and Philosophies

How do business decision makers decide whether a given action is the "right" one for their firms? What ethical standards should be applied? Broadly speaking, **ethical reasoning**—the application of moral convictions or ethical standards to a situation—applies to businesses just as it does to individuals. As businesses make decisions, they must analyze the alternatives in a variety of ways, one of which is from an ethical perspective. In analyzing alternatives in this way, businesses may take one of two approaches.

Generally, the study of ethics is divided into two major categories—duty-based ethics and outcome-based ethics. **Duty-based ethics** is rooted in the idea that every person (and business) has certain duties to others, including humans and the planet. **Outcome-based ethics** determines what is ethical by looking at the consequences, or outcomes, of any given action. Most companies have written codes or policies that outline their approach to ethics.

3–2a Duty-Based Ethics

Duty-based ethics focuses on the obligations of the corporation. It deals with standards for behavior that traditionally were derived from revealed truths, religious authorities, and philosophical reasoning. These standards involve concepts of right and wrong, duties owed, and rights to be protected. Corporations today often describe these values or duties in their mission statements or strategic plans. Some companies base their statements on a nonreligious rationale. Others still derive their values from religious doctrine.

Religious Ethical Principles Nearly every religion has principles or beliefs about how one should treat others. In the Judeo-Christian tradition, which is the dominant religious tradition in the United States, the Ten Commandments of the Old Testament establish these fundamental rules for moral action. The principles of the Muslim faith are set out in the Qur'an, and Hindus find their principles in the four Vedas.

Religious rules generally are absolute with respect to the behavior of their adherents. **Example 3.7** The commandment "Thou shalt not steal" is an absolute mandate for a person who believes that the Ten Commandments reflect revealed truth. Even a benevolent motive for stealing (such as Robin Hood's) cannot justify the act, because the act itself is inherently immoral and thus wrong.

6. *Gandhi v. Sonal Furniture and Custom Draperies, LLC*, 192 So.3d 783 (La.App. 2015).

Learning Objective 2

How do duty-based ethical standards differ from outcome-based ethical standards?

Ethical Reasoning A reasoning process in which an individual links his or her moral convictions or ethical standards to the situation at hand.

Duty-Based Ethics An ethical philosophy rooted in the idea that every person (and every business) has certain duties to others, including both humans and the planet.

Outcome-Based Ethics An ethical philosophy that focuses on the consequences of any given action in order to maximize benefits and minimize harms.

"When I do good, I feel good. When I do bad, I feel bad. And that's my religion."

Abraham Lincoln
1809–1865
(Sixteenth president of the United States, 1861–1865)

How can religious beliefs complicate or enhance a business owner's operations and decisions?

Principle of Rights The belief that human beings have certain fundamental rights.

For businesses, religious principles can be a unifying force for employees or a rallying point to increase employee motivation. They can also present problems, however, when owners, suppliers, employees, and customers have varying religious backgrounds. Taking an action based on religious principles, especially when those principles address socially or politically controversial topics, can lead to negative publicity and even to protests or boycotts.

Example 3.8 Bright Futures, a family-owned educational supply business in California, hires Jamie as a bookkeeper. When Jamie tells the owners that she is transgender, she is fired because of their religious beliefs. When Jamie's story is published in the local media, Bright Futures loses many customers. Eventually, Bright Futures closes down. ▪

The Principle of Rights Another view of duty-based ethics focuses on basic rights. The principle that human beings have certain fundamental rights (to life, freedom, and the pursuit of happiness, for instance) is deeply embedded in Western culture. As discussed in Chapter 1, the natural law tradition embraces the concept that certain actions (such as killing another person) are morally wrong because they are contrary to nature (the natural desire to continue living).

Those who adhere to the **principle of rights,** or "rights theory," believe that a key factor in determining whether a business decision is ethical is how that decision affects the rights of others. These others include the firm's owners, its employees, the consumers of its products or services, its suppliers, the community in which it does business, and society as a whole.

Conflicting Rights. A potential dilemma for those who support rights theory is that they may disagree on which rights are most important. When considering all those affected by a business decision to downsize a firm, for instance, how much weight should be given to employees relative to shareholders? Which employees should be laid off first—those with the highest salaries or those who have worked for the firm for a shorter time (and have less seniority)? How should the firm weigh the rights of customers relative to the community, or of employees relative to society as a whole?

Resolving Conflicts. In general, rights theorists believe that whichever right is stronger in a particular circumstance takes precedence. **Example 3.9** Murray Chemical Corporation has to decide whether to keep a chemical plant in Utah open, thereby saving the jobs of a hundred and fifty workers, or shut it down. Closing the plant will prevent the contamination of a river with pollutants that would endanger the health of tens of thousands of people. In this situation, a rights theorist can easily choose which group to favor because the value of the right to health and well-being is obviously stronger than the basic right to work. Not all choices are so clear-cut, however. ▪

Kantian Ethical Principles Duty-based ethical standards may be derived solely from philosophical reasoning. The German philosopher Immanuel Kant (1724–1804) identified some general guiding principles for moral behavior based on what he thought to be the fundamental nature of human beings. Kant believed that human beings are qualitatively different from other physical objects and are endowed with moral integrity and the capacity to reason and conduct their affairs rationally.

People Are Not a Means to an End. Based on his view of human beings, Kant said that when people are treated merely as a means to an end, they are being treated as the equivalent of objects and are being denied their basic humanity. For instance, a manager who treats subordinates as mere profit-making tools is less likely to retain motivated and loyal employees than a manager who respects subordinates. Management research has shown that employees who feel empowered to share their thoughts, opinions, and solutions to problems are happier and more productive.

The Categorical Imperative. When a business makes unethical decisions, it often rationalizes its actions by saying that the company is "just one small part" of the problem or that its decision would have "only a small impact." A central theme in Kantian ethics is that individuals should evaluate their actions in light of the consequences that would follow if everyone in society acted in the same way. This **categorical imperative** can be applied to any action.

Example 3.10 CHS Fertilizer is deciding whether to invest in expensive equipment that will decrease profits but will also reduce pollution from its factories. If CHS has adopted Kant's categorical imperative, the decision makers will consider the consequences if every company invested in the equipment (or if no company did so). If the result would make the world a better place (less polluted), CHS's decision would be clear.

Categorical Imperative An ethical guideline developed by Immanuel Kant under which an action is evaluated in terms of what would happen if everybody else in the same situation, or category, acted the same way.

3–2b Outcome-Based Ethics: Utilitarianism

In contrast to duty-based ethics, outcome-based ethics focuses on the consequences of an action, not on the nature of the action itself or on any set of preestablished moral values or religious beliefs. Outcome-based ethics looks at the impacts of a decision in an attempt to maximize benefits and minimize harms.

The premier philosophical theory for outcome-based decision making is **utilitarianism,** a philosophical theory developed by Jeremy Bentham (1748–1832) and modified by John Stuart Mill (1806–1873)—both British philosophers. "The greatest good for the greatest number" is a paraphrase of the major premise of the utilitarian approach to ethics.

How might a company use Kant's categorical imperative to decide whether to voluntarily reduce pollution?

Cost-Benefit Analysis Under a utilitarian model of ethics, an action is morally correct, or "right," when, among the people it affects, it produces the greatest amount of good for the greatest number (or creates the least amount of harm). When an action affects the majority adversely, it is morally wrong. Applying the utilitarian theory thus requires the following steps:

1. A determination of which individuals will be affected by the action in question.

2. A **cost-benefit analysis,** which involves an assessment of the negative and positive effects of alternative actions on these individuals.

3. A choice among alternative actions that will produce maximum societal utility (the greatest positive net benefits for the greatest number of individuals).

For instance, assume that expanding a factory would provide hundreds of jobs but generate pollution that could endanger the lives of thousands of people. A utilitarian analysis would find that saving the lives of thousands creates greater good than providing jobs for hundreds.

Utilitarianism An approach to ethical reasoning in which an action is evaluated in terms of its consequences for those whom it will affect. A "good" action is one that results in the greatest good for the greatest number of people.

Cost-Benefit Analysis A decision-making technique that involves weighing the costs of a given action against the benefits of that action.

Problems with the Utilitarian Approach There are problems with a strict utilitarian analysis. In some situations, an action that produces the greatest good for the most people may not seem to be the most ethical.

Example 3.11 Phazim Company is producing a drug that will cure a disease in 99 percent of patients, but the other 1 percent will experience agonizing side effects and a horrible, painful death. A quick utilitarian analysis would suggest that the drug should be produced and marketed because the majority of patients will benefit. Many people, however, have significant concerns about manufacturing a drug that will cause serious harm to anyone.

3–2c Corporate Social Responsibility

Corporate Social Responsibility (CSR) The idea that corporations can and should act ethically and be accountable to society for their actions.

In pairing duty-based concepts with outcome-based concepts, strategists and theorists developed the idea of the corporate citizen, which we touched on earlier, and the concept of corporate social responsibility. **Corporate social responsibility (CSR)** combines a commitment to good citizenship with a commitment to making ethical decisions, improving society, and minimizing environmental impact. CSR is not imposed on a corporation by law but is instead a form of self-regulation by the company.

CSR is a relatively new concept in the history of business, but it is a concept that becomes more important every year. A survey of U.S. executives undertaken by the Boston College Center for Corporate Citizenship found that more than 70 percent of those polled agreed that corporate citizenship must be treated as a priority. More than 60 percent said that good corporate citizenship added to their companies' profits.

CSR can be a successful strategy for companies, but corporate decision makers must not lose track of the two descriptors in the title: *corporate* and *social*. The company must link the responsibility of citizenship with the strategy and key principles of the business. Incorporating both the social and the corporate components of CSR and making ethical decisions can help companies grow and prosper.

CSR is most successful when a company undertakes activities that are significant and related to its business operations. Some types of activities that businesses are practicing today include the following:

1. Environmental efforts, such as using efficient building materials and reducing the size of the firm's carbon footprint.

2. Ethical labor practices, including treating all employees fairly and ethically in international as well as domestic operations.

3. Charitable donations to local and national causes.

4. Volunteering for specific issues and organizations. As an incentive, many companies now pay employees to perform volunteer work.

How did Ben & Jerry's benefit from promoting sustainability in its operations?

Ken Wolter/Shutterstock.com

The Corporate Aspects of CSR Arguably, any socially responsible activity will benefit a corporation. A corporation may see an increase in goodwill from the local community for creating a sports park, for instance. A corporation that is viewed as a good citizen may see a rise in sales. **Example 3.12** Sales have increased for Ben & Jerry's ice cream since the 1980s when the company became known for its socially responsible business practices. The company uses only fair trade ingredients and opposes the use of growth hormones in cows. It promotes sustainability programs for dairy farmers and supports family farms. ▪

At times, the benefit may not be immediate. It may cost more initially to construct a new plant that meets the high standards necessary to be certified as environmentally friendly by the LEED program, for example. (LEED stands for Leadership in Energy and Environmental Design.) Nevertheless, over the life of the building, the savings in maintenance and utilities may more than make up for the extra cost of construction.

Surveys of college students about to enter the job market confirm that young people are looking for socially responsible employers. While socially responsible activities may cost a corporation now, they may also lead to more talented and more committed employees. Corporations that engage in meaningful social activities retain workers longer, particularly younger ones. **Example 3.13** Google's focus on social responsibility attracts many young workers. Google has worked to reduce its carbon footprint and to make its products and services better for the environment. The company promotes green commuting, recycling, and reducing energy consumption at its data centers. ▪

The Social Aspects of CSR Because business controls so much of the wealth and power in this country, it has a responsibility to use that wealth and power in socially beneficial ways. Thus, the social aspect requires that corporations demonstrate that they are promoting goals that society deems worthwhile and are moving toward solutions to social problems. Companies may be judged on how much they donate to social causes, as well as how they conduct their operations with respect to employment discrimination, human rights, environmental concerns, and similar issues. Millennials, in particular, are concerned about corporate social responsibility.

Some corporations publish annual social responsibility reports, which may also be called citizenship or sustainability reports. **Example 3.14** The multinational technology company Cisco Systems, Inc., issues corporate responsibility reports to demonstrate its focus on people, society, and the planet. In a recent report, Cisco outlined its commitment to developing its employees' skills, ethical conduct, and charitable donations (including matching employee contributions and giving employees time off for volunteer work). Cisco also reported on the social and economic impact of its business globally, in the areas of human rights, labor, privacy and data security, and responsible manufacturing. The report indicated that Cisco had completed more than a hundred energy-efficient projects and was on track to meet its goals of reducing emissions from its worldwide operations by 40 percent. ▪

Stakeholders and CSR One view of CSR stresses that corporations have a duty not just to shareholders, but also to other groups affected by corporate decision making, called **stakeholders.** The rationale for this "stakeholder view" is that, in some circumstances, one or more of these groups may have a greater stake in company decisions than the shareholders do.

Stakeholders Groups that are affected by corporate decisions. Stakeholders include employees, customers, creditors, suppliers, and the community in which the corporation operates.

A corporation's stakeholders include its employees, customers, creditors, suppliers, and the community in which it operates. Advocacy groups, such as environmental groups and animal rights groups, may also be stakeholders. Under the stakeholder approach, a corporation considers the impact of its decision on these stakeholders, which helps it to avoid making a decision that may appear unethical and may result in negative publicity.

The most difficult aspect of the stakeholder analysis is determining which group's interests should receive greater weight if the interests conflict. For instance, companies that are struggling financially sometimes lay off workers to reduce labor costs. But some corporations have found ways to avoid slashing their workforces and to prioritize their employees' interests. Companies finding alternatives to layoffs include Dell (extended unpaid holidays), Cisco (four-day end-of-year shutdowns), Motorola (salary cuts), and Honda (voluntary unpaid vacation time). These alternatives not only benefit the employees who get to keep their jobs, but also the community as whole. Working people can afford to go out to local restaurants and shops and use local service providers. Thus, other businesses in the community benefit.

3–3 Sources of Ethical Issues in Business Decisions

A key to avoiding unethical conduct is to recognize how certain situations may lead individuals to act unethically. In this section, we first consider some specific areas in which ethical decisions may often arise. We then discuss some additional problems in making ethical business decisions.

Learning Objective 3

What is short-term profit maximization, and why does it lead to ethical problems?

3–3a Short-Term Profit Maximization

Businesspersons often commit ethical violations because they are too focused on one issue or one needed result, such as increasing profits or outperforming the competition. Some studies indicate that top-performing companies may actually be more likely to behave unethically than less successful companies, because employees feel they are expected to continue performing at a high level. Thus, abnormally high profits and stock prices may lead to unethical behavior.

In attempting to maximize profits, corporate executives and employees have to distinguish between *short-run* and *long-run* profit maximization. In the short run, a company may increase its profits by continuing to sell a product even though it knows that the product is defective. In the long run, though, because of lawsuits, large settlements, and bad publicity, such unethical conduct will cause profits to suffer. An overemphasis on short-run profit maximization is perhaps the most common reason that ethical problems occur in business.

How did short-term profit maximization backfire on German car manufacturer Volkswagen?

ollo/iStock Unreleased/Getty Images

Case Example 3.15 Volkswagen's corporate executives were accused of cheating on the pollution emissions tests of millions of vehicles that were sold in the United States. Volkswagen (VW) eventually admitted that it had installed "defeat device" software in its diesel models. The software detected when the car was being tested and changed its performance to improve the test outcome. As a result, the diesel cars showed low emissions—a feature that made the cars more attractive to today's consumers.

Ultimately, Volkswagen agreed to plead guilty to criminal charges and pay $2.8 billion in fines. The company also agreed to pay $1.5 billion to the Environmental Protection Agency to settle the federal investigation into its "clean diesel" emissions fraud. Overall, the scandal has cost VW nearly $15 billion (in fines and to compensate consumers or buy back their vehicles). Even though the company has settled, six top executives at VW were charged with criminal wire fraud, conspiracy, and violations of the Clean Air Act. In the end, the company's focus on maximizing profits in the short run (with increased sales) led to unethical conduct that will hurt profits in the long run.[7]

In the following case, a drug manufacturer was accused of fabricating the "average wholesale prices" for its drugs to maximize its profits and receive an overpayment from Medicaid.

---

7. *In re Volkswagen "Clean Diesel" Marketing, Sales Practices, and Product Liability Litigation,* 229 F.Supp.3d 1052 and 2017 WL 66281 (N.D.Cal. 2017).

■ Case 3.2

Watson Laboratories, Inc. v. State of Mississippi

Supreme Court of Mississippi, __ So.3d __, 2018 WL 372297 (2018).

Background and Facts Watson Laboratories, Inc., makes generic drugs, which are provided by pharmacies to Medicaid patients. In the state of Mississippi, a claim is submitted for the cost of the drug to Mississippi Medicaid. The claim is paid according to a percentage of the drug's average wholesale price (AWP). Like other drug makers, Watson published its products' AWPs. But for more than a dozen years, Watson set each AWP to meet the requirements to obtain a generic designation for the drug, without regard to the actual price.

When Mississippi Medicaid learned that the actual prices were much lower than the published AWPs, the state filed a lawsuit in a Mississippi state court against Watson, alleging fraud.

The court concluded that Watson caused the state to overpay for the drugs and ordered the payment of more than $30 million in penalties, damages, and interest. Watson appealed.

In the Words of the Court . . .

CHAMBERLIN, Justice, for the court:

* * * *

* * * The elements of an intentional * * * fraudulent representation are:

(1) a representation, (2) its falsity, (3) its materiality, (4) the speaker's knowledge of its falsity or ignorance of its truth, (5) his intent that it should be acted on by the hearer and in the manner reasonably contemplated, (6) the hearer's ignorance of its falsity, (7) his reliance on its truth, (8) his right to rely thereon, and (9) his consequent and proximate injury.

* * * *

* * * *The numbers [published] by Watson * * * were not "suggested wholesale prices" or "list prices." They were fabricated numbers tied to nothing more than a ceiling amount it was necessary to stay under in order to obtain a generic designation.* [Emphasis added.]

* * * Thus, Watson did make a false representation.

* * * *

* * * Watson knew that Mississippi Medicaid would rely on its false statements and benefitted from this reliance. It is evident that Watson intended to deceive Mississippi Medicaid.

* * * *

Mississippi Medicaid had every right to rely on AWP [average wholesale price] as a "starting point" or "benchmark" for determining appropriate reimbursement rates. They were held out as a "suggested wholesale price."

* * * *

Evidence in the record is sufficient to show the overpayment for the drugs in question. The extent of the damages, through just and reasonable inference, has been supported by the evidence. [Emphasis added.]

* * * *

In sum, * * * Watson defrauded the State. For years, Watson intentionally published its AWPs * * * with the knowledge and intent that Mississippi Medicaid would rely on the figures for its reimbursement formulas. * * * Mississippi Medicaid did not know that the AWPs had no relation to the actual prices paid for the drugs. As such, Mississippi Medicaid continued to reasonably rely on the AWPs * * * . All the while, Watson * * * exploited Mississippi Medicaid's lack of knowledge at the expense of the taxpayers of the State of Mississippi.

Decision and Remedy
The Mississippi Supreme Court affirmed the lower court's order. Watson falsely misrepresented its AWPs, and it "knew that Mississippi Medicaid would rely on its false statements, and [Watson] benefitted from this reliance."

Critical Thinking

• **Economic** *What marketing tool did Watson gain by inflating its AWPs?*

• **What If the Facts Were Different?** *Watson argued that AWP was a term of art in the pharmaceutical industry that meant "suggested price." Suppose that the court had accepted this argument. What might have been the effect of this decision?*

3–3b Social Media

Advancements in technology have created various new ethical issues for companies. Here, we focus on those involving social media. Most people think of social media—Facebook, Flickr, Instagram, Snapchat, Tumblr, Twitter, Pinterest, WhatsApp, LinkedIn, and the like—as simply ways to communicate rapidly. But everyone knows that they can quickly encounter ethical and legal disputes for posting statements that others interpret as harassing, inappropriate, insulting, or racist. Businesses often face ethical issues with respect to these social media platforms.

The Use of Social Media to Make Hiring Decisions In the past, to learn about a prospective employee, an employer would ask the candidate's former employers for references. Today, employers are likely to also conduct Internet searches to discover what job candidates have posted on their Facebook pages, blogs, and tweets.

On the one hand, job candidates may be judged by what they post on social media. On the other hand, though, they may be judged because they *do not participate* in social media. Given that the vast majority of younger people use social media, some employers have decided that the failure to do so raises a red flag. In either case, many people believe that judging a job candidate based on what she or he does outside the work environment is unethical.

The Use of Social Media to Discuss Work-Related Issues Because so many Americans use social media daily, they often discuss work-related issues there. Numerous companies have strict guidelines about what is appropriate and inappropriate for employees to say when posting on their own or others' social media accounts. A number of companies have fired employees for such activities as criticizing other employees or managers through social media outlets. Until recently, such disciplinary measures were considered ethical and legal.

The Responsibility of Employers. A ruling by the National Labor Relations Board (NLRB— the federal agency that investigates unfair labor practices) has changed the legality of such actions. **Example 3.16** At one time, Costco's social media policy specified that its employees should not make statements that would damage the company, harm another person's reputation, or violate the company's policies. Employees who violated these rules were subject to discipline and could be fired.

The NLRB ruled that Costco's social media policy violated federal labor law, which protects employees' right to engage in "concerted activities." Employees can freely associate with each other and have conversations about common workplace issues without employer interference. This right extends to social media posts. Therefore, an employer cannot broadly prohibit its employees from criticizing the company or co-workers, supervisors, or managers via social media.

The Responsibility of Employees. While most of the discussion in this chapter concerns the ethics of business management, employee ethics is also an important issue. For instance, is it ethical for employees to make negative posts in social media about other employees or, more commonly, about managers? After all, negative comments about managers reflect badly on those managers, who often are reluctant to respond via social media to such criticism. Disgruntled employees may exaggerate the negative qualities of managers whom they do not like.

Some may consider the decision by the National Labor Relations Board outlined in *Example 3.16* to be too lenient toward employees and too stringent toward management. There is likely to be an ongoing debate about how to balance employees' right to free expression against employers' right to prevent the spreading of inaccurate negative statements online.

3-3c Awareness

Regardless of the context in which a decision is called for, sometimes businesspersons are not even aware that the decision has ethical implications. Perhaps they are focused on something else, for instance, or perhaps they do not take the time to think through their actions.

Takata Corporation knew about its defective airbags, yet it continued to use them in production. How can business managers learn from Takata's situation?

Case Example 3.17 Japanese airbag maker Takata Corporation manufactured some airbags that used an ammonium nitrate-based propellant without a chemical drying agent. It was later discovered that these airbags tended to deploy explosively, especially in higher temperatures, higher humidity, and older vehicles. When the airbags deployed, metal inflator cartridges inside them sometimes ruptured, sending metal shards into the passenger cabin.

By the beginning of 2017, these defective airbags had caused 11 deaths and 180 injuries in the United States. The federal government ordered recalls of the devices in nearly 42 million vehicles nationwide. Takata executives likely did not intend to hurt consumers and may not even have considered the ethics of their decision. Takata, however, continued to produce airbags with this defect for years. A class-action lawsuit has been filed against the company. (Takata filed for bankruptcy protection in 2017.)[8]

---

8. *In re Takata Airbag Products Liability Litigation,* 84 F.Supp.3d 1371 (2015).

3–3d **Rationalization**

Assuming that is unacceptable to claim ignorance of the ethical dimensions of a business decision, the difficult challenge of making an ethical decision still exists. Sometimes, businesspersons make a decision that benefits them or their company that they know is ethically questionable. Afterward, they rationalize their bad behavior. For instance, an employee might rationalize that it is acceptable to take company property for personal use or to lie to a client just this one time, because she or he normally does not steal and is usually honest. An executive might rationalize that unethical conduct directed against a certain competitor is acceptable because that company deserves it. Individuals might rationalize that their conduct is simply a part of doing business and is not personal or unethical.

One suggestion that is useful in counteracting rationalization is for businesspersons to *first decide the right thing to do on an ethical level before making a business decision.* Then they can figure out how to mitigate the costs of doing the right thing. This works much better to prevent unethical conduct than making decisions based solely on a financial or business basis and then trying to make that result seem ethical (by rationalizing).

3–3e **Uncertainty**

One common denominator identified by businesspersons who have faced ethical problems is the feeling of uncertainty. They may be uncertain as to what they should do, what they should have done, or (as mentioned) whether there was even an ethical issue or ethical breach involved. Such uncertainty is practically unavoidable, but it should be treated as an indicator of a potential ethical problem.

When employees or executives express uncertainty about a particular decision, it is therefore best to treat the situation as involving an ethical issue. Decision makers should try to identify what the ethical dilemma is and why the individual or group is feeling uneasy. They should also take the time to think through the decision completely and discuss various options. They might want to consider whether the company would be pleased if the decision were reported to its clients or to the public. Building a process that supports and assists those facing ethical dilemmas can be key to avoiding unethical business practices (and any corresponding negative publicity).

> "If you are uncertain about an issue, it's useful to ask yourself, 'Would I be absolutely comfortable for my actions to be disclosed on the front page of my hometown newspaper?'"
>
> **Warren E. Buffett**
> 1930–present
> (American businessperson and philanthropist)

3–4 **Making Ethical Business Decisions**

Even if officers, directors, and others in a company want to make ethical decisions, it is not always clear what is ethical in a given situation. Thinking beyond things that are easily measured, such as profits, can be challenging. Although profit projections are not always accurate, they may be more objective than considering the personal impacts of decisions on employees, shareholders, customers, and the community. But this subjective component of decision making can be equally important to a company's long-run profits.

Individuals entering the global corporate community, even in entry-level positions, must be prepared to make hard decisions. Sometimes, there is no "good" answer to the questions that arise. Therefore, it is important to have tools to help in the decision-making process and a framework for organizing those tools.

Several frameworks exist to help businesspersons make ethical decisions. Some frameworks, for instance, focus more on legal than ethical implications. This approach tends to be primarily outcome-based and, as such, may not be appropriate for a company that is values driven or committed to corporate social responsibility (or has a consumer or investor base that is focused on CSR). Other models, such as the Business Process Pragmatism™ procedure developed by ethics consultant Leonard H. Bucklin, set out a series of steps to follow. In this text, we present a modified version of this system that we call IDDR. ("I Desire to Do Right" is a useful mnemonic device for remembering the name.)

Learning Objective 4

What are the four steps in the IDDR approach to ethical decision making?

3–4a A Systematic Approach: IDDR ("I Desire to Do Right")

Using the IDDR approach involves organizing the issues and approaching them systematically. This process can help eliminate various alternatives and identify the strengths and weaknesses of the remaining alternatives. Often, the best approach is for a group (rather than an individual) to carry out the process, which comprises the following steps. Thus, if an individual employee is facing an ethical issue, she or he should talk with her or his supervisor, and then they should perform the following steps together.

Step 1: Inquiry The first step in making an ethical decision is to understand the problem. If an employee feels uneasy about a particular decision, pay attention. Ask questions. People generally know when something does not "feel" right, and this is often a good indicator that there may be an ethical problem. The decision makers must identify the ethical problem and all the parties involved—the stakeholders. It is important that they *not* frame the issue in a way that gives them the answer they might prefer. After gathering the relevant facts, the decision makers can also consider which ethical theories can help them analyze the problem thoroughly. Making a list of the ethical principles that will guide the decision may be helpful at this point.

Step 2: Discussion Once the ethical problem or problems have been clarified, a list of possible actions can be compiled. In discussing these alternatives, the decision makers should take time to think through each alternative completely and analyze its potential impact on various groups of stakeholders. They must evaluate the strengths and weaknesses of each option, along with its ethical and legal consequences. It is helpful to discuss with management the ultimate goals for the decision. At this point, too, the decision makers need to consider what they *should* do (what is the most ethical) before considering what they can or will do.

Step 3: Decision With all the relevant facts collected and the alternatives thoroughly analyzed and discussed, it's time to make a decision. Those participating in the decision-making process now work together to craft a consensus decision or plan of action for the company. Once the decision has been made, the decision makers should use the analysis from the discussion step to articulate the reasons they arrived at the decision. This results in documentation that can be shared with stakeholders to explain why the course of action is an ethical solution to the problem.

Step 4: Review After the decision has been made and implemented, it is important for the decision maker(s) to review the outcome to determine whether the solution was effective. Did the action solve the ethical problem? Were the stakeholders satisfied with the result? Could anything have been handled better? The results of this evaluation can be used in making future decisions. Successful decision makers learn from their mistakes and continue to improve.

3–4b Applying the IDDR Approach—A Sample Scenario

To really understand the IDDR approach, it is helpful to work through the process by analyzing an ethical problem. Here, as a sample, we present a scenario that is based on a real story but contains fictional elements as well. The conversations and analyses included in the scenario are fictional. Because any discussions that may have happened took place behind closed doors, we cannot know if any ethical analysis or discussions about ethics occurred.

Example 3.18 Assume that you are an intern working on a social media campaign for Duane Reade, a New York pharmacy chain. As part of your internship, you follow several celebrity gossip Web pages and do regular Internet searches looking for any picture or mention of the stores. In the course of these searches, you find a picture of Katherine Heigl leaving a Duane Reade store carrying bags imprinted with the company logo. (Katherine Heigl is a recognizable actress from television's *Grey's Anatomy* and several major movies.) You can easily copy the picture to the company's Twitter account and add a caption about her shopping at one of the stores. Having customers or potential customers seeing this well-known person carrying Duane Reade bags and leaving the store could increase store visits and sales.

The question is this: Is it appropriate to use Heigl's photo without her permission as part of an advertising campaign? Use the IDDR approach to analyze what you should do. Assume that you, your supervisor, and a few other members of the marketing department engage in this analysis.

Step 1: Inquiry To begin, clarify the nature of the problem. You want to use a picture of Heigl from a celebrity gossip Web page to potentially increase profits for the company. The problem could be phrased in this way: "Is it ethical to use a picture of a famous person to try to improve sales without contacting her or the photographer first?" Note that the way you frame the question will affect how you answer it. For example, if the question was phrased, "Should we steal this picture?" the answer would be obvious. Remember *not* to frame the issue in a way that gives you the answer you might want.

You also need to identify the stakeholders. Here, the stakeholders include Heigl, the photographer who took the picture, Heigl's fans, and the potential customers of Duane Reade. Other stakeholders include your boss (who will get credit if sales increase due to the marketing campaign), Duane Reade stockholders, and store employees (who might see an increase in customers).

When gathering the facts, determine whether there are any legal issues. Given these facts, there may be state and federal laws that would guide a decision. For instance, reproducing a photograph without the owner's permission might violate federal copyright laws. In addition, most states have laws (sometimes called *right to publicity* laws) that protect a person's name, voice, or likeness (image or picture) from being used for advertising without the person's consent.

You can also consider which ethical theories can help you analyze the problem. The ethical theories may include religious values, rights theory, the categorical imperative, and utilitarianism. Ask yourself whether it is right, or ethical, to use Heigl's name or face without her permission as part of an advertising campaign.

Step 2: Discussion Several actions could be taken in this sample situation. Each action should be thoroughly analyzed using the various ethical approaches identified by the decision makers. The ultimate goals for the decision are to increase sales and do the least amount of harm to the business and its reputation without compromising the values of the business. We will analyze three alternatives here, though it is important as a decision maker to brainstorm and find as many options as possible. Exhibit 3–1 shows how our three alternatives could be analyzed.

It is important to note that different ethical perspectives will be more or less helpful in different situations. In the sample scenario, a strong argument can be made that Heigl's rights to privacy and to control her image are very important. Under other circumstances, however, the right to privacy might be outweighed by some other right, such as another person's right to safety. Using multiple theories will help ensure that the decision maker can work through the analytical process and find a result.

Step 3: Decision After a lively discussion concerning Heigl's rights to privacy and to compensation for the use of her image, the decisions makers come to a consensus. Given the potential for increased income, the company decides to use the picture. It will be posted on the company's Twitter account with a caption that reads, "Love a quick #DuaneReade run? Even @KatieHeigl can't resist shopping #NYC's favorite drugstore."

Exhibit 3–1 An Analysis of Ethical Approaches to the Sample Dilemma

ALTERNATIVE	LEGAL IMPLICATIONS	RELIGIOUS VALUES	CATEGORICAL IMPERATIVE	RIGHTS THEORY	UTILITARIANISM
1. Use the Picture without Permission	How does this alternative comply with copyright law? Are there any exceptions to copyright law that would allow this use?	Is this stealing? If so, it violates religious principles. Is it stealing to use a picture taken on a public street?	If everyone did this, then the images and names of famous people would often be used to promote products. Is this a good thing or not?	Using the picture may negatively impact the Web page or Heigl's ability to make money using her image. It also may violate some right to privacy.	If we use the picture, we may see an increase in sales and an improvement in reputation. We may, however, be sued for using her image without permission.
2. Contact the Web Page and/ or Heigl for Permission	Are there any laws that would make this alternative illegal? Are there any precautions we should take when asking for permission to avoid any appearance of threat or intimidation?	This alternative clearly is not stealing and thus would align with religious principles.	If everyone asked for permission, then such material would not be used without permission. This would seem to make the world a better place.	Getting permission would not seem to violate anyone's rights. In fact, giving someone the opportunity to decide might enhance that person's rights.	If we contact the parties for permission, we may be able to use the image, make more money, and improve our reputation. But the parties might refuse to give permission or demand payment, which would cost the company money.
3. Do Not Use the Picture	There are no legal implications to not using the picture.	This alternative clearly is not stealing and thus would align with religious principles.	If companies never used public, candid images of famous people, then all advertising would be staged. This might not make the world a better place.	Not using the picture may damage the stockholders' right to maximum income or the company's right to advertise as it sees fit.	If we do not use the picture, we avoid potential lawsuits. Alternatively, we won't have the potential increase in sales associated with the use of the famous face.

Make sure to articulate the reasons you arrived at the decision to serve as documentation explaining why the plan of action was ethical. In this meeting, the persuasive evidence was the projection for increased revenue balanced by the minimal harm to Heigl. Because the picture was taken on a public street, the people in the room did not feel that it involved a violation of any privacy right. The company would not have paid Heigl to do an advertisement. Also, because only people who followed Duane Reade on Twitter could view the tweet, the group felt the likelihood of any damage to Heigl was small. Most people felt that the worst that could happen would be that Heigl would ask them to remove it.

Step 4: Review You and the other decision makers at Duane Reade need to review the effectiveness of your decision. Assume that after the picture and caption are posted on Twitter, Heigl sees it and sues Duane Reade for "no less than $6 million." She argues that the company violated her rights by falsely claiming that she had endorsed its stores and that it misappropriated her name and likeness for a profit. The case is settled out of court, with Duane Reade paying an undisclosed amount to a foundation that Heigl created.

Here, the decision did not solve the ethical problem and, in fact, led to liability. Decision makers need to determine what they could have done better. Perhaps they should change their practices and obtain legal counsel for their marketing department—or at least hire a legal consultant when ethical issues arise. Perhaps they need to establish an internal process for getting permission to use pictures from social media or other sources. In any event, it is likely that the company should change some of its policies and practices related to social media marketing.

The decision-making process is not easy or precise. It may entail repeating steps as decision makers recognize new alternatives or as unforeseen stakeholders appear. Sometimes, the analysis will lead to a clear decision, and other times it will not. Even if it does not, the process will allow decision makers to enter the public phase of the decision (action) with a better idea of what consequences to expect.

For more on the IDDR approach to ethical decision making, see the *Business Law Analysis* feature.

Applying the IDDR Framework

Business Law Analysis

Pfizer, Inc., developed a new antibiotic called Trovan (trovafloxacinmesylate). Tests in animals showed that Trovan had life-threatening side effects, including joint disease, abnormal cartilage growth, liver damage, and a degenerative bone condition. Pfizer was seeking approval from the Food and Drug Administration (FDA) to market Trovan for use in the United States when an epidemic of bacterial meningitis swept across Nigeria.

Pfizer sent three U.S. physicians to test Trovan on children who were patients in Nigeria's Infectious Disease Hospital. Pfizer's representatives obtained all necessary approvals from the Nigerian government and had Nigerian nurses explain the details of the study to parents and inform them that participation was voluntary. They did not, however, alert the parents or patients about the serious risks involved, or tell them about an effective conventional treatment that Doctors without Borders was providing at the same site. The results of the study showed that Trovan had a success rate of 94.4 percent in treating the children's condition. Nevertheless, eleven children died in the experiment, and others were left blind, deaf, paralyzed, or brain damaged. Rabi Abdullahi and other Nigerian children filed a suit in a U.S. federal court against Pfizer, alleging a violation of a customary international law norm prohibiting involuntary medical experimentation on humans.

Analysis: Pfizer could have applied the IDDR approach to review the ethical conflicts in a test of Trovan. (1) In the inquiry step, decision makers ask questions to understand the ethical dilemma, identify the stakeholders, gather relevant facts, and articulate the ethical principles at issue. (2) In the discussion step, the decision makers further explore potential actions and their effects. (3) The next step is to come to a consensus decision as to what to do. This consensus should withstand moral scrutiny and fulfill corporate, community, and individual values. (4) The last step is to review the outcome to determine whether it was effective and what the company could do better. In this instance, for example, fully informing the patients and their parents about the risks of the treatment would have been a better course of action.

Result and Reasoning: It seems unlikely that a proposed Trovan test on children, based on the facts described here, would have survived an IDDR analysis, under either a duty-based or an outcome-based ethical standard. It also would appear that Pfizer was rushing to test and market Trovan as soon as possible. This focus on short-run profit maximization took precedence over any ethical considerations. It is often easier to see ethical lapses in retrospect than it is to identify potential ethical problems in advance, however.

3–5 Business Ethics on a Global Level

Just as individual religions have different moral codes, individual countries and regions have different ethical expectations and priorities. Some of these differences are based on religious values, whereas others are cultural in nature. Such differences can make it even more difficult to determine what is ethical in a particular situation.

3–5a World Religions, Cultural Norms, and Ethics

Global businesses need to be conscious of the impact of different religious principles and cultural norms on ethics. For instance, in certain countries the consumption of alcohol is forbidden for religious reasons. It would be considered unethical for a U.S. business to produce alcohol in those countries and employ local workers to assist in alcohol production.

In other countries, women may not be treated as equals because of cultural norms or religion. In contrast, discrimination against employees on the basis of sex (or race, national origin, age, or disability) is prohibited in the United States. The varying roles of women can give rise to ethical issues regarding how women working for a U.S. company should dress or behave in certain regions of the world. Should female executives have to cover their heads? Should they avoid involvement in certain business transactions? How will various stakeholders react to whatever decisions companies make in these situations?

How far should companies go to cater to business partners in other nations? Going too far to please clients in another country can alienate a firm's employees and domestic customers and generate bad press. Decision makers in charge of global business operations should consider these ethical issues and make some decisions from the outset.

3–5b Outsourcing

Outsourcing The practice by which a company hires an outside firm or individual to perform work rather than hiring employees to do it.

Outsourcing is the practice by which a company hires an outside firm or individual to perform work rather than hiring employees to do it. Ethical problems involving outsourcing most often arise when global companies outsource work to other countries in an attempt to save on labor costs. This type of outsourcing elicits an almost automatic negative reaction in the U.S. public. Some people feel that companies should protect American jobs above all else. Furthermore, ethical questions often arise as to the employment practices of the foreign companies to which the work is outsourced.

Outsourcing covers a wide spectrum of ethical gray areas and is not always clearly unethical. Outsourcing domestically, for instance—such as when companies hire outside firms to transport goods—generally does not raise ethical issues. Nonetheless, companies involved in global operations need to be careful when outsourcing to make sure that employees in other nations are being treated fairly.

catastrophe_OL/Shutterstock.com

Outsourcing is not inherently unethical, but under what circumstances could the practice cause problems for a company?

3–5c Avoiding Corruption

Another ethical problem in global business dealings has to do with corruption in foreign governments. Under the Foreign Corrupt Practices Act,[9] U.S. businesses are prohibited from

---

9. 15 U.S.C. Sections 78dd-1 *et seq.* This act will be discussed in more detail in the context of criminal law.

making payments to (bribing) foreign officials to secure beneficial contracts, with certain exceptions. If such payments are lawful within the foreign country, then they are permitted. It is also acceptable to pay small amounts to minor officials to facilitate or speed up the performance of administrative services (such as approval of construction). Payments to private foreign companies or other third parties are also permissible.

Corruption is widespread in some nations, however, and it can be the norm in dealing with both government and private businesses in certain locations. Global companies must take special care when doing business in countries where corruption is common. Discuss potential ethical problems with employees in advance and again when situations arise. The company's goal should be to ensure that it supports management and employees in doing the right thing and following the firm's anticorruption policies.

3–5d Monitoring the Employment Practices of Foreign Suppliers

Many businesses contract with companies in developing nations to produce goods, such as shoes and clothing, because the wage rates in those nations are significantly lower than those in the United States. But what if one of those contractors hires women and children at below-minimum-wage rates or requires its employees to work long hours in a workplace full of health hazards? What if the company's supervisors routinely engage in workplace conduct that is offensive to women? What if factories located abroad routinely violate U.S. labor and environmental standards?

Wages and Working Conditions Allegations that a business allows its suppliers to engage in unethical practices hurt the firm's reputation. **Example 3.19** Noi Supalai, a garment worker in Thailand, came forward in 2016 with reports about how harshly she and other workers had been treated at Eagle Speed factory, which produced apparel for Nike Corporation. Because the workers did not produce all of the "Just Do the Right Thing" line of products by a set deadline, Nike fined the factory and barred it from paying its workers. The factory then forced some two thousand employees to work sixteen-hour days or longer, and to take turns going home to shower. Workers eventually formed a union and named Supalai as president, but they were unsuccessful in getting the conditions improved. A meeting was set up between Supalai and a Nike representative, but Nike did not even show up. Supalai later learned that Nike chose to use other suppliers. ■

Corporate Watch Groups Given today's global communications network, few companies can assume that their actions in other nations will go unnoticed by "corporate watch" groups that discover and publicize unethical corporate behavior. As a result, U.S. businesses today usually take steps to avoid such adverse publicity—either by refusing to deal with certain suppliers or by arranging to monitor their suppliers' workplaces to make sure that employees are not being mistreated.

Example 3.20 A Chinese factory supplied parts for certain Apple products. After Apple discovered that the factory had violated labor and environmental standards, it began evaluating the practices at all the companies in its supply chain. Apple's audits revealed numerous violations, such as withholding worker pay as a disciplinary measure, falsifying pay records, and forcing workers to use unsafe machines. Apple terminated its relationship with one foreign supplier and turned over its findings to the Fair Labor Association, a nonprofit organization that promotes adherence to national and international labor laws, for further inquiry. ■

"Never doubt that a small group of committed citizens can change the world; indeed, it is the only thing that ever has."

Margaret Mead
1901–1978
(American anthropologist)

Practice and Review

James Stilton is the chief executive officer (CEO) of RightLiving, Inc., a company that buys life insurance policies at a discount from terminally ill persons and sells the policies to investors. RightLiving pays the terminally ill patients a percentage of the future death benefit (usually 65 percent) and then sells the policies to investors for 85 percent of the value of the future benefit. The patients receive the cash to use for medical and other expenses, and the investors are "guaranteed" a positive return on their investment. The difference between the purchase and sale prices is Right Living's profit. Stilton is aware that some sick patients may obtain insurance policies through fraud (by not revealing their illness on the insurance application). An insurance company that discovers such fraud will cancel the policy and refuse to pay. Stilton believes that most of the policies he has purchased are legitimate, but he knows that some probably are not. Using the information presented in this chapter, answer the following questions.

1. Would a person who adheres to the principle of rights consider it ethical for Stilton not to disclose the potential risk of cancellation to investors? Why or why not?

2. Using Immanuel Kant's categorical imperative, are the actions of RightLiving ethical? Why or why not?

3. Under utilitarianism, are Stilton's actions ethical? Why or why not? If most of the policies are, in fact, legitimate, does this make a difference in your analysis?

4. Using the IDDR approach, discuss the decision process Stilton should use in deciding whether to disclose the risk of fraudulent policies to potential investors.

Debate This

Executives in large corporations are ultimately rewarded if their companies do well, particularly as evidenced by rising stock prices. Consequently, shouldn't those who run corporations be able to decide what level of negative side effects is "acceptable" for their companies' products?

Key Terms

business ethics 58
categorical imperative 67
corporate social responsibility
   (CSR) 68
cost-benefit analysis 67

duty-based ethics 65
ethical reasoning 65
ethics 58
moral minimum 60
outcome-based ethics 65

outsourcing 78
principle of rights 66
stakeholders 69
triple bottom line 61
utilitarianism 67

Chapter Summary: Ethics in Business

| Ethics and the Role of Business | 1. *The relationship of law and ethics*—The government has created some ethical rights and duties through the passage of laws and regulations. Many laws are designed to prevent fraudulent conduct, including the Dodd-Frank Wall Street Reform and Consumer Protection Act and the Sarbanes-Oxley Act.
a. *Gray areas in the law*—Sometimes legislation includes language that is overly broad or provisions that are ambiguous. Such gray areas make it difficult to predict how the law will apply or should be applied to a situation, complicating determinations of what is legal or ethical. |

    b. *The moral minimum*—Lawful behavior is the moral minimum. The law has its limits, though, and some actions may be legal but not ethical. The study of ethics goes beyond legal requirements to evaluate what is right for society.

    c. *Codes of ethics*—Most large firms have internal ethical codes. Many industry associations also have codes of ethics for their members. Because these internal codes are not laws, their effectiveness is determined by the commitment of the company leadership or industry to enforcing the codes.

2. *The role of business in society*— The public perception of corporations has changed from entities that primarily generate profits for their owners to entities that participate in society as corporate citizens. Whether one believes in profit maximization or corporate citizenship, ethics is important in making business decisions—such as by looking to the *triple bottom line*. Decision makers must evaluate (a) the legal implications, (b) the public relations impact, (c) any safety risks, and (d) the financial implications.

3. *Ethical issues in business*—A fundamental ethical issue for business is developing integrity and trust. Businesspersons should exhibit integrity in their dealings with other people in the company, other businesses, clients, and the community.

4. *The importance of ethical leadership*—Management's commitment and behavior are essential in creating an ethical workplace. Management's behavior, more than anything else, sets the ethical tone of a firm and influences the behavior of employees.

Ethical Principles and Philosophies

1. *Duty-based ethics*—Ethics based on religious beliefs; the basic rights of human beings (the principle of rights); and philosophical reasoning, such as that of Immanuel Kant. A potential problem for those who support this ethical approach is deciding which rights are more important in a given situation. Management constantly faces ethical conflicts and trade-offs when considering all those affected by a business decision.

2. *Outcome-based ethics (utilitarianism)*—Ethics based on philosophical reasoning, such as that of Jeremy Bentham and John Stuart Mill. Applying this theory requires a cost-benefit analysis, weighing the negative effects against the positive and deciding which course of action produces the better outcome.

3. *Corporate social responsibility*—Corporate social responsibility (CSR) combines a commitment to good citizenship with a commitment to making ethical decisions, improving society, and minimizing environmental impact. Although there are different theories, the basic idea is that corporations can and should act ethically and be accountable to society for their actions. One view of CSR stresses that corporations have a duty not just to shareholders, but also to other groups affected by corporate decisions, called stakeholders.

Sources of Ethical Issues in Business Decisions

1. *Short-term profit maximization*—Executives should distinguish between short-run and long-run profit goals and focus on maximizing profits over the long run. An overemphasis on short-run profit maximization is perhaps the most common reason that ethical problems occur in business.

2. *Social media*—Advances in technology have created new ethical problems for companies. Issues involving social media include how to use social media in the hiring process and how to monitor employees' online activities.

3. *Awareness*—Whatever the context, businesspersons must be aware of the possibility that ethical issues will arise.

4. *Rationalization*—Sometimes, businesspersons make a decision that they know is not particularly ethical but that will benefit them or their company. After the fact, they rationalize their bad behavior and unethical decision.

5. *Uncertainty*—When making a business decision, businesspersons may be uncertain as to what they should do, what they should have done, or whether an ethical issue or breach is even involved. Such uncertainty is unavoidable, but it should be treated as an indicator of a potential ethical problem.

(Continues)

Making Ethical Business Decisions	Making ethical business decisions is crucial in today's legal environment. Business decisions can be complex. Several frameworks exist to help businesspersons make ethical decisions. One such framework is the four-step IDDR ("I Desire to Do Right") approach.
	1. *I = Inquiry*—Involves identifying the ethical problem and all of the stakeholders, gathering the relevant facts, and considering which ethical theories can help in analyzing the problem.
	2. *D = Discussion*—Involves making a list of possible actions and evaluating the strengths and weaknesses of each option, including its ethical and legal consequences.
	3. *D = Decision*—Involves crafting a consensus decision or a company's plan of action. Decision makers should use the analysis from Step 2 to articulate the reasons behind the decision.
	4. *R = Review*—Involves reviewing the decision outcome to determine whether the solution was effective and satisfied the stakeholders. The results of this evaluation may be used in making future decisions.
Business Ethics on a Global Level	Global businesses need to be conscious of the impact of different religious principles and cultural norms on ethics. In addition, ethical concerns may arise in the areas of outsourcing, avoiding corruption, and monitoring the employment practices of foreign suppliers.

Issue Spotters

1. Acme Corporation decides to respond to what it sees as a moral obligation to correct for past discrimination by adjusting pay differences among its employees. Does this raise an ethical conflict between Acme and its employees? Between Acme and its shareholders? Explain your answers. (See *Ethical Principles and Philosophies*.)

2. Delta Tools, Inc., markets a product that under some circumstances is capable of seriously injuring consumers. Does Delta have an ethical duty to remove this product from the market, even if the injuries result only from misuse? Why or why not? (See *Making Ethical Business Decisions*.)

—**Check your answers to the *Issue Spotters* against the answers provided in Appendix D at the end of this text.**

Business Scenarios and Case Problems

3–1. Business Ethics. Jason Trevor owns a commercial bakery in Blakely, Georgia, that produces a variety of goods sold in grocery stores. Trevor is required by law to perform internal tests on food produced at his plant to check for contamination. On three occasions, tests of food products containing peanut butter were positive for salmonella contamination. Trevor was not required to report the results to U.S. Food and Drug Administration officials, however, so he did not. Instead, Trevor instructed his employees to simply repeat the tests until the results were negative. Meanwhile, the products that had originally tested positive for salmonella were eventually shipped out to retailers. Five people who ate Trevor's baked goods that year became seriously ill, and one person died from a salmonella infection. Even though Trevor's conduct was legal, was it unethical for him to sell goods that had once tested positive for salmonella? Why or why not? (See *Ethics and the Role of Business*.)

3–2. Ethical Conduct. Internet giant Zoidle, a U.S. company, generated sales of £2.5 billion in the United Kingdom (UK) in 2013 (roughly $4 billion in U.S. dollars). The U.K. corporate tax rate is usually between 20 percent and 24 percent, but Zoidle paid only 3 percent (£6 million). At a press conference, company officials touted how the company took advantage of tax loopholes and sheltered profits to avoid paying the full corporate income tax. They justified their practices as ethical, declaring that it would be verging on illegal to tell shareholders that the company paid more taxes than it should.

Zoidle receives significant benefits for doing business in the UK, including large sales tax exemptions and some property tax breaks. The UK relies on the corporate income tax to provide services to the poor and to help run the agency that regulates corporations. Is it ethical for Zoidle to avoid paying taxes? Why or why not? (See *Ethics and the Role of Business*.)

3–3. Consumer Rights. Best Buy, a national electronics retailer, offered a credit card that allowed users to earn "reward points" that could be redeemed for discounts on Best Buy goods. After reading a newspaper advertisement for the card, Gary Davis applied for, and was given, a credit card. As part of the application process, he visited a Web page containing Frequently Asked Questions as well as terms and conditions for the card. He clicked on a button affirming that he understood the terms and conditions. When Davis received his card, it came with seven brochures about the card and the reward point program. As he read the brochures, he discovered that a $59 annual fee would be charged for the card. Davis went back to the Web pages he had visited and found a statement that the card "may" have an annual fee. Davis sued, claiming that the company did not adequately disclose the fee. Is it unethical for companies to put terms and conditions, especially terms that may cost the consumer money, in an electronic document that is too long to read on one screen? Why or why not? Assuming that the Best Buy credit-card materials were legally sufficient, discuss the ethical aspects of businesses strictly following the language of the law as opposed to following the intent of the law. [*Davis v. HSBC Bank Nevada, N.A.*, 691 F.3d 1152 (9th Cir. 2012)] (See *Ethics and the Role of Business*.)

3–4. Business Ethics. Mark Ramun worked as a manager for Allied Erecting and Dismantling Co., where he had a tense relationship with his father, who was Allied's president. After more than ten years, Mark left Allied, taking 15,000 pages of Allied's documents on DVDs and CDs, which constituted trade secrets. Later, he joined Allied's competitor, Genesis Equipment & Manufacturing, Inc. Genesis soon developed a piece of equipment that incorporated elements of Allied equipment. How might business ethics have been violated in these circumstances? Discuss. [*Allied Erecting and Dismantling Co. v. Genesis Equipment & Manufacturing, Inc.*, 511 Fed.Appx. 398 (6th Cir. 2013)] (See *Making Ethical Business Decisions*.)

3–5. Ethical Principles. Stephen Glass made himself infamous as a dishonest journalist by fabricating material for more than forty articles for *The New Republic* magazine and other publications. He also fabricated supporting materials to delude *The New Republic's* fact checkers. At the time, he was a law student at Georgetown University. Once suspicions were aroused, Glass tried to avoid detection. Later, Glass applied for admission to the California bar. The California Supreme Court denied his application, citing "numerous instances of dishonesty and disingenuousness" during his "rehabilitation" following the exposure of his misdeeds. How do these circumstances underscore the importance of ethics? Discuss. [*In re Glass*, 58 Cal.4th 500, 316 P.3d 1199 (2014)] (See *Ethical Principles and Philosophies*.)

3–6. Business Case Problem with Sample Answer—Business Ethics. Operating out of an apartment in Secane, Pennsylvania, Hratch Ilanjian convinced Vicken Setrakian, the president of Kenset Corp., that he was an international businessman who could help turn around Kenset's business in the Middle East. At Ilanjian's insistence, Setrakian provided confidential business documents. Claiming that they had an agreement, Ilanjian demanded full, immediate payment and threatened to disclose the confidential

information to a Kenset supplier if payment was not forthcoming. Kenset denied that there was a contract and filed a suit in a federal district court against Ilanjian, seeking return of the documents. During discovery, Ilanjian was uncooperative. Who behaved unethically in these circumstances? Explain. [*Kenset Corp. v. Ilanjian*, 600 Fed.Appx. 827 (3d Cir. 2015)] (See *Making Ethical Business Decisions*.)

—For a sample answer to Problem 3–6, go to Appendix E at the end of this text.

3–7. Spotlight on Bed, Bath & Beyond—Ethics and the Role of Business. Bed Bath & Beyond Inc. sold a ceramic pot, called the "FireBurners" Pot, with a stainless steel fuel reservoir at its center and a bottle of gelled fuel for use with the fire pot called "FireGel." A red sticker on the fire pot warned, "DON'T REFILL UNTIL FLAME IS OUT & CUP IS COOL." "CARE AND USE INSTRUCTIONS" with the product cautioned, in a "WARNINGS" section, "Do not add fuel when lit and never pour gel on an open fire or hot surface." The label on the back of the fuel gel bottle instructed, "NEVER add fuel to a burning fire," and under a bold "WARNING" stated, "DANGER, FLAMMABLE LIQUID & VAPOR." M.H., a minor, was injured when a fire pot in one of the products—bought from Bed Bath & Beyond—was refueled with the gel and an explosion occurred. Safer alternatives for the design of the fire pot existed, but its manufacturer chose not to use them. In these circumstances, is Bed, Bath & Beyond ethically responsible for the injury to M.H.? Discuss. [*M.H. v. Bed, Bath & Beyond, Inc.*, 156 A.D.3d 33, 64 N.Y.S.3d 205 (1 Dept. 2017)] (See *Ethics and the Role of Business*.)

3–8. A Question of Ethics—Applying the IDDR Framework. *Priscilla Dickman worked as a medical technologist at the University of Connecticut Health Center for twenty-eight years. Early in her career at the Health Center, Dickman sustained a back injury while at work. The condition eventually worsened, causing her significant back pain and disability. Her physician ordered restrictions on her work duties for several years. Then Dickman's supervisor received complaints that Dickman was getting personal phone calls and was frequently absent from her work area. Based on e-mails and other documents found on her work computer, it appeared that she had been running two side businesses (selling jewelry and providing travel agent services) while at work. The state investigated, and she was convicted of a civil ethics violation for engaging in "personal business for financial gain on state time utilizing state resources." Separate investigations resulted in criminal convictions for forgery and the filing of an unrelated fraudulent insurance claim. Dickman "retired" from her job (after she obtained approval for disability retirement) and filed a claim with the state of Connecticut against the health center. She alleged that her former employer* *had initiated the investigations to harass her and force her to quit. She claimed that the Health Center was unlawfully retaliating against her for being disabled and being put on workplace restrictions.* [Dickman v. University of Connecticut Health Center, *162 Conn.App. 441, 132 A.3d 739 (2016)*] (See *Making Ethical Business Decisions.*)

1. Assume that you are Dickman's supervisor and have been informed that she is frequently away from her desk and often makes personal phone calls. The first step of using the IDDR method is *inquiry*, so you start asking questions. Several people tell you that that Dickman has offered to sell them jewelry. Others say she has offered to make travel arrangements for them. You have not spoken to Dickman directly about the complaints, though, and are not sure if you should. You also know that the Health Center would need more evidence of wrongdoing to justify firing Dickman but are uncertain as to whether you can search her computer. Should you report your findings to management? Is there any ethical problem involved in investigating and possibly firing a long-term employee? Is it fair to terminate an employee who is under disability restrictions? How would you frame the ethical dilemma that the Health Center faced in this case, and who are the stakeholders? What ethical theories would you use to guide your decision?

2. Now suppose that you are Dickman. You have been a medical technologist for a long time but now experience severe back pain while at your desk at the Health Center. You find that you have less pain if you get up and move around during the day, rather than just sitting. That is why you are often away from your desk. You know that you will not be able to do this job much longer, and that is why you recently started a jewelry business and began providing travel services. Sure, you have made a few personal phone calls related to those businesses while at the Health Center, but other employees make personal calls, and they have not been fired. You feel that the Health Center's investigation was intended to force you to quit because you are disabled and cannot perform the tasks that you used to perform. Using the inquiry portion of the IDDR method, how might you frame the ethical issue you face, and who are the stakeholders? What ethical principles can help you analyze the problem thoroughly?

Critical Thinking and Writing Assignments

3–9. Business Law Writing. Assume that you are a high-level manager for a shoe manufacturer. You know that your firm could increase its profit margin by producing shoes in Indonesia, where you could hire women for $100 a month to assemble them. You also know that human rights advocates recently accused a competing shoe manufacturer of engaging in exploitative labor practices because the manufacturer sold shoes made by Indonesian women for similarly low wages. You personally do not believe that paying $100 a month to Indonesian women is unethical because you know that in their country, $100 a month is a better-than-average wage rate.

Write one page explaining whether you would have the shoes manufactured in Indonesia and make higher profits for the company, or avoid the risk of negative publicity and its potential adverse consequences for the firm's reputation. Are there other alternatives? Discuss fully. (See *Business Ethics on a Global Level.*)

3–10. Time-Limited Group Assignment—Corporate Social Responsibility. Methamphetamine (meth) is an addictive drug made chiefly in small toxic labs (STLs) in homes, tents, barns, and hotel rooms. The manufacturing process is dangerous, often resulting in explosions, burns, and toxic fumes. Government entities spend time and resources to find and destroy STLs, imprison meth dealers and users, treat addicts, and provide services for affected families.

Meth cannot be made without ingredients that are also used in cold and allergy medications. Arkansas has one of the highest numbers of STLs in the United States. To recoup the costs of fighting the meth epidemic, twenty counties in Arkansas filed a suit against Pfizer, Inc., which makes cold and allergy medications. They argued that it was Pfizer's ethical responsibility to either stop using the ingredients in their cold and allergy medications that can be used to make meth or to compensate the government for the amount it spends closing down meth labs. (See *Ethics and the Role of Business, Ethical Principles and Philosophies,* and *Making Ethical Business Decisions.*)

1. The first group will outline Pfizer's ethical responsibility under the corporate social responsibility doctrine. To whom does Pfizer owe duties?

2. The second group will formulate an argument on behalf of Pfizer that the company has not breached any of its ethical responsibilities.

3. The third group will assume that they work for Pfizer and that the company is trying to determine the best course of action to prevent its medications from being used to make meth. The group will apply the IDDR approach and explain the steps in the reasoning used.

4. The fourth group will adopt a utilitarian point of view and perform a cost-benefit analysis to determine what the company should do. Specifically, should the company pay compensation to the state, or should it stop using certain ingredients in its medications?

Costco Wholesale Corporation takes a strong position on behaving ethically in all transactions and relationships. It also expects employees to behave ethically, according to domestic ethical standards, in any country in which it operates. Costco's Code of Ethics outlines its commitment to business ethics.

CODE OF ETHICS

By Jim Sinegal

OBEY THE LAW

The law is irrefutable! Absent a moral imperative to challenge a law, we must our business in total compliance with the laws of every community where we do business.

- Comply with all statutes.
- Cooperate with authorities.
- Respect all public officials and their positions.
- Avoid all conflict of interest issues with public officials.
- Comply with all disclosure and reporting requirements.
- Comply with safety and security standards for all products sold.
- Exceed ecological standards required in every community where we do business.
- Comply with all applicable wage and hour laws.
- Comply with all applicable anti-trust laws.
- Protect "inside information" that has not been released to the general public.

TAKE CARE OF OUR MEMBERS

The member is our key to success. If we don't keep our members happy, little else that we do will make a difference.

- Provide top-quality products at the best prices in the market.
- Provide a safe shopping environment in our warehouses.
- Provide only products that meet applicable safety and health standards.
- Sell only products from manufacturers who comply with "truth in advertising/packaging" standards.
- Provide our members with a 100% satisfaction guaranteed warranty on every product and service we sell, including their membership fee.
- Assure our members that every product we sell is authentic in make and in representation of performance.
- Make our shopping environment a pleasant experience by making our members feel welcome as our guests.
- Provide products to our members that will be ecologically sensitive.

> Our member is our reason for being. If they fail to show up, we cannot survive. Our members have extended a "trust" to Costco by virtue of paying a fee to shop with us. We can't let them down or they will simply go away. We must always operate in the following manner when dealing with our members:
> Rule #1 – The member is always right.
> Rule #2 – In the event the member is ever wrong, refer to rule #1.
>
> There are plenty of shopping alternatives for our members. We will succeed only if we do not violate the trust they have extended to us. We must be committed at every level of our company, with every once of energy and grain of creativity we have, to constantly strive to "bring goods to market at a lower price."

If we do these four things throughout our organization, we will realize our ultimate goal, which is to REWARD OUR SHAREHOLDERS.

TAKE CARE OF OUR EMPLOYEES

To claim "people are our most important asset" is true and an understatement. Each employee has been hired for a very important job. Jobs such as stocking the shelves, ringing members' orders, buying products, and paying our bills are jobs we would all choose to perform because of their importance. The employees hired to perform these jobs are performing as management's "alter egos." Every employee, whether they are in a Costco warehouse, or whether they work in the regional or corporate offices, is a Costco ambassador trained to give our members professional, courteous treatment.

Today we have warehouse managers who were once stockers and callers, and vice presidents who were once in clerical positions for Costco. We believe that Costco's future executive officers are currently working in our warehouses, depots, buying offices, and accounting departments, as well as in our home offices.

To that end, we are committed to these principles:

- Provide a safe work environment.
- Pay a fair wage.
- Make every job challenging, but make it fun!
- Consider the loss of any employee as a failure on the part of the company and a loss to the organization.
- Teach our people how to do their jobs and how to improve personally and professionally.
- Promote from within the company to achieve the goal of a minimum of 80% of management positions being filled by current employees.
- Create an "open door" attitude at all levels of the company that is dedicated to "fairness and listening."

RESPECT OUR VENDORS

Our vendors are our partners in business and for us to prosper as a company, they must proper with us. It is important that our vendors understand that we will be tough negotiators, but fair in our treatment of them.

- Treat all vendors and their representatives as you would expect to be treated if visiting their places of business.
- Pay all bills within the allocated time frame.
- Honor all commitments.
- Protect all vendor property assigned to Costco as though it were our own.
- Always be thoughtful and candid in negotiations.
- Provide a careful review process with at least two levels of authorization before terminating business with an existing vendor of more than two years.
- Do not accept gratuities of any kind from a vendor.

> These guidelines are exactly that - guidelines, some common sense rules for the conduct of our business. Intended to simplify our jobs, not complicate our lives, these guidelines will not answer every question or solve every problem. At the core of our philosophy as a company must be the implicit understanding that not one of us is required to lie or cheat on behalf of PriceCostco. In fact, dishonest conduct will not be tolerated. To do any less would be unfair to the overwhelming majority of our employees who support and respect Costco's commitment to ethical business conduct.
>
> If your are ever in doubt as to what course of action to take on a business matter that is open to varying ethical interpretations, take the high road and do what is right.
>
> If you want our help, we are always available for advice and counsel. That's our job and we welcome your questions or comments.
>
> Our continued success depends on you. We thank each of you for your contribution to our past success and for the high standards you have insisted upon in our company.

RichLegg/E+/Getty Images

4 Courts and Alternative Dispute Resolution

Learning Objectives

The six Learning Objectives below are designed to help improve your understanding. After reading this chapter, you should be able to answer the following questions:

1. What is judicial review? How and when was the power of judicial review established?

2. How are the courts applying traditional jurisdictional concepts to cases involving Internet transactions?

3. What is the difference between the focus of a trial court and that of an appellate court?

4. What is discovery, and how does electronic discovery differ from traditional discovery?

5. What is an electronic court filing system?

6. What are three alternative methods of resolving disputes?

"An eye for an eye will make the whole world blind."

Mahatma Gandhi
1869–1948
(Indian political and spiritual leader)

Every society needs to have an established method for resolving disputes. Without one, as Mahatma Gandhi implied in the chapter-opening quotation, the biblical "eye for an eye" would lead to anarchy. This is particularly true in the business world—almost every businessperson will face a lawsuit at some time in his or her career. For this reason, anyone involved in business needs to have an understanding of court systems in the United States, as well as the various methods of dispute resolution that can be pursued outside the courts.

Assume that Evan Heron is a top executive at Des Moines Semiconductor Manufacturing Company, Inc. (DSMC), and that DSMC is one of the largest U.S. makers of mobile phone processors. Heron negotiates some of its most lucrative contracts, under which DSMC provides companies like Apple, Inc., with the chips they use in smartphones.

A dispute arises between DSMC and one of its customers, a Canadian smartphone company, concerning the price the Canadian company was charged for chips. The Canadian firm threatens litigation, but Heron convinces his colleagues at DSMC to agree to arbitrate, rather than litigate, the dispute. The arbitration panel ends up deciding that DSMC overcharged for the chips and awards the Canadian company $800 million. Heron and DSMC are dissatisfied with the result. Is the panel's decision binding? Can DSMC appeal the arbitration award to a court? These are a few of the concerns discussed in this chapter. (This chapter's *Business Web Log* feature deals with an arbitration clause Samsung sought to impose on buyers of its smartphones.)

Samsung and Forced Arbitration

Samsung, like other smartphone manufacturers, does not want to go to court to address every consumer complaint. Consequently, in each new smartphone box, it includes a Product Safety & Warranty Information brochure containing the following statement:

> ALL DISPUTES WITH SAMSUNG ARISING IN ANY WAY FROM THIS LIMITED WARRANTY OR THE SALE, CONDITION, OR PERFORMANCE OF THE PRODUCTS SHALL BE RESOLVED EXCLUSIVELY THROUGH FINAL AND BINDING ARBITRATION, AND NOT BY A COURT OR JURY.

In the same 101-page brochure, Samsung explains the procedures for arbitration and notes that purchasers can opt out of the arbitration agreement by calling a toll-free number or sending an e-mail within thirty days of purchase. The lead plaintiff in what became a class-action suit against Samsung did not take any steps to opt out.

The class-action suit alleged that the company misrepresented its smartphone's storage capacity and "rigged the phone to operate at a higher speed when it was being tested." Samsung moved to compel arbitration by invoking the arbitration provision in its Product Safety & Warranty Information brochure. A federal district court denied Samsung's motion to compel arbitration. On appeal, the trial court's reasoning was accepted. There was no evidence that the plaintiff had expressly agreed to submit to arbitration. The mere fact that an arbitration clause was included in the Product Safety & Warranty Information brochure did not create a binding contract between the plaintiff and Samsung. Further, even though the plaintiff had signed a Customer Agreement with the seller of the smartphone (Verizon Wireless), Samsung was not a signatory to that agreement.[a]

---

a. *Norcia v. Samsung Telecommunications America, LLC,* 845 F.3d 1279 (9th Cir. 2017).

Key Point

It is understandable that companies wish to avoid the high cost of going to court for every customer grievance. Binding arbitration offers businesses numerous advantages over litigation. A business must be certain, though, that a binding arbitration requirement is part of an actual contractual agreement between the business and its customers. Placing an arbitration clause, even in all capital letters, in a multi-page document that customers may never read is usually not sufficient.

4–1 The Judiciary's Role in American Government

The body of American law includes the federal and state constitutions, statutes passed by legislative bodies, administrative law, and the case decisions and legal principles that form the common law. These laws would be meaningless, however, without the courts to interpret and apply them. This is the essential role of the judiciary—the courts—in the American governmental system: to interpret and apply the law.

4–1a Judicial Review

As the branch of government entrusted with interpreting the laws, the judiciary can decide, among other things, whether the laws or actions of the other two branches are constitutional. The process for making such a determination is known as **judicial review.**

Leszek Kobusinski/Shutterstock.com

Each Samsung phone comes with a brochure requiring arbitration.

Judicial Review The process by which a court decides on the constitutionality of legislative enactments and actions of the executive branch.

Learning Objective 1

What is judicial review? How and when was the power of judicial review established?

The power of judicial review enables the judicial branch to act as a check on the other two branches of government, in line with the checks-and-balances system established by the U.S. Constitution. (Today, nearly all nations with constitutional democracies, including Canada, France, and Germany, have some form of judicial review.)

4–1b The Origins of Judicial Review in the United States

The U.S. Constitution does not mention judicial review (although many constitutional scholars believe that the founders intended the judiciary to have this power). How was the doctrine of judicial review established? See this chapter's *Landmark in the Law* feature for the answer.

Marbury v. Madison (1803)

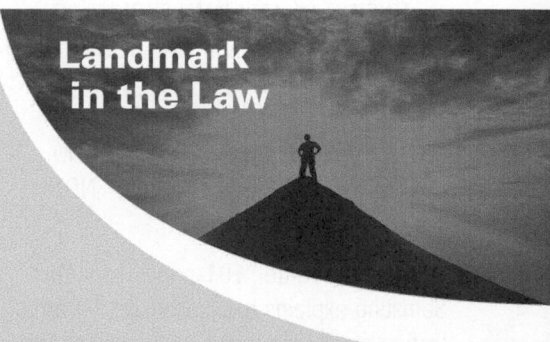

Landmark in the Law

The power of judicial review was established in the Supreme Court's decision in the case of *Marbury v. Madison*.[a] Although the decision is widely viewed as a cornerstone of constitutional law, the case had its origins in early U.S. politics.

When Thomas Jefferson defeated the incumbent president, John Adams, in the presidential elections of 1800, Adams feared the Jeffersonians' antipathy toward business and toward a strong national government. Adams thus rushed to "pack" the judiciary with loyal Federalists (those who believed in a strong national government) by appointing what came to be called "midnight judges" just before he left office.

But Adams's secretary of state (John Marshall) was able to deliver only forty-two of the fifty-nine judicial appointment letters by the time Jefferson took over as president. Jefferson refused to order his secretary of state, James Madison, to deliver the remaining commissions.

Marshall's Dilemma William Marbury and three others to whom the commissions had not been delivered sought a writ of *mandamus* (an order directing a government official to fulfill a duty) from

the United States Supreme Court, as authorized by the Judiciary Act in 1789.

As fate would have it, John Marshall had just been appointed as chief justice of the Supreme Court. Marshall faced a dilemma: If he ordered the commissions delivered, the new secretary of state (Madison) could simply refuse to deliver them—and the Court had no way to compel him to act. At the same time, if Marshall simply allowed the new administration to do as it wished, the Court's power would be severely eroded.

Marshall's Decision Marshall masterfully fashioned his decision to enlarge the power of the Supreme Court by affirming the Court's power of judicial review. He stated, "It is emphatically the province and duty of the Judicial Department to say what the law is. . . . If two laws conflict with each other, the Courts must decide on the operation of each. . . . [I]f both [a] law and the Constitution apply to a particular case, . . . the Court must determine which of these conflicting rules governs the case."

Marshall's decision did not require anyone to do anything. He concluded that the highest court did not have the power to issue a writ of *mandamus* in this particular case. Although the Judiciary Act specified that the Supreme Court could issue writs of

mandamus as part of its original jurisdiction, Article III of the Constitution, which spelled out the Court's original jurisdiction, did not mention such writs. Because Congress did not have the right to expand the Supreme Court's jurisdiction, this section of the Judiciary Act was unconstitutional—and thus void. The *Marbury* decision stands to this day as a judicial and political masterpiece.

Application to Today's World *Since the* Marbury v. Madison *decision, the power of judicial review has remained unchallenged and today is exercised by both federal and state courts. If the courts did not have the power of judicial review, the constitutionality of Congress's acts could not be challenged in court—a congressional statute would remain law unless changed by Congress. The courts of other countries that have adopted a constitutional democracy often cite this decision as a justification for judicial review.*

a. 5 U.S. (1 Cranch) 137, 2 L.Ed. 60 (1803).

4–2 Basic Judicial Requirements

Before a court can hear a lawsuit, certain requirements must be met. These requirements relate to jurisdiction, venue, and standing to sue. We examine each of these important concepts here.

4–2a Jurisdiction

In Latin, *juris* means "law," and *diction* means "to speak." Thus, "the power to speak the law" is the literal meaning of the term **jurisdiction**. Before any court can hear a case, it must have jurisdiction over the person or company against whom the suit is brought (the defendant) or over the property involved in the suit. The court must also have jurisdiction over the subject matter of the dispute.

In 1803, James Madison was a party in the *Marbury v. Madison* case. What did that case say about judicial review?

Jurisdiction over Persons or Property Generally, a court with jurisdiction over a particular geographic area can exercise personal jurisdiction (*in personam* jurisdiction) over any person or business that resides in that area. A state trial court, for instance, normally has jurisdictional authority over residents (including businesses) in a particular area of the state, such as a county or district. A state's highest court (often called the state supreme court)[1] has jurisdiction over all residents of that state.

A court can also exercise jurisdiction over property that is located within its boundaries. This kind of jurisdiction is known as *in rem* jurisdiction, or "jurisdiction over the thing." **Example 4.1** A dispute arises over the ownership of a boat in dry dock in Fort Lauderdale, Florida. The boat is owned by an Ohio resident, over whom a Florida court normally cannot exercise personal jurisdiction. The other party to the dispute is a resident of Nebraska. In this situation, because the boat is in Florida, a lawsuit concerning the boat could be brought in a Florida state court on the basis of the court's *in rem* jurisdiction.

Jurisdiction The authority of a court to hear and decide a specific case.

Long Arm Statutes. Under the authority of a state **long arm statute,** a court can exercise personal jurisdiction over certain out-of-state defendants based on activities that took place within the state. Before exercising long arm jurisdiction over a nonresident, however, the court must be convinced that the defendant had sufficient contacts, or *minimum contacts*, with the state to justify the jurisdiction.[2] Generally, this means that the defendant must have enough of a connection to the state for the judge to conclude that it is fair for the state to exercise power over the defendant.

If an out-of-state defendant caused an automobile accident or sold defective goods within the state, for instance, a court will usually find that minimum contacts exist to exercise jurisdiction over that defendant. **Spotlight Case Example 4.2** An Xbox game system caught fire in Bonnie Broquet's home in Texas and caused substantial personal injuries. Broquet filed a lawsuit in a Texas court against Ji-Haw Industrial Company, a nonresident company that made the Xbox components. Broquet alleged that Ji-Haw's components were defective and had caused the fire. Ji-Haw argued that the Texas court lacked jurisdiction over it, but a state appellate court held that the Texas long arm statute authorized the exercise of jurisdiction over the out-of-state defendant.[3]

Similarly, a state may exercise personal jurisdiction over a nonresident defendant who is sued for breaching a contract that was formed within the state. This is true even when that contract was negotiated over the phone or through correspondence.

Long Arm Statute A state statute that permits a state to exercise jurisdiction over nonresident defendants.

---

1. As will be discussed shortly, a state's highest court is frequently referred to as the state supreme court, but there are exceptions. For example, in New York, the supreme court is a trial court.
2. The minimum-contacts standard was established in *International Shoe Co. v. State of Washington*, 326 U.S. 310, 66 S.Ct. 154, 90 L.Ed. 95 (1945).
3. *Ji-Haw Industrial Co. v. Broquet*, 2008 WL 441822 (Tex.App.—San Antonio 2008).

Corporate Contacts. Because corporations are considered legal persons, courts use the same principles to determine whether it is fair to exercise jurisdiction over a corporation. A corporation normally is subject to personal jurisdiction in the state in which it is incorporated, has its principal office, and is doing business. Courts apply the minimum-contacts test to determine if they can exercise jurisdiction over out-of-state corporations.

In the past, corporations were usually subject to jurisdiction in states in which they were doing business, such as advertising or selling products. The United States Supreme Court has now clarified that large corporations that do business in many states are not automatically subject to jurisdiction in all of them. A corporation is subject to jurisdiction only in states where it does such substantial business that it is "at home" in that state.[4] The courts look at the amount of business the corporation does within the state relative to the amount it does elsewhere.

Is the presence of a railroad company's tracks in one state enough to satisfy the minimum-contacts requirement?

Case Example 4.3 Norfolk Southern Railway Company is a Virginia corporation. Russell Parker, a resident of Indiana and a former employee of Norfolk, filed a lawsuit against the railroad in Missouri. Parker claimed that while working for Norfolk in Indiana he had sustained a cumulative injury. Norfolk argued that Missouri courts did not have jurisdiction over the company. The Supreme Court of Missouri agreed. Simply having train tracks running through Missouri was not enough to meet the minimum-contacts requirement. Norfolk also had tracks and operations in twenty-one other states. The plaintiff worked and was allegedly injured in Indiana, not Missouri. Even though Norfolk did register its corporation in Missouri, the amount of business that it did in Missouri was not so substantial that it was "at home" in that state.[5]

Jurisdiction over Subject Matter

Jurisdiction over subject matter is a limitation on the types of cases a court can hear. In both the federal and the state court systems, there are courts of *general* (unlimited) *jurisdiction* and courts of *limited jurisdiction*. An example of a court of general jurisdiction is a state trial court or a federal district court.

An example of a state court of limited jurisdiction is a probate court. **Probate courts** are state courts that handle only matters relating to the transfer of a person's assets and obligations after that person's death, including matters relating to the custody and guardianship of children. An example of a federal court of limited subject-matter jurisdiction is a bankruptcy court. **Bankruptcy courts** handle only bankruptcy proceedings, which are governed by federal bankruptcy law.

A court's jurisdiction over subject matter is usually defined in the statute or constitution creating the court. In both the federal and the state court systems, a court's subject-matter jurisdiction can be limited by any of the following:

1. The subject of the lawsuit.

2. The sum in controversy.

3. Whether the case involves a felony (a more serious type of crime) or a misdemeanor (a less serious type of crime).

4. Whether the proceeding is a trial or an appeal.

Probate Court A state court of limited jurisdiction that conducts proceedings relating to the settlement of a deceased person's estate.

Bankruptcy Court A federal court of limited jurisdiction that handles only bankruptcy proceedings, which are governed by federal bankruptcy law.

---

4. *Daimler AG v. Bauman,* 571 U.S. 117, 134 S.Ct. 746, 187 L.Ed. 624 (2014).
5. *State ex rel. Norfolk Southern Railway Co. v. Dolan,* 512 S.W.3d 41 (Sup.Ct. Mo. 2017).

Original and Appellate Jurisdiction The distinction between courts of original jurisdiction and courts of appellate jurisdiction normally lies in whether the case is being heard for the first time. Courts having original jurisdiction are courts of the first instance, or trial courts—that is, courts in which lawsuits begin, trials take place, and evidence is presented. In the federal court system, the *district courts* are trial courts. In the various state court systems, the trial courts are known by various names, as will be discussed shortly.

The key point here is that any court having original jurisdiction is normally known as a trial court. Courts having appellate jurisdiction act as reviewing courts, or appellate courts. In general, cases can be brought before appellate courts only on appeal from an order or a judgment of a trial court or other lower court.

Jurisdiction of the Federal Courts Because the federal government is a government of limited powers, the jurisdiction of the federal courts is limited. Federal courts have subject-matter jurisdiction in two situations: those involving federal questions and diversity of citizenship.

Federal Questions. Article III of the U.S. Constitution establishes the boundaries of federal judicial power. Section 2 of Article III states that "[t]he judicial Power shall extend to all Cases, in Law and Equity, arising under this Constitution, the Laws of the United States, and Treaties made, or which shall be made, under their Authority." This clause means that whenever a plaintiff's cause of action is based, at least in part, on the U.S. Constitution, a treaty, or a federal law, then a **federal question** arises, and the federal courts have jurisdiction.

Any lawsuit involving a federal question, such as a person's rights under the U.S. Constitution, can originate in a federal court. Note that in a case based on a federal question, a federal court will apply federal law.

Diversity of Citizenship. Federal district courts can also exercise original jurisdiction over cases involving **diversity of citizenship**. The most common type of diversity jurisdiction requires *both* of the following:[6]

1. The plaintiff and defendant must be residents of different states.

2. The dollar amount in controversy must exceed $75,000.

For purposes of diversity jurisdiction, a corporation is a citizen of both the state in which it is incorporated and the state in which its principal place of business is located. A case involving diversity of citizenship can be filed in the appropriate federal district court. If the case starts in a state court, it can sometimes be transferred, or "removed," to a federal court. A large percentage of the cases filed in federal courts each year are based on diversity of citizenship.

As noted, a federal court will apply federal law in cases involving federal questions. In a case based on diversity of citizenship, in contrast, a federal court will apply the relevant state law (which is often the law of the state in which the court sits).

Case Example 4.4 Kelley Mala, a U.S. citizen of the Virgin Islands, was driving his powerboat near St. Thomas, Virgin Islands. When he stopped at Crown Bay Marina to buy gas, a pump malfunctioned, and gas overflowed and spilled into Mala's boat. Later, when he left the dock, Mala's engine caught fire and exploded, severely burning him and destroying the boat.

Mala sued the marina for negligence in a federal district court in the Virgin Islands. He claimed that the court had diversity jurisdiction (which would mean that the court would apply state law and he would be entitled to a jury trial). The court found that it did *not* have diversity jurisdiction because Crown Bay and the plaintiff were both citizens of the Virgin

Federal Question A question that pertains to the U.S. Constitution, an act of Congress, or a treaty and provides a basis for federal jurisdiction in a case.

Diversity of Citizenship A basis for federal court jurisdiction over a lawsuit between citizens of different states or a lawsuit involving a U.S. citizen and a citizen of a different country.

---

6. Diversity jurisdiction also exists in cases between (1) a foreign country and citizens of a state or of different states and (2) citizens of a state and citizens or subjects of a foreign country. These bases for diversity jurisdiction are less commonly used.

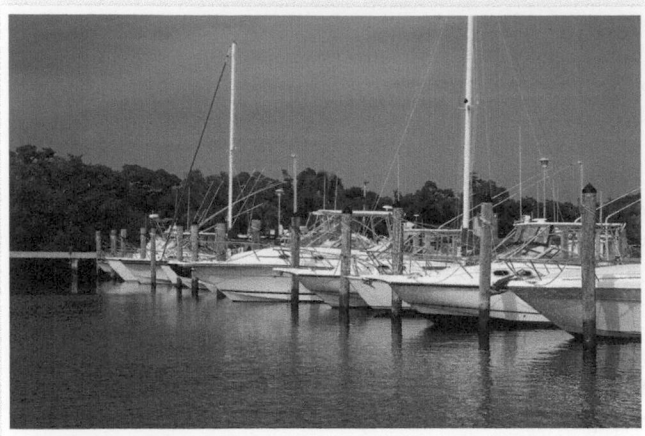

If a marina employee commits a negligent act while servicing a boat owned by someone whose legal residence is nearby, can the injured boat owner have the case removed to a federal court?

Concurrent Jurisdiction
Jurisdiction that exists when two different courts have the power to hear a case.

Exclusive Jurisdiction
Jurisdiction that exists when a case can be heard only in a particular court or type of court.

Islands. A federal appellate court affirmed. Therefore, Mala had to sue the marina under admiralty law (law governing transportation on the seas and ocean waters) and did not have a right to a jury trial.[7]

Exclusive versus Concurrent Jurisdiction When both federal and state courts have the power to hear a case, as is true in lawsuits involving diversity of citizenship, **concurrent jurisdiction** exists. When cases can be tried only in federal courts or only in state courts, **exclusive jurisdiction** exists.

Federal courts have exclusive jurisdiction in cases involving federal crimes, bankruptcy, most patent and copyright claims, suits against the United States, and some areas of admiralty law. State courts also have exclusive jurisdiction over certain subject matter—for instance, divorce and adoption.

When concurrent jurisdiction exists, a party may bring a suit in either a federal court or a state court. A number of factors can affect the decision of whether to litigate in a federal or a state court, such as the availability of different remedies, the distance to the respective courthouses, or the experience or reputation of a particular judge.

A resident of a state other than the one with jurisdiction might also choose a federal court over a state court if he or she is concerned that a state court might be biased against an out-of-state plaintiff. In contrast, a plaintiff might choose to litigate in a state court if it has a reputation for awarding substantial amounts of damages or if the judge is perceived as being pro-plaintiff. The concepts of exclusive and concurrent jurisdiction are illustrated in Exhibit 4–1.

---

7. *Mala v. Crown Bay Marina, Inc.*, 704 F.3d 239 (2013).

Exhibit 4–1 Exclusive and Concurrent Jurisdiction

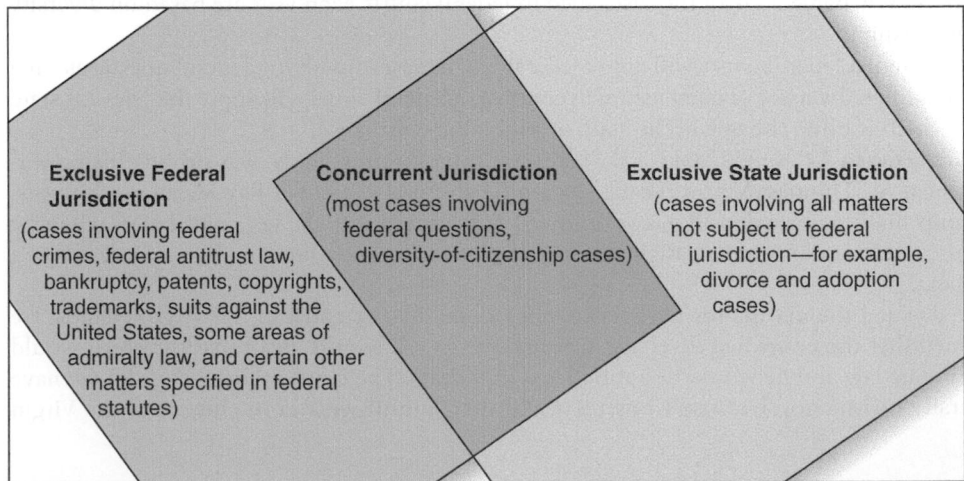

Exclusive Federal Jurisdiction
(cases involving federal crimes, federal antitrust law, bankruptcy, patents, copyrights, trademarks, suits against the United States, some areas of admiralty law, and certain other matters specified in federal statutes)

Concurrent Jurisdiction
(most cases involving federal questions, diversity-of-citizenship cases)

Exclusive State Jurisdiction
(cases involving all matters not subject to federal jurisdiction—for example, divorce and adoption cases)

4–2b Jurisdiction in Cyberspace

The Internet's capacity to bypass political and geographic boundaries undercuts the traditional basis on which courts assert personal jurisdiction. As already discussed, for a court to compel a defendant to come before it, there must be at least minimum contacts—the presence of a salesperson within the state, for example. Today, however, courts frequently have to decide what constitutes sufficient minimum contacts when a defendant's only connection to a jurisdiction is through an ad on a website.

The "Sliding-Scale" Standard The courts have developed a standard—called a "sliding-scale" standard—for determining when the exercise of jurisdiction over an out-of-state defendant is proper. The sliding-scale standard identifies three types of Internet business contacts and outlines the following rules for jurisdiction:

1. When the defendant conducts *substantial business* over the Internet (such as contracts and sales), jurisdiction is proper. This is true whether the business is conducted with traditional computers, smartphones, or other means of Internet access.

2. When there is *some interactivity* through a website, jurisdiction may be proper, depending on the circumstances. It is up to the courts to decide how much online interactivity is enough to satisfy the minimum-contacts requirement. **Case Example 4.5** Dr. Arthur Delahoussaye, a Louisiana resident, bought a special racing bicycle he saw listed on eBay from Frederick Boelter, who lived in Wisconsin. Later, while Delahoussaye was riding the bike, he had to "bunny hop" (jump) over a gap in the pavement. When he landed, the front wheel disconnected, pushing the forks of the bicycle into the ground and propelling him over the handlebars and onto the pavement. Delahoussaye suffered serious injuries. He sued Boelter in a Louisiana court, alleging that Boelter had negligently removed the secondary retention devices designed to prevent the detachment of the front wheel.

    The Louisiana court ruled that the state did not have jurisdiction over Boelter, and a state appellate court affirmed. Boelter did not have any prior relationship with Delahoussaye, did not initiate communications with Delahoussaye, and discussed the transaction with Delahoussaye only over the Internet. Payment was made through an intermediary, PayPal, and Boelter shipped the bicycle to Louisiana. The sale of a single bicycle to Delahoussaye over eBay was not enough to give Louisiana state jurisdiction over Boelter, so the plaintiff's case was dismissed.[8]

3. When a defendant merely engages in *passive advertising* on the Web, jurisdiction is never proper.[9]

International Jurisdictional Issues Because the Internet is global in scope, it raises international jurisdictional issues. The world's courts seem to be developing a standard that echoes the minimum-contacts requirement applied by U.S. courts.

Most courts are indicating that minimum contacts—doing business within the jurisdiction, for instance—are enough to compel a defendant to appear. The effect of this standard is that a business firm has to comply with the laws in any jurisdiction in which it targets customers for its products. This situation is complicated by the fact that many countries' laws on particular issues—such as free speech—are very different from U.S. laws.

The following case illustrates how federal courts apply a sliding-scale standard to determine if they can exercise jurisdiction over a foreign defendant whose only contact with the United States is through a website.

8. *Delahoussaye v. Boelter*, 199 So.3d 633 (La.App. 2016).
9. For a leading case on this issue, see *Zippo Manufacturing Co. v. Zippo Dot Com, Inc.*, 952 F.Supp. 1119 (W.D.Pa. 1997).

Spotlight on Gucci: Case 4.1

Gucci America, Inc. v. Wang Huoqing

United States District Court, Northern District of California, 2011 WL 30972 (2011).

Background and Facts Wang Huoqing, a resident of the People's Republic of China, operates numerous websites. When Gucci discovered that Huoqing's websites were selling counterfeit goods—products that carried Gucci's trademarks but were not genuine Gucci articles—it hired a private investigator (Robert Holmes) in San Jose, California, to buy goods from the websites. The investigator purchased a wallet that was labeled Gucci but was counterfeit.

*Gucci luxury leather products
are often counterfeited.
Can Gucci sue an
Asian company in the
United States nonetheless?*

Gucci filed a trademark infringement lawsuit against Huoqing in a federal district court in California seeking damages and an injunction to prevent further infringement. Huoqing was notified of the lawsuit via e-mail but did not appear in court. Gucci asked the court to enter a default judgment—that is, a judgment entered when the defendant fails to appear. The court first had to determine whether it had personal jurisdiction over Huoqing based on the Internet sales.

In the Words of the Court
Joseph C. *SPERO,* United States Magistrate Judge.

* * * *

* * * Under California's long-arm statute, federal courts in California may exercise jurisdiction to the extent permitted by the Due Process Clause of the Constitution. The Due Process Clause allows federal courts to exercise jurisdiction where * * * the defendant has had sufficient minimum contacts with the forum to subject him or her to the specific jurisdiction of the court. The courts apply a three-part test to determine whether specific jurisdiction exists:

(1) The nonresident defendant must do some act or consummate some transaction with the forum or perform some act by which he purposefully avails himself of the privilege of conducting activities in the forum, thereby invoking the benefits and protections of its laws; (2) the claim must be one which arises out of or results from the defendant's forum-related activities; and (3) exercise of jurisdiction must be reasonable.

* * * *

In order to satisfy the first prong of the test for specific jurisdiction, a defendant must have either purposefully availed itself

of [taken advantage of] the privilege of conducting business activities within the forum or purposefully directed activities toward the forum. *Purposeful availment [advantage] typically consists of action taking place in the forum that invokes the benefits and protections of the laws of the forum, such as executing or performing a contract within the forum.* To show purposeful availment, a plaintiff must show that the defendant "engage[d] in some form of affirmative conduct allowing or promoting the transaction of business within the forum state." [Emphasis added.]

"In the Internet context, the Ninth Circuit utilizes a sliding scale analysis under which 'passive' websites do not create sufficient contacts to establish purposeful availment, whereas interactive websites may create sufficient contacts, depending on how interactive the website is." * * * *Personal jurisdiction is appropriate where an entity is conducting business over the Internet and has offered for sale and sold its products to forum [California] residents.* [Emphasis added.]

Here, the allegations and evidence presented by Plaintiffs in support of the Motion are sufficient to show purposeful availment on the part of Defendant Wang Huoqing. Plaintiffs have alleged that Defendant operates "fully interactive Internet websites operating under the Subject Domain Names" and have presented evidence in the form of copies of web pages showing that the websites are, in fact, interactive.

* * * Additionally, Plaintiffs allege Defendant is conducting counterfeiting and infringing activities within this Judicial District and has advertised and sold his counterfeit goods in the State of California. * * * Plaintiffs have also presented evidence of one actual sale within this district, made by investigator Robert Holmes from the website bag2do.cn.

* * * Finally, Plaintiffs have presented evidence that Defendant Wang Huoqing owns or controls the twenty-eight websites listed in the Motion for Default Judgment. * * * Such commercial activity in the forum amounts to purposeful availment of the privilege of conducting activities within the forum, thus invoking the benefits and protections of its laws. Accordingly, the Court concludes

that Defendant's contacts with California are sufficient to show purposeful availment.

Decision and Remedy   The U.S. District Court for the Northern District of California held that it had personal jurisdiction over the foreign defendant, Huoqing. The court entered a default judgment against Huoqing and granted Gucci an injunction.

4–2c Venue

Jurisdiction has to do with whether a court has authority to hear a case involving specific persons, property, or subject matter. **Venue**[10] is concerned with the most appropriate physical location for a trial. Two state courts (or two federal courts) may have the authority to exercise jurisdiction over a case, but it may be more appropriate or convenient to hear the case in one court than in the other.

Venue The geographic district in which a legal action is tried and from which the jury is selected.

Basically, the concept of venue reflects the policy that a court trying a suit should be in the geographic neighborhood (usually the county) where the incident leading to the lawsuit occurred or where the parties involved in the lawsuit reside. Venue in a civil case typically is where the defendant resides, whereas venue in a criminal case normally is where the crime occurred. Pretrial publicity or other factors, though, may require a change of venue to another community, especially in criminal cases when the defendant's right to a fair and impartial jury has been impaired.

Note that venue has lost some significance in today's world because of the Internet and 24/7 news reporting. Courts now rarely grant requests for a change of venue. Because everyone has instant access to the same information about a purported crime, courts reason that no community is more or less informed about the matter or prejudiced for or against the defendant.

In a criminal trial involving comedian Bill Cosby, the venue was changed from his hometown of Philadelphia to western Pennsylvania. Why do courts sometimes change venue?

4–2d Standing to Sue

Before a person can bring a lawsuit before a court, the party must have **standing to sue,** or a sufficient "stake" in the matter to justify seeking relief through the court system. Standing means that the party that filed the action in court has a legally protected interest at stake in the litigation. The party bringing the lawsuit must have suffered a harm, such as physical injury or economic loss, as a result of the action about which she or he has complained.

At times, a person can have standing to sue on behalf of another person, such as a minor (child) or a mentally incompetent person. Standing to sue also requires that the controversy at issue be a **justiciable**[11] **controversy**—a controversy that is real and substantial, as opposed to hypothetical or academic.

Case Example 4.6   Harold Wagner obtained a loan through M.S.T. Mortgage Group to buy a house in Texas. After the sale, M.S.T. transferred its interest in the loan to another lender,

Standing to Sue The legal requirement that an individual must have a sufficient stake in a controversy before he or she can bring a lawsuit.

Justiciable Controversy A controversy that is not hypothetical or academic but real and substantial. It is a requirement that must be satisfied before a court will hear a case.

---

10. Pronounced *ven*-yoo.
11. Pronounced jus-*tish*-uh-bul.

which assigned it to another lender, as is common in the mortgage industry. Eventually, when Wagner failed to make the loan payments, CitiMortgage, Inc., notified him that it was going to foreclose on the property and sell the house. Wagner filed a lawsuit claiming that the lenders had improperly assigned the mortgage loan. A federal district court ruled that Wagner lacked standing to contest the assignment. Under Texas law, only the parties directly involved in an assignment can challenge its validity. In this case, the assignment was between two lenders and did not directly involve Wagner.[12] ■

4–3 The State and Federal Court Systems

Each state has its own court system. Additionally, there is a system of federal courts. Even though there are fifty-two court systems—one for each of the fifty states, one for the District of Columbia, and a federal system—similarities abound. Exhibit 4–2 illustrates the basic organizational structure characteristic of the court systems in many states. The exhibit also shows how the federal court system is structured.

Keep in mind that the federal courts are not superior to the state courts. They are simply an independent system of courts, which derives its authority from Article III, Sections 1 and 2, of the U.S. Constitution.

4–3a The State Court Systems

No two state court systems are exactly the same. Typically, a state court system will include several levels, or tiers, of courts. As indicated in Exhibit 4–2, state courts may include (1) trial courts of limited jurisdiction, (2) trial courts of general jurisdiction, (3) appellate courts, and (4) the state's highest court (often called the state supreme court).

---

12. *Wagner v. CitiMortgage, Inc.*, 995 F.Supp.2d 621 (N.D.Tex. 2014).

Exhibit 4–2 The State and Federal Court Systems

Generally, any person who is a party to a lawsuit has the opportunity to plead the case before a trial court and then, if he or she loses, before at least one level of appellate court. If the case involves a federal statute or a federal constitutional issue, the decision of a state supreme court on that issue may be further appealed to the United States Supreme Court.

Trial Courts Trial courts are courts in which trials are held and testimony taken. State trial courts have either general or limited jurisdiction. Trial courts that have general jurisdiction as to subject matter may be called county, district, superior, or circuit courts.[13] These courts have jurisdiction over a wide variety of subjects, including both civil disputes and criminal prosecutions. (In some states, trial courts of general jurisdiction may hear appeals from courts of limited jurisdiction.)

Courts of limited jurisdiction may be called special inferior trial courts or minor judiciary courts. Limited jurisdiction courts might include local municipal courts (which could include separate traffic courts and drug courts) and domestic relations courts (which handle divorce and child-custody disputes). **Small claims courts** are inferior trial courts that hear only civil cases involving claims of less than a certain amount, such as $5,000 (the amount varies from state to state). Suits brought in small claims courts are generally conducted informally, and lawyers are not required (in a few states, lawyers are not even allowed). Decisions of small claims courts and municipal courts may sometimes be appealed to a state trial court of general jurisdiction.

A few states have even tried to establish Islamic law courts, which are courts of limited jurisdiction that serve the American Muslim community. (See this chapter's *Beyond Our Borders* feature for a discussion of Islamic law courts.)

> **Small Claims Court** A special court in which parties can litigate small claims without an attorney.

> **Learning Objective 3**
> What is the difference between the focus of a trial court and that of an appellate court?

---

13. The name in Ohio is court of common pleas, and the name in New York is supreme court.

Islamic Law Courts Abroad and at Home

Beyond Our Borders

Islamic law is one of the world's three most common legal systems, along with civil law and common law systems. In most Islamic countries, the law is based on *sharia*, a system of law derived from the Qur'an and the sayings and doings of Muhammad and his companions. Today, many non-Islamic countries are establishing Islamic courts for their Muslim citizens.

Islamic Law in Britain, Canada, and Belgium

For several years, Great Britain has had councils that arbitrate disputes between British Muslims involving child custody, property, employment, and housing. These councils do not deal with criminal law or with any civil issues that would put *sharia* in direct conflict with British statutory law. Most Islamic law cases involve marriage or divorce. Britain officially sanctioned the authority of *sharia* judges to rule on divorce and financial disputes of Muslim individuals. Britain now has more than one hundred officially recognized *sharia* courts that have the full power of equivalent courts within the traditional British judicial system.

In Ontario, Canada, a group of Canadian Muslims established a judicial tribunal using *sharia*. To date, this tribunal has resolved only marital disagreements and some other civil disputes. Under Ontario law, the regular judicial system must uphold such agreements as long as they are voluntary and negotiated through an arbitrator. Any agreements that violate Canada's Charter of Rights and Freedoms will not be upheld.

Belgium has also established a *sharia* court that handles primarily family law matters for Muslim immigrants. Other

(Continues)

European nations, including France, Germany, and Sweden, allow their courts to consider *sharia* law when deciding disputes involving Muslims.

Islamic Law Courts in the United States

The use of Islamic courts in the United States has been controversial. The legality of arbitration clauses that require disputes to be settled in Islamic courts has been upheld by regular state courts in some states, including Minnesota and Texas. In some other states, however, there has been a public backlash against the use of Islamic courts.

For instance, in Detroit, Michigan, which has a large American Muslim population, a controversy erupted over the community's attempt to establish Islamic courts. Legislators in Michigan and many other states started introducing bills to limit consideration of foreign or religious laws in state court decisions. Voters in Oklahoma enacted a referendum banning courts from considering *sharia* law, but the ban was later held to be unconstitutional.[a]

---

a. *Awad v. Zirax*, 670 F.3d 1111 (10th Cir. 2012). A lower court later issued a permanent injunction to prevent the ban from being enforced. *Awad v. Zirax*, 966 F.Supp.2d 1198 (2013).

Legislation enacted in Arizona, Kansas, Louisiana, North Carolina, Oklahoma, South Dakota, and Tennessee bans judicial consideration of foreign law. (These laws do not explicitly mention Islamic, or *sharia*, law, because that might be ruled unconstitutional.)

Critical Thinking

One of the arguments against allowing sharia *courts in the United States is that we would no longer have a common legal framework within our society. Do you agree or disagree? Why?*

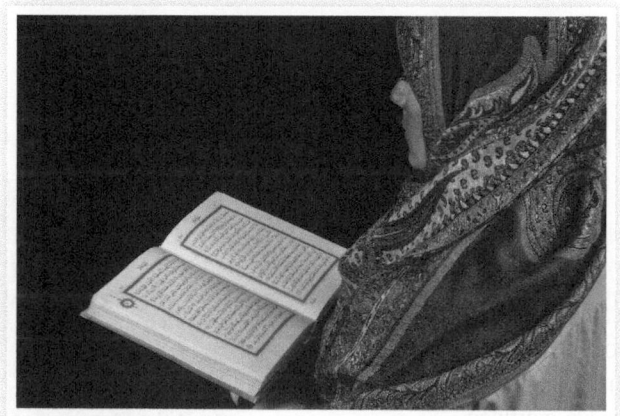

Can a U.S. court ever use the Qur'an as a basis for reaching a decision?

Mehmet Hilmi Barcin/iStock/Getty Images

Question of Fact In a lawsuit, an issue that involves only disputed facts, and not what the law is on a given point.

Question of Law In a lawsuit, an issue involving the application or interpretation of a law.

Appellate, or Reviewing, Courts Every state has at least one court of appeals (appellate court, or reviewing court), which may be an intermediate appellate court or the state's highest court. About three-fourths of the states have intermediate appellate courts. Generally, courts of appeals do not conduct new trials, in which evidence is submitted and witnesses are examined. Rather, an appellate court panel of three or more judges reviews the record of the case on appeal, which includes a transcript of the trial proceedings, and determines whether the trial court committed an error.

Focus on Questions of Law. Appellate courts generally focus on questions of law, not questions of fact. A **question of fact** deals with what really happened in regard to the dispute being tried—such as whether a party actually burned a flag. A **question of law** concerns the application or interpretation of the law—such as whether flag-burning is a form of speech protected by the First Amendment to the U.S. Constitution. Only a judge, not a jury, can rule on questions of law.

Defer to the Trial Court's Findings of Fact. Appellate courts normally defer (give significant weight) to a trial court's findings on questions of fact, because the trial court judge and jury were in a better position to evaluate testimony. The trial court could directly observe witnesses' gestures, demeanor, and nonverbal behavior during the trial. An appellate court cannot. At the appellate level, the judges review the written transcript of the trial.

An appellate court will challenge a trial court's finding of fact only when the finding is clearly erroneous (that is, when it is contrary to the evidence presented at trial or when no evidence was presented to support the finding). In the following case, neither the administrative agency that initially ruled on the dispute nor the trial court to which the agency's decision was appealed made a finding on a crucial question of fact. Faced with that circumstance, what should a state appellate court do?

Case 4.2

Johnson v. Oxy USA, Inc.

Court of Appeals of Texas, Houston—14th District, 533 S.W.3d 395 (2016).

Background and Facts Jennifer Johnson was working as a finance analyst for Oxy USA, Inc., when Oxy changed the job's requirements. To meet the new standards, Johnson took courses to become a certified public accountant. Johnson and Oxy signed an agreement regarding reimbursement from Oxy to Johnson for the cost of the courses.

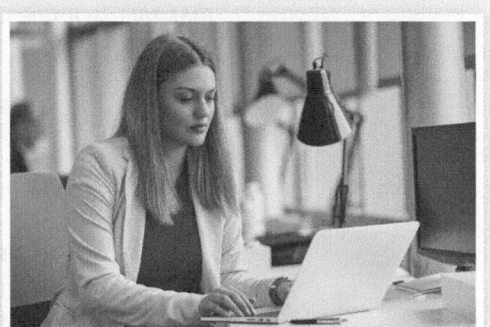

When Johnson resigned less than a year after having been reimbursed for the coursework, Oxy withheld the amount of the reimbursement from her last check. Oxy argued that under the agreement, it was entitled to do this because Johnson had worked less than a year from the date of reimbursement.

Johnson contended that the agreement did not apply because the funds should have been classified as a business expense, which did not have to be repaid under Oxy's Educational Assistance Policy. Johnson filed a claim for the amount with the Texas Workforce Commission (TWC). The TWC ruled that she was not entitled to the unpaid wages. She filed a suit in a Texas state court against Oxy, alleging breach of contract. The court affirmed the TWC's ruling. Johnson appealed.

In the Words of the Court
Ken *WISE*, Justice

* * * *

* * * The trial court * * * held that Johnson's [claim for breach of contract was] barred by *res judicata* ["a matter judged"]. In a court of law, a claimant typically cannot pursue one remedy to an unfavorable outcome and then seek the same remedy in another proceeding before the same or a different tribunal. *Res judicata bars the relitigation of claims that have been finally adjudicated or that could have been litigated in the prior action.* [Emphasis added.]

Johnson argues that *res judicata* does not apply here because the TWC did not render a final judgment on the merits of her claim that Oxy misinterpreted its Educational Assistance Policy. Specifically, Johnson claims she was "denied the right of full adjudication of her claim because the TWC refused to consider her arguments at the administrative level as beyond its jurisdiction."

To support this contention, Johnson points to the following excerpt from the * * * decision:

> * * * The TWC does not interpret contracts between employers and employee but only enforces the Texas Payday Law [the Texas state law that governs the timing of employees' paychecks]. * * * The question of whether the employer properly interpreted their policy on reimbursed educational expenses versus a business expense is a question for a different forum.

According to Johnson, this language shows that the TWC refused to consider the merits of the issue she raised as "beyond its reach." In contrast, the defendants contend that Johnson's claims are barred by *res judicata* because they are based on claims previously decided by the TWC.

* * * *

In Johnson's case, however, the TWC did not decide the key question of fact in dispute—whether Oxy violated its own Educational Assistance Policy when it withheld Johnson's final wages as reimbursement for the CPA courses. In fact, the TWC explicitly refused to do so, stating that the agency "does not interpret contracts between employers and employee." * * * Because this question goes to the heart of Johnson's breach of contract * * * claim, we hold that res judicata does not bar [that] claim. [Emphasis added.]

The defendants argue that because Johnson seeks to recover the same wages in this suit as she did in her claim with the TWC, *res judicata* must bar her common law cause of action. However, * * * *res judicata* would only bar a claim if TWC's order is considered final. * * * Here, the order in Johnson's case made no such findings with regard to the Educational Assistance Policy. The order expressly declined to address that issue. Therefore, * * * *res judicata* will not bar Johnson's breach of contract * * * claim.

Decision and Remedy A state intermediate appellate court reversed the lower court's decision. "The TWC did not decide the key question of fact in dispute—whether Oxy violated its own Educational Assistance Policy when it withheld Johnson's final wages.

(Continues)

In fact, the TWC explicitly refused to do so, stating that the agency 'does not interpret contracts between employers and employee.'" The appellate court remanded the case for a trial on the merits.

Critical Thinking

• **Legal Environment** *Who can decide questions of fact? Who can rule on questions of law? Why?*

• **Global** *In some cases, a court may be asked to determine and interpret the law of a foreign country. Some states consider the issue of what the law of a foreign country requires to be a question of fact. Federal rules of procedure provide that this is a question of law. Which position seems more appropriate? Why?*

Trial decisions are normally determined by juries. Under what types of circumstances might an appellate court reverse a jury's decision?

Highest State Courts The highest appellate court in a state is usually called the supreme court but may be called by some other name. For instance, in both New York and Maryland, the highest state court is called the court of appeals. The decisions of each state's highest court are final on all questions of state law. Only when issues of federal law are involved can a decision made by a state's highest court be overruled by the United States Supreme Court.

Example 4.7 A city enacts an ordinance that prohibits citizens from engaging in door-to-door advocacy without first registering with the mayor's office and receiving a permit. A religious group then sues the city, arguing that the law violates the freedoms of speech and religion guaranteed by the First Amendment. If the state supreme court upholds the law, the group could appeal the decision to the United States Supreme Court, because a constitutional (federal) issue is involved. ■

4–3b The Federal Court System

The federal court system is basically a three-tiered model consisting of (1) U.S. district courts (trial courts of general jurisdiction) and various courts of limited jurisdiction, (2) U.S. courts of appeals (intermediate courts of appeals), and (3) the United States Supreme Court.

Unlike state court judges, who are usually elected, federal court judges—including the justices of the Supreme Court—are appointed by the president of the United States and confirmed by the U.S. Senate. Under Article III, federal judges "hold their offices during Good Behavior." In the entire history of the United States, only seven federal judges have been removed from office through impeachment proceedings.

Certain federal court officers are not appointed by the president and approved by the Senate. This chapter's *Managerial Strategy* feature describes how U.S. magistrate judges are selected.

U.S. District Courts At the federal level, the equivalent of a state trial court of general jurisdiction is the district court. There is at least one federal district court in every state. The number of judicial districts can vary over time, primarily owing to population changes and corresponding caseloads. Today, there are ninety-four federal judicial districts.

U.S. district courts have original jurisdiction in federal matters. Federal cases typically originate in district courts. Federal courts with original, but specialized (or limited), jurisdiction include the bankruptcy courts and others that were shown in Exhibit 4–2.

Should You Consent to Have Your Business Case Decided by a U.S. Magistrate Judge?

Managerial Strategy

You have a strong case in a contract dispute with one of your business's suppliers. The supplier is located in another state. Your attorney did everything necessary to obtain your "day in court." The court in question is a federal district court. But you have just found out that your case may not be heard for several years—or even longer. Your attorney tells you that the case can be heard in just a few months if you consent to place it in the hands of a U.S. magistrate judge.[a] Should you consent?

A Short History of U.S. Magistrate Judges

Congress authorized the creation of a new federal judicial officer, the U.S. magistrate, in 1968 to help reduce delays in the U.S. district courts.[b] These junior federal officers were to conduct a wide range of judicial proceedings as set out by statute and as assigned by the district judges under whom they served. In 1979, Congress gave U.S. magistrates consent jurisdiction, which authorized them to conduct all civil trials as long as the parties

consented.[c] Currently, magistrate judges dispose of over one million civil and criminal district court matters, which include motions and hearings.

The Selection and Quality of Magistrate Judges

As mentioned, federal district judges are nominated by the president, confirmed by the Senate, and appointed for life. In contrast, U.S. magistrate judges are selected by federal district court judges based on the recommendations of a screening committee. They serve an eight-year term (which can be renewed).

By statute, magistrate judges must be chosen through a merit selection process. Applicants are interviewed by a screening committee of lawyers and others from the district in which the position will be filled.[d] The committee is not allowed to consider an applicant's political party affiliation.

A variety of experienced attorneys, administrative law judges, state court judges, and others apply for magistrate judge positions. A typical opening receives about a hundred applicants. The merit

selection panel selects the five most qualified, who are then voted on by federal district court judges.

Because the selection process for a magistrate judge is not the same as for a district judge, some critics have expressed concerns about the quality of magistrate judges. Some groups, such as People for the American Way, are not in favor of allowing magistrate judges the power to decide cases. These critics believe that because of their limited terms, they are not completely immune from outside pressure.

Business Questions

1. *If you were facing an especially complex legal dispute—one involving many facets and several different types of law—would you consent to allowing a U.S. magistrate judge to decide the case? Why or why not?*

2. *If you had to decide whether to allow a U.S. magistrate judge to hear your case, what information might you ask your attorney to provide concerning that individual?*

---

a. 28 U.S.C. Sec 636(c); see also *Coleman v. Labor and Industry Review Commission of Wisconsin*, 830 F.3d 461 (7th Cir. 2017).
b. Federal Magistrates Act, 82 Stat. 1107, October 17, 1968.
c. U.S.C. Section 636(c)(1).
d. 28 U.S.C. Section 631(b)(5).

U.S. Courts of Appeals In the federal court system, there are thirteen U.S. courts of appeals—also referred to as U.S. circuit courts of appeals. The federal courts of appeals for twelve of the circuits, including the U.S. Court of Appeals for the District of Columbia Circuit, hear appeals from the federal district courts located within their respective judicial circuits.

The Court of Appeals for the Thirteenth Circuit is called the Federal Circuit. It has national appellate jurisdiction over certain types of cases, such as cases involving patent law and cases in which the U.S. government is a defendant.

The decisions of the circuit courts of appeals are final in most cases, but appeal to the United States Supreme Court is possible. Exhibit 4–3 shows the boundaries of both the district courts and the U.S. courts of appeals within each circuit.

Exhibit 4–3 Boundaries of the U.S. Courts of Appeals and U.S. District Courts

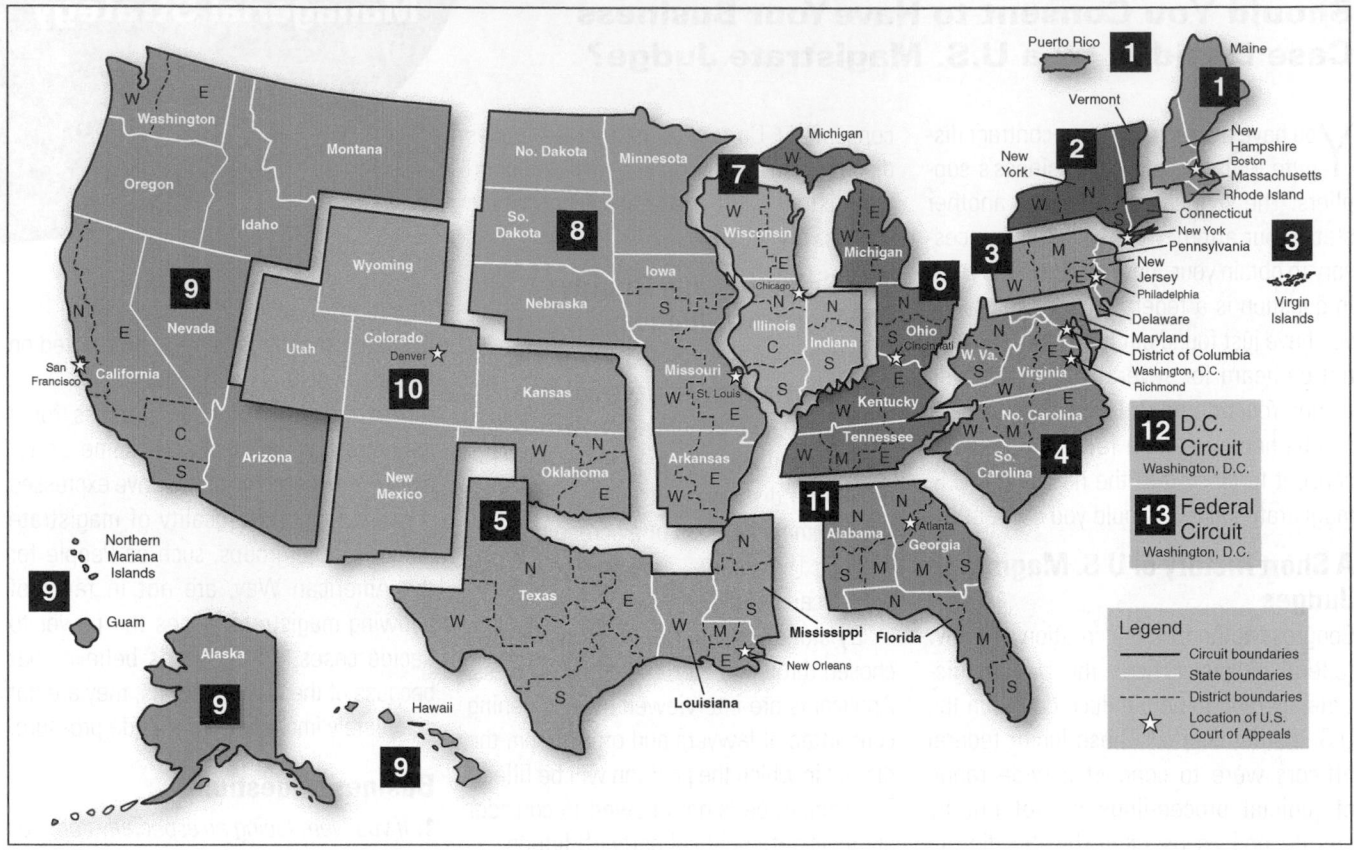

Source: Administrative Office of the United States Courts.

The United States Supreme Court The highest level of the three-tiered model of the federal court system is the United States Supreme Court. According to Article III of the U.S. Constitution, there is only one national Supreme Court. All other courts in the federal system are considered "inferior." Congress is empowered to create inferior courts as it deems necessary. The inferior courts that Congress has created include the second tier in our model—the U.S. courts of appeals—as well as the district courts and any other courts of limited, or specialized, jurisdiction.

The United States Supreme Court consists of nine justices. Although the Supreme Court has original, or trial, jurisdiction in rare instances (set forth in Article III, Section 2), most of its work is as an appeals court. The Supreme Court can review any case decided by any of the federal courts of appeals, and it also has appellate authority over some cases decided in the state courts.

Appeals to the Supreme Court. To bring a case before the Supreme Court, a party requests that the Court issue a writ of *certiorari*. A **writ of *certiorari***[14] is an order issued by the Supreme Court to a lower court requiring that court to send the record of the case for review. Under the **rule of four,** the Court will not issue a writ unless at least four of the nine justices approve.

Whether the Court will issue a writ of *certiorari* is entirely within its discretion. The Court is not required to issue one, and most petitions for writs are denied. (Although thousands of cases are filed with the Supreme Court each year, it hears, on average, fewer than one

Writ of *Certiorari* A writ from a higher court asking a lower court for the record of a case.

Rule of Four A rule of the United States Supreme Court under which the Court will not issue a writ of *certiorari* unless at least four justices approve of the decision to issue the writ.

14. Pronounced sur-shee-uh-*rah*-ree.

hundred of these cases.)[15] A denial is not a decision on the merits of a case, nor does it indicate agreement with the lower court's opinion. Furthermore, a denial of the writ has no value as a precedent.

Petitions Granted by the Court. Typically, the Court grants petitions when cases raise important constitutional questions or when the lower courts are issuing conflicting decisions on a significant issue. The justices, however, never explain their reasons for hearing certain cases and not others, so it is difficult to predict which type of case the Court might select.

Ethical Issue

Should Supreme Court justices follow the *Code of Conduct for United States Judges*? Every member of the U.S. judiciary is subject to the published *Code of Conduct for United States Judges,* except the nine justices of the United States Supreme Court. There is no code of conduct for them, except their consciences. Two main ethical issues are often in question with respect to Supreme Court justices.

The first ethical issue involves accepting gifts and payments from outside sources other than the U.S. government. Just before his death, Justice Antonin Scalia took seventeen international trips, Justice Stephen Breyer took fourteen, and Justice Ruth Bader Ginsburg took six. Someone else paid for all of these trips. Do the individuals or organizations paying for those trips anticipate getting favorable treatment if a case involving them ever comes before the Court?

The other ethical issue involves when it is appropriate for a Supreme Court justice to remove (recuse) herself or himself from a case because of a conflict of interest. Certain members of the Court have investments in private corporations that have, at times, written *amicus* briefs (legal arguments submitted by friends of the court). Should a justice recuse herself or himself in such a situation? Because there is no code of conduct for the Court, we will never know.

U.S. representative Louise Slaughter (D-NY) wants to change this situation. Every year since 2013, she has introduced a bill called The Supreme Court Ethics Act. She wants the Court to "adopt clear, written rules that establish standards by which justices' behavior can be guided and assessed by both themselves and the American people."

4–4 Following a State Court Case

To illustrate the procedures that would be followed in a civil lawsuit brought in a state court, we present a hypothetical case and follow it through the state court system. The case involves an automobile accident in which Kevin Anderson, driving a Lexus, struck Lisa Marconi, driving a Hyundai Genesis. The accident occurred at the intersection of Wilshire Boulevard and Rodeo Drive in Beverly Hills, California. Marconi suffered personal injuries and incurred medical and hospital expenses as a result, as well as lost wages for four months. Anderson and Marconi are unable to agree on a settlement, and Marconi sues Anderson. Marconi is the plaintiff, and Anderson is the defendant. Both are represented by lawyers.

During each phase of the **litigation** (the process of working a lawsuit through the court system), Marconi and Anderson will have to observe strict procedural requirements. A large body of law—procedural law—establishes the rules and standards for determining disputes in courts.

> "Lawsuit: A machine which you go into as a pig and come out of as a sausage."
>
> **Ambrose Bierce**
> 1842–1914
> (American journalist)

Litigation The process of resolving a dispute through the court system.

---

15. From the mid-1950s through the early 1990s, the United States Supreme Court reviewed more cases per year than it has in the last few years. In the Court's 1982–1983 term, for instance, the Court issued opinions in 151 cases. In contrast, in its 2016–2017 term, the Court issued opinions in only 70 cases.

Procedural rules are very complex, and they vary from court to court and from state to state. In addition to the various sets of rules for state courts, the federal courts have their own rules of procedure. Additionally, the applicable procedures will depend on whether the case is a civil or criminal proceeding. Generally, the Marconi-Anderson civil lawsuit will involve the procedures discussed in the following subsections. Keep in mind that attempts to settle the case may be ongoing throughout the trial.

4–4a **The Pleadings**

The complaint and answer (and other legal documents discussed here) are known as the **pleadings**. The pleadings inform each party of the other's claims and specify the issues (disputed questions) involved in the case. The style and form of the pleadings may be quite different in different states.

Pleadings Statements by the plaintiff and the defendant that detail the facts, charges, and defenses of a case.

The Plaintiff's Complaint

Marconi's suit against Anderson commences when her lawyer files a **complaint** with the appropriate court. The complaint contains statements alleging:

1. *Jurisdiction.* The facts necessary for the court to take *jurisdiction.*

2. *Legal theory.* A brief summary of the *facts* necessary to show that the plaintiff is entitled to relief (a remedy).[16]

3. *Remedy.* A statement of the *remedy* the plaintiff is seeking.

Complaints may be lengthy or brief, depending on the complexity of the case and the rules of the jurisdiction.

Complaint The pleading made by a plaintiff alleging wrongdoing on the part of the defendant. When filed with a court, the complaint initiates a lawsuit.

Service of Process

Before the court can exercise personal jurisdiction over the defendant (Anderson)—in effect, before the lawsuit can begin—the court must have proof that the defendant was notified of the lawsuit. Formally notifying the defendant of a lawsuit is called **service of process**. The plaintiff must deliver, or serve, a copy of the complaint and a **summons** (a notice requiring the defendant to appear in court and answer the complaint) to the defendant.

The summons notifies Anderson that he must file an answer to the complaint within a specified time period (twenty days in the federal courts) or suffer a default judgment against him. A **default judgment** in Marconi's favor would mean that she would be awarded the damages alleged in her complaint because Anderson failed to respond to the allegations. In our legal system, no case can proceed to trial unless the plaintiff can prove that he or she has properly served the defendant.

Service of Process The delivery of the complaint and summons to a defendant.

Summons A document informing a defendant that a legal action has been commenced against her or him and that the defendant must appear in court on a certain date to answer the plaintiff's complaint.

Method of Service. How service of process occurs depends on the rules of the court or jurisdiction in which the lawsuit is brought. Under the Federal Rules of Civil Procedure, anyone who is at least eighteen years of age and is not a party to the lawsuit can serve process in federal court cases. In state courts, the process server is often a county sheriff or an employee of an independent company that provides process service in the local area.

Usually, the server hands the summons and complaint to the defendant personally or leaves it at the defendant's residence or place of business. In cases involving corporate defendants, the summons and complaint may be served on an officer or on a *registered agent* (representative) of the corporation. The name of a corporation's registered agent can usually be obtained from the secretary of state's office in the state where the company incorporated its business. Process can be served by mail in some states if the defendant consents (accepts service). When the defendant cannot be reached, special rules provide for alternative means of service, such as publishing a notice in the local newspaper.

Default Judgment A judgment entered by a court against a defendant who has failed to appear in court to answer or defend against the plaintiff's claim.

---

16. The factual allegations in a complaint must be enough to raise a right to relief above the speculative level. They must plausibly suggest that the plaintiff is entitled to a remedy. See *Bell Atlantic Corp. v. Twombly,* 550 U.S. 544, 127 S.Ct. 1955, 167 L.Ed.2d 929 (2007).

In some situations, courts allow service of process via e-mail, as long as it is reasonably calculated to provide notice and an opportunity to respond. **Case Example 4.8** A county in New York filed a petition to remove a minor child, J.T., from his mother's care due to neglect. The child's father had been deported to Jordan, and the county sought to terminate the father's parental rights. Although the father's exact whereabouts were unknown, the county caseworker had been in contact with him via e-mail. Therefore, the court allowed the father to be served via e-mail because it was reasonably calculated to inform him of the proceedings and allow him an opportunity to respond.[17]

Today, some judges have even allowed defendants to be served legal documents via social media, as discussed in this chapter's *Adapting the Law to the Online Environment* feature.

17. *In re J.T.*, 53 Misc.3d 888, 37 N.Y.S.3d 846 (2016).

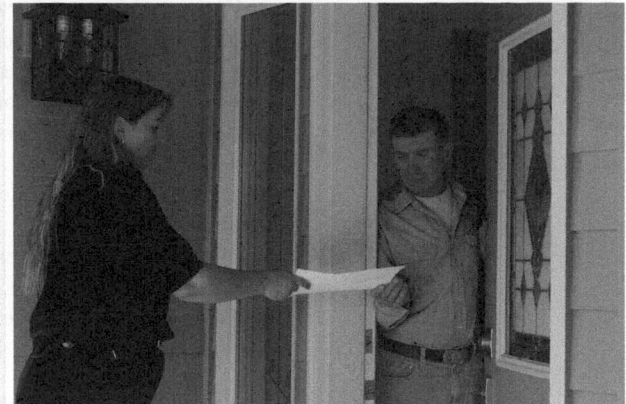

Usually, a summons is hand-delivered to the defendant. What other ways could a summons be served using today's technologies?

Adapting the Law to the Online Environment

Using Social Media for Service of Process

Historically, when process servers failed to reach a defendant at home, they attempted to serve process at the defendant's workplace, by mail, and by publication. In our digital age, does publication via social media qualify as legitimate service of process?

Facebook has over 2 billion active users per month. Assume that a man has a Facebook account and so does his spouse. He has moved out and is intentionally avoiding service of a divorce summons. Even a private investigator has not been able to deliver that summons. What to do? According to some courts today, the lawyer for the woman can serve the divorce summons through a private message from her Facebook account.

An Increasing Use of Social Media for Service of Process

More and more courts are allowing service of process via Facebook and other social media. One New York City family court judge ruled that a divorced man could serve his ex-wife through her active Facebook account. She had moved out of the house and provided no forwarding address. A U.S. District Court in Virginia allowed a plaintiff in a trademark case to serve a defendant residing in Turkey using Facebook, LinkedIn, and e-mail.[a] A federal judge in San Francisco allowed a plaintiff to use Twitter accounts to serve several defendants located in Kuwait who had allegedly financed terrorism using their Twitter accounts.[b]

The key requirement appears to be that the plaintiff has diligently and reasonably attempted to serve process by traditional means. Once the plaintiff has exhausted the usual means to effect service, then a court is likely to allow service via social media.[c]

a. *WhosHere, Inc. v. Orun*, 2014 WL 670817 (E.D. Virginia 2014).
b. *St. Francis Assisi v. Kuwait Finance House*, 2016 WL 5725002 (N.D.Cal. 2016).
c. *MetroPCS v. Devor*, 256 F.Supp.3d 807 (N.D.Ill. 2017).

Not All Courts Agree, Though

In spite of these examples, the courts have not uniformly approved of using social media to serve process. After all, it is relatively simple to create a fake Facebook account and nearly impossible to verify the true owner of that account. Some judges have voiced concerns that serving process via Facebook and other social media raises significant questions of whether that service comports with due process.[d]

Critical Thinking

In our connected world, is there any way a defendant could avoid service of process via social media?

d. *FTC v. PCCare247, Inc.*, 2013 WL 841037 (S.D.N.Y. 2013); and *In re Adoption of K.P.M.A.*, 341 P.3d 38 (Sup.Ct.Okla. 2014).

Waiver of Formal Service of Process. In many instances, the defendant is already aware that a lawsuit is being filed and is willing to waive (give up) her or his right to be served personally. The Federal Rules of Civil Procedure (FRCP) and many states' rules allow defendants to waive formal service of process, provided that certain procedures are followed.

In the Marconi-Anderson case, for instance, Marconi's attorney could mail a copy of the complaint to defendant Anderson, along with "Waiver of Service of Summons" forms for Anderson to sign. If Anderson signs and returns the forms within thirty days, formal service of process is waived.

Under the FRCP, defendants who agree to waive formal service of process receive additional time to respond to the complaint (sixty days, instead of twenty days). Some states provide similar incentives to encourage defendants to waive formal service of process, and thereby reduce associated costs and foster cooperation between the parties.

Answer Procedurally, a defendant's response to the plaintiff's complaint.

The Defendant's Answer

The defendant's **answer** either admits the statements or allegations set forth in the complaint or denies them and outlines any defenses that the defendant may have. If Anderson admits to all of Marconi's allegations in his answer, the court will enter a judgment for Marconi. If Anderson denies any of Marconi's allegations, the litigation will go forward.

Counterclaim A claim made by a defendant in a civil lawsuit against the plaintiff. In effect, the defendant is suing the plaintiff.

Reply Procedurally, a plaintiff's response to a defendant's answer.

Anderson can deny Marconi's allegations and set forth his own claim that Marconi was negligent and therefore owes him compensation for the damage to his Lexus. This is appropriately called a **counterclaim.** If Anderson files a counterclaim, Marconi will have to answer it with a pleading, normally called a **reply,** which has the same characteristics as an answer.

Anderson can also admit the truth of Marconi's complaint but raise new facts that may result in dismissal of the action. This is called raising an *affirmative defense.* For instance, Anderson could assert that Marconi was driving negligently at the time of the accident and thus was partially responsible for her own injuries. In some states, a plaintiff's contributory negligence operates as a complete defense, whereas in others it simply reduces the amount of damages that Marconi can recover.

Motion to Dismiss A pleading in which a defendant admits the facts as alleged by the plaintiff but asserts that the plaintiff's claim to state a cause of action has no basis in law.

Motion to Dismiss

A *motion* is a procedural request submitted to the court by an attorney on behalf of her or his client. A **motion to dismiss** requests the court to dismiss the case for stated reasons. Grounds for dismissal of a case include improper delivery of the complaint and summons, improper venue, and the plaintiff's failure to state a claim for which a court could grant relief. For instance, suppose that Marconi had suffered no injuries or losses as a result of Anderson's negligence. In that situation, Anderson could move to have the case dismissed because Marconi would not have stated a claim for which relief could be granted.

If the judge grants the motion to dismiss, the plaintiff generally is given time to file an amended complaint. If the judge denies the motion, the suit will go forward, and the defendant must then file an answer. Note that if Marconi wishes to discontinue the suit because, for instance, an out-of-court settlement has been reached, she can likewise move for dismissal. The court can also dismiss the case on its own motion.

Case Example 4.9 Espresso Disposition Corporation 1 entered into a contract with Santana Sales & Marketing Group, Inc. The agreement included a mandatory *forum-selection clause*, which was a provision designating that any disputes arising under the contract would be decided by a court in Illinois. When Santana Sales filed a lawsuit against Espresso in a Florida state court, Espresso filed a motion to dismiss based on the agreement's forum selection clause. Santana claimed that the forum-selection clause had been a mistake. The court denied Espresso's motion to dismiss. Espresso appealed. A state intermediate appellate court reversed the trial court's denial of Espresso's motion to dismiss and remanded the case to the lower court for the entry of an order of dismissal.[18]

---

18. *Espresso Disposition Corp. 1 v. Santana Sales & Marketing Group, Inc.,* 105 So.3d 592 (Fla.App. 3 Dist. 2013).

4–4b Pretrial Motions

Either party may attempt to get the case dismissed before trial through the use of various pretrial motions. We have already mentioned the motion to dismiss. Two other important pretrial motions are the motion for judgment on the pleadings and the motion for summary judgment.

At the close of the pleadings, either party may make a **motion for judgment on the pleadings,** or on the merits of the case. The judge will grant the motion only when there is no dispute over the facts of the case and the sole issue to be resolved is a question of law. In deciding on the motion, the judge may consider only the evidence contained in the pleadings.

In contrast, in a **motion for summary judgment,** the court may consider evidence outside the pleadings, such as sworn statements (*affidavits*) by parties or witnesses, or other documents relating to the case. Either party can make a motion for summary judgment. Like the motion for judgment on the pleadings, a motion for summary judgment will be granted only if there are no genuine questions of fact and the sole question is a question of law. When a party appeals a court's grant or denial of a summary judgment motion, the appellate court engages in a *de novo* review, which means it applies the same standard that the trial court applied.

4–4c Discovery

Before a trial begins, each party can use a number of procedural devices to obtain information and gather evidence about the case from the other party or from third parties. The process of obtaining such information is known as **discovery.** Discovery includes gaining access to witnesses, documents, records, and other types of evidence.

The Federal Rules of Civil Procedure and similar rules in the states set forth the guidelines for discovery. Generally, discovery is allowed regarding any matter that is not privileged and is relevant to the claim or defense of any party. Discovery rules also attempt to protect witnesses and parties from undue harassment and to safeguard privileged or confidential material from being disclosed.

If a discovery request involves privileged or confidential business information, a court can deny the request and can limit the scope of discovery in a number of ways. For instance, a court can require the party to submit the materials to the judge in a sealed envelope so that the judge can decide if they should be disclosed to the opposing party.

Discovery prevents surprises at trial by giving parties access to evidence that might otherwise be hidden. This allows both parties to learn what to expect during a trial before they reach the courtroom. Discovery also serves to narrow the issues so that trial time is spent on the main questions in the case.

Depositions and Interrogatories Discovery can involve the use of depositions, interrogatories, or both. A **deposition** is sworn testimony by a party to the lawsuit or any witness. The person being deposed (the deponent) answers questions asked by the attorneys, and the questions and answers are recorded by an authorized court official and sworn to and signed by the deponent. (Occasionally, written depositions are taken when witnesses are unable to appear in person.) The answers given to depositions will, of course, help the attorneys prepare for the trial. They can also be used in court to impeach (challenge the credibility of) a party or a witness who changes her or his testimony at the trial. In addition, a witness's deposition can be used as testimony if he or she is not available for the trial.

Interrogatories are written questions for which written answers are prepared and then signed under oath. The main difference between interrogatories and written depositions is that interrogatories are directed to a party to the lawsuit (the plaintiff or the defendant), not to a witness, and the party can prepare answers with the aid of an attorney. In addition, the scope of interrogatories is broader because parties are obligated to answer the questions, even if that means disclosing information from their records and files.

Motion for Judgment on the Pleadings A motion by either party to a lawsuit at the close of the pleadings requesting the court to decide the issue solely on the pleadings without proceeding to trial. The motion will be granted only if no facts are in dispute.

Motion for Summary Judgment A motion requesting the court to enter a judgment without proceeding to trial. The motion can be based on evidence outside the pleadings and will be granted only if no facts are in dispute.

Learning Objective 4
What is discovery, and how does electronic discovery differ from traditional discovery?

Discovery A method by which the opposing parties obtain information from each other to prepare for trial.

Deposition The testimony of a party to a lawsuit or a witness taken under oath before a trial.

Interrogatories A series of written questions for which written answers are prepared by a party to a lawsuit, usually with the assistance of the party's attorney, and then signed under oath.

Note that, as with other discovery requests, a court can impose sanctions on a party who fails to answer interrogatories. **Case Example 4.10** Construction Laborers Trust Funds for Southern California Administrative Company (the plaintiff), which administers various Southern California employee benefit plans, sued Mario Miguel Montalvo in a federal district court in California. The plaintiff alleged that the defendant, Montalvo, had failed to pay required benefit contributions for every hour that his employees worked (as required under federal law). The plaintiff also claimed that Montalvo refused to allow an audit of his payroll and business records and failed to submit monthly employment records needed to determine the amounts due.

Montalvo did not respond to plaintiff's interrogatories. The court ordered Montalvo to answer the interrogatories and produce the necessary documents three times. The defendant continued to disobey the court's orders and told the plaintiff's attorney that he was "too busy" to comply with the discovery requests. Eventually, the court entered a default judgment against Montalvo noting that he had willfully disobeyed multiple court orders.[19]

Requests for Other Information

A party can serve a written request on the other party for an admission of the truth on matters relating to the trial. Any matter admitted under such a request is conclusively established for the trial. For instance, Marconi can ask Anderson to admit that he was driving at a speed of forty-five miles an hour. A request for admission saves time at trial because the parties will not have to spend time proving facts on which they already agree.

A party can also gain access to documents and other items not in her or his possession in order to inspect and examine them. Likewise, a party can gain "entry upon land" to inspect the premises. Anderson's attorney, for instance, normally can gain permission to inspect and photocopy Marconi's car repair bills.

When the physical or mental condition of one party is in question, the opposing party can ask the court to order a physical or mental examination, but the court will do so only if the need for the information outweighs the right to privacy of the person to be examined. If the court issues the order, the opposing party can obtain the results of the examination.

Electronic Discovery

Any relevant material, including information stored electronically, can be the object of a discovery request. The federal rules and most state rules now specifically allow all parties to obtain electronic "data compilations." Electronic evidence, or **e-evidence,** includes all types of computer-generated or electronically recorded information. This might include e-mail, voice mail, tweets, blogs, social media posts, and spreadsheets, as well as documents and other data stored on computers.

E-Evidence A type of evidence that consists of computer-generated or electronically recorded information.

E-evidence can reveal significant facts that are not discoverable by other means. Computers, smartphones, cameras, and other devices automatically record certain information about files—such as who created a file and when, and who accessed, modified, or transmitted it—on their hard drives. This information is called **metadata,** which can be thought of as "data about data." Metadata can be obtained only from the file in its electronic format—not from printed-out versions.

Metadata Data that are automatically recorded by electronic devices and provide information about who created a file and when, and who accessed, modified, or transmitted the file. It can be described as data about data.

Example 4.11 John McAfee, the programmer responsible for creating McAfee antivirus software, was wanted for questioning in the murder of his neighbor in Belize. McAfee left Belize and was on the run from police, but he allowed a journalist to come with him and photograph him. When the journalist posted photos of McAfee online, some metadata were attached to a photo. The police used the metadata to pinpoint the latitude and longitude of the image and subsequently arrested McAfee in Guatemala.

E-Discovery Procedures. The Federal Rules of Civil Procedure deal specifically with the preservation, retrieval, and production of electronic data. Although parties may still use traditional means, such as interrogatories and depositions, to find out about the e-evidence,

---

19. *Construction Laborers Trust Funds for Southern California Administrative Co. v. Montalvo,* 2011 WL 1195892 (C.D.Cal. 2011); see also, *Loop AI Labs Inc. v. Gatti,* 2017 WL 934599 (N.D.Cal. 2017).

they must usually hire an expert to retrieve evidence in its electronic format. The expert uses software to reconstruct e-mail exchanges and establish who knew what and when they knew it. The expert can even recover files that the user thought had been deleted from a computer.

Advantages and Disadvantages. E-discovery has significant advantages over paper discovery. Back-up copies of documents and e-mail can provide useful—and often quite damaging—information about how a particular matter progressed over several weeks or months. E-discovery can uncover the proverbial smoking gun that will win the lawsuit, but it is also time consuming and expensive, especially when lawsuits involve large firms with multiple offices. Many companies have found it challenging to fulfill their duty to preserve electronic evidence from a vast number of sources. Failure to do so, however, can lead to sanctions and even force companies to agree to settlements that are not in their best interests.

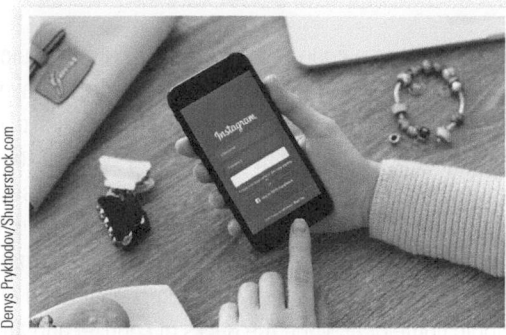

E-discovery may involve examining social media accounts, such as those on Instagram.

A failure to provide e-evidence in response to a discovery request does not always arise from an unintentional failure to preserve documents and e-mail. The following case involved a litigant that delayed a response to gain time to intentionally alter and destroy data. At issue was the amount of sanctions imposed for this spoliation. (*Spoliation of evidence* occurs when a document or information that is required for discovery is destroyed or altered significantly.)

■ Case 4.3

Klipsch Group, Inc. v. ePRO E-Commerce Limited

United States Court of Appeals, Second Circuit, 880 F.3d 620 (2018).

Background and Facts Klipsch Group, Inc., makes sound equipment, including headphones. Klipsch filed a suit in a federal district court against ePRO E-Commerce Limited, a Chinese corporation. Klipsch alleged that ePRO had sold $5 million in counterfeit Klipsch products. ePRO claimed that the sales of relevant products amounted to less than $8,000 worldwide. In response to discovery requests, ePRO failed to timely disclose the majority of the responsive documents in its possession. In addition, ePRO restricted Klipsch's access to its e-data. The court directed ePRO to impose a litigation hold on the custodians of the data to preserve evidence, but the defendant failed to do so. This led to the deletion of thousands of documents and significant quantities of data. To determine what data had been blocked or lost, and what might and might not be recovered, Klipsch spent $2.7 million on a forensic examination.

The federal district court concluded that ePRO had willingly engaged in spoliation of e-evidence. For this misconduct, the court imposed sanctions, including an order to pay Klipsch the entire $2.7 million for its restorative discovery efforts. ePRO appealed, contending that the sanctions were "disproportionate."

In the Words of the Court
Gerard E. *LYNCH*, Circuit Judge:
* * * *

ePRO argues that the monetary sanctions imposed against it are so out of proportion to the value of the evidence uncovered by Klipsch's efforts or to the likely ultimate value of the case as to be impermissibly punitive [punishing] and a violation of due process. That position, although superficially sympathetic given the amount of the sanction, overlooks the fact that ePRO caused Klipsch to accrue those costs by failing to comply with its discovery obligations. *Such compliance is not optional or negotiable; rather, the integrity of our civil litigation process requires that the parties before us, although adversarial to one another, carry out their duties to maintain and disclose the relevant information in their possession in good faith.* [Emphasis added.]

The extremely broad discovery permitted by the Federal Rules depends on the parties' voluntary participation. The system functions because, in the vast majority of cases, we can rely on each side to preserve evidence and to disclose relevant information when asked (and sometimes even before then) without being forced to proceed

(Continues)

at the point of a court order. The courts are ill-equipped to address parties that do not voluntarily comply: we do not have our own investigatory powers, and even if we did, the spoliation of evidence would frequently be extremely difficult for any outsider to detect.

Moreover, noncompliance vastly increases the cost of litigation * * * . Accordingly, we have held that discovery sanctions are proper * * * , because an alternative rule would encourage dilatory tactics, and compliance with discovery orders would come only when the backs of counsel and the litigants were against the wall.

When we apply those principles to the case at hand, it is clear that the district court did not abuse its discretion by imposing monetary sanctions calculated to make Klipsch whole for the extra cost and efforts it reasonably undertook in response to ePRO's recalcitrance. * * * *

In sum, we see nothing in ePRO's proportionality arguments compelling us to conclude that the district court abused its discretion by awarding full compensation for efforts that were * * *

a reasonable response to ePRO's own evasive conduct. The proportionality that matters here is that the amount of the sanctions was plainly proportionate—indeed, it was exactly equivalent—to the costs ePRO inflicted on Klipsch in its reasonable efforts to remedy ePRO's misconduct.

Decision and Remedy The U.S. Court of Appeals for the Second Circuit affirmed the sanctions. "The district court's award properly reflects the additional costs ePRO imposed on its opponent by refusing to comply with its discovery obligations."

Critical Thinking

• **Economic** *Should the cost of corrective discovery efforts be imposed on an uncooperative party if those efforts turn up nothing of real value to the case? Explain.*

• **Legal Environment** *Should it be inferred from a business's failure to keep backup copies of its database that the business must therefore have destroyed the data? Discuss.*

4–4d Pretrial Conference

Either party or the court can request a pretrial conference, or hearing. Usually, the hearing consists of an informal discussion between the judge and the opposing attorneys after discovery has taken place. The purpose of the hearing is to explore the possibility of a settlement without a trial and, if this is not possible, to identify the matters that are in dispute and to plan the course of the trial.

4–4e Jury Selection

Know This

Picking the "right" jury is often an important aspect of litigation strategy, and a number of firms now specialize in jury-selection consulting services.

Voir Dire An important part of the jury selection process in which the attorneys question prospective jurors about their backgrounds, attitudes, and biases to ascertain whether they can be impartial jurors.

A trial can be held with or without a jury. The Seventh Amendment to the U.S. Constitution guarantees the right to a jury trial for cases in *federal* courts when the amount in controversy exceeds $20, but this guarantee does not apply to state courts. Most states have similar guarantees in their own constitutions (although the threshold dollar amount is higher than $20). The right to a trial by jury does not have to be exercised, and many cases are tried without a jury. In most states and in federal courts, one of the parties must request a jury in a civil case, or the judge presumes that the parties waive the right.

Before a jury trial commences, a jury must be selected. The jury selection process is known as **voir dire**.[20] During *voir dire* in most jurisdictions, attorneys for the plaintiff and the defendant ask prospective jurors oral questions to determine whether a potential jury member is biased or has any connection with a party to the action or with a prospective witness. In some jurisdictions, the judge may do all or part of the questioning based on written questions submitted by counsel for the parties.

During *voir dire*, a party may challenge a prospective juror *peremptorily*—that is, ask that an individual not be sworn in as a juror without providing any reason. Alternatively, a party may challenge a prospective juror *for cause*—that is, provide a reason why an individual should not be sworn in as a juror. If the judge grants the challenge, the individual is asked to step down. A prospective juror may not be excluded from the jury by the use of discriminatory challenges, however, such as those based on racial criteria or gender.

---

20. Pronounced vwahr *deehr.*

4–4f At the Trial

Once the trial begins, it follows the specific procedures discussed next.

Opening Arguments and Examination of Witnesses At the beginning of the trial, the attorneys present their opening arguments, setting forth the facts that they expect to prove during the trial. Then the plaintiff's case is presented. In our hypothetical case, Marconi's lawyer would introduce evidence (relevant documents, exhibits, and the testimony of witnesses) to support Marconi's position. The defendant has the opportunity to challenge any evidence introduced and to cross-examine any of the plaintiff's witnesses.

At the end of the plaintiff's case, the defendant's attorney has the opportunity to ask the judge to direct a verdict for the defendant on the ground that the plaintiff has presented no evidence that would justify the granting of the plaintiff's remedy. This is called a **motion for a directed verdict** (known in federal courts as a *motion for judgment as a matter of law*).

If the motion is not granted (it seldom is granted), the defendant's attorney then presents the evidence and witnesses for the defendant's case. At the conclusion of the defendant's case, the defendant's attorney has another opportunity to make a motion for a directed verdict. The plaintiff's attorney can challenge any evidence introduced and cross-examine the defendant's witnesses.

Motion for a Directed Verdict A motion for the judge to take the decision out of the hands of the jury and to direct a verdict for the party making the motion on the ground that the other party has not produced sufficient evidence to support her or his claim.

Closing Arguments and Awards After the defense concludes its presentation, the attorneys present their closing arguments, each urging a verdict in favor of her or his client. The judge instructs the jury in the law that applies to the case (these instructions are often called *charges*), and the jury retires to the jury room to deliberate a verdict. Typically, jurors are instructed that they must decide the case based only on the information that they learned during the trial.

In the Marconi-Anderson case, the jury will decide in favor of either the plaintiff or the defendant. In addition, if the jury finds for the plaintiff, it will also decide on the amount of the **award** (the monetary compensation to be paid to her).

Award The monetary compensation given to a party at the end of a trial or other proceeding.

4–4g Posttrial Motions

After the jury has rendered its verdict, either party may make a posttrial motion. If Marconi wins and Anderson's attorney has previously moved for a directed verdict, Anderson's attorney may make a **motion for judgment** *n.o.v.* (from the Latin *non obstante veredicto,* which means "notwithstanding the verdict"—called a *motion for judgment as a matter of law* in the federal courts). Such a motion will be granted only if the jury's verdict was unreasonable and erroneous. If the judge grants the motion, the jury's verdict will be set aside, and a judgment will be entered in favor of the opposite party (Anderson).

Alternatively, Anderson could make a **motion for a new trial,** asking the judge to set aside the adverse verdict and to hold a new trial. The motion will be granted if, after looking at all the evidence, the judge is convinced that the jury was in error but does not feel that it is appropriate to grant judgment for the other side. A judge can also grant a new trial on the basis of newly discovered evidence, misconduct by the participants or the jury during the trial, or error by the judge.

Motion for Judgment *n.o.v.* A motion requesting the court to grant judgment in favor of the party making the motion on the ground that the jury's verdict against him or her was unreasonable and erroneous.

Motion for a New Trial A motion asserting that the trial was so fundamentally flawed (because of error, newly discovered evidence, prejudice, or another reason) that a new trial is necessary to prevent a miscarriage of justice.

4–4h The Appeal

Assume here that any posttrial motion is denied and that Anderson appeals the case. (If Marconi wins but receives a smaller monetary award than she sought, she can appeal also.) Keep in mind, though, that a party cannot appeal a trial court's decision simply because he or she is dissatisfied with the outcome of the trial.

A party must have legitimate grounds to file an appeal. In other words, he or she must be able to claim that the lower court committed an error. If Anderson has grounds to appeal the case, a notice of appeal must be filed with the clerk of the trial court within a prescribed time. Anderson now becomes the appellant, or petitioner, and Marconi becomes the appellee, or respondent.

Filing the Appeal Anderson's attorney files the record on appeal with the appellate court. The record includes the pleadings, the trial transcript, the judge's rulings on motions made by the parties, and other trial-related documents. Anderson's attorney will also provide the reviewing court with a condensation of the record, known as an *abstract*, and a brief. The **brief** is a formal legal document outlining the facts and issues of the case, the judge's rulings or jury's findings that should be reversed or modified, the applicable law, and arguments on Anderson's behalf (citing applicable statutes and relevant cases as precedents).

Marconi's attorney will file an answering brief. Anderson's attorney can file a reply to Marconi's brief, although it is not required. The reviewing court then considers the case.

Appellate Review As explained earlier, a court of appeals does not hear evidence. Instead, the court reviews the record for errors of law. Its decision concerning a case is based on the record on appeal, the abstracts, and the attorneys' briefs. The attorneys can present oral arguments, after which the case is taken under advisement.

After reviewing a case, an appellate court has the following options:

> **Brief** A written summary or statement prepared by one side in a lawsuit to explain its case to the judge.

1. The court can *affirm* the trial court's decision.
2. The court can *reverse* the trial court's judgment if it concludes that the trial court erred or that the jury did not receive proper instructions.
3. The appellate court can *remand* (send back) the case to the trial court for further proceedings consistent with its opinion on the matter.
4. The court might also affirm or reverse a decision in *part*. For instance, the court might affirm the jury's finding that Anderson was negligent but remand the case for further proceedings on another issue (such as the extent of Marconi's damages).
5. An appellate court can also *modify* a lower court's decision. If the appellate court decides that the jury awarded an excessive amount in damages, for instance, the court might reduce the award to a more appropriate, or fairer, amount.

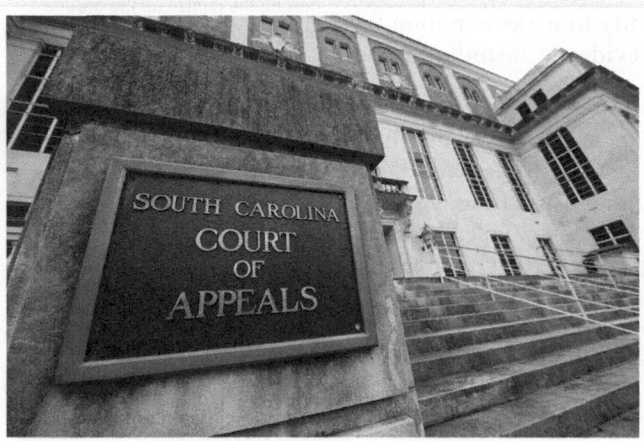

Do parties to a trial decision always have a right to appeal that decision?

thepixelchef/E+/Getty Images

Appeal to a Higher Appellate Court If the reviewing court is an intermediate appellate court, the losing party may decide to appeal to the state supreme court (the highest state court). Such a petition corresponds to a petition for a writ of *certiorari* from the United States Supreme Court. Although the losing party has a right to ask (petition) a higher court to review the case, the party does not have a right to have the case heard by the higher appellate court.

Appellate courts normally have discretionary power and can accept or reject an appeal. Like the United States Supreme Court, state supreme courts generally deny most appeals. If the appeal is granted, new briefs must be filed before the state supreme court, and the attorneys may be allowed or requested to present oral arguments. Like the intermediate appellate court, the supreme court may reverse or affirm the appellate court's decision or remand the case. At this point, the case typically has reached its end (unless a federal question is at issue and one of the parties has legitimate grounds to seek review by a federal appellate court).

4–4i Enforcing the Judgment

The uncertainties of the litigation process are compounded by the lack of guarantees that any judgment will be enforceable. Even if a plaintiff wins an award of damages in court, the defendant may not have sufficient assets or insurance to cover that amount. Usually, one of the factors considered before a lawsuit is initiated is whether the defendant will be able to pay the damages sought, should the plaintiff win the case.

4–5 Courts Online

Most courts today have websites. Of course, each court decides what to make available at its site. Some courts display only the names of court personnel and office phone numbers. Others add court rules and forms. Many appellate court sites include judicial decisions, although the decisions may remain online for only a limited time. In addition, in some states, including California and Florida, court clerks offer information about the court's **docket** (its schedule of cases to be heard) and other searchable databases online.

Docket The list of cases entered on a court's calendar and thus scheduled to be heard by the court.

Appellate court decisions are often posted online immediately after they are rendered. Recent decisions of the U.S. courts of appeals, for instance, are available online at their websites. The United States Supreme Court also has an official website and publishes its opinions there immediately after they are announced to the public. In fact, even decisions that are designated as "unpublished" opinions by the appellate courts are usually published (posted) online.

4–5a Electronic Filing

A number of state and federal courts now allow parties to file litigation-related documents with the courts via the Internet or other electronic means. In fact, the federal court system has implemented its electronic filing system, Case Management/Electronic Case Files (CM/ECF), in nearly all federal courts. The system is available in federal district, appellate, and bankruptcy courts, as well as the U.S. Court of International Trade and the U.S. Court of Federal Claims. More than 41 million cases are on the CM/ECF system. Access to the electronic documents filed on CM/ECF is available through a system called PACER (Public Access to Court Electronic Records), which is a service of the U.S. courts.

Learning Objective 5
What is an electronic court filing system?

A majority of the states have some form of electronic filing, although often it is not yet available in state appellate courts. Some states, including Arizona, California, Colorado, Delaware, Mississippi, New Jersey, New York, and Nevada, offer statewide e-filing systems. Generally, when electronic filing is made available, it is optional. Nonetheless, some state courts have now made e-filing mandatory in certain types of disputes, such as complex civil litigation.

4–5b Cyber Courts and Proceedings

Eventually, litigants may be able to use cyber courts, in which judicial proceedings take place only on the Internet. The parties to a case could meet online to make their arguments and present their evidence. Cyber proceedings might use e-mail submissions, video cameras, designated chat rooms, closed sites, or other Internet facilities. The promise of these virtual proceedings is greater efficiency and lower costs.

Electronic courtroom projects have already been developed in some federal and state courts. The state of Michigan has cyber courts that hear cases involving technology issues and high-tech businesses. Other states that have introduced cyber courts include California, Delaware, Louisiana, and North Carolina. The Federal Rules of Civil Procedure also authorize video conferencing, and some federal bankruptcy courts offer online chatting at their websites.

4–6 Alternative Dispute Resolution

Litigation is expensive. It is also time consuming. Because of the backlog of cases pending in many courts, several years may pass before a case is actually tried. For these and other reasons, more and more businesspersons are turning to **alternative dispute resolution (ADR)** as a means of settling their disputes.

Alternative Dispute Resolution (ADR) The resolution of disputes in ways other than those involved in the traditional judicial process, such as negotiation, mediation, and arbitration.

The great advantage of ADR is its flexibility. Methods of ADR range from the parties sitting down together and attempting to work out their differences to multinational corporations agreeing to resolve a dispute through a formal hearing before a panel of experts. Normally, the parties themselves can control how they will attempt to settle their dispute, what procedures will be used, whether a neutral third party will be present or make a decision, and whether that decision will be legally binding or nonbinding.

Today, more than 90 percent of cases are settled before trial through some form of ADR. Indeed, most states either require or encourage parties to undertake ADR prior to trial. Many federal courts have instituted ADR programs as well.

4–6a Negotiation

Negotiation A process in which parties attempt to settle their dispute informally, with or without attorneys to represent them.

The simplest form of ADR is **negotiation**, in which the parties attempt to settle their dispute informally, with or without attorneys to represent them. Attorneys frequently advise their clients to negotiate a settlement voluntarily before they proceed to trial. Parties may even try to negotiate a settlement during a trial or after the trial but before an appeal.

Negotiation traditionally involves just the parties themselves and (if attorneys are involved) their attorneys. The attorneys still act as advocates—they are obligated to put their clients' interests first. In contrast, other forms of ADR typically also involve neutral third parties.

4–6b Mediation

Mediation A method of settling disputes outside the courts by using the services of a neutral third party, who acts as a communicating agent between the parties and assists them in negotiating a settlement.

In **mediation,** a neutral third party acts as a mediator and works with both sides in the dispute to facilitate a resolution. The mediator talks with the parties separately as well as jointly and emphasizes their points of agreement in an attempt to help them evaluate their options. Although the mediator may propose a solution (called a *mediator's proposal*), he or she does not make a decision resolving the matter. States that require parties to undergo ADR before trial often offer mediation as one of the ADR options or (as in Florida) the only option.

One of the biggest advantages of mediation is that it is not as adversarial as litigation. In a trial, the parties "do battle" with each other in the courtroom, trying to prove each other wrong, while the judge is usually a passive observer. In mediation, the mediator takes an active role and attempts to bring the parties together so that they can come to a mutually satisfactory resolution. The mediation process tends to reduce the hostility between the disputants, allowing them to resume their former relationship without bad feelings. For this reason, mediation is often the preferred form of ADR for disputes involving business partners, employers and employees, or other parties involved in long-term relationships.

Example 4.12 Two business partners, Mark Shalen and Charles Rowe, have a dispute over how the profits of their firm should be distributed. If the dispute is litigated, Shalen and Rowe will be adversaries, and their respective attorneys will emphasize how the parties' positions differ, not what they have in common. In contrast, if the dispute is mediated, the mediator will emphasize the common ground shared by Shalen and Rowe and help them work toward agreement. The two men can work out the distribution of profits without damaging their continuing relationship as partners. ▪

Learning Objective 6

What are three alternative methods of resolving disputes?

4–6c Arbitration

Arbitration The settling of a dispute by submitting it to a disinterested third party (other than a court), who renders a decision.

In **arbitration,** a more formal method of ADR, an arbitrator (a neutral third party or a panel of experts) hears a dispute and imposes a resolution on the parties. Arbitration differs from other forms of ADR in that the third party hearing the dispute makes a decision for the parties. Exhibit 4–4 outlines the basic differences among the three traditional forms of ADR.

Exhibit 4–4 Basic Differences in the Traditional Forms of ADR

	Type of ADR		
	Negotiation	**Mediation**	**Arbitration**
Description	Parties meet informally with or without their attorneys and attempt to agree on a resolution. This is the simplest and least expensive method of ADR.	A neutral third party meets with the parties and emphasizes points of agreement to bring them toward resolution of their dispute, reducing hostility between the parties.	The parties present their arguments and evidence before an arbitrator at a formal hearing. The arbitrator renders a decision to resolve the parties' dispute.
Neutral Third Party Present?	No	Yes	Yes
Who Decides the Resolution?	The parties themselves reach a resolution.	The parties, but the mediator may suggest or propose a resolution.	The arbitrator imposes a resolution on the parties that may be either binding or nonbinding.

Usually, the parties in arbitration agree that the third party's decision will be *legally binding*, although the parties can also agree to *nonbinding* arbitration. (Arbitration that is mandated by the courts often is nonbinding.) In nonbinding arbitration, the parties can go forward with a lawsuit if they do not agree with the arbitrator's decision.

In some respects, formal arbitration resembles a trial, although usually the procedural rules are much less restrictive than those governing litigation. In the typical arbitration, the parties present opening arguments and ask for specific remedies. Both sides present evidence and may call and examine witnesses. The arbitrator then renders a decision.

The Arbitrator's Decision The arbitrator's decision is called an award. It is usually the final word on the matter. Although the parties may appeal an arbitrator's decision, a court's review of the decision will be much more restricted in scope than an appellate court's review of a trial court's decision. The general view is that because the parties were free to frame the issues and set the powers of the arbitrator at the outset, they cannot complain about the results. A court will set aside an award only in the event of one of the following:

1. The arbitrator's conduct or "bad faith" substantially prejudiced the rights of one of the parties.

2. The award violates an established public policy.

3. The arbitrator exceeded her or his powers—that is, arbitrated issues that the parties did not agree to submit to arbitration.

What are the steps in a typical arbitration proceeding?

Arbitration Clauses Just about any commercial matter can be submitted to arbitration. Parties can agree to arbitrate a dispute after it arises. Frequently, though, parties include an **arbitration clause** in a contract. The clause provides that any dispute that arises under the contract will be resolved through arbitration rather than through the court system.

Arbitration Statutes Most states have statutes (often based in part on the Uniform Arbitration Act) under which arbitration clauses will be enforced. Some state statutes compel arbitration of certain types of disputes, such as those involving public employees.

Arbitration Clause A clause in a contract that provides that, in the event of a dispute, the parties will submit the dispute to arbitration rather than litigate the dispute in court.

At the federal level, the Federal Arbitration Act (FAA) enforces arbitration clauses in contracts involving maritime activity and interstate commerce (though its applicability to employment contracts has been controversial, as discussed later). Because of the breadth of the commerce clause, arbitration agreements involving transactions only slightly connected to the flow of interstate commerce may fall under the FAA.

Case Example 4.13 Cable subscribers sued Cox Communications, Inc., in federal court. They claimed that Cox violated antitrust law by tying premium cable service to the rental of set-top cable boxes. Cox filed a motion to compel arbitration based on an agreement it had sent to its subscribers. A district court granted the motion to compel, and the subscribers appealed. A federal appellate court affirmed, based on the Federal Arbitration Act. The subscribers' antitrust claims fell within the scope of the arbitration agreement.[21]

The Issue of Arbitrability The terms of an arbitration agreement can limit the types of disputes that the parties agree to arbitrate. Disputes can arise, however, when the parties do not specify limits or when the parties disagree on whether a particular matter is covered by their arbitration agreement.

When one party files a lawsuit to compel arbitration, it is up to the court to resolve the issue of *arbitrability*. That is, the court must decide whether the matter is one that must be resolved through arbitration. If the court finds that the subject matter in controversy is covered by the agreement to arbitrate, then it may compel arbitration. Usually, a court will allow the claim to be arbitrated if the court finds that the relevant statute (the state arbitration statute or the FAA) does not exclude such claims.

No party, however, will be ordered to submit a particular dispute to arbitration unless the court is convinced that the party has consented to do so. Additionally, the courts will not compel arbitration if it is clear that the arbitration rules and procedures are inherently unfair to one of the parties.

Mandatory Arbitration in the Employment Context A significant question for businesspersons concerns mandatory arbitration clauses in employment contracts. Many employees claim they are at a disadvantage when they are forced, as a condition of being hired, to agree to arbitrate all disputes and thus waive their rights under statutes designed to protect employees. The United States Supreme Court, however, has held that mandatory arbitration clauses in employment contracts are generally enforceable.

Classic Case Example 4.14 In a landmark decision, *Gilmer v. Interstate/Johnson Lane Corp.*,[22] the Supreme Court held that a claim brought under a federal statute prohibiting age discrimination could be subject to arbitration. The Court concluded that the employee had waived his right to sue when he agreed, as part of a required registration application to be a securities representative with the New York Stock Exchange, to arbitrate "any dispute, claim, or controversy" relating to his employment.

Since the *Gilmer* decision, some courts have refused to enforce one-sided arbitration clauses. Nevertheless, the policy favoring enforcement of mandatory arbitration agreements remains strong.[23]

4–6d Other Types of ADR

The three forms of ADR just discussed are the oldest and traditionally the most commonly used. In addition, a variety of newer types of ADR have emerged, including those described here.

---

21. *In re Cox Enterprises, Inc. Set-top Cable Television Box Antitrust Litigation*, 835 F.3d 1195 (10th Cir. 2016).
22. 500 U.S. 20, 111 S.Ct. 1647, 114 L.Ed.2d 26 (1991).
23. See, for example, *Cruise v. Kroger Co.*, 233 Cal.App.4th 390, 193 Cal.Rptr.3d 17 (2015).

1. In *early neutral case evaluation*, the parties select a neutral third party (generally an expert in the subject matter of the dispute) and then explain their respective positions to that person. The case evaluator assesses the strengths and weaknesses of each party's claims.

2. In a *mini-trial*, each party's attorney briefly argues the party's case before the other party and a panel of representatives from each side who have the authority to settle the dispute. Typically, a neutral third party (usually an expert in the area being disputed) acts as an adviser. If the parties fail to reach an agreement, the adviser renders an opinion as to how a court would likely decide the issue.

3. Numerous federal courts now hold **summary jury trials (SJTs),** in which the parties present their arguments and evidence and the jury renders a verdict. The jury's verdict is not binding, but it does act as a guide to both sides in reaching an agreement during the mandatory negotiations that immediately follow the trial.

4–6e Providers of ADR Services

ADR services are provided by both government agencies and private organizations. A major provider of ADR services is the American Arbitration Association (AAA), which handles more than 200,000 claims a year in its numerous offices worldwide. Most of the largest U.S. law firms are members of this nonprofit association. Cases brought before the AAA are heard by an expert or a panel of experts in the area relating to the dispute and are usually settled quickly. The AAA has a special team devoted to resolving large, complex disputes across a wide range of industries.

Hundreds of for-profit firms around the country also provide various dispute-resolution services. Typically, these firms hire retired judges to conduct arbitration hearings or otherwise assist parties in settling their disputes. The judges follow procedures similar to those of the federal courts and use similar rules. Usually, each party to the dispute pays a filing fee and a designated fee for a hearing session or conference.

4–6f Online Dispute Resolution

An increasing number of companies and organizations offer dispute-resolution services using the Internet. The settlement of disputes in these online forums is known as **online dispute resolution (ODR).** The disputes have most commonly involved disagreements over the rights to domain names or over the quality of goods sold via the Internet, including goods sold through Internet auction sites.

Rules being developed in online forums may ultimately become a code of conduct for everyone who does business in cyberspace. Most online forums do not automatically apply the law of any specific jurisdiction. Instead, results are often based on general, universal legal principles. As with most offline methods of dispute resolution, any party may appeal to a court at any time.

ODR may be best suited for resolving small- to medium-sized business liability claims, which may not be worth the expense of litigation or traditional ADR. In addition, some local governments are using ODR to resolve claims. **Example 4.15** New York City has used Cybersettle.com to resolve auto accident, sidewalk, and other personal-injury claims made against the city. Parties with complaints submit their demands, and the city submits its offers confidentially online. If an offer exceeds a demand, the claimant keeps half the difference as a bonus.

Summary Jury Trial (SJT) A method of settling disputes by holding a trial in which the jury's verdict is not binding but instead guides the parties toward reaching an agreement during the mandatory negotiations that immediately follow.

Online Dispute Resolution (ODR) The resolution of disputes with the assistance of organizations that offer dispute-resolution services via the Internet.

Practice and Review

Stan Garner resides in Illinois and promotes boxing matches for SuperSports, Inc., an Illinois corporation. Garner created the promotional concept of the "Ages" fights—a series of three boxing matches pitting an older fighter (George Foreman) against a younger fighter, such as John Ruiz or Riddick Bowe. The concept included titles for each of the three fights ("Challenge of the Ages," "Battle of the Ages," and "Fight of the Ages"), as well as promotional epithets to characterize the two fighters ("the Foreman Factor").

Garner contacted George Foreman and his manager, who both reside in Texas, to sell the idea, and they arranged a meeting at Caesar's Palace in Las Vegas, Nevada. At some point in the negotiations, Foreman's manager signed a nondisclosure agreement prohibiting him from disclosing Garner's promotional concepts unless they signed a contract. Nevertheless, after negotiations between Garner and Foreman fell through, Foreman used Garner's "Battle of the Ages" concept to promote a subsequent fight. Garner filed a lawsuit against Foreman and his manager in a federal district court in Illinois, alleging breach of contract. Using the information presented in the chapter, answer the following questions.

1. On what basis might the federal district court in Illinois exercise jurisdiction in this case?

2. Does the federal district court have original or appellate jurisdiction?

3. Suppose that Garner had filed his action in an Illinois state court. Could an Illinois state court have exercised personal jurisdiction over Foreman or his manager? Why or why not?

4. What if Garner had filed his action in a Nevada state court? Would that court have had personal jurisdiction over Foreman or his manager? Explain.

Debate This

In this age of the Internet, when people communicate via e-mail, tweets, social media, and Skype, is the concept of jurisdiction losing its meaning?

Key Terms

Chapter Summary: Courts and Alternative Dispute Resolution

The Judiciary's Role in American Government	The role of the judiciary—the courts—in the American governmental system is to interpret and apply the law. Through the process of judicial review—determining the constitutionality of laws—the judicial branch acts as a check on the executive and legislative branches of government.
Basic Judicial Requirements	**1.** *Jurisdiction*—Before a court can hear a case, it must have jurisdiction over the person against whom the suit is brought or the property involved in the suit, as well as jurisdiction over the subject matter.

a. Limited versus general jurisdiction—Limited jurisdiction exists when a court is limited to a specific subject matter, such as probate or divorce. General jurisdiction exists when a court can hear any kind of case.

b. Original versus appellate jurisdiction—Original jurisdiction exists when courts have authority to hear a case for the first time (trial courts). Appellate jurisdiction is exercised by courts of appeals, or reviewing courts, which generally do not have original jurisdiction.

c. Federal jurisdiction—Arises (1) when a federal question is involved (when the plaintiff's cause of action is based, at least in part, on the U.S. Constitution, a treaty, or a federal law), or (2) when a case involves diversity of citizenship (citizens of different states, for example) and the amount in controversy exceeds $75,000.

d. Concurrent versus exclusive jurisdiction—Concurrent jurisdiction exists when both federal and state courts have authority to hear the same case. Exclusive jurisdiction exists when only state courts or only federal courts have authority to hear a case.

2. *Jurisdiction in cyberspace*—Because the Internet does not have physical boundaries, traditional jurisdictional concepts have been difficult to apply in cases involving activities conducted via the Web. Gradually, the courts are developing standards to use in determining when jurisdiction over an Internet business operator located in another state (or even another country) is proper.

3. *Venue*—Venue has to do with the most appropriate location for a trial, which is usually the geographic area where the event leading to the dispute took place or where the parties reside.

4. *Standing to sue*—A requirement that a party must have a legally protected interest at stake sufficient to justify seeking relief through the court system. The controversy at issue must also be a justiciable controversy—one that is real and substantial, as opposed to hypothetical or academic.

The State and Federal Court Systems	**1.** *Trial courts*—Courts of original jurisdiction, in which legal actions are initiated.

a. State—Courts of general jurisdiction can hear any case. Courts of limited jurisdiction include domestic relations courts, probate courts, traffic courts, and small claims courts.

b. Federal—The federal district court is the equivalent of the state trial court of general jurisdiction. Federal courts of limited jurisdiction include the U.S. Tax Court, the U.S. Bankruptcy Court, and the U.S. Court of Federal Claims.

2. *Appellate courts*—Courts of appeals, or reviewing courts, which generally do not have original jurisdiction. Every state has at least one court of appeals, and many have intermediate appellate courts. In the federal court system, the U.S. circuit courts of appeals are the intermediate appellate courts.

3. *Supreme (highest) courts*—Each state has a supreme court, although it may be called by some other name. Appeal from the state supreme court to the United States Supreme Court is possible only if the case involves a federal question. As the highest court in the federal court system, the United States Supreme Court is the final arbiter of the U.S. Constitution and federal law, as well as resolving conflicting decisions by lower courts on a significant issue.

(Continues)

Following a State Court Case

Rules of procedure prescribe the way in which disputes are handled in the courts. Rules differ from court to court, and separate sets of rules exist for federal and state courts, as well as for criminal and civil cases. A civil court case in a state court would involve the following procedures:

1. *The pleadings—*
   a. Complaint—Filed by the plaintiff with the court to initiate the lawsuit. The complaint is served with a summons on the defendant.
   b. Answer—A response to the complaint in which the defendant admits or denies the allegations made by the plaintiff. The answer may assert a counterclaim or an affirmative defense.
   c. Motion to dismiss—A request to the court to dismiss the case for stated reasons, such as the plaintiff's failure to state a claim for which relief can be granted.

2. *Pretrial motions (in addition to the motion to dismiss)—*
   a. Motion for judgment on the pleadings—May be made by either party. It will be granted if the parties agree on the facts and the only question is how the law applies to the facts. The judge bases the decision solely on the pleadings.
   b. Motion for summary judgment—May be made by either party. It will be granted if the parties agree on the facts and the sole question is a question of law. The judge can consider evidence outside the pleadings when evaluating the motion.

3. *Discovery*—The process of gathering evidence concerning the case and obtaining information from the opposing party. Discovery involves depositions (sworn testimony by a party to the lawsuit or any witness), interrogatories (written questions and answers to these questions made by parties to the action with the aid of their attorneys), and various requests (for admissions, documents, and medical examinations, for instance). Discovery may also involve electronically recorded information, such as e-mail, voice mail, social media posts, and other data compilations. Although electronic discovery has significant advantages over paper discovery, it is also more time consuming and expensive and often requires the parties to hire experts.

4. *Pretrial conference*—Either party or the court can request a pretrial conference to identify the matters in dispute after discovery has taken place and to plan the course of the trial. Also, the conference may explore the possibility of a settlement without a trial.

5. *Trial*—Following jury selection (*voir dire*), the trial begins with opening statements from both parties' attorneys. The following events then occur:
   a. The plaintiff's introduction of evidence (including the testimony of witnesses) supporting the plaintiff's position. The defendant's attorney can challenge evidence and cross-examine witnesses.
   b. The defendant's introduction of evidence (including the testimony of witnesses) supporting the defendant's position. The plaintiff's attorney can challenge evidence and cross-examine witnesses.
   c. Closing arguments by the attorneys in favor of their respective clients, the judge's instructions to the jury, and the jury's verdict.

6. *Posttrial motions—*
   a. Motion for judgment *n.o.v.* ("notwithstanding the verdict")—Will be granted if the judge is convinced that the jury's verdict was in error.
   b. Motion for a new trial—Will be granted if the judge is convinced that the jury's verdict was in error. The motion can also be granted on the grounds of newly discovered evidence, misconduct by the participants during the trial, or error by the judge.

7. *Appeal*—Either party can appeal the trial court's judgment to an appropriate court of appeals. After reviewing the record on appeal, the abstracts, and the attorneys' briefs, the appellate court holds a hearing and renders its opinion.

Courts Online

Almost every court has a website offering information about the court and its procedures, and increasingly courts are publishing their opinions online. In the future, we may see cyber courts, in which all trial proceedings are conducted online. A number of state and federal courts allow parties to file litigation-related documents with the courts via the Internet or other electronic means. Nearly all of the federal appellate courts and bankruptcy courts and a majority of the federal district courts have implemented electronic filing systems.

Alternative Dispute Resolution	1. *Negotiation*—The parties come together, with or without attorneys to represent them, to try to reach a settlement without the involvement of a third party.
	2. *Mediation*—The parties themselves reach an agreement with the help of a neutral third party, called a mediator. The mediator may propose a solution but does not make a decision resolving the matter.
	3. *Arbitration*—The parties submit their dispute to a neutral third party, the arbitrator, who renders a decision. The decision may or may not be legally binding, depending on the circumstances.
	4. *Other types of ADR*—These include early neutral case evaluation, mini-trials, and summary jury trials (SJTs).
	5. *Providers of ADR services*—The leading nonprofit provider of ADR services is the American Arbitration Association. Hundreds of for-profit firms also provide ADR services.
	6. *Online dispute resolution*—A number of organizations and firms are now offering negotiation, mediation, and arbitration services through online forums. These forums have been a practical alternative for the resolution of domain name disputes and e-commerce disputes in which the amount in controversy is relatively small.

Issue Spotters

1. At the trial, after Sue calls her witnesses, offers her evidence, and otherwise presents her side of the case, Tom has at least two choices between courses of action. Tom can call his first witness. What else might he do? (See *Following a State Court Case.*)

2. Lexi contracts with Theo to deliver a quantity of computers to Lexi's Computer Store. They disagree over the amount, the delivery date, the price, and the quality. Lexi files a suit against Theo in a state court. Their state requires that their dispute be submitted to mediation or nonbinding arbitration. If the dispute is not resolved, or if either party disagrees with the decision of the mediator or arbitrator, will a court hear the case? Explain. (See *Alternative Dispute Resolution.*)

—Check your answers to the *Issue Spotters* against the answers provided in Appendix D at the end of this text.

Business Scenarios and Case Problems

4–1. Standing to Sue. Jack and Maggie Turton bought a house in Jefferson County, Idaho, located directly across the street from a gravel pit. A few years later, the county converted the pit to a landfill. The landfill accepted many kinds of trash that cause harm to the environment, including major appliances, animal carcasses, containers with hazardous content warnings, leaking car batteries, and waste oil. The Turtons complained to the county, but the county did nothing. The Turtons then filed a lawsuit against the county alleging violations of federal environmental laws pertaining to groundwater contamination and other pollution. Do the Turtons have standing to sue? Why or why not? (See *Basic Judicial Requirements.*)

4–2. Discovery. Advance Technology Consultants, Inc. (ATC), contracted with RoadTrac, LLC, to provide software and client software systems for products using global positioning satellite (GPS) technology being developed by RoadTrac. RoadTrac agreed to provide ATC with hardware with which ATC's software would interface. Problems soon arose, however, and RoadTrac filed a lawsuit against ATC alleging breach of contract. During discovery, RoadTrac requested ATC's customer lists and marketing procedures. ATC objected to providing this information because RoadTrac and ATC had become competitors in the GPS industry. Should a party to a lawsuit have to hand over its confidential business secrets as part of a discovery request? Why or why not? What limitations might a court consider imposing before requiring ATC to produce this material? (See *Following a State Court Case.*)

4–3. Arbitration. Horton Automatics and the Industrial Division of the Communications Workers of America—the union that represented Horton's workers—negotiated a collective bargaining agreement. If an employee's discharge for a workplace-rule violation was submitted to arbitration, the agreement limited the arbitrator to determining whether the rule was reasonable and whether the employee had violated it. When Horton discharged its employee Ruben de la Garza, the union appealed to arbitration. The arbitrator found that de la Garza had violated a reasonable safety rule, but "was not totally convinced" that Horton should have treated the violation more seriously than other rule violations. The arbitrator ordered de la Garza reinstated to his job. Can a court set aside this order from the arbitrator? Explain. [*Horton Automatics v. The Industrial Division of the Communications Workers of America, AFL-CIO,* 506 Fed.Appx. 253 (5th Cir. 2013)] (See *Alternative Dispute Resolution.*)

4–4. Discovery. Jessica Lester died from injuries suffered in an auto accident caused by the driver of a truck owned by Allied Concrete Co. Jessica's widower, Isaiah, filed a suit against Allied for damages. The defendant requested copies of all of Isaiah's Facebook photos and other postings. Before responding, Isaiah "cleaned up" his Facebook page. Allied suspected that some of the items had been deleted, including a photo of Isaiah holding a beer can while wearing a T-shirt that declared "I [heart] hotmoms." Can this material be recovered? If so, how?

What effect might Isaiah's "misconduct" have on the result in this case? Discuss. [*Allied Concrete Co. v. Lester*, 736 S.E.2d 699 (Va. 2013)] (See *Following a State Court Case.*)

4–5. Electronic Filing. Betsy Faden worked for the U.S. Department of Veterans Affairs. Faden was removed from her position in April 2012 and was given until May 29 to appeal the removal decision. She submitted an appeal through the Merit Systems Protection Board's e-filing system seven days after the deadline. Ordered to show good cause for the delay, Faden testified that she had attempted to e-file the appeal while the board's system was down. The board acknowledged that its system had not been functioning on May 27, 28, and 29. Was Faden sufficiently diligent in ensuring a timely filing? Discuss. [*Faden v. Merit Systems Protection Board*, 553 Fed.Appx. 991 (Fed. Cir. 2014)] (See *Courts Online.*)

4–6. Business Case Problem with Sample Answer— Corporate Contacts. LG Electronics, Inc., a South Korean company, and nineteen other foreign companies participated in the global market for cathode ray tube (CRT) products. CRTs were integrated as components in consumer goods, including television sets, and sold for many years in high volume in the United States, including the state of Washington. The state filed a suit against LG and the others, alleging a conspiracy to raise prices and set production levels in the market for CRTs in violation of a state consumer protection statute. The defendants filed a motion to dismiss the suit for lack of personal jurisdiction. Should this motion be granted? Explain your answer. [*State of Washington v. LG Electronics, Inc.*, 185 Wash. App. 394, 341 P.3d 346 (2015)] (See *Basic Judicial Requirements.*)

—**For a sample answer to Problem 4–6, go to Appendix E at the end of this text.**

4–7. Appellate, or Reviewing, Courts. Angelica Westbrook was employed as a collector for Franklin Collection Service, Inc. During a collection call, Westbrook told a debtor that a $15 processing fee was an "interest" charge. This violated company policy, and Westbrook was fired. She filed a claim for unemployment benefits, which the Mississippi Department of Employment Security (MDES) approved. Franklin objected. At an MDES hearing, a Franklin supervisor testified that she had heard Westbrook make the false statement, although she admitted that there had been no

similar incidents with Westbrook. Westbrook denied making the statement but added that, if she had said it, she did not remember it. The agency found that Franklin's reason for terminating Westbrook did not amount to the misconduct required to disqualify her for benefits and upheld the approval. Franklin appealed to a state intermediate appellate court. Is the court likely to uphold the agency's findings of fact? Explain. [*Franklin Collection Service, Inc. v. Mississippi Department of Employment Security*, 184 So.3d 330 (Miss.App. 2016)] (See *The State and Federal Court Systems.*)

4–8. Service of Process. Bentley Bay Retail, LLC, filed a suit in a Florida state court against Soho Bay Restaurant LLC, and its corporate officers, Luiz and Karine Queiroz, in their individual capacities. The charge against the Queirozes was for a breach of their personal guaranty for Soho Bay's debt to Bentley Bay. The plaintiff filed notices with the court to depose the Queirozes, who reside in Brazil. The Queirozes argued that they could not be deposed in Brazil. The court ordered them to appear in Florida to provide depositions in their *corporate* capacity. Witnesses appearing in court outside the jurisdiction of their residence are immune from service of process while in court. On the Queirozes' appearance in Florida, can they be served with process in their *individual* capacities? Explain. [*Queiroz v. Bentley Bay Retail, LLC*, 43 Fla.L.Weekly D85, ___ So.3d ___ (3 Dist. 2018)] (See *The State and Federal Court Systems.*)

4–9. A Question of Ethics—The IDDR Approach and Complaints. *John Verble worked as a financial advisor for Morgan Stanley Smith Barney, LLC. After nearly seven years, Verble was fired. He filed a suit in a federal district court against his ex-employer. In his complaint, Verble alleged that he had learned of illegal activity by Morgan Stanley and its clients. He claimed that he had reported the activity to the Federal Bureau of Investigation, and that he was fired in retaliation. His complaint contained no additional facts.* [Verble v. Morgan Stanley Smith Barney LLC, *676 Fed.Appx. 421 (6th Cir. 2017)*] (See *Following a State Court Case.*)

1. To avoid a dismissal of his suit, does Verble have a *legal* obligation to support his claims with more facts? Explain.

2. Does Verble owe an *ethical* duty to back up his claims with more facts? Use the IDDR approach to express your answer.

Critical Thinking and Writing Assignments

4–10. Time-Limited Group Assignment—Access to Courts. Assume that a statute in your state requires that all civil lawsuits involving damages of less than $50,000 be arbitrated. Such a case can be tried in court only if a party is dissatisfied with the arbitrator's decision. The statute also provides that if a trial does not result in an improvement of more than 10 percent in the position of the party who demanded the trial, that party must pay the entire cost of the arbitration proceeding. (See *Alternative Dispute Resolution.*)

1. One group will argue that the state statute violates litigants' rights of access to the courts and trial by jury.

2. Another group will argue that the statute does not violate litigants' right of access to the courts.

3. A third group will evaluate how the determination on right of access would be changed if the statute was part of a pilot program that affected only a few judicial districts in the state.

Tort Law

"Two wrongs do not make a right."

English Proverb

Most of us agree with the chapter-opening quotation—two wrongs do not make a right. In this chapter, we consider a particular type of wrongful actions called **torts** (the word *tort* is French for "wrong").

Part of doing business today—and indeed, part of everyday life—is the risk of being involved in a lawsuit. The list of circumstances in which business-persons can be sued is long and varied. Anytime one party's allegedly wrongful conduct causes injury to another, an action may arise under the law of torts. Through tort law, society compensates those who have suffered injuries as a result of the wrongful conduct of others.

Sheila Dearning is a reporter for the *National Post* who has gained notoriety by writing a number of articles that exposed the misconduct of powerful public officials. A competing publication, the *Tribunal*, knows that Dearning has a five-year contract with her current employer. Neverthe-less, the *Tribunal* offers to hire Dearning as a reporter and to pay her twice the amount she is being paid at the *National Post*. Dearning accepts. Has the *Tribunal* committed a tort? As you will learn in this chapter, the tort of wrongful interference with a contractual relationship is one of many that can lead to liability for businesses. In this situation, the *Tribunal* can be sued for wrongfully interfering with Dearning's contract with her employer. (The *National Post* can also sue Dearning personally for breaching the contract, as will be discussed in a later chapter.)

Learning Objectives

The five Learning Objectives *below are designed to help improve your understand-ing. After reading this chapter, you should be able to answer the following questions:*

1. What types of damages are available in tort lawsuits?

2. What is defamation? Name two types of defamation.

3. What conduct constitutes conversion?

4. Identify the four elements of negligence.

5. What is meant by strict liabil-ity? In what circumstances is strict liability applied?

5–1 The Basis of Tort Law

Two notions serve as the basis of all torts: wrongs and compensation. Tort law is designed to compensate those who have suffered a loss or injury due to another person's wrongful act. In a tort action, one person or group brings a personal suit against another person or group to obtain compensation (monetary damages) or other relief for the harm suffered.

Tort A wrongful act (other than a breach of contract) that results in harm or injury to another and leads to civil liability.

5–1a The Purpose of Tort Law

Generally, the purpose of tort law is to provide remedies for the invasion of various *protected interests*. Society recognizes an interest in personal physical safety, and tort law provides remedies for acts that cause physical injury or interfere with physical security and freedom. Society also recognizes an interest in protecting property, and tort law provides remedies for acts that cause destruction of or damage to property.

Note that in legal usage, the singular *damage* is used to refer to harm or injury to persons or property. The plural **damages** is used to refer to monetary compensation for such harm or injury.

5–1b Damages Available in Tort Actions

Because the purpose of tort law is to compensate the injured party for the damage suffered, it is important to have a basic understanding of the types of damages that plaintiffs seek in tort actions.

Compensatory Damages Plaintiffs are awarded **compensatory damages** to compensate or reimburse them for actual losses. Thus, the goal is to make the plaintiffs whole and put them in the same position that they would have been in had the tort not occurred. Compensatory damages awards are often broken down into *special damages* and *general damages*.

Special damages compensate plaintiffs for quantifiable monetary losses, such as medical expenses, lost wages and benefits (now and in the future), extra costs, the loss of irreplaceable items, and the costs of repairing or replacing damaged property. **General damages** compensate individuals (not companies) for the nonmonetary aspects of the harm suffered, such as pain and suffering. A court might award general damages for physical or emotional pain and suffering, loss of companionship, loss of consortium (losing the emotional and physical benefits of a spousal relationship), disfigurement, loss of reputation, or loss or impairment of mental or physical capacity.

Case Example 5.1 While working as a seaman in Louisiana, Chedrick Starks was injured when a piece of equipment broke free and struck him. After undergoing several surgeries, Starks sued his employer for past and future medical expenses, and pain and suffering. At trial, a jury awarded him damages for past and future medical expenses and past pain and suffering, but did not award him damages for future pain and suffering. Starks appealed, claiming that the damages awarded were inadequate. A federal district court held that the jury's damages award was inconsistent. Starks had presented sufficient proof that his injuries and future medical treatment could result in future pain and suffering. Therefore, Starks was entitled to a new trial on the issue of damages.[1]

Punitive Damages Occasionally, the courts also award **punitive damages** in tort cases to punish the wrongdoers and deter others from similar wrongdoing. Punitive damages are appropriate only when the defendant's conduct was particularly egregious (flagrant) or reprehensible (blameworthy).

Thus, punitive damages are normally available mainly in intentional tort actions and only rarely in negligence lawsuits (*intentional torts* and *negligence* will be explained later in the chapter). They may be awarded, however, in suits involving *gross negligence*, which can be defined as an intentional failure to perform a manifest duty in reckless disregard of the effect on the life or property of another.

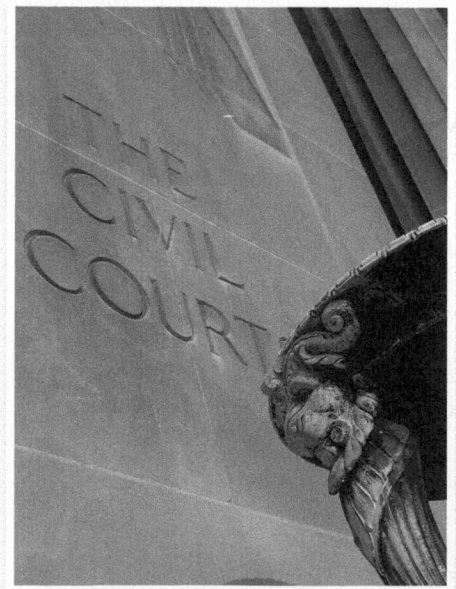

Do tort lawsuits end up in civil or criminal courts?

DHuss/E+/Getty Images

---

1. *Starks v. Advantage Staffing, LLC*, 217 F.Supp.3d 917 (E.D.La. 2016).

Courts exercise great restraint in granting punitive damages to plaintiffs in tort actions because punitive damages are subject to the limitations imposed by the due process clause of the U.S. Constitution. In a landmark decision, the United States Supreme Court held that when an award of punitive damages is grossly excessive, it furthers no legitimate purpose and violates due process requirements.[2] Consequently, an appellate court will sometimes reduce the amount of punitive damages awarded to a plaintiff because the amount was excessive and thereby violates the due process clause.

Legislative Caps on Damages State laws may limit the amount of damages—both punitive and general—that can be awarded to the plaintiff. More than half of the states have placed caps ranging from $250,000 to $750,000 on noneconomic general damages (such as for pain and suffering), especially in medical malpractice suits. More than thirty states have limited punitive damages, with some imposing outright bans.

5–1c Classifications of Torts

There are two broad classifications of torts: *intentional torts* and *unintentional torts* (torts involving negligence). Intentional torts result from the intentional violation of person or property (fault with intent). Negligence results from the breach of a duty to act reasonably (fault without intent). The classification of a particular tort depends largely on how the tort occurs (intentionally or negligently) and the surrounding circumstances.

5–1d Defenses

Even if a plaintiff proves all the elements of a tort, the defendant can raise a number of legally recognized **defenses**—reasons why the plaintiff should not obtain damages. The defenses available may vary depending on the specific tort involved. A successful defense releases the defendant from partial or full liability for the tortious act.

A common defense to intentional torts against persons, for instance, is *consent*. When a person consents to the act that damages her or him, there is generally no tort liability. The most widely used defense in negligence actions is *comparative negligence* (discussed later in this chapter).

Most states also have a *statute of limitations* that establishes the time limit (often two years from the date of discovering the harm) within which a particular type of lawsuit can be filed. After that time period, the plaintiff can no longer file a claim.

5–2 Intentional Torts against Persons

An **intentional tort,** as just mentioned, requires *intent*. The **tortfeasor** (the one committing the tort) must intend to commit an act, the consequences of which interfere with the personal or business interests of another in a way not permitted by law. An evil or harmful motive is not required—in fact, the person committing the action may even have a beneficial motive for committing what turns out to be a tortious act.

In tort law, intent means only that the person intended the consequences of his or her act or knew with substantial certainty that certain consequences would result from the act. The law generally assumes that individuals intend the *normal* consequences of their actions. Thus, forcefully pushing another—even if done in jest and without any evil motive—is an intentional tort if injury results, because the object of a strong push can ordinarily be expected to fall down.

Know This
Damage refers to harm or injury to persons or property. *Damages* is a legal term that refers to the monetary compensation awarded to a plaintiff who has suffered such harm or injury.

Defense A reason offered by a defendant in an action or lawsuit as to why the plaintiff should not recover or establish what she or he seeks.

Intentional Tort A wrongful act knowingly committed.

Tortfeasor One who commits a tort.

---

2. *State Farm Mutual Automobile Insurance Co. v. Campbell*, 538 U.S. 408, 123 S.Ct. 1513, 155 L.Ed.2d 585 (2003).

Intent can be transferred when a defendant intends to harm one individual but unintentionally harms a different person. This is called **transferred intent**. **Example 5.2** Alex swings a bat intending to hit Blake but misses and hits Carson instead. Carson can sue Alex for the tort of battery (discussed shortly) because Alex's intent to harm Blake can be transferred to Carson. ▪

5–2a **Assault**

An **assault** is any intentional and unexcused threat of immediate harmful or offensive contact—words or acts that create in another person a reasonable apprehension of harmful contact. An assault can be completed even if there is no actual contact with the plaintiff, provided the defendant's conduct causes the plaintiff to have a reasonable apprehension of imminent harm. Tort law aims to protect individuals from having to expect harmful or offensive contact.

5–2b **Battery**

If the act that created the apprehension is *completed* and results in harm to the plaintiff, it is a **battery**, which is defined as an unexcused and harmful or offensive physical contact *intentionally* performed. **Example 5.3** Ivan threatens Jean with a gun and then shoots her. The pointing of the gun at Jean is an assault. The firing of the gun (if the bullet hits Jean) is a battery. ▪

The contact can be harmful, or it can be merely offensive (such as an unwelcome kiss). Physical injury need not occur. The contact can be made by the defendant or by some force set in motion by the defendant, such as a rock thrown by the defendant. Whether the contact is offensive or not is determined by the *reasonable person standard*.[3]

If the plaintiff shows that there was contact, and the jury (or judge, if there is no jury) agrees that the contact was offensive, the plaintiff has a right to compensation. A plaintiff may be compensated for the emotional harm resulting from a battery, as well as for physical harm. The defendant may raise a number of legally recognized defenses to justify his or her conduct, including self-defense and defense of others.

5–2c **False Imprisonment**

False imprisonment is the intentional confinement or restraint of another person's activities without justification. False imprisonment interferes with the freedom to move without restraint. The confinement can be accomplished through the use of physical barriers, physical restraint, or threats of physical force. It is essential that the person under restraint does not wish to be restrained. (The plaintiff's consent to the restraint bars any liability.)

Businesspersons may face suits for false imprisonment after they have attempted to confine a suspected shoplifter for questioning. Under the "privilege to detain" granted to merchants in most states, a merchant can use *reasonable force* to detain or delay a person suspected of shoplifting the merchant's property. Although the details of the privilege vary from state to state, generally laws require that any detention be conducted in a *reasonable* manner and for only a *reasonable* length of time. Undue force or unreasonable detention can lead to liability for the business.

Case Example 5.4 Justin Mills was playing blackjack at the Maryland Live! Casino when two casino employees approached him, grabbed his arm, and led him into a back hallway. The employees (who were off-duty police officers moonlighting for the casino) accused Mills of counting cards and

Under what circumstances can a person in jail sue for false imprisonment?

© Photobank gallery/Shutterstock.com

---

3. The reasonable person standard is an objective test of how a reasonable person would have acted under the same circumstances. See "The Duty of Care and Its Breach" later in this chapter.

demanded his identification. They detained Mills and told him that they would not let him go unless he produced his ID so that the casino could ban him from the premises.

Mills gave the employees his passport and was eventually allowed to leave, but he secretly recorded the audio from the interaction using the smartphone in his pocket. Mills later filed a lawsuit alleging, in part, false imprisonment. A federal district court granted Mills a summary judgment on the false imprisonment claim, because the casino personnel had no legal justification for detaining him.[4] ▓ Cities and counties may also face liability for false imprisonment if they detain individuals without reason.

5–2d Intentional Infliction of Emotional Distress

The tort of *intentional infliction of emotional distress* can be defined as extreme and outrageous conduct resulting in severe emotional distress to another. To be **actionable** (capable of serving as the ground for a lawsuit), the conduct must be so extreme and outrageous that it exceeds the bounds of decency accepted by society.

Actionable Capable of serving as the basis of a lawsuit. An actionable claim can be pursued in a lawsuit or other court action.

Outrageous Conduct Courts in most jurisdictions are wary of emotional distress claims and confine them to truly outrageous behavior. Generally, repeated annoyances (such as those experienced by a person who is being stalked), coupled with threats, are sufficient to support a claim. (See this chapter's *Business Law Analysis* feature for details of how courts analyze these types of claims.) Acts that cause indignity or annoyance alone usually are not enough.

---

4. *Mills v. PPE Casino Resorts Maryland, LLC*, 2017 WL 2930460 (D.Md. 2017).

Analyzing Intentional Infliction of Emotional Distress Claims

Business Law Analysis

While living in her home country of Tanzania, Sophia Kiwanuka signed an employment contract with Anne Bakilana, a Tanzanian living in the United States. Kiwanuka came to Washington, D.C., to work as a babysitter and maid in Bakilana's house. When Kiwanuka arrived, Bakilana confiscated her passport, held her in isolation, and forced her to work long hours under threat of having her deported. Kiwanuka worked seven days a week without breaks and was subjected to regular verbal and psychological abuse by Bakilana.

Kiwanuka filed a complaint against Bakilana for intentional infliction of emotional distress. Bakilana asked the court to dismiss the claim. Are Kiwanuka's allegations sufficient to show outrageous intentional conduct that resulted in severe emotional distress?

Analysis: In deciding whether the alleged conduct was sufficiently outrageous, a court would look at the repeated conduct of the purported tortfeasor. The complaint stated that Bakilana, on a daily basis, used her position of power and control over Kiwanuka to engage in an intentional pattern of outrageous verbal abuse against her. The complaint also alleged that Bakilana intentionally interfered with Kiwanuka's attempts to form relationships or acquaintances, which deepened Kiwanuka's suffering of isolation and distress.

Result and Reasoning: These allegations were sufficient to show extreme and outrageous conduct, intentionally committed, that resulted in severe emotional distress to Kiwanuka. Therefore, Kiwanuka was entitled to a trial on her claim for intentional infliction of emotional distress.

Is it legal to create a parody of a public figure, such as the late Reverend Jerry Falwell?

© Ron Galella/Getty Images

Learning Objective 2

What is defamation? Name two types of defamation.

Defamation Anything published or publicly spoken that causes injury to another's good name, reputation, or character.

Libel Defamation in writing or another permanent form (such as a digital recording).

Slander Defamation in oral form.

Example 5.5 A father attacks a man who has had consensual sexual relations with the father's nineteen-year-old daughter. The father handcuffs the man to a steel pole and threatens to kill him unless he leaves town immediately. The father's conduct may be sufficiently extreme and outrageous to be actionable as an intentional infliction of emotional distress.

Limited by the First Amendment When the outrageous conduct consists of speech about a public figure, the First Amendment's guarantee of freedom of speech limits emotional distress claims. ★ **Spotlight Case Example 5.6** *Hustler* magazine once printed a fake advertisement that showed a picture of the Reverend Jerry Falwell and described him as having lost his virginity to his mother in an outhouse while he was drunk. Falwell sued the magazine for intentional infliction of emotional distress and won, but the United States Supreme Court overturned the decision. The Court held that creators of parodies of public figures are protected under the First Amendment from claims of intentional infliction of emotional distress. (The Court applied the same standards that apply to public figures in defamation lawsuits, discussed next.)[5]

5–2e Defamation

The freedom of speech guaranteed by the First Amendment to the U.S. Constitution is not absolute. In interpreting the First Amendment, the courts must balance free speech rights against other strong social interests, including society's interest in preventing and redressing attacks on reputation.

The tort of **defamation** involves wrongfully hurting a person's good reputation. The law has imposed a general duty on all persons to refrain from making false, defamatory statements of fact about others. Breaching this duty in writing or another permanent form (such as a digital recording) constitutes the tort of **libel**. Breaching the duty orally is the tort of **slander**. The tort of defamation also arises when a false statement of fact is made about a person's product, business, or legal ownership rights to property.

To establish defamation, a plaintiff normally must prove the following:

1. The defendant made a false statement of fact.
2. The statement was understood as being about the plaintiff and tended to harm the plaintiff's reputation.
3. The statement was published to at least one person other than the plaintiff.
4. In addition, if the plaintiff is a public figure, she or he must prove *actual malice*.

Statement of Fact Requirement Often at issue in defamation lawsuits (including online defamation) is whether the defendant made a *statement of fact* or *a statement of opinion*. Statements of opinion normally are not actionable because they are protected under the First Amendment. In other words, making a negative statement about another person is not defamation unless the statement is false and represents something as a fact. **Example 5.7** Vickie's statement "Lane cheats on his taxes," if false, can lead to liability for defamation because it is a statement of fact. The statement "Lane is a jerk" cannot constitute defamation because it is clearly an opinion.

The Publication Requirement The basis of the tort of defamation is the publication of a statement or statements that hold an individual up to contempt, ridicule, or hatred. *Publication* here means that the defamatory statements are communicated to persons other than the defamed party.

The following case involved the application of free speech guarantees to reviews of professional services posted online.

---

5. *Hustler Magazine, Inc. v. Falwell*, 485 U.S. 46, 108 S.Ct. 876, 99 L.Ed.2d 41 (1988). For another example of how the courts protect parody, see *Busch v. Viacom International, Inc.*, 477 F.Supp.2d 764 (N.D.Tex. 2007), involving a fake endorsement of televangelist Pat Robertson's diet shake.

Case 5.1

Blake v. Giustibelli

District Court of Appeal of Florida, Fourth District, 41 Fla.L.Weekly D122, 182 So.3d 881 (2016).

Background and Facts Copia Blake retained attorney Ann-Marie Giustibelli to represent Blake in a divorce proceeding against Peter Birzon. Blake agreed to pay Giustibelli $300 an hour. After the marriage was dissolved and the related issues were resolved, Giustibelli sought payment for her services. Blake balked at the amount. She posted negative reviews of Giustibelli online, including the following:

> SHE MISREPRESENTED HER FEES WITH REGARDS TO THE CONTRACT I INITIALLY SIGNED. THE CONTRACT SHE SUBMITTED TO THE COURTS FOR HER FEES WERE 4 TIMES HER ORIGINAL QUOTE AND PAGES OF THE ORIGINAL HAD BEEN EXCHANGED TO SUPPORT HER CLAIMS.

Giustibelli filed a suit in a Florida state court against Blake, alleging libel. During the trial, Blake admitted that Giustibelli had not charged four times more than what was quoted in the agreement. The court entered a judgment in Giustibelli's favor and awarded punitive damages of $350,000. Blake appealed.

In the Words of the Court
CIKLIN, C.J. [Chief Judge]
* * * *

On appeal, Blake and Birzon argue that their Internet reviews constituted statements of opinion and thus were protected by the First Amendment and not actionable as defamation. We disagree. *An action for libel will lie for a false and unprivileged publication by letter, or otherwise, which exposes a person to distrust, hatred, contempt, ridicule or obloquy [censure or disgrace] or which causes such person to be avoided, or which has a tendency to injure such person in their office, occupation, business or employment.* [Emphasis added.]

Here, all the reviews contained allegations that Giustibelli lied to Blake regarding the attorney's fee. Two of the reviews contained the allegation that Giustibelli falsified a contract. These are factual allegations, and the evidence showed they were false.

* * * *

Affirmed.

Decision and Remedy The state intermediate appellate court affirmed the lower court's judgment and award. Blake's online reviews focused on her contract with Giustibelli and were particularly critical of the amount of Giustibelli's fee. The evidence, however, showed that Blake had agreed to pay the amount stated in the contract, which is the amount that Giustibelli sought after the divorce proceedings were completed.

Critical Thinking

• **Ethical** *If false statements of fact were not actionable at law, would they be unethical? Explain.*

• **E-Commerce** *How does posting a false statement online magnify its effect on a person's reputation?*

The courts have generally held that even dictating a letter to a secretary constitutes publication, although the publication may be privileged (as discussed shortly). If a third party overhears defamatory statements by chance, the courts usually hold that this also constitutes publication. Defamatory statements made via the Internet are actionable as well. Note also that anyone who republishes or repeats defamatory statements is liable even if that person reveals the source of the statements.

Case Example 5.8 Eddy Ramirez, a meat cutter at Costco Wholesale Corporation, was involved in a workplace incident with a co-worker, and Costco gave him a notice of suspension. After an investigation in which co-workers were interviewed, Costco fired Ramirez. Ramirez sued, claiming that the suspension notice was defamatory. The court ruled in Costco's favor. Ramirez could not establish defamation, because he had not shown that the suspension notice was published to any third parties. Costco did nothing beyond what was necessary to investigate the events that led to Ramirez's termination.[6]

---

6. *Ramirez v. Costco Wholesale Corp.,* 2014 WL 2696737 (Ct.Sup.Ct. 2014).

Damages for Libel Once a defendant's liability for libel is established, a plaintiff is normally entitled to general damages. General damages are designed to compensate the plaintiff for nonspecific harms such as disgrace or dishonor in the eyes of the community, humiliation, injured reputation, and emotional distress—harms that are difficult to measure. In other words, to recover general damages in a libel case, the plaintiff need not prove that she or he was actually harmed in any specific way as a result of the libelous statement.

Damages for Slander In contrast to cases involving libel, in a case alleging slander, the plaintiff must prove *special damages* (defined earlier) to establish the defendant's liability. In other words, the plaintiff must show that the slanderous statement caused the plaintiff to suffer actual economic or monetary losses.

Unless this initial hurdle of proving special damages is overcome, a plaintiff alleging slander normally cannot go forward with the suit and recover any damages. This requirement is imposed in cases involving slander because slanderous statements have a temporary quality. In contrast, a libelous (written) statement has the quality of permanence, can be circulated widely, especially through social media, and usually results from some degree of deliberation on the part of the author.

Slander *Per Se* Exceptions to the burden of proving special damages in cases alleging slander are made for certain types of slanderous statements. If a false statement constitutes "slander *per se*," no proof of special damages is required for it to be actionable. The following four types of false utterances are considered to be slander *per se*:

1. A statement that another has a loathsome disease (such as a sexually transmitted diseases) or serious mental defect.
2. A statement that another has committed improprieties while engaging in a profession or trade.
3. A statement that another has committed or has been imprisoned for a serious crime.
4. A statement that a person is unchaste or has engaged in serious sexual misconduct. (This category of slander *per se* usually applies only to unmarried persons and sometimes only to women.)

Defenses to Defamation Truth is normally an absolute defense against a defamation charge. In other words, if the defendant in a defamation suit can prove that his or her allegedly defamatory statements were true, normally no tort has been committed.

Other defenses to defamation may exist if the statement is privileged or concerns a public figure. Note that the majority of defamation actions in the United States are filed in state courts, and the states may differ both in how they define defamation and in the particular defenses they allow, such as privilege (discussed shortly).

Privileged Communications. In some circumstances, a person will not be liable for defamatory statements because she or he enjoys a **privilege,** or immunity. Privileged communications are of two types: absolute and qualified.[7] Only in judicial proceedings and certain government proceedings is an absolute privilege granted. Thus, statements made in a courtroom by attorneys and judges during a trial are absolutely privileged, as are statements made by government officials during legislative debate.

In other situations, a person will not be liable for defamatory statements because he or she has a *qualified*, or conditional, privilege. An employer's statements in written evaluations of employees are an example of a qualified privilege. Generally, if the statements are made in good faith and the publication is limited to those who have a legitimate interest in the communication, the statements fall within the area of qualified privilege.

> "My initial response was to sue her for defamation of character, but then I realized that I had no character."
>
> **Charles Barkley,**
> 1963–present
> (National Basketball Association player, 1984–2000)

Privilege A special right, advantage, or immunity that enables a person or a class of persons to avoid liability for defamation.

---

7. Note that the term *privileged communication* in this context is *not* the same as privileged communication between a professional, such as an attorney, and his or her client.

When does an online criticism of a physician become defamation? | Ethical Issue

Just as there are online rating sites for college professors, there are rating sites for practicing physicians. A posting at such a site formed the basis for a defamation lawsuit brought by neurologist Dr. David McKee.

McKee went to examine a patient who had been transferred from the intensive care unit (ICU) to a private room. In the room were family members of the patient, including his son. The patient's son later made the following post on a physician-rating website: "[Dr. McKee] seemed upset that my father had been moved [into a private room]. Never having met my father or his family, Dr. McKee said 'When you weren't in ICU, I had to spend time finding out if you transferred or died.' When we gaped at him, he said 'Well, 44 percent of hemorrhagic strokes dies within 30 days. I guess this is the better option.'"[8]

McKee filed suit for defamation but lost. The court found that all the statements made by the son were essentially true, and truth is a complete defense to a defamation action. In other words, true statements, however disparaging, are not actionable. Even the presence of minor inaccuracies of expression or detail does not render basically true statements false. As long as the "sting of the libelous charge is justified," defamation has not occurred.

Example 5.9 Jorge has worked at Google for five years and is being considered for a management position. His supervisor, Lydia, writes an e-mail about Jorge's performance to those evaluating him for the management position. The message contains certain negative statements, which Lydia honestly believes are true. If Lydia limits the disclosure of the contents of the message to company representatives, her statements will likely be protected by a qualified privilege. ▪

Public Figures. Politicians, entertainers, professional athletes, and other persons who are in the public eye are considered *public figures.* In general, public figures are considered fair game, and false and defamatory statements about them that appear in the media will not constitute defamation unless the statements are made with **actual malice.**[9] To be made with actual malice, a statement must be made *with either knowledge of its falsity or a reckless disregard of the truth.*

Statements about public figures, especially when made via a public medium, are usually related to matters of general interest. They are made about people who substantially affect all of us. Furthermore, public figures generally have some access to a public medium for answering disparaging (belittling) falsehoods about themselves, whereas private individuals do not. For these reasons, public figures have a greater burden of proof in defamation cases (they must prove actual malice) than do private individuals.

Case Example 5.10 *In Touch Weekly* magazine published a story about a former call girl who claimed to have slept with legendary soccer player David Beckham more than once. Beckham sued *In Touch* for libel, seeking $25 million in damages. He said that he had never met the woman, had not cheated on his wife with her, and had not paid her for sex. After months of litigation, a federal district court dismissed the case because Beckham could not show that the magazine had acted with actual malice. Whether or not the statements in the article were accurate, there was no evidence that the defendants had made the statements with knowledge of their falsity or reckless disregard for the truth.[10] ▪

Actual Malice The deliberate intent to cause harm that exists when a person makes a statement with either knowledge of its falsity or reckless disregard of the truth. It is required to establish defamation against public figures.

A publication printed statements by a woman who claimed that she had slept with David Beckham on several occasions. In order for Beckham to prevail in a lawsuit against the publication for defamatory statements, what legal barrier must he overcome?

---

8. *McKee v. Laurion*, 825 N.W.2d 725 (Minn. 2013).
9. The landmark case establishing the actual malice requirement is *New York Times Co. v. Sullivan*, 376 U.S. 254, 84 S.Ct. 710, 11 L.Ed.2d 686 (1964).
10. *Beckham v. Bauer Pub. Co., L.P.*, 2011 WL 977570 (C.D.Cal. 2011).

5–2f Invasion of the Right to Privacy and Appropriation

A person has a right to solitude and freedom from prying public eyes—in other words, to privacy. The Supreme Court has held that a fundamental right to privacy is implied by various amendments to the U.S. Constitution. Some state constitutions also explicitly provide for privacy rights. In addition, a number of federal and state statutes have been enacted to protect individual rights in specific areas.

Tort law also safeguards these rights through the torts of *invasion of privacy* and *appropriation*. Generally, to sue successfully for an invasion of privacy, a person must have a reasonable expectation of privacy, and the invasion must be highly offensive. (See this chapter's *Adapting the Law to the Online Environment* feature for a discussion of how invasion of privacy claims can arise when someone posts pictures or videos taken with digital devices.)

Revenge Porn and Invasion of Privacy

Adapting the Law to the Online Environment

Nearly every digital device today takes photos and videos and has software that allows the recording of conversations via Skype. Many couples immortalize their "private moments" using such digital devices. One partner may take a racy selfie and send it as an attachment to a text message to the other partner, for instance.

Occasionally, after a relationship ends, one partner seeks a type of digital revenge. The result, called revenge porn, involves the online distribution of sexually explicit images of a nonconsenting individual with the intent to humiliate that person.

State Statutes

Thirty-five states have enacted statutes that make revenge porn a crime. But each state's law is different. (In some states, it is a misdemeanor with less serious consequences, and in other states, it is a felony with more serious penalties.) In addition, most of these criminal statutes do not provide victims with a right to obtain damages. Therefore, victims have sued in civil courts on the basis of (1) invasion of privacy, (2) public disclosure of private facts, and (3) intentional infliction of emotional distress.

A Case Example

Nadia Hussain had dated Akhil Patel on and off for seven years since high school. After they broke up, Patel hounded her with offensive and threatening phone calls, texts, and e-mails—often twenty to thirty per day. He did this for several years. He even came to her workplace a few times. Hussain filed police reports and changed her phone number multiple times, but the harassment continued. Patel also hacked or attempted to hack into her accounts (she had received alerts).

Eventually, Patel posted secretly recorded sexual videos of Hussain on the Internet. (He had recorded, without her consent, a Skype conversation they once had in which Hussain had undressed and masturbated.) Hussain sued Patel claiming invasion of privacy, public disclosure of private facts, and intentional infliction of emotional distress. A jury found in her favor and awarded $500,000 in damages for mental anguish and damage to her reputation. An appellate court affirmed but reduced the damages to $345,000 (because the intentional infliction of emotional distress claim was not supported by the evidence).[a]

It Is More Than Just Pictures and Videos

Perhaps the worst form of revenge porn occurs when the perpetrator provides detailed information about the victim. The information posted online may include the victim's name, Facebook page, address, and phone number, as well as the victim's photos and videos. Many of the hosting websites have been shut down, but others are still active.

Perpetrators also use social media sites, such as Facebook, Twitter, Instagram, and Reddit, to disseminate revenge porn. Even though Facebook and other companies have explicit policies against pornography and will take content down once it is reported, users often hide it within restricted or closed groups. For example, the Senate Armed Services Committee held hearings in 2017 on a private Facebook group called Marines United. Marines United circulated nude photos of women (including fellow marines, ex-girlfriends, and strangers) without their consent. The group was closed down after one member reported it to the Marine Corps. At least one member was court-martialed.

Critical Thinking

Why might the appellate court have decided that the evidence did not support Nadia Hussain's intentional infliction of emotional distress claim?

---

a. *Patel v. Hussain*, 485 S.W.3d 153 (Tex.App.—Houston 2016); also see *Doe v. Doe*, 2017 WL 3025885 (S.D.N.Y. 2017).

Invasion of Privacy Four acts qualify as an invasion of privacy:

1. *Intrusion into an individual's affairs or seclusion.* Invading someone's home or illegally searching someone's briefcase is an invasion of privacy. The tort has been held to extend to eavesdropping by wiretap, the unauthorized scanning of a bank account, compulsory blood testing, and window peeping. **Example 5.11** A female sports reporter for ESPN is digitally videoed while naked through the peephole in the door of her hotel room. If she sues, she will likely win a lawsuit against the man who took the video and posted it on the Internet.

2. *False light.* Publication of information that places a person in a false light is also an invasion of privacy. For instance, writing a story about a person that attributes ideas and opinions not held by that person is an invasion of privacy. (Publishing such a story could involve the tort of defamation as well.) **Case Example 5.12** Police received a report from a customer of West Gate Bank that his debit card had been stolen and used to withdraw funds from his account at the bank's ATM. The ATM video depicted a female walking up to an ATM and using a debit card to withdraw cash. To identify the person, the police posted still images from the video on the Crime Stoppers website and Facebook page. The caption said, "This young lady doesn't look like your typical crook, but she is! She used someone's stolen credit card.... If you know who she is, leave us a tip here."

   Police received tips that the woman in the video was Shayla Funk. Funk, as it turned out, was not a criminal and was simply withdrawing funds with her own card from her own bank account. Nevertheless, as a result of the posting, she lost her job as an occupational therapist. Funk sued the city and Crime Stoppers organization for defamation and for violating her privacy by false light, and won. The court awarded Funk more than $259,000 in damages, which was affirmed on appeal by the state's highest court.[11]

3. *Public disclosure of private facts.* This type of invasion of privacy occurs when a person publicly discloses private facts about an individual that an ordinary person would find objectionable or embarrassing. A newspaper account about a private citizen's sex life or financial affairs could be an actionable invasion of privacy, even if the information revealed is true, because it should not be a matter of public concern.

4. *Appropriation of identity.* Under the common law, using a person's name, picture, or other likeness for commercial purposes without permission is a tortious invasion of privacy. An individual's right to privacy normally includes the right to the exclusive use of her or his identity. **Example 5.13** An advertising agency asks a singer with a distinctive voice and stage presence to do a marketing campaign for a new automobile. The singer rejects the offer. If the agency then uses someone who imitates the singer's voice and dance moves in the ad, this would be actionable as an appropriation of identity.

Appropriation Most states today have codified the common law tort of appropriation of identity in statutes that establish the distinct tort of **appropriation,** or right of publicity. States differ as to the degree of likeness that is required to impose liability for appropriation, however.

Some courts have held that even when an animated character in a video or a video game is made to look like an actual person, there are not enough similarities to constitute appropriation. � **Spotlight Case Example 5.14** The Naked Cowboy, Robert Burck, was a street entertainer in New York City who had achieved some fame performing for tourists. He performed wearing only a white cowboy hat, white cowboy boots, and white underwear and carrying a guitar strategically placed to give the illusion of nudity. Burck sued Mars, Inc., the maker of M&Ms candy, over a video it showed on billboards in Times Square that depicted a blue M&M dressed exactly like The Naked Cowboy. The court, however, held that the use of Burck's signature costume did not amount to appropriation.[12]

Appropriation In tort law, the use by one person of another person's name, likeness, or other identifying characteristic without permission and for the benefit of the user.

Under what circumstances, if any, could the use of the image of The Naked Cowboy in an ad constitute appropriation?

---

11. *Funk v. Lincoln-Lancaster County Crime Stoppers, Inc.*, 294 Neb. 715, 885 N.W.2d 1 (2016).
12. *Burck v. Mars, Inc.*, 571 F.Supp.2d 446 (S.D.N.Y. 2008). Also see *Beastie Boys v. Monster Energy Co.*, 66 F.Supp.3d 424 (S.D.N.Y. 2014).

Fraudulent Misrepresentation Any misrepresentation, either by misstatement or by omission of a material fact, knowingly made with the intention of deceiving another and on which a reasonable person would and does rely to his or her detriment.

Puffery A salesperson's exaggerated claims concerning the quality of property offered for sale. Such claims involve opinions rather than facts and are not legally binding promises or warranties.

If a home seller claims that a new septic system was installed when it wasn't, does that constitute fraud?

5–2g Fraudulent Misrepresentation

A misrepresentation leads another to believe in a condition that is different from the condition that actually exists. This is often accomplished through a false or incorrect statement. Although persons sometimes make misrepresentations accidentally because they are unaware of the existing facts, the tort of **fraudulent misrepresentation**, or fraud, involves *intentional* deceit for personal gain. The tort includes several elements:

1. The misrepresentation of facts or conditions with knowledge that they are false or with reckless disregard for the truth.
2. An intent to induce another to rely on the misrepresentation.
3. Justifiable reliance by the deceived party.
4. Damage suffered as a result of the reliance.
5. A causal connection between the misrepresentation and the injury suffered.

For fraud to occur, more than mere **puffery**, or *seller's talk*, must be involved. Fraud exists only when a person represents as a fact something she or he knows is untrue. For instance, it is fraud to claim that a roof does not leak when one knows it does. Facts are objectively ascertainable, whereas seller's talk (such as "I am the best accountant in town") is not.

Case Example 5.15 Joseph Guido bought nine rental houses in Stillwater, New York. The houses shared a waste disposal system that was not functioning. Guido hired someone to design and install a new system. When town officials later discovered sewage on the property, Guido had the system partially replaced. He then represented to prospective buyers of the property, including Danny Revell, that the "Septic system [was] totally new—each field totally replaced." In response to a questionnaire from the buyers' bank, Guido denied any knowledge of environmental problems.

A month after the sale of the houses, the septic system failed and required substantial repairs. The buyers sued Guido for fraud. A jury found in favor of the plaintiffs and awarded damages. A state intermediate appellate court affirmed the judgment on appeal. Guido knew that the septic system was not totally new and that sewage had been released on the property (an environmental problem). He had misrepresented these facts to the buyers. The buyers' reliance on Guido's statements was justifiable because a visual inspection of the property did not reveal any problems.[13] ■

Statement of Fact versus Opinion Normally, the tort of misrepresentation or fraud occurs only when there is reliance on a *statement of fact*. Sometimes, however, the tort may involve reliance on a *statement of opinion* if the individual making the statement has a superior knowledge of the subject matter. For instance, when a lawyer makes a statement of opinion about the law in a state in which the lawyer is licensed to practice, a court would treat it as a statement of fact.

Negligent Misrepresentation Sometimes, a tort action can arise from misrepresentations that are made negligently rather than intentionally. The key difference between intentional and negligent misrepresentation is whether the person making the misrepresentation had actual knowledge of its falsity. Negligent misrepresentation requires only that the person making the statement or omission did not have a reasonable basis for believing its truthfulness.

Liability for negligent misrepresentation usually arises when the defendant who made the misrepresentation owed a duty of care to the plaintiff to supply correct information. Statements or omissions made by attorneys and accountants to their clients, for instance, can lead to liability for negligent misrepresentation.

---

13. *Revell v. Guido*, 124 A.D.3d 1006, 2 N.Y.S.3d 252 (3d Dept. 2015).

5–2h Wrongful Interference

The torts known as **business torts** generally involve wrongful interference with another's business rights. Business torts involving wrongful interference are generally divided into two categories: wrongful interference with a contractual relationship and wrongful interference with a business relationship.

Business Tort Wrongful interference with another's business rights and relationships.

Wrongful Interference with a Contractual Relationship Three elements are necessary for wrongful interference with a contractual relationship to occur:

1. A valid, enforceable contract must exist between two parties.

2. A third party must know that this contract exists.

3. The third party must *intentionally* induce a party to breach the contract.

   Classic Case Example 5.16 A classic case involved an opera singer, Johanna Wagner, who was under contract to sing for a man named Lumley for a specified period of years. A man named Gye, who knew of this contract, nonetheless "enticed" Wagner to refuse to carry out the agreement, and Wagner began to sing for Gye. Gye's action constituted a tort because it wrongfully interfered with the contractual relationship between Wagner and Lumley.[14] (Of course, Wagner's refusal to carry out the agreement also entitled Lumley to sue Wagner for breach of contract.)

   The body of tort law relating to intentional interference with a contractual relationship has expanded greatly in recent years. In principle, any lawful contract can be the basis for an action of this type. The contract could be between a firm and its employees or a firm and its customers. Sometimes, for instance, a competitor draws away one of a firm's key employees. Only if the original employer can show that the competitor knew of the contract's existence, and intentionally induced the breach, can damages be recovered from the competitor.

Opera singer Johanna Wagner is shown here in one of her many roles. She was under contract to sing for one person, but was enticed to break the contract and sing for someone else. Was a tort committed? If so, by whom?

Wrongful Interference with a Business Relationship Businesspersons devise countless schemes to attract customers, but they are prohibited from unreasonably interfering with another's business in their attempts to gain a share of the market. There is a difference between *competitive methods* and *predatory behavior*—actions undertaken with the intention of unlawfully driving competitors completely out of the market. Attempting to attract customers in general is a legitimate business practice, whereas specifically targeting the customers of a competitor is more likely to be predatory.

   Example 5.17 A shopping mall contains two athletic shoe stores: Joe's and Ultimate Sport. Joe's cannot station an employee at the entrance of Ultimate Sport to divert customers by telling them that Joe's will beat Ultimate Sport's prices. This type of activity constitutes the tort of wrongful interference with a business relationship, which is commonly considered to be an unfair trade practice. If this activity were permitted, Joe's would reap the benefits of Ultimate Sport's advertising.

Defenses to Wrongful Interference A person will not be liable for the tort of wrongful interference with a contractual or business relationship if it can be shown that the interference was justified or permissible. Bona fide competitive behavior is a permissible interference even if it results in the breaking of a contract.

   Example 5.18 If Antonio's Meats advertises so effectively that it induces Sam's Restaurant to break its contract with Burke's Meat Company, Burke's will be unable to recover against Antonio's Meats on a wrongful interference theory. After all, the public policy that favors free competition in advertising outweighs any possible instability that such competitive activity might cause in contractual relations.

---

14. *Lumley v. Gye*, 118 Eng.Rep. 749 (1853).

5–3 Intentional Torts against Property

Intentional torts against property include trespass to land, trespass to personal property, conversion, and disparagement of property. These torts are wrongful actions that interfere with individuals' legally recognized rights with regard to their land or personal property. The law distinguishes real property from personal property. *Real property* is land and things "permanently" attached to the land. *Personal property* consists of all other items, which are basically movable. Thus, a house and lot are real property, whereas the furniture inside the house is personal property. Cash, stocks, and bonds are also personal property.

5–3a Trespass to Land

A **trespass to land** occurs anytime a person, without permission, does any of the following:

1. Enters onto, above, or below the surface of land that is owned by another.
2. Causes anything to enter onto land owned by another.
3. Remains on land owned by another or permits anything to remain on it.

Actual harm to the land is not an essential element of this tort, because the tort is designed to protect the right of an owner to exclusive possession.

Common types of trespass to land include walking or driving on another's land, shooting a gun over the land, and throwing rocks at a building that belongs to someone else. Another common form of trespass involves constructing a building so that part of it is on an adjoining landowner's property.

Establishing Trespass Before a person can be a trespasser, the real property owner (or other person in actual and exclusive possession of the property) must establish that person as a trespasser. For instance, "posted" trespass signs expressly establish as a trespasser a person who ignores these signs and enters onto the property. Any person who enters onto property to commit an illegal act (such as a thief entering a lumberyard at night to steal lumber) is established impliedly as a trespasser, without posted signs. In contrast, a guest in your home is not a trespasser unless she or he has been asked to leave but refuses.

Liability for Harm At common law, a trespasser is liable for any damage caused to the property and generally cannot hold the owner liable for injuries sustained on the premises. This common law rule is being abandoned in many jurisdictions in favor of a *reasonable duty of care* rule that varies depending on the status of the parties.

For instance, a landowner may have a duty to post a notice that guard dogs patrol the property. Also, if young children are likely to be attracted to the property by some object, such as a swimming pool or a sand pile, and are injured, the landowner may be held liable under the *attractive nuisance doctrine*. An owner can normally use reasonable force to remove a trespasser from the premises—or detain the trespasser for a reasonable time—without liability for damages, however.

Defenses against Trespass to Land One defense to a claim of trespass to land is to show that the trespass was warranted. This may occur, for instance, when the trespasser entered the property to assist someone in danger.

Another defense is for the trespasser to show that he or she had a license to come onto the land. A *licensee* is one who is invited (or allowed to enter) onto the property of another for the licensee's benefit. A person who enters another's property to read an electric meter, for example, is a licensee. Another example of a licensee is someone who is camping on another person's land with the owner's permission but without paying for the privilege.

Note that licenses to enter are *revocable* by the property owner. If a property owner asks a meter reader to leave and the meter reader refuses to do so, the meter reader at that point becomes a trespasser.

Know This
What society and the law consider permissible often depends on the circumstances.

Trespass to Land Entry onto, above, or below the surface of land owned by another without the owner's permission or legal authorization.

What are some common types of trespass to land?

Konstantin L/Shutterstock.com

5–3b Trespass to Personal Property

Whenever an individual wrongfully takes or harms the personal property of another or otherwise interferes with the lawful owner's possession of personal property, **trespass to personal property** (also called *trespass to chattels* or *trespass to personalty*[15]) occurs. In this context, harm means not only destruction of the property, but also anything that diminishes its value, condition, or quality.

Trespass to personal property involves intentional meddling with a possessory interest (the right to possess), including barring an owner's access to personal property. **Example 5.19** Kelly takes Ryan's business law book as a practical joke and hides it so that Ryan is unable to find it for several days before the final examination. Here, Kelly has engaged in a trespass to personal property. (Kelly has also committed the tort of *conversion*—to be discussed next.)

If it can be shown that trespass to personal property was warranted, then a complete defense exists. Most states, for instance, allow automobile repair shops to retain a customer's car (under what is called an *artisan's lien*) when the customer refuses to pay for repairs already completed.

> **Trespass to Personal Property** Wrongfully taking or harming the personal property of another or otherwise interfering with the lawful owner's possession of personal property.

5–3c Conversion

Any act that deprives an owner of personal property or of the use of that property without the owner's permission and without just cause can constitute **conversion.** Even the taking of electronic records and data can form the basis of a conversion claim. Often, when conversion occurs, a trespass to personal property also occurs. The original taking of the personal property from the owner was a trespass, and wrongfully retaining the property is conversion.

> **Conversion** Wrongfully taking or retaining possession of an individual's personal property and placing it in the service of another.

Failure to Return Goods Conversion is the civil side of crimes related to theft, but it is not limited to theft. Even if the rightful owner consented to the initial taking of the property, so there was no theft or trespass, a failure to return the personal property may still be conversion. **Example 5.20** Chen borrows Mark's iPad Pro to use while traveling home from school for the holidays. When Chen returns to school, Mark asks for his iPad Pro back. Chen tells Mark that she gave it to her little brother for Christmas. In this situation, Mark can sue Chen for conversion, and Chen will have to either return the iPad Pro or pay damages equal to its replacement value.

> **Learning Objective 3**
> What conduct contitutes conversion?

Intention Conversion can occur even when a person mistakenly believes that she or he was entitled to the goods. In other words, good intentions are not a defense against conversion. Someone who buys stolen goods, for instance, can be sued for conversion even if he or she did not know that the goods were stolen. If the true owner of the goods sues the buyer and wins, the buyer must either return the property to the owner or pay the owner the full value of the property.

Case Example 5.21 Nicholas Mora worked for Welco Electronics, Inc., but had also established his own company, AQM Supplies. Mora used Welco's credit card without permission and deposited more than $375,000 into AQM's account, which he then transferred to his personal account. Welco sued. A California court held that Mora was liable for conversion. The court reasoned that when Mora misappropriated Welco's credit card and used it, he took part of Welco's credit balance with the credit-card company.[16]

> **Know This**
> It is the *intent* to do an act that is important in tort law, not the motive behind the intent.

> **Disparagement of Property** An economically injurious falsehood about another's product or property.

5–3d Disparagement of Property

Disparagement of property occurs when economically injurious falsehoods are made about another's product or property, rather than about another's reputation (as in the tort of defamation). Disparagement of property is a general term for torts specifically referred to as *slander of quality* or *slander of title*.

How can a portable credit-card terminal be used for conversion?

---

15. Pronounced *per-sun-ul-tee.*
16. *Welco Electronics, Inc. v. Mora,* 223 Cal.App.4th 202, 166 Cal.Rptr.3d 877 (2014).

Slander of Quality (Trade Libel) The publication of false information about another's product, alleging that it is not what its seller claims.

Publication of false information about another's product, alleging that it is not what its seller claims, constitutes the tort of **slander of quality,** or **trade libel.** To establish trade libel, the plaintiff must prove that the improper publication caused a third party to refrain from dealing with the plaintiff and that the plaintiff sustained economic damages (such as lost profits) as a result. An improper publication may be both a slander of quality and defamation of character. For example, a statement that disparages the quality of a product may also, by implication, disparage the character of the person who would sell such a product.

Slander of Title The publication of a statement that denies or casts doubt on another's legal ownership of property, causing financial loss to that property's owner.

When a publication denies or casts doubt on another's legal ownership of property, and the property's owner suffers financial loss as a result, the tort of **slander of title** may exist. Usually, this is an intentional tort that occurs when someone knowingly publishes an untrue statement about property with the intent of discouraging a third party from dealing with the property's owner. For instance, a car dealer would have difficulty attracting customers if competitors publish a notice that the dealer's stock consists of stolen automobiles.

5–4 Negligence

Negligence The failure to exercise the standard of care that a reasonable person would exercise in similar circumstances.

The tort of **negligence** occurs when someone suffers injury because of another's failure to fulfill a required *duty of care*. In contrast to intentional torts, in torts involving negligence, the tortfeasor neither wishes to bring about the consequences of the act nor believes that they will occur. The person's conduct merely creates a risk of such consequences. If no risk is created, there is no negligence. Moreover, the risk must be foreseeable—that is, it must be such that a reasonable person engaging in the same activity would anticipate the risk and guard against it. In determining what is reasonable conduct, courts consider the nature of the possible harm.

Many of the actions giving rise to the intentional torts discussed earlier in the chapter constitute negligence if the element of intent is missing (or cannot be proved). **Example 5.22** Juan walks up to Maya and intentionally shoves her. Maya falls and breaks an arm as a result. In this situation, Juan has committed an intentional tort (assault and battery). If Juan carelessly bumps into Maya, however, and she falls and breaks an arm as a result, Juan's action will constitute negligence. In either situation, Juan has committed a tort. ■

To succeed in a negligence action, the plaintiff must prove each of the following:

1. *Duty.* The defendant owed a duty of care to the plaintiff.
2. *Breach.* The defendant breached that duty.
3. *Causation.* The defendant's breach caused the plaintiff's injury.
4. *Damages.* The plaintiff suffered a legally recognizable injury.

Learning Objective 4
Identify the four elements of negligence.

We discuss each of these four elements of negligence next.

5–4a The Duty of Care and Its Breach

Duty of Care The duty of all persons, as established by tort law, to exercise a reasonable amount of care in their dealings with others. Failure to exercise due care, which is normally determined by the reasonable person standard, constitutes the tort of negligence.

Central to the tort of negligence is the concept of a **duty of care.** The basic principle underlying the duty of care is that people in society are free to act as they please so long as their actions do not infringe on the interests of others. When someone fails to comply with the duty to exercise reasonable care, a potentially tortious act may result.

Failure to live up to a standard of care may be an act (setting fire to a building) or an omission (neglecting to put out a campfire). It may be a careless act or a carefully performed but nevertheless dangerous act that results in injury. In determining whether the duty of care has been breached, courts consider several factors:

1. The nature of the act (whether it is outrageous or commonplace).
2. The manner in which the act was performed (cautiously versus heedlessly).
3. The nature of the injury (whether it is serious or slight).

Creating even a very slight risk of a dangerous explosion might be unreasonable, whereas creating a distinct possibility of someone's burning his or her fingers on a stove might be reasonable.

The question in the following case was whether a fraternity's local chapter and its officers owed a duty of care to their pledges.

Case 5.2

Bogenberger v. Pi Kappa Alpha Corporation, Inc.

Supreme Court of Illinois, 2018 IL 120951, ___ N.E.3d ___ (2018).

Background and Facts David Bogenberger attended a pledge event at the Pi Kappa Alpha fraternity house at Northern Illinois University (NIU). The NIU Chapter officers planned an evening of hazing, during which the pledges were required to consume vodka provided by the fraternity's members. By the end of the night, Bogenberger's blood-alcohol level was more than five times the legal limit. He lost consciousness. The NIU Chapter officers failed to seek medical attention, and Bogenberger died during the night.

Bogenberger's father, Gary, filed a complaint in an Illinois state court against the NIU Chapter of the fraternity and its officers, on a theory of negligence. Gary alleged that the defendants required the pledges—including his son, David—to participate in the pledge event and to consume excessive and dangerous amounts of alcohol in violation of the state's hazing statute.[a] The court dismissed the complaint. A state intermediate appellate court reversed the dismissal. The defendants appealed to the Illinois Supreme Court.

In the Words of the Court

Justice *FREEMAN* delivered the judgment of the court, with opinion.

* * * *

* * * Every person owes a duty of ordinary care to all others to guard against injuries which naturally flow as a reasonably probable and foreseeable consequence of an act * * *. *Where an individual's course of action creates a foreseeable risk of injury, the individual has a duty to protect others from such injury.* [Emphasis added.]

* * * *

To determine whether the NIU Chapter and officers owed a duty to the pledges, *we look to the reasonable foreseeability of the injury, the likelihood of the injury, the magnitude of the burden of guarding against the injury, and the consequences of placing*

---

a. As a result of the pledge event, the Pi Kappa Alpha national organization revoked the NIU Chapter's charter, and criminal charges were brought against those who participated in the hazing.

that burden on the defendant. In deciding reasonable foreseeability, an injury is not reasonably foreseeable where it results from freakish, bizarre, or fantastic circumstances. Regarding the first two factors, we cannot say that * * * an injury resulting from hazing is freakish, bizarre, or occurs under fantastic circumstances. The existence of hazing statutes across the country, including the [national Pi Kappa Alpha organization's] written policy against hazing as well as Illinois's hazing statute, indicates that injury due to hazing is reasonably foreseeable. We also find that injuries resulting from hazing events, especially those involving the consumption of large amounts of alcohol, are likely to occur. When pledges are required to consume large quantities of alcohol in short periods of time, their risk of injury is great—not only physical injury due to their inebriated condition but injury or death resulting from alcohol poisoning. [Emphasis added.]

Regarding the last two factors, we find that the magnitude of the burden of guarding against injury is small and the consequences of placing that burden on the NIU Chapter and officers are reasonable. To require the NIU Chapter and officers to guard against hazing injuries is infinitesimal. Hazing is not only against the law in Illinois, it is against the university's rules as well as the Pi Kappa Alpha fraternity's rules. There can be no real burden to require the NIU Chapter and officers to comply with the law and the university's and fraternity's rules. And it seems quite reasonable to place that burden on the very people who are in charge of planning and carrying out the pledge event. We find that the NIU Chapter and the officers owed a duty to the pledges, including David, and plaintiff has sufficiently alleged a claim for negligence against them.

Decision and Remedy The Illinois Supreme Court affirmed the intermediate appellate court's reversal of the trial court's dismissal. Gary's complaint against the NIU Chapter of Pi Kappa Alpha (and its officers) could proceed.

(Continues)

Critical Thinking

• **Legal Environment** *The NIU Chapter invited nonmember sorority women to participate in the hazing event by filling the pledges' cups with vodka and directing them to drink it. Did these women owe a duty of care to the pledges? Discuss.*

• **What If the Facts Were Different?** *Suppose that the pledges' attendance at the hazing event had been optional, and the NIU Chapter had furnished alcohol, but not required its consumption. Would the result have been different? Explain.*

Reasonable Person Standard The standard of behavior expected of a hypothetical "reasonable person." It is the standard against which negligence is measured and that must be observed to avoid liability for negligence.

> "A little neglect may breed great mischief."
>
> **Benjamin Franklin,**
> 1706–1790
> (American politician and inventor)

Business Invitee A person, such as a customer or a client, who is invited onto business premises by the owner of those premises for business purposes.

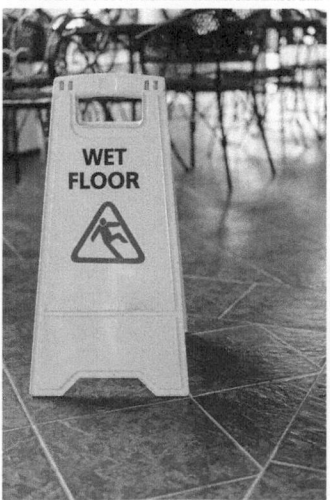

Does a "Wet Floor" sign relieve a restaurant owner from being held negligent if a customer slips?

The Reasonable Person Standard Tort law measures duty by the **reasonable person standard.** In determining whether a duty of care has been breached, the courts ask how a reasonable person would have acted in the same circumstances. The reasonable person standard is said to be (though in an absolute sense it cannot be) objective. It is not necessarily how a particular person *would* act. It is society's judgment on how people *should* act. If the so-called reasonable person existed, he or she would be careful, conscientious, even tempered, and honest.

The degree of care to be exercised varies, depending on the defendant's occupation or profession, her or his relationship with the plaintiff, and other factors. Generally, whether an action constitutes a breach of the duty of care is determined on a case-by-case basis. The outcome depends on how the judge (or jury, in a jury trial) decides a reasonable person in the position of the defendant would act in the particular circumstances of the case.

Note that the courts frequently use the reasonable person standard in other areas of law as well as in negligence cases. Indeed, the principle that individuals are required to exercise a reasonable standard of care in their activities is a pervasive concept in many areas of business law.

The Duty of Landowners Landowners are expected to exercise reasonable care to protect persons coming onto their property from harm. In some jurisdictions, landowners are held to owe a duty to protect even trespassers against certain risks. Landowners who rent or lease premises to tenants are expected to exercise reasonable care to ensure that the tenants and their guests are not harmed in common areas, such as stairways, entryways, and laundry rooms.

Duty to Warn Business Invitees of Risks. Retailers and other firms that explicitly or implicitly invite persons to come onto their premises have a duty to exercise reasonable care to protect these **business invitees.** The duty normally requires storeowners to warn business invitees of foreseeable risks, such as construction zones and wet floors, about which the owners knew or *should have known.*

Example 5.23 Liz enters a Crown Market, slips on a wet floor, and sustains injuries as a result. If there was no sign warning that the floor was wet when Liz slipped, the owner of Crown Market would be liable for damages. A court would hold that the business owner was negligent because the owner failed to exercise a reasonable degree of care in protecting the store's customers against foreseeable risks about which the owner knew or should have known. That a patron might slip on the wet floor and be injured was a foreseeable risk, and the owner should have taken care to avoid this risk or to warn the customer of it (by posting a sign or setting out orange cones, for instance). ▪

The business owner also has a duty to discover and remove any hidden dangers that might injure a customer or other invitee. Hidden dangers might include uneven surfaces or defects in the pavement of a parking lot or walkway, or merchandise that has fallen off a store shelf.

Obvious Risks Are an Exception. Some risks, of course, are so obvious that the owner need not warn of them. For instance, a business owner does not need to warn customers to open a door before attempting to walk through it. Other risks, however, may seem obvious to a business owner but may not be so to someone else, such as a child. In addition, even an obvious risk does not necessarily excuse a business owner from the duty to protect customers from foreseeable harm.

Case Example 5.24 During a trip to a Costco warehouse store in Nevada, Stephen Foster tripped and fell over a wooden pallet and sustained injuries. A Costco employee who was restocking the shelves had placed the pallet in the aisle without any barricades. When Foster sued Costco for negligence, Costco argued that it had not breached its duty by failing to warn customers because the pallet was open and obvious. A lower court agreed and granted a summary judgment in Costco's favor, but the Supreme Court of Nevada reversed. The court held that the open and obvious nature of a dangerous condition does not *automatically* relieve a business owner from the general duty of reasonable care. Every situation is different. Therefore, Foster was entitled to proceed to trial and argue that Costco should have used barricades or warnings to protect customers.[17]

The Duty of Professionals Persons who possess superior knowledge, skill, or training are held to a higher standard of care than others. Professionals—such as physicians, dentists, architects, engineers, accountants, and lawyers—are required to have a standard minimum level of special knowledge and ability. In determining what constitutes reasonable care, the law takes their training and expertise into account. Thus, an accountant's conduct is judged not by the reasonable person standard, but by the reasonable accountant standard.

If a professional violates her or his duty of care toward a client, the professional may be sued for **malpractice,** which is essentially professional negligence. For instance, a patient might sue a physician for *medical malpractice.* A client might sue an attorney for *legal malpractice.*

> **Malpractice** Professional misconduct or the lack of the requisite degree of skill as a professional. Negligence on the part of a professional, such as a physician, is commonly referred to as malpractice.

5–4b Causation

Another element necessary in a negligence action is *causation.* If a person breaches a duty of care and someone suffers an injury, the wrongful act must have caused the harm for it to constitute the tort of negligence.

Courts Ask Two Questions In deciding whether there is causation, the court must address two questions:

1. *Is there causation in fact?* Did the injury occur because of the defendant's act, or would it have occurred anyway? If an injury would not have occurred without the defendant's act, then there is **causation in fact.**

   Causation in fact can usually be determined by the use of the *but for* test: "but for" the wrongful act, the injury would not have occurred. Theoretically, causation in fact is limitless. One could claim, for example, that "but for" the creation of the world, a particular injury would not have occurred. Thus, as a practical matter, the law has to establish limits, and it does so through the concept of proximate cause.

> **Causation in Fact** An act or omission without which an event would not have occurred.

2. *Was the act the proximate cause of the injury?* **Proximate cause,** or legal cause, exists when the connection between an act and an injury is strong enough to justify imposing liability. Courts use proximate cause to limit the scope of the defendant's liability to a subset of the total number of potential plaintiffs that might have been harmed by the defendant's actions.

   Example 5.25 Ackerman carelessly leaves a campfire burning. The fire not only burns down the forest but also sets off an explosion in a nearby chemical plant that spills chemicals into a river,

> **Proximate Cause** Legal cause. It exists when the connection between an act and an injury is strong enough to justify imposing liability.

---

17. *Foster v. Costco Wholesale Corp.,* 128 Nev.Adv.Op. 71, 291 P.3d 150 (2012).

killing all the fish for a hundred miles downstream and ruining the economy of a tourist resort. Should Ackerman be liable to the resort owners? To the tourists whose vacations were ruined? These are questions of proximate cause that a court must decide.

Both questions concerning causation must be answered in the affirmative for tort liability to arise. If a defendant's action constitutes causation in fact but a court decides that the action was not the proximate cause of the plaintiff's injury, the causation requirement has not been met—and the defendant normally will not be liable to the plaintiff.

Know This

Proximate cause can be thought of in terms of social policy. Should the defendant be made to bear the loss instead of the plaintiff?

Foreseeability   Questions of proximate cause are linked to the concept of foreseeability. It would be unfair to impose liability on a defendant unless the defendant's actions created a foreseeable risk of injury. Probably the most cited case on proximate cause is the *Palsgraf* case, which is discussed in this chapter's *Landmark in the Law* feature. In determining the issue of proximate cause, the court addressed the following question: Does a defendant's duty of care extend only to those who may be injured as a result of a foreseeable risk, or does it also extend to a person whose injury could not reasonably have been foreseen?

Palsgraf v. Long Island Railroad Co. (1928)

Landmark in the Law

In 1928, the New York Court of Appeals (that state's highest court) issued its decision in *Palsgraf v. Long Island Railroad Co.,*[a] a case that has become a landmark in negligence law and proximate cause.

The Facts of the Case   The plaintiff, Helen Palsgraf, was waiting for a train on a station platform. A man carrying a small package wrapped in newspaper was rushing to catch a train that had begun to move away from the platform. As the man attempted to jump aboard the moving train, he seemed unsteady and about to fall. A railroad guard on the train car reached forward to grab him, and another guard on the platform pushed him from behind to help him board the train. In the process, the man's package fell on the railroad tracks and exploded, because it contained fireworks. The repercussions of the explosion caused scales at the other end of the train platform to fall on Palsgraf, who was injured as a result. She sued the railroad company for damages in a New York state court.

The Question of Proximate Cause   At the trial, the jury found that the railroad guards were negligent in their conduct. On appeal, the question before the New York Court of Appeals was whether the conduct of the railroad guards was the proximate cause of Palsgraf's injuries. In other words, did the guards' duty of care extend to Palsgraf, who was outside the zone of danger and whose injury could not reasonably have been foreseen?

The court stated that the question of whether the guards were negligent *with respect to Palsgraf* depended on whether her injury was *reasonably foreseeable* by the railroad guards. Although the guards may have acted negligently with respect to the man boarding the train, this had no bearing on the question of their negligence with respect to Palsgraf. This was not a situation in which a person committed an act so potentially harmful (for example, firing a gun at a building) that he or she would be held responsible for any harm that resulted. The court stated that here "there was nothing in the situation to suggest to the most cautious mind that

the parcel wrapped in newspaper would spread wreckage through the station." The court thus concluded that the railroad guards were not negligent with respect to Palsgraf, because her injury was not reasonably foreseeable.

Application to Today's World   *The* Palsgraf *case established foreseeability as the test for proximate cause. Today, the courts continue to apply this test in determining proximate cause—and thus tort liability for injuries. Generally, if the victim of a harm or the consequences of a harm done are unforeseeable, there is no proximate cause. Note, though, that in the online environment, distinctions based on physical proximity, such as the "zone of danger" cited by the court in this case, are largely inapplicable.*

a. 248 N.Y. 339, 162 N.E. 99 (1928).

5–4c The Injury Requirement and Damages

For a tort to have been committed, the plaintiff must have suffered a *legally recognizable* injury. To recover damages (receive compensation), the plaintiff must have suffered some loss, harm, wrong, or invasion of a protected interest. If no harm or injury results from a given negligent action, there is nothing to compensate—and no tort exists. **Example 5.26** If you carelessly bump into a passerby, who stumbles and falls as a result, you may be liable in tort if the passerby is injured in the fall. If the person is unharmed, however, there normally cannot be a suit for damages because no injury was suffered.

Essentially, the purpose of tort law is to compensate for legally recognized injuries resulting from wrongful acts. Thus, compensatory damages are the norm in negligence cases. As noted earlier, a court will award punitive damages only if the defendant's conduct was grossly negligent, reflecting an intentional failure to perform a duty with reckless disregard of the consequences to others.

Snowleopard1/E+/Getty Images

Injuries from car accidents can cause handicaps that last a lifetime. Do such injuries satisfy the injury requirement for a finding of negligence?

5–4d Good Samaritan Statutes

Most states now have what are called **Good Samaritan statutes.**[18] Under these statutes, someone who is aided voluntarily by another cannot turn around and sue the "Good Samaritan" for negligence. These laws were passed largely to protect physicians and medical personnel who volunteer their services in emergency situations to those in need, such as individuals hurt in car accidents.

Good Samaritan Statute A state statute stipulating that persons who provide emergency services to, or rescue, someone in peril cannot be sued for negligence unless they act recklessly and cause further harm.

5–4e Dram Shop Acts

Many states have also passed **dram shop acts,**[19] under which a bar owner or bartender may be held liable for injuries caused by a person who became intoxicated while drinking at the bar. The owner or bartender may also be held responsible for continuing to serve a person who was already intoxicated.

Some states' statutes also impose liability on *social hosts* (persons hosting parties) for injuries caused by guests who became intoxicated at the hosts' homes. Under these statutes, it is unnecessary to prove that the bar owner, bartender, or social host was negligent. **Example 5.27** Monica hosts a Super Bowl party at which Brett, a minor, sneaks alcoholic drinks. Monica is potentially liable for damages resulting from Brett's drunk driving after the party, even if she was not negligent in serving the alcoholic beverages.

Dram Shop Act A state statute that imposes liability on bar owners, as well as bartenders and social hosts who serve alcohol, for injuries resulting from accidents caused by intoxicated persons when the sellers or servers of alcoholic drinks contributed to the intoxication.

5–4f Defenses to Negligence

Defendants often defend against negligence claims by asserting that the plaintiffs failed to prove the existence of one or more of the required elements for negligence. Additionally, there are three basic *affirmative* defenses in negligence cases (defenses that a defendant can use to avoid liability even if the facts are as the plaintiff states): (1) assumption of risk, (2) superseding cause, and (3) contributory and comparative negligence.

---

18. These laws derive their name from the Good Samaritan story in the Bible. In the story, a traveler who had been robbed and beaten lay along the roadside, ignored by those passing by. Eventually, a man from the region of Samaria (the "Good Samaritan") stopped to render assistance to the injured person.

19. Historically, a *dram* was a small unit of liquid, and spirits were sold in drams. Thus, a dram shop was a place where liquor was sold in drams.

Assumption of Risk A defense to negligence that bars a plaintiff from recovering for injuries or damage suffered as a result of risks he or she knew of and voluntarily assumed.

Assumption of Risk A plaintiff who voluntarily enters into a risky situation, knowing the risk involved, will not be allowed to recover. This is the defense of **assumption of risk,** which requires two elements:

1. Knowledge of the risk.
2. Voluntary assumption of the risk.

This defense is frequently asserted when a plaintiff is injured during recreational activities that involve known risk, such as skiing and skydiving. Courts do not apply the assumption of risk doctrine in certain situations, such as those involving emergencies, however.

Assumption of risk can apply not only to participants in sporting events, but also to spectators and bystanders who are injured while attending those events. In the following *Spotlight Case*, the issue was whether a spectator at a baseball game voluntarily assumed the risk of being hit by an errant ball thrown while the players were warming up before the game.

✳ Spotlight on the Seattle Mariners: Case 5.3

Taylor v. Baseball Club of Seattle, L.P.

Court of Appeals of Washington, 132 Wash.App. 32, 130 P.3d 835 (2006).

Background and Facts Delinda Middleton Taylor went to a Mariners baseball game at Safeco Field with her boyfriend and two minor sons. Their seats were four rows up from the field along the right field foul line. They arrived more than an hour before the game began so that they could see the players warm up and get their autographs. When she walked in, Taylor saw that Mariners pitcher Freddy Garcia was throwing a ball back and forth with José Mesa right in front of their seats.

As Taylor stood in front of her seat, she looked away from the field, and a ball thrown by Mesa got past Garcia and struck her in the face, causing serious injuries. Taylor sued the Mariners for the allegedly negligent warm-up throw. The Mariners filed a motion for a summary judgment in which they argued that Taylor, a Mariners fan, was familiar with baseball and the inherent risk of balls entering the stands, and therefore assumed the risk of her injury. The trial court granted the motion and dismissed Taylor's case. Taylor appealed.

In the Words of the Court
DWYER, J. [Judge]
* * * *

* * * For many decades, courts have required baseball stadiums to screen some seats—generally those behind home plate—to provide protection to spectators who choose it.

Many fans arrive at baseball games early so they can watch the players warm up.

© Alan C. Heison/Shutterstock.com

A sport spectator's assumption of risk and a defendant sports team's duty of care are accordingly discerned under the doctrine of primary assumption of risk. * * * "Implied *primary* assumption of risk arises where a plaintiff has impliedly consented (often in advance of any negligence by defendant) to relieve defendant of a duty to plaintiff regarding specific known and appreciated risks." [Emphasis in original.]
* * * *

Under this implied primary assumption of risk, defendant must show that plaintiff had full subjective understanding of the specific risk, both its nature and presence, and that he or she voluntarily chose to encounter the risk.

* * * It is undisputed that the warm-up is part of the sport, that spectators such as Taylor purposely attend that portion of the event, and that the Mariners permit ticket-holders to view the warm-up.

* * * We find the fact that Taylor was injured during warm-up is not legally significant because that portion of the event is necessarily incident to the game.
* * * *

Here, there is no evidence that the circumstances leading to Taylor's injury constituted an unusual danger. It is undisputed that it is the normal, everyday practice at all levels of baseball for pitchers to warm up in the manner that led to this incident. *The risk of injuries such as Taylor's are within the normal comprehension of a spectator who is familiar with the game.* Indeed, the possibility of an errant ball entering the stands is part of the game's attraction for many spectators. [Emphasis added.]

* * * The record contains substantial evidence regarding Taylor's familiarity with the game. She attended many of her sons' baseball games, she witnessed balls entering the stands, she had watched Mariners' games both at the Kingdome and on television, and she knew that there was no screen protecting her seats, which were close to the field. In fact, as she walked to her seat she saw the players warming up and was excited about being in an unscreened area where her party might get autographs from the players and catch balls.

Decision and Remedy The state intermediate appellate court affirmed the lower court's judgment. As a spectator who chose to sit in an unprotected area of seats, Taylor voluntarily undertook the risk associated with being hit by an errant baseball thrown during warm-ups before the start of the game.

Critical Thinking

• **What If the Facts Were Different?** *Would the result in this case have been different if Taylor's minor son, rather than Taylor herself, had been struck by the ball? Should courts apply the doctrine of assumption of risk to children? Discuss.*

Superseding Cause An unforeseeable intervening event may break the connection between a wrongful act and an injury to another. If so, the event acts as a *superseding cause*—that is, it relieves a defendant of liability for injuries caused by the intervening event.

Example 5.28 While riding his bicycle, Derrick negligently hits Julie, who is walking on the sidewalk. As a result of the impact, Julie falls and fractures her hip. While she is waiting for help to arrive, a small plane crashes nearby and explodes, and some of the fiery debris hits her, causing her to sustain severe burns. Derrick will be liable for Julie's fractured hip because the risk of hitting her with his bicycle was foreseeable. Normally, though, Derrick will not be liable for the burns caused by the plane crash, because the risk of a plane's crashing nearby and injuring Julie was not foreseeable.

Contributory Negligence All individuals are expected to exercise a reasonable degree of care in looking out for themselves. In the past, under the common law doctrine of **contributory negligence,** a plaintiff who was also negligent (who failed to exercise a reasonable degree of care) could not recover anything from the defendant. Under this rule, no matter how insignificant the plaintiff's negligence was relative to the defendant's negligence, the plaintiff was precluded from recovering any damages. Today, only a few jurisdictions still follow this doctrine.

Contributory Negligence A rule in tort law, used in only a few states, that completely bars the plaintiff from recovering any damages if the harm suffered is partly the plaintiff's own fault.

Comparative Negligence In most states, the doctrine of contributory negligence has been replaced by a **comparative negligence** standard. Under this standard, both the plaintiff's and the defendant's negligence are computed, and the liability for damages is distributed accordingly.

Some jurisdictions have adopted a "pure" form of comparative negligence that allows a plaintiff to recover, even if the extent of his or her fault is greater than that of the defendant. For instance, if a plaintiff was 80 percent at fault and the defendant 20 percent at fault, the plaintiff may recover 20 percent of his or her damages.

Many states' comparative negligence statutes, however, contain a "50 percent" rule that prevents a plaintiff from recovering any damages if she or he was more than 50 percent at fault. Under this rule, a plaintiff who is 35 percent at fault could recover 65 percent of his or her damages, but a plaintiff who is 65 percent at fault could recover nothing.

Comparative Negligence A rule in tort law, used in the majority of states, that reduces the plaintiff's recovery in proportion to the plaintiff's degree of fault, rather than barring recovery completely.

5–5 Strict Liability

Another category of torts is called **strict liability,** or *liability without fault.* Intentional torts and torts of negligence involve acts that depart from a reasonable standard of care and cause injuries. Under the doctrine of strict liability, liability for injury is imposed for reasons other than fault.

Strict Liability Liability regardless of fault, which is imposed on those engaged in abnormally dangerous activities, on persons who keep dangerous animals, and on manufacturers or sellers that introduce into commerce defective and unreasonably dangerous goods.

5–5a Abnormally Dangerous Activities

Strict liability for damages proximately caused by an abnormally dangerous or exceptional activity is one application of this doctrine. Courts apply the doctrine of strict liability in such cases because of the extreme risk of the activity. For instance, even if blasting with dynamite is performed with all reasonable care, there is still a risk of injury. Because of the potential for harm, the person who is engaged in an abnormally dangerous activity—and benefits from it—is responsible for paying for any injuries caused by that activity. Although there is no fault, there is still responsibility because of the dangerous nature of the undertaking.

5–5b Other Applications of Strict Liability

Learning Objective 5

What is meant by strict liability? In what circumstances is strict liability applied?

The strict liability principle is also applied in other situations. Persons who keep wild animals, for instance, are strictly liable for any harm inflicted by the animals. In addition, an owner of domestic animals may be strictly liable for harm caused by those animals if the owner knew, or should have known, that the animals were dangerous or had a propensity to harm others.

A significant application of strict liability is in the area of *product liability*—liability of manufacturers and sellers for harmful or defective products. Liability here is a matter of social policy. Manufacturers and sellers can better bear the cost of injuries, and because they profit from making and selling the products, they should be responsible for the injuries the products cause.

Practice and Review

Elaine Sweeney went to Ragged Mountain Ski Resort in New Hampshire with a friend. Elaine went snow tubing down a run designed exclusively for snow tubers. No Ragged Mountain employees were present in the snow-tube area to instruct Elaine on the proper use of a snow tube. On her fourth run down the trail, Elaine crossed over the center line between snow-tube lanes, collided with another snow tuber, and was injured. Elaine filed a negligence action against Ragged Mountain seeking compensation for the injuries that she sustained. Two years earlier, the New Hampshire state legislature had enacted a statute that prohibited a person who participates in the sport of skiing from suing a ski-area operator for injuries caused by the risks inherent in skiing. Using the information presented in the chapter, answer the following questions.

1. What defense will Ragged Mountain probably assert?

2. The central question in this case is whether the state statute establishing that skiers assume the risks inherent in the sport applies to Elaine's suit. What would your decision be on this issue? Why?

3. Suppose that the court concludes that the statute applies only to skiing and not to snow tubing. Will Elaine's lawsuit be successful? Explain.

4. Now suppose that the jury concludes that Elaine was partly at fault for the accident. Under what theory might her damages be reduced in proportion to how much her actions contributed to the accident and her resulting injuries?

Debate This

Each time a state legislature enacts a law that applies the assumption of risk doctrine to a particular sport, participants in that sport suffer.

Key Terms

actionable 127

actual malice 131

appropriation 133

assault 126

assumption of risk 144

battery 126

business invitee 140

business tort 135

causation in fact 141

comparative negligence 145

compensatory damages 124

contributory negligence 145

conversion 137

damages 124

defamation 128

defense 125

disparagement of property 137

dram shop act 143

duty of care 138

fraudulent misrepresentation 134

general damages 124

Good Samaritan statute 143

intentional tort 125

libel 128

malpractice 141

negligence 138

privilege 130

proximate cause 141

puffery 134

punitive damages 124

reasonable person standard 140

slander 128

slander of quality (trade libel) 138

slander of title 138

special damages 124

strict liability 145

tort 123

tortfeasor 125

transferred intent 126

trespass to land 136

trespass to personal property 137

Chapter Summary: Tort Law

Intentional Torts against Persons	1. *Assault and battery*—An assault is an unexcused and intentional act that causes another person to be apprehensive of immediate physical harm. A battery is an assault that results in actual physical contact.
	2. *False imprisonment*—The intentional confinement or restraint of another person's movement without justification.
	3. *Intentional infliction of emotional distress*—An extreme and outrageous act, intentionally committed, that results in severe emotional distress to another.
	4. *Defamation (libel or slander)*—A false statement of fact, not made under privilege, that is communicated to a third person and that causes damage to a person's reputation. For public figures, the plaintiff must also prove actual malice.
	5. *Invasion of the right to privacy*—Includes four types: wrongful intrusion into a person's private activities; publication of information that places a person in a false light; public disclosure of private facts that an ordinary person would find objectionable; and appropriation of identity, which involves the use of a person's name, likeness, or other identifying characteristic, without permission and for a commercial purpose. Most states have enacted statutes establishing appropriation of identity as the tort of *appropriation*, or right of publicity. Courts differ on the degree of likeness required.
	6. *Fraudulent misrepresentation*—A false representation made by one party, through misstatement of facts or through conduct, with the intention of deceiving another and on which the other reasonably relies to his or her detriment. Negligent misrepresentation occurs when a person supplies information without having a reasonable basis for believing its truthfulness.
	7. *Wrongful interference*—The knowing, intentional interference by a third party with an enforceable contractual relationship or an established business relationship between other parties for the purpose of advancing the economic interests of the third party.
Intentional Torts against Property	1. *Trespass to land*—The invasion of another's real property without consent or privilege.
	2. *Trespass to personal property*—Unlawfully damaging or interfering with the owner's right to use, possess, or enjoy her or his personal property.
	3. *Conversion*—Wrongfully taking, retaining, or using the personal property of another without permission.
	4. *Disparagement of property*—Any economically injurious falsehood that is made about another's product or property. The term includes the torts of *slander of quality* and *slander of title*.

(*Continues*)

Negligence	Negligence is the failure to exercise the standard of care that a reasonable person would apply in similar circumstances. A plaintiff must prove that a legal duty of care existed, that the defendant breached that duty, that the breach caused the plaintiff's injury, and that the plaintiff suffered a legally recognizable injury. 1. *Good Samaritan statutes*—State laws that protect those who voluntarily aid another from being sued for negligence. 2. *Dram shop acts*—State laws that impose liability on bar owners, bartenders, or persons hosting parties for injuries caused by intoxicated persons when the sellers or servers contributed to the intoxication. 3. *Defenses to negligence*—The basic affirmative defenses in negligence cases are assumption of risk, superseding cause, and contributory or comparative negligence.
Strict Liability	Under the doctrine of strict liability, parties may be held liable, regardless of the degree of care exercised, for damages or injuries caused by their products or activities. Strict liability includes liability for harms caused by abnormally dangerous activities, by dangerous animals, and by defective products (product liability).

Issue Spotters

1. Jana leaves her truck's motor running while she enters a Kwik-Pik Store. The truck's transmission engages, and the vehicle crashes into a gas pump, starting a fire that spreads to a warehouse on the next block. The warehouse collapses, causing its billboard to fall and injure Lou, a bystander. Can Lou recover from Jana? Why or why not? (See *Negligence*.)

2. A water pipe bursts, flooding a Metal Fabrication Company utility room and tripping the circuit breakers on a panel in the room. Metal Fabrication contacts Nouri, a licensed electrician with five years' experience, to check the damage and turn the breakers back on. Without testing for short circuits, which Nouri knows that he should do, he tries to switch on a breaker. He is electrocuted, and his wife sues Metal Fabrication for damages, alleging negligence. What might the firm successfully claim in defense? (See *Negligence*.)

   —Check your answers to the *Issue Spotters* against the answers provided in Appendix D at the end of this text.

Business Scenarios and Case Problems

5–1. Defamation. Richard is an employee of the Dun Construction Corp. While delivering materials to a construction site, he carelessly backs Dun's truck into a passenger vehicle driven by Green. This is Richard's second accident in six months. When the company owner, Dun, learns of this latest accident, a heated discussion ensues, and Dun fires Richard. Dun is so angry that he immediately writes a letter to the union of which Richard is a member and to all other construction companies in the community. In it, Dun states that Richard is the "worst driver in the city" and that "anyone who hires him is asking for legal liability." Richard files a suit against Dun, alleging libel on the basis of the statements made in the letters. Discuss. (See *Intentional Torts Against Persons*.)

5–2. Liability to Business Invitees. Kim went to Ling's Market to pick up a few items for dinner. It was a stormy day, and the wind had blown water through the market's door each time it opened. As Kim entered through the door, she slipped and fell in the rainwater that had accumulated on the floor. The manager knew of the weather conditions but had not posted any sign to warn customers of the water hazard. Kim injured her back as a result of the fall and sued Ling's for damages. Can Ling's be held liable for negligence? Discuss. (See *Negligence*.)

5–3. Spotlight on Intentional Torts—Defamation. Sharon Yeagle was an assistant to the vice president of student affairs at Virginia Polytechnic Institute and State University (Virginia Tech). As part of her duties, Yeagle helped students participate in the Governor's Fellows Program. The *Collegiate Times*, Virginia Tech's student newspaper, published an article about the university's success in placing students in the program. The article's text surrounded a block quotation attributed to Yeagle with the phrase "Director of Butt Licking" under her name. Yeagle sued the *Collegiate Times* for defamation. She argued that the phrase implied the commission of sodomy and was therefore actionable. What is *Collegiate Times*'s defense to this claim? [*Yeagle v. Collegiate Times*, 497 S.E.2d 136 (Va. 1998)] (See *Intentional Torts Against Persons*.)

**5–4. Business Case Problem with Sample Answer—
Negligence.** At the Weatherford Hotel in Flagstaff, Arizona, in Room 59, a balcony extends across thirty inches of the room's only window, leaving a twelve-inch gap with a three-story drop to the concrete below. A sign prohibits smoking in the room but invites guests to "step out onto the balcony" to smoke. Toni Lucario was a guest in Room 59 when she climbed out of the window and fell to her death. Patrick McMurtry, her estate's personal representative, filed a suit against the Weatherford. Did the hotel breach a duty of care to Lucario? What might the Weatherford assert in its defense? Explain. [*McMurtry v. Weatherford Hotel, Inc.*, 293 P.3d 520 (Ariz. App. 2013)] (See *Negligence*.)

—**For a sample answer to Problem 5–4, go to Appendix E at the end of this text.**

5–5. Negligence. Ronald Rawls and Zabian Bailey were in an auto accident in Bridgeport, Connecticut. Bailey rear-ended Rawls at a stoplight. Evidence showed it was more likely than not that Bailey failed to apply his brakes in time to avoid the collision, failed to turn his vehicle to avoid the collision, failed to keep his vehicle under control, and was inattentive to his surroundings. Rawls filed a suit in a Connecticut state court against his insurance company, Progressive Northern Insurance Co., to obtain benefits under an underinsured motorist clause, alleging that Bailey had been negligent. Could Rawls collect? Discuss. [*Rawls v. Progressive Northern Insurance Co.*, 310 Conn. 768, 83 A.3d 576 (2014)] (See *Negligence*.)

5–6. Negligence. Charles Robison, an employee of West Star Transportation, Inc., was ordered to cover an unevenly loaded flatbed trailer with a 150-pound tarpaulin. The load included uncrated equipment and pallet crates of different heights, about thirteen feet off the ground at its highest point. While standing on the load, manipulating the tarpaulin without safety equipment or assistance, Robison fell headfirst and sustained a traumatic head injury. He filed a suit against West Star to recover for his injury. Was West Star "negligent in failing to provide a reasonably safe place to work," as Robison claimed? Explain. [*West Star Transportation, Inc. v. Robison*, 457 S.W.3d 178 (Tex.App.—Amarillo 2015)] (See *Negligence*.)

5–7. Negligence. DSC Industrial Supply and Road Rider Supply are located in North Kitsap Business Park in Seattle, Washington. Both firms are owned by Paul and Suzanne Marshall. The Marshalls had outstanding commercial loans from Frontier Bank. The bank dispatched one of its employees, Suzette Gould, to North Kitsap to "spread Christmas cheer" to the Marshalls as an expression of appreciation for their business. Approaching the entry to Road Rider, Gould tripped over a concrete "wheel stop" and fell, suffering a broken arm and a dislocated elbow. The stop was not clearly visible, it had not been painted a contrasting color, and it was not marked with a sign. Gould had not been aware of the stop before she tripped over it. Is North Kitsap liable to Gould for negligence? Explain. [*Gould v. North Kitsap Business Park Management, LLC*, 192 Wash.App. 1021 (2016)] (See *Negligence*.)

5–8. Defamation. Jonathan Martin, an offensive lineman with the Miami Dolphins, abruptly quit the team and checked himself into a hospital seeking psychological treatment. Later, he explained that he left because of persistent taunting from other Dolphins players. The National Football League hired attorney Theodore Wells to investigate Martin's allegations of bullying. After receiving Wells's report, the Dolphins fired their offensive line coach, James Turner. Turner was a prominent person on the Dolphins team, and during his career he chose to thrust himself further into the public arena. He was the subject of articles discussing his coaching philosophy, and the focus of one season of HBO's "Hard Knocks," showcasing his coaching style. Turner filed a suit in a federal district court against Wells, alleging defamation. He charged that Wells failed to properly analyze certain information. Is Turner likely to succeed on his claim? Explain. [*Turner v. Wells*, 879 F.3d 1254 (11th Cir. 2018)] (See *Intentional Torts Against Persons*.)

5–9. A Question of Ethics—The IDDR Approach and Wrongful Interference. *Julie Whitchurch was an employee of Vizant Technologies, LLC. After she was fired, she created a website falsely accusing Vizant of fraud and mismanagement to discourage others from doing business with the company. Vizant filed a suit in a federal district court against her, alleging wrongful interference with a business relationship. The court concluded that Whitchurch's online criticism of Vizant adversely affected its employees and operations, forced it to accept reduced compensation to obtain business, and deterred outside investment. The court ordered Whitchurch to stop her online efforts to discourage others from doing business with Vizant.* [Vizant Technologies, LLC v. Whitchurch, *675 Fed.Appx. 201 (3d Cir. 2017)*] (*See* Intentional Torts Against Persons.)

1. How does the motivation for Whitchurch's conduct differ from other cases that involve wrongful interference? What does this suggest about the ethics in this situation? Discuss.

2. Using the IDDR approach, analyze and evaluate Vizant's decision to file a suit against Whitchurch.

Critical Thinking and Writing Assignments

5–10. Time-Limited Group Assignment—Negligence.
Donald and Gloria Bowden hosted a cookout at their home in South Carolina, inviting mostly business acquaintances. Justin Parks, who was nineteen years old, attended the party. Alcoholic beverages were available to all of the guests, even those who, like Parks, were between the ages of eighteen and twenty-one.

Parks consumed alcohol at the party and left with other guests. One of these guests detained Parks at the guest's home to give Parks time to "sober up." Parks then drove himself from this guest's home and was killed in a one-car accident. At the time of death, he had a blood alcohol content of 0.291 percent, which exceeded the state's limit for driving a motor vehicle. Linda Marcum, Parks's mother, filed a suit in a South Carolina state court against the Bowdens and others, alleging negligence. (See *Negligence*.)

1. The first group will present arguments in favor of holding the social hosts (Donald and Gloria Bowden) liable in this situation.

2. The second group will formulate arguments against holding the social hosts liable.

3. The states vary widely in assessing liability and imposing sanctions in the circumstances described in this problem. The third group will analyze the possible reasons why some courts treat social hosts who serve alcohol differently than parents who serve alcohol to their underage children.

4. The fourth group will decide whether the guest who detained Parks at his home to give Parks time to sober up could be held liable for negligence. What defense might this guest raise?

Product Liability

"You only have to do a very few things right in your life so long as you don't do too many things wrong."

Warren Buffett
1930–present
(American businessman and the most successful investor in the twentieth century)

An area of tort law of particular importance to business-persons is product liability. As Warren Buffett implies in the chapter-opening quote, to be successful, a business cannot make too many mistakes. This is especially true for businesses that make or sell products. The manufacturers and sellers of products may incur product liability when product defects cause injury or property damage to consumers, users, or bystanders (people in the vicinity of the product when it fails).

Suppose that Braden is injured when his Samsung Galaxy Note 7 smartphone explodes into flames. Under product liability laws, he could sue Samsung. Indeed, Samsung is facing numerous product liability lawsuits as a result of exploding lithium batteries in its Galaxy Note 7s. Some plaintiffs claim that Samsung knew that its smartphones could explode. Eventually, the company recalled all Galaxy Note 7 phones and halted production of the model.

In this chapter, you will learn about various theories of product liability under which plaintiffs can sue. Remember that although multimillion-dollar product liability lawsuits often involve big automakers, pharmaceutical companies, and the tobacco industry, many businesses face potential liability for the products they sell.

Learning Objectives

The four Learning Objectives *below are designed to help improve your understanding. After reading this chapter, you should be able to answer the following questions:*

1. Can a manufacturer be held liable to any person who suffers an injury proximately caused by the manufacturer's negligently made product?

2. What are the elements of a cause of action in strict product liability?

3. What are three types of product defects?

4. What defenses to liability can be raised in a product liability lawsuit?

Product Liability The legal liability of manufacturers, sellers, and lessors of goods for injuries or damage caused by the goods to consumers, users, or bystanders.

6–1 Product Liability Claims

Those who make, sell, or lease goods can be held liable for physical harm or property damage caused by those goods to a consumer, user, or bystander. This is called **product liability.** Product liability claims may be based on the tort theories of negligence, fraudulent misrepresentation,

151

Johnson & Johnson Faces Continuing Lawsuits Over Its Talcum Powder

In 1892, the director of scientific affairs of Johnson & Johnson (J&J) invented scented talcum powder. Talcum, or talc, is a soft mineral found in rock deposits. This invention quickly became J&J's Baby Powder, known throughout the world. Over time, the product expanded beyond being used on babies after a diaper change. In the early 1900s, women began applying the powder to their bodies and undergarments for a fresh scent.

In the 1970s, several studies suggested that using talc around the female genital area increased a woman's risk of ovarian cancer. Despite these studies, J&J denied the findings and did not include any warning labels on its talc-based products. By 2016, several female plaintiffs had been awarded tens of millions of dollars—mainly in punitive damages. Why punitive damages? Juries were convinced J&J had withheld critical information about a possible relationship between ovarian cancer and talcum powder for more than four decades. By 2017, J&J faced more than 2,500 lawsuits in state and federal courts.

In its defense, J&J contends that the National Toxicology Program has not yet fully reviewed talc. Moreover, the International Agency for Research on Cancer classifies genital use of talc as only "possibly" carcinogenic—that is, having the potential to cause cancer. After all, talc is found in a wide variety of cosmetic products and has other uses, such as in paints and plastics.

Key Point

Product liability lawsuits are common for large corporations. Note that in the talcum powder cases, 90 percent or more of the jury awards were for "failure to warn." J&J could have warned consumers of a potential link between genital use of talcum powder and ovarian cancer, but it did not. Of course, sales of talc-based products would not have grown so rapidly had such a warning been evident on each J&J Baby Powder container.

The talc mineral used in Johnson's Baby Powder has been linked to certain cancers in women. Should the company be liable for not warning consumers about this possibility? Why or why not?

Raihana Asral/Shutterstock

and strict liability. Sometimes, a business faces multiple product liability lawsuits over the same product, as discussed in this chapter's *Business Web Log* feature.

6–1a Negligence

Negligence is the failure to exercise the degree of care that a reasonable, prudent person would have exercised under the circumstances. If a manufacturer fails to exercise "due care" to make a product safe, a person who is injured by the product may sue the manufacturer for negligence.

Due Care Must Be Exercised The manufacturer must exercise due care in all of the following areas:

1. Designing the product.
2. Selecting the materials.
3. Using the appropriate production process.
4. Assembling and testing the product.
5. Placing adequate warnings on the label to inform the user of dangers of which an ordinary person might not be aware.
6. Inspecting and testing any purchased components used in the final product.

Privity of Contract Not Required A product liability action based on negligence does not require privity of contract between the injured plaintiff and the defendant manufacturer. **Privity of contract** refers to the relationship that exists between the promisor and the promisee of a contract. Privity is the reason that normally only the parties to a contract can enforce that contract.

In the context of product liability law, privity is not required. A person who is injured by a defective product can bring a negligence suit even though he or she was not the one who actually purchased the product—and thus is not in privity. A manufacturer is liable for its failure to exercise due care to *any person* who sustains an injury proximately caused by a negligently made (defective) product.

Relative to the long history of the common law, this exception to the privity requirement is a fairly recent development, dating to the early part of the twentieth century. A leading case in this respect is *MacPherson v. Buick Motor Co.*, which is presented as this chapter's *Landmark in the Law* feature.

"Cause in Fact" and Proximate Cause In a product liability suit based on negligence, as in any action alleging that the defendant was negligent, the plaintiff must show that the defendant's conduct was the "cause in fact" of an injury. Cause in fact requires showing that but for the defendant's action, the injury would not have occurred.

> **Learning Objective 1**
> Can a manufacturer be held liable to any person who suffers an injury proximately caused by the manufacturer's negligently made product?

Privity of Contract The relationship that exists between the promisor and the promisee of a contract.

MacPherson v. Buick Motor Co. (1916)

Landmark in the Law

In the landmark case of *MacPherson v. Buick Motor Co.*,[a] the New York Court of Appeals—New York's highest court—considered the liability of a manufacturer that had failed to exercise reasonable care in manufacturing a finished product.

Case Background Donald MacPherson suffered injuries while riding in a Buick automobile that suddenly collapsed because one of the wheels was made of defective wood. The spokes crumbled into fragments, throwing MacPherson out of the vehicle and injuring him.

MacPherson had purchased the car from a Buick dealer, but he brought a lawsuit against the manufacturer, Buick Motor Company. Buick itself had not made the wheel but had bought it from another manufacturer. There was evidence, though, that the defects could have been discovered by a reasonable inspection by Buick and that no such inspection had taken

a. 217 N.Y. 382, 111 N.E. 1050 (1916).

place. MacPherson charged Buick with negligence for putting a human life in imminent danger.

The Issue Before the Court and the Court's Ruling The primary issue was whether Buick owed a duty of care to anyone except the immediate purchaser of the car—that is, the Buick dealer. In deciding the issue, Justice Benjamin Cardozo stated that "if the nature of a thing is such that it is reasonably certain to place life and limb in peril when negligently made, it is then a thing of danger. . . . If to the element of danger there is added knowledge that the thing will be used by persons other than the purchaser, and used without new tests, then, irrespective of contract, the manufacturer of this thing of danger is under a duty to make it carefully."

The court concluded that "beyond all question, the nature of an automobile gives warning of probable danger if its construction is defective. This automobile was designed to go 50 miles an hour. Unless its

wheels were sound and strong, injury was almost certain." Although Buick itself had not manufactured the wheel, the court held that Buick had a duty to inspect the wheels and that Buick "was responsible for the finished product." Therefore, Buick was liable to MacPherson for the injuries he sustained when he was thrown from the car.

Application to Today's World *This landmark decision was a significant step in creating the legal environment of the modern world. As often happens, technological developments necessitated changes in the law. Today, automobile manufacturers are commonly held liable when their negligence causes automobile users to be injured.*

It must also be determined that the defendant's act was the *proximate cause* of the injury. This determination focuses on the foreseeability of the consequences of the act and whether the defendant should be held legally responsible.

For proximate cause to become a relevant issue, however, a plaintiff must establish cause in fact. The issue in the following case was whether a "silent" alarm bell could be a product defect that was the cause in fact and the proximate cause of the deaths of two sisters.

■ Case 6.1

Schwarck v. Arctic Cat, Inc.

Court of Appeals of Michigan, 2016 WL 191992 (2016).

Background and Facts Karen Schwarck was operating an Arctic Cat 660 snowmobile on Mackinac Island in Michigan with her sister, Edith Bonno, as a passenger. The sisters were killed when the Cat went backward through a fence and over a bluff. Their spouses filed a suit in a Michigan state court against the manufacturer, Arctic Cat, Inc., alleging negligent design.

The vehicle was equipped with a reverse alarm that did not sound the entire time the vehicle was in reverse. The plaintiffs asserted that in executing a turn, Schwarck stopped the Cat, shifted forward, and, not hearing the alarm, accelerated. Still in reverse, however, the Cat crashed through the fence. The court ruled that there was no dispute the alarm was "operational" and issued a summary judgment in the defendant's favor. The plaintiffs appealed, arguing that the alarm, though "operational," was defective because it caused Schwarck to be confused about whether she was in forward or reverse gear.

In the Words of the Court
PER CURIAM [By the Whole Court].
* * * *

[The plaintiffs' expert, John Frackelton, an accident reconstructionist and snowmobile mechanic] observed that the shift lever traveled from full reverse to full forward in a distance of four inches. * * * Frackelton experimented with the lever, shifting it up toward forward gear, an inch at a time. For the next two inches of shift travel forward, the reverse alarm did not sound, but the snowmobile was still in reverse. Frackelton observed that it was only in the last or fourth inch of shift travel that the snowmobile was in full forward.
* * * *

* * * Defendant argues that the alarm served its intended purpose, which is to notify bystanders and not operators that the snowmobile is in reverse and that it was unreasonable for decedent [Karen] Schwarck to rely on the alarm to determine the gear of the snowmobile. *The fact that the manufacturer's intended purpose for the alarm was to warn third-parties is not dispositive [does not settle the issue] of whether decedent*

Schwarck relied on the alarm to determine her gear or whether that reliance was reasonable or a foreseeable misuse of the alarm and snowmobile. [Emphasis added.]

Reasonable minds could differ as to whether a reverse alarm that does not sound throughout the reverse trajectory or only operates in a partial manner is defective.

* * * *

* * * It is foreseeable that an operator of the Arctic Cat may rely on the sound of the reverse alarm to indicate when the snowmobile is no longer in reverse and experience unexpected travel backward because the alarm does not sound during the entire reverse gear. It is further foreseeable that unanticipated reverse travel may cause a risk of harm to the operator.

A jury could infer that traveling backward when one thought he or she would go forward is an unexpected stimulus. It is also a reasonable inference * * * that it was foreseeable that the operator would be surprised by the rearward motion. Given the evidence, reasonable minds may differ as to whether decedent Schwarck did not or could not correct the snowmobile's rearward direction in the time allotted.

Decision and Remedy A state intermediate appellate court vacated the lower court's judgment. The fact that the alarm was "operational" did not determine whether its operation constituted a product defect. The appellate court remanded the case to be submitted to a jury to make this determination.

Critical Thinking

- **Ethical** *Does a manufacturer have an ethical obligation to warn the buyers of its products of defects? Explain.*

- **What If the Facts Were Different?** *Suppose that the Arctic Cat 660 did not have an alarm, and that occasionally, when the gearshift was pushed forward, the vehicle did not shift into forward as expected. Is this a feature that the plaintiffs might have asserted as a defect? Discuss.*

6–1b Misrepresentation

When a user or consumer is injured as a result of a manufacturer's or seller's fraudulent misrepresentation, the basis of liability may be the tort of fraud. In this situation, the misrepresentation must have been made knowingly or with reckless disregard for the facts. The intentional mislabeling of packaged cosmetics, for instance, or the intentional concealment of a product's defects constitutes fraudulent misrepresentation.

The misrepresentation must be of a material fact, and the seller must have intended to induce the buyer's reliance on the misrepresentation. Misrepresentation on a label or advertisement is enough to show the intent to induce reliance. Of course, to bring a lawsuit on this ground, the buyer must have relied on the misrepresentation.

6–2 Strict Product Liability

Under the doctrine of strict liability, people may be liable for the results of their acts regardless of their intentions or their exercise of reasonable care. In addition, liability does not depend on privity of contract. The injured party does not have to be the buyer or a *third party beneficiary* (one for whose benefit a contract is made). In the 1960s, courts applied the doctrine of strict liability in several landmark cases involving manufactured goods, and this doctrine has since become a common method of holding manufacturers liable.

6–2a Strict Product Liability and Public Policy

The law imposes strict product liability as a matter of public policy. The public policy concerning strict product liability may be expressed in a statute or in the common law. This public policy rests on a threefold assumption:

1. Consumers should be protected against unsafe products.

2. Manufacturers and distributors should not escape liability for faulty products simply because they are not in privity of contract with the ultimate user of those products.

3. Manufacturers, sellers, and lessors of products are generally in a better position than consumers to bear the costs associated with injuries caused by their products. They can ultimately pass on these costs to all consumers in the form of higher prices.

California was the first state to impose strict product liability in tort on manufacturers. **⊞ Classic Case Example 6.1** William Greenman was injured when his Shopsmith combination power tool threw off a piece of wood that struck him in the head. He sued the manufacturer, claiming that he had followed the product instructions and that the product must be defective.

In a landmark decision, *Greenman v. Yuba Power Products, Inc.*,[1] the California Supreme Court set out the reason for applying tort law rather than contract law in cases involving consumers who were injured by defective products. According to the *Greenman* court, the "purpose of such liability is to [e]nsure that the costs of injuries resulting from defective products are borne by the manufacturers . . . rather than by the injured persons who are powerless to protect themselves." ■ Today, the majority of states recognize strict product liability, although some state courts limit its application to situations involving personal injuries (rather than property damage).

If a power tool is defective and injures a user, does the user sue under contract law or tort law?

6–2b Requirements for Strict Product Liability

After the *Restatement (Second) of Torts* was issued in 1964, Section 402A became a widely accepted statement of how the doctrine of strict liability should be applied to sellers of goods. These sellers include manufacturers, processors, assemblers, packagers, bottlers, wholesalers, distributors, retailers, and lessors.

Learning Objective 2

What are the elements of a cause of action in strict product liability?

---

1. 59 Cal.2d 57, 377 P.2d 897, 27 Cal.Rptr. 697 (1962); see also, *Okoye v. Bristol-Myers Squibb Co.*, ___ F.Supp.3d ___, 2017 WL 1435886 (N.D.Cal. 2017).

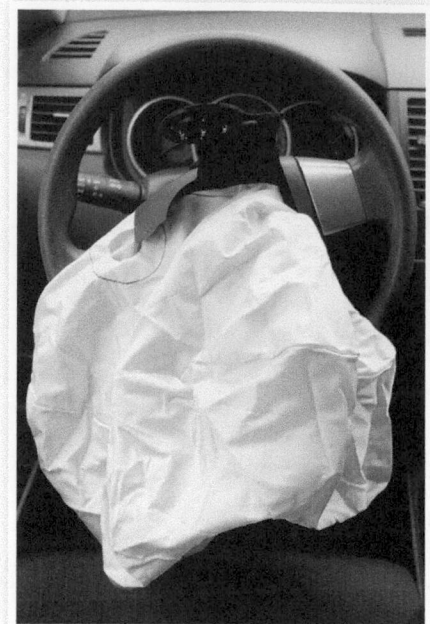

Does a person injured by a defective air bag have to prove that it was defective when the car was manufactured?

nikkytok/iStock/Getty Images

The bases for an action in strict liability that are set forth in Section 402A can be summarized as the following six requirements. Depending on the jurisdiction, if these requirements are met, a manufacturer's liability to an injured party can be almost unlimited.

1. The product must have been in a *defective condition* when the defendant sold it.
2. The defendant must normally be engaged in the *business of selling* (or otherwise distributing) that product.
3. The product must be *unreasonably dangerous* to the user or consumer because of its defective condition.
4. The plaintiff must incur *physical harm* to self or property by use or consumption of the product.
5. The defective condition must be the *proximate cause* of the injury or damage.
6. The *goods must not have been substantially changed* from the time the product was sold to the time the injury was sustained.

Proving a Defective Condition Under these requirements, in any action against a manufacturer, seller, or lessor, the plaintiff does not have to show why or how the product became defective. The plaintiff does, however, have to prove that the product was defective at the time it left the seller or lessor and that this defective condition made it "unreasonably dangerous" to the user or consumer.

Unless evidence can be presented that will support the conclusion that the product was defective when it was sold or leased, the plaintiff normally will not succeed. If the product was delivered in a safe condition and subsequent mishandling made it harmful to the user, the seller or lessor usually is not strictly liable.

Unreasonably Dangerous Products The *Restatement* recognizes that many products cannot possibly be made entirely safe for all uses. Thus, sellers or lessors of these products are held liable only when the products are *unreasonably* dangerous. A court may consider a product so defective as to be an **unreasonably dangerous product** in either of the following situations.

1. The product is dangerous beyond the expectation of the ordinary consumer.
2. A less dangerous alternative was economically feasible for the manufacturer, but the manufacturer failed to produce it.

A product may be unreasonably dangerous due to a flaw in its manufacturing, design, or warning.

Unreasonably Dangerous Product A product that is so defective that it is dangerous beyond the expectation of an ordinary consumer, or a product for which a less dangerous alternative was feasible but the manufacturer failed to produce it.

6–2c Product Defects

The *Restatement (Third) of Torts: Products Liability* defines the three types of product defects that have traditionally been recognized in product liability law—manufacturing defects, design defects, and inadequate warnings.

Manufacturing Defects According to Section 2(a) of the *Restatement (Third) of Torts: Products Liability*, a product "contains a manufacturing defect when the product departs from its intended design even though all possible care was exercised in the preparation and marketing of the product." Basically, a manufacturing defect is a departure from design specifications that results in products that are physically flawed, damaged, or incorrectly assembled. A glass bottle that is made too thin, causing it to explode in a consumer's face, is an example of a product with a manufacturing defect.

Learning Objective 3

What are three types of product defects?

Quality Control. Usually, manufacturing defects occur when a manufacturer fails to assemble, test, or check the quality of a product adequately. In fact, the idea behind holding defendants strictly liable for manufacturing defects is to encourage greater investment in product safety and stringent quality control standards.

Note that liability is imposed on a manufacturer (and on the wholesaler and retailer) regardless of whether the manufacturer's quality control efforts were "reasonable." For more information on how effective quality control procedures can help businesses reduce their potential legal liability for defective products, see the *Linking Business Law to Corporate Management* feature.

Quality Control

Linking Business Law to Corporate Management

Manufacturing and design defects can give rise to expensive lawsuits and substantial liability, which is a major concern for managers in every organization. The legal issues surrounding product liability relate directly to quality control. Companies that have cost-effective quality control systems produce products with fewer manufacturing and design defects. As a result, these companies incur fewer potential and actual product liability lawsuits.

Three Types of Quality Control

Most management systems involve three types of quality control—preventive, concurrent, and feedback. They apply at different stages of the manufacturing process. Preventive quality control occurs before the process begins, concurrent control takes place during the process, and feedback control occurs after it is finished.

Preventive quality control, for instance, might involve inspecting raw materials before they are used in the manufacturing process. During production, measuring and monitoring devices constantly assess quality standards as part of a concurrent quality control system. When the standards are not being met, employees can correct the problem.

Once the manufacturing is complete, the products can undergo a final quality inspection as part of the feedback quality control system. Of course, there are economic limits to how extensive the final inspection will be. Management faces a trade-off. The less a product is tested, the sooner it gets to market and the faster the company receives its payment. With a shorter testing period, however, comes a higher risk of a defect that could cost the manufacturer.

Total Quality Management (TQM)

Some managers attempt to reduce product liability costs by relying on a concurrent quality control system known as total quality management (TQM). TQM attempts to infuse quality into every activity in a company through continuous improvement.

Quality circles are a popular TQM technique. Groups of six to twelve employees volunteer to meet regularly to discuss problems and possible solutions. A quality circle might consist of workers from different phases in the production process, so that workers in various stages of production have input on changes. Quality circles force changes in the production process that affect workers who are actually on the production line.

Benchmarking is a TQM technique in which a company continuously measures its products against those of its competitors or the industry leaders in order to identify areas for improvement. In the automobile industry, benchmarking enabled several Japanese firms to overtake U.S. automakers in terms of quality.

Another TQM system is called Six Sigma, a quality control approach based on a five-step methodology: define, measure, analyze, improve, and control. Six Sigma controls emphasize discipline and a relentless attempt to achieve higher quality (and lower costs). A Six Sigma program requires a major commitment from management, however, because it involves widespread changes throughout the entire organization.

Critical Thinking

Quality control leads to fewer defective products and fewer lawsuits, which is important for a company's long-term financial health. At the same time, the more quality control that managers impose on their organization, the higher the average cost per unit of whatever is produced and sold. How does a manager decide how much quality control to undertake?

The Role of Expert Testimony. Cases involving allegations of a manufacturing defect are often decided based on the opinions and testimony of experts. **Case Example 6.2** Kevin Schmude purchased an eight-foot stepladder and used it to install radio-frequency shielding in a hospital room. While Schmude was standing on the ladder, it collapsed, and he was seriously injured. He filed a lawsuit against the ladder's maker, Tricam Industries, Inc., based on a manufacturing defect.

Experts testified that when the ladder was assembled during manufacturing, the preexisting holes in the top cap did not properly line up with the holes in the rear right rail and backing plate. As a result of the misalignment, the rear legs of the ladder were not securely fastened in place, causing the ladder to fail. A jury concluded that this manufacturing defect made the ladder unreasonably dangerous and awarded Schmude more than $677,000 in damages.[2]

> "Almost all quality improvement comes via simplification of design, manufacturing . . . layout, processes, and procedures."
>
> **Tom Peters**
> 1942–present
> (American business writer)

Design Defects Unlike a product with a manufacturing defect, a product with a design defect is made in conformity with the manufacturer's design specifications. Nevertheless, it results in injury to the user because the design itself is flawed. The product's design creates an unreasonable risk to the user.

A product "is defective in design when the foreseeable risks of harm posed by the product could have been reduced or avoided by the adoption of a reasonable alternative design by the seller or other distributor, or a predecessor in the commercial chain of distribution, and the omission of the alternative design renders the product not reasonably safe."[3] See this chapter's *Business Law Analysis* feature for an example of how courts analyze design defects.

Test for Design Defects. To successfully assert a design defect, a plaintiff has to show that:

1. A reasonable alternative design was available.

2. As a result of the defendant's failure to adopt the alternative design, the product was not reasonably safe.

In other words, a manufacturer or other defendant is liable only when the harm was reasonably preventable. **Example 6.3** Gillespie accidentally cuts off several of his fingers while operating a table saw. He later files a lawsuit against the maker of the saw, claiming that the blade guards on the saw were defectively designed. At trial, however, an expert testifies that the alternative design for blade guards used for table saws could not have been used for the particular cut that Gillespie was performing at the time he was injured. In this situation, Gillespie's claim will likely fail because there is no proof that the "better" guard design would have prevented his injury.

---

2. *Schmude v. Tricam Industries, Inc.*, 550 F.Supp.2d 846 (E.D.Wis. 2008); see also *Stuhlmacher v. Home Depot, U.S.A., Inc.*, 2013 WL 3201572 (N.D.Ind. 2013).
3. *Restatement (Third) of Torts: Products Liability*, Section 2(b).

How State Legislation Can Limit Recovery for Design Defects

David Dobrovolny bought a new Ford F-350 pickup truck. A year later, the truck spontaneously caught fire in Dobrovolny's driveway. The truck was destroyed, but no other property was damaged, and no one was injured. Dobrovolny filed a suit in a Nebraska state court against Ford Motor Company on a theory of strict product liability to recover the cost of the truck. Nebraska limits the application of strict product liability to situations involving personal injuries. Will Dobrovolny's lawsuit succeed? Why or why not?

Analysis: The majority of states recognize strict product liability. The purpose of strict product liability is to ensure that the costs of injuries resulting from defective products are borne by the manufacturers rather than by the injured persons. The law imposes this liability as a matter of public policy. Some state courts limit the application of the tort theory of strict product liability to situations involving personal injuries rather than property damage.

Nebraska recognizes strict product liability, but the state's courts limit its application. The issue is whether these limits apply when a product self-destructs without causing damage to persons or other property.

Result and Reasoning: Because Nebraska limits strict product liability suits to situations involving personal injury, a court will most likely dismiss Dobrovolny's design defect claim. When a product injures only itself, the reasons for imposing strict product liability lose their significance. The consumer has not been injured, and the loss concerns the consumer's benefit of the bargain from the contract with the seller of the product. Although a consumer with only a damaged product may not recover in tort, the consumer is not without other remedies. Dobrovolny may attempt to recover for the loss of his truck under contract theories for breach of warranty.

According to the Official Comments accompanying the *Restatement (Third) of Torts*, a court can consider a broad range of factors in deciding claims of design defects. These factors include the magnitude and probability of the foreseeable risks, as well as the relative advantages and disadvantages of the product as it was designed and as it alternatively could have been designed.

Ethical Issue

Can a Taser be considered unreasonably dangerous as designed? Taser International, Inc., located in Scottsdale, Arizona, provides nonlethal devices that police personnel can use to "stun" aggressors. When officer Jeremy Baird of the Moberly, Missouri, Police Department used a Taser device after a routine traffic stop, the victim fell to the ground, lost consciousness, and died two hours later. The victim's mother sued the city of Moberly and several police officers. That case was settled for $2.4 million.

The victim's mother then sued Taser International. The claim was that the company did not provide adequate warnings that using the device directly on the chest could lead to cardiac arrest. The lawsuit also argued that the Taser was defectively designed. A federal trial court dismissed the case.

On appeal, the reviewing court pointed out that the plaintiff would have had to prove that additional warnings on the use of the Taser "would have altered the behavior of the officers involved in the incident." But, concluded the court, there was "no dispute on this record that Officer Baird would not have read any additional warning Taser may have added about the cardiac danger" of its device. As to the defective design claim, the court noted that "under strict liability, a manufacturer is not intended to be an ensurer of any and all injuries caused by its products."[4] Just showing a link between the use of the Taser and the victim's injury was insufficient to establish strict liability.

Is showing that a Taser caused the death of a victim sufficient under the doctrine of strict liability?

---

4. *Bachtel v. Taser International, Inc.*, 747 F.3d 967 (2014).

Risk-Utility Analysis. Most courts engage in a risk-utility analysis, determining whether the risk of harm from the product as designed outweighs its utility to the user and to the public. **Case Example 6.4** Benjamin Riley, a county sheriff, was driving his Ford F-150 pickup truck near Ehrhardt, South Carolina, when it collided with another vehicle. The impact caused Riley's truck to leave the road and roll over. The driver's door of the truck opened in the collision, and Riley was ejected and killed. Riley's widow, Laura, as the representative of his estate, filed a product liability suit against Ford Motor Company. She claimed that the design of the door-latch system of the truck allowed the door to open in the collision. A state court held in her favor and awarded the estate $900,000 in damages.

Ford appealed, but the court found that a reasonable alternative design was available for the door-latch system. Evidence showed that Ford was aware of the safety problems presented by the current system (a rod-linkage system). After conducting a risk-utility analysis of a different system (a cable-linkage system), Ford had concluded that the alternative system was feasible and perhaps superior. The state's highest court affirmed the damages award.[5]

How can a plaintiff prove that a truck's door latch was defectively designed?

Mark Scheuern/Alamy

Consumer-Expectation Test. Instead of the risk-utility test, some courts apply the consumer-expectation test to determine whether a product's design was defective. Under this test, a product is unreasonably dangerous when it fails to perform in the manner that would reasonably be expected by an ordinary consumer.

Case Example 6.5 A representative from Wilson Sporting Goods Company gave Edwin Hickox an umpire's mask that was designed to be safer than other umpire's masks. The mask had a newly designed throat guard that angled forward instead of extending straight down. While Hickox was working as an umpire during a game and wearing the mask, he was was struck by a foul ball and injured. He suffered a concussion and damage to his inner ear, which caused permanent hearing loss. Hickox and his wife sued the manufacturer for product liability based on a defective design and won. A jury awarded $750,000 to Hickox and $25,000 to his wife. Wilson appealed.

The reviewing court affirmed the jury's verdict. The design was defective because "an ordinary consumer would have expected the mask to perform more safely than it did." The evidence presented to the jury had shown that Wilson's mask was more dangerous than comparable masks sold at the time. The new "masks could concentrate energy at the point of impact, rather than distribute energy evenly throughout the padded area of the mask," as an ordinary consumer would have expected a baseball mask to do.[6]

Inadequate Warnings

A product may also be deemed defective because of inadequate instructions or warnings. A product will be considered defective "when the foreseeable risks of harm posed by the product could have been reduced or avoided by the provision of reasonable instructions or warnings by the seller or other distributor, or a predecessor in the commercial chain of distribution, and the omission of the instructions or warnings renders the product not reasonably safe."[7] Generally, a seller must also warn consumers of the harm that can result from the *foreseeable misuse* of its product.

Note that the plaintiff must show that the inadequate warning was the proximate cause of the injuries that she or he sustained. In the following case, a drug manufacturer argued that an injured plaintiff failed to prove an inadequate warning was the cause of his injuries.

5. *Riley v. Ford Motor Co.,* 414 S.C. 185, 777 S.E.2d 824 (2015).
6. *Wilson Sporting Goods Co. v. Hickox,* 59 A.3d 1267 (D.C.App. 2013).
7. *Restatement (Third) of Torts: Products Liability,* Section 2(c).

Case 6.2

Stange v. Janssen Pharmaceuticals, Inc.

Superior Court of Pennsylvania, 2018 PA Super 4, 179 A.3d 45 (2018).

Background and Facts Timothy Stange was twelve years old when he was prescribed Risperdal, an antipsychotic drug, for Tourette's syndrome. Stange subsequently developed female breasts, a condition known as gynecomastia. Surgery successfully removed Stange's breasts but left him with permanent scars and pain. Janssen Pharmaceuticals, Inc., manufactures Risperdal. Janssen knew that gynecomastia was a frequent adverse event in children and adolescents who took Risperdal. Its label, however, significantly downplayed the risk, for instance, stating that the disorder's occurrence was "rare."

Stange filed a suit in a Pennsylvania state court against Janssen, alleging that the maker negligently failed to adequately warn of the risk of gynecomastia associated with Risperdal use. The court entered a judgment in favor of the plaintiff for more than $500,000. Janssen appealed to a state intermediate appellate court.

In the Words of the Court
Opinion by Ford *ELLIOTT*, P.J.E. [President Judge Emeritus]

* * * *

* * * Janssen argues that Stange failed to prove proximate cause, [meaning] that an inadequate warning was the cause of Stange's injuries. * * * Janssen argues that it was entitled to [a judgment notwithstanding the verdict (JNOV) because] Stange failed to prove that additional risk information would have changed Dr. Kovnar's prescribing decision.

To support his claim of negligence, Stange must establish that Janssen breached its duty to warn, and that the breach caused his injuries.

A plaintiff who has established both a duty and a failure to warn must also establish causation by showing that, if properly warned, he or she would have altered behavior and avoided injury. * * * Absent proof that a more complete or explicit warning would have prevented Stange's use of Risperdal, he cannot establish that Janssen's alleged failure to warn was the proximate cause of his injuries. [Emphasis added.]

In cases involving the failure to warn of risks associated with prescription drugs, * * * a manufacturer will be held liable only where it fails to exercise reasonable care to inform a physician of the facts which make the drug likely to be dangerous. The

manufacturer has the duty to disclose risks to the physician, as opposed to the patient, because it is the duty of the prescribing physician to be fully aware of (1) the characteristics of the drug he is prescribing, (2) the amount of the drug which can be safely administered, and (3) the different medications the patient is taking. It is also the duty of the prescribing physician to advise the patient of any dangers or side effects associated with the use of the drug as well as how and when to take the drug.

* * * There was substantial evidence that Janssen intentionally downplayed the risk of gynecomastia for adolescent boys using Risperdal. * * * The * * * label * * * reported that gynecomastia occurred in less than 1% of adult patients and less than 5% of pediatric patients treated with Risperdal. Both of these warnings were inaccurate based on the scientific evidence that the Defendants possessed [which] indicated that gynecomastia was a frequent adverse event, not "rare." * * * These warnings were not accurate, strong, or clear. Instead, the warnings, to the extent they warned at all, were inaccurate and misleading about the risks of gynecomastia.

Furthermore, Dr. Kovnar, Stange's pediatric neurologist, testified that * * * he would not have prescribed Risperdal to Stange had he been aware of the increased risk.

* * * The trial court did not err in refusing to grant JNOV.

Decision and Remedy The appellate court affirmed the judgment in favor of Stange. The court stated, "Due to Janssen's inadequate labeling and failure to warn, Dr. Kovnar was unaware of the specific heightened risks associated with the use of Risperdal." Had the doctor known about Risperdal's risks for children, he would have prescribed a different drug for Stange.

Critical Thinking

• **Economic** *Why did Janssen downplay the risks of Risperdal in the warnings to physicians? Discuss.*

• **What If the Facts Were Different?** *Suppose that instead of suffering harm through a prescription drug's legitimate use, the plaintiff had been injured by a drug's illegal abuse. Would the result have been different? Explain.*

Content of Warnings. Important factors for a court to consider include the risks of a product, the "content and comprehensibility" and "intensity of expression" of warnings and instructions, and the "characteristics of expected user groups."[8] Courts apply a "reasonableness" test to determine if the warnings adequately alert consumers to the product's risks. For instance, children will likely respond more readily to bright, bold, simple warning labels, while educated adults might need more detailed information. For more on tips on making sure a product's warnings are adequate, see this chapter's *Managerial Strategy* feature.

8. *Restatement (Third) of Torts: Products Liability*, Section 2, Comment h.

When Is a Warning Legally Bulletproof?

Managerial Strategy

A company can develop and sell a perfectly manufactured and designed product, yet still face product liability lawsuits for defective warnings. A product may be defective because of inadequate instructions or warnings when the foreseeable risks of harm posed by the product could have been reduced by reasonable warnings offered by the seller or other distributor. Manufacturers and distributors have a duty to warn users of any hidden dangers of their products. Additionally, they have a duty to instruct users in how to use the product to avoid any dangers. Warnings generally must be clear and specific. They must also be conspicuous.

When No Warning Is Required

Not all manufacturers have to provide warnings. People are expected to know that knives can cut fingers, for instance, so a seller need not place a bright orange label on each knife sold reminding consumers of this danger. Most household products are generally safe when used as intended.

In a New Jersey case, a ten-year-old boy was injured when he fell and struck his face on a Razor A kick scooter's handlebars. The padded end caps on the handlebars had deteriorated, and the boy's mother had thrown them away, exposing the handlebars' metal ends.

The boy and his mother sued, claiming that the manufacturer was required to provide a warning to prevent injuries of this type. The appellate court noted, however, that the plaintiffs were not able to claim that the

Razor A was defective. "Lacking evidence that Razor A's end-cap design was defective, plaintiffs cannot show that Razor A had a duty to warn of such a defect, and therefore cannot make out their failure to warn claim."[a]

In an Indiana case, an employee of a concrete contractor was injured at a construction site when his head was struck by a sixteen-foot-long two-by-four board that had dislodged from a concrete formwork system. The employee sued the construction manager and the manufacturer of the formwork system for failure to warn. The court decided that the danger that lumber used in this formwork system could eject and strike a person was open and obvious. Therefore, neither the construction manager nor the manufacturer of the system was liable for failing to warn the employee.[b]

Warnings on Medication

In a case involving prescription medication, a woman suffered neurological disorders after taking a generic drug to treat her gastroesophageal reflux disease. Part of her complaint asserted strict liability for failure to warn. The plaintiff claimed that the manufacturer had not updated its label to indicate that usage should not exceed twelve weeks. The reviewing court reasoned that "The adequacy of the instructions . . . made no difference to the outcome . . . because [the plaintiff alleges

that her prescribing physician] did not read those materials."[c]

In contrast, in a Pennsylvania case, a family was awarded over $10 million in a lawsuit against Johnson & Johnson for defective warnings on bottles of children's Motrin. A three-year-old girl suffered burns over 84 percent of her skin, experienced brain damage, and went blind after suffering a reaction to the drug. The drug did have a specific warning label that instructed consumers to stop taking the medication and contact a physician in the event of an allergic reaction. Nonetheless, Johnson & Johnson was found liable for failing to warn about the known risk of severe side effects.[d]

Business Questions

1. *To protect themselves, manufacturers have been forced to include lengthy safety warnings for their products. What might be the downside of such warnings?*

2. *Does a manufacturer have to create safety warnings for every product? Why or why not?*

---

a. *Vann v. Toys R Us*, 2014 WL3537937 (N.J.Sup.A.D. 2014).
b. *Gleaves v. Messer Construction Co.*, 77 N.E.3d 1244 (Ind. App. 2017).
c. *Brinkley v. Pfizer, Inc.*, 772 F.3d 1133 (8th Cir. 2014). For another situation in which the alleged warning defect did not cause the plaintiff's injury, see *Bock v. Novartis Pharmaceuticals Corp.*, 661 Fed.Appx. 227 (3d Cir. 2016).
d. *Maya v. Johnson and Johnson*, 2014 Pa.Super. 152, 97 A.3d 1203 (2014).

Case Example 6.6 Jeffrey Johnson was taken to the emergency room for an episode of atrial fibrillation, a heart rhythm disorder. Dr. David Hahn used a defibrillator manufactured by Medtronic, Inc., to deliver electric shocks to Johnson's heart. The defibrillator had synchronous and asynchronous modes, and it reverted to the asynchronous mode after each use. Hahn intended to deliver synchronized shocks, which required him to select the synchronous mode for each shock. Hahn did not read the device's instructions, which Medtronic had provided both in a manual and on the device itself. As a result, he delivered one synchronized shock, followed by twelve asynchronous shocks that endangered Johnson's life.

Johnson and his wife filed a product liability suit against Medtronic asserting that Medtronic had provided inadequate warnings about the defibrillator and that the device had a design defect. A Missouri appellate court held that the Johnsons could not pursue a claim based on the inadequacy of Medtronic's warnings, but they could pursue a claim alleging a design defect. The court reasoned that in some cases, "a manufacturer may be held liable where it chooses to warn of the danger . . . rather than preclude the danger by design."[9]

Obvious Risks. There is no duty to warn about risks that are obvious or commonly known. Warnings about such risks do not add to the safety of a product and could even detract from it by making other warnings seem less significant. The obviousness of a risk and a user's decision to proceed in the face of that risk may be a defense in a product liability suit based on an inadequate warning.

Example 6.7 Sixteen-year-old Lana White attempts to do a back flip on a trampoline and fails. She is paralyzed as a result. There are nine warning labels affixed to the trampoline, an instruction manual with safety warnings, and a placard attached at the entrance advising users not to do flips. If White sues the manufacturer for inadequate warnings, she is likely to lose. The warning labels are probably sufficient to make the risks obvious and insulate the manufacturer from liability for her injuries.

Risks that may seem obvious to some users will not be obvious to all users. This is a particular problem when users are likely to be children. A young child may not be able to read or understand warning labels or comprehend the risk of certain activities. To avoid liability, the manufacturer would have to prove that the warnings it provided were adequate to make the risk of injury obvious to a young child.

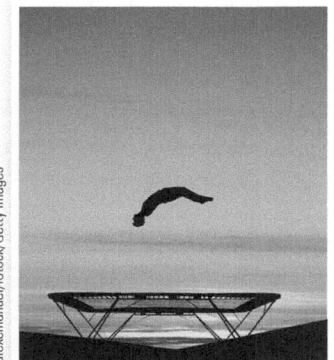

How can a manufacturer adequately warn users against doing back flips on a trampoline?

State Laws and Constitutionality. An action alleging that a product is defective due to an inadequate label can be based on state law, but that law must not violate the U.S. Constitution. **Case Example 6.8** California once enacted a law imposing restrictions and a labeling requirement on the sale or rental of "violent video games" to minors. Although the video game industry had adopted a voluntary rating system for games, the legislators deemed those labels inadequate. The Video Software Dealers Association immediately filed a suit in federal court to invalidate the law, and the law was struck down. The court found that the definition of a violent video game in California's law was unconstitutionally vague and violated the First Amendment.[10]

6–2d Market-Share Liability

Generally, in cases involving product liability, a plaintiff must prove that the defective product that caused her or his injury was made by a specific defendant. In a few situations, however, courts have dropped this requirement when a plaintiff cannot prove which of many distributors of a harmful product supplied the particular product that caused the injury. Under a theory of **market-share liability,** a court can hold each manufacturer responsible for a percentage of the plaintiff's damages that is equal to the percentage of its market share.

Market-Share Liability A theory under which liability is shared among all firms that manufactured and distributed a particular product during a certain period of time. This form of liability sharing is used only when the specific source of the harmful product is unidentifiable.

---

9. *Johnson v. Medtronic, Inc.,* 365 S.W.3d 226 (Mo.App. 2012).

10. *Video Software Dealers Association v. Schwarzenegger,* 556 F.3d 950 (9th Cir. 2009); *Brown v. Entertainment Merchants Association,* 564 U.S. 786, 131 S.Ct. 2729, 180 L.Ed.2d 708 (2011).

Case Example 6.9 Suffolk County Water Authority (SCWA) is a municipal water supplier in Suffolk County, New York. SCWA discovered the presence of a toxic chemical, perchloroethylene (PCE), used by dry cleaners and others in its local water. SCWA filed a product liability lawsuit against Dow Chemical Corporation and other companies that manufactured and distributed PCE. Dow filed a motion to dismiss the case for failure to state a claim, since SCWA could not identify each defendant whose allegedly defective product caused the water contamination.

A state trial court refused to dismiss the action, holding that SWCA's allegations were sufficient to invoke market-share liability. Under market-share liability, the burden of identification shifts to defendants if the plaintiff establishes a *prima facie* case on every element of the claim except identification of the specific defendant. (A *prima facie* case is one in which the plaintiff has presented sufficient evidence for the claim to go forward.)[11]

Courts in many jurisdictions do not recognize market-share liability, believing that it deviates too significantly from traditional legal principles. Jurisdictions that do recognize this theory of liability apply it only when it is difficult or impossible to determine which company made a particular product.

6–2e Other Applications of Strict Liability

Almost all courts extend the strict liability of manufacturers and other sellers to injured bystanders. **Example 6.10** A forklift that Trent is operating will not go into reverse, and as a result, it runs into a bystander. In this situation, the bystander can sue the manufacturer of the defective forklift under strict liability (and possibly bring a negligence action against the forklift operator as well).

Strict liability also applies to suppliers of component parts. **Example 6.11** Toyota buys brake pads from a subcontractor and puts them in Corollas without changing their composition. If those pads are defective, both the supplier of the brake pads and Toyota will be held strictly liable for injuries caused by the defects.

6–3 Defenses to Product Liability

Defendants in product liability suits can raise a number of defenses. One defense, of course, is to show that there is no basis for the plaintiff's claim. For instance, in a product liability case based on negligence, if a defendant can show that the plaintiff has not met the requirements (such as causation) for an action in negligence, generally the defendant will not be liable. A defendant may also assert that the *statute of limitations* for a product liability claim has lapsed.[12]

In a case involving strict product liability, a defendant can claim that the plaintiff failed to meet one of the requirements. If the defendant establishes that goods were altered after they were sold, for instance, the defendant normally will not be held liable.

6–3a Preemption

Learning Objective 4

What defenses to liability can be raised in a product liability lawsuit?

A defense that has been successfully raised by defendants in recent years is preemption—that government regulations preempt claims for product liability. An injured party may not be able to sue a manufacturer of defective products that are subject to comprehensive federal regulatory schemes.

Medical devices, for instance, are subject to extensive government regulation and undergo a rigorous premarket approval process. **Case Example 6.12** The United States Supreme Court decided in *Riegel v. Medtronic, Inc.*, that a man who was injured by an approved medical device (a balloon catheter) could not sue its maker for product liability. The Court reasoned that Congress had created a comprehensive scheme of federal safety oversight for medical

---

11. *Suffolk County Water Authority v. Dow Chemical Co.*, 44 Misc.3d 569, 987 N.Y.S.2d 819 (N.Y.Sup. 2014).
12. Similar state statutes, called *statutes of repose*, place outer time limits on product liability actions.

devices. The U.S. Food and Drug Administration is required to review the design, labeling, and manufacturing of medical devices before they are marketed to make sure that they are safe and effective. Because premarket approval is a "rigorous process," it preempts all common law claims challenging the safety or effectiveness of a medical device that has been approved.[13]

Since the *Medtronic* decision, some courts have extended the preemption defense to other product liability actions.[14] Other courts have been unwilling to deny an injured party relief simply because the federal government was supposed to ensure the product's safety.

In the following *Spotlight Case*, the United States Supreme Court had to decide if the preemption defense barred a plaintiff's claim for injuries caused by vaccination.

---

13. *Riegel v. Medtronic, Inc.*, 552 U.S. 312, 128 S.Ct. 999, 169 L.Ed.2d 892 (2008).
14. See, for example, *Fortner v. Bristol-Myers Squibb Co.*, __ F.Supp.3d __, 2017 WL 3193928 (S.D.N.Y. 2017).

✳ Spotlight on Injuries from Vaccinations: Case 6.3

Bruesewitz v. Wyeth, LLC

Supreme Court of the United States, 562 U.S. 223, 131 S.Ct. 1068, 179 L.Ed.2d 1 (2011).

Background and Facts When Hannah Bruesewitz was six months old, her pediatrician administered a dose of the diphtheria, tetanus, and pertussis (DTP) vaccine according to the Centers for Disease Control and Prevention's recommended childhood immunization schedule. Within twenty-four hours, Hannah began to experience seizures. She suffered more than one hundred seizures during the next month. Her doctors diagnosed her with "residual seizure disorder" and "developmental delay."

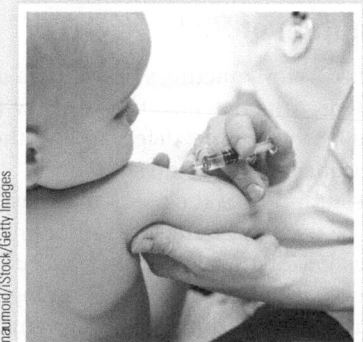
What happens when a vaccine causes adverse side effects?

Hannah's parents, Russell and Robalee Bruesewitz, filed a claim for relief in the U.S. Court of Federal Claims under the National Childhood Vaccine Injury Act (NCVIA). The NCVIA set up a no-fault compensation program for persons injured by vaccines. The claim was denied. The Bruesewitzes then filed a suit in a Pennsylvania state court against Wyeth, LLC, the maker of the vaccine, alleging strict product liability. The suit was moved to a federal district court. The court held that the claim was preempted by the NCVIA, which includes provisions protecting manufacturers from liability for "a vaccine's unavoidable, adverse side effects." A federal appellate court affirmed the district court's judgment. The Bruesewitzes appealed to the United States Supreme Court.

In the Words of the Court
Justice *SCALIA* delivered the opinion of the Court.
* * * *

In the 1970's and 1980's vaccines became, one might say, victims of their own success. They had been so effective in preventing infectious diseases that the public became much less alarmed at the threat of those diseases, and much more concerned with the risk of injury from the vaccines themselves.

Much of the concern centered around vaccines against * * * DTP, which were blamed for children's disabilities * * * . This led to a massive increase in vaccine-related tort litigation. * * * This destabilized the DTP vaccine market, causing two of the three domestic manufacturers to withdraw.
* * * *

To stabilize the vaccine market and facilitate compensation, Congress enacted the NCVIA in 1986. The Act establishes a no-fault compensation program designed to work faster and with greater ease than the civil tort system. A person injured by a vaccine, or his legal guardian, may file a petition for compensation in the United States Court of Federal Claims.

(Continues)

* * * *

Successful claimants receive compensation for medical, rehabilitation, counseling, special education, and vocational training expenses; diminished earning capacity; pain and suffering; and $250,000 for vaccine-related deaths. Attorneys' fees are provided * * * . These awards are paid out of a fund created by a * * * tax on each vaccine dose.

The *quid pro quo* [something done in exchange] for this, designed to stabilize the vaccine market, was the provision of significant tort-liability protections for vaccine manufacturers. * * * *Manufacturers are generally immunized from liability * * * if they have complied with all regulatory requirements * * * . And most relevant to the present case, the Act expressly eliminates liability for a vaccine's unavoidable, adverse side effects.* [Emphasis added.] * * * *

The Act's structural *quid pro quo* leads to the * * * conclusion: The vaccine manufacturers fund from their sales an informal,

efficient compensation program for vaccine injuries; in exchange they avoid costly tort litigation.

Decision and Remedy The United States Supreme Court affirmed the federal appellate court's judgment. The NCVIA preempted the Bruesewitzes' claim against Wyeth for compensation for the injury to their daughter caused by the DTP vaccine's side effects. In the Court's opinion, the NCVIA's compensation program strikes a balance between paying victims harmed by vaccines and protecting the vaccine industry from collapsing under the costs of tort liability.

Critical Thinking

• **Political** *If the public wants to change the policy outlined in this case, which branch of the government—and at what level—should be lobbied to make the change? Explain.*

• **Economic** *What is the public policy expressed by the provisions of the NCVIA?*

6–3b Assumption of Risk

Assumption of risk can sometimes be used as a defense in a product liability action. To establish such a defense, the defendant must show that (1) the plaintiff knew and appreciated the risk created by the product defect and (2) the plaintiff voluntarily assumed the risk, even though it was unreasonable to do so.

Although assumption of the risk is a defense in product liability actions, some courts do not allow it to be used as a defense to strict product liability claims. **Case Example 6.13** When Savannah Boles became a customer of Executive Tans, she signed a contract. One clause stated that signers used the company's tanning booths at their own risk. It also released the manufacturer and others from liability for any injuries. Later, Boles's fingers were partially amputated when they came into contact with a tanning booth's fan. Boles sued the manufacturer, claiming strict product liability. The Colorado Supreme Court held that assumption of risk was not applicable because strict product liability is driven by public-policy considerations. The theory focuses on the nature of the product rather than the conduct of either the manufacturer or the person injured.[15]

Under what circumstances can a tanning salon customer sue for injuries even though she or he signed a release?

6–3c Product Misuse

Similar to the defense of voluntary assumption of risk is that of product misuse, which occurs when a product is used for a purpose for which it was not intended. The courts have severely limited this defense. Today, product misuse is recognized as a defense *only when the particular use was not reasonably foreseeable.* If the misuse is foreseeable, the seller must take measures to guard against it.

Case Example 6.14 David Stults developed "popcorn lung" (bronchiolitis obliterans) from consuming multiple bags of microwave popcorn daily for several years. When he filed suit against the manufacturers of the popcorn and butter flavorings, the defendants asked the court for a summary judgment in their favor. The court denied defendants' motion and found that a manufacturer has a duty to warn of dangers associated with reasonably foreseeable

---

15. *Boles v. Sun Ergoline, Inc.*, 223 P.3d 724 (Co.Sup.Ct. 2010).

misuses of a product. If it is foreseeable that a person might consume several bags of the popcorn a day, then the manufacturer might have to warn users about the potential health risks associated with doing so.[16]

6–3d Comparative Negligence (Fault)

Developments in the area of comparative negligence, or fault (discussed in the torts chapter), have also affected the doctrine of strict liability. Today, courts in many jurisdictions consider the negligent or intentional actions of both the plaintiff and the defendant when apportioning liability and awarding damages. A defendant may be able to limit at least some liability for injuries caused by a defective product if it can show that the plaintiff's misuse of the product contributed to the injuries.

When proved, comparative negligence differs from other defenses in that it does not completely absolve the defendant of liability. It can, however, reduce the amount of damages that will be awarded to the plaintiff. Note that some jurisdictions allow only intentional conduct to affect a plaintiff's recovery, whereas others allow ordinary negligence to be used as a defense to product liability.

6–3e Commonly Known Dangers

As mentioned, the dangers associated with certain products (such as sharp knives and guns) are so commonly known that manufacturers need not warn users of those dangers. If a defendant succeeds in convincing the court that a plaintiff's injury resulted from a *commonly known danger*, the defendant normally will not be liable.

Classic Case Example 6.15 In a case from 1957, Marguerite Jamieson was injured when an elastic exercise rope slipped off her foot and struck her in the eye, causing a detachment of the retina. Jamieson claimed that the manufacturer should be liable because it had failed to warn users that the exerciser might slip off a foot in such a manner.

The court stated that to hold the manufacturer liable in these circumstances "would go beyond the reasonable dictates of justice in fixing the liabilities of manufacturers." After all, stated the court, "almost every physical object can be inherently dangerous or potentially dangerous in a sense. . . . A manufacturer cannot manufacture a knife that will not cut or a hammer that will not mash a thumb or a stove that will not burn a finger. The law does not require [manufacturers] to warn of such common dangers."[17]

6–3f Knowledgeable User

A related defense is the *knowledgeable user* defense. If a particular danger (such as electrical shock) is or should be commonly known by particular users of the product (such as electricians), the manufacturer of electrical equipment need not warn these users of the danger.

Spotlight Case Example 6.16 The parents of a group of teenagers who had become overweight and developed health problems filed a product liability lawsuit against McDonald's. The plaintiffs claimed that the well-known fast-food chain should be held liable for failing to warn customers of the adverse health effects of eating its food products. The court rejected this claim, however, based on the knowledgeable user defense.

According to the court, it is well known that the food at McDonald's contains high levels of cholesterol, fat, salt, and sugar, and is therefore unhealthful. The court's opinion, which thwarted numerous future lawsuits against fast-food restaurants, stated, "If consumers know (or reasonably should know) the potential ill health effects of eating at McDonald's, they cannot blame McDonald's if they, nonetheless, choose to satiate [satisfy] their appetite with a surfeit [excess] of supersized McDonald's products."[18]

---

16. *Stults v. International Flavors and Fragrances, Inc.*, 31 F.Supp.3d 1015 (N.D. Iowa 2014).
17. *Jamieson v. Woodward & Lothrop*, 247 F.2d 23, 101 D.C.App. 32 (1957).
18. *Pelman v. McDonald's Corp.*, 237 F.Supp.2d 512 (S.D.N.Y. 2003).

Toll To temporarily suspend the running of a prescribed time period, such as a statute of limitations.

Statute of Repose A statute that places outer time limits on product liability actions. Such statutes cut off absolutely the right to bring an action after a specified period of time following some event (often the product's manufacture or purchase) other than the occurrence of an injury.

6–3g Statutes of Limitations and Repose

As mentioned previously, statutes of limitations restrict the time within which an action may be brought. The statute of limitations for product liability cases varies according to state law. Usually, the injured party must bring a product liability claim within two to four years. Often, the running of the prescribed period is **tolled** (that is, suspended) until the party suffering an injury has discovered it or should have discovered it.

To ensure that sellers and manufacturers will not be left vulnerable to lawsuits indefinitely, many states have passed **statutes of repose**, which place outer time limits on product liability actions. For instance, a statute of repose may require that claims be brought within twelve years from the date of sale or manufacture of the defective product. If the plaintiff does not bring an action before the prescribed period expires, the seller cannot be held liable.

Practice and Review

Shalene Kolchek bought a Great Lakes Spa from Val Porter, a dealer who was selling spas at the state fair. After Kolchek signed the contract, Porter handed her the manufacturer's paperwork and arranged for the spa to be delivered and installed for her. Three months later, Kolchek left her six-year-old daughter, Litisha, alone in the spa. While exploring the spa's hydromassage jets, Litisha got her index finger stuck in one of the jet holes.

Litisha yanked hard, injuring her finger, and then panicked and screamed for help. Kolchek was unable to remove Litisha's finger, and the local police and rescue team were called to assist. After a three-hour operation that included draining the spa, sawing out a section of the spa's plastic molding, and slicing the jet casing, Litisha's finger was freed. Following this procedure, the spa was no longer functional. Litisha was taken to the local emergency room, where she was told that a bone in her finger was broken in two places. Using the information presented in the chapter, answer the following questions.

1. Under which theories of product liability can Kolchek sue Porter to recover for Litisha's injuries?

2. Would privity of contract be required for Kolchek to succeed in a product liability action against Great Lakes? Explain.

3. For an action in strict product liability against Great Lakes, what six requirements must Kolchek meet?

4. What defenses to product liability might Porter or Great Lakes be able to assert?

Debate This

All liability suits against tobacco companies for causing lung cancer should be thrown out of court now and forever.

Key Terms

Chapter Summary: Product Liability

Product Liability Claims	1. *Negligence*—The manufacturer must use due care in designing the product, selecting materials, using the appropriate production process, assembling and testing the product, placing adequate warnings on the label or product, and inspecting and testing its components. Privity of contract is not required. A manufacturer is liable for failure to exercise due care to any person who sustains an injury proximately caused by a negligently made (defective) product. 2. *Misrepresentation*—Fraudulent misrepresentation of a product may result in product liability based on the tort of fraud. The misrepresentation must have been made knowingly or with reckless disregard for the facts.

Strict Product Liability	1. *Requirements*—
	  a. The defendant must have sold the product in a defective condition.
	  b. The defendant must normally be engaged in the business of selling that product.
	  c. The product must be unreasonably dangerous to the user or consumer because of its defective condition (in most states).
	  d. The plaintiff must incur physical harm to self or property by use or consumption of the product.
	  e. The defective condition must be the proximate cause of the injury or damage.
	  f. The goods must not have been substantially changed from the time the product was sold to the time the injury was sustained.
	2. *Product defects*—A product may be defective in three basic ways: in its manufacture, in its design, or in the instructions or warnings that come with it.
	3. *Market-share liability*—When plaintiffs cannot prove which of many distributors of a defective product supplied the particular product that caused the plaintiffs' injuries, some courts apply market-share liability. All firms that manufactured and distributed the harmful product during the period in question are then held liable for the plaintiffs' injuries in proportion to the firms' respective share of the market, as directed by the court.
	4. *Other applications*—Manufacturers and other sellers are liable for harms suffered by bystanders as a result of defective products. Suppliers of component parts are strictly liable for defective parts that, when incorporated into a product, cause injuries to users.

Defenses to Product Liability	1. *Preemption*—An injured party may not be able to sue the manufacturer of a product that is subject to comprehensive federal safety regulations, such as medical devices. 2. *Assumption of risk*—The user or consumer knew of the risk of harm and voluntarily assumed it. 3. *Product misuse*—The user or consumer misused the product in a way unforeseeable by the manufacturer. 4. *Comparative negligence*—Liability may be distributed between the plaintiff and the defendant under the doctrine of comparative negligence if the plaintiff's misuse of the product contributed to the risk of injury. 5. *Commonly known dangers*—If a defendant succeeds in convincing the court that a plaintiff's injury resulted from a commonly known danger, such as the danger associated with using a sharp knife, the defendant will not be liable. 6. *Knowledgeable user*—If a particular danger is or should be commonly known by particular users of the product, the manufacturer of the product need not warn these users of the danger.

Issue Spotters

1. Rim Corporation makes tire rims and sells them, to Superior Vehicles, Inc., which installs them on cars. One set of rims is defective, which an inspection would reveal. Superior does not inspect the rims. The car with the defective rims is sold to Town Auto Sales, which sells the car to Uri. Soon, the car is in an accident caused by the defective rims, and Uri is injured. Is Superior Vehicles liable? Explain your answer. (See *Product Liability Claims*.)

2. Bensing Company manufactures generic drugs for the treatment of heart disease. A federal law requires generic drug makers to use labels that are identical to the labels on brand-name versions of the drugs. Hunter Rothfus purchased Bensing's generic drugs in Ohio and wants to sue Bensing for defective labeling based on its failure to comply with Ohio state common law (rather than the federal labeling requirements). What defense might Bensing assert to avoid liability under state law? (See *Defenses to Product Liability*.)

—**Check your answers to the *Issue Spotters* against the answers provided in Appendix D at the end of this text.**

Business Scenarios and Case Problems

6–1. Product Liability. Carmen buys a television set manufactured by AKI Electronics. She is going on vacation, so she takes the set to her mother's house for her mother to use. Because the set is defective, it explodes, causing considerable damage to her mother's house. Carmen's mother sues AKI for the damage to her house. Discuss the theories under which Carmen's mother can recover from AKI. (See *Product Liability Claims*.)

6–2. Product Liability. Jason Clark, an experienced hunter, bought a paintball gun. Clark practiced with the gun and knew how to screw in the carbon dioxide cartridge, pump the gun, and use its safety and trigger. Although Clark was aware that he could purchase protective eyewear, he chose not to do so. Clark had taken gun safety courses and understood that it was "common sense" not to shoot anyone in the face. Clark's friend, Chris Wright, also owned a paintball gun and was similarly familiar with the gun's use and its risks.

Clark, Wright, and their friends played a game that involved shooting paintballs at cars whose occupants also had the guns. One night, while Clark and Wright were cruising with their guns, Wright shot at Clark's car but hit Clark in the eye. Clark filed a product liability lawsuit against the manufacturer of Wright's paintball gun to recover for the injury. Clark claimed that the gun was defectively designed. During the trial, Wright testified that his gun "never malfunctioned." In whose favor should the court rule? Why? (See *Product Liability Claims*.)

6–3. Product Misuse. Five-year-old Cheyenne Stark was riding in the backseat of her parents' Ford Taurus. Cheyenne was not sitting in a booster seat. Instead, she was using a seatbelt designed by Ford but was wearing the shoulder belt behind her back. The car was involved in a collision. As a result, Cheyenne suffered a spinal cord injury and was paralyzed from the waist down. The family filed a suit against Ford Motor Co., alleging that the seatbelt was defectively designed. Could Ford successfully claim that Cheyenne had misused the seatbelt? Why or why not? [*Stark v. Ford Motor Co.*, 365 N.C. 468, 723 S.E.2d 753 (2012)] (See *Defenses to Product Liability*.)

6–4. Business Case Problem with Sample Answer— Product Liability. While driving on Interstate 40 in North Carolina, Carroll Jett became distracted by a texting system in the cab of his tractor-trailer truck. He smashed into several vehicles that were slowed or stopped in front of him, injuring Barbara and Michael Durkee and others. The injured motorists filed a suit in a federal district court against Geologic Solutions, Inc., the maker of the texting system, alleging product liability. Was the accident caused by Jett's inattention or the texting device? Should a manufacturer be required to design a product that is incapable of distracting a driver? Discuss. [*Durkee v. Geologic Solutions, Inc.*, 502 Fed. Appx. 326 (4th Cir. 2013)] (See *Product Liability Claims*.)

—**For a sample answer to Problem 6–4, go to Appendix E at the end of this text.**

6–5. Strict Product Liability. Medicis Pharmaceutical Corp. makes Solodyn, a prescription oral antibiotic. Medicis warns physicians that "autoimmune syndromes, including drug-induced lupus-like syndrome," may be associated with use of the drug. Amanda Watts had chronic acne. Her physician prescribed Solodyn. Information included with the drug did not mention the risk of autoimmune disorders, and Watts was not otherwise advised of it. She was prescribed the drug twice, each time for twenty weeks. Later, she experienced debilitating joint pain and, after being hospitalized, was diagnosed with lupus. On what basis could Watts recover from Medicis in an action grounded in product liability? Explain. [*Watts v. Medicis Pharmaceutical Corp.*, 236 Ariz. 19, 365 P.3d 944 (2016)] (See *Strict Product Liability*.)

6–6. Strict Product Liability. Duval Ford, LLC, sold a new Ford F-250 pickup truck to David Sweat. Before taking delivery, Sweat ordered a lift kit to be installed on the truck by a Duval subcontractor. Sweat also replaced the tires and modified the suspension system to increase the towing capacity. Later, through Burkins Chevrolet, Sweat sold the truck to Shaun Lesnick. Sweat had had no problems with the truck's steering or suspension, but Lesnick did. He had the steering repaired and made additional changes, including installing a steering stabilizer and replacing the tires. Two months later, Lesnick was driving the truck when the steering and suspension suddenly failed, and the truck flipped over, causing Lesnick severe injuries. Could Lesnick successfully claim that Duval and Burkins had failed to warn him of the risk of a lifted truck? Explain. [*Lesnick v. Duval Ford, LLC*, 41 Fla.L.Weekly D281, 185 So.3d 577 (1 Dist. 2016)] (See *Product Liability Claims*.)

6–7. Spotlight on Pfizer, Inc.—Defenses to Product Liability. Prescription drugs in the United States must be approved by the Food and Drug Administration (FDA) before they can be sold. A drug maker whose product is approved through the FDA's "abbreviated new drug application" (ANDA) process cannot later change the label without FDA approval. Pfizer Inc. makes and sells by prescription Depo-T, a testosterone replacement drug classified as an ANDA-approved drug. Rodney Guilbeau filed a claim in a federal district court against Pfizer, alleging that he sustained a "cardiovascular event" after taking Depo-T. He sought recovery on a state-law product liability theory, arguing that Pfizer failed to warn patients adequately about the risks. He claimed that after the drug's approval its maker had become aware of a higher incidence of heart attacks, strokes, and other cardiovascular events among those who took it but had not added a warning to its label. What is Pfizer's best defense to this claim? Explain. [*Guilbeau v. Pfizer, Inc.*, 80 F.3d 304 (7th Cir. 2018)] (See *Defenses to Product Liability*.)

6–8. A Question of Ethics—The IDDR Approach and Product Liability. *While replacing screws in a gutter, John Baugh fell off a ladder and landed headfirst on his concrete driveway. He sustained a severe brain injury, which permanently limited his ability to perform routine physical and intellectual functions. He filed a suit in a federal district court against Cuprum S.A. de C.V., the company that designed and made the ladder, alleging a design defect under product liability theories. Baugh weighed nearly 200 pounds, which was the stated weight limit on this ladder. Kevin Smith, a mechanical engineer, testified on Baugh's behalf that the gusset (bracket) on the ladder's right front side was too* short to support Baugh's weight. This caused the ladder's leg to fail and Baugh to fall. In Smith's opinion, a longer gusset would have prevented the accident. Cuprum argued that the accident occurred because Baugh climbed too high on the ladder and stood on its fourth step and pail shelf, neither of which were intended for the purpose. No other person witnessed Baugh using the ladder prior to his fall, however, so there was no evidence to support Cuprum's argument. [Baugh v. Cuprum S.A. de C.V., *845 F.3d 838 (7th Cir. 2017)*] (See *Strict Product Liability*.)

1. What is a manufacturer's legal and ethical duty when designing and making products for consumers? Did Cuprum meet this standard? Discuss.

2. Did the mechanical engineer's testimony establish that a reasonable alternative design was available for Cuprum's ladder? Explain.

Critical Thinking and Writing Assignments

6–9. Time-Limited Group Assignment. Bret D'Auguste was an experienced skier when he rented equipment to ski at Hunter Mountain Ski Bowl in New York. When D'Auguste entered an extremely difficult trail, he noticed immediately that the surface consisted of ice with almost no snow. He tried to exit the steeply declining trail by making a sharp right turn, but in the attempt, his left ski snapped off. D'Auguste lost his balance, fell, and slid down the mountain, striking his face and head against a fence along the trail. According to a report by a rental shop employee, one of the bindings on D'Auguste's skis had a "cracked heel housing." D'Auguste filed a lawsuit against the bindings' manufacturer on a theory of strict product liability. The manufacturer filed a motion for summary judgment. (See *Product Liability Claims*.)

1. The first group will take the position of the manufacturer and develop an argument why the court should *grant* the summary judgment motion and dismiss the strict product liability claim.

2. The second group will take the position of D'Auguste and formulate a basis for why the court should *deny* the motion and allow the strict product liability claim.

3. The third group will evaluate whether D'Auguste assumed the risk of this type of injury.

4. The fourth group will analyze whether the manufacturer could claim that D'Auguste's negligence (under the comparative negligence doctrine) contributed to his injury.

7 Intellectual Property Rights

Learning Objectives

The five Learning Objectives *below are designed to help improve your understanding. After reading this chapter, you should be able to answer the following questions:*

1. Why is the protection of trademarks important?

2. How does the law protect patents?

3. What laws protect authors' rights in the works they create?

4. What are trade secrets, and what laws offer protection for this form of intellectual property?

5. How does the TRIPS agreement protect intellectual property worldwide?

Intellectual Property Property resulting from intellectual and creative processes.

"My words and my ideas are my property, and I'll keep and protect them as surely as I do my stable of unicorns."

Jarod Kintz
1982–present
(American author)

Intellectual property is any property resulting from intellectual, creative processes—the products of an individual's mind, as suggested in the chapter-opening quotation. Although it is an abstract term for an abstract concept, intellectual property is nonetheless familiar to almost everyone. The apps for your iPhone or Samsung Galaxy, the movies you see, and the music you listen to are all forms of intellectual property.

More than two hundred years ago, the framers of the U.S. Constitution recognized the importance of protecting creative works in Article I, Section 8. Statutory protection of these rights began in the 1940s and continues to evolve to meet the needs of modern society. Suppose that JD Beverage Company makes and sells a line of flavored vodkas called "Hot Lips Vodka." The name Hot Lips Vodka, along with an image of puckered lips, appears on the label of each bottle. The color of the lips logo depends on the vodka's flavor—red for chili pepper, green for apple, and so on. JD Beverage has registered trademarks for the name Hot Lips Vodka and the puckered lips logo, and the company heavily markets the vodka using hot lips as a theme. Sales of Hot Lips Vodka are at an all-time high.

Now another alcoholic beverage company begins to distribute a line of flavored vodkas called "Kiss Vodka." Like the Hot Lips label, the new vodka's label features the product's name and a puckered lips logo, and the company uses the lips in its marketing. JD Beverage believes that Kiss Vodka's use of the lips logo is diminishing the value of its Hot Lips brand and cutting into its sales. What can JD Beverage do? The answer lies in intellectual property law.

7-1 Trademarks

A **trademark** is a distinctive word, symbol, sound, or design that identifies the manufacturer as the source of particular goods and distinguishes its products from those made or sold by others. At common law, the person who used a symbol or mark to identify a business or product was protected in the use of that trademark. Clearly, if another company used the trademark, it could lead consumers to believe that its goods were made by the trademark owner. The law seeks to avoid this kind of confusion. (For information on how companies use trademarks and service marks, see the *Linking Business Law to Marketing* feature.)

Learning Objective 1
Why is the protection of trademarks important?

Trademark A distinctive word, symbol, sound, or design that identifies the manufacturer as the source of particular goods and distinguishes its products from those made or sold by others.

Linking Business Law to Marketing

Trademarks and Service Marks

Trademarks and service marks consist of much more than well-known brand names, such as Apple and Amazon. If you become a marketing manager, you will be involved in creating trademarks or service marks for your firm, protecting the firm's existing marks, and ensuring that you do not infringe on anyone else's marks. You will need to be aware that parts of a brand name or other forms of product identification may qualify for trademark protection.

- **Catchy phrases**—Certain brands have established phrases that are associated with the brands, such as Nike's "Just Do It!" Take care to avoid using another brand's catchy phrase in your own program. Note, too, that not all phrases can become part of a trademark or service mark. When a phrase is extremely common, the courts normally will not grant it trademark or service mark protection.
- **Abbreviations**—The public sometimes abbreviates a well-known trademark. For example, Budweiser beer is known as Bud and Coca-Cola as Coke. Do not use any name for a product or service that closely resembles a well-known abbreviation, such as Koke for a cola drink.
- **Shapes**—The shape of a brand name, a service mark, or a container can take on exclusivity if the shape clearly aids in product or service identification. Just about everyone recognizes the shape of a Coca-Cola bottle, for example. Avoid using a similar shape for competing products.
- **Ornamental colors**—Sometimes, color combinations can become part of a service mark or trademark. For example, FedEx established its unique identity with the use of bright orange and purple. The courts have protected this color combination. The same holds for the black-and-copper color combination of Duracell batteries.
- **Ornamental designs**—Symbols and designs associated with a particular mark are normally protected, so do not attempt to copy them. For example, Levi's places a small tag on the left side of the rear pocket of its jeans. Cross uses a cutoff black cone on the top of its pens.
- **Sounds**—Sounds can also be protected. For example, the familiar roar of the Metro-Goldwyn-Mayer (MGM) lion is protected.

When to Protect Trademarks and Service Marks

Once your company has established trademarks or service marks, it must decide how aggressively to protect those marks. If it fails to protect them, it faces the possibility that the marks will become generic. As discussed later, *aspirin*, *cellophane*, *thermos*, *dry ice*, *shredded wheat*, and many other familiar terms were once legally protected trademarks.

EVERETT COLLECTION, INC.

Should the roar of the MGM lion be protected under trademark law?

Protecting exclusive rights to a mark can be expensive, however, and a company must determine how much it is worth to protect its rights. Major expenditures to protect a small company's trademarks and service marks might not be cost-effective.

Critical Thinking

The U.S. Patent and Trademark Office requires that a registered trademark or service mark be put into commercial use within six months. Extensions can be granted but the mark must be put into commercial use within three years after the application has been approved. Why do you think the federal government established this requirement?

In the following *Classic Case* concerning Coca-Cola, the defendants argued that the Coca-Cola trademark was not entitled to protection under the law because the term did not accurately represent the product.

Classic Case 7.1

Coca-Cola Co. v. Koke Co. of America

Supreme Court of the United States, 254 U.S. 143, 41 S.Ct. 113, 65 L.Ed. 189 (1920).

Background and Facts John Pemberton, an Atlanta pharmacist, invented a caramel-colored, carbonated soft drink in 1886. His bookkeeper, Frank Robinson, named the beverage Coca-Cola after two of the ingredients, coca leaves and kola nuts. Asa Candler bought the Coca-Cola Company in 1891 and made the soft drink available throughout the United States and in parts of Canada and Mexico. Candler continued to sell Coke aggressively and to open up new markets in Europe and elsewhere, attracting numerous competitors, some of whom tried to capitalize directly on the Coke name.

How is Coca-Cola protected?

© Rob Wilson/ShutterStock.com

The Coca-Cola Company brought an action in a federal district court to enjoin (prevent) other beverage companies (including Koke Company of America) from using the names *Koke* and *Dope* for their products. The defendants contended that the Coca-Cola trademark was a fraudulent representation and that Coca-Cola was therefore not entitled to any help from the courts. By using the Coca-Cola name, the defendants alleged, the Coca-Cola Company represented that the beverage contained cocaine (from coca leaves). The district court granted the injunction, but the federal appellate court reversed. The Coca-Cola Company appealed to the United States Supreme Court.

In the Words of the Court

Mr. Justice *HOLMES* delivered the opinion of the Court.

* * * *

* * * Before 1900 the beginning of [Coca-Cola's] good will was more or less helped by the presence of cocaine, a drug that, like alcohol or opium, may be described as a deadly poison or as a valuable item of the pharmacopoea [collection of pharmaceuticals] according to the [purposes of the speaker]. * * * After the Food and Drug Act of June 30, 1906, if not earlier, long before this suit was brought, it was eliminated from the plaintiff's compound.

* * * Since 1900 the sales have increased at a very great rate corresponding to a like increase in advertising. The name now characterizes a beverage to be had at almost any soda fountain. It means a single thing coming from a single source, and well known to the community. It hardly would be too much to say that the drink characterizes the name as much as the name the drink. In other words, *Coca-Cola probably means to most persons the plaintiff's familiar product to be had everywhere rather than a compound of particular substances.* [Emphasis added.]

* * * Before this suit was brought the plaintiff had advertised to the public that it must not expect and would not find cocaine, and had eliminated everything tending to suggest cocaine effects except the name and the picture of the leaves and nuts, which probably conveyed little or nothing to most who saw it. It appears to us that it would be going too far to deny the plaintiff relief against a palpable fraud because possibly here and there an ignorant person might call for the drink with the hope for incipient cocaine intoxication. The plaintiff's position must be judged by the facts as they were when the suit was begun, not by the facts of a different condition and an earlier time.

Decision and Remedy The United States Supreme Court upheld the district court's injunction. The competing beverage companies were prevented from calling their products *Koke.* The Court did not prevent them from calling their products *Dope,* however.

Critical Thinking

• **What If the Facts Were Different?** *Suppose that Coca-Cola had been trying to make the public believe that its product*

contained cocaine. Would the result in the case likely have been different? Explain your answer.

• **Impact of This Case on Today's Law** *In this early case, the United States Supreme Court made it clear that trademarks and trade names (and nicknames for those marks and names, such as "Coke" for "Coca-Cola") that are in common use receive protection under the common law. This holding is significant historically because it is the predecessor to the federal statute later passed to protect trademark rights (the Lanham Act, discussed next).*

7–1a Statutory Protection of Trademarks

Statutory protection of trademarks and related property is provided at the federal level by the Lanham Act of 1946.[1] The Lanham Act was enacted in part to protect manufacturers from losing business to rival companies that used confusingly similar trademarks. The Lanham Act incorporates the common law of trademarks and provides remedies for owners of trademarks who wish to enforce their claims in federal court. Many states also have trademark statutes.

Trademark Dilution The Federal Trademark Dilution Act[2] amended the Lanham Act to allow trademark owners to bring suits in federal court for **trademark dilution.** Later, Congress further amended the law on trademark dilution by passing the Trademark Dilution Revision Act (TDRA).[3]

Under the TDRA, to state a claim for trademark dilution, a plaintiff must prove the following:

1. The plaintiff owns a famous mark that is distinctive.

2. The defendant has begun using a mark in commerce that allegedly is diluting the famous mark.

3. The similarity between the defendant's mark and the famous mark gives rise to an *association* between the marks.

4. The association is likely to impair the distinctiveness of the famous mark or harm its reputation.

Trademark dilution laws protect "distinctive" or "famous" trademarks (such as Rolls-Royce, McDonald's, Starbucks, and Apple) from certain unauthorized uses. Such a mark is protected even when the unauthorized use is on noncompeting goods or is unlikely to confuse. More than half of the states have also enacted trademark dilution laws.

The Marks Need Not Be Identical A famous mark may be diluted not only by the use of an identical mark but also by the use of a *similar* mark, provided that it reduces the value of the famous mark. A similar mark is more likely to lessen the value of a famous mark when the companies using the marks provide related goods or compete against each other in the same market.

Trademark Dilution The unauthorized use of a distinctive and famous mark in a way that impairs the mark's distinctiveness or harms its reputation.

Know This
Trademark dilution laws protect the owners of distinctive marks from unauthorized uses even when the defendants' use involves noncompeting goods or is unlikely to cause confusion.

---

1. 15 U.S.C. Sections 1051–1128.
2. 15 U.S.C. Section 1125.
3. Pub. L. No. 103-312, 120 Stat. 1730 (2006).

✳ **Spotlight Case Example 7.1** When Samantha Lundberg opened Sambuck's Coffeehouse in Astoria, Oregon, she knew that Starbucks was one of the largest coffee chains in the nation. Starbucks Corporation filed a dilution lawsuit, and a federal court ruled that use of the Sambuck's mark constituted trademark dilution because it created confusion for consumers. Not only was there a "high degree" of similarity between the marks, but also both companies provided coffee-related services through stand-alone retail stores. Therefore, the use of the similar mark (Sambuck's) reduced the value of the famous mark (Starbucks).[4] ◼

7–1b Trademark Registration

Trademarks may be registered with the state or with the federal government. To register for protection under federal trademark law, a person must file an application with the U.S. Patent and Trademark Office in Washington, D.C. A mark can be registered (1) if it is currently in commerce or (2) if the applicant intends to put it into commerce within six months.

In special circumstances, the six-month period can be extended by thirty months. Thus, the applicant would have a total of three years from the date of notice of trademark approval to make use of the mark and to file the required use statement. Registration is postponed until the mark is actually used.

During this waiting period, an applicant can legally protect his or her trademark against a third party who has neither used the mark previously nor filed an application for it. Registration is renewable between the fifth and sixth years after the initial registration and every ten years thereafter (every twenty years for trademarks registered before 1990).

Ethical Issue

Should the law allow offensive trademark names? It is settled law that the First Amendment generally protects people's use of offensive words. Until recently, though, free speech did not necessarily extend to trademarking a word or name that some Americans find offensive. Under Section 2(a) of the Lanham Act (also known as the disparagement clause), the federal government could prohibit applicants from trademarking offensive (or disparaging) terms. The disparagement clause bars any trademark that "may disparage . . . or bring into contempt, or disrepute" any persons, institutions, beliefs, or national symbols. The U.S. Patent and Trademark Office (USPTO) used this clause to cancel the Washington Redskins football team's trademarks, which were deemed offensive to Native Americans.[5] Then came another case involving a musical group called The Slants, which consisted of only Asians.

The members of The Slants picked the name because it was offensive. They claimed they wanted to turn the phrase upside down "to reappropriate it into something positive and empowering." When the trademark registration was reviewed by the USPTO, however, the USPTO cited Section 2(a) of the Lanham Act to deny registration. The band contested the ruling, noting that it could not get a record label deal unless it had a federally registered trademark. The case eventually was heard by the United States Supreme Court. In arguing before the Court, the band's attorney pointed out the numerous inconsistencies in the USPTO's decisions concerning potentially offensive names. For instance, the USPTO had approved a hip-hop group's registration of N.W.A.—which stands for Niggaz Wit Attitudes.

Some people find the term "Redskins" offensive, while others do not. Who should prevail when it comes to providing trademark protection to such offensive terms or names, and why?

dean bertoncelj/Shutterstock.com

---

4. *Starbucks Corp. v. Lundberg,* 2005 WL 3183858 (D.Or. 2005).
5. See *Pro-Football, Inc. v. Amanda Blackhorse,* 62 F.Supp.3d 498 (E.D.Va. 2014) and 112 F.Supp.3d 439 (E.D.Va. 2015).

In 2017, the United States Supreme Court decided that the disparagement clause of the Lanham Act was an unconstitutional restraint on free speech. In a unanimous opinion, Justice Samuel Alito wrote, "It offends a bedrock First Amendment principle: Speech may not be banned on the ground that it expresses ideas that offend." Under this ruling, the federal government can no longer cancel or refuse to register trademarks—such as The Slants or the Redskins—that officials deem to be offensive or disparaging.[6]

7–1c Trademark Infringement

Registration of a trademark with the U.S. Patent and Trademark Office gives notice on a nationwide basis that the trademark belongs exclusively to the registrant. The registrant is also allowed to use the symbol ® to indicate that the mark has been registered. Whenever that trademark is copied to a substantial degree or used in its entirety by another, intentionally or unintentionally, the trademark has been *infringed* (used without authorization).

When a trademark has been infringed, the owner has a cause of action against the infringer. To succeed in a lawsuit for trademark infringement, the owner must show that the defendant's use of the mark created a likelihood of confusion about the origin of the defendant's goods or services. (See this chapter's *Beyond Our Borders* feature for a discussion of how confusion can arise from product packaging.) The owner need not prove that the infringer acted intentionally or that the trademark was registered (although registration does provide proof of the date of inception of the trademark's use).

---

6. *Matal v. Tam*, ___ U.S. ___, 137 S.Ct. 1744, 198 L.Ed.2d 366 (2017).

Beyond Our Borders

ALEVE versus FLANAX—Same Pain Killer, But in Different Countries

How many U.S. residents have not heard of the pain relief drug Aleve? Not many, because the product is so heavily advertised. The same could be said about the painkiller Flanax in Mexico. And in fact, Aleve and Flanax are the same drug, owned by the same company, Bayer AG. Bayer has been selling Flanax in Mexico and Latin America since the 1970s.

Trademark Rights versus the Lanham Act

Traditionally, trademark rights have been territorial. Consequently, Bayer did not register the Flanax brand name in the United States. After all, Bayer never sold or marketed any products under the Flanax name in this country. Here, it chose to use the name Aleve. Taking advantage of this lack of trademark registration in the United States, a small pharmaceutical company named Belmora applied for and obtained a U.S. trademark registration for Flanax in 2005.

Since then, Belmora has used packaging identical to that used for Bayer's Flanax in Mexico, including color schemes and type style. Within the United States, it has targeted the Mexican American community with such advertising copy as "Flanax products have been used [for] many, many years in Mexico [and are] now being produced in the United States by Belmora." Clearly, such practices make it difficult, if not impossible, for consumers to distinguish between Bayer's Mexican product and the product offered by Belmora. Bayer petitioned the U.S. Patent and Trademark Office to cancel Belmora's Flanax trademark registration under the provisions of the Lanham Act.[a]

A Long Road to Redemption

The Trademark Trial and Appeal Board cancelled Belmora's trademark registration, citing obvious misuse of the Flanax mark. A Virginia district court reversed the

---

a. Section 14(3).

(*Continues*)

trademark registration cancellation, and Bayer appealed.

The U.S. Court of Appeals for Fourth Circuit sided with Bayer.[b] It held that Bayer had standing under Section 43(a) of the Lanham Act, which did not require that Bayer hold a U.S. trademark registration. Rather, Bayer had clearly been damaged by Belmora's activities in the United States, and that was sufficient under the plain

language of the statute. The court further ruled that Bayer's claims were sufficient under a test established by the Supreme Court several years earlier.[c] Bayer's claim came "within the zone of interest in a suit for false advertising."

The U.S. Supreme Court denied *certiorari.*[d] That means that, at least in the Fourth

Circuit, the owner of a non-U.S. trademark can bring an action under the Lanham Act for the unauthorized use of a brand that the plaintiff never marketed in this country.

The federal district court in Virginia, in upholding Belmora's registered trademark, held that "Bayer could not have an economic loss for a market it did not use in U.S. commerce." Why did the appellate court not accept this reasoning?

b. *Belmora, LLC v. Bayer Consumer Care, A.G.,* 819 F.3d 697 (4th Cir. 2016).

c. *Lexmark International, Inc. v. Static Control Components, Inc.,* ___ U.S. ___, 134 S.Ct. 1377, 188 L.Ed.2d 392 (2014).
d. *Cert.* denied, *Belmora, LLC v. Bayer Consumer Care, A.G.,* ___ U.S. ___, 137 S.Ct. 1202, 197 L.Ed.2d 246 (2017).

Know This

To prove trademark infringement, the trademark owner must show that the other party's use of the mark has created a likelihood of confusion about the origin of that party's goods or services.

The most commonly granted remedy for trademark infringement is an *injunction* to prevent further infringement. Under the Lanham Act, a trademark owner that successfully proves infringement can recover actual damages, plus the profits that the infringer wrongfully received from the unauthorized use of the mark. A court can also order the destruction of any goods bearing the unauthorized trademark. In some situations, the trademark owner may also be able to recover attorneys' fees.

At the center of the following case was an injunction granted in an earlier dispute between two brothers. The injunction prohibited one of the brothers from using trademarks owned by the other, including a mark featuring their shared last name.

■ Case 7.2

LFP IP, LLC v. Hustler Cincinnati, Inc.
United States Court of Appeals, Sixth Circuit, 810 F.3d 424 (2016).

Background and Facts Brothers Jimmy and Larry Flynt owned "The Hustler Club," a bar and nightclub, in Cincinnati, Ohio. Larry opened Hustler clubs in other Ohio cities and, within a few years, began publishing *Hustler*, a sexually explicit magazine. Larry formed LFP IP, Inc., and other corporations to conduct his enterprises. Many of these used "HUSTLER" or "LARRY FLYNT" as trademarks, which LFP owned. Jimmy opened his own store, "Hustler Cincinnati," and paid LFP licensing fees to use the "HUSTLER" mark.

When Hustler Cincinnati stopped paying the fees, LFP filed a suit in a federal district court against the store's corporate owner, alleging trademark infringement. The court issued an injunction prohibiting Jimmy from using the "HUSTLER" mark. Later, he opened a store called "FLYNT Sexy Gifts." LFP claimed that this name was likely to cause confusion with the "LARRY FLYNT" mark. The court modified the injunction to limit Jimmy's use of the "Flynt" name without "Jimmy." Jimmy appealed.

In the Words of the Court
SUTTON, Circuit Judge.
* * * *

Courts * * * may exercise their sound judicial discretion to modify an injunction if the circumstances, whether of law or fact, obtaining at the time of its issuance have changed, or new ones have since arisen.

* * * The [district] court * * * applied the traditional test for trademark infringement under federal law, asking whether (1) Larry and his companies owned the LARRY FLYNT trademark, (2) Jimmy used the mark in commerce, and (3) the use was likely to cause confusion. The court found all three elements satisfied * * *. Because the original injunction was tailored to prevent trademark infringement by [Jimmy] and because Jimmy had committed new violations, the district court acted appropriately when it modified its initial grant of relief to cover Jimmy's conduct at the [new] outlet.

The district court's modified injunction was also suitably tailored to the changed circumstances. Balancing the competing interests of Larry and Jimmy, the court permitted Jimmy to use his full name while protecting Larry's interest in the LARRY FLYNT trademark.

* * * *

Jimmy * * * takes issue with some of the factual findings that the district court used to justify the modified injunction.

But none of the district court's factual findings is clearly erroneous. * * * Larry * * * presented evidence that he used the mark in connection with a wide range of adult entertainment products, including the kinds of products sold at Jimmy's store. Because *product use * * * marks the salient [most noticeable] indicator of ownership in trademark-infringement actions,* the district court reasonably found that Larry * * * owned the LARRY FLYNT trademark with respect to retail goods. The court also reasonably found that Larry began using the mark on adult entertainment products before Jimmy did. * * * And * * * Larry's company * * * continued to use that mark in commerce. [Emphasis added.]

In claiming an absence of evidence of consumer confusion, Jimmy missteps. Some of the evidence comes from Jimmy himself. When asked about instances where a consumer has been confused, in terms of whether or not Jimmy was the owner of the store, Jimmy responded, "I have experienced the confusion in the names, you know. Jimmy and Larry Flynt, in this market area, is somewhat synonymous with Hustler or with Flynt. You're not going to get around that."

Decision and Remedy The federal appellate court affirmed the lower court's modification of the injunction. The injunction was initially tailored to prevent Jimmy's infringement of his brother's marks. When Jimmy committed a new violation by opening "FLYNT Sexy Gifts," the district court acted appropriately in modifying the injunction to cover this conduct.

Critical Thinking

• **E-Commerce** *Can Jimmy use his last name—the name that he shares with his brother—as a domain name? Why or why not?*

• **What If the Facts Were Different?** *Suppose that Jimmy had used the marks at the center of this case on an entirely different line of goods, not adult entertainment products. Would the result have been the same? Explain.*

7–1d Distinctiveness of the Mark

A central objective of the Lanham Act is to reduce the likelihood that consumers will be confused by similar marks. For that reason, only those trademarks that are deemed sufficiently distinctive from all competing trademarks will be protected.

To determine a mark's strength, courts classify it on a spectrum of five categories, ranging from strongest to weakest. *Fanciful* and *arbitrary marks* employ words and phrases with no commonly understood connection to the product. These are the two strongest categories and trigger the highest degree of trademark protection. *Suggestive marks,* which suggest a product's features and require consumers to use some imagination to associate the suggestive mark with the product, are in the middle of the spectrum. The two weakest categories are *descriptive* and *generic marks. Descriptive marks* define a particular characteristic of the product in a way that does not require any imagination. *Generic marks* describe the product in its entirety and are not entitled to trademark protection.

Strong Marks As the most distinctive (strongest) trademarks, fanciful and arbitrary marks receive automatic protection because they serve to identify a particular product's source, as opposed to describing the product itself. Fanciful trademarks often include invented words. Examples include *Xerox* for one company's copiers and *Google* for another company's search engine.

Arbitrary trademarks use words and phrases with no commonly understood connection to the product, such as *Dutch Boy* as a name for paint. Even a single letter used in a particular style can be an arbitrary trademark, such as the stylized X mark that Quiksilver, Inc., uses on its clothing.

Suggestive trademarks, representing the middle of the spectrum, indicate something about a product's nature, quality, or characteristics without describing the product directly. For instance, "Dairy Queen" suggests an association between its products and milk, but it does not directly describe ice cream. Suggestive marks can be transformed into strong marks by achieving a high degree of marketplace recognition, such as through substantial advertising.

Secondary Meaning Descriptive terms, geographic terms, and personal names are not inherently distinctive and do not receive protection under the law until they acquire a secondary meaning. Whether a secondary meaning becomes attached to a term or name usually depends on how extensively the product is advertised, the market for the product, the number of sales, and other factors.

A secondary meaning may arise when customers begin to associate a specific term or phrase (such as Calvin Klein) with specific trademarked items made by a particular company (designer clothing and goods). Once a secondary meaning is attached to a term or name, a trademark is considered distinctive and is protected. Even a color can qualify for trademark protection, such as the color schemes used by college sports teams.

Why should a company's distinctive colors, such those for FedEx, be protected under trademark law?

Case Example 7.2 Federal Express Corporation (FedEx) provides transportation and delivery services worldwide using the logo FedEx in a specific color combination. FedEx sued a competitor, JetEx Management Services, Inc., for using the same color combination and a similar name and logo. JetEx also mimicked FedEx's trademarked slogan ("The World on Time" for FedEx, and "Keeping the World on Time" for JetEx). FedEx alleged trademark infringement and dilution, among other claims.

A federal district court in New York granted a permanent injunction to block JetEx from using the infringing mark in FedEx colors. When JetEx (now operating as JetEx Air Express) continued to use the infringing mark on its vehicles, FedEx went back to the court to enforce the injunction. The court entered a default judgment against JetEx and awarded FedEx an additional $25,000 in attorney's fees and court costs.[7]

Generic Terms Generic terms that refer to an entire class of products, such as *bicycle* and *computer*, receive no protection, even if they acquire secondary meanings. A particularly thorny problem for a business arises when its trademark acquires generic use. For instance, *aspirin* and *thermos* were originally trademarked products, but today the words are used generically. Other trademarks that have acquired generic use include *escalator*, *trampoline*, *raisin bran*, *dry ice*, *lanolin*, *linoleum*, *nylon*, and *cornflakes*.

A trademark that is commonly used does not automatically become generic, though. **Case Example 7.3** David Elliot and Chris Gillespie sought to register numerous domain names (Internet addresses), including "googledisney.com" and "googlenewstvs.com." They were unable to register the names because all of them used the word *google*, a trademark of Google, Inc.

Elliot and Gillespie brought an action in federal court to have the Google trademark canceled because it had become a generic term. They argued that because most people now use *google* as a verb ("to google") when referring to searching the Internet with any search engine (not just Google), the term should no longer be protected. The court held that even if people do use the word *google* as a verb, it is still a protected trademark if consumers associate the noun with one company. The court concluded that "the primary significance of the word *google* to a majority of the public who utilize Internet search engines is a designation of the Google search engine."[8]

---

7. *Federal Express Corp. v. JetEx Air Express, Inc.,* ___ F.Supp.3d ___, 2017 WL 816479 (E.D.N.Y. 2017).
8. *Elliot v. Google, Inc.,* 45 F.Supp.3d 1156 (D.Ariz. 2014).

7–1e Service, Certification, and Collective Marks

A **service mark** is essentially a trademark that is used to distinguish the services (rather than the products) of one person or company from those of another. For instance, each airline has a particular mark or symbol associated with its name. Titles and character names used in radio and television are frequently registered as service marks.

Other marks protected by law include certification marks and collective marks. A **certification mark** is used by one or more persons, other than the owner, to certify the region, materials, mode of manufacture, quality, or other characteristic of specific goods or services. Certification marks include such marks as "Good Housekeeping Seal of Approval" and "UL Tested."

When used by members of a cooperative, association, labor union, or other organization, a certification mark is referred to as a **collective mark**. **Example 7.4** Collective marks appear at the end of a movie's credits to indicate the various associations and organizations that participated in making the movie. The mark "CPA" is a collective mark used by members of the Society of Certified Public Accountants. ▮

7–1f Trade Dress

The term **trade dress** refers to the image and overall appearance of a product. Trade dress is a broad concept that can include all or part of the total image or overall impression created by a product or its packaging. **Example 7.5** The distinctive decor, menu, and style of service of a particular restaurant may be regarded as the restaurant's trade dress. Similarly, trade dress can include the layout and appearance of a catalogue, the use of a lighthouse as part of a golf hole, the fish shape of a cracker, or the G-shaped design of a Gucci watch. ▮

Basically, trade dress is subject to the same protection as trademarks. In cases involving trade dress infringement, as in trademark infringement cases, a major consideration is whether consumers are likely to be confused by the allegedly infringing use. **Example 7.6** Converse makes All-Star shoes, which were the first shoes ever endorsed by a famous basketball player, Chuck Taylor. Nike, Inc., which now owns Converse, sued thirty-one companies, including Ralph Lauren, for manufacturing very similar versions of these shoes, claiming that consumers are likely to be confused. The knockoffs use the same white rubber soles, rubber cap on the toes, canvas tops, and conspicuous stitching as used on All-Stars. Ralph Lauren ultimately agreed to settle its dispute with Nike by destroying all remaining fake All-Stars and paying Nike an undisclosed sum. ▮

7–1g Counterfeit Goods

Counterfeit goods copy or otherwise imitate trademarked goods but are not genuine. The importation of goods bearing counterfeit trademarks poses a significant problem for U.S. businesses, consumers, and law enforcement (see the *Business Web Log* feature for an example). In addition to having negative financial effects on legitimate businesses, sales of certain counterfeit goods, such as pharmaceuticals and nutritional supplements, can present serious public health risks.

Stop Counterfeiting in Manufactured Goods Act The Stop Counterfeiting in Manufactured Goods Act[9] (SCMGA) was enacted to combat counterfeit goods. The act made it a crime to intentionally traffic in, or attempt to traffic in, counterfeit goods or services, or to knowingly use a counterfeit mark on or in connection with goods or services.

Service Mark A trademark that is used to distinguish the services (rather than the products) of one person or company from those of another.

Certification Mark A mark used by one or more persons, other than the owner, to certify the region, materials, mode of manufacture, quality, or other characteristic of specific goods or services.

Collective Mark A mark used by members of a cooperative, association, union, or other organization to certify the region, materials, mode of manufacture, quality, or other characteristic of specific goods or services.

Trade Dress The image and overall appearance of a product.

---

9. Pub. L. No. 109-181 (2006), which amended 18 U.S.C. Sections 2318–2320.

Amazon Faces Fake Products

The world's largest online retailer is facing at least one lawsuit alleging trademark infringement, copyright infringement, and other torts. Electronic cable designer and manufacturer Fuse Chicken, LLC, discovered that Amazon consumers were frequently being sold fake Fuse Chicken cables for their smartphones.

The reality today is that when any branded product becomes well known, cheap imitations become a problem. Amazon apparently did not do enough to prevent the sale of such inferior copies of Fuse Chicken's trademarked and copyrighted products. For example, Amazon sold Fuse Chicken's Bobine Auto iPhone Lightning Car Dock to a customer who gave it a one-star review because it broke within a week. The product was clearly a counterfeit version.

Fuse Chicken attempted to resolve the issue of counterfeit products with Amazon. When Fuse Chicken received little satisfaction, it filed suit.[a] In its lawsuit, Fuse Chicken pointed out that Amazon does not control the products sold via its "Sell Yours Here" listing site. Anybody can sell a trademarked or copyrighted product via this site. According to the lawsuit, "Amazon makes no effort to determine whether the products sold by such third-party sellers are authentic."

Another disgruntled trademark and copyright holder is Randy Hetrick, the seller of the TRX Training System. He claims that fake TRX systems are costing him $100 million a year—twice his annual sales. Currently, he and his employees scour the Amazon website regularly to inform the online retailer about third-party sellers of fake items that should be eliminated from Amazon's system.

---

a. *Fuse Chicken, LLC. v. Amazon.com, Inc.*, Case: 5:17-c-b-01538-SL Doc # 1 Filed July 21, 2017 in Northern District Ohio Court.

Key Point

Large-scale online retailing continues to grow, and Amazon continues to dominate this sector. The number of counterfeit products is growing, too. Amazon has decided to fight back. It has built teams in the United States and Europe that work with major brands. Together, they are developing a registry to help prevent fakes. Amazon is asking brand owners to register with its online store. Then Amazon requires any marketplace merchant who lists registered products to prove that it has the brands' permission to sell them online. Other online resellers, such as Alibaba and eBay, also face counterfeit issues. It's a multibillion-dollar problem that won't go away soon.

Before this act, the law did not prohibit the creation or shipment of counterfeit labels that were not attached to products. Therefore, counterfeiters would make labels and packaging bearing a counterfeit trademark, ship the labels to another location, and then affix them to inferior products to deceive buyers. The SCMGA closed this loophole by making it a crime to traffic in counterfeit labels, stickers, packaging, and the like, whether or not they are attached to goods.

Penalties for Counterfeiting Persons found guilty of violating the SCMGA may be fined up to $2 million or imprisoned for up to ten years (or more if they are repeat offenders). If a court finds that the statute was violated, it must order the defendant to forfeit the counterfeit products (which are then destroyed), as well as any property used in the commission of the crime. The defendant must also pay restitution to the trademark holder or victim in an amount equal to the victim's actual loss.

Case Example 7.7 Charles Anthony Jones pleaded guilty to trafficking in counterfeit prescription drugs for erectile dysfunction. The court sentenced Jones to thirty-seven months in prison and ordered him to pay more than $600,000 in restitution. Jones appealed, arguing that the amount awarded was more than the pharmaceutical companies' actual losses. The court agreed. The pharmaceutical companies were entitled only to their lost net profits rather than the retail price of the genuine drugs.[10] ◼

---

10. *United States v. Jones*, 616 Fed.Appx. 726 (5th Cir. 2015).

Combating Online Sales of Counterfeit Goods The United States cannot prosecute foreign counterfeiters under U.S. laws, because our national laws do not apply to them. One effective tool that U.S. officials are using to combat online sales of counterfeit goods is to obtain a court order to close down the domain names of websites that sell such goods.

Example 7.8 U.S. agents have shut down hundreds of domain names on the Monday after Thanksgiving ("Cyber Monday"). Shutting down the websites, particularly on key shopping days, prevents some counterfeit goods from entering the United States. Europol, an international organization, has also used this tactic. ▪

What are the limits on restitution as a penalty for selling counterfeit prescription pills, such as Viagra?

7–1h Trade Names

Trademarks apply to *products*. The term **trade name** refers to part or all of a *business's name*, whether the business is a sole proprietorship, a partnership, or a corporation. Generally, a trade name is directly related to a business and its goodwill.

A trade name may be protected as a trademark if the trade name is the same as the company's trademarked product—for instance, Coca-Cola. Unless it is also used as a trademark or service mark, a trade name cannot be registered with the federal government. Trade names are protected under the common law, but only if they are unusual or fancifully used. The word *Safeway*, for instance, was sufficiently fanciful to obtain protection as a trade name for a grocery chain.

Trade Name A name that a business uses to identify itself and its brand. A trade name is directly related to a business's reputation and goodwill, and is protected under trademark law.

7–1i Licensing

One way to avoid litigation and still make use of another's trademark or other form of intellectual property is to obtain a license to do so. A **license** in this context is an agreement permitting the use of a trademark, copyright, patent, or trade secret for certain limited purposes. The party that owns the intellectual property rights and issues the license is the *licensor*, and the party obtaining the license is the *licensee*.

A license grants only the rights expressly described in the license agreement. A licensor might, for instance, allow the licensee to use a trademark as part of its company or domain name, but not otherwise use the mark on any products or services. Disputes frequently arise over licensing agreements, particularly when the license involves Internet use.[11]

License An agreement by the owner of intellectual property to permit another to use a trademark, copyright, patent, or trade secret for certain limited purposes.

7–2 Patents

A **patent** is a grant from the government that gives an inventor the exclusive right to make, use, and sell an invention for a period of twenty years. Patents for designs, as opposed to inventions, are given for a fourteen-year period. The applicant must demonstrate to the satisfaction of the U.S. Patent and Trademark Office that the invention, discovery, process, or design is novel, useful, and not obvious in light of current technology.

Until recently, patent law in the United States differed from the laws of many other countries because the first person to invent a product or process obtained the patent rights, rather than the first person to file for a patent. It was often difficult to prove who invented an item first, however, which prompted Congress to change the system by passing the

Patent A property right granted by the federal government that gives an inventor an exclusive right to make, use, and sell an invention for a limited time.

Learning Objective 2
How does the law protect patents?

---

11. See, for instance, *Diebold Incorporated v. QSI, Inc.*, ___F.Supp. 3d ___, 2017 WL 3219866 (N.D. Ohio 2017).

America Invents Act.[12] Now, the first person to file an application for a patent on a product or process will receive patent protection. In addition, the law established a nine-month limit for challenging a patent on any ground.

The period of patent protection begins on the date when the patent application is filed, rather than when the patent is issued, which can sometimes be years later. After the patent period ends (either fourteen or twenty years later), the product or process enters the public domain, and anyone can make, sell, or use the invention without paying the patent holder.

7–2a Searchable Patent Databases

A significant development relating to patents is the availability online of the world's patent databases. The website of the U.S. Patent and Trademark Office (www.uspto.gov) provides searchable databases covering U.S. patents granted since 1976. The website the European Patent Office (www.epo.org) provides online access to 50 million patent documents in more than seventy nations through a searchable network of databases.

Businesses use these searchable databases in many ways. Companies may conduct patent searches to list or inventory their patents, which are valuable assets. Patent searches also enable companies to study trends and patterns in a specific technology or to gather information about competitors in the industry.

7–2b What Is Patentable?

Know This

A patent is granted to inventions that are novel (new) and not obvious in light of prior discoveries.

Under the Patent Act, "[w]hoever invents or discovers any new and useful process, machine, manufacture, or composition of matter, or any new and useful improvement thereof, may obtain a patent therefor, subject to the conditions and requirements of this title."[13] Thus, to be patentable, an invention must be *novel*, *useful*, and *not obvious* in light of current technology.

Almost anything is patentable, except the laws of nature, natural phenomena, and abstract ideas (including algorithms[14]). Even artistic methods and works of art, certain business processes, and the structures of storylines are patentable, provided that they are novel and not obvious.[15] Plants that are reproduced asexually (by means other than from seed), such as hybrid or genetically engineered plants, are patentable in the United States, as are genetically engineered (or cloned) microorganisms and animals.

As mentioned, abstract ideas (including theories and concepts) are not patentable. For this reason, ideas that involve analyzing information and displaying results have often been found ineligible for patents. Such an idea becomes patentable only if particular aspects or combinations of elements transform it into a patent-eligible claim. **Case Example 7.9** West View Research, LLC (WVR), holds numerous patents in a range of technologies, including speech recognition, wireless mobile devices, and medical devices. WVR filed a suit in federal court against several automakers, including Audi, Hyundai, Nissan, Tesla, and Volkswagen, alleging patent infringement.

WVR claimed that the carmakers had infringed two of its patents by selling vehicles with touch-screen displays that offered navigation, traffic, and weather information. A federal district court held in favor of the defendants, and a federal appellate court affirmed. The appellate court reasoned that the two patents simply described abstract ideas (analyzing

---

12. The full title of this law is the Leahy-Smith America Invents Act, Pub. L. No. 112-29 (2011), which amended 35 U.S.C. Sections 1, 41, and 321.
13. 35 U.S.C. Section 101.
14. An *algorithm* is a step-by-step procedure, formula, or set of instructions for accomplishing a specific task. An example is the set of rules used by a search engine to rank the listings contained within its index in response to a particular query.
15. For a United States Supreme Court case discussing the obviousness requirement, see *KSR International Co. v. Teleflex, Inc.*, 550 U.S. 398, 127 S.Ct. 1727, 167 L.Ed.2d 705 (2007). For a discussion of business process patents, see *In re Bilski*, 545 F3d 943 (Fed. Cir. 2008).

information and displaying results) and lacked an inventive element that could transform them into patent-eligible inventions. WVR's two patents were thus invalid.[16]

7–2c Patent Infringement

If a firm makes, uses, or sells another's patented design, product, or process without the patent owner's permission, it commits the tort of patent infringement. Patent infringement may occur even though the patent owner has not put the patented product in commerce. Patent infringement may also occur even though not all features or parts of an invention are copied. (To infringe the patent on a process, however, all steps or their equivalent must be copied.)

Syda Productions/Shutterstock.com

Why are abstract ideas, such as the in-dash navigation system in new cars, ineligible for patent protection?

Patent Infringement Suits and High-Tech Companies

Obviously, companies that specialize in developing new technology stand to lose significant profits if someone "makes, uses, or sells" devices that incorporate their patented inventions. Because these firms are the holders of numerous patents, they are frequently involved in patent infringement lawsuits (as well as other types of intellectual property disputes).

A complication in many such lawsuits is their global scope. Many companies that make and sell electronics and computer software and hardware are based in foreign nations (for instance, Sony is a Japanese firm). Foreign firms can apply for and obtain U.S. patent protection on items that they sell within the United States, just as U.S. firms can obtain protection in foreign nations where they sell goods. In the United States, however, no patent infringement occurs when a patented product is made and sold in another country.

Apple, Inc. versus Samsung Electronics Company
Apple sued Samsung in federal court alleging that Samsung's Galaxy smartphones and tablets using Google's HTC Android operating system infringe on Apple's patents. Apple has design patents that cover its devices' graphical user interface (the display of icons on the home screen), shell, and screen and button design. Apple has also patented the way information is displayed on iPhones and other devices, the way windows pop open, and the way information is scaled and rotated.

In 2014, a jury found that Samsung had willfully infringed five of Apple's patents and awarded $399 million in damages. The parties appealed. A judge later reduced the amount of damages awarded on the patent claims. Litigation between the two companies continued. In 2015, a federal appellate court held that elements of the physical design of these two manufacturers' mobile devices and their on-screen icons were functional. Therefore, they were not protected as trade dress under the Lanham Act.

In 2016, the United States Supreme Court reversed and remanded. The Court held that the Patent Act provision governing damages for design patent infringement encompasses both a product sold to a consumer and a component of that product. Therefore, components of the infringing smartphones could be considered relevant to the damages, even though consumers could not purchase those components separately from the smartphones. The Court left it up to the lower courts to determine the appropriate amount of damages. In 2017, a federal appellate court sent the case back to the trial court.[17]

"To invent, you need a good imagination and a pile of junk."

Thomas Edison
1847–1931
(American inventor)

---

16. *West View Research, LLC v. Audi AG, Volkswagen AG*, 685 Fed.Appx. 923 (Fed.Cir. 2017).

17. *Apple, Inc. v. Samsung Electronics Co.*, 678 Fed.Appx. 1012 (Fed.Cir. 2017); *Samsung Electronics Co. v. Apple, Inc.*, ___ U.S. ___, 137 S.Ct. 429, 196 L.Ed.2d 363 (2016).

How did the Supreme Court rule on Apple's claim that Samsung should pay damages for Samsung's patent infringement on Apple's product components?

7–2d Remedies for Patent Infringement

If a patent is infringed, the patent holder may sue for relief in federal court. The patent holder can seek an injunction against the infringer and can also request damages for royalties and lost profits. (A royalty is a payment made to a patent or copyright holder for the privilege of using the patent or the copyrighted work.) In some cases, the court may grant the winning party reimbursement for attorneys' fees and costs. If the court determines that the infringement was willful, the court can triple the amount of damages awarded (treble damages).

In the past, permanent injunctions were routinely granted to prevent future infringement. Today, however, a patent holder must prove that it has suffered irreparable injury and that the public interest would not be *disserved* by a permanent injunction. Thus, courts have the discretion to decide what is equitable in the circumstances and to consider the public interest rather than just the interests of the parties.

Spotlight Case Example 7.10 Cordance Corporation developed some of the technology and software that automates Internet communications. Cordance sued Amazon.com, Inc., for patent infringement, claiming that Amazon's one-click purchasing interface infringed on one of Cordance's patents. After a jury found Amazon guilty of infringement, Cordance requested the court to issue a permanent injunction against Amazon's infringement or, alternatively, to order Amazon to pay Cordance an ongoing royalty.

The court refused to issue a permanent injunction, because Cordance had not proved that it would otherwise suffer irreparable harm. Cordance and Amazon were not direct competitors in the relevant market. Cordance had never sold or licensed the technology infringed by Amazon's one-click purchasing interface and had presented no market data or evidence to show how the infringement negatively affected Cordance. The court also refused to impose an ongoing royalty on Amazon.[18]

7–3 Copyrights

Copyright The exclusive right of an author or originator of a literary or artistic production to publish, print, sell, or otherwise use that production for a statutory period of time.

Learning Objective 3
What laws protect authors' rights in the works they create?

A **copyright** is an intangible property right granted by federal statute to the author or originator of certain literary or artistic productions. The 1976 Copyright Act,[19] as amended, governs copyrights. Works created after January 1, 1978, are automatically given statutory copyright protection for the life of the author plus 70 years. For copyrights owned by publishing companies, the copyright expires 95 years from the date of publication or 120 years from the date of creation, whichever is first. For works by more than one author, the copyright expires 70 years after the death of the last surviving author.

Case Example 7.11 The popular character Sherlock Holmes originated in stories written by Arthur Conan Doyle and published from 1887 through 1927. Over the years, elements of the characters and stories created by Doyle have appeared in books, movies, and television series, including *Elementary* on CBS and *Sherlock* on BBC. Before 2013, those who wished to use the copyrighted Sherlock material had to pay a licensing fee to Doyle's estate. Then, in 2013, the editors of a book of Holmes-related stories filed a lawsuit in federal court claiming that the basic Sherlock Holmes story elements introduced before 1923 should no longer

---

18. *Cordance Corp. v. Amazon.com, Inc.*, 730 F.Supp.2d 333 (D.Del. 2010).
19. 17 U.S.C. Sections 101 *et seq.*

be protected. The court agreed and ruled that these elements have entered the public domain—that is, the copyright has expired, and they can be used without permission.[20]

7-3a Registration

Copyrights can be registered with the U.S. Copyright Office (www.copyright.gov) in Washington, D.C. Registration is not required, however. A copyright owner need not place a © or *Copr.* or *Copyright* on the work to have the work protected against infringement. Chances are that if somebody created it, somebody owns it.

Generally, copyright owners are protected against the following:

1. Reproduction of the work.
2. Development of derivative works.
3. Distribution of the work.
4. Public display of the work.

7-3b What Is Protected Expression?

Works that are copyrightable include books, records, films, artworks, architectural plans, menus, music videos, product packaging, and computer software. To be protected, a work must be "fixed in a durable medium" from which it can be perceived, reproduced, or communicated. As noted, protection is automatic, and registration is not required.

To obtain protection under the Copyright Act, a work must be original and fall into one of the following categories:

1. Literary works (including newspaper and magazine articles, computer and training manuals, catalogues, brochures, and print advertisements).
2. Musical works and accompanying words (including advertising jingles).
3. Dramatic works and accompanying music.
4. Pantomimes and choreographic works (including ballets and other forms of dance).
5. Pictorial, graphic, and sculptural works (including cartoons, maps, posters, statues, and even stuffed animals).
6. Motion pictures and other audiovisual works (including multimedia works).
7. Sound recordings.
8. Architectural works.

Section 102 Exclusions Generally, anything that is not an original expression will not qualify for copyright protection. Facts widely known to the public are not copyrightable. Page numbers are not copyrightable because they follow a sequence known to everyone. Mathematical calculations are not copyrightable.

In addition, it is not possible to copyright an idea. Section 102 of the Copyright Act specifically excludes copyright protection for any "idea, procedure, process, system, method of operation, concept, principle, or discovery, regardless of the form in which it is described, explained, illustrated, or embodied." Thus, others can freely use the underlying ideas or principles embodied in a work. What is copyrightable is the particular way in which an idea is *expressed.* Whenever an idea and an expression are inseparable, the expression cannot be copyrighted.

Why have the story elements from the famous Sherlock Holmes books entered the public domain?

HARTSWOOD FILMS/BBC WALES/Album/Newscom

Know This

A creative work that is not copyrightable may be protected by other intellectual property law.

---

20. *Klinger v. Conan Doyle Estate, Ltd.,* 988 F.Supp.2d 879 (N.D.Ill. 2013).

An idea and its expression, then, must be separable to be copyrightable. Thus, for the design of a useful item to be copyrightable, the sculptural features—that is, the way it looks—must be separate from its utilitarian (functional) purpose. **Case Example 7.12** A hookah is a device for smoking tobacco by filtering the smoke through water held in a container at the base of the hookah. Inhale, Inc., claimed to hold a registered copyright on a hookah that covered the shape of the hookah's water container.

Inhale filed a suit in a federal district court against Starbuzz Tobacco, Inc., for copyright infringement, alleging that Starbuzz sold hookahs with water containers shaped exactly like the Inhale containers. The district court held that the shape of the water container on Inhale's hookahs was not copyrightable, and issued a summary judgment in Starbuzz's favor. A federal appellate court affirmed. "The shape of a container is not independent of the container's utilitarian function—to hold the contents within its shape—because the shape accomplishes the function."[21]

Compilations of Facts

As mentioned, facts widely known to the public are not copyrightable. Compilations of facts, however, may be copyrightable. Under Section 103 of the Copyright Act, a compilation is a work formed by the collection and assembling of pre-existing materials or of data that are selected, coordinated, or arranged in such a way that the resulting work as a whole constitutes an original work of authorship.

The key requirement for the copyrightability of a compilation is originality. For instance, a template form used by emergency room physicians to record patient information is not original and does not qualify for copyright protection.

7–3c Copyright Infringement

Whenever the form or expression of an idea is copied, an infringement of copyright occurs. The reproduction does not have to be exactly the same as the original, nor does it have to reproduce the original in its entirety. If a substantial part of the original is reproduced, copyright infringement has occurred.

Example 7.13 Ed Sheeran was accused of copyright infringement over his hit song "Photograph." Sheeran allegedly copied much of the song note for note from "Amazing," a single released a few years earlier by X Factor winner Matt Cardle. The songwriters of "Amazing" sued Sheeran, who reportedly settled the case for $20 million in 2017.

Note that when a copyright owner grants to another a license to use the work, the owner waives his or her right to sue that party (the licensee) for copyright infringement. See this chapter's *Business Law Analysis* feature for an example of how a license can be used as a defense to copyright infringement claims.

Remedies for Copyright Infringement

Those who infringe copyrights may be liable for damages or criminal penalties. These range from actual damages or statutory damages, imposed at the court's discretion, to criminal proceedings for willful violations. Actual damages are based on the harm caused to the copyright holder by the infringement, while statutory damages, not to exceed $150,000, are provided for under the Copyright Act. In addition, criminal proceedings may result in fines and/or imprisonment. In some instances, a court may grant an injunction against the infringer.

⭐ **Spotlight Case Example 7.14** Rusty Carroll operated an online term paper business, R2C2, Inc., that offered up to 300,000 research papers for sale on nine different websites. Individuals whose work was posted on these websites without their permission filed a lawsuit against Carroll for copyright infringement. Because Carroll repeatedly failed to comply with court orders regarding discovery, the court found that the copyright infringement was likely

Is the shape of this hookah's water container copyrightable?

©Megastocker/Shutterstock.com

"Don't worry about people stealing an idea. If it's original and it's any good, you'll have to ram it down their throats."

Howard Aiken
1900–1973
(Engineer and pioneer in computing)

---

21. *Inhale, Inc. v. Starbuzz Tobacco, Inc.*, 755 F.3d 1038 (9th Cir. 2014).

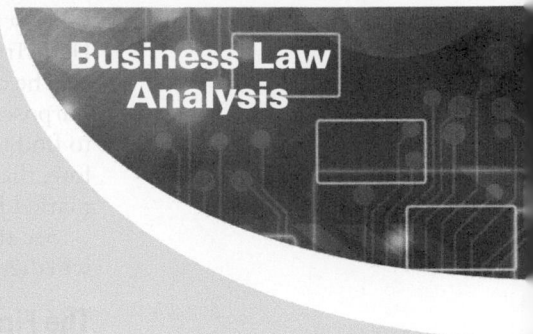

Licensing Is a Defense to Copyright Infringement

Redwin Wilchcombe composed, performed, and recorded a song called "Tha Weedman" at the request of Lil Jon. Lil Jon, who was then a member of Lil Jon & the East Side Boyz (LJESB), wanted to use "Tha Weedman" for LJESB's album *Kings of Crunk*.

Wilchcombe was not paid but was given credit on the album as a producer. After the album had sold 2 million copies, Wilchcombe filed a suit against LJESB, alleging copyright infringement. The defendants claimed that they had a license to use the song. Which party should win the lawsuit? Explain.

Analysis: A license is permission granted by a property owner to another to make, sell, or use the item. If the property is a copyrighted work, the copyright owner waives the right to sue the licensee for copyright infringement while the license is in effect.

Result and Reasoning: In this situation, the parties' conduct established that Wilchcombe gave LJESB a license to use his song. He created the song at Lil Jon's request. He knew that it would be used on LJESB's album and that it would be widely distributed. Wilchcombe never indicated to the defendants that their use of the song would constitute copyright infringement. Thus, the license constitutes a valid defense to Wilchcombe's allegation of copyright infringement, and the defendants (LJESB) should win the lawsuit.

---

to continue unless an injunction was issued. The court therefore issued a permanent injunction prohibiting Carroll and R2C2 from selling any term paper without sworn documentary evidence that the paper's author had given permission.[22]

The "Fair Use" Exception An exception to liability for copyright infringement is made under the "fair use" doctrine. In certain circumstances, a person or organization can reproduce copyrighted material without paying royalties. Section 107 of the Copyright Act provides as follows:

> [T]he fair use of a copyrighted work, including such use by reproduction in copies or phonorecords or by any other means specified by [Section 106 of the Copyright Act], for purposes such as criticism, comment, news reporting, teaching (including multiple copies for classroom use), scholarship, or research, is not an infringement of copyright. In determining whether the use made of a work in any particular case is a fair use the factors to be considered shall include—
>
> (1) the purpose and character of the use, including whether such use is of a commercial nature or is for nonprofit educational purposes;
> (2) the nature of the copyrighted work;
> (3) the amount and substantiality of the portion used in relation to the copyrighted work as a whole; and
> (4) the effect of the use upon the potential market for or value of the copyrighted work.

What Is Fair Use? Because the fair use guidelines are very broad, the courts determine whether a particular use is fair on a case-by-case basis. Thus, anyone reproducing copyrighted material may be committing a violation. In determining whether a use is fair, courts have often considered the fourth factor to be the most important. **Case Example 7.15** A number of research universities, in partnership with Google, Inc., agreed to digitize books from their libraries and create a repository for them. Eighty member institutions (including many colleges and universities) contributed more than 10 million works to the HathiTrust Digital

---

22. *Weidner v. Carroll*, 2010 WL 310310 (S.D.Ill. 2010).

Library. Some authors complained that this book scanning violated their rights and sued the HathiTrust and several associated entities for copyright infringement.

The court, however, sided with the defendants and held that making digital copies for the purposes of online search was a fair use. The library's searchable database enabled researchers to find terms of interest in the digital volumes—but not to read the volumes online. Therefore, the court concluded that the digitization did not provide a substitute that damaged the market for the original works.[23]

See this chapter's *Adapting the Law to the Online Environment* feature for a discussion of whether Beyoncé's use of three phrases written by another artist constituted fair use.

The First Sale Doctrine Section 109(a) of the Copyright Act provides that the owner of a particular item that is copyrighted can, without the authority of the copyright owner, sell or otherwise dispose of it. This rule is known as the first sale doctrine.

Under this doctrine, once a copyright owner sells or gives away a particular copy of a work, the copyright owner no longer has the right to control the distribution of that copy.

---

23. *Authors Guild, Inc. v. HathiTrust*, 755 F.3d 87 (2d Cir. 2014). See also *Authors Guild v. Google, Inc.*, 804 F.3d 202 (2d Cir. 2015).

Adapting the Law to the Online Environment

Beyoncé, Sampling, and a $20 Million Lawsuit

To date, Beyoncé's single "Formation" has been legally downloaded millions times. The video and the song itself were nominated for Grammy awards in the following categories: Record of the Year, Song of the Year, and Best Music Video.

What Does Sampling Involve?

In the song "Formation," Beyoncé sampled several phrases attributed to street performer and music artist Anthony Barré, popularly known as Messy Mya. (Sampling is taking a part of a sound recording and reusing it in a different recording.) Messy Mya became famous on YouTube by filming himself in New Orleans' gay, lesbian, and transgender communities in the aftermath of Hurricane Katrina. The three phrases that Beyoncé sampled are:

- "I like that."
- "What happened at the New Orleans."
- "Bitch, I'm back by popular demand."

Was It Fair Use?

Copyright law requires payment to copyright owners except for fair use. But what constitutes fair use? Typically, courts tend to measure fair use by looking at whether the use in question is of a commercial nature. Additionally, courts look at the amount and substantiality of the portion used in relation to the copyrighted work as a whole and the effect of the use on the potential market for the copyrighted work. Beyoncé claimed that her sampled use of Messy Mya's words fell under the fair use doctrine.

A Lawsuit Nonetheless

Messy Mya was shot and killed in 2010, and his estate would not accept the fair use doctrine defense offered by Beyoncé's attorneys. Rather, the estate sued for $20 million in back royalties, as well as proper credit for Messy Mya "as a writer, composer, producer, and performer." The suit alleged that "the verbatim copying of [Messy Mya's] voice and words by

defendant is so blatant in both scale and degree that it raises this matter to an unusual level of striking similarity."

Are the three phrases that Beyoncé sampled worth $20 million? After losing a motion to dismiss the case based on a fair use defense in a federal district court, Beyoncé agreed to settle the case for the full $20 million.[a]

Critical Thinking

Beyoncé also used footage from a 2013 documentary called That B.E.A.T. *Why might international entertainment stars choose to use sampled words and sampled video footage without the permission of the copyright holders?*

---

a. *Estate of Barré v. Carter*, 272 F.Supp.3d 906 (E.D.La. 2017).

Thus, for instance, a person who buys a copyrighted book can sell it to someone else. The first sale doctrine also applies to copyrighted CDs and DVDs.

The United States Supreme Court has ruled that the first sale doctrine protects lawfully made copies no matter where in the world those copies were made. **Case Example 7.16** Supap Kirtsaeng, a citizen of Thailand, was a graduate student at the University of Southern California. He enlisted friends and family in Thailand to buy copies of textbooks there and ship them to him in the United States. Kirtsaeng resold the textbooks on eBay, where he eventually made about $100,000.

John Wiley & Sons, Inc., had printed some of those textbooks in Asia. Wiley sued Kirtsaeng in federal district court for copyright infringement. Kirtsaeng argued that Section 109(a) of the Copyright Act allows the first purchaser-owner of a book to sell it without the copyright owner's permission. The trial court held in favor of Wiley, and that decision was affirmed on appeal. Kirtsaeng then appealed to the United States Supreme Court, which ruled in Kirtsaeng's favor. The first sale doctrine applies even to goods purchased abroad and resold in the United States.[24]

Kevin Winter/WireImage/Getty Images

Beyoncé sampled several phrases from another musician in one of her new songs. Why might a court conclude that this use was not a fair use under copyright law?

7–3d Copyright Protection for Software

The Computer Software Copyright Act amended the Copyright Act to include computer programs in the list of creative works protected by federal copyright law. Generally, copyright protection extends to those parts of a computer program that can be read by humans, such as the high-level language of a source code. Protection also extends to the binary-language object code, which is readable only by the computer, and to such elements as the overall structure, sequence, and organization of a program.

Not all aspects of software are protected, however. Courts typically have not extended copyright protection to the "look and feel"—the general appearance, command structure, video images, menus, windows, and other screen displays—of computer programs. (Note that copying the "look and feel" of another's product may be a violation of trade dress or trademark laws, however.) Sometimes it can be difficult for courts to decide which particular aspects of software are protected.

Case Example 7.17 Oracle America, Inc., is a software company that owns numerous application programming interfaces, or API packages. Oracle grants licenses to others to use these API packages to write applications in the Java programming language. Java is open and free for anyone to use, but using it requires an interface.

When Google began using some of Oracle's API packages to run Java on its Android mobile devices, Oracle sued for copyright infringement. Google argued that the software packages were command structure and, as such, not protected under copyright law. Ultimately, a federal appellate court concluded that the API packages were source code and were entitled to copyright protection.[25]

The dispute in the following case was whether a third-party software support service infringed the copyright of the owner of the software that the service supported.

---

24. *Kirtsaeng v. John Wiley & Sons, Inc.*, 568 U.S. 519, 133 S.Ct. 1351, 185 L.Ed.2d 392 (2013). See also *Geophysical Service, Inc. v. TGS-NOPEC Geophysical Co.*, 850 F.3d 785 (5th Cir. 2017).
25. *Oracle America, Inc. v. Google, Inc.*, 750 F.3d 1339 (Fed.Cir. 2014).

Case 7.3

Oracle USA, Inc. v. Rimini Street, Inc.

United States Court of Appeals, Ninth Circuit, 879 F.3d 948 (2018).

Background and Facts Oracle USA, Inc., licenses its proprietary enterprise software for a one-time payment. Oracle also sells its licensees maintenance contracts for the software. The maintenance work includes software updates. Rimini Street, Inc., provided third-party support for Oracle's enterprise software, in competition with Oracle's maintenance services. To compete effectively, Rimini also needed to provide software updates to its customers. Creating these updates required copying Oracle's copyrighted software.

Oracle filed a suit in a federal district court against Rimini, alleging copyright infringement. Oracle alleged that Rimini copied Oracle's software under the license of one customer for work for other customers, or for unknown or future customers, instead of restricting the copying to work for the licensee. A jury found in Oracle's favor. The court entered a judgment for Oracle, awarding damages of more than $50 million. Rimini appealed the judgment to the U.S. Court of Appeals for the Ninth Circuit.

In the Words of the Court
*FOGEL, * * * Judge:*
* * * *

Work produced by humans is rarely if ever perfect, and computer software is no exception. Even casual users of computers are familiar with regular software patches and updates intended to correct glitches and to modify software in light of changing circumstances.

However, unlike the off-the-shelf consumer software used by individuals in everyday life, enterprise software employed by large organizations is customized around the organizations' specific needs. While producers of consumer software generally design updates around standard use cases and make them available for end users to download and install directly, updates to enterprise software must be tested and modified to fit with bespoke [specially made] customizations before being put to actual use.

This testing process requires the creation of "development environments." A "development environment," sometimes called a "sandbox," is * * * a software environment that contains a copy of the software program which is then modified to develop and test software updates.

In other words, the very work of maintaining customized software requires copying the software, which without a license to do so is a violation of the exclusive right of the copyright owner. Here,

it is undisputed that the licenses generally permit Oracle's licensees to maintain the software and make development environments for themselves. However, some licensees of the software, lacking either the capability or the interest, opt to outsource the work of maintenance to others, such as Rimini or even Oracle itself.
* * * *

* * * Rimini argues * * * that: 1) each of Rimini's customers had its own license; 2) each license permits copies to be made for archival and support purposes; 3) the licenses authorize the customers to outsource the archival and support work to third parties; and 4) such archival and support work includes the creation of development environments. Rimini dismisses evidence showing that it created development environments for future customers using the license of an existing customer on the basis that future customers presumably would have licenses that would permit them to hire Rimini to create development environments.

Oracle properly responds that * * * the licenses at issue here "pointedly limits copying and use to supporting the *Licensee*." The licenses do not authorize Rimini to "develop products *Rimini* could sell for *Rimini's* financial gain." *Any work that Rimini performs under color of a license held by a customer for other existing customers cannot be considered work in support of that particular customer. The same logic applies to work Rimini performs for unknown, future customers.* The licensees may hire a third party such as Rimini to maintain their software for them, but nothing in the licenses permits them to grant a non-party to the license a general right to copy proprietary software. [Emphasis added.]

Decision and Remedy The U.S. Court of Appeals for the Ninth Circuit affirmed the judgment of the lower court. The court stated, "Absent an applicable license, Rimini's accused acts violated the exclusive right Oracle enjoys as owner of the software copyright to copy or to modify the software."

Critical Thinking

• **Economic** *Rimini argued that Oracle was misusing the copyright in its proprietary software to stifle competition. Do you agree? Explain.*

• **What If the Facts Were Different?** *Suppose that Rimini had bought one of Oracle's licenses for itself. Would the result have been different? Why or why not?*

7–4 Trade Secrets

The law of trade secrets protects some business processes and information that are not or cannot be protected under patent, copyright, or trademark law. A **trade secret** is basically information of commercial value. A company's customer lists, plans, and research and development are trade secrets. Trade secrets may also include pricing information, marketing techniques, and production methods—anything that makes an individual company unique and that would have value to a competitor.

Unlike copyright and trademark protection, protection of trade secrets extends both to ideas and to their expression. (For this reason, and because there are no registration or filing requirements for trade secrets, trade secret protection may be well suited for software.) Of course, the secret formula, method, or other information must be disclosed to some persons, particularly to key employees. Businesses generally attempt to protect their trade secrets by having all employees who use the process or information agree in their contracts, or in confidentiality agreements, never to divulge it.

> **Trade Secret** A formula, device, idea, process, or other information used in a business that gives the owner a competitive advantage in the marketplace.

> **Learning Objective 4**
> What are trade secrets, and what laws offer protection for this form of intellectual property?

7–4a State and Federal Law on Trade Secrets

Under Section 757 of the *Restatement of Torts*, those who disclose or use another's trade secret, without authorization, are liable to that other party if either of the following is true:

1. They discovered the secret by improper means.
2. Their disclosure or use constitutes a breach of a duty owed to the other party.

Stealing of confidential business data by industrial espionage, as when a business taps into a competitor's computer, is a theft of trade secrets without any contractual violation and is actionable in itself.

Trade secrets have long been protected under the common law. Today, nearly every state has enacted trade secret laws based on the Uniform Trade Secrets Act. Additionally, the Economic Espionage Act made the theft of trade secrets a federal crime.

7–4b Trade Secrets in Cyberspace

Today's computer technology undercuts a business firm's ability to protect its confidential information, including trade secrets. For instance, a dishonest employee could e-mail trade secrets in a company's server to a competitor or a future employer. If e-mail is not an option, the employee might walk out with the information on a flash drive.

Misusing a company's social media accounts is yet another way in which employees may appropriate trade secrets. **Case Example 7.18** Noah Kravitz worked for a company called PhoneDog for four years as a product reviewer and video blogger. PhoneDog provided him with the Twitter account "@PhoneDog_Noah." Kravitz's popularity grew, and he had approximately 17,000 followers by the time he quit the company in 2010. PhoneDog requested that Kravitz stop using the Twitter account. Although Kravitz changed his handle to "@noahkravitz," he continued to use the account. PhoneDog subsequently sued Kravitz for misappropriation of trade secrets, among other things. Kravitz moved for a dismissal, but the court found that the complaint adequately stated a cause of action for misappropriation of trade secrets and allowed the suit to continue.[26] ■

For a summary of trade secrets and other forms of intellectual property, see Exhibit 7–1.

7–5 International Protections

For many years, the United States has been a party to various international agreements relating to intellectual property rights. For instance, the Paris Convention of 1883, to which about 180 countries are signatory, allows parties in one country to file for patent and trademark

---

26. *PhoneDog v. Kravitz*, 2011 WL 5415612 (N.D.Cal. 2011).

Exhibit 7–1 Forms of Intellectual Property

	DEFINITION	HOW ACQUIRED	DURATION	REMEDY FOR INFRINGEMENT
Trademark (service, certification, and collective marks, and trade dress)	Any distinctive word, symbol, sound, or design that an entity uses to distinguish its goods or services from those of others. The owner has the exclusive right to use that mark or trade dress.	1. At common law, ownership created by use of the mark. 2. Registration with the appropriate federal or state office gives notice and is permitted if the mark is currently in commercial use or will be within the next six months.	Unlimited, as long as it is in use. To continue notice by registration, the owner must renew by filing between the fifth and sixth years, and thereafter, every ten years.	1. Injunction prohibiting the future use of the mark. 2. Actual damages plus profits received by the party who infringed (can be increased under the Lanham Act). 3. Destruction of articles that infringed. 4. *Plus* attorneys' fees.
Patent	A grant from the government that gives an inventor exclusive rights to make, use, and sell an invention.	By filing a patent application with the U.S. Patent and Trademark Office and receiving its approval.	Twenty years from the date of the application; for design patents, fourteen years.	1. Injunction against infringer. 2. Possible monetary damages, including royalties and lost profits, plus attorneys' fees. 3. Damages may be tripled for intentional infringement.
Copyright	The right of an author or originator of a literary or artistic work, or other production that falls within a specified category, to have the exclusive use of that work for a given period of time.	Automatic (once the work or creation is put in tangible form). Only the *expression* of an idea (and not the idea itself) can be protected by copyright.	For authors: the life of the author plus 70 years. For publishers: 95 years after the date of publication or 120 years after creation.	Actual damages plus profits received by the party who infringed, *or* statutory damages under the Copyright Act. Courts may impose fines and/or imprisonment, as well as an injunction.
Trade Secret	Any information that a business possesses and that gives the business an advantage over competitors (including customer lists, plans, pricing information, and production methods).	Through the originality and development of the information and processes that constitute the business secret and are unknown to others.	Unlimited, so long as not revealed to others. Once revealed to others, it is no longer a trade secret.	Monetary damages for misappropriation (the Uniform Trade Secrets Act also permits punitive damages if willful), *plus* costs and attorneys' fees.

protection in any of the other member countries. Other international agreements include the Berne Convention, the Trade-Related Aspects of Intellectual Property Rights (known as the TRIPS agreement), the Madrid Protocol, and the Anti-Counterfeiting Trade Agreement.

7–5a The Berne Convention

Under the Berne Convention of 1886, if a U.S. citizen writes a book, every country that has signed the convention must recognize her or his copyright in the book. Also, if a citizen of a country that has not signed the convention first publishes a book in one of the 169 countries that have signed, all other countries that have signed the convention must recognize that author's copyright. Copyright notice is not needed to gain protection under the Berne Convention for works published after March 1, 1989.

The European Union altered its copyright rules under the Berne Convention by agreeing to extend the period of royalty protection for musicians from fifty years to seventy years. This decision aids major record labels as well as performers and musicians. The profits of musicians and record companies have been shrinking in recent years because of the sharp decline in sales of compact discs and the rise in digital downloads (both legal and illegal).

7–5b The TRIPS Agreement

The Berne Convention and other international agreements have given some protection to intellectual property on a worldwide level. None of them, however, has been as significant and far reaching in scope as the Trade-Related Aspects of Intellectual Property Rights (TRIPS) agreement. Representatives from more than one hundred nations signed the TRIPS agreement in 1994.

Learning Objective 5
How does the TRIPS agreement protect intellectual property worldwide?

Established Standards and Procedures The TRIPS agreement established, for the first time, standards for the international protection of intellectual property rights, including patents, trademarks, and copyrights for movies, computer programs, books, and music. The TRIPS agreement provides that each member country must include in its domestic laws broad intellectual property rights and effective remedies (including civil and criminal penalties) for violations of those rights.

Each member nation must ensure that legal procedures are available for parties who wish to bring actions for infringement of intellectual property rights. Additionally, a related document established a mechanism for settling disputes among member nations.

Prohibits Discrimination Generally, the TRIPS agreement forbids member nations from discriminating against foreign owners of intellectual property rights in the administration, regulation, or adjudication of such rights. In other words, a member nation cannot give its own nationals (citizens) favorable treatment without offering the same treatment to nationals of all member countries. **Example 7.19** A U.S. software manufacturer brings a suit for the infringement of intellectual property rights under Germany's national laws. Because Germany is a member of the TRIPS agreement, the U.S. manufacturer is entitled to receive the same treatment as a German manufacturer. ■

7–5c The Madrid Protocol

In the past, one of the difficulties in protecting U.S. trademarks internationally was that it was time consuming and expensive to apply for trademark registration in foreign countries. The filing fees and procedures for trademark registration vary significantly among individual countries. The Madrid Protocol, which was signed into law in 2003, may help to resolve these problems.

The Madrid Protocol is an international treaty that has been signed by about a hundred countries. Under its provisions, a U.S. company wishing to register its trademark abroad can submit a single application and designate other member countries in which it would like to register the mark. The treaty was designed to reduce the costs of obtaining international trademark protection by more than 60 percent.

Although the Madrid Protocol may simplify and reduce the cost of trademark registration in foreign nations, it remains to be seen whether it will provide significant benefits to trademark owners. Even with an easier registration process, the question of whether member countries will enforce the law and protect the mark still remains.

7–5d The Anti-Counterfeiting Trade Agreement

In 2011, Australia, Canada, Japan, Korea, Morocco, New Zealand, Singapore, and the United States signed the Anti-Counterfeiting Trade Agreement (ACTA), an international treaty to combat global counterfeiting and piracy. Other nations have since signed the agreement. Once a nation has adopted appropriate procedures, it can ratify the treaty.

Provisions and Goals The goals of the treaty are to increase international cooperation, facilitate the best law enforcement practices, and provide a legal framework to combat counterfeiting. The treaty has its own governing body.

The ACTA applies not only to counterfeit physical goods, such as medications, but also to pirated copyrighted works being distributed via the Internet. The idea is to create a new standard of enforcement for intellectual property rights that goes beyond the TRIPS agreement and encourages international cooperation and information sharing among signatory countries.

Border Searches Under ACTA, member nations are required to establish border measures that allow officials, on their own initiative, to search commercial shipments of imports and exports for counterfeit goods. The treaty neither requires nor prohibits random border searches of electronic devices, such as laptops and iPads, for infringing content.

If border authorities reasonably believe that any goods in transit are counterfeit, the treaty allows them to keep the suspect goods unless the owner proves that the items are authentic and noninfringing. The treaty allows member nations, in accordance with their own laws, to order online service providers to furnish information about (including the identity of) suspected trademark and copyright infringers.

Practice and Review

Two computer science majors, Trent and Xavier, have an idea for a new video game, which they propose to call "Hallowed." They form a business and begin developing their idea. Several months later, Trent and Xavier run into a problem with their design and consult with a friend, Brad, who is an expert in creating computer source codes. After the software is completed but before Hallowed is marketed, a video game called Halo 2 is released for both the Xbox and the PlayStation 3 systems. Halo 2 uses source codes similar to those of Hallowed and imitates Hallowed's overall look and feel, although not all the features are alike. Using the information presented in the chapter, answer the following questions.

1. Would the name Hallowed receive protection as a trademark or as trade dress?

2. If Trent and Xavier had obtained a business process patent on Hallowed, would the release of Halo 2 infringe on their patent? Why or why not?

3. Based only on the facts presented above, could Trent and Xavier sue the makers of Halo 2 for copyright infringement? Why or why not?

4. Suppose that Trent and Xavier discover that Brad took the idea of Hallowed and sold it to the company that produced Halo 2. Which type of intellectual property issue does this raise?

Debate This

Congress has amended the Copyright Act several times. Copyright holders now have protection for many decades. Was Congress justified in extending the copyright time periods? Why or why not?

Key Terms

Chapter Summary: Intellectual Property Rights

Trademarks	1. A *trademark* is a distinctive word, symbol, sound, or design that identifies the manufacturer as the source of the goods and distinguishes its products from those made or sold by others.
	2. The major federal statutes protecting trademarks and related property are the Lanham Act and the Federal Trademark Dilution Act. Generally, to be protected, a trademark must be sufficiently distinctive from all competing trademarks.
	3. *Trademark infringement* occurs when one party uses a mark that is the same as, or confusingly similar to, the protected trademark, service mark, certification mark, collective mark, or trade name of another party without permission when marketing goods or services.
Patents	1. A *patent* is a grant from the government that gives an inventor the exclusive right to make, use, and sell an invention for a period of twenty years (fourteen years for a design patent) from the date when the application for a patent is filed. To be patentable, an invention (or a discovery, process, or design) must be novel, useful, and not obvious in light of current technology. Computer software may be patented.
	2. Almost anything is patentable, except the laws of nature, natural phenomena, and abstract ideas (including algorithms). Even artistic methods and works of art, certain business processes, and the structures of storylines may be patentable.
	3. *Patent infringement* occurs when someone uses or sells another's patented design, product, or process without the patent owner's permission. The patent holder can sue the infringer in federal court and request an injunction, but must prove irreparable injury to obtain a permanent injunction against the infringer. The patent holder can also request damages and attorneys' fees. If the infringement was willful, the court can grant treble damages.
Copyrights	1. A *copyright* is an intangible property right granted by federal statute to the author or originator of certain literary or artistic productions. The Copyright Act, as amended, governs copyrights. Works created after January 1, 1978, are automatically given statutory protection for the life of the author plus seventy years.
	2. *Copyright infringement* occurs whenever the form or expression of an idea is copied without the permission of the copyright holder. An exception applies if the copying is deemed a "fair use."
	3. The Computer Software Copyright Act amended the Copyright Act to include computer programs in the list of creative works protected by federal copyright law.
Trade Secrets	1. *Trade secrets* are basically information of commercial value and include customer lists, plans, research and development, and pricing information.
	2. Trade secrets are protected under the common law and by statute in nearly all of the states against misappropriation by competitors. Unlike copyright and trademark protection, protection of trade secrets extends both to ideas and to their expression. The Economic Espionage Act made the theft of trade secrets a federal crime.
International Protections	Various international agreements provide international protection for intellectual property. A landmark agreement is the Trade-Related Aspects of Intellectual Property Rights (TRIPS) agreement, which provides for enforcement procedures in all countries signatory to the agreement.

Issue Spotters

1. Roslyn, a food buyer for Organic Cornucopia Food Company, decides to go into business for herself as Roslyn's Kitchen. She contacts Organic's suppliers, offering to buy their entire harvest for the next year. She also contacts Organic's customers, offering to sell her products for less than Organic. Has Roslyn violated any of the intellectual property rights discussed in this chapter? Explain. (See *Trade Secrets.*)

2. Global Products develops, patents, and markets software. World Copies, Inc., sells Global's software without the maker's permission. Is this patent infringement? If so, how might Global save the cost of suing World for infringement and at the same time profit from World's sales? (See *Patents.*)

    —**Check your answers to the *Issue Spotters* against the answers provided in Appendix D at the end of this text.**

Business Scenarios and Case Problems

7–1. Patent Infringement. John and Andrew Doney invented a hard-bearing device for balancing rotors. Although they obtained a patent for their invention from the U.S. Patent and Trademark Office, it was never used as an automobile wheel balancer. Some time later, Exetron Corp. produced an automobile wheel balancer that used a hard-bearing device similar to the Doneys' device. Given that the Doneys had not used their device for automobile wheel balancing, does Exetron's use of a similar device infringe on the Doneys' patent? (See *Patents.*)

7–2. Fair Use. Professor Wise is teaching a summer seminar in business torts at State University. Several times during the course, he makes copies of relevant sections from business law texts and distributes them to his students. Wise does not realize that the daughter of one of the textbook authors is a member of his seminar. She tells her father about Wise's copying activities, which have taken place without her father's or his publisher's permission. Her father sues Wise for copyright infringement. Wise claims protection under the fair use doctrine. Who will prevail? Explain. (See *Copyrights.*)

7–3. Spotlight on Macy's—Copyright Infringement. United Fabrics International, Inc., bought a fabric design from an Italian designer and registered a copyright to the design with the U.S. Copyright Office. When Macy's, Inc., began selling garments with a similar design, United filed a copyright infringement suit against Macy's. Macy's argued that United did not own a valid copyright to the design and so could not claim infringement. Does United have to prove that the copyright is valid to establish infringement? Explain. [*United Fabrics International, Inc. v. C & J Wear, Inc.*, 630 F.3d 1255 (9th Cir. 2011)] (See *Copyrights.*)

7–4. Copyright Infringement. SilverEdge Systems Software hired Catherine Conrad to perform a singing telegram. SilverEdge arranged for James Bendewald to record Conrad's performance of her copyrighted song to post on the company's website. Conrad agreed to wear a microphone to assist in the recording, told Bendewald what to film, and asked for an additional fee only if SilverEdge used the video for a commercial purpose. Later, the company chose to post a video of a different performer's singing telegram instead. Conrad filed a suit in a federal district court against SilverEdge and Bendewald for copyright infringement. Are the defendants liable? Explain. [*Conrad v. Bendewald*, 500 Fed.Appx. 526 (7th Cir. 2013)] (See *Copyrights.*)

7–5. Business Case Problem with Sample Answer—Patents. The U.S. Patent and Trademark Office (PTO) denied Raymond Gianelli's application for a patent for a "Rowing Machine"—an exercise machine on which a user *pulls* on handles to perform a rowing motion against a selected resistance. The PTO considered the device obvious in light of a previously patented "Chest Press Apparatus for Exercising Regions of the Upper Body"—an exercise machine on which a user *pushes* on handles to overcome a selected resistance. On what ground might this result be reversed on appeal? Discuss. [*In re Gianelli*, 739 F.3d 1375 (Fed. Cir. 2014)] (See *Patents.*)

—**For a sample answer to Problem 7–5, go to Appendix E at the end of this text.**

7–6. Patents. Rodney Klassen was employed by the U.S. Department of Agriculture (USDA). Without the USDA's authorization, Klassen gave Jim Ludy, a grape grower, plant material for two unreleased varieties of grapes. For almost two years, most of Ludy's plantings bore no usable fruit, none of the grapes were sold, and no plant material was given to any other person. The plantings were visible from publicly accessible roads, but none of the vines were labeled, and the variety could not be identified by simply viewing the vines. Under patent law, an applicant may not obtain a patent for an invention that is in public use more than one year before the date of the application. Could the USDA successfully apply for patents on the two varieties given to Ludy? Explain. [*Delano Farms Co. v. California Table Grape Commission*, 778 F.3d 1243 (Fed.Cir. 2015)] (See *Patents.*)

7–7. Copyright Infringement. Savant Homes, Inc., is a custom home designer and builder. Using what it called the Anders Plan, Savant built a model house in Windsor, Colorado. This was a ranch house with two bedrooms on one side and a master suite on the other, separated by a combined family room, dining room, and kitchen. Ron and Tammie Wagner toured the Savant house. The same month, the Wagners hired builder Douglas Collins and his firm, Douglas Consulting, to build a house for them. After it was built, Savant filed a lawsuit in a federal district court against Collins for copyright infringement, alleging that the builder had copied the Anders Plan in the design and construction of the Wagner house. Collins showed that the Anders Plan consisted of standard elements and standard arrangements of elements. In these circumstances, has infringement occurred? Explain. [*Savant Homes, Inc. v. Collins*, 809 F.3d 1133 (10th Cir. 2016)] (See *Copyrights*.)

7–8. Patent Infringement. Finjan, Inc., owns a patent—U.S. Patent No. 7,418,731, or "the '731 patent"—for a system and method that provide computer security from malicious software embedded in websites on the Internet. The system consists of a gateway that compares security profiles associated with requested files to the security policies of requesting users. The method includes scanning an incoming file to create the profile, which comprises a list of computer commands the file is programmed to perform. The '731 patent required "a list of computer commands." Blue Coat Systems, Inc., sold a competing product. Blue Coat's product scanned an incoming file for certain commands and created a new file called Cookie2 that contained a field showing whether, and how often, those commands appeared. Finjan filed a suit against Blue Coat, alleging

patent infringement. Blue Coat argued that its profiles did not contain the '731 patent's required "list of computer commands." Did Blue Coat's product infringe Finjan's patent? Explain. [*Finjan, Inc. v. Blue Cost Systems, Inc.*, 879 F.3d 1299 (Fed. Cir. 2018)] (See *Patents*.)

7–9. A Question of Ethics—The IDDR Approach and Copyright Infringement. *Usenet is an online bulletin board network. A user gains access to Usenet posts through a commercial service, such as Giganews, Inc. Giganews deletes or blocks posts that contain child pornography. Otherwise, the service does not monitor content. Perfect 10, Inc. owns the copyrights to tens of thousands of images, many of which have been illegally posted on Usenet through Giganews. When Perfect 10 notified Giganews of posts that contained infringing images, the service took them down. Despite these efforts, illegal posting continued. Perfect 10 filed a suit in a federal district court against Giganews, alleging copyright infringement.* [Perfect 10, Inc. v. Giganews, Inc., *847 F.3d 657 (9th Cir. 2017)] (See* Copyrights.*)*

1. Is Giganews liable for copyright infringement? Do Internet service providers have an ethical duty to do more to prevent infringement? Why or why not?

2. Using the IDDR approach, decide whether a copyright owner has an ethical duty to protect against infringement.

Critical Thinking and Writing Assignments

7–10. Time-Limited Group Assignment—Patents. After years of research, your company has developed a product that might revolutionize the green (environmentally conscious) building industry. The product is made from relatively inexpensive and widely available materials combined in a unique way that can substantially lower the heating and cooling costs of residential and commercial buildings. The company has registered the trademark it intends to use for the product and has filed a patent application with the U.S. Patent and Trademark Office. (See *Patents*.)

1. One group will provide three reasons why this product does or does not qualify for patent protection.

2. A second group will develop a four-step plan for how the company can best protect its intellectual property rights (trademark, trade secret, and patent) and prevent domestic and foreign competitors from producing counterfeit goods or cheap knockoffs.

3. The third group will list and explain three ways in which the company can utilize licensing.

8 | Internet Law, Social Media, and Privacy

Learning Objectives

The five Learning Objectives *below are designed to help improve your understanding. After reading this chapter, you should be able to answer the following questions:*

1. What is cybersquatting, and when is it illegal?

2. What law protects copyrights in the digital age?

3. When does the law protect a person's electronic communications from being intercepted or accessed?

4. What law governs whether Internet service providers are liable for online defamatory statements made by users?

5. How do online retailers track their users' Web browsing activities?

"The Internet is just the world passing around notes in a classroom."

Jon Stewart
1962–present
(American comedian and former host of *The Daily Show*)

The Internet has changed our lives and our laws. Technology has put the world at our fingertips and now allows even the smallest business to reach customers around the globe. Because the Internet allows the world to "pass around notes" so quickly, as Jon Stewart joked in the chapter-opening quotation, it presents a variety of challenges for the law.

Courts are often in uncharted waters when deciding disputes that involve the Internet, social media, and online privacy. Judges may have no common law precedents to rely on when resolving cases. Long-standing principles of justice may be inapplicable. New rules are evolving, but often not as quickly as technology.

Alex Jones is a talk show host who promotes conspiracy theories online through his website, Twitter feed, and YouTube channel. Suppose that Jones posts a video online accusing Chobani, LLC, of bringing in "migrant rapists" to work at its new facility in Twin Falls, Idaho. The statements in Jones's video are false. Understandably, the statements anger the owners and employees of Chobani, a company that was founded by a Turkish immigrant in New York. Chobani spent $450 million expanding to the Twin Falls location, where it employs more than a thousand workers, a few hundred of whom are refugees (but not illegal immigrants or rapists).

Can Chobani succeed in a lawsuit against Jones for online defamation? Proving online defamation can be difficult. In addition, several laws protect those who post online defamatory statements made by a third party. In this chapter, you will read about the rules pertaining to online defamation, as well as other legal challenges presented by the Internet and social media.

8–1 Internet Law

A number of laws specifically address issues that arise only on the Internet. These issues include unsolicited e-mail, domain names, cybersquatting, and meta tags, as we discuss here. We also discuss how the law is dealing with problems of trademark dilution online, as well as licensing.

8–1a Spam

Businesses and individuals alike are targets of **spam**.[1] Spam is the unsolicited "junk e-mail" that floods virtual mailboxes with advertisements, solicitations, and similar communications. Considered relatively harmless in the early days of the Internet, spam has become a serious problem. By 2019, it accounted for roughly 75 percent of all e-mails.

Spam Bulk, unsolicited (junk) e-mail.

State Regulation of Spam In an attempt to combat spam, thirty-seven states have enacted laws that prohibit or regulate its use. Many state laws that regulate spam require the senders of e-mail ads to instruct the recipients on how they can "opt out" of further e-mail ads from the same sources. For instance, in some states, an unsolicited e-mail must include a toll-free phone number or return e-mail address that the recipient can use to ask the sender not to send unsolicited e-mails.

The Federal CAN-SPAM Act In 2003, Congress enacted the Controlling the Assault of Non-Solicited Pornography and Marketing (CAN-SPAM) Act.[2] The legislation applies to any "commercial electronic mail messages" that are sent to promote a commercial product or service. Significantly, the statute preempts state antispam laws except those provisions in state laws that prohibit false and deceptive e-mailing practices.

Generally, the act permits the sending of unsolicited commercial e-mail but prohibits certain types of spamming activities. Prohibited activities include the use of a false return address and the use of false, misleading, or deceptive information when sending e-mail. The statute also prohibits the use of "dictionary attacks"—sending messages to randomly generated e-mail addresses—and the "harvesting" of e-mail addresses from websites through the use of specialized software.

Example 8.1 Sanford Wallace, known as the "Spam King," is considered to be one of the world's most prolific spammers. He has operated several businesses over the years that used *botnets* (automated spamming networks) to send out hundreds of millions of unwanted e-mails. Wallace also infected computers with spyware and then sold consumers the software to fix it. He infiltrated Facebook accounts to spam 27 million Facebook users.

As a result, Wallace was sued by Facebook and the Federal Trade Commission, and ordered to pay millions of dollars in fines. The Federal Bureau of Investigation ultimately filed criminal charges against Wallace, and he pleaded guilty to fraud, spam, and violating a court order not to access Facebook. Arresting prolific spammers, however, has done little to curb spam, which continues to flow at a rate of many billions of messages per day.

©Feng Yu/Shutterstock.com

Have state and federal laws against spam reduced its use?

---

1. The term *spam* is said to come from the lyrics of a Monty Python song that repeats the word *spam* over and over.
2. 15 U.S.C. Sections 7701 *et seq.*

The U.S. Safe Web Act After the CAN-SPAM Act, spamming from servers located in other nations increased. These cross-border spammers generally were able to escape detection and legal sanctions because the Federal Trade Commission (FTC) lacked the authority to investigate foreign spamming.

Congress sought to rectify the situation by enacting the U.S. Safe Web Act (also known as the Undertaking Spam, Spyware, and Fraud Enforcement with Enforcers beyond Borders Act).[3] The act allows the FTC to cooperate and share information with foreign agencies in investigating and prosecuting those involved in spamming, spyware, and various Internet frauds and deceptions.

The Safe Web Act also provides a "safe harbor" for **Internet service providers (ISPs)**—organizations that provide access to the Internet. The safe harbor gives ISPs immunity from liability for supplying information to the FTC concerning possible unfair or deceptive conduct in foreign jurisdictions.

Internet Service Provider (ISP) A business or organization that offers users access to the Internet and related services.

8–1b Domain Names

As e-commerce expanded worldwide, one issue that emerged involved the rights of a trademark owner to use the mark as part of a domain name. A **domain name** is part of an Internet address, such as "cengage.com."

Domain Name The series of letters and symbols used to identify a site operator on the Internet (an Internet address).

Structure of Domain Names Every domain name ends with a top-level domain (TLD), which is the part of the name to the right of the period. This part of the name often indicates the type of entity that operates the site. For instance, com is an abbreviation for commercial, and edu is a shortened term for education.

The second-level domain (SLD)—the part of the name to the left of the period—is chosen by the business entity or individual registering the domain name. Competition for SLDs among firms with similar names and products has led to numerous disputes. By using an identical or similar domain name, one company may attempt to profit from a competitor's **goodwill** (the intangible value of a business). For instance, a party might use a similar domain name to sell pornography or otherwise infringe on another's trademarks.

Goodwill In the business context, the valuable reputation of a business viewed as an intangible asset.

Domain Name Distribution System The Internet Corporation for Assigned Names and Numbers (ICANN), a nonprofit corporation, oversees the distribution of domain names and operates an online arbitration system. Due to numerous complaints, ICANN overhauled the domain name distribution system in 2012.

ICANN now sells new *generic top-level domain names* (gTLDs) for an initial price of $185,000 plus an annual fee of $25,000. Whereas TLDs previously had been limited to only a few terms (including com, net, and org), gTLDs can take any form. By 2019, many companies and corporations had acquired gTLDs based on their brands, such as aol, bmw, target, and walmart. Some companies have numerous gTLDs. Google's gTLDs, for instance, include android, chrome, gmail, goog, and YouTube.

Because gTLDs have greatly increased the potential number of domain names, domain name registrars have proliferated. Registrar companies charge a fee to businesses and individuals to register new names and to renew annual registrations (often through automated software). Many of these companies also buy and sell expired domain names.

> "Almost overnight, the Internet's gone from a technical wonder to a business must."
>
> **Bill Schrader**
> 1953–present
> (Internet pioneer and co-founder of the first commercial Internet service provider)

8–1c Cybersquatting

One of the goals of the new gTLD system was to alleviate the problem of cybersquatting. **Cybersquatting** occurs when a party registers a domain name that is the same as, or confusingly similar to, the trademark of another and then offers to sell the domain name back to the trademark owner.

Cybersquatting The act of registering a domain name that is the same as, or confusingly similar to, the trademark of another and then offering to sell that domain name back to the trademark owner.

---

3. Pub. L. No. 109–455, 120 Stat. 3372 (2006), codified in various sections of 15 U.S.C. and 12 U.S.C. Section 3412.

Example 8.2 Apple, Inc., has repeatedly sued cybersquatters that registered domain names similar to the names of its products, such as iphone8.com and ipods.com. ■

Anticybersquatting Legislation Because cybersquatting has led to so much litigation, Congress enacted the Anticybersquatting Consumer Protection Act (ACPA).[4] The act amended the Lanham Act—the federal law protecting trademarks. The ACPA makes cybersquatting illegal when both of the following are true:

1. The domain name is identical or confusingly similar to the trademark of another.

2. The one registering, trafficking in, or using the domain name has a "bad faith intent" to profit from that trademark.

Despite the ACPA, cybersquatting continues to present a problem for businesses. **Case Example 8.3** CrossFit, Inc., is a Delaware corporation that provides personal fitness services and products. CrossFit is well known in the fitness industry and licenses affiliates to operate individual CrossFit-branded programs. CrossFit granted a license to Andres Del Cueto Davalos to operate a location in Mexico and allowed him to use the domain name "CrossFitAlfa." Davalos later registered the domain name CrossFitBeta without CrossFit's permission and then used both of these domain names to redirect website visitors to a third website, www.woodbox.com. Davalos was attempting to siphon off CrossFit customers to another business that he co-owned, Woodbox Training Centers, which operated in twenty-five locations across Mexico. CrossFit sued under the ACPA. Because of Davalos's bad faith intent, the court awarded CrossFit the maximum amount of statutory damages available ($100,000 for each domain name), plus costs and attorneys' fees.[5] ■

All domain name registrars are supposed to relay information about registrations and renewals to ICANN and other companies that keep a master list of domain names, but this does not always occur. The speed at which domain names change hands and the difficulty in tracking mass automated registrations have created an environment in which cybersquatting can flourish.

Typosquatting Cybersquatters have also developed new tactics, such as **typosquatting,** or registering a name that is a misspelling of a popular brand name, such as googl.com or appple.com. Because many Internet users are not perfect typists, Web pages using these misspelled names may receive a lot of traffic. More traffic generally means increased profits (advertisers often pay websites based on the number of unique visits, or hits).

Case Example 8.4 Counter Balance Enterprises, Ltd., registered and used domain names that misspelled Facebook, such as "facebobk.com" and "facemonk.com." Facebook, Inc., filed suit in a California federal court under the ACPA against Counter Balance (and ten other defendants, including Banana Ads, LLC) for typosquatting. The defendants failed to appear, and the court entered a default judgment in favor of Facebook. The court permanently enjoined the defendants from using the infringing domain names and awarded Facebook a total of $2.8 million in damages (ranging from $5,000 to $1.3 million per individual defendant).[6] ■

Learning Objective 1
What is cybersquatting, and when is it illegal?

How did the Anticybersquatting Consumer Protection Act affect a dispute involving the physical fitness program, CrossFit, and its affiliates?

Andrew Errington/Moment Mobile/Getty Images

Typosquatting A form of cybersquatting that relies on mistakes, such as typographical errors, made by Internet users when entering information into a Web browser.

4. 15 U.S.C. Section 1129.
5. *CrossFit, Inc. v. Davalos,* ___ F.Supp.3d ___, 2017 WL 733213 (N.D.Cal. 2017).
6. *Facebook, Inc. v. Banana Ads, LLC,* 2013 WL 1873289 (N.D.Cal. 2013).

Typosquatters may sometimes fall beyond the reach of the ACPA. If the misspelling that they use is significant, the trademark owner may have difficulty proving that the name is identical or confusingly similar to the trademark of another, as the ACPA requires.

Typosquatting adds costs for businesses seeking to protect their domain name rights. Companies must attempt to register not only legitimate variations of their domain names but also potential misspellings. Large corporations may have to register thousands of domain names across the globe just to protect their basic brands and trademarks.

Applicability and Sanctions of the ACPA The ACPA applies to all domain name registrations of trademarks. Successful plaintiffs in suits brought under the act can collect actual damages and profits, or they can elect to receive statutory damages ranging from $1,000 to $100,000.

Although some companies have been successful suing under the ACPA, there are roadblocks to pursuing such lawsuits. Some domain name registrars offer privacy services that hide the true owners of websites, making it difficult for trademark owners to identify cybersquatters. Thus, before bringing a suit, a trademark owner has to ask the court for a subpoena to discover the identity of the owner of the infringing website. Because of the high costs of court proceedings, discovery, and even arbitration, many disputes over cybersquatting are settled out of court.

To facilitate dispute resolution, ICANN offers two dispute resolution forums: the Uniform Domain-Name Dispute-Resolution Policy (UDRP) and the Uniform Rapid Suspension (URS) system. More disputes are resolved through the UDRP, which allows common law trademark claims and has fewer procedural requirements. The newer URS system can be used by only registered trademark owners with clear-cut infringement claims. The URS has other limitations as well, but it is faster. **Example 8.5** IBM once filed a complaint with the URS against an individual who registered the domain names IBM.guru and IBM.ventures. A week later, the URS panel decided in IBM's favor and suspended the two domain names. ■

8–1d Meta Tags

Meta tags are key words that give Internet browsers specific information about a Web page. Meta tags can be used to increase the likelihood that a site will be included in search engine results, even if the site has nothing to do with the key words. In effect, one website can appropriate the key words of other sites with more frequent hits so that the appropriating site will appear in the same search engine results as the more popular sites.

Using another's trademark in a meta tag without the owner's permission normally constitutes trademark infringement. Some uses of another's trademark as a meta tag may be permissible, however, if the use is reasonably necessary and does not suggest that the owner authorized or sponsored the use.

Case Example 8.6 Nespresso USA, Inc., is a well-known espresso and coffee machine producer, and owner of the federally registered trademark "Nespresso." Nespresso also makes and sells espresso capsules for use with its machines. Africa America Coffee Trading Company, which does business as Libretto, makes espresso capsules that are compatible with Nespresso machines. Libretto's capsules are the same shape and size as Nespresso's, but they are made of plastic (not aluminum like Nespresso's). Libretto used Nespresso's trademark on its boxes and also used the word "Nespresso" as a meta tag in the source code for its website.

Nespresso attempted to contact Libretto and request that it stop producing and selling espresso capsules that infringed on its trademark, but Libretto did not respond. Nespresso filed a suit in a federal court in New York. The court concluded that Libretto had been infringing on Nespresso's trademark and permanently enjoined (prohibited) Libretto from using Nespresso's mark—including its meta tags.[7] ■

---

7. *Nespresso USA, Inc. v. Africa America Coffee Trading Co., LLC,* 2016 WL 3162118 (S.D.N.Y. 2016).

8–1e Trademark Dilution in the Online World

As previously explained, trademark *dilution* occurs when a trademark is used, without authorization, in a way that diminishes the distinctive quality of the mark. Unlike trademark infringement, a claim of dilution does not require proof that consumers are likely to be confused by a connection between the unauthorized use and the mark. For this reason, the products involved need not be similar, as the following *Spotlight Case* illustrates.

 Spotlight on Internet Porn: Case 8.1

Hasbro, Inc. v. Internet Entertainment Group, Ltd.

United States District Court, Western District of Washington, 1996 WL 84853 (1996).

Background and Facts In 1949, Hasbro, Inc.—then known as the Milton Bradley Company—published its first version of Candy Land, a children's board game. Hasbro is the owner of the trademark "CANDY LAND," which has been registered with the U.S. Patent and Trademark Office since 1951. Over the years, Hasbro has produced several versions of the game, including Candy Land puzzles, a computer game, and a handheld electronic version.

Candy Land is a children's board game. Why did its parent company, Hasbro, Inc., sue a website?

In the mid-1990s, Brian Cartmell and his employer, the Internet Entertainment Group, Ltd., used the term *candyland.com* as a domain name for a sexually explicit Internet site. Anyone who performed an online search using the word *candyland* was directed to this adult website. Hasbro filed a trademark dilution claim in a federal court, seeking a permanent injunction to prevent the defendants from using the CANDY LAND trademark.

In the Words of the Court
DWYER, U.S. District Judge.
* * * *

2. Hasbro has demonstrated a probability of proving that defendants Internet Entertainment Group, Ltd., Brian Cartmell and Internet Entertainment Group, Inc. (collectively referred to as "defendants") have been diluting the value of Hasbro's CANDY LAND mark by using the name CANDYLAND to identify a sexually explicit Internet site, and by using the name string "candyland.com" as an Internet domain name which, when typed

into an Internet-connected computer, provides Internet users with access to that site.
* * * *

4. Hasbro has shown that defendants' use of the CANDY LAND name and the domain name candyland.com in connection with their Internet site is causing irreparable injury to Hasbro.

5. *The probable harm to Hasbro from defendants' conduct outweighs any inconvenience that defendants will experience if they are required to stop using the CANDYLAND name.* [Emphasis added.]
* * * *

THEREFORE, IT IS HEREBY ORDERED that Hasbro's motion for preliminary injunction is granted.

Decision and Remedy The federal district court granted Hasbro an injunction against the defendants, agreeing that the domain name *candyland.com* was "causing irreparable injury to Hasbro." The judge ordered the defendants to immediately remove all content from the *candyland.com* website and to stop using Habro's CANDY LAND trademark.

Critical Thinking

• **What If the Facts Were Different?** *Suppose that the* candyland.com *website had not been sexually explicit but had sold candy. Would the result have been the same? Explain.*

• **Economic** *How can companies protect themselves from situations such as the one described in this case? What limits each company's ability to be fully protected?*

8–1f Licensing

Recall that a company may permit another party to use a trademark (or other intellectual property) under a license. A licensor might grant a license allowing its trademark to be used as part of a domain name, for instance.

Another type of license involves the use of a product such as software. This sort of licensing is ubiquitous in the online world. When you download an application on your smartphone or other mobile device, for instance, you are typically entering into a license agreement. You are obtaining only a *license* to use the software and not ownership rights in it. Apps published on Google Play, for instance, may use its licensing service to prompt users to agree to a license at the time of installation and use.

Licensing agreements frequently include restrictions that prohibit licensees from sharing the file and using it to create similar software applications. The license may also limit the use of the application to a specific device or give permission to the user for a certain time period.

8–2 Copyrights in Digital Information

Learning Objective 2

What law protects copyrights in the digital age?

Copyright law is probably the most important form of intellectual property protection on the Internet. This is because much of the material on the Internet (including software and database information) is copyrighted, and in order for that material to be transferred online, it must be "copied." Generally, whenever a party downloads software, movies, or music into a computer's random access memory, or RAM, without authorization, a copyright is infringed.

In 1998, Congress passed additional legislation to protect copyright holders—the Digital Millennium Copyright Act (DMCA).[8] Because of its significance in protecting against the piracy of copyrighted materials in the online environment, this act is presented as this chapter's *Landmark in the Law* feature.

Donald Miralle/Getty Images

Was the use of a Prince song in a YouTube video considered a "fair use" under the DMCA?

8–2a Copyright Infringement

Technology has vastly increased the potential for copyright infringement. Even using a small portion of another's copyrighted sound recording (digital sampling) can constitute copyright infringement. Fair use can be asserted as a defense to copyright infringement. ✖ **Spotlight Case Example 8.7** Stephanie Lenz posted a short video on YouTube of her toddler son dancing with the Prince song "Let's Go Crazy" playing in the background. Universal Music Group (UMG) sent YouTube a take-down notice that stated that the video violated copyright law under the DMCA. YouTube removed the "dancing baby" video and notified Lenz of the allegations of copyright infringement, warning her that repeated incidents of infringement could lead it to delete her account.

Lenz filed a lawsuit against UMG claiming that accusing her of infringement constituted a material misrepresentation (fraud) because UMG knew that Lenz's video was a fair use of the song. The district court held that UMG should have considered the fair use doctrine before sending the take-down notice. UMG appealed, and the U.S. Court of Appeals for the Ninth Circuit affirmed. Lenz was allowed to pursue nominal damages from UMG for sending the notice without considering whether her use was fair.[9] ■

---

8. 17 U.S.C. Sections 512, 1201–1205, 1301–1332; and 28 U.S.C. Section 4001.

9. *Lenz v. Universal Music Group,* 815 F.3d 1145 (9th Cir. 2015).

The Digital Millennium Copyright Act

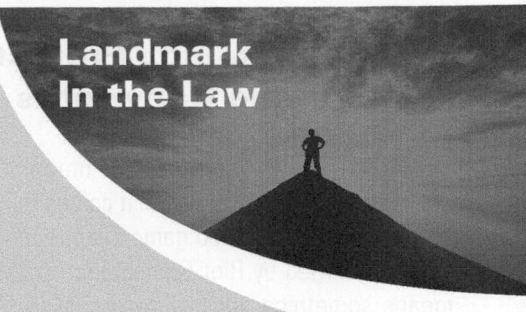

The United States leads the world in the production of creative products, including books, films, videos, recordings, and software. Exports of U.S. creative products surpass those of every other U.S. industry in value.

Given the importance of intellectual property to the U.S. economy, the United States has actively supported international efforts to protect ownership rights in intellectual property, including copyrights. In 1996, to curb unauthorized copying of copyrighted materials, the member nations of the World Intellectual Property Organization (WIPO) adopted a treaty to upgrade global standards of copyright protection, particularly for the Internet.

Implementing the WIPO Treaty

Congress implemented the provisions of the WIPO treaty by enacting a new statute to update U.S. copyright law in 1998. The law—the Digital Millennium Copyright Act (DMCA)—is a landmark step in the protection of copyright owners. Because of the leading position of the United States in the creative industries, the law also serves as a model for other nations.

Among other things, the DMCA established civil and criminal penalties for anyone who circumvents (bypasses) encryption software or other technological antipiracy protection. Also prohibited are the manufacture, import, sale, and distribution of devices or services for circumvention.

Allowing Fair Use The act provides for exceptions to fit the needs of libraries, scientists, universities, and others. In general, the law does not restrict the "fair use" of circumvention methods for educational and other noncommercial purposes. For instance, circumvention is allowed to test computer security, conduct encryption research, protect personal privacy, and enable parents to monitor their children's use of the Internet. The exceptions are to be reconsidered every three years.

Limiting the Liability of Internet Service Providers The DMCA also includes a safe-harbor provision that limits the liability of Internet service providers (ISPs). Under the act, an ISP is not liable for any copyright infringement by its customer *unless* the ISP is aware of the subscriber's violation. An ISP may be held liable only if it fails to take action to shut the subscriber down after learning of the violation. A copyright holder has to act promptly, however, by pursuing a claim in court, or the subscriber has the right to be restored to online access.

Application to Today's World

Without the DMCA, copyright owners would have a more difficult time obtaining legal redress against those who, without authorization, decrypt or copy copyrighted materials. Nevertheless, problems remain, particularly because of the global nature of the Internet.

Initially, criminal penalties for copyright violations could be imposed only if unauthorized copies were exchanged for financial gain. Then, Congress amended the law and extended criminal liability for the piracy of copyrighted materials to persons who exchange unauthorized copies of copyrighted works without realizing a profit.

See this chapter's *Adapting the Law to the Online Environment* feature for a discussion of copyright law in the context of video games.

8–2b File-Sharing Technology

Soon after the Internet became popular, a few enterprising programmers created software to compress large data files, particularly music files. The best-known compression and decompression system is MP3, which enables music fans to download songs or entire CDs onto their computers or onto portable listening devices, such as smartphones. The MP3 system also made it possible for music fans to access other fans' files by engaging in file-sharing via the Internet.

"We're into a whole new world with the Internet, and whenever we sort of cross another plateau in our development, there are those who seek to take advantage of it. So this is a replay of things that have happened throughout our history."

Bill Clinton
1946–present
(Forty-second president of the United States)

Riot Games, Inc., Protects Its Online Video Game Copyrights

The acronym LoL generally means "laugh out loud." But when it comes to the popular online video game *League of Legends* owned by Riot Games, Inc., *LoL* means something much different. More than 100 million people use this free multi-player video game online each month. Of course, competitors have eyed that large market for years.

Taking on a Chinese Competitor

To protect its *LoL* copyrights, U.S.-based Riot Games has filed a lawsuit against a Chinese company, Shanghai MoBai Computer Technology (Moby). Riot Games alleges that Moby has "blatantly and slavishly copied *LoL* in [Moby's online video game called] *Arena of Battle*."[a] In particular, Moby's copycat game features nearly sixty champions with similar names, sound effects, icons, and abilities as those used in *LoL*. Moby has marketed *Arena of Battle* through the Apple App Store as well as Google Play, and it has used alternative titles and aliases in order to sell its game.

Note that under current case law, video gameplay is not protected by copyright law. *Gameplay* describes how players interact with a video game, such as through its plot and its rules. Specific expressions of that gameplay, however—as measured by look, settings, stories, characters, and sound—are protected.

The Mobile Game Market in China

While *LoL* has been China's top computer desktop game for years, millions of Chinese online game players use only mobile platforms, such as smartphones or tablets. As a result, Tencent, the parent company of Riot Games, created a mobile version of *LoL* called *King of Glory*. It is almost an exact copy of *LoL*. *King of Glory* is now China's top-grossing Apple mobile game. Of course, there are no copyright issues with *King of Glory* because Tencent can copy its own video game.

Taking on a Cheating Software Developer

In addition to suing Moby, as mentioned earlier, Riot Games accused the makers of LeagueSharp of violating the Digital Millennium Copyright Act.[b] The plaintiff claimed that the defendants had violated the Digital Millennium Copyright Act[c] by circumventing *LoL*'s anti-cheating software. Customers had paid a monthly fee to use LeagueSharp. Among other things, the service enabled them to see hidden information, automate gameplay to perform with enhanced accuracy, and accumulate certain rewards at a rate not possible for a normal human player.

The obvious question is why anybody would have wanted to pay for LeagueSharp services—recall that *LoL* is a free online game. The reason is the advantage the cheating players gained over ordinary players. They could, for instance, more quickly and easily win "swords," which they could use to buy new characters with which to play. LeagueSharp's makers ultimately agreed to pay $10 million to Riot Games.[d]

Critical Thinking

If LoL is free to players, why would a Chinese company want to copy it?

---

a. *Riot Games, Inc., v. Shanghai MoBai Computer Technology Co., Ltd. et al*, Case No. 3:17-CV-00331 (N.D.Cal. 2017).

b. *Riot Games, Inc. v. Argote*, Case No. 2:16-CV-5871 (C.D.Cal. 2017).

c. Pub. L. No. 105–304, 112 Stat. 2860 (1998).

d. Chalk, Andy. "Riot awarded $10 million in Leaguesharp lawsuit settlement." *pcgamer.com*. 03 Mar. 2017. Web.

Peer-to-Peer (P2P) Networking The sharing of resources among multiple DVDs without the requirement of a central network server.

Distributed Network A network that can be used by persons located (distributed) around the country or the globe to share computer files.

Methods of File-Sharing File-sharing can be accomplished through **peer-to-peer (P2P) networking**. The concept is simple. Rather than going through a central network, P2P networking uses numerous computers or other devices that are connected to one another, often via the Internet.

A P2P network is a type of **distributed network**, which may include devices distributed all over the country or the world. Persons located almost anywhere can work together on the same project by using file-sharing programs on distributed networks.

A newer method of sharing files via the Internet is **cloud computing,** which is essentially a subscription-based or pay-per-use service that extends a computer's software or storage capabilities. Cloud computing can deliver a single application through a browser to multiple users. Alternatively, cloud computing might provide data storage and virtual servers that can be accessed on demand. Amazon, Facebook, Google, IBM, and Sun Microsystems are using and developing more cloud computing services.

Cloud Computing The delivery to users of on-demand services from third-party servers over a network.

As more individuals and companies store their data on "the cloud," what security issues might arise?

Sharing Stored Music Files When file-sharing is used to download others' stored music files, copyright issues arise. Recording artists and their labels stand to lose large amounts of royalties and revenues if relatively few digital downloads are purchased and then made available on distributed networks. These concerns have prompted recording companies to pursue not only companies involved in file-sharing but also individuals who have file-shared copyrighted works.

Case Example 8.8 Maverick Recording Company and other recording companies sued Whitney Harper in federal court for copyright infringement. Harper had used a file-sharing program to download a number of copyrighted songs from the Internet and had then shared the audio files with others via a P2P network. The plaintiffs sought $750 per infringed work—the minimum amount of statutory damages available under the Copyright Act.

Harper claimed that she was an "innocent" infringer because she was unaware that her actions constituted copyright infringement. Under the act, innocent infringement can result in a reduced penalty. The court, however, noted that a copyright notice appeared on all the songs that Harper had downloaded. She therefore could not assert the innocent infringer defense, and the court ordered her to pay damages of $750 per infringed work.[10]

In the following case, the owner of copyrights in musical compositions sought to recover from an Internet service provider, some of whose subscribers used a P2P network to share the owner's copyrighted compositions without permission.

---

10. *Maverick Recording Co. v. Harper,* 598 F.3d 193 (5th Cir. 2010).

■ Case 8.2

BMG Rights Management (US), LLC v. Cox Communications, Inc.

United States Court of Appeals, Fourth Circuit, 881 F.3d 293 (2018).

Background and Facts Cox Communications, Inc., is an Internet service provider (ISP), with 4.5 million subscribers. Some of Cox's subscribers shared copyrighted files, including music files, without the copyright owners' permission, using BitTorrent. (BitTorrent is a peer-to-peer file transfer protocol for sharing large amounts of data online.) Cox's stated policy is to suspend or terminate subscribers who use the service to "infringe the . . . copyrights . . . of any party." Despite this policy, Cox declined to terminate infringing subscribers so as not to lose revenue.

BMG Rights Management (US), LLC, owned copyrights in some of the music shared by the subscribers. BMG sent millions of notices to Cox to alert the ISP to the infringing activity. Cox deleted the notices without acting on them. BMG filed a suit in a federal district court against Cox, seeking to hold the ISP liable under the Digital Millennium Copyright Act (DMCA) for its subscribers' infringement of BMG's copyrights. Cox claimed a "safe harbor" under the act. The court issued a judgment in BMG's favor. Cox appealed to the U.S. Court of Appeals for the Fourth Circuit.

In the Words of the Court
Diana Gribbon *motz,* Circuit Judge:
  * * * *

[The Digital Millennium Copyright Act (DMCA)] requires that, to obtain the benefit of the * * * safe harbor, Cox must have reasonably implemented "a policy that provides for the termination in appropriate circumstances" of its subscribers who repeatedly infringe copyrights. * * * Cox formally adopted a repeat infringer "policy," but * * * made every effort to avoid reasonably implementing that

(Continues)

policy. Indeed, * * * Cox very clearly determined *not* to terminate subscribers who in fact repeatedly violated the policy.

The words of Cox's own employees confirm this conclusion. In [an] email, Jason Zabek, the executive managing the Abuse Group, a team tasked with addressing subscribers' violations of Cox's policies, explained to his team that "if a customer is terminated for DMCA, you are able to reactivate them." * * * This would allow Cox to "collect a few extra weeks of payments for their account." * * * As a result of this practice, * * * Cox *never* terminated a subscriber for infringement without reactivating them.

Cox nonetheless contends that it lacked "actual knowledge" of its subscribers' infringement and therefore did not have to terminate them. That argument misses the mark. The evidence shows that Cox *always* reactivated subscribers after termination, regardless of its knowledge of the subscriber's infringement. * * * *An ISP* [Internet service provider] *cannot claim the protections of the DMCA safe harbor provisions merely by terminating customers as a symbolic gesture before indiscriminately reactivating them within a short timeframe.* [Emphasis added.]

* * * *

Moreover, Cox dispensed with terminating subscribers who repeatedly infringed *BMG's* copyrights in particular when it decided to delete automatically all infringement notices received from [BMG]. As a result, Cox received none of the millions of infringement notices that [BMG] sent to Cox.

* * * *

* * * Cox suggests that because the DMCA merely requires termination of repeat infringers in "appropriate circumstances," Cox decided not to terminate certain subscribers only when "appropriate circumstances" were lacking. But Cox failed to provide evidence that a determination of "appropriate circumstances" played *any* role in its decisions to terminate (or not to terminate). * * * Instead, the evidence shows that Cox's decisions not to terminate * * * were based on one goal: not losing revenue from paying subscribers.

Decision and Remedy The federal appellate court affirmed the judgment of the lower court. To qualify for the DMCA safe-harbor defense, an ISP must implement a repeat-infringer policy. The court stated, "Cox failed to qualify . . . because it failed to implement its policy."

Critical Thinking

• **Technology** *Should an ISP be liable for copyright infringement by its subscribers regardless of whether the ISP is aware of the violation? Why or why not?*

• **Legal Environment** *Could Cox legitimately claim that it had no knowledge of subscribers who infringed BMG's copyrights, since the ISP was deleting all of BMG's infringement notices? Explain.*

Pirated Movies and Television File-sharing also creates problems for the motion picture industry, which loses significant amounts of revenue annually as a result of pirated DVDs. Numerous websites offer software that facilitates the illegal copying of movies. Bit-Torrent, for instance, enables users to download high-quality files from the Internet. Popcorn Time is a BitTorrent site that offers streaming services that allow users to watch pirated movies and television shows without downloading them.

Case Example 8.9 Malibu Media, LLC, produces and distributes adult erotic films through its website X-Art.com. Customers pay a monthly or yearly subscription fee to access an online library of copyrighted pornographic content. Malibu hires investigators to identify individuals who use BitTorrent to illegally download, reproduce, and distribute content from its website. After investigators named Jonathan Gonzales as a suspect, Malibu filed a copyright infringement action against him. A federal district court in Texas ruled in favor of Malibu Media. Gonzales had infringed on fifteen of Malibu's copyrighted films. Thus, Malibu was entitled to damages and to an injunction prohibiting Gonzales from future infringement.[11]

Social Media Forms of communication through which users create and share information, ideas, messages, and other content via the Internet.

8–3 Social Media

Social media provide a means by which people can create, share, and exchange ideas and comments via the Internet. Social networking sites, such as Facebook, Google+, LinkedIn, Pinterest, and Tumblr, have become ubiquitous. Other social media platforms, including

---

11. *Malibu Media, LLC v. Gonzales,* ___ F.Supp.3d ___, 2017 WL 2985641 (S.D.Tex.—Houston 2017).

Instagram, Snapchat, and Twitter, have also gained popularity. Studies show that Internet users spend more time on social networks than at any other sites. The amount of time people spend on social media is constantly increasing.

8–3a Legal Issues

The emergence of Facebook and other social networking sites has affected the legal process in various ways. Here, we explain some uses of social media posts in the litigation process, as well as in the investigations that precede prosecutions or other actions. We also discuss what can happen when employees violate their employers' social media policies.

Impact on Litigation Social media posts now are routinely included in discovery in litigation. Such posts can provide damaging information that establishes a person's intent or what she or he knew at a particular time. Like e-mail, posts on social networks can be the smoking gun that leads to liability.

In some situations, social media posts have been used to reduce damages awards. **Example 8.10** Jil Daniels sues for injuries she sustained in a car accident, claiming that her injuries make it impossible for her to continue working as a hairstylist. The jury initially determines that her damages were $237,000, but when the jurors see Daniels's tweets and photographs of her partying in New Orleans and vacationing on the beach, they reduce the damages award to $142,000. ■

Impact on Settlement Agreements Social media posts have been used to invalidate settlement agreements that contained confidentiality clauses. **Case Example 8.11** Patrick Snay was the headmaster of Gulliver Preparatory School in Florida. When Gulliver did not renew Snay's employment contract, Snay sued the school for age discrimination. During mediation, Snay agreed to settle the case for $80,000 and signed a confidentiality clause that required his wife and he not to disclose the "terms and existence" of the agreement. Nevertheless, Snay and his wife told their daughter, Dana, that the dispute had been settled and that they were happy with the results.

Dana, a college student, had recently graduated from Gulliver and, according to Snay, had suffered retaliation at the school. Dana posted a Facebook comment that said, "Mama and Papa Snay won the case against Gulliver. Gulliver is now officially paying for my vacation to Europe this summer. SUCK IT." The comment went out to 1,200 of Dana's Facebook friends, many of whom were Gulliver students, and school officials soon learned of it. The school immediately notified Snay that he had breached the confidentiality clause and refused to pay the settlement amount. Ultimately, a state intermediate appellate court agreed and held that Snay could not enforce the settlement agreement.[12] ■

Criminal Investigations Law enforcement uses social media to detect and prosecute criminals. A surprising number of criminals boast about their illegal activities on social media. **Example 8.12** A nineteen-year-old posts a message on Facebook bragging about how drunk he was on New Year's Eve and apologizing to the owner of the parked car that he hit. The next day, police officers arrest him for drunk driving and leaving the scene of an accident. ■

Police may also use social media to help them to locate a particular suspect or to determine the identity of other suspects within a criminal network. In fact, police officers in New York City and other locations have even assumed fake identities on Facebook in order to "friend" suspects and obtain information. According to at least one court, it is legally acceptable for law enforcement officers to set up a phony social media account to catch a suspect.[13]

Administrative Agencies Federal regulators also use social media posts in their investigations into illegal activities. **Example 8.13** Reed Hastings, the top executive of Netflix, stated on Facebook that Netflix subscribers had watched a billion hours of video the previous

> "Twitter is just a multiplayer notepad."
>
> **Ben Maddox**
> (Chief instructional technology officer at New York University)

---

12. *Gulliver Schools, Inc. v. Snay*, 137 So.3d 1045 (Fla.App. 2014).
13. *United States v. Gatson*, 2014 WL 7182275 (D.N.J. 2014). See also *United States v. Tutis*, 216 F.Supp.3d 467 (D.N.J. 2016).

month. As a result, Netflix's stock price rose, which prompted a federal agency investigation. Under securities laws, such a statement is considered to be material information to investors. Thus, it must be disclosed to all investors, not just a select group, such as those who had access to Hastings's Facebook post.

The agency ultimately concluded that it could not hold Hastings responsible for any wrong-doing because the agency's policy on social media use was not clear. The agency then issued new guidelines that allow companies to disclose material information through social media if investors have been notified in advance. ■

An administrative law judge can base his or her decision on the content of social media posts. **Case Example 8.14** Jennifer O'Brien was a tenured teacher at a public school in New Jersey when she posted two messages on her Facebook page. "I'm not a teacher—I'm a warden for future criminals!" and "They had a scared straight program in school—why couldn't I bring first graders?" Not surprisingly, outraged parents protested. The deputy superintendent of schools filed a complaint against O'Brien with the state's commissioner of education, charging her with conduct unbecoming a teacher.

After a hearing, an administrative law judge ordered that O'Brien be removed from her teaching position. O'Brien appealed to a state court, claiming that her Facebook postings were protected by the First Amendment and could not be used by the school district to discipline or discharge her. The court found that O'Brien had failed to establish that her Facebook postings were protected speech and that the seriousness of O'Brien's conduct warranted removal from her position.[14] ■

Can a public school teacher be fired for making derogatory comments about students on Facebook?

© 1000 Words/Shutterstock.com

Employers' Social Media Policies Many large corporations have established specific guidelines on using social media in the workplace. Employees who use social media in a way that violates their employer's stated policies may be disciplined or fired from their jobs. Courts and administrative agencies usually uphold an employer's right to terminate a person based on his or her violation of a social media policy.

Case Example 8.15 Virginia Rodriquez worked for Walmart Stores, Inc., for almost twenty years and had been promoted to management. Then she was disciplined for violating the company's policies by having a fellow employee use Rodriquez's password to alter the price of an item that she purchased. Under Walmart's rules, another violation within a year would mean termination.

Nine months later, on Facebook, Rodriquez publicly chastised employees under her supervision for calling in sick to go to a party. The posting violated Walmart's "Social Media Policy," which was "to avoid public comment that adversely affects employees." Walmart terminated Rodriquez. She filed a lawsuit, alleging discrimination, but the court issued a summary judgment in Walmart's favor.[15] ■ Note, though, that some employees' posts on social media may be protected under labor law.

8–3b The Electronic Communications Privacy Act

The Electronic Communications Privacy Act (ECPA)[16] amended federal wiretapping law to cover electronic forms of communications. Although Congress enacted the ECPA many years before social media networks existed, it nevertheless applies to communications through social media.

The ECPA prohibits the intentional interception of any wire, oral, or electronic communication. It also prohibits the intentional disclosure or use of the information obtained by the interception.

Exclusions Excluded from the ECPA's coverage are any electronic communications through devices that an employer provides for its employee to use "in the ordinary course

---

14. *In re O'Brien*, 2013 WL 132508 (N.J.App. 2013). See also *Grutzmacher v. Howard County*, 851 F.3d 332 (4th Cir. 2017).
15. *Rodriquez v. Wal-Mart Stores, Inc.*, 2013 WL 102674 (N.D.Tex. 2013).
16. 18 U.S.C. Sections 2510–2521.

of its business." Consequently, if a company provides the electronic device (cell phone, laptop, tablet) to the employee for ordinary business use, the company is not prohibited from intercepting business communications made on it.

This "business-extension exception" to the ECPA permits employers to monitor employees' electronic communications made in the ordinary course of business. It does not permit employers to monitor employees' personal communications. Another exception allows an employer to avoid liability under the act if the employees consent to having the employer monitor their electronic communications.

Stored Communications Part of the ECPA is known as the Stored Communications Act (SCA).[17] The SCA prohibits intentional and unauthorized access to *stored* electronic communications, and sets forth criminal and civil sanctions for violators. A person can violate the SCA by intentionally accessing a stored electronic communication.

The SCA also prevents "providers" of communication services (such as cell phone companies and social media networks) from divulging private communications to certain entities and individuals. **Case Example 8.16** As part of an investigation into disability fraud, the New York County District Attorney's Office sought from Facebook the data and stored communications of 381 retired police officers and firefighters. The government suspected that these individuals had faked illness after 9/11 in order to obtain disability.

Facebook challenged the warrants in court, arguing that they were unconstitutional because they were overly broad and lacked particularity. The court ruled against Facebook and ordered it to comply. It also ordered the company not to notify the users that it was disclosing their data to government investigators. Facebook complied but appealed the decision. The reviewing court held that only the individuals, not Facebook, could challenge the warrants as violations of privacy. Thus, the government was allowed to seize all of Facebook's digital data pertaining to these users.[18]

Why did a court rule that stored data from Facebook accounts of certain police officers and firefighters could be accessed by a third party?

8–3c Protection of Social Media Passwords

Employees and applicants for jobs or colleges have occasionally been asked to divulge their social media passwords. An employer or school may look at an individual's Facebook or other account to see if it includes controversial postings, such as racially discriminatory remarks or photos of parties where drugs were being used. Such postings can have a negative effect on a person's prospects even if they were made years earlier or are taken out of context.

By 2019, more than half of the states had enacted legislation to protect individuals from having to disclose their social media passwords. These laws vary. Some states, such as Michigan, prohibit employers from taking adverse action against an employee or job applicant based on what the person has posted online. Michigan's law also applies to e-mail and cloud storage accounts.

Legislation will not completely prevent employers and others from taking actions against employees or applicants based on their social network postings, though. Management and human resources personnel are unlikely to admit that they based a hiring decision on what they saw on someone's Facebook page. They may not even have to admit to looking at the Facebook page if they use private browsing, which enables people to keep their Web browsing activities confidential. How, then, would a person who does not get the job prove that he or she was rejected because the employer accessed social media postings?

"My favorite thing about the Internet is that you get to go into the private world of real creeps without having to smell them."

Penn Jillette
1955–present
(American illusionist, comedian, and author)

---

17. 18 U.S.C. Sections 2701–2711.
18. *In re 381 Search Warrants Directed to Facebook, Inc.,* 29 N.Y.3d 231, 78 N.E.3d 141, 55 N.Y.S.3d 696 (2017).

8–3d Company-wide Social Media Networks

Many companies, including Dell, Inc., and Nikon Instruments, form their own internal social media networks. Software companies offer a variety of systems, including Salesforce.com's Chatter, Microsoft's Yammer, and WebEx Meetings. Posts on these internal networks, or *intranets*, are quite different from the typical posts on Facebook, LinkedIn, and Twitter. Employees use them to exchange messages about topics related to their work, such as deals that are closing, new products, production flaws, how a team is solving a problem, and the details of customer orders. Thus, the tone is businesslike.

An important advantage to using an internal system for employee communications is that the company can better protect its trade secrets. The company usually decides which employees can see particular intranet files and which employees will belong to each "social group" within the company. Generally, the company will keep the data in its system on its own secure server.

Internal social media systems also offer additional benefits. They provide real-time information about important issues, such as production glitches, along with information about products, customers, and competitors. Another major benefit is a significant reduction in e-mail. Rather than wasting fellow employees' time on mass e-mailings, workers can post messages or collaborate on presentations via the company's social network.

8–4 Online Defamation

Cyber Tort A tort committed via the Internet.

Cyber torts are torts that arise from online conduct. One of the most prevalent cyber torts is online defamation. Recall that defamation is wrongfully hurting a person's reputation by communicating false statements about that person to others. Because the Internet enables individuals to communicate with large numbers of people simultaneously (via tweets, for instance), online defamation is a common problem in today's legal environment.

Example 8.17 Singer-songwriter Courtney Love was sued for defamation based on remarks she posted about fashion designer Dawn Simorangkir on Twitter. Love claimed that her statements were opinion (rather than statements of fact, as required) and therefore were not actionable as defamation. Nevertheless, Love ended up paying $430,000 to settle the case out of court. ■

8–4a Identifying the Author of Online Defamation

"In cyberspace, the First Amendment is a local ordinance."

John Perry Barlow
1947–present
(American poet and essayist)

An initial issue raised by online defamation is simply discovering who is committing it. In the real world, identifying the author of a defamatory remark generally is an easy matter. Suppose, though, that a business firm has discovered that defamatory statements about its policies and products are being posted in an online forum. Such forums allow anyone—customers, employees, or crackpots—to complain about a firm that they dislike while remaining anonymous.

Therefore, a threshold barrier to anyone who seeks to bring an action for online defamation is discovering the identity of the person who posted the defamatory message. An Internet service provider (ISP) can disclose personal information about its customers only when ordered to do so by a court. Consequently, businesses and individuals are increasingly bringing lawsuits against "John Does" (John Doe, Jane Doe, and the like are fictitious names used in lawsuits when the identity of a party is not known or when a party wishes to conceal his or her name for privacy reasons). Then, using the authority of the courts, the plaintiffs can obtain from the ISPs the identity of the persons responsible for the defamatory messages.

Note that courts have occasionally refused to order companies to disclose the identity of their users. **Case Example 8.18** Yelp, Inc., is a California company that operates a social networking website for consumer reviews. Seven users of Yelp posted negative reviews of Hadeed Carpet Cleaning, Inc., in Alexandria, Virginia. Hadeed brought a defamation suit against the "John Doe" reviewers in a Virginia state court, claiming that because these individuals were not actual customers, their comments were false and defamatory. Yelp failed to comply with a court order to reveal the users' identities and was held in contempt.

Yelp appealed, claiming that releasing the identities would violate the defendants' First Amendment right to free speech. A state intermediate appellate court affirmed the lower court's judgment, but that decision was reversed on appeal. The Supreme Court of Virginia ruled that even though the state trial court had jurisdiction, it did not have subpoena power over Yelp, a nonresident defendant. According to the court, "Enforcement of a subpoena seeking out-of-state discovery is generally governed by the courts and the law of the state in which the witness resides or where the documents are located."[19]

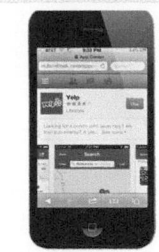

Can a business that receives poor reviews on Yelp force Yelp to disclose the reviewers' identities in a lawsuit for online defamation?

8–4b Liability of Internet Service Providers

Normally, those who repeat or otherwise republish a defamatory statement are subject to liability. Thus, newspapers, magazines, and television and radio stations are subject to liability for defamatory content that they publish or broadcast, even though the content was prepared or created by others.

Applying this rule to cyberspace, however, raises an important issue: Should ISPs be regarded as publishers and therefore be held liable for defamatory messages that are posted by their users in online forums or other arenas?

General Rule The Communications Decency Act (CDA) states that "no provider or user of an interactive computer service shall be treated as the publisher or speaker of any information provided by another information content provider."[20] Thus, under the CDA, ISPs usually are treated differently from publishers in print and other media and are not liable for publishing defamatory statements that come from a third party.

The CDA's broad protection for ISPs extends beyond republication of defamatory statements. This chapter's *Business Law Analysis* feature illustrates the CDA's general rule.

Learning Objective 4

What law governs whether Internet service providers are liable for online defamatory statements made by users?

---

19. *Yelp, Inc. v. Hadeed Carpet Cleaning, Inc.*, 289 Va. 426, 770 S.E.2d 440 (2015).
20. 47 U.S.C. Section 230.

Immunity of ISPs under the Communications Decency Act

Business Law Analysis

CyberConnect, Inc., is an Internet service provider (ISP). Emma is a CyberConnect subscriber. Market Reach, Inc., is an online advertising company.

Using sophisticated software, Market Reach directs its ads to those users most likely to be interested in a particular product. When Emma receives one of the ads, she objects to the content. Furthermore, she claims that CyberConnect should pay damages for "publishing" the ad. Is Cyber-Connect liable for the content of Market Reach's ad?

Analysis: The Communications Decency Act (CDA) states that "no provider . . . of an interactive computer service shall be treated as the publisher or speaker of any information provided by another information content provider." In other words, under the CDA, CyberConnect and other ISPs are not liable for the content of published statements that come from a third party, such as the statements in Market Reach's ad.

Result and Reasoning: Because CyberConnect is not regarded as a publisher under the CDA, the company is not liable for the content of Market Reach's ad (even if Emma could prove that the content was defamatory). ISPs are not liable for third party content that they have no ability to control.

Exceptions Although the courts generally have construed the CDA as providing a broad shield to protect ISPs from liability for third party content, some courts have started establishing limits to this immunity. **Case Example 8.19** Roommate.com, LLC, operates an online roommate-matching website that helps individuals find roommates based on their descriptions of themselves and their roommate preferences. Users respond to a series of online questions, choosing from answers in drop-down and select-a-box menus. Some of the questions asked users to disclose their sex, family status, and sexual orientation—which is not permitted under the federal Fair Housing Act.

When a nonprofit housing organization sued Roommate.com, the company claimed it was immune from liability under the CDA. A federal appellate court disagreed and ordered Roommate.com to pay nearly $500,000. By creating the website and the questionnaire and answer choices, Roommate.com prompted users to express discriminatory preferences and matched users based on these preferences in violation of federal law.[21]

8-4c Other Actions Involving Online Posts

Online conduct can give rise to a wide variety of legal actions. E-mails, tweets, posts, and every sort of online communication may form the basis for almost any type of tort. For instance, in addition to defamation, suits relating to online conduct may involve allegations of wrongful interference or infliction of emotional distress.

Besides actions grounded in the common law, online conduct may give rise to a cause of action based on a statute. In the following case, the court was asked to issue an injunction to prohibit speech that was alleged to constitute *cyberstalking*. The applicable statute defined this term to require in part "substantial emotional distress."

---

21. *Fair Housing Council of San Fernando Valley v. Roommate.com, LLC,* 666 F.3d 1216 (9th Cir. 2012).

■ Case 8.3

David v. Textor

District Court of Appeal of Florida, Fourth District, 41 Fla.L.Weekly D131, 189 So.3d 871 (2016).

Background and Facts Hologram USA, Inc., and Pulse Entertainment are companies that produce holograms. When Pulse announced that it would produce a Michael Jackson hologram for a Billboard Music Awards ceremony, Hologram filed a lawsuit in a federal district court against Pulse, alleging patent infringement. Pulse's owner, John Textor, then made a counterclaim in a California state court against Hologram's owner, Alkiviades David, alleging a business tort.

While these suits were pending, David sent two e-mails to Textor demanding (1) that Hologram be credited for the Jackson hologram, and (2) that Textor drop his lawsuit against David and settle Hologram's suit against Pulse. In an online magazine article, David was quoted as joking that he "would have killed [Textor] if he could." In addition, on his website, David posted references to articles criticizing Textor and his business.

Textor filed a suit in a Florida state court against David, alleging cyberstalking. The court issued an injunction prohibiting David from communicating with or posting anything about Textor. David appealed.

In the Words of the Court
WARNER, J. [Judge].
* * * *

David claims that none of the allegations in the petition constitute cyberstalking but are merely heated rhetoric over a business dispute. Further, he claims that the injunction constitutes a prior restraint on speech, which violates the First Amendment.

[Under Florida law,] "Cyberstalk" means to engage in a course of conduct to communicate, or to cause to be communicated, words, images, or language by or through the use of electronic mail or electronic communication, directed at a specific person, causing substantial emotional distress to that person and serving no legitimate purpose.

*Whether a communication causes substantial emotional distress * * * is governed by the reasonable person standard.*

* * * Whether a communication serves a legitimate purpose * * * will cover a wide variety of conduct. * * * Where comments are made on an electronic medium to be read by others, they cannot be said to be directed to a particular person. [Emphasis added.]

In this case, Textor alleged that two communications came directly from David to him, both of which were demands that Textor drop his lawsuit. In neither of them did David make any threat to Textor's safety. * * * Moreover, nothing in the e-mails should have caused substantial emotional distress to Textor, himself a sophisticated businessman.

The postings online are also not communications [that] would cause substantial emotional distress. Most of them are simply re-tweets of articles or headlines involving Textor. That they may be embarrassing to Textor is not at all the same as causing him substantial emotional distress sufficient to obtain an injunction.

Even the alleged physical threat made by David in an online interview, that David would have killed Textor if he could have, would not cause a reasonable person substantial emotional distress. In the online article the author stated that "David joked" when stating that he would have killed Textor. Spoken to a journalist for publication, it hardly amounts to an actual and credible threat of violence to Textor.

In sum, none of the allegations in Textor's petition show acts constituting cyberstalking, in that a reasonable person would not suffer substantial emotional distress over them. Those communications made directly to Textor served a legitimate purpose.

An injunction in this case would also violate [the freedom of speech under the U.S. Constitution's First Amendment. An] injunction directed to speech is a classic example of prior restraint on speech triggering First Amendment concerns. * * * *Prior restraints on speech and publication are the most serious and the least tolerable infringement on First Amendment rights.* [The Florida Statute] itself recognizes the First Amendment rights of individuals by concluding that a "course of conduct" for purposes of the statute does not include protected speech. [Emphasis added.]

Decision and Remedy A state intermediate appellate court reversed the injunction and remanded the case with a direction to dismiss Textor's petition. David's conduct did not constitute cyberstalking under the relevant Florida statute, and the injunction was a prior restraint that violated the First Amendment.

Critical Thinking

• **Legal Environment** *What could these parties have done to avoid spending so much time and money on litigation? Discuss.*

• **What If the Facts Were Different?** *Suppose that David's posts and other online communications had amounted to extreme and outrageous conduct. Would the result in this case have been different? Explain.*

8–5 Privacy

In recent years, Facebook, Google, and Yahoo have all been accused of violating users' privacy rights. The right to privacy is guaranteed by the Bill of Rights and some state constitutions. (See this chapter's *Beyond Our Borders* feature for a discussion of how the European Union now recognizes a "right to be forgotten.") To maintain a suit for the invasion of privacy, though, a person must have a reasonable expectation of privacy in the particular situation.

8–5a Reasonable Expectation of Privacy

People clearly have a reasonable expectation of privacy when they enter their personal banking or credit-card information online. They also have a reasonable expectation that online companies will follow their own privacy policies. But it is probably not reasonable to expect privacy in statements made on Twitter—or photos posted on Twitter, Flickr, or Instagram, for that matter.

Sometimes, people mistakenly believe that they are making statements or posting photos in a private forum. **Example 8.20** Randi Zuckerberg, the older sister of Mark Zuckerberg (the founder of Facebook), used a mobile app called Poke to post a photo on Facebook of their family gathering during the holidays. Poke allows the sender to decide how long the photo can be seen by others. Facebook allows users to configure their privacy settings to limit access to photos, which Randi thought she had done. Nonetheless, the photo showed up in the Facebook feed of Callie Schweitzer, who then put it on Twitter, where it eventually "went viral." Schweitzer apologized and removed the photo, but it had already gone public for the world to see. ■

"Science fiction does not remain fiction for long. And certainly not on the Internet."

Vinton Cerf
1943–present
(American Internet pioneer and author)

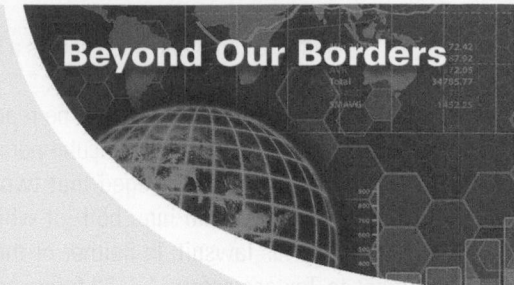

"The Right to Be Forgotten" in the European Union

Beyond Our Borders

As the saying goes, the Internet never forgets. If fifteen years ago you had some financial problems and had to sell your house at auction, that information about you remains available forever. A Spanish lawyer, Mario Costeja Gonzàlez, found himself in just that situation. If anyone Googled his name, they discovered that his house had gone into foreclosure when he was a younger man.

Taking Google to Court

Costeja Gonzàlez requested that Google's search engine no longer access those old court records. Google refused. The case ultimately ended up in the European Union Court of Justice. Google lost.[a] The company had to remove the links to publicly available information that Costeja Gonzàlez considered damaging and an invasion of his privacy.

_____

a. *SL, Google Inc. v. Agencia Española de Protección de Datos, Mario Costeja Gonzalez,* Court of Justice for the European Union (Grand Chamber), Case C-131/12, May 13, 2014.

What "The Right to Be Forgotten" Means

The new "right to be forgotten" in the European Union allows individuals to petition Google to remove search result links that are personal in nature and that have become "outdated" or "irrelevant." Does that mean that anyone in Europe can ask that links to old information be removed? Not really. Right now, a European wishing to remove a link to older personal data needs a lawyer to make the request. Moreover, the original "offensive" documents are not removed—only the Google search link to those documents. According to Viviane Reading, vice president of the European Commission, "It is clear that the right to be forgotten cannot amount to a right of the total erasure of history."

Can the Ruling Be Applied Outside Europe?

The Court of Justice's ruling applies only within the member countries of the European Union. None-theless, the French Data Protection Authority is seeking to expand the ruling. France has ordered Google to remove links from its database entirely, in all locations worldwide. Google thus far has refused.

According to Google, the right to be forgotten should be limited to the European Union. Google argues that the framework used in Europe would not work in the United States because of the First Amendment. Still, several countries in Asia and Latin America are considering enacting their own delinking rules.

Critical Thinking

How could the "right to be forgotten" affect free speech?

8–5b Data Collection and Cookies

Cookie A small file sent from a website and stored in a user's Web browser to track the user's Web browsing activities.

Whenever a consumer purchases items online from a retailer, the retailer collects information about the consumer. **Cookies** are invisible files that computers, smartphones, and other mobile devices create to track a user's Web browsing activities. Cookies provide detailed information to marketers about an individual's behavior and preferences, which is then used to personalize online services.

Over time, a retailer can amass considerable data about a person's shopping habits. Does collecting this information violate the person's right to privacy? Should retailers be able to pass on the data they have collected to their affiliates? Should they be able to use the information to predict what a consumer might want and then create online "coupons" customized to fit the person's buying history?

Learning Objective 5

How do online retailers track their users' Web browsing activities?

Example 8.21 Facebook, Inc., once used a targeted advertising technique called "Sponsored Stories." An ad would display a Facebook friend's name and profile picture, along with a statement that the friend "likes" the company sponsoring the advertisement. A group of plaintiffs filed suit, claiming that Facebook had used their pictures for advertising without their permission. When a federal court refused to dismiss the case, Facebook agreed to settle. ■

Should smart-TV manufacturers collect consumer-use data?   Ethical Issue

Any device connected to the Internet is capable of transmitting a multitude of information about not only the device, but also its use. Using integrated software, smart TVs allow consumers to access the Internet and on-demand services, including Hulu, Netflix, and Pandora. One manufacturer, Los Angeles–based Vizio, Inc., preinstalls such software, or it is installed through software updates. That software uses automatic content recognition to collect and report customers' content-viewing histories. Such histories are associated with each customer's digital identity, including an IP address, a zip code, a region, and language settings. This information is transmitted to Vizio's data service platform and then sold to advertisers. Advertisers can then specifically target advertising to Vizio smart TVs and to any computers, tablets, or smartphones connected to the same network.

A number of purchasers of Vizio's smart TVs filed a class-action suit against the company for, at a minimum, violating the Video Privacy Protection Act.[22] In response, Vizio issued the following statement: "Nonpersonal identifiable information may be shared with select partners . . . to permit these companies to make, for example, better-informed decisions regarding content production, programming, and advertising." Certainly, the plaintiffs in the numerous lawsuits against Vizio are not satisfied with that reasoning. They do not believe that Vizio's marketing or privacy policies clearly stated that their viewing information was going to be collected and then sold to advertisers. Is it ethical for Vizio to do this? Does it matter that purchasers of Vizio's smart TVs can buy them at relatively low prices because the company is able to profit from selling consumer-viewing data to advertisers?

8–5c Internet Companies' Privacy Policies

The Federal Trade Commission (FTC) investigates consumer complaints of privacy violations. The FTC has forced many companies, including Google, Facebook, and Twitter, to enter into agreements consenting to give the FTC broad power to review their privacy and data practices. It can then sue companies that violate the terms of the agreements.

Example 8.22 Google settled a suit brought by the FTC alleging that it had misrepresented its use of tracking cookies to users of Apple's Safari Internet browser. Google allegedly had used cookies to trick the Safari browser on Macs, iPhones, and iPads so that Google could monitor users who believed they had blocked such tracking. This violated a consent decree with the FTC. Google agreed to pay $22.5 million to settle the suit without admitting liability. ■

Facebook has had to deal with a number of complaints about its privacy policy and has changed its policy several times to satisfy its critics and ward off potential government investigations. Other companies, including mobile app developers, have also changed their privacy policies to provide more information to consumers. Consequently, it is frequently companies, rather than courts or legislatures, that define the privacy rights of their online users.

Robert Daly/Getty Images

Smart TVs have software designed to collect consumers' program habits and other identifying data. If manufacturers sell this data to advertisers, does this violate the Video Privacy Protection Act?

22. *In re Vizio, Inc., Consumer Privacy Litigation*, 238 F.Supp.3d 1204 (D.Ca. 2017); Video Privacy Protection Act, 18 U.S.C. Section 2710(a).

Practice and Review

While he was in high school, Joel Gibb downloaded numerous songs to his smartphone from an unlicensed file-sharing service. He used portions of the copyrighted songs when he recorded his own band and posted videos on YouTube and Facebook. He also used BitTorrent to download several movies from the Internet. Now Gibb has applied to Boston University. The admissions office has requested access to his Facebook password, and he has complied. Using the information presented in the chapter, answer the following questions.

1. What laws, if any, did Gibb violate by downloading the music and videos from the Internet?
2. Was Gibb's use of portions of copyrighted songs in his own music illegal? Explain.
3. Can individuals legally post copyrighted content on their Facebook pages? Why or why not?
4. Did Boston University violate any laws when it asked Joel to provide his Facebook password? Explain.

Debate This

Internet service providers should be subject to the same defamation laws as newspapers, magazines, and television and radio stations.

Key Terms

cloud computing 209
cookie 218
cybersquatting 202
cyber tort 214

distributed network 208
domain name 202
goodwill 202
Internet service provider (ISP) 202

peer-to-peer (P2P) networking 208
social media 210
spam 201
typosquatting 203

Chapter Summary: Internet Law, Social Media, and Privacy

Internet Law	1. *Spam*—Unsolicited junk e-mail accounts for about three-quarters of all e-mails. Laws to combat spam have been enacted, but the flow of spam continues.
	  a. The Controlling the Assault of Non-Solicited Pornography and Marketing (CAN-SPAM) Act prohibits false and deceptive e-mails originating in the United States.
	  b. The U.S. Safe Web Act allows U.S. authorities to cooperate and share information with foreign agencies in investigating and prosecuting those involved in spamming, spyware, and various Internet frauds and deceptions. The act includes a "safe harbor" for Internet service providers.
	2. *Domain names*—Trademark owners often use their mark as part of a domain name (Internet address). The Internet Corporation for Assigned Names and Numbers (ICANN) oversees the distribution of domain names. ICANN has expanded the available domain names to include new generic top-level domain names (gTLDs).
	3. *Cybersquatting*—Registering a domain name that is the same as, or confusingly similar to, the trademark of another and then offering to sell the domain name back to the trademark owner is known as cybersquatting. Anticybersquatting legislation makes this practice illegal if the one registering, trafficking in, or using the domain name has a "bad faith intent" to profit from that mark.

4. *Meta tags*—Search engines compile their results by looking through a website's *meta tags*, or key words. Using another's trademark in a meta tag without the owner's permission normally constitutes trademark infringement.

5. *Trademark dilution*—When a trademark is used online, without authorization, in a way that diminishes the distinctive quality of the mark, it constitutes trademark dilution. Unlike infringement actions, trademark dilution claims do not require proof that consumers are likely to be confused by a connection between the unauthorized use and the mark.

6. *Licensing*—Many companies choose to permit others to use their trademarks and other intellectual property online through licensing. The purchase of software generally involves a license agreement. These agreements frequently include restrictions that prohibit licensees from sharing the file and using it to create similar software applications.

Copyrights in Digital Information	1. *Copyrighted works online*—Much of the material on the Internet (including software and database information) is copyrighted. In order for that material to be transferred online, it must be "copied." Generally, whenever a party downloads software or music without authorization, a copyright is infringed. 2. *Digital Millennium Copyright Act*—The Digital Millennium Copyright Act (DMCA) protects copyrights online and establishes civil and criminal penalties for anyone who bypasses encryption software or other technologies. The DMCA provides exceptions for certain educational and nonprofit uses. It also limits the liability of Internet service providers for infringement unless the ISP is aware of the user's infringement and fails to take action. 3. *File-sharing*—When file-sharing is used to download others' stored music files or illegally copy movies, copyright issues arise. Individuals who download music or movies in violation of copyright laws are liable for infringement. Companies that distribute file-sharing software or provide such services have been held liable for the copyright infringement of their users if the software or technology involved promoted copyright infringement.

Social Media	1. *Legal issues*—The emergence of Facebook and other social networking sites has had a number of effects on the legal process. Social media posts have had an impact on litigation and settlement agreements. Law enforcement and administrative agencies now routinely use social media to detect illegal activities and conduct investigations, as do many businesses.
	
	2. *The Electronic Communications Privacy Act (ECPA)*—The ECPA prohibits the intentional interception or disclosure of any wire, oral, or electronic communication.
	  a. The ECPA includes a "business-extension exception" that permits employers to monitor employees' electronic communications made in the ordinary course of business (but not their personal communications).
	  b. The Stored Communications Act (SCA) is part of the ECPA and prohibits intentional unauthorized access to stored electronic communications (such as backup data stored by an employer).
	
	3. *Social media passwords*—Private employers and schools have sometimes looked at an individual's Facebook or other social media account to see if it included controversial postings. A number of states have enacted legislation that protects individuals from having to divulge their social media passwords. Such laws may not be completely effective in preventing employers from rejecting applicants or terminating workers based on their social media postings.
	
	4. *Company-wide social media networks*—Many companies today form their own internal social media networks through which employees can exchange messages about topics related to their work.

Online Defamation	Federal and state statutes apply to certain forms of cyber torts, or torts that occur in cyberspace, such as online defamation. Under the federal Communications Decency Act (CDA), Internet service providers generally are not liable for defamatory messages posted by their subscribers.
Privacy	1. *Expectation of privacy*—Numerous Internet companies have been accused of violating users' privacy rights. To sue for invasion of privacy, though, a person must have a reasonable expectation of privacy in the particular situation. It is often difficult to determine how much privacy can reasonably be expected on the Internet. 2. *Data collection and cookies*—Whenever a consumer purchases items online from a retailer, the retailer collects information about the consumer through "cookies." Consequently, retailers have gathered large amounts of data about individuals' shopping habits. It is not always clear whether collecting such information violates a person's right to privacy. 3. *Internet companies' privacy policies*—Many companies establish Internet privacy policies, which typically inform users what types of data they are gathering and for what purposes it will be used.

Issue Spotters

1. Karl self-publishes a cookbook titled *Hole Foods*, in which he sets out recipes for donuts, Bundt cakes, tortellini, and other foods with holes. To publicize the book, Karl designs the website holefoods.com. Karl appropriates the key words of other cooking and cookbook sites with more frequent hits so that holefoods.com will appear in the same search engine results as the more popular sites. Has Karl done anything wrong? Explain. (See *Internet Law*.)

2. Eagle Corporation began marketing software in 2010 under the mark "Eagle." In 2019, Eagle.com, Inc., a different company selling different products, begins to use *eagle* as part of its URL and registers it as a domain name. Can Eagle Corporation stop this use of *eagle*? If so, what must the company show? (See *Internet Law*.)

   —**Check your answers to the *Issue Spotters* against the answers provided in Appendix D at the end of this text.**

Business Scenarios and Case Problems

8–1. Privacy. SeeYou, Inc., is an online social network. SeeYou's members develop personalized profiles to share information—photos, videos, stories, activity updates, and other items—with other members. Members post the information that they want to share and decide with whom they want to share it. SeeYou launched a program to allow members to share with others what they do elsewhere online. For example, if a member rents a movie through Netflix, SeeYou will broadcast that information to everyone in the member's online network. How can SeeYou avoid complaints that this program violates its members' privacy? (See *Privacy*.)

8–2. Copyrights in Digital Information. When she was in college, Jammie Thomas-Rasset wrote a case study on Napster, the online peer-to-peer (P2P) file-sharing network, and knew that it had been shut down because it was illegal. Later, Capitol Records, Inc., which owns the copyrights to a large number of music recordings, discovered that "tereastarr"—a user name associated with Thomas-Rasset's Internet protocol address—had made twenty-four songs available for distribution on KaZaA, another P2P network. Capitol notified Thomas-Rasset that she had been identified as engaging in the unauthorized trading of music. She replaced the hard drive on her computer with a new drive that did not contain the songs in dispute. Is Thomas-Rasset liable for copyright infringement? Explain. [*Capitol Records, Inc. v. Thomas-Rasset*, 692 F.3d 899 (8th Cir. 2012)] (See *Copyrights in Digital Information*.)

8–3. Privacy. Using special software, South Dakota law enforcement officers found a person who appeared to possess child pornography at a specific Internet protocol address. The officers subpoenaed Midcontinent Communications, the service that assigned the address, for the personal information of its subscriber. With this information, the officers obtained a search warrant for the residence of John Rolfe, where they found a laptop that contained child pornography. Rolfe argued that the subpoenas violated his "expectation of privacy." Did Rolfe have a privacy interest in the information obtained by the subpoenas issued to Midcontinent? Discuss. [*State of South Dakota v. Rolfe*, 825 N.W.2d 901 (S.Dak. 2013)] (See *Privacy*.)

8–4. File-Sharing. Dartmouth College professor M. Eric Johnson, in collaboration with Tiversa, Inc., a company that monitors peer-to-peer networks to provide security services, wrote an article titled "Data Hemorrhages in the Health-Care Sector." In preparing the article, Johnson and Tiversa searched the networks for data that could be used to commit medical or financial identity theft. They found a document that contained the Social Security numbers, insurance information, and treatment codes for patients of LabMD, Inc. Tiversa notified LabMD of the find in order to solicit its business. Instead of hiring Tiversa, however, LabMD filed a suit in a federal district court against the company, alleging trespass, conversion, and violations of federal statutes. What do these facts indicate about the security of private information? Explain. How should the court rule? [*LabMD, Inc. v. Tiversa, Inc.*, 2013 WL 425983 (11th Cir. 2013)] (See *Copyrights in Digital Information*.)

8–5. Business Case Problem with Sample Answer— Social Media. Mohammad Omar Aly Hassan and nine others were indicted in a federal district court on charges of conspiring to advance violent jihad (holy war against enemies of Islam) and other offenses related to terrorism. The evidence at Hassan's trial included postings he made on Facebook concerning his adherence to violent jihadist ideology. Convicted, Hassan appealed, contending that the Facebook items had not been properly authenticated (established as his own comments). How might the government show the connection between postings on Facebook and those who post them? Discuss. [*United States v. Hassan*, 742 F.3d 104 (4th Cir. 2014)] (See *Social Media*.)

   —**For a sample answer to Problem 8–5, go to Appendix E at the end of this text.**

8–6. Social Media. Kenneth Wheeler was angry at certain police officers in Grand Junction, Colorado, because of a driving-under-the-influence arrest that he viewed as unjust. While in Italy, Wheeler posted a statement to his Facebook page urging his "religious followers" to "kill cops, drown them in the blood of their children, hunt them down and kill their entire bloodlines" and provided names. Later, Wheeler added a post to "commit a massacre in the Stepping Stones Preschool and day care, just walk in and kill everybody." Could a reasonable person conclude that Wheeler's posts were true threats? How might law enforcement officers use Wheeler's posts? Explain. [*United States v. Wheeler*, 776 F.3d 736 (10th Cir. 2015)] (See *Social Media*.)

8–7. Social Media. Irvin Smith was charged in a Georgia state court with burglary and theft. Before the trial, during the selection of the jury, the state prosecutor asked the prospective jurors whether they knew Smith. No one responded affirmatively. Jurors were chosen and sworn in, without objection. After the trial, during deliberations, the jurors indicated to the court that they were deadlocked. The court charged them to try again. Meanwhile, the prosecutor learned that "Juror 4" appeared as a friend on the defendant's Facebook page and filed a motion to dismiss her. The court replaced Juror 4 with an alternate. Was this an appropriate action, or was it an "abuse of discretion"? Should the court have admitted evidence that Facebook friends do not always actually know each other? Discuss. [*Smith v. State of Georgia*, 335 Ga.App. 497, 782 S.E.2d 305 (2016)] (See *Social Media*.)

8–8. Internet Law. Jason Smathers, an employee of America Online (AOL), misappropriated an AOL customer list with 92 million screen names. He sold the list for $28,000 to Sean Dunaway, who sold it to Braden Bournival. Bournival used it to send AOL customers more than 3 billion unsolicited, deceptive e-mail ads. AOL estimated the cost of processing the ads to be at least $300,000. Convicted of conspiring to relay deceptive e-mail in violation of federal law, Smathers was ordered to pay AOL restitution of $84,000 (treble the amount for which he had sold the AOL customer list). Smathers appealed, seeking to reduce the amount. He cited a judgment in a civil suit for a different offense against Bournival and others for which AOL had collected $95,000. Smathers also argued that his obligation should be reduced by restitution payments made by Dunaway. Which federal law did Smathers violate? Should the amount of his restitution be reduced? Explain. [*United States v. Smathers*, 879 F.3d 453 (2d. Cir. 2018)] (See *Internet Law*.)

8–9. A Question of Ethics—The IDDR Approach and Social Media. *One August morning, around 6:30 A.M., a fire occurred at Ray and Christine Nixon's home in West Monroe, Louisiana. The Nixons told Detective Gary Gilley of the Ouachita Parish Sheriff's Department that they believed the fire was deliberately set by Matthew Alexander, a former employee of Ray's company. Ray gave Alexander's phone number to Gilley, who contacted the number's service provider, Verizon Wireless Services, L.L.C. Gilley said that he was investigating a house fire that had been started with the victims inside the dwelling, and wanted to know where the number's subscriber had been that day. He did not present a warrant, but he did certify that Verizon's response would be considered an "emergency disclosure."* [*Alexander v. Verizon Wireless Services, L.L.C.*, 875 F.3d 243 (5th Cir. 2017)] *(See Social Media.)*

1. Using the *Inquiry* and *Discussion* steps in the IDDR approach, identify the ethical dilemma that Verizon faced in this situation and actions that the company might have taken to resolve that issue.

2. Suppose that Verizon gave Gilley the requested information, and that later Alexander filed a suit against the provider, alleging a violation of the Stored Communications Act. Could Verizon successfully plead "good faith" in its defense?

Critical Thinking and Writing Assignments

8–10. Time-Limited Group Assignment—File-Sharing. James, Chang, and Braden are roommates. They are music fans and frequently listen to the same artists and songs. They regularly exchange MP3 music files that contain songs from their favorite artists. (See *Copyrights in Digital Information*.)

1. One group of students will decide whether the fact that the roommates are transferring files among themselves for no monetary benefit protects them from being subject to copyright law.

2. The second group will consider whether it would be legal for each roommate to buy music on CD and then, after downloading a copy on to their hard drive, give the CD to the other roommates to do the same. Does this violate copyright law? Is it the same as file-sharing digital music? Explain.

3. A third group will consider streaming music services. If one roommate subscribes to a streaming service and the other roommates use the service for free, would this violate copyright law? Why or why not?

9 | Criminal Law and Cyber Crime

Learning Objectives

The six Learning Objectives below are designed to help improve your understanding. After reading this chapter, you should be able to answer the following questions:

1. How does the burden of proof differ in criminal versus civil cases?

2. What two elements normally must exist before a person can be held liable for a crime?

3. What are five broad categories of crimes? What is white-collar crime?

4. What defenses can be raised to avoid liability for criminal acts?

5. What constitutional safeguards exist to protect persons accused of crimes?

6. How has the Internet expanded opportunities for identity theft?

"The crime problem is getting really serious. The other day, the Statue of Liberty had both hands up."

Jay Leno
1950–present
(American comedian and former television host)

The "crime problem" is of concern to all Americans, as suggested in the chapter-opening quotation. Not surprisingly, laws dealing with crime are an important part of the legal environment of business.

Society imposes a variety of sanctions to protect businesses from harm so that they can compete and flourish. These sanctions include damages for tortious conduct, damages for breach of contract, and various equitable remedies. Additional sanctions are imposed under criminal law.

Many statutes regulating business provide for criminal as well as civil sanctions. For instance, federal statutes that protect the environment often include criminal sanctions. Businesses that violate environmental laws can be criminally prosecuted. Walmart stores, Inc., for example, was charged with illegally handling and disposing of hazardous materials (such as pesticides) at its retail stores across the nation. Walmart ultimately pleaded guilty to six counts of violating the Clean Water Act and was sentenced to pay over $81 million in fines as a result.

9–1 Civil Law and Criminal Law

Civil law pertains to the duties that exist between persons or between persons and their governments. Criminal law, in contrast, has to do with crime. A **crime** can be defined as a wrong against society proclaimed in a statute and, if committed, punishable by society through fines and/or imprisonment—and, in some cases, death.

Because crimes are *offenses against society* as a whole, they are prosecuted by a public official, such as a district attorney (D.A.) or an attorney general (A.G.), not by the crime victims. Once a crime has been reported, the D.A.'s office decides whether to file criminal charges and to what extent to pursue the prosecution or carry out additional investigation.

Crime A wrong against society proclaimed in a statute and, if committed, punishable by society through fines, imprisonment, or death.

9–1a Key Differences Between Civil Law and Criminal Law

Because the state has extensive resources at its disposal when prosecuting criminal cases, and because the sanctions can be so severe, there are numerous procedural safeguards to protect the rights of defendants. We look here at one of these safeguards—the higher burden of proof that applies in a criminal case—and at the sanctions imposed for criminal acts. Exhibit 9–1 summarizes these and other key differences between civil law and criminal law.

Burden of Proof In a civil case, the plaintiff usually must prove his or her case by a *preponderance of the evidence*. Under this standard, the plaintiff must convince the court that, based on the evidence presented by both parties, it is more likely than not that the plaintiff's allegation is true.

In a criminal case, in contrast, the state must prove its case **beyond a reasonable doubt.** If the jury views the evidence in the case as reasonably permitting either a guilty or a not guilty verdict, then the jury's verdict must be *not* guilty. In other words, the prosecutor must prove beyond a reasonable doubt that the defendant has committed every essential element of the offense with which she or he is charged. If the jurors are not convinced of the defendant's guilt beyond a reasonable doubt, they must find the defendant not guilty.

Note also that in a criminal case, the jury's verdict normally must be unanimous—agreed to by all members of the jury—to convict the defendant.[1] In a civil trial by jury, in contrast, typically only three-fourths of the jurors need to agree.

Beyond a Reasonable Doubt The standard of proof used in criminal cases.

Learning Objective 1
How does the burden of proof differ in criminal versus civil cases?

Criminal Sanctions The sanctions imposed on criminal wrongdoers are also harsher than those applied in civil cases. Remember that the purpose of tort law is to allow persons harmed by the wrongful acts of others to obtain compensation from the wrongdoer rather than to punish the wrongdoer.

In contrast, criminal sanctions are designed to punish those who commit crimes and to deter others from committing similar acts in the future. Criminal sanctions include fines as well as the much harsher penalty of the loss of liberty by incarceration in a jail or prison. Most criminal sanctions also involve probation and sometimes require restitution, community service, or an educational or treatment program. The harshest criminal sanction is, of course, the death penalty.

---

1. Note that two states, Louisiana and Oregon, allow jury verdicts that are not unanimous.

Exhibit 9–1 Key Differences between Civil Law and Criminal Law

ISSUE	CIVIL LAW	CRIMINAL LAW
Party who brings suit	The person who suffered harm.	The state.
Wrongful act	Causing harm to a person or to a person's property.	Violating a statute that prohibits some type of activity.
Burden of proof	Preponderance of the evidence.	Beyond a reasonable doubt.
Verdict	Three-fourths majority (typically).	Unanimous (almost always).
Remedy	Damages to compensate for the harm or a decree to achieve an equitable result.	Punishment (fine, imprisonment, or death).

9–1b Civil Liability for Criminal Acts

Some torts, such as assault and battery, provide a basis for a criminal prosecution as well as a tort action. **Example 9.1** Carlos is walking down the street, minding his own business, when suddenly a person attacks him. In the ensuing struggle, the attacker stabs Carlos several times, seriously injuring him. A police officer restrains and arrests the wrongdoer. In this situation, the attacker may be subject both to criminal prosecution by the state and to a tort lawsuit brought by Carlos. ■ Exhibit 9–2 illustrates how the same act can result in both a tort action and a criminal action against the wrongdoer.

9–1c Classification of Crimes

Depending on their degree of seriousness, crimes are classified as felonies or misdemeanors. **Felonies** are serious crimes punishable by death or by imprisonment for more than one year.[2] Many states also define several degrees of felony offenses and vary the punishment according to the degree.[3] For instance, most jurisdictions punish a burglary that involves forced entry into a home at night more harshly than a burglary that involves breaking into a nonresidential building during the day.

Felony A serious crime—such as arson, murder, rape, or robbery—that carries the most severe sanctions, ranging from more than one year in a state or federal prison to the death penalty.

---

2. Federal law and most state laws use this definition, but there is some variation among states as to the length of imprisonment associated with a felony conviction.
3. Although the American Law Institute issued the Model Penal Code in 1962, it is not a uniform code, and each state has developed its own set of laws governing criminal acts. Thus, types of crimes and prescribed punishments may differ from one jurisdiction to another.

Exhibit 9–2   Tort Lawsuit and Criminal Prosecution for the Same Act

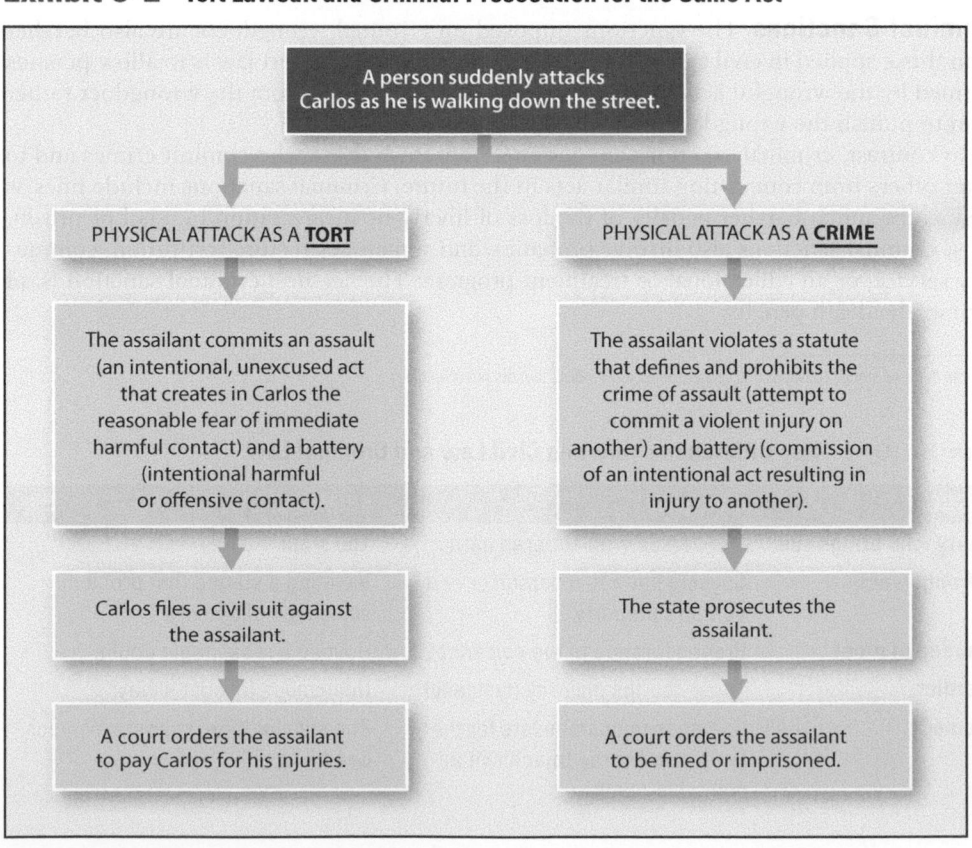

A person suddenly attacks Carlos as he is walking down the street.

PHYSICAL ATTACK AS A **TORT**	PHYSICAL ATTACK AS A **CRIME**
The assailant commits an assault (an intentional, unexcused act that creates in Carlos the reasonable fear of immediate harmful contact) and a battery (intentional harmful or offensive contact).	The assailant violates a statute that defines and prohibits the crime of assault (attempt to commit a violent injury on another) and battery (commission of an intentional act resulting in injury to another).
Carlos files a civil suit against the assailant.	The state prosecutes the assailant.
A court orders the assailant to pay Carlos for his injuries.	A court orders the assailant to be fined or imprisoned.

Misdemeanors are less serious crimes, punishable by a fine or by confinement in jail for up to a year. **Petty offenses** are minor violations, such as jaywalking or violations of building codes, considered to be a subset of misdemeanors. Even for petty offenses, however, a guilty party can be put in jail for a few days, fined, or both, depending on state or local law. Whether a crime is a felony or a misdemeanor can determine in which court the case is tried and, in some states, whether the defendant has a right to a jury trial.

> **Misdemeanor** A lesser crime than a felony, punishable by a fine or incarceration in jail for up to one year.
>
> **Petty Offense** The least serious kind of criminal offense, such as a traffic or building-code violation.

9–2 Criminal Liability

Two elements normally must exist simultaneously for a person to be convicted of a crime:

1. The performance of a prohibited act *(actus reus).*
2. A specified state of mind or intent on the part of the actor *(mens rea).*

> **Learning Objective 2**
> What two elements normally must exist before a person can be held liable for a crime?

9–2a The Criminal Act

Every criminal statute prohibits certain behavior. Most crimes require an act of *commission.* That is, a person must *do* something in order to be accused of a crime. In criminal law, a prohibited act is referred to as the **actus reus,**[4] or guilty act. In some instances, an act of *omission* can be a crime, but only when a person has a legal duty to perform the omitted act, such as filing a tax return.

> **Actus Reus** A guilty (prohibited) act. It is one of the two essential elements required to establish criminal liability.

The *guilty act* requirement is based on one of the premises of criminal law—that a person is punished for harm done to society. For a crime to exist, the guilty act must cause some harm to a person or to property. Thinking about killing someone or about stealing a car may be wrong, but the thoughts do no harm until they are translated into action. Of course, a person can be punished for *attempting* murder or robbery, but normally only if he or she took substantial steps toward the criminal objective. Additionally, the person must have specifically intended to commit the crime to be convicted of an attempt. (Can a person commit a crime by sending a flashing video via Twitter to an epileptic? See this chapter's *Adapting the Law to the Online Environment* feature for a discussion.)

---

4. Pronounced *ak*-tuhs *ray*-uhs.

Using Twitter to Cause Seizures—A Crime?

Adapting the Law to the Online Environment

Vanity Fair contributing editor and *Newsweek* senior writer Kurt Eichenwald has on occasion written about his battle with epilepsy. For many suffering from this condition, strobe lights can spark seizures. A few decades ago, for instance, a *Pokémon* episode apparently sent hundreds of Japanese children to the hospital because of the strobe-light effects.

Using Twitter to Create a Seizure

John Rayne Rivello apparently did not like Eichenwald's political views. He therefore created a strobe-light image within a tweet sent to Eichenwald. In that tweet, Rivello said, "You deserve a seizure for your posts." When Eichenwald clicked on the embedded .gif file, the resulting flashing images it contained did, in fact, cause a seizure in its intended victim.

Arrested for Cyberstalking

Rivello was arrested by the Federal Bureau of Investigation at his residence in Salisbury, Maryland, on a charge of cyberstalking. The federal cyberstalking law criminalizes the intentional use of electronic communications systems to place another in reasonable fear of death or serious bodily injury.[a] This was thought to be the first criminal arrest for the use of electronic communications to create a seizure in a recipient.

Critical Thinking

What other types of cyberstalking crimes might involve the use of tweets?

a. 18 U.S.C. Section 875.

9–2b State of Mind

Mens Rea A wrongful mental state ("guilty mind"), or intent. It is one of the two essential elements required to establish criminal liability.

A wrongful mental state *(mens rea)*[5] is generally required to establish criminal liability. The required mental state, or intent, is indicated in the applicable statute or law. Theft, for example, involves the guilty act of taking another person's property. The guilty mental state involves both the awareness that the property belongs to another and the intent to deprive the owner of it. A court can also find that the required mental state is present when a defendant's acts are reckless or criminally negligent.

A criminal conspiracy exists when two or more people agree to commit an unlawful act, and then take some action toward its completion. The required intent involves purposely agreeing with others and intending to commit the underlying crime. In the following case, the issue was whether the evidence was sufficient to prove that the defendant had "knowingly and voluntarily" participated in a conspiracy to commit health-care fraud.

---

5. Pronounced *mehns ray*-uh.

Case 9.1

United States v. Crabtree

United States Court of Appeals, Eleventh Circuit, 878 F.3d 1274 (2018).

Background and Facts Health Care Solutions Network, Inc. (HCSN), operated mental health centers to provide psychiatric therapy as a partial hospitalization program—a bridge between restrictive inpatient care and routine outpatient care. HCSN organized its business around procuring, retaining, and readmitting patients to maximize billing potential, without respect to their health needs. It ensured patient files complied with strict Medicare requirements by editing intake information, fabricating treatment plans, and falsifying therapy and treatment notes. The scheme spanned seven years and amounted to more than $63 million in fraudulent claims.

At one of HCSN's facilities, Doris Crabtree was responsible for patient therapy notes. The notes were systematically altered and falsified to support Medicare claims. Convicted in a federal district court of conspiracy to commit health-care fraud, Crabtree appealed to the U.S. Court of Appeals for the Eleventh Circuit. She argued that she had only been negligent and careless.

In the Words of the Court
WILSON, Circuit Judge:
* * * *

* * * According to Crabtree, * * * the evidence against [her] was primarily circumstantial and * * * did not show that [she] knowingly and voluntarily joined a conspiracy to defraud Medicare.
* * * *

* * * The very nature of conspiracy frequently requires that the existence of an agreement be proved by inferences from the conduct of the alleged participants or from circumstantial evidence of a scheme. *The government need only prove that the defendant knew of the essential nature of the conspiracy, and we will affirm a conspiracy conviction when the circumstances surrounding a person's presence at the scene of conspiratorial activity are so obvious that knowledge of its character can fairly be attributed to [her].* The government can show that a defendant voluntarily joined a conspiracy through proof of surrounding circumstances such as acts committed by the defendant which furthered the purpose of the conspiracy. [Emphasis added.]
* * * *

The government put forth considerable evidence that Crabtree [was] directly aware of the essential nature of the conspiracy and that the circumstances at HCSN were so obvious that knowledge of the fraud's character can fairly be attributed to [her]. Multiple former-employees testified that Crabtree * * * complied with their requests to doctor patient notes so that they would pass Medicare review. * * * Numerous witnesses spoke of the overwhelming evidence that patients were unqualified for * * * treatment [at HCSN]: that it was obvious, and widely observed, that patients at HCSN suffered from Alzheimer's, dementia, autism, and forms of mental retardation that rendered treatment ineffective; that this was evidenced, for example, by patients * * * who were unable to engage in group therapy sessions; and that Crabtree [was] involved in multiple conversations about the unsuitability of [the] patients for * * * treatment [at HCSN]. One former-employee put it simply: "everybody was aware of the fraud."

Likewise, a reasonable jury could have found that Crabtree * * * voluntarily joined the conspiracy, given the substantial evidence of [her] role in furthering the fraud. The government put forth evidence that Crabtree * * * complied with requests to alter and fabricate notes for billing and Medicare auditing purposes; * * * and that [she] misrepresented the therapy that patients received when, for example, they * * * were * * * absent but notes indicated that they participated fully.

Decision and Remedy The federal appellate court affirmed Crabtree's conviction. The court concluded that Crabtree "had knowledge of the conspiracy at HCSN" and that she had "voluntarily joined the conspiracy, given the substantial evidence of [her] role in furthering the fraud."

Critical Thinking

• **Legal Environment** *Could Crabtree have successfully avoided her conviction by arguing that her only "crime" was naively trusting her co-workers? Why or why not?*

• **Ethical** *It seems reasonable to assume that one of the purposes of any business is to maximize billing potential. When does conduct to accomplish that purpose become unethical?*

Recklessness A defendant is *criminally reckless* if he or she consciously disregards a substantial and unjustifiable risk. **Example 9.2** A fourteen-year-old New Jersey girl posts a Facebook message saying that she is going to launch a terrorist attack on her high school and asks if anyone wants to help. The police arrest the girl for the crime of making a terrorist threat, which requires the intent to commit an act of violence with "the intent to terrorize" or "in reckless disregard of the risk of causing" terror or inconvenience. Although the girl claims that she does not intend to cause harm, she can be prosecuted under the "reckless disregard" part of the statute. ▪

Criminal Negligence *Criminal negligence* occurs when the defendant takes an unjustified, substantial, and foreseeable risk that results in harm. A defendant can be negligent even if she or he was not actually aware of the risk but *should have been aware* of it.[6]

A homicide is classified as *involuntary manslaughter* when it results from an act of criminal negligence and there is no intent to kill. **Example 9.3** Dr. Conrad Murray, the personal physician of pop star Michael Jackson, was convicted of involuntary manslaughter for prescribing the drug that led to Jackson's sudden death. Murray had given Jackson propofol, a powerful anesthetic normally used in surgery, as a sleep aid on the night of his death, even though Murray knew that Jackson had already taken other sedatives. ▪

Strict Liability and Overcriminalization An increasing number of laws and regulations have imposed criminal sanctions for strict liability crimes—that is, offenses that do not require a wrongful mental state, or malice, to establish criminal liability. Critics say that such laws lead to overcriminalization.

Federal Crimes. The federal criminal code now lists more than four thousand criminal offenses, many of which do not require a specific mental state. In addition, several hundred thousand federal rules can be enforced through criminal sanctions, and many of these rules do not require intent. See this chapter's *Managerial Strategy* feature for a discussion of how these laws and rules affect American businesspersons.

Strict liability crimes are particularly common in environmental laws, laws aimed at combatting illegal drugs, and other laws affecting public health, safety, and welfare. **Case Example 9.4** Paul Kenner was a commercial cattle rancher in Nebraska. Due to a faulty fence, three hundred of Kenner's cattle wandered onto a national wildlife refuge, where they grazed for ten days. A Kenner ranch hand also unknowingly drove an all-terrain vehicle onto the wildlife refuge. Kenner was convicted of four separate crimes involving failing to comply with the National Wildlife Refuge System.[7] ▪

RachelKolokoffHopper/Shutterstock.com

Why do some strict liability crimes—such as cowboys or cattle wandering onto a national wildlife refuge—not require a specific mental state?

---

6. Model Penal Code Section 2.02(2)(d).
7. *United States v. Kenner*, 238 F.Supp.3d 1157 (D.Neb. 2017).

State Crimes. Many states have also enacted laws that punish behavior as criminal without the need to show criminal intent. **Example 9.5** In Arizona, a hunter who shoots an elk outside the area specified by the hunting permit has committed a crime. The hunter can be convicted of the crime regardless of her or his intent or knowledge of the law. ■

9–2c Corporate Criminal Liability

A *corporation* is a legal entity created under the laws of a state. At one time, it was thought that a corporation could not incur criminal liability because, although a corporation is a legal person, it can act only through its agents (corporate directors, officers, and employees). Therefore, the corporate entity itself could not "intend" to commit a crime. Over time, this view has changed. Obviously, corporations cannot be imprisoned, but they can be fined or denied certain legal privileges (such as necessary licenses).

The Criminalization of American Business

Managerial Strategy

What do Bank of America, Citigroup, JPMorgan Chase, and Goldman Sachs have in common? All paid hefty fines for purportedly misleading investors about mortgage-backed securities. In fact, these companies paid the government a total of $50 billion in fines. The payments were made in lieu of criminal prosecutions.

Today, several hundred thousand federal rules that apply to businesses carry some form of criminal penalty. That is in addition to more than four thousand federal laws, many of which carry criminal sanctions for their violation. From 2000 to 2019, about 3,200 corporations either were convicted or pleaded guilty to violating federal statutes or rules.

Criminal Convictions

The first successful criminal conviction in a federal court against a company—the New York Central and Hudson River Railroad—was upheld by the Supreme Court in 1909 (the violation: cutting prices).[a] Many other successful convictions followed.

One landmark case developed the *aggregation test*, now called the Doctrine

of Collective Knowledge.[b] This test aggregates the omissions and acts of two or more persons in a corporation, thereby constructing an *actus reus* and a *mens rea* out of the conduct and knowledge of several individuals.

Not all government attempts at applying criminal law to corporations survive. Courts have sometimes found insufficient evidence to show that a company acted with specific intent to commit a crime.[c] Often, however, companies choose to reach settlement agreements with the government rather than fight criminal indictments.

Many Pay Substantial Fines in Lieu of Prosecution

More than four hundred corporations reached so-called nonprosecution agreements with the government from 2000 to the beginning of 2019. These agreements typically involve multimillion- or multibillion-dollar fines. This number does not include fines

paid to the Environmental Protection Agency or to the Fish and Wildlife Service.

According to law professors Margaret Lemos and Max Minzner, "Public enforcers often seek large monetary awards for self-interested reasons divorced from the public interest and deterrents. The incentives are strongest when enforcement agencies are permitted to retain all or some of the proceeds of enforcement."[d]

Business Questions

1. *Why might a corporation's managers agree to pay a large fine rather than to be indicted and proceed to trial?*

2. *How does a manager determine the optimal amount of legal research to undertake to prevent her or his company from violating the many thousands of federal regulations?*

a. *New York Central and Hudson River Railroad v. United States,* 212 U.S. 481, 29 S.Ct. 304, 53 L.Ed. 613 (1909).

b. *United States v. Bank of New England,* 821 F.2d 844 (1st Cir. 1987).

c. See, for example, *McGee v. Sentinel Offender Services, LLC,* 719 F.3d 1236 (11th Cir. 2013); *Golden v. FNF Servicing, Inc.,* 2015 WL 5302703 (M.D.Ga. 2015); and *United States ex rel. Salters v. American Family Care, Inc.,* 262 F.Supp.3d 1266 (N.D.Ala. 2017).

d. Margaret Lemos and Max Minzner, "For-Profit Public Enforcement," *Harvard Law Review* 127, 17 Jan. 2014.

Liability of the Corporate Entity Today, corporations are normally liable for the crimes committed by their agents and employees within the course and scope of their employment.[8] For liability to be imposed, the prosecutor typically must show that the corporation could have prevented the act or that a supervisor within the corporation authorized or had knowledge of the act. In addition, corporations can be criminally liable for failing to perform specific duties imposed by law (such as duties under environmental laws or securities laws).

★ **Spotlight Case Example 9.6** A prostitution ring, the Gold Club, was operating out of motels in West Virginia. A motel manager, who was also an officer in the corporation that owned the motels, gave discounted rates to Gold Club prostitutes, and they paid him in cash. The corporation received a portion of the funds generated by the Gold Club's illegal operations. At trial, the jury found that the corporation was criminally liable because a supervisor within the corporation—the motel manager—had knowledge of the prostitution ring and profited from it, and the corporation had allowed it to continue.[9]

Liability of Corporate Officers and Directors Corporate directors and officers are personally liable for the crimes they commit, regardless of whether the crimes were committed for their personal benefit or on the corporation's behalf. Additionally, corporate directors and officers may be held liable for the actions of employees under their supervision. Under the *responsible corporate officer doctrine*, a court may impose criminal liability on a corporate officer regardless of whether she or he participated in, directed, or even knew about a given criminal violation.[10]

Case Example 9.7 Austin DeCoster owned and controlled Quality Egg, LLC, an egg-production and processing company with facilities across Iowa. His son, Peter DeCoster, was the chief operating officer. Due to unsanitary conditions in some of its facilities, Quality shipped and sold eggs that contained salmonella bacteria, which sickened thousands of people across the United States.

The federal government prosecuted the DeCosters under the responsible corporate officer doctrine, in part for Quality's failure to comply with regulations on egg-production facilities. The DeCosters ultimately pleaded guilty to violating three criminal statutes. But when they were ordered to serve three months in jail, the DeCosters challenged the sentence as unconstitutional. The court held that the sentence of incarceration was appropriate because the evidence suggested that the defendants knew about the unsanitary conditions in their processing plants.[11]

If unsanitary conditions at an egg-production facility spark sickness among consumers, can the corporate owner be held criminally liable?

9–3 Types of Crimes

Federal, state, and local laws provide for the classification and punishment of hundreds of thousands of different criminal acts. Traditionally, though, crimes have been grouped into five broad categories: violent crime (crimes against persons), property crime, public order crime, white-collar crime, and organized crime. In addition, when crimes are committed in cyberspace rather than the physical world, we often refer to them as cyber crimes.

Learning Objective 3

What are five broad categories of crimes? What is white-collar crime?

---

8. See Model Penal Code Section 2.07.

9. As a result of the convictions, the motel manager was sentenced to fifteen months in prison, and the corporation was ordered to forfeit the motel property. *United States v. Singh*, 518 F.3d 236 (4th Cir. 2008). For an example involving environmental laws, see *United States v. House of Raeford Farms, Inc.*, 2013 WL 179185 (M.D.N.C. 2013).

10. For a landmark case in this area, see *United States v. Park*, 421 U.S. 658, 95 S.Ct. 1903, 44 L.Ed.2d 489 (1975).

11. *United States v. Quality Egg, LLC*, 99 F.Supp.3d 920 (N.D. Iowa 2015).

9–3a Violent Crime

Certain crimes are called *violent crimes*, or crimes against persons, because they cause others to suffer harm or death. Murder is a violent crime. So, too, is sexual assault. **Robbery**—defined as the taking of cash, personal property, or any other article of value from a person by means of force or fear—is another violent crime. Typically, states have more severe penalties for *aggravated robbery*—robbery with the use of a deadly weapon.

Assault and battery, which were discussed in the context of tort law, are also classified as violent crimes. **Example 9.8** Former rap star Flavor Flav (whose real name is William Drayton) was arrested in Las Vegas on assault and battery charges. During an argument with his fiancée, Drayton allegedly threw her to the ground and then grabbed two kitchen knives and chased her son. ■

Each of these violent crimes is further classified by degree, depending on the circumstances surrounding the criminal act. These circumstances include the intent of the person committing the crime and whether a weapon was used. For crimes other than murder, the level of pain and suffering experienced by the victim is also a factor.

9–3b Property Crime

The most common type of criminal activity is property crime—crimes in which the goal of the offender is some form of economic gain or the damaging of property. Robbery is a form of property crime, as well as a violent crime, because the offender seeks to gain the property of another. We look here at a number of other crimes that fall within the general category of property crime.

Burglary Traditionally, **burglary** was defined under the common law as breaking and entering the dwelling of another at night with the intent to commit a felony. Originally, the definition was aimed at protecting an individual's home and its occupants. Most state statutes have eliminated some of the requirements found in the common law definition. The time of day at which the breaking and entering occurs, for example, is usually immaterial. State statutes frequently omit the element of breaking, and some states do not require that the building be a dwelling. When a deadly weapon is used in a burglary, the person can be charged with *aggravated burglary* and punished more severely.

Larceny Under the common law, the crime of **larceny** involved the unlawful taking and carrying away of someone else's personal property with the intent to permanently deprive the owner of possession. Put simply, larceny is stealing, or theft. (For a discussion of proving theft, see this chapter's *Business Law Analysis* feature.)

Whereas robbery involves force or fear, larceny does not. Therefore, picking pockets is larceny, not robbery. Similarly, an employee who takes company products and supplies home for personal use without authorization commits larceny.

Most states have expanded the definition of property that is subject to larceny statutes. Stealing computer programs may constitute larceny even though the "property" is not physical (see the discussion of cyber crime later in this chapter). The theft of natural gas, Internet access, and television cable service can also constitute larceny.

Obtaining Goods by False Pretenses Obtaining goods by means of false pretenses is a form of theft that involves trickery or fraud, such as using someone else's credit-card number without permission to purchase an iPad. Statutes dealing with such illegal activities vary widely from state to state. They often apply not only to property, but also to services and cash.

Case Example 9.9 While Matthew Steffes was incarcerated, he devised a scheme to make free collect calls from prison. (A *collect call* is a telephone call in which the calling party places

Proof of Credit-Card Theft

Jacqueline Barden was shopping for school clothes with her children when her purse and automobile were taken. In Barden's purse were her car keys, her credit and debit cards, and her children's Social Security cards and birth certificates, which were needed for enrollment at school.

Immediately after the purse and car were stolen, Rebecca Mary Turner attempted to use Barden's credit card at a local Exxon gas station, but the card was declined. The gas station attendant recognized Turner because she had previously written bad checks and used credit cards that did not belong to her. Turner was later arrested while attempting to use one of Barden's checks to pay for merchandise at a Walmart—where the clerk also recognized Turner from prior criminal activity.

Turner claimed that she had not stolen Barden's purse or car. Instead, she said that a friend had told her he had some checks and credit cards and asked her to try using them at Walmart. Is there sufficient evidence that Turner committed theft to convince a jury of her guilt beyond a reasonable doubt?

Analysis: Theft involves the wrongful taking and carrying away of another person's property with the intent of permanently depriving the owner of the property. Although there were no eyewitnesses to say they saw Turner take Barden's purse, there was sufficient circumstantial evidence suggesting that she was a thief. Turner attempted to use Barden's credit card immediately after the purse was taken. Turner also had Barden's credit and debit cards at

the time of her arrest—and she had a long history of theft-related offenses.

Result and Reasoning: Yes, there was sufficient evidence to convince a jury beyond a reasonable doubt that Turner had wrongfully taken and carried away Barden's credit cards with the intent of permanently depriving her of them. A jury could reasonably have believed the circumstantial evidence of Turner's guilt and doubted the truth of her story about a friend's having given her the credit cards.

---

a call at the called party's expense.) Steffes had his friends and family members set up new phone number accounts by giving false information to AT&T. This information included fictitious business names, as well as personal identifying information stolen from a health-care clinic. Once a new phone number was working, Steffes made unlimited collect calls to it without paying the bill until AT&T eventually shut down the account. For nearly two years, Steffes used sixty fraudulently obtained phone numbers to make hundreds of collect calls. The loss to AT&T was more than $28,000.

Steffes was convicted in a state court of theft by fraud. He appealed, arguing that he had not made false representations to AT&T. The Wisconsin Supreme Court affirmed his conviction. The court held that Steffes had made false representations to AT&T by providing it with fictitious business names and stolen personal identifying information. He made these false representations so that he could make phone calls without paying for them, which deprived the company of its "property"—its electricity.[12]

Receiving Stolen Goods It is a crime to receive goods that a person knows or should have known were stolen or illegally obtained. To be convicted, the recipient of such goods need not know the true identity of the owner or the thief, and need not have paid for the goods. All that is necessary is that the recipient knows or should have known that the goods were stolen, which implies an intent to deprive the true owner of those goods.

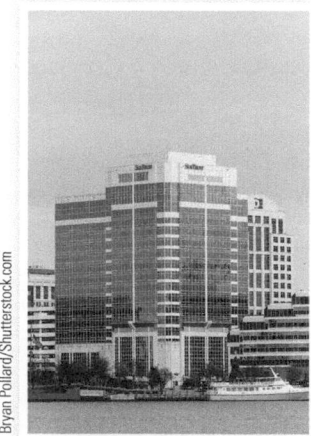

Bryan Pollard/Shutterstock.com

Some U.S. corporations commit crimes, such as fraud. What are some ways a court can prove criminal intent? What do some corporations do to avoid criminal prosecution?

---

12. *State of Wisconsin v. Steffes*, 347 Wis.2d 683, 832 N.W.2d 101 (2013).

If this fire was started to obtain insurance money, what type of crime was committed?

Arson The intentional burning of a building.

Forgery The fraudulent making or altering of any writing in a way that changes the legal rights and liabilities of another.

Arson The willful and malicious burning of a building (and, in some states, vehicles and other items of personal property) is the crime of **arson**. At common law, arson traditionally applied only to burning down another person's house. The law was designed to protect human life. Today, arson statutes have been extended to cover the destruction of any building, regardless of ownership, by fire or explosion.

Every state has a special statute that covers the act of burning a building for the purpose of collecting insurance. **Example 9.10** Benton owns an insured apartment building that is falling apart. If he sets fire to it or pays someone else to do so, he is guilty not only of arson but also of defrauding the insurer, which is attempted larceny. ■ Of course, the insurer need not pay the claim when insurance fraud is proved.

Forgery The fraudulent making or altering of any writing (including electronic records) in a way that changes the legal rights and liabilities of another is **forgery**. **Example 9.11** Without authorization, Severson signs Bennett's name to the back of a check made out to Bennett and attempts to cash it. Severson has committed the crime of forgery. ■ Forgery also includes changing trademarks, falsifying public records, counterfeiting, and altering a legal document.

9–3c Public Order Crime

Historically, societies have always outlawed activities considered to be contrary to public values and morals. Today, the most common public order crimes include public drunkenness, prostitution, gambling, and illegal drug use. These crimes are sometimes referred to as victimless crimes because they normally harm only the offender. From a broader perspective, however, they are detrimental to society as a whole because they may create an environment that gives rise to property and violent crimes.

Example 9.12 A flight attendant observed a man and woman engaging in sex acts while on a flight to Las Vegas. A criminal complaint was filed, and the two defendants pleaded guilty in federal court to the public order crime of misdemeanor disorderly conduct. ■

9–3d White-Collar Crime

Crimes occurring in the business context are popularly referred to as *white-collar crimes*, although this is not an official legal term. Ordinarily, **white-collar crime** involves an illegal act or series of acts committed by an individual or business entity using some nonviolent means to obtain a personal or business advantage.

Usually, this kind of crime is committed in the course of a legitimate occupation. Corporate crimes fall into this category. In addition, certain property crimes, such as larceny and forgery, may also be white-collar crimes if they occur within the business context.

White-Collar Crime Nonviolent crime committed by individuals or business entities to obtain a personal or business advantage.

Embezzlement The fraudulent appropriation of funds or other property by a person who was entrusted with the funds or property.

Embezzlement When a person who is entrusted with another person's funds or property fraudulently appropriates it, embezzlement occurs. **Embezzlement** is not larceny, because the wrongdoer does not physically take the property from another's possession, and it is not robbery, because force or fear is not used.

Typically, embezzlement is carried out by an employee who steals funds. Banks are particularly prone to this problem, but embezzlement can occur in any firm. In a number of businesses, corporate officers or accountants have fraudulently converted funds for their own benefit and then "fixed" the books to cover up their crime. Embezzlement occurs whether the embezzler takes the funds directly from the victim or from a third person. If the financial officer of a corporation pockets checks from third parties that were given to her to deposit into the corporate account, she is embezzling.

Frequently, an embezzler takes relatively small amounts repeatedly over a long period. This might be done by underreporting income or deposits and embezzling the remaining amount, or by creating fictitious persons or accounts and writing checks to them from the corporate account. An employer's failure to remit state withholding taxes that were collected from employee wages can also constitute embezzlement.

The intent to return embezzled property—or its actual return—is not a defense to the crime of embezzlement, as the following *Spotlight Case* illustrates.

Spotlight on White-Collar Crime: Case 9.2

People v. Sisuphan

Court of Appeal of California, First District, 181 Cal.App.4th 800, 104 Cal.Rptr.3d 654 (2010).

Background and Facts Lou Sisuphan was the director of finance at a Toyota dealership. Sisuphan complained repeatedly to management about another employee, Ian McClelland. The general manager, Michael Christian, would not terminate McClelland "because he brought a lot of money into the dealership." In an attempt to get McClelland fired, Sisuphan took and kept an envelope containing a payment of nearly $30,000 from one of McClelland's customers. McClelland believed the envelope had been deposited in the company safe's drop slot, but after it got stuck, Sisuphan wriggled the envelope free and kept it in the company's safe.

Later, Sisuphan told the dealership what he had done and returned the money, adding that he had "no intention of stealing the money." Christian fired Sisuphan the next day, and the district attorney later charged Sisuphan with embezzlement. After a jury trial, Sisuphan was found guilty. Sisuphan appealed.

In the Words of the Court
JENKINS, J. [Judge]
* * * *

Fraudulent intent is an essential element of embezzlement. Although restoration of the property is not a defense, evidence of repayment may be relevant to the extent it shows that a defendant's intent at the time of the taking was not fraudulent. Such evidence is admissible "only when [a] defendant shows a relevant and probative [supporting] link in his subsequent actions from which it might be inferred his original intent was innocent." The question before us, therefore, is whether evidence that Sisuphan returned the money reasonably tends to prove he lacked the requisite intent at the time of the taking. [Emphasis added.]

Section 508 [of the California Penal Code], which sets out the offense of which Sisuphan was convicted, provides: "Every clerk, agent, or servant of any person who fraudulently appropriates to his own use,

A Toyota dealership employee committed embezzlement but returned the funds. Is this a crime?

or secretes with a fraudulent intent to appropriate to his own use, any property of another which has come into his control or care by virtue of his employment * * * is guilty of embezzlement." Sisuphan denies he ever intended "to use the [money] to financially better himself, even temporarily" and contends the evidence he sought to introduce showed "he returned the [money] without having appropriated it to his own use in any way." He argues that this evidence negates fraudulent intent because it supports his claim that he took the money to get McClelland fired and acted "to help his company by drawing attention to the inadequacy and incompetency of an employee." We reject these contentions.

In determining whether Sisuphan's intent was fraudulent at the time of the taking, the issue is not whether he intended to spend the money, but whether he intended to use it for a purpose other than that for which the dealership entrusted it to him. *The offense of embezzlement contemplates a principal's entrustment of property to an agent for certain purposes and the agent's breach of that trust by acting outside his authority in his use of the property.* * * * Sisuphan's undisputed purpose—to get McClelland fired— was beyond the scope of his responsibility and therefore outside the trust afforded him by the dealership. Accordingly, even if the proffered evidence shows he took the money for this purpose, it does not tend to prove he lacked fraudulent intent, and the trial court properly excluded this evidence. [Emphasis added.]

Decision and Remedy The California appellate court affirmed the trial court's decision. The fact that Sisuphan had returned the payment was irrelevant. He was guilty of embezzlement.

Critical Thinking

• **Legal Environment** *Why was Sisuphan convicted of embezzlement instead of larceny? What is the difference between these two crimes?*

Mail and Wire Fraud One of the most potent weapons against white-collar criminals are the federal laws that prohibit mail fraud[13] and wire fraud.[14] These laws make it a federal crime to devise any scheme that uses the U.S. mail, commercial carriers (such as FedEx or UPS), or wire (including telegraph, telephone, television, e-mail, and online social media) with the intent to defraud the public. These laws are often applied when persons send advertisements via e-mail or social media with the intent to obtain cash or property by false pretenses.

Case Example 9.13 Cisco Systems, Inc., offers a warranty program to authorized resellers of Cisco parts. Iheanyi Frank Chinasa and Robert Kendrick Chambliss formulated a scheme to use this program to defraud Cisco by obtaining replacement parts to which they were not entitled. The two men sent numerous e-mails and Internet service requests to Cisco to convince the company to ship them new parts via commercial carriers. Ultimately, Chinasa and Chambliss were convicted of mail and wire fraud, as well as conspiracy to commit mail and wire fraud.[15]

The maximum penalty under these statutes is substantial. Persons convicted of mail or wire fraud may be imprisoned for up to twenty years and/or fined. If the violation affects a financial institution or involves fraud in connection with emergency disaster-relief funds, the violator may be fined up to $1 million, imprisoned for up to thirty years, or both.

Bribery The crime of bribery involves offering something of value to someone in an attempt to influence that person—who is usually, but not always, a public official—to act in a way that serves a private interest. Three types of bribery are considered crimes: bribery of public officials, commercial bribery, and bribery of foreign officials. As an element of the crime of bribery, intent must be present and proved. The bribe itself can be anything the recipient considers to be valuable, but the defendant must have intended it as a bribe. Realize that the *crime of bribery occurs when the bribe is offered*—it is not required that the bribe be accepted. *Accepting a bribe* is a separate crime.

Commercial bribery involves corrupt dealings between private persons or businesses. Typically, people make commercial bribes to obtain proprietary information, cover up an inferior product, or secure new business. Industrial espionage sometimes involves commercial bribes. Example 9.14 Kent works at the firm of Jacoby & Meyers. He offers to pay Laurel, an employee in a competing firm, if she will give him her firm's trade secrets and pricing schedules. Kent has committed commercial bribery. So-called kickbacks, or payoffs for special favors or services, are a form of commercial bribery in some situations.

The Foreign Corrupt Practices Act In many foreign countries, government officials make the decisions on most major construction and manufacturing contracts. Side payments to government officials in exchange for favorable business contracts are not unusual in such countries. The Foreign Corrupt Practices Act[16] (FCPA) prohibits U.S. businesspersons from bribing foreign officials to secure beneficial contracts. Firms that violate the FCPA can be fined up to $2 million. Individuals can be fined up to $100,000 and imprisoned for up to five years.

Prohibition against the Bribery of Foreign Officials. The first part of the FCPA applies to all U.S. companies and their directors, officers, shareholders, employees, and agents. This part of the act prohibits the bribery of most officials of foreign governments if the purpose of the payment is to motivate the official to act in an official capacity to provide business opportunities.

The FCPA does not prohibit payments to minor officials whose duties are ministerial. A ministerial action is a routine activity, such as the processing of paperwork, with little or no discretion involved in the action. These payments, often referred to as "grease," are meant to expedite the performance of administrative services. Thus, a firm that makes a payment to a minor official to speed up an import licensing process has not violated the FCPA.

---

13. The Mail Fraud Act of 1990, 18 U.S.C. Sections 1341–1342.
14. 18 U.S.C. Section 1343.
15. *United States v. Chinasa*, 789 F.Supp.2d 691 (E.D.Va. 2011).
16. 15 U.S.C., Sections 78dd-1, *et seq.*

> "It was beautiful and simple as all truly great swindles are."
>
> **O. Henry**
> 1862–1910
> (American writer)

Generally, the act also permits payments to foreign officials if such payments are lawful within the foreign country. Payments to private foreign companies or other third parties are permissible unless the U.S. firm knows that the payments will be passed on to a foreign government in violation of the FCPA.

Accounting Requirements. In the past, bribes were often concealed in corporate financial records. Thus, the second part of the FCPA is directed toward accountants. All companies must keep detailed accounting records that provide "reasonable assurance" that their transactions are accounted for and legal. The FCPA prohibits any person from making false statements to accountants or false entries in any record or account.

Case Example 9.15 Noble Corporation operated some drilling rigs offshore in Nigeria. Mark Jackson and James Ruehlen were officers at Noble. The U.S. government accused Noble of bribing Nigerian government officials and charged Jackson and Ruehlen individually with violating the FCPA's accounting provisions. Jackson and Ruehlen allegedly approved numerous "special handling" and "procurement" payments to the Nigerian government, knowing that those payments were actually bribes. Allowing illegal payments to be listed on the books as legitimate operating expenses violates the FCPA.[17]

What type of payments to foreign officials are allowed under the Foreign Corrupt Practices Act?

Bankruptcy Fraud Federal bankruptcy law allows individuals and businesses to be relieved of oppressive debt through bankruptcy proceedings. Numerous white-collar crimes may be committed during the many phases of a bankruptcy proceeding. A creditor may file a false claim against the debtor. Also, a debtor may attempt to protect assets from creditors by fraudulently concealing property or by fraudulently transferring property to favored parties. For instance, a company-owned automobile may be "sold" at a bargain price to a trusted friend or relative.

Theft of Trade Secrets Trade secrets constitute a form of intellectual property that can be extremely valuable for many businesses. The Economic Espionage Act[18] made the theft of trade secrets a federal crime. The act also made it a federal crime to buy or possess the trade secrets of another person, knowing that the trade secrets were stolen or otherwise acquired without the owner's authorization.

Violations of the act can result in steep penalties. An individual who violates the act can be imprisoned for up to ten years and fined up to $500,000. A corporation or other organization can be fined up to $5 million. Additionally, any property acquired as a result of the violation, such as airplanes and automobiles, is subject to criminal forfeiture, or seizure by the government. Similarly, any property used in the commission of the violation, such as servers and other electronic devices, is subject to forfeiture. A theft of trade secrets conducted via the Internet, for instance, could result in the forfeiture of every computer or other device used to commit or facilitate the crime.

Insider Trading An individual who obtains "inside information" about the plans of a publicly listed corporation can often make stock-trading profits by purchasing or selling corporate securities based on the information. **Insider trading** is a violation of securities law. Generally, the rule is that a person who possesses inside information and has a duty not to disclose it to outsiders may not profit from the purchase or sale of securities based on that information until the information is made available to the public.

Insider Trading The purchase or sale of securities on the basis of information that has not been made available to the public.

17. *Securities Exchange Commission v. Jackson*, 908 F.Supp.2d 834 (S.D.Tex.—Houston 2012).
18. 18 U.S.C. Sections 1831–1839.

9–3e Organized Crime

As mentioned, white-collar crime takes place within the confines of the legitimate business world. *Organized crime*, in contrast, operates *illegitimately* by, among other things, providing illegal goods and services, such as illegal drugs, gambling, and prostitution. Today, organized crime is heavily involved in cyber crime.

How do criminals launder money?

Money Laundering Engaging in financial transactions to conceal the identity, source, or destination of illegally gained funds.

Money Laundering Organized crime and other illegal activities generate many billions of dollars in profits each year. Under federal law, banks and other financial institutions are required to report currency transactions involving more than $10,000. Consequently, those who engage in illegal activities face difficulties when they try to deposit their cash profits from illegal transactions.

As an alternative to simply storing cash from illegal transactions somewhere outside of the banking system, wrongdoers and racketeers often launder their "dirty" money through a legitimate business to make it "clean." **Money laundering** is engaging in financial transactions to conceal the identity, source, or destination of illegally gained funds.

Example 9.16 Leo Harris, a successful drug dealer, becomes a partner with a restaurateur. Little by little, the restaurant shows increasing profits. As a partner in the restaurant, Harris is able to report the "profits" of the restaurant as legitimate income on which he pays federal and state taxes. He can then spend those funds without worrying that his lifestyle may exceed the level possible with his reported income. ■

Racketeering To curb the entry of organized crime into the legitimate business world, Congress enacted the Racketeer Influenced and Corrupt Organizations Act (RICO).[19] The statute makes it a federal crime to:

1. Use income obtained from racketeering activity to purchase any interest in an enterprise.
2. Acquire or maintain an interest in an enterprise through racketeering activity.
3. Conduct or participate in the affairs of an enterprise through racketeering activity.
4. Conspire to do any of the preceding activities.

Broad Application of RICO. The broad language of RICO has allowed it to be applied in cases that have little or nothing to do with organized crime. RICO incorporates by reference twenty-six separate types of federal crimes and nine types of state felonies.[20] If a person commits two of these offenses, he or she is guilty of "racketeering activity."

Under the criminal provisions of RICO, any individual found guilty is subject to a fine of up to $25,000 per violation, imprisonment for up to twenty years, or both. Additionally, any assets (property or cash) that were acquired as a result of the illegal activity or that were "involved in" or an "instrumentality of" the activity are subject to government forfeiture.

Civil Liability. In the event of a RICO violation, the government can seek not only criminal penalties but also civil penalties, such as the divestiture of a defendant's interest in a business or the dissolution of the business. (Divestiture refers to the taking of possession—or forfeiture—of the defendant's interest and its subsequent sale.)

Moreover, in some cases, the statute allows private individuals to sue violators and potentially to recover three times their actual losses (treble damages), plus attorneys' fees, for business injuries caused by a RICO violation. This is perhaps the most controversial aspect of

---

19. 18 U.S.C. Sections 1961–1968.
20. See 18 U.S.C. Section 1961(1)(A).

RICO and one that continues to cause debate in the nation's federal courts. The prospect of receiving treble damages in civil RICO lawsuits has given plaintiffs a financial incentive to pursue businesses and employers for violations.

9–4 Defenses to Criminal Liability

Persons charged with crimes may be relieved of criminal liability if they can show that their criminal actions were justified under the circumstances. In certain circumstances, the law may also allow a person to be excused from criminal liability because she or he lacks the required mental state. We look at several of the defenses to criminal liability here.

Note that procedural violations, such as obtaining evidence without a valid search warrant, may also operate as defenses. Evidence obtained in violation of a defendant's constitutional rights normally may not be admitted in court. If the evidence is suppressed, then there may be no basis for prosecuting the defendant.

> **Learning Objective 4**
> What defenses can be raised to avoid liability for criminal acts?

9–4a Justifiable Use of Force

Probably the best-known defense to criminal liability is **self-defense**. Other situations, however, also justify the use of force: the defense of one's dwelling, the defense of other property, and the prevention of a crime. In all of these situations, it is important to distinguish between deadly and nondeadly force. *Deadly force* is likely to result in death or serious bodily harm. *Nondeadly force* is force that reasonably appears necessary to prevent the imminent use of criminal force.

Generally speaking, people can use the amount of nondeadly force that seems necessary to protect themselves, their dwellings, or other property or to prevent the commission of a crime. Deadly force can be used in self-defense if the defender *reasonably believes* that imminent death or grievous bodily harm will otherwise result. In addition, normally the attacker must be using unlawful force, and the defender must not have initiated or provoked the attack.

Many states are expanding the situations in which the use of deadly force can be justified. Florida, for instance, allows the use of deadly force to prevent the commission of a "forcible felony," including robbery, carjacking, and sexual battery.

> **Self-Defense** The legally recognized privilege to do what is reasonably necessary to protect oneself, one's property, or someone else against injury by another.

9–4b Necessity

Sometimes, criminal defendants are relieved of liability if they can show that a criminal act was necessary to prevent an even greater harm. **Example 9.17** Jake Trevor is a convicted felon and, as such, is legally prohibited from possessing a firearm. While he and his wife are in a convenience store, a man draws a gun, points it at the cashier, and demands all the cash. Afraid that the man will start shooting, Trevor grabs the gun and holds on to it until police arrive. In this situation, if Trevor is charged with possession of a firearm, he can assert the defense of necessity. ▪

9–4c Insanity

A person who suffers from a mental illness may be incapable of the state of mind required to commit a crime. Thus, insanity can be a defense to a criminal charge. Note that an insanity defense does not allow a person to avoid imprisonment. It simply means that if the defendant successfully proves insanity, she or he will be placed in a mental institution.

Example 9.18 James Holmes opened fire with an automatic weapon in a crowded Colorado movie theater during the screening of *The Dark Knight Rises*, killing twelve people and

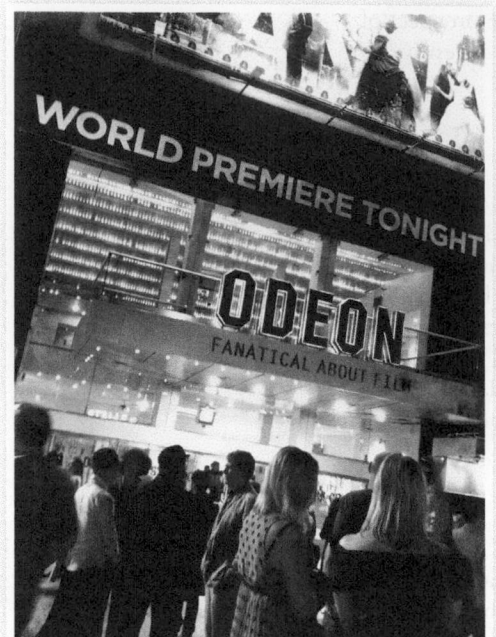

If a person suffers from mental health problems and opens fire inside a movie theater, can that person use the defense of insanity?

track5/iStock Unreleased/Getty Images

injuring more than fifty. Holmes had been a graduate student but had increasingly suffered from mental health problems and had left school. Before the incident, he had no criminal history. Holmes's attorneys asserted the defense of insanity in an attempt to avoid a possible death penalty. Although a jury ultimately rejected the defense and convicted Holmes of multiple counts of murder, he was sentenced to life in prison rather than death. If the defense had been successful, Holmes would have been confined to a mental institution, not a prison.

9–4d Mistake

Everyone has heard the saying "ignorance of the law is no excuse." Ordinarily, ignorance of the law or a mistaken idea about what the law requires is not a valid defense. A *mistake of fact*, as opposed to a *mistake of law*, can excuse criminal responsibility if it negates the mental state necessary to commit a crime.

Example 9.19 If Oliver Wheaton mistakenly walks off with Julie Tyson's briefcase because he thinks it is his, there is no crime. Theft requires knowledge that the property belongs to another. (If Wheaton's act causes Tyson to incur damages, however, she may sue him in a civil action for the tort of trespass to personal property or conversion.)

9–4e Duress

Duress exists when the *wrongful threat* of one person induces another person to perform an act that she or he would not otherwise perform. In such a situation, duress is said to negate the mental state necessary to commit a crime because the defendant was forced or compelled to commit the act.

Duress can be used as a defense to most crimes except murder. The states vary in how duress is defined and what types of crimes it can excuse, however. Generally, to successfully assert duress as a defense, the defendant must reasonably believe that he or she is in immediate danger, and the jury (or judge) must conclude that the defendant's belief was reasonable.

9–4f Entrapment

Entrapment is a defense designed to prevent police officers or other government agents from enticing persons to commit crimes so that they can later be prosecuted for criminal acts. In the typical entrapment case, an undercover agent *suggests* that a crime be committed and pressures or induces an individual to commit it. The agent then arrests the individual for the crime.

For entrapment to succeed as a defense, both the suggestion and the inducement must take place. The defense is not intended to prevent law enforcement agents from ever setting a trap for an unwary criminal. Rather, its purpose is to prevent them from pushing the individual into a criminal act. The crucial issue is whether the person who committed a crime was predisposed to commit the illegal act or did so only because the agent induced it.

9–4g Statute of Limitations

With some exceptions, such as for the crime of murder, statutes of limitations apply to crimes just as they do to civil wrongs. In other words, the state must initiate criminal prosecution within a certain number of years. If a criminal action is brought after the statutory time period has expired, the accused person can raise the statute of limitations as a defense.

Know This

"Ignorance" is a lack of information. "Mistake" is a confusion of information, which can sometimes negate criminal intent.

Duress Unlawful pressure brought to bear on a person, causing the person to perform an act that she or he would not otherwise perform.

Entrapment A defense in which a defendant claims that he or she was induced by a public official to commit a crime that he or she would otherwise not have committed.

The running of the time period in a statute of limitations may be *tolled*—that is, suspended or stopped temporarily—if the defendant is a minor or is not in the jurisdiction. When the defendant reaches the age of majority or returns to the jurisdiction, the statutory time period begins to run again.

9–4h Immunity

Accused persons are understandably reluctant to give information if it will be used to prosecute them, and they cannot be forced to do so. The privilege against **self-incrimination** is granted by the Fifth Amendment to the U.S. Constitution. The clause reads "nor shall [any person] be compelled in any criminal case to be a witness against himself."

When the state wishes to obtain information from a person accused of a crime, the state can grant *immunity* from prosecution or agree to prosecute for a less serious offense in exchange for the information. Once immunity is given, the person can no longer refuse to testify on Fifth Amendment grounds because he or she now has an absolute privilege against self-incrimination.

Often, a grant of immunity from prosecution for a serious crime is part of the **plea bargaining** between the defendant and the prosecuting attorney. The defendant may be convicted of a lesser offense, while the state uses the defendant's testimony to prosecute accomplices for serious crimes carrying heavy penalties.

> **Self-Incrimination** Giving testimony in a trial or other legal proceeding that could expose the person testifying to criminal prosecution.

> **Plea Bargaining** The process by which a criminal defendant and the prosecutor work out an agreement to dispose of the criminal case, subject to court approval.

9–5 Constitutional Safeguards and Criminal Procedures

Criminal law brings the power of the state, with all its resources, to bear against the individual. Criminal procedures are designed to protect the constitutional rights of individuals and to prevent the arbitrary use of power by the government.

The U.S. Constitution provides specific safeguards for those accused of crimes. Most of these safeguards protect individuals not only against federal government actions but also, by virtue of the due process clause of the Fourteenth Amendment, against state government actions. These protections are set forth in the Fourth, Fifth, Sixth, and Eighth Amendments.

> **Learning Objective 5**
> What constitutional safeguards exist to protect persons accused of crimes?

9–5a Fourth Amendment Protections

The Fourth Amendment protects the "right of the people to be secure in their persons, houses, papers, and effects." Before searching or seizing private property, law enforcement officers must obtain a **search warrant**—an order from a judge or other public official authorizing the search or seizure.

Advances in technology have allowed authorities to track phone calls and vehicle movements with greater ease and precision. The use of such technology can constitute a search within the meaning of the Fourth Amendment. **Case Example 9.20** Antoine Jones owned and operated a nightclub in the District of Columbia. Government agents suspected that he was also trafficking in narcotics. As part of their investigation, agents obtained a warrant to attach a global positioning system (GPS) to Jones's wife's car, which he used regularly. The warrant authorized installation in the District of Columbia and within ten days, but agents installed the device on the eleventh day and in Maryland.

The agents then tracked the vehicle's movement for about a month, eventually arresting Jones for possession and intent to distribute cocaine. Jones was convicted. He appealed, arguing that the government did not have a valid warrant for the GPS tracking. The United

> **Search Warrant** An order granted by a public authority, such as a judge, that authorizes law enforcement personnel to search particular premises or property.

States Supreme Court held that the attachment of a GPS tracking device to a suspect's vehicle does constitute a Fourth Amendment search. The Court did not rule on whether the search in this case was unreasonable, however, and allowed Jones's conviction to stand.[21]

Probable Cause To obtain a search warrant, law enforcement officers must convince a judge that they have reasonable grounds, or **probable cause,** to believe a search will reveal a specific illegality. Probable cause requires the officers to have trustworthy evidence that would convince a reasonable person that the proposed search or seizure is more likely justified than not.

Case Example 9.21 Based on a tip that Oscar Gutierrez was involved in drug trafficking, law enforcement officers went to his home with a drug-sniffing dog. The dog alerted officers to the scent of narcotics at the home's front door. Officers knocked for fifteen minutes, but no one answered. Eventually, they entered and secured the men inside the home. They then obtained a search warrant based on the dog's positive alert. Officers found eleven pounds of methamphetamine in the search, and Gutierrez was convicted. The evidence of the drug-sniffing dog's positive alert for the presence of drugs established probable cause for the warrant.[22]

Furthermore, the Fourth Amendment prohibits general warrants. It requires a particular description of what is to be searched or seized. General searches through a person's belongings are not permissible. The search cannot extend beyond what is described in the warrant. Although search warrants require specificity, if a search warrant is issued for a person's residence, items in that residence may be searched even if they do not belong to that individual.

Because of the strong governmental interest in protecting the public, a warrant normally is not required for seizures of spoiled or contaminated food. Nor are warrants required for searches of businesses in such highly regulated industries as liquor, guns, and strip mining.

Reasonable Expectation of Privacy The Fourth Amendment protects only against searches that violate a person's *reasonable expectation of privacy*. A reasonable expectation of privacy exists if (1) the individual actually expects privacy, and (2) the person's expectation is one that society as a whole would think is legitimate.

Case Example 9.22 Angela Marcum was the drug court coordinator responsible for collecting money for the District County Court of Pittsburg County, Oklahoma. She was romantically involved with James Miller, an assistant district attorney. The state charged Marcum with obstructing an investigation of suspected embezzlement and offered in evidence text messages sent and received by her and Miller. The state had obtained a search warrant and collected the records of the messages from U.S. Cellular, Miller's phone company.

Marcum filed a motion to suppress the messages, which the court granted. The state appealed. A state intermediate appellate court reversed the lower court's judgment. Marcum had no reasonable expectation of privacy in U.S. Cellular's records of her text messages in Miller's account. "Once the messages were both transmitted and received, the expectation of privacy was lost."[23]

9–5b Fifth Amendment Protections

The Fifth Amendment offers significant protections for accused persons. One is the guarantee that no one can be deprived of "life, liberty, or property without due process of law." Two other important Fifth Amendment provisions protect persons against double jeopardy and self-incrimination.

Probable Cause Reasonable grounds for believing that a search or seizure should be conducted.

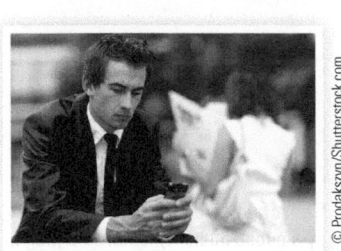

Is there an absolute right to privacy for text messages?

---

21. *United States v. Jones,* 565 U.S. 945, 132 S.Ct. 945, 181 L.Ed.2d 911 (2012).
22. *United States v. Gutierrez,* 760 F.3d 750 (7th Cir. 2014).
23. *State of Oklahoma v. Marcum,* 319 P.3d 681 (Okla.Crim.App. 2014).

Due Process of Law Remember that *due process of law* has both procedural and substantive aspects. Procedural due process requirements underlie criminal procedures. The law must be carried out in a fair and orderly way. In criminal cases, due process means that defendants should have an opportunity to object to the charges against them before a fair, neutral decision maker, such as a judge. Defendants must also be given the opportunity to confront and cross-examine witnesses and accusers, and to present their own witnesses.

Double Jeopardy The Fifth Amendment also protects persons from **double jeopardy** (being tried twice for the same criminal offense). The prohibition against double jeopardy means that once a criminal defendant is acquitted (found "not guilty") of a particular crime, the government may not retry him or her for the same crime.

The prohibition against double jeopardy does not preclude the crime victim from bringing a civil suit against that same defendant to recover damages, however. In other words, a person found "not guilty" of assault and battery in a state criminal case can be sued for damages by the victim in a civil tort case. Additionally, a state's prosecution of a crime will not prevent a separate federal prosecution relating to the same activity (and vice versa), provided the activity can be classified as a different crime.

Self-Incrimination The Fifth Amendment grants a privilege against self-incrimination. Thus, in any criminal proceeding, an accused person cannot be compelled to give testimony that might subject her or him to criminal prosecution.

The Fifth Amendment's guarantee against self-incrimination extends only to natural persons. Because a corporation is a legal entity and not a natural person, the privilege against self-incrimination does not apply to it. Similarly, the business records of a partnership do not receive Fifth Amendment protection. When a partnership is required to produce these records, it must do so even if the information incriminates the persons who constitute the business entity.

Double Jeopardy The Fifth Amendment requirement that prohibits a person from being tried twice for the same criminal offense.

Know This
The Fifth Amendment protection against self-incrimination does not cover partnerships or corporations.

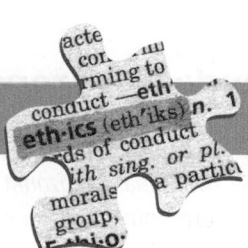

Ethical Issue

Should police be able to force you to unlock your mobile phone? Today's cell phones can store countless pages of text, thousands of pictures, and hundreds of videos. Such data can remain on a mobile phone for years. Also, since the advent of the "cloud," much of the data viewable on a mobile phone is stored on a remote server. Should police nonetheless be able to force you to unlock your phone? Or does this practice violate the Fifth Amendment protection against self-incrimination?

In *Riley v. California*,[24] the United States Supreme Court unanimously held that warrantless search and seizure of digital contents of a mobile phone during an arrest is unconstitutional. Chief Justice John Roberts stated, "The fact that technology now allows for an individual to carry [the privacies of life] in his hand does not make the information any less worthy of the protection for which the Founders fought." Nevertheless, a number of federal courts have allowed evidence obtained from cell phones to be used against a defendant even when there was no search warrant.[25]

---

24. 573 U.S. ___, 134 S.Ct. 2473, 189 L.Ed.2d 430 (2014). See also *United States v. Caballero*, 178 F.Supp.3d 1008 (S.D.Cal. 2016).
25. See, for instance, *Ly v. Beard*, 652 Fed.Appx. 550 (9th Cir. 2016); and *U.S. v. Miller*, 641 Fed.Appx. 242 (4th Cir. 2016).

Exclusionary Rule A rule that prevents evidence that is obtained illegally or without a proper search warrant from being admissible in court.

Know This

Once a suspect has been informed of his or her rights, anything that person says can be used as evidence in a trial.

9–5c The Exclusionary Rule

Under what is known as the **exclusionary rule,** any evidence obtained in violation of the constitutional rights spelled out in the Fourth, Fifth, and Sixth Amendments generally is not admissible at trial. All evidence derived from the illegally obtained evidence is known as the "fruit of the poisonous tree," and normally must also be excluded from the trial proceedings. For instance, if a confession is obtained after an illegal arrest, the arrest is the "poisonous tree," and the confession, if "tainted" by the arrest, is the "fruit."

The purpose of the exclusionary rule is to deter police from conducting warrantless searches and engaging in other misconduct. The rule can sometimes lead to injustice, however. If evidence of a defendant's guilt was obtained improperly (without a valid search warrant, for instance), it normally cannot be used against the defendant in court.

9–5d The *Miranda* Rule

In *Miranda v. Arizona,* a case decided in 1966, the United States Supreme Court established the rule that individuals who are arrested must be informed of certain constitutional rights. Suspects must be informed of their Fifth Amendment right to remain silent and their Sixth Amendment right to counsel. If the arresting officers fail to inform a criminal suspect of these constitutional rights, any statements the suspect makes normally will not be admissible in court. Because of its importance in criminal procedure, the *Miranda case* is presented as this chapter's *Landmark in the Law* feature.

Although the Supreme Court's *Miranda* ruling was controversial, the decision has survived attempts by Congress to overrule it. Over time, however, the Supreme Court has made a number of exceptions to the *Miranda* ruling. For instance, the Court has recognized a "public safety" exception that allows certain statements to be admitted even if the defendant was not given *Miranda* warnings. A defendant's statements that reveal the location of a weapon would be admissible under this exception.

Landmark in the Law

Miranda v. Arizona (1966)

The United States Supreme Court's decision in *Miranda v. Arizona*[a] has been cited in more court decisions than any other case in the history of U.S. law. Through television shows and other media, the case has also become familiar to most of the adult population in the United States.

The case arose after Ernesto Miranda was arrested in his home on March 13, 1963, for the kidnapping and rape of an eighteen-year-old woman. Miranda was taken to a police station in Phoenix, Arizona, and questioned by two police officers. Two hours later, the officers

emerged from the interrogation room with a written confession signed by Miranda.

Rulings by the Lower Courts The confession was admitted into evidence at the trial, and Miranda was convicted and sentenced to prison for twenty to thirty years. Miranda appealed his conviction, claiming that he had not been informed of his constitutional rights. He did not assert that he was innocent of the crime or that his confession was false or made under duress. He claimed only that he would not have confessed if he had been advised of his right to remain silent and to have an attorney.

The Supreme Court of Arizona held that Miranda's constitutional rights had not

been violated and affirmed his conviction. In its decision, the court emphasized that Miranda had not specifically requested an attorney.

The Supreme Court's Decision The *Miranda* case was subsequently consolidated with three other cases involving similar issues and reviewed by

a. 384 U.S. 436, 86 S.Ct. 1602, 16 L.Ed.2d 694 (1966).

the United States Supreme Court. In its decision, the Court stated that whenever an individual is taken into custody, "the following measures are required: He must be warned prior to any questioning that he has the right to remain silent, that anything he says can be used against him in a court of law, that he has the right to the presence of an attorney, and that if he cannot afford an attorney one will be appointed for him prior to any questioning if he so desires." If the accused waives his or her rights to remain silent and to have counsel present, the government must be able to demonstrate that the waiver was made knowingly, intelligently, and voluntarily.

Application to Today's World

Today, both on television and in the real world, police officers routinely advise suspects of their "Miranda rights" on arrest. When Ernesto Miranda himself was later murdered, the suspected murderer was "read his Miranda rights." Interestingly, *this decision has also had ramifications for criminal procedure in Great Britain. British police officers are required, when making arrests, to inform suspects, "You do not have to say anything. But if you do not mention now something which you later use in your defense, the court may decide that your failure to mention it now strengthens the case against you. A record will be made of everything you say, and it may be given in evidence if you are brought to trial."*

Additionally, a suspect must unequivocally and assertively ask to exercise her or his right to counsel in order to stop police questioning. Saying, "Maybe I should talk to a lawyer" during an interrogation after being taken into custody is not enough.

9–5e Criminal Process

A criminal prosecution differs from a civil case in several respects. These differences reflect the desire to safeguard the rights of individuals against the state. Exhibit 9–3 summarizes the major procedural steps in processing a criminal case. Here, we discuss three phases of the criminal process—arrest, indictment or information, and trial—in more detail.

Arrest Before a warrant for arrest can be issued, there must be probable cause to believe that the individual in question has committed a crime. *Probable cause* can be defined as a substantial likelihood that the person has committed or is about to commit a crime. Note that probable cause involves a likelihood, not just a possibility. An arrest can be made without a warrant if there is no time to get one, but the action of the arresting officer is still judged by the standard of probable cause.

Indictment or Information Individuals must be formally charged with having committed specific crimes before they can be brought to trial. If issued by a grand jury, this charge is called an **indictment**.[26] A **grand jury** usually consists of more jurors than the ordinary trial jury. A grand jury does not determine the guilt or innocence of an accused party. Rather, its function is to hear the state's evidence and to determine whether a reasonable basis (probable cause) exists for believing that a crime has been committed and that a trial ought to be held.

Usually, grand juries are used in cases involving serious crimes, such as murder. For lesser crimes, an individual may be formally charged with a crime by what is called an **information,** or criminal complaint. An information will be issued by a government prosecutor if the prosecutor determines that there is sufficient evidence to justify bringing the individual to trial.

Trial At a criminal trial, the accused person does not have to prove anything. The entire burden of proof is on the prosecutor (the state). The prosecution must show that, based on all the evidence presented, the defendant's guilt has been established *beyond a reasonable doubt.*

Indictment A charge by a grand jury that a reasonable basis (probable cause) exists for believing that a crime has been committed and that a trial should be held.

Grand Jury A group of citizens who decide, after hearing the state's evidence, whether a reasonable basis (probable cause) exists for believing that a crime has been committed and that a trial ought to be held.

Information A formal accusation or complaint (without an indictment) issued in certain types of actions (usually criminal actions involving lesser crimes) by a government prosecutor.

In a criminal trial, does the defendant have to prove anything?

---

26. Pronounced in-*dyte*-ment.

Exhibit 9–3 Major Procedural Steps in a Criminal Case

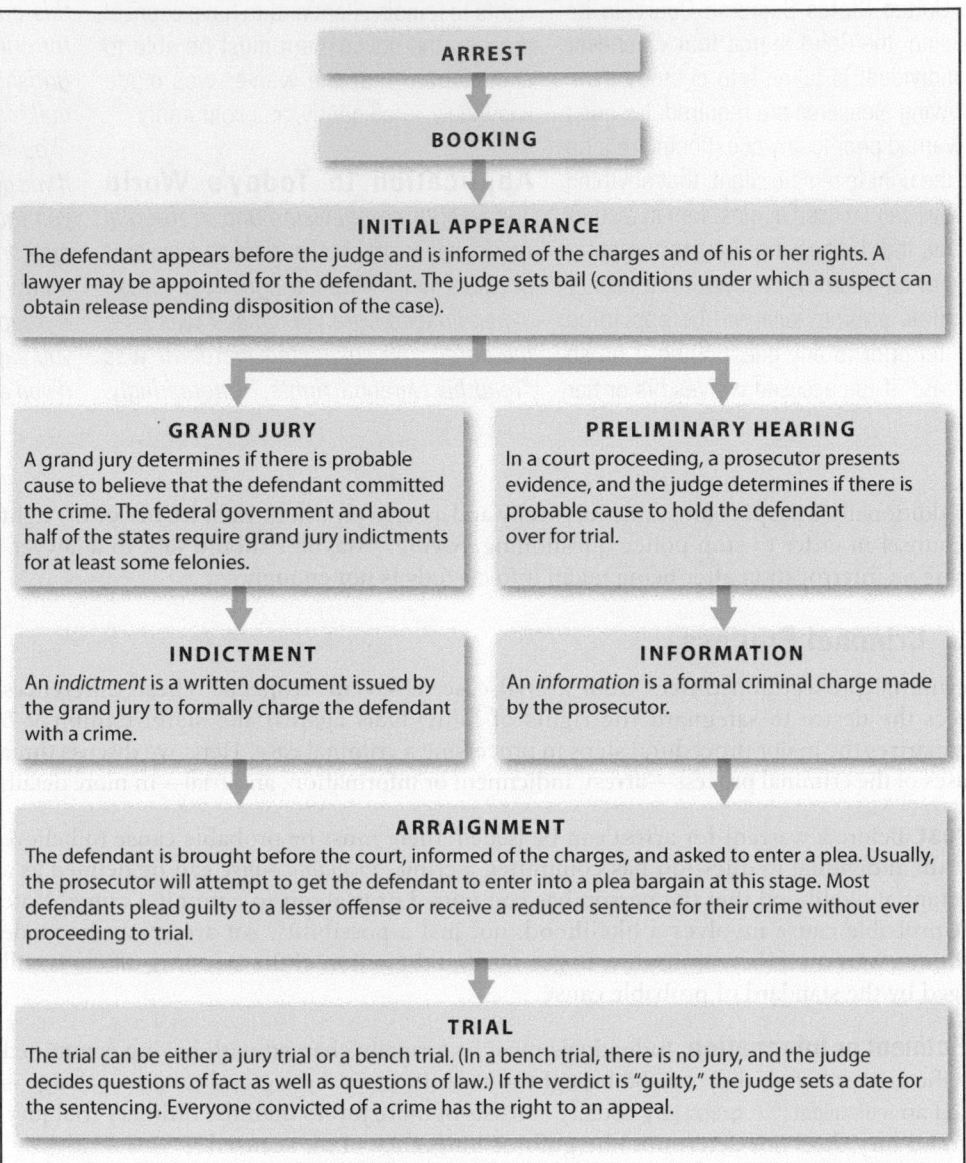

If there is a reasonable doubt as to whether a criminal defendant committed the crime with which she or he has been charged, then the verdict must be "not guilty." A verdict of "not guilty" is not the same as stating that the defendant is innocent. It merely means that not enough evidence was properly presented to the court to prove guilt beyond a reasonable doubt.

At the conclusion of the trial, a court will sentence a convicted defendant. The U.S. Sentencing Commission performs the task of standardizing sentences for *federal* crimes. The commission's guidelines establish a range of possible penalties, but judges are allowed to depart from the guidelines if circumstances warrant (such as when an individual has no prior criminal offenses).

Sentencing guidelines also provide for enhanced punishment for white-collar crimes, violations of the Sarbanes-Oxley Act, and violations of securities laws. When sentencing business firms, judges may consider any past violations and the extent to which the firm has undertaken specific programs and procedures to prevent criminal activities by its employees.

> "In school, every period ends with a bell. Every sentence ends with a period. Every crime ends with a sentence."
>
> **Steven Wright**
> 1955–present
> (American comedian)

9–6 Cyber Crime

The U.S. Department of Justice broadly defines **computer crime** as any violation of criminal law that involves knowledge of computer technology for its perpetration, investigation, or prosecution. Many computer crimes fall under the broad label of **cyber crime,** which describes any criminal activity occurring in the virtual community of the Internet.

Most cyber crimes are simply existing crimes, such as fraud and theft of intellectual property, in which the Internet is the instrument of wrongdoing. Here we look at several types of activities that constitute cyber crimes against persons or property.

9–6a Cyber Fraud

Fraud is any misrepresentation knowingly made with the intention of deceiving another and on which a reasonable person would and does rely to her or his detriment. **Cyber fraud** is fraud committed over the Internet. Scams that were once conducted solely by mail or phone can now be found online, and new technology has led to increasingly creative ways to commit fraud.

Two widely reported forms of cyber crime are *advance fee fraud* and *online auction fraud*. In the simplest form of advance fee fraud, consumers order and pay for items, such as automobiles or antiques, that are never delivered. Online auction fraud is also fairly straightforward. A person lists an expensive item for auction, on either a legitimate or a fake auction site, and then refuses to send the product after receiving payment. Or, as a variation, the wrongdoer may send the purchaser an item that is worth less than the one offered in the auction.

The larger online auction sites, such as eBay, try to protect consumers against such schemes by providing warnings or offering various forms of insurance. Nonetheless, it is nearly impossible to completely eliminate online fraud potential because users can assume multiple identities.

Case Example 9.23 Jeremy Jaynes grossed more than $750,000 per week selling nonexistent or worthless products such as "penny stock pickers" and "Internet history erasers." By the time he was arrested, he had amassed an estimated $24 million from his various fraudulent schemes.[27]

9–6b Cyber Identity Theft

In cyberspace, thieves are not subject to the physical limitations of the "real" world. A thief can steal data stored in a networked computer with Internet access from anywhere on the globe. Only the speed of the connection and the thief's computer equipment limit the quantity of data that can be stolen.

Identity Theft **Identity theft** occurs when the wrongdoer steals a form of identification—such as a name, date of birth, or Social Security number—and uses the information to access and steal the victim's financial resources. Widespread use of the Internet has caused a marked increase in identity theft, and many millions of Americans have been victimized.

Easy Access to Personal Information. The Internet has provided relatively easy access to private data. Frequent Web surfers and social media users surrender a wealth of personal information. Websites use so-called "cookies" to collect data on their customers and visitors. Often, sites store information such as names, e-mail addresses, and credit-card numbers. Identity thieves may be able to steal this information by fooling a website into thinking that they are the true account holders. Identity thieves may also be able to use personal information that people disclose on social media sites (such as birthdays, children's names, hometowns, employers) to gain access to financial information.

---

27. *Jaynes v. Commonwealth of Virginia*, 276 Va. 443, 666 S.E.2d 303 (2008).

Know This

When determining the appropriate sentence for a business firm, courts focus on three things: previous violations, cooperation with authorities, and good faith efforts to avoid violations.

Computer Crime Any violation of criminal law that involves knowledge of computer technology for its perpetration, investigation, or prosecution.

Cyber Crime A crime that occurs in the online environment.

Cyber Fraud Any misrepresentation knowingly made over the Internet with the intention of deceiving another for the purpose of obtaining property or funds.

Identity Theft The illegal use of someone else's personal information to access the victim's financial resources.

Learning Objective 6

How has the Internet expanded opportunities for identity theft?

Stolen Credit-Card Numbers. More than half of identity thefts involve the misappropriation of credit-card accounts. In most situations, the legitimate holders of credit cards are not held responsible for the costs of purchases made with a stolen number. The loss is borne by the businesses and banks.

Example 9.24 A security breach at Target Corporation exposed the personal information of 70 million Target customers. Hackers stole credit- and debit-card numbers and debit-card PINs from the embedded code on the magnetic strips of the cards, as well as customers' names, addresses, and phone numbers. JPMorgan Chase Bank, the world's largest issuer of credit cards, had to replace 2 million credit and debit cards as a result of the breach. ■

Other Criminal Objectives. Identity theft can be committed in the course of pursuing other criminal objectives. In the following case, for instance, the defendant was charged with identity theft in connection with the filing of five thousand false income tax returns to obtain refunds.

Case 9.3

United States v. Warner
United States Court of Appeals, Eleventh Circuit, 638 Fed.Appx. 961 (2016).

Background and Facts Mauricio Warner was indicted on charges of obtaining individuals' identities and using those identities to file more than five thousand false federal income tax returns with the U.S. Department of Revenue. As a result, millions of dollars in federal tax refunds were deposited in bank accounts that Warner controlled. At trial, the court admitted into evidence spreadsheets of fraudulently submitted tax returns.

Convicted of the charges, Warner appealed to the U.S. Court of Appeals for the Eleventh Circuit. He sought a new trial, in part, on the ground that the court had abused its discretion by admitting into evidence, as business records, government exhibits consisting of spreadsheets detailing fraudulently submitted tax returns.

In the Words of the Court
PER CURIAM [By the Whole Court]:
* * * *

Federal Rule of Evidence 1006 authorizes the admission into evidence of a summary of voluminous business records but only where the originals or duplicates of those originals are available for examination or copying by the other party.
* * * *

Rule 803(6) requires that both the underlying records and the report summarizing those records be prepared and maintained for business purposes in the ordinary course of business and not for purposes of litigation. * * * *The touchstone of admissibility under Rule 803(6) is reliability, and a trial judge has broad discretion to determine the admissibility of such evidence.* [Emphasis added.]

Computer-generated business records are admissible under the following circumstances: (1) the records must be kept pursuant to some routine procedure designed to assure their accuracy, (2) they must be created for motives that would tend to assure accuracy (preparation for litigation, for example, is not such a motive), and (3) they must not themselves be mere accumulations of hearsay or uninformed opinion.

* * * A typed summary of handwritten business records created solely for litigation [is] inadmissible hearsay evidence. [This is] distinguishable from * * * records [that consist of] electronically stored information and the summary [is] simply a printout of that information.
* * * *

We find no abuse of discretion in admitting government Exhibits 500 and 500A under Rule 803(6). Although the spreadsheets were formatted to be easier to understand and printed for litigation, the underlying records were kept in the ordinary course of business and the data was not modified or combined when entered into the spreadsheet.

Decision and Remedy The federal appellate court concluded that the lower court's rulings at issue were not an abuse of discretion and affirmed Warner's convictions. Computer-generated business records are admissible if they were kept according to a routine procedure designed to assure their accuracy.

Critical Thinking

• **Legal Environment** *Why is a computer-generated summary of business records created solely for a trial generally not admissible? How were the spreadsheets in this case different?*

• **Ethical** *Is filing a false tax return to obtain a refund unethical? If so, is filing more than five thousand false returns more unethical? Explain.*

Password Theft The more personal information a cyber criminal obtains, the easier it is for him or her to find a victim's online user name at a particular website. Once the online user name has been compromised, it is easier to steal the victim's password, which is often the last line of defense to financial information.

Numerous software programs aid identity thieves in illegally obtaining passwords. A technique called *keystroke logging*, for instance, relies on software that embeds itself in a victim's computer and records every keystroke made on that computer. User names and passwords are then recorded and sold to the highest bidder. Internet users should also be wary of any links contained within e-mails sent from unknown sources. These links can sometimes be used to illegally obtain personal information.

Phishing In a distinct form of identity theft known as **phishing,** the perpetrators "fish" for financial data and passwords from consumers by posing as a legitimate business such as a bank or credit-card company. The "phisher" may send an e-mail asking the recipient to "update" or "confirm" vital information. Often, the e-mail includes a threat that an account or some other service will be discontinued if the information is not provided. Once the unsuspecting individual enters the information, the phisher can sell it or use it to masquerade as that person or to drain his or her bank or credit account.

Example 9.25 Customers of Wells Fargo Bank receive official-looking e-mails telling them to enter personal information in an online form to complete mandatory installation of a new Internet security certificate. But the website is bogus. When the customers complete the forms, their computers are infected and funnel their data to a computer server. The cyber criminals then sell the data. ▪ Phishing scams have also spread to text messages and social networking sites.

9–6c **Hacking**

A **hacker** is someone who uses one computer, smartphone, or other device to break into another. The danger posed by hackers has increased significantly because of **botnets,** or networks of computers that have been appropriated by hackers without the knowledge of their owners. A hacker may secretly install a program on thousands, if not millions, of personal computer "robots," or "bots."

Example 9.26 After Apple, Inc., introduced its mobile-payment system, cyber thieves began hacking into Apple mobile devices to make purchases with stolen credit-card numbers. At about the same time, cyber criminals were stealing the credit-card data of at least 60 million Home Depot customers and illegally accessing the financial information of 76 million JPMorgan Chase clients. Hackers have also demonstrated that they can take over the dashboard computer systems that control cars. Additionally, the risk of takeover extends to numerous wireless-enabled medical devices, such as pacemakers and insulin pumps. ▪

Malware Botnets are one form of **malware,** a term that refers to any program that is harmful to a computer or, by extension, its user. One type of malware is a **worm**—a software program that is capable of reproducing itself as it spreads from one computer to the next. The Conficker worm, for instance, spread to more than a million personal computers around the world within a three-week period. It was transmitted to some computers through the use of Facebook and Twitter.

Phishing A form of identity theft in which the perpetrator sends e-mails purporting to be from legitimate businesses to induce recipients to reveal their personal financial data, passwords, or other information.

Hacker A person who uses computers to gain unauthorized access to data.

Botnet A network of compromised computers connected to the Internet that can be used to generate spam, relay viruses, or cause servers to fail.

Malware Malicious software programs, such as viruses and worms, that are designed to cause harm to a computer, network, or other device.

Worm A software program that automatically replicates itself over a network but does not alter files and is usually invisible to the user until it has consumed system resources.

Josie Elias/Alamy

Hackers can potentially take over automobile computer systems. What other everyday products and services are susceptible to hacking?

Virus A software program that can replicate itself over a network and spread from one device to another, altering files and interfering with normal operations.

"A hacker does for love what others would not do for money."

Laura Creighton
(Computer programmer and entrepreneur)

Cyberterrorist Criminals who use technology and the Internet to cause fear, violence, and extreme financial harm.

A **virus,** another form of malware, is also able to reproduce itself but must be attached to an "infested" host file to travel from one computer network to another. For instance, hackers can corrupt banner ads that use Adobe's Flash Player or send bogus Flash Player updates. When an Internet user clicks on the banner ad or installs the update, a virus is installed. Worms and viruses can be programmed to perform a number of functions, such as prompting host computers to continually "crash" and reboot, or to otherwise infect the system.

Service-Based Hacking Today, many companies offer "software as a service." Instead of buying software to install on a computer, the user connects to Web-based software. The user can then write e-mails, edit spreadsheets, and the like using a Web browser.

Cyber criminals have adapted this method and now offer "crimeware as a service." A would-be thief no longer has to be a computer hacker to create a botnet or steal banking information and credit-card numbers. He or she can rent the online services of cyber criminals to do the work for a small price. The thief can even target individual groups, such as U.S. physicians or British attorneys.

9–6d Cyberterrorism

Cyberterrorists use technology and the Internet to cause fear, violence, or extreme financial harm. Cyberterrorists, as well as hackers, may target businesses. The goals of a hacking operation might include a wholesale theft of data, such as a merchant's customer files, or the monitoring of a computer to discover a business firm's plans and transactions. A cyberterrorist might also want to insert false codes or data into a computer. For instance, the processing control system of a food manufacturer could be changed to alter the levels of ingredients so that consumers of the food would become ill.

A cyberterrorist attack on a major financial institution, such as the New York Stock Exchange or a large bank, could leave securities or money markets in flux. Such an attack could seriously affect the daily lives of U.S. citizens, business operations, and national security.

9–6e Prosecution of Cyber Crime

Cyber crime has raised new issues in the investigation of crimes and the prosecution of offenders. Determining the "location" of a cyber crime and identifying a criminal in cyberspace are two significant challenges for law enforcement.

Jurisdiction and Identification Challenges A threshold issue is, of course, jurisdiction. Jurisdiction is normally based on physical geography, and each state and nation has jurisdiction over crimes committed within its boundaries. But geographic boundaries simply do not apply in cyberspace. A person who commits an act against a business in California, where the act is a cyber crime, might never have set foot in California but might instead reside in, say, Canada, where the act may not be a crime.

Identifying the wrongdoer can also be difficult. Cyber criminals do not leave physical traces, such as fingerprints or DNA samples, as evidence of their crimes. Even electronic "footprints" (digital evidence) can be hard to find and follow. For instance, cyber criminals may employ software, such as Tor, to mask their IP addresses—codes that identify individual computers on the Internet—and the IP addresses of those with whom they communicate. Law enforcement must hire computer forensic experts to bypass the software and track down the criminals. For these reasons, laws written to protect physical property are often difficult to apply in cyberspace.

The Computer Fraud and Abuse Act Perhaps the most significant federal statute specifically addressing cyber crime is the Counterfeit Access Device and Computer Fraud and Abuse Act.[28] This act is commonly known as the Computer Fraud and Abuse Act, or CFAA.

Among other things, the CFAA provides that a person who accesses a computer online, without authority, to obtain classified, restricted, or protected data (or attempts to do so) is subject to criminal prosecution. Such data could include financial and credit records, medical records, legal files, military and national security files, and other confidential information. The data can be located in government or private computers. The crime has two elements: accessing a computer without authority and taking the data.

This theft is a felony if it is committed for a commercial purpose or for private financial gain, or if the value of the stolen information exceeds $5,000. Penalties include fines and imprisonment for up to twenty years. A victim of computer theft can also bring a civil suit against the violator to obtain damages, an injunction, and other relief.

---

28. 18 U.S.C. Section 1030.

Practice and Review

Edward Hanousek worked for Pacific & Arctic Railway and Navigation Company (P&A) as a road-master of the White Pass & Yukon Railroad in Alaska. As an officer of the corporation, Hanousek was responsible "for every detail of the safe and efficient maintenance and construction of track, structures, and marine facilities of the entire railroad," including special projects. One project was a rock quarry, known as "6-mile," above the Skagway River. Next to the quarry, and just beneath the surface, ran a high-pressure oil pipeline owned by Pacific & Arctic Pipeline, Inc., P&A's sister company. When the quarry's backhoe operator punctured the pipeline, an estimated one thousand to five thousand gallons of oil were discharged into the river. Hanousek was charged with negligently discharging a harmful quantity of oil into a navigable water of the United States in violation of the criminal provisions of the Clean Water Act (CWA). Using the information presented in the chapter, answer the following questions.

1. Did Hanousek have the required mental state *(mens rea)* to be convicted of a crime? Why or why not?

2. Which theory discussed in the chapter would enable a court to hold Hanousek criminally liable for violating the statute regardless of whether he participated in, directed, or even knew about the specific violation?

3. Could the quarry's backhoe operator who punctured the pipeline also be charged with a crime in this situation? Explain.

4. Suppose that, at trial, Hanousek argued that he could not be convicted because he was not aware of the requirements of the CWA. Would this defense be successful? Why or why not?

Debate This

Because of overcriminalization, particularly by the federal government, Americans may be breaking the law regularly without knowing it. Should Congress rescind many of the more than four thousand federal crimes now on the books?

Key Terms

actus reus 227
arson 234
beyond a reasonable doubt 225
botnet 249
burglary 232
computer crime 247
crime 225
cyber crime 247
cyber fraud 247
cyberterrorist 250
double jeopardy 243
duress 240
embezzlement 234

entrapment 240
exclusionary rule 244
felony 226
forgery 234
grand jury 245
hacker 249
identity theft 247
indictment 245
information 245
insider trading 237
larceny 232
malware 249
mens rea 228

misdemeanor 227
money laundering 238
petty offense 227
phishing 249
plea bargaining 241
probable cause 242
robbery 232
search warrant 241
self-defense 239
self-incrimination 241
virus 250
white-collar crime 234
worm 249

Chapter Summary: Criminal Law and Cyber Crime

Civil Law and Criminal Law	1. *Civil law*—Pertains to the duties that exist between persons or between persons and their governments, excluding the duty not to commit crimes. 2. *Criminal law*—Has to do with crimes, which are wrongs against society proclaimed in statutes and, if committed, punishable by society through fines and/or imprisonment—or in some cases, death. Because crimes are *offenses against society as a whole*, they are prosecuted by a public official, not by the victims. 3. *Key differences*—An important difference between civil and criminal law is that the standard of proof is higher in criminal cases. 4. *Civil liability for criminal acts*—A criminal act may give rise to both criminal liability and tort liability. 5. *Classification of crimes*—Crimes may also be classified according to their degree of seriousness. Felonies are serious crimes usually punishable by death or by imprisonment for more than one year. Misdemeanors are less serious crimes punishable by fines or by confinement for up to one year.
Criminal Liability	1. *Guilty act*—In general, some form of harmful act to a person or property must be committed for a crime to exist. 2. *State of mind*—An intent to commit a crime, or a wrongful mental state, is also required for a crime to exist. 3. *Corporate criminal liability*—Corporations are normally liable for crimes committed by their agents or employees within the course and scope of their employment.
Types of Crimes	1. *Violent crimes*—Crimes that cause others to suffer harm or death, including murder, assault and battery, sexual assault, and robbery. 2. *Property crimes*—The most common form of crime. The offender's goal is to obtain some economic gain or to damage property. This category includes burglary, larceny, obtaining goods by false pretenses, receiving stolen property, arson, and forgery. 3. *Public order crimes*—Acts, such as public drunkenness, prostitution, gambling, and illegal drug use, that a statute has established are contrary to public values and morals. 4. *White-collar crimes*—Illegal acts committed by a person or business using nonviolent means to obtain a personal or business advantage. Usually, such crimes are committed in the course of a legitimate occupation. Examples include embezzlement, mail and wire fraud, bribery, bankruptcy fraud, theft of trade secrets, and insider trading. 5. *Organized crimes*—A form of crime conducted by groups operating illegitimately to satisfy the public's demand for illegal goods and services (such as illegal drugs, gambling, and prostitution). Organized crime is heavily involved in cyber crime, money laundering, and racketeering (RICO) violations.

Defenses to Criminal Liability	Defenses to criminal liability include justifiable use of force, necessity, insanity, mistake, duress, entrapment, and the statute of limitations. In some cases, defendants may be relieved of criminal liability, at least in part, if they are given immunity.
Constitutional Safeguards and Criminal Procedures	1. *Fourth Amendment*—Provides protection against unreasonable searches and seizures and requires that probable cause exist before a warrant for a search or seizure can be issued. 2. *Fifth Amendment*—Requires due process of law, prohibits double jeopardy, and protects against self-incrimination. 3. *Exclusionary rule*—A criminal procedural rule that prohibits the introduction at trial of all evidence obtained illegally or without a proper search warrant. 4. Miranda *rule*—A rule set forth by the Supreme Court in *Miranda v. Arizona* holding that individuals who are arrested must be informed of certain constitutional rights, including their right to counsel. 5. *Criminal process*—Procedures governing arrest, indictment or information, and trial for a crime that are designed to safeguard the rights of the individual against the government (see Exhibit 9–3).
Cyber Crime	1. *Cyber fraud*—Misrepresentations are knowingly made over the Internet to deceive another. Two widely reported forms are online auction fraud and advance fee fraud. 2. *Cyber identity theft*—In cyberspace, identity theft is made easier by the fact that many e-businesses store information such as consumers' names, e-mail addresses, and credit-card numbers. Password theft and phishing are variations of cyber identity theft. 3. *Hacking*—A hacker is a person who uses one computer to break into another. Malware is any program that is harmful to a computer or, by extension, a computer user. Worms and viruses are examples. 4. *Cyberterrorism*—A cyberterrorist attack on a major U.S. financial institution or telecommunications system could have serious repercussions, including jeopardizing national security. 5. *Prosecution of cyber crime*—Prosecuting cyber crime is more difficult than prosecuting traditional crime. Identifying the wrongdoer is complicated, and jurisdictional issues may arise. A significant federal statute addressing cyber crime is the Computer Fraud and Abuse Act.

Issue Spotters

1. Dana takes her roommate's credit card, intending to charge expenses that she incurs on a vacation. Her first stop is a gas station, where she uses the card to pay for gas. With respect to the gas station, has she committed a crime? If so, what is it? (See *Types of Crimes.*)

2. Without permission, Ben downloads consumer credit files from a computer belonging to Consumer Credit Agency. He then sells the data to Dawn. Has Ben committed a crime? If so, what is it? (See *Cyber Crime.*)

—**Check your answers to the *Issue Spotters* against the answers provided in Appendix D at the end of this text.**

Business Scenarios and Case Problems

9–1. Types of Cyber Crimes. The following situations are similar, but each represents a variation of a particular crime. Identify the crime and point out the differences in the variations. (See *Cyber Crime.*)

1. Chen, posing fraudulently as Diamond Credit Card Co., sends an e-mail to Emily, stating that the company has observed suspicious activity in her account and has frozen the account. The e-mail asks her to reregister her credit-card number and password to reopen the account.

2. Claiming falsely to be Big Buy Retail Finance Co., Conner sends an e-mail to Dino, asking him to confirm or update his personal security information to prevent his Big Buy account from being discontinued.

9–2. Cyber Scam. Kayla, a student at Learnwell University, owes $20,000 in unpaid tuition. If Kayla does not pay the tuition, Learnwell will not allow her to graduate. To obtain the funds to pay the debt, she sends e-mails to people that she does not know asking them for financial help to send her child, who has a disability, to a special school. In reality, Kayla has no children. Is this a crime? If so, which one? (See *Cyber Crime.*)

9–3. Business Case Problem with Sample Answer—White-Collar Crime. Matthew Simpson and others created and operated a series of corporate entities to defraud telecommunications companies, creditors, credit reporting agencies, and others. Through these entities, Simpson and his confederates used routing codes and spoofing services to make long-distance calls appear to be local. They stole other firms' network capacity and diverted payments to themselves. They leased goods and services without paying for them. To hide their association with their corporate entities and with each other, they used false identities, addresses, and credit histories, and issued false bills, invoices, financial statements, and credit references. Did these acts constitute mail and wire fraud? Discuss. [*United States v. Simpson*, 741 F.3d 539 (5th Cir. 2014)] (See *Types of Crimes*.)

—For a sample answer to Problem 9–3, go to Appendix E at the end of this text.

9–4. Defenses to Criminal Liability. George Castro told Ambrosio Medrano that a bribe to a certain corrupt Los Angeles County official would buy a contract with the county hospitals. To share in the deal, Medrano recruited Gustavo Buenrostro. In turn, Buenrostro contacted his friend James Barta, the owner of Sav–Rx, which provides prescription benefit management services. Barta was asked to pay a "finder's fee" to Castro. He did not pay, even after frequent e-mails and calls with deadlines and ultimatums delivered over a period of months. Eventually, Barta wrote Castro a Sav–Rx check for $6,500, saying that it was to help his friend Buenrostro. Castro was an FBI agent, and the county official and contract were fictional. Barta was charged with conspiracy to commit bribery. At trial, the government conceded that Barta was not predisposed to commit the crime. Could he be absolved of the charge on a defense of entrapment? Explain. [*United States v. Barta*, 776 F.3d 931 (7th Cir. 2015)] (See *Defenses to Criminal Liability*.)

9–5. Criminal Process. Gary Peters fraudulently told an undocumented immigrant that Peters could help him obtain lawful status. Peters said that he knew immigration officials and asked for money to aid in the process. The victim paid Peters at least $25,000 in wire transfers and checks. Peters had others call the victim, falsely represent that they were agents with the U.S. Department of Homeland Security, and induce continued payments. He threatened to contact authorities to detain or deport the victim and his wife. Peters was charged with wire fraud and convicted in a federal district court. Peters's attorney argued that his client's criminal history was partially due to "difficult personal times" caused by divorce, illness, and job loss. Despite this claim, Peters was sentenced to forty-eight months imprisonment, which exceeded the federal sentencing guidelines but was less than the statutory maximum of twenty years. Was this sentence too harsh? Was it too lenient? Discuss. [*United States v. Peters*, 597 Fed.Appx. 1033 (11th Cir. 2015)] (See *Constitutional Safeguards and Criminal Procedures*.)

9–6. Criminal Procedures. Federal officers obtained a warrant to arrest Kateena Norman on charges of credit-card fraud and identity theft. Evidence of the crime included videos, photos, and a fingerprint on a fraudulent check. A previous search of Norman's house had uncovered credit cards, new merchandise, and identifying information for other persons. An Internet account registered to the address had been used to apply for fraudulent credit cards, and a fraudulently obtained rental car was parked on the property. As the officers arrested Norman outside her house, they saw another woman and a caged pit bull inside. They further believed that Norman's boyfriend, who had a criminal record and was also suspected of identify theft, could be there. In less than a minute, the officers searched only those areas within the house in which a person could hide. Would it be reasonable to admit evidence revealed in this "protective sweep" during Norman's trial on the arrest charges? Discuss. [*United States v. Norman*, 637 Fed.Appx. 934 (11th Cir. 2016)] (See *Constitutional Safeguards and Criminal Procedures*.)

9–7. Types of Crimes. In Texas, Chigger Ridge Ranch, L.P., operated a 700-acre commercial hunting area called Coyote Crossing Ranch (CCR). Chigger Ridge leased CCR and its assets for twelve months to George Briscoe's company, VPW Management, LLC. The lease identified all of the vehicles and equipment that belonged to Chigger Ridge, which VPW could use in the course of business, but the lease did not convey any ownership interest. During the lease term, however, Briscoe told his employees to sell some of the vehicles and equipment. Briscoe did nothing to correct the buyers' false impression that he owned the property and was authorized to sell it. The buyers paid with checks, which were deposited into an account to which only Briscoe and his spouse had access. Which crime, if any, did Briscoe commit? Explain. [*Briscoe v. State of Texas*, 542 S.W.3d 100 (Tex.App.—Texarkana 2018)] (See *Types of Crimes*.)

9–8. A Question of Ethics—The IDDR Approach and Identity Theft. *Heesham Broussard obtained counterfeit money instruments. To distribute them, he used account information and numbers on compromised FedEx accounts procured from hackers. Text messages from Broussard indicated that he had participated previously in a similar scam and that he knew the packages would be delivered only if the FedEx accounts were "good." For his use of the accounts, Broussard was charged with identity theft. In defense, he argued that the government could not prove he knew the misappropriated accounts belonged to real persons* *or businesses. [United States v. Broussard, 675 Fed.Appx. 454 (5th Cir. 2017)] (See Cyber Crime.)*

1. Does the evidence support Broussard's assertion? From an ethical perspective, does it matter whether he knew that the accounts belonged to real customers? Why or why not?

2. Assuming that FedEx knew its customers' account information had been compromised, use the IDDR approach to consider whether the company had an ethical obligation to take steps to protect those customers from theft.

Critical Thinking and Writing Assignments

9–9. Critical Legal Thinking. Ray steals a purse from an unattended car at a gas station. Because the purse contains money and a handgun, Ray is convicted of grand theft of property (cash) and grand theft of a firearm. On appeal, Ray claims that he is not guilty of grand theft of a firearm because he did not know that the purse contained a gun. Can Ray be convicted of grand theft of a firearm even though he did not know that the gun was in the purse? Explain. (See *Types of Crimes.*)

9–10. Time-Limited Group Assignment—Cyber Crime. Cyber crime costs consumers millions of dollars every year. It costs businesses, including banks and other credit-card issuers even more. Nonetheless, when cyber criminals are caught and convicted, they are rarely ordered to pay restitution or sentenced to long prison terms. (See *Cyber Crime.*)

1. One group should formulate an argument that stiffer sentences would reduce the amount of cyber crime.

2. A second group should determine how businesspersons can best protect themselves from cyber crime and avoid the associated costs.

3. A third group should decide how and when a court should order a cyber criminal to pay restitution to his or her victims. Should victims whose computers have been infected with worms or viruses be entitled to restitution, or only victims of theft who have experienced financial loss? What should the measure of restitution be? Should large companies that are victims of cyber crime be entitled to the same restitution as individuals?

Unit One—Task-Based Simulation

iStockPhoto.com/lisafx

CompTac, Inc., which is headquartered in San Francisco, California, is one of the leading software manufacturers in the United States. The company invests millions of dollars to research and develop new software applications and computer games that are sold worldwide. It also has a large service department and takes great pains to offer its customers excellent support services.

1. **Jurisdiction.** CompTac routinely purchases some of the materials necessary to produce its computer games from a New York firm, Electrotex, Inc. A dispute arises between the two firms, and CompTac wants to sue Electrotex for breach of contract. Can CompTac bring the suit in a California state court? Can CompTac bring the suit in a federal court? Explain.

2. **Negligence.** A customer at one of CompTac's retail stores stumbles over a crate in the parking lot and breaks her leg. Just moments earlier, the crate had fallen off a CompTac truck that was delivering goods from a CompTac warehouse to the store. The customer sues CompTac, alleging negligence. Will she succeed in her suit? Why or why not?

3. **Wrongful Interference.** Roban Electronics, a software manufacturer and one of CompTac's major competitors, has been trying to convince one of CompTac's key employees, Jim Baxter, to come to work for Roban. Roban knows that Baxter has a written employment contract with CompTac, which Baxter would breach if he left CompTac before the contract expired. Baxter goes to work for Roban, and the departure of its key employee causes CompTac to suffer substantial losses due to delays in completing new software. Can CompTac sue Roban to recoup some of these losses? If so, on what ground?

4. **Cyber Crime.** One of CompTac's employees in its accounting division, Alan Green, has a gambling problem. To repay a gambling debt of $10,000, Green decides to "borrow" from CompTac to cover the debt. Using his knowledge of Comp-Tac account numbers, Green electronically transfers $10,000 from a CompTac account into his personal checking account. A week later, he is luckier at gambling and uses the same electronic procedures to transfer funds from his personal checking account back to the CompTac account. Has Green committed any crimes? If so, what are they?

5. **Ethical Decision Making.** One of CompTac's best-selling products is a computer game that includes some extremely violent actions. Groups of parents, educators, and consumer activists have bombarded CompTac with letters and e-mail messages calling on the company to stop selling the product. CompTac executives are concerned about the public outcry, but at the same time, they realize that the game is CompTac's major source of profits. If it ceased marketing the game, the company could go bankrupt. If you were a CompTac decision maker, what would your decision be in this situation? How would you justify your decision from an ethical perspective?

6. **Intellectual Property.** CompTac wants to sell one of its best-selling software programs to An Phat Company, a firm located in Ho Chi Minh City, Vietnam. CompTac is concerned, however, that after an initial purchase, An Phat will duplicate the software without permission (and in violation of U.S. copyright laws) and sell the illegal bootleg software to other firms in Vietnam. How can CompTac protect its software from being pirated by An Phat Company?

7. **Social Media.** CompTac seeks to hire fourteen new employees. Its human resources (HR) department asks all candidates during their interview to disclose their social media passwords so that the company can access their social media accounts. Is it legal for employers to ask prospective employees for their social media passwords? Explain. If CompTac does not ask for passwords, can it legally look at a person's online posts when evaluating whether to hire or fire the person?

Michal Kalasek/Shutterstock.com

Unit 2
Contracts and E-Contracts

Vladstudioraw/iStock/Getty Images

10

Nature and Classification

Learning Objectives

The five Learning Objectives *below are designed to help improve your understanding. After reading this chapter, you should be able to answer the following questions:*

1. What is the objective theory of contracts?

2. What are the four basic elements necessary to the formation of a valid contract?

3. What is the difference between express and implied contracts?

4. When will a court impose a quasi contract?

5. What rules guide the courts in interpreting contracts?

Promise A declaration that binds a person who makes the promisor do or not do a certain act.

Promisor A person who makes a promise.

Promisee A person to whom a promise is made.

"All sensible people are selfish, and nature is tugging at every contract to make the terms of it fair."

Ralph Waldo Emerson
1803–1882
(American poet)

As Ralph Waldo Emerson observed in the chapter-opening quotation, people tend to act in their own self-interest, and this influences the terms they seek in their contracts. Contract law must therefore provide rules to determine which contract terms will be enforced.

A contract is based on a **promise**—a declaration by a person (the **promisor**) that binds the person to do or not to do a certain act. As a result, the person to whom the promise is made (the **promisee**) has a right to expect or demand that something either will or will not happen in the future.

Like other types of law, contract law reflects our social values, interests, and expectations at a given point in time. It shows what kinds of promises our society thinks should be legally binding. For instance, licensing agreements that a person clicks on to download software on a smartphone are among the kinds of promises that should be legally binding. If Dave Reynolds agrees to Snapchat's terms of service but then reverse-engineers Snapchat's software to create competing software, he has breached his contract with Snapchat. Contract law also distinguishes between promises that create only moral obligations (such as a promise to take a friend to lunch) and promises that are legally binding (such as a promise to pay for items ordered online).

10–1 An Overview of Contract Law

Before we look at the numerous rules that courts use to determine whether a particular promise will be enforced, it is necessary to understand some fundamental concepts of contract law. In this section, we describe the sources and general function of contract law and introduce the objective theory of contracts.

10–1a Sources of Contract Law

The common law governs all contracts except when it has been modified or replaced by statutory law, such as the Uniform Commercial Code (UCC), or by administrative agency regulations. Contracts relating to services, real estate, employment, and insurance, for instance, generally are governed by the common law of contracts. Contracts for the sale and lease of goods, however, are governed by the UCC—to the extent that the UCC has modified general contract law.

House purchases always are completed with explicit contracts. Why?

10–1b The Function of Contracts

No aspect of modern life is entirely free of contractual relationships. You acquire rights and obligations, for instance, when you borrow funds, buy or lease a house, obtain insurance, form a business, or purchase goods or services. Contract law is designed to provide stability and predictability, as well as certainty, for both buyers and sellers in the marketplace.

Contract law assures the parties to private agreements that the promises they make will be enforceable. Clearly, many promises are kept because the parties involved feel a moral obligation to keep them or because keeping a promise is in their mutual self-interest. Nevertheless, in business agreements, the rules of contract law are often followed to avoid potential disputes.

By supplying procedures for enforcing private agreements, contract law provides an essential condition for the existence of a market economy. Without a legal framework of reasonably assured expectations within which to make long-run plans, businesspersons would be able to rely only on the good faith of others. Duty and good faith are usually sufficient to obtain compliance with a promise. When price changes or adverse economic factors make contract compliance costly, however, these elements may not be enough. Contract law is necessary to ensure compliance with a promise or to entitle the innocent party to some form of relief.

10–1c The Definition of a Contract

A **contract** is an agreement that can be enforced in court. It is formed by two or more parties who agree to perform or to refrain from performing some act now or in the future.

Generally, contract disputes arise when there is a promise of future performance. If the contractual promise is not fulfilled, the party who made it is subject to the sanctions of a court. That party may be required to pay damages for failing to perform the contractual promise. In a few instances, the party may be required to perform the promised act.

Contract A set of promises constituting an agreement between parties, giving each a legal duty to the other and the right to seek a remedy for the breach of the promises or duties.

10–1d The Objective Theory of Contracts

In determining whether a contract has been formed, the element of intent is of prime importance. In contract law, intent is determined by what is referred to as the **objective theory of contracts**. Under this theory, a party's intention to enter into a contract is judged by outward, objective facts as interpreted by a *reasonable person*, rather than by the party's secret, subjective intentions. Objective facts may include:

1. What the party said when entering into the contract.
2. How the party acted or appeared.
3. The circumstances surrounding the transaction.

Objective Theory of Contracts The view that contracting parties shall be bound only by terms that can be objectively inferred from promises made.

Learning Objective 1

What is the objective theory of contracts?

Under what circumstances can a property owner prevail when a prospective lessee "backs out" of a lease agreement?

Case Example 10.1 Pan Handle Realty, LLC, built a luxury home in Westport, Connecticut. Robert Olins signed a lease for the property and gave Pan Handle a check for the amount of the annual rent—$138,000. Olins planned to move into the home on January 28, but on January 27, Olins's bank informed Pan Handle that payment had been stopped on the rental check. Olins then told Pan Handle that he was "unable to pursue any further interest in the property."

When Pan Handle was not able to find a new tenant, it filed a lawsuit in a Connecticut state court against Olins, alleging that he had breached the lease. Olins argued that when he signed the lease, he did not intend to be bound by it. The court ruled in Pan Handle's favor and awarded $138,000 in damages, plus $8,000 for utilities, interest, and attorneys' fees. The decision was affirmed on appeal. Under the objective theory of contracts, the parties intended to be bound by the lease when they signed it. The fact that Olins had a change of heart after signing the contract was irrelevant.[1]

10–2 Elements of a Contract

The many topics that will be discussed in the following chapters on contract law require an understanding of the basic elements of a valid contract and the way in which a contract is created. Also important is an understanding of the types of circumstances in which even legally valid contracts will not be enforced.

10–2a Requirements of a Valid Contract

The following list briefly describes the four requirements that must be met for a valid contract to exist. If any of these elements is lacking, no contract will have been formed. (Each item will be explained more fully in subsequent chapters.)

Learning Objective 2

What are the four basic elements necessary to the formation of a valid contract?

1. *Agreement.* An agreement to form a contract includes an *offer* and an *acceptance*. One party must offer to enter into a legal agreement, and another party must accept the terms of the offer.

2. *Consideration.* Any promises made by the parties must be supported by legally sufficient and bargained-for consideration (something of value received or promised to convince a person to make a deal).

3. *Contractual capacity.* Both parties entering into the contract must have the contractual capacity to do so. The law must recognize them as possessing characteristics that qualify them as competent parties.

4. *Legality.* The contract's purpose must be to accomplish some goal that is legal and not against public policy.

An agreement to form a contract can modify the terms of a previous contract. When a dispute concerns whether this has occurred, the offer and acceptance of both agreements can be reviewed to determine their effect. If the terms are ambiguous, evidence outside the expression of an agreement can be considered to determine what the parties intended at the time.

Of course, as in every case involving a contract, the parties' *subjective* beliefs with respect to the terms are irrelevant, particularly in the absence of any evidence to support those beliefs. At issue in the following case was the effect of an offer and acceptance between a university and an associate professor on a previous agreement between the same parties.

---

1. *Pan Handle Realty, LLC v. Olins,* 140 Conn.App. 556, 59 A.3d 842 (2013).

Case 10.1

Weston v. Cornell University

New York Supreme Court, Appellate Division, Third Department, 116 A.D.3d 1094, 24 N.Y.S.3d 448 (2016).

Background and Facts Cornell University, located in Ithaca, New York, sent a letter to Leslie Weston, offering her an associate professorship for a term of five years. The offer stated that the position came "with tenure" subject to a review of Weston's performance early in the term. Weston accepted the position but delayed her submission for tenure until the end of the five years. At that time, the university declined to award her tenure, but in a second offer letter, it extended her appointment for two years "without tenure" and gave her the opportunity to improve and resubmit. She agreed, but again delayed her submission until the end of the term. The university again denied her tenure and eventually terminated her position.

Weston filed a suit in a New York state court against Cornell University, alleging breach of contract. The university filed a motion for summary judgment to dismiss Weston's cause of action, but the court (called the Supreme Court in New York) denied the motion. The university appealed.

In the Words of the Court
ROSE, J. [Judge]

* * * *

Contrary to defendant's [Cornell University's] argument, Supreme Court properly found that issues of fact exist as to whether defendant's [original] offer letter reflects an intent to assure plaintiff [Weston] that she would be granted tenure. * * * The terms of the letter are ambiguous. Accordingly, Supreme Court properly relied upon extrinsic evidence [evidence outside of the contract itself] to determine the parties' intent. Based upon the affidavit of the then-chair of defendant's department who hired plaintiff and wrote the [original] offer letter, as well as correspondence from the dean and associate dean of the college in which plaintiff's department was located, Supreme Court appropriately declined to award summary judgment to defendant with respect to the [original] offer of tenure.

However, we must agree with defendant's alternative argument that the terms of its original offer were materially modified by plaintiff's acceptance of its [second] offer to extend her appointment. *Defendant's [second] letter offering to extend her appointment unambiguously replaced the "with tenure" language contained in the [original] offer letter by restating her job title as "associate professor without tenure."* Defendant also points to plaintiff's deposition testimony, in which she explicitly acknowledged that she understood the [second] letter to be a modification of the original terms of her employment agreement and agreed—albeit reluctantly—to the new terms. Significantly, plaintiff further admitted that defendant was "not guaranteeing her tenure in any case after this letter." [Emphasis added.]

In response * * *, plaintiff contends that, regardless of what she agreed to in [the second offer letter], her oft-repeated assertions of her belief that defendant still owed her tenure based upon the original letter suffice to preclude [bar] summary judgment. Aside from plaintiff's own opinions on the matter, however, there is nothing in the record to indicate that any alleged guarantee of tenure remained beyond the date of the [second] letter.

Decision and Remedy A state intermediate appellate court reversed the trial court's denial of Cornell University's motion for summary judgment on Weston's claim for breach of contract. Despite Weston's opinion that the university owed her tenure, there was no evidence to support an alleged guaranty of tenure.

Critical Thinking

• **E-Commerce** *Written, hard-copy correspondence between the parties provided most of the evidence to support the courts' conclusions in this case. Can an exchange of e-mail serve the same purpose? Why or why not?*

• **What If the Facts Were Different?** *Suppose that Weston had resigned from a tenured position at a different university to accept Cornell's original offer. Would the result in this case have been different? Explain.*

10–2b Defenses to the Enforceability of a Contract

Even if all of the requirements listed above are satisfied, a contract may be unenforceable if the following requirements are not met. These requirements typically are raised as *defenses* to the enforceability of an otherwise valid contract.

1. *Voluntary consent.* The consent of both parties must be voluntary. For instance, if a contract was formed as a result of fraud, mistake, or duress (coercion), the contract may not be enforceable.

2. *Form.* The contract must be in whatever form the law requires. Some contracts must be in writing to be enforceable.

10–3 Types of Contracts

There are many types of contracts. They may be categorized based on legal distinctions as to their *formation*, *performance*, and *enforceability*.

10–3a Contract Formation

Contracts may be classified based on how and when they are formed. Exhibit 10–1 shows three such classifications, and the following subsections explain them in greater detail.

Offeror A person who makes an offer.

Offeree A person to whom an offer is made.

Bilateral Contract A type of contract that arises when a promise is given in exchange for a return promise.

Bilateral versus Unilateral Contracts Every contract involves at least two parties. The **offeror** is the party making the offer (promising to do or not to do something). The **offeree** is the party to whom the offer is made. A contract is classified as *bilateral* or *unilateral* depending on what the offeree must do to accept the offer and bind the offeror to a contract.

Bilateral Contracts. If the offeree can accept simply by promising to perform, the contract is a **bilateral contract.** Hence, a bilateral contract is a "promise for a promise." An example of a bilateral contract is a contract in which one person agrees to buy another person's automobile for a specified price. No performance, such as the payment of funds or delivery of goods, need take place for a bilateral contract to be formed. The contract comes into existence at the moment the promises are exchanged.

Example 10.2 Javier offers to buy Ann's smartphone for $200. Javier tells Ann that he will give her the cash for the phone on the following Friday, when he gets paid. Ann accepts Javier's offer and promises to give him the phone when he pays her on Friday. Javier and Ann have formed a bilateral contract.

Unilateral Contract A type of contract that results when an offer can be accepted only by the offeree's performance.

Unilateral Contracts. If the offer is phrased so that the offeree can accept only by completing the contract performance, the contract is a **unilateral contract.** Hence, a unilateral contract

Exhibit 10–1 **Classifications Based on Contract Formation**

CONTRACT FORMATION

Bilateral
A promise for a promise

Unilateral
A promise for an act

Formal
Requires a special form for creation

Informal
Requires no special form for creation

Express
Formed by words

Implied
Formed by the conduct of the parties

is a "promise for an act." In other words, the contract is formed not at the moment when promises are exchanged but rather when the contract is *performed*.

Example 10.3 Reese says to Kay, "If you drive my car from New York to Los Angeles, I'll give you $1,000." Only on Kay's completion of the act—bringing the car to Los Angeles—does she fully accept Reese's offer to pay $1,000. If she chooses not to accept the offer to drive the car to Los Angeles, there are no legal consequences. ■

Contests, lotteries, and other competitions offering prizes are also examples of offers for unilateral contracts. If a person complies with the rules of the contest—such as by submitting the right lottery number at the right place and time—a unilateral contract is formed. The organization offering the prize is then bound to a contract to perform as promised in the offer. If the person fails to comply with the contest rules, however, no binding contract is formed.

Ethical Issue

Does a "You break it, you buy it" sign create a unilateral contract? It is not unusual to see posted in retail stores signs that say, "You break it, you buy it." The implication, of course, is that you are legally obligated to buy something if you break it while inspecting it prior to a potential purchase. This "rule" is often known as the "Pottery Barn Rule," even though that retailer has no such rule.

Some argue that posted signs of this nature create unilateral contracts. It is difficult to prove the validity of such contracts, however. After all, for a contract to be formed, the accepting party has to demonstrate acceptance of the terms purposed. Few courts would uphold the notion that every customer agrees to every proposition posted on the walls of retail establishments. Moreover, where is the consideration? That is, what does the retailer give customers in return for their acceptance of a unilateral contract that says, "You break it, you buy it"?

Consider also that every customer in a retail establishment is an *invitee*. Consequently, the retailer accepts the risk that customers may accidentally damage items on display, regardless of posted warnings. Simply stating that once a customer reads a sign and chooses to continue shopping constitutes an acceptance is not only legally problematic, it is ethically bothersome. Merchants cannot transfer the risk of breakage to customers just by posting notices.

Revocation of Offers for Unilateral Contracts. A problem arises in unilateral contracts when the promisor attempts to *revoke* (cancel) the offer after the promisee has begun performance but before the act has been completed. **Example 10.4** Seiko offers to buy Jin's sailboat, moored in San Francisco, on delivery of the boat to Seiko's dock in Newport Beach, three hundred miles south of San Francisco. Jin rigs the boat and sets sail. Shortly before his arrival at Newport Beach, Jin receives a message from Seiko withdrawing her offer. Is the offer terminated?

In contract law, offers are normally *revocable* (capable of being taken back, or canceled) until accepted. Under the traditional view of unilateral contracts, Seiko's revocation would terminate the offer. Because Seiko's offer was to form a unilateral contract, only Jin's delivery of the sailboat at her dock would have been an acceptance. ■

Because of the harsh effect on the offeree of the revocation of an offer to form a unilateral contract, the modern-day view is different. Today, once performance has been *substantially* undertaken, the offeror cannot revoke the offer. In fact, as illustrated by the following case, the rule in some states is that as soon as the offeree begins performing, the offeror is precluded from revoking or modifying the offer.

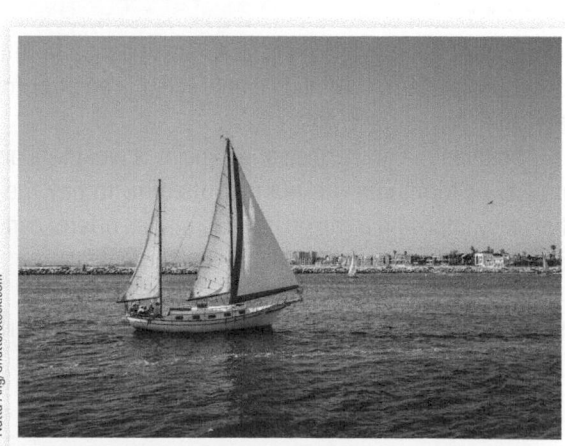

Can a party withdraw from an offer to buy a sailboat just before it is delivered to the agreed-upon location? Why or why not?

■ Case 10.2

Boswell v. Panera Bread Co.

United States Court of Appeals, Eighth Circuit, 879 F.3d 296 (2018).

Background and Facts To recruit and retain managers for its restaurants, Panera Bread Company created a program under which managers were eligible to receive a one-time bonus. A manager who signed an agreement to participate in the program would be paid the bonus five years later, provided he or she was still working for Panera at that time. The amount of the bonus depended on the profitability of the manager's restaurant. Later, a change in general business conditions led Panera to conclude that the bonuses would be too costly. The employer set a $100,000 cap on the amount.

Mark Boswell, and sixty-six other Panera managers, filed a suit in a federal district court, maintaining that by imposing the cap, the company had committed breach of contract. The court issued a summary judgment in favor of the managers. Panera appealed to the U.S. Court of Appeals for the Eighth Circuit.

In the Words of the Court
ARNOLD, Circuit Judge:

* * * *

The managers here were * * * at-will employees when they signed their respective agreements, and those documents expressly recognized that the managers would remain at-will employees during the five-year bonus period. * * * *Employment at-will can be characterized as a unilateral contract because there is an express or implied promise that the employer will pay if the employee works as directed.* [Emphasis added.]

* * * *

* * * An employer's promise to pay a bonus in return for an at-will employee's continued employment is an offer for a unilateral contract.

The question that arises at this point is whether Panera could modify or terminate the terms of its offer to pay the one-time bonus by imposing a cap on it. Generally, an offeror can withdraw an offer at any time before the offeree accepts it.

* * * The offeree of a unilateral-contract offer * * * to make the offer irrevocable * * * must merely begin performance.

* * * [Because] each of the managers * * * here had at least begun performing under the offer, we conclude that Panera could not modify the offer terms.

* * * *

Panera maintains, though, that no matter when a unilateral-contract offer becomes irrevocable as a general matter, in this specific instance Panera expressly reserved the power to revoke or modify its offer. It argues that it reserved that power by conditioning the payment of the bonus on the managers' continued employment, a matter that Panera controlled since the employment was at will.

* * * We do not think that the reservation of power here accomplishes the goal that Panera hopes. Keeping in mind that *the purpose of the rule precluding an offeror from modifying or terminating a unilateral-contract offer after the offeree begins performance is to protect the offeree in justifiable reliance on the offeror's promise,* the alleged reservation of power here adds nothing beyond what the at-will relationship already provides * * * . Panera could have terminated the managers if it chose and precluded them from receiving the bonus, but it did not. * * * [Because] the managers had begun performing the unilateral-contract offer, Panera was not entitled to move the goalposts on them by imposing a bonus cap, which was outside the contemplation of the unilateral-contract offer. [Emphasis added.]

Decision and Remedy The U.S. Court of Appeals for the Eighth Circuit affirmed the judgment of the lower court. Panera's promise to pay bonuses in return for the managers' continued employment was an offer for a unilateral contract.

Critical Thinking

• **Economic** *Could Panera have successfully argued that a drop in its revenue allowed it to impose the cap? Why or why not?*

• **Legal Environment** *Does the fact that the managers continued to work for Panera after it imposed the cap undercut their claim? Explain.*

Formal versus Informal Contracts Another classification system divides contracts into formal contracts and informal contracts. **Formal contracts** are contracts that require a special form or method of creation (formation) to be enforceable.[2] One example is *negotiable instruments*, which include checks, drafts, promissory notes, and certificates of deposit. Negotiable instruments are formal contracts because, under the Uniform Commercial Code, a special form and language are required to create them. *Letters of credit*, which are frequently used in international sales contracts, are another type of formal contract.

Informal contracts (also called *simple contracts*) include all other contracts. No special form is required (except for certain types of contracts that must be in writing or evidenced by an electronic record). The contracts are usually based on their substance rather than their form. Typically, though, businesspersons put their contracts in writing (including electronic records) to ensure that there is some proof of a contract's existence should problems arise.

Express versus Implied Contracts Contracts may also be categorized as express or implied. In an **express contract,** the terms of the agreement are fully and explicitly stated in words, oral or written. A signed lease for an apartment or a house is an express written contract. If a classmate accepts your offer to sell your textbooks from last semester for $200, an express oral contract has been made.

A contract that is implied from the conduct of the parties is called an **implied contract** (or sometimes an *implied-in-fact contract*). This type of contract differs from an express contract in that the *conduct* of the parties, rather than their words, creates and defines at least some of the terms of the contract. For an implied contract to arise, certain requirements must be met.

Requirements for Implied Contracts. Normally, if the following conditions exist, a court will hold that an implied contract was formed:

1. The plaintiff furnished some service or property.
2. The plaintiff expected to be paid for that service or property, and the defendant knew or should have known that payment was expected.
3. The defendant had a chance to reject the services or property and did not.

Example 10.5 Ryan, a small-business owner, needs an accountant to complete his tax return. He drops by a local accountant's office, explains his situation to the accountant, and learns what fees she charges. The next day, he returns and gives the receptionist all of the necessary documents to complete his tax return. Then he walks out without saying anything further. In this situation, Ryan has entered into an implied contract to pay the accountant the usual fees for her services. The contract is implied because of Ryan's conduct and hers. She expects to be paid for completing the tax return, and by bringing in the records she will need to do the job, Ryan has implied an intent to pay her. ▪

Mixed Contracts with Express and Implied Terms. Note that a contract can be a mixture of an express contract and an implied contract. In other words, a contract may contain some express terms, while others are implied. During the construction of a home, for instance, the homeowner often asks the builder to make changes in the original specifications.

Case Example 10.6 Lamar Hopkins hired Uhrhahn Construction & Design, Inc., for several projects in the construction of his home. For each project, the parties signed a written contract that was based on a cost estimate and specifications and that required changes to the agreement to be in writing. While the work was in progress, however, Hopkins repeatedly asked Uhrhahn to deviate from the contract specifications, which Uhrhahn did. None of these requests was made in writing.

One day, Hopkins asked Uhrhahn to use Durisol blocks instead of the cinder blocks specified in the original contract, indicating that the cost would be the same. Uhrhahn used the Durisol blocks but demanded extra payment when it became clear that the Durisol blocks

Formal Contract An agreement that by law requires a specific form for its validity.

Informal Contract A contract that does not require a specific form or method of creation to be valid.

Express Contract A contract in which the terms of the agreement are stated in words, oral or written.

Implied Contract A contract formed in whole or in part from the conduct of the parties.

Learning Objective 3
What is the difference between express and implied contracts?

---

2. See *Restatement (Second) of Contracts,* Section 6. Remember that *Restatements of the Law* are books that summarize court decisions on a particular topic and that courts often refer to for guidance.

Under what circumstances can an owner be liable for additional costs due to a request for a change in materials even though no written contract modification was created?

Executed Contract A contract that has been fully performed by both parties.

Executory Contract A contract that has not yet been fully performed.

Valid Contract A contract that results when the elements necessary for contract formation (agreement, consideration, capacity, and legality) are present.

were more complicated to install. Although Hopkins had paid for the other orally requested deviations from the contract, he refused to pay Uhrhahn for the substitution of the Durisol blocks. Uhrhahn sued for breach of contract. The court found that Hopkins, through his conduct, had waived the provision requiring written contract modification and created an implied contract to pay the extra cost of installing the Durisol blocks.[3]

10–3b Contract Performance

Contracts are also classified according to their state of performance. A contract that has been fully performed on both sides is called an **executed contract.** A contract that has not been fully performed by the parties is called an **executory contract.** If one party has fully performed but the other has not, the contract is said to be executed on the one side and executory on the other, but the contract is still classified as executory.

Example 10.7 Jackson, Inc., agreed to buy ten tons of coal from the Northern Coal Company. Northern has delivered the coal to Jackson's steel mill, but Jackson has not yet paid. At this point, the contract is executed on the part of Northern and executory on Jackson's part. After Jackson pays Northern, the contract will be executed on both sides. ■

10–3c Contract Enforceability

A **valid contract** has the four elements necessary to entitle at least one of the parties to enforce it in court. Those elements, as mentioned earlier, consist of (1) an agreement (offer and acceptance), (2) supported by legally sufficient consideration, (3) made by parties who have the legal capacity to enter into the contract, and (4) for a legal purpose.

As you can see in Exhibit 10–2, valid contracts may be enforceable, voidable, or unenforceable. Additionally, a contract may be referred to as a *void contract*. We look next at the meaning of the terms *voidable*, *unenforceable*, and *void* in relation to contract enforceability.

---

3. *Uhrhahn Construction & Design, Inc. v. Hopkins,* 179 P.3d 808 (Utah App. 2008).

Exhibit 10–2 Enforceable, Voidable, Unenforceable, and Void Contracts

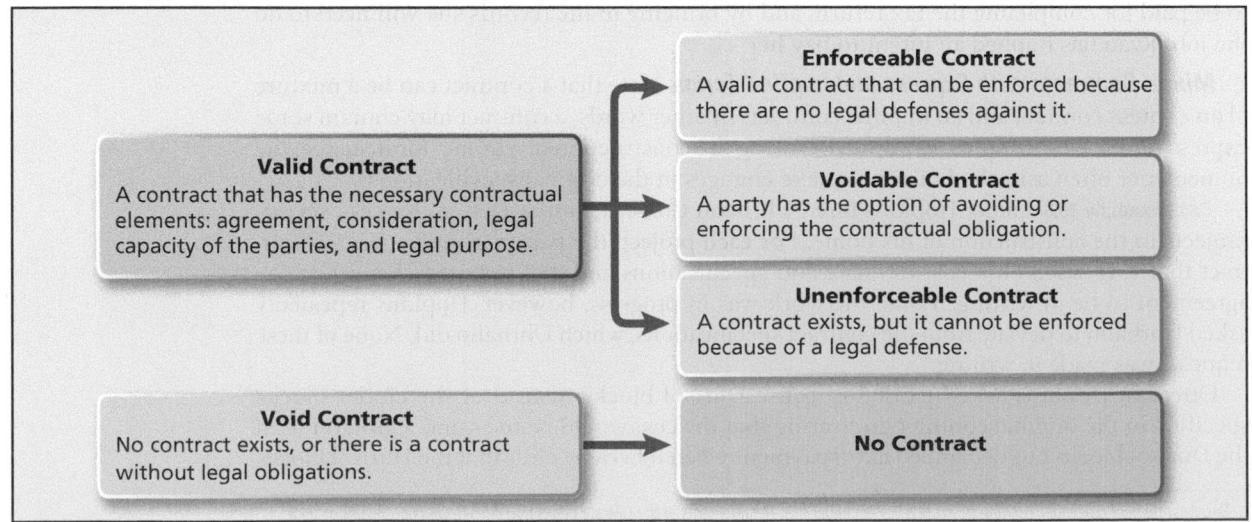

Valid Contract
A contract that has the necessary contractual elements: agreement, consideration, legal capacity of the parties, and legal purpose.

Enforceable Contract
A valid contract that can be enforced because there are no legal defenses against it.

Voidable Contract
A party has the option of avoiding or enforcing the contractual obligation.

Unenforceable Contract
A contract exists, but it cannot be enforced because of a legal defense.

Void Contract
No contract exists, or there is a contract without legal obligations.

No Contract

Voidable Contracts A **voidable contract** is a valid contract but one that can be avoided at the option of one or both of the parties. The party having the option can elect either to avoid any duty to perform or to *ratify* (make valid) the contract. If the contract is avoided, both parties are released from it. If it is ratified, both parties must fully perform their respective legal obligations.

For instance, contracts made by minors generally are voidable at the option of the minor (with certain exceptions). Contracts made by incompetent persons and intoxicated persons may also be voidable. Additionally, contracts entered into under fraudulent conditions are voidable at the option of the defrauded party. Contracts entered into under legally defined duress or undue influence are also voidable.

Unenforceable Contracts An **unenforceable contract** is one that cannot be enforced because of certain legal defenses against it. It is not unenforceable because a party failed to satisfy a legal requirement of the contract. Rather, it is a valid contract rendered unenforceable by some statute or law. For instance, some contracts must be in writing. If they are not, they will not be enforceable except in certain exceptional circumstances.

Void Contracts A **void contract** is no contract at all. The terms *void* and *contract* are contradictory. None of the parties has any legal obligations if a contract is void. A contract can be void because one of the parties was previously determined by a court to be mentally incompetent, for instance, or because the purpose of the contract was illegal.

10–4 Quasi Contracts

Express contracts and implied contracts are actual or true contracts formed by the words or actions of the parties. **Quasi contracts,** or contracts *implied in law*, are not actual contracts because they do not arise from any agreement, express or implied, between the parties themselves. Rather, they are fictional contracts that courts can impose on the parties "as if" the parties had entered into an actual contract. (The word *quasi* is Latin for "as if.")

Quasi contracts are equitable rather than legal contracts. Usually, they are imposed to avoid the *unjust enrichment* of one party at the expense of another. The doctrine of unjust enrichment is based on the theory that individuals should not be allowed to profit or enrich themselves inequitably at the expense of others. **Case Example 10.8** Seawest Services Association operated a water distribution system that served homes inside a housing development (full members) and some homes located outside the subdivision (limited members). Both full and limited members paid water bills and assessments for work performed on the water system when necessary.

The Copenhavers purchased a home outside the housing development. They did not have an express contract with Seawest, but they paid water bills for eight years and paid one $3,950 assessment for water system upgrades. After a dispute arose, the Copenhavers refused to pay their water bills and assessments. Seawest sued. The court found that the Copenhavers had a quasi contract with Seawest and were liable. The Copenhavers had enjoyed the benefits of Seawest's water services and even paid for them prior to their dispute. In addition, "the Copenhavers would be unjustly enriched if they could retain benefits provided by Seawest without paying for them."[4] For an example of when a court would most likely not impose a quasi contract, see this chapter's *Business Law Analysis* feature.

When the court imposes a quasi contract, a plaintiff may recover in *quantum meruit*,[5] a Latin phrase meaning "as much as he or she deserves." *Quantum meruit* essentially describes the extent of compensation owed under a quasi contract.

Voidable Contract A contract that may be legally avoided at the option of one or both of the parties.

Unenforceable Contract A valid contract rendered unenforceable by some statute or law.

Void Contract A contract having no legal force or binding effect.

Quasi Contract An obligation or contract imposed by law (a court), in the absence of an agreement, to prevent the unjust enrichment of one party.

Learning Objective 4
When will a court impose a quasi contract?

Quantum Meruit A Latin phrase meaning "as much as he or she deserves." The expression describes the extent of compensation owed under a quasi contract.

4. *Seawest Services Association v. Copenhaver,* 166 Wash.App. 1006 (2012).
5. Pronounced *kwahn*-tuhm *mehr*-oo-wit.

Deciding If a Court Would Impose a Quasi Contract

Robert Gutkowski, a sports marketing expert, met with George Steinbrenner, the owner of the New York Yankees, many times to discuss the Yankees Entertainment and Sports Network (YES). Gutkowski was paid as a consultant. Later, he filed a suit seeking an ownership share in YES under a quasi contract theory. There was no written contract for the share, but he claimed that there were discussions about his being a part owner. Does Gutkowski have a valid claim for payment?

Analysis: Quasi contracts are not actual contracts. They are obligations imposed by courts on parties in the interest of fairness and justice. Usually, courts impose a quasi contract to avoid the unjust enrichment of one party at the expense of another. In this situation, it is not clear that any party was unjustly enriched at the expense of another.

Result and Reasoning: Gutkowski does not have a valid claim for payment, nor should he recover on the basis of a quasi contract. Gutkowski was compensated as a consultant. To establish a claim that he is due more compensation based on unjust enrichment, he must have proof. As it is, he has only his claim that there were discussions about his being a part owner of YES. Discussions and negotiations are not a basis for recovery on a quasi contract. It is not clear that any party was unjustly enriched at the expense of Gutkowski. Therefore, a court is unlikely to allow him to recover under the theory of quasi contract.

10–4a Limitations on Quasi-Contractual Recovery

Although quasi contracts exist to prevent unjust enrichment, in some situations, the party who obtains a benefit is not liable for its fair value. Basically, a party who has conferred a benefit on someone else unnecessarily or as a result of misconduct or negligence cannot invoke the doctrine of quasi contract. The enrichment in those situations will not be considered "unjust."

Case Example 10.9 Michael Plambeck owned two chiropractic clinics in Kentucky that treated many patients injured in car accidents, including some who were customers of State Farm Automobile Insurance Company. All of the clinics' treating chiropractors were licensed to practice in Kentucky, but Plambeck (the owner) was not. Plambeck was a licensed chiropractor in another state but had allowed his Kentucky license to lapse because he was not treating any patients. Plambeck did not realize that Kentucky state law required him to be licensed as the owner of the clinics.

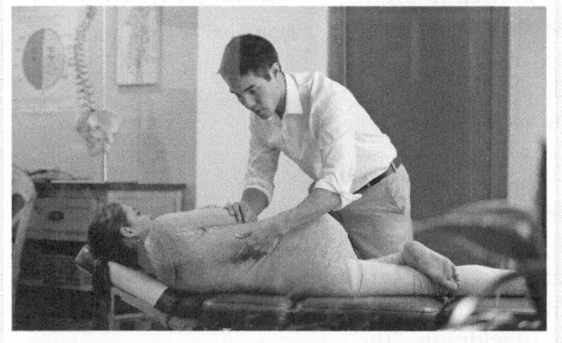

Is it unjust enrichment if a chiropractor, who is licensed in one state, receives payment from an insurance company for treatment given to clients living in another state?

When State Farm discovered that Plambeck was not licensed in Kentucky, it filed a suit against the clinics seeking to recover payments it had made on behalf of its customers. The trial court awarded State Farm $577,124 in damages for unjust enrichment, but the appellate court reversed. The court reasoned that State Farm had a legal duty to pay for the chiropractic treatment of its customers and could not avoid paying for the services because the clinics' owner was not licensed. The payments did not constitute unjust enrichment, because the patients had, in fact, received treatment by licensed chiropractors.[6]

10–4b When an Actual Contract Exists

The doctrine of quasi contract generally cannot be used when an actual contract covers the area in controversy. In this situation, a remedy already exists if a party is unjustly enriched because the other fails to perform. The nonbreaching party can sue the breaching party for breach of contract.

---

6. *State Farm Automobile Insurance Co. v. Newburg Chiropractic, P.S.C.*, 741 F.3d 661 (6th Cir. 2013).

Case Example 10.10 R & M Trucking-Intermodal, Inc., is a trucking company that provides transportation and warehousing services in the Chicago area. Richard Lombardi is a top executive at DRM Holdings, Inc., which, along with Dr. Miracle's, Inc., produces and distributes hair care products. Lombardi contracted with R & M to transport a large amount of inventory (773 pallets, or 20 full-size trailer loads) of hair relaxer kits for DRM. Lombardi then requested that R & M store the inventory until DRM could pick it up.

R & M agreed to store the goods for a weekly storage fee, but DRM never came to remove the pallets, despite repeated requests. DRM owed nearly $430,000 on the account, and payments were sporadic. Eventually, R & M filed a lawsuit, asserting a number of claims, including both breach of contract and quasi contract. Lombardi filed a motion to dismiss. The court held that R & M's quasi-contract claim must be dismissed under state law, because an express contract already existed that governed the parties' relationship.[7]

10–5 Interpretation of Contracts

Parties may sometimes agree that a contract has been formed but disagree on its meaning or legal effect. One reason that this may happen is the technical legal terminology traditionally used in contracts, sometimes referred to as *legalese*. Today, many contracts are written in "plain," nontechnical language. Even then, though, a dispute may arise over the meaning of a contract simply because the rights or obligations under the contract are not expressed clearly—no matter how "plain" the language used.

In this section, we look at some common law rules of contract interpretation. These rules provide the courts with guidelines for deciding disputes over how contract terms or provisions should be interpreted. Exhibit 10–3 provides a brief graphic summary of how these rules are applied.

10–5a Plain Language Laws

The federal government and a majority of the states have enacted *plain language laws* to regulate legal writing and eliminate legalese. All federal agencies are required to use plain language in most of their forms and written communications. Plain language requirements have been extended to agency rulemaking as well. States frequently have plain language laws that apply to consumer contracts—contracts made primarily for personal, family, or household purposes. The legal profession has also moved toward plain English, and court rules in many jurisdictions require attorneys to use plain language in court documents.

---

7. *R & M Trucking-Intermodal, Inc. v. Dr. Miracle's, Inc.,* ___ F.Supp.3d ___, 2017 WL 3034673 (N.D.Ill. 2017).

Exhibit 10–3 Rules of Contract Interpretation

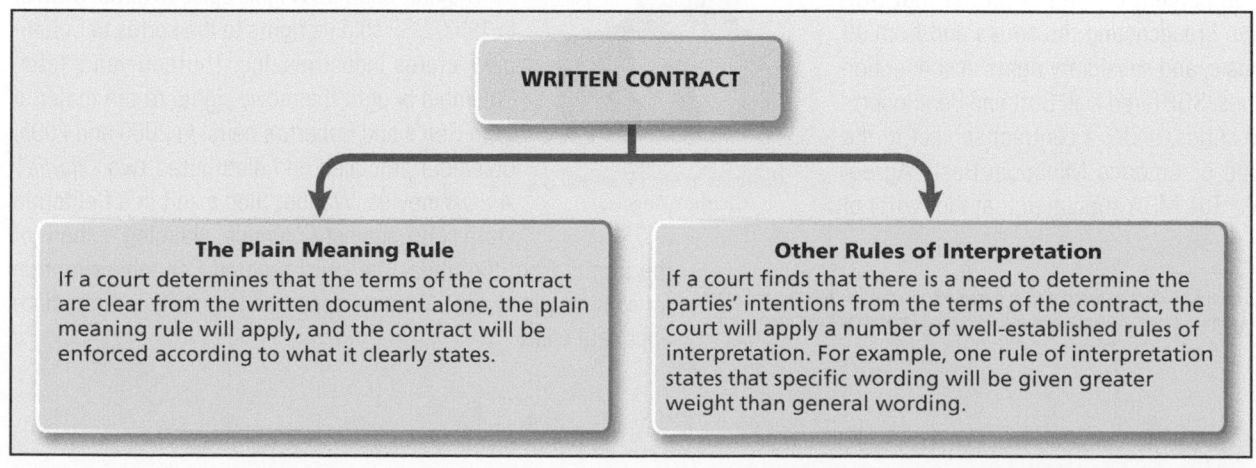

WRITTEN CONTRACT

The Plain Meaning Rule
If a court determines that the terms of the contract are clear from the written document alone, the plain meaning rule will apply, and the contract will be enforced according to what it clearly states.

Other Rules of Interpretation
If a court finds that there is a need to determine the parties' intentions from the terms of the contract, the court will apply a number of well-established rules of interpretation. For example, one rule of interpretation states that specific wording will be given greater weight than general wording.

Know This

No one can avoid contractual obligations by claiming that she or he did not read the contract. A contract normally is interpreted as if each party had read every word carefully.

10–5b The Plain Meaning Rule

When a contract's language is clear and unequivocal, a court will enforce it according to its obvious terms. The meaning of the terms must be determined from *the face of the instrument*—from the written document alone. This is sometimes referred to as the *plain meaning rule*. The words—and their plain, ordinary meanings—determine the intent of the parties at the time they entered into the contract. A court is bound to give effect to the contract according to this intent.

Ambiguity What if a contract's language is not clear and unequivocal? A court will consider a contract to be unclear, or ambiguous, in the following situations:

1. When the intent of the parties cannot be determined from its language.
2. When it lacks a provision on a disputed issue.
3. When a term is susceptible to more than one interpretation.
4. When there is uncertainty about a provision.

Extrinsic Evidence If a contract term is ambiguous, a court may interpret the ambiguity against the party who drafted the contract term, as discussed shortly. Sometimes, too, a court may consider **extrinsic evidence**—evidence not contained in the document itself—in interpreting ambiguous contract terms. Such evidence may include the testimony of the parties, additional agreements or communications, or other information relevant to determining the parties' intent.

Extrinsic Evidence Any evidence not contained in the contract itself, which may include the testimony of the parties, additional agreements or communications, or other information relevant to determining the parties' intent.

The admissibility of extrinsic evidence can significantly affect the court's interpretation of ambiguous contractual provisions and thus the outcome of litigation. But when the contract is clear and unambiguous, a court normally cannot consider evidence outside the contract. The following *Spotlight Case* illustrates these points.

Spotlight on Columbia Pictures: Case 10.3

Wagner v. Columbia Pictures Industries, Inc.

California Court of Appeal, Second District, 146 Cal.App.4th 586, 52 Cal.Rptr.3d 898 (2007).

Background and Facts Actor Robert Wagner entered into an agreement with Spelling-Goldberg Productions (SGP) "relating to *Charlie's Angels* (herein called the 'series')." The contract entitled Wagner to 50 percent of the net profits that SGP received from broadcasting the series and from all ancillary, music, and subsidiary rights in connection with the series. SGP hired Ivan Goff and Ben Roberts to write the series, under a contract subject to the Writers Guild of America Minimum Basic Agreement (MBA).[a] The MBA stipulated that the writer of

Actor Robert Wagner had the rights to the TV series, Charlie's Angels.

a television show retains the right to make and market films based on the material, subject to the producer's right to buy this right if the writer decides to sell it within five years.

The first *Charlie's Angels* episode aired in 1976. In 1982, SGP sold its rights to the series to Columbia Pictures Industries, Inc. Thirteen years later, Columbia bought the movie rights to the material from Goff's and Roberts's heirs. In 2000 and 2003, Columbia produced and distributed two *Charlie's Angels* movies. Wagner filed a suit in a California state court against Columbia, claiming a share of the profits from the films. The court granted Columbia's motion for summary judgment. Wagner appealed to a state intermediate appellate court.

---

a. The Writers Guild of America is an association of screen and television writers that negotiates industry-wide agreements with motion picture and television producers to cover the rights of its members.

In the Words of the Court
JOHNSON, Acting P.J. [Presiding Judge]
* * * *

Wagner contends the "subsidiary rights" provision in the agreement with SGP entitles him * * * to 50 percent of the net profits from the two "Charlie's Angels" films.
* * * *

Wagner introduced evidence of the history of the negotiations underlying the "Charlie's Angels" contract in support of his [contention].

This history begins with a contract the Wagners [Robert and his wife, Natalie Wood] entered into with SGP to star in a television movie-of-the-week, "Love Song." As compensation for Wagner and Wood acting in "Love Song," SGP agreed to pay them a fixed amount plus one-half the net profits * * * .
* * * *

In the * * * "Love Song" contract net profits were not limited to monies received "for the right to exhibit the Photoplay." Instead they were defined as the net of "all monies received by Producer as consideration for the right to exhibit the Photoplay, and exploitation of all ancillary, music and subsidiary rights in connection therewith."
* * * *

Wagner's argument is simple and straightforward. The net profits provision in the "Love Song" agreement was intended to give the Wagners a one-half share in the net profits received by SGP "from all sources" without limitation as to source or time. * * * The "Charlie's Angels" agreement was based on the "Love Song" agreement and defines net profits in identical language. Therefore, the "Charlie's Angels" agreement should also be interpreted as providing the Wagners with a 50 percent share in SGP's income "from all sources" without limitation as to source or time. Since Columbia admits it stands in SGP's shoes with respect to SGP's obligations under the "Charlie's Angels" agreement, Columbia is obligated to pay Wagner * * * 50 percent of the net profits derived from the "Charlie's Angels" movies.
* * * *

The problem with Wagner's extrinsic evidence is that it does not explain the ["Charlie's Angels"] contract language, it contradicts it. *Under the parol evidence rule,[b] extrinsic evidence is not admissible to contradict express terms in a written contract or to explain what the agreement was. The agreement is the writing itself. Parol evidence cannot be admitted to show intention independent of an unambiguous written instrument.* [Emphasis added.]

Even if the Wagners and SGP intended the Wagners would share in the net profits "from any and all sources" they did not say so in their contract. What they said in their contract was the Wagners would share in "all monies actually received by Producer, as consideration for the right to exhibit photoplays of the series, and from the exploitation of all ancillary, music and subsidiary rights in connection therewith." For a right to be "subsidiary" or "ancillary," meaning supplementary or subordinate, there must be a primary right to which it relates. The only primary right mentioned in the contract is "the right to exhibit photoplays of the series."

Thus the Wagners were entitled to share in the profits from the exploitation of the movie rights to "Charlie's Angels" if those rights were exploited by Columbia as ancillary or subsidiary rights of its primary "right to exhibit photoplays of the series" but not if those rights were acquired by Columbia independently from its right to exhibit photoplays.

Decision and Remedy The state intermediate appellate court affirmed the lower court's summary judgment in favor of Columbia. The contract "unambiguously" stated the conditions under which the parties were to share the films' profits, and those conditions had not occurred.

Critical Thinking

• **Legal Environment** *How might the result in this case have been different if the court had allowed Wagner's extrinsic evidence of the prior contract regarding* Love Song *to be used as evidence in this dispute?*

b. The parol evidence rule prohibits the parties from introducing in court evidence of an oral agreement that contradicts the written terms of a contract.

10–5c Other Rules of Interpretation

Generally, as mentioned, a court will interpret contract language to give effect to the parties' intent *as expressed in the contract*. This is the primary purpose of the rules of interpretation—to determine the parties' intent from the language used in their agreement and to give effect to that intent. A court normally will not make or remake a contract, nor will it normally interpret the language according to what the parties *claim* their intent was when they made the contract.

Rules the Courts Use The courts use the following rules in interpreting contractual terms:

1. Insofar as possible, a reasonable, lawful, and effective meaning will be given to all of a contract's terms.

2. A contract will be interpreted as a whole. Individual, specific clauses will be considered subordinate to the contract's general intent. All writings that are a part of the same transaction will be interpreted together.

3. Terms that were the subject of separate negotiation will be given greater consideration than standardized terms and terms that were not negotiated separately.

4. A word will be given its ordinary, commonly accepted meaning, and a technical word or term will be given its technical meaning, unless the parties clearly intended something else.

5. Specific and exact wording will be given greater consideration than general language.

6. Written or typewritten terms prevail over preprinted terms.

7. Because a contract should be drafted in clear and unambiguous language, a party that uses ambiguous expressions is held to be responsible for the ambiguities. Thus, when the language has more than one meaning, it will be interpreted *against* the party that drafted the contract.

8. Evidence of *trade usage*, *prior dealing*, and *course of performance* may be admitted to clarify the meaning of an ambiguously worded contract. (We will define and discuss these terms in the chapter on sales and lease contracts.)

Express Terms Usually Given Most Weight In situations in which trade usage, prior dealing, and course of performance come into play, the courts observe certain priorities in interpreting contracts. Express terms (terms expressly stated in the contract) are given the greatest weight, followed by course of performance, course of dealing, and custom and usage of trade—in that order. When considering custom and usage, a court will look at the trade customs and usage common to the particular business or industry and to the locale in which the contract was made or is to be performed.

Case Example 10.11 When Elizabeth Eberbach and Christopher Eberbach got divorced, they entered into a marital dissolution agreement. The contract specified that if either party had to go back to court to enforce the provisions of their agreement, the prevailing party would be entitled to attorneys' fees.

Three years after the divorce was final, the parties ended up in court in a dispute over provisions in the agreement concerning parenting time, parental relocation, and medical expenses. Elizabeth won, and the trial court awarded her attorneys' fees. Christopher appealed, and the appellate court affirmed the trial court's decision but then denied Elizabeth the additional attorneys' fees she incurred in the appeal. Elizabeth appealed to the Supreme Court of Tennessee, which held that a marital dissolution agreement should be treated like a contract. Under the express terms of the parties' agreement, Elizabeth was the prevailing party and was therefore entitled to attorneys' fees.[8]

> "The difference between the almost right word and the right word is really a large matter—'tis the difference between the lightning-bug and the lightning."
>
> **Mark Twain**
> 1835–1910
> (American author and humorist)

---

8. *Eberbach v. Eberbach*, 535 S.W.3d 467 (Tenn. 2017).

Practice and Review

Mitsui Bank hired Ross Duncan as a branch manager in one of its Southern California locations. At that time, Duncan received an employee handbook informing him that Mitsui would review his performance and salary level annually. In 2018, Mitsui decided to create a new lending program to help financially troubled businesses stay afloat. It promoted Duncan to be the credit development officer (CDO) and gave him a written compensation plan. Duncan's compensation was to be based on the new program's success and involved a bonus and commissions based on new loans and sales volume. The written plan also stated, "This compensation plan will be reviewed and potentially amended after one year and will be subject to such review and amendment annually thereafter."

Duncan's efforts as CDO were successful, and the business-lending program he developed grew to represent 25 percent of Mitsui's business in 2019 and 40 percent by 2020. Nevertheless, Mitsui refused to give Duncan a raise in 2019. Mitsui also amended Duncan's compensation plan to significantly reduce his compensation and to change his performance evaluation schedule to every six months. When he had still not received a raise by 2020, Duncan resigned as CDO and filed a lawsuit claiming breach of contract. Using the information presented in the chapter, answer the following questions.

1. What are the four requirements of a valid contract?

2. Did Duncan have a valid contract with Mitsui for employment as credit development officer? If so, was it a bilateral or a unilateral contract?

3. What are the requirements of an implied contract?

4. Can Duncan establish an implied contract based on the employment manual or the written compensation plan? Why or why not?

Debate This
Companies should be able to make or break employment contracts whenever and however they wish.

Key Terms

Chapter Summary: Nature and Classification

An Overview of Contract Law	1. *Sources of contract law*—The common law governs all contracts except when it has been modified or replaced by statutory law, such as the Uniform Commercial Code (UCC), or by administrative agency regulations. The UCC governs contracts for the sale and lease of goods. 2. *The function of contracts*—Contract law establishes what kinds of promises will be legally binding and supplies procedures for enforcing legally binding promises, or agreements. 3. *The definition of a contract*—A contract is an agreement that can be enforced in court. It is formed by two or more parties who agree to perform or to refrain from performing some act now or in the future. Each party has a legal duty to the other and the right to seek a remedy for breach of the promise or duty. 4. *The objective theory of contracts*—In contract law, intent is determined by objective facts, not by the personal or subjective intent or belief of a party.
Elements of a Contract	1. *Requirements of a valid contract*—The four requirements of a valid contract are agreement, consideration, contractual capacity, and legality. 2. *Defenses to the enforceability of a contract*—Even if the four requirements of a valid contract are met, a contract may be unenforceable if it lacks voluntary consent or is not in the required form.
Types of Contracts	1. *Bilateral*—A promise for a promise. 2. *Unilateral*—A promise for an act (acceptance is the completed or substantial performance of the contract by the offeree). 3. *Formal*—Requires a special form for contract formation. 4. *Informal*—Requires no special form for contract formation. 5. *Express*—Formed by words (oral or written). 6. *Implied*—Formed at least in part by the conduct of the parties. 7. *Executed*—A fully performed contract. 8. *Executory*—A contract not yet fully performed. 9. *Valid*—A contract that has the four necessary contractual elements of agreement, consideration, capacity, and legality. 10. *Voidable*—A contract in which a party has the option of avoiding or ratifying the contractual obligation. 11. *Unenforceable*—A valid contract that cannot be enforced because of some statute or law. 12. *Void*—No contract exists.
Quasi Contracts	A quasi contract, or a contract implied in law, is a fictional contract that is imposed by a court to prevent unjust enrichment of one party at the expense of another.
Interpretation of Contracts	Increasingly, plain language laws require contracts to be written in nontechnical language so that the terms are clear and understandable to the parties. Under the plain meaning rule, a court will enforce the contract according to its obvious terms, the meaning of which must be determined from the written document alone. Other rules applied by the courts when interpreting contracts include giving greater consideration to specific wording and holding a party that uses vague terms responsible for the ambiguities.

Issue Spotters

1. Kerin sends a letter to Joli telling her that he has a book to sell at a certain price. Joli signs and returns the letter. When Kerin delivers the book, Joli sends it back, claiming that they do not have a contract. Kerin claims they do. What standard determines whether these parties have a contract? (See *An Overview of Contract Law*.)

2. Dyna tells Ed that she will pay him $1,000 to set fire to her store so that she can collect under a fire insurance policy. Ed sets fire to the store, but Dyna refuses to pay. Can Ed recover? Why or why not? (See *Types of Contracts*.)

   —**Check your answers to the *Issue Spotters* against the answers provided in Appendix D at the end of this text.**

Business Scenarios and Case Problems

10–1. Unilateral Contract. Rocky Mountain Races, Inc., sponsors the "Pioneer Trail Ultramarathon," with an advertised first prize of $10,000. The rules require the competitors to run one hundred miles from the floor of Blackwater Canyon to the top of Pinnacle Mountain. The rules also provide that Rocky reserves the right to change the terms of the race at any time. Monica enters the race and is declared the winner. Rocky offers her a prize of $1,000 instead of $10,000. Did Rocky and Monica have a contract? Explain. (See *Types of Contracts*.)

10–2. Implied Contract. Janine was hospitalized with severe abdominal pain and placed in an intensive care unit. Her doctor told hospital personnel to order around-the-clock nursing care for Janine. At the hospital's request, a nursing services firm, Nursing Services Unlimited, provided two weeks of in-hospital care and, after Janine was sent home, two additional weeks of at-home care. During the at-home period of care, Janine was fully aware that she was receiving the benefit of the nursing services. Nursing Services later billed Janine $4,000 for the nursing care, but Janine refused to pay on the ground that she had never contracted for the services, either orally or in writing. In view of the fact that no express contract was ever formed, can Nursing Services recover the $4,000 from Janine? If so, under what legal theory? Discuss. (See *Types of Contracts*.)

10–3. Contract Classification. For employment with the Firestorm Smokejumpers—a crew of elite paratroopers who parachute into dangerous situations to fight fires—applicants must complete a series of tests. The crew chief sends the most qualified applicants a letter stating that they will be admitted to Firestorm's training sessions if they pass a medical exam. Jake Kurzyniec receives the letter and passes the exam, but a new crew chief changes the selection process and rejects him. Is there a contract between Kurzyniec and Firestorm? If there is a contract, what type of contract is it? (See *Types of Contracts*.)

10–4. Spotlight on Taco Bell—Implied Contract. Thomas Rinks and Joseph Shields developed Psycho Chihuahua, a caricature of a Chihuahua dog with a "do-not-back-down" attitude. They promoted and marketed the character through their company, Wrench, LLC. Ed Alfaro and Rudy Pollak, representatives of Taco Bell Corp., learned of Psycho Chihuahua and met with Rinks and Shields to talk about using the character as a Taco Bell "icon." Wrench sent artwork, merchandise, and marketing ideas to Alfaro, who promoted the character within Taco Bell. Alfaro asked Wrench to propose terms for Taco Bell's use of Psycho Chihuahua. Taco Bell did not accept Wrench's terms, but Alfaro continued to promote the character within the company.

Meanwhile, Taco Bell hired a new advertising agency, which proposed an advertising campaign involving a Chihuahua. When Alfaro learned of this proposal, he sent the Psycho Chihuahua materials to the agency. Taco Bell made a Chihuahua the focus of its marketing but paid nothing to Wrench. Wrench filed a suit against Taco Bell in a federal court claiming that it had an implied contract with Taco Bell and that Taco Bell breached that contract. Do these facts satisfy the requirements for an implied contract? Why or why not? [*Wrench, LLC. v. Taco Bell Corp.*, 256 F.3d 446 (6th Cir. 2001), *cert.* denied, 534 U.S. 1114, 122 S.Ct. 921, 151 L.Ed.2d 805 (2002)] (See *Types of Contracts*.)

10–5. Business Case Problem with Sample Answer— Implied Contracts. Ralph Ramsey insured his car with Allstate Insurance Co. He also owned a house on which he maintained a homeowner's insurance policy with Allstate. Bank of America had a mortgage on the house and paid the insurance premiums on the homeowner's policy from Ralph's account. After Ralph died, Allstate canceled the car insurance. Ralph's son Douglas inherited the house. The bank continued to pay the premiums on the homeowner's policy, but from Douglas's account, and Allstate continued to renew the insurance. When a fire destroyed the house, Allstate denied coverage, however, claiming that the policy was still in Ralph's name. Douglas filed a suit in a federal district court against the insurer. Was Allstate liable under the homeowner's policy? Explain. [*Ramsey v. Allstate Insurance Co.*, 514 Fed.Appx. 554 (6th Cir. 2013)] (See *Types of Contracts*.)

—For a sample answer to Problem 10–5, go to Appendix E at the end of this text.

10–6. Quasi Contracts. Lawrence M. Clarke, Inc., was the general contractor for construction of a portion of a sanitary sewer system in Billings, Michigan. Clarke accepted Kim Draeger's proposal to do the work for a certain price. Draeger arranged with two subcontractors to work on the project. The work provided by Draeger and the subcontractors proved unsatisfactory. All of the work fell under Draeger's contract with Clarke. Clarke filed a suit in a Michigan state court against Draeger, seeking to recover damages on a theory of quasi contract. The court awarded Clarke $900,000 in damages on that theory. A state intermediate appellate court reversed this award. Why? [*Lawrence M. Clarke, Inc. v. Draeger*, 2015 WL 205182 (Mich. App. 2015)] (See *Quasi Contracts*.)

10–7. Interpretation of Contracts. Lehman Brothers, Inc. (LBI), wrote a letter to Mary Ortegón offering her employment as LBI's "Business Chief Administrative Officer in Its Fixed Income Division." The offer included a salary of $150,000 per year and an annual "minimum bonus" of $350,000. The letter stated that the bonus would be paid unless Ortegón resigned or was terminated for certain causes. In other words, the bonus was not a "signing" bonus—it was clearly tied to her performance on the job. Ortegón accepted the offer. Before she started work, however, LBI rescinded it. Later, LBI filed for bankruptcy in a federal court. Ortegón filed a claim with the court for the amount of the bonus on the ground that LBI had breached its contract with her by not paying it. Can extrinsic evidence be admitted to interpret the meaning of the bonus term? Explain. [*Ortegón v. Giddens*, 638 Fed.Appx. 47 (2d Cir. 2016)] (See *Interpretation of Contracts*.)

10–8. Quasi Contracts. In New Jersey, a patient admitted to a medical care facility through the regular admissions process is responsible for applying to the state for assistance in paying the bill. In contrast, a patient admitted on an emergency basis is not responsible for applying to the state—the facility is. Of course, to obtain assistance, the patient must be indigent. D.B., a diagnosed schizophrenic, experienced a psychotic episode. The Warren County, New Jersey, psychiatric emergency screening service determined that he was a danger to himself and others. He was involuntarily committed to Newton Medical Center, a mental health-care facility. Newton did not apply to the state for financial assistance for D.B.'s treatment. Instead, Newton billed the patient $6,745.50. D.B., who was indigent, did not pay. Can Newton recover the amount of the unpaid bill from D.B. on a theory of quasi contract? Discuss. [*Newton Medical Center v. D.B.*, 452 N.J.Super. 615, 178 A.3d 1281 (App.Div. 2018)] (See *Quasi Contracts*.)

10–9. A Question of Ethics—The IDDR Approach and Contract Requirements. *Mark Carpenter, a certified financial planner, contracted to recruit investors for GetMoni.com, which owned a defunct gold mine in Arizona. Carpenter then contracted with clients to invest their funds, sending more than $2 million to GetMoni.com. Only about 20 percent of the money went to developing the mine. The rest was used to run a Ponzi scheme. Carpenter collected another $1 million, but instead of sending it to GetMoni.com, he deposited it into his own account. A federal investigation unraveled the scheme. Carpenter was charged with two counts of fraud— one for his deal with GetMoni.com and one for his misrepresentations to clients after he stopped dealing with GetMoni.com. [United States v. Carpenter, 676 Fed.Appx. 397 (6th Cir. 2017)] (See An Overview of Contract Law.)*

1. Which elements do Carpenter's contracts lack, preventing them from being enforced? Can he argue successfully that he acted ethically? Discuss.

2. Using the IDDR approach, discuss whether a certified financial planner has an ethical obligation to contract in the best interests of his or her clients.

Critical Thinking and Writing Assignments

10–10. Time-Limited Group Assignment—Contracts. Review the basic requirements for a valid contract listed at the beginning of this chapter. Now consider the relationship entered into when a student enrolls in a college or university. (See *Elements of a Contract*.)

1. One group should analyze and discuss whether a contract has been formed between the student and the college or university.

2. A second group should assume that there is a contract and explain whether it is bilateral or unilateral.

3. The third group will consider the documents that each of you signed when enrolling in college. Did you read and understand the provisions? Would the plain meaning rule apply even if you did not understand some parts?

Agreement

"It is necessity that makes laws."

Voltaire
1694–1778
(French intellectual and writer)

Voltaire's statement that it is "necessity that makes laws" is particularly true in regard to contracts. Contract law developed over time to meet society's need to know with certainty what kinds of promises, or contracts, will be enforced and the point at which a valid and binding contract is formed. For a contract to be considered valid and enforceable, four basic requirements—agreement, consideration, contractual capacity, and legality—must be met.

In this chapter, we look closely at the first of these requirements, **agreement**. The parties must agree on the terms of the contract and manifest to each other their *mutual assent* (agreement) to the same bargain. Ordinarily, agreement is evidenced by two events: an *offer* and an *acceptance*. One party offers a certain bargain to another party, who then accepts that bargain. An agreement does not necessarily have to be in writing. Both parties, however, must manifest their assent, or voluntary consent, to the same bargain.

Agreement is required to form a contract, whether it is formed in the traditional way (on paper) or online. In today's world, numerous contracts are formed via the Internet. When someone enters an online agreement with a cellphone company to purchase a smartphone and data plan, for instance, she or he has entered into an electronic contract, or e-contract.

11–1 Offer

An **offer** is a promise or commitment to perform or refrain from performing some specified act in the future. The party making an offer is called the *offeror*, and the party to whom the offer is made is called the *offeree*.

Learning Objectives

The four Learning Objectives *below are designed to help improve your understanding. After reading this chapter, you should be able to answer the following questions:*

1. What three elements are necessary for an effective offer?
2. What are the elements that are necessary for an effective acceptance?
3. How do click-on and shrink-wrap agreements differ?
4. What is the primary purpose of the Uniform Electronic Transactions Act?

Agreement A mutual understanding or meeting of the minds between two or more individuals regarding the terms of a contract.

Offer A promise or commitment to perform or refrain from performing some specified act in the future.

Three elements are necessary for an offer to be effective:

1. There must be a serious, objective intention by the offeror.
2. The terms of the offer must be reasonably certain, or definite, so that the parties and the court can ascertain the terms of the contract.
3. The offer must be communicated to the offeree.

Once an effective offer has been made, the offeree's acceptance of that offer creates a legally binding contract (providing the other essential elements for a valid and enforceable contract are present).

11–1a Intention of the Offer

The first requirement for an effective offer is serious, objective intent on the part of the offeror. Intent is not determined by the *subjective* intentions, beliefs, or assumptions of the offeror. Rather, it is determined by what a reasonable person in the offeree's position would conclude that the offeror's words and actions meant. Offers made in obvious anger, jest, or undue excitement do not meet the requirement of serious, objective intent. Because these offers are not effective, an offeree's acceptance does not create an agreement.

Example 11.1 You ride to school each day with Spencer in his new automobile, which has a market value of $25,000. One cold morning, the car will not start. Spencer yells in anger, "I'll sell this car to anyone for $500!" You drop $500 in his lap. A reasonable person—taking into consideration Spencer's frustration and the obvious difference in value between the car's market price and the purchase price—would realize that Spencer's offer was not made with serious and objective intent. Therefore, no agreement is formed. ■

In the *Classic Case* presented next, the court considered whether an offer made "after a few drinks" met the serious-intent requirement.

Classic Case 11.1

Lucy v. Zehmer
Supreme Court of Appeals of Virginia, 196 Va. 493, 84 S.E.2d 516 (1954).

Background and Facts W. O. Lucy and A. H. Zehmer had known each other for fifteen to twenty years. For some time, Lucy had wanted to buy Zehmer's farm, but Zehmer had always said that he was not interested in selling. One night, Lucy stopped in to visit with the Zehmers at a restaurant they operated. Lucy said to Zehmer, "I bet you wouldn't take $50,000 for that place." Zehmer replied, "Yes, I would, too; you wouldn't give fifty." Throughout the evening, the conversation returned to the sale of the farm. All the while, the parties were drinking whiskey.

Can an intoxicated person's offer to sell his farm for a specific price meet the serious-intent requirement?

Eventually, Zehmer wrote up an agreement on the back of a restaurant check for the sale of the farm, and he asked his wife, Ida, to sign it—which she did. When Lucy brought an action in a Virginia state court to enforce the agreement, Zehmer argued that he had been "high as a Georgia pine" at the time and that the offer had been made in jest: "two doggoned drunks bluffing to see who could talk the biggest and say the most." Lucy claimed that he had not been intoxicated and did not think Zehmer had been, either, given the way Zehmer handled the transaction. The trial court ruled in favor of the Zehmers, and Lucy appealed.

In the Words of the Court

BUCHANAN, J. [Justice] delivered the opinion of the court.

* * * *

In his testimony, Zehmer claimed that he "was high as a Georgia pine," and that the transaction "was just a bunch of two doggoned drunks bluffing to see who could talk the biggest and say the most." That claim is inconsistent with his attempt to testify in great detail as to what was said and what was done.

* * * *

The appearance of the contract, the fact that it was under discussion for forty minutes or more before it was signed; Lucy's objection to the first draft because it was written in the singular, and he wanted Mrs. [Ida] Zehmer to sign it also; the rewriting to meet that objection and the signing by Mrs. Zehmer; the discussion of what was to be included in the sale, the provision for the examination of the title, the completeness of the instrument that was executed, the taking possession of it by Lucy with no request or suggestion by either of the defendants that he give it back, are facts which furnish persuasive evidence that the execution of the contract was a serious business transaction rather than a casual, jesting matter as defendants now contend.

* * * *

In the field of contracts, as generally elsewhere, *we must look to the outward expression of a person as manifesting his intention rather than to his secret and unexpressed intention.* The law imputes to a person an intention corresponding to the reasonable meaning of his words and acts. [Emphasis added.]

* * * *

Whether the writing signed by the defendants and now sought to be enforced by the complainants was the result of a serious offer by Lucy and a serious acceptance by the defendants, or was a serious offer by Lucy and an acceptance in secret jest by the defendants, in either event it constituted a binding contract of sale between the parties.

Decision and Remedy The Supreme Court of Appeals of Virginia determined that the writing was an enforceable contract and reversed the ruling of the lower court. The Zehmers were required by court order to follow through with the sale of the Ferguson Farm to Lucy.

Critical Thinking

• **What If the Facts Were Different?** *Suppose that after Lucy signed the agreement, he decided he did not want the farm after all, and that Zehmer sued Lucy to perform the contract. Would this change in the facts alter the court's decision that Lucy and Zehmer had created an enforceable contract? Why or why not?*

• **Impact of This Case on Today's Law** *This is a classic case in contract law because it so clearly illustrates the objective theory of contracts with respect to determining whether an offer was intended. Today, the courts continue to apply the objective theory of contracts and routinely cite the* Lucy v. Zehmer *decision as a significant precedent in this area.*

When Intent May Be Lacking The concept of intention can be further clarified by looking at statements that are *not* offers and situations in which the parties' intent to be bound might be questionable.

1. *Expressions of opinion.* An expression of opinion is not an offer. It does not indicate an intention to enter into a binding agreement.

2. *Statements of future intent.* A statement of an intention to do something in the future (such as "I plan to sell my Verizon stock") is not an offer.

3. *Preliminary negotiations.* A request or invitation to negotiate is not an offer. It only expresses a willingness to discuss the possibility of entering into a contract. Statements such as "Will you sell your farm?" or "I wouldn't sell my car for less than $8,000" are examples.

4. *Invitations to bid.* When a government entity or private firm needs to have construction work done, contractors are invited to submit bids. The invitation to submit bids is not an offer. The bids that contractors submit are offers, however, and the government entity or private firm can bind the contractor by accepting the bid.

Know This
An opinion is not an offer and not a contract term. Goods or services can be "perfect" in one party's opinion and "poor" in another's.

5. *Advertisements and price lists*. In general, representations made in advertisements and price lists are treated not as offers to contract but as invitations to negotiate.[1] Only rarely are such materials construed as offers. On some occasions, courts have considered advertisements to be offers because they contained definite terms that invited acceptance. (An example is an ad offering a reward for a lost dog.)

6. *Live and online auctions*. In a live auction, a seller "offers" goods for sale through an auctioneer, but this is not an offer to form a contract. Rather, it is an invitation asking bidders to submit offers. In the context of an auction, a bidder is the offeror, and the auctioneer is the offeree. The offer is accepted when the auctioneer strikes the hammer.

    The most familiar type of auction today takes place online through websites like eBay and eBid. "Offers" to sell an item on these sites generally are treated as invitations to negotiate. Unlike live auctions, online auctions are automated. Buyers can enter incremental bids on an item (without approving each price increase) up to a specified amount or without a limit.

Agreements to Agree Traditionally, agreements to agree—that is, agreements to agree to the material terms of a contract at some future date—were not considered to be binding contracts. The modern view, however, is that agreements to agree may be enforceable agreements (contracts) if it is clear that the parties intended to be bound by the agreements. In other words, under the modern view the emphasis is on the parties' intent rather than on form.

✦ **Spotlight Case Example 11.2** After a person was injured and nearly drowned on a water ride at one of its amusement parks, Six Flags, Inc., filed a lawsuit against the manufacturer that had designed the ride. The manufacturer claimed that the parties did not have a binding contract but had only engaged in preliminary negotiations that were never formalized in a construction contract.

How did intention affect the outcome of a lawsuit between Six Flags and the manufacturer of a water ride?

The court, however, held that the evidence was sufficient to show an intent to be bound. The evidence included a faxed document specifying the details of the water ride, along with the parties' subsequent actions (having begun construction and written notes on the faxed document). The manufacturer was required to provide insurance for the water ride at Six Flags. In addition, its insurer was required to defend Six Flags in the personal-injury lawsuit that arose from the incident.[2] ▇

Preliminary Agreements Increasingly, the courts are holding that a preliminary agreement constitutes a binding contract if the parties have agreed on all essential terms and no disputed issues remain to be resolved. In contrast, if the parties agree on certain major terms but leave other terms open for further negotiation, a preliminary agreement is binding only in the sense that the parties have committed themselves to negotiate the undecided terms in good faith in an effort to reach a final agreement.

In the following *Spotlight Case*, a dispute arose over an agreement to settle a case during the trial. One party claimed that the agreement, which was formed via e-mail, was binding. The other party claimed that the e-mail exchange was merely an agreement to work out the terms of a settlement in the future. Can an exchange of e-mails create a complete and unambiguous agreement?

---

1. *Restatement (Second) of Contracts*, Section 26, Comment b.
2. *Six Flags, Inc. v. Steadfast Insurance Co.*, 474 F.Supp.2d 201 (D.Mass. 2007).

Spotlight on Amazon.com: Case 11.2

Basis Technology Corp. v. Amazon.com, Inc.

Appeals Court of Massachusetts, 71 Mass.App.Ct. 29, 878 N.E.2d 952 (2008).

Background and Facts Basis Technology Corporation created software and provided technical services for a Japanese-language website operated by Amazon.com, Inc. The agreement between the two companies allowed for separately negotiated contracts for additional services that Basis might provide to Amazon. Later, Basis sued Amazon for various claims, including failure to pay for services not included in the original agreement.

During the trial, the two parties appeared to reach an agreement to settle out of court via a series of e-mail exchanges outlining the settlement. When Amazon reneged, Basis served a motion to enforce the proposed settlement. The trial judge entered a judgment against Amazon, which appealed.

In the Words of the Court

SIKORA, J. [Judge]

* * * *

* * * On the evening of March 23, after the third day of evidence and after settlement discussions, Basis counsel sent an e-mail with the following text to Amazon counsel:

[Amazon counsel]—This e-mail confirms the essential business terms of the settlement between our respective clients * * *. Basis and Amazon agree that they promptly will take all reasonable steps to memorialize in a written agreement, to be signed by individuals authorized by each party, the terms set forth below, as well as such other terms that are reasonably necessary to make these terms effective.

* * * *

[Amazon counsel], please contact me first thing tomorrow morning if this e-mail does not accurately summarize the settlement terms reached earlier this evening. See you tomorrow morning when we report this matter settled to the Court.

At 7:26 A.M. on March 24, Amazon counsel sent an e-mail with a one-word reply: "correct." Later in the morning, in open court

Can Amazon.com, Inc., be held to an agreement arrived at via e-mail exchanges?

and on the record, both counsel reported the result of a settlement without specification of the terms.

On March 25, Amazon's counsel sent a [fax] of the first draft of a settlement agreement to Basis's counsel. The draft comported with all the terms of the e-mail exchange, and added some implementing and boilerplate [standard contractual] terms.

* * * *

[Within a few days, though,] the parties were deadlocked. On April 21, Basis served its motion to enforce the settlement agreement. Amazon opposed. * * * The motion and opposition presented the issues whether the e-mail terms were sufficiently complete and definite to form an agreement and whether Amazon had intended to be bound by them.

* * * *

We examine the text of the terms for the incompleteness and indefiniteness charged by Amazon. *Provisions are not ambiguous simply because the parties have developed different interpretations of them.* [Emphasis added.]

* * * *

We must interpret the document as a whole. In the preface to the enumerated [mentioned one by one] terms, Basis counsel stated that the "e-mail confirms the essential business terms of the settlement between our respective clients," and that the parties "agree that they promptly will take all reasonable steps to memorialize" those terms. Amazon counsel concisely responded, "correct." Thus the "essential business terms" were resolved. The parties were proceeding to "memorialize" or record the settlement terms, not to create them.

* * * *

To ascertain intent, a court considers the words used by the parties, the agreement taken as a whole, and surrounding facts

(Continues)

and circumstances. The essential circumstance of this disputed agreement is that it concluded a trial.

* * * As the trial judge explained in her memorandum of decision, she "terminated" the trial; she did not suspend it for exploratory negotiations. She did so in reliance upon the parties' report of an accomplished agreement for the settlement of their dispute.

Decision and Remedy The Appeals Court of Massachusetts affirmed the trial court's finding that Amazon intended to be bound by the terms of the March 23 e-mail. That e-mail constituted a complete and unambiguous statement of the parties' desire to be bound by the settlement terms.

Critical Thinking

• **What If the Facts Were Different?** *Assume that, instead of exchanging e-mails, the attorneys for both sides had completed a phone conversation that included all of the terms to which they actually agreed in their e-mail exchanges. Would the court have ruled differently? Why or why not?*

11–1b Definiteness of the Offer

The second requirement for an effective offer involves the definiteness of its terms. An offer must have reasonably definite terms so that a court can determine if a breach has occurred and give an appropriate remedy.[3] The specific terms required depend, of course, on the type of contract. Generally, a contract must include the following terms, either expressed in the contract or capable of being reasonably inferred from it:

1. The identification of the parties.

2. The identification of the object or subject matter of the contract (also the quantity, when appropriate), including the work to be performed, with specific identification of such items as goods, services, and land.

3. The consideration to be paid.

4. The time of payment, delivery, or performance.

An offer may invite an acceptance to be worded in such specific terms that the contract is made definite. **Example 11.3** Nintendo of America, Inc., contacts your Play 2 Win Games store and offers to sell "from one to twenty-five Nintendo 3DS gaming systems for $75 each. State number desired in acceptance." You agree to buy twenty systems. Because the quantity is specified in the acceptance, the terms are definite, and the contract is enforceable. ■

When the parties have clearly manifested their intent to form a contract, courts sometimes are willing to supply a missing term in a contract, especially a sales contract. But a court will not rewrite a contract if the parties' expression of intent is too vague or uncertain to be given any precise meaning.

> "I fear explanations explanatory of things explained."
>
> **Abraham Lincoln**
> 1809–1865
> (Sixteenth president of the United States, 1861–1865)

11–1c Communication of the Offer

A third requirement for an effective offer is communication—the offer must be communicated to the offeree. Ordinarily, one cannot agree to a bargain without knowing that it exists. **Case Example 11.4** Adwoa Gyabaah was hit by a bus owned by Rivlab Transportation Corporation. Gyabaah filed a suit in a New York state court against the bus company. Rivlab's insurer offered to tender the company's policy limit of $1 million in full settlement of Gyabaah's claims. On the advice of her attorney, Jeffrey Aronsky, Gyabaah signed a release (a contract forfeiting the right to pursue a legal claim) to obtain the settlement funds.

The release, however, was not sent to Rivlab or its insurer, National Casualty. Moreover, Gyabaah claimed that she had not decided whether to settle. Two months later, Gyabaah changed lawyers and changed her mind about signing the release. Her former

---

3. *Restatement (Second) of Contracts*, Section 33. The UCC has relaxed the requirements regarding the definiteness of terms in contracts for the sale of goods. See UCC 2–204(3).

attorney, Aronsky, filed a motion to enforce the release so that he could obtain his fees from the settlement funds. The court denied the motion, and Aronsky appealed. The reviewing court held that there was no binding settlement agreement. The release was never delivered to Rivlab or its insurer, nor was acceptance of the settlement offer otherwise communicated to them.[4]

(See this chapter's *Business Law Analysis* feature for an example of how courts deal with offers of a reward.)

11–1d Termination of the Offer

The communication of an effective offer to an offeree gives the offeree the power to transform the offer into a binding, legal obligation (a contract) by an acceptance. This power of acceptance does not continue forever, though. It can be terminated either by the *action of the parties* or by *operation of law*. Termination by the action of the parties can involve a revocation by the offeror or a rejection or counteroffer by the offeree.

How did the requirement of communication affect a dispute between a woman hit by a bus and the bus company's insurer?

Termination by Action of the Parties An offer can be terminated by action of the parties in any of three ways: by revocation, by rejection, or by counteroffer.

> *Revocation.* The offeror's act of withdrawing an offer is referred to as **revocation**. Unless an offer is irrevocable, the offeror usually can revoke the offer (even if he or she has promised

Revocation The withdrawal of a contract offer by the offeror. Unless an offer is irrevocable, it can be revoked at any time prior to acceptance without liability.

---

4. *Gyabaah v. Rivlab Transportation Corp.*, 102 A.D.3d 451, 958 N.Y.S.2d 109 (2013).

Offers of a Reward

Business Law Analysis

The Baton Rouge Crime Stoppers (BCS) offered a reward for information about the "South Louisiana Serial Killer." The information was to be provided via a hotline. Dianne Alexander had survived an attack by a person suspected of being the killer. She identified a suspect in a police photo lineup and later sought to collect the reward. BCS refused to pay because she had not provided information to them via the hotline. Had Alexander complied with the terms of the offer?

Analysis: One of the requirements for an effective offer is communication, resulting in the offeree's knowledge of the offer. One of the requirements

for an effective acceptance is also communication—in most situations, the offeror must be notified of the acceptance. In a unilateral contract, the full performance of some act is called for. If acceptance is evident, notification may be unnecessary, unless of course, the offeror asks for it.

Result and Reasoning: In this situation, the offer consisted of a reward. To obtain the reward, an offeree was asked to provide information regarding the "South Louisiana Serial Killer" to the Baton Rouge Crime Stoppers via a hotline. Alexander did not comply with the terms of this offer, and thus the offerors were

not bound to pay her. She provided information to the police related to the arrest and indictment of the killer. But there was no indication in the offer that the police were the offerors or that they were authorized to accept the requested information on behalf of the offerors. Therefore, a court would not require BCS to pay the reward to Alexander.

A crime-stopper organization offers a reward for information leading to the capture of a certain criminal. How should communication between the offeror and offeree be made for the offer to be effective?

Option Contract A contract under which the offeror cannot revoke the offer for a stipulated time period (because the offeree has given consideration for the offer to remain open).

Know This

The way in which a response to an offer is phrased can determine whether the offer is accepted or rejected.

Counteroffer An offeree's response to an offer in which the offeree rejects the original offer and at the same time makes a new offer.

Mirror Image Rule A common law rule that requires that the terms of the offeree's acceptance adhere exactly to the terms of the offeror's offer for a valid contract to be formed.

to keep it open), as long as the revocation is communicated to the offeree before the offeree accepts. Revocation may be accomplished by either of the following:

1. Express repudiation of the offer (such as "I withdraw my previous offer of October 17").
2. Performance of acts that are inconsistent with the existence of the offer and are made known to the offeree (for instance, selling the offered property to another person in the offeree's presence).

The general rule followed by most states is that a revocation becomes effective when the offeree or the offeree's *agent* (a person acting on behalf of the offeree) actually receives it. Therefore, a statement of revocation sent via FedEx on April 1 and delivered at the offeree's residence or place of business on April 2 becomes effective on April 2. An offer made to the general public (such as through a website) may be revoked in the same manner in which it was originally communicated (through the same website).

Irrevocable Offers. Although most offers are revocable, some can be made irrevocable. Increasingly, courts refuse to allow an offeror to revoke an offer when the offeree has changed position because of justifiable reliance on the offer (under the doctrine of *promissory estoppel*). In some circumstances, "firm offers" made by merchants may also be considered irrevocable.

Another form of irrevocable offer is an option contract. An **option contract** is created when an offeror promises to hold an offer open for a specified period of time in return for a payment (consideration) given by the offeree. An option contract takes away the offeror's power to revoke an offer for the period of time specified in the option. If no time is specified, then a reasonable period of time is implied.

Option contracts are frequently used in conjunction with the sale of real estate. **Example 11.5** Tyler agrees to lease a house from Jackson, the property owner. The lease contract includes a clause stating that Tyler is paying an additional $15,000 for an option to purchase the property within a specified period of time. If Tyler decides not to purchase the house after the specified period has lapsed, he loses the $15,000, and Jackson is free to sell the property to another buyer. ▪

Termination by Action of the Offeree
If the offeree rejects the offer, either by words or by conduct, the offer is terminated. Any subsequent attempt by the offeree to accept will be construed as a new offer, giving the original offeror (now the offeree) the power of acceptance.

Rejection. Like a revocation, a rejection is effective only when it is actually received by the offeror or the offeror's agent. **Example 11.6** Goldfinch Farms offers to sell specialty Maitake mushrooms to a Japanese buyer, Kinoko Foods. If Kinoko rejects the offer by sending a letter via U.S. mail, the rejection will not be effective (and the offer will not be terminated) until Goldfinch receives the letter. ▪

Merely inquiring about an offer does not constitute rejection. **Example 11.7** Ray offers to buy Fran's digital pen for $100. Fran responds, "Is that your best offer?" A reasonable person would conclude that Fran has not rejected the offer but has merely made an inquiry. She could still accept and bind Ray to the $100 price. ▪

Counteroffers. A **counteroffer** is a rejection of the original offer and the simultaneous making of a new offer. **Example 11.8** Burke offers to sell his home to Lang for $270,000. Lang responds, "Your price is too high. I'll offer to purchase your house for $250,000." Lang's response is a counteroffer because it rejects Burke's offer to sell at $270,000 and creates a new offer by Lang to purchase the home at a price of $250,000. ▪

At common law, the **mirror image rule** requires that the offeree's acceptance match the offeror's offer exactly. In other words, the terms of the acceptance must "mirror" those of the offer. If the acceptance materially changes or adds to the terms of the original offer, it will be considered not an acceptance but a counteroffer—which, of course, need not be accepted. The original offeror can, however, accept the terms of the counteroffer and create a valid contract.[5]

---

5. The mirror image rule has been greatly modified in regard to sales contracts. Section 2–207 of the UCC provides that a contract is formed if the offeree makes a definite expression of acceptance (such as signing the form in the appropriate location), even though the terms of the acceptance modify or add to the terms of the original offer.

Termination by Operation of Law The power of the offeree to transform the offer into a binding, legal obligation can be terminated by operation of law through the occurrence of any of the following events:

1. Lapse of time.
2. Destruction of the specific subject matter of the offer.
3. Death or incompetence of the offeror or the offeree.
4. Supervening illegality of the proposed contract.

Lapse of Time. An offer terminates automatically by law when the period of time *specified in the offer* has passed. If the offer states that it will be left open until a particular date, then the offer will terminate at midnight on that day. If the offer states that it will be left open for a number of days, this time period normally begins to run when the offer is actually *received* by the offeree, not when it is formed or sent.

If the offer does not specify a time for acceptance, the offer terminates at the end of a *reasonable* period of time. A reasonable period of time is determined by the subject matter of the contract, business and market conditions, and other relevant circumstances. An offer to sell farm produce, for instance, will terminate sooner than an offer to sell farm equipment because produce is perishable and subject to greater fluctuations in market value.

Destruction, Death, or Incompetence. An offer is automatically terminated if the specific subject matter of the offer (such as a smartphone or a house) is destroyed before the offer is accepted. An offeree's power of acceptance is also terminated when the offeror or offeree dies or becomes legally incapacitated, *unless the offer is irrevocable.* **Example 11.9** Sybil Maven offers to sell commercial property to Westside Investments for $2 million. In June, Westside pays Maven $5,000 in exchange for her agreement to hold the offer open for ten months (forming an option contract). If Maven dies in July, her offer is not terminated, because it is irrevocable. Westside can purchase the property from Maven's estate at any time within the ten-month period.

In contrast, a revocable offer is personal to both parties and cannot pass to the heirs, guardian, or estate of either party. This rule applies whether or not the other party had notice of the death or incompetence.

Supervening Illegality. A statute or court decision that makes an offer illegal automatically terminates the offer. **Example 11.10** Lee offers to lend Kim $10,000 at an annual interest rate of 15 percent. Before Kim can accept the offer, a law is enacted that prohibits interest rates higher than 8 percent. Lee's offer is automatically terminated. (If the statute is enacted after Kim accepts the offer, a valid contract is formed, but the contract may still be unenforceable.)

11–2 Acceptance

An **acceptance** is a voluntary act by the offeree that shows assent, or agreement, to the terms of an offer. The offeree's act may consist of words or conduct. The acceptance must be unequivocal and must be communicated to the offeror. Generally, only the person to whom the offer is made or that person's agent can accept the offer and create a binding contract. (See this chapter's *Adapting the Law to the Online Environment* feature for a discussion of how parties can sometimes inadvertently accept a contract via e-mail or instant messages.)

Jeff Greenberg/Universal Images Group/Getty Images

If the owner of a commercial property dies before the end of the time period specified in an option contract, what happens to the deal?

Acceptance The act of voluntarily agreeing, through words or conduct, to the terms of an offer, thereby creating a contract.

Can Your E-Mails or Instant Messages Create a Valid Contract?

Adapting the Law to the Online Environment

Instant messaging and e-mailing are among the most common forms of informal communication. Not surprisingly, parties considering an agreement often exchange offers and counteroffers via e-mail (and, to a lesser extent, instant messaging). The parties may believe that these informal electronic exchanges are for negotiation purposes only. But such communications can lead to the formation of valid contracts.

E-Mails and Settlements

After automobile accidents, the parties' attorneys sometimes exchange e-mails as part of the negotiation process. Consider the case of Jose Jimenez and Tanya Morales, who were allegedly injured in an automobile accident with Patrick Yanne, an employee of RMC Industrial Supplies, Inc. Jimenez and Morales filed a personal injury lawsuit against Yanne and the company. After a series of e-mails negotiating a settlement, the defendant's attorney sent the following e-mail to the plaintiffs' attorney: "Ok, we can agree to settle this matter for $13,000 to Jimenez and $17,000 to Morales. Please confirm. Thanks." The plaintiffs' attorney confirmed.

Morales then changed her mind about settling and claimed that the e-mail did not constitute a contract. A New York trial court refused to enforce the terms of the e-mail agreement on Morales, but a reviewing court reversed on appeal. The state intermediate appellate court held that the e-mail set forth an enforceable

agreement to settle Morales's personal injury claim.[a]

"Accidental" Contracts via E-Mail

When a series of e-mails signal intent to be bound, a contract may be formed, even though some language in the e-mails may be careless or accidental. Even if a party later claims to have had unstated objections to the terms, the e-mails will prevail. What matters is whether a court determines that it is reasonable for the receiving party to believe that there is an agreement.

Indeed, e-mail contracting has become so common that only unusually strange circumstances will cause a court to reject such contracts.[b] Furthermore, under the Uniform Electronic Transactions Act, a contract "may not be denied legal effect solely because an electronic record was used in its formation." Most states have adopted this act, at least in part.

Valid Contract Modifications via Instant Messaging

Like e-mail exchanges, instant messaging conversations between individuals in the process of negotiations can result in the formation (or modification) of a contract. One case involved an online marketing service, CX Digital Media, Inc.,

which provides clients with advertising referrals from its network of affiliates.

CX Digital charges a fee for its services based on the number of referrals. One of its clients was Smoking Everywhere, Inc., a seller of electronic cigarettes. While the two companies were negotiating a change in contract terms via instant messaging, the issue of the maximum number of referrals per day came up. A CX Digital employee sent an instant message to a Smoking Everywhere executive asking about the maximum number. The executive responded, "NO LIMIT," and CX Digital's employee replied, "awesome!"

After that, CX Digital referred a higher volume of sales leads than previously. Smoking Everywhere refused to pay for these additional referrals, claiming that the instant messaging chat did not constitute an enforceable modification of the initial contract. At trial, CX Digital prevailed. Smoking Everywhere had to pay more than $1 million for the additional sales leads.[c]

Critical Thinking

How can a company structure e-mail negotiations to avoid "accidentally" forming a contract?

---

a. *Jimenez v. Yanne*, 152 A.D.3d 434, 55 N.Y.S.3d 434 (2017). See also *Forcelli v. Gelco Corp.*, 109 A.D.3d 244, 972 N.Y.S.2d 570 (2013).

b. See, for example, *Beastie Boys v. Monster Energy Co.*, 983 F.Supp.2d 338 (S.D.N.Y. 2013).

c. *CX Digital Media, Inc. v. Smoking Everywhere, Inc.*, 2011 WL 1102782 (S.D.Fla. 2011). See also *Verde Media Corp. v. Levi*, 2015 WL 374934 (N.D.Cal. 2015).

11–2a Unequivocal Acceptance

To exercise the power of acceptance effectively, the offeree must accept unequivocally. This is the mirror image rule previously discussed. An acceptance may be unequivocal even though the offeree expresses dissatisfaction with the contract. For instance, "I accept the offer, but can you give me a better price?" or "I accept, but please send a written contract" is an effective acceptance. (Notice how important each word is!)

An acceptance cannot impose new conditions or change the terms of the original offer. If it does, the acceptance may be considered a counteroffer, which is a rejection of the original offer. For instance, the statement "I accept the offer but only if I can pay on ninety days' credit" is a counteroffer and not an unequivocal acceptance.

Note, though, that even when the additional terms are construed as a counteroffer, the other party can accept the terms by words or by conduct. **Case Example 11.11** Sonja Brown made a written offer to Lagrange Development to buy a particular house for $79,900. Lagrange's executive director, Terry Glazer, penciled in modifications to the offer—an increased purchase price of $84,200 and a later date for acceptance. Glazer initialed the changes and signed the document. Brown initialed the date change but not the price increase, and did not sign the revised contract. Nevertheless, Brown went through with the sale and received ownership of the property. When a dispute later arose as to the purchase price, a court found that Glazer's modification of the terms had constituted a counteroffer, which Brown had accepted by performance. Therefore, the contract was enforceable for the modified price of $84,200.[6]

11–2b Silence as Acceptance

Ordinarily, silence cannot constitute acceptance, even if the offeror states, "By your silence and inaction, you will be deemed to have accepted this offer." This general rule applies because an offeree should not be put under a burden of liability to act affirmatively in order to reject an offer. No consideration—that is, nothing of value—has passed to the offeree to impose such a liability.

In some instances, however, the offeree does have a duty to speak. If so, his or her silence or inaction will operate as an acceptance. Silence may be an acceptance when an offeree takes the benefit of offered services even though he or she had an opportunity to reject them and knew that they were offered with the expectation of compensation.

Silence can also operate as an acceptance when the offeree has had prior dealings with the offeror. **Example 11.12** Marabel's restaurant routinely receives shipments of produce from a certain supplier. That supplier notifies Marabel's that it is raising its prices because its crops were damaged by a late freeze. If the restaurant does not respond in any way, the silence may operate as an acceptance, and the supplier will be justified in continuing regular shipments.

andresr/E+/Getty Images

Why can silence operate as an acceptance to changes in contract terms between a restaurant and its regular produce supplier?

11–2c Communication of Acceptance

Whether the offeror must be notified of the acceptance depends on the nature of the contract. In a unilateral contract, the full performance of some act is called for. Acceptance is usually evident, and notification is therefore unnecessary (unless the law requires it or the offeror asks for it). In a bilateral contract, in contrast, communication of acceptance is necessary,

---

6. *Brown v. Lagrange Development Corp.*, 2015 -Ohio- 133, 2015 WL 223877 (Ohio App. 2015).

because acceptance is in the form of a promise. The bilateral contract is formed when the promise is made rather than when the act is performed.

Case Example 11.13 Powerhouse Custom Homes, Inc., owed $95,260.42 to 84 Lumber Company under a credit agreement. When Powerhouse failed to pay, 84 Lumber filed a suit to collect. During mediation, the parties agreed to a deadline for objections to whatever agreement they might reach. If there were no objections, the agreement would be binding.

Powerhouse then offered to pay less than the amount owed, but 84 Lumber did not respond. Powerhouse argued that 84 Lumber had accepted the offer by not objecting to it within the deadline. The court ruled in 84 Lumber's favor for the entire amount of the debt. To form a contract, an offer must be accepted unequivocally. Powerhouse made an offer, but 84 Lumber did not communicate acceptance. Therefore, the parties did not reach an agreement on settlement.[7]

11–2d Mode and Timeliness of Acceptance

Acceptance in bilateral contracts must be timely. The general rule is that acceptance in a bilateral contract is timely if it is made before the offer is terminated. Problems may arise, though, when the parties involved are not dealing face to face. In such situations, the offeree should use an authorized mode of communication.

The Mailbox Rule. Acceptance takes effect, and thus completes formation of the contract, at the time the offeree sends or delivers the acceptance via the mode of communication expressly or impliedly authorized by the offeror. This is the so-called **mailbox rule,** also called the *deposited acceptance rule*, which the majority of courts follow. Under this rule, if the authorized mode of communication is the mail, then an acceptance becomes valid when it is dispatched (placed in the control of the U.S. Postal Service)—not when it is received by the offeror. (Note, however, that if the offer stipulates when acceptance will be effective, then the offer will not be effective until the time specified.)

The mailbox rule does not apply to instantaneous forms of communication, such as when the parties are dealing face to face, by phone, by fax, and usually by e-mail. Under the Uniform Electronic Transactions Act (UETA—discussed later in this chapter), e-mail is considered sent when it either leaves the sender's control or is received by the recipient. This rule, which takes the place of the mailbox rule if the parties have agreed to conduct transactions electronically, allows an e-mail acceptance to become effective when sent.

Authorized Means of Communication. A means of communicating acceptance can be expressly authorized by the offeror or impliedly authorized by the facts and circumstances of the situation. An acceptance sent by means not expressly or impliedly authorized normally is not effective until it is received by the offeror.

When an offeror specifies how acceptance should be made, such as by overnight delivery, the contract is not formed unless the offeree uses that mode of acceptance. Both the offeror and the offeree are bound in contract the moment the specified means of acceptance is employed. **Example 11.14** Motorola Mobility, Inc., offers to sell 144 Atrix 4G smartphones and 72 Lapdocks to Call Me Plus phone stores. The offer states that Call Me Plus must accept the offer via FedEx overnight delivery. The acceptance is effective (and a binding contract is formed) the moment that Call Me Plus gives the overnight envelope containing the acceptance to the FedEx driver.

If the offeror does not expressly authorize a certain mode of acceptance, then acceptance can be made by *any reasonable means*.[8] Courts look at the prevailing business usages and the surrounding circumstances to determine whether the mode of acceptance used was

---

7. *Powerhouse Custom Homes, Inc. v. 84 Lumber Co.*, 307 Ga.App. 605, 705 S.E.2d 704 (2011).

8. Note that UCC 2–206(1)(a) states specifically that an acceptance of an offer for the sale of goods can be made by any medium that is *reasonable* under the circumstances.

reasonable. Usually, the offeror's choice of a particular means in making the offer implies that the offeree can use the *same or a faster means* for acceptance. **Example 11.15** If the offer is made via USPS Priority Mail, it would be reasonable to accept the offer via Priority Mail or by a faster method, such as signed scanned documents sent as attachments via e-mail. ▪

Substitute Method of Acceptance. Sometimes, the offeror authorizes a particular method of acceptance, but the offeree accepts by a different means. In that situation, the acceptance may still be effective if the substituted method serves the same purpose as the authorized means. Acceptance by a substitute method is not effective on dispatch, though. No contract will be formed until the acceptance is received by the offeror. **Example 11.16** Bennion's offer specifies acceptance via FedEx overnight delivery but the offeree accepts instead by overnight delivery from UPS. The substitute method of acceptance will still be effective, but not until the offeror (Bennion) receives it from UPS. ▪

11–3 E-Contracts

Numerous contracts are formed online. Electronic contracts, or **e-contracts,** must meet the same basic requirements (agreement, consideration, contractual capacity, and legality) as paper contracts. Disputes concerning e-contracts, however, tend to center on contract terms and whether the parties voluntarily agreed to those terms.

E-Contract A contract that is formed electronically.

Online contracts may be formed not only for the sale of goods and services, but also for *licensing*. The "sale" of software generally involves a license, or a right to use the software, rather than the passage of title (ownership rights) from the seller to the buyer. **Example 11.17** When Lauren downloads an app on her smartphone, she has to select "I agree" several times to the terms and conditions under which she will use the software. After she agrees to these terms (the licensing agreement), she can use the application. ▪

As you read through the following subsections, keep in mind that although we typically refer to the offeror and the offeree as a *seller* and a *buyer*, in many online transactions these parties would be more accurately described as a *licensor* and a *licensee*.

Do online "I agree" click-ons validate software licensing agreements?

11–3a Online Offers

Sellers doing business via the Internet can protect themselves against contract disputes and legal liability by creating offers that clearly spell out the terms that will govern their transactions if the offers are accepted. All important terms should be conspicuous and easy to view.

Displaying the Offer The seller's website should include a hypertext link to a page containing the full contract so that potential buyers are made aware of the terms to which they are assenting. The contract generally must be displayed online in a readable format such as in a twelve-point typeface. All provisions should be reasonably clear.

Example 11.18 Netquip sells a variety of heavy equipment, such as trucks and trailers, online at its website. Because Netquip's pricing schedule is very complex, the schedule must be fully provided and explained on the website. In addition, the terms of the sale (such as any warranties and the refund policy) must be fully disclosed. ▪

Provisions to Include An important rule to keep in mind is that the offeror (seller) controls the offer and thus the resulting contract. The seller should therefore anticipate the terms she or he wants to include in a contract and provide for them in the offer. In some instances, a standardized contract form may suffice. At a minimum, an online offer should include the following provisions:

1. *Acceptance of terms.* A clause that clearly indicates what constitutes the buyer's agreement to the terms of the offer, such as a box containing the words "I accept" that the buyer can click on to indicate acceptance. (Mechanisms for accepting online offers will be discussed in detail later in this chapter.)

2. *Payment.* A provision specifying how payment for the goods (including any applicable taxes) must be made.

3. *Return policy.* A statement of the seller's refund and return policies.

4. *Disclaimer.* Disclaimers of liability for certain uses of the goods. For instance, an online seller of business forms may add a disclaimer that the seller does not accept responsibility for the buyer's reliance on the forms rather than on an attorney's advice.

5. *Limitation on remedies.* A provision specifying the remedies available to the buyer if the goods are found to be defective or if the contract is otherwise breached. Any limitation of remedies should be clearly spelled out.

6. *Privacy policy.* A statement indicating how the seller will use the information gathered about the buyer. (See this chapter's *Linking Business Law to Marketing* feature for a discussion of how the information may be used.)

7. *Dispute resolution.* Provisions relating to dispute settlement, such as an arbitration clause.

Linking Business Law to Marketing

Customer Relationship Management

Increasingly, the contracting process is moving online. Websites offer to sell millions of goods and services and collect vast amount of data from online shoppers. *Customer relationship management (CRM)* is key. CRM is a marketing strategy that allows companies to acquire information about customers' wants, needs, and behaviors. The companies can then use that information to build customer relationships and loyalty. The focus of CRM is understanding customers as individuals rather than simply as a group of consumers.

Two Examples—Netflix and Amazon

If you are a customer of Netflix.com, you choose which movies and video games you want to rent based on your individual tastes and preferences. Netflix asks you to rate movies that you have rented on a scale of one to five stars. Using a computer algorithm, Netflix then creates an individualized rating system that predicts how you will rate other movies. Over time, the system's predictions become more accurate, and Netflix is able to suggest movies and games that you might like.

Amazon.com uses similar technology to recommend books, music, and other products that you might wish to buy. Amazon sends out numerous "personalized" e-mails to its customers with suggestions based on those customers' individual buying habits.

Thus, CRM allows both Netflix and Amazon to focus their marketing efforts. Such focused efforts are much more effective than the typical shotgun approach used in spam advertising on the Internet.

CRM in Online versus Traditional Companies

For online companies such as Amazon and Netflix, all customer information has some value because the cost of obtaining it, analyzing it, and utilizing it is so small. In contrast, traditional companies often must use a much more costly process to obtain data for CRM. An automobile company, for example, obtains customer information from a variety of sources, including dealers, customer surveys, online inquiries, and the like. Integrating, storing, and managing such information generally makes CRM much more expensive for traditional companies than for online companies.

Critical Thinking

Online companies such as Amazon not only target individual customers, but also utilize each customer's buying habits to create generalized marketing campaigns. What privacy issues, if any, might arise as an online company creates a database to be used for generalized marketing campaigns?

Dispute-Settlement Provisions Online offers frequently include provisions relating to dispute settlement. For instance, the offer might include an arbitration clause specifying that any dispute arising under the contract will be arbitrated in a designated forum.

Case Example 11.19 Scott Rosendahl enrolled in an online college, Ashford University. He claimed that the school's adviser had told him that Ashford offered one of the cheapest undergraduate degree programs in the country. In fact, it did not. Rosendahl later sued the school, claiming that it had violated false advertising laws and had engaged in fraud and negligent misrepresentation. The university argued that the enrollment agreement clearly contained a requirement that all disputes be arbitrated. Rosendahl, like other students, had electronically assented to this agreement when he enrolled. Ashford presented the online application forms to the court, and the court dismissed Rosendahl's lawsuit. Rosendahl had agreed to arbitrate any disputes he had with Ashford.[9]

Forum-Selection Clause. Many online contracts also contain a **forum-selection clause** indicating the forum, or location (such as a court or jurisdiction), for the resolution of any dispute arising under the contract. Significant jurisdictional issues can occur when parties are at a great distance, as they often are when they form contracts via the Internet. A forum-selection clause will help to avert future jurisdictional problems and also help to ensure that the seller will not be required to appear in court in a distant state.

Case Example 11.20 Lisa Zaltz subscribed to JDATE.com, an online dating website. Later, she sued JDATE in a federal district court in New York, claiming that it had repeatedly billed her for months without her consent. JDATE argued that its contract with Zaltz included a forum-selection clause requiring any disputes to be litigated in the central district of California. The district court in New York agreed with JDATE that the forum-selection clause was enforceable and granted a motion transferring the case to California.[10]

Choice-of-Law Clause. Some online contracts may also include a *choice-of-law clause*, specifying that any dispute arising out of the contract will be settled in accordance with the law of a particular jurisdiction, such as a state or country. Choice-of-law clauses are particularly common in international contracts, but they may also appear in e-contracts to specify which state's laws will govern in the United States.

Sometimes, the same contract will include all three of these types of clauses (arbitration, forum-selection, and choice-of-law).

Case Example 11.21 Xlibris Publishing provides services to authors

Forum-Selection Clause
A provision in a contract designating the court, jurisdiction, or tribunal that will decide any disputes arising under the contract.

How can a forum-selection clause affect those who agree to use an online-dating service but then file a lawsuit against the company?

9. *Rosendahl v. Bridgepoint Education, Inc.*, 2012 WL 667049 (S.D.Cal. 2012).
10. *Zaltz v. JDATE*, 952 F.Supp.2d 439 (E.D.N.Y. 2013).

who wish to self-publish their work. It offers, through its website, a variety of publishing packages to facilitate editing, publishing, and marketing. Avis Smith, a New York resident, had previously submitted his manuscript to Xlibris. Smith received an e-mail from Xlibris offering him a program at half price that would "provide the book what it deserves when it comes to exposure and publicity." Four days later, Smith contracted to purchase the Platinum Service Package from Xlibris for around $7,500 to be paid over three months.

A clause in the contract stated that any disputes between the parties would be arbitrated in Indianapolis, under the laws of Indiana. Communications between Smith and Xlibris deteriorated, and Smith ultimately filed a lawsuit against the company in a federal court in New York. Xlibris asked the court to compel arbitration in Indiana. The court ruled that Smith had consented to the arbitration, forum-selection, and choice-of-law clauses, which were enforceable. Smith was required to arbitrate the dispute in Indiana.[11]

11–3b Online Acceptances

The *Restatement (Second) of Contracts* states that parties may agree to a contract "by written or spoken words or by other action or by failure to act."[12] The Uniform Commercial Code (UCC), which governs sales contracts, has a similar provision. Section 2–204 of the UCC states that any contract for the sale of goods "may be made in any manner sufficient to show agreement, including conduct by both parties which recognizes the existence of such a contract." The courts have used these provisions in determining what constitutes an online acceptance.

Click-On Agreements The courts have concluded that the act of clicking on a box labeled "I accept" or "I agree" can indicate acceptance of an online offer. The agreement resulting from such an acceptance is often called a **click-on agreement** (sometimes, a *click-on license* or *click-wrap agreement*).

Generally, the law does not require that the parties have read all of the terms in a contract for it to be effective. Therefore, clicking on a box that states "I agree" to certain terms can be enough to bind a party to these terms. The terms may be contained on a website through which the buyer is obtaining goods or services, or they may appear on the screen of a computer, smartphone, or other device when software is downloaded from the Internet.

Case Example 11.22 Any person who agrees to work as an Uber driver must enter into a services agreement and driver addendum contract with Uber Technologies, Inc. The contracts include an arbitration provision. New drivers must click the "Yes, I agree" button to use the Uber App and to start working by picking up passengers.

A group of Chinese-speaking Uber drivers filed a breach of contract suit against the company. Uber responded with a motion to compel arbitration, which a federal district court granted. The plaintiffs had downloaded the Chinese version of the Uber App and could read the arbitration provision in their native language. Each had clicked on the button and agreed to arbitrate any disputes (whether or not they had actually read the clause). Thus, the arbitration clause was enforceable, and the lawsuit was dismissed.[13]

In the following case, the court had to determine whether a lottery entrant was disqualified from winning an online contest because he had failed to comply with the rules of the contest.

Learning Objective 3
How do click-on and shrink-wrap agreements differ?

Click-On Agreement An agreement that arises when an online buyer clicks on "I agree" or otherwise indicates her or his assent to be bound by the terms of an offer.

By clicking on the "I agree" button of Uber's downloadable service agreement, does a user validate its arbitration clause?

11. *Smith v. Xlibris Publishing*, 2016 WL 5678566 (E.D.N.Y. 2016).
12. *Restatement (Second) of Contracts*, Section 19.
13. *Kai Peng v. Uber Technologies, Inc.*, 237 F.Supp.3d 36 (E.D.N.Y. 2017).

■ Case 11.3

Bailey v. Kentucky Lottery Corp.

Kentucky Court of Appeals, __ S.W.3d __, 2018 WL 910824 (2018).

Background and Facts Kentucky Lottery Corporation (the Lottery) operates the state's lottery. In one of the Lottery's contests, a scratch-off ticket that revealed a "Final Top Prize" symbol could be entered into an online drawing to win $175,000. The Lottery operates a website at which individuals could register for an online account and enter the contest. The contest's rules required an entrant to provide a valid phone number and mailing address and to keep them current. If the contest's winner could not be reached within seven days after the drawing, he or she would be disqualified.

Brett Bailey established an online account and entered several scratch-off tickets in the contest. He provided a mailing address, which was not correct, and before the drawing, he changed his phone number without notifying the Lottery. Bailey's ticket won the drawing, but the Lottery was unable to reach him. After expiration of the contest's seven-day period, the $175,000 prize was awarded to an eligible alternate. Later, Bailey filed a suit in a Kentucky state court against the Lottery, claiming breach of contract. The court granted a summary judgment to the defendant. Bailey appealed.

In the Words of the Court
COMBS, Judge:

* * * *

* * * Bailey joined the Fun Club Rewards program and entered several eligible scratch-off lottery tickets as chances to win the "Final Top Prize" ["FTP"] promotion. He did so by providing information on the lottery's website and by agreeing to the terms of use and to all other rules and regulations that applied to online account holders.

* * * *The purchase of a lottery ticket is the acceptance of an offer to contract and* * * * *the terms of the contract are the rules and regulations of the lottery.* Furthermore, Bailey expressly agreed to the rules and regulations of the "FTP" promotion upon entry of his * * * ticket into the * * * drawing. Pursuant to the rules of the "FTP" promotion, players were required to keep their telephone number and mailing address current so that the lottery could notify second-chance winners on a timely basis. The rules provided that any drawing winner would be disqualified if the lottery could not reach him within seven business days. [Emphasis added.]

There is no dispute that Bailey failed to keep his telephone number current and that he never provided the lottery [organization] with a valid mailing address. As a result, the lottery was unable to contact him pursuant to the rules. While the lottery reserved the right to change or extend any of the dates set out in the rules, it did not reserve the right to award a prize based upon a nonqualified entry. Based upon his own acts and omissions, Bailey was properly disqualified from the drawing; the lottery did not breach the contract by refusing to award him a prize. There is no genuine issue of material fact, and the court did not err when it granted summary judgment to the lottery with respect to Bailey's breach-of-contract claim.

Decision and Remedy A state intermediate appellate court affirmed the judgment of the lower court in favor of the Lottery. The Lottery had a contractual right to disqualify Bailey's drawing entry because he had not complied with the rules of the contest. Bailey could not collect his $175,000 lottery prize.

Critical Thinking

- **Legal Environment** *The Lottery's rules did not provide for entrants to be notified by e-mail, but contracts generally impose on the parties a duty to do everything necessary to carry them out. Did the Lottery breach its contract with Bailey by failing to notify him by e-mail? Explain.*

- **What If the Facts Were Different?** *Suppose that Bailey had complied with the Lottery's rules by keeping his address and phone number current, but that the Lottery had not tried to notify him before the expiration of the seven-day period. Would the result have been different? Why or why not?*

Ethical Issue

How enforceable are click-on agreements to donate funds to a charity? Millions of online shoppers use PayPal as a convenient payment method. But PayPal can also be used to donate to a favorite charity. PayPal offers its users a Giving Fund platform. By going to PayPal's charity-giving platform, a potential contributor can choose from a list of charities. The Giving Fund platform requires two steps: clicking on the donation button for the charity and specifying the amount.

Many of the listed charities, though, have not yet actually signed up with PayPal to receive these donated funds. What happens when a contributor clicks on a listed charity that has not signed up? Apparently, neither the contributor nor the charity is notified, and PayPal sends the funds to other listed charities that are signed up with its service. Consequently, contributors' funds may go to charities that they did not choose, and charities may fail to receive donations meant for them. A number of individuals have filed a class-action lawsuit against PayPal based on this practice. The suit alleges that PayPal misled those making charitable contributions on its Giving Fund platform.[14]

Shrink-Wrap Agreement An agreement whose terms are expressed in a document located inside a box in which goods (usually software) are packaged.

Shrink-Wrap Agreements A **shrink-wrap agreement** (or *shrink-wrap license*) is an agreement whose terms are expressed inside a box in which goods are packaged. (The term *shrink-wrap* refers to the plastic that covers the box.) Usually, the party who opens the box is told that she or he agrees to the terms by keeping the goods. Similarly, when the purchaser opens a software package, he or she agrees to abide by the terms of the limited license agreement.

Example 11.23 Arial orders a new iPhone from Best Electronics, which ships it to her. Along with the iPhone, the box contains an agreement setting forth the terms of the sale, including what remedies are available. The document also states that Arial's retention of the iPhone for longer than thirty days will be construed as an acceptance of the terms.

In most instances, a shrink-wrap agreement is not between a retailer and a buyer, but is between the manufacturer of the hardware or software and the ultimate buyer-user of the product. The terms generally concern warranties, remedies, and other issues associated with the use of the product. ■

Shrink-Wrap Agreements and Enforceable Contract Terms. In some cases, the courts have enforced the terms of shrink-wrap agreements in the same way as the terms of other contracts. These courts have reasoned that by including the terms with the product, the seller proposed a contract that the buyer could accept by using the product after having an opportunity to read the terms. Thus, a buyer's failure to object to terms contained within a shrink-wrapped software package may constitute an acceptance of the terms by conduct.

Shrink-Wrap Terms That May Not Be Enforced. Sometimes, courts have refused to enforce certain terms included in shrink-wrap agreements because the buyer did not expressly consent to them. An important factor is when the parties form their contract.

If a buyer orders a product over the telephone, for instance, and the seller does not mention terms such as an arbitration clause or a forum-selection clause, clearly the buyer has not expressly agreed to these terms. If the buyer discovers the clauses *after* the parties entered into a contract, a court may conclude that those clauses were proposals for additional terms and not part of the contract.

---

14. *Friends for Health v. PayPal, Inc.*, 2017 WL 782249 (N.D.Ill. 2017).

Case Example 11.24 David Noble purchased a Samsung Smartwatch from an AT&T store after seeing ads saying that its battery life was twenty-four to forty-eight hours with typical use. But Noble's Smartwatch battery lasted only about four hours, so he returned the Smartwatch and received a new one. The second Smartwatch suffered from the same battery problem. Noble again went back to the AT&T store and, this time, was directed to ship the Smartwatch to Samsung. Samsung then sent Noble a third Smartwatch with equally poor battery life. Noble then filed a suit against Samsung in a federal district court. Samsung filed a motion to compel arbitration, which the district court denied. Samsung appealed.

Inside each of the Smartwatch boxes that Noble received was a tiny booklet titled "Health and Safety and Warranty Guide" that included a standard Limited Warranty. On page ninety-seven of the guide, a boldface question read "What is the procedure for resolving disputes?" Under that was a statement saying that any disputes would be resolved exclusively through binding arbitration, and not by a court or jury. The federal appellate court held that this language "tucked away in a brochure" was not sufficient to show that Noble had agreed to arbitration. Because consumers were not given reasonable notice of the arbitration clause (on the outside of the guide or somewhere obvious in the packaging), it was unenforceable.[15]

Browse-Wrap Terms Like the terms of a click-on agreement, **browse-wrap terms** can occur in a transaction conducted over the Internet. Unlike a click-on agreement, however, browse-wrap terms do not require the buyer or user to assent to the terms before, say, downloading or using certain software. **Case Example 11.25** James McCants bought dietary supplements over the Internet that allegedly seriously damaged his liver. When he sued the seller, Vitacost.com, Inc., the company moved for arbitration based on a clause in the browse-wrap terms. To see the arbitration clause, a purchaser would have had to scroll to the bottom of the seller's Web page and click on a hyperlink labeled "Terms and Conditions." The court held that these browse-wrap terms were not part of the sales agreement and were thus unenforceable.[16]

> **Browse-Wrap Term** A term or condition of use that is presented when an online buyer downloads a product but to which the buyer does not have to agree before installing or using the product.

11–3c Federal Law on E-Signatures and E-Documents

An **e-signature** has been defined as "an electronic sound, symbol, or process attached to or logically associated with a record and executed or adopted by a person with the intent to sign the record."[17] Electronic documents can be signed in a number of ways. Thus, e-signatures include encrypted digital signatures, names (intended as signatures) at the ends of e-mail messages, and "clicks" on a Web page if the clicks include some means of identification.

> **E-Signature** An electronic sound, symbol, or process attached to or logically associated with a record and adopted by a person with the intent to sign the record.

Under the Electronic Signatures in Global and National Commerce Act (E-SIGN Act),[18] no contract, record, or signature may be "denied legal effect" solely because it is in electronic form. An electronic signature is as valid as a signature on paper, and an e-document can be as enforceable as a paper one.

For an e-signature to be enforceable, however, the contracting parties must have agreed to use electronic signatures. For an electronic document to be valid, it must be in a form that can be retained and accurately reproduced.

The E-SIGN Act does not apply to all types of documents. Contracts and documents that are exempt include court papers, divorce decrees, evictions, foreclosures, health-insurance terminations, prenuptial agreements, and wills. Also, the only agreements governed by the UCC that fall under this law are those covered by Articles 2 and 2A and UCC 1–107 and 1–206. Despite these limitations, the E-SIGN Act significantly expanded contracting online.

©Farbled/ShutterStock.com

Why are many e-signatures binding today?

---

15. *Noble v. Samsung Electronics Company, Inc.*, 682 Fed.Appx. 113 (3d Cir. 2017).
16. *Vitacost.com, Inc. v. McCants*, 210 So.3d 761 (Fla.App. 2017).
17. This definition is from the Uniform Electronic Transactions Act.
18. 15 U.S.C. Sections 7001 *et seq.*

11–3d Partnering Agreements

One way online sellers and buyers can prevent disputes over signatures in their e-contracts, as well as disputes over the terms and conditions of those contracts, is to form partnering agreements. In a **partnering agreement,** a seller and a buyer who frequently do business with each other agree in advance on the terms and conditions that will apply to all transactions subsequently conducted electronically. The partnering agreement can also establish special access and identification codes to be used by the parties when transacting business electronically.

A partnering agreement reduces the likelihood that disputes will arise under the contract because the buyer and the seller have agreed in advance to the terms and conditions that will accompany each sale. Furthermore, if a dispute does arise, a court or arbitration forum will be able to refer to the partnering agreement when determining the parties' intent.

Partnering Agreement An agreement between a seller and a buyer who frequently do business with each other concerning the terms and conditions that will apply to all subsequently formed electronic contracts.

11–4 The Uniform Electronic Transactions Act

Learning Objective 4

What is the primary purpose of the Uniform Electronic Transactions Act?

The National Conference of Commissioners on Uniform State Laws and the American Law Institute promulgated the Uniform Electronic Transactions Act (UETA). The UETA has been adopted, at least in part, by forty-eight states.

The primary purpose of the UETA is to remove barriers to e-commerce by giving the same legal effect to electronic records and signatures as is given to paper documents and signatures. The UETA broadly defines an *e-signature* as "an electronic sound, symbol, or process attached to or logically associated with a record and executed or adopted by a person with the intent to sign the record."[19] A **record** is "information that is inscribed on a tangible medium or that is stored in an electronic or other medium and is retrievable in perceivable [visual] form."[20]

Record Information that is either inscribed on a tangible medium or stored in an electronic or other medium and is retrievable in visual form.

11–4a The Scope and Applicability of the UETA

The UETA does not create new rules for electronic contracts. Rather, it establishes that records, signatures, and contracts may not be denied enforceability solely due to their electronic form.

The UETA does not apply to all writings and signatures. It covers only electronic records and electronic signatures *relating to a transaction*. A *transaction* is defined as an interaction between two or more parties relating to business, commercial, or governmental activities.[21] The act specifically does not apply to wills or testamentary trusts or to transactions governed by the UCC (other than those covered by Articles 2 and 2A).[22] In addition, the provisions of the UETA allow the states to exclude its application to other areas of law.

11–4b The Federal E-SIGN Act and the UETA

Congress passed the E-SIGN Act a year after the UETA was presented to the states for adoption. Thus, a significant issue was to what extent the federal E-SIGN Act preempted the UETA as adopted by the states.

The E-SIGN Act[23] explicitly provides that if a state has enacted the uniform version of the UETA, it is not preempted by the E-SIGN Act. In other words, if the state has enacted the UETA without modification, state law will govern.

The problem is that many states have enacted nonuniform (modified) versions of the UETA, largely for the purpose of excluding other areas of state law from the UETA's terms. The E-SIGN Act specifies that those exclusions will be preempted to the extent that they are inconsistent with the E-SIGN Act's provisions.

---

19. UETA 102(8).
20. UETA 102(15).
21. UETA 2(12) and 3.
22. UETA 3(b).
23. 15 U.S.C. Section 7002(2)(A)(i).

The E-SIGN Act explicitly allows the states to enact alternative requirements for the use of electronic records or electronic signatures. Generally, however, the requirements must be consistent with the provisions of the E-SIGN Act, and the state must not give greater legal status or effect to one specific type of technology. Additionally, if a state enacts alternative requirements *after* the E-SIGN Act was adopted, the state law must specifically refer to the E-SIGN Act.

The relationship between the E-SIGN Act and the UETA is illustrated in Exhibit 11–1.

11–4c Highlights of the UETA

The UETA will not apply to a transaction unless the parties have agreed to conduct transactions by electronic means. The agreement may be explicit, or it may be implied by the conduct of the parties and the surrounding circumstances.[24] It may be reasonable, for instance, to infer that a person who gives out a business card with an e-mail address on it has consented to transact business electronically.[25] Agreement may also be inferred from a letter or other writing, as well as from verbal communication. Furthermore, a person who has previously agreed to an electronic transaction can withdraw his or her consent and refuse to conduct further business electronically.

Attribution Under the UETA, if an electronic record or signature is the act of a particular person, the record or signature may be attributed to that person. If a person types her or his name at the bottom of an e-mail purchase order, for instance, that name will qualify as a "signature" and be attributed to the person whose name appears.

---

24. UETA 5(b).
25. UETA 5, Comment 4B.

Exhibit 11–1 The E-SIGN Act and the UETA

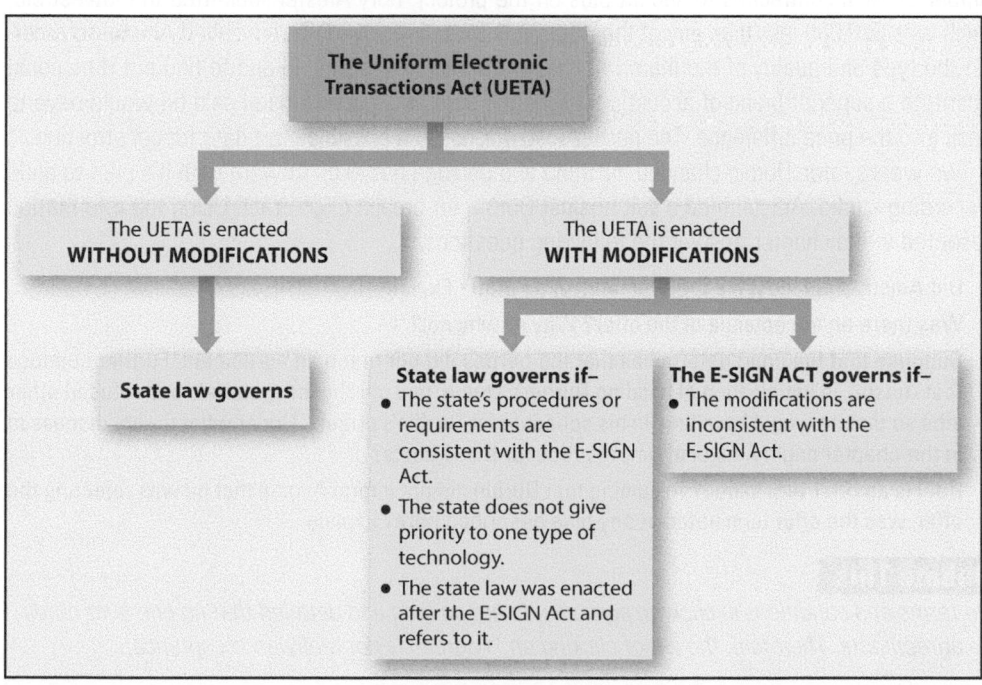

The UETA contains no express provisions about what constitutes fraud or whether an agent is authorized to enter a contract. Under the UETA, other state laws control if any issues relating to agency, authority, forgery, or contract formation arise. If existing state law requires a document to be notarized, the electronic signature of a notary public or other person authorized to verify signatures satisfies this requirement.

The Effect of Errors The UETA encourages, but does not require, the use of security procedures (such as encryption) to verify changes to electronic documents and to correct errors. If the parties have agreed to a security procedure and one party does not detect an error because he or she did not follow the procedure, the conforming party can legally avoid the effect of the change or error.

To avoid the effect of errors, a party must promptly notify the other party of the error and of her or his intent not to be bound by the error. In addition, the party must take reasonable steps to return any benefit received. Parties cannot avoid a transaction if they have benefited.

Timing An electronic record is considered *sent* when it is properly directed to the intended recipient in a form readable by the recipient's computer system. Once the electronic record leaves the control of the sender or comes under the control of the recipient, the UETA deems it to have been sent. An electronic record is considered *received* when it enters the recipient's processing system in a readable form—*even if no individual is aware of its receipt.*

Practice and Review

Shane Durbin wanted to have a recording studio custom-built in his home. He sent invitations to a number of local contractors to submit bids on the project. Rory Amstel submitted the lowest bid, which was $20,000 less than any of the other bids Durbin received. Durbin called Amstel to ascertain the type and quality of the materials that were included in the bid and to find out if he could substitute a superior brand of acoustic tiles for the same bid price. Amstel said he would have to check into the price difference. The parties also discussed a possible start date for construction.

Two weeks later, Durbin changed his mind and decided not to go forward with his plan to build a recording studio. Amstel filed a suit against Durbin for breach of contract. Using the information presented in the chapter, answer the following questions.

1. Did Amstel's bid meet the requirements of an offer? Explain.
2. Was there an acceptance of the offer? Why or why not?
3. Suppose that the court determines that the parties did not reach an agreement. Further suppose that Amstel, in anticipation of building Durbin's studio, had purchased materials and refused other jobs so that he would have time in his schedule for Durbin's project. Under what theory discussed in the chapter might Amstel attempt to recover these costs?
4. How is an offer terminated? Assuming that Durbin did not inform Amstel that he was rejecting the offer, was the offer terminated at any time described here? Explain.

Debate This

The terms and conditions in click-on agreements are so long and detailed that no one ever reads the agreements. Therefore, the act of clicking on "I agree" is not really an acceptance.

Key Terms

acceptance 285
agreement 277
browse-wrap term 295
click-on agreement 292
counteroffer 284
e-contract 289

e-signature 295
forum-selection clause 291
mailbox rule 288
mirror image rule 284
offer 277
option contract 284

partnering
 agreement 296
record 296
revocation 283
shrink-wrap
 agreement 294

Chapter Summary: Agreement

Offer

1. *Intention*—There must be a serious, objective intent by the offeror to become bound by the offer. Nonoffer situations include (a) expressions of opinion; (b) statements of future intent; (c) preliminary negotiations; (d) invitations to bid; (e) advertisements and price lists; and (f) live and online auctions.
2. *Definiteness*—The terms of the offer must be sufficiently definite to be ascertainable by the parties or by a court.
3. *Communication*—The offer must be communicated to the offeree.
4. *Termination of the offer*—The offer can be terminated either by the action of the parties or by operation of law.
   a. The parties can either revoke or reject the offer. Some offers, such as a merchant's firm offer and option contracts, are irrevocable. A counteroffer is a rejection of the original offer and the making of a new offer.
   b. An offer terminates by operation of law through a lapse of time, destruction of the specific subject of the offer, death or incompetence of the parties, or the supervening illegality of the proposed contract.

Acceptance

1. Can be made only by the offeree or the offeree's agent.
2. Must be unequivocal. Under the common law (mirror image rule), if new terms or conditions are added to the acceptance, it will be considered a counteroffer.
3. Except in a few situations, an offeree's silence does not constitute an acceptance.
4. Communication of acceptance depends on the nature of the contract. In a unilateral contract, full performance is called for. In a bilateral contract, communication of acceptance is necessary because acceptance is in the form of a promise.
5. Acceptance in bilateral contracts must be timely and takes effect when the offeree sends or delivers the acceptance via the mode of communication authorized by the offeror.

E-Contract

1. *Online offers*—The terms of contract offers presented via the Internet should be as inclusive as the terms in an offer made in a written (paper) document. The offer should be displayed in an easily readable format and should include some mechanism, such as an "I agree" or "I accept" box, by which the customer may accept the offer. Because jurisdictional issues frequently arise with online transactions, the offer should include dispute-settlement provisions and may include a forum-selection clause.
2. *Online acceptances*—
   a. Click-on agreements are created when a buyer, completing an online transaction, is required to indicate her or his assent to be bound by the terms of an offer by clicking on a box that says, for instance, "I agree." The terms of the agreement may appear on the website through which the buyer is obtaining goods or services, or they may appear on a computer screen when software is downloaded.
   b. The terms of a shrink-wrap agreement are expressed inside a box in which goods are packaged. The party who opens the box is informed that, by keeping the goods, he or she agrees to the terms of the shrink-wrap agreement.
   c. Browse-wrap terms do not require the buyer or user to assent to the terms before, say, downloading or using certain software.

(Continues)

3. *Federal law on e-signatures and e-documents—*
   a. The Uniform Electronic Transactions Act (UETA) defines an e-signature as "an electronic sound, symbol, or process attached to or logically associated with a record and executed or adopted by a person with the intent to sign the record." E-signatures may include encrypted digital signatures, names at the ends of e-mail messages, and clicks on a Web page.
   b. The Electronic Signatures in Global and National Commerce Act (E-SIGN Act) gave validity to e-signatures by providing that no contract, record, or signature may be "denied legal effect" solely because it is in an electronic form.
4. *Partnering agreements*—A seller and a buyer who frequently do business with each other agree in advance on the terms and conditions that will apply to all transactions subsequently conducted electronically.

The Uniform Electronic Transactions Act (UETA)	The Uniform Electronic Transactions Act (UETA) has been adopted, at least in part, by most states, to create rules to support the enforcement of e-contracts. Under the UETA, contracts entered into online, as well as other documents, are presumed to be valid. The UETA does not apply to certain transactions governed by the UCC or to wills or testamentary trusts.

Issue Spotters

1. Fidelity Corporation offers to hire Ron to replace Monica, who has given Fidelity a month's notice of her intent to leave the company. Fidelity gives Ron a week to decide whether to accept. Two days later, Monica decides not to leave and signs an employment contract with Fidelity for another year. The next day, Monica tells Ron of the new contract. Ron immediately e-mails a formal letter of acceptance to Fidelity. Do Fidelity and Ron have a contract? Why or why not? (See *Offer.*)

2. Applied Products, Inc., does business with Beltway Distributors, Inc., online. Under the Uniform Electronic Transactions Act, what determines the effect of the electronic documents evidencing the parties' deal? Is a party's "signature" necessary? Explain. (See *The Uniform Electronic Transactions Act.*)

—**Check your answers to the *Issue Spotters* against the answers provided in Appendix D at the end of this text.**

Business Scenarios and Case Problems

11–1. Offer. Ball writes to Sullivan and inquires how much Sullivan is asking for a specific forty-acre tract of land Sullivan owns. Ball then receives a letter from Sullivan stating, "I will not take less than $60,000 for the forty-acre tract as specified." Ball immediately sends Sullivan a fax stating, "I accept your offer for $60,000 for the forty-acre tract as specified." Discuss whether Ball can hold Sullivan to a contract for sale of the land. (See *Offer.*)

11–2. Shrink-Wrap Agreements. TracFone Wireless, Inc., sells phones and wireless service. The phones are sold for less than their cost, and TracFone recoups this loss by selling prepaid airtime for their use on its network. Software in the phones prohibits their use on other networks. The phones are sold subject to the condition that the buyer agrees "not to tamper with or alter the software." This condition is printed on the packaging. Bequator Corp. bought at least 18,616 of the phones, disabled the software so that they could be used on other networks, and resold them. Is Bequator liable for breach of contract? Explain. [*TracFone Wireless, Inc. v. Bequator Corp., Ltd.*, 2011 WL 1427635 (S.D.Fla. 2011)] (See *E-Contracts.*)

11–3. Online Acceptances. Heather Reasonover opted to try Internet service from Clearwire Corp. Clearwire sent her a confirmation e-mail that included a link to its website. Clearwire also sent her a modem. In the enclosed written materials, at the bottom of a page,

in small type was the website URL. When Reasonover plugged in the modem, an "I accept terms" box appeared. Without clicking on the box, Reasonover quit the page. A clause in Clearwire's "Terms of Service," accessible only through its website, required its subscribers to submit any dispute to arbitration. Is Reasonover bound to this clause? Why or why not? [*Kwan v. Clearwire Corp.*, 2012 WL 32380 (W.D.Wash. 2012)] (See *E-Contracts.*)

11–4. Acceptance. Judy Olsen, Kristy Johnston, and their mother, Joyce Johnston, owned seventy-eight acres of real property on Eagle Creek in Meagher County, Montana. When Joyce died, she left her interest in the property to Kristy. Kristy wrote to Judy, offering to buy Judy's interest or to sell her own interest to Judy. She requested that Judy "please respond to Bruce Townsend." In a letter to Kristy—not to Bruce—Judy accepted the offer to buy Kristy's interest in the property. By that time, however, Kristy had offered to sell her interest to their brother, Dave, and he had accepted. Did Judy and Kristy have an enforceable binding contract, entitling Judy to specific performance? Or did Kristy's offer so limit its acceptance to one exclusive mode that Judy's reply was not effective? Discuss. [*Olsen v. Johnston*, 368 Mont. 347, 301 P.3d 791 (2013)] (See *Acceptance.*)

11–5. Acceptance. Amy Kemper was seriously injured when her motorcycle was struck by a vehicle driven by Christopher Brown. Kemper's attorney wrote to Statewide Claims Services, the administrator for Brown's insurer, asking for "all the insurance money that Mr. Brown had under his insurance policy." In exchange, the letter indicated that Kemper would sign a "limited release" on Brown's liability, provided that it did not include any language requiring her to reimburse Brown or his insurance company for any of their incurred costs. Statewide then sent a check and release form to Kemper, but the release demanded that Kemper "place money in an escrow account in regards to any and all liens pending." Kemper refused the demand, claiming that Statewide's response was a counteroffer rather than an unequivocal acceptance of the settlement offer. Did Statewide and Kemper have an enforceable agreement? Discuss. [*Kemper v. Brown*, 325 Ga.App. 806, 754 S.E.2d 141 (2014)] (See *Acceptance*.)

11–6. Business Case Problem with Sample Answer—

Requirements of the Offer. Technical Consumer Products, Inc. (TCP), makes and distributes energy-efficient lighting products. Emily Bahr was TCP's district sales manager in Minnesota, North Dakota, and South Dakota when the company announced the details of a bonus plan. A district sales manager who achieved 100 percent year-over-year sales growth and a 42 percent gross margin would earn 200 percent of his or her base salary as a bonus. TCP retained absolute discretion to modify the plan. Bahr's base salary was $42,500. Her final sales results for the year showed 113 percent year-over-year sales growth and a 42 percent gross margin. She anticipated a bonus of $85,945, but TCP could not afford to pay the bonuses as planned, and Bahr received only $34,229. In response to Bahr's claim for breach of contract, TCP argued that the bonus plan was too indefinite to be an offer. Is TCP correct? Explain. [*Bahr v. Technical Consumer Products, Inc.*, 601 Fed.Appx. 359 (6th Cir. 2015)] (See *Offer*.)

—For a sample answer to Problem 11–6, go to Appendix E at the end of this text.

11–7. Acceptance. Altisource Portfolio Solutions, Inc., is a global corporation that provides real property owners with services, such as property preservation—repairs, debris removal, and so on. Lucas Contracting, Inc., is a small trade contractor in Carrollton, Ohio. On behalf of Altisource, Berghorst Enterprises, LLC, hired Lucas to perform preservation work on certain foreclosed properties in eastern Ohio. When Berghorst did not pay for the work, Lucas filed a suit in an Ohio state court against Altisource. Before the trial, Lucas e-mailed the terms of a settlement. The same day, Altisource e-mailed a response that did not challenge or contradict Lucas's proposal and indicated agreement to it. Two days later, however, Altisource forwarded a settlement document that contained additional terms. Which proposal most likely satisfies the element of agreement to establish a contract? Explain. [*Lucas Contracting, Inc. v. Altisource Portfolio Solutions, Inc.*, 2016 -Ohio- 474 (2016)] (See *Acceptance*.)

11–8. Online Acceptances. Airbnb, Inc., maintains a website that lists, advertises, and takes fees or commissions for property rentals posted on the site. To offer or book accommodations on the site, a party must register and create an account. The sign-up screen states, "By clicking 'Sign Up' . . . you confirm that you accept the Terms of Service" (TOS). The TOS, which are hyperlinked, include a mandatory arbitration provision. Francesco Plazza registered with Airbnb and created an account but did not read the TOS. Later, Plazza filed a suit in a federal district court against Airbnb, alleging that the defendant was acting as an unlicensed real estate broker and committing deceptive trade practices in violation of New York state law. Airbnb filed a motion to compel arbitration, pursuant to the TOS. Can Plazza avoid arbitration? Explain. [*Plazza v. Airbnb, Inc.*, 289 F.Supp.3d 537 (S.D.N.Y. 2018)] (See *E-Contracts*.)

11–9. A Question of Ethics—The IDDR Approach and

Intention. *The Prince Hall Grand Lodge of Washington is a fraternal association incorporated in the state of Washington. The Grand Lodge Constitution provides that the Grand Master "shall decide all questions of . . . Masonic law." Grand Master Gregory Wraggs suspended the membership of Lonnie Traylor for "un-Masonic conduct." Traylor asked Wraggs to revoke the suspension and prepared a "Memo of Understanding." Wraggs agreed to talk but declined to revoke the suspension and did not sign the memo. Traylor filed a suit in a Washington state court against the Grand Lodge and Wraggs, alleging that the Grand Master's failure to revoke Traylor's suspension was a breach of contract. [*Traylor v. Most Worshipful Prince Hall Grand Lodge, 197 Wash.App. 1026 (Div. 2 2017)] (See Offer.)*

1. Was it ethical of Wraggs to agree to talk to Traylor but decline to revoke his suspension? Use the IDDR approach to decide.

2. On what basis would the court likely hold that there was no contract between Wraggs and Traylor? Is it unethical of Traylor to assert otherwise? Discuss, using the IDDR approach.

Critical Thinking and Writing Assignments

11–10. Time-Limited Group Assignment—E-Contracts. To download a specific app to your smartphone or tablet device, you usually have to check a box indicating that you agree to the company's terms and conditions. Most individuals do so without ever reading those terms and conditions. Print out a specific set of terms and conditions from a downloaded app to use in this assignment. All group members should print out the same set of terms and conditions. (See *E-Contracts*.)

1. One group will determine which of these terms and conditions are favorable to the company.

2. Another group will determine which of these terms and conditions could conceivably be favorable to the individual.

3. A third group will determine which terms and conditions, on net, favor the company too much.

Hero Images/Getty Images

12 Consideration

Learning Objectives

The four Learning Objectives *below are designed to help improve your understanding. After reading this chapter, you should be able to answer the following questions:*

1. What is required for consideration to be legally sufficient?

2. What are some examples of contracts that lack consideration?

3. What is an accord and satisfaction?

4. In what circumstances might a promise be enforced despite a lack of consideration?

Consideration The value given in return for a promise or performance in a contractual agreement.

> "No cause of action arises from a bare promise."
>
> **Legal Maxim**

As the chapter-opening quotation infers, a "bare promise" is not enforceable. Before a court will enforce a contractual promise, it must be convinced that there was some exchange of *consideration* underlying the bargain.

In this chapter, we first examine the basic elements of consideration and the requirement that consideration be legally sufficient. We then describe certain types of contracts in which consideration is lacking. Next, we discuss the requirement of consideration with respect to the settlement of claims. Lastly, we conclude with a discussion of a doctrine under which promises may be enforceable despite the lack of consideration.

12–1 Elements of Consideration

The simple fact that a party has made a promise does not necessarily mean that the promise is enforceable. Under the common law, a primary basis for the enforcement of promises is consideration. **Consideration** usually is defined as the value given in return for a promise. Often, consideration is broken down into two parts: (1) something of *legally sufficient value* must be given in exchange for the promise, and (2) there must be a *bargained-for exchange*.

12–1a Legally Sufficient Value

To be legally sufficient, consideration must be something of value in the eyes of the law. The "something of legally sufficient value" may consist of any of the following:

1. A promise to do something that one has no prior legal duty to do.
2. The performance of an action that one is otherwise not obligated to undertake (such as providing accounting services).
3. The refraining from an action that one has a legal right to undertake (called a **forbearance**).

Consideration in bilateral contracts normally consists of a promise in return for a promise. In a contract for the sale of goods, for instance, the seller promises to ship specific goods to the buyer, and the buyer promises to pay for those goods when they are received. Each of these promises constitutes consideration for the contract.

In contrast, unilateral contracts involve a promise in return for a performance. **Example 12.1** Anita says to her neighbor, "If you paint my garage, I will pay you $800." Anita's neighbor paints the garage. The act of painting the garage is the consideration that creates Anita's contractual obligation to pay her neighbor $800. ▪

What if, in return for a promise to pay, a person refrains from pursuing harmful habits, such as the use of tobacco and alcohol? Does such forbearance create consideration for the contract? This was the issue in the 1891 case *Hamer v. Sidway*, which we present as this chapter's *Landmark in the Law* feature.

> **Learning Objective 1**
> What is required for consideration to be legally sufficient?

forbearance The act of refraining from an action that one has a legal right to undertake.

Hamer v. Sidway (1891)

Landmark in the Law

In *Hamer v. Sidway*,[a] the issue before the court arose from a contract created in 1869 between William Story, Sr., and his nephew, William Story II. The uncle promised his nephew that if the nephew refrained from drinking alcohol, using tobacco, and playing billiards and cards for money until he reached the age of twenty-one, the uncle would pay him $5,000 (about $75,000 in today's dollars). The nephew, who indulged occasionally in all of these "vices," agreed to refrain from them and did so for the next six years.

Following his twenty-first birthday in 1875, the nephew wrote to his uncle that he had performed his part of the bargain and was thus entitled to the promised $5,000 (plus interest). A few days later, the uncle wrote the nephew a letter stating, "[Y]ou shall have the five thousand dollars, as I promised you." The uncle said that the money was in the bank and that the nephew could "consider this money on interest."

The Issue of Consideration The nephew left the money in the care of his uncle, who held it for the next twelve years. When the uncle died in 1887, however, the executor of the uncle's estate refused to pay the $5,000 (plus interest) claim brought by Hamer, a third party to whom the promise had been *assigned*. (The law allows parties to assign, or transfer, rights in contracts to third parties.)

The executor, Sidway, contended that the contract was invalid because there was insufficient consideration to support it. The uncle had received nothing, and the nephew had actually benefited by fulfilling the uncle's wishes. Therefore, no contract existed.

The Court's Conclusion Although a lower court upheld Sidway's position, the New York Court of Appeals reversed and ruled in favor of the plaintiff, Hamer. "The promisee used tobacco, occasionally drank liquor, and he had a legal right to do so," the court stated. "That right he abandoned for a period of years upon the strength of the promise of the testator [one who makes a will] that for such forbearance he would give him $5,000. We need not speculate on the effort which may have been required to give up the use of those stimulants. It is sufficient that he restricted his lawful freedom of action within certain prescribed limits upon the faith of his uncle's agreement."

Application to Today's World *Although this case was decided more than a century ago, the principles enunciated by the court remain applicable to contracts formed today, including online contracts. For a contract to be valid and binding, consideration must be given, and that consideration must be something of legally sufficient value.*

a. 124 N.Y. 538, 27 N.E. 256 (1891).

12–1b Bargained-for Exchange

The second element of consideration is that it must provide the basis for the bargain struck between the contracting parties. The item of value must be given or promised by the promisor (offeror) in return for the promisee's promise or performance.

This element of bargained-for exchange distinguishes contracts from gifts. **Case Example 12.2** Rachel Thomas was admitted to a hospital emergency room with pregnancy-related complications. The attending physician, Dr. Archer, recommended that she be transported by medevac (helicopter) to a different facility. The woman and her husband informed the physician that they needed their insurer's preauthorization for that course of action or they could be personally liable for the costs. Dr. Archer allegedly promised to call the insurer and, if it would not approve the medevac, have the hospital bear the costs itself. But the physician failed to contact the insurer until much later, and the insurer declined coverage.

The couple sued the hospital, claiming breach of contract by Dr. Archer. The court ruled in favor of the hospital, and the case was appealed to the Alaska Supreme Court. The court held that the physician's alleged promise about insurance and payment did not give rise to an enforceable contract. There was no evidence that the hospital sought any consideration from the Thomases for the physician's alleged promise. Thus, there was no "bargained-for" consideration. The court affirmed the dismissal of the Thomases' contract claim (but remanded the case on the issue of promissory estoppel, a concept that will be discussed shortly)[1]. ■

Sometimes, employers offer to cover the costs of employment-related education for their employees. The employees may then be required to repay their employers for all or a portion of the costs. At the center of the dispute in the following case was an agreement signed by an employee to reimburse his employer for educational costs. The question was whether the agreement met the requirement of a bargained-for exchange.

---

1. *Thomas v. Archer*, 384 P.3d 791 (Alaska 2016).

Case 12.1

USS–POSCO Industries v. Case
California Court of Appeal, First District, Division 1, 244 Cal.App.4th 197, 197 Cal.Rptr.3d 791 (2016).

Background and Facts Floyd Case was an employee of USS–POSCO Industries (UPI) in Pittsburg, California. While an employee, Case voluntarily enrolled in a three-year, employer-sponsored educational program to become a maintenance technical electrical worker. UPI agreed to pay the upfront costs of the program. Under a one-page written reimbursement agreement, Case agreed that if he quit his job within thirty months of completing the program, he would reimburse UPI a prorated portion of the $46,000 cost of the program.

Two months after completing the program, Case left UPI to work for Lawrence Livermore National Laboratory as a high-voltage electrician. When he refused to reimburse UPI for the cost of his education, the company filed a suit in a California

state court against him for breach of contract. Case filed a cross-complaint, asserting that the reimbursement agreement was unenforceable, because it lacked consideration. The court granted UPI's motion for summary judgment on both complaints. Case appealed.

In the Words of the Court
BANKE, J. [Judge]
* * * *

Case maintains the [written] reimbursement agreement [he signed] * * * lacked consideration because UPI had no obligation to keep Case employed and, thus, no obligation to provide education, which Case views as "the only possible consideration listed in the Reimbursement Agreement." Case's view of the bargained-for exchange is too constrained.

On entering the program, Case held a new position of Learner, which meant he would remain on UPI's payroll while *additionally* getting classroom and on-the-job training, the costs of which UPI would front. While Case was not guaranteed a promotion, transfer, or continued employment, exactly the same had been true with respect to his previous position. The exchange, frankly, is obvious: Case got continued wages and fronted education costs, and UPI got Case's agreement to repay those costs if he both completed the training and left the company before it could benefit from the investment. *That either Case or UPI could have terminated the agreement by ending the employment relationship at some point during the educational program does not render illusory the parties' bargained-for exchange—or require us to ignore the substantial benefits Case obtained every day he spent on the payroll*

receiving advanced training with no upfront cost and potentially no cost at all to him. [Emphasis added.]

Decision and Remedy A state intermediate appellate court affirmed the lower court's summary judgment in favor of UPI. There was sufficient bargained-for consideration in the written reimbursement agreement between the parties. Case was in breach of contract and liable to UPI for part of the cost of his education to become a maintenance electrical technician.

Critical Thinking

• **What If the Facts Were Different?** *Suppose that UPI had simply offered to pay its employees wages and training expenses during their participation in a program of instruction "subject entirely and exclusively to UPI's approval." Would the element of bargained-for exchange have been met? Explain.*

12–1c Adequacy of Consideration

Adequacy of consideration involves "how much" consideration is given. Essentially, adequacy of consideration concerns the fairness of the bargain.

The General Rule On the surface, when the items exchanged are of unequal value, fairness would appear to be an issue. Normally, however, a court will not question the adequacy of consideration based solely on the comparative value of the things exchanged.

In other words, the determination of whether consideration exists does not depend on the values of the things exchanged. Something need not be of direct economic or financial value to be considered legally sufficient consideration. In many situations, the exchange of promises and potential benefits is deemed to be sufficient consideration.

Under the doctrine of freedom of contract, courts leave it up to the parties to decide what something is worth, and parties are usually free to bargain as they wish. If people could sue merely because they had entered into an unwise contract, the courts would be overloaded with frivolous suits.

When Voluntary Consent May Be Lacking Occasionally, an exception may be made to the general rule just discussed. A large disparity in the amount or value of the consideration exchanged may raise a red flag for a court to look more closely at the bargain. Shockingly inadequate consideration can indicate that fraud, duress, or undue influence was involved. **Example 12.3** Spencer pays $500 for an iPhone 8 that he later discovers is a fake (counterfeit). Because the device is not authentic, he could claim that there was no valid contract because of inadequate consideration and fraud. ■ (Disparity in the consideration exchanged may also cause a judge to question whether the contract is so one-sided that it is *unconscionable.*[2])

"Understanding does not necessarily mean agreement."

Vernon Howard
1918–1992
(American author)

Know This
A consumer's signature on a contract does not always guarantee that the contract will be enforced. The contract must also comply with state and federal consumer protection laws.

---

2. Pronounced un-*kon*-shun-uh-bul.

12–2 Agreements That Lack Consideration

Sometimes, one or both of the parties to a contract may think that they have exchanged consideration when in fact they have not. Here, we look at some situations in which the parties' promises or actions do not qualify as contractual consideration.

12–2a Preexisting Duty

Under most circumstances, a promise to do what one already has a legal duty to do does not constitute legally sufficient consideration. A sheriff, for instance, cannot collect a reward for information leading to the capture of a criminal if the sheriff already has a legal duty to capture the criminal.

Likewise, if a party is already bound by contract to perform a certain duty, that duty cannot serve as consideration for a second contract. **Example 12.4** Bauman-Bache, Inc., begins construction on a seven-story office building and after three months demands an extra $75,000 on its contract. If the extra $75,000 is not paid, the firm will stop working. The owner of the land, finding no one else to complete construction, agrees to pay the extra $75,000. The agreement is not enforceable because it is not supported by legally sufficient consideration—Bauman-Bache had a preexisting contractual duty to complete the building. ■

Unforeseen Difficulties The preexisting duty rule is intended to prevent extortion and the so-called holdup game. Nonetheless, if, during performance of a contract, extraordinary difficulties arise that were totally unforeseen at the time the contract was formed, a court may allow an exception to the rule. The key is whether the court finds that the modification is fair and equitable in view of circumstances not anticipated by the parties when the contract was made.[3]

Are there circumstances under which a contractor can legally demand a payment amount that is greater than what was stated in the contract?

Suppose that in *Example 12.4*, Bauman-Bache asked for the extra $75,000 because it encountered a rock formation that no one knew existed. Suppose, too, that the landowner agreed to pay the extra amount to excavate the rock. In this situation, if the court finds that it is fair to do so, it may enforce the agreement. If rock formations are common in the area, however, the court may determine that the contractor should have known of the risk. In that situation, the court may choose to apply the preexisting duty rule and prevent Bauman-Bache from obtaining the extra $75,000.

Rescission and New Contract The law recognizes that two parties can mutually agree to rescind, or cancel, their contract, at least to the extent that it is *executory* (still to be carried out). **Rescission**[4] is the unmaking of a contract so as to return the parties to the positions they occupied before the contract was made.

Sometimes, parties rescind a contract and make a new contract at the same time. When this occurs, it is often difficult to determine whether there was consideration for the new contract or whether the parties had a preexisting duty under the previous contract. If a court finds there was a preexisting duty, then the new contract will be invalid because there was no consideration.

Rescission A remedy whereby a contract is canceled and the parties are returned to the positions they occupied before the contract was made.

12–2b Past Consideration

Promises made in return for actions or events that have already taken place are unenforceable. These promises lack consideration in that the element of bargained-for exchange is missing. In short, you can bargain for something to take place now or in the future but not for something that has already taken place. Therefore, **past consideration** is no consideration.

⭐ **Spotlight Case Example 12.5** Jamil Blackmon became friends with Allen Iverson when Iverson was a high school student who showed tremendous promise as an athlete. Blackmon suggested that Iverson use "The Answer" as a nickname in the league tournaments, and said

Past Consideration Something given or some act done in the past, which cannot ordinarily be consideration for a later bargain.

---

3. *Restatement (Second) of Contracts*, Section 73.
4. Pronounced reh-sih-zhen.

that Iverson would be "The Answer" to the National Basketball Association's declining attendance. Later, Iverson said that he would give Blackmon 25 percent of any proceeds from the merchandising of products that used "The Answer" as a logo or a slogan. Because Iverson's promise was made in return for past consideration (Blackmon's earlier suggestion), it was unenforceable. In effect, Iverson stated his intention to give Blackmon a gift.[5]

Often, an employer will ask an employee to sign a noncompete agreement. Under these agreements, the employee agrees not to compete with the employer for a certain period of time after the employment relationship ends. When a current employee is required to sign a noncompete agreement, his or her employment is not sufficient consideration for the agreement, because he or she is already employed. The agreement requires new consideration.

In the following case, the court had to decide if new consideration supported a noncompete agreement between physicians and a medical clinic.

5. *Blackmon v. Iverson*, 324 F.Supp.2d 602 (E.D.Pa. 2003).

Case 12.2

Baugh v. Columbia Heart Clinic, P.A.[a]
Court of Appeals of South Carolina, 402 S.C. 1, 738 S.E.2d 480 (2013).

Background and Facts Columbia Heart Clinic, P.A., in Columbia, South Carolina, provides comprehensive cardiology services. Its physicians are all cardiologists. When Kevin Baugh, M.D., and Barry Feldman, M.D., became employees and shareholders of Columbia Heart, and again several years later, they signed noncompete agreements. Under these agreements, Baugh and Feldman would forfeit certain payments if they competed with Columbia Heart within a year after their employment ended. Specifically, they were not to practice cardiology within twenty miles of any Columbia Heart office where they routinely provided services.

Later, Baugh and Feldman left Columbia Heart and opened a new cardiology practice near one of Columbia Heart's offices. They then filed a suit in a South Carolina state court against Columbia Heart, seeking a ruling that their noncompete agreements were unenforceable. From a judgment in favor of Baugh and Feldman, Columbia Heart appealed.

In the Words of the Court
THOMAS, J. [Judge]
* * * *

* * * Article 5 [of the agreements] says the following:

Physician, in the event of termination * * * for any reason, during the twelve (12) month period immediately following the date of termination * * * shall not Compete * * * with Columbia Heart * * * within a twenty (20) mile radius of any Columbia Heart office at

which Physician routinely provided services during the year prior to the date of termination.

No separate monetary consideration was paid to any shareholder-physician to sign the Agreements, nor did the Agreements change the [established] compensation system.
* * * *

[Baugh and Feldman] contend * * * that the Agreements are unenforceable because they are not supported by new consideration. We disagree.

When a covenant not to compete [noncompete agreement] is entered into after the inception of employment, separate consideration, in addition to continued at-will employment, is necessary in order for the covenant to be enforceable. There is no consideration when the contract containing the covenant is exacted after several years' employment and the employee's duties and position are left unchanged. [Emphasis added.]

[Baugh and Feldman] executed the Agreements after they became employed by Columbia Heart, and the Agreements did not change the general compensation system agreed to by the parties under their prior employment contracts. However, * * * Article 4 of the Agreements provides the following:

Physician shall be paid Five Thousand and No/100 Dollars ($5,000.00) per month for each of the twelve (12) months following termination, so long as the Physician is not in violation of Article 5 of this Agreement.

(Continues)

This language established that Columbia Heart promised to pay [Baugh and Feldman] each * * * a total of $60,000 over twelve months after termination so long as they did not violate the noncompetition provision in Article 5. * * * Consequently, the Agreements are supported by new consideration.

Decision and Remedy   A state intermediate appellate court reversed the lower court's finding that the noncompete provisions were unenforceable. The agreements were supported by new consideration because they provided for compensation to shareholders who left Columbia Heart so long as they did not compete with the clinic's cardiology practice.

Critical Thinking

• **Social** *When a noncompete agreement is entered into after employment has begun, is continued employment sufficient consideration for the agreement? Explain.*

12–2c Illusory Promises

If the terms of the contract express such uncertainty of performance that the promisor has not definitely promised to do anything, the promise is said to be *illusory*—without consideration and unenforceable. **Example 12.6** The president of Tuscan Corporation says to his employees, "All of you have worked hard, and if profits remain high, a 10 percent bonus at the end of the year will be given—if management thinks it is warranted." This is an *illusory promise*, or no promise at all, because performance depends solely on the discretion of the president (the management). There is no bargained-for consideration. The statement declares merely that management may or may not do something in the future.

Option-to-cancel clauses in contracts for specified time periods sometimes present problems because of illusory promises. **Example 12.7** Abe contracts to hire Chris for one year at $5,000 per month, reserving the right to cancel the contract at any time. On close examination of these words, you can see that Abe has not actually agreed to hire Chris, as Abe can cancel without liability before Chris starts performance. Abe has not given up the opportunity of hiring someone else. This contract is therefore illusory.

But if, instead, Abe reserves the right to cancel the contract at any time *after* Chris has begun performance by giving Chris *thirty days' notice*, the promise is not illusory. Abe, by saying that he will give Chris thirty days' notice, is relinquishing the opportunity (legal right) to hire someone else instead of Chris for a thirty-day period. If Chris works for one month and Abe then gives him thirty days' notice, Chris has an enforceable claim for two months' salary ($10,000).

Exhibit 12–1 illustrates some common situations in which promises or actions do not constitute contractual consideration.

Exhibit 12–1 Examples of Agreements That Lack Consideration

PREEXISTING DUTY	PAST CONSIDERATION	ILLUSORY PROMISES
When a person already has a legal duty to perform an action, a promise to perform that action is not legally sufficient consideration.	When a person makes a promise in return for actions or events that have already taken place, there is no consideration.	When contract terms are so uncertain that there is no definite promise, the promise is illusory.
Example: A firefighter cannot receive a cash reward from a business owner for putting out a fire in a downtown commercial district. As a city employee, the firefighter had a duty to extinguish the fire.	*Example:* A real estate agent sells a friend's house without charging a commission, and in return, the friend promises to give the agent $1,000. The friend's promise is simply an intention to give a gift.	*Example:* A man promises to stop by soon to look at his neighbor's riding lawn mower. If he likes it, he will pay $900. The promise to purchase is simply a statement of something he might do in the future.

12–3 Settlement of Claims

Businesspersons and others often enter into contracts to settle legal claims. It is important to understand the nature of the consideration given in these settlement agreements. Commonly used settlement agreements include the *accord and satisfaction*, the *release*, and the *covenant not to sue*.

12–3a Accord and Satisfaction

In an **accord and satisfaction**, a debtor offers to pay, and a creditor accepts, a lesser amount than the creditor originally claimed was owed. The *accord* is the agreement. In the accord, one party undertakes to give or perform, and the other to accept, in satisfaction of a claim, something other than that on which the parties originally agreed. *Satisfaction* is the performance (usually payment) that takes place after the accord is executed.

A basic rule is that there can be no satisfaction unless there is first an accord. In addition, for accord and satisfaction to occur, the amount of the debt *must be in dispute*.

Liquidated Debts If a debt is *liquidated*, accord and satisfaction cannot take place. A **liquidated debt** is one whose amount has been ascertained, fixed, agreed on, settled, or exactly determined. **Example 12.8** Barbara Kwan signs an installment loan contract with her banker. In the contract, Kwan agrees to pay a specified rate of interest on a specified amount of borrowed funds at monthly intervals for two years. Because both parties know the precise amount of the total obligation, it is a liquidated debt. ▪

In the majority of states, a creditor's acceptance of a lesser sum than the entire amount of a liquidated debt is not satisfaction, and the balance of the debt is still legally owed. The reason for this rule is that the debtor has given no consideration to satisfy the obligation of paying the balance to the creditor. The debtor has a preexisting legal obligation to pay the entire debt. (Of course, even with liquidated debts, creditors often do negotiate debt settlement agreements with debtors for a lesser amount than was originally owed. Creditors sometimes even forgive or write off a liquidated debt as uncollectable.)

Unliquidated Debts An **unliquidated debt** is the opposite of a liquidated debt. The amount of the debt is not settled, fixed, agreed on, ascertained, or determined, and reasonable persons may differ over the amount owed. In these circumstances, acceptance of payment of the lesser sum operates as a satisfaction, or discharge, of the debt because there is valid consideration. The parties give up a legal right to contest the amount in dispute.

12–3b Release

A **release** is a contract in which one party forfeits the right to pursue a legal claim against the other party. It bars any further recovery beyond the terms stated in the release.

A release will generally be binding if it meets the following requirements:

1. The agreement is made in good faith.
2. The release contract is in a signed writing (required in many states).
3. The contract is accompanied by consideration.[6]

A person involved in an automobile accident may be asked to sign a release. Clearly, the person is better off knowing the extent of his or her injuries or damages before signing. **Example 12.9** Kara's car is damaged in an accident caused by Raoul's negligence. Raoul offers to give Kara $3,000 if she will release him from further liability resulting from the accident. Kara agrees and signs the release.

Accord and Satisfaction A common means of settling a disputed claim, whereby a debtor offers to pay a lesser amount than the creditor purports to be owed.

Liquidated Debt A debt whose amount has been ascertained, fixed, agreed on, settled, or exactly determined.

Unliquidated Debt A debt that is uncertain in amount.

Release An agreement in which one party gives up the right to pursue a legal claim against another party.

---

6. Under the Uniform Commercial Code (UCC), a written, signed waiver by an aggrieved party discharges any further liability for a breach, even without consideration.

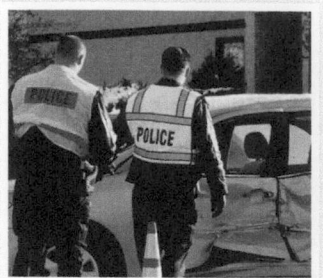

Is it possible to limit one's liability after a car accident?

Covenant Not to Sue An agreement to substitute a contractual obligation for another legal action based on a valid claim.

If Kara later discovers that the repairs will cost $4,200, she cannot recover the additional amount from Raoul. Kara is limited to the $3,000 specified in the release because a valid contract was formed. Kara and Raoul both voluntarily agreed to the terms in a signed writing, and sufficient consideration was present. The consideration was the legal right to recover damages that Kara forfeited should her damages be more than $3,000, in exchange for Raoul's promise to give her $3,000.

12–3c Covenant Not to Sue

Unlike a release, a **covenant not to sue** does not always prevent further recovery. The parties simply substitute a contractual obligation for some other type of legal action based on a valid claim. Suppose in *Example 12.9* that Kara agrees not to sue Raoul for damages in a tort action if he will pay for the damage to her car. If Raoul fails to pay, Kara can bring an action for breach of contract.

As the following *Spotlight Case* illustrates, a covenant not to sue can form the basis for a dismissal of the claims of either party to the covenant.

★ Spotlight on Nike: Case 12.3

Already, LLC v. Nike, Inc.
Supreme Court of the United States, 568 U.S. 85, 133 S.Ct. 721, 184 L.Ed.2d 553 (2013).

Background and Facts Nike, Inc., designs, makes, and sells athletic footwear, including a line of shoes known as "Air Force 1." Already, LLC, also designs and markets athletic footwear, including the "Sugar" and "Soulja Boy" lines. Nike filed a suit in a federal district court against Already, alleging that Soulja Boys and Sugars infringed the Air Force 1 trademark. Already filed a counterclaim, contending that the Air Force 1 trademark was invalid.

While the suit was pending, Nike issued a covenant not to sue. Nike promised not to raise any trademark claims against Already based on Already's existing footwear designs or any future Already designs that constituted a "colorable imitation" of Already's current products. Nike then filed a motion to dismiss its own claims and to dismiss Already's counterclaim. Already opposed the dismissal of its counterclaim, but the court granted Nike's motion. The U.S. Court of Appeals for the Second Circuit affirmed. Already appealed to the United States Supreme Court.

In the Words of the Court
Chief Justice *ROBERTS* delivered the opinion of the Court.
* * * *
* * * A defendant cannot automatically moot a case simply by ending its unlawful conduct once sued. [A matter is *moot* if it

Will a plaintiff's covenant not to sue prevent the defendant from pursuing a counterclaim against the plaintiff?

involves no actual controversy for the court to decide, and federal courts will dismiss moot cases.] Otherwise, a defendant could engage in unlawful conduct, stop when sued to have the case declared moot, then pick up where he left off, repeating this cycle until he achieves all his unlawful ends. Given this concern, * * * *a defendant claiming that its voluntary compliance moots a case bears the formidable burden of showing that it is absolutely clear the allegedly wrongful behavior could not reasonably be expected to recur.* [This is the voluntary cessation test. Emphasis added.]
* * * *

We begin our analysis with the terms of the covenant:

[Nike] unconditionally and irrevocably covenants to refrain from making *any* claim(s) or demand(s) * * * against Already or *any* of its * * * related business entities * * * [including] distributors * * * and employees of such entities and all customers * * * on account of any *possible* cause of action based on or involving trademark infringement * * * relating to the NIKE Mark based on the appearance of *any* of Already's current and/or previous footwear product designs, and *any* colorable imitations thereof, regardless of whether that footwear is produced * * * or otherwise used in commerce.

The breadth of this covenant suffices to meet the burden imposed by the voluntary cessation test. In addition, Nike originally argued that the Sugars and Soulja Boys infringed its trademark; in other words, Nike believed those shoes were "colorable imitations" of the Air Force 1s. Nike's covenant now allows Already to produce all of its existing footwear designs—including the Sugar and Soulja Boy—and any "colorable imitation" of those designs. * * * It is hard to imagine a scenario that would potentially infringe Nike's trademark and yet not fall under the covenant. Nike, having taken the position in court that there is no prospect of such a shoe, would be hard pressed to assert the contrary down the road. If such a shoe exists, the parties have not pointed to it, there is no evidence that Already has dreamt of it, and we cannot conceive of it. It sits, as far as we can tell, on a shelf between Dorothy's ruby slippers and Perseus's winged sandals.

* * * *

* * * Given the covenant's broad language, and given that Already has asserted no concrete plans to engage in conduct not covered by the covenant, we can conclude the case is moot because the challenged conduct cannot reasonably be expected to recur.

Decision and Remedy The United States Supreme Court affirmed the judgment of the lower court. Under the covenant not to sue, Nike could not file a claim for trademark infringement against Already, and Already could not assert that Nike's trademark was invalid.

Critical Thinking

• **Economic** *Why would any party agree to a covenant not to sue?*

• **Legal Environment** *Which type of contracts are similar to covenants not to sue?*

12–4 Promissory Estoppel

Sometimes, individuals rely on promises, and their reliance may form a basis for a court to infer contract rights and duties. Under the doctrine of **promissory estoppel** (also called *detrimental reliance*), a person who has reasonably and substantially relied on the promise of another can obtain some measure of recovery. Promissory estoppel allows a party to recover on a promise even though it was made *without consideration*. Under this doctrine, a court may enforce an otherwise unenforceable promise to avoid an injustice that would otherwise result.

> **Promissory Estoppel** A doctrine that can be used to enforce a promise when the promisee has justifiably relied on the promise and when justice will be better served by enforcing the promise.

12–4a Requirements to Establish Promissory Estoppel

For the doctrine of promissory estoppel to be applied, the following elements are required:

1. There must be a clear and definite promise.
2. The promisor should have expected that the promisee would rely on the promise.
3. The promisee reasonably relied on the promise by acting or refraining from some act.
4. The promisee's reliance was definite and resulted in substantial detriment.
5. Enforcement of the promise is necessary to avoid injustice.

> **Learning Objective 4**
>
> In what circumstances might a promise be enforced despite a lack of consideration?

If these requirements are met, a promise may be enforced even though it is not supported by consideration. In essence, the promisor (the offeror) will be **estopped** (barred or prevented) from asserting lack of consideration as a defense.

> **Estopped** Barred, impeded, or precluded.

Promissory estoppel is similar in some ways to the doctrine of quasi contract that was discussed in a previous chapter. In both situations, a court is acting in the interests of equity and imposes contract obligations on the parties to prevent unfairness even though no actual contract exists. The difference is that with quasi contract, no promise was made at all. In contrast, with promissory estoppel, an otherwise unenforceable promise was made and relied on.

12–4b Application of Promissory Estoppel

Promissory estoppel was originally applied to situations involving gifts (I promise to pay you $1,000 a week so that you will not have to work) and donations to charities (I promise to contribute $50,000 a year to the All Saints orphanage). Later, courts began to apply the doctrine in other situations, including business transactions, employment relationships, and disputes among family members.

Case Example 12.10 CBRE, Inc., was selling commercial real estate owned by API Foils, Inc. BH 329 NB, LLC, offered to buy the property for $7.5 million, which CBRE accepted. BH 329 NB signed a letter of intent setting forth the sale's terms, including the purchase price and an agreement to lease back the property to API for one year. API signed the letter of intent, showing its agreement in principle to the deal. The letter specified that it was not a sales contract.

CBRE promised it would not market or accept other purchase offers while the parties were closing the deal. Despite its promise, CBRE continued to market the property and eventually received a higher offer from a different buyer. CBRE then notified BH 329 NB that it no longer had a deal with API.

BH 329 NB sued CBRE for breach of contract and promissory estoppel. A federal district court dismissed the contract claim but allowed the promissory estoppel claim to go forward. CBRE clearly had promised not to market the property in exchange for the plaintiff's agreement not to lower its offer price. BH 329 NB reasonably relied on CBRE's promise by continuing to negotiate the deal with API, and by doing so, incurred costs and lost other business opportunities as a result.[7]

---

7. *BH 329 NB, LLC v. CBRE, Inc.,* 2017 WL 3641566 (D.N.J. 2017).

Practice and Review

John operates a motorcycle repair shop from his home but finds that his business is limited by the small size of his garage. Driving by a neighbor's property, he notices a for-sale sign on a large, metal-sided garage. John contacts the neighbor and offers to buy the building, hoping that it can be dismantled and moved to his own property. The neighbor accepts John's payment and makes a generous offer in return. If John will help him dismantle the garage, which will take a substantial amount of time, he will help John reassemble it after it has been transported to John's property. They agree to have the entire job completed within two weeks.

John then spends every day for a week working with his neighbor to disassemble the building. In his rush to acquire a larger workspace, he turns down several lucrative repair jobs. Once the disassembled building has been moved to John's property, however, the neighbor refuses to help John reassemble it as he originally promised. Using the information presented in the chapter, answer the following questions.

1. Are the basic elements of consideration present in the neighbor's promise to help John reassemble the garage? Why or why not?

2. Suppose that the neighbor starts to help John but then realizes that putting the building back together will take much more work than dismantling it. Under which principle might the neighbor be allowed to ask for additional compensation?

3. What if John's neighbor made his promise to help reassemble the garage at the time he and John were moving it? Suppose he said, "Since you helped me take it down, I will help you put it back up." Would John be able to enforce this promise? Why or why not?

4. Under what doctrine might John seek to recover the profits he lost when he turned down repair jobs for one week?

Debate This

Courts should not be able to rule on adequacy of consideration. A deal is a deal.

Key Terms

Chapter Summary: Consideration

Elements of Consideration	Consideration is broken down into two parts: (1) something of *legally sufficient value* must be given in exchange for the promise, and (2) there must be a *bargained-for exchange*. (The *adequacy of consideration* relates to how much consideration is given and whether a fair bargain was reached.)
Agreements That Lack Consideration	Consideration is lacking in the following situations: 1. *Preexisting duty*—In general, a promise to do what one already has a legal or contractual duty to do does not constitute legally sufficient consideration. 2. *Past consideration*—Actions or events that have already taken place do not constitute legally sufficient consideration. 3. *Illusory promises*—When the nature or extent of performance is too uncertain, the promise is rendered illusory (without consideration and unenforceable).
Settlement of Claims	1. *Accord and satisfaction*—An accord is an agreement in which a debtor offers to pay a lesser amount than the creditor claims is owed. Satisfaction takes place when the accord is executed. 2. *Release*—An agreement in which, for consideration, a party forfeits the right to pursue further recovery beyond the terms specified in the release. 3. *Covenant not to sue*—An agreement not to sue on a present, valid claim.
Promissory Estoppel	The equitable doctrine of promissory estoppel applies when a promisor makes a clear and definite promise on which the promisee reasonably relies, and the promise substantially alters the promisee's actions. The court will enforce such promises only if an injustice would occur otherwise.

Issue Spotters

1. In September, Sharyn agrees to work for Totem Productions, Inc., at $500 a week for a year beginning January 1. In October, Sharyn is offered $600 a week for the same work by Umber Shows, Ltd. When Sharyn tells her boss at Totem about the other offer, he tears up their contract and agrees that Sharyn will be paid $575. Is the new contract binding? Explain. (See *Consideration*.)

2. Before Maria starts her first year of college, Fred promises to give her $5,000 when she graduates. She goes to college, borrowing and spending far more than $5,000. At the beginning of the spring semester of her senior year, she reminds Fred of the promise. Fred sends her a note that says, "I revoke the promise." Is Fred's promise binding? Explain. (See *Promissory Estoppel*.)

   —**Check your answers to the *Issue Spotters* against the answers provided in Appendix D at the end of this text.**

Business Scenarios and Case Problems

12–1. Preexisting Duty. Ben hired Lewis to drive his racing car in a race. Tuan, a friend of Lewis, promised to pay Lewis $3,000 if he won the race. Lewis won the race, but Tuan refused to pay the $3,000. Tuan contended that no legally binding contract had been formed because he had received no consideration from Lewis for his promise to pay the $3,000. Lewis sued Tuan for breach of contract, arguing that winning the race was the consideration given in exchange for Tuan's promise to pay the $3,000. What rule of law discussed in this chapter supports Tuan's claim? Explain. (See *Agreements That Lack Consideration*.)

12–2. Accord and Satisfaction. Merrick grows and sells blueberries. Maine Wild Blueberry Co. agreed to buy all of Merrick's crop under a contract that left the price unliquidated. Merrick delivered the berries, but a dispute arose over the price. Maine Wild sent Merrick a check with a letter stating that the check was the "final settlement." Merrick cashed the check but filed a suit for breach of contract, claiming that he was owed more. What will the court likely decide in this case, and why? (See *Settlement of Claims*.)

12–3. Rescission. Farrokh and Scheherezade Sharabianlou agreed to buy a building owned by Berenstein Associates for $2 million. They deposited $115,000 toward the purchase. Before the deal closed, an environmental assessment of the property indicated the presence of chemicals used in dry cleaning. This substantially reduced the property's value. Do the Sharabianlous have a good argument for the return of their deposit and rescission of the contract? Explain. [*Sharabianlou v. Karp*, 181 Cal.App.4th 1133, 105 Cal.Rptr.3d 300 (2010)] (See *Agreements That Lack Consideration*.)

12–4. Spotlight on Kansas City Chiefs—Consideration. On Brenda Sniezek's first day of work for the Kansas City Chiefs Football Club, she signed a document that purported to compel arbitration of any disputes that she might have with the Chiefs. In the document, Sniezek agreed to comply at all times with and be bound by the constitution and bylaws of the National Football League (NFL). She agreed to refer all disputes to the NFL commissioner for a binding decision and to release the Chiefs and others from any related claims. Nowhere in the document did the Chiefs agree to do anything. Was there consideration for the arbitration provision? Explain. [*Sniezek v. Kansas City Chiefs Football Club*, 402 S.W.3d 580 (Mo.App. W.D. 2013)] (See *Consideration*.)

12–5. Consideration. Citynet, LLC, established an employee incentive plan "to enable the Company to attract and retain experienced individuals." The plan provided that a participant who left Citynet's employment was entitled to "cash out" his or her entire vested balance. (When an employee's rights to a particular benefit become *vested*, they belong to that employee and cannot be taken away. The vested balance refers to the part of an account that goes with the employee if he or she leaves the company.)

When Citynet employee Ray Toney terminated his employment, he asked to redeem his $87,000.48 vested balance. Citynet refused, citing a provision of the plan that limited redemptions to no more than 20 percent annually. Toney filed a suit in a West Virginia state court against Citynet, alleging breach of contract. Citynet argued that the plan was not a contract but a discretionary bonus over which Citynet had sole discretion. Was the plan a contract? If so, was it bilateral or unilateral, and what was the consideration? [*Citynet, LLC v. Toney*, 235 W.Va.79, 772 S.E.2d 36 (2015)] (See *Consideration*.)

12–6. Business Case Problem with Sample Answer— Agreements That Lack Consideration. Arkansas-Missouri Forest Products, LLC (Ark-Mo), sells supplies to make wood pallets. Blue Chip Manufacturing (BCM) makes pallets. Mark Garnett, an owner of Ark-Mo, and Stuart Lerner, an owner of BCM, went into business together. Garnett and Lerner agreed that Ark-Mo would have a 30-percent ownership interest in their future projects. When Lerner formed Blue Chip Recycling, LLC (BCR), to manage a pallet repair facility in California, however, he allocated only a 5 percent interest to Ark-Mo. Garnett objected.

In a "Telephone Deal," Lerner then promised Garnett that Ark-Mo would receive a 30 percent interest in their future projects in the Midwest, and Garnett agreed to forgo an ownership interest in BCR. But when Blue Chip III, LLC (BC III), was formed to operate a repair facility in the Midwest, Lerner told Garnett that he "was not getting anything." Ark-Mo filed a suit in a Missouri state court against Lerner, alleging breach of contract. Was there consideration to support the Telephone Deal? Explain. [*Arkansas-Missouri Forest Products, LLC v. Lerner*, 486 S.W.3d 438 (Mo.App. E.D. 2016)] (See *Consideration*.)

—For a sample answer to Problem 12–6, go to Appendix E at the end of this text.

12–7. Elements of Consideration. Carmen White signed a lease with Sienna Ridge Apartments in San Antonio, Texas. The lease required White to reimburse Sienna Ridge for any damage to the apartment not caused by the landlord's negligence or fault. After moving in, White received a new washer and dryer from her parents. She did not read the instruction manual before overloading the dryer with bedding, including an unwashed pillow, which started a fire. Sienna Ridge filed a claim for the resulting damage with Philadelphia Indemnity Insurance Company. Philadelphia paid the claim and filed a suit in a Texas state court against White, alleging that she had breached the lease by failing to reimburse Sienna Ridge for the damage. White argued that the lease was unenforceable for lack of consideration. Is White correct? Discuss. [*Philadelphia Indemnity Insurance Co. v. White*, 2017 WL 32899 (Tex.App.—San Antonio 2017)] (See *Consideration*.)

12–8. A Question of Ethics—Promissory Estoppel.

 Claudia Aceves borrowed $845,000 from U.S. Bank to buy a home. Less than two years into the loan, she could no longer afford the monthly payments. The bank notified her that it planned to foreclose on her home.

(Foreclosure is a process that allows a lender to repossess and sell the property that secures a loan.) The bank offered to modify Aceves's mortgage if she would forgo bankruptcy. In reliance on the bank's promise, she agreed. Once she withdrew the filing, however, the bank foreclosed and began eviction proceedings. Aceves filed a suit against the bank for promissory estoppel. [Aceves v. U.S. Bank, N.A., 192 Cal.App.4th 218, 120 Cal.Rptr.3d 507 (2011)] (See Promissory Estoppel.*)*

1. Could Aceves succeed in her claim of promissory estoppel? Why or why not?

2. Did Aceves or U.S. Bank behave unethically? Discuss.

Critical Thinking and Writing Assignments

12–9. Time-Limited Group Assignment—Preexisting Duty. Melissa Faraj owns a lot and wants to build a house according to a particular set of plans and specifications. She solicits bids from building contractors and receives three bids: one from Carlton for $160,000, one from Feldberg for $158,000, and one from Siegel for $153,000. She accepts Siegel's bid. One month after beginning construction of the house, Siegel contacts Faraj and tells her that because of inflation and a recent price hike for materials, his costs have gone up. He says he will not finish the house unless Faraj agrees to pay an extra $13,000. Faraj reluctantly agrees to pay the additional sum. (See *Agreements That Lack Consideration*.)

1. One group will evaluate whether a contractor can ever raise the price of completing construction based on inflation and the rising cost of materials.

2. A second group will assume that after the house is finished, Faraj refuses to pay the extra $13,000. The group will decide whether Faraj is legally required to pay this additional amount.

3. A third group will determine what types of extraordinary difficulties could arise during construction that would justify a contractor's charging more than the original bid.

4. A fourth group will consider what would happen if Faraj and Siegel had rescinded the initial contract and entered a new construction contract that included the extra $13,000. Would a court be likely to find that there was no consideration because of a preexisting duty? Explain.

13 | Capacity and Legality

Learning Objectives

The four Learning Objectives *below are designed to help improve your understanding. After reading this chapter, you should be able to answer the following questions:*

1. Does a minor have the capacity to enter into an enforceable contract? What does it mean to disaffirm a contract?

2. When does an intoxicated person have the capacity to enter into an enforceable agreement?

3. Under what circumstances will courts enforce a covenant not to compete?

4. What are the consequences of entering an illegal agreement?

Contractual Capacity The capacity required by the law for a party who enters into a contract to be bound by that contract.

"Liberty of contract is not an absolute concept. It is relative to many conditions of time and place and circumstance."

Benjamin Cardozo
1870–1938
(Associate justice of the United States Supreme Court, 1932–1938)

The first two of the four requirements for a valid contract are agreement and consideration. This chapter examines the third and fourth requirements—*contractual capacity* and *legality*. As indicated in the chapter-opening quotation, "liberty of contract" is not absolute. In other words, not all people can make legally binding contracts at all times. Contracts entered into by persons lacking the capacity to do so may be voidable. Similarly, contracts calling for the performance of an illegal act are illegal and thus void—they are not contracts at all.

13–1 Contractual Capacity

Contractual capacity is the legal ability to enter into a contractual relationship. Courts generally presume the existence of contractual capacity, but in some situations, capacity is lacking or may be questionable. A person who has been determined by a court to be mentally incompetent, for instance, cannot form a legally binding contract. In other situations, a party may have the capacity to enter into a valid contract but may also have the right to avoid liability under it. For instance, minors—or *infants*, as they are commonly referred to in the law—usually are not legally bound by contracts.

In this section, we look at the effect of youth, intoxication, and mental incompetence on contractual capacity.

13–1a Minors

Today, in almost all states, the **age of majority** (when a person is no longer a minor) for contractual purposes is eighteen years.[1] In addition, some states provide for the termination of minority on marriage.

Minority status may also be terminated by a minor's **emancipation,** which occurs when a child's parent or legal guardian relinquishes the legal right to exercise control over the child. Normally, minors who leave home to support themselves are considered emancipated. Several jurisdictions permit minors to petition a court for emancipation. For business purposes, a minor may petition a court to be treated as an adult.

The general rule is that a minor can enter into any contract that an adult can, provided that the contract is not one prohibited by law for minors (such as a contract involving the sale of alcoholic beverages or tobacco products). A contract entered into by a minor, however, is voidable at the option of that minor, subject to certain exceptions (to be discussed shortly). To exercise the option to avoid a contract, a minor need only manifest (clearly show) an intention not to be bound by it. The minor "avoids" the contract by disaffirming it.

Disaffirmance The legal avoidance, or setting aside, of a contractual obligation is referred to as **disaffirmance.** To disaffirm, a minor must express, through words or conduct, his or her intent not to be bound to the contract. The minor must disaffirm the entire contract, not merely a portion of it. For instance, a minor cannot decide to keep part of the goods purchased under a contract and return the remaining goods.

Note that an adult who enters into a contract with a minor cannot avoid his or her contractual duties on the ground that the minor can do so. Unless the minor exercises the option to disaffirm the contract, the adult party normally is bound by it.

The question in the following *Spotlight Case* was whether a minor had effectively disaffirmed an agreement to arbitrate with her employer.

---

1. The age of majority may still be twenty-one for other purposes, such as the purchase and consumption of alcohol.

Age of Majority The age (eighteen years, in most states) at which a person, formerly a minor, is recognized by law as an adult and is legally responsible for his or her actions.

Emancipation In regard to minors, the act of being freed from parental control.

> ### Learning Objective 1
> Does a minor have the capacity to enter into an enforceable contract? What does it mean to disaffirm a contract?

Disaffirmance The legal avoidance, or setting aside, of a contractual obligation.

✸ Spotlight on KFC: Case 13.1

PAK Foods Houston, LLC v. Garcia
Court of Appeals of Texas, Houston (14th District), 433 S.W.3d 171 (2014).

Background and Facts S.L., a female sixteen-year-old minor, worked at a KFC Restaurant operated by PAK Foods Houston, LLC. PAK Foods' policy was to resolve any dispute with an employee through arbitration. At the employer's request, S.L. signed an acknowledgment of this policy. S.L was injured on the job and subsequently terminated her employment. S.L.'s mother, Marissa Garcia, filed a suit on S.L.'s behalf in a Texas state court against PAK Foods to recover the medical expenses for the injury. PAK Foods filed a motion to compel arbitration. The court

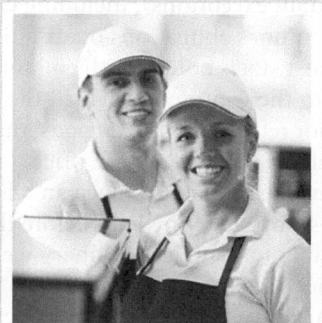

When minors sign employment agreements with fast-food restaurants, how can they disaffirm those agreements?

zokara/E+/Getty Images

denied the motion. "To the extent any agreement to arbitrate existed between S.L. and PAK Foods Houston, LLC, S.L. voided such agreement by filing this suit." PAK Foods appealed.

In the Words of the Court
Martha Hill *JAMISON*, Justice.

* * * *

* * * It is undisputed S.L. was a 16-year-old minor when the arbitration agreement was executed and she remained a minor during her employment by PAK Foods, including at the time of her injury. In Texas, the age of majority is 18 years.

(Continues)

It has long been the law in Texas that a contract executed by a minor is not void, but it is voidable by the minor. * * * They may be either disaffirmed by the minor or ratified after the minor reaches majority. This means that the minor may set aside the entire contract at her option. [Emphasis added.]

Appellees assert that S.L. elected to void any agreement to arbitrate by filing the underlying suit.

* * * *

PAK Foods argues that * * * S.L. was an at-will employee and did not execute an employment contract. PAK Foods also notes that S.L. did not notify PAK Foods prior to filing suit that she was voiding the arbitration agreement. These distinctions do not alter the settled law that a minor may void a contract at her election. The arbitration agreement is a contract with a minor, S.L., who had the option to disaffirm the contract.

While appellees assert that S.L. voided the agreement by filing suit, the mere filing of suit may not necessarily disaffirm an arbitration agreement. A party may file suit but later determine arbitration is appropriate. Here, appellees' original petition does not expressly disaffirm an agreement to arbitrate; the petition is silent about arbitration. However, appellees' response filed in opposition to the motion to compel arbitration is a definitive disaffirmance of any agreement to arbitrate. The response states in relevant part:

S.L. was a minor at the time of her employment. * * * Contracts such as this Arbitration Agreement are voidable at her instance, and may be disaffirmed or repudiated by her or her guardian, * * * . Thus as S.L.'s disaffirmance of the Arbitration agreement has manifestly occurred with her termination of employment and election to file suit, she cannot be bound by the terms of the Arbitration Agreement.

S.L. was still a minor when she objected to arbitration and elected to void the contract. The record contains sufficient evidence of her election to support the trial court's fact finding. The trial court also did not abuse its discretion in concluding as a matter of law that S.L.'s action voided the contract.

Decision and Remedy A state intermediate appellate court affirmed the decision of the lower court. A minor may disaffirm a contract at his or her option. S.L. opted to disaffirm the agreement to arbitrate by terminating her employment and filing the lawsuit.

Critical Thinking

• **Legal Environment** *Could PAK Foods successfully contend that S.L.'s minority does not bar enforcement of the arbitration agreement because medical expenses are necessaries? Discuss.*

Disaffirmance within a Reasonable Time. A contract can ordinarily be disaffirmed at any time during minority[2] or for a reasonable time after the minor reaches the age of majority. What constitutes a "reasonable" time may vary. If an individual fails to disaffirm an executed contract within a reasonable time after reaching the age of majority, a court will likely hold that the contract has been ratified (*ratification* will be discussed shortly).

A Minor's Obligations on Disaffirmance. All states' laws permit minors to disaffirm contracts (with certain exceptions), including executed contracts. However, state laws differ on the extent of a minor's obligations on disaffirmance.

Courts in most states hold that the minor need only return the goods (or other consideration) subject to the contract, provided the goods are in the minor's possession or control. Even if the minor returns damaged goods, the minor often is entitled to disaffirm the contract and obtain a refund of the purchase price.

A growing number of states place an additional duty on the minor to restore the adult party to the position she or he held before the contract was made. These courts may hold a minor responsible for damage, ordinary wear and tear, and depreciation of goods that the minor used prior to disaffirmance. **Example 13.1** Sixteen-year-old Jay Dodd buys a truck for $5,900 from a used-car dealer. The truck develops mechanical problems nine months later,

---

2. In some states, however, a minor who enters into a contract for the sale of land cannot disaffirm the contract until she or he reaches the age of majority.

but Dodd continues to drive it until the engine blows up and the truck stops running. Dodd then disaffirms the contract and attempts to return the truck to the dealer for a refund of the full purchase price. In states that hold minors responsible for damage, Dodd can still disaffirm the contract, but he may only recover the depreciated value—not the purchase price—of the truck.

Exceptions to a Minor's Right to Disaffirm State courts and legislatures have carved out several exceptions to the minor's right to disaffirm. Some contracts, such as marriage contracts and contracts to enlist in the armed services, cannot be avoided. These exceptions are made for reasons of public policy.

In addition, although ordinarily minors can disaffirm contracts even when they have misrepresented their age, a growing number of states have enacted laws to prohibit disaffirmance in such situations. Other states prohibit disaffirmance by minors who misrepresented their age while engaged in business as adults.

Finally, a minor who enters into a contract for necessaries may disaffirm the contract but remains liable for the reasonable value of the goods. **Necessaries** include whatever is reasonably needed to maintain the minor's standard of living. In general, food, clothing, shelter, and medical services are necessaries. What is a necessary for one minor, however, may be a luxury for another, depending on the minors' customary living standard. Contracts for necessaries are enforceable only to the level of value needed to maintain the minor's standard of living.

Necessaries Necessities required to maintain a standard of living, such as food, shelter, clothing, and medical attention.

Ratification In contract law, **ratification** is the act of accepting and giving legal force to an obligation that previously was not enforceable. A minor who has reached the age of majority can ratify a contract expressly or impliedly. *Express* ratification occurs when the individual, on reaching the age of majority, states orally or in writing that she or he intends to be bound by the contract. *Implied* ratification takes place when the minor, on reaching the age of majority, behaves in a manner inconsistent with disaffirmance.

Ratification The acceptance or confirmation of an act or agreement that gives legal force to an obligation that previously was not enforceable.

Example 13.2 Lindsay posts an ad on Craigslist offering to sell her grandmother's Yamaha Grand Piano for $6,000. Axel, who is seventeen years old, agrees to purchase the piano by making monthly payments of $200 over the next two and a half years. Axel does not disaffirm the contract, and six months into the agreement, he turns eighteen (the age of majority in his state). When Axel stops by Lindsay's house to make his seventh payment, he states, "I love the piano and will continue making payments." Axel's oral statement to Lindsay is an express ratification of their contract. He can no longer disaffirm it. Even if Axel never expressly tells Lindsay he will continue making payments but continues to do so well after reaching the age of majority, he has impliedly ratified the contract.

If a minor fails to disaffirm a contract within a reasonable time after reaching the age of majority, then a court must determine whether the conduct constitutes implied ratification or disaffirmance. Generally, courts presume that executed contracts are ratified and that executory contracts are disaffirmed.

Parents' Liability As a general rule, parents are not liable for the contracts made by minor children acting on their own, except contracts for necessaries, which the parents are legally required to provide. This is why businesses ordinarily require parents to cosign any contract made with a minor. The parents then become personally obligated to perform the conditions of the contract, even if their child avoids liability.

How can a minor imply ratification of an agreement to purchase a grand piano?

Know This

A minor's station in life (including financial position, social status, and lifestyle) is important in determining whether an item is a necessary or a luxury. For instance, clothing is a necessary, but if a minor from a low-income family contracts to purchase a $2,000 leather coat, a court may deem the coat a luxury. In this situation, the contract would not be for "necessaries."

13–1b Intoxicated Persons

Intoxication is a condition in which a person's normal capacity to act or think is inhibited by alcohol or some other drug. A contract entered into by an intoxicated person can be either voidable or valid (and thus enforceable).

If the person was sufficiently intoxicated to lack mental capacity and the other party had reason to know it, then the transaction may be voidable at the option of the intoxicated person, even if the intoxication was purely voluntary. The intoxicated person has the option of disaffirming the contract while intoxicated or for a reasonable time after becoming sober. If, despite intoxication, the person understood the legal consequences of the agreement, the contract is enforceable. (Note that an intoxicated person may ratify a contract expressly or impliedly after becoming sober.)

Courts look at objective indications of the intoxicated person's condition to determine if he or she possessed or lacked the required capacity. It is difficult to prove that a person's judgment was so severely impaired that he or she could not comprehend the legal consequences of entering into a contract. Therefore, courts rarely permit contracts to be avoided due to intoxication.

13–1c Mentally Incompetent Persons

Contracts made by mentally incompetent persons can be void, voidable, or valid. If a court has previously determined that a person is mentally incompetent and has appointed a guardian to represent the person, any contract made by that person is *void*—no contract exists. Only the guardian can enter into a binding contract on behalf of the mentally incompetent person.

If a court has not previously judged a person to be mentally incompetent but the person was incompetent at the time the contract was formed, the contract is *voidable* in most states. A contract is voidable if the person did not know that he or she was entering into the contract or lacked the mental capacity to comprehend its nature, purpose, and consequences. In such situations, the contract is voidable (or can be ratified) at the option of the mentally incompetent person but not at the option of the other party.

Case Example 13.3 Annabelle Duffie was mildly mentally retarded and, at age seventy, had the beginning of dementia. For her entire life, she had lived with her brother, Jerome. When Jerome died, he left Annabelle his property, including 180 acres of timberland near Hope, Arkansas, valued at more than $400,000. Less than three months later, Annabelle signed a deed granting her interest in the tract to Charles and Joanne Black. The Blacks agreed to pay Annabelle $150,000 in monthly payments of $1,000.

Later, Annabelle's nephew, Jack, was appointed to be her legal guardian. On her behalf, Jack filed a lawsuit in an Arkansas state court against the Blacks, seeking to void the land deal because of Annabelle's lack of mental competence. The court ordered the Blacks to return the property to Annabelle. They appealed. A state intermediate appellate court affirmed. The evidence showed that Annabelle had been incompetent her entire life. She lacked the cognitive ability to make the complex financial decisions involved in selling property. Therefore, the contract was voidable.[3]

A contract entered into by a mentally ill person (whom a court has not previously declared incompetent) may also be *valid* if the person had capacity *at the time the contract was formed*. Some people who are incompetent due to age or illness have *lucid intervals*—temporary periods of sufficient intelligence, judgment, and will. During such intervals, they will be considered to have legal capacity to enter into contracts in the majority of states.

---

3. *Black v. Duffie*, 2016 Ark.App. 584, 508 S.W.3d 40 (2016).

13–2 **Legality**

Legality is the fourth requirement for a valid contract to exist. For a contract to be valid and enforceable, it must be formed for a legal purpose. A contract to do something that is prohibited by federal or state statutory law is illegal and, as such, is void from the outset and thus unenforceable. Additionally, a contract to commit a tortious act (such as engage in fraudulent misrepresentation) or to commit an action that is contrary to public policy is illegal and unenforceable.

13–2a **Contracts Contrary to Statute**

Statutes often prescribe the terms of contracts. Some statutes set forth rules specifying which terms and clauses may be included in certain contracts and which are prohibited. Others prohibit certain contracts on the basis of their subject matter, the status of the contracting parties, or other factors. Next, we examine several ways in which contracts may be contrary to statute.

Contracts to Commit a Crime Any contract to commit a crime is in violation of a statute. Thus, a contract to sell illegal drugs in violation of criminal laws is unenforceable, as is a contract to hide a corporation's violation of securities laws or environmental regulations.

Sometimes, the object or performance of a contract is rendered illegal by statute *after* the contract has been formed. In that situation, the contract is considered discharged (terminated) by law.

Usury Almost every state has a statute that sets the maximum rate of interest that can be charged for different types of transactions, including ordinary loans. A lender who makes a loan at an interest rate above the lawful maximum commits **usury**.

Although usurious contracts are illegal, most states simply limit the interest that the lender may collect on the contract to the lawful maximum interest rate in that state. In a few states, the lender can recover the principal amount of the loan but no interest. In addition, states can make exceptions to facilitate business transactions. For instance, many states exempt corporate loans from the usury laws, and nearly all states allow higher interest rate loans for borrowers who could not otherwise obtain loans.

Usury Charging an illegal rate of interest.

Gambling Gambling is the creation of risk for the purpose of assuming it. Traditionally, the states have deemed gambling contracts illegal and thus void. Today, many states allow (and regulate) certain forms of gambling, such as horse racing, video poker machines, and charity-sponsored bingo. In addition, nearly all states allow state-operated lotteries and gambling on Native American reservations.

Licensing Statutes All states require members of certain professions—including physicians, lawyers, real estate brokers, accountants, architects, electricians, and stockbrokers—to have licenses. Some licenses are obtained only after extensive schooling and examinations, which indicate to the public that a special skill has been acquired. Others require only that the person obtaining the license be of good moral character and pay a fee.

Whether a contract with an unlicensed person is legal and enforceable depends on the purpose of the licensing statute. If the statute's purpose is to protect the public from unauthorized practitioners, then a contract involving an unlicensed practitioner generally is illegal and unenforceable. If the purpose is merely to raise government revenues, however, a contract with an unlicensed person may be enforced (and the unlicensed practitioner fined). See this chapter's *Business Law Analysis* feature for an example.

Determining If a Contract with an Unlicensed Party Is Enforceable

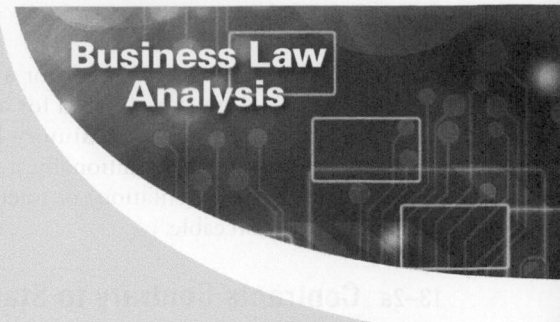
PEMS Co. International, Inc., agreed to find a buyer for Rupp Industries, Inc., for a commission of 2 percent of the purchase price, which was to be paid by the buyer. Using PEMS's services, an investment group bought Rupp for $20 million and changed its name to Temp-Air, Inc. PEMS asked Temp-Air to pay a commission on the sale. Temp-Air refused, arguing that PEMS had acted as a broker in the deal without a license. The applicable statute defines a broker as any person who deals with the sale of a business. Can PEMS collect its commission?

Analysis: Whether a contract with an unlicensed person is legal and

enforceable depends on the purpose of the statute. If the purpose is to protect the public from unauthorized practitioners, then a contract involving an unlicensed practitioner is generally illegal and unenforceable.

Result and Reasoning: The applicable statute defined a broker as any person who deals with the sale of a business. It seems clear that this definition covers PEMS. The purpose of this statute is to protect the public from potentially serious consequences related to having unlicensed parties handle business sales transactions that often involve millions of dollars.

PEMS's efforts toward the sale constituted the action of a broker. PEMS did not have a broker's license. Thus, if PEMS was acting as a broker, the unlicensed firm forfeited its right to collect a commission for its services. Using PEMS's services, an investment group made a successful purchase of Rupp. Therefore, PEMS is barred from maintaining this suit to collect the unpaid commission.

A Minnesota state real-estate licensing statute declares it a crime for any person to provide unlicensed real-estate broker's services for compensation. The statute also prohibits any party from maintaining an action in a state court to collect compensation for providing unlicensed real-estate broker's services. The question in the following case was whether this statute rendered invalid a contract between a mobile-home park owner and an unlicensed "mortgage broker."

Case 13.2

Woischke v. Stursberg & Fine, Inc.

Minnesota Court of Appeals, 906 N.W.2d 586 (2018).

Background and Facts Woischke Enterprises, LLC, owned a mobile-home park in Pine County, Minnesota. Woischke contracted with Stursberg & Fine, Inc., for Stursberg & Fine to act "as a mortgage broker." Through Stursberg & Fine, Woischke obtained new financing for the park, presumably allowing the owner to pay off a high-interest mortgage by means of a new, lower-interest loan.

Later, Woischke discovered that no Stursberg & Fine employee was a real-estate broker, mortgage broker, or loan broker licensed under Minnesota's real-estate licensing statute. Woischke refused to pay Stursberg & Fine's $60,000 fee and filed a complaint in a Minnesota state court against the firm, claiming that their agreement was void. The court held that the agreement was valid and dismissed the complaint. Woischke appealed.

In the Words of the Court
ROSS, Judge

* * * *

* * * *When a party contracts to perform services that are prohibited and penalized by statute, whether the contracted duty to pay for those services is void depends entirely on whether the legislature intended that a contract imposing the duty to pay should be void, and that intent is inferred if the objective of the law is to protect the public rather than merely to raise revenue.* [Emphasis added.]

* * * *

* * * A real-estate broker is someone who charges a commission or fee to attempt to negotiate a real-estate sale or a loan to be secured by a mortgage. By the terms of the contract, these are the primary services Stursberg & Fine agreed to perform for a fee. Performing these broker services in Minnesota requires a license. And performing the services without a broker's license is a crime. The real-estate-licensing statute prohibits persons from performing specified, unlicensed real-estate services for a fee and applies to Stursberg & Fine's contract.

* * * The * * * licensing requirement * * * rests on public-policy concerns and does not merely fulfill an administrative objective. * * * [The] provisions were enacted in the public interest to prevent abuses by unqualified or unreliable real estate brokers and salesmen.

* * * In addition to prohibiting and penalizing the unlicensed brokering of real estate sales and mortgage loans, [the legislature] has expressly declared that "no person shall bring or maintain any action in the courts of this state for the collection of compensation for the performance of any of the acts for which a license is required * * * without alleging and proving that the person was a duly licensed real estate broker, salesperson, or closing agent at the time the alleged cause of action arose." The primary obligation that the agreement places on Woischke is to compensate Stursberg & Fine for its service in negotiating a real-estate sale or a mortgaged loan. *The legislative intent about contractual enforceability in this context is explicit and unmistakable: persons who engage in this service without a license cannot enforce their contractual right to compensation in court.* Given the statutory language, we have no difficulty concluding that the legislature has expressly declared its intent that contracts under which unlicensed persons broker real-estate sales or mortgage loans for compensation be held invalid as to the violating party. [Emphasis added.]

Decision and Remedy A state intermediate appellate court reversed the judgment of the lower court. "Contracts made in violation of a licensing statute are void as a matter of law when the legislature has expressly or impliedly directed this outcome."

Critical Thinking

• **What If the Facts Were Different?** *Suppose that the Minnesota legislature had not expressly declared in the state's real-estate licensing statute that unlicensed brokers could not collect fees for their broker services. Would the result in the Woischke case have been different? Discuss.*

13–2b Contracts Contrary to Public Policy

Although contracts involve private parties, some are not enforceable because of the negative impact they would have on society. These contracts are said to be *contrary to public policy.* Examples include a contract to commit an immoral act, such as selling a child, and a contract that prohibits marriage (such as a contract to pay someone not to marry one's daughter). Business contracts that may be contrary to public policy include contracts in restraint of trade and unconscionable contracts or clauses.

Contracts in Restraint of Trade The United States has a strong public policy favoring competition in the economy. Thus, contracts in restraint of trade (anticompetitive agreements) generally are unenforceable because they are contrary to public policy. Typically, such contracts also violate one or more federal or state antitrust laws.

An exception is recognized when the restraint is reasonable and is an ancillary (secondary, or subordinate) part of the contract. Such restraints often are included in contracts for the sale of an ongoing business and employment contracts.

Covenants Not to Compete and the Sale of an Ongoing Business. Many contracts involve a type of restraint called a **covenant not to compete,** or a restrictive covenant (promise). A covenant not to compete may be created when a merchant who sells a store agrees not to open a new store in a certain geographic area surrounding the old store. Such an agreement enables the seller to sell, and the purchaser to buy, the goodwill and reputation of an ongoing business without having to worry that the seller will open a competing business a block away. Provided the restrictive covenant is reasonable and is an ancillary part of the sale of an ongoing business, it is enforceable.

Covenant Not to Compete A contractual promise of one party to refrain from conducting business similar to that of another party for a certain period of time and within a specified geographical area.

Employment Contract A contract between an employer and an employee in which the terms and conditions of employment are stated.

Learning Objective 3
Under what circumstances will courts enforce a covenant not to compete?

Covenants Not to Compete in Employment Contracts. Sometimes, agreements not to compete (also referred to as *noncompete agreements*) are included in **employment contracts.** People in middle-level and upper-level management positions commonly agree not to work for competitors and not to start a competing business for a specified period of time after terminating employment.

Noncompete agreements are generally legal in most states so long as the specified period of time (of restraint) is not excessive in duration and the geographic restriction is reasonable. To be reasonable, a restriction on competition must protect a legitimate business interest and must not be any greater than necessary to protect that interest. What constitutes a reasonable time period may be different in the online environment than in conventional employment contracts. Because the geographical restrictions apply worldwide, the time restrictions may be shorter.

Case Example 13.4 An insurance firm in New York City, Brown & Brown, Inc., hired Theresa Johnson to perform actuarial analysis. On her first day of work, Johnson was asked to sign a nonsolicitation covenant, which prohibited her from soliciting or servicing any of Brown's clients for two years after the termination of her employment. Less than five years later, when Johnson's employment with Brown was terminated, she went to work for Lawley Benefits Group, LLC. Brown sued to enforce the covenant. A state appellate court ruled that the covenant was overly broad and unenforceable because it attempted to restrict Johnson from working for any of Brown's clients, without regard to whether she had had a relationship with those clients.[4] ■

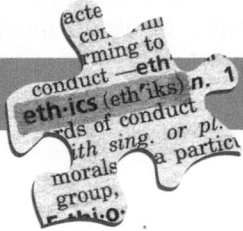

Ethical Issue

Are expansive noncompete agreements reducing worker mobility? You would probably expect workers to be asked to sign noncompete agreements that prevented them from, say, taking proprietary software code to a competitor. But would you expect a sandwich chain to require a worker to sign a noncompete agreement related to sandwich making? In the past, such agreements would not have been upheld in court. Today, they increasingly are. James Bessen, a writer for *The Atlantic*, estimates that the number of lawsuits over noncompete agreements and trade secrets has nearly tripled in the last twenty years.

Employees in high-tech firms seem to be the most affected. They often sign noncompete agreements that "freeze" them out of their industry for two years after they leave a high-tech employer, forcing them to seek jobs in other industries where they cannot use key skills and knowledge. The result is that noncompete agreements tend to limit job opportunities for highly skilled workers. In addition, noncompete agreements are increasingly being used with employees at lower levels (including blue-collar workers).

The negative impact of such agreements can be devastating on persons who lose or leave their jobs to find other employment. In other words, job mobility may be suffering from the pervasive use of noncompete agreements.

Enforcement Problems. The laws governing the enforceability of covenants not to compete vary significantly from state to state. California prohibits the enforcement of all covenants not to compete. In some states, such as Texas, such a covenant will not be enforced unless the employee has received some benefit in return for signing the noncompete agreement. This is true even if the covenant is reasonable as to time and area. If the employee receives no benefit, the covenant will be deemed void.

---

4. *Brown & Brown, Inc. v. Johnson*, 980 N.Y.S.2d 631 (2014).

Reformation. Occasionally, depending on the jurisdiction, courts will *reform* covenants not to compete. If a covenant is found to be unreasonable in time or geographic area, the court may convert the terms into reasonable ones and then enforce the reformed covenant. This presents a problem, however, in that the judge has implicitly become a party to the contract. Consequently, courts usually resort to contract **reformation** only when necessary to prevent undue burdens or hardships.

Unconscionable Contracts or Clauses
Ordinarily, a court does not look at the fairness or equity of a contract (or inquire into the adequacy of consideration). Persons are assumed to be reasonably intelligent, and the courts will not come to their aid just because they have made unwise or foolish bargains.

In certain circumstances, however, bargains are so oppressive that the courts relieve innocent parties of part or all of their duties. Such bargains are deemed **unconscionable**[5] because they are so unscrupulous or grossly unfair as to be "void of conscience."

The Uniform Commercial Code (UCC) incorporates the concept of unconscionability in its provisions with regard to the sale and lease of goods.[6] A contract can be unconscionable on either procedural or substantive grounds, as discussed in the following subsections and illustrated graphically in Exhibit 13–1.

Procedural Unconscionability. Procedural unconscionability often involves inconspicuous print, unintelligible language ("legalese"), or the lack of an opportunity to read the contract or ask questions about its meaning. This type of unconscionability typically arises when a party's lack of knowledge or understanding of the contract terms deprive him or her of any meaningful choice.

Procedural unconscionability can also occur when there is such a disparity in bargaining power between the two parties that the weaker party's consent is not voluntary. This type of situation often involves an **adhesion contract,** which is a standard-form contract written

Reformation A court-ordered correction of a written contract so that it reflects the true intentions of the parties.

Unconscionable A contract or clause that is void on the basis of public policy because one party was forced to accept terms that are unfairly burdensome and that unfairly benefit the other party.

Adhesion Contract A standard-form contract in which the stronger party dictates the terms.

---

5. Pronounced un-*kon*-shun-uh-bul.
6. See UCC 2–302 and 2–719.

Exhibit 13–1 Unconscionability

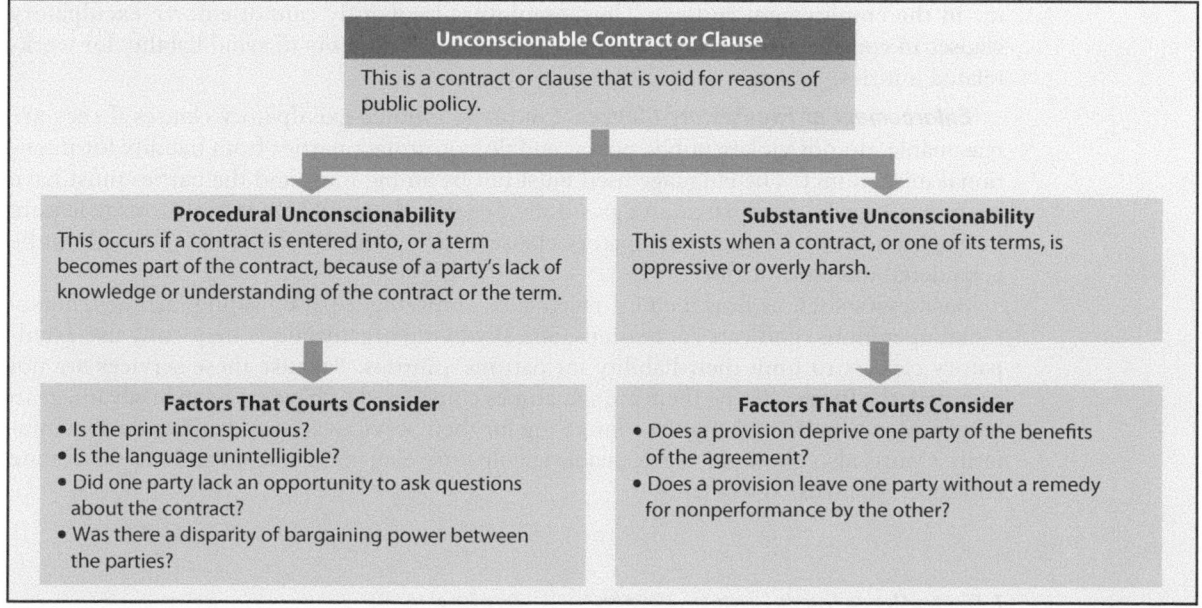

exclusively by one party (the dominant party) and presented to the other (the adhering party) on a take-it-or-leave-it basis. In other words, the adhering party (usually a buyer or borrower) has no opportunity to negotiate the terms of the contract. Not all adhesion contracts are unconscionable—only those that unreasonably favor the drafter.

Case Example 13.5 Tiffany Brinkley committed to take six real estate investment training sessions at a cost of $4,195. She paid $850 and signed a retail installment contract promising to pay monthly payments on the balance to Monterey Financial Services. The contract contained an arbitration agreement. When a dispute arose, Brinkley stopped making payments and filed a lawsuit against Monterey in a California state court.

Monterey filed a motion to arbitrate, which the trial court granted. Brinkley appealed. She argued that the arbitration clause was procedurally unconscionable because it was part of an adhesion contract. The court, though, found that the arbitration clause was enforceable and dismissed the lawsuit. The court held that the "purported lack of meaningful choice did not render the arbitration provision in the retail installment contract procedurally unconscionable."[7]

Substantive Unconscionability. Substantive unconscionability occurs when contracts, or portions of contracts, are oppressive or overly harsh. Courts generally focus on provisions that deprive one party of the benefits of the agreement or leave that party without remedy for nonperformance by the other. Sometimes, courts will find that the same contract is both substantively and procedurally unconscionable.

Substantive unconscionability can arise in a wide variety of business contexts. For instance, a contract clause that gives a business entity unrestricted access to the courts but requires the other party to arbitrate any dispute with the firm may be unconscionable.

Exculpatory Clauses Often closely related to the concept of unconscionability are **exculpatory clauses,** which release a party from liability in the event of monetary or physical injury, *no matter who is at fault.* Indeed, courts sometimes refuse to enforce such clauses because they deem them to be unconscionable.

> **Exculpatory Clause** A clause that releases a contractual party from liability in the event of monetary or physical injury, no matter who is at fault.

Violation of Public Policy. Most courts view exculpatory clauses with disfavor. Exculpatory clauses found in rental agreements for commercial property are frequently held to be contrary to public policy, and such clauses are almost always unenforceable in residential property leases. Courts also usually hold that exculpatory clauses are against public policy in the employment context. Thus, employers frequently cannot enforce exculpatory clauses in contracts with employees or independent contractors to avoid liability for work-related injuries.

Enforcement of Exculpatory Clauses. Courts do enforce exculpatory clauses if they are reasonable, do not violate public policy, and do not protect parties from liability for intentional misconduct. The language used must not be ambiguous, and the parties must have been in relatively equal bargaining positions. See this chapter's *Managerial Strategy* feature for suggestions on drafting exculpatory clauses, such as liability waivers, that will not be considered unconscionable.

Businesses such as health clubs, racetracks, amusement parks, skiing facilities, horse-rental operations, golf-cart concessions, and skydiving organizations frequently use exculpatory clauses to limit their liability for patrons' injuries. Because these services are not essential, the firms offering them are sometimes considered to have no relative advantage in bargaining strength, and anyone contracting for their services is considered to do so voluntarily. Courts also may enforce reasonable exculpatory clauses in loan documents, real estate contracts, and trust agreements.

---

7. *Brinkley v. Monterey Financial Services, Inc.,* 242 Cal.App.4th 314, 196 Cal.Rptr.3d 1 (2015).

Managerial Strategy

Creating Liability Waivers That Are Not Unconscionable

Blanket liability waivers that absolve a business from virtually every event, even those caused by the business's own negligence, are usually unenforceable because they are unconscionable. Exculpatory waivers are common, nonetheless. We observe such waivers in gym memberships, on admissions tickets to sporting events, and in simple contracts for the use of campgrounds.

Typically, courts view liability waivers as voluntarily bargained for whether or not they have been read. Thus, a waiver included in the fine print on the back of an admission ticket or on an entry sign to a stadium may be upheld. In general, if such waivers are unambiguous and conspicuous, the assumption is that patrons have had a chance to read them and have accepted their terms.

Activities with Inherent Risks

Cases challenging liability waivers have been brought against skydiving businesses, ski resorts, bobsledding operations, whitewater rafting companies, and health clubs. For example, in *Bergin v. Wild Mountain, Inc.*,[a] an appellate court in Minnesota upheld a ski resort's liability waiver. In that case, the plaintiff hit a snowmaking mound, which was "an inherent risk of skiing." Before the accident, the plaintiff had stated that he knew "that an inherent risk of serious injury in downhill skiing was hitting snowmaking mounds." Furthermore, he had not rejected the season pass that contained the resort's exculpatory clause. Thus, the ski resort prevailed.

In a similar case, Teresa Brigance fell and broke her leg when her ski boot caught on the chairlift as she was attempting to get off the lift. She sued the owner, Vail Summit Resorts, Inc., for her injuries. Brigance had signed a liability waiver before taking ski lessons at the resort, however. The waiver stated that she understood the inherent dangers and risks of skiing, and it specifically mentioned lift loading and unloading. The court found the waiver was valid and enforceable, and therefore dismissed Brigance's suit against Vail Summit. Brigance appealed, but a federal appellate court affirmed the lower court's dismissal.[b]

Overly Broad Waivers

While most liability waivers have survived legal challenges, some have not. In *Bagley v. Mt. Bachelor, Inc.*,[c] the Supreme Court of Oregon ruled against a ski resort's "very broad" liability waiver. The case involved an eighteen-year-old, Myles Bagley, who was paralyzed from the waist down after a snowboarding accident at Mt. Bachelor ski resort. The season pass that Bagley signed included a liability waiver. The waiver stated that the signer agreed not to sue the resort for injury even if "caused by negligence."

Bagley argued that the resort had created a dangerous condition because of the way it had set up a particular ski jump. He sued for $21.5 million and eventually won the right to go forward with his lawsuit. The Oregon Supreme Court found that, for various reasons, enforcement of the release would have been unconscionable. "Because the release is unenforceable, genuine issues of fact exist that preclude summary judgment in defendant's favor."

Business Questions

1. *If you are running a business, why would you opt to include overly broad waivers in your contracts with customers?*

2. *Under what circumstances would you, as a business owner, choose to aggressively defend your business against a customer's liability lawsuit?*

---

a. 2014 WL 996788 (Minn.App. 2014).

b. *Brigance v. Vail Summit Resorts, Inc.*, 883 F.3d 1243 (10th Cir. 2018).

c. 356 Or. 543, 340 P.3d 27 (Or. 2014). See also *Emerson v. Mt. Bachelor, Inc.*, 273 Or.App. 524, 359 P.3d 510 (2015).

In the following case, the court considered whether an exculpatory clause that released "any Event sponsors and their agents and employees" from liability for future negligence was ambiguous.

Case 13.3

Holmes v. Multimedia KSDK, Inc.

Missouri Court of Appeals, Eastern District, Division 2, 395 S.W.3d 557 (2013).

Background and Facts Colleen Holmes signed an entry form for the Susan G. Komen Race for the Cure to be held in June 2009 in St. Louis, Missouri. The form included a "RACE WAIVER AND RELEASE" clause under which Holmes agreed to release "any Event sponsors and their agents and employees . . . for any injury or damages" that Holmes might suffer in connection with her participation in the race. Among other causes, the release applied to injury or damages caused by "negligence of the [sponsors]."

Is a waiver of negligence liability that appears on an entry form for a foot race enforceable?

Multimedia KSDK, Inc., was one of the race sponsors and also broadcasted the race. During the event, Holmes was injured when she tripped and fell over a Multimedia audiovisual box. Multimedia employees had placed the box on the ground without barricades or warnings of its presence. Holmes filed a suit in a Missouri state court against Multimedia, alleging negligence. The court entered a judgment in Multimedia's favor, and Holmes appealed.

In the Words of the Court

Kathianne Knaup *CRANE*, Presiding Judge.

* * * *

The release described the individuals and entities to be released in the following language:

The St. Louis Affiliate of Susan G. Komen for the Cure, their affiliates, and any affiliated individuals, any Event sponsors and their agents and employees, and all other persons or entities associated with this Event.

Plaintiffs argue that the * * * language is ambiguous because it does not specifically name the individuals and entities being released. They contend that such specificity is required in a prospective release.

We have routinely held that the word "any" when used with a class in a release is all-inclusive, it excludes nothing, and it is not ambiguous. * * * *A release that releases claims against "any and all persons" is unambiguous and enforceable to bar claims against third parties who were not parties to the release, and it is not necessary that the release identify those persons by name or otherwise.* Thus, * * * the release of "any Event sponsors" unambiguously releases all Event sponsors without exclusion, and

it is not necessary that each sponsor be named. [Emphasis added.]

However, plaintiffs argue that this reasoning does not apply to the use of "any" with classes of persons in a prospective release for future acts of negligence because courts require more specificity in a prospective release. We disagree.

Public policy disfavors but does not prohibit releases of future negligence. * * * To be enforceable in Missouri, exculpatory clauses must contain clear, unambiguous, unmistakable, and conspicuous language in order to release a party from his or her own future negligence. The exculpatory language must effectively notify a party that he or she is releasing the other party from claims arising from the other party's own negligence. * * * The words "negligence" or "fault" or their equivalents must be used conspicuously so that a clear and unmistakable waiver and shifting of risk occurs. There must be no doubt that a reasonable person agreeing to an exculpatory clause actually understands what future claims he or she is waiving.

* * * *

* * * [It is] not required that for a release of liability for future negligence to be effective, it must identify every individual sought to be released by name.

The release of "any Event sponsors and their agents and employees" from liability for future negligence clearly releases all Event sponsors and their agents and employees without exclusion. It is not ambiguous because it does not name each individual Event sponsor it purported to release from liability.

Decision and Remedy A state intermediate appellate court affirmed the lower court's judgment in favor of KSDK. The appellate court held that the language used in the exculpatory clause clearly released all sponsors and their agents and employees without exclusion from liability for future negligence.

Critical Thinking

• **Social** *At the time Holmes signed the release, Multimedia had not yet become a sponsor of the event. Should this fact have rendered the clause unenforceable? Explain.*

13–3 The Effect of Illegality

In general, an illegal contract is void—that is, the contract is deemed never to have existed, and the courts will not aid either party. In most illegal contracts, both parties are considered to be equally at fault—*in pari delicto*.[8] If the contract is executory, neither party can enforce it. If it has been executed, neither party can recover damages.

The courts usually are not concerned if one wrongdoer in an illegal contract is unjustly enriched at the expense of the other. The main reason for this hands-off attitude is a belief that a plaintiff who has broken the law by entering into an illegal bargain should not be allowed to obtain help from the courts. Another justification is the hoped-for deterrent effect: a plaintiff who suffers a loss because of an illegal bargain will presumably be deterred from entering into similar illegal bargains in the future.

There are exceptions to the general rule that neither party to an illegal bargain can sue for breach and neither party can recover for performance rendered. We look at these exceptions here.

Learning Objective 4

What are the consequences of entering an illegal agreement?

13–3a Justifiable Ignorance of the Facts

Sometimes, one of the parties to a contract has no reason to know that the contract is illegal and thus is relatively innocent. That party can often recover any benefits conferred in a partially executed contract. The courts will not enforce the contract but will allow the parties to return to their original positions.

A court may sometimes permit an innocent party who has fully performed under a contract to enforce the contract against the guilty party. **Example 13.6** A trucking company contracts with Gillespie to carry crates filled with goods to a specific destination for a normal fee of $5,000. The trucker delivers the crates and later finds out that they contained illegal goods. Although the shipment, use, and sale of the goods are illegal under the law, the trucker, being an innocent party, can normally still legally collect the $5,000 from Gillespie. ■

13–3b Members of Protected Classes

When a statute is clearly designed to protect a certain class of people, a member of that class can enforce a contract in violation of the statute even though the other party cannot. **Example 13.7** Statutes prohibit certain employees (such as flight attendants or pilots) from working more than a specified number of hours per month. An employee who is required to work more than the maximum can recover for those extra hours of service. ■

Other examples of statutes designed to protect a particular class of people are state statutes that regulate the sale of insurance. If an insurance company violates a statute when selling insurance, the purchaser can still enforce the policy and recover from the insurer.

13–3c Withdrawal from an Illegal Agreement

If the illegal part of a bargain has not yet been performed, the party rendering performance can withdraw from the contract and recover the performance or its value. **Example 13.8** Marta and Andy decide to wager (illegally) on the outcome of a boxing match. Each deposits $1,000 with a stakeholder, who agrees to pay the winner of the bet. At this point, each party has performed part of the agreement. Before payment occurs, either party is entitled to withdraw from the agreement by giving notice to the stakeholder of his or her withdrawal. ■

13–3d Severable, or Divisible, Contracts

A contract that is *severable*, or divisible, consists of distinct parts that can be performed separately, with separate consideration provided for each part. With an *indivisible* contract, in contrast, complete performance by each party is essential, even if the contract contains a number of seemingly separate provisions.

When two persons place an illegal bet on the outcome of a boxing match, can either withdraw from the wager?

---

8. Pronounced in-*pah*-ree deh-*lick*-tow.

If a contract is divisible into legal and illegal portions, a court may enforce the legal portion but not the illegal one, so long as the illegal portion does not affect the essence of the bargain. This approach is consistent with the basic policy of enforcing the legal intentions of the contracting parties whenever possible.

Example 13.9 Cole signs an employment contract that is valid but includes an overly broad and thus illegal covenant not to compete. In that situation, a court might find the employment contract enforceable but reform the unreasonably broad covenant by converting its terms into reasonable ones. Alternatively, the court could declare the covenant illegal (and thus void) and enforce the remaining employment terms. ■

13–3e Fraud, Duress, or Undue Influence

Often, one party to an illegal contract is more at fault than the other. When one party uses fraud, duress, or undue influence to induce the other party to enter into an agreement, the second party will be allowed to recover for the performance or its value.

Practice and Review

Renee Beaver started racing go-karts competitively in 2017, when she was fourteen. Many of the races required her to sign an exculpatory clause to participate. She or her parents regularly signed such clauses. In 2019, right before her birthday, Renee participated in the annual Elkhart Grand Prix, a series of races in Elkhart, Indiana. During the event in which she drove, a piece of foam padding used as a course barrier was torn from its base and ended up on the track. A portion of the padding struck Beaver in the head, and another portion was thrown into oncoming traffic, causing a multikart collision during which she sustained severe injuries. Beaver filed an action against the race organizers for negligence. The organizers could not locate the exculpatory clause that Beaver had supposedly signed. Race organizers argued that she must have signed one to enter the race, but even if she had not signed one, her actions showed her intent to be bound by its terms. Using the information presented in the chapter, answer the following questions.

1. Did Beaver have the contractual capacity to enter into a contract with an exculpatory clause? Why or why not?

2. Assuming that Beaver did, in fact, sign the exculpatory clause, did she later disaffirm or ratify the contract? Explain.

3. Now assume that Beaver had stated that she was eighteen years old at the time she signed the exculpatory clause. How might this affect her ability to disaffirm or ratify the contract?

4. Suppose Beaver can prove that she did not actually sign an exculpatory clause and this fact convinces race organizers to pursue a settlement. They offer to pay Beaver one-half of the amount that she is claiming in damages if she now signs a release of all claims. Because Beaver is young and the full effect of her injuries may not yet be clear, what other type of settlement agreement might she prefer? What is the consideration to support any settlement agreement that Beaver enters into with the race organizers?

Debate This

After agreeing to an exculpatory clause or purchasing some item, minors often seek to avoid the contracts. Today's minors are far from naïve and should not be allowed to avoid their contractual obligations.

Key Terms

Chapter Summary: Capacity and Legality

CONTRACTUAL CAPACITY	

Minors	1. *General rule*—Contracts with minors are voidable at the option of the minor.
	 2. *Emancipation*—Occurs when a child's parent or legal guardian relinquishes the legal right to exercise control over the child. Normally, minors who leave home to support themselves are considered emancipated. In some jurisdictions, minors are permitted to petition a court for emancipation.
	 3. *Disaffirmance*—The legal avoidance of a contractual obligation.
	   a. Disaffirmance can take place (in most states) at any time during minority and within a reasonable time after the minor has reached the age of majority.
	   b. The minor must disaffirm the entire contract, not just part of it.
	   c. When disaffirming executed contracts, the minor has a duty to return the received goods if they are still in the minor's control or (in some states) to pay their reasonable value.
	   d. A minor who has misrepresented her or his age will be denied the right to disaffirm by some courts.
	   e. A minor may disaffirm a contract for necessaries but remains liable for the reasonable value of the goods.
	 4. *Ratification*—The acceptance, or affirmation, of a legal obligation.
	   a. Express ratification—Occurs when the minor, in writing or orally, explicitly assumes the obligations imposed by the contract.
	   b. Implied ratification—Occurs when the conduct of the minor is inconsistent with disaffirmance or when the minor fails to disaffirm an executed contract within a reasonable time after reaching the age of majority.
	 5. *Parents' liability*—Generally, except for contracts for necessaries, parents are not liable for the contracts made by minor children acting on their own.

Intoxicated Persons	1. A contract entered into by an intoxicated person is voidable at the option of the intoxicated person if the person was sufficiently intoxicated to lack mental capacity, even if the intoxication was voluntary. 2. A contract with an intoxicated person is enforceable if, despite being intoxicated, the person understood the legal consequences of entering into the contract.
Mentally Incompetent Persons	1. A contract made by a person previously judged by a court to be mentally incompetent is void. 2. A contract made by a person who is mentally incompetent, but has not been previously declared incompetent by a court, is voidable at the option of that person.
LEGALITY	
Contracts Contrary to Statute	1. *Usury*—Usury occurs when a lender makes a loan at an interest rate above the lawful maximum, which varies from state to state. 2. *Gambling*—Gambling contracts that violate state statutes are deemed illegal and thus void. 3. *Licensing statutes*—Contracts entered into by persons who do not have a license, when one is required by statute, will not be enforceable unless the underlying purpose of the statute is to raise government revenues (and not to protect the public from unauthorized practitioners).

(Continues)

Contracts Contrary to Public Policy	1. *Contracts in restraint of trade*—Contracts to restrain free competition are illegal and prohibited by statutes. An exception is a *covenant not to compete*. Such covenants usually are enforced by the courts if the terms are secondary to a contract (such as a contract for the sale of a business or an employment contract) and are reasonable as to time and area of restraint. Courts tend to scrutinize covenants not to compete closely and, at times, may reform them if they are overly broad rather than declaring the entire covenant unenforceable. 2. *Unconscionable contracts and clauses*—When a contract or contract clause is so unfair that it is oppressive to one party, it may be deemed unconscionable. As such, it is illegal and cannot be enforced. 3. *Exculpatory clauses*—An exculpatory clause releases a party from liability in the event of monetary or physical injury, no matter who is at fault. In certain situations, exculpatory clauses may be contrary to public policy and thus unenforceable.
EFFECT OF ILLEGALITY	
General Rule	In general, an illegal contract is void, and the courts will not aid either party when both parties are considered to be equally at fault (*in pari delicto*). If the contract is executory, neither party can enforce it. If the contract is executed, neither party can recover damages.
Exceptions	Several exceptions exist to the general rule that neither party to an illegal bargain will be able to recover. The court may grant recovery in the following situations: 1. *Justifiable ignorance of the facts*—When one party has no reason to know that the contract is illegal and so is relatively innocent. 2. *Members of protected classes*—When one party to the contract is a member of a group of persons protected by a particular statute. 3. *Withdrawal from an illegal agreement*—When either party seeks to recover consideration given for an illegal contract before the illegal act is performed. 4. *Severable, or divisible, contracts*—When the court can divide the contract into illegal and legal portions, and the illegal portion is not essential to the bargain. 5. *Fraud, duress, or undue influence*—When one party was induced by the other party to enter into an illegal bargain through fraud, duress, or undue influence.

Issue Spotters

1. Cedric, a minor, enters into a contract with Diane. How might Cedric effectively ratify this contract? (See *Contractual Capacity*.)

2. Sun Airlines, Inc., prints on its tickets that it is not liable for any injury to a passenger caused by the airline's negligence. If the cause of an accident is found to be the airline's negligence, can it use the clause as a defense to liability? Why or why not? (See *Legality*.)

   —**Check your answers to the *Issue Spotters* against the answers provided in Appendix D at the end of this text.**

Business Scenarios and Case Problems

13–1. Contracts by Minors. Kalen is a seventeen-year-old minor who has just graduated from high school. He is attending a university two hundred miles from home and has contracted to rent an apartment near the university for one year at $500 per month. He is working at a convenience store to earn enough income to be self-supporting. After living in the apartment and paying monthly rent for four months, he becomes involved in a dispute with his landlord. Kalen, still a minor, moves out and returns the key to the landlord. The landlord wants to hold Kalen liable for the balance of the payments due under the lease. Discuss fully Kalen's liability in this situation. (See *Contractual Capacity*.)

13–2. Intoxication. After Kira had had several drinks one night, she sold Charlotte a diamond necklace worth thousands of dollars for one hundred dollars. The next day, Kira offered the one hundred dollars to Charlotte and requested the return of her necklace. Charlotte refused to accept the money or return the necklace, claiming that she and Kira had a valid contract of sale. Kira explained that she had been intoxicated at the time the bargain was made and thus the contract was voidable at her option. Was Kira correct? Explain. (See *Contractual Capacity*.)

13–3. Disaffirmance. J.T., a minor, is a motocross competitor. At Monster Mountain MX Park, he signed a waiver of liability to "hold harmless the park for any loss due to negligence." Riding around the Monster Mountain track, J.T. rode over a blind jump, became airborne, and crashed into a tractor that he had not seen until he was in the air. To recover for his injuries, J.T. filed a suit against Monster Mountain, alleging negligence for its failure to remove the tractor from the track. Does the liability waiver bar this claim? Explain. [*J.T. v. Monster Mountain, LLC*, 754 F.Supp.2d 1323 (M.D.Ala. 2010)] (See *Contractual Capacity*.)

13–4. Business Case Problem with Sample Answer—Minors. D.V.G. (a minor) was injured in a one-car auto accident in Hoover, Alabama. The vehicle was covered by an insurance policy issued by Nationwide Mutual Insurance Co. Stan Brobston, D.V.G.'s attorney, accepted Nationwide's offer of $50,000 on D.V.G.'s behalf. Before the settlement could be submitted to an Alabama state court for approval, D.V.G. died from injuries received in a second, unrelated auto accident. Nationwide argued that it was not bound to the settlement because a minor lacks the capacity to contract and cannot enter into a binding settlement without court approval. Should Nationwide be bound to the settlement? Why or why not? [*Nationwide Mutual Insurance Co. v. Wood*, 121 So.3d 982 (Ala. 2013)] (See *Contractual Capacity*.)

—For a sample answer to Problem 13–4, go to Appendix E at the end of this text.

13–5. Adhesion Contracts. David Desgro hired Paul Pack to inspect a house that Desgro wanted to buy. Pack had Desgro sign a standard-form contract that included a twelve-month limit for claims based on the agreement. Pack reported that the house had no major problems, but after Desgro bought it, he discovered issues with the plumbing, insulation, heat pump, and floor support. Thirteen months after the inspection, Desgro filed a suit in a Tennessee state court against Pack. Was Desgro's complaint filed too late, or was the contract's twelve-month limit unenforceable? Discuss. [*Desgro v. Pack*, 2013 WL 84899 (Tenn. App. 2013)] (See *Legality*.)

13–6. Minors. Bonney McWilliam's father deeded a house in Norfolk County, Massachusetts, to Bonney and her daughter, Mechelle. Each owned a one-half interest. Described as "an emotionally troubled teenager," Mechelle had a history of substance abuse and a fractured relationship with her mother. At age sixteen, in the presence of her mother and her mother's attorney, Mechelle signed a deed transferring her interest in the house to Bonney. Later, still at odds with her mother, Mechelle learned that she did not have a right to enter the house to retrieve her belongings. Bonney claimed sole ownership. Mechelle filed a lawsuit in a Massachusetts state court against her mother to declare the deed void. Could the transfer of Mechelle's interest be disaffirmed? Explain. [*McWilliam v. McWilliam*, 46 N.E.3d 598 (Mass.App.Ct. 2016)] (See *Contractual Capacity*.)

13–7. Legality. Sue Ann Apolinar hired a guide through Arkansas Valley Adventures, LLC, for a rafting excursion on the Arkansas River. At the outfitter's office, Apolinar signed a release that detailed potential hazards and risks, including "overturning," "unpredictable currents," "obstacles" in the water, and "drowning." The release clearly stated that her signature discharged Arkansas Valley from liability for all claims arising in connection with the trip. On the river, while attempting to maneuver around a rapid, the raft capsized. The current swept Apolinar into a logjam where, despite efforts to save her, she drowned. Her son, Jesus Espinoza, Jr., filed a suit in a federal district court against the rafting company, alleging negligence. What are the arguments for and against enforcing the release that Apolinar signed? Discuss. [*Espinoza v. Arkansas Valley Adventures, LLC*, 809 F.3d 1150 (10th Cir. 2016)] (See *Legality*.)

13–8. Contracts Contrary to Public Policy. P.M. and C.M. are married (the "Ms") and live in Iowa. Unable to conceive their own child, they signed a contract with T.B., who, in exchange for $13,000 and medical expenses, agreed to be impregnated with embryos fertilized with P.M.'s sperm and the ova (eggs) of an anonymous donor. T.B. agreed to carry the pregnancy to term, and she and her spouse D.B. (the "Bs") promised to deliver the baby at birth to the Ms. During the pregnancy, the relations between the parties deteriorated. When the baby was born, T.B. refused to honor the agreement to give up the child. Meanwhile, genetic testing excluded T.B. and D.B. as the biological parents, and established P.M. as the father. Iowa exempts "surrogacy" from a state criminal statute that prohibits selling babies. There is no other state law on point. Is the contract between the Ms and the Bs enforceable? Discuss. [*P.M. v. T.B.*, 907 N.W.2d 522 (Iowa 2018)] (See *Legality*.)

13–9. A Question of Ethics—The IDDR Approach and Minors. *Sky High Sports Nashville Operations, LLC operated a trampoline park in Nashville, Tennessee. At the park, during a dodgeball tournament, Jacob Blackwell, a minor, suffered a torn tendon and a broken tibia. His mother Crystal filed a suit on his behalf in a Tennessee state court against Sky High, alleging negligence and seeking $500,000 to cover medical and other expenses. Sky High asserted that the claim was barred by a waiver of liability in a contract between the parties, which the defendant asked the court to enforce. The waiver released Sky High from liability for any "negligent acts or omissions."* [Blackwell v. Sky High Sports Nashville Operations, LLC, *523 S.W.3d 624 (Tenn.App. 2017)*] *(See* Contractual Capacity.*)*

1. Should Sky High offer a defense to the suit? What might Sky High argue as a reason for enforcing the waiver? Use the IDDR approach to answer these questions.

2. Would it be unethical to allow Jacob to recover? Apply the IDDR approach to explain.

Critical Thinking and Writing Assignments

13–10. Time-Limited Group Assignment. Assume that you are a group of executives at a large software corporation. The company is considering whether to add covenants not to compete to its employment contracts. You know that there are some issues with the enforceability of these covenants and want to make an informed decision. (See *Legality*.)

1. One group should make a list of interests that are served by enforcing covenants not to compete.

2. A second group should create a list of interests that are served by refusing to enforce covenants not to compete.

3. third group should discuss whether a court that determines that a covenant not to compete is illegal should reform (and then enforce) the covenant. The group should present arguments for and against reformation.

Voluntary Consent

"Understanding is a two-way street."

Eleanor Roosevelt
1884–1962
(First Lady of the United States, 1933–1945)

An otherwise valid contract may still be unenforceable if the parties have not genuinely agreed to its terms. The lack of voluntary consent is a *defense* to the enforcement of a contract. As Eleanor Roosevelt stated in the chapter-opening quotation, "Understanding is a two-way street." If one party does not voluntarily consent to the terms of a contract, then there is no genuine "meeting of the minds," and the law will not normally enforce the contract, as we discuss in the first part of this chapter.

Voluntary consent (assent) may be lacking because of mistake, fraudulent misrepresentation, undue influence, or duress. Generally, a party who demonstrates that he or she did not genuinely agree to the terms of a contract can choose either to carry out the contract or to rescind (cancel) it and thus avoid the entire transaction.

A contract that is otherwise valid may also be unenforceable if it is not in the proper form. For instance, if a contract is required by law to be in writing and there is no written evidence or electronic record of it, the contract will not be enforced.

14–1 Mistakes

We all make mistakes, so it is not surprising that mistakes are made when contracts are created. In certain circumstances, contract law allows a contract to be avoided on the basis of mistake.

It is important to distinguish between *mistakes of fact* and *mistakes of value or quality*. Only a mistake of fact makes a contract voidable. Also, the mistake must involve some *material fact*—a fact that a reasonable person would consider important when determining his or her course of action.

Learning Objectives

The three Learning Objectives *below are designed to help improve your understanding. After reading this chapter, you should be able to answer the following questions:*

1. What is the difference between a unilateral and a bilateral mistake?

2. What are the elements of fraudulent misrepresentation?

3. What is the essential feature of undue influence?

Voluntary Consent Knowledge of and genuine assent to the terms of a contract.

Mistakes of fact occur in two forms—*unilateral* and *bilateral (mutual)*. A unilateral mistake is made by only one of the contracting parties, whereas a mutual mistake is made by both. We look at these two types of mistakes next and illustrate them graphically in Exhibit 14–1.

14–1a Unilateral Mistakes

Unilateral Mistake A mistake that occurs when one party to a contract is mistaken as to a material fact.

A **unilateral mistake** occurs when only one party is mistaken as to a material fact. Generally, a unilateral mistake does not give the mistaken party any right to relief from the contract. In other words, the contract normally is enforceable against the mistaken party.

Example 14.1 Elena intends to sell her jet ski for $2,500. When she learns that Chin is interested in buying a used jet ski, she sends him an e-mail offering to sell the jet ski to him. When typing the e-mail, however, she mistakenly keys in the price of $1,500. Chin immediately sends Elena an e-mail reply accepting her offer. Even though Elena intended to sell her jet ski for $2,500, she has made a unilateral mistake and is bound by the contract to sell it to Chin for $1,500. ■

This rule has at least two exceptions.[1] The contract may not be enforceable in either of the following situations.

1. The *other* party to the contract knows or should have known that a mistake of fact was made.
2. The error was due to a *substantial* mathematical mistake in addition, subtraction, division, or multiplication and was made inadvertently and without gross (extreme) negligence. If, for instance, a contractor's bid was significantly low because he or she made a mistake in addition when totaling the estimated costs, any contract resulting from the bid normally may be rescinded.

In both situations, the mistake must still involve some material fact.

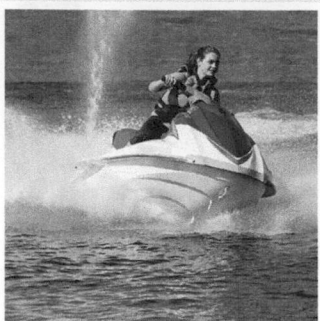

If this young woman wants to sell her jet ski for one price but mistakenly types a lower price in her e-mail offer, is she bound by the lower price?

MrPants/Getty Images

14–1b Bilateral (Mutual) Mistakes

Bilateral Mistake A mistake that occurs when both parties to a contract are mistaken about the same material fact.

A **bilateral mistake** is a "mutual misunderstanding concerning a basic assumption on which the contract was made."[2] When both parties are mistaken about the same material fact, the contract can be rescinded, or canceled, by either party. Note that, as with unilateral mistakes, the mistake must be about a material fact.

Either Party Can Rescind the Contract When a bilateral mistake occurs, normally the contract is voidable by the adversely affected party and can be rescinded. **Case Example 14.2** Coleman

---

1. The *Restatement (Second) of Contracts*, Section 153, liberalizes the general rule to take into account the modern trend of allowing avoidance in some circumstances even though only one party has been mistaken.
2. *Restatement (Second) of Contracts*, Section 152.

Exhibit 14–1 Mistakes of Fact

Material Mistake of Fact

Bilateral Mistake
Both parties mistaken

→ Contract Can Be Rescinded by Either Party

Unilateral Mistake
One party mistaken

→ Contract Enforceable Unless—
- Other party knew or should have known that mistake was made *or*
- Mistake was due to substantial mathematical error, made inadvertently and without gross negligence

Holdings LP bought a parcel of real estate subject to setback restrictions imposed by a document entitled "Partial Release of Restrictions." The release effectively precluded building a structure on the property. Lance and Joanne Eklund offered to buy the parcel from Coleman, intending to combine it with an adjacent parcel and build a home. Coleman gave the Eklunds a title report that referred to the "Partial Release of Restrictions," but they were not given a copy of the release.

Mistakenly believing that the document released restrictions on the property, the Eklunds did not investigate further. Meanwhile, Coleman mistakenly believed that the setback restrictions had been removed. After buying the property and discovering the restrictions, the Eklunds filed a suit in a Nevada state court against Coleman, seeking rescission of the sale. The court ordered the deal rescinded. The Nevada Supreme Court affirmed the order. "The parties made a mutual mistake in their mutual belief that the parcel had no setback restrictions."[3]

When the Parties Reasonably Interpret a Term Differently A word or term in a contract may be subject to more than one reasonable interpretation. If the parties to the contract attach materially different meanings to the term, their mutual misunderstanding may allow the contract to be rescinded or reformed. **Case Example 14.3** Offshore Energy Services (OES) contracted with companies to provide workers at offshore oil drilling operations. In its contract with rig operators, OES had an indemnity provision stating that it would insure the companies for tort claims filed against them by an OES employee. Raylin Richard, an OES employee, was injured while working on an oil rig. Richard filed a personal injury suit against Anadarko Petroleum, the head of that drilling project.

OES paid $2.5 million to Richard to settle the lawsuit, but OES's insurance company, Liberty Mutual, denied coverage. Liberty took the position that the indemnity clause in the contract between OES and Anadarko explicitly covered "subcontractors" but did not mention "contractors" like Anadarko. Both OES and Anadarko had thought that the indemnity provision applied to subcontractors and contractors, so they claimed that there had been a mutual mistake. The district court agreed and reformed the contract to include the words *contractors* as well as *subcontractors*. Thus, Liberty Mutual had to cover the amounts OES paid.[4]

Learning Objective 1
What is the difference between a unilateral and a bilateral mistake?

"Mistakes are the inevitable lot of mankind."

Sir George Jessel
1824–1883
(English jurist)

Should a surviving member of Lynyrd Skynyrd abide by a thirty-year-old consent decree? One of the biggest songs of the 1970s was "Free Bird" by the southern rock group Lynyrd Skynyrd. Not too long after its release, the group's touring plane crashed, killing band members Ronnie Van Zant and Steve Gaines, among others. A decade later, all surviving band members became bound by a consent decree allowing the surviving musicians to tell only their personal *individual* stories rather than the story of the band. The order also prohibited the use of the group's name by any surviving member.

Ethical Issue

Flash forward three decades. Former Lynyrd Skynyrd drummer Artimus Pyle, along with Cleopatra Films, went into production of a biopic about the plane crash entitled *Street Survivors: The True Story of the Lynyrd Skynyrd Plane Crash*. Van Zant's brother, Johnny, and others sought a permanent injunction blocking the production and distribution of the film. The president of Cleopatra Films argued that the company had First Amendment rights to make the movie. The presiding judge ruled otherwise. "None of the defendants received the requisite authorization under the terms of the consent order in depiction of [Ronnie] Van Zant or Gaines or in the use of the Lynyrd Skynyrd name, and therefore all have violated the consent order."[5]

---

3. *Coleman Holdings Limited Partnership v. Eklund*, 2015 WL 428567 (Nev.Sup.Ct. 2015).
4. *Richard v. Anadarko Petroleum Corp.*, 850 F.3d 701 (5th Cir. 2017).
5. *Ronnie Van Zant Inc. v. Pyle*, 270 F.Supp.3d 656 311C (S.D.N.Y. 2017).

Ronnie Van Zant, the founder of the rock band Lynyrd Skynyrd, died in a plane crash in 1977. How did a consent decree limit how his story could be told in the future?

Pictorial Press Ltd/Alamy

14–1c Mistakes of Value

If a mistake concerns the future market value or quality of the object of the contract, the mistake is one of *value*, and the contract normally is enforceable. **Example 14.4** Pablo buys a violin from Bev for $250. Although the violin is very old, neither party believes that it is valuable. Later, however, an antiques dealer informs the parties that the violin is rare and worth thousands of dollars. Here, both parties were mistaken, but the mistake is a mistake of *value* rather than a mistake of *fact*. Because mistakes of value do not warrant contract rescission, Bev cannot rescind the contract. ■

The reason that mistakes of value do not affect the enforceability of contracts is that value is variable. Depending on the time, place, and other circumstances, the same item may be worth considerably different amounts. When parties form a contract, their agreement establishes the value of the object of their transaction—for the moment. Each party is considered to have assumed the risk that the value will change in the future or prove to be different from what he or she thought. Without this rule, almost any party who did not receive what she or he considered a fair bargain could argue mistake.

14–2 Fraudulent Misrepresentation

Although fraud is a tort, the presence of fraud also affects the authenticity of the innocent party's consent to a contract. When an innocent party is fraudulently induced to enter into a contract, the contract usually can be avoided because that party has not *voluntarily* consented to the terms.[6] Normally, the innocent party can either rescind the contract and be restored to her or his original position, or enforce the contract and seek damages for any harms resulting from the fraud.

Generally, fraudulent misrepresentation refers only to misrepresentation that is consciously false and is intended to mislead another. That is, the person making a fraudulent misrepresentation knows or believes that the assertion is false or knows that she or he does not have a basis (stated or implied) for the assertion.[7]

Typically, fraud involves the following elements:

1. A misrepresentation of a material fact must occur.

2. There must be an intent to deceive.

3. The innocent party must justifiably rely on the misrepresentation.

4. To collect damages, a party must have been harmed as a result of the misrepresentation.

14–2a Misrepresentation Has Occurred

The first element of proving fraud is to show that misrepresentation of a material fact has occurred. This misrepresentation can occur by words or actions. For instance, an art gallery owner's statement "This painting is a Picasso" is a misrepresentation of fact if the painting was done by another artist. Similarly, if a customer asks to see only Jasper Johns paintings and the owner immediately leads the customer over to paintings that were not done by Johns, the owner's actions can be a misrepresentation.

Learning Objective 2

What are the elements of fraudulent misrepresentation?

Know This

To collect damages in almost any lawsuit, there must be some sort of injury.

---

6. *Restatement (Second) of Contracts,* Sections 163 and 164.

7. *Restatement (Second) of Contracts,* Section 162.

Sometimes, a party agrees to enter into a contract on the basis of a promise that is not included in the document evidencing the agreement. And the document includes a *merger clause*, which states, "This agreement contains the entire agreement between the parties. There are no understandings or agreements between the parties except as expressly set forth."

The issue in the following case concerned the effect of a merger clause on an allegation that the contract containing it was procured by fraud.

■ Case 14.1

McCullough v. Allstate Property and Casualty Insurance Co.

Alabama Court of Civil Appeals, __ So.3d __, 2018 WL 387844 (2018).

Background and Facts Allstate Property and Casualty Insurance Company issued a policy to Jerry McCullough, insuring his pickup truck. McCullough loaned the truck to an acquaintance, who returned it damaged. McCullough filed a claim on the policy. Allstate treated the claim as involving multiple different claims (each with a $250 deductible). Allstate also reported these claims to an insurance exchange, Verisk Analytics Automobile Property Loss Underwriting Service (A-PLUS).[a]

Contending that the damage had resulted from only one claim, McCullough filed a suit in a federal district court against Allstate. The insurer agreed to settle the suit for $8,000. McCullough agreed to this amount, but only if Allstate corrected the report to reflect that he was making only one insurance claim and that Allstate paid nothing on that claim. (McCullough felt that the $8,000 was not a payment for the damage to his truck.) Allstate's lawyer sent McCullough an e-mail agreeing to these terms, but the promise was not included in the release and settlement agreement that the parties signed. The release had a merger clause saying that there were no other agreements, verbal or otherwise, between the parties except as set forth in the contract.

Later, McCullough learned that Allstate had reported to A-PLUS that it had paid $8,000 to him on his claim. He filed a suit in an Alabama state court against Allstate, seeking damages for fraud. Both parties filed motions for summary judgment. The court granted Allstate's motion and denied McCullough's. McCullough appealed.

In the Words of the Court

MOORE, Judge.

* * * *

---

a. A-PLUS reports information received from insurance companies regarding claims. The reports can affect a claimant's insurance costs.

On appeal, McCullough argues that the trial court erred in granting Allstate's motion for a summary judgment * * *. Allstate simply argued that McCullough's claim was barred by * * * the release. McCullough argues, though, that he should be permitted to present * * * evidence to prove that the release was procured by fraud.

The law in this state renders [a] merger clause ineffective to bar * * * evidence of fraud in the inducement or procurement of a contract. * * * Such a holding is required. To hold otherwise is to encourage deliberate fraud. [Emphasis added.]

* * * Allstate was incorrect in its argument that McCullough's claim * * * was barred * * * by the language of the release. * * * Therefore, Allstate's summary-judgment motion was due to be denied.

* * * *

McCullough also argues that the trial court erred in denying his motion for * * * summary judgment on his claim.

According to McCullough, he informed Allstate, through its attorney, that he would not settle the federal lawsuit unless Allstate reported no payment on the claim. McCullough averred [declared] that Allstate's attorney * * * informed McCullough that Allstate had reported * * * that it had paid nothing on the claim. According to McCullough, that fact * * * led McCullough to settle the federal lawsuit because he believed that no reported payment on the claim would be on record; however, Allstate subsequently reported the $8,000 payment to * * * A–PLUS.

Although McCullough presented evidence of fraud, the release contained a merger clause * * *. Considering that the release did not specify that Allstate must report that nothing was paid on the claim, coupled with * * * the merger clause, we conclude that *there is a genuine issue of material fact as to whether Allstate, willfully to deceive, or recklessly without knowledge, agreed to*

(Continues)

report an amount of $0 on the claim and whether McCullough reasonably relied on any representation outside those contained in the release. [Emphasis added.]

Based on the foregoing, McCullough's motion for * * * summary judgment on his claim * * * was properly denied.

Decision and Remedy A state intermediate appellate court reversed the lower court's summary judgment in favor of Allstate, affirmed the court's denial of McCullough's motion for summary judgment, and remanded the case. Genuine issues of material fact precluded summary judgment on McCullough's claim for fraud.

Critical Thinking

• **Legal Environment** *In most cases involving the interpretation and application of a contract, a party is not allowed to present evidence outside of the document expressing the parties' agreement. Why not?*

Misrepresentation by Conduct Misrepresentation also occurs when a party takes specific action to conceal a fact that is material to the contract.[8] Therefore, if a seller, by her or his actions, prevents a buyer from learning of some fact that is material to the contract, the seller's behavior constitutes misrepresentation by conduct. It would also be misrepresentation by conduct for a seller to untruthfully deny knowledge of facts that are material to the contract when a buyer requests such information.

✳ Spotlight Case Example 14.5 Actor Tom Selleck contracted to purchase a horse named Zorro for his daughter from Dolores Cuenca. Cuenca acted as though Zorro were fit to ride in competitions, when in reality the horse was unfit for this use because of a medical condition. Selleck filed a lawsuit against Cuenca for wrongfully concealing the horse's condition, and a jury awarded Selleck more than $187,000 for Cuenca's misrepresentation by conduct.[9]

How did misrepresentation by conduct affect an agreement between the television actor Tom Selleck and the owner of a horse?

Kathy Hutchins/Shutterstock.com

Statements of Opinion Statements of opinion and representations of future facts (predictions) are generally not subject to claims of fraud. Statements such as "This land will be worth twice as much next year" and "This car will last for years and years" are statements of opinion, not fact. Contracting parties should recognize them as opinions and not rely on them. A fact is objective and verifiable, whereas an opinion is usually subject to debate. Therefore, a seller is allowed to use *puffery* to sell her or his goods without being liable for fraud.

Nevertheless, in certain situations, such as when a naïve purchaser relies on an opinion from an expert, the innocent party may be entitled to rescission or reformation. (Recall that reformation is an equitable remedy by which a court alters the terms of a contract to reflect the true intentions of the parties.)

Misrepresentation of Law Misrepresentation of law *ordinarily* does not entitle a party to be relieved of a contract. **Example 14.6** Cameron has a parcel of property that she is trying to sell to Levi. Cameron knows that a local ordinance prohibits building anything higher than three stories on the property. Nonetheless, she tells Levi, "You can build a condominium one hundred stories high if you want to." Levi buys the land and later discovers that Cameron's statement is false. Levi generally cannot avoid the contract, because under the common law, people are assumed to know state and local laws.

Exceptions to this rule occur when the misrepresenting party is in a profession known to require greater knowledge of the law than the average citizen possesses. For instance, if Cameron, in *Example 14.6*, had been a lawyer or a real estate broker, her willful misrepresentation of the area's zoning laws probably would have constituted fraud.

---

8. *Restatement (Second) of Contracts*, Section 160.
9. *Selleck v. Cuenca*, Case No. GIN056909, North County of San Diego, California, decided September 9, 2009.

Misrepresentation by Silence Ordinarily, neither party to a contract has a duty to come forward and disclose facts, and a contract normally will not be set aside because certain pertinent information has not been volunteered. **Example 14.7** Jude is selling a car that has been in an accident and has been repaired. He does not need to volunteer this information to a potential buyer. If, however, the buyer asks him if the car has had extensive bodywork and he lies, Jude has committed fraudulent misrepresentation.

In general, if the seller knows of a serious potential problem that the buyer cannot reasonably be expected to discover, the seller may have a duty to speak. Normally, the seller must disclose only **latent defects**—that is, defects that could not readily be ascertained. Because a buyer of a house could easily discover the presence of termites through an inspection, for instance, termites may not qualify as a latent defect. Also, when the parties are in a *fiduciary relationship*—one of trust, such as partners, physician and patient, or attorney and client—there is a duty to disclose material facts. Failure to do so may constitute fraud.

> **Latent Defect** A defect that is not obvious or cannot readily be ascertained.

14–2b Intent to Deceive

The second element of fraud is knowledge on the part of the misrepresenting party that facts have been misrepresented. This element, usually called *scienter,*[10] or "guilty knowledge," generally signifies that there was an intent to deceive.

Scienter clearly exists if a party knows that a fact is not as stated. **Example 14.8** Richard Wright applies for a position as a business law professor two weeks after his release from prison. On his résumé, he lies and says that he was a corporate president for fourteen years and taught business law at another college. After he is hired, his probation officer alerts the school to Wright's criminal history. The school immediately fires him. If Wright sues the school for breach of his employment contract, he is unlikely to succeed. Because Wright clearly exhibited an intent to deceive the college by not disclosing his personal history, the school can rescind his employment contract without incurring liability.

Scienter also exists if a party makes a statement that he or she believes not to be true or makes a statement recklessly, without regard to whether it is true or false. Finally, this element is met if a party says or implies that a statement is made on some basis, such as personal knowledge or personal investigation, when it is not.

> **Scienter** Knowledge on the part of a misrepresenting party that material facts have been falsely represented or omitted with an intent to deceive.

Innocent Misrepresentation If a person makes a statement that she or he believes to be true but that actually misrepresents material facts, the person is guilty only of an **innocent misrepresentation,** not of fraud. When an innocent misrepresentation occurs, the aggrieved party can rescind the contract but usually cannot seek damages. **Example 14.9** Parris tells Roberta that a tract of land contains 250 acres. Parris is mistaken—the tract contains only 215 acres—but Parris had no knowledge of the mistake. Roberta relies on the statement and contracts to buy the land. Even though the misrepresentation is innocent, Roberta can avoid the contract if the misrepresentation is material.

> **Innocent Misrepresentation** A misrepresentation that occurs when a person makes a false statement of fact that he or she believes is true.

Negligent Misrepresentation Sometimes, a party will make a misrepresentation through carelessness, believing the statement is true. Such a misrepresentation may constitute **negligent misrepresentation** if the party did not exercise reasonable care in uncovering or disclosing the facts or did not use the skill and competence that her or his business or profession requires. **Example 14.10** Dirk, an operator of a weight scale, certifies the weight of Sneed's commodity. If Dirk knows that the scale's accuracy has not been checked for more than three years, his action may constitute negligent misrepresentation.

In almost all states, negligent misrepresentation is equal to *scienter,* or knowingly making a misrepresentation. In effect, negligent misrepresentation is treated as fraudulent

> **Negligent Misrepresentation** A misrepresentation that occurs when a person makes a false statement of fact because he or she did not exercise reasonable care or use the skill and competence required by her or his business or profession.

---

10. Pronounced sy-*en*-ter.

misrepresentation, even though the misrepresentation was not purposeful. In negligent misrepresentation, culpable ignorance of the truth supplies the intention to mislead, even if the defendant can claim, "I didn't know."

14–2c Justifiable Reliance on the Misrepresentation

Know This

A statement of opinion is neither a contract offer, nor a contract term, nor fraud.

The third element of fraud is reasonably justifiable reliance on the misrepresentation of fact. The deceived party must have a justifiable reason for relying on the misrepresentation. Also, the misrepresentation must be an important factor (but not necessarily the sole factor) in inducing the deceived party to enter into the contract.

Reliance is not justified if the innocent party knows the true facts or relies on obviously extravagant statements (such as "this pickup truck will get fifty miles to the gallon"). The same rule applies to defects in property sold. If the defects would be obvious on inspection, the buyer cannot justifiably rely on the seller's representations. If the defects are hidden or latent, however, the buyer is justified in relying on the seller's statements.

In the following case, the buyer of a car wash relied on the seller's representations that the property would be "appropriately winterized" to protect it from damage, but it was not. Was the buyer justified in relying on the seller's representations?

Case 14.2

Cronkelton v. Guaranteed Construction Services, LLC

Court of Appeals of Ohio, Third District, 988 N.E.2d 656, 2013-Ohio-328 (2013).

Background and Facts A court appointed Patrick Shivley to be the receiver of a foreclosed car wash that was being sold in Bellefontaine, Ohio. (A receiver is an independent, impartial party appointed by a bankruptcy court to manage property in bankruptcy proceedings and dispose of it in an orderly manner for the benefit of the creditors.) The buyer, Clifford Cronkelton, inspected the car wash in November 2009. He knew that some equipment would have to be replaced, but he was concerned that the property needed to be winterized to protect it from damage. In phone calls and e-mails, Shivley assured him that the winterizing would be done.

Shivley contacted Guaranteed Construction Services, which hired Strayer Company to winterize the property. Strayer told Shivley that the only way to avoid problems was to leave the heat on at the car wash, but Shivley knew that the bank had shut off the heat because the property was not generating income. In March 2010, Shivley informed the bank of damage to the property caused by freezing. Shivley did not share this information with Cronkelton, who did not become aware of the damage until after he had bought the car wash in June.

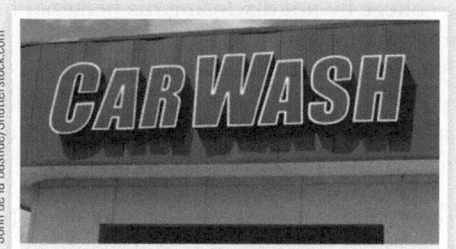
Is it reasonable for the buyer of a car wash to rely on the seller's statements that the property has been properly winterized?

Cronkelton filed a suit in an Ohio state court against Guaranteed and Shivley, asserting fraud. The jury returned a verdict in Cronkelton's favor, and he was awarded more than $140,000 in damages and attorneys' fees. The defendants appealed.

In the Words of the Court
PRESTON, P.J. [Presiding Judge]
* * * *

* * * Appellants argue Cronkelton unjustifiably relied on Shivley's statements about the car wash's condition because Cronkelton had the opportunity to inspect the property prior to closing.
* * * *

* * * Whether or not reliance on a material misrepresentation was justified under the facts of a case is a question for the trier of fact. Consequently, we must determine whether the jury's decision is supported by competent, credible evidence.

In the present case, it is undisputed that the damage caused by freezing was open and obvious upon inspection, that Cronkelton did inspect the property in November 2009, and that he could have inspected the property again before signing the purchase agreement. Cronkelton testified regarding why he did not inspect the property after November 2009:

> * * * [Shivley] wrote me this e-mail, guaranteed me it was taken care of in detail what he was going to do, so I had no reason. And because * * * he was appointed by the Court, I don't know how much more I could have done to know that I could trust him.

* * * The jury found that Cronkelton had reasonably relied on Shivley's representations.

The jury's finding was supported by competent, credible evidence. * * * *When determining whether reliance is justifiable courts consider the various circumstances involved, such as the nature of the transaction, the form and materiality of the transaction, the form and materiality of the representation, the relationship of the parties, the respective intelligence, experience, age, and mental and physical condition of the parties, and their respective knowledge and means of knowledge.* [Emphasis added.]

Cronkelton relied on representations made by Shivley * * *. As a receiver, Shivley had a fiduciary duty to the assets under his control. Under the circumstances of this case, Cronkelton had a reasonable basis to believe that Shivley, who was acting as an arm of the court, would take the promised steps to winterize the property.

Decision and Remedy A state intermediate appellate court affirmed the lower court's judgment in Cronkelton's favor. The appellate court found that the jury verdict was supported by "competent, credible evidence" indicating that Cronkelton reasonably relied on Shivley's representations.

Critical Thinking

• **Legal Environment** *Did Shivley's misrepresentations rise to the level of fraud? Explain.*

14–2d Injury to the Innocent Party

Most courts do not require a showing of harm in an action to rescind a contract. These courts hold that because rescission returns the parties to the positions they held before the contract was made, a showing of injury to the innocent party is unnecessary.

In contrast, to recover damages caused by fraud, proof of harm is universally required. The measure of damages is ordinarily equal to the property's value had it been delivered as represented, less the actual price paid for the property. (What if someone pretends to be someone else online? Can the victim of the hoax prove injury sufficient to recover for fraudulent misrepresentation? See this chapter's *Adapting the Law to the Online Environment* feature for a discussion of this topic.)

"Catfishing": Is That Online "Friend" for Real?

Adapting the Law to the Online Environment

When you are communicating with a person you have met only online, how do you know who that person really is? After all, the person could turn out to be a "catfish."

The term *catfish* comes from a 2010 film of the same name about a fake online persona. According to a story told in the film, when live cod were shipped long distances,

they were inactive, and their flesh became mushy. When catfish were added to the tanks, the cod swam around and stayed in good condition. At the end of the film, a character says of the creator of the fake persona, "There are those people who are catfish in life. And they keep you on your toes. They keep you guessing, they keep you thinking, they keep you fresh."

Catfishing Makes National Headlines

Catfishing made headlines when a popular Notre Dame football star supposedly fell

(Continues)

victim to it in 2012. Linebacker Manti Te'o said that his girlfriend, Lennay Kekua, a student at Stanford, had died of leukemia after a near-fatal car accident. Although Kekua had Facebook and Twitter accounts and Te'o had communicated with her online and by telephone for several years, reporters could find no evidence of her existence. Te'o later claimed that he had been a victim of a catfishing hoax. Others suggested that his friends had created the persona and her tragic death to provide an inspirational story that would increase Te'o's chances of winning the Heisman trophy.

Is Online Fraudulent Misrepresentation Actionable?

Some victims of catfishing have turned to the courts, but they have had little success. A few have attempted to sue Internet service providers for allowing fake personas, but the courts have generally dismissed these suits.[a] Laws in some states make it a crime to impersonate someone online,

but these laws generally do not apply to those who create totally fictional personas.[b]

Attempts to recover damages for fraudulent misrepresentation have generally failed to meet the requirement that there must be proof of actual injury. For instance, Paula Bonhomme developed an online romantic relationship with a man called Jesse. Jesse was actually a woman named Janna St. James, who also communicated with Bonhomme using her own name and pretending to be a friend of Jesse's.

St. James created a host of fictional characters, including an ex-wife and a son, for Jesse. Bonhomme in turn sent gifts totaling more than $10,000 to Jesse and the other characters. After being told by St. James that Jesse had attempted suicide, Bonhomme suffered such emotional distress that she incurred more than $5,000 in bills for a therapist. Eventually, she was told that Jesse had died of liver cancer. When Bonhomme finally learned the truth, she suffered additional emotional distress,

resulting in more expenses for a therapist and lost earnings due to her "affected mental state."

Although Bonhomme had incurred considerable expenses, the Illinois Supreme Court ruled that she could not bring a suit for fraudulent misrepresentation. The case involved a "purely personal relationship" without any "commercial, transactional, or regulatory component." Bonhomme and St. James "were not engaged in any kind of business dealings or bargaining." The truth of representations "made in the context of purely private personal relationships is simply not something the state regulates or in which the state possesses any kind of valid public policy interest."[c]

Critical Thinking

So far, victims of catfishing have had little success in the courts. Under what circumstances might a person be able to collect damages for fraudulent misrepresentation involving online impersonation?

a. See, for example, *Beckman v. Match.com, LLC,* 668 Fed.Appx. 759 (9th Cir. 2016), 2017 WL 1424899 (D.Nev. 2017); and *Robinson v. Match.com, LLC,* 2012 WL 3263992 (N.D.Tex. 2012).

b. See *LeBlanc v. State of Texas,* 2017 WL 1086575 (Tex.App. —Houston 2017).

c. *Bonhomme v. St. James,* 970 N.E.2d 1 (Ill. 2012).

Because fraud actions necessarily involve wrongful conduct, courts may also award *punitive,* or *exemplary, damages,* which compensate a plaintiff over and above the amount of the actual loss. Because of the potential for punitive damages, which normally are not available in contract actions, plaintiffs often include a claim for fraudulent misrepresentation in their contract disputes.

In the following case, a real estate investor claimed that a seller's failure to disclose material facts about the property affected its value. The court had to determine not only if the seller's conduct constituted fraud, but also whether the fraud had caused harm to the property value.

■ Case 14.3

Fazio v. Cypress/GR Houston I, LP

Court of Appeals of Texas, First District, 403 S.W.3d 390 (2013).

Background and Facts Peter Fazio began talks with Cypress/GR Houston I, LP, to buy retail property whose main tenant was a Garden Ridge store. In performing a background investigation, Fazio and his agents became concerned about Garden Ridge's financial health. Nevertheless, after being assured that Garden Ridge had a positive financial outlook, Fazio sent Cypress a letter of intent to buy the property for $7.67 million "[b]ased on the currently reported absolute net income of $805,040.00." Cypress then agreed to provide all information in its possession, but it failed to disclose the following:

1. A consultant for Garden Ridge had recently requested a $240,000 reduction in the annual rent as part of a restructuring of the company's real estate leases.
2. Cypress's bank was so concerned about Garden Ridge's financial health that it had required a personal guaranty of the property's loan.

The parties entered into a purchase agreement, but Garden Ridge went into bankruptcy shortly after the deal closed. Fazio, along with other members of his family, sued Cypress for fraud after he was forced to sell the property three years later for only $3.75 million. A jury found in Fazio's favor. Although the jury agreed that Cypress had failed to disclose a material fact, however, it determined that Fazio was not entitled to any damages. The jury concluded that the fraud had not negatively affected the value of the property at the time it was sold to Fazio. Thus, no damages had been proximately caused by the fraud. The trial court entered a judgment notwithstanding the verdict in favor of Cypress, and Fazio appealed.

In the Words of the Court
Jane *BLAND*, Justice.

In this suit arising from the sale of land, we examine the appropriate measure of damages for a sale obtained through fraudulent inducement. A jury concluded that the seller of the land had failed to disclose material information to the buyer about the financial state of a commercial tenant who leased the land. But the jury further concluded that the buyers suffered nothing in damages proximately caused by the fraud, measured at the time of the sale, and it awarded no damages * * * . The trial court entered a take-nothing judgment [a judgment in which the plaintiff will receive no damages or other relief] in favor of the seller.

* * * *

The Fazios appeal the trial court's judgment against them on their claim for fraudulent inducement, contending that the trial court erred in disregarding the jury's * * * findings in their favor.

* * * *

There are two measures of direct damages in a fraud case: out-of-pocket and benefit-of-the-bargain. Out-of-pocket damages measure the difference between the amount the buyer paid and the value of the property the buyer received. Benefit-of-the-bargain damages measure the difference between the value of the property as represented and the actual value of the property. Both measures are determined at the time of the sale induced by the fraud. [Emphasis added.]

Losses that arise after the time of sale may be recoverable as consequential damages in appropriate cases. Consequential damages must be foreseeable and directly traceable to the misrepresentation and result from it. * * * Consequential damages must be explicitly premised on findings that the losses were foreseeable and directly traceable to the misrepresentation.

* * * *

* * * [The jury was] instructed * * * to determine the difference between the fraud-induced price that the Fazios paid for the property and the actual value of the property they received when they purchased it. * * * The question correctly focused the jury on the time of the sale, *because direct damages for fraud, including out-of-pocket damages, are properly measured at the time of the sale induced by the fraud—in this case, when the purchase agreement was executed—and not at some future time.* The jury responded that such damages were $0. It found other sorts of incidental and consequential damage to be $0 as well. [Emphasis added.]

* * * *

* * * The trial court properly * * * accorded judgment based on the jury's zero damages finding.

Decision and Remedy *A state intermediate appellate court affirmed the trial court's judgment based on the jury's finding. Fazio was not entitled to damages, because the misrepresentation (fraud) had not negatively affected the property's value at the time Fazio purchased the property.*

Critical Thinking

- **Ethical** *Was Cypress's conduct unethical? Why or why not?*

- **Social** *What does the decision in this case suggest to sellers of commercial real estate and others who engage in business negotiations?*

14–3 Undue Influence and Duress

A contract lacks voluntary consent and is unenforceable if *undue influence* or *duress* is present.

14–3a Undue Influence

Undue Influence Persuasion that is less than actual force but more than advice and that induces a person to act according to the will or purposes of the dominating party.

Undue influence arises from relationships in which one party can greatly influence another party, thus overcoming that party's free will. A contract entered into under excessive or undue influence lacks voluntary consent and is therefore voidable.[11]

One Party Dominates the Other In various types of relationships, one party may have an opportunity to dominate and unfairly influence another party. Minors and elderly people, for instance, are often under the influence of guardians (persons who are legally responsible for others). If a guardian induces a young or elderly ward (the person whom the guardian looks after) to enter into a contract that benefits the guardian, the guardian may have exerted undue influence. Undue influence can arise from a number of confidential or fiduciary relationships, including attorney-client, physician-patient, guardian-ward, parent-child, husband-wife, and trustee-beneficiary.

The essential feature of undue influence is that the party being taken advantage of does not exercise free will in entering into a contract. It is not enough that a person is elderly or suffers from some mental or physical impairment. There must be clear and convincing evidence that the person did not act out of her or his free will. Similarly, the existence of a fiduciary relationship alone is insufficient to prove undue influence.

Learning Objective 3

What is the essential feature of undue influence?

A Presumption of Undue Influence in Certain Situations The dominant party in a fiduciary relationship must exercise the utmost good faith in dealing with the other party. When the dominant party benefits from the relationship, a presumption of undue influence may arise. Thus, when a contract enriches the dominant party in a fiduciary relationship, the court will often *presume* that the contract was made under undue influence.

Example 14.11 Erik is the guardian for Kinsley, his ward. On her behalf, he enters into a contract from which he benefits financially. If Kinsley challenges the contract, the court will likely presume that the guardian has taken advantage of his ward. To rebut (refute) this presumption, Erik has to show that he made full disclosure to Kinsley and that consideration was present. He must also show that Kinsley received, if available, independent and competent advice before completing the transaction. Unless the presumption can be rebutted, the contract will be rescinded.

14–3b Duress

Agreement to the terms of a contract is not voluntary if one of the parties is *forced* into the agreement. The use of threats to force a party to enter into a contract constitutes *duress,* as does the use of blackmail or extortion to induce consent. Duress is both a defense to the enforcement of a contract and a ground for rescission of a contract.

To establish duress, there must be proof of a threat to do something that the threatening party has no right to do. Generally, for duress to occur, the threatened act must be wrongful or illegal, and it must render the person who receives the threat incapable of exercising free will. A threat to exercise a legal right, such as the right to sue someone, ordinarily does not constitute duress.

When a person is forced to enter into a contract, what can that person claim as a defense to avoid being bound by it?

Phovoir/Shutterstock.com

---

11. *Restatement (Second) of Contracts,* Section 177.

Practice and Review

Chelene had been a caregiver for Marta's elderly mother, Janis, for nine years. Shortly before Janis passed away, Chelene convinced her to buy Chelene's house for Marta. Janis died before the papers were signed, however. Four months later, Marta used her inheritance to buy Chelene's house without having it inspected. The house was built in the 1950s, and Chelene said it was in "perfect condition." Nevertheless, one year after the purchase, the basement started leaking. Marta had the paneling removed from the basement walls and discovered that the walls were bowed inward and cracked. Marta then had a civil engineer inspect the basement walls, and he found that the cracks had been caulked and painted over before the paneling was installed. He concluded that the "wall failure" had existed "for at least thirty years" and that the basement walls were "structurally unsound." Using the information presented in the chapter, answer the following questions.

1. Can Marta avoid the contract on the ground that both parties made a mistake about the condition of the house? Explain.

2. Can Marta sue Chelene for fraudulent misrepresentation? Why or why not? What element (or elements) might be lacking?

3. Now assume that Chelene knew that the basement walls were cracked and bowed and that she hired someone to install paneling before offering to sell the house. Did she have a duty to disclose this defect to Marta? Could a court find that Chelene's silence in this situation constituted misrepresentation? Explain.

4. Can Marta obtain rescission of the contract based on undue influence? If the sale to Janis had been completed before her death, could Janis have obtained rescission based on undue influence? Explain.

Debate This

The concept of caveat emptor ("let the buyer beware") should be applied to all sales, including those of real property.

Key Terms

bilateral mistake 336
innocent misrepresentation 341
latent defect 341

negligent misrepresentation 341
scienter 341
undue influence 346

unilateral mistake 336
voluntary consent 335

Chapter Summary: Voluntary Consent

Mistakes	
	1. *Unilateral*—Generally, the mistaken party is bound by the contract *unless* (a) the other party knows or should have known of the mistake or (b) the mistake is a substantial mathematical error—such as an error in addition or subtraction—made inadvertently and without gross negligence.
	2. *Bilateral (mutual)*—When both parties are mistaken about the same material fact, such as identity, either party can avoid the contract.

(Continues)

Fraudulent Misrepresentation	When fraud occurs, usually the innocent party can enforce or avoid the contract. The following elements are necessary to establish fraud: 1. A misrepresentation of a material fact must occur. 2. There must be an intent to deceive. 3. The innocent party must justifiably rely on the misrepresentation. 4. To collect damages, a party must have been harmed as a result of the misrepresentation.
Undue Influence and Duress	1. *Undue influence*—Arises from special relationships, such as fiduciary relationships, in which one party's free will has been overcome by the undue influence exerted by the other party. The contract is voidable because it lacks voluntary consent. 2. *Duress*—The tactic of forcing a party to enter a contract under the fear of a threat—for instance, the threat of violence or serious economic loss. The party forced to enter the contract can rescind the contract.

Issue Spotters

1. In selling a house, Matt tells Ann that the wiring, fixtures, and appliances are of a certain quality. Matt knows nothing about the quality, but it is not as specified. Ann buys the house. On learning the true quality, Ann confronts Matt. He says he wasn't trying to fool her, he was only trying to make a sale. Can she rescind the deal? Why or why not? (See *Fraudulent Misrepresentation*.)

2. Brad, an accountant, files Dina's tax returns. When the Internal Revenue Service assesses a large tax against Dina, she retains Brad to contest the assessment. The day before the deadline for replying to the IRS, Brad tells Dina that unless she pays a higher fee, he will withdraw. If Dina agrees to pay, is the contract enforceable? Explain your answer. (See *Undue Influence and Duress*.)

   —Check your answers to the *Issue Spotters* against the answers provided in Appendix D at the end of this text.

Business Scenarios and Case Problems

14–1. Voluntary Consent. Jerome is an elderly man who lives with his nephew, Philip. Jerome is totally dependent on Philip's support. Philip tells Jerome that unless Jerome transfers a tract of land he owns to Philip for a price 30 percent below market value, Philip will no longer support and take care of him. Jerome enters into the contract. Discuss fully whether Jerome can set aside this contract. (See *Undue Influence and Duress*.)

14–2. Fraudulent Misrepresentation. Grano owns a forty-room motel on Highway 100. Tanner is interested in purchasing the motel. During the course of negotiations, Grano tells Tanner that the motel netted $30,000 last year and that it will net at least $45,000 next year. The motel books, which Grano turns over to Tanner before the purchase, clearly show that Grano's motel netted only $15,000 last year. Also, Grano fails to tell Tanner that a bypass to Highway 100 is being planned that will redirect most traffic away from the front of the motel. Tanner purchases the motel. During the first year under Tanner's operation, the motel nets $18,000. At this time, Tanner learns of the previous low profitability of the motel and the planned bypass. Tanner wants his money back from Grano. Discuss fully Tanner's probable success in getting his money back. (See *Fraudulent Misrepresentation*.)

14–3. Fraudulent Misrepresentation. Ricky Wilcox contracted with Fireside Log Homes to build a house. The logs were to be delivered precut and predrilled, but they arrived unfinished. Fireside told Wilcox that cutting and drilling the logs would take only two or three days. In fact, this process slowed the project by five months. To cover costs caused by the delay, Wilcox borrowed an additional $200,000. When the house was finally built, he filed a suit against Fireside. Did Fireside commit fraud? Explain. [*Esprit Log and Timber Frame Homes, Inc. v. Wilcox*, 302 Ga.App. 550, 691 S.E.2d 344 (2010)] (See *Fraudulent Misrepresentation*.)

14–4. Fraudulent Misrepresentation. Marguerite Eaton and Bobby Joe Waldrop moved into a mobile home on land owned by her son, James. Bobby Joe asked James to transfer that portion of the land to him and Marguerite, stating falsely that they had married. James agreed. Marguerite soon transferred her interest in the land to Bobby Joe. When James learned of this transfer and that his mother and Bobby Joe were not married, he filed a suit against Bobby Joe, alleging fraud. Bobby Joe asserted that James had not proved intent to deceive. Do these facts indicate intent to deceive? Explain. [*Eaton v. Waldrop*, 45 So.3d 371 (Ala. Civ.App. 2010)] (See *Fraudulent Misrepresentation*.)

14–5. Misrepresentation. Charter One Bank owned a fifteen-story commercial building. A fire inspector told Charter that the building's drinking-water and fire-suppression systems were linked, which violated building codes. Without disclosing this information, Charter sold the building to Northpoint Properties, Inc. Northpoint spent $280,000 to repair the water and fire-suppression systems and filed a suit against Charter One. Is the seller liable for not disclosing the building's defects? Discuss. [*Northpoint Properties, Inc. v. Charter One Bank,* 2011-Ohio- 2512 (Ohio App. 8 Dist. 2011) (See *Fraudulent Misrepresentation.*)

14–6. Business Case Problem with Sample Answer—Fraudulent Misrepresentation. Joy Pervis and Brenda Pauley worked together as talent agents in Georgia. When Pervis "discovered" actress Dakota Fanning, Pervis sent Fanning's audition tape to Cindy Osbrink, a talent agent in California. Osbrink agreed to represent Fanning in California and to pay 3 percent of Osbrink's commissions to Pervis and Pauley, who agreed to split the payments equally. Six years later, Pervis told Pauley that their agreement with Osbrink had expired and there would be no more payments. Nevertheless, Pervis continued to receive payments from Osbrink. Each time Pauley asked about commissions, however, Pervis replied that she was not receiving any. Do these facts evidence fraud? Explain. [*In re Pervis,* 512 Bankr. 348 (N.D.Ga. 2014)] (See *Fraudulent Misrepresentation.*)

—**For a sample answer to Problem 14–6, go to Appendix E at the end of this text.**

14–7. A Question of Ethics—The IDDR Approach and Fraudulent Misrepresentation. *Data Consulting Group contracted with Weston Medsurg Center, PLLC, a health-care facility in Charlotte, North Carolina, to install, maintain, and manage Weston's computers and software. At about the same time, Ginger Blackwood began to work for Weston as a medical billing and coding specialist. Soon, she was submitting false time reports and converting Weston documents and data to her own purposes. On her request, Data Consulting manager Nasko Dinev removed evidence of her actions from her work computer. [*Weston Medsurg Center, PLLC v. Blackwood,* 795 S.E.2d 829 (2017)] (See* Fraudulent Misrepresentation.*)*

1. What should Weston do when it learns of these activities? With respect to this situation, identify and consider the firm's primary ethical dilemma using the IDDR approach.

2. Suppose that despite Dinev's efforts, Weston is later able to recover the data that was removed from Blackwood's work computer. How might this affect Weston's choices? Discuss.

Critical Thinking and Writing Assignments

14–8. Time-Limited Group Assignment—Fraudulent Misrepresentation. Radiah Givens was involved romantically with Joseph Rosenzweig. She moved into an apartment on which he made the down payment. She signed the mortgage, but he made the payments and paid household expenses. They later married. She had their marriage annulled, however, when she learned that he was married to someone else. Rosenzweig then filed a suit against her to collect on the mortgage. (See *The Fraudulent Misrepresentation.*)

1. The first group should decide whether Rosenzweig committed fraud.

2. The second group should evaluate whether Rosenzweig's conduct was deceitful, and if so, whether his deceitfulness should affect the decision in this case.

3. The third group should consider how fraud is related to ethics. Can a contracting party act ethically and still commit fraud? How?

15

The Statute of Frauds— Writing Requirement

Learning Objectives

The four Learning Objectives *below are designed to help improve your understanding. After reading this chapter, you should be able to answer the following questions:*

1. What types of contracts must be in writing to be enforceable?

2. What are three exceptions to the Statute of Frauds?

3. If a written contract is required, what terms must it contain?

4. What is parol evidence? When is it admissible to clarify the terms of a written contract?

Statute of Frauds A state statute that requires certain types of contracts to be in writing to be enforceable.

"A verbal contract isn't worth the paper it's written on."

Samuel Goldwyn
1879–1974
(Hollywood motion picture producer)

A contract that is otherwise valid may still be unenforceable if it is not in the proper form. Certain types of contracts are required to be in writing or evidenced by a memorandum or an electronic record. After all, as Samuel Goldwyn implies in the chapter-opening quotation, verbal contracts are not as reliable as those whose terms are reduced to a writing.

An agreement subject to the writing requirement does not necessarily have to be written on paper. An exchange of e-mails that evidences the parties' contract can be sufficient, provided that they are "signed," or agreed to, by the party against whom enforcement is sought.

In this chapter, we examine the kinds of contracts that require a writing and some exceptions to the writing requirement. We also discuss the *parol evidence rule*, which courts follow when determining whether evidence that is extraneous, or external, to written contracts may be admissible at trial.

15–1 The Writing Requirement

Another defense to the enforceability of a contract is *form*—specifically, some contracts must be in writing. All states require certain types of contracts to be in writing or evidenced by a written memorandum or an electronic record. In addition, the party or parties against whom enforcement is sought must have signed the contract, unless certain exceptions apply (as discussed later in this chapter). In this text, we refer to these state statutes collectively as the **Statute of Frauds**.

The following types of contracts are said to fall "within" or "under" the Statute of Frauds and therefore require a writing:

1. Contracts involving interests in land.
2. Contracts that cannot *by their terms* be performed within one year from the day after the date of formation.
3. Collateral, or secondary, contracts, such as promises to answer for the debt or duty of another.
4. Promises made in consideration of marriage.
5. Under the Uniform Commercial Code, contracts for the sale of goods priced at $500 or more.

The actual name of the Statute of Frauds is misleading because it does not apply to fraud. Rather, in an effort to prevent fraud, the statute denies enforceability to certain contracts that do not comply with its requirements. The name derives from an English act passed in 1677 that was titled "An Act for the Prevention of Frauds and Perjuries."

15–1a Contracts Involving Interests in Land

A contract calling for the sale of land is not enforceable unless it is in writing or evidenced by a written or electronic memorandum. Land is *real property* and includes all physical objects that are permanently attached to the soil, such as buildings, fences, trees, and the soil itself. The Statute of Frauds operates as a defense to the enforcement of an oral contract for the sale of land. **Example 15.1** Skylar contracts orally to sell his property in Fair Oaks to Beth. If he later decides not to sell, under most circumstances, Beth cannot enforce the contract. ■

The Statute of Frauds also requires written evidence of contracts for the transfer of other interests in land, such as mortgage agreements and leases. Similarly, an agreement that includes an option to purchase real property must be in writing for the option to be enforced. The issue in the following case was whether a contract for a sale of land met this requirement.

Learning Objective 1
What types of contracts must be in writing to be enforceable?

■ Case 15.1

Sloop v. Kiker

Court of Appeals of Arkansas, Division III, 2016 Ark.App. 125, 484 S.W.3d 696 (2016).

Background and Facts Russell and Sally Kiker owned a house in Newton County, Arkansas. Mona Sloop agreed to buy it for $850,000. The parties signed a contract that identified the property by its street address and stipulated a $350,000 down payment, which was nonrefundable if closing did not occur by August 31. On the same day, they executed a deed containing a formal, legal description of the property by metes and bounds. (Metes and bounds is a way of describing the boundary lines of property according to the distance between two points.) They also agreed that Sloop could live in the house as caretaker until the August 31 deadline.

When the closing had not occurred by September 6, the Kikers filed a suit in an Arkansas state court against Sloop, seeking an order to remove her from the property and a declaration that they were entitled to keep the down payment. Sloop filed

a counterclaim for the return of the $350,000. She argued that their contract violated the Statute of Frauds. The court issued a summary judgment in the favor of the Kikers. Sloop appealed.

In the Words of the Court
Cliff *Hoofman*, Judge
* * * *

* * * Sloop argues that the circuit court erred in determining that the parties' real-estate contract satisfied the Statute of Frauds. We see no error on this point.

The Statute of Frauds provides that a contract for the sale of land must be in writing to be enforceable. Additionally, the contract must contain certain essential information, such as the terms and conditions of the sale, the price to be paid, the time for payment, and a description of the property. [Emphasis added.]

(Continues)

Sloop contends that the contract in this case was deficient because it did not name the Kikers * * * as sellers of the property and did not contain a sufficient description of the property. However, as noted by the circuit court, the warranty deed that the parties executed on the same day as the real-estate contract named the Kikers * * * as grantors and provided a formal, legal description of the property. Generally, instruments executed at the same time by the same parties, for the same purpose, and in the course of the same transaction, are, in the eyes of the law, one instrument and will be read and construed together. Moreover, if a contract furnishes a means by which realty can be identified—a key to the property's location—the Statute of Frauds is satisfied. Here, the contract's designation of the premises by street address met this requirement.

* * * *

Affirmed.

Decision and Remedy A state intermediate appellate court affirmed the judgment of the lower court. The Statute of Frauds was satisfied because the deed that the parties executed on the same day as the contract identified the Kikers as "grantors" and included a legal description of the property. In addition, the designation in the contract of the premises by its street address met the requirement of the Statute of Frauds that the property being transferred be described with sufficient certainty for it to be identified.

Critical Thinking

• **Legal Environment** *Why does the Statute of Frauds require that a contract for a sale of land contain a sufficient description of the property?*

• **What If the Facts Were Different?** *Suppose that the court in the* Sloop *case had not construed the deed and the contract as one instrument but as separate documents. How might that have affected the result? Explain.*

15–1b The One-Year Rule

Contracts that cannot, *by their own terms*, be performed within one year *from the day after* the contract is formed must be in writing to be enforceable. The reason for this rule is that the parties' memory of their contract's terms is not likely to be reliable for longer than a year.

Time Period Starts the Day after the Contract Is Formed   The one-year period begins to run *the day after the contract is made.* **Example 15.2** Superior University forms a contract with Kimi San stating that San will teach three courses in history during the coming academic year (September 15 through June 15). If the contract is formed in March, it must be in writing to be enforceable—because it cannot be performed within one year. If the contract is formed in July, in contrast, it will not have to be in writing to be enforceable—because it can be performed within one year.

Contract Must Be Objectively Impossible to Perform within One Year   The test for determining whether an oral contract is enforceable under the one-year rule is whether performance is *possible* within one year from the day after the date of contract formation. It does not matter whether the agreement is *likely* to be performed during that period.

When performance of a contract is objectively impossible during the one-year period, the contract must be in writing to be enforceable. **Example 15.3** A contract to provide five crops of tomatoes to be grown on a specific farm in Illinois would be objectively impossible to perform within one year. No farm in Illinois can produce five crops of tomatoes in a single year.

If performance is possible within one year under the contract's terms, the contract does not fall under the Statute of Frauds and need not be in writing. **Case Example 15.4** Robert and Lynette Knigge owned a B&L Food Store in Redfield, South Dakota. When Robert was diagnosed with brain cancer and given five months to live, he entered into an oral contract with his brother, David, to manage the store. Robert died five months after the date of the contract.

Exhibit 15–1 The One-Year Rule

Under the Statute of Frauds, contracts that by their terms are impossible to perform within one year from the day after the date of contract formation must be in writing to be enforceable. Put another way, if it is at all possible to perform an oral contract within one year from the day after the contract is made, the contract will fall outside the Statute of Frauds and be enforceable.

Lynette terminated David's employment two months later. David filed a suit in a South Dakota state court against his sister-in-law. He claimed that, under his oral contract with Robert, he was entitled to a severance payment if he lost the job at the store. A state court dismissed David's suit, but the South Dakota Supreme Court reversed and remanded. Because the oral contract between David and Robert could have been performed within one year, it did not have to be in writing to be enforceable.[1]

Exhibit 15–1 graphically illustrates the one-year rule.

15–1c Collateral Promises

A **collateral promise,** or secondary promise, is one that is ancillary (subsidiary) to a principal transaction or primary contractual relationship. In other words, a collateral promise is one made by a third party to assume the debts or obligations of a primary party to a contract if that party does not perform. Any collateral promise of this nature falls under the Statute of Frauds and therefore must be in writing to be enforceable.

How did the one-year rule affect the outcome of a lawsuit regarding the management of a local food store?

Primary versus Secondary Obligations An understanding of this concept requires the ability to distinguish between primary and secondary promises and obligations. A promise to pay another person's debt (or other obligation) that is *not conditioned on the person's failure to pay (or perform)* is a primary obligation. A promise to pay another's debt *only if that party fails to pay* is a secondary obligation. A contract in which a party assumes a primary obligation normally does not need to be in writing to be enforceable, whereas a contract assuming a secondary obligation does. **Example 15.5** Nigel tells Dr. Lu, an orthodontist, that he will pay for the services provided for Nigel's niece. Because Nigel has assumed direct financial responsibility for his niece's debt, this is a primary obligation and need not be in writing to be enforceable. In contrast, if Nigel commits to paying his niece's orthodontist bill only if her mother does not, it is a secondary obligation. In that situation, Lu must have a signed writing or record proving that Nigel assumed this obligation for it to be enforced.

Exhibit 15–2 illustrates the concept of a collateral promise.

Collateral Promise A secondary promise to a primary transaction, such as a promise made by one person to pay the debts of another if the latter fails to perform. A collateral promise normally must be in writing to be enforceable.

---

1. *David Knigge v. B&L Food Stores, Inc.,* 2017 S.D. 4, 890 N.W.2d 570 (2017).

Exhibit 15–2 Collateral Promises

A collateral (secondary) promise is one made by a third party (C, in this exhibit) to a creditor (B, in this exhibit) to pay the debt of another (A, in this exhibit), who is primarily obligated to pay the debt. Under the Statute of Frauds, collateral promises must be in writing to be enforceable.

An Exception—The "Main Purpose" Rule An oral promise to answer for the debt of another is covered by the Statute of Frauds *unless* the guarantor's purpose in accepting secondary liability is to secure a personal benefit. Under the "main purpose" rule, this type of contract need not be in writing.[2] The assumption is that a court can infer from the circumstances of a case whether a "leading objective" of the promisor was to secure a personal benefit.

Example 15.6 Carrie Braswell contracts with Custom Manufacturing Company to have some machines custom made for her factory. She promises Newform Supply, Custom's supplier, that if Newform continues to deliver the materials to Custom for the production of the custom-made machines, she will guarantee payment. This promise need not be in writing, even though the effect may be to pay the debt of another, because Braswell's main purpose is to secure a benefit for herself. ■

Another typical application of the main purpose doctrine occurs when one creditor guarantees a debtor's debt to another creditor to forestall litigation. The purpose is to allow the debtor to remain in business long enough to generate profits sufficient to pay *both* creditors. In this situation, the guaranty does not need to be in writing to be enforceable.

15–1d Promises Made in Consideration of Marriage

A unilateral promise to make a monetary payment or to give property in consideration of marriage must be in writing. **Example 15.7** Evan promises to buy Celeste a house in Maui if she marries him. Celeste would need written evidence of Evan's promise to enforce it. ■

Prenuptial Agreement An agreement made before marriage that defines each partner's ownership rights in the other partner's property. Prenuptial agreements must be in writing to be enforceable.

The same rule applies to **prenuptial agreements**—agreements made before marriage that define each partner's ownership rights in the other partner's property. **Example 15.8** Before marrying country singer Keith Urban, actress Nicole Kidman entered into a prenuptial agreement with him. Kidman agreed that if the couple divorced, she would pay Urban $640,000 for every year they had been married, unless Urban had begun to use drugs again. In that event, he would receive nothing. ■

15–1e Contracts for the Sale of Goods

The Uniform Commercial Code (UCC) includes Statute of Frauds provisions that require written evidence or an electronic record of a contract for the sale of goods priced at $500 or more. (This low threshold amount may be increased in the future.)

---

2. *Restatement (Second) of Contracts*, Section 116.

A writing that will satisfy the UCC requirement need only state the quantity term (six thousand boxes of cotton gauze, for instance). The contract will not be enforceable for any quantity greater than that set forth in the writing.

Other agreed-on terms can be omitted or even stated imprecisely in the writing, as long as they adequately reflect both parties' intentions. A written memorandum or series of communications (including e-mail) evidencing a contract will suffice, provided that the writing is signed by the party against whom enforcement is sought. (See this chapter's *Beyond Our Borders* feature to learn whether other countries have requirements similar to those in the Statute of Frauds.)

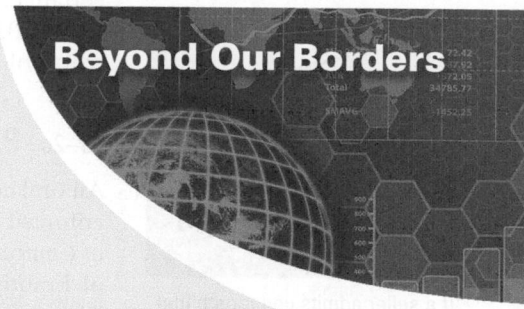

Henry Martin/The New Yorker Collection/cartoonbank.com

"*Wallace, have you forgotten our prenuptial contract? No whistling!*"

15–2 Exceptions to the Statute of Frauds

Exceptions to the applicability of the Statute of Frauds are made in certain situations. We describe those situations in the following subsections.

15–2a Partial Performance

When a contract has been partially performed and the parties cannot be returned to their positions prior to the contract's formation, a court may grant *specific performance*. Specific performance is an equitable remedy that requires that a contract be performed according to its precise terms. The parties still must prove that an oral contract existed, of course.

Learning Objective 2

What are three exceptions to the Statute of Frauds?

Beyond Our Borders

The Statute of Frauds and International Sales Contracts

The Convention on Contracts for the International Sale of Goods (CISG) provides rules that govern international sales contracts between citizens of countries that have ratified the convention (agreement). Article 11 of the CISG does not incorporate any Statute of Frauds provisions. Rather, it states that a "contract for sale need not be concluded in or evidenced by writing and is not subject to any other requirements as to form."

Article 11 accords with the legal customs of most nations, which no longer require contracts to meet certain formal or writing requirements to be enforceable. Ironically, even England, the nation that enacted the original Statute of Frauds in 1677, has repealed all of it except the provisions relating to collateral promises and to transfers of interests in land. Many other countries that once had such statutes have also repealed all or parts of them. Civil law countries, such as France, have never required certain types of contracts to be in writing. Obviously, without a writing requirement, contracts can take any form.

Critical Thinking

If a country does not have a Statute of Frauds and a dispute arises over an oral agreement, how can the parties substantiate their positions?

In cases involving oral contracts for the transfer of interests in land, courts usually look at whether justice is better served by enforcing the oral contract when partial performance has taken place. For instance, if the purchaser has paid part of the price, taken possession, and made valuable improvements to the property, a court may grant specific performance.

In some states, mere reliance on certain types of oral contracts is enough to remove them from the Statute of Frauds. Under the UCC, an oral contract for goods priced at $500 or more is enforceable to the extent that a seller accepts payment or a buyer accepts delivery of the goods.[3]

Case Example 15.9 Pacific Fruit, Inc., exports cargo from Ecuador. NYKCool, based in Sweden, provides maritime transportation. NYKCool and Pacific entered into a written contract with a two-year duration, under which NYKCool agreed to transport weekly shipments of bananas from Ecuador to California and Japan.

At the end of the period, the parties agreed to extend the deal, but a new contract was never signed. The parties continued making weekly shipments for four more years until a dispute arose over unused cargo capacity and unpaid freight charges. An international arbitration panel found that Pacific Fruit was liable to NYKCool for $8.7 million for breach of contract. Pacific Fruit appealed, arguing that there was no contract in place. The court affirmed the award in favor of NYKCool. "The parties' substantial partial performance on the contract weighs strongly in favor of contract formation."[4]

15–2b Admissions

If a party against whom enforcement of an oral contract is sought "admits" under oath that a contract for sale was made, the contract will be enforceable.[5] The party's admission can occur at any stage of the court proceedings, such as during a deposition or other discovery, pleadings, or testimony.

If a party admits a contract subject to the UCC, the contract is enforceable, but only to the extent of the quantity admitted.[6] **Example 15.10** Rachel, the president of Bistro Corporation, admits under oath that an oral agreement was made with Commercial Kitchens, Inc., to buy certain equipment for $10,000. A court will enforce the agreement only to the extent admitted ($10,000), even if Commercial Kitchens claims that the agreement involved $20,000 worth of equipment.

If a seller admits under oath that a contract was for only $10,000 of commercial kitchen equipment, does the buyer owe more if additional equipment was installed?

15–2c Promissory Estoppel

An oral contract that would otherwise be unenforceable under the Statute of Frauds may be enforced under the doctrine of *promissory estoppel*. Section 139 of the *Restatement (Second) of Contracts* provides that an oral promise can be enforceable, notwithstanding the Statute of Frauds, if the promisee has justifiably relied on the promise to his or her detriment. The promisee's reliance must have been foreseeable to the person making the promise, and enforcing the promise must be the only way to avoid injustice.

Note the similarities between promissory estoppel and the doctrine of partial performance discussed previously. Both require reasonable reliance and operate to estop, or prevent, a party from claiming that no contract exists.

3. UCC 2–201(3)(c).
4. *NYKCool A.B. v. Pacific Fruit, Inc.*, 2013 WL 163621 (2d Cir. 2013). The initials *A.B.* stand for *Aktiebolag*, which is the Swedish term for "limited company."
5. *Restatement (Second) of Contracts*, Section 133.
6. UCC 2–201(3)(b).

15–2d Special Exceptions under the UCC

Special exceptions to the applicability of the Statute of Frauds exist for sales contracts. Oral contracts for customized goods may be enforced in certain circumstances. Another exception has to do with oral contracts *between merchants* that have been confirmed in a written memorandum. We will examine this exception when we discuss the UCC's Statute of Frauds provisions.

Exhibit 15–3 graphically summarizes the types of contracts that fall under the Statute of Frauds and the various exceptions that apply.

15–3 Sufficiency of the Writing or Electronic Record

A written contract will satisfy the writing requirement of the Statute of Frauds, as will a written memorandum or an electronic record that evidences the agreement and is signed by the party against whom enforcement is sought. The signature need not be placed at the end of the document but can be anywhere in the writing. A signature can consist of a typed name or even just initials rather than the full name.

15–3a What Constitutes a Writing?

A writing can consist of any confirmation, invoice, sales slip, check, fax, or e-mail—or such items in combination. The written contract need not be contained in a single document to constitute an enforceable contract. One document may incorporate another document by expressly referring to it. Several documents may form a single contract if they are physically attached—such as by staple, paper clip, or glue—or even if they are only placed in the same envelope.

Example 15.11 Simpson orally agrees to sell some land next to a shopping mall to Terro Properties. Simpson gives Terro an unsigned memo that contains a legal description of the property, and Terro gives Simpson an unsigned first draft of their contract. Simpson sends Terro a signed letter that refers to the memo and to the first and final drafts of the contract. Terro sends Simpson an unsigned copy of the final draft of the contract with a signed check stapled to it. Together, the documents can constitute a writing sufficient to satisfy the Statute of Frauds and bind both parties to the terms of the contract as evidenced by the writings. ■

Exhibit 15–3 Contracts Subject to the Statute of Frauds

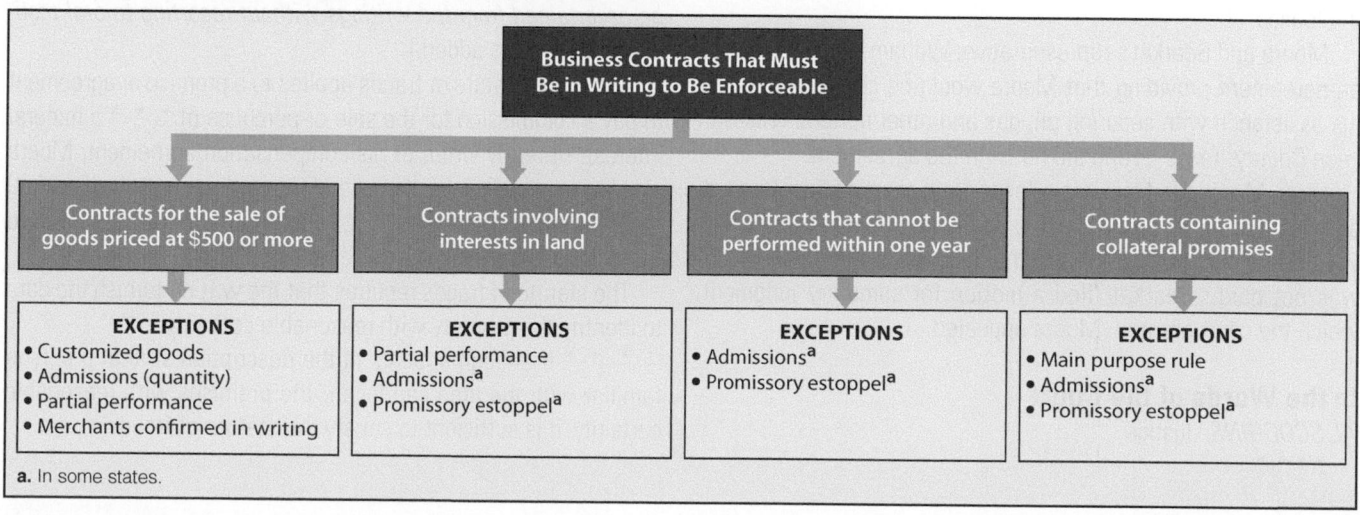

```
                     ┌──────────────────────────────┐
                     │  Business Contracts That Must │
                     │   Be in Writing to Be Enforceable │
                     └──────────────────────────────┘
```

Contracts for the sale of goods priced at $500 or more	Contracts involving interests in land	Contracts that cannot be performed within one year	Contracts containing collateral promises
EXCEPTIONS • Customized goods • Admissions (quantity) • Partial performance • Merchants confirmed in writing	**EXCEPTIONS** • Partial performance • Admissions[a] • Promissory estoppel[a]	**EXCEPTIONS** • Admissions[a] • Promissory estoppel[a]	**EXCEPTIONS** • Main purpose rule • Admissions[a] • Promissory estoppel[a]

a. In some states.

15–3b What Must Be Contained in the Writing?

A memorandum or note evidencing an oral contract need only contain the essential terms of the contract, not every term. There must, of course, also be some indication that the parties voluntarily agreed to the terms. As mentioned, under the UCC, a writing evidencing a contract for the sale of goods need only state the quantity and be signed by the party against whom enforcement is sought.

Under most state laws, the writing must also name the parties and identify the subject matter, the consideration, and the essential terms with reasonable certainty. In addition, contracts for the sale of land usually must state the price and describe the property with sufficient clarity to allow these terms to be determined without reference to outside sources.

Note that because only the party against whom enforcement is sought must have signed the writing, a contract may be enforceable by one of its parties but not by the other. **Example 15.12** Rock orally agrees to buy Betty Devlin's lake house and lot for $350,000. Devlin writes Rock a letter confirming the sale by identifying the parties and the essential terms of the sales contract—price, method of payment, and legal address—and signs the letter. Devlin has made a written memorandum of the oral land contract. Because she signed the letter, she normally can be held to the oral contract by Rock. Devlin cannot enforce the agreement against Rock, however. Because he has not signed or entered into a written contract or memorandum, Rock can plead the Statute of Frauds as a defense. ■

In the following case, the plaintiff sought to obtain payment for his performance under a written agreement to assist in acquiring mineral leases. The description of the property to be acquired was vague.

■ Case 15.2

Moore v. Bearkat Energy Partners, LLC

Court of Appeals of Texas, Waco, 2018 WL 683754 (2018).

Background and Facts Jason Lane hired Bearkat Energy Partners, LLC, to buy mineral leases in Leon County, Texas. Lane intended to package the leases to sell to other buyers. He provided the funding for Bearkat's purchases, and when the leases were resold, Bearkat received a percentage of the profit. Without telling Lane, Bearkat hired Larry Moore to help acquire the leases.

Moore and Bearkat's representative, William Bramlett, signed an agreement providing that Moore would be compensated "for his assistance with securing oil, gas and other mineral leases in Leon County, Texas." Lane did not sign the agreement.

Later, Moore filed a suit in a Texas state court against Bearkat, alleging that his efforts under the agreement resulted in the conveyance of numerous leases to the defendant, for which Moore was not paid. Bearkat filed a motion for summary judgment, which the court granted. Moore appealed.

In the Words of the Court
AL SCOGGINS, Justice.
* * * *

Under the statute of frauds, certain promises and agreements are unenforceable unless they are in writing and signed by the person sought to be charged. Moreover, *the statute of frauds requires that a memorandum of an agreement * * * must be complete within itself in every material detail and contain all of the essential elements of the agreement so that the contract can be ascertained from the writings without resorting to oral testimony.* [Emphasis added.]

* * * The statute of frauds applies to a promise or agreement to pay a commission for the sale or purchase of * * * a mineral interest. Here, by virtue of his compensation agreement, Moore sought commissions for the sale of mineral interests by [Bearkat] to third parties. Therefore, * * * the statute of frauds applies to Moore's compensation agreement.

The statute of frauds requires that the writing furnish the data to identify the property with reasonable certainty.

* * * If enough appears in the description so that a person familiar with the area can locate the premises with reasonable certainty, it is sufficient to satisfy the statute of frauds.

* * * *

Here, the compensation agreement does not contain within itself, or by reference to some other identified writing then in existence, a sufficient description of the properties Moore believes he should be compensated for based on his efforts in the leasing process. Rather, the compensation agreement merely refers to "oil, gas and other mineral leases in Leon County, Texas." The compensation agreement does not provide any information regarding the size, shape, or boundaries of the land subject to the leases for which Moore was to be compensated. We do not believe that this language sufficiently describes the property in question such that a person familiar with the area could locate the premises that are the subject of the compensation agreement with reasonable certainty.

* * * *

And because we have concluded that Moore's compensation agreement did not sufficiently describe the leases subject to the agreement, we hold that the agreement is void and unenforceable under the statute of frauds.

Decision and Remedy A state intermediate appellate court affirmed the judgment of the trial court. Bearkat was not liable on the agreement to compensate Moore.

Critical Thinking

• **Legal Environment** *Could Moore have presented leases purportedly entered into as a result of his performance under the compensation agreement to provide a property description sufficient to satisfy the Statute of Frauds? Why or why not?*

• **What If the Facts Were Different?** *Suppose that Moore had filed his suit against Lane instead of Bearkat and that the court had held the compensation agreement to be enforceable. Would Lane have been liable on the agreement? Explain.*

15–4 The Parol Evidence Rule

Sometimes, a written contract does not include—or contradicts—an oral understanding reached by the parties before or at the time of contracting. For instance, a landlord might tell a person who agrees to rent an apartment that she or he can have a cat, whereas the lease contract clearly states that no pets are allowed. In determining the outcome of such disputes, the courts look to a common law rule called the **parol evidence rule.**

Under this rule, if a court finds that a written contract represents the complete and final statement of the parties' agreement, then it will not allow either party to present parol evidence. *Parol evidence* is testimony or other evidence of communications between the parties that is not contained in the contract itself. Thus, a party normally cannot present evidence of the parties' "prior or contemporaneous agreements or negotiations" if that evidence contradicts or varies the terms of the parties' written contract.[7]

15–4a Exceptions to the Parol Evidence Rule

Because of the rigidity of the parol evidence rule, courts make several exceptions. These exceptions include the following:

1. *Contracts subsequently modified.* Evidence of a *subsequent modification* (oral or written) of a written contract can be introduced in court. Oral modifications may not be enforceable, however, if they come under the Statute of Frauds (such as a modification that increases the price of the goods being sold to more than $500). Also, oral modifications will not be enforceable if the original contract provides that any modification must be in writing.[8]

2. *Voidable or void contracts.* Oral evidence can be introduced in all cases to show that the contract was voidable or void (for instance, induced by mistake, fraud, or misrepresentation). The reason is simple: if deception led one of the parties to agree to the terms of a written contract, oral evidence

Learning Objective 4

What is parol evidence? When is it admissible to clarify the terms of a written contract?

Parol Evidence Rule A rule of contracts under which a court will not receive into evidence prior or contemporaneous external agreements that contradict the terms of the parties' written contract.

Know This

The parol evidence rule and its exceptions relate to the rules concerning the *interpretation* of contracts.

---

7. *Restatement (Second) of Contracts*, Section 213.
8. UCC 2–209(2), (3).

indicating fraud should not be excluded. Courts frown on bad faith and are quick to allow the introduction at trial of parol evidence when it establishes fraud.

3. *Contracts containing ambiguous terms.* When the terms of a written contract are ambiguous, evidence is admissible to show the meaning of the terms. **Case Example 15.13** Howard and Eleanor Windows owned a home in Pennsylvania. When raw sewage backed up in the city's sewer system and infiltrated their home, they filed a claim with their homeowner's insurance company, Erie Insurance Exchange. Erie denied coverage, under the insurance policy's general exclusion for water damage caused by "water or sewage which backs up through sewers and drains." The Windowses sued Erie for breach of contract.

Erie claimed that the parol evidence rule applied and prevented the Windowses from presenting evidence that contradicted the water-damage exclusion in the policy. The court disagreed and allowed the Windowses to present their case to a jury, which awarded them more than $75,000 in damages. Erie appealed. The appellate court affirmed the jury's verdict, reasoning that the term "backs up" was not defined in the contract and was subject to more than one reasonable interpretation.[9]

Which exception to the parol evidence rule applied in a dispute regarding an insurance claim for water and sewer damage?

4. *Incomplete contracts.* Evidence is admissible when the written contract is incomplete in that it lacks one or more of the essential terms. The courts allow evidence to "fill in the gaps" in the contract.

5. *Prior dealing, course of performance, or usage of trade.* Under the UCC, evidence can be introduced to explain or supplement a written contract by showing a prior dealing, course of performance, or usage of trade.[10] This is because when buyers and sellers deal with each other over extended periods of time, certain customary practices develop. These practices are often overlooked in the writing of the contract, so courts allow the introduction of evidence to show how the parties have acted in the past. Usage of trade—the practices and customs generally followed in a particular industry—can also shed light on the meaning of certain contract provisions, and thus evidence of trade usage may be admissible.

6. *Contracts subject to an orally agreed-on condition precedent.* Sometimes the parties agree that a condition must be fulfilled before a party is required to perform the contract. This is called a *condition precedent.* If the parties have orally agreed on a condition precedent and the condition does not conflict with the terms of a written agreement, then a court may allow parol evidence to prove the oral condition. The parol evidence rule does not apply here because the existence of the entire written contract is subject to an orally agreed-on condition. Proof of the condition does not alter or modify the written terms but affects the *enforceability* of the written contract.

7. *Contracts with an obvious or gross clerical (or typographic) error.* When an *obvious* or *gross* clerical (or typographic) error exists that clearly would not represent the agreement of the parties, parol evidence is admissible to correct the error. **Example 15.14** Davis agrees to lease office space from Stone Enterprises for $3,000 per month. The signed written lease provides for a monthly lease payment of $300 rather than the $3,000 agreed to by the parties. Because the error is obvious, Stone Enterprises would be allowed to admit parol evidence to correct the mistake.

In the following case, an appellate court considered whether the trial court should have admitted parol evidence regarding the terms of an apartment lease.

9. *Windows v. Erie Insurance Exchange,* 161 A.3d 953 (Pa.Sup.Ct. 2017).
10. UCC 1–205, 2–202.

Case 15.3

Frewil, LLC v. Price

Court of Appeals of South Carolina, 411 S.C. 525, 769 S.E.2d 250 (2015).

Background and Facts Madison Price and Carter Smith were planning to attend the College of Charleston in South Carolina. They contacted Frewil, LLC, about renting an apartment at the beginning of the fall semester. They asked if the apartment had a washer/dryer and dishwasher, and were told yes. The lease did not expressly state that the unit contained those appliances, but it provided that any overflow from a washing machine or dishwasher was the responsibility of the tenant and that the dishwasher had to be clean for a refund of the security deposit.

When Price and Smith arrived to move in, the apartment had no washer/dryer or dishwasher and no connections for them. The students found housing elsewhere. Frewil filed a suit in a South Carolina state court against Price and Smith, claiming breach of contract. The defendants sought to introduce parol evidence to challenge Frewil's claim. The court denied the request and issued a judgment in Frewil's favor. Price and Smith appealed.

In the Words of the Court

Konduros, [judge]

* * * *

* * * If a writing, on its face, appears to express the whole agreement between the parties, parol evidence cannot be admitted to add another term thereto. However, *where a contract is silent as to a particular matter, and ambiguity thereby arises, parol evidence may be admitted to supply the deficiency and establish the true intent. For, generally, parol evidence is admissible to show the true meaning of an ambiguous written contract.* Such a contract is one capable of being understood in more ways than just one, or an agreement unclear in meaning because it expresses its purpose in an indefinite manner. When an agreement is ambiguous, the court may consider the circumstances surrounding its execution in determining the intent. Where the contract is susceptible of more than one interpretation, the ambiguity will be resolved against the party who prepared the contract. It would be virtually impossible for a contract to encompass all of the many possibilities which may be encountered by the parties. Indeed, neither law, nor equity, requires every term or condition to be set forth in a contract. If a situation is unaddressed in a contract, the court may look to the circumstances surrounding the bargain as an aid in determining the parties' intent. [Emphasis added.]

In this case, the [lower] court relied upon * * * the lease itself to conclude the girls had breached the lease as a matter of law. However, if a contract is subject to more than one interpretation, it is ambiguous and parol evidence is admissible. Frewil contends, and the [lower] court found, the lease unambiguously states the unit does not contain a washer/dryer or dishwasher. However, the lease states any overflow from washing machines or dishwashers is the responsibility of the tenant. Additionally, the Security Deposit Agreement * * * indicates the dishwasher must be clean in order for the tenant to receive a return of the security deposit. The lease does not explicitly indicate what appliances are or are not in the unit. Because the lease is ambiguous on this point, parol evidence was admissible. As these appliances are mentioned and Price and Smith allege they were told the washer/dryer and dishwasher were included, the [lower] court erred in concluding the lease * * * precluded any challenge to Frewil's breach of contract claim as a matter of law.

Decision and Remedy A state intermediate appellate court reversed the judgment of the lower court. The court noted that, "the lease was ambiguous thereby permitting the introduction of parol evidence."

Critical Thinking

• **Economic** *How does the parol evidence rule save time and money for the parties to a dispute and the court that hears it? Discuss.*

15–4b Integrated Contracts

In determining whether to allow parol evidence, courts consider whether the written contract is intended to be a complete and final statement of the terms of the agreement. If it is, the contract is referred to as an **integrated contract**, and extraneous evidence (evidence from outside the contract) is excluded.

Integrated Contract A written contract that constitutes the final expression of the parties' agreement. Evidence extraneous to the contract that contradicts or alters the meaning of the contract in any way is inadmissible.

Case Example 15.15 Volvo Trucks makes heavy-duty trucks. Andy Mohr Truck Center was one of its dealers for a few years, until the relationship soured and they ended up in litigation. Volvo sought to terminate Mohr's dealership, claiming that Mohr had misrepresented a material fact in connection with its dealership application.

Mohr supposedly had orally promised Volvo that it would build a new long-term facility for the dealership if Volvo awarded the contract to Mohr (the "new-facility claim"). Mohr claimed that Volvo had orally promised to give Mohr a Mack Truck dealership franchise because Volvo owned Mack Truck (the "Mack claim"). Neither of these alleged promises was written in the parties' contract, which contained an integration clause. A federal district court dismissed the new-facility claim and the Mack claim. A federal appellate court affirmed, noting that both Volvo and Mohr were sophisticated parties and had experience with franchises and dealer agreements. The existence of an integration clause in their contract made it unreasonable for them to rely on any representations made outside of the contract.[11] ■

A contract can be either completely or partially integrated. If it contains all of the terms of the parties' agreement, then it is completely integrated. If it contains only some of the terms and not others, it is partially integrated. If the contract is only partially integrated, evidence of consistent additional terms is admissible to supplement the written agreement.[12] Note that parol evidence is admitted only to add to the terms of a partially integrated contract. For both completely and partially integrated contracts, courts exclude any evidence that *contradicts* the writing.

Exhibit 15–4 illustrates the relationship between integrated contracts and the parol evidence rule.

---

11. *Andy Mohr Truck Center, Inc. v. Volvo Trucks North America*, 869 F.3d 598 (7th Cir. 2017).
12. *Restatement (Second) of Contracts*, Section 216.

Exhibit 15–4 The Parol Evidence Rule

Written Contract

Fully Integrated
Intended to be a complete and final embodiment of the terms of the parties' agreement

Not Fully Integrated
Omits an agreed-on term that is consistent with the parties' agreement

Parol Evidence Inadmissible
For instance, evidence of a prior negotiation that contradicts a term of the written contract would not be admitted.

Parol Evidence Admissible
For instance, if the contract is incomplete and lacks one or more of the essential terms, parol evidence may be admitted.

Practice and Review

Evelyn Vollmer orally agreed to loan Danny Lang $150,000 to make an investment in a local nightclub. The loan was to be repaid from the profits received from the investment. Their agreement was never memorialized in writing, however. Eighteen months later, Lang had paid only $15,000 on the loan from the profits from the business. Vollmer filed a lawsuit alleging breach of contract. Using the information presented in the chapter, answer the following questions.

1. Lang claimed that repayment of the loan would "almost certainly" take over a year and that his agreement with Vollmer was therefore unenforceable because it was not in writing. Is he correct? Explain.

2. Suppose that a week after Vollmer gave Lang the funds, she sent him an e-mail containing the terms of their loan agreement with her named typed at the bottom. Lang did not respond to the e-mail. Is this sufficient as a writing under the Statute of Frauds?

3. Assume that at trial the court finds that the contract falls within the Statute of Frauds. Further assume that the state in which the court sits recognizes every exception to the Statute of Frauds discussed in the chapter. What exception provides Vollmer with the best chance of enforcing the oral contract in this situation?

4. Suppose that at trial, Lang never raises the argument that the parties' agreement violates the Statute of Frauds, and the court rules in favor of Vollmer. Then Lang appeals and raises the Statute of Frauds for the first time. What exception can Vollmer now argue?

Debate This

Many countries have eliminated the Statute of Frauds except for sales of real estate. The United States should do the same.

Key Terms

collateral promise 353
integrated contract 362

parol evidence rule 359
prenuptial agreements 354

Statute of Frauds 350

Chapter Summary: The Statute of Frauds—Writing Requirement

The Writing Requirement	1. *Applicability*—The following types of contracts fall under the Statute of Frauds and must be in writing to be enforceable: **a.** Contracts involving interests in land, such as sales, leases, or mortgages. **b.** Contracts that cannot by their terms be fully performed within one year from (the day after) the contract's formation. **c.** Collateral promises, such as contracts made between a guarantor and a creditor whose terms make the guarantor secondarily liable. *Exception:* the "main purpose" rule. **d.** Promises made in consideration of marriage, including promises to make a monetary payment or give property in consideration of a promise to marry and prenuptial agreements made in consideration of marriage. **e.** Contracts for the sale of goods priced at $500 or more under the Statute of Frauds provision in Section 2–201 of the Uniform Commercial Code.

(*Continues*)

Exceptions to the Writing Requirement	Partial performance, admissions, and promissory estoppel. Oral contracts for customized goods may be enforced in certain circumstances. Another exception concerns oral contracts between merchants that have been confirmed in writing.
Sufficiency of the Writing or Electronic Record	To constitute an enforceable contract under the Statute of Frauds, under most state laws a writing must be signed by the party against whom enforcement is sought, name the parties, identify the subject matter and the consideration, and state with reasonable certainty the essential terms of the contract. Under the UCC, a contract for a sale of goods is not enforceable beyond the quantity of goods shown in the contract.
The Parol Evidence Rule	The parol evidence rule prohibits the introduction at trial of evidence of the parties' prior or contemporaneous negotiations or agreements if this evidence contradicts or varies the terms of the parties' written contract. The written contract is assumed to be the complete embodiment of the parties' agreement. Because of the rigidity of the parol evidence rule, courts make a number of exceptions. For instance, courts may allow parol evidence when a contract is void or voidable, contains ambiguous terms, or is incomplete.

Issue Spotters

1. GamesCo orders $800 worth of game pieces from Midstate Plastic, Inc. Midstate delivers, and GamesCo pays for $450 worth. GamesCo then says it wants no more pieces from Midstate. GamesCo and Midstate have never dealt with each other before and have nothing in writing. Can Midstate enforce a deal for the full $800? Explain your answer. (See *The Writing Requirement*.)

2. Paula orally agrees to work with Next Corporation in New York City for two years. Paula moves her family to the city and begins work. Three months later, Paula is fired for no stated cause. She sues for reinstatement and back pay. Next Corporation argues that there is no written contract between them. What will the court say? (See *The Writing Requirement*.)

—**Check your answers to the *Issue Spotters* against the answers provided in Appendix D at the end of this text.**

Business Scenarios and Case Problems

15–1. The One-Year Rule. On May 1, by telephone, Yu offers to hire Benson to perform personal services. On May 5, Benson returns Yu's call and accepts the offer. Discuss fully whether this contract falls under the Statute of Frauds in the following circumstances: (See *The Writing Requirement*.)

1. The contract calls for Benson to be employed for one year, with the right to begin performance immediately.

2. The contract calls for Benson to be employed for nine months, with performance of services to begin on September 1.

3. The contract calls for Benson to submit a written research report, with a deadline of two years for submission.

15–2. Statute of Frauds. Gemma promises a local hardware store that she will pay for a lawn mower that her brother is purchasing on credit if the brother fails to pay the debt. Must this promise be in writing to be enforceable? Why or why not? (See *The Writing Requirement*.)

15–3. Collateral Promises. Mallory promises a local hardware store that she will pay for a lawn mower that her brother is purchasing on credit if the brother fails to pay the debt. Must this promise be in writing to be enforceable? Why or why not? (See *The Writing Requirement*.)

15–4. Promises Made in Consideration of Marriage. After twenty-nine years of marriage, Robert and Mary Lou Tuttle were divorced. They admitted in court that before they were married, they had signed a prenuptial agreement. They both acknowledged that the agreement had stated that each would keep his or her own property and anything derived from that property. Robert came into the marriage owning farmland, while Mary Lou owned no real estate. During the marriage, ten different parcels of land, totaling about six hundred acres, were acquired, and two corporations, Tuttle Grain, Inc., and Tuttle Farms, Inc., were formed. A copy of the prenuptial agreement could not be found. Can the court enforce the agreement without a writing? Why or why not? [*In re Marriage of Tuttle*, 2015.WL 164035 (Ill.App. 5 Dist. 2015.] (See *The Writing Requirement*.)

15–5. Business Case Problem with Sample Answer—The Parol Evidence Rule. Rimma Vaks and her husband, Steven Mangano, executed a written contract with Denise Ryan and Ryan Auction Co. to auction their furnishings. The six-page contract provided a detailed summary of the parties' agreement. It addressed the items to be auctioned, how reserve prices would be determined, and the amount of Ryan's commission. When a dispute arose between the parties,

Vaks and Mangano sued Ryan for breach of contract. Vaks and Mangano asserted that, before they executed the contract, Ryan had made various oral representations that were inconsistent with the terms of their written agreement. Assuming that their written contract was valid, can Vaks and Mangano recover for breach of an oral contract? Why or why not? [*Vaks v. Ryan*, 2014 Mass.App.Div. 37 (2014)]. (See *The Parol Evidence Rule*.)

—For a sample answer to Problem 15–5, go to Appendix E at the end of this text.

15–6. Promises Made in Consideration of Marriage. Before their marriage, Linda and Gerald Heiden executed a prenuptial agreement. The agreement provided that "no spouse shall have any right in the property of the other spouse, even in the event of the death of either party." The description of Gerald's separate property included a settlement from a personal injury suit. Twenty-four years later, Linda filed for divorce. The court ruled that the prenuptial agreement applied only in the event of death, not divorce, and entered a judgment that included a property division and spousal support award. The ruling disparately favored Linda, whose monthly income with spousal support would be $4,467, leaving Gerald with only $1,116. Did the court interpret the Heidens' prenuptial agreement correctly? Discuss. [*Heiden v. Heiden*, 2015 WL 849006 (Mich.App. 2015)] (See *The Writing Requirement*.)

15–7. The Statute of Frauds. Michael Brannon filed a suit in an Ohio state court against Derrick and Nancy Edman, claiming breach of an alleged oral contract for the sale of certain real property in Akron. Brannon asserted that he moved onto the property and made significant improvements to the house, investing time and money in anticipation of receiving ownership of the property after all of the payments had been made. Brannon asserted that he diligently made the payments, and the Edmans accepted them, crediting each against the remaining balance, until about half of the price had been paid. But when he attempted to make a payment in the third year of his occupancy, the Edmans refused it and threatened him with eviction. The Edmans argued that the Statute of Frauds barred Brannon's claim. Is this alleged contract enforceable? Explain. [*Brannon v. Edman*, 2018 -Ohio- 70, __ Ohio App.3d __, __ N.E.3d __ (9th Dist. 2018)] (See *The Writing Requirement*.)

15–8. A Question of Ethics—Exceptions to the Writing Requirement. *Madeline Castellotti was the sole shareholder of Whole Pies, Inc., which owns John's Pizzeria in New York City. Her other assets included a 51 percent interest in a real estate partnership, a residence on Staten Island, and various bank accounts. When Madeline's son, Peter Castellotti, was going through a divorce, Madeline wanted to prevent Peter's then-wife Rea from benefiting from any of Madeline's assets. With this purpose in mind, she removed Peter from her will, leaving her daughter Lisa Free as the sole beneficiary. Lisa orally agreed to provide Peter with half of the income generated by the assets after their mother's death if his divorce was still pending and to transfer half of the assets after the divorce was final. In reliance on those promises, Peter agreed to pay the property taxes for the estate. Madeline died and Peter paid the taxes, but Lisa reneged on the deal. Peter filed a suit in a New York state court against his sister to recover. [Castellotti v. Free, 138 A.D.3d 198, 27 N.Y.S.3d 507 (1 Dept. 2016)] (See Exceptions to the Writing Requirement.)*

1. Should the court enforce the promise? On what legal theory?
2. If the court enforces the promise, should Rea get a share of what Peter and his mother and sister were "hiding"? Discuss.

Critical Thinking and Writing Assignments

15–9. Time-Limited Group Assignment—The Writing Requirement. Jason Novell, doing business as Novell Associates, hired Barbara Meade as an independent contractor. The parties orally agreed on the terms of employment, including payment of a share of the company's income to Meade, but they did not put anything in writing. Two years later, Meade quit. Novell then told Meade that she was entitled to $9,602—25 percent of the difference between the accounts receivable and the accounts payable as of Meade's last day of work. Meade disagreed and demanded more than $63,500—25 percent of the revenue from all invoices, less the cost of materials and outside processing, for each of the years that she had worked for Novell. Meade filed a lawsuit against Novell for breach of contract. (See *The Writing Requirement*.)

1. The first group will evaluate whether the parties had an enforceable contract.
2. The second group will decide whether the parties' oral agreement falls within any exception to the Statute of Frauds.
3. The third group will discuss how the lawsuit would be affected if Novell admitted that the parties had an oral contract under which Meade was entitled to a share of the company's income, but claimed that they had agreed she would receive only 15 percent of the income from invoices, not 25 percent.

shapecharge/iStock/Getty Images

16 | Performance and Discharge

Learning Objectives

The four Learning Objectives *below are designed to help improve your understanding of the chapter. After reading this chapter, you should be able to answer the following questions:*

1. What is a condition precedent, and how does it affect a party's duty to perform a contract?

2. What is substantial performance?

3. When does an accord and satisfaction discharge a contractual obligation?

4. In what situations will a court discharge a contract based on impossibility of performance?

Discharge The termination of an obligation, such as occurs when the parties to a contract have fully performed their contractual obligations.

"There are occasions and causes and why and wherefore in all things."

William Shakespeare
1564–1616
(English dramatist and poet)

In a perfect world, every party who signed a contract would perform his or her duties completely and in a timely fashion, thereby discharging the contract. In the real world, however, as William Shakespeare suggests in the chapter-opening quotation, things frequently become complicated. Certainly, events often occur that may affect our performance or our ability to perform contractual duties.

In this chapter, we examine how a contract is discharged. The most common way to **discharge,** or terminate, one's contractual duties is by the **performance** of those duties. The duty to perform under a contract may be *conditioned* on the occurrence or nonoccurrence of a certain event, or the duty may be *absolute*.

In addition to performance, a contract can be discharged in numerous other ways, including discharge by agreement of the parties and discharge by operation of law (see Exhibit 16–1.)

16–1 Conditions of Performance

In most contracts, promises of performance are not expressly conditioned or qualified. Instead, they are *absolute promises*. They must be performed, or the party making the promise will be in breach of contract. **Example 16.1** Paloma Enterprises contracts to sell a truckload of organic produce to Tran for $10,000. The parties' promises are unconditional: Paloma will deliver the produce to Tran, and Tran will pay $10,000 to Paloma. The payment does not have to be made if the produce is not delivered. ▮

Exhibit 16–1 Contract Discharge

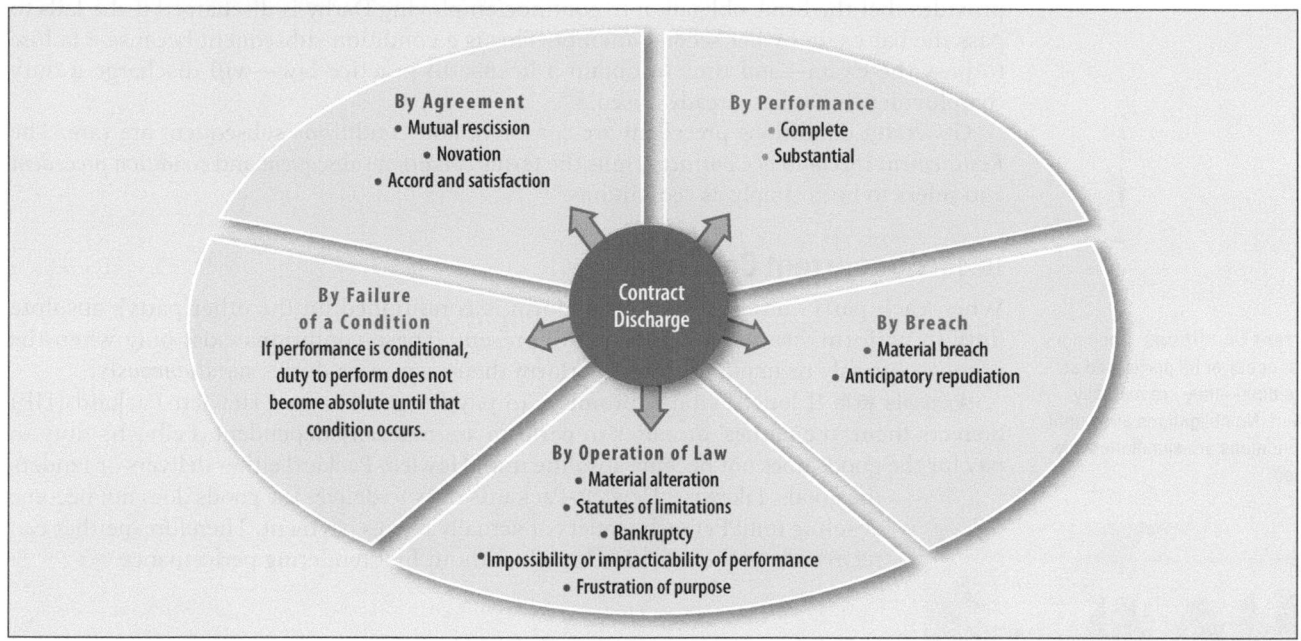

In some situations, however, contractual promises are conditioned. A **condition** is a qualification in a contract based on a possible future event, the occurrence or nonoccurrence of which will trigger or suspend the performance of a legal obligation or terminate an existing obligation under a contract. If the condition is not satisfied, the obligations of the parties are discharged.

Three types of conditions can be present in any given contract: *conditions precedent, conditions subsequent*, and *concurrent conditions*.

16–1a Conditions Precedent

A condition that must be fulfilled before a party's promise becomes absolute is called a **condition precedent.** The condition precedes the absolute duty to perform. Life insurance contracts frequently specify that certain conditions, such as passing a physical examination, must be met before the insurance company will be obligated to perform under the contract. A contract to lease university housing, for instance, may be conditioned on the person being a student at the university.

Many contracts are conditioned on an independent appraisal of value. **Example 16.2** Restoration Motors offers to buy Charlie's 1959 Thunderbird only if an expert appraiser estimates that it can be restored for less than a certain price. Thus, the parties' obligations are conditioned on the outcome of the appraisal. If the condition is not satisfied—that is, if the appraiser deems the cost to be significantly above that price—their obligations are discharged. ■

16–1b Conditions Subsequent

When a condition operates to terminate a party's absolute promise to perform, it is called a **condition subsequent.** The condition follows, or is subsequent to, the absolute duty to perform. If the condition occurs, the party need not perform any further.

Learning Objective 1

What is a condition precedent, and how does it affect a party's duty to perform a contract?

Performance The fulfillment of one's duties under a contract—the normal way of discharging one's contractual obligations.

Condition A qualification, provision, or clause in a contractual agreement, the occurrence or nonoccurrence of which creates, suspends, or terminates the obligations of the contracting parties.

Condition Precedent A condition in a contract that must be met before a party's promise becomes absolute.

Condition Subsequent A condition in a contract that, if it occurs, operates to terminate a party's absolute promise to perform.

Example 16.3 A law firm hires Julia Darby, a recent law school graduate. Their contract provides that the firm's obligation to continue employing Darby is discharged if she fails to pass the bar exam by her second attempt. This is a condition subsequent because a failure to pass the exam—and thus to obtain a license to practice law—will discharge a duty (employment) that has already arisen. ▪

Generally, conditions precedent are common, and conditions subsequent are rare. The *Restatement (Second) of Contracts* omits the terms *condition subsequent* and *condition precedent* and refers to both simply as "conditions."[1]

16–1c Concurrent Conditions

Concurrent Conditions Conditions that must occur or be performed at the same time—they are mutually dependent. No obligations arise until these conditions are simultaneously performed.

When each party's absolute duty to perform is conditioned on the other party's absolute duty to perform, **concurrent conditions** are present. These conditions exist only when the parties expressly or impliedly are to perform their respective duties *simultaneously*.

Example 16.4 If Janet Feibush promises to pay for goods when Hewlett-Packard (HP) delivers them, the parties' promises to perform are mutually dependent. Feibush's duty to pay for the goods does not become absolute until Hewlett-Packard either delivers or tenders the goods. Likewise, Hewlett-Packard's duty to deliver the goods does not become absolute until Feibush tenders or actually makes payment. Therefore, neither can recover from the other for breach without first tendering performance. ▪

If HP agrees to sell and deliver goods to someone who agrees to pay for them, what are the concurrent conditions?

David McNew/Getty Images

16–2 Discharge by Performance

The contract comes to an end when both parties fulfill their respective duties by performing the acts they have promised. Performance can also be accomplished by tender. **Tender** is an unconditional offer to perform by a person who is ready, willing, and able to do so. Therefore, a seller who places goods at the disposal of a buyer has tendered delivery and can demand payment according to the terms of the agreement. A buyer who offers to pay for goods has tendered payment and can demand delivery of the goods.

Once performance has been tendered, the party making the tender has done everything possible to carry out the terms of the contract. If the other party then refuses to perform, the party making the tender can consider the duty discharged and sue for breach of contract.

Tender An unconditional offer to perform an obligation by a person who is ready, willing, and able to do so.

16–2a Complete Performance

When a party performs exactly as agreed, there is no question as to whether the contract has been performed. When a party's performance is perfect, it is said to be complete.

Normally, conditions expressly stated in the contract must fully occur in all aspects for complete performance (strict performance) of the contract to take place. Any deviation breaches the contract and discharges the other party's obligations to perform.

For instance, most construction contracts require the builder to meet certain specifications. If the specifications are conditions, complete performance is required to avoid material breach. (*Material breach* will be discussed shortly.) If the conditions are met, the other party to the contract must then fulfill her or his obligation to pay the builder.

If the parties to the contract did not expressly make the specifications a condition, however, and the builder fails to meet the specifications, performance is not complete. What effect does that failure have on the other party's obligation to pay? The answer is part of the doctrine of *substantial performance*.

---

1. *Restatement (Second) of Contracts*, Section 224. Note that a plaintiff must prove a condition precedent, whereas the defendant normally proves a condition subsequent.

16–2b Substantial Performance

A party who in good faith performs substantially all of the terms of a contract can enforce the contract against the other party under the doctrine of substantial performance. Note that good faith is required. Intentionally failing to comply with the terms is a breach of the contract.

Learning Objective 2
What is substantial performance?

The basic requirements for performance to qualify as substantial performance are as follows:

1. The party must have performed in good faith. Intentional failure to comply with the contract terms is a breach of the contract.

2. The performance must not vary greatly from the performance promised in the contract. An omission, variance, or defect in performance is considered minor if it can easily be remedied by compensation (monetary damages).

3. The performance must create substantially the same benefits as those promised in the contract.

Courts decide whether performance was substantial on a case-by-case basis, examining all of the facts of the particular situation. **Case Example 16.5** Angele Jackson Guient and Borjius Guient hired Sterling Doucette and Doucette & Associated Contractors, Inc., to construct a new home for them in New Orleans. The original contract price was $177,000. The Guients paid Doucette a total of $159,300 for the work. They withheld the final $17,700 payment because of alleged deficiencies in the work, delays in construction, and Doucette's failure to complete the home.

Doucette filed a breach of contract action, seeking to recover the $17,700 balance. A state appellate court held that Doucette was not entitled to recover the balance. When the Guients took possession of the home from Doucette, it failed to pass inspections, and before they could move in, they had to hire other subcontractors to complete the work. Therefore, Doucette could not claim substantial performance.[2]

Effect on Duty to Perform If one party's performance is substantial, the other party's duty to perform—for instance, to make payment—remains absolute. (The party can, however, sue for damages due to the minor deviations.) In other words, the parties must continue performing under the contract. If performance is not substantial, there is a material breach, and the nonbreaching party is excused from further performance.

Measure of Damages Because substantial performance is not perfect, the other party is entitled to damages to compensate for the failure to comply with the contract. The measure of the damages is the cost to bring the object of the contract into compliance with its terms, if that cost is reasonable under the circumstances. If the cost is unreasonable, the measure of damages is the difference in value between the performance that was rendered and the performance that would have been rendered if the contract had been performed completely.

16–2c Performance to the Satisfaction of Another

Contracts often state that completed work must personally satisfy one of the parties or a third person. The question is whether this satisfaction becomes a condition precedent, requiring actual personal satisfaction or approval for discharge, or whether the test of satisfaction is performance that would satisfy a *reasonable person* (substantial performance).

When the subject matter of the contract is *personal*, a contract to be performed to the satisfaction of one of the parties is conditioned, and performance must actually satisfy that party. For instance, contracts for portraits and works of art are considered personal. Therefore, only the personal satisfaction of the party fulfills the condition (unless a court finds that the party is expressing dissatisfaction to avoid payment or otherwise is not acting in good faith).

---

2. *Doucette v. Guient*, 208 So.3d 444 (La.App. 4 Cir. 2016).

Most other contracts need be performed only to the satisfaction of a reasonable person unless they *expressly state otherwise*. When such contracts require performance to the satisfaction of a third party (such as "to the satisfaction of Robert Ames, the supervising engineer"), the courts are divided. A majority of courts require the work to be satisfactory to a reasonable person. But some courts do require the personal satisfaction of the third party designated in the contract (here, Robert Ames). Again, the personal judgment must be made honestly, or the condition will be excused.

16–2d Material Breach of Contract

Breach of Contract The failure, without legal excuse, of a promisor to perform the obligations of a contract.

A **breach of contract** is the nonperformance of a contractual duty. A breach is *material* when performance is not at least substantial.[3] If there is a material breach, the nonbreaching party is excused from the performance of contractual duties and can sue for damages caused by the breach.

If the breach is *minor* (not material), the nonbreaching party's duty to perform may sometimes be suspended until the breach is remedied, but the duty is not entirely excused. Once the minor breach is cured (corrected), the nonbreaching party must resume performance of the contractual obligations.

Any breach entitles the nonbreaching party to sue for damages, but only a material breach discharges the nonbreaching party from the contract. The policy underlying these rules is that contracts should go forward when only minor problems occur, but that contracts should be terminated if major problems arise. (See this chapter's *Business Law Analysis* feature for further explanation of how courts determine whether there has been a material breach.)

---

3. *Restatement (Second) of Contracts*, Section 241.

Determining When a Breach Is Material

Business Law Analysis

The Northeast Independent School District in Bexar County, Texas, hired STR Constructors, Ltd., to renovate a middle school. STR subcontracted the tile work in the school's kitchen to Newman Tile, Inc. (NTI). The project had already fallen behind schedule. As a result, STR allowed its workers and other subcontractors' employees to walk on and damage the newly installed tile before it had cured, forcing NTI to constantly redo its work.

Despite NTI's requests for payment, STR remitted only half the amount due under their contract. When the school district refused to accept the kitchen, including the tile work, STR told NTI to quickly make repairs. A week later, STR terminated their contract. Did STR breach the contract with NTI?

Analysis: A breach of contract is the nonperformance of a contractual duty.

A breach is *material* when performance is not at least substantial. On a material breach, the nonbreaching party is excused from performance. If a breach is *minor*, the nonbreaching party's duty to perform can sometimes be suspended until the breach has been remedied, but the duty to perform is not entirely excused. Once a minor breach has been cured, the nonbreaching party must resume performance. Any breach—material or minor—entitles the nonbreaching party to sue for damages.

Result and Reasoning: Yes, STR breached the contract with NTI. Because STR permitted its employees and other subcontractors to walk over and damage the newly installed tile, NTI had to redo its work constantly. Furthermore, despite NTI's requests for payment, STR remitted

only half the amount due under the contract. Therefore, STR's performance was not substantial, and its breach was material.

Although NTI could have chosen to stop performing the contract right away and sue STR for breach, it did not. In fact, NTI continued to perform until STR terminated the contract. The termination apparently was done wrongfully and without good cause. The tile work would have been completed satisfactorily if STR had not allowed other workers to trample the newly installed tile before it had cured.

Both parties in the following case were arguably in breach of their contract. The court had to determine which party's breach was material.

Case 16.1

Kohel v. Bergen Auto Enterprises, LLC
Superior Court of New Jersey, Appellate Division, 2013 WL 439970 (2013).

Background and Facts Marc and Bree Kohel agreed to buy a used 2009 Mazda from Bergen Auto Enterprises, LLC, doing business as Wayne Mazda, Inc. The Kohels were credited $7,000 as a trade-in for their 2005 Nissan Altima. They still owed about $8,000 on the Nissan, which Wayne Mazda agreed to pay. The Kohels took possession of the Mazda with temporary plates.

When is it considered a material breach for a car dealer to refuse to go through with a sale?

Sometime later, Wayne Mazda discovered that the Nissan was missing a vehicle identification number (VIN) tag. The dealer therefore refused to make the payment for the Nissan and also refused to give the Kohels permanent plates for the Mazda. The Kohels applied and paid for a replacement VIN tag for the Nissan, but Wayne Mazda refused to take their calls on the matter and continued to refuse to supply permanent plates for the Mazda. The Kohels filed a complaint against the dealer in a New Jersey state court, alleging breach of contract. The court ruled in the plaintiffs' favor, and Wayne Mazda appealed.

In the Words of the Court
PER CURIAM [By the Whole Court].
* * * *

Defendant [Wayne Mazda] argues that plaintiffs' delivery of the Nissan without a VIN tag was, itself, a breach of the contract of sale and precludes a finding that defendant breached the contract. However, the trial court found that plaintiffs were not aware that the Nissan lacked a VIN tag when they offered it in trade. Moreover, defendant's representatives examined the car twice before accepting it in trade and did not notice the missing VIN tag until they took the car to an auction where they tried to sell it. *There is a material distinction in plaintiffs' conduct, which the court found unintentional, and defendant's refusal to release the permanent plates for which the plaintiffs had paid, an action the court concluded was done to maintain "leverage."* [Emphasis added.]

* * * The evidence * * * indicated that * * * the problem with the missing VIN tag could be rectified. Marc Kohel applied and paid [$35.31] for a replacement VIN tag at Meadowlands [Nissan]. While he initially made some calls to Meadowlands, he did not follow up in obtaining the VIN tag after the personnel at Wayne Mazda began refusing to take his calls.

* * * The court concluded that "Wayne Mazda didn't handle this as—as adroitly [skillfully] as they could * * * ." Kevin DiPiano, identified in the complaint as the owner and/or CEO of Wayne Mazda, would not even take [the plaintiffs'] calls to discuss this matter. The court found:

Mr. DiPiano could have been a better businessman, could have been a little bit more compassionate or at least responsive, you know? He was not. He acted like he didn't care. That obviously went a long way to infuriate the plaintiffs. I don't blame them for being infuriated.

* * * *

* * * Here, plaintiffs attempted to remedy the VIN tag issue but this resolution was frustrated by defendant's unreasonable conduct. We thus reject defendant's argument that plaintiffs' failure to obtain the replacement VIN tag amounted to a repudiation of the contract.

Decision and Remedy A state intermediate appellate court affirmed the judgment in the Kohels' favor. While both parties were arguably in breach of their contract, "there is a material distinction in plaintiffs' conduct," which was unintentional, "and defendant's refusal to release the permanent plates for which the plaintiffs had paid."

Critical Thinking

• **Legal Consideration** *What is a material breach of contract? When a material breach occurs, what are the nonbreaching party's options?*

Ethical Issue

Is it a material breach of contract for a hospital to accept a donation and then refuse to honor part of its commitment?

Country singer Garth Brooks was born in Yukon, Oklahoma, and has made generous contributions to charities in that town. When his mother, Colleen Brooks, died, he donated $500,000 to Integris Rural Health, Inc., in that town. Brooks believed that he and the hospital's president had agreed verbally that the donation would be used to build a new women's health center in Yukon, which would be named after his mother. Several years passed, but the health center was not built. Integris claimed that it intended to do something to honor Colleen Brooks but insisted that it had never promised to build a new health center. When Integris refused to return the $500,000, Garth Brooks sued for breach of contract.

Was the hospital's failure to build a women's health center and name it after Brooks's mother a material breach of the verbal contract between Brooks and hospital management? A jury in Rogers County, Oklahoma, thought so and awarded Brooks $500,000 in actual damages for breach of contract. The jury also awarded Brooks another $500,000 because it found the hospital guilty of reckless disregard and intentional malice.

16–2e Anticipatory Repudiation of a Contract

Before either party to a contract has a duty to perform, one of the parties may refuse to perform her or his contractual obligations. This is called **anticipatory repudiation**.[4]

Anticipatory Repudiation An assertion or action by a party indicating that he or she will not perform a contractual obligation.

Repudiation Is a Material Breach When anticipatory repudiation occurs, it is treated as a material breach of the contract, and the nonbreaching party is permitted to bring an action for damages immediately. The nonbreaching party can file suit even though the scheduled time for performance under the contract may still be in the future. Until the nonbreaching party treats this early repudiation as a breach, however, the breaching party can retract the anticipatory repudiation by proper notice and restore the parties to their original obligations.[5]

An anticipatory repudiation is treated as a present, material breach for two reasons. First, the nonbreaching party should not be required to remain ready and willing to perform when the other party has already repudiated the contract. Second, the nonbreaching party should have the opportunity to seek a similar contract elsewhere. Indeed, that party may have the duty to do so to minimize his or her loss.

Repudiation May Occur When Market Prices Fluctuate Quite often, an anticipatory repudiation occurs when performance of the contract would be extremely unfavorable to one of the parties because of a sharp fluctuation in market prices.

Know This

The risks that prices will fluctuate and values will change are ordinary business risks for which the law does not provide relief.

Example 16.6 Mobile X enters into an e-contract to manufacture and sell 100,000 smartphones to Best Com, a global telecommunications company. Delivery is to be made two months from the date of the contract. One month later, three inventory suppliers raise their prices to Mobile X. Because of these higher prices, Mobile X stands to lose $500,000 if it sells the smartphones to Best Com at the contract price.

Mobile X immediately sends an e-mail to Best Com, stating that it cannot deliver the 100,000 phones at the contract price. Even though you may sympathize with Mobile X, its e-mail is an anticipatory repudiation of the contract. Best Com can treat the repudiation as

---

4. *Restatement (Second) of Contracts*, Section 253; and UCC 2–610.
5. See UCC 2–611.

a material breach and immediately pursue remedies, even though the contract delivery date is still a month away. ▓

16–3 Discharge by Agreement

Any contract can be discharged by agreement of the parties. The agreement can be contained in the original contract, or the parties can form a new contract for the express purpose of discharging the original contract.

16–3a Discharge by Mutual Rescission

As mentioned in previous chapters, rescission occurs when the parties cancel the contract and are returned to the positions they occupied prior to the contract's formation. For *mutual rescission* to take place, the parties must make another agreement that also satisfies the legal requirements for a contract—there must be an *offer*, an *acceptance*, and *consideration*. Ordinarily, if the parties agree to rescind the original contract, their promises not to perform those acts promised in the original contract will be legal consideration for the second contract.

A smartphone manufacturer learns its supply costs will suddenly increase and cancels its upcoming delivery to clients. What is this action called?

Generally, a rescission agreement may be written or oral. Oral agreements to rescind most executory contracts (that neither party has performed) are enforceable even if the original agreement was in writing. A writing (or electronic record) is required to rescind a contract for the sale of goods under the Uniform Commercial Code when the contract requires a written rescission. Also, agreements to rescind contracts involving transfers of realty must be evidenced by a writing or record.

When one party has fully performed, an agreement to rescind the original contract usually is not enforceable unless additional consideration or restitution is made. Because the performing party has received no consideration for the promise to call off the original bargain, additional consideration is necessary.

16–3b Discharge by Novation

The process of **novation** substitutes a third party for one of the original parties. Essentially, the parties to the original contract and one or more new parties get together and agree to the substitution. The requirements of a novation are as follows:

Novation The substitution, by agreement, of a new contract for an old one, with the rights under the old one being terminated.

1. A previous valid obligation.

2. An agreement by all of the parties to a new contract.

3. The extinguishing of the old obligation (discharge of the prior party).

4. A new, valid contract.

Example 16.7 Union Corporation contracts to sell its pharmaceutical division to British Pharmaceuticals, Ltd. Before the transfer is completed, Union, British Pharmaceuticals, and a third company, Otis Chemicals, execute a new agreement to transfer all of British Pharmaceuticals' rights and duties in the transaction to Otis Chemicals. As long as the new contract is supported by consideration, the novation will discharge the original contract (between Union and British Pharmaceuticals) and replace it with the new contract (between Union and Otis Chemicals). ▓

A novation expressly or impliedly revokes and discharges a prior contract. The parties involved may expressly state in the new contract that the old contract is now discharged. If the parties do not expressly discharge the old contract, it will be impliedly discharged if the new contract's terms are inconsistent with the old contract's terms.

Dan Grytsku/Alamy

16–3c Discharge by Accord and Satisfaction

In an *accord and satisfaction*, the parties agree to accept performance different from the performance originally promised. An *accord* is a contract to perform some act to satisfy an existing contractual duty that has not yet been discharged. A *satisfaction* is the performance of the accord agreement. An accord and its satisfaction discharge the original contractual obligation.

Once the accord has been made, the original obligation is merely suspended until the accord agreement is fully performed. If it is not performed, the party to whom performance is owed can bring an action on the original obligation or for breach of the accord. **Example 16.8** Shea obtains a judgment of $8,000 against Marla. Later, both parties agree that the judgment can be satisfied by Marla's transfer of her automobile to Shea. This agreement to accept the auto in lieu of $8,000 in cash is the accord. If Marla transfers her automobile to Shea, the accord agreement is fully performed, and the $8,000 debt is discharged. If Marla refuses to transfer her car, the accord is breached. Because the original obligation is merely suspended, Shea can sue to enforce the judgment for $8,000 in cash or bring an action for breach of the accord. ■

In the following case, two commercial lessees insisted on an accord and satisfaction to discharge their potential liability for damage to the leased premises.

Learning Objective 3

When does an accord and satisfaction discharge a contractual obligation?

When may an automobile be a valid part of a discharge by accord and satisfaction?

■ Case 16.2

DWB, LLC v. D&T Pure Trust

Arkansas Court of Appeals, 2018 Ark. App. 283 (2018).

Background and Facts DWB, LLC, and its member Danny Brown operated Mayflower RV, an RV business, in Arkansas. Doug Boydston and D&T Pure Trust leased the land on which Mayflower operated to DWB and Brown. The lease required Brown and DWB to obtain insurance coverage in the amount of the replacement value of the structures and other improvements on the property. This was the amount and type of insurance that had previously been carried on the property. Instead, DWB obtained cash-value insurance covering only the market value—$450,000.

Less than a year later, a tornado struck the property, causing substantial damage. The insurance company tendered a $450,000 check payable to DWB. Brown refused to release the funds to D&T and Boydston unless they accepted the amount as an accord and satisfaction for any claim they might have against DWB and Brown for the damage. D&T and Boydston did not agree, and filed a claim in an Arkansas state court against DWB and Brown. The check was deposited with the court. After a trial, the court found that Brown and DWB had converted the insurance proceeds. The defendants appealed.

In the Words of the Court
LARRY D. VAUGHT, Judge

* * * *

Conversion is the wrongful possession or disposition of another's property. This tort is committed when one wrongfully commits a distinct act of dominion over another's property that is inconsistent with the owner's rights.

* * * *

After the * * * tornado, the insurance company issued a $450,000 check to DWB as payment for the damage to the Mayflower property. Although the check was payable to DWB, Brown admitted that neither he nor DWB had a legal claim to the money and that it rightfully belonged to appellees. Nevertheless, appellants placed conditions on appellees' acceptance of the money by requiring that the check be accepted as an accord and satisfaction of all the parties' claims. Appellees declined, and the money was eventually [deposited with] the court pending the outcome of this litigation. Throughout the litigation, appellants maintained that they would not approve the release of the money unless it was accepted as an accord and satisfaction despite admitting they had no legal claim to the money. Ultimately, the * * * court found that appellants converted the $450,000 because they resisted its release despite having no right to place conditions on its release.

* * * Appellants argue that they could not have committed conversion because, on receipt, Brown endorsed the check and sent it to appellees with an accord-and-satisfaction letter, to which appellees refused to agree. Appellants argue that these acts do not demonstrate an intent to control the money. We disagree. *The intent required to commit conversion is not conscious wrongdoing but rather an intent to exercise dominion or control over the goods that is inconsistent with the plaintiff's rights.* The * * * court found that appellants exercised dominion and control over money to which they were not entitled, and these findings are supported by the evidence. [Emphasis added.]

Decision and Remedy A state intermediate appellate court affirmed the lower court's finding of conversion. "The money belonged to appellees, and throughout the litigation, appellants exercised control over the money by placing conditions on its release."

Critical Thinking

• **Legal Environment** *Did Brown and DWB breach the lease? If so, was the breach material? Discuss.*

• **What If the Facts Were Different?** *Suppose that Boydston and D&T had agreed to the cash-value policy in lieu of the lease's required replacement-value coverage, and that they had subsequently accepted the insurance check. Would the result have been different? Explain.*

16–4 Discharge by Operation of Law

Under specified circumstances, contractual duties may be discharged by operation of law. These circumstances include material alteration of the contract, an applicable statute of limitations, bankruptcy, impossibility or impracticability of performance, and frustration of purpose.

16–4a Material Alteration

To discourage parties from altering written contracts, the law allows an innocent party to be discharged from a contract that has been materially altered. If one party alters a material term of the contract—such as the quantity term or the price term—without the other party's knowledge the party who was unaware of the alteration can treat the contract as discharged or terminated.

> "Law is a practical matter."
>
> **Roscoe Pound**
> 1870–1964
> (American jurist)

16–4b Statutes of Limitations

Statutes of limitations limit the period during which a party can sue on a particular cause of action. After the applicable limitations period has passed, a suit can no longer be brought.

The period for bringing lawsuits for breach of oral contracts is usually two to three years and for written contracts, four to five years. Lawsuits for breach of a contract for the sale of goods must be brought within four years after the cause of action has accrued.[6] In their original contract, the parties can agree to reduce this four-year period to not less than one year. They cannot, however, agree to extend it beyond four years.

16–4c Bankruptcy

A proceeding in bankruptcy attempts to allocate a debtor's assets to the creditors in a fair and equitable fashion. Once the assets have been allocated, the debtor receives a *discharge in bankruptcy*. A discharge in bankruptcy ordinarily prevents the creditors from enforcing most of the debtor's contracts. Partial payment of a debt *after* discharge in bankruptcy will not revive the debt.

---

6. See UCC 2-725.

16–4d Impossibility of Performance

Impossibility of Performance
A doctrine under which a party to a contract is relieved of his or her duty to perform when performance becomes objectively impossible or totally impracticable.

Learning Objective 4

In what situations will a court discharge a contract based on impossibility of performance?

After a contract has been made, supervening events (such as a fire) may make performance impossible in an objective sense. This so-called **impossibility of performance** can discharge the contract. The doctrine of impossibility of performance is applied only when the parties could not have reasonably foreseen, at the time the contract was formed, the event or events that rendered performance impossible.

Objective impossibility ("It cannot be done") must be distinguished from subjective impossibility ("I'm sorry, I personally cannot do it"). An example of subjective impossibility occurs when a person cannot deliver goods on time or make payment on time because the person has to have an emergency surgery. In effect, the nonperforming party is saying, "It is impossible for *me* to perform" rather than "It is impossible for *anyone* to perform." Accordingly, such excuses do not discharge a contract, and the nonperforming party is normally held in breach of contract.

When Performance Is Impossible Three basic types of situations may qualify as grounds for the discharge of contractual obligations based on impossibility of performance:[7]

1. *When a party whose personal performance is essential to the completion of the contract dies or becomes incapacitated prior to performance.* **Example 16.9** Fred, a famous dancer, contracts with Ethereal Dancing Guild to play a leading role in its new ballet. Before the ballet can be performed, Fred becomes ill and dies. His personal performance was essential to the completion of the contract. Thus, his death discharges the contract and his estate's liability for his nonperformance.

2. *When the specific subject matter of the contract is destroyed.* **Example 16.10** A-1 Farm Equipment agrees to sell Gunther the green tractor on its lot and promises to have the tractor ready for Gunther to pick up on Saturday. On Friday night, however, a truck veers off the nearby highway and smashes into the tractor, destroying it beyond repair. Because the contract was for this specific tractor, A-1's performance is rendered impossible owing to the accident.

3. *When a change in the law renders performance illegal.* **Example 16.11** Russo contracts with Playlist, Inc., to create a website through which users can post and share movies, music, and other forms of digital entertainment. Russo goes to work. Before the site is operational, however, Congress passes the No Online Piracy in Entertainment (NOPE) Act. The NOPE Act makes it illegal to operate a website on which copyrighted works are posted without the copyright owners' consent. In this situation, the contract is discharged by operation of law. The purpose of the contract has been rendered illegal, and contract performance is objectively impossible.

The following case involved a financial institution participating in the federal Troubled Assets Relief Program (TARP). Could the institution assert TARP's prohibition on "golden parachute" payments as a defense to a breach of contract action brought by one of its former senior executive officers?

This dancer has a contract to dance the lead role in a famous ballet that will run for a month. What happens if he breaks a leg before the shows start?

---

7. *Restatement (Second) of Contracts,* Sections 261–266; and UCC 2–615.

■ Case 16.3

Hampton Road Bankshares, Inc. v. Harvard

Virginia Supreme Court, 291 Va. 42, 781 S.E.2d 172 (2016).

Background and Facts Scott Harvard was a senior executive officer of Hampton Roads Bankshares (HRB) in Virginia. Harvard's employment contract included a "golden parachute"—a payment of approximately three times his average annual compensation if he quit.

During the 2008 recession, Congress created the Troubled Assets Relief Program (TARP), which allowed the government to buy "troubled assets" from financial institutions to promote market stability. TARP barred participating institutions from making golden parachute payments, defined as "any payment to a senior executive officer for departure from a company for any reason."

HRB participated in TARP. Later, when Harvard quit the firm, HRB refused to pay him the golden parachute amount in the belief that TARP had made such payments illegal. Harvard filed a suit in a Virginia state court against HRB to obtain his golden parachute. The court ordered HRB to make the payment. HRB appealed to the Virginia Supreme Court.

In the Words of the Court
Opinion by Justice William C. *MIMS.*
* * * *

The defense of impossibility of performance is an established principle of contract law. In Virginia, *it is well settled that where impossibility is due to domestic law, to the death or illness of one who by the terms of the contract was to do an act requiring his personal performance, or to the fortuitous destruction or change in the character of something to which the contract related, or which by the terms of the contract was made a necessary means of performance, the promisor will be excused, unless he either expressly agreed in the contract to assume the risk of performance, whether possible or not, or the impossibility was due to his fault.* [Emphasis added.]

Harvard does not dispute that EESA directly bars HRB from making the severance payment to Harvard upon the termination of his employment, because the payment falls within the definition of a prohibited "golden parachute payment." Moreover, Harvard does not suggest that HRB expressly agreed in the contract to assume the risk of performance, whether possible or not. Nor could he; the * * * Employment Agreement clearly places the risk of * * * the law regulating golden parachute payments on Harvard.

On December 31, 2008, Harvard agreed [with HRB to amend] the Employment Agreement [to provide that it] "will be interpreted, administered and construed to, comply with EESA."

By its plain language, the amended Employment Agreement must be read to comply with EESA. Nothing therein exempts the agreement from * * * EESA * * * or places the risk of performance * * * on HRB.
* * * *

There is nothing in the record that would suggest HRB refused to make the golden parachute payment in bad faith. After Harvard terminated his employment, HRB sought guidance from [the U.S. Department of the] Treasury regarding its contractual obligation to make the disputed golden parachute payment, and whether it could perform that obligation in light of EESA. In response, Treasury provided informal guidance indicating that HRB could not make the payment and comply with EESA. Where, as here, the government has clearly expressed its intent to enforce the law, and the promisor cannot in good faith perform its contractual obligation without violating the law, the promisor is discharged from its obligation.

Decision and Remedy The Virginia Supreme Court reversed the order of the lower court, which "erred when it ordered HRB to make the golden parachute payment despite the federal prohibition on such payments found in EESA." Under EESA, payment of the golden parachute would violate the law.

Critical Thinking

• **Ethical** *Did HRB violate any ethical duty by refusing to pay Harvard's golden parachute? Explain.*

Temporary Impossibility An occurrence or event that makes performance temporarily impossible operates to suspend performance until the impossibility ceases. Once the temporary event ends, the parties ordinarily must perform the contract as originally planned.

Example 16.12 Mindy and Lyn Carr contract to rent a sailboat from Key West Rentals for a month-long trip. The day before their trip is scheduled to begin, Hurricane Irma hits the coast where the boat is docked, causing damage. The hurricane makes performance temporarily impossible, and the Carrs postpone their trip. Once the repairs are made to the dock and the boat, however, Key West Rentals will be required to perform the contract as originally planned. The Carrs have a right to rent the boat for a month for the previously agreed-on price. ■

Sometimes, however, the lapse of time and the change in circumstances surrounding such a contract make it substantially more burdensome for the parties to perform the promised acts. In that situation, the contract may be discharged. **Classic Case Example 16.13** In 1942, actor Gene Autry was drafted into the U.S. Army. Being drafted rendered his contract with a Hollywood movie company temporarily impossible to perform, and it was suspended until the end of World War II in 1945. When Autry got out of the army, the purchasing power of the dollar had declined so much that performance of the contract would have been substantially burdensome to him. Therefore, the contract was discharged.[8] ■

Know This
The doctrine of commercial impracticability does not provide relief from such events as ordinary price increases or easily predictable changes in the weather.

---

8. *Autry v. Republic Productions*, 30 Cal.2d 144, 180 P.2d 888 (1947).

Impossibility or Impracticability of Performance in Germany

Beyond Our Borders

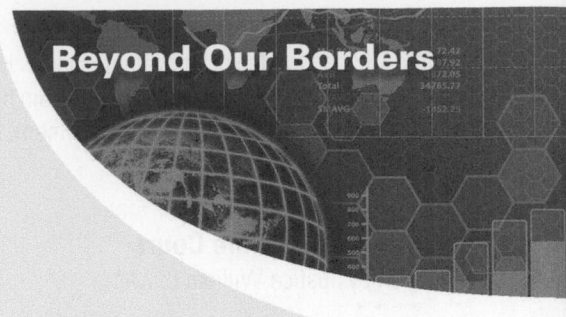

In the United States, when a party alleges that contract performance is impossible or impracticable because of circumstances unforeseen at the time the contract was formed, a court will either discharge the party's contractual obligations or hold the party to the contract.

In other words, if a court agrees that the contract is impossible or impracticable to perform, the remedy is to rescind (cancel) the contract.

Under German law, however, a court may reform (adjust the terms of) a contract in light of economic developments. If an unforeseen event affects the foundation of the agreement, the court can alter the contract's terms to align with the parties' original expectations, thus making the contract fair to the parties.

Critical Thinking

When a contract becomes impossible or impracticable to perform, what options does a businessperson have?

Commercial Impracticability Courts may also excuse parties from their performance obligations when the performance becomes much more difficult or expensive than the parties originally contemplated. In one classic case, for instance, a court held that a contract could be discharged because a party would have to pay ten times more than the original estimate to excavate a certain amount of gravel.[9]

For someone to invoke the doctrine of **commercial impracticability** successfully, however, the anticipated performance must become *extremely difficult or costly*.[10] Furthermore, the added burden of performing *must not have been foreseeable by the parties when the contract was made*. (See this chapter's *Beyond Our Borders* feature for a discussion of Germany's approach to impracticability and impossibility of performance.)

Commercial Impracticability
A doctrine that may excuse the duty to perform a contract when performance becomes much more difficult or costly due to forces that neither party could control or foresee at the time the contract was formed.

Frustration of Purpose A court-created doctrine under which a party to a contract will be relieved of her or his duty to perform when the objective purpose for performance no longer exists due to reasons beyond that party's control.

Frustration of Purpose Closely allied with the doctrine of commercial impracticability is the doctrine of **frustration of purpose**. In principle, a contract will be discharged if supervening circumstances make it impossible to attain the purpose both parties had in mind when making the contract. As with commercial impracticability, the supervening event must not have been foreseeable at the time of the contracting.

There are some differences between the doctrines, however. Commercial impracticability usually involves an event that increases the cost or difficulty of performance. In contrast, frustration of purpose typically involves an event that decreases the value of what a party receives under the contract.

9. *Mineral Park Land Co. v. Howard*, 172 Cal. 289, 156 P. 458 (1916).
10. *Restatement (Second) of Contracts*, Section 264.

Practice and Review

Val's Foods signs a contract to buy 1,500 pounds of basil from Sun Farms, a small organic herb grower, if an independent organization inspects the crop and certifies that it contains no pesticide or herbicide residue. Val's has a contract with several restaurant chains to supply pesto and intends to use Sun Farms' basil in the pesto to fulfill these contracts. When Sun Farms is preparing to harvest the basil, an unexpected hailstorm destroys half the crop. Sun Farms attempts to purchase additional basil from other farms, but it is late in the season, and the price is twice the normal market price.

Sun Farms is too small to absorb this cost and immediately notifies Val's that it will not fulfill the contract. Using the information presented in the chapter, answer the following questions.

1. Suppose that Sun Farms supplies the basil that survived the storm but the basil does not pass the chemical-residue inspection. Which concept discussed in the chapter might allow Val's to refuse to perform the contract in this situation?

2. Under which legal theory or theories might Sun Farms claim that its obligation under the contract has been discharged by operation of law? Discuss fully.

3. Suppose that Sun Farms contacts every basil grower in the country and buys the last remaining chemical-free basil anywhere. Nevertheless, Sun Farms is able to ship only 1,475 pounds to Val's. Would this fulfill Sun Farms' obligations to Val's? Why or why not?

4. Now suppose that Sun Farms sells its operations to Happy Valley Farms. As part of the sale, all three parties agree that Happy Valley will provide the basil as stated under the original contract. What is this type of agreement called?

Debate This

The doctrine of commercial impracticability should be abolished.

Key Terms

anticipatory repudiation 372
breach of contract 370
commercial impracticability 378
concurrent conditions 368
condition 367

condition precedent 367
condition subsequent 367
discharge 366
frustration of purpose 378

impossibility of performance 376
novation 373
performance 367
tender 368

Chapter Summary: Performance and Discharge

Conditions of Performance	Contract obligations may be subject to the following types of conditions: 1. *Condition precedent*—A condition that must be fulfilled before a party's promise becomes absolute. 2. *Condition subsequent*—A condition that, if it occurs, operates to terminate a party's absolute promise to perform. 3. *Concurrent conditions*—Conditions that must be performed simultaneously. Each party's absolute duty to perform is conditioned on the other party's absolute duty to perform.
Discharge by Performance	A contract may be discharged by complete (strict) performance or by substantial performance. In some instances, performance must be to the satisfaction of another. Totally inadequate performance constitutes a material breach of the contract. An anticipatory repudiation of a contract allows the other party to sue immediately for breach of contract.
Discharge by Agreement	Parties may agree to discharge their contractual obligations in several ways: 1. *By rescission*—The parties mutually agree to rescind (cancel) the contract. 2. *By novation*—A new party is substituted for one of the primary parties to a contract. 3. *By accord and satisfaction*—The parties agree to render and accept performance different from that on which they originally agreed.

(Continues)

Discharge by Operation of Law	Parties' obligations under contracts may be discharged by operation of law owing to one of the following: 1. Material alteration. 2. Statutes of limitations. 3. Bankruptcy. 4. Impossibility of performance. 5. Commercial impracticability. 6. Frustration of purpose.

Issue Spotters

1. Ready Foods contracts to buy two hundred carloads of frozen pizzas from Stealth Distributors. Before Ready or Stealth starts performing, can the parties call off the deal? What if Stealth has already shipped the pizzas? Explain your answers. (See *Discharge by Performance.*)

2. C&D Services contracts with Ace Concessions, Inc., to service Ace's vending machines. Later, C&D wants Dean Vending Services to assume the duties under a new contract. Ace consents. What type of agreement is this? Are Ace's obligations discharged? Why or why not? (See *Discharge by Agreement.*)

— **Check your answers to the *Issue Spotters* against the answers provided in Appendix D at the end of this text.**

Business Scenarios and Case Problems

16–1. Conditions of Performance. The Caplans con-tract with Faithful Construction, Inc., to build a house for them for $360,000. The specifications state "all plumbing bowls and fixtures . . . to be Crane brand." The Caplans leave on vacation, and during their absence, Faithful is unable to buy and install Crane plumbing fixtures. Instead, Faithful installs Kohler brand fixtures, an equivalent in the industry. On completion of the building contract, the Caplans inspect the work, discover the substitution, and refuse to accept the house, claiming Faithful has breached the conditions set forth in the specifications. Discuss fully the Caplans' claim. (See *Conditions of Performance.*)

16–2. Discharge by Agreement. Junior owes creditor Iba $1,000, which is due and payable on June 1. Junior has been in a car accident, has missed a great deal of work, and con-se-quently will not have the funds on June 1. Junior's father, Fred, offers to pay Iba $1,100 in four equal installments if Iba will discharge Junior from any further liability on the debt. Iba accepts. Is this transaction a novation or an accord and satisfaction? Explain. (See *Discharge by Agreement.*)

16–3. Impossibility of Performance. In the follow-ing situations, certain events take place after the contracts are formed. Discuss which of these contracts are discharged because the events render the contracts impossible to perform. (See *Discharge by Operation of Law.*)

1. Jimenez, a famous singer, contracts to perform in your nightclub. He dies prior to performance.

2. Raglione contracts to sell you her land. Just before title is to be transferred, she dies.

3. Oppenheim contracts to sell you one thousand bushels of apples from her orchard in the state of Washington. Because of a severe frost, she is unable to deliver the apples.

4. Maxwell contracts to lease a service station for ten years. His principal income is from the sale of gasoline. Because of an oil embargo by foreign oil-producing nations, gaso-line is rationed, cutting sharply into Maxwell's gasoline sales. He cannot make his lease payments.

16–4. Conditions of Performance. Russ Wyant owned Humble Ranch in Perkins County, South Dakota. Edward Humble, whose parents had previously owned the ranch, was Wyant's uncle. Humble held a two-year option to buy the ranch. The option included specific conditions. Once it was exercised, the parties had thirty days to enter into a purchase agreement, and the seller could become the buyer's lender by matching the terms of the proposed financing. After the option was exercised, the parties engaged in lengthy negotiations, but Humble did not respond to Wyant's proposed purchase agreement nor advise him of available financing terms before the option expired. Six months later, Humble filed a suit against Wyant to enforce the option. Is Humble entitled to specific performance? Explain. [*Humble v. Wyant*, 843 N.W.2d 334 (S.Dak. 2014)] (See *Conditions of Performance.*)

16–5. Discharge by Operation of Law. Dr. Jake Lambert signed an employment agreement with Baptist Health Services, Inc., to provide cardiothoracic-surgery services to Baptist Memorial Hospital–North Mississippi, Inc., in Oxford, Mississippi. Complaints about Lambert's behavior arose almost immediately. He was evaluated by a team of doctors and psychologists, who diagnosed him as suffering from obsessive-compulsive personality disorder and concluded that he was unfit to practice medicine. Based on this conclusion, the hospital suspended his staff privileges. Citing the suspension, Baptist Health Services claimed that Lambert had breached his employment contract. What is Lambert's best defense to this claim? Explain. [*Baptist Memorial Hospital–North Mississippi, Inc. v. Lambert,* 157 So.3d 109 (Miss.App. 2015)] (See *Discharge by Operation of Law.*)

16–6. Business Case Problem with Sample Answer— Conditions of Performance. H&J Ditching & Excavating, Inc., was hired by JRSF, LLC, to perform excavating and grading work on Terra Firma, a residential construction project in West Knox County, Tennessee. Cornerstone Community Bank financed the project with a loan to JRSF. As the work progressed, H&J received payments totaling 90 percent of the price on its contract. JRSF then defaulted on the loan from Cornerstone, and Cornerstone foreclosed and took possession of the property. H&J filed a suit in a Tennessee state court against the bank to recover the final payment on its contract. The bank responded that H&J had not received its payment because it had failed to obtain an engineer's certificate of final completion, a condition under its contract with JRSF. H&J responded that it had completed all the work it had contracted to do. What type of contract condition does obtaining the engineer's certificate represent? Is H&J entitled to the final payment? Discuss. [*H&J Ditching & Excavating, Inc. v. Cornerstone Community Bank,* __ S.W.3d __, 2016 WL 675554 (Tenn.App. 2016)] (See *Conditions of Performance.*)

—**For a sample answer to Problem 16–6, go to Appendix E at the end of this text.**

16–7. Substantial Performance. Melissa Gallegos bought a used 1996 Saturn automobile for $2,155 from Raul Quintero, doing business as JR's Motors. Their written contract focused primarily on the transfer of physical possession of the vehicle and did not mention who would pay the taxes on the sale. Gallegos paid Quintero $2,200, believing that this amount included the taxes. When she asked him for the title to the vehicle, he told her that only the state could provide the title and only after the taxes were paid. Quintero added that they had orally agreed Gallegos would pay the taxes. Without the title, Gallegos could not obtain license plates and legally operate the vehicle. More than six years later, she filed a suit in a Texas state court against Quintero, alleging breach of contract. Did Quintero substantially perform his obligation under the contract? Explain. [*Gallegos v. Quintero,* 2018 WL 655539 (Tex.App.—Corpus Christi-Edinburg 2018)] (See *Discharge by Performance.*)

16–8. A Question of Ethics—The IDDR Approach and Discharge by Operation of Law. *Lisa Goldstein reserved space for a marriage ceremony in a building owned by Orensanz Events, LLC, in New York City. The rental agreement provided that on cancellation of the event "for any reason beyond Owner's control," the client's sole remedy was another date for the event or a refund. Shortly before the wedding, the New York City Department of Buildings found Orensanz's building to be structurally unstable and ordered it vacated. The owner closed it and told Goldstein to find another venue. She filed a suit in a New York state court against Orensanz for breach of contract, arguing that the city's order had been for a cause within the defendant's control. [Goldstein v. Orensanz Events, LLC, 146 A.D.3d 492, 44 N.Y.S.3d 437 (1 Dept. 2017)] (See* Discharge by Operation of Law.)

1. Is the owner of a commercial building ethically obligated to keep it structurally sound? Apply the IDDR approach in the context of the *Goldstein* case to answer this question.

2. Is a contracting party ethically obligated to "relax" the terms of the deal if the other party encounters "trouble" in performing them? Discuss.

Critical Thinking and Writing Assignments

16–9. Critical Legal Thinking. The concept of substantial performance permits a party to be discharged from a contract even though the party has not fully performed her or his obligations according to the contract's terms. Is this fair? Why or why not? What policy interests are at issue here? (See *Discharge by Performance.*)

16–10. Time-Limited Group Assignment—Anticipatory Repudiation. ABC Clothiers, Inc., has a contract with John Taylor, owner of Taylor & Sons, a retailer, to deliver one thousand summer suits to Taylor's place of business on or before May 1. On April 1, John receives a letter from ABC informing him that ABC will not be able to make the delivery as scheduled. John is very upset, as he had planned a big ad campaign. (See *Discharge by Performance.*)

1. The first group will decide whether John Taylor can immediately sue ABC for breach of contract (on April 2).

2. Now suppose that John Taylor's son, Tom, tells his father that they cannot file a lawsuit until ABC actually fails to deliver the suits on May 1. The second group will determine who is correct, John or Tom.

3. Assume that Taylor & Sons can either file immediately or wait until ABC fails to deliver the goods. The third group will evaluate which course of action is better, given the circumstances.

17

Breach and Remedies

Learning Objectives

The four Learning Objectives *below are designed to help improve your understanding. After reading this chapter, you should be able to answer the following questions:*

1. What is the standard measure of compensatory damages when a contract is breached?

2. When do courts grant specific performance as a remedy?

3. What remedy is available when a court imposes a quasi contract?

4. What is a limitation-of-liability clause, and when will courts enforce it?

> "There's a remedy for everything except death."
>
> **Miguel de Cervantes**
> 1547–1616
> (Spanish author)

When one party breaches a contract, the other party—the nonbreaching party—can choose one or more of several remedies. A *remedy* is the relief provided to an innocent party when the other party has breached the contract. It is the means employed to enforce a right or to redress an injury. Although it may be an exaggeration to say there is a remedy for "everything" in life, as Cervantes claimed in the chapter-opening quotation, there is a remedy available for nearly every contract breach.

The most common remedies available to a nonbreaching party under contract law include damages, rescission and restitution, specific performance, and reformation. Courts distinguish between *remedies at law* and *remedies in equity*. Today, the remedy at law is normally monetary damages. Usually, a court will not award an equitable remedy unless the remedy at law is inadequate.

Suppose Daren Liotta, an orthodontist, is having a new office built for his orthodontic practice. He contracts with Bryan Phillips, doing business as Desert Sun Landscaping, to build a fountain in front of the new office for $14,000. Desert Sun installs the fountain while the office building is still under construction. Three weeks later, the fountain stops working properly. Desert Sun repairs the problem, which Phillips claims was caused by dirt and debris coming from the office construction.

The fountain continues to have problems, however. Within a month, the concrete slab underneath it irreparably cracks, and a pipe leading to the spray nozzles comes loose. Liotta hires another landscaper to remove the defective fountain from the front of his new office building. Can Liotta sue Phillips for breach of contract? If he sues and is successful, can he recover the $14,000 he paid for the fountain, as well as the cost of removing the fountain? These are the kinds of issues concerning breach and damages that we consider in this chapter.

17–1 Damages

A breach of contract entitles the nonbreaching party to sue for monetary damages. In contract law, damages compensate the nonbreaching party for the loss of the bargain (whereas in tort law, damages compensate for harm suffered as a result of another's wrongful act). Often, courts say that innocent parties are to be placed in the position they would have occupied had the contract been fully performed.[1]

17–1a Types of Damages

There are basically four broad categories of damages:

1. Compensatory (to cover direct losses and costs).
2. Consequential (to cover indirect and foreseeable losses).
3. Punitive (to punish and deter wrongdoing).
4. Nominal (to recognize wrongdoing when no monetary loss is shown).

Compensatory and punitive damages were discussed in the context of tort law. Here, we look at these types of damages, as well as consequential and nominal damages, in the context of contract law.

Compensatory Damages Damages that compensate the nonbreaching party for the *loss of the bargain* are known as *compensatory damages*. These damages compensate the injured party only for damages actually sustained and proved to have arisen directly from the loss of the bargain caused by the breach of contract. They simply replace what was lost because of the wrong or damage, and, for this reason, are often said to "make the person whole."

Case Example 17.1 Janet Murley was the vice president of marketing at Hallmark Cards, Inc., until Hallmark eliminated her position as part of a corporate restructuring. Murley and Hallmark entered into a separation agreement under which she agreed not to work in the greeting card industry for eighteen months and not to disclose or use any of Hallmark's confidential information. In exchange, Hallmark gave Murley a $735,000 severance payment.

After eighteen months, Murley took a job with Recycled Paper Greetings (RPG) for $125,000 and disclosed confidential Hallmark information to RPG. Hallmark sued for breach of contract and won. The jury awarded $860,000 in damages (the $735,000 severance payment plus the $125,000 that Murley received from RPG). Murley appealed. The appellate court held that Hallmark was entitled only to the return of the $735,000 severance payment. Hallmark was not entitled to the other $125,000 because that additional award would have left Hallmark better off than if Murley had not breached the contract.[2] ■

There is a two-step process to determine whether a breach of contract has resulted in compensatory damages. Initially, it must be established that there is a contract between the parties and that the contract has been breached. Next, it must be proved that the breach caused damages. The following case concerned the second step of this process.

When a former Hallmark employee breaches a term in her separation contract, how much can Hallmark recover as damages?

1. *Restatement (Second) of Contracts*, Section 347.
2. *Hallmark Cards, Inc. v. Murley*, 703 F.3d 456 (8th Cir. 2013).

Case 17.1

Baird v. Owens Community College

Court of Appeals of Ohio, Tenth District, Franklin County, 2016 -Ohio- 537 (2016).

Background and Facts Owens Community College in Ohio maintains a registered nursing program approved by the Ohio Board of Nursing, which permits graduates to take the National Council Licensure Examination (NCLEX) for their nursing license. Owens lost its accreditation from the National League for Nursing Accreditation Commission (NLNAC) in July 2009, but the school did not tell its students until after classes for the fall semester had begun in September.

Carrianne Baird and sixty-one other students from the program filed a suit in an Ohio state court against the college, alleging breach of contract. The court concluded that the students suffered no damages because the loss of accreditation did not affect their ability to take the state licensing examination, and issued a summary judgment in favor of the defendant. The students appealed.

In the Words of the Court
BRUNNER, J. [Judge]

* * * *

[Carrianne Baird and the other sixty-one] plaintiffs-appellants * * * are former students in the registered nursing program of defendant-appellee, Owens Community College.

* * * *

Kelsey Darbyshire testified * * * that Lima Memorial Hospital required applicants to have graduated from an accredited nursing school. She indicated on her application that she did not graduate from an accredited program, and had no response.

* * * *

* * * None of the appellants submitted sufficient evidence of economic damages based on their rejection from specific employment or a higher degree program. *However, a claimant's inability to demonstrate a specific denial of employment due to the program's loss of accreditation does not defeat damages on account of lost earning capacity* * * *. *The measure of damages for impairment of earning capacity is the difference between the amount which the plaintiff was capable of earning before his injury and that which he is capable of earning thereafter.* The claimant must offer sufficient proof of any future impairment and also sufficient evidence of the extent of prospective damages flowing from the

impairment. In order to recover for impaired earning capacity, the plaintiff must prove by sufficient evidence that he is reasonably certain to incur such damages in the future. * * * The [lower] court * * * should have considered whether each of the appellants suffered impaired earning capacity or other compensable damages and what those damages would be to place them in the same position that they would have enjoyed if appellee had performed its contract. [Emphasis added.]

Since there exists a genuine issue of material fact concerning damages, the [lower] court * * * must also determine, in addition to whether any appellant can prove diminished earning capacity, whether any appellant produced sufficient evidence that appellee breached its contract with her or him.

When a student enrolls in a college or university, pays his or her tuition and fees, and attends such school, the resulting relationship may reasonably be construed as being contractual in nature. The terms of such a contract may be found in the college or university catalog, handbook, and/or other guidelines supplied to the students.

On the first page of the registered nursing section of the course book appellee provided to students, appellee listed its NLNAC accreditation foremost, and according to appellants, providing an NLNAC accredited education was part and parcel of appellee's "deal" with each of them.

Decision and Remedy A state intermediate appellate court reversed the judgment of the lower court and remanded the case for trial. If the plaintiffs prove that the defendant (Owens) breached its contract by failing to be an accredited nursing school, the plaintiffs are entitled to damages for the loss of the bargain.

Critical Thinking

• **What If the Facts Were Different?** *Suppose that a plaintiff establishes diminished earning capacity in the nursing field but has opted for a different career that is more financially rewarding. Is he or she still entitled to recover damages? Explain.*

Standard Measure. The standard measure of compensatory damages is the difference between the value of the breaching party's promised performance under the contract and the value of her or his actual performance. This amount is reduced by any loss that the injured party has avoided.

Example 17.2 Randall contracts to perform certain services exclusively for Hernandez during the month of March for $4,000. Hernandez cancels the contract and is in breach. Randall is able to find another job during March but can earn only $3,000. He can sue Hernandez for breach and recover $1,000 as compensatory damages. Randall can also recover from Hernandez the amount that he spent to find the other job. ■ Expenses that are directly incurred because of a breach of contract—such as those incurred to obtain performance from another source—are called **incidental damages.**

Note that the measure of compensatory damages often varies by type of contract. Certain types of contracts deserve special mention and are discussed next.

Sale of Goods. In a contract for the sale of goods, the usual measure of compensatory damages is the difference between the contract price and the market price.[3] **Example 17.3** Medik Laboratories contracts to buy ten model UTS 400 network servers from Cal Industries for $4,000 each, but Cal Industries fails to deliver the servers. The market price of the servers at the time Medik learns of the breach is $4,500. Therefore, Medik's measure of damages is $5,000 (10 × $500), plus any incidental damages (expenses) caused by the breach. ■

Sometimes, the buyer breaches when the seller has not yet produced the goods. In that situation, compensatory damages normally equal the seller's lost profits on the sale, not the difference between the contract price and the market price.

Sale of Land. Ordinarily, because each parcel of land is unique, the remedy for a seller's breach of a contract for a sale of real estate is specific performance. The buyer is awarded the parcel of property for which he or she bargained (specific performance will be discussed more fully later in the chapter). The majority of states follow this rule.

A minority of states apply a different rule when the seller breaches a land-sale contract unintentionally (for instance, when the seller cannot deliver good title to the land for a reason he or she had previously been unaware of). In these states, a prospective buyer is limited to a refund of any down payment made plus any expenses incurred (such as fees for title searches, attorneys, and escrows). Thus, the minority rule effectively returns purchasers to the positions they occupied prior to the sale, rather than giving them the benefit of the bargain.

When the *buyer* is the party in breach, the measure of damages is typically the difference between the contract price and the market price of the land. The same measure is used when specific performance is not available (because the seller has sold the property to someone else, for instance).

Construction Contracts. The measure of damages in a building or construction contract depends on which party breaches and when the breach occurs.

1. *Breach by owner.* The owner may breach at three different stages—before performance has begun, during performance, or after performance has been completed. If the owner breaches *before performance has begun,* the contractor can recover only the profits that would have been made on the contract. (Profits equal the total contract price less the cost of materials and labor.) If the owner breaches *during performance,* the contractor can recover the profits plus the costs incurred in partially constructing the building. If the owner breaches *after construction has been completed,* the contractor can recover the entire contract price, plus interest.

2. *Breach by contractor.* When the contractor breaches the contract—either by failing to begin construction or by stopping work partway through the project—the measure of damages is the cost of completion. The cost of completion includes reasonable compensation for any delay in performance. If the contractor finishes late, the measure of damages is the loss of use.

---

3. This amount is the difference between the contract price and the market price at the time and place at which the goods were to be delivered or tendered. See Sections 2–708, 2–713, and 2–715(1) of the Uniform Commercial Code (UCC).

Learning Objective 1
What is the standard measure of compensatory damages when a contract is breached?

Incidental Damages Damages that compensate for expenses directly incurred because of a breach of contract, such as those incurred to obtain performance from another source.

"A long dispute means that both parties are wrong."

Voltaire
1694–1778
(French author)

When a woodworking contractor breaches a contract, how is the measure of damages calculated?

Case Example 17.4 To remodel his home in Connecticut, Richard Viola hired J. S. Benson of J. S. Benson Woodworking & Design as his contractor. Over a period of five years, Viola paid Benson more than $500,000 to fabricate and install windows and doors, nearly $50,000 for the purchase of lumber, $10,000 to ship and store the lumber, as well as $111,000 toward the contract price. Nevertheless, Benson failed to complete the project and would not give Viola the lumber that he had purchased despite repeated requests. Viola eventually sued Benson for breaching the contract. A state court held that Benson had breached the contract and ordered him to pay $848,000 in damages. The damages awarded included additional amounts to reimburse Viola for attorneys' fees, rental costs (because he was unable to live in the home), and property taxes.[4]

3. *Breach by both owner and contractor.* When the performance of both parties—the construction contractor and the owner—falls short of what their contract required, the courts attempt to strike a fair balance in awarding damages.

Exhibit 17–1 summarizes the rules for the measure of damages in breached construction contracts.

Consequential Damages

Foreseeable damages that result from a party's breach of contract but are caused by special circumstances beyond the contract itself.

Consequential Damages Foreseeable damages that result from a party's breach of contract are called **consequential damages**, or *special damages*. They differ from compensatory damages in that they are caused by special circumstances beyond the contract itself. They flow from the consequences, or results, of a breach. When a seller fails to deliver goods, knowing that the buyer is planning to use or resell those goods immediately, a court may award consequential damages for the loss of profits from the planned resale.

Example 17.5 Mason contracts to buy six hundred cases of a specialty sports drink from Nathan. Nathan knows that Mason has contracted with Ruthie to resell and ship the sports drink within hours of its receipt. The beverage will then be sold to fans attending the Super Bowl. Nathan fails to deliver the sports drink on time. Mason can recover the consequential damages—the loss of profits from the planned resale to Ruthie—caused by the nondelivery. (If Mason purchases the beverage from another vendor, he can also recover compensatory damages for the difference between the contract price and the market price.)

For the nonbreaching party to recover consequential damages, the breaching party must know (or have reason to know) that special circumstances will cause the nonbreaching party to suffer an additional loss.[5] See this chapter's *Landmark in the Law* feature for a discussion of the nineteenth-century English case that established this rule on consequential damages.

Know This

To avoid the risk of consequential damages, a seller can limit the buyer's remedies via contract.

Punitive Damages Punitive damages generally are not awarded in lawsuits for breach of contract. Because punitive damages are designed to punish the wrongdoer and set an

---

4. *Viola v. J. S. Benson*, 2017 WL 2817404 (Conn.Super.Ct. 2017).
5. UCC 2–715(2).

Exhibit 17–1 Measure of Damages—Breach of Construction Contracts

PARTY IN BREACH	TIME OF BREACH	MEASURE OF DAMAGES
Owner	Before construction has begun	Profits (contract price less cost of materials and labor)
Owner	During construction	Profits plus costs incurred up to time of breach
Owner	After construction is completed	Full contract price, plus interest
Contractor	Before construction has begun	Cost in excess of contract price to complete work
Contractor	Before construction is completed	Generally, all costs incurred by owner to complete

Hadley v. Baxendale (1854)

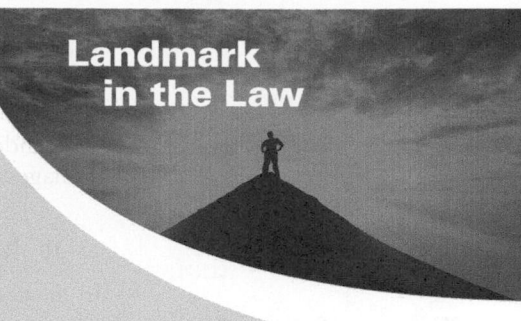

Landmark in the Law

The rule that requires a breaching party to have notice of special ("consequential") circumstances that will result in additional loss to the nonbreaching party before consequential damages can be awarded was first enunciated in *Hadley v. Baxendale*,[a] a landmark case decided in 1854.

Case Background The case involved a broken crankshaft used in a flour mill run by the Hadley family in Gloucester, England. The crankshaft attached to the steam engine in the mill broke, and the shaft had to be sent to a foundry in Greenwich so that a new shaft could be made to fit the engine.

The Hadleys hired Baxendale, a common carrier, to transport the shaft from Gloucester to Greenwich. Baxendale received payment in advance and promised to deliver the shaft the following day. It was not delivered for several days, however. The Hadleys had no extra crankshaft on hand to use, so they had to close the mill during those days. The Hadleys sued Baxendale to recover the profits they lost during that time. Baxendale contended that the loss of profits was "too remote."

———————————
a. 9 Exch. 341, 156 Eng. Rep. 145 (1854).

In the mid-1800s, it was common knowledge that large mills, such as that run by the Hadleys, normally had more than one crankshaft in case the main one broke and had to be repaired. It is against this background that the parties presented their arguments on whether the damages resulting from the loss of profits while the crankshaft was out for repair were "too remote" to be recoverable.

The Issue Before the Court and the Court's Ruling The crucial issue for the court was whether the Hadleys had informed the carrier, Baxendale, of the special circumstances surrounding the crankshaft's repair. Specifically, did Baxendale know at the time of the contract that the mill would have to shut down while the crankshaft was being repaired?

In the court's opinion, the only circumstances communicated by the Hadleys to Baxendale at the time the contract was made were that the item to be transported was a broken crankshaft of a mill and that the Hadleys were the owners and operators of that mill. The court concluded that these circumstances did not reasonably indicate that the mill would have to stop operations if the delivery of the crankshaft was delayed.

Application to Today's World
Today, the rule enunciated by the court in this case still applies. When damages are awarded, compensation is given only for those injuries that the defendant could reasonably have foreseen as a probable result of the usual course of events following a breach. If the alleged injury is outside the usual and foreseeable course of events, the plaintiff must show specifically that the defendant had reason to know the facts and foresee the injury.

This rule applies to contracts in the online environment as well. For example, suppose that an online merchant loses business (and profits) due to a computer system's failure. If the failure was caused by malfunctioning software, the merchant normally may recover the lost profits from the software maker if these consequential damages were foreseeable.

example to deter similar conduct in the future, they have no legitimate place in contract law. A contract is simply a civil relationship between the parties. The law may compensate one party for the loss of the bargain—no more and no less. In a few situations, when a person's actions cause both a breach of contract and a tort, punitive damages may be available.

Nominal Damages When no actual damage or financial loss results from a breach of contract and only a technical injury is involved, the court may award **nominal damages** to the innocent party. Nominal damages awards are often small, such as one dollar, but they do establish that the defendant acted wrongfully. Most lawsuits for nominal damages are brought as a matter of principle under the theory that a breach has occurred and some damages must be imposed regardless of actual loss.

Nominal Damages A small monetary award (often one dollar) granted to a plaintiff when no actual damage was suffered.

Example 17.6 Hernandez contracts to buy potatoes from Stanley at fifty cents a pound. Stanley breaches the contract and does not deliver the potatoes. Meanwhile, the price of potatoes falls. Hernandez is able to buy them in the open market at half the price he agreed to pay Stanley. Hernandez is clearly better off because of Stanley's breach. Thus, if Hernandez sues for breach of contract and wins, the court will likely award only nominal damages. ■

17–1b Mitigation of Damages

Mitigation of Damages The requirement that a plaintiff do whatever is reasonable to minimize the damages caused by the defendant's breach of contract.

In most situations, when a breach of contract occurs, the injured party is held to a duty to mitigate, or reduce, the damages that he or she suffers. Under this doctrine of **mitigation of damages,** the required action depends on the nature of the situation.

Employment Contracts In the majority of states, a person whose employment has been wrongfully terminated has a duty to mitigate damages incurred because of the employer's breach of the employment contract. In other words, a wrongfully terminated employee has a duty to take a similar job if one is available.

If the employee fails to do this, the damages received will be equivalent to the person's former salary less the income he or she would have received in a similar job obtained by reasonable means. The employer has the burden of proving that such a job existed and that the employee could have been hired. Normally, a terminated employee is under no duty to take a job that is not of the same type and rank.

Example 17.7 Susan De La Concha works as a librarian at Brigham Young University. When she is fired, she claims that she has been terminated in retaliation for filing an employment discrimination claim. Suppose that De La Concha succeeds in her employment discrimination claim but that Brigham Young can show that she has failed to take another librarian position when several comparable positions were available. Brigham Young can assert that she has failed to mitigate damages. In that situation, any compensation she is awarded for wrongful termination will be reduced by the amount she *could have obtained* from other employment. ■

Assume that a librarian is wrongfully fired for filing an employment discrimination claim. Is she obligated to mitigate damages by taking another librarian position?

iphotoj/iStock/Getty Images

Rental Agreements Some states require a landlord to use reasonable means to find a new tenant if a tenant abandons the premises and fails to pay rent. If an acceptable tenant becomes available, the landlord is required to lease the premises to this tenant to mitigate the damages recoverable from the former tenant.

The former tenant is still liable for the difference between the amount of the rent under the original lease and the rent received from the new tenant. If the landlord has not taken reasonable steps to find a new tenant, a court will likely reduce any award by the amount of rent the landlord could have received had he or she done so.

17–1c Liquidated Damages versus Penalties

Liquidated Damages An amount, stipulated in a contract, that the parties to the contract believe to be a reasonable estimation of the damages that will occur in the event of a breach.

A **liquidated damages** provision in a contract specifies that a certain dollar amount is to be paid in the event of a *future* default or breach of contract. (*Liquidated* means determined, settled, or fixed.)

Liquidated damages differ from penalties. Although a **penalty** also specifies a certain amount to be paid in the event of a default or breach of contract, it is designed to penalize the breaching party, not to make the innocent party whole. Liquidated damages provisions normally are enforceable. In contrast, if a court finds that a provision calls for a penalty, the agreement as to the amount will not be enforced, and recovery will be limited to actual damages.

Penalty A sum specified in a contract not as a measure of compensation for its breach but rather as a punishment for a default. The agreement as to the amount will not be enforced, and recovery will be limited to the actual damages.

Enforceability To determine whether a particular provision is for liquidated damages or a penalty, the court must answer two questions:

1. At the time the contract was formed, was it apparent that damages would be difficult to estimate in the event of a breach?

2. Was the amount set as damages a reasonable estimate and not excessive?[6]

If the answers to both questions are yes, the provision normally will be enforced. If either answer is no, the provision usually will not be enforced.

In the following *Spotlight Case*, the court had to decide whether a clause in a contract was an enforceable liquidated damages provision or an unenforceable penalty.

---

6. *Restatement (Second) of Contracts*, Section 356(1).

✳ Spotlight on Liquidated Damages: Case 17.2

Kent State University v. Ford

Court of Appeals of Ohio, Eleventh District, Portage County, 2015-Ohio-41, 26 N.E.3d 868 (2015).

Background and Facts Gene Ford signed a five-year contract with Kent State University in Ohio to work as the head coach for the men's basketball team. The contract provided that if Ford quit before the end of the term, he would pay to the school liquidated damages in an amount equal to his salary ($300,000), multiplied by the number of years remaining on the contract. Laing Kennedy, Kent State's athletic director, told Ford that the contract would be renegotiated within a few years.

Four years before the contract expired, however, Ford left Kent State and began to coach for Bradley University at an annual salary of $700,000. Kent State filed a suit in an Ohio state court against Ford, alleging breach of contract. The court enforced the liquidated damages clause and awarded the university $1.2 million. Ford appealed, arguing that the liquidated damages clause in his employment contract was an unenforceable penalty.

If a college coach quits before the end of his contract, can the university recover liquidated damages?

Debby Wong/Shutterstock.com

In the Words of the Court . . .

Diane V. *GRENDELL*, J. [Judge]

* * * *

* * * The parties agreed on an amount of damages, stated in clear terms in Ford's * * * employment contract. * * * *It is apparent that such damages were difficult, if not impossible, to determine.* * * * The departure of a university's head basketball coach may result in a decrease in ticket sales, impact the ability to successfully recruit players and community support for the team, and require a search for both a new coach and additional coaching staff. Many of these damages cannot be easily measured or proven. This is especially true given the nature of how such factors may change over the course of different coaches' tenures with a sports program or team. [Emphasis added.]

* * * *

* * * Kennedy's statements to Ford that the contract would be renegotiated within a few years made it clear that Kent State desired Ford to have long-term employment, which was necessary to establish the stability in the program that would benefit recruitment, retention of assistant coaching staff, and community participation and involvement. The breach of the contract impacted all of these areas.

* * * *

Regarding the alleged unreasonableness of the damages, * * * based on the record, we find that the damages were reasonable. * * * Finding a coach of a similar skill and experience level as Ford, which was gained based partially on the investment of Kent State in his development, would have an increased cost. This is evident from the fact that Ford was able to more than double his yearly salary when hired by Bradley University. The salary Ford earned at Bradley shows the loss of market value in coaching experienced by Kent State, $400,000 per year, for four years. Although this may not have been known at the time the contract was executed, it could have been anticipated, and was presumably why Kent State wanted to renegotiate the contract * * * . There was also an asserted decrease in ticket sales, costs associated with the trips for the coaching search, and additional potential sums that may be expended.

(Continues)

* * * *

As discussed extensively above, there was justification for seeking liquidated damages to compensate for Kent State's losses, and, thus, there was a valid compensatory purpose for including the clause. * * * Given all of the circumstances and facts in this case, and the consideration of the factors above, we cannot find that the liquidated damages clause was a penalty. [Emphasis added.]

Decision and Remedy A state intermediate appellate court affirmed the lower court's award. At the time Ford's contract was entered into, ascertaining the damages resulting from a breach was "difficult, if not impossible." The court found, "based on the record, . . . that the damages were reasonable." Thus, the clause was not a penalty—it had "a valid compensatory purpose."

Critical Thinking

• **Cultural** *How does a college basketball team's record of wins and losses, and its ranking in its conference, support the court's decision in this case?*

Common Uses of Liquidated Damages Provisions Liquidated damages provisions are frequently used in construction contracts. For instance, a provision requiring a construction contractor to pay $300 for every day he or she is late in completing the project is a liquidated damages provision. Such provisions are also common in contracts for the sale of goods[7] and in certain loan contracts (see the example discussed in this chapter's *Business Law Analysis*). In addition, contracts with entertainers and professional athletes often include liquidated damages provisions.

---

7. Section 2–718(1) of the UCC specifically authorizes the use of liquidated damages provisions.

Enforceability of Liquidated Damages Provisions

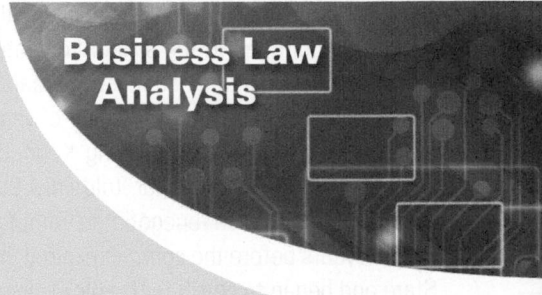

Business Law Analysis

Planned Pethood Plus, Inc. (PPP), is a veterinarian-owned clinic. It borrowed $389,000 from KeyBank at an interest rate of 9.3 percent per year for ten years. The loan had a "prepayment penalty" clause that clearly stated that if the loan was repaid early, a specific formula would be used to assess a lump-sum payment to extinguish the obligation. The sooner the loan was paid off, the higher the prepayment penalty.

After a year, the veterinarians decided to pay off the loan. KeyBank invoked a prepayment penalty of $40,525.92, which was equal to 10.7 percent of the balance due. PPP sued, contending that the prepayment requirement was unenforceable because it was a penalty. The bank countered that the amount was not a penalty but liquidated damages and that the sum was reasonable. Was the loan's prepayment penalty clause enforceable?

Analysis: A liquidated damages provision in a contract specifies a certain amount of money to be paid in the event of a future default or breach of contract. In contrast, a penalty provision specifies a certain amount to be paid in the event of a default or breach of contract and is designed to penalize the breaching party. Liquidated damages provisions normally are enforceable, but penalty provisions are not.

To determine whether a provision is for liquidated damages or a penalty, ask (1) when the contract was formed, were the potential damages that would be incurred on its breach difficult to estimate, and (2) was the amount set as damages a reasonable estimate of those potential damages? If both answers are yes, the provision is for liquidated damages. If either answer is no, the provision is a penalty.

Result and Reasoning: PPP's loan included a prepayment penalty clause common to many loan agreements. If PPP decided to repay its loan early, an amount would be added to the balance due according to a specific formula. When the contract was formed, the potential loss to the lender on the loan's prepayment was difficult to estimate because the time of the prepayment could not be reasonably foreseen. The formula provided a reasonable estimate of that loss.

In other words, the answers to both questions in the Analysis section are yes. Thus, the provision in PPP's loan was for liquidated damages and enforceable.

17–2 Equitable Remedies

Sometimes, damages are an inadequate remedy for a breach of contract. In these situations, the nonbreaching party may ask the court for an equitable remedy. Equitable remedies include rescission and restitution, specific performance, and reformation.

17–2a Rescission and Restitution

As previously discussed, rescission is essentially an action to undo, or cancel, a contract—to return nonbreaching parties to the positions that they occupied prior to the transaction.[8] When fraud, mistake, duress, undue influence, lack of capacity, or failure of consideration is present, rescission is available. Rescission may also be available by statute.[9] The failure of one party to perform under a contract entitles the other party to rescind the contract. The rescinding party must give prompt notice to the breaching party.

Rescission of a contract on the basis of a breach is appropriate where the breach is found to be material and willful. A party seeking rescission must also show that the contracting parties can be restored to the *status quo*. In the following case, a landlord overcharged its tenant certain fees and did not explain how the amount was calculated, as the lease required. The question was whether these circumstances entitled the tenant to rescind the lease.

Was a prepayment penalty clause in a loan from KeyBank to a local veterinarian clinic considered an enforceable liquidated damages provision? Why or why not?

---

8. The rescission discussed here refers to *unilateral* rescission, in which only one party wants to undo the contract. In *mutual* rescission, both parties agree to undo the contract. Mutual rescission discharges the contract, whereas unilateral rescission is generally available as a remedy for breach of contract.

9. Many states have laws that allow individuals who enter into "home solicitation contracts" to rescind these contracts within three business days for any reason. See, for example, California Civil Code Section 1689.5.

■ Case 17.3

Cipriano Square Plaza Corp. v. Munawar

Maryland Court of Special Appeals, __ Md.App. __, 2018 WL 1040020 (2018).

Background and Facts Haseeb and Razia Munawar entered into a lease to rent space in a shopping center in Greenbelt, Maryland, owned by Cipriano Square Plaza Corporation. The lease obligated the Munawars to pay a pro rata (proportionate) share of the real estate taxes. The new tenants were assessed with property tax charges shortly after occupying the leased space. Asserting that the amount was excessive, they asked Cipriano for an explanation.

The lease required the landlord to provide certain documents (such as tax bills) and explain how the tenants' share was calculated. After repeated requests, the Munawars received a partial reduction but no explanation. They filed a suit in a Maryland state court against Cipriano, alleging a breach of the lease. The court rescinded the deal. Cipriano appealed.

In the Words of the Court

Opinion by *KEHOE*, J. [Judge]

* * * *

The trial court found that Cipriano had breached its duties to the Munawars regarding payment of their pro rata share of real

(Continues)

estate taxes, that the breach was material, * * * and that rescission would restore the parties to their positions before the lease agreement was executed.

* * * *

* * * The trial court based its finding of breach on the initial overcharges and Cipriano's refusal to explain the basis by which it calculated the Munawars' share of the taxes * * * . Cipriano had ample opportunities to explain how its determination of the Munawars' portion was fair and reasonable but it declined to do so. For these reasons, we conclude that the trial court's finding that Cipriano breached the lease agreement was supported by clear and convincing evidence.

* * * "Willful" means voluntary and intentional * * * [according to *Black's Law Dictionary* (10th Ed.)]. There was evidence before the court that Cipriano's alleged overbilling and refusal to provide information to the Munawars was both voluntary and intentional, and Cipriano doesn't argue otherwise on appeal.

* * * *A breach is material if it leaves the subject of the contract substantially different from what was contracted.* The unrebutted evidence was that Cipriano was charging the Munawars about 30 percent more than [their pro rata share]. A lease agreement that calls for a tenant to pay 130 percent of its pro rata share of taxes assessed to a shopping center is substantially different from a lease that requires the tenant to pay its pro rata share. The court's finding as to materiality was not clearly erroneous. [Emphasis added.]

* * * *

Finally, Cipriano argues that the trial court erred in finding that rescission would restore the parties to the status quo prior to the contract. Cipriano asserts that rescission will leave it "without the benefit of a ten-year commercial lease" that it had with the Munawars. Cipriano misapprehends the purpose of [this] requirement. It is not to give the breaching party the benefit of the bargain that it would have had but for its breach. Instead, *the purpose * * * is to return the parties to their positions before they entered into the contract.* Before the lease agreement was signed, Cipriano had an empty storefront. As a result of the judgment rescinding the lease, Cipriano was free to lease the space to someone else. [Emphasis added.]

Decision and Remedy A state intermediate appellate court affirmed the judgment of the trial court. The landlord had materially breached the lease, and its rescission was an appropriate remedy.

Critical Thinking

• **Legal Environment** *Cipriano designated Nicholas Vassello to testify on its behalf. Vassello was unable to explain how the Munawars' share of the property taxes was calculated. What effect might this testimony have had on the trial court's decision?*

• **Economic** *The lease provided that any monetary judgment in favor of the tenant could be recovered only on the landlord's sale of the shopping center. As a practical matter, how might this provision have affected the result in the* Cipriano *case?*

Restitution An equitable remedy under which a person is restored to his or her original position prior to loss or injury, or placed in the position he or she would have been in had the breach not occurred.

Restitution To rescind a contract, both parties generally must make **restitution** to each other by returning goods, property, or funds previously conveyed.[10] If the property or goods can be returned, they must be. If the property or goods have been consumed, restitution must be made in an equivalent dollar amount. Essentially, restitution involves the recapture of a benefit conferred on the defendant that has unjustly enriched her or him.

Example 17.8 Katie contracts with Mikhail to design a house for her. Katie pays Mikhail $9,000 and agrees to make two more payments of $9,000 (for a total of $27,000) as the design progresses. The next day, Mikhail calls Katie and tells her that he has taken a position with a large architectural firm in another state and cannot design the house. Katie decides to hire another architect that afternoon. Katie can obtain restitution of the $9,000. ■

Restitution Is Not Limited to Rescission Cases Restitution may be required when a contract is rescinded, but the right to restitution is not limited to rescission cases. Because an award of restitution basically returns something to its rightful owner, a party can seek restitution in actions for breach of contract, tort actions, and other types of actions.

---

10. *Restatement (Second) of Contracts,* Section 370.

Restitution can be obtained when funds or property has been transferred by mistake or because of fraud or incapacity. Similarly, restitution might be available when there has been misconduct by a party with a special relationship with the other party. Even in criminal cases, a court can order restitution of funds or property obtained through embezzlement, conversion, theft, or copyright infringement.

Case Example 17.9 Clara Lee contracted to purchase Rosalina Robles's dental practice in Chicago, Illinois, for $267,000. Nearly half of the practice's market value was attributed to the business's good reputation. After Lee took over the practice, however, *Chicago Magazine* and other local media revealed that one of the dentists at Robles's practice had treated underage prostitutes in the offices after hours. Federal authorities were investigating that dentist for this and other misconduct.

Lee sued Robles for fraud, alleging that she had deliberately withheld information about the dentist and the investigation. An Illinois state court awarded rescission, and the holding was affirmed on appeal. The appellate court reasoned that the parties' agreement for the sale of the dental practice required Robles to disclose "any material information." The duty to disclose included actions by a "governmental agency that materially alters the desirability or economic potential of the assets."[11]

17–2b Specific Performance

The equitable remedy of **specific performance** calls for the performance of the act promised in the contract. This remedy is attractive to a nonbreaching party because it provides the exact bargain promised in the contract. It also avoids some of the problems inherent in a suit for monetary damages, such as collecting a judgment and arranging another contract. Moreover, the actual performance may be more valuable (to the promisee) than the monetary damages.

Normally, however, specific performance will not be granted unless the party's legal remedy (monetary damages) is inadequate.[12] For this reason, contracts for the sale of goods rarely qualify for specific performance. Monetary damages ordinarily are adequate in sales contracts because substantially identical goods can be bought or sold in the market. Only if the goods are unique will a court grant specific performance. For instance, paintings, sculptures, and rare books and coins are often unique, and monetary damages will not enable a buyer to obtain substantially identical substitutes in the market.

Sale of Land A court may grant specific performance to a buyer in an action for a breach of contract involving the sale of land. In this situation, the legal remedy of monetary damages may not compensate the buyer adequately because every parcel of land is unique. The same land in the same location obviously cannot be obtained elsewhere. Only when specific performance is unavailable (such as when the seller has sold the property to someone else) will damages be awarded instead.

Case Example 17.10 Developer Charles Ghidorzi formed Crabtree Ridge, LLC, for the sole purpose of purchasing twenty-three acres of vacant land from Cohan Lipp, LLC. Crabtree signed a contract agreeing to pay $3.1 million for the land, which would be developed and paid for in three phases. When an environmental survey showed that the land might contain some wetlands that could not be developed, Crabtree backed out of the deal. Lipp sued Crabtree for breach of contract, seeking specific performance. The court held that Lipp was entitled to specific performance of the land-sale contract.[13]

Know This

Restitution offers several advantages over traditional damages. First, restitution may be available in situations when damages cannot be proved or are difficult to prove. Second, restitution can be used to recover specific property. Third, restitution sometimes results in a greater overall award.

What determines the value of the reputation of a dental office?

Learning Objective 2

When do courts grant specific performance as a remedy?

Specific Performance An equitable remedy in which a court orders the parties to perform as promised in the contract. This remedy normally is granted only when the legal remedy (monetary damages) is inadequate.

---

11. *Clara Wonjung Lee, DDS, Ltd. v. Robles*, 2014 WL 976776 (Ill.App. 2014). *DDS* stands for Doctor of Dental Surgery.
12. *Restatement (Second) of Contracts*, Section 359.
13. *Cohan Lipp, LLC v. Crabtree Ridge, LLC*, 358 Wis.2d 711, 856 N.W.2d 346 (2014).

Contracts for Personal Services Contracts for personal services require one party to work personally for another party. Courts normally refuse to grant specific performance of personal-service contracts. One reason is that ordering a party to perform personal services against his or her will would amount to a type of involuntary servitude.[14]

Moreover, the courts do not want to monitor contracts for personal services, which usually require the exercise of personal judgment or talent. **Example 17.11** Nicole contracts with a surgeon to remove a tumor on her brain. If he refuses to perform the surgery, the court will not compel (nor would Nicole want) him to perform. A court cannot ensure meaningful performance in such a situation.[15]

If a contract is not deemed personal, the remedy at law of monetary damages may be adequate if a substantially identical service (for instance, lawn mowing) is available from other persons.

17–2c Reformation

Reformation is an equitable remedy used when the parties have *imperfectly* expressed their agreement in writing. Reformation allows a court to rewrite the contract to reflect the parties' true intentions.

Fraud or Mutual Mistake Courts order reformation most often when fraud or mutual mistake is present. **Example 17.12** If Carson contracts to buy a forklift from Yoshie but the written contract refers to a crane, a mutual mistake has occurred. Accordingly, a court could reform the contract so that the writing conforms to the parties' original intention as to which piece of equipment is being sold.

What happens when a contract mistakenly specifies a crane instead of a forklift?

Incorrect Written Statement of the Parties' Oral Agreement A court will also reform a contract when two parties enter into a binding oral contract but later make an error when they attempt to put the terms into writing. Usually, the court will allow into evidence the correct terms of the oral contract, thereby reforming the written contract.

Covenants Not to Compete Courts also may reform contracts involving written covenants not to compete, or restrictive covenants. Such covenants are often included in contracts for the sale of ongoing businesses and in employment contracts. The agreements restrict the area and time in which one party can directly compete with the other party.

If a covenant not to compete is for a valid and legitimate purpose, but the area or time restraints are unreasonable, some courts will reform the restraints by making them reasonable and will then enforce the entire contract as reformed. Other courts will throw out the entire restrictive covenant as illegal. Thus, when businesspersons create restrictive covenants, they must make sure that the restrictions imposed are reasonable.

Case Example 17.13 Cardiac Study Center, Inc., a medical practice group, hired Dr. Robert Emerick. Later, Emerick became a shareholder of Cardiac and signed an agreement that included a covenant not to compete. The covenant stated that a physician who left the group promised not to practice competitively in the surrounding area for a period of five years. After Cardiac began receiving complaints from patients and other physicians about Emerick, it terminated his employment.

Emerick sued Cardiac, claiming that the covenant not to compete that he had signed was unreasonable and should be declared illegal. Ultimately, a state appellate court reformed the geographic and temporal restraints, and held that the covenant was both reasonable and

---

14. Involuntary servitude, or slavery, is contrary to the public policy expressed in the Thirteenth Amendment to the U.S. Constitution.
15. Similarly, courts often refuse to order specific performance of construction contracts because courts are not set up to operate as construction supervisors or engineers.

Exhibit 17–2 Remedies for Breach of Contract

enforceable. Cardiac had a legitimate interest in protecting its existing client base and prohibiting Emerick from taking its clients.[16]

Exhibit 17–2 graphically presents the remedies that are available to the nonbreaching party.

17–3 Recovery Based on Quasi Contract

In some situations, when no actual contract exists, a court may step in to prevent one party from being unjustly enriched at the expense of another party. As previously discussed, *quasi contract* is a legal theory under which an obligation is imposed in the absence of an agreement.

The legal obligation arises because the law considers that the party accepting the benefits has made an implied promise to pay for them. Generally, when one party has conferred a benefit on another party, justice requires that the party receiving the benefit pay the reasonable value for it. The party conferring the benefit can recover in *quantum meruit*, which means "as much as he or she deserves."

17–3a When Quasi Contract Is Used

Quasi contract allows a court to act as if a contract exists when there is no actual contract or agreement between the parties. Therefore, if the parties have entered into a contract concerning the matter in controversy, a court normally will not impose a quasi contract. A court can also use the doctrine when the parties entered into a contract, but it is unenforceable for some reason.

Quasi-contractual recovery is often granted when one party has partially performed under a contract that is unenforceable. Quasi contracts provide an alternative to suing for damages and allow the party to recover the reasonable value of the partial performance. Depending on the case, the amount of the recovery may be measured either by the benefit received or by the detriment suffered.

Example 17.14 Ericson contracts to build two oil derricks for Petro Industries. The derricks are to be built over a period of three years, but the parties do not create a written contract. Therefore, the writing requirement will bar the enforcement of the contract.[17] After Ericson completes one derrick, Petro Industries informs him that it will not pay for the derrick. Ericson can sue Petro Industries under the theory of quasi contract.

Learning Objective 3
What remedy is available if a court imposes a quasi contract?

Know This
The function of a quasi contract is to impose a legal obligation on a party who made no actual promise.

---

16. *Emerick v. Cardiac Study Center, Inc.*, 189 Wash.App. 711, 357 P.3d 696 (2015).
17. Contracts that by their terms cannot be performed within one year from the day after the date of contract formation must be in writing to be enforceable under the Statute of Frauds.

Assume that it takes several years to build two oil derricks, but no written contract exists. If one is built, does the purchaser have to pay for it?

17–3b The Requirements of Quasi Contract

To recover on a quasi contract theory, the party seeking recovery must show the following:

1. The party conferred a benefit on the other party.
2. The party conferred the benefit with the reasonable expectation of being paid.
3. The party did not act as a volunteer in conferring the benefit.
4. The party receiving the benefit would be unjustly enriched if allowed to retain the benefit without paying for it.

Applying these requirements to *Example 17.14*, Ericson can sue in quasi contract because all of the conditions for quasi-contractual recovery have been fulfilled. Ericson conferred a benefit on Petro Industries by building the oil derrick. Ericson built the derrick with the reasonable expectation of being paid. He did not intend to act as a volunteer. Petro Industries would be unjustly enriched if it was allowed to keep the derrick without paying Ericson for the work. Therefore, Ericson should be able to recover in *quantum meruit* the reasonable value of the oil derrick that was built, which is ordinarily equal to the fair market value.

17–4 Contract Provisions Limiting Remedies

A contract may include provisions stating that no damages can be recovered for certain types of breaches or that damages will be limited to a maximum amount. A contract may also provide that the only remedy for breach is replacement, repair, or refund of the purchase price. In addition, a contract may provide that one party can seek injunctive relief if the other party breaches the contract. Provisions stating that no damages can be recovered are called *exculpatory clauses*. Provisions that affect the availability of certain remedies are called *limitation-of-liability clauses*.

Ethical Issue

Can contracts for mixed martial arts fighters limit a fighter's right to stop fighting? If you are a mixed martial arts champion, the highest-profile league to work for is the Ultimate Fighting Championship, or UFC. But a contract with UFC's parent company, Zuffa, LLC, includes numerous restrictions on your behavior.

The UFC's exclusivity clause, for instance, prevents you from competing in other mixed martial arts leagues. Another clause states that if you refuse a fight—or are injured or disabled—Zuffa can choose to extend the term of your contract. The term may be extended for any period when a fighter is unable or unwilling to compete or train for any reason. Zuffa can even retain the rights to a fighter who wants to retire from mixed martial arts.

You probably also signed an agreement that has a "champions clause." That means that if you become a champion, your contract with the UFC is automatically extended. If you get really famous, you do not even have rights to your likeness. You have signed those away to the UFC. So if a video game is based on your likeness, the UFC obtains the profits, and you do not. Therefore, you will have trouble negotiating with sponsors outside of the UFC, because you really do not own much of yourself to "sell."

A group of current and former mixed martial arts fighters have filed a lawsuit against Zuffa. They claim that these contract limitations are fundamentally unfair. Because the contracts prevent fighters from working with other promoters, profiting from individual marketing deals, and signing with outside sponsors, the suit alleges that the UFC is violating antitrust laws. Litigation is ongoing.[18]

---

18. See *Cung Le v. Zuffa, LLC*, 2017 WL 2803171 (D.Nev. 2017); and *Le v. Zuffa, LLC*, 216 F.Supp.3d 1154 (D.Nev. 2016).

17–4a Sales Contracts

The Uniform Commercial Code (UCC) provides that remedies can be limited in a contract for the sale of goods. We will examine the UCC provisions on limitation-of-liability clauses again in the context of the remedies available on the breach of a contract for the sale or lease of goods.[19]

17–4b Enforceability of Limitation-of-Liability Clauses

Whether a limitation-of-liability clause in a contract will be enforced depends on the type of breach that is excused by the provision. Clauses that normally will not be enforced include provisions excluding liability for fraudulent or intentional injury or for illegal acts or other violations of law. Clauses excluding liability for negligence may be enforced in certain situations, however. When an exculpatory clause for negligence is contained in a contract made between parties who have roughly equal bargaining positions, the clause usually will be enforced.

Case Example 17.15 2010-1 SFG Venture, LLC, was the main lender on a commercial real estate loan for $15 million to fund construction of a hotel in Wisconsin. Lee Bank & Trust Co. purchased a 3.36 percent interest in the loan. Lee Bank signed a contract with SFG that included a clause limiting SFG's liability "except in the case of gross negligence or willful misconduct."

When the borrower made payments on the loan, SFG remitted 3.36 percent of each payment to Lee Bank. Eventually, however, the borrower stopped making payments, and litigation followed. Lee Bank sued SFG, which argued that it was protected by the contract provisions limiting its liability. The lower court refused to enforce the limitation-of-liability clause, but a state appellate court reversed. The court held that the clause was enforceable. It was sufficiently prominent in the contract and represented a reasonable allocation of risks in an arms-length business transaction.[20]

19. UCC 2–719.
20. *2010-1 SFG Venture, LLC v. Lee Bank & Trust Co.*, 332 Ga.App. 894, 775 S.E.2d 243 (2015).

Learning Objective 4
What is a limitation-of-liability clause, and when will courts enforce it?

Why did a court enforce the limitation-of-liability clause in a dispute over a hotel construction contract?

Practice and Review

Kyle Bruno enters into a contract with X Entertainment to be a stuntman in a movie. Bruno is widely known as the best motorcycle stuntman in the business, and the movie, *Xtreme Riders*, has numerous scenes involving high-speed freestyle street-bike stunts. Filming is set to begin August 1 and end by December 1 so that the film can be released the following summer. Both parties to the contract have stipulated that the filming must end on time in order to capture the profits from the summer movie market.

The contract states that Bruno will be paid 10 percent of the net proceeds from the movie for his stunts. The contract also includes a liquidated damages provision, which specifies that if Bruno breaches the contract, he will owe X Entertainment $1 million. In addition, the contract includes a

(Continues)

limitation-ofliability clause stating that if Bruno is injured during filming, X Entertainment's liability is limited to nominal damages. Using the information presented in the chapter, answer the following questions.

1. One day, while Bruno is preparing for a difficult stunt, he gets into an argument with the director and refuses to perform any stunts. Can X Entertainment seek specific performance of the contract? Why or why not?
2. Suppose that while performing a high-speed wheelie on a motorcycle, Bruno is injured by an intentionally reckless act of an X Entertainment employee. Will a court be likely to enforce the limitation-of-liability clause? Why or why not?
3. What factors would a court consider to determine if the $1 million liquidated damages clause is valid or is a penalty?
4. Suppose that there was no liquidated damages clause (or the court refused to enforce it) and X Entertainment breached the contract. The breach caused the release of the film to be delayed by many months. Could Bruno seek consequential (special) damages for lost profits from the summer movie market in that situation? Explain.

Debate This

Courts should always uphold limitation-of-liability clauses, whether or not the two parties to the contract had equal bargaining power.

Key Terms

Chapter Summary: Breach and Remedies

Damages	In contract law, the legal remedy designed to compensate the nonbreaching party for the loss of the bargain. The nonbreaching party frequently has a duty to *mitigate* (lessen or reduce) the damages suffered. There are four broad categories of damages. In addition, a contract may contain a provision for liquidated damages.

1. *Compensatory damages*—Damages that compensate the nonbreaching party for injuries actually sustained and proved to have arisen directly from the loss of the bargain resulting from the breach of contract.
   a. In breached contracts for the sale of goods, the usual measure of compensatory damages is the difference between the contract price and the market price.
   b. In a seller's breach of a contract for the sale of land, the measure of damages is ordinarily specific performance. For a buyer's breach, the measure of damages is typically the same as in contracts for the sale of goods.
   c. In breached construction contracts, the measure of damages depends on which party breaches and at what stage of construction the breach occurs.

2. *Consequential damages*—Foreseeable damages that result from special circumstances beyond the contract itself (also called *special damages*). The damages flow only from the consequences of a breach. For a party to recover consequential damages, the breaching party must have known at the time the contract was formed that special circumstances existed that would cause the nonbreaching party to incur additional loss on breach of the contract.
3. *Punitive damages*—Damages awarded to punish the breaching party. Usually not awarded in an action for breach of contract unless a tort is involved.
4. *Nominal damages*—Damages small in amount (such as one dollar) that are awarded when a breach has occurred but no actual injury has been suffered. Awarded only to establish that the defendant acted wrongfully.
5. *Liquidated damages*—Damages specified in a contract as the amount to be paid to the nonbreaching party in the event the contract is breached. Clauses providing for liquidated damages are enforced if the damages were difficult to estimate at the time the contract was formed and if the amount stipulated is reasonable. If the amount is construed to be a penalty, the clause will not be enforced.

| **Equitable Remedies** | 1. *Rescission*—A remedy whereby a contract is canceled and the parties are restored to the original positions that they occupied prior to the transaction. Available when fraud, mistake, duress, undue influence, lack of capacity, or failure of consideration is present. The rescinding party must give prompt notice of the rescission to the breaching party.
2. *Restitution*—When a contract is rescinded, both parties must make restitution to each other by returning the goods, property, or funds previously conveyed. Restitution prevents the unjust enrichment of the parties.
3. *Specific performance*—An equitable remedy calling for the performance of the act promised in the contract. This remedy is available only in special situations—such as those involving contracts for the sale of unique goods or land—when monetary damages would be an inadequate remedy. Specific performance is not available as a remedy for breached contracts for personal services.
4. *Reformation*—An equitable remedy allowing a contract to be "reformed," or rewritten, to reflect the parties' true intentions. Available when an agreement is imperfectly expressed in writing. |
|---|---|
| **Recovery Based on Quasi Contract** | An equitable theory imposed by the courts to obtain justice and prevent unjust enrichment in a situation in which no enforceable contract exists. The party seeking recovery must show the following:
1. A benefit was conferred on the other party.
2. The party conferring the benefit did so with the expectation of being paid.
3. The party conferring the benefit did not volunteer the benefit.
4. The party receiving the benefit would be unjustly enriched if allowed to retain the benefit without paying for it. |
| **Contract Provisions Limiting Remedies** | A contract may provide that no damages (or only a limited amount of damages) can be recovered in the event the contract is breached. Under the Uniform Commercial Code, remedies may be limited in contracts for the sale of goods. Clauses excluding liability for fraudulent or intentional injury or for illegal acts cannot be enforced. Clauses excluding liability for negligence may be enforced if both parties hold roughly equal bargaining power. |

Issue Spotters

1. Greg contracts to build a storage shed for Haney. Haney pays Greg in advance, but Greg completes only half the work. Haney pays Ipswich $500 to finish the shed. If Haney sues Greg, what would be the measure of recovery? (See *Damages*.)

2. Lyle contracts to sell his ranch to Marley, who is to take possession on June 1. Lyle delays the transfer until August 1. Marley incurs expenses in providing for cattle that he bought for the ranch. When they made the contract, Lyle had no reason to know of the cattle. Is Lyle liable for Marley's expenses in providing for the cattle? Why or why not? (See *Damages*.)

—**Check your answers to the *Issue Spotters* against the answers provided in Appendix D at the end of this text.**

Business Scenarios and Case Problems

17–1. Liquidated Damages. Carnack contracts to sell his house and lot to Willard for $100,000. The terms of the contract call for Willard to make a deposit of 10 percent of the purchase price as a down payment. The terms further stipulate that if the buyer breaches the contract, Carnack will retain the deposit as liquidated damages. Willard makes the deposit, but because her expected financing of the $90,000 balance falls through, she breaches the contract. Two weeks later, Carnack sells the house and lot to Balkova for $105,000. Willard demands her $10,000 back, but Carnack refuses, claiming that Willard's breach and the contract terms entitle him to keep the deposit. Discuss who is correct. (See *Damages*.)

17–2. Measure of Damages. Before buying a house, Dean and Donna Testa hired Ground Systems, Inc. (GSI), to inspect the sewage and water disposal system. GSI reported a split system with a watertight septic tank, a wastewater tank, a distribution box, and a leach field. The Testas bought the house. Later, Dean saw that the system was not as GSI described—there was no distribution box or leach field, and there was only one tank, which was not watertight. The Testas arranged for the installation of a new system and sold the house. Assuming that GSI is liable for breach of contract, what is the measure of damages? [*Testa v. Ground Systems, Inc.*, 206 N.J. 330, 20 A.3d 435 (App. Div. 2011)] (See *Damages*.)

17–3. Consequential Damages. After submitting the high bid at a foreclosure sale, David Simard entered into a contract to purchase real property in Maryland for $192,000. Simard defaulted (failed to pay) on the contract, so a state court ordered the property to be resold at Simard's expense, as required by state law. The property was then resold for $163,000, but the second purchaser also defaulted on his contract. The court then ordered a second resale, resulting in a final price of $130,000. Assuming that Simard is liable for consequential damages, what is the extent of his liability? Is he liable for losses and expenses related to the first resale? If so, is he also liable for losses and expenses related to the second resale? Why or why not? [*Burson v. Simard*, 35 A.3d 1154 (Md. 2012)] (See *Damages*.)

17–4. Liquidated Damages. Cuesport Properties, LLC, sold a condominium in Anne Arundel County, Maryland, to Critical Developments, LLC. As part of the sale, Cuesport agreed to build a wall between Critical Developments' unit and an adjacent unit within thirty days of closing. If Cuesport failed to do so, it was to pay $126 per day until completion. This was an estimate of the amount of rent that Critical Developments would lose until the wall was finished and the unit could be rented. Actual damages were otherwise difficult to estimate at the time

of the contract. The wall was built on time, but without a county permit, and it did not comply with the county building code. Critical Developments did not modify the wall to comply with the code until 260 days after the date of the contract deadline for completion of the wall. Does Cuesport have to pay Critical Developments $126 for each of the 260 days? Explain. [*Cuesport Properties, LLC v. Critical Developments, LLC*, 209 Md.App. 607, 61 A.3d 91 (2013)] (See *Damages*.)

17–5. Business Case Problem with Sample Answer— Limitation-of-Liability Clauses. Mia Eriksson was a seventeen-year-old competitor in horseback-riding events. Her riding coach was Kristi Nunnink. Eriksson signed an agreement that released Nunnink from all liability except for damages caused by Nunnink's "direct, willful and wanton negligence." During an event at Galway Downs in Temecula, California, Eriksson's horse struck a hurdle. She fell from the horse and the horse fell on her, causing her death. Her parents, Karan and Stan Eriksson, filed a suit in a California state court against Nunnink for wrongful death. Is the limitation-of-liability agreement that Eriksson signed likely to be enforced in her parents' case? If so, how would it affect their claim? Explain. [*Eriksson v. Nunnink*, 233 Cal.App.4th 708, 183 Cal.Rptr.3d 234 (4 Dist. 2015)] (See *Contract Provisions Limiting Remedies*.)

—For a sample answer to Problem 17–5, go to Appendix E at the end of this text.

17–6. Damages. Robert Morris was a licensed insurance agent working for his father's independent insurance agency when he contacted Farmers Insurance Exchange in Alabama about becoming a Farmers agent. According to Farmers' company policy, Morris was an unsuitable candidate due to his relationship with his father's agency. But no Farmers representative told Morris of this policy, and none of the documents that he signed expressed it. Farmers trained Morris and appointed him its agent. About three years later, however, Farmers terminated the appointment for "a conflict of interest because his father was in the insurance business." Morris filed a suit in an Alabama state court against Farmers, claiming that he had been fraudulently induced to leave his father's agency to work for Farmers. If Morris was successful, what type of damages was he most likely awarded? What was the measure of damages? Discuss. [*Farmers Insurance Exchange v. Morris*, 228 So.3d 971 (Ala. 2016)] (See *Damages*.)

17–7. Reformation. Dr. John Holm signed a two-year employment agreement with Gateway Anesthesia Associates PLLC. During negotiations for the agreement, Gateway's president Dr. Jon Nottingham told Holm that on completion of the contract he would become a partner in the firm, and during the term he would be paid "like a partner." The written agreement did not reflect this promise—the contract read that Holm would be paid based on "net collections" for his services and did not state that at the end of the term he would become a partner. Later, Gateway told Holm that it did not intend to make him a partner. Holm filed a complaint in an Arizona state court against Gateway, alleging breach. Before the trial, Holm filed a motion to reform the contract to express what he had been told. Nottingham did not dispute Holm's account. What is the basis for the reformation of a contract? Is it appropriate in this case? Why or why not? [*Holm v. Gateway Anesthesia Associates PLLC*, 2018 WL 770503 (Ariz. Div. 1 2018)] (See *Equitable Remedies*.)

17–8. A Question of Ethics—The IDDR Approach and

Damages. *Dr. John Braun conceived a cutting-edge device to treat adolescent scoliosis, a severe deformity of the spine. As consideration for the assignment* of his intellectual property in the invention, Medtronic Sofamor Danek, Inc., a medical device manufacturer, offered Braun a higher-than-typical royalty and upfront payment. Medtronic also promised to fund expensive human trials for the device to obtain Food and Drug Administration (FDA) approval. But Medtronic never applied for permission to conduct human clinical studies. Finally, frustrated with the lack of performance on the contract, Braun filed a suit in a federal district court against Medtronic, seeking damages for breach. [Braun v. Medtronic Sofamor Danek, Inc., 719 Fed.Appx. 782 (10th Cir. 2017)] (See Damages.)*

1. Why would Medtronic make expensive promises and fail to perform? Is this ethical? Discuss, using the IDDR approach.

2. What would be the measure of damages that Braun seeks? Do the circumstances warrant an award of punitive damages? Explain.

Critical Thinking and Writing Assignments

17–9. Critical Legal Thinking. Review the discussion of the doctrine of mitigation of damages in this chapter. What are some of the advantages and disadvantages of this doctrine? (See *Damages*.)

17–10. Time-Limited Group Assignment—Remedies. Frances Morelli agreed to sell Judith Bucklin a house in Rhode Island for $177,000. The sale was supposed to be closed by September 1. The contract included a provision that "if Seller is unable to convey good, clear, insurable, and marketable title, Buyer shall have the option to (a) accept such title as Seller is able to convey without reduction of the Purchase Price, or (b) cancel this Agreement and receive a return of all Deposits."

An examination of the public records revealed that the house did not have marketable title. Bucklin offered Morelli additional time to resolve the problem, and the closing did not occur as scheduled. Morelli decided that "the deal was over" and offered to return the deposit. Bucklin refused and, in mid-October, decided to exercise her option to accept the house without marketable title. She notified Morelli, who did not respond. She then filed a lawsuit against Morelli in a state court. (See *Equitable Remedies*.)

1. One group will discuss whether Morelli has breached the contract and will decide in whose favor the court should rule.

2. A second group will assume that Morelli did breach the contract and will determine what the appropriate remedy is in this situation.

3. A third group will list some possible reasons why Bucklin wanted to go through with the transaction even when faced with not receiving marketable title.

18 | Third Party Rights

Learning Objectives

The four Learning Objectives *below are designed to help improve your understanding of the chapter. After reading this chapter, you should be able to answer the following questions:*

1. What is an assignment?

2. What rights can be assigned despite a contract clause expressly prohibiting assignment?

3. In what situations is the delegation of duties prohibited?

4. What factors indicate that a third party beneficiary is an intended beneficiary?

Privity of Contract The relationship that exists between the promisor and the promisee of a contract.

"The laws of a state change with the changing times."

Aeschylus
525–456 B.C.E.
(Greek dramatist)

Once it has been determined that a valid and legally enforceable contract exists, attention can turn to the rights and duties of the parties to the contract. A contract is a private agreement between the parties who have entered into it, and traditionally these parties alone have rights and liabilities under the contract. This principle is referred to as **privity of contract**, and it establishes the basic principle that third parties have no rights in contracts to which they are not parties.

You may expect by now that for every rule of contract law, there is an exception. As times change, so must the laws, as indicated in the chapter-opening quotation. When justice cannot be served by adherence to a rule of law, exceptions to the rule must be made. For instance, privity of contract is not required for an injured person to recover damages under product liability laws.

In this chapter, we look at some exceptions to the rule of privity of contract. One exception allows a party to contract to transfer the rights or duties arising from the contract to another person through an *assignment* (of rights) or a *delegation* (of duties). The other exception involves a *third party beneficiary contract*—a contract intended to benefit a third party.

18–1 Assignments

In a bilateral contract, the two parties have corresponding rights and duties. One party has a *right* to require the other to perform some task, and the other has a *duty* to perform it. Sometimes, though, a party will transfer her or his rights under the contract to someone else.

The transfer of contract *rights* to a third person is known as an **assignment.** (The transfer of contract duties is a *delegation*, as will be discussed later in this chapter.)

Assignments are important because they are often used in business financing. Lending institutions, such as banks, frequently assign the rights to receive payments under their loan contracts to other firms, which pay for those rights. **Example 18.1** Kendra Vasey obtains a loan from a bank to finance an online business venture. Later, she receives a notice from the bank stating that it has transferred (assigned) its rights to receive payments on the loan to another firm. When it is time to repay the loan, Vasey must make the payments to that other firm. █

Note also that lenders that make *mortgage loans* (loans that enable prospective home buyers to purchase real estate) often assign their rights to collect the mortgage payments to a third party. Following an assignment, the home buyer is notified that future payments must be made to the third party, rather than to the original lender. Billions of dollars change hands daily in the business world in the form of assignments of rights in contracts. If it were not possible to transfer contractual rights, many businesses could not continue to operate.

18–1a **Effect of an Assignment**

In an assignment, the party assigning the rights to a third party is known as the **assignor,**[1] and the party receiving the rights is the **assignee.**[2] Other terms traditionally used to describe the parties in assignment relationships are **obligee** (the person to whom a duty, or obligation, is owed) and **obligor** (the person who is obligated to perform the duty).

In general, an assignment can take any form, oral or written, although it is advisable to put all assignments in writing. Of course, assignments covered by the Statute of Frauds— such as an assignment of an interest in land—must be in writing to be enforceable. In addition, most states require contracts for the assignment of wages to be in writing.[3] There are other assignments that must be in writing as well.

Extinguishes the Rights of the Assignor
When rights under a contract are assigned unconditionally, the rights of the assignor are extinguished.[4] The assignee has a right to demand performance from the other original party to the contract, the obligor.

Example 18.2 Brenda is obligated by contract to pay Alex $1,000. Brenda is the obligor because she owes an obligation, or duty, to Alex. Alex is the obligee, the one to whom the obligation is owed. If Alex then assigns his right to receive the $1,000 to Charles, Alex is the assignor and Charles is the assignee. Charles now becomes the obligee because Brenda owes Charles the $1,000. Here, a valid assignment of a debt exists. Charles (the assignee-obligee) is entitled to enforce payment in court if Brenda (the obligor) does not pay him the $1,000. (Alex is no longer entitled to enforce payment because the assignment extinguished his original contract rights.) █ These concepts are illustrated in Exhibit 18–1.

Assignee Takes Rights Subject to Defenses
The assignee obtains only those rights that the assignor originally had. In addition, the assignee's rights are subject to the defenses that the obligor has against the assignor.

Example 18.3 Returning to *Example 18.2*, suppose that Brenda owes Alex the $1,000 under a contract in which she agreed to buy Alex's Microsoft Surface Pro. When Brenda decided to purchase the tablet, she relied on Alex's fraudulent misrepresentation that it had an Intel Core i7 processor. When Brenda discovers that its processor is an Intel i3, she tells Alex that she is

Assignment The transfer to another of all or part of one's rights arising under a contract.

Learning Objective 1
What is an assignment?

Assignor A party who transfers (assigns) his or her rights under a contract to another party (the *assignee*).

Assignee A party to whom the rights under a contract are transferred, or assigned.

Obligee One to whom an obligation is owed.

Obligor One who owes an obligation to another.

---

1. Pronounced uh-*sye*-nore.
2. Pronounced uh-*sye*-nee.
3. See, for example, California Labor Code Section 300.
4. *Restatement (Second) of Contracts*, Section 317.

Exhibit 18–1 Assignment Relationships

In the assignment relationship illustrated here, Alex assigns his *rights* under a contract that he made with Brenda to a third party, Charles. Alex thus becomes the *assignor* and Charles the *assignee* of the contractual rights. Brenda, the *obligor*, now owes performance to Charles instead of Alex. Alex's original contractual rights are extinguished after assignment.

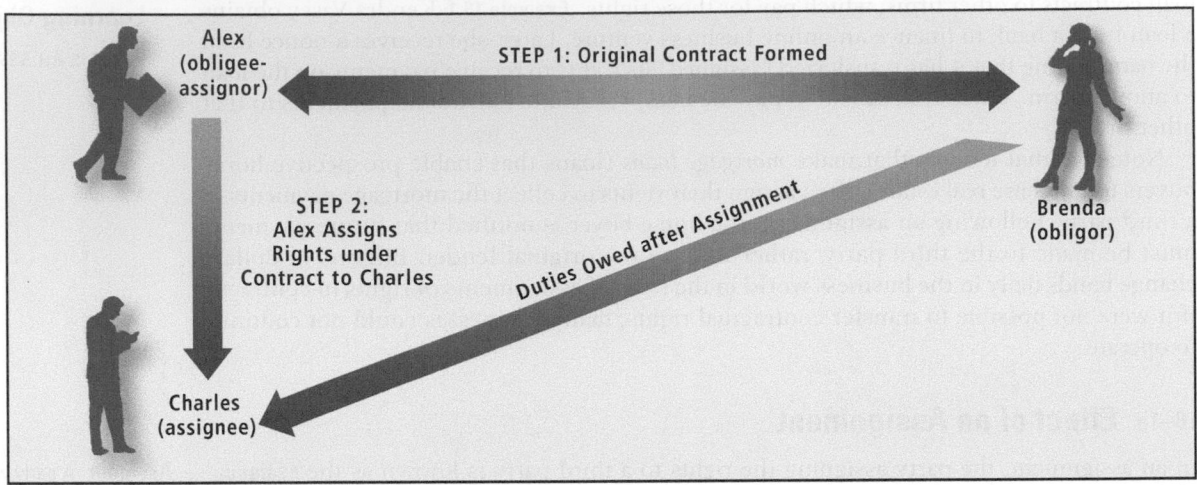

Alex
(obligee-
assignor)

STEP 1: Original Contract Formed

Brenda
(obligor)

STEP 2:
Alex Assigns
Rights under
Contract to Charles

Duties Owed after Assignment

Charles
(assignee)

going to return the device to him and cancel the contract. Even though Alex has assigned his "right" to receive the $1,000 to Charles, Brenda need not pay Charles the $1,000. Brenda can raise the defense of Alex's fraudulent misrepresentation to avoid payment. ▪

18–1b Rights That Cannot Be Assigned

As a general rule, all rights can be assigned. Exceptions are made, however, in the following special circumstances.

When a Statute Expressly Prohibits Assignment If a statute expressly prohibits assignment, the right in question cannot be assigned. For instance, in many states, workers' compensation statutes prohibit an employee who is receiving benefits from assigning them to another.

Can the right to receive piano lessons be assigned to another student?

yenwen/E+/Getty Images

When a Contract Is Personal in Nature When a contract is for personal services, the rights under the contract normally cannot be assigned unless all that remains is a monetary payment.[5] **Example 18.4** Anton signs a contract to be a tutor for Marisa's children. Marisa then attempts to assign to Roberto her right to Anton's services. Roberto cannot enforce the contract against Anton. Roberto's children may be more difficult to tutor than Marisa's. Thus, if Marisa could assign her rights to Anton's services to Roberto, it would change the nature of Anton's obligation. Because personal services are unique to the person rendering them, rights to receive personal services are likewise unique and cannot be assigned. ▪

When an Assignment Will Significantly Change the Risk or Duties of the Obligor A right cannot be assigned if assignment will significantly alter the risks or the duties of the obligor.[6] **Example 18.5** Alice has a hotel, and to insure it, she takes out a policy with Northwest Insurance Company. The policy insures against fire, theft, floods, and vandalism. Alice attempts to assign the insurance policy to Carmen, who owns a hotel in another city.

The assignment is ineffective because it may substantially alter the insurance company's duty of performance and the risk that the company undertakes. An insurance company

---

5. *Restatement (Second) of Contracts*, Sections 317 and 318.
6. See Section 2–210(2) of the Uniform Commercial Code (UCC).

evaluates the particular risk associated with a specific party and tailors its policy to fit that risk. If the policy were assigned to a third party, the insurance risk would be materially altered.

When the Contract Prohibits Assignment If a contract stipulates that the right cannot be assigned, then *ordinarily* it cannot be assigned. This restraint operates only against the parties themselves. It does not prohibit an assignment by operation of law, such as an assignment pursuant to bankruptcy or death.

Whether an *antiassignment clause* is effective depends, in part, on how it is phrased. A contract that states that *any* assignment is void effectively prohibits any assignment. **Example 18.6** Ramirez agrees to build a house for Amy. Their contract states, "This contract cannot be assigned by Amy without Ramirez's consent. Any assignment without such consent renders the contract void." This antiassignment clause is effective, and Amy cannot assign her rights without obtaining Ramirez's consent.

The rule that a contract can prohibit assignments has several exceptions:

1. A contract cannot prevent an assignment of the right to receive funds. This exception exists to encourage the free flow of funds and credit in modern business settings.

2. The assignment of ownership rights in real estate often cannot be prohibited because such a prohibition is contrary to public policy in most states. Prohibitions of this kind are called restraints against **alienation** (the voluntary transfer of land ownership).

3. The assignment of negotiable instruments (such as checks and promissory notes) cannot be prohibited.

4. In a contract for the sale of goods, the right to receive payments on an account or damages for breach of contract may be assigned even though the sales contract prohibits such an assignment.[7]

The lease and purchase agreement in the following case contained an antiassignment clause. The court had to decide whether the clause was enforceable.

Learning Objective 2

What rights can be assigned despite a contract clause expressly prohibiting assignment?

Alienation The transfer of title to real property (which "alienates" the real property from the former owner).

---

7. UCC 2–210(2).

■ Case 18.1

Bass-Fineberg Leasing, Inc. v. Modern Auto Sales, Inc.

Court of Appeals of Ohio, Ninth District, Medina county, 2015 -Ohio- 46 (2015).

Background and Facts Bass-Fineberg Leasing, Inc., leased a tour bus to Modern Auto Sales, Inc., and Michael Cipriani. The lease included an option to buy the bus. The lease prohibited Modern Auto and Cipriani from assigning their rights without Bass-Fineberg's written consent. Later, Cipriani left the bus with Anthony Allie at BVIP Limo Services, Ltd., for repairs. Modern Auto and Cipriani did not pay for the repairs. At the same time, they defaulted on the lease payments to Bass-Fineberg. While BVIP retained possession of the bus, Allie signed an agreement with Cipriani to buy it and to make an initial $5,000 payment to Bass-Fineberg. Bass-Fineberg filed an action in an Ohio state court against Modern Auto, Cipriani, BVIP, and Allie to regain possession of the bus. The court ordered the bus returned to Bass-Feinberg and the $5,000 payment refunded to Allie. All of the parties appealed.

In the Words of the Court
WHITMORE, Judge

* * * *

* * * Bass-Fineberg argues that the purported contract between Cipriani and Allie was void because Cipriani could not assign his rights or obligations under the lease without the written consent of Bass-Fineberg. * * * BVIP responds that if the contract was void, then the parties should be returned to their pre-contract status, including refunding its $5,000 payment. We agree with Bass-Fineberg that there was not a valid contract between Allie and Cipriani, but we agree with BVIP as to the effect of that invalidity, namely that it was entitled to have its $5,000 returned.]

Ohio enforces anti-assignment clauses where there is clear contractual language prohibiting an assignment. Violations of a non-assignment provision in a contract render the resulting agreement null and void. [Emphasis added.]

* * * *

The lease between Bass-Fineberg and Modern Auto and Cipriani contained the following provision:

> MODERN AUTO AND CIPRIANI ACKNOWLEDGE THAT MODERN AUTO AND CIPRIANI MAY NOT ASSIGN OR IN ANY WAY TRANSFER OR DISPOSE OF ALL OR ANY PART OF MODERN AUTO AND CIPRIANI'S RIGHTS OR OBLIGATIONS UNDER THIS LEASE * * * WITHOUT BASS-FINEBERG'S PRIOR WRITTEN CONSENT.

This clear contractual language prohibited Modern Auto and Cipriani from transferring their rights or obligations under the lease agreement unless Bass-Fineberg consented in writing.

The purported agreement between Cipriani and Allie attempted to transfer Cipriani's right to purchase the bus to Allie and some of Cipriani's payment obligations to Allie. [David] Libman,

Bass-Fineberg's lease sales manager, did not sign the agreement between Allie and Cipriani. Nor did the parties introduce evidence of anyone else from Bass-Fineberg providing written consent to the attempted assignment.

As the lease agreement prohibited an assignment without Bass-Fineberg's consent, the agreement between Cipriani and Allie was void. If a contract is void, then an obligation under it never existed. In such circumstances, the one who made a payment is entitled to a refund.

Decision and Remedy A state intermediate appellate court affirmed the lower court's order. The contract between Cipriani and Allie was void because Cipriani could not assign his rights under the lease without Bass-Fineberg's written consent. Because the contract was void, the parties were to be returned to their pre-contract status, which included a refund of the $5,000 payment.

Critical Thinking

• **Economic** *The repairs to the bus cost $1,341.50. Who should pay this amount? Why?*

18–1c Notice of Assignment

Once a valid assignment of rights has been made to a third party, the third party should notify the obligor of the assignment (for instance, in *Example 18.2*, Charles should notify Brenda). Giving notice is not legally necessary to establish the validity of the assignment because an assignment is effective immediately, whether or not notice is given. Two major problems arise, however, when notice of the assignment is *not* given to the obligor.

Priority Issues If the assignor assigns the same right to two different persons, the question arises as to which one has priority—that is, which one has the right to the performance by the obligor. The rule most often observed in the United States is that the first assignment in time is the first in right. Some states, though, follow the English rule, which basically gives priority to the first assignee who gives notice.

Example 18.7 Jason owes Alexis $5,000 under a contract. Alexis first assigns the claim to Louisa, who does not give notice to Jason. Then Alexis assigns it to Dorman, who notifies Jason. In most states, Louisa would have priority because the assignment to her was first in time. In some states, however, Dorman would have priority because he gave first notice. ▮

Potential for Discharge by Performance to the Wrong Party Until the obligor has notice of an assignment, the obligor can discharge his or her obligation by performance to the assignor, and this performance constitutes a discharge to the assignee. Once the obligor receives proper notice, only performance to the assignee can discharge the obligor's obligations.

Example 18.8 Recall that Alexis, the obligee in Example 18.7, assigned to Louisa her right to collect $5,000 from Jason, and Louisa did not give notice to Jason. What will happen if Jason later pays Alexis the $5,000? Although the assignment was valid, Jason's payment to

Alexis will discharge the debt. Louisa's failure to notify Jason of the assignment will cause her to lose the right to collect the $5,000 from Jason. (Note that Louisa will still have a claim against Alexis for the $5,000.) If Louisa had given Jason notice of the assignment, Jason's payment to Alexis would not have discharged the debt.

18–2 Delegations

Just as a party can transfer rights to a third party through an assignment, a party can also transfer duties. Duties are not assigned, however. They are *delegated*. Normally, a **delegation of duties** does not relieve the party making the delegation (the **delegator**) of the obligation to perform in the event that the party to whom the duty has been delegated (the **delegatee**) fails to perform.

No special form is required to create a valid delegation of duties. As long as the delegator expresses an intention to make the delegation, it is effective. The delegator need not even use the word *delegate*. Exhibit 18–2 illustrates delegation relationships.

18–2a Duties That Cannot Be Delegated

As a general rule, any duty can be delegated. This rule has some exceptions, however. Delegation is prohibited in the following circumstances:

1. When performance depends on the personal skill or talents of the obligor.
2. When special trust has been placed in the obligor.
3. When performance by a third party will vary materially from that expected by the obligee.
4. When the contract expressly prohibits delegation.

Delegation of Duties The transfer to another of a contractual duty.

Delegator A party who transfers (delegates) her or his obligations under a contract to another party (the *delegatee*).

Delegatee A party to whom contractual obligations are transferred, or delegated.

Learning Objective 3
In what situations is the delegation of duties prohibited?

Exhibit 18–2 Delegation Relationships

In the delegation relationship illustrated here, Brower delegates her *duties* under a contract that she made with Horton to a third party, Kuhn. Brower thus becomes the *delegator* and Kuhn the *delegatee* of the contractual duties. Kuhn now owes performance of the contractual duties to Horton. Note that a delegation of duties normally does not relieve the delegator (Brower) of liability if the delegatee (Kuhn) fails to perform the contractual duties.

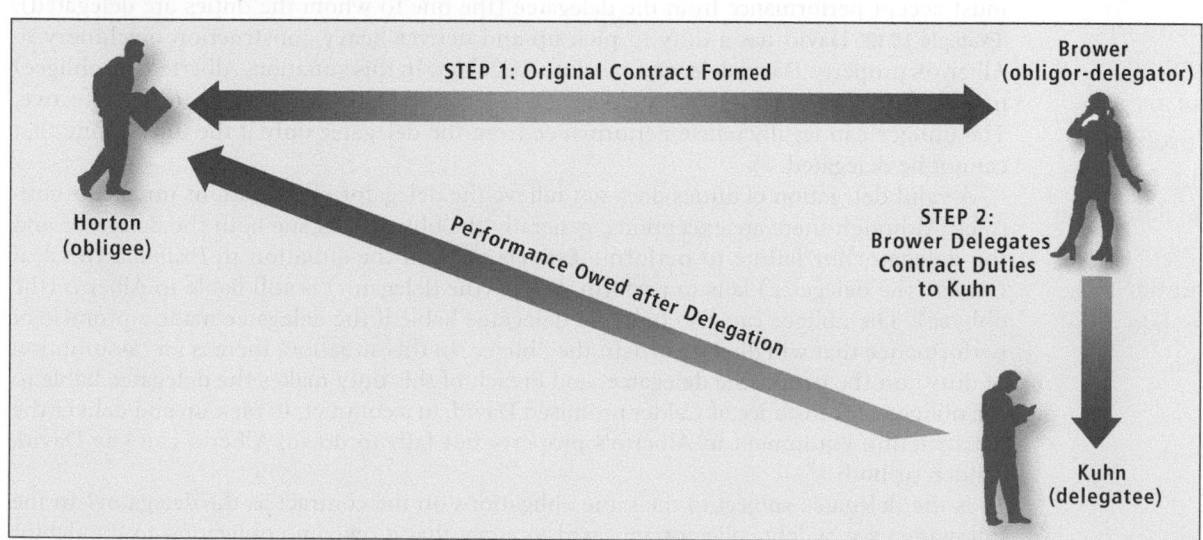

When the Duties Are Personal in Nature When special trust has been placed in the obligor or when performance depends on the obligor's personal skill or talents, contractual duties cannot be delegated. **Example 18.9** O'Brien, who is impressed with Brodie's ability to perform veterinary surgery, contracts with Brodie to have her perform surgery on O'Brien's prize-winning stallion in July. Brodie later decides that she would rather spend the summer at the beach, so she delegates her duties under the contract to Lopez, who is also a competent veterinary surgeon. The delegation is not effective without O'Brien's consent, no matter how competent Lopez is, because the contract is for *personal* performance.

In contrast, nonpersonal duties may be delegated. Suppose that, in *Example 18.9*, Brodie contracts with O'Brien to pick up a large horse trailer and deliver it to O'Brien's property. Brodie delegates this duty to Lopez, who owns a towing business. This delegation is effective because the performance required is of a *routine* and *nonpersonal* nature.

When Performance by a Third Party Will Vary Materially from That Expected by the Obligee When performance by a third party will vary materially from that expected by the obligee under the contract, contractual duties cannot be delegated. **Example 18.10** Jared, a wealthy investor, establishes the company Heaven Sent to provide grants of capital to struggling but potentially successful businesses. Jared contracts with Merilyn, whose judgment Jared trusts, to select the recipients of the grants. Later, Merilyn delegates this duty to Donald. Jared does not trust Donald's ability to select worthy recipients. This delegation is not effective because it materially alters Jared's expectations under the contract with Merilyn.

When the Contract Prohibits Delegation When the contract expressly prohibits delegation by including an *antidelegation clause*, the duties cannot be delegated. **Example 18.11** Dakota Company contracts with Belisario, a certified public accountant, to perform its audits. Because the contract prohibits delegation, Belisario cannot delegate the duty to perform the audits to another accountant—not even an accountant at the same firm.

18–2b Effect of a Delegation

If a delegation of duties is enforceable, the obligee (the one to whom performance is owed) must accept performance from the delegatee (the one to whom the duties are delegated). **Example 18.12** David has a duty to pick up and deliver heavy construction machinery to Alberto's property. David delegates his duty to Calder. In this situation, Alberto (the obligee) must accept performance from Calder (the delegatee) because the delegation is effective. The obligee can legally refuse performance from the delegatee only if the duty is one that cannot be delegated.

A valid delegation of duties does not relieve the delegator of obligations under the contract. Although there are exceptions, generally the obligee can sue both the delegatee and the delegator for failure to perform. **Example 18.13** In the situation in *Example 18.12*, if Calder (the delegatee) fails to perform, David (the delegator) is still liable to Alberto (the obligee). The obligee can also hold the delegatee liable if the delegatee made a promise of performance that will directly benefit the obligee. In this situation, there is an "assumption of duty" on the part of the delegatee, and breach of this duty makes the delegatee liable to the obligee. For instance, if Calder promised David, in a contract, to pick up and deliver the construction equipment to Alberto's property but fails to do so, Alberto can sue David, Calder, or both.

Is the delegatee subject to the same obligations on the contract as the delegator? In the following case, a debt collector appeared to argue that it owed no obligation to the debtor arising from the acceptance of the delegation of the duty to service a student loan.

Under what circumstances may a veterinary surgeon delegate her duties to another veterinarian?

baranozdemir/iStock/Getty Images

Know This

In an assignment, the assignor's original contract rights are extinguished after the assignment. In a delegation, the delegator remains liable for performance under the contract if the delegatee fails to perform.

Case 18.2

Mirandette v. Nelnet, Inc.
United States Court of Appeals, Sixth Circuit, 720 Fed.Appx. 288 (2018).

Background and Facts To pay for his daughter's education, Kurt Mirandette borrowed the funds. As a condition of the loan, Mirandette signed a "Master Promissory Note" (MPN). The MPN did not specify when payments on the loan were to be credited. Nelnet, Inc. and Nelnet Servicing, LLC, credited Mirandette's payments ten to thirty days after he mailed the checks. Mirandette filed a suit in a federal district court against the Nelnet companies, claiming breach of contract. He alleged that the defendants manipulated the date on which they credited the payments, resulting in the wrongful accrual of interest and late fees. The defendants responded that the MPN did not obligate them to credit payments as of a certain date. The court dismissed the suit. Mirandette appealed.

In the Words of the Court
Helene N. *WHITE*, Circuit Judge.
* * * *

Defendants present two arguments in support of the district court's dismissal: 1) that they could not have breached the MPN because the MPN is a contract between Mirandette and a separate lender; and 2) even if they are bound by the MPN, there is no provision obligating them to credit Mirandette's payments as of a certain date. Both arguments fail.

In essence, Defendants argue that a third-party lender contracted with Mirandette to provide a loan. Then, instead of dealing with the service requirements of that loan, the lender contracted with Defendants and delegated those duties to Defendants in exchange for a servicing fee. * * * *Defendants have not shown that they have no obligation to the debtor arising from their acceptance of the asserted delegation of the duty to service the loan.* [Emphasis added.]

Defendants' second argument, that they are under no obligation to credit Mirandette's payments at any particular time because there is no term describing when they must credit Mirandette's payments, also fails.

Although the MPN does not specify when payments must be credited, * * * Defendants' interpretation of the MPN is untenable. Under their logic, Defendants are entitled to withhold crediting Mirandette's account indefinitely, thus allowing Defendants to charge interest on the full principal for the entire duration of the loan. Defendants' reading would suggest that even if Mirandette walked into their office and paid his monthly installments in cash, Defendants still would not be required to credit his account until they chose to do so. Such an absurdity cannot have been intended by the parties signing this contract * * *. Rather, the more natural reading of the contract is that when Mirandette fulfills his obligation to make timely payments, *Defendants have the reciprocal obligation to acknowledge those payments by crediting his * * * account.* The question is when Defendants must credit those payments. [Emphasis added.]
* * * *

Mirandette's * * * theory is that Defendants should credit his payments upon receipt. * * * The district court did not address this aspect of Mirandette's breach-of-contract claim. We therefore remand.

Decision and Remedy The U.S. Court of Appeals for the Sixth Circuit reversed the district court's dismissal of Mirandette's suit, and remanded the case for the lower court to consider Mirandette's payment-on-receipt theory.

Critical Thinking

• **Legal Environment** *The MPN stated that "applicable state law … may provide for certain borrower rights." The Nelnet companies are based in Nebraska. Nebraska's commercial code provides that the delivery of a check marks the date of payment. How might this provision affect the decision of the lower court on remand?*

• **Economic** *According to the defendants' reasoning, borrowers would have no contract remedies if loan servicers overcharged them. What effect might this circumstance have in the market for credit? Discuss.*

18–2c "Assignment of All Rights"

Sometimes, a contract provides for an "assignment of all rights." This wording may create both an assignment of rights and a delegation of duties.[8] Typically, this situation occurs when general words are used, such as "I assign the contract" or "I assign all my rights under the

8. See UCC 2-210(1), (4); and *Restatement (Second) of Contracts*, Section 328.

contract." A court normally will construe such words as implying both an assignment of rights and a delegation of any duties of performance. Thus, the assignor remains liable if the assignee fails to perform the contractual obligations.

18–3 Third Party Beneficiaries

Third Party Beneficiary One who is not a party to the contract but who stands to benefit from the contract's performance.

Intended Beneficiary A third party for whose benefit a contract is formed. An intended beneficiary can sue the promisor if the contract is breached.

Another exception to the doctrine of privity of contract arises when the contract is intended to benefit a third party. The original parties to a contract can agree that the contract performance should be rendered to or directly benefit a third person. When this happens, the third person becomes an *intended* **third party beneficiary** of the contract. As the **intended beneficiary** of the contract, the third party has legal rights and can sue the promisor directly for breach of the contract.

18–3a Who Is the Promisor?

Who, though, is the promisor? In a bilateral contract, both parties to the contract make promises that can be enforced, so the court has to determine which party made the promise that benefits the third party. That person is the promisor.

In effect, allowing a third party to sue the promisor directly circumvents the "middle person" (the promisee) and thus reduces the burden on the courts. Otherwise, the third party would sue the promisee, who would then sue the promisor.

🏛 Classic Case Example 18.14 The classic case that gave third party beneficiaries the right to bring a suit directly against a promisor was decided in 1859. The case involved three parties—Holly, Lawrence, and Fox. Holly had borrowed $300 from Lawrence. Shortly thereafter, Holly loaned $300 to Fox, who in return promised Holly that he would pay Holly's debt to Lawrence on the following day. When Lawrence failed to obtain the $300 from Fox, he sued Fox to recover the funds. The court had to decide whether Lawrence could sue Fox directly (rather than suing Holly). The court held that when "a promise [is] made for the benefit of another, he for whose benefit it is made may bring an action for its breach."[9]

In the following case, the third party beneficiary was the former lead singer for a 1980s New Wave band. The promisor was the band's recording company and distributor. The promisee was a corporation formed by the band members to receive the band's royalties. The contract involved the payment of those royalties. The question before the court was whether the third party beneficiary could sue for breach of contract when the promisee lacked the capacity to bring the suit.

---

9. *Lawrence v. Fox*, 20 N.Y. 268 (1859).

■ Case 18.3

Bozzio v. EMI Group, Ltd.

United States Court of Appeals, Ninth Circuit, 811 F.3d 1144 (2016).

Background and Facts In the 1980s, Dale Bozzio was the front woman of the Los Angeles–based New Wave band, Missing Persons. The members of the band formed Missing Persons, Inc. (MPI), a "loan-out" corporation through which to provide their artistic services.[a] Capitol Records (the promisor) entered into a

contract with MPI (the promisee) to produce and market the band's recordings. The band members agreed to look solely to MPI for payment of all royalties and not to bring any claims against Capitol Records. After the group disbanded, MPI's corporate status was suspended for nonpayment of state corporate taxes.

Two decades later, Bozzio filed a suit in a federal district court against Capitol Records and others (including EMI Group, Ltd.),

---

a. A *loan-out corporation* is a corporation formed for the financial benefit of artists and entertainers. Normally, its only function is to provide the services of an artist to producers and others.

(Continues)

seeking royalties on their licensing for sale of "digital downloads, ringtones . . . , and streaming music" featuring the recordings of Missing Persons. Bozzio asserted that she was a third party beneficiary of the contract between Capitol Records and MPI with a right to sue directly for its enforcement.

The court dismissed the complaint on the ground that MPI, as a suspended corporation, lacked the capacity to sue. Bozzio appealed.

In the Words of the Court
CHRISTEN, Circuit Judge:
* * * On appeal, Bozzio argues that the suspended status of the contracting corporate party is irrelevant when the party bringing the action is a third-party beneficiary of the contract, and the district court's dismissal of the * * * complaint on that basis constitutes reversible error. We agree with Bozzio that the district court erred in holding that, even if Bozzio is a third-party beneficiary, she cannot bring an action while Missing Persons, Inc. is suspended.
* * * *

The parties have not cited, and we have not found, any California case holding that a third-party beneficiary cannot sue the promisor for breach of contract when the promisee is a suspended corporation.
* * * *

* * * California courts do not consider the incapacity of the promisee to a contract to be an absolute bar to a lawsuit by a third-party beneficiary. [Emphasis added.]
* * * *

When sitting in diversity jurisdiction, this court will follow a state supreme court's interpretation * * * . Where the state's highest court has not decided an issue, this court looks for guidance to decisions by intermediate appellate courts of the state * * * . Here, the California Supreme Court has not decided whether a promisee corporation's suspended status precludes suit by a third-party beneficiary of the contract, but * * * the California Court of Appeal [has] suggested that a third-party beneficiary

suit may go forward notwithstanding the promisee's incapacity to sue. Therefore, the district court erred in its determination that a third-party beneficiary cannot state a claim if the promisee is a suspended corporation.
* * * *

Capitol strenuously argues that by agreeing "not to assert any claims * * * against Capitol," Bozzio waived her right to sue as a third-party beneficiary. Bozzio counters that this "look solely to" clause was intended to prohibit an artist from asserting a claim against Capitol only "when there is a dispute among individual band members over the internal allocation and distribution of royalties that have already been properly accounted for and paid by the record label to the artists' musical group or loan-out corporation." Nothing in the record forecloses Bozzio's reading of this contract language.

We agree with Bozzio that whether she forfeited the ability to sue as a third-party beneficiary is a fact-bound inquiry ill-suited to resolution at the motion to dismiss stage. On remand, a record can be developed that will allow consideration of Bozzio's claim that she was an intended third-party beneficiary of the Agreement.

Decision and Remedy The U.S. Court of Appeals for the Ninth Circuit reversed the lower court's dismissal of the complaint and remanded the case. MPI's corporate status was irrelevant with respect to Bozzio's right to assert a third party claim and the lower court must consider her arguments.

Critical Thinking

• **Legal Environment** *Capitol Records will, of course, contend that Bozzio's agreement to look solely to MPI for payment of all royalties and not to bring any claims against Capitol Records bars her suit in this case. What would be Bozzio's best response to this contention? Discuss.*

• **E-Commerce** *What effect might an ultimate decision in the plaintiff's favor in this case have on the licensing and sale of digital music? Explain.*

18–3b Types of Intended Beneficiaries

Intended beneficiaries can be further classified as *creditor beneficiaries* or *donee beneficiaries*.

Creditor Beneficiary Like the plaintiff in *Classic Case Example 18.14*, a *creditor beneficiary* benefits from a contract in which one party (the promisor) promises another party (the promisee) to perform a duty that the promisee owes to a third party (the creditor beneficiary). As an intended beneficiary, the creditor beneficiary can sue the promisor directly to enforce the contract.

Case Example 18.15 Autumn Allan owned a condominium unit in a Texas complex. Her unit was located directly beneath a unit owned by Aslan Koraev. Over the course of two years, Allan's unit suffered eight incidents of water and sewage incursion as a result of plumbing problems and misuse of appliances in Koraev's unit. Allan sued Koraev for breach of contract and won.

Koraev appealed, arguing that he had no contractual duty to Allan. The court, however, found that Allan was an intended third party beneficiary of the contract between Koraev and the condominium owners' association. Because the governing documents stated that each owner had to comply strictly with their provisions, failure to comply created grounds for an action by either the condominium association or an aggrieved (wronged) owner. Here, Allan was an aggrieved owner and could sue Koraev directly for his failure to perform his contractual duties to the condominium association.[10]

Donee Beneficiary When a contract is made for the express purpose of giving a *gift* to a third party, the third party is a *donee beneficiary*. A donee beneficiary can sue the promisor directly to enforce the promise.

The most common donee beneficiary contract is a life insurance contract. **Example 18.16** Ben (the promisee) pays premiums to Standard Life, a life insurance company, and Standard Life (the promisor) promises to pay a certain amount on Ben's death to anyone Ben designates as a beneficiary. The designated beneficiary is a donee beneficiary under the life insurance policy and can enforce the promise made by the insurance company to pay her or him on Ben's death.

18–3c When the Rights of an Intended Beneficiary Vest

An intended third party beneficiary cannot enforce a contract against the original parties until the third party's rights have *vested*, meaning that the rights have taken effect and cannot be taken away. Until these rights have vested, the original parties to the contract—the promisor and the promisee—can modify or rescind the contract without the consent of the third party.

When do the rights of third parties vest? Generally, the rights vest when any of the following occurs:

1. When the third party demonstrates express consent to the agreement, such as by sending a letter, a note, or an e-mail acknowledging awareness of, and consent to, a contract formed for her or his benefit.

2. When the third party materially alters his or her position in detrimental reliance on the contract, such as when a donee beneficiary contracts to have a home built in reliance on the receipt of funds promised to him or her in a donee beneficiary contract.

3. When the conditions for vesting are satisfied. For instance, the rights of a beneficiary under a life insurance policy vest when the insured person dies.

18–3d Incidental Beneficiaries

Sometimes, a third person receives a benefit from a contract even though that person's benefit is not the reason the contract was made. Such a person is known as an **incidental beneficiary.** Because the benefit is *unintentional*, an incidental beneficiary cannot sue to enforce the contract. Only intended beneficiaries acquire legal rights in a contract.

Classic Case Example 18.17 Spectators who attended an automobile race (the Grand Prix) sued the organizations that presented the event. The spectators were upset because fourteen of the twenty cars that were supposed to race dropped out at the last minute due to tire failures. The plaintiffs claimed that they were third party beneficiaries of the contract between the teams of drivers and the race promoters. They sought compensation for traveling to and

Incidental Beneficiary A third party who benefits from a contract even though the contract was not formed for that purpose. An incidental beneficiary has no rights in the contract and cannot sue to have it enforced.

---

10. *Allan v. Nersesova*, 307 S.W.3d 564 (Tx.App—Dallas 2010).

attending the race. The court dismissed the plaintiffs' claims, however. "A failure to satisfy the subjective expectations of spectators at a sporting event is not actionable." The defendants did not have a contract with the spectators, and the spectators could not sue as third party beneficiaries.[11]

Why can't spectators of an automobile race make legal claims as third party beneficiaries?

Pascal Rondeau/Getty Images

18–3e Identifying Intended versus Incidental Beneficiaries

In determining whether a party is an intended or an incidental beneficiary, the courts focus on the parties' intent, as expressed in the contract language and implied by the surrounding circumstances. Any beneficiary who is not deemed an intended beneficiary is considered incidental. Exhibit 18–3 graphically illustrates the distinction between intended and incidental beneficiaries.

Although no single test can embrace all possible situations, courts often apply the *reasonable person* test: Would a reasonable person in the position of the beneficiary believe that the promisee intended to confer on the beneficiary the right to enforce the contract? In addition, the presence of one or more of the following factors strongly indicates that the third party is an intended beneficiary of the contract:

1. Performance is rendered directly to the third party.
2. The third party has the right to control the details of performance.
3. The third party is expressly designated as a beneficiary in the contract.

Learning Objective 4
What factors indicate that a third party beneficiary is an intended beneficiary?

Case Example 18.18 New York City decided to build a fifteen-story forensic biology (DNA testing) laboratory next to Bellevue Hospital in Manhattan. The city turned the project over to the Dormitory Authority of the State of New York (DASNY), which oversees public projects. DASNY contracted with Perkins Eastman Architects, P.C., which hired Samson Construction Company to excavate the site and lay the foundation. Unfortunately, Samson's excavation of the site caused adjacent structures, including a building, sidewalks, roadbeds, sewers, and water systems, to "settle," causing about $37 million in damage.

---

11. *Bowers v. Federation Internationale de L'Automobile,* 461 F.Supp.2d 855 (S.D.Ind. 2006).

Exhibit 18–3 Third Party Beneficiaries

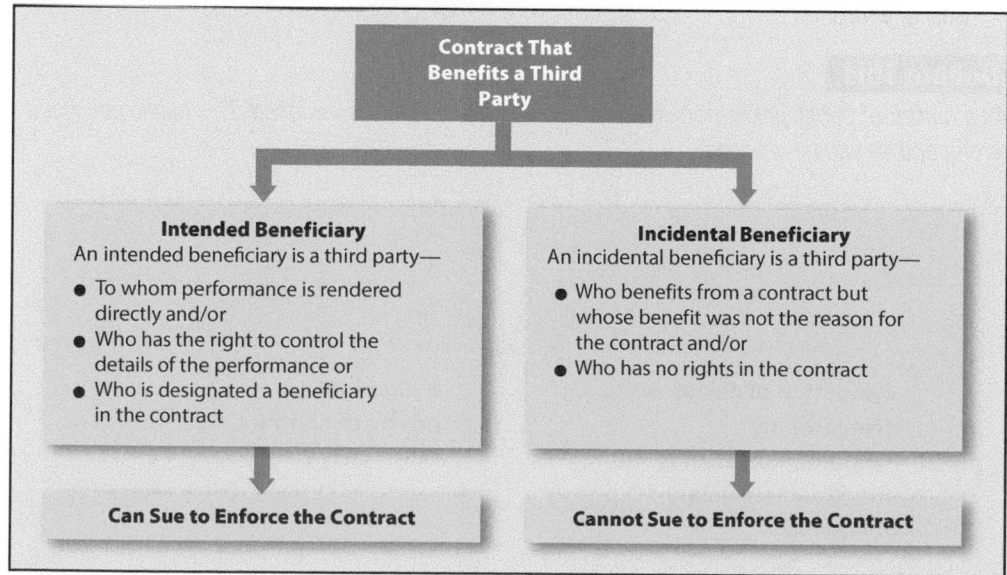

Contract That Benefits a Third Party

Intended Beneficiary
An intended beneficiary is a third party—
- To whom performance is rendered directly and/or
- Who has the right to control the details of the performance or
- Who is designated a beneficiary in the contract

Can Sue to Enforce the Contract

Incidental Beneficiary
An incidental beneficiary is a third party—
- Who benefits from a contract but whose benefit was not the reason for the contract and/or
- Who has no rights in the contract

Cannot Sue to Enforce the Contract

DASNY and the city sued Samson and Perkins, alleging breach of contract. Even though the city was not named in the contract between Samson and Perkins, a state appellate court held that the city was an intended third party beneficiary. "The contract expressly states that a City agency will operate the DNA laboratory, and the City retained control over various aspects of the project."[12]

---

12. *Dormitory Authority of the State of New York v. Samson Construction Co.*, 137 A.D.3d 433, 27 N.Y.S.3d 114 (1 Dept. 2016).

Practice and Review

Myrtle Jackson owns several commercial buildings that she leases to businesses, one of which is a restaurant. The lease states that tenants are responsible for securing all necessary insurance policies but the landlord is obligated to keep the buildings in good repair. The owner of the restaurant, Joe McCall, tells his restaurant manager to purchase insurance, but the manager never does so. Jackson tells her son-in-law, Rob Dunn, to perform any necessary maintenance for the buildings. Dunn knows that the ceiling in the restaurant needs repair but fails to do anything about it.

One day a customer, Ian Faught, is dining in the restaurant when a chunk of the ceiling falls on his head and fractures his skull. Faught files suit against the restaurant and discovers that there is no insurance policy in effect. Faught then files a suit against Jackson. He argues that he is an intended third party beneficiary of the lease provision requiring the restaurant to carry insurance and thus can sue Jackson for failing to enforce that provision. Using the information presented in the chapter, answer the following questions.

1. Can Jackson delegate her duty to maintain the buildings to Dunn? Why or why not?
2. Who can be held liable for Dunn's failure to fix the ceiling, Jackson or Dunn? Why?
3. Was Faught an intended third party beneficiary of the lease between Jackson and McCall? Why or why not?
4. Suppose that Jackson tells Dan Stryker, a local builder to whom she owes $50,000, that he can collect the rents from the buildings' tenants until the debt is satisfied. Is this a valid assignment? Why or why not?

Debate This

As a matter of public policy, personal-injury tort claims cannot be assigned. This public policy is wrong and should be changed.

Key Terms

alienation 405
assignee 403
assignment 403
assignor 403
delegatee 407

delegation of duties 407
delegator 407
incidental beneficiary 412
intended beneficiary 410
obligee 403

obligor 403
privity of contract 402
third party beneficiary 410

Chapter Summary: Third Party Rights

Assignments	1. An assignment is the transfer of rights under a contract to a third party. The person assigning the rights is the *assignor,* and the party to whom the rights are assigned is the *assignee.* The assignee has a right to demand performance from the other original party to the contract, the *obligor.*
	
	2. Generally, all rights can be assigned *unless:*
	  a. A statute expressly prohibits assignment.
	  b. The contract is for personal services.
	  c. The assignment will significantly alter the obligor's risk or duties.
	  d. The contract prohibits assignment. (Exception: Contracts cannot generally prohibit assignment of the right to receive funds, of ownership rights in real property, of negotiable instruments, or of certain payments on account or damages for breach of contract.)
	
	3. The assignee should notify the obligor of the assignment. Although not legally required, notification avoids two potential problems:
	  a. If the assignor assigns the same right to two different persons, the first assignment in time is generally the first in right, but in some states the first assignee to give notice takes priority.
	  b. Until the obligor is notified of the assignment, the obligor can tender performance to the assignor. If the assignor accepts the performance, the obligor's duties under the contract are discharged without benefit to the assignee.

Delegations	1. A delegation is the transfer of duties under a contract to a third party (the *delegatee*), who then assumes the obligation of performing the contractual duties previously held by the one making the delegation (the *delegator*).
	
	2. As a general rule, any duty can be delegated *unless:*
	  a. Performance depends on the obligor's personal skills or talents.
	  b. Special trust has been placed in the obligor.
	  c. Performance by a third party will vary materially from that expected by the obligee.
	  d. The contract expressly prohibits delegation.
	
	3. A valid delegation of duties does not relieve the delegator of obligations under the contract. If the delegatee fails to perform, the delegator is still liable to the obligee.
	
	4. An "assignment of all rights" is often construed to mean that both the rights and the duties arising under the contract are transferred to a third party.

Third Party Beneficiaries	A third party beneficiary contract is one made for the purpose of benefiting a third party. 1. *Intended beneficiary*—A third party for whose benefit a contract is created. When the promisor (the one making the contractual promise that benefits a third party) fails to perform as promised, the intended beneficiary can sue the promisor directly. Types of intended beneficiaries are creditor and donee beneficiaries. 2. *Incidental beneficiary*—A third party who indirectly (incidentally) benefits from a contract but for whose benefit the contract was not specifically intended. Incidental beneficiaries have no rights to the benefits received and cannot sue to have the contract enforced.

Issue Spotters

1. Eagle Company contracts to build a house for Frank. The contract states that "any assignment of this contract renders the contract void." After Eagle builds the house, but before Frank pays, Eagle assigns its right to payment to Good Credit Company. Can Good Credit enforce the contract against Frank? Why or why not? (See *Assignments*.)

2. Brian owes Jeff $1,000. Ed tells Brian to give him the $1,000 and he will pay Jeff. Brian gives Ed the $1,000, but Ed never pays Jeff. Can Jeff successfully sue Ed for the $1,000? Why or why not? (See *Assignments*.)

—**Check your answers to the *Issue Spotters* against the answers provided in Appendix D at the end of this text.**

Business Scenarios and Case Problems

18–1. Third Party Beneficiaries. Wilken owes Rivera $2,000. Howie promises Wilken that he will pay Rivera the $2,000 in return for Wilken's promise to give Howie's children guitar lessons. Is Rivera an intended beneficiary of the Howie-Wilken contract? Explain. (See *Third Party Beneficiaries.*)

18–2. Assignment. Aron, a college student, signs a one-year lease agreement that runs from September 1 to August 31. The lease agreement specifies that the lease cannot be assigned without the landlord's consent. In late May, Aron decides not to go to summer school and assigns the balance of the lease (three months) to a close friend, Erica. The landlord objects to the assignment and denies Erica access to the apartment. Aron claims that Erica is financially sound and should be allowed the full rights and privileges of an assignee. Discuss fully whether the landlord or Aron is correct. (See *Assignments.*)

18–3. Delegation. Inez has a specific set of plans to build a sailboat. The plans are detailed, and any boatbuilder can construct the boat. Inez secures bids, and the low bid is made by the Whale of a Boat Corp. Inez contracts with Whale to build the boat for $4,000. Whale then receives unexpected business from elsewhere. To meet the delivery date in the contract with Inez, Whale delegates its obligation to build the boat, without Inez's consent, to Quick Brothers, a reputable boatbuilder. When the boat is ready for delivery, Inez learns of the delegation and refuses to accept delivery, even though the boat is built to her specifications. Discuss fully whether Inez is obligated to accept and pay for the boat. Would your answer be any different if Inez had not had a specific set of plans but had instead contracted with Whale to design and build a sailboat for $4,000? Explain. (See *Delegations.*)

18–4. Business Case Problem with Sample Answer—Third Party Beneficiary. David and Sandra Dess contracted with Sirva Relocation, LLC, to assist in selling their home. In their contract, the Desses agreed to disclose all information about the property on which Sirva "and other prospective buyers may rely in deciding whether and on what terms to purchase the Property." The Kincaids contracted with Sirva to buy the house. After the closing, they discovered dampness in the walls, defective and rotten windows, mold, and other undisclosed problems. Can the Kincaids bring an action against the Desses for breach of their contract with Sirva? Why or why not? [*Kincaid v. Dess,* 48 Kan. App.2d 640, 298 P.3d 358 (2013)] (See *Third Party Beneficiaries.*)

—For a sample answer to Problem 18–4, go to Appendix E at the end of this text.

18–5. Third Party Beneficiaries. Randy Jones is an agent for Farmers Insurance Co. of Arizona. Through Jones, Robert and Marcia Murray obtained auto insurance with Farmers. On Jones's advice, the Murrays increased the policy's limits over the minimums required by the state of Arizona, except for uninsured/underinsured motorist coverage, for which Jones made no recommendation. Later, the Murrays' seventeen-year-old daughter, Jessyka, was in an accident that involved both an uninsured motorist and an underinsured motorist. She sustained a traumatic brain injury that permanently incapacitated her. Does Jessyka have standing to bring a claim against Jones and Farmers as a third party to her parents' contract for auto insurance? Explain. [*Lucas Contracting, Inc. v. Altisource Portfolio Solutions, Inc.,* 2016 -Ohio- 474 (Ohio App. 2016)] (See *Third Party Beneficiaries.*)

18–6. Third Party Beneficiaries. The Health Care Providers Self Insurance Trust (the trust) provided workers' compensation coverage to the employees of its members, including Accredited Aides Plus, Inc. The trust contracted with Program Risk Management, Inc. (PRM), to serve as the program administrator. The contract obligated PRM to reimburse the trust for "claims, losses, and liabilities . . . arising out of" PRM's acts or omissions. When the trust became insolvent, the state of New York assessed the trust's employer-members for some of its debts. These employer-members filed a suit against PRM for breach of contract. Were the trust's employer-members third party beneficiaries of the trust's contract with PRM? If so, could the employer-members maintain this action against PRM? Explain. [*Accredited Aides Plus, Inc. v. Program Risk Management, Inc.,* 147 A.D.3d 122, 46 N.Y.S.3d 246 (N.Y.A.D. 3 Dept. 2017)] (See *Third Party Beneficiaries.*)

18–7. Assignments. State Farm Insurance Co. issued a policy to David Stulberger to insure a Nissan Rogue for collision damage. The policy provided, "No assignment . . . is binding upon us unless approved by us." When the Nissan was involved in an accident, State Farm agreed that the vehicle should be repaired. M.V.B. Collision, Inc., performed the repairs at a cost of $14,101.80. State Farm offered to pay $9,960.36. Stulberger assigned to M.V.B. the right to pursue State Farm for the difference, or $4,141.44. The assignee filed a suit in a New York state court against the insurer to recoup this amount. The defendant responded with a motion to dismiss, arguing that the plaintiff lacked the capacity to sue because the defendant had not consented to the transfer by Stulberger. Is the assignment valid? Why or why not? [*M.V.B. Collision, Inc. v. State Farm Insurance Co.,* 59 Misc.3d 406, 72 N.Y.S.3d 407 (2018)] (See *Assignments.*)

18–8. A Question of Ethics—Intended Third Party Beneficiaries. *The Health Care Providers Self Insurance Trust (the trust) provided workers' compensation coverage to the employees of its members, including Accredited Aides Plus, Inc. The trust contracted with Program Risk Management, Inc. (PRM), to serve as the program administrator. The contract obligated PRM to reimburse the trust for "claims, losses, and liabilities . . . arising out of" PRM's acts or omissions. When the trust became insolvent, the state of New York assessed the trust's employer-members for some of its debts. These employer-members filed a suit against PRM for breach of contract. [Accredited Aides Plus, Inc. v. Program Risk Management, Inc.,* 147 A.D.3d 122, 46 N.Y.S.3d 246 (3 Dept. 2017)] *(See* Third Party Beneficiaries.*)*

1. Were the trust's employer-members third party beneficiaries of the trust's contract with PRM? If so, could the employer-members maintain this action against PRM?

2. Did the members have an ethical duty to pursue this claim? Explain.

Critical Thinking and Writing Assignments

18–9. Critical Legal Thinking. If intended third party beneficiaries could not sue the promisor directly to enforce a contract, what would their legal remedy be? (See *Third Party Beneficiaries.*)

18–10. Time-Limited Group Assignment—Assignment. The Smiths buy a house. They borrow 80 percent of the purchase price from the local ABC Savings and Loan. Before they make their first payment, ABC transfers the right to receive mortgage payments to Citibank. (See *Assignments.*)

1. The first group will outline what would happen if the Smiths continued to make all their payments to ABC Savings and Loan because ABC never notified them of the assignment.

2. The second group will describe what would happen if the Smiths were notified by ABC of the assignment, but continued to make payments to ABC.

3. A third group will determine what would happen if the Smiths failed to make any payments on the loan. Which financial institution would have the right to repossess their house?

Unit Two—Task-Based Simulation

Alberto Corelli offers to pay $2,500 to purchase a painting titled *Moonrise* from Tara Shelley, an artist whose works have been causing a stir in the art world. Shelley accepts Corelli's offer. Assuming that the contract has met all of the requirements for a valid contract, answer the following questions.

1. **Minors**. Corelli is a minor when he purchases the painting. Is the contract void? Is it voidable? What is the difference between these two conditions? A month after his eighteenth birthday, Corelli decides that he would rather have the $2,500 than the painting. He informs Shelley that he is disaffirming the contract and requests that Shelley return the $2,500 to him. When she refuses to do so, Corelli brings a court action to recover the $2,500. What will the court likely decide in this situation? Why?

2. **Statute of Frauds**. Both parties are adults, the contract is oral, and the painting is still in progress. Corelli pays Shelley the $2,500 in return for her promise to deliver the painting to his home when it is finished. A week later, after Shelley finishes the painting, a visitor to her gallery offers her $3,500 for it. Shelley sells the painting to the visitor and sends Corelli a signed letter explaining that she is "canceling" their contract for the sale of the *Moonrise* painting. Corelli sues Shelley to enforce the contract. Is the contract enforceable? Explain.

3. **Capacity**. Both parties are adults, and the contract, which is in writing, states that Corelli will pay Shelley the $2,500 the following day. In the meantime, Shelley allows Corelli to take the painting home with him. The next day, Corelli's son returns the painting to Shelley, stating that he is canceling the contract. He explains that his father has been behaving strangely lately, that he seems to be mentally incompetent at times, and that he clearly was not acting rationally when he bought the painting, which he could not afford. Is the contract enforceable? Discuss fully.

4. **Impossibility of Performance**. Both parties are adults, and the contract is in writing. The contract calls for Shelley to deliver the painting to Corelli's gallery in two weeks. Corelli has already arranged to sell the painting to a third party for $4,000 (a $1,500 profit), but it must be available for the third party in two weeks, or the sale will not go through. Shelley knows this but does not deliver the painting at the time promised. Corelli sues Shelley for $1,500 in damages. Shelley claims that performance was impossible because her mother fell seriously ill and required Shelley's care. Who will win this lawsuit, and why?

5. **Agreement in E-Contracts**. Both parties are adults. Shelley, on her website, offers to sell the painting for $2,500. Corelli accepts the offer by clicking on an "I accept" box on the computer screen displaying the offer. Among other terms, the online offer includes a forum-selection clause stating that any disputes under the contract are to be resolved by a court in California, the state in which Shelley lives. After Corelli receives the painting, he notices a smear of paint across the lower corner that was not visible in the digitized image that appeared on Shelley's website. Corelli calls Shelley, tells her about the smear, and says that he wants to cancel the contract and return the painting.

    When Shelley refuses to cooperate, Corelli sues her in a Texas state court, seeking to rescind the contract. Shelley claims that any suit against her must be filed in a California court in accordance with the forum-selection clause. Corelli maintains that the forum-selection clause is unconscionable and should not be enforced. What factors will the court consider in deciding this case? What will the court likely decide? Would it matter whether Corelli read the terms of the online offer before clicking on "I accept"?

Unit 3
Commercial Transactions

Michal Kalasek/Shutterstock.com

419

Image Source/Getty Images

19 | The Formation of Sales and Lease Contracts

Learning Objectives

The four Learning Objectives *below are designed to help improve your understanding. After reading this chapter, you should be able to answer the following questions:*

1. If a contract involves both goods and services, when does the UCC apply?

2. What happens if an acceptance to a sales contract includes terms additional to or different from those in the offer?

3. When exceptions to the writing requirement of the Statute of Frauds are provided in Article 2 and 2A of the UCC?

4. What law governs contracts for the international sale of goods?

> "I am for free commerce with all nations."
>
> **George Washington**
> 1732–1799
> (First president of the United States, 1789–1797)

When we turn to contracts for the sale and lease of goods, we move away from common law principles and into the area of statutory law. State statutory law governing sales and lease transactions is based on the Uniform Commercial Code (UCC), which has been adopted as law by all of the states.[1] (See this chapter's *Landmark in the Law* feature for more information on the UCC.)

The chapter-opening quotation echoes a sentiment that most Americans believe—free commerce will benefit our nation. The UCC seeks to promote commerce. Its goal is to simplify and to streamline commercial transactions. The UCC allows parties to form sales and lease contracts, including those entered into online, without observing the same degree of formality used in forming other types of contracts.

The UCC applies not only to transactions between merchants, but also to sales and leases that consumers enter into with merchants. Suppose that Peter Foster wants an electric car. He would like a Tesla Model S, but a lease on a Tesla typically costs more than $1,000 a month. After some research, Foster is considering the less expensive Chevy Volt. He can lease the Volt for $294 a month for thirty-nine months and only has to make a $500 down payment up front. The Volt is not as sleek as the Tesla, but with the Volt, he has the benefit of an electric car.

Foster goes to the dealership, signs a lease, and is driving his new electric car that same day. At the end of the lease period, Foster simply returns the car to the dealership. The lease agreement between Foster and the dealership is governed by the UCC.

---

1. Louisiana has not adopted Articles 2 and 2A, however.

The Uniform Commercial Code

Of all the attempts to produce a uniform body of laws relating to commercial transactions in the United States, none has been as successful or comprehensive as the Uniform Commercial Code (UCC).

The Origins of the UCC In the early years of this nation, sales law varied from state to state, and this lack of uniformity complicated the formation of multistate sales contracts. To remedy this situation, the National Conference of Commissioners on Uniform State Laws (NCCUSL) began drafting the UCC in 1945.

The most significant individual involved in the project was its chief editor, Karl N. Llewellyn of the Columbia University Law School. Llewellyn's intellect, continuous efforts, and ability to compromise made the first version of the UCC—completed in 1949—a legal landmark. Over the next several years, the UCC was substantially accepted by almost every state in the nation.

Comprehensive Coverage The concepts of *good faith* and *commercial reasonableness* permeate the UCC. It attempts to provide a consistent, integrated framework of rules to deal with all phases ordinarily arising in a commercial sales or lease transaction. For instance, consider the following events, all of which may occur during a single transaction:

1. *A contract for the sale or lease of goods is formed and executed.* Article 2 and Article 2A of the UCC provide rules governing all aspects of this transaction.
2. *The transaction may involve a payment—by check, electronic fund transfer, or other means.* Article 3 (on negotiable instruments), Article 4 (on bank deposits and collections), Article 4A (on fund transfers), and Article 5 (on letters of credit) cover this part of the transaction.
3. *The transaction may involve a bill of lading or a warehouse receipt that covers goods when they are shipped or stored.* Article 7 (on documents of title) deals with this subject.
4. *The transaction may involve a demand by the seller or lender for some form of security for the remaining balance owed.* Article 9 (on secured transactions) covers this part of the transaction.

Periodic Changes and Updates Various articles and sections of the UCC are periodically changed or supplemented to clarify certain rules or to establish new rules when changes in business customs render the existing UCC provisions inapplicable.

For instance, when leases of goods in the commercial context became important, Article 2A governing leases was added to the UCC. To clarify the rights of parties to commercial fund transfers, particularly electronic fund transfers, Article 4A was issued. Articles 3 and 4, on negotiable instruments and banking relationships, have undergone significant revisions. The NCCUSL also substantially revised Article 9 on secured transactions, and the revised Article 9 has been adopted by all of the states.

Application to Today's World *By periodically revising the UCC's articles, the NCCUSL has been able to adapt its provisions to changing business customs and practices. UCC provisions governing sales and lease contracts have also been extended to contracts formed in the online environment.*

19–1 The Scope of Articles 2 and 2A

Article 2 of the UCC sets forth the requirements for *sales contracts*, as well as the duties and obligations of the parties involved in the sales contract. Article 2A covers similar issues for *lease contracts*. Bear in mind, however, that the parties to sales or lease contracts are free to agree to terms different from those stated in the UCC.

19–1a Article 2—Sales

Article 2 of the UCC governs **sales contracts,** or contracts for the sale of goods. To facilitate commercial transactions, Article 2 modifies some of the common law contract requirements that were discussed in previous chapters.

Sales Contract A contract for the sale of goods.

To the extent that it has not been modified by the UCC, however, the common law of contracts also applies to sales contracts. In other words, the common law requirements for a valid contract—agreement, consideration, capacity, and legality—are also applicable to sales contracts.

In general, the rule is that when a UCC provision addresses a certain issue, the UCC governs, but when the UCC is silent, the common law governs. The relationship between general contract law and the law governing sales of goods is illustrated in Exhibit 19–1.

In regard to Article 2, keep two points in mind.

1. Article 2 deals with the sale of *goods.* It does not deal with real property (real estate), services, or intangible property such as stocks and bonds. Thus, if the subject matter of a dispute is goods, the UCC governs. If it is real estate or services, the common law applies.

2. In some situations, the rules can vary depending on whether the buyer or the seller is a *merchant.*

Sale The passing of title to property from the seller to the buyer for a price.

When does title pass in a sale of personal property at a bar?

What Is a Sale? The UCC defines a **sale** as "the passing of title [evidence of ownership rights] from the seller to the buyer for a price" [UCC 2–106(1)]. The price may be payable in cash (or its equivalent) or in other goods or services. **Case Example 19.1** Blasini, Inc., contracted to buy the business assets of the Attic Bar & Grill in Omaha, Nebraska, from Cheran Investments, LLC. Blasini obtained insurance and was making monthly payments on the assets. A fire broke out and damaged the business assets (such as furniture and equipment) involved in the sale. Because the purchase price had not yet been fully paid, a dispute arose concerning who was entitled to the insurance proceeds for the damage.

The insurance company asked a Nebraska state court to resolve the matter. Ultimately, a state appellate court held that the sale of the Attic's business assets involved goods, and thus the agreement was governed by the UCC. Under UCC 2–401, title to the goods passed to

Exhibit 19–1 The Law Governing Contracts

This exhibit graphically illustrates the relationship between general contract law and statutory law (UCC Articles 2 and 2A) governing contracts for the sale and lease of goods. Sales contracts are not governed exclusively by Article 2 of the UCC but are also governed by general contract law whenever it is relevant and has not been modified by the UCC.

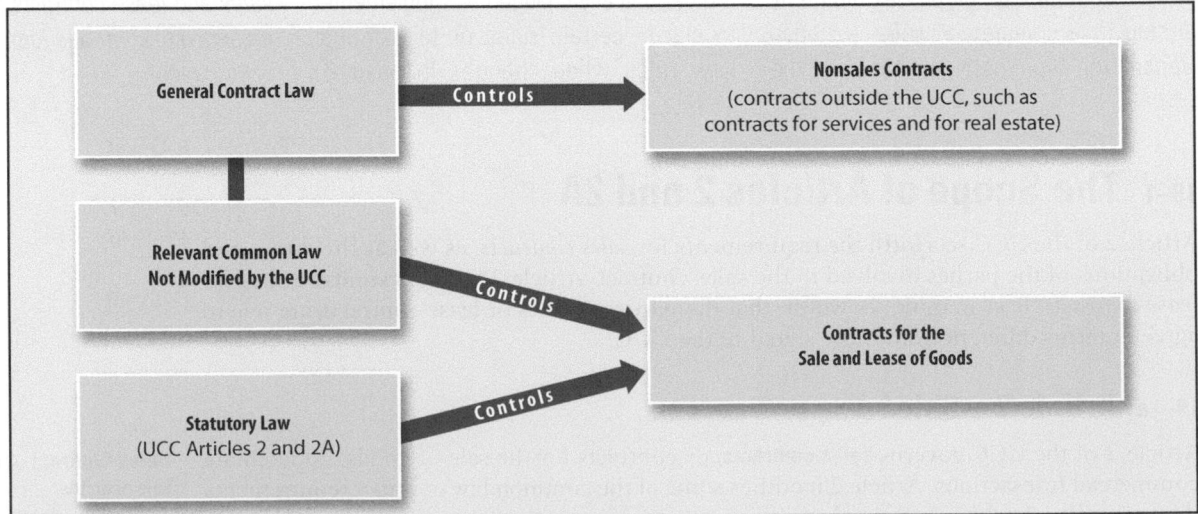

Blasini at the time of the contract, regardless of whether the entire purchase price had been paid. Therefore, Blasini was entitled to the insurance proceeds.[2]

(For a discussion of how states can impose taxes on online sales, see this chapter's *Adapting the Law to the Online Environment* feature.)

---

2. *Nautilus Insurance Co. v. Cheran Investments, LLC,* 2014 WL 292809 (Neb.Ct.App. 2014).

Adapting the Law to the Online Environment

Taxing Web Purchases

In 1992, the United States Supreme Court ruled that an individual state cannot compel an out-of-state business that lacks a substantial physical presence within that state to collect and remit state taxes.[a] Congress has the power to pass legislation requiring out-of-state corporations to collect and remit state sales taxes, but it has not yet done so. Thus, until 2018, only online retailers that also had a physical presence within a state were required to collect state taxes on Internet sales made to residents of that state. (State residents are supposed to self-report their purchases and pay use taxes to the state, but they rarely do.)

Redefining Physical Presence

A number of states found a way to circumvent the Supreme Court's 1992 ruling—they simply redefined *physical presence*. New York started the trend in 2008 when it changed its tax laws in this manner. Now, an online retailer that pays any party within New York to solicit business for its products is considered to have a physical presence in the state and must collect state taxes. Since then, around half of the states have made similar changes in an effort to increase their revenues by collecting sales tax from online retailers.

These laws, often called "Amazon tax" laws because they are aimed largely at Amazon.com, affect all online sellers, especially retailers that pay affiliates to direct traffic to their websites. The laws have been upheld by several courts.[b]

The Supreme Court Changes Course

In 2018, in *South Dakota v. Wayfair, Inc.,*[c] the United States Supreme Court overruled its earlier decision and opened the door to state taxation of online sales. The South Dakota legislature had enacted a statute that required certain out-of-state sellers to collect and remit sales tax "as if the seller had a physical presence in the state." The law applied only to sellers that annually sell more than $100,000 worth of goods or services within the state. South Dakota then sued three large retailers, Wayfair, Inc., Overstock.com, Inc., and Newegg, Inc., for failing to collect taxes as required under this law. The lower courts and the state's highest court ruled in favor of the retailers because of the Court's precedent requiring physical presence.

When the case reached the Court, however, the justices reexamined the earlier decision, and five out of nine of them chose to overrule it. The majority found that the case's focus on physical presence created an "online sales tax loophole" that gave out-of-state businesses an advantage. The justices concluded that in today's online environment, physical presence in a taxing state is not necessary for the seller to have a substantial connection with the state.

Chief Justice John Roberts wrote the dissenting opinion. He noted, "E-Commerce has grown into a significant and vibrant part of our national economy against the backdrop of established rules, including the physical-presence rule. Any alteration to those rules with the potential to disrupt the development of such a critical segment of the economy should be undertaken by Congress."

Critical Thinking

Does the Supreme Court's decision in South Dakota v. Wayfair, Inc., *make it more or less likely that Congress will enact legislation that requires out-of-state corporations to collect and pay taxes to states for online sales?*

---

a. *Quill Corp. v. North Dakota,* 504 U.S. 298, 112 S.Ct. 1904, 119 L.Ed.2d 91 (1992).

b. *Direct Marketing Association v. Brohl,* 814 F.3d 1129 (10th Cir. 2016). See also *D & H Distributing Company v. Commissioner of Revenue,* 477 Mass. 538, 79 N.E.3d 409 (2017).

c. ___ U.S. ___, ___ S.Ct. ___, ___ L.Ed.2d ___, 2018 WL 3058015 (2018).

Why would local and state governments sue online companies, such as Priceline.com, for payment of state sales taxes?

Learning Objective 1

If a contract involves both goods and services, when does the UCC apply?

Tangible Property Property that has physical existence and can be distinguished by the senses of touch and sight.

Intangible Property Property that cannot be seen or touched but exists only conceptually, such as corporate stocks. Such property is not governed by Article 2 of the UCC.

Predominant-Factor Test A test courts use to determine whether a contract is primarily for the sale of goods or for the sale of services.

What Are Goods? To be characterized as a *good,* the item of property must be *tangible,* and it must be *movable.* **Tangible property** has physical existence—it can be touched or seen. **Intangible property**—such as corporate stocks and bonds, patents and copyrights, and ordinary contract rights—has only conceptual existence and thus does not come under Article 2. A *movable* item can be carried from place to place.

Goods Associated with Real Estate. Because real estate cannot be carried from place to place, it is excluded from Article 2. Goods *associated* with real estate often fall within the scope of Article 2, however [UCC 2–107]. For instance, a contract for the sale of minerals, oil, or natural gas is a contract for the sale of goods if *severance, or separation, is to be made by the seller.* In contrast, a contract for the sale of growing crops or timber to be cut is a contract for the sale of goods *regardless of who severs them from the land.*

Goods and Services Combined. When contracts involve a combination of goods and services, courts generally use the **predominant-factor test** to determine whether a contract is primarily for the sale of goods or for the sale of services. If a court decides that a mixed contract is primarily a goods contract, *any* dispute, even a dispute over the services portion, will be decided under the UCC.

Case Example 19.2 N111KJ, LLC, contracted to buy a jet from Cessna Aircraft Company for $7.2 million. As part of the agreement, Cessna promised to manage the jet—that is, rent it out on N111KJ's behalf—for five years to help recoup some of the purchase price. Three years later, Cessna informed N111KJ that the jet was being dropped from the management program. Because of this decision, N111KJ was forced to sell the jet for less than 80 percent of the purchase price. Later, N111KJ filed a suit in a federal district court against Cessna, claiming breach of contract under the UCC. The court dismissed the claim, ruling that the contract was not subject to the UCC because managing a jet was a service. N111KJ appealed.

The U.S. Court of Appeals for the Eleventh Circuit reversed the lower court's dismissal of the suit. The contract involved a sale of goods (the jet) and a sale of services (its management). Under the predominant-factor test, the clear purpose of the agreement was the sale of the jet to N111KJ. Its management was a secondary purpose.[3]

Who Is a Merchant? Article 2 governs the sale of goods in general. It applies to sales transactions between all buyers and sellers. In a limited number of instances, though, the UCC presumes that certain special business standards ought to be imposed on merchants because of their relatively high degree of commercial expertise.[4] Such standards do not apply to the casual or inexperienced seller or buyer (consumer).

Section 2–104 sets out three ways in which merchant status can arise:

1. A merchant is a person who *deals in goods of the kind* involved in the sales contract. Thus, a retailer, a wholesaler, or a manufacturer is a merchant of those goods sold in the business. A merchant for one type of goods is not necessarily a merchant for another type. For instance, a sporting equipment retailer is a merchant when selling tennis rackets but not when selling a used iPad.

2. A merchant is a person who, by occupation, *holds himself or herself out as having special knowledge and skill* related to the practices or goods involved in the transaction. This broad definition may include banks or universities as merchants.

3. A person who *employs a merchant as a broker, agent, or other intermediary* has the status of merchant in that transaction. Hence, if an art collector hires a broker to purchase or sell art for her, the collector is considered a merchant in the transaction.

---

3. *Sack v. Cessna Aircraft Co.,* 676 Fed.Appx. 887 (11th Cir. 2017).

4. The provisions that apply only to merchants deal principally with the Statute of Frauds, firm offers, confirmatory memoranda, warranties, and contract modifications. These special rules reflect expedient business practices commonly known to merchants in the commercial setting. They will be discussed later in this chapter.

In summary, a **merchant** is someone who is in the business of buying or selling particular goods and who possesses or uses an expertise specifically related to those goods. This basic distinction is not always clear-cut. For instance, state courts appear to be split on whether farmers should be considered merchants.

19–1b Article 2A—Leases

Leases of personal property (goods such as automobiles and industrial equipment) have become increasingly common. In this context, a **lease** is a transfer of the right to possess and use goods for a period of time in exchange for payment. Article 2A of the UCC was created to fill the need for uniform guidelines in this area.

Article 2A covers any transaction that creates a lease of goods, as well as subleases of goods [UCC 2A–102, 2A–103(1)(k)]. Article 2A is essentially a repetition of Article 2, except that it applies to leases of goods rather than sales of goods and thus varies to reflect differences between sales and lease transactions. (Note that Article 2A does not apply to leases of real property, such as land or buildings.)

Definition of a Lease Agreement Article 2A defines a **lease agreement** as the bargain between a lessor and a lessee with respect to the lease of goods, as found in their language and as implied by other circumstances, including course of dealing and usage of trade or course of performance [UCC 2A–103(1)(k)]. A **lessor** is one who transfers the right to the possession and use of goods under a lease [UCC 2A–103(1)(p)]. A **lessee** is one who acquires the right to the temporary possession and use of goods under a lease [UCC 2A–103(1)(o)]. In other words, the lessee is the party who is leasing the goods from the lessor.

Article 2A applies to all types of leases of goods, including commercial leases and consumer leases. Special rules apply to certain types of leases, however, including consumer leases.

Consumer Leases Under UCC 2A–103(1)(e), a *consumer lease* involves three elements:

1. A lessor who regularly engages in the business of leasing or selling.
2. A lessee (except an organization) who leases the goods "primarily for a personal, family, or household purpose."
3. Total lease payments that are less than a dollar amount set by state statute.

To ensure special protection for consumers, certain provisions of Article 2A apply only to consumer leases. For instance, one provision states that a consumer may recover attorneys' fees if a court finds that a term in a consumer lease contract is unconscionable [UCC 2A–108(4)(a)].

19–2 The Formation of Sales and Lease Contracts

As mentioned, Article 2 and Article 2A of the UCC modify common law contract rules in several ways. Remember, though, that parties to sales contracts are normally free to establish whatever terms they wish. The UCC comes into play only when the parties have failed to provide in their contract for a contingency that later gives rise to a dispute. The UCC makes this clear time and again by using such phrases as "unless the parties otherwise agree" or "absent a contrary agreement by the parties."

19–2a Offer

In general contract law, the moment a definite offer is met by an unqualified acceptance, a binding contract is formed. In commercial sales transactions, the verbal exchanges, correspondence, and actions of the parties may not reveal exactly when a binding contractual obligation arises. The UCC states that an agreement sufficient to constitute a contract can exist even if the moment of its making is undetermined [UCC 2–204(2), 2A–204(2)].

Merchant Under the UCC, a person who deals in goods of the kind involved in the sales contract or who holds herself or himself out as having skill or knowledge peculiar to the practices or goods being purchased or sold.

Lease Under Article 2A of the UCC, a transfer of the right to possess and use goods for a period of time in exchange for payment.

Lease Agreement An agreement in which one person (the lessor) agrees to transfer the right to the possession and use of property to another person (the lessee) in exchange for rental payments.

Lessor A person who transfers the right to the possession and use of goods to another in exchange for rental payments.

Lessee A person who acquires the right to the possession and use of another's goods in exchange for rental payments.

Know This

Under the UCC, it is the actions of the parties that determine whether they intended to form a contract.

Open Terms Remember that under the common law of contracts, an offer must be definite enough for the parties (and the courts) to ascertain its essential terms when it is accepted. In contrast, the UCC states that a sales or lease contract will not fail for indefiniteness even if one or more terms are left open as long as *both* of the following are true:

1. The parties intended to make a contract.
2. There is a reasonably certain basis for the court to grant an appropriate remedy [UCC 2–204(3), 2A–204(3)].

The UCC provides numerous *open-term* provisions (discussed next) that can be used to fill the gaps in a contract. Thus, if a dispute occurs, all that is necessary to prove the existence of a contract is an indication (such as a purchase order) that there is a contract. Missing terms can be proved by evidence, or a court can presume that the parties intended whatever is reasonable under the circumstances.

Keep in mind, though, that if too many terms are left open, a court may find that the parties did not intend to form a contract. In addition, the *quantity* of goods involved must be expressly stated in the contract. If the quantity term is left open, the courts will have no basis for determining a remedy.

In the following case, one company orally agreed to store another company's goods in anticipation of forming a contract, but they did not agree on how long that arrangement would last. The question was whether the open term in their agreement rendered the contract unenforceable.

■ Case 19.1

Toll Processing Services, LLC v. Kastalon, Inc.

United States Court of Appeals, Seventh Circuit, 880 F.3d 820 (2018).

Background and Facts Toll Processing Services, a subsidiary of International Steel Services, Inc., was formed to own and operate a pickle line. A pickle line is a machine used in the steel industry to process hot-rolled steel coil through acid tanks to remove rust and impurities. Toll Processing purchased a used pickle line from Ryerson & Sons that had been serviced by Kastalon, Inc., which provides equipment and repairs for the steel industry. Toll Processing was planning to reinstall the used pickle line somewhere else but did not have a facility. Kastalon agreed to move the pickle rolls to its facility and store them, at no cost, until Toll Processing could issue a purchase order to Kastalon to recondition the rolls. Both parties believed that Toll Processing would complete its plan to reinstall the pickle line within months, but they did not discuss the time frame.

Kastalon moved fifty-seven pickle rolls to its facility over a period of three months, but then had no further contact with Toll Processing for two years. Believing that the pickle rolls were of little value and that Toll Processing had gone out of business, Kastalon eventually scrapped the rolls and received $6,300 from a recycler. The following year, Toll Processing contacted Kastalon and requested a price quote for reconditioning the rolls, at which point Kastalon informed Toll that the rolls had been scrapped.

Toll sued Kastalon for breach of contract (in addition to several other claims). A district court granted summary judgment in favor of Kastalon, finding that the oral agreement between the parties did not have a specific duration, and lacked consideration. Toll Processing appealed.

In the Words of the Court

PEPPER, District Judge.

* * * *

Under Illinois law, oral agreements are enforceable "so long as there is an offer, an acceptance, and a meeting of the minds as to the terms of the agreement." *To be enforceable, such an oral agreement must be sufficiently definite as to its material terms.* The parties do not dispute that the duration of Kastalon's obligation to store the rolls was a material term of their agreement; their dispute relates to the length of the duration. [Emphasis added.]

* * * Toll Processing argued that Kastalon agreed to store the rolls until Toll Processing issued a purchase order for Kastalon to refurbish the rolls—whenever that might be. Kastalon confirmed that it had agreed to store the rolls until Toll Processing found a location for the pickle line and issued the purchase order for the refurbishment of the rolls, but insisted that this was to be for a

short time—a period of three or four months. This discrepancy, the district court found, showed that the parties did not have a mutual understanding as to the duration of the storage agreement.

On appeal, Toll Processing argues that "the parties' conduct established an agreement on the material terms, and the undisputed facts of record established that there was consideration to support the agreement." Toll Processing also argues that the district court erred because the duration of the contract either was tied to the reinstallation of the pickle line, or presented a genuine dispute of material fact regarding the parties' mutual intent.

Kastalon responded that [Toll Processing's in-house attorney] admitted that the parties did not reach an agreement that Kastalon was to hold the rolls indefinitely, and that he admitted that the alleged oral agreement placed no obligations on Toll Processing other than to advise Kastalon that it had received a purchase order for the pickle line and was ready to proceed with work involving the rolls. According to Kastalon, the spare and vague terms of this oral agreement were too indefinite to be enforced under Illinois law.

Kastalon's expectation that Toll Processing would hire it to repair and refurbish the rolls constitutes consideration. But we conclude that the district court correctly entered judgment in Kastalon's favor as to Toll Processing's breach of contract claim, because the evidence shows that the parties did not have a mutual understanding that Kastalon would store the rolls indefinitely.

The duration of the agreement was to be determined by the date on which Toll Processing issued a purchase order to Kastalon to repair and refurbish the rolls for use in the newly installed pickle line. When Kastalon agreed to store the rolls, however, Toll Processing did not know when—or even if—it would issue that purchase order. The parties hoped and anticipated that Toll Processing would issue the purchase order within months, but Toll Processing conceded that it was possible it might never have issued a purchase order.

Decision and Remedy A federal appellate court affirmed the judgment of the district court on the breach of contract claim. Although the parties may have attempted to form a contract, they did not reach a mutual understanding that Kastalon would store the pickle rolls for any certain period of time. Because there was no meeting of the minds on this term, the agreement was unenforceable. The appellate court reversed and remanded the district court's decision on Toll Processing's other claims, however.

Critical Thinking

• **What If the Facts Were Different?** *Suppose that the parties admitted that they had agreed Kastalon would store the rolls for up to one year. How would this have affected the court's decision on breach of contract?*

• **Ethical** *Was it unethical for Kastalon to scrap the rolls without attempting to contact Toll Processing? Explain.*

Open Price Term. If the parties have not agreed on a price, the court will determine a "reasonable price at the time for delivery" [UCC 2–305(1)]. If either the buyer or the seller is to determine the price, the price is to be fixed (set) in good faith [UCC 2–305(2)]. Under the UCC, *good faith* means honesty in fact and the observance of reasonable commercial standards of fair dealing in the trade [UCC 2–103(1)(b)].

Sometimes, the price fails to be fixed through the fault of one of the parties. In that situation, the other party can treat the contract as canceled or fix a reasonable price. **Example 19.3** Perez and Merrick enter into a contract for the sale of unfinished doors and agree that Perez will determine the price. Perez refuses to specify the price. Merrick can either treat the contract as canceled or set a reasonable price [UCC 2–305(3)]. ▪

Open Payment Term. When parties do not specify payment terms, payment is due at the time and place at which the buyer is to receive the goods [UCC 2–310(a)]. The buyer can tender payment using any commercially normal or acceptable means, such as a check or credit card. If the seller demands payment in cash, the buyer must be given a reasonable time to obtain it [UCC 2–511(2)].

Example 19.4 Max Angel agrees to purchase hay from Wagner's farm. Angel leaves his truck and trailer at the farm for the seller to load the hay. Nothing is said about when payment is due, and the parties are unaware of the UCC's rules. Nevertheless, because the parties did not specify when payment was due, UCC 2–310(a) controls, and payment is due at the time Angel picks up the hay. Therefore, Wagner can refuse to release the hay (or the vehicles on which the hay is loaded) to Angel until he pays for it. ▪

Know This
The common law requires that the parties make their terms definite before they have a contract. The UCC applies general commercial standards to make the terms of a contract definite.

If no time for payment for hay is specified in a sales contract, when is payment due?

"Business, more than any other occupation, is a continual dealing with the future. It is a continual calculation, an instinctive exercise in foresight."

Henry R. Luce
1898–1967
(U.S. editor and publisher)

Requirements Contract An agreement in which a buyer agrees to purchase and a seller agrees to sell all or up to a stated amount of what the buyer needs or requires.

Output Contract An agreement in which a seller agrees to sell and a buyer agrees to buy all or up to a stated amount of what the seller produces.

Open Delivery Term. When no delivery terms are specified, the buyer normally takes delivery at the seller's place of business [UCC 2–308(a)]. If the seller has no place of business, the seller's residence is used. When goods are located in some other place and both parties know it, delivery is made there. If the time for shipment or delivery is not clearly specified in the sales contract, the court will infer a "reasonable" time for performance [UCC 2–309(1)].

Duration of an Ongoing Contract. A single contract might specify successive performances but not indicate how long the parties are required to deal with each other. In this situation, either party may terminate the ongoing contractual relationship. Principles of good faith and sound commercial practice call for reasonable notification before termination, however, to give the other party time to make substitute arrangements [UCC 2–309(2), (3)].

Options and Cooperation Regarding Performance. When the contract contemplates shipment of the goods but does not specify the shipping arrangements, the *seller* has the right to make these arrangements in good faith, using commercial reasonableness in the situation [UCC 2–311].

When a sales contract omits terms relating to the assortment of goods, the *buyer* can specify the assortment. **Example 19.5** Petry Drugs, Inc., enters an e-contract to purchase one thousand toothbrushes from Marconi's Dental Supply. The toothbrushes come in a variety of colors, but the contract does not specify color. Petry, the buyer, has the right to take six hundred blue toothbrushes and four hundred green ones, if it wishes. Petry, however, must exercise good faith and commercial reasonableness in making its selection [UCC 2–311]. ■

Open Quantity Terms. Normally, if the parties do not specify a quantity, no contract is formed. A court will have no basis for determining a remedy because there is almost no way for a court to determine objectively what is a reasonable quantity of goods for someone to buy. (In contrast, a court can objectively determine a reasonable price for particular goods by looking at the market for like goods.) Nevertheless, the UCC recognizes two exceptions to this rule in *requirements* and *output contracts* [UCC 2–306(1)].

1. *Requirements Contracts.* Requirements contracts are common in the business world and normally are enforceable. In a **requirements contract**, the buyer agrees to purchase and the seller agrees to sell all or up to a stated amount of what the buyer *needs* or *requires.* **Example 19.6** Umpqua Cannery forms a contract with Al Garcia. The cannery agrees to purchase from Garcia, and Garcia agrees to sell to the cannery, all of the green beans that the cannery needs or requires during the following summer. ■ There is implicit consideration in this contract because the buyer (the cannery) gives up the right to buy goods (green beans) from any other seller. This forfeited right creates a legal *detriment*—that is, consideration.

   If, however, the buyer promises to purchase only if the buyer *wishes* to do so, the promise is illusory (without consideration) and unenforceable by either party. Similarly, if the buyer reserves the right to buy the goods from someone other than the seller, the promise is unenforceable (illusory) as a requirements contract.

2. *Output Contracts.* In an **output contract**, the seller agrees to sell and the buyer agrees to buy all or up to a stated amount of what the seller *produces.* **Example 19.7** Ruth Sewell has planted two acres of organic tomatoes. Bella Union, a local restaurant, agrees to buy all of the tomatoes that Sewell produces that year to use at the restaurant. ■ Again, because the seller essentially forfeits the right to sell goods to another buyer, there is implicit consideration in an output contract.

The UCC imposes a *good faith limitation* on requirements and output contracts. The quantity under such contracts is the amount of requirements or the amount of output that occurs during a *normal* production year. The actual quantity purchased or sold cannot be unreasonably disproportionate to normal or comparable prior requirements or output [UCC 2–306(1)].

Merchant's Firm Offer Under regular contract principles, an offer can be revoked at any time before acceptance. The major common law exception is an *option contract,* in which the offeree pays consideration for the offeror's irrevocable promise to keep the offer open for a stated period. The UCC creates a second exception for firm offers made by a merchant to sell, buy, or lease goods.

A **firm offer** arises when a merchant-offeror gives *assurances* in a *signed writing* that the offer will remain open. A merchant's firm offer is irrevocable without the necessity of consideration[5] for the stated period or, if no definite period is stated, a reasonable period (neither period to exceed three months) [UCC 2–205, 2A–205].

Example 19.8 Osaka, a used-car dealer, e-mails Saucedo on January 1, stating, "I have a used 2018 Toyota RAV4 on the lot that I'll sell you for $26,000 any time between now and January 31." This e-mail creates a firm offer, and Osaka will be liable for breach if he sells that Toyota RAV4 to someone other than Saucedo before January 31. ■

19–2b Acceptance

Acceptance of an offer to buy, sell, or lease goods generally can be made in any reasonable manner and by any reasonable means. The UCC permits acceptance of an offer to buy goods "either by a prompt *promise* to ship or by the prompt or current shipment of conforming or nonconforming goods" [UCC 2–206(1)(b)]. *Conforming goods* accord with the contract's terms, whereas *nonconforming goods* do not.

Shipment of Nonconforming Goods The prompt shipment of nonconforming goods constitutes both an acceptance, which creates a contract, and a breach of that contract. This rule does not apply if the seller **seasonably** (within a specified time period or a reasonable amount of time) notifies the buyer that the nonconforming shipment is offered only as an *accommodation,* or a favor. The notice of accommodation must clearly indicate to the buyer that the shipment does not constitute an acceptance and that, therefore, no contract has been formed.

Example 19.9 McCleary orders one thousand blue smart fitness watches from Halderson. Halderson ships one thousand *black* smart fitness watches to McCleary. If Halderson notifies McCleary that it has only black watches in stock, and the black watches are being sent as an accommodation, then the shipment is an offer. A contract will be formed only if McCleary accepts the black watches.

If, however, Halderson ships black watches *without* notifying McCleary that the goods are being sent as an accommodation, the shipment is both an acceptance and a breach of the resulting contract. McCleary can sue Halderson for any appropriate damages. ■

Communication of Acceptance Required Under the common law, a unilateral offer can be accepted by beginning performance. The offeree need not notify the offeror of performance unless the offeror would not otherwise know about it. Under the UCC, however, the offeror must be notified within a reasonable time that the offeree has accepted the contract by beginning performance. Otherwise, the offeror can treat the offer as having lapsed before acceptance [UCC 2–206(2), 2A–206(2)].

Additional Terms Recall that under the common law, the *mirror image rule* requires that the terms of the acceptance exactly match those of the offer. **Example 19.10** Adderson e-mails an offer to sell twenty Samsung Galaxy Tab S2 9.7 tablets to Beale. If Beale accepts the offer but changes it to require Tab S3 tablets, then there is no contract if the mirror image rule applies. ■

Firm Offer An offer (by a merchant) that is irrevocable without the necessity of consideration for a stated period of time or, if no definite period is stated, for a reasonable time (neither period to exceed three months).

Know This

The UCC provides that acceptance can be made by any means that is reasonable under the circumstances—including prompt shipment of the goods.

Seasonably Within a specified time period or, if no period is specified, within a reasonable time.

Alexey Boldin/Shutterstock.com

If a retailer orders blue smart fitness watches, but instead the shipper sends black ones, is this an acceptance, a breach, or an accommodation?

---

5. If the offeree pays consideration, then an option contract (not a merchant's firm offer) is formed.

To avoid such situations, the UCC dispenses with the mirror image rule. Under the UCC, a contract is formed if the offeree's response indicates a *definite* acceptance of the offer, *even if the acceptance includes terms additional to or different from those contained in the offer* [UCC 2–207(1)]. Whether the additional terms become part of the contract depends, in part, on whether the parties are nonmerchants or merchants.

Rules When One Party or Both Parties Are Nonmerchants. If one (or both) of the parties is a *nonmerchant*, the contract is formed according to the terms of the original offer submitted by the original offeror and not according to the additional terms of the acceptance [UCC 2–207(2)].

Example 19.11 BettyBloom.com sells plants and gardening supplies online. Employees of a school district in Oregon order $10,000 worth of goods for a school project—without the authority or approval of their employer—from the website. The invoices that accompany the goods contain a *forum-selection clause* requiring all disputes to be resolved in California.

When the school district fails to pay, BettyBloom.com files suit in a California court. The court is likely to find that the forum-selection clause is unenforceable. The clause is an additional term included in invoices delivered to a nonmerchant buyer (the school district) with the purchased goods. The clause cannot become part of the contract unless the school district expressly agrees to it.

Rules When Both Parties Are Merchants. The drafters of the UCC created a special rule for merchants to avoid the "battle of the forms," which occurs when two merchants exchange separate standard forms containing different contract terms. Under UCC 2–207(2), in contracts *between merchants,* the additional terms *automatically* become part of the contract unless one of the following conditions exists:

1. The original offer expressly limited acceptance to its terms.
2. The new or changed terms materially alter the contract.
3. The offeror objects to the new or changed terms within a reasonable period of time.

When determining whether an alteration is material, courts consider several factors. Generally, if the modification does not involve an unreasonable element of surprise or hardship for the offeror, the court will hold that the modification did not materially alter the contract.

As shown in the following case, however, what constitutes a material alteration is frequently a question of fact that only a court can decide.

■ Case 19.2

C. Mahendra (N.Y.), LLC v. National Gold & Diamond Center, Inc.

New York Supreme Court, Appellate Division, First Department, 125 A.D.3d 454, 3 N.Y.S.3d 27 (2015).

Background and Facts C. Mahendra (N.Y.), LLC, is a New York wholesaler of loose diamonds. National Gold & Diamond Center, Inc., is a California seller of jewelry. Over a ten-year period, National placed orders, totaling millions of dollars, with Mahendra by phoning and negotiating the terms. Mahendra shipped diamonds "on memorandum" for National to examine. Mahendra then sent invoices for the diamonds that National chose to keep. Both

What happens if one party to an ongoing contract inserts a forum-selection clause without approval?

the memoranda and the invoices stated, "You consent to the exclusive jurisdiction of the . . . courts situated in New York County." When two orders totaling $64,000 went unpaid, Mahendra filed a suit in a New York state court against National, alleging breach of contract. National filed a motion to dismiss the complaint for lack of personal jurisdiction, contending that the forum-selection clause was not binding. The court granted the motion. Mahendra appealed.

In the Words of the Court
SWEENY, P.J. [Presiding Judge], *MOSKOWITZ, DEGRASSE, MANZANET–DANIELS, CLARK*, JJ. [Judges]

* * * *

* * * Defendant argued the forum-selection clause in the * * * memorandums was not binding because its president never signed the memorandums' terms and conditions. Defendant thus maintained that it had not signed or agreed to the forum-selection clause, nor had it otherwise consented to being sued in New York. Likewise, defendant asserted that because it had negotiated for and ordered the diamonds from California and did not sign or agree to the forum-selection clause, the consent to jurisdiction contained in the memorandums would materially alter the parties' agreements in contravention of UCC 2–207(2)(b). Thus, defendant concluded, it was not bound by the unsigned provision on the back of the * * * memorandums.

* * * *

* * * The [lower] court found the forum-selection clause invalid, noting that defendant did not sign the invoices. The court further found that under UCC 2–207(2), forum-selection clauses are additional terms that materially alter a contract, and must be construed as mere proposals for additions to the contract. Thus, the court concluded, the forum-selection clause was nonbinding absent an express agreement. Indeed, the court noted, the complaint did not allege that defendant affirmatively expressed consent, either orally or in writing, to the forum-selection clause when it retained the invoices.

* * * *

The [lower] court correctly found that defendant is not bound by the forum-selection clause on plaintiff's invoices. UCC 2–207 contemplates situations like the one here, where parties do business through an exchange of forms such as purchase orders and invoices. As the parties did here, *merchants frequently include terms in their forms that were not discussed with the other side. UCC 2–207(2) addresses that scenario, providing, "the additional terms are to be construed as proposals for addition to the contract. Between merchants such terms become part of the contract unless: * * * (b) they materially alter it."* [Emphasis added.]

Here, during telephone discussions, the parties negotiated the essential terms required for contract formation, and the invoices were merely confirmatory. Thus, the forum-selection clause is an additional term that materially altered the parties' oral contracts, and defendant did not give its consent to that additional term.

Decision and Remedy A state intermediate appellate court agreed that "the forum-selection clause is an additional term that materially altered the parties' . . . contracts, and defendant did not give its consent to that additional term." But the court reversed the dismissal of Mahendra's complaint on the ground that National's phone calls with Mahendra were sufficient contacts to subject the defendant to personal jurisdiction in New York under the state's longarm statute.

Critical Thinking

• **Legal Environment** *What is Mahendra's best argument that the forum-selection clause was, in fact, binding on National? Discuss.*

Prior Dealings between Merchants. Courts also consider the parties' prior dealings in determining whether the added terms become part of contracts between merchants. See this chapter's *Business Law Analysis* feature for an example.

Conditioned on Offeror's Assent. The offeree's expression cannot be construed as an acceptance if it contains additional or different terms that are explicitly conditioned on the offeror's assent to those terms [UCC 2–207(1)]. This rule applies whether or not the parties are merchants. **Example 19.12** Philips offers to sell ninety boxes of peaches at a specified price to Foodland. Dawn Koker, Foodland's owner, responds, "I accept your offer *on the condition that you give me thirty more boxes.*" Foodland's response will be construed not as an acceptance but as a counteroffer, which Philips may or may not accept. ■

Additional Terms May Be Stricken. The UCC provides yet another option for dealing with conflicting terms in the parties' writings. Section 2–207(3) states that conduct by both parties that recognizes the existence of a contract is sufficient to establish a contract for the sale of goods. This is so even if the parties' writings contain different terms. In this situation, "the terms of the particular contract will consist of those terms on which the writings of the

Additional Terms between Merchants

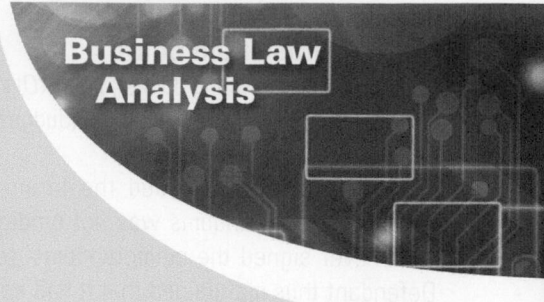

B.S. International (BSI), makes costume jewelry. Jayco, Inc., is a wholesaler of costume jewelry. Jayco sent BSI a letter outlining the terms for orders, including the necessary procedure for obtaining credit for items that customers rejected. The letter stated, "By signing below, you agree to the terms." Steven Brown, BSI's owner, signed the letter and returned it. For six years, BSI made jewelry for Jayco, which resold it. Items rejected by customers were sent back to Jayco but never returned to BSI.

BSI eventually filed a suit against Jayco, claiming $41,000 for the unreturned items. BSI showed the court a copy of Jayco's terms. Across the bottom had been typed a "P.S." (postscript) requiring the return of rejected merchandise. Was this P.S. part of the contract?

Analysis: Under the common law, variations in terms between the offer and the acceptance violate the mirror image rule, which requires that the terms of an acceptance exactly mirror the terms of the offer. The UCC dispenses with this rule. Under the UCC, a contract is formed if the offeree makes a definite expression of acceptance even though the terms of the acceptance modify or add to the terms of the offer.

When both parties to a sales contract are merchants, the additional terms become part of their contract unless (1) the original offer expressly required acceptance of its terms, (2) the new or changed terms materially alter the contract, or (3) the offeror rejects the new or changed terms within a reasonable time.

In this situation, the original offer stated, "By signing below, you agree to the terms." This statement could be construed to expressly require acceptance of the terms to make the offer a binding contract. The contract stated that Jayco was to receive credit for any rejected merchandise. Nothing indicated that the merchandise would be returned to BSI.

Result and Reasoning: When Brown (BSI's owner and the offeree) signed Jayco's (the offeror's) letter, it indicated BSI's agreement to the terms. Thus, BSI made a definite expression of acceptance. The practice of the parties—for six years rejected items were not returned—supports the conclusion that their contract did not contemplate the return of those items. The P.S. could be interpreted as materially altering the contract. Therefore, the P.S. is not part of the contract, and a court should dismiss BSI's lawsuit.

TatyanaMishchenko/iStock/Getty Images

Should prior dealings between a costume jewelry manufacturer and a buyer be considered if a contract dispute arises over additional terms? Why or why not?

parties agree, together with any supplementary terms incorporated under any other provisions of this Act."

In a dispute over contract terms, this provision allows a court simply to strike from the contract those terms on which the parties do not agree. **Example 19.13** SMT Marketing orders goods over the phone from Brigg Sales, Inc., which ships the goods with an acknowledgment form (confirming the order) to SMT. SMT accepts and pays for the goods. The parties' writings do not establish a contract, but there is no question that a contract exists. If a dispute arises over the terms, such as the extent of any warranties, UCC 2–207(3) provides the governing rule. ▮

As noted previously, the fact that a merchant's acceptance frequently contains terms that add to or even conflict with those of the offer is often referred to as the "battle of the forms." Although the UCC tries to eliminate this battle, the problem of differing contract terms still arises in commercial settings, particularly when standard forms for placing and confirming orders are used.

19–2c Consideration

The common law rule that a contract requires consideration also applies to sales and lease contracts. Unlike the common law, however, the UCC does not require a contract modification to be supported by new consideration. An agreement modifying a contract for the sale or lease of goods "needs no consideration to be binding" [UCC 2–209(1), 2A–208(1)]. Of course, a contract modification must be sought in good faith [UCC 1–304].

In some situations, an agreement to modify a sales or lease contract without consideration must be in writing to be enforceable. If the contract itself prohibits any changes to the contract unless they are in a signed writing, for instance, then only those changes agreed to in a signed writing are enforceable.

Sometimes, when a consumer (nonmerchant buyer) is dealing with a merchant, the merchant supplies the form that contains a clause prohibiting oral modification. In those situations, the consumer must sign a separate acknowledgment of the clause for it to be enforceable [UCC 2–209(2), 2A–208(2)]. Also, any modification that brings a sales contract under Article 2's Statute of Frauds provision usually must be in writing to be enforceable.

19–2d The Statute of Frauds

The UCC contains Statute of Frauds provisions covering sales and lease contracts. Under these provisions, sales contracts for goods priced at $500 or more and lease contracts requiring payments of $1,000 or more must be in writing to be enforceable [UCC 2–201(1), 2A–201(1)]. E-mails and other electronic records satisfy the writing requirement.

Sufficiency of the Writing A writing will be sufficient to satisfy the UCC's Statute of Frauds as long as it meets the following requirements:

1. It indicates that the parties intended to form a contract.
2. It is signed by the party (or agent of the party) against whom enforcement is sought. (Remember that a typed name can qualify as a signature.)

The contract normally will not be enforceable beyond the quantity of goods shown in the writing, however. All other terms can be proved in court by oral testimony. For leases, the writing or record must reasonably identify and describe the goods leased and the lease term.

Special Rules for Contracts between Merchants Once again, the UCC provides a special rule for merchants in sales transactions. (There is no corresponding rule that applies to leases under Article 2A.) Merchants can satisfy the Statute of Frauds if, after the parties have agreed orally, one of the merchants sends a signed written confirmation to the other merchant within a reasonable time.

The communication must indicate the terms of the agreement, and the merchant receiving the confirmation must have reason to know of its contents. Unless the merchant who receives the confirmation gives written notice of objection to its contents within ten days after receipt, the writing or record is sufficient, even though she or he has not signed anything [UCC 2–201(2)].

Example 19.14 Alfonso is a merchant-buyer in Cleveland. He contracts over the telephone to purchase $6,000 worth of spare aircraft parts from Goldstein, a merchant-seller in New York City. Two days later, Goldstein e-mails a signed confirmation detailing the terms of the oral contract, and Alfonso receives it. Alfonso does not notify Goldstein in writing of any objection to the contents of the confirmation within ten days of receipt. Therefore, Alfonso cannot raise the Statute of Frauds as a defense against the enforcement of the oral contract. ∎

Exceptions In addition to the special rules for merchants, the UCC defines three exceptions to the writing requirements of the Statute of Frauds. An oral contract for the sale of goods priced at $500 or more—or the lease of goods involving total payments of $1,000 or more—will be enforceable despite the absence of a writing in the circumstances described next [UCC 2–201(3), 2A–201(4)].

Know This

It has been proposed that the UCC be revised to eliminate the Statute of Frauds.

Learning Objective 3

What exceptions to the writing requirements of the Statute of Frauds are provided in Article 2 and Article 2A of the UCC?

Specially Manufactured Goods. An oral contract for the sale or lease of custom-made goods will be enforceable if the following conditions exist:

1. The goods are *specially manufactured* for a particular buyer or specially manufactured or obtained for a particular lessee.

2. The goods are *not suitable for resale or lease* to others in the ordinary course of the seller's or lessor's business.

3. The seller or lessor has *substantially started to manufacture* the goods or has made commitments for the manufacture or procurement of the goods.

Under these conditions, once the seller or lessor has taken action, the buyer or lessee cannot repudiate the agreement claiming the Statute of Frauds as a defense. **Example 19.15** Womach orders custom window treatments from Hunter Douglas to use at her day spa business. The contract is oral, and the price is $6,000. When Hunter Douglas manufactures the window coverings and tenders delivery to Womach, she refuses to pay for them, even though the job is completed on time. Womach claims that she is not liable because the contract is oral. If the unique style, size, and color of the window treatments make it improbable that Hunter Douglas can find another buyer, Womach is liable to Hunter Douglas. ■

Admissions. An oral contract for the sale or lease of goods is enforceable if the party against whom enforcement of the contract is sought admits in pleadings, testimony, or other court proceedings that a contract for sale or lease was made. In this situation, the contract will be enforceable even though it was oral, but enforceability will be limited to the quantity of goods admitted.

Example 19.16 Gerald Lingman, a farmer, agrees by phone to sell his crops to Great Plains Cooperative. The parties reach two oral agreements for the delivery of corn. Lingman then reneges on the deal and sells his corn to another dealer. Great Plains pays a higher price to buy corn elsewhere and then sues Lingman for breach of contract. In court, Lingman acknowledges the first oral agreement but not the second. The court will apply the admissions exception to enforce the agreement admitted by Lingman, but the other agreement will be unenforceable under this exception. ■

Can two oral agreements for delivery of corn be enforced if the seller admits that only the first agreement occurred?

Partial Performance. An oral contract for the sale or lease of goods is enforceable if payment has been made and accepted or goods have been received and accepted. This is the "partial performance" exception. The oral contract will be enforced at least to the extent that performance *actually* took place.

Example 19.17 Jamal orally contracts to lease to Opus Enterprises one thousand chairs at $2 each to be used during a one-day concert. Before delivery, Opus sends Jamal a check for $1,000, which Jamal cashes. Later, when Jamal attempts to deliver the chairs, Opus refuses delivery, claiming the Statute of Frauds as a defense, and demands the return of its $1,000.

Under the UCC's partial performance rule, Jamal can enforce the oral contract by tender of delivery of five hundred chairs for the $1,000 accepted. Similarly, if Opus had made no payment but had accepted the delivery of five hundred chairs from Jamal, the oral contract would have been enforceable against Opus for $1,000, the lease payment due for the five hundred chairs delivered. ■

These exceptions and other ways in which sales law differs from general contract law are summarized in Exhibit 19–2.

19–2e Parol Evidence

Recall that *parol evidence* consists of evidence outside the contract, such as evidence of the parties' prior negotiations, prior agreements, or oral agreements made at the time of contract formation. When a contract completely sets forth all the terms and conditions agreed to by

Exhibit 19–2 **Major Differences between Contract Law and Sales Law**

TOPIC	CONTRACT LAW	SALES LAW
Contract Terms	The contract must contain all material terms.	Open terms are acceptable, if the parties intended to form a contract, but the quantity term normally must be specified, and the contract is not enforceable beyond the quantity term.
Acceptance	Mirror image rule applies. If additional terms are added in acceptance, a counteroffer is created.	Additional terms will not negate acceptance unless acceptance is made expressly conditional on assent to the additional terms.
Contract Modification	Modification requires consideration.	Modification does not require consideration.
Irrevocable Offers	Option contracts (with consideration) are irrevocable.	Merchants' firm offers (without consideration) are irrevocable.
Statute of Frauds Requirements	All material terms must be included in the writing.	Writing is required only for the sale of goods priced at $500 or more, but the contract is not enforceable beyond the quantity specified. Merchants can satisfy the requirement by a confirmatory memorandum evidencing their agreement. Exceptions exist for (1) specially manufactured goods, (2) admissions, and (3) partial performance.

the parties and is intended as a final statement of their agreement, it is considered *fully integrated*. The terms of a fully integrated contract cannot be contradicted by evidence outside the contract.

If, however, the writing (or record) contains some of the terms the parties agreed on but not others, the contract is *not fully integrated*. In this situation, a court may allow evidence of *consistent additional terms* to explain or supplement the terms stated in the contract. The court may also allow the parties to submit evidence of *course of dealing, usage of trade*, or *course of performance* [UCC 2–202, 2A–202]. A court will not under any circumstances allow the parties to submit evidence that contradicts the contract's stated terms, however. (This is also the rule under the common law.)

Course of Dealing and Usage of Trade Under the UCC, the meaning of any agreement, evidenced by the language of the parties and by their actions, must be interpreted in light of commercial practices and other surrounding circumstances. In interpreting a commercial agreement, the court will assume that the course of prior dealing between the parties and the usage of trade were taken into account when the agreement was phrased.

Course of Dealing. A **course of dealing** is a sequence of actions and communications between the parties to a particular transaction that establishes a common basis for their understanding [UCC 1–303(b)]. A course of dealing is restricted to the sequence of conduct between the parties in their transactions prior to the agreement.

Under the UCC, a course of dealing between the parties is relevant in ascertaining the meaning of the parties' agreement. It "may give particular meaning to specific terms of the agreement, and may supplement or qualify the terms of the agreement" [UCC 1–303(d)].

Usage of Trade. Any practice or method of dealing that is so regularly observed in a place, vocation, or trade as to justify an expectation by the parties that it will be observed in their transaction is a **usage of trade** [UCC 1–303(c)].

Example 19.18 United Loans, Inc., hires Fleet Title Review to search the public records for prior claims on potential borrowers' assets. Fleet's invoice states, "Liability limited to amount

Course of Dealing Prior conduct between the parties to a contract that establishes a common basis for their understanding.

Usage of Trade Any practice or method of dealing that is so regularly observed in a place, vocation, or trade that parties justifiably expect it will be observed in their transaction.

of fee." In the search industry, liability limits are common. After conducting many searches for United, Fleet reports that there are no claims with respect to Main Street Autos. United loans $100,000 to Main, with payment guaranteed by Main's assets.

When Main defaults on the loan, United learns that another lender has priority to Main's assets under a previous claim. If United sues Fleet Title for breach of contract, Fleet's liability will normally be limited to the amount of its fee. The statement in the invoice was part of the contract between United and Fleet Title, according to the usage of trade in the industry and the parties' course of dealing.

Course of Performance A **course of performance** is the conduct that occurs under the terms of a particular agreement [UCC 1–303(a)]. Presumably, the parties themselves know best what they meant by their words. Thus, the course of performance actually carried out under their agreement is the best indication of what they meant [UCC 2–208(1), 2A–207(1)].

Example 19.19 Janson's Lumber Company contracts with Lopez to sell Lopez a specified number of two-by-fours. The lumber in fact does not measure exactly 2 inches by 4 inches but rather 1⅞ inches by 3¾ inches. Janson's agrees to deliver the lumber in five deliveries, and Lopez, without objection, accepts the lumber in the first three deliveries. On the fourth delivery, however, Lopez objects that the two-by-fours do not measure 2 inches by 4 inches.

The course of performance in this transaction—that is, Lopez's acceptance of three deliveries without objection under the agreement—is relevant in determining that here the term *two-by-four* actually means "1⅞ by 3¾." Janson's can also prove that *two-by-fours* need not be exactly 2 inches by 4 inches by applying course of prior dealing, usage of trade, or both. Janson's can, for example, show that in previous transactions, Lopez took 1⅞-by-3¾-inch lumber without objection. In addition, Janson's can show that in the lumber trade, two-by-fours are commonly 1⅞ inches by 3¾ inches.

Rules of Construction The UCC provides *rules of construction* for interpreting contracts. Express terms, course of performance, course of dealing, and usage of trade are to be construed to be consistent with each other whenever reasonable. When such a construction is unreasonable, however, the UCC establishes the following order of priority [UCC 1–303(e), 2–208(2), 2A–207(2)]:

1. Express terms.
2. Course of performance.
3. Course of dealing.
4. Usage of trade.

19–2f Unconscionability

As previously discussed, an unconscionable contract is one that is so unfair and one-sided that it would be unreasonable to enforce it. Under the UCC, if a court deems a contract or a clause to have been unconscionable *at the time it was made*, the court can do any of the following [UCC 2–302, 2A–108]:

1. Refuse to enforce the contract.
2. Enforce the remainder of the contract without the unconscionable part.
3. Limit the application of the unconscionable term to avoid an unconscionable result.

The following *Classic Case* illustrates an early application of the UCC's unconscionability provisions.

Course of Performance The conduct that occurs under the terms of a particular agreement, which indicates what the parties to that agreement intended the agreement to mean.

Do two-by-fours actually measure 2 inches by 4 inches?

Classic Case 19.3

Jones v. Star Credit Corp.

Supreme Court of New York, Nassau County, 59 Misc.2d 189, 298 N.Y.S.2d 264 (1969).

Background and Facts The Joneses agreed to purchase a freezer for $900 as the result of a sales-person's visit to their home. Tax and financing charges raised the total price to $1,234.80. Later, the Joneses, who had made payments totaling $619.88, brought a suit in a New York state court to have the purchase contract declared unconscionable under the UCC. At trial, the freezer was found to have a maximum retail value of approximately $300.

Can a retailer sell a freezer at four times its wholesale price?

JazzIRT/E+/Getty Images

In the Words of the Court

Sol M. *WACHTLER*, Justice.

* * * *

* * * [Section 2–302 of the UCC] authorizes the court to find, as a matter of law, that a contract or a clause of a contract was "unconscionable at the time it was made," and upon so finding the court may refuse to enforce the contract, excise the objectionable clause or limit the application of the clause to avoid an unconscionable result.

* * * *

* * * The question which presents itself is whether or not, under the circumstances of this case, the sale of a freezer unit having a retail value of $300 for $900 ($1,439.69 including credit charges and $18 sales tax) is unconscionable as a matter of law.

Concededly, deciding [this case] is substantially easier than explaining it. No doubt, the mathematical disparity between $300, which presumably includes a reasonable profit margin, and $900, which is exorbitant on its face, carries the greatest weight. Credit charges alone exceed by more than $100 the retail value of the freezer. These alone may be sufficient to sustain the decision. Yet, a caveat [warning] is warranted lest we reduce the import of

Section 2–302 solely to a mathematical ratio formula. It may, at times, be that; yet it may also be much more. The very limited financial resources of the purchaser, known to the sellers at the time of the sale, is entitled to weight in the balance. Indeed, the value disparity itself leads inevitably to the felt conclusion that knowing advantage was taken of the plaintiffs. In addition, *the meaningfulness of choice essential to the making of a contract can be negated by a gross inequality of bargaining power.* [Emphasis added.]

* * * *

* * * The defendant has already been amply compensated. In accordance with the statute, the application of the payment provision should be limited to amounts already paid by the plaintiffs and the contract be reformed and amended by changing the payments called for therein to equal the amount of payment actually so paid by the plaintiffs.

Decision and Remedy The court held that the contract was not enforceable and reformed the contract so that the Joneses were not required to make further payments on the freezer.

Critical Thinking

• **Social** *Why would the seller's knowledge of the buyers' limited resources support a finding of unconscionability?*

• **Impact of This Case on Today's Law** *This early case illustrates the approach that many courts today take when deciding whether a sales contract is unconscionable—an approach that focuses on excessive price and unequal bargaining power.*

19–3 Contracts for the International Sale of Goods

Today, businesses often engage in sales and lease transactions on a global scale. International sales contracts between firms or individuals located in different countries are governed by the 1980 United Nations Convention on Contracts for the International Sale of Goods (CISG). The CISG governs international contracts only if the countries of the parties to the contract have ratified the CISG and if the parties have not agreed that some other law will govern their contract. As of 2019, the CISG had been adopted by eighty-four countries, including the

Learning Objective 4

What law governs contracts for the international sale of goods?

United States, Canada, some Central and South American countries, China, most European nations, Japan, and Mexico. That means that the CISG is the uniform international sales law of countries that account for more than two-thirds of all global trade.

19–3a Applicability of the CISG

Essentially, the CISG is to international sales contracts what Article 2 of the UCC is to domestic sales contracts. As discussed earlier, in domestic transactions the UCC applies when the parties to a contract for a sale of goods have failed to specify in writing some important term concerning price, delivery, or the like. Similarly, whenever the parties subject to the CISG have failed to specify in writing the precise terms of a contract for the international sale of goods, the CISG will be applied.

Unlike *the UCC, the CISG does not apply to consumer sales.* Neither the UCC nor the CISG applies to contracts for services.

19–3b A Comparison of CISG and UCC Provisions

The provisions of the CISG, although similar for the most part to those of the UCC, differ from them in certain respects. If the CISG and the UCC conflict, the CISG applies (because it is a treaty of the U.S. national government and therefore takes precedence over state laws under the U.S. Constitution). We look here at some differences with respect to contract formation.

The appendix at the end of this chapter—which shows an actual international sales contract used by Starbucks Coffee Company—illustrates many of the special terms and clauses that are typically contained in international contracts for the sale of goods. Annotations in the appendix explain the meaning and significance of specific contract clauses.

Statute of Frauds Unlike the UCC, the CISG does not include any Statute of Frauds provisions. Under Article 11 of the CISG, an international sales contract does not need to be evidenced by a writing or to be in any particular form.

Offers UCC 2–205 provides that a merchant's firm offer is irrevocable, even without consideration, if the merchant gives assurances in a signed writing or record. In contrast, under the CISG, an offer can become irrevocable without a signed writing or record. Article 16(2) of the CISG provides that an offer will be irrevocable in either of the following circumstances:

1. The offeror states orally that the offer is irrevocable.
2. The offeree reasonably relies on the offer as being irrevocable.

In both of these situations, the offer will be irrevocable without a writing or record and without consideration.

Another difference is that, under the UCC, if the price term is left open, the court will determine "a reasonable price at the time for delivery" [UCC 2–305(1)]. Under the CISG, however, the price term must be specified, or at least provisions for its specification must be included in the agreement. Otherwise, normally no contract will exist.

Acceptances Under the UCC, a definite expression of acceptance that contains additional terms can still result in the formation of a contract, unless the additional terms are conditioned on the assent of the offeror. In other words, the UCC does away with the mirror image rule in domestic sales contracts.

Article 19 of the CISG provides that a contract can be formed even though the acceptance contains additional terms, unless the additional terms materially alter the contract. Under the CISG, however, a "material alteration" includes almost any change in the terms. If an additional term relates to payment, quality, quantity, price, time and place of delivery, extent of one party's liability to the other, or the settlement of disputes, the CISG considers the added term a material alteration. In effect, then, the CISG requires that the terms of the acceptance mirror those of the offer.

Case Example 19.20 VLM Food Trading International, Inc., a Canadian agricultural supplier, sold frozen potatoes to Illinois Trading Co., an American buyer and seller of produce. For each of their transactions, Illinois Trading sent a purchase order setting out the terms, and VLM responded with a confirming e-mail. VLM then shipped the order, Illinois Trading accepted it, and VLM followed up with a "trailing" invoice. Only the trailing invoice included a provision that the buyer would be liable for attorneys' fees if it breached the contract.

Nine transactions occurred without incident. Illinois Trading ran into financial difficulties, however, and did not pay for the next nine shipments. VLM filed a suit in a federal district court against the buyer, seeking to recover the unpaid amount plus attorneys' fees. Illinois Trading admitted that it owed the price for the potatoes but contested liability for the attorneys' fees. A federal appellate court agreed with Illinois Trading that under the CISG, the attorneys' fee provision in the trailing invoice did not become part of the parties' contract. The attorneys' fee provision was a material alteration to the contract terms, and Illinois Trading did not agree to the additional term.[6]

How did Article **19** of the CISG affect the court's decision regarding a dispute over the international sale of potatoes?

---

6. *VLM Food Trading International, Inc. v. Illinois Trading Co.,* 811 F.3d 247 (7th Cir. 2016).

Practice and Review

Guy Holcomb owns and operates Oasis Goodtime Emporium, an adult entertainment establishment. Holcomb wanted to create an adult Internet system for Oasis that would offer customers adult theme videos and live chat room programs using performers at the club. On May 10, Holcomb signed a work order authorizing Thomas Consulting Group (TCG) "to deliver a working prototype of a customer chat system, demonstrating the integration of live video and chatting in a Web browser." In exchange for creating the prototype, Holcomb agreed to pay TCG $64,697. On May 20, Holcomb signed an additional work order in the amount of $12,943 for TCG to install a customized firewall system. The work orders stated that Holcomb would make monthly installment payments to TCG, and both parties expected the work would be finished by September.

Due to unforeseen problems largely attributable to system configuration and software incompatibility, the project required more time than anticipated. By the end of the summer, the website was still not ready, and Holcomb had fallen behind in the payments to TCG. TCG was threatening to cease work and file suit for breach of contract unless the bill was paid. Rather than make further payments, Holcomb wanted to abandon the website project. Using the information presented in the chapter, answer the following questions.

1. Would a court be likely to decide that the transaction between Holcomb and TCG was covered by the Uniform Commercial Code (UCC)? Why or why not?

2. Would a court be likely to consider Holcomb a merchant under the UCC? Why or why not?

3. Did the parties have a valid contract under the UCC? Explain.

(Continues)

4. Suppose that Holcomb and TCG meet in October in an attempt to resolve their problems. At that time, the parties reach an oral agreement that TCG will continue to work without demanding full payment of the past-due amounts and Holcomb will pay TCG $5,000 per week. Assuming that the contract falls under the UCC, is the oral agreement enforceable? Why or why not?

Debate This

The UCC should require the same degree of definiteness of terms, especially with respect to price and quantity, as general contract law does.

Key Terms

course of dealing 435	lessee 425	sale 422
course of performance 436	lessor 425	sales contract 421
firm offer 429	merchant 425	seasonably 429
intangible property 424	output contract 428	tangible property 424
lease 425	predominant-factor test 424	usage of trade 435
lease agreement 425	requirements contract 428	

Chapter Summary: The Formation of Sales and Lease Contracts

The Scope of Articles 2 and 2A	1. *The Uniform Commercial Code (UCC)*—Attempts to provide a consistent, uniform, and integrated framework of rules to deal with all phases ordinarily arising in a commercial sales or lease transaction, including contract formation, passage of title, and risk of loss. The concepts of good faith and commercial reasonableness permeate the UCC.
	2. *Article 2 (sales)*—Governs contracts for the sale of goods (tangible, movable personal property). Rules can vary if the buyer or seller is a merchant. The common law of contracts also applies to sales contracts to the extent that the common law has not been modified by the UCC. If there is a conflict between a common law rule and the UCC, the UCC controls.
	3. *Article 2A (leases)*—Governs contracts for the lease or sublease of goods. Except that it applies to leases, instead of sales, of goods, Article 2A is essentially a repetition of Article 2 and varies only to reflect differences between sales and lease transactions.
The Formation of Sales and Lease Contracts	1. *Offer*—
	a. Not all terms have to be included for a contract to be formed (only the subject matter and quantity term normally must be specified).
	b. The price does not have to be included for a contract to be formed.
	c. Particulars of performance can be left open.
	d. A written and signed offer by a *merchant*, covering a period of three months or less, is irrevocable without payment of consideration.
	2. *Acceptance*—
	a. Acceptance may be made by any reasonable means of communication. It is effective when dispatched.
	b. An offer can be accepted by a promise to ship or by prompt shipment of conforming goods, or by prompt shipment of nonconforming goods if accompanied by a notice of accommodation.
	c. Acceptance by performance requires notice within a reasonable time. Otherwise, the offer can be treated as lapsed before acceptance.
	d. A definite expression of acceptance creates a contract even if the terms of the acceptance differ from those of the offer, unless the additional or different terms in the acceptance are expressly conditioned on the offeror's assent to those terms.

3. *Consideration*—A modification of a contract for the sale of goods does not require consideration.
4. *The Statute of Frauds*—
   a. All contracts for the sale of goods priced at $500 or more, and lease contracts requiring payments of $1,000 or more, must be in writing. A writing is sufficient as long as it indicates the parties' intention to form a contract and is signed by the party against whom enforcement is sought. A contract normally is not enforceable beyond the quantity shown in the writing.
   b. When written confirmation of an oral contract *between merchants* is not objected to in writing by the receiver within ten days, the contract is enforceable.
   c. For exceptions to the Statute of Frauds, see Exhibit 19–2.
5. *Parol evidence rule*—
   a. The terms of a clear and complete written contract cannot be contradicted by evidence of prior agreements or contemporaneous oral agreements.
   b. Evidence is admissible to clarify the terms of a writing if the contract terms are ambiguous or if evidence of course of dealing, usage of trade, or course of performance is necessary to learn or to clarify the parties' intentions.
6. *Unconscionability*—An unconscionable contract is one that is so unfair and one-sided that it would be unreasonable to enforce it. If the court deems a contract or a clause in a contract to have been unconscionable at the time it was made, the court can (a) refuse to enforce the contract, (b) refuse to enforce the unconscionable clause, or (c) limit the application of any unconscionable clauses to avoid an unconscionable result.

Contracts for the International Sale of Goods
International sales contracts are governed by the United Nations Convention on Contracts for the International Sale of Goods (CISG) if the countries of the parties to the contract have ratified the CISG and if the parties have not agreed that some other law will govern their contract. Essentially, the CISG is to international sales contracts what Article 2 of the UCC is to domestic sales contracts. Unlike the UCC, however, the CISG does not apply to consumer sales. Whenever parties who are subject to the CISG have failed to specify in writing the precise terms of a contract for the international sale of goods, the CISG will be applied.

Issue Spotters

1. E-Design, Inc., orders 150 computer desks. Fav-O-Rite Supplies, Inc., ships 150 printer stands. Is this an acceptance of the offer or a counteroffer? If it is an acceptance, is it a breach of the contract? What if Fav-O-Rite told E-Design it was sending the printer stands as "an accommodation"? (See *The Formation of Sales and Lease Contracts*.)

2. Truck Parts, Inc. (TPI), often sells supplies to United Fix-It Company (UFC), which services trucks. Over the phone, they negotiate for the sale of eighty-four sets of tires. TPI sends a letter to UFC detailing the terms and two weeks later ships the tires. Is there an enforceable contract between them? Why or why not? (See *The Formation of Sales and Lease Contracts*.)

   —**Check your answers to the *Issue Spotters* against the answers provided in Appendix D at the end of this text.**

Business Scenarios and Case Problems

19–1. Additional Terms. Strike offers to sell Bailey one thousand shirts for a stated price. The offer declares that shipment will be made by Dependable Truck Line. Bailey replies, "I accept your offer for one thousand shirts at the price quoted. Delivery to be by Yellow Express Truck Line." Both Strike and Bailey are merchants. Three weeks later, Strike ships the shirts by Dependable Truck Line, and Bailey refuses to accept delivery. Strike sues for breach of contract. Bailey claims that there never was a contract because his reply, which included a modification of carriers, did not constitute an acceptance. Bailey further claims that even if there had been a contract, Strike would have been in breach because Strike shipped the shirts by Dependable, contrary to the contract terms. Discuss fully Bailey's claims. (See *The Formation of Sales and Lease Contracts*.)

19–2. Merchant's Firm Offer. On May 1, Jennings, a car dealer, e-mails Wheeler and says, "I have a 1955 Thunderbird convertible in mint condition that I will sell you for $13,500 at any time before June 9. [Signed] Peter Jennings." By May 15, having heard nothing from Wheeler, Jennings sells the car to another. On May 29, Wheeler accepts Jennings's offer and tenders $13,500. When told Jennings has sold the car to another, Wheeler claims Jennings has breached their contract. Is Jennings in breach? Explain. (See *The Formation of Sales and Lease Contracts*.)

19–3. Spotlight on Goods and Services—The Statute of Frauds. Fallsview Glatt Kosher Caterers ran a business that provided travel packages, including food, entertainment, and lectures on religious subjects, to customers during the Passover holiday at a New York resort. Willie Rosenfeld verbally agreed to pay Fallsview $24,050 for the Passover package for himself and his family. Rosenfeld did not appear at the resort and never paid the money owed. Fallsview sued Rosenfeld for breach of contract. Rosenfeld claimed that the contract was unenforceable because it was not in writing and violated the UCC's Statute of Frauds. Is the contract valid? Explain. [*Fallsview Glatt Kosher Caterers, Inc. v. Rosenfeld*, 7 Misc.3d 557, 794 N.Y.S.2d 790 (2005)] (See *The Formation of Sales and Lease Contracts*.)

19–4. Partial Performance and the Statute of Frauds. After a series of e-mails, Jorge Bonilla, the sole proprietor of a printing company in Uruguay, agreed to buy a used printer from Crystal Graphics Equipment, Inc., in New York. Crystal Graphics, through its agent, told Bonilla that the printing press was fully operational, contained all of its parts, and was in excellent condition except for some damage to one of the printing towers. Bonilla paid $95,000. Crystal Graphics sent him a signed, stamped invoice reflecting this payment. The invoice was dated six days after Bonilla's conversation with the agent.

When the printing press arrived, Bonilla discovered that it was missing parts and was damaged. Crystal Graphics sent replacement parts, but they did not work. Crystal Graphics was never able to make the printer operational. Bonilla sued, alleging breach of contract, breach of the implied covenant of good faith and fair dealing, breach of express warranty, and breach of implied warranty. Crystal Graphics claimed that the contract was not enforceable because it did not satisfy the Statute of Frauds. Can Crystal Graphics prevail on this basis? Why or why not? [*Bonilla v. Crystal Graphics Equipment, Inc.*, 2012 WL 360145 (S.D.Fla. 2012)] (See *The Formation of Sales and Lease Contracts*.)

19–5. The Statute of Frauds. Kendall Gardner agreed to buy from B&C Shavings a specially built shaving mill to produce wood shavings for poultry processors. B&C faxed an invoice to Gardner reflecting a purchase price of $86,200, with a 30 percent down payment and the "balance due before shipment." Gardner paid the down payment. B&C finished the mill and wrote Gardner a letter telling him to "pay the balance due or you will lose the down payment." By then, Gardner had lost his customers for the wood shavings, could not pay the balance due, and asked for the return of his down payment. Did these parties have an enforceable contract under the Statute of Frauds? Explain. [*Bowen v. Gardner*, 2013 Ark.App. 52, 425 S.W.3d 875 (2013)] (See *The Formation of Sales and Lease Contracts*.)

19–6. Business Case Problem with Sample Answer—Goods and Services Combined. Allied Shelving and Equipment, Inc., sells and installs shelving systems. National Deli, LLC, contracted with Allied to provide and install a parallel rack system (a series of large shelves) in National's warehouse. Both parties were dissatisfied with the result. National filed a suit in a Florida state court against Allied, which filed a counterclaim. Each contended that the other had materially breached the contract. The court applied common law contract principles to rule in National's favor on both claims. Allied appealed, arguing that the court should have applied the UCC. When does a court apply common law principles to a contract that involves both goods and services? In this case, why might an appellate court rule that the UCC should be applied instead? Explain. [*Allied Shelving and Equipment, Inc. v. National Deli, LLC*, 40 Fla.L.Weekly D145, 154 So.3d 482 (Dist.App. 2015)] (See *The Scope of Articles 2 and 2A*.)

—For a sample answer to Problem 19–6, go to Appendix E at the end of this text.

19–7. Acceptance. New England Precision Grinding, Inc. (NEPG), sells precision medical parts in Massachusetts. NEPG agreed to supply Kyphon, Inc., with certain medical parts. NEPG contracted with Simply Surgical, LLC, to obtain the parts from Iscon Surgicals, Ltd. The contract did not mention Kyphon or require Kyphon's acceptance of the parts. Before shipping, Iscon would certify that the parts conformed to NEPG's specifications. On receiving the parts, NEPG would certify that they conformed to Kyphon's specifications. On delivery, Kyphon would also inspect the parts.

After about half a dozen transactions, NEPG's payments to Simply Surgical lagged, and the seller refused to make further deliveries. NEPG filed a suit in a Massachusetts state court against Simply Surgical, alleging breach of contract. NEPG claimed that Kyphon had rejected some of the parts, which gave NEPG the right not to pay for them. Do the UCC's rules with respect to acceptance support or undercut the parties' actions? Discuss. [*New England Precision Grinding, Inc. v. Simply Surgical, LLC*, 89 Mass.App.Ct.176, 46 N.E.3d 590 (2016)] (See *The Formation of Sales and Lease Contracts*.)

19–8. Requirements Contracts. Medalist Golf, Inc., a high-end golf course builder, was working on a new golf course project in Missouri. Chris Williams, doing business as Cane Creek Sod, submitted a bid with Medalist to provide Meyer Zoysia grass sod for the project. Williams and Medalist executed a "grass supplier agreement" that specified the type and quality of grass to be used, stated the price, and gave Medalist a right to inspect and reject the sod. The parties estimated the quantity of sod needed for the project to be twenty-one acres. Williams had approximately sixty-five acres of Meyer Zoysia

CHAPTER 19: The Formation of Sales and Lease Contracts

growing at the time. The agreement did not specify the amount of sod that Medalist would purchase from Williams, nor did it say that Medalist would buy Williams's sod exclusively. Later, when Medalist had an expert inspect William's sod (before it was harvested), the expert concluded that it did not meet the quality standards required for the project. Medalist therefore rejected the sod. Williams sued for breach of contract. Was the "grass supplier agreement" enforceable as a requirements contract? Why or why not? [*Williams v. Medalist Golf, Inc.*, ___ F.Supp.3d ___, 2018 WL 1046889 (E.D.Mo. 2018)] (See *The Formation of Sales and Lease Contracts.*)

19–9. A Question of Ethics—The IDDR Approach and Sales and Lease Contracts. *Camal Terry signed a "Sales Contract" to buy a 1995 BMW 3 Series from Robin Drive Auto, a car dealership in Delaware. Terry agreed to pay $4,995, and Robin Drive agreed to hold the BMW on layaway for him in contemplation of a sale* within twenty-one days. Also specified were a down payment of $1,200 and the timing of other payments. But under the payment schedule, Terry was to pay $100 a week for six weeks (forty-two days) even though the sale was to take place twenty-one days later. In addition, the contract provided that the payments were fees for storage and "prep" and were not deductible from the price of the car. Terry paid more than $1,000 before asking Robin Drive to refund the money. When the dealership refused, Terry filed a suit in a Delaware state court against Robin Drive. Testimony about the mismatched contract terms was conflicting. [Terry v. Robin Drive Auto, *2017 WL 65842 (Del.Com.Pl. 2017)] (See* The Formation of Sales and Lease Contracts.*)*

1. Ethically, what is wrong with this deal? Explain.

2. Using the IDDR approach, consider whether Robin Drive has an ethical obligation to use a different contract in its sales to consumers.

Critical Thinking and Writing Assignments

19–10. Time-Limited Group Assignment—Parol Evidence. Mountain Stream Trout Co. agreed to buy "market size" trout from trout grower Lake Farms, LLC. Their five-year contract did not define *market size*. At the time, in the trade, *market size* referred to fish of one-pound live weight. After three years, Mountain Stream began taking fewer, smaller deliveries of larger fish, claiming that *market size* varied according to whatever its customers demanded and that its customers now demanded larger fish. Lake Farms filed a suit for breach of contract. (See *The Formation and of Sales and Lease Contracts.*)

1. The first group will decide whether parol evidence is admissible to explain the terms of this contract. Are there any exceptions that could apply?

2. A second group will determine the impact of course of dealing and usage of trade on the interpretation of contract terms.

3. A third group will discuss how parties to a commercial contract can avoid the possibility that a court will interpret the contract terms in accordance with trade usage.

Appendix to Chapter 19
An Example of a Contract for the International Sale of Coffee

1 **2**
OVERLAND COFFEE IMPORT CONTRACT
OF THE
GREEN COFFEE ASSOCIATION
OF
NEW YORK CITY, INC.*

Contract Seller's No.: __504617__
Buyer's No.: __P9264__
Date: __10/11/20__

SOLD BY: __XYZ Co.__
TO: __Starbucks__

3 QUANTITY: __Five Hundred__ (__500__) Tons of __Mexican__ coffee (Bags)
weighing about __152.117 lbs.__ per bag.

4 PACKAGING: Coffee must be packed in clean sound bags of uniform size made of sisal, henequen, jute, burlap, or similar woven material, without inner lining or outer covering of any material properly sewn by hand and/or machine. Bulk shipments are allowed if agreed by mutual consent of Buyer and Seller.

5 DESCRIPTION: __High grown Mexican Altura__

PRICE: At __Ten/$10.00 dollars__ U.S. Currency, per __1b.__ net, (U.S. Funds)
Upon delivery in Bonded Public Warehouse at __Laredo, TX__
(City and State)

6 PAYMENT: __Cash against warehouse receipts__

Bill and tender to DATE when all import requirements and governmental regulations have been satisfied, and coffee delivered or discharged (as per contract terms). Seller is obliged to give the Buyer two (2) calendar days free time in Bonded Public Warehouse following but not including date of tender.

7 ARRIVAL: During __December__ via __truck__
(Period) (Method of Transportation)
from __Mexico__ for arrival at __Laredo, TX, USA__
(Country of Exportation) (Country of Importation)
Partial shipments permitted.

8 ADVICE OF ARRIVAL: Advice of arrival with warehouse name and location, together with the quantity, description, marks and place of entry, must be transmitted directly, or through Seller's Agent/Broker, to the Buyer or his Agent/ Broker. Advice will be given as soon as known but not later than the fifth business day following arrival at the named warehouse. Such advice may be given verbally with written confirmation to be sent the same day.

9 WEIGHTS: (1) DELIVERED WEIGHTS: Coffee covered by this contract is to be weighed at location named in tender. Actual tare to be allowed.
(2) SHIPPING WEIGHTS: Coffee covered by this contract is sold on shipping weights. Any loss in weight exceeding __1/2__ percent at location named in tender is for account of Seller at contract price.
(3) Coffee is to be weighed within fifteen (15) calendar days after tender. Weighing expenses, if any, for account of __Seller__ (Seller or Buyer)

10 MARKINGS: Bags to be branded in English with the name of Country of Origin and otherwise to comply with laws and regulations of the Country of Importation, in effect at the time of entry, governing marking of import merchandise. Any expense incurred by failure to comply with these regulations to be borne by Exporter/Seller.

11 RULINGS: The "Rulings on Coffee Contracts" of the Green Coffee Association of New York City, Inc., in effect on the date this contract is made, is incorporated for all purposes as a part of this agreement, and together herewith, constitute the entire contract. No variation or addition hereto shall be valid unless signed by the parties to the contract.
Seller guarantees that the terms printed on the reverse hereof, which by reference are made a part hereof, are identical with the terms as printed in By-Laws and Rules of the Green Coffee Association of New York City, Inc., heretofore adopted.
Exceptions to this guarantee are:

ACCEPTED:
__XYZ Co.__
BY _____*Dm*_____ Seller
Agent

__Starbucks__
BY _____ Buyer
Agent

COMMISSION TO BE PAID BY:
__Seller__

__ABC Brokerage__
Broker(s)

12

13 When this contract is executed by a person acting for another, such person hereby represents that he is fully authorized to commit his principal.

* Reprinted with permission of The Green Coffee Association of New York City, Inc.

1 This is a contract for a sale of coffee to be *imported* internationally. If the parties have their principal places of business located in different countries, the contract may be subject to the United Nations Convention on Contracts for the International Sale of Goods (CISG). If the parties' principal places of business are located in the United States, the contract may be subject to the Uniform Commercial Code (UCC).

2 Quantity is one of the most important terms to include in a contract. Without it, a court may not be able to enforce the contract.

3 Weight per unit (bag) can be exactly stated or approximately stated. If it is not so stated, usage of trade in international contracts determines standards of weight.

4 Packaging requirements can be conditions for acceptance and payment. Bulk shipments are not permitted without the consent of the buyer.

5 A description of the coffee and the "Markings" constitute express warranties. International contracts rely more heavily on descriptions and models or samples.

6 Under the UCC, parties may enter into a valid contract even though the price is not set. Under the CISG, a contract must provide for an exact determination of the price.

7 The terms of payment may take one of two forms: credit or cash. Credit terms can be complicated. A cash term can be simple, and payment can be made by any means acceptable in the ordinary course of business (for example, a personal check or a letter of credit). If the seller insists on actual cash, the buyer must be given a reasonable time to get it.

8 *Tender* means the seller has placed goods that conform to the contract at the buyer's disposition. This contract requires that the coffee meet all import regulations and that it be ready for pickup by the buyer at a "Bonded Public Warehouse." (A *bonded warehouse* is a place in which goods can be stored without payment of taxes until the goods are removed.)

9 The delivery date is significant because, if it is not met, the buyer may hold the seller in breach of the contract. Under this contract, the seller is given a "period" within which to deliver the goods, instead of a specific day. The seller is also given some time to rectify goods that do not pass inspection (see the "Guarantee" clause on the second page of the contract).

10 As part of a proper tender, the seller (or its agent) must inform the buyer (or its agent) when the goods have arrived at their destination.

11 In some contracts, delivered and shipping weights can be important. During shipping, some loss can be attributed to the type of goods (spoilage of fresh produce, for example) or to the transportation itself. A seller and buyer can agree on the extent to which either of them will bear such losses.

12 Documents are often incorporated in a contract by reference, because including them word for word can make a contract difficult to read. If the document is later revised, the entire contract might have to be reworked. Documents that are typically incorporated by reference include detailed payment and delivery terms, special provisions, and sets of rules, codes, and standards.

13 In international sales transactions, and for domestic deals involving certain products, brokers are used to form the contracts. When so used, the brokers are entitled to a commission.

(Continues)

TERMS AND CONDITIONS

14   ARBITRATION: All controversies relating to, in connection with, or arising out of this contract, its modification, making or the authority or obligations of the signatories hereto, and whether involving the principals, agents, brokers, or others who actually subscribe hereto, shall be settled by arbitration in accordance with the "Rules of Arbitration" of the Green Coffee Association of New York City, Inc., as they exist at the time of the arbitration (including provisions as to payment of fees and expenses). Arbitration is the sole remedy hereunder, and it shall be held in accordance with the law of New York State, and judgment of any award may be entered in the courts of that State, or in any other court of competent jurisdiction. All notices or judicial service in reference to arbitration or enforcement shall be deemed given if transmitted as required by the aforesaid rules.

15   GUARANTEE: (a) If all or any of the coffee is refused admission into the country of importation by reason of any violation of governmental laws or acts, which violation existed at the time the coffee arrived at Bonded Public Warehouse, seller is required, as to the amount not admitted and as soon as possible, to deliver replacement coffee in conformity to all terms and conditions of this contract, excepting only the Arrival terms, but not later than thirty (30) days after the date of the violation notice. Any payment made and expenses incurred for any coffee denied entry shall be refunded within ten (10) calendar days of denial of entry, and payment shall be made for the replacement delivery in accordance with the terms of this contract. Consequently, if Buyer removes the coffee from the Bonded Public Warehouse, Seller's responsibility as to such portion hereunder ceases.
(b) Contracts containing the overstamp "No Pass-No Sale" on the face of the contract shall be interpreted to mean: If any or all of the coffee is not admitted into the country of Importation in its original condition by reason of failure to meet requirements of the government's laws or Acts, the contract shall be deemed null and void as to that portion of the coffee which is not admitted in its original condition. Any payment made and expenses incurred for any coffee denied entry shall be refunded within ten (10) calendar days of denial of entry.

16   CONTINGENCY: This contract is not contingent upon any other contract.

CLAIMS: Coffee shall be considered accepted as to quality unless within *fifteen* (15) calendar days after delivery at Bonded Public Warehouse or within *fifteen* (15) calendar days after all Government clearances have been received, whichever is later, either:
(a) Claims are settled by the parties hereto, or,
(b) Arbitration proceedings have been filed by one of the parties in accordance with the provisions hereof.
17 (c) If neither (a) nor (b) has been done in the stated period or if any portion of the coffee has been removed from the Bonded Public Warehouse before representative sealed samples have been drawn by the Green Coffee Association of New York City, Inc., in accordance with its rules, Seller's responsibility for quality claims ceases for that portion so removed.
(d) Any question of quality submitted to arbitration shall be a matter of allowance only, unless otherwise provided in the contract.

18   DELIVERY: (a) No more than three (3) chops may be tendered for each lot of 250 bags.
(b) Each chop of coffee tendered is to be uniform in grade and appearance. All expense necessary to make coffee uniform shall be for account of seller.
(c) Notice of arrival and/or sampling order constitutes a tender, and must be given not later than the fifth business day following arrival at Bonded Public Warehouse stated on the contract.

INSURANCE: Seller is responsible for any loss or damage, or both, until Delivery and Discharge of coffee at the Bonded Public Warehouse in the Country of Importation.

All Insurance Risks, costs and responsibility are for Seller's Account until Delivery and Discharge of coffee at the Bonded Public Warehouse in the Country of Importation.

Buyer's insurance responsibility begins from the day of importation or from the day of tender, whichever is later.

19   FREIGHT: Seller to provide and pay for all transportation and related expenses to the Bonded Public Warehouse in the Country of Importation.

20   EXPORT DUTIES/TAXES: Exporter is to pay all Export taxes, duties or other fees or charges, if any, levied because of exportation.

IMPORT DUTIES/TAXES: Any Duty or Tax whatsoever, imposed by the government or any authority of the Country of Importation, shall be borne by the Importer/Buyer.

21   INSOLVENCY OR FINANCIAL FAILURE OF BUYER OR SELLER: If, at any time before the contract is fully executed, either party hereto shall meet with creditors because of inability generally to make payment of obligations when due, or shall suspend such payments, fail to meet his general trade obligations in the regular course of business, shall file a petition in bankruptcy or, for an arrangement, shall become insolvent, or commit an act of bankruptcy, then the other party may at his option, expressed in writing, declare the aforesaid to constitute a breach and default of this contract, and may, in addition to other remedies, decline to deliver further or make payment or may sell or purchase for the defaulter's account, and may collect damage for any injury or loss, or shall account for the profit, if any, occasioned by such sale or purchase.

This clause is subject to the provisions of (11 USC 365 (e) 1) if invoked.

22   BREACH OR DEFAULT OF CONTRACT: In the event either party hereto fails to perform, or breaches or repudiates this agreement, the other party shall subject to the specific provisions of this contract be entitled to the remedies and relief provided for by the Uniform Commercial Code of the State of New York. The computation and ascertainment of damages, or the determination of any other dispute as to relief, shall be made by the arbitrators in accordance with the Arbitration Clause herein.

Consequential damages shall not, however, be allowed.

23

14 Arbitration is the settling of a dispute by submitting it to a disinterested party (other than a court), which renders a decision. The procedures and costs can be provided for in an arbitration clause or incorporated through other documents. To enforce an award rendered in an arbitration, the winning party can "enter" (submit) the award in a court "of competent jurisdiction."

15 When goods are imported internationally, they must meet certain import requirements before being released to the buyer. Because of this, buyers frequently want a guaranty clause that covers the goods not admitted into the country and that either requires the seller to replace the goods within a stated time or allows the contract for those goods not admitted to be void.

16 In the "Claims" clause, the parties agree that the buyer has a certain time within which to reject the goods. The right to reject is a right by law and does not need to be stated in a contract. If the buyer does not exercise the right within the time specified in the contract, the goods will be considered accepted.

17 Many international contracts include definitions of terms so that the parties understand what they mean. Some terms are used in a particular industry in a specific way. Here, the word *chop* refers to a unit of like-grade coffee beans. The buyer has a right to inspect ("sample") the coffee. If the coffee does not conform to the contract, the seller must correct the nonconformity.

18 The "Delivery," "Insurance," and "Freight" clauses, with the "Arrival" clause on the first page of the contract, indicate that this is a destination contract. The seller has the obligation to deliver the goods to the destination, not simply deliver them into the hands of a carrier. Under this contract, the destination is a "Bonded Public Warehouse" in a specific location. The seller bears the risk of loss until the goods are delivered at their destination. Typically, the seller will have bought insurance to cover the risk.

19 Delivery terms are commonly placed in all sales contracts. Such terms determine who pays freight and other costs and, in the absence of an agreement specifying otherwise, who bears the risk of loss. International contracts may use these delivery terms, or they may use INCOTERMS, which are published by the International Chamber of Commerce. For example, the INCOTERM DDP (delivered duty paid) requires the seller to arrange shipment, obtain and pay for import or export permits, and get the goods through customs to a named destination.

20 Exported and imported goods are subject to duties, taxes, and other charges imposed by the governments of the countries involved. International contracts spell out who is responsible for these charges.

21 This clause protects a party if the other party should become financially unable to fulfill the obligations under the contract. Thus, if the seller cannot afford to deliver, or the buyer cannot afford to pay, for the stated reasons, the other party can consider the contract breached. This right is subject to "11 USC 365(e)(1)," which refers to a specific provision of the U.S. Bankruptcy Code dealing with executory contracts.

22 In the "Breach or Default of Contract" clause, the parties agree that the remedies under this contract are the remedies (except for consequential damages) provided by the UCC, as in effect in the state of New York. The amount and "ascertainment" of damages, as well as other disputes about relief, are to be determined by arbitration.

23 Three clauses frequently included in international contracts are *omitted* here. There is no choice-of-language clause designating the official language to be used in interpreting the contract terms. There is no choice-of-forum clause designating the place in which disputes will be litigated, except for arbitration (law of New York State). Finally, there is no *force majeure* clause relieving the sellers or buyers from nonperformance due to events beyond their control.

20 | Title and Risk of Loss

Learning Objectives

The four Learning Objectives *below are designed to help improve your understanding. After reading this chapter, you should be able to answer the following questions:*

1. What is the significance of identifying goods to a contract?

2. Under what circumstances is a seller's title to goods being sold voidable?

3. When does risk of loss pass in a shipment contract?

4. Can both the buyer and the seller have an insurable interest in the goods simultaneously?

"To win, you have to risk loss."

Jean-Claude Killy
1943–present
(French Alpine skier)

Entrepreneurs, as well as many other business owners and managers, understand the reality of the chapter-opening quotation. To get ahead, it is sometimes necessary to risk loss. The risk of loss arises, for instance, when goods are transferred from sellers to buyers.

In business, a sale of goods transfers ownership rights in (title to) the goods from the seller to the buyer. Often, a sales contract is signed before the actual goods are available. For instance, a sales contract for oranges might be signed in May, but the oranges may not be ready for picking and shipment until October.

Any number of factors can happen between the time the sales contract is signed and the time the goods are actually transferred into the buyer's possession. Fire, flood, or frost may destroy the orange groves, or the oranges may be lost or damaged in transit. The same problems may occur under a lease contract. Because of these possibilities, it is important to know the rights and liabilities of the parties between the time the contract is formed and the time the goods are actually received by the buyer or lessee.

Before the creation of the UCC, *title*—the right of ownership—was the central concept in sales law and controlled all issues of rights and remedies of the parties to a sales contract. In some situations, title is still relevant under the UCC, and the UCC has special rules for determining who has title. (These rules do not apply to leased goods, obviously, because title remains with the lessor, or owner, of the goods.) In most situations, however, as you will discover, the UCC focuses less on title than on the concepts of *identification, risk of loss,* and *insurable interest.*

20-1 Identification

Before any interest in specific goods can pass from the seller or lessor to the buyer or lessee, the goods must exist and must be identified as the specific goods designated in the contract. **Identification** takes place when specific goods are designated as the subject matter of a sales or lease contract.

Identification allows title to pass from the seller to the buyer. (Remember that title to leased goods does not pass to the lessee.) In addition, it allows risk of loss to pass from the seller or lessor to the buyer or lessee. This is important because it gives the buyer or lessee the right to insure the goods and the right to recover from third parties who damage the goods.

For goods already in existence, the parties can agree in their contract on when identification will take place. If the parties do not so specify, the UCC provisions discussed here determine when identification takes place [UCC 2–501(1), 2A–217].

Identification In a sale of goods, the express designation of the goods provided for in the contract.

> ## Learning Objective 1
> What is the significance of identifying goods to a contract?

20-1a Existing Goods

If the contract calls for the sale or lease of specific goods that are already in existence, identification takes place at the time the contract is made. **Example 20.1** Litco Company contracts to lease a fleet of five cars designated by their vehicle identification numbers (VINs). Because the cars are identified by their VINs, identification has taken place, and Litco acquires an insurable interest in the cars at the time of contracting. ▪

20-1b Future Goods

Any goods that are not in existence at the time of contracting are known as *future goods*. Various rules apply to identification of future goods, depending on the goods.

- If a sale or lease involves unborn animals to be born within twelve months after contracting, identification takes place when the animals are conceived.

- If a sale involves crops that are to be harvested within twelve months (or the next harvest season occurring after contracting, whichever is longer), identification takes place when the crops are planted. Otherwise, identification takes place when the crops begin to grow.

- In a sale or lease of any other future goods, identification occurs when the goods are shipped, marked, or otherwise designated by the seller or lessor as the goods to which the contract refers.

20-1c Goods That Are Part of a Larger Mass

As a general rule, goods that are part of a larger mass are identified when the goods are marked, shipped, or somehow designated by the seller or lessor as the particular goods that are the subject of the contract. **Example 20.2** Carlos orders 10,000 pairs of men's jeans from a lot that contains 90,000 articles of clothing for men, women, and children. Until the seller separates the 10,000 pairs of men's jeans from the other items, title and risk of loss remain with the seller. ▪

A common exception to this rule involves fungible goods. **Fungible goods** are goods that are alike naturally, by agreement, or by trade usage. Typical examples include specific grades or types of wheat, petroleum, and cooking oil, which usually are stored in large containers. If the owners of these goods hold title as *tenants in common* (owners with undivided shares of the whole), a seller-owner can pass title and risk of loss to the buyer without actually separating the goods. The buyer replaces the seller as an owner in common [UCC 2–105(4)].

Fungible Goods Goods that are alike by physical nature, agreement, or trade usage.

If an order for men's blue jeans is part of a larger shipment of men's clothing from a seller, when does the risk of loss become the buyer's?

Shotshop GmbH/Alamy

It is important to emphasize that what makes goods fungible is not simply that they are alike, but that they are of an *identical* grade or type. This distinction is illustrated by the facts in the following case.

Case 20.1

BMW Group, LLC v. Castle Oil Corp.

New York Supreme Court, Appellate Division, First Department, 139 A.D.3d 78, 29 N.Y.S. 3d 253 (2016).

Background and Facts BMW Group, LLC, ordered No. 4 fuel oil from Castle Oil Corporation for delivery to BMW's building in Manhattan. BMW paid the retail price for No. 4 fuel oil, but Castle's delivered product did not conform to the order—it appeared to have been mixed with waste oil. Meanwhile, Mid Island L.P. and Carnegie Park Associates, L.P., ordered No. 4 and No. 6 fuel oil for their buildings in New York City from Hess Corporation but also received a blend containing waste oil.

BMW and the other property owners filed a suit in a New York state court against Castle and Hess, alleging that the defendants had delivered goods of lesser value that did not meet the standards governing the parties' contracts.

The court dismissed the complaint on the ground that the plaintiffs did not allege an injury caused by the use of the blended oil. The plaintiffs appealed.

In the Words of the Court
SAXE, J. [Judge]
* * * *

The issue is whether * * * plaintiffs' claims amount to merely "theoretical nonconformities" that do not justify a claim for breach of warranty or breach of contract.
* * * *

* * * *If the goods that are delivered do not conform to the goods contemplated by the sale contract, the purchaser has a cause of action under the Uniform Commercial Code.* [Emphasis added.]

An issue is raised as to whether plaintiffs successfully alleged that the delivered goods were nonconforming.

* * * The Administrative Code of the City of New York * * * defines "heating oil" as "oil refined for the purpose of use as a fuel for combustion in a heating system and that meets the specifications of the American Society for Testing and Materials * * *." The applicable American Society of Testing and Materials (ASTM) specifications for fuel oil * * * establish detailed requirements for the different grades of oil, using such categories as minimum flash point temperature, viscosity, density, and maximum percentages of ash and sulfur.

Plaintiffs essentially allege that, consistent with the ASTM specifications, as well as common commercial usage, and pursuant to the UCC, customers purchasing goods described as No. 4 and No. 6 fuel oil are entitled to presume that they are receiving 100% fuel oil of the specified grade, and not a product consisting of a blend of No. 4 or No. 6 fuel oil with some other types of oil that do not meet the criteria of those ASTM specifications.

[Plaintiffs] allege that "Castle intentionally adulterates its fuel oil products by using other, cheaper oils (primarily used motor and lubricating oil) as filler, resulting in an inferior blended petroleum product." They explain that lubricating oil and fuel oil are different chemical substances, and that lubricating oils are designed with a higher boiling point than fuel oil and do not burn efficiently at temperatures typical in non-industrial heating systems. Additionally, because lubricating oils contain chemical additives not found in fuel oil, burning them in heating systems such as those in plaintiffs' buildings will tend to produce more soot and particulate matter pollution, reducing the efficiency of the heating system and creating an increased risk of fire.
* * * *

* * * *Since we must infer from the complaint that plaintiffs received nonconforming oil deliveries of lesser value than those they contracted and paid for, causes of action for breach of contract and breach of warranty—including plaintiffs' damages— are stated in each action.* [Emphasis added.]

Decision and Remedy A state intermediate appellate court reversed the lower court's dismissal of the plaintiffs' complaint. The appellate court concluded that in their complaint the "plaintiffs successfully alleged that the delivered goods were nonconforming." When used in the plaintiffs' heating systems, the mixed oils produced more pollution, increased the risk, and reduced the systems' efficiency.

Critical Thinking

• **Legal Environment** *State and federal law allows and encourages the use of certain forms of used oil for fuel in* high-temperature industrial settings and other situations. Should the court in the BMW *case have considered these policies in its opinion? Explain.*

• **Ethical** *The defendants did not inform the plaintiffs that the delivered oil was a blend. How does this reflect on the ethics of the defendants' conduct in this case? Discuss.*

20–2 Passage of Title

Once goods are identified, the provisions of UCC 2–401 apply to the passage of title. Parties can expressly agree when and how title will pass. Throughout UCC 2–401, the words "unless otherwise explicitly agreed" appear, meaning that any explicit understanding between the buyer and the seller determines when title passes.

Without an explicit agreement to the contrary, *title passes to the buyer at the time and the place the seller performs by delivering the goods* [UCC 2–401(2)]. For instance, if a person buys cattle at a livestock auction, title will pass to the buyer when the cattle are physically delivered to him or her (unless, of course, the parties agree otherwise).

⭐ **Spotlight Case Example 20.3** Timothy Allen contracted with Indy Route 66 Cycles, Inc., to have a motorcycle custom built for him. Indy built the motorcycle and issued a "Certificate of Origin." Two years later, federal law enforcement officers arrested Allen on drug charges and seized his home and other property. The officers also seized the Indy-made motorcycle from the garage of the home of Allen's sister, Tena. Indy filed a claim against the government, arguing that it owned the motorcycle because it still possessed the "Certificate of Origin."

The court applied UCC Section 2–401(2) and ruled in favor of the government. Testimony by Indy's former vice president was "inconclusive" but implied that Indy had delivered the motorcycle to Allen. Because Indy had given up possession of the cycle to Allen, this was sufficient to pass title even though Indy had kept a "Certificate of Origin."[1]

When does title pass to the buyer of a motorcycle?

(In the future, the delivery of goods may sometimes be accomplished by drones. This chapter's *Managerial Strategy* feature discusses the use of drones in commerce.)

---

1. *United States v. 2007 Custom Motorcycle*, 2011 WL 232331 (D.Ariz. 2011).

Commercial Use of Drones

Managerial Strategy

The commercial use of drones—small, pilotless aerial vehicles—has been on hold for several years in the United States. Possible commercial uses of drones are numerous. They can be used for railroad track inspections, oil and gas pipeline reviews, real estate videos, discovery for land boundary disputes, and wildfire and disaster assessment, among others.

In addition, businesses have started developing drones for delivery of goods. Amazon created Amazon Prime Air, a drone-based delivery service, which has been used experimentally in the

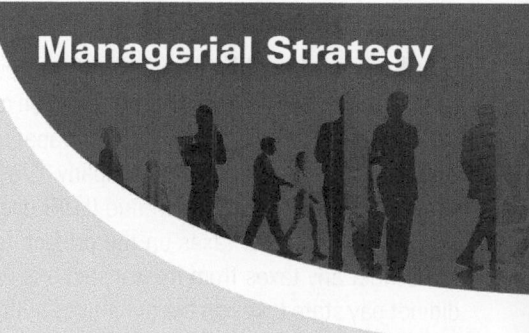

(Continues)

United Kingdom. Prime Air is scheduled to become operational in the United States in 2020. Google's Project Wing is another drone-based service that is under development.

The Federal Aviation Administration Rules

Commercial drone delivery service is widely available in other parts of the world, including Australia and China. The delay in the United States has been because the Federal Aviation Administration (FAA) took a long time creating and finalizing regulations. The FAA has authority to regulate *all* unmanned aircraft systems (UASs). It first proposed rules on commercial drone use in 2015, and these rules were not finalized until 2016.[a]

The FAA's rules require operators to apply for a license to use drones commercially. Drone flights are limited to daylight hours, and drones are not allowed to go above four hundred feet or fly faster than one hundred miles per hour. The rules also require that licensed drone operators maintain a continuous visual line of sight with the drones during operation. Drones cannot be operated over anyone who is not directly participating in the operation.

Court Actions

In the past, the FAA has attempted to fine other-than-recreational users of drones. One case involved Texas EquuSearch, a group that searches for missing persons. The organization requested an emergency injunction after receiving an e-mail from an FAA employee indicating that its drone use was illegal. A federal appellate court in the District of Columbia refused to grant an injunction, however. The court found that the FAA's e-mail was not subject to judicial review.[b] (That same federal appellate court

also held that the FAA's "registration rule," which requires recreational operators of model aircraft drones to register with the FAA, was invalid.[c])

In a case involving an administrative hearing, the FAA assessed a civil penalty against Raphael Pirker for careless and reckless operation of an unmanned aircraft. Pirker flew a drone over the University of Virginia while filming a video advertisement for the medical school. Pirker appealed to the National Transportation Safety Board Office of Administrative Law Judges, and the board ruled in his favor.[d]

Business Questions

1. *What benefits can delivery by commercial drone provide to consumers?*

2. *Why might the United States be slow to adopt commercial drone delivery in comparison with some other nations?*

---

a. 14 C.F.R. Part 107.

b. *Texas EquuSearch Mounted Search and Recovery Team, RP Search Services, Inc., v. Federal Aviation Administration,* 2014 WL 2860332 (D.C. Cir. 2014).

c. *Taylor v. Huerta,* 856 F.3d 1089 (D.C. Cir. 2017).

d. *Huerta v. Pirker,* Decisional Order of National Transportation Safety Board Office of Administrative Judges, 2014 WL 3388631 (N.T.S.B., March 6, 2014).

A dispute over when title to certain goods passed between a seller and a buyer was at the center of the following case.

■ Case 20.2

Louisiana Department of Revenue v. Apeck Construction, LLC

Louisiana Court of Appeal, Third Circuit, 238 So.3d 1045. (2018).

Background and Facts Apeck Construction, LLC (AC), delivered and installed building and construction materials on a federal government job site in Fort Polk, Louisiana, under a contract with Graybar Electrical Equipment Company. Graybar told AC that the Louisiana Department of Revenue (LDR) exempted Graybar from the payment of state taxes on the project. Consequently, AC did not collect any taxes from its transactions with Graybar. AC also did not pay state taxes on the purchases of the materials delivered to the site. LDR filed an action in a Louisiana state court against AC to collect those taxes. The court found that AC's purchases

of materials for the Graybar project were sales for re-sales, and therefore not taxable, and that title to the materials transferred on their delivery from AC to Graybar. LDR appealed.

In the Words of the Court

SAUNDERS, Judge.

* * * *

* * * According to LDR, the trial court erred in finding that title of the tangible personal property transferred from AC to Graybar upon delivery of the property to Fort Polk.

* * * *

LDR argues that the contract between AC and Graybar mandated that the property belonged to AC up until installation because they were construction contracts. Our reading of the contract between AC and Graybar finds no language related to when property 4 ownership would transfer from AC to Graybar.

LDR reaches its conclusion based on language regarding when Graybar would pay AC for the property it delivered to Fort Polk. That language was such that Graybar would pay AC for the property "within thirty (30) days after Final Acceptance of Project." While it is true that the contract has this language, there is uncontradicted testimony in the record by Joseph Williams, the owner of AC, that the custom between the parties was not this way at all.

* * * Regardless of when AC was paid for the materials, there is no language in the contract between AC and Graybar that dictates who owns the property after it is delivered and prior to installation. Rather, there are references to * * * the contract between Graybar and the Government. Under that contract, it is written * * * that:

* * * Risk of loss or damage to the supplies provided under this contract shall remain with the contractor until, and shall pass to the government upon:

(1) Delivery of the supplies to a carrier, if transportation is f.o.b. origin, or

(2) Delivery of the supplies to the Government at the destination specified in the contract, if transportation is f.o.b. destination.

The plain meaning of this language is that the risk of loss was no longer AC's once the property was delivered. This, coupled with [Williams's] uncontroverted testimony that AC was customarily paid for materials prior to their installation after invoicing Graybar upon delivery * * * , makes the trial court's finding * * * correct and reasonable. [Emphasis added.]

Decision and Remedy A state intermediate appellate court affirmed the lower court's judgment. Title to the materials that AC delivered to the job site transferred to Graybar on delivery, and thus AC did not owe taxes on their purchase. "We find no error by the trial court in its judgment regarding AC's transactions with Graybar."

Critical Thinking

• **Legal Environment** *At the time of AC's work for Graybar, AC bought, delivered, and installed materials for projects overseen by contractors who were not exempt from state taxes. According to the reasoning of the court in this case, would AC owe taxes on the purchases of those materials? Discuss.*

• **What If the Facts Were Different?** *Suppose that AC's contract with Graybar provided that materials purchased for the project were the property of the subcontractor until they were installed. Would the result have been different? Explain.*

20–2a Shipment and Destination Contracts

Unless otherwise agreed, delivery arrangements can determine when title passes from the seller to the buyer. In a **shipment contract,** the seller is required or authorized to ship goods by carrier, such as a trucking company. Under a shipment contract, the seller is required only to deliver conforming goods into the hands of a carrier, and title passes to the buyer at the time and place of shipment [UCC 2–401(2) (a)]. Generally, *all contracts are assumed to be shipment contracts if nothing to the contrary is stated in the contract.*

In a **destination contract,** the seller is required to deliver the goods to a particular destination, usually directly to the buyer, but sometimes to another party designated by the buyer. Title passes to the buyer when the goods are *tendered* at that destination [UCC 2–401(2) (b)]. *Tender of delivery* occurs when the seller places or holds conforming goods at the buyer's disposal (with any necessary notice), enabling the buyer to take possession [UCC 2–503(1)].

20–2b Delivery without Movement of the Goods

When the sales contract does not call for the seller to ship or deliver the goods (when the buyer is to pick up the goods), the passage of title depends on whether the seller must deliver a **document of title,** such as a bill of lading or a warehouse receipt, to the buyer. A *bill of lading* is a receipt for goods that is signed by a carrier and serves as a contract for the transport of the goods. A *warehouse receipt* is a receipt issued by a warehouser for goods stored in a warehouse.

Shipment Contract A contract for the sale of goods in which the seller is required or authorized to ship the goods by carrier. The seller assumes liability for any losses or damage to the goods until they are delivered to the carrier.

Destination Contract A contract for the sale of goods in which the seller is required or authorized to ship the goods by carrier and tender delivery of the goods at a particular destination. The seller assumes liability for any losses or damage to the goods until they are tendered at the destination specified in the contract.

Document of Title A paper exchanged in the regular course of business that evidences the right to possession of goods (for example, a bill of lading or a warehouse receipt).

When a Title Document Is Required When a document of title is required, title passes to the buyer *when and where the document is delivered*. Thus, if the goods are stored in a warehouse, title passes to the buyer when the appropriate documents are delivered to the buyer. The goods never move. In fact, the buyer can choose to leave the goods at the same warehouse for a period of time, and the buyer's title to those goods will be unaffected.

When a Title Document Is Not Required When no documents of title are required and delivery is made without moving the goods, title passes at the time and place the sales contract is made, if the goods have already been identified. If the goods have not been identified, title does not pass until identification occurs [UCC 2–401(3)].

> **Example 20.4** Greg sells lumber to Bodan. They agree that Bodan will pick up the lumber at the lumberyard. If the lumber has been identified (segregated, marked, or in any other way distinguished from all other lumber), title passes to Bodan when the contract is signed. If the lumber is still in large storage bins at the lumberyard, title does not pass to Bodan until the particular pieces of lumber to be sold under this contract are identified.

20–2c Sales or Leases by Nonowners

Problems occur when a person who acquires goods with *imperfect* title attempts to sell or lease them. Sections 2–402 and 2–403 of the UCC deal with the rights of two parties who lay claim to the same goods, sold with imperfect title. Generally, a buyer acquires at least whatever title the seller has to the goods sold.

Void Title A buyer may unknowingly purchase goods from a seller who is not the owner of the goods. If the seller is a thief, the seller's title is *void*—legally, no title exists. Thus, the buyer acquires no title, and the real owner can reclaim the goods from the buyer. If the goods were leased, the same result would occur, because the lessor has no leasehold interest to transfer.

> **Example 20.5** If Saki steals diamonds owned by Bruce, Saki has a *void title* to those diamonds. If Saki sells the diamonds to Shannon, Bruce can reclaim them from Shannon even though Shannon acted in good faith and honestly was not aware that the goods were stolen. Article 2A contains similar provisions for leases.

Voidable Title A seller has *voidable title* to the goods in the following circumstances:

1. The goods were obtained by fraud.
2. The goods were paid for with a check that is later *dishonored* (returned for insufficient funds).
3. The goods were purchased on credit when the seller was **insolvent**. Under the UCC, insolvency occurs when a person ceases to pay his or her debts in the ordinary course of business, cannot pay debts as they become due, or is insolvent under federal bankruptcy law [UCC 1–201(23)].

In contrast to a seller with *void title*, a seller with *voidable title* has the power to transfer good title to a good faith purchaser for value. A **good faith purchaser** is one who buys without knowledge of circumstances that would make a person of ordinary prudence inquire about the validity of the seller's title to the goods. One who purchases *for value* gives legally sufficient consideration (value) for the goods purchased. The original owner cannot recover goods from a good faith purchaser for value [UCC 2–403(1)].[2]

If the buyer is not a good faith purchaser for value, the actual owner can reclaim them from the buyer (or from the seller, if the goods are still in the seller's possession). Exhibit 20–1 illustrates these concepts.

Learning Objective 2

Under what circumstances is a seller's title to goods being sold voidable?

Insolvent A condition in which a person cannot pay his or her debts as they become due or ceases to pay debts in the ordinary course of business.

Good Faith Purchaser A purchaser who buys without notice of any circumstance that would cause a person of ordinary prudence to inquire as to whether the seller has valid title to the goods being sold.

---

2. The real owner can sue the person who initially obtained voidable title to the goods.

Exhibit 20–1 Void and Voidable Titles

If goods are transferred from their owner to another by theft, the thief acquires no ownership rights. Because the thief's title is *void*, a later buyer can acquire no title, and the owner can recover the goods. If the transfer occurs by fraud, the transferee acquires a *voidable* title. A later good faith purchaser for value can acquire good title, and the original owner cannot recover the goods.

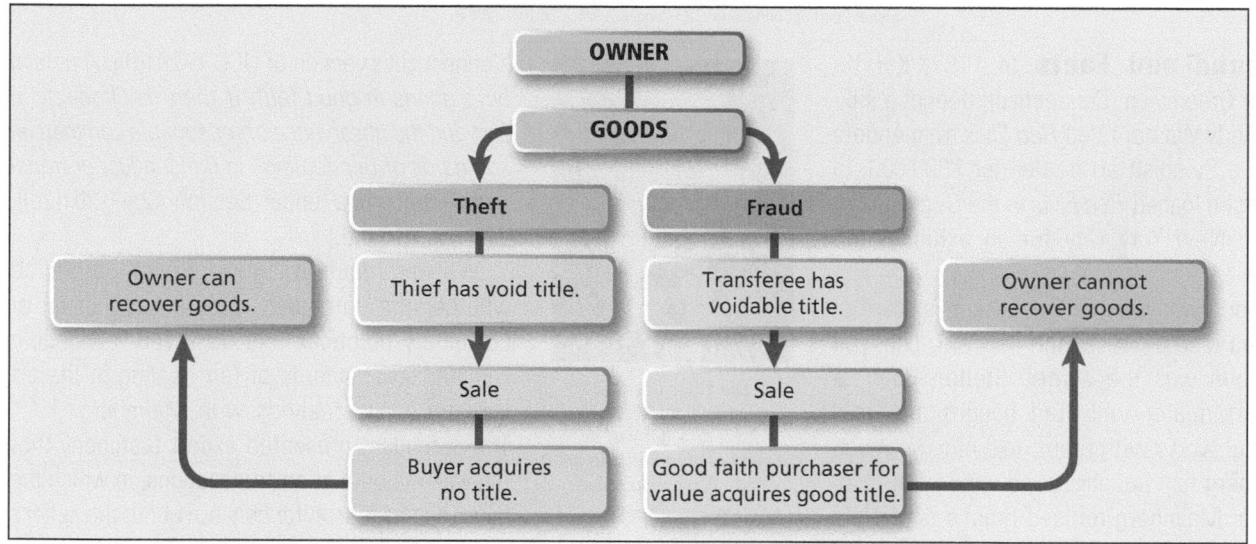

20–2d The Entrustment Rule

According to Section 2–403(2), when goods are entrusted to a merchant *who deals in goods of that kind*, the merchant has the power to transfer all rights to *a buyer in the ordinary course of business*. This is known as the **entrustment rule**. Entrusted goods include both goods that are turned over to the merchant and purchased goods left with the merchant for later delivery or pickup [UCC 2–403(3)]. Article 2A provides a similar rule for leased goods [UCC 2A–305(2)].

Under the UCC, a person is a **buyer in the ordinary course of business** in the following circumstances:

1. She or he buys goods in good faith (honestly).

2. The goods are purchased without knowledge that the sale violates the rights of another person in the goods.

3. The goods are purchased in the ordinary course from a merchant (other than a pawnbroker) in the business of selling goods of that kind.

4. The sale to that person is consistent with the usual or customary practices in the kind of business in which the seller is engaged [UCC 1–201(9)].

The entrustment rule basically allows innocent buyers to obtain legitimate title to goods purchased from merchants even if the merchants do not have good title. **Example 20.6** Jan leaves her watch with a jeweler to be repaired. The jeweler sells both new and used watches. The jeweler sells Jan's watch to Kim, a customer, who is unaware that the jeweler has no right to sell it. Kim, as a good faith buyer, gets good title against Jan's claim of ownership.[3] Kim, however, obtains only those rights held by the person entrusting the goods (here, Jan).

Now suppose that Jan stole the watch from Greg and left it with the jeweler to be repaired. The jeweler then sells it to Kim. In this situation, Kim gets good title against Jan, who entrusted the watch to the jeweler, but not against Greg (the real owner), who neither entrusted the watch to Jan nor authorized Jan to entrust it. ▪

A nonowner's sale of *Red Elvis*, an artwork by Andy Warhol, was at the center of the dispute over title in the following *Spotlight Case*.

Entrustment Rule The rule that entrusting goods to a merchant who deals in goods of that kind gives that merchant the power to transfer those goods and all rights to them to a buyer in the ordinary course of business.

Buyer in the Ordinary Course of Business A buyer who, in good faith and without knowledge that the sale violates the ownership rights or security interest of a third party in the goods, purchases goods in the ordinary course of business from a person in the business of selling goods of that kind.

Know This
The purpose of holding most goods in inventory is to turn those goods into revenues by selling them. That is one of the reasons for the entrustment rule.

---

3. Jan, of course, can sue the jeweler for the tort of trespass to personalty or conversion for the equivalent cash value of the watch.

⭐ **Spotlight on Andy Warhol: Case 20.3**

Lindholm v. Brant

Supreme Court of Connecticut, 283 Conn. 65, 925 A.2d 1048 (2007).

Background and Facts In 1987, Kerstin Lindholm of Greenwich, Connecticut, bought a silkscreen by Andy Warhol titled *Red Elvis* from Anders Malmberg, a Swedish art dealer, for $300,000. In 1998, Lindholm loaned *Red Elvis* to the Guggenheim Museum in New York City for an exhibition to tour Europe.

Peter Brant, who was on the museum's board of trustees and also a Greenwich resident, believed that Lindholm was the owner. Stellan Holm, a Swedish art dealer who had bought and sold other Warhol works with Brant, told him, however, that Malmberg had bought it and would sell it for $2.9 million. Malmberg refused Brant's request to provide a copy of an invoice between Lindholm and himself on the ground that such documents normally and customarily are not disclosed in art deals.

To determine whether Malmberg had good title, Brant hired an attorney to search the Art Loss Register (an international database of stolen and missing artworks) and other sources. No problems were found, but Brant was cautioned that this provided only "minimal assurances." Brant's attorney drafted a formal contract, which conditioned payment on the delivery of *Red Elvis* to a warehouse in Denmark. The exchange took place in April 2000.[a] Lindholm filed a suit in a Connecticut state court against Brant, alleging conversion, among other things. The court issued a judgment in Brant's favor. Lindholm appealed to the Connecticut Supreme Court.

In the Words of the Court

SULLIVAN, J. [Justice]

* * * *

* * * "A person buys goods in the ordinary course if the sale to the person comports with the usual or customary practices in the kind of business in which the seller is engaged or with the seller's own usual or customary practices * * *" [according to Connecticut General Statutes Annotated Section 42a-1-201(9),

Did Peter Brant, a Guggenheim Museum trustee, do what was necessary to obtain title to an Andy Warhol painting?

Astrid Stawiarz/Getty Images

(Connecticut's version of UCC 1–201(9)]. *A person buys goods in good faith if there is "honesty in fact and the observance of reasonable commercial standards of fair dealing" in the conduct or transaction concerned* [under Section 42a-1-201(20)]. [Emphasis added.]

We are required, therefore, to determine whether the defendant followed the usual or customary practices and observed reasonable commercial standards of fair dealing in the art industry in his dealings with Malmberg. * * * The defendant presented expert testimony that the vast majority of art transactions, in which the buyer has no reason for concern about the seller's ability to convey good title, are "completed on a handshake and an exchange of an invoice." It is not customary for sophisticated buyers and sellers to obtain a signed invoice from the original seller to the dealer prior to a transaction, nor is it an ordinary or customary practice to request the underlying invoice or corroborating information as to a dealer's authority to convey title. Moreover, it is not customary to approach the owner of an artwork if the owner regularly worked with a particular art dealer because any inquiries about an art transaction customarily are presented to the art dealer rather than directly to the [owner]. *It is customary to rely upon representations made by respected dealers regarding their authority to sell works of art.* A dealer customarily is not required to present an invoice establishing when and from whom he bought the artwork or the conditions of the purchase. [Emphasis added.]

We are compelled to conclude, however, that the sale from Malmberg to the defendant was unlike the vast majority of art transactions. * * * Under such circumstances, a handshake and an exchange of invoice is not sufficient to confer status as a buyer in the ordinary course.

* * * *

* * * A merchant buyer has a heightened duty of inquiry when a reasonable merchant would have doubts or questions regarding the seller's authority to sell. * * * In the present case, the defendant had concerns about Malmberg's ability to convey good title to *Red Elvis* because he believed that Lindholm might have had

---

a. Unaware of this deal, Lindholm accepted a Japanese buyer's offer of $4.6 million for *Red Elvis*. The funds were wired to Malmberg, who kept them. Lindholm filed a criminal complaint against Malmberg in Sweden. In 2003, a Swedish court convicted Malmberg of "gross fraud embezzlement." The court awarded Lindholm $4.6 million and other relief.

a claim to the painting. The defendant also was concerned that Malmberg had not yet acquired title to the painting * * * .

Because of his concern that Lindholm might make a claim to *Red Elvis*, the defendant took the extraordinary step of hiring counsel to conduct an investigation and to negotiate a formal contract of sale on his behalf. * * * Such searches typically are not conducted during the course of a normal art transaction and, therefore, provided the defendant with at least some assurance that Lindholm had no claims to the painting.

Moreover, * * * both Malmberg and Holm had reputations as honest, reliable, and trustworthy art dealers. * * * The defendant had little reason to doubt Malmberg's claim that he was the owner of *Red Elvis*, and any doubts that he did have reasonably were allayed [reduced] by relying on Holm's assurances that Malmberg had bought the painting from the plaintiff * * * .

The defendant's concerns were further allayed when Malmberg delivered *Red Elvis* to a * * * warehouse in Denmark, the delivery location the parties had agreed to in the contract of sale. At the time of the sale, the painting was on loan to the Guggenheim, whose policy it was to release a painting on loan only to the true owner, or to someone the true owner had authorized to take possession. * * * We conclude that these steps were sufficient to conform to reasonable commercial standards for the sale of artwork under the circumstances and, therefore, that the defendant had status as a buyer in the ordinary course of business.

Decision and Remedy The Connecticut Supreme Court affirmed the judgment of the lower court. The state supreme court concluded that "on the basis of all the circumstances surrounding this sale," Brant was a buyer in the ordinary course of business and, therefore, took all rights to *Red Elvis* under UCC 2–403(2).

Critical Thinking

• **Ethical** *How did the "usual and customary" methods of dealing in the art business help Malmberg deceive the other parties in this case? What additional steps might those parties have taken to protect themselves from such deceit?*

20–3 Risk of Loss

Under the UCC, risk of loss does not necessarily pass with title. When risk of loss passes from a seller or lessor to a buyer or lessee is generally determined by the contract between the parties. Sometimes, the contract states expressly when the risk of loss passes. At other times, it does not, and a court must interpret the performance and delivery terms of the contract to determine whether the risk has passed.

Like risk of loss, the risk of liability that arises from the goods does not necessarily require the passage of title. In addition, as with risk of loss, when this risk passes from a seller to a buyer is generally determined by the contract between the parties. **Case Example 20.7** Tammy Herring contracted to buy a horse named Toby from Stacy and Gregory Bowman, who owned Summit Stables in Washington. The contract required Herring to make monthly payments until she paid $2,200 in total for Toby. Additionally, Herring agreed to pay Toby's monthly boarding fee at Summit Stables until the purchase price balance was paid. The Bowmans were to provide Toby's registration papers to Herring only when she had paid in full.

One day, another stable boarder, Diana Person, was injured when she was thrown from a buggy drawn by Toby and driven by Herring's daughter. Person sued the Bowmans to recover for her injuries, but the court held that Herring (not the Bowmans) owned Toby at the time of the accident. Herring argued that she did not own the horse because she did not yet have its registration papers, but the court found that the contract clearly showed that Herring owned Toby. Therefore, the Bowmans were not liable for the injuries that Toby caused.[4]

ProjectB/iStock/Getty Images

When does the risk of loss pass to the buyer in the sale of a horse?

---

4. *Person v. Bowman*, 173 Wash.App. 1024 (2013).

20–3a Delivery with Movement of the Goods—Carrier Cases

When the contract involves movement of the goods through a common carrier but does not specify when risk of loss passes, the courts first look for specific delivery terms in the contract. The terms that have traditionally been used in contracts within the United States are listed and defined in Exhibit 20–2. *Unless the parties agree otherwise*, these terms determine which party will pay the costs of delivering the goods and who bears the risk of loss. If the contract does not include these terms, then the courts must decide whether the contract is a shipment or a destination contract.

Shipment Contracts In a shipment contract, the seller or lessor is required or authorized to ship goods by carrier but is not required to deliver them to a particular final destination. The risk of loss in a shipment contract passes to the buyer or lessee when the goods are delivered to the carrier [UCC 2–319(1)(a), 2–509(1)(a), 2A–219(2)(a)].

Example 20.8 Pitman, a seller in Texas, sells five hundred cases of grapefruit to a buyer in New York, F.O.B. Houston (free on board in Houston—see Exhibit 20–2). The contract authorizes shipment by carrier. It does not require that the seller tender the grapefruit in New York. Risk passes to the buyer when conforming goods are properly placed in the possession of the carrier in Houston. If the goods are damaged in transit, the loss is the buyer's. (Actually, buyers have recourse against carriers, subject to certain limitations, and buyers usually insure the goods from the time the goods leave the seller.)

Destination Contracts In a destination contract, the risk of loss passes to the buyer or lessee when the goods are tendered to the buyer or lessee at the specified destination [UCC 2–319(1)(b), 2–509(1)(b), 2A–219(2)(b)]. In *Example 20.8*, if the contract had been F.O.B. New York, the risk of loss during transit to New York would have been the seller's. Risk of loss would not have passed to the buyer until the carrier tendered the grapefruit to the buyer in New York.

20–3b Delivery without Movement of the Goods

The UCC also addresses situations in which the contract does not require the goods to be shipped or moved. Frequently, the buyer or lessee is to pick up the goods from the seller or lessor, or the goods are held by a bailee.

Exhibit 20–2 Contract Terms—Definitions

These contract terms help to determine which party will bear the costs of delivery and when risk of loss will pass from the seller to the buyer.

TERM	DEFINITION
F.O.B. (free on board)	Indicates that the selling price of goods includes transportation costs to the specific F.O.B. place named in the contract. The seller pays the expenses and carries the risk of loss to the F.O.B. place named [UCC 2–319(1)]. If the named place is the place from which the goods are shipped (for example, the seller's city or place of business), the contract is a shipment contract. If the named place is the place to which the goods are to be shipped (for example, the buyer's city or place of business), the contract is a destination contract.
F.A.S. (free alongside ship)	Requires that the seller, at his or her own expense and risk, deliver the goods alongside the carrier before risk passes to the buyer [UCC 2–319(2)]. An F.A.S. contract is essentially an F.O.B. contract for ships.
C.I.F. or C.&F. (cost, insurance, and freight, or just cost and freight)	Requires, among other things, that the seller "put the goods in the possession of a carrier" before risk passes to the buyer [UCC 2–320(2)]. (These are basically pricing terms, and the contracts remain shipment contracts, not destination contracts.)
Delivery ex-ship (delivery from the carrying vessel)	Means that risk of loss does not pass to the buyer until the goods are properly unloaded from the ship or other carrier [UCC 2–322].

A **bailment** is a temporary delivery of personal property, without passage of title, into the care of another, called a *bailee*. Under the UCC, a *bailee* is a party who, by a bill of lading, warehouse receipt, or other document of title, acknowledges possession of goods and/or contracts to deliver them. For instance, a warehousing company or a trucking company may be a bailee.

> **Bailment** A situation in which the personal property of one person (a bailor) is entrusted to another (a bailee), who is obligated to return the bailed property to the bailor or dispose of it as directed.

Goods Held by the Seller

When the seller keeps the goods for pickup, a document of title usually is not used. If the seller is a merchant, risk of loss to goods held by the seller passes to the buyer when the buyer *actually takes physical possession of the goods* [UCC 2–509(3)]. In other words, the merchant bears the risk of loss between the time the contract is formed and the time the buyer picks up the goods. **Case Example 20.9** Roger Adams bought a preassembled table saw that weighed 288 pounds from Sears Roebuck and Company. When Adams went to the loading area to pick up the saw, a Sears employee used a hydraulic lift to elevate it to the height of Adams's pickup bed. Adams then pulled the saw onto the truck, and the employee went back inside the store (and did not secure the saw).

Adams, who was standing in the bed of his truck, took a step and lost his balance. He grabbed the saw to steady himself. Both he and the saw fell off the truck, and he was injured. Adams sued Sears, alleging negligence, but the court granted summary judgment in favor of Sears. Sears was under no duty to help Adams secure the saw in the truck, so the employee had not been negligent. Once the truck was loaded, the risk of loss (or injury) passed to Adams under the UCC because he had taken physical possession of the goods.[5]

If the seller is not a merchant, the risk of loss to goods held by the seller passes to the buyer on *tender of delivery* [UCC 2–509(3)]. This means that the seller bears the risk of loss until he or she makes the goods available to the buyer and notifies the buyer that the goods are ready to be picked up.

With respect to leases, similar rules apply. The risk of loss passes to the lessee on the lessee's receipt of the goods if the lessor is a merchant. Otherwise, the risk passes to the lessee on tender of delivery [UCC 2A–219(2)(c)].

Goods Held by a Bailee

When a bailee is holding goods for a person who has contracted to sell them and the goods are to be delivered without being moved, the goods are usually represented by a document of title. The title document may be written, such as a bill of lading or a warehouse receipt, or evidenced by an electronic record.

When goods are held by a bailee, risk of loss passes to the buyer when one of the following occurs:

1. The buyer receives a negotiable document of title for the goods.
2. The bailee acknowledges the buyer's right to possess the goods.
3. The buyer receives a nonnegotiable document of title, *and* the buyer has a *reasonable time* to present the document to the bailee and demand the goods. If the bailee refuses to honor the document, the risk of loss remains with the seller [UCC 2–503(4)(b), 2–509(2)].

With respect to leases, if goods held by a bailee are to be delivered without being moved, the risk of loss passes to the lessee on acknowledgment by the bailee of the lessee's right to possession of the goods [UCC 2A–219(2)(b)].

While securing his purchases in his truck bed at a store's loading area, a customer falls and is injured. Who is liable, and why?

Monty Rakusen/Cultura/Getty Images

20–3c Risk of Loss When the Contract Is Breached

When a sales or lease contract is breached, the transfer of risk operates differently depending on which party breaches. Generally, the party in breach bears the risk of loss.

---

5. *Adams v. Sears Roebuck and Co.*, 2014 WL 670630 (D. Utah 2014).

When the Seller or Lessor Breaches If the seller or lessor breaches by supplying goods that are so nonconforming that the buyer has the right to reject them, the risk of loss does not pass to the buyer. **Example 20.10** A buyer orders ten stainless steel refrigerators from a seller, F.O.B. the seller's plant. The seller ships white refrigerators instead. The white refrigerators (nonconforming goods) are damaged in transit. The risk of loss falls on the seller. Had the seller shipped stainless steel refrigerators (conforming goods) instead, the risk would have fallen on the buyer [UCC 2–510(1)].

With nonconforming goods, the risk of loss does not pass to the buyer until one of the following occurs:

1. The defects are **cured** (that is, the goods are repaired, replaced, or discounted in price by the seller).

2. The buyer accepts the goods in spite of their defects (thus waiving the right to reject).

If a buyer accepts a shipment of goods and later discovers a defect, acceptance can be revoked. Revocation allows the buyer to pass the risk of loss back to the seller, at least to the extent that the buyer's insurance does not cover the loss [UCC 2–510(2)]. Article 2A provides similar rules for leases.

When the Buyer or Lessee Breaches The general rule is that when a buyer or lessee breaches a contract, the risk of loss immediately shifts to the buyer or lessee. This rule has three important limitations:

1. The seller or lessor must already have identified the contract goods.

2. The buyer or lessee bears the risk for only a commercially reasonable time after the seller or lessor has learned of the breach.

3. The buyer or lessee is liable only to the extent of any deficiency in the seller's insurance coverage [UCC 2–510(3), 2A–220(2)].

20–4 Insurable Interest

Parties to sales and lease contracts often obtain insurance coverage to protect against damage, loss, or destruction of goods. Any party purchasing insurance must have a sufficient interest in the insured item to obtain a valid policy. Insurance laws—not the UCC—determine sufficiency. The UCC is helpful, however, because it contains certain rules regarding insurable interests in goods.

20–4a Insurable Interest of the Buyer or Lessee

A buyer or lessee has an **insurable interest** in *identified* goods. The moment the contract goods are identified by the seller or lessor, the buyer or lessee has a property interest in them. That allows the buyer or lessee to obtain necessary insurance coverage for those goods even before the risk of loss has passed [UCC 2–501(1), 2A–218(1)]. When the parties do not explicitly agree on identification in their contract, then the UCC provisions on identification discussed earlier in this chapter apply.

20–4b Insurable Interest of the Seller or Lessor

A seller has an insurable interest in goods as long as she or he retains title to the goods. Even after title passes to the buyer, a seller who has a *security interest* in the goods (a right to secure payment) still has an insurable interest [UCC 2–501(2)]. Thus, both a buyer and a seller can have an insurable interest in the same goods at the same time. Of course, the buyer or seller must sustain an actual loss to recover from an insurance company. In regard to leases, the lessor retains an insurable interest in leased goods until the lessee exercises an option to buy and the risk of loss has passed to the lessee [UCC 2A–218(3)].

Cure The right of a party who tenders nonconforming performance to correct his or her performance within the contract period.

Insurable Interest A property interest in goods being sold or leased that is sufficiently substantial to permit a party to insure against damage to the goods.

Learning Objective 4

Can both the buyer and seller have an insurable interest in the goods simultaneously?

Practice and Review

In December, Mendoza agreed to buy the broccoli grown on one hundred acres of Willow Glen's one-thousand-acre broccoli farm. The sales contract specified F.O.B. Willow Glen's field by Falcon Trucking. The broccoli was to be planted in February and harvested in March of the following year. Using the information presented in the chapter, answer the following questions.

1. At what point is a crop of broccoli identified to the contract under the Uniform Commercial Code? Why is identification significant?

2. When does title to the broccoli pass from Willow Glen to Mendoza under the contract terms? Why?

3. Suppose that while in transit, Falcon's truck overturns and spills the entire load. Who bears the loss, Mendoza or Willow Glen?

4. Suppose that instead of buying fresh broccoli, Mendoza contracted with Willow Glen to purchase one thousand cases of frozen broccoli from Willow Glen's processing plant. The highest grade of broccoli is packaged under the "FreshBest" label, and everything else is packaged under the "FamilyPac" label. Further suppose that although the contract specified that Mendoza was to receive FreshBest broccoli, Falcon Trucking delivered FamilyPac broccoli to Mendoza. If Mendoza refuses to accept the broccoli, who bears the loss?

Debate This

The distinction between shipment and destination contracts for the purpose of deciding who will bear the risk of loss should be eliminated in favor of a rule that always requires the buyer to obtain insurance for the goods being shipped.

Key Terms

bailment 459
buyer in the ordinary course
  of business 455
cure 460
destination contract 453

document of title 453
entrustment rule 455
fungible goods 449
good faith purchaser 454

identification 449
insolvent 454
insurable interest 460
shipment contract 453

Chapter Summary: Title and Risk of Loss

Passage of Title

1. *For shipment and destination contracts—*
   a. In the absence of an agreement, title and risk pass on the seller's or lessor's delivery of conforming goods to the carrier [UCC 2–319(1)(a), 2–401(2)(a), 2–509(1)(a), 2A–219(2)(a)]
   b. In the absence of an agreement, title and risk pass on the seller's or lessor's tender of delivery of conforming goods to the buyer or lessee at the point of destination [UCC 2–319(1)(b), 2–401(2)(b), 2–509(1)(b), 2A–219(2)(b)].

2. *For delivery without movement of the goods—*In the absence of an agreement, if the goods are not represented by a document of title, title passes on the formation of the contract. Risk passes when the goods are delivered to a merchant or when the seller or lessor tenders delivery to a nonmerchant.

(Continues)

3. *For sales or leases by nonowners*—Between the owner and a good faith purchaser or between the lessee and a sublessee:

    a. *Void title*—Owner prevails [UCC 2–403(1)].

    b. *Voidable title*—Buyer prevails [UCC 2–403(1)].

    c. *The entrustment rule*—Buyer or sublessee prevails [UCC 2–403(2), (3); 2A–305(2)].

Risk of Loss	When the contract is breached:
	1. If the seller or lessor breaches by tendering nonconforming goods that are rejected by the buyer or lessee, the risk of loss does not pass to the buyer or lessee until the defects are cured (unless the buyer or lessee accepts the goods in spite of their defects, thus waiving the right to reject) [UCC 2–510(1), 2A–220(1)].
	2. If the buyer or lessee breaches the contract, the risk of loss immediately shifts to the buyer or lessee. Limitations to this rule are as follows [UCC 2–510(3), 2A–220(2)]:
	a. The seller or lessor must already have identified the contract goods.
	b. The buyer or lessee bears the risk for only a commercially reasonable time after the seller or lessor has learned of the breach.
	c. The buyer or lessee is liable only to the extent of any deficiency in the seller's or lessor's insurance coverage.
Insurable Interest	1. Buyers and lessees have an insurable interest in goods the moment the goods are identified to the contract by the seller or the lessor [UCC 2–501(1), 2A–218(1)].—
	2. Sellers have an insurable interest in goods as long as they have (1) title to the goods or (2) a security interest in the goods [UCC 2–501(2)]. Lessors have an insurable interest in leased goods until the lessee exercises an option to buy and the risk of loss has passed to the lessee [UCC 2A–218(3)].

Issue Spotters

1. Under a contract between Great Products, Inc., in New York and National Sales Corporation in Dallas, if delivery is "F.O.B. New York," the risk passes when Great Products puts the goods in a carrier's hands. If delivery is "F.O.B. Dallas," the risk passes when the goods reach Dallas. What happens if the contract says only that Great Products is "to ship goods at the seller's expense"? (See *Risk of Loss*.)

2. Chocolate, Inc., sells five hundred cases of cocoa mix to Dessert Company, which pays with a bad check. Chocolate does not discover that the check is bad until after Dessert sells the cocoa to Eden Food Stores, which suspects nothing. Can Chocolate recover the cocoa from Eden? Explain. (See *Passage of Title*.)

    —**Check your answers to the *Issue Spotters* against the answers provided in Appendix D at the end of this text.**

Business Scenarios and Case Problems

20–1. Sales by Nonowners. In the following situations, two parties lay claim to the same goods sold. Explain which party would prevail in each situation. (See *Passage of Title*.)

    1. Terry steals Dom's iPad and sells it to Blake, an innocent purchaser, for value. Dom learns that Blake has the iPad and demands its return.

    2. Karlin takes her laptop computer for repair to Orken, a merchant who sells new and used computers. By accident, one of Orken's employees sells Karlin's laptop computer to Grady, an innocent purchaser-customer, who takes possession. Karlin wants her laptop back from Grady.

20–2. Risk of Loss. When will risk of loss pass from the seller to the buyer under each of the following contracts, assuming the parties have not expressly agreed on when risk of loss will pass? (See *Risk of Loss*.)

    1. A New York seller contracts with a San Francisco buyer to ship goods to the buyer F.O.B. San Francisco.

    2. A New York seller contracts with a San Francisco buyer to ship goods to the buyer in San Francisco. There is no indication as to whether the shipment will be F.O.B. New York or F.O.B. San Francisco.

    3. A seller contracts with a buyer to sell goods located on the seller's premises. The buyer pays for the goods and arranges to pick them up the next week at the seller's place of business.

    4. A seller contracts with a buyer to sell goods located in a warehouse.

20–3. Sales by Nonowners. Julian Makepeace, who had been declared mentally incompetent by a court, sold his diamond ring to Golding for value. Golding later sold the ring to Carmichael for value. Neither Golding nor Carmichael knew that Makepeace had been adjudged mentally incompetent by a court. Farrel, who had been appointed as Makepeace's guardian, subsequently learned that the diamond ring was in Carmichael's possession and demanded its return from Carmichael. Who has legal ownership of the ring? Why? (See *Passage of Title.*)

20–4. Business Case Problem with Sample Answer—

Passage of Title. Kenzie Godfrey was a passenger in a taxi when it collided with a car driven by Dawn Altieri. Altieri had originally leased the car from G.E. Capital Auto Lease, Inc. By the time of the accident, she had bought it, but she had not fully paid for it or completed the transfer-of-title paperwork. Godfrey suffered a brain injury and sought to recover damages from the owner of the car that Altieri was driving. Who had title to the car at the time of the accident? Explain. [*Godfrey v. G.E. Capital Auto Lease, Inc.*, 89 A.D.3d 471, 933 N.Y.S.2d 208 (1 Dept. 2011)] (See *Passage of Title.*)

—For a sample answer to Problem 20–4, go to Appendix E at the end of this text.

20–5. Goods Held by the Seller or Lessor.
Douglas Singletary bought a manufactured home from Andy's Mobile Home and Land Sales. The contract stated that the buyer accepted the home "as is where is." Singletary paid the full price, and his crew began to ready the home to relocate it to his property. The night before the home was to be moved, however, it was destroyed by fire. Who suffered the loss? Explain. [*Singletary, III v. P&A Investments, Inc.*, 712 S.E.2d 681 (N.C.App. 2011)] (See *Risk of Loss.*)

20–6. Risk of Loss.
Ethicon, Inc., a pharmaceutical company, entered into an agreement with UPS Supply Chain Solutions, Inc., to transport pharmaceuticals. The drivers were provided by International Management Services Co. under a contract with a UPS subsidiary, Worldwide Dedicated Services, Inc. During the transport of a shipment from Ethicon's facility in Texas to buyers "F.O.B. Tennessee," one of the trucks collided with a concrete barrier near Little Rock, Arkansas, and caught fire, damaging the goods. Who was liable for the loss? Why? [*Royal & Sun Alliance Insurance, PLC v. International Management Services Co.*, 703 F.3d 604 (2d Cir. 2013)] (See *Risk of Loss.*)

Critical Thinking and Writing Assignments

20–9. Time-Limited Group Assignment—Shipment

Contracts. Professional Products, Inc. (PPI), bought three pallets of computer wafers from Omneon Video Graphics. (A computer wafer is a thin, round slice of silicon from which microchips are made.) Omneon agreed to ship the wafers to the City University of New York "FOB Omneon's dock." Shipment was arranged through Haas Industries, Inc. The "conditions of carriage" on the back of the bill of lading stated that Haas's liability for lost goods was limited to fifty cents per pound. When the shipment arrived, it included only two pallets. (See *Passage of Title.*)

20–7. When Title Passes.
James McCoolidge, a Nebraska resident, saw a used Honda Element for sale online. He contacted the seller, Daniel Oyvetsky, who offered to sell the vehicle for $7,500 on behalf of Car and Truck Center, LLC, a dealership in Nashville, Tennessee. McCoolidge paid the price and received the car and a certificate of title. Before he registered the certificate with the Nebraska Department of Motor Vehicles, he learned that the state of Tennessee had issued numerous certificates of title to the Element. Based on these documents, title could ultimately be traced to McCoolidge. But he chose to file a suit in a Nebraska state court against Oyvetsky, claiming that he had not received "clear" title. What does the UCC provide with respect to the passage of title under a sales contract? How does that rule impact McCoolidge's claim? Discuss. [*McCoolidge v. Oyvetsky*, 292 Neb. 955, 874 N.W.2d 892 (2016)] (See *Passage of Title.*)

20–8. A Question of Ethics—Passage of Title.
Indiana enacted the Vapor Pens and E-Liquid Act to regulate the manufacture and distribution of e-cigarettes. The act was based on the state's interest in public health and safety. Requirements included childproof packaging and labels designating active ingredients, nicotine content, and expiration dates. The act covered in-state and out-of-state production and sales. Legato Vapors, LLC, an out-of-state maker of e-liquid products, filed a lawsuit in a federal district court against David Cook, head of the Indiana Alcohol and Tobacco Commission, seeking an injunction. Legato argued that the state's act violated the U.S. Constitution, which prohibits the application of a state statute to commerce that takes places completely outside of the state. Specifically, Legato noted that direct online sales by out-of-state manufacturers to Indiana consumers could not be regulated by the state act. [Legato Vapors, LLC v. Cook, 847 F.3d 825 (7th Cir. 2017)] (See Passage of Title.)

1. Under the UCC, when does title to goods pass from the seller to the buyer?

2. Does this UCC provision support Legato's argument for an injunction of the state act? In any event, should Legato follow the act's requirements for ethical reasons? Discuss.

1. The first group will determine who suffers the loss in this situation.

2. The second group will discuss whether it is it fair for a carrier to limit its liability for lost goods.

3. A third group will analyze whether this is a shipment or a destination contract.

4. The fourth group will decide at what point the buyer (PPI) obtained an insurable interest in the goods.

21

Performance and Breach of Sales and Lease Contracts

Learning Objectives

The five Learning Objectives *below are designed to help improve your understanding. After reading this chapter, you should be able to answer the following questions:*

1. What is the perfect tender rule? What are some important exceptions to this rule?

2. When will a buyer or lessee be deemed to have accepted the goods?

3. What remedies are available to a seller or lessor when the buyer or lessee breaches the contract?

4. When can a buyer or lessee revoke acceptance?

5. What implied warranties arise under the UCC?

"Gratitude is as the good faith of merchants: it holds commerce together."

François de la Rochefoucauld
1613–1680
(French author)

The performance required of the parties under a sales or lease contract consists of the duties and obligations each party has under the terms of the contract. The basic obligation of the seller or lessor is to *transfer and deliver conforming goods.* The basic obligation of the buyer or lessee is to *accept and pay for conforming goods* in accordance with the contract [UCC 2–301, 2A–516(1)]. Overall performance of a sales or lease contract is controlled by the agreement between the parties. If Reyes contracts with Nike to buy five shipments of soccer balls for his store, he is obligated to pay for them according to the terms of his contract (within thirty days of receiving each shipment, for instance).

When the contract is unclear and disputes arise, the courts look to the UCC and impose standards of good faith and commercial reasonableness. The obligations of good faith and commercial reasonableness underlie every sales and lease contract. The UCC's good faith provision, which can never be disclaimed, reads as follows: "Every contract or duty within this Act imposes an obligation of good faith in its performance or enforcement" [UCC 1–304]. *Good faith* means honesty in fact. For a merchant, it means both honesty in fact and the observance of reasonable commercial standards of fair dealing in the trade [UCC 2–103(1)(b)]. In other words, merchants are held to a higher standard of performance or duty than are nonmerchants.

Sometimes, circumstances make it difficult for a party to carry out the promised performance, leading to a breach of the contract. When a breach occurs, the aggrieved (wronged) party looks for remedies. At other times, a problem arises concerning the goods that are purchased or leased. In those situations, the buyer or lessee may sometimes be able to recover against the seller or lessor under a warranty.

21–1 Obligations of the Seller or Lessor

The major obligation of the seller or lessor under a sales or lease contract is to deliver or tender delivery of conforming goods to the buyer or lessee. **Conforming goods** are goods that conform to the contract description in every way.

21–1a Tender of Delivery

Tender of delivery occurs when the seller or lessor makes conforming goods available to the buyer or lessee and provides whatever notification is reasonably necessary to enable the buyer or lessee to take delivery [UCC 2–503(1), 2A–508(1)].

Tender must occur at a *reasonable hour* and in a *reasonable manner.* In other words, a seller cannot call the buyer at 2:00 A.M. and say, "The goods are ready. I'll give you twenty minutes to get them." Unless the parties have agreed otherwise, the goods must be tendered for delivery at a reasonable hour and kept available for a reasonable period of time to enable the buyer to take possession of them [UCC 2–503(1)(a)].

Normally, all goods called for by a contract must be tendered in a single delivery, unless the parties have agreed that the goods may be delivered in several lots or *installments* [UCC 2–307, 2–612, 2A–510]. **Example 21.1** An order for one thousand Under Armour men's shirts cannot be delivered two shirts at a time. If, however, the parties agree that the shirts will be delivered in four orders of 250 each as they are produced (for summer, fall, winter, and spring inventory), then tender of delivery may occur in this manner.

How does the Uniform Commercial Code's good faith provision affect everyday business transactions?

Conforming Goods Goods that conform to contract specifications.

Tender of Delivery A seller's or lessor's act of placing conforming goods at the disposal of the buyer or lessee and providing whatever notification is reasonably necessary to enable the buyer or lessee to take delivery.

21–1b Place of Delivery

The UCC provides for the place of delivery under a contract only if the contract does not indicate the place where the buyer or lessee will take possession. If the contract does not indicate where the goods will be delivered, then the place for delivery will be one of the following:

1. The *seller's place of business.*
2. The *seller's residence,* if the seller has no business location [UCC 2–308(a)].
3. The *location of the goods,* if both parties know at the time of contracting that the goods are located somewhere other than the seller's business [UCC 2–308(b)].

Example 21.2 Li Wan and Jo Boyd both live in Los Angeles. Li Wan contracts to sell to Boyd five shipping containers that both parties know are located in San Francisco. If nothing more is specified in the contract, the place of delivery for the shipping containers is San Francisco. Li Wan may tender delivery by giving Boyd a negotiable or nonnegotiable document of title. Alternatively, Li Wan may obtain the bailee's (warehouser's) acknowledgment that the buyer is entitled to possession.[1]

21–1c Delivery via Carrier

In many instances, circumstances or delivery terms in the contract (such as F.O.B. or F.A.S. terms) make it apparent that the parties intended the goods to be moved by a carrier. In carrier contracts, the seller fulfills the obligation to deliver the goods through either a shipment contract or a destination contract.

---

1. Unless the buyer objects, the seller may also tender delivery by instructing the bailee in writing to release the goods to the buyer without a bailee's acknowledgment of the buyer's rights [UCC 2–503(4)]. Risk of loss, however, does not pass until the buyer has a reasonable amount of time in which to present the document or to give the bailee instructions for delivery.

Know This

Documents of title include bills of lading, warehouse receipts, and any other documents that, in the regular course of business, entitle a person holding these documents to obtain possession of, and title to, the goods covered.

Shipment Contracts Recall that a *shipment contract* requires or authorizes the seller to ship goods by a carrier, rather than to deliver them at a particular destination [UCC 2–319, 2–509(1)(a)]. Under a shipment contract, unless otherwise agreed, the seller must do the following:

1. Put the goods into the hands of the carrier.

2. Make a contract for their transportation that is reasonable according to the nature of the goods and their value. (For instance, certain types of goods require refrigeration in transit.)

3. Obtain and promptly deliver or tender to the buyer any documents necessary to enable the buyer to obtain possession of the goods from the carrier.

4. Promptly notify the buyer that shipment has been made [UCC 2–504].

If the seller fails to make a reasonable contract for transportation or notify the buyer of the shipment, the buyer can reject the shipment, but only if a *material loss* or a *significant delay* results. **Example 21.3** Zigi's Organic Fruits sells strawberries to Lozier under a shipment contract. If Zigi's does not arrange for refrigerated transportation and the berries spoil during transport, a material loss to Lozier will likely result. ■ Of course, the parties can agree in their contract that a lesser amount of loss or delay will be grounds for rejection.

Destination Contracts In a *destination contract,* the seller agrees to deliver conforming goods to the buyer at a particular destination. The seller must give the buyer appropriate notice about the delivery and hold the goods at the buyer's disposal for a reasonable length of time. The seller must also provide the buyer with any documents of title necessary to enable the buyer to obtain delivery from the carrier [UCC 2–503].

Learning Objective 1

What is the perfect tender rule? What are some important exceptions to this rule?

21–1d The Perfect Tender Rule

As previously noted, the seller or lessor has an obligation to ship or tender *conforming goods.* The buyer or lessee is then required to accept and pay for the goods according to the terms of the contract [UCC 2–507]. Under the common law, the seller was not necessarily obligated to deliver goods that conformed to the terms of the contract in every detail. Minor defects in performance were compensable under the substantial performance doctrine.

In contrast, the UCC adopted the perfect tender rule. The **perfect tender rule** states that if the goods or tender of delivery fail *in any respect* to conform to the contract, the buyer or lessee has the right to accept the goods, reject the entire shipment, or accept part and reject part [UCC 2–601, 2A–509].

Perfect Tender Rule The legal right of a buyer or lessee of goods to insist on perfect tender by the seller or lessor. If the goods fail to conform to the contract, the buyer may accept the goods, reject the goods, or accept part and reject part of the goods tendered.

Photo 12/Alamy

How did the perfect tender rule affect a dispute over a sales contract involving a McDonnell Douglas aircraft?

Case Example 21.4 First Technology Capital, Inc., contracted to purchase a McDonnell Douglas DC-9-83 aircraft from Airborne, Inc. A technical summary report was attached and incorporated into the parties' contract. The report listed specifications for the plane that First Technology intended to buy, which, as it turned out, described a McDonnell Douglas MD-83 rather than the aircraft Airborne was selling. When First Technology refused to accept the DC-9-83 aircraft, Airborne sued for breach of contract.

A federal district court in New York held in First Technology's favor and dismissed the case. The specifications listed in the contract (the technical summary report) were clear. The DC-9-83 did not comply with those specifications. Therefore, under the perfect tender rule, the buyer had a right to reject the goods.[2] ■ (Note that the corollary to this rule is that if the goods conform in every respect, the buyer or lessee does not have a right to reject the goods.)

---

2. *First Technology Capital, Inc. v. Airborne, Inc.,* 261 F.Supp.3d 371 (W.D.N.Y. 2017).

In the following case, a company ordered a custom-built tow truck from a manufacturer, but when it was delivered, the truck did not function properly. The question was whether the seller's tender of a truck that did not function properly gave the buyer a right to reject the truck under the perfect tender rule.

■ Case 21.1

All the Way Towing, LLC v. Bucks County International, Inc.

Superior Court of New Jersey, Appellate Division, 452 N.J.Super. 565, 178 A.3d 97 (2018).

Background and Facts After extensive discussions, Bucks County International, Inc., contracted with All the Way Towing, LLC, to manufacture and sell a tow truck with particular specifications. The contract specified that the custom-made truck would be "an International 7300 4×4 with a Dynamic 801 tow body mounted."

The truck was supposed to be delivered by April 15, but the first attempt at delivery occurred months later, in October. At that time, the tow truck's forks did not move correctly, and there were other significant problems. Bucks made two more attempts at delivery in October, but the towing function was not operational, and the truck spewed hydraulic fluid. The fourth attempt at delivery occurred in November. At that time, metal fell out from beneath the truck, and the wheel lift failed to close properly.

All the Way rejected the truck and, believing that Bucks would never be able to deliver a properly functioning truck, demanded return of the $10,000 deposit. When Bucks did not refund the deposit, All the Way sued. The trial court granted a summary judgment to the defendant dismissing the complaint because Bucks had tendered a tow truck as specified in the contract. All the Way appealed.

In the Words of the Court

FISHER, P.J.A.D. [Presiding Judge of a part of the Appellate Division]

* * * *

The [trial court] judge dismissed plaintiffs' breach of contract claim because, in his view, Bucks produced and tendered a tow truck. In support of this conclusion, the judge cited in his written opinion only [New Jersey's version of the UCC 2–106(2)], which, in defining terms relevant to sales contracts, declares that "goods" are " 'conforming' or conform to the contract when they are in accordance with the obligations under the contract." In other words, as the judge explained, the contract called for the delivery of "an International 7300 4×4 with a Dynamic 801 tow body mounted" and that's what was tendered; the judge did not

consider plaintiffs' allegations that the tow truck failed to function properly and, for that reason alone, we must reverse.

Had he viewed the evidence in the light most favorable to plaintiffs, the judge would have been required to assume that Bucks attempted delivery on four occasions—all well beyond the stipulated delivery date—and on each occasion failed to deliver a truck that adequately performed its essential functions. If plaintiffs' allegations regarding the tow truck's apparent problems, which were identified at each of four attempted deliveries, are ultimately proven, plaintiffs would have demonstrated the tow truck was nonconforming, [and] its failure to conform authorized plaintiffs' rejection of delivery * * *. *In short, the record reveals a central factual dispute as to whether the tow truck conformed to the contract and that dispute alone precludes summary judgment.* [Emphasis added.]

Decision and Remedy The state intermediate appellate court reversed the lower court's decision and remanded the case for a trial. When deciding a defendant's summary judgment motion, a court is required to view the evidence in the light most favorable to the plaintiff. Thus, the lower court should have considered All the Way's allegations that Bucks had failed to deliver a tow truck that adequately performed its essential functions. If All the Way's allegations are true, then the tow truck was nonconforming, and All the Way had a right to reject the truck under the perfect tender rule and to pursue remedies under the UCC.

Critical Thinking

• **What If the Facts Were Different?** *Suppose that Bucks had completely fixed the truck by the fourth time it was tendered. Could All the Way continue to reject delivery of the truck? Why or why not?*

• **Legal Environment** *What provisions might the parties in this situation have included in their contract to protect themselves from this type of dispute?*

21–1e **Exceptions to the Perfect Tender Rule**

Because of the rigidity of the perfect tender rule, several exceptions to the rule have been created, some of which are discussed here.

Agreement of the Parties Exceptions to the perfect tender rule may be established by agreement. If the parties have agreed, for instance, that defective goods or parts will not be rejected if the seller or lessor is able to repair or replace them within a reasonable period of time, the perfect tender rule does not apply.

The Right to Cure The UCC does not specifically define the term *cure*, but it refers to the right of the seller or lessor to repair, adjust, or replace defective or nonconforming goods [UCC 2–508, 2A–513]. The seller or lessor can attempt to cure a defect when the following are true:

1. A delivery is rejected because the goods were nonconforming.
2. The time for performance has not yet expired.
3. The seller or lessor provides timely notice to the buyer or lessee of the intention to cure.
4. The cure can be made within the contract time for performance.

Reasonable Grounds. Even if the contract time for performance has expired, the seller or lessor can still cure if he or she had *reasonable grounds to believe that the nonconforming tender would be acceptable to the buyer or lessee* [UCC 2–508(2), 2A–513(2)]. **Example 21.5** In the past, Reddy Electronics frequently allowed Topps Company to substitute gray keyboards when the silver keyboards that Reddy ordered were not available. Under a new contract for silver keyboards, Reddy rejects a shipment of gray keyboards. In this situation, Topps had reasonable grounds to believe Reddy would accept a substitute. Therefore, Topps can cure within a reasonable time even if conforming delivery will occur after the contract time for performance has ended.

A seller or lessor may tender nonconforming goods with a price allowance (discount). This may also serve as "reasonable grounds" for the seller or lessor to believe that the buyer or lessee will accept the nonconforming tender.

Limits the Right to Reject Goods. The right to cure substantially restricts the right of the buyer or lessee to reject goods. To reject, the buyer or lessee must inform the seller or lessor of the particular defect. If the defect is not disclosed, and if it is one that the seller or lessor could have cured, the buyer or lessee cannot later assert the defect as a defense. Generally, buyers and lessees must act in good faith and state specific reasons for refusing to accept goods [UCC 2–605, 2A–514].

Substitution of Carriers An agreed-on manner of delivery (such as the use of a particular carrier) may become impracticable or unavailable through no fault of either party. In that situation, if a commercially reasonable substitute is available, this substitute must be used and will constitute sufficient tender to the buyer [UCC 2–614(1)]. The seller or lessor is required to arrange for the substitute carrier and normally is responsible for any additional shipping costs (unless the contract states otherwise).

Example 21.6 A sales contract calls for a large generator to be delivered via Roadway Trucking Corporation on or before June 1. The contract terms clearly state the importance of the delivery date. The employees of Roadway Trucking go on strike. The seller must make a reasonable substitute tender, by another trucking company or perhaps by rail, if it is available. The seller normally will be responsible for any additional shipping costs.

Installment Contracts An **installment contract** is a single contract that requires or authorizes delivery in two or more separate lots to be accepted and paid for separately.

Installment Contract A contract that requires or authorizes delivery in two or more separate lots to be accepted and paid for separately.

With an installment contract, a buyer or lessee can reject an installment *only if the nonconformity substantially impairs the value* of the installment and cannot be cured [UCC 2–307, 2–612(2), 2A–510(1)]. **Example 21.7** A seller, Emmy's Appliances, is to deliver fifteen freezers in lots of five each. In the first lot, four of the freezers have defective cooling units that cannot be repaired. In these circumstances, the buyer can reject the entire lot. If the buyer or lessee fails to notify the seller or lessor of the rejection, however, and subsequently accepts a nonconforming installment, the contract is reinstated [UCC 2–612(3), 2A–510(2)].

Unless the contract provides otherwise, the entire installment contract is breached only when one or more nonconforming installments *substantially* impair the value of the *whole contract*. The point to remember is that the UCC significantly alters the right of the buyer or lessee to reject the entire contract if the contract requires delivery to be made in several installments. The UCC strictly limits rejection to cases of *substantial* nonconformity.

> "Obstacles are those frightful things you see when you take your eyes off your goal."
>
> **Henry Ford**
> 1863–1947
> (Founder of Ford Motor Company)

Commercial Impracticability

Occurrences unforeseen by either party when a contract was made may make performance commercially impracticable. When this occurs, the rule of perfect tender no longer applies. The seller or lessor must, however, notify the buyer or lessee as soon as practicable that there will be a delay or nondelivery.

The doctrine of commercial impracticability does not extend to problems that could have been foreseen, such as an increase in cost resulting from inflation. The nonoccurrence of the contingency must have been a basic assumption on which the contract was made [UCC 2–615, 2A–405].

Classic Case Example 21.8 Maple Farms, Inc., entered a contract to supply a school district in New York with milk for one school year. The contract price was the market price of milk in June, but by December, the price of raw milk had increased by 23 percent. Maple Farms stood to lose $7,350 on this contract (and more on similar contracts with other school districts).

To avoid performing the contract, Maple Farms filed a suit and claimed that the unanticipated increases in a seller's costs made performance "impracticable." A New York trial court disagreed. Because inflation and fluctuating prices could have been foreseen, they did not render performance of this contract impracticable. The court ruled in favor of the school district.[3]

Commercial Impracticability and Partial Performance

Sometimes, an unforeseen event only *partially* affects the capacity of the seller or lessor to perform. Therefore, the seller or lessor can *partially* fulfill the contract but cannot tender total performance. In this situation, the seller or lessor is required to distribute any remaining goods or deliveries fairly and reasonably among the parties to whom it is contractually obligated to deliver the goods [UCC 2–615(b), 2A–405(b)]. The buyer or lessee must receive notice of the allocation and has the right to accept or reject it [UCC 2–615(c), 2A–405(c)].

Example 21.9 A Florida orange grower, Best Citrus, Inc., contracts to sell this season's crop to a number of customers, including Martin's grocery chain. Martin's contracts to purchase two thousand crates of oranges. Best Citrus has sprayed some of its orange groves with a chemical called Karmoxin. When studies show that persons who eat products sprayed with Karmoxin may develop cancer, the Department of Agriculture issues an order prohibiting the sale of these products. Best Citrus picks only those oranges not sprayed with Karmoxin, but there are not enough to meet all the contracted-for deliveries.

In this situation, Best Citrus is required to allocate its production. It notifies Martin's that it cannot deliver the full quantity specified in the contract and indicates the amount it will be able to deliver. Martin's can either accept or reject the allocation, but Best Citrus has no further contractual liability.

School districts often make long-term contracts for milk deliveries. Under what circumstances can a milk supplier claim commercial impracticability when it fails to deliver the milk?

---

3. *Maple Farms, Inc. v. City School District of Elmira,* 76 Misc.2d 1080, 352 N.Y.S.2d 784 (1974).

Destruction of Identified Goods Sometimes, an unexpected event, such as a fire, totally destroys goods through no fault of either party and before risk passes to the buyer or lessee. In such a situation, *if the goods were identified at the time the contract was formed,* the parties are excused from performance [UCC 2–613, 2A–221]. If the goods are only partially destroyed, however, the buyer or lessee can inspect them and either treat the contract as void or accept the goods with a reduction of the contract price.

Example 21.10 Atlas Sporting Equipment agrees to lease to River Bicycles sixty bicycles of a particular model that has been discontinued. No other bicycles of that model are available. River specifies that it needs the bicycles to rent to tourists. Before Atlas can deliver the bicycles, they are destroyed by a fire. In this situation, Atlas is not liable to River for failing to deliver the bicycles. The goods were destroyed through no fault of either party, before the risk of loss passed to the lessee. The loss was total, so the contract is avoided. Clearly, Atlas has no obligation to tender the bicycles, and River has no obligation to make the lease payments for them.

Assurance and Cooperation If one party has "reasonable grounds" to believe that the other party will not perform as contracted, he or she may *in writing* "demand adequate assurance of due performance" from the other party. Until such assurance is received, he or she may "suspend" further performance (such as payments due under the contract) without liability. What constitutes "reasonable grounds" is determined by commercial standards. If such assurances are not forthcoming within a reasonable time (not to exceed thirty days), the failure to respond may be treated as a *repudiation* of the contract [UCC 2–609, 2A–401].

Sometimes, the performance of one party depends on the cooperation of the other. The UCC provides an exception to the perfect tender doctrine if one party fails to cooperate. When cooperation is not forthcoming, the other party can suspend her or his own performance without liability and hold the uncooperative party in breach or proceed to perform the contract in any reasonable manner [UCC 2–311(3)].

Example 21.11 Aman is required by contract to deliver 1,200 Samsung washing machines to various locations in California on or before October 1. Farrell, the buyer, is to specify the locations for delivery. Aman repeatedly requests the delivery locations, but Farrell does not respond. The washing machines are ready for shipment on October 1, but Farrell still refuses to give Aman the delivery locations. If Aman does not ship on October 1, he cannot be held liable. Aman is excused for any resulting delay of performance because of Farrell's failure to cooperate.

21–2 Obligations of the Buyer or Lessee

The main obligation of the buyer or lessee under a sales or lease contract is to pay for the goods tendered in accordance with the contract. Once the seller or lessor has adequately tendered delivery, the buyer or lessee is obligated to accept the goods and pay for them according to the terms of the contract.

21–2a Payment

In the absence of any specific agreement, the buyer or lessee must make payment at the time and place the goods are *received* [UCC 2–310(a), 2A–516(1)]. When a sale is made on credit, the buyer is obligated to pay according to the specified credit terms (for instance, 60, 90, or 120 days), not when the goods are received. The credit period usually begins on the *date*

Who is liable for nondelivery of washing machines if the buyer does not provide delivery locations?

deepblue4you/E+/Getty Images

of shipment [UCC 2–310(d)]. Under a lease contract, a lessee must make the lease payment that was specified in the contract [UCC 2A–516(1)].

Payment can be made by any means agreed on by the parties—cash or any other method generally acceptable in the commercial world. If the seller demands cash, the seller must give the buyer reasonable time to obtain it [UCC 2–511].

21–2b Right of Inspection

Unless the parties otherwise agree, or for C.O.D. (collect on delivery) transactions, the buyer or lessee has an absolute right to inspect the goods before making payment. This right allows the buyer or lessee to verify, before making payment, that the goods tendered or delivered are what were contracted for or ordered. If the goods are *not* what were ordered, the buyer or lessee has no duty to pay. *An opportunity for inspection is therefore a condition precedent to the right of the seller or lessor to enforce payment* [UCC 2–513(1), 2A–515(1)].

Inspection can take place at any reasonable place and time and in any reasonable manner. Generally, what is reasonable is determined by custom of the trade, past practices of the parties, and the like. The buyer bears the costs of inspecting the goods (unless otherwise agreed), but if the goods are rejected because they are not conforming, the buyer can recover the costs of inspection from the seller [UCC 2–513(2)].

21–2c Acceptance

After having had a reasonable opportunity to inspect the goods, the buyer or lessee can demonstrate acceptance in any of the following ways:

1. The buyer or lessee indicates (by words or conduct) to the seller or lessor that the goods are conforming or that he or she will retain them in spite of their nonconformity [UCC 2–606(1)(a), 2A–515(1)(a)].

2. The buyer or lessee *fails to reject* the goods within a reasonable period of time [UCC 2–602(1), 2–606(1)(b), 2A–515(1)(b)].

3. In sales contracts, the buyer *performs any act inconsistent with the seller's ownership.* For instance, any use or resale of the goods—except for the limited purpose of testing or inspecting the goods—generally constitutes an acceptance [UCC 2–606(1)(c)].

Case Example 21.12 Hemacare Plus, Inc., ordered more than $660,000 in specialty pharmaceutical products from Cardinal Health 108, LLC. Cardinal supplied the products, which Hemacare used and did not reject or return. Hemacare did not pay the invoices for the goods delivered, however, so Cardinal filed a breach action in a federal district court. Because Hemacare had used the pharmaceutical products it had received, the court found it had accepted the goods. Therefore, the court granted a summary judgment to Cardinal awarding $688,920 in damages (including interest, attorneys' fees, and costs).[4] ▪

21–2d Partial Acceptance

If some of the goods delivered do not conform to the contract and the seller or lessor has failed to cure, the buyer or lessee can make a *partial* acceptance [UCC 2–601(c), 2A–509(1)]. The same is true if the nonconformity was not reasonably discoverable before acceptance. (In the latter situation, the buyer or lessee may be able to revoke the acceptance, as will be discussed later in this chapter.)

A buyer or lessee cannot accept less than a single commercial unit, however. The UCC defines a *commercial unit* as a unit of goods that, by commercial usage, is viewed as a

Learning Objective 2

When will a buyer or lessee be deemed to have accepted the goods?

"Death, they say, acquits us of all obligations."

Michel de Montaigne
1533–1592
(French writer and philosopher)

---

4. *Cardinal Health 108, LLC v. Hemacare Plus, Inc.,* 2017 WL 114405 (S.D.Ala. 2017).

"single whole" that cannot be divided without material impairment of the character of the unit, its market value, or its use [UCC 2–105(6), 2A–103(1)(c)]. A commercial unit can be a single article (such as a machine), a set of articles (such as a suite of furniture or an assortment of sizes), a quantity (such as a bale, a gross, or a carload), or any other unit treated in the trade as a single whole for purposes of sale.

21–2e Anticipatory Repudiation

What if, before the time for contract performance, one party clearly communicates to the other the intention not to perform? As discussed earlier in this text, such an action is a breach of the contract by anticipatory repudiation.

Possible Responses to Repudiation When anticipatory repudiation occurs, the nonbreaching party has a choice of two responses:

1. Treat the repudiation as a final breach by pursuing a remedy.
2. Wait to see if the repudiating party will decide to perform the contract despite the avowed intention to renege [UCC 2–610, 2A–402].

In either situation, the nonbreaching party may *suspend performance.*

A Repudiation May Be Retracted The UCC permits the breaching party to "retract" his or her repudiation (subject to some limitations). This retraction can be done by any method that clearly indicates the party's intent to perform. Once retraction is made, the rights of the repudiating party under the contract are reinstated. There can be no retraction, however, if since the time of the repudiation the other party has canceled or materially changed position or otherwise indicated that the repudiation is final [UCC 2–611, 2A–403].

Example 21.13 On April 1, Cora Lyn, who owns a small inn, purchases a suite of furniture from Tom Horton, proprietor of Horton's Furniture Warehouse. The contract states that "delivery must be made on or before May 1." On April 10, Horton informs Lyn that he cannot make delivery until May 10 and asks her to consent to the modified delivery date.

In this situation, Lyn has two options. She can either treat Horton's notice of late delivery as a final breach of contract and pursue a remedy or agree to the later delivery date. Suppose that Lyn does neither for two weeks. On April 24, Horton informs Lyn that he will be able to deliver the furniture by May 1 after all. In effect, Horton has retracted his repudiation, reinstating the rights and obligations of the parties under the original contract. Note that if Lyn had told Horton that she was canceling the contract after he repudiated, he would not have been able to retract his repudiation. ▪

An inn owner buys new bedroom furniture, but the seller modifies the delivery date of the shipment. What are the inn owner's options?

Christian Delbert/Shutterstock

21–3 Remedies of the Seller or Lessor

Remedies under the UCC are *cumulative,* meaning that the aggrieved (wronged) party is not limited to one exclusive remedy. (Of course, a party still may not recover twice for the same harm.) When the buyer or lessee is in breach, the remedies available to the seller or lessor depend on the circumstances existing at the time of the breach. The most pertinent considerations are which party has possession of the goods, whether the goods are in transit, and whether the buyer or lessee has rejected or accepted the goods.

21–3a When the Goods Are in the Possession of the Seller or Lessor

If the breach occurs *before the goods have been delivered to the buyer or lessee,* the seller or lessor has the right to pursue a number of remedies, which are listed below and discussed in the following subsections.

1. Cancel (rescind) the contract.
2. Withhold delivery of the goods.
3. Resell or dispose of the goods and sue to recover damages.
4. Sue to recover the purchase price or lease payments due.
5. Sue to recover damages for the buyer's nonacceptance.

The Right to Cancel the Contract If the buyer or lessee breaches the contract, the seller or lessor can choose to cancel (rescind) the contract [UCC 2–703(f), 2A–523(1)(a)]. The seller must notify the buyer or lessee of the cancellation, and at that point all remaining obligations of the seller or lessor are discharged. The buyer or lessee is not discharged from all remaining obligations, however. She or he is in breach, and the seller or lessor can pursue remedies available under the UCC for breach.

The Right to Withhold Delivery In general, sellers and lessors can withhold or discontinue performance of their obligations under sales or lease contracts when the buyers or lessees are in breach. This is true whether a buyer or lessee has wrongfully rejected or revoked acceptance of contract goods (rejection and revocation of acceptance will be discussed later), failed to make a payment, or repudiated the contract [UCC 2–703(a), 2A–523(1)(c)]. The seller or lessor can also refuse to deliver the goods to a buyer or lessee who is insolvent (unable to pay debts as they become due), unless the buyer or lessee pays in cash [UCC 2–702(1), 2A–525(1)].

The Right to Resell or Dispose of the Goods When a buyer or lessee breaches or repudiates the contract while the seller or lessor is still in possession of the goods, the seller or lessor can resell or dispose of the goods. Any resale of the goods must be made in good faith and in a commercially reasonable manner. The seller must give the original buyer reasonable notice of the resale, unless the goods are perishable or will rapidly decline in value [UCC 2–706(2), (3)].

The seller or lessor can retain any profits made as a result of the sale or disposition and can hold the buyer or lessee liable for any loss [UCC 2–703(d), 2–706(1), 2A–523(1)(e), 2A–527(1)]. In sales transactions, the seller can recover any deficiency between the resale price and the contract price, and can also recover *incidental damages,* defined as the costs to the seller resulting from the breach [UCC 2–706(1), 2–710]. In lease transactions, the lessor can lease the goods to another party and recover damages from the original lessee. Damages include any unpaid lease payments up to the time the new lease begins. The lessor can also recover any deficiency between the lease payments due under the original lease and those due under the new lease, along with incidental damages [UCC 2A–527(2)].

When the goods are unfinished at the time of breach, the seller or lessor can do either of the following:

1. Cease manufacturing the goods and resell them for scrap or salvage value.
2. Complete the manufacture, resell or dispose of the goods, and hold the buyer or lessee liable for any difference between the contract price and the sale.

In choosing between these two alternatives, the seller or lessor must exercise reasonable commercial judgment to mitigate the loss and obtain maximum value from the unfinished goods [UCC 2–704(2), 2A–524(2)].

Learning Objective 3

What remedies are available to a seller or lessor when the buyer or lessee breaches the contract?

Know This

A buyer or lessee breaches a contract by wrongfully rejecting the goods, wrongfully revoking acceptance, refusing to pay, or repudiating the contract.

The Right to Sue to Recover the Purchase Price or the Lease Payments Due

Under the UCC, an unpaid seller or lessor can bring an action to recover the purchase price or payments due under the lease contract, plus incidental damages [UCC 2–709(1), 2A–529(1)]. If a seller or lessor is unable to resell or dispose of goods and sues for the contract price or lease payments due, the goods must be held for the buyer or lessee. The seller or lessor can resell or dispose of the goods at any time before collecting the judgment from the buyer or lessee. If the goods are resold, the net proceeds from the sale must be credited to the buyer or lessee because of the duty to mitigate damages.

Example 21.14 Canyonville Academy contracts with Stickme.com to purchase ten thousand bumper stickers with the school's name and logo on them. Stickme tenders delivery of the stickers, but Canyonville wrongfully refuses to accept them. In this situation, Stickme can bring an action for the purchase price. Stickme has delivered conforming goods, and Canyonville has refused to accept or pay for the goods. Obviously, Stickme will not likely be able to resell the stickers, so this situation falls under UCC 2–709. Stickme is required to make the bumper stickers available for Canyonville. In the unlikely event that it can find another buyer, it can sell the stickers at any time prior to collecting the judgment from Canyonville.

If a school orders special merchandise with its school name and mascot printed on it and then refuses the shipment of conforming goods, what can the seller do to recoup payment?

monkeybusinessimages/iStock/Getty Images

The Right to Sue to Recover Damages for the Buyer's Non-acceptance

If a buyer or lessee repudiates a contract or wrongfully refuses to accept the goods, a seller or lessor can bring an action to recover the damages sustained. Ordinarily, the amount of damages equals the difference between the contract price or lease payments and the market price or lease payments at the time and place of tender of the goods, plus incidental damages [UCC 2–708(1), 2A–528(1)].

When the ordinary measure of damages is insufficient to put the seller or lessor in the same position as the buyer's or lessee's performance would have, the UCC provides an alternative. In that situation, the proper measure of damages is the lost profits of the seller or lessor, including a reasonable allowance for overhead and other expenses [UCC 2–708(2), 2A–528(2)].

21–3b When the Goods Are in Transit

If the seller or lessor has delivered the goods to a carrier or a bailee, but the buyer or lessee has not yet received them, the goods are said to be *in transit*. In limited situations, the seller or lessor can prevent goods in transit from being delivered to the buyer or lessee.

Effect of Insolvency and Breach If the seller or lessor learns that the buyer or lessee is insolvent, the seller or lessor can stop the carrier or bailee from delivering the goods regardless of the quantity of goods shipped. If the buyer or lessee is in breach but is not insolvent, however, the seller or lessor can stop delivery of goods in transit only if the quantity shipped is at least a carload, a truckload, a planeload, or a larger shipment [UCC 2–705(1), 2A–526(1)].

Example 21.15 Arturo Ortega orders a truckload of lumber from Timber Products, Inc., to be shipped to Ortega six weeks later. Ortega, who owes payment to Timber Products for a past shipment, promises to pay the debt immediately and to pay for the current shipment as soon as it is received. After the lumber has been shipped, a bankruptcy court judge notifies Timber Products that Ortega has filed a petition in bankruptcy and listed Timber Products as one of his creditors. If the goods are still in transit, Timber Products can stop the carrier from delivering the lumber to Ortega.

Requirements for Stopping Delivery To stop delivery, the seller or lessor must *timely notify* the carrier or other bailee that the goods are to be returned or held for the seller or lessor. If the carrier has sufficient time to stop delivery, it must hold and deliver the goods according to the instructions of the seller or lessor. The seller or lessor is liable to the carrier for any additional costs incurred [UCC 2–705(3), 2A–526(3)].

The seller or lessor has the right to stop delivery of the goods under UCC 2–705(2) and 2A–526(2) until the time when the following occurs:

1. The buyer or lessee obtains possession of the goods.

2. The carrier or the bailee acknowledges the rights of the buyer or lessee in the goods (by reshipping or holding the goods for the buyer or lessee, for instance).

3. A negotiable document of title covering the goods has been properly transferred to the buyer (in sales transactions only), giving the buyer ownership rights in the goods [UCC 2–702].

Once the seller or lessor reclaims the goods in transit, she or he can pursue the remedies allowed to sellers and lessors when the goods are in their possession.

21–3c When the Goods Are in the Possession of the Buyer or Lessee

When the buyer or lessee breaches the contract while the goods are in his or her possession, the seller or lessor can sue. The seller or lessor can sue to recover the purchase price of the goods or the lease payments due, plus incidental damages [UCC 2–709(1), 2A–529(1)].

In some situations, a seller may also have a right to reclaim the goods from the buyer. For instance, in a sales contract, if the buyer has received the goods on credit and the seller discovers that the buyer is insolvent, the seller can demand return of the goods [UCC 2–702(2)]. Ordinarily, the demand must be made within ten days of the buyer's receipt of the goods.[5] The seller's right to reclaim the goods is subject to the rights of a good faith purchaser or other subsequent buyer in the ordinary course of business who purchases the goods from the buyer before the seller reclaims them.

A lessor may also have a right to reclaim goods. If the lessee is in default (fails to make payments that are due, for instance), the lessor may reclaim leased goods that are in the lessee's possession [UCC 2A–525(2)].

21–4 Remedies of the Buyer or Lessee

When the seller or lessor breaches the contract, the buyer or lessee has numerous remedies available under the UCC. Like the remedies available to sellers and lessors, the remedies of buyers and lessees depend on the circumstances existing at the time of the breach. Relevant factors include whether the seller has refused to deliver conforming goods or has delivered nonconforming goods.

21–4a When the Seller or Lessor Refuses to Deliver the Goods

If the seller or lessor refuses to deliver the goods, or the buyer or lessee has rightfully rejected the goods, the remedies available to the buyer or lessee include the right to:

1. Cancel (rescind) the contract.

2. Obtain goods that have been paid for if the seller or lessor is insolvent.

3. Sue to obtain specific performance if the goods are unique or damages are an inadequate remedy.

4. Buy other goods (obtain *cover*), and obtain damages from the seller.

Know This
Incidental damages include all reasonable expenses incurred because of a breach of contract.

---

5. The seller can demand and reclaim the goods at any time, though, if the buyer misrepresented his or her solvency in writing within three months prior to the delivery of the goods.

5. Sue to obtain identified goods held by a third party (*replevy* goods).

6. Sue to obtain damages.

The Right to Cancel the Contract When a seller or lessor fails to make proper delivery or repudiates the contract, the buyer or lessee can cancel, or rescind, the contract. On notice of cancellation, the buyer or lessee is relieved of any further obligations under the contract but retains all rights to other remedies against the seller [UCC 2–711(1), 2A–508(1)(a)]. (The right to cancel the contract is also available to a buyer or lessee who has rightfully rejected goods or revoked acceptance, as will be discussed shortly.)

The Right to Obtain the Goods on Insolvency If a buyer or lessee has made a partial or full payment for goods that are in the possession of a seller or lessor who is or becomes insolvent, the buyer or lessee has a right to obtain the goods. For this right to be exercised, the goods must be identified to the contract, and the buyer or lessee must pay any remaining balance of the price to the seller or lessor [UCC 2–502, 2A–522].

The Right to Obtain Specific Performance A buyer or lessee can obtain specific performance when the goods are unique and the remedy at law is inadequate [UCC 2–716(1), 2A–521(1)]. Ordinarily, a successful suit for monetary damages is sufficient to place a buyer or lessee in the position he or she would have occupied if the seller or lessor had fully performed. When the contract is for the purchase of a particular work of art or a similarly unique item, however, monetary damages may not be sufficient. Under these circumstances, equity requires that the seller or lessor perform exactly by delivering the goods identified to the contract (a remedy of specific performance).

★ **Spotlight Case Example 21.16** Doreen Houseman and Eric Dare together bought a house and a pedigreed dog. When the couple separated, they agreed that Dare would keep the house (and pay Houseman for her interest in it) and Houseman would keep the dog. Houseman allowed Dare to take the dog for visits. After one such visit, Dare failed to return the dog. Houseman filed a lawsuit seeking specific performance of their agreement. The court found that because pets have special, subjective value to their owners, a dog can be considered a unique good. Thus, an award of specific performance was appropriate.[6]

Will a court consider a pedigreed dog a unique good?

fotoiagodka/iStock/Getty Images

The Right to Obtain Cover In certain situations, buyers and lessees can protect themselves by obtaining **cover**—that is, by purchasing or leasing other goods to substitute for those due under the contract. This option is available when the seller or lessor repudiates the contract or fails to deliver the goods, or when a buyer or lessee has rightfully rejected goods or revoked acceptance. In purchasing or leasing substitute goods, the buyer or lessee must act in good faith and without unreasonable delay [UCC 2–712, 2A–518].

After obtaining substitute goods, the buyer or lessee can recover the following from the seller or lessor:

1. The difference between the cost of cover and the contract price (or lease payments).

2. Incidental damages that resulted from the breach.

3. Consequential damages to compensate for indirect losses (such as lost profits) resulting from the breach that were reasonably foreseeable at the time of contract formation.

Buyers and lessees are not required to cover, and failure to do so will not bar them from using any other remedies available under the UCC. A buyer or lessee who fails to cover, however, may not be able to collect consequential damages that he or she could have avoided by purchasing or leasing substitute goods.

Cover A remedy that allows the buyer or lessee, on the seller's or lessor's breach, to obtain substitute goods from another seller or lessor.

---

6. *Houseman v. Dare,* 405 N.J.Super. 538, 966 A.2d 24 (2009).

The Right to Replevy Goods Buyers and lessees also have the right to replevy goods. Replevin[7] is an action that a buyer or lessee can use to recover specific goods from a third party, such as a bailee, who is wrongfully withholding them. Under the UCC, the buyer or lessee can replevy goods subject to the contract if the seller or lessor has repudiated or breached the contract. To maintain an action to replevy goods, buyers and lessees usually must show that they are unable to cover for the goods after a reasonable effort [UCC 2–716(3), 2A–521(3)].

The Right to Recover Damages If a seller or lessor repudiates the contract or fails to deliver the goods, the buyer or lessee can sue for damages. For the buyer (or lessee), the measure of recovery is the difference between the contract price (or lease payments) and the market price (or lease payments) at the time the buyer (or lessee) *learned* of the breach. The market price or market lease payments are determined at the place where the seller or lessor was supposed to deliver the goods. The buyer or lessee can also recover incidental and consequential damages, less the expenses that were saved as a result of the breach [UCC 2–713, 2A–519].

> **Example 21.17** Jason & Fils, Inc., contracts to buy a thirty-thousand-gallon industrial tank from Burbank Equipment Corporation for $70,000. Jason & Fils hires Zach's Transport to pick up the tank, but when Zach's arrives at the pickup location, there is no tank. Jason & Fils pays Zach's $7,500 for its services and sues Burbank Equipment to recover.
>
> In this situation, Jason & Fils is entitled to recover the difference between the contract price and the market price of the tank. In addition, Jason & Fils is entitled to incidental damages of at least $7,500 for the cost of transport, as well as any consequential damages that were reasonably foreseeable. ◼

21–4b When the Seller or Lessor Delivers Nonconforming Goods

When the seller or lessor delivers nonconforming goods, the buyer or lessee has several remedies available under the UCC. The buyer or lessee may reject the goods, revoke acceptance of the goods, and recover damages for accepted goods.

The Right to Reject the Goods If either the goods or the tender of the goods by the seller or lessor fails to conform to the contract *in any respect,* the buyer or lessee can reject the goods in whole or in part [UCC 2–601, 2A–509]. If the buyer or lessee rejects the goods, she or he may then obtain cover, cancel the contract, or sue for damages for breach of contract, just as if the seller or lessor had refused to deliver the goods.

Timeliness and Reason for Rejection Required. The buyer or lessee must reject the goods within a reasonable amount of time after delivery and must *seasonably* (timely) notify the seller or lessor [UCC 2–602(1), 2A–509(2)]. If the buyer or lessee fails to reject the goods within a reasonable amount of time, acceptance will be presumed.

When rejecting goods, the buyer or lessee must also designate specific defects that would have been apparent to the seller or lessor on reasonable inspection. Failure to do so precludes the buyer or lessee from using such defects to justify rejection or to establish breach when the seller could have cured the defects if they had been disclosed in a timely fashion [UCC 2–605, 2A–514].

Replevin An action that can be used by a buyer or lessee to recover identified goods from a third party, such as a bailee, who is wrongfully withholding them.

Know This
Consequential damages compensate for a loss (such as lost profits) that is not direct but was reasonably foreseeable at the time of the breach.

vincent noel/Shutterstock

If a supplier of industrial storage tanks fails to provide a tank when and where specified in the sales contract, can the buyer recover funds paid to a transport company for its shipment?

---

7. Pronounced ruh-*pleh*-vun. Note that outside the UCC, the term *replevin* refers to a prejudgment process that permits the seizure of specific personal property in which a party claims a right or an interest.

Duties of Merchant Buyers and Lessees When Goods Are Rejected. What happens if a *merchant buyer or lessee* rightfully rejects goods and the seller or lessor has no agent or business at the place of rejection? In that situation, the merchant buyer or lessee has a good faith obligation to follow any reasonable instructions received from the seller or lessor with respect to the goods [UCC 2–603, 2A–511]. The buyer or lessee is entitled to be reimbursed for the care and cost entailed in following the instructions. The same requirements hold if the buyer or lessee rightfully revokes his or her acceptance of the goods at some later time [UCC 2–608(3), 2A–517(5)]. (Revocation of acceptance will be discussed shortly.)

If no instructions are forthcoming and the goods are perishable or threaten to decline in value quickly, the buyer can resell the goods in good faith. The buyer can then take the appropriate reimbursement from the proceeds and a selling commission (not to exceed 10 percent of the gross proceeds) [UCC 2–603(1), (2); 2A–511(1), (2)]. If the goods are not perishable, the buyer or lessee may store them for the seller or lessor or reship them to the seller or lessor [UCC 2–604, 2A–512].

Revocation of Acceptance

Acceptance of the goods precludes the buyer or lessee from exercising the right of rejection, but it does not necessarily prevent the buyer or lessee from pursuing other remedies. In certain circumstances, a buyer or lessee is permitted to *revoke* her or his acceptance of the goods.

Revoking Acceptance of a Lot or Commercial Unit. Acceptance of a lot or a commercial unit can be revoked if the nonconformity *substantially* impairs the value of the lot or unit *and* if one of the following factors is present:

1. Acceptance was predicated on the reasonable assumption that the nonconformity would be cured, and it was not cured within a reasonable time [UCC 2–608(1)(a), 2A–517(1)(a)].

2. The buyer or lessee did not discover the nonconformity before acceptance, either because it was difficult to discover before acceptance or because assurances made by the seller or lessor that the goods were conforming kept the buyer or lessee from inspecting the goods [UCC 2–608(1)(b), 2A–517(1)(b)].

Case Example 21.18 Armadillo Distribution Enterprises, Inc., is a major distributor of musical instruments. Armadillo contracted with a Chinese corporation, Hai Yun Musical Instruments Manufacture Co., Ltd., to manufacture one thousand drum kits. Hai Yun had made drums for Armadillo in the past. Hai Yun furnished samples for Armadillo's approval prior to manufacturing the kits. After Armadillo inspected and approved the samples, Hai Yun delivered five shipping containers of drum kits, and Armadillo began distribution.

Armadillo soon started receiving complaints from its retail outlet customers concerning product returns due to cosmetic and structural defects in the drum kits. Armadillo immediately inspected the remaining four shipment containers and discovered that a high percentage of the drum kits were defective and unfit for commercial distribution. Armadillo revoked its acceptance of the kits and filed a suit in federal court for breach of contract. The district court ruled that Hai Yun had breached the contract by delivering nonconforming goods. The court awarded Armadillo nearly $90,000 in direct and incidental damages.[8] ■

Notice of Revocation. Revocation of acceptance is not effective until notice is given to the seller or lessor. Notice must occur within a reasonable time after the buyer or lessee either discovers or *should have discovered* the grounds for revocation. Additionally, revocation must occur before the goods have undergone any substantial change (such as spoilage) not caused by their own defects [UCC 2–608(2), 2A–517(4)]. Once acceptance is revoked, the buyer or lessee can pursue remedies just as if the goods had been rejected.

If a company accepts a large lot of drum sets but many of the drum sets are later returned by customers who complain of defects, can the company revoke acceptance of the goods? Why or why not?

Ryan McVay/Getty Images

---

8. *Armadillo Distribution Enterprises, Inc. v. Hai Yun Musical Instruments Manufacture Co. Ltd.*, 142 F.Supp.3d 1245 (M.D.Fla. 2015).

Note that to effectively revoke acceptance, a buyer must "relinquish dominion over the goods." This requires a buyer to return the goods or at least to stop using them, unless the use is necessary to avoid substantial hardship. **Case Example 21.19** Genesis Health Clubs, Inc., contracted with LED Solar & Light Company to furnish replacement lighting for its building. When Genesis experienced problems with the lights, LED Solar offered to fix or replace them or to refund the price. Genesis responded that it wanted a refund and would return all of the lights "in stages so the club would not go dark."

Genesis returned one shipment of the lights but then disputed the way that LED Solar credited its account for the lights. After that, Genesis made no additional returns. In a lawsuit between the parties, a federal district court concluded that Genesis could not recover the purchase price for the lights. A federal appellate court affirmed. Genesis had not effectively revoked acceptance because it did not return the lights (beyond the first shipment) to LED Solar and because it continued to use them.[9] ■ (See this chapter's *Beyond Our Borders* feature for a glimpse at how international sales law deals with revocation of acceptance.)

The Right to Recover Damages for Accepted Goods A buyer or lessee who has accepted nonconforming goods may also keep the goods and recover damages caused by the breach. To do so, the buyer or lessee must notify the seller or lessor of the breach within a reasonable time after the defect was or should have been discovered. Failure to give notice of the defect (breach) to the seller or lessor bars the buyer or lessee from pursuing any remedy [UCC 2–607(3), 2A–516(3)]. In addition, the parties to a sales or lease contract can insert a provision requiring the buyer or lessee to give notice of any defects in the goods within a set period.

When the goods delivered are not as promised, the measure of damages equals the difference between the value of the goods as accepted and their value if they had been delivered as warranted [UCC 2–714(2), 2A–519(4)]. The buyer or lessee is also entitled to incidental and consequential damages when appropriate [UCC 2–714(3), 2A–519(3)]. The UCC also permits the buyer or lessee, with proper notice to the seller or lessor, to deduct all or any part of the damages from the price or lease payments still due under the contract [UCC 2–717, 2A–516(1)].

---

9. *Genesis Health Clubs, Inc. v. LED Solar & Light Co.,* 639 Fed.Appx. 550 (10th Cir. 2016).

The CISG's Approach to Revocation of Acceptance

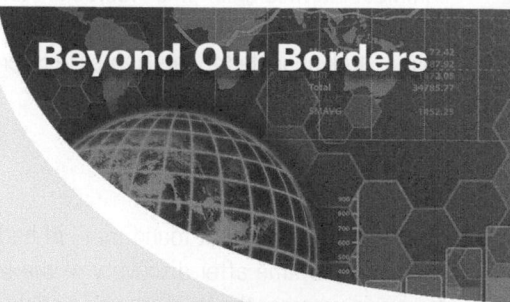

Beyond Our Borders

Under the UCC, a buyer or lessee who has accepted goods may be able to revoke acceptance under the circumstances mentioned in the text. The United Nations Convention on Contracts for the International Sale of Goods (CISG) also allows buyers to rescind their contracts after they have accepted the goods. The CISG, however, takes a somewhat different—and more direct—approach to the problem.

Under the CISG, the buyer can simply declare that the seller has *fundamentally* breached the contract and proceed to sue the seller for the breach. Article 25 of the CISG states that a "breach of contract committed by one of the parties is fundamental if it results in such detriment to the other party as substantially to deprive him [or her] of what he [or she] is entitled to expect under the contract." For example, to revoke acceptance of a shipment under the CISG, a buyer need not prove that the nonconformity of one shipment substantially impaired the value of the whole lot.

The buyer can simply file a lawsuit alleging that the seller is in breach.

Critical Thinking

What is the essential difference between revoking acceptance and bringing a suit for breach of contract?

Is two years after a sale of goods a reasonable time period in which to discover a defect in the goods and notify the seller of a breach? That was the question in the following *Spotlight Case*.

✴ Spotlight on Baseball Cards: Case 21.2

Fitl v. Strek
Supreme Court of Nebraska, 269 Neb. 51, 690 N.W.2d 605 (2005).

Background and Facts In 1995, James Fitl attended a sports-card show in San Francisco, California, where he met Mark Strek, doing business as Star Cards of San Francisco, an exhibitor at the show. Later, on Strek's representation that a certain 1952 Mickey Mantle Topps baseball card was in near-mint condition, Fitl bought the card from Strek for $17,750. Strek delivered the card to Fitl in Omaha, Nebraska, and Fitl placed it in a safe-deposit box.

In May 1997, Fitl sent the card to Professional Sports Authenticators (PSA), a sports-card grading service. PSA told Fitl that the card was ungradable because it had been discolored and doctored. Fitl complained to Strek, who replied that Fitl should have returned the card within "a typical grace period for the unconditional return of a card, … 7 days to 1 month" of its receipt. In August, Fitl sent the card to ASA Accugrade, Inc. (ASA), another grading service, for a second opinion of the value. ASA also concluded that the card had been refinished and trimmed. Fitl filed a suit in a Nebraska state court against Strek, seeking damages. The court awarded Fitl $17,750, plus his court costs. Strek appealed to the Nebraska Supreme Court.

What is a reasonable time period to discover that a purchased baseball card is not authentic?

In the Words of the Court
WRIGHT, J. [Judge]
* * * *

* * * The [trial] court found that Fitl had notified Strek within a reasonable time after discovery of the breach. Therefore, our review is whether the [trial] court's finding as to the reasonableness of the notice was clearly erroneous.

Section 2–607(3)(a) states: "Where a tender has been accepted * * * the buyer must within a reasonable time after he discovers or should have discovered any breach notify the seller of breach or be barred from any remedy." [Under UCC 1–204(2)] *"what is a reasonable time for taking any action depends on the nature, purpose and circumstances of such action."* [Emphasis added.]

The notice requirement set forth in Section 2–607(3)(a) serves three purposes. * * *

* * * The most important one is to enable the seller to make efforts to cure the breach by making adjustments or replacements in order to minimize the buyer's damages and the seller's liability. A second policy is to provide the seller a reasonable opportunity to learn the facts so that he may adequately prepare for negotiation and defend himself in a suit. A third policy * * * is the same as the policy behind statutes of limitation: to provide a seller with a terminal point in time for liability.

* * * *A party is justified in relying upon a representation made to the party as a positive statement of fact when an investigation would be required to ascertain its falsity.* In order for Fitl to have determined that the baseball card had been altered, he would have been required to conduct an investigation. We find that he was not required to do so. Once Fitl learned that the baseball card had been altered, he gave notice to Strek. [Emphasis added.]

* * * One of the most important policies behind the notice requirement * * * is to allow the seller to cure the breach by making adjustments or replacements to minimize the buyer's damages and the seller's liability. However, even if Fitl had learned immediately upon taking possession of the baseball card that it was not authentic and had notified Strek at that time, there is no evidence that Strek could have made any adjustment or taken any action that would have minimized his liability. In its altered condition, the baseball card was worthless.

* * * Earlier notification would not have helped Strek prepare for negotiation or defend himself in a suit because the damage to Fitl could not be repaired. Thus, the policies behind the notice requirement, to allow the seller to correct a defect, to prepare for negotiation and litigation, and to protect against stale claims at a time beyond which an investigation can be completed, were not unfairly prejudiced by the lack of an earlier notice to Strek. Any problem Strek may have had with the party from whom he obtained the baseball card was a separate matter from his transaction with Fitl, and an investigation into the source of the altered card would not have minimized Fitl's damages.

Decision and Remedy The state supreme court affirmed the decision of the lower court. Under the circumstances, notice of a defect in the card two years after its purchase was reasonable. The buyer had reasonably relied on the seller's representation that the card was "authentic" (which it was not), and when the defects were discovered, the buyer had given timely notice.

Critical Thinking

• **What If the Facts Were Different?** *Suppose that Fitl and Strek had included in their deal a written clause requiring Fitl to give notice of any defect in the card within "7 days to 1 month" of its receipt. Would the result have been different? Why or why not?*

21–4c Provisions That Affect or Limit Remedies

The parties to a sales or lease contract can vary their respective rights and obligations by contractual agreement. For instance, a seller and buyer can expressly provide for remedies in addition to those provided in the UCC. They can also specify remedies in lieu of those provided in the UCC, or they can change the measure of damages. Any agreed-on remedy is in addition to those provided in the UCC unless the parties expressly agree that the remedy is exclusive of all others [UCC 2–719(1), 2A–503(1), (2)].

Exclusive Remedies If the parties state that a remedy is exclusive, then it is the sole, or exclusive, remedy. **Example 21.20** Standard Tool Company agrees to sell a pipe-cutting machine to United Pipe & Tubing Corporation. The contract limits United's remedy exclusively to repair or replacement of any defective parts. Thus, repair or replacement of defective parts is the buyer's exclusive remedy under this contract.

When circumstances cause an exclusive remedy to fail in its essential purpose, however, it is no longer exclusive, and the buyer or lessee may pursue other remedies available under the UCC [UCC 2–719(2), 2A–503(2)]. In *Example 21.20*, suppose that Standard Tool Company is unable to repair a defective part, and no replacement parts are available. In this situation, because the exclusive remedy failed in its essential purpose, the buyer normally will be entitled to seek other remedies provided by the UCC.

Limitations on Consequential Damages As discussed previously, *consequential damages* are special damages that compensate for indirect losses (such as lost profits) resulting from a breach of contract that were reasonably foreseeable. Under the UCC, parties to a contract can limit or exclude consequential damages, provided the limitation is not unconscionable.

When the buyer or lessee is a consumer, any limitation of consequential damages for personal injuries resulting from consumer goods is *prima facie* (presumptively, or on its face) unconscionable. The limitation of consequential damages is not necessarily unconscionable when the loss is commercial in nature—such as lost profits and property damage [UCC 2–719(3), 2A–503(3)].

Statute of Limitations An action for breach of contract under the UCC must be commenced *within four years after the cause of action accrues*—that is, a buyer or lessee must file the lawsuit within four years after the breach occurs [UCC 2–725(1)]. In addition, a buyer or lessee who has accepted nonconforming goods usually must notify the breaching party of the breach within a reasonable time, or the aggrieved party is barred from pursuing any remedy [UCC 2–607(3)(a), 2A–516(3)].

The parties can agree in their contract to reduce this period to not less than one year, but cannot extend it beyond four years [UCC 2–725(1), 2A–506(1)]. A cause of action accrues for breach of warranty (discussed next) when the seller or lessor tenders delivery. This is the rule even if the aggrieved party is unaware that the cause of action has accrued [UCC 2–725(2), 2A–506(2)].

If this pipe-cutting machine has defective parts, can the buyer insist on replacement of the entire machine?

snezniok/iStock/Getty Images

21–5 **Warranties**

The UCC has numerous rules governing product warranties as they occur in sales and lease contracts. Article 2 and Article 2A designate several types of warranties that can arise in a sales or lease contract, including warranties of title, express warranties, and implied warranties. If the seller or lessor breaches a warranty, the buyer or lessee can sue to recover damages.

21–5a **Warranties of Title**

Under the UCC, three types of title warranties—*good title, no liens,* and *no infringements*—can automatically arise in sales and lease contracts.

Good Title In most sales, sellers warrant that they have good and valid title to the goods sold and that transfer of the title is rightful [UCC 2–312(1)(a)]. If the buyer subsequently learns that the seller did not have good title to goods that were purchased, the buyer can sue the seller for breach of this warranty.

Example 21.21 Alexis steals two iPads from Camden and sells them to Emma, who does not know that they are stolen. If Camden discovers that Emma has the iPads, then he has the right to reclaim them from her. When Alexis sold Emma the iPads, Alexis automatically warranted to Emma that the title conveyed was valid and that its transfer was rightful. Because a thief has no title to stolen goods, Alexis breached the warranty of title imposed by the UCC and became liable to Emma for appropriate damages. ■

There is no warranty of good title in lease contracts because title to the goods does not pass to the lessee.

No Liens A second warranty of title shields buyers and lessees who are unaware of any encumbrances, or **liens** (claims, charges, or liabilities), against goods at the time the contract is made [UCC 2–312(1)(b), 2A–211(1)]. This warranty protects buyers who unknowingly purchase goods that are subject to a creditor's *security interest* (an interest in the goods that secures payment or performance). If a buyer knows (or has reason to know from the language in the contract) that the goods are subject to a prior claim, then the buyer cannot sue the seller for breach of warranty.[10]

> **Lien** An encumbrance on a property to satisfy a debt or protect a claim for payment of a debt.

Example 21.22 Henderson buys a used boat from Loring for cash. A month later, Barish proves that she has a valid security interest in the boat and that Loring, who has missed five payments, is in default. Barish then repossesses the boat from Henderson. Henderson demands his cash back from Loring. Under Section 2–312(1)(b), Henderson has legal grounds to recover from Loring. As a seller of goods, Loring warrants that the goods are delivered free from any security interest or other lien of which the buyer has no knowledge. ■

No Infringements A third type of title warranty is a warranty against infringement of any patent, trademark, or copyright. When the seller or lessor is a merchant, he or she automatically warrants that the buyer or lessee takes the goods *free of infringements*. In other words, a merchant promises that the goods delivered are free from any copyright, trademark, or patent claims of a third person [UCC 2–312(3), 2A–211(2)]. If a buyer or lessee is subsequently sued by a third party holding copyright, trademark, or patent rights in the goods, then this warranty has been breached.

If a person buys a used boat that has a lien on it, but the buyer knows nothing about the lien, what section of the UCC provides a remedy for the buyer if the boat is taken away to satisfy the prior claim?

xbrchx/Shutterstock.com

---

10. Note that a *buyer in the ordinary course of business* from a merchant seller generally takes the goods free of the security interest even if he or she knows of it. For instance, when a merchant has a loan that is secured by all the inventory of the business, this does not prevent a buyer in the ordinary course from obtaining clear title to the goods.

21–5b Express Warranties

A seller or lessor can create an **express warranty** by making representations concerning the quality, condition, description, or performance potential of the goods. Under UCC 2–313 and 2A–210, express warranties arise when a seller or lessor indicates any of the following:

1. That the goods conform to any *affirmation* (declaration that something is true) or *promise* of fact that the seller or lessor makes to the buyer or lessee about the goods. Such affirmations or promises are usually made during the bargaining process. **Example 21.23** D. J. Vladick, a salesperson at Home Depot, tells a customer, "These drill bits will easily penetrate stainless steel—and without dulling." Vladick's statement is an express warranty.

2. That the goods conform to any *description* of them. **Example 21.24** A label reads, "Crate contains one Kawasaki Brute Force 750 4X4i EPS ATV." A contract calls for the delivery of a "wool coat." Both statements create express warranties that the goods sold conform to the descriptions.

3. That the goods conform to any *sample* or *model* of the goods shown to the buyer or lessee. **Example 21.25** Melissa Faught orders a stainless steel 5500 Super Angel juicer for $1,100 after seeing a dealer demonstrate its use at a health fair. The Super Angel is shipped to her. When the juicer arrives, it is an older model, not the 5500 model. This is a breach of an express warranty because the dealer warranted that the juicer would be the same model used in the demonstration.

> **Express Warranty** A seller's or lessor's promise as to the quality, condition, description, or performance of the goods being sold or leased.

Express warranties can be found in a seller's or lessor's advertisement, e-mail, brochure, or other promotional materials, in addition to being made orally or set forth in a provision of a contract.

Basis of the Bargain To create an express warranty, a seller or lessor does not have to use words such as *warrant* or *guarantee* [UCC 2–313(2), 2A–210(2)]. It is only necessary that a reasonable buyer or lessee would regard the representation of fact as part of the basis of the bargain [UCC 2–313(1), 2A–210(1)]. The UCC does not define *basis of the bargain*, however, and it is a question of fact in each case whether a representation was made at such a time and in such a way that it induced the buyer or lessee to enter into the contract.

Statements of Opinion and Value Only statements of fact create express warranties. If the seller or lessor makes a statement about the supposed value or worth of the goods, or offers an opinion or recommendation about the goods, the seller or lessor is not creating an express warranty [UCC 2–313(2), 2A–210(2)].

Case Example 21.26 Kathleen Arthur underwent a surgical procedure for neck pain. Her surgeon implanted an Infuse Bone Graft device made by Medtronic, Inc. Although the device was not approved for this use, a sales representative for Medtronic allegedly had told the surgeon that the Infuse device could be appropriate for this surgery. The surgery did not resolve Arthur's neck pain, and she developed numbness in her arm and fingers. She filed a breach of warranty claim against Medtronic, alleging that the salesperson's statement created an express warranty. The court dismissed Arthur's case, however. The alleged statement of a sales representative on whether it was "appropriate" to use the Infuse device in such a procedure was an opinion and did not create an express warranty.[11]

Opinions by Experts. Ordinarily, statements of opinion do not create warranties. If the seller or lessor is an expert, however, and gives an opinion as an expert to a layperson, then a warranty may be created. **Example 21.27** Stephen is an art dealer and an expert in seventeenth-century paintings. If Stephen tells Lauren, a purchaser, that in his opinion a particular painting is by Rembrandt, Stephen has warranted the accuracy of his opinion.

Reasonable Reliance. It is not always easy to determine whether a statement constitutes an express warranty or puffery (seller's talk). The reasonableness of the buyer's or lessee's reliance appears to be the controlling criterion in many cases. For instance, a salesperson's

---

11. *Arthur v. Medtronic, Inc.*, 123 F.Supp.3d 1145 (E.D.Mo. 2015).

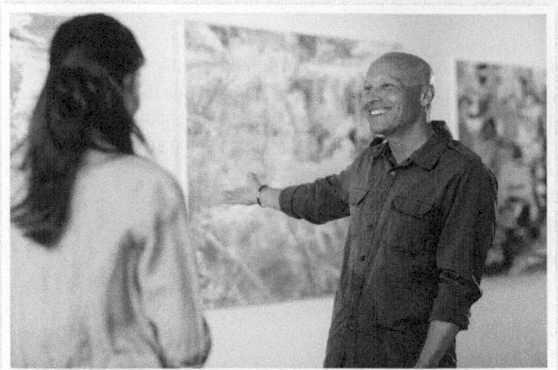

An expert art dealer claims a painting is by Rembrandt. Does his statement create an express warranty? Why or why not?

statements that a ladder "will never break" and will "last a lifetime" are so clearly improbable that no reasonable buyer should rely on them.

A reasonable person is more likely to rely on specific statements made in a product's advertisement than on a statement made orally by a salesperson, however. **Case Example 21.28** Lennox International, Inc., makes heating, ventilating, and air conditioning (HVAC) systems. T & M Solar and Air Conditioning, Inc., installs HVAC systems in California. T & M became interested in Lennox solar panel systems because Lennox advertised that the systems could run through an existing HVAC system, rather than through an electrical panel. This meant that the systems, unlike traditional solar panel systems, could be installed without modifying the electrical panels in a residence.

Lennox representatives repeatedly assured T & M that their systems would operate as advertised. T & M ordered and paid for six Lennox systems for customers. The systems could not be operated or installed as promised, however, and T & M ultimately had to remove them from customers' homes at its own expense. T & M sued for breach of an express warranty. A federal court found that T & M had ordered the Lennox systems precisely because they could operate through an HVAC system without modification of existing electrical panels. That was sufficient evidence of reasonable reliance to justify a trial.[12]

21–5c Implied Warranties

Implied Warranty A warranty that arises by law because of the circumstances of a sale and not from the seller's express promise.

An express warranty is based on the seller's express promise. In contrast, an **implied warranty** is one that *the law derives* by implication or inference because of the circumstances of a sale. In an action based on breach of implied warranty, it is necessary to show that an implied warranty existed and that the breach of the warranty proximately caused[13] the damage sustained. We look here at some of the implied warranties that arise under the UCC.

Implied Warranty of Merchantability A warranty that goods being sold or leased are reasonably fit for the general purpose for which they are sold or leased, are properly packaged and labeled, and are of proper quality.

Implied Warranty of Merchantability Every sale or lease of goods made *by a merchant who deals in goods of the kind sold or leased* automatically gives rise to an **implied warranty of merchantability** [UCC 2–314, 2A–212]. Thus, a merchant who is in the business of selling ski equipment makes an implied warranty of merchantability every time she sells a pair of skis. A neighbor selling his skis at a garage sale does not (because he is not in the business of selling goods of this type).

Merchantable Goods. Goods that are merchantable are "reasonably fit for the ordinary purposes for which such goods are used." They must be of at least average, fair, or medium-grade quality—quality adequate to pass without objection in the trade or market for goods of the same description. The goods must also be adequately packaged and labeled, and they must conform to the promises or affirmations of fact made on the container or label, if any. The warranty of merchantability may be breached even though the merchant did not know or could not have discovered that a product was defective (not merchantable).

Learning Objective 5

What implied warranties arise under the UCC?

Case Example 21.29 Joy Pipe, USA, L.P., is in the business of selling quality steel couplings for use in oil field drilling operations. Joy Pipe entered into a contract with Fremak Industries (a broker) to purchase grade P-110 steel made in India by ISMT Limited. When the steel arrived, Joy Pipe machined it into couplings, which it then sold to its customers.

---

12. *T & M Solar and Air Conditioning, Inc. v. Lennox International, Inc.,* 83 F.Supp.3d 855 (N.D.Cal. 2015).
13. Proximate, or legal, cause exists when the connection between an act and an injury is strong enough to justify imposing liability.

Two companies that used these couplings in oil wells had well failures and notified Joy Pipe. Joy Pipe then discovered that the ISMT steel it had purchased was of a much lower grade than P-110, which is what caused the couplings to fail. After Joy Pipe paid another company to locate and replace the nonconforming steel, it sued ISMT for breach of the implied warranty of merchantability. A jury awarded Joy Pipe nearly $3 million in damages. An appellate court affirmed and also awarded court costs and interest, and remanded the case back to the trial court to calculate the amount of interest.[14]

Of course, merchants are not absolute insurers against all accidents occurring in connection with their goods. For instance, a bar of soap is not unmerchantable merely because stepping on it could cause a user to slip and fall.

Merchantable Food. The UCC recognizes the serving of food or drink to be consumed on or off the premises as a sale of goods subject to the implied warranty of merchantability [UCC 2–314(1)]. "Merchantable" food means food that is fit to eat.

Courts generally determine whether food is fit to eat on the basis of consumer expectations. The courts assume that consumers should reasonably expect on occasion to find bones in fish fillets, cherry pits in cherry pie, or a nutshell in a package of shelled nuts, for example—because such substances are natural parts of the food. In contrast, consumers would not reasonably expect to find an inchworm in a can of peas or a piece of glass in a soft drink.

In the following *Classic Case,* the court had to determine whether a diner should reasonably expect to find a fish bone in fish chowder.

---

14. *Joy Pipe, USA, L.P. v. ISMT Limited,* 703 Fed.Appx. 253 (5th Cir. 2017).

Classic Case 21.3

Webster v. Blue Ship Tea Room, Inc.
Supreme Judicial Court of Massachusetts, 347 Mass. 421, 198 N.E.2d 309 (1964).

Background and Facts Blue Ship Tea Room, Inc., was located in Boston in an old building overlooking the ocean. Priscilla Webster, who had been born and raised in New England, went to the restaurant and ordered fish chowder. The chowder was milky in color. After three or four spoonfuls, she felt something lodged in her throat. As a result, she underwent two esophagoscopies (a procedure in which a telescope-like instrument is used to look into the throat). In the second esophagoscopy, a fish bone was found and removed. Webster filed a lawsuit against the restaurant in a Massachusetts state court for breach of the implied warranty of merchantability. The jury rendered a verdict for Webster, and the restaurant appealed to the state's highest court.

Who is liable for fish bones in seafood chowder?

In the Words of the Court
REARDON, Justice.

[The plaintiff] ordered a cup of fish chowder. Presently, there was set before her "a small bowl of fish chowder." * * * After 3 or 4 [spoonfuls] she was aware that something had lodged in her throat because she "couldn't swallow and couldn't clear her throat by gulping and she could feel it." This misadventure led to two esophagoscopies [procedures in which a telescope-like instrument is used to look into the throat] at the Massachusetts General Hospital, in the second of which, on April 27, 1959, a fish bone was found and removed. The sequence of events produced injury to the plaintiff which was not insubstantial.

(Continues)

We must decide whether a fish bone lurking in a fish chowder, about the ingredients of which there is no other complaint, constitutes a breach of implied warranty under applicable provisions of the Uniform Commercial Code * * *. As the judge put it in his charge [jury instruction], "Was the fish chowder fit to be eaten and wholesome? * * * Nobody is claiming that the fish itself wasn't wholesome. * * * But the bone of contention here—I don't mean that for a pun—but was this fish bone a foreign substance that made the fish chowder unwholesome or not fit to be eaten?" [Emphasis added.]

* * *

[We think that it] is not too much to say that a person sitting down in New England to consume a good New England fish chowder embarks on a gustatory [taste-related] adventure which may entail the removal of some fish bones from his bowl as he proceeds. We are not inclined to tamper with age-old recipes by any amendment reflecting the plaintiff's view of the effect of the Uniform Commercial Code upon them. We are aware of the heavy body of case law involving foreign substances in food, but we sense a strong distinction between them and those relative to unwholesomeness of the food itself [such as] tainted mackerel, and a fish bone in a fish chowder. * * * We consider that the joys of life in New England include the ready availability of fresh fish chowder. We should be prepared to cope with the hazards of fish bones, the occasional presence of which in chowders is, it seems to us, to be anticipated, and which, in the light of a hallowed tradition, do not impair their fitness or merchantability.

Decision and Remedy The Supreme Judicial Court of Massachusetts "sympathized with a plaintiff who has suffered a peculiarly New England injury" but entered a judgment for the defendant, Blue Ship Tea Room. A fish bone in fish chowder is not a breach of the implied warranty of merchantability.

Critical Thinking

• **What If the Facts Were Different?** *If Webster had made the chowder herself from a recipe that she had found on the Internet, could she have successfully brought an action against its author for a breach of the implied warranty of merchantability? Explain.*

• **Impact of This Case on Today's Law** *This classic case, phrased in memorable language, was an early application of the UCC's implied warranty of merchantability to food products. The case established the rule that consumers should expect to occasionally find elements of food products that are natural to the product (such as fish bones in fish chowder). Courts today still apply this rule.*

Implied Warranty of Fitness for a Particular Purpose A warranty that goods sold or leased are fit for the particular purpose for which the buyer or lessee will use the goods.

Implied Warranty of Fitness for a Particular Purpose The implied warranty of fitness for a particular purpose arises in the sale or lease of goods when a seller or lessor (merchant or nonmerchant) knows *both* of the following:

1. The particular purpose for which a buyer or lessee will use the goods.

2. That the buyer or lessee is relying on the skill and judgment of the seller or lessor to select suitable goods [UCC 2–315, 2A–213].

A "particular purpose" of the buyer or lessee differs from the "ordinary purpose for which goods are used" (merchantability). Goods can be merchantable but unfit for a particular purpose. **Example 21.30** Cheryl needs a gallon of paint to match the color of her living room walls—a light shade of green. She takes a sample to the local hardware store and requests a gallon of paint of that color. Instead, she is given a gallon of bright blue paint. Here, the salesperson has not breached any warranty of implied merchantability—the bright blue paint is of high quality and suitable for interior walls. The salesperson has breached an implied warranty of fitness for a particular purpose, though, because the paint is not the right color for Cheryl's purpose (to match her living room walls). ▪

A seller or lessor need not have actual knowledge of the buyer's or lessee's particular purpose. It is sufficient if the seller or lessor "has reason to know" the purpose. For an implied warranty to be created, however, the buyer or lessee must have relied on the skill or judgment of the seller or lessor in selecting or furnishing suitable goods. For further illustration of how courts analyze implied warranties, see this chapter's *Business Law Analysis* feature.

Implied Warranties

Bariven, S.A. (S.A. stands for Société Anonyme, a French business form), agreed to buy 26,000 metric tons of powdered milk for $123.5 million from Absolute Trading Corp. The powdered milk was to be delivered in shipments from China to Venezuela.

After the first three shipments, China halted dairy exports due to the presence of melamine (a chemical used in plastics and adhesives) in some products. Absolute assured Bariven that its milk was safe, and when China resumed dairy exports, Absolute delivered sixteen more shipments. Tests of samples of the milk revealed that it contained dangerous levels of melamine. Did Absolute breach any implied warranties?

Analysis: Under the UCC, merchants impliedly warrant that the goods they sell or lease are merchantable and, in certain circumstances, fit for a particular purpose.

To be merchantable, goods must be "reasonably fit for the ordinary purposes for which such goods are used." They must be at least average, fair, or medium-grade quality— quality that will pass without objection in the trade or market for the goods. To be fit for a particular purpose, the seller must know (or have reason to know) the purpose for which the buyer will use the goods and that the buyer is relying on the judgment of the seller to select suitable goods.

Result and Reasoning: Absolute Trading breached the implied warranties of merchantability and fitness for a particular purpose. Bariven agreed to buy a substantial quantity of powdered milk from Absolute that was to be delivered in shipments. Absolute assured Bariven that its milk was safe, but tests of samples from the shipments Bariven received revealed that it was contaminated. Therefore, the milk was not

of a quality that would pass without objection in the market for the goods. Nor is milk contaminated with melamine "reasonably fit for the ordinary purposes for which such goods are used." The value of the milk as food was impaired because it was potentially lethal and thus not fit to be consumed.

Absolute had reason to know the purpose for which Bariven bought the milk (for human consumption). Absolute also knew that the buyer was relying on it to provide safe milk. In view of the potential hazards and liabilities of consuming the contaminated milk, Absolute was in breach of both of these implied warranties.

Warranties Implied from Prior Dealings or Trade Custom Implied warranties can also arise (or be excluded or modified) as a result of course of dealing or usage of trade [UCC 2–314(3), 2A–212(3)]. In the absence of evidence to the contrary, when both parties to a sales or lease contract have knowledge of a well-recognized trade custom, the courts will infer that both parties intended for that trade custom to apply to their contract.

Example 21.31 Industry-wide custom is to lubricate new cars before they are delivered to buyers. If a dealer fails to lubricate a car, the dealer can be held liable to a buyer for damages resulting from the breach of an implied warranty. (This, of course, would also be negligence on the part of the dealer.) ▪

Chris Ratcliffe/
Bloomberg/Getty Images

How did the UCC's warranty of fitness for a particular purpose affect the outcome in a dispute over a sales contract involving powdered milk?

21–5d Overlapping Warranties

Sometimes, two or more warranties are made in a single transaction. Thus, an implied warranty of merchantability, an implied warranty of fitness for a particular purpose, or both can exist in addition to an express warranty. **Example 21.32** A sales contract for a new car states that "this car engine is warranted to be free from defects for 36,000 miles or thirty-six months, whichever occurs first." This statement creates an express warranty against all defects, as well as an implied warranty that the car will be fit for normal use. ▪

The rule under the UCC is that express and implied warranties are construed as *cumulative* if they are consistent with one another [UCC 2–317, 2A–215]. If the warranties are inconsistent, courts apply the following rules to establish which warranty has priority:

1. *Express* warranties displace inconsistent *implied* warranties, except for implied warranties of fitness for a particular purpose.

2. Samples take precedence over inconsistent general descriptions.

3. Exact or technical specifications displace inconsistent samples or general descriptions.

21–5e Warranty Disclaimers

The UCC generally permits warranties to be disclaimed or limited by specific and unambiguous language, provided that the buyer or lessee is protected from surprise. Because each type of warranty is created in a different way, the manner in which a seller or lessor can disclaim warranties varies with the type of warranty.

Express Warranties A seller or lessor can disclaim all oral express warranties by including a statement in the written contract. The disclaimer must be in language that is clear and conspicuous, and is called to the buyer's or lessee's attention [UCC 2–316(1), 2A–214(1)]. This allows the seller or lessor to avoid false allegations that oral warranties were made, and it ensures that only representations made by properly authorized individuals are included in the bargain.

Note, however, that a buyer or lessee must be made aware of any warranty disclaimers or modifications *at the time the contract is formed*. In other words, the seller or lessor cannot modify any warranties or disclaimers made during the bargaining process without the consent of the buyer or lessee.

Implied Warranties Generally, unless circumstances indicate otherwise, the implied warranties of merchantability and fitness are disclaimed by the expressions "as is," "with all faults," or other similar phrases. Both parties must be able to clearly understand from the language used that there are no implied warranties [UCC 2–316(3)(a), 2A–214(3)(a)].

Case Example 21.33 Brett Silver contracted with Porsche of the Main Line, where he was a regular customer, to purchase a used 2009 Ferrari 599 GTB for $232,630. The dealer did not have a Ferrari on the lot but located one at Silver's request, and Silver selected the particular Ferrari. The sales contract stated that the vehicle was being sold "AS IS" without any warranty either express or implied. Silver signed the contract right below this statement. After Silver took possession of the Ferrari, he noticed several spots where there was damage to its clear coat. He contacted the dealer, who offered to accept the Ferrari back for full market value as long as Silver used the credit to purchase another vehicle there. Silver refused and sued the dealer. The court held that the "AS IS" clause was valid and precluded Silver from suing the dealer.[15]

Know This

Express and implied warranties do not necessarily displace each other. More than one warranty can cover the same goods in the same transaction.

A consumer buys a used Ferrari but later discovers spots on its exterior paint. How will the "as is" clause in the sales contract affect the buyer's ability to get his money back?

dimcars/Shutterstock.com

---

15. *Silver v. Porsche of the Main Line*, 2015 WL 7424848 (Pa.Super.Ct. 2015).

Note that some states have laws that forbid "as is" sales. Other states do not allow disclaimers of warranties of merchantability for consumer goods.

Disclaimer of the Implied Warranty of Merchantability. To specifically disclaim an implied warranty of merchantability, a seller or lessor must mention the word *merchantability* [UCC 2–316(2), 2A–214(2)]. The disclaimer need not be written, but if it is, the writing must be conspicuous [UCC 2–316(2), 2A–214(4)].

Under the UCC, a term or clause is conspicuous when it is written or displayed in such a way that a reasonable person would notice it. Words are conspicuous when they are in capital letters or are in a larger font size or a different color than the surrounding text.

Disclaimer of the Implied Warranty of Fitness. To specifically disclaim an implied warranty of fitness for a particular purpose, the disclaimer must be in a writing and must be conspicuous. The word *fitness* does not have to be mentioned. It is sufficient if, for instance, the disclaimer states, "THERE ARE NO WARRANTIES THAT EXTEND BEYOND THE DESCRIPTION ON THE FACE HEREOF."

Buyer's or Lessee's Examination or Refusal to Inspect. If a buyer or lessee examines the goods (or a sample or model) as fully as desired, *there is no implied warranty with respect to defects that a reasonable examination would reveal or defects that are found on examination* [UCC 2–316(3)(b), 2A–214(2)(b)]. Therefore, no disclaimer of warranty would be necessary with respect to such defects. Also, if a buyer or lessee refuses to examine the goods on the seller's or lessor's request that he or she do so, there is no implied warranty with respect to reasonably evident defects.

Example 21.34 Janna buys a table at Gershwin's Home Store. No express warranties are made. Gershwin asks Janna to inspect the table before buying it, but she refuses. Had Janna inspected the table, she would have noticed that one of its legs was obviously cracked, which made it unstable. Janna takes the table home and sets a lamp on it. The table later collapses, and the lamp starts a fire that causes significant damage. Janna normally will not be able to hold Gershwin's liable for breach of the warranty of merchantability, because she refused to examine the table as Gershwin requested. Janna therefore assumed the risk that the table was defective.

21–5f Lemon Laws

Purchasers of defective automobiles—called "lemons"—may pursue remedies in addition to those provided by the UCC under state *lemon laws*. Basically, state lemon laws provide remedies to consumers who buy automobiles that repeatedly fail to meet standards of quality and performance because they are "lemons."

Although lemon laws vary by state, typically they apply to automobiles under warranty that are defective in a way that significantly affects their value or use. Lemon laws do not necessarily cover used-car purchases (unless the car is covered by a manufacturer's extended warranty) or vehicles that are leased.

Generally, the seller or manufacturer of the automobile is given a number of opportunities to remedy the defect (usually four). If the seller fails to cure the problem despite a reasonable number of attempts (as specified by state law), the buyer is entitled to a new car, replacement of defective parts, or return of all consideration paid.

Typically, buyers must submit their complaint to the arbitration program specified in the manufacturer's warranty before taking the case to court. Buyers who prevail in a lemon-law dispute may also be entitled to reimbursement of their attorneys' fees.

Know This
Courts generally view warranty disclaimers unfavorably, especially when consumers are involved.

Practice and Review

GFI, Inc., a Hong Kong company, makes audio decoder chips, one of the essential components used in the manufacture of MP3 players. Egan Electronics contracts with GFI to buy 10,000 chips on an installment contract, with 2,500 chips to be shipped every three months, F.O.B. Hong Kong via Air Express. At the time for the first delivery, GFI delivers only 2,400 chips but explains to Egan that even though the shipment is 4 percent short, the chips are of a higher quality than those specified in the contract and are worth 5 percent more than the contract price. Egan accepts the shipment and pays GFI the contract price. At the time for the second shipment, GFI makes a shipment identical to the first. Egan again accepts and pays for the chips. At the time for the third shipment, GFI ships 2,400 of the same chips, but this time GFI sends them via Hong Kong Air instead of Air Express. While in transit, the chips are destroyed. When it is time for the fourth shipment, GFI again sends 2,400 chips, but this time Egan rejects the chips without explanation. Using the information presented in the chapter, answer the following questions.

1. Did GFI have a legitimate reason to expect that Egan would accept the fourth shipment? Why or why not?

2. Does the substitution of carriers for the third shipment constitute a breach of the contract by GFI? Explain.

3. Suppose that the silicon used for the chips becomes unavailable for a period of time and that GFI cannot manufacture enough chips to fulfill the contract but does ship as many as it can to Egan. Under what doctrine might a court release GFI from further performance of the contract?

4. Under the UCC, does Egan have a right to reject the fourth shipment? Why or why not?

Debate This

If a contract specifies a particular carrier, then the shipper must use that carrier or be in breach of the contract—no exceptions should ever be allowed.

Key Terms

conforming goods 465
cover 476
express warranty 483
implied warranty 484
implied warranty of fitness for a particular purpose 486

implied warranty of merchantability 484
installment contract 468
lien 482

perfect tender rule 466
replevin 477
tender of delivery 465

Chapter Summary: Performance and Breach of Sales and Lease Contracts

Obligations of the Seller or Lessor

1. *Tender of delivery*—The seller or lessor must tender *conforming* goods to the buyer or lessee. Tender must take place at a *reasonable hour* and in a *reasonable manner*.
2. *Place of delivery*—If the contract does not indicate where the goods are to be delivered, the place of delivery will be either the seller's place of business, the seller's residence, or the location of the goods.
3. *Delivery via carrier*—In carrier contracts, the seller fulfills the obligation to deliver the goods through either a shipment contract or a destination contract.
4. *The perfect tender rule*—If the goods or tender of delivery fail in any respect to conform to the contract, the buyer or lessee has the right to accept the goods, reject the entire shipment, or accept part and reject part [UCC 2-601, 2A-509].
5. *Exceptions to the perfect tender rule*—Exceptions may be established by the following:
   a. Agreement of the parties.
   b. If the seller or lessor tenders nonconforming goods prior to the performance date and the buyer or lessee rejects them, the seller or lessor may *cure* (repair or replace the goods) within the contract time for performance [UCC 2–508(1), 2A–513(1)]. If the seller or lessor had reasonable grounds to believe that the buyer or lessee would accept the tendered goods, on the buyer's or lessee's rejection the seller or lessor has a reasonable time to substitute conforming goods without liability [UCC 2–508(2), 2A–513(2)].
   c. If the agreed-on means of delivery becomes impracticable or unavailable, the seller must substitute an alternative means (such as a different carrier), if one is available [UCC 2–614(1)].
   d. If a seller or lessor tenders nonconforming goods in any one installment under an installment contract, the buyer or lessee may reject the installment only if its value is substantially impaired and cannot be cured. The entire installment contract is breached only when one or more nonconforming installments *substantially* impair the value of the *whole* contract [UCC 2–612, 2A–510].
   e. When performance becomes commercially impracticable owing to circumstances that were not foreseeable when the contract was formed, the perfect tender rule no longer holds [UCC 2–615, 2A–405].

Obligations of the Buyer or Lessee

1. *Payment*—On tender of delivery by the seller or lessor, the buyer or lessee must pay for the goods at the time and place the goods are *received*, unless the sale is made on credit. Payment may be made by any method generally acceptable in the commercial world unless the seller demands cash [UCC 2–310, 2–511]. In lease contracts, the lessee must make lease payments in accordance with the contract [UCC 2A–516(1)].
2. *Right of inspection*—Unless otherwise agreed, the buyer or lessee has an absolute right to inspect the goods before acceptance [UCC 2–513(1), 2A–515(1)].
3. *Acceptance*—The buyer or lessee can manifest acceptance of delivered goods expressly in words or by conduct, or by failing to reject the goods after a reasonable period of time following inspection or after having had a reasonable opportunity to inspect them [UCC 2–606(1), 2A–515(1)]. A buyer will be deemed to have accepted goods if he or she performs any act inconsistent with the seller's ownership [UCC 2–606(1)(c)].
4. *Partial acceptance*—The buyer or lessee can make a partial acceptance if some of the goods do not conform to the contract and the seller or lessor failed to cure [UCC 2–601(c), 2A–509(1)].
5. *Anticipatory repudiation*—If, before the time for performance, one party clearly indicates to the other an intention not to perform, under UCC 2–610 and 2A–402, the nonbreaching party may do the following:
   a. Treat the repudiation as a final breach by pursuing a remedy.
   b. Await performance by the repudiating party for a commercially reasonable time.
   c. In either situation, suspend performance.
   In addition, the breaching party may retract the repudiation by any method that clearly indicates the party's intent to perform.

(Continues)

| **Remedies of the Seller or Lessor** | 1. *When the goods are in the possession of the seller or lessor*—The seller or lessor may do the following: |

Remedies of the Seller or Lessor

1. *When the goods are in the possession of the seller or lessor*—The seller or lessor may do the following:
   a. Cancel the contract [UCC 2–703(f), 2A–523(1)(a)].
   b. Withhold delivery [UCC 2–703(a), 2A–523(1)(c)].
   c. Resell or dispose of the goods [UCC 2–703(d), 2–706(1), 2A–523(1)(e), 2A–527(1)].
   d. Sue to recover the purchase price or lease payments due [UCC 2–709(1), 2A–529(1)].
   e. Sue to recover damages [UCC 2–708, 2A–528].
2. *When the goods are in transit*—The seller or lessor may stop the carrier or bailee from delivering the goods under certain conditions [UCC 2–705, 2A–526].
3. *When the goods are in the possession of the buyer or lessee*—The seller or lessor may do the following:
   a. Sue to recover the purchase price or lease payments due [UCC 2–709(1), 2A–529(1)].
   b. Reclaim the goods. A seller may reclaim goods received by an insolvent buyer if the demand is made within ten days of the buyer's receipt (reclaiming goods excludes all other remedies) [UCC 2–702(2)]. A lessor may repossess goods if the lessee is in default [UCC 2A–525(2)].

Remedies of the Buyer or Lessee

1. *When the seller or lessor refuses to deliver the goods*—The buyer or lessee may do the following:
   a. Cancel the contract [UCC 2–711(1), 2A–508(1)(a)].
   b. Recover the goods if the seller or lessor becomes insolvent and the goods are identified to the contract [UCC 2–502, 2A–522].
   c. Sue to obtain specific performance (when the goods are unique and the remedy at law is inadequate) [UCC 2–716(1), 2A–521(1)].
   d. Obtain cover [UCC 2–712, 2A–518].
   e. Replevy the goods (if cover is unavailable) [UCC 2–716(3), 2A–521(3)].
   f. Sue to recover damages [UCC 2–713, 2A–519].
2. *When the seller or lessor delivers or tenders delivery of nonconforming goods*—The buyer or lessee may do the following:
   a. Reject the goods [UCC 2–601, 2A–509].
   b. Revoke acceptance if the nonconformity *substantially* impairs the value of the unit or lot and if one of the following factors is present:
      (1) Acceptance was predicated on the reasonable assumption that the nonconformity would be cured, and it was not cured within a reasonable time [UCC 2–608(1)(a), 2A–517(1)(a)].
      (2) The buyer or lessee did not discover the nonconformity before acceptance, either because it was difficult to discover before acceptance or because the seller's or lessor's assurance that the goods were conforming kept the buyer or lessee from inspecting the goods [UCC 2–608(1)(b), 2A–517(1)(b)].
   c. Accept the goods and recover damages [UCC 2–607, 2–714, 2–717, 2A–519].
3. *Provisions that affect or limit remedies*—
   a. Remedies may be limited in sales or lease contracts by agreement of the parties. If the contract states that a remedy is exclusive, then that is the sole remedy unless the remedy fails in its essential purpose. Sellers and lessors can also limit the rights of buyers and lessees to consequential damages unless the limitation is unconscionable [UCC 2–719, 2A–503].
   b. The UCC has a four-year statute of limitations for actions involving breach of contract. By agreement, the parties to a sales or lease contract can reduce this period to not less than one year, but they cannot extend it beyond four years [UCC 2–725(1), 2A–506(1)].

Warranties

1. *Warranties of title*—Under the UCC, three types of title warranties can automatically arise in sales and lease contracts.
   a. In most sales, sellers warrant that they have good and valid title to the goods sold and that transfer of the title is rightful [UCC 2–312(1)(a)].
   b. The seller or lessor warrants that the goods are free of any encumbrances, or liens, of which the buyer or lessee is unaware [UCC 2–312(1)(b), 2A–211(1)].
   c. When the seller or lessor is a merchant, he or she warrants that the buyer or lessee takes the goods free of infringements [UCC 2–312(3), 2A–211(2)].

2. *Express warranties*—Under the UCC, an express warranty arises under the UCC when a seller or lessor provides, as part of the basis of the bargain, any of the following [UCC 2–313, 2A–210]:
   a. An affirmation or promise of fact.
   b. A description of the goods.
   c. A sample shown as conforming to the contract goods.
3. *Implied warranties*—Under the UCC, an implied warranty arises by law because of the circumstances of a sale.
   a. An implied warranty of merchantability occurs when a seller or lessor who deals in goods of the kind sold or leased (a merchant) warrants that the goods sold or leased are properly packaged and labeled, are of proper quality, and are reasonably fit for the ordinary purposes for which such goods are used [UCC 2–314, 2A–212].
   b. An implied warranty of fitness for a particular purpose arises when the buyer's or lessee's purpose or use is expressly or impliedly known by the seller or lessor, and the buyer or lessee purchases or leases the goods in reliance on the seller's or lessor's skill and judgment [UCC 2–315, 2A–213].
   c. Warranties implied from prior dealings or trade custom can arise as a result of course of dealing or usage of trade [UCC 2–314(3), 2A–212(3)].
4. *Overlapping warranties*—When warranties are consistent with each other, they are considered cumulative under the UCC [UCC 2–317, 2A–215]. If warranties are inconsistent, then express warranties take precedence over implied warranties, except for the implied warranty of fitness for a particular purpose. Also, samples take precedence over general descriptions, and exact or technical specifications displace inconsistent samples or general descriptions.
5. *Warranty disclaimers*—The effectiveness of disclaimers varies with the type of warranty.
   a. Express warranties can be disclaimed if the disclaimer is written in clear language, is conspicuous, and is called to the buyer's or lessee's attention at the time the contract is formed.
   b. A disclaimer of the implied warranty of merchantability must specifically mention the word *merchantability*. The disclaimer need not be in writing, but if it is written, it must be conspicuous.
   c. A disclaimer of the implied warranty of fitness *must* be in writing and must be conspicuous, though it need not mention the word *fitness*.
   d. There is no implied warranty with respect to defects that a reasonable examination would reveal or defects that are found on examination.
6. *Lemon laws*—State statutes may allow purchasers of defective automobiles to pursue remedies in addition to those provided by the UCC. The seller or manufacturer is given opportunities to remedy the defect. If the seller or manufacturer fails to cure the problem, the buyer is entitled to a new car, replacement of defective parts, or return of all consideration paid.

Issue Spotters

1. Country Fruit Stand orders eighty cases of peaches from Down Home Farms. Without stating a reason, Down Home untimely delivers thirty cases instead of eighty. Does Country have the right to reject the shipment? Explain. (See *Obligations of the Seller or Lessor*.)

2. Brite Images, Inc. (BI), agrees to sell Catalog Corporation (CC) five thousand posters of celebrities, to be delivered on May 1. On April 1, BI repudiates the contract. CC informs BI that it expects delivery. Can CC sue BI without waiting until May 1? Why or why not? (See *Obligations of the Buyer or Lessee*.)

   —**Check your answers to the *Issue Spotters* against the answers provided in Appendix D at the end of this text.**

Business Scenarios and Case Problems

21–1. Remedies. Genix, Inc., has contracted to sell Larson five hundred washing machines of a certain model at list price. Genix is to ship the goods on or before December 1. Genix produces one thousand washing machines of this model but has not yet prepared Larson's shipment. On November 1, Larson repudiates the contract. Discuss the remedies available to Genix in this situation. (See *Remedies of the Seller or Lessor*.)

21–2. Anticipatory Repudiation. Moore contracted in writing to sell her 2010 Hyundai Santa Fe to Hammer for $16,500.

(Continues)

Moore agreed to deliver the car on Wednesday, and Hammer promised to pay the $16,500 on the following Friday. On Tuesday, Hammer informed Moore that he would not be buying the car after all. By Friday, Hammer had changed his mind again and tendered $16,500 to Moore. Although Moore had not sold the car to another party, she refused the tender and refused to deliver. Hammer claimed that Moore had breached their contract. Moore contended that Hammer's repudiation had released her from her duty to perform under the contract. Who is correct, and why? (See *Obligations of the Buyer or Lessee.*)

21–3. Spotlight on Apple—Implied Warranties. Alan Vitt purchased an iBook G4 laptop computer from Apple, Inc. Shortly after the one-year warranty expired, the laptop stopped working due to a weakness in the product manufacture. Vitt sued Apple, arguing that the laptop should have lasted "at least a couple of years," which Vitt believed was a reasonable consumer expectation for a laptop. Vitt claimed that Apple's descriptions of the laptop as "durable," "rugged," "reliable," and "high performance" were affirmative statements concerning the quality and performance of the laptop, which Apple did not meet. How should the court rule? Why? [*Vitt v. Apple Computer, Inc.*, 469 Fed.Appx. 605 (9th Cir. 2011)] (See *Warranties.*)

21–4. The Right of Rejection. Erb Poultry, Inc., is a distributor of fresh poultry products in Lima, Ohio. CEME, LLC, does business as Bank Shots, a restaurant in Trotwood, Ohio. CEME ordered chicken wings and "dippers" from Erb, which were delivered and for which CEME issued a check in payment. A few days later, CEME stopped payment on the check. When contacted by Erb, CEME alleged that the products were beyond their freshness date, mangled, spoiled, and the wrong sizes. CEME did not provide any evidence to support the claims or arrange to return the products. Is CEME entitled to a full refund of the amount paid for the chicken? Explain. [*Erb Poultry, Inc. v. CEME, LLC*, 2014 -Ohio-4504, 20 N.E.3d 1228 (Ohio App. 2014)] (See *Remedies of the Buyer or Lessee.*)

21–5. Remedies for Breach. LO Ventures, LLC, doing business as Reefpoint Brewhouse in Racine, Wisconsin, contracted with Forman Awnings and Construction, LLC, for the fabrication and installation of an awning system over an outdoor seating area. After the system was complete, Reefpoint expressed concerns about the workmanship but did not give Forman a chance to make repairs. The brewhouse used the awning for two months and then had it removed so that siding on the building could be replaced. The parties disagreed about whether cracked and broken welds observed after the removal of the system were due to shoddy workmanship. Reefpoint paid only $400 on the contract price of $8,161. Can Reefpoint rescind the contract and obtain a return of its $400? Is Forman entitled to recover the difference between Reefpoint's payment and the contract price? Discuss. [*Forman Awnings and Construction, LLC v. LO Ventures, LLC*, 360 Wis.2d 492, 864 N.W.2d 121 (2015)] (See *Remedies of the Buyer or Lessee.*)

21–6. Business Case Problem with Sample Answer—Remedies of the Buyer or Lessee. M. C. and Linda Morris own a home in Gulfport, Mississippi, that was extensively damaged in Hurricane Katrina. The Morrises contracted with Inside Outside, Inc. (IO), to rebuild their kitchen. When the new kitchen cabinets were delivered, some defects were apparent, and as installation progressed, others were revealed. IO ordered replacement parts to cure the defects. Before the parts arrived, however, the parties' relationship deteriorated, and IO offered to remove the cabinets and refund the price. The Morrises also asked to be repaid for the installation fee. IO refused but emphasized that it was willing to fulfill its contractual obligations. At this point, are the Morrises entitled to revoke their acceptance of the cabinets? Why or why not? [*Morris v. Inside Outside, Inc.*, 185 So.3d 413 (Miss.Ct.App. 2016)] (See *Remedies of the Buyer or Lessee.*)

—For a sample answer to Problem 21–6, go to Appendix E at the end of this text.

21–7. Warranty Disclaimers. Charity Bell bought a used Toyota Avalon from Awny Gobran of Gobran Auto Sales, Inc. The odometer showed that the car had been driven 147,000 miles. Bell asked whether it had been in any accidents, and Gobran replied that it was in good condition. The parties signed a warranty disclaimer that the vehicle was sold "as is." Problems with the car arose the same day as the purchase. Gobran made a few ineffectual attempts to repair it before refusing to do more. Meanwhile, Bell obtained a vehicle history report from CARFAX, which showed that the Avalon had been damaged in an accident and that its last reported odometer reading was 237,271.

Was the "as is" disclaimer sufficient to put Bell on notice that the odometer reading could be false and that the car might have been in an accident? Can Gobran avoid any liability that might otherwise be imposed because Bell did not obtain the CARFAX report until *after* she bought the car? Discuss. [*Gobran Auto Sales, Inc. v. Bell*, 335 Ga.App. 873, 783 S.E.2d 389 (2016)] (See *Warranties.*)

21–8. Implied Warranties. Harold Moore bought a barrel-racing horse named Clear Boggy for $100,000 for his daughter from Betty Roper, who appraises barrel-racing horses. (Barrel racing is a rodeo event in which a horse and rider attempt to complete a cloverleaf pattern around preset barrels in the fastest time.)

Clear Boggy was promoted for sale as a competitive barrel-racing horse. On inquiry, Roper represented that Clear Boggy did not have any performance issues or medical problems, and that the only medications the horse had been given were hock injections, a common treatment.

Shortly after the purchase, Clear Boggy began exhibiting significant performance problems, including nervousness, unwillingness to practice, and stalling on the first barrel during runs. Roper then disclosed that the horse had been given shoulder injections prior to the sale and had previously stalled in competition. Moore took the horse to a veterinarian and discovered that it suffered from arthritis, impinged vertebrae, front-left foot problems, and a right-hind leg fracture. The vet recommended, and Moore paid for, surgery to repair the hind leg fracture, but Clear Boggy remained unfit for competition. Moore also discovered that the horse had been scratched from competition prior to the sale because it was injured. Can Moore prevail in a lawsuit against Roper for breach of the implied warranty of fitness for a particular purpose? Why or why not? [*Moore v. Roper*, ___ F.Supp.3d ___, 2018 WL 1123868 (E.D.Okla. 2018)] (See *Warranties*.)

21–9. A Question of Ethics—The IDDR Approach and Buyer's Remedies. Samsung Telecommunications America, LLC, makes Galaxy phones. Daniel Norcia bought a Galaxy S4 in a Verizon store in San Francisco, California. A Verizon employee opened the box, unpacked the phone, and helped Norcia transfer his contacts to the new phone. Norcia took the phone, and its charger and headphones, and left the store. Less than a year later, he filed an action on behalf of himself and other Galaxy S4 buyers in a federal district court against Samsung, alleging that the manufacturer misrepresented the phone's storage capacity and rigged it to operate at a higher speed when it was being tested. [Norcia v. Samsung Telecommunications America, LLC, 845 *F.3d 1279 (9th Cir. 2017)*] (See Remedies of the Buyer or Lessee.)

1. Samsung included an arbitration provision in a brochure in the Galaxy S4 box. Would it be ethical of Samsung to assert the arbitration clause?

2. Why would corporate decision makers choose to misrepresent their product? Explain, using the *Discussion* and *Review* steps of the IDDR approach.

Critical Thinking and Writing Assignments

21–10. Business Law Writing. Suppose that you are a collector of antique cars and you need to purchase spare parts for a 1938 engine. These parts are not made anymore and are scarce. You discover that Beem has the spare parts that you need. You contract with Beem to buy the parts and agree to pay 50 percent of the purchase price in advance. You send the payment on May 1, and Beem receives it on May 2. On May 3, Beem, having found another buyer willing to pay substantially more for the parts, informs you that he will not deliver as contracted. That same day, you learn that Beem is insolvent. Write three paragraphs fully discussing any possible remedies that would enable you to take possession of the parts. (See *Remedies of the Buyer or Lessee*.)

21–11. Time-Limited Group Assignment—Warranties. Milan purchased saffron extract, marketed as "America's Hottest New Way to a Flat Belly," online from Dr. Chen. The website stated that recently published studies showed a significant weight loss (more than 25 percent) for people who used pure saffron extract as a supplement *without diet or exercise*. Dr. Chen said that the saffron suppresses appetite by increasing levels of serotonin, which reduces emotional eating. Milan took the extract as directed without any resulting weight loss. (See *Warranties*.)

1. The first group will determine whether Dr. Chen's website made any express warranty on the saffron extract or its effectiveness in causing weight loss.

2. The second group will discuss whether the implied warranty of merchantability applies to the purchase of weight-loss supplements.

3. The third group will decide if Dr. Chen's sale of saffron extract breached the implied warranty of fitness for a particular purpose.

4. The fourth group will determine if current common knowledge that weight loss can only occur if one burns more calories than one consumes makes it impossible to sue any company that offers weight-loss products that require no dieting and no exercise.

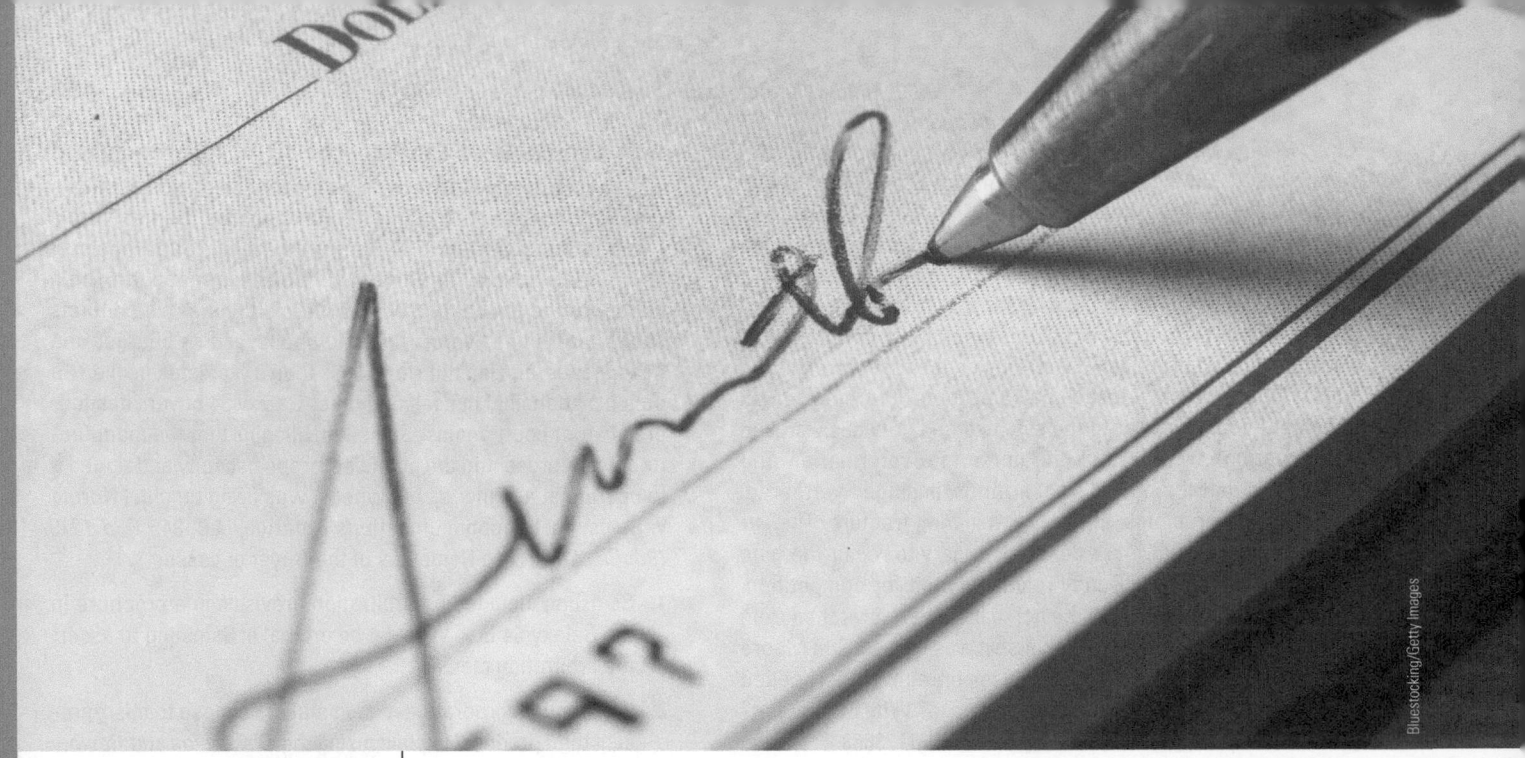

22 | Negotiable Instruments

Learning Objectives

The five Learning Objectives *below are designed to help improve your understanding. After reading this chapter, you should be able to answer the following questions:*

1. What requirements must an instrument meet to be negotiable?

2. How does the negotiation of order instruments differ from the negotiation of bearer instruments?

3. What are three basic requirements for attaining the status of a holder in due course (HDC)?

4. What is the difference between signature liability and warranty liability?

5. What four defenses can be used against an ordinary holder that are not effective against an HDC?

"It took many generations for people to feel comfortable accepting paper in lieu of gold or silver."

Alan Greenspan
1926–present
(Chair of the Board of Governors of the Federal Reserve System, 1987–2006)

Most commercial transactions would be inconceivable without negotiable instruments. A **negotiable instrument** is a signed writing that contains an unconditional promise or order to pay an exact amount, either on demand or at a specified future time. The promise can be made to the order of a specific person or to a bearer. Because negotiable instruments originally were (and often still are) paper documents, they are sometimes referred to as *commercial paper*. As indicated in the chapter-opening quotation, it took many years for paper money to be fully accepted as a substitute for gold or silver in commerce.

A negotiable instrument can function as a substitute for cash or as an extension of credit. For a negotiable instrument to operate *practically* as either a substitute for cash or a credit device, or both, it is essential that the instrument be *easily transferable without danger of being uncollectible*. This is a fundamental function of negotiable instruments.

When her bank will not loan Kyra Plack the capital she needs to start a company, her wealthy uncle, Martin Kohl, agrees to loan her the funds. Plack signs a promissory note for $300,000 and promises to pay back the money, with 5 percent interest, exactly two years from today's date. Because the promissory note is a negotiable instrument, it can be sold to another. Therefore, if Kohl needs access to the funds before the date set for payment, he can negotiate, or transfer, the promissory note to a third party in exchange for cash. When the note becomes due, Plack will repay the then-current holder of the note.

22–1 Formation of Negotiable Instruments

The law governing negotiable instruments grew out of commercial necessity. In the medieval world, merchants developed their own set of rules, which eventually became known as the *Lex Mercatoria* (Law Merchant). The Law Merchant was later codified in England and is the forerunner of Article 3 of the Uniform Commercial Code (UCC). Article 3 imposes special requirements for the form and content of negotiable instruments. It also governs their negotiation, or transfer.

22–1a Types of Negotiable Instruments

The UCC specifies four types of negotiable instruments: *drafts, checks, promissory notes*, and *certificates of deposit* (CDs). These instruments, which are summarized briefly in Exhibit 22–1, are frequently divided into the two classifications that we will discuss in the following subsections: *orders to pay* (drafts and checks) and *promises to pay* (promissory notes and CDs).

Negotiable instruments may also be classified as either demand instruments or time instruments. A *demand instrument* is payable on demand. In other words, it is payable immediately after it is issued and for a reasonable period of time thereafter. A *time instrument* is payable at a future date.

Note that Section 3–104(b) of the UCC defines *instrument* as a "negotiable instrument."[1] For that reason, whenever the term *instrument* is used in this book, it refers to a negotiable instrument.

Drafts and Checks (Orders to Pay) A **draft** is an unconditional written order that involves three parties. The party creating the draft (the **drawer**) orders another party (the **drawee**) to pay funds, usually to a third party (the **payee**). The most common type of draft is a check, but drafts other than checks may be used in commercial transactions.

Time Drafts versus Sight Drafts. A *time draft* is payable at a definite future time. A *sight draft* (or demand draft) is payable on sight—that is, when it is presented to the drawee (usually a bank or financial institution) for payment. A draft can be both a time and a sight draft. Such a draft is payable at a stated time after sight (a draft that states it is payable ninety days after sight, for instance).

Negotiable Instrument A signed writing (record) that contains an unconditional promise or order to pay an exact sum on demand or at a specified future time to a specific person or order, or to bearer.

Draft Any instrument drawn on a drawee that orders the drawee to pay a certain amount of funds, usually to a third party (the payee), on demand or at a definite future time.

Drawer The party that initiates a draft (such as a check), thereby ordering the drawee to pay.

Drawee The party that is ordered to pay a draft or check. With a check, a bank or a financial institution is always the drawee.

Payee A person to whom an instrument is made payable.

---

1. Note that all of the references to Article 3 of the UCC in this chapter are to the 1990 version of Article 3, which has been adopted by nearly every state. One-fifth of the states have adopted an amended version of Article 3, issued in 2002.

Exhibit 22–1 Basic Types of Negotiable Instruments

INSTRUMENTS	CHARACTERISTICS	PARTIES
ORDERS TO PAY:		
Draft	An order by one person to another person or to bearer.	*Drawer*—The person who signs or makes the order to pay.
Check	A draft drawn on a bank and payable on demand. (With certain types of checks, such as cashier's checks, the bank is both the drawer and the drawee.)	*Drawee*—The person to whom the order to pay is made. *Payee*—The person to whom payment is ordered.
PROMISES TO PAY:		
Promissory note	A promise by one party to pay funds to another party or to bearer.	*Maker*—The person who promises to pay.
Certificate of deposit	A note issued by a bank acknowledging a deposit of funds made payable to the holder of the note.	*Payee*—The person to whom the promise is made.

Exhibit 22–2 shows a typical time draft. For the drawee to be obligated to honor (pay) the order, the drawee must be obligated to the drawer either by agreement or through a debtor-creditor relationship. **Example 22.1** On January 16, OurTown Real Estate orders $1,000 worth of office supplies from Eastman Supply Company, with payment due in ninety days. Also on January 16, OurTown sends Eastman a draft drawn on its account with the First National Bank of Whiteacre as payment. In this scenario, the drawer is OurTown, the drawee is OurTown's bank (First National Bank of Whiteacre), and the payee is Eastman Supply Company. ▪

Acceptances. A drawee's written promise to pay a draft when it comes due is called an **acceptance.** Usually, the drawee accepts the instrument by writing the word *accepted* on its face, with a signature and a date. A drawee who has accepted an instrument becomes an **acceptor.**

A *trade acceptance* is a type of draft commonly used in the sale of goods. In this draft, the seller is both the drawer and the payee. The buyer to whom credit is extended is the drawee. **Example 22.2** Jackson Street Bistro buys its restaurant supplies from Osaka Industries. When Jackson requests supplies, Osaka creates a draft ordering Jackson to pay Osaka for the supplies within ninety days. Jackson accepts the draft by signing its face, which obligates it to make the payment. This is a trade acceptance, and Osaka can sell it to a third party at any time before the payment is due. ▪

When a draft orders the buyer's bank to pay, it is called a *banker's acceptance.* Banker's acceptances are often used in international trade.

Checks. As mentioned, the most commonly used type of draft is a **check.** Although fewer checks are written today and most transactions are electronic, checks are still more common than promissory notes or other types of negotiable instruments. (For a discussion of mobile payment apps, which are increasingly popular as alternatives to checks, see this chapter's *Adapting the Law to the Online Environment* feature.)

Checks are demand instruments because they are payable on demand. Most commonly, the writer of the check is the drawer, the bank on which the check is drawn is the drawee, and the person to whom the check is made payable is the payee. On certain types of checks, such as *cashier's checks,* the bank is both the drawer and the drawee. A cashier's check functions the same as cash because the bank has committed itself to paying the stated amount on demand.

Acceptance In negotiable instruments law, a drawee's signed agreement to pay a draft when it is presented.

Acceptor A drawee that accepts, or promises to pay, an instrument when it is presented later for payment.

Check A draft drawn by a drawer ordering the drawee bank or financial institution to pay a certain amount of funds to the payee on demand.

Exhibit 22–2 A Typical Time Draft

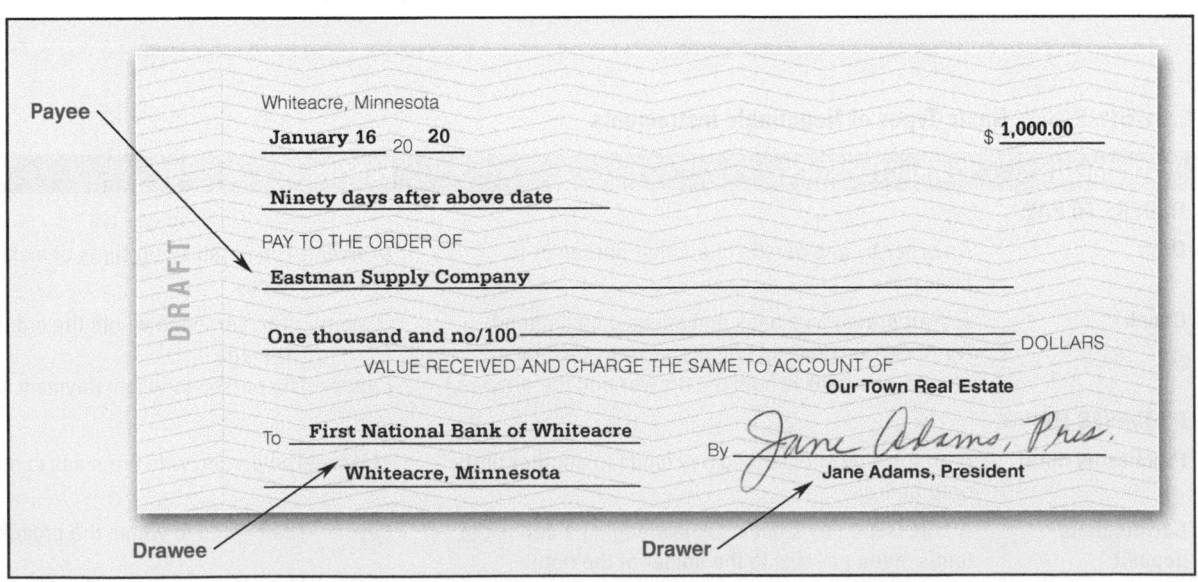

Pay with Your Smartphone

A payment revolution is going on right now. Customers at certain Starbucks locations in New York, San Francisco, and Seattle first started using an iPhone app to pay for their lattes in 2009. By 2019, thousands of Starbucks locations were accepting payments from all types of smartphone-based operating systems. Some experts estimate that smartphone point-of-sale payments will total more than $1 trillion in 2021. Growth of such payments is greatest in Indonesia, India, China, and Turkey.

Apple Enters the Mobile Payments Arena

Apple, Inc., provides its own mobile payment and "digital wallet" service, called Apple Pay. Owners of Apple iPhones and iPads sold after 2014, along with its Apple Watch, have access to the service. Apple Pay enables these devices to communicate wirelessly with special point-of-sale systems using near field communication (NFC) technology. A person using an iPhone holds it close to the point-of-sale terminal and authenticates the transaction by holding a fingerprint to the phone's Touch ID sensor. Customers' payment information is kept private from the retailer. The system generates a "dynamic security code" for each transaction.

Google and Samsung Provide Competition

Google created the Google Wallet wireless payment system even before Apple Pay was launched. Then, in 2015, Google and the mobile payments company Softcard contracted with AT&T, T-Mobile USA, and Verizon Wireless to preinstall Google Wallet in smartphones sold by those three companies.

Google's Android system is used on most Samsung smartphones. Samsung, a fierce competitor of Apple, purchased LoopPay, a mobile payments start-up. In addition, Samsung created a direct competitor to Apple Pay called Samsung Pay. It was designed to work with existing magnetic-strip credit-card machines, as well as the newer NFC technology.

Linking Digital Wallets to Other Apps on a Smartphone

The ultimate goal in this modern-payment system is a link from a digital wallet to another app within a single smartphone. For instance, Google allows its Google Wallet to link to its Google Offers, which is a discount-deal app. Mobile payment systems will eventually be tied to rewards programs and special offers at individual stores.

Critical Thinking

Does having a digital wallet in a smartphone entail more security risks than carrying a physical wallet? Explain.

Promissory Notes (Promises to Pay) A **promissory note** is a written promise made by one person (the **maker** of the promise to pay) to another (usually a payee). A promissory note, which is often referred to simply as a *note*, can be made payable at a definite time or on demand. It can name a specific payee or merely be payable to bearer (bearer instruments will be discussed later in this chapter). **Example 22.3** On April 30, Laurence and Margaret Roberts sign a writing unconditionally promising to pay "to the order of" the First National Bank of Whiteacre $3,000 (with 5 percent interest) on or before June 29. This writing is a promissory note. (See Exhibit 22–3.)

Promissory notes are used in a variety of credit transactions. Often, a promissory note will carry the name of the transaction involved. A note secured by personal property, such as an automobile, is referred to as a *collateral note* because property pledged as security for the satisfaction of a debt is called *collateral*.[2] A note payable in installments, such as installment payments for a 65-inch OLED 4K UHD television over a twelve-month period, is called an *installment note*.

Promissory Note A written promise made by one person (the maker) to pay a fixed amount of funds to another person (the payee or a subsequent holder) on demand or on a specified date.

Maker One who promises to pay a fixed amount of funds to the holder of a promissory note or a certificate of deposit (CD).

2. To minimize the risk of loss when making a loan, a creditor often requires the debtor to provide some *collateral*, or security, beyond a promise that the debt will be repaid. When this security takes the form of personal property (such as a motor vehicle), the creditor has an interest in the property that is known as a *security interest*.

Exhibit 22–3 A Typical Promissory Note

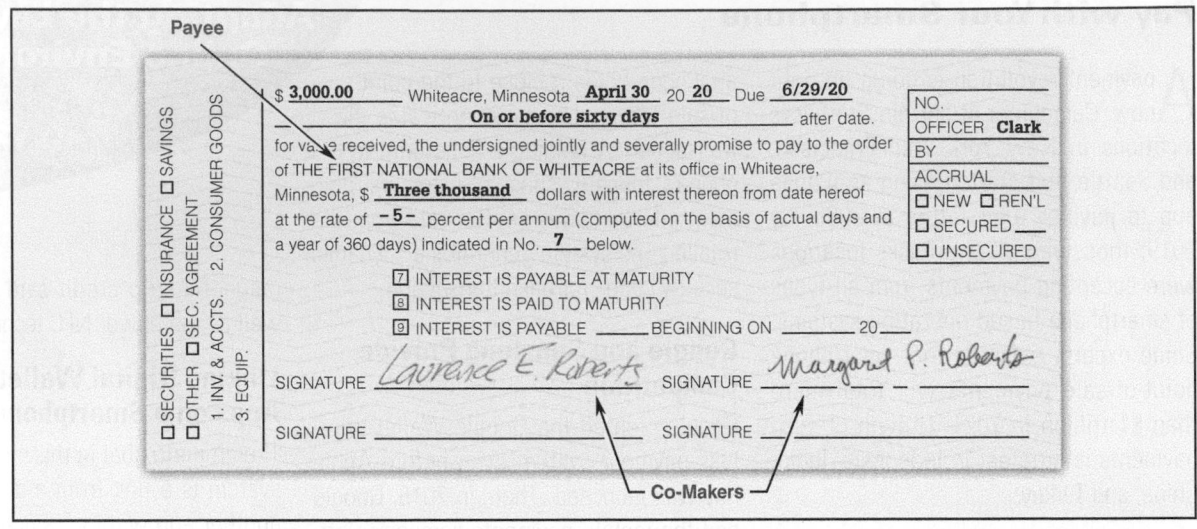

A promissory note is not a debt—it is only the evidence of a debt. **Case Example 22.4** Miracle Faith World Outreach borrowed $1,962,000 to buy buildings and land in Connecticut, signing a note payable to Silicon Valley Bank. In the seventh year of the note's ten-year term, with more than $1,600,000 owed on the principal and almost $60,000 owed on unpaid interest, Miracle Faith defaulted. Silicon Valley Bank filed a lawsuit but only had a copy of the promissory note, not the original (which had been in a storage facility). The court held in favor of the bank, and an appellate court affirmed. Even when a promissory note is lost, impaired, or destroyed (in good faith), the owner still retains rights and may prove its existence through other evidence, such as a copy.[3] ▪

Certificate of Deposit (CD) A note issued by a bank in which the bank acknowledges the receipt of funds from a party and promises to repay that amount, with interest, to the party on a certain date.

Certificates of Deposit (Promises to Pay)
A **certificate of deposit (CD)** is a type of note issued when a party deposits funds with a bank that the bank promises to repay, with interest, on a certain date [UCC 3–104(j)]. The bank is the maker of the note, and the depositor is the payee. **Example 22.5** On February 15, Sara Levin deposits $5,000 with the First National Bank of Whiteacre. The bank issues a CD, in which it promises to repay the $5,000, plus 1.85 percent annual interest, on August 15. (See Exhibit 22–4.) ▪

Because CDs are time deposits, the purchaser-payee typically is not allowed to withdraw the funds before the date of maturity. Banks usually charge a sizable penalty for early withdrawal (except in limited circumstances, such as disability or death). Certificates of deposit are often sold by savings and loan associations, commercial banks, and credit unions. Small CDs are for amounts up to $100,000.

22–1b Requirements for Negotiability

Learning Objective 1

What requirements must an instrument meet to be negotiable?

For an instrument to be negotiable, it must meet the following requirements:

1. Be in writing.
2. Be signed by the maker or the drawer.
3. Be an unconditional promise or order to pay.
4. State a fixed amount of money.
5. Be payable on demand or at a definite time.
6. Be payable to order or to bearer, unless the instrument is a check.

---

3. *Silicon Valley Bank v. Miracle Faith World Outreach, Inc.*, 140 Conn.App. 827, 60 A.3d 343 (2013).

Exhibit 22–4 **A Sample Certificate of Deposit**

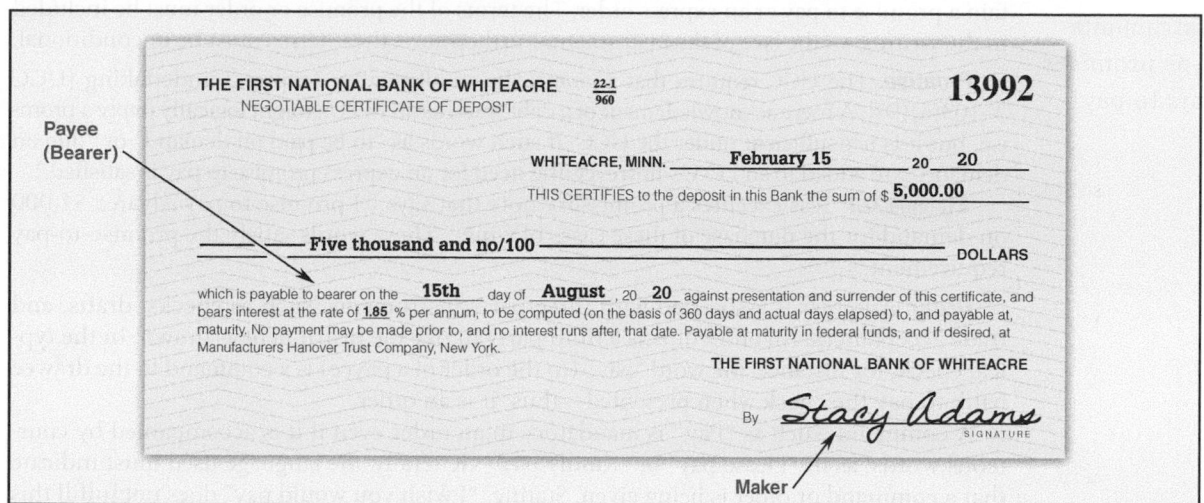

Payee
(Bearer)

THE FIRST NATIONAL BANK OF WHITEACRE   22-1 / 960   **13992**
NEGOTIABLE CERTIFICATE OF DEPOSIT

WHITEACRE, MINN.   **February 15**   20 **20**

THIS CERTIFIES to the deposit in this Bank the sum of $ **5,000.00**

———— **Five thousand and no/100** ———————————————————— DOLLARS

which is payable to bearer on the ___ **15th** ___ day of **August** , 20 **20** against presentation and surrender of this certificate, and bears interest at the rate of **1.85** % per annum, to be computed (on the basis of 360 days and actual days elapsed) to, and payable at, maturity. No payment may be made prior to, and no interest runs after, that date. Payable at maturity in federal funds, and if desired, at Manufacturers Hanover Trust Company, New York.

THE FIRST NATIONAL BANK OF WHITEACRE

By *Stacy Adams*
SIGNATURE

Maker

Written Form Negotiable instruments must be in written form (but may be evidenced by an electronic record) [UCC 3–103(a)(6), (9)].[4] This is because negotiable instruments must possess the quality of certainty that only formal, written expression can give. The writing must have the following qualities:

1. The writing must be on material that lends itself to *permanence*. Instruments carved in blocks of ice or etched in sand would not qualify as negotiable instruments. The UCC nevertheless gives considerable leeway as to what can be a negotiable instrument. Courts have found checks and notes written on napkins, menus, tablecloths, shirts, and a variety of other materials to be negotiable.

2. The writing must also have *portability*. Although the UCC does not explicitly state this requirement, if an instrument is not movable, it obviously cannot meet the requirement that it be freely transferable. **Example 22.6** Charles writes on the side of a cow, "I promise to pay $500 to the order of Jason." Technically, this would meet the requirements of a negotiable instrument—except for portability. A cow cannot easily be transferred in the ordinary course of business. Thus, the "instrument" is nonnegotiable. ■

Signatures For an instrument to be negotiable, it must be signed by (1) the maker, if it is a note or a certificate of deposit, or (2) the drawer, if it is a draft or a check [UCC 3–103(a)(3)]. If a person signs an instrument as an authorized agent of the maker or drawer, the maker or drawer has effectively signed the instrument.

The UCC is quite lenient with regard to what constitutes a signature. Nearly any symbol executed or adopted by a person with the intent to authenticate a written or electronic document can be a signature [UCC 1–201(37)]. A signature can be made by a device, such as a rubber stamp, or by a thumbprint. In addition, it can consist of any name, including a trade name, or a word, mark, or symbol [UCC 3–401(b)]. If necessary, parol evidence is admissible to identify the signer.

The location of the signature on the document is unimportant, although the usual place is the lower right-hand corner. A *handwritten* statement on the body of the instrument, such as "I, Jerome Garcia, promise to pay Elena Greer," is sufficient to act as a signature.

> "I'm a writer. I write checks. They're not very good."
>
> **Wendy Liebman**
> 1961–present
> (American comedian)

Would a promise to pay written on the side of this calf be negotiable? Why or why not?

Karpiyon/Getty Images

---

4. Under the Uniform Electronic Transactions Act (UETA) and the 2002 amendments to Article 3, an electronic record may be sufficient to constitute a writing. Note, however, that the amendments to Article 3 do not expressly authorize electronic negotiable instruments.

Know This

Negotiable instruments are classified as promises to pay or orders to pay.

Unconditional Promise or Order to Pay For an instrument to be negotiable, it must contain a promise to pay or an express order. The terms of the promise or order must be included in the writing on the face of the instrument. Furthermore, these terms must be unconditional.

Promise. The UCC requires that a *promise* be an affirmative (express) undertaking [UCC 3–103(a)(9)]. A mere acknowledgment of a debt, such as an I.O.U., might logically *imply* a promise, but it is *not* sufficient under the UCC. If such words as "to be paid on demand" or "due on demand" are added to an I.O.U., however, the need for an express promise to pay is satisfied.[5]

Example 22.7 Tess executes a promissory note that says, "I promise to pay Alvarez $1,000 on demand for the purchase of these cases of wine." These words satisfy the promise-to-pay requirement.

Order. An *order* is associated with three-party instruments, such as checks, drafts, and trade acceptances. An order directs a third party to pay the instrument as drawn. In the typical check, for instance, the word "pay" (to the order of a payee) is a command to the drawee bank to pay the check when presented—thus, it is an order.

A command, such as "Pay," is mandatory in an order even if it is accompanied by courteous words, as in "Please pay" or "Kindly pay." Generally, the language used must indicate that a command or order is being given. Stating, "I wish you would pay" does not fulfill this requirement. An order may be addressed to one party or to more than one party, either jointly ("to A *and* B") or alternatively ("to A *or* B") [UCC 3–103(a)(6)].

Unconditionality of Promise or Order. Only *unconditional* promises or orders can be negotiable [UCC 3–106(a)]. A promise or order is conditional (and therefore *not* negotiable) if it states *any* of the following:

1. An express condition to payment.
2. That the promise or order is subject to or governed by another writing or record.
3. That the rights or obligations with respect to the promise or order are stated in another writing or record.

A mere reference to another writing, however, does not make the promise or order conditional [UCC 3–106(a)]. For instance, the words "As per contract" or "This debt arises from the sale of goods X and Y" do not render an instrument nonnegotiable. Similarly, a statement in the instrument that payment can be made only out of a particular fund or source will not render the instrument nonnegotiable [UCC 3–106(b)(ii)].

Case Example 22.8 Sam and Odalis Groome entered into two contracts to buy a pair of alpacas from Alpacas of America, LLC (AOA). To finance the purchases, the buyers signed two notes, one for $18,750 and one for $20,250. Each note included a reference to a contract, a payment schedule, and a security agreement, which provided an interest in the alpacas to secure payment. Within a few months, the Groomes stopped making payments. When AOA sued to collect the unpaid amounts, the Groomes argued that the notes were nonnegotiable because they referred to and were governed by other writings (the contracts). Ultimately, a state appellate court ruled that the Groomes' notes did contain unconditional promises to pay and thus were negotiable.[6]

In contrast, if the payment is to be made from a fund that does not yet exist, or is conditioned on the occurrence of some future event, the instrument will be nonnegotiable. **Example 22.9** Duffy's note promises to pay Sherman from the trust account that Duffy will establish when he receives the proceeds from his father's estate. This promise is conditional, and the note is nonnegotiable.

In the following case, the court considered the negotiability of a promissory note that included a reference to a mortgage. The makers of the note argued that this reference rendered the note nonnegotiable.

Is a note for funds to purchase alpacas negotiable?

---

5. A certificate of deposit (CD) is an exception in this respect. A CD does not have to contain an express promise, because the bank's acknowledgment of the deposit and the other terms of the instrument clearly indicate a promise by the bank to repay the funds [UCC 3–104(j)].

6. *Alpacas of America, LLC v. Groome*, 179 Wash.App. 391, 317 P.3d 1103 (2014).

Case 22.1

OneWest Bank, FSB[a] v. Nunez

District Court of Appeal of Florida, Fourth District, 41 Fla.L.Weekly D540, 193 So.3d 13 (2016).

Background and Facts To buy property in Hallandale, Florida, Jose and Jessica Nunez signed a promissory note and mortgage payable to Countrywide Home Loans, Inc. The note contained a reference to the mortgage, and described how and under what conditions its payment could be accelerated. Countrywide transferred the note to OneWest Bank. The Nunezes defaulted on the payments. OneWest filed a suit in a Florida state court to collect. The Nunezes claimed that OneWest was not entitled to enforce the note because it was not a negotiable instrument. They contended that the reference to the mortgage and the conditions for acceleration destroyed the note's negotiability. The court agreed with the Nunezes and dismissed the complaint. OneWest appealed.

In the Words of the Court

WARNER, J. [Judge]

* * * The trial court erred in concluding that the note in question was non-negotiable. Florida has adopted the Uniform Commercial Code, including its provision on negotiability and enforcement of negotiable instruments.

* * * *

Florida Statutes Section 673.1061 [UCC 3–106(a)] defines "unconditional" by stating those conditions that prevent it from being unconditional:

(1) Except as provided in this section, for the purposes of [Florida Statutes] Section 673.1041(1), a promise or order is unconditional unless it states:
(a) An express condition to payment;
(b) That the promise or order is subject to or governed by another writing; or
(c) That rights or obligations with respect to the promise or order are stated in another writing. A reference to another writing does not of itself make the promise or order conditional.
(2) A promise or order is not made conditional:
(a) By a reference to another writing for a statement of rights with respect to collateral, prepayment, or acceleration.

The UCC comments to this section address the inclusion of language regarding collateral and acceleration, and confirm that the inclusion of such language does not make the note conditional:

Many notes issued in commercial transactions are secured by collateral, are subject to acceleration in the event of default, or are subject to prepayment, or acceleration does not prevent the note from being an instrument if the statement is in the note itself. * * * In some cases it may be convenient not to include a statement concerning collateral, prepayment, or acceleration in the note, but rather to refer to an accompanying loan agreement, security agreement or mortgage for that statement. [Florida Statutes Section 673.1061(2)(a)] allows a reference to the appropriate writing for a statement of these rights. * * *

*Thus, the mention of the mortgage instrument as to the * * * rights of acceleration in the promissory note does not destroy the unconditional nature of the note.* [Emphasis added.]

Two cases from other jurisdictions have considered the exact language contained in the promissory note in this case and concluded that it did not render the note non-negotiable. In [the first case], the court relied on the UCC comment to the statutory provision to conclude that "the reference to the mortgage, in Section 11 of the note, with respect to rights of acceleration does not render the note nonnegotiable." * * * [The second case] * * * dealt with nearly identical language, including the incorporation of the acceleration on transfer provisions of the mortgage in the note. The bankruptcy judge found that the provisions were conditions regarding acceleration, permissible under Section 3-106(b) of the UCC and not destroying negotiability. *We agree with the foregoing authority that Section 11 of the note refers to the mortgage for a statement of rights with respect to * * * acceleration and thus does not render the note nonnegotiable.* [Emphasis added.]

Decision and Remedy Yes. A state intermediate appellate court reversed the dismissal of OneWest's complaint. The note's reference to the Nunez's mortgage for a statement of rights concerning acceleration did not render the note conditional and nonnegotiable.

Critical Thinking

• **What If the Facts Were Different?** *Suppose that the note in this case had stated, "The terms of the mortgage are by this reference made a part hereof." Would the result have been different?*

---

a. The initials *FSB* mean Federal Savings Bank.

A Fixed Amount of Money   Negotiable instruments must state with certainty a fixed amount of money to be paid at any time the instrument is payable [UCC 3–104(a)]. This requirement ensures that the value of the instrument can be determined with clarity and certainty.

The term *fixed amount* means an amount that is ascertainable from the face of the instrument. A demand note payable with 8 percent interest meets the requirement of a fixed amount because its amount can be determined at the time it is payable or at any time thereafter [UCC 3–104(a)].

The rate of interest may also be determined from information that is not contained in the instrument itself but described by it, such as a formula or a source [UCC 3–112(b)]. For instance, an instrument that is payable at the *legal rate of interest* (a rate of interest fixed by statute) is negotiable. Mortgage notes tied to a variable rate of interest (a rate that fluctuates as a result of market conditions) are also negotiable.

The fixed amount must be *payable in money*. The UCC defines money as "a medium of exchange authorized or adopted by a domestic or foreign government as a part of its currency" [UCC 1–201(24)]. Gold is not a medium of exchange adopted by the U.S. government, so a note payable in gold is nonnegotiable. An instrument payable in the United States with a face amount stated in a foreign currency is negotiable, however, and can be paid in the foreign currency or in the equivalent amount of U.S. dollars [UCC 3–107].

Payable on Demand or at a Definite Time   A negotiable instrument must "be payable on demand or at a definite time" [UCC 3–104(a)(2)]. To determine the instrument's value, it is necessary to know when the maker, drawee, or acceptor is required to pay. It is also necessary to know when the obligations of secondary parties, such as *indorsers*,[7] will arise.

Furthermore, it is necessary to know when an instrument is due in order to calculate when the statute of limitations may apply [UCC 3–118(a)]. Finally, with an interest-bearing instrument, it is necessary to know the exact interval during which interest will accrue to determine the instrument's present value.

Payable on Demand.   Instruments that are payable on demand include those that contain the words "Payable at sight" or "Payable upon presentment." **Presentment** is a demand made by or on behalf of a person entitled to enforce an instrument to either pay or accept the instrument [UCC 3–501]. Thus, presentment occurs when a person offers the instrument to the appropriate party for payment or acceptance. Presentment can by made by any commercially reasonable means, including oral, written, or electronic communication.

The very nature of the instrument may indicate that it is payable on demand. For instance, a check, by definition, is payable on demand [UCC 3–104(f)]. If no time for payment is specified and the person responsible for payment must pay on the instrument's presentment, the instrument is payable on demand [UCC 3–108(a)]. (See the *Business Law Analysis* feature for further illustration.)

Case Example 22.10   National City Bank gave Reger Development, LLC, a line of credit to finance potential development opportunities. Reger signed a promissory note requiring it to "pay this loan in full immediately upon Lender's demand." About a year later, the bank asked Reger to pay down the loan and stated that it would be reducing the amount of cash available through the line of credit. Reger sued, alleging that the bank had breached the terms of the note. The court ruled in the bank's favor. The promissory note was a demand instrument because it explicitly set forth the lender's right to demand payment at any time. Thus, National City had the right to collect payment from Reger at any time on demand.[8]

---

7. We should note that the UCC uses the spelling *indorse* (*indorsement*, and the like), rather than the more common spelling *endorse* (*endorsement*, and the like). We follow the UCC's spelling here and in other chapters in this text.

8. *Reger Development, LLC v. National City Bank*, 592 F.3d 759 (7th Cir. 2010).

Deciding If an Instrument Is Negotiable

Abby Novel signed a promissory note to her stepfather to obtain funds to manufacture and market a patented jewelry display design. The note read, "Glen Gallwitz 1-8-2016 loaned me $5,000 at 6 percent interest for a total of $10,000.00." The note did not state a time for repayment. More than seven years after Novel signed the note, Gallwitz filed a suit to recover the stated amount. Novel claimed that she did not have to pay because the note was not negotiable—it was incomplete. Is she correct?

Analysis: For an instrument to be negotiable under UCC 3–104, it must meet the following requirements: (1) be in writing, (2) be signed by the maker or the drawer, (3) be an unconditional promise or order to pay, (4) state a fixed amount of money, (5) be payable on demand or at a definite time, and (6) be payable to order or to bearer unless it is a check. When no time for payment is stated on an instrument, the instrument is payable on demand.

Result and Reasoning: Novel is not correct. All of the requirements to establish the instrument as negotiable are met: (1) the instrument is in writing, (2) it is signed by Novel, (3) there are no conditions or promises other than the unconditional promise to pay, (4) the instrument states a fixed amount—$10,000, (5) the instrument does not include a definite repayment date, which means that it is payable on demand, and (6) the instrument is payable to Gallwitz.

Therefore, the instrument is negotiable, and Novel is bound to pay it.

Payable at a Definite Time. If an instrument is not payable on demand, to be negotiable it must be payable at a definite time. An instrument is payable at a definite time if it states *any* of the following:

1. That it is payable on a specified date.

2. That it is payable within a definite period of time (such as thirty days) after being presented for payment.

3. That it is payable on a date or time readily ascertainable at the time the promise or order is issued [UCC 3–108(b)].

The maker or drawee in a time draft is under no obligation to pay until the specified time.

When an instrument is payable by the maker or drawer *on or before* a stated date, it is clearly payable at a definite time. The maker or drawer has the *option* of paying before the stated maturity date, but the payee can still rely on payment being made by the maturity date. **Example 22.11** Ari gives Ernesto an instrument dated May 1, 2019, that indicates on its face that it is payable *on or before* May 1, 2020. This instrument satisfies the definite-time requirement. ▪

In contrast, an instrument that is undated and made payable "one month after date" is clearly nonnegotiable. There is no way to determine the maturity date from the face of the instrument. If the date is uncertain, the instrument is not payable at a definite time. **Example 22.12** An instrument that states, "One year after the death of my grandfather, Jerome Adams, I promise to pay $5,000 to the order of Lucy Harmon. [Signed] Jacqueline Wells," is nonnegotiable. The date on which the instrument becomes payable is uncertain. ▪

Acceleration Clause. An **acceleration clause** allows a payee or other holder of a time instrument to demand payment of the entire amount due, with interest, if a certain event occurs. (A **holder** is any person in possession of an instrument drawn, issued, or indorsed to him or her, to his or her order, to bearer, or in blank [UCC 1–201(20)].)

Acceleration Clause A clause that allows a payee or other holder of a time instrument to demand payment of the entire amount due, with interest, if a certain event occurs, such as a default in the payment of an installment when due.

Holder Any person in possession of an instrument drawn, issued, or indorsed to him or her, to his or her order, to bearer, or in blank.

Can a note made in exchange for funds contain an acceleration clause and still be negotiable?

Example 22.13 Marta lends $1,000 to Ruth, who makes a negotiable note promising to pay $100 per month (plus interest) for ten months. The note contains an acceleration provision that permits Marta or any holder to immediately demand all the payments plus the interest owed to date if Ruth fails to pay an installment. Ruth fails to make the third payment. Marta accelerates the unpaid balance, and the note becomes due and payable in full. Ruth owes Marta the remaining principal plus any unpaid interest to that date. ■

Instruments that include acceleration clauses are negotiable because the exact value of the instrument can be ascertained. In addition, the instrument will be payable on a specified date if the event allowing acceleration does not occur [UCC 3–108(b)(ii)]. Thus, the specified date is the outside limit used to determine the value and negotiability of the instrument.

Extension Clause A clause in a time instrument that allows the instrument's date of maturity to be extended into the future.

Extension Clause. The reverse of an acceleration clause is an **extension clause**, which allows the date of maturity to be extended into the future [UCC 3–108(b)(iii), (iv)]. If the right to extend the time of payment is given to the maker or drawer, the interval of the extension must be specified to keep the instrument negotiable. If, however, the holder can extend the time of payment, the extended maturity date need not be specified for the instrument to be negotiable.

Example 22.14 Alek's note reads, "The holder of this note at the date of maturity, January 1, 2021, can extend the time of payment until the following June 1 or later, if the holder so wishes." This note is negotiable. The length of the extension does not have to be specified, because only the holder has the option to extend. After January 1, 2021, the note is, in effect, a demand instrument. ■

Payable to Order or to Bearer

Because one of the functions of a negotiable instrument is to serve as a substitute for cash, freedom to transfer is essential. To ensure a proper transfer, the instrument must be "payable to order or to bearer" at the time it is issued or first comes into the possession of the holder [UCC 3–104(a)(1)]. An instrument is not negotiable unless it meets this requirement.

Order Instrument A negotiable instrument that is payable "to the order of an identified person" or "to an identified person or order."

Order Instruments. An **order instrument** is an instrument that is payable (1) "to the order of an identified person" or (2) "to an identified person or order" [UCC 3–109(b)]. An identified person is the person "to whom the instrument is initially payable" as determined by the intent of the maker or drawer [UCC 3–110(a)]. The identified person, in turn, may transfer the instrument to whomever he or she wishes. In this way, the instrument retains its transferability.

Note that with order instruments, the person specified must be identified with *certainty*, because the transfer of the instrument requires the *indorsement*, or signature, of the payee (indorsements will be discussed later in this chapter). An order instrument made "Payable to the order of my nicest cousin," for instance, is not negotiable, because it does not clearly specify the payee.

Bearer Instrument Any instrument that is not payable to a specific person, including instruments payable to bearer or to cash.

Bearer A person in possession of an instrument payable to bearer or indorsed in blank.

Bearer Instruments. A **bearer instrument** is an instrument that does not designate a specific payee [UCC 3–109(a)]. The term **bearer** refers to a person in possession of an instrument that is payable to bearer or indorsed in blank (with a signature only, as will be discussed shortly) [UCC 1–201(5), 3–109(a), 3–109(c)]. This means that the maker or drawer agrees to pay anyone who presents the instrument for payment.

Any instrument containing terms such as the following is a bearer instrument:

1. "Payable to the order of bearer."
2. "Payable to Simon Reed or bearer."

3. "Payable to bearer."

4. "Payable to X" or "Payable to Captain America" (can be payable to a *nonexistent person*, but not to a company that does not exist).

5. "Pay to the order of cash."

Spotlight Case Example 22.15 Amine Nehme applied for credit at the Venetian Resort Hotel Casino in Las Vegas, Nevada, and was granted $500,000 in credit. He signed a marker—that is, a promise to pay a gambling debt—for $500,000. Nehme quickly lost that amount gambling. The Venetian presented the marker for payment to Nehme's bank, Bank of America, which returned it for insufficient funds. The casino's owner, Las Vegas Sands, LLC, filed a suit against Nehme for failure to pay a negotiable instrument.

The court held that the marker fit the UCC's definitions of negotiable instrument and check. It was a means for payment of $500,000 from Bank of America to the order of the Venetian. It did not state a time for payment and thus was payable on demand. It was also unconditional—that is, it stated no promise by Nehme other than the promise to pay a fixed amount of money.[9]

Factors That Do Not Affect Negotiability Certain ambiguities or omissions will not affect the negotiability of an instrument. The UCC provides the following rules for clearing up ambiguous terms:

1. Unless the date of an instrument is necessary to determine a definite time for payment, the fact that an instrument is *undated* does not affect its negotiability. A typical example is an undated check, which is still negotiable. If a check is not dated, its date is the date of its issue, meaning the date the maker first delivers the check to another person to give that person rights in the check [UCC 3–113(b)].

2. Antedating or postdating an instrument (using a date before or after the actual current date) does not affect the instrument's negotiability [UCC 3–113(a)]. **Example 22.16** Crenshaw draws a check on his account at First Bank, payable to Sirah Imports. He postdates the check by fifteen days. Sirah Imports can immediately negotiate the check, and, unless Crenshaw tells First Bank otherwise, the bank can charge the amount of the check to Crenshaw's account [UCC 4–401(c)].

3. Handwritten terms outweigh typewritten and printed terms (preprinted terms on forms, for instance), and typewritten terms outweigh printed terms [UCC 3–114]. **Example 22.17** Most checks are preprinted "Pay to the order of" followed by a blank line, indicating an order instrument. In handwriting, Chad inserts in the blank, "Anita Delgado or bearer." The handwritten terms will outweigh the printed form, and the check will be a bearer instrument.

4. Words outweigh figures unless the words are ambiguous [UCC 3–114]. This rule is important when the numerical amount and the written amount on a check differ. **Example 22.18** Megan Jefferies issues a check payable to Reliable Appliance Company. For the amount, she fills in the number "$100" but writes out the words "One thousand and 00/100" dollars. The check is payable in the amount of $1,000.

5. When an instrument does not specify a particular interest rate but simply states "with interest," the interest rate is the *judgment rate of interest* (a rate of interest fixed by statute that is applied to court judgments) [UCC 3–112(b)].

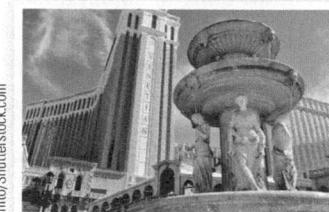

Can a gambling marker be a negotiable instrument?

Know This
An instrument that purports to be payable both to order and to bearer contains a contradiction in terms. Such an instrument is a bearer instrument.

---

9. *Las Vegas Sands, LLC v. Nehme*, 632 F.3d 526 (9th Cir. 2011).

6. A check is negotiable even if a notation on it states that it is "nonnegotiable" or "not governed by Article 3." Any other instrument, in contrast, can be made nonnegotiable if the maker or drawer conspicuously notes on it that it is "nonnegotiable" or "not governed by Article 3" [UCC 3–104(d)].

In the following case, the court was asked to compare the words and figures in a note to determine its amount.

■ Case 22.2

Charles R. Tips Family Trust v. PB Commercial, LLC

Court of Appeals of Texas, Houston, First District, 459 S.W.3d 147 (2015).

Background and Facts The Charles R. Tips Family Trust signed a promissory note in favor of Patriot Bank to obtain a loan to buy a house in Harris County, Texas. The note identified the principal amount of the loan as "ONE MILLION SEVEN THOUSAND AND NO/100 ($1,700,000.00) DOLLARS." The family trust made payments totaling only $595,586. PB Commercial, LLC (PBC), acquired the note, sold the residence for $874,125, and pursued litigation in a Texas state court against the borrower, alleging default.

The defendant argued that the written words in an instrument control. Thus, the note had been satisfied in full by the amount of the payments plus the sale price of the house. In fact, the trust pointed out that PBC had collected a surplus of $189,111. The court entered a judgment in PBC's favor. The trust appealed, arguing one issue—that the amount of the loan must be determined from the printed words in the note.

In the Words of the Court

Michael *MASSENGALE*, Justice.

* * * *

* * * To recover on a promissory note on which the borrower has defaulted, PBC was required to prove that * * * a certain balance was due and owing on the note.

* * * *

* * * Under the Uniform Commercial Code, which governs negotiable instruments such as the Note, "if an instrument contains contradictory terms, * * * words prevail over numbers." * * * *This rule derives from the principle that writing words more likely represents the parties' true intentions than writing numbers.* [Emphasis added.]

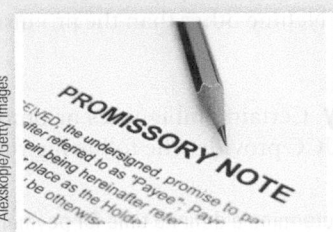

What happens when the numbers in a promissory note differ from the written amount?

The Note * * * describes the original amount of the loan obligation as "ONE MILLION SEVEN THOUSAND AND NO/100 ($1,700,000.00) DOLLARS." The phrase "one million seven thousand and no/100 dollars" has a plain, unambiguous meaning, namely the sum of $1,007,000.00. Thus, the words and the numerals in the [Note] are in conflict, differing by $693,000.

* * * *

* * * It does not matter that the discrepancy between the words and numbers here is a large one. Neither [Texas Business & Commercial Code] Section 3.114 [Texas's version of UCC 3–114] nor Texas case law makes a distinction on the basis of the size of the obligation or the significance of the conflict in terms.

PBC argues that this case presents a unique circumstance in that the omission of a single word transforms "one million seven hundred thousand" into "one million seven thousand." If the former phrase were modified in any other way, according to PBC, we would be faced with either an ambiguous term or an unambiguous but absurd one. For example, PBC [proposes] a scenario in which a [clerk's] error rendered the phrase as "one seven hundred thousand," omitting the word "million." According to PBC, such an amount would be ambiguous, and the court would have to refer to the numerals and extrinsic [outside] evidence to resolve the ambiguity. But this hypothetical scenario has no bearing on this case because there is no ambiguity in the text here.

* * * *

Here, the words "one million seven thousand" control over the numerals "$1,700,000" to set the amount of the promissory note.

Decision and Remedy A state intermediate appellate court reversed the judgment of the lower court. Under the UCC, "if an instrument contains contradictory terms, . . . words prevail over numbers." In this case, the note's words and numerals were in conflict. Thus, the words of "one million seven thousand" control over the numerals "$1,700,000" as the amount of the promissory note.

Critical Thinking

• **What If the Facts Were Different?** *Suppose that the note had described the amount of the loan as "ONE MILLION SEVEN HUNDRED THOUSAND AND NO/100 ($1,007,000.00) DOLLARS." What would have been the result?*

22–2 Transfer of Instruments

Once issued, a negotiable instrument can be transferred by *assignment* or by *negotiation*. The party receiving the instrument obtains the rights of a holder only if the transfer is by negotiation.

22–2a Transfer by Assignment

Recall that an assignment is a transfer of rights under a contract. Under general contract principles, a transfer by assignment gives the assignee only those rights that the assignor possessed. Any defenses that can be raised against an assignor can normally be raised against the assignee. This same principle applies when a negotiable instrument, such as a promissory note, is transferred by assignment. The transferee is an *assignee* rather than a *holder*.

22–2b Transfer by Negotiation

Negotiation is the transfer of an instrument in such a way that the transferee (the person to whom the instrument is transferred) becomes a holder [UCC 3–201(a)]. Under UCC principles, a transfer by negotiation creates a holder who, at the very least, receives the rights of the previous possessor [UCC 3–203(b)].

Unlike an assignment, a transfer by negotiation can make it possible for a holder to receive more rights in the instrument than the prior possessor had [UCC 3–202(b), 3–305, 3–306]. A holder who receives greater rights is known as a *holder in due course*, a concept we will discuss later in this chapter.

There are two methods of negotiating an instrument so that the receiver becomes a holder. The method used depends on whether the instrument is an *order instrument* or a *bearer instrument*.

Negotiating Order Instruments An order instrument contains the name of a payee capable of indorsing it, as in "Pay to the order of Lloyd Sorenson." If the instrument is an order instrument, it is negotiated by delivery with any necessary indorsements.

Example 22.19 Welpac Corporation issues a payroll check "to the order of Lloyd Sorenson." Sorenson takes the check to the bank, signs his name on the back (an indorsement), gives it to the teller (a delivery), and receives cash. Sorenson has *negotiated* the check to the bank [UCC 3–201(b)]. ■

Negotiating order instruments requires both delivery and indorsement. If Sorenson had taken the check to the bank and delivered it to the teller without signing it, the transfer would not qualify as a negotiation. In that situation, the transfer would be treated as an assignment, and the bank would become an assignee rather than a holder.

Negotiating Bearer Instruments If an instrument is payable to bearer, it is negotiated by delivery—that is, by transfer into another person's possession. Indorsement is not necessary

"Money has little value to its possessor unless it also has value to others."

Leland Stanford
1824–1893
(U.S. senator and founder of Stanford University)

Negotiation The transfer of an instrument in such form that the transferee (the person to whom the instrument is transferred) becomes a holder.

Learning Objective 2
How does the negotiation of order instruments differ from the negotiation of bearer instruments?

[UCC 3–201(b)]. The use of bearer instruments thus involves more risk through loss or theft than the use of order instruments.

Example 22.20 Richard Kray writes a check "payable to cash" and hands it to Jessie Arnold (a delivery). Kray has issued the check (a bearer instrument) to Arnold. Arnold places the check in her wallet, which is subsequently stolen. The thief has possession of the check. At this point, the thief has no rights to the check. If the thief "delivers" the check to an innocent third person, however, negotiation will be complete. All rights to the check will be passed absolutely to that third person, and Arnold will lose all rights to recover the proceeds of the check from that person [UCC 3–306]. Of course, Arnold can attempt to recover the amount from the thief if the thief can be found. ▪

22–2c Indorsements

Indorsement A signature placed on an instrument for the purpose of transferring ownership rights in the instrument.

An indorsement is required whenever an order instrument is negotiated. An **Indorsement** is a signature with or without additional words or statements. It is most often written on the back of the instrument itself. If there is no room on the instrument, the indorsement can be on a separate piece of paper that is firmly affixed to the instrument, such as with staples [UCC 3–204(a)]. (See this chapter's *Beyond Our Borders* feature for a discussion of the approach to indorsements in France.)

A person who transfers an instrument by signing (indorsing) it and delivering it to another person is an *indorser*. The person to whom the check is indorsed and delivered is the *indorsee*. **Example 22.21** Luisa Perez receives a graduation check for $100. She can transfer the check to her mother (or to anyone) by signing it on the back. Luisa is an indorser. If Luisa indorses the check by writing "Pay to Avery Perez," Avery Perez is the indorsee. ▪

There are four main categories of indorsements: blank, special, qualified, and restrictive. Note that a single indorsement may have characteristics of more than one category.

Blank Indorsement An indorsement on an instrument that specifies no indorsee. An order instrument that is indorsed in blank becomes a bearer instrument.

Blank Indorsements A **blank indorsement** does not specify a particular indorsee and can consist of a mere signature [UCC 3–205(b)]. **Example 22.22** A check payable "to the order of Alan Luberda" is indorsed in blank if Luberda simply writes his signature on the back of the check. A blank indorsement is shown in Exhibit 22–5. ▪

An order instrument indorsed in blank becomes a bearer instrument and can be negotiated by delivery alone, as already discussed. In other words, a blank indorsement converts an order instrument to a bearer instrument, which anybody can cash.

Exhibit 22–5 A Blank Indorsement

Alan Luberda

Severe Restrictions on Check Indorsements in France

Beyond Our Borders

If you were reading a business law textbook in France, you would find very little on check indorsements. The reason is that checks rarely, if ever, can be indorsed. That means that almost all checks must be deposited in a bank account, rather than transferred to another individual or entity. The French government says that these restrictions on indorsements reduce the risk of loss and theft.

Critical Thinking

What would be the cost to individuals and businesses that use checks if a similar rule was passed in this country?

Case Example 22.23 To buy a house, Tonya Bass signed a note with Mortgage Lenders Network USA, Inc., to borrow $139,988, repayable with interest in monthly installments of $810.75. The note was transferred by a rubber-stamp indorsement to Emax Financial Group, LLC, then to Residential Funding Corporation, and finally to U.S. Bank, N.A.

When Bass stopping paying on the note, U.S. Bank filed a suit in a North Carolina state court. Bass claimed that the bank's rubber stamp was not sufficient to qualify as a proper indorsement. A lower court holding in her favor was reversed by the state's highest court. The stamp was a valid signature and an indorsement sufficient to transfer the note.[10]

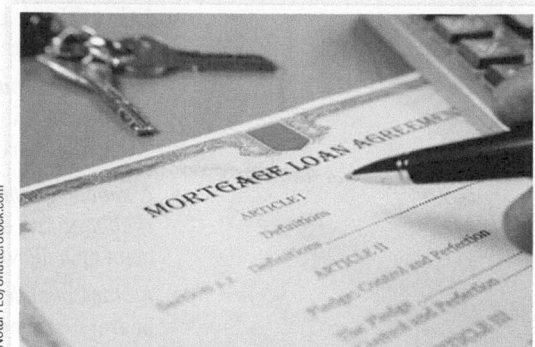

Can a signature stamp constitute a valid indorsement on a negotiable instrument?

Special Indorsements A **special indorsement** contains the signature of the indorser and identifies the person to whom the instrument is made payable—that is, it names the indorsee [UCC 3–205(a)]. Words such as "Pay to the order of Rick Clay" or "Pay to Rick Clay," followed by the signature of the indorser, create a special indorsement. An instrument indorsed in this way is an order instrument.

To avoid the risk of loss from theft, a holder may convert a blank indorsement to a special indorsement by writing, above the signature of the indorser, words identifying the indorsee [UCC 3–205(c)]. This changes the bearer instrument back to an order instrument.

Example 22.24 A check is made payable to Peter Rabe. He indorses the check in blank by signing his name on the back and delivers the check to Anthony Bartomo. Anthony is unable to cash the check immediately and wants to avoid any risk should he lose the check. He therefore prints "Pay to Anthony Bartomo" above Peter's blank indorsement (see Exhibit 22–6). By doing this, Anthony has converted Peter's blank indorsement into a special indorsement. Further negotiation now requires Anthony's indorsement plus delivery.

Qualified Indorsements Generally, an indorser, *merely by indorsing*, impliedly promises to pay the holder or any subsequent indorser the amount of the instrument in the event that the drawer or maker defaults on the payment [UCC 3–415(a)]. Usually, then, indorsements are *unqualified indorsements*, which means that the indorser is guaranteeing payment of the instrument in addition to transferring title to it.

An indorser who does not wish to be liable on an instrument can use a **qualified indorsement** to disclaim this liability [UCC 3–415(b)]. The notation "without recourse" is commonly used to create a qualified indorsement. If an instrument with such an indorsement is later dishonored, the holder cannot recover from the qualified indorser unless the indorser has breached one of the transfer warranties discussed later.

Example 22.25 A check is made payable to the order of Bridgett Cage. Cage wants to negotiate the check to Evelyn Ling but does not want to assume liability for the check's payment. Cage could create a qualified indorsement by indorsing the check as follows: "Pay to Evelyn Ling, without recourse, [signed] Bridgett Cage" (see Exhibit 22–7).

The Effect of Qualified Indorsements. Qualified indorsements are often used by persons (agents) acting in a representative capacity. Insurance agents sometimes receive checks payable to them that are really intended as payment to the insurance company. The agent is merely indorsing the payment through to the insurance company

Special Indorsement An indorsement on an instrument that identifies the specific person to whom the indorser intends to make the instrument payable.

Exhibit 22–6 A Special Indorsement

> Pay to Anthony Bartomo
> Peter Rabe

Qualified Indorsement An indorsement on a negotiable instrument in which the indorser disclaims any contract liability on the instrument. The notation "without recourse" is commonly used to create a qualified indorsement.

Exhibit 22–7 A Qualified Indorsement

> Pay to Evelyn Ling, without recourse.
> Bridgett Cage

---

10. *In re Bass*, 738 S.E.2d 173 (N.C. 2013).

and should not be required to make good on a check if it is later dishonored. The "without recourse" indorsement relieves the agent from any liability on a check.

Special versus Blank Qualified Indorsements. A qualified indorsement can be accompanied by either a special indorsement or a blank indorsement. In either situation, the instrument can be further negotiated.

- A *special qualified indorsement* includes the name of the indorsee as well as the words *without recourse*. The special indorsement makes the instrument an order instrument requiring an indorsement plus delivery for negotiation.

- A *blank qualified indorsement* ("without recourse, [signed] Jennie Cole") makes the instrument a bearer instrument, and only delivery is required for negotiation.

Case Example 22.26 Thomas Brandt executed a promissory note with MortgageIT, Inc., to finance a home. Seven years later, Brandt still owed $132,000 on the note, and Green Tree Servicing, LLC, filed a suit to foreclose on the property.

Brandt argued that MortgageIT had canceled the note because the note included an undated indorsement—"without recourse" to Wells Fargo Bank, NA—that had been crossed out and marked "VOID." Another paper was attached to the note, however. It contained indorsements without recourse from MortgageIT to Countrywide Bank FSB, from Countrywide Bank FSB to Countrywide Home Loans, and from Countrywide Home Loans to blank.

A state appellate court held that the note was payable to bearer. Because Green Tree Servicing was in possession of the note, it had title to, and was a holder of, the note. Therefore, the court ordered foreclosure on the property to pay Brandt's debt on the note to Green Tree.[11]

Restrictive Indorsements A **restrictive indorsement** requires the indorsee to comply with certain instructions regarding the funds involved, but it does not generally prohibit further negotiation of the instrument [UCC 3–206(a)]. Although most indorsements are nonrestrictive, many forms of restrictive indorsements do exist, including those discussed here.

Conditional Indorsements. When payment depends on the occurrence of some event specified in the indorsement, the indorsement is conditional. **Example 22.27** Ken Barton indorses a check, "Pay to Lars Johansen if he completes the renovation of my kitchen by June 1, 2020. [Signed] Ken Barton." Barton has created a conditional indorsement.

Indorsements for Deposit or Collection. A common type of restrictive indorsement is one that makes the indorsee (almost always a bank) a collecting agent of the indorser [UCC 3–206(c)]. **Example 22.28** Stephanie Mallak has received a check and wants to deposit it into her checking account at the bank. She can indorse the check "For deposit [or collection] only. [Signed] Stephanie Mallak" (see Exhibit 22–8). She may also wish to write her bank account number on the check. A "For deposit" or "For collection" indorsement prohibits further negotiation except by the bank. Following this indorsement, only the bank can acquire the rights of a holder.

Restrictive Indorsement An indorsement on a negotiable instrument that requires the indorsee to comply with certain instructions regarding the funds involved.

Exhibit 22–8 "For Deposit" and "For Collection" Indorsements

For deposit only Stephanie Mallak   or   For Collection only Stephanie Mallak

11. *Green Tree Servicing, LLC v. Brandt*, 2015 -Ohio- 4636 (Ohio Ct. App. 2015).

Exhibit 22–9 Trust (Agency) Indorsements

| Pay to Anna Johnson in trust for Sarah Emerson *Robert Emerson* | or | Pay to Anna Johnson as Agent for Sarah Emerson *Robert Emerson* |

Trust (Agency) Indorsements. Indorsements to persons who are to hold or use the funds for the benefit of the indorser or a third party are called **trust indorsements** (also known as *agency indorsements*) [UCC 3–206(d), (e)]. **Example 22.29** Robert Emerson asks his accountant, Anna Johnson, to pay some bills for his invalid wife, Sarah, while he is out of the country. He indorses a check as follows: "Pay to Anna Johnson as Agent for Sarah Emerson." This agency indorsement obligates Johnson to use the funds only for the benefit of Sarah Emerson. ■ Exhibit 22–9 shows sample trust (agency) indorsements.

Trust Indorsements An indorsement to a person who is to hold or use funds for the benefit of the indorser or a third person. It is also known as an *agency indorsement.*

Misspelled Names A payee or indorsee whose name is misspelled can indorse with the misspelled name, the correct name, or both [UCC 3–204(d)]. The usual practice is to indorse with the name as it appears on the instrument, followed by the correct name.

Alternative or Joint Payees An instrument payable to two or more persons *in the alternative* (for example, "Pay to the order of Ramirez or Johnson") requires the indorsement of only one of the payees. In contrast, if an instrument is made payable to two or more persons *jointly* (for example, "Pay to the order of Shari and Bob Covington"), all of the payees' indorsements are necessary for negotiation.

Sometimes, an instrument payable to two or more persons does not clearly indicate whether it is payable in the alternative or jointly ("Pay to the order of John and/or Sara Fitzgerald" or "Pay to the order of J&D Landscaping, Bryson Maintenance"). In that situation, the instrument is payable to the persons alternatively [UCC 3–110(d)]. The same principles apply to special indorsements that identify more than one person to whom the indorser intends to make the instrument payable [UCC 3–205(a)].

22–3 Holder in Due Course (HDC)

Often, whether a holder is entitled to obtain payment will depend on whether the holder is a *holder in due course.* An ordinary holder obtains only those rights that the transferor had in the instrument and normally is subject to any defenses that could be asserted against the transferor. In contrast, a **holder in due course (HDC)** takes an instrument *free* of most of the defenses and claims that could be asserted against the transferor. To become an HDC, a holder must meet certain acquisition requirements.

Example 22.30 Shanna Morrison buys a BMW X3 SUV for her business from Heritage Motors in Irvine, California, signing a promissory note for $50,000 as part of the deal. Heritage negotiates the note to Apollo Financial Services, which promises to pay Heritage for it in six months. During the next two months, Morrison has significant problems with the SUV and sues Heritage for breach of contract. She also refuses to make further payments on the note.

Whether Apollo can hold Morrison liable on the note depends on whether it has met the requirements for HDC status. If Apollo has met these requirements and thus has HDC status, it is entitled to payment on the note. If Apollo has not met these requirements, it has the status of an ordinary holder, and Morrison's defense against payment to Heritage will also be effective against Apollo. ■

Holder in Due Course (HDC) A holder who acquires a negotiable instrument for value, in good faith, and without notice that the instrument is defective.

Learning Objective 3

What are three basic requirements for attaining the status of a holder in due course (HDC)?

22–3a Requirements for HDC Status

The basic requirements for attaining HDC status are set forth in UCC 3–302. A holder of a negotiable instrument is an HDC if she or he takes the instrument (1) for value, (2) in good faith, and (3) without notice that it is defective. Next, we examine each of these requirements.

Taking for Value An HDC must have given *value* for the instrument [UCC 3–302(a)(2)(i)]. A person who receives an instrument as a gift or inherits it has not met the requirement of value. In these situations, the person becomes an ordinary holder and does not possess the rights of an HDC.

Under UCC 3–303(a), a holder takes an instrument for value if the holder has done any of the following:

1. Performed the promise for which the instrument was issued or transferred.

2. Acquired a security interest or other lien in the instrument, excluding a lien obtained by a judicial proceeding.

3. Taken the instrument in payment of, or as security for, a preexisting claim. **Example 22.31** Zon owes Dwyer $2,000 on a past-due account. If Zon negotiates a $2,000 note signed by Gordon to Dwyer and Dwyer accepts it to discharge the overdue account balance, Dwyer has given value for the instrument. ▪

4. Given a negotiable instrument as payment for the instrument. **Example 22.32** Justin issues a six-month, $5,000 negotiable promissory note to Paige. Paige needs cash and does not want to wait for the maturity date to collect. She negotiates the note to her friend Kristen, who pays her $2,000 in cash and writes her a check—a negotiable instrument—for the balance of $3,000. Kristen has given full value for the note. ▪

5. Given an irrevocable commitment (such as a letter of credit) as payment for the instrument.

Value Is Distinguishable from Consideration. The concept of *value* in the law of negotiable instruments is not the same as the concept of *consideration* in the law of contracts. Although a promise to give value in the future is valid consideration to support a contract, it does not constitute sufficient value to make the promisor an HDC. If a person promises to perform or give value in the future, that person is not an HDC.

A holder takes an instrument for value *only to the extent that the promise has been performed* [UCC 3–303(a)(1)]. Let's return to *Example 22.30*, in which Heritage Motors negotiates Shanna Morrison's promissory note to Apollo Financial Services in return for Apollo's promise to pay in six months. In this example, Apollo is not an HDC. At the time of Morrison's breach of contract lawsuit against Heritage, Apollo has not yet paid Heritage for the note. Thus, it did not take the note for value. If Apollo had paid Heritage for the note at the time of transfer (given value), it would be an HDC and could have held Morrison liable on the note. Exhibit 22–10 illustrates these concepts further.

Exceptions. In a few situations, the holder may pay for the instrument but not acquire HDC status. For instance, when the instrument is purchased at a judicial sale, such as a bankruptcy or creditor's sale, the holder will not be an HDC. Similarly, if the instrument is acquired as a result of taking over a trust or an estate (as administrator), or as part of a corporate purchase of assets, the holder will have only the rights of an ordinary holder [UCC 3–302(c)].

Taking in Good Faith To qualify as an HDC, a holder must take the instrument in *good faith* [UCC 3–302(a)(2)(ii)]. This means that the holder must have acted honestly and observed reasonable commercial standards of fair dealing in the process of acquiring the instrument [UCC 3–103(a)(4)].

"Carpe per diem—seize the check.*"*

Robin Williams
1951–2014
(American comedian and actor)

Exhibit 22–10 Taking for Value

By exchanging defective goods (a defective BMW X3 SUV) for a promissory note, Heritage Motors breached its contract with Morrison. Morrison could assert this breach as a defense if Heritage presented the note to her for payment. Heritage exchanged the note for Apollo Financial Services' promise to pay in six months, however. Because Apollo did not take the note for value, it is not a holder in due course. Thus, Morrison can assert against Apollo the defense of Heritage's breach when Apollo submits the note to Morrison for payment. In contrast, if Apollo had taken the note for value, Morrison could not assert that defense and would be liable to pay the note.

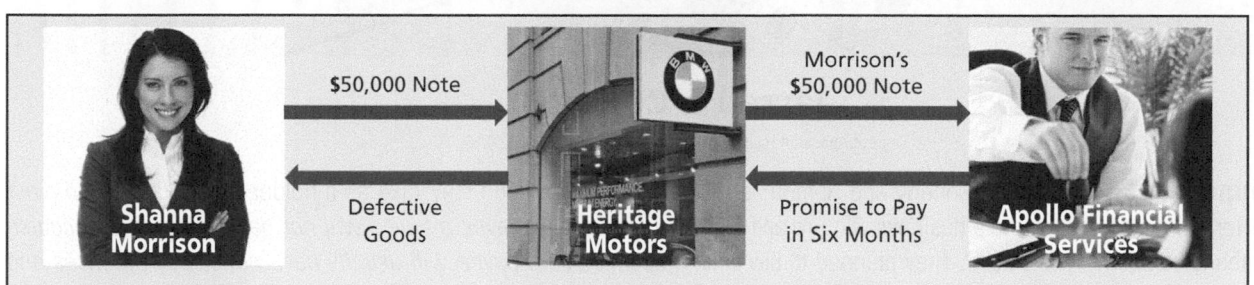

Jacob Wackerhausen/E+/Getty Images; Tupungato/Shutterstock; Wavebreakmedia/Getty Images

The good faith requirement applies only to the *holder*. It is immaterial whether the transferor acted in good faith. Thus, even a person who takes a negotiable instrument from a thief may become an HDC if the person acquired the instrument in good faith and honestly had no reason to be suspicious of the transaction.

✴ Spotlight Case Example 22.33 Cassandra Demery worked as a bookkeeper at Freestyle until the owner, Clinton Georg, discovered that she had embezzled more than $200,000. Georg fired Demery and demanded repayment. Demery went to work for her parents' firm, Metro Fixtures, where she had some authority to write checks. Without specific authorization, she wrote a check for $189,000 to Freestyle on Metro's account and deposited it in Freestyle's account. She told Georg that the check was a loan to her from her family.

When Metro discovered Demery's theft, it filed a suit against Georg and Freestyle. Freestyle argued that it had taken the check in good faith and was an HDC. The Colorado Supreme Court agreed. Demery was the wrongdoer. She had the authority to issue checks for Metro, and Georg had no reason to know that Demery had lied about this check. Therefore, Freestyle was an HDC, and Metro would bear the loss.[12]

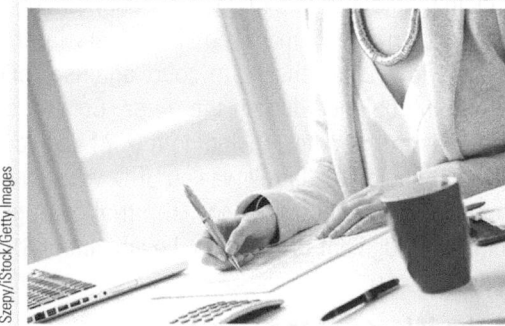

Szepy/iStock/Getty Images

Can a recipient of a check become an HDC when the person providing the check has check-writing authority?

Taking without Notice The final requirement for HDC status involves *notice* [UCC 3–302]. A person will not qualify for HDC protection if he or she is *on notice* (knows or has reason to know) that the instrument being acquired is defective in any one of the following ways [UCC 3–302(a)]:

1. It is overdue.

2. It has been dishonored.

3. It is part of a series of which at least one instrument has an uncured (uncorrected) default.

4. It contains an unauthorized signature or has been altered.

5. There is a defense against the instrument or a claim to it.

6. The instrument is so irregular or incomplete as to call its authenticity into question.

Typically, disputes involving the status of an HDC involve persons that acquire negotiable instruments from others. Therefore, taking without notice is a matter of whether the holder

---

12. *Georg v. Metro Fixtures Contractors, Inc.,* 178 P.3d 1209 (Colo. 2008).

has reason to know of a defect in the instrument. Sometimes, however, a person who is a party to the instrument claims HDC status. In the following case, the original payee on promissory notes issued to him when he contributed capital to a business that he co-owned claimed to be an HDC.

Case 22.3

Jarrell v. Conerly

Court of Appeal of Louisiana Fourth Circuit, 240 So.3d 266 (2018).

Background and Facts Jessie Conerly and Ramon Jarrell signed a letter of intent to enter into a business venture and form a limited liability company, K & M, LLC. They planned to buy land from Marion Clay & Gravel, LLC, and extract and sell the natural resources of sand, gravel, and clay from it. Jarrell would own 48 percent of the company and secure $6.8 million in start-up capital for the purpose of buying out the four members of Marion Clay. Jarrell would also receive 50 percent of the profits, provide oversight, and have access to all records and aspects of the operation. Conerly would own 52 percent of K & M, be responsible for daily operational management and oversight, and receive 50 percent of the profits.

After the letter-of-intent agreement, Jarrell began advancing capital to Conerly. Conerly issued four promissory notes (for the principal amounts of $40,000, $20,000, $22,000, and $22,000) naming Jarrell as the payee. Two years later, Jarrell filed a lawsuit in a Louisiana state court against Conerly for failing to pay the balance due on the notes. Conerly claimed several defenses to the notes, including lack of consideration, but the trial court held that Jarrell was an HDC, which precluded Conerly from asserting these defenses. The trial court granted a partial summary judgment to Jarrell in the amount of $104,000. Conerly appealed.

In the Words of the Court

MCKAY III, Chief Judge

* * * *

* * * Conerly argues that Jarrell is a holder, but not a holder in due course of the promissory notes in question. We find that assertion to have merit.

* * * *

Jarrell is the original payee on the four notes. However, *it is well settled in our jurisprudence that a payee on a note is not automatically a holder in due course.* [Emphasis added.]

* * * When the payee deals with the maker through an intermediary * * * and does not have notices of defenses, such an isolated payee may take as a holder in due course. *In most instances, however, a payee will not be a holder in due course because said payee will usually have notices of defenses and claims by virtue of the fact that he has dealt directly with the maker.* [Emphasis added.]

Here, the record reflects that Jarrell was closely involved in the original business venture. The Letter of Intent, which Jarrell signed, provides that: 1) Jarrell and Conerly agreed to form an LLC in order to acquire the Marion property and extract materials from the land; 2) Jarrell would be responsible to secure the $6.8 million in start-up capital; 3) Jarrell would own 48% of the LLC; 4) Jarrell would receive 50% of the profits from the venture; and 5) Jarrell would oversee the operation and have access to all records in connection with the operation. Given Jarrell's status as a payee, and his personal involvement in the formation and operation of the business venture, Jarrell is not a holder in due course. At the very least, there are questions of material fact on this issue. Moreover, because Jarrell is not a holder in due course, the notes are subject to the defenses advanced by Conerly, such as failure of consideration * * *.

* * * Conerly presented his sworn affidavit in support of his defenses to the notes [in which he stated:]

- Conerly informed Jarrell that the mortgage on the Marion Property was in danger of default;
- Conerly previously spent significant sums to prevent foreclosure;
- Conerly and Jarrell verbally agreed that in order to secure the Marion Property, the venture would have to prevent a foreclosure;
- Jarrell would provide Conerly with funds to pay the mortgage until Jarrell fulfilled his obligation to obtain financing for the venture;
- Jarrell asked Conerly to sign promissory notes as a formal means of recording and accounting for each of the mortgage payments, and that such recording would reflect Jarrell's personal investment in the business;

- Jarrell stated that the money provided to Conerly was an advancement of funds made in anticipation of the venture, and that it was understood that the funds would be paid back to Jarrell through the financing or from the profits of the venture, but not from Conerly personally;

* * * We find that the evidence presented by Conerly * * * casts doubt on the consideration for the notes * * *.

Decision and Remedy The state intermediate appellate court reversed the lower court's summary judgment and remanded the case for further proceedings. Because Jarrell was not an HDC on the four promissory notes, Conerly is entitled to present his legitimate defenses.

Critical Thinking

- **What If the Facts Were Different?** *If Jarrell had simply invested in K & M, but was not a co-owner and did not interact with Conerly, how might this have affected the outcome of this case?*

What Constitutes Notice? Under UCC 1–201(25), a person is considered to have notice in the following circumstances:

1. The person has actual knowledge of the defect.

2. The person has received a notice or notification concerning the defect (such as a letter from a bank identifying the serial numbers of stolen bearer instruments).

3. The person has reason to know that a defect exists, given all the facts and circumstances known at the time in question.

The holder must also have received notice "at a time and in a manner that gives a reasonable opportunity to act on it" [UCC 3–302(f)]. A purchaser's knowledge of certain facts, such as insolvency proceedings against the maker or drawer of the instrument, does not constitute notice that the instrument is defective [UCC 3–302(b)].

Overdue Instruments. What constitutes notice that an instrument is overdue depends on whether it is a demand instrument or a time instrument.

A purchaser has notice that a *demand instrument* is overdue in two situations. One situation occurs when a person takes the instrument knowing that demand already has been made. The other situation is when a person takes a demand instrument an unreasonable length of time after its date. For a check, a "reasonable time" is within ninety days after the date of the check. For all other demand instruments, what will be considered a reasonable time depends on the circumstances [UCC 3–304(a)].

Normally, a *time instrument* is overdue on the day after its due date. Anyone who takes a time instrument after the due date is on notice that it is overdue [UCC 3–304(b)(2)]. Thus, if a promissory note due on May 15 is purchased on May 16, the purchaser is an ordinary holder, not an HDC. If an instrument states that it is "Payable in thirty days," counting begins the day after the instrument is dated. Thus, a note dated December 1 that is payable in thirty days is due by midnight on December 31. If the payment date falls on a Sunday or holiday, the instrument is payable on the next business day.

Dishonored Instruments. An instrument is **dishonored** when the party to whom the instrument is presented refuses to pay it. If a holder knows or has reason to know that an instrument has been dishonored, the holder is on notice and cannot claim HDC status [UCC 3–302(a)(2)]. Thus, a person who takes a check clearly stamped "insufficient funds" is put on notice.

Conversely, if a person purchasing an instrument does not know and has no reason to know that it has been dishonored, the person is *not* put on notice and therefore can become an HDC. **Example 22.34** Leah Gonzalez holds a demand note dated September 1 issued by Apex, Inc., a local business firm. On September 17, she demands payment, and

Dishonor To refuse to pay or to accept a negotiable instrument that has been presented in a timely and proper manner.

Apex refuses (that is, dishonors the instrument). On September 22, Gonzalez negotiates the note to Brenner, a purchaser who lives in another state. Brenner does not know, and has no reason to know, that the note has been dishonored. Because Brenner is not put on notice, Brenner can become an HDC. ■

Notice of Claims or Defenses. A holder cannot become an HDC if she or he has notice of any claim to the instrument or any defense against it [UCC 3–302(a)(2)]. A purchaser has notice if the claims or defenses are apparent on the instrument's face or if the purchaser had reason to know of them from facts surrounding the transaction. Instruments with irregularities and incomplete instruments fall under this rule.

Any *irregularity* on the face of an instrument (such as an obvious forgery or alteration) that calls into question its validity or ownership will bar HDC status. A good forgery of a signature or the careful alteration of an instrument, however, can go undetected by reasonable examination. In that situation, the purchaser can qualify as an HDC.

In addition, a purchaser cannot become an HDC of an instrument so *incomplete* on its face that an element of negotiability is lacking (for instance, the amount is not filled in) [UCC 3–302(a)(1)]. Minor omissions (such as the omission of the date) are permissible, because these do not call into question the validity of the instrument [UCC 3–113(b)].

22–3b Holder through an HDC

A person who does not qualify as an HDC but who derives his or her title through an HDC can acquire the rights and privileges of an HDC. This rule, which is sometimes called the **shelter principle,** is set out in UCC 3–203(b). Under this rule, anyone—no matter how far removed from an HDC—who can ultimately trace his or her title back to an HDC may acquire the rights of an HDC. By extending the benefits of HDC status, the shelter principle promotes the marketability and free transferability of negotiable instruments.

There are some limitations on the shelter principle, though. If a holder participated in fraud or illegality affecting the instrument, that holder is not allowed to improve his or her status by repurchasing the instrument from a later HDC [UCC 3–203(b)]. Similarly, a holder who had notice of a claim or defense against an instrument cannot gain the benefits of HDC status by later reacquiring the instrument from an HDC.

22–4 Signature and Warranty Liability

Liability on negotiable instruments can arise either from a person's signature or from the warranties that are implied when the person presents the instrument for negotiation. A person who signs a negotiable instrument is potentially liable for payment of the amount stated on the instrument. Unlike signature liability, warranty liability does not require a signature and extends to both signers and nonsigners.

22–4a Signature Liability

The general rule is that every party, except a qualified indorser,[13] who signs a negotiable instrument is either primarily or secondarily liable for payment of that instrument when it comes due. Signature liability is contractual liability—no person will be held contractually liable for an instrument that he or she has not signed.

Know This
A difference between the handwriting in the body of a check and the handwriting in the signature does not affect the validity of the check.

Shelter Principle The principle that the holder of a negotiable instrument who cannot qualify as a holder in due course (HDC), but who derives his or her title through an HDC, acquires the rights of an HDC.

"Most men are admirers of justice—when justice happens to be on their side."

Richard Whately
1787–1863
(English theologian and logician)

---

13. A qualified indorser—one who indorses "without recourse"—undertakes no contractual obligation to pay. A qualified indorser merely assumes warranty liability.

Primary Liability Primary liability is unconditional. A person who is primarily liable on a negotiable instrument is absolutely required to pay the instrument—unless, of course, he or she has a valid defense to payment [UCC 3–305]. Only *makers* and *acceptors* of instruments are primarily liable.

The maker of a promissory note unconditionally promises to pay the note. It is the maker's promise to pay that makes the note a negotiable instrument. If the instrument was incomplete when the maker signed it, the maker is obligated to pay it according to its stated terms or according to terms that were agreed on and later filled in to complete the instrument [UCC 3–115, 3–407(a), 3–412].

Example 22.35 Tristan executes a preprinted promissory note to Sharon, without filling in the blank for a due date. If Sharon does not complete the form by adding the date, the note will be payable on demand. If Sharon subsequently fills in a due date that Tristan authorized, the note is payable on the stated due date. In either situation, Tristan (the maker) is obligated to pay the note.

As mentioned earlier, an acceptor is a drawee, such as a bank, that promises to pay an instrument when it is presented for payment. Once a drawee accepts a draft, the drawee is obligated to pay the draft when it is presented for payment [UCC 3–409(a)]. Failure to pay an accepted draft when presented leads to primary signature liability.

Secondary Liability *Drawers* and *indorsers* are secondarily liable. On a negotiable instrument, secondary liability is *contingent liability* (similar to that of a guarantor in a contract). In other words, a drawer or an indorser will be liable only if the party that is responsible for paying the instrument dishonors it by refusing to pay.

Parties are secondarily liable on a negotiable instrument *only if* the following events occur:[14]

1. The instrument is properly and timely presented.

2. The instrument is dishonored.

3. Timely notice of dishonor is given to the secondarily liable party.

Proper and Timely Presentment. Presentment occurs when a person presents an instrument either to the party liable on the instrument for payment or to a drawee for acceptance. The holder must present the instrument to the appropriate party in a proper and timely fashion and must give reasonable identification if requested [UCC 3–414(f), 3–415(e), 3–501]. The party to whom the instrument must be presented depends on the type of instrument involved. A note or CD is presented to the maker for payment. A draft is presented to the drawee for acceptance, payment, or both. A check is presented to the drawee for payment [UCC 3–501(a), 3–502(b)].

Presentment can be made by any commercially reasonable means, including oral, written, or electronic communication [UCC 3–501(b)]. Ordinarily, it is effective when received. (If presentment takes place after an established cutoff hour, though, it may be treated as occurring the next business day.)

Timeliness is important for proper presentment [UCC 3–414(f), 3–415(e), 3–501(b)(4)]. Failure to present an instrument on time is the most common reason for improper presentment. If the instrument is payable on demand, the holder should present it for payment or acceptance within a reasonable time. The holder of a domestic check must present that check for payment or collection within thirty days

Know This
A drawee is the party ordered to pay a draft or check, such as a bank or financial institution.

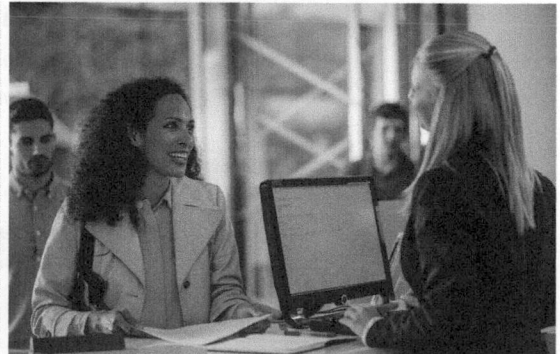
If this bank customer bought a certificate of deposit, how would she obtain payment for it when it comes due?

---

14. These requirements are necessary for a secondarily liable party to have signature liability on a negotiable instrument, but they are not necessary for a secondarily liable party to have warranty liability.

of its *date* to hold the drawer secondarily liable. With respect to indorsers, the holder must present a check within thirty days after its indorsement to hold the indorser secondarily liable. The time for proper presentment for various types of instruments is shown in Exhibit 22–11.

Dishonor. As mentioned, an instrument is dishonored when the required acceptance or payment is refused. It is also dishonored when acceptance or payment cannot be obtained within the prescribed time or when the required presentment is excused (as it would be, for instance, if the maker had died) and the instrument is not properly accepted or paid [UCC 3–502(e), 3–504].

In certain situations, a delay in payment or a refusal to pay an instrument will *not dishonor* the instrument.

1. When presentment is made after an established cutoff hour (not earlier than 2:00 P.M.), a bank can postpone payment until the following business day without dishonoring the instrument [UCC 3–501(b)(4)].

2. When the holder refuses (a) to exhibit the instrument, (b) to give reasonable identification, or (c) to sign a receipt for the payment on the instrument, then a bank's refusal to pay does not dishonor the instrument [UCC 3–501(b)(2)].

3. When an instrument is returned because it lacks a proper indorsement, the instrument is not dishonored [UCC 3–501(b)(3)(i)].

Proper Notice of Dishonor. Once an instrument has been dishonored, proper notice must be given to secondary parties (drawers and indorsers) for them to be held liable. **Example 22.36** Oscar writes a check on his account at People's Bank payable to Bess. Bess indorses the check in blank and cashes it at Midwest Grocery, which transfers it to People's Bank for payment. If People's Bank refuses to pay it, Midwest must timely notify Bess to hold her liable. ▪

Notice can be given in any reasonable manner, including an oral, written, or electronic communication, as well as notice written or stamped on the instrument itself. A bank must give any necessary notice before its midnight deadline (midnight of the next banking day after receipt). Notice by any party other than a bank must be given within thirty days following the day of dishonor or the day on which the person who is secondarily liable receives notice of dishonor [UCC 3–503].

Unauthorized Signatures   Unauthorized signatures arise in two situations:

1. When a person forges another person's name on a negotiable instrument.

2. When an agent who lacks the authority signs an instrument on behalf of a principal.

Exhibit 22–11 Time for Proper Presentment

TYPE OF INSTRUMENT	FOR ACCEPTANCE	FOR PAYMENT
Time	On or before due date.	On due date.
Demand	Within a reasonable time (after date of issue or after secondary party becomes liable on the instrument).	Within a reasonable time.
Check	Not applicable.	Within thirty days of its date, to hold drawer secondarily liable. Within thirty days of indorsement, to hold indorser secondarily liable.

The General Rule. The general rule is that an unauthorized signature is wholly inoperative and will not bind the person whose name is signed or forged. **Example 22.37** Parker finds Dolby's checkbook lying in the street, writes out a check to himself, and forges Dolby's signature. Banks normally have a duty to determine whether a person's signature on a check is forged. If a bank fails to determine that Dolby's signature is not genuine and cashes the check for Parker, the bank will generally be liable to Dolby for the amount.

The general rule also may apply to agents' signatures. If an agent lacks the authority to sign the principal's name or has exceeded the authority given by the principal, the signature does not bind the principal but will bind the "unauthorized signer" [UCC 3–403(a)].

Exceptions to the General Rule. There are two exceptions to the general rule that an unauthorized signature will not bind the person whose name is signed:

1. *Ratification.* When the person whose name is signed ratifies (affirms) the signature, he or she will be bound [UCC 3–403(a)]. For instance, a mother may ratify her daughter's forgery of the mother's signature so that the daughter will not be prosecuted. A person can ratify an unauthorized signature either expressly (by affirming the signature) or impliedly (by other conduct, such as keeping any benefits received in the transaction or failing to repudiate the signature).

2. *Negligence.* When the negligence of the person whose name was forged substantially contributed to the forgery, a court may not allow the person to deny the effectiveness of an unauthorized signature [UCC 3–115, 3–406, 4–401(d)(2)]. For instance, a person who signs a check but leaves blank the amount and payee's name and then leaves the check in a public place may be unable to deny liability for it.

Someone finds a checkbook on the sidewalk, writes out a check to himself, and forges the signature of the account holder. Is the bank liable to the true account holder if it cashes the forged check?

Special Rules for Unauthorized Indorsements

Generally, when an instrument has a forged or unauthorized indorsement, the burden of loss falls on the first party to take the instrument. The reason for this general rule is that the first party to take an instrument is in the best position to prevent the loss.

Example 22.38 Jen Nilson steals a check drawn on Universal Bank that is payable to the order of Inga Leed. Nilson indorses the check "Inga Leed" and presents the check to Universal Bank for payment. The bank, without asking Nilson for identification, pays the check, and Nilson disappears. Leed will not be liable on the check, because her indorsement was forged. The bank will bear the loss, which it might have avoided if it had asked Nilson for identification.

This general rule has two important exceptions that cause the loss to fall on the maker or drawer. These exceptions arise when an indorsement is made by an imposter or by a fictitious payee.

Imposter Rule. An **imposter** is one who, through deception, induces a maker or drawer to issue an instrument in the name of an impersonated payee. If the maker or drawer believes the imposter to be the named payee at the time of issue, the indorsement by the imposter is not treated as unauthorized when the instrument is transferred to an innocent party. This is because the maker or drawer *intended* the imposter to receive the instrument. In these situations, the unauthorized indorsement of a payee's name can be as effective as if the real payee had signed. The *imposter rule* provides that an imposter's indorsement will be effective—that is, not a forgery—insofar as the drawer or maker is concerned [UCC 3–404(a)].

Example 22.39 Carol impersonates Donna and induces Edward to write a check payable to the order of Donna. Carol, continuing to impersonate Donna, negotiates the check to First National Bank as payment on her loan there. As the drawer of the check, Edward is liable for its amount to First National.

Imposter One who induces a maker or drawer to issue a negotiable instrument in the name of an impersonated payee. Indorsements by imposters are treated as authorized indorsements under UCC Article 3.

Fictitious Payee A payee on a negotiable instrument whom the maker or drawer did not intend to have an interest in the instrument. Indorsements by fictitious payees are treated as authorized indorsements under UCC Article 3.

Fictitious Payee Rule. When a person causes an instrument to be issued to a payee who will have *no interest* in the instrument, the payee is referred to as a **fictitious payee**. A fictitious payee can be a person or firm that does not exist, or it may be an identifiable party that will not acquire any interest in the instrument. Under the UCC's *fictitious payee rule*, the payee's indorsement is not treated as a forgery, and an innocent holder can hold the maker or drawer liable on the instrument [UCC 3–404(b), 3–405]. Basically, the loss falls on the maker or drawer of the instrument rather than on the third party that accepts it or on the bank that cashes it.

Fictitious payees most often arise in two situations:

1. When a dishonest employee deceives the employer into signing an instrument payable to a party with no right to receive payment on the instrument.

2. When a dishonest employee or agent has the authority to issue an instrument on behalf of the employer and issues a check to a party who has no interest in the instrument.

Case Example 22.40 Braden Furniture Company gave its bookkeeper, Bonnie Manning, general authority to create checks. Over the course of seven years, Manning created more than two hundred unauthorized checks, totaling $470,000, which she deposited in her own account at Union State Bank. Braden Furniture was not a customer of the bank. Most of the checks did not identify a payee (the payee line was left blank). Braden Furniture (the drawer) sued Union State Bank for the loss, claiming that the bank had been negligent in accepting and paying the blank checks. The court, however, held that the fictitious payee rule applied. Therefore, under Alabama's version of the UCC, the loss fell on Braden Furniture, not on Union State Bank.[15]

A furniture company's bookkeeper created several unauthorized business checks for her personal use. How did the fictitious payee rule affect the dispute that arose over who suffered the loss of funds?

22–4b Warranty Liability

In addition to signature liability, transferors make certain implied warranties regarding the instruments that they are negotiating. Warranty liability arises even when a transferor does not sign the instrument [UCC 3–416, 3–417].

Warranty liability is particularly important when a holder cannot hold a party liable on her or his signature, such as when a person delivers a bearer instrument. *Unlike secondary signature liability, warranty liability is not subject to the conditions of proper presentment, dishonor, or notice of dishonor.*

Warranties fall into two categories: those that arise on the *transfer* of a negotiable instrument and those that arise on *presentment*. Both transfer and presentment warranties attempt to shift liability back to a wrongdoer or to the person who dealt face to face with the wrongdoer and thus was in the best position to prevent the wrongdoing.

Transfer Warranties A person who transfers an instrument *for consideration* makes the following five **transfer warranties** to all subsequent transferees and holders who take the instrument in good faith [UCC 3–416]:[16]

1. The transferor is entitled to enforce the instrument.

2. All signatures are authentic and authorized.

3. The instrument has not been altered.

Learning Objective 4

What is the difference between signature liability and warranty liability?

Transfer Warranty An implied warranty made by any person who transfers an instrument for consideration that the person is entitled to enforce the instrument, the signatures are authentic, it has not been altered, there are no defenses, and the transferor is unaware of any bankruptcy proceedings of parties to the instrument.

---

15. *Braden Furniture Co. v. Union State Bank*, 109 So.3d 625 (Ala. 2012). See also *State of Vermont v. Stewart*, 176 A.3d 1120 (Vt. 2017).

16. An amendment to UCC 3–416(a) adds a sixth warranty "with respect to a remotely created consumer item," such as an electronic check drawn on a consumer account, that is not created by the payor bank and does not contain the drawer's handwritten signature. Under this amendment, which fifteen states have adopted, a bank that accepts and pays the instrument warrants to the next bank in the collection chain that the consumer authorized the item in that amount.

4. The instrument is not subject to a defense or claim of any party that can be asserted against the transferor.

5. The transferor has no knowledge of any bankruptcy proceedings of the maker, the acceptor, or the drawer of the instrument.

Presentment Warranties A person who presents an instrument for payment or acceptance makes the following **presentment warranties** to anyone who in good faith pays or accepts the instrument [UCC 3–417(a), 3–417(d)]:

1. The person obtaining payment or acceptance is entitled to enforce the instrument or is authorized to obtain payment or acceptance on behalf of a person who is entitled to enforce the instrument. (This is, in effect, a warranty that there are no missing or unauthorized indorsements.)

2. The instrument has not been altered.

3. The person obtaining payment or acceptance has no knowledge that the signature of the issuer of the instrument is unauthorized.[17]

The second and third presentment warranties do not apply to makers, acceptors, and drawers when the presenter is an HDC. It is assumed that a drawer or a maker will recognize his or her own signature and that a maker or an acceptor will recognize whether an instrument has been materially altered.

Presentment warranties generally protect the person to whom the instrument is presented. They often have the effect of shifting liability back to the party that was in the best position to prevent the wrongdoing.

> **Presentment Warranty**
> An implied warranty made by any person who presents an instrument for payment or acceptance that he or she is entitled to enforce the instrument, that the instrument has not been altered, and that he or she is unaware of any unauthorized signatures.

22–5 Defenses, Limitations, and Discharge

Defenses can bar collection from persons who would otherwise be primarily or secondarily liable on a negotiable instrument. There are two general categories of defenses—*universal defenses* and *personal defenses*.

22–5a Universal Defenses

Universal defenses (also called *real defenses*) are valid against *all* holders, including HDCs and holders who take through an HDC. Universal defenses include those described here.

1. *Forgery of a signature on the instrument.* A forged signature will not bind the person whose name is used. Thus, when an instrument is forged, the person whose name is forged normally has no liability to pay any holder the value of the instrument. If the person whose name is forged ratifies the signature, however, he or she may be liable, as discussed earlier.

2. *Fraud in the execution.* If a person is deceived into signing a negotiable instrument by being told that it is something else, *fraud in the execution* is committed against the signer [UCC 3–305(a)(1)]. This defense cannot be raised, however, if reasonable inquiry would have revealed the nature and terms of the instrument.

   Example 22.41 Connor, a salesperson, asks Javier, a customer, to sign a paper. Connor says that it is a receipt for goods that Javier is picking up from the store. In fact, it is a promissory note, but Javier is unfamiliar with English and does not realize this. Here, even if the note is negotiated to an HDC, Javier has a valid defense against payment. (Note that the result might be different if Javier was an English speaker and could have read the words saying it was a promissory note.) ▪

3. *Material alteration.* An alteration is *material* if it changes the obligations of the parties in the instrument *in any way*. Material alterations include completing an incomplete instrument, adding

> **Universal Defense** A defense that can be used to avoid payment to all holders of a negotiable instrument, including a holder in due course (HDC) or a holder with the rights of an HDC. It is also called a real defense.

---

17. Amendments to Article 3 of the UCC provide additional protection for "remotely created" consumer items in the context of presentment also [see Amended UCC 3–417(a)(4)].

words or numbers, or making any unauthorized changes that affect the obligation of a party [UCC 3–407(a)]. Making any change in the instrument's amount, date, or rate of interest—even if the change is only 1 percent—is material. It is not a material alteration, however, to correct the maker's address or to change the figures on a check so that they agree with the written amount.

Material alteration is a *complete defense* against an ordinary holder, but only a *partial defense* against an HDC. Thus, an ordinary holder can recover nothing on an instrument that has been materially altered. An HDC can enforce the instrument against the maker or drawer according to its original terms but not for the altered amount.

4. *Discharge in bankruptcy.* Discharge in bankruptcy is an absolute defense on any instrument regardless of the status of the holder, because the purpose of bankruptcy is to settle all of the insolvent party's debts [UCC 3–305(a)(1)].

5. *Minority.* Minority, or infancy, is a universal defense only to the extent that state law recognizes it as a defense to a simple contract [UCC 3–305(a)(1)(i)].

6. *Illegality, mental incapacity, or extreme duress.* When the law declares an instrument to be void because it was issued in connection with illegal conduct, illegality is a universal defense. Similarly, if a court has declared a person who signed the instrument to be mentally incompetent, the instrument is void. If a person was under an immediate threat of force or violence (extreme duress, such as being held at gunpoint), the defense is universal, and the instrument is unenforceable by any holder or HDC [UCC 3–305(a)(1)(ii)].

Personal Defense A defense that can be used to avoid payment to an ordinary holder of a negotiable instrument but not a holder in due course (HDC) or a holder with the rights of an HDC. It is also called a *limited defense.*

22–5b Personal Defenses

Personal defenses (sometimes called *limited defenses*) are used to avoid payment to an ordinary holder of a negotiable instrument. They are not a defense against an HDC or a holder through an HDC. Personal defenses include the following:

1. *Breach of contract or breach of warranty.* When there is a breach of the underlying contract for which the negotiable instrument was issued, the maker of a note can refuse to pay it, or the drawer of a check can stop payment.

Learning Objective 5

What four defenses can be used against an ordinary holder that are not effective against an HDC?

2. *Lack or failure of consideration.* The absence of consideration may be a successful personal defense in some instances [UCC 3–303(b), 3–305(a)(2)]. **Example 22.42** Tara gives Clem, as a gift, a note that states, "I promise to pay you $100,000." Clem accepts the note. Because there is no consideration for Tara's promise, a court will not enforce the promise. ▪

3. *Fraud in the inducement (ordinary fraud).* A person who issues a negotiable instrument based on false statements by the other party will be able to avoid payment to an ordinary holder of that instrument.

4. *Illegality, mental incapacity, or ordinary duress.* If the law declares that an instrument is voidable because of illegality, mental incapacity, or ordinary duress, the defense is personal [UCC 3–305(a)(1)(ii)].

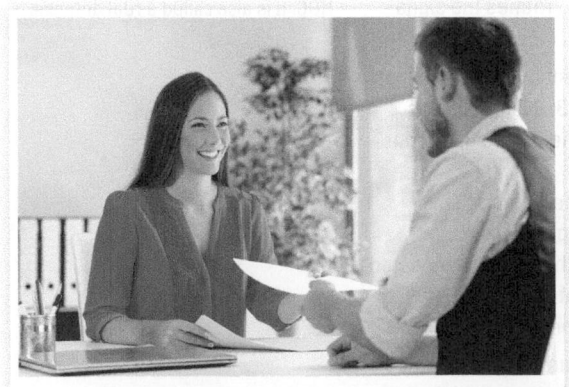

If a woman makes a gift to another person by writing out a note that says, "I promise to pay you $100,000," is the note enforceable? Why or why not?

22–5c Federal Limitations on the Rights of HDCs

The federal government limits the rights of HDCs in certain circumstances because of the harsh effects that the HDC rules can sometimes have on consumers. Under the HDC doctrine, a consumer who purchased a defective product (such as a defective automobile) would continue to be liable to HDCs even if the consumer returned the defective product to the retailer.

To protect consumers who purchase defective products, the Federal Trade Commission (FTC) adopted Rule 433, which effectively abolished the HDC doctrine in consumer transactions. How does this rule curb the rights of HDCs? See this chapter's *Landmark in the Law* feature to learn more.

Federal Trade Commission Rule 433

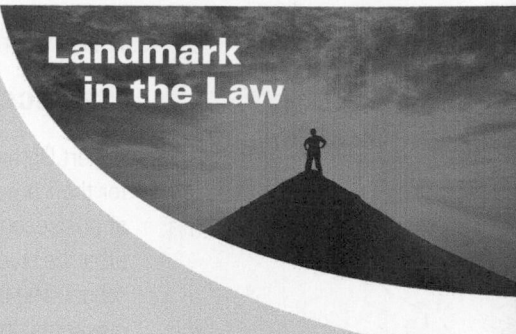

In 1976, the Federal Trade Commission (FTC) issued Rule 433,[a] which severely limited the rights of HDCs that purchase instruments arising out of consumer credit transactions. The rule, entitled "Preservation of Consumers' Claims and Defenses," applies to any seller or lessor of goods or services who takes or receives a consumer credit contract. The rule also applies to a seller or lessor who accepts as full or partial payment for a sale or lease the proceeds of any purchase-money loan[b] made in connection with any consumer credit contract.

Under the rule, these parties must include the following provision in the consumer credit contract:

Notice

ANY HOLDER OF THIS CONSUMER CREDIT CONTRACT IS SUBJECT TO

---

a. 16 C.F.R. Section 433.2. The rule was enacted pursuant to the FTC's authority under the Federal Trade Commission Act, 15 U.S.C. Sections 41–58.

b. In a *purchase-money loan*, a seller or lessor advances funds to a buyer or lessee, through a credit contract, for the purchase or lease of goods.

ALL CLAIMS AND DEFENSES WHICH THE DEBTOR COULD ASSERT AGAINST THE SELLER OF GOODS OR SERVICES OBTAINED PURSUANT HERETO OR WITH THE PROCEEDS HEREOF. RECOVERY HEREUNDER BY THE DEBTOR SHALL NOT EXCEED AMOUNTS PAID BY THE DEBTOR HEREUNDER.

Thus, a consumer who is a party to a consumer credit transaction can bring any defense she or he has against the seller of a product against a subsequent holder as well. In essence, the FTC rule places an HDC of the negotiable instrument in the position of a contract assignee. The rule makes the buyer's duty to pay conditional on the seller's full performance of the contract. Finally, the rule clearly reduces the degree of transferability of negotiable instruments resulting from consumer credit contracts.

What if the seller does not include the notice in a promissory note and then sells the note to a third party, such as a bank? In this situation, the seller has violated the rule, but the bank has not. Because the FTC rule does not prohibit third parties from purchasing notes or credit contracts that do not contain the required provision, the third party does not become subject to the buyer's defenses against the seller. Thus, a few consumers remain unprotected by the FTC rule.

Application to Today's World *The FTC rule has been invoked in many cases involving automobiles that turned out to be "lemons," even when the consumer credit contract did not contain the FTC notice. In these and similar actions, when the notice was not included in the contract, the courts have generally inferred its presence as a contract term.*

22–5d Discharge from Liability

Discharge from liability on an instrument can come from payment, cancellation, or material alteration. The liability of all parties is discharged when the party primarily liable on the instrument pays to the holder the full amount due [UCC 3–602, 3–603]. Payment by any other party (such as an indorser) discharges only the liability of that party and subsequent parties.

Intentional cancellation by the holder discharges the liability of all parties [UCC 3–604]. Intentionally writing "Paid" across the face of an instrument cancels it, as does intentionally tearing it up. If a holder intentionally crosses out a party's signature, that party's liability and the liability of subsequent indorsers who have already indorsed the instrument are discharged.

Materially altering an instrument may discharge the liability of any party affected by the alteration, as previously discussed [UCC 3–407(b)]. An HDC may be able to enforce a materially altered instrument against its maker or drawer according to the instrument's original terms, however.

Discharge of liability can also occur when a holder impairs another party's right of recourse (right to seek reimbursement) on the instrument [UCC 3–605]. This occurs when, for instance, the holder releases, or agrees not to sue, a party against whom the indorser has a right of recourse.

Practice and Review

Robert Durbin, a student, borrowed funds from a bank for his education and signed a promissory note for their repayment. The bank loaned the funds under a federal program designed to assist students at postsecondary institutions. Under this program, repayment ordinarily begins nine to twelve months after the student borrower fails to carry at least one-half of the normal full-time course load at his or her school. The federal government guarantees that the note will be fully paid. If the student defaults on the payments, the lender presents the current balance—principal, interest, and costs—to the government. When the government pays the balance, it becomes the lender, and the borrower owes the government directly. After Durbin defaulted on his note, the government paid the lender the balance due and took possession of the note. Durbin then refused to pay the government, claiming that the government was not the holder of the note. The government filed a suit in a federal district court against Durbin to collect the amount due. Using the information presented in the chapter, answer the following questions.

1. Was the note that Durbin signed an order to pay or a promise to pay? Explain.

2. Suppose that the note did not state a specific interest rate but instead referred to a statute that established the maximum interest rate for government-guaranteed student loans. Would the note fail to meet the requirements for negotiability in that situation? Why or why not?

3. How does a party who is not named in a negotiable instrument (in this situation, the government) obtain a right to enforce the instrument?

4. Now suppose that the school Durbin attended closed down before he could finish his education. In court, Durbin argues that this resulted in a failure of consideration: he did not get something of value in exchange for his promise to pay. Assuming that the government is a holder of the promissory note, will this argument likely be successful against it? Why or why not?

Debate This

We should eliminate the status of holder in due course for those who possess negotiable instruments.

Key Terms

acceleration clause 505
acceptance 498
acceptor 498
bearer 506
bearer instrument 506
blank indorsement 510
certificate of deposit (CD) 500
check 498
dishonor 517
draft 497
drawee 497
drawer 497

extension clause 506
fictitious payee 522
holder 505
holder in due course (HDC) 513
imposter 521
indorsement 510
maker 499
negotiable instrument 497
negotiation 509
order instrument 506
payee 497

personal defense 524
presentment 504
presentment warranty 523
promissory note 499
qualified indorsement 511
restrictive indorsement 512
shelter principle 518
special indorsement 511
transfer warranty 522
trust indorsement 513
universal defense 523

Chapter Summary: Negotiable Instruments

Formation of Negotiable Instruments	1. *Types of negotiable instruments*—The UCC specifies four types of negotiable instruments: drafts, checks, promissory notes, and certificates of deposit (CDs). These instruments fall into two basic classifications:

     a. *Demand instruments versus time instruments*—A demand instrument is payable on demand (when the holder presents it to the maker or drawer). A time instrument is payable at a future date.

     b. *Orders to pay versus promises to pay*—Checks and drafts are orders to pay. Promissory notes and CDs are *promises* to pay.

2. *Requirements for negotiability*—To be negotiable, an instrument must meet the following requirements.

     a. *Be in writing*—A writing can be on anything that is readily transferable and has a degree of permanence [UCC 3–103(a) (6), (9)].

     b. *Be signed by the maker or drawer*—The signature can be anyplace on the face of the instrument, can be in any form (including a rubber stamp), can consist of any name (including a trade name), and can be made in a representative capacity [UCC 3–103(a)(3), 3–401(b)].

     c. *Be an unconditional promise or order to pay*—

       1. A promise must be more than a mere acknowledgment of a debt [UCC 3–103(a)(6), (9)].

       2. Such words as "pay on demand" meet this criterion.

       3. Only unconditional promises or orders can be negotiable [UCC 3–106(a)].

     d. *State a fixed amount of money*—

       1. An amount is considered a fixed sum if it is ascertainable from the face of the instrument or (for an interest rate) readily determinable by a formula described by the instrument [UCC –104(a), 3–112(b)].

       2. Any medium of exchange recognized as the currency of a government is money [UCC 3–201(24)].

     e. *Be payable on demand or at a definite time*—

       1. Any instrument that is payable on sight, presentation, or issue, or that does not state any time for payment, is a demand instrument [UCC 3—104(a)(2)].

       2. An instrument is payable at a definite time if it states that it is payable on a stated date, within a fixed period after presentment, or on a date or time readily ascertainable at the time of issue. [UCC 3–108(a), (b), (c)].

       3. Acceleration clauses allow a payee or other holder of a time instrument to demand payment of the entire amount due, with interest, if a certain event occurs. Extension clauses allow the date of maturity to be extended into the future [UCC 3-108(b)(iii), (iv)].

     f. *Be payable to order or bearer*—

       1. An order instrument must identify the payee with certainty.

       2. An instrument that indicates it is not payable to an identified person is payable to bearer [UCC 3–109(a)(3)].

3. *Factors that do not affect negotiability*—Certain ambiguities (such as differences between words and figures) or omissions (such as when an instrument is undated) normally will not affect an instrument's negotiability.

Transfer of Instruments	1. *Transfer by assignment*—A transfer by assignment to an assignee gives the assignee only those rights that the assignor possessed. Any defenses against payment that can be raised against an assignor normally can be raised against the assignee.

2. *Transfer by negotiation*—An order instrument is negotiated by indorsement and delivery. A bearer instrument is negotiated by delivery only.

3. *Indorsements*—

     a. Blank indorsements do not specify a particular indorsee and can consist of a mere signature (see Exhibit 22–5).

     b. Special indorsements contain the signature of the indorser and identify the indorsee (see Exhibit 22–6).

(Continues)

    c. Qualified indorsements contain language, such as "without recourse," that indicates the indorser is not guaranteeing payment of the instrument (see Exhibit 22–7).

    d. Restrictive indorsements, such as "For deposit only," require the indorsee to comply with certain instructions regarding the funds involved, but do not prohibit further negotiation of the instrument (see Exhibit 22–8).

    e. An instrument payable to two or more persons in the alternative requires the indorsement of only one of the payees. An instrument payable to two or more individuals jointly must be indorsed by all of the payees.

Holder in Due Course (HDC)	**1.** *Holder*—A person in possession of an instrument drawn, issued, or indorsed to him or her, to his or her order, to bearer, or in blank. A holder obtains only those rights that the transferor had in the instrument.
	
	2. *Holder in due course (HDC)*—A holder who, by meeting certain acquisition requirements, takes an instrument free of most defenses and claims to which the transferor was subject.
	
	3. *Requirements for HDC status*—To be an HDC, a holder must take the instrument:
	  a. For value—A holder can take an instrument for value in five ways: by performing the promise, acquiring a security interest or other lien in the instrument, taking the instrument as payment (or security) for a preexisting obligation, giving the instrument as payment, or giving an irrevocable commitment as payment [UCC 3–303].
	  b. In good faith—A holder can take an instrument in good faith by acting honestly and observing commercial standards of fair dealing.
	  c. Without notice—To be an HDC, a holder must not be on notice that the instrument is defective because it is overdue, has been dishonored, is part of a series of which at least one instrument has a uncured defect, contains an unauthorized signature or has been altered, has a defense against it or a claim to it, or is so irregular or incomplete as to call its authenticity into question.
	
	4. *Shelter principle*—A holder who cannot qualify as an HDC has the *rights* of an HDC if the holder derives her or his title through an HDC, unless the holder engaged in fraud or illegality affecting the instrument [UCC 3–203(b)] or had notice of a claim or defense against an instrument.

Signature and Warranty Liability	Liability on negotiable instruments can arise either from a person's signature or from the warranties that are implied when a person presents the instrument for negotiation.
	
	1. *Signature liability*—Every party (except a qualified indorser) who signs a negotiable instrument is either primarily (unconditionally) or secondarily liable for payment of the instrument when it comes due.
	  a. Primary liability—Makers and acceptors are primarily liable [UCC 3–115, 3–407, 3–409, 3–412].
	  b. Secondary liability—Drawers and indorsers are secondarily liable [UCC 3–412, 3–414, 3–415, 3–501, 3–502, 3–503]. Parties are secondarily liable on an instrument only if presentment is proper and timely, the instrument is dishonored, and they received timely notice of dishonor.
	
	2. *Transfer warranties*—Any person who transfers an instrument for consideration makes five warranties to subsequent transferees and holders [UCC 3–416].
	  a. The transferor is entitled to enforce the instrument.
	  b. All signatures are authentic and authorized.
	  c. The instrument has not been altered.
	  d. The instrument is not subject to a defense or claim of any party that can be asserted against the transferor.
	  e. The transferor has no knowledge of any bankruptcy proceedings against the maker, the acceptor, or the drawer of the instrument.
	
	3. *Presentment warranties*—Any person who presents an instrument for payment or acceptance makes three warranties to any person who in good faith pays or accepts the instrument [UCC 3–417(a), 3–417(d)].
	  a. The person is entitled to enforce the instrument or is authorized to act on behalf of a person who is so entitled.
	  b. The instrument has not been altered.
	  c. The person has no knowledge that the drawer's signature is unauthorized.

Defenses, Limitations, and Discharge	1. *Universal (real) defenses*—The following defenses are valid against all holders, including HDCs and holders with the rights of HDCs [UCC 3–305, 3–403, 3–407]:
	  a. Forgery.
	  b. Fraud in the execution.
	  c. Material alteration.
	  d. Discharge in bankruptcy.
	  e. Minority—if the contract is voidable under state law.
	  f. Illegality, mental incapacity, or extreme duress—if the contract is void under state law.
	2. *Personal (limited) defenses*—The following defenses are valid against ordinary holders but not against HDCs or holders with the rights of HDCs [UCC 3–303, 3–305]:
	  a. Breach of contract or breach of warranty.
	  b. Lack or failure of consideration.
	  c. Fraud in the inducement.
	  d. Illegality, mental incapacity, or ordinary duress—if the contract is voidable.
	3. *Federal limitations on the rights of HDCs*—Rule 433 of the Federal Trade Commission limits the rights of HDCs who purchase instruments arising out of consumer transactions. The rule allows a consumer who is a party to such a transaction to bring any defense he or she has against the seller against a subsequent holder as well, even if the subsequent holder is an HDC.
	4. *Discharge from liability*—All parties to a negotiable instrument will be discharged when the party primarily liable on it pays to the holder the full amount due. Discharge can also occur in other circumstances (if the instrument has been canceled or materially altered, for example) [UCC 3–602 through 3–605].

Issue Spotters

1. Sabrina owes $600 to Yale, who asks Sabrina to sign an instrument for the debt. If written on the instrument by Sabrina, which of the following would prevent its negotiability: "I.O.U. $600," "I promise to pay $600," or an instruction to the bank stating, "I wish you would pay $600 to Yale"? Why? (See *Formation of Negotiable Instruments.*)

2. Rye signs corporate checks for Suchin Corporation. Rye writes a check payable to U-All Company, even though Suchin does not owe U-All anything. Rye signs the check, forges U-All's indorsement, and cashes the check at Viceroy Bank, the drawee. Does Suchin have any recourse against the bank for the payment? Why or why not? (See *Signature and Warranty Liability.*)

—**Check your answers to the *Issue Spotters* against the answers provided in Appendix D at the end of this text.**

Business Scenarios and Case Problems

22–1. Negotiable Instruments. Muriel Evans writes the following note on the back of an envelope: "I, Muriel Evans, promise to pay Karen Marvin or bearer $100 on demand." Is this a negotiable instrument? Discuss fully. (See *Formation of Negotiable Instruments.*)

22–2. Material Alteration. Williams purchased a used car from Stein for $1,000. Williams paid for the car with a check (written in pencil) payable to Stein for $1,000. Stein, through careful erasures and alterations, changed the amount on the check to read $10,000 and negotiated the check to Boz. Boz took the check for value, in good faith, and without notice of the alteration and thus met the Uniform Commercial Code's requirements for the status of a holder in due course. Can Williams successfully raise the universal (real) defense of material alteration to avoid payment on the check? Explain. (See *Defenses, Limitations, and Discharge.*)

22–3. Indorsements. Angela Brock borrowed $544,000 and signed a note payable to Amerifund Mortgage Services, LLC, to buy a house in Silver Spring, Maryland. The note was indorsed in blank and transferred several times "without recourse" before Brock fell behind on the payments. On behalf of Deutsche Bank National Trust Co., BAC Home Loans Servicing LP initiated foreclosure. Brock filed an action in a Maryland state court to block it, arguing that BAC could not foreclose because Deutsche Bank, not BAC, owned the note. Can BAC enforce the note? Explain. [*Deutsche Bank National Trust Co. v. Brock*, 63 A.3d 40 (Md. 2013)] (See *Transfer of Instruments.*)

22–4. Transfer by Negotiation. Thao Thi Duong signed a note in the amount of $200,000 in favor of Country Home Loans, Inc., to obtain a loan to buy a house in Marrero, Louisiana. The note was indorsed "PAY TO THE ORDER OF [blank space] WITHOUT RECOURSE COUNTRY HOME LOANS, INC." Almost five years later, Duong defaulted on the payments. The Federal National Mortgage Association (Fannie Mae) had come into possession of the note. Fannie Mae wanted to foreclose on the house and sell it to recover the balance due. Duong argued that the words "to the order of [blank space]" in the indorsement made the note an incomplete order instrument and that Fannie Mae thus could not enforce it. What is Fannie Mae's best response to this argument? [*Federal National Mortgage Association v. Thao Thi Duong*, 167 So.3d 920 (La.App. 5 Cir. 2015)] (See *Transfer of Instruments*.)

22–5. Payable to Order or to Bearer. Thomas Caraccia signed a note and mortgage in favor of VirtualBank to obtain funds to buy property in Palm Beach Gardens, Florida. VirtualBank indorsed the note in blank, making it bearer paper, and transferred possession of the note to Bank of America. Bank of America transferred the note to U.S. Bank, which later gave the note back to Bank of America to collect Caraccia's payments on behalf of U.S. Bank. When Caraccia defaulted on the payments, U.S. Bank filed a suit in a Florida state court against him, seeking to enforce the note and foreclose on the property. Caraccia contended that because the note was indorsed in blank and was not in the physical possession of U.S. Bank, the bank could not enforce it. Could the bank successfully argue that although it did not *physically* possess the note, it *constructively* possessed (exercised legal control over) it? Explain. [*Caraccia v. U.S. Bank, National Association*, 41 Fla.L.Weekly D476, 185 So.3d 1277 (Dist.Ct.App. 2016)] (See *Formation of Negotiable Instruments*.)

22–6. Business Case Problem with Sample Answer— Indorsements. Denise and Nick Purificato signed a note secured by real property in Florida. The note was transferred through several parties to Aurora Loan Services, LLC. The Purificatos defaulted on the payments. Aurora filed a suit in a Florida state court against them, seeking a judgment of foreclosure to recover the unpaid debt. While proceedings were pending, Nationstar Mortgage, LLC, succeeded Aurora and became the plaintiff in the suit. At trial, Nationstar provided a screenshot of the note and an attachment, which had been imaged as a single document before Aurora filed the complaint against the Purificatos. Nationstar also provided the original note and attachment, which had a series of indorsements that ended in a blank indorsement. The attachment stated that it was "affixed and a permanent part of said note." Did this evidence establish that the attachment was sufficiently affixed to the note to prove Nationstar's status as the holder with the right to enforce it? Discuss. [*Purificato v. Nationstar Mortgage, LLC*, 41 Fla.L.Weekly D104, 182 So.3d 821 (Dist.Ct.App. 2016)] (See *Transfer of Instruments*.)

—For a sample answer to Problem 22–6, go to Appendix E at the end of this text.

22–7. Signature Liability. Guillermo and Guadalupe Albarran and their sons, Ruben and Rolando, owned R Cleaning Impact, Inc. (RCI). Neresh Kumar owned Amba II, Inc., a check-cashing business. The Albarrans cashed checks through Amba on a regular basis, often delivering a stack of employee paychecks to Amba for cashing. Later, the Albarrans' bank refused payment on some of the checks. Kumar learned that some of these items were payable to fictitious payees with fictitious addresses. Others had been filled out for amounts greater than real employees' pay. Meanwhile, RCI became insolvent and closed its account, and Guillermo and Guadalupe filed for bankruptcy. Amba was left with many unpaid checks. Among these parties, who can be held liable for the loss on the unpaid checks? Explain. [*Albarran v. Amba II, Inc.*, 2016 WL 688924 (Md. 2016)] (See *Signature and Warranty Liability*.)

22–8. Holder in Due Course. Robert Triffin purchased a dishonored payroll check from Fair Law Financial Services (doing business as United Check Cashing) and filed a complaint against the maker seeking to collect on the check. The check was issued by Extensis Group, LLC, to Maria Pagan in the amount of $610. The face of the check clearly stated "THE FACE OF THIS DOCUMENT HAS A COLORED BACKGROUND NOT A WHITE BACKGROUND." But the check that Triffin introduced into evidence had a white background. The check also stated "THE BACK OF THIS DOCUMENT CONTAINS A UNIQUE IDENTITY BARCODE AND AN ARTIFICIAL WATERMARK— HOLD AT AN ANGLE TO VIEW," but Triffin's check did not have this barcode or watermark. Was Triffin an HDC? Why or why not? [*Triffin v. Extensis Group, LLC*, 2018 WL 548613 (N.J.Super. Ct.App.Div. 2018)] (*See Holder in Due Course.*)

22–9. A Question of Ethics—The IDDR Approach and Unconditional Promise or Order to Pay. *Carlos Pardo signed a note to obtain $627,500 to buy a house in Stamford, Connecticut. The note was secured by a mortgage. Later, Pardo signed a loan modification agreement that increased the balance due. The modification was not referenced in the note. Deutsche Bank National Trust Company came to possess the note. When Pardo defaulted on the payments, Deutsche Bank filed a suit in a Connecticut state court against him to recover the unpaid balance. Pardo maintained that the bank could not enforce the note. He argued that the bank was not a holder because the note was not a negotiable instrument—the loan modification agreement rendered it conditional. [Deutsche Bank National Trust Co. v. Pardo, 170 Conn.App. 642, 155 A.3d 764 (2017)] (See Formation of Negotiable Instruments.)*

1. Was it ethical of Deutsche Bank to sue to recover the unpaid balance on Pardo's note? Explain, using the steps of the IDDR approach.

2. Is Pardo correct about the status of the note? Was it ethical to make this argument? Discuss.

Critical Thinking and Writing Assignments

22–10. Time-Limited Group Assignment—Negotiability.

Peter Gowin was an employee of a granite counter-top business owned by Joann Stathis. In November 2019, Gowin signed a promissory note agreeing to pay $12,500 in order to become a co-owner of the business. The note was dated January 15, 2019 (ten months before it was signed), and required him to make installment payments starting in February 2019. Stathis told Gowin not to worry about the note and never requested any payments. Gowin continued to work at the business until 2021, when he quit, claiming that he owned half of the business. Stathis argued that Gowin was not a co-owner because he had never paid the $12,500 into the business. (See *Formation of Negotiable Instruments*.)

1. The first group will argue in favor of Stathis that Gowin did not own any interest in the business.
2. The second group will evaluate the strength of Gowin's argument. Gowin claimed that because compliance with the stated dates was impossible, the note effectively did not state a date for its payment. It therefore was a demand note under UCC 3–108(a). Because no demand for payment had been made, Gowin's obligation to pay had not arisen, and the termination of his ownership interest was improper.
3. The third group will create a list with expanation and examples detailing under what circumstances oral statements by Stathis to Gowin can be enforced or can be used as a defense by Gowin.

23 | International and Space Law

Learning Objectives

The five Learning Objectives *below are designed to help improve your understanding. After reading this chapter, you should be able to answer the following questions:*

1. What is the act of state doctrine? In what circumstances is this doctrine applied?

2. Why would a U.S. firm enter into a distribution agreement?

3. What does it mean for the World Trade Organization to grant "normal trade relations status"?

4. What federal law allows U.S. citizens, as well as citizens of foreign nations, to file civil actions in U.S. courts for torts that were committed overseas?

5. What treaty provides a framework for international space law?

International Law Law—based on international customs, organizations, and treaties—that governs relations among nations.

"The merchant has no country."

Thomas Jefferson
1743–1826
(Third president of the United States, 1801–1809)

Commerce has always crossed national borders, as President Thomas Jefferson noted in the chapter-opening quotation. But technology has fueled dramatic growth in world trade and the emergence of a global business community. Because exchanges of goods, services, and intellectual property on a global level are now routine, students of business law and the legal environment should be familiar with the laws pertaining to international business transactions.

Suppose that Ryan, a popular Olympic snowboarder, starts an outdoor-wear business and begins manufacturing his own snowboarding gear. The business grows, and Ryan's factory is no longer able to keep up with the demand for his products. Ryan is considering opening a manufacturing plant in China, where labor costs are lower and there are fewer government regulations. Before he decides, he needs to understand the relevant laws. He also needs to know how the business will be taxed when his goods are imported back into the United States or shipped to other nations. This chapter introduces you to some of the legal considerations involved in doing business globally, including the emerging area of space law.

23-1 International Law

Laws affecting the international legal environment of business include both international law and national law. **International law** can be defined as a body of law—formed as a result of international customs, treaties, and organizations—that governs relations among or between nations. **National law** is the law of a particular nation, such as Brazil, Germany, Japan, or the United States. In some ways, national laws that involve restrictions applied at a nation's borders effectively become international law. (Can officials legally search electronic devices, including laptops and smartphones, of persons who cross national borders? See this chapter's *Beyond Our Borders* feature for the answer.)

National Law Law that pertains to a particular nation.

Border Searches of Your Electronic Devices

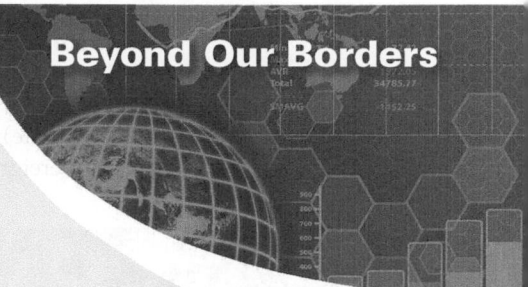

Beyond Our Borders

Every year, tens of millions of travelers arrive at U.S. borders, where they are subject to a search. Of these travelers, about 12 million undergo a secondary screening, and approximately five thousand of these screenings involve an electronic device. About three hundred devices—laptops, tablets, and smartphones—are sent to the Immigration and Customs Enforcement forensics laboratory in Fairfax, Virginia, for further examination.

The U.S. government has historically had broad power to search travelers and their property when they enter this country. That power includes the right to inspect papers and other physical documents in the possession of anyone entering the United States, including U.S. citizens.

Increasingly, however, instead of being carried in physical form, documents are carried on the hard drives of laptop computers, in tablets, or in smartphones. Indeed, a person might have thousands of photos, e-mails, video clips, and documents on the hard drive of a laptop. Does the government's power to conduct border searches give it the right to rummage through all of the data on an electronic device?

A Legal Challenge to Extensive Searches of Electronic Devices

When Pascal Abidor, a Ph.D. student who has dual U.S. and French citizenship, traveled by train from Canada to New York, U.S. Customs and Border Control agents pulled him aside and required him to log on to his computer. They then examined much

of its contents. Abidor was released after a few hours, but the Department of Homeland Security kept his laptop for eleven days.

Abidor challenged the search. His complaint alleged that the suspicionless search of U.S. citizens' electronic devices at international borders violates their constitutional right to privacy. The lawsuit was dismissed when a federal court concluded that Abidor lacked standing to challenge the government's border search policies.[a]

Routine versus Forensic Searches of Electronic Devices

In another case, Ali Saboonchi and his wife were stopped at the border on returning from a day trip to the Canadian side of Niagara Falls. Saboonchi was a dual citizen of the United States and Iran. His name had been flagged in the Homeland Security database because of information from the FBI concerning inquiries he had made about specialized technology with possible medical or military applications. Customs officials performed a secondary search of Saboonchi's vehicle and questioned him and his wife. The officials allowed the couple to reenter the country, but seized two of Saboonchi's smartphones and a flash drive and sent them to Virginia for further testing.

A week later, customs officials returned Saboonchi's electronics. The government then filed criminal charges against Saboonchi in federal court for violating

U.S. export restrictions on trade with Iran. The indictment alleged that he had sold specialized equipment to a company in the United Arab Emirates that was linked to a company in Iran. His digital devices had contained contact information about the companies involved, along with other evidence.

Saboonchi argued that the evidence had been illegally seized and that the information obtained from his electronic devices should be excluded from trial. The court recognized a difference between routine border searches and forensic border searches, which involve experts using specialized software. Forensic searches, according to the court, require reasonable suspicion. Nevertheless, the court concluded that the government had reasonable suspicion that Saboonchi was involved in violations of export restrictions.[b]

Critical Thinking

What are some steps that businesspersons can take to avoid issues at the border with respect to the contents of their electronic devices?

a. *Abidor v. Napolitano*, 990 F.Supp.2d 260 (E.D.N.Y. 2013).

b. *United States v. Saboonchi*, 990 F.Supp.2d 536 (D. Md. 2014). See also *United States v. Kolsuz*, 185 F.Supp.3d 843 (E.D.Va. 2016); and *United States v. Molina-Isidoro*, 884 F.3d 287 (5th Cir. 2018).

The major difference between international law and national law is that a nation's government authorities can enforce its national law. What government, however, can enforce international law? By definition, a *nation* is a sovereign entity—meaning that there is no higher authority to which that nation must submit.

If a nation violates an international law and persuasive tactics fail, other countries or international organizations have no recourse except to take coercive actions. Coercive actions may include economic sanctions, severance of diplomatic relations, boycotts, and, as a last resort, war against the violating nation. **Example 23.1** Russia sent troops into the neighboring nation of Ukraine and supported an election that allowed Crimea (part of Ukraine) to secede from Ukraine. Because Russia's actions violated Ukraine's independent sovereignty, the United States and the European Union imposed economic sanctions on Russia. Nevertheless, Russia continued to support military action in Eastern Ukraine. ■

In essence, international law is the result of centuries-old attempts to reconcile the need of each country to be the final authority over its own affairs with the desire of nations to benefit economically from trade and harmonious relations with one another. Sovereign nations can, and do, voluntarily agree to be governed in certain respects by international law for the purpose of facilitating international trade and commerce, as well as civilized discourse. As a result, a body of international law has evolved.

When Russia sent troops into Ukraine, what did the United States and Western Europe do?

23–1a Sources of International Law

Basically, there are three sources of international law: international customs, treaties and international agreements, and international organizations.

International Customs One important source of international law consists of the customs that have evolved among nations in their relations with one another. Article 38(1) of the Statute of the International Court of Justice refers to an international custom as "evidence of a general practice accepted as law." The legal principles and doctrines that you will read about shortly are rooted in international customs and traditions that have evolved over time in the international arena.

Treaties and International Agreements Treaties and other explicit agreements between or among foreign nations provide another important source of international law. A **treaty** is an agreement or contract between two or more nations that must be authorized and ratified by the supreme power of each nation. Under Article II, Section 2, of the U.S. Constitution, the president has the power "by and with the Advice and Consent of the Senate, to make Treaties, provided two thirds of the Senators present concur."

Treaty A formal international agreement negotiated between two nations or among several nations.

A *bilateral* agreement, as the term implies, is an agreement formed by two nations to govern their commercial exchanges or other relations with one another. A *multilateral* agreement is formed by several nations. For instance, regional trade associations such as the Andean Common Market (ANCOM), the Association of Southeast Asian Nations (ASEAN), and the European Union (EU) are the result of multilateral trade agreements.

International Organization An organization composed mainly of member nations and usually established by treaty—for instance, the United Nations. More broadly, the term also includes nongovernmental organizations (NGOs), such as the Red Cross.

International Organizations In international law, the term **international organization** generally refers to an organization that is composed mainly of member nations and usually established by treaty. The United States is a member of more than one hundred bilateral and multilateral organizations, including at least twenty through the United Nations.

Adopt Standards. International organizations adopt resolutions, declarations, and other types of standards that often require nations to behave in a particular manner. The General Assembly of the United Nations, for instance, has adopted numerous nonbinding resolutions and declarations that embody principles of international law. Disputes involving these resolutions and declarations may be brought before the International Court of Justice. That court, however, normally has authority to settle legal disputes only when nations voluntarily submit to its jurisdiction.

Create Uniform Rules. International organizations may also create uniform rules. The United Nations Commission on International Trade Law has made considerable progress in establishing uniformity in international law as it relates to trade. One of the commission's most significant creations to date is the 1980 Convention on Contracts for the International Sale of Goods (CISG).

The CISG is similar to Article 2 of the Uniform Commercial Code. It is designed to settle disputes between parties to sales contracts if the parties have not agreed otherwise in their contracts. The CISG governs only sales contracts between trading partners in nations that have ratified the CISG, however.

23–1b International Principles and Doctrines

Over time, a number of legal principles and doctrines have evolved and have been employed by the courts of various nations to resolve or reduce conflicts that involve a foreign element. The three important legal principles and doctrines discussed next are based primarily on courtesy and respect, and are applied in the interests of maintaining harmonious relations among nations.

Comity The principle by which one nation defers to and gives effect to the laws and judicial decrees of another nation. This recognition is based primarily on respect.

Act of State Doctrine A doctrine providing that the judicial branch of one country will not examine the validity of public acts committed by a recognized foreign government within its own territory.

The Principle of Comity Under the principle of **comity,** one nation will defer to and give effect to the laws and judicial decrees of another country, as long as they are consistent with the law and public policy of the accommodating nation. For instance, a U.S. court ordinarily will recognize and enforce a default judgment from an Australian court because the legal procedures in Australia are compatible with those in the United States. Nearly all nations recognize the validity of marriage decrees (at least, those between a man and a woman) issued in another country.

Case Example 23.2 Karen Goldberg's husband was killed in a terrorist bombing in Israel. She filed a lawsuit in a federal court in New York against UBS AG, a Switzerland-based global financial services company with many offices in the United States. Goldberg claimed that UBS was liable under the U.S. Anti-Terrorism Act for aiding and abetting the murder of her husband because it provided financial services to the terrorist organizations responsible.

UBS argued that the case should be transferred to a court in Israel, which would offer a remedy "substantially the same" as the one available in the United States. The court refused, however. Transferring the case would require an Israeli court to take evidence and judge the emotional damage suffered by Goldberg, "raising distinct concerns of comity and enforceability."[1]

The Act of State Doctrine The **act of state doctrine** provides that the judicial branch of one country will not examine the validity of public acts committed by a recognized foreign government within its own territory.

Case Example 23.3 Spectrum Stores, Inc., a gasoline retailer in the United States, filed a lawsuit in a U.S. court against Citgo Petroleum Corporation, which is owned by the government of Venezuela. Spectrum alleged that Citgo had conspired with other oil companies in Venezuela and Saudi Arabia to limit production of crude oil and thereby fix the prices of petroleum products sold in the United States. Because Citgo is owned by a foreign

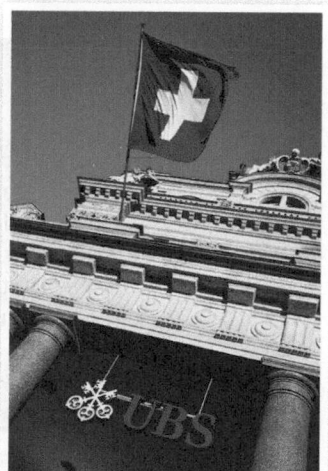

Can a U.S. citizen sue Swiss-based bank UBS for providing financial support to a terrorist organization somewhere else in the world?

1. *Goldberg v. UBS AG,* 690 F.Supp.2d 92 (E.D.N.Y. 2010).

Learning Objective 1

What is the act of state doctrine? In what circumstances is this doctrine applied?

Expropriation A government's seizure of a privately owned business or personal property for a proper public purpose and with just compensation.

Confiscation A government's taking of a privately owned business or personal property without a proper public purpose or an award of just compensation.

Sovereign Immunity A doctrine that immunizes foreign nations from the jurisdiction of U.S. courts when certain conditions are satisfied.

In the 1930s, Germany's Nazi regime forced a group of Jewish art dealers to sell a famous collection of medieval art. Years later, was Germany entitled to sovereign immunity when Jewish descendants sued to have the artworks returned?

government, the U.S. court dismissed the case under the act of state doctrine. A government controls the natural resources, such as oil reserves, within its territory. A U.S. court will not rule on the validity of a foreign government's acts within its own territory.[2]

When a Foreign Government Takes Private Property. The act of state doctrine can have important consequences for individuals and firms doing business with, and investing in, other countries. This doctrine is frequently employed in situations involving expropriation or confiscation.

Expropriation occurs when a government seizes a privately owned business or privately owned goods for a proper public purpose and awards just compensation. When a government seizes private property for an illegal purpose or without just compensation, the taking is referred to as a **confiscation**. The line between these two forms of taking is sometimes blurred because of differing interpretations of what is illegal and what constitutes just compensation.

Example 23.4 Flaherty, Inc., a U.S. company, owns a mine in Brazil. The government of Brazil seizes the mine for public use and claims that the profits that Flaherty realized from the mine in preceding years constitute just compensation. Flaherty disagrees, but the act of state doctrine may prevent the company's recovery in a U.S. court. ▮ Note that in a case alleging that a foreign government has wrongfully taken the plaintiff's property, the defendant government has the burden of proving that the taking was an expropriation, not a confiscation.

Doctrine May Immunize a Foreign Government's Actions. When applicable, both the act of state doctrine and the doctrine of *sovereign immunity* (to be discussed next) tend to shield foreign nations from the jurisdiction of U.S. courts. As a result, firms or individuals who own property overseas generally have little legal protection against government actions in the countries in which they operate.

Case Example 23.5 In 2017, a federal district court ruled that the United States had jurisdiction over an art theft claim against Germany that dated back to the Nazi regime. The plaintiffs, including Alan Philipp, were descendants of Jewish art dealers in Frankfurt who had owned the Welfenschatz collection of medieval art. The plaintiffs argued that the art dealers had been terrorized by the Nazis and forced to sell the collection in 1935 for much less than its market price. (Adolf Hitler had allegedly discussed in letters how Nazis should take action to "save the Welfenschatz.") Germany claimed that the U.S. court did not have jurisdiction, but the federal judge disagreed. The court was convinced by the plaintiffs that Germany was not entitled to sovereign immunity in this case.[3] ▮

The Doctrine of Sovereign Immunity When certain conditions are satisfied, the doctrine of **sovereign immunity** immunizes foreign nations from the jurisdiction of U.S. courts. In 1976, Congress codified this rule in the Foreign Sovereign Immunities Act (FSIA).[4] The FSIA exclusively governs the circumstances in which an action may be brought in the United States against a foreign nation, including attempts to attach a foreign nation's property. Because the law is jurisdictional in nature, a plaintiff has the burden of showing that a defendant is not entitled to sovereign immunity. See Exhibit 23–1 for a graphic illustration of the three principles of international law under discussion.

---

2. *Spectrum Stores, Inc. v. Citgo Petroleum Corp.*, 632 F.3d 938 (5th Cir. 2011).
3. *Philipp v. Federal Republic of Germany*, 248 F.Supp.3d 59 (D.D.C. 2017).
4. 28 U.S.C. Sections 1602–1611.

Exhibit 23–1 Examples of International Principles and Doctrines

The Principle of Comity	The Act of State Doctrine	The Doctrine of Sovereign Immunity
Nations will defer and give effect to the laws and judicial decrees of other nations when those laws are consistent with their own.	U.S. courts will avoid passing judgment on the validity of public acts committed by a recognized foreign government within its own territory.	Foreign nations are immune from U.S. jurisdiction under the Foreign Sovereign Immunities Act when certain circumstances are satisfied. Some major exceptions apply.
Example: A U.S. court will most likely uphold the validity of a contract created in England, because England's legal procedures are compatible with those in the United States.	*Example:* A U.S. gas company files a lawsuit against a Saudi Arabian petroleum company, claiming a price-fixing conspiracy. A U.S. court will dismiss the case under the act of state doctrine because Saudi Arabia controls its own natural resources.	*Example:* A German governmental agency engages in commercial activity in New York. If a party in New York files a lawsuit against the agency, the foreign state is not immune from U.S. jurisdiction.

When a Foreign State Will Not Be Immune. Section 1605 of the FSIA sets forth the major exceptions to the jurisdictional immunity of a foreign state. A foreign state is not immune from the jurisdiction of U.S. courts in the following situations:

1. When the foreign state has waived its immunity either explicitly or by implication.
2. When the foreign state has engaged in commercial activity within the United States or in commercial activity outside the United States that has "a direct effect in the United States."
3. When the foreign state has committed a tort in the United States or has violated certain international laws.
4. When a foreign state that has been designated "a state sponsor of terrorism" is sued under the FSIA for "personal injury or death that was caused by an act of torture" or a related act of terrorism.

The following case involved an action to attach and execute a judgment against the property of a foreign state that had been held liable for the results of acts of terrorism.

■ **Case 23.1**

Rubin v. Islamic Republic of Iran

United States Supreme Court, __ U.S. __, 138 S.Ct. 816, __ L.Ed.2d __ (2018).

Background and Facts Hamas, a terrorist organization sponsored by the Islamic Republic of Iran, carried out three suicide bombings in Jerusalem, causing the deaths of five people and injuring nearly two hundred others. Jenny Rubin and other U.S. citizens who were injured or related to those injured obtained a judgment under Section 1605A of the Foreign Sovereign Immunities Act (FSIA) against Iran for $71.5 million in damages.

To collect on the judgment, the plaintiffs sued Iran in a federal district court under Section 1610(g) of the FSIA. The plaintiffs sought to attach and execute against a collection of ancient art owned by Iran that was currently being housed at the University of Chicago. The court ruled in the defendant's favor, finding that Section 1610(g) did not deprive the art collection of the immunity typically afforded to the property of a foreign sovereign. The

(Continues)

plaintiffs appealed. The U.S. Court of Appeals for the Seventh Circuit affirmed. The plaintiffs petitioned the United States Supreme Court.

In the Words of the Court
Justice *SONYA SOTOMAYER* delivered the opinion of the Court.
* * * *

* * * Section 1610(g) provides: * * * "The property of a foreign state against which a judgment is entered under Section 1605A * * * is subject to attachment in aid of execution, and execution, upon that judgment as provided in this section."

* * * The issue at hand is whether Section 1610(g) * * * allows a Section 1605A judgment holder to attach and execute against *any* property of the foreign state.
* * * *

* * * The most natural reading is that "this section" refers to Section 1610 as a whole, so that Section 1610(g) will govern the attachment and execution of property that is exempted from the grant of immunity as provided elsewhere in Section 1610.

Other provisions of Section 1610 unambiguously revoke the immunity of property of a foreign state, including specifically where a plaintiff holds a judgment under Section 1605A, provided certain express conditions are satisfied. For example, [Section 1610(a)] provides that "property in the United States * * * used for a commercial activity in the United States * * * shall not be immune" from attachment and execution in seven enumerated circumstances * * *. [Section 1610(b), (d), (e), and (f)] similarly set out circumstances in which certain property of a foreign state "shall not be immune."

Section 1610(g) conspicuously lacks the textual markers, "shall not be immune" or "notwithstanding any other provision of law," that would have shown that it serves as an independent avenue

for abrogation [abolition] *of immunity.* In fact, its use of the phrase "as provided in this section" signals the opposite: A judgment holder seeking to take advantage of Section 1610(g) must identify a basis under one of Section 1610's express immunity-abrogating provisions to attach and execute against a relevant property. [Emphasis added.]
* * * *

Throughout the FSIA, special avenues of relief to victims of terrorism exist * * *. Where the FSIA goes so far as to divest a foreign state or property of immunity in relation to terrorism-related judgments, however, it does so expressly. Out of respect for the delicate balance that Congress struck in enacting the FSIA, we decline to read into the statute a blanket abrogation of attachment and execution immunity for Section 1605A judgment holders absent a clearer indication of Congress' intent.

Decision and Remedy The United States Supreme Court concluded that Section 1610(g) does not provide "a freestanding basis for parties holding a judgment under Section 1605A to attach and execute against the property of a foreign state, where the immunity of the property is not otherwise rescinded under a separate provision within Section 1610." The Court affirmed the judgment of the federal appellate court.

Critical Thinking

• **Legal Environment** *Is the Court's interpretation of Section 1610(g) consistent with the purpose of the FSIA? Explain.*

• **Economic** *What practical lesson might be learned from the decision and result in the Rubin case? Discuss.*

Application of the Act. When courts apply the FSIA, questions frequently arise as to whether an entity is a "foreign state" and what constitutes a "commercial activity." Under Section 1603 of the FSIA, a *foreign state* includes both a political subdivision of a foreign state and an instrumentality of a foreign state. An *instrumentality* includes any department or agency of any branch of a government.

Section 1603 broadly defines a *commercial activity* as a regular course of commercial conduct, transaction, or act that is carried out by a foreign state within the United States. Section 1603, however, does not describe the particulars of what constitutes a commercial activity. Thus, the courts are left to decide whether a particular activity is governmental or commercial in nature. (This chapter's *Business Law Analysis* feature illustrates how courts decide whether an activity is commercial.)

Sovereign Immunity Claims

Taconic Plastics, Ltd., is a manufacturer incorporated in Ireland with its principal place of business in New York. Taconic enters into a contract with a German firm, Werner Voss Architects and Engineers, which is acting as an agent for the government of Saudi Arabia. The contract calls for Taconic to supply special materials for tents designed to shelter religious pilgrims visiting holy sites in Saudi Arabia. Most of the material is made in, and shipped from, New York. When the German company does not pay Taconic and files for bankruptcy, Taconic sues the government of Saudi Arabia in a U.S. court, seeking to collect $3 million. Is Saudi Arabia entitled to sovereign immunity?

Analysis: Under the doctrine of sovereign immunity, foreign nations are presumed to be immune from the jurisdiction of U.S. courts unless one of the exceptions in the Foreign Sovereign Immunity Act (FSIA) applies. One of the main exceptions under the FSIA (when a U.S. court will have jurisdiction) is the commercial activity exception. A government undertaking qualifies as commercial activity when the government acts as a "private player" in the marketplace. Here, the German firm was acting as an agent for Saudi Arabia. The agency relationship allowed Saudi Arabia to "step into the shoes" of a private player—the German construction firm—to complete the tent project.

Result and Reasoning: Based on these facts, Saudi Arabia should not be entitled to sovereign immunity. The government of Saudi Arabia was acting as a private company through its German agent to contract with Taconic in the United States. Also, substantial parts of the contract were performed in the United States because the materials for the tents were made in New York and shipped to Germany. Thus, the U.S. courts should have jurisdiction over this claim against Saudi Arabia.

23–2 Doing Business Internationally

A U.S. domestic firm can engage in international business transactions in a number of ways. The simplest way is for U.S. firms to **export** their goods and services to markets abroad. Alternatively, a U.S. firm can establish foreign production facilities so as to be closer to the foreign market or markets in which its products are sold.

Export The sale of goods and services by domestic firms to buyers located in other countries.

Is it ethical (and legal) to brew "imported" beer brands domestically? One-quarter of the beer sold in the United States is imported. Imported beer typically costs more than domestic beer, but the people who buy and drink it believe that its superior taste justifies the higher price. Many consumers are unaware that beers marketed as imported are often made in the United States. For instance, people think of Beck's beer as German, but for a number of years, Beck's has been brewed in St. Louis, Missouri. Foster's beer ads feature Australian countryside scenes, yet Foster's is brewed in Fort Worth, Texas. Killian's Irish Red is brewed in Colorado, not in Ireland. The Japanese beer Sapporo sold in the United States is actually brewed in Canada.

A number of lawsuits have been filed against the owners of imported beer brands made in the United States for misleading country-of-origin labels. One such suit was filed against

Ethical Issue

(Continues)

Anheuser-Busch Companies, LLC, for mislabeling the origin of Beck's beer. The plaintiffs argued that labels, such as "brewed under the German Purity Law" and "originated in Bremen, German," were misleading because the beer was brewed in the United States. The defendants pointed out that each beer bottle stated that it was a "Product of U.S.A." The case was ultimately settled out of court, and the company gave purchasers a right to apply for up to $50 in refunds.[5] Another case was filed in New York against Sapporo U.S.A., Inc., for misleading labels. A federal district court dismissed that action, however, because the beer label clearly stated it was "Brewed and canned [or bottled] by Sapporo Brewing Company, Guelph, Ontario, Canada."[6]

23–2a Exporting

Exporting can take two forms: direct and indirect. In *direct exporting,* a U.S. company signs a sales contract with a foreign purchaser that provides for the conditions of shipment and payment for the goods. If sufficient business develops in a foreign country, a U.S. company may set up a specialized marketing organization in that country. This is called *indirect exporting* and may be accomplished through the use of an agency relationship or a distributorship.

Agency Relationships When a U.S. firm prefers to limit its involvement in an international market, it will typically establish an *agency relationship* with a foreign firm. The foreign firm then acts as the U.S. firm's agent and can enter into contracts in the foreign location on behalf of the principal (the U.S. company).

Distributorships When a foreign country represents a substantial market, a U.S. firm may wish to appoint a distributor located in that country. The U.S. firm and the distributor enter into a **distribution agreement**. This is a contract setting out the terms and conditions of the distributorship, such as price, currency of payment, guarantee of supply availability, and method of payment. Disputes concerning distribution agreements may involve jurisdictional or other issues, as well as contract law.

23–2b Manufacturing Abroad

An alternative to direct or indirect exporting is the establishment of foreign manufacturing facilities. The advantages of manufacturing abroad may include lower costs, fewer government regulations, and lower taxes and trade barriers.

Typically, U.S. firms establish manufacturing plants abroad if they believe that doing so will reduce their costs—particularly for labor, shipping, and raw materials. Lower costs will enable the firms to compete more effectively in foreign markets. Japanese manufacturers, such as Canon, Hitachi, and Toyota, have established U.S. plants to avoid import duties that the U.S. Congress may impose on Japanese products entering this country.

A domestic firm may engage in manufacturing abroad by licensing its technology to an existing foreign company. Alternatively, it may establish overseas subsidiaries or participate in joint ventures.

Licensing A U.S. firm may license a foreign manufacturing company to use its copyrighted, patented, or trademarked intellectual property or trade secrets. A licensing agreement with a foreign-based firm is much the same as any other licensing agreement. Its terms require a payment of royalties on some basis—such as so many cents per unit produced or a certain percentage of profits from units sold in a particular geographic territory. **Example 23.6** The

To reduce exporting costs, some international companies have their beer produced in U.S.-based facilities. How might this situation upset import-beer enthusiasts?

Steve Cukrov/Alamy

Distribution Agreement A contract between a seller and a distributor of the seller's products setting out the terms and conditions of the distributorship.

Learning Objective 2

Why would a U.S. firm enter into a distribution agreement?

---

5. *Marty v. Anheuser-Busch Companies, LLC,* 43 F.Supp.3d 1333 (S.D. Fl. 2014), and 2016 WL 397593 (S.D. Fl. 2016).
6. *Bowring v. Sapporo U.S.A., Inc.,* 234 F.Supp.3d 386 (E.D.N.Y. 2017).

Coca-Cola Bottling Company licenses firms worldwide to use (and keep confidential) its secret formula for the syrup used in its soft drink. In return, the foreign firms licensed to make the syrup pay Coca-Cola a percentage of the income earned from the sale of the soft drink.

The firm that receives the license can take advantage of an established reputation for quality. The firm that grants the license receives income from the foreign sales of its products and also establishes a global reputation. Once a firm's trademark is known worldwide, the demand for other products manufactured or sold by that firm may increase. Franchising is a well-known form of licensing.

Subsidiaries A U.S. firm can also expand into a foreign market by establishing a wholly owned subsidiary firm in a foreign country. When a wholly owned subsidiary is established, the parent company, which remains in the United States, retains complete ownership of all the facilities in the foreign country, as well as complete authority and control over all phases of the operation.

Joint Ventures A *joint venture* provides another method that a U.S. firm can use to expand into international markets. In a joint venture, the U.S. company owns only part of the operation. The rest is owned either by local owners in the foreign country or by another foreign entity. All of the firms involved in a joint venture share responsibilities, as well as profits and liabilities.

23–2c International Dispute Resolution

International contracts frequently include arbitration clauses. By means of such clauses, the parties agree in advance to be bound by the decision of a specified third party in the event of a dispute.

The New York Convention The United Nations Convention on the Recognition and Enforcement of Foreign Arbitral Awards (often referred to as the *New York Convention*) assists in the enforcement of arbitration clauses, as do provisions in specific treaties among nations. The New York Convention has been implemented in nearly one hundred countries, including the United States.

Under the New York Convention, a court will compel the parties to arbitrate their dispute if all of the following are true:

1. There is a written (or electronically recorded) agreement to arbitrate the matter.
2. The agreement provides for arbitration in a convention signatory nation.
3. The agreement arises out of a commercial legal relationship.
4. One party to the agreement is not a U.S. citizen. In other words, both parties cannot be U.S. citizens.

Case Example 23.7 Juridica Investments, Ltd. (JIL), entered into a financing contract with S&T Oil Equipment & Machinery, Ltd., a U.S. company. The contract was signed and performed in Guernsey, which is a British Crown dependency located in the English Channel. The contract included an arbitration clause. When a dispute arose between the parties, JIL initiated arbitration in Guernsey, and S&T filed a suit in a U.S. court. JIL filed a motion to dismiss in favor of arbitration, which the court granted. S&T appealed.

A federal appellate court affirmed and compelled arbitration under the New York Convention. The court explained that all of the necessary requirements for compelling arbitration had been met.[7]

Effect of Choice-of-Law and Forum-Selection Clauses If an international contract does not include an arbitration clause, litigation may occur. When the contract contains forum-selection and choice-of-law clauses, the lawsuit will be heard by a court in the specified forum and decided according to that forum's law.

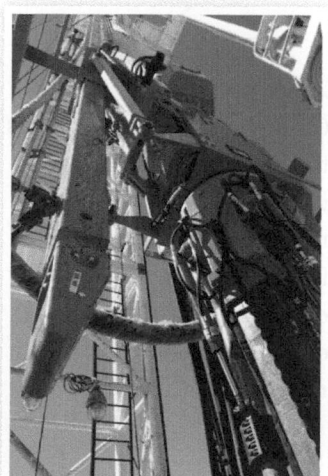

How did the New York Convention affect S&T Oil's contract with an investment company?

---

7. *S&T Oil Equipment & Machinery, Ltd. v. Juridica Investments, Ltd.*, 456 Fed.Appx. 481 (5th Cir. 2012).

Forum-Selection Clause A provision in a contract designating the court, jurisdiction, or tribunal that will decide any disputes arising under the contract.

Choice-of-Law Clause A clause in a contract designating the law (such as the law of a particular state or nation) that will govern the contract.

"The notion dies hard that in some sort of way exports are patriotic but imports are immoral."

Lord Harlech
1918–1985
(British writer)

As you may recall, a **forum-selection clause** indicates what court, jurisdiction, or tribunal will decide any disputes arising under the contract. A **choice-of-law clause** designates the applicable law. Both are useful additions to international contracts.

23–3 Regulation of Specific Business Activities

Doing business abroad can affect the economies, foreign policies, domestic policies, and other national interests of the countries involved. For this reason, nations impose laws to restrict or facilitate international business. Controls may also be imposed by international agreements. Here, we discuss how different types of international activities are regulated.

23–3a Investment Protections

Firms that invest in foreign nations face the risk that the foreign government may take possession of the investment property. Expropriation, as already mentioned, occurs when property is taken and the owner is paid just compensation. Expropriation generally does not violate observed principles of international law.

Confiscation occurs when property is taken without compensation (or without adequate compensation). Unlike expropriation, confiscation normally violates international law. Few remedies are available for confiscation of property by a foreign government, however. Claims are often resolved by lump-sum settlements after negotiations between the United States and the taking nation.

Because the possibility of confiscation may deter potential investors, many countries guarantee that foreign investors will be compensated if their property is taken. A guaranty can take the form of statutory laws or provisions in international treaties. As further protection for foreign investments, some countries provide insurance for their citizens' investments abroad.

23–3b Export Controls

The U.S. Constitution provides in Article I, Section 9, that "No Tax or Duty shall be laid on Articles exported from any State." Thus, Congress cannot impose export taxes. Congress can, however, use a variety of other methods to restrict or encourage exports, including the following:

1. *Export quotas.* Congress sets export quotas on various items, such as grain being sold abroad.

2. *Restrictions on technology exports.* Under the Export Administration Act,[8] the flow of technologically advanced products and technical data can be restricted.

3. *Incentives and subsidies.* Incentives and subsidies are used to stimulate some exports and thereby aid domestic businesses. **Example 23.8** The Export Trading Company Act[9] encouraged U.S. banks to invest in export trading companies, which are formed when exporting firms join together to export a line of goods. The Export-Import Bank of the United States has provided financial assistance, primarily in the form of credit guaranties given to commercial banks that, in turn, lend funds to U.S. exporting companies. ■

23–3c Import Controls

Import restrictions include strict prohibitions, quotas, and tariffs. Under the Trading with the Enemy Act,[10] for instance, no goods may be imported from nations that have been designated enemies of the United States. Other laws prohibit the importation of illegal drugs and agricultural products that pose dangers to domestic crops or animals. The import of

Know This
Countries restrict exports for several reasons, including to protect national security, to further foreign policy objectives, and to conserve resources (or raise their prices).

---

8. 50 U.S.C. Sections 2401–2420.
9. 15 U.S.C. Sections 4001, 4003.
10. 12 U.S.C. Section 95a.

goods that infringe U.S. patents is also prohibited. The International Trade Commission investigates allegations that imported goods infringe U.S. patents. The commission imposes penalties if necessary.

Quotas Limits on the amounts of goods that can be imported are known as **quotas.** At one time, the United States had legal quotas on the number of automobiles that could be imported from Japan. Today, Japan "voluntarily" restricts the number of automobiles exported to the United States. (But Japanese automakers build most cars sold in the United States in U.S. factories.)

Quota A set limit on the amount of goods that can be imported.

Tariffs Taxes on imports are called **tariffs.** A tariff usually is a percentage of the value of the import, but it can be a flat rate per unit (such as, per barrel of oil). Tariffs raise the prices of imported goods. The effect is to cause some consumers to purchase more domestically manufactured goods. **Example 23.9** In 2017, President Donald Trump imposed tariffs on foreign steel and aluminum. In 2018, the president announced that those tariffs would extend to goods imported to the United States from Canada and Mexico. Opponents argued that the tariffs would start a trade war. Canada, China, the European Union, and Mexico retaliated by levying tariffs on U.S. goods that they import. ■

Tariff A tax on imported goods.

Antidumping Duties The United States has specific laws directed at what it sees as unfair international trade practices. **Dumping,** for instance, is the sale of imported goods at "less than fair value." *Fair value* is usually based on the price of those goods in the exporting country. Foreign firms that engage in dumping in the United States hope to undersell U.S. businesses to obtain a larger share of the U.S. market. To prevent this, an extra tariff—known as an *antidumping duty*—may be assessed on the imports. The duty may be retroactive to cover past dumping.

Two U.S. government agencies are instrumental in imposing antidumping duties: the International Trade Commission (ITC) and the International Trade Administration (ITA). The ITC assesses the effects of dumping on domestic businesses and then makes recommendations to the president concerning temporary import restrictions. The ITA, which is part of the Department of Commerce, decides whether imports were sold at less than fair value. The ITA's determination establishes the amount of antidumping duties, which equals the difference between the price charged in the United States and the price charged in the exporting country.

In the following case, a Chinese producer and importer challenged the ITC's determination that the import of their products into the United States materially injured the domestic industry.

What are some potential consequences if President Donald Trump announces new tariffs on imported goods?

Dumping The sale of goods in a foreign country at a price below the price charged for the same goods in the domestic market.

■ Case 23.2

Changzhou Trina Solar Energy Co., Ltd. v. International Trade Commission

United States Court of Appeals, Federal Circuit, 879 F.3d 1377 (2018).

Background and Facts Changzhou Trina Solar Energy Company, Ltd., a Chinese firm, makes crystalline silicon photovoltaic (CSPV) cells and related products. Trina Solar (U.S.), Inc., imported Changzhou's CSPV products into the United States. The U.S. Department of Commerce found that the imports were subsidized by the Chinese government and sold in the United States at less than fair value. The International Trade Commission (ITC) determined that the domestic CSPV industry was materially

(Continues)

injured by reason of the imports from China. Changzhou and Trina challenged this determination in the U.S. Court of International Trade. The court rejected the challenge and sustained the ITC's determination. Changzhou and Trina appealed this decision to the U.S. Court of Appeals for the Federal Circuit.

In the Words of the Court

TARANTO, Circuit Judge.

* * * *

In this case, [Changzhou and Trina] * * * argue * * * that the Commission failed to make findings, supported by substantial evidence, that the domestic industry would have been materially better off * * * if the subject imports had not been introduced into the market.

* * * *

[Changzhou and Trina] argue that * * * the domestic industry would have been materially as badly off * * * even had there been no unfairly priced and subsidized subject imports. * * * *The question is whether the Commission found, with adequate reasons and substantial-evidence support, that the difference between the state of the domestic industry as it actually was * * * and the state of the domestic industry as it would have been without the subject imports was more than inconsequential, immaterial, or unimportant.* [Emphasis added.]

* * * The Commission's summary * * * rested on detailed findings about demand conditions and the business cycle in the domestic market, the roles of conventional and renewable sources of electricity, government incentives and regulations at federal, state, and local levels, domestic consumption trends, market segments, who was supplying the domestic market, what happened to prices and market shares * * * , and the ways in which the domestic industry's financial performance was very poor and deteriorating. The findings rested on various types of evidence, including the answers to questionnaires addressed to market participants such as purchasers.

* * * *

* * * The Commission recognized "there may have been additional factors exerting downward pricing pressure on CSPV products," but it found "that subject imports were a significant cause of the decline in prices.

"* * * In sum, the significant and growing volume of low-priced subject imports from China competed directly with the domestic like product, was sold in the same channels of distribution to the same segments of the U.S. market, and undersold the domestic like product at significant margins, causing domestic producers to lose revenue and market share and leading to significant depression and suppression of the domestic industry's prices."

Decision and Remedy The U.S. Court of Appeals for the Federal Circuit affirmed the decision of the lower court. The ITC's explanation for the determination that the imported products unfairly impacted the domestic industry provided substantial evidence that supported imposition of antidumping duties.

Critical Thinking

• **Economic** *How does the Changzhou case illustrate that dumping is an unfair international trade practice? Discuss.*

• **What If the Facts Were Different?** *Suppose that the ITC had not issued detailed findings supported by a variety of evidence, but had only released a statement that the subject imports seemed to have a negative effect on the domestic industry. Would the result have been different? Explain.*

Learning Objective 3

What does it mean for the World Trade Organization to grant a nation "normal trade relations status"?

Normal Trade Relations (NTR) Status A legal trade status granted to member countries of the World Trade Organization.

23–3d Minimizing Trade Barriers

Restrictions on imports are also known as *trade barriers*. The elimination of trade barriers is sometimes seen as essential to the world's economic well-being. Various regional trade agreements and associations work to reduce trade barriers among nations. (The Trump administration may attempt to modify some of these existing trade agreements.)

The World Trade Organization Most of the world's leading trading nations are members of the World Trade Organization (WTO), which was established in 1995. To minimize trade barriers among nations, each member country is required to grant **normal trade relations (NTR) status** to other member countries. This means that each member must treat other members at least as well as it treats the country that receives its most favorable treatment with regard to imports or exports.

The European Union (EU) The European Union (EU) arose out the 1957 Treaty of Rome, which created the Common Market, a free trade zone comprising the nations of Belgium, France, Italy, Luxembourg, the Netherlands, and West Germany. Today, the EU is a single integrated trading unit made up of twenty-eight European nations.

The EU has gone a long way toward creating a new body of law to govern all of the member nations. The EU's council and commission issue regulations, or directives, that define EU law in various areas, such as environmental law, product liability, anticompetitive practices, and corporations. The directives normally are binding on all member countries. Nevertheless, some of the EU's efforts to create uniform laws have been confounded by nationalism. An example is Brexit, which refers to Britain's decision to withdraw from the EU.

The North American Free Trade Agreement (NAFTA) The North American Free Trade Agreement (NAFTA) created a regional trading unit consisting of Canada, Mexico, and the United States. The goal of NAFTA is to eliminate tariffs among these three countries on substantially all goods by reducing the tariffs incrementally over a period of time.

NAFTA gives the three countries a competitive advantage by retaining tariffs on goods imported from countries outside the NAFTA trading unit. Additionally, NAFTA provides for the elimination of barriers that traditionally have prevented the cross-border movement of services, such as financial and transportation services. NAFTA also attempts to eliminate citizenship requirements for the licensing of accountants, attorneys, physicians, and other professionals.

The Central America–Dominican Republic–United States Free Trade Agreement (CAFTA-DR) The Central America–Dominican Republic–United States Free Trade Agreement (CAFTA-DR) was formed by Costa Rica, the Dominican Republic, El Salvador, Guatemala, Honduras, Nicaragua, and the United States. Its purpose is to reduce tariffs and improve market access among all of the signatory nations. Legislatures in all seven countries have approved the CAFTA-DR, despite significant opposition in certain nations.

The Republic of Korea–United States Free Trade Agreement (KORUS FTA) The United States ratified its first free trade agreement with South Korea in 2011. This agreement, called the Republic of Korea–United States Free Trade Agreement (KORUS FTA), is aimed at eliminating 95 percent of each nation's tariffs on industrial and consumer exports.

KORUS is the largest free trade agreement the United States has entered into since NAFTA. It was expected to boost U.S. exports and benefit U.S. automakers, farmers, ranchers, and manufacturers. To date, however, exports have not increased as much as predicted, and the agreement is likely to be renegotiated.

23–4 U.S. Laws in a Global Context

The internationalization of business raises questions about the extraterritorial application of a nation's laws—that is, the effect of the country's laws outside its boundaries. To what extent do U.S. domestic laws apply to other nations' businesses? To what extent do U.S. domestic laws apply to U.S. firms doing business abroad? Here, we discuss the extraterritorial application of certain U.S. laws, including antitrust laws, tort laws, and laws prohibiting employment discrimination.

23–4a U.S. Antitrust Laws

U.S. antitrust laws have a wide application. They may *subject* firms in foreign nations to their provisions, as well as *protect* foreign consumers and competitors from violations committed by U.S. citizens. Section 1 of the Sherman Act—the most important U.S. antitrust law— provides for the extraterritorial effect of the U.S. antitrust laws.

Any conspiracy that has a *substantial effect* on U.S. commerce is within the reach of the Sherman Act. The law applies even if the violation occurs outside the United States, and foreign governments as well as businesses can be sued for violations.

Example 23.10 A Tokyo-based auto parts supplier, Furukawa Electric Company, and its executives had conspired with competitors in an international price-fixing agreement (an agreement to set prices) that lasted more than ten years. As a result of the conspiracy, automobile manufacturers had paid noncompetitive and higher prices for parts in cars sold to U.S. consumers.

Because the conspiracy had a substantial effect on U.S. commerce, the United States had jurisdiction to prosecute the case. Ultimately, Furukawa agreed to plead guilty and pay a $200 million fine. The Furukawa executives from Japan also agreed to serve up to eighteen months in a U.S. prison and to cooperate fully with the ongoing investigation.

23–4b International Tort Claims

Learning Objective 4

What federal law allows U.S. citizens, as well as citizens of foreign nations, to file civil actions in U.S. courts for torts that were committed overseas?

The international application of tort liability has grown in significance and controversy. An increasing number of U.S. plaintiffs have sued foreign (or U.S.) entities for torts that these entities allegedly committed overseas. Often, these cases involve human rights violations by foreign governments. The Alien Tort Statute (ATS),[11] adopted in 1789, allows even foreign citizens to bring civil suits in U.S. courts for injuries caused by violations of international law or a treaty of the United States.

Since 1980, plaintiffs increasingly used the ATS to bring actions against private companies operating in foreign nations, including Colombia, Egypt, Nigeria, and Saudi Arabia. Critics argued that allowing such suits extended the application of the ATS too far. In 2018, however, the United States Supreme Court limited the application of the ATS when it ruled that foreign corporations could no longer be defendants in suits brought under the ATS.[12]

In the following *Spotlight Case,* the United States Supreme Court considered the parameters of the ATS. The question was whether the statute allows U.S. courts to exercise jurisdiction over a cause of action that occurred outside the United States.

---

11. 28 U.S.C. Section 1350.
12. *Jesner v. Arab Bank, PLC,* ___ U.S. ___, 138 S.Ct. 1386, 200 L.Ed.2d 612 (2018).

✳ Spotlight on International Torts: Case 23.3

Daimler AG v. Bauman

United States Supreme Court, 571 U.S. 117, 134 S.Ct. 746, 187 L.Ed.2d 624 (2014).

Background and Facts Barbara Bauman and twenty-one other residents of Argentina filed a suit in a federal district court in California against Daimler AG,[a] a German company. They alleged that Mercedes-Benz (MB) Argentina, a subsidiary of Daimler, had collaborated with state security forces to kidnap, detain, torture, and kill certain MB

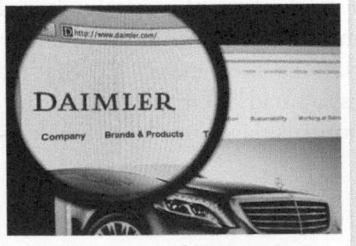
Can victims of Argentina's "dirty war" sue a German company in a U.S. court?

Argentina workers during Argentina's "dirty war." These workers included the plaintiffs and some of their relatives. Their claims were asserted under the Alien Tort Statute.

Personal jurisdiction was based on the California contacts of Mercedes-Benz USA (MBUSA), a Daimler subsidiary incorporated in Delaware with its principal place of business in New Jersey. MBUSA distributes Daimler-made vehicles to dealerships throughout the

---

a. The initials *A.G.* stand for "Automotive Group."

United States, including California. The district court dismissed the suit for lack of jurisdiction. The U.S. Court of Appeals for the Ninth Circuit reversed this ruling. Daimler appealed to the United States Supreme Court.

In the Words of the Court
Justice *GINSBURG* delivered the opinion of the Court.
* * * *

Even if we were to assume that MBUSA is at home in California, and further to assume MBUSA's contacts are imputable [attributable] to Daimler, there would still be no basis to subject Daimler to general jurisdiction in California, for Daimler's slim contacts with the State hardly render it at home there.

* * * Only a limited set of affiliations with a forum will render a defendant amenable to all-purpose jurisdiction there. For an individual, the paradigm forum [the typical forum] for the exercise of general jurisdiction is the individual's domicile; for a corporation, it is an equivalent place, one in which the corporation is fairly regarded as at home. *With respect to a corporation, the place of incorporation and principal place of business are paradigm * * * bases for general jurisdiction.* Those affiliations have the virtue of being unique—that is, each ordinarily indicates only one place—as well as easily ascertainable. These bases afford plaintiffs recourse to at least one clear and certain forum in which a corporate defendant may be sued on any and all claims. [Emphasis added.]

[This does not mean] that a corporation may be subject to general jurisdiction *only* in a forum where it is incorporated or has its principal place of business * * *. [But] plaintiffs would have us look beyond the exemplar bases identified [above] and approve the exercise of general jurisdiction in every State in which a corporation engages in a substantial, continuous, and systematic course of business. That formulation, we hold, is unacceptably grasping.

* * * The inquiry * * * is not whether a foreign corporation's in-forum contacts can be said to be in some sense continuous and systematic; it is whether that corporation's affiliations with the State are so continuous and systematic as to render it essentially at home in the forum State.

Here, neither Daimler nor MBUSA is incorporated in California, nor does either entity have its principal place of business there. If Daimler's California activities sufficed to allow adjudication of this Argentina-rooted case in California, the same global reach would presumably be available in every other State in which MBUSA's sales are sizable. Such exorbitant exercises of all-purpose jurisdiction would scarcely permit out-of-state defendants to structure their primary conduct with some minimum assurance as to where that conduct will and will not render them liable to suit.

It was therefore [an] error for the Ninth Circuit to conclude that Daimler, even with MBUSA's contacts attributed to it, was at home in California, and hence subject to suit there on claims by foreign plaintiffs having nothing to do with anything that occurred or had its principal impact in California.

Decision and Remedy The United States Supreme Court reversed the decision of the appellate court. The federal district court could not exercise jurisdiction over Daimler given the absence of any California connection to the atrocities, perpetrators, or victims described in the complaint.

Critical Thinking

• **Legal Environment** *What are the consequences for Daimler of the decision in this case?*

23–4c Antidiscrimination Laws

As you probably know, federal laws in the United States prohibit discrimination on the basis of race, color, national origin, religion, gender, age, and disability. These laws, as they affect employment relationships, generally apply extraterritorially.

Thus, U.S. employees working abroad for U.S. employers are protected under the Age Discrimination in Employment Act. Similarly, the Americans with Disabilities Act, which requires employers to accommodate the needs of workers with disabilities, applies to U.S. nationals working abroad for U.S. firms.

In addition, the major law regulating employment discrimination—Title VII of the Civil Rights Act—applies extraterritorially to all U.S. employees working for U.S. employers abroad. U.S. employers must abide by U.S. discrimination laws unless to do so would violate the laws of the country where their workplaces are located. This "foreign laws exception" prevents employers from being subjected to conflicting laws.

23–5 Space Law

Space Law Law consisting of the international and national laws that govern activities in outer space.

Space law consists of the international and national laws that govern activities in outer space. For the first fifty years of space exploration, national governments conducted most of those activities. Thus, space law was directed primarily at governments and government activities. In the last decade, private companies have been preparing to undertake some space-related activities and broaden access to outer space for the rest of us. Space law, accordingly, faces new challenges.

23–5a International Space Law

International space law consists of international treaties—primarily negotiated by the United Nations (U.N.)—and U.N. resolutions. These sources recognize fundamentally that activities conducted in outer space and the benefits derived from those activities should improve the welfare of all nations and all humanity.

The major space law treaties were concluded by the U.N. Committee on the Peaceful Uses of Outer Space (COPUOS). COPUOS also administers the treaties and advises the international community on space policy matters.

Learning Objective 5

What treaty provides a framework for international space law?

Exploration and Exploitation The foundation of international space law is the U.N. Treaty on Principles Governing the Activities of States in the Exploration and Use of Outer Space, including the Moon and Other Celestial Bodies.[13] This treaty—generally referred to as the *Outer Space Treaty*—established the framework for later international agreements and U.N. resolutions.

The Outer Space Treaty expresses general principles that have been expanded and applied in subsequent treaties. In Article I and Article II, outer space is declared to be free for exploration and use by all nations. The moon, the planets, asteroids, and other celestial bodies are not subject to appropriation by any single nation.[14] In addition, space objects are to be used exclusively for peaceful purposes. No weapons of mass destruction are permitted in outer space under Article IV. [15]

According to Article VI, each nation is responsible for its activities in outer space, whether they are conducted by the government or by a private entity. In fact, the activities of private entities require authorization and supervision by a government. Article VII imposes on each nation liability for damage caused by its space objects. Article VIII provides that each nation retains jurisdiction and control over its space objects and the personnel on them. Finally, Article IX requires that space exploration be conducted so as to avoid "harmful contamination."[16]

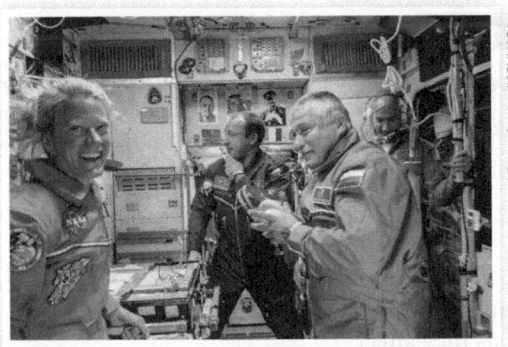

Expedition 36, International Space Station (ISS)/NASA

The international space station orbits the earth with crews from different countries. How do international treaties and space law policies affect the way we explore outer space?

Astronauts and Space Objects The Outer Space Treaty was followed by several other agreements, including the following:

- The Agreement on the Rescue of Astronauts, the Return of Astronauts and the Return of Objects Launched into Outer Space (the Rescue Agreement).[17]

- The Convention on International Liability for Damage Caused by Space Objects (the Liability Convention).[18]

- The Convention on Registration of Objects Launched into Outer Space (the Registration Convention).[19]

---

13. 18 U.S.T. 2410, T.I.A.S. 6347, 610 U.N.T.S. 205.
14. After the treaty went into effect, the United States and Russia conducted joint space activities.
15. Establishing military bases, testing weapons, and conducting military maneuvers are prohibited.
16. Other articles promote further international cooperation in the exploration and use of space.
17. 19 U.S.T. 7570, T.I.A.S. 6599, 672 U.N.T.S. 119.
18. 24 U.S.T. 2389, T.I.A.S. 7762, 961 U.N.T.S. 187.
19. 28 U.S.T. 695, T.I.A.S. 8480, 1023 U.N.T.S. 15.

The Rescue Agreement expands on Articles V and VIII of the Outer Space Treaty. It provides that each nation will undertake to rescue and assist astronauts in distress and return them to their "launching State." All nations are to assist in recovering space objects that return to earth outside the territory of the launching state.

The Liability Convention elaborates on Article VII of the Outer Space Treaty. This agreement provides that a launching state is absolutely liable for personal injury and property damage caused by its space objects on the surface of the earth or to aircraft in flight. Liability for injury or damage in space is subject to a determination of fault. The convention also prescribes procedures for the settlement of claims for damages.

The Registration Convention provides for the mandatory registration of objects launched into outer space. Each launching state is to maintain a registry of the objects that it launches into space. The intent is to assist in the objects' identification.

Space Debris An estimated 600,000 objects made by humans are in orbit around the earth. Most of these objects are no longer under any party's control and are classified as *space debris*. In 2009, two orbiting satellites collided for the first time. Fragments generated by such collisions are expected to be a significant source of space debris in the future. As noted previously, the Liability Convention sets out principles of liability to apply in instances of injury or damage in space.

The United Nations has endorsed guidelines to reduce space debris.[20] The guidelines, which reflect the current practices of a number of national and international organizations, apply to the planning, design, manufacture, and operational phases of spacecraft. Among other points, the guidelines suggest that systems should be designed not to release debris during normal operations. They also recognize that some objects no longer in operation should be removed from orbit, if this can be accomplished in a controlled manner.

23–5b U.S. Space Law

In the United States, each government agency that operates or authorizes spacecraft is responsible for complying with U.S. law and international treaties. Federal law, state law, and more than half a century of common practices in space-related industries also affect government and private space activities.

Commercial Spaceflight The Federal Aviation Administration (FAA) regulates private spaceports, as well as the launch and reentry of private spacecraft under the Commercial Space Launch Act.[21] The FAA is working to establish licensing and safety criteria for private spacecraft. Some states, including Florida, New Mexico, Texas, and Virginia, limit the liability of space tourism providers under state tort law. But state legislatures and, ultimately, courts will need to consider other issues in this context, including insurance requirements and the enforceability of liability waivers.

In 2015, Congress passed landmark legislation aimed at encouraging commercial spaceflight companies. The U.S. Commercial Space Launch Competitiveness Act[22] streamlines regulatory processes and promotes safety standards. In addition, the new law provides that if a U.S. citizen or company retrieves minerals or other resources from an asteroid or other space location, that person or company owns them.

Exports of Space Technology Currently, under U.S. regulations, all spacecraft are classified as "defense articles." The defense classification restricts the transfer of space technology and related information to any foreign person or nation under the U.S.

---

20. Space Debris Mitigation Guidelines of the Committee on the Peaceful Uses of Outer Space, G.A. Res. 62/217, U.N. GAOR, 50th Sess., U.N.Doc. A/62/20 (Dec. 22, 2007).
21. 51 U.S.C. Sections 50901 *et seq.*
22. Pub. L. No. 114-90, 129 Stat. 704, Nov. 25, 2015.

Department of State's International Traffic in Arms Regulations.[23] This restriction makes it difficult for U.S. space companies to compete in global space markets.

Property Rights to Space Resources Article II of the Outer Space Treaty bans the national appropriation of territory in space. If the United States cannot appropriate territory in space, then it cannot give U.S. citizens title to property associated with this territory. Under U.S. law, the government must have sovereignty over territory before it can confer title to associated property to its citizens.

Article VIII, however, provides that a state party to the treaty retains jurisdiction over objects on its space registry that are launched into space. In addition, Article IX prohibits interference with space activities. In effect, these provisions confer the protections associated with property rights on private space activities.

The 2015 U.S. Commercial Space Launch Competitiveness Act changed the law somewhat by granting private citizens property rights over asteroid resources that they obtain from space. The act specifically recognizes that the United States is not attempting to assert an exclusive right to or sovereignty over any celestial body.

---

23. 22 C.F.R. Sections 120.1 *et seq.*

Practice and Review

Robco, Inc., was a Florida arms dealer. The armed forces of Honduras contracted to purchase weapons from Robco over a six-year period. After the government was replaced and a democracy installed, the Honduran government sought to reduce the size of its military, and its relationship with Robco deteriorated.

Honduras refused to honor the contract by purchasing the inventory of arms, which Robco could sell only at a much lower price. Robco filed a suit in a federal district court in the United States to recover damages for this breach of contract by the government of Honduras. Using the information provided in the chapter, answer the following questions.

1. Should the Foreign Sovereign Immunities Act preclude this lawsuit? Why or why not?

2. Does the act of state doctrine bar Robco from seeking to enforce the contract? Explain.

3. Suppose that before Robco filed its lawsuit, the new government of Honduras had enacted a law making it illegal to purchase weapons from foreign arms dealers. What doctrine might lead a U.S. court to dismiss Robco's case in that situation?

4. Now suppose that the U.S. court hears the case and awards damages to Robco, but the government of Honduras has no assets in the United States that can be used to satisfy the judgment. Under which doctrine might Robco be able to collect the damages by asking another nation's court to enforce the U.S. judgment?

Debate This

The U.S. federal courts are accepting too many lawsuits initiated by foreigners that concern matters not relevant to this country.

Key Terms

act of state doctrine 535
choice-of-law clause 542
comity 535
confiscation 536
distribution agreement 540
dumping 543

export 539
expropriation 536
forum-selection clause 542
international law 532
international organization 534
national law 533

normal trade relations (NTR) status 544
quota 543
sovereign immunity 536
space law 548
tariff 543
treaty 534

Chapter Summary: International and Space Law

International Law	1. *Principle of comity*—Under this principle, nations give effect to the laws and judicial decrees of other nations, as long as they are consistent with the law and public policy of the accommodating nation. It is based primarily on respect. 2. *Act of state doctrine*—Under this doctrine, U.S. courts avoid passing judgment on the validity of public acts committed by a recognized foreign government within its own territory. 3. *Doctrine of sovereign immunity*—When certain conditions are satisfied, foreign nations are immune from U.S. jurisdiction under the Foreign Sovereign Immunities Act. Exceptions are made when a foreign state (a) has waived its immunity either explicitly or by implication, (b) has engaged in commercial activity within the United States or that has a direct effect on the United States, (c) has committed a tort within the United States, or (d) has been designated "a state sponsor of terrorism" and is sued for "personal injury or death" caused by an act of terrorism.
Doing Business Internationally	U.S. domestic firms may engage in international business transactions in several ways, including (1) exporting, which may involve foreign agents or distributors, and (2) manufacturing abroad through licensing arrangements, wholly owned subsidiaries, or joint ventures. International business contracts often include arbitration clauses and forum-selection clauses to reduce the uncertainties associated with dispute resolution. The New York Convention assists in the enforcement of arbitration clauses and requires signatory nations to honor private agreements to arbitrate. If the parties have signed a forum-selection clause, the dispute will be tried (or arbitrated) in the specified forum.
Regulation of Specific Business Activities	In the interests of their economies, foreign policies, domestic policies, and other national priorities, nations impose laws that restrict or facilitate international business. Such laws regulate foreign investments, exporting, and importing. Various regional trade agreements and associations, including the World Trade Organization and the European Union, attempt to minimize trade barriers among nations.
U.S. Laws in a Global Context	1. *Antitrust laws*—U.S. antitrust laws may be applied beyond the borders of the United States. Any conspiracy that has a substantial effect on commerce within the United States may be subject to the Sherman Act, even if the violation occurs outside the United States. 2. *International tort claims*—U.S. tort laws may be applied to wrongful acts that take place in foreign jurisdictions under the Alien Tort Statute. This act allows even foreign citizens to bring civil suits in U.S. courts for injuries caused by violations of international law or a treaty of the United States. 3. *Antidiscrimination laws*—The major U.S. laws prohibiting employment discrimination, including Title VII of the Civil Rights Act, the Age Discrimination in Employment Act, and the Americans with Disabilities Act, cover U.S. employees working abroad for U.S. firms—*unless* to apply the U.S. laws would violate the laws of the host country.
Space Law	Space law consists of international and national laws that govern activities in outer space. International treaties and resolutions (mostly through the United Nations) cover space exploration and exploitation, astronauts, space objects, and space debris. National laws in the United States deal with commercial space flights (regulated by the Federal Aviation Administration), space technology, and property rights.

Issue Spotters

1. Café Rojo, Ltd., an Ecuadoran firm, agrees to sell coffee beans to Dark Roast Coffee Company, a U.S. firm. Dark Roast accepts the beans but refuses to pay. Café Rojo sues Dark Roast in an Ecuadoran court and is awarded damages, but Dark Roast's assets are in the United States. Under what circumstances would a U.S. court enforce the judgment of the Ecuadoran court? (See *International Law.*)

2. Gems International, Ltd., is a foreign firm that has a 12 percent share of the U.S. market for diamonds. To capture a larger share, Gems offers its products at a below-cost discount to U.S. buyers (and inflates the prices in its own country to make up the difference). How can this attempt to undersell U.S. businesses be defeated? (See *Regulation of Specific Business Activities.*)

—**Check your answers to the *Issue Spotters* against the answers provided in Appendix D at the end of this text.**

Business Scenarios and Case Problems

23–1. Doing Business Internationally. Macrotech, Inc., develops an innovative computer chip and obtains a patent on it. The firm markets the chip under the trademarked brand name "Flash." Macrotech wants to sell the chip to Nitron, Ltd., in Pacifica, a foreign country. Macrotech is concerned, however, that after an initial purchase Nitron will duplicate the chip, pirate it, and sell the pirated version to computer manufacturers in Pacifica. To avoid this possibility, Macrotech could establish its own manufacturing facility in Pacifica, but it does not want to do this. How can Macrotech, without establishing a manufacturing facility in Pacifica, protect Flash from being pirated by Nitron? (See *Doing Business Internationally.*)

23–2. Dumping. U.S. pineapple producers alleged that producers of canned pineapple from the Philippines were selling their canned pineapple in the United States for less than its fair market value (dumping). The Philippine producers also exported other products, such as pineapple juice and juice concentrate, which used separate parts of the same pineapple used for the canned pineapple. All these products shared raw material costs, according to the producers' own financial records. To determine fair value and antidumping duties, the plaintiffs argued that a court should calculate the Philippine producers' cost of production and allocate a portion of the shared fruit costs to the canned fruit. The result of this allocation showed that more than 90 percent of the canned fruit sales were below the cost of production. Is this a reasonable approach to determining the production costs and fair market value of canned pineapple in the United States? Why or why not? (See *Regulation of Specific Business Activities.*)

23–3. Sovereign Immunity. Bell Helicopter Textron, Inc., designs, makes, and sells helicopters with distinctive and famous trade dress that identifies them as Bell aircraft. Bell also owns the helicopters' design patents. Bell's Model 206 Series includes the Jet Ranger. Thirty-six years after Bell developed the Jet Ranger, the Islamic Republic of Iran began to make and sell counterfeit Model 206 Series helicopters and parts. Iran's counterfeit versions—the Shahed 278 and the Shahed 285—used Bell's trade dress. The Shahed aircraft was promoted at an international air show in Iran to aircraft customers. Bell filed a suit in a U.S. district court against Iran, alleging violations of trademark and patent laws. Is Iran—a foreign nation—exempt in these circumstances from the jurisdiction of U.S. courts? Explain. [*Bell Helicopter Textron, Inc. v. Islamic Republic of Iran,* 734 F.3d 1175 (C.A.D.C. 2013)] (See *International Law.*)

23–4. Sovereign Immunity. In 1954, the government of Bolivia began expropriating land from Francisco Loza for public projects, including an international airport. The government directed the payment of compensation in exchange for at least some of his land. But the government never paid the full amount. Decades later, his heirs, Genoveva and Marcel Loza, who were both U.S. citizens, filed a suit in a federal district court in the United States against the government of Bolivia, seeking damages for the taking. Can the court exercise jurisdiction? Explain. [*Santivanez v. Estado Plurinacional de Bolivia,* 512 Fed.Appx. 887 (11th Cir. 2013)] (See *International Law.*)

23–5. Business Case Problem with Sample Answer—Import Controls. The Wind Tower Trade Coalition is an association of domestic manufacturers of utility-scale wind towers. The coalition filed a suit in the U.S. Court of International Trade against the U.S. Department of Commerce. It challenged the Commerce Department's decision to impose only *prospective* antidumping duties, rather than *retrospective* (retroactive) duties, on imports of utility-scale wind towers from China and Vietnam. The department had found that the domestic industry had not suffered any "material injury" or "threat of material injury" from such imports and that it would be protected by a prospective assessment. Can an antidumping duty be assessed retrospectively? If so, should it be assessed here? Discuss. [*Wind Tower Trade Coalition v. United States,* 741 F.3d 89 (Fed. Cir. 2014)] (See *Regulation of Specific Business Activities.*)

—For a sample answer to Problem 23–5, go to Appendix E at the end of this text.

23–6. The Principle of Comity. Holocaust survivors and the heirs of Holocaust victims filed a suit in a federal district court in the United States against the Hungarian national railway, the Hungarian national bank, and several private Hungarian banks. The plaintiffs alleged that the defendants had participated in expropriating the property of Hungarian Jews who were victims of the Holocaust. The claims arose from events in Hungary seventy years ago. The plaintiffs had not exhausted remedies available through Hungarian courts. Indeed, they had not even attempted to seek remedies in Hungarian courts, and they did not provide a legally compelling reason for their failure to do so. The defendants asked the court to dismiss the suit. Does the principle of comity support the defendants' request? Explain. [*Fischer v. Magyar Államvasutak Zrt.*, 777 F.3d 847 (7th Cir. 2015)] (See *International Law.*)

23–7. International Law. For fifty years, the Soviet Union made and sold Stolichnaya vodka. At the time, VVO-SPI, a Soviet state enterprise, licensed the Stolichnaya trademark in the United States. When the Soviet Union collapsed, VVO-SPI was purportedly privatized and fell under the control of Spirits International B.V. (SPI). In 2000, a Russian court held that VVO-SPI had not been validly privatized under Russian law. Thus, ownership of the Stolichnaya mark remained with the Soviet Union's successor, the Russian Federation. The Russian Federation assigned the mark to Federal Treasury Enterprise Sojuzplodoimport, OAO (FTE). FTE then filed a suit in a U.S. federal district court against SPI, asserting unlawful misappropriation and commercial exploitation of the mark in violation of federal law. Is the validity of the assignment of the mark to FTE a question to be determined by the court? Why or why not? [*Federal Treasury Enterprise Sojuzplodoimport v. Spirits International B.V.*, 809 F.3d 737 (2d Cir. 2016)] (See *International Law.*)

23–8. Import Controls. Goods exported to a foreign country for repair or alteration can qualify for tariff-free or reduced-tariff treatment when they re-enter the United States. But the goods do not qualify for favorable import-duty treatment if, in the foreign country, they are transformed into commercially different goods. Daimler-Chrysler AG Sprinter vans are marketed in the United States as cargo vans. Pleasure-Way Industries, Inc., bought 144 Sprinter vans and exported them to Canada for conversion into motorhomes. This included the installation of fully plumbed and furnished kitchens, bathrooms, and sleeping quarters. After the conversion, Pleasure-Way sought to import the vehicles back into the United States to market the motorhomes under new model names as upscale leisure vehicles at prices double or triple the price for Sprinter vans. Do the converted vans qualify for favorable import-tariff treatment? Discuss. [*Pleasure-Way Industries, Inc. v. United States*, 878 F.3d 1348 (Fed. Cir. 2018)] (See *Regulation of Specific Business Activities.*)

23–9. A Question of Ethics—The IDDR Approach and Doing Business Internationally. *Incorporated under Venezuelan law, a subsidiary of U.S.-based Helmerich & Payne International Drilling Co. supplied oil-drilling rigs to entities that were part of the government of Venezuela. The government fell behind in payment on contracts for the use of the rigs. When the overdue amounts topped $100 million, the government nationalized the rigs and took possession. Helmerich filed a suit in a U.S. federal district court against Venezuela, claiming expropriation of property in violation of international law. Helmerich asserted that the U.S. court had jurisdiction under the Foreign Sovereign Immunities Act (FSIA). [Bolivarian Republic of Venezuela v. Helmerich & Payne International Drilling Co., ___ U.S. ___, 137 S.Ct. 1312, 197 L.Ed.2d 663 (2017)] (See International Law.)*

1. Venezuela argued that the FSIA did not apply because Helmerich did not have rights in the rigs, which were the subsidiary's property. Does that fact make Helmerich's claim frivolous and unethical? Explain.

2. Using the IDDR approach, determine whether a company is ethically obligated to become familiar with the political situation before doing business in another country.

Critical Thinking and Writing Assignments

23–10. Time-Limited Group Assignment—Globalization. Assume that you are manufacturing tablet accessories and that your business is becoming more successful. You are now considering expanding operations into another country. (See *Doing Business Internationally.*)

1. One group will explore the costs and benefits of advertising internationally on the Internet.

2. Another group will consider whether to take in a partner from a foreign nation and examine the benefits and risks of doing so.

3. A third group will discuss what problems may arise if you want to manufacture in a foreign location.

24

Banking in the Digital Age

Learning Objectives

The five Learning Objectives *below are designed to help improve your understanding. After reading this chapter, you should be able to answer the following questions:*

1. What type of check does a bank agree in advance to accept when the check is presented for payment?

2. When may a bank properly dishonor a customer's check without being liable to the customer?

3. What is electronic check presentment, and how does it differ from the traditional check-clearing process?

4. What are the four most common types of electronic fund transfers?

5. What is the difference between a stored-value card and a smart card?

"Money is just what we use to keep tally."

Henry Ford
1863–1947
(American automobile manufacturer)

Many people today use debit cards rather than checks for their retail transactions, and payments are increasingly being made via smartphones, tablets, and other mobile devices. Nonetheless, checks remain an integral part of the U.S. economic system and are the most common type of negotiable instrument. Because checks serve as a substitute for cash, we use them to "keep tally," a phrase used by Henry Ford in the chapter-opening quotation.

Many businesses still use checks to pay bills because they facilitate record keeping. But on some occasions, employers have fallen victim to a dishonest employee who embezzles funds using company checks. For instance, assume that Closetmakers, Inc., hired Carter Triplett as a bookkeeper. Triplett was responsible for maintaining the company checkbook and reconciling it with the monthly statements from TD Financial Bank. He also wrote checks to pay invoices, which Closetmakers' president, Denise Rose, reviewed and signed, but no other employee checked Triplett's work.

By the end of his first full month of employment, Triplett had forged six checks, amounting to more than $22,000. By the following year, Triplett had forged fifty-nine more checks, totaling more than $475,000. A TD Financial Bank employee became suspicious about an item and notified Closetmakers. Triplett left work and did not return. Closetmakers sued TD Financial Bank for reimbursement, alleging that it had been negligent in not detecting the forgeries. The bank argued that it was not liable because Closetmakers had been negligent. Who bears the loss resulting from forged checks is one of the many important topics covered in this chapter.

24–1 Checks and the Bank-Customer Relationship

Articles 3 and 4 of the Uniform Commercial Code (UCC) govern issues relating to checks. Article 4 of the UCC governs bank deposits and collections as well as bank-customer relationships. Article 4 also regulates the relationships of banks with one another as they process checks for payment, and it establishes a framework for deposit and checking agreements between a bank and its customers. A check therefore may fall within the scope of Article 3 as a negotiable instrument and yet be subject to the provisions of Article 4 while in the course of collection. If a conflict between Article 3 and Article 4 arises, Article 4 controls [UCC 4–102(a)].

24–1a Checks

A *check* is a special type of draft that is drawn on a bank, ordering the bank to pay a fixed amount of funds on demand [UCC 3–104(f)]. Article 4 defines a *bank* as "a person engaged in the business of banking, including a savings bank, savings and loan association, credit union or trust company" [UCC 4–105(1)]. If any other institution (such as a brokerage firm) handles a check for payment or for collection, the check is *not* covered by Article 4.

A person who writes a check is called the *drawer.* The drawer is a depositor in the bank on which the check is drawn. The person to whom the check is payable is the *payee.* The bank or financial institution on which the check is drawn is the *drawee.* **Example 24.1** When Anita Cruzak writes a check from her checking account to pay her college tuition, she is the drawer. Her bank is the drawee, and her college is the payee.

Between the time a check is drawn and the time it reaches the drawee, the effectiveness of the check may be altered in some way. For instance, the account on which the check is drawn may no longer have sufficient funds to pay the check. To avoid such problems, a payee may insist on payment by an instrument that has already been accepted by the drawee, such as a cashier's check, a traveler's check, or a certified check.

Cashier's Checks Checks usually are three-party instruments, but on certain types of checks, the bank can serve as both the drawer and the drawee. For instance, when a bank draws a check on itself, the check is called a **cashier's check** and is a negotiable instrument at the moment it is issued (see Exhibit 24–1) [UCC 3–104(g)]. Normally, a

Cashier's Check A check drawn by a bank on itself.

Exhibit 24–1 A Cashier's Check

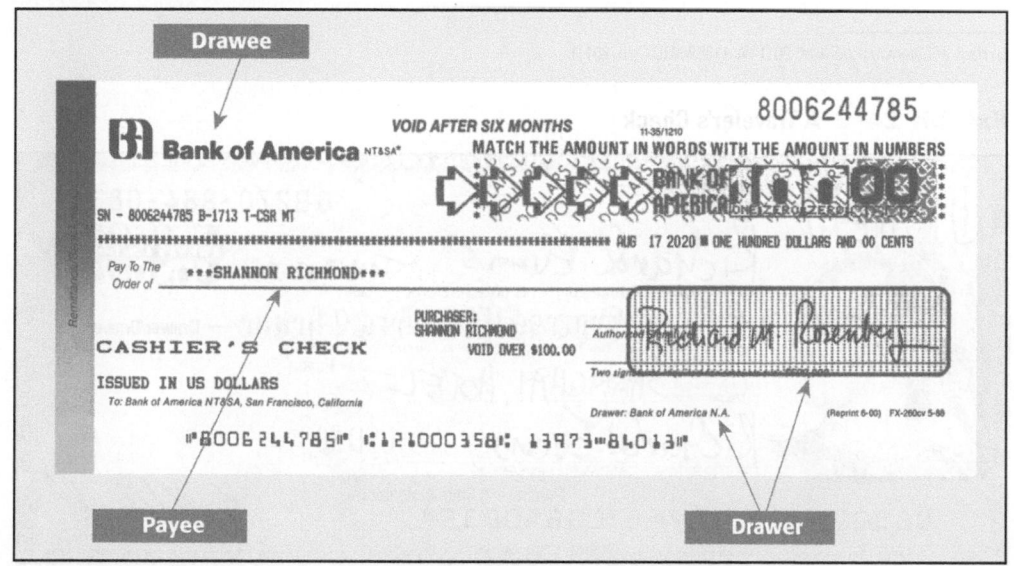

cashier's check indicates a specific payee. In effect, with a cashier's check, the bank assumes responsibility for paying the check, thus making the check more readily acceptable as a substitute for cash.

Example 24.2 Kramer needs to pay a moving company $8,000 for moving his household goods to his new home in another state. The moving company requests payment in the form of a cashier's check. Kramer goes to a bank (he need not have an account at the bank) and purchases a cashier's check, payable to the moving company, in the amount of $8,000. Kramer has to pay the bank the $8,000 for the check, plus a small service fee. He then gives the check to the moving company. ■

Cashier's checks are sometimes used in the business community as the near equivalent of cash. Except in very limited circumstances, the issuing bank *must* honor its cashier's checks when they are presented for payment. If a bank wrongfully dishonors a cashier's check, a holder can recover from the bank all expenses incurred, interest, and consequential damages [UCC 3–411]. **Case Example 24.3** James Berwick purchased a $250,000 cashier's check from Bank of Colorado that was made payable to Ron Bryant. Berwick instructed the bank to give the check to James Kalhorn, who was to deliver the check to Bryant. The next day, Bryant presented the cashier's check to a Las Vegas Sands casino, which called Bank of Colorado to verify that it had issued the cashier's check. Las Vegas Sands then deposited the check into its bank account.

Before the cashier's check was returned to Bank of Colorado for payment, however, Berwick claimed that it was lost and requested the bank to stop payment on it. The bank refused to pay the cashier's check, and litigation followed. A court found that Bank of Colorado had improperly honored Berwick's stop-payment order and was liable for wrongfully refusing to pay the cashier's check.[1] ■

Traveler's Check A check that is payable on demand, drawn on or payable through a financial institution, and designated as a traveler's check.

Traveler's Checks A **traveler's check** is an instrument that is payable on demand, drawn on or payable at or through a financial institution (such as a bank), and designated as a traveler's check. The issuing institution is directly obligated to accept and pay its traveler's check according to the check's terms.

Traveler's checks are designed to be a safe substitute for cash for people who are on vacation or traveling. They are issued for fixed amounts, such as $20, $50, or $100. The purchaser is required to sign the check at the time it is bought and again at the time it is used [UCC 3–104(i)]. Most major banks today do not issue their own traveler's checks but, instead, purchase and issue American Express traveler's checks for their customers (see Exhibit 24–2).

---

1. *Bank of Colorado v. Berwick,* 2011 WL 1135349 (D.Colo. 2011).

Exhibit 24–2 A Traveler's Check

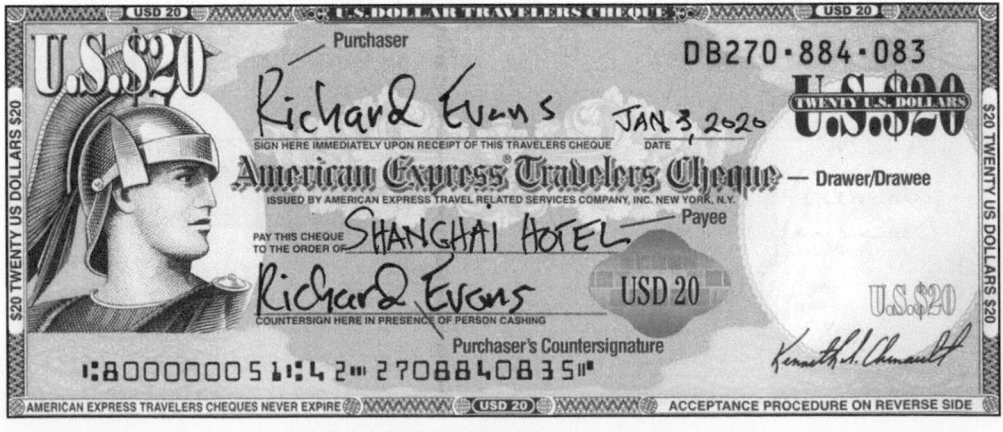

Certified Checks A **certified check** is a check that has been accepted in writing by the bank on which it is drawn [UCC 3–409(d)]. When a drawee bank *certifies* a check, it immediately charges the drawer's account with the amount of the check and transfers those funds to its own certified check account. In effect, the bank is agreeing in advance to accept that check when it is presented for payment and to make payment from those funds reserved in its certified check account. Essentially, certification prevents the bank from denying liability. It is a promise that sufficient funds are on deposit *and have been set aside* to cover the check.

To certify a check, the bank writes or stamps the word *certified* on the face of the check and typically writes the amount that it will pay.[2] Once a check is certified, the drawer and any prior indorsers are completely discharged from liability on the check [UCC 3–414(c), 3–415(d)]. Only the certifying bank is required to pay the instrument.

Either the drawer or the holder (payee) of a check can request certification. The drawee bank is not required to certify the check, however, and the bank's refusal to certify a check is not a dishonor of the check [UCC 3–409(d)].

> **Certified Check** A check that has been accepted in writing by the bank on which it is drawn. By certifying (accepting) the check, the bank promises to pay the check at the time it is presented.

> **Learning Objective 1**
> What type of check does a bank agree in advance to accept when the check is presented for payment?

24–1b The Bank-Customer Relationship

The bank-customer relationship begins when the customer opens a checking account and deposits funds that the bank will use to pay for checks written by the customer. The customer becomes the signatory, or authorized party, on the account. That is, he or she is the only person from whom the bank should take instructions regarding the account. Essentially, three types of relationships are established at this time between the bank and the customer:

1. A *creditor-debtor relationship* is created when, for instance, a customer makes cash deposits into a checking account. When a customer makes a deposit, the customer becomes a creditor, and the bank a debtor, for the amount deposited.

2. An *agency relationship* arises between the customer and the bank when the customer writes a check. In an agency relationship, one party (an agent) agrees to represent or act for the other party (a principal). In effect, the customer orders the bank to pay the amount on the check. The bank becomes the customer's (principal's) agent and is obligated to honor the customer's request.

3. Finally, a *contractual relationship* exists when certain rights and duties arise. The contractual rights and duties of the bank and the customer depend on the nature of the transaction. For instance, a bank has specific contractual duties when honoring checks, accepting deposits, and transferring funds.

Case Example 24.4 Royal Arcanum Hospital Association of Kings County, Inc., required all of its corporate checks to be signed by two of three corporate officers. These officers were Frank Vassallo, Joseph Rugilio, and William Herrnkind. The three were also named as signatories on the firm's account with Capital One Bank, but the terms of the account did not include the two-signature requirement.

After Vassallo and Rugilio died, Herrnkind opened a new account in the corporate name that expressly permitted checks to be drawn on it with only his signature. Over the next four years, a series of transactions reduced the balance of the account from nearly $200,000 to zero. Royal Arcanum sued Herrnkind and Capital One in a New York state court to recover the funds. The court dismissed the complaint against Capital One, and Royal Arcanum appealed. A state intermediate appellate court affirmed. Capital One was not liable for the payment of unauthorized withdrawals on the firm's corporate accounts because the contract terms never included a two-signature requirement for the transactions.[3] ■

Can a customer account require two signatures for any check?

---

2. If the certification does not state an amount, and the amount is later increased and the instrument negotiated to a holder in due course (HDC), the obligation of the certifying bank is the amount of the instrument when it was taken by the HDC [UCC 3–413(b)].

3. *Royal Arcanum Hospital Association of Kings County, Inc. v. Herrnkind,* 113 A.D.3d 672, 978 N.Y.S.2d 355 (2014).

Learning Objective 2

When may a bank properly dishonor a customer's check without being liable to the customer?

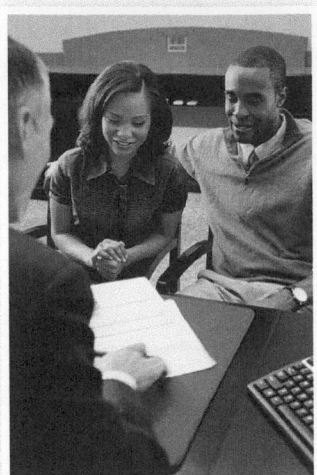

When you open a checking account, do you establish a contractual relationship?

Overdraft A check that is paid by a bank when the checking account on which the check is written contains insufficient funds to cover the check.

24–2 The Bank's Duty to Honor Checks

When a banking institution provides checking services, it agrees to honor the checks written by its customers, with the usual stipulation that the account must have sufficient funds available to pay each check [UCC 4–401(a)]. When a drawee bank *wrongfully* fails to honor a check, it is liable to its customer for damages resulting from its refusal to pay [UCC 4–402(b)]. The customer does not have to prove that the bank breached its contractual commitment or was negligent.

The customer's agreement with the bank includes a general obligation to keep sufficient funds on deposit to cover all checks written. The customer is liable to the payee or to the holder of a check in a civil suit if a check is dishonored for insufficient funds. If intent to defraud can be proved, the customer can also be subject to criminal prosecution for writing a bad check.

When the bank properly dishonors a check for insufficient funds, it has no liability to the customer. The bank may rightfully refuse payment on a customer's check in other circumstances as well.

24–2a Overdrafts

When the bank receives an item properly payable from its customer's checking account but the account contains insufficient funds to cover the amount of the check, the bank has two options. It can dishonor the item, or it can pay the item and charge the customer's account, thus creating an **overdraft.** The bank can subtract the amount of the overdraft (plus a service charge) from the customer's next deposit or other customer funds, because a check carries with it an enforceable implied promise to reimburse the bank.

With a joint account, however, the bank cannot hold any joint-account owner liable for payment of the overdraft unless that customer signed the check or benefited from its proceeds [UCC 4–401(b)]. **Example 24.5** Aaron and Sarah are married and have a joint bank account. Aaron writes a check to pay the electric bill for their apartment. If the check results in an overdraft, both Aaron and Sarah will be liable, because both obviously benefited from having electricity in their apartment.

A bank can expressly agree with a customer to accept overdrafts through an "overdraft protection agreement." If such an agreement is formed, any failure of the bank to honor a check because it would create an overdraft breaches this agreement and is considered a wrongful dishonor [UCC 4–402(a), (b)].

If a bank posts items to a customer's account only once a day, several items of different amounts may accumulate before the posting. Depending on the order in which the items are posted, an overdraft may occur earlier or later in the sequence. If the bank charges its customer a separate fee for honoring each item after an overdraft occurs, the sequencing of items can significantly impact the amount of fees that the customer is charged. At the center of the following case was one bank's decision to switch its sequencing to post items of the highest amount first.

■ Case 24.1

Legg v. West Bank
Supreme Court of Iowa, 873 N.W.2d 763 (2016).

Background and Facts Darla and Jason Legg had a joint checking account with West Bank in Iowa. When they first opened the account, West Bank provided them with a Deposit Account Agreement stating that the bank had an obligation to exercise good faith and ordinary care in connection with each account.

Without notifying its customers, West Bank changed its posting sequence of transactions from low-to-high to high-to-low check amounts. This sequencing change caused eight overdrafts in the Leggs' account, resulting in eight overdraft fees. Had the bank not changed its sequencing order, the Leggs would have been

Image Source/Getty Images

charged only three overdraft fees. The Leggs filed a suit in an Iowa state court against West Bank, in part, claiming that the bank had breached its duty to act in good faith. The bank filed a motion for summary judgment, which the court denied. West Bank appealed.

In the Words of the Court
ZAGER, Justice.
* * * *

When the Leggs opened their account with West Bank, they were provided with a [Deposit Account] Agreement that included the statement that West Bank "shall have an obligation to Depositor to exercise good faith and ordinary care in connection with each account." Before West Bank initiated the sequencing change, it consulted with an Iowa Bankers Association Compliance Officer. After this consultation, West Bank concluded in an internal memo that the previous practice of posting low-to-high created a business expectation with customers and it would be necessary to notify them of the change. Although West Bank's memo specifically discussed notifying its customers of the sequencing change with regard to bank card transactions, West Bank nonetheless made the change without notifying customers. [Emphasis added.]

The [lower] court, relying on the opinions of other courts that have heard similar issues, concluded that the plaintiffs could pursue their good-faith claim. One case the * * * court discussed addressed whether express contract terms were being carried out in good faith. In [another case,] the plaintiffs argued that the banks violated express contractual provisions to act in good faith by reordering postings to high-to-low sequencing. The court found that the plaintiffs were not asking to vary the terms of the express contract. Rather, they were asking that the bank carry out its express agreement to exercise its discretion regarding the posting sequencing in good faith. The court cited to a number of cases where other courts held that when one party is given discretion to act under a contract, said discretion must be exercised in good faith.

Similarly, West Bank has discretion with regard to the sequencing order of bank card transactions in its agreements with the Leggs and its other customers. *The bank wrote the duty of good faith into its contract with customers.* The Leggs could reasonably argue that the change in sequencing of bank card transactions, coupled with the lack of notification, violated the reasonable expectations of customers that the bank act in good faith when exercising its discretion to sequence transactions. [Emphasis added.]

Decision and Remedy The state intermediate appellate court affirmed the lower court's ruling that there were fact issues precluding summary judgment on the Leggs' good faith claim, and remanded the case for further proceedings. The court reversed the decision as to the other claims (which included unjust enrichment and usury), however, finding that they should have been dismissed by summary judgment.

Critical Thinking

• **What If the Facts Were Different?** *Suppose that West Bank's Deposit Account Agreement had not included "an obligation to Depositor to exercise good faith and ordinary care in connection with each account." How might the result have been different?*

24–2b Postdated Checks

A bank may charge a postdated check against a customer's account unless the customer notifies the bank, in a timely manner, not to pay the check until the stated date. (In fact, a check is usually paid without respect to its date.) The notice of postdating must be given in time to allow the bank to act on the notice before it pays the check. A bank that fails to act on the customer's notice and charges the customer's account before the date on the postdated check may be liable for any damages incurred by the customer [UCC 4–401(c)].

24–2c Stale Checks

Commercial banking practice regards a check that is presented for payment more than six months from its date as a **stale check.** A bank is not obligated to pay an uncertified check presented more than six months from its date [UCC 4–404].

When it receives a stale check for payment, the bank has the option of paying or not paying the check. The bank may consult the customer before paying the check. If a bank pays a stale check in good faith without consulting the customer, the bank has the right to charge the customer's account for the amount of the check.

Stale Check A check, other than a certified check, that is presented for payment more than six months after its date.

24–2d Stop-Payment Orders

Stop-Payment Order An order by a bank customer to his or her bank not to pay or certify a certain check.

A **stop-payment order** is an order by a customer to his or her bank not to pay or certify a certain check. Only a customer (or a person authorized to draw on the account) can order the bank not to pay the check when it is presented for payment [UCC 4–403(a)].[4] A customer has no right to stop payment on a check that has been certified or accepted by a bank, however. In addition, the customer-drawer must have a *valid legal ground* for issuing such an order, or the holder can sue the customer-drawer for payment.

Reasonable Time and Manner The customer must issue the stop-payment order within a reasonable time and in a reasonable manner to permit the bank to act on it [UCC 4–403(a)]. Although a stop-payment order can be given orally over the phone (in most states), it is binding on the bank for only fourteen calendar days unless confirmed in writing. (Recall that an electronic record, such as a stop-payment order submitted via the bank's website, is a writing.) A written or electronic stop-payment order is effective for six months, at which time it may be renewed [UCC 4–403(b)].

Bank's Liability for Wrongful Payment If the bank pays the check in spite of a stop-payment order, the bank will be obligated to recredit the customer's account. In addition, if the bank's payment over a stop-payment order causes subsequent checks written on the drawer's account to "bounce" (be returned for nonsufficient funds), the bank will be liable for the resultant costs the drawer incurs. The bank is liable only for the amount of actual damages suffered by the drawer because of the wrongful payment, however [UCC 4–403(c)].

Example 24.6 Mike Murano orders one hundred smartphones from Advanced Communications, Inc., at $100 each. Murano pays in advance with a check for $10,000. Later that day, Advanced Communications tells Murano that it will not deliver the smartphones as arranged. Murano immediately calls the bank and stops payment on the check, which he then confirms in writing. Two days later, in spite of this stop-payment order, the bank inadvertently honors Murano's check to Advanced Communications for the undelivered phones. The bank will be liable to Murano for the full $10,000.

The result would be different, however, if Advanced Communications had delivered and Murano had accepted ninety phones. Because Murano would have owed Advanced Communications $9,000 for the goods delivered, Murano's actual loss would be only $1,000. Consequently, the bank would be liable to Murano for only $1,000. ■

An individual tells his bank to stop payment on a check he wrote to buy a computer. What happens if the bank honors that check?

Paul Rapson / Alamy

24–2e Incompetence or Death of a Customer

A customer's mental incompetence or death does not automatically revoke a bank's authority to accept, pay, or collect an item. Only after the bank is notified of the customer's incompetence or death and has reasonable time to act on the notice will the bank's authority be ineffective [UCC 4–405]. Without this provision, banks would constantly be required to verify the continued competence and life of their drawers.

Thus, if a bank is unaware that a customer who wrote a check has been declared incompetent or has died, the bank can pay the item without incurring liability [UCC 4–405]. Even when a bank knows of the death of its customer, for ten days after the *date of death,* it can pay

---

4. Note that the right to stop payment is not limited to checks. It extends to any item payable by any bank. (See Official Comment 3 to UCC 4–403.) Also, any person claiming a legitimate interest in the account of a deceased customer may issue a stop-payment order [UCC 4–405].

or certify checks drawn on or before the date of death. An exception to this rule is made if a person claiming an interest in the account, such as an heir, orders the bank to stop payment.

24–2f Checks with Forged Drawers' Signatures

When a bank pays a check on which the drawer's signature is forged, generally the bank is liable. A forged signature on a check has no legal effect as the signature of a customer-drawer [UCC 3–403(a)]. A bank may be able to recover at least some of the loss from a customer whose negligence substantially contributed to the forgery, from the forger, or from the holder who cashed the check.

The general rule is that the bank must recredit the customer's account when it pays a check with a forged signature. A bank may contractually shift to the customer the risk of forged checks created electronically or by the use other nonmanual signatures. For instance, the contract might stipulate that the customer is solely responsible for maintaining security over any signature stamp.

Customer Negligence When the customer's negligence substantially contributed to the forgery, the bank normally will *not* be obligated to recredit the customer's account for the amount of the check [UCC 3–406].[5] To avoid liability for negligence, a customer must examine monthly bank statements and canceled checks promptly and with reasonable care, and report any forged signatures [UCC 4–406].

In addition, the customer has a duty to make sure there are no unauthorized items—such as unfamiliar purchases or suspicious withdrawals—on the account statement. The failure to examine statements and report forged drawer signatures—or any carelessness by the customer that results in a loss to the bank—makes the customer liable for the loss.

Discovery of a forged drawer's signature and notice to the bank must take place within one year from the date that the statement was made available for inspection. Otherwise, the customer loses the legal right to have the bank recredit his or her account [UCC 4–406(f)].

Sometimes, the same wrongdoer forges a customer's signature on a series of checks. To recover for all the forged, unauthorized items, the customer must discover and report the *first* forged check to the bank within thirty calendar days of the receipt of the bank statement. Failure to notify the bank within this period of time discharges the bank's liability for all similar forged checks and unauthorized items that it pays before notification.

At the center of the following case is the effect of these provisions and of an agreement between the bank and its customer concerning the time periods. The unauthorized item in dispute was not a check but a withdrawal of all of the funds in the account.

> "Canceled checks will be to future historians and cultural anthropologists what the Dead Sea Scrolls and hieroglyphics are to us."
>
> **Brent Staples**
> 1951–present
> (American journalist)

---

5. The customer's liability may be reduced, however, by the amount of the loss caused by negligence on the part of the bank [UCC 3–406(b)].

■ Case 24.2

Horton v. JPMorgan Chase Bank, N.A.
Court of Appeals of Texas, Dallas, 2018 WL 494776 (2018).

Background and Facts Robbie Horton, a paralegal for Stovall & Associates, P.C., opened an individual checking account with JPMorgan Chase Bank (Chase) and provided a signature card. The terms of the account agreement required Horton to notify Chase, in writing, of any unauthorized item within thirty days of when a statement showing the item was mailed or made available. A failure to provide the notice would prevent a claim based on the item. Two months later, Chase received a second signature card purportedly signed by Horton and Kimberly Stovall, an attorney with Stovall & Associates, to convert the account to a joint account.

(Continues)

Less than a year later, the law firm terminated Horton's employment, and on the same day, Stovall withdrew all of the funds in the joint account. Almost two years after the withdrawal, Horton filed a suit in a Texas state court against Chase, alleging breach of contract. Horton asserted that she had not agreed to the withdrawal by Stovall. Chase filed a motion for summary judgment, which the court granted. Horton appealed.

In the Words of the Court
Opinion by Justice *BOATRIGHT*

* * * *

* * * Article 4 of the UCC establishes the rights and duties of banks and their customers regarding deposits and collections. Section 4–401 provides that a bank can only charge against a customer's account "an item that is properly payable." To be properly payable, an item must be "authorized by the customer and * * * in accordance with any agreement between the customer and the bank." *A bank is liable to its customer if it charges the customer's account for an item that is not properly payable from the account.* [Emphasis added.]

Section 4–406 imposes corresponding obligations on the customer and provides the bank with certain defenses should the customer fail to comply with its obligations. To summarize, if a bank sends or makes available to the customer an account statement that reasonably identifies the items paid, the customer must exercise reasonable promptness in examining the statement and must promptly notify the bank of the relevant facts regarding any unauthorized payments due to the alteration of an item or an unauthorized signature. * * * *A customer's claim is absolutely barred if she fails to provide the requisite notice within one year.* [Emphasis added.]

The parties' obligations under Article 4 may be varied by their agreement * * *. The Account Terms required [Horton] to review each monthly account statement and to notify Chase in writing—within 30 days of when the statement was mailed or otherwise made available—of any unauthorized items or errors * * * identified in the statement. The Terms precluded [Horton] from asserting a claim relating to an unauthorized item or error for which she failed to provide the requisite notice.

* * * *

* * * [The] evidence demonstrates that [Horton] did not timely notify Chase in writing of the purported errors regarding the * * * account.

* * * Chase routinely mailed monthly account statements to its customers within six business days of the end date reflected on the statement. * * * Additionally, * * * Chase's online banking interface permitted customers to view their account statements as well as images of items drawn on their account.

* * * Notwithstanding [Horton's] receipt of these statements, she did not notify Chase in writing of any errors regarding the * * * account until her * * * petition [twenty months later] in which she alleged that Chase breached the account agreement by permitting the * * * withdrawal.

Decision and Remedy A state intermediate appellate court affirmed the summary judgment of the trial court. Chase required thirty days' written notice of any errors in its monthly account statements. Because Horton did not notify the bank in writing until long after the thirty-day deadline, the summary judgment dismissing her claim was appropriate.

Critical Thinking

• **Legal Environment** *Horton claimed that she had not agreed to the conversion of the account or to the withdrawal of the funds. These contentions did not affect the court's decision. Why not?*

• **Economic** *Why does the UCC "absolutely" limit the time that a customer has to report an altered check or unauthorized signature?*

Bank Negligence In one situation, a bank customer can escape liability, at least in part, for failing to notify the bank of forged checks within the required time period. When the customer can prove that the bank was also negligent—that is, that the bank failed to exercise ordinary care—then the bank, too, will be liable.

Ordinary care means that a bank must observe reasonable banking standards prevalent in that geographical area [UCC3–103]. If the customer can show the bank did not use ordinary care, the loss will be allocated between the bank and the customer on the basis of comparative negligence [UCC 4–406(e)].

Other Parties from Whom the Bank May Recover As noted earlier, a forged signature on a check has no legal effect as the signature of a drawer. Instead, the person who forged the signature is liable [UCC 3–403(a)]. Therefore, when a bank pays a check on which the drawer's signature is forged, the bank has a right to recover from the party who forged the signature (if he or she can be found). The bank may also have a right to recover from a party who transferred a check bearing a forged drawer's signature and received payment.

24–2g Checks Bearing Forged Indorsements

A bank that pays a customer's check bearing a forged indorsement must recredit the customer's account or be liable to the customer-drawer for breach of contract. **Example 24.7** Simon issues a $500 check "to the order of Antonio." Juan steals the check, forges Antonio's indorsement, and cashes the check. When the check reaches Simon's bank, the bank pays it and debits Simon's account. The bank must recredit the $500 to Simon's account because it failed to carry out Simon's order to pay "to the order of Antonio" [UCC 4–401(a)].

Eventually, the loss usually falls on the first party to take the instrument bearing the forged indorsement because a forged indorsement does not transfer title. Thus, whoever takes an instrument with a forged indorsement cannot become a holder. In *Example 24.7*, Simon's bank can recover—for breach of warranty—from the bank that cashed the check when Juan presented it [UCC 4–207(a)(2)].

The customer, in any event, has a duty to report forged indorsements promptly. Failure to report forged indorsements within a three-year period after the forged items have been made available to the customer relieves the bank of liability [UCC 4–111].

24–2h Altered Checks

The customer's instruction to the bank is to pay the exact amount on the face of the check to the holder. The bank has a duty to examine each check before making final payment. If the bank fails to detect an alteration, normally it is liable to its customer for the loss because it did not pay as the customer ordered.

The bank's loss is the difference between the original amount of the check and the amount actually paid [UCC 4–401(d)(1)]. **Example 24.8** Hailey Lyonne writes a check for $11 that is altered to $111. Lyonne's account will be charged $11 (the amount the customer ordered the bank to pay). The bank normally will be responsible for the $100 difference.

Customer Negligence As in a situation involving a forged drawer's signature, a customer's negligence can shift the loss when payment is made on an altered check (unless the bank was also negligent). For instance, a person may carelessly write a check and leave large gaps in it where additional numbers and words can be inserted (see Exhibit 24–3).

Similarly, a person who signs a check and leaves the dollar amount for someone else to fill in is barred from protesting when the bank unknowingly and in good faith pays whatever amount is shown [UCC 4–401(d)(2)]. Finally, if the bank can trace its loss on successive altered checks to the customer's failure to discover the initial alteration, the bank can reduce its liability for reimbursing the customer's account [UCC 4–406].

In every situation involving a forged drawer's signature or an alteration, a bank must observe reasonable commercial (banking) standards of care in paying on a customer's checks [UCC 4–406(e)]. The customer's negligence can be used as a defense only if the bank has exercised ordinary care.

Exhibit 24–3 A Poorly Filled-Out Check

XYZ CORPORATION
10 INDUSTRIAL PARK
ST. PAUL, MINNESOTA 56561

2206

June 8, 20 20   22-1/960

PAY TO THE ORDER OF _John Duncan_ $ 100.00

One hundred and 00/100 ———— DOLLARS

THE FIRST NATIONAL BANK OF MYTOWN
332 MINNESOTA STREET
MYTOWN, MINNESOTA 55555

Stephanie Roe, President

⑈94⑈77577⑈ 0885

Other Parties from Whom the Bank May Recover The bank is entitled to recover the amount of loss from the transferor who presented the check for payment. A transferor, by presenting a check for payment, warrants that the check has not been altered.

There are two exceptions to this rule. First, if the bank is also the drawer (as it is on a cashier's check), it cannot recover from the presenting party if the party is a holder in due course (HDC) acting in good faith [UCC 3–417(a)(2), 4–208(a)(2)]. The reason is that an instrument's drawer is in a better position than an HDC to know whether the instrument has been altered.

Second, an HDC who presents a certified check for payment in good faith will not be held liable under warranty principles if the check was altered before the HDC acquired it [UCC 3–417(a)(2), 4–207(a)(2)]. **Example 24.9** Jordan draws a check for $500 payable to David. David alters the amount to $5,000. The drawee bank, First National, certifies the check for $5,000. David negotiates the check to Ethan, an HDC. The drawee bank pays Ethan $5,000. On discovering the mistake, the bank cannot recover from Ethan the $4,500 paid by mistake, even though the bank was not in a superior position to detect the alteration. This is in accord with the purpose of certification, which is to obtain the definite obligation of a bank to honor a definite instrument. ■

24–3 The Bank's Duty to Accept Deposits

A bank has a duty to its customer to accept the customer's deposits of cash and checks. When checks are deposited, the bank must make the funds represented by those checks available within certain time frames. A bank also has a duty to collect payment on any checks payable or indorsed to its customers and deposited by them into their accounts. Cash deposits made in U.S. currency are received into customers' accounts without being subject to further collection procedures.

24–3a Availability Schedule for Deposited Checks

The Expedited Funds Availability Act[6] and Regulation CC[7] (the regulation implementing the act) establish when funds from deposited checks must be made available to the customer. The rules are as follows:

1. Any local check (drawn on a bank in the same area) deposited must be available for withdrawal by check or as cash within one business day from the date of deposit.

---

6. 12 U.S.C. Sections 4001–4010.
7. 12 C.F.R. Sections 229.1–229.42.

2. For nonlocal checks, the funds must be available for withdrawal within not more than five business days.

3. Under the Check Clearing for the 21st Century Act[8] (Check 21, which will be discussed in this chapter's *Landmark in the Law* feature), a bank must credit a customer's account as soon as the bank receives the funds.

4. For cash deposits, wire transfers, and government checks, funds must be available on the next business day.

5. The first $100 of any deposit must be available for cash withdrawal on the opening of the next business day after deposit.

A different availability schedule applies to deposits made at *nonproprietary* automated teller machines (ATMs). These are ATMs that are not owned or operated by the bank receiving the deposits. Basically, a five-day hold is permitted on all deposits, including cash deposits, made at nonproprietary ATMs. Other exceptions also exist. For instance, a banking institution has eight days to make funds available in new accounts (those open less than thirty days).

A bank that places a longer hold on a deposited check than that specified by the rules must notify the customer. A credit union's failure to provide this notice to its customer was at the center of the following case.

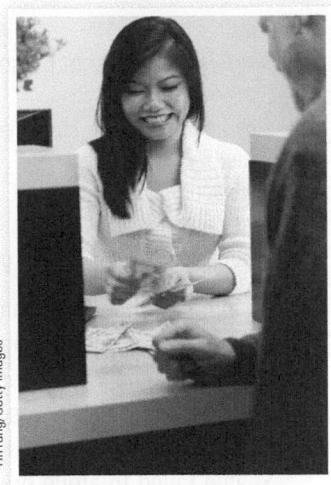

If you deposit a check at your bank that is written on another bank, can you withdraw those funds in cash immediately? Why or why not?

---

8. 12 U.S.C. Sections 5001–5018.

■ Case 24.3

Shahin v. Delaware Federal Credit Union

United States Court of Appeals, Third Circuit, 602 Fed.Appx. 50 (2015).

Background and Facts Nina Shahin deposited a check in the amount of $2,500 into her checking account at the Delaware Federal Credit Union (DelOne). DelOne placed a two-business-day "local hold" on the check pending verification. Concerned that the drawer's signature did not match the handwriting on the rest of the check, the bank placed it on a fifteen-day "nonverified" hold. Meanwhile, a payment from Shahin's checking account to Bank of America was denied for nonsufficient funds (NSF), and DelOne transferred funds from her savings account to cover other payments. DelOne then imposed two $30 penalties for NSF, as well as transfer fees totaling $6.

Shahin filed a suit in a federal district court against DelOne, alleging that the credit union had failed to give her proper notice of the extended hold. The court issued a summary judgment in

Is the bank liable when it incorrectly returns a check for nonsufficient funds? If so, what is the proper amount of damages?

Shahin's favor, awarding her the amount of the NSF and transfer fees, plus $1,000, the maximum amount of liability for a notice violation under Regulation CC. Shahin appealed, claiming that the amount of damages was insufficient.

In the Words of the Court
PER CURIAM [By the Whole Court].

* * * *

* * * *Proper notice of the extended hold [is] required under 12 C.F.R. Section 229.13 [of Regulation CC].* [Emphasis added.]

* * * *

Shahin claims on appeal that the District Court failed to award sufficient * * * damages. * * * Pursuant to 12 C.F.R. Section 229.21, a depository institution that fails to comply with the notice provision of Section 229.13 with respect to any person:

(Continues)

(a) * * * is liable to that person in an amount equal to the sum of—

(1) Any actual damage sustained by that person as a result of the failure;

(2) Such additional amount as the court may allow, except that—

(i) In the case of an individual action, liability under this paragraph shall not be less than $100 nor greater than $1,000 * * * .

* * * In her motion for summary judgment, Shahin asserted * * * that DelOne imposed $60 in NSF charges and $6.00 in transfer fees. The summary judgment record supported the District Court's finding that DelOne was liable to Shahin for the NSF and "overdraft" fees it imposed; those actual damages totaled $66.00. * * * Shahin failed to argue or provide evidence to support any other claim for actual damages.

DelOne was subject to liability to Shahin for penalties under Section 229.21(a)(2). * * * The amount of $1,000 was the maximum amount allowable under that provision.

Decision and Remedy The U.S. Court of Appeals for the Third Circuit affirmed the judgment of the lower court and the award to Shahin of the amount of DelOne's NSF and transfer fees, plus $1,000. The federal appellate court denied Shahin's claim for further damages.

Critical Thinking

• **Economic** *Is $1,000 an appropriate penalty for the failure of a depository institution to comply with Regulation CC's notice provision? Why or why not?*

24–3b The Traditional Collection Process

The bank collection process is the process by which a bank that accepts a check for deposit collects the amount from the issuing bank. Usually, deposited checks involve parties that do business at different banks, but sometimes checks are written between customers of the same bank. Either situation is governed by the statutory framework of Article 4 of the UCC.

Depositary Bank The first bank to receive a check for payment.

Payor Bank The bank on which a check is drawn (the drawee bank).

Collecting Bank Any bank handling an item for collection, except the payor bank.

Intermediary Bank Any bank to which an item is transferred in the course of collection, except the depositary or payor bank.

Designations of Banks The first bank to receive a check for payment is the **depositary bank**.[9] For instance, when a person deposits a tax-refund check into a personal checking account at the local bank, that bank is the depositary bank. The bank on which a check is drawn (the drawee bank) is the **payor bank**. Any bank except the payor bank that handles a check during some phase of the collection process is a **collecting bank**. Any bank except the payor bank or the depositary bank to which an item is transferred in the course of this collection process is an **intermediary bank**.

During the collection process, any bank can take on one or more of the various roles of depositary, payor, collecting, and intermediary bank. **Example 24.10** A buyer in New York writes a check on her New York bank and sends it to a seller in San Francisco. The seller deposits the check in her San Francisco bank account. The seller's bank is both a *depositary bank* and a *collecting bank*. The buyer's bank in New York is the *payor bank*. As the check travels from San Francisco to New York, any collecting bank handling the item in the collection process (other than the depositary bank and the payor bank) is also called an *intermediary bank*. Exhibit 24–4 illustrates how various banks function in the collection process in the context of this example. ■

Check Collection Between Customers of the Same Bank An item that is payable by the same bank that receives it (which in this situation is both the depositary bank and the payor bank) is called an "on-us item." Usually, the bank issues a "provisional credit" for on-us items within the same day. If the bank does not dishonor the check by the opening of the second banking day following its receipt, the check is considered paid [UCC 4–215(e)(2)].

---

9. All definitions in this section are found in UCC 4–105. The terms *depositary* and *depository* have different meanings in the banking context. A depository bank refers to a *physical place* (a bank or other institution) in which deposits or funds are held or stored.

Exhibit 24–4 The Check-Collection Process

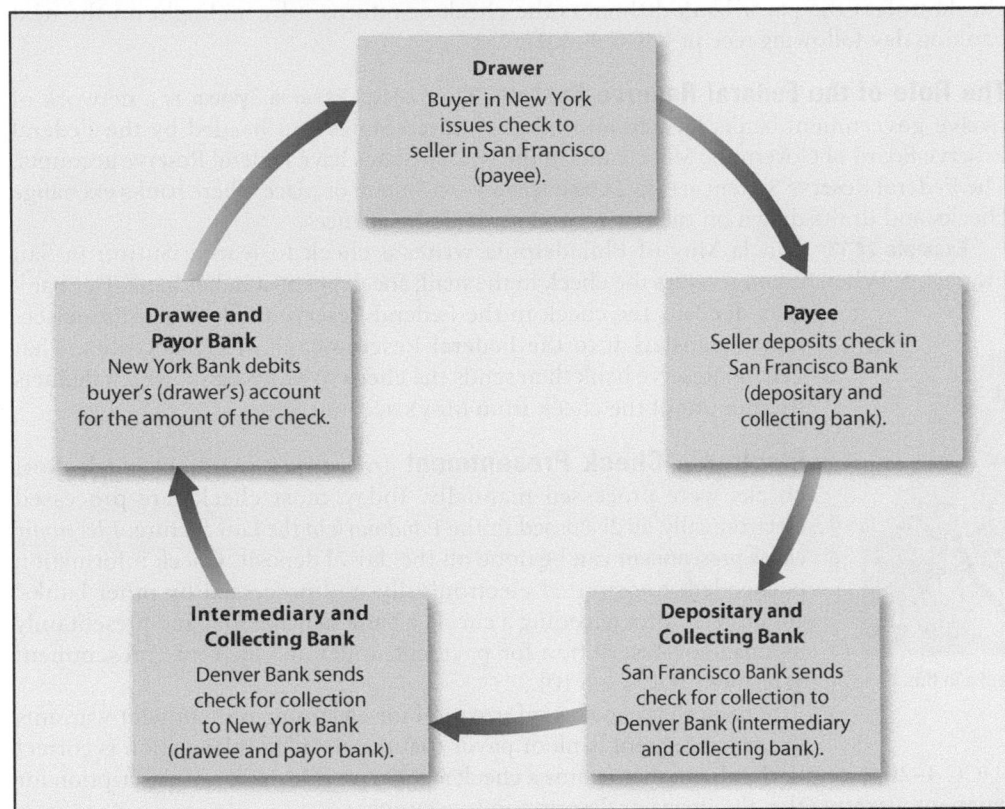

Example 24.11 Pam Otterley and Jenna Merkowitz have checking accounts at First State Bank. On Monday, Merkowitz deposits into her checking account a $300 check from Otterley. That same day, the bank issues Merkowitz a provisional (temporary) credit for $300. When the bank opens on Wednesday, Otterley's check is considered honored, and Merkowitz's provisional credit becomes a final payment.

Check Collection between Customers of Different Banks Once a depositary bank receives a check payable to another bank, it must arrange to present the check, either directly or through intermediary banks, to the appropriate payor bank. Each bank in the collection chain must pass the check on before midnight of the next banking day following its receipt [UCC 4–202(b)].[10] A "banking day" is any part of a day that the bank is open to carry on substantially all of its banking functions. Thus, if only a bank's drive-through facilities are open, a check deposited on Saturday will not trigger the bank's midnight deadline until the following Monday.

The UCC permits what is called *deferred posting*. According to UCC 4–108, "a bank may fix an afternoon hour of 2:00 P.M. or later as a cutoff hour for the handling of money and items and the making of entries on its books." Any checks received after that hour "may be treated as being received at the opening of the next banking day." Thus, if a depositary bank's cutoff hour is 3:00 P.M., a check received by that bank at 4:00 P.M. on Monday will be deferred for posting until Tuesday. In this situation, the bank's deadline will be midnight Wednesday.

"I saw a bank that said '24-Hour Banking,' but I don't have that much time."

Steven Wright
1955–present
(American comedian)

---

10. A bank may take a "reasonably longer time" in certain circumstances, such as when the bank's computer system is down due to a power failure, but the bank must show that its action is still timely [UCC 4–202(b)].

Federal Reserve System A network of twelve district banks and related branches located around the country and headed by the Federal Reserve Board of Governors. Most banks in the United States have Federal Reserve accounts.

Clearinghouse A system or place where banks exchange checks and drafts drawn on each other and settle daily balances.

Do bank customers directly deposit checks in the closest Federal Reserve Bank?

Learning Objective 3

What is electronic check presentment, and how does it differ from the traditional check-clearing process?

When the check reaches the payor bank, that bank is liable for the face amount of the check, unless the payor bank dishonors the check or returns it by midnight on the next banking day following receipt [UCC 4–302].[11]

The Role of the Federal Reserve System The **Federal Reserve System** is a network of twelve government banks located around the United States and headed by the Federal Reserve Board of Governors. Most banks in the United States have Federal Reserve accounts. The Federal Reserve System acts as a **clearinghouse**—a system or place where banks exchange checks and drafts drawn on each other and settle daily balances.

Example 24.12 Pamela Moy of Philadelphia writes a check to Jeanne Sutton in San Francisco. When Sutton receives the check in the mail, she deposits it in her bank. Her bank then deposits the check in the Federal Reserve Bank of San Francisco, which transfers it to the Federal Reserve Bank of Philadelphia. That Federal Reserve bank then sends the check to Moy's bank, which deducts the amount of the check from Moy's account.

Electronic Check Presentment In the past, as mentioned, most checks were processed manually. Today, most checks are processed electronically, as discussed in the *Landmark in the Law* feature. *Electronic check presentment* can be done on the day of deposit. Check information is encoded, transmitted electronically, and processed by other banks' computers. After encoding a check, a bank may retain it and present only its image or description for payment under an electronic presentment agreement [UCC 4–110].

A bank that encodes information for electronic presentment warrants to any subsequent bank or payor that the encoded information is correct [UCC 4–209]. Similarly, a bank that retains a check and presents its image or description for payment warrants that the image or description is accurate.

Regulation CC provides that a returned check must be encoded with the routing number of the depositary bank, the amount of the check, and other information. The regulation further states that a check must still be returned within the deadlines required by the UCC.

11. A bank may be excused from liability for failing to meet its midnight deadline under certain conditions, such as when there is an electrical outage or equipment failure and the bank has exercised "such diligence as the circumstances require" [UCC 4–109(d)].

Landmark in the Law

Check Clearing for the 21st Century Act (Check 21)

In the traditional collection process, paper checks had to be processed manually and physically transported before they could be cleared. Although the UCC allowed banks to use *electronic presentment*—that is, to transmit check information electronically instead of sending actual paper checks—this method was not widely adopted because it required agreements among individual banks.

Purpose of Check 21 To streamline the costly and time-consuming collection process and improve the overall efficiency of the nation's payment system, Congress passed the Check Clearing for the 21st Century Act (Check 21), which went into effect in 2004. Check 21 changed the collection process by creating a new negotiable instrument called a *substitute check*. Although the act did not require banks to change their check-collection practices, the creation of substitute checks has facilitated the use of electronic check processing.

Substitute Checks A substitute check is a paper reproduction of the front and back of an original check that contains all of the information required for automated processing. A bank creates substitute checks from digital images of original checks. It can then process the check information electronically or deliver substitute checks to banks that wish to continue receiving paper checks.

The original check can be destroyed after a substitute check is created, helping to prevent the check from being paid twice and reducing expenses. Nevertheless, at least for a while, not all checks will be converted to substitute checks.

Faster Access to Funds The Expedited Funds Availability Act requires the Federal Reserve Board to revise the availability schedule for funds from deposited checks to correspond to reductions in check-processing time. Therefore, as the speed of check processing continues to increase under Check 21, the Federal Reserve Board will reduce the maximum time that a bank can hold funds from deposited checks before making them available to the depositors.

That means, of course, that account holders will have faster access to their deposited funds. But it also means that they will have less *float time*—the time between when a check is written and when the amount is deducted from the account. Consequently, to avoid overdrafts, account holders need to make sure that funds are available to cover checks when they are written.

Application to Today's World *As more financial institutions transfer digital images of checks, the check-processing system becomes more efficient. Customers are increasingly unable to rely on banking float when they are low on funds, so they should make sure that funds are available to cover checks when they are written. Customers cannot opt out of Check 21. Nor can they refuse to accept a substitute check as proof of payment.*

24–4 Electronic Fund Transfers

An **electronic fund transfer (EFT)** is a transfer of funds through the use of an electronic terminal, smartphone, tablet, computer, or telephone. The law governing EFTs depends on the type of transfer involved. Consumer fund transfers are governed by the Electronic Fund Transfer Act (EFTA).[12] Commercial fund transfers are governed by Article 4A of the UCC.

Although electronic banking offers numerous benefits, it also poses difficulties on occasion. For instance, it is difficult to issue stop-payment orders with electronic banking. Also, fewer records are available to prove or disprove that a transaction took place. The possibilities for tampering with a person's private banking information have increased.

Electronic Fund Transfer (EFT) A transfer of funds through the use of an electronic terminal, smartphone, tablet, telephone, or computer.

24–4a Types of EFT Systems

Most banks offer EFT services. The following are the most common types of EFT systems used by bank customers:

1. *Automated teller machines (ATMs)*—The machines are connected online to the bank's computers. A customer inserts a plastic card (called an ATM or debit card) issued by the bank and keys in a *personal identification number (PIN)* to access her or his accounts and conduct banking transactions.

2. *Point-of-sale systems*—Online terminals allow consumers to transfer funds to merchants to pay for purchases using a debit card.

3. *Direct deposits and withdrawals*—Customers can authorize the bank to allow another party, such as the government or an employer, to make direct deposits into their accounts. Similarly, customers can request the bank to make automatic payments to a third party at regular, recurrent intervals from the customer's funds (insurance premiums or loan payments, for instance).

4. *Online payment systems*—Many financial institutions permit their customers to access the institution's computer system via the Internet and direct a transfer of funds between accounts or pay a particular bill. Payments can be made on a one-time or a recurring basis.

Know This
The EFTA does not provide for the reversal of an electronic transfer of funds once it has occurred.

Learning Objective 4
What are the four most common types of electronic fund transfers?

---

12. 15 U.S.C. Sections 1693–1693r. The EFTA amended Title IX of the Consumer Credit Protection Act.

Regulation E A set of rules issued by the Federal Reserve System's Board of Governors to protect users of electronic fund transfer systems.

24–4b Consumer Fund Transfers

The Electronic Fund Transfer Act (EFTA) provides a basic framework for the rights, liabilities, and responsibilities of users of EFT systems. Additionally, the act gave the Federal Reserve Board authority to issue rules and regulations to help implement the act's provisions. The Federal Reserve Board's implemental regulation is called **Regulation E.**

The EFTA governs financial institutions that offer electronic fund transfers involving consumer accounts. The types of accounts covered include checking accounts, savings accounts, and any other asset accounts established for personal, family, or household purposes.

Disclosure Requirements The EFTA is essentially a disclosure law benefiting consumers. The act requires financial institutions to inform consumers of their rights and responsibilities, including those listed here, with respect to EFT systems.

1. The bank must provide a monthly statement for every month in which there is an electronic transfer of funds. The statement must show the amount and date of the transfer, the names of the retailers or other third parties involved, the location or identification of the terminal, and the fees.

2. If a customer's debit card is lost or stolen and used without his or her permission, the customer will be required to pay no more than $50 if he or she notifies the bank of the loss or theft within two days of learning about it. Otherwise, the liability increases to $500. The customer may be liable for more than $500 if he or she fails to report the unauthorized use within sixty days after it appears on the customer's statement. (If a customer voluntarily gives her or his debit card to another, who then uses it improperly, the protections just mentioned do not apply.)

3. The customer must discover any error on the monthly statement within sixty days and notify the bank. The bank then has ten days to investigate and must report its conclusions to the customer in writing. If the bank takes longer than ten days, it must return the disputed amount to the customer's account until it finds the error. If there is no error, the customer has to return the disputed funds to the bank.

4. The bank must make receipts available for transactions made through computer terminals, but it is not obligated to do so for telephone transfers.

Violations and Damages EFT systems are vulnerable to fraud when someone uses another's card or code or other means to make unauthorized transfers. Unauthorized access to an EFT system constitutes a federal felony, and those convicted may be fined up to $10,000 and sentenced to as long as ten years in prison. Banks must strictly comply with the terms of the EFTA and are liable for any failure to adhere to its provisions.

For a bank's violation of the EFTA, a consumer may recover both actual damages (including attorneys' fees and costs) and punitive damages of not less than $100 and not more than $1,000. Even when a customer has sustained no actual damage, the bank may be liable for legal costs and punitive damages if it fails to follow the proper procedures outlined by the EFTA in regard to error resolution.

Know This

If any part of an electronic fund transfer is covered by the EFTA, the entire transfer is excluded from UCC Article 4A.

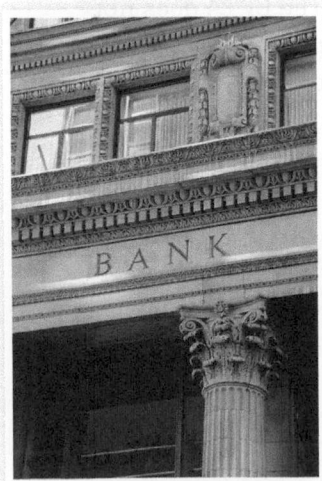

How do businesses transfer large sums of funds among themselves?

24–4c Commercial Fund Transfers

Funds are also transferred electronically "by wire" between commercial parties. In fact, the dollar volume of payments by wire transfer is more than $1 trillion a day—an amount that far exceeds the dollar volume of payments made by other means. The two major wire payment systems are the Federal Reserve's wire transfer network (Fedwire) and the New York Clearing House Interbank Payments Systems (CHIPS).

Commercial wire transfers are governed by Article 4A of the UCC, which has been adopted by most states. Article 4A uses the term *funds transfer* rather than *wire transfer* to describe the overall payment transaction. **Example 24.13** Jellux, Inc., owes $5 million to Perot Corporation. Instead of sending Perot a check or some other instrument that would enable Perot to obtain payment, Jellux instructs its bank, East Bank, to credit $5 million to Perot's account in West Bank. East Bank debits Jellux's East Bank account and wires $5 million to Perot's West Bank account. In more complex transactions, additional banks would be involved. ■

24–5 Online Banking and E-Money

Online banking is common in today's world. In a few minutes, anyone with the proper software can access his or her account, transfer funds, write "checks," pay bills, monitor investments, and even buy and sell stocks. Also commonplace today is the use of **e-money** (also called *digital cash*), which consists of funds stored on microchips in laptops, smartphones, tablets, and other devices. E-money replaces *physical* cash—coins and paper currency—with *virtual* cash in the form of electronic impulses.

E-Money Prepaid funds stored on microchips in laptops, smartphones, tablets, and other devices.

All these developments are part of a general trend toward making payments electronically. Electronic payment systems are often replacing checks, as discussed in this chapter's *Adapting the Law to the Online Environment* feature.

24–5a Online Banking

Most customers use three kinds of online banking services: consolidating bills and making payments, transferring funds among accounts, and applying for loans and credit cards.

Withdrawing and depositing funds are two banking functions not yet widely available online. Nevertheless, there are software applications (apps) that enable customers to make deposits into their accounts using electronic devices. For instance, JPMorgan Chase has an app that allows customers to deposit checks via their smartphones or tablets. The customer

---

Electronic Payment Systems and the Use of Checks

Adapting the Law to the Online Environment

Most young people no longer use checks. Businesses, in contrast, use checks regularly. Indeed, businesses are still using checks for more than half of their transactions. Issuing checks is costly. A typical business spends $5 to $25 to issue a paper check. That same transaction, if done electronically, costs between $1 and $2. Nevertheless, U.S. businesses account for more than two-thirds of the 22 billion checks written each year worldwide.

eBills on the Rise

In some areas of the world, such as within the European Union and parts of Latin America, businesses have been required to switch to digital invoices. That has not been the case in the United States.

Still, the use of electronic billing is on the rise in the United States. An electronic bill, or eBill, is simply an electronic version of a paper bill. eBills contain the same information as paper bills. The difference is that they can be viewed and paid online.

An increasing number of banks offer online banking services that enable customers to pay bills online. Such services include electronic bill payment and presentment (EBPP). One type of EBPP is offered directly by the company that provides goods or services to consumers. Another type allows consumers to pay multiple bills electronically through their bank's online banking system.

Business-to-Business (B2B) Bill Paying and the Cloud

As U.S. businesses have grown more comfortable with cloud computing, they have also grown more comfortable with digital payments. The Association of Financial Professionals estimates that approximately 60 percent of today's businesses are very likely or somewhat likely to convert to electronic payments for their suppliers within the next few years. Whereas the use of checks for business-to-business payments was 80 percent of all transactions in 2004, it is estimated that by 2020, that figure will drop to 40 percent.

Several companies offer Internet-based payment systems for B2B bill paying. Typical companies of this kind charge a monthly subscription cost plus a small per-unit transaction fee. These companies carry out the payment process without any additional input from the firms requesting the transaction payments. A growing number of cloud-based companies, such as Zoho Invoice and inHANCE, offer these services.

Critical Thinking

What are some additional risks in using electronic payment systems instead of checks?

simply takes a photo of the check's front and back (showing proper indorsement) with a smartphone or tablet and then sends that image to the bank.

Mobile payment apps, such as Apple Pay, Android Pay, and Samsung Pay, are also popular. These apps allow people to use a smartphone, smart watch, or tablet to make purchases at a growing number of establishments. The person simply holds a smartphone or other device close to the point-of-sale terminal to authenticate the transaction. Customers' payment information is kept private while the system generates a "dynamic security code" for each transaction.

24–5b Stored-Value Cards and Smart Cards

Stored-Value Card A card bearing a magnetic strip that holds magnetically encoded data providing access to stored funds.

The simplest kind of e-money system uses **stored-value cards.** These are plastic cards embossed with magnetic strips containing magnetically encoded data. Frequently, a stored-value card can be used only to purchase specific goods and services offered by the card issuer. An example is a gift card that is only redeemable at a particular retail store or restaurant.

Smart cards are plastic cards containing tiny microchips that can hold more information than a magnetic strip can. A smart card carries and processes security programming. This capability gives smart cards a technical advantage over stored-value cards. The microprocessors on smart cards can also authenticate the validity of transactions. Retailers can program electronic cash registers to confirm the authenticity of a smart card by examining a unique digital signature stored on its microchip. Common uses for smart cards are as credit cards and ATM cards.

Learning Objective 5

What is the difference between a stored-value card and a smart card?

Smart Card A card containing a microprocessor with security programming that is typically used for financial transactions, personal identification, and other purposes.

Practice and Review

RPM Pizza, Inc., issued a check for $96,000 to Systems Marketing for an advertising campaign. A few days later, RPM decided not to go through with the deal and placed a written stop-payment order on the check. RPM and Systems had no further contact for many months. Three weeks after the stop-payment order expired, however, Toby Rierson, an employee at Systems, cashed the check. Bank One Cambridge, RPM's bank, paid the check with funds from RPM's account. Because the check was more than six months old, it was stale. Thus, according to standard banking procedures as well as Bank One's own policies, the signature on the check should have been specially verified, but it was not. RPM filed a suit in a federal district court against Bank One to recover the amount of the check. Using the information presented in the chapter, answer the following questions.

1.   How long is a written stop-payment order effective? What else could RPM have done to prevent this check from being cashed?

2.   What would have happened if RPM had not had a legitimate reason for stopping payment on the check?

3.   What are a bank's obligations with respect to stale checks?

4.   Would a court be likely to hold the bank liable for the amount of the check because it failed to verify the signature on the check? Why or why not?

Debate This

To reduce fraud, checks that utilize mechanical or electronic signature systems should not be honored.

Key Terms

Chapter Summary: Banking in the Digital Age

Checks and the Bank-Customer Relationship	**1.** *Checks—* **a.** Cashier's check—A check drawn by a bank on itself (the bank is both the drawer and the drawee) and purchased by a customer. In effect, the bank assumes responsibility for paying the check, thus making the check nearly the equivalent of cash. **b.** Traveler's check—An instrument on which a financial institution is both the drawer and the drawee. The purchaser is required to sign the check at the time it is bought and again at the time it is used as a negotiable instrument. **c.** Certified check—A check for which the drawee bank certifies in writing that it has set aside funds from the drawer's account to ensure payment of the check on presentation. On certification, the drawer and all prior indorsers are completely discharged from liability on the check. **2.** *The bank-customer relationship—*When a customer opens an account, three types of relationships are established with the bank: a creditor-debtor relationship, an agency relationship, and a contractual relationship.
The Bank's Duty to Honor Checks	Generally, a bank has a duty to honor its customers' checks, provided that the customers have sufficient funds on deposit to cover the checks [UCC 4–401(a)]. The bank is liable to its customers for actual damages proved to be due to wrongful dishonor [UCC 4–402(b)]. **1.** *Overdraft—*The bank has a right to charge a customer's account for any item properly payable, even if the charge results in an overdraft [UCC 4–401]. **2.** *Postdated check—*The bank may charge a postdated check against a customer's account, unless the customer notifies the bank, in a timely manner, not to pay the check until the stated date [UCC 4–401]. **3.** *Stale check—*The bank is not obligated to pay an uncertified check presented more than six months after its date, but the bank may do so in good faith without liability [UCC 4–404]. **4.** *Stop-payment order—*The customer (or a person authorized to draw on the account) must make a stop-payment order in time for the bank to have a reasonable opportunity to act. Oral orders are binding for only fourteen days unless they are confirmed in writing. Written or electronic orders are effective for six months unless renewed in writing [UCC 4–403(b)]. The bank is liable for wrongful payment over a timely stop-payment order to the extent that the customer suffers a loss. **5.** *Incompetence or death of a customer—*So long as the bank does not know of the death or incompetence of a customer, the bank can pay an item without liability. Even with knowledge of a customer's death, a bank can honor or certify checks (in the absence of a stop-payment order) for ten days after the date of the customer's death [UCC 4–405]. **6.** *Checks with forged drawers' signatures—*The customer has a duty to examine account statements with reasonable care on receipt and to notify the bank promptly of any forged signatures. On a series of forged signatures by the same wrongdoer, examination and report must be made within thirty calendar days of receipt of the first statement containing a forged item [UCC 4–406]. The customer's failure to comply with these rules releases the bank from liability unless the bank failed to exercise ordinary care, in which case liability may be apportioned according to a comparative negligence standard. Regardless of care or lack of care, the customer is barred from holding the bank liable after one year for forged customer signatures.

(Continues)

7. *Checks bearing forged indorsements*—A bank that pays a customer's check bearing a forged indorsement must recredit the customer's account or be liable to the customer for breach of contract. A customer's failure to report a forged indorsement within a three-year period after the forged items are available to the customer relieves the bank of liability [UCC 4-111].

8. *Altered checks*—If the bank fails to detect an alteration, normally it is liable to its customer because it did not pay as the customer ordered. Customer negligence can shift the loss.

The Bank's Duty to Accept Deposits

A bank has a duty to accept deposits made by its customers into their accounts. Funds from deposited checks must be made available to customers according to a schedule mandated by the Expedited Funds Availability Act and Regulation CC. A bank also has a duty to collect payment on any checks deposited by its customers. When checks deposited by customers are drawn on other banks, the check-collection process comes into play.

1. *Designations of banks*—UCC 4–105 provides the following definitions of banks involved in the collection process:
   a. Depository bank—The first bank to accept a check for payment.
   b. Payor bank—The bank on which a check is drawn.
   c. Collecting bank—Any bank except the payor bank that handles a check during the collection process.
   d. Intermediary bank—Any bank except the payor bank or the depositary bank to which an item is transferred in the course of the collection process.

2. *Check collection between customers of the same bank*—A check payable by the depositary bank that receives it is an "on-us item." If the bank does not dishonor the check by the opening of the second banking day following its receipt, the check is considered paid [UCC 4–215(e)(2)].

3. *Check collection between customers of different banks*—Each bank in the collection process must pass the check on to the next appropriate bank before midnight of the next banking day following its receipt [UCC 4–108, 4–202(b), 4–302].

4. *The role of the Federal Reserve System*—The Federal Reserve System facilitates the check-clearing process by serving as a clearinghouse for checks.

5. *Electronic check presentment*—Check information may be encoded, transmitted electronically, and processed by other banks' computers. After encoding a check, a bank may retain it and present only its image or description for payment under an electronic presentment agreement [UCC 4-209, 4–110].

Electronic Fund Transfers

1. *Types of EFT systems*—
   a. Automated teller machines (ATMs).
   b. Point-of-sale systems.
   c. Direct deposits and withdrawals.
   d. Online payment systems.

2. *Consumer fund transfers*—Consumer fund transfers are governed by the Electronic Fund Transfer Act (EFTA). The EFTA is basically a disclosure law that sets forth the rights and duties of the bank and the customer with respect to EFT systems. Banks must comply strictly with EFTA requirements.

3. *Commercial fund transfers*—Article 4A of the UCC, which has been adopted by almost all of the states, governs fund transfers not subject to the EFTA or other federal or state statutes.

Online Banking and E-Money

1. *Online banking*—Most customers use three kinds of online banking services:
   a. Consolidating bills and making payments.
   b. Transferring funds among accounts.
   c. Applying for loans and credit cards.

2. *Stored-value cards and smart cards*—
   a. Stored-value cards hold magnetically encoded data providing access to stored funds (for instance, a gift card).
   b. Smart cards contain microchips with security programming. They are typically used for financial transactions, personal identification, and other purposes (for instance, ATM cards).

Issue Spotters

1. Lyn writes a check for $900 to Mac, who indorses the check in blank and transfers it to Jan. She presents the check to Omega Bank, the drawee bank, for payment. Omega does not honor the check. Is Lyn liable to Jan? Could Lyn be subject to criminal prosecution? Why or why not? (See *The Bank's Duty to Honor Checks*.)

2. Herb steals a check from Kay's checkbook, forges Kay's signature, and transfers the check to Will for value. Unaware that the signature is not Kay's, Will presents the check to First State Bank, the drawee. The bank cashes the check. Two weeks later, Kay discovers the forgery and insists that the bank recredit her account. Can the bank refuse to recredit Kay's account? If not, can the bank recover the amount paid to Will? Why or why not? (See *The Bank's Duty to Honor Checks*.)

—**Check your answers to the *Issue Spotters* against the answers provided in Appendix D at the end of this text.**

Business Scenarios and Case Problems

24–1. Forged Checks. Roy Supply, Inc., and R. M. R. Drywall, Inc., had checking accounts at Wells Fargo Bank. Both accounts required all checks to carry two signatures—that of Edward Roy and that of Twila June Moore, both of whom were executive officers of both companies. Between January 2018 and March 2019, the bank honored hundreds of checks on which Roy's signature was forged by Moore. On January 31, 2020, Roy and the two corporations notified the bank of the forgeries and then filed a suit in a California state court against the bank, alleging negligence. Who is liable for the amounts of the forged checks? Why? (See *The Bank's Duty to Honor Checks*.)

24–2. Customer Negligence. Gary goes grocery shopping and carelessly leaves his checkbook in his shopping cart. His checkbook, with two blank checks remaining, is stolen by Dolores. On May 5, Dolores forges Gary's name on a check for $100 and cashes the check at Gary's bank, Citizens Bank of Middletown. Gary has not reported the loss of his blank checks to his bank. On June 1, Gary receives his monthly bank statement from Citizens Bank that includes the forged check, but he does not notice the item, nor does he examine his bank statement. On June 20, Dolores forges Gary's last check. This check is for $1,000 and is cashed at Eastern City Bank, a bank with which Dolores has previously done business. Eastern City Bank puts the check through the collection process, and Citizens Bank honors it. On July 1, on receipt of his bank statement and canceled checks covering June transactions, Gary discovers both forgeries and immediately notifies Citizens Bank. Dolores cannot be found. Gary claims that Citizens Bank must recredit his account for both checks, as his signature was forged. Discuss fully Gary's claim. (See *The Bank's Duty to Honor Checks*.)

24–3. Forged Indorsements. Adley Abdulwahab (Wahab) opened an account on behalf of W Financial Group, LLC, with Wells Fargo Bank. Wahab was one of three authorized signers on the account. Five months later, Wahab withdrew $1,701,250 from W Financial's account to buy a cashier's check payable to Lubna Lateef. Wahab visited a different Wells Fargo branch and deposited the check into the account of CA Houston Investment Center, LLC. Wahab was the only authorized signer on this account. Lateef never received or indorsed the check. W Financial filed a suit to recover the amount. Applying the rules for payment on a forged indorsement, who is liable? [*Jones v. Wells Fargo Bank, N.A.*, 666 F.3d 955 (5th Cir. 2012)] (See *The Bank's Duty to Honor Checks*.)

24–4. Business Case Problem with Sample Answer—Consumer Fund Transfers. Stephen Patterson held an account with Suntrust Bank in Alcoa, Tennessee. Juanita Wehrman—with whom Patterson was briefly involved in a romantic relationship—stole his debit card and used it for sixteen months (well beyond the length of their relationship) to make unauthorized purchases in excess of $30,000. When Patterson learned what was happening, he closed his account. The bank refused to reimburse him more than $677.46—the amount of unauthorized transactions that occurred within sixty days of the transmittal of the bank statement that revealed the first unauthorized transaction. Is the bank's refusal justifiable? Explain. [*Patterson v. Suntrust Bank*, 2013 WL 139315 (Tenn.App. 2013)] (See *Electronic Fund Transfers*.)

—**For a sample answer to Problem 24–4, go to Appendix E at the end of this text.**

24–5. Forged Drawers' Signatures. Victor Nacim had a checking account at Compass Bank. The "Deposit Agreement" required him to report an unauthorized transaction within thirty days of his receipt of the statement on which it appeared to obtain a recredit. When Nacim moved to a new residence, he asked the bank to update the address on his account. Compass continued to mail his statements to his previous address, however, and Nacim did not receive them. In the meantime, Compass officer David Peterson made an unauthorized withdrawal of $34,000 from Nacim's account. A month later, Peterson told Nacim what he had done. The next month, Nacim asked the bank for a recredit. Compass refused on the ground that he reported the withdrawal more than thirty days after the bank mailed the statement on which it appeared—a statement that Nacim never received. Is Nacim entitled to a recredit? Explain. [*Compass Bank v. Nacim*, 459 S.W.3d 95 (Tex. App.—El Paso 2015)] (See *The Bank's Duty to Honor Checks*.)

24–6. Checks Bearing Forged Indorsements. The law firm of Levy Baldante Finney & Rubenstein, P.C., had a checking account at TD Bank, N.A. The account agreement required notice to the bank of "any problem with a check" within thirty days from when a statement showing the item was mailed. Jack Cohen, a partner at the law firm, stole more than three hundred thousand dollars from the account by fraudulently indorsing twenty-nine checks that had been made payable to clients and other third parties. More than two years after the first item appeared in an account statement, Susan Huffington, the firm's bookkeeper, discovered one of the fraudulently indorsed checks. She reviewed previous statements with images of the back of each check, compiled a list of fraudulently indorsed items, and notified the bank to recredit the account. Is the bank obligated to honor this request? Why or why not?

[*Levy Baldante Finney & Rubenstein, P.C. v. Wells Fargo Bank, N.A.*, 2018 WL 847756 (Pa.Super. 2018)] (See *The Bank's Duty to Honor Checks*.)

24–7. A Question of Ethics—The IDDR Approach and Unauthorized Items. *While working as an executive assistant to David Ducote, Michelle Freytag fraudulently obtained a credit card in Ducote's name from Whitney National Bank in New Orleans, Louisiana. Freytag told Whitney to pay the credit card balances with funds from Ducote's bank account. The bank included a "debit memo" of each payment with the monthly account statements sent to Ducote. But Ducote never contacted the bank about any unauthorized items. Freytag's scheme was not discovered until, more than five years later, the bank contacted Ducote to ask about some of the charges to the credit card. [Ducote v. Whitney National Bank, 212 So.3d 729 (La.App. 5 Cir. 2017)] (See* The Bank's Duty to Honor Checks.*)*

1. Does a bank customer in Ducote's position have an ethical duty to examine his or her account statements? Discuss.
2. Is the bank ethically obligated to recredit Ducote's account? Explain.

Critical Thinking and Writing Assignments

24–8. Critical Legal Thinking. Under the revised Article 4, a bank is no longer required to include the customer's canceled checks when it sends monthly statements to the customer. A bank may simply itemize the checks (by number, date, and amount). It may provide photocopies of the checks as well but is not required to do so. What implications do these rules have for bank customers in terms of liability for unauthorized signatures and indorsements? (See *The Bank's Duty to Honor Checks*.)

24–9. Time-Limited Group Assignment—Death of a Customer. On January 5, Brian drafts a check for $3,000 drawn on Southern Marine Bank and payable to his assistant, Shanta. Brian puts last year's date on the check by mistake. On January 7, before Shanta has had a chance to go to the bank, Brian is killed in an automobile accident. Southern Marine Bank is aware of Brian's death. On January 10, Shanta presents the check to the bank, and the bank honors the check by payment to Shanta. Later,

Brian's widow, Joyce, claims that because the bank knew of Brian's death and also because the check was by date over one year old, the bank acted wrongfully when it paid Shanta. Joyce, as executor of Brian's estate and sole heir by his will, demands that Southern Marine Bank recredit Brian's estate for the check paid to Shanta. (See *The Bank's Duty to Honor Checks*.)

1. The first group will determine whether the bank acted wrongfully by honoring Brian's check and paying Shanta.
2. The second group will assess whether Joyce has a valid claim against Southern Marine Bank for the amount of the check paid to Shanta.
3. The third group will assume that the check Brian drafted was on his business account rather than on his personal account and that he had two partners in the business. Would a business partner be in a better position to force Southern Marine Bank to recredit Brian's account than his widow? Why or why not?

Security Interests and Creditors' Rights

25

> "I will pay you some, and, as most debtors do, promise you infinitely."

William Shakespeare
1564–1616
(English dramatist and poet)

When buying or leasing goods, debtors frequently pay some portion of the price now and promise to pay the remainder in the future, as William Shakespeare observed in the chapter-opening quotation. Logically, sellers and lenders do not want to risk nonpayment, so they usually will not sell goods or lend funds unless the payment is somehow guaranteed.

Whenever the payment of a debt is guaranteed, or *secured*, by personal property owned or held by the debtor, the transaction becomes known as a **secured transaction**. Indeed, business as we know it could not exist without laws permitting and governing secured transactions. When Stone Investments, Ltd., wants to buy a Learjet 70 for executive travel, it borrows funds from Capital Bank. Capital obtains a security interest in the plane to guarantee that Stone will repay the debt.

Article 9 of the Uniform Commercial Code (UCC) governs secured transactions in personal property. Personal property includes accounts, agricultural liens, *chattel paper* (documents or records evidencing a debt secured by personal property), and fixtures (certain property that is attached to land). Personal property also includes other types of intangible property, such as negotiable instruments and patents. Article 9 does not cover creditor-collection devices such as liens and garnishments.

Learning Objectives

The five Learning Objectives *below are designed to help improve your understanding. After reading this chapter, you should be able to answer the following questions:*

1. What is required to create a security interest?

2. How can a security interest extend to a debtor's newly acquired inventory?

3. If two parties have perfected security interests in the debtor's collateral, which party has priority on default?

4. When is a creditor required to sell or otherwise dispose of the repossessed collateral?

5. What is a suretyship, and how does it differ from a guaranty?

25–1 Creating and Perfecting a Security Interest

A creditor has two main concerns if the debtor **defaults** (fails to pay the debt as promised). The first is whether the debt can be satisfied through the possession and (usually) sale of the collateral. The second concern is whether the creditor will have priority over any other

Secured Transaction Any transaction in which the payment of a debt is guaranteed, or secured, by personal property owned by the debtor or in which the debtor has a legal interest.

Default Failure to pay a debt when it is due.

Secured Party A creditor who has a security interest in the debtor's collateral, including a seller, lender, cosigner, or buyer of accounts or chattel paper.

Debtor Under Article 9 of the UCC, any party who owes payment or performance of a secured obligation.

Security Interest Any interest in personal property or fixtures that secures payment or performance of an obligation.

Security Agreement An agreement that creates or provides for a security interest between the debtor and a secured party.

Collateral Under Article 9 of the UCC, the property subject to a security interest.

Financing Statement A document filed by a secured creditor with the appropriate official to give notice to the public of the creditor's security interest in collateral belonging to the debtor named in the statement.

Learning Objective 1

What is required to create a security interest?

creditors or buyers who may have rights in the same collateral. These two concerns are met through the creation and perfection of a security interest.

25–1a Definitions

Before we examine the creation and perfection of security interests, however, you need to understand the UCC's terminology, which is uniformly used by every state. The following is a brief summary of the UCC's definitions relating to secured transactions.

1. A **secured party** is any creditor who has a *security interest* in the *debtor's collateral*. This creditor can be a seller, a lender, a cosigner, or even a buyer of accounts or chattel paper [UCC 9–102(a)(72)].

2. A **debtor** is a person who *owes payment* or other performance of a secured obligation [UCC 9–102(a)(28)].

3. A **security interest** is the *interest* in the collateral (such as personal property or fixtures) that *secures payment or performance of an obligation* [UCC 1–201(37)].

4. A **security agreement** is an *agreement* that *creates* or provides for a *security interest* [UCC 9–102(a) (73)]. In other words, it is the contract in which a debtor agrees to give a creditor the right to take his or her property in the event of default.

5. **Collateral** is the *subject* of the *security interest* [UCC 9–102(a)(12)].

6. A **financing statement**—referred to as the UCC-1 form—is the *instrument normally filed to give public notice to third parties* of the *secured party's security interest* [UCC 9–102(a)(39)].

Together, these basic definitions form the concept under which a debtor-creditor relationship becomes a secured transaction relationship (see Exhibit 25–1).

25–1b Requirements to Create a Security Interest

To become a secured party, a creditor must obtain a security interest in the collateral of the debtor. Three requirements must be met for a creditor to have an enforceable security interest:

1. Unless the creditor has possession of the collateral, there must be a written or authenticated security agreement that clearly describes the collateral subject to the security interest and that is signed or authenticated by the debtor.

2. The secured party must give something of value to the debtor.

3. The debtor must have "rights" in the collateral.

Exhibit 25–1 The Secured Transactions Relationship

In a security agreement, a debtor and a creditor agree that the creditor will have a security interest in collateral in which the debtor has rights. In essence, the collateral secures the loan and ensures the creditor of payment should the debtor default.

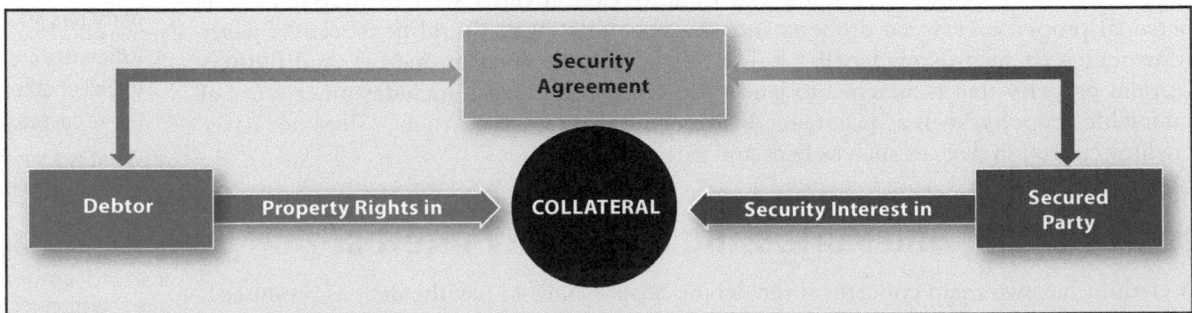

Once these requirements have been met, the creditor's rights are said to attach to the collateral. **Attachment** gives the creditor an enforceable security interest in the collateral [UCC 9–203].[1]

Example 25.1 To furnish his new office suite, Bryce applies for a credit card at an office supply store. The application contains a clause stating that the store will retain a security interest in the goods that he buys with the card until he has paid for them in full. This application is a *written security agreement*, which is the first requirement for an enforceable security interest. The goods that Bryce buys with the card are the *something of value* from the secured party (the second requirement). His ownership interest in those goods is the *right* that he has in them (the third requirement). Thus, the requirements for an enforceable security interest are met. When Bryce buys something with the card, the store's rights attach to the purchased goods. ▪

Attachment In a secured transaction, the process by which a secured creditor's interest "attaches" to the collateral and the creditor's security interest becomes enforceable.

Written or Authenticated Security Agreement
When the collateral is not in the possession of the secured party, the security agreement must be either written or authenticated. It must also describe the collateral.

Here, **authenticate** means to sign, execute, or adopt any symbol on an electronic record that verifies that the person signing has the intent to adopt or accept the record [UCC 9–102(a)(7)(69)]. Authentication provides for electronic filing (the filing process will be discussed later). See this chapter's *Adapting the Law to the Online Environment* feature for a discussion of a type of secured transaction that is performed online.

A security agreement must contain a description of the collateral that reasonably identifies it. Generally, such phrases as "all the debtor's personal property" or "all the debtor's assets" would *not* constitute a sufficient description [UCC 9–108(c)].

If the debtor signs or otherwise authenticates a security agreement, does he or she also have to sign an attached list of the collateral to create a valid security interest? That was the question before the court in the following case.

If you use a store-provided credit card at that store, does the store automatically have a security interest in what you purchase?

Authenticate To sign, execute, or adopt any symbol on an electronic record that verifies the intent to adopt or accept the record.

---

1. The term *attachment* has a different meaning in secured transactions than in the context of judicial liens, where it refers to a court-ordered seizure of property.

✳ Spotlight on Wedding Rings: Case 25.1

Royal Jewelers, Inc. v. Light
Supreme Court of North Dakota, 2015 ND 44, 859 N.W.2d 921 (2015).

Background and Facts Steven Light bought a $55,050 wedding ring for his wife, Sherri Light, on credit from Royal Jewelers, Inc., a store in Fargo, North Dakota. The receipt granted Royal a security interest in the ring. Later, Royal assigned its interest to GRB Financial Corp. Steven and GRB signed a modification agreement changing the repayment terms. An attached exhibit listed the

Who retains a security interest in a wedding ring when the buyer dies?

items pledged as security for the modification, including the ring. Steven did not separately sign the exhibit.

A year later, Steven died. Royal and GRB filed a suit in a North Dakota state court against Sherri, alleging that GRB had a valid security interest in the ring. Sherri cited UCC 9–203, under which there is an enforceable interest only if "the debtor has authenticated a security

(Continues)

agreement that provides a description of the collateral." Sherri argued that the modification agreement did not "properly authenticate" the description of the collateral, including the ring, because Steven had not signed the attached exhibit. The court issued a judgment in GRB's favor. Sherri appealed.

In the Words of the Court
CROTHERS, Justice.

* * * *

Sherri Light * * * claims the * * * modification agreement signed by Steven Light * * * did not properly authenticate the agreement describing the collateral under [North Dakota Commercial Code (NDCC)] Section 41–09–13(2)(c)(1) [North Dakota's version of UCC 9–203] because he did not separately sign the exhibit identifying secured collateral, including the ring.

Section 41–09–13(2)(c)(1) provides:

2. * * * A security interest is enforceable against the debtor and third parties with respect to the collateral only if:

* * * *

c. One of the following conditions is met:

(1) The debtor has authenticated a security agreement that provides a description of the collateral * * *.

The plain language of that statute requires a debtor to authenticate a security agreement providing a description of the collateral. [Under NDCC Section 41–09–02(1)(g) [North Dakota's version of UCC 9–102(1)(g),] "authenticate" means "to sign" or "to execute or otherwise adopt a symbol, or encrypt or similarly process a record in whole or in part, with the present intent of the authenticating person to identify the person and adopt or accept a record." NDCC Section 41–09–08(2) [North Dakota's version of

UCC 9–108(2)] says a description of collateral is sufficient if it reasonably identifies the collateral and may include a specific listing or any other method by which the collateral is objectively determinable.

* * * No authority [requires] a debtor to separately sign an exhibit attached to and referenced in a signed security agreement * * *. *A security agreement is not unenforceable merely because a description of collateral in an exhibit was attached to the security agreement * * * Several documents may be considered together as a security agreement.* [Emphasis added.]

Steven Light signed the * * * modification agreement which referenced an attached exhibit listing assets pledged as security for the note. * * * The attached exhibit listing the ring was part of the * * * agreement signed by Steven Light, and the [lower] court determined the modification agreement was properly executed by Steven Light. Evidence establishes Steven Light initially granted a valid security interest in the ring and the ring had not been fully paid for * * *. GRB Financial received an assignment of the security interest from Royal Jewelers * * *, and the court did not err in finding GRB Financial had a valid and enforceable security interest in the ring.

Decision and Remedy The North Dakota Supreme Court affirmed the lower court's judgment. The court stated, "No authority [requires] a debtor to separately sign an exhibit attached to and referenced in a signed security agreement."

Critical Thinking

• **Ethical** *Under the circumstances, is it ethical for GRB to enforce its security interest in the ring to recover the unpaid amount of the price? Discuss.*

Secured Party Must Give Value The secured party must give something of value to the debtor. Some examples of value include a binding commitment to extend credit or consideration to support a simple contract [UCC 1–204]. Normally, the value given by a secured party is in the form of a direct loan or a commitment to sell goods on credit.

Debtor Must Have Rights in the Collateral The debtor must have rights in the collateral. That means that the debtor must have some ownership interest or right to obtain possession of the collateral. For instance, a retail seller-debtor can give a secured party a security interest not only in existing inventory owned by the retailer but also in *future* inventory to be acquired by the retailer. (A common misconception is that the debtor must have title to the collateral to have rights in it, but this is not a requirement.)

Secured Transactions Online

When you buy something online, you typically must use your credit card, make an electronic fund transfer, or send a check before the goods that you bought are sent to you. If you are buying an expensive item, such as a car, you are not likely to send funds without being assured that you will receive the item in the condition promised. Enter the concept of escrow.

Escrow Accounts

Escrow accounts are commonly used in real estate transactions, but they are also useful for smaller transactions, particularly those done on the Internet. An escrow account involves three parties—the buyer, the seller, and a trusted third party that collects, holds, and disperses funds according to instructions from the buyer and seller. Escrow services are provided by licensed and regulated escrow companies. For instance, if you buy a car on the Internet, you and the seller will agree on an escrow company to which you will send the funds. When you receive the car and are satisfied with it, the escrow company will release the funds to the seller. This is a type of secured transaction.

Escrow.com

One of the best-known online escrow firms is Escrow.com, which had provided escrow services for more than $3.5 billion in secured transactions by 2019. All of its escrow services are offered via its website and provided independently by Internet Escrow Services, one of its operating subsidiaries. Escrow.com is particularly useful for transactions that involve an international buyer or seller. It has become the recommended transaction settlement service for Autotrader, Resale Weekly, Cars.com, eBay Motors, and Flippa.com.

Critical Thinking

How could online escrow services reduce Internet fraud?

25–1c Perfecting a Security Interest

Perfection is the legal process by which secured parties protect themselves against the claims of third parties who may wish to have their debts satisfied out of the same collateral. Whether a secured party's security interest is perfected or unperfected can have serious consequences for the secured party.

What if a debtor has borrowed from two different creditors, for instance, using the same property as collateral for both loans? If the debtor defaults on both loans, which of the two creditors has first rights to the collateral? In this situation, the creditor with a perfected security interest will prevail.

Perfection usually is accomplished by filing a financing statement. In some circumstances, however, a security interest becomes perfected even though no financing statement is filed.

Perfection by Filing The most common means of perfection is by filing a *financing statement* with the office of the appropriate government official. A financing statement gives public notice to third parties of the secured party's security interest. The security agreement itself can also be filed to perfect the security interest. The financing statement must provide the names of the debtor and the secured party, and must identify the collateral covered by the financing statement. A uniform financing statement form is now used in all states [see UCC 9–521].

Communication of the financing statement to the appropriate filing office, together with the correct filing fee, or the acceptance of the financing statement by the filing officer constitutes a filing [UCC 9–516(a)]. The filing can

Perfection The legal process by which secured parties protect themselves against the claims of third parties who may wish to have their debts satisfied out of the same collateral. It is usually accomplished by filing a financing statement with the appropriate government official.

When a bank finances the purchase of a tractor, how does it normally perfect its security interest in that tractor?

be accomplished electronically [UCC 9–102(a)(18)]. In fact, most states use electronic filing systems. A financing statement may be filed even before a security agreement is made or a security interest attaches [UCC 9–502(d)].

The Debtor's Name. The UCC requires that a financing statement be filed under the name of the debtor [UCC 9–502(a)(1)]. Filings are indexed by the name of the debtor so that they can be located by subsequent searchers. Slight variations in names normally will not be considered misleading if a search of the filing office's records, using a standard computer search engine routinely used by that office, would disclose the filings [UCC 9–506(c)].[2]

UCC 9–503 sets out some detailed rules for determining when the debtor's name as it appears on a financing statement is sufficient.

1. *Corporations.* For corporations, which are organizations that have registered with the state, the debtor's name on the financing statement must be "the name of the debtor indicated on the public record of the debtor's jurisdiction of organization" [UCC 9–503(a)(1)].

2. *Trusts.* If the debtor is a trust or a trustee for property held in trust, the financing statement must disclose this information and provide the trust's name as specified in its official documents [UCC 9–503(a)(3)].

3. *Individuals and organizations.* For all others, the financing statement must disclose "the individual or organizational name of the debtor" [UCC 9–503(a)(4)(A)]. The word *organization* includes unincorporated associations, such as clubs, churches, joint ventures, and general partnerships. If an organizational debtor does not have a group name, the names of the individuals in the group must be listed.

4. *Trade names.* When the debtor's trade name is not the legal name of the business, providing only the trade name in a financing statement is *not* sufficient for perfection [UCC 9–503(c)]. The financing statement must also include the owner-debtor's actual name. **Example 25.2** Pete Hanson is a plumber who does business under the name HoneyPot Plumbing. Hanson obtains a loan from North Bank to purchase some equipment for his business. For North Bank to perfect its security interest in the equipment, the filed financing statement must include the owner's name, Pete Hanson, rather than just his trade name.

If the debtor's name changes, the financing statement remains effective for collateral the debtor acquired before or within four months after the name change. Unless an amendment to the financing statement is filed within this four-month period, a security interest in collateral acquired by the debtor after the four-month period is unperfected [UCC 9–507(b) and (c)]. A one-page uniform financing statement amendment form is available for filing name changes and for other purposes.

Description of the Collateral. Both the security agreement and the financing statement must describe the collateral in which the secured party has a security interest. The security agreement must describe the collateral because no security interest in goods can exist unless the parties agree on which goods are subject to the security interest.

The financing statement must describe the collateral to provide public notice of the fact that certain goods of the debtor are subject to a security interest. Other parties who might later wish to lend funds to the debtor or buy the collateral can thus learn of the security interest by checking with the office in which a financing statement would be filed. For land-related security interests, a legal description of the realty is also required [UCC 9–502(b)].

---

2. If the name listed in the financing statement is so inaccurate that a search using a standard search engine will not disclose the debtor's name, then the financing statement is deemed seriously misleading under UCC 9–506. See also UCC 9–507, which governs the effectiveness of financing statements found to be seriously misleading.

Sometimes, the descriptions in the two documents vary. The description in the security agreement must be more precise than the description in the financing statement. The UCC permits broad, general descriptions in the financing statement, such as "all assets" or "all personal property," as long as they are accurate [UCC 9–504].

Example 25.3 A security agreement for a commercial loan to Casey Manufacturing lists all of Casey's equipment subject to the loan by serial number. The financing statement for the equipment simply refers to "all equipment owned or hereafter acquired." ▪ (This chapter's *Business Law Analysis* feature provides an additional illustration.)

Where to File. Normally, a financing statement must be filed centrally in the appropriate state office, such as the office of the secretary of state, in the state where the debtor is located. An exception occurs when the collateral consists of timber to be cut, fixtures, or items to be extracted—such as oil, coal, gas, and minerals [UCC 9–301(3) and (4), 9–502(b)]. In those circumstances, the financing statement is filed in the county where the collateral is located.

Note that the state in which a financing statement should be filed usually depends on the *debtor's location,* not the location of the collateral (but not for the exception just mentioned) [UCC 9–301]. The debtor's location is determined as follows [UCC 9–307]:

1. For *individual debtors,* it is the state of the debtor's principal residence.

2. For an *organization that is registered with the state,* such as a corporation or limited liability company, it is the state in which the organization is registered. Thus, if a debtor is incorporated in Maryland and has its chief executive office in New York, a secured party would file the financing statement in Maryland.

3. For *all other entities,* it is the state in which the business is located or, if the debtor has more than one office, the place from which the debtor manages its business operations and affairs.

Tom Cheney The New Yorker Collection/The Cartoon Bank

"O.K., folks, let's move along. I'm sure you've all seen someone qualify for a loan before."

Perfecting a Security Interest

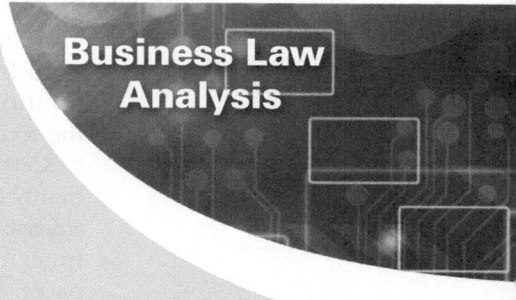

Business Law Analysis

Thomas Tille owned M.A.T.T. Equipment Company. To operate the business, Tille borrowed funds from Union Bank. For each loan, Union filed a financing statement that included Tille's signature and address, the bank's address, and a description of the collateral.

The first loan covered all of Tille's equipment, including "any after-acquired property." The second loan covered a truck crane "whether owned now or acquired later." The third loan covered a "Bobcat mini-excavator." Did these financing statements perfect Union's security interests?

Analysis: In most situations, perfection is accomplished by filing a financing statement with the appropriate official. To effectively perfect a security interest, a financing statement must contain (1) the debtor's signature, (2) the debtor's and creditor's addresses, and (3) a description of the collateral by type or item. Under the UCC, the financing statement can contain broad, general descriptions of the collateral, whereas the security agreement must be more precise.

Result and Reasoning: All of Union Bank's financing statements were sufficient to perfect its security interests in Tille's equipment. They each provided the name and address of the debtor (Tille), and the name and address of the secured party (Union Bank). They also included a description of the collateral covered by the financing statement. For one loan, it was all of Tille's equipment, including after-acquired property; for another, the truck crane; and for the third, a Bobcat mini-excavator. These descriptions were clearly sufficient to put a prospective creditor on notice that the collateral was the subject of a security interest.

Consequences of an Improper Filing. Improper filing renders the security interest unperfected and reduces the secured party's claim in bankruptcy to that of an unsecured creditor. For instance, if the debtor's name on the financing statement is seriously misleading or if the collateral is not sufficiently described in the financing statement, the filing may not be effective.

Example 25.4 Arthur Mendez Juarez, a strawberry farmer, leases farmland from Morona Fruits, Inc., and borrows funds from Morona for payroll and production expenses. The sublease and other documents set out Juarez's full name, but Juarez generally goes by the name "Mendez" and signs the sublease "Arthur Mendez." To perfect its interests, Morona files financing statements that identify the debtor as "Arthur Mendez."

Then Juarez contracts to sell strawberries to Frozun Foods, Inc., which also advances him funds secured by a financing statement that identifies the debtor as "Arthur Juarez." By the following year, Juarez is unable to pay his debts and owes Morona more than $200,000 and Frozun nearly $50,000. Both Morona and Frozun file a suit against Juarez claiming to have priority under a perfected security interest. In this situation, a properly filed financing statement would identify the debtor's true name (Arthur Juarez). Because a debtor name search for "Arthur Juarez" would not disclose a financing statement in the name of "Arthur Mendez," Morona's financing statement is seriously misleading. Therefore, Frozun's security interest would have priority because its financing statement was recorded properly. ▪

Perfection without Filing

A few types of security interests can be perfected without filing a financing statement. One occurs when the collateral is transferred into the possession of the secured party. A second occurs when the security interest can be perfected on attachment (without a filing and without having to possess the goods) [UCC 9–309].

The phrase *perfected on attachment* means that these security interests are automatically perfected at the time of their creation. Two of the more common security interests that are perfected on attachment are a *purchase-money security interest* in consumer goods (discussed shortly) and an assignment of a beneficial interest in a decedent's estate [UCC 9–309(1), (13)].

Perfection by Possession. In the past, one of the most common means of obtaining financing was to **pledge** certain collateral as security for the debt and transfer the collateral into the creditor's possession. When the debt was paid, the collateral was returned to the debtor. Article 9 of the UCC retained the common law pledge and the principle that the security agreement need not be in writing to be enforceable if the collateral is transferred to the secured party [UCC 9–310, 9–312(b), 9–313].

Certain items, such as stocks, bonds, negotiable instruments, and jewelry, are commonly transferred into the creditor's possession when they are used as collateral for loans. **Example 25.5** Sheila needs cash to pay for a medical procedure. She obtains a loan for $4,000 from Trent. As security for the loan, she gives him a promissory note on which she is the payee. Even though the agreement to hold the note as collateral was oral, Trent has a perfected security interest and does not need to file a financing statement. No other creditor of Sheila's can attempt to recover the promissory note from Trent in payment for other debts. ▪

For most collateral, however, possession by the secured party is impractical because it denies the debtor the right to use or derive income from the property to pay off the debt. **Example 25.6** Jeb, a farmer, takes out a loan to finance the purchase of a large corn harvester and uses the equipment as collateral. Clearly, the purpose of the purchase would be defeated if Jeb transferred the collateral into the creditor's possession, because he would not be able to use the equipment to harvest his corn. ▪

Perfection by Attachment—The Purchase-Money Security Interest in Consumer Goods. Under the UCC, fourteen types of security interests are perfected automatically at the time they are created [UCC 9–309]. The most common is the **purchase-money security interest (PMSI)** in *consumer goods* (items bought primarily for personal, family, or household purposes). A PMSI in consumer goods is created when a person buys goods on credit. The entity

Pledge A security device in which personal property is transferred into the possession of the creditor as security for the payment of a debt and retained by the creditor until the debt is paid.

Purchase-Money Security Interest (PMSI) A security interest that arises when a seller or lender extends credit for part or all of the price of goods purchased by a buyer.

that extends the credit and obtains the PMSI can be either the seller (a store, for instance) or a financial institution that lends the buyer the funds with which to purchase the goods [UCC 9–102(a)(2)].

Automatic Perfection. A PMSI in consumer goods is perfected automatically at the time of a credit sale—that is, at the time the PMSI is created. The seller in this situation does not need to do anything more to perfect her or his interest. **Example 25.7** Jami purchases an LG washer and dryer from West Coast Appliance for $2,500. Unable to pay the entire amount in cash, Jami signs a purchase agreement to pay $1,000 down and $100 per month until the balance, plus interest, is fully paid. West Coast Appliance is to retain a security interest in the appliances until full payment has been made. Because the security interest was created as part of a purchase agreement with a consumer, it is a PMSI, and West Coast Appliance's security interest is automatically perfected. ▪

If this couple buys a 4K UHD television on credit, is a PMSI automatically perfected?

Exceptions to the Rule of Automatic Perfection. There are two exceptions to the rule of automatic perfection for PMSIs:

1. Certain types of security interests that are subject to other federal or state laws may require additional steps to be perfected [UCC 9–311]. Many jurisdictions, for instance, have certificate-of-title statutes that establish perfection requirements for security interests in certain goods, including automobiles, trailers, boats, mobile homes, and farm tractors.

   Example 25.8 Martin Sedek purchases a boat at a Florida dealership. Florida has a certificate-of-title statute. Sedek obtains financing for his purchase through General Credit Corporation. General Credit Corporation will need to file a certificate of title with the appropriate state official to perfect the PMSI. ▪

2. PMSIs in nonconsumer goods, such as a business's inventory or livestock, are not automatically perfected [UCC 9–324]. These types of PMSIs will be discussed later in this chapter in the context of priorities.

Perfection and the Classification of Collateral

Where or how to perfect a security interest sometimes depends on the classification or definition of the collateral. Collateral is generally divided into two classifications: *tangible collateral* (collateral that can be seen, felt, and touched) and *intangible collateral* (collateral that consists of or generates rights). Exhibit 25–2 summarizes the various classifications of collateral and the methods of perfecting a security interest in collateral falling within each of those classifications.[3]

Effective Time Duration of Perfection

A financing statement is effective for five years from the date of filing [UCC 9–515]. If a **continuation statement** is filed within six months *prior to* the expiration date, the effectiveness of the original statement is continued for another five years, starting with the expiration date of the first five-year period [UCC 9–515(d), (e)]. The effectiveness of the statement can be continued in the same manner indefinitely. Any attempt to file a continuation statement outside the six-month window will render the continuation ineffective, however, and the perfection will lapse at the end of the five-year period.

If a financing statement lapses, the security interest that had been perfected by the filing becomes unperfected. A purchaser for value can acquire the collateral as if the security interest had never been perfected [UCC 9–515(c)].

Continuation Statement A statement that, if filed within six months prior to the expiration date of the original financing statement, continues the perfection of the security interest for another five years.

---

3. There are additional classifications, such as agricultural liens, commercial tort claims, and investment property. For definitions of these types of collateral, see UCC 9–102(a)(5), (a)(13), and (a)(49).

Exhibit 25–2 Selected Types of Collateral and Their Methods of Perfection

TANGIBLE COLLATERAL		METHOD OF PERFECTION
All things that are movable at the time the security interest attaches or that are attached to land, including timber to be cut and growing crops.		
1. Consumer Goods [UCC 9–301, 9–303, 9–309(1), 9–310(a), 9–313(a)]	Goods used or bought primarily for personal, family, or household purposes—for example, household furniture [UCC 9–102(a)(23)].	For purchase-money security interest, attachment (that is, the creation of a security interest) is sufficient. For boats, motor vehicles, and trailers, filing or compliance with a certificate-of-title statute is required. For other consumer goods, general rules of filing or possession apply.
2. Equipment [UCC 9–301, 9–310(a), 9–313(a)]	Goods bought for or used primarily in business (and not part of inventory or farm products)—for example, a delivery truck [UCC 9–102(a)(33)].	Filing or (rarely) possession by secured party.
3. Farm Products [UCC 9–301, 9–310(a), 9–313(a)]	Crops (including aquatic goods), livestock, or supplies produced in a farming operation—for example, ginned cotton, milk, eggs, and maple syrup [UCC 9–102(a)(34)].	Filing or (rarely) possession by secured party.
4. Inventory [UCC 9–301, 9–310(a), 9–313(a)]	Goods held by a person for sale or under a contract of service or lease; raw materials held for production and work in progress [UCC 9–102(a)(48)].	Filing or (rarely) possession by secured party.

INTANGIBLE COLLATERAL		METHOD OF PERFECTION
Nonphysical property that exists only in connection with something else.		
1. Chattel Paper [UCC 9–301, 9–310(a), 9–312(a), 9–313(a), 9–314(a)]	A writing or electronic record that evidences both a monetary obligation and a security interest in goods and software used in goods—for example, a security agreement [UCC 9–102(a)(11), (a)(31), and (a)(78)].	Filing or possession or control by secured party.
2. Instruments [UCC 9–301, 9–309(4), 9–310(a), 9–312(a) and (e), 9–313(a)]	A negotiable instrument, such as a check, note, certificate of deposit, draft, or other writing that evidences a right to the payment of money and is not a security agreement or lease, but rather a type that can ordinarily be transferred (after indorsement, if necessary) by delivery [UCC 9–102(a)(47)].	Normally filing or possession. For the sale of promissory notes, perfection can be by attachment (automatically on the creation of the security interest).
3. Accounts [UCC 9–301, 9–309(2) and (5), 9–310(a)]	Any right to receive payment for property (real or personal), including intellectual licensed property, services, insurance policies, and certain other receivables [UCC 9–102(a)(2) and (a)(46)].	Filing required except for certain assignments that can be perfected by attachment (automatically on the creation of the security interest).
4. Deposit Accounts [UCC 9–104, 9–304, 9–312(b), 9–314(a)]	Any demand, time, savings, passbook, or similar account maintained with a bank [UCC 9–102(a)(29)].	Perfection by control, such as when the secured party is the bank in which the account is maintained or when the parties have agreed that the secured party can direct the disposition of funds in a particular account.

25–2 Scope of a Security Interest

A security interest can cover property in which the debtor has either present or future ownership or possessory rights. Therefore, security agreements can cover not only collateral in the present possession or control of the debtor but also proceeds from the sale of collateral, after-acquired property, and future advances, as discussed next.

25–2a Proceeds

Proceeds are whatever cash or property is received when collateral is sold or disposed of in some other way [UCC 9–102(a)(64)]. A security interest in the collateral gives the secured party a security interest in the proceeds acquired from the sale of that collateral.

A security interest in proceeds perfects automatically on the perfection of the secured party's security interest in the original collateral. It remains perfected for twenty days after the debtor receives the proceeds. The parties can agree to extend the twenty-day automatic perfection period in their original security agreement [UCC 9–315(c), (d)]. This is typically done when the collateral is the type that is likely to be sold, such as a retailer's inventory of tablets or smartphones. The UCC also permits a security interest in identifiable cash proceeds to remain perfected after twenty days [UCC 9–315(d)(2)].

The dispute in the following case focused on proceeds. The court was asked to decide whether the actions taken by the debtor and another creditor had stripped a secured creditor of its interest in certain proceeds.

Proceeds Under Article 9 of the UCC, whatever is received when collateral is sold or disposed of in some other way.

■ Case 25.2

In re Tusa–Expo Holdings, Inc.

United States Court of Appeals, Fifth Circuit, 811 F.3d 786 (2016).

Background and Facts Tusa Office Solutions, Inc., a subsidiary of Tusa–Expo Holdings, Inc., was the largest retail dealer in new furniture made by Knoll, Inc. A customer placed an order for Knoll furniture from Tusa Office, which, in turn, ordered the furniture from Knoll, who delivered it to the customer. The customer paid Tusa Office, which then paid Knoll. Knoll set a limit on the amount of the payments that could be outstanding before it would stop filling new orders. As part of the deal, Tusa Office granted Knoll a first-priority security interest in specified accounts receivable.

Meanwhile, Tusa Office obtained a loan from Textron Financial, Inc. Knoll and Textron agreed separately that Textron would have a first-priority security interest in all of Tusa Office's assets, except for Knoll's collateral (the furniture).

The terms of the loan required Tusa Office to establish a bank account—called the lockbox—into which its customers made payments directly. Textron could withdraw funds from the lockbox and use them to increase the credit available to Tusa Office on its loan. Tusa Office used the increased credit to pay Knoll. By paying Knoll, Tusa Office kept its debt to Knoll below the furniture maker's limit, which enabled Tusa Office to fill new orders for its customers.

Ultimately, Tusa Office filed a bankruptcy petition in a federal bankruptcy court. Marilyn Garner, the bankruptcy trustee, sought to recapture some of the funds that Knoll had received through the lockbox.[a] To do this, Garner had to prove that Knoll had received more by these transfers than it would receive on Tusa Office's bankruptcy. The court issued a ruling against the trustee, who appealed.

In the Words of the Court
WIENER, Circuit Judge:

* * * *

* * * *A creditor who merely recovers its own collateral receives no more * * * than it would have received anyway.* [Emphasis added.]

The Trustee asserts that the transfers from Tusa Office to Knoll were not made from the proceeds of Knoll's collateral.

* * * *

The Trustee does not dispute that the payments Tusa Office's customers deposited into the lockbox were proceeds of Tusa Office's accounts receivable. She argues * * * that * * * Knoll's first-priority security interest in the payments was stripped by operation of [Texas Business and Commerce Code] Section 9.332(a) [Texas's version of UCC 9–332(a)]: "A transferee of money takes the money free of a security interest * * * ." Section 9.332(a)

---

a. A debtor files a petition in a federal bankruptcy court to liquidate its assets, pay its creditors with the proceeds, and obtain a discharge of any remaining debt. It is the job of the bankruptcy trustee to collect those assets and distribute them fairly among the debtor's creditors.

(Continues)

does not apply if such a transfer of money was made to the debtor. The Trustee therefore insists that Textron, not Tusa Office, was the transferee. In so doing, the Trustee contends that the lockbox was "owned * * * by Textron."

* * * *

* * * The Loan Agreement is clear. It specifies that * * * "Tusa Office shall have established a * * * lockbox * * * for its collections and the transfer thereof to Textron * * *." The Loan Agreement also states that "Tusa Office shall have possession of Textron's Collateral."

Because Tusa Office, not Textron, owned the lockbox, Section 9.332(a) does not apply. Therefore, Knoll's first-priority security interest in the proceeds of Tusa Office's accounts receivable survived the deposit into the lockbox.

* * * *

The Trustee next contends that Section 9.332(b) [Texas's version of UCC 9–332(b)] stripped Knoll's first-priority security interest when they were transferred from the lockbox to Textron.

* * * *

The plain language of Section 9.332(b) states that a "transferee of funds from a deposit account takes the funds free of a security interest in the deposit account."

* * * *

The plain language of Section 9.332(b) is unambiguous. Knoll's first-priority security interest in the proceeds of Tusa Office's accounts receivable survived the transfer from the lockbox to Textron. Not only is this consistent with Section 9.332(b), but it is also consistent with the * * * Agreement between Knoll and Textron.

Decision and Remedy The U.S. Court of Appeals for the Fifth Circuit affirmed the ruling of the lower court. The trustee could not recover the funds that were transferred to Knoll from Tusa Office through the lockbox because those funds were the proceeds of Knoll's own collateral.

Critical Thinking

• **Legal Environment** *Why does the UCC permit transferees to take funds "free of a security interest"? How did this provision work to protect the parties in this case?*

• **Ethical** *Office Expo, Inc., a dealer in used furniture, was, like Tusa Office, a subsidiary of Tusa–Expo Holdings. Tusa Office operated profitably, but Office Expo did not. To bolster Office Expo, funds were transferred from Tusa Office to Office Expo on a regular basis, which caused problems for Tusa Office. Were these transfers unethical? Discuss.*

25–2b After-Acquired Property

After-Acquired Property Property that is acquired by the debtor after the execution of a security agreement.

After-acquired property is property that the debtor acquired after the execution of the security agreement. The security agreement may provide for a security interest in after-acquired property, such as a debtor's inventory [UCC 9–204(1)]. Generally, the debtor will purchase new inventory to replace the inventory sold. The secured party wants this newly acquired inventory to be subject to the original security interest. Thus, the after-acquired property clause continues the secured party's claim to any inventory acquired thereafter. (This is not to say that the original security interest will always take priority over the rights of all other creditors with regard to this after-acquired inventory, as will be discussed later.)

Learning Objective 2

How can a security interest extend to a debtor's newly acquired inventory?

Example 25.9 Amato buys factory equipment from Bronson on credit, giving as security an interest in all of her equipment—both what she is buying and what she already owns. The security interest with Bronson contains an after-acquired property clause. Six months later, Amato pays cash to another seller of factory equipment for more equipment. Six months after that, Amato goes out of business before she has paid off her debt to Bronson. Bronson has a security interest in all of Amato's equipment, even the equipment bought from the other seller. ▪

25–2c Future Advances

Often, a debtor will arrange with a bank to have a *continuing line of credit* under which the debtor can borrow funds intermittently. Advances against lines of credit can be subject to a properly perfected security interest in certain collateral.

The security agreement may provide that any future advances made against that line of credit are also subject to the security interest in that collateral [UCC 9–204(c)]. Future advances do not have to be of the same type or otherwise related to the original advance to benefit from this type of **cross-collateralization.**[4] Cross-collateralization occurs when an asset that is not the subject of a loan is used to secure that loan.

Cross-Collateralization The use of an asset that is not the subject of a loan to collateralize that loan.

Example 25.10 Stroh is the owner of a small manufacturing plant with equipment valued at $1 million. He has an immediate need for $50,000 of working capital, so he obtains a loan from Midwestern Bank and signs a security agreement, putting up all of his equipment as security. The bank properly perfects its security interest. The security agreement provides that Stroh can borrow up to $500,000 in the future, using the same equipment as collateral for any future advances. In this situation, Midwestern Bank does not have to execute a new security agreement and perfect a security interest in the collateral each time an advance is made, up to a cumulative total of $500,000. For priority purposes, each advance is perfected as of the date of the *original* perfection. ■

25–2d The Floating-Lien Concept

A security agreement that provides for a security interest in proceeds, in after-acquired property, or in collateral subject to future advances by the secured party (or in all three) is often characterized as a **floating lien.** This type of security interest continues in the collateral or proceeds even if the collateral is sold, exchanged, or disposed of in some other way.

Can equipment be used as collateral for future advances?

A Floating Lien in Inventory
Floating liens commonly arise in the financing of inventories. A creditor is not interested in *specific* pieces of inventory, which are constantly changing, so the lien "floats" from one item to another as the inventory changes.

Floating Lien A security interest in proceeds, after-acquired property, or collateral subject to future advances by the secured party (or all three). The security interest is retained even when the collateral changes in character, classification, or location.

Example 25.11 Cascade Sports, Inc., an Oregon corporation, operates as a cross-country ski dealer and has a line of credit with Portland First Bank to finance its inventory of cross-country skis. Cascade and Portland First enter into a security agreement that provides for coverage of proceeds, after-acquired inventory, present inventory, and future advances. Portland First perfects its security interest in the inventory by filing centrally with the office of the secretary of state in Oregon.

One day, Cascade sells a new pair of the latest cross-country skis and receives a used pair in trade. That same day, Cascade purchases two new pairs of cross-country skis from a local manufacturer for cash. Later that day, to meet its payroll, Cascade borrows $8,000 from Portland First Bank under the security agreement.

Portland First gets a perfected security interest in the used pair of skis under the proceeds clause and a perfected security interest in the two new pairs of skis under the after-acquired property clause. This collateral, as well as other inventory, secures the new funds advanced to Cascade under the future-advances clause. All of this is accomplished under the original perfected security interest. The various items in the inventory have changed, but Portland First still has a perfected security interest in Cascade's inventory. Hence, it has a floating lien in the inventory. ■

A Floating Lien in a Shifting Stock of Goods
The concept of the floating lien can also apply to a shifting stock of goods. The lien can start with raw materials, follow them as they become finished goods and inventories, and continue as the goods are sold and are turned into accounts receivable, chattel paper, or cash.

Know This
Secured creditors—perfected or not—have priority over unsecured creditors.

---

4. See official Comment 5 to UCC 9–204.

25–3 Priorities, Rights, and Duties

When more than one party claims an interest in the same collateral, which has priority? The UCC sets out detailed rules to answer this question. Although in many situations the party who has a perfected security interest will have priority, there are exceptions. The UCC also provides certain rights and duties to debtors and secured parties.

25–3a General Rules of Priority

The basic rule is that when more than one security interest has been perfected in the same collateral, the first security interest to be perfected (or filed) has priority over any security interests that are perfected later. If only one of the conflicting security interests has been perfected, then that security interest has priority. If none of the security interests have been perfected, then the first security interest that attaches has priority.

The UCC's rules of priority can be summarized as follows:

1. *Perfected security interest versus unsecured creditors and unperfected security interests.* When two or more parties have claims to the same collateral, a perfected secured party's interest has priority over the interests of most other parties [UCC 9–322(a)(2)]. This includes priority to the proceeds from a sale of collateral resulting from a bankruptcy (giving the perfected secured party rights superior to that of a bankruptcy trustee).

2. *Conflicting perfected security interests.* When two or more secured parties have perfected security interests in the same collateral, the first to perfect (by filing or taking possession of the collateral) generally has priority [UCC 9–322(a)(1)].

3. *Conflicting unperfected security interests.* When two conflicting security interests are unperfected, the first to attach (be created) has priority [UCC 9–322(a)(3)]. This is sometimes called the "first-in-time" rule.

Example 25.12 Rick Morales and his wife and son own a dairy farm called Lost Creek Heifers (LCH) that has received multiple loans through Ag Services, Inc. To obtain the loans, Morales executes a $800,000 promissory note and security agreement in favor of Ag Services. The note lists all of LCH's accounts, equipment, farm products, inventory, livestock, and proceeds as collateral. A year later, Morales and his wife separate, and he signs a separation agreement giving her some cash and land.

The following year, Morales buys out his son's interest in LCH by giving him a promissory note for $100,000. The note lists all of LCH's equipment, inventory, livestock, and proceeds as collateral. Morales also sells a herd of dairy cows for $500,000 and gives his former wife a check for $240,000. LCH files for bankruptcy shortly thereafter. A dispute arises over which party (Ag Services, Morales's son, or Morales's former wife) is entitled to the proceeds from the sale of the cows. In this situation, a court will likely find that because Ag Services' security interest in the proceeds was the first in time to *attach*, Ag Services has first priority to the proceeds. ■

A family dairy farm operation is sold and a dispute arises over who has priority to part of the proceeds. What are three rules of priority the court will follow?

25–3b Exceptions to the General Priority Rules

Under some circumstances, on the debtor's default, the perfection of a security interest will not protect a secured party against certain other third parties having claims to the collateral. For instance, the UCC provides that in some situations a PMSI, properly perfected,[5]

---

5. Recall that, with some exceptions (such as motor vehicles), a PMSI in *consumer goods* is automatically perfected—no filing is necessary. A PMSI that is *not* in consumer goods must still be perfected, however.

will prevail over another security interest in after-acquired collateral, even though the other was perfected first. We discuss some significant exceptions to the general rules of priority next.

Buyers in the Ordinary Course of Business Under the UCC, a person who buys "in the ordinary course of business" takes the goods free from any security interest created by the seller even if the security interest is perfected and the buyer knows of its existence [UCC 9–320(a)]. A *buyer in the ordinary course of business* is a person who in good faith, and without knowledge that the sale violates the rights of another in the goods, buys goods in the ordinary course from a person in the business of selling goods of that kind [UCC 1–201(9)].[6] The rationale for this rule is obvious. If buyers could not obtain the goods free and clear of any security interest the merchant had created—for instance, in inventory—the free flow of goods in the marketplace would be hindered.

Example 25.13 Dubbs Auto grants a security interest in its inventory to Heartland Bank for a $300,000 line of credit. Heartland perfects its security interest by filing financing statements with the appropriate state offices. Dubbs uses $9,000 of its credit to buy two used trucks and delivers the certificates of title, which designate Dubbs as the owner, to Heartland.

Later, Dubbs sells one of the trucks to Shea Murdoch and another to Michael Laxton. National City Bank finances both purchases. New certificates of title are issued in the buyers' names, but Heartland receives none of the funds from the sales.

If Heartland sues National City, claiming that its security interest in the vehicles takes priority, it will lose. Because Murdoch and Laxton are buyers in the ordinary course of business, Heartland's security interest in the motor vehicles was extinguished when the vehicles were sold to them. (Dubbs still owes Heartland the $9,000, of course.) ▪

PMSI in Inventory Another important exception to the first-in-time rule has to do with security interests in inventory. (Remember that a PMSI that is *not* in consumer goods must be perfected.) A perfected PMSI in inventory has priority over a conflicting security interest in the same inventory. To maintain this priority, the holder of the PMSI must notify the holder of the conflicting security interest on or before the time the debtor takes possession of the inventory [UCC 9–324(b)].

Buyers of the Collateral The UCC recognizes that there are certain types of buyers whose interests in purchased goods could conflict with those of a perfected secured party on the debtor's default. These include not only buyers in the ordinary course of business (as just discussed), but also buyers of farm products, chattel paper, instruments, documents, or securities. The UCC sets down special rules of priority for these types of buyers.

25–3c Rights and Duties of Debtors and Creditors

The security agreement itself determines most of the rights and duties of the debtor and the secured party. The UCC, however, imposes some rights and duties that are applicable unless the security agreement states otherwise.

Information Requests At the time of filing, a secured party can furnish a copy of the financing statement and request that the filing officer note the file number, date, and hour of the original filing on the copy [UCC 9–523(a)]. The filing officer must send this copy to the person designated by the secured party.

The filing officer must also give information to a person who is contemplating obtaining a security interest from a prospective debtor [UCC 9–523(c), (d)]. If requested, the filing officer must issue a certificate (for a fee) that provides information on possible perfected financing statements with respect to the named debtor.

"A man who pays his bills on time is soon forgotten."

Oscar Wilde
1854–1900
(Irish author, playwright, and poet)

---

6. Note that even though a buyer may know about the existence of a perfected security interest, he or she must not know that buying the goods violates the rights of any third party.

Release, Assignment, and Amendment A secured party can release all or part of any collateral described in the financing statement, thereby terminating its security interest in that collateral. The release is recorded by filing a uniform amendment form [UCC 9–512, 9–521(b)].

A secured party can also assign all or part of the security interest to a third party (the assignee). The assignee becomes the secured party of record if the assignment is filed by use of a uniform amendment form [UCC 9–514, 9–521(a)].

If the debtor and the secured party agree, they can amend the filing—to add or substitute new collateral, for example—by filing a uniform amendment form that indicates the file number of the initial financing statement [UCC 9–512(a)]. The amendment does not extend the time period of perfection, but if new collateral is added, the perfection date (for priority purposes) for the new collateral begins on the date the amendment is filed [UCC 9–512(b), (c)].

Confirmation or Accounting Request by Debtor The debtor may believe that the amount of the unpaid debt or the list of collateral subject to the security interest is inaccurate. The debtor has the right to request a confirmation of the unpaid debt or list of collateral [UCC 9–210]. The debtor is entitled to one request without charge every six months.

The secured party must comply with the debtor's confirmation request by authenticating and sending to the debtor an accounting within fourteen days after the request is received. Otherwise, the secured party will be held liable for any loss suffered by the debtor, plus $500 [UCC 9–210, 9–625(f)].

Termination Statement When the debtor has fully paid the debt, if the secured party perfected the security interest by filing, the debtor is entitled to have a termination statement filed. Such a statement demonstrates to the public that the filed perfected security interest has been terminated [UCC 9–513].

Whenever consumer goods are involved, the secured party *must* file a termination statement (or, alternatively, a release). The statement must be filed within one month of the final payment or within twenty days of receiving the debtor's demand, whichever is earlier [UCC 9–513(b)]. When the collateral is not consumer goods, the secured party is not required to file or to send a termination statement unless the debtor demands one [UCC 9–513(c)].

25–4 Default

Article 9 defines the rights, duties, and remedies of the secured party and of the debtor on the debtor's default. If the secured party fails to comply with his or her duties, the debtor is afforded particular rights and remedies under the UCC.

25–4a What Constitutes Default?

What constitutes default is not always clear. In fact, Article 9 does not define the term. Instead, the UCC encourages parties to include in their security agreements the standards under which their rights and duties will be measured [UCC 9–601, 9–603]. In so doing, parties can stipulate the conditions that will constitute a default. Often, these critical terms are shaped by creditors in an attempt to provide themselves with the maximum protection possible. The terms may not, however, run counter to the UCC's provisions regarding good faith and unconscionability.

Any breach of the terms of the security agreement can constitute default. Nevertheless, default occurs most commonly when the debtor fails to meet the scheduled payments or becomes bankrupt.

25–4b Basic Remedies

UCC 9–601(a) and (b) set out rights and remedies for secured parties, and these rights and remedies are *cumulative* [UCC 9–601(c)]. Therefore, if a creditor is unsuccessful in enforcing rights by one method, he or she can pursue another method. Generally, a secured party's remedies can be divided into the two basic categories discussed next.

Repossession of the Collateral—The Self-Help Remedy On the debtor's default, a secured party can take peaceful possession of the collateral without the use of judicial process [UCC 9–609(b)]. This provision is often referred to as the "self-help" provision of Article 9.

The UCC does not define *peaceful possession*. The general rule is that the collateral has been taken peacefully if the secured party can take possession without trespassing, assaulting, or breaking and entering.

On taking possession, the secured party may either retain the collateral for satisfaction of the debt [UCC 9–620] or resell the goods and apply the proceeds toward the debt [UCC 9–610].

Judicial Remedies Alternatively, a secured party can relinquish the security interest and use any judicial remedy available, such as obtaining a judgment on the underlying debt, followed by execution and levy [UCC 9–601(a)]. (**Execution** is the implementation of a court's decree or judgment. **Levy** is the legal process of obtaining funds through the seizure and sale of nonexempt property, usually done after a writ of execution has been issued.)

25–4c Disposition of Collateral

Once default has occurred and the secured party has obtained possession of the collateral, the secured party can:

1. Retain the collateral in full or partial satisfaction of the debt (subject to limitations, discussed next).
2. Sell, lease, license, or otherwise dispose of the collateral in any commercially reasonable manner, and apply the proceeds toward satisfaction of the debt [UCC 9–602(7), 9–603, 9–610(a), 9–613, 9–620]. Any sale is always subject to procedures established by state law.

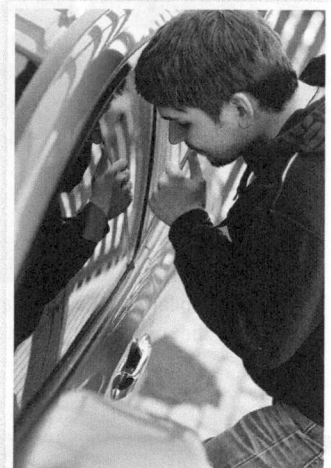

This man is not stealing this car. What UCC remedy might he be exercising instead?

Execution The implementation of a court's decree or judgment.

Levy The legal process of obtaining funds through the seizure and sale of nonexempt property, usually done after a writ of execution has been issued.

Retention of Collateral by the Secured Party Parties are sometimes better off if they do not sell the collateral. Therefore, the UCC generally allows secured parties to choose not to sell. A secured party may retain the collateral unless it consists of consumer goods and the debtor has paid 60 percent or more of the purchase price or loan amount (see the discussion of consumer goods for specifics). This general right to retain the collateral is subject to several limitations.

Notice Requirements. The secured party must notify the debtor of its proposal to retain the collateral. Notice is required unless the debtor has signed a statement renouncing or modifying her or his rights *after default* [UCC 9–620(a), 9–621].

If the collateral is consumer goods, the secured party does not need to give any other notice. In all other situations, the secured party must also send notice to any other secured party from whom the secured party has received notice of a claim of interest in the collateral.

Objections. The debtor or other party notified of the retention has the right to object. If, within twenty days after the notice is sent, the secured party receives a written objection, the secured party must sell or otherwise dispose of the collateral. If no written objection is received, the secured party may retain the collateral in full or partial satisfaction of the debtor's obligation [UCC 9–620(a), 9–621].

©Haveseen/Shutterstock.com

Learning Objective 4

When is a creditor required to sell or otherwise dispose of the repossessed collateral?

Consumer Goods When the collateral is consumer goods and the debtor has paid 60 percent of the purchase price on a PMSI or loan amount on a non-PMSI, the secured party cannot retain the goods. Instead, the secured party is required to sell or otherwise dispose of the repossessed collateral within ninety days [UCC 9–620(e), (f)]. Failure to comply opens the secured party to an action for conversion or other liability under UCC 9–625(b) and (c). A secured party will not be liable, however, if the consumer-debtor signed a written statement *after default* renouncing or modifying the right to demand the sale of the goods [UCC 9–624].

Disposition Procedures A secured party who does not choose to retain the collateral or who is required to sell it must follow the disposition procedures prescribed in the UCC. The sale can be public or private. The collateral can be disposed of in its present condition or following any commercially reasonable preparation or processing [UCC 9–610(a)].

Notice Requirement. The secured party must notify the debtor and other specified parties in writing ahead of time about the sale or disposition of the collateral. If the collateral is consumer goods, the notice must specify the method of intended disposition. Notification is not required if the collateral is perishable, will decline rapidly in value, or is a type customarily sold on a recognized market [UCC 9–611(b), (c)].

Commercially Reasonable Manner. Every aspect of the disposition's method, manner, time, and place must be *commercially reasonable* [UCC 9–610(b)]. If the secured party does not dispose of the collateral in a commercially reasonable manner, the price paid for the collateral at the sale may be negatively affected. In that situation, a court can reduce the amount of any deficiency that the debtor owes to the secured party [UCC 9–626(a)(3)].

The issue in the following case was whether the creditor's disposition of the collateral was commercially reasonable.

Is the sale of collateral at auction a reasonable means of disposing of that collateral?

Cameron Spencer/Getty Images

■ Case 25.3

SunTrust Bank v. Monroe

Court of Appeals of Texas, Fort Worth, 2018 WL 651198 (2018).

Background and Facts Liberty Redevelopment Group, LLC, financed the purchase of an Aston Martin for $233,305.46 with a loan from the dealer, Aston Martin of Dallas. Mark Monroe, a Liberty officer and the owner and operator of Delta Bail Bonds, co-signed for the loan. The dealer assigned the loan to SunTrust Bank. Seven months later, Liberty defaulted on the payments. SunTrust repossessed the car and sold it at auction for $115,000.

The bank filed a suit in a Texas state court against Monroe to recover the deficiency between the auction price and the balance of the loan, plus $38,000 in repossession expenses. Monroe responded that the sale was not made in a commercially reasonable manner. A jury agreed with Monroe and found that he owed SunTrust nothing. The bank appealed.

In the Words of the Court
Bonnie *SUDDERTH,* Chief Justice
* * * *

"Commercial reasonableness" at its core is a fact-based inquiry that requires a balance of Article 9's two competing policies—protecting debtors against creditor dishonesty and minimizing interference in honest dispositions. Courts have considered a number of non-exclusive factors when addressing the term "commercial reasonableness," such as (1) whether the secured party endeavored to obtain the best price possible; (2) whether the collateral was sold in bulk or piecemeal; (3) whether it was sold via private or public sale; (4) whether it was available for inspection before sale; (5) whether it was sold at a propitious time;

(6) whether the expenses incurred during the sale were reasonable and necessary; (7) whether the sale was advertised; (8) whether multiple bids were received; (9) what state the collateral was in; and (10) where the sale was conducted. The inquiry's ultimate purpose is to ensure the creditor realizes a satisfactory price, which is not necessarily the highest price, and it is recognized that secured creditors frequently sell in the low end of the wholesale markets. [Emphasis added.]

* * * *

* * * SunTrust presented little evidence to support its contention that the collateral's sale was made in a commercially reasonable manner. Monroe testified that he had not received anything from SunTrust to tell him the time, date, place, or anything else about the sale or to show SunTrust's other attempts to sell the vehicle; that he had not seen any documents about the actual sale; that he had looked at Kelly Blue Book's retail value and NADA Black Book's wholesale value, as well as online research, to reach his own valuation of $165,000 to $175,000; and that he was astounded that the vehicle had been sold for $115,000. As to the $38,000 in repossession expenses, Monroe testified that in his experience as a bail bondsman, this was higher than any repossession fee he had ever seen.

* * * *

* * * [Given] the lack of any evidence for the jury's fact-based inquiry to determine whether SunTrust endeavored to obtain the best price possible for the vehicle, * * * and the lack of evidence with regard to the state of the collateral and whether the expenses incurred in the sale were reasonable and necessary, we conclude that the jury could have reasonably determined that SunTrust did not dispose of the collateral in a commercially reasonable manner.

Decision and Remedy A state intermediate appellate court affirmed the lower court's judgment. "Because the jury found that SunTrust did not dispose of the collateral in a commercially reasonable manner, Monroe's liability for a deficiency was limited. . . . The trial court entered a take-nothing judgment. . . . We affirm."

Critical Thinking

• **Legal Environment** *Is a low price sufficient to establish that a sale of collateral was not made in a commercially reasonable manner? Explain.*

• **Economic** *A jury has broad discretion to identify the value of collateral in a commercially reasonable transaction. What evidence might provide a rational basis for this determination?*

Distribution of Proceeds from the Disposition Proceeds from the disposition of collateral after default on the underlying debt are distributed in the following order:

1. Reasonable expenses incurred by the secured party in repossessing, storing, and reselling the collateral are paid first.
2. The balance of the debt owed to the secured party is then paid.
3. Other lienholders who have made written or authenticated demands are paid.
4. Any surplus goes to the debtor, unless the collateral consists of accounts, payment intangibles, promissory notes, or chattel paper [UCC 9–608(a); 9–615(a), (e)].

Noncash Proceeds Sometimes the secured party receives noncash proceeds from the disposition of collateral after default. Whenever that occurs, the secured party must make a value determination and apply this value in a commercially reasonable manner [UCC 9–608(a)(3), 9–615(c)].

Deficiency Judgment Often, after proper disposition of the collateral, the secured party has not collected all that the debtor still owes. Unless otherwise agreed, the debtor normally is liable for any deficiency, and the creditor can obtain a **deficiency judgment** from a court to collect this amount. Practically speaking, though, debtors who have defaulted on a loan rarely have the cash to pay any deficiency.

Note that if the underlying transaction was a sale of accounts, chattel paper, or promissory notes, the debtor is *not* liable for any deficiency. The debtor normally is entitled to any surplus from the disposition of these types of collateral, however [UCC 9–615(e)].

"If you think nobody cares if you're alive, try missing a couple of car payments."

Earl Wilson
1907–1987
(American journalist)

Deficiency Judgment A judgment against a debtor for the amount of a debt remaining unpaid after the collateral has been repossessed and sold.

Redemption Rights The debtor or any other secured party can exercise the right of *redemption* of the collateral. Redemption may occur at any time before the secured party disposes of the collateral, enters into a contract for its disposition, or discharges the debtor's obligation by retaining the collateral. The debtor or other secured party exercises the redemption right by tendering performance of all obligations secured by the collateral and by paying the expenses reasonably incurred by the secured party in retaking and maintaining the collateral [UCC 9–623].

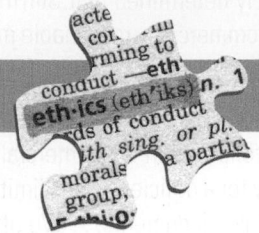

Ethical Issue

How long should a secured party have to seek a deficiency judgment? Because of depreciation, the amount received from the sale of collateral is frequently less than the amount the debtor owes to the secured party. In this situation, the secured party can file a suit against the debtor in an attempt to collect the balance due. UCC Article 9 does not contain a statute of limitations provision, though, so it is not clear how long a secured party has after default to file a deficiency suit against a debtor. If the secured party waits until the debtor becomes solvent again, though, the court may not allow the suit. When creditors have sued debtors for deficiencies owed on repossessed cars, for instance, courts have sometimes applied the four-year limitation period specified in UCC Article 2 because the transaction was a sale of goods, even though a security interest was involved.[7] Is this fair?

25–5 Other Laws Assisting Creditors

Both the common law and statutory laws other than Article 9 of the Uniform Commercial Code create rights and remedies for creditors. These remedies are available regardless of whether a creditor is secured or unsecured. Here, we discuss some of these rights and remedies.

25–5a Liens

A *lien* is an encumbrance on (claim against) property to satisfy a debt or protect a claim for the payment of a debt. Creditors' liens may arise under the common law or under statutory law. Statutory liens include *mechanic's liens,* whereas *artisan's liens* were recognized by common law. *Judicial liens* arise when a creditor attempts to collect on a debt before or after a judgment is entered by a court.

Liens can be useful because a lien creditor generally has priority over an unperfected secured party. In other words, if a creditor obtains a lien *before* another party perfects a security interest in the same property, the lienholder has priority. If the lien is obtained *after* another's security interest in the property is perfected, the perfected security interest has priority. Mechanic's and artisan's liens are exceptions to this rule. They normally take priority *even over perfected security interests,* unless a statute provides otherwise.

Mechanic's Lien Sometimes, a person who has contracted for labor, services, or materials to be furnished for making improvements on real property does not immediately pay for the improvements. When that happens, the creditor can place a **mechanic's lien** on the property.

A mechanic's lien creates a special type of debtor-creditor relationship in which the real estate itself becomes security for the debt. If the property owner fails to pay the debt, the lienholder is technically entitled to foreclose on the real estate and sell it. (*Foreclosure* is

Mechanic's Lien A nonpossessory, filed lien on an owner's real estate for labor, services, or materials furnished for making improvements on the realty.

---

7. See, for example, *Price Automotive II, LLC v. Mass Management, LLC,* 2015 WL 300418 (W.D.Va. 2015).

the process by which a creditor legally takes a debtor's property to satisfy a debt.) The sale proceeds are then used to pay the debt and the costs of the legal proceedings. The surplus, if any, is paid to the former owner.

In the real world, however, small-amount mechanic's liens are rarely the basis of foreclosure. Rather, these liens simply remain on the books of the state until the property is sold. At closing (when the sale is finalized), the seller agrees to pay all mechanic's liens out of the proceeds of the sale before the seller receives any of the funds. In contrast, mechanic's liens for significant amounts, such as when a contractor is owed millions for building an apartment complex, sometimes do lead to foreclosure.[8]

State law governs the procedures that must be followed to create a mechanic's lien. Generally, the lienholder must file a written notice of lien within a specific time period (usually 60 to 120 days) from the last date that labor or materials were provided.

Artisan's Lien
When a debtor fails to pay for labor and materials furnished for the repair or improvement of personal property, a creditor can recover payment through an **artisan's lien**.

Artisan's Lien A possessory lien held by a party who has made improvements and added value to the personal property of another party as security for payment for services performed.

Lienholder Must Retain Possession. Unlike a mechanic's lien, an artisan's lien is *possessory*. The lienholder ordinarily must have retained possession of the property and expressly or impliedly agreed to provide the services on a cash, not a credit, basis. The lien remains in existence as long as the lienholder maintains possession of the property, and the lien is terminated once possession is voluntarily surrendered, unless the surrender is only temporary.

Case Example 25.14 Carrollton Exempted Village School District (in Ohio) hired Clean Vehicle Solutions America, LLC (CVSA, based in New York), to convert ten school buses from diesel to compressed natural gas. The contract price was $660,000. The district paid a $400,000 deposit and agreed to pay installments of $26,000 to CVSA after the delivery of each converted bus. After the first two buses were delivered, the district refused to continue the contract, claiming that the conversion made the two buses unsafe to drive.

Both parties filed breach of contract lawsuits. CVSA also asserted an artisan's lien over two other buses that it still had in its possession because it had started converting them to natural gas and had spent $65,000 doing so. CVSA has an artisan's lien that gives it a priority claim to those two buses as long as they remain in its possession. The buses act as security for the district's payment of the amount that CVSA has spent converting them to natural gas.[9]

A dispute over payment arose in a contract to convert school buses to natural gas. For the lien on the buses to remain in effect, what must the lienholder do?

Foreclosure on Personal Property. Modern statutes permit the holder of an artisan's lien to foreclose and sell the property subject to the lien to satisfy payment of the debt. As with a mechanic's lien, the holder of an artisan's lien must give notice to the owner of the property prior to foreclosure and sale. The sale proceeds are used to pay the debt and the costs of the legal proceedings, and the surplus, if any, is paid to the former owner.

Judicial Lien
When a debt is past due, a creditor can bring a legal action against the debtor to collect the debt. If the creditor is successful, the court awards the creditor a judgment against the debtor (usually for the amount of the debt plus any interest and legal costs incurred). Frequently, however, the creditor is unable to collect the awarded amount.

To ensure that a judgment will be collectible, the creditor can request that certain nonexempt property of the debtor be seized to satisfy the debt. (Under state or federal statutes,

8. See, for example, *Picerne Construction Corp. v. Villas*, 244 Cal.App.4th 1201, 199 Cal.Rptr.3d 257 (2016).
9. *Clean Vehicle Solutions America, LLC v. Carrollton Exempted Village School District Board of Education*, 2015 WL 5459852 (S.D.N.Y. 2015).

certain property is exempt from attachment by creditors.) A court's order to seize the debtor's property is known as a *writ of attachment* if it is issued before a judgment. If the order is issued after a judgment, it is referred to as a *writ of execution.*

Writ of Attachment. In the context of judicial liens, *attachment* is a court-ordered seizure of property before a judgment is secured for a past-due debt. Attachment rights are created by state statutes. Because attachment is a *prejudgment* remedy, it occurs at the time a lawsuit is filed or immediately afterward. The due process clause of the Fourteenth Amendment to the U.S. Constitution requires that the debtor be given notice and an opportunity to be heard before property can be seized.

To use attachment, a creditor must comply with the specific state's statutory restrictions and requirements. The creditor must have an enforceable right to payment of the debt under law and must follow certain procedures. Otherwise, the creditor may be liable for damages for wrongful attachment. The typical procedures for attachment are as follows:

1. The creditor files with the court an *affidavit* (a written statement, made under oath) stating that the debtor has failed to pay. The affidavit must indicate the statutory grounds for seeking attachment.

2. The creditor must post a bond to cover at least the court costs, the value of the property attached, and the value of the loss of use of that property suffered by the debtor.

3. When the court is satisfied that all the requirements have been met, it issues a **writ of attachment.** The writ directs the sheriff or other officer to seize the debtor's nonexempt property. If the creditor prevails at trial, the seized property can be sold to satisfy the judgment.

Writ of Execution. If the creditor wins a judgment against a debtor and the debtor will not or cannot pay the amount due, the creditor can request a **writ of execution.** A writ of execution is an order that directs the sheriff to seize (levy) and sell any of the debtor's nonexempt real or personal property. The writ applies only to property that is within the court's geographic jurisdiction (usually the county in which the courthouse is located).

The proceeds of the sale are used to pay off the judgment, accrued interest, and the costs of the sale. Any excess is paid to the debtor. The debtor can pay the judgment and redeem the nonexempt property any time before the sale takes place. (Because of exemption laws and bankruptcy laws, however, many judgments are uncollectible.)

25–5b Garnishment

An order for **garnishment** permits a creditor to collect a debt by seizing property of the debtor that is being held by a third party. As a result of a garnishment proceeding, for instance, a debtor's employer may be ordered by the court to turn over a portion of the debtor's wages to pay the debt. Many other types of property can be garnished as well, including funds in a bank account, tax refunds, pensions, and trust funds. It is only necessary that the property not be exempt from garnishment and be in the possession of a third party.

Case Example 25.15 When Edward G. Tinsley divorced Michelle Townsend, they entered into a marital settlement contract. They agreed to sell the marital home and split the proceeds evenly. But Tinsley refused to cooperate with the sale. A court therefore appointed a trustee to sell the house for them and ordered the sheriff to evict Tinsley. Tinsley then conveyed the house to a trust established in his name. Although the sheriff evicted Tinsley from the house and changed the locks, Tinsley managed to move back in and change the locks again.

Tinsley was arrested for trespassing and charged with contempt of court (for disobeying court orders). In the meantime, Tinsley secretly sold the home for $150,000 and deposited the proceeds into a bank

Writ of Attachment A court order to seize a debtor's nonexempt property prior to a court's final determination of a creditor's rights to the property.

Writ of Execution A court order directing the sheriff to seize (levy) and sell a debtor's nonexempt real or personal property to satisfy a court's judgment in the creditor's favor.

Garnishment A legal process whereby a creditor collects a debt by seizing property of the debtor that is in the hands of a third party.

When can property—such as proceeds from a house sale—be garnished from a trust?

Artazum/Shutterstock.com

account held in the name of Edward G. Tinsley Living Trust at SunTrust Bank. After learning of the sale, the court-appointed trustee obtained a writ of garnishment on all of Tinsley's and his trust's accounts at SunTrust Bank. Despite Tinsley's objections, SunTrust Bank eventually complied with the garnishment order and sent all the funds to the trustee.[10]

Procedures Garnishment can be a prejudgment remedy, requiring a hearing before a court, but it is most often a postjudgment remedy. State law governs garnishment, so the procedure varies.

In some states, the creditor needs to obtain only one order of garnishment, which will then apply continuously to the debtor's wages until the entire debt is paid. In other states, the judgment creditor must go back to court for a separate order of garnishment for each pay period.

Limitations Both federal and state laws limit the amount that can be taken through garnishment proceedings.[11] Federal law provides a framework to protect debtors from suffering unduly when paying judgment debts by setting limits on how much can be garnished per pay period.[12] State laws also provide dollar exemptions, and these amounts are often larger than those provided by federal law. In addition, under federal law, an employer cannot dismiss an employee because his or her wages are being garnished.

25–5c Creditors' Composition Agreements

Creditors may contract with a debtor for discharge of the debtor's liquidated debts (debts that are definite, or fixed, in amount) on payment of a sum less than that owed. These agreements are called **creditors' composition agreements**, or simply *composition agreements*, and usually are held to be enforceable.

25–5d Suretyship and Guaranty

When a third person promises to pay a debt owed by another in the event that the debtor does not pay, either a *suretyship* or a *guaranty* relationship is created. Exhibit 25–3 illustrates these relationships. The third person's income and assets become the security for the debt owed.

Creditors' Composition Agreement A contract between a debtor and his or her creditors in which the creditors agree to discharge the debts on the debtor's payment of a sum less than the amount actually owed.

Learning Objective 5
What is a suretyship, and how does it differ from a guaranty?

---

10. *Tinsley v. SunTrust Bank*, 2016 WL 687545 (Md.App. 2016).
11. Some states (for example, Texas) do not permit garnishment of wages by private parties except under a child-support order.
12. For instance, the federal Consumer Credit Protection Act, 15 U.S.C. Sections 1601–1693r, provides that a debtor can retain either 75 percent of disposable earnings per week or a sum equivalent to thirty hours of work paid at federal minimum-wage rates, whichever is greater.

Exhibit 25–3 Suretyship and Guaranty Relationships

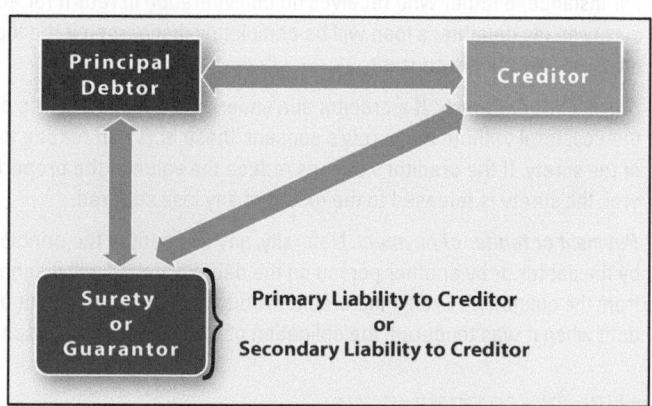

Suretyship and guaranty provide creditors with the right to seek payment from the third party if the primary debtor defaults on her or his obligations. At common law, there were significant differences in the liability of a surety and a guarantor, as discussed in the following subsections. Today, however, the distinctions outlined here have been abolished in some states.

Suretyship A promise made by a third party to be responsible for a debtor's obligation.

Surety A third party who agrees to be primarily responsible for the debt of another.

Surety

A contract of strict **suretyship** is a promise made by a third person to be responsible for the debtor's obligation. It is an express contract between the **surety** (the third party) and the creditor. The surety in the strictest sense is primarily liable for the debt of the principal. The creditor need not exhaust all legal remedies against the principal debtor before holding the surety responsible for payment. The creditor can demand payment from the surety from the moment the debt is due.

Example 25.16 Roberto Delmar wants to borrow from the bank to buy a used car. Because Roberto is still in college, the bank will not lend him the funds unless his father, José Delmar, who has dealt with the bank before, will cosign the note (add his signature to the note, thereby becoming a surety and thus jointly liable for payment of the debt). When José cosigns the note, he becomes primarily liable to the bank. On the note's due date, the bank can seek payment from either Roberto or José, or both jointly.

Guarantor A third party who agrees to be secondarily liable for the debt of another (the debtor) only after the principal debtor defaults.

Guaranty

With a suretyship arrangement, the surety is *primarily* liable for the debtor's obligation. With a guaranty arrangement, the **guarantor**—the third person making the guaranty—is *secondarily* liable. The guarantor can be required to pay the obligation *only after the principal debtor defaults,* and default usually takes place only after the creditor has made an attempt to collect from the debtor.

Case Example 25.17 To finance a development project in Delaware, Brandywine Partners, LLC, borrowed $15.9 million from HSBC Realty Credit Corp. (USA). As part of the deal, Brian O'Neill, an executive at Brandywine, signed a guaranty on the loan. The guaranty expressly stated that O'Neill was familiar with the value of the property and that he was not relying on it as an inducement to sign. Brandywine defaulted, and HSBC filed a suit in a federal district court against O'Neill to recover. O'Neill tried to claim that he had been fraudulently induced into signing the guaranty, but the court found that argument unconvincing given the language of the guaranty. Therefore, the guaranty was enforceable, and O'Neill had to pay HSBC.[13]

Actions That Release the Surety and Guarantor

Basically, the same actions will release a surety or a guarantor from an obligation. In general, the following rules apply to both sureties and guarantors, but for simplicity, we refer just to sureties:

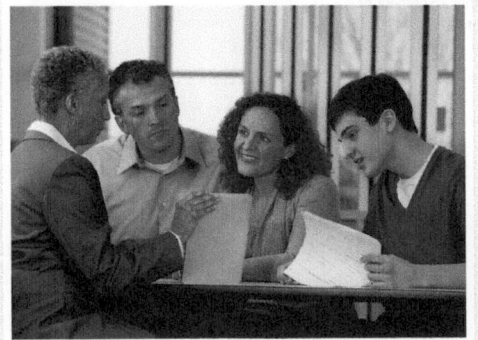

Many parents are sureties for their children's student loans. If the student loan is materially modified without the parents' knowledge, why can the loan be completely discharged?

1. *Material modification.* Making any material modification to the terms of the original contract without the surety's consent will discharge the surety's obligation. The extent to which the surety is discharged depends on whether he or she was compensated and the amount of the loss suffered as a result of the modification. For instance, a father who receives no consideration in return for acting as a surety on his daughter's loan will be completely discharged if the loan contract is modified without his consent.

2. *Surrender of property.* If a creditor surrenders the collateral to the debtor or impairs the collateral without the surety's consent, these acts can reduce the obligation of the surety. If the creditor's actions reduce the value of the property used as collateral, the surety is released to the extent of any loss suffered.

3. *Payment or tender of payment.* Naturally, any payment of the principal obligation by the debtor or by another person on the debtor's behalf will discharge the surety from the obligation. Even if the creditor refused to accept payment of the principal debt when it was tendered, the obligation of the surety can be discharged.

---

13. *HSBC Realty Credit Corp. (USA) v. O'Neill,* 745 F.3d 564 (1st Cir. 2014).

Defenses of the Surety and the Guarantor Generally, the surety (or guarantor) can also assert any of the defenses available to the principal debtor to avoid liability on the obligation to the creditor. A few exceptions do exist, however. The surety cannot assert the principal debtor's incapacity or bankruptcy as a defense. Nor can the surety assert the statute of limitations as a defense.

Obviously, a surety (or guarantor) may also have her or his own defenses. For instance, the surety can assert her or his own incapacity or bankruptcy as a defense. Furthermore, if the creditor fraudulently induced the surety to guarantee the debt of the debtor, the surety can assert fraud as a defense. In most states, the creditor has a legal duty to inform the surety, before the formation of the suretyship contract, of material facts known by the creditor that would substantially increase the surety's risk. Failure to so inform may constitute fraud and render the suretyship obligation voidable.

Rights of the Surety and the Guarantor Usually, when the surety (or guarantor) pays the debt owed to the creditor, the surety (or guarantor) is entitled to certain rights.

The Right of Subrogation. The surety has the legal **right of subrogation,** which means that any right the creditor had against the debtor now becomes the right of the surety. Included are creditor rights in bankruptcy, rights to collateral possessed by the creditor, and rights to judgments secured by the creditor. In short, the surety stands in the shoes of the creditor and may pursue any remedies that were available to the creditor against the debtor.

The Right of Reimbursement. The surety has a **right of reimbursement** from the debtor. Basically, the surety is entitled to receive from the debtor all outlays made on behalf of the suretyship arrangement. Such outlays can include expenses incurred as well as the actual amount of the debt paid to the creditor.

The Right of Contribution. Two or more sureties are called **co-sureties.** When one co-surety pays more than her or his proportionate share on a debtor's default, she or he is entitled to recover from the other co-sureties the amount paid above her or his obligation. This is the **right of contribution.** Generally, a co-surety's liability either is determined by agreement between the co-sureties or, in the absence of an agreement, is specified in the suretyship contract itself.

Example 25.18 Two co-sureties—Yasser and Itzhak—are obligated under a suretyship contract to guarantee the debt of Jules. Itzhak's maximum liability is $15,000, and Yasser's is $10,000. Jules owes $10,000 and is in default. Itzhak pays the creditor the entire $10,000.

In the absence of an agreement to the contrary, Itzhak can recover $4,000 from Yasser. The amount of the debt that Yasser agreed to cover is divided by the total amount that Itzhak and Yasser together agreed to cover. The result is multiplied by the amount of the default, yielding the amount that Yasser owes: ($10,000 ÷ $25,000) × $10,000 = $4,000.

Right of Subrogation The right of a party to stand in the place of another, giving the substituted party the same legal rights that the original party had.

Right of Reimbursement The right of a party to be repaid for costs, expenses, or losses incurred on behalf of another.

Co-Surety A party who assumes liability jointly with another surety for the payment of a debtor's obligation under a suretyship arrangement.

Right of Contribution The right of a co-surety who pays more than his or her proportionate share on a debtor's default to recover the excess paid from other co-sureties.

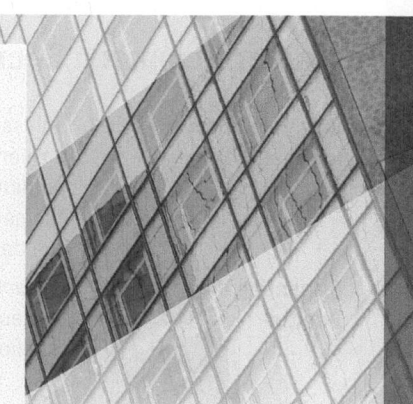

Practice and Review

Paul Barton owned a small property-management company, doing business as Brighton Homes. In October, Barton went on a spending spree. First, he bought a Bose surround-sound system for his home from KDM Electronics. The next day, he purchased a Wilderness Systems kayak from Outdoor Outfitters, and the day after that he bought a new Toyota 4-Runner financed through Bridgeport Auto. Two weeks later, Barton purchased six new iMac computers for his office, also from KDM Electronics. Barton bought all of these items under installment sales contracts. Six months later, Barton's property-management

(Continues)

business was failing. He could not make the payments due on any of these purchases and thus defaulted on the loans. Using the information presented in the chapter, answer the following questions.

1. For which of Barton's purchases (the surround-sound system, the kayak, the 4-Runner, and the six iMacs) would the creditor need to file a financing statement to perfect its security interest?

2. Suppose that Barton's contract for the office computers mentioned only the name *Brighton Homes*. What would be the consequences if KDM Electronics filed a financing statement that listed only Brighton Homes as the debtor's name?

3. Which of these purchases would qualify as a PMSI in consumer goods?

4. Suppose that after KDM Electronics repossesses the surround-sound system, it decides to keep the system rather than sell it. Can KDM do this under Article 9? Why or why not?

Debate This

A financing statement that does not have the debtor's exact name should still be effective because creditors should always be protected when debtors default.

Key Terms

after-acquired property 588
artisan's lien 597
attachment 579
authenticate 579
collateral 578
continuation statement 585
co-surety 601
creditors' composition agreement 599
cross-collateralization 589
debtor 578
default 578
deficiency judgment 595

execution 593
financing statement 578
floating lien 589
garnishment 598
guarantor 600
levy 593
mechanic's lien 596
perfection 581
pledge 584
proceeds 587
purchase-money security interest (PMSI) 584

right of contribution 601
right of reimbursement 601
right of subrogation 601
secured party 578
secured transaction 577
security agreement 578
security interest 578
surety 600
suretyship 600
writ of attachment 598
writ of execution 598

Chapter Summary: Security Interests and Creditors' Rights

Creating a Security Interest	1. Unless the creditor has possession of the collateral, there must be a written or authenticated security agreement that clearly describes the collateral subject to the security interest and is signed or authenticated by the debtor. 2. The secured party must give value to the debtor. 3. The debtor must have rights in the collateral.
Perfecting a Security Interest	1. *Perfection by filing*—The most common method of perfection is by filing a financing statement containing the names of the secured party and the debtor and identifying the collateral covered by the financing statement. The financing statement must be filed under the name of the debtor. Trade names normally are not sufficient.

2. *Perfection without filing*—
  a. By possession—The debtor can transfer possession of the collateral to the secured party. A *pledge* is an example of this type of transfer.
  b. By attachment—Fourteen types of security interests are perfected automatically when they are created. The most common is the purchase-money security interest (PMSI) in consumer goods.
3. *Classification of collateral*—The classification of collateral determines how and where a security interest is perfected (see Exhibit 25–2).

Scope of a Security Interest	A security agreement can cover the following types of property: 1. *Collateral in the present possession or control of the debtor.* 2. *Proceeds from a sale, exchange, or disposition of secured collateral.* 3. *After-acquired property*—A security agreement may provide that property acquired after execution of the agreement will also be secured by the agreement. This provision is often included in security agreements covering a debtor's inventory. 4. *Future advances*—A security agreement may provide that any future advances made against a line of credit will be subject to the initial security interest in the same collateral. 5. *The floating-lien concept*—This type of security interest continues in the collateral or proceeds even if the collateral changes in character, classification, or location.

Priorities	1. *General rules*—
	  a. Perfected security interest versus unsecured creditors and unperfected security interests—A perfected secured party's interest has priority over the interests of most other parties.
	  b. Conflicting perfected security interests—When two or more secured parties have perfected security interests in the same collateral, the first to perfect generally has priority [UCC 9–322(a)(1)].
	  c. Conflicting unperfected security interests—When two conflicting security interests are unperfected, the first to attach (be created) has priority [UCC 9–322(a)(3)].
	2. *Exceptions*—
	  a. In some instances, a PMSI, properly perfected, will prevail over another security interest in after-acquired collateral, even though the other was perfected first.
	  b. A buyer of goods in the ordinary course of the seller's business prevails over a secured party's security interest, even if the security interest is perfected and even if the buyer knows of its existence [UCC 9–320(a)].
	  c. A perfected PMSI in inventory has priority over a conflicting security interest in the same inventory.
	  d. Exceptions also exist for buyers of farm products, chattel paper, instruments, documents, or securities.

Rights and Duties	1. *Information request*—On request by the filing party, the filing officer must send a statement listing the file number, the date, and the hour of the filing of the financing statement to the person making the request. 2. *Release, assignment, and amendment*—A secured party may (a) release part or all of the collateral described in a filed financing statement, thus ending the creditor's security interest, or (b) assign part or all of the security interest to another party. If the debtor and the secured party agree, they can also amend the filed statement. 3. *Confirmation or accounting request by debtor*—If the debtor requests a confirmation of the unpaid debt or a list of the collateral, the secured party must send the debtor an authenticated accounting within fourteen days. 4. *Termination statement*—When a debt is paid, the secured party generally must file a termination statement. If the financing statement covers consumer goods, the termination statement must be filed by the secured party within one month after the debt is paid or within twenty days of receiving the debtor's demand, whichever is earlier.
Default	Parties can stipulate the conditions that will constitute a default, so long as they do not run counter to the UCC's provisions regarding good faith and unconscionability. Default occurs most commonly when the debtor fails to meet scheduled payments or becomes bankrupt. 1. *Basic Remedies*—The secured party's remedies are the self-help remedy (repossession of the collateral) and judicial remedies (such as obtaining a judgment on the underlying debt, followed by execution and levy).

(Continues)

2. *Disposition of collateral*—On the debtor's default, and once the secured party has possession of the collateral, the secured party may do either of the following:
   a. Retain the collateral in full or partial satisfaction of the debt (subject to limitations).
   b. Sell, lease, license, or otherwise dispose of the collateral in any commercially reasonable manner and apply the proceeds toward satisfaction of the debt [UCC 9–602(7), 9–603, 9–610(a), 9–613, 9–620]. Any sale is subject to procedures established by state law.

Other Laws Assisting Creditors

1. *Mechanic's lien*—A nonpossessory, filed lien on an owner's real estate for labor, services, or materials furnished for making improvements on the realty.
2. *Artisan's lien*—A possessory lien on an owner's personal property for labor performed or value added.
3. *Judicial lien*—
   a. Writ of attachment—A court order to seize a debtor's nonexempt property prior to a court's final determination of a creditor's rights to the property. Attachment is available only if the creditor complies with the applicable state statutes.
   b. Writ of execution—A court order directing the sheriff to seize (levy) and sell a debtor's nonexempt real or personal property to satisfy a court's judgment in the creditor's favor.
4. *Garnishment*—A collection remedy that allows a creditor to collect a debt by seizing property of the debtor that is being held by a third party.
5. *Creditors' composition agreements*—Contracts between a debtor and his or her creditors in which the creditors agree to discharge the debts on the debtor's payment of a sum less than the amount actually owed.
6. *Suretyships and guaranty*—Arrangements by which, under contract, a third person agrees to be primarily or secondarily liable for the debt owed by the principal debtor. A creditor can turn to this third person for satisfaction of the debt.

Issue Spotters

1. Liberty Bank loans Michelle $5,000 to buy a car, which is used as collateral to secure the loan. After repaying less than 50 percent of the loan, Michelle defaults. Liberty could repossess and keep the car, but the bank does not want it. What are the alternatives? (See *Priorities, Rights, and Duties*.)
2. Jorge contracts with Midwest Roofing to fix his roof. Jorge pays half of the contract price in advance. Midwest completes the job, but Jorge refuses to pay the rest of the price. What can Midwest do? (See *Other Laws Assisting Creditors*.)
   —**Check your answers to the *Issue Spotters* against the answers provided in Appendix D at the end of this text.**

Business Scenarios and Case Problems

25–1. Priority Disputes. Redford is a seller of electric generators. He purchases a large quantity of generators from a manufacturer, Mallon Corp., by making a down payment and signing an agreement to pay the balance over a period of time. The agreement gives Mallon Corp. a security interest in the generators and the proceeds. Mallon Corp. properly files a financing statement on its security interest. Redford receives the generators and immediately sells one of them to Garfield on an installment contract with payment to be made in twelve equal installments. At the time of the sale, Garfield knows of Mallon's security interest. Two months later, Redford goes into default on his payments to Mallon. Discuss Mallon's rights against purchaser Garfield in this situation. (See *Priorities, Rights, and Duties*.)

25–2. Perfection. Marsh has a prize horse named Arabian Knight. In need of working capital, Marsh borrows $5,000 from Mendez, who takes possession of Arabian Knight as security for the loan. No written agreement is signed. Discuss whether, in the absence of a written agreement, Mendez has a security interest in Arabian Knight. If Mendez does have a security interest, is it a perfected security interest? Explain. (See *Creating and Perfecting a Security Interest*.)

25–3. Guaranty. Timothy Martinez, owner of Koenig & Vits, Inc. (K&V), guaranteed K&V's debt to Community Bank & Trust. The guaranty stated that the bank was not required to seek payment of the debt from any other source before enforcing the guaranty. K&V defaulted. Through a Wisconsin state court, the bank sought payment of $536,739.40, plus interest at the contract rate of 7.5 percent, from Martinez. Martinez argued that the bank could not enforce his guaranty while other funds were available to satisfy K&V's debt. For instance, the debt might be paid out of the proceeds of a sale of corporate assets. Is this an effective defense to a guaranty? Why or why not? [*Community Bank & Trust v. Koenig & Vits, Inc.*, 346 Wis.2d 279, 827 N.W.2d 279 (2013)] (See *Other Laws Assisting Creditors*.)

25–4. Liens. Daniel and Katherine Balk asked Jirak Construction, LLC, to remodel their farmhouse in Lawler, Iowa. Jirak provided the Balks with an initial estimate of $45,975 for the cost. Over the course of the work, the Balks made significant changes to the plan. Jirak agreed to the changes and regularly advised the Balks about the increasing costs. In mid-project, Jirak provided an itemized breakdown at their request. The Balks paid Jirak $67,000 but refused to pay more. Jirak claimed that they still owed $55,000 in labor and materials. Jirak filed a suit in an Iowa state court against the Balks to collect. Which of the liens discussed in this chapter would be most effective to Jirak in its attempt to collect? How does that type of lien work? Is the court likely to enforce it in this case? Explain. [*Jirak Construction, LLC v. Balk*, 863 N.W.2d 35 (Iowa App. 2015)] (See *Other Laws Assisting Creditors*.)

25–5. Business Case Problem with Sample Answer—Perfection of a Security Interest. G&K Farms, a North Dakota partnership, operated a farm in Texas. G&K was insured under the Supplemental Revenue Assistance Payments Program (SURE), through which the federal government provides financial assistance for crop losses caused by natural disasters. PHI Financial Services, Inc., loaned G&K $6.6 million. PHI filed a financing statement that described the collateral as the debtor's interest in "Government Payments." The document did not refer to the farm's crops. G&K defaulted on the loan. Later, G&K received a SURE payment for crop losses and transferred some of the funds to its law firm, Johnston Law Office, P.C., in payment for services. PHI brought an action against Johnston to recover those funds as partial payment on its loan to G&K. Johnston argued that PHI did not have a perfected security interest in the SURE payment because the financing statement did not identify the crops. Was the description of the collateral in the financing statement sufficient? Why or why not? [*PHI Financial Services, Inc. v. Johnston Law Office, P.C.*, 2016 ND 20, 874 N.W.2d 910 (Dakota 2016)] (See *Creating and Perfecting a Security Interest*.)

—For a sample answer to Problem 25–5, go to Appendix E at the end of this text.

25–6. Laws Assisting Creditors. Grand Harbour Condominium Owners Association, Inc., obtained a judgment in an Ohio state court against Gene and Nancy Grogg for $45,458.86. To satisfy the judgment, Grand Harbour filed a notice of garnishment

with the court, seeking funds held by the Groggs in various banks. The Groggs disputed Grand Harbour's right to garnish the funds. They claimed that the funds were exempt Social Security and pension proceeds, but they offered no proof of this claim. The banks responded by depositing $23,911.97 with the court. These funds were delivered to Grand Harbour. Later, the Groggs filed a petition for bankruptcy in a federal bankruptcy court. After they were granted a discharge, they filed a "motion to return funds to debtors" but provided no evidence that their debt to Grand Harbour had been included in the discharge. What is Grand Harbour's best argument in response to the Groggs' motion? [*Grand Harbour Condominium Owners Association, Inc. v. Grogg*, 2016 -Ohio- 1386 (Ohio Ct.App. 2016)] (See *Other Laws Assisting Creditors*.)

25–7. Disposition of Collateral. Dustin Mosely financed the purchase of two cars with a loan from Show-Me Credit Union (SMCU). When Mosely stopped making payments on the loan, SMCU notified him that it intended to repossess the cars and dispose of them at a "private or public" sale. After the sale, the creditor filed a suit in a Missouri state court to recover the difference between the sale price and the outstanding debt. Mosely counterclaimed that SMCU had failed to give proper notice before repossessing the vehicles. Public and private sales of collateral are significantly different methods of disposition. Did SMCU's failure to specify the type of sale, either public or private, at which the creditor would dispose of the collateral violate the UCC's notice requirement? Explain. [*Show-Me Credit Union v. Mosely*, 541 S.W.3d 28 (Mo.Ct.App. 2018)] (See *Default*.)

25–8. A Question of Ethics—The IDDR Approach and Defenses of the Guarantor. Woodsmill Park Limited Partnership borrowed $6.2 million secured by real property in Chicago, Illinois. Bill and Brian Bruce and Matthew O'Malley signed guaranties to meet Woodsmill's obligation on the loan. Woodsmill defaulted on the payments. Northbrook Bank & Trust Company filed an action in an Illinois state court against Woodsmill and the Bruces to foreclose on the property. The defendants agreed to resolve the claim in exchange for a deed in lieu of foreclosure and a promise to pay the difference between the value of the property and the unpaid amount of the loan. The parties stipulated, "Nothing in this Agreement shall release or reduce O'Malley's obligations under O'Malley's Guaranty." [Northbrook Bank & Trust Co. v. O'Malley, *2017 IL App (1st) 160438-U (2017)*] (See Other Laws Assisting Creditors.)

1. What is the effect on O'Malley's guaranty of the agreement between Northbrook, Woodsmill, and the Bruces? Explain.

2. Using the IDDR approach, evaluate the ethics of Northbrook, Woodsmill, and the Bruces in agreeing to the stipulation concerning O'Malley.

Critical Thinking and Writing Assignments

25–9. Business Law Writing. Write a few sentences describing the circumstances in which a creditor would resort to each of the following remedies when trying to collect on debt. (See *Other Laws Assisting Creditors.*)

1. Mechanic's lien
2. Artisan's lien
3. Writ of attachment

25–10. Time-Limited Group Assignment—Validity of a Security Interest. Nick Sabol, doing business in the recording industry as Sound Farm Productions, applied to Morton Community Bank for a $58,000 loan to expand his business. Besides the loan application, Sabol signed a promissory note that referred to the bank's rights in "any collateral." Sabol also signed a letter authorizing Morton Community Bank to execute, file, and record all financing statements, amendments, and other documents required by Article 9 to establish a security interest. Sabol did not sign any other documents, including the financing statement, which contained a description of the collateral. Two years later, without having repaid the loan, Sabol filed for bankruptcy. The bank claimed a security interest in Sabol's sound equipment. (See *Creating and Perfecting a Security Interest.*)

1. The first group will list all the requirements of an enforceable security interest and explain why each of these elements is necessary.
2. The second group will determine if Morton Community Bank had a valid security interest.
3. The third group will discuss whether a bank should be able to execute financing statements on a debtor's behalf without the debtor being present or signing them. Are there are any drawbacks to this practice?

Bankruptcy

"Capitalism without bankruptcy is like Christianity without hell."

Frank Borman
1928–present
(U.S. astronaut and businessman)

Many people and businesses in today's economy are struggling to pay their monthly bills. In the old days, debtors were punished and sometimes sent to jail for failing to pay their debts. Today, the law provides debtors with numerous options, including bankruptcy—a last resort in resolving debtor-creditor problems.

As implied by the chapter-opening quotation, bankruptcy is an essential aspect of our capitalistic society. Individuals and businesses in our nation have great opportunities for financial success but may also encounter financial difficulties. For instance, many retail chains (The Limited, Wet Seal, Gymboree) have filed for bankruptcy in recent years, in part due to the increase in online shopping. (See this chapter's *Business Web Log* feature for further discussion.) Therefore, every businessperson should have some understanding of the bankruptcy process.

26–1 The Bankruptcy Code

Bankruptcy relief is provided under federal law. Nevertheless, state laws on property, secured transactions, liens, and judgments also play a role in federal bankruptcy proceedings.

Article I, Section 8, of the U.S. Constitution gave Congress the power to establish "uniform laws on the subject of bankruptcies throughout the United States." Federal bankruptcy

Learning Objectives

The four Learning Objectives *below are designed to help improve your understanding. After reading this chapter, you should be able to answer the following questions:*

1. What are the two main goals of bankruptcy?

2. In a Chapter 7 bankruptcy, what happens if a court finds that there was "substantial abuse"? How is the means test used?

3. In a Chapter 11 reorganization, what is the role of the debtor in possession?

4. How does a Chapter 13 bankruptcy differ from bankruptcy under Chapter 7 and Chapter 11?

Online Retail Competition Causes Yet Another Brick-and-Mortar Retailer to File for Bankruptcy

Business Web Log

The online world did not significantly affect consumers and brick-and-mortar competitors for quite a few years after the invention of the Internet. But as online retailers become more aggressive and consumers become more comfortable ordering online, the inevitable is finally happening. More and more large retailers are filing for bankruptcy. One of the latest is Toys R Us. Toys R Us is just one of more than thirty-five major retailers that have filed for either Chapter 7 or Chapter 11 bankruptcy in recent years. Others include Radio Shack, Payless ShoeSource, and Vitamin World.

Toys R Us initially filed for Chapter 11 bankruptcy protection, indicating that it wanted to come to terms with its debt holders and other creditors. At issue was $5 billion of debt. The company promised consumers that its stores would stay open for the 2017 Christmas holidays, which they did, but its holiday sales were disappointing. Ultimately, the company's enormous debt and growing losses proved too much to overcome with reorganization. Toys R Us then announced that it was filing for Chapter 7 liquidation and was closing (or selling) all of its retail stores in the United States.

Shopping malls throughout America are struggling, too. Many of their anchor stores, such as Nordstrom, are closing money-losing locations. Others are filing for bankruptcy. Retailers in malls are not suffering because of cyclical downturns in spending. The reality is that many younger purchasers do not frequent shopping malls and instead do their shopping primarily on the Internet.

Although online competition has affected department stores more than any other retail sector, other retailers are feeling pressure as well, as shown by the example of Toys R Us. As one commentator stated, "Virtually every sub-segment of retail, other than auto retail and pharmacy, is caught in the cross-hairs of Amazon's growing online presence."

Key Point

We can expect to see brick-and-mortar retailers forced into Chapter 11 reorganization for many years to come. Not only is Amazon, the Internet's biggest retailer, expanding every year, but traditional retailers are shifting resources away from physical stores and learning how to increase their online presence.

What are some factors that can cause large retail chains, such as Toys R Us, to file for bankruptcy?

QualityHD/Shutterstock.com

legislation was first enacted in 1898 and since then has undergone several modifications, most recently in the Bankruptcy Reform Act.[1] Federal bankruptcy laws are called the Bankruptcy Code or, more simply, the Code.

26–1a Goals of Bankruptcy Law

Bankruptcy law in the United States has two main goals:

1. To protect a debtor by giving him or her a fresh start without creditors' claims.

2. To ensure equitable treatment of creditors who are competing for a debtor's assets.

Thus, the law attempts to balance the rights of the debtor and the creditors.

Although the twin goals of bankruptcy remained the same, the balance between them shifted somewhat after the reform legislation. Because of its significance for creditors and debtors alike, we present the Bankruptcy Reform Act as this chapter's *Landmark in the Law* feature.

Learning Objective 1

What are the two main goals of bankruptcy?

---

1. The full title of the act is the Bankruptcy Abuse Prevention and Consumer Protection Act of 2005, Pub. L. No. 109-8, 119 Stat. 23 (April 20, 2005).

The Bankruptcy Abuse Prevention and Consumer Protection Act

When Congress enacted the first Bankruptcy Reform Act in 1978, many claimed that the law made it too easy for debtors to file for bankruptcy protection. The 2005 Bankruptcy Abuse Prevention and Consumer Protection Act (BAPCPA) was passed, in part, in response to businesses' concerns about the rise in personal bankruptcy filings.

From 1978 to 2005, personal bankruptcy filings increased dramatically. Various business groups—including credit-card companies, retailers, and banks—claimed that the bankruptcy process was being abused and that reform was necessary.

More Repayment Plans, Fewer Liquidation Bankruptcies One of the major goals of the BAPCPA is to require consumers to pay as many of their debts as they possibly can instead of having those debts fully discharged in bankruptcy. Before the reforms, the vast majority of bankruptcies were filed under Chapter 7 of the Bankruptcy Code, which permits debtors, with some exceptions, to have *all* of their debts

discharged in bankruptcy. Only about 20 percent of personal bankruptcies were filed under Chapter 13 of the Bankruptcy Code.

As you will read later in this chapter, Chapter 13 of the Bankruptcy Code requires the debtor to establish a repayment plan and pay off as many of his or her debts as possible over a maximum period of five years. Under the BAPCPA, more debtors have to file for bankruptcy under Chapter 13.

Other Significant Provisions of the Act The BAPCPA also made a number of other changes. One important provision involves the homestead exemption. Before the passage of the act, some states allowed debtors petitioning for bankruptcy to exempt all of the *equity* (the market value minus the outstanding mortgage owed) in their homes during bankruptcy proceedings. The act leaves these exemptions in place but puts some limits on their use.

Another BAPCPA provision gives child-support obligations priority over other debts and allows enforcement agencies to

continue efforts to collect child-support payments.

Application to Today's World
Under the 2005 bankruptcy reforms, fewer debtors are allowed to have their debts discharged in Chapter 7 liquidation proceedings. At the same time, the act makes it more difficult for debtors to obtain a "fresh start" financially—one of the major goals of bankruptcy law in the United States. Today, more debtors are forced to file under Chapter 13.

Additionally, the bankruptcy process has become more time consuming and costly because it requires more extensive documentation and certification. These changes in the law have left many Americans unable to obtain relief from their debts.

26–1b Bankruptcy Courts

Bankruptcy proceedings are held in federal bankruptcy courts, which are under the authority of U.S. district courts. Rulings by bankruptcy courts can be appealed to the district courts.

A bankruptcy court can conduct a jury trial if the appropriate district court has authorized it and the parties to the bankruptcy consent. Bankruptcy courts follow the Federal Rules of Bankruptcy Procedure rather than the Federal Rules of Civil Procedure. Bankruptcy court judges are appointed for terms of fourteen years.

26–1c Types of Bankruptcy Relief

The Bankruptcy Code is contained in Title 11 of the *United States Code* (U.S.C.) and has eight "chapters." Chapters 1, 3, and 5 of the Code include general definitions and provisions governing case administration and procedures, creditors, the debtor, and the estate. These three chapters of the Code normally apply to all types of bankruptcies.

Four chapters of the Code set forth the most important types of relief that debtors can seek.

Know This
Congress regulates the jurisdiction of the federal courts within the limits set by the U.S. Constitution. Congress can expand or reduce the number of federal courts at any time.

1. Chapter 7 provides for *liquidation* proceedings—that is, the selling of all non-exempt assets and the distribution of the proceeds to the debtor's creditors.
2. Chapter 11 governs reorganizations.
3. Chapter 12 (for family farmers and family fishermen) and Chapter 13 (for individuals) provide for adjustment of the debts of parties with regular income.[2]

Note that a debtor (except for a municipality) need not be insolvent[3] to file for bankruptcy relief under the Bankruptcy Code. Anyone obligated to a creditor can declare bankruptcy.

26–1d Special Treatment of Consumer-Debtors

A **consumer-debtor** is a debtor whose debts result primarily from the purchase of goods for personal, family, or household use. The Bankruptcy Code requires that the clerk of the court give all consumer-debtors written notice of the general purpose, benefits, and costs of each chapter of bankruptcy under which they may proceed. In addition, the clerk must provide consumer-debtors with information on the types of services available from credit counseling agencies. Consumer-debtors are also required to confirm the accuracy of certain information filed with the court (their attorney must do so if they are represented).

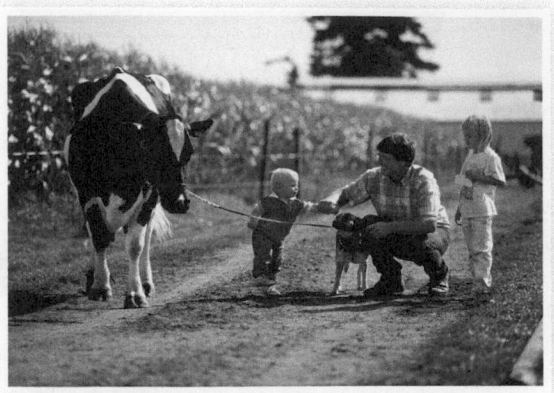

Under which chapter of the Code may family farmers seek bankruptcy relief?

Consumer-Debtor One whose debts result primarily from the purchase of goods for personal, family, or household use.

Liquidation The sale of the nonexempt assets of a debtor and the distribution of the funds received to creditors.

Bankruptcy Trustee A person appointed by the court to manage the debtor's funds.

Discharge The termination of a bankruptcy debtor's obligation to pay debts.

Petition in Bankruptcy The document that is filed with a bankruptcy court to initiate bankruptcy proceedings.

26–2 Chapter 7—Liquidation

Liquidation under Chapter 7 is the most familiar type of bankruptcy proceeding and is often referred to as an *ordinary*, or *straight, bankruptcy*. Put simply, a debtor in a liquidation bankruptcy turns all assets over to a **bankruptcy trustee,** a person appointed by the court to manage the debtor's funds. The trustee sells the nonexempt assets and distributes the proceeds to creditors. With certain exceptions, the remaining debts are then **discharged** (extinguished), and the debtor is relieved of the obligation to pay the debts.

Any "person"—defined as including individuals, partnerships, and corporations[4]—may be a debtor under Chapter 7. Railroads, insurance companies, banks, savings and loan associations, investment companies licensed by the U.S. Small Business Administration, and credit unions *cannot* be Chapter 7 debtors. Other chapters of the Code or other federal or state statutes apply to them. A husband and wife may file jointly for bankruptcy under a single petition.

A straight bankruptcy may be commenced by the filing of either a voluntary or an involuntary **petition in bankruptcy**—the document that is filed with a bankruptcy court to initiate bankruptcy proceedings. If a debtor files the petition, then it is a *voluntary bankruptcy*. If one or more creditors file a petition to force the debtor into bankruptcy, then it is an *involuntary bankruptcy*.

26–2a Voluntary Bankruptcy

To bring a voluntary petition in bankruptcy, the debtor files official forms designated for that purpose in the bankruptcy court. The law now requires that before debtors can file a petition, they must receive credit counseling from an approved nonprofit agency. Debtors

---

2. There are no Chapters 2, 4, 6, 8, or 10 in Title 11. Such "gaps" are not uncommon in the *United States Code.* They occur because, when a statute is enacted, chapter numbers (or other subdivisional unit numbers) are sometimes reserved for future use. (A gap may also appear if a law has been repealed.)
3. The inability to pay debts as they come due is known as *equitable* insolvency. A *balance-sheet* insolvency, which exists when a debtor's liabilities exceed assets, is not the test. Thus, it is possible for debtors to petition voluntarily for bankruptcy even though their assets far exceed their liabilities. This situation may occur when a debtor's cash-flow problems become severe.
4. The definition of *corporation* includes unincorporated companies and associations. It also covers labor unions.

filing a Chapter 7 petition must thus include a certificate proving that they have received individual or group counseling from an approved agency within the last 180 days (roughly six months).

A consumer-debtor who is filing a voluntary petition must confirm the accuracy of the petition's contents. The debtor must also state in the petition, at the time of filing, that he or she understands the relief available under other chapters of the Code and has chosen to proceed under Chapter 7.

Attorneys representing consumer-debtors must file an affidavit stating that they have informed the debtors of the relief available under each chapter of the Code. In addition, the attorneys must reasonably attempt to verify the accuracy of the consumer-debtors' petitions and schedules (described next). Failure to do so is considered perjury.

Chapter 7 Schedules The voluntary petition contains the following schedules:

1. A list of both secured and unsecured creditors, their addresses, and the amount of debt owed to each.
2. A statement of the financial affairs of the debtor.
3. A list of all property owned by the debtor, including property claimed by the debtor to be exempt.
4. A list of current income and expenses.
5. A certificate of credit counseling (as mentioned previously).
6. Proof of payments received from employers within sixty days prior to the filing of the petition.
7. A statement of the amount of monthly income, itemized to show how the amount is calculated.
8. A copy of the debtor's federal income tax return for the most recent year ending immediately before the filing of the petition.

The official forms must be completed accurately, sworn to under oath, and signed by the debtor. To conceal assets or knowingly supply false information on these schedules is a crime under the bankruptcy laws.

With the exception of tax returns, failure to file the required schedules within forty-five days after the filing of the petition (unless an extension is granted) will result in an automatic dismissal of the petition. The debtor has up to seven days before the date of the first creditors' meeting to provide a copy of the most recent tax returns to the trustee.

Tax Returns during Bankruptcy A debtor may be required to file a tax return at the end of each tax year while the case is pending and to provide a copy to the court. A request for a copy of the debtor's tax return may be made by the court or the **U.S. Trustee**—a government official who performs administrative tasks that a bankruptcy judge would otherwise have to perform. In addition, any *party in interest* (a party, such as a creditor, who has a valid interest in the outcome of the proceedings) may make this request. Debtors may also be required to file tax returns during Chapter 11 and 13 bankruptcies.

U.S. Trustee A government official who performs administrative tasks that a bankruptcy judge would otherwise have to perform.

Substantial Abuse and the Means Test A bankruptcy court can dismiss a Chapter 7 petition if the use of Chapter 7 constitutes a "substantial abuse" of bankruptcy law. The revised Code provides a *means test* to determine a debtor's eligibility for Chapter 7. The purpose of the test is to keep higher-income people from abusing the bankruptcy process, as was thought to have happened in the past. The test forces more people to file for Chapter 13 bankruptcy rather than have their debts discharged under Chapter 7.

The Basic Formula. A debtor wishing to file for bankruptcy must complete the means test to determine whether she or he qualifies for Chapter 7. The debtor's average monthly income in recent months is compared with the median income in the geographic area in which the person lives. (The U.S. Trustee Program provides these data at its website, www.justice.gov/ust.)

Learning Objective 2

In a Chapter 7 bankruptcy, what happens if a court finds that there was "substantial abuse"? How is the means test used?

If the debtor's income is below the median income, the debtor usually is allowed to file for Chapter 7 bankruptcy, as there is no presumption of bankruptcy abuse.

Applying the Means Test to Future Disposable Income. If the debtor's income is above the median income, then further calculations must be made to determine the debtor's future disposable income. As a basis for the calculations, it is presumed that the debtor's recent monthly income will continue for the next sixty months. *Disposable income* is then calculated by subtracting living expenses and interest payments on secured debt, such as mortgage payments, from monthly income.

Living expenses are the amounts allowed under formulas used by the Internal Revenue Service (IRS). The IRS allowances include modest allocations for food, clothing, housing, utilities, transportation (including car payments), health care, and other necessities. (The U.S. Trustee Program's website also provides these amounts.) The allowances do not include expenditures for items such as cell phones and cable television service.

Can the Debtor Afford to Pay Unsecured Debts? Once future disposable income has been estimated, that amount is used to determine whether the person will have sufficient income in the future to repay at least some of his or her unsecured debts. The court may also consider the debtor's bad faith or other circumstances indicating abuse.

Case Example 26.1 John and Sarah Buoy filed for Chapter 7 bankruptcy. For the past three months, John's gross monthly income was $4,900, and Sarah's was $6,761. They had five children. They owed secured debts of $34,321 on a Subaru Impreza and a BMW 328i, on which they intended to continue making loan payments (this is called reaffirmation, as will be discussed later). They owed $123,000 on a mortgage and $19,000 in student loans, and their unsecured debts were $4,900.

An auditor for the U.S. Trustee Program reviewed the Buoys' Chapter 7 schedule and concluded that the family's gross income figures were understated. Because of a mistake in the math, the Buoys had miscalculated their biweekly income by approximately $800 a month (or nearly $650 after taxes). The debtors claimed that they had incurred additional expenses after the petition, including orthodontic braces and another car. Even with those expenses, however, the court found that they would have an additional $400 a month in future disposable income and would receive sizeable tax refunds. The court concluded that the Buoys could afford to pay their debts and dismissed the Chapter 7 petition for substantial abuse.[5]

Order for Relief A court's grant of assistance to a debtor in bankruptcy that relieves the debtor of the immediate obligation to pay debts.

How does family size affect the calculation and application of the means test?

Blend Images/Alamy

Additional Grounds for Dismissal

As noted, a debtor's voluntary petition for Chapter 7 relief may be dismissed for substantial abuse or for failure to provide the necessary documents (such as schedules and tax returns) within the specified time. In addition, a motion to dismiss a Chapter 7 filing may be granted in two other situations.

1. If the debtor has been convicted of a violent crime or a drug-trafficking offense, the victim can file a motion to dismiss the voluntary petition.[6]

2. If the debtor fails to pay postpetition domestic-support obligations (which include child and spousal support), the court may dismiss the petition.

Order for Relief

If the voluntary petition for bankruptcy is found to be proper, the filing of the petition will itself constitute an **order for relief**. (An order for relief is the court's grant of assistance to a debtor.)

5. *In re Buoy*, ___ Bankr. ___, 2017 WL 3194755 (N.D. Ohio 2017).

6. Note that the court may not dismiss a case on this ground if the debtor's bankruptcy is necessary to satisfy a claim for a domestic-support obligation.

Once a consumer-debtor's voluntary petition has been filed, the clerk of the court (or other appointee) must give the trustee and creditors notice of the order for relief by mail not more than twenty days after the entry of the order.

26–2b Involuntary Bankruptcy

An involuntary bankruptcy occurs when the debtor's creditors force the debtor into bankruptcy proceedings. An involuntary petition cannot be filed against a charitable institution or a farmer (an individual or business that receives more than 50 percent of its gross income from farming operations).

An involuntary petition should not be used as an everyday debt-collection device. The Code provides penalties for the filing of frivolous (unjustified) petitions against debtors. If the court dismisses an involuntary petition, the petitioning creditors may be required to pay the costs and attorneys' fees incurred by the debtor in defending against the petition. If the petition was filed in bad faith, damages can be awarded for injury to the debtor's reputation. Punitive damages may also be awarded.

Requirements For an involuntary action to be filed, the following requirements must be met:

1. If the debtor has twelve or more creditors, three or more of those creditors having unsecured claims totaling at least $15,775 must join in the petition.

2. If the debtor has fewer than twelve creditors, one or more creditors having a claim of $15,775 or more may file.[7]

Order for Relief If the debtor challenges the involuntary petition, a hearing will be held. The bankruptcy court will enter an order for relief if it finds either of the following:

1. The debtor generally is not paying debts as they become due.

2. A general receiver, assignee, or custodian took possession of, or was appointed to take charge of, substantially all of the debtor's property within 120 days before the filing of the involuntary petition.

If the court grants an order for relief, the debtor will be required to supply the same information in the bankruptcy schedules as in a voluntary bankruptcy.

26–2c Automatic Stay

The moment a petition, either voluntary or involuntary, is filed, an **automatic stay,** or suspension, of almost all actions by creditors against the debtor or the debtor's property normally goes into effect. Until the bankruptcy proceeding is closed or dismissed, the automatic stay prohibits a creditor from taking any act to collect, assess, or recover a claim against the debtor that arose before the filing of the petition.

If the debtor had two or more bankruptcy petitions dismissed during the prior year, the Code presumes bad faith. In such a situation, the automatic stay does *not* go into effect until the court determines that the petition was filed in good faith.

If a creditor *knowingly* violates the automatic stay (a willful violation), any injured party, including the debtor, is entitled to recover actual damages, costs, and attorneys' fees and may be entitled to punitive damages as well. **Example 26.2** Richard Anderson and his wife filed for bankruptcy. One of the debts listed on their Chapter 7 schedule was a JCPenney credit card with a balance of $630. Even after it is notified of the bankruptcy, Recovery Management

> "I hope that after I die, people will say of me: 'That guy sure owed me a lot of money.'"
>
> **Jack Handey**
> 1949–present
> (American humorist)

Automatic Stay In bankruptcy proceedings, the suspension of almost all litigation and other actions by creditors against the debtor or the debtor's property. The stay is effective the moment the debtor files a petition in bankruptcy.

---

7. 11 U.S.C. Section 303. The amounts stated in this chapter are in accordance with those computed on April 1, 2016. The dollar amounts are adjusted every three years on April 1.

Systems Corporation (RMSC), a debt collection service, continues to send letters to Richard Anderson in an attempt to collect the balance on the card. In this situation, RMSC is willfully violating the automatic stay. The Andersons are entitled to seek actual damages, costs, attorneys' fees, and even punitive damages for RMSC's conduct. ▇ (See this chapter's *Business Law Analysis* feature for further clarification.)

The Adequate Protection Doctrine Underlying the Code's automatic-stay provision for a secured creditor is a concept known as *adequate protection*. The **adequate protection doctrine**, among other things, protects secured creditors from losing their security as a result of the automatic stay. The bankruptcy court can provide adequate protection by requiring the debtor or trustee to make periodic cash payments or a one-time cash payment. If the stay may cause the value of the property to decrease, the court can also require the debtor or trustee to provide additional collateral or replacement liens.

Adequate Protection Doctrine
A doctrine that protects secured creditors from losing the value of their security (because the collateral depreciates, for instance) as a result of an automatic stay in a bankruptcy proceeding.

Exceptions to the Automatic Stay The Code provides the following exceptions to the automatic stay:

1. Collection efforts can continue for domestic-support obligations, which include any debt owed to or recoverable by a spouse, a former spouse, a child of the debtor, that child's parent or guardian, or a governmental unit.

2. Proceedings against the debtor related to divorce, child custody or visitation, domestic violence, and support enforcement are not stayed.

3. Investigations by a securities regulatory agency can continue.

4. Certain statutory liens for property taxes are not stayed.

Requests for Relief from the Automatic Stay A secured creditor or other party in interest can petition the bankruptcy court for relief from the automatic stay. If a creditor

---

Violations of the Automatic Stay

Business Law Analysis

Michelle Gholston leased a Chevy Impala from EZ Auto Van Rentals. On November 8, Gholston filed for bankruptcy. On November 21, the bankruptcy court notified EZ Auto of Gholston's bankruptcy and the imposition of an automatic stay. Nevertheless, because Gholston had fallen behind on her payments, EZ Auto repossessed the vehicle on November 28.

Gholston's attorney reminded EZ Auto that it could not take this action because of the automatic stay, but the company failed to return the car. As a result of the car's repossession, Gholston suffered damages that included emotional distress, lost wages, attorneys' fees, and car rental

expenses. Can Gholston recover from EZ Auto?

Analysis: A debtor may be entitled to recover damages if a creditor knowingly or willfully violates the automatic stay. The test is whether EZ Auto knew about Gholston's bankruptcy at the time it repossessed her car. The bankruptcy court and the debtor's attorney had, in fact, notified EZ Auto about the bankruptcy and the automatic stay a week before the car was repossessed.

Result and Reasoning: Gholston can recover damages because EZ Auto willfully violated the automatic stay. EZ Auto repossessed the car even though it received

notice of the automatic stay from the bankruptcy court. In addition, EZ Auto refused to return the car even after Gholston's attorney had reminded it of the stay. Thus, EZ Auto knew about the automatic stay and violated it willfully. Because Gholston suffered direct damages as a result, she can recover from EZ Auto. She may also be awarded punitive damages for EZ Auto's wrongful conduct.

or other party requests relief from the stay, the stay will automatically terminate sixty days after the request, unless the court grants an extension or the parties agree otherwise.

Secured Property The automatic stay on secured property terminates forty-five days after the creditors' meeting unless the debtor redeems or reaffirms certain debts. (Creditors' meetings and reaffirmation will be discussed later in this chapter.) In other words, the debtor cannot keep secured property (such as a financed automobile), even if she or he continues to make payments on it, without reinstating the rights of the secured party to collect on the debt.

If a collection agency knowingly repossesses a car when there is an automatic stay in effect, what can a debtor do?

26–2d Estate in Bankruptcy

On the commencement of a liquidation proceeding under Chapter 7, an **estate in bankruptcy** is created. The estate consists of all the debtor's interests in property currently held, wherever located. The estate in bankruptcy includes all of the following:

1. *Community property* (property jointly owned by a husband and wife in certain states).
2. Property transferred in a transaction voidable by the trustee.
3. Proceeds and profits from the property of the estate.

Certain after-acquired property to which a debtor becomes entitled *within 180 days after filing* may also become part of the estate. Such after-acquired property includes gifts, inheritances, property settlements (from divorce), and life insurance death proceeds. Generally, though, the filing of a bankruptcy petition fixes a dividing line. Property acquired prior to the filing of the petition becomes property of the estate, and property acquired after the filing of the petition, except as just noted, remains the debtor's.

Estate in Bankruptcy All of the property owned by a person, including real estate and personal property.

26–2e The Bankruptcy Trustee

Promptly after the order for relief has been entered, a trustee is appointed. The basic duty of the trustee is to collect the debtor's available estate and reduce it to cash for distribution, preserving the interests of both the debtor and the unsecured creditors. This requires that the trustee be accountable for administering the debtor's estate. To enable the trustee to accomplish this duty, the Code gives the trustee certain powers. These powers must be exercised within two years after the order for relief has been entered.

Review for Substantial Abuse The trustee is required to review promptly all materials filed by the debtor to determine if there is substantial abuse. Within ten days after the first meeting of the creditors, the trustee must file a statement as to whether the case is presumed to be an abuse under the means test. The trustee must provide all creditors with a copy of this statement.

When there is a presumption of abuse, the trustee must either file a motion to dismiss the petition (or convert it to a Chapter 13 proceeding) or file a statement explaining why a motion would not be appropriate. If the debtor owes a domestic-support obligation (such as child support), the trustee must provide written notice of the bankruptcy to the claim holder (a former spouse, for instance).

Trustee's Powers The trustee has the power to require persons holding the debtor's property at the time the petition is filed to deliver the property to the trustee.[8] To enable the trustee to implement this power, the Code provides that the trustee has rights *equivalent* to those of certain other parties, such as a creditor who has a judicial lien. This power of a trustee, which is equivalent to that of a lien creditor, is known as the *strong-arm power.*

---

8. Usually, the trustee takes constructive, rather than actual, possession of the debtor's property. For instance, to obtain possession of a business's inventory, a trustee might change the locks on the doors and hire a security guard.

In addition, the trustee has specific *powers of avoidance*. They enable the trustee to set aside (avoid or cancel) a sale or other transfer of the debtor's property and take the property back for the debtor's estate. These powers apply to voidable rights available to the debtor, preferences, and fraudulent transfers by the debtor (as discussed in more detail next). The trustee can also avoid certain statutory liens.

The debtor shares most of the trustee's avoidance powers. Thus, if the trustee does not take action to enforce one of these rights, the debtor in a liquidation bankruptcy can enforce it.

Voidable Rights   A trustee steps into the shoes of the debtor. Thus, any reason that a debtor can use to obtain the return of his or her property can be used by the trustee as well. The grounds for recovery include fraud, duress, incapacity, and mutual mistake.

Example 26.3   Ben sells his RV trailer to Inga. Inga gives Ben a check, knowing that she has insufficient funds in her bank account to cover the check. Inga has committed fraud. Ben has the right to avoid that transfer and recover the RV trailer from Inga. If Ben files for bankruptcy relief under Chapter 7, the trustee can exercise the same right to recover the RV trailer from Inga, and the RV trailer becomes part of the debtor's estate. ■

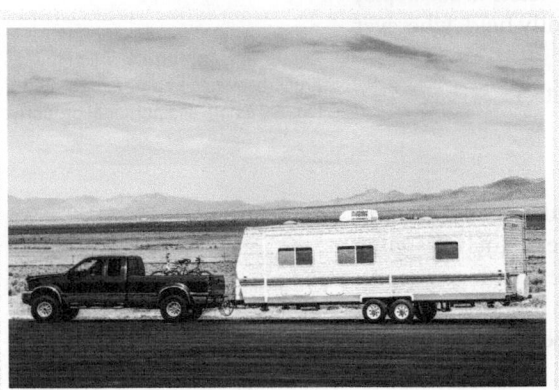

Just before filing Chapter 7 bankruptcy, a debtor sells his RV trailer, but the buyer's check is no good. What, if anything, can the trustee do to recover the RV trailer on the debtor's estate's behalf?

turtix/Shutterstock.com

Preferences   A debtor is not permitted to make a property transfer or a payment that favors—or gives a **preference** to—one creditor over others. The trustee is allowed to recover such payments whether they were made voluntarily or involuntarily.

To have made a recoverable preferential payment, an *insolvent* debtor generally must have transferred property for a *preexisting* debt during the *ninety days* before the filing of the petition in bankruptcy. The transfer must have given the creditor more than the creditor would have received as a result of the bankruptcy proceedings. The Code presumes that the debtor is insolvent during the ninety-day period before filing a petition.

Preference   In bankruptcy proceedings, a property transfer or payment made by the debtor that favors one creditor over others.

Preferred Creditor   In the context of bankruptcy, a creditor who has received a preferential transfer from a debtor.

Insider   In bankruptcy proceedings, any individual, partnership, or corporation with a close personal or business relation with the debtor.

If a **preferred creditor** (one who has received a preferential transfer from the debtor) has sold the property to an innocent third party, the trustee cannot recover the property from the innocent party. The trustee can generally force the preferred creditor to pay the value of the property, however.

Preferences to Insiders.   Sometimes, a creditor receiving a preference is an *insider*. An **insider** is any individual (such as a relative or partner), partnership, or corporation with a close relationship with the debtor. In this situation, the avoidance power of the trustee is extended to transfers made within *one year* before filing. (If the transfer was fraudulent, as will be discussed shortly, the trustee can avoid transfers made within *two years* before filing.) However, the trustee must prove that the debtor was insolvent at the time the earlier transfer occurred.

Transfers That Do Not Constitute Preferences.   Not all transfers are preferences. To be a preference, the transfer must be made in exchange for something other than current consideration. Most courts do not consider a debtor's payment for services rendered within fifteen days prior to the payment to be a preference. If a creditor receives payment in the ordinary course of business, such as payment of last month's cell phone bill, the trustee in bankruptcy cannot recover the payment. In contrast, a transfer for a preexisting debt, such as a year-old landscaping bill, would be a recoverable preference.

Case Example 26.4   David Tidd operated a business performing small home repairs as well as house-building projects. Tidd and his son regularly purchased supplies for his business on credit from S.W. Collins. Eventually, Tidd filed for Chapter 7 bankruptcy. Within ninety days preceding his petition, Tidd had made four payments for materials to S.W. Collins, totaling $46,000. The trustee filed a motion seeking to avoid this transfer as a preference. The court, however, concluded that the transfer was a substantially contemporaneous exchange of value (current consideration) and not a preference. The payments were made in the ordinary course of business. Therefore, the court found in Tidd's favor and denied the trustee's motion.[9]

In addition, the Code permits a consumer-debtor to transfer any property to a creditor up to a total value of $6,425 without the transfer constituting a preference. Payments of domestic-support debts do not constitute a preference. Neither do payments required under a plan created by an approved credit-counseling agency.

Fraudulent Transfers A trustee can avoid fraudulent transfers or obligations if (1) they were made within two years of the filing of the petition or (2) they were made with actual intent to hinder, delay, or defraud a creditor. **Case Example 26.5** David Dearmond was a real estate developer who owned interests in two development companies—Briartowne, LLC, and Hillside, LLC. He also owned one-third of Bluffs of Sevier County, LLC, which operated Bluff's Bar & Grill. When Briartowne defaulted on a $623,499 promissory note, SmartBank filed an action against Briartowne, Dearmond, and others.

Five months later, Dearmond sold Boyds Creek Market and Garage, a property he had paid $400,000 for the previous year, to his fiancée, Patricia Harper, for $90,000. Two days after that, Dearmond created two irrevocable trust agreements and transferred all of his interest in Hillside and Bluffs of Sevier County into those trusts. The trusts named Harper as the primary beneficiary. Although SmartBank obtained a judgment against Dearmond (and the other owners of Briartowne), it was unable to collect from these assets.

A year and a half later, Dearmond filed a petition for bankruptcy. The trustee filed a motion seeking to avoid the fraudulent transfers made to benefit Harper. Harper claimed that Dearmond had given her the interest in Hillside as a wedding present. The court concluded that the transfers should be set aside because they were made with actual intent to hinder, delay, or defraud a creditor. Therefore, the trusts no longer owned the properties. The court entered judgment for the trustee in an amount equivalent to the value of the fraudulent transfers.[10]

26–2f **Exemptions**

An individual debtor is entitled to exempt certain property from the bankruptcy under federal or state exemption schemes.

Federal Exemptions The Bankruptcy Code exempts the following property up to a specified dollar amount that changes automatically every three years:

1. A portion of equity in the debtor's home (not to exceed $160,375[11] under the federal homestead exemption, even if state law would permit a higher amount).
2. Motor vehicles, up to a certain value (usually just one vehicle).
3. Reasonably necessary clothing, household goods and furnishings, and household appliances (the aggregate value not to exceed a specified amount).
4. Jewelry, up to a specified value.
5. Tools of the debtor's trade or profession, up to a specified value.

During bankruptcy proceedings, when can a trustee claim that the sale of a restaurant was a fraudulent transfer?

---

9. *In re Tidd,* ___ Bankr. ___, 2017 WL 4011014 (D.Me. 2017).
10. *In re Dearmond,* 2017 WL 4220396 (Bankr. E.D.Tenn. 2017).
11. The amounts stated in this chapter are in accordance with those computed from the Consumer Price Index as of April 1, 2016.

6. A portion of unpaid but earned wages.

7. Pensions.

8. Public benefits, including public assistance (welfare), Social Security, and unemployment compensation, accumulated in a bank account.

9. Damages awarded for personal injury, up to a specified amount.

Property that is *not* exempt under federal law includes bank accounts, cash, family heirlooms, collections of stamps and coins, second cars, and vacation homes.

State Exemptions Individual states have the power to pass legislation precluding debtors from using the federal exemptions within the state. A majority of the states have done this. In those states, debtors may use only state, not federal, exemptions. In the rest of the states, an individual debtor (or a husband and wife filing jointly) may choose either the exemptions provided under state law or the federal exemptions.

Homestead Exemption A law permitting a debtor to retain the family home, either in its entirety or up to a specified dollar amount, free from the claims of unsecured creditors or trustees in bankruptcy.

Limitations on the Homestead Exemption Probably the most familiar real property exemption is the **homestead exemption,** the purpose of which is to ensure that the debtor will retain some form of shelter. Each state permits the debtor to retain the family home, either in its entirety or up to a specified dollar amount. The Bankruptcy Code limits the amount that can be claimed in bankruptcy under the homestead exemption of any state, however. In general, if the debtor acquired the home within three years and four months preceding the date of filing, the maximum equity exempted is $160,375, even if state law would permit a higher amount.

In addition, the state homestead exemption is available only if the debtor has lived in the state for two years before filing the petition. A debtor who has violated securities law, been convicted of a felony, or engaged in certain other intentional misconduct may not be permitted to claim the homestead exemption at all.

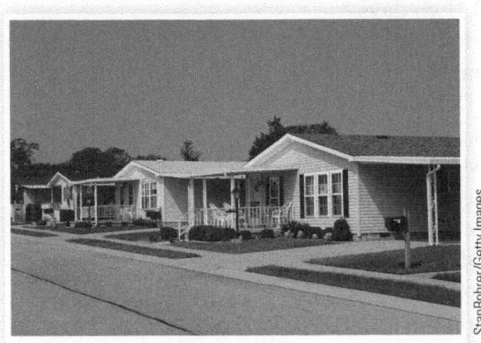

How does the homestead exemption help debtors who go into bankruptcy?

26–2g Creditors' Meeting and Claims

Within a reasonable time after the order of relief has been granted (not more than forty days), the trustee must call a meeting of the creditors listed in the schedules filed by the debtor. The bankruptcy judge does not attend this meeting, but the debtor must attend and submit to an examination under oath. At the meeting, the trustee ensures that the debtor is aware of the potential consequences of bankruptcy and the possibility of filing under a different chapter of the Code.

To be entitled to receive a portion of the debtor's estate, each creditor normally files a *proof of claim* with the bankruptcy court clerk within ninety days of the creditors' meeting. The proof of claim lists the creditor's name and address, as well as the amount that the creditor asserts is owed to the creditor by the debtor.

When the debtor has no assets—called a "no-asset case"—creditors are notified of the debtor's petition for bankruptcy but are instructed not to file a claim. In no-asset cases, the unsecured creditors will receive no payment, and most, if not all, of these debts will be discharged.

26–2h Distribution of Property

The Code provides specific rules for the distribution of the debtor's property to secured and unsecured creditors. If any amount remains after the priority classes of creditors have been satisfied, it is turned over to the debtor.

Distribution to Secured Creditors Secured creditors have priority. The Code requires that consumer-debtors file a statement of intention with respect to the secured collateral. They can choose to pay off the debt and redeem the collateral, claim that it is exempt, reaffirm the debt and continue making payments, or surrender the property to the secured party.

If the collateral is surrendered to the secured party, the secured creditor can either (1) accept the collateral in full satisfaction of the debt or (2) sell the collateral and use the proceeds to pay off the debt. Thus, the secured party has priority over unsecured parties as to the proceeds from the disposition of the collateral. Should the collateral be insufficient to cover the secured debt owed, the secured creditor becomes an unsecured creditor for the difference.

There are limited exceptions to these rules. For instance, certain unsecured creditors can sometimes step into the shoes of secured tax creditors in Chapter 7 liquidation proceedings. In such situations, when the collateral securing the tax claims is sold, the unsecured creditors are paid first. This exception does *not* include holders of unsecured claims for administrative expenses incurred in Chapter 11 cases that are converted to Chapter 7 liquidations. In the following case, the plaintiff argued that it should.

■ Case 26.1

In re Anderson

United States Court of Appeals, Fourth Circuit, 811 F.3d 166 (2016).

Background and Facts Henry Anderson filed a voluntary petition in a federal bankruptcy court for relief under Chapter 11 of the Bankruptcy Code (which governs reorganizations of the debtor's estate). The Internal Revenue Service (IRS) filed a proof of claim against the bankruptcy estate for unpaid taxes of nearly $1 million. This claim was secured by Anderson's property. Stubbs & Perdue, P.A., served as Anderson's counsel. The court approved compensation of $200,000 to Stubbs for its services. These fees constituted an unsecured claim against the estate for administrative expenses.

Later, Anderson's case was converted to a Chapter 7 liquidation. The trustee accumulated more than $700,000 for distribution to the estate's creditors—but this was not enough to pay the claims of both the IRS and Stubbs. The trustee excluded Stubbs's claim. Stubbs objected. The court dismissed Stubbs's objection. A federal district court upheld the exclusion. Stubbs appealed, arguing that the IRS's claim should be subordinated to Stubbs's claim for fees.

In the Words of the Court
Pamela *HARRIS,* Circuit Judge:

* * * *

* * * Before any of the events at issue here, Section 724(b)(2) * * * provided all holders of administrative expense claims, like Stubbs, with the right to subordinate secured tax creditors in Chapter 7 liquidations. But that statutory scheme was criticized on the ground that it created perverse incentives, encouraging Chapter 11 debtors and their representatives to incur administrative expenses even where there was no real hope for a successful reorganization, to the detriment of secured tax creditors when Chapter 7 liquidation ultimately proved necessary.

* * * Congress responded with a fix * * * to limit the class of administrative expenses covered by Section 724(b)(2) * * *. *In order to provide greater protection for holders of tax liens * * *, unsecured Chapter 11 administrative expense claims would no longer take priority over secured tax claims in Chapter 7 liquidations.* [Emphasis added.]

* * * *

* * * The Bankruptcy Technical Corrections Act [BTCA] * * * clarified that Chapter 11 administrative expense claimants do not hold subordination rights under Section 724(b)(2).

* * * Eleven months later, the Debtor's bankruptcy case converted from Chapter 11 to Chapter 7, implicating Section 724(b)(2) for the first time.

* * * *

* * * *As a general rule, a court is to apply the law in effect at the time it renders its decision.* [Emphasis added.]

* * * *

Stubbs argues, however, that it would be unjust to apply the BTCA version of Section 724(b)(2) * * * to disallow payment on its unsecured claim for Chapter 11 fees. Prior to the BTCA, Stubbs contends, it was entitled to subordinate the IRS's secured claim.

The problem with Stubbs's argument is its premise: that Stubbs held subordination rights under Section 724(b)(2) before the BTCA was enacted * * *. Before the BTCA was enacted, Section 724(b)(2) had no application to the Debtor's case at all. It afforded Stubbs no entitlement to subordinate the IRS's secured tax claim for the threshold reason that it simply did not apply in the Chapter 11 proceedings that began in this case * * * and did not end until * * * eleven months *after* the BTCA's passage. The pre-BTCA

(Continues)

version of Section 724(b)(2) that Stubbs invokes, in other words, never controlled this case.

Decision and Remedy The U.S. Court of Appeals for the Fourth Circuit affirmed the dismissal of Stubbs's claim. Under Section 724(b)(2), "it is clear that Stubbs is not entitled to subordinate the IRS's secured tax claim in favor of its unsecured claim to Chapter 11 administrative expenses."

Critical Thinking

• **Legal Environment** *Why, as a general rule, should a court apply the law that is in effect at the time the court renders its decision?*

• **Ethical** *If Anderson had filed his initial bankruptcy petition under Chapter 7, not under Chapter 11, the result would have been different—Stubbs would have been able to subordinate the IRS claim. Is this fair?*

Distribution to Unsecured Creditors Bankruptcy law establishes an order of priority for classes of debts owed to unsecured creditors, and they are paid in the order of their priority. Each class must be fully paid before the next class is entitled to any of the remaining proceeds. If there is any balance remaining after all the creditors are paid, it is returned to the debtor.

In almost all Chapter 7 bankruptcies, the funds will be insufficient to pay all creditors. If there are insufficient proceeds to pay the full amount to all the creditors in a class, the proceeds are distributed *proportionately* to the creditors in that class. Creditors in classes lower in priority receive nothing. Claims for domestic-support obligations, such as child support and alimony, have the highest priority among unsecured claims, so these debts must be paid first. In almost all Chapter 7 bankruptcies, the funds will be insufficient to pay all creditors. Exhibit 26–1 illustrates the collection and distribution of property in most voluntary bankruptcies.

26–2i Discharge

From the debtor's point of view, the primary purpose of liquidation is to obtain a fresh start through the discharge of debts. A discharge voids, or sets aside, any judgment on a discharged debt and prevents any action to collect it. Certain debts, however, are not dischargeable in bankruptcy. Also, certain debtors may not qualify to have all debts discharged in bankruptcy. These situations are discussed next.

Exhibit 26–1 Collection and Distribution of Property in Most Voluntary Bankruptcies

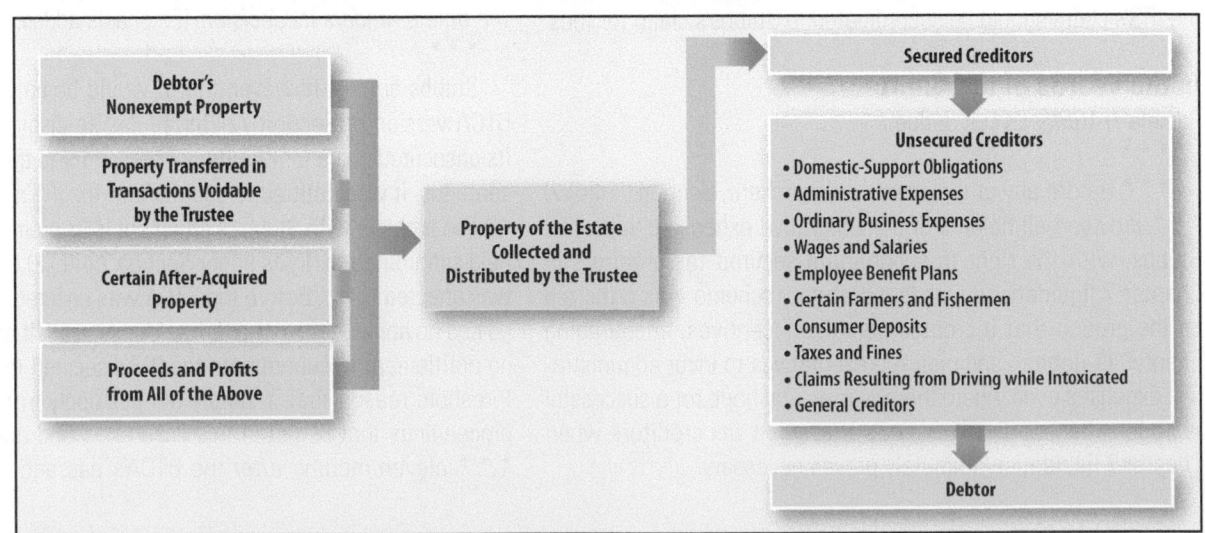

Debts That Are Not Dischargeable The most important claims that are not dischargeable under Chapter 7 include the following:

1. Claims for back taxes accruing within two years prior to bankruptcy.

2. Claims for amounts borrowed by the debtor to pay federal taxes or any nondischargeable taxes.

3. Claims against property or funds obtained by the debtor under false pretenses or by false misrepresentations.

4. Claims by creditors who were not notified of the bankruptcy. These claims did not appear on the schedules the debtor was required to file.

5. Claims based on fraud or misuse of funds by the debtor or claims involving the debtor's embezzlement or larceny.

6. Domestic-support obligations and property settlements.

7. Claims for amounts due on a retirement loan account.

8. Claims based on willful or malicious conduct by the debtor toward another or toward the property of another.

9. Certain government fines and penalties.

10. Student loans, unless payment of the loans causes an undue hardship for the debtor and the debtor's dependents (when paying the loan would leave the debtor unable to maintain a minimal standard of living, for instance).

11. Consumer debts of more than $675 for luxury goods or services owed to a single creditor incurred within ninety days of the order for relief.

Case Example 26.6 Anthony Mickletz owned a pizza restaurant that employed John Carmello. One night after Carmello had finished his shift, Mickletz called him back into the restaurant and accused him of stealing. An argument ensued, and Mickletz shoved Carmello, causing him to fall and injure his back. Because Mickletz did not provide workers' compensation coverage as required by law, the state prosecuted him criminally. He was ordered to pay more than $45,000 in restitution to Carmello for his injuries.

Carmello also filed a civil suit against Mickletz, which the parties agreed to settle for $175,000. Later, Mickletz filed a petition for bankruptcy. Carmello argued that these debts were nondischargeable, and the court agreed. The exceptions from discharge include any debts for willful (deliberate or intentional) injury, and Mickletz's actions were deliberate.[12]

---

12. *In re Mickletz*, 544 Bankr. 804 (E.D. Pa. 2016).

A pizza restaurant owner intentionally injures one of his employees, who then sues and is awarded damages by a civil court. If the owner files for Chapter 7 bankruptcy, can his debt to the injured worker be discharged? Why or why not?

Know This

Often, a discharge in bankruptcy—even under Chapter 7—does not free a debtor of *all* of her or his debts.

Ethical Issue

Should there be more relief for student loan defaults? Outstanding student loan balances total $1.4 *trillion* nationally and are growing by approximately $3,000 *per second*. About 20 percent of these loans are ninety or more days' delinquent or are in default. That is the highest delinquency rate among all forms of debt, including credit cards, automobile loans, and mortgages. The average student loan debt is more than $35,000. Any student borrower who has not made regular payments for nine months is in default. The U.S. Department of Education can keep the debtor's tax refund or garnish his

(Continues)

or her paychecks or other federal benefits (such as disability benefits) without obtaining a court order. The government can also sue to collect a judgment from the debtor's bank accounts or place a lien on real property.

Politicians and society are increasingly discussing student loan debt and the costs of higher education. Some are suggesting reducing the interest rates that can be charged and imposing student loan debt forgiveness after a certain period of time, such as twenty years. Others advocate making college education free or at least reducing the costs charged to certain students. Another proposal is to prohibit the federal government from profiting from student loan debt (the government brings in more than $41 billion a year from student loans). In addition, some are asking Congress to allow federal student loans to be discharged in most bankruptcy proceedings, rather than only in cases of undue hardship.

Reasons That a Court Can Deny a Discharge A bankruptcy court may also deny the discharge based on the debtor's *conduct*. Grounds for denial of discharge of the debtor include the following:

1. The debtor's concealment or destruction of property with the intent to hinder, delay, or defraud a creditor.
2. The debtor's fraudulent concealment or destruction of financial records.
3. The granting of a discharge to the debtor within eight years prior to the filing of the petition.
4. The debtor's failure to complete the required consumer education course.
5. Proceedings in which the debtor could be found guilty of a felony. (Basically, a court may not discharge any debt until the completion of the felony proceedings against the debtor.)

When a discharge is denied under any of these circumstances, the debtor's assets are still distributed to the creditors. After the bankruptcy proceeding, however, the debtor remains liable for the unpaid portions of all claims.

A discharge may be revoked (taken back) within one year if it is discovered that the debtor acted fraudulently or dishonestly during the bankruptcy proceeding. If that occurs, a creditor whose claim was not satisfied in the distribution of the debtor's property can proceed with his or her claim against the debtor.

Whether a bankruptcy court properly denied a discharge based on the debtors' conduct was the issue in the following case.

■ Case 26.2

In re Cummings
United States Court of Appeals, Ninth Circuit, 595 Fed.Appx. 707 (2015).

Background and Facts Clarence and Pamela Cummings filed a petition for a Chapter 7 bankruptcy in a federal bankruptcy court. After the debtors filed two amended versions of the required schedules, the trustee asked for additional time to investigate. The court granted the request. The debtors then filed a third amended schedule. In it, they disclosed

What constitutes a false oath in Chapter 7 proceedings?

for the first time the existence of First Beacon Management Company, a corporation that they planned to use as part of their postbankruptcy "fresh start." The trustee then claimed that the Cummingses' failure to disclose their interest in First Beacon as debtor property was a "false oath relating to a material fact made knowingly and fraudulently" in violation of the Bankruptcy

Code. The court agreed and denied the debtors a discharge. The Bankruptcy Appellate Panel (BAP) affirmed the court's decision. The Cummingses appealed.

In the Words of the Court
MEMORANDUM.
* * * *

Chapter 7 debtors Clarence Thomas Cummings and Pamela K. Cummings appeal the judgment of the Bankruptcy Appellate Panel ("BAP") affirming * * * the bankruptcy court's order denying discharge on the ground that the debtors made false oaths * * *. The bankruptcy court rejected the explanatory testimony of Mr. Cummings as "not credible" and "beyond not credible" and the BAP found that "there is ample evidence to support the bankruptcy court's findings.
* * * *

* * * Debtors claim that the bankruptcy court failed to consider other "voluminous independent and undisputed documentary evidence" introduced at trial that, they assert, "completely obliterated any suggestion of fraudulent intent."

* * * These materials do not advance debtors' claim of inadvertence [lack of intent] or otherwise suggest bankruptcy court error. To the contrary, *the documents corroborate the obviousness of debtors' fraud and the objective it advanced, [namely], to insulate First Beacon Management Co., * * * the new corporate anchor* of their post-petition fresh start, from the stigma of bankruptcy. [Emphasis added.]
* * * *

Debtors' eventual disclosure of their interest in First Beacon on their third amended Schedule * * * does not negate their initial fraud. To the contrary, the sequence of debtors' filings substantiates the presence of fraud: they elected, twice, to amend their Schedule * * * without adding First Beacon, and disclosed First Beacon only after the issuance of an order granting the Trustee additional time to investigate.
* * * *

The Trustee fully carried its burden of proving by a preponderance of the evidence * * * that under the circumstances, debtors' failure to disclose their interest in First Beacon as debtor property was a "false oath" relating to a material fact made knowingly and fraudulently.

Decision and Remedy The U.S. Court of Appeals for the Ninth Circuit affirmed the ruling of the BAP. "The sequence of debtors' filings substantiates the presence of fraud." Thus, the debtors' Chapter 7 petition was denied.

Critical Thinking

• **Economic** *Why would a debtor risk the denial of a discharge to conceal assets? Discuss.*

26–2j Reaffirmation of Debt

An agreement to pay a debt dischargeable in bankruptcy is called a **reaffirmation agreement**. A debtor may wish to pay a debt—for instance, a debt owed to a family member, physician, bank, or some other creditor—even though the debt could be discharged in bankruptcy. Also, as noted previously, a debtor cannot retain secured property while continuing to make payments on the underlying debt without entering into a reaffirmation agreement.

Reaffirmation Agreement An agreement between a debtor and a creditor in which the debtor voluntarily agrees to pay a debt dischargeable in bankruptcy.

Procedures To be enforceable, the reaffirmation agreement must be made before the debtor is granted a discharge. The agreement must be signed and filed with the court (along with disclosure documents, as described next). Court approval is required when the debtor is not represented by an attorney. Even when the debtor is represented by an attorney, court approval may be required if it appears that the reaffirmation will result in undue hardship to the debtor.

When court approval is required, a separate hearing will take place. The court will approve the reaffirmation only if it finds that the agreement is consistent with the debtor's best interests and will not result in undue hardship.

Required Disclosures To discourage creditors from engaging in abusive reaffirmation practices, the law provides specific language for disclosures that must be given to debtors entering reaffirmation agreements. Among other things, these disclosures explain that the debtor is not required to reaffirm any debt, but that liens on secured property, such as mortgages and cars, will remain in effect even if the debt is not reaffirmed.

The reaffirmation agreement must disclose the amount of the debt reaffirmed, the rate of interest, the date payments begin, and the right to rescind. The disclosures also caution the debtor: "Only agree to reaffirm a debt if it is in your best interest. Be sure you can afford the payments you agree to make."

The original disclosure documents must be signed by the debtor, certified by the debtor's attorney, and filed with the court at the same time as the reaffirmation agreement. A reaffirmation agreement that is not accompanied by the original signed disclosures will not be effective.

Case Example 26.7 The owner of a seafood import business, Howard Lapides, signed a secured promissory note for $400,000 with Venture Bank for a revolving line-of-credit loan. Part of the collateral for that loan was a third mortgage on the Lapideses' home (two other banks held prior mortgages). Eventually, Howard and his wife filed for Chapter 7 bankruptcy protection, and their personal debts were discharged.

Afterward, Venture Bank convinced the Lapideses to sign a reaffirmation agreement by telling them that it would refinance all three mortgages so that they could keep their house. The Lapideses made twelve $3,500 payments to Venture Bank, but the bank did not refinance the other mortgages, so they stopped making payments. Venture Bank filed suit, but a court refused to enforce the reaffirmation agreement because it violated the Bankruptcy Code. The agreement had never been signed by Lapideses' attorney or filed with the bankruptcy court.[13]

26–3 Chapter 11—Reorganization

The type of bankruptcy proceeding used most commonly by corporate debtors is the Chapter 11 *reorganization*. In a reorganization, the creditors and the debtor formulate a plan under which the debtor pays a portion of its debts and the rest of the debts are discharged. The debtor is allowed to continue in business. Although this type of bankruptcy is generally a corporate reorganization, any debtor (except a stockbroker or commodities broker) who is eligible for Chapter 7 relief is normally eligible for relief under Chapter 11. Railroads are also eligible.

Congress has established a "fast-track" Chapter 11 procedure for small-business debtors whose liabilities do not exceed $2.56 million and who do not own or manage real estate. The fast track enables a debtor to avoid the appointment of a creditors' committee and also shortens the filing periods and relaxes certain other requirements. Because the process is shorter and simpler, it is less costly. (See the *Linking Business Law to Corporate Management* feature for suggestions on how small businesses can prepare for Chapter 11.)

The same principles that govern the filing of a liquidation (Chapter 7) petition apply to reorganization (Chapter 11) proceedings. The case may be brought either voluntarily or involuntarily. The automatic-stay provision and its exceptions apply in reorganizations as well, as do the provisions regarding substantial abuse and additional grounds for dismissal (or conversion) of bankruptcy petitions.

26–3a Workouts

Workout An agreement outlining the respective rights and responsibilities of a borrower and a lender as they try to resolve the borrower's default.

In some instances, to avoid bankruptcy proceedings, creditors may prefer private, negotiated adjustments of creditor-debtor relations, known as **workouts.** Often, these out-of-court agreements are much more flexible and thus conducive to a speedy settlement. Speed is critical because delay is one of the most costly elements in any bankruptcy proceeding. Another advantage of workout agreements is that they avoid the various administrative costs of bankruptcy proceedings.

13. *Venture Bank v. Lapides*, 800 F.3d 442 (8th Cir. 2015).

Chapter 11 of the Bankruptcy Code expresses the broad public policy of encouraging commerce. To this

What Can You Do to Prepare for a Chapter 11 Reorganization?

end, Chapter 11 allows a financially troubled business firm to petition for reorganization in bankruptcy while it is still solvent so that the firm's business can continue. Small businesses, however, do not fare very well under Chapter 11. Although some corporations that enter into Chapter 11 emerge as functioning entities, only a small number of companies survive the process.

Plan Ahead

If you ever are a small-business owner contemplating Chapter 11 reorganization, you can improve your chances of being among the survivors by planning ahead. To ensure the greatest possibility of success, you should take action before, not after, entering bankruptcy proceedings. Discuss your financial troubles openly and cooperatively with creditors to see if you can agree on a workout or some other arrangement.

   If you appear to have no choice but to file for Chapter 11 protection, try to persuade a lender to loan you funds to see you through the bankruptcy. If your business is a small corporation, you might try to negotiate a favorable deal with a major investor. For instance, a small business could offer to transfer ownership of stock to the investor in return for a loan to pay the costs of the bankruptcy proceedings and an option to repurchase the stock when the firm becomes profitable again.

Consult with Creditors

Most important, you should form a Chapter 11 plan before entering bankruptcy proceedings. Consult with creditors in advance to see what kind of plan would be acceptable to them, and prepare your plan accordingly. Having an acceptable plan prepared before you file will expedite the proceedings and thus save substantially on costs.

What are some strategies a small-business debtor can use to prepare for Chapter 11?

Critical Thinking

Filing for bankruptcy under Chapter 11 may involve a time-consuming process. How might this affect the likelihood that a firm will be able to negotiate some type of agreement with its creditors?

26–3b Best Interests of the Creditors

Once a petition for Chapter 11 has been filed, a bankruptcy court can dismiss or suspend all proceedings in a case at any time if dismissal or suspension would better serve the interests of the creditors. Before taking such an action, the court must give notice and conduct a hearing. The Code also allows a court, after notice and a hearing, to dismiss a reorganization case "for cause" when there is no reasonable likelihood that the business can successfully remain in operation. Similarly, a court can dismiss a Chapter 11 petition when the debtor's reorganization plan cannot be effected or when an unreasonable delay by the debtor may harm the interests of creditors. A debtor whose petition is dismissed for these reasons can file another Chapter 11 petition in the future.[14]

---

14. See 11 U.S.C. Section 1112(b).

26–3c Debtor in Possession

On entry of the order for relief, the debtor in Chapter 11 generally continues to operate the business as a **debtor in possession (DIP)**. The court, however, may appoint a trustee (often referred to as a *receiver*) to operate the debtor's business if gross mismanagement of the business is shown or if appointing a trustee is in the best interests of the estate.

The DIP's role is similar to that of a trustee in a liquidation. The DIP is entitled to avoid preferential payments made to creditors and fraudulent transfers of assets. The DIP can also exercise a trustee's strong-arm powers. The DIP has the power to decide whether to cancel or assume prepetition executory contracts (contracts not yet performed) or unexpired leases.

Cancellation of executory contracts or unexpired leases can be of substantial benefit to a Chapter 11 debtor. **Example 26.8** Five years ago, APT Corporation leased an office building for a twenty-year term. Now, APT can no longer pay the rent due under the lease and has filed for Chapter 11 reorganization. In this situation, the debtor in possession can cancel the lease so that APT will not be required to continue paying the substantial rent due for fifteen more years.

26–3d Creditors' Committees

As soon as practicable after the entry of the order for relief, a committee of unsecured creditors is appointed.[15] The business's supplier may serve on the committee. The committee can consult with the trustee or the debtor concerning the administration of the case or the formulation of the plan. Additional creditors' committees may be appointed to represent special interest creditors. Generally, no orders affecting the estate will be entered without the consent of the committee or a hearing in which the judge is informed of the position of the committee.

As mentioned earlier, businesses with debts of less than $2.56 million that do not own or manage real estate can avoid creditors' committees. In these fast-track proceedings, orders can be entered without a committee's consent.

26–3e The Reorganization Plan

A reorganization plan is established to conserve and administer the debtor's assets in the hope of an eventual return to successful operation and solvency. The plan must be fair and equitable and must do the following:

1. Designate classes of claims and interests.
2. Specify the treatment to be afforded the classes. (The plan must provide the same treatment for all claims in a particular class.)
3. Provide an adequate means for execution. (Individual debtors must utilize postpetition assets as necessary to execute the plan.)
4. Provide for payment of tax claims over a five-year period.

The plan need not provide for full repayment to unsecured creditors. Instead, creditors receive a percentage of each dollar owed to them by the debtor.

Filing the Plan Only the debtor may file a plan within the first 120 days after the date of the order for relief. This period may be extended, but not beyond eighteen months from the date of the order for relief. If the debtor does not meet the 120-day deadline or obtain an extension, or if the debtor fails to obtain the required creditor consent (discussed next)

---

15. If the debtor has filed a plan accepted by the creditors, the trustee may decide not to call a meeting of the creditors.

within 180 days, any party may propose a plan. If a small-business debtor chooses to avoid a creditors' committee, the time for the debtor's filing is 180 days.

Acceptance and Confirmation of the Plan Once the plan has been developed, it is submitted to each class of creditors for acceptance. For the plan to be adopted, each class must accept it. A class has accepted the plan when a majority of the creditors, representing two-thirds of the amount of the total claim, vote to approve it.

Even when all classes of creditors accept the plan, the court may refuse to confirm it if it is not "in the best interests of the creditors." In addition, confirmation is conditioned on the debtor's certifying that all postpetition domestic-support obligations have been paid in full. For small-business debtors, if the plan meets the listed requirements, the court must confirm the plan within forty-five days (unless this period is extended).

The plan can also be modified upon the request of the debtor, DIP, trustee, U.S. trustee, or holder of an unsecured claim. If an unsecured creditor objects to the plan, specific rules apply to the value of property to be distributed under the plan. Tax claims must be paid over a five-year period.

Even if only one class of creditors has accepted the plan, the court may still confirm the plan under the Code's so-called **cram-down provision.** In other words, the court may confirm the plan over the objections of a class of creditors. Before the court can exercise this right of cram-down confirmation, it must be demonstrated that the plan is fair and equitable.

Discharge The plan is binding on confirmation. Nevertheless, the law provides that confirmation of a plan does not discharge an individual debtor. *For individual debtors, the plan must be completed before discharge will be granted,* unless the court orders otherwise. For all other debtors, the court may order discharge at any time after the plan is confirmed.

On completion of the plan, the debtor is given a reorganization discharge from all claims not protected under the plan. This discharge does not apply to any claims that would be denied discharge under liquidation.

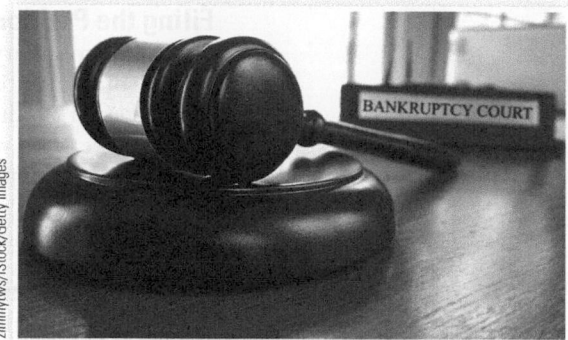

What are some basic criteria a bankruptcy court uses to confirm a Chapter 11 reorganization plan?

zimmytws/iStock/Getty Images

Cram-Down Provision A provision of the Bankruptcy Code that allows a court to confirm a debtor's Chapter 11 reorganization plan even though only one class of creditors has accepted it.

26–4 Bankruptcy Relief under Chapter 13 and Chapter 12

In addition to bankruptcy relief through liquidation (Chapter 7) and reorganization (Chapter 11), the Code also provides for individuals' repayment plans (Chapter 13) and family-farmer and family-fisherman debt adjustments (Chapter 12).

26–4a Individuals' Repayment Plan—Chapter 13

Chapter 13 of the bankruptcy code provides for the "adjustment of debts of an individual with regular income." Individuals (not partnerships or corporations) with regular income who owe fixed unsecured debts of less than $394,725 or fixed secured debts of less than $1,184,200 may take advantage of bankruptcy repayment plans.

Among those eligible are salaried employees and sole proprietors, as well as individuals who live on welfare, Social Security, fixed pensions, or investment income. Many small-business debtors have a choice of filing under either Chapter 11 or Chapter 13. Repayment plans offer some advantages because they are typically less expensive and less complicated than reorganization or liquidation proceedings.

Learning Objective 4

How does a Chapter 13 bankruptcy differ from bankruptcy under Chapter 7 and Chapter 11?

Filing the Petition A Chapter 13 repayment plan case can be initiated only by the debtor's filing of a voluntary petition or by court conversion of a Chapter 7 petition (because of a finding of substantial abuse, for instance). Certain liquidation and reorganization cases may be converted to Chapter 13 with the consent of the debtor.[16]

A trustee, who will make payments under the plan, must be appointed. On the filing of a repayment plan petition, an automatic stay takes effect. Although the stay applies to all or part of the debtor's consumer debt, it does not apply to any business debt incurred by the debtor or to any domestic-support obligations.

Good Faith Requirement The Bankruptcy Code imposes the requirement of good faith on a debtor in both the filing of the petition and the filing of the plan. The Code does not define good faith, but if the circumstances as a whole indicate bad faith (such as when a debtor lies about available assets), a court can dismiss a debtor's Chapter 13 petition.

The Repayment Plan A plan of rehabilitation by repayment must provide for the following:

1. The turning over to the trustee of future earnings or income of the debtor as necessary for execution of the plan.

2. Full payment through deferred cash payments of all claims entitled to priority, such as taxes.[17]

3. Identical treatment of all claims within a particular class. (The Code permits the debtor to list co-debtors, such as guarantors or sureties, as a separate class.)

The repayment plan may provide either for payment of all obligations in full or for payment of a lesser amount. The debtor applies the means test to determine the amount of disposable income that is available to repay creditors. The debtor is allowed to deduct certain expenses from monthly income to arrive at this amount.

The debtor must begin making payments under the proposed plan within thirty days after the plan has been filed and must continue to make "timely" payments. If the debtor fails to make timely payments or does not commence payments within the thirty-day period, the court can convert the case to a liquidation bankruptcy or dismiss the petition.

The Length of the Plan. The length of the payment plan can be three or five years, depending on the debtor's family income. If the debtor's family income is greater than the median family income in the relevant geographic area under the means test, the term of the proposed plan must be three years.[18] The term may not exceed five years.

Confirmation of the Plan. After the plan is filed, the court holds a confirmation hearing, at which interested parties (such as creditors) may object to the plan. The hearing must be held at least twenty days, but no more than forty-five days, after the meeting of the creditors. The debtor must have filed all prepetition tax returns and paid all postpetition domestic-support obligations before a court will confirm the plan.

The court will confirm a plan with respect to each claim of a secured creditor under any of the following circumstances:

1. If the secured creditors have accepted the plan.

2. If the plan provides that secured creditors retain their liens until there is payment in full or until the debtor receives a discharge.

3. If the debtor surrenders the property securing the claims to the creditors.

In addition, for a motor vehicle purchased within 910 days before the petition is filed, the plan must provide that a creditor with a purchase-money security interest (PMSI) retains its

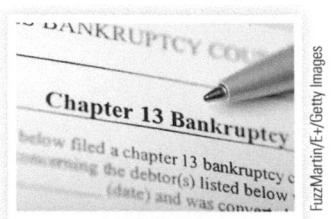

How does good faith play a role in Chapter 13 reorganization plans?

Know This

Courts, trustees, and creditors carefully monitor Chapter 13 debtors. If payments are not made, a court can require that the debtor explain why and may allow a creditor to take back the property.

---

16. A Chapter 13 repayment plan may be converted to a Chapter 7 liquidation either at the request of the debtor or, under certain circumstances, "for cause" by a creditor. A Chapter 13 petition may be converted to a Chapter 11 reorganization after a hearing.

17. As with a Chapter 11 reorganization plan, full repayment of all claims is not always required.

18. See 11 U.S.C. Section 1322(d) for details on when a court will find that the Chapter 13 plan should extend to a five-year period.

lien until the entire debt is paid. For PMSIs on other personal property, the payment plan must cover debts incurred within a one-year period preceding the filing.

Discharge After the debtor has completed all payments, the court grants a discharge of all debts provided for by the repayment plan. Generally, all debts are dischargeable except the following:

1. Allowed claims not provided for by the plan.
2. Certain long-term debts provided for by the plan.
3. Certain tax claims and payments on retirement accounts.
4. Claims for domestic-support obligations.
5. Debts related to injury or property damage caused while driving under the influence of alcohol or drugs.

An order granting discharge is final as to the debts listed in the repayment plan. A creditor that willfully continues to attempt to collect on a debt that a court has ordered discharged under Chapter 13 is in violation of the law and can be sanctioned.[19]

In the following case, a Chapter 13 debtor's domestic-support obligations were at issue. Under the Bankruptcy Code, a debt constitutes a domestic-support obligation if it is "in the nature of alimony, maintenance, or support." Did a parent's promise to pay his children's college expenses meet this requirement?

---

19. See, for example, *In re Vanamann*, 561 Bankr. 106 (D.Nev. 2017).

■ **Case 26.3**

In re Chamberlain

United States Court of Appeals, Tenth Circuit, 721 Fed.Appx. 826 (2018).

Background and Facts When Stephen and Judith Chamberlain were divorced, their marital settlement agreement included a "College Education" provision. Stephen promised to "pay the costs of tuition, room and board, books, registration fees, and reasonable application fees incident to . . . an undergraduate college education" for each of their three children, Sarah, Kate, and John. Stephen did not meet this obligation.

Judith obtained an order in a Maryland state court to enforce the agreement and initiated an effort to collect. Stephen filed a petition for bankruptcy under Chapter 13. Judith filed a creditor's claim with the bankruptcy court, contending that the college expenses were domestic-support obligations and thus created priority claims that had to be fully paid. The court agreed. Stephen appealed.

In the Words of the Court
Robert E. *BACHARACH*, Circuit Judge

* * * *

* * * Stephen argued that his obligation to pay his children's college expenses did not constitute a domestic support obligation because it was not "in the nature of * * * support."

* * * The court properly conducted a dual inquiry to determine whether these obligations involved support, looking first to the intent of the parties at the time they entered into their agreement, and then to the substance of the obligation.

* * * With respect to the initial issue of intent, the court appropriately considered [1] the language and structure of the college expense obligation in the marital settlement agreement and [2] the parties' testimony regarding surrounding circumstances, including the disparity in Stephen and Judith's financial circumstances at the time of the divorce.

The bankruptcy court found that the parties had intended Stephen's college expense obligation to constitute support because [of the following:]

- the evidence established that Stephen and Judith had viewed a college education as an important part of their children's upbringing,

- the couple had long intended to provide for the children's education, and

- this intent could not be carried out at the time of the divorce, given the couple's relative financial capabilities, without Stephen assuming this obligation.

* * * *

(Continues)

* * * In determining whether Stephen's obligation involved support, the bankruptcy court also considered the substance of Stephen's obligation. The critical question in determining whether the obligation is, in substance, support is the function served by the obligation at the time of the divorce. In turn, *the function of the obligation is affected by the parties' relative financial circumstances at the time of the divorce.* [Emphasis added.]

Here, the bankruptcy court reasonably determined that Stephen was the only parent financially able to pay for the children's college education. Thus, the court was justified in regarding Stephen's obligation, in substance, as support.

Decision and Remedy The U.S. Court of Appeals for the Tenth Circuit affirmed the judgment of the bankruptcy court.

"Stephen's college expense obligation was 'in the nature of support' as required for a domestic support obligation under the Bankruptcy Code."

Critical Thinking

• **Legal Environment** *Maryland law arguably does not include postsecondary education expenses in the definition of "child support." Should this state law have governed the court's conclusion in the* Chamberlain *case? Why or why not?*

• **What If the Facts Were Different?** *Suppose that the marital settlement agreement had obligated Stephen to assume the mortgage debt on the family home. If all other facts were the same, would the result have been different?*

26–4b Family Farmers and Fishermen—Chapter 12

To help relieve economic pressure on small farmers, Congress created Chapter 12 of the Bankruptcy Code. In 2005, Congress extended this protection to family fishermen, modified its provisions somewhat, and made it a permanent chapter in the Bankruptcy Code (previously, it had to be periodically renewed by Congress).

For purposes of Chapter 12, a *family farmer* is one whose gross income is at least 50 percent farm dependent and whose debts are at least 50 percent farm related. The total debt must not exceed $4,153,150. A partnership or a close corporation that is at least 50 percent owned by the farm family can also qualify as a family farmer.[20]

A *family fisherman* is one whose gross income is at least 50 percent dependent on commercial fishing operations and whose debts are at least 80 percent related to commercial fishing. The total debt for a family fisherman must not exceed $1,924,550. As with family farmers, a partnership or close corporation can also qualify.

John Wollwerth/Shutterstock.com

Under Chapter 12, what is the definition of a "family fisherman"?

Filing the Petition The procedure for filing a family-farmer or family-fisherman bankruptcy plan is similar to the procedure for filing a repayment plan under Chapter 13. The debtor must file a plan not later than ninety days after the order for relief has been entered. The filing of the petition acts as an automatic stay against creditors' and co-obligors' actions against the estate.

A farmer or fisherman who has already filed a reorganization or repayment plan may convert the plan to a Chapter 12 plan. The debtor may also convert a Chapter 12 plan to a liquidation plan.

Content and Confirmation of the Plan The content of a plan under Chapter 12 is basically the same as that of a Chapter 13 repayment plan. Generally, the plan must be confirmed or denied within forty-five days of filing. The plan must provide for payment of secured debts at the

---

20. Note that for a corporation or partnership to qualify for bankruptcy under Chapter 12, at least 80 percent of the value of the firm's assets must consist of assets related to the farming operation.

value of the collateral. If the secured debt exceeds the value of the collateral, the remaining debt is unsecured.

For unsecured debtors, the plan must be confirmed if either (1) the value of the property to be distributed under the plan equals the amount of the claim or (2) the plan provides that all of the debtor's disposable income to be received in a three-year period (or longer, by court approval) will be applied to making payments. Completion of payments under the plan discharges all debts provided for by the plan.

Practice and Review

Three months ago, Janet Hart's husband of twenty years died of cancer. Although he had medical insurance, he left Janet with outstanding medical bills of more than $50,000. Janet has worked at the local library for the past ten years, earning $1,500 per month. Since her husband's death, Janet also has received $1,500 in Social Security benefits and $1,100 in life insurance proceeds every month, giving her a monthly income of $4,100. After she pays the mortgage payment of $1,500 and the amounts due on other debts each month, Janet barely has enough left over to buy groceries for her family (she has two teenage daughters at home). She decides to file for Chapter 7 bankruptcy, hoping for a fresh start. Using the information provided in the chapter, answer the following questions.

1. Under the Bankruptcy Code after the reform act, what must Janet do before filing a petition for relief under Chapter 7?

2. How much time does Janet have after filing the bankruptcy petition to submit the required schedules? What happens if Janet does not meet the deadline?

3. Assume that Janet files a petition under Chapter 7. Further assume that the median family income in the state in which Janet lives is $49,300. What steps would a court take to determine whether Janet's petition is presumed to be substantial abuse under the means test?

4. Suppose the court determines that no presumption of substantial abuse applies in Janet's case. Nevertheless, the court finds that Janet does have the ability to pay at least a portion of the medical bills out of her disposable income. What would the court likely order in that situation?

Debate This

Rather than being allowed to file Chapter 7 bankruptcy petitions, individuals and couples should always be forced to make an effort to pay off their debts through Chapter 13.

Key Terms

adequate protection doctrine 614	discharge 610	petition in bankruptcy 610
automatic stay 613	estate in bankruptcy 615	preference 616
bankruptcy trustee 610	homestead exemption 618	preferred creditor 616
consumer-debtor 610	insider 616	reaffirmation agreement 623
cram-down provision 627	liquidation 610	U.S. Trustee 611
debtor in possession (DIP) 626	order for relief 612	workout 624

Chapter Summary: Bankruptcy

The Bankruptcy Code	1. *Goals of bankruptcy law*—The law attempts to balance the rights of the debtor and the creditors by giving the debtor a fresh start and ensuring equitable treatment of creditors. 2. *Bankruptcy courts*—Bankruptcy proceedings are held in federal bankruptcy courts (under the authority of U.S. district courts). They follow the Federal Rules of Bankruptcy Procedure. Bankruptcy court judges are appointed for fourteen-year terms. 3. *Types of bankruptcy relief*—Chapter 7 provides for liquidation proceedings, Chapter 11 governs reorganizations, and Chapter 13 (for individuals) and Chapter 12 (for family farmers and family fishermen) provide for adjustment of debts of parties with regular income. 4. *Special treatment of consumer-debtors*—The Bankruptcy Code requires that all consumer-debtors receive written notice of the purpose, benefits, and costs of each chapter of bankruptcy, as well as information on the types of services available from credit counseling agencies.

BANKRUPTCY—A COMPARISON OF CHAPTERS 7, 11, 12, AND 13

Issue	Chapter 7	Chapter 11	Chapters 12 and 13
Who Can Petition	Debtor (voluntary) or creditors (involuntary).	Debtor (voluntary) or creditors (involuntary).	Debtor (voluntary) only.
Who Can Be a Debtor	Any "person" (including partnerships and corporations) except railroads, insurance companies, banks, savings and loan institutions, investment companies licensed by the U.S. Small Business Administration, and credit unions. Farmers and charitable institutions cannot be involuntarily petitioned.	Any debtor eligible for Chapter 7 relief; railroads are also eligible.	*Chapter 12*—Any family farmer (one whose gross income is at least 50 percent farm dependent and whose debts are at least 50 percent farm related) or family fisherman (one whose gross income is at least 50 percent dependent on and whose debts are at least 80 percent related to commercial fishing) or any partnership or close corporation at least 50 percent owned by a family farmer or fisherman, when total debt does not exceed a specified amount ($4,153,150 for farmers and $1,924,550 for fishermen). *Chapter 13*—Any individual (not partnerships or corporations) with regular income who owes fixed (liquidated) unsecured debts of less than $394,175 or fixed secured debts of less than $1,184,200.
Procedure Leading to Discharge	Nonexempt property is sold with proceeds to be distributed (in order) to priority groups. Dischargeable debts are terminated.	Plan is submitted. If it is approved and followed, debts are discharged.	Plan is submitted and must be approved if the value of the property to be distributed equals the amount of the claims or if the debtor turns over disposable income for a three-year or five-year period. If the plan is followed, debts are discharged.
Advantages	On liquidation and distribution, most debts are discharged, and the debtor has an opportunity for a fresh start.	Debtor continues in business. Creditors can either accept the plan, or it can be "crammed down" on them. The plan allows for the reorganization and liquidation of debts over the plan period.	Debtor continues in business or possession of assets. If the plan is approved, most debts are discharged after the specified period.

Issue Spotters

1. After graduating from college, Tina works briefly as a salesperson and then files for bankruptcy. As part of her petition, Tina reveals that her only debts are student loans, taxes accruing within the last year, and a claim against her based on her misuse of funds during her employment. Are these debts dischargeable in bankruptcy? Explain. (See *Chapter 7—Liquidation*.)

2. Ogden is a vice president of Plumbing Service, Inc. (PSI). On May 1, Ogden loans PSI $10,000. On June 1, the firm repays the loan. On July 1, PSI files for bankruptcy. Quentin is appointed trustee. Can Quentin recover the $10,000 paid to Ogden on June 1? Why or why not? (See *Chapter 7—Liquidation*.)

—**Check your answers to the *Issue Spotters* against the answers provided in Appendix D at the end of this text.**

Business Scenarios and Case Problems

26–1. Voluntary versus Involuntary Bankruptcy. Burke has been a rancher all her life, raising cattle and crops. Her ranch is valued at $500,000, almost all of which is exempt under state law. Burke has eight creditors and a total indebtedness of $70,000. Two of her largest creditors are Oman ($30,000 owed) and Sneed ($25,000 owed). The other six creditors have claims of less than $5,000 each. A drought has ruined all of Burke's crops and forced her to sell many of her cattle at a loss. She cannot pay off her creditors. (See *Chapter 7—Liquidation*.)

1. Under the Bankruptcy Code, can Burke, with a $500,000 ranch, voluntarily petition herself into bankruptcy? Explain.

2. Could either Oman or Sneed force Burke into involuntary bankruptcy? Explain.

26–2. Distribution of Property. Montoro petitioned himself into voluntary bankruptcy. There were three major claims against his estate. One was made by Carlton, a friend who held Montoro's negotiable promissory note for $2,500. Another was made by Elmer, Montoro's employee, who claimed that Montoro owed him three months' back wages of $4,500. The last major claim was made by the United Bank of the Rockies on an unsecured loan of $5,000. In addition, Dietrich, an accountant retained by the trustee, was owed $500, and property taxes of $1,000 were owed to Rock County. Montoro's nonexempt property was liquidated, with proceeds of $5,000. Discuss fully what amount each party will receive, and why. (See *Chapter 7—Liquidation*.)

26–3. Discharge in Bankruptcy. Like many students, Barbara Hann financed her education partially through loans. These loans included three federally insured Stafford Loans of $7,500 each ($22,500 in total). Hann believed that she had repaid the loans, but later, when she filed a Chapter 13 petition, Educational Credit Management Corp. (ECMC) filed an unsecured proof of claim based on the loans. Hann objected. At a hearing at which ECMC failed to appear, Hann submitted correspondence from the lender that indicated the loans had been paid. The court entered an order sustaining Hann's objection. Despite the order, can ECMC resume its effort to collect on Hann's loans? Explain. [*In re Hann,* 711 F.3d 235 (1st Cir. 2013)] (See *Bankruptcy Relief under Chapter 13 and Chapter 12.*)

26–4. Business Case Problem with Sample Answer— Discharge. Michael and Dianne Shankle divorced. An Arkansas state court ordered Michael to pay Dianne alimony and child support, as well as half of the $184,000 in their investment accounts. Instead, Michael withdrew more than half of the investment funds and spent them. Over the next several years, the court repeatedly held Michael in contempt for failing to pay Dianne. Six years later, Michael filed for Chapter 7 bankruptcy, including in the petition's schedule the debt to Dianne of unpaid alimony, child support, and investment funds. Is Michael entitled to a discharge of this debt? Explain. [*In re Shankle,* 554 Fed.Appx. 264 (5th Cir. 2014)] (See *Chapter 7—Liquidation*.)

—**For a sample answer to Problem 26–4, go to Appendix E at the end of this text.**

26–5. Discharge under Chapter 13. James Thomas and Jennifer Clark married and had two children. They bought a home in Ironton, Ohio, with a loan secured by a mortgage. Later, they took out a second mortgage. On their divorce, the court gave Clark custody of the children and required Clark to pay the first mortgage. The divorce decree also required Thomas and Clark to make equal payments on the second mortgage and provided that Clark would receive all proceeds on the sale of the home. Thomas failed to make any payments, and Clark sold the home. At that point, she learned that Auto Now had a lien on the home because Thomas had not made payments on his car. Clark used all the sale proceeds to pay off the lien and the mortgages. When Thomas filed a petition for a Chapter 13 bankruptcy in a federal bankruptcy court, Clark filed a proof of claim for the mortgage and lien debts. Clark claimed that Thomas should not be able to discharge these debts because they were part of his domestic-support obligations. Are these debts dischargeable? Explain. [*In re Thomas,* 591 Fed.Appx. 443 (6th Cir. 2015)] (See *Bankruptcy Relief under Chapter 13 and Chapter 12.*)

26–6. Liquidation Proceedings. Jeffrey Krueger and Michael Torres, shareholders of Cru Energy, Inc., were embroiled in litigation in a Texas state court. Both claimed to act on Cru's behalf, and each charged the other with attempting to obtain control of Cru through fraud and other misconduct. Temporarily prohibited from participating in Cru's business, Krueger formed Kru, a company with the same business plan and many of the same shareholders as Cru. Meanwhile, to delay state court proceedings, Krueger filed a petition for a Chapter 7 liquidation in a federal bankruptcy court. He did not reveal his interest in Kru to the bankruptcy court. Ownership of Krueger's Cru shares passed to the bankruptcy trustee, but Krueger ignored this. He called a meeting of Cru's shareholders—except Torres—and voted those shares to remove Torres from the board and elect himself chairman, president, chief executive officer, and treasurer. The Cru board then dismissed all of Cru's claims against Krueger in his suit with Torres. Are there sufficient grounds for the bankruptcy court to dismiss Krueger's bankruptcy petition? Discuss. [*In re Krueger,* 812 F.3d 365 (5th Cir. 2016)] (See *Chapter 7—Liquidation.*)

26–7. The Reorganization Plan. Under the "plain language" of the Bankruptcy Code, at least one class of creditors must accept a Chapter 11 plan for it to be confirmed. Transwest Resort Properties, Inc., and four related companies filed a petition for bankruptcy under Chapter 11. The five debtors filed a joint reorganization plan. Several classes of their creditors approved the plan. Grasslawn Lodging, LLC, filed a claim based on its loan to two of the companies, and objected to the plan. Grasslawn further asserted that the Code's confirmation requirement applied on a "per debtor," not a "per plan," basis, and because Grasslawn was the only class member for two of the debtors, the plan in this case did not meet the test. Can the court order a "cram-down"? Why or why not? [*In the Matter of Transwest Resort Properties, Inc.,* 881 F.3d 724 (9th Cir. 2018)] (See *Chapter 11—Reorganization.*)

26–8. A Question of Ethics—The IDDR Approach and Reorganization. *Jevic Transportation Corporation filed a petition in a federal bankruptcy court for a Chapter 11 reorganization. A group of former Jevic truck drivers filed a suit and won a judgment against the firm for unpaid wages. This judgment entitled the workers to payment from Jevic's estate ahead of its unsecured creditors. Later, some of Jevic's unsecured creditors filed a suit against some of its other unsecured creditors. The plaintiffs won a judgment on the ground that the firm's payments to the defendants constituted fraudulent transfers and preferences. These parties then negotiated, without the truck drivers' consent, a settlement agreement that called for the workers to receive nothing on their claims while the creditors were to be paid proportionately. [Czyzewski v Jevic Holding Corp, __ U.S. __, 137 S.Ct. 973, 197 L.Ed.2d 398 (2017)] (See Chapter 11—Reorganization.)*

1. Was it ethical of the truck drivers to obtain a judgment entitling them to payment ahead of the unsecured creditors? Why or why not?

2. Was it ethical of the unsecured creditors to agree that the workers would receive nothing on their claims? Use the IDDR approach to decide.

Critical Thinking and Writing Assignments

26–9. Time-Limited Group Assignment—Student Loan Debt. Cathy Coleman took out loans to complete her college education. After graduation, Coleman was irregularly employed as a teacher. Eventually, she filed a petition in a federal bankruptcy court under Chapter 13. The court confirmed a five-year plan under which Coleman was required to commit all of her disposable income to paying the student loans. Less than a year later, when Coleman was laid off, she still owed more than $100,000 to Educational Credit Management Corp. Coleman asked the court to discharge the debt on the ground that it would be an undue hardship for her to pay it. (See *Bankruptcy Relief under Chapter 13 and Chapter 12.*)

1. The first group will explain when a debtor normally is entitled to a discharge under Chapter 13.

2. The second group will discuss whether student loans are dischargeable and when "undue hardship" is a legitimate ground for an exception.

3. The third group will outline the goals of bankruptcy law and make an argument, based on these facts and principles, in support of Coleman's request.

Unit Three—Task-Based Simulation

Amin Akhavan/Shutterstock.com

Sonja owns a bakery in San Francisco.

1. **Performance of Sales Contracts.** Sonja orders two new model X23 McIntyre ovens from Western Heating Appliances for $16,000. Sonja and Western Heating agree orally, on the telephone, that Western will deliver the ovens within two weeks and that Sonja will pay for the ovens when they are delivered. Two days later, Sonja receives a fax from Western confirming her order. Before delivery, Sonja learns that she can obtain the same ovens from another company at a much lower price. Sonja wants to cancel her order, but Western refuses. Is the contract enforceable against Sonja? Why or why not?

2. **Banking.** To pay a supplier, Sonja issues a check to Milled Grains Co. that is drawn on United First Bank. A Milled Grains employee, with authorization, indorses the check and transfers it to Milled Grains' financial institution, Second Federal Bank. Second Federal puts the check into the regular bank collection process. If United First refuses to honor the check, who will ultimately suffer the loss? Could Sonja be subject to criminal prosecution if United First refuses to honor the check?

3. **Security Interests.** Sonja wants to borrow $40,000 from Credit National Bank to buy coffee-brewing equipment. If Credit National accepts Sonja's equipment as collateral for the loan, how does it let other potential creditors know of its interest? If Sonja fails to repay the loan, what are Credit National's alternatives with respect to collecting the amount due?

4. **Creditors' Rights.** Sonya borrows $20,000 from Ace Loan Co. to remodel the bakery and gives it to Jones Construction, a contractor, to do the work. The amount covers only half of the cost, but when Jones finishes the work, Sonja fails to pay the rest. Sonja also does not repay Ace for the loan. What can Jones do to collect what it is owed? What can Ace do?

Unit 4
Agency and Employment Law

Michal Kabsek/Shutterstock.com

637

27 | Agency Relationships in Business

Learning Objectives

The six Learning Objectives *below are designed to help improve your understanding. After reading this chapter, you should be able to answer the following questions:*

1. What is the difference between an employee and an independent contractor?

2. How do agency relationships arise?

3. What duties do agents and principals owe to each other?

4. How does a person acquire apparent authority to act as someone's agent?

5. When is a principal liable for an agent's negligence?

6. What are some of the ways in which an agency relationship can be terminated?

"[It] is a universal principle in the law of agency, that the powers of the agent are to be exercised for the benefit of the principal only, and not of the agent or of third parties."

Joseph Story
1779–1845
(Associate justice of the United States Supreme Court, 1811–1844)

One of the most common, important, and pervasive legal relationships is that of **agency**. In an agency relationship between two parties, one of the parties, called the *agent,* agrees to represent or act for the other, called the *principal.* The principal has the right to control the agent's conduct in matters entrusted to the agent. The agent must exercise his or her powers "for the benefit of the principal only," as Justice Joseph Story indicated in the chapter-opening quotation.

Agency relationships are crucial to the business world. Indeed, the only way that some business entities—including corporations and limited liability companies—can function is through their agents. Using agents provides clear benefits to principals, but agents can also create liability for their principals.

Amelia works as the on-site leasing agent for an apartment complex owned by Premier Properties. As part of her job, she signs leases with tenants and accepts rent on behalf of Premier. She also contracts with companies that do routine maintenance and landscaping at the complex. Is Amelia, as an agent, liable if a maintenance worker is injured while working at the apartment complex? Is Premier (the principal) liable if Amelia makes fraudulent statements to tenants? What happens if Amelia signs a contract for a major renovation of the complex that Premier did not authorize? These are just a few of the legal issues that can arise in agency relationships.

27-1 Agency Law

Section 1(1) of the *Restatement (Third) of Agency*[1] defines agency as "the fiduciary relation which results from the manifestation of consent by one person to another that the other shall act in his [or her] behalf and subject to his [or her] control, and consent by the other so to act." In other words, in a principal-agent relationship, the parties have agreed that the agent will act *on behalf and instead of* the principal in negotiating and transacting business with third parties.

The term **fiduciary** is at the heart of agency law. The term can be used both as a noun and as an adjective. When used as a noun, it refers to a person having a duty created by her or his undertaking to act primarily for another's benefit in matters connected with the undertaking. When used as an adjective, as in "fiduciary relationship," it means that the relationship involves trust and confidence.

Agency relationships commonly exist between employers and employees. Agency relationships may sometimes also exist between employers and independent contractors who are hired to perform special tasks or services.

Agency A relationship between two parties in which one party (the agent) agrees to represent or act for the other (the principal).

Fiduciary As a noun, a person having a duty created by his or her undertaking to act primarily for another's benefit in matters connected with the undertaking. As an adjective, a relationship founded on trust and confidence.

27-1a Employer-Employee Relationships

Normally, all employees who deal with third parties are deemed to be agents. A salesperson in a department store, for instance, is an agent of the store's owner (the principal) and acts on the owner's behalf. Any sale of goods made by the salesperson to a customer is binding on the principal. Similarly, most representations of fact made by the salesperson with respect to the goods sold are binding on the principal.

Because employees who deal with third parties are generally deemed to be agents of their employers, agency law and employment law overlap considerably. Agency relationships, however, can exist outside an employer-employee relationship, so agency law has a broader reach than employment law. Additionally, agency law is based on the common law, whereas much employment law is statutory law.

Note that employment laws (state and federal) apply only to the employer-employee relationship. Statutes governing Social Security, withholding taxes, workers' compensation, unemployment compensation, workplace safety, and employment discrimination are applicable only if employer-employee status exists.

The person on the left works for the owner of this fabric store. Is she an agent of the owner?

27-1b Employer–Independent Contractor Relationships

Independent contractors are not employees because, by definition, those who hire them have no control over the details of their physical performance. Section 2 of the *Restatement (Third) of Agency* defines an **independent contractor** as follows:

> [An independent contractor is] a person who contracts with another to do something for him [or her] but who is not controlled by the other nor subject to the other's right to control with respect to his [or her] physical conduct in the performance of the undertaking. *He [or she] may or may not be an agent.* [Emphasis added.]

Building contractors and subcontractors are independent contractors. A property owner does not control the acts of either of these professionals. Truck drivers who own their equipment and hire themselves out on a per-job basis are independent contractors, whereas truck drivers who drive company trucks on a regular basis are usually employees.

Independent Contractor One who works for, and receives payment from, an employer but whose working conditions and methods are not controlled by the employer. An independent contractor is not an employee but may be an agent.

Learning Objective 1

What is the difference between an employee and an independent contractor?

---

1. The *Restatement (Third) of Agency* is an authoritative summary of the law of agency and is often referred to by judges and other legal professionals.

The relationship between a person or firm and an independent contractor may or may not involve an agency relationship. To illustrate: A homeowner who hires a real estate broker to sell the property has contracted with an independent contractor (the broker). The homeowner also has established an agency relationship with the broker for the specific purpose of selling the property. Another example is an insurance agent, who is both an independent contractor and an agent of the insurance company for which she or he sells policies. (Note that an insurance *broker*, in contrast, normally is an agent of the person obtaining insurance and not of the insurance company.)

Ethical Issue

Is it fair to classify Uber and Lyft drivers as independent contractors? Uber services are available in about sixty countries and over three hundred cities worldwide. Its main competitor, Lyft, operates in more than two hundred U.S. cities. Drivers for Lyft, Uber, and similar companies present new challenges for a system of categorizing workers as employees or independent contractors. Drivers get to choose when and where they work, but not how much they will be paid. They have no benefits and are not entitled to protections provided by employment law statutes. They must electronically accept the companies' platform terms to obtain work assignments. For them, employment is a take-it-or-leave-it proposition.

A number of former and current Uber and Lyft drivers have pursued legal remedies to change their job classification and to obtain better benefits. In California, for instance, two federal court judges allowed separate lawsuits to go before juries on the question of whether on-demand drivers should be considered employees rather than independent contractors.[2] In a similar case, rather than go to court, Lyft settled a worker-misclassification lawsuit for $12.25 million.[3] The settlement did not reclassify Lyft drivers as employees, however. Instead, Lyft agreed to change its terms of service to conform to California's regulations governing independent-contractor status. Even though the lawsuit and the agreement were California based, the new terms of service will apply to all Lyft drivers nationwide.

27–1c Determining Employee Status

The courts are frequently asked to determine whether a particular worker is an employee or an independent contractor. How a court decides this issue can have a significant effect on the rights and liabilities of the parties. For instance, employers are required to pay certain taxes, such as Social Security and unemployment insurance taxes, for employees but not for independent contractors.

Criteria Used by the Courts In determining whether a worker has the status of an employee or an independent contractor, the courts often consider the following questions:

1. How much control can the employer exercise over the details of the work? (If an employer can exercise considerable control over the details of the work, this indicates employee status. The employer's degree of control is perhaps the most important factor weighed by the courts in determining employee status.)

2. Is the worker engaged in an occupation or business distinct from that of the employer? (If so, this points to independent-contractor status.)

Why would drivers working for Uber or Lyft want to be reclassified as employees?

---

2. *Cotter v. Lyft, Inc.*, 60 F.Supp.3d 1067 (N.D.Cal. 2015); *O'Connor v. Uber Technologies, Inc., et al.*, Case No. C-13-3826 EMC (N.D.Cal. 2015), and 201 F.Supp.3d 1110 (2016).
3. *Cotter v. Lyft, Inc.*, 193 F.Supp.3d 1030 (N.D.Cal. 2016); and *Cotter v. Lyft, Inc.*, 2017 WL 1033527 (N.D.Cal. 2017).

3. Is the work usually done under the employer's direction or by a specialist without supervision? (If the work is usually done under the employer's direction, this indicates employee status.)

4. Does the employer supply the tools at the place of work? (If so, this indicates employee status.)

5. For how long is the person employed? (If the person is employed for a long, continuous period, this indicates employee status.)

6. What is the method of payment—by time period or at the completion of the job? (Regular payment by time period, such as once a month, indicates employee status.)

7. What degree of skill is required of the worker? (Independent contractors are more likely to be highly skilled or to have unique skills than to be unskilled, so these types of skills may indicate independent-contractor status.)

"I'd like to think of you as a person, David, but it's my job to think of you as personnel."

Dean Vietor/The New Yorker Collection/The Cartoon Bank

Sometimes, workers may benefit from having employee status—for tax purposes and to be protected under certain employment laws, for instance. As mentioned earlier, federal statutes governing employment discrimination apply only when an employer-employee relationship exists. Protection under antidiscrimination statutes provides a significant incentive for workers to claim that they are employees rather than independent contractors.

An employer normally is not responsible for the actions of an independent contractor. **Case Example 27.1** AAA North Jersey, Inc., contracted with Five Star Auto Service to perform towing and auto repair services for AAA. One night, Terence Pershad, a Five Star tow-truck driver, responded to an AAA call for assistance by the driver of a car involved in an accident. While at the scene, Pershad got into a fight with Nicholas Coker, a passenger in the disabled car, and assaulted him with a knife.

Coker filed a suit against Pershad, Five Star, and AAA, alleging that AAA was responsible for Pershad's tortious conduct. The court ruled that Pershad was Five Star's employee and that Five Star was an independent contractor, not AAA's employee. An appellate court affirmed the ruling. Because AAA did not control Five Star's work, it was not liable for a tort committed by Five Star's employee.[4] ▪

Criteria Used by the IRS The Internal Revenue Service (IRS) has established its own criteria for determining whether a worker is an independent contractor or an employee. The most important factor in this determination is the degree of control the business exercises over the worker.

The IRS tends to closely scrutinize a firm's classification of its workers because employers can avoid certain tax liabilities by hiring independent contractors instead of employees. Even when a firm classifies a worker as an independent contractor, the IRS may decide that the worker is actually an employee. If the IRS decides that an employee is misclassified, the employer will be responsible for paying any applicable Social Security, withholding, and unemployment taxes due for that employee.

Employee Status and "Works for Hire" Ordinarily, a person who creates a copyrighted work is the owner of it—unless it is a "work for hire." Under the Copyright Act, any copyrighted work created by an employee within the scope of her or his employment at the request of the employer is a "work for hire." The *employer* owns the copyright to the work.

In contrast, when an employer hires an independent contractor—a freelance artist, writer, or computer programmer, for instance—the *independent contractor* normally owns the copyright. An exception is made if the parties agree in writing that the work is a "work for hire" and the work falls into specified categories, including audiovisual and other works.

---

4. *Coker v. Pershad*, 2013 WL 1296271 (N.J.App. 2013).

Case Example 27.2 As a freelance (independent) contractor, Brian Cooley created two sculptures of dinosaur eggs for the National Geographic Society to use in connection with an article in *National Geographic* magazine. Cooley spent hundreds of hours researching, designing, and constructing the sculptures. National Geographic hired Louis Psihoyos to photograph Cooley's sculptures for the article. Cooley and Psihoyos had separate contracts with National Geographic in which each transferred the copyrights in their works to National Geographic for a limited time.

How are copyrights on artwork and photographs affected by a person's employee status?

The rights to the works were returned to the artists at different times after publication. Psihoyos then began licensing his photographs of Cooley's sculptures to third parties in return for royalties. He digitized the photographs and licensed them to various online stock photography companies, and they appeared in several books published by Penguin Group. Cooley sued Psihoyos for copyright infringement. A federal district court held that Psihoyos did not have an unrestricted right to use and license the photos. When Psihoyos reproduced an image of a Cooley sculpture, he reproduced the sculpture, which infringed on Cooley's copyright. Therefore, the court granted a summary judgment to Cooley.[5]

27–2 Formation of an Agency

Agency relationships normally are consensual. They come about by voluntary consent and agreement between the parties. Normally, the agreement need not be in writing, and consideration is not required.

A person must have contractual capacity to be a principal. Those who cannot legally enter into contracts directly generally are not allowed to do so indirectly through an agent. (In some states, however, a minor can be a principal.) Any person can be an agent regardless of whether he or she has the capacity to enter a contract (including minors).

An agency relationship can be created for any legal purpose. An agency relationship that is created for an illegal purpose or that is contrary to public policy is unenforceable. **Example 27.3** Sharp (as principal) contracts with McKenzie (as agent) to sell illegal narcotics. The agency relationship here is unenforceable because selling illegal narcotics is a felony and is contrary to public policy. ■ It is also illegal for physicians and other licensed professionals to employ unlicensed agents to perform professional actions.

Generally, an agency relationship can arise in four ways: by agreement of the parties, by ratification, by estoppel, or by operation of law.

27–2a Agency by Agreement

Most agency relationships are based on an express or implied agreement that the agent will act for the principal and that the principal agrees to have the agent so act. An agency agreement can take the form of an express written contract or be created by an oral agreement, such as when a person hires a neighbor to mow his lawn on a regular basis.

An agency agreement can also be implied by conduct. ✷ **Spotlight Case Example 27.4** Gilbert Bishop was admitted to Laurel Creek Health Care Center suffering from various physical ailments. During an examination, Bishop told Laurel Creek staff that he could not use his hands well enough to write or hold a pencil, but he was otherwise found to be mentally competent. Bishop's sister offered to sign the admissions forms, but it was Laurel Creek's policy to have the patient's spouse sign the admissions papers if the patient was unable to do so.

Learning Objective 2
How do agency relationships arise?

---

5. *Cooley v. Penguin Group (USA), Inc.*, 31 F.Supp.3d 599 (S.D.N.Y. 2014).

Bishop's sister then brought his wife, Anna, to the hospital to sign the paperwork, which included a mandatory arbitration clause. Later, when the family filed a lawsuit against Laurel Creek, the nursing home sought to enforce the arbitration clause. Ultimately, a state appellate court held that Bishop was bound by the contract and the arbitration clause his wife had signed. Bishop's conduct had indicated that he was giving his wife authority to act as his agent in signing the admissions papers.[6]

27–2b Agency by Ratification

On occasion, a person who is in fact not an agent (or who is an agent acting outside the scope of her or his authority) may make a contract on behalf of another (a principal). If the principal affirms that contract by word or by action, an agency relationship is created by **ratification.** Ratification involves a question of intent, and intent can be expressed by either words or conduct. The basic requirements for ratification will be discussed later in this chapter.

27–2c Agency by Estoppel

When a principal causes a third person to believe that another person is his or her agent, and the third person deals with the supposed agent, the principal is "estopped to deny" the agency relationship. In such a situation, the principal's actions create the *appearance* of an agency that does not in fact exist.

The third person must prove that she or he *reasonably* believed that an agency relationship existed. Facts and circumstances must show that an ordinary, prudent person familiar with business practice and custom would have been justified in concluding that the agent had authority.

Note that the acts or declarations of a purported *agent* in and of themselves do not create an agency by estoppel. Rather, it is the deeds or statements of the *principal* that create an agency by estoppel. The question in the following case was whether this exception applied to a hospital whose emergency room physician was an independent contractor.

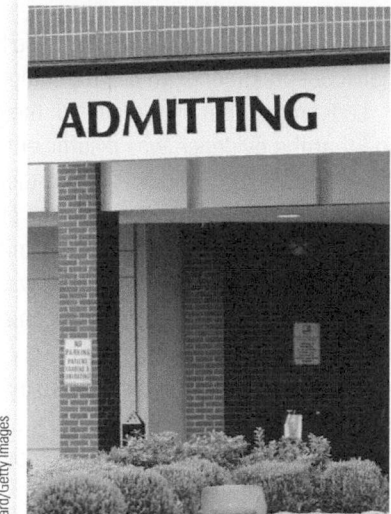

Can a new hospital patient designate someone else to sign all of the "paperwork"?

Ratification A party's act of accepting or giving legal force to a contract or other obligation entered into on his or her behalf by another that previously was not enforceable.

---

6. *Laurel Creek Health Care Center v. Bishop*, 2010 WL 985299 (Ky.App. 2010).

■ Case 27.1

Reidel v. Akron General Health System

Ohio Court of Appeals, Eighth District, 2018 -Ohio- 840, 97 N.E.3d 508 (2018).

Background and Facts Akron General Health System owns and operates health-care centers, including Lodi Community Hospital, in Ohio. Aaron Reidel was experiencing severe back pain when he visited the emergency room at Lodi. Attending physician Chris Kalapodis failed to timely diagnose the problem—a spinal epidural abscess—in spite of the presence of an active methicillin-resistant staphylococcus aureus (MRSA) infection.

Reidel filed a suit in an Ohio state court against the hospital, alleging that the physician's negligence was the proximate cause of Reidel's subsequent paraplegia and seeking to recover medical expenses and the cost of future care. Lodi argued that it was

not liable because Kalapodis was not the hospital's employee or agent. Based on the findings of a jury, the court ordered an award of damages to Reidel of $5.2 million. Lodi appealed.

In the Words of the Court
Anita Laster *MAYS*, J. [Judge]:

* * * *

* * * A hospital may be held liable under the doctrine of agency by estoppel for the negligence of independent medical practitioners practicing in the hospital if it holds itself out to the public as a provider of medical services and in the absence of notice or knowledge

(Continues)

to the contrary, the patient looks to the hospital, as opposed to the individual practitioner, to provide competent medical care.

Lodi argues that both prongs of the requirements must be met and that the evidence was insufficient to meet the second prong of the test because Riedel did not testify that he "looked to the hospital, as opposed to the individual practitioner, to provide competent medical care" and that he admitted that he was "going to be treated by a doctor" upon his arrival at the hospital.

The emergency room has become the community medical center, serving as the portal of entry to the myriad of services available at the hospital. As an industry, hospitals spend enormous amounts of money advertising in an effort to compete with each other for the health care dollar, thereby inducing the public to rely on them in their time of medical need. The public, in looking to the hospital to provide such care, is unaware of and unconcerned with the technical complexities and nuances surrounding the contractual and employment arrangements between the hospital and the various medical personnel operating therein. Indeed, often the very nature of a medical emergency precludes choice. *Public policy dictates that the public has every right to assume and expect that the hospital is the medical provider it purports to be.* [Emphasis added.]

* * * *

Unless the patient merely viewed the hospital as the *situs* where [his] physician would treat [him], [he] had the right to assume and expect that the treatment was being rendered through hospital employees and that any negligence associated therewith would render the hospital liable.

There is no evidence in the record that Riedel had a doctor-patient relationship with Dr. Kalapodis prior to the Lodi emergency room encounter. Riedel testified that Lodi was close to his daughters' home and he was seeking emergency medical care. Riedel had no information that Dr. Kalapodis was not directly employed by Lodi. We agree with [Reidel] that it is hardly unusual for a person seeking emergency medical care to expect to be treated by a physician employed by a hospital.

Decision and Remedy A state intermediate appellate court affirmed the order of the trial court. The court stated, "The record contains substantial competent evidence to support the jury's finding of liability by estoppel." As for the remedy, the amount of the damages fell within the range of estimates in expert analyses submitted by the parties supporting the cost of the life care plan for Riedel's permanent disability.

Critical Thinking

• **Legal Environment** *An unconscious individual transported to a hospital would be unable to demonstrate that he or she was seeking care from the hospital and not a particular physician. Would the public policy considerations stated in the* Reidel *case apply? Why or why not?*

• **What If the Facts Were Different?** *Suppose that a sign had been posted in the Lodi emergency room spelling out the legal relationship between the hospital and the attending physician. Would the result have been different? Explain.*

27–2d Agency by Operation of Law

The courts may find an agency relationship in the absence of a formal agreement in other situations as well. This can occur in family relationships, such as when one spouse purchases certain necessaries and charges them to the other spouse's account. The courts will often rule that a spouse is liable for necessaries purchased by the other spouse because of either a social policy or a legal duty to supply necessaries to family members.

Agency by operation of law may also occur in emergency situations. If the agent is unable to contact the principal and failure to act would cause the principal substantial loss, the agent may take steps beyond the scope of her or his authority. For instance, a railroad engineer may contract on behalf of her or his employer for medical care for an injured motorist hit by the train.

Learning Objective 3

What duties do agents and principals owe to each other?

27–3 Duties of Agents and Principals

Once the principal-agent relationship has been created, both parties have duties that govern their conduct. Because an agency relationship is *fiduciary* (one of trust), each party owes the other the duty to act with the utmost good faith. In general, for every duty of the principal, the agent has a corresponding right, and vice versa.

27–3a Agent's Duties to the Principal

Generally, the agent owes the principal five duties—performance, notification, loyalty, obedience, and accounting (see Exhibit 27–1).

Performance An implied condition in every agency contract is the agent's agreement to use reasonable diligence and skill in performing the work. When an agent fails to perform her or his duties, liability for breach of contract may result. The degree of skill or care required of an agent is usually that expected of a reasonable person under similar circumstances. Generally, this is interpreted to mean ordinary care. If an agent has claimed to possess special skill, however, failure to exercise that degree of skill constitutes a breach of the agent's duty.

Not all agency relationships are based on contract. In some situations, an agent acts gratuitously—that is, not for monetary compensation. A gratuitous agent cannot be liable for breach of contract, as there is no contract, but he or she can be subject to tort liability. Once a gratuitous agent has begun to act in an agency capacity, he or she has the duty to continue to perform in that capacity. In addition, a gratuitous agent must perform in an acceptable manner and is subject to the same standards of care and duty to perform as other agents.

Example 27.5 Bryan's friend Alice is a real estate broker. Alice offers to sell Bryan's vacation home at no charge. If Alice never attempts to sell the home, Bryan has no legal cause of action to force her to do so. If Alice does attempt to sell the home, but then performs so negligently that the sale falls through, Bryan can sue Alice for negligence. ■

Notification An agent is required to notify the principal of all matters that come to her or his attention concerning the subject matter of the agency. This is the duty of notification, or the duty to inform. **Example 27.6** Lang, an artist, is about to negotiate a contract to sell a series of paintings to Barber's Art Gallery for $25,000. Lang's agent learns that Barber is insolvent and will be unable to pay for the paintings. The agent has a duty to inform Lang of this fact because it is relevant to the subject matter of the agency—the sale of Lang's paintings ■

Generally, the law assumes that the principal knows of any information acquired by the agent that is relevant to the agency—regardless of whether the agent actually passes on this information to the principal. It is a basic tenet of agency law that notice to the agent is notice to the principal.

"If God had an agent, the world wouldn't be built yet. It'd only be about Thursday."

Jerry Reynolds
1944–present
(National Basketball Association executive)

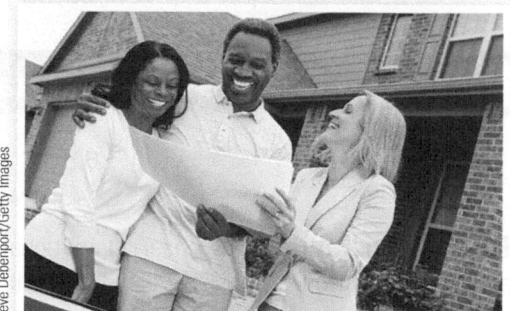

If a friend who is a licensed real estate broker agrees to sell your house at no charge, can you sue for nonperformance?

Exhibit 27–1 Duties of the Agent

Duties of the Agent				
Performance	**Notification**	**Loyalty**	**Obedience**	**Accounting**
Agent must use reasonable diligence and skill when performing duties.	Agent is required to notify the principal of all matters that concern the subject of the agency.	Agent has a duty to act solely for the principal's benefit.	Agent must follow all lawful and stated instructions from the principal.	Agent must provide records of all property and funds received or paid out on the principal's behalf.

Know This

An agent's disclosure of confidential information could constitute the business tort of misappropriation of trade secrets.

Loyalty Loyalty is one of the most fundamental duties in a fiduciary relationship. Basically, the agent has the duty to act *solely for the benefit of the principal* and not in the interest of the agent or a third party. For instance, an agent cannot represent two principals in the same transaction unless both know of the dual capacity and consent to it.

The duty of loyalty also means that any information or knowledge acquired through the agency relationship is considered confidential. It would be a breach of loyalty to disclose such information either during the agency relationship or after its termination. Typical examples of confidential information are trade secrets and customer lists compiled by the principal.

In short, the agent's loyalty must be undivided. The agent's actions must be strictly for the benefit of the principal and must not result in any secret profit for the agent. **Example 27.7** Don contracts with Leo, a real estate agent, to negotiate the purchase of an office building. Leo discovers that the property owner will sell the building only as a package deal with another parcel, so he buys the two properties, intending to resell the building to Don. Leo has breached his fiduciary duty. As a real estate agent, Leo has a duty to communicate all offers to his principal and not to purchase the property secretly and then resell it to his principal. Leo is required to act in Don's best interests and can become the purchaser in this situation only with Don's knowledge and approval.

In the following case, an employer alleged that a former employee had breached his duty of loyalty by planning a competing business while still working for the employer.

Spotlight on Taser International: Case 27.2

Taser International, Inc. v. Ward

Court of Appeals of Arizona, Division 1, 224 Ariz. 389, 231 P.3d 921 (2010).

Background and Facts Taser International, Inc., develops and makes electronic control devices—stun guns—as well as accessories for them, including a personal video and audio recording device called the TASER CAM.

Steve Ward was Taser's vice president of marketing when he began to explore the possibility of developing and marketing devices of his own design, including a clip-on camera. Ward talked to patent attorneys and a product development company and completed most of a business plan.

After he resigned from Taser, Ward formed Vievu, LLC, to market his clip-on camera. Ten months later, Taser announced the AXON, a product that provides an audio-video record of an incident from the visual perspective of the person involved. Taser then filed a suit in an Arizona state court against Ward, alleging that he had breached his duty of loyalty to Taser. The court granted Taser's motion for a summary judgment in the employer's favor. Ward appealed.

In the Words of the Court
PORTLEY, Judge.

* * * *

* * * An agent is under the duty to act with entire good faith and loyalty for the furtherance of the interests of his principal in all matters concerning or affecting the subject of his agency.

One aspect of this broad principle is that an employee is precluded from actively competing with his or her employer during the period of employment.

Although an employee may not compete prior to termination, the employee may take action during employment, not otherwise wrongful, to prepare for competition following termination of the agency relationship. Preparation cannot take the form of acts in direct competition with the employer's business. [Emphasis added.]

* * * *

It is undisputed that, prior to his resignation, Ward did not solicit or recruit any Taser employees, distributors, customers, or vendors; he did not buy, sell, or incorporate any business; he did not acquire office space or other general business services; he did not contact or enter into any agreements with suppliers or manufacturers for his proposed clip-on camera; and he did not sell any products. However, Ward did begin developing a business plan, counseled with several attorneys, explored and abandoned the concept of an eyeglass-mounted camera device, and engaged, to some extent, in the exploration and development of a clip-on camera device.

Ward argues that his pre-termination activities did not constitute active competition but were merely lawful preparation for a future business venture. Taser contends, however, that "this case is * * * about developing a rival design during employment, knowing full well TASER has sold such a device and continues to develop a second-generation product."

* * * *

* * * Assuming Taser was engaged in the research and development of a recording device during Ward's employment, assuming Ward knew or should have known of those efforts, and assuming Taser's device would compete with Ward's concept, substantial design and development efforts by Ward during his employment would constitute direct competition with the business activities of Taser and would violate his duty of loyalty. In the context of a business which engages in research, design, development, manufacture, and marketing of products, we cannot limit "competition" to just actual sales of competing products.

Decision and Remedy A state intermediate appellate court agreed with Taser that an employee might not actively compete with his employer before his employment is terminated. But the parties disputed the extent of Ward's pre-termination efforts, creating a genuine issue of material fact that could not be resolved on a motion for summary judgment. The appellate court thus reversed the lower court's decision in Taser's favor and remanded the case for further proceedings.

Critical Thinking

• **Legal Environment** *Did Ward breach any duties owed to his employer in addition to his alleged breach of the duty of loyalty? Discuss.*

• **What If the Facts Were Different?** *Suppose that Ward's pre-termination activities focused on a product that was not designed to compete with Taser's products. Would these efforts have breached the duty of loyalty? Why or why not?*

Obedience When acting on behalf of a principal, an agent has a duty to follow all lawful and clearly stated instructions of the principal. Any deviation from such instructions is a violation of this duty. During emergency situations, however, when the principal cannot be consulted, the agent may deviate from the instructions without violating this duty. Whenever instructions are not clearly stated, the agent can fulfill the duty of obedience by acting in good faith and in a manner reasonable under the circumstances.

Accounting Unless an agent and a principal agree otherwise, the agent has the duty to keep and make available to the principal an account of all property and funds received and paid out on behalf of the principal. This includes gifts from third parties in connection with the agency. **Example 27.8** Marta is a salesperson for Roadway Supplies. Knife River Construction gives Marta a new tablet as a gift for prompt deliveries of Roadway's paving materials. The tablet belongs to Roadway. ▮ The agent has a duty to maintain separate accounts for the principal's funds and for the agent's personal funds, and the agent must not intermingle these accounts.

27–3b Principal's Duties to the Agent

The principal also owes certain duties to the agent (as shown in Exhibit 27–2). These duties relate to compensation, reimbursement and indemnification, cooperation, and safe working conditions.

Compensation In general, when a principal requests services from an agent, the agent reasonably expects payment. The principal therefore has a duty to pay the agent for services rendered. For instance, when an accountant or an attorney is asked to act as an agent, an agreement to compensate the agent for service is implied. The principal also has a duty to pay that compensation in a timely manner.

Unless the agency is gratuitous and the agent does not act in exchange for payment, the principal must pay the agreed-on value for the agent's services. If no amount has been expressly agreed on, the principal owes the agent the customary compensation for such services.

Exhibit 27–2 Duties of the Principal

Compensation	Reimbursement and Indemnification	Cooperation	Safe Working Conditions
Principal must pay the agreed-on (or reasonable) value for the agent's services.	Principal must reimburse the agent for any funds paid out at the principal's request, as well as for necessary expenses.	Principal must cooperate with and assist an agent in performing his or her duties.	Principal must provide a safe working environment for agents and employees.

Case Example 27.9 Keith Miller worked as a sales representative for Paul M. Wolff Company, a subcontractor specializing in concrete finishing services. Sales representatives at Wolff are paid a 15 percent commission on projects that meet a 35 percent gross profit threshold. The commission is paid after the projects are completed. When Miller resigned, he asked for commissions on fourteen projects for which he had secured contracts but which had not yet been completed. Wolff refused, so Miller sued.

The court found that "an agent is entitled to receive commissions on sales that result from the agent's efforts," even after the employment or agency relationship ends. Miller had met the gross profit threshold on ten of the unfinished projects, and therefore he was entitled to more than $21,000 in commissions.[7]

Reimbursement and Indemnification Whenever an agent disburses funds at the request of the principal, the principal has the duty to reimburse the agent. The principal must also reimburse the agent for any necessary expenses incurred in the court of the reasonable performance of agency duties. Agents cannot recover for expenses incurred through their own misconduct or negligence, however.

Subject to the terms of the agency agreement, the principal has the duty to compensate, or *indemnify*, an agent for liabilities incurred because of authorized acts and transactions. For instance, if the principal fails to perform a contract formed by the agent with a third party and the third party then sues the agent, the principal must compensate the agent for any costs incurred in defending against the lawsuit.

Additionally, the principal must indemnify the agent for the value of benefits that the agent confers on the principal. The amount of indemnification is usually specified in the agency contract. If it is not, the courts will look to the nature of the benefits and the type of expenses to determine the amount. Note that this rule applies to acts by gratuitous agents as well. Suppose that a person finds a dog that becomes sick, takes the dog to a veterinarian, and pays

A salesperson works for commission based on concrete-finishing services sold. If that salesperson quits, is she or he still entitled to commissions owed on previous sales?

7. *Miller v. Paul M. Wolff Co.*, 178 Wash.App. 957, 316 P.3d 1113 (2014).

for the veterinarian's services. The finder is a gratuitous agent and is entitled to be reimbursed by the dog's owner for those costs.

Cooperation A principal has a duty to cooperate with the agent and to assist the agent in performing her or his duties. The principal must do nothing to prevent that performance. When a principal grants an agent an exclusive territory, for instance, the principal creates an exclusive agency and cannot compete with the agent or assign or allow another agent to compete. If the principal does so, he or she violates the exclusive agency and can be held liable for the agent's lost profits.

Example 27.10 Penny (the principal) creates an exclusive agency by granting Andrew (the agent) an exclusive territory within which Andrew may sell Penny's organic skin care products. If Penny starts to sell the products herself within Andrew's territory—or permits another agent to do so—Penny has failed to cooperate with the agent. Because she has violated the exclusive agency, Penny can be held liable for Andrew's lost sales or profits.

Safe Working Conditions A principal is required to provide safe working premises, equipment, and conditions for all agents and employees. The principal has a duty to inspect the working conditions and to warn agents and employees about any hazards. When the agent is an employee, the employer's liability is frequently covered by state workers' compensation insurance, and federal and state statutes often require the employer to meet certain safety standards.

27–4 Agent's Authority

An agent's authority to act can be either *actual* (express or implied) or *apparent*. If an agent contracts outside the scope of his or her authority, the principal may still become liable by ratifying the contract.

27–4a Express Authority

Express authority is actual authority declared in clear, direct, and definite terms. Express authority can be given orally or in writing.

Equal Dignity Rule In most states, the **equal dignity rule** requires that if the contract being executed is or must be in writing, then the agent's authority must also be in writing. Failure to comply with the equal dignity rule can make a contract voidable *at the option of the principal*. The law regards the contract at that point as a mere offer. If the principal decides to accept the offer, the agent's authority must be ratified, or affirmed, in writing.

Example 27.11 Parker (the principal) orally asks Austin (the agent) to sell a ranch that Parker owns. Austin finds a buyer and signs a sales contract on behalf of Parker to sell the ranch. Because a contract for an interest in realty must be in writing, the equal dignity rule applies here. Thus, the buyer cannot enforce the contract unless Parker subsequently ratifies Austin's agency status in writing. Once Austin's agency status is ratified, either party can enforce rights under the contract.

Modern business practice allows several exceptions to the equal dignity rule. An executive officer of a corporation normally is not required to obtain written authority from the corporation to conduct *ordinary* business transactions. The equal dignity rule also does not apply when an agent acts in the presence of a principal or when the agent's act of signing is merely a formality. Thus, if the principal negotiates a contract but is called out of town the day it is to be signed and orally authorizes his or her assistant to act as agent to sign the contract, the oral authorization is sufficient.

> "Let every eye negotiate for itself and trust no agent."
>
> **William Shakespeare**
> 1546–1616
> (English poet and playwright)

Equal Dignity Rule A rule requiring that an agent's authority be in writing if the contract to be made on behalf of the principal must be in writing.

Power of Attorney Authorization for another to act as one's agent or attorney either in specified circumstances (special) or in all situations (general).

Notary Public A public official authorized to attest to the authenticity of signatures.

Power of Attorney Giving an agent a **power of attorney** confers express authority on the agent.[8] The power of attorney is a written document that is usually notarized. (A document is notarized when a **notary public**—a person authorized by the state to attest to the authenticity of signatures—signs and dates the document and imprints it with his or her seal of authority.) Most states have statutory provisions for creating a power of attorney.

A power of attorney can be special (permitting the agent to do specified acts only), or it can be general (permitting the agent to transact all business for the principal). Because a general power of attorney grants extensive authority to an agent to act on behalf of the principal in many ways, it should be used with great caution. Ordinarily, a power of attorney terminates on the incapacity or death of the person giving the power.[9]

27–4b Implied Authority

An agent has the *implied authority* to do what is reasonably necessary to carry out his or her express authority and accomplish the objectives of the agency. Actual authority can also be implied by custom or inferred from the position the agent occupies.

Example 27.12 Adam is employed by Pete's Supermarket to manage one of its stores. Pete's has not expressly stated that Adam has authority to contract with third persons. Nevertheless, authority to manage a business implies authority to do what is reasonably required (as is customary or can be inferred from a manager's position) to operate the business. It is reasonable to infer that Adam has the authority to form contracts to hire employees, to buy merchandise and equipment, and to advertise the products sold in the store. ■

27–4c Apparent Authority

Apparent Authority Authority that is only apparent, not real. An agent's apparent authority arises when the principal causes a third party to believe that the agent has authority, even though she or he does not.

Actual authority (express or implied) arises from what the principal manifests *to the agent*. An agent has **apparent authority** when the principal, by either words or actions, causes a *third party* to reasonably believe that an agent has authority to act, even though the agent has no express or implied authority. If the third party changes his or her position in reliance on the principal's representations, the principal may be estopped (prevented) from denying that the agent had authority.

Learning Objective 4

How does a person acquire apparent authority to act as someone's agent?

Apparent authority usually comes into existence through a principal's pattern of conduct over time. ✖ **Spotlight Case Example 27.13** Gilbert Church owned Church Farm, Inc., a horse breeding farm in Illinois managed by Herb Bagley. Church Farm's advertisements for the breeding rights to one of its stallions, Imperial Guard, directed all inquiries to "Herb Bagley, Manager." Vern and Gail Lundberg contacted Bagley and executed a preprinted contract giving them breeding rights to Imperial Guard "at Imperial Guard's location." Bagley handwrote a statement on the contract that guaranteed the Lundbergs "six live foals in the first two years." He then signed it "Gilbert G. Church by H. Bagley."

The Lundbergs bred four mares, which resulted in one live foal. Church then moved Imperial Guard from Illinois to Oklahoma. The Lundbergs sued Church for breaching the contract by moving the horse. Church claimed that Bagley was not authorized to sign contracts for Church or to change or add terms, but only to present preprinted contracts to potential buyers. The jury found in favor of the Lundbergs and awarded $147,000 in damages. A state appellate court affirmed. Church was bound by Bagley's actions because Church had allowed circumstances to lead the Lundbergs to believe Bagley had the authority. In other words, Bagley had apparent authority to modify and execute the contract on behalf of Church.[10] ■

---

8. An agent who holds the power of attorney is called an *attorney-in-fact* for the principal. The holder does not have to be an attorney-at-law (and often is not).

9. A *durable* power of attorney, however, continues to be effective despite the principal's incapacity. An elderly person, for example, might grant a durable power of attorney to provide for the handling of property and investments or specific health-care needs should she or he become incompetent.

10. *Lundberg v. Church Farm, Inc.*, 502 N.E.2d 806, 151 Ill.App.3d (1986).

27–4d Emergency Powers

Sometimes, an unforeseen emergency demands action by the agent to protect or preserve the principal's property or rights, but the agent is unable to communicate with the principal. In that situation, the agent has emergency power. **Example 27.14** Rob Fulsom is an engineer for Pacific Drilling Company. While Fulsom is acting within the scope of his employment, he is severely injured in an accident on an oil rig many miles from home. Acosta, the rig supervisor, directs Thompson, a physician, to give medical aid to Fulsom and to charge Pacific for the medical services.

Acosta, an agent, has no express or implied authority to bind the principal, Pacific Drilling, for Thompson's medical services. Because of the emergency situation, however, the law recognizes Acosta as having authority to act appropriately under the circumstances. ■

27–4e Ratification

Ratification occurs when the principal affirms an agent's *unauthorized act*. When ratification occurs, the principal is bound to the agent's act, and the act is treated as if it had been authorized by the principal *from the outset*. Ratification can be either express or implied.

If the principal does not ratify the contract, the principal is not bound, and the third party's agreement with the agent is viewed as merely an unaccepted offer. Because the third party's agreement is an unaccepted offer, the third party can revoke the offer at any time, without liability, before the principal ratifies the contract.

The requirements for ratification can be summarized as follows:

1. The agent must have acted on behalf of an identified principal who subsequently ratifies the action.
2. The principal must know of all material facts involved in the transaction. If a principal ratifies a contract without knowing all of the facts, the principal can rescind (cancel) the contract.
3. The principal must affirm the agent's act in its entirety.
4. The principal must have the legal capacity to authorize the transaction at the time the agent engages in the act and at the time the principal ratifies. The third party must also have the legal capacity to engage in the transaction.
5. The principal's affirmation (ratification) must occur before the third party withdraws from the transaction.
6. The principal must observe the same formalities when approving the act done by the agent as would have been required to authorize it initially.

27–5 Liability in Agency Relationships

Frequently, a question arises as to which party, the principal or the agent, should be held liable for contracts formed by the agent or for torts or crimes committed by the agent. We look here at these aspects of agency law.

27–5a Liability for Contracts

Liability for contracts formed by an agent depends on how the principal is classified and on whether the actions of the agent were authorized or unauthorized. Principals are classified as disclosed, partially disclosed, or undisclosed.[11]

A **disclosed principal** is a principal whose identity is known by the third party at the time the contract is made by the agent. A **partially disclosed principal** is a principal whose identity is not known by the third party, but the third party knows that the agent is or may be acting for a principal at the time the contract is made. **Example 27.15** Sarah has contracted with a real

Can the manager of a horse-breeding farm make guarantees about foals on the owner's behalf?

Know This
An agent who exceeds his or her authority and enters into a contract that the principal does not ratify may be liable to the third party on the ground of misrepresentation.

Disclosed Principal A principal whose identity is known to a third party at the time the agent makes a contract with the third party.

Partially Disclosed Principal A principal whose identity is unknown by a third party, but the third party knows that the agent is or may be acting for a principal at the time the agent and the third party form a contract.

---

11. *Restatement (Third) of Agency*, Section 1.04(2).

estate agent to sell certain property. She wishes to keep her identity a secret, but the agent makes it clear to potential buyers of the property that the agent is acting in an agency capacity. In this situation, Sarah is a partially disclosed principal. An **undisclosed principal** is a principal whose identity is totally unknown by the third party, and the third party has no knowledge that the agent is acting in an agency capacity at the time the contract is made.

Undisclosed Principal A principal whose identity is unknown by a third party, and the third party has no knowledge that the agent is acting for a principal at the time the agent and the third party form a contract.

Authorized Acts If an agent acts within the scope of her or his authority, normally the principal is obligated to perform the contract regardless of whether the principal was disclosed, partially disclosed, or undisclosed. Whether the agent may also be held liable under the contract, however, depends on the status of the principal.

Disclosed or Partially Disclosed Principal. A disclosed or partially disclosed principal is liable to a third party for a contract made by an agent who is acting within the scope of her or his authority. (See this chapter's *Business Law Analysis* feature for illustration.) If the principal is disclosed, an agent has no contractual liability for the nonperformance of the principal or the third party. If the principal is partially disclosed, in most states the agent is also treated as a party to the contract, and the third party can hold the agent liable for contractual nonperformance.[12]

Case Example 27.16 Stonhard, Inc., makes epoxy and urethane flooring and installs it in industrial and commercial buildings. Marvin Sussman contracted with Stonhard to install flooring at a Blue Ridge Farms food-manufacturing facility in Brooklyn, New York. Sussman did not disclose at that time that he was acting as an agent for the facility's owner, Blue Ridge Foods, LLC.

---

12. *Restatement (Third) of Agency*, Section 6.02.

Liabililty of Disclosed Principals

Business Law Analysis

To display desserts in restaurants, Mario Sclafani ordered refrigeration units from Felix Storch, Inc. Felix faxed a credit application to Sclafani. The application was faxed back with a signature that appeared to be Sclafani's. Felix delivered the units, but Sclafani did not pay for them. Felix sued Sclafani to collect, but Sclafani denied that he saw the credit application or signed it. Sclafani claimed that he referred all credit questions to "the woman in the office." Who was liable on the contract?

Analysis: First, you need to identify the agent and the principal. In this situation, with respect to the refrigeration-unit contract with Felix, Sclafani was the

principal and "the woman in the office" was his agent. Who is liable for contracts formed by an agent depends on how the principal is classified and on whether the actions of the agent were authorized. If the agent acts within the scope of authority, normally the principal is obligated to perform the contract. If the principal is disclosed—that is, if the principal's identity is known by the third party at the time the contract is made—the agent has no contractual liability for the principal's nonperformance.

Result and Reasoning: Sclafani referred all credit questions to "the woman in the office." Sclafani's referral of credit matters to this woman established

that she was his agent. He gave her the authority to enter into legally binding credit contracts on his behalf. Thus, if Sclafani or "the woman in the office" signed Felix's credit application to guarantee payment, Sclafani is bound to the contract. Sclafani was a disclosed principal—Felix knew his identity at the time the contract was made. Therefore, Sclafani is liable on the contract and his agent is not.

When Stonhard was not paid for the installed flooring, it filed a suit against the Blue Ridge Farms facility, its owner, and Sussman to recover damages for breach of contract. The lower court dismissed the complaint against Sussman personally, but on appeal a reviewing court reversed that decision. The contract had been signed by Sussman "of Blue Ridge Farms." That evidence indicated that Sussman was acting as an agent for a partially disclosed principal, in that the agency relationship was known, but not the principal's identity. As an agent for a partially disclosed principal, Sussman became personally liable under the contract.[13]

Undisclosed Principal. Sometimes, neither the fact of agency nor the identity of the principal is disclosed, and the agent is acting within the scope of his or her authority. In this situation, the undisclosed principal is bound to perform just as if the principal had been fully disclosed at the time the contract was made.

The agent is also liable as a party to the contract. When a principal's identity is undisclosed and the agent is forced to pay the third party, however, the agent is entitled to be indemnified (compensated) by the principal. The principal had a duty to perform, even though his or her identity was undisclosed, and failure to do so will make the principal ultimately liable.

Once the undisclosed principal's identity is revealed, the third party generally can elect to hold either the principal or the agent liable on the contract. At the same time, the undisclosed principal can require the third party to fulfill the contract, except under any of the following circumstances:

1. The undisclosed principal was expressly excluded as a party in the contract.

2. The contract is a negotiable instrument signed by the agent with no indication of signing in a representative capacity.

3. The performance of the agent is personal to the contract, allowing the third party to refuse the principal's performance.

Unauthorized Acts If an agent has no authority but nevertheless contracts with a third party, the principal cannot be held liable on the contract. It does not matter whether the principal was disclosed, partially disclosed, or undisclosed.

In general, the agent is liable on the contract. **Example 27.17** Scranton signs a contract for the purchase of a truck, purportedly acting as an agent under authority granted by Johnson. In fact, Johnson has not given Scranton any such authority. Johnson refuses to pay for the truck, claiming that Scranton had no authority to purchase it. The seller of the truck is entitled to hold Scranton liable for payment.

If the principal is disclosed or partially disclosed, the agent is liable to the third party only if the third party relied on the agency status. The agent's liability here is based on the breach of an *implied warranty of authority*, not on the breach of contract itself.[14] If the third party knows at the time the contract is made that the agent does not have authority—or if the agent expresses to the third party *uncertainty* as to the extent of her or his authority—then the agent is not personally liable.

27–5b **Liability for Torts and Crimes**

Obviously, any person, including an agent, is liable for her or his own torts and crimes. Whether a principal can also be held liable for an agent's torts and crimes depends on several factors. In some situations, a principal may be held liable for the torts of an agent.

Principal's Tortious Conduct A principal conducting an activity through an agent may be liable for harm resulting from the principal's own negligence or recklessness. Thus, a principal may be liable for giving improper instructions, authorizing the use of improper materials or tools, or establishing improper rules that resulted in the agent's committing a tort.

Is an agent for a partially disclosed principal liable when the installer of food-plant flooring is not paid?

Know This

An agent who signs a negotiable instrument on behalf of a principal may be personally liable on the instrument. Liability depends, in part, on whether the identity of the principal is disclosed and whether the parties intend the agent to be bound by her or his signature.

---

13. *Stonhard, Inc. v. Blue Ridge Farms, LLC*, 114 A.D.3d 757, 980 N.Y.S.2d 507 (2 Dept. 2014).
14. The agent is not liable on the contract because the agent was never intended personally to be a party to the contract.

Example 27.18 Paul knows that Audra is not qualified to drive large trucks. Paul nevertheless tells her to use the company truck to deliver some equipment to a customer. If Audra causes an accident that injures someone, Paul (the principal) will be liable for his own negligence in giving improper instructions to Audra.

Principal's Authorization of Agent's Tortious Conduct
A principal who authorizes an agent to commit a tort may be liable to persons or property injured thereby, because the act is considered to be the principal's. **Example 27.19** Preston directs his agent, Ames, to cut the corn on specific acreage, which neither of them has the right to do. The harvest is therefore a trespass (a tort), and Preston is liable to the owner of the corn.

A principal instructs an agent to harvest corn on land that the principal does not own. Is the agent liable to the legal owner of the land?

Note also that an agent acting at the principal's direction can be liable as a tortfeasor (one who commits a tort), along with the principal, for committing the tortious act even if the agent was unaware of the wrongfulness of the act. Assume in *Example 27.19* that Ames, the agent, was unaware that Preston had no right to harvest the corn. Ames can nevertheless be held liable to the owner of the field for damages, along with Preston.

Liability for Agent's Misrepresentation
A principal is exposed to tort liability whenever a third person sustains a loss due to the agent's misrepresentation. The principal's liability depends on whether the agent was actually or apparently authorized to make representations and whether the representations were made within the scope of the agency. The principal is always directly responsible for an agent's misrepresentation made within the scope of the agent's authority.

Example 27.20 Arnett is a demonstrator for Moore's products. Moore sends Bassett to a home show to demonstrate the products and to answer questions from consumers. Moore has given Arnett authority to make statements about the products. If Arnett makes only true representations, all is fine, but if she makes false claims, Moore will be liable for any injuries or damages sustained by third parties in reliance on Arnett's false representations.

Learning Objective 5

When is a principal liable for an agent's negligence?

Respondeat Superior A doctrine under which a principal or an employer is held liable for the wrongful acts committed by agents or employees while acting within the course and scope of their agency or employment.

Vicarious Liability Indirect liability imposed on a supervisory party (such as an employer) for the actions of a subordinate (such as an employee) because of the relationship between the two parties.

Liability for Agent's Negligence
A principal may also be liable for harm an agent caused to a third party under the doctrine of ***respondeat superior***,[15] a Latin term meaning "let the master respond." This doctrine, which is discussed in this chapter's *Landmark in the Law* feature, is similar to the theory of strict liability. It imposes **vicarious liability,** or indirect liability, on the employer—that is, liability without regard to the personal fault of the employer—for torts committed by an employee in the course or scope of employment.

When an agent commits a negligent act, *both* the agent and the principal are liable. **Example 27.21** BDI Communications hires Pinnacle to provide landscaping services for its property. An herbicide sprayed by Pinnacle employee David Hoggatt enters BDI's building through the air-conditioning system and caused Catherine Warner, an BDI employee, to suffer a heart attack. If Warner sues, both Pinnacle (principal) and Hoggatt (agent) can be held liable for negligence. As Pinnacle's agent, Hoggatt is not excused from responsibility for tortious conduct just because he is working for a principal.

Determining the Scope of Employment. The key to determining whether a principal may be liable for an agent's torts under the doctrine of *respondeat superior* is whether the torts are committed within the scope of employment. In determining whether a

---

15. Pronounced ree-*spahn*-dee-uht soo-*peer*-ee-uhr.

particular act occurred within the course and scope of employment, the courts consider the following factors:

1. Whether the employee's act was authorized by the employer.
2. The time, place, and purpose of the act.
3. Whether the act was one commonly performed by employees on behalf of their employers.
4. The extent to which the employer's interest was advanced by the act.
5. The extent to which the private interests of the employee were involved.
6. Whether the employer furnished the means or instrumentality (for instance, a truck or a machine) by which the injury was inflicted.
7. Whether the employer had reason to know that the employee would do the act in question and whether the employee had ever done it before.
8. Whether the act involved the commission of a serious crime.

The Distinction between a "Detour" and a "Frolic." A useful insight into the "scope of employment" concept may be gained from the judge's classic distinction between a "detour" and a "frolic" in the case of *Joel v. Morison*.[16] In this case, the English court held that if a servant merely took a detour from his master's business, the master is responsible. If, however, the servant was on a "frolic of his own" and not in any way "on his master's business," the master is not liable.

16. 6 Car. & P. 501, 172 Eng.Rep. 1338 (1834).

The Doctrine of *Respondeat Superior*

Landmark in the Law

The idea that a master (employer) must respond to third persons for losses negligently caused by the master's servant (employee) first appeared in Lord Holt's opinion in *Jones v. Hart* (1698).[a] By the early nineteenth century, this maxim had been adopted by most courts and was referred to as the doctrine of *respondeat superior*.

Theories of Liability The vicarious (indirect) liability of the master for the acts of the servant has been supported primarily by two theories. The first theory rests on the issue of *control*, or *fault*—the master has control over the acts of the servant and is thus responsible for injuries arising out of such service. The second theory is economic in nature—the master receives the benefits or profits of the servant's service and therefore should also suffer the losses. Moreover, the master is better able than the servant to absorb such losses.

a. K.B. 642, 90 Eng.Rep. 1255 (1698).

The control theory is clearly recognized in the *Restatement (Third) of Agency*, which defines a master as "a principal who employs an agent to perform service in his [or her] affairs and who controls, or has the right to control, the physical conduct of the other in the performance of the service." Accordingly, a servant is defined as "an agent employed by a master to perform service in his [or her] affairs whose physical conduct in his [or her] performance of the service is controlled, or is subject to control, by the master."

Limitations on the Employer's Liability There are limitations on the master's liability for the acts of the servant. As discussed in the text, an employer (master) is responsible only for the wrongful conduct of an employee (servant) that occurs in "the scope of employment." Generally, the act must be of a kind that the servant was employed to do, it must

have occurred within "authorized time and space limits," and it must have been "activated, at least in part, by a purpose to serve the master."

Application to Today's World *The courts have accepted the doctrine of respondeat superior for some two centuries. This theory of vicarious liability has practical implications in all situations in which a principal-agent (master-servant, employer-employee) relationship exists. Today, the small-town grocer with one clerk and the multinational corporation with thousands of employees are equally subject to the doctrine.*

Example 27.22 While driving his employer's vehicle to call on a customer, Mandel decides to stop at a store—which is one block off his route—to take care of a personal matter. Mandel then negligently runs into a parked vehicle owned by Chan. In this situation, because Mandel's detour from the employer's business is not substantial, he is still acting within the scope of employment, and the employer is liable.

But suppose instead that Mandel decides to pick up a few friends for cocktails in another city and in the process negligently runs into Chan's vehicle. In this situation, the departure from the employer's business is substantial—Mandel is on a "frolic" of his own. Thus, the employer normally is not liable to Chan for damages.

Employee Travel Time. The time an employee spends going to and from work or to and from meals is usually considered outside the scope of employment. If travel is part of a person's position, however, as it is for a traveling salesperson or a regional representative of a company, then travel time is normally considered within the scope of employment. Thus, for such an employee, the duration of the business trip, including the return trip home, is within the scope of employment unless there is a significant departure from the employer's business.

Notice of Dangerous Conditions. The employer is charged with knowledge of any dangerous conditions discovered by an employee and pertinent to the employment situation. **Example 27.23** Brad, a maintenance employee in Martin's apartment building, notices a lead pipe protruding from the ground in the building's courtyard. Brad neglects either to fix the pipe or to inform Martin of the danger. John trips on the pipe and is injured. The employer is charged with knowledge of the dangerous condition regardless of whether or not Brad actually informed him. That knowledge is imputed to Martin by virtue of the employment relationship. ▪

When can an employer be held liable for an employee's negligence while driving?

RobertCrum/Getty Images

Liability for Agent's Intentional Torts

Most intentional torts that employees commit have no relation to their employment. Thus, their employers will not be held liable. Nevertheless, under the doctrine of *respondeat superior*, the employer can be liable for an employee's intentional torts that are committed within the course and scope of employment, just as the employer is liable for negligence. For instance, a department store owner is liable when a security guard who is a store employee commits the tort of false imprisonment while acting within the scope of employment. Similarly, a nightclub owner is liable when a "bouncer" commits the tort of assault and battery while on the job.

In addition, an employer who knows or should know that an employee has a propensity for committing tortious acts is liable for the employee's acts even if they ordinarily would not be considered within the scope of employment. For instance, if the employer hires a bouncer knowing that he has a history of arrests for assault and battery, the employer may be liable if the employee viciously attacks a patron in the parking lot after hours.

An employer may also be liable for permitting an employee to engage in reckless actions that can injure others. **Example 27.24** The owner of Bates Trucking observes an employee smoking while filling containerized trucks with highly flammable liquids. Failure to stop the employee will cause the owner to be liable for any injuries that result if a truck explodes. ▪ (See this chapter's *Beyond Our Borders* feature for a discussion of another approach to an employer's liability for an employee's acts.)

Know This

An agent-employee going to or from work or meals usually is not considered to be within the scope of employment. An agent-employee whose job requires travel, however, is considered to be within the scope of employment for the entire trip, including the return.

Islamic Law and *Respondeat Superior*

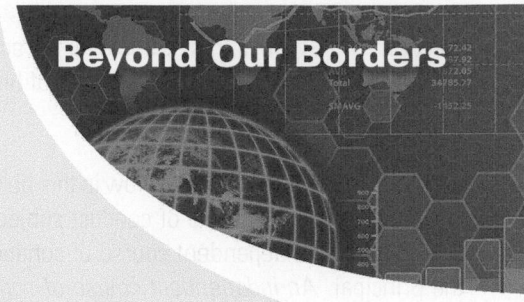

The doctrine of *respondeat superior* is well established in the legal systems of the United States and most Western countries. As you have already read, under this doctrine employers can be held liable for the acts of their employees. The doctrine of *respondeat superior* is not universal, however. Most Middle Eastern countries, for example, do not follow this doctrine.

Codification of Islamic Law

Islamic law, as codified in the *sharia*, holds to a strict belief that responsibility for human actions lies with the individual and cannot be vicariously extended to others. This belief and other concepts of Islamic law are based on the writings of Muhammad, the seventh-century prophet whose revelations form the basis of the Islamic religion and, by extension, the *sharia*. Muhammad's prophecies are documented in the Koran (Qur'an), which is the principal source of the *sharia*.

An Exception under Islamic Law

Islamic law does allow for an employer to be responsible for an employee's actions when the actions result from a direct order given by the employer to the employee. This principle also applies to contractual obligations. Note that the employer is responsible *only* if direct orders were given.

Otherwise stated, unless an employee is obeying a direct order of the employer, liability for the employee's actions does not extend to the employer.

Critical Thinking

How would U.S. society be affected if employers could not be held vicariously liable for their employees' torts?

Whether an agent's allegedly intentional tort fell within the scope of the agent's employment, making the principal vicariously liable, was at the heart of the dispute in the following case.

■ Case 27.3

M.J. v. Wisan

Utah Supreme Court, 2016 UT 13, 371 P.3d 21 (2016).

Background and Facts M.J. was a member of the Fundamentalist Church of Jesus Christ of Latter-Day Saints (FLDS) and a beneficiary of the church's United Effort Plan Trust. The trust was formed for the express purpose of furthering the church's doctrines, including the practice of marriage involving underage girls. When M.J. was fourteen years old, Warren Jeffs—who headed the church and the trust at that time—forced her to marry Allen Steed, her first cousin. M.J. claimed that Steed repeatedly raped her and that Jeffs refused to permit her to separate from or divorce Steed.

Later, M.J. filed a lawsuit in a Utah state court against Bruce Wisan, who was the trust's current leader. M.J. sought to hold the trust liable under the doctrine of *respondeat superior* for Jeffs's allegedly tortious conduct, including intentional infliction of emotional distress. The trust filed a motion for summary judgment, claiming that it could not be vicariously liable for Jeffs's conduct, which the court denied. The trust appealed.

In the Words of the Court

Associate Chief Justice *LEE* * * *:

* * * *

* * * Under [Utah Code Section 75–7–1010, Utah's version of Section 1010 of the Uniform Trust Code,] a trust is liable for the trustee's acts performed "in the course of administering the trust."

* * * The terms of the statute, in context, are quite clear. "In the course of" *is the traditional formulation of the standard for vicarious liability under the doctrine of* respondeat superior. *We accordingly interpret the Uniform Trust Act as incorporating the established standard of* respondeat superior *liability. Thus, under*

(Continues)

[Section 75–7–1010] a trust is liable for the acts of a trustee when the trustee was acting within the scope of his responsibility as a trustee. [Emphasis added.]

* * * *

The difficult question for the law in this field has been to define the line between a course of conduct subject to the employer's control and an independent course of conduct not connected to the principal. *An independent course of conduct is a matter so removed from the agent's duties that the law, in fairness, eliminates the principal's vicarious liability.* Such a course of conduct is one that represents a departure from, not an escalation of, conduct involved in performing assigned work or other conduct that an employer permits or controls. [Emphasis added.]

Our cases have identified three factors of relevance to this inquiry: (1) whether the agent's conduct is of the general kind the agent is employed to perform; (2) whether the agent is acting within the hours of the agent's work and the ordinary spatial boundaries of the employment; and (3) whether the agent's acts were motivated, at least in part, by the purpose of serving the principal's interest.

* * * In the case law of a number of states, spatial and time boundaries are no longer essential hallmarks of an agency relationship. Instead, the law now recognizes that agents may interact on an employer's behalf with third parties although the employee is neither situated on the employer's premises nor continuously or exclusively engaged in performing assigned work.

A number of courts have also questioned the viability of the requirement that an agent's acts be motivated in some part by an intention to serve the principal's purposes.

* * * *

* * * To resolve this case we need not choose * * * between the purpose or motive test * * * and the alternative formulations

* * * because we find that the Trust's attempts to defeat its liability on summary judgment fail under any of the * * * formulations.

We [also specifically find] * * * that an agent need not be acting within the hours of the employee's work and the ordinary spatial boundaries of the employment in order to be acting within the course of his employment. * * * We acknowledge that in today's business world much work is performed for an employer away from a defined work space and outside of a limited work shift. And we accordingly reject the Trust's attempt to escape liability on the ground that Jeffs's acts as a trustee were not performed while he was on the Trust's clock or at a work space designated for his work for the Trust. Instead we hold that the key question is whether Jeffs was acting within the scope of employment when performing work assigned by the employer or engaging in a course of conduct subject to the employer's control.

Decision and Remedy The Utah Supreme Court affirmed the lower court's denial of the trust's motion for summary judgment. Because Jeffs was the church's leader, "a reasonable fact finder could conclude that Jeffs was acting within the scope of his role as a trustee in directing Steed to engage in sexual activity with M.J."

Critical Thinking

• **Legal Environment** *Why do some courts apply a standard for imposing vicarious liability that does not rely on motive or purpose to determine whether an agent's tortious conduct falls within the scope of employment?*

• **Ethical** *When Jeffs was the head of the trust, none of the other trustees on its board questioned his actions. Was this a breach of ethics? Discuss.*

Liability for Independent Contractor's Torts Generally, an employer is not liable for physical harm caused to a third person by the negligent act of an independent contractor in the performance of the contract. This is because the employer does not have the right to control the details of an independent contractor's performance.

Courts make an exception to this rule when the contract involves unusually hazardous activities, such as blasting operations, the transportation of highly volatile chemicals, or the use of poisonous gases. In such situations, strict liability is imposed, and an employer cannot be shielded from liability merely by using an independent contractor.

Liability for Agent's Crimes An agent is liable for his or her own crimes. A principal or employer is not liable for an agent's crime even if the crime was committed within the scope of authority or employment, unless the principal participated by conspiracy or other action. In some jurisdictions, under specific statutes, a principal may be liable for an agent's violation in the course and scope of employment. For instance, a principal might be liable when an agent, during work, violates criminal regulations governing sanitation, prices, weights, or the sale of liquor.

27–6 Termination of an Agency

Agency law is similar to contract law in that both an agency and a contract can be terminated *by an act of the parties* or *by operation of law*. Once the relationship between the principal and the agent has ended, the agent no longer has the right (*actual* authority) to bind the principal. For an agent's *apparent* authority to be terminated, third persons may also need to be notified that the agency has been terminated.

27–6a Termination by Act of the Parties

An agency may be terminated by certain acts of the parties. Bases for termination by acts of the parties include lapse of time, achievement of the purpose of the agency, occurrence of a specific event, mutual agreement, and at the option of one party (see Exhibit 27–3).

When an agency agreement specifies the time period during which the agency relationship will exist, the agency ends when that time period expires. If no definite time is stated, then the agency continues for a reasonable time and can be terminated at will by either party. What constitutes a reasonable time depends on the circumstances and the nature of the agency relationship.

The parties can, of course, mutually agree to end their agency relationship. In addition, as a general rule, either party can terminate the agency relationship without the agreement of the other. The act of termination is called *revocation* if done by the principal and *renunciation* if done by the agent. Note, however, that the terminating party may face liability if the termination is wrongful.

Wrongful Termination Although both parties have the *power* to terminate an agency relationship, they may not always possess the *right* to do so. Wrongful termination can subject the canceling party to a suit for breach of contract. **Case Example 27.25** Smart Trike, Ltd., a Singapore manufacturing company based in Israel, contracted with a New Jersey firm, Piermont Products, LLC, to distribute its products in the United States and Canada. The parties' contract required six months' notice of termination, during which time Smart Trike was to continue paying commissions to Piermont for products that were sold. When Smart Trike

Learning Objective 6
What are some of the ways in which an agency relationship can be terminated?

Exhibit 27–3 Termination by Act of Parties

METHOD	RULES	ILLUSTRATION
1. Lapse of time	Agency terminates automatically at the end of the stated time.	Page lists her property for sale with Alex, a real estate agent, for six months. The agency ends in six months.
2. Purpose achieved	Agency terminates automatically on the completion of the purpose for which it was formed.	Calvin, a cattle rancher, hires Abe as his agent in the purchase of fifty head of breeding stock. The agency ends when the cattle have been purchased.
3. Occurrence of a specific event	Agency normally terminates automatically on the event's occurrence.	Meredith appoints Allen to handle her business affairs while she is away. The agency terminates when Meredith returns.
4. Mutual agreement	Agency terminates when both parties consent to end the agency relationship.	Linda and Greg agree that Greg will no longer be her agent in procuring business equipment.
5. At the option of one party (*revocation*, if by principal; *renunciation*, if by agent)	Either party normally has a right to terminate the agency relationship. Wrongful termination can lead to liability for breach of contract.	When Patrick becomes ill, he informs Alice that he is revoking her authority to be his agent.

terminated the agreement without providing the required notice, Piermont sued for breach of contract. The court held in favor of Piermont. Under the terms of the agreement, Piermont was entitled to receive commissions for products of Smart Trike that it had sold during the six months after the notice of termination.[17]

Agency Coupled with an Interest An agency, created for the benefit of the agent, in which the agent has some legal right (interest) in the property that is the subject of the agency

Agency Coupled with an Interest A special rule applies to an **agency coupled with an interest,** in which the agent has some legal right (an interest) in the property that is the subject of the agency. Because the agent has an additional interest in the property beyond the normal commission for selling it, the agent's position cannot be terminated until the agent's interest ends.

An agency coupled with an interest is not an agency in the usual sense because it is created for the agent's benefit instead of for the principal's benefit. **Example 27.26** Sylvia owns Harper Hills. She needs some cash right away, so she enters into an agreement with Rob under which Rob will lend her $10,000. In return, she will grant Rob a one-half interest in Harper Hills and "the exclusive right to sell" it. The loan is to be repaid out of the sale's proceeds. Rob is Sylvia's agent, and their relationship is an agency coupled with an interest. The agency was created when the loan agreement was made for the purpose of securing the loan. Therefore, Rob's agency power is irrevocable.

An agency coupled with an interest should not be confused with a situation in which the agent merely derives proceeds or profits from the sale of the subject matter. Many agents are paid a commission for their services, but the agency relationship involved does not constitute an agency coupled with an interest. For instance, a real estate agent who merely receives a commission from the sale of real property does not have a beneficial interest in the property itself.

Notice of Termination No particular form is required for notice of agency termination to be effective. If the agent's authority is written, however, it normally must be revoked in writing. The principal can personally notify the agent, or the agent can learn of the termination through some other means.

When an agency is terminated by act of the parties, it is the principal's duty to inform any third parties who know of the existence of the agency that it has been terminated. If the principal knows that a third party has dealt with the agent, the principal is expected to notify that person *directly*.

Although an agent's actual authority ends when the agency is terminated, an agent's *apparent authority* continues until the third party receives notice (from any source) that such authority has been terminated. **Example 27.27** Manning bids on a shipment of steel, and Stone is hired as an agent to arrange transportation of the shipment. When Stone learns that Manning has lost the bid, Stone's authority to make the transportation arrangement terminates.

27–6b Termination by Operation of Law

Termination of an agency by operation of law occurs in the circumstances discussed here. Note that when an agency terminates by operation of law, there is no duty to notify third persons.

1. *Death or insanity.* The general rule is that the death or mental incompetence of either the principal or the agent automatically and immediately terminates an ordinary agency relationship. Knowledge of the death is not required. **Example 27.28** Gary sends Tyron to China to purchase a rare painting. Before Tyron makes the purchase, Gary dies. Tyron's agent status is terminated at the moment of Gary's death, even though Tyron does not know that Gary has died. (Some states have enacted statutes that change this common law rule to require an agent's knowledge of the principal's death before termination.)

---

17. *Smart Trike, MND, PTE, Ltd. v. Piermont Products, LLC,* 147 A.D.3d 477, 48 N.Y.S.3d 23 (2017).

2. *Impossibility.* When the specific subject matter of an agency is destroyed or lost, the agency terminates. **Example 27.29** Blake employs Pedro to sell Blake's house, but before any sale takes place, the house is destroyed by fire. In this situation, Pedro's agency and authority to sell Blake's house terminate. ▪ Similarly, when it is impossible for the agent to perform the agency lawfully because of a change in the law, the agency terminates.

3. *Changed circumstances.* When an event occurs that has such an unusual effect on the subject matter of the agency that the agent can reasonably infer that the principal will not want the agency to continue, the agency terminates. **Example 27.30** Robert hires Miles to sell a tract of land for $40,000. Subsequently, Miles learns that there is oil under the land and that the land is worth $1 million. The agency and Miles's authority to sell the land for $40,000 are terminated. ▪

4. *Bankruptcy.* If either the principal or the agent petitions for bankruptcy, the agency is usually terminated. In certain circumstances, as when the agent's financial status is irrelevant to the purpose of the agency, the agency relationship may continue. Insolvency (the inability to pay debts when they become due or when liabilities exceed assets), as distinguished from bankruptcy, does not necessarily terminate the relationship.

5. *War.* When the principal's country and the agent's country are at war with each other, the agency is terminated. In this situation, the agency is automatically suspended or terminated because there is no way to enforce the legal rights and obligations of the parties.

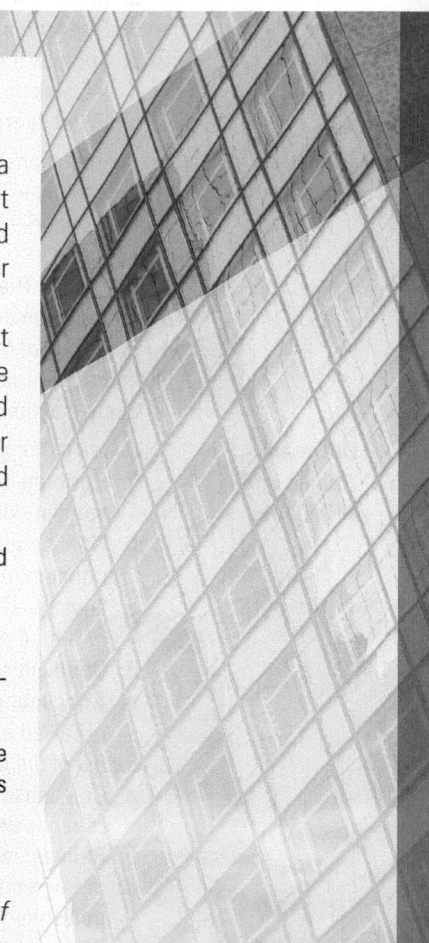

Practice and Review

Lynne Meyer, on her way to a business meeting and in a hurry, stopped by a Buy-Mart store for a new car charger for her smartphone. There was a long line at one of the checkout counters, but a cashier, Valerie Watts, opened another counter and began loading the cash drawer. Meyer told Watts that she was in a hurry and asked Watts to work faster. Watts, however, only slowed her pace. At this point, Meyer hit Watts.

It is not clear whether Meyer hit Watts intentionally or, in an attempt to retrieve the car charger, hit her inadvertently. In response, Watts grabbed Meyer by the hair and hit her repeatedly in the back of the head, while Meyer screamed for help. Management personnel separated the two women and questioned them about the incident. Watts was immediately fired for violating the store's no-fighting policy. Meyer subsequently sued Buy-Mart, alleging that the store was liable for the tort (assault and battery) committed by its employee. Using the information presented in the chapter, answer the following questions.

1. Under what doctrine discussed in this chapter might Buy-Mart be held liable for the tort committed by Watts?

2. What is the key factor in determining whether Buy-Mart is liable under this doctrine?

3. Did Watts's behavior constitute an intentional tort or a tort of negligence? How would this difference affect Buy-Mart's potential liability?

4. Suppose that when Watts applied for the job at Buy-Mart, she disclosed in her application that she had previously been convicted of felony assault and battery. Nevertheless, Buy-Mart hired Watts as a cashier. How might this fact affect Buy-Mart's liability for Watts's actions?

Debate This

The doctrine of respondeat superior *should be modified to make agents solely liable for some of their own tortious (wrongful) acts.*

Key Terms

Chapter Summary: Agency Relationships in Business

Agency Law	In a *principal-agent* relationship, an agent acts on behalf of and instead of the principal in dealing with third parties.
	1. *Employer-employee relationships*—An employee who deals with third parties is normally an agent of the employer.
	2. *Employer–independent contractor relationships*—An independent contractor is not an employee because the employer has no control over the details of the independent contractor's physical performance. An independent contractor may or may not be an agent.
	3. *Determining employee status*—The criteria used by courts includes the following:
	a. How much control can the employer exercise over the details of the work?
	b. Is the worker engaged in an occupation or business distinct from that of the employer?
	c. Is the work usually done under the employer's direction or by a specialist without supervision?
	d. Does the employer supply the tools at the place of work?
	e. For how long is the person employed?
	f. What is the method of payment—by time period or at the completion of the job?
	g. What degree of skill is required of the worker?
Formation of an Agency	Agency relationships may be formed by the following methods:
	1. *Agreement*—The agency relationship is formed through express consent (oral or written) or implied by conduct.
	2. *Ratification*—The principal either by act or by agreement ratifies the conduct of a person who is not in fact an agent.
	3. *Estoppel*—The principal causes a third person to believe that another person is the principal's agent, and the third person deals with the supposed agent in the reasonable belief that an agency exists.
	4. *Operation of law*—The agency relationship is based on social policy (as in family relationships) or formed in an emergency situation when the agent is unable to contact the principal and failure to act outside the scope of the agent's authority would cause the principal substantial loss.
Duties of Agents and Principals	1. *Duties of the agent*—
	a. Performance—In performing her or his duties, the agent must use reasonable diligence and skill or use the special skills that the agent has claimed to possess.
	b. Notification—The agent is required to notify the principal of all matters that come to his or her attention concerning the subject matter of the agency.
	c. Loyalty—The agent has a duty to act solely for the benefit of the principal and not in the interest of the agent or a third party.
	d. Obedience—The agent must follow all lawful and clearly stated instructions of the principal.
	e. Accounting—The agent has a duty to make available to the principal records of all property and funds received and paid out on behalf of the principal.
	2. *Duties of the principal*—
	a. Compensation—Except in a gratuitous agency relationship, the principal must pay the agreed-on value (or reasonable value) for the agent's services.
	b. Reimbursement and indemnification—The principal must reimburse the agent for all funds disbursed at the request of the principal, as well as for funds disbursed for necessary expenses in the reasonable performance of agency duties.
	c. Cooperation—A principal must cooperate with and assist an agent in performing her or his duties.
	d. Safe working conditions—A principal must provide safe working conditions for agents and employees.

Agent's Authority	1. *Express authority*—Can be given orally or in writing. Authorization must be in writing if the agent is to execute a contract that must be in writing.
	2. *Implied authority*—Authority deemed necessary for the agent to carry out expressly authorized tasks or customarily associated with the agent's position.
	3. *Apparent authority*—Exists when the principal, by word or action, causes a third party to reasonably believe that an agent has authority to act, even though the agent has no express or implied authority.
	4. *Ratification*—The affirmation by the principal of an agent's unauthorized action or promise. For the ratification to be effective, the principal must be aware of all material facts.
Liability in Agency Relationships	1. *Liability for contracts*—If the principal's identity is disclosed or partially disclosed at the time the agent forms a contract with a third party, the principal is liable to the third party under the contract if the agent acted within the scope of his or her authority. If the principal's identity is undisclosed at the time of contract formation, the agent is personally liable to the third party, but if the agent acted within the scope of his or her authority, the principal is also bound by the contract.
	2. *Liability for torts and crimes*—
	a. A principal conducting an activity through an agent may be liable for harm resulting from the principal's own negligence or recklessness.
	b. Under the doctrine of *respondeat superior*, the principal is liable for any harm caused to another through the agent's torts if the agent was acting within the scope of her or his employment at the time the harmful act occurred.
	c. Liability for agent's intentional torts—Usually, employers are not liable for the intentional torts that their agents commit, unless the acts are committed within the scope of employment, the employer knows or should know that the employee has a propensity for committing tortious acts, or the employer allowed the employee to engage in reckless acts that caused injury to another.
	d. Liability for independent contractor's torts—A principal is not liable for harm caused by an independent contractor's negligence, unless unusually hazardous activities are involved.
	e. Liability for agent's crimes—An agent is responsible for his or her own crimes, even if the crimes were committed while the agent was acting within the scope of authority or employment. A principal will be liable for an agent's crime only if the principal participated by conspiracy or other action or (in some jurisdictions) if the agent violated certain government regulations in the course of employment.
Termination of an Agency	1. *By act of the parties* (see *Exhibit 27–3*)
	a. Lapse of time.
	b. Purpose achieved.
	c. Occurrence of a specific event.
	d. Mutual agreement.
	e. At the option of one party.
	Notice to third parties is required when an agency is terminated by act of the parties.
	2. *By operation of law*—
	a. Death or insanity.
	b. Impossibility.
	c. Changed circumstances.
	d. Bankruptcy.
	e. War.

Issue Spotters

1. Dimka Corporation wants to build a new mall on a specific tract of land. Dimka contracts with Nadine to act as its agent in buying the property. When Nadine learns of the difference between the price that Dimka is willing to pay and the price at which the owner is willing to sell, she wants to buy the land and sell it to Dimka herself. Can she do this? Discuss. (See *Duties of Agents and Principals*.)

2. Davis contracts with Estee to buy a certain horse on her behalf. Estee asks Davis not to reveal her identity. Davis makes a deal with Farmland Stables, the owner of the horse, and makes a down payment. Estee does not pay the rest of the price. Farmland Stables sues Davis for breach of contract. Can Davis hold Estee liable for whatever damages he has to pay? Why or why not? (See *Liability in Agency Relationships*.)

—**Check your answers to the *Issue Spotters* against the answers provided in Appendix D at the end of this text.**

Business Scenarios and Case Problems

27–1. Ratification by Principal. Springer, who was running for Congress, instructed his campaign staff not to purchase any campaign materials without his explicit authorization. In spite of these instructions, one of his campaign workers contracted with Dubychek Printing Co. to print some promotional materials for Springer's campaign. When the printed materials arrived, Springer did not return them but instead used them during his campaign.

When Springer failed to pay for the materials, Dubychek sued for recovery of the price. Springer contended that he was not liable on the sales contract because he had not authorized his agent to purchase the printing services. Dubychek argued that the campaign worker was Springer's agent and that the worker had authority to make the printing contract. Additionally, Dubychek claimed that even if the purchase was unauthorized, Springer's use of the materials constituted ratification of his agent's unauthorized purchase. Is Dubychek correct? Explain. (See *Formation of an Agency.*)

27–2. Employee versus Independent Contractor. Stephen Hemmerling was a driver for the Happy Cab Co. Hemmerling paid certain fixed expenses and abided by a variety of rules relating to the use of the cab, the hours that could be worked, and the solicitation of fares, among other things. Rates were set by the state. Happy Cab did not withhold taxes from Hemmerling's pay. While driving the cab, Hemmerling was injured in an accident and filed a claim against Happy Cab in a Nebraska state court for workers' compensation benefits. Such benefits are not available to independent contractors. On what basis might the court hold that Hemmerling is an employee? Explain. (See *Agency Law.*)

27–3. Liability for Contracts. Thomas Huskin and his wife entered into a contract to have their home remodeled by House Medic Handyman Service. Todd Hall signed the contract as an authorized representative of House Medic. It turned out that House Medic was a fictitious name for Hall Hauling, Ltd. The contract did not indicate this, however, and Hall did not inform the Huskins about Hall Hauling. When a contract dispute later arose, the Huskins sued Todd Hall personally for breach of contract. Can Hall be held personally liable? Why or why not? [*Huskin v. Hall*, 2012 -Ohio- 653 (Ohio Ct.App. 2012)] (See *Liability in Agency Relationships.*)

27–4. Agent's Authority. Basic Research, LLC, advertised its products on television networks owned by Rainbow Media Holdings, Inc., through an ad agency, Icebox Advertising, Inc. As Basic's agent, Icebox had the express authority to buy ads from Rainbow on Basic's behalf, but the authority was limited to buying ads with cash in advance. Despite this limit, Rainbow sold ads to Basic through Icebox on credit. Basic paid Icebox

for the ads, but Icebox did not pass all of the payments on to Rainbow. Icebox filed for bankruptcy. Can Rainbow recoup the unpaid amounts from Basic? Explain. [*American Movie Classics v. Rainbow Media Holdings,* 508 Fed.Appx. 826 (10th Cir. 2013)] (See *Agent's Authority.*)

27–5. Business Case Problem with Sample Answer— Determining Employee Status. Nelson Ovalles worked as a cable installer for Cox Rhode Island Telecom, LLC, under an agreement with a third party, M&M Communications, Inc. The agreement stated that no employer-employee relationship existed between Cox and M&M's technicians, including Ovalles. Ovalles was required to designate his affiliation with Cox on his work van, clothing, and identification badge, but Cox had minimal contact with him and limited power to control the manner in which he performed his duties. Cox supplied cable wire and similar items, but the equipment was delivered to M&M, not to Ovalles. On a workday, while Ovalles was fulfilling a work order, his van rear-ended a car driven by Barbara Cayer. Is Cox liable to Cayer? Explain. [*Cayer v. Cox Rhode Island Telecom, LLC*, 85 A.3d 1140 (R.I. 2014)] (See *Agency Law.*)

—For a sample answer to Problem 27–5, go to Appendix E at the end of this text.

27–6. Agent's Authority. Terry Holden's stepmother, Rosie, was diagnosed with amyotrophic lateral sclerosis (ALS), and Terry's wife, Susan, became Rosie's primary caregiver. Rosie executed a durable power of attorney appointing Susan as her agent. Susan opened a joint bank account with Rosie at Bank of America, depositing $9,643.62 of Rosie's funds. Susan used some of the money to pay for "household expenses to keep us going while we were taking care of her." Rosie died three months later. Terry's father, Charles, as executor of Rosie's estate, filed a petition in a Texas state court against Susan for an accounting. What general duty did Susan owe Rosie as her agent? What does an agent's duty of accounting require? Did Susan breach either of these duties? Explain. [*Holden v. Holden*, 456 S.W.3d 642 (Tex.App.—Tyler 2015)] (See *Agent's Authority.*)

27–7. Agency Relationships. Standard Oil of Connecticut, Inc., sells home heating, cooling, and security systems. Standard schedules installation and service appointments with its customers and then contracts with installers and technicians to do the work. The company requires an installer or technician to complete a project by a certain time but to otherwise "exercise independent judgment and control in the execution of any work." The installers and technicians are licensed and certified by the state. Standard does not train them, provide instruction manuals, supervise them at customers' homes, or inspect their work. The installers and technicians use their own equipment and tools, and they can choose which days they work. Standard pays a set rate per project. According to criteria used by the courts, are these installers and technicians independent contractors or employees? Why? [*Standard Oil of Connecticut, Inc. v. Administrator, Unemployment Compensation Act*, 320 Conn. 611, 134 A.3d 581 (2016)] (See *Agency Law*.)

27–8. Scope of Agent's Authority. Kindred Nursing Centers East, LLC, owns and operates Whitesburg Gardens, a long-term care and rehabilitation facility, in Huntsville, Alabama. Lorene Jones was admitted to the facility following knee-replacement surgery. Jones's daughter, Yvonne Barbour, signed the admission forms required by Whitesburg Gardens as her mother's representative in her presence. Jones did not object. The forms included an "Alternative Dispute Resolution Agreement," which provided for binding arbitration in the event of a dispute between "the Resident" (Jones) and "the Facility" (Whitesburg Gardens). Six days later, Jones was transferred to a different facility. After recovering from the surgery, she filed a suit in an Alabama state court against Kindred, alleging substandard care on a claim of negligence. Can Jones be compelled to submit her claim to arbitration? Explain. [*Kindred Nursing Centers East, LLC v. Jones*, 201 So.3d 1146 (Ala. 2016)] (See *Agent's Authority*.)

27–9. Agency Relationships. Jane Westmas was killed when a tree branch cut by Creekside Tree Service, Inc., fell on her while she was walking on a public path through the private property of Conference Point Center on the shore of Lake Geneva in Wisconsin. Conference Point had contracted with Creekside to trim and remove trees from its property, but the owner had no control of (and no right to control) the details of Creekside's work. Jane's husband, John, and her son, Jason, filed a suit in a Wisconsin state court against Creekside, alleging that the service's negligence caused her death. Creekside contended it was immune from the suit under a state statute that provides "no . . . agent of an owner is liable for the death of . . . a person engaging in a recreational activity on the owner's property." Could Creekside be held liable for Jane's death? Why or why not? [*Westmas v. Creekside Tree Service, Inc.*, 2018 WI 12, 379 Wis.2d 471, 907 N.W.2d 68 (2018)] (See *Agency Law*.)

27–10. A Question of Ethics—The IDDR Approach and Agent's Authority. *Devin Fink was the manager of Precision Tune Auto Care in Charlotte, North Carolina. Randall Stywall brought her car to the shop to replace the rear shocks. Fink filled out the service order with an estimate of the cost. Later, Stywall returned to pick up her car, and Fink collected payment for the work. When Stywall started to drive away, however, the car bounced as if the shocks had not been replaced. A complaint to Precision's corporate office resulted in the discovery that in fact the work had not been done and Fink had kept the payment. He was charged with larceny against his employer. He argued that he had not committed this crime because the victim was Stywall, not Precision.* [State of North Carolina v. Fink, *798 S.E.2d 537 (N.C.App. 2017)*] *(See* Agent's Authority.*)*

1. Which agency principles support the charge against Fink? Explain.

2. Using the IDDR approach, determine whether Fink had an ethical duty to offer a defense to the crime with which he was charged. What does Fink's stated defense suggest about his ethics?

Critical Thinking and Writing Assignments

27–11. Critical Legal Thinking. What policy is served by the law that employers do not own the copyrights for works created by independent contractors (unless there is a written "work for hire" agreement)? (See *Agency Law*.)

27–12. Time-Limited Group Assignment—Liability for Independent Contractor's Torts. Dean Brothers Corp. owns and operates a steel-drum manufacturing plant. Lowell Wyden, the plant superintendent, hired Best Security Patrol, Inc. (BSP), a security company, to guard the property and "deter thieves and vandals." Some BSP security guards, as Wyden knew, carried firearms. Pete Sidell, a BSP security guard, was not certified as an armed guard but nevertheless took his gun to work. While working at the Dean plant on October 31, 2014, Sidell fired his gun at Tyrone Gaines, in the belief that Gaines was an intruder. The bullet struck and killed Gaines. Gaines's mother filed a lawsuit claiming that her son's death was the result of BSP's negligence, for which Dean was responsible. (See *Liability in Agency Relationships*.)

1. The first group will determine what the plaintiff's best argument is to establish that Dean is responsible for BSP's actions.

2. The second group will discuss Dean's best defense and formulate arguments in support of it.

3. The third group will consider slightly different facts. Suppose that Dean Brothers had an express policy that prohibited all security guards from carrying firearms on its property, which Wyden had conveyed to BSP. Despite knowing about this policy, Sidell had brought his weapon to work, and then fired it, killing Gaines. Could Dean be held responsible for negligence in that situation? Explain.

28 | Employment, Immigration, and Labor Law

Learning Objectives

The five Learning Objectives *below are designed to help improve your understanding. After reading this chapter, you should be able to answer the following questions:*

1. What is the employment-at-will doctrine?

2. Under the Family and Medical Leave Act, in what circumstances may an employee take family or medical leave?

3. What is the purpose of state workers' compensation laws?

4. What are the two most important federal statutes governing immigration and employment today?

5. What federal statute gave employees the right to engage in collective bargaining and to strike?

"The employer generally gets the employees he deserves."

Sir Walter Gilbey
1831–1914
(English merchant)

Until the early 1900s, most employer-employee relationships were governed by the common law. Even today, private employers have considerable freedom to hire and fire workers under the common law. (This is one reason that employers generally get the employees they deserve, as the chapter-opening quotation observed.)

Numerous statutes and administrative agency regulations now govern the workplace, however. Thus, to a large extent, statutory law has displaced common law doctrines. Note that the distinction made under agency law between employee status and independent-contractor status is important here. The employment laws that will be discussed apply only to the employer-employee relationship. They do not apply to independent contractors.

Suppose that Randall works as an activities director for Valley Manor, a retirement community that offers several independent- and assisted-living options. As director, Randall normally spends his days at the Manor, where he hires and supervises other employees. One day, though, when another employee calls in sick, Randall accompanies residents on an excursion to a local art museum.

During the trip, Randall falls down some cement stairs and breaks his pelvis. He is taken by ambulance to a hospital, where he is told that he will need surgery and likely have a long recovery time. Does Randall qualify for workers' compensation coverage, or did this injury occur outside the scope of his employment? What about the time he will need to take off from work—is Randall entitled to take unpaid medical leave under federal law? If he takes unpaid leave, can he return to his original position afterward? You will learn about these and other important employment-related issues in this chapter.

28–1 Employment at Will

Employment relationships have traditionally been governed by the common law doctrine of **employment at will.** Under this doctrine, either party may terminate the employment relationship at any time and for any reason, unless doing so would violate an employee's statutory or contractual rights.

Today, the majority of U.S. workers continue to have the legal status of "employees at will." In other words, this common law doctrine is still in widespread use. Only one state (Montana) does not apply it. Nonetheless, federal and state statutes governing employment relationships prevent the doctrine from being applied in a number of circumstances, and the courts have created several exceptions.

28–1a Exceptions to the Employment-at-Will Doctrine

Because of the sometimes harsh effects of the employment-at-will doctrine for employees, the courts have carved out various exceptions to it. These exceptions are based on contract theory, tort theory, and public policy.

Exceptions Based on Contract Theory Some courts have held that an *implied* employment contract exists between an employer and an employee. If an employee is fired outside the terms of the implied contract, he or she may succeed in an action for breach of contract even though no written employment contract exists. **Example 28.1** Innova Enterprise's employment manual and personnel bulletin both state that, as a matter of policy, workers will be dismissed only for good cause. If the language is clear so that an employee reasonably expects Innova to follow this policy, a court may find that there is an implied contract based on the terms stated in the manual and bulletin. ▪ Generally, the employee's reasonable expectations are the key to whether an employment manual creates an implied contractual obligation.

An employer's oral promises to employees regarding discharge policy may also be considered part of an implied contract. If the employer fires a worker in a manner contrary to what was promised, a court may hold that the employer has violated the implied contract and is liable for damages. Most state courts will judge a claim of breach of an implied employment contract by traditional contract standards.

Exceptions Based on Tort Theory In a few situations, the discharge of an employee may give rise to an action for wrongful discharge under tort theories. Abusive discharge procedures may result in a suit for intentional infliction of emotional distress or defamation.

In addition, some courts have permitted workers to sue their employers under the tort theory of fraud. **Example 28.2** Goldfinch, Inc., induces Jarvis to leave a lucrative job and move to another state by offering "a long-term job with a thriving business." In fact, Goldfinch not only is having significant financial problems but also is planning a merger that will result in the elimination of the position offered to Jarvis. If Jarvis takes the job in reliance on Goldfinch's representations and is fired shortly thereafter, she may be able to bring an action against the employer for fraud. ▪

Tulenkov/Shutterstock.com

Why are there some exceptions to the employment-at-will doctrine?

Exceptions Based on Public Policy The most common exception to the employment-at-will doctrine is made on the basis that the employer's reason for firing the worker violates a fundamental public policy of the jurisdiction. Generally, the public policy involved must be expressed clearly in the jurisdiction's statutory law.

The public-policy exception may also apply to an employee who is discharged for **whistleblowing**—that is, telling government authorities, upper-level managers, or the media

Employment at Will A common law doctrine under which either party may terminate an employment relationship at any time for any reason, unless it would violate a contract or statute.

Learning Objective 1
What is the employment-at-will doctrine?

Whistleblowing An employee's disclosure to government authorities, upper-level managers, or the media that the employer is engaged in unsafe or illegal activities.

that an employer is engaged in some unsafe or illegal activity. Normally, however, whistleblowers seek protection from retaliatory discharge under federal and state statutory laws, such as the Whistleblower Protection Act.[1]

Once an employee establishes a claim under the Whistleblower Protection Act, that statute is the employee's exclusive remedy. **Case Example 28.3** Dale Yurk was employed at Application Software Technology (AST) Corp. He discovered that AST was planning to reuse and resell software that it had developed for the city of Detroit. Yurk contacted his superiors—including the company's chief executive officer—and told them that he believed the resale infringed on the city's intellectual property rights. Shortly afterward, AST terminated Yurk's employment. Yurk sued AST, alleging that the company had violated both the Whistleblower Protection Act and public policy. A federal district court held that Yurk had stated a claim under the Whistleblower Protection Act and therefore dismissed the public policy claim.[2]

The issue in the following case was whether the public-policy exception to the employment-at-will doctrine could be applied to support the discharge of an employee who brought a handgun to work but left it locked in his vehicle—in plain sight.

---

1. 5 U.S.C. Section 1201.
2. *Yurk v. Application Software Technology Corp.*, ___ F.Supp.3d ___, 2017 WL 661014 (E.D.Mich. 2017).

■ Case 28.1

Caterpillar, Inc. v. Sudlow

Court of Appeals of Indiana, 52 N.E.3d 19 (2016).

Background and Facts The firearms policy at a Caterpillar, Inc., facility in Indiana allowed employees who were legally permitted to possess firearms to store the weapons in their vehicles "in line with state law." The state firearms statute required firearms stored in vehicles to be locked in a trunk, kept in the glove compartment, or otherwise placed out of sight.

William Sudlow, an employee at Caterpillar, drove to work one day with a loaded Ruger .357 Magnum handgun—for which he had a permit—stuffed between the center console and the driver's seat. Sudlow left the gun there when he parked and entered the building to begin his workday. Another Caterpillar employee was walking through the parking lot, noticed the handgun in Sudlow's vehicle, and reported it to the head of security.

Two days later, Sudlow was fired for violating the company's firearms policy. The same day, Caterpillar posted a new firearms policy that explicitly stated that firearms in employees' vehicles must be kept "secured and out of sight." Sudlow filed a complaint in an Indiana state court against Caterpillar, alleging *wrongful discharge*. The trial court found in Sudlow's favor, and a jury awarded him $85,000 in damages. Caterpillar appealed, agruing that the public-policy exception did not apply to Sudlow's firing.

In the Words of the Court
BAKER, Judge.

* * * *

Here, Caterpillar's Firearms Policy did not prohibit conduct that is protected by the [Indiana's] Firearms Statute. * * * Indeed, * * * Caterpillar could have enacted a more restrictive policy * * * but it chose not to do so. It is readily apparent that neither the Firearms Policy nor Caterpillar's interpretation thereof violated the Firearms Statute. *As a cause of action under the Firearms Statute is authorized only when an employer violates the statute, Sudlow has no right to recover on this basis.* [Emphasis added.]

* * * *

If Sudlow does not have a cause of action under the Firearms Statute, his only recourse would be something akin to a wrongful termination claim. It is undisputed that he was an at-will employee, meaning that his employment could have been terminated by either party at will, with or without a reason. There are three exceptions to the employment-at-will doctrine, but the parties discuss only the public policy exception: we have recognized a public policy exception to the employment-at-will doctrine if a clear statutory expression of a right or duty is contravened [violated].

The Firearms Statute is the best expression of Indiana's public policy regarding the right to transport and store firearms at work. And while this statute does confer a right to store a weapon in a trunk, glove compartment, or out of sight in a locked vehicle, it simply does not confer a right to store a weapon in a vehicle in plain sight. It is apparent, therefore, that in this case, *there was no contravention [violation] of a clear statutory expression of a right.* As a result, the public policy exception to the employment-at-will doctrine does not apply [to Sudlow's claim of wrongful discharge], and Sudlow is not entitled to relief under the common law. [Emphasis added.]

Decision and Remedy The state appellate court found in favor of Caterpillar and reversed and remanded the case to the trial court. Caterpillar had not violated a "clear statutory expression of a right," because Indiana's firearms statute did not grant a right to store a gun in a vehicle in plain sight.

Critical Thinking

• **Ethical** *Is the employment-at-will doctrine fair to employees? Why or why not?*

28–1b Wrongful Discharge

Whenever an employer discharges an employee in violation of an employment contract or a statute protecting employees, the employee may bring an action for **wrongful discharge.** For instance, an employee who is terminated in retaliation for some protected activity, such as whistleblowing or participating in an employment-discrimination investigation, can sue for wrongful discharge.

Even if an employer's actions do not violate any provisions in an employment contract or a statute, the employer may still be subject to liability. An employee can sue for wrongful discharge under a common law doctrine such as an agency or tort theory. For instance, if while firing an employee, an employer publicly discloses private facts about that employee's sex life to her co-workers, the employee could claim wrongful discharge based on invasion of privacy. Similarly, if a salesperson is fired because she refuses to participate in falsifying consumers' credit applications as instructed by her employer, she can sue for wrongful discharge as a matter of public policy.[3]

Wrongful Discharge An employer's termination of an employee's employment in violation of the law or an employment contract.

28–2 Wages, Hours, and Leave

In the 1930s, Congress enacted several laws regulating the wages and working hours of employees.

1. The Davis-Bacon Act[4] requires contractors and subcontractors working on federal government construction projects to pay "prevailing wages" to their employees.

2. The Walsh-Healey Act[5] applies to U.S. government contracts. It requires that a minimum wage, as well as overtime pay at 1.5 times regular pay rates, be paid to employees of manufacturers or suppliers entering into contracts with agencies of the federal government.

3. The Fair Labor Standards Act (FLSA)[6] extended wage-hour requirements to cover all employers engaged in interstate commerce or in producing goods for interstate commerce. Certain other types of businesses are included as well. The FLSA, as amended, provides the most comprehensive federal regulation of wages and hours today.

Know This

In today's business world, an employment contract may be established or modified via e-mail exchanges.

28–2a Child Labor

The FLSA prohibits oppressive child labor. Restrictions on child labor differ by age group. Children under fourteen years of age are allowed to do certain types of work. They can deliver newspapers, work for their parents, and be employed in entertainment and (with some exceptions) agriculture. Children aged fourteen and fifteen are allowed to work, but not in hazardous occupations. There are also numerous restrictions on how many hours per day and per week children can work.

---

3. See *Anderson v. Reeds Jewelers, Inc.,* ___ F.Supp.3d ___, 2017 WL 1987249 (E.D.Va. 2017).
4. 40 U.S.C. Sections 276a–276a-5.
5. 41 U.S.C. Sections 35–45.
6. 29 U.S.C. Sections 201–260.

Minimum Wage The lowest wage, either by government regulation or by union contract, that an employer may pay an hourly worker.

Working times and hours are not restricted for persons between the ages of sixteen and eighteen, but they cannot be employed in hazardous jobs or in jobs detrimental to their health and well-being. None of these restrictions apply to individuals over the age of eighteen.

28–2b Minimum Wage Requirement

The FLSA provides that a **minimum wage** of $7.25 per hour must be paid to covered, nonexempt employees. More than half of the states (and some cities) also have minimum wage laws. When the state (or city) minimum wage is greater than the federal minimum wage, the employee is entitled to the higher wage.

Example 28.4 The Oakland Raiders paid $1.25 million to settle wage claims made by the team's cheerleading squad (the Raiderettes) filed as a class-action lawsuit. The cheerleaders had complained that they were not being paid for the hours that they spent attending other events and performing other tasks required of them by contract. After the time spent performing these other tasks was factored in, the cheerleaders were receiving wages well below California's minimum wage, persuading the Raiders to settle the dispute. ■

Why did the Oakland Raiders cheerleaders file a class-action lawsuit?

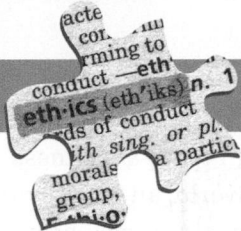

Ethical Issue

Are employees entitled to receive wages for all the time they spend at work, including times when they are taking a personal break? For some employees, "punching a time clock" means accounting for all of the time that they are not working. These employees must "punch in" when they arrive and "punch out" when they leave for the day, of course, but they also must clock out when they take personal breaks, including bathroom, coffee, and smoking breaks.

The Fair Labor Standards Act does not require that an employer offer personal breaks to its employees. If an employer does offer them, though, employees must be compensated during those breaks. Otherwise, the employer may effectively be in violation of federal minimum wage laws. The issue of unpaid bathroom breaks came to the fore when the U.S. Department of Labor (DOL) filed a lawsuit against American Future Systems, Inc. (doing business as Progressive Business Publications). The DOL alleged that American Future Systems had created a compensation system in which none of its six thousand employees were compensated for bathroom breaks. The DOL argued that under federal regulations implementing the FLSA, all workday breaks of twenty minutes or less are compensable time.[7] A federal district court agreed. Because the employees had not been paid for their break time, the court ordered the company to pay past and current employees nearly $2 million in unpaid wages. A federal appellate court affirmed the decision.[8]

> "By working faithfully eight hours a day, you may eventually get to be a boss and work twelve hours a day."
>
> **Robert Frost**
> 1875–1963
> (American poet)

Overtime Provisions and Exemptions Under the FLSA, employees who work more than forty hours per week normally must be paid 1.5 times their regular pay for all hours over forty. The FLSA overtime provisions apply only after an employee has worked more than forty hours per *week*. Thus, employees who work for ten hours a day, four days per week, are not entitled to overtime pay, because they do not work more than forty hours per week. (Smartphones and similar technologies have raised new issues concerning overtime wages, as discussed in this chapter's *Beyond Our Borders* feature.)

---

7. 29 C.F.R. Section 785.18.

8. *Secretary United States Department of Labor v. American Future Systems, Inc.*, 873 F.3d 420 (3d Cir. 2017).

Brazil Requires Employers to Pay Overtime for Use of Smartphones after Work Hours

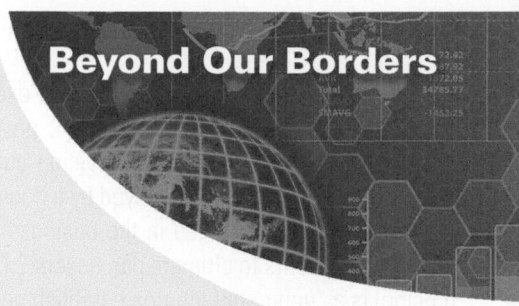

Beyond Our Borders

Workers in the United States are increasingly arguing that they should receive overtime pay for the time they spend staying connected to work through their iPads, smartphones, or other electronic devices. Indeed, many employers require their employees to carry a mobile device to keep in contact.

Checking e-mail, responding to text messages, tweeting, and using LinkedIn or other employment-related apps can be considered work. If employees who are not exempt under the overtime regulations are required to use mobile devices after office hours, the workers may have a valid claim

to overtime wages. The FLSA is not clear about what constitutes work, however, so workers have difficulty showing they are entitled to overtime wages.

In Brazil, though, workers who answer work e-mails on their smartphones or other electronic devices after work are entitled to receive overtime wages. E-mail from an employer is considered the equivalent of orders given directly to an employee, so it constitutes work. A few other nations also require payment to workers for staying connected through smartphones and other devices after hours. France has even gone one step further and banned employers

from sending e-mail and other electronic communications to their employees' smartphones and tablets after 6:00 P.M.

Critical Thinking

What are the pros and cons of paying overtime wages to workers who check e-mail and perform other work-related tasks electronically after hours?

Certain employees are exempt from the FLSA's overtime provisions. These employees generally include executive, administrative, and professional employees, as well as outside salespersons and employees who create computer code. Executive and administrative employees are those whose primary duty is management and who exercise discretion and independent judgment.

Employers are not required to pay overtime wages to exempt employees. Regulations also provide that employers are not required to pay overtime to workers who make more than a specified amount. (Although the Department of Labor raised the threshold amount to $50,440 in 2016, an injunction has kept it from taking effect.) An employer can voluntarily pay overtime to ineligible employees but cannot waive or reduce the overtime requirements of the FLSA.

The question in the following case was whether an auto dealer's service advisors fit within the FLSA overtime-pay exemption.

■ Case 28.2

Encino Motorcars, LLC v. Navarro

Supreme Court of the United States, __ U.S. __, 138 S.Ct. 1134, 200 L.Ed.2d 433 (2018).

Background and Facts Encino Motorcars, LLC, owned a Mercedes-Benz dealership in California. Encino employed service advisors whose duties included listening to customer concerns about their vehicles, suggesting repair and maintenance services, and selling new accessories or parts. They also record service orders, follow up with customers as the services are performed, and explain all the work performed.

Some of Encino's service advisors, including Hector Navarro, filed a suit against Encino in a federal district court, alleging that

the dealership had violated the Fair Labor Standards Act (FLSA) by failing to pay them overtime. Encino argued that the FLSA's exemption from the overtime-pay requirement applied to Navarro and its other service advisors. The court agreed and dismissed the complaint. The U.S. Court of Appeals for the Ninth Circuit reversed the dismissal. Encino appealed to the United States Supreme Court.

In the Words of the Court

Justice *THOMAS* delivered the opinion of the Court.

(Continues)

* * * *

The FLSA [Fair Labor Standards Act] exempts from its overtime-pay requirement "any salesman, partsman, or mechanic primarily engaged in selling or servicing automobiles, trucks, or farm implements, if he is employed by a nonmanufacturing establishment primarily engaged in the business of selling such vehicles or implements to ultimate purchasers." The parties agree that [Encino] is a "nonmanufacturing establishment primarily engaged in the business of selling [automobiles] to ultimate purchasers." The parties also agree that a service advisor is not a "partsman" or "mechanic," and that a service advisor is not "primarily engaged * * * in selling automobiles." The question, then, is whether service advisors are "salesmen * * * primarily engaged in * * * servicing automobiles." We conclude that they are.

* * * *

A service advisor is obviously a "salesman." The term "salesman" is not defined in the statute, so we give the term its ordinary meaning. *The ordinary meaning of "salesman" is someone who sells goods or services. Service advisors do precisely that. * * * Service advisors sell customers services for their vehicles.* [Emphasis added.]

* * * *

Service advisors are also "primarily engaged in * * * servicing automobiles." The word "servicing" in this context can mean either the action of maintaining or repairing a motor vehicle, or the action of providing a service. Service advisors satisfy both definitions. Service advisors are integral to the servicing process. * * * If you ask the average customer who services his car, the primary, and perhaps only, person he is likely to identify is his service advisor.

True, service advisors do not spend most of their time physically repairing automobiles. But the statutory language is not so constrained. All agree that partsmen, for example, are "primarily engaged in * * * servicing automobiles." But partsmen, like service advisors, do not spend most of their time under the hood. Instead, they obtain the vehicle parts * * * and provide those parts to the mechanics. In other words, the phrase "primarily engaged in * * * servicing automobiles" must include some individuals who do not physically repair automobiles themselves but who are integrally involved in the servicing process. That description applies to partsmen and service advisors alike.

Decision and Remedy The United States Supreme Court reversed the federal appellate court's decision and remanded the case. Navarro and the other service advisors were exempt from the overtime-pay requirement of the FLSA and thus not entitled to overtime pay.

Critical Thinking

• **Legal Environment** *The salesmen, mechanics, and partsmen identified in the FLSA exemption work irregular hours, sometimes away from their principal work site. Service advisors typically work ordinary, fixed schedules on-site. Should the Court have considered these attributes in making its decision in the* Encino *case? Discuss.*

• **What If the Facts Were Different?** *Suppose that the FLSA exemption covered "any salesman or mechanic primarily engaged in selling or servicing automobiles" but not "any partsman." Would the result have been different? Explain.*

> "All I've ever wanted was an honest week's pay for an honest day's work."
>
> **Steve Martin**
> 1945–present
> (American actor and comedian)

Interaction of State and Federal Wage and Overtime Laws Note that state legislation may include rules that impact federal wage and overtime laws. For instance, if a state requires employers to give employees one day off per week, an employee who works that day may be entitled to overtime wages.

Case Example 28.5 Christopher Mendoza and Meagan Gordon were Nordstrom employees at different locations in California. Nordstrom had asked both Mendoza and Gordon to fill in for other employees. As a result, both had worked more than six consecutive days without receiving a day off. California state law prohibits employers from causing employees "to work more than six days in seven." The employees filed suit against Nordstrom, Inc., and the case ultimately came before the California Supreme Court.

At issue was whether the law applies on a calendar basis, with each workweek considered a fixed unit, or on a rolling basis. If the rolling basis was used, as Nordstrom argued that it should be, employees could work more than six consecutive days if on average they had one day off per seven. The state's highest court held that Nordstrom had violated California's law. Employees are entitled to one day off each workweek, not one day in seven on a rolling basis. Employees could choose not to take the seventh day off (as they are entitled to do), but employers could not force them to do so, the court said.[9]

---

9. *Mendoza v. Nordstrom, Inc.*, 2 Cal.5th 1074, 393 P.3d 375, 216 Cal.Rptr.3d 889 (2017).

28–2c Family and Medical Leave

The Family and Medical Leave Act (FMLA)[10] allows employees to take time off from work for family or medical reasons or in certain situations that arise from military service. A majority of the states have similar legislation. The FMLA does not supersede any state or local law that provides more generous protection.

Coverage and Applicability The FMLA requires employers who have fifty or more employees to provide employees with up to twelve weeks of unpaid family or medical leave during any twelve-month period. The FMLA expressly covers private and public (government) employees who have worked for their employers for at least a year.

An eligible employee may take up to *twelve weeks of leave* within a twelve-month period for any of the following reasons:

1. To care for a newborn baby within one year of birth.
2. To care for an adopted or foster child within one year of the time the child is placed with the employee.
3. To care for the employee's spouse, child, or parent who has a serious health condition.
4. If the employee suffers from a serious health condition and is unable to perform the essential functions of her or his job.
5. For any qualifying exigency (nonmedical emergency) arising out of the fact that the employee's spouse, son, daughter, or parent is a covered military member on active duty.[11] For instance, an employee can take leave to arrange for child care or to deal with financial or legal matters when a spouse is being deployed overseas.

In addition, an employee may take up to *twenty-six weeks of military caregiver leave* within a twelve-month period to care for a family member with a serious injury or illness incurred as a result of military duty.[12]

Under what circumstances can this wife take family leave to care for her sick husband?

Benefits and Protections When an employee takes FMLA leave, the employer must continue the worker's health-care coverage on the same terms as if the employee had continued to work. On returning from FMLA leave, most employees must be restored to their original positions or to comparable positions (with nearly equivalent pay and benefits, for instance).

An important exception allows the employer to avoid reinstating a *key employee*—defined as an employee whose pay falls within the top 10 percent of the firm's local workforce—if doing so would cause "substantial and grievous economic injury" to the employer. The employer must also notify the employee of its intention to deny reinstatement.

Violations An employer that violates the FMLA can be required to provide various remedies, including the following:

1. Damages to compensate an employee for lost benefits, denied compensation, and actual monetary losses (such as the cost of providing for care of the family member) up to an amount equivalent to the employee's wages for twelve weeks (twenty-six weeks for military caregiver leave).
2. Job reinstatement.
3. Promotion, if a promotion has been denied.

A successful plaintiff is also entitled to court costs and attorneys' fees. In addition, if the plaintiff shows that the employer acted in bad faith, the plaintiff can receive double the amount of damages awarded by a judge or jury. Supervisors can also be held personally liable, as employers, for violations of the act.

10. 29 U.S.C. Sections 2601, 2611–2619, 2651–2654.
11. 29 C.F.R. Section 825.126.
12. 29 C.F.R. Section 825.200.

Learning Objective 2

Under the Family and Medical Leave Act, in what circumstances may an employee take family or medical leave?

Employers generally are required to notify employees when an absence will be counted against leave authorized under the act. If an employer fails to provide such notice, and the employee suffers an injury as a result, the employer may be sanctioned.

28-3 Health, Safety, Income Security, and Privacy

Under the common law, employees who were injured on the job had to file lawsuits against their employers to obtain recovery. Today, numerous state and federal statutes protect employees and their families from the risk of accidental injury, disease, or death resulting from employment. In addition, the government protects employees' income through programs such as Social Security and unemployment insurance, and protects employees' privacy rights to a certain extent.

28-3a The Occupational Safety and Health Act

At the federal level, the primary legislation protecting employees' health and safety is the Occupational Safety and Health Act,[13] which is administered by the Occupational Safety and Health Administration (OSHA). The act imposes on employers a general duty to keep workplaces safe. To this end, OSHA has established specific safety standards for various industries that employers must follow. For instance, OSHA regulations require the use of safety guards on certain mechanical equipment and set maximum levels of exposure to substances in the workplace that may be harmful to a worker's health.

Case Example 28.6 James Bobo worked at the Tennessee Valley Authority (TVA) nuclear power plant for more than twenty-two years. He eventually contracted asbestos-induced lung cancer. After his death, his wife, Barbara, was diagnosed with malignant mesothelioma. She sued TVA in federal court, alleging that its negligence had resulted in her being exposed to "take-home" asbestos when she washed her husband's work clothes over the years. Although she died prior to trial, her children continued the suit.

At trial, the plaintiffs proved that TVA knew about OSHA regulations—adopted during the time of James's employment—to protect not only workers but also their families. These rules were aimed at preventing asbestos fibers from clinging to an employee's street clothes, skin, or hair and being taken off TVA property. The court held in favor of the plaintiffs and awarded $3.3 million. TVA appealed. A federal appellate court affirmed that TVA was liable for failing to follow OSHA regulations but remanded the case for a recalculation of the damages awarded.[14] ■

Preventing workplace accidents and employee injuries is the goal of the Occupational Safety and Health Act. What are some employer requirements under the act?

Notices, Records, and Reports The act requires that employers post certain notices in the workplace, maintain specific records, and submit reports. Employers with eleven or more employees are required to keep records of occupational injuries and illnesses. Each record must be made available for inspection when requested by an OSHA compliance officer. Some employers are required to electronically post their workplace injury and illness records from the prior year on OSHA's website.

Whenever a work-related fatality or serious injury requiring hospitalization occurs, employers must report directly to OSHA. The employer must notify OSHA within eight hours if an employee dies and submit a report within twenty-four hours for any inpatient hospitalization, amputation, or loss of an eye. A company that fails to do so will be fined.

Inspections and Employee Complaints OSHA compliance officers may enter and inspect the facilities of any establishment

---

13. 29 U.S.C. Sections 553, 651–678.
14. *Bobo v. Tennessee Valley Authority*, 855 F.3d 1294 (11th Cir. 2017).

covered by the Occupational Safety and Health Act. Employees may also file complaints of violations and cannot be fired by their employers for doing so. Under the act, an employer cannot discharge an employee who files a complaint or who, in good faith, refuses to work in a high-risk area if bodily harm or death might result.

28–3b State Workers' Compensation Laws

State **workers' compensation laws** establish an administrative procedure for compensating workers injured on the job. Instead of suing, an injured worker files a claim with the administrative agency or board that administers local workers' compensation claims.

All states require employers to provide workers' compensation insurance, but the specific rules vary by state. Typically, employers pay into a state fund for workers' compensation or, alternatively, purchase insurance from a private insurer. Most states also allow certain employers to be *self-insured*—that is, employers that show an ability to pay claims do not need to buy insurance.

No state covers all employees under its workers' compensation statute. Frequently, domestic workers, agricultural workers, temporary employees, and employees of common carriers (companies that provide transportation services to the public) are excluded. Minors are covered.

Requirements for Receiving Workers' Compensation In general, only two requirements must be met for an employee to receive benefits under a state workers' compensation law:

1. The existence of an employment relationship.

2. *An accidental injury that occurred on the job or in the course of employment,* regardless of fault. (An injury that occurs while an employee is commuting to or from work usually is not considered to have occurred on the job or in the course of employment and hence is not covered.) This chapter's *Business Law Analysis* feature illustrates these requirements.

An injured employee must notify her or his employer promptly (usually within thirty days of the accident). Generally, an employee must also file a workers' compensation claim with the appropriate state agency or board within a certain period (sixty days to two years) from the time the injury is first noticed, rather than from the time of the accident.

> **Workers' Compensation Laws**
> State statutes that establish an administrative process for compensating workers for injuries that arise in the course of their employment, regardless of fault.

> **Learning Objective 3**
> What is the purpose of state workers' compensation laws?

Workers' Compensation Claims

Business Law Analysis

As a safety measure, Dynea USA, Inc., required an employee, Tony Schrader, to wear steel-toed boots. One of the boots caused a sore on Schrader's leg. The skin over the sore broke, and within a week, Schrader was hospitalized with a methicillin-resistant staphylococcus aureus (MRSA) infection. He filed a workers' compensation claim. Dynea argued that the MRSA bacteria that caused the infection had been on Schrader's skin before he came to work. Does Schrader's claim meet the requirements to recover workers' compensation benefits?

Analysis: To recover benefits under state workers' compensation laws, an employee must show that an injury (1) was accidental and (2) occurred on the job or in the course of employment. Fault is not an issue. The employee must file a claim with the state agency or board that administers local workers' compensation claims, which Schrader did. The issue here is whether the injury occurred on the job or in the course of employment.

Result and Reasoning: Schrader is entitled to workers' compensation benefits. Dynea required its employees to wear the boots that caused the sore on Schrader's leg, which subsequently became infected with MRSA. Even if the bacteria had been on Schrader's skin before he came to work, it was the rubbing of the boot at work that caused the sore through which the bacteria entered his body. Therefore, the second requirement for the recovery of workers' compensation benefits—that the injury occurred on the job—is fulfilled.

Workers' Compensation versus Litigation An employee's acceptance of workers' compensation benefits bars the employee from suing for injuries caused by the employer's negligence. By barring lawsuits for negligence, workers' compensation laws also prevent employers from raising common law defenses to negligence, such as contributory negligence and assumption of risk. A worker may sue an employer who has *intentionally* injured the worker, however.

28–3c Income Security

Federal and state governments participate in insurance programs designed to protect employees and their families by covering the financial impact of retirement, disability, death, hospitalization, and unemployment. The key federal law on this subject is the Social Security Act.[15]

Know This

Social Security covers almost all jobs in the United States. Nine out of ten workers "contribute" to this protection for themselves and their families.

Social Security The Social Security Act provides for old-age (retirement), survivors', and disability insurance. Hence, the act is often referred to as OASDI. Both employers and employees must "contribute" under the Federal Insurance Contributions Act (FICA)[16] to help pay for Social Security retirement benefits. Retired workers are then eligible to receive monthly payments from the Social Security Administration, which administers the Social Security Act. Social Security benefits are fixed by statute but increase automatically with increases in the cost of living.

Medicare Medicare is a federal government health-insurance program that is administered by the Social Security Administration for people sixty-five years of age and older and for some under the age of sixty-five who are disabled. Medicare originally had two parts, one pertaining to hospital costs and the other to nonhospital medical costs, such as visits to physicians' offices. It now offers additional coverage options and a prescription-drug plan. People who have Medicare hospital insurance can also obtain additional federal medical insurance by paying small monthly premiums, which increase as the cost of medical care increases.

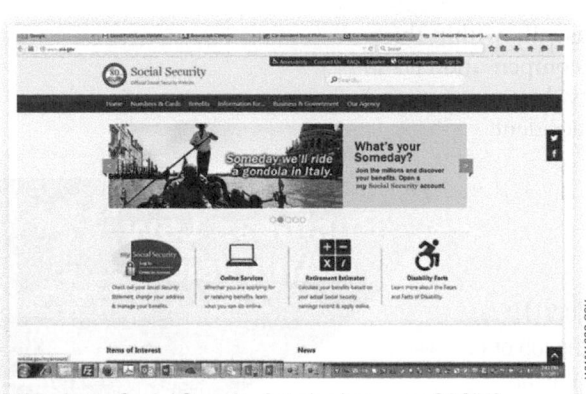

Why is the Social Security Act also known as OASDI?

www.ssa.gov

Tax Contributions Under FICA, both employers and employees contribute to Social Security and Medicare, although the contributions are determined differently. The employer withholds the employee's FICA contributions from the employee's wages and ordinarily matches the contributions.

For Social Security, the basis for the contributions is the employee's annual wage base—the maximum amount of the employee's wages that is subject to the tax. As of 2018, that amount was $128,400, and the tax rate was 12.4 percent.

The Medicare tax rate is 2.9 percent. Unlike Social Security, Medicare has no cap on the amount of wages subject to the tax. So even if an employee's salary is well above the cap for Social Security, he or she will still owe Medicare tax on the total earned income.

For Social Security and Medicare together, typically the employer and the employee each pay 7.65 percent—6.2 percent (half of 12.4 percent) for Social Security plus 1.45 percent (half of 2.9 percent) for Medicare—up to the maximum wage base. Any earned income above that threshold is taxed at 2.9 percent for Medicare. Self-employed persons pay both the employer's and the employee's portions of the Social Security and Medicare taxes.

---

15. 42 U.S.C. Sections 301–1397e.
16. 26 U.S.C. Sections 3101–3125.

Additionally, under the Affordable Care Act, high-income earners are subject to an additional Medicare tax of 0.9 percent (for a total rate of 3.8 percent).

Private Retirement Plans The major federal act regulating employee retirement plans is the Employee Retirement Income Security Act (ERISA).[17] This act empowers the U.S. Department of Labor to enforce its provisions. ERISA does not require an employer to establish a pension plan. When a plan exists, however, ERISA specifies standards for its management, including establishing rules on how funds must be invested and records kept.

ERISA created the Pension Benefit Guaranty Corporation (PBGC), an independent federal agency, to provide timely and uninterrupted payment of voluntary private pension benefits. The pension plans pay annual insurance premiums (at set rates adjusted for inflation) to the PBGC, which then pays benefits to participants in the event that a plan is unable to do so.

A key provision of ERISA concerns vesting. **Vesting** gives an employee a legal right to receive pension benefits at some future date when he or she stops working. Before ERISA was enacted, some employees who had worked for companies for as long as thirty years received no pension benefits when their employment terminated because those benefits had not vested. Under ERISA, generally all employee contributions to pension plans vest immediately, and employee rights to employer contributions to a plan vest after five years of employment.

Vesting The creation of an absolute or unconditional right or power.

Unemployment Insurance The Federal Unemployment Tax Act (FUTA)[18] created a state-administered system that provides unemployment compensation to eligible individuals. Under this system, employers that fall under the provisions of the act to pay unemployment taxes at regular intervals. The proceeds from these taxes are then paid out to qualified unemployed workers.

To be eligible for unemployment compensation, a worker must be willing and able to work. Workers who have been fired for misconduct or who have voluntarily left their jobs are not eligible for benefits. Normally, workers must be actively seeking employment to continue receiving benefits.

Example 28.7 Martha works for Baily Snowboards in Vermont. One day at work, Martha receives a text from her son saying that he has been taken to the hospital. Martha rushes to the hospital and does not return to work for several days. Bailey hires someone else for Martha's position, and Martha files for unemployment benefits. Martha's claim will be denied because she left her job voluntarily and made no effort to maintain contact with her employer. ◼

COBRA The Consolidated Omnibus Budget Reconciliation Act (COBRA)[19] enables workers to continue, for a limited time, their health-care coverage after they are no longer eligible for their employers' group health-insurance plans. The workers—not the employers—pay the premiums for the continued coverage.

COBRA prohibits an employer from eliminating a worker's medical, optical, or dental insurance when the worker's employment is terminated or when a reduction in the worker's hours would affect coverage. Termination of employment may be voluntary or involuntary. Only workers fired for gross misconduct are excluded from protection.

Know This
If an employer does not pay unemployment taxes, a state government can place a lien (claim) on the business's property to secure the debt.

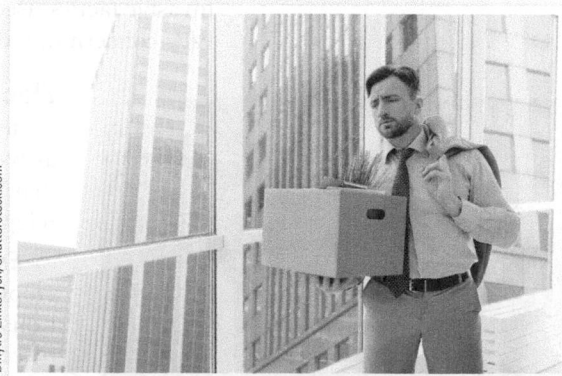

Dmytro Zinkevych/Shutterstock.com

How does the Federal Unemployment Tax Act benefit employees?

---

17. 29 U.S.C. Sections 1001 *et seq.*
18. 26 U.S.C. Sections 3301–3310.
19. 29 U.S.C. Sections 1161–1169.

Employers, with some exceptions, must inform an employee of COBRA's provisions when the employee faces termination or a reduction of hours that would affect his or her eligibility for coverage under the employer's health-insurance plan. An employer that does not comply with COBRA risks substantial penalties, such as a tax of up to 10 percent of the annual cost of the group plan or $500,000, whichever is less.

Employer-Sponsored Group Health Plans The Health Insurance Portability and Accountability Act (HIPAA)[20] contains provisions that affect employer-sponsored group health plans. HIPAA does not require employers to provide health insurance, but it does establish requirements for those that do. For instance, HIPAA restricts the manner in which covered employers collect, use, and disclose the health information of employees and their families. Employers must designate privacy officials, distribute privacy notices, and train employees to ensure that employees' health information is not disclosed to unauthorized parties.

Failure to comply with HIPAA regulations can result in civil penalties of up to $100 per person per violation (with a cap of $25,000 per year). The employer is also subject to criminal prosecution for certain types of HIPAA violations and can face up to $250,000 in criminal fines and imprisonment for up to ten years if convicted.

Affordable Care Act The Affordable Care Act[21] (ACA, commonly referred to as Obamacare) requires most employers with fifty or more full-time employees to offer health-insurance benefits. Under the act, any business offering health benefits to its employees, even if it is not legally required to do so, may be eligible for tax credits of up to 35 percent to offset the costs.

An employer who fails to provide health benefits as required under the statute can be fined up to $2,000 for each employee after the first thirty. (This is known as the 50/30 rule—employers with fifty employees must provide insurance, and those failing to do so will be fined for each employee after the first thirty.) An employer who offers a plan that costs an employee more than 9.5 percent of the employee's income may have to pay a penalty of $3,000 per insured worker.

28–3d Employee Privacy Rights

Concerns about the privacy rights of employees have arisen in response to the sometimes invasive tactics used by employers to monitor and screen workers. Perhaps the greatest privacy concern in today's employment arena has to do with electronic monitoring.

Can employees refuse to be video-monitored?

Electronic Monitoring More than half of employers engage in some form of surveillance of their employees. Many employers review employees' e-mail, as well as their social media posts and other Internet messages. Employers may also make video recordings of their employees at work, monitor their telephone conversations, and listen to their voice mail.

Employee Privacy Protection. Employees of private (nongovernment) employers have some privacy protection under tort law and state constitutions. In addition, state and federal statutes may limit an employer's conduct in certain respects. For instance, the Electronic Communications Privacy Act prohibits employers from intercepting an employee's personal electronic communications unless they are made on devices and systems furnished by the employer.

---

20. 29 U.S.C.A. Sections 1181 *et seq.*
21. Pub. L. No. 111–148, 124 Stat. 119, March 23, 2010, codified in various sections of 42 U.S.C.

Nonetheless, employers do have considerable leeway to monitor employees in the workplace. In addition, private employers generally are free to use filtering software to block access to certain websites, such as sites containing sexually explicit images. The First Amendment's protection of free speech prevents only *government employers* from restraining speech by blocking websites.

Reasonable Expectation of Privacy. When determining whether an employer is liable for violating an employee's privacy rights, the courts generally weigh the employer's interests against the employee's reasonable expectation of privacy.

Normally, if employees have been informed that their communications are being monitored, they cannot reasonably expect those interactions to be private. In addition, a court will typically hold that employees do not have a reasonable expectation of privacy when using a system (such as an e-mail system) provided by the employer.

If employees are *not* informed that certain communications are being monitored, however, the employer may be held liable for invading their privacy. Most employers that engage in electronic monitoring notify their employees about the monitoring. Nevertheless, notifying employees of a general policy may not sufficiently protect an employer who monitors forms of communications that the policy fails to mention. For instance, notifying employees that their e-mails and phone calls may be monitored does not necessarily protect an employer who also monitors social media posts or text messages.

For a discussion of how some employers are creating their own social media networks, see this chapter's *Adapting the Law to the Online Environment* feature.

> "We are rapidly entering the age of no privacy, where everyone is open to surveillance at all times; where there are no secrets from government."
>
> **William O. Douglas**
> 1898–1980
> (Associate justice of the United States Supreme Court, 1939–1975)

Adapting the Law to the Online Environment

Social Media in the Workplace Come of Age

What do corporate giant Dell, Inc., and relatively small Nikon Instruments have in common? They—and many other companies—have created internal social media networks using enterprise social networking software and systems, such as Igloo, Slack, Yammer, and Basecamp. A glance at the posts on these internal networks reveals that they are quite different from typical posts on Facebook, LinkedIn, and Twitter. Rather than being personal, the tone is businesslike, and the posts deal with workplace concerns such as how a team is solving a problem or how to sell a new product.

Benefits and Pitfalls of Internal Social Media Networks

Internal social media networks offer businesses several advantages. Perhaps the most important is that employees can obtain real-time information about important issues such as production glitches. They can also exchange tips about how to deal with problems, such as difficult customers. News about the company's new products or those of a competitor is available immediately. Furthermore, employees spend much less time sorting through e-mail. Rather than wasting their fellow employees' time by sending mass e-mailings, workers can post messages or collaborate on presentations via the company's internal network.

The downside is that these networks may become polluted with annoying "white noise." If employees start posting comments about what they ate for lunch, for instance, the system will lose much of its utility. Companies can prevent this from happening by establishing explicit guidelines on what can be posted.

Keeping the Data Safe

Another concern is how to keep data and corporate secrets safe. When a company sets up a social media network, it usually decides which employees can see which files and which employees will belong to each specific "social" group within the company. Often, the data created through a social media network are kept on the company's own servers in secure "clouds."

Critical Thinking

What problems might arise if data from an internal social media system are stored on third party servers?

Other Types of Monitoring In addition to monitoring their employees' activities electronically, employers also engage in other types of monitoring. These practices, which have included lie-detector tests and drug tests, have often been subject to challenge as violations of employee privacy rights.

Lie-Detector Tests. At one time, many employers required employees or job applicants to take polygraph examinations (lie-detector tests). Today, the Employee Polygraph Protection Act[22] generally prohibits employers from requiring or requesting that employees or job applicants take lie-detector tests. It also prevents employers from asking about the results of a polygraph or taking any negative employment action based on the results.

Certain employers are exempt from these prohibitions. Federal, state, and local government employers, as well as certain security service firms, may conduct polygraph tests. In addition, companies that manufacture and distribute controlled substances may perform lie-detector tests. Other employers may use polygraph tests when investigating losses attributable to theft, including embezzlement and the theft of trade secrets.

Does current federal law allow security service firms to use lie-detector tests?

Drug Testing. In the interests of public safety, many employers, including government employers, require their employees to submit to drug testing. Government (public) employers are constrained in drug testing by the Fourth Amendment to the U.S. Constitution, which prohibits unreasonable searches and seizures. Drug testing of public employees is allowed by statute for transportation workers. Courts normally uphold drug testing of certain employees when drug use in a particular job may threaten public safety. Also, when there is a reasonable basis for suspecting government employees of using drugs, courts often find that drug testing does not violate the Fourth Amendment.

The Fourth Amendment does not apply to drug testing conducted by private employers. Hence, the privacy rights and drug testing of private-sector employees is governed by state law, which varies widely. Many states have statutes that allow drug testing by private employers but place restrictions on when and how the testing may be performed. A collective bargaining agreement may also provide protection against drug testing (or authorize drug testing under certain conditions).

The permissibility of a private employee's drug test often hinges on whether the employer's testing was reasonable. Random drug tests and even "zero-tolerance" policies (which deny a "second chance" to employees who test positive for drugs) have been held to be reasonable.

28–4 Immigration Law

The United States did not have any laws restricting immigration until the late nineteenth century. Today, the most important laws governing immigration and employment are the Immigration Reform and Control Act[23] (IRCA) and the Immigration Act.[24]

Immigration law has become increasingly important in recent years. An estimated 12 million undocumented immigrants now live in the United States. Many of them came to find jobs. Because U.S. employers face serious penalties if they hire undocumented immigrants, businesspersons need to understand our immigration laws.

28–4a Immigration Reform and Control Act (IRCA)

When the IRCA was enacted in 1986, it provided amnesty to certain groups of illegal aliens living in the United States at the time. It also established a system that sanctions employers who

---

22. 29 U.S.C. Sections 2001 *et seq.*
23. 29 U.S.C. Section 1802.
24. This act amended various provisions of the Immigration and Nationality Act, 8 U.S.C. Sections 1101 *et seq.*

hire immigrants lacking work authorization. The IRCA makes it illegal to hire, recruit, or refer for a fee someone not authorized to work in this country. Through Immigration and Customs Enforcement (ICE) officers, the federal government conducts random compliance audits and engages in enforcement actions against employers who hire undocumented immigrants.

I-9 Employment Verification To comply with the IRCA, an employer must perform **I-9 verifications** for new hires, including those hired as "contractors" or "day workers" if they work under the employer's direct supervision. Form I-9, Employment Eligibility Verification, which is available from U.S. Citizenship and Immigration Services, must be completed *within three days* of a worker's commencement of employment. The three-day period is to allow the employer to check the form's accuracy and to review and verify documents establishing the prospective worker's identity and eligibility for employment in the United States.

Documentation Requirements The employer must declare, under penalty of perjury, that an employee produced documents establishing his or her identity and legal employability. A U.S. passport establishing the person's citizenship is acceptable documentation, as is a document authorizing a foreign citizen to work in the United States, such as a Permanent Resident Card (discussed shortly).

Most legal actions for violations of I-9 rules are brought against employees who provide false information or documentation. If an employee enters false information on an I-9 form or presents false documentation, the employer can fire the worker, who then may be subject to deportation. Nevertheless, employers must be honest when verifying an employee's documentation. If an employer "should have known" that the worker was unauthorized, the employer has violated the rules.

Enforcement U.S. Immigration and Customs Enforcement (ICE) is the largest investigative arm of the U.S. Department of Homeland Security. ICE has a general inspection program that conducts random compliance audits. Other audits may occur if the agency receives a written complaint alleging an employer's violations. Government inspections include a review of an employer's file of I-9 forms. The government does not need a subpoena or a warrant to conduct such an inspection.

If an investigation reveals a possible violation, ICE will bring an administrative action and issue a Notice of Intent to Fine, which sets out the charges against the employer. The employer has a right to a hearing on the enforcement action if a request is filed within thirty days. This hearing is conducted before an administrative law judge, and the employer has a right to counsel and to discovery. The typical defense in such actions is good faith or substantial compliance with the documentation provisions.

Penalties An employer who violates the law by hiring an unauthorized alien is subject to substantial penalties. The employer may be fined up to $2,200 for each unauthorized employee for a first offense, $5,000 per employee for a second offense, and up to $11,000 for subsequent offenses.

Employers who have engaged in a "pattern or practice of violations" are subject to criminal penalties, which include additional fines and imprisonment for up to ten years. A company may also be barred from future government contracts for violations. In determining the penalty, ICE considers the seriousness of the violation (such as intentional falsification of documents), the employer's past compliance, and whether the employer cooperated with authorities during the investigation.

28–4b The Immigration Act

Often, U.S. businesses find that they cannot hire enough domestic workers with specialized skills. For this reason, U.S. immigration laws have long made provisions for businesses to hire specially qualified foreign workers.

I-9 Verification The process of verifying the employment eligibility and identity of a new worker. It must be completed within three days after the worker commences employment.

Know This
If an employer had any reason to suspect that a worker's documents were forged or inaccurate at the time of hiring, the employer can be fined for violating the IRCA.

diego_cervo/Getty Images

What are the penalties for employing an unauthorized immigrant?

The Immigration Act placed caps on the number of visas (entry permits) that can be issued to immigrants each year, including employment-based visas. Employment-based visas may be classified as permanent (immigrant) or temporary (nonimmigrant). Employers who wish to hire workers with either type of visa must comply with detailed government regulations.[25]

I-551 Permanent Resident Card

I-551 Permanent Resident Card A company seeking to hire a noncitizen worker on a permanent basis may do so if the worker is self-authorized—that is, if the worker either is a lawful permanent resident or has a valid temporary Employment Authorization Document. A lawful permanent resident can prove his or her status to an employer by presenting an **I-551 Permanent Resident Card**, known as a "green card," or a properly stamped foreign passport.

Many immigrant workers are not already self-authorized, and an employer that wishes to hire them can attempt to obtain labor certification, or green cards, for them. A limited number of new green cards are issued each year. A green card can be obtained only for a person who is being hired for a permanent, full-time position. (A separate authorization system provides for the temporary entry and hiring of nonimmigrant visa workers.)

To gain authorization for hiring a foreign worker, an employer must show that no U.S. worker is qualified, willing, and able to take the job. The government has detailed regulations governing the advertising of positions as well as the certification process. Any U.S. applicants who meet the stated job qualifications must be interviewed for the position. The employer must also be able to show that the qualifications required for the job are a business necessity.

The H-1B Visa Program

The H-1B Visa Program A relatively common and sometimes controversial temporary visa program is the H-1B visa system. To obtain an H-1B visa, the potential employee must be qualified in a "specialty occupation," meaning that the individual has highly specialized knowledge and has attained a bachelor's or higher degree or its equivalent. Individuals with H-1B visas can stay in the United States for three to six years and can work only for the sponsoring employer.

The recipients of H1B visas include many high-tech workers. A maximum of sixty-five thousand H-1B visas are set aside each year for new immigrants. That limit is typically reached within the first few weeks of the year. Consequently, technology companies complain that Congress needs to expand the number of H-1B visas available in order to encourage the best and the brightest minds to work in the United States.

An employer who wishes to submit an H-1B application must first file a Labor Condition Application on a form known as ETA 9035. The employer must agree to provide a wage level at least equal to the wages offered to other individuals with similar experience and qualifications. The employer must also show that the hiring will not adversely affect other workers similarly employed. The employer is required to inform U.S. workers of the intent to hire a foreign worker by posting the form. The U.S. Department of Labor reviews the applications and may reject them for omissions or inaccuracies.

H-2, O, L, and E Visas

H-2, O, L, and E Visas Other specialty temporary visas are available for other categories of employees. H-2A visas provide for workers performing agricultural labor of a seasonal nature; H-2B visas are used for workers in nonagricultural positions. O visas provide entry for persons who have "extraordinary ability in the sciences, arts, education, business or athletics which has been demonstrated by sustained national or international acclaim." L visas allow a company's foreign managers or executives to work inside the United States. E visas permit the entry of certain foreign investors and entrepreneurs.

---

25. The most relevant regulations can be found at 20 C.F.R. Section 655 (for temporary employment) and 20 C.F.R. Section 656 (for permanent employment).

28–4c State Immigration Legislation

Until 2010, immigration and the treatment of illegal immigrants were governed exclusively by federal laws. Then Arizona enacted a law that required Arizona law enforcement officials to identify and charge immigrants in Arizona who were there illegally, potentially leading to the immigrants' deportation. Among other things, that law required immigrants to carry their papers at all times and allowed police to check a person's immigration status during any law enforcement action.

In *Arizona v. United States,*[26] the United States Supreme Court upheld the controversial "show-me-your-papers" provision that requires police to check the immigration status of persons stopped for another violation. All other provisions of Arizona's law were struck down because they were preempted by federal laws. The Supreme Court's decision does not prohibit states from enacting laws related to immigration, but it does set some limits.

28–5 Labor Law

In the 1930s, in addition to wage-hour laws, the government also enacted the first of several labor laws. These laws protect employees' rights to join labor unions, to bargain with management over the terms and conditions of employment, and to conduct strikes.

28–5a Federal Labor Laws

Federal labor laws governing union-employer relations have developed considerably since the first law was enacted in 1932. Initially, the laws were concerned with protecting the rights and interests of workers. Subsequent legislation placed some restraints on unions and granted rights to employers. We look next at four major federal statutes regulating union-employer relations.

Norris-LaGuardia Act In 1932, Congress protected peaceful strikes, picketing, and boycotts in the Norris-LaGuardia Act.[27] The statute restricted the power of federal courts to issue injunctions against unions engaged in peaceful strikes. In effect, this act established a national policy permitting employees to organize.

National Labor Relations Act One of the foremost statutes regulating labor is the National Labor Relations Act (NLRA), enacted in 1935.[28] This act established the rights of employees to engage in collective bargaining and to strike.

Unfair Labor Practices. The NLRA also specifically defined a number of employer practices as unfair to labor:

1. Interference with the efforts of employees to form, join, or assist labor organizations or to engage in concerted activities for mutual aid or protection.

2. An employer's domination of a labor organization or contribution of financial or other support to it.

3. Discrimination in the hiring of or awarding of tenure to employees based on union affiliation.

4. Discrimination against employees for filing charges under the act or giving testimony under the act.

5. Refusal to bargain collectively with the duly designated representative of the employees.

The National Labor Relations Board. The NLRA also created the National Labor Relations Board (NLRB) to oversee union elections and to prevent employers from engaging in unfair and illegal union activities and unfair labor practices.

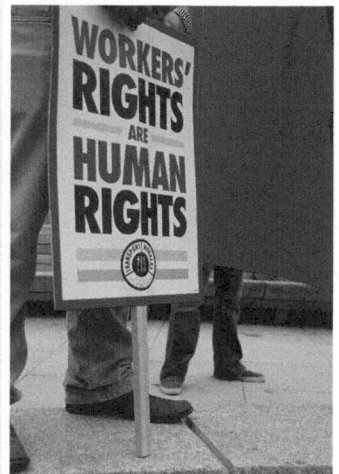

FireAtDusk/Getty Images

When were many labor union laws created?

Learning Objective 5

What federal statute gave employees the right to engage in collective bargaining and to strike?

---

26. 567 U.S. 387, 132 S.Ct. 2492, 183 L.Ed.2d 351 (2012).
27. 29 U.S.C. Sections 101–110, 113–115.
28. 20 U.S.C. Section 151.

The NLRB has the authority to investigate employees' charges of unfair labor practices and to file complaints against employers in response to these charges. When violations are found, the NLRB may issue a cease-and-desist order compelling the employer to stop engaging in the unfair practices. Cease-and-desist orders can be enforced by a federal appellate court if necessary. After the NLRB rules on claims of unfair labor practices, its decision may be appealed to a federal court.

Case Example 28.8 Roundy's, Inc., which operates a chain of stores in Wisconsin, became involved in a dispute with a local construction union. When union members started distributing "extremely unflattering" flyers outside the stores, Roundy's ejected them from the property. The NLRB filed a complaint against Roundy's for unfair labor practices. An administrative law judge ruled that Roundy's had violated the law by discriminating against the union, and a federal appellate court affirmed. It is an unfair labor practice for an employer to prohibit union members from distributing flyers outside a store when it allows nonunion members to do so.[29]

Good Faith Bargaining. Under the NLRA, employers and unions have a duty to bargain in good faith. Bargaining over certain subjects (such as wages, hours, and benefits) is mandatory, and a party's refusal to bargain over these subjects is an unfair labor practice that can be reported to the NLRB. An employer may be required to bargain with the union over the use of hidden video surveillance cameras, for instance.

Workers Protected by the NLRA. To be protected under the NLRA, an individual must be an *employee,* as that term is defined in the statute. Courts have long held that job applicants fall within the definition (otherwise, the NLRA's ban on discrimination in hiring would mean nothing). Additionally, individuals who are hired by a union to organize a company are to be considered employees of the company for NLRA purposes.

Even a temporary worker hired through an employment agency may qualify for protection under the NLRA. **Case Example 28.9** Matthew Faush was an African American employee of Labor Ready, which provides temporary employees to businesses. Faush was assigned to a job stocking shelves at a Tuesday Morning store in Pennsylvania. After he was fired by Tuesday Morning, Faush filed a suit alleging discrimination. Tuesday Morning argued that Faush was not its employee. A federal court, however, found that the NLRA's protections may extend to temporary workers and that Faush was entitled to a trial.[30]

Labor Management Relations Act The Labor Management Relations Act (LMRA), also called the Taft-Hartley Act,[31] was passed in 1947 to proscribe certain unfair union practices, such as the *closed shop*. A **closed shop** requires union membership as a condition of employment.

Although the act made the closed shop illegal, it preserved the legality of the union shop. A **union shop** does not require membership as a prerequisite for employment but can, and usually does, require that workers join the union after a specified amount of time on the job.

The LMRA also prohibited unions from refusing to bargain with employers, engaging in certain types of picketing, and *featherbedding*—causing employers to hire more employees than necessary. The act also allowed individual states to pass their own **right-to-work laws,** which make it illegal for union membership to be required for *continued* employment in any establishment. Thus, union shops are technically illegal in the twenty-eight states that have right-to-work laws.

Labor-Management Reporting and Disclosure Act The Labor-Management Reporting and Disclosure Act (LMRDA)[32] established an employee bill of rights and

Closed Shop A firm that requires union membership as a condition of employment.

Union Shop A firm that requires all workers, once employed, to become union members within a specified period of time as a condition of their continued employment.

Right-to-Work Law A state law providing that employees may not be required to join a union as a condition of retaining employment.

---

29. *Roundy's, Inc. v. NLRB,* 674 F.3d 638 (7th Cir. 2012).
30. *Faush v. Tuesday Morning, Inc.,* 808 F.3d 208 (3d Cir. 2015).
31. 29 U.S.C. Sections 141 *et seq.*
32. 29 U.S.C. Sections 401 *et seq.*

reporting requirements for union activities. The act also outlawed **hot-cargo agreements,** in which employers voluntarily agree with unions not to handle, use, or deal in goods produced by nonunion employees working for other employers.

Hot-Cargo Agreement An illegal agreement in which employers voluntarily agree with unions not to handle, use, or deal in the nonunion-produced goods of other employers.

The LMRDA strictly regulates unions' internal business procedures, including union elections. For instance, it requires a union to hold regularly scheduled elections of officers using secret ballots. Ex-convicts are prohibited from holding union office. Moreover, union officials are accountable for union property and funds. Members have the right to attend and to participate in union meetings, to nominate officers, and to vote in most union proceedings.

The LMRDA holds union officers to a high standard of responsibility and ethical conduct in administering the affairs of their union. **Case Example 28.10** The Services Employees International Union (SEIU) consists of 2.2 million members who work in health care, public services, and property services. United Health Workers (UHW) is affiliated with SEIU and represents 150,000 health-care workers in California. The SEIU proposed moving 150,000 long-term care workers from three separate unions, including 65,000 from the UHW, into a new union chartered by the SEIU. The UHW opposed the move.

How can a labor union's officer breach his or her fiduciary duties to members?

Meanwhile, the UHW officials, while still on the UHW payroll, created and promoted a new union—the National Union of Healthcare Workers (NUHW). The SEIU sued the NUHW and the UHW officials for breach of fiduciary duties. The SEIU claimed that union officials had a duty under the LMRDA to act primarily for the benefit of the union. The court agreed and a federal appellate court affirmed. Officials who diverted union resources to establish a competing union breached their duty under the LMRDA.[33] ■

28–5b **Union Organization**

Typically, the first step in organizing a union at a particular firm is to have the workers sign authorization cards. An **authorization card** usually states that the worker wishes to have a certain union, such as the United Auto Workers, represent the workforce.

Authorization Card A card signed by an employee that gives a union permission to act on his or her behalf in negotiations with management.

If a majority of the workers sign authorization cards, the union organizers (unionizers) present the cards to the employer and ask for formal recognition of the union. The employer is not required to recognize the union at this point in the process, but it may do so voluntarily on a showing of majority support.

Union Elections If the employer does not voluntarily recognize the union—or if less than a majority of the workers sign authorization cards—the union organizers can petition for an election. The organizers present the authorization cards to the NLRB with a petition to hold an election on unionization. For an election to be held, they must demonstrate that at least 30 percent of the workers to be represented support a union or an election on unionization.

Appropriate Bargaining Unit. Not every group of workers can form a single union. The proposed union must represent an *appropriate bargaining unit.* One key requirement of an appropriate bargaining unit is a *mutuality of interest* among all the workers to be represented by the union. Factors considered in determining whether there is a mutuality of interest include the similarity of the jobs of all the workers to be unionized and their physical location.

NLRB Rules Expedite Elections. NLRB rules that took effect early in 2015 have significantly reduced the time between the filing of a petition and the ensuing election—from an average of thirty-eight days to as little as ten days. This change favors unions because it gives employers less time to respond to organizing campaigns that unions often spend months preparing.

In most instances, the parties agree on the voting unit and other issues. If the parties do not agree, the NLRB holds a pre-election hearing shortly after it receives a petition to

---

33. *Services Employees International Union v. National Union of Healthcare Workers,* 718 F.3d 1036 (9th Cir. 2013).

resolve issues and determine whether an election should be conducted. On the day before the hearing, the company must submit a "statement of position" laying out every argument it intends to make against the union. Any argument that the company does not include in its position paper can be excluded from evidence at the hearing. Once the hearing is held, an election can be scheduled right away.

Voting. If an election is held, the NLRB supervises the election and ensures secret voting and voter eligibility. If the proposed union receives majority support in a fair election, the NLRB certifies the union as the bargaining representative for the employees.

Union Election Campaigns   Many disputes between labor and management arise during union election campaigns. Generally, the employer has control over unionizing activities that take place on company property during working hours. Employers may thus limit the campaign activities of union supporters as long as the employer has a legitimate business reason for doing so. The employer may also reasonably limit the times and places that union solicitation occurs so long as the employer is not discriminating against the union. (Can union organizers use company e-mail during campaigns? See this chapter's *Managerial Strategy* feature for a discussion of this topic.)

Union Organizing Using a Company's E-Mail System

Managerial Strategy

When union organizers start an organizing drive, there are certain restrictions on what they can do, particularly within the workplace. Both employers and employees must comply with Section 7 of the National Labor Relations Act (NLRA).

Protected Concerted Activities

Under Section 7, employees have certain rights to communicate among themselves. Section 7 states, "Employees shall have the right to self-organization, . . . and to engage in other concerted activities for the purpose of collective bargaining or other mutual aid or protection."

What about communication via e-mail? Can union organizers use a company-operated e-mail system for organizing purposes? Companies typically provide e-mail systems so that employees can communicate with outsiders and among themselves as part of their jobs. Generally, company policies have prohibited the use of company-owned and -operated e-mail systems for other than job-related communications.

Some union organizers have challenged this prohibition.

The NLRB's Perspective Evolves

At first, the National Labor Relations Board (NLRB) allowed an employer's written policy that prohibited the use of a company-provided e-mail system for non-job-related solicitations.[a] Then the NLRB reversed its position. "[W]e decide today that employee use of e-mail for statutorily protected communications on non-working time must presumptively be permitted by employers who have chosen to give employees access to their e-mail systems."[b] The NLRB claimed that its earlier decision had failed to adequately protect "employees' rights under the NLRA." The board also stated that it had a responsibility "to adapt the Act to the changing patterns of industrial life."

---

a. See *Guard Publishing v. NLRB,* 571 F.3d 53 (D.C. Cir. 2009).
b. *Purple Communications, Inc. and Communication Workers of America, AFL-CIO,* Cases 21-CA-095151, 21-RC-091531, and 21-RC-091584, March 16, 2015.

The rules are clear. Once an organizing election is scheduled, a company must turn over all telephone numbers and home and e-mail addresses of the company's employees to union organizers within two days. The organizers can then communicate with employees via the company's e-mail system.

Business Questions

1. *Employees meeting around the water cooler or coffee machine have always had the right to discuss work-related matters. Is an employer-provided e-mail system or social media outlet simply a digital water cooler? Why or why not?*

2. *If your company instituted a policy stating that employees should "think carefully about 'friending' co-workers," would that policy be lawful? Why or why not?*

Example 28.11 A union is seeking to organize clerks at a department store owned by Amanti Enterprises. Amanti can prohibit all union solicitation in areas of the store open to the public because that activity could seriously interfere with the store's business. If Amanti allows solicitation for charitable causes in the workplace, however, it may not prohibit union solicitation. ■

An employer may campaign among its workers against the union, but the NLRB carefully monitors and regulates the tactics used by management. Otherwise, management might use its economic power to coerce the workers into voting against unionization. If an employer issued threats ("If the union wins, you'll all be fired") or engaged in other unfair labor practices, the NLRB could certify the union even though it lost the election. Alternatively, the NLRB could ask a court to order a new election.

Whether an employer violated its employees' rights under the National Labor Relations Act during a union election campaign was at issue in the following case.

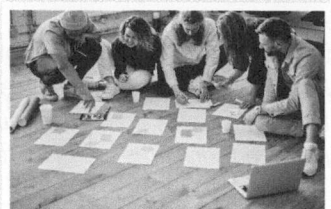

When workers wish to organize a union, what types of activities are allowed on the employer's premises? What types of activities are not allowed?

Case 28.3

Contemporary Cars, Inc. v. National Labor Relations Board

United States Court of Appeals, Seventh Circuit, 814 F.3d 859 (2016).

Background and Facts Contemporary Cars, Inc., sells and services cars. AutoNation owns this dealership, along with others. The International Association of Machinists began a campaign to organize the company's service technicians. During the election campaign, Contemporary engaged in various activities to monitor and perhaps affect the campaign. AutoNation's vice president, who opposed the union, held group meetings with the service technicians. Afterwards, Bob Berryhill, Contemporary's manager, called individual employees into his office to ask about union activity. He also promised that the dealership was working on finding solutions for various workplace problems the technicians had. In addition, the dealership fired an employee, Anthony Roberts, who was a leader in the union campaign. An administrative law judge ordered Contemporary to stop interfering with its employees' union activities and to reinstate Roberts. The NLRB affirmed the order. The dealership petitioned for a review of the order.

In the Words of the Court

HAMILTON, Circuit Judge.

* * * *

* * * The dealership violated [the National Labor Relations Act] in the run-up to the election by coercively creating an impression of surveillance of union activity, interrogating employees about union activity, and soliciting and promising to remedy employee grievances.

* * * *

* * * Berryhill coercively interrogated employees [when he] called them individually into his office and asked them about union activity.

The dealership's service director was also present. * * * The setting of the meetings in Berryhill's office, Berryhill's and the director's positions of authority, and the fact that each technician was alone and outnumbered by managers all support the finding of coercion.

* * * *

* * * At the * * * meetings, Berryhill asked the technicians how the dealership could improve. * * * Berryhill [stated] that he was "working on" the problems and "in progress" on the solutions. * * * The * * * meetings also included inquiries about the union effort. * * * This was an effort to frustrate the union organizing drive by soliciting and at least implicitly promising to adjust grievances.

* * * *

* * * AutoNation vice president * * * [Brian] Davis coercively interrogated a * * * technician, Tumeshwar Persaud * * *. Davis * * * asked him how he felt about the union election. * * * The question forced Persaud, who had not previously disclosed his union support, either to disclose his own union sympathies or to report on his perception of his fellow employees' union support.

* * * Davis held a meeting with employees at which he solicited employee complaints and, upon hearing that management had been unresponsive to employee complaints in the past, said that employees could call him or talk to him at any time. This meeting was part of a series of * * * meetings that management held in the run-up to the union election. * * * Davis was implicitly promising to remedy grievances with the goal of frustrating the union effort.

* * * *

* * * AutoNation * * * promulgated [publicized] an overly broad no-solicitation policy in the employee handbook used at all of its

(Continues)

facilities. * * * AutoNation's policy prohibited any solicitation on AutoNation property at any time. * * * *The policy * * * amounted to an unfair labor practice because of the likelihood it would chill protected concerted activity.* [Emphasis added.]

* * * *

* * * The dealership's discharge of Anthony Roberts * * * a week before the election was motivated by anti-union animus.

* * * *

* * * Berryhill's identification of Roberts as a troublemaker and instigator of the organizational campaign established that anti-union animus was a substantial factor motivating Roberts's layoff. * * * The dealership's stated reason for firing Roberts—that he lacked sufficient electronic diagnostic skills—failed to establish that Roberts would have been laid off in the absence of anti-union animus. * * * Roberts was more productive and had a higher skill rating than many technicians who were retained.

Decision and Remedy The U.S. Court of Appeals for the Seventh Circuit affirmed the administrative law judge's order. The dealership and AutoNation violated the National Labor Relations Act by interfering with their employees' protected rights to engage in concerted activity and to organize a union.

Critical Thinking

• **Legal Environment** *What might the dealership have asserted in defense to the charge that its actions violated its employees' rights?*

• **What If the Facts Were Different?** *Suppose that the dealership had taken no steps to change any of the terms or conditions of employment until well after the union election. Would the result have been different in this case? Explain.*

28–5c Collective Bargaining

Collective Bargaining The process by which labor and management negotiate the terms and conditions of employment, including working hours and workplace conditions.

If the NLRB certifies the union, the union becomes the *exclusive bargaining representative* of the workers. The central legal right of a union is to engage in collective bargaining on the members' behalf. **Collective bargaining** is the process by which labor and management negotiate the terms and conditions of employment, such as wages, benefits, and working conditions. Collective bargaining allows union representatives elected by union members to speak on behalf of the members at the bargaining table.

Once an employer and a union sit down at the conference table, they must negotiate in good faith and make a reasonable effort to come to an agreement. They are not obligated to reach an agreement. They must, however, approach the negotiations with the idea that an agreement is possible. Both parties may engage in hard bargaining, but the bargaining process itself must be geared toward reaching a compromise—not avoiding a compromise.

Although good faith is a matter of subjective intent, a party's actions can be used to evaluate the party's good or bad faith. Excessive delaying tactics may be proof of bad faith, as may insistence on obviously unreasonable contract terms. If an employer (or a union) refuses to bargain in good faith without justification, it has committed an unfair labor practice. Exhibit 28–1 illustrates some differences between good faith and bad faith bargaining.

28–5d Strikes

Strike An action undertaken by unionized workers when collective bargaining fails. The workers leave their jobs, refuse to work, and (typically) picket the employer's workplace.

Even when labor and management have bargained in good faith, they may be unable to reach a final agreement. When extensive collective bargaining has been conducted and an impasse results, the union may call a strike against the employer to pressure it into making concessions.

In a **strike,** the unionized workers leave their jobs and refuse to work. The workers also typically picket the workplace, standing outside the facility with signs stating their complaints. A strike is an extreme action. Striking workers lose their rights to be paid, and management loses production and may lose customers when orders cannot be filled. Labor law regulates the circumstances and conduct of strikes.

Most strikes take the form of "economic strikes," which are initiated because the union wants a better contract. **Example 28.12** Teachers in Eagle Point, Oregon, engage in an economic strike after contract negotiations with the school district fail to bring an agreement on pay, working hours, and subcontracting jobs. The unionized teachers picket outside the

Exhibit 28–1 Good Faith versus Bad Faith in Collective Bargaining

Good Faith Bargaining	Bad Faith Bargaining
1. Negotiating with the belief that an agreement is possible	1. Excessive delaying tactics
2. Seriously considering the other side's positions	2. Insistence on unreasonable contract terms
3. Making reasonable proposals	3. Rejecting a proposal without offering a counterproposal
4. Being willing to compromise	4. Engaging in a campaign among workers to undermine the union
5. Sending bargainers who have the authority to enter into agreements for the company	5. Constantly shifting positions on disputed contract terms
	6. Sending bargainers who lack authority to commit the company to a contract

Eagle Point school building. Classes are canceled for a few weeks until the district can find substitute teachers who will fill in during the strike.

The Right to Strike The right to strike is guaranteed by the NLRA, within limits. In addition, certain strike activities, such as picketing, are protected by the free speech guarantee of the First Amendment to the U.S. Constitution. Nonworkers have a right to participate in picketing an employer, and workers have the right to refuse to cross a picket line of fellow workers who are engaged in a lawful strike.

Strikers are not allowed to use (or threaten to use) violence against anyone or to prevent others from entering a facility. Furthermore, a strike may be illegal if it contravenes a no-strike clause that was in the previous collective bargaining agreement between the employer and the union.

After a Strike Ends In a typical strike, the employer has a right to hire permanent replacements during the strike. The employer need not terminate the replacement workers when the economic strikers seek to return to work. In other words, striking workers are not guaranteed the right to return to their jobs after the strike if satisfactory replacement workers have been found.

If the employer has not hired replacement workers to fill the strikers' positions, however, then the employer must rehire the economic strikers to fill any vacancies. Employers may not discriminate against former economic strikers, and those who are rehired retain their seniority rights.

Practice and Review

Rick Saldona began working as a traveling salesperson for Aimer Winery in 2009. Sales constituted 90 percent of Saldona's work time. Saldona worked an average of fifty hours per week but received no overtime pay. In June 2019, Saldona's new supervisor, Caesar Braxton, claimed that Saldona had been inflating his reported sales calls and required Saldona to submit to a polygraph test. Saldona reported Braxton to the U.S. Department of Labor, which prohibited Aimer from requiring Saldona to take a polygraph test for this purpose. In August 2019, Saldona's wife, Venita, fell from a ladder and sustained a head injury while employed as a full-time agricultural harvester. Saldona

(Continues)

delivered to Aimer's human resources department a letter from his wife's physician indicating that she would need daily care for several months, and Saldona took leave until December 2019. Aimer had sixty-three employees at that time. When Saldona returned to Aimer, he was informed that his position had been eliminated because his sales territory had been combined with an adjacent territory. Using the information presented in the chapter, answer the following questions.

1. Would Saldona have been legally entitled to receive overtime pay at a higher rate? Why or why not?

2. What is the maximum length of time Saldona would have been allowed to take leave to care for his injured spouse?

3. Under what circumstances would Aimer have been allowed to require an employee to take a lie-detector test?

4. Would Aimer likely be able to avoid reinstating Saldona under the *key employee* exception? Why or why not?

Debate This

The U.S. labor market is highly competitive, so state and federal laws that require overtime pay are unnecessary and should be abolished.

Key Terms

authorization card 685	I-551 Permanent Resident Card 682	union shop 684
closed shop 684	I-9 verification 681	vesting 677
collective bargaining 688	minimum wage 670	whistleblowing 667
employment at will 667	right-to-work law 684	workers' compensation laws 675
hot-cargo agreement 685	strike 688	wrongful discharge 669

Chapter Summary: Employment, Immigration, and Labor Law

Employment at Will	Under this common law doctrine, either party may terminate the employment relationship at any time and for any reason ("at will"). 1. *Exceptions to the employment-at-will doctrine*—Courts have made exceptions to the doctrine on the basis of contract theory, tort theory, and public policy. The public policy exception may sometimes apply to whistleblowers. 2. *Wrongful discharge*—Whenever an employer discharges an employee in violation of an employment contract or statutory law protecting employees, the employee may bring a suit for wrongful discharge.
Wages, Hours, and Leave	1. *Davis-Bacon Act*—Requires contractors and subcontractors working on federal government construction projects to pay their employees "prevailing wages." 2. *Walsh-Healey Act*—Requires firms that contract with federal agencies to pay their employees a minimum wage and overtime pay. 3. *Fair Labor Standards Act*—Extended wage and hour requirements to cover all employers whose activities affect interstate commerce plus certain other businesses. The act has specific requirements in regard to child labor, maximum hours, minimum wages, and overtime. 4. *The Family and Medical Leave Act (FMLA)*—Requires employers with fifty or more employees to provide employees with up to twelve weeks of unpaid leave (twenty-six weeks for military caregiver leave) during any twelve-month period. An eligible employee: a. May take family leave to care for a newborn baby, an adopted child, or a foster child. b. May take medical leave when the employee or the employee's spouse, child, or parent has a serious health condition requiring care.

c. May take military caregiver leave to care for a family member with a serious injury or illness incurred as a result of military duty.

d. May take qualifying exigency leave to handle specified nonmedical emergencies when a spouse, parent, or child is in, or called to, active military duty

Health, Safety, Income Security, and Privacy	1. *Occupational Safety and Health Act*—Requires employers to meet specific safety and health standards that are established and enforced by the Occupational Safety and Health Administration (OSHA).

1. *Occupational Safety and Health Act*—Requires employers to meet specific safety and health standards that are established and enforced by the Occupational Safety and Health Administration (OSHA).

2. *State workers' compensation laws*—Establish an administrative procedure for compensating workers who are injured in accidents that occur on the job, regardless of fault.

3. *Social Security and Medicare*—The Social Security Act provides for old-age (retirement), survivors', and disability insurance. Both employers and employees must make contributions under the Federal Insurance Contributions Act (FICA). The Social Security Administration also administers Medicare, a health-insurance program for older or disabled persons.

4. *Private retirement plans*—The federal Employee Retirement Income Security Act (ERISA) establishes standards for the management of employer-provided pension plans.

5. *Unemployment insurance*—The Federal Unemployment Tax Act (FUTA) created a system that provides unemployment compensation to eligible individuals. Employers are taxed to cover the costs.

6. *COBRA*—The Consolidated Omnibus Budget Reconciliation Act (COBRA) requires employers to give employees, on termination of employment, the option of continuing their medical, optical, or dental insurance coverage for a certain period at their own expense.

7. *HIPAA*—The Health Insurance Portability and Accountability Act (HIPAA) establishes requirements for employer-sponsored group health plans. The plans must also comply with various safeguards to ensure the privacy of employees' health information.

8. *Affordable Care Act*—The Affordable Care Act requires most employers with fifty or more full-time employees to offer health-insurance benefits. It also provides tax credits to employers who provide benefits even if they are not required to do so.

9. *Employee privacy rights*—Tort law, state constitutions, and federal and state statutes, as well as the U.S. Constitution, provide some protection for employees' privacy rights. Employer practices that have been challenged by employees as violations of their privacy rights include electronic monitoring, lie-detector tests, and drug testing.

Immigration Law

1. *Immigration Reform and Control Act*—Prohibits employers from hiring illegal immigrants. The act is administered by U.S. Citizenship and Immigration Services. Compliance audits and enforcement actions are conducted by U.S. Immigration and Customs Enforcement.

2. *Immigration Act*—Limits the number of legal immigrants entering the United States by capping the number of visas (entry permits) that are issued each year.

Labor Law

1. *Federal labor laws*—
   a. Norris-LaGuardia Act—Protects peaceful strikes, picketing, and boycotts.
   b. National Labor Relations Act—Established the rights of employees to engage in collective bargaining and to strike. It also defined specific employer practices as unfair to labor. The National Labor Relations Board (NLRB) was created to administer and enforce the act.
   c. Labor Management Relations Act—Proscribes certain unfair union practices, such as the closed shop.
   d. Labor-Management Reporting and Disclosure Act—Established an employee bill of rights and reporting requirements for union activities.

2. *Union organization*—Union campaign activities and elections must comply with the requirements established by federal labor laws and the NLRB.

3. *Collective bargaining*—The process by which labor and management negotiate the terms and conditions of employment (such as wages, benefits, and working conditions). The central legal right of a labor union is to engage in collective bargaining on the members' behalf.

4. *Strikes*—When collective bargaining reaches an impasse, union members may use their ultimate weapon in labor-management struggles—the strike. A strike occurs when unionized workers leave their jobs, refuse to work, and typically picket the employer's workplace.

Issue Spotters

1. Erin, an employee of Fine Print Shop, is injured on the job. For Erin to obtain workers' compensation, does her injury have to have been caused by Fine Print's negligence? Does it matter whether the action causing the injury was intentional? Explain. (See *Health, Safety, Income Security, and Privacy.*)

2. Onyx applies for work with Precision Design Company, which tells her that it requires union membership as a condition of employment. She applies for work with Quality Engineering, Inc., which does not require union membership as a condition of employment but requires employees to join a union after six months on the job. Are these conditions legal? Why or why not? (See *Labor Law.*)

   —**Check your answers to the *Issue Spotters* against the answers provided in Appendix D at the end of this text.**

Business Scenarios and Case Problems

28–1. Unfair Labor Practices. Consolidated Stores is undergoing a unionization campaign. Prior to the union election, management states that the union is unnecessary to protect workers. Management also provides bonuses and wage increases to the workers during this period. The employees reject the union. Union organizers protest that the wage increases during the election campaign unfairly prejudiced the vote. Should these wage increases be regarded as an unfair labor practice? Discuss. (See *Labor Law.*)

28–2. Wrongful Discharge. Denton and Carlo were employed at an appliance plant. Their job required them to do occasional maintenance work while standing on a wire mesh twenty feet above the plant floor. Other employees had fallen through the mesh, and one was killed by the fall. When Denton and Carlo were asked by their supervisor to do work that would likely require them to walk on the mesh, they refused due to their fear of bodily harm or death. Because of their refusal to do the requested work, the two employees were fired. Was their discharge wrongful? If so, under what federal employment law? To what federal agency or department should they turn for assistance? (See *Employment at Will.*)

28–3. Exceptions to the Employment-at-Will Doctrine. Li Li worked for Packard Bioscience, and Mark Schmeizl was her supervisor. In March 2000, Schmeizl told Li Li to call Packard's competitors, pretend to be a potential customer, and request "pricing information and literature." Li Li refused to perform the assignment. She told Schmeizl that she thought the work was illegal and recommended that he contact Packard's legal department. Although a lawyer recommended against the practice, Schmeizl insisted that Li Li perform the calls. Moreover, he later wrote negative performance reviews because she was unable to get the requested information when she called competitors and identified herself as a Packard employee. On June 1, 2000, Li Li was terminated on Schmeizl's recommendation. Can Li Li bring a claim for wrongful discharge? Why or why not? [*Li Li v. Canberra Industries,* 134 Conn.App. 448, 39 A.3d 789 (2012)] (See *Employment at Will.*)

28–4. Collective Bargaining. SDBC Holdings, Inc., acquired Stella D'oro Biscuit Co., a bakery in New York City. At the time, a collective bargaining agreement existed between Stella D'oro and Local 50 of the Bakery, Confectionary, Tobacco Workers and Grain Millers International Union. During negotiations to renew the agreement, Stella D'oro allowed Local 50 to examine and take notes on the company's financial statement but would not give Local 50 a copy of the statement. Did Stella D'oro engage in an unfair labor practice? Discuss. [*SDBC Holdings, Inc. v. National Labor Relations Board,* 711 F.3d 281 (2d Cir. 2013)] (See *Labor Law.*)

28–5. Business Case Problem with Sample Answer— Unemployment Compensation. Fior Ramirez worked as a housekeeper for Remington Lodging & Hospitality, a hotel in Atlantic Beach, Florida. After her father in the Dominican Republic suffered a stroke, she asked her employer for time off to be with him. Ramirez's manager, Katie Berkowski, refused the request. Two days later, Berkowski received a call from Ramirez to say that she was with her father. He died about a week later, and Ramirez returned to work, but Berkowski told her that she had abandoned her position. Ramirez applied for unemployment compensation. Under the applicable state statute, "an employee is disqualified from receiving benefits if he or she voluntarily left work without good cause." Does Ramirez qualify for benefits? Explain. [*Ramirez v. Reemployment Assistance Appeals Commission,* 135 So.3d 408 (Fla.App. 1 Dist. 2014)] (See *Health, Safety, Income Security, and Privacy.*)

   —**For a sample answer to Problem 28–5, go to Appendix E at the end of this text.**

28–6. Labor Unions. Carol Garcia and Pedro Salgado, bus drivers for Latino Express, Inc., a transportation company, began soliciting signatures from other drivers to certify the Teamsters Local Union No. 777 as the official representative of the employees. Latino Express fired Garcia and Salgado. The two drivers filed a claim with the National Labor Relations Board (NLRB) alleging that the employer had committed an unfair labor practice. Which employer practice defined by the National Labor Relations Act did the plaintiffs most likely charge Latino Express with committing? Is the employer's discharge of Garcia and

Salgado likely to be construed as a legitimate act in opposition to union solicitation? If a violation is found, what can the NLRB do? Discuss. [*Ohr v. Latino Express, Inc.*, 776 F.3d 469 (7th Cir. 2015)] (See *Labor Law*.)

28–7. Income Security. Jefferson Partners LP entered into a collective bargaining agreement (CBA) with the Amalgamated Transit Union. Under the CBA, drivers had to either join the union or pay a fair share—85 percent—of union dues, which were used to pay for administrative costs incurred by the union. An employee who refused to pay was subject to discharge. Jefferson hired Tiffany Thompson to work as a bus driver. When told of the CBA requirement, she said that she thought it was unfair. She asserted that it was illegal to compel her to join the union and that it would be illegal to discharge her for not complying. She refused either to join the union or to pay the dues. More than two years later, she was fired on the ground that her continued refusal constituted misconduct. Is Thompson eligible for unemployment compensation? Explain. [*Thompson v. Jefferson Partners LP*, 2016 WL 953038 (Minn. App. 2016)] (See *Health, Safety, Income Security, and Privacy.*)

28–8. Family and Medical Leave. To qualify for leave under the Family and Medical Leave Act (FMLA), an employee must comply with his or her employer's usual and customary notice requirements, including call-in policies. Robert Stein, an employee of Atlas Industries, Inc., tore his meniscus at work. Stein took medical leave to have surgery on the knee. Ten weeks into his recovery, Stein's doctor notified Atlas that Stein could return to work with light-duty restrictions in two days. Stein, however,

thought he was on leave for several more weeks. Atlas company policy provided that employees who missed three workdays without notification were subject to automatic termination. Stein did not return to work or call in as Atlas expected. Four days later, he was fired. Did Stein's discharge violate the FMLA? Discuss. [*Stein v. Atlas Industries, Inc.*, ___ Fed. Appx. ___, 2018 WL 1719097 (6th Cir. 2018)] (See *Wages, Hours, and Leave.*)

28–9. A Question of Ethics—The IDDR Approach and **Immigration Law.** *Split Rail Fence Company sells and installs fencing materials in Colorado. U.S. Immigration and Customs Enforcement (ICE) sent Split Rail a list of the company's employees whose documentation did not satisfy the Form I-9 employment eligibility verification requirements. The list included long-term workers who had been involved in company activities, parties, and picnics. They had bank accounts, driver's licenses, cars, homes, and mortgages. At Split Rail's request, the employees orally verified that they were eligible to work in the United States. Unwilling to accept the oral verifications, ICE filed a complaint against Split Rail for its continued employment of the individuals.* [Split Rail Fence Co. v. United States, *852 F.3d 1228 (10th Cir. 2017)] (See* Immigration Law.*)*

1. Using the IDDR approach, identify Split Rail's ethical dilemma. What steps might the company take to resolve it? Explain.

2. Is penalizing employers the best approach to take in attempting to curb illegal immigration? Discuss.

Critical Thinking and Writing Assignments

28–10. Time-Limited Group Assignment—Immigration. Nicole Tipton and Sadik Seferi owned and operated a restaurant in Iowa. Acting on a tip from the local police, agents of Immigration and Customs Enforcement executed search warrants at the restaurant and at an apartment where some restaurant workers lived. The agents discovered six undocumented aliens working at the restaurant and living together. When the I-9 forms for the restaurant's employees were reviewed, none were found for the six aliens. They were paid in cash while other employees were paid by check. Tipton

and Seferi were charged with hiring and harboring illegal aliens. (See *Immigration Law*.)

1. The first group will develop an argument that Tipton and Seferi were guilty of hiring and harboring illegal aliens.

2. The second group will assess whether Tipton and Seferi can assert a defense by claiming that they did not know that the workers were unauthorized aliens.

3. The third group will determine the potential penalties that Tipton and Seferi could face for violating the Immigration Reform and Control Act by hiring six unauthorized workers.

kupicoo/iStock/Getty Images

29 | Employment Discrimination

"Equal rights for all, special privileges for none."

Thomas Jefferson
1743–1826
(Third president of the
United States, 1801–1809)

Out of the civil rights movement of the 1960s grew a body of law protecting employees against discrimination in the workplace. Legislation, judicial decisions, and administrative agency actions restrict employers from discriminating against workers on the basis of race, color, religion, national origin, gender, age, disability, or military status. A class of persons defined by one or more of these criteria is known as a **protected class.** The laws designed to protect these individuals embody the sentiment expressed by Thomas Jefferson in the chapter-opening quotation.

Suppose that Marta Brown had been a medical assistant for a group of physicians for five years before she married a Turkish man and became a Muslim. She began wearing a hijab (head scarf) and taking several breaks each day to pray. The physicians, who had given Brown positive job evaluations in the past, began treating her differently. They forbade her from wearing the hijab at work, and told her that she could only perform prayers during her lunch break if she left the building. The physicians also started finding problems with her work performance and gave her a poor evaluation.

Eventually, Brown was let go from her position. Can she sue for employment discrimination? What evidence would she need to prove her case? Do private employers have to accommodate their employees' religious practices even if they are different from the employers' beliefs? These are some of the questions that will be answered in this chapter.

Several federal statutes prohibit *employment discrimination* against members of protected classes. Although this chapter focuses on federal statutes, many states have their own laws that protect employees against discrimination, and some provide more protection to employees than federal laws do.

29–1 Title VII of the Civil Rights Act

The most important statute covering employment discrimination is Title VII of the Civil Rights Act.[1] Title VII prohibits both intentional and unintentional discrimination against employees, applicants, and union members on the basis of race, color, national origin, religion, or gender at any stage of employment.

Title VII applies to employers with fifteen or more employees and labor unions with fifteen or more members. Title VII also applies to labor unions that operate hiring halls (where members go regularly to be assigned jobs as they become available), to employment agencies, and to state and local governing units or agencies. A special section of the act prohibits discrimination in most federal government employment. When Title VII applies to an employer, any employee—including an undocumented worker—can bring an action for employment discrimination.

Protected Class A group of persons protected by specific laws because of the group's defining characteristics, including race, color, religion, national origin, gender, age, disability, and military status.

29–1a The Equal Employment Opportunity Commission

Compliance with Title VII is monitored by the Equal Employment Opportunity Commission (EEOC). A victim of alleged discrimination must file a claim with the EEOC before bringing a suit against the employer. The EEOC may investigate the dispute and attempt to arrange an out-of-court settlement. **Example 29.1** Jacqueline Cote met her wife, Diana Smithson, in Maine while they were both employees at Walmart. They moved to Massachusetts and were married a few days after the state legalized same-sex marriage. They continued working at a Walmart there.

Smithson eventually quit work to take care of Cote's elderly mother. Cote tried to enroll her partner in Walmart's health plan, but coverage was denied. Five years later, Smithson was diagnosed with cancer. Cote filed a claim with the EEOC arguing that Walmart had intentionally discriminated against her on the basis of sex. The EEOC agreed that Cote was treated differently and denied benefits because of her sex and ordered Walmart to work with Cote to help pay Smithson's medical bills. ■

If a female employee's wife is denied coverage through the employer's health-care plan because of her sex, what action can the employee take to seek a remedy for the discrimination?

If a voluntary agreement cannot be reached, the EEOC may file a suit against the employer on the employee's behalf. If the EEOC decides not to investigate the claim, the EEOC issues a "right to sue" that allows the victim to bring her or his own lawsuit against the employer.

The EEOC does not investigate every claim of employment discrimination, regardless of the merits of the claim. Generally, it investigates only "priority cases," such as cases involving retaliatory discharge (firing an employee in retaliation for submitting a claim to the EEOC) and cases involving types of discrimination that are of particular concern to the EEOC.

29–1b Limitations on Class Actions

The United States Supreme Court issued an important decision that limited the rights of employees—as a group, or class—to bring discrimination claims against their employer. The Court held that to bring a class action, employees must prove a company-wide policy of discrimination that had a common effect on all the plaintiffs covered by the action.[2]

---

1. 42 U.S.C. Sections 2000e–2000e-17.

2. *Wal-Mart Stores, Inc. v. Dukes,* 564 U.S 338, 131 S.Ct. 2541, 180 L.Ed.2d 374 (2011). See also *Chen-Oster v. Goldman, Sachs & Co.,* 251 F.Supp.3d 579 (S.D.N.Y. 2017).

29–1c **Intentional and Unintentional Discrimination**

Title VII prohibits both intentional and unintentional discrimination.

Disparate-Treatment Discrimination A form of employment discrimination that results when an employer intentionally discriminates against employees who are members of protected classes.

Intentional Discrimination Intentional discrimination by an employer against an employee is known as **disparate-treatment discrimination.** Because intent can be difficult to prove, courts have established certain procedures for resolving disparate-treatment cases.

A plaintiff who sues on the basis of disparate-treatment discrimination must first make out a *prima facie* case. *Prima facie* is Latin for "at first sight." Legally, it refers to a fact that is presumed to be true unless contradicted by evidence.

Prima Facie Case A case in which the plaintiff has produced sufficient evidence of his or her claim that the case will be decided for the plaintiff unless the defendant produces evidence to rebut the claim.

Establishing a **Prima Facie** *Case.* To establish a *prima facie* case of disparate-treatment discrimination in hiring, a plaintiff must show all of the following:

1. The plaintiff is a member of a protected class.
2. The plaintiff applied and was qualified for the job in question.
3. The plaintiff was rejected by the employer.
4. The employer continued to seek applicants for the position or filled the position with a person not in a protected class.

Learning Objective 1

What is required to establish a *prima facie* case of disparate-treatment discrimination?

A plaintiff who can meet these relatively easy requirements has made out a *prima facie* case of illegal discrimination and will win in the absence of a legally acceptable employer defense.

Sometimes, a current or former employee makes a claim of discrimination. When the plaintiff alleges that the employer fired or took some other adverse employment action against him or her, similar requirements apply. To establish a *prima facie* case, the plaintiff must show that he or she was fired or treated adversely for discriminatory reasons.

Burden-Shifting Procedure. Once a *prima facie* case has been established, the burden then shifts to the employer-defendant, who must articulate a legal reason for not hiring the plaintiff or for taking some other adverse employment action. If the employer did not have a legal reason for taking the action, the plaintiff wins.

If the employer can articulate a legitimate reason for the action, the burden shifts back to the plaintiff. To prevail, the plaintiff must then show that the employer's reason is a *pretext* (not the true reason) and that the employer's decision was actually motivated by discriminatory intent.

Disparate-Impact Discrimination Discrimination that results from certain employer practices or procedures that, although not discriminatory on their face, have a discriminatory effect.

Unintentional Discrimination Employers often use interviews and tests to choose among a large number of applicants for job openings. Minimum educational requirements are also common. These practices and procedures may have an unintended discriminatory impact on a protected class. **Disparate-impact discrimination** occurs when a protected group is adversely affected by an employer's practices, procedures, or tests, even though they do not appear to be discriminatory. (For tips on how human resource managers can prevent these types of discrimination claims, see this chapter's *Linking Business Law to Corporate Management* feature.)

Linking Business Law to Corporate Management

Human Resource Management   Your career may lead to running a small business, managing a small part of a larger business, or making decisions for the operations of a big business. You may be responsible for employment decisions. As a manager, you must also ensure that employees do not practice discrimination on the job. Enter the human resource management specialist.

Human Resource Management

Human resource management (HRM) is concerned with the acquisition, maintenance, and development of an organization's employees. All managers need to be skilled in HRM. Some firms require managers to play an active role in recruiting and selecting personnel, as well as in developing training programs. Anyone engaging in these practices—especially those working in the company's human resource department—should be aware of the potential for employment discrimination claims.

The Acquisition Phase of HRM

Acquiring talented employees is the first step in an HRM system. All recruitment must be done without violating any of the laws and regulations outlined in this chapter. Obviously, recruitment must be colorblind, as well as indifferent to gender, religion, national origin, and age.

Recruitment methods must not have even the slightest hint of discriminatory basis. For instance, when evaluating a disabled job applicant, managers must make sure to consider only her or his training and qualifications, not the disability.

On-the-Job HRM Issues

In addition, the HRM professional must monitor the working environment. Sexual harassment is a major concern. It may be necessary to work closely with an employment law specialist to develop antiharassment rules and policies. The company must publish these rules and policies and provide training to ensure that all employees are familiar with them. In addition, the company should create and supervise a grievance system so that any harassment can be stopped before it becomes actionable.

Employee Termination and HRM

Even in employment-at-will jurisdictions, lawsuits can arise for improper termination. The company should develop a system to protect itself from lawsuits. The system should create procedures for documenting an employee's misconduct and the employer's warnings and other disciplinary actions. There should be an established policy for dealing with employees' improper or incompetent behavior, and guidelines for determining the amount of severance pay that terminated employees will receive. Sometimes, it is better to err on the side of generosity to maintain the goodwill of terminated employees.

Critical Thinking

What are some types of actions that an HRM professional can take to reduce the probability of harassment lawsuits against her or his company?

In a disparate-impact discrimination case, the complaining party must first show statistically that the employer's practices, procedures, or tests are discriminatory in effect. Once the plaintiff has made out a *prima facie* case, the burden of proof shifts to the employer to show that the practices or procedures in question were justified.

There are two ways of showing that an employer's practices, procedures, or tests are effectively discriminatory—that is, that disparate-impact discrimination exists.

Pool of Applicants. A plaintiff can prove a disparate impact by comparing the employer's workforce with the pool of qualified individuals available in the local labor market. The plaintiff must show that (1) as a result of educational or other job requirements or hiring procedures, (2) the percentage of nonwhites, women, or members of other protected classes in the employer's workforce (3) does not reflect the percentage of that group in the pool of qualified applicants. If the plaintiff can show a connection between the practice and the disparity, he or she has made out a *prima facie* case and need not provide evidence of discriminatory intent.

Rate of Hiring. A plaintiff can also prove disparate-impact discrimination by comparing the employer's selection rates of members and nonmembers of a protected class (for instance, whites and nonwhites). When a job requirement or hiring procedure excludes members of a protected class from an employer's workforce at a substantially higher rate than nonmembers, discrimination occurs, regardless of the balance in the employer's workforce.

The EEOC has devised a test, called the "four-fifths rule," to determine whether an employment selection procedure is discriminatory on its face. Under this rule, a selection rate for protected classes that is less than four-fifths, or 80 percent, of the rate for the group with the highest rate generally is regarded as evidence of disparate impact.

Example 29.2 Shady Cove District Fire Department administers an exam to applicants for the position of firefighter. At the exam session, one hundred white applicants take the test, and fifty pass and are hired—a selection rate of 50 percent. At the same exam session, sixty minority applicants take the test, but only twelve pass and are hired—a selection rate of 20 percent. Because 20 is less than four-fifths (80 percent) of 50, the test will be considered discriminatory under the EEOC guidelines. ▪

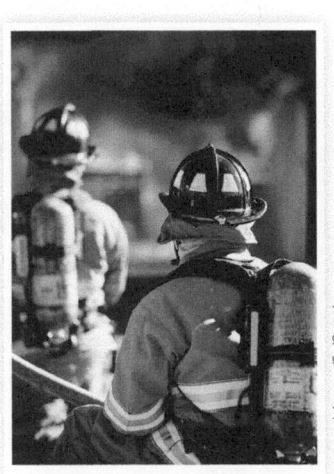

How might the "four-fifths rule" apply to the results of a fire department's entrance exam?

stevecoleimages/E+/Getty Images

29–1d Discrimination Based on Race, Color, and National Origin

Title VII prohibits employers from discriminating against employees or job applicants on the basis of race, color, or national origin. If an employer's standards for selecting or promoting employees have a discriminatory effect on job applicants or employees in these protected classes, then a presumption of illegal discrimination arises. To avoid liability, the employer must then show that its standards have a substantial, demonstrable relationship to realistic qualifications for the job in question.

Example 29.3 Hai Chang is an instructor at a university in Arkansas. When the university terminates his employment and hires a white male instructor, he files a lawsuit for employment discrimination. Chang is able to make out a *prima facie* case of discrimination because he (1) is a member of a protected class, (2) is qualified for the job, (3) suffered an adverse employment action, and (4) was replaced by a non-Asian instructor.

Nonetheless, the university can avoid liability for discrimination by showing that it discharged Chang for legitimate and nondiscriminatory reasons. For example, if Chang was terminated because he had argued with a university vice president and refused to comply with her instructions, the university is not liable for unlawful discrimination. ▪

Reverse Discrimination Note that discrimination based on race can also take the form of *reverse discrimination,* or discrimination against "majority" individuals, such as white males. **Case Example 29.4** Montana's Department of Transportation receives federal funds for transportation projects. As a condition of receiving the funds, Montana was required to set up a program to avoid discrimination in awarding contracts to disadvantaged business enterprises (DBEs). DBEs are businesses owned by members of historically disadvantaged groups, such as minorities. Mountain West Holding Company, Inc., installs signs, guardrails, and concrete barriers on highways in Montana and competes against DBEs for contracts.

Mountain West sued the state in federal court for violating Title VII by giving preference to these DBEs. At trial, the court pointed out that any classifications based on race are permissible "only if they are narrowly tailored measures that further compelling governmental interests." Montana thus had the burden of showing that its DBE program met this requirement. To show that the program addressed actual discrimination, the state presented a study that reported disparities in state-awarded contracts and provided anecdotal evidence of a "good ol' boys" network within the state's contracting industry. The district court accepted this evidence and concluded that Montana had satisfied its burden. A federal appellate court reversed, finding that the evidence was insufficient to prove a history of discrimination that would justify the preferences given to DBEs.[3]

Potential Section 1981 Claims Victims of racial or ethnic discrimination may also have a cause of action under 42 U.S.C. Section 1981. This section, which was enacted in 1866 to protect the rights of freed slaves, prohibits discrimination on the basis of race or ethnicity in the formation or enforcement of contracts. Because employment is often a contractual relationship, Section 1981 can provide an alternative basis for a plaintiff's action and is potentially advantageous because it does not place a cap on damages. (There is a cap placed on Title VII damages from small employers, as will be discussed later.)

29–1e Discrimination Based on Religion

Title VII also prohibits government employers, private employers, and unions from discriminating against persons because of their religion. (This chapter's *Adapting the Law to the Online Environment* feature discusses how employers who examine prospective employees' social media posts, including posts concerning religion, might engage in unlawful discrimination.)

Employers cannot treat their employees more or less favorably based on the employees' religious beliefs or practices and cannot require employees to participate in any religious activity (or forbid them from participating in one). **Example 29.5** Jason Sewell, a salesperson for TC Chevy, does not attend the weekly prayer meetings of dealership employees for several months. Then he is discharged by his employer. If he can show that the dealership required its employees to attend prayer gatherings and fired him for not attending, he has a valid claim of religious discrimination.

Reasonable Accommodation An employer must "reasonably accommodate" the religious practices of its employees, unless to do so would cause undue hardship to the employer's business. This means that an employer may need to make reasonable adjustments to the work environment to allow an employee to practice his or her religion. Reasonable accommodation is required even if the employee's belief is not based on the doctrines of a traditionally recognized religion, such as Christianity or Judaism, or a particular denomination, such as Baptist. The only requirement is that the belief be sincerely held by the employee.

Example 29.6 Syed Sahad is a Muslim who works at Rheitan Company, which manufactures snowblowers and lawn tractors. For years, Rheitan has allowed its Muslim employees to take prayer breaks at traditional prayer times if they have received permission from a supervisor. Now Rheitan decides to change its policy and will no longer allow Muslim prayer breaks at the traditional times. All employees receive two ten-minute breaks per eight-hour shift, however.

In this situation, if Sahad sues for religious discrimination, it will be difficult for the employer to establish a legitimate reason for not reasonably accommodating its Muslim employees. Rheitan has accommodated Muslim prayers in the past, after all. To accommodate its Muslim employees in the future, Rheitan could be more flexible in scheduling breaks, or it could require Muslim employees who take prayer breaks to make up the time spent in prayer.

Undue Hardship An employer is not required to make an accommodation that would cause the employer undue hardship. A reasonable attempt to accommodate does not necessarily require the employer to make every change an employee requests or to make a permanent change for an employee's benefit.

How can an employer make reasonable accommodations for Muslim employees who wish to take prayer breaks?

---

3. *Mountain West Holding Co., Inc. v. State of Montana*, 691 Fed.Appx. 326 (9th Cir. 2017).

Adapting the Law to the Online Environment

Hiring Discrimination Based on Social Media Posts

Human resource officers in most companies routinely check job candidates' social media posts when deciding whom to hire. Certainly, young people are warned not to post photos that they might later regret having made available to potential employers. But a more serious issue involves standard reviewing of job candidates' social media information. Specifically, do employers discriminate based on such information?

An Experiment in Hiring Discrimination via Online Social Networks

Two researchers at Carnegie-Mellon University conducted an experiment to determine whether social media information posted by prospective employees influences employers' hiring decisions.[a] The researchers created false résumés and social media profiles. They submitted job applications on behalf of the fictional "candidates" to about four thousand U.S. employers. They then compared employers' responses to different groups—for instance, to Muslim candidates versus Christian candidates.

The researchers found that candidates whose public profiles indicated that they were Muslim were less likely to be called for interviews than Christian applicants. The difference was particularly pronounced in parts of the country with more conservative residents. In those locations, Muslims received callbacks only 2 percent of the time, compared with 17 percent for Christian applicants. According to the authors of the study, "Hiring discrimination via online searches of candidates may not be widespread, but online disclosures of personal traits can significantly influence the hiring decisions of a self-selected set of employers."

Job Candidates' Perception of the Hiring Process

Job candidates frequently view the hiring process as unfair when they know that their social media profiles have been used in the selection process. This perception may make litigation more likely. Nevertheless, 84 percent of employers report using social media to recruit job applicants. One-third of those who recruit in this manner admit that they have disqualified applicants based on content found in their social media accounts.[b]

The EEOC Speaks Up

The Equal Employment Opportunity Commission (EEOC) has investigated how prospective employers can use social media to engage in discrimination in the hiring process. Given that the Society for Human Resource Management estimates that more than three-fourths of its members use social media in their employment screening process, the EEOC is interested in regulating this procedure.

Social media sites, examined closely, can provide information to a prospective employer on the applicant's race, color, national origin, disability, religion, and other protected characteristics. The EEOC has reminded employers that such information—whether it comes from social media postings or other sources—may not legally be used to make employment decisions on prohibited bases, such as race, gender, and religion.

Critical Thinking

Can you think of a way a company could use information from an applicant's social media posts without running the risk of being accused of hiring discrimination?

---

a. A. Acquisti and C. N. Fong, "An Experiment in Hiring Discrimination via Online Social Networks," *Social Service Research Network*, October 26, 2014.

b. Alexia Elejalde-Ruiz, "Using Social Media to Disqualify Job Candidates Is Risky," *Chicago Tribune*, January 11, 2016.

Case Example 29.7 Leontine K. Robinson worked as an administrative assistant in the emergency department at the Children's Hospital Boston. The hospital started requiring all employees who worked in or had access to patient-care areas to receive the influenza (flu) vaccine. When Robinson, who had taken a tetanus vaccine, refused to get the flu vaccine based on her religious beliefs, the hospital terminated her employment. Robinson filed a lawsuit alleging religious discrimination. The hospital argued that allowing Robinson to keep her patient-care position without receiving the vaccine would create an undue hardship. The court agreed and granted a summary judgment for the hospital.[4]

29–1f Discrimination Based on Gender

Under Title VII, as well as other federal acts, employers are forbidden from discriminating against employees on the basis of gender. Employers are prohibited from classifying jobs as male or female and from advertising positions as male or female unless they can prove that the gender of the applicant is essential to the job. In addition, employers cannot have separate male and female seniority lists and cannot refuse to promote employees based on gender.

Gender Must Be a Determining Factor Generally, to succeed in a suit for gender discrimination, a plaintiff must demonstrate that gender was a determining factor in the employer's decision to fire or refuse to hire or promote her or him. Typically, this involves looking at all of the surrounding circumstances.

Case Example 29.8 Wanda Collier worked for Turner Industries Group, LLC, in the maintenance department. She complained to her supervisor that Jack Daniell, the head of the department, treated her unfairly. Her supervisor told her that Daniell had a problem with her gender and was harder on women. The supervisor talked to Daniell but did not take any disciplinary action.

A month later, Daniell confronted Collier, pushing her up against a wall and berating her. After this incident, Collier filed a formal complaint and kept a male co-worker with her at all times. A month later, she was fired. She subsequently filed a lawsuit alleging gender discrimination. The court concluded that there was enough evidence that gender was a determining factor in Daniell's conduct to allow Collier's claims to go to a jury.[5]

In the following case, the court had to determine whether differing physical fitness standards for males and females constituted gender discrimination.

> "A sign that says 'men only' looks very different on a bathroom door than a courthouse door."
>
> **Thurgood Marshall**
> 1908–1993
> (Associate justice of the United States Supreme Court, 1967–1991)

---

4. *Robinson v. Children's Hospital Boston,* 2016 WL 1337255 (D.Mass. 2016).
5. *Collier v. Turner Industries Group, LLC,* 797 F.Supp.2d 1029 (D. Idaho 2011).

■ Case 29.1

Bauer v. Lynch

United States Court of Appeals, Fourth Circuit, 812 F.3d 340 (2016).

Background and Facts The Federal Bureau of Investigation (FBI) trains its recruits at the FBI Academy in Quantico, Virginia. All recruits must pass a physical fitness test (PFT) twice, once to gain admission and once to graduate.

Jay Bauer was admitted to the academy after passing the PFT on a second attempt, three months after his initial application. At the academy, Bauer passed all academic tests, demonstrated proficiency in firearms and defensive tactics, and met all expectations for practical applications and skills. He was unable, however, to pass the PFT's minimum requirement of thirty push-ups

for men after five attempts. (For women, the minimum was only fourteen push-ups.) Following this PFT failure, Bauer resigned and did not graduate from the acadamy. Two weeks later, the FBI offered him a position as an intelligence analyst, which he accepted.

Bauer filed a suit in a federal district court against Loretta Lynch, the U.S. attorney general, alleging that the FBI's use of the gender-normed PFT standards constituted discrimination on the basis of gender in violation of Title VII. The court issued a summary judgment in Bauer's favor. The attorney general appealed.

(Continues)

In the Words of the Court
KING, Circuit Judge.

* * * *

Title VII requires that any "personnel actions affecting employees or applicants for employment" taken by federal employers "shall be made free from any discrimination based on * * * sex." * * * *A plaintiff is entitled to demonstrate discrimination by showing that the employer uses a facially discriminatory employment practice. [The Supreme Court has outlined] a "simple test" for identifying facial sex discrimination: such discrimination appears "where the evidence shows treatment of a person in a manner which but for that person's sex would be different."* [Emphasis added.]

* * * The district court applied [this] test and concluded that, because Bauer would have been held to a lower minimum number of push-ups had he been a woman, the gender-normed PFT standards constitute facial sex discrimination. The Attorney General maintains on appeal, however, that because the PFT assesses an overall level of physical fitness, and equally fit men and women possess innate physiological differences that lead to different performance outcomes, the PFT's gender-normed standards actually require the same level of fitness for all Trainees. In that way, the Attorney General contends, the PFT standards do not treat the sexes differently and therefore do not contravene Title VII.

* * * *

* * * The Attorney General * * * maintains that * * * some differential treatment of men and women based upon inherent physiological differences is not only lawful but also potentially required.

* * * *

Men and women simply are not physiologically the same for the purposes of physical fitness programs. * * * Physical fitness standards suitable for men may not always be suitable for women, and accommodations addressing physiological differences between the sexes are not necessarily unlawful.

* * * The physiological differences between men and women impact their relative abilities to demonstrate the same levels of physical fitness. In other words, equally fit men and women demonstrate their fitness differently. Whether physical fitness standards discriminate based on sex, therefore, depends on whether they require men and women to demonstrate different levels of fitness.

Put succinctly, *an employer does not contravene [violate] Title VII when it utilizes physical fitness standards that distinguish between the sexes on the basis of their physiological differences but impose an equal burden of compliance on both men and women, requiring the same level of physical fitness of each.* Because the FBI purports to assess physical fitness by imposing the same burden on both men and women, this rule applies to Bauer's Title VII claims. Accordingly, the district court erred in failing to apply the rule in its disposition of Bauer's motion for summary judgment. [Emphasis added.]

Decision and Remedy The U.S. Court of Appeals for the Fourth Circuit vacated the lower court's judgment and remanded the case for further proceedings. The FBI did not violate Title VII by requiring PFT standards that distinguish between the sexes.

Critical Thinking

• **Legal Environment** *In what other circumstances might the use of different employment standards for men and women be acceptable and not violate Title VII's requirement for equality?*

• **Global** *How could global economic integration affect gender equality? Discuss.*

Pregnancy Discrimination The Pregnancy Discrimination Act[6] expanded Title VII's definition of gender discrimination to include discrimination based on pregnancy. Women affected by pregnancy, childbirth, or related medical conditions must be treated the same as other persons not so affected but similar in ability to work. For instance, an employer cannot discriminate against a pregnant woman by withholding benefits available to others under employee benefit programs.

An employer is required to reasonably accommodate a worker who is pregnant. In the following case, an employer accommodated many of its employees who had lifting restrictions due to disabilities. The employer refused to accommodate a pregnant employee with a similar restriction. Did this refusal constitute a violation of the Pregnancy Discrimination Act?

---

6. 42 U.S.C. Section 2000e(k).

■ Case 29.2

Young v. United Parcel Service, Inc.
Supreme Court of the United States, ___ U.S. ___, 135 S.Ct. 1338, 191 L.Ed.2d 279 (2015).

Background and Facts Peggy Young was a driver for United Parcel Service, Inc. (UPS). When she became pregnant, her doctor advised her not to lift more than twenty pounds. UPS required drivers to lift up to seventy pounds and told Young that she could not work under a lifting restriction. She filed a suit in a federal district court against UPS, claiming an unlawful refusal to accommodate her pregnancy-related lifting restriction.

Is UPS required to offer a pregnant employee a less physically demanding job?

Young alleged that UPS had multiple light-duty-for-injury categories to accommodate individuals whose non-pregnancy-related disabilities created work restrictions similar to hers. UPS responded that, because Young did not fall into any of those categories, it had not discriminated against her. The court issued a summary judgment in UPS's favor. The U.S. Court of Appeals of the Fourth Circuit affirmed the judgment. Young appealed to the United States Supreme Court.

In the Words of the Court
Justice *BREYER* delivered the opinion of the Court.
* * * *

* * * A plaintiff alleging that the denial of an accommodation constituted disparate treatment under the Pregnancy Discrimination Act * * * may make out a *prima facie* case by showing that she belongs to the protected class, that she sought accommodation, that the employer did not accommodate her, and that the employer did accommodate others similar in their ability or inability to work.

The employer may then seek to justify its refusal to accommodate the plaintiff by relying on legitimate, nondiscriminatory reasons for denying her accommodation. If the employer offers an apparently legitimate, nondiscriminatory reason for its actions, the plaintiff may in turn show that the employer's proffered reasons are in fact pretextual [false]. We believe that the plaintiff may reach a jury on this issue by providing sufficient evidence that the employer's policies impose a significant burden on pregnant workers, and that the employer's legitimate, nondiscriminatory reasons are not sufficiently strong to justify the burden, but rather—when considered along with the burden imposed—give rise to an inference of intentional discrimination. [Emphasis added.]

The plaintiff can create a genuine issue of material fact as to whether a significant burden exists by providing evidence that the employer accommodates a large percentage of nonpregnant workers while failing to accommodate a large percentage of pregnant workers. Here, for example, if the facts are as Young says they are, she can show that UPS accommodates most nonpregnant employees with lifting limitations while categorically failing to accommodate pregnant employees with lifting limitations. Young might also add that the fact that UPS has multiple policies that accommodate nonpregnant employees with lifting restrictions suggests that its reasons for failing to accommodate pregnant employees with lifting restrictions are not sufficiently strong— to the point that a jury could find that its reasons for failing to accommodate pregnant employees give rise to an inference of intentional discrimination.

* * * *

* * * A party is entitled to summary judgment if there is no genuine dispute as to any material fact and the movant [the one who applies to a court for a ruling in his or her favor] is entitled to judgment as a matter of law. * * * *Viewing the record in the light most favorable to Young, there is a genuine dispute as to whether UPS provided more favorable treatment to at least some employees whose situation cannot reasonably be distinguished from Young's.* [Emphasis added.]

Decision and Remedy The United States Supreme Court vacated the judgment of the U.S. Court of Appeals for the Fourth Circuit and remanded the case for further proceedings. Young had identified a genuine dispute as to whether UPS provided more favorable treatment to employees whose situation could not reasonably be distinguished from hers. On remand, the court must determine whether Young had also identified a genuine issue of material fact as to whether UPS's reasons for treating her less favorably were a pretext.

Critical Thinking

• **Legal Environment** *Could UPS have succeeded in this case if it had claimed simply that it would be more expensive or less convenient to include pregnant women among those whom it accommodates? Explain.*

Protections Extend to Employees' Post-Pregnancy. An employer must continue to reasonably accommodate medical conditions of an employee related to pregnancy and childbirth, even after the pregnancy has ended. **Case Example 29.9** Professional Ambulance, LLC, hired Allison Mayer as an emergency medical technician (EMT) while she was still breastfeeding an infant. She was supposed to work three twelve-hour shifts a week, but Professional did not provide her with a schedule so that she could arrange childcare. Mayer informed Professional that she needed to take short breaks to use a pump to express breast milk (lactation breaks). At first, her supervisor told her to take these breaks in the restroom, but Mayer objected because the conditions were unsanitary. Then the employer made Mayer take lactation breaks in an office that was not private or secure and made Mayer uncomfortable because the male EMTs could hear her pumping.

A few weeks later, Professional fired Mayer, claiming that it was because other employees had complained about her being rude and abusive. The employer refused to provide her with further explanation and replaced her with a male EMT with fewer qualifications. Mayer sued. A federal district court found that Mayer had established a *prima facie* case of discrimination on the basis of pregnancy, childbirth, or related medical conditions.[7] ◼

Wage Discrimination

The Equal Pay Act[8] requires equal pay for male and female employees doing similar work at the same establishment. To determine whether the Equal Pay Act has been violated, a court will look to the primary duties of the two jobs—the job content rather than the job description controls. If the wage differential is due to "any factor other than gender," such as a seniority or merit system, then it does not violate the Equal Pay Act.

The Lilly Ledbetter Fair Pay Act[9] made discriminatory wages actionable under federal law regardless of when the discrimination began. Previously, plaintiffs had had to file a complaint within a limited time period. Today, if a plaintiff continues to work for the employer while receiving discriminatory wages, the time period for filing a complaint is basically unlimited.

Ethical Issue

Should corporations be forced to publicize the ratio of CEO-to-worker pay? As part of wide-ranging changes in U.S. financial regulation, the Dodd-Frank Wall Street Reform and Consumer Protection Act[10] set forth new rules intended to hold corporate executives more accountable for their companies' performance. The Securities and Exchange Commission (SEC) was tasked with creating a regulation that forces certain companies not only to disclose how much the chief executive officer (CEO) makes, but also to establish a ratio of that pay to the median pay of the workforce. For instance, if the median employee makes $45,790 and the CEO makes $12,260,000, then the pay ratio is 1 to 268. Otherwise stated, the CEO's total compensation is 268 times that of the median annual compensation for all employees.

In announcing this rule, the SEC indicated that it was unsure what potential economic benefits, "if any," would be realized from making this information public. The SEC estimates that the regulation will cost companies, in total, almost 550,000 annual paperwork hours, plus about $75 million per year to hire outside professionals. Supporters of the new regulation, however, argue that it will help investors evaluate the relative value a CEO creates. In other words, pay ratio information is supposed to act as a check against insiders paying themselves "too much."

---

7. *Mayer v. Professional Ambulance, LLC,* 211 F.Supp.3d 408 (D.R.I. 2016).

8. 29 U.S.C. Section 206(d).

9. Pub. L. No. 111-2, 123 Stat. 5 (January 5, 2009), amending 42 U.S.C. Section 2000e-5[e].

10. Pub. L. No. 111-203, 124 Stat. 1376, 2010 H.R. 4173.

Discrimination against Transgender Persons In the past, most courts held that federal law (Title VII) does not protect transgender persons from discrimination. The situation may be changing, however. A growing number of federal courts are interpreting Title VII's protections against gender discrimination to apply to transsexuals.

Case Example 29.10 Dr. Deborah Fabian applied for a position as an on-call orthopedic surgeon at the Hospital of Central Connecticut. The hospital apparently declined to hire Fabian because she disclosed her identity as a transgender woman. Fabian sued the hospital alleging violations of Title VII of the Civil Rights Act and the Connecticut Fair Employment Practices Act (CFEPA).

The hospital filed a motion for summary judgment, arguing that neither Title VII nor the Connecticut statute prohibits discrimination on the basis of transgender identity. The federal district court rejected this argument, however, finding that discrimination on the basis of transgender identity is discrimination on the basis of gender for Title VII purposes. Fabian was entitled to take her case to a jury and to argue violations of Title VII and the CFEPA.[11]

If a hospital does not hire a physician because she identifies as a transgender woman, does Title VII protect that person from gender discrimination?

29–1g Constructive Discharge

The majority of Title VII complaints involve unlawful discrimination in decisions to hire or fire employees. In some situations, however, employees who leave their jobs voluntarily can claim that they were "constructively discharged" by the employer. **Constructive discharge** occurs when the employer causes the employee's working conditions to be so intolerable that a reasonable person in the employee's position would feel compelled to quit.

When constructive discharge is claimed, the employee can pursue damages for loss of income, including back pay. These damages ordinarily are not available to an employee who left a job voluntarily.

Constructive Discharge A termination of employment brought about by making the employee's working conditions so intolerable that the employee reasonably feels compelled to leave.

Proving Constructive Discharge To prove constructive discharge, an employee must present objective proof of intolerable working conditions. The employee must also show that the employer knew or had reason to know about the conditions, yet failed to correct them within a reasonable period. In addition, courts generally require the employee to show causation—that the employer's unlawful discrimination caused the working conditions to be intolerable. Put in a different way, the employee's resignation must be a foreseeable result of the employer's discriminatory action. Courts weigh the facts on a case-by-case basis.

Employee demotion is one of the most frequently cited reasons for a finding of constructive discharge, particularly when the employee was subjected to humiliation. **Example 29.11** Khalil's employer humiliates him in front of his co-workers by informing him that he is being demoted to an inferior position. Khalil's co-workers continually insult and harass him about his national origin (he is from Iran). The employer is aware of this discriminatory treatment but does nothing to remedy the situation, despite repeated complaints from Khalil. After several months, Khalil quits his job and files a Title VII claim. In this situation, Khalil would likely have sufficient evidence to maintain an action for constructive discharge in violation of Title VII.

Learning Objective 2

What is a constructive discharge? To which employment discrimination claims does the theory of constructive discharge apply?

11. *Fabian v. Hospital of Central Connecticut*, 172 F.Supp.3d 509 (D.Conn. 2016). See also *Christiansen v. Omnicom Group, Incorporated*, 852 F.3d 195 (2d Cir. 2017).

Constructive Discharge Applies to All Title VII Discrimination Note that constructive discharge is a theory that plaintiffs can use to establish any type of discrimination claims under Title VII, including race, color, national origin, religion, and gender. It is most commonly asserted in cases involving sexual harassment. Constructive discharge has also been successfully used in situations involving discrimination based on age or disability.

29–1h Sexual Harassment

Sexual Harassment The demanding of sexual favors in return for job promotions or other benefits, or language or conduct that is so sexually offensive that it creates a hostile working environment.

Title VII protection against **sexual harassment** in the workplace can take two forms:

1. *Quid pro quo* harassment occurs when sexual favors are demanded in return for job opportunities, promotions, salary increases, or other benefits. *Quid pro quo* is a Latin phrase that is often translated as "something in exchange for something else."

2. *Hostile-environment* harassment occurs when a pattern of sexually offensive conduct runs throughout the workplace and the employer has not taken steps to prevent or discourage it. In this situation, the workplace is permeated with discriminatory intimidation, ridicule, and insult, and this behavior is so severe or pervasive that it alters the conditions of employment.

In 2017, several high-profile claims of sexual harassment made national headlines, including one involving Bill O'Reilly of Fox News. What legal hurdles do plaintiffs face when they make such claims?

Reuters/Brendan McDermid

Harassment by Supervisors For an employer to be held liable for a supervisor's sexual harassment, the supervisor normally must have taken a *tangible employment action* against the employee. A **tangible employment action** is a significant change in employment status or benefits, such as when an employee is fired, refused a promotion, demoted, or reassigned to a position with significantly different responsibilities. Only a supervisor, or another person acting with the authority of the employer, can cause this sort of injury. A constructive discharge also qualifies as a tangible employment action.

Tangible Employment Action A significant change in employment status or benefits, such as occurs when an employee is fired, refused a promotion, or reassigned to a lesser position.

The United States Supreme Court has issued several important rulings in cases alleging sexual harassment by supervisors that established what is known as the "*Ellerth/Faragher* affirmative defense."[12] The defense has two elements:

1. The employer took reasonable care to prevent and promptly correct any sexually harassing behavior (by establishing effective antiharassment policies and complaint procedures, for instance).

2. The plaintiff-employee unreasonably failed to take advantage of any preventive or corrective opportunities provided by the employer to avoid harm.

An employer that can prove both elements normally will not be liable for a supervisor's harassment.

"Sexual harassment at work: Is it a problem for the self-employed?"

Victoria Wood
1953–2016
(English comedian and actor)

Retaliation by Employers Employers sometimes retaliate against employees who complain about sexual harassment or other Title VII violations. Retaliation can take many forms. An employer might demote or fire the person, or otherwise change the terms, conditions, and benefits of employment. Title VII prohibits retaliation, and employees can sue their employers on that basis. This chapter's *Business Law Analysis* feature exemplifies how courts analyze retaliation claims.

---

12. *Burlington Industries, Inc. v. Ellerth,* 524 U.S. 742, 118 S.Ct. 2257, 141 L.Ed.2d 633 (1998); and *Faragher v. City of Boca Raton,* 524 U.S. 775, 118 S.Ct. 2275, 141 L.Ed.2d 662 (1998).

Retaliation Claims

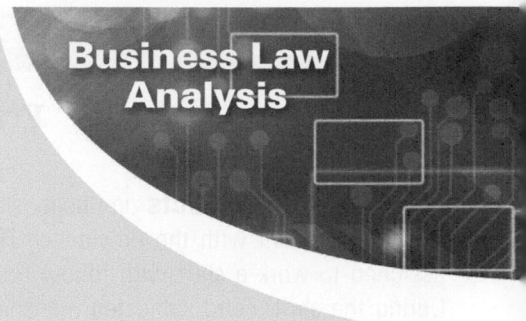

Shane Dawson, a male homosexual, worked for Entek International. Some of Dawson's co-workers, including his supervisor, made derogatory comments about his sexual orientation. Dawson's work deteriorated. He filed a complaint with Entek's human resource department. Two days later, he was fired. State law made it unlawful for an employer to discriminate against an individual based on sexual orientation. Can Dawson establish a claim for retaliation?

Analysis: Title VII prohibits retaliation. In a retaliation claim, an individual asserts that he or she suffered harm as a result of making a charge, testifying, or participating in a Title VII investigation or proceeding. To prove retaliation, a plaintiff must show that the challenged action was one that would likely have dissuaded a reasonable worker from making or supporting a charge of discrimination.

Result and Reasoning: Dawson can establish a claim for retaliation in his state. Under the applicable state law, it was unlawful for an employer to discriminate against an individual based on sexual orientation. Dawson was subjected to derision on the part of co-workers, including his supervisor, based on his sexual orientation. He filed a complaint with his employer's human resource department. Two days later, he was fired. The fact that the firing occurred so soon after the complaint filing would support a retaliation claim, as would the other circumstances, especially the supervisor's conduct. Also, the discharge would likely have tended to dissuade others from making claims of discrimination. Therefore, it is likely that Dawson offered enough evidence to establish a claim for retaliation.

In a *retaliation claim*, an individual asserts that she or he has suffered a harm as a result of making a charge, testifying, or participating in a Title VII investigation or proceeding. Plaintiffs do not have to prove that the challenged action adversely affected their workplace or employment. Instead, to prove retaliation, plaintiffs must show that the challenged action was one that would likely have dissuaded a reasonable worker from making or supporting a charge of discrimination. Title VII's retaliation protection extends to an employee who speaks out about discrimination during an employer's internal investigation of another employee's complaint.

Harassment by Co-Workers and Nonemployees When the harassment of co-workers, rather than supervisors, creates a hostile working environment, an employee may still have a cause of action against the employer. Normally, though, the employer will be held liable only if the employer knew, or should have known, about the harassment and failed to take immediate remedial action.

Occasionally, a court may also hold an employer liable for harassment by *nonemployees* if the employer knew about the harassment and failed to take corrective action. **Example 29.12** Gordon, who owns and manages a Great Bites restaurant, knows that one of his regular customers, Dean, repeatedly harasses Sharon, a waitress. If Gordon does nothing and permits the harassment to continue, he may be liable under Title VII even though Dean is not an employee of the restaurant.

In the following case, a female firefighter claimed that her male co-workers subjected her to a hostile working environment and that the fire department knew about the harassment but failed to act. The city (the defendant) responded that there was no evidence to support this claim.

Case 29.3

Franchina v. City of Providence

United States Court of Appeals, First Circuit, 881 F.3d 32 (2018).

Background and Facts In Rhode Island, Lori Franchina, a rescue lieutenant with the Providence Fire Department, was assigned to work a shift with fellow firefighter Andre Ferro. During the shift, Ferro subjected Franchina to unprofessional sexual comments and conduct. Based on Franchina's account of Ferro's actions, the fire chief, Curt Varone, filed an intradepartment complaint, charging Ferro with sexual harassment. No action was taken. Other firefighters then began to treat Franchina with contempt. She was subjected to insubordination and verbal assaults, and was spit on and shoved, among other negative actions. She submitted forty separate complaints of harassment to her superiors.

Franchina filed a suit in a federal district court against the city of Providence, asserting that she had been subjected to a hostile work environment as a result of her gender in violation of Title VII of the Civil Rights Act. The city argued that Franchina had presented no evidence to support her claim. A jury issued a verdict in her favor and awarded damages. The city appealed.

In the Words of the Court

THOMPSON, Circuit Judge.

Sticks and stones may break some bones, but harassment can hurt forever.

* * * *

Here, Franchina presented a plethora [excess] of evidence showing that the impetus [motivation] for the discrimination she sustained was based in part on her being a female. *In gender discrimination cases premised on a hostile work environment, Title VII permits a plaintiff to prove unlawful discrimination by demonstrating that the workplace is permeated with discriminatory intimidation, ridicule, and insult that is sufficiently severe or pervasive to alter the conditions of the victim's employment and create an abusive working environment.* Evidence of sexual remarks, innuendos, ridicule, and intimidation may be sufficient to support a jury verdict for a hostile work environment. Here, there was repeated evidence that Franchina was called a "bitch" and "Frangina" [a combination of her last name and the word "vagina"]. The use of these words is inherently gender-specific and their repeated and hostile use * * * can reasonably be considered evidence of sexual harassment. In fact a raft of case law

* * * establishes that the use of sexually degrading, gender-specific epithets, such as "slut," * * * "whore," and "bitch" * * *, has been consistently held to constitute harassment based upon sex. This case is no different. In fact, there was more. [Emphasis added.]

There was also evidence that [within the department] women were treated as less competent; a treatment barred by Title VII. The critical issue, Title VII's text indicates, is whether members of one sex are exposed to disadvantageous terms or conditions of employment to which members of the other sex are not exposed. There was evidence that men treated women better when they were perceived as willing to have sex with them. There was evidence that Franchina was subjected to humiliating sexual remarks and innuendos by Ferro, including asking the plaintiff if she wanted to have babies and if he could help her conceive. This type of sexually based *animus* [hostility] is a hallmark of Title VII.

In sum, the jury heard evidence of repeated hostile, gender-based epithets, ill treatment of women as workers, sexual innuendoes, and preferential treatment for women who were more likely to sleep with the men of the department. This sampling of evidence demonstrates that the accumulated effect * * * taken together constitutes a hostile work environment.

Decision and Remedy The U.S. Court of Appeals for the First Circuit affirmed the jury's decision. The federal appellate court concluded that the abuse Franchina had suffered from her co-workers was "nothing short of abhorrent." The court stated, "Employers should be cautioned that turning a blind eye to blatant discrimination does not generally fare well under antidiscrimination laws like Title VII."

Critical Thinking

• **Economic** *Because of the constant harassment, Franchina had to be placed on injured-on-duty status. Later, diagnosed with severe post-traumatic stress disorder and unable to work again as a rescue lieutenant, she "retired." What is the appropriate measure of damages for this result? Discuss.*

• **Legal Environment** *What steps might an employer take to avoid the circumstances that occurred in the* Franchina *case?*

Same-Sex Harassment In *Oncale v. Sundowner Offshore Services, Inc.*,[13] the United States Supreme Court held that Title VII protection extends to individuals who are sexually harassed by members of the same sex. Proving that the harassment in same-sex cases is "based on sex" can be difficult, though. It is usually easier to establish a case of same-sex harassment when the harasser is homosexual.

Sexual-Orientation Harassment Federal law (Title VII) does not prohibit discrimination or harassment based on a person's sexual orientation. A growing number of states, however, have enacted laws that prohibit sexual orientation discrimination in private employment. Some states, such as Michigan, explicitly prohibit discrimination based on a person's gender identity or expression. In addition, many companies and organizations, such as the National Football League, have voluntarily established nondiscrimination policies that include sexual orientation. Workers in the United States often have more protection against sexual harassment in the workplace than workers in other countries, as this chapter's *Beyond Our Borders* feature explains.

29–1i Online Harassment

Employees' online activities can create a hostile working environment in many ways. Racial jokes, ethnic slurs, or other comments contained in e-mail, texts, blogs, or social media posts can become the basis for a claim of hostile-environment harassment or other forms of discrimination. Similarly, a worker who regularly sees sexually explicit and offensive images on a co-worker's computer screen or tablet device may claim that they create a hostile working environment.

Nevertheless, employers may be able to avoid liability for online harassment if they take prompt remedial action. **Example 29.13** While working at TriCom, Shonda Dean receives

---

13. 523 U.S. 75, 118 S.Ct. 998, 140 L.Ed.2d 207 (1998).

Sexual Harassment in Other Nations

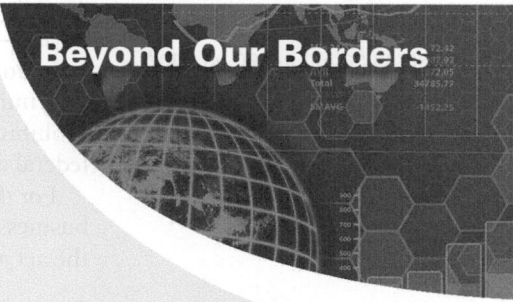

Beyond Our Borders

The problem of sexual harassment in the workplace is not confined to the United States. Indeed, it is a worldwide problem for female workers.

In Argentina, Brazil, Egypt, Turkey, and many other countries, there is no legal protection against any form of employment discrimination. Even in countries that do have laws prohibiting discriminatory employment practices, including gender-based discrimination, those laws often do not specifically include sexual harassment as a discriminatory practice.

Several countries have attempted to remedy this omission by passing new laws or amending others to specifically prohibit sexual harassment in the workplace. Japan, for instance, has amended its Equal Employment Opportunity Law to include a provision making sexual harassment illegal. Thailand has also passed a sexual-harassment law. The European Union has adopted a directive that specifically identifies sexual harassment as a form of discrimination.

Nevertheless, women's groups throughout Europe contend that corporations in European countries tend to view sexual harassment with "quiet tolerance." They contrast this attitude with that of most

U.S. corporations, which have implemented specific procedures to deal with harassment claims.

Critical Thinking

Why do you think U.S. corporations are more aggressive than European companies in taking steps to prevent sexual harassment in the workplace?

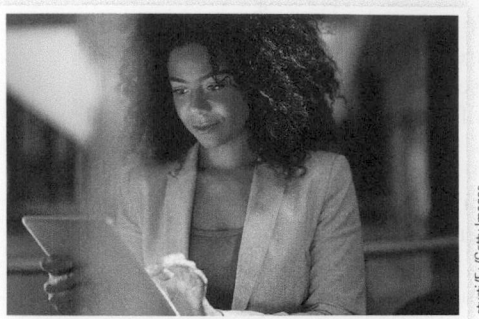

sturti/E+/Getty Images

If this employee receives racially harassing tweets from another employee, why might she not prevail in a lawsuit for racial discrimination?

racially harassing tweets from another employee. Shortly afterward, the company issues a warning to the offending employee about the proper use of the Internet at work and holds two meetings to discuss company policy on the use of social media. If Dean sues TriCom for racial discrimination, a court may find that because the employer took prompt remedial action, TriCom should not be held liable for its employee's racially harassing tweets. ■

29–1j Remedies under Title VII

Employer liability under Title VII may be extensive. If the plaintiff successfully proves that unlawful discrimination occurred, he or she may be awarded reinstatement, back pay, retroactive promotions, and damages. Compensatory damages are available in cases of intentional discrimination. Punitive damages may be recovered against a private employer only if the employer acted with malice or reckless indifference to an individual's rights.

The total amount of compensatory and punitive damages that plaintiffs can recover depends on the size of the employer. For instance, there is a $50,000 cap on damages from employers with one hundred or fewer employees.

29–2 Discrimination Based on Age, Disability, or Military Status

Certain types of employment discrimination that are not banned by Title VII of the Civil Rights Act are prohibited under other statutes. These include discrimination based on age, disability, and military status.

29–2a Discrimination Based on Age

Learning Objective 3

What federal act prohibits discrimination based on age?

Age discrimination is potentially the most widespread form of discrimination, because anyone—regardless of race, color, national origin, or gender—could be a victim at some point in life. The Age Discrimination in Employment Act (ADEA)[14] prohibits employment discrimination on the basis of age against individuals forty years of age or older. The act also prohibits mandatory retirement for nonmanagerial workers. In addition, the act protects federal and private-sector employees from retaliation based on age-related complaints.

For the act to apply, an employer must have twenty or more employees, and the employer's business activities must affect interstate commerce. The EEOC administers the ADEA, but the act also permits private causes of action against employers for age discrimination.

Procedures under the ADEA The burden-shifting procedure under the ADEA differs from the procedure under Title VII. As explained earlier, if the plaintiff in a Title VII case can show that the employer was motivated, at least in part, by unlawful discrimination, the burden of proof shifts to the employer to articulate a legitimate nondiscriminatory reason. Thus, in cases in which the employer has a "mixed motive" for discharging an employee, the employer has the burden of proving that its reason was legitimate.

Under the ADEA, in contrast, a plaintiff must show that the unlawful discrimination was not just a reason but *the* reason for the adverse employment action. In other words, the employee has the burden of establishing "but for" causation—but for the plaintiff's age, the adverse action would not have happened.

---

14. 29 U.S.C. Sections 621–634.

Prima Facie *Age Discrimination Case.* To establish a *prima facie* case, the plaintiff must show that he or she was the following:

1. A member of the protected age group.
2. Qualified for the position from which he or she was discharged.
3. Discharged because of age discrimination.

Then the burden shifts to the employer to give a legitimate nondiscriminatory reason for the adverse action.

Pretext. If the employer offers a legitimate reason for its action, then the plaintiff must show that the stated reason is only a pretext (a false reason) and that the plaintiff's age was the real reason for the employer's decision. **Case Example 29.14** Jerry Stever was a financial adviser at US Bancorp, Inc. He was terminated at age sixty-eight for "deficient performance." Stever sued US Bancorp in federal court alleging age discrimination and claiming that deficient performance was a pretext. The plaintiff proved that he was in the protected age group (over forty) and was qualified for the position, but he lacked proof that he had been discharged because of his age.

Stever argued that two younger financial advisers had received more favorable treatment from the company than he had. Showing that "similarly situated" younger employees were treated more favorably would have given rise to an inference of discrimination. The court found no evidence of preferential treatment, however. One of the men had generated considerably more revenue than Stever, and the other man differed from Stever in terms of seniority and prior performance. Thus, they were not similarly situated to Stever.

Stever also claimed that his manager had made the comment, "we old dogs had to learn new tricks." The district court found that this single stray remark was not sufficient to demonstrate age discrimination and granted summary judgment to US Bancorp. A federal appellate court affirmed the decision on appeal.[15]

State Employees Not Covered by the ADEA

Generally, the states are immune from lawsuits brought by private individuals in federal court, unless a state consents to the suit. This immunity stems from the United States Supreme Court's interpretation of the Eleventh Amendment.

State immunity under the Eleventh Amendment is not absolute, however. When fundamental rights are at stake, Congress has the power to abolish state immunity through legislation. For instance, Congress has chosen to subject states to private lawsuits under the Family and Medical Leave Act. State employers are usually immune from suits brought by employees under the ADEA, the Americans with Disabilities Act, and the Fair Labor Standards Act, however.

29–2b Discrimination Based on Disability

The Americans with Disabilities Act (ADA)[16] prohibits disability-based discrimination in workplaces with fifteen or more workers (with the exception of state government employers, who are generally immune). Basically, the ADA requires that employers reasonably accommodate the needs of persons with disabilities unless to do so would cause undue hardship. The ADA Amendments Act broadened the ADA's coverage.[17]

> "Growing old is like being increasingly penalized for a crime you have not committed."
>
> **Anthony Powell**
> 1905-2000
> (English novelist)

A male bank employee who is over sixty years old is fired for not performing well. If he believes the reason was a pretext, what must he do to establish a *prima facie* case for age discrimination?

---

15. *Stever v. US Bancorp, Inc.,* 690 Fed.Appx. 491 (9th Cir. 2017).
16. 42 U.S.C. Sections 12102–12118.
17. 42 U.S.C. Sections 12103 and 12205a.

Procedures under the ADA

To prevail on a claim under the ADA, a plaintiff must show all of the following:

1. The plaintiff has a disability.
2. The plaintiff is otherwise qualified for the employment in question.
3. The plaintiff was excluded from the employment solely because of the disability.

As in Title VII cases, a plaintiff must pursue her or his claim through the EEOC before filing an action in court for a violation of the ADA.

The EEOC may decide to investigate and perhaps even sue the employer on behalf of the employee. If the EEOC decides not to sue, then the employee is entitled to sue in court. The EEOC can bring a suit against an employer for disability-based discrimination even though the employee previously agreed to submit any job-related disputes to arbitration.

Plaintiffs in lawsuits brought under the ADA may seek many of the same remedies available under Title VII. These include reinstatement, back pay, a limited amount of compensatory and punitive damages (for intentional discrimination), and certain other forms of relief. Repeat violators may be ordered to pay fines of up to $100,000.

What Is a Disability?

The ADA is broadly drafted to cover persons with a wide range of disabilities. Specifically, the ADA defines *disability* to include any of the following:

1. A physical or mental impairment that substantially limits one or more of an individual's major life activities.
2. A record of such an impairment.
3. Being regarded as having such an impairment.

Health conditions that have been considered disabilities under the federal law include alcoholism, acquired immune deficiency syndrome (AIDS), blindness, cancer, cerebral palsy, diabetes, heart disease, muscular dystrophy, and paraplegia. Testing positive for the human immunodeficiency virus (HIV) has qualified as a disability, as has morbid obesity. (A morbidly obese person weighs twice the normal weight for his or her height.)

Note that obesity does not qualify as a disability under the ADA unless it involves physical impairment. **Case Example 29.15** Melvin Morriss applied for a machinist posi-

An estimated 160 million Americans are either obese or overweight. Is being morbidly obese considered a disability under the ADA? Why or why not?

tion at BNSF Railway. He was offered the position conditioned on a medical review, which was required because the position was considered safety sensitive. BNSF physicians found that Morriss's body mass index, or BMI, exceeded 40, identifying him as seriously obese. (BMI is a typical method of evaluating a person's body fat.) BNSF had a policy of not employing workers with BMIs of 40 or more in safety-sensitive positions. Thus, the company rescinded its offer of employment.

Morriss sued, alleging discrimination on the basis of disability, but the court found that Morriss's obesity was not a physical impairment under the ADA. Morriss was otherwise in good health and did not suffer from any medical condition that caused his obesity or any medical condition associated with obesity. Therefore, the court granted a summary judgment to BNSF Railway. A federal appellate court affirmed.[18]

Association with Disabled Persons. A separate provision in the ADA prevents employers from taking adverse employment actions based on stereotypes or assumptions about

---

18. *Morriss v. BNSF Railway Co.*, 817 F.3d 1104 (8th Cir. 2016).

individuals who associate with people who have disabilities.[19] **Example 29.16** Joan, an employer, refuses to hire Edward, who has a daughter with a physical disability. She bases her decision on the assumption that, because of his daughter's disability, Edward will miss work too often or be unreliable. Edward can sue Joan for violating the ADA's provisions.

Mitigating Measures. At one time, the courts focused on whether a person was disabled *after* the use of corrective devices or medication. Then Congress amended the ADA to strengthen its protections and prohibit employers from considering mitigating measures, such as medications, when determining if an individual has a disability.

Disability is now determined on a case-by-case basis. A condition may fit the definition of disability in one set of circumstances, but not in another. **Case Example 29.17** Larry Rohr, a welding specialist for a power district in Arizona, was diagnosed with type 2 diabetes. If he fails to follow a complex regimen of daily insulin injections and blood tests, as well as a strict diet, his blood sugar will rise to a level that aggravates his disease. Therefore, Rohr's physician forbade him from taking work assignments that involved overnight, out-of-town travel, which were common in his job.

Because of these limitations, the power district asked him to transfer, apply for disability, or take early retirement. Rohr sued for disability discrimination. The lower court granted summary judgment for the employer. Rohr appealed. A federal appellate court reversed. The court held that under the amended ADA, diabetes is a disability if it significantly restricts an individual's eating (a major life activity), as it did for Rohr. Therefore, Rohr was entitled to a trial on his discrimination claim.[20]

Disclosure of Confidential Medical Information. ADA provisions also require employers to keep their employees' medical information confidential. An employee who discovers that an employer has disclosed the employee's confidential medical information has a right to sue the employer—even if the employee was not technically disabled. The prohibition against disclosure also applies to other employees acting on behalf of the employer.

Case Example 29.18 George Shoun was working at his job at Best Formed Plastics, Inc., when he fell and injured his shoulder. Another Best Formed employee, Jane Stewart, prepared an accident report for the incident and processed Shoun's workers' compensation claim. As a result of the injury, Shoun had to take several months off work and received workers' compensation.

Stewart posted on her Facebook page a statement about how Shoun's shoulder injury "kept him away from work for 11 months and now he is trying to sue us." Shoun sued Best Formed under the ADA for wrongfully disclosing confidential information about his medical condition to other people via Facebook. He claimed the action resulted in loss of employment and impairment of his earning capacity. The court allowed Shoun's claim to go forward to trial.[21]

Reasonable Accommodation
The ADA does not require that employers accommodate the needs of job applicants or employees with disabilities who are not otherwise qualified for the work. If a job applicant or an employee with a disability can perform essential job functions with a reasonable accommodation, however, the employer must make the accommodation.

Required modifications may include installing ramps for a wheelchair, establishing more flexible working hours, creating or modifying job assignments, and creating or improving training materials and procedures. Generally, employers should give primary consideration to employees' preferences in deciding what accommodations should be made.

"Jobs are physically easier, but the worker now takes home worries instead of an aching back."

Homer Bigart
1907–1991
(American journalist)

---

19. 42 U.S.C. Section 12112(b)(4).
20. *Rohr v. Salt River Project Agricultural Improvement and Power District,* 555 F.3d 850 (9th Cir. 2009). For another decision in which a court found that diabetes was a disability, see *Hensel v. City of Utica,* ___ F.Supp.3d ___, 2017 WL 2589355 (N.D.N.Y. 2017).
21. *Shoun v. Best Formed Plastics, Inc.,* 28 F.Supp.3d 786 (N.D.Ind. 2014).

Undue Hardship. Employers who do not accommodate the needs of persons with disabilities must demonstrate that the accommodations will cause "undue hardship" in terms of being significantly difficult or expensive for the employer. Usually, the courts decide whether an accommodation constitutes an undue hardship on a case-by-case basis by looking at the employer's resources in relation to the specific accommodation.

Example 29.19 Bryan Lockhart, who uses a wheelchair, works for a cell phone company that provides parking for its employees. Lockhart informs company supervisors that the parking spaces are so narrow that he is unable to extend the ramp that allows him to get in and out of his van. Lockhart requests that the company reasonably accommodate his needs by paying a monthly fee for him to use a larger parking space in an adjacent lot. In this situation, a court would likely find that it would not be an undue hardship for the employer to pay for additional parking for Lockhart.

Job Applications and Preemployment Physical Exams. Employers must modify their job-application process so that those with disabilities can compete for jobs with those who do not have disabilities. For instance, a job announcement might be modified to allow job applicants to respond by e-mail or letter, as well as by telephone, so that it does not discriminate against potential applicants with hearing impairments.

Employers are restricted in the kinds of questions they may ask on job-application forms and during preemployment interviews. Furthermore, they cannot require persons with disabilities to submit to preemployment physicals unless such exams are required of all other applicants. Employers can condition an offer of employment on the applicant's successfully passing a medical examination, but can disqualify the applicant only if the medical problems discovered would render the applicant unable to perform the job.

Substance Abuse. Drug addiction is a disability under the ADA because it is a substantially limiting impairment. The act does not protect those who are actually using illegal drugs. The ADA protects only persons with *former* drug addictions—those who have completed or are now in a supervised drug-rehabilitation program. Individuals who have used drugs casually in the past are not protected under the act. They are not considered addicts and therefore do not have a disability (addiction).

People suffering from alcoholism are protected by the ADA. Of course, employers have the right to prohibit the use of alcohol in the workplace and can require that employees not be under the influence of alcohol while working. Employers can also fire or refuse to hire a person who is an alcoholic if (1) he or she poses a *substantial risk of harm* either to himself or herself or to others, and (2) the risk cannot be reduced by reasonable accommodation.

Health-Insurance Plans. Workers with disabilities must be given equal access to any health insurance provided to other employees and cannot be excluded from coverage for preexisting health conditions. An employer can put a limit, or cap, on health-care payments under its group health policy, but such caps must be "applied equally to all insured employees" and must not "discriminate on the basis of disability."

29–2c Discrimination Based on Military Status

The Uniformed Services Employment and Reemployment Rights Act (USERRA) prohibits discrimination against persons who have served in the military.[22] In effect, the USERRA makes military service and status a protected class and gives members of this class a right to sue an employer for violations.

Broad Application and Provisions The USERRA covers *all* employers, public and private, large and small. Even an employer with only one employee is subject to its provisions. The act also applies to United States employers operating in foreign countries.

Know This
Preemployment screening procedures must be applied equally in regard to all job applicants.

---

22. Pub. L. No. 103–353, codified at 38 U.S.C. Sections 4301–4335.

Under the USERRA, military plaintiffs can sue not only the employer but also individual employees who were acting in an official capacity for the employer. In other words, these employees—supervisors, for instance—can be held personally liable for violations. Additionally, there is no statute of limitations for bringing a lawsuit. The cause of action could have arisen ten weeks or ten years before the suit was filed.

The USERRA specifies that veterans can be terminated from their employment only "for cause." The employer is obligated to give employees a list of all the behaviors that would trigger a for-cause termination.

Prima Facie Case of Discrimination under the USERRA

To establish a *prima facie* case under the USERRA, the plaintiff must establish that the employer took an adverse employment action based in part on the employee's connection with the military. If another similarly situated person who did not serve in the military or engage in a protected activity was treated more favorably than the plaintiff, the employer has violated the USERRA.

Are reserve and former members of the military considered a protected class? Why or why not?

Case Example 29.20 Baldo Bello, a staff sergeant with the United States Marine Corps Reserve, was employed by the Village of Skokie as a police officer. Police officers in Skokie normally have nine regular days off (RDO) per month and eight sick days per year. Skokie officers who are in the Reserve receive two weeks of paid leave for annual training each summer, but they do not receive pay for the required weekend military training.

During his first four years as an officer in Skokie, Bello always requested RDOs to cover his weekend training drills. After that, he started requesting military leave for the two to four days of drills per month, in addition to his nine RDO days. Skokie at first granted Bello military leave for monthly drills but later began to deny the requests. When Skokie officials told Bello that he needed to schedule his RDOs to cover his weekend military training, he filed suit in a federal district court alleging violations of the USERRA. Skokie filed a motion for summary judgment, which the court denied. The court found that Bello was meeting his employer's legitimate expectations. He was therefore entitled to a trial on the issue of whether Skokie had treated his leave requests less favorably than requests from other employees.[23]

Plaintiffs May Be Entitled to Promotions

Under the USERRA, returning service members are to be reemployed in the jobs that they would have attained had they not been absent for military service. Reinstatement could affect their seniority, status, pay, and other rights and benefits (such as health and pension plans). In essence, this means that if a returning service member sues an employer for violations of the USERRA and is successful, she or he could receive not only damages and reinstatement but also a promotion.

Exhibit 29–1 illustrates the coverage of the employment discrimination laws discussed in this chapter.

---

23. *Bello v. Village of Skokie*, 151 F.Supp.3d 849 (N.D.Ill. 2015).

Exhibit 29–1 Coverage of Employment Discrimination Laws

TITLE VII OF THE CIVIL RIGHTS ACT	AGE DISCRIMINATION IN EMPLOYMENT ACT	AMERICANS WITH DISABILITIES ACT (AS AMENDED)	UNIFORMED SERVICES EMPLOYMENT AND REEMPLOYMENT RIGHTS ACT
Prohibits discrimination based on race, color, national origin, religion, gender, and pregnancy; prohibits sexual harassment.	Prohibits discrimination against persons over forty years of age.	Prohibits discrimination against persons with a mental or physical impairment that substantially limits a major life activity or who have a record of such an impairment, or who are regarded as having such an impairment, or who are associated with a disabled person.	Prohibits discrimination against persons who have served in the military.
Applies to employers with fifteen or more employees.	Applies to employers with twenty or more employees.	Applies to employers with fifteen or more employees.	Applies to all employers, even if they have only one employee.

29–3 Defenses to Employment Discrimination

The first line of defense for an employer charged with employment discrimination is to assert that the plaintiff has failed to meet his or her initial burden of proving that discrimination occurred. Once a plaintiff succeeds in proving discrimination, the burden shifts to the employer to justify the discriminatory practice.

Possible justifications include that the discrimination resulted from a business necessity, a bona fide occupational qualification, or a seniority system. In addition, as noted earlier, an effective antiharassment policy and prompt remedial action when harassment occurs can sometimes shield employers from liability for sexual harassment under Title VII.

29–3a Business Necessity

Business Necessity A defense to an allegation of employment discrimination in which the employer demonstrates that an employment practice that discriminates against members of a protected class is related to job performance.

An employer may defend against a claim of disparate-impact (unintentional) discrimination by asserting that a practice that has a discriminatory effect is a **business necessity.** **Example 29.21** EarthFix, Inc., an international consulting agency, requires its applicants to be fluent in at least two languages. If this requirement is shown to have a discriminatory effect, EarthFix can argue that its workers need to know more than one language to perform the job at a required level of competence. If EarthFix can demonstrate a definite connection between multilingualism and job performance, it normally will succeed in this business necessity defense. ▪

29–3b Bona Fide Occupational Qualification

Bona Fide Occupational Qualification (BFOQ) An identifiable characteristic reasonably necessary to the normal operation of a particular business. Such characteristics can include gender, national origin, and religion, but not race.

Another defense applies when discrimination against a protected class is essential to a job—that is, when a particular trait is a **bona fide occupational qualification (BFOQ).** Race, however, can never be a BFOQ.

Generally, courts have restricted the BFOQ defense to instances in which the employee's gender is essential to the job. For instance, a women's clothing store might legitimately hire only female sales attendants if part of an attendant's job involves assisting clients in the store's dressing rooms. Similarly, the Federal Aviation Administration can legitimately impose age limits for airline pilots—but an airline cannot impose weight limits only on female flight attendants.

29–3c Seniority Systems

Seniority System A system in which those who have worked longest for an employer are first in line for promotions, salary increases, and other benefits, and are last to be laid off if the workforce must be reduced.

An employer with a history of discrimination may have no members of protected classes in upper-level positions. Nevertheless, the employer may have a defense against a discrimination suit if promotions or other job benefits have been distributed according to a fair *seniority system.* In a **seniority system,** workers with more years of service are promoted first or laid off last.

Case Example 29.22 Cathalene Johnson, an African American woman, was a senior service agent for Federal Express Corporation (FedEx) for more than seventeen years. She resigned and filed a suit against FedEx for discrimination based on race and gender, as well as for violation of the Equal Pay Act. Johnson claimed that FedEx had paid a white male co-worker about two dollars more per hour than she received for basically the same position. FedEx argued that the man had seniority. He had worked for FedEx seven years longer, was the most senior employee at the station where Johnson worked, and had been a courier in addition to being a service agent. The court ruled that FedEx's seniority system was fair and provided a defense to Johnson's claims.[24] ▪

---

24. *Johnson v. Federal Express Corp.,* 996 F.Supp.2d 302 (M.D.Pa. 2014).

29–3d After-Acquired Evidence of Employee Misconduct

In some situations, employers have attempted to avoid liability for employment discrimination on the basis of *after-acquired evidence* of an employee's misconduct—that is, evidence that the employer discovered after the employee had filed a lawsuit. **Example 29.23** Pratt Legal Services fires Lucy, who then sues Pratt for employment discrimination. During pretrial investigation, Pratt discovers that Lucy made material misrepresentations on her job application. Had Pratt known of these misrepresentations, it would have had grounds to fire Lucy. ▪

After-acquired evidence of wrongdoing cannot shield an employer entirely from liability for discrimination. It may, however, be used to limit the amount of damages for which the employer is liable.

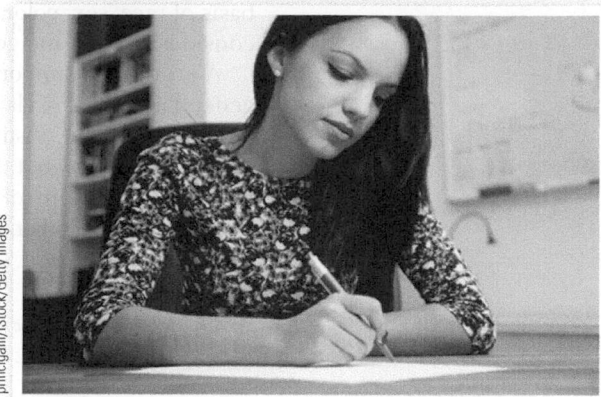

If this job candidate makes material misrepresentations on her application and is hired, can her employer use after-acquired evidence to shield itself from a discrimination lawsuit?

29–4 Affirmative Action

Federal statutes and regulations providing for equal opportunity in the workplace were designed to reduce or eliminate discriminatory practices with respect to hiring, retaining, and promoting employees. **Affirmative action** programs go further and attempt to "make up" for past patterns of discrimination by giving members of protected classes preferential treatment in hiring or promotion. During the 1960s, all federal and state government agencies, private companies that contracted to do business with the federal government, and institutions that received federal funding were required to implement affirmative action policies.

Title VII of the Civil Rights Act neither requires nor prohibits affirmative action. Thus, most private firms have not been required to implement affirmative action policies, though many have voluntarily done so. Affirmative action programs have been controversial, however, particularly when they have resulted in reverse discrimination.

Affirmative Action Job-hiring policies that give special consideration to members of protected classes in an effort to overcome present effects of past discrimination.

29–4a Equal Protection Issues

Because of their inherently discriminatory nature, affirmative action programs may violate the equal protection clause of the Fourteenth Amendment to the U.S. Constitution. Any federal, state, or local affirmative action program that uses racial or ethnic classifications as the basis for making decisions is subject to strict scrutiny (the highest standard to meet) by the courts.

Today, an affirmative action program normally is constitutional only if it attempts to remedy past discrimination and does not make use of quotas or preferences. Furthermore, once such a program has succeeded in the goal of remedying past discrimination, it must be changed or eliminated.

Learning Objective 5

Why are affirmative action programs often found to be unconstitutional?

Know This

The Fourteenth Amendment prohibits any state from denying any person "the equal protection of the laws." This prohibition applies to the federal government through the due process clause of the Fifth Amendment.

29–4b State Laws Prohibiting Affirmative Action Programs

Some states, including California, Maryland, Michigan, New Hampshire, Oklahoma, Virginia, and Washington, have enacted laws that prohibit affirmative action programs at public institutions (colleges, universities, and state agencies) within their borders. The United States Supreme Court has recognized that states have the power to enact such bans. **Case Example 29.24** Michigan voters passed an initiative to amend the state's constitution to prohibit publicly funded colleges from granting preferential treatment to any group on the basis of race, sex, color, ethnicity, or national origin. The law also prohibited Michigan from considering race and gender in public hiring and contracting decisions.

A group that supports affirmative action programs in education sued the state's attorney general and others, claiming that the initiative deprived minorities of equal protection and violated the U.S. Constitution. A federal appellate court agreed that the law violated the equal protection clause, but the United States Supreme Court reversed. The Court did not rule on the constitutionality of any specific affirmative action program but held that a state has the inherent power to ban affirmative action within that state.[25]

---

25. *Schuette v. Coalition to Defend Affirmative Action, Integration and Immigrant Rights*, 572 U.S. 291, 134 S.Ct. 1623, 188 L.Ed.2d 613 (2014).

Practice and Review

Amaani Lyle, an African American woman, took a job as a scriptwriters' assistant at Warner Brothers Television Productions. She worked for the writers of *Friends,* a popular, adult-oriented television series. One of her essential job duties was to type detailed notes for the scriptwriters during brainstorming sessions in which they discussed jokes, dialogue, and story lines. The writers then combed through Lyle's notes after the meetings for script material.

During the meetings, the three male scriptwriters told lewd and vulgar jokes and made sexually explicit comments and gestures. They often talked about their personal sexual experiences and fantasies, and some of these conversations were later used in episodes of *Friends.* During the meetings, Lyle never complained that she found the writers' conduct offensive.

After four months, Lyle was fired because she could not type fast enough to keep up with the writers' conversations during the meetings. She filed a suit against Warner Brothers alleging sexual harassment and claiming that her termination was based on racial discrimination. Using the information presented in the chapter, answer the following questions.

1. Would Lyle's claim of racial discrimination be for intentional (disparate-treatment) or unintentional (disparate-impact) discrimination? Explain.

2. Can Lyle establish a *prima facie* case of racial discrimination? Why or why not?

3. When she was hired, Lyle was told that typing speed was extremely important to her position. At the time, she maintained that she could type eighty words per minute, so she was not given a typing test. It later turned out that Lyle could type only fifty words per minute. What impact might typing speed have on Lyle's lawsuit?

4. Lyle's sexual-harassment claim was based on the hostile work environment created by the writers' sexually offensive conduct at meetings that she was required to attend. The writers, however, argued that their behavior was essential to the "creative process" of writing *Friends,* a show that routinely contained sexual innuendos and adult humor. Which defense discussed in the chapter might Warner Brothers assert using this argument?

Debate This

Members of minority groups and women no longer need special legislation to protect them from employment discrimination.

Key Terms

affirmative action 717

bona fide occupational qualification (BFOQ) 716

business necessity 716

constructive discharge 705

disparate-impact discrimination 696

disparate-treatment discrimination 696

prima facie case 696

protected class 695

seniority system 716

sexual harassment 706

tangible employment action 706

Chapter Summary: Employment Discrimination

Title VII of the Civil Rights Act	Title VII prohibits employment discrimination based on race, color, national origin, religion, or gender.
	1. *Procedures*—Employees alleging discrimination must file a claim with the Equal Employment Opportunity Commission (EEOC). The EEOC may sue the employer on the employee's behalf. If it does not, the EEOC may allow the employee to sue the employer directly.
	2. *Types of discrimination*—Title VII prohibits both intentional (disparate-treatment) and unintentional (disparate-impact) discrimination. Disparate-impact discrimination occurs when an employer's practices, tests, or procedures, such as requiring a certain level of education, have the effect of discriminating against a protected class. Title VII extends to discriminatory practices, such as various forms of harassment, in the online environment.
	3. *Remedies for discrimination under Title VII*—Remedies include reinstatement, back pay, and retroactive promotions. Damages (both compensatory and punitive) may be awarded for intentional discrimination.
Discrimination Based on Age, Disability, or Military Status	1. *The Age Discrimination in Employment Act (ADEA)*—Prohibits employment discrimination on the basis of age against individuals forty years of age or older. Procedures for bringing a case under the ADEA are similar to those for bringing a case under Title VII.
	2. *The Americans with Disabilities Act (ADA)*—Prohibits employment discrimination against persons with disabilities who are otherwise qualified to perform the essential functions of the jobs for which they apply.
	a. To prevail on a claim, the plaintiff must show that she or he has a disability, is otherwise qualified for the employment in question, and was excluded from it solely because of the disability. Procedures and remedies under the ADA are similar to those in Title VII cases.
	b. The ADA defines the term *disability* as a physical or mental impairment that substantially limits one or more of an individual's major life activities, a record of such impairment, or being regarded as having such an impairment.
	c. Employers are required to reasonably accommodate the needs of qualified persons with disabilities through such measures as modifying the physical work environment and permitting more flexible work schedules.
	3. *The Uniformed Services Employment and Reemployment Rights Act (USERRA)*—Prohibits discrimination against persons who have served in the military. The USERRA applies to *all* employers regardless of their size.
Defenses to Employment Discrimination	As defenses to claims of employment discrimination, employers may assert that the discrimination was required for reasons of business necessity, to meet a bona fide occupational qualification, or to maintain a legitimate seniority system. Evidence of prior employee misconduct acquired after the employee has been fired is not a defense to discrimination.
Affirmative Action	Affirmative action programs attempt to "make up" for past patterns of discrimination by giving members of protected classes preferential treatment in hiring or promotion. Such programs are subject to strict scrutiny by the courts and are often struck down for violating the Fourteenth Amendment.

Issue Spotters

1. Ruth is a supervisor for a Subs & Suds restaurant. Tim is a Subs & Suds employee. The owner announces that some employees will be discharged. Ruth tells Tim that if he has sex with her, he can keep his job. Is this sexual harassment? Why or why not? (See *Title VII of the Civil Rights Act.*)

2. Koko, a person with a disability, applies for a job at Lively Sales Corporation for which she is well qualified, but she is rejected. Lively continues to seek applicants and eventually fills the position with a person who does not have a disability. Could Koko succeed in a suit against Lively for discrimination? Explain. (See *Discrimination Based on Age, Disability, or Military Status.*)

   —**Check your answers to the *Issue Spotters* against the answers provided in Appendix D at the end of this text.**

Business Scenarios and Case Problems

29–1. Title VII Violations. Discuss fully whether either of the following actions would constitute a violation of Title VII of the Civil Rights Act.

1. Tennington, Inc., is a consulting firm with ten employees. These employees travel on consulting jobs in seven states. Tennington has an employment record of hiring only white males. (See *Title VII of the Civil Rights Act.*)

2. Novo Films, Inc., is making a film about Africa and needs to employ approximately one hundred extras for this picture. To hire these extras, Novo advertises in all major newspapers in Southern California. The ad states that only African Americans need apply. (See *Defenses to Employment Discrimination.*)

29–2. Religious Discrimination. Gina Gomez, a devout Roman Catholic, worked for Sam's Department Stores, Inc., in Phoenix, Arizona. Sam's considered Gomez a productive employee because her sales exceeded $200,000 per year. The store gave its managers the discretion to grant unpaid leave to employees but prohibited vacations or leave during the holiday season—October through December. Gomez felt that she had a "calling" to go on a "pilgrimage" in October to a location in Bosnia where some persons claimed to have had visions of the Virgin Mary. The Catholic Church had not designated the site an official pilgrimage site, the visions were not expected to be stronger in October, and tours were available at other times. The store managers denied Gomez's request for leave, but she had a nonrefundable ticket and left anyway. Sam's terminated her employment, and she could not find another job. Can Gomez establish a *prima facie* case of religious discrimination? Explain. (See *Title VII of the Civil Rights Act.*)

29–3. Spotlight on Dress Code Policies—Discrimination Based on Gender. Burlington Coat Factory Warehouse, Inc., had a dress code that required male sales clerks to wear business attire consisting of slacks, shirt, and necktie. Female salesclerks, by contrast, were required to wear a smock so that customers could readily identify them. Karen O'Donnell and other female employees refused to wear the smock. Instead, they reported to work in business attire and were suspended. After numerous suspensions, the female employees were fired for violating Burlington's dress code policy. All other conditions of employment, including salary, hours, and benefits, were the same for female and male employees. Was the dress code policy discriminatory? Why or why not? [*O'Donnell v. Burlington Coat Factory Warehouse, Inc.*, 656 F.Supp. 263 (S.D.Ohio 1987)] (See *Title VII of the Civil Rights Act.*)

29–4. Age Discrimination. Beginning in 1986, Paul Rangel was a sales professional for pharmaceutical company Sanofi-Aventis U.S., LLC (S-A). Rangel had satisfactory performance reviews until 2006, when S-A issued new expectations guidelines with sales call quotas and other standards that he failed to meet. After two years of negative performance reviews, Rangel—who was then more than forty years old—was terminated as part of a nationwide reduction of sales professionals who had not met the expectations guidelines. This sales force reduction also included younger workers. Did S-A engage in age discrimination? Discuss. [*Rangel v. Sanofi Aventis U.S. LLC,* 507 Fed.Appx. 782 (10th Cir. 2013)] (See *Discrimination Based on Age, Disability, or Military Status.*)

29–5. Discrimination Based on Disability. Cynthia Horn worked for Knight Facilities Management–GM, Inc., in Detroit, Michigan, as a janitor. When Horn developed a sensitivity to cleaning products, her physician gave her a "no exposure to cleaning solutions" restriction. Knight discussed possible accommodations with Horn. She suggested that restrooms be eliminated from her cleaning route or that she be provided with a respirator. Knight explained that she would be exposed to cleaning solutions in any situation and concluded that there was no work available within her physician's restriction. Has Knight violated the Americans with Disabilities Act by failing to provide Horn with the requested accommodations? Explain. [*Horn v. Knight Facilities Management–GM, Inc.,* 556 Fed.Appx.

452 (6th Cir. 2014)] (See *Discrimination Based on Age, Disability, or Military Status.*)

29–6. Business Case Problem with Sample Answer— Sexual Harassment. Jamel Blanton, a male employee at a Pizza Hut restaurant operated by Newton Associates, Inc., in San Antonio, Texas, was subjected to sexual and racial harassment by the general manager, who was female. Newton had a clear, straightforward antidiscrimination policy and complaint procedure. The policy provided that in such a situation, an employee should complain to the harasser's supervisor. Blanton alerted a shift leader and an assistant manager about the harassment, but they were subordinate to the general manager and did not report the harassment to higher-level management. When Blanton finally complained to a manager with authority over the general manager, the employer investigated and fired the general manager within four days. Blanton filed a suit in a federal district court against Newton, seeking to impose liability on the employer for the general manager's actions. What is Newton's best defense? Discuss. [*Blanton v. Newton Associates, Inc.,* 593 Fed.Appx. 389 (5th Cir. 2015)] (See *Title VII of the Civil Rights Act.*)

—**For a sample answer to Problem 29–6, go to Appendix E at the end of this text.**

29–7. Discrimination Based on Disability. Dennis Wallace was a deputy sheriff for Stanislaus County, California, when he injured his left knee. After surgery, he was subject to limits on prolonged standing, walking, and running. The county assigned him to work as a bailiff. The sergeants who supervised him rated his performance above average. Less than a year later, without consulting those supervisors, the county placed him on an unpaid leave of absence, under the mistaken belief that he could not safely perform the essential functions of the job. Wallace filed an action in a California state court against the county, alleging discrimination based on disability. Under state law, discriminatory intent is shown by evidence that an actual or perceived disability was a "substantial motivating factor or reason" for an employer's adverse employment action. An employee is not required to show that the action was motivated by animosity or ill will. Could Wallace likely prove the "substantial motivating factor or reason" element? Explain. [*Wallace v. County of Stanislaus,* 245 Cal.App.4th 109, 199 Cal.Rptr.3d 462

(5 Dist. 2016)] (See *Discrimination Based on Age, Disability, or Military Status.*)

29–8. Discrimination Based on Gender. The Fresno County Office of Education hired Aileen Rizo as a math consultant. She had previously worked as a middle and high school math teacher, earning about $50,000 a year. Fresno based the salary of its new hires on the individual's prior salary, according to the county's Standard Operating Procedure (SOP). When Rizo learned that she was being paid less than comparable male employees for the same work, she filed a complaint. The county responded that all salaries were set under the SOP. Rizo filed a suit against Jim Yovino, the Fresno superintendent, claiming a violation of the Equal Pay Act. She asserted that under the Equal Pay Act, an employer should not be able to justify a wage differential between men and women on the basis of prior salary. Yovino argued that basing pay on a prior salary was permissible under an exception in the act for "any factor other than gender." Did the county violate the Equal Pay Act? Discuss. [*Rizo v. Yovino,* 887 F.3d 453 (9th Cir. 2018)] (See *Title VII of the Civil Rights Act.*)

29–9. A Question of Ethics—The IDDR Approach and Unintentional Discrimination. *McLane Company is a supply-chain services company that distributes goods to retailers. McLane requires employees with physically demanding jobs to have physical evaluations, both when they start work and when they return after medical leave. After working in a physically demanding job for McLane for eight years, Damiana Ochoa took maternity leave. When she returned to work, she failed the physical evaluation and was fired. She filed a discrimination complaint with the Equal Employment Opportunity Commission (EEOC). The agency issued a subpoena—an order to appear in court—seeking the names and contact information of McLane employees who had been asked to have evaluations throughout the company's national operations.* [McLane Co. v. Equal Employment Opportunity Commission, __ U.S. __, 137 S.Ct. 1159, 197 L.Ed.2d 500 (2017)] (See Title VII of the Civil Rights Act.)

1. On what legal ground might McLane legitimately refuse to comply with the EEOC's subpoena? What practical factors could affect the choice not to comply? Discuss.

2. Using the IDDR approach, consider whether McLane has an ethical duty to comply with the subpoena.

Critical Thinking and Writing Assignments

29–10. Critical Legal Thinking. Why has the federal government limited the application of the statutes discussed in this chapter to firms with a specified number of employees, such as fifteen or twenty? Should these laws apply to all employers regardless of size? Why or why not? (See *Title VII of the Civil Rights Act*.)

29–11. Time-Limited Group Assignment—Discrimination Based on Race. Two African American plaintiffs sued the producers of the reality television series *The Bachelor* and *The Bachelorette* for racial discrimination. The plaintiffs claimed that the shows had never featured a person of color in the lead role. Plaintiffs also alleged that the producers had failed to provide people of color who auditioned for lead roles with the same opportunities to compete

as white people who auditioned. (See *Title VII of the Civil Rights Act*.)

1. The first group will assess whether the plaintiffs can establish a *prima facie* case of disparate-treatment discrimination.

2. The second group will consider what the plaintiffs would have to show to establish disparate-impact discrimination.

3. The third group will assume that the plaintiffs established a *prima facie* case and that the burden has shifted to the employer to articulate a legal reason for not hiring the plaintiffs. What legitimate reasons might the employer assert for not hiring the plaintiffs in this situation? Should the law require television producers to hire persons of color for lead roles in reality television shows? Explain your answer.

Unit Four—Task-Based Simulation

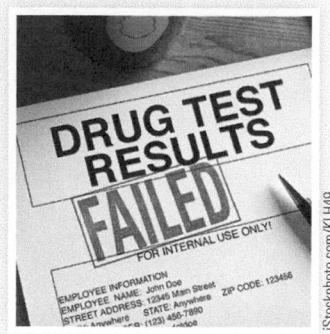

Two brothers, Ray and Paul Ashford, start a business—Ashford Brothers, Inc.—manufacturing a new type of battery system for hybrid automobiles. The batteries hit the market at the perfect time and are in great demand.

1. **Agency.** Loren, one of Ashford's salespersons, anxious to make a sale, intentionally quotes a price to a customer that is $500 lower than Ashford has authorized for the product. The customer purchases the product at the quoted price. When Ashford learns of the deal, it claims that it is not legally bound to the sales contract because it has not authorized Loren to sell the product at that price. Is Ashford bound to the contract? Discuss fully.

2. **Workers' Compensation.** One day, Gina, an Ashford employee, suffered a serious burn when she accidentally spilled some acid on her hand. The accident occurred because another employee, who was suspected of using illegal drugs, carelessly bumped into her. Gina's hand required a series of skin grafts before it healed sufficiently to allow her to return to work. Gina wants to obtain compensation for her lost wages and medical expenses. Can she do that? If so, how?

3. **Drug Testing.** After Gina's injury, Ashford decides to conduct random drug tests on all of its employees. Several employees claim that the testing violates their privacy rights and bring a lawsuit. What factors will the court consider in deciding whether the random drug testing is legally permissible?

4. **COBRA.** Ashford provides health insurance for its two hundred employees, including Dan. For personal medical reasons, Dan takes twelve weeks' leave. During this period, can Dan continue his coverage under Ashford's health-insurance plan? After Dan returns to work, Ashford closes Dan's division and terminates the employees, including Dan. Can Dan continue his coverage under Ashford's health-insurance plan after the termination? Explain.

5. **Sexual Harassment.** Aretha, another employee at Ashford, is disgusted by the sexually offensive behavior of several male employees. She has complained to her supervisor on several occasions about the behavior, but the supervisor merely laughs at her concerns. Aretha decides to bring a legal action against the company for sexual harassment. Does Aretha's complaint concern *quid pro quo* harassment or hostile-environment harassment? What federal statute protects employees from sexual harassment? What remedies are available under that statute? What procedures must Aretha follow in pursuing her legal action?

Unit 5
Business Organizations

30

Sole Proprietorships and Franchises

Learning Objectives

The four Learning Objectives below are designed to help improve your understanding. After reading this chapter, you should be able to answer the following questions:

1. What advantages and disadvantages are associated with the sole proprietorship?

2. What is required by the Franchise Rule, and why?

3. What might happen if a franchisor exercises too much control over the operations of a franchise?

4. When will a court decide that a franchisor has wrongfully terminated a franchise?

Entrepreneur One who initiates and assumes the financial risk of a new business enterprise and undertakes to provide or control its management.

> "Why not go out on a limb? Isn't that where the fruit is?"

Frank Scully
1892–1964
(American author)

Many Americans would agree with Frank Scully's comment in the chapter-opening quotation that to succeed in business one must "go out on a limb." Certainly, an entrepreneur's primary motive for "going out on a limb" to start a business enterprise is to make profits.

An **entrepreneur** is one who initiates and assumes the financial risks of a new enterprise and undertakes to provide or control its management. Keep in mind that many of the biggest corporations today, such as Apple, Alphabet (Google), and Amazon, were originally very small companies. Jeff Bezos, founder of Amazon, and Steve Jobs, founder of Apple, started their companies in their garages.

One of the first decisions an entrepreneur must make is which form of business organization will be most appropriate for the new endeavor. In selecting an organizational form, the entrepreneur will consider a number of factors, including (1) ease of creation, (2) the liability of the owners, (3) tax considerations, and (4) the ability to raise capital. Keep these factors in mind as you read this unit and learn about the various forms of business organization. In considering these business forms, remember, too, that the primary motive of an entrepreneur is to make profits.

Traditionally, entrepreneurs have used three major forms to structure their business enterprises—the sole proprietorship, the partnership, and the corporation. In this chapter, we examine sole proprietorships. We also discuss franchises. Although the franchise is not, strictly speaking, a separate business organizational form, it is widely used today by entrepreneurs.

30–1 Sole Proprietorships

The simplest form of business is a **sole proprietorship.** In this form, the owner is the business. Thus, anyone who does business without creating a separate business organization has a sole proprietorship.

More than two-thirds of all U.S. businesses are sole proprietorships. Sole proprietors can own and manage any type of business from an informal home office or Web-based undertaking to a large restaurant or construction firm. Most sole proprietorships are small enterprises, however. About 99 percent of the sole proprietorships in the United States have revenues of less than $1 million per year.

30–1a Advantages of the Sole Proprietorship

A major advantage of the sole proprietorship is that the proprietor owns the entire business and has a right to receive all of the profits (because he or she assumes all of the risk). In addition, starting a sole proprietorship is often easier and less costly than starting any other kind of business, as few legal formalities are involved. Generally, no documents need to be filed with the government to start a sole proprietorship.[1]

Taxes A sole proprietor pays only personal income taxes (including Social Security and Medicare taxes) on the business's profits. The profits are reported as personal income on the proprietor's personal income tax return. In other words, the business itself need not file an income tax return. Sole proprietors are allowed to establish retirement accounts that are tax-exempt until the funds are withdrawn.

Like any form of business enterprise, a sole proprietorship can be liable for other taxes, such as those collected and applied to the disbursement of unemployment compensation. The unpaid unemployment compensation taxes of a sole proprietorship were at issue in the following case.

> **Sole Proprietorship** The simplest form of business organization, in which the owner is the business. The owner reports business income on his or her personal income tax return and is legally responsible for all debts and obligations incurred by the business.

> **Learning Objective 1**
> What advantages and disadvantages are associated with the sole proprietorship?

---

1. Sole proprietorships may need to comply with certain zoning requirements, obtain a business license or other appropriate license from the state, and the like.

■ Case 30.1

A. Gadley Enterprises, Inc. v. Department of Labor and Industry Office of Unemployment Compensation Tax Services

Commonwealth Court of Pennsylvania, 2016 WL 55591 (2016).

Background and Facts Julianne Gresh operated Romper Room Day Care, as a sole proprietorship in Pennsylvania. Gresh owed the state's Department of Labor and Industry Office of Unemployment Compensation Tax Services $43,000 in unpaid unemployment compensation contributions, interest, and penalties. Because she was about to lose her license to operate, Gresh sold her business to A. Gadley Enterprises, Inc. A. Gadley agreed to pay Gresh $38,000 for her business assets—$10,000 for the use of the name "Romper Room," $10,790 for a covenant not to compete, and $17,210 for items on an "Inventory List."

The state's unemployment compensation law contains a "bulk sales provision." It requires a buyer of 51 percent or more of an employer's assets to obtain a state-issued certificate from the seller showing that all amounts owed to the state have been paid. A failure to obtain the certificate renders the buyer liable for any unpaid amount. A. Gadley did not obtain this certificate from Gresh. As a result, the Department of Labor and Industry notified A. Gadley that it was liable for Gresh's unpaid debt. A. Gadley asked a Pennsylvania court to review the assessment of liability.

(Continues)

In the Words of the Court

SIMPSON, Judge.

* * * *

Purchaser [A. Gadley argues that the state] erred in construing the term "assets" in the bulk sales provision to include only business assets when determining whether a sale met the 51 percent threshold. Purchaser asserts the provision does not differentiate between business and personal assets of an employer and there is no legal distinction when the employer is a sole proprietor.

* * * *

* * * The definition of "employer" [in the Unemployment Compensation Law] includes a sole proprietor like [Gresh]. The word "assets" is not defined in the Law. [In Section 788.3(a)] the term "assets" precedes a list of examples, followed by the phrase "including but not limited to."

* * * *

* * * The examples * * * indicate that the term "assets" refers to business assets. This conclusion is buttressed [reinforced] by the context of the statute as a whole, which pertains to employers operating businesses and paying employees as part of their business operations.

The factual circumstances surrounding the sale also indicate the term "assets" means "business assets." Here, the context is the sale of a business, in the childcare industry, to another business engaged in the same industry that intends to operate a childcare facility at the location of the former business. The Agreement reflects the intention of the parties that Purchaser would operate the childcare facility as a satellite location. [Emphasis added.]

* * * *

Moreover, Purchaser's interpretation does not consider *the purpose of the bulk sales provision. That purpose is to ensure an employer does not divest itself of assets without satisfying outstanding liabilities, either itself or by the purchaser.* [Emphasis added.]

Decision and Remedy The Pennsylvania state court affirmed the Department of Labor and Industry's decision that A. Gadley was liable for the unpaid taxes. Gresh's sale of her business assets triggered the certificate requirement. A. Gadley's failure to obtain the certificate rendered it liable for Gresh's unpaid unemployment compensation contributions.

Critical Thinking

• **Legal Environment** *What action can A. Gadley take now to avoid suffering the loss of the funds required to cover Gresh's unpaid taxes?*

• **Ethical** *Did A. Gadley act unethically by not obtaining from Gresh the certificate required by the state's unemployment compensation law? Discuss.*

Flexibility A sole proprietorship also offers more flexibility than does a partnership or a corporation. The sole proprietor is free to make any decision she or he wishes concerning the business—including whom to hire, when to take a vacation, and what kind of business to pursue. The sole proprietor can sell or transfer all or part of the business to another party at any time without seeking approval from anyone else. In contrast, approval is typically required from partners in a partnership and from shareholders in a corporation.

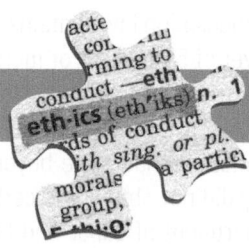

Ethical Issue

Can the religious beliefs of a small business owner justify the business refusing to provide services to members of the LGBT community? In recent years, American society has come a long way in accepting that persons in the LGBT (lesbian, gay, bisexual, and transgender) community should be treated fairly. Nevertheless, many business owners' religious beliefs prevent them from wanting to have these individuals as customers. In a number of cases, business owners refuse to provide services to gay or lesbian couples based on their religious beliefs. This is particularly apparent in the wedding industry, when same-sex couples are planning to marry.

For example, the owners of a wedding-photography business in New Mexico refused to photograph a ceremony held by clients who were gay. They based this refusal on their religious beliefs.

New Mexico's highest court ruled against the owners. Additionally, a New York court imposed a $10,000 fine on the owners of a small business that refused to rent a wedding venue to a gay couple for their ceremony.[2]

Currently, federal law does not provide protection against discrimination based on sexual orientation in the same way that it protects against discrimination based on race, color, and some other "protected" characteristics. Many states, though, do have laws prohibiting discrimination based on sexual orientation, as do many cities.

The intersection of business owners' religious beliefs and the rights of gays and lesbians is certain to be an area in which there will be continuing litigation, and additional laws may need to be created.

30–1b Disadvantages of the Sole Proprietorship

The major disadvantage of the sole proprietorship is that the proprietor alone bears the burden of any losses or liabilities incurred by the business enterprise. In other words, the sole proprietor has unlimited liability, or legal responsibility, for all obligations incurred in doing business.

Case Example 30.1 Michael Sark operated a logging business as a sole proprietorship. To acquire equipment for the business, Sark and his wife, Paula, borrowed funds from Quality Car & Truck Leasing, Inc. Eventually, the logging business failed, and Sark was unable to pay his creditors, including Quality. The Sarks filed a bankruptcy petition and sold their house (valued at $203,500) to their son, Michael, Jr., for one dollar but continued to live in it.

Three months later, Quality obtained a judgment in an Ohio state court against the Sarks for $150,480. Quality also filed a claim to set aside the transfer of the house to Michael, Jr., as a fraudulent conveyance. The trial court ruled in Quality's favor, and the Sarks appealed. A state intermediate appellate court affirmed. The Sarks were personally liable for the debts of the sole proprietorship.[3] ▪

Personal Assets at Risk Because of the sole proprietor's unlimited liability, creditors can go after his or her personal assets to satisfy any business debts. Although sole proprietors may obtain insurance to protect the business, liability can easily exceed policy limits. This unlimited liability is a major factor to be considered in choosing a business form.

Example 30.2 Sheila Fowler operates a golf shop near a world-class golf course as a sole proprietorship. One of Fowler's employees fails to secure a display of golf clubs, and they fall on Dean Maheesh, a professional golfer, and seriously injure him. If Maheesh sues Fowler's shop and wins, Fowler's personal liability could easily exceed the limits of her insurance policy. Fowler could lose not only her business, but also her house, her car, and any other personal assets that can be attached to pay the judgment. ▪

Lack of Continuity and Limited Ability to Raise Capital The sole proprietorship also has the disadvantage of lacking continuity after the death of the proprietor. When the owner dies, so does the business—it is automatically dissolved.

Another disadvantage is that in raising capital, the proprietor is limited to his or her personal funds and any loans that he or she can obtain for the business. Lenders may be unwilling to make loans to sole proprietorships, particularly start-ups, because the sole proprietor risks unlimited personal liability and may not be able to pay. (See this chapter's *Adapting the Law to the Online Environment* feature for a discussion of one court's refusal to discharge a loan made to a sole proprietor who had declared bankruptcy.)

"Always tell yourself: The difference between running a business and ruining a business is I."

Anonymous

Can a person who owns a logging business as a sole proprietorship avoid liability for the business's debts?

---

2. See *Elane Photography, LLC. v. Willock*, 2013 -NMSC- 040, 309 P.3d 53 (2013); and *Gifford v. McCarthy*, 137 A.D.3d 30, 23 N.Y.S.3d 422 (Dept. 3 2016).

3. *Quality Car & Truck Leasing, Inc. v. Sark*, 2013 -Ohio- 44 (Ohio Ct.App. 2013).

A Sole Proprietorship, Facebook Poker, and Bankruptcy

One major downside of a sole proprietorship is that it is more difficult for a sole proprietor to obtain funding for start-up and expansion. Moreover, if funding is obtained through loans, the sole proprietor is exposed to personal liability.

Personal Liability Exposure for an Online Start-up

A case in point went before the United States bankruptcy court in Massachusetts in 2015.[a] Michael Dewhurst, living in Raynham, Massachusetts, sometimes did computer work for Gerald Knappik. Dewhurst decided to start a new business venture—the commercial development of an online poker-playing application. Dewhurst envisioned an application that would enable multiple individuals to play poker together over the Internet through Facebook. Dewhurst informed Knappik of his business plan and predicted that his Facebook poker application "was going to be something very big."

a. *In re Dewhurst*, 528 Bankr. 211 (D.Mass. 2015). See also, *In re Zutrau*, 563 Bankr. 431 (1st Cir. 2017).

Knappik initially loaned $50,000 to Dewhurst for the project. The loan agreement stated, "The sole purpose of this loan agreement is to provide funds on a personal level for the start-up of said business project, in conjunction with borrower's personal funds, not limited to start-up costs, operating expenses, advertising costs." That was the first of a series of personal loans that ultimately totaled $220,000.

Dewhurst had repaid only $9,000 on the total outstanding debt when he filed for bankruptcy. Ultimately, the bankruptcy court ascertained that at least $120,000 of the loans that were supposed to be used exclusively for the Facebook poker project had been used for other activities. Furthermore, Dewhurst kept "no contemporaneous records of his disbursements and uses of this cash, no cash journal, ledger, or disbursement slips of any kind."

The Lender Objects to a Discharge of the Debt in Bankruptcy

During bankruptcy proceedings, Knappik requested that the bankruptcy court deny discharge of Dewhurst's debts to him. Upon review, the court stated that "Dewhurst's failure to keep and preserve adequate records makes it impossible to reconstruct an accurate and complete account of financial affairs and business transactions." The bankruptcy judge ultimately denied discharge of $120,000 of the debt owed to Knappik. Thus, a sole proprietor's failed attempt to create an online poker-playing application led to personal liability even after he had filed for bankruptcy.

Critical Thinking

Sole proprietorships, as well as other businesses, routinely seek funding for online projects. How can the individuals involved avoid personal liability?

Franchise Any arrangement in which the owner of a trademark, trade name, or copyright licenses another to use that trademark, trade name, or copyright in the selling of goods or services.

Franchisee One receiving a license to use another's (the franchisor's) trademark, trade name, or copyright in the sale of goods and services.

Franchisor One licensing another (the franchisee) to use the owner's trademark, trade name, or copyright in the selling of goods or services.

30–2 Franchises

Instead of setting up a completely independent business, many entrepreneurs opt to purchase a franchise. A **franchise** is an arrangement in which the owner of intellectual property—such as a trademark, a trade name, or a copyright—licenses others to use it in the selling of goods or services. A **franchisee** (a purchaser of a franchise) is generally legally independent of the **franchisor** (the seller of the franchise). At the same time, the franchisee is economically dependent on the franchisor's integrated business system. In other words, a franchisee can operate as an independent businessperson and choose any business form but still obtain the advantages of a regional or national organization.

Today, franchising companies and their franchisees account for a significant portion of all retail sales in this country. Well-known franchises include McDonald's, 7-Eleven, and Holiday Inn. Franchising has also become a popular way for businesses to expand their operations internationally, as discussed in this chapter's *Beyond Our Borders* feature.

Franchising in Foreign Nations

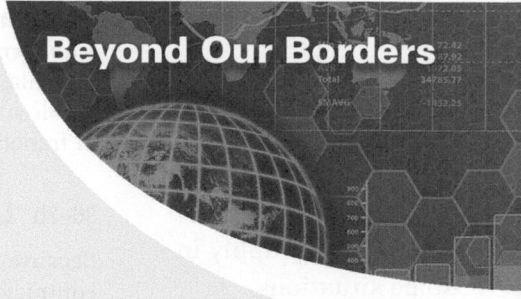

In the last twenty-five years, many U.S. companies (particularly fast-food chains and coffeehouses) have successfully expanded through franchising in nations around the globe. Targeted locations include Asia and Central and South America, as well as Canada and Mexico in North America. Franchises offer businesses a way to expand internationally without violating the legal restrictions that many nations impose on foreign ownership of businesses.

Cultural and Legal Differences Are Important

Businesspersons must exercise caution when entering international franchise relationships, however. Differences in language, culture, laws, and business practices can seriously complicate the franchising relationship. If a U.S. franchisor's quality control standards do not mesh with local business practices, for instance,

how can the franchisor maintain the quality of its product and protect its good reputation? If the law in, say, China does not provide for a high level of intellectual property protection, how can a U.S. franchisor protect its trademark rights or prevent its secret recipe or formula from being copied?

The Need to Assess the Market

Because of the complexities of international franchising, a company seeking to franchise overseas needs to conduct thorough research to determine whether its business will be well received in the target country. It is important to know the political and cultural climate, as well as current economic trends. Marketing surveys to assess the potential success of the franchise location are crucial.

Because compliance with U.S. disclosure laws may not satisfy the legal requirements of other nations, most successful franchisors retain attorneys knowledgeable

in the laws of the prospective location. The attorneys can draft dispute-settlement provisions (such as an arbitration clause) for international franchising contracts and advise the franchisor about the tax implications of operating a foreign franchise (such as import taxes and customs duties).

Critical Thinking

Should a U.S.-based franchisor be allowed to impose contract terms and quality control standards on franchisees in foreign nations that are different from those imposed on domestic franchisees? Why or why not?

30–2a Types of Franchises

Many different kinds of businesses now sell franchises, and numerous types of franchises are available. Generally, though, most franchises fall into one of three classifications: distributorships, chain-style business operations, or manufacturing or processing-plant arrangements.

Distributorships In a *distributorship*, a manufacturer (the franchisor) licenses a dealer (the franchisee) to sell its product. Often, a distributorship covers an exclusive territory. Automobile dealerships and beer distributorships are examples of this type of franchise.

Example 30.3 Black Snow Beer Company distributes its beer brands through a network of authorized wholesale distributors, each with an assigned territory. Marik signs a distributorship contract for the area from Gainesville to Ocala, Florida. If the contract states that Marik is the exclusive distributor in that area, then no other franchisee may distribute Black Snow beer in that region. ■

Chain-Style Business Operations In a *chain-style business operation*, a franchise operates under a franchisor's trade name and is identified as a member of a select group of dealers that engage in the franchisor's business. The franchisee is generally required to follow standardized or prescribed methods of operation. In addition, the franchisee may be required to obtain materials and supplies exclusively from the franchisor.

McDonald's and most other fast-food chains are examples of chain-style franchises. This type of franchise is also common in service-related businesses, including real estate brokerage firms such as Century 21 and tax-preparing services such as H&R Block, Inc.

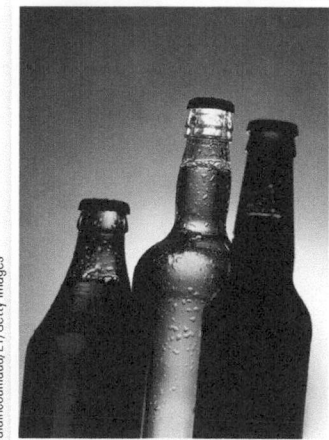

alaincouillaud/E+/Getty Images

If these brands of beer are sold through authorized wholesale distributors only, can a potential distributor obtain an exclusive territory?

Manufacturing or Processing-Plant Arrangements In a *manufacturing or processing-plant arrangement*, the franchisor transmits to the franchisee the essential ingredients or formula to make a particular product. The franchisee then markets the product either at wholesale or at retail in accordance with the franchisor's standards. Examples of this type of franchise are Pepsi-Cola and other soft-drink bottling companies.

30–2b Laws Governing Franchising

Because a franchise relationship is primarily a contractual relationship, it is governed by contract law. If the franchise exists primarily for the sale of products manufactured by the franchisor, the law governing sales contracts as expressed in Article 2 of the Uniform Commercial Code applies.

Additionally, the federal government and most states have enacted laws governing certain aspects of franchising. Generally, these laws are designed to protect prospective franchisees from dishonest franchisors and to prohibit franchisors from terminating franchises without good cause.

Federal Regulation of Franchising The federal government regulates franchising through laws that apply to specific industries and through the Franchise Rule, created by the Federal Trade Commission (FTC).

Industry-Specific Standards. Congress has enacted laws that protect franchisees in certain industries, such as automobile dealerships and service stations. These laws protect the franchisee from unreasonable demands and bad-faith terminations of the franchise by the franchisor.

An automobile manufacturer-franchisor cannot make unreasonable demands of dealer-franchisees or set unrealistically high sales quotas, for instance. If an automobile manufacturer-franchisor terminates a franchise because of a dealer-franchisee's failure to comply with unreasonable demands, the manufacturer may be liable for damages.[4]

Similarly, federal law prescribes the conditions under which a franchisor of service stations can terminate a franchise.[5] In addition, federal antitrust laws sometimes apply to prohibit certain types of anticompetitive agreements involving service-station franchises.

The Franchise Rule. The FTC's Franchise Rule requires franchisors to disclose certain material facts that a prospective franchisee needs in order to make an informed decision concerning the purchase of a franchise.[6] Those who violate the Franchise Rule are subject to substantial civil penalties, and the FTC can sue on behalf of injured parties to recover damages.

The rule requires the franchisor to make numerous written disclosures to prospective franchisees (see Exhibit 30–1). All representations made to a prospective franchisee must have a reasonable basis. For instance, if a franchisor provides projected earnings figures, the franchisor must indicate whether the figures are based on actual data or hypothetical examples. If a franchisor makes sales or earnings projections based on actual data for a specific franchise location, the franchisor must disclose the number and percentage of its existing franchises that have achieved this result. The Franchise Rule does not require franchisors to provide potential earnings figures, however.

State Regulation of Franchising State legislation varies but generally is aimed at protecting franchisees from unfair practices and bad-faith terminations by franchisors.

---

4. Automobile Dealers' Franchise Act of 1965, also known as the Automobile Dealers' Day in Court Act, 15 U.S.C. Sections 1221 *et seq.*
5. Petroleum Marketing Practices Act (PMPA) of 1979, 15 U.S.C. Sections 2801 *et seq.*
6. 16 C.F.R. Part 436.

Exhibit 30–1 The FTC's Franchise Rule Requirements

REQUIREMENTS	EXPLANATION
Written (or electronic) disclosures	The franchisor must make numerous disclosures, such as the range of goods and services included, as well as the value and estimated profitability of the franchise. Disclosures can be delivered on paper or electronically. Prospective franchisees must be able to download or save any electronic disclosure documents.
Reasonable basis for any representations	To prevent deception, all representations made to a prospective franchisee must have a reasonable basis at the time they are made.
Projected earnings figures	If a franchisor provides projected earnings figures, the franchisor must indicate whether the figures are based on actual data or hypothetical examples. The Franchise Rule does not require franchisors to provide potential earnings figures, however.
Actual data	If a franchisor makes sales or earnings projections based on actual data for a specific franchise location, the franchisor must disclose the number and percentage of its existing franchises that have achieved this result.
Explanation of terms	Franchisors are required to explain termination, cancellation, and renewal provisions of the franchise contract to potential franchisees before the agreement is signed.

State Disclosures. A number of states have laws similar to the federal rules requiring franchisors to provide presale disclosures to prospective franchisees.[7] Many state laws also require that a disclosure document (known as the Franchise Disclosure Document, or FDD) be registered or filed with a state official. State laws may also require that a franchisor submit advertising aimed at prospective franchisees to the state for approval.

To protect franchisees, a state law may require the disclosure of information such as the actual costs of operation, recurring expenses, and profits earned, along with data substantiating these figures. State deceptive trade practices acts may also apply and may prohibit certain actions on the part of franchisors.

Requirements for Termination. To prevent arbitrary or bad-faith terminations, state law may prohibit termination without "good cause" or require that certain procedures be followed in terminating a franchising relationship. **Case Example 30.4** FMS, Inc., entered into a franchise agreement to become an authorized dealership for the sale of Samsung brand construction equipment. Samsung then sold its construction-equipment business to Volvo Construction Equipment North America, Inc., which was to continue selling Samsung brand equipment. Later, Volvo rebranded the construction equipment under its own name and canceled FMS's franchise.

FMS sued, claiming that Volvo had terminated the franchise without good cause in violation of state law. Because Volvo was no longer manufacturing the Samsung brand equipment, however, the court found that Volvo could legally terminate FMS's franchise. If Volvo had continued making the Samsung brand equipment, it could not have terminated the franchise.[8] ▪

Can a construction-equipment franchisor terminate the franchise of an authorized dealer after a change in equipment brands?

---

7. These states include California, Florida, Hawaii, Illinois, Indiana, Maryland, Michigan, Minnesota, New York, North Dakota, Oregon, Rhode Island, South Dakota, Texas, Utah, Virginia, Washington, and Wisconsin.

8. *FMS, Inc. v. Volvo Construction Equipment North America, Inc.,* 557 F.3d 758 (7th Cir. 2009). See also *Southern Track & Pump, Inc. v. Terex Corp.,* 618 Fed.Appx. 99 (3rd Cir. 2015).

30–3 The Franchise Contract

The franchise relationship is defined by a contract between the franchisor and the franchisee. The franchise contract specifies the terms and conditions of the franchise and spells out the rights and duties of both parties. If either party fails to perform the contractual duties, that party may be subject to a lawsuit for breach of contract. Generally, statutes and case law governing franchising emphasize the importance of good faith and fair dealing in franchise relationships.

Because each type of franchise relationship has its own characteristics, franchise contracts tend to differ. Nonetheless, certain major issues typically are addressed in a franchise contract.

30–3a Payment for the Franchise

The franchisee ordinarily pays an initial fee or lump-sum price for the franchise license (the privilege of being granted a franchise). This fee is separate from the various products that the franchisee purchases from or through the franchisor. The franchise agreement may also require the franchisee to pay a percentage of advertising costs and certain administrative expenses.

In some industries, the franchisor relies heavily on the initial sale of the franchise for realizing a profit. In other industries, the continued dealing between the parties brings profit to both. Generally, the franchisor receives a stated percentage of the annual (or monthly) sales or volume of business done by the franchisee.

30–3b Business Premises

The franchise agreement may specify whether the premises for the business must be leased or purchased outright. Sometimes, a building must be constructed or remodeled to meet the terms of the agreement. The agreement usually specifies whether the franchisor supplies equipment and furnishings for the premises or whether this is the responsibility of the franchisee.

30–3c Location of the Franchise

Typically, the franchisor determines the territory to be served. Some franchise contracts give the franchisee exclusive rights, or "territorial rights," to a certain geographic area. Other franchise contracts, though they define the territory allotted to a particular franchise, either specifically state that the franchise is nonexclusive or are silent on the issue of territorial rights.

Many franchise cases involve disputes over territorial rights, and the implied covenant of good faith and fair dealing often comes into play in this area of franchising. If the franchise contract does not grant exclusive territorial rights to a franchisee and the franchisor allows a competing franchise to be established nearby, the franchisee may suffer a significant loss in profits. In this situation, a court may hold that the franchisor's actions breached an implied covenant of good faith and fair dealing.

"You have written more than a book, Ms. McBean— you have written a franchise."

William Hamilton/The New Yorker Collection/www.cartoonbank.com

30–3d Quality Control by the Franchisor

The day-to-day operation of the franchise business normally is left up to the franchisee. Nonetheless, the franchise agreement may specify that the franchisor will provide some degree of supervision and control so that it can protect the franchise's name and reputation.

Means of Control When the franchise prepares a product, such as food, or provides a service, such as motel accommodations, the contract often states that the franchisor will establish certain standards for the facility. Typically, the contract will state that the franchisor is permitted to make periodic inspections to ensure that the standards are being maintained.

As a means of controlling quality, franchise agreements also typically limit the franchisee's ability to sell the franchise to another party. **Example 30.5** Mark Keller, an authorized Jaguar franchise, contracts to sell its dealership to Henrique Autos West. A Jaguar franchise generally cannot be sold without Jaguar Cars' permission. Prospective franchisees must meet Jaguar's customer satisfaction standards. If Henrique Autos fails to meet those standards, Jaguar can refuse to allow the sale and can terminate the franchise. ■

Degree of Control As a general rule, the validity of a provision permitting the franchisor to establish and enforce certain quality standards is unquestioned. The franchisor has a legitimate interest in maintaining the quality of the product or service to protect its name and reputation.

If a franchisor exercises too much control over the operations of its franchisees, however, the franchisor risks potential liability. A franchisor may also occasionally be held liable—under the doctrine of *respondeat superior*—for the tortious acts of the franchisees' employees. **Example 30.6** The National Labor Relations Board (NLRB) received nearly two hundred employee complaints that certain McDonald's restaurants had engaged in unfair labor practices. Employees alleged that the restaurants had fired or penalized workers for participating in protests over wages and working conditions. Investigators found that at least some of the complaints had merit. The NLRB ruled that McDonald's USA, LLC, could be held jointly liable along with several of its franchisees for labor and wage violations. The NLRB reasoned that McDonald's exerts sufficient control over its franchisees to be found liable for the franchisees' employment law violations. ■

Learning Objective 3
What might happen if a franchisor exercises too much control over the operations of a franchise?

Know This
Under the doctrine of *respondeat superior*, an employer may be liable for the torts of employees if they occur within the scope of employment, without regard to the personal fault of the employer.

30–3e Pricing Arrangements

Franchises provide the franchisor with an outlet for the firm's goods and services. Depending on the nature of the business, the franchisor may require the franchisee to purchase certain supplies from the franchisor at an established price.[9] A franchisor cannot, however, set the prices at which the franchisee will resell the goods, because such price setting may be a violation of state or federal antitrust laws, or both. A franchisor can suggest retail prices but cannot mandate them.

30–4 Franchise Termination

The duration of the franchise is a matter to be determined between the parties. Sometimes, a franchise will start out for a short period, such as a year, so that the franchisor can determine whether it wants to stay in business with the franchisee. Other times, the duration of the franchise contract correlates with the term of the lease for the business premises, and both are renewable at the end of that period.

30–4a Grounds for Termination

Usually, the franchise agreement specifies that termination must be "for cause" and then defines the grounds for termination. Cause might include, for instance, the death or disability of the franchisee, insolvency of the franchisee, breach of the franchise agreement, or failure to meet specified sales quotas.

In the following case, a franchisee contended that its franchisor did not have good cause to terminate the franchise.

---

9. Although a franchisor can require franchisees to purchase supplies from it, requiring a franchisee to purchase exclusively from the franchisor may violate federal antitrust laws.

Case 30.2

S&P Brake Supply, Inc. v. Daimler Trucks North America, LLC

Montana Supreme Court, 2018 MT 25, 390 Mont. 243, 411 P.3d 1264 (2018).

Background and Facts S&P Brake Supply, Inc., was the sole authorized dealer of Western Star Trucks in Yellowstone County, Montana. S&P operated its franchise under an agreement with Daimler Trucks North America, LLC. The agreement required that S&P sell a certain number of trucks in its area of responsibility (Yellowstone County). Over a three-year period, S&P sold only two trucks. Daimler advised its franchisee to use more effective marketing strategies and to hire more sales staff, among other things.

The next year, primarily because of S&P's failure to meet its sales goals, Daimler notified S&P that the franchise was being terminated. S&P objected, but the Montana Department of Justice, Motor Vehicle Division, ruled in Daimler's favor, and a state court upheld the department's decision. S&P appealed to the Montana Supreme Court.

In the Words of the Court

Justice Jim *RICE* delivered the Opinion of the Court.

* * * *

S&P argues * * * the [lower] court erred in its assessment of the [Montana Department of Justice, Motor Vehicle Division's] determination.

* * * *

S&P argues that an analysis of its sales performance [should have been] restricted to evidence related to Yellowstone County. Daimler established that S&P had failed to meet new truck sales objectives * * *, which are set for all Western Star dealers using an algorithm that considers market factors and the population of a dealer's area of responsibility. * * * Daimler offered its analysis of S&P's "dealer market share," which compared how many trucks S&P sold in its AOR [area of responsibility] to how many Western Star trucks were annually registered in Yellowstone County, to measure how well S&P was reaching and serving local customers. Of the seven Western Star trucks registered in Yellowstone County [during the last four years of S&P's franchise,] only two had been sold by S&P, an indicator to Daimler that S&P was not well serving

its market, as the majority of customers were purchasing their Western Star trucks elsewhere. This evidence was premised upon S&P's performance in Yellowstone County.

Daimler also argued S&P's "dealer market share" was low compared to Western Star's "regional market share," a factor which is compiled from national truck registration data to compare S&P's sales performance in its AOR with Western Star's regional performance. While this assessment included evidence from outside the Yellowstone County franchise location, the [lower] court properly noted that *limiting the evidence to only Yellowstone County would not allow a comparison to other dealers where there is only one dealer in a county,* reasoning that "when only one franchisee exists in a market, expanded data must be considered. Otherwise, a lone franchisee could never be terminated." [Emphasis added.]

* * * The Department found, "The bottom line is that S&P's sales were deficient no matter which way one analyzed the data," and this determination was supported by substantial evidence.

Decision and Remedy The Montana Supreme Court affirmed the judgment of the lower court. The court concluded, "The evidence focused on S&P's performance in Yellowstone County and was properly considered." Thus, Daimler had the grounds to terminate S&P's franchise.

Critical Thinking

• **Economic** *The department concluded that S&P's failure to use more effective marketing strategies and to hire more sales staff breached the franchise agreement. S&P argued that these were not material breaches because the agreement's fundamental purpose was to sell trucks. Is S&P correct? Discuss.*

• **Legal Environment** *Considering that S&P was the only Western Star truck dealer in Yellowstone County, did discontinuing the franchise injure the public interest? Explain.*

Notice Requirements Most franchise contracts provide that notice of termination must be given. If no set time for termination is specified, then a reasonable time, with notice, is implied. A franchisee must be given reasonable time to wind up the business—that is, to do the accounting and return the copyright or trademark or any other property of the franchisor.

Opportunity to Cure a Breach A franchise agreement may give the franchisee the right to attempt to cure an ordinary, curable breach within a certain period of time after notice so as to postpone, or even avoid, the termination of the contract. Even when a contract contains a notice-and-cure provision, however, a franchisee's breach of the duty of honesty and fidelity may be enough to allow the franchisor to terminate the franchise.

Case Example 30.7 Milind and Minaxi Upadhyaya entered into a franchise contract with 7-Eleven, Inc., to operate a store in Pennsylvania. The contract included a notice-and-cure provision. Under 7-Eleven's usual contract, franchisees lease the store and equipment, and receive a license to use 7-Eleven's trademarks and other intellectual property. 7-Eleven receives a percentage of the store's gross profit (net sales less the cost of goods sold).

A 7-Eleven manager noticed a high rate of certain questionable transactions at the Upadhyayas' store and began investigating. The investigation continued for nearly two years and revealed that the store had been misreporting its sales to 7-Eleven so as to conceal sales proceeds. Evidence indicated that nearly one-third of the store's sales transactions had not been properly recorded.

7-Eleven sent a "non-curable" notice of material breach and termination of the franchise to the Upadhyayas. The franchisees argued that they had not been given an opportunity to cure the breach. The court found there was sufficient evidence of fraud to warrant immediate termination without an opportunity to cure.[10]

Why did a court prevent 7-Eleven franchisees from curing a breach in their franchise agreement?

30–4b Wrongful Termination

Because a franchisor's termination of a franchise often has adverse consequences for the franchisee, much franchise litigation involves claims of wrongful termination. Generally, the termination provisions of contracts are more favorable to the franchisor. This means that the franchisee, who normally invests a substantial amount of time and funds to make the franchise operation successful, may receive little or nothing for the business on termination. The franchisor owns the trademark and hence the business.

It is in this area that statutory and case law become important. The federal and state laws discussed earlier attempt, among other things, to protect franchisees from arbitrary or unfair termination of their franchises by the franchisors.

> **Learning Objective 4**
>
> When will a court decide that a franchisor has wrongfully terminated a franchise?

30–4c The Importance of Good Faith and Fair Dealing

Generally, both statutory law and case law emphasize the importance of good faith and fair dealing in terminating a franchise relationship. In determining whether a franchisor has acted in good faith when terminating a franchise agreement, the courts generally try to balance the rights of both parties.

If a court perceives that a franchisor has arbitrarily or unfairly terminated a franchise, the franchisee will be provided with a remedy for wrongful termination. When a franchisor's decision to terminate a franchise was made in the normal course of the franchisor's business operations, however, that weighs in favor of the franchisor. In that situation, a court generally will not consider termination wrongful as long as reasonable notice of termination was given to the franchisee.

The importance of good faith and fair dealing in a franchise relationship is underscored by the consequences of the franchisor's acts in the following case.

---

10. *7-Eleven, Inc. v. Upadhyaya*, 926 F.Supp.2d 614 (E.D.Penn. 2013).

Spotlight on Holiday Inns: Case 30.3

Holiday Inn Franchising, Inc. v. Hotel Associates, Inc.

Court of Appeals of Arkansas, 2011 Ark.App. 147, 382 S.W.3d 6 (2011).

Background and Facts Buddy House was in the construction business. For decades, he collaborated on projects with Holiday Inn Franchising, Inc. Their relationship was characterized by good faith—many projects were undertaken without written contracts. At Holiday Inn's request, House inspected a hotel in Wichita Falls, Texas, to estimate the cost of getting it into shape. Holiday Inn wanted House to renovate the hotel and operate it as a Holiday Inn. House estimated that recovering the cost of renovation would take him more than ten years, so he asked for a franchise term longer than Holiday Inn's usual ten years. Holiday Inn refused, but said that if he ran the hotel "appropriately," the term would be extended at the end of ten years. House bought the hotel, renovated it, and operated it as Hotel Associates, Inc. (HAI), generating substantial profits. He refused offers to sell it for as much as $15 million.

Before the ten years had passed, Greg Aden, a Holiday Inn executive, developed a plan to license a different local hotel as a Holiday Inn instead of renewing House's franchise license. Aden stood to earn a commission from licensing the other hotel. No one informed House of Aden's plan. When the time came, HAI applied for an extension of its franchise, and Holiday Inn asked for major renovations. HAI spent $3 million to comply with this request. Holiday Inn did not renew the term for HAI, however, and granted a franchise to the other hotel instead. HAI sold its hotel for $5 million and filed a suit against Holiday Inn, asserting fraud. The court awarded HAI compensatory and punitive damages. Holiday Inn appealed.

In the Words of the Court
Raymond R. *ABRAMSON*, Judge.

    * * * *

Generally, a mere failure to volunteer information does not constitute fraud. But *silence can amount to actionable fraud in some circumstances where the parties have a relation of trust or confidence, where there is inequality of condition and knowledge, or where there are other attendant circumstances.* [Emphasis added.]

In this case, substantial evidence supports the existence of a duty on Holiday Inn's part to disclose the Aden [plan] to HAI. Buddy House had a long-term relationship with Holiday Inn characterized by honesty, trust, and the free flow of pertinent information. He testified that [Holiday Inn's] assurances at the onset of licensure [the granting of the license] led him to believe that he would be relicensed after ten years if the hotel was operated appropriately. Yet, despite Holiday Inn's having provided such an assurance to House, it failed to apprise House of an internal business plan * * * that advocated licensure of another facility instead of the renewal of his license. *A duty of disclosure may exist where information is peculiarly within the knowledge of one party and is of such a nature that the other party is justified in assuming its nonexistence.* Given House's history with Holiday Inn and the assurance he received, we are convinced he was justified in assuming that no obstacles had arisen that jeopardized his relicensure. [Emphasis added.]

Holiday Inn asserts that it would have provided Buddy House with the Aden [plan] if he had asked for it. But, Holiday Inn cannot satisfactorily explain why House should have been charged with the responsibility of inquiring about a plan that he did not know existed. Moreover, several Holiday Inn personnel testified that Buddy House in fact should have been provided with the Aden plan. Aden himself stated that * * * House should have been given the plan. * * * In light of these circumstances, we see no ground for reversal on this aspect of HAI's cause of action for fraud.

Decision and Remedy The state intermediate appellate court affirmed the lower court's judgment and its award of compensatory damages. The appellate court increased the amount of punitive damages, however, citing Holiday Inn's "degree of reprehensibility."

Critical Thinking

• **Legal Environment** *Why should House and HAI have been advised of Holiday Inn's plan to grant a franchise to a different hotel in their territory?*

Practice and Review

Carlos Del Rey decided to open a fast-food Mexican restaurant and signed a franchise contract with a national chain called La Grande Enchilada. Under the franchise agreement, Del Rey purchased the building, and La Grande Enchilada supplied the equipment. The contract required the franchisee to strictly follow the franchisor's operating manual and stated that failure to do so would be grounds for terminating the franchise contract. The manual set forth detailed operating procedures and safety standards, and provided that a La Grande Enchilada representative would inspect the restaurant monthly to ensure compliance.

Nine months after Del Rey began operating his restaurant, a spark from the grill ignited an oily towel in the kitchen. No one was injured, but by the time firefighters put out the fire, the kitchen had sustained extensive damage. The cook told the fire department that the towel was "about two feet from the grill" when it caught fire, which was in compliance with the franchisor's manual that required towels to be at least one foot from the grills. Nevertheless, the next day La Grande Enchilada notified Del Rey that his franchise would terminate in thirty days for failure to follow the prescribed safety procedures. Using the information presented in the chapter, answer the following questions.

1. What type of franchise was Del Rey's La Grande Enchilada restaurant?

2. If Del Rey operates the restaurant as a sole proprietorship, who bears the loss for the damaged kitchen? Explain.

3. Assume that Del Rey files a lawsuit against La Grande Enchilada, claiming that his franchise was wrongfully terminated. What is the main factor a court would consider in determining whether the franchise was wrongfully terminated?

4. Would a court be likely to rule that La Grande Enchilada had good cause to terminate Del Rey's franchise in this situation? Why or why not?

Debate This
All franchisors should be required by law to provide a comprehensive estimate of the profitability of a prospective franchise based on the experiences of their existing franchisees.

Key Terms

entrepreneur 726   franchisee 730   sole proprietorship 727
franchise 730   franchisor 730

Chapter Summary: Sole Proprietorships and Franchises

Sole Proprietorships	The simplest form of business organization, the sole proprietorship is used by anyone who does business without creating a separate organization. The owner is the business. The owner pays personal income taxes on all profits and is personally liable for all business debts.

Franchises	1. *Types of franchises*—
	    a. Distributorships (for example, automobile dealerships).
	    b. Chain-style business operations (for example, fast-food chains).
	    c. Manufacturing or processing-plant arrangements (for example, soft-drink bottling companies).
	 2. *Laws governing franchising*—Franchises are governed by contract law. They are also governed by federal and state statutory laws, as well as agency regulations.

The Franchise Contact	The franchise relationship is defined by a contract between the franchisor and the franchisee. The contract normally spells out the following terms: 1. *Payment for the franchise*—Ordinarily, the contract requires the franchisee (purchaser) to pay an initial fee or lump-sum price for the franchise license. 2. *Business premises*—The contract may specify whether the business premises will be leased or purchased by the franchisee and which party will provide the equipment and furnishings. 3. *Location of the franchise*—The franchisor typically specifies the territory to be served by the franchisee. 4. *Quality control*—The franchisor may require the franchisee to abide by certain standards of quality relating to the product or service offered. 5. *Pricing arrangements*—The franchisor may require the franchisee to purchase certain supplies from the franchisor at an established price but cannot set retail resale prices.
Franchise Termination	Usually, the contract specifies the duration and conditions of termination of the franchise arrangement. Both federal and state statutes attempt to protect franchisees from franchisors who unfairly or arbitrarily terminate franchises.

Issue Spotters

1. Frank plans to open a sporting goods store and to hire Gogi and Hap. Frank will invest only his own funds. He expects that he will not make a profit for at least eighteen months and will make only a small profit in the three years after that. He hopes to expand eventually. Would a sole proprietorship be an appropriate form for Frank's business? Why or why not? (See *Sole Proprietorships*.)

2. Thirsty Bottling Company and U.S. Beverages, Inc. (USB), enter into a franchise agreement that states that the franchise may be terminated at any time "for cause." Thirsty fails to meet USB's specified sales quota. Does this constitute "cause" for termination? Why or why not? (See *Franchise Termination*.)

   —**Check your answers to the *Issue Spotters* against the answers provided in Appendix D at the end of this text.**

Business Scenarios and Case Problems

30–1. Franchising. Maria, Pablo, and Vicky are recent college graduates who would like to go into business for themselves. They are considering purchasing a franchise. If they enter into a franchising arrangement, they would have the support of a large company that could answer any questions they might have. Also, a firm that has been in business for many years would be experienced in dealing with some of the problems that novice businesspersons might encounter. These and other attributes of franchises can lessen some of the risks of the marketplace. What other aspects of franchising—positive and negative—should Maria, Pablo, and Vicky consider before committing themselves to a particular franchise? (See *Franchises*.)

30–2. Control of a Franchise. National Foods, Inc., sells franchises to its fast-food restaurants, known as Chicky-D's. Under the franchise agreement, franchisees agree to hire and train employees strictly according to Chicky-D's standards. In addition, Chicky-D's regional supervisors must approve all new hires and policies, which they generally do. Chicky-D's reserves the right to terminate a franchise for violating the franchisor's rules. After several incidents of racist comments and conduct by Tim, a recently hired assistant manager at a Chicky-D's, Sharon, a counterperson at the restaurant, resigns. Sharon files a suit against National. National files a motion for summary judgment, arguing that it is not liable for harassment by franchise employees. Will the court grant National's motion? Why or why not? (See *The Franchise Contract*.)

30–3. Spotlight on McDonald's—Franchise Termination. C.B. Management, Inc., had a franchise agreement with McDonald's Corp. to operate McDonald's restaurants in Cleveland, Ohio. The agreement required C.B. to make monthly payments of certain percentages of the gross sales to McDonald's. If any payment was more than thirty days late, McDonald's had the right to terminate the franchise. The agreement also stated that even if McDonald's accepted a late payment, that would not "constitute a waiver of any subsequent breach." McDonald's sometimes accepted C.B.'s late payments, but when C.B. defaulted on the payments in July, McDonald's gave notice of thirty days to comply or surrender possession of the restaurants. C.B. missed the deadline. McDonald's demanded that C.B. vacate the restaurants, but C.B. refused. McDonald's alleged that C.B. had violated the franchise agreement. C.B. claimed that McDonald's had breached the implied covenant of good faith and fair dealing. Which party should prevail, and why? [*McDonald's Corp. v. C.B. Management Co.*, 13 F.Supp.2d 705 (N.D.Ill. 1998)] (See *Franchise Termination*.)

30–4. Business Case Problem with Sample Answer—Quality Control. JTH Tax, Inc., doing business as Liberty Tax Service, provides tax preparation and related loan services throughout the United States in more than two thousand company-owned and franchised stores. Liberty's agreement with its franchisees reserved the right to control their ads. In company operations manuals, Liberty provided step-by-step instructions, directions, and limitations to its franchisees regarding their ads. Liberty retained the right to unilaterally modify the steps at any time. The California Attorney General filed a suit in a California state court against Liberty, alleging misleading or deceptive ads by its franchisees regarding refund anticipation loans and e-refund checks. Can Liberty be held liable? Discuss. [*People v. JTH Tax, Inc.*, 212 Cal.App.4th 1219, 151 Cal. Rptr.3d 728 (1 Dist. 2013)] (See *The Franchise Contract*.)

—For a sample answer to Problem 30–4, go to Appendix E at the end of this text.

30–5. Quality Control. The franchise agreement of Domino's Pizza, LLC, sets out operational standards, including safety requirements, for a franchisee to follow but provides that the franchisee is an independent contractor. Each franchisee is free to use its own means and methods. For example, Domino's does not know whether a franchisee's delivery drivers are complying with vehicle safety requirements. MAC Pizza Management, Inc., operates a Domino's franchise. A vehicle driven by Joshua Balka, a MAC delivery driver, hydroplaned due to a bald tire and wet pavement, and struck the vehicle of Devavaram and Ruth Christopher, killing Ruth and injuring Devavaram. Is Domino's liable for negligence? Explain. [*Domino's Pizza, LLC v. Reddy*, 2015 WL 1247349 (Tex. App.—Beaumont 2015)] (See *The Franchise Contract*.)

30–6. Franchise Termination. Executive Home Care Franchising, LLC, sells in-home health-care franchises. Clint, Massare, and Greer Marshall entered into a franchise agreement with Executive Home Care. The agreement provided that the franchisees' failure to comply with the agreement's terms would likely cause irreparable harm to the franchisor, entitling it to an injunction. About two years later, the Marshalls gave up their franchise. They returned thirteen boxes of documents, stationery, operating manuals, marketing materials, and other items—everything in their possession that featured Executive Home Care trademarks. They quit operating out of the franchised location. They transferred the phone number back to the franchisor and informed their clients that they were no longer associated with Executive Home Care. They continued to engage in the home health-care business, however, under the name "Well-Being Home Care Corp." Is Executive Home Care entitled to an injunction against the Marshalls and their new company? Discuss. [*Executive Home Care Franchising, LLC v. Marshall Health Corp.*, 642 Fed.Appx. 181 (3d Cir. 2016)] (See *Franchise Termination*.)

30–7. Location of the Franchise. Chrysler, LLC, awarded a Chrysler-Jeep franchise in Billings, Montana, to Lithia Motors, Inc. Lithia exceeded the sales goals and other expectations expressed in the franchise agreement. Later, Chrysler approved an application by Rimrock Chrysler, Inc., to open an additional Chrysler-Jeep franchise less than a mile from Lithia's location. Lithia's agreement was silent on the issue of territorial rights, but the dealer protested Chrysler's approval of Rimrock's application. Could Chrysler's actions be considered a breach of the franchisor's deal with Lithia? Discuss. [*Rimrock Chrysler, Inc. v. State of Montana Department of Justice, Motor Vehicle Division*, 2018 MT 24, 390 Mont. 235, 411 P.3d 1278 (2018)] (See *The Franchise Contract*.)

30–8. A Question of Ethics—The IDDR Approach and Sole Proprietorships. *Tom George was the sole owner of Turbine Component Super Market, LLC (TCSM), when its existence was terminated by the state of Texas. A TCSM creditor, Turbine Resources Unlimited, filed and won a suit in a Texas state court against George for breach of contract. The plaintiff sought to collect the amount of the judgment through a sale of George's property. Instead of turning his assets over to the court, however, George tried to hide them by reforming TCSM. Without telling the court, he paid an unrelated debt with $100,000 of TCSM's funds. George* claimed that the funds were a loan and that he was merely an employee of TCSM. [Mitchell v. Turbine Resources Unlimited, Inc., 523 S.W.3d 189 (Tex.App.—Houston [14th Dist.] 2017)] (See Sole Proprietorships.)

1. Is it more likely that the court will recognize TCSM as an LLC or a sole proprietorship? Why?

2. Using the *Discussion* step of the IDDR approach, consider whether the owner of a business has an ethical obligation to represent the character and purpose of the organization truthfully.

Critical Thinking and Writing Assignments

30–9. Business Law Writing. Jordan Mendelson is interested in purchasing a franchise in a meal-preparation business. Customers will come to the business to assemble gourmet dinners and then take the prepared meals to their homes for cooking. The franchisor requires each store to use a specific layout and provides the recipes for various dinners, but the franchisee is not required to purchase the food products from the franchisor. What general factors should Mendelson consider before entering into a contract to buy such a franchise? Is location important? Are there any laws that Mendelson should consider, given that this franchise involves food preparation and sales? Should Mendelson operate this business as a sole proprietorship? Why or why not? (See *The Franchise Contract.*)

30–10. Time-Limited Group Assignment—Franchise Termination. Walid Elkhatib, an Arab American, bought a Dunkin' Donuts franchise in Illinois. Ten years later, Dunkin' Donuts began offering breakfast sandwiches with bacon, ham, or sausage through its franchises. Elkhatib refused to sell these items at his store on the ground that his religion forbade the handling of pork. Elkhatib then opened a second franchise, at which he also refused to sell pork products. The next year, at both locations, Elkhatib began selling meatless sandwiches. He also opened a third franchise. When he proposed to relocate this franchise, Dunkin' Donuts refused to approve the new location and informed him that it would not renew any of his franchise agreements because he did not carry the full sandwich line. Elkhatib filed a lawsuit against Dunkin' Donuts. (See *Franchise Termination.*)

1. The first group will argue on behalf of Elkhatib that Dunkin' Donuts wrongfully terminated his franchises.

2. The second group will take the side of Dunkin' Donuts and justify its decision to terminate the franchises.

3. The third group will assess whether Dunkin' Donuts acted in good faith in its relationship with Elkhatib. It will also consider whether Dunkin' Donuts should be required to accommodate Elkhatib's religious beliefs and allow him to not serve pork in these three locations.

Pgiam/iStock/Getty Images

All Forms of Partnership

31

> "All men's gains
> are the fruit of
> venturing."
>
> **Herodotus**
> Fifth Century B.C.E.
> (Greek historian)

Historically, the two most common forms of business organization selected by two or more persons going into business together have been the partnership and the corporation. A *partnership* arises from an agreement, express or implied, between two or more persons to carry on a business for profit. Partners are co-owners of a business and have joint control over its operation and the right to share in its profits. As the chapter-opening quotation indicates, all gains are the "fruit of venturing," and partnerships—to the extent that they encourage business ventures—contribute to those gains.

Suppose that, after graduating with a fine arts degree, Coralee Linde starts an online business that sells handmade jewelry and crafts. Her business grows, and she hires employees. Then she meets an app developer, Derek LaRue, who wants to invest in her business. He also wants to work with her to create an app that will enable people to easily place orders for her goods from their smartphones and from devices such as Alexa and Google Home.

Linde agrees to give LaRue a 25 percent share of her business profits in exchange for the cash he is contributing and for building the app. Although they sign a contract to that effect, the contract does not identify a particular business form. Is LaRue now Linde's partner? Does LaRue have a right to control any aspects of Linde's business? If LaRue never creates the app, or if the app does not function properly, does Linde still have to give him 25 percent of the profits? Is she liable for his actions? In this chapter, you will learn the answers to questions such as these.

Learning Objectives

The five Learning Objectives *below are designed to help improve your understanding. After reading this chapter, you should be able to answer the following questions:*

1. What are the three essential elements of a partnership?

2. What are the fiduciary duties of partners in a general partnership?

3. What is dissociation? What happens when a partner dissociates from a partnership?

4. What advantages do limited liability partnerships offer to businesspersons that are not offered by general partnerships?

5. What are the key differences between the rights and liabilities of general partners and those of limited partners?

31–1 Basic Partnership Concepts

The traditional partnership is an ordinary, or *general*, partnership. General partnerships are governed both by common law concepts—in particular, those relating to agency—and by statutory law. As in so many other areas of business law, the National Conference of Commissioners on Uniform State Laws has drafted uniform law for partnerships, and these uniform laws have been widely adopted by the states.

31–1a Agency Concepts and Partnership Law

When two or more persons agree to do business as partners, they enter into a special relationship with one another. To an extent, their relationship is similar to an agency relationship because each partner is deemed to be the agent of the other partners and of the partnership. Thus, the common law agency concepts apply. Specifically, each partner is charged with knowledge of, and responsibility for, acts done within the scope of the partnership relationship. In their relationships with one another, partners, like agents, are bound by fiduciary ties.

In one important way, however, partnership law is distinct from agency law. A partnership is based on a voluntary contract between two or more competent persons who agree to commit financial capital, labor, and skill to a business with the understanding that profits and losses will be shared. In a nonpartnership agency relationship, the agent usually does not have an ownership interest in the business, and he or she is not obliged to bear a portion of the ordinary business losses.

31–1b The Uniform Partnership Act

The Uniform Partnership Act (UPA) governs the operation of partnerships *in the absence of an express agreement*. In other words, the partners are free to establish rules for their partnership that differ from those stated in the UPA. The majority of the states have adopted the most recent version of the UPA (completed in 1997 and last amended in 2013).

31–1c Definition of a Partnership

Partnership An agreement by two or more persons to carry on, as co-owners, a business for profit.

The UPA defines a **partnership** as "an association of two or more persons to carry on as co-owners a business for profit" [UPA 101(6)]. Note that the UPA's definition of *person* includes corporations, so a corporation can be a partner in a partnership [UPA 101(10)]. The *intent* to associate is a key element of a partnership, and a person cannot join a partnership unless all of the other partners consent [UPA 401(i)].

31–1d Essential Elements of a Partnership

Learning Objective 1

What are the three essential elements of a partnership?

Questions may sometimes arise as to whether a business enterprise is a legal partnership, especially when there is no formal, written partnership agreement. In determining whether a partnership exists, courts usually look for three essential elements, which are implicit in the UPA's definition of a general partnership:

1. A sharing of profits and losses.
2. A joint ownership of the business.
3. An equal right to be involved in the management of the business.

If the evidence in a particular case is insufficient to establish all three factors, the UPA provides a set of guidelines to be used.

The court in the following case considered these and other factors to determine whether a partnership existed between two participants in a new restaurant venture.

Case 31.1

Harun v. Rashid

Texas Court of Appeals, Dallas, 2018 WL 329292 (2018).

Background and Facts Mohammed Harun was interested in opening a new restaurant, Spice-N-Rice, in Irving, Texas, but lacked the financial resources. He asked Sharif Rashid if Rashid was interested in funding the venture. Rashid said that he was and provided $60,000. Rashid also helped negotiate a lease for the restaurant, was a signatory on its bank account, dealt with contractors, paid for advertising, and bought furniture, equipment, and supplies. In addition, Rashid hired a bookkeeper to perform the restaurant's accounting.

When the bookkeeper expressed concern about Harun's reporting of Spice-N-Rice's income on his tax return, Harun removed Rashid from the bank account and locked him out of the restaurant's premises. Rashid filed a suit in a Texas state court against Harun and Spice-N-Rice, alleging the existence of a partnership and a breach of fiduciary duty. Harun denied that he and Rashid had ever been partners. The court ruled that a partnership existed and awarded damages to Rashid. The defendants appealed.

In the Words of the Court
Opinion by Justice *SCHENCK*.

* * * *

In determining whether a partnership was created, we consider several factors, including (1) the parties' receipt or right to receive a share of profits of the business; (2) any expression of an intent to be partners in the business; (3) participation or right to participate in control of the business; (4) any agreement to share or sharing losses of the business or liability for claims by third parties against the business; and (5) any agreement to contribute or contributing money or property to the business. *Proof of each of these factors is not necessary to establish a partnership.* [Emphasis added.]

* * * *

At trial, Rashid presented evidence through his testimony that: (a) Harun approached him indicating he had found a good location to open a restaurant and needed a partner to finance the operation; (b) Harun asked him to be his partner; (c) he and Harun were equal business partners in the restaurant; (d) he and Harun agreed to share equally in the profits and losses; (e) he and Harun met with the leasing agents to negotiate the lease of the restaurant space; (f) he and Harun had equal access to the restaurant's bank account; (g) he hired and communicated with the bookkeeper; (h) he was very involved in preparing paperwork for the restaurant; (i) he paid restaurant-related bills, and purchased furniture and equipment for the restaurant; (j) he was not an employee of the restaurant or Harun, nor did he receive any pay for the work he performed on behalf of the restaurant; and (k) he invested approximately $60,000 in the business. We conclude the trial court's finding a partnership existed between Harun and Rashid is supported by more than a scintilla [speck] of evidence.

Finally, * * * appellants argue Rashid was not entitled to an award of damages because there was no partnership and thus there could be no breach of fiduciary duty. As we have concluded there is sufficient evidence Harun and Rashid were partners in Spice-N-Rice, we overrule appellants' * * * issue.

Decision and Remedy Decision and Remedy A state intermediate appellate court affirmed the lower court's award to Rashid of actual damages of $36,000 (the difference between Rashid's investment of $60,000 and the amount Harun had repaid), punitive damages of $36,000, and attorneys' fees of $79,768, plus interest and costs.

Critical Thinking

• **Legal Environment** *Harun's income tax return and other documents prepared by the bookkeeper on behalf of Spice-N-Rice identified the business as a sole proprietorship. Should the appellate court have reversed the finding of a partnership on this basis? Explain.*

• **What If the Facts Were Different?** *Suppose that the appellants had complained there was a lack of evidence of an agreement between Harun and Rashid to share losses. Would the result have been different? Why or why not?*

The Sharing of Profits and Losses   The sharing of *both profits and losses* from a business creates a presumption (legal inference) that a partnership exists.   **Case Example 31.1**   David Tubb, representing Superior Shooting Systems, Inc., entered into an agreement with Aspect International, Inc., to create a business that would make and sell ammunition to the public. Their contract stated that both companies would participate in the business and split the profits equally, but it did not say explicitly that they would share the losses. It also did not specify what type of entity the business would be. A dispute arose between the two companies, and the matter ended up in court.

A Texas appellate court held that the two corporations had created a partnership even though there was no express agreement to share in losses. Because they had agreed to share control and ownership of the business and to split the profits equally, they would also have to share the losses equally.[1]

A court will *not presume* that a partnership exists, however, if shared profits are received as payment of any of the following [UPA 202(c)(3)]:

1. A debt by installments or interest on a loan.

2. Wages of an employee or payment for the services of an independent contractor.

3. Rent to a landlord.

4. An annuity to a surviving spouse or representative of a deceased partner.

5. A sale of the goodwill (valuable reputation) of a business or property.

Example 31.2   A debtor, Mason Snopel, owes a creditor, Alice Burns, $5,000 on an unsecured debt. They agree that Mason will pay 10 percent of his monthly business profits to Alice until the loan with interest has been paid. Although Mason and Alice are sharing profits from the business, they are not presumed to be partners.

Joint Property Ownership   Joint ownership of property does not in and of itself create a partnership [UPA 202(c)(1), (2)]. The parties' intentions are key.   **Example 31.3**   Chiang and Burke jointly own farmland and lease it to a farmer for a share of the profits from the farming operation in lieu of fixed rental payments. This arrangement normally would not make Chiang, Burke, and the farmer partners.

Equal Management Rights   In general, every partner in a partnership has an equal say in managing the partnership's affairs. In other words, each partner has a single vote in the management decisions, regardless of her or his proportional interest in the business (unless the partners have agreed otherwise).

31–1e Entity versus Aggregate Theory of Partnerships

At common law, a partnership was treated only as an aggregate of individuals and never as a separate legal entity. Thus, at common law a lawsuit could never be brought by or against the firm in its own name. Each individual partner had to sue or be sued.

Today, in contrast, a majority of the states follow the UPA and treat a partnership as an entity for most purposes. For instance, a partnership usually can sue or be sued, collect judgments, and have all accounting procedures performed in the name of the partnership entity [UPA 201, 307(a)].

As an entity, a partnership may hold the title to real or personal property in its name rather than in the names of the individual partners. Additionally, federal procedural laws permit the partnership to be treated as an entity in lawsuits in federal courts and bankruptcy proceedings.

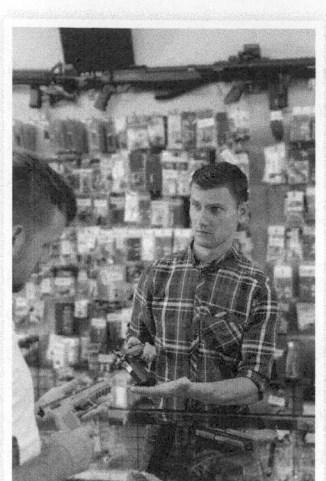

Two firms agree to form a partnership to sell ammunition to the public. Are they indeed partners if they do not expressly agree to share the losses of the business?

Iakov Filimonov/Shutterstock.com

---

1. *Tubb v. Aspect International, Inc.*, 2017 WL 192919 (Tex.App.—Tyler 2017).

31–1f Tax Treatment of Partnerships

Modern law does treat a partnership as an aggregate of the individual partners rather than as a separate legal entity in one situation—for federal income tax purposes. The partnership is a pass-through entity and not a taxpaying entity.

A **pass-through entity** is a business entity that has no tax liability—the entity's income is passed through to the owners of the entity, who pay income taxes on it. Thus, the income or losses a partnership incurs are "passed through" the entity framework and attributed to the partners on their individual tax returns. The partnership itself pays no taxes and is responsible only for filing an **information return** with the Internal Revenue Service.

A partner's profit from the partnership (whether distributed or not) is taxed as individual income to the individual partner. Similarly, partners can deduct a share of the partnership's losses on their individual tax returns (in proportion to their partnership interests).

Pass-Through Entity A business entity that has no tax liability. The entity's income is passed through to the owners, and they pay taxes on the income.

Information Return A tax return submitted by a partnership that reports the business's income and losses. The partnership itself does not pay taxes on the income received by the partnership.

31–2 Formation and Operation

A partnership is a voluntary association of individuals. As such, it is formed by the agreement of the partners.

31–2a The Partnership Agreement

As a general rule, agreements to form a partnership can be oral, written, or implied by conduct. Some partnership agreements, however, such as one authorizing the transfer of interests in real property, must be in writing to be legally enforceable. (Recall that a writing may be an electronic record.)

A written partnership agreement, often called **articles of partnership**, sets forth each partner's rights and obligations in the partnership. Such an agreement can include any terms that the parties wish, unless the terms are illegal or contrary to public policy or statute [UPA 103]. The terms commonly included in a partnership agreement are listed in Exhibit 31–1. (Creating a partnership agreement in another country may involve additional requirements, as this chapter's *Beyond Our Borders* feature explains.)

Articles of Partnership A written agreement that sets forth each partner's rights and obligations with respect to the partnership.

Exhibit 31–1 Common Terms Included in a Partnership Agreement

TERM	DESCRIPTION
Basic Structure	1. Name of the partnership and names of the partners. 2. Location of the business and the state law under which the partnership is organized. 3. Purpose and duration of the partnership.
Capital Contributions	1. Amount of capital that each partner is contributing. 2. The agreed-on value of any real or personal property that is contributed instead of cash. 3. How losses and gains on contributed capital will be allocated, and whether contributions will earn interest.
Sharing of Profits and Losses	1. Percentage of the profits and losses of the business that each partner will receive. 2. When distributions of profit will be made and how net profit will be calculated.
Management and Control	1. How management responsibilities will be divided among the partners. 2. Name(s) of the managing partner(s) and whether other partners have voting rights.
Dissociation and Dissolution	1. Events that will cause the dissociation of a partner or dissolve the firm, such as the retirement, death, or incapacity of any partner. 2. How partnership property will be valued and apportioned on dissociation and dissolution. 3. Whether an arbitrator will determine the value of partnership property on dissociation and dissolution, and whether that determination will be binding.

Doing Business with Foreign Partners

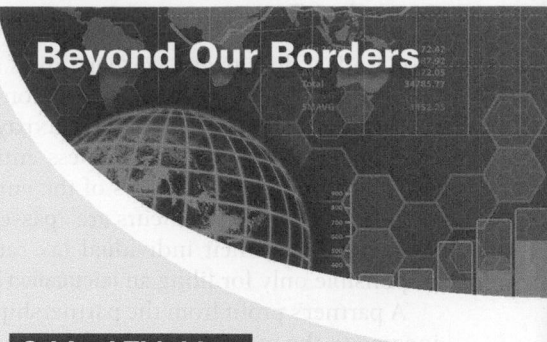
Beyond Our Borders

U.S. businesspersons who wish to operate a partnership in another country often discover that the country requires local participation. That is, nationals of the host country must own a specific share of the business. In other words, the partnership will have to include one or more partners who live in the host country. Sometimes, U.S. businesspersons are reluctant to establish partnerships in a country that requires local participation. They fear that if the partnership breaks up, the technology and expertise developed by the partnership business may end up in the hands of a future competitor. In that event, the U.S. parties may have little recourse under the host country's laws against their former partners' use of the intellectual property.

Critical Thinking

Do local participation rules benefit host countries in the long run? Explain.

The rights and duties of partners are governed largely by the specific terms of their partnership agreement. In the absence of provisions to the contrary in the agreement, the law imposes certain rights and duties, as discussed in the following subsections. The character and nature of the partnership business generally influence the application of these rights and duties.

31–2b Duration of the Partnership

The partnership agreement can specify the duration of the partnership by stating that it will continue until a certain date or the completion of a particular project. A partnership that is specifically limited in duration is called a *partnership for a term*. Generally, withdrawing prematurely (before the expiration date) from a partnership for a term constitutes a breach of the agreement. The responsible partner can be held liable for any resulting losses [UPA 602(b)(2)].

If no fixed duration is specified, the partnership is a *partnership at will*. A partnership at will can be dissolved at any time without liability.

31–2c Partnership by Estoppel

When a third person has reasonably and detrimentally relied on a representation that a nonpartner was part of a partnership, a court may conclude that a **partnership by estoppel** exists.

Liability Imposed A partnership by estoppel may arise when a person who is not a partner holds himself or herself out as a partner and makes representations that third parties rely on. In this situation, a court may impose liability—but not partnership rights—on the alleged partner.

Nonpartner as Agent A partnership by estoppel may also be imposed when a partner represents, expressly or impliedly, that a nonpartner is a member of the firm. In this situation, the nonpartner may be regarded as an agent whose acts are binding on the partnership [UPA 308].

Case Example 31.4 Jackson Paper Manufacturing Company makes paper that is used by Stonewall Packaging, LLC. Jackson and Stonewall have officers and directors in common, and they share employees, property, and equipment. In reliance on Jackson's business reputation, Best Cartage, Inc., agreed to provide transportation services for Stonewall and bought thirty-seven tractor-trailers to use in fulfilling the contract. Best provided the services until Stonewall terminated the agreement.

Best filed a suit for breach of contract against both Stonewall and Jackson. Best argued that Stonewall and Jackson had a partnership by estoppel. The court agreed, finding that

Partnership by Estoppel
A partnership imposed by a court when nonpartners have held themselves out to be partners, or have allowed themselves to be held out as partners, and others have detrimentally relied on their misrepresentations.

"defendants combined labor, skills, and property to advance their alleged business partnership." Jackson had negotiated the agreement with Best on Stonewall's behalf. Jackson had also bought real estate, equipment, and general supplies for Stonewall with no expectation that Stonewall would repay these expenditures. This was sufficient to prove a partnership by estoppel.[2]

31–2d Rights of Partners

The rights of partners in a partnership relate to the following areas: management, interest in the partnership, compensation, inspection of books, accounting, and property.

Why was a partnership by estoppel imposed on two companies involved in the paper industry?

Management Rights In a general partnership, all partners have equal rights in managing the partnership [UPA 401(f)]. Unless the partners agree otherwise, each partner has one vote in management matters *regardless of the proportional size of his or her interest in the firm*. In a large partnership, partners often agree to delegate daily management responsibilities to a management committee made up of one or more of the partners.

The majority rule controls decisions in ordinary matters connected with partnership business, unless otherwise specified in the agreement. Decisions that significantly change the nature of the partnership or its ordinary course of business, however, require the *unanimous* consent of the partners [UPA 301(2), 401(i), (j)]. For instance, unanimous consent is likely required for a partnership to admit new partners, to amend the partnership agreement, or to enter a new line of business.

Interest in the Partnership Each partner is entitled to the proportion of business profits and losses designated in the partnership agreement. If the agreement does not apportion profits (indicate how the profits will be shared), the UPA provides that profits will be shared equally. If the agreement does not apportion losses, losses will be shared in the same ratio as profits [UPA 401(b)].

> "Forty for you, sixty for me—and equal partners we will be."
>
> **Anonymous**

Example 31.5 The partnership agreement for Rick and Brent provides for capital contributions of $60,000 from Rick and $40,000 from Brent. If the agreement is silent as to how Rick and Brent will share profits or losses, they will share both profits and losses equally. In contrast, if the agreement provides for profits to be shared in the same ratio as capital contributions, 60 percent of the profits will go to Rick, and 40 percent will go to Brent. Unless the agreement provides otherwise, losses will be shared in the same ratio as profits.

Compensation Devoting time, skill, and energy to partnership business is a partner's duty and generally is not a compensable service. Rather, as mentioned, a partner's income from the partnership takes the form of a distribution of profits according to the partner's share in the business.

Partners can, of course, agree otherwise. For instance, the managing partner of a law firm often receives a salary—in addition to her or his share of profits—for performing special administrative or managerial duties.

Inspection of Books Partnership books and records must be accessible to all partners. Each partner has the right to receive full and complete information concerning the conduct of all aspects of partnership business [UPA 403]. Partners have a duty to provide the information to the firm, which has a duty to preserve it and keep accurate records.

The partnership's books must be kept at the firm's principal business office (unless partners agree otherwise) and cannot be removed without the consent of all of the partners. Every partner is entitled to inspect all books and records on demand and to make copies of

---

2. *Best Cartage, Inc. v. Stonewall Packaging, LLC,* 727 S.E.2d 291 (N.C.App. 2012).

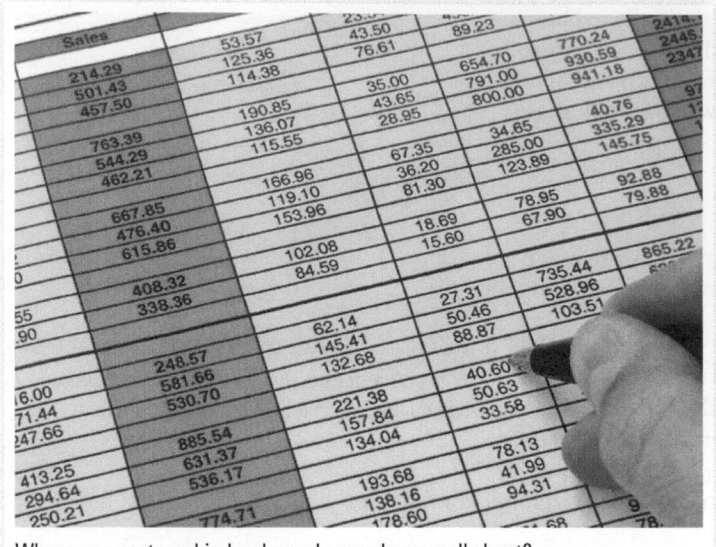

Where are partnership books and records normally kept?

jasantiso/E+/Getty Images

the materials. The personal representative of a deceased partner's estate has the same right of access to partnership books and records that the decedent would have had [UPA 403].

Accounting of Partnership Assets or Profits An accounting of partnership assets or profits is required to determine the value of each partner's share. An accounting can be performed voluntarily, or it can be compelled by court order. Under UPA 405(b), a partner has the right to bring an action for an accounting during the term of the partnership, as well as on the partnership's dissolution.

Property Rights Property acquired by a partnership is the property of the partnership and not of the partners individually [UPA 203]. Partnership property includes all property that was originally contributed to the partnership and anything later purchased by the partnership or in the partnership's name (except in rare circumstances) [UPA 204].

A partner may use or possess partnership property only on behalf of the partnership [UPA 401(g)]. A partner is *not* a co-owner of partnership property and has no right to sell, mortgage, or transfer it.

Because partnership property is owned by the partnership as an entity and not by the individual partners, the property cannot be used to satisfy the personal debts of individual partners. A partner's creditor, however, can petition a court for a **charging order** to attach the partner's *interest* in the partnership (her or his proportionate share of any profits that are distributed) to satisfy the partner's obligation. (A partner can also assign her or his right to a share of the partnership profits to another to satisfy a debt.)

Charging Order In partnership law, an order granted by a court to a judgment creditor that entitles the creditor to attach a partner's interest in the partnership.

31–2e Duties and Liabilities of Partners

The duties and liabilities of partners are basically derived from agency law. Each partner is an agent of every other partner and acts as both a principal and an agent in any business transaction within the scope of the partnership agreement.

Each partner is also a general agent of the partnership in carrying out the usual business of the firm "or business of the kind carried on by the partnership" [UPA 301(1)]. Thus, every act of a partner concerning partnership business, or "business of the kind," and every contract signed in the partnership's name bind the firm.

Learning Objective 2

What are the fiduciary duties of partners in a general partnership?

Fiduciary Duties The fiduciary duties a partner owes to the partnership and to the other partners are the duty of care and the duty of loyalty [UPA 404(a)]. Under the UPA, a partner's *duty of care* involves refraining from "grossly negligent or reckless conduct, intentional misconduct, or a knowing violation of law" [UPA 404(c)]. A partner is not liable to the partnership for simple negligence or honest errors in judgment in conducting partnership business.

The *duty of loyalty* requires a partner to account to the partnership for "any property, profit, or benefit" derived by the partner from the partnership's business or the use of its property [UPA 404(b)]. A partner must also refrain from competing with the partnership in business or dealing with the firm as an adverse party.

The duty of loyalty can be breached by self-dealing, misusing partnership property, disclosing trade secrets, or usurping a partnership business opportunity, as the following *Classic Case* illustrates.

Classic Case 31.2

Meinhard v. Salmon

Court of Appeals of New York, 249 N.Y. 458, 164 N.E. 545 (1928).

Background and Facts Background and Facts Walter Salmon negotiated a twenty-year lease for the Hotel Bristol in New York City. To pay for the conversion of the building into shops and offices, Salmon entered into an agreement with Morton Meinhard to assume half of the cost. They agreed to share the profits and losses from the joint venture. (A *joint venture* is similar to a partnership but typically is created for a single project, whereas a partnership usually involves an ongoing business.) Salmon, however, was to have the sole power to manage the building.

Less than four months before the end of the lease term, the building's owner, Elbridge Gerry, approached Salmon about a project to raze the converted structure, clear five adjacent lots, and construct a single building across the whole property. Salmon agreed and signed a new lease in the name of his own business, Midpoint Realty Company, without telling Meinhard. When Meinhard learned of the deal, he filed a suit in a New York state court against Salmon. From a judgment in Meinhard's favor, Salmon appealed.

In the Words of the Court

CARDOZO, C.J. [Chief Justice]

* * * *

Joint adventurers, like copartners, owe to one another, while the enterprise continues, the duty of the finest loyalty. Many forms of conduct permissible in a work-a-day world for those acting at arm's length are forbidden to those bound by fiduciary ties. * * * Not honesty alone, but the punctilio [strict observance of details] of an honor the most sensitive, is then the standard of behavior. As to this there has developed a tradition that is unbending and inveterate [entrenched]. Uncompromising rigidity has been the attitude of courts * * * when petitioned to undermine the rule of undivided loyalty.

* * * The trouble about [Salmon's] conduct is that he excluded his co-adventurer from any chance to compete, from any chance to enjoy the opportunity for benefit. * * * The very fact that Salmon was in control with exclusive powers of direction charged him

What fiduciary duties does a partner have with respect to renewing a hotel lease?

the more obviously with the duty of disclosure, [because] only through disclosure could opportunity be equalized.

* * * Authority is, of course, abundant that one partner may not appropriate to his own use a renewal of a lease, though its term is to begin at the expiration of the partnership. The lease at hand with its many changes is not strictly a renewal. Even so, the standard of loyalty for those in trust relations is without the fixed divisions of a graduated scale. * * * *A man obtaining [an] * * * opportunity * * * by the position he occupies as a partner is bound by his obligation to his copartners in such dealings not to separate his interest from theirs, but, if he acquires any benefit, to communicate it to them. Certain it is also that there may be no abuse of special opportunities growing out of a special trust as manager or agent.* [Emphasis added.]

* * * Very likely [Salmon] assumed in all good faith that with the approaching end of the venture he might ignore his coadventurer and take the extension for himself. He had given to the enterprise time and labor as well as money. He had made it a success. Meinhard, who had given money, but neither time nor labor, had already been richly paid. * * * [But] Salmon had put himself in a position in which thought of self was to be renounced, however hard the abnegation [self-denial]. He was much more than a co-adventurer. He was a managing co-adventurer. For him and for those like him the rule of undivided loyalty is relentless and supreme.

Decision and Remedy The Court of Appeals of New York held that Salmon had breached his fiduciary duty by failing to inform Meinhard of Gerry's business opportunity and secretly taking advantage of it himself. The court granted Meinhard an interest "measured by the value of half of the entire lease."

Critical Thinking

• **What If the Facts Were Different?** *Suppose that Salmon had disclosed the proposed deal to Meinhard, who had said that he was not interested. Would the result in this case have been different? Explain.*

(*Continues*)

Breach and Waiver of Fiduciary Duties A partner's fiduciary duties may not be waived or eliminated in the partnership agreement. In fulfilling her or his duties, each partner must act consistently with the obligation of good faith and fair dealing [UPA 103(b), 404(d)]. The agreement can specify acts that the partners agree will violate a fiduciary duty.

Note that a partner may pursue his or her own interests without automatically violating fiduciary duties [UPA 404(e)]. The key is whether the partner has disclosed the interest to the other partners. **Example 31.6** Jayne Trell, a partner at Jacoby & Meyers, owns a shopping mall. Trell may vote against a partnership proposal to open a competing mall, provided that she has fully disclosed her interest in the existing shopping mall to the other partners at the firm. ▮ A partner cannot make secret profits or put self-interest before his or her duty to the interest of the partnership, however.

Authority of Partners The UPA affirms general principles of agency law that pertain to the authority of a partner to bind a partnership in contract. If a partner acts within the scope of her or his authority, the partnership is legally bound to honor the partner's commitments to third parties.

A partner may also subject the partnership to tort liability under agency principles. When a partner is carrying on partnership business with third parties in the usual way, both the partner and the firm share liability. The partnership will not be liable, however, if the third parties *know* that the partner had no authority to commit the partnership.

Limitations on Authority. A partnership may limit the capacity of a partner to act as the firm's agent or transfer property on its behalf by filing a "statement of partnership authority" in a designated state office [UPA 105, 303]. Such limits on a partner's authority normally are effective only with respect to third parties who are notified of the limitations. (An exception is made in real property transactions when the statement of authority has been recorded with the appropriate state office.)

The Scope of Implied Powers. The agency concepts relating to apparent authority, actual authority, and ratification also apply to partnerships. *The extent of implied authority is generally broader for partners than for ordinary agents.*

In an ordinary partnership, the partners can exercise all implied powers reasonably necessary and customary to carry on that particular business. Some customarily implied powers include the authority to make warranties on goods in a retail sales business and the power to enter into contracts consistent with the firm's ordinary course of business.

Example 31.7 Jamie Schwab, a partner in a firm that operates a retail tire store, regularly promises that "each tire will be warranted for normal wear for 40,000 miles." Because Schwab has authority to make warranties, the partnership is bound to honor them. Schwab would not, however, have the authority to sell the partnership's office equipment, fixtures, or other property without the consent of all of the other partners. ▮

> "Surround yourself with partners who are better than you are."
>
> **David Ogilvy**
> 1911–1999
> (Scottish advertising executive)

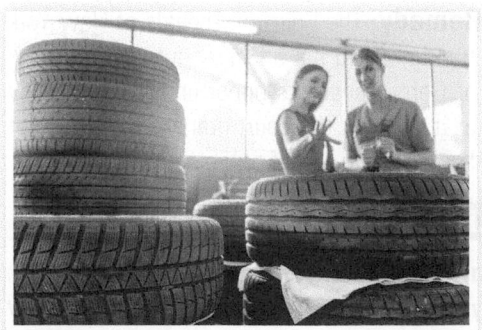

A partner in a tire store tells customers that every tire comes with a specific type of warranty. How could the partner's words affect the partnership as a whole?

Kzenon/Alamy Stock Photo

Liability of Partners in a General Partnership One significant disadvantage associated with a traditional partnership is that partners are *personally* liable for the debts of the partnership. In most states, the liability is essentially unlimited because the acts of one partner in the ordinary course of business subject the other partners to personal liability [UPA 305].

Joint Liability. Each partner in a partnership is jointly liable for the partnership's obligations. **Joint liability** means that a third party must sue all of the partners as a group, but each partner can be held liable for the full amount.[3]

If, for instance, a third party sues one individual partner on a partnership contract, that partner has the right to demand that the other partners be sued with her or him. In fact, if the third party does not name all of the partners in the lawsuit, the assets of the partnership cannot be used to satisfy the judgment. With joint liability, the partnership's assets must be exhausted before creditors can reach the partners' individual assets.

Joint and Several Liability. In the majority of the states, under UPA 306(a), partners are jointly and severally (separately or individually) liable for all partnership obligations. **Joint and several liability** means that a third party has the option of suing all of the partners together (jointly) or one or more of the partners separately (severally).

All the partners in a partnership can be held liable even if a particular partner did not participate in, know about, or ratify the conduct that gave rise to the lawsuit. Normally, though, the partnership's assets must be exhausted before a creditor can enforce a judgment against a partner's personal assets [UPA 307(d)]. In addition, a partner who commits a tort may be required to indemnify (reimburse) the partnership for any damages it pays unless the tort was committed in the ordinary course of the partnership's business.

A judgment against one partner severally (separately) does not extinguish the others' liability. (Similarly, a release of one partner does not discharge the partners' several liability.) Those not sued in the first action may be sued subsequently, unless the court in the first action held that the partnership was not liable.

If a plaintiff is successful in a suit against a partner or partners, he or she may collect on the judgment only against the assets of those partners named as defendants. **Example 31.8** Brian and Julie are partners. If Tom sues Brian for a debt on a partnership contract and wins, Tom can collect the amount of the judgment against Brian only. If Tom cannot collect enough from Brian, however, Tom can later sue Julie for the difference. ▪

Liability of Incoming Partners. A partner newly admitted to an existing partnership is not personally liable for any partnership obligations incurred before the person became a partner [UPA 306(b)]. The new partner's liability to existing creditors of the partnership is limited to her or his capital contribution to the firm.

Example 31.9 Smartclub, an existing partnership with four members, admits a new partner, Alex Jaff. He contributes $100,000 to the partnership. Smartclub has debts amounting to $600,000 at the time Jaff joins the firm. Although Jaff's capital contribution of $100,000 can be used to satisfy Smartclub's prior obligations, Jaff is not personally liable for debts incurred before he became a partner. If, however, the partnership incurs additional debts after Jaff becomes a partner, he will be personally liable for those amounts, along with all other partners. ▪

31–3 Dissociation and Termination

Dissociation occurs when a partner ceases to be associated in the carrying on of the partnership business. Dissociation normally entitles the partner to have his or her interest purchased by the partnership. It also terminates the partner's actual authority to act for the partnership and to participate with the partners in running the business.

Joint Liability In partnership law, the partners' shared liability for partnership obligations and debts. A third party must sue all of the partners as a group, but each partner can be held liable for the full amount.

Joint and Several Liability In partnership law, a doctrine under which a plaintiff may sue, and collect a judgment from, all of the partners together (jointly) or one or more of the partners separately (severally, or individually). A partner can be held liable even if she or he did not participate in, ratify, or know about the conduct that gave rise to the lawsuit.

Dissociation The severance of the relationship between a partner and a partnership.

Learning Objective 3

What is dissociation? What happens when a partner dissociates from a partnership?

---

3. Under the prior version of the UPA, which is still in effect in a few states, partners were subject to joint liability on partnership debts and contracts, but not on partnership debts arising from torts.

Once dissociation occurs, the partnership normally can continue to do business without the dissociating partner.[4] If the partners no longer wish to (or are unable to) continue the business, the partnership may be terminated (dissolved).

31–3a Events That Cause Dissociation

Under UPA 601, a partner can be dissociated from a partnership in any of the following ways:

If a partner is convicted of a crime, he or she can be dissociated from a partnership. What other events can cause a partner's dissociation?

Rich Legg/E+/Getty Images

1. By the partner's voluntarily giving notice of an "express will to withdraw." (When a partner gives notice of intent to withdraw, the remaining partners must decide whether to continue the partnership business. If they decide not to continue, the voluntary dissociation of a partner will dissolve the firm [UPA 801(1)].)

2. By the occurrence of an event agreed to in the partnership agreement.

3. By a unanimous vote of the other partners under certain circumstances, such as when a partner transfers substantially all of her or his interest in the partnership.

4. By order of a court or arbitrator if the partner has engaged in wrongful conduct that affects the partnership business. The court can order dissociation if a partner breached the partnership agreement or violated a duty owed to the partnership or to the other partners. Dissociation may also be ordered if the partner engaged in conduct that makes it "not reasonably practicable to carry on the business in partnership with the partner" [UPA 601(5)].

5. By the partner's declaring bankruptcy, assigning his or her interest in the partnership for the benefit of creditors, becoming physically or mentally incapacitated, or by the partner's dying.

Wrongful Dissociation A partner always has the *power* to dissociate from the firm, but he or she may not have the *right* to do so. If the partner lacks the right to dissociate, then the dissociation is considered wrongful under the law [UPA 602]. When a partner's dissociation is in breach of the partnership agreement, for instance, it is wrongful.

Example 31.10 Jensen & Whalen's partnership agreement states that it is a breach of the agreement for any partner to assign partnership property to a creditor without the consent of the other partners. If Janis, a partner, makes such an assignment, she not only has breached the agreement but also has wrongfully dissociated from the partnership. ■

A partner who wrongfully dissociates is liable to the partnership and to the other partners for damages caused by the dissociation. This liability is in addition to any other obligation to the partnership or to the partners.

Effects of Dissociation Dissociation (rightful or wrongful) terminates some of the rights of the dissociated partner, requires that the partnership purchase his or her interest, and alters the liability of the parties to third parties.

Rights and Duties. On a partner's dissociation, his or her right to participate in the management and conduct of the partnership business terminates [UPA 603]. The partner's duty of loyalty also ends. A partner's duty of care continues only with respect to events that occurred before dissociation, unless the partner participates in *winding up* the partnership's business (discussed shortly).

Example 31.11 Tanya Pearson, a partner who leaves an accounting firm, Bubb & Ferngold, can immediately compete with that firm for new clients. She must exercise care in completing ongoing client transactions, however, and must account to Bubb & Ferngold for any fees received from the former clients based on those transactions. ■

---

4. Under the previous version of the UPA, when a partner withdrew from a partnership, the partnership was considered dissolved, its business had to be wound up, and the proceeds had to be distributed to creditors and among the partners. The new UPA dramatically changed the law governing partnership breakups and does not require that a partnership be dissolved just because one partner has left the firm.

Buyouts. After a partner's dissociation, the partnership must purchase his or her partnership interest according to the rules in UPA 701. The **buyout price** is based on the amount that would have been distributed to the partner if the partnership had been wound up on the date of dissociation. Offset against the price are any amounts owed by the partner to the partnership, including any damages to the firm if the dissociation was wrongful.

Liability to Third Parties. For two years after a partner dissociates from a continuing partnership, the partnership may be bound by the acts of the dissociated partner based on apparent authority [UPA 702]. In other words, if a third party reasonably believed at the time of a transaction that the dissociated partner was still a partner, the partnership may be liable. In addition, a dissociated partner may be liable for partnership obligations entered into during a two-year period following dissociation [UPA 703].

To avoid this possible liability, a partnership should notify its creditors, customers, and clients of a partner's dissociation. Also, either the partnership or the dissociated partner can file a *statement of dissociation* in the appropriate state office to limit the dissociated partner's authority to ninety days after the filing [UPA 704].

31–3b Partnership Termination

The same events that cause dissociation can result in the end of the partnership if the remaining partners no longer wish to (or are unable to) continue the business. A partner's departure will not necessarily end the partnership, though. The partnership can continue if the remaining partners consent.

The termination of a partnership is referred to as **dissolution,** which essentially means the commencement of the winding up process. **Winding up** is the actual process of collecting, liquidating, and distributing the partnership assets. If the partners entered into a *buy-sell agreement* (discussed shortly) at the time they formed the partnership, that agreement will govern the specific procedures used.

Dissolution Dissolution of a partnership generally can be brought about by acts of the partners, by operation of law, or by judicial decree [UPA 801]. Any partnership (including one for a fixed term) can be dissolved by the partners' agreement. Similarly, if the partnership agreement states that it will dissolve on a certain event, such as a partner's death or bankruptcy, then the occurrence of that event will dissolve the partnership. A partnership for a fixed term or a particular undertaking is dissolved by operation of law at the expiration of the term or on the completion of the undertaking.

Case Example 31.12 Clyde Webster, James Theis, and Larry Thomas formed T&T Agri-Partners Company to own and farm 180 acres in Illinois for a fixed term. Under the partnership agreement, the death of any partner would dissolve the partnership. Nevertheless, when Webster died, Theis and Thomas did not liquidate T&T and distribute its assets. Webster's estate filed a complaint in state court seeking to dissolve the partnership. The court ordered the defendants to dissolve the partnership and liquidate its assets in accord with the clear provisions of the partnership agreement.[5]

Illegality or Impracticality. Any event that makes it unlawful for the partnership to continue its business will result in dissolution [UPA 801(4)]. Under the UPA, a court may order dissolution when it becomes obviously impractical for the firm to continue—for instance, if the business can only be operated at a loss [UPA 801(5)]. Even when one partner has brought a court action seeking to dissolve a partnership, the partnership continues to exist until it is legally dissolved by the court or by the parties' agreement.

Buyout Price The amount payable to a partner on his or her dissociation from a partnership, based on the amount distributable to that partner if the partnership had been wound up on that date and offset by any damages for wrongful dissociation.

Dissolution The formal disbanding of a partnership or a corporation. Partnerships can be dissolved by acts of the partners, by operation of law, or by judicial decree.

Winding Up The second of two stages in the termination of a partnership or corporation, in which the firm's assets are collected, liquidated, and distributed, and liabilities are discharged.

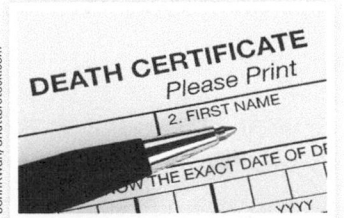

What happens when a partnership that was supposed to dissolve after one partner's death continues to operate?

---

5. *Estate of Webster v. Thomas,* 2013 WL 164041 (Ill.App. 2013).

Case Example 31.13 Members of the Russell family began operating Russell Realty Associates (RRA) as a partnership. Eddie Russell had decision-making authority over the partnership's business, which involved buying, holding, leasing, and selling investment properties. After several years, Eddie and his sister, Nina Russell, became involved in disputes, and Nina began to routinely question Eddie's business decisions. Because of their disagreements, RRA experienced two years of delays before it could sell one piece of property. Although the firm continued to profit, Eddie filed a complaint seeking a judicial dissolution of the partnership, which the court granted. Nina appealed.

The Virginia Supreme Court affirmed the lower court's decision that Russell Realty must be judicially dissolved. The partners' relationship had deteriorated to the point where the partnership was unable to function effectively. As a result, the firm had incurred substantial and unnecessary added costs, which frustrated the partnership's economic purpose and made it impracticable to continue.[6]

Good Faith. Each partner must exercise good faith during the dissolution of a partnership. Some state statutes allow partners injured by another partner's bad faith to file a tort claim for wrongful dissolution.

Case Example 31.14 Attorneys Randall Jordan and Mary Helen Moses formed a two-member partnership for an indefinite term. Jordan ended the partnership three years later and asked the court for declarations concerning the partners' financial obligations. Moses, who had objected to ending the partnership, filed a claim against Jordan for wrongful dissolution and for appropriating $180,000 in fees that should have gone to the partnership.

Ultimately, the court held in favor of Moses. A claim for wrongful dissolution of a partnership may be based on damages arising from the excluded partner's loss of "an existing, or continuing, business opportunity" or of income and material assets. Because Jordan had attempted to appropriate partnership assets through dissolution, Moses could sue for wrongful dissolution.[7]

Winding Up and Distribution of Assets

After dissolution, the partnership continues for the limited purpose of the winding up process. The partners cannot create new obligations on behalf of the partnership. They have authority only to complete transactions begun but not finished at the time of dissolution and to wind up the partnership's business [UPA 803, 804(1)].

Duties and Compensation. Winding up includes collecting and preserving partnership assets, discharging liabilities (paying debts), and accounting to each partner for the value of her or his interest in the partnership. Partners continue to have fiduciary duties to one another and to the firm during this process. UPA 401(h) provides that a partner is entitled to compensation for services in winding up partnership affairs (and reimbursement for expenses incurred in the process) above and apart from his or her share in the partnership profits.

Creditors' Claims. Both creditors of the partnership and creditors of the individual partners can make claims on the partnership's assets. In general, partnership creditors and the partners' personal creditors share proportionately in the partners' assets, which include their interests in the partnership.

A partnership's assets are distributed according to the following priorities [UPA 807]:

1. Payment of debts, including those owed to partner and nonpartner creditors.

2. Return of capital contributions and distribution of profits to partners.

If the partnership's liabilities are greater than its assets, the partners bear the losses—in the absence of a contrary agreement—in the same proportion in which they shared the profits (rather than, for instance, in proportion to their contributions to the partnership's capital).

Know This

Secured creditors have priority over unsecured creditors in any assets that serve as collateral for a partnership's debts.

---

6. *Russell Realty Associates v. Russell,* 724 S.E.2d 690 (Va.Sup.Ct. 2012).
7. *Jordan v. Moses,* 291 Ga. 39, 727 S.E.2d 460 (2012).

Partnership Buy-Sell Agreements Before entering into a partnership, partners may agree on how the assets will be valued and divided in the event that the partnership dissolves. Such an agreement may eliminate costly negotiations or litigation later.

The agreement may provide for one or more partners to buy out the other or others, should the situation warrant. This is called a **buy-sell agreement,** or simply a *buyout agreement.* Alternatively, the agreement may specify that one or more partners will determine the value of the interest being sold and that the other or others will decide whether to buy or sell.

Under UPA 701(a), if a partner's dissociation does not result in a dissolution of the partnership, a buyout of the partner's interest is mandatory. The UPA contains an extensive set of buyout rules that apply when the partners do not have a buy-sell agreement. Basically, a withdrawing partner receives the same amount through a buyout that he or she would receive if the business were winding up [UPA 701(b)].

> **Buy-Sell Agreement** An agreement made at the time of partnership formation providing for one or more of the partners to buy out the other or others, in the event the firm is dissolved. It is also called a *buyout agreement.*

31–4 Limited Liability Partnerships

The **limited liability partnership (LLP)** is a hybrid form of business designed mostly for professionals who normally do business as partners in a partnership. Almost all of the states have enacted LLP statutes.

The major advantage of the LLP is that it allows a partnership to continue as a pass-through entity for tax purposes but limits the personal liability of the partners. The LLP is especially attractive for professional service firms and family businesses. All of the "Big Four" accounting firms—the four largest international accountancy and professional services firms—are organized as LLPs, including Ernst & Young, LLP, and PricewaterhouseCoopers, LLP.

> **Limited Liability Partnership (LLP)** A hybrid form of business organization that is used mainly by professionals who normally do business in a partnership. An LLP is a pass-through entity for tax purposes, but a partner's personal liability for the malpractice of other partners is limited.

31–4a Formation of an LLP

LLPs must be formed and operated in compliance with state statutes, which may include provisions of the UPA. The appropriate form must be filed with a central state agency, usually the secretary of state's office, and the business's name must include either "Limited Liability Partnership" or "LLP" [UPA 1001, 1002]. An LLP must file an annual report with the state to remain qualified as an LLP in that state [UPA 1003].

In most states, it is relatively easy to convert a traditional partnership into an LLP because the firm's basic organizational structure remains the same. Additionally, all of the statutory and common law rules governing partnerships still apply (apart from those modified by the LLP statute). Normally, LLP statutes are simply amendments to a state's already existing partnership law.

> **Learning Objective 4**
> What advantages do limited liability partnerships offer to businesspersons that are not offered by general partnerships?

31–4b Liability in an LLP

An LLP allows professionals, such as attorneys and accountants, to avoid personal liability for the malpractice of other partners. A partner in an LLP is still liable for her or his own wrongful acts, such as negligence, of course. Also liable is the partner who supervised the individual who committed a wrongful act. (This supervisory liability generally applies to all types of partners and partnerships, not just LLPs.)

Example 31.15 Five lawyers operate a law firm as a limited liability partnership. One of the attorneys, Dan Kolcher, is sued for malpractice and loses. The firm's malpractice insurance is insufficient to pay the judgment. If the firm had been organized as a general partnership, the personal assets of the other attorneys could be used to satisfy the obligation. Because the firm is organized as an LLP, however, no other partner at the law firm can be held

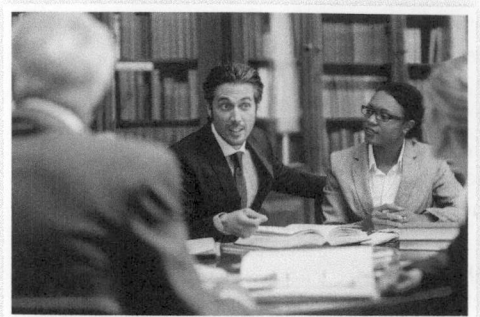

What is the advantage for professionals, such as attorneys, who decide to form a limited liability partnership?

personally liable for Kolcher's malpractice, unless she or he acted as Kolcher's supervisor. In the absence of a supervisor, only Kolcher's personal assets can be used to satisfy the judgment.

Although LLP statutes vary from state to state, generally each state statute limits the liability of partners in some way. For instance, Delaware law protects each innocent partner from the "debts and obligations of the partnership arising from negligence, wrongful acts, or misconduct." The UPA more broadly exempts partners in an LLP from personal liability for any partnership obligation, "whether arising in contract, tort, or otherwise" [UPA 306(c)].

Liability outside the State of Formation   When an LLP formed in one state wishes to do business in another state, it may be required to register in the second state—for instance, by filing a Statement of Foreign Qualification [UPA 1102]. Because state LLP statutes are not uniform, a question sometimes arises as to which law applies if the LLP statutes in the two states provide different liability protection. Most states apply the law of the state in which the LLP was formed, which is also the rule under UPA 1101.

Sharing Liability among Partners   When more than one partner in an LLP is negligent, there is a question as to how liability is to be shared. Is each partner jointly and severally liable for the entire result, as a general partner would be in most states?

Some states provide instead for proportionate liability—that is, for separate determinations of the negligence of the partners. **Example 31.16** Accountants Zach and Lyla are partners in an LLP, with Zach supervising Lyla. Lyla negligently fails to file a tax return for a client, Centaur Tools. Centaur files a suit against Zach and Lyla. Under a proportionate liability statute, Zach will be liable for no more than his portion of the responsibility for the missed tax deadline. In a state that does not allow for proportionate liability, Zach can be held liable for the entire loss.

Learning Objective 5

What are the key differences between the rights and liabilities of general partners and those of limited partners?

Limited Partnership (LP)
A partnership consisting of one or more general partners and one or more limited partners.

General Partner   In a limited partnership, a partner who assumes responsibility for the management of the partnership and has full liability for all partnership debts.

Limited Partner   In a limited partnership, a partner who contributes capital to the partnership but has no right to participate in its management and has no liability for partnership debts beyond the amount of her or his investment.

31–5 Limited Partnerships

A **limited partnership (LP)** limits the liability of *some* of its owners. Limited partnerships originated in medieval Europe and have been in existence in the United States since the early 1800s. Today, most states and the District of Columbia have adopted laws based on the Revised Uniform Limited Partnership Act (RULPA).

Limited partnerships differ from general partnerships in several ways.[8] A limited partnership consists of at least one **general partner** and one or more **limited partners.** A general partner assumes management responsibility for the partnership and so has full responsibility for the partnership and for all of its debts. A limited partner contributes cash or other property and owns an interest in the firm but does not undertake any management responsibilities and is not personally liable for partnership debts beyond the amount of his or her investment. A limited partner can forfeit limited liability by taking part in the management of the business.

In the following case, two firms—a corporation and a limited partnership—were involved in the construction of a residential development. One individual served as the president of the corporation and the sole general partner of the partnership, and took charge of the activities at the construction site. How did this individual's status affect his responsibility for those activities?

---

8. Under the UPA, a general partnership can be converted into a limited partnership and vice versa [UPA 902, 903]. The UPA also provides for the merger of a general partnership with one or more general or limited partnerships under rules that are similar to those governing corporate mergers [UPA 905].

Case 31.3

DeWine v. Valley View Enterprises, Inc.

Court of Appeals of Ohio, Eleventh District, Trumbull County, 2015 -Ohio- 1222 (2015).

Background and Facts Valley View Enterprises, Inc., built Pine Lakes Golf Club and Estates in Trumbull County, Ohio, in two phases—Phase I and Phase II. Valley View Properties, Ltd., a limited partnership, cut out the roadways and constructed sewer, water, and storm-water lines with water inlets. Joseph Ferrara was the owner and the president of Valley View Enterprises and the sole general partner of Valley View Properties. Ferrara failed to obtain the proper permits and to comply with their requirements for each phase of the development in a timely manner.

Michael DeWine, the state's attorney general, filed a lawsuit in an Ohio court against the Valley View entities and Ferrara, alleging violations of the state's water pollution–control laws and seeking civil penalties. The court entered a judgment in the defendants' favor, holding with respect to Ferrara that "a corporate officer cannot be held liable merely by virtue of his status as a corporate officer." DeWine appealed.

In the Words of the Court
Timothy J. *CANNON*, P.J. [Presiding Judge]
* * * *

Here, the state sought civil penalties from three entities: the property owner and Phase II permit holder, Valley View Properties, Ltd.; the Phase I permit holder, Valley View Enterprises, Inc.; and the sole general partner of the property owner, Mr. Ferrara. * * * The state alleges the trial court erred in its finding that "Valley View Properties is the only party against whom civil penalties can be assessed." The trial court also found Mr. Ferrara was not liable based on his "good faith" actions and Valley View Enterprises, Inc. was not liable because it had no relationship to Pine Lakes Estates; [and] the state failed to present evidence that Mr. Ferrara ordered activities that caused pollution.

Can a general partner be liable for failing to obtain wetlands-fill permits prior to creating roadways for a subdivision?

* * * Although the trial court found that Valley View Enterprises, Inc. had no relationship to Pine Lake Estates, the evidence establishes that Valley View Enterprises, Inc. applied for and was granted the [Phase I] Permit and, as the permittee, was required to ensure compliance with the permit. The [Phase I] Permit explicitly states, "the permittee must comply with all conditions of this permit, any permit noncompliance constitutes a violation of [state law]." Additionally, * * * *the evidence demonstrates that Mr. Ferrara personally was in charge of the activities performed at the sites; authorized the construction activities at the sites; and failed to obtain necessary certifications and permits.* [Emphasis added.]

Moreover, the trial court's finding that "a corporate officer cannot be held liable merely by virtue of his status as a corporate officer" is erroneous and not supported by the evidence. Admittedly, Mr. Ferrara is the sole general partner of Valley View Properties, Ltd., an Ohio limited partnership. He is not, in relation to Valley View Properties, Ltd., a "corporate officer." Therefore, he is not, in the course of his conduct as the general partner of that limited partnership, entitled to the insulation from liability of a corporate officer.

Decision and Remedy A state intermediate appellate court reversed the lower court's judgment in favor of the defendants. With respect to Ferrara's status in relation to Valley View Properties, he was the general partner and therefore not "entitled to the insulation from liability of a corporate officer." On remand, the trial court was to determine the number of violations established by the state, and issue and apportion penalties among the liable parties.

Critical Thinking

• **Legal Environment** *How are the penalties likely to be apportioned among the three defendants? Explain.*

31–5a Formation of an LP

In contrast to the informal, private, and voluntary agreement that usually suffices for a general partnership, the formation of a limited partnership is a public and formal proceeding. The partners must strictly follow statutory requirements. See Exhibit 31–2 for a comparison

Exhibit 31–2 A Comparison of General Partnerships and Limited Partnerships

CHARACTERISTIC	GENERAL PARTNERSHIP (UPA)	LIMITED PARTNERSHIP (RULPA)
Creation	By agreement of two or more persons to carry on a business as co-owners for profit.	By agreement and by filing a certificate of limited partnership with the secretary of state. There must be at least one general partner and one limited partner.
Sharing of Profits and Losses	By agreement. In the absence of agreement, profits are shared equally by the partners, and losses are shared in the same ratio as profits.	Profits are shared as stated in the certificate. Losses are also shared, up to the amount of the limited partners' capital contributions. In the absence of a provision in the certificate, profits and losses are shared on the basis of percentages of capital contributions.
Liability	Unlimited personal liability of all partners.	Unlimited personal liability of all general partners; limited partners liable only to the extent of their capital contributions.
Capital Contribution	No minimum or mandatory amount; set by agreement.	Set by agreement.
Management	By agreement. In the absence of agreement, all partners have an equal voice.	Only the general partner (or the general partners). Limited partners have no voice. A limited partner who participates in management will be just as liable as a general partner to third parties.
Duration	A fixed term can be set by the agreement. If no duration is specified, the partners can continue to do business even when a partner dissociates from the partnership.	As specified in the certificate. An LP may be dissolved by a court or by the general partner's bankruptcy, retirement, mental incompetence, or death. Death of a limited partner does not terminate the partnership, unless he or she is the only remaining limited partner.

of the characteristics of general and limited partnerships. Not only must a limited partnership have at least one general partner and one limited partner, but the partners must also sign a **certificate of limited partnership.**

The certificate of limited partnership must include certain information, such as the name, mailing address, and capital contribution of each general and limited partner. The certificate must be filed with the designated state official—under the RULPA, the secretary of state. The certificate is usually open to public inspection.

Certificate of Limited Partnership
The document that must be filed with a designated state official to form a limited partnership.

Know This

A limited partner is liable only to the extent of any contribution that she or he made to the partnership, but can lose this limited liability by participating in management.

31–5b Liabilities of Partners in an LP

General partners, unlike limited partners, are personally liable to the partnership's creditors. Thus, at least one general partner is necessary in a limited partnership so that someone has personal liability. This policy can be circumvented in states that allow a corporation to be the general partner in a partnership. Because the corporation has limited liability by virtue of corporate laws, if a corporation is the general partner, no one in the limited partnership has personal liability.

The liability of a limited partner, as mentioned, is limited to the capital that she or he contributes or agrees to contribute to the partnership [RULPA 502]. Limited partners enjoy this limited liability only so long as they do not participate in management [RULPA 303].

A limited partner who participates in management will be just as liable as a general partner to any creditor who does business with the limited partnership. Liability arises when the creditor believes, based on the limited partner's conduct, that the limited partner is a general partner [RULPA 303]. How much review and advisement a limited partner can engage in before being exposed to liability is not always clear, however.

Should an innocent general partner be jointly liable for fraud?	Ethical Issue

When general partners in a limited partnership jointly engage in fraud, there is usually no question that they are jointly liable. But if one general partner engages in fraud and the other is unaware of the wrongdoing, is it fair to make the innocent partner share in the liability? Many states' limited partnership laws protect innocent general partners from suits for fraud brought by limited partners. The law is less clear, however, in some other situations.

For example, Robert Bisno and James Coxeter formed two limited partnerships to develop property in Berkeley, California. Without Coxeter's knowledge, Bisno took almost $500,000 from one of the partnerships to buy a personal home. He also made material misrepresentations to potential investors. One of those investors, George Miske—after purchasing an interest in the limited partnership—discovered the fraud and brought suit. Coxeter argued that Miske was a limited partner, not an innocent third party. Under the state's limited partnership law, that meant Coxeter should be protected from liability.

The court disagreed. The fraud at issue had induced Miske to purchase the limited partnership interest. Therefore, at the time the fraud was perpetrated by Bisno, Miske was an innocent third party. As a result, Coxeter, though innocent of any wrongdoing, was jointly liable.[9]

31–5c Dissociation and Dissolution in an LP

A general partner has the power to voluntarily dissociate, or withdraw, from a limited partnership unless the partnership agreement specifies otherwise. A limited partner can withdraw from the partnership by giving six months' notice *unless* the partnership agreement specifies a term, which most do. Also, some states have passed laws prohibiting the withdrawal of limited partners.

Events That Cause Dissolution A limited partnership can be dissolved by court decree [RULPA 802]. In addition, a general partner's voluntary dissociation from the firm normally will lead to dissolution unless all partners agree to continue the business. Similarly, the bankruptcy, retirement, death, or mental incompetence of a general partner will cause the dissociation of that partner and the dissolution of the limited partnership unless the other members agree to continue the firm [RULPA 801].

Bankruptcy of a limited partner, however, does not dissolve the partnership unless it causes the bankruptcy of the firm. Death or an assignment of the interest of a limited partner does not dissolve a limited partnership [RULPA 702, 704, 705].

Distribution of Assets On dissolution, creditors' claims, including those of partners who are creditors, take first priority. After that, partners and former partners receive unpaid distributions of partnership assets and, except as otherwise agreed, amounts representing returns of their capital contributions and proportionate distributions of profits [RULPA 804].

> "A friendship founded on business is a good deal better than a business founded on friendship."
>
> **John D. Rockefeller**
> 1839–1937
> (American industrialist)

---

9. *Miske v. Bisno*, 204 Cal.App.4th 1249, 139 Cal.Rptr.3d 626 (2012). See also *In re Barlaam*, 2014 WL 3398381 (9th Cir. 2014).

Can a limited partner in actor
Kevin Costner's limited partnership
force the sale of the entity?

Valuation of Assets Disputes commonly arise about how the partnership's assets should be valued and distributed on dissolution and whether the business should be sold. ⚡ **Spotlight Case Example 31.17** Actor Kevin Costner was a limited partner in Midnight Star Enterprises, LP, which runs a casino, bar, and restaurant in South Dakota. There were two other limited partners, Carla and Francis Caneva, who owned a small percentage of the partnership (3.25 units each) and received salaries for managing its operations. Another company owned by Costner, Midnight Star Enterprises, Limited (MSEL), was the general partner. Costner thus controlled a majority of the partnership (93.5 units).

When communications broke down between the partners, MSEL asked a court to dissolve the partnership. MSEL's accountant determined that the firm's fair market value was $3.1 million. The Canevas presented evidence that a competitor would buy the business for $6.2 million. The Canevas wanted the court to force Costner to either buy the business for that price or sell it on the open market to the highest bidder. Ultimately, the state's highest court held in favor of Costner. A partner cannot force the sale of a limited partnership when the other partners want to continue the business. The court also accepted the $3.1 million buyout price of MSEL's accountant and ordered Costner to pay the Canevas the value of their 6.5 partnership units.[10]

---

10. *In re Dissolution of Midnight Star Enterprises, LP,* 2006 S.D. 98, 724 N.W.2d 334 (2006).

Practice and Review

Grace Tarnavsky and her sons, Manny and Jason, bought a ranch known as the Cowboy Palace in March 2016. The three orally agreed to share the business for five years. Grace contributed 50 percent of the investment, and each son contributed 25 percent. Manny agreed to handle the livestock, and Jason agreed to do the bookkeeping. The Tarnavskys took out joint loans and opened a joint bank account into which they deposited the ranch's proceeds and from which they made payments for property, cattle, equipment, and supplies.

In September 2018, Manny severely injured his back while baling hay and became permanently unable to handle livestock. Manny therefore hired additional laborers to tend the livestock, causing the Cowboy Palace to incur significant debt. In September 2019, Al's Feed Barn filed a lawsuit against Jason to collect $32,400 in unpaid debts. Using the information presented in the chapter, answer the following questions.

1. Was this relationship a partnership for a term or a partnership at will?

2. Did Manny have the authority to hire additional laborers to work at the ranch after his injury? Why or why not?

3. Under the UPA, can Al's Feed Barn bring an action against Jason individually for the Cowboy Palace's debt? Why or why not?

4. Suppose that after his back injury in 2018, Manny sent his mother and brother a notice indicating his intent to withdraw from the partnership. Can he still be held liable for the debt to Al's Feed Barn? Why or why not?

Debate This

A partnership should automatically end when one partner dissociates from the firm.

Key Terms

Chapter Summary: All Forms of Partnership

Basic Partnership Concepts	1. *Agency concepts and partnership law*—A partnership is similar to an agency relationship except that partners have an ownership interest in the business and are obliged to bear a portion of ordinary business losses.
	2. *The Uniform Partnership Act (UPA)*—Governs the operation of partnerships in the absence of an express agreement.
	3. *Definition of a partnership*—An agreement by two or more persons to carry on, as co-owners, a business for profit.
	4. *Essential elements of a partnership*—A sharing of profits and losses, a joint ownership of the business, and an equal right to be involved in the management of the business are essential partnership elements.
	5. *Entity versus aggregate theory of partnerships*—A majority of the states follows the UPA and treat a partnership as an entity for most purposes.
	6. *Tax treatment of partnerships*—Partnerships are treated as an aggregate of the individual partners rather than as a separate legal entity for federal income tax purposes. The partnership is a pass-through entity and not a tax-paying entity.
Formation and Operation	1. *The partnership agreement*—Also called articles of partnership, the written agreement sets forth each partner's rights and obligations with respect to the partnership.
	2. *Duration of the partnership*—A partnership specifically limited in duration is called a partnership for a term. If no fixed duration is specified, the partnership is called a partnership at will.
	3. *Partnership by estoppel*—Imposed by a court when a third person has reasonably and detrimentally relied on a representation that a nonpartner was part of a partnership.
	4. *Rights of partners*—Rights include (a) management, (b) interest in the partnership, (c) compensation, (d) inspection of books, (e) accounting, and (f) property.
	5. *Duties and liabilities of partners*—
	a. Fiduciary duties (duty of care and duty of loyalty) may not be waived. Each partner must act consistently with good faith and fair dealing.
	b. A partner has the authority to bind the partnership in a contract. A partner may also subject the partnership to tort liability under agency principles. The extent of implied authority is generally broader for partners than for ordinary agents.
	c. In a traditional partnership, partners are personally liable for the debts of the partnership.
Dissociation and Termination	1. *Events that cause dissociation*—
	a. A partner's voluntarily giving notice of an "express will to withdraw."
	b. The occurrence of an event agreed to in the partnership agreement.
	c. Unanimous vote of the other partners under certain circumstances.
	d. The order of a court or arbitrator if the partner engaged in wrongful conduct that affects the business.
	e. The partner's declaring bankruptcy, assigning his or her interest in the partnership for the benefit of creditors, becoming physically or mentally incapacitated, or dying.
	2. *Partnership termination*—Referred to as dissolution. Winding up is the actual process of collecting, liquidating, and distributing the partnership assets. A buy-sell agreement provides for one or more of the partners to buy out the other or others, and may specify how the assets will be valued in the event the firm is dissolved.

(Continues)

Limited Liability Partnerships (LLPs)	1. *Formation*—The appropriate form must be filed with a state agency, usually the secretary of state's office. Typically, an LLP is formed by professionals who work together as partners in a partnership. Under most state LLP statutes, it is relatively easy to convert a traditional partnership into an LLP. 2. *Liabilities of partners*—LLP statutes vary, but under the UPA, professionals generally can avoid personal liability for acts committed by other partners. Partners in an LLP continue to be liable for their own wrongful acts and for the wrongful acts of those whom they supervise.
Limited Partnerships (LPs)	1. *Formation*—A certificate of limited partnership must be filed with the secretary of state's office or other designated state official. The certificate must include information about the business. The partnership consists of one or more general partners and one or more limited partners. 2. *Liabilities of partners*—General partners have unlimited liability for partnership obligations. Limited partners are liable only to the extent of their contributions. Limited partners have no voice in management. If they do participate in management, they risk having general-partner liability. 3. *Dissociation and dissolution*—A limited partnership can be dissolved by court decree. In addition, a general partner's voluntary dissociation, bankruptcy, death, or mental incompetence will cause the dissociation of that partner and the partnership's dissolution unless all partners agree to continue the business. The death or assignment of the interest of a limited partner does not dissolve the partnership. Bankruptcy of a limited partner also does not dissolve the partnership unless it causes the bankruptcy of the firm.

Issue Spotters

1. Darnell and Eliana are partners in D&E Designs, an architectural firm. When Darnell dies, his widow claims that as Darnell's heir, she is entitled to take his place as Eliana's partner or to receive a share of the firm's assets. Is she right? Why or why not? (See *Dissociation and Termination*.)

2. Finian and Gloria are partners in F&G Delivery Service. When business is slow, without Gloria's knowledge, Finian leases the delivery vehicles as moving vans. Because the delivery vehicles would otherwise be sitting idle in a parking lot, can Finian keep the income that results from leasing the vehicles? Explain your answer. (See *Formation and Operation*.)

—**Check your answers to the *Issue Spotters* against the answers provided in Appendix D at the end of this text.**

Business Scenarios and Case Problems

31–1. Partnership Formation. Daniel is the owner of a chain of shoe stores. He hires Rubya to be the manager of a new store, which is to open in Grand Rapids, Michigan. Daniel, by written contract, agrees to pay Rubya a monthly salary and 20 percent of the profits. Without Daniel's knowledge, Rubya represents himself to Classen as Daniel's partner, showing Classen the agreement to share profits. Classen extends credit to Rubya. Rubya defaults. Discuss whether Classen can hold Daniel liable as a partner. (See *Formation and Operation*.)

31–2. Limited Partnership. Dorinda, Luis, and Elizabeth form a limited partnership. Dorinda is a general partner, and Luis and Elizabeth are limited partners. Discuss fully whether each of the

separate events below constitutes a dissolution of the limited partnership. (See *Limited Partnerships*.)

1. Luis assigns his partnership interest to Ashley.

2. Elizabeth is petitioned into involuntary bankruptcy.

3. Dorinda dies.

31–3. Winding Up. Dan and Lori Cole operated a Curves franchise exercise facility in Angola, Indiana, as a partnership. The firm leased commercial space from Flying Cat, LLC, for a renewable three-year term. The Coles renewed the lease for a second three-year term. Two years later, however, the Coles divorced. By the end of the second term, the Coles owed Flying

Cat more than $21,000 on the lease. Without telling the landlord about the divorce, Lori signed another extension. More rent went unpaid. Flying Cat obtained a judgment in an Indiana state court against the partnership for almost $50,000. Can Dan be held liable? Why or why not? [*Curves for Women Angola v. Flying Cat, LLC,* 983 N.E.2d 629 (Ind.App. 2013)] (See *Dissociation and Termination.*)

31–4. Business Case Problem with Sample Answer—Partnerships. Karyl Paxton asked Christopher Sacco to work with her interior design business, Pierce Paxton Collections, in New Orleans. At the time, they were in a romantic relationship. Sacco was involved in every aspect of the business—bookkeeping, marketing, and design—but was not paid a salary. He was reimbursed, however, for expenses charged to his personal credit card, which Paxton also used. Sacco took no profits from the firm, saying that he wanted to "grow the business" and "build sweat equity." When Paxton and Sacco's personal relationship soured, she fired him. Sacco objected, claiming that they were partners. Is Sacco entitled to 50 percent of the profits of Pierce Paxton Collections? Explain. [*Sacco v. Paxton,* 133 So.3d 213 (La.App. 2014)] (See *Formation and Operation.*)

—**For a sample answer to Problem 31–4, go to Appendix E at the end of this text.**

31–5. Formation. Leisa Reed and Randell Thurman lived together in Spring City, Tennessee. Randell and his father, Leroy, formed a cattle-raising operation and opened a bank account in the name of L&R Farm. Within a few years, Leroy quit the operation. Leisa and Randell each wrote a personal check for $5,000 to buy his cattle. Leisa picked up supplies, fed and administered medicine to cattle, collected hay, and participated in the bookkeeping for L&R. Later, checks drawn on her personal account for $12,000 to buy equipment and $35,000 to buy cattle were deposited into the L&R account. After several years, Leisa decided that she no longer wanted to associate with Randell, but they could not agree on a financial settlement. Was Leisa a partner in L&R? Is she entitled to half of the value of L&R's assets? Explain. [*Reed v. Thurman,* 2015 WL 1119449 (Tenn.App. 2015)] (See *Formation and Operation.*)

31–6. Formation and Operation. FS Partners is a general partnership whose partners are Jerry Stahlman, a professional engineer, and Fitz & Smith, Inc., a corporation in the business of excavating and paving. Timothy Smith signed the partnership agreement on Fitz & Smith's behalf and deals with FS matters on Fitz & Smith's behalf. Stahlman handles the payment of FS's bills, including its tax bills, and is the designated partner on FS's federal tax return. FS was formed to buy and develop twenty acres of unoccupied, wooded land in York County, Pennsylvania. The deed to the property lists the owner as "FS Partners, a

general partnership." When the taxes on the real estate were not paid, the York County Tax Claim Bureau published notice that the property would be sold at a tax sale. The bureau also mailed a notice to FS's address of record and posted a notice on the land. Is this sufficient notice of the tax sale? Discuss. [*FS Partners v. York County Tax Claim Bureau,* 132 A.3d 577 (Pa. 2016)] (See *Formation and Operation.*)

31–7. Dissociation and Dissolution. Marc Malfitano and seven others formed Poughkeepsie Galleria as a partnership to own and manage a shopping mall in New York. The partnership agreement stated that "all decisions to be made by the Partners shall be made by the casting of votes" with "no less than fifty-one percent" of the partners "required to approve any matter." The agreement also provided that the partnership would dissolve on "the election of the Partners" or "the happening of any event which makes it unlawful for the business . . . to be carried on." Later, Malfitano decided to dissociate from the firm and wrote to the other partners, "I hereby elect to dissolve the Partnership." Did Malfitano have the power and the right to dissociate from Poughkeepsie Galleria? Could he unilaterally dissolve the partnership? Can the other partners continue the business? Which, if any, of these actions violate the partnership agreement? Discuss. [*Congel v. Malfitano,* 31 N.Y.3d 272, __ N.E.3d __ (2018)] (See *Dissociation and Termination.*)

31–8. A Question of Ethics—The IDDR Approach and a Partner's Fiduciary Duty. *Floyd Finch and Bruce Campbell were partners in a law firm. They did not have a written partnership agreement, but they shared the firm's expenses and profits equally. The partnership operated on a cash basis, using billing software to track time spent on client matters. Instead of using the software, however, Finch would review e-mails and other work product to create and generate bills months or years after the work had been performed. As a result, large amounts of the firm's accounts receivable were uncollectable. Upset over the lost revenue, Campbell filed a claim in a Missouri state court against Finch. Campbell argued that failing to bill clients in a timely manner was a breach of a partner's fiduciary duty. He alleged that Finch was trying to lower his income because he was involved in divorce proceedings. Finch responded that billing clients was a matter of partnership management and operation reserved to the judgment of each partner. [Finch v. Campbell, 541 S.W.3d 616 (Mo.App.W.D. 2017)] (See Formation and Operation.)*

1. Is Finch's billing practice a breach of ethics? Explain, using the IDDR approach.

2. Finch asserted that there must be self-dealing for a partner's act to be a breach of fiduciary duty. Is he correct? Discuss.

Critical Thinking and Writing Assignments

31–9. Business Law Writing. Sandra Lerner and Patricia Holmes were friends. One evening, while applying nail polish to Lerner, Holmes layered a raspberry color over black to produce a new color, which Lerner liked. Later, the two created other colors with names like "Bruise," "Smog," and "Oil Slick," and titled their concept "Urban Decay." Lerner and Holmes started a firm to produce and market the polishes but never discussed the sharing of profits and losses. They agreed to build the business and then sell it. Together, they did market research, worked on a logo and advertising, obtained capital, and hired employees. Then Lerner began scheming to edge Holmes out of the firm. (See *Formation and Operation*.)

1. Lerner claimed that there was no partnership agreement because there was no agreement on how to divide profits. Was Lerner right? Why or why not?

2. Suppose that Lerner, but not Holmes, had contributed a significant amount of personal funds to developing and marketing the new nail polish. Would this entitle Lerner to receive more of the profit? Explain.

3. Did Lerner violate her fiduciary duty? Why or why not?

31–10. Time-Limited Group Assignment—Partnership Formation and Operation. At least six months before the Summer Olympic Games in Atlanta, Georgia, a group made up of Stafford Fontenot, Steve Turner, Mike Montelaro, Joe Sokol, and Doug Brinsmade agreed to sell Cajun food at the games and began making preparations. On May 19, the group (calling themselves Prairie Cajun Seafood Catering of Louisiana) applied for a business license with the county health department.

Ted Norris sold members of the group a mobile kitchen in return for an $8,000 check drawn on the "Prairie Cajun Seafood Catering of Louisiana" account and two promissory notes, one for $12,000 and the other for $20,000. The notes, which were dated June 12, listed only Fontenot "d/b/a Prairie Cajun Seafood" as the maker (*d/b/a* is an abbreviation for "doing business as").

On July 31, Fontenot and his friends signed a partnership agreement, which listed specific percentages of profits and losses. They drove the mobile kitchen to Atlanta, but business was disastrous. When the notes were not paid, Norris filed a suit in a Louisiana state court against Fontenot, seeking payment. (See *Formation and Operation*.)

1. The first group will discuss the elements of a partnership and determine whether there was a partnership among Fontenot and the others.

2. The second group will determine who can be held liable on the notes and why.

3. The third group will discuss the concept of "d/b/a," or "doing business as." Does a person who uses this designation when signing checks or promissory notes avoid liability on the checks or notes?

Limited Liability Companies and Special Business Forms

"To play it safe is not to play."

Robert Altman
1925–2006
(American film director)

Our government allows entrepreneurs to choose from a variety of business organizational forms. Many businesspersons would agree with the chapter-opening quotation that in business "to play it safe is not to play." Because risk is associated with the potential for higher profits, businesspersons are motivated to choose organizational forms that limit their liability while allowing them to take risks that may lead to greater profits.

A relatively new and increasingly common form of business organization is the *limited liability company (LLC)*. LLCs have become the organizational form of choice among many small businesses. Other special business forms outlined in this chapter include joint ventures, syndicates, joint stock companies, business trusts, and cooperatives.

32–1 The Limited Liability Company

A **limited liability company (LLC)** is a hybrid business form that combines the limited liability aspects of a corporation and the tax advantages of a partnership. This chapter's *Landmark in the Law* feature discusses the evolution of laws authorizing LLCs in the United States.

LLCs are governed by state LLC statutes, which vary, of course, from state to state. In an attempt to create more uniformity, the National Conference of Commissioners on Uniform State Laws (NCCUSL) issued the Uniform Limited Liability Company Act (ULLCA). Fewer than one-fifth of the states have adopted it, however. Thus, the law governing LLCs remains far from uniform.

Nevertheless, some provisions are common to most state statutes. We base our discussion of LLCs on these common elements.

Learning Objectives

The four Learning Objectives *below are designed to help improve your understanding. After reading this chapter, you should be able to answer the following questions:*

1. What advantages do limited liability companies offer to businesspersons that are not offered by sole proprietorships or partnerships?

2. What are the two options for managing limited liability companies?

3. What happens when a member dissociates from an LLC?

4. What is a joint venture? How is it similar to a partnership? How is it different?

Limited Liability Company (LLC)
A hybrid form of business enterprise that offers the limited liability of a corporation and the tax advantages of a partnership.

Limited Liability Company (LLC) Statutes

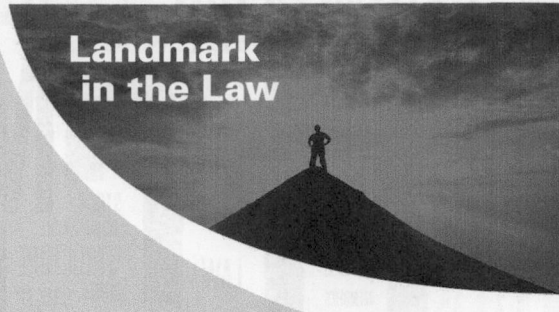

Limited liability companies (LLCs) have been used for more than a century in various foreign jurisdictions, including several European and South American nations. They did not emerge in the United States, however, until the late 1970s. Wyoming became the first state to pass legislation authorizing the creation of LLCs in 1977.

Taxation Rules Encouraged States to Pass Legislation After Wyoming's adoption of its LLC statute, it still was unclear how the Internal Revenue Service (IRS) would treat LLCs for tax purposes. In 1988, however, the IRS ruled that Wyoming LLCs could be taxed as partnerships instead of corporations, providing that certain requirements were met. This ruling was favorable toward LLCs because it meant that, like a partnership, an LLC could pass through profits to its owners without paying taxes on them. Before the ruling, only one other state—Florida, in 1982—had authorized LLCs. The 1988 ruling encouraged additional states to enact LLC statutes, and in less than a decade, all states had done so.

Other IRS rules also encouraged more widespread use of LLCs in the business world. Under these rules, any unincorporated business with more than one owner is automatically taxed as a partnership unless it indicates otherwise on the tax form or fits into one of the exceptions. The exceptions involve publicly traded companies, companies formed under a state incorporation statute, and certain foreign-owned companies. If a business chooses to be taxed as a corporation, it can indicate this preference by checking a box on the IRS form.

Foreign Entities May Be LLC Members Another factor that has encouraged the creation of LLCs in this country is that foreign investors are allowed to become LLC members. In an era increasingly characterized by global business efforts and investments, the LLC often offers U.S. firms and potential investors from other countries greater flexibility and opportunities than are available through partnerships or corporations.

Application to Today's World *Once it became clear that LLCs could be taxed as partnerships, the LLC form of business organization was widely adopted. Members could avoid the personal liability associated with the partnership form of business, as well as the double taxation of the corporate form of business. Today, LLCs are a common form of business organization.*

32–1a The Nature of the LLC

LLCs share many characteristics with corporations. Like corporations, LLCs are creatures of the state. In other words, they must be formed and operated in compliance with state law. Like shareholders in a corporation, owners of an LLC, who are called **members,** enjoy limited liability [ULLCA 303].

Member A person who has an ownership interest in a limited liability company.

Know This

A uniform law is a "model" law. It does not become the law of any state until the state legislature adopts it, either in part or in its entirety.

Limited Liability of Members Members of LLCs are shielded from personal liability in most situations. In other words, the liability of members is normally limited to the amount of their investments.

An exception arises when a member has significantly contributed to the LLC's tortious conduct. **Case Example 32.1** Randy Coley, the sole member and manager of East Coast Cablevision, LLC, installed cable television systems for many hotels and resorts. Coley established a DIRECTV Satellite Master Antenna Television (SMATV) account in the name of Massanutten Resort. The system provided programming to 168 timeshare units, as well as to the resort's bar, golf shop, lobbies, and waterpark. The bill for the resort's account was sent to (and paid by) East Coast Cablevision, which in turn billed the customers.

Over time, East Coast Cablevision began providing cable services to additional customers using the resort's SMATV account but did not pay DIRECTV for these other customers. Ultimately, another cable dealer affiliated with DIRECTV sued Coley for not paying for all of the DIRECTV programming transmissions that East Coast's customers had received. The court held that because Coley had played a direct role in the unauthorized transmissions, he could be held personally liable for them.[1]

When Liability May Be Imposed The members of an LLC, like the shareholders in a corporation, can lose their limited personal liability in certain circumstances. For instance, when an individual guarantees payment of a business loan to the LLC, that individual is personally liable for the business's obligation. In addition, if an LLC member fails to comply with certain formalities, such as by commingling personal and business funds, a court can impose personal liability.

Under various principles of corporate law, courts may hold the owners of a business liable for its debts. On rare occasions, for instance, courts ignore the corporate structure ("pierce the corporate veil") to expose the shareholders to personal liability when it is required to achieve justice. Similarly, courts will sometimes pierce the veil of an LLC to hold its members personally liable. Note, however, that courts have reserved piercing the veil of an LLC for circumstances that are clearly extraordinary. There must normally be some flagrant disregard of the LLC formalities, as well as fraud or malfeasance on the part of the LLC member.

Case Example 32.2 Tom and Shannon Brown purchased a new home in Hattiesburg, Mississippi, from Ray Richard and Nick Welch. Richard had hired Waldron Properties, LLC (WP), to build the home. Several years later, cracks began to develop in the walls of the Browns' home as a result of defects in the construction of the foundation. The Browns sued Murray Waldron, the sole member of WP, for breach of warranty under the state's New Home Warranty Act (NHWA). Because Waldron had signed the notice required by the NHWA that the Browns had received when they bought the home, they claimed that Waldron was liable personally.

The trial court found that WP (the LLC), not Waldron individually, was the builder of the Browns' home. The Browns appealed. They contended that even if WP was the builder, the court should pierce the veil of the LLC and hold Waldron personally liable. A state appellate court affirmed the lower court's ruling. The Browns had not entered into a contract with either Waldron or WP. There was not sufficient evidence that Waldron had disregarded LLC formalities or had engaged in fraud or other misconduct to justify piercing the LLC's veil to hold him personally liable.[2]

Other Similarities to Corporations Like corporations, LLCs are legal entities apart from their members. As a legal person, an LLC can sue or be sued, enter into contracts, and hold title to property [ULLCA 201]. The terminology used to describe LLCs formed in other states or nations is also similar to the terminology used in corporate law. For instance, an LLC formed in one state but doing business in another state is referred to in the second state as a *foreign LLC*.

32–1b The Formation of the LLC

LLCs are creatures of statute and thus must follow state statutory requirements.

Articles of Organization To form an LLC, **articles of organization** must be filed with a central state agency—usually the secretary of state's office [ULLCA 202].[3] Typically, the articles must include the name of the business, its principal address, the name and address of a registered agent, the members' names, and information on how the LLC will be managed [ULLCA 203]. The business's name must include the words *Limited Liability Company* or the initials *LLC* [ULLCA 105(a)]. Although a majority of the states permit one-member LLCs, some states require at least two members.

Articles of Organization The document filed with a designated state official by which a limited liability company is formed.

---

1. *Sky Cable, LLC v. Coley*, 2013 WL 3517337 (W.D.Va. 2013). See also *DIRECTV, LLC v. OLCR, Inc.*, 2016 WL 4679037 (E.D.Pa. 2016).
2. *Brown v. Waldron*, 186 So.3d 955 (Miss.App. 2016).
3. In addition to requiring the filing of articles of organization, a few states require that a notice of the intention to form an LLC be published in a local newspaper.

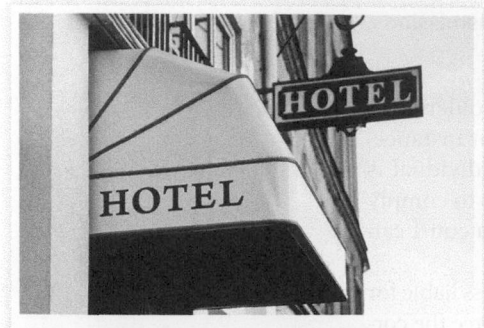

Many hotel chains are franchised as limited liability companies (LLCs). What is the document required to form an LLC?

Nikada/E+/Getty Images

Preformation Contracts Businesspersons sometimes enter into contracts on behalf of a business organization that is not yet formed. For instance, persons forming a corporation may enter into contracts during the process of incorporation but before the corporation becomes a legal entity. These contracts are referred to as *preincorporation contracts*. Once the corporation is formed and adopts the preincorporation contract (by means of a *novation,* which substitutes a new contract for the old contract), it can then enforce the contract terms.

In dealing with the preorganization contracts of LLCs, courts may apply the well-established principles of corporate law relating to preincorporation contracts. That is, when the promoters of an LLC enter preformation contracts, the LLC, once formed, can adopt the contracts through novation and then enforce them.

⭐ **Spotlight Case Example 32.3** 607 South Park, LLC, entered into an agreement to sell a hotel to 607 Park View Associates, Ltd., which then assigned the rights to the purchase to another company, 02 Development, LLC. At the time, 02 Development did not yet exist—it was legally created several months later. 607 South Park subsequently refused to sell the hotel to 02 Development, and 02 Development sued for breach of the purchase agreement.

A California appellate court ruled that LLCs should be treated the same as corporations with respect to preorganization contracts. Although 02 Development did not exist when the agreement was executed, once it came into existence, it could enforce any preorganization contract made on its behalf.[4]

> "Business is the salt of life."
>
> **Voltaire**
> 1694–1778
> (French author and intellectual)

32–1c Jurisdictional Requirements

A significant difference between LLCs and corporations involves federal jurisdictional requirements. Under federal law, a corporation is deemed to be a citizen of the state where it is incorporated and maintains its principal place of business.[5] Federal law does not mention the citizenship of partnerships, LLCs, and other unincorporated associations, but the courts have tended to regard these entities as citizens of every state of which their members are citizens.

The state citizenship of LLCs may come into play when a party sues an LLC based on diversity of citizenship. Remember that when parties to a lawsuit are from different states, a federal court can exercise diversity jurisdiction if the amount in controversy exceeds $75,000. *Total* diversity of citizenship must exist, however.

Example 32.4 Jen Fong, a citizen of New York, wishes to bring a lawsuit against Skycel, an LLC formed under the laws of Connecticut. One of Skycel's members also lives in New York. Fong will not be able to bring the action against Skycel in federal court on the basis of diversity jurisdiction because the defendant LLC is also considered a citizen of New York. The same would be true if Fong was filing a suit against multiple defendants and one of the defendants lived in New York.

Learning Objective 1

What advantages do limited liability companies offer to businesspersons that are not offered by sole proprietorships or partnerships?

32–1d Advantages of the LLC

The LLC offers many advantages to businesspersons, which is why this form of business organization has become increasingly popular.

Limited Liability A key advantage of the LLC is that the liability of members is limited to the amount of their investments. The LLC as an entity can be held liable for any loss or injury caused by the wrongful acts or omissions of its members, but members themselves generally are not personally liable.

---

4. *02 Development, LLC v. 607 South Park, LLC,* 159 Cal.App.4th 609, 71 Cal.Rptr.3d 608 (2008).
5. 28 U.S.C. Section 1332.

In the following case, a consumer died as a result of using an allegedly defective product made and sold by an LLC. The consumer's children sought to hold the LLC's sole member and manager liable for the actions of the firm.

Case 32.1

Hodge v. Strong Built International, LLC

Court of Appeal of Louisiana, Third Circuit, 159 So.3d 1159 (2015).

Background and Facts Donald Hodge was hunting on a ladder-style deer stand when its straps failed and it fell to the ground, killing Hodge. Louisiana-based Strong Built International, LLC, was the maker and seller of the deer stand, and Ken Killen was the company's sole member and manager. Hodge's children, Donald and Rachael Hodge, filed a lawsuit in a Louisiana state court against Strong Built and Killen. They claimed that the defendants were liable under product liability law for selling a defective deer stand to their father. Killen filed a motion for summary judgment, asserting that he was not personally liable to the Hodges. The court granted the motion and issued a summary judgment in Killen's favor, dismissing the claims against him. The Hodges appealed, asserting that Killen was personally liable.

Can a member-manager of an LLC that built a defective deer stand be held liable for its collapse?

Steve Oehlenschlager/ShutterStock.com

In the Words of the Court

AMY, Judge.

* * * *

* * * An LLC member or manager's liability to third parties is delineated in [Louisiana Revised Statute (La.R.S.)] 12:1320, which states:

* * * *

* * * no member, manager, employee, or agent of a limited liability company is liable in such capacity for a debt, obligation, or liability of the limited liability company.

* * * *

* * * That protection is not unlimited. Pursuant to La.R.S. 12:1320(D), *a member or manager may be subjected to personal liability for claims involving * * * breach of a professional duty or other negligent or wrongful act.* [Emphasis added.]

* * * In an affidavit, Mr. Killen asserted that he is "not an engineer, nor a licensed professional in any profession in Louisiana or any other state." Mr. Killen also asserts that he:

was a participant in the creation of the deer stand which * * * Strong Built International, L.L.C. manufactured and sold, but he

never personally dictated or participated in the design, selection of materials used in the manufacture, or the manufacture of, or the selection of any warnings to any deer stand for the use or consumption by any consumer beyond my input and work as a manager * * * and member of * * * Strong Built International, L.L.C.

The plaintiffs offered no evidence to contradict Mr. Killen's affidavit in this regard. Accordingly, we find no basis for Mr. Killen's personal liability under the "breach of professional duty" exception.

Neither do we find sufficient evidence in the record to create a genuine issue of material fact with regard to the "other negligent or wrongful act" exception.

* * * With regard to [this exception], the member (or manager) must have a duty of care to the plaintiff. * * * That duty must be "something more" than the duties arising out of the LLC's contract with the plaintiff.

* * * *

* * * Mr. Killen states in his affidavit that not only was he not personally responsible for the design and manufacture of the deer stands while involved with Strong Built International * * * but that any involvement that he may have had was in his capacity as a member and manager. *The plaintiffs have submitted nothing to show that Mr. Killen's actions are "something more" than his duties as a member/manager of the LLC.* [Emphasis added.]

Decision and Remedy A state intermediate appellate court affirmed the judgment in Killen's favor. Under the applicable state LLC statute, no member or manager of an LLC is liable in that capacity for the liability of the company. There are exceptions, but the Hodges failed to show that Killen's actions were anything more than his duties as a member and manager of Strong Built.

Critical Thinking

• **Economic** *Why does the law allow—and even encourage—limits on the liability of a business organization's owners and managers for the firm's actions? Discuss.*

Flexibility in Taxation Another advantage of the LLC is the flexibility in regard to taxation. An LLC that has *two or more members* can choose to be taxed either as a partnership or as a corporation. A corporate entity normally must pay income taxes on its profits, and the shareholders must then pay personal income taxes on any of those profits that are distributed as dividends. An LLC that wants to distribute profits to its members may prefer to be taxed as a partnership to avoid the "double taxation" that is characteristic of the corporate entity.

Unless an LLC indicates that it wishes to be taxed as a corporation, the Internal Revenue Service (IRS) automatically taxes it as a partnership. This means that the LLC, as an entity, pays no taxes. Rather, as in a partnership, profits are "passed through" the LLC to the members, who then personally pay taxes on the profits. If an LLC's members want to reinvest profits in the business rather than distribute the profits to members, however, they may prefer to be taxed as a corporation. Corporate income tax rates also may be lower than personal tax rates.

An LLC that has only *one member* cannot be taxed as a partnership. For federal income tax purposes, one-member LLCs are automatically taxed as sole proprietorships unless they indicate that they wish to be taxed as corporations. With respect to state taxes, most states follow the IRS rules.

Management and Foreign Investors One more advantage of the LLC for businesspersons is the flexibility it offers in terms of business operations and management, as will be discussed shortly. Foreign investors are allowed to become LLC members, so organizing as an LLC can enable a business to attract investors from other countries. For a discussion of business organizations in other nations that are similar to the LLC, see this chapter's *Beyond Our Borders* feature.

Limited Liability Companies in Other Nations

Beyond Our Borders

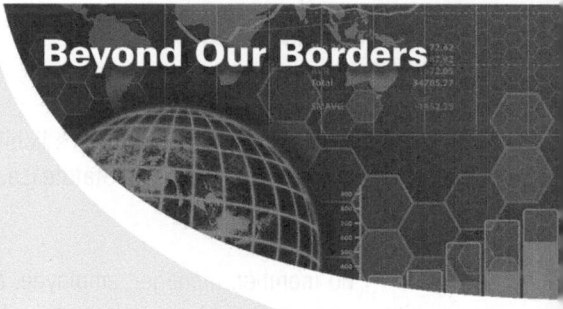

Limited liability companies did not originate in the United States. Many nations have business forms that provide limited liability, although these organizations may differ significantly from our domestic limited liability companies (LLCs).

In Germany, the *GmbH*, or *Gesellschaft mit beschränkter Haftung* (which means "company with limited liability"), is a type of business entity that resembles the LLC. The GmbH is now the most widely used business form in Germany. A GmbH, however, is owned by shareholders and thus resembles a U.S. corporation in certain respects. German laws also impose numerous restrictions on the operations and

business transactions of GmbHs, whereas LLCs in many U.S. states are not even required to have an operating agreement.

Business forms that limit the liability of owners can also be found in various other countries. Limited liability companies known as *limitadas* are common in many Latin American nations. In France, a *société à responsabilité limitée* (SARL, meaning "society with limited liability") is an entity that provides business owners with limited liability.

Although laws in the United Kingdom and Ireland use the term *limited liability partnership*, the entities described by the term are similar to our domestic LLCs.

Japan has created a new type of business organization called the *Godo Kaisha (GK)*, which is also quite similar to an LLC in the United States.

Critical Thinking
Clearly, limited liability is an important aspect of doing business globally. Why might a nation limit the number of member-owners in a limited liability entity?

32–1e Disadvantages of the LLC

The main disadvantage of the LLC is that state LLC statutes are not uniform. Therefore, businesses that operate in more than one state may not receive consistent treatment. Generally, most states apply to a foreign LLC (an LLC formed in another state) the law of the state where the LLC was formed. Difficulties can arise, though, when one state's court must interpret and apply another state's laws.

32–2 LLC Operation and Management

The members of an LLC have considerable flexibility in operating and managing the business. Here, we discuss management options for an LLC, the fiduciary duties owed, and the operating agreement and general operating procedures.

32–2a Management of an LLC

Basically, LLC members have two options for managing the firm, as shown in Exhibit 32–1. It can be either a member-managed LLC or a manager-managed LLC. In a *member-managed* LLC, all of the members participate in management, and decisions are made by majority vote [ULLCA 404(a)]. In a *manager-managed* LLC, the members designate a person or group of persons to manage the firm. The management group may consist of only members, both members and nonmembers, or only nonmembers. Most LLC statutes and the ULLCA provide that unless the articles of organization specify otherwise, an LLC is assumed to be member managed [ULLCA 203(a)(6)].

However an LLC is managed, its managers need to be aware of the firm's potential liability under employment-discrimination laws. Those laws may sometimes extend to individuals who are not members of a protected class, as discussed in this chapter's *Managerial Strategy* feature.

32–2b Fiduciary Duties

Under the ULLCA, managers in a manager-managed LLC owe fiduciary duties (the duty of loyalty and the duty of care) to the LLC and to its members, just as corporate directors and officers owe fiduciary duties to the corporation and to its shareholders [ULLCA 409(a), (h)]. Because not all states have adopted the ULLCA, though, some state statutes provide that managers owe fiduciary duties only to the LLC and not to its members.

To whom a fiduciary duty is owed may seem insignificant at first glance, but it can have a dramatic effect on the outcome of litigation. In North Carolina and Virginia, for instance, LLC statutes do not explicitly state that managers owe fiduciary duties to members.[6] Thus, in those two states, a manager-member owes fiduciary duties only to the LLC and not to its members.[7] In contrast, laws in Idaho and Kentucky provide that a manager-member owes fiduciary duties to the LLC's members and that the members can sue the manager for breaching fiduciary duties.[8]

Learning Objective 2

What are the two options for managing limited liability companies?

Exhibit 32–1 Management of an LLC

LLC Management Options

Member Managed
- All members vote on decisions; majority vote controls.
- Most LLC statutes assume the firm will be member managed unless the articles state otherwise.

Manager Managed
- Members designate a person or group of persons to manage the LLC, which may include nonmembers.
- Members normally specify that the LLC is manager managed in the articles of organization.

---

6. North Carolina General Statutes Section 57C-3-22(b); and Virginia Code Section 13.1-1024.1.
7. See, for instance, *Atkinson v. Lackey*, 2015 WL 867181 (N.C.Super. 2015).
8. Idaho Code Sections 30-25-101 *et seq.*; and Kentucky Revised Statutes Section 275.170.

Can a Person Who Is Not a Member of a Protected Class Sue for Discrimination?

Under federal law and the laws of most states, discrimination in employment based on race, color, religion, national origin, gender, age, or disability is prohibited. Persons who are members of these protected classes can sue if they are subjected to discrimination.

But can a person subjected to discrimination bring a lawsuit if he is not a member of a protected class, even though managers and other employees believe that he is? This somewhat unusual situation occurred in New Jersey.

A New Jersey Case

Myron Cowher worked at Carson & Roberts Site Construction & Engineering, Inc. For more than a year, at least two of his supervisors directed almost daily barrages of anti-Semitic remarks at him. They believed that he was Jewish, although his actual background was German-Irish and Lutheran.

Cowher brought a suit against the supervisors and the construction company, claiming a hostile work environment. The trial court, however, ruled that he did not

have standing to sue under New Jersey law because he was not Jewish and, thus, was not a member of a protected class. Cowher appealed.

The appellate court disagreed with the trial court. The court ruled that if Cowher could prove that the discrimination "would not have occurred but for the perception that he was Jewish," his claim was covered by New Jersey's antidiscrimination law.[a] In the appellate court's view, the nature of the discriminatory remarks—and not the actual characteristics of the plaintiff—determines whether the remarks are actionable.

A Second New Jersey Court Follows the Precedent

Another New Jersey court followed the precedent set by the *Cowher* case to allow Shi-Juan Lin, a Chinese worker whose fiancé and child were black, to recover for racial discrimination. The employer created a hostile work environment by allowing

Lin's supervisor to constantly use the "n" word at work. The employer knew that even though Lin was not black, she was hurt by the supervisor's remarks. Therefore, the court affirmed an administrative law judge's award of damages for pain and suffering, plus attorneys' fees.[b]

Business Questions

1. *Should a manager for an LLC respond to employee complaints of discrimination any differently than a manager at a corporation, a partnership, or a sole proprietorship? Why or why not?*

2. *How can a company, whether an LLC or some other business form, reduce the possibility of discrimination lawsuits?*

---

a. *Cowher v. Carson & Roberts,* 425 N.J.Super. 285, 40 A.3d 1171 (2012). See also *Sheridan v. Egg Harbor Township Board of Education,* 2015 WL 9694404 (N.J.Sup.Ct. 2016), involving a plaintiff who alleged discrimination based on obesity.

b. *Lin v. Dane Construction Co.,* 2014 WL 8131876 (N.J.Super.A.D. 2015). See also *Norton v. Karistos Corp.,* 2015 WL 8485157 (N.J.Super.A.D. 2015).

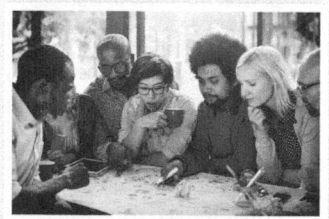

What should managers of limited liability companies do to avoid discrimination lawsuits by members of a protected class?

Operating Agreement An agreement in which the members of a limited liability company set forth the details of how the business will be managed and operated.

32–2c The LLC Operating Agreement

The members of an LLC can decide how to operate the various aspects of the business by forming an **operating agreement** [ULLCA 103(a)]. In many states, an operating agreement is not required for an LLC to exist, and if there is one, it need not be in writing. Generally, though, LLC members should protect their interests by creating a written operating agreement.

Operating agreements typically contain provisions relating to the following areas:

1. Management and how future managers will be chosen or removed. (Although most LLC statutes are silent on this issue, the ULLCA provides that members may choose and remove managers by majority vote [ULLCA 404(b)(3)].)

2. How profits will be divided.

3. How membership interests may be transferred.

4. Whether the dissociation of a member, such as by death or departure, will trigger dissolution of the LLC.

5. Whether formal members' meetings will be held.

6. How voting rights will be apportioned. (If the agreement does not cover voting, LLC statutes in most states provide that voting rights are apportioned according to each member's capital contributions. Some states provide that, in the absence of an agreement to the contrary, each member has one vote.)

7. How a buyout price will be calculated in the event of a member's dissociation.

If a dispute arises and there is no agreement covering the topic under dispute, the state LLC statute will govern the outcome. For instance, most LLC statutes provide that if the members have not specified how profits will be divided, they will be divided equally among the members. When an issue is not covered by an operating agreement or by an LLC statute, the courts often apply principles of partnership law.

Sometimes, as in the following case, an operating agreement and the state's LLC statutes are applied together to determine the outcome of a dispute between the members of an LLC.

■ Case 32.2

Schaefer v. Orth
Court of Appeals of Wisconsin, 2018 WI App 35 (2018).

Background and Facts Jason Schaefer and Randy Orth created Grilled Cheese, LLC, to own and operate a Tom and Chee franchise, a casual restaurant specializing in grilled cheese sandwiches and soups. The operating agreement provided that Schaefer would be responsible for the restaurant's day-to-day operations, for which the LLC would pay him a monthly salary and bonuses. Orth would be responsible for the LLC's business and financial decisions, but he would not receive any compensation.

The restaurant reported a profit only in its first full month of operations. Five months later, when Schaefer was not paid his salary and bonuses, he quit. Later, Orth closed the restaurant and worked to wind up the business. Both Schaefer and Orth lost everything they had invested in the LLC. Schaefer filed a suit in a Wisconsin state court against Orth, claiming breach of contract for failure to pay his salary. The court directed a verdict in Orth's favor. Schaefer appealed.

In the Words of the Court
PER CURIAM [By the Whole Court].
  * * * *

  * * * The [lower] court granted Orth's motion for a directed verdict because it determined there was no credible evidence to support a conclusion that Orth was personally liable to Schaefer for the unpaid wages and bonuses to which Schaefer was entitled under the operating agreement.

At trial, both Orth and Schaefer testified it was the LLC's responsibility to pay Schaefer the wages and bonuses set forth in the operating agreement, and Orth was not personally required to pay Schaefer those amounts.

The operating agreement's unambiguous language confirms that the LLC, not Orth, was responsible for paying Schaefer's wages and bonuses. The section of the agreement pertaining to "Distributions" specifically lists Schaefer's wages and bonuses as distributions to be paid to Schaefer before other distributions to the LLC's members. The agreement specifies that distributions are made from *the LLC's* available funds. The section of the agreement pertaining to "Profits" similarly states that, in the case of any profit resulting from the LLC's operations, "the LLC shall, as the first priority, allocate Profit to Schaefer to the extent, if any, that (A) all service compensation accruing in his favor through the date of the relevant allocation, exceeds (B) all prior allocations under this Clause." The agreement defines the term profit as *the LLC's* profit.

The language cited above plainly demonstrates that the LLC was responsible for paying Schaefer's wages and bonuses. Wisconsin's LLC statutes provide that "the debts, obligations and liabilities of a limited liability company, whether arising in contract, tort or otherwise, shall be solely the debts, obligations and liabilities of the limited liability company." With certain exceptions not applicable here, "*a member or manager of a limited liability company is not personally liable for any debt, obligation or liability of the limited liability company, except that a member or manager may become personally liable by his or her acts or conduct other than as a member or manager.*" There is no evidence Orth was acting outside his capacity as a member or manager of the LLC when he failed to pay Schaefer's wages and bonuses. [Emphasis added.]

Decision and Remedy A state intermediate appellate court affirmed the lower court's judgment. "The evidence presented at trial does not permit a legal conclusion that Orth was personally liable to Schaefer for" his unpaid salary and bonuses.

(Continues)

32–3 Dissociation and Dissolution of an LLC

Recall that in a partnership, *dissociation* occurs when a partner ceases to be associated in the carrying on of the business. The same concept applies to LLCs. Like a partner in a partnership, a member of an LLC has the *power* to dissociate at any time but may not have the *right* to dissociate.

Under the ULLCA, the events that may trigger a member's dissociation from an LLC are similar to the events causing a partner to be dissociated under the Uniform Partnership Act (UPA). These include voluntary withdrawal, expulsion by other members or by court order, bankruptcy, incompetence, and death. Generally, if a member dies or otherwise dissociates from an LLC, the other members may continue to carry on the LLC's business, unless the operating agreement provides otherwise.

32–3a The Effects of Dissociation

When a member dissociates from an LLC, he or she loses the right to participate in management and the right to act as an agent for the LLC. The member's duty of loyalty to the LLC also terminates, and the duty of care continues only with respect to events that occurred before dissociation.

Generally, the dissociated member also has a right to have his or her interest in the LLC bought out by the other members. The LLC's operating agreement may contain provisions establishing a buyout price. If it does not, the member's interest is usually purchased at a fair value. In states that have adopted the ULLCA, the LLC must purchase the interest at fair value within 120 days after the dissociation.

If the member's dissociation violates the LLC's operating agreement, it is considered legally wrongful, and the dissociated member can be held liable for damages caused by the dissociation. **Example 32.5** Chadwick and Barrel are members of an LLC. Chadwick manages the accounts, and Barrel, who has many connections in the community and is a skilled investor, brings in the business. If Barrel wrongfully dissociates from the LLC, the LLC's business will suffer, and Chadwick can hold Barrel liable for the loss of business resulting from her withdrawal.

32–3b Dissolution

Regardless of whether or not a member's dissociation was wrongful, normally the dissociated member has no right to force the LLC to dissolve. The remaining members can opt to either continue or dissolve the business.

Members can also stipulate in their operating agreement that certain events will cause dissolution, or they can agree that they have the power to dissolve the LLC by vote. As with partnerships, a court can order an LLC to be dissolved in certain circumstances. For instance, a court might order dissolution when the members have engaged in illegal or oppressive conduct, or when it is no longer feasible to carry on the business.

Case Example 32.6 Three men—Walter Perkins, Gary Fordham, and David Thompson—formed Venture Sales, LLC, to develop a subdivision in Mississippi. Each of them contributed land and funds, resulting in total holdings of 466 acres of land and about $158,000 in cash. Perkins was busy as an assistant coach for the Cleveland Browns, so he trusted Fordham and Thompson to develop the property. More than ten years later, however, they still had not done so, although they had formed two other LLCs and developed two other subdivisions in the area.

Fordham and Thompson claimed that they did not know when they could develop Venture's property and suggested selling it at a discounted price, but Perkins disagreed. Perkins then sought a judicial dissolution of Venture Sales. The court ordered the dissolution. Because Venture Sales was not meeting the economic purpose for which it was established (developing a subdivision), continuing the business was impracticable.[9] ■ (See this chapter's *Business Law Analysis* feature for an illustration of when a court will not dissolve an LLC.)

A judge's exercise of discretion to order the dissolution of an LLC was disputed in the following case.

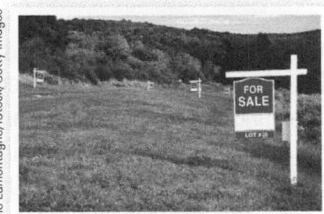

What happens when the members fail to develop a subdivision that the LLC was created to develop?

---

9. *Venture Sales, LLC v. Perkins*, 86 So.3d 910 (2012).

■ Case 32.3

Reese v. Newman

District of Columbia Court of Appeals, 131 A.3d 880 (2016).

Background and Facts Allison Reese and Nicole Newman, the owners of ANR Construction Management, LLC, could not reconcile their difference of opinion over the company's direction. Newman told Reese that she was going to dissolve and wind up the firm. Reese wanted Newman to dissociate from ANR, so that Reese could continue the business. This dispute led to Newman's filing a suit in a District of Columbia court against Reese.

Following a trial, a jury found grounds for both ANR's dissolution and Newman's dissociation. The court chose to exercise its discretion under the state statutes governing the dissociation of members and the dissolution of LLCs. The court ordered dissolution. Reese appealed.

In the Words of the Court
KING, Senior Judge.

* * * *

* * * Reese argues that the [District of Columbia (D.C.)] statute [governing dissociation from an LLC] does not allow for any discretion by the court, and that, in fact, the statute mandates that the court order dissociation of Newman based on the jury's findings.

* * * Our analysis starts with the plain language of the statute * * *. To that end, *the words of the statute should be construed according to their ordinary sense and with the meaning commonly attributed to them.* [Emphasis added.]

Reese argues that the court was required to dissociate Newman from the LLC under [D.C. Code] Section 29–806.02(5) which reads:

A person *shall* be dissociated as a member from a limited liability company when:

* * * *

(5) On application by the company, the person is expelled as a member by judicial order because the person has:
(A) Engaged, or is engaging, in wrongful conduct that has adversely and materially affected, or will adversely and materially affect, the company's activities and affairs;
(B) Willfully or persistently committed, or is willfully and persistently committing, a material breach of the operating agreement or the person's duties or obligations under Section 29–804.09; or
(C) Engaged in, or is engaging, in conduct relating to the company's activities which makes it not reasonably practicable to carry on the activities with the person as a member.

Reese's interpretation of the statute is that, upon application to the court by a company, a judge shall dissociate a member of an LLC, when that member commits any one of the actions described in subsections (5)(A)-(C).

* * * While the introductory language of Section 29–806.02 does use the word "shall"—that command is in no way directed at the trial judge. It reads, "a person shall be dissociated * * * when," and then goes on to recite fifteen separate circumstances describing different occasions when a person shall be dissociated from an LLC. That is to say, when one of the events described in subparagraphs (1) through (15) occurs, the member shall be dissociated. Subparagraph (5), however, is merely one instance for which a person shall be dissociated; that is, when and if a judge

(Continues)

has ordered a member expelled because she finds that any conditions under (5)(A)-(C) have been established. In other words, the command in the introductory language is not directed at the trial judge, it is directed at all the circumstances set forth in subparagraphs (1) through (15) * * * . There is nothing in the language of Section 29–806.02(5) that strips a judge of her discretion because it does not require the judge to expel the member if any of the enumerated conditions are established. In short, Section 29–806.02(5) means: *when a judge has used her discretion to expel a member of an LLC by judicial order, under any of the enumerated circumstances in (5)(A)-(C), that member shall be dissociated.*

* * * *

In sum, we hold that Section 29–806.02(5) can only be interpreted to mean: when a judge finds that any of the events in (5)(A)-(C) have taken place, she may (*i.e.*, has discretion to) expel by judicial order a member of an LLC, and when a judge has done so the member shall be dissociated. *Moreover, when both grounds for dissociation of a member and dissolution of the LLC exist, the trial judge has discretion to choose either alternative.* [Emphasis added.]

Decision and Remedy A state intermediate appellate court affirmed the lower court's order. The trial court acted within its discretion in ordering dissolution rather than dissociation.

Critical Thinking

• **Legal Environment** *Newman alleged that after she delivered her notice to dissolve ANR, Reese locked her out of the LLC's bank accounts, blocked her access to the LLC's files and e-mail, and ended her salary and health benefits. Do these allegations, if proved, support or refute the court's decision to dissolve the firm? Explain.*

Business Law Analysis

When Will a Court Order the Dissolution of an LLC?

Walter Van Houten and John King formed 1545 Ocean Avenue, LLC, with each managing 50 percent of the business. Its purpose was to renovate an existing building and construct a new commercial building. Van Houten and King quarreled over many aspects of the work on the properties. King claimed that Van Houten paid the contractors too much for the work performed. As the projects neared completion, King demanded that the LLC be dissolved and that Van Houten agree to a buyout. Because the parties could not agree on a buyout, King sued for dissolution. The trial court enjoined (prevented) further work on the projects until the dispute was settled.

As the ground for dissolution, King cited the fights over management decisions. There was no claim of fraud or frustration of purpose. The trial court ordered that the LLC be dissolved, and Van Houten appealed. Should either of the owners be forced to dissolve the LLC before the completion of its purpose—that is, before the building projects are finished?

Analysis: The issue here is whether disagreements over management decisions are a sufficient reason for a court to dissolve an LLC. Normally, the grounds for dissolution are specified in the operating agreement. If not, then a court will consider several factors. Usually, the petitioning member must establish that (1) the management of the entity is unable or unwilling to reasonably permit or promote the stated purpose of the entity to be realized or achieved, or (2) continuing the entity is financially unfeasible.

A court will not dissolve a LLC merely because events have not turned out exactly as the LLC's owners originally envisioned or because the LLC has failed to be profitable. Dissolution is reserved for situations in which the LLC's management has become so dysfunctional or its business purpose so thwarted that it is no longer practicable to operate the business. For instance, when there is a voting deadlock among members or when the LLC's defined purpose has become impossible to fulfill, a court will order dissolution.

Result and Reasoning: Here, there was disagreement about the work being done (and the price), but the project was moving toward completion. Thus, there is no reason that the purpose of the LLC should not be fulfilled. Also, there is no evidence that the LLC is financially unfeasible. Therefore, a court is not likely to order dissolution of the LLC.

32–3c Winding up

When an LLC is dissolved, any members who did not wrongfully dissociate may participate in the winding up process. To wind up the business, members must collect, liquidate, and distribute the LLC's assets.

Members may preserve the assets for a reasonable time to optimize their return, and they continue to have the authority to perform reasonable acts in conjunction with winding up. In other words, the LLC will be bound by the reasonable acts of its members during the winding up process.

Once all the LLC's assets have been sold, the proceeds are distributed. Debts to creditors are paid first (including debts owed to members who are creditors of the LLC). The members' capital contributions are returned next. Any remaining amounts are then distributed to members in equal shares or according to their operating agreement.

32–4 Special Business Forms

Besides the business forms already discussed in this unit, several other forms can be used to organize a business. For the most part, these special business forms are hybrid organizations—that is, they combine features of other organizational forms, such as partnerships and corporations. These forms include joint ventures, syndicates, joint stock companies, business trusts, and cooperatives.

32–4a Joint Ventures

In a **joint venture**, two or more persons or business entities combine their efforts or their property for a single transaction or project or for a related series of transactions or projects. For instance, when several contractors combine their resources to build and sell houses in a single development, their relationship is a joint venture. Unless otherwise agreed, joint venturers share profits and losses equally.

Joint ventures range in size from very small activities to multimillion-dollar joint actions carried out by some of the world's largest corporations. Large organizations often investigate new markets or new ideas by forming joint ventures with other enterprises. **Example 32.7** BMW enters into a joint venture with JLR's Range Rover Division. Under the agreement, the companies work together and use the S63, a twin-turbo V8 engine, to manufacture certain automobiles. ■

Similarities to Partnerships The joint venture resembles a partnership and is taxed like a partnership. For this reason, most courts apply the same principles to joint ventures as they apply to partnerships. Joint venturers owe each other the same fiduciary duties, including the duty of loyalty, that partners owe each other. Thus, if one of the venturers secretly buys land that was supposed to be acquired by the joint venture, the other joint venturers may be awarded damages for the breach of loyalty. Joint venturers have some authority as agents to enter into contracts for business purposes that will bind the joint venture.

A joint venturer can be held personally liable for the venture's debts (because joint venturers share losses as well as profits). Like partners, joint venturers have equal rights to manage the activities of the enterprise, but they can agree to give control of the operation to one of the members.

Differences from Partnerships Joint ventures differ from partnerships in several important ways. A joint venture is typically created for a single project or series of transactions, whereas a partnership usually (though not always) involves an ongoing business. Also, unlike most partnerships, a joint venture normally terminates when the project or the transaction for which it was formed has been completed.

Joint Venture A joint undertaking by two or more persons or business entities to combine their efforts or their property for a single transaction or project or for a related series of transactions or projects. A joint venture is generally treated like a partnership for tax and other legal purposes.

Learning Objective 4

What is a joint venture? How is it similar to a partnership? How is it different?

Know This
A partnership involves a continuing relationship of the partners. A joint venture is often a one-time association.

Because the activities of a joint venture are more limited than the business of a partnership, the members of a joint venture are presumed to have less power to bind their co-venturers. Accordingly, the members of a joint venture have less implied and apparent authority than the partners in a partnership (each of whom is treated as an agent of the other partners).

32–4b Syndicates

Syndicate A group of individuals or firms that join together to finance a project. A syndicate is also called an *investment group*.

In a **syndicate**, or *investment group*, several individuals or firms join together to finance a particular project. Syndicates can finance projects such as the construction of a shopping center or the purchase of a professional basketball franchise. The form of such groups varies considerably.

A syndicate may be organized as a corporation or as a general or limited partnership. In some instances, the members do not have a legally recognized business arrangement but merely purchase and own property jointly.

32–4c Joint Stock Companies

Joint Stock Company A hybrid form of business organization that combines characteristics of a corporation and a partnership. Usually, a joint stock company is regarded as a partnership for tax and other legal purposes.

A **joint stock company** is a true hybrid of a partnership and a corporation. It has many characteristics of a corporation in that (1) its ownership is represented by transferable shares of stock, (2) it is managed by directors and officers of the company or association, and (3) it can have a perpetual existence.

Most of its other features, however, are more characteristic of a partnership, and it is usually treated like a partnership. Like a partnership, a joint stock company is formed by agreement (not statute). Property is usually held in the names of the members, who are called shareholders, and they have personal liability. In a joint stock company, however, shareholders are not considered to be agents of one another, as they are in a partnership.

32–4d Business Trusts

Business Trust A form of business organization, created by a written trust agreement, that resembles a corporation. Legal ownership and management of the trust's property stay with the trustees, and the profits are distributed to the beneficiaries, who have limited liability.

A **business trust** is created by a written trust agreement that sets forth the interests of the beneficiaries and obligations and powers of the trustee. This form of organization was started in Massachusetts in an attempt to obtain the limited liability advantage of a corporation while avoiding restrictions on real property ownership. With a business trust, legal ownership and management of the trust's property stay with one or more of the trustees, and the profits are distributed to the beneficiaries.

A business trust resembles a corporation in many respects. Beneficiaries of the trust, for instance, are not personally responsible for the trust's debts or obligations. In fact, in a number of states, business trusts must pay corporate taxes.

Cooperative An association, which may or may not be incorporated, that is organized to provide an economic service to its members. Unincorporated cooperatives are often treated like partnerships for tax and other legal purposes.

32–4e Cooperatives

A **cooperative** (co-op) is an association that is organized to provide an economic service to its members (or shareholders). It may or may not be incorporated. Most cooperatives are organized under state statutes for cooperatives, general business corporations, or LLCs. Co-ops range in size from small, local consumer cooperatives to national businesses such as Ace Hardware and Land O'Lakes, a well-known producer of dairy products.

Generally, an incorporated cooperative distributes dividends, or profits, to its owners on the basis of their transactions with the cooperative rather than on the basis of the amount of capital they contributed. Members of incorporated cooperatives have limited liability, as do shareholders of corporations and members of LLCs. Cooperatives that are unincorporated are often treated like partnerships, and members have joint liability for the cooperative's acts.

Most people believe that cooperatives are small enterprises, but not all are. Ace Hardware is a nationwide co-op that was formed over eighty years ago. What is the benefit of forming a co-op?

RiverNorthPhotography/iStock Unreleased/Getty Images

The cooperative form of business is generally adopted by groups of individuals who wish to pool their resources to gain some advantage in the marketplace. *Consumer purchasing co-ops*, for instance, are formed to obtain lower prices through quantity discounts. *Seller marketing co-ops* are formed to control the market and thereby enable members to sell their goods at higher prices.

Practice and Review

The city of Papagos, Arizona, had a deteriorating bridge in need of repair on a prominent public roadway. The city posted notices seeking proposals for an artistic bridge design and reconstruction. Davidson Masonry, LLC—owned and managed by Carl Davidson and his wife, Marilyn Rowe— decided to submit a bid for a decorative concrete project that incorporated artistic metalwork. They contacted Shana Lafayette, a local sculptor who specialized in large-scale metal creations, to help them design the bridge. The city selected their bridge design and awarded them the contract for a commission of $184,000.

Davidson Masonry and Lafayette then entered into an agreement to work together on the bridge project. Davidson Masonry agreed to install and pay for concrete and structural work, and Lafayette agreed to install the metalwork at her expense. They agreed that overall profits would be split, with 25 percent going to Lafayette and 75 percent going to Davidson Masonry. Lafayette designed numerous metal salmon sculptures that were incorporated into colorful decorative concrete forms designed by Rowe, while Davidson performed the structural engineering. The group worked together successfully until the completion of the project. Using the information presented in the chapter, answer the following questions.

1. Would Davidson Masonry automatically be taxed as a partnership or a corporation? Explain.

2. Is Davidson Masonry member managed or manager managed?

3. When Davidson Masonry and Lafayette entered into an agreement to work together, what kind of special business form was created? Explain.

4. Suppose that during construction, Lafayette entered into an agreement to rent space in a warehouse that was close to the bridge so that she could work on her sculptures near the location where they would be installed. She entered into the contract without the knowledge or consent of Davidson Masonry. In this situation, would a court be likely to hold that Davidson Masonry was bound by the contract? Why or why not?

Debate This

Because LLCs are essentially just partnerships with limited liability for members, all partnership laws should apply.

Key Terms

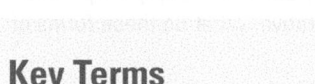

articles of organization 769	**joint stock company** 780	**member** 768
business trust 780	**joint venture** 779	**operating agreement** 774
cooperative 780	**limited liability company (LLC)** 767	**syndicate** 780

Chapter Summary: Limited Liability Companies and Special Business Forms

The Limited Liability Company	A limited liability company (LLC) is a hybrid form of business enterprise that offers the limited liability of a corporation and the tax advantages of a partnership.
	1. *Formation*—Articles of organization must be filed with the appropriate state office—usually the office of the secretary of state—setting forth the name of the business, its principal address, the name and address of a registered agent, the names of the owners (called *members*), and information on how the LLC will be managed.
	2. *Advantages and disadvantages of the LLC*—Advantages of the LLC include limited liability, the option to be taxed as a partnership or as a corporation, and flexibility in deciding how the business will be managed and operated. It allows foreign investors to be members. The main disadvantage is the absence of uniformity in state LLC statutes.
LLC Operation and Management	1. *Management*—An LLC can be member managed or manager managed. The management group may consist of members only, both members and nonmembers, or nonmembers only.
	2. *Fiduciary duties*—In some states, managers in a manager-managed LLC owe fiduciary duties (the duty of loyalty and the duty of care) to the LLC and to its members.
	3. *Operating agreement*—When an LLC is formed, the members decide, in an operating agreement, how the business will be managed and what rules will apply to the organization.
Dissociation and Dissolution of an LLC	Members of an LLC have the power to dissociate from the LLC at any time, but they may not have the right to dissociate. Dissociation does not always result in the dissolution of an LLC. The remaining members can choose to continue the business. Dissociated members have a right to have their interest purchased by the other members. If the LLC is dissolved, the business must be wound up and the assets sold. Creditors are paid first, and then members' capital investments are returned. Any remaining proceeds are distributed to members.
Special Business Forms	1. *Joint venture*—An organization created by two or more persons in contemplation of a single transaction or project or a related series of transactions or projects. A joint venture is similar to a partnership in many respects.
	2. *Syndicate*—An investment group that undertakes to finance a particular project. A syndicate may be organized as a corporation or as a general or limited partnership.
	3. *Joint stock company*—A business form similar to a corporation in some respects (transferable shares of stock, management by directors and officers, perpetual existence) but otherwise resembling a partnership.
	4. *Business trust*—A business form created by a written trust agreement that sets forth the interests of the beneficiaries and the obligations and powers of the trustees. Beneficiaries are not personally liable for the debts or obligations of the business trust, which is similar to a corporation in many respects.
	5. *Cooperative*—An association organized to provide an economic service, without profit, to its members. A co-op may or may not be incorporated.

Issue Spotters

1. Gabriel, Harry, and Ida are members of Jeweled Watches, LLC. What are their options with respect to the management of their firm? (See *LLC Operation and Management*.)

2. Greener Delivery Company and Hiway Trucking, Inc., form a business trust. Insta Equipment Company and Jiffy Supply Corporation form a joint stock company. Kwik Mart, Inc., and Luscious Produce, Inc., form an incorporated cooperative. What do these forms of business organization have in common? (See *Special Business Forms*.)

—**Check your answers to the *Issue Spotters* against the answers provided in Appendix D at the end of this text.**

Business Scenarios and Case Problems

32–1. Limited Liability Companies. John, Lesa, and Trevor form a limited liability company. John contributes 60 percent of the capital, and Lesa and Trevor each contribute 20 percent. Nothing is decided about how profits will be divided. John assumes that he will be entitled to 60 percent of the profits, in accordance with his contribution. Lesa and Trevor, however, assume that the profits will be divided equally. A dispute over the profits arises, and ultimately a court has to decide the issue. What law will the court apply? In most states, what will result? How could this dispute have been avoided in the first place? Discuss fully. (See *The Limited Liability Company.*)

32–2. Special Business Forms. Faraway Corp. supplies business equipment. Faraway is considering entering into two contracts, one with a joint stock company east of the Mississippi River and the other with a business trust formed by a number of sole proprietors on the West Coast. Both contracts require Faraway to make large capital outlays in order to supply the businesses with restaurant equipment. In both business organizations, at least two shareholders or beneficiaries are personally wealthy, but each organization has limited financial resources. The owner-managers of Faraway are not familiar with either form of business organization. Because each form resembles a corporation, they are concerned about whether they will be able to collect payments from the wealthy members of the business organizations in the event that either organization breaches the contract by failing to make the payments. Discuss fully Faraway's concern. (See *Special Business Forms.*)

32–3. Jurisdiction. Joe, a resident of New Jersey, wants to open a restaurant. He asks his friend Kay, who is an experienced attorney and a New Yorker, for her business and legal advice in exchange for a 20 percent ownership interest in the restaurant. Kay helps Joe negotiate a lease for the restaurant premises and advises Joe to organize the business as a limited liability company (LLC). Joe forms Café Olé, LLC, and, with Kay's help, obtains financing. Then, the night before the restaurant opens, Joe tells Kay that he is "cutting her out of the deal." The restaurant proves to be a success. Kay wants to file a suit in a federal district court against Joe and the LLC. Can a federal court exercise jurisdiction over the parties based on diversity of citizenship? Explain. (See *The Limited Liability Company.*)

32–4. Business Case Problem with Sample Answer— LLC Operation. James Williford, Patricia Mosser, Marquetta Smith, and Michael Floyd formed Bluewater Logistics, LLC, to bid on construction contracts after Hurricane Katrina struck the Gulf Coast. Under Mississippi law, every member of a member-managed LLC is entitled to participate in managing the business. The operating agreement provided for a "supermajority" 75 percent vote to remove a member who "has either committed a felony or under any other circumstances that would jeopardize the company status" as a contractor. After Bluewater had completed more than $5 million in contracts, Smith told Williford that she, Mosser, and Floyd were exercising their "supermajority" vote to fire him. No reason was provided. Williford sued Bluewater and the other members. Did Smith, Mosser, and Floyd breach the state LLC statute, their fiduciary duties, or the Bluewater operating agreement? Discuss. [*Bluewater Logistics, LLC v. Williford*, 55 So.3d 148 (Miss. 2011)] (See *LLC Operation and Management.*)

—For a sample answer to Problem 32–4, go to Appendix E at the end of this text.

32–5. Jurisdictional Requirements. Fadal Machining Centers, LLC, and MAG Industrial Automation Centers, LLC, sued a New Jersey–based corporation, Mid-Atlantic CNC, Inc., in federal district court. Ten percent of MAG was owned by SP MAG Holdings, a Delaware LLC. SP MAG had six members, including a Delaware limited partnership called Silver Point Capital Fund and a Delaware LLC called SPCP Group III. In turn, Silver Point and SPCP Group had a common member, Robert O'Shea, who was a New Jersey citizen. Assuming that the amount in controversy exceeds $75,000, does the district court have diversity jurisdiction? Why or why not? [*Fadal Machining Centers, LLC v. Mid-Atlantic CNC, Inc.*, 464 Fed.Appx. 672 (9th Cir. 2012)] (See *The Limited Liability Company.*)

32–6. Jurisdictional Requirements. Siloam Springs Hotel, LLC, operates a Hampton Inn in Siloam Springs, Arkansas. Siloam bought insurance from Century Surety Co. to cover the hotel. When guests suffered injuries due to a leak of carbon monoxide from the heating element of an indoor swimming pool, Siloam filed a claim with Century. Century denied coverage. Siloam disputed the denial. Century asked a federal district court to resolve the dispute. In asserting that the federal court had jurisdiction, Century noted that the amount in controversy exceeded $75,000 and that the parties had complete diversity of citizenship: Century is "a corporation organized under the laws of Ohio, with its principal place of business in Michigan," and Siloam is "a corporation organized under the laws of Oklahoma, with its principal place of business in Arkansas." Can the court exercise diversity jurisdiction in this case? Discuss. [*Siloam Springs Hotel, L.L.C. v. Century Surety Co.*, 781 F.3d 1233 (10th Cir. 2015)] (See *The Limited Liability Company.*)

32–7. Special Business Forms. Randall and Peggy Norman operated a dairy farm in Pine River, Minnesota. About ten years after the operation was begun, the cows started to experience health issues. Over the next eighteen years, the herd suffered many serious health problems. Eventually, stray electrical voltage—which can use cow hooves as an unintended pathway, causing health issues—was detected. By then, milk production in the Normans' herd had declined from 27 percent above the state average to 20 percent below it. The Normans filed a suit in a Minnesota state court against Crow Wing Cooperative Power & Light Company, a member-owned electrical cooperative that provided electricity to the Normans' farm. If Crow Wing is found to have acted negligently, can its members be held jointly liable for the cooperative's acts? Explain. [*Norman v. Crow Wing Cooperative Power & Light Co.*, 2016 WL 687472 (Minn.App. 2016)] (See *Special Business Forms*.)

32–8. Limited Liability. Vision Metals, Inc., owned and operated a pipe manufacturing facility that caused groundwater contamination. The Texas Commission on Environmental Quality (TCEQ) issued a plan that obligated Vision to treat the water and monitor the treatment. Later, Vision sold the property to White Lion Holdings, LLC. Bernard Morello, the sole member of White Lion, knew of the environmental obligations accompanying the property. When White Lion failed to comply with the TCEQ plan, the agency filed a suit in a Texas state court against Morello, asserting violations of the state's environmental rules. Morello was charged with personally removing the facility's treatment plant and monitoring system. Considering the nature of an LLC, what is Morello's best argument that he is not liable? Is this argument likely to succeed? Explain. [*State of Texas v. Morello*, 61 Tex.Sup.Ct.J. 381, 547 S.W.3d 881 (2018)] (See *Limited Liability Companies*.)

32–9. A Question of Ethics—The IDDR Approach and LLC Operation and Management. *Q Restaurant Group Holdings, LLC, owns and operates Q-BBQ restaurants. Michael Lapidus managed the restaurants and conducted the day-to-day operations. This included bargaining with the restaurants' vendors, buying the supplies, keeping the books and records of account, and handling the company's money. Lapidus dealt with the staff and made the hiring and firing decisions. He was expected to use his best efforts to grow the profitability of the restaurants. The LLC discovered, however, that Lapidus was misappropriating and converting company funds to his own use. He was also exposing the LLC to liability by mistreating female employees and vendors. When the members voted to terminate Lapidus, he changed the passwords on the Q-BBQ social media accounts, interfered with the employees during their work hours, and refused to return company property in his possession. [Q Restaurant Group Holdings, LLC v. Lapidus, 2017 IL App (2d) 170804-U (2017)] (See LLC Operation and Management.)*

1. What action should the LLC take against Lapidus? Consider the ethics of the options, using the IDDR approach.

2. Suppose that Lapidus was in the midst of a contentious divorce, experiencing severe financial problems, and undergoing psychological distress as a consequence. Could these issues excuse his conduct at work? Discuss.

Critical Thinking and Writing Assignments

32–10. Time-Limited Group Assignment—Fiduciary Duties. Newbury Properties Group owns, manages, and develops real property. Jerry Stoker and the Stoker Group, Inc. (the Stokers), also develop real property. Newbury entered into agreements with the Stokers concerning a large tract of property in Georgia. The parties formed Bellemare, LLC, to develop various parcels of the tract for residential purposes. The operating agreement of Bellemare indicated that "no Member shall be accountable to the LLC or to any other Member with respect to any other business or activity even if the business or activity competes with the LLC's business." Later, when the Newbury group contracted with other parties to develop parcels within the tract in competition with Bellemare, LLC, the Stokers sued, alleging breach of fiduciary duty. (See *LLC Operation and Management*.)

1. The first group will discuss and outline the fiduciary duties that the members of an LLC owe to each other.

2. The second group will determine whether the terms of an operating agreement can alter these fiduciary duties.

3. The last group will decide in whose favor the court should rule in this situation.

Bob Daemmrich/Alamy Stock Photo

Corporate Formation and Financing | **33**

"A corporation is
an artificial being,
invisible, intangible,
and existing only
in contemplation
of law."

John Marshall
1755–1835
(Chief justice of the United States
Supreme Court, 1801–1835)

A **corporation** is a creature of statute—a legal entity created and recognized by state law. As John Marshall indicated in the chapter-opening quotation, a corporation is an artificial being, existing only in law and neither tangible nor visible. Its existence generally depends on state law. Each state has its own body of corporate law, and these laws are not entirely uniform.

The Model Business Corporation Act (MBCA) is a codification of modern corporate law that has been influential in shaping state corporation statutes. Today, the majority of state statutes are guided by the most recent version of the MBCA, often referred to as the Revised Model Business Corporation Act (RMBCA).

Keep in mind, however, that there is considerable variation among the laws of states that have used the MBCA or the RMBCA as a basis for their statutes. In addition, several states do not follow either act. Consequently, individual state corporation laws should be relied on to determine corporate law, rather than the MBCA or RMBCA.

33–1 Nature and Classification

A corporation is a legal entity created and recognized by state law. This business entity can have one or more owners (called shareholders), and it operates under a name distinct from the names of its owners. Both individuals and other businesses can be shareholders. The corporation substitutes itself for its shareholders when conducting corporate business and incurring liability. Its authority to act and the liability for its actions, however, are separate and apart from the shareholders who own it.

Learning Objectives

The four Learning Objectives *below are designed to help improve your understanding. After reading this chapter, you should be able to answer the following questions:*

1. What is a close corporation?

2. What four steps are involved in bringing a corporation into existence?

3. In what circumstances might a court disregard the corporate entity ("pierce the corporate veil") and hold the shareholders personally liable?

4. What is the difference between stocks and bonds?

Corporation A legal entity formed in compliance with statutory requirements that is distinct from its shareholder-owners.

785

A corporation is recognized under U.S. law as a person—an artificial *legal person,* as opposed to a *natural person.* As a "person," it enjoys many of the same rights and privileges under state and federal law that U.S. citizens enjoy. For instance, corporations possess the same right of access to the courts as citizens and can sue or be sued. The constitutional guarantees of due process, free speech, and freedom from unreasonable searches and seizures also apply to corporations.

33–1a Corporate Personnel

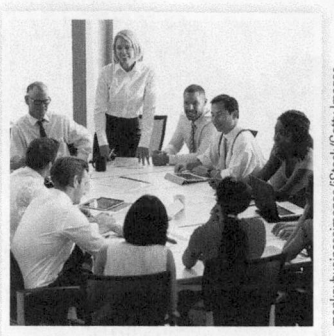

Who hires corporate officers?

In a corporation, the responsibility for the overall management of the firm is entrusted to a *board of directors,* whose members are elected by the shareholders. The board of directors hires *corporate officers* and other employees to run the corporation's daily business operations.

When an individual purchases a share of stock (an equity interest) in a corporation, that person becomes a shareholder and thus an owner of the corporation. Unlike the members of a partnership, the body of shareholders can change constantly without affecting the continued existence of the corporation. A shareholder can sue the corporation, the corporation can sue a shareholder, and in certain situations, a shareholder can sue "on behalf of" the corporation.

33–1b The Limited Liability of Shareholders

The major advantage of the corporate form is the limited liability of its owners (shareholders). Corporate shareholders' liability is limited to the amount of their investments. Shareholders usually are not otherwise liable for the debts of the corporation. To enable the firm to obtain credit, however, shareholders in small companies sometimes voluntarily assume personal liability, as guarantors, for corporate obligations.

33–1c Corporate Earnings and Taxation

Dividend A distribution of corporate profits to the corporation's shareholders in proportion to the number of shares held.

Retained Earnings The portion of a corporation's profits that has not been paid out as dividends to shareholders.

When a corporation earns profits, it can either pass them on to its shareholders in the form of **dividends** or retain them as profits. These **retained earnings,** if invested properly, will yield higher corporate profits in the future and cause the price of the company's stock to rise. Individual shareholders can then reap the benefits in the capital gains that they receive when they sell their stock.

Whether a corporation retains its profits or passes them on to the shareholders as dividends, those profits are subject to income taxation by various levels of government. Failure to pay taxes can lead to severe consequences. The state can suspend the entity's corporate status until the taxes are paid or even dissolve the corporation for failing to pay taxes.

Another important aspect of corporate taxation is that corporate profits can be subject to double taxation. The company pays tax on its profits, and then if the profits are passed on to the shareholders as dividends, the shareholders must also pay income tax on them. The corporation normally does not receive a tax deduction for dividends it distributes to shareholders. This double-taxation feature is one of the major disadvantages of the corporate business form.

In late 2017, Congress voted to reduce the federal corporate tax rate, which had taxed income over $10 million at 35 percent, to a flat rate of 21 percent. These changes will boost corporate profits, but do not affect the potential for double taxation.

33–1d Torts and Criminal Acts

Under modern criminal law, a corporation may be held liable for the criminal acts of its agents and employees. Although corporations cannot be imprisoned, they can be fined. (Of course, corporate directors and officers can be imprisoned, and many have been in recent years.) In addition, under sentencing guidelines for crimes committed by corporate employees (white-collar crimes), corporations can face fines amounting to hundreds of millions of dollars.

A corporation is also liable for the torts committed by its agents or officers within the course and scope of their employment. The doctrine of *respondeat superior* applies to corporations in the same way as it does to other agency relationships.

Case Example 33.1 Mark Bloom was an officer and a director of MB Investment Partners, Inc. (MB), at the time that he formed North Hills, LP, a stock investment fund. Bloom and other MB employees used MB's offices and equipment to administer investments in North Hills. Later, investors in North Hills requested a full redemption of their investments. By that time, however, most of the funds that had been invested were gone. North Hills had, in fact, been a Ponzi scheme that Bloom had used to finance his lavish personal lifestyle, taking at least $20 million from North Hills for his personal use.

Barry Belmont and other North Hills investors filed a suit in a federal district court against MB, alleging fraud. The court held that MB was liable for Bloom's fraud. MB appealed, and the appellate court affirmed. Tort liability can be attributed to a corporation for the acts of its agent that were committed within the scope of the agent's employment.[1] ▪

Because corporations can be liable for their employees' fraud and other misconduct, companies need to be careful about whom they hire and how much they monitor or supervise their employees. Some companies are using special software designed to predict employee misconduct before it occurs, as discussed in this chapter's *Adapting the Law to the Online Environment* feature.

---

1. *Belmont v. MB Investment Partners, Inc.*, 708 F.3d 470 (3d Cir. 2013).

Adapting the Law to the Online Environment

Programs That Predict Employee Misconduct

Monitoring employees' e-mails and phone conversations at work is generally legal.[a] But what about using software to analyze employee behavior with the goal of predicting, rather than observing, wrongdoing? We are now entering into the digital realm of predictive analytics.

Spy agencies around the world today use analytic software to predict who will engage in a terrorist act, where it will happen, and when. Software applied to data mining of employee behavior (usually only online) actually has been around for several years as well. For instance, Amazon started using employee-monitoring programs to predict who might quit. But only recently have such programs been used to predict misconduct.

JPMorgan Chase Attempts to Reduce Its Legal Bills

JPMorgan Chase, the world's largest private financial institution, is perhaps the world's largest purchaser of legal services in that business sector. Its legal bills have exceeded $36 billion since the financial crisis in 2008. The company's management found that employees had engaged in dubious mortgage bond sales and rigged foreign exchange and energy markets, among many other transgressions. The company hired 2,500 extra compliance officers and spent almost $750 million on compliance operations during a recent three-year period.

Today, JPMorgan is using new software to identify—in advance of any wrongdoing—"rogue" employees. The software analyzes a wide range of inputs on employees' behavior in an attempt to identify patterns that point to future misconduct. If successful, the program will certainly be copied by other financial institutions.

An Ethical Problem?

Former Federal Reserve Bank examiner Mark Williams has raised an important issue with respect to predictive analytics: "Policing intentions can be a slippery slope. Do people get a scarlet letter for something they have yet to do?" In other words, will employees be labeled as wrongdoers before they have actually done anything wrong?

Critical Thinking

Is thinking about committing a crime illegal? Is it unethical? Explain your answers.

---

a. Electronic Communications Privacy Act, 18 U.S.C. Section 2511(2)(d).

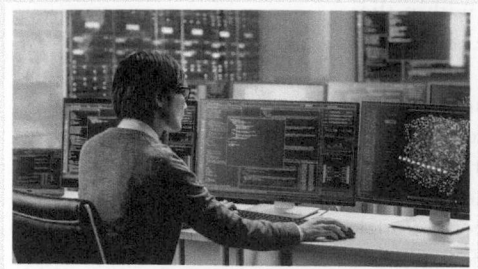

What are some of the pitfalls employers face when they use software that attempts to predict employee misconduct?

Domestic Corporation In a given state, a corporation that is organized under the law of that state.

Foreign Corporation In a given state, a corporation that does business in that state but is not incorporated there.

Alien Corporation A corporation formed in another country but doing business in the United States.

33–1e Classification of Corporations

Corporations can be classified in several ways. The classification of a corporation normally depends on its location, purpose, and ownership characteristics, as described in the following subsections.

Domestic, Foreign, and Alien Corporations A corporation is referred to as a **domestic corporation** by its home state (the state in which it incorporates). A corporation formed in one state but doing business in another is referred to in the second state as a **foreign corporation**. A corporation formed in another country (say, Mexico) but doing business in the United States is referred to in the United States as an **alien corporation**.

A corporation does not have an automatic right to do business in a state other than its state of incorporation. In some instances, it must obtain a *certificate of authority* in any state in which it plans to do business. Once the certificate has been issued, the corporation generally can exercise in that state all of the powers conferred on it by its home state. If a foreign corporation does business in a state without obtaining a certificate of authority, the state can impose substantial fines and sanctions on the corporation, and sometimes even on its officers, directors, or agents.

Note that most state statutes specify certain activities, such as soliciting orders via the Internet, that are not considered doing business within the state. Thus, a foreign corporation normally does not need a certificate of authority to sell goods or services via the Internet or by mail.

What constitutes doing business within a state? In the following case, the court answered that question.

■ Case 33.1

Drake Manufacturing Co. v. Polyflow, Inc.

Superior Court of Pennsylvania, 2015 PA Super 16, 109 A.3d 250 (2015).

Background and Facts Drake Manufacturing Company, a Delaware corporation, entered into a contract to sell certain products to Polyflow, Inc., headquartered in Pennsylvania. Drake promised to ship the goods from Drake's plant in Sheffield, Pennsylvania, to Polyflow's place of business in Oaks, Pennsylvania, as well as to addresses in California, Canada, and Holland.

When Polyflow withheld payment of about $300,000 for some of the goods, Drake filed a breach of contract suit in a Pennsylvania state court against Polyflow seeking to collect the unpaid amount. But Drake had failed to obtain a certificate of authority to do business in Pennsylvania as a foreign corporation. Polyflow asserted that this failure to register with the state meant that Drake could not bring an action against Polyflow in the state's courts. The court issued a judgment in Drake's favor. Polyflow appealed.

In the Words of the Court
Opinion by *JENKINS*, J. [Judge]:

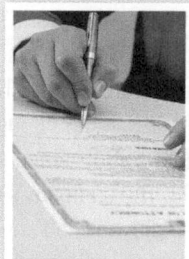

If a company fails to obtain the required foreign corporation certificate of authority, can it still undertake legal actions?

* * * *

[15 Pennsylvania Consolidated Statutes (Pa.C.S.)] Section 4121 provides: "A foreign business corporation, before doing business in this Commonwealth, shall procure a certificate of authority to do so from the Department of State."

* * * Typical conduct requiring a certificate of authority includes maintaining an office to conduct local intrastate business [and] entering into contracts relating to local business or sales. *A corporation is not "doing business" solely because it resorts to the courts of this Commonwealth to recover an indebtedness.* [Emphasis added.]

* * * *

[15 Pa.C.S.] Section 4141(a) provides in relevant part that "a nonqualified foreign business corporation doing business in this Commonwealth * * * shall not be permitted to maintain any action or proceeding in any court of this Commonwealth until the corporation has obtained a certificate of authority."

* * * *

* * * The evidence demonstrates that Drake failed to submit a certificate of authority into evidence prior to the verdict in violation of 15 Pa.C.S. Section 4121. Therefore, the trial court should not have permitted Drake to prosecute its action.

The trial court contends that Drake is exempt from the certificate of authority requirement because it merely commenced suit in Pennsylvania to collect a debt * * * . Drake did much more, however, than file suit or attempt to collect a debt. Drake maintains an office in Pennsylvania to conduct local business, conduct which typically requires a certificate of authority. Drake also entered into a contract with Polyflow, and * * * shipped couplings and portable swaging machines to Polyflow's place of business in Pennsylvania * * * . In short, *Drake's conduct was * * * regular, systematic, and extensive, * * * thus constituting the transaction of business and requiring Drake to obtain a certificate of authority.* [Emphasis added.]

We also hold that Drake needed a certificate of authority to sue Polyflow in Pennsylvania for Polyflow's failure to pay for out-of-state shipments in California, Canada and Holland. A foreign corporation that "does business" in Pennsylvania * * * must obtain a certificate in order to prosecute a lawsuit in this Commonwealth, regardless of whether the lawsuit itself concerns in-state conduct or out-of-state conduct.

Decision and Remedy A state intermediate appellate court reversed the judgment in Drake's favor. Under Pennsylvania state statutes, Drake was required to obtain a certificate of authority to do business in that state. Drake failed to do so. The court should not have allowed Drake to prosecute its action against Polyflow.

Critical Thinking

• **Legal Environment** *Why would the appellate court permit Polyflow to get away with not paying for delivered and presumably merchantable goods?*

Public and Private Corporations

A **public corporation** is one formed by the government to meet some political or governmental purpose. Cities and towns that incorporate are common examples. In addition, many federal government organizations—such as the U.S. Postal Service, the Tennessee Valley Authority, and AMTRAK—are public corporations.

Note that a public corporation is not the same as a *publicly held* corporation (often called a *public company*). A **publicly held corporation** is any corporation whose shares are publicly traded in securities markets, such as the New York Stock Exchange or the NASDAQ. (The NASDAQ is an electronic stock exchange founded by the National Association of Securities Dealers.)

Private corporations, in contrast, are created either wholly or in part for private benefit. Most corporations are private. Although private corporations may serve a public purpose, as a public electric or gas utility does, they are owned by private persons rather than by the government.[2]

Nonprofit Corporations

Corporations that are formed without a profit-making purpose are called *nonprofit* or *not-for-profit corporations*. Private hospitals, educational institutions, charities, and religious organizations, for instance, are frequently organized as nonprofit corporations. The nonprofit corporation is a convenient form of organization that allows various groups to own property and to form contracts without exposing the individual members to personal liability.

In some circumstances, a nonprofit corporation and its members may also be immune from liability for a personal injury caused by its negligence. Whether those circumstances were present in the following case was the question before the court.

Public Corporation A corporation owned by a federal, state, or municipal government to meet a political or governmental purpose.

Publicly Held Corporation A corporation whose shares are publicly traded in securities markets, such as the New York Stock Exchange or the NASDAQ.

---

2. The United States Supreme Court first recognized the property rights of private corporations and clarified the distinction between public and private corporations in the landmark case *Trustees of Dartmouth College v. Woodward,* 17 U.S. (4 Wheaton) 518, 4 L.Ed. 629 (1819).

Case 33.2

Pantano v. Newark Museum

Superior Court of New Jersey, Appellate Division, 2016 WL 528771 (2016).

Background and Facts Loredana Pantano was an immigration attorney for La Casa de Don Pedro, a nonprofit organization in Newark, New Jersey. La Casa's director of personal development told Pantano to go to the Newark Museum for a panel discussion being held in the museum's auditorium as part of La Casa's fortieth anniversary celebration. The museum—a nonprofit association organized exclusively for charitable, artistic, scientific, educational, historical, and cultural purposes—hosted the discussion but charged La Casa a fee for the use of its auditorium.

At a museum entrance, Pantano slipped and fell on icy steps, sustaining injuries to her back. She filed a lawsuit in a New Jersey state court against the museum, alleging that it was negligent in its maintenance of the premises. The museum filed a motion for summary judgment, contending that as a nonprofit corporation, it was immune to liability under the state's Charitable Immunity Act (CIA). The court granted the museum's motion. Pantano appealed.

In the Words of the Court
PER CURIAM.

* * * *

In pertinent part, the [state Charitable Immunity Act (CIA)] provides:

No nonprofit corporation * * * shall * * * be liable to respond in damages to any person who shall suffer damage from the negligence * * * of such corporation * * * where such person is a beneficiary, to whatever degree, of the works of such nonprofit corporation * * * ; provided, however, that such immunity from liability shall not extend to any person * * * where such person is one unconcerned in and unrelated to and outside of the benefactions of such corporation.

The CIA serves two primary purposes. *First, immunity preserves a charity's assets. Second, immunity recognizes that a beneficiary of the services of a charitable organization has entered into a relationship that exempts the benefactor from liability.* [Emphasis added.]

* * * The established test for determining whether a party is a beneficiary of the works of a charity has two prongs. The first is that the institution pleading the immunity, at the time in question, was engaged in the performance of the charitable objectives it was organized to advance. The second is that the injured party must have been a direct recipient of those good works.

* * * *

As to the first prong, * * * a qualifying organization does not lose its statutory immunity merely because it charges money for its services, unless it makes a profit or collects fees for services totally unrelated to its organizational pursuits. * * * Hosting an educational panel discussion in the auditorium was entirely consistent with the Museum's charitable endeavors.

The second prong of the test * * * distinguishes between persons benefiting from the charity, and persons who contribute to the charity by virtue of their attendance or participation.

* * * *

* * * *[Thus, under the CIA] to be a beneficiary under the second prong, the injured party must be a direct recipient of the Museum's good works. Only those unconcerned in and unrelated to the benefactions of the organization are not beneficiaries.* [Emphasis added.]

* * * [Pantano], as an employee of La Casa who was ordered on the day of her fall to attend the panel discussion at the Museum, was not a direct beneficiary of the Museum's charitable endeavors.

Decision and Remedy A state intermediate appellate court reversed the lower court's judgment and remanded the case. The museum could be held liable for Pantano's injuries.

Critical Thinking

• **What If the Facts Were Different?** *Suppose that the museum had not been hosting an educational panel in its auditorium but instead had rented the facility to an organization for a sales conference. Would the result have been different? Discuss.*

Close Corporation A corporation whose shareholders are limited to a small group of persons, often family members.

Close Corporations Most corporate enterprises in the United States fall into the category of close corporations. A **close corporation** is one whose shares are held by relatively few persons, often members of a family. Close corporations are also referred to as *closely held, family,* or *privately held* corporations.

Usually, the members of the small group constituting a close corporation are personally known to one another. Because the number of shareholders is so small, there is no trading market for the shares. In practice, close corporations often operate somewhat like a partnership. The statutes in many states allow them to depart significantly from certain formalities required by traditional corporation law.[3]

Learning Objective 1
What is a close corporation?

Under the RMBCA, close corporations have considerable flexibility in determining their operating rules [RMBCA 7.32]. If all of a corporation's shareholders agree in writing, the corporation can operate without directors and bylaws. In addition, a close corporation need not hold annual or special shareholders' or directors' meetings, issue stock certificates, or keep formal records of shareholders' and directors' decisions.[4]

Management of Close Corporations. Management of a close corporation resembles that of a sole proprietorship or a partnership in that a single shareholder or a tightly knit group of shareholders usually hold the positions of directors and officers. As a corporation, however, the firm must meet all specific legal requirements set forth in state statutes.

To prevent a majority shareholder from dominating a close corporation, a close corporation may require that more than a simple majority of the directors approve any action taken by the board. In a larger corporation, such a requirement would typically apply only to extraordinary actions (such as selling all the corporate assets) and not to ordinary business decisions.

Transfer of Shares in Close Corporations. By definition, a close corporation has a small number of shareholders. Thus, the transfer of one shareholder's shares to someone else can cause serious management problems. The other shareholders may find themselves required to share control with someone they do not know or like.

How is a close corporation usually managed?

To avoid this situation, the corporation could restrict the transferability of shares to outside persons. Shareholders could be required to offer their shares to the corporation or the other shareholders before selling them to an outside purchaser. In fact, a few states have statutes that prohibit the transfer of close corporation shares unless certain persons—including shareholders, family members, and the corporation—are first given the opportunity to purchase the shares for the same price.

Misappropriation of Close Corporation Funds. Sometimes, a majority shareholder in a close corporation takes advantage of his or her position and misappropriates company funds. In such situations, the normal remedy for the injured minority shareholders is to have their shares appraised and to be paid the fair market value for them.

S Corporations
A close corporation that meets the qualifying requirements specified in Subchapter S of the Internal Revenue Code can operate as an **S corporation.** (A corporation will automatically be taxed under Subchapter C unless it elects S corporation status.) If a corporation has S corporation status, it can avoid the imposition of income taxes at the corporate level while retaining many of the advantages of a corporation, particularly limited liability. Among the numerous requirements for S corporation status, the following are the most important:

1. The corporation must be a domestic corporation.

2. The corporation must not be a member of an affiliated group of corporations.

3. The shareholders must be individuals, estates, or certain trusts. Partnerships and nonqualifying trusts cannot be shareholders. Corporations can be shareholders under certain circumstances.

S Corporation A close business corporation that has most corporate attributes, including limited liability, but qualifies under the Internal Revenue Code to be taxed as a partnership.

---

3. For example, in some states (such as Maryland), a close corporation need not have a board of directors.

4. Shareholders cannot agree, however, to eliminate certain rights of shareholders, such as the right to inspect corporate books and records and the right to bring lawsuits on behalf of the corporation.

4. The corporation must have no more than one hundred shareholders.

5. The corporation must have only one class of stock, although all shareholders do not have to have the same voting rights.

6. No shareholder of the corporation may be a nonresident alien.

An S corporation is treated differently from a regular corporation for tax purposes. It is taxed like a partnership, so the corporate income passes through to the shareholders, who pay personal income tax on it. This treatment enables the S corporation to avoid the double taxation that is imposed on regular corporations. In addition, the shareholders' tax brackets may be lower than the tax bracket that the corporation would have been in if the tax had been imposed at the corporate level.

In spite of these benefits, the S corporation has lost much of its appeal. The newer limited liability business forms (such as LLCs, LPs, and LLPs) offer similar tax advantages and greater flexibility.

Know This

The shareholders of professional corporations generally must be licensed professionals.

Professional Corporations Professionals such as physicians, lawyers, dentists, and accountants can incorporate. Professional corporations typically are identified by the letters *S.C.* (service corporation), *P.C.* (professional corporation), or *P.A.* (professional association). In general, the laws governing the formation and operation of professional corporations are similar to those governing ordinary business corporations. There are some differences in terms of liability, however.

For liability purposes, some courts treat a professional corporation somewhat like a partnership and hold each professional liable for any malpractice committed by others in the firm within the scope of the firm's business. With the exception of malpractice or a breach of duty to clients or patients, a shareholder in a professional corporation generally cannot be held liable for torts committed by other professionals at the firm.

Benefit Corporation A for-profit corporation that seeks to have a material positive impact on society and the environment. It is available by statute in a number of states.

Benefit Corporations A growing number of states have enacted legislation that creates a new corporate form called a *benefit corporation*. A **benefit corporation** is a for-profit corporation that seeks to have a material positive impact on society and the environment. Benefit corporations differ from traditional corporations in the following ways:

1. *Purpose.* Although the corporation is designed to make a profit, its purpose is to benefit the public as a whole (rather than just to provide long-term shareholder value, as in ordinary corporations). The directors of a benefit corporation must, during the decision-making process, consider the impact of their decisions on society and the environment.

2. *Accountability.* Shareholders of a benefit corporation determine whether the company has achieved a material positive impact. Shareholders also have a right of private action, called a *benefit enforcement proceeding,* enabling them to sue the corporation if it fails to pursue or create public benefit.

3. *Transparency.* A benefit corporation must issue an annual benefit report on its overall social and environmental performance that uses a recognized third-party standard to assess its performance. The report must be delivered to the shareholders and posted on a public website.

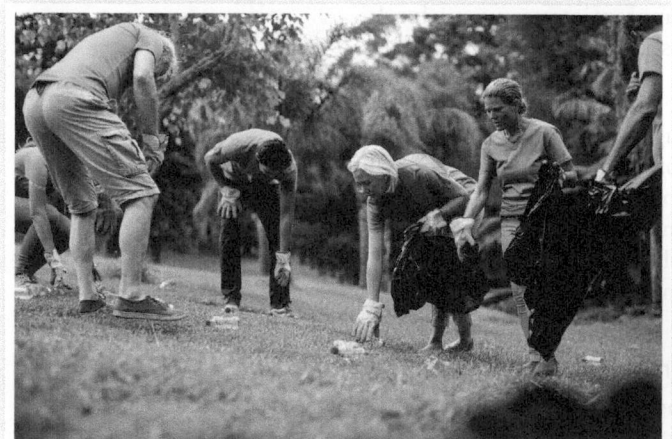
Benefit corporations strive to have a positive impact on society. How do they differ from traditional, for-profit corporations?

wavebreakmedia/Shutterstock.com

In the following case, a benefit corporation took an action that it believed would have a positive impact on those it was established to serve. Two of those affected by the action disagreed and filed a suit to challenge the action.

Case 33.3

Greenfield v. Mandalay Shores Community Association

California Court of Appeal, Second District, Division 6, 21 Cal.App.5th 896, 230 Cal.Rptr.3d 827 (2018).

Background and Facts Mandalay Shores is a beach community in California's Oxnard Coastal Zone, where nonresidents have vacationed for decades, renting homes on a short-term basis. Robert and Demetra Greenfield owned a single-family residence at Mandalay Shores that they rented to families for periods of less than thirty days. Mandalay Shores Community Association is a mutual benefit corporation established for the development of the community. The association adopted a resolution banning short-term rentals (STRs), claiming that it was necessary to reduce parking, noise, and trash problems. Homeowners who rented their homes "for less than 30 consecutive days" were subjected to fines of up to $5,000 per offense.

The Greenfields filed a suit in a California state court against the association, contending that the STR ban violated the California Coastal Act. The court denied the plaintiffs' request for a preliminary injunction to stay the enforcement of the association's resolution. The Greenfields appealed.

In the Words of the Court

YEGAN, Acting P.J. [Presiding Judge].

* * * *

* * * The California Coastal Act is intended to, among other things, "maximize public access to and along the coast and maximize public recreational opportunities to the coastal zone consistent with sound resources conservation principles and constitutionally protected right of private property owners." The Coastal Act requires that any person who seeks to undertake a "development" in the coastal zone to obtain a coastal development permit. "Development" is broadly defined to include, among other things, any "change in the density or intensity of use of land." * * * *"Development" under the Coastal Act is not restricted to activities that physically alter the land or water.* [Emphasis added.]

* * * *

* * * The STR ban changes the intensity of use and access to single-family residences in the Oxnard Coastal Zone. STRs were common in [Mandalay Shores] before the STR ban; now they are prohibited. Respondent asserts that the STR ban is necessary to curtail the increasing problem of short-term rentals which cause parking, noise, and trash problems. *STR bans, however, are a matter for the City and Coastal Commission to address.* STRs may not be regulated by private actors where it affects the intensity of use or access to single-family residences in a coastal zone. The question of whether a seven-day house rental is more of a neighborhood problem than a 31-day rental must be decided by the City and the Coastal Commission, not a homeowner's association. [Emphasis added.]

* * * Respondent's STR ban affects 1,400 [housing] units and cuts across a wide swath of beach properties that have historically been used as short-term rentals. A *prima facie* showing has been made to issue a preliminary injunction staying enforcement of the STR ban until trial.

Decision and Remedy A state intermediate appellate court reversed the lower court's denial of the Greenfields' motion, and ordered the issuance of a preliminary injunction. The court concluded that "Mandalay Shores Community Association . . . has erected a monetary barrier to the beach. It has no right to do so."

Critical Thinking

• **Legal Environment** *Did the STR ban adopted by the association comport with or contravene its status as a benefit corporation? Discuss.*

• **What If the Facts Were Different?** *Suppose that instead of adopting an STR ban on its own, the association had petitioned the city and the Coastal Commission to impose one. Would the result have been different? Explain.*

33–2 Formation and Powers

Incorporating a business is much simpler today than it was twenty years ago. Many states allow businesses to incorporate via the Internet.

Learning Objective 2
What four steps are involved in bringing a corporation into existence?

33–2a Promotional Activities

In the past, preliminary steps were taken to organize and promote a business prior to incorporating. Contracts were made with investors and others on behalf of the future corporation. Today, due to the relative ease of forming a corporation in most states, persons incorporating a business rarely, if ever, engage in preliminary promotional activities.

Nevertheless, businesspersons need to understand that they are personally liable for any preincorporation contracts made with investors, accountants, or others on behalf of the future corporation. Liability continues until the corporation is formed and explicitly assumes the contract by novation.

33–2b Incorporation Procedures

Each state has its own set of incorporation procedures, which most often are listed on the secretary of state's website. Generally, however, all incorporators follow four basic steps, discussed next.

Select the State of Incorporation Because state corporate laws differ, individuals may look for the states that offer the most advantageous tax or other provisions. Many corporations, for instance, have chosen to incorporate in Delaware because it has historically had the least restrictive laws, along with provisions that favor corporate management. For reasons of convenience and cost, though, businesses often choose to incorporate in the state in which the corporation's business will primarily be conducted.

Secure an Appropriate Corporate Name The choice of a corporate name is subject to state approval to ensure against duplication or deception. In today's online world, what matters most is to secure a corporate name that can be used as a domain name. A new corporation's name cannot be the same as (or deceptively similar to) the name of an existing corporation. Therefore, the incorporators usually must perform a search to confirm that the corporate name they choose is available as a domain name. State approval of the name may also be required. In addition, all states require the corporation name to include the word *Corporation, Incorporated, Company,* or *Limited,* or an abbreviation of one of these terms.

Articles of Incorporation The document that is filed with the appropriate state official, usually the secretary of state, when a business is incorporated and that contains basic information about the corporation.

Prepare the Articles of Incorporation The primary document needed to incorporate a business is the **articles of incorporation**. The articles include basic information about the corporation and serve as a primary source of authority for its future organization and business functions. The person or persons who execute (sign) the articles are the *incorporators.* Articles of incorporation vary widely depending on the jurisdiction and the size and type of the corporation. Generally, though, the articles *must* include the following information [RMBCA 2.02]:

1. The name of the corporation.
2. The number of shares of stock the corporation is authorized to issue [RMBCA 2.02(a)]. (Large corporations often also state a par value for each share, such as $0.20 per share, and specify the various types or classes of stock authorized for issuance.)
3. The name and street address of the corporation's initial registered agent and registered office. The registered agent is the person who can receive legal documents (such as orders to appear in court) on behalf of the corporation. The registered office is usually the main corporate office.
4. The name and address of each incorporator.

In addition, the articles *may* set forth other information, such as the names and addresses of the initial members of the board of directors and the duration and purpose of the corporation. A corporation has perpetual existence unless the articles state otherwise.

As to the corporation's purpose, a corporation can be formed for any lawful purpose, and the RMBCA does not require the articles to include a specific statement of purpose. Consequently, the articles often include only a general statement of purpose. By not mentioning specifics, the corporation avoids the need for future amendments to the corporate articles [RMBCA 2.02(b)(2)(i), 3.01]. Similarly, the articles do not provide much detail about the firm's operations, which are spelled out in the company's *bylaws* (discussed shortly).

File the Articles of Incorporation Once the articles of incorporation have been prepared and signed by the incorporators, they are sent to the appropriate state official. They are most often filed with the secretary of state's office, along with the required filing fee. In most states, the secretary of state then stamps the articles as "Filed" and returns a copy of the articles to the incorporators. Once this occurs, the corporation officially exists.

33–2c First Organizational Meeting to Adopt Bylaws

After incorporation, the first organizational meeting must be held. If the articles of incorporation named the initial board of directors (as is typical), then the directors, by majority vote, call the meeting. If the articles did not name the directors, then the incorporators hold the meeting to elect the directors and conduct any other necessary business.

Bylaws The internal rules of management adopted by a corporation at its first organizational meeting.

Usually, the most important function of the first organizational meeting is the adoption of the **bylaws,** which are the corporation's internal rules of management. The bylaws cannot conflict with the state corporate statute or the articles of incorporation [RMBCA 2.06].

Under the RMBCA, the shareholders may amend or repeal the bylaws. The board of directors may also amend or repeal the bylaws, unless the articles of incorporation or provisions of the state corporate statute reserve this power to the shareholders exclusively [RMBCA 10.20]. The bylaws typically describe such matters as voting requirements for shareholders, the election and replacement of the board of directors, and the manner and time of holding shareholders' and board meetings.

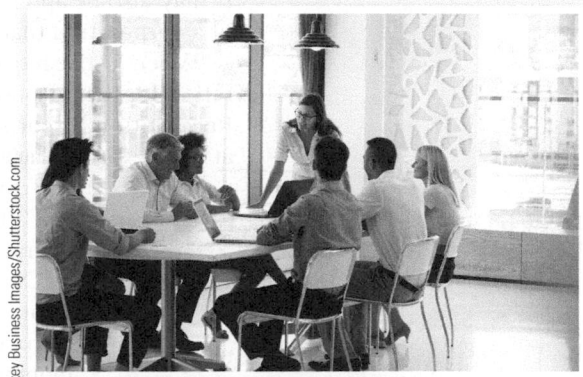

What are some of the important functions of a corporation's first organizational meeting?

33–2d Improper Incorporation

The procedures for incorporation are very specific. If they are not followed precisely, others may be able to challenge the existence of the corporation. Errors in the incorporation procedures can become important when, for instance, a third party who is attempting to enforce a contract or bring a suit for a tort injury learns of them.

Know This

Unlike the articles of incorporation, bylaws do not need to be filed with a state official.

***De Jure* Corporations** If a corporation has substantially complied with all conditions precedent to incorporation, the corporation is said to have *de jure* (rightful and lawful) existence. In most states and under the RMBCA 2.03(b), the secretary of state's filing of the articles of incorporation is conclusive proof that all mandatory statutory provisions have been met.

Sometimes, the incorporators fail to comply with all statutory mandates. If the defect is minor, such as an incorrect address listed on the articles of incorporation, most courts will overlook the defect and find that a *de jure* corporation exists.

***De Facto* Corporations** If a defect in formation is substantial, such as a corporation's failure to hold an organizational meeting to adopt bylaws, the outcome will vary depending on the court. Some states, including Mississippi, New York, Ohio, and Oklahoma, recognize the common law doctrine of *de facto* corporation. In those states, the courts will treat a corporation as a legal corporation despite the defect in its formation if all three of the following requirements are met:

1. A state statute exists under which the corporation can be validly incorporated.

2. The parties have made a good faith attempt to comply with the statute.

3. The parties have already undertaken to do business as a corporation.

Many states' courts, however, have interpreted their states versions of the RMBCA as abolishing the common law doctrine of *de facto* corporation. These states include Alaska, Arizona, Minnesota, New Mexico, Oregon, South Dakota, Tennessee, Utah, and Washington, as well as the District of Columbia. In those states, if there is a substantial defect in complying with the statutory mandates, the corporation does not legally exist, and the incorporators are personally liable.

Corporation by Estoppel　Sometimes, a business association holds itself out to others as being a corporation when it has made no attempt to incorporate. In those situations, the firm normally will be estopped (prevented) from denying corporate status in a lawsuit by a third party. The estoppel doctrine most commonly applies when a third party contracts with an entity that claims to be a corporation but has not filed articles of incorporation. It may also be applied when a third party contracts with a person claiming to be an agent of a corporation that does not, in fact, exist.

When justice requires, the courts treat an alleged corporation as if it were an actual corporation for the purpose of determining the rights and liabilities in a particular circumstance. Recognition of corporate status does not extend beyond the resolution of the problem at hand. **Case Example 33.2** Dale Ross bought a farm and formed Big Little Farms, Inc. (BLF), in Trumbull County, Ohio, to breed and train race horses. Dale failed to pay BLF's taxes, and the state cancelled BLF's corporate status. Dale continued operating the farm business, however.

Over a number of years, Dale's brother, Gene, loaned him funds to make improvements to BLF. At one point, Dale signed—as president of BLF Corporation—a promissory note to Gene and a mortgage on the farm. A few months after the mortgage was signed, Gene died. Gene's wife filed a claim against Dale and his wife seeking, in part, to foreclose on the mortgage. Then Dale died.

Dale's wife claimed that the mortgage note her husband had signed was void because the corporation did not legally exist at the time he had signed it. Gene's wife argued that Dale's estate should not be able to avoid paying a note that Dale had knowingly signed as president of a corporation whose legal status had been revoked. Ultimately, a state appellate court ruled that the mortgage note was valid. BLF was estopped from denying its corporate status for the purpose of invalidating the loan contract.[5] ■

What are some potential consequences if a farming operation loses its corporate status by failing to pay its taxes?

33–2e　Corporate Powers

When a corporation is created, the express and implied powers necessary to achieve its purpose also come into existence. Corporations cannot engage in acts that are beyond their powers, nor can a corporation's owners (shareholders) avoid liability if they misuse the corporate entity for their own personal benefit.

Express Powers　The express powers of a corporation are found in its articles of incorporation, in the law of the state of incorporation, and in the state and federal constitutions. Corporate bylaws also establish the express powers of the corporation. Because state

---

5. *Lamancusa v. Big Little Farms, Inc.*, 2013 -Ohio- 5815, 5 N.E.3d 1080 (Ohio App. 2013).

corporation statutes frequently provide default rules that apply if the company's bylaws are silent on an issue, it is important that the bylaws set forth the specific operating rules of the corporation. In addition, after the bylaws are adopted, the corporation's board of directors will pass resolutions that grant or restrict corporate powers.

On occasion, the U.S. government steps in to challenge what a corporation may consider one of its express powers. This chapter's *Beyond Our Borders* feature discusses a dispute between the government and Microsoft Corporation over a demand that the company provide the government with access to e-mail stored in servers on foreign soil.

Does Cloud Computing Have a Nationality?

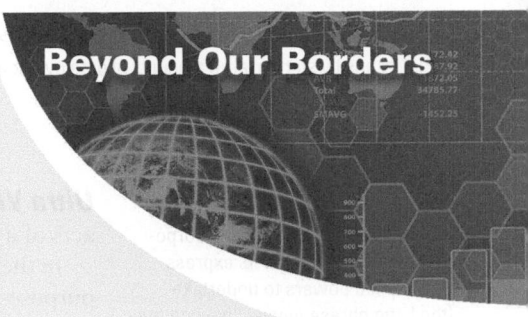

Beyond Our Borders

Most people use "the cloud" for the storage of their digital data—photos, e-mails, music, documents, and just about anything else. Not surprisingly, major global digital players such as Apple, Amazon, Google, and Microsoft have spent billions to create "clouds" of servers all over the world. In the clouds are stored confidential, organized, and secure data. The revenues generated by the U.S. cloud-computing industry exceed $100 billion a year.

Microsoft and Google Battle Federal Warrants

The U.S. government issued a warrant to Microsoft to produce e-mails related to a narcotics case from a Hotmail account. That e-mail account was hosted in a Microsoft cloud location in Ireland. Microsoft refused, arguing that the U.S. government did not have the power to issue a warrant for information stored in a foreign country and that doing so would threaten the privacy of U.S. citizens.

Some industry experts predicted that if Microsoft was forced to comply with the government's warrant, U.S. technology companies could lose up to $35 billion a year from their cloud storage businesses. Foreign corporations and individuals would no longer trust U.S. companies to keep their data secret. A federal district court in New York confirmed the government's right to the Ireland-located e-mails, but that decision was reversed on appeal. Ultimately, the United States Supreme Court granted *certiorari* to resolve the dispute.[a]

A subsequent case was brought against Google. In relation to a criminal investigation, the government issued a warrant to access e-mails that Google had stored outside the United States. Google made the same arguments that Microsoft had, but a federal district court ruled in the government's favor. The court reasoned that there were differences in the way the two corporations stored the cloud data overseas. Microsoft had stored the data exclusively in Ireland, so it "resided" in that location. Google had separated its cloud data into components and constantly moved it around the globe to improve network efficiency.[b]

Congress Enacts the CLOUD Act

In March 2018, Congress enacted the Clarifying Lawful Overseas Use of Data Act (CLOUD Act), which amended existing law.[c] The CLOUD Act requires service providers to preserve, backup, or disclose the contents of wire or electronic communications—as well as any record pertaining to a customer or subscriber within such provider's possession, custody, or control. Under the act, service providers have a duty to preserve this information, regardless of whether it is located inside or outside the United States.

After the CLOUD Act was passed, the government in the *Microsoft* case obtained a new warrant pursuant to the act. By the time the case reached the United States Supreme Court, there was no longer any dispute to resolve. The Court found that the government had the authority under the CLOUD Act to issue warrants to access information extraterritorially (and vacated the appellate court's decision).[d]

Critical Thinking

How might the CLOUD Act affect the privacy of U.S. citizens who store their information in the cloud?

---

a. *United States v. Microsoft Corp.*, 583 U.S. ___, 138 S.Ct. 356, 199 L.Ed.2d 261 (2017).

b. *In the Matter of the Search of Content Stored at Premises Controlled by Google, Inc.*, ___ F.Supp.3d ___, 2017 WL 1487625 (N.D.Cal. 2017).

c. 18 U.S.C. Section 2703.

---

d. *United States v. Microsoft Corp.*, ___ U.S. ___ 138 S.Ct. 1186, 200 L.Ed.2d 610 (2018).

Why are large companies, such as Google, encountering legal issues by storing large amounts of data overseas?

Implied Powers When a corporation is created, it acquires certain implied powers. Barring express constitutional, statutory, or other prohibitions, the corporation has the implied power to perform all acts reasonably appropriate and necessary to accomplish its corporate purposes. For this reason, a corporation has the implied power to borrow funds within certain limits, to lend funds, and to extend credit to those with whom it has a legal or contractual relationship.

Most often, the president or chief executive officer of the corporation will execute the necessary papers on behalf of the corporation. In so doing, corporate officers have the implied power to bind the corporation in matters directly connected with the *ordinary* business affairs of the enterprise. There is a limit to what a corporate officer can do, though. A corporate officer does not have the authority to bind the corporation to an action that will greatly affect the corporate purpose or undertaking, such as the sale of substantial corporate assets.

Ultra Vires Acts Acts of a corporation that are beyond its express and implied powers to undertake (the Latin phrase means "beyond the powers").

***Ultra Vires* Doctrine** The term *ultra vires* means "beyond the powers." In corporate law, acts of a corporation that are beyond its express and implied powers are ***ultra vires* acts.**

In the past, most cases dealing with *ultra vires* acts involved contracts made for unauthorized purposes. Now, however, most private corporations are organized for "any legal business" and not for a specific purpose, so the *ultra vires* doctrine has declined in importance. Today, cases that allege *ultra vires* acts usually involve nonprofit corporations or municipal (public) corporations.[6]

Under Section 3.04 of the RMBCA, shareholders can seek an injunction from a court to prevent (or stop) the corporation from engaging in *ultra vires* acts. The attorney general in the state of incorporation can also bring an action to obtain an injunction against the *ultra vires* transactions or seek dissolution of the corporation.

33–3 Piercing the Corporate Veil

Occasionally, the owners use a corporate entity to perpetrate a fraud, circumvent the law, or in some other way accomplish an illegitimate objective. In these situations, the court will ignore the corporate structure by **piercing the corporate veil** and exposing the shareholders to personal liability [RMBCA 2.04].

Piercing the Corporate Veil The action of a court to disregard the corporate entity and hold the shareholders personally liable for corporate debts and obligations.

Generally, courts pierce the veil when corporate privilege is abused for personal benefit or when the corporate business is treated so carelessly that it is indistinguishable from that of a controlling shareholder. In short, when the facts show that great injustice would result from a shareholder's use of a corporation to avoid individual responsibility, a court will look behind the corporate structure to the individual shareholder. The shareholder/owner is then required to assume personal liability to creditors for the corporation's debts.

Learning Objective 3

In what circumstances might a court disregard the corporate entity ("pierce the corporate veil") and hold the shareholders personally liable?

33–3a Factors That Lead Courts to Pierce the Corporate Veil

The following are some of the factors that frequently cause the courts to pierce the corporate veil:

1. A party is tricked or misled into dealing with the corporation rather than the individual.

2. The corporation is set up to never make a profit or always be insolvent, or it is too thinly capitalized—that is, it has insufficient capital at the time of formation to meet its prospective debts or other potential liabilities.

---

6. See, for instance, *Xcel Energy Services, Inc. v. Federal Energy Regulatory Commission*, 815 F.3d 947 (D.C.Cir. 2016).

3. Statutory corporate formalities, such as holding required corporation meetings, are not followed.

4. Personal and corporate interests are **commingled** to such an extent that the corporation has no separate identity.

> **Commingle** To mix funds or goods together to such a degree that they no longer have separate identities.

Case Example 33.3 Dog House Investments, LLC, operated a dog "camp" in Nashville, Tennessee. Dog House leased the property from Teal Properties, Inc., which was owned by Jerry Teal, its sole shareholder. Under the lease, the landlord promised to repair damage from fire or other causes that rendered the property "untenantable" (unusable). Following a flood, Dog House notified Jerry that the property was untenantable. Jerry assured Dog House that the flood damage was covered by insurance but took no steps to restore the property. The parties then agreed that Dog House would undertake the repairs and be reimbursed by Teal Properties.

Dog House spent $39,000 to repair the damage and submitted invoices for reimbursement. Teal Properties recovered $40,000 from its insurance company but did not pay Dog House. Close to bankruptcy, Dog House sued Teal Properties and Jerry. The court pierced the corporate veil and held Jerry personally liable for the repair costs. An appellate court affirmed. Teal Properties owned no property and had no assets. It received rent but paid it immediately to Jerry. The court concluded that the company was not operated as an entity separate from its sole shareholder.[7] (See this chapter's *Business Law Analysis* feature, which illustrates a situation in which a court may decide not to pierce the corporate veil.)

If a leased property for dog kennels floods, what is the landlord's responsibility?

33–3b A Potential Problem for Close Corporations

The potential for corporate assets to be used for personal benefit is especially great in a close corporation. In such a corporation, the separate status of the corporate entity and the shareholders must be carefully preserved. Certain practices invite trouble for a close corporation,

---

7. *Dog House Investments, LLC v. Teal Properties, Inc.*, 448 S.W.3d 905 (Tenn.App. 2014).

Business Law Analysis

Piercing the Corporate Veil

Country Contractors, Inc., contracted to provide excavation services for Westside Storage of Indianapolis, Inc., but did not complete the job and later filed for bankruptcy. Stephen Songer and Jahn Songer were Country's sole shareholders. The Songers had not misused the corporate form to engage in fraud. The firm had not been undercapitalized, personal and corporate funds had not been commingled, and Country had kept accounting records and minutes of its annual board meetings. Are the Songers personally liable for Country's failure to complete its contract?

Analysis: A hallmark of the corporate form of business organization is that shareholders are not personally liable for the debts of the corporation. If the corporation fails, the shareholders can lose their investments, but that is generally the limit of their liability. A court may pierce the corporate veil to hold the shareholders personally liable in certain instances of fraud, undercapitalization, or a failure to observe corporate formalities. But these situations are exceptions.

Result and Reasoning: The Songers are not personally liable for Country's failure to complete its contract with Westside Storage. They had not misused the corporate form to engage in misconduct, the firm had not been undercapitalized, and personal and corporate funds had not been commingled. In addition, Country had kept accounting records and minutes of its annual board meetings, thus observing the formalities required by law. These circumstances fall under none of the exceptions to the limit on shareholders' liability for corporate obligations. Thus, as shareholders, the Songers are not personally liable for the failure of their company to complete its job.

such as the commingling of corporate and personal funds or the shareholders' continuous personal use of corporate property (for instance, vehicles).

Typically, courts are reluctant to hold shareholders in close corporations personally liable unless there is some evidence of fraud or wrongdoing. ✴ **Spotlight Case Example 33.4** Pip, Jimmy, and Theodore Brennan are brothers and shareholders of Brennan's, Inc., which owns and operates New Orleans's famous Brennan's Restaurant. As a close corporation, Brennan's, Inc., did not hold formal corporate meetings with agendas and minutes, but it did maintain corporate books, hold corporate bank accounts, and file corporate tax returns.

The Brennan brothers retained attorney Edward Colbert to represent them in a family matter, and the attorney's bills were sent to the restaurant and paid from the corporate account. Later, when Brennan's, Inc., sued Colbert for malpractice, Colbert argued that the court should pierce the corporate veil because the Brennan brothers did not observe corporate formalities. The court refused to do so, however, because there was no evidence of fraud or other wrongdoing by the Brennan brothers. There is no requirement for small, close corporations to operate with the formality usually expected of larger corporations.[8]

33–4 Corporate Financing

Part of the process of corporate formation involves financing. Corporations normally are financed by the issuance and sale of corporate securities. **Securities**—stocks and bonds—evidence the right to participate in earnings and the distribution of corporate property or the obligation to pay funds.

33–4a Bonds

Bonds (*debentures* or *debt securities*) represent the borrowing of funds. Bonds are issued by business firms and by governments at all levels as evidence of the funds they are borrowing from investors.

Bonds normally have a designated *maturity date*—the date when the principal, or face, amount of the bond is returned to the bondholder. Bondholders also receive fixed-dollar interest payments, usually semiannually, during the period of time before maturity. For that reason, bonds are sometimes referred to as *fixed-income securities*. Because debt financing represents a legal obligation on the part of the corporation, various features and terms of a particular bond issue are specified in a lending agreement.

Of course, not all debt is in the form of debt securities. For instance, some debt is in the form of accounts payable and notes payable, which typically are short-term debts. Bonds are simply a way for the corporation to split up its long-term debt so that it can be more easily marketed.

33–4b Stocks

Issuing stock is another way that corporations can obtain financing. **Stocks,** or *equity securities*, represent the purchase of ownership in the business firm. The true ownership of a corporation is represented by **common stock**. Common stock provides a proportionate interest in the corporation with regard to (1) control (voting rights), (2) earnings, and (3) net assets. A shareholder's interest is generally in proportion to the number of shares he or she owns out of the total number of shares issued.

Securities Generally, stocks, bonds, or other items that represent an ownership interest in a corporation or a promise of repayment of debt by a corporation.

Bond A security that evidences a corporate (or government) debt.

Learning Objective 4

What is the difference between stocks and bonds?

Stock An ownership (equity) interest in a corporation, measured in units of shares.

Common Stock Shares of ownership in a corporation that give the owner a proportionate interest in the corporation with regard to control, earnings, and net assets. Common stock is lowest in priority with respect to payment of dividends and distribution of the corporation's assets on dissolution.

---

8. *Brennan's, Inc. v. Colbert*, 85 So.3d 787 (La.App.4th Cir. 2012).

An issuing firm is not obligated to return a principal amount per share to each holder of its common stock, nor does the firm have to guarantee a dividend. Indeed, some corporations never pay dividends. Holders of common stock are investors who assume a *residual* position in the overall financial structure of a business. They benefit when the market price of the stock increases. In terms of receiving payment for their investments, they are last in line.

Preferred stock is stock with *preferences*. Holders of preferred stock usually have priority over holders of common stock as to dividends and payment on dissolution of the corporation, but may not have the right to vote. Although holders of preferred stock have a stronger position than common shareholders with respect to dividends and claims on assets, they will not share in the full prosperity of the firm if it grows successfully over time. Preferred stockholders do receive fixed dividends periodically, however, and they may benefit to some extent from changes in the market price of the shares.

Preferred Stock Stock that has priority over common stock as to payment of dividends and distribution of assets on the corporation's dissolution.

33–4c **Venture Capital**

Start-up businesses and high-risk enterprises often obtain venture capital financing. **Venture capital** is capital provided to new business ventures by professional, outside investors (*venture capitalists*, usually groups of wealthy investors and securities firms). Venture capital investments are high risk—the investors must be willing to lose their invested funds—but offer the potential for well-above-average returns at some point in the future.

To obtain venture capital financing, the start-up business typically gives up a share of its ownership to the venture capitalists. In addition to funding, venture capitalists may provide managerial and technical expertise, and they nearly always are given some control over the new company's decisions. Many Internet-based companies, such as Amazon and Google, were initially financed by venture capital.

Venture Capital Financing provided by professional, outside investors (venture capitalists) to new business ventures.

33–4d **Private Equity Capital**

Private equity firms pool funds from wealthy investors and use this **private equity capital** to invest in existing corporations. Usually, a private equity firm buys an entire corporation and then reorganizes it. Sometimes, divisions of the purchased company are sold off to pay down debt. Ultimately, the private equity firm may sell shares in the reorganized (and perhaps more profitable) company to the public in an *initial public offering (IPO)*. In this way, the private equity firm can make profits by selling its ownership rights in the company to the public.

Private Equity Capital Funds invested in an existing corporation by a private equity firm, usually to purchase and reorganize it.

33–4e **Crowdfunding**

Start-up businesses can also attempt to obtain financing through *crowdfunding*. **Crowdfunding** is a cooperative activity in which people network and pool funds and other resources via the Internet to assist a cause or invest in a venture. Sometimes, crowdfunding is used to raise funds for charitable purposes, such as disaster relief, but increasingly it is being used to finance budding entrepreneurs. Basic crowdfunding websites include NextSeed and StartEngine.

In 2016, new Securities and Exchange Commission rules went into effect to allow companies to offer and sell securities through crowdfunding. The rules removed a decades-old ban on public solicitation for private investments. In essence, this means that companies can advertise investment opportunities to the public, which will encourage more crowdfunding in the future. The new rules are intended to help smaller companies raise capital while providing investors with additional protections.

Crowdfunding A cooperative activity in which people network and pool funds and other resources via the Internet to assist a cause (such as disaster relief) or invest in a venture (business).

Practice and Review

William Sharp was the sole shareholder and manager of Chickasaw Club, Inc., an S corporation that operated a popular nightclub of the same name in Columbus, Georgia. Sharp maintained a corporate checking account but paid the club's employees, suppliers, and entertainers in cash out of the club's proceeds. Sharp owned the property on which the club was located. He rented it to the club but made mortgage payments out of the club's proceeds and often paid other personal expenses with Chickasaw corporate funds.

At 12:45 A.M. on July 31, eighteen-year-old Aubrey Lynn Pursley, who was already intoxicated, entered the Chickasaw Club. Chickasaw employees did not check Pursley's identification to verify her age, as required by a city ordinance. Pursley drank more alcohol at Chickasaw and was visibly intoxicated when she left the club at 3:00 A.M. with a beer in her hand. Shortly afterward, Pursley lost control of her car, struck a tree, and was killed. Joseph Dancause, Pursley's stepfather, filed a tort lawsuit against Chickasaw Club and William Sharp. Using the information presented in the chapter, answer the following questions.

1. Under what theory might the court in this case make an exception to the limited liability of shareholders and hold Sharp personally liable for the damages? What factors would be relevant to the court's decision?

2. Suppose that Chickasaw's articles of incorporation failed to describe the corporation's purpose or management structure as required by state law. Would the court be likely to rule that Sharp is personally liable to Dancause on that basis? Why or why not?

3. Suppose that the club extended credit to its regular patrons in an effort to maintain a loyal clientele, although neither the articles of incorporation nor the corporate bylaws authorized this practice. Would the corporation likely have the power to engage in this activity? Explain.

4. How would the court classify Chickasaw Club, Inc.—domestic or foreign, public or private?

Debate This

The sole shareholder of an S corporation should not be able to avoid liability for the torts of her or his employees.

Key Terms

Chapter Summary: Corporate Formation and Financing

Nature and Classification	A corporation is a legal entity distinct from its owners. Formal statutory requirements, which vary somewhat from state to state, must be followed in forming a corporation. Under U.S. law, a corporation is recognized as an artificial legal person and enjoys the same rights that U. S. citizens enjoy.

1. *Corporate personnel*—Shareholders, whose liability is limited to the amount of their investments, own the corporation. They elect a board of directors to govern the corporation. The board of directors hires corporate officers and other employees to run the firm's daily business.
2. *Corporate taxation*—The corporation pays income tax on net profits, and shareholders pay income tax on the disbursed dividends that they receive from the corporation (double-taxation feature).
3. *Torts and criminal acts*—The corporation is liable for the torts committed by its agents or officers within the course and scope of their employment (under the doctrine of *respondeat superior*). A corporation can be held liable (and be fined) for the criminal acts of its agents and employees.
4. *Domestic, foreign, and alien corporations*—A corporation is referred to as a *domestic corporation* within its home state (the state in which it incorporates), as a *foreign corporation* by any state that is not its home state, and as an *alien corporation* if it originates in another country but does business in the United States.
5. *Public and private corporations*—A public corporation is formed by a government (for example, a city or town). A private corporation is formed wholly or in part for private benefit. Most corporations are private corporations.
6. *Nonprofit corporations*—Corporations formed without a profit-making purpose.
7. *Close corporations*—Corporations owned by a family or a relatively small number of individuals, often members of the same family. Transfer of shares is usually restricted.
8. *S corporations*—Small domestic corporations that receive special tax treatment under Subchapter S of the Internal Revenue Code. Shareholders enjoy limited liability while avoiding double taxation.
9. *Professional corporations*—Corporations formed by professionals (such as physicians and lawyers). For liability purposes, some courts disregard the corporate form and treat the shareholders as partners.
10. *Benefit corporations*—Corporations formed to benefit the public as a whole and have a material positive impact on society and the environment.

Formation and Powers	

1. *Promotional activities*—A person who enters contracts on behalf of the future corporation is personally liable on all preincorporation contracts until the corporation is formed and assumes the contracts by novation.
2. *Incorporation procedures*—Procedures vary among the states, but the basic steps are as follows:
    a. Select a state of incorporation.
    b. Secure an appropriate corporate name.
    c. Prepare the articles of incorporation. The articles must include the corporate name, the number of shares of stock the corporation is authorized to issue, the names and addresses of the registered office and agent, and the name and address of each incorporator.
    d. File the articles with the secretary of state. The state's filing of the articles authorizes the corporation to conduct business.
3. *First organizational meeting*—The main function of the meeting is to adopt the bylaws, or internal rules of the corporation, but other business, such as election of the board of directors, may also take place.
4. *Improper incorporation*—A corporation that has complied with the conditions for incorporation has *de jure* status. A minor defect in formation generally does not affect this status. If a defect is substantial, courts in some states may hold that the corporation has *de facto* status and treat it as a corporation despite the defect.
5. *Corporation by estoppel*—If a firm is not incorporated but represents itself to be a corporation and is sued as such by a third party, it may be held to be a corporation by estoppel.

(Continues)

    6. *Corporate powers—*

        a. Express and implied powers—The express powers of a corporation are found in its articles of incorporation, in the law of the state of incorporation, and in the state and federal constitutions. Barring express constitutional, statutory, or other prohibitions, the corporation has the implied power to perform all acts reasonably appropriate and necessary to accomplish its corporate purposes.

        b. *Ultra vires* doctrine—Any act of a corporation that is beyond its express or implied powers is an *ultra vires* act and may lead to a lawsuit by the shareholders or the state attorney general.

Piercing the Corporate Veil	To avoid injustice, courts may "pierce the corporate veil" and hold a shareholder or shareholders personally liable. This usually occurs when the corporate privilege is abused for personal benefit or when the corporate business is treated so carelessly that it is indistinguishable from that of a controlling shareholder.
Corporate Financing	**1.** *Bonds*—Securities representing corporate debt—funds borrowed by a corporation.
	2. *Stocks*—Equity securities issued by a corporation that represent the purchase of ownership in the firm. Exhibit 33–1 describes how stocks differ from bonds.
	3. *Venture capital*—Capital provided to new business ventures by professional, outside investors (venture capitalists, usually groups of wealthy investors and securities firms). Venture capital investments are high risk but offer the potential for well-above-average returns at some point in the future.
	4. *Private equity capital*—Private equity firms pool funds from wealthy investors and use this capital to invest in existing corporations. Usually, a private equity firm buys an entire corporation and then reorganizes it.
	5. *Crowdfunding*—A cooperative activity in which people network and pool funds and other resources via the Internet to assist a cause or invest in a venture.

Issue Spotters

1. Name Brand, Inc., is a small business. Twelve members of a single family own all of its stock. Ordinarily, corporate income is taxed at the corporate and shareholder levels. How can Name Brand avoid this double taxation of income? (See *Nature and Classification*.)

2. The incorporators of Consumer Investments, Inc., want their new corporation to have the authority to transact nearly any conceivable type of business. Can they grant this authority to their firm? If so, how? If not, why? (See *Corporation Formation and Powers*.)

    —Check your answers to the *Issue Spotters* against the answers provided in Appendix D at the end of this text.

Business Scenarios and Case Problems

33–1. Preincorporation. Cummings, Okawa, and Taft are recent college graduates who want to form a corporation to manufacture and sell personal computers. Peterson tells them he will set in motion the formation of their corporation. First, Peterson makes a contract with Owens for the purchase of a piece of land for $20,000. Owens does not know of the prospective corporate formation at the time the contract is signed. Second, Peterson makes a contract with Babcock to build a small plant on the property being purchased. Babcock's contract is conditional on the corporation's formation. Peterson secures all necessary capitalization and files the articles of incorporation. Discuss whether the newly formed corporation, Peterson, or both are liable on the contracts with Owens and Babcock. Is the corporation automatically liable to Babcock on formation? Explain. (See *Formation and Powers*.)

33–2. *Ultra Vires* Doctrine. Kora Nayenga and two business associates formed a corporation called Nayenga Corp. for the purpose of selling computer services. Kora, who owned 50 percent of the corporate shares, served as the corporation's president. Kora wished to obtain a personal loan from his bank for $250,000, but the bank required the note to be cosigned by a third party. Kora cosigned the note in the name of the corporation. Later, Kora defaulted on the note, and the bank sued the corporation for payment. The corporation asserted, as a defense, that Kora had exceeded his authority when he cosigned the note. Had he? Explain. (See *Formation and Powers.*)

33–3. Spotlight on Smart Inventions—Piercing the Corporate Veil.
Thomas Persson and Jon Nokes founded Smart Inventions, Inc., to market household consumer products. The success of their first product, the Smart Mop, continued with later products, which were sold through infomercials. Persson and Nokes were the firm's officers and equal shareholders, with Persson responsible for product development and Nokes in charge of day-to-day activities. By 1998, they had become dissatisfied with each other's efforts. Nokes represented the firm as financially "dying," and "in a grim state, . . . worse than ever." He offered to buy all of Persson's shares for $1.6 million, and Persson accepted.

On the day that they signed the agreement to transfer the shares, Smart Inventions began marketing a new product— the Tap Light. It was an instant success, generating millions of dollars in revenues. In negotiating with Persson, Nokes had intentionally kept the Tap Light a secret. Persson sued Smart Inventions, asserting fraud and other claims. Under what principle might Smart Inventions be liable for Nokes's fraud? Is Smart Inventions liable in this case? Explain. [*Persson v. Smart Inventions, Inc.,* 125 Cal.App.4th 1141, 23 Cal.Rptr.3d 335 (2 Dist. 2005)] (See *Formation and Powers.*)

33–4. Business Case Problem with Sample Answer— Piercing the Corporate Veil.
Scott Snapp contracted with Castlebrook Builders, Inc., which was owned by Stephen Kappeler, to remodel a house. Kappeler estimated that the remodeling would cost around $500,000. Eventually, however, Snapp paid Kappeler more than $1.3 million. Snapp filed a suit in an Ohio state court against Castlebrook, alleging breach of contract and fraud, among other things. During the trial, it was revealed that Castlebrook had issued no shares of stock and had commingled personal and corporate funds. The minutes of the corporate meetings all looked exactly the same. In addition, Kappeler could not provide an accounting for the Snapp project. In particular, he could not explain evidence of double and triple billing nor demonstrate that the amount Snapp paid had actually been spent on the remodeling project. Are these sufficient grounds to pierce the corporate veil? Explain. [*Snapp v. Castlebrook Builders, Inc.,* 2014 -Ohio- 163, 7 N.E.3d 574 (2014)] (See *Formation and Powers.*)

—For a sample answer to Problem 33–4, go to Appendix E at the end of this text.

33–5. Torts.
Jennifer Hoffman took her cell phone to a store owned by R&K Trading, Inc., for repairs. Later, Hoffman filed a suit in a New York state court against R&K, Verizon Wireless, Inc., and others, seeking to recover damages for a variety of torts, including infliction of emotional distress and negligent hiring and supervision. She alleged that an R&K employee, Keith Press, had examined her phone in a back room, accessed private photos of her stored on her phone, and disseminated the photos to the public. Hoffman testified that "after the incident, she learned from another R&K employee that personal information and pictures had been removed from the phones of other customers." Can R&K be held liable for the torts of its employees? Explain. [*Hoffman v. Verizon Wireless, Inc.,* 5 N.Y.S.3d 123, 125 A.D.3d 806 (2015)] (See *Nature and Classification.*)

33–6. Piercing the Corporate Veil.
In New York City, 2406-12 Amsterdam Associates, LLC, brought an action in a New York state court against Alianza Dominicana and Alianza, LLC, to recover unpaid rent. The plaintiff asserted cause to pierce the corporate veil, alleging that Alianza Dominicana had made promises to pay its rent while discreetly forming Alianza, LLC, to avoid liability for it. According to 2406-12, Alianza, LLC, was 90 percent owned by Alianza Dominicana, had no employees, and had no function but to hold Alianza Dominicana's assets away from its creditors. The defendants filed a motion to dismiss the plaintiff's claim. Assuming that 2406-12's allegations are true, are there sufficient grounds to pierce Alianza, LLC's corporate veil? Discuss. [*2406-12 Amsterdam Associates, LLC v. Alianza, LLC,* 136 A.D.3d 512, 25 N.Y.S.2d 167 (1 Dept. 2016)] (See *Formation and Powers.*)

33–7. Certificate of Authority.
Armour Pipe Line Company assigned leases to its existing oil wells in Texas to Sandel Energy, Inc. The assignment included royalties for the oil produced from the wells. Armour specified that the assignment "does not pertain to production attributable to these leases from any new wells," reserving for itself an interest in those royalties. Later, Armour—a foreign corporation in Texas—forfeited its certificate of authority to do business in the state. More than three years later, the certificate was reissued. Meanwhile, new wells were drilled on the leases. Sandel filed a suit in a Texas state court against Armour, claiming that the reservation of a royalty interest in those wells was "ineffective" because of the temporary forfeiture. When and why does a corporation need a certificate of authority? Is Armour entitled to the royalties from the new wells? Discuss. [*Armour Pipeline Co. v. Sandel Energy, Inc.,* 546 S.W.3d 455 (Tex.App.—Houston (14th Dist.) 2018)] (See *Nature and Classification.*)

33–8. A Question of Ethics—Piercing the Corporate Veil.

Lester Fulmer sold H2O Lifts and Ramps, LLC (H2O), to Hurt-Hoover Investments, LLC (HHI). HHI agreed to pay $550,000 of the price by a note in thirty-six installments. From the installments, HHI deducted offsets, including charges for expenses incurred before the sale. Meanwhile, HHI incurred annual losses. Its owners, William Hurt and Michael Hoover, contributed funds to keep the firm in business. They followed the statutory business formalities. To collect on the note, Fulmer obtained a judgment in an Arkansas state court against HHI for the unpaid amount. Hurt and Hoover did not dissolve HHI or form another entity to avoid the judgment, but offered to pay it when the profits from H2O became sufficient.[Fulmer v. Hurt, 2017 Ark.App. 117, 515 S.W.3d 129 (2017)] (See Piercing the Corporate Veil.)

1. Should HHI's corporate veil be pierced to hold Hurt and Hoover liable? Why or why not?

2. Did Hurt and Hoover conduct their business according to ethical standards? Explain.

Critical Thinking and Writing Assignments

33–9. Critical Legal Thinking.
If you had started a business, under what circumstances would you be willing to give up a substantial percentage of its ownership to obtain venture capital financing? (See Corporate Financing.)

33–10. Time-Limited Group Assignment—Corporate versus LLC Form of Business.
Although a limited liability company (LLC) may be the best organizational form for most businesses, a significant number of firms may be better off as a corporation or some other form of organization. (See Nature and Classification.)

1. The first group will outline several reasons why a firm might be better off as a corporation than as an LLC.

2. The second group will discuss the differences between corporations and LLCs in terms of their management structure.

Corporate Directors, Officers, and Shareholders

34

> "They [Corporations] cannot commit treason, nor be outlawed nor excommunicated, because they have no soul."

Sir Edward Coke
1552–1634
(English jurist and legal scholar)

When Sir Edward Coke observed, in the chapter-opening quotation, that a corporation has no "soul," he was referring to the fact that a corporation is not a "natural" person but a legal fiction. No one individual shareholder or director bears sole responsibility for the corporation and its actions. Rather, a corporation joins the efforts and resources of a large number of individuals for the purpose of producing greater returns than those persons could have obtained individually.

Corporate directors, officers, and shareholders all play different roles within the corporate entity. Sometimes, actions that benefit the corporation as a whole do not coincide with the separate interests of the individuals making up the corporation. In such situations, it is important to know the rights and duties of all participants in the corporate enterprise.

This chapter focuses on the rights and duties of directors, officers, and shareholders and the ways in which conflicts among them are resolved. You will also read about the ongoing debate over whether shareholders should be able to access corporate proxy materials effortlessly and without cost.

Learning Objectives

The four Learning Objectives *below are designed to help improve your understanding. After reading this chapter, you should be able to answer the following questions:*

1. What three rights do corporate directors possess?

2. What must directors do to avoid liability for honest mistakes of judgment and poor business decisions?

3. What is a voting proxy?

4. If a group of shareholders perceives that the corporation has suffered a wrong and the directors refuse to take action, can the shareholders compel the directors to act? If so, how?

34–1 Directors and Officers

The board of directors is the ultimate authority in every corporation. Directors have responsibility for all policymaking decisions necessary to the management of corporate affairs. The board selects and removes the corporate officers, determines the capital structure of the corporation, and declares dividends.

Directors are sometimes inappropriately characterized as *agents* because they act on behalf of the corporation. No *individual* director, however, can act as an agent to bind the corporation. As a group, directors collectively control the corporation in a way that no agent is able to control a principal.

Few qualifications are legally required for directors. Only a handful of states impose minimum age and residency requirements. A director may be a shareholder, but this is not necessary (unless the articles of incorporation or bylaws require it).

34–1a Election of Directors

Subject to statutory limitations, the number of directors is set forth in the corporation's articles or bylaws. Historically, the minimum number of directors has been three, but today many states permit fewer. Normally, the incorporators appoint the first board of directors at the time the corporation is created. The initial board serves until the first annual shareholders' meeting. Subsequent directors are elected by a majority vote of the shareholders.

Directors usually serve for a term of one year—from annual meeting to annual meeting. Most state statutes permit longer and staggered terms. A common practice is to elect one-third of the board members each year for a three-year term. In this way, there is greater management continuity.

A director can be removed *for cause*—that is, for failing to perform a required duty—either as specified in the articles or bylaws or by shareholder action. When a vacancy occurs or a new position is created through amendment of the articles or bylaws, how the vacancy is filled depends on state law or the provisions of the bylaws. Usually, either the shareholders or the board itself can fill the vacant position by an election. The board cannot attempt to manipulate the election in order to reduce the shareholders' influence, however. If it does, the shareholders can challenge the election in court.

Know This
The articles of incorporation may provide that a director can be removed only for cause.

34–1b Compensation of Directors

In the past, corporate directors rarely were compensated. Today, they are often paid at least nominal sums and may receive more substantial compensation in large corporations because of the time, the work, the effort, and especially the risk involved. Most states permit the corporate articles or bylaws to authorize compensation for directors. In fact, the RMBCA states that unless the articles or bylaws provide otherwise, the board of directors itself may set directors' compensation [RMBCA 8.11].

In many corporations, directors are also chief corporate officers (president or chief executive officer, for instance) and receive compensation in their managerial positions. A director who is also an officer of the corporation is referred to as an **inside director,** whereas a director who does not hold a management position is an **outside director.** Typically, a corporation's board of directors includes both inside and outside directors.

Inside Director A person on the board of directors who is also an officer of the corporation.

Outside Director A person on the board of directors who does not hold a management position at the corporation.

34–1c Board of Directors' Meetings

The board of directors conducts business by holding formal meetings with recorded minutes. The dates of regular meetings are usually established in the articles or bylaws or by board resolution, and ordinarily no further notice is required. Special meetings can be called as well, with notice sent to all directors. Today, most states allow directors to participate in board meetings from remote locations via telephone, Web conferencing, or Skype, provided that all the directors can simultaneously hear each other during the meeting [RMBCA 8.20].

Normally, a majority of the board of directors constitutes a quorum [RMBCA 8.24]. (A **quorum** is the minimum number of members of a body of officials or other group that must be present in order for business to be validly transacted.) Some state statutes, including those

Quorum The number of members of a decision-making body that must be present before business may be transacted.

of Delaware and New York, specifically allow corporations to set a quorum at less than a majority but not less than one-third of the directors.

Once a quorum is present, the directors transact business and vote on issues affecting the corporation. Each director present at the meeting has one vote.[1] Ordinary matters generally require a simple majority vote, but certain extraordinary issues may require a greater-than-majority vote.

34–1d Committees of the Board of Directors

When a board of directors has a large number of members and must deal with myriad complex business issues, meetings can become unwieldy. Therefore, the boards of large publicly held corporations typically create committees of directors and delegate certain tasks to these committees. Committees focus on individual subjects and increase the efficiency of the board.

What are the two most common committees that a board of directors of a large corporation creates?

Two of the most common types of committees are the *executive committee* and the *audit committee*. An executive committee handles interim management decisions between board meetings. It is limited to making decisions about ordinary business matters and does not have the power to declare dividends, amend the bylaws, or authorize the issuance of stock. The Sarbanes-Oxley Act requires all publicly held corporations to have an audit committee. The audit committee is responsible for the selection, compensation, and oversight of the independent public accountants that audit the firm's financial records.

34–1e Rights of Directors

A corporate director must have certain rights to function properly in that position and make informed policy decisions for the company.

1. *Right to participation.* Directors are entitled to participate in all board of directors' meetings and to be notified of these meetings. Because the dates of regular board meetings are usually specified in the bylaws, no notice of these meetings is required. If special meetings are called, however, notice is required unless waived by the director.

2. *Right of inspection.* Each director can access the corporation's books and records, facilities, and premises. Inspection rights are essential for directors to make informed decisions and to exercise the necessary supervision over corporate officers and employees. This right of inspection is almost absolute and cannot be restricted (by the articles, bylaws, or any act of the board).

3. *Right to indemnification.* When a director becomes involved in litigation by virtue of her or his position or actions, the director may have a right to be indemnified (reimbursed) for legal costs, fees, and damages incurred. Most states allow corporations to indemnify and purchase liability insurance for corporate directors [RMBCA 8.51].

Case Example 34.1 NavLink, Inc., a Delaware corporation, provides high-end data management for customers and governments in Saudi Arabia, Qatar, Lebanon, and the United Arab Emirates. NavLink's co-founders, George Chammas and Laurent Delifer, serve on its board of directors.

Chammas and Delifer were concerned about the company's 2015 annual budget and three-year operating plan. Despite repeated requests, Chammas was never given the minutes from several board meetings in 2015. Chammas and Delifer believed that the other directors were withholding information and holding secret "pre-board meetings" at which plans and decisions were being made without them. They filed a lawsuit in a Delaware state court seeking inspection rights.

Learning Objective 1
What three rights do corporate directors possess?

"Executive ability is deciding quickly and getting somebody else to do the work."

John G. Pollard
1871–1937
(American lawyer and politician)

---

1. Except in Louisiana, which allows a director to authorize another person to cast a vote in his or her place under certain circumstances.

The court ordered NavLink to provide the plaintiffs with board meeting minutes and with communications from NavLink's secretary regarding the minutes. The plaintiffs were also entitled to inspect corporate documents and communications concerning NavLink's 2015 budget and three-year plan.[2]

34–1f Corporate Officers and Executives

Corporate officers and other executive employees are hired by the board of directors. At a minimum, most corporations have a president, one or more vice presidents, a secretary, and a treasurer. In most states, an individual can hold more than one office, such as president and secretary, and can be both an officer and a director of the corporation. In addition to carrying out the duties articulated in the bylaws, corporate and managerial officers act as agents of the corporation, and the ordinary rules of agency normally apply to their employment.

Corporate officers and other high-level managers are employees of the company, so their rights are defined by employment contracts. The board of directors, though, normally can remove corporate officers at any time with or without cause. If the directors remove an officer in violation of an employment contract, however, the corporation may be liable for breach of contract.

34–2 Duties and Liabilities of Directors and Officers

Directors and officers are considered fiduciaries of the corporation because their relationship with the corporation and its shareholders is one of trust and confidence. As fiduciaries, directors and officers owe ethical—and legal—duties to the corporation and to the shareholders as a whole. These fiduciary duties include the duty of care and the duty of loyalty.

34–2a Duty of Care

Directors and officers must exercise due care in performing their duties. The standard of due care generally requires a director or officer to act in good faith (honestly) and to exercise the care that an ordinarily prudent person would exercise in similar circumstances. In addition, a director or officer is expected to act in what he or she considers to be the best interests of the corporation [RMBCA 8.30]. Directors or officers whose failure to exercise due care results in harm to the corporation or its shareholders can be held liable for negligence (unless the *business judgment rule* applies, as discussed shortly).

Duty to Make Informed and Reasonable Decisions Directors and officers are expected to be informed on corporate matters and to conduct a reasonable investigation of the relevant situation before making a decision. They must do what is necessary to keep adequately informed: attend meetings and presentations, ask for information from those who have it, read reports, and review other written materials. They cannot make decisions on the spur of the moment without adequate research.

Although directors and officers are expected to act in accordance with their own knowledge and training, they are also normally entitled to rely on information given to them by certain other persons. Most states and Section 8.30(b) of the RMBCA allow a director to make decisions in reliance on information furnished by competent officers or employees. The director may also rely on information provided by professionals (such as attorneys and accountants) and by committees of the board of directors (on which the director does not serve).

---

2. *Chammas v. NavLink, Inc.*, 2016 WL 767714 (Del.Ch.Ct. 2016).

Duty to Exercise Reasonable Supervision Directors are also expected to exercise a reasonable amount of supervision when they delegate work to corporate officers and employees. **Example 34.2** Dale, a corporate bank director, has not attended a board of directors' meeting for five years. In addition, Dale never inspects any of the corporate books or records and generally fails to supervise the efforts of the bank president and the loan committee. Meanwhile, Brennan, the bank president, makes various improper loans and permits large overdrafts. In this situation, Dale can be held liable to the corporation for losses resulting from the unsupervised actions of the bank president and the loan committee. ▪

34–2b The Business Judgment Rule

Directors and officers are expected to exercise due care and to use their best judgment in guiding corporate management, but they are not insurers of business success. Under the **business judgment rule,** a corporate director or officer will not be liable to the corporation or to its shareholders for honest mistakes of judgment or bad business decisions made in good faith.

Courts give significant deference to the decisions of corporate directors and officers, and consider the reasonableness of a decision at the time it was made, *without the benefit of hindsight.* Thus, corporate decision makers are not subjected to second-guessing by shareholders or others in the corporation.

When the Rule Applies The business judgment rule will apply as long as the director or officer did the following:

1. Took reasonable steps to become informed about the matter.
2. Had a rational basis for his or her decision.
3. Did not have a conflict of interest between his or her personal interest and that of the corporation.

Whether these conditions were met formed the basis for the court's decision in the following case.

Business Judgment Rule A rule under which courts will not hold corporate officers and directors liable for honest mistakes of judgment and bad business decisions that were made in good faith.

Learning Objective 2
What must directors do to avoid liability for honest mistakes of judgment and poor business decisions?

■ Case 34.1

Oliveira v. Sugarman
Court of Special Appeals of Maryland, 226 Md.App. 524, 130 A.3d 1085 (2016).

Background and Facts iStar, Inc., a Maryland corporation, promised to award shares of company stock to employees for their performance if the stock averaged a certain target price per share over a specific period. The stock price rose 300 percent, but the target was missed. The board changed the basis for an award from performance to service—an employee who had been with iStar for a certain period was entitled to an award. It then issued additional shares to pay the awards.

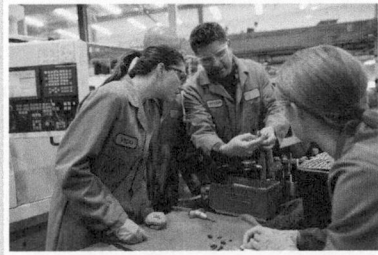
How did the business judgment rule help iStar employees receive a stock award for their tenure with the company?

Albert and Lena Oliveira, iStar shareholders, demanded that the board rescind the awards. The Oliveiras alleged misconduct and demanded that the board file a suit on the company's behalf to seek damages or other relief. The board appointed Barry Ridings, an outside director, to investigate the allegation. Ridings recommended that the board refuse the demand. The board acted on his recommendation.

The Oliveiras filed a suit in a Maryland state court against Jay Sugarman, the board

(Continues)

chairman, and the other directors, including Ridings, alleging a breach of fiduciary duty. The court dismissed the claim. The Oliveiras appealed.

In the Words of the Court
BURGER, J. [Judge]

* * * *

Judicial review of a demand refusal is subject to the business judgment rule, and the court * * * limits its review to whether the board acted independently, in good faith, and within the realm of sound business judgment. [Emphasis added.]

* * * *

* * * The Shareholders [the Oliveiras] assert that [Ridings's] investigation of the Shareholders' demand was rife with improper procedure. The Shareholders argue that * * * Ridings lacked sufficient corporate experience to make a proper recommendation to the Board and that Ridings was not sufficiently disinterested. Both contentions are baseless. Ridings has forty years of business experience, including service on the boards of several public companies, including the American Stock Exchange. Furthermore, Ridings hired highly respected and experienced legal counsel to assist him and conducted multiple interviews.

We further reject the Shareholders' contention that Ridings was interested or lacked independence. Ridings joined the Board after the challenged conduct and had no business, personal, social, or other relationships with any other member of the Board. Although Ridings's employer [Lazard Freres & Company, where Ridings was vice chairman of investment banking] performed banking services for iStar [for two years], Lazard has no ongoing business relationship with iStar. *Furthermore, allegations of*

mere personal friendship or a mere outside business relationship, standing alone, are insufficient to raise a reasonable doubt about a director's independence. [Emphasis added.]

The Shareholders' contention that Ridings lacks independence because he is compensated for his service as a Director is similarly unfounded. The Shareholders further contend that Ridings lacks independence because he is a named defendant in this lawsuit. This assertion is contrary to established law. Accordingly, we reject the Shareholders' contentions that Ridings was interested or lacked independence.

* * * *

In conclusion, the Shareholders have failed to surmount the presumption of the business judgment rule. In failing to do so, they have failed to state a claim upon which relief may be granted.

Decision and Remedy A state intermediate appellate court affirmed the lower court's dismissal of the Oliveiras' claim. "The Shareholders' bald allegations of impropriety are plainly insufficient to overcome the presumption of the business judgment rule."

Critical Thinking

• **Legal Environment** *In a letter to the Oliveiras, the board explained that it saw "no upside—and much downside—to the action and lawsuit proposed in the Demand." What would the "downside" consist of ?*

• **What If the Facts Were Different?** *Only one member of the iStar board—Sugarman—received an award as an employee. The others who made the decision to change the award were, like Ridings, outside directors. Suppose that the opposite had been true. Would the result have been the same?*

The Rule Provides Broad Protections The business judgment rule provides broad protections to corporate decision makers. In fact, most courts will apply the rule unless there is evidence of bad faith, fraud, or a clear breach of fiduciary duties. Consequently, if there is a reasonable basis for the business decision, a court is unlikely to interfere with that decision, even if the corporation suffers as a result. The business judgment rule does not apply, however, when a director engages in fraud, dishonesty, or other intentional or reckless misconduct. For instance, if a director acts without board approval, ignores board rules, and personally mistreats other directors, shareholders, and employees, the business judgment rule may not protect that director.

34–2c Duty of Loyalty

Loyalty can be defined as faithfulness to one's obligations and duties. In the corporate context, the duty of loyalty requires directors and officers to subordinate their personal interests to the welfare of the corporation. Directors cannot use corporate funds or confidential corporate information for personal advantage and must refrain from self-dealing. For instance, a director should not personally take advantage of a business opportunity that is offered to the corporation and is in the corporation's best interest.

Cases dealing with the duty of loyalty typically involve one or more of the following:

1. Competing with the corporation.
2. Usurping (taking advantage of) a corporate opportunity.
3. Having an interest that conflicts with the interest of the corporation.
4. Engaging in insider trading (using information that is not public to make a profit trading securities).
5. Authorizing a corporate transaction that is detrimental to minority shareholders.
6. Selling control over the corporation.

The following *Classic Case* illustrates the conflict that can arise between a corporate official's personal interests and his or her duty of loyalty.

🏛 Classic Case 34.2

Guth v. Loft, Inc.
Supreme Court of Delaware, 23 Del.Ch. 255, 5 A.2d 503 (1939).

Background and Facts In 1930, Charles Guth became the president of Loft, Inc., a candy and restaurant chain. At the time, Guth and his family owned Grace Company, which made syrups for soft drinks in a plant in Baltimore, Maryland. Coca-Cola Company supplied Loft with cola syrup. Unhappy with what he felt was Coca-Cola's high price, Guth entered into an agreement with Roy Megargel to acquire the trademark and formula for Pepsi-Cola and form Pepsi-Cola Corporation.

Neither Guth nor Megargel could finance the new venture, and Grace Company was insolvent. Without the knowledge of Loft's board of directors, Guth used Loft's capital, credit, facilities, and employees to further the Pepsi enterprise. At Guth's direction, a Loft employee made the concentrate for the syrup, which was sent to Grace Company to add sugar and water. Loft charged Grace Company for the concentrate but allowed forty months' credit. Grace charged Pepsi for the syrup but also granted substantial credit. Grace sold the syrup to Pepsi's customers, including Loft, which paid on delivery or within thirty days. Loft also paid for Pepsi's advertising.

Finally, losing profits at its stores as a result of switching from Coca-Cola, Loft filed a suit in a Delaware state court against Guth, Grace, and Pepsi, seeking their Pepsi stock and an accounting. The court entered a judgment in the plaintiff's favor. The defendants appealed to the Delaware Supreme Court.

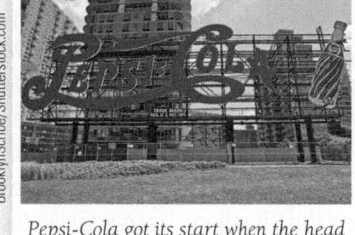

Pepsi-Cola got its start when the head of Loft Candy Company usurped a corporate opportunity.

In the Words of the Court

LAYTON, Chief Justice, delivering the opinion of the court:

* * * *

Corporate officers and directors are not permitted to use their position of trust and confidence to further their private interests. * * * They stand in a fiduciary relation to the corporation and its stockholders. A public policy, existing through the years, and derived from a profound knowledge of human characteristics and motives, has established *a rule that demands of a corporate officer or director, peremptorily [absolutely] and inexorably [unavoidably], the most scrupulous observance of his duty, not only affirmatively to protect the interests of the corporation committed to his charge, but also to refrain from doing anything that would work injury to the corporation* * * *. The rule that requires an undivided and unselfish loyalty to the corporation demands that there shall be no conflict between duty and self-interest. [Emphasis added.]

* * * *

* * * *If there is presented to a corporate officer or director a business opportunity which the corporation is financially able to undertake [that] is* * * * *in the line of the corporation's business and is of practical advantage to it* * * * *and, by embracing the opportunity, the self-interest of the officer or director will be brought into*

(Continues)

*conflict with that of his corporation, the law will not permit him to seize the opportunity for himself. * * * In such circumstances, * * * the corporation may elect to claim all of the benefits of the transaction for itself, and the law will impress a trust in favor of the corporation upon the property, interests and profits so acquired.* [Emphasis added.]

* * * *

* * * The appellants contend that no conflict of interest between Guth and Loft resulted from his acquirement and exploitation of the Pepsi-Cola opportunity [and] that the acquisition did not place Guth in competition with Loft * * * . [In this case, however,] Guth was Loft, and Guth was Pepsi. He absolutely controlled Loft. His authority over Pepsi was supreme. As Pepsi, he created and controlled the supply of Pepsi-Cola syrup, and he determined the price and the terms. What he offered, as Pepsi, he had the power, as Loft, to accept. Upon any consideration of human characteristics and motives, he created a conflict between self-interest and duty. He made himself the judge in his own cause. * * * Moreover, a reasonable probability of injury to Loft resulted from the situation forced upon it. Guth was in the same position to impose his terms upon Loft as had been the Coca-Cola Company.

* * * The facts and circumstances demonstrate that Guth's appropriation of the Pepsi-Cola opportunity to himself placed him in a competitive position with Loft with respect to a commodity essential to it, thereby rendering his personal interests incompatible with the superior interests of his corporation; and this situation was accomplished, not openly and with his own resources, but secretly and with the money and facilities of the corporation which was committed to his protection.

Decision and Remedy The Delaware Supreme Court upheld the judgment of the lower court. The state supreme court was "convinced that the opportunity to acquire the Pepsi-Cola trademark and formula, goodwill and business belonged to [Loft], and that Guth, as its President, had no right to appropriate the opportunity to himself."

Critical Thinking

• **What If the Facts Were Different?** *Suppose that Loft's board of directors had approved Pepsi-Cola's use of its personnel and equipment. Would the court's decision have been different? Discuss.*

• **Impact of This Case on Today's Law** *This early Delaware decision was one of the first to set forth a test for determining when a corporate officer or director has breached the duty of loyalty. The test has two basic parts—whether the opportunity was reasonably related to the corporation's line of business, and whether the corporation was financially able to undertake the opportunity. The court also considered whether the corporation had an interest or expectancy in the opportunity and recognized that when the corporation had "no interest or expectancy, the officer or director is entitled to treat the opportunity as his own."*

34–2d Disclosure of Conflicts of Interest

Corporate directors often have many business affiliations, and a director may sit on the board of more than one corporation. Of course, directors are precluded from entering into or supporting businesses that operate in direct competition with corporations on whose boards they serve. Their fiduciary duty requires them to make a full disclosure of any potential conflicts of interest that might arise in any corporate transaction [RMBCA 8.60].

Sometimes, a corporation enters into a contract or engages in a transaction in which an officer or director has a personal interest. The director or officer must make a *full disclosure* of that interest and must abstain from voting on the proposed transaction.

Example 34.3 Southwood Corporation needs office space. Lambert Alden, one of its five directors, owns the building adjoining the corporation's main office building. He negotiates a lease with Southwood for the space, making a full disclosure to Southwood and the other four directors. The lease arrangement is fair and reasonable, and it is unanimously approved by the other four directors. In this situation, Alden has not breached his duty of loyalty to the corporation, and thus the lease contract is valid. If it were otherwise, directors would be prevented from ever transacting business with the corporations they serve. ▪

34–2e Liability of Directors and Officers

Directors and officers are exposed to liability on many fronts. They are, of course, liable for their own crimes and torts. They also may be held liable for the crimes and torts committed by corporate employees under their supervision.

Additionally, if shareholders perceive that the corporate directors are not acting in the best interests of the corporation, they may sue the directors on behalf of the corporation. (This is known as a *shareholder's derivative suit,* which will be discussed later in this chapter.) Directors and officers can also be held personally liable under a number of statutes, such as those enacted to protect consumers or the environment.

If a director owns this unrented office space, can she offer it for rent to the corporation for which she is a director?

34–3 Shareholders

The acquisition of a share of stock makes a person an owner and shareholder in a corporation. Shareholders thus own the corporation, but they generally are not responsible for its daily management. Although they have no legal title to corporate property, such as buildings and equipment, they do have an equitable (ownership) interest in the firm.

34–3a Shareholders' Powers

Shareholders must approve fundamental changes affecting the corporation before the changes can be implemented. Hence, shareholders are empowered to amend the articles of incorporation and bylaws, approve a merger or the dissolution of the corporation, and approve the sale of all or substantially all of the corporation's assets. Some of these powers are subject to prior board approval. Shareholder approval may also be requested (though it is not required) for certain other actions, such as to approve an independent auditor.

Shareholders also have the power to elect or remove members of the board of directors. As mentioned earlier, the incorporators normally choose the first directors, who serve until the first shareholders' meeting. From that time on, the selection and retention of directors are exclusively shareholder functions.

Directors usually serve their full terms. If the shareholders judge them unsatisfactory, they are simply not reelected. Shareholders have the inherent power, however, to remove a director from office for cause (such as for breach of duty or misconduct) by a majority vote. Some state statutes (and some corporate articles) permit removal of directors without cause by the vote of a majority of the shareholders entitled to vote.

34–3b Shareholders' Meetings

Shareholders' meetings must occur at least annually. In addition, special meetings can be called to deal with urgent matters. A corporation must notify its shareholders of the date, time, and place of an annual or special shareholders' meeting at least ten days, but not more than sixty days, before the meeting date [RMBCA 7.05].[3] Notice of a special meeting must include a statement of the purpose of the meeting, and business transacted at the meeting is limited to that purpose.

Know This
Shareholders normally are not agents of the corporation.

"If it is not in the interest of the public, it is not in the interest of the business."

Joseph H. Defrees
1812–1885
(Member of U.S. Congress, 1865–1867)

Learning Objective 3
What is a voting proxy?

---

3. A shareholder can waive the requirement of written notice by signing a waiver form or, in some states, by attending a meeting without protesting the lack of notice.

Proxies

Proxy In corporate law, formal authorization to serve as a corporate shareholder's agent and vote his or her shares in a certain manner.

Proxies It is usually not practical for owners of only a few shares of stock of publicly traded corporations to attend shareholders' meetings. Therefore, the law allows stockholders to either vote in person or appoint another person as their agent to vote their shares at the meeting. The agent's formal authorization to vote the shares is called a **proxy** (from the Latin *procurare,* meaning "to manage, take care of"). Proxy materials are sent to all shareholders before shareholders' meetings.

Management often solicits proxies, but any person can solicit proxies to concentrate voting power. Proxies have been used by groups of shareholders as a device for taking over a corporation. Proxies normally are revocable (that is, they can be withdrawn), unless they are specifically designated as irrevocable. Under RMBCA 7.22(c), proxies last for eleven months, unless the proxy agreement provides for a longer period.

Shareholder Proposals When shareholders want to change a company policy, they can put their idea up for a shareholder vote. They can do this by submitting a shareholder proposal to the board of directors and asking the board to include the proposal in the proxy materials that are sent to all shareholders before meetings.

Rules for Proxies and Shareholder Proposals The Securities and Exchange Commission (SEC), which regulates the purchase and sale of securities, has special provisions relating to proxies and shareholder proposals. SEC Rule 14a-8 provides that all shareholders who own stock worth at least $1,000 are eligible to submit proposals for inclusion in corporate proxy materials. The corporation is required to include information on whatever proposals will be considered at the shareholders' meeting along with proxy materials.

Under the SEC's e-proxy rules,[4] all public companies must post their proxy materials on the Internet and notify shareholders how to find that information. Although the law requires proxy materials to be posted online, public companies may still choose among several options—including paper documents and DVDs sent by mail—for delivering the materials to shareholders.

34–3c Shareholder Voting

Shareholders exercise ownership control through the power of their votes. Corporate business matters are presented in the form of *resolutions,* which shareholders vote to approve or disapprove. Each common shareholder is entitled to one vote per share. The articles of incorporation can exclude or limit voting rights, particularly for certain classes of shares. For instance, owners of *preferred stock* usually are denied the right to vote.

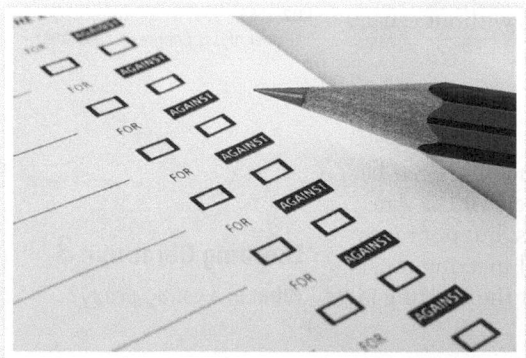

Why is shareholder voting important in the management of a corporation?

Quorum Requirements For shareholders to act during a meeting, a quorum must be present. Generally, a quorum exists when shareholders holding more than 50 percent of the outstanding shares are present, but state laws often permit the articles of incorporation to set higher or lower quorum requirements.

Case Example 34.4 Sink & Rise, Inc., had eighty-four shares of voting common stock outstanding. James Case owned twenty shares. In addition, he and his estranged wife, Shirley, jointly owned another sixteen shares. Three different individuals owned sixteen shares each. During a shareholders' meeting, James was the only shareholder present. He elected himself and another shareholder to be directors, replacing Shirley as Sink & Rise's secretary. Shirley sued to set aside the election, claiming the sixteen shares that she owned jointly with James should not have been counted for quorum purposes.

kenneth-cheung/iStock/Getty Images

---

4. 17 C.F.R. Parts 240, 249, and 274.

A court, however, held that the shares Shirley owned jointly with James counted for purposes of quorum. The Wyoming Supreme Court affirmed the lower court's judgment. Corporate bylaws required that, in determining a quorum, the shares had to be entitled to vote and represented in person or by proxy. Because the sixteen shares that were jointly held were represented in person by James at the shareholders' meeting, they could be counted for quorum purposes. Consequently, the actions taken at the meeting were accomplished with authority, and Shirley was no longer the company's secretary.[5]

Voting Requirements Once a quorum is present, voting can proceed. If a state statute requires specific voting procedures, the corporation's articles or bylaws must be consistent with the statute.

Normally, a majority vote of the shares represented at the meeting is required to pass resolutions. At times, more than a simple majority vote is required, either by a state statute or by the corporate articles. Extraordinary corporate matters, such as a merger, consolidation, or dissolution of the corporation, require approval by a higher percentage of all corporate shares entitled to vote [RMBCA 7.27].

Cumulative Voting Most states permit, and some require, shareholders to elect directors by *cumulative voting*. This voting method is designed to allow minority shareholders to be represented on the board of directors.[6]

With cumulative voting, each shareholder is entitled to a total number of votes equal to the number of board members to be elected multiplied by the number of voting shares the shareholder owns. The shareholder can cast all of these votes for one candidate or split them among several candidates. All candidates stand for election at the same time.

Example 34.5 Nak Corporation has 10,000 shares issued and outstanding. The minority shareholders hold 3,000 shares, and the majority shareholders hold the other 7,000 shares. Three members of the board are to be elected. The majority shareholders' nominees are Acevedo, Barkley, and Craycik. The minority shareholders' nominee is Drake. Can Drake be elected by the minority shareholders?

If cumulative voting is allowed, the answer is yes. Together, the minority shareholders have 9,000 votes (3 directors to be elected times 3,000 shares held by minority shareholders equals 9,000 votes). All of these votes can be cast to elect Drake. The majority shareholders have 21,000 votes (3 times 7,000 equals 21,000), but these votes have to be distributed among their three nominees. No matter how the majority shareholders cast their 21,000 votes, they will not be able to elect all three directors if the minority shareholders cast all of their 9,000 votes for Drake, as illustrated in Exhibit 34–1.

In contrast, in "regular" voting, each candidate is elected by a simple majority. A shareholder cannot give more than one vote per share to any single nominee.

> **Know This**
> Once a quorum is present, a vote can be taken even if some shareholders leave without casting their votes.

---

5. *Case v. Sink & Rise, Inc.*, 2013 WY 19, 297 P.3d 762 (2013).

6. See, for instance, California Corporations Code Section 708. Under RMBCA 7.28, however, no cumulative voting rights exist unless the articles of incorporation provide for them.

Exhibit 34–1 Results of Cumulative Voting

BALLOT	MAJORITY SHAREHOLDERS' VOTES			MINORITY SHAREHOLDERS' VOTES	DIRECTORS ELECTED
	Acevedo	**Barkley**	**Craycik**	**Drake**	
1	10,000	10,000	1,000	9,000	Acevedo/Barkley/Drake
2	9,001	9,000	2,999	9,000	Acevedo/Barkley/Drake
3	6,000	7,000	8,000	9,000	Barkley/Craycik/Drake

Other Voting Techniques Before a shareholders' meeting, a group of shareholders can agree in writing to vote their shares together in a specified manner. Such agreements, called *shareholder voting agreements,* usually are held to be valid and enforceable. As noted earlier, a shareholder can also appoint a voting agent and vote by proxy.

34–4 Rights and Duties of Shareholders

Shareholders possess numerous rights in addition to the right to vote their shares, and we examine several here.

34–4a Stock Certificates

Stock Certificate A certificate issued by a corporation evidencing the ownership of a specified number of shares in the corporation.

In the past, shareholders had a right to **stock certificates** that evidenced ownership of a specified number of shares in the corporation. Only a few jurisdictions still require physical stock certificates. Shareholders there have the right to demand that the corporation issue certificates (or replace those that were lost or destroyed). Stock is intangible personal property, however, and the ownership right exists independently of the certificate itself.

In most states today and under RMBCA 6.26, boards of directors may provide that shares of stock will be uncertificated, or "paperless"—that is, no physical stock certificates will be issued. Notice of shareholders' meetings, dividends, and operational and financial reports are distributed according to the ownership lists recorded in the corporation's books.

34–4b Preemptive Rights

Preemptive Right The right of a shareholder in a corporation to have the first opportunity to purchase a new issue of that corporation's stock in proportion to the amount of stock already owned by the shareholder.

Sometimes, the articles of incorporation grant preemptive rights to shareholders [RMBCA 6.30]. With **preemptive rights,** a shareholder receives a preference over all other purchasers to subscribe to or purchase a prorated share of a new issue of stock. Generally, preemptive rights apply only to additional, newly issued stock and must be exercised within a specified time period (usually thirty days).

A shareholder who is given preemptive rights can purchase a percentage of the new shares being issued that is equal to the percentage of shares she or he already holds in the company. This allows each shareholder to maintain her or his proportionate control, voting power, and financial interest in the corporation.

Example 34.6 Alisha is a shareholder who owns 10 percent of a company. Because she has preemptive rights, she can buy 10 percent of any new issue (to maintain her 10 percent position). Thus, if the corporation issues one thousand more shares, Alisha can buy one hundred of them. ■

Preemptive rights are most important in close corporations because each shareholder owns a relatively small number of shares but controls a substantial interest in the corporation. Without preemptive rights, it would be possible for a shareholder to lose his or her proportionate control over the firm.

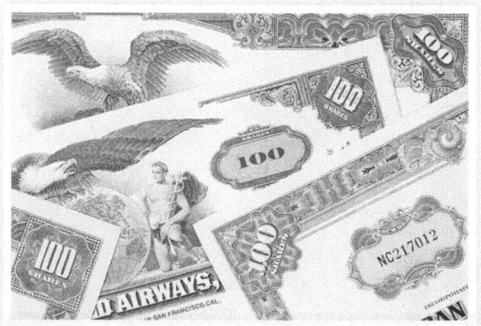

Does the number of shares you hold determine your rights as a shareholder?

34–4c Dividends

As mentioned, a *dividend* is a distribution of corporate profits or income ordered by the directors and paid to the shareholders in proportion to their shares in the corporation. Dividends can be paid in cash, property, stock of the corporation that is paying the dividends, or stock of other corporations.[7] On one occasion, a distillery declared and paid a "dividend" in bonded whiskey.

---

7. Technically, dividends paid in stock are not dividends. They maintain each shareholder's proportionate interest in the corporation.

State laws vary, but each state determines the general circumstances and legal requirements under which dividends are paid. State laws also control the sources of revenue to be used. All states allow dividends to be paid from the undistributed net profits earned by the corporation, for instance, and a number of states allow dividends to be paid out of any surplus.

Illegal Dividends Dividends are illegal if they are improperly paid from an unauthorized account, or if their payment causes the corporation to become insolvent (unable to pay its debts as they come due). Whenever dividends are illegal or improper, the board of directors can be held personally liable for the amount of the payment.

Directors' Failure to Declare a Dividend When directors fail to declare a dividend, shareholders can ask a court to compel the directors to do so. To succeed, the shareholders must show that the directors have acted so unreasonably in withholding the dividend that their conduct is an abuse of their discretion. The mere fact that the firm has sufficient earnings or surplus available to pay a dividend is not enough to compel directors to distribute funds that, in the board's opinion, should not be distributed. There must be a clear abuse of discretion.

34–4d Inspection Rights

Shareholders in a corporation enjoy both common law and statutory inspection rights. The RMBCA provides that every shareholder is entitled to examine specified corporate records for a *proper purpose,* provided the request is made in advance. The shareholder can inspect in person or have an attorney, accountant, or other authorized agent do so. In some states, a shareholder must have held shares for a minimum period of time immediately preceding the demand to inspect or must hold a minimum number of outstanding shares.

The power of inspection is fraught with potential abuses, and the corporation is allowed to protect itself from them. For instance, a corporation can properly deny a shareholder access to corporate records to prevent harassment or to protect trade secrets or other confidential corporate information.

Case Example 34.7 Trading Block Holdings, Inc., offers online brokerage services. On April 1, some Trading Block shareholders, including Sunlitz Holding Company, sent a letter (through an attorney) asking to inspect specific items in the corporation's books and records. This letter indicated that the purpose was to determine the company's financial condition, how it was being managed, and whether its financial practices were appropriate. The letter also stated that the shareholders wanted to know whether Trading Block's management had engaged in any self-dealing that had negatively impacted the company as a whole.

On April 30, Trading Block responded with a letter stating that the plaintiffs were on a "fishing expedition" and did not have a proper purpose for inspecting the corporate records. Eventually, the shareholders filed a motion to compel inspection in an Illinois state court. The trial court denied the plaintiffs' motion. On appeal, the reviewing court reversed. The court held that the plaintiffs' allegations of self-dealing constituted a proper purpose for their inspection request.[8] ■

In the following case, the court considered whether a corporation can deny a shareholder access to its records based on the circumstances under which the shareholder acquired the shares.

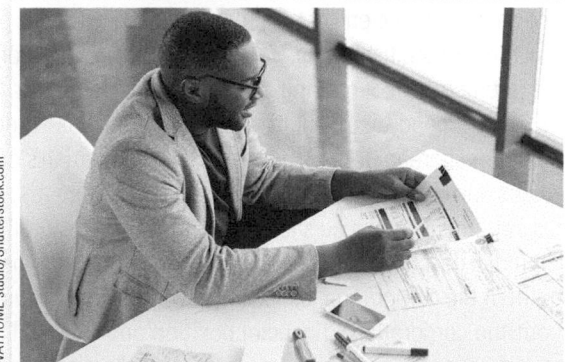

How does a shareholder's right to inspect corporate books help or hurt a corporation?

---

8. *Sunlitz Holding Co., v. Trading Block Holdings, Inc.,* 2014 IL App(1st) 133938, 17 N.E.3d 715 (4 Dist. 2014).

Case 34.3

Hammoud v. Advent Home Medical, Inc.
Michigan Court of Appeals, 2018 WL 1072988 (2018).

Background and Facts Advent Home Medical, Inc., is a family-owned close corporation. Carlia Cichon is Advent's president. Her daughter Amanda Hammoud owns 400 shares of Advent stock, representing 40 percent of the total shares. Hammoud submitted a written request to Cichon to review Advent's financial records. Advent did not respond. Hammoud filed a complaint in a Michigan state court against the corporation, seeking an order to compel the firm to permit an inspection of the materials. Advent asserted that Hammoud had procured her shares through fraud, threats, and duress. Hammoud filed a motion to compel Advent to permit the inspection. She attached a notarized transfer of stock certificate verifying her status as a shareholder. The court granted the motion, ordering the production of the information that Hammoud sought. Advent appealed.

In the Words of the Court
PER CURIAM. [By the Whole Court]

The Michigan Business Corporation Act (MBCA) grants shareholders certain rights to examine corporate books and records. *A simple written request suffices to compel the production of some records. To review others, a shareholder must advance a proper purpose.* [Emphasis added.]

* * * *

* * * Hammoud sent a letter to Cichon seeking Advent's balance sheet from the end of the preceding fiscal year, "its statement of income for the fiscal year," "and, if prepared by the corporation, its statement of source and application for funds for the fiscal year." Hammoud also sought to inspect Advent's "stock ledger and list of shareholders" as well as "the corporation's accounting records, including its general ledgers, bank statements, profit and loss statements, balance sheets, tax returns and payroll records." Hammoud described that her interest was "to monitor the financial health of the corporation, especially given recent communications about the corporation's financial position and financial decisions reducing benefits and payments to shareholders and employees." Hammoud additionally asserted that she needed the records "to

affirm" her "ownership/shareholder share" and to ensure that Advent was "in compliance with its Articles of Incorporation, Bylaws, and Policies and Procedures."

* * * *

Advent's fraud-related defenses to Hammoud's records request are simply irrelevant. *The [MBCA] is unambiguous: a "shareholder" has a right to inspect corporate books if certain prerequisites are met.* Hammoud easily satisfied the definition of a shareholder; she presented documents verifying that status. Advent produced no evidence to the contrary. How or why Hammoud became a shareholder is not probative [indicative] of whether she is, in fact, a shareholder. Nor does such evidence create a material issue in an action brought to enforce shareholder rights. [Emphasis added.]

* * * *

* * * A shareholder who has a genuine, good faith interest in the corporation's welfare or her own as a shareholder is entitled to inspect those corporate books that bear on her concerns. Hammoud's letter satisfied that standard.

Decision and Remedy A state intermediate appellate court affirmed the lower court's order compelling Advent to produce the records that Hammoud sought to inspect. "Hammoud was a shareholder when she sent her written request [and she] supplied a proper purpose for all the records she requested."

Critical Thinking

• **Legal Environment** *Cichon insisted that she had transferred shares in Advent to Hammoud only because her daughter had threatened to prevent Cichon from visiting her grandchildren. Should the court have been persuaded by this argument to deny Hammoud's motion? Explain.*

• **What If the Facts Were Different?** *Suppose that Hammoud had stated her purpose for an inspection of Advent's records as "speculation of mismanagement." Would the result have been different? Discuss.*

34–4e **Transfer of Shares**

Corporate stock represents an ownership right in intangible personal property. The law generally recognizes the right to transfer stock to another person unless there are valid restrictions on its transferability, such as frequently occur with close corporation stock.

Restrictions must be reasonable and can be set out in the bylaws or in a shareholder agreement.

When shares are transferred, a new entry is made in the corporate stock book to indicate the new owner. Until the corporation is notified and the entry is complete, all rights—including voting rights and the right to dividend distributions—remain with the currently recorded owner.

34–4f The Shareholder's Derivative Suit

When the corporation is harmed by the actions of a third party, the directors can bring a lawsuit in the name of the corporation against that party. If the corporate directors fail to bring a lawsuit, shareholders can do so "derivatively" in what is known as a **shareholder's derivative suit.**

The right of shareholders to bring a derivative action is especially important when the wrong suffered by the corporation results from the actions of corporate directors or officers. For obvious reasons, the directors and officers would probably be unwilling to take any action against themselves.

Shareholder's Derivative Suit
A suit brought by a shareholder to enforce a corporate cause of action against a third person.

Written Demand Required Before shareholders can bring a derivative suit, they must submit a written demand to the corporation, asking the board of directors to take appropriate action [RMBCA 7.40]. The directors then have ninety days in which to act. Only if they refuse to do so can the derivative suit go forward. In addition, a court will dismiss a derivative suit if the majority of directors or an independent panel determines in good faith that the lawsuit is not in the best interests of the corporation [RMBCA 7.44].

Damages Recovered Go into Corporate Funds When shareholders bring a derivative suit, they are not pursuing rights or benefits for themselves personally but are acting as guardians of the corporate entity. Therefore, if the suit is successful, any damages recovered normally go into the corporation's treasury, not to the shareholders personally.

Learning Objective 4
If a group of shareholders perceives that the corporation has suffered a wrong and the directors refuse to take action, can the shareholders compel the directors to act? If so, how?

Example 34.8 Zeon Corporation is owned by two shareholders, each holding 50 percent of the corporate shares. One of the shareholders wants to sue the other for misusing corporate assets. In this situation, the plaintiff-shareholder will have to bring a shareholder's derivative suit (not a suit in his or her own name) because the alleged harm was suffered by Zeon, not by the plaintiff personally. Any damages awarded will go to the corporation, not to the plaintiff-shareholder.

34–4g Duties of Majority Shareholders

In some instances, a majority shareholder is regarded as having a fiduciary duty to the corporation and to the minority shareholders. This occurs when a single shareholder (or a few shareholders acting in concert) owns a sufficient number of shares to exercise *de facto* (actual) control over the corporation. In these situations, which commonly involve close corporations, majority shareholders owe a fiduciary duty to the minority shareholders.

When a majority shareholder breaches her or his fiduciary duty to a minority shareholder, the minority shareholder can sue for damages. A breach of fiduciary duties by those who control a close corporation normally constitutes what is known as *oppressive conduct*. A common example of a breach of fiduciary duty occurs when the majority shareholders "freeze out" the minority shareholders and exclude them from certain benefits of participating in the firm.

Example 34.9 Brodie, Jordan, and Barbara form a close corporation to operate a machine shop. Brodie and Jordan own 75 percent of the shares in the company, but all three are directors. After disagreements arise, Brodie asks the company to purchase his shares, but his requests are refused. A few years later, Brodie dies, and his wife, Ella, inherits his shares. Jordan and Barbara refuse to perform a valuation of the company, deny Ella access to the corporate information she requests, do not declare any dividends, and refuse to elect Ella as a director. In this situation, the majority shareholders have violated their fiduciary duty to Ella.

Practice and Review

David Brock was on the board of directors of Firm Body Fitness, Inc., which owned a string of fitness clubs in New Mexico. Brock owned 15 percent of the Firm Body stock and was also employed as a tanning technician at one of the fitness clubs. After the January financial report showed that Firm Body's tanning division was operating at a substantial net loss, the board of directors, led by Marty Levinson, discussed terminating the tanning operations. Brock successfully convinced a majority of the board that the tanning division was necessary to market the clubs' overall fitness package. By April, the tanning division's financial losses had risen. The board hired a business analyst, who conducted surveys and determined that the tanning operations did not significantly increase membership.

A shareholder, Diego Peñada, discovered that Brock owned stock in Sunglow, Inc., the company from which Firm Body purchased its tanning equipment. Peñada notified Levinson, who privately reprimanded Brock. Shortly thereafter, Brock and Mandy Vail, who owned 37 percent of the Firm Body stock and also held shares of Sunglow, voted to replace Levinson on the board of directors. Using the information presented in the chapter, answer the following questions.

1. What duties did Brock, as a director, owe to Firm Body?

2. Does the fact that Brock owned shares in Sunglow establish a conflict of interest? Why or why not?

3. Suppose that Firm Body brought an action against Brock claiming that he had breached the duty of loyalty by not disclosing his interest in Sunglow to the other directors. What theory might Brock use in his defense?

4. Now suppose that Firm Body did not bring an action against Brock. What type of lawsuit might Peñada be able to bring based on these facts?

Debate This

Because most shareholders never bother to vote for directors, shareholders have no real control over corporations.

Key Terms

business judgment rule 811
inside director 808
outside director 808

preemptive rights 818
proxy 816
quorum 808

shareholder's derivative suit 821
stock certificate 818

Chapter Summary: Corporate Directors, Officers, and Shareholders

Directors and Officers	1. *Directors*—Directors are responsible for all policymaking decisions necessary to the management of corporate affairs. Directors are elected by the shareholders and usually serve a one-year term. Compensation is usually specified in the corporate articles or bylaws. The board conducts business by holding formal meetings with recorded minutes. Directors' rights include the rights of participation, inspection, and indemnification. 2. *Corporate officers and executives*—Corporate officers and other executive employees are normally hired by the board of directors and have the rights defined by their employment contracts.
Duties and Liabilities of Directors and Officers	1. *Duty of care*—Directors and officers are obligated to act in good faith, to use prudent business judgment in the conduct of corporate affairs, and to act in the corporation's best interests. If a director fails to exercise this duty of care, she or he can be answerable to the corporation and to the shareholders. 2. *The business judgment rule*—This rule immunizes directors and officers from liability for honest mistakes of judgment or bad business decisions made in good faith. 3. *Duty of loyalty*—Directors and officers have a fiduciary duty to subordinate their own interests to those of the corporation in matters relating to the corporation. 4. *Conflicts of interest*—To fulfill their duty of loyalty, directors and officers must make a full disclosure of any potential conflicts between their personal interests and those of the corporation. 5. *Liability*—Directors and officers are liable for their own crimes and torts, and may be liable for the crimes and torts committed by corporate employees under their supervision.

Shareholders	1. *Shareholders' powers*—Shareholders must approve all fundamental changes affecting the corporation and elect the board of directors.
	
	2. *Shareholders' meetings*—Shareholders' meetings must occur at least annually. Special meetings can be called when necessary. Notice of the date, time, and place of the meeting (and its purpose, if it is specially called) must be sent to shareholders. Shareholders may vote by proxy and may submit proposals to be included in the proxy materials sent to shareholders before meetings.
	
	3. *Shareholder voting*—Shareholder voting requirements and procedures are as follows:
	  a. A minimum number of shareholders (a quorum) must be present at a meeting for business to be conducted. Resolutions are usually passed by simple majority vote.
	  b. Cumulative voting may be required or permitted. Cumulative voting gives minority shareholders a better chance to be represented on the board of directors.
	  c. A shareholder voting agreement (in which shareholders agree to vote their shares together) is usually held to be valid and enforceable.

Rights and Duties of Shareholders	Shareholders have numerous rights, which may include preemptive rights, the right to dividends, inspection rights, the right to transfer shares, and the right to sue on behalf of the corporation (bring a shareholder's derivative suit). A majority shareholder may be regarded as having a fiduciary duty to the corporation and to minority shareholders. A breach of fiduciary duties by those who control a close corporation normally constitutes oppressive conduct.

Issue Spotters

1. Wonder Corporation has an opportunity to buy stock in XL, Inc. The directors decide that instead of buying the stock in the name of the corporation, they will buy it for themselves. Yvon, a Wonder shareholder, learns of the purchase and wants to sue the directors on Wonder's behalf. Can she do it? Explain. (See *Shareholders*.)

2. Nico is Omega Corporation's majority shareholder. He owns enough stock in Omega that if he were to sell it, the sale would be a transfer of control of the firm. Discuss whether Nico owes a duty to Omega or the minority shareholders in selling his shares. (See *Rights and Duties of Shareholders*.)

   —Check your answers to the *Issue Spotters* against the answers provided in Appendix D at the end of this text.

Business Scenarios and Case Problems

34–1. Conflicts of Interest. Oxy Corp. is negotiating with the Wick Construction Co. for the renovation of the Oxy corporate headquarters. Wick, the owner of the Wick Construction Co., is also one of the five members of Oxy's board of directors. The contract terms are standard for this type of contract. Wick has previously informed two of the other directors of his interest in the construction company. Oxy's board approves the contract by a three-to-two vote, with Wick voting with the majority. Discuss whether this contract is binding on the corporation. (See *Directors and Officers*.)

34–2. Liability of Directors. AstroStar, Inc., has approximately five hundred shareholders. Its board of directors consists of three members—Eckhart, Dolan, and Macero. At a regular board meeting, the board selects Galiard as president of the corporation by a two-to-one vote, with Eckhart dissenting. The minutes of the meeting do not register Eckhart's dissenting vote. Later, an audit reveals that Galiard is a former convict and has embezzled $500,000 from the corporation that is not covered by insurance. Can the corporation hold directors Eckhart, Dolan, and Macero personally liable? Discuss. (See *Duties and Liabilities of Directors and Officers*.)

34–3. Voting Techniques. Algonquin Corp. has issued and has outstanding 100,000 shares of common stock. Four stockholders own 60,000 of these shares, and for the past six years they have nominated a slate of candidates for membership on the board, all of whom have been elected. Sergio and twenty other shareholders, owning 20,000 shares, are dissatisfied with corporate management and want a representative on the board who shares their views. Explain under what circumstances Sergio and the twenty other shareholders can elect their representative to the board. (See *Shareholders*.)

34–4. Duties of Majority Shareholders. Bill McCann was the president and chief executive officer of McCann Ranch & Livestock Co. He and his brother Ron each owned 36.7 percent of the stock. Ron had been removed from the board of directors on their father's death, however, and was not authorized to work for the firm. Their mother, Gertrude, owned the rest of the stock, which was to pass to Bill on her death. The corporation paid Gertrude's personal expenses in an amount that represented about 75 percent of the net corporate income. Bill received regular salary increases. The corporation did not issue a dividend. Was Ron the victim of a freeze-out? Discuss. [*McCann v. McCann*, 152 Idaho 809, 275 P.3d 824 (2012)] (See *Rights and Duties of Shareholders*.)

34–5. Business Case Problem with Sample Answer—Business Judgment Rule. Country Contractors, Inc., contracted to provide excavation services for A Westside Storage of Indianapolis, Inc., but did not complete the job and later filed for bankruptcy. Stephen Songer and Jahn Songer were Country's sole shareholders. The Songers had not misused the corporate form to engage in fraud. The firm had not been undercapitalized, personal and corporate funds had not been commingled, and Country had kept accounting records and minutes of its annual board meetings. Are the Songers personally liable for Country's failure to complete its contract? Explain. [*Country Contractors, Inc. v. A Westside Storage of Indianapolis, Inc.*, 4 N.E.3d 677 (Ind.App. 2014)] (See *Duties and Liabilities of Directors and Officers*.)

—For a sample answer to Problem 34–5, go to Appendix E at the end of this text.

34–6. Rights of Shareholders. FCR Realty, LLC, and Clifford B. Green & Sons, Inc., were co-owned by three brothers—Frederick, Clifford Jr., and Richard Green. Each brother was a shareholder of the corporation. Frederick was a controlling shareholder, as well as president. Each brother owned a one-third interest in the LLC. Clifford believed that Frederick had misused LLC and corporate funds to pay nonexistent debts and liabilities and had diverted LLC assets to the corporation. He also contended that Frederick had disbursed about $1.8 million in corporate funds to Frederick's own separate business. Clifford hired an attorney and filed an action on behalf of the two companies against Frederick for a breach of fiduciary duty. Frederick argued that Clifford lacked the knowledge necessary to adequately represent the companies' interest because he did not understand financial statements. Can Clifford maintain the action against Frederick? If so, and if the suit is successful, who recovers the damages? Explain. [*FCR Realty, LLC v. Green*, 2016 WL 571449 (Conn. Super. 2016)] (See *Shareholders*.)

34–7. Duties and Liabilities of Directors and Officers. M&M Country Store, Inc. operated a gas station and convenience store. Debra Kelly bought M&M from Mary Millett. Under the purchase agreement, Millett was to remain as the corporation's sole shareholder until the price was fully paid. A default on any payment would result in the return of M&M to Millett. During Kelly's management of M&M, taxes were not remitted, vendors were not paid, repairs were not made, and the store's gas tanks and shelves were often empty. Kelly commingled company and personal funds, kept inaccurate records, and allowed M&M's business licenses and insurance policies to lapse. After she defaulted on her payments to Millett and surrendered M&M, the company incurred significant expenses to pay outstanding bills and replenish the inventory. Can M&M recover these costs from Kelly? Explain. [*M&M Country Store, Inc. v. Kelly,* 159 A.D.3d 1102, 71 N.Y.S.3d 707 (3 Dept. 2018)] (See *Duties and Liabilities of Directors and Officers.*)

34–8. A Question of Ethics—The IDDR Approach and Duties of Directors and Officers. *Hewlett-Packard Company (HP) hired detectives to secretly monitor the phones and e-mail accounts of its directors to find the sources of leaks of company information to the media. When the government learned of the monitoring, criminal charges were brought against HP's then-chairwoman and general counsel. Mark Hurd, HP's chief executive officer, was found free of wrongdoing. The scandal had the effect of bolstering Hurd's reputation for integrity, and he became both chairman and CEO. In congressional testimony, press releases, and investor briefings, Hurd proclaimed HP's integrity and its intent to enforce violations of its corporate code of ethics, the Standards of Business Conduct (SBC). Hurd's statements concerning HP's commitment to ethics and compliance with the SBC reassured investors and the public, and kept HP's stock prices from falling.*

Meanwhile, an independent contractor for HP accused Hurd of sexual harassment. An investigation by HP's board found no harassment, but revealed that Hurd lied about his personal relationship with the woman and falsified expense reports to cover it up. Hurd resigned, causing the price of HP stock to drop. A group of shareholders sued HP claiming that Hurd's unethical behavior while promoting HP's commitment to ethics constituted fraud. [Retail Wholesale and Department Store Union Local 338 Retirement Fund v. Hewlett-Packard Co., 845 F.3d 1268 (9th Cir. 2017)] (See Directors and Officers.*)*

1. Using the *Discussion* step of the IDDR approach, consider whether Hurd's conduct constituted an ethical violation against HP and its shareholders.

2. Using the *Review* step of the IDDR approach, evaluate HP's decision to monitor its directors' phones.

Critical Thinking and Writing Assignments

34–9.Time-Limited Group Assignment—Shareholders' Duties. Milena Weintraub and Larry Griffith were shareholders in Grand Casino, Inc., which operated a casino in South Dakota. Griffith owned 51 percent of the stock and Weintraub 49 percent. Weintraub managed the casino, which Griffith typically visited once a week. At the end of 2012, an accounting audit showed that the cash on hand was less than the amount posted in the casino's books. Later, more shortfalls were discovered. In October 2014, Griffith did a complete audit. Weintraub was unable to account for $200,500 in missing cash. Griffith kept all of the casino's most recent profits, including Weintraub's $90,447.20 share, and, without telling Weintraub, sold the casino for $400,000 and kept all of the proceeds. Weintraub filed a suit against Griffith, asserting a breach of fiduciary duty. Griffith countered with evidence of Weintraub's misappropriation of corporate cash. (See *Shareholders.*)

1. The first group will discuss the duties that these parties owed to each other and determine whether Weintraub or Griffith, or both, breached those duties.

2. The second group will decide how this dispute should be resolved and who should pay what to whom to reconcile the finances.

3. The third group will discuss whether Weintraub or Griffin violated any ethical duties to each other or to the corporation.

Stock photo © Maxiphoto

35

Corporate Mergers, Takeovers, and Termination

Learning Objectives

The four Learning Objectives *below are designed to help improve your understanding of the chapter. After reading this chapter, you should be able to answer the following questions:*

1. What are the basic differences between a merger, a consolidation, and a share exchange?

2. Under what circumstances is a corporation that purchases the assets of another corporation responsible for the liabilities of the selling corporation?

3. What actions might a target corporation take to resist a takeover attempt?

4. What are the two ways in which a corporation can be voluntarily dissolved?

"Business is a combination of war and sport."

André Maurois
1885–1967
(French author and historian)

During the later part of the twentieth century, the acquisition of corporations by other corporations became a common phenomenon, and corporate takeovers have continued into the twenty-first century. Observers of the numerous corporate takeovers occurring in the business world today might well conclude, as André Maurois did in the chapter-opening quotation, that business is indeed a "combination of war and sport."

A corporation often extends its operations by combining with another corporation through a merger, a consolidation, a share exchange, a purchase of assets, or a purchase of a controlling interest in the other corporation. This chapter will examine these types of corporate expansion. Dissolution and winding up (liquidation) are the combined processes by which a corporation terminates its existence. The latter part of this chapter will discuss the typical reasons for—and methods used in—terminating a corporation's existence.

35–1 Merger, Consolidation, and Share Exchange

A corporation may extend its operations by combining with another corporation through a merger, a consolidation, or a share exchange. The terms *merger* and *consolidation* traditionally referred to two legally distinct proceedings, but some people today use the term *consolidation* to refer to all types of combinations. Whether a combination is a merger, a consolidation, or a share exchange, the rights and liabilities of shareholders, the corporation, and the corporation's creditors are the same.

35–1a Merger

A **merger** involves the legal combination of two or more corporations in such a way that only one of the corporations continues to exist. **Example 35.1** Corporation A and Corporation B decide to merge. They agree that A will absorb B. Therefore, on merging, B ceases to exist as a separate entity, and A continues as the *surviving corporation*. ▮ Exhibit 35–1 graphically illustrates this process.

One of the Firms Survives Continuing with *Example 35.1*, after the merger, Corporation A—*the surviving corporation*—is recognized as a single corporation, and B no longer exists as an entity. A's articles of incorporation are deemed amended to include any changes stated in the *articles of merger* (a document setting forth the terms and conditions of the merger). Corporation A will issue shares or pay some fair consideration to the shareholders of B.

It Inherits All Legal Rights and Obligations of the Other Firm After the merger, Corporation A possesses all of the rights, privileges, and powers of itself and B. It automatically acquires all of B's property and assets without the necessity of a formal transfer. In addition, it becomes liable for all of B's debts and obligations, and it inherits B's preexisting legal rights. Thus, if Corporation B had a right of action against a third party under tort or property law, Corporation A can bring a suit after the merger to recover B's damages.

35–1b Consolidation

In a **consolidation,** two or more corporations combine in such a way that each corporation ceases to exist and a new one emerges. **Example 35.2** Corporation A and Corporation B consolidate to form an entirely new organization, Corporation C. In the process, A and B both terminate, and C comes into existence as an entirely new entity. ▮ Exhibit 35–2 graphically illustrates this process.

A New Corporation Is Formed The results of a consolidation are similar to those of a merger—only one company remains—but it is a completely new entity (the *consolidated corporation*). In terms of *Example 35.2*, Corporation C is recognized as a new corporation, while A and B cease to exist. C's *articles of consolidation* take the place of A's and B's original corporate articles and are thereafter regarded as C's corporate articles. As with a merger, the newly formed corporation will issue shares or pay some fair consideration to the shareholders of the disappearing corporations.

It Inherits All Rights and Liabilities of Both Predecessors Corporation C inherits all of the rights, privileges, and powers previously held by A and B. Title to any property and assets owned by A and B passes to C without a formal transfer. C assumes liability for all debts and obligations owed by A and B.

True consolidations have become less common among for-profit corporations because it is often advantageous for one of the combining firms to survive. In contrast, nonprofit corporations and associations may prefer consolidation because it suggests a new beginning in which neither of the two initial entities is dominant.

35–1c Share Exchange

In a **share exchange,** some or all of the shares of one corporation are exchanged for some or all of the shares of another corporation, but both companies continue to exist. Share exchanges are often used to create *holding companies*—that is, a company whose business activities is holding shares in another company. For instance, UAL Corporation is a large

---

Merger The legal combination of two or more corporations in such a way that only one corporation (the surviving corporation) continues to exist.

Exhibit 35–1 Merger

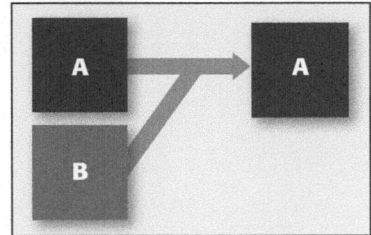

Consolidation The legal combination of two or more corporations in such a way that the original corporations cease to exist, and a new corporation emerges with all their assets and liabilities.

Exhibit 35–2 Consolidation

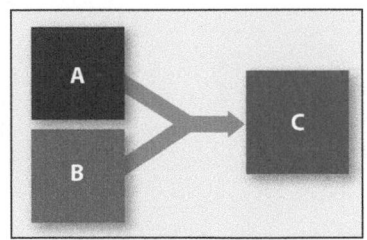

Learning Objective 1

What are the basic differences between a merger, a consolidation, and a share exchange?

Share Exchange A transaction in which some or all of the shares of one corporation are exchanged for some or all of the shares of another corporation, but both corporations continue to exist.

holding company that owns United Airlines. If one corporation owns *all* of the shares of another corporation, it is referred to as the *parent corporation,* and the wholly owned company is the *subsidiary corporation.*

35–1d Merger, Consolidation, and Share Exchange Procedures

All states have statutes authorizing mergers, consolidations, and share exchanges for domestic (in-state) and foreign (out-of-state) corporations. The procedures vary somewhat among jurisdictions. In some states, a consolidation resulting in an entirely new corporation simply follows the initial incorporation procedures, whereas other business combinations must follow the procedures outlined below.

The Revised Model Business Corporation Act (RMBCA) is used by the majority of states to govern corporate formation and operations. The RMBCA sets forth the following basic requirements:

1. The board of directors of *each* corporation involved must approve the merger or consolidation plan.

2. The plan must specify any terms and conditions of the merger. It also must state how the value of the shares of each merging corporation will be determined and how they will be converted into shares or other securities, cash, property, or other interests in another corporation.

3. The majority of the shareholders of *each* corporation must vote to approve the plan at a shareholders' meeting. If any class of stock is entitled to vote as a separate group, the majority of each separate voting group must approve the plan.

   Although RMBCA 11.04(e) requires the approval of only a simple majority of the shareholders entitled to vote once a quorum is present, frequently a corporation's articles of incorporation or bylaws require approval by more than a simple majority. In addition, some state statutes require the approval of two-thirds of the outstanding shares of voting stock, and others require a four-fifths vote.

4. Once the plan is approved by the directors and the shareholders of both corporations, the surviving corporation files the plan (articles of merger, consolidation, or share exchange) with the appropriate official, usually the secretary of state.

5. When state formalities are satisfied, the state issues a certificate of merger to the surviving corporation or a certificate of consolidation to the newly consolidated corporation.

Note that when a merger or consolidation takes place, the surviving corporation or newly formed corporation will issue shares or pay some fair consideration to the shareholders of the corporation or corporations that cease to exist.

In the following case, the attorneys for a group of shareholders argued that the plaintiffs had not been given enough information before they were asked to vote on a proposed merger.

■ **Case 35.1**

In re Trulia, Inc. Stockholder Litigation
Court of Chancery of Delaware, 129 A.3d 884 (2016).

Background and Facts Trulia, Inc. is an online provider of information on homes for sale or rent in the United States. Zillow, Inc. is a real estate marketplace that helps house buyers, sellers, landlords, and others find and share information. Zillow proposed to acquire Trulia. When the deal was announced publicly, complaints filed in a Delaware state court on behalf of Trulia shareholders alleged that the company's directors had breached their fiduciary duties in approving the proposed merger. Attorneys for a group of shareholders argued that the plaintiffs had not been given enough information before they were asked to vote on the proposal. The court was asked to enjoin Zillow's acquisition. The parties agreed to settle. Trulia would supplement the proxy materials provided to the shareholders before the vote to include additional information. In exchange, the plaintiffs would drop their request for an injunction and agree to release any claims arising from the transaction that they, as a class, might otherwise have.

In the Words of the Court
BOUCHARD, C. [Chancellor]
* * * *

Under Delaware law, when directors solicit stockholder action, they must disclose fully and fairly all material information within the board's control. * * * Information is material if there is a substantial likelihood that a reasonable shareholder would consider it important in deciding how to vote. In other words, *information is material if, from the perspective of a reasonable stockholder, there is a substantial likelihood that it significantly alters the total mix of information made available.* [Emphasis added.]

Here, the * * * Proxy that Trulia and Zillow stockholders received in advance of their respective stockholders' meetings to consider whether to approve the proposed transaction ran 224 pages in length, excluding annexes. It contained extensive discussion concerning, among other things, the background of the mergers, each board's reasons for recommending approval of the proposed transaction, prospective financial information concerning the companies that had been reviewed by their respective boards and financial advisors, and explanations of the opinions of each company's financial advisor.

The Supplemental Disclosures plaintiffs obtained in this case solely concern the section of the Proxy summarizing J.P. Morgan's financial analysis, which the Trulia board cited as one of the factors it considered in deciding to recommend approval of the proposed merger. Specifically, these disclosures provided additional details concerning * * * J.P. Morgan's * * * analysis.

* * * Under Delaware law, when the board relies on the advice of a financial advisor in making a decision that requires

stockholder action, those stockholders are entitled to receive in the proxy statement a fair summary of the substantive work performed by the investment bankers upon whose advice the recommendations of their board as to how to vote on a merger or tender rely.

A fair summary, however, is a *summary*. By definition, it need not contain all information underlying the financial advisor's opinion or contained in its report to the board. * * * A fair summary is not a cornucopia [abundance] of financial data, but rather an accurate description of the advisor's methodology and key assumptions. * * * Disclosures that provide extraneous [inessential] details do not contribute to a fair summary and do not add value for stockholders.

* * * *

* * * The disclosures in the original Proxy already provided a fair summary of J.P. Morgan's methodology and assumptions * * *. Inserting additional minutiae [intricacies] underlying some of the assumptions could not reasonably have been expected to significantly alter the total mix of information and thus was not material. * * * The supplemental information was not even helpful to stockholders.

Decision and Remedy The court denied approval of the settlement. The additional information in the supplemental disclosures did not warrant a release of all claims against the defendants. "Accordingly, * * * the proposed settlement is not fair or reasonable to Trulia's stockholders."

Critical Thinking

• **Legal Environment** *When the parties to a dispute agree to a settlement, they share the same interest in obtaining the court's approval. What are the advantages and disadvantages of this situation?*

• **Economic** *In the* Trulia *case, the settlement, if approved, would not have yielded any genuine benefit for the shareholders. If the court had approved the settlement, however, who would have benefited?*

35–1e Short-Form Mergers

RMBCA 11.04 provides a simplified procedure for the merger of a substantially owned subsidiary corporation into its parent corporation. Under these provisions, a **short-form merger**—also referred to as a *parent-subsidiary merger*—can be accomplished *without* the approval of the shareholders of either corporation.

Short-Form Merger A merger that can be accomplished without the approval of the shareholders of either corporation because one company (the parent corporation) owns at least 90 percent of the outstanding shares of each class of stock of the other corporation (the subsidiary corporation).

The short-form merger can be used only when the parent corporation owns at least 90 percent of the outstanding shares of each class of stock of the subsidiary corporation. Once the board of directors of the parent corporation approves the plan, it is filed with the state, and copies are sent to each shareholder of record in the subsidiary corporation.

35–1f Shareholder Approval

As mentioned, except in a short-form merger, the shareholders of both corporations must approve a merger or consolidation plan. Shareholders invest in a corporation with the expectation that the board of directors will manage the enterprise and make decisions on ordinary business matters. For *extraordinary* matters, normally both the board of directors and the shareholders must approve the transaction.

Mergers and other combinations are extraordinary business matters, meaning that the board of directors must normally obtain the shareholders' approval and provide *appraisal rights* (discussed next). Amendments to the articles of incorporation and the dissolution of the corporation also generally require shareholder approval.

Sometimes, a transaction can be structured in such a way that shareholder approval is not required, but if the shareholders challenge the transaction, a court might use its equity powers to require shareholder approval. For this reason, the board of directors may request shareholder approval even when it might not be legally required.

35–1g Appraisal Rights

What if a shareholder disapproves of a merger or a consolidation but is outvoted by the other shareholders? The law recognizes that a dissenting shareholder should not be forced to become an unwilling shareholder in a corporation that is new or different from the one in which the shareholder originally invested. Dissenting shareholders therefore are given a statutory right to be paid the fair value of the shares they held on the date of the merger or consolidation. This right is referred to as the shareholder's **appraisal right.** So long as the transaction does not involve fraud or other illegal conduct, appraisal rights are the exclusive remedy for a shareholder who is dissatisfied with the price received for the stock.

When Appraisal Rights Apply Appraisal rights normally extend to regular mergers, consolidations, share exchanges, short-form mergers, and sales of substantially all of the corporate assets not in the ordinary course of business. Such rights can be particularly important in a short-form merger because the minority stockholders do not receive advance notice of the merger, the directors do not consider or approve it, and there is no vote. Appraisal rights are often the only recourse available to shareholders who object to parent-subsidiary mergers.

Procedures Each state establishes the procedures for asserting appraisal rights in that jurisdiction. Shareholders may lose their appraisal rights if they do not adhere precisely to the procedures prescribed by statute. When they lose the right to an appraisal, dissenting shareholders must go along with the transaction despite their objections.

35–2 Purchase of Assets

When a corporation acquires all or substantially all of the assets of another corporation by direct purchase, the purchasing, or *acquiring,* corporation simply extends its ownership and control over more physical assets. Because no change in the legal entity occurs, the acquiring corporation is not generally required to obtain shareholder approval for the purchase.

Know This
State statutes, articles of incorporation, and corporate bylaws can require the approval of more than a simple majority of shares for some extraordinary matters.

Appraisal Right The right of a dissenting shareholder, who objects to a merger or consolidation of the corporation, to have his or her shares appraised and to be paid the fair value of those shares by the corporation.

35–2a When Shareholder Approval May Be Required

Shareholder approval may be required in a few situations, however. If the acquiring corporation plans to pay for the assets with its own corporate stock and not enough authorized unissued shares are available, the shareholders must vote to approve the issuance of additional shares by amendment of the corporate articles. Also, if the acquiring corporation's stock is traded on a national stock exchange and it will be issuing a significant number (at least 20 percent) of its outstanding shares, shareholder approval can be required.

Note that the corporation that is *selling* all of its assets is substantially changing its business position and perhaps its ability to carry out its corporate purposes. For that reason, the corporation whose assets are being sold must obtain the approval of both the board of directors and the shareholders. In most states and under RMBCA 13.02, a dissenting shareholder of the selling corporation can demand appraisal rights.

Both the U.S. Department of Justice and the Federal Trade Commission have guidelines that significantly constrain and often prohibit mergers that could result from a purchase of assets. (These guidelines will be discussed in the materials covering federal antitrust laws.)

35–2b Successor Liability in Purchases of Assets

Generally, a corporation that purchases the assets of another corporation is not responsible for the liabilities of the selling corporation. Exceptions to this rule are made in certain circumstances, however. In any of the following situations, the acquiring corporation will be held to have assumed *both* the assets and the liabilities of the selling corporation.

> **Learning Objective 2**
>
> Under what circumstances is a corporation that purchases the assets of another corporation responsible for the liabilities of the selling corporation?

1. *Express or implicit agreement.* The purchasing corporation impliedly or expressly assumes the seller's liabilities.

2. De facto *merger.* The sale transaction amounts to a merger or consolidation of the two companies.

3. *Continuation.* The purchaser continues the seller's business and retains the same shareholders, directors, and officers.

4. *Fraud exception.* The sale is entered into fraudulently for the purpose of escaping liability.

Case Example 35.3 American Standard, Inc., sold its Kewanee Boiler division to OakFabco, Inc. The agreement stated that OakFabco would purchase Kewanee assets subject to Kewanee liabilities. "Kewanee liabilities" were defined as "all the debts, liabilities, obligations, and commitments (fixed or contingent) connected with or attributable to Kewanee existing and outstanding at the Closing Date."

Because the boilers manufactured by Kewanee had been insulated with asbestos, many tort claims arose in the years following the purchase of the business. Some of those claims were brought by plaintiffs who had suffered injuries after the closing of the transaction that were allegedly attributable to boilers manufactured and sold before the closing.

American Standard filed an action against OakFabco in New York, asking the court for a declaratory judgment on the issue of whether liabilities for such injuries were among the "Kewanee liabilities" that OakFabco had assumed. The court held that OakFabco had expressly assumed the liabilities of the selling corporation in the contract, including claims that arose after the closing date. A state appellate court affirmed that decision. According to the reviewing court, "nothing in the nature of the transaction suggested that the parties intended OakFabco, which got all the assets, to escape any of the related obligations."[1]

When does the purchase of a boiler division create ongoing liabilities for past acts?

---

1. *American Standard, Inc. v. OakFabco, Inc.,* 14 N.Y.3d 399, 901 N.Y.S.2d 572 (2010).

Does a purchasing corporation assume the liability of the selling corporation if the buyer has constructive notice of potential liability? That was the issue in the following case.

Case 35.2

Heavenly Hana, LLC v. Hotel Union & Hotel Industry of Hawaii Pension Plan

United States Court of Appeals, Ninth Circuit, 891 F.3d 839 (2018).

Background and Facts The Hotel Union & Hotel Industry of Hawaii Pension Plan is a multiemployer plan that represents more than 12,000 members who work at unionized hotels in Hawaii. Ohana Hotel Company, which operated Ohana Hotel on the island of Maui, contributed to the plan for its hotel employees but had underfunded the contributions for years. The plan's annual funding notices revealed Ohana's underfunding and were publicly available online. Ohana agreed to sell the hotel to Heavenly Hana, LLC, and its parent company, Amstar-39. Amstar had previously owned and operated a hotel that participated in a multiemployer pension plan. The purchase agreement stated that Ohana contributed to such a plan. Before the deal closed, however, Ohana withdrew from the plan without informing Amstar. The plan's administrators demanded that the new owner cover the unfunded "withdrawal" liability. Amstar filed a suit in a federal district court against the plan, contesting the demand. The court entered a judgment in Amstar's favor. The plan appealed.

In the Words of the Court
THOMAS, Chief Judge:

* * * *

* * * *Under a constructive notice standard, purchasers are deemed to have notice of any facts that one using reasonable care or diligence should have.* [Emphasis added.]

* * * *

* * * *Requiring purchasers to make reasonable inquiries into the existence of withdrawal liability advances the * * * interest in preventing underfunding in multiemployer pension plans.* Imposing this burden [has] little negative impact on the fluid transfer of corporate assets. *Purchasers [can] simply investigate the possible liability and negotiate a purchase price [or other accommodation] that would take it into account.* [Emphasis added.]

* * * Of the three relevant parties to successor withdrawal liability—the seller, the purchaser, and the pension plan— purchasers are in the best position to ensure withdrawal liability is accounted for during an asset sale. Sellers have no incentive to disclose potential liabilities because such liabilities are likely to drive the sale price in one direction only: down. Pension plans cannot be asked to investigate sales rumors, track down the identity of all potential purchasers, avoid confidentiality or contract interference concerns, and send notice of its publicly available funding status directly to potential purchasers. Rather, pension plans are only responsible for (1) determining the amount of the employer's withdrawal liability, (2) notifying the employer of the amount of the withdrawal liability, and (3) collecting the amount of the withdrawal liability from the employer. Purchasers, in contrast, have the incentive to inquire about potential withdrawal liability in order to avoid unexpected post-transaction liabilities.

* * * *

Applying a constructive notice standard in this case leads us to conclude that Amstar had constructive notice because a reasonable purchaser would have discovered Ohana's withdrawal liability.

Amstar previously operated a hotel that participated in a multiemployer pension plan * * *. The Agreement [between Amstar and Ohana] plainly informed Amstar that * * * Ohana had contributed to a multiemployer pension plan. Finally, the Plan's annual funding notices, which indicated a state of underfunding, were publicly available.

Decision and Remedy The U.S. Court of Appeals for the Ninth Circuit reversed the lower court's judgment. "The undisputed facts indicate that Amstar should have determined that . . . Ohana would incur withdrawal liability."

Critical Thinking

• **Legal Environment** *What actions might a purchasing corporation take to determine if withdrawal liability exists?*

• **What If the Facts Were Different?** *Suppose that Amstar's lawyers had advised, "Absent an express assumption of liability, a purchasing corporation does not assume a selling corporation's withdrawal liability." Would the result have been different? Why or why not?*

35–3 Takeovers

An alternative to the purchase of another corporation's assets is the purchase of a substantial number of the voting shares of its stock. This enables the acquiring corporation to control the *target corporation* (the corporation being acquired). The process of acquiring control over a corporation in this way is commonly referred to as a corporate **takeover.**

35–3a Tender Offers

The acquiring corporation deals directly with the target company's shareholders in seeking to purchase the shares they hold. It does this by making a **tender offer** to all of the shareholders of the target corporation. The tender offer can be conditioned on receipt of a specified number of shares by a certain date.

To induce shareholders to accept the tender offer, the acquiring corporation generally offers them a price higher than the market price of the target corporation's shares before the announcement of the offer. In a merger of two Fortune 500 pharmaceutical companies, for instance, Pfizer, Inc., paid $68 billion to acquire its rival Wyeth. Wyeth shareholders reportedly received approximately $50.19 per share (part in cash and part in Pfizer stock), which amounted to a 15 percent premium over the market price of the stock.

Federal securities laws strictly control the terms, duration, and circumstances under which most tender offers are made. In addition, many states have passed antitakeover statutes.

35–3b Responses to Takeover Attempts

A firm may respond to a takeover attempt in many ways. Sometimes, a target firm's board of directors will see a tender offer as favorable and will recommend to the shareholders that they accept it. Frequently, though, the target corporation's management opposes the proposed takeover.

To resist a takeover, a target company can make a *self-tender,* which is an offer to acquire stock from its own shareholders and thereby retain corporate control. Alternatively, the target corporation might resort to one of several other defensive tactics. Several of these tactics are described in Exhibit 35–3.

In a hostile takeover attempt, sometimes directors' duties of care and loyalty collide with their self-interest. Then the shareholders, who would have received a premium for their shares as a result of the takeover, file lawsuits. Such lawsuits frequently allege that the directors breached their fiduciary duties in defending against the tender offer.

Business Judgment Rule Courts apply the *business judgment rule* when analyzing whether the directors acted reasonably in resisting the takeover attempt. The directors must show that they had reasonable grounds to believe that the tender offer posed a danger to the corporation's policies and effectiveness.

In addition, the board's response must have been rational in relation to the threat posed. Basically, the defensive tactics used must have been reasonable, and the board of directors must have been trying to protect the corporation and its shareholders from a perceived danger. If the directors' actions were reasonable under the circumstances, then they are not liable for breaching their fiduciary duties.

An Example—The Poison Pill Defense One technique to avoid takeovers is the poison pill defense. With this defensive measure, a board gives shareholders the right to buy additional shares at low prices. The right is triggered when a party acquires a certain proportion of the target corporation's stock—often between 15 and 20 percent. (This party, of course, does not have the right to purchase shares at a discount.) With more shares outstanding, the

Takeover The acquisition of control over a corporation through the purchase of a substantial number of the voting shares of the corporation.

Tender Offer An offer made by one company directly to the shareholders of another (target) company to purchase their shares of stock.

Learning Objective 3
What actions might a target corporation take to resist a takeover attempt?

"In the takeover business, if you want a friend, you buy a dog."

Carl Icahn
1936–present
(American financier)

Exhibit 35–3 The Terminology of Takeover Defenses

TERM	DEFINITION
Crown Jewel	When threatened with a takeover, management makes the company less attractive to the raider by selling the company's most valuable asset (the "crown jewel") to a third party.
Golden Parachute	When a takeover is successful, top management usually is changed. With this in mind, a company may establish special termination or retirement benefits that must be paid to top managers if they are "retired." In other words, a departing high-level manager's parachute will be "golden" when he or she is forced to "bail out" of the company.
Greenmail	To regain control, a target company may pay a higher-than-market price to repurchase the stock that the acquiring corporation bought. When a takeover is attempted through a gradual accumulation of target stock rather than a tender offer, the intent may be to get the target company to buy back the shares at a premium price—a concept similar to blackmail.
Pac-Man	Named after the Atari video game, this is an aggressive defense in which the target corporation attempts its own takeover of the acquiring corporation.
Poison Pill	The target corporation issues to its stockholders rights to purchase additional shares at low prices when there is a takeover attempt. This makes the takeover undesirably or even prohibitively expensive for the acquiring corporation.
White Knight	The target corporation solicits a merger with a third party, which then makes a better (often simply a higher) tender offer to the target's shareholders. The third party that "rescues" the target is the "white knight."

acquiring party's interest is diluted. The tactic is meant to make a takeover too expensive for the acquiring party.

Example 35.4 Back in 2012, Netflix, Inc., used the poison pill defense to effectively block a takeover attempt by billionaire investor Carl Icahn. Netflix gave its shareholders the right to acquire newly issued stock if any individual acquired more than 10 percent of the company. At the time, Icahn held 9.98 percent of the shares. If his interest had risen to 10 percent, new shares would have flooded the market, and his interest in the corporation would have been immediately diluted. Consequently, he was effectively prevented from buying more shares. ■

35–4 Corporate Termination

The termination of a corporation's existence has two phases—dissolution and winding up. **Dissolution** is the legal death of the artificial "person" of the corporation. Dissolution can be brought about by the following:

1. An act of the state.

2. An agreement of the shareholders and the board of directors.

3. The expiration of a time period stated in the certificate of incorporation.

4. A court order.

Winding up is the process by which corporate assets are liquidated, or converted into cash and distributed among creditors and shareholders. Some prefer to call this phase

Dissolution The formal disbanding of a corporation.

liquidation. Here, we use the term *winding up* to mean all acts needed to bring the legal and financial affairs of the business to an end, including but not necessarily limited to liquidation of assets.

Dissolution can be either voluntary or involuntary. Winding up may differ to some extent based on whether voluntary or involuntary dissolution has occurred.

35–4a Voluntary Dissolution

Dissolution can be brought about voluntarily by the directors and the shareholders. State corporation statutes establish the procedures required to voluntarily dissolve a corporation. Basically, there are two possible methods:

1. By the shareholders' unanimous vote to initiate dissolution proceedings. **Example 35.5** Dee and Jim form Home Remodeling, Inc. They are Home Remodeling's only shareholders and directors. After three years, they decide to cease business, dissolve the corporation, and go their separate ways.

2. By a proposal of the board of directors that is submitted to the shareholders at a shareholders' meeting.

When a corporation is dissolved voluntarily, the corporation must file *articles of dissolution* with the state and notify its creditors of the dissolution. The corporation must also establish a date (at least 120 days after the date of dissolution) by which all claims against the corporation must be received [RMBCA 14.06].

35–4b Involuntary Dissolution

Because corporations are creatures of statute, the state can also dissolve a corporation in certain circumstances. The secretary of state or the state attorney general can bring an action to dissolve a corporation that has failed to pay its annual taxes or to submit required annual reports, for example. A state court can also dissolve a corporation that has engaged in *ultra vires* acts or committed fraud or misrepresentation to the state during incorporation.

Sometimes, a shareholder or a group of shareholders petitions a court for corporate dissolution. In such a situation, the court may dissolve the corporation if the controlling shareholders or directors have engaged in fraudulent, illegal, or oppressive conduct. **Example 35.6** The Miller family—Todd, Otilia, and Breanna—operates Seven Oaks Farm in rural Virginia, as a close corporation. When Todd and Otilia are arrested for stealing from the farm's financial accounts, Breanna petitions the court for dissolution so that she can wind up Seven Oaks's business. Shareholders may also petition a court for dissolution when the board of directors is deadlocked and the affairs of the corporation can no longer be conducted because of the deadlock.

35–4c Winding Up

When dissolution takes place by voluntary action, the members of the board of directors act as trustees of the corporate assets. As trustees, they are responsible for winding up the affairs of the corporation for the benefit of corporate creditors and shareholders. This makes the board members personally liable for any breach of their fiduciary trustee duties.

When the dissolution is involuntary—or if board members do not wish to act as trustees of the assets—the court will appoint a **receiver** to wind up the corporate affairs and liquidate corporate assets. Courts may also appoint a receiver when shareholders or creditors can show that the board of directors should not be permitted to act as trustees of the corporate assets.

Learning Objective 4
What are the two ways in which a corporation can be voluntarily dissolved?

Receiver In a corporate dissolution, a court-appointed person who winds up corporate affairs and liquidates corporate assets.

35–5 Major Business Forms Compared

When deciding which form of business organization would be most appropriate, business-persons normally take into account several factors, including the liability of the owners, tax considerations, and the need for capital. Each major form of business organization offers advantages and disadvantages with respect to these and other factors.

Exhibit 35–4 summarizes the essential advantages and disadvantages of each form of business organization discussed in this unit.

Exhibit 35–4 Major Business Forms Compared

CHARACTERISTIC	SOLE PROPRIETORSHIP	PARTNERSHIP	CORPORATION
Method of Creation	Created at will by owner.	Created by agreement of the parties.	Authorized by the state under the state's corporation law.
Legal Position	Not a separate entity; owner is the business.	A general partnership is a separate legal entity in most states.	Always a legal entity separate and distinct from its owners—a legal fiction for the purposes of owning property and being a party to litigation.
Liability	Unlimited liability.	Unlimited liability.	Limited liability of shareholders—shareholders are not liable for the debts of the corporation.
Duration	Determined by owner; automatically dissolved on owner's death.	Terminated by agreement of the partners, but can continue to do business even when a partner dissociates from the partnership.	Can have perpetual existence.
Transferability of Interest	Interest can be transferred, but individual's proprietorship then ends.	Although partnership interest can be assigned, assignee does not have full rights of a partner.	Shares of stock can be transferred.
Management	Completely at owner's discretion.	Each partner has a direct and equal voice in management unless expressly agreed otherwise in the partnership agreement.	Shareholders elect directors, who set policy and appoint officers.
Taxation	Owner pays personal taxes on business income.	Each partner pays pro rata share of income taxes on net profits, whether or not they are distributed.	Double taxation—corporation pays income tax on net profits, with no deduction for dividends, and shareholders pay income tax on disbursed dividends they receive.
Organizational Fees, Annual License Fees, and Annual Reports	None or minimal.	None or minimal.	All required.
Transaction of Business in Other States	Generally no limitation.	Generally no limitation.[a]	Normally must qualify to do business and obtain certificate of authority.

a. A few states have enacted statutes requiring that foreign partnerships qualify to do business there.

CHARACTERISTIC	LIMITED PARTNERSHIP	LIMITED LIABILITY COMPANY	LIMITED LIABILITY PARTNERSHIP
Method of Creation	Created by agreement to carry on a business for a profit. Must include at least one general partner and at least one limited partner. Certificate of limited partnership is filed. Charter must be issued by the state.	Created by an agreement of the member-owners of the company. Articles of organization are filed. Charter must be issued by the state.	Created by agreement of the partners. A statement of qualification for the limited liability partnership is filed.
Legal Position	Treated as a legal entity.	Treated as a legal entity.	Generally, treated same as a general partnership.
Liability	Unlimited liability of all general partners; limited partners are liable only to the extent of capital contributions.	Member-owners' liability is limited to the amount of capital contributions or investments.	Varies, but under the Uniform Partnership Act, liability of a partner for acts committed by other partners is limited.
Duration	By agreement in certificate, or by termination of the last general partner (retirement, death, and the like) or last limited partner.	Unless a single-member LLC, can have perpetual existence (same as a corporation).	Remains in existence until cancellation or revocation.
Transferability of Interest	Interest can be assigned (same as in a general partnership), but if assignee becomes a member with consent of other partners, certificate must be amended.	Member interests are freely transferable.	Interest can be assigned same as in a general partnership.
Management	General partners have equal voice or by agreement. Limited partners may not retain limited liability if they actively participate in management.	Member-owners can fully participate in management, or can designate a group of persons to manage on behalf of the members.	Same as a general partnership.
Taxation	Generally taxed as a partnership.	LLC is not taxed, and members are taxed personally on profits "passed through" the LLC.	Same as a general partnership.
Organizational Fees, Annual License Fees, and Annual Reports	Organizational fee required; usually not others.	Organizational fee required; others vary with states.	Fees are set by each state for filing statements of qualification, foreign qualification, and annual reports.
Transaction of Business in Other States	Generally no limitation.	Generally no limitation, but may vary depending on state.	Must file a statement of foreign qualification before doing business in another state.

Practice and Review

Mario Bonsetti and Rico Sanchez incorporated Gnarly Vulcan Gear, Inc. (GVG), to manufacture windsurfing equipment. Bonsetti owned 60 percent of the corporation's stock, and Sanchez owned 40 percent. Both men served on the board of directors. Hula Boards, Inc., owned solely by Mai Jin Li, made a public offer to buy GVG stock. Hula offered 30 percent more than the market price per share for the stock, and Bonsetti and Sanchez each sold 20 percent of their stock to Hula. Jin Li became the third member of the GVG board of directors. An irreconcilable dispute soon arose between Bonsetti and Sanchez over design modifications of their popular Baked Chameleon board. Despite Bonsetti's dissent, Sanchez and Jin Li voted to merge GVG with Hula Boards under the latter name, Gnarly Vulcan Gear was dissolved, and production of the Baked Chameleon ceased. Using the information presented in the chapter, answer the following questions.

1. What rights does Bonsetti have (in most states) as a minority shareholder dissenting to the merger of GVG and Hula Boards?

2. Could the parties have used a short-form merger procedure in this situation? Why or why not?

3. What is the term used for Hula's offer to purchase GVG stock?

4. Suppose that after the merger, a person who was injured on the Baked Chameleon board sued Hula (the surviving corporation). Can Hula be held liable for the injury? Why or why not?

Debate This

Corporate law should be changed to prohibit management from using most of the legal methods currently used to fight takeovers.

Key Terms

appraisal right 830   merger 827   short-form merger 829
consolidation 827   receiver 835   takeover 833
dissolution 834   share exchange 827   tender offer 833

Chapter Summary: Corporate Mergers, Takeovers, and Termination

Merger, Consolidation, and Share Exchange	1. *Merger*—The legal combination of two or more corporations, with the result that the surviving corporation acquires all the assets and obligations of the other corporation, which then ceases to exist.
	2. *Consolidation*—The legal combination of two or more corporations, with the result that each corporation ceases to exist and a new one emerges. The new corporation assumes all the assets and obligations of the former corporations.
	3. *Share exchange*—Some or all of the shares of one corporation are exchanged for some or all of the shares of another corporation, but both corporations continue to exist.
	4. *Procedure*—Determined by state statutes.
	5. *Short-form merger*—Possible when the parent corporation owns at least 90 percent of the outstanding shares of each class of stock of the subsidiary corporation. Shareholder approval is not required. The merger need be approved only by the board of directors of the parent corporation.
	6. *Appraisal rights*—Rights of dissenting shareholders (given by state statute) to receive the fair value for their shares when a merger or consolidation takes place.
Purchase of Assets	A purchase of assets occurs when one corporation acquires all or substantially all of the assets of another corporation.
	1. *Acquiring corporation*—The acquiring (purchasing) corporation is generally not required to obtain shareholder approval. The corporation is merely increasing its assets, and no fundamental business change occurs.
	2. *Acquired corporation*—The acquired (purchased) corporation is required to obtain the approval of both its directors and its shareholders for the sale of its assets, because the sale will substantially change the corporation's business position.

Takeovers	1. *Purchase of stock*—A purchase of stock occurs when one corporation acquires a substantial number of the voting shares of the stock of another (target) corporation.
	2. *Tender offer*—A public offer to all shareholders of the target corporation to purchase its stock at a price that generally is higher than the market price of the target stock prior to the announcement of the tender offer. Federal and state securities laws strictly control the terms, duration, and circumstances under which most tender offers are made.
	3. *Target responses*—Target corporations may respond to takeover bids in various ways, including self-tender (the target firm's offer to acquire its shareholders' stock.) Other strategies are listed in Exhibit 35–3.
Corporate Termination	The termination of a corporation involves the following two phases:
	1. *Dissolution*—The legal death of the artificial "person" of the corporation. Dissolution can be brought about voluntarily by the directors and shareholders or involuntarily by the state or through a court order.
	2. *Winding up (liquidation)*—The process by which corporate assets are converted into cash and distributed to creditors and shareholders according to specified rules of preference. May be supervised by members of the board of directors (when dissolution is voluntary) or by a receiver appointed by the court to wind up corporate affairs.

Issue Spotters

1. Macro Corporation and Micro Company combine, and a new organization, MM, Inc., takes their place. What is the term for this type of combination? What happens to the assets, property, and liabilities of Micro? (See *Merger, Consolidation, and Share Exchange.*)

2. Peppertree, Inc., hired Robert McClellan, a licensed contractor, to repair a condominium complex that was damaged in an earthquake. McClellan completes the work, but Peppertree fails to pay. McClellan is awarded $181,000 in an arbitration proceeding. Peppertree then forms another corporation and transfers all of its assets to the new corporation without notifying McClellan. Can McClellan hold Peppertree's shareholders personally liable for the debt? Why or why not? (See *Takeovers.*)

   —**Check your answers to the *Issue Spotters* against the answers provided in Appendix D at the end of this text.**

Business Scenarios and Case Problems

35–1. Corporate Merger. Alir owns 10,000 shares of Ajax Corp. Her shares represent a 10 percent ownership interest in Ajax. Zeta Corp. wishes to acquire Ajax in a merger, and the board of directors of each corporation has approved. The shareholders of Zeta have already approved as well, and Ajax has called for a shareholders' meeting to vote on the merger. Alir disapproves of the merger and does not want to accept Zeta shares for the Ajax shares she holds. The market price of Ajax shares is $20 per share the day before the Ajax shareholder vote. On the day of the vote, the shareholders approve the merger, and the share price drops to $16. Discuss Alir's rights in this matter, beginning with the notice of the proposed merger. (See *Merger, Consolidation, and Share Exchange.*)

35–2. Purchase of Assets. Paradise Pools, Inc. (PPI) entered into a contract with Vittorio, LLP, to build a pool as part of a hotel being developed by Takahashi Development. PPI built the pool, but Vittorio, the general contractor, defaulted on other parts of the project. Takahashi completed the construction. Litigation followed, and Takahashi was awarded $18,656 against PPI. Meanwhile, Paradise Corp. (PC) was incorporated with the same management as PPI, but different shareholders. PC acquired PPI's assets, without assuming its liabilities, and soon became known as "Paradise Pools and Spas." Takahashi sought to obtain a writ of garnishment against PC to enforce the judgment against PPI. Is PC liable for PPI's obligation to Takahashi? Why or why not? (See *Purchase of Assets.*)

35–3. Corporate Takeover. Alitech Corp. is a small midwestern business that owns a valuable patent. Alitech has approximately 1,000 shareholders with 100,000 authorized and outstanding shares. Block Corp. would like to have the use of the patent, but Alitech refuses to give Block a license. Block has tried to acquire Alitech by purchasing Alitech's assets, but Alitech's board of directors has refused to approve the acquisition. Alitech's shares are selling for $5 per share. Discuss how Block Corp. might proceed to gain the control and use of Alitech's patent. (See *Takeovers.*)

35–4. Successor Liability. In 2004, the Watergate Hotel in Washington, D.C., obtained a loan from PB Capital. At this time, hotel employees were represented by a union. Under a collective bargaining agreement, the hotel had agreed to make contributions to an employees' pension fund run by the union. In 2007, the hotel was closed due to poor business, although the owner stated that the hotel would reopen in 2010. Despite this expectation, PB Capital—which was still owed $40 million by the hotel owner—instituted foreclosure proceedings. At the foreclosure sale, PB Capital bought the hotel and reopened it under new management and with a new workforce.

The union sued PB Capital, contending that it should pay $637,855 owed by the previous owner into the employees' pension fund. Should PB Capital, as the hotel's new owner, have to incur the previous owner's obligation to pay into the pension fund under the theory of successor liability? Why or why not? [*Board of Trustees of Unite Here Local 25 v. MR Watergate, LLC,* 677 F.Supp.2d 229 (D.D.C. 2010)] (See *Merger, Consolidation, and Share Exchange.*)

35–5. Purchase of Assets. Grand Adventures Tour & Travel Publishing Corp. (GATT) provided travel services. Duane Boyd, a former GATT director, incorporated Interline Travel & Tour, Inc. At a public sale, Interline bought GATT's assets. Interline moved into GATT's office building, hired former GATT employees, and began to serve former GATT customers. A GATT creditor, Call Center Technologies, Inc., sought to collect the unpaid amount on a contract with GATT from Interline. Is Interline liable? Why or why not? [*Call Center Technologies, Inc. v. Grand Adventures Tour & Travel Publishing Corp.,* 635 F.3d 48 (2d Cir. 2011)] (See *Merger, Consolidation, and Share Exchange.*)

35–6. Business Case Problem with Sample Answer— Purchase of Assets. Lockheed Martin Corporation owned an aluminum refinery in St. Croix, Virgin Islands, that produced hazardous waste. Lockheed sold the refinery to Glencore Ltd. Their contract provided that Glencore would indemnify Lockheed for "pre-closing" environmental conditions. Alcoa World Alumina LLC bought the refinery from Glencore. Their contract stated that the buyer assumed only certain liabilities, including those relating to two specific contracts. Glencore's contract with Lockheed was not on the list. A decade later, the government of the Virgin Islands brought actions against the current and former owners of the refinery to recover for the environmental damage. In a settlement, Lockheed agreed to pay for certain remediation costs. Lockheed then filed a suit against Glencore to recover costs related to the settlement. Does Alcoa have to indemnify Glencore for costs related to Lockheed's suit? Why or why not?

[*Alcoa World Alumina LLC v. Glencore Ltd.,* 2016 WL 521193 (Del.Super.Ct. 2016)] (See *Purchase of Assets.*)

—For a sample answer to Problem 35–6, go to Appendix E at the end of this text.

35–7. Tender Offers. Apollo Global Management made a tender offer to the shareholders of Diamond Resorts International. Stephen Cloobeck, the founder of Diamond and the chairman of its board, did not approve of the deal because "he was disappointed with the price and the company's management for not having run the business in a manner that would command a higher price, and that in his view, it was not the right time to sell the company." The directors voted, with Cloobeck abstaining, to recommend that the shareholders accept the offer. The recommendation did not state Cloobeck's concerns. Apollo acquired a sufficient number of Diamond's shares to take control of the company. Did the Diamond board's failure to disclose its chairman's views render the recommendation to accept Apollo's offer materially misleading? Discuss. [*Appel v. Berkman,* 180 A.3d 1055 (Del. 2018)] (See *Takeovers.*)

35–8. A Question of Ethics—Successor Liability. Ian Bell loaned $250,000 to Bio Defense Corporation, a waste management company in Massachusetts. Before Bell's loan came due, Boston Local Development Corp. (BLDC) foreclosed on its own loan to Bio Defense, forcing Bio Defense to cease operations and be sold. At the foreclosure sale, BLDC bought Bio Defense's property, including three very valuable patents (assets). BLDC then sold these patents to Oneighty C Technologies Corporation (OCTC). Bell, who had not been paid back for his loan to Bio Defense, learned of these events and filed a lawsuit against OCTC claiming that OCTC was the corporate successor to Bio Defense. [Bell v. Oneighty C Technologies Corp., *91 Mass.App.Ct. 1112, 81 N.E.3d 825 (2017)] (*See *Purchase of Assets.*)

1. Could OCTC be held legally liable on the unpaid loan to Bell?
2. Could OCTC owe an ethical duty to assume liability for the debt? Why or why not?

Critical Thinking and Writing Assignments

35–9. Time-Limited Group Assignment—Mergers and Acquisitions. Angie Jolson is the chair of the board of directors of Artel, Inc., and Sam Douglas is the chair of the board of directors of Fox Express, Inc. Jolson and Douglas meet to consider the possibility of combining their corporations and activities into a single corporate entity. They consider two alternative courses of action: Artel could acquire all of the stock and assets of Fox Express, or the corporations could combine to form a new corporation, called A&F Enterprises, Inc. Both Jolson and Douglas are concerned about the necessity of a formal transfer of property, liability for

existing debts, and the need to amend the articles of incorporation. (See *Merger, Consolidation, and Share Exchange.*)

1. The first group will identify the first proposed combination and outline its legal effect on the transfer of property, the liabilities of the combined corporations, and the need to amend the articles of incorporation.
2. The second group will do the same for the second proposed combination—determine its identity and describe its legal effect on the transfer of property, the liabilities of the combined corporations, and the need to amend the articles of incorporation.

Investor Protection, Insider Trading, and Corporate Governance

36

"You are remembered for the rules you break."

General Douglas MacArthur
1880–1964
(U.S. Army general)

After the stock market crash of 1929, Congress enacted legislation to regulate securities markets. **Securities** generally include any instruments representing corporate ownership (stock) or debts (bonds). The goal of regulation was to provide investors with more information to help them make buying and selling decisions about securities and to prohibit deceptive, unfair, and manipulative practices.

Today, the sale and transfer of securities are heavily regulated by federal and state statutes and by government agencies. The Securities and Exchange Commission (SEC) is the main independent regulatory agency that administers securities regulations. The SEC continually updates its rules in response to legislation, such as the Dodd-Frank Wall Street Reform and Consumer Protection Act.[1]

Despite all efforts to regulate the securities markets, people continue to break the rules and are often remembered for it, as observed in the chapter-opening quotation. Consider what happened to Billy Walters, a high-rolling sports gambler living in Nevada who was convicted of insider trading in 2017. Walters reportedly made $43 million by making trades based on inside information about Dean Foods Company that he had received from his long-time friend Thomas Davis, a director at Dean Foods. (Dean Foods is a Delaware corporation based in Texas that distributes dairy products under many brand names nationwide.) Walters also shared some of this inside information with professional golfer Phil Mickelson, who later agreed to pay more than $1 million in fines for profiting from the tips.

In this chapter, we explore securities regulations and laws on insider trading so that you understand how to avoid breaking the rules. We also discuss corporate governance and accountability.

Learning Objectives

The four Learning Objectives *below are designed to help improve your understanding. After reading this chapter, you should be able to answer the following questions:*

1. What is meant by the term *securities*?

2. What is insider trading? Why is it prohibited?

3. What are some of the features of state securities laws?

4. What certification requirements does the Sarbanes-Oxley Act impose on corporate executives?

Securities Generally, any instruments representing corporate ownership (stock) or debt (bonds).

---

1. Pub. L. No. 111-203, July 21, 2010, 124 Stat. 1376; 12 U.S.C. Sections 5301 *et seq.*

36–1 Securities Act of 1933

The Securities Act of 1933[2] governs initial sales of stock by businesses. The act was designed to prohibit various forms of fraud and to stabilize the securities industry by requiring that all essential information concerning the issuance of securities be made available to the investing public. Basically, the purpose of the 1933 act is to require disclosure. The act provides that all securities transactions must be registered with the SEC unless they qualify for an exemption.

During the stock market crash of 1929, hordes of investors crowded Wall Street to find out the latest news. How did the "crash" affect stock trading in the years thereafter?

Investment Contract In securities law, a transaction in which a person invests in a common enterprise reasonably expecting profits that are derived primarily from the efforts of others.

36–1a What Is a Security?

Section 2(1) of the Securities Act contains a broad definition of *securities*, which generally include the following:[3]

1. Instruments and interests commonly known as securities, such as preferred and common stocks, treasury stocks, bonds, debentures, and stock warrants.

2. Any interests, such as stock options, puts, calls, or other types of privilege on a security or on the right to purchase a security or a group of securities on a national security exchange.

3. Notes, instruments, or other evidence of indebtedness, including certificates of interest in a profit-sharing agreement and certificates of deposit.

4. Any fractional undivided interest in oil, gas, or other mineral rights.

5. Investment contracts, which include interests in limited partnerships and other investment schemes.

The *Howey* Test In interpreting the act, the United States Supreme Court has held that an **investment contract** is any transaction in which a person (1) invests (2) in a common enterprise (3) reasonably expecting profits (4) derived *primarily* or *substantially* from others' managerial or entrepreneurial efforts.[4] Known as the *Howey* test, this definition continues to guide the determination of what types of contracts can be considered securities.

Case Example 36.1 James Nistler and his wife bought undeveloped land in Jackson County, Oregon, and created a limited liability company to develop it. The property, called Tennessee Acres, was divided into six lots. Nistler obtained investors for the development by telling them that they would earn 12 to 15 percent interest on their investment and be repaid in full within a specified time. The property was never developed, the investors were never paid, and a substantial part of the funds provided by investors were used to pay Nistler and his wife.

Nistler was convicted of securities fraud. He appealed, claiming that the investments at issue did not involve "securities," but a state appellate court affirmed his conviction. The court found that there had been a pooling of funds from a group of investors, whose interests had been secured by the same land. The value of that land had been highly dependent on Nistler's use of the investors' funds to develop the land. In other words, the investors had engaged in a common enterprise from which they reasonably expected to profit, and that profit would be derived from the development efforts of Nistler.[5]

Many Types of Securities For our purposes, it is probably convenient to think of securities in their most common forms—stocks and bonds issued by corporations. Bear in mind, though, that securities can take many forms, including interests in whiskey, cosmetics, worms, beavers, boats, vacuum cleaners, muskrats, and cemetery lots. Almost any stake in

---

2. 15 U.S.C. Sections 77–77aa.
3. 15 U.S.C. Section 77b(1). Amendments in 1982 added stock options.
4. *Securities and Exchange Commission v. W. J. Howey Co.*, 328 U.S. 293, 66 S.Ct. 1100, 90 L.Ed. 1244 (1946).
5. *State of Oregon v. Nistler*, 286 Or.App. 470, 342 P.3d 1035 (2015).

the ownership or debt of a company can be considered a security. Investment contracts in condominiums, franchises, limited partnerships in real estate, and oil or gas or other mineral rights have qualified as securities as well.

36–1b Registration Statement

Section 5 of the Securities Act of 1933 broadly provides that a security must be *registered* before being offered to the public unless it qualifies for an exemption. The issuing corporation must file a *registration statement* with the SEC and must provide all investors with a *prospectus*. In principle, the registration statement and the prospectus supply sufficient information to enable unsophisticated investors to evaluate the financial risk involved.

A **prospectus** is a written disclosure document that describes the security being sold, the financial operations of the issuing corporation, and the investment or risk attaching to the security. The prospectus also serves as a selling tool for the issuing corporation. The SEC now allows an issuer to deliver its prospectus to investors electronically.[6]

Prospectus A written document required by securities laws when a security is being sold. The prospectus describes the security, the financial operations of the issuing corporation, and the risk attaching to the security.

Contents of the Registration Statement The registration statement must be written in plain English and must fully describe the following:

1. The securities being offered for sale, including their relationship to the issuer's other securities.
2. The corporation's properties and business (including a financial statement certified by an independent public accounting firm).
3. The management of the corporation, including managerial compensation, stock options, pensions, and other benefits. (See this chapter's *Managerial Strategy* feature for a discussion of a new SEC rule that imposes additional requirements on the disclosure of management compensation.) Any interests of directors or officers in any material transactions with the corporation must be disclosed.
4. How the corporation intends to use the proceeds of the sale.
5. Any pending lawsuits or special risk factors.

All companies, both domestic and foreign, must file their registration statements electronically so that they can be posted on the SEC's EDGAR (Electronic Data Gathering, Analysis, and Retrieval) database. The EDGAR database includes material on initial public offerings, proxy statements, corporations' annual reports, registration statements, and other documents that have been filed with the SEC. Investors can access the database online to obtain information that they can use to make investment decisions.

Know This
The purpose of the Securities Act of 1933 is disclosure. The SEC does not consider whether a security is worth the investment price.

The Registration Process The registration statement does not become effective until after it has been reviewed and approved by the SEC (unless it is filed by a *well-known seasoned issuer*, as will be discussed shortly). The process includes several stages, and the 1933 act restricts the types of activities that an issuer can engage in at each stage.

Prefiling Period. During the *prefiling period* (before the registration statement is filed), the issuer normally cannot sell or offer to sell the securities. Once the registration statement has been filed, a waiting period begins while the SEC reviews the registration statement for completeness.[7]

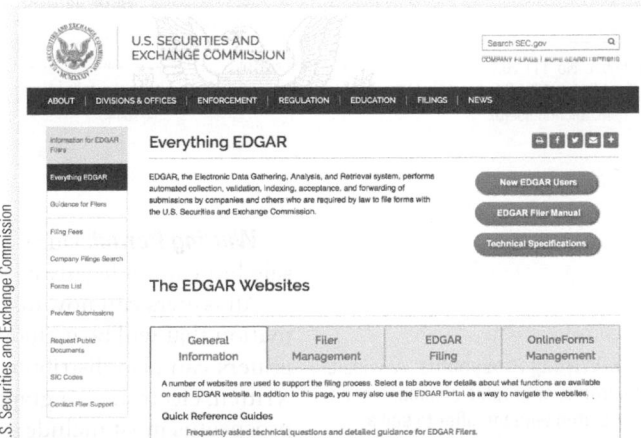

U.S. Securities and Exchange Commission

What type of information is posted on the Securities and Exchange Commission's EDGAR database?

---

6. Basically, an electronic prospectus must meet the same requirements as a printed prospectus. The SEC has special rules that address situations in which the graphics, images, or audio files in a printed prospectus cannot be reproduced in an electronic form. 17 C.F.R. Section 232.304.

7. The waiting period must last at least twenty days but always extends much longer because the SEC invariably requires numerous changes and additions to the registration statement.

The SEC's New Pay-Ratio Disclosure Rule

After the financial meltdown of recent years, Congress passed the Dodd-Frank Wall Street Reform and Consumer Protection Act.[a] One of the goals of the act was to improve accountability and transparency in the financial system. A brief section[b] in the lengthy bill requires a publicly held company to disclose the ratio of the total compensation of its chief executive officer (CEO) to the compensation of its "median" worker. For instance, if the annual pay of the median employee is $45,790 and the total compensation of the CEO is $12,260,000, then the pay ratio is 1 to 268. Otherwise stated, the CEO's income is 268 times greater than the income of the median employee.

Five Years in the Making

For five years, the Securities and Exchange Commission (SEC) hesitated to adopt a disclosure rule, as mandated by the Dodd-Frank act. The SEC received almost 300,000 comments and issued its own comments on the proposed rule.[c] The commissioners indicated that they were unsure what potential economic benefits, "if any," would be realized from making this information public. The SEC has estimated that the regulation will cost companies almost 550,000 annual paperwork hours, plus about $75 million per year to hire outside professionals.

Dealing with the New Rule

The new rule is 1,800 words long, and managers initially may find it difficult to implement. Fortunately for them, the SEC realizes that it can only ask for "reasonable estimates" of the CEO-worker pay ratio.

The CEO's measured compensation includes salary, bonuses, stocks and options, incentive plans, and other compensation. In theory, calculating this amount is fairly straightforward.

Calculating the median income of the company's labor force is more difficult. Note that the median income is not the average income of employees. Rather, the rule requires the company to identify a "median" employee as the basis for comparison.

The rule gives companies flexibility in determining how to identify this median employee. Statistical sampling can be used, for instance. And the rule states, "Since identifying the median involves finding the employee in the middle, it may not be necessary to determine the exact compensation amounts for every employee paid more or less than that employee in the middle." The rule also permits companies to make the median employee determination only once every three years.

Business Questions

1. *Why might the new SEC pay-ratio disclosure rule cause certain businesses to eliminate low-wage workers?*

2. *How might the new SEC pay-ratio disclosure rule help shareholders?*

---

a. Pub. L. No. 111-203, July 21, 2010, 124 Stat. 1376 (2010); codified at 12 U.S.C. Sections 5301 *et seq.*
b. *Ibid.*, Section 953(b).

c. 2013 WL 6503197 (2013, S.E.C. Release Nos. 33-9452 and 34-70443).

Waiting Period. During the *waiting period*, or *quiet period*, the securities can be offered for sale but cannot legally be sold. Only certain types of offers are allowed during this period.

All issuers can now distribute a *preliminary prospectus*, which contains most of the information that will be included in the final prospectus but often does not include a price. Most issuers can also distribute a *free-writing prospectus*.[8] A **free-writing prospectus** is any type of written, electronic, or graphic offer that describes the issuer or its securities. The free-writing prospectus must include a legend indicating that the issuer has filed a registration statement (including a prospectus) with the SEC and that these documents can be obtained at the SEC website.

> **Free-Writing Prospectus** A written, electronic, or graphic communication associated with the offer to sell a security and used during the waiting period to supplement other information about the security.

Posteffective Period. Once the SEC has reviewed and approved the registration statement and the waiting period is over, the registration is effective, and the *posteffective period* begins. The issuer can now offer and sell the securities without restrictions. If the company issued

---

8. See SEC Rules 164 and 433.

a preliminary or free-writing prospectus to investors, it must provide those investors with a final prospectus either before or at the time they purchase the securities. The issuer can require investors to download the final prospectus from a website if it notifies them of the appropriate Internet address.

Well-Known Seasoned Issuers A *well-known seasoned issuer* (WKSI) is a firm that has issued at least $1 billion in securities in the last three years or has outstanding stock valued at $700 million or more in the hands of the public.[9] WKSIs have greater flexibility than other issuers. They can file registration statements the day they announce a new offering and are not required to wait for SEC review and approval. They can also use a free-writing prospectus at any time, even during the prefiling period.

36–1c Exempt Securities

Certain types of securities are exempt from the registration requirements of the Securities Act because they are low-risk investments or are regulated by other statutes.[10] Exempt securities maintain their exempt status forever and can also be resold without being registered. Exempt securities include the following:

- Government-issued securities.
- Bank and financial institution securities.
- Short-term notes and drafts (negotiable instruments that have a maturity date that does not extend beyond nine months).
- Securities of nonprofit, educational, and charitable organizations.
- Securities issued by common carriers (railroads and trucking companies).
- Insurance policies, endowments, and annuity contracts.
- Securities issued in a corporate reorganization in which one security is exchanged for another or in a bankruptcy proceeding.
- Securities issued in stock dividends and stock splits.

36–1d Exempt Transactions

The Securities Act of 1933 also exempts certain transactions from registration requirements (see Exhibit 36–1 for a summary of these exemptions.) The transaction exemptions are very broad and can enable an issuer to avoid the high cost and complicated procedures associated with registration. For instance, private (nonpublic) offerings that involve a small number of investors generally are exempt. Securities offered and sold only to residents of the state in which the issuing firm is incorporated and does business are also exempt. In addition, crowdfunding is allowed without SEC registration, as discussed in this chapter's *Adapting the Law to the Online Environment* feature.

Note, however, that even when a transaction is exempt from the registration requirements, the offering is still subject to the antifraud provisions of the 1933 act (and the 1934 act).

Know This
The issuer of an exempt security does not have to disclose the same information as other issuers.

Exhibit 36–1 Exempt Transactions under the 1933 Securities Act

Exempt Transactions

Regulation A

Securities issued by an issuer that has offered less than $50 million in securities during any twelve-month period if the issuer meets specific requirements:

- Tier 1 for offerings of up to $20 million in a twelve-month period. (Unlimited number of investors, both accredited and unaccredited.)

- Tier 2 for offerings of up to $50 million with additional review requirements in a twelve-month period. (Unlimited number of investors, but unaccredited investors may not invest more than 10 percent of their annual income or net worth.)

Regulation D

- **Rule 504:** Noninvestment company offerings up to $5 million in any twelve-month period.

- **Rule 506:** Private, noninvestment company offerings in unlimited amounts that are not generally advertised or solicited. Unlimited number of accredited investors and thirty-five unaccredited investors.

Unregistered Restricted Securities

Restricted securities must be registered before resale *unless* they qualify for a safe harbor under Rule 144 or 144A.

---

9. Securities Offering Reform, codified at 17 C.F.R. Sections 200, 228, 229, 230, 239, 240, 243, 249, and 274.
10. 15 U.S.C. Section 77c.

Investment Crowdfunding—Regulations and Restrictions

Today, small entrepreneurs can gain access to public funds through crowdfunding without filing a registration statement with the Securities and Exchange Commission (SEC). Generally, crowdfunding refers to raising small sums of money from a large number of individuals via the Internet. Crowdfunding as a way for businesses to raise equity capital was made possible by the Jumpstart Our Business Startups Act, or JOBS Act—specifically, by Title III, also known as the Crowdfund Act.[a]

Restrictions on Those Who Invest

The Crowdfund Act imposes certain restrictions on investors. The aggregate amount sold to any investor cannot exceed the greater of $2,000 or 5 percent of the investor's annual income or net worth if that net worth is less than $100,000. For those investors with higher incomes or net worth, the limit is 10 percent.

Other Restrictions

Companies seeking investment funds through crowdfunding cannot offer shares directly to investors. They must go through an online fundraising platform registered with the SEC. Some companies that provide such platforms, such as Venture.com, take an active role in the crowdfunding process, drafting paperwork and soliciting investors. Others, such as NetSeed and StartEngine, take a more hands-off approach. An increasing number of approved crowdfunding portals are available. They usually impose a fee of 5 to 9 percent of the funds raised.

Of course, a potential start-up entrepreneur does not simply create a video and ask people to send money via the Internet. Paperwork must be filed prior to the start of a crowdfunding campaign, and detailed financial statements must be available for potential investors. Indiegogo, Inc., an international crowdfunding website, has estimated that companies spend at least $7,000 on compliance and other regulatory matters before starting a crowdfunding campaign.

The Success Rate?

Investors who provide funds to crowdfunded start-ups naturally expect a return on their investment. Consider, though, that half of all new companies are not in business five years after start-up. Consider further that many companies offering investment opportunities via crowdfunding have already been rejected by professional investors. Otherwise stated, these investors did not believe that the companies' products, services, or management warranted investment.

Thus, the fact that you have shares in a company because you invested in its crowdfunding campaign does not mean that you can do much with them. Those shares are not publicly traded. It may be difficult, if not impossible, to cash out the shares unless the new firm is acquired by a larger company or goes public through an initial public offering.

Critical Thinking

What alternatives are there to crowdfunding for a start-up business?

---

a. Pub. L. No. 112-106, April 5, 2012, 126 Stat 306; and 17 C.F.R. Section 227.

Regulation A Offerings Securities issued by an issuer that has offered less than $50 million in securities during any twelve-month period are exempt from registration.[11] Under Regulation A,[12] the issuer must file with the SEC a notice of the issue and an offering circular, which must also be provided to investors before the sale. This is a much simpler and less expensive process than full registration.

There are two types of public offerings under this regulation:

- Tier 1, for securities offerings of up to $20 million in a twelve-month period.

- Tier 2, for securities offerings of up to $50 million in a twelve-month period. (Legislation has been proposed that would raise the Tier 2 limit to $75 million.)

---

11. 15 U.S.C. Section 77c(b).
12. 17 C.F.R. Sections 230.251–230.263.

An issuer of $20 million or less of securities can elect to proceed under either Tier 1 or Tier 2. Both tiers are subject to certain basic requirements, and Tier 2 offerings are subject to additional requirements. Purchasers under Tier 2 who are not *accredited investors* cannot purchase shares that cost more than 10 percent of their annual income or net worth. (**Accredited investors** are sophisticated investors, such as banks, insurance companies, and people whose income or net worth exceeds a certain amount.)

    Important Rule Changes. Note that the cap for Regulation A—which, as noted, is now $50 million—was $5 million until 2015. At that time, the SEC approved rule changes (commonly known as Reg A+) to make it easier for small and mid-sized businesses to raise capital. This chapter's *Landmark in the Law* feature discusses these important changes.

Accredited Investor In the context of securities offerings, sophisticated investors, such as banks, insurance companies, investment companies, the issuer's executive officers and directors, and persons whose income or net worth exceeds certain limits.

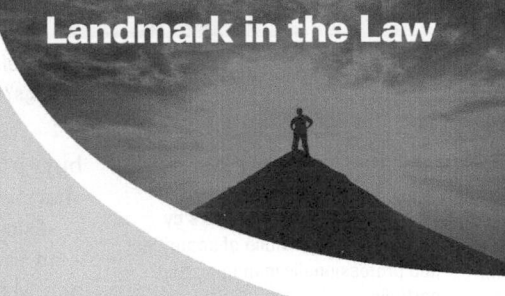

Landmark in the Law

Changes to Regulation A: "Reg A+"

Under the Securities Act of 1933, before offering or selling securities, a corporation must register the securities with the SEC unless the securities qualify for an exemption.

    Traditionally, most of the exempt transactions have involved offers and sales made to *accredited investors* (sophisticated investors, such as banks, insurance companies, and people whose income or net worth exceeds a certain amount). As a result, members of the general public were unable to invest in smaller, growth-stage companies and start-ups.

    In addition, small businesses and start-ups were at a relative disadvantage in raising capital through initial public offerings (IPOs) if they could not qualify for an exemption or afford the cost of SEC registration. Start-ups were forced to seek financing from other sources, often giving up some degree of control in the business in exchange for funds.

Legislation Led to Amended Rules
Congress passed the Jumpstart Our Business Startups Act (JOBS Act)[a] to encourage small business growth and to bolster employment. The goal was to provide more funding and reduce the regulatory hurdles for companies trying to go public. In 2015, the SEC adopted final rules (Regulation A+ or Reg A+) to implement the JOBS Act. These rules establish an IPO process that is less expensive and complicated than the procedures associated with normal SEC registration.

Reg A+ Provides Benefits Reg A+ expands the number of issuers that qualify for exemption by raising the limit from $5 to $50 million. It also creates a two-tier system—one for companies seeking to raise less than $20 million, and another for those seeking to raise between $20 and $50 million. Small and mid-sized businesses can now raise up to $50 million a year selling stock by using a simple, streamlined, and cost-efficient process. A bill proposed in Congress, if passed, will further raise the maximum to $75 million a year.[b]

    Moreover, anyone in the world can invest in Reg A+ offerings, not just accredited investors, although some restrictions apply to certain offerings.[c] Companies can also advertise their stock to the general public. (This is not possible with transactions exempted under Regulation D, however.)

Application to Today's Law *The SEC's changes to Regulation A offer average investors enhanced opportunities to invest in companies that they believe in and hope to profit from financially. Reg A+ also helps start-ups and growing companies reach a bigger pool of potential investors and still retain control of their operations. Because it provides a simpler, lower-cost IPO process for small businesses, Reg A+ is likely to decrease the significance of all the other exemptions over time.*

---

a. Pub. L. No. 112-106, April 5, 2012, 126 Stat 306.

b. Regulation A+ Improvement Act, H.R. 4263.

c. For Tier 2 offerings, unaccredited investors cannot invest more than to 10 percent of their annual income or net worth.

Example 36.2 Myomo, Inc., is a company based in Massachusetts that makes robotic medical devices for people with upper-body paralysis. The company relied on venture capital funding for a number of years but decided to take advantage of the amended Regulation A when it became available. Seeking to raise $15 million, Myomo became the first company to issue an initial public offering under Regulation A+.

Testing the Waters. Before preparing a Regulation A offering circular, companies are allowed to "test the waters" for potential interest. To *test the waters* means to determine potential interest without actually selling any securities or requiring any commitment on the part of those who express interest.

Small Offerings—Regulation D   The SEC's Regulation D contains exemptions from registration requirements (Rules 504 and 506) for offers that either involve a small dollar amount or are made in a limited manner.

Rule 504. Rule 504 is the exemption used by most small businesses. It provides that noninvestment company offerings up to $5 million in any twelve-month period are exempt. Noninvestment companies are firms that are not engaged primarily in the business of investing or trading in securities. (In contrast, an **investment company** is a firm that buys a large portfolio of securities and professionally manages it on behalf of many smaller shareholders-owners. A **mutual fund** is a type of investment company.)

Example 36.3 Zeta Enterprises is a limited partnership that develops commercial property. Zeta intends to offer $600,000 of its limited partnership interests for sale between June 1 and May 31. According to the definition of a security, this offering would be subject to the registration and prospectus requirements of the 1933 Securities Act.

Under Rule 504, however, the sales of Zeta's interests are exempt from these requirements because Zeta is a noninvestment company making an offering of less than $1 million in a twelve-month period. Therefore, Zeta can sell its limited partnership interests without filing a registration statement with the SEC or issuing a prospectus to any investor.

Rule 506—Private Placement Exemption. Rule 506 exempts private, noninvestment company offerings in unlimited amounts if these offerings are not generally solicited or advertised. This exemption is often referred to as the *private placement exemption* because it exempts "transactions not involving any public offering."[13] The offering can involve an unlimited number of accredited investors and no more than thirty-five unaccredited investors. The issuer must believe that each unaccredited investor has sufficient knowledge or experience in financial matters to be capable of evaluating the investment's merits and risks.[14]

The private placement exemption is perhaps most important to firms that want to raise funds through the sale of securities without registering them. **Example 36.4** Citco Corporation needs to raise capital to expand its operations. Citco decides to make a private $10 million offering of its common stock directly to two hundred accredited investors and thirty highly sophisticated, but unaccredited, investors. Citco provides all of these investors with a prospectus and material information about the firm, including its most recent financial statements.

As long as Citco notifies the SEC of the sale, this offering will likely qualify for the private placement exemption. The offering is nonpublic and not generally advertised.

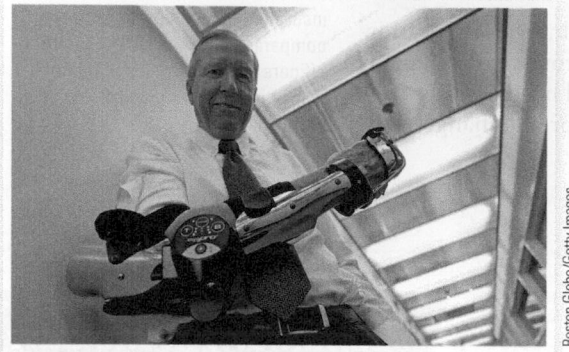

How did Myomo, Inc., in Massachusetts, benefit from recent rule changes to Regulation A offerings?

Boston Globe/Getty Images

Investment Company A company that acts on the behalf of many smaller shareholders-owners by buying a large portfolio of securities and professionally managing that portfolio.

Mutual Fund A specific type of investment company that continually buys or sells to investors shares of ownership in a portfolio.

Know This

An investor can be "sophisticated" by virtue of his or her education and experience or by virtue of investing through a knowledgeable, experienced representative.

---

13. 15 U.S.C. Section 77d(2).
14. 17 C.F.R. Section 230.506.

There are fewer than thirty-five unaccredited investors, and each of them possesses sufficient knowledge and experience to evaluate the risks involved. The issuer has provided all purchasers with the necessary material information. Thus, Citco will *not* be required to comply with the registration requirements of the Securities Act. ■

Resales and Safe Harbor Rules Most securities can be resold without registration. The Securities Act provides exemptions for resales by most persons other than issuers or underwriters. Thus, the average investor who sells shares of stock does not have to file a registration statement with the SEC.

Different rules apply to resales of *restricted securities*—securities acquired in an unregistered private sale. Resales of restricted securities trigger the registration requirements unless the party selling them complies with Rule 144 or Rule 144A. These rules are sometimes referred to as "safe harbors."

How does the Securities and Exchange Commission's Regulation D exemption help small businesses with small offerings?

mavo/Shutterstock.com

Rule 144. Rule 144 exempts restricted securities from registration on resale if all of the following conditions are met:

1. There is adequate current public information about the issuer. ("Adequate current public information" refers to the reports that certain companies are required to file under the 1934 Securities Exchange Act.)

2. The person selling the securities has owned them for at least six months, if the issuer is subject to the reporting requirements of the 1934 act. If the issuer is not subject to the 1934 act's reporting requirements, the seller must have owned the securities for at least one year.

3. The securities are sold in certain limited amounts in unsolicited brokers' transactions.

4. The SEC is notified of the resale.[15]

Rule 144A. Rule 144A allows the resale of unregistered securities that, at the time of issue, are not of the same class as securities listed on a national securities exchange or quoted in a U.S. automated interdealer quotation system.[16] The securities may be sold only to qualified institutional buyers (institutions, such as insurance companies or banks, that hold and manage at least $100 million in securities). The seller must take reasonable steps to ensure that the buyer knows that the seller is relying on the exemption under Rule 144A.

36–1e **Violations of the 1933 Act**

It is a violation of the Securities Act to intentionally defraud investors by misrepresenting or omitting facts in a registration statement or prospectus. Liability may also be imposed on those who are negligent with respect to the preparation of these publications. Selling securities before the effective date of the registration statement or under an exemption for which the securities do not qualify also results in liability.

Can the omission of a fact make a statement of opinion misleading to an ordinary investor? That was the question before the United States Supreme Court in the following case.

Know This
Securities do not have to be held for a specific period (six months) to be exempt from registration on a resale under Rule 144A, as they do under Rule 144.

---

15. 17 C.F.R. Section 230.144.
16. 17 C.F.R. Section 230.144A.

■ Case 36.1

Omnicare, Inc. v. Laborers District Council Construction Industry Pension Fund

Supreme Court of the United States __ U.S. __, 135 S.Ct. 1318, 191 L.Ed.2d 253 (2015).

Background and Facts Omnicare, Inc., a pharmacy services company, filed a registration statement in connection with a public offering. The statement expressed the company's opinion that it was in compliance with federal and state laws. Later, the federal government accused Omnicare of receiving kickbacks from pharmaceutical manufacturers. The Laborers District Council Construction Industry Pension Fund and others (the Funds), who had bought the stock, filed a suit in a federal district court against Omnicare.

What requirements does a drug company need to satisfy to file an accurate registration statement?

The plaintiffs alleged that Omnicare's legal-compliance opinion was "untrue" and that Omnicare had, in violation of the Securities Act, "omitted to state [material] facts necessary" to make that opinion not misleading. Omnicare claimed that "no reasonable person, in any context, can understand a pure statement of opinion to convey anything more than the speaker's own mindset." The court dismissed the plaintiff's suit. The U.S. Court of Appeals for the Sixth Circuit reversed the dismissal in part and affirmed in part. The Funds appealed to the United States Supreme Court.

In the Words of the Court

Justice *KAGAN* delivered the opinion of the Court.

* * * *

* * * Whether a statement is "misleading" depends on the perspective of a reasonable investor: The inquiry * * * is objective.

* * * *

* * * A reasonable person understands, and takes into account, the difference * * * between a statement of fact and one of opinion. She recognizes the import of words like "I think" or "I believe," and grasps that they convey some lack of certainty as to the statement's content.

But Omnicare takes its point too far, because a reasonable investor may, depending on the circumstances, understand an opinion statement to convey facts about how the speaker has formed the opinion—or, otherwise put, about the speaker's basis for holding that view. And if the real facts are otherwise, but not provided, the opinion statement will mislead its audience. Consider

an unadorned statement of opinion about legal compliance: "We believe our conduct is lawful." * * * If the issuer made the statement in the face of its lawyers' contrary advice, or with knowledge that the Federal Government was taking the opposite view, the investor * * * has cause to complain: He expects not just that the issuer believes the opinion (however irrationally), but that it fairly aligns with the information in the issuer's possession at the time. Thus, *if a registration statement omits material facts about the issuer's inquiry into or knowledge concerning a statement of opinion, and if those facts conflict with what a reasonable investor would take from the statement itself, then [the Securities Act] creates liability.* [Emphasis added.]

An opinion statement, however, is not necessarily misleading when an issuer knows, but fails to disclose, some fact cutting the other way. * * * A reasonable investor does not expect that *every* fact known to an issuer supports its opinion statement. [Emphasis in the original.]

Moreover, *whether an omission makes an expression of opinion misleading always depends on context.* Registration statements as a class are formal documents, filed with the SEC as a legal prerequisite for selling securities to the public. Investors do not, and are right not to, expect opinions contained in those statements to reflect baseless, off-the-cuff judgments, of the kind that an individual might communicate in daily life. At the same time, an investor reads each statement within such a document, whether of fact or opinion, in light of all its surrounding text, including hedges, disclaimers, and apparently conflicting information. And the investor takes into account the customs and practices of the relevant industry. * * * The reasonable investor understands a statement of opinion in its full context, and [the Securities Act] creates liability only for the omission of material facts that cannot be squared with such a fair reading. [Emphasis added.]

Decision and Remedy The United States Supreme Court concluded that "neither [lower court] considered the Funds' omissions theory with the right standard in mind." The Court therefore vacated the decision of the lower court and remanded the case "for a determination of whether the Funds have stated a viable omissions claim (or, if not, whether they should have a chance to replead)."

• **Legal Environment** *Would a reasonable investor have cause to complain if an issuer, without having consulted a lawyer, states, "We believe our conduct is lawful"? Explain.*

Remedies Criminal violations are prosecuted by the U.S. Department of Justice. Violators may be fined anywhere from $10,000 to $2 million, depending on circumstances, and imprisoned for up to five years.

The SEC is authorized to seek civil sanctions against those who willfully violate the 1933 act. It can request an injunction to prevent further sales of the securities involved or ask the court to grant other relief, such as an order to a violator to refund profits. Parties who purchase securities and suffer harm as a result of false or omitted statements may also bring suits in a federal court to recover their losses and other damages.

Defenses There are three basic defenses to charges of violations under the 1933 act. A defendant can avoid liability by proving any of the following:

1. The statement or omission was not material.

2. The plaintiff knew about the misrepresentation at the time of purchasing the stock.

3. The defendant exercised *due diligence* in preparing the registration and reasonably believed at the time that the statements were true and there were no omissions of material facts.

✦ **Spotlight Case Example 36.5** In preparation for an initial public offering (IPO), Blackstone Group, LP, filed a registration statement with the SEC. At the time, Blackstone's corporate private equity investments included FGIC Corporation (which insured investments in subprime mortgages) and Freescale Semiconductor, Inc. Before the IPO, FGIC's customers began to suffer large losses, and Freescale lost an exclusive contract to make wireless 3G chipsets for Motorola, Inc. (its largest customer). The losses suffered by these two companies would affect Blackstone. Nevertheless, Blackstone's registration statement did not mention the impact on its revenues of the investments in FGIC and Freescale.

Martin Litwin and others who invested in Blackstone's IPO filed a suit in a federal district court against Blackstone and its officers, alleging material omissions from the statement. Blackstone argued as a defense that the omissions were not material, and the lower court dismissed the case. The plaintiffs appealed. A federal appellate court ruled in favor of the plaintiffs that the alleged omissions were reasonably likely to be material, and remanded the case. The plaintiffs were entitled to the opportunity to prove at a trial that Blackstone had omitted material information that it was required to disclose.[17]

Blackstone Group, LP, owned a large interest in Freescale Semiconductor, Inc. Should Blackstone have revealed in its registration statement that Freescale had lost a major 3G chipset order?

36–2 Securities Exchange Act of 1934

The 1934 Securities Exchange Act provides for the regulation and registration of securities exchanges, brokers, dealers, and national securities associations, such as the National Association of Securities Dealers (NASD). Unlike the 1933 act, which is a one-time disclosure law, the 1934 act provides for continuous periodic disclosures by publicly held corporations to enable the SEC to regulate subsequent trading.

---

17. *Litwin v. Blackstone Group, LP,* 634 F.3d 706 (2d Cir. 2011).

The Securities Exchange Act applies to companies that have assets in excess of $10 million and either two thousand or more shareholders or five hundred or more shareholders who are unaccredited. These corporations are referred to as *Section 12 companies* because they are required to register their securities under Section 12 of the 1934 act. Section 12 companies must file reports with the SEC annually and quarterly, and sometimes even monthly if specified events occur (such as a merger). Other provisions in the 1934 act require all securities brokers and dealers to be registered, to keep detailed records of their activities, and to file annual reports with the SEC.

The act also authorizes the SEC to engage in market surveillance to deter undesirable market practices such as fraud, market manipulation (attempts at illegally influencing stock prices), and misrepresentation. In addition, the act provides for the SEC's regulation of proxy solicitations for voting.

36–2a Section 10(b), SEC Rule 10b-5, and Insider Trading

Section 10(b) is an especially important section of the Securities Exchange Act. This section proscribes the use of any manipulative or deceptive mechanism in violation of SEC rules and regulations. Among the rules that the SEC has promulgated pursuant to Section 10(b) is **SEC Rule 10b-5,** which prohibits the commission of fraud in connection with the purchase or sale of any security.

SEC Rule 10b-5 applies to almost all cases concerning the trading of securities, whether on organized exchanges, in over-the-counter markets, or in private transactions. Generally, the rule covers just about any form of security, and the securities need not be registered under the 1933 act for the 1934 act to apply.

Private parties can sue for securities fraud under the 1934 act and SEC Rule 10b-5. The basic elements of a securities fraud action are as follows:

1. A *material misrepresentation* (or omission) in connection with the purchase and sale of securities.
2. *Scienter* (a wrongful state of mind).
3. *Reliance* by the plaintiff on the material misrepresentation.
4. An *economic loss*.
5. *Causation,* meaning that there is a causal connection between the misrepresentation and the loss.

Insider Trading One of the major goals of Section 10(b) and SEC Rule 10b-5 is to prevent so-called **insider trading,** which occurs when persons buy or sell securities on the basis of information that is not available to the public. Corporate directors, officers, and majority shareholders, among others, often have advance inside information about events that can affect the future market value of the corporate stock. Obviously, acting on this information would give them a trading advantage over the general public and other shareholders.

The 1934 act defines inside information and extends liability to those who take advantage of such information in their personal transactions when they know that the information is unavailable to those with whom they are dealing. Section 10(b) of the act and SEC Rule 10b-5 apply to anyone who has access to or receives information of a nonpublic nature on which trading is based—not just to corporate "insiders."

Disclosure under SEC Rule 10b-5 Any material omission or misrepresentation of material facts in connection with the purchase or sale of a security may violate not only the Securities Act of 1933 but also the antifraud provisions of Section 10(b) of the 1934 act and SEC Rule 10b-5. The key to liability (which can be civil or criminal) under Section 10(b) and SEC Rule 10b-5 is whether the insider's information is *material*.

SEC Rule 10b-5 A rule of the Securities and Exchange Commission that prohibits the commission of fraud in connection with the purchase or sale of any security.

Know This

A required element in any fraud claim is reliance. The innocent party must justifiably have relied on the misrepresentation.

Insider Trading The purchase or sale of securities on the basis of information that has not been made available to the public.

Learning Objective 2

What is insider trading? Why is it prohibited?

The following are some examples of material facts calling for disclosure under SEC Rule 10b-5:

1. Fraudulent trading in the company's stock by a broker-dealer.

2. A dividend change (whether up or down).

3. A contract for the sale of corporate assets.

4. A new discovery, a new process, or a new product.

5. A significant change in the firm's financial condition.

6. Potential litigation against the company.

Note that any one of these facts, by itself, is not *automatically* considered a material fact. Rather, it will be regarded as a material fact if it is significant enough that it would likely affect an investor's decision as to whether to purchase or sell the company's securities.

What are some examples of material facts that should be disclosed according to SEC Rule 10b-5?

Example 36.6 Sheen, Inc., is the defendant in a class-action product liability suit that its attorney, Paula Frasier, believes that the company will lose. Frasier has advised Sheen's directors, officers, and accountants that the company will likely have to pay a substantial damages award. Sheen plans to make a $5 million offering of newly issued stock before the date when the trial is expected to end. Sheen's potential liability and the financial consequences to the firm are material facts that must be disclosed, because they are significant enough to affect an investor's decision as to whether to purchase the stock. ▪

The following is a *Classic Case* interpreting materiality under SEC Rule 10b-5.

🏛 Classic Case 36.2

Securities and Exchange Commission v. Texas Gulf Sulphur Co.

United States Court of Appeals, Second Circuit, 401 F.2d 833 (1968).

Background and Facts In the late 1950s, Texas Gulf Sulphur Company (TGS) conducted aerial geophysical surveys over more than fifteen thousand square miles of Eastern Canada. The operations indicated concentrations of commercially exploitable minerals. At one site near Timmins, Ontario, TGS drilled a hole that appeared to yield a core with an exceedingly high mineral content. The company did not disclose the results of the sample to the public. After learning of the sample, officers and employees of the company made substantial purchases of TGS's stock or accepted stock options (rights to purchase stock).

On April 11, 1964, an unauthorized report of the mineral find appeared in the newspapers. On the following day, TGS issued a press release that played

After sample drilling revealed potential mineral deposits, company executives made large stock purchases. Did they violate insider trading laws?

down the discovery and stated that it was too early to tell whether the ore discovery would be significant. Several months later, TGS announced that the strike was expected to yield at least 25 million tons of ore. Subsequently, the price of TGS stock rose substantially.

The Securities and Exchange Commission (SEC) brought a suit in a federal district court against the officers and employees of TGS for violating the insider-trading prohibition of SEC Rule 10b-5. The officers and employees argued that the information on which they traded had not been material at the time of the trades because the strike had not been commercially proved. The trial court held that most of the defendants had not violated SEC Rule 10b-5, and the SEC appealed.

(Continues)

In the Words of the Court
WATERMAN, Circuit Judge.

* * * *

* * * Whether facts are material within Rule 10b-5 when the facts relate to a particular event and are undisclosed by those persons who are knowledgeable thereof *will depend at any given time upon a balancing of both the indicated probability that the event will occur and the anticipated magnitude of the event in light of the totality of the company activity.* Here, * * * knowledge of the possibility, which surely was more than marginal, of the existence of a mine of the vast magnitude indicated by the remarkably rich drill core located rather close to the surface (suggesting mineability by the less expensive open-pit method) within the confines of a large anomaly (suggesting an extensive region of mineralization) might well have affected the price of TGS stock and would certainly have been an important fact to a reasonable, if speculative, investor in deciding whether he should buy, sell, or hold. [Emphasis added.]

* * * *

* * * A major factor in determining whether the * * * discovery was a material fact is the importance attached to the drilling results by those who knew about it. * * * The timing by those who knew of it of their stock purchases * * * —purchases in some cases by individuals who had never before purchased * * * TGS stock—virtually compels the inference that the insiders were influenced by the drilling results.

Decision and Remedy The appellate court ruled in favor of the SEC. All of the trading by insiders who knew of the mineral find before its true extent had been publicly announced had violated SEC Rule 10b-5.

Critical Thinking

• **What If the Facts Were Different?** *Suppose that further drilling revealed that there was not enough ore at this site for it to be mined commercially. Would the defendants still have been liable for violating SEC Rule 10b-5? Why or why not?*

• **Impact of This Case on Today's Law** *This landmark case affirmed the principle that the test of whether information is "material," for SEC Rule 10b-5 purposes, is whether it would affect the judgment of reasonable investors. The corporate insiders' acquisition of stock and stock options indicated that they were influenced by the results—in other words, that the information about the drilling results was material. The courts continue to cite this case when applying SEC Rule 10b-5 to cases of alleged insider trading.*

Outsiders and SEC Rule 10b-5 The traditional insider-trading case involves true insiders—corporate officers, directors, and majority shareholders who have access to (and trade on) inside information. Increasingly, liability under Section 10(b) of the 1934 act and SEC Rule 10b-5 is being extended to certain "outsiders"—persons who trade on inside information acquired indirectly. Two theories have been developed under which outsiders may be held liable for insider trading: the *tipper/tippee theory* and the *misappropriation theory*.

Tippee A person who receives inside information.

Tipper/Tippee Theory. Anyone who acquires inside information as a result of a corporate insider's breach of his or her fiduciary duty can be liable under SEC Rule 10b-5. This liability extends to **tippees** (those who receive "tips" from insiders) and even remote tippees (tippees of tippees).

The key to liability under this theory is that the inside information must be obtained as a result of someone's breach of a fiduciary duty to the corporation whose shares are involved in the trading. The tippee is liable under this theory only if the following requirements are met:

1. There is a breach of a duty not to disclose inside information.
2. The disclosure is in exchange for personal benefit.
3. The tippee knows (or should know) of this breach and benefits from it.

Case Example 36.7 Eric McPhail was a member of the same country club as an executive at American Superconductor. While they were golfing, the executive shared information with McPhail about the company's expected earnings, contracts, and other major developments, trusting that McPhail would keep the information confidential. Instead, McPhail repeatedly tipped six of his other golfing buddies at the country club, and they all used the nonpublic information to their advantage in trading. In this situation, the executive breached his duty not to disclose the information, which McPhail knew. McPhail (the tippee) is liable under SEC Rule 10b-5, and so are his other golfing buddies (remote tippees). All traded on inside information to their benefit.[18]

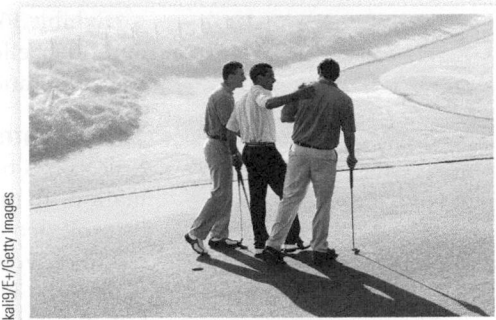

kali9/E+/Getty Images

A golfer obtains inside information while playing with an executive of a listed company. The golfer then tells his friends about this valuable information. When can friends be liable for insider trading under securities law?

Misappropriation Theory. Liability for insider trading may also be established under the misappropriation theory. Under this theory, an individual who wrongfully obtains (misappropriates) inside information and trades on it for her or his personal gain should be held liable because, in essence, she or he stole information rightfully belonging to another.

The misappropriation theory has been controversial because it significantly extends the reach of SEC Rule 10b-5 to outsiders who ordinarily would *not* be deemed fiduciaries of the corporations in whose stock they trade. It is not always wrong to disclose material, nonpublic information about a company to another person. Nevertheless, a person who obtains the information and trades securities on it can be liable.

Case Example 36.8 Robert Bray, a real estate developer, first met Patrick O'Neill, an executive at Eastern Bank, at the Oakley Country Club, and the two men became good friends. One day, Bray told O'Neill that he needed cash to fund a project and asked O'Neill if he had any "bank stock tips" for him. O'Neill rattled off a few names of local banks. Then Bray wrote the word "Wainwright" on a napkin and slid it across the bar to O'Neill.

O'Neill, who knew that Eastern Bank was in the process of buying Wainwright Bank, told Bray, "this could be a good one." The next day, Bray bought 25,000 shares of Wainwright stock, and he bought another 31,000 shares a few weeks later. Then, Eastern publicly announced that it was buying Wainwright, and the stock price doubled. Bray eventually sold the stock at a profit of $300,000.

The SEC prosecuted Bray for insider trading using the misappropriation theory. He was convicted after a jury trial. On appeal, the conviction was affirmed. Bray and O'Neill had been good friends for many years. The jury could reasonably have concluded that Bray not only knew that he had traded on material, nonpublic information, but also knew that O'Neill owed Eastern a duty of loyalty and confidentiality.[19]

"The way to stop financial 'joy-riding' is to arrest the chauffeur, not the automobile."

Woodrow Wilson
1856–1924
(Twenty-eighth president of the United States, 1913–1921)

Insider Reporting and Trading—Section 16(b)

Section 16(b) of the 1934 act provides for the recapture by the corporation of all profits realized by an insider on a purchase and sale, or sale and purchase, of the corporation's stock within any six-month period.[20] It is irrelevant whether the insider actually uses inside information—all such **short-swing profits** must be returned to the corporation.

In this context, *insiders* means officers, directors, and large stockholders of Section 12 corporations. (Large stockholders are those owning at least 10 percent of the class of equity securities registered under Section 12 of the 1934 act.) To discourage such insiders from using nonpublic information about their companies for their personal benefit in the stock market, the SEC requires them to file reports concerning their ownership and trading of the corporation's securities.

Short-Swing Profits Profits earned by a purchase and sale, or sale and purchase, of the same security within a six-month period.

Section 16(b) applies not only to stock but also to stock warrants, options, and securities convertible into stock. In addition, the courts have fashioned complex rules for determining profits. Note, however, that the SEC exempts a number of transactions under Rule 16b-3.[21]

---

18. Three of the defendants in this case agreed to settle with the SEC and return the trading profits. See SEC press release 2014-134, "SEC Charges Group of Amateur Golfers in Insider Trading Ring."

19. *United States v. Bray,* 853 F.3d 18 (1st Cir. 2017).

20. A person who expects the price of a particular stock to decline can realize profits by "selling short"—selling at a high price and repurchasing later at a lower price to cover the "short sale."

21. 17 C.F.R. Section 240.16b-3.

Exhibit 36–2 compares the effects of SEC Rule 10b-5 and Section 16(b). Because of these and other effects, corporate insiders are wise to seek specialized counsel before trading in the corporation's stock.

The Private Securities Litigation Reform Act The disclosure requirements of SEC Rule 10b-5 had the unintended effect of deterring the disclosure of forward-looking information. To understand why, consider an example. **Example 36.9** BT Company announces that its projected earnings in a future time period will be a certain amount, but the forecast turns out to be wrong. The earnings are, in fact, much lower, and the price of BT's stock is affected negatively. The shareholders then file a suit against BT, claiming that its directors violated SEC Rule 10b-5 by disclosing misleading financial information. ▮

To encourage companies to make earnings projections, Congress passed the Private Securities Litigation Reform Act (PSLRA) in 1995.[22] The PSLRA provides a "safe harbor" for publicly held companies that make forward-looking statements, such as financial forecasts. Those who make such statements are protected against liability for securities fraud if they include "meaningful cautionary statements identifying important factors that could cause actual results to differ materially from those in the forward-looking statement."[23]

The PSLRA also affects the level of detail required in securities fraud complaints. Plaintiffs must specify each purportedly misleading statement and say how it led them to a mistaken belief.

36–2b Regulation of Proxy Statements

Section 14(a) of the Securities Exchange Act of 1934 regulates the solicitation of proxies (authorization to vote shares) from shareholders of Section 12 companies. The SEC regulates the content of proxy statements. Whoever solicits a proxy must fully and accurately disclose in the proxy statement all of the facts that are pertinent to the matter on which the shareholders are to vote. SEC Rule 14a-9 is similar to the antifraud provisions of SEC Rule 10b-5. Remedies for violations range from injunctions to prevent a vote from being taken to monetary damages.

---

22. Pub. L. No. 104-67, 109 Stat. 737 (codified in scattered sections of Title 15 of the *United States Code*).
23. 15 U.S.C. Sections 77z-2, 78u-5.

Exhibit 36–2 Comparison of Coverage, Application, and Liability under SEC Rule 10b-5 and Section 16(b)

AREA OF COMPARISON	SEC RULE 10b-5	SECTION 16(b)
What is the subject matter of the transaction?	Any security (does not have to be registered).	Any security (does not have to be registered).
What transactions are covered?	Purchase or sale.	Short-swing purchase and sale or short-swing sale and purchase.
Who is subject to liability?	Almost anyone with inside information under a duty to disclose—including officers, directors, controlling shareholders, and tippees.	Officers, directors, and shareholders who own 10 percent or more of the relevant class of securities.
Is omission or misrepresentation necessary for liability?	Yes.	No.
Are there any exempt transactions?	No.	Yes, there are a number of exemptions.
Who may bring an action?	A person transacting with an insider, the SEC, or a purchaser or seller damaged by a wrongful act.	A corporation or a shareholder by derivative action.

36–2c Violations of the 1934 Act

As mentioned earlier, violations of Section 10(b) of the Securities Exchange Act and SEC Rule 10b-5, including insider trading, may be subject to criminal or civil liability.

Scienter Requirement For either criminal or civil sanctions to be imposed, *scienter* must exist—that is, the violator must have had an intent to defraud or knowledge of her or his misconduct. *Scienter* can be proved by showing that the defendant made false statements or wrongfully failed to disclose material facts. In some situations, *scienter* can even be proved by showing that the defendant was consciously reckless as to the truth or falsity of his or her statements.

Case Example 36.10 Etsy, Inc., a Brooklyn-based company, operates a website that connects buyers and sellers of handmade and vintage goods. When Etsy went public, it filed a prospectus and registration statement that set forth its commitment to working solely with "responsible, small-batch manufacturing partners" that adhere to Etsy's ethical expectations. Further, it described the company as "a mindful, transparent, and humane business." The statement also explained the company's methods for safeguarding against counterfeit goods and goods that infringe on another's copyright or trademark rights.

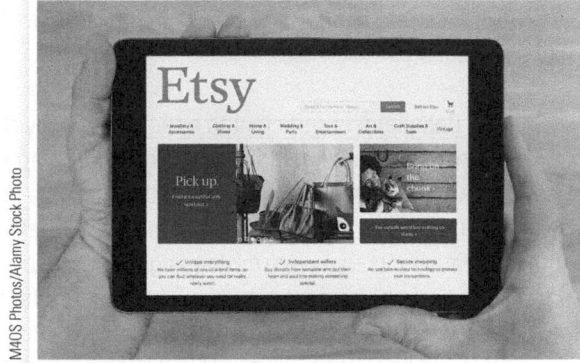

Saleh Altayyar and several other investors sued Etsy, alleging that it had misrepresented or omitted material facts in its registration statement. The plaintiffs claimed that Etsy had made false and misleading statements about its values and that nearly 5 percent of its goods were counterfeit or infringing. Etsy argued that it had exercised due diligence and reasonably believed that the statements were true and contained no omissions of material facts. A federal district court in New York ruled in Etsy's favor and dismissed the case. The court found that the plaintiffs did not establish *scienter*. "The plaintiffs may disagree with the defendants' opinions [statements about the company], but disagreement does not render the opinions false."[24]

Did Etsy violate the 1933 act by omitting material facts on its registration statement? Why or why not?

The plaintiff must state facts giving rise to an inference of *scienter*—knowledge that an action was illegal or that statements were false—in his or her complaint. The dispute in the following case was whether, as part of an allegation of securities fraud under Section 10(b) of the 1934 act, the plaintiffs adequately alleged the required elements of the claim, including *scienter*.

---

24. *Altayyar v. Etsy, Inc.*, 242 F.Supp.3d 161 (E.D.N.Y. 2017).

■ Case 36.3

Singer v. Reali

United States Court of Appeals, Fourth Circuit, 883 F.3d 425 (2018).

Background and Facts TranS1, Inc., a medical device company, sold the "System," a spinal surgical procedure. TranS1's financial success hinged on reimbursement by health insurers and government health-care programs of the claims of the surgeons who used the System. When the American Medical Association designated the System to be "experimental," surgeons could no longer count on being reimbursed for its use. TranS1 then coached surgeons to file fraudulent claims that would allow for full reimbursement. The company's officers publicly stated that they were "assisting surgeons in obtaining appropriate reimbursement" but did not reveal the fraudulent scheme.

(Continues)

When TranS1 disclosed that the government was investigating the firm, the value of its stock dropped. Phillip Singer and other shareholders filed a suit in a federal district court against Kenneth Reali and other TranS1 officers, alleging a violation of Section 10(b). The court dismissed the complaint. The plaintiffs appealed.

In the Words of the Court
KING, Circuit Judge:

* * * *

* * * *The material misrepresentation element * * * of a Section 10(b) claim requires an allegation that the defendant acted deceptively, i.e., that the defendant engaged in deceptive acts such as misstatements and omissions by those with a duty to disclose. Furthermore, the deceptive act must concern a material fact.* [Emphasis added.]

* * * *

* * * The Complaint is sufficient to establish that, by choosing to speak about its reimbursement practices, the Company possessed a duty to disclose its alleged illegal conduct. The Company violated that duty and acted deceptively by way of false statements and statements that were misleading because they omitted the fraudulent reimbursement scheme. Furthermore, the facts of that scheme were material, in that a reasonable investor would have considered the scheme important in deciding whether to buy or sell TranS1 stock.

* * * *

* * * To allege the *scienter* element, a plaintiff must demonstrate that the defendant acted with a mental state embracing intent to deceive, manipulate, or defraud.

* * * *

By alleging that the fraudulent reimbursement scheme was known to the Officers, clearly illegal, and fundamental to TranS1's financial success, the Complaint * * * gives rise to a strong inference that TranS1 and the Officers intended to deceive the market, or at the very least acted recklessly, when they made false and misleading statements about the Company's reimbursement practices that omitted the fraudulent reimbursement scheme.

* * * *

* * * The * * * causation element requires the pleading of a sufficiently direct relationship between the plaintiff's economic loss and the defendant's fraudulent conduct, which may be accomplished by alleging facts establishing that the defendant's misrepresentation or omission was one substantial cause of the investment's decline in value.

* * * *

[After the government began its investigation, TranS1] revealed enough facts for the market to finally recognize what the Officers' previous statements had materially omitted: the existence of the Company's fraudulent reimbursement scheme.

* * * According to the Complaint, the revelations * * * caused the value of TranS1's stock to plummet more than 40 percent * * *. Such an allegation is wholly adequate to demonstrate that the exposure of the Company's fraud was at least one substantial cause of the investment's decline in value.

Decision and Remedy   The U.S. Court of Appeals for the Fourth Circuit vacated the judgment of the district court and remanded the case. The complaint sufficiently alleged the misrepresentation, *scienter*, and cause of the plaintiffs' loss.

Critical Thinking

• **Legal Environment** *In documents available to the public, TranS1 included general warnings about "the risks of regulatory scrutiny and litigation." Did this satisfy the company's duty to disclose its allegedly fraudulent scheme? Why or why not?*

• **Economic** *If the plaintiffs can prove the elements of their claim, what should be the measure of their damages? Explain.*

***Scienter* Not Required for Section 16(b) Violations**   Violations of Section 16(b) include the sale by insiders of stock acquired less than six months before the sale (or less than six months after the sale if selling short). These violations are subject to civil sanctions. Liability under Section 16(b) is strict liability. Neither *scienter* nor negligence is required.

Criminal Penalties   For violations of Section 10(b) and Rule 10b-5, an individual may be fined up to $5 million, imprisoned for up to twenty years, or both. A partnership or a corporation may be fined up to $25 million. The Sarbanes-Oxley Act increased the penalties for securities fraud. Section 807 of the act provides that for a *willful* violation of the 1934 act, the violator may be imprisoned for up to twenty-five years in addition to being fined.

For a defendant to be convicted in a criminal prosecution under the securities laws, there can be no reasonable doubt that the defendant knew he or she was acting wrongfully. A jury is not allowed merely to speculate that the defendant may have acted willfully.

Case Example 36.11 Douglas Newton was the president and sole director of Real American Brands, Inc. (RLAB). RLAB owned the Billy Martin's USA brand and operated a Billy Martin's retail boutique at the Trump Plaza in New York City. (Billy Martin's, a Western wear store, was co-founded by Billy Martin, the one-time manager of the New York Yankees.)

Newton agreed to pay kickbacks to Chris Russo, whom he believed to be the manager of a pension fund, to induce the fund to buy shares of RLAB stock. Newton later arranged for his friend Yan Skwara to pay similar kickbacks for the fund's purchase of stock in U.S. Farms, Inc. In reality, the pension fund was fictitious, and Newton and Skwara had been dealing with agents of the Federal Bureau of Investigation (FBI). Newton was charged with securities fraud and convicted by a jury (Skwara pled guilty). Newton appealed, but a federal appellate court upheld his conviction.

According to the court, the evidence established that in each transaction, the amount of the kickback was added to the price of the stock, which artificially increased the stock price. The evidence sufficiently proved that Newton had engaged in a scheme to defraud the supposed pension fund. His words and conduct, which were revealed on video at the trial, showed his intent to defraud the pension fund investors.[25]

Civil Sanctions The SEC can also bring suit in a federal district court against anyone violating or aiding in a violation of the 1934 act or SEC rules by purchasing or selling a security while in the possession of material nonpublic information.[26] The violation must occur on or through the facilities of a national securities exchange or through a broker or dealer. A court may assess a penalty for as much as triple the profits gained or the loss avoided by the guilty party. In addition, the Insider Trading and Securities Fraud Enforcement Act increased the number of persons who may be subject to civil liability for insider trading and gave the SEC authority to pay monetary rewards to informants.[27]

Private parties may also sue violators of Section 10(b) and Rule 10b-5. A private party may obtain rescission (cancellation) of a contract to buy securities or damages to the extent of the violator's illegal profits. Those found liable have a right to seek contribution from those who share responsibility for the violations, including accountants, attorneys, and corporations. For violations of Section 16(b), a corporation can bring an action to recover the short-swing profits.

36–2d **Online Securities Fraud**

A problem facing the SEC today is how to enforce the antifraud provisions of the securities laws in the online environment. Internet-related forms of securities fraud include many types of investment scams. Spam, online newsletters and bulletin boards, chat rooms, blogs, social media, and tweets can all be used to spread false information and perpetrate fraud. For a relatively small cost, fraudsters can even build sophisticated Web pages to facilitate their investment scams.

In addition, the SEC has filed an increasing number of enforcement actions against perpetrators of *Ponzi schemes*. (Ponzi schemes are fraudulent investment operations that pay returns to investors from new capital paid to the fraudsters rather than from a legitimate investment.)

Investment Newsletters Hundreds of online investment newsletters provide information on stocks. Legitimate online newsletters can help investors gather valuable information, but some e-newsletters are used for fraud. The law allows companies to pay the people who write

---

25. *United States v. Newton,* 559 Fed.Appx. 902 (11th Cir. 2014).
26. The Insider Trading Sanctions Act, 15 U.S.C. Section 78u(d).
27. 15 U.S.C. Section 78u-1.

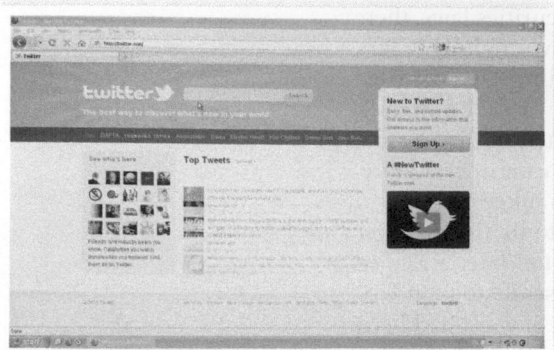

How do social media, such as Twitter and Facebook, complicate securities fraud?

these newsletters to tout their securities, but the newsletters are required to disclose who paid for the advertising. Many newsletters do not follow that law, however. Thus, an investor reading an online newsletter may believe that the information is unbiased, when in fact the fraudsters will directly profit by convincing investors to buy or sell particular stocks.

Social Media Social media sites have presented a particularly difficult problem for the SEC. Using sites such as Twitter and Facebook, anonymous fraudsters can quickly disseminate information to millions of people at little or no cost. Again, their aim is to convince others to trade in specific stocks. It can be difficult for the SEC to access social media accounts to investigate potential violations. The government must subpoena the sites to determine the user behind particular messages. In addition, social media sites are constantly being updated and changed, which adds another wrinkle for enforcement.

36–3 State Securities Laws

Learning Objective 3

What are some of the features of state securities laws?

Today, every state has its own corporate securities laws, or "blue sky laws," that regulate the offer and sale of securities within its borders. (The phrase *blue sky laws* dates to a 1917 decision by the United States Supreme Court in which the Court declared that the purpose of such laws was to prevent "speculative schemes which have no more basis than so many feet of 'blue sky.'")[28] Article 8 of the Uniform Commercial Code, which has been adopted by all of the states, also imposes various requirements relating to the purchase and sale of securities.

36–3a Requirements under State Securities Laws

State securities laws apply mainly to intrastate transactions (transactions within one state). Typically, state laws have disclosure requirements and antifraud provisions, many of which are patterned after Section 10(b) of the Securities Exchange Act and SEC Rule 10b-5. State laws also provide for the registration of securities offered or issued for sale within the state and impose disclosure requirements.

Case Example 36.12 Randall Fincke was the founder, director, and officer of Access Cardiosystems, Inc., a small start-up company that sold portable automated external heart defibrillators. Fincke prepared a business plan that stated Access's "patent counsel" had advised him that Access's product did not infringe any patents. This statement was false—patent counsel never offered Access any opinion on the question of infringement.

Fincke gave this plan to potential investors, including Joseph Zimmel, who bought $1.5 million in Access shares. When the company later filed for Chapter 11 bankruptcy protection, Zimmel filed a complaint with the federal bankruptcy court, alleging that Fincke had violated the Massachusetts blue sky law. The court awarded Zimmel $1.5 million in damages, and the award was affirmed on appeal. Fincke had solicited investors by means of a false statement of material fact, in violation of the fraud provisions in the state's securities laws.[29]

Methods of registration, required disclosures, and exemptions from registration vary among states. Unless an exemption from registration is applicable, issuers must register or qualify their stock with the appropriate state official, often called a *corporations commissioner.* Additionally, most state securities laws regulate securities brokers and dealers.

---

28. *Hall v. Geiger-Jones Co.*, 242 U.S. 539, 37 S.Ct. 217, 61 L.Ed. 480 (1917).
29. *In re Access Cardiosystems, Inc.*, 776 F.3d 30 (1st Cir. 2015).

36–3b Concurrent Regulations

Since the adoption of the 1933 and 1934 federal securities acts, the state and federal governments have regulated securities concurrently. Issuers must comply with both federal and state securities laws, and exemptions from federal law are not exemptions from state laws.

The dual federal and state system has not always worked well, particularly during the early 1990s, when the securities markets underwent considerable expansion. Today, most duplicate regulations have been eliminated, and the SEC has exclusive power to regulate most national securities activities. The National Conference of Commissioners on Uniform State Laws also substantially revised the Uniform Securities Act to coordinate state and federal securities regulation and enforcement efforts. Nineteen states have adopted the most recent version of the Uniform Securities Act.[30]

Know This
Federal securities laws do not take priority over state securities laws.

36–4 Corporate Governance

Corporate governance can be narrowly defined as the relationship between a corporation and its shareholders. Some argue for a broader definition—that corporate governance specifies the rights and responsibilities among different participants in the corporation, such as the board of directors, managers, shareholders, and other stakeholders, and spells out the rules and procedures for making decisions on corporate affairs. Regardless of the way it is defined, effective corporate governance requires more than just compliance with laws and regulations. (For a discussion of corporate governance in other nations, see this chapter's *Beyond Our Borders* feature.)

Effective corporate governance is essential in large corporations because corporate ownership (by shareholders) is separated from corporate control (by officers and managers). Under these circumstances, officers and managers may attempt to advance their own interests at the expense of the shareholders. The well-publicized corporate scandals in the first decade of the 2000s clearly illustrate the reasons for concern about managerial opportunism.

Corporate Governance A set of policies specifying the rights and responsibilities of the various participants in a corporation and spelling out the rules and procedures for making corporate decisions.

---

30. At the time this book went to press, the Uniform Securities Act had been adopted in Georgia, Hawaii, Idaho, Indiana, Iowa, Kansas, Maine, Michigan, Minnesota, Mississippi, Missouri, New Hampshire, New Mexico, Oklahoma, South Carolina, South Dakota, Vermont, Wisconsin, and Wyoming, as well as the U.S. Virgin Islands.

Corporate Governance in Other Nations

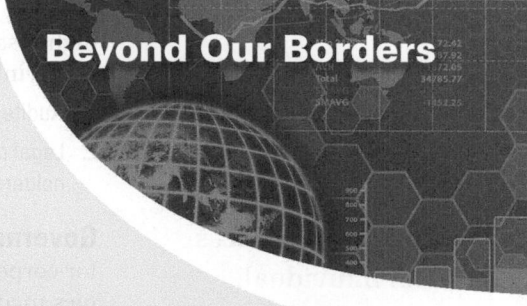

Beyond Our Borders

Corporate governance has become an issue of concern not only for U.S. corporations, but also for corporate entities around the world. With the globalization of business, a corporation's bad acts (or lack of control systems) can have far-reaching consequences.

Different models of corporate governance exist in different nations, often depending on the degree of capitalism in the particular nation. In the United States, corporate governance tends to give priority to shareholders' interests. This approach encourages significant innovation, as well as cost and quality competition.

In contrast, the coordinated model of governance that prevails in continental Europe and Japan gives priority to the interests of so-called stakeholders—employees, managers, suppliers, customers, and the community. The coordinated model still encourages innovation and cost and quality competition, but not to the same extent as the U.S. model.

Critical Thinking
Why does the presence of a capitalist system affect a nation's perspective on corporate governance?

36–4a Aligning the Interests of Officers and Shareholders

Stock Option A right to buy a given number of shares of stock at a set price, usually within a specified time period.

Some corporations have sought to align the financial interests of their officers with those of the company's shareholders by providing the officers with **stock options,** which enable them to purchase shares of the corporation's stock at a set price. When the market price rises above that level, the holders can sell their shares for a profit. Because a stock's market price generally increases as the corporation prospers, stock options give the officers a financial stake in the corporation's well-being and supposedly encourage them to work hard for the benefit of the shareholders.

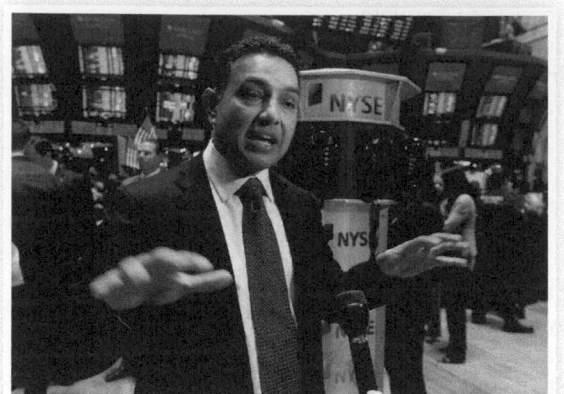

Stock options are valuable when the market price of a company's shares rises greatly. Why?

Problems with Stock Options Options have turned out to be an imperfect device for encouraging effective governance, however. Executives in some companies have been tempted to "cook" the company's books in order to keep share prices higher so that they could sell their stock for a profit. Executives in other corporations have experienced no losses when share prices dropped because their options were "repriced" so that they did not suffer from the share price decline. Thus, although stock options theoretically can motivate officers to protect shareholder interests, stock option plans have sometimes become a way for officers to take advantage of shareholders.

Outside Directors With stock options generally failing to work as planned, there has been an outcry for more outside directors (those with no formal employment affiliation with the company). The theory is that independent directors will more closely monitor the actions of corporate officers. Hence, today we see more boards with outside directors. Note, though, that outside directors may not be truly independent of corporate officers. They may be friends or business associates of the leading officers.

36–4b Promoting Accountability

Effective corporate governance standards are designed to address problems and to motivate officers to make decisions that promote the financial interests of the company's shareholders. Generally, corporate governance entails corporate decision-making structures that monitor employees (particularly officers) to ensure that they are acting for the benefit of the shareholders. Firms that are more accountable to shareholders typically report higher profits, higher sales growth, higher firm value, and other economic advantages. Corporate governance involves, at a minimum:

1. Audited reporting of the corporation's financial progress, so that managers can be evaluated.

2. Legal protections for shareholders so that violators of the law who attempt to take advantage of shareholders can be punished for misbehavior and victims can recover damages for any associated losses.

Governance and Corporate Law State corporation statutes set up the legal framework for corporate governance. Under the corporate law of Delaware, where most major companies incorporate, all corporations must have certain structures of corporate governance in place. The most important structure, of course, is the board of directors, because the board makes the major decisions about the future of the corporation.

"Honesty is the single most important factor having a direct bearing on the final success of an individual, corporation, or product."

Ed McMahon
1923–2009
(American entertainer)

The Board of Directors Under corporate law, a corporation must have a board of directors elected by the shareholders. Directors are responsible for ensuring that the corporation's officers are operating wisely and in the exclusive interest of shareholders. The directors receive reports from the officers and give them managerial direction. In reality, though, corporate directors devote a relatively small amount of time to monitoring officers.

Ideally, shareholders would monitor the directors' supervision of the officers. In practice, however, it can be difficult for shareholders to monitor directors and hold them responsible for corporate failings. Although the directors can be sued for failing to do their jobs effectively, directors are rarely held personally liable.

The Audit Committee. A crucial committee of the board of directors is the *audit committee,* which oversees the corporation's accounting and financial reporting processes, including both internal and outside auditors. Unless the committee members have sufficient expertise and are willing to spend the time to carefully examine the corporation's bookkeeping methods, however, the audit committee may be ineffective.

The audit committee also oversees the corporation's "internal controls." These controls, carried out largely by the company's internal auditing staff, are measures taken to ensure that reported results are accurate. For instance, internal controls help to determine whether a corporation's debts are collectible. If the debts are not collectible, it is up to the audit committee to make sure that the corporation's financial officers do not simply pretend that payment will eventually be made.

The Compensation Committee. Another important committee of the board of directors is the *compensation committee.* This committee monitors and determines the compensation of the company's officers. As part of this process, it is responsible for assessing the officers' performance and for designing a compensation system that will better align the officers' interests with those of the shareholders.

36–4c The Sarbanes-Oxley Act

In 2002, following a series of corporate scandals, Congress passed the Sarbanes-Oxley Act,[31] which addresses certain issues relating to corporate governance. Generally, the act attempts to increase corporate accountability by imposing strict disclosure requirements and harsh penalties for violations of securities laws. The act requires chief corporate executives to take responsibility for the accuracy of financial statements and reports that are filed with the SEC.

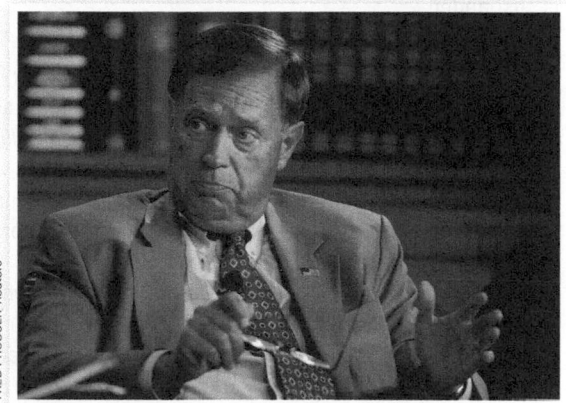

Additionally, the act requires that certain financial and stock-transaction reports be filed with the SEC earlier than was required under the previous rules. The act also created a new entity, called the Public Company Accounting Oversight Board, to regulate and oversee public accounting firms. Other provisions of the act established private civil actions and expanded the SEC's remedies in administrative and civil actions.

Michael Oxley, a former member of the U.S. House of Representatives, was a co-sponsor of the Sarbanes-Oxley Act.

Because of the importance of this act for corporate leaders and for those dealing with securities transactions, we highlight some of its key provisions relating to corporate accountability in Exhibit 36–3.

More Internal Controls and Accountability The Sarbanes-Oxley Act introduced direct *federal* corporate governance requirements for public companies (companies whose shares are traded in the public securities markets). The law addressed many of the corporate governance procedures discussed here and created new requirements in an attempt to make the system work more effectively. The requirements deal with independent monitoring of company officers by both the board of directors and auditors.

Sections 302 and 404 of Sarbanes-Oxley require high-level managers (the most senior officers) to establish and maintain an effective system of internal controls. The system must include "disclosure controls and procedures" to ensure that company financial reports are accurate and timely and to document financial results prior to reporting.

---

31. 15 U.S.C. Sections 7201 *et seq.*

Exhibit 36–3 Some Key Provisions of the Sarbanes-Oxley Act Relating to Corporate Accountability

Certification Requirements—Under Section 906 of the Sarbanes-Oxley Act, the chief executive officers (CEOs) and chief financial officers (CFOs) of most major companies listed on public stock exchanges must certify financial statements that are filed with the SEC. CEOs and CFOs must certify that filed financial reports "fully comply" with SEC requirements and that all of the information reported "fairly represents in all material respects, the financial conditions and results of operations of the issuer."

Under Section 302 of the act, CEOs and CFOs of reporting companies are required to certify that a signing officer reviewed each quarterly and annual filing with the SEC and that none contained untrue statements of material fact. Also, the signing officer or officers must certify that they have established an internal control system to identify all material information and that any deficiencies in the system were disclosed to the auditors.

Effectiveness of Internal Controls on Financial Reporting—Under Section 404(a), all public companies are required to assess the effectiveness of their internal control over financial reporting. Section 404(b) requires independent auditors to report on management's assessment of internal controls, but companies with a public float (price times total shares publicly owned) of less than $75 million are exempted from this requirement.

Loans to Directors and Officers—Section 402 prohibits any reporting company, as well as any private company that is filing an initial public offering, from making personal loans to directors and executive officers (with a few limited exceptions, such as for certain consumer and housing loans).

Protection for Whistleblowers—Section 806 protects whistleblowers—employees who report ("blow the whistle" on) securities violations by their employers—from being fired or in any way discriminated against by their employers.

Blackout Periods—Section 306 prohibits certain types of securities transactions during "blackout periods"—periods during which the issuer's ability to purchase, sell, or otherwise transfer funds in individual account plans (such as pension funds) is suspended.

Enhanced Penalties for—

- *Violations of Section 906 Certification Requirements*—A CEO or CFO who certifies a financial report or statement filed with the SEC knowing that the report or statement does not fulfill all of the requirements of Section 906 will be subject to criminal penalties of up to $1 million in fines, ten years in prison, or both. *Willful* violators of the certification requirements may be subject to $5 million in fines, twenty years in prison, or both.
- *Violations of the 1934 Securities Exchange Act*—Penalties for securities fraud under the 1934 act were increased. Individual violators may be fined up to $5 million, imprisoned for up to twenty years, or both. *Willful* violators may be imprisoned for up to twenty-five years in addition to being fined.
- *Destruction or Alteration of Documents*—Anyone who alters, destroys, or conceals documents or otherwise obstructs any official proceeding will be subject to fines, imprisonment for up to twenty years, or both.
- *Other Forms of White-Collar Crime*—The act stiffened the penalties for certain criminal violations, such as federal mail and wire fraud, and ordered the U.S. Sentencing Commission to revise the sentencing guidelines for white-collar crimes.

Statute of Limitations for Securities Fraud—Section 804 provides that a private right of action for securities fraud may be brought no later than two years after the discovery of the violation or five years after the violation, whichever is earlier.

Senior management must reassess the system's effectiveness annually. Some companies had to take expensive steps to bring their internal controls up to the new federal standard. After the act was passed, hundreds of companies reported that they had identified and corrected shortcomings in their internal control systems.

Exemptions for Smaller Companies The Sarbanes-Oxley Act initially required all public companies to have an independent auditor file a report with the SEC on management's assessment of internal controls. Later, however, Congress enacted an exemption for smaller companies in an effort to reduce compliance costs. Public companies with a market capitalization, or public float (price times total shares publicly owned), of less than $75 million no longer need to have an auditor report on management's assessment of internal controls.

Certification and Monitoring Requirements Section 906 requires that chief executive officers (CEOs) and chief financial officers (CFOs) certify that the information in the corporate financial statements "fairly represents in all material respects, the financial conditions and results of operations of the issuer." This requirement makes officers directly accountable for the accuracy of their financial reporting and avoids any "ignorance defense" if shortcomings are later discovered.

The act also includes requirements to improve directors' monitoring of officers' activities. All members of the corporate audit committee for public companies must be outside directors. The audit committee must have a written charter that sets out its duties and provides for performance appraisal. At least one "financial expert" must serve on the audit committee, which must hold executive meetings without company officers present. In addition to reviewing the internal controls, the committee also monitors the actions of the outside auditor.

Learning Objective 4
What certification requirements does the Sarbanes-Oxley Act impose on corporate executives?

Practice and Review

Dale Emerson served as the chief financial officer for Reliant Electric Company, a distributor of electricity serving portions of Montana and North Dakota. Reliant was in the final stages of planning a takeover of Dakota Gasworks, Inc., a natural gas distributor that operated solely within North Dakota. On a weekend fishing trip with his uncle, Ernest Wallace, Emerson mentioned that he had been putting in a lot of extra hours at the office planning a takeover of Dakota Gasworks. When he returned from the fishing trip, Wallace purchased $20,000 worth of Reliant stock. Three weeks later, Reliant made a tender offer to Dakota Gasworks stockholders and purchased 57 percent of Dakota Gasworks stock. Over the next two weeks, the price of Reliant stock rose 72 percent before leveling out. Wallace sold his Reliant stock for a gross profit of $14,400. Using the information presented in the chapter, answer the following questions.

1. Would registration with the SEC be required for Dakota Gasworks securities? Why or why not?
2. Did Emerson violate Section 10(b) of the Securities Exchange Act of 1934 and SEC Rule 10b-5? Why or why not?
3. What theory or theories might a court use to hold Wallace liable for insider trading?
4. Under the Sarbanes-Oxley Act, who would be required to certify the accuracy of the financial statements Reliant filed with the SEC?

Debate This
Insider trading should be legalized.

Key Terms

accredited investor 847
corporate governance 861
free-writing prospectus 844
insider trading 852
investment company 848

investment contract 842
mutual fund 848
prospectus 843
SEC Rule 10b-5 852
securities 841

short-swing profits 855
stock option 862
tippee 854

Chapter Summary: Investor Protection, Insider Trading, and Corporate Governance

Securities Act of 1933	Prohibits fraud and stabilizes the securities industry by requiring disclosure of all essential information relating to the issuance of securities to the investing public.
	
	1. *Registration requirements*—Securities, unless exempt, must be registered with the SEC before being offered to the public.
	   a. The *registration statement* must include detailed financial information about the securities being offered for sale; the issuing corporation's properties, business, and management; the intended use of the proceeds of the sale of the securities being issued; and any pending lawsuits or special risk factors.
	   b. The issuer must provide investors with a *prospectus* that describes the security being sold, the financial operations of the issuing corporation, and the investment or risk attaching to the security.
	2. *Exemptions*—The SEC has exempted certain offerings from the requirements of the Securities Act of 1933. Exemptions may be determined on the basis of the size of the issue, whether the offering is private or public, and whether advertising is involved.

Securities Exchange Act of 1934	Provides for the regulation and registration of securities exchanges, brokers, dealers, and national securities associations. Maintains a continuous disclosure system for publicly held corporations to enable the SEC to regulate subsequent trading. Applies to companies that have assets in excess of $10 million and either two thousand or more shareholders or five hundred or more shareholders who are unaccredited (Section 12 companies).
	
	1. *SEC Rule 10b-5 [under Section 10(b) of the 1934 act]*—This rule prohibits the commission of fraud in connection with the purchase or sale of any security.
	   a. Applies to almost all trading of securities—a firm's securities do not have to be registered under the 1933 act for the 1934 act to apply.
	   b. Applies to insider trading by corporate officers, directors, majority shareholders, and any persons receiving inside information (information not available to the public) who base their trading on this information. Liability for insider trading may be based on the tipper/tippee or the misappropriation theory.
	   c. May be violated by omitting or misrepresenting "material facts" related to the purchase or sale of a security.
	   d. Liability for violations can be civil or criminal.
	2. *Insider trading [under Section 16(b) of the 1934 act]*—To prevent corporate insiders from taking advantage of inside information, the 1934 act requires officers, directors, and shareholders owning 10 percent or more of the issued stock of a corporation to turn over to the corporation all short-term profits (called *short-swing profits*) realized from the purchase and sale or sale and purchase of corporate stock within any six-month period.
	3. *Regulation of proxies*—Section 14(a) of the 1934 act regulates the solicitation of proxies from shareholders of Section 12 companies.
	4. *Online securities fraud*—The SEC today faces the problem of enforcing the antifraud provisions of the securities laws in the online environment. Internet-related forms of securities fraud include fraudulent newsletters and social media posts.

State Securities Laws	Regulate the offer and sale of securities within state borders (also known as *blue sky laws*). States regulate securities concurrently with the federal government. The Uniform Securities Act is designed to promote coordination of state and federal securities regulation and enforcement efforts.
Corporate Governance	Involves a set of policies specifying the rights and responsibilities of the various participants in a corporation and spelling out the rules and procedures for making decisions on corporate affairs. Corporate governance is necessary in large corporations because corporate ownership (by the shareholders) is separated from corporate control (by officers and managers). This separation of corporate ownership and control can often result in conflicting interests. Corporate governance standards address such issues. **1.** *Aligning the interests of officers and shareholders*—Some corporations attempt to align the financial interests of their officers with those of their shareholders by providing the officers with stock options. **2.** *Sarbanes-Oxley Act*—This act attempts to increase corporate accountability by imposing strict disclosure requirements and harsh penalties for violations of securities laws.

Issue Spotters

1. When a corporation wishes to issue certain securities, it must provide sufficient information for an unsophisticated investor to evaluate the financial risk involved. Specifically, the law imposes liability for making a false statement or omission that is "material." What sort of information would an investor consider material? (See *Securities Exchange Act of 1934*.)

2. Lee is an officer of Magma Oil, Inc. Lee knows that a Magma geologist has just discovered a new deposit of oil. Can Lee take advantage of this information to buy and sell Magma stock? Why or why not? (See *Securities Exchange Act of 1934*.)

—**Check your answers to the *Issue Spotters* against the answers provided in Appendix D at the end of this text.**

Business Scenarios and Case Problems

36–1. Registration Requirements. Langley Brothers, Inc., a corporation incorporated and doing business in Kansas, decides to sell common stock worth $1 million to the public. The stock will be sold only within the state of Kansas. Joseph Langley, the chair of the board, says the offering need not be registered with the Securities and Exchange Commission. His brother, Harry, disagrees. Who is right? Explain. (See *Securities Act of 1933*.)

36–2. Insider Trading. David Gain is the chief executive officer (CEO) of Forest Media Corp., which is interested in acquiring RS Communications, Inc. To initiate negotiations, Gain meets with RS's CEO, Gill Raz, on Friday, July 12. Two days later, Gain phones his brother, Mark, who buys 3,800 shares of RS stock on the following Monday. Mark discusses the deal with their father, Jordan, who buys 20,000 RS shares on Thursday. On July 25, the day before the RS bid is due, Gain phones his parents' home, and Mark buys another 3,200 RS shares. Over the next few days, Gain periodically phones Mark and Jordan, both of whom continued to buy RS shares. On August 5, RS refuses Forest's bid and announces that it is merging with another company. The price of RS stock rises 30 percent, increasing the value of Mark's and Jordan's shares by nearly $660,000 and $400,000, respectively. Is Gain guilty of insider trading? What is required to impose sanctions for this offense? Could a court hold Gain liable? Why or why not? (See *Securities Exchange Act of 1934*.)

36–3. Violations of the 1934 Act. Matrixx Initiatives, Inc., makes and sells over-the-counter pharmaceutical products. Its core brand is Zicam, which accounts for 70 percent of its sales. Matrixx received reports that some consumers had lost their sense of smell (a condition called *anosmia*) after using Zicam Cold Remedy. Four product liability suits were filed against Matrixx, seeking damages for anosmia. In public statements relating to revenues and product safety, however, Matrixx did not reveal this information.

James Siracusano and other Matrixx investors filed a suit in a federal district court against the company and its executives under Section 10(b) of the Securities Exchange Act of 1934 and SEC Rule 10b-5, claiming that the statements were misleading because they did not disclose the information about the product liability suits. Matrixx argued that to be material, information must consist of a statistically significant number of adverse events that require disclosure. Because Siracusano's claim did not allege that Matrixx

knew of a statistically significant number of adverse events, the company contended that the claim should be dismissed. What is the standard for materiality in this context? Should Siracusano's claim be dismissed? Explain. [*Matrixx Initiatives, Inc. v. Siracusano*, 563 U.S. 27, 131 S.Ct. 1309, 179 L.Ed.2d 398 (2011)] (See *Securities Exchange Act of 1934*.)

36–4. Business Case Problem with Sample Answer— Disclosure under SEC Rule 10b-5. Dodona I, LLC, invested $4 million in two securities offerings from Goldman, Sachs & Co. The investments were in collateralized debt obligations (CDOs). Their value depended on residential mortgage-backed securities (RMBSs), whose value in turn depended on the performance of subprime residential mortgages. Before marketing the CDOs, Goldman had noticed several "red flags" relating to investments in the subprime market, in which it had invested heavily.

To limit its risk, Goldman began betting against subprime mortgages, RMBSs, and CDOs, including the CDOs it had sold to Dodona. In other words, Goldman made investments based on the assumption that subprime mortgages and the securities instruments built upon them would decrease in value. In an internal e-mail, one Goldman official commented that the company had managed to "make some lemonade from some big old lemons." Nevertheless, Goldman's marketing materials provided only boilerplate statements about the risks of investing in the securities. The CDOs were later downgraded to junk status, and Dodona suffered a major loss while Goldman profited. Assuming that Goldman did not affirmatively misrepresent any facts about the CDOs, can Dodona still recover under SEC Rule 10b-5? If so, how? [*Dodona I, LLC v. Goldman, Sachs & Co.*, 847 F.Supp.2d 624 (S.D.N.Y. 2012)] (See *Securities Exchange Act of 1934*.)

—**For a sample answer to Problem 36–4, go to Appendix E at the end of this text.**

36–5. Violations of the 1933 Act. Three shareholders of iStorage sought to sell their stock through World Trade Financial Corp. The shares were *restricted securities*—that is, securities acquired in an unregistered, private sale. Restricted securities typically bear a "restrictive" legend clearly stating that they cannot be resold in the public marketplace. This legend had been wrongly removed from the iStorage shares, however. Information about the company that was publicly available included the fact that, despite a ten-year life, it had no operating history or earnings. In addition, it had net losses of about $200,000, and its stock was thinly traded. Without investigating the company or the status of its stock, World Trade sold more than 2.3 million shares to the public on behalf of the three customers. Did World Trade violate the Securities Act of 1933? Discuss. [*World Trade Financial Corp. v. U.S. Securities and Exchange Commission*, 739 F.3d 1243 (9th Cir. 2014)] (See *Securities Act of 1933.*)

36–6. Securities Act of 1933. Big Apple Consulting USA, Inc., provided small publicly traded companies with a variety of services, including marketing, business planning, and website development and maintenance. CyberKey Corp. sold customizable USB drives. CyberKey falsely informed Big Apple that CyberKey had been awarded a $25 million contract with the Department of Homeland Security (DHS). Big Apple used this information in aggressively promoting CyberKey's stock and was compensated for the effort in the form of CyberKey shares. When the Securities and Exchange Commission (SEC) began to investigate, Big Apple sold its shares for $7.8 million. The SEC filed an action in a federal district court against Big Apple, alleging a violation of the Securities Act of 1933. Can liability be imposed on a seller for a false statement that was made by someone else? Explain. [*U.S. Securities and Exchange Commission v. Big Apple Consulting USA, Inc.*, 783 F.3d 786 (11th Cir. 2015)] (See *Securities Act of 1933.*)

36–7. The Securities Exchange Act of 1934. Dilean Reyes-Rivera was the president of Global Reach Trading (GRT), a corporation registered in Puerto Rico. His brother Jeffrey was the firm's accountant. Along with GRT sales agents and other promoters, the brothers solicited funds from individuals by promising to invest the funds in low-risk, short-term, high-yield securities. The investors were guaranteed a rate of return of up to 20 percent. Through this arrangement, more than 230 persons provided the brothers with about $22 million. This money was not actually invested. Instead, the funds received from later investors were used to pay "returns" to earlier investors. The Reyes-Riveras spent $4.6 million of the proceeds to buy luxury vehicles, houses, furniture, jewelry, and trips

for themselves. What is this type of scheme called? What are the potential consequences? Discuss. [*United States v. Reyes-Rivera*, 812 F.3d 79 (1st Cir. 2016)] (See *Securities Exchange Act of 1934.*)

36–8. Securities Fraud. First Solar, Inc., is one of the world's largest producers of photovoltaic solar panel modules. When First Solar revealed to the market that the company had discovered defects in its products, the price of the company's stock fell, causing the shareholders to suffer an economic loss. Mineworkers' Pension Scheme and other First Solar shareholders filed a suit in a federal district court against the firm and its officers, alleging a violation of Section 10(b). The plaintiffs contended that for more than two years, First Solar had wrongfully concealed its discovery, misrepresented the cost and scope of the defects, and reported false information on financial statements. On these facts, can the plaintiffs successfully plead the causation element of a securities fraud action under Section 10(b)? Explain. [*Mineworkers' Pension Scheme. v. First Solar, Inc.*, 881 F.3d 750 (9th Cir. 2018)] (See *Securities Exchange Act of 1934.*)

36–9. A Question of Ethics—The IDDR Approach and **Insider Trading.** *Nan Huang was a senior data analyst for Capital One Financial Corporation. In violation of the company's confidentiality policies, Huang downloaded and analyzed confidential information regarding* purchases made with Capital One credit cards at more than 200 consumer retail companies and used that information to conduct more than 2,000 trades in the securities of those companies. Capital One terminated Huang due to his violation of the company's policies. The next day, Huang boarded a flight to his home country of China. Four days later, the Securities and Exchange Commission filed a complaint against Huang, alleging violations of Section 10(b) and Rule 10b-5. [Securities and Exchange Commission v. Huang, *684 Fed.Appx. 167 (3d Cir. 2017)] (See* Securities Exchange Act of 1934.*)*

1. Evaluate the ethics of Huang's actions, as an employee of Capital One, using the IDDR approach.

2. When Capital One learned what Huang had done, was the company ethically obligated to terminate him? Explain.

Critical Thinking and Writing Assignments

36–10. Time-Limited Group Assignment—Violations of Securities Laws. Karel Svoboda, a credit officer for Rogue Bank, evaluated and approved his employer's extensions of credit to clients. These responsibilities gave Svoboda access to nonpublic information about the clients' earnings, performance, acquisitions, and business plans from confidential memos, e-mail, and other sources. Svoboda devised a scheme with Alena Robles, an independent accountant, to use this information to trade securities. Pursuant to their scheme, Robles traded in the securities of more than twenty different companies and profited by more than $2 million. Svoboda also executed trades for his own profit of more than $800,000, despite their agreement that Robles would do all of the trading. Aware that

their scheme violated Rogue Bank's policy, they attempted to conduct their trades in such a way as to avoid suspicion. When the bank questioned Svoboda about his actions, he lied, refused to cooperate, and was fired. (See *Securities Exchange Act of 1934.*)

1. The first group will determine whether Svoboda or Robles committed any crimes.

2. The second group will decide whether Svoboda or Robles is subject to civil liability. If so, who could file a suit and on what ground? What are the possible sanctions?

3. A third group will identify any defenses that Svoboda or Robles could raise and determine whether the defenses would be likely to succeed.

Unit Five—Task-Based Simulation

Devonyu/iStock/Getty Images

John leases an office and buys computer equipment. Initially, to pay for the lease and the equipment, he goes into the business of designing applications for smartphones. He also has an idea for a new software product that he hopes will be more profitable than designing apps. Whenever he has time, he works on the software.

1. **Selecting a Business Organization.** After six months, Mary and Paul come to work in the office to help develop John's idea. John continues to pay the rent and other expenses, including salaries for Mary and Paul. John does not expect to make a profit until the software is developed, which could take months. Even then, there may be very little profit unless the product is marketed successfully. If the software is successful, though, John believes that the firm will be able to follow up with other products. In choosing a form of business organization for this firm, what are the important considerations? What are the advantages and disadvantages of each basic option?

2. **Corporate Nature and Classification.** It is decided that the organizational form for this firm should provide limited liability for the owners. The owners will include John, Mary, Paul, and some members of their respective families. Limited liability is one of the features of the corporate form. Ordinarily, however, corporate income is taxed at both the corporate level and the shareholder level. Which corporate form could the firm use to avoid this double taxation? Which other forms of business organization provide limited liability? What factors, other than liability and taxation, influence a firm's choice among these forms?

3. **Duties of Corporate Directors.** The firm is incorporated as Digital Software, Inc. (DSI). The software is developed and marketed successfully, and DSI prospers. John, Mary, and Paul become directors of DSI. At a board meeting, Paul proposes a marketing strategy for DSI's next product, and John and Mary approve it. Implementing the strategy causes DSI's profits to drop. If the shareholders accuse Paul of breaching his fiduciary duty to DSI, what is Paul's most likely defense? If the shareholders accuse John and Mary of the same breach, what is their best defense? In either case, if the shareholders file a suit, how is a court likely to rule?

4. **Securities Regulation.** Mary and Paul withdraw from DSI to set up their own firm. To obtain operating capital, they solicit investors, who agree to become "general partners." Mary and Paul designate themselves "managing partners." The investors are spread over a wide area geographically and learn about Mary and Paul's business only through contact from Mary and Paul. Are Mary and Paul truly soliciting partners, or are they selling securities? What are the criteria for determining whether an investment is a security? What are the advantages and disadvantages of selling securities versus soliciting partners?

Unit 6
Government Regulation

37 | Administrative Law

Learning Objectives

The five Learning Objectives *below are designed to help improve your understanding. After reading this chapter, you should be able to answer the following questions:*

1. What is the difference between how statutory law and administrative law are created?

2. How do the three branches of government limit the power of administrative agencies?

3. What sequence of events must normally occur before an agency rule becomes law?

4. What is the importance of the *Chevron* case?

5. In what way has federal legislation made agencies more accountable to the public?

Administrative Law The body of law created by administrative agencies in order to carry out their duties and responsibilities.

"Perhaps more values today are affected by [administrative] decisions than by those of all the courts."

Robert H. Jackson
1892–1954
(Associate justice of the United States Supreme Court, 1941–1954)

As the chapter-opening quotation suggests, government agencies established to administer the law have a significant impact on the day-to-day operation of the government and the economy. In its early years, the United States had a simple, nonindustrial economy with little regulation. As the economy has grown and become more complex, the size of government has also increased, and so has the number of administrative agencies.

Sometimes, new agencies have been created in response to a crisis. For instance, after the latest financial crisis, Congress enacted the Dodd-Frank Wall Street Reform and Consumer Protection Act. Among other things, this statute created the Financial Stability Oversight Council to identify and respond to emerging risks in the financial system. It also created the Consumer Financial Protection Bureau to protect consumers from abusive practices by financial institutions, including mortgage lenders and credit-card companies.

As the number of agencies has multiplied, so have the rules, orders, and decisions that they issue. Today, there are rules covering almost every aspect of a business's operations. These regulations make up the body of **administrative law.**

37–1 Practical Significance

Whereas statutory law is created by legislatures, administrative law is created by administrative agencies. When Congress—or a state legislature—enacts legislation, it typically adopts a rather general statute and leaves the statute's implementation to an

administrative agency. The agency then creates the detailed rules and regulations necessary to carry out the statute. The administrative agency, with its specialized personnel, has the time, resources, and expertise to make the detailed decisions required for regulation.

Administrative Agency
A federal or state government agency established to perform a specific function.

37–1a Administrative Agencies Exist at All Levels of Government

Administrative agencies are spread throughout the government. At the national level the two basic types of administrative agencies are executive agencies and independent regulatory agencies.

Executive agencies exist within the cabinet departments of the executive branch. For instance, the Food and Drug Administration is within the U.S. Department of Health and Human Services. Executive agencies are subject to the authority of the president, who has the power to appoint and remove officers of federal agencies. Exhibit 37–1 lists the cabinet departments and their most important subagencies.

Learning Objective 1

What is the difference between how statutory law and administrative law are created?

Exhibit 37–1 Executive Departments and Important Subagencies

DEPARTMENT NAME	SELECTED SUBAGENCIES
State	Passport Office; Bureau of Diplomatic Security; Foreign Service; Bureau of Human Rights and Humanitarian Affairs; Bureau of Consular Affairs; Bureau of Intelligence and Research
Treasury	Internal Revenue Service; U.S. Mint
Interior	U.S. Fish and Wildlife Service; National Park Service; Bureau of Indian Affairs; Bureau of Land Management
Justice[a]	Federal Bureau of Investigation; Drug Enforcement Administration; Bureau of Prisons; U.S. Marshals Service
Agriculture	Soil Conservation Service; Agricultural Research Service; Food Safety and Inspection Service; Forest Service
Commerce[b]	Bureau of the Census; Bureau of Economic Analysis; Minority Business Development Agency; U.S. Patent and Trademark Office; National Oceanic and Atmospheric Administration
Labor[b]	Occupational Safety and Health Administration; Bureau of Labor Statistics; Employment Standards Administration; Office of Labor-Management Standards; Employment and Training Administration
Defense[c]	National Security Agency; Joint Chiefs of Staff; Departments of the Air Force, Navy, Army; service academies
Housing and Urban Development	Office of Community Planning and Development; Government National Mortgage Association; Office of Fair Housing and Equal Opportunity
Transportation	Federal Aviation Administration; Federal Highway Administration; National Highway Traffic Safety Administration; Federal Transit Administration
Energy	Office of Civilian Radioactive Waste Management; Office of Nuclear Energy; Energy Information Administration
Health and Human Services[d]	Food and Drug Administration; Centers for Medicare and Medicaid Services; Centers for Disease Control and Prevention; National Institutes of Health
Education[d]	Office of Special Education and Rehabilitation Services; Office of Elementary and Secondary Education; Office of Postsecondary Education; Office of Vocational and Adult Education
Veterans Affairs	Veterans Health Administration; Veterans Benefits Administration; National Cemetery Administration
Homeland Security	U.S. Citizenship and Immigration Services; Directorate of Border and Transportation Services; U.S. Coast Guard; Federal Emergency Management Agency

a. Formed from the Office of the Attorney General.
b. Formed from the Department of Commerce and Labor.
c. Formed from the Department of War and the Department of the Navy.
d. Formed from the Department of Health, Education, and Welfare.

Independent regulatory agencies are outside the cabinet departments and include the Federal Trade Commission, the Securities and Exchange Commission, and the Federal Communications Commission. The president's power is less pronounced in regard to independent agencies, whose officers serve for fixed terms and cannot be removed without just cause. See Exhibit 37–2 for a list of selected independent regulatory agencies and their principal functions.

There are administrative agencies at the state and local levels as well. Commonly, a state agency (such as a state pollution-control agency) is created as a parallel to a federal agency (such as the Environmental Protection Agency). Just as federal statutes take precedence over conflicting state statutes, so do federal agency regulations take precedence over conflicting state regulations. Because the rules of state and local agencies vary widely, we focus here on federal administrative law.

37–1b Agencies Provide a Comprehensive Regulatory Scheme

Often, administrative agencies at various levels of government work together and share the responsibility of creating and enforcing particular regulations.

Example 37.1 When Congress enacted the Clean Air Act, it provided only general directions for the prevention of air pollution. The specific pollution-control requirements imposed on business are almost entirely the product of decisions made by the Environmental Protection Agency (EPA), which was created seven years later. Moreover, the EPA works with parallel environmental agencies at the state level to analyze existing data and determine the appropriate pollution-control standards. ■

Legislation and regulations have benefits. At the same time, these benefits entail considerable costs for business. The EPA has estimated the costs of compliance with the Clean Air Act at many tens of billions of dollars yearly. Although the agency has calculated that the overall benefits of its regulations often exceed their costs, the burden on business is substantial. (See this chapter's *Linking Business Law to Corporate Management* feature.)

Exhibit 37–2 Selected Independent Regulatory Agencies

NAME OF AGENCY	PRINCIPAL DUTIES
Federal Reserve System Board of Governors (the Fed)	Determines policy with respect to interest rates, credit availability, and the money supply.
Federal Trade Commission (FTC)	Prevents businesses from engaging in purported unfair trade practices; stops the formation of monopolies in the business sector; protects consumer rights.
Securities and Exchange Commission (SEC)	Regulates the nation's stock exchanges, in which shares of stock are bought and sold; enforces the securities laws, which require full disclosure of the financial profiles of companies that wish to sell stock and bonds to the public.
Federal Communications Commission (FCC)	Regulates all communications by telegraph, cable, telephone, radio, satellite, and television.
National Labor Relations Board (NLRB)	Protects employees' rights to join unions and bargain collectively with employers; attempts to prevent unfair labor practices by both employers and unions.
Equal Employment Opportunity Commission (EEOC)	Works to eliminate discrimination in employment based on religion, gender, race, color, disability, national origin, or age; investigates claims of discrimination.
Environmental Protection Agency (EPA)	Undertakes programs aimed at reducing air and water pollution; works with state and local agencies to help fight environmental hazards.
Nuclear Regulatory Commission (NRC)	Ensures that electricity-generating nuclear reactors in the United States are built and operated safely; regularly inspects operations of such reactors.

Dealing with Administrative Law

Whether you work for a large corporation or own a small business, you will be dealing with multiple aspects of administrative law. All federal, state, and local government administrative agencies create rules that have the force of law. As a manager, you probably will need to pay more attention to administrative rules and regulations than to laws passed by local, state, and federal legislatures.

The three levels of government create three levels of rules and regulations through their respective administrative agencies. As a manager, you will have to learn about agency regulations that pertain to your business activities. It will be up to you, as a corporate manager or a small-business owner, to discern which of those regulations are most important and could create significant liability if you violate them.

Critical Thinking

Why are owner/operators of small businesses at a disadvantage relative to those of large corporations when they attempt to decipher complex regulations that apply to their businesses?

37–2 Agency Creation and Powers

Congress creates federal administrative agencies. By delegating some of its authority to make and implement laws, Congress can indirectly monitor a particular area in which it has passed legislation. Delegation enables Congress to avoid becoming bogged down in the details relating to enforcement—details that are often best left to specialists.

To create an administrative agency, Congress passes **enabling legislation,** which specifies the name, purposes, functions, and powers of the agency being created. Federal administrative agencies can exercise only those powers that Congress has delegated to them in enabling legislation. Through similar enabling acts, state legislatures create state administrative agencies.

Enabling Legislation A statute enacted by Congress that authorizes the creation of an administrative agency and specifies the name, composition, and powers of the agency.

37–2a Enabling Legislation—An Example

Congress created the Federal Trade Commission (FTC) in the Federal Trade Commission Act.[1] The act prohibits unfair and deceptive trade practices. It also describes the procedures that the agency must follow to charge persons or organizations with violations of the act, and it provides for judicial review of agency orders. The act grants the FTC the power to do the following:

1. Create "rules and regulations for the purpose of carrying out the Act."
2. Conduct investigations of business practices.
3. Obtain reports from interstate corporations concerning their business practices.
4. Investigate possible violations of federal antitrust statutes. (The FTC shares this task with the Antitrust Division of the U.S. Department of Justice.)
5. Publish findings of its investigations.
6. Recommend new legislation.
7. Hold trial-like hearings to resolve certain kinds of trade disputes that involve FTC regulations or federal antitrust laws.

"Laws and institutions, like clocks, must occasionally be cleaned, wound up, and set to true time."

Henry Ward Beecher
1813–1887
(American clergyman and abolitionist)

---

1. 15 U.S.C. Sections 41–58.

The commission that heads the FTC is composed of five members. Each is appointed by the president, with the advice and consent of the Senate, for a term of seven years. The president designates one of the commissioners to be the chair. Various offices and bureaus of the FTC undertake different administrative activities for the agency.

37–2b Agency Powers and the Constitution

Administrative agencies occupy an unusual niche in the U.S. governmental structure, because they exercise powers that are normally divided among the three branches of government. Agencies' powers include functions associated with the legislature (*rulemaking*), the executive branch (*enforcement*), and the courts (*adjudication*).

The constitutional principle of *checks and balances* allows each branch of government to act as a check on the actions of the other two branches. Furthermore, the U.S. Constitution authorizes only the legislative branch to create laws. Yet administrative agencies, to which the Constitution does not specifically refer, can make **legislative rules** that are as legally binding as laws that Congress passes.

Legislative Rule An administrative agency rule that carries the same weight as a congressionally enacted statute.

The Delegation Doctrine
Courts generally hold that Article I of the U.S. Constitution is the basis for administrative law. Section 1 of that article grants all legislative powers to Congress and requires Congress to oversee the implementation of all laws. Article I, Section 8, gives Congress the power to make all laws necessary for executing its specified powers. Under what is known as the **delegation doctrine,** the courts interpret these passages as granting Congress the power to establish administrative agencies and delegate to them the power to create rules for implementing those laws.

Delegation Doctrine A doctrine, based on the U.S. Constitution, which has been construed to allow Congress to delegate some of its power to make and implement laws to administrative agencies.

The three branches of government exercise certain controls over agency powers and functions, as discussed next, but in many ways administrative agencies function independently. For this reason, administrative agencies, which constitute the **bureaucracy,** are sometimes referred to as the fourth branch of the U.S. government.

Bureaucracy The organizational structure, consisting of government bureaus and agencies, through which the government implements and enforces the laws.

Executive Controls
The executive branch of government exercises control over agencies both through the president's power to appoint federal officers and through the president's veto power. The president may veto enabling legislation presented by Congress or congressional attempts to modify an existing agency's authority.

Legislative Controls
Congress exercises authority over agency powers through legislation. Congress gives power to an agency through enabling legislation and can take power away— or even abolish an agency altogether—through subsequent legislation. Legislative authority is required to fund an agency, and enabling legislation usually sets certain time and monetary limits on the funding of particular programs. Congress can always revise these limits.

In addition to its power to create and fund agencies, Congress has the authority to investigate the implementation of its laws and the agencies that it has created. Congress also has the power to "freeze" the enforcement of most federal regulations before the regulations take effect. (Another legislative check on agency actions is the Administrative Procedure Act (APA), discussed shortly.)

Learning Objective 2

How do the three branches of government limit the power of administrative agencies?

Judicial Controls
The judicial branch exercises control over agency powers through the courts' review of agency actions. The Administrative Procedure Act, discussed shortly, provides for judicial review of most agency decisions. Agency actions are not automatically subject to judicial review, however. The party seeking court review must first exhaust all administrative remedies under what is called the **exhaustion doctrine.**

Exhaustion Doctrine In administrative law, the principle that a complaining party normally must have exhausted all available administrative remedies before seeking judicial review.

Example 37.2 The Federal Trade Commission (FTC) claims that Sysco Industries used deceptive advertising and orders it to run new ads correcting the misstatements. Sysco contends that its ads were not deceptive. Under the exhaustion doctrine, Sysco must go through the entire FTC process before it can bring a suit against the FTC in federal court to challenge the order.

37–2c The Administrative Procedure Act

Sometimes, Congress specifies certain procedural requirements in an agency's enabling legislation. In the absence of directives from Congress concerning a particular agency procedure, the Administrative Procedure Act (APA)[2] applies. The APA sets forth rules and regulations that govern the procedures administrative agencies follow in performing their duties.

The Arbitrary and Capricious Test One of Congress's goals in enacting the APA was to provide for more judicial control over administrative agencies. To that end, the APA provides that courts should "hold unlawful and set aside" agency actions found to be "arbitrary, capricious, an abuse of discretion, or otherwise not in accordance with law."[3] Under this standard, parties can challenge regulations as contrary to law or so irrational as to be arbitrary and capricious.

The arbitrary and capricious standard does not have a precise definition, but in applying it, courts typically consider whether the agency has done any of the following:

1. Failed to provide a rational explanation for its decision.
2. Changed its prior policy without justification.
3. Considered legally inappropriate factors.
4. Failed to consider a relevant factor.
5. Rendered a decision plainly contrary to the evidence.

The following case involved a challenge to the boundaries of a protected wild and scenic river established by the National Park Service. The plaintiff—an owner of land that fell within those boundaries—claimed that the boundaries were set arbitrarily and capriciously.

---

2. 5 U.S.C. Sections 551–706.
3. 5 U.S.C. Section 706(2)(A).

■ Case 37.1

Simmons v. Smith

United States Court of Appeals, Eighth Circuit, 888 F.3d 994 (2018).

Background and Facts The Niobrara River runs through northern Nebraska before flowing into the Missouri River along the border between Nebraska and South Dakota. Pursuant to the Niobrara Scenic River Designation Act, the National Park Service (NPS)—led by Paul Hedren, an NPS superintendent—established the boundaries of the Niobrara Scenic River Area (NSRA). The process involved public meetings, conversations with local landowners and other stakeholders, and scientific evidence. The statute required the agency to focus on protecting five "outstandingly remarkable values" (ORVs)—scenic, recreational, geologic, fish and wildlife, and paleontological.

Lee Simmons operates a recreational outfitter business on the Niobrara River. At least twenty-five acres of his land is within the NSRA's boundaries. Arguing that the NPS acted arbitrarily and capriciously in drawing those boundaries, Simmons filed a suit in a federal district court against Paul Smith, the NPS's acting director. The court issued a judgment in Smith's favor. Simmons appealed.

In the Words of the Court
KELLY, Circuit Judge:
* * * *

Simmons * * * argues that NPS acted arbitrarily and capriciously in setting the boundary on his property because it did not identify specific ORVs that existed in that area. We agree with Simmons's premise to a certain extent, but, based on the facts of this case, we

(Continues)

reach the opposite conclusion. In crafting the boundaries, NPS *is* required to use the ORV determinations as a guide to decide which land should be included within the boundary in order to protect and enhance the ORVs. But * * * *NPS is not required to include only land with outstandingly remarkable values.* * * * NPS explained that [the placement of the] boundary * * * sought to balance the various ORVs "as equitably as possible" * * * . Thus, *as long as the boundary placement was rationally connected to the protection of ORVs, NPS was not required to identify a specific ORV on any specific piece of property.* And Simmons does not allege that NPS acted contrary to its stated objective of protecting these values. [Emphasis added.]

Moreover, the record amply demonstrates that multiple ORVs were identified within the boundary line in question. Specifically, Simmons's land contains a large portion of viewshed [a geographical area that includes all line-of-site property viewable from that location] that is directly downstream from Berry Bridge, which is a common launch point for recreational canoeists on the river. His land also contains a large and particularly impressive stand of ponderosa pine trees and habitats that support bald eagle foraging. Indeed, the final boundary line on Simmons's property tracks quite closely the extent of the viewshed and the ponderosa stand. Simmons does not dispute these facts. Instead, he relies on a statement by [Paul] Hedren [of the National Park Service]—made during a lengthy deposition—in which he said that he could not identify specific features on Simmons's property. But, read in context, that statement indicates confusion about the location of Simmons's property, not confusion about the existence of ORVs. At various other points in the deposition, Hedren clearly and specifically identified which ORVs motivated his boundary determination on this property.

In sum, we see no flaw—either generally or related specifically to Simmons's property—in the public, thorough, and comprehensive process that NPS undertook to establish the boundaries of the NSRA.

Decision and Remedy The U.S. Court of Appeals for the Eighth Circuit affirmed the judgment of the lower court. The federal appellate court determined that the NPS engaged "in a methodical, time-consuming boundary-drawing process" and that it used "the appropriate statutory standard" when identifying ORVs and drawing the boundary lines to protect those ORVs.

Critical Thinking

- **Economic** *Why would an owner of land that falls within the boundaries of a wild and scenic river area challenge those boundaries?*

- **What If the Facts Were Different?** *Suppose that instead of establishing the boundaries of the NSRA to protect ORVs, the NPS had drawn the boundaries to maintain the area's acreage at a certain number. Would the result in this case have been different? Explain.*

Fair Notice The APA also includes many requirements concerning the notice that regulatory agencies must give to those affected by its regulations. For example, an agency may change the way it applies a certain regulatory principle. Before the change can be carried out, the agency must give fair notice of what conduct will be expected in the future.

⚡ **Spotlight Case Example 37.3** The 1934 Communications Act established a system of limited-term broadcast licenses subject to various conditions. One condition was the indecency ban, which prohibits the uttering of "any obscene, indecent, or profane language by means of radio communication." For nearly thirty years, the Federal Communications Commission (FCC) invoked this ban only when the offensive language had been repeated, or "dwelled on," in the broadcast. It was not applied to "fleeting expletives" (offensive words used only briefly).

Then the FCC changed its policy, declaring that an offensive term was actionably indecent even if it was used only once. In 2006, the FCC applied this rule to two Fox Television broadcasts, each of which contained a single use of the F-word. The broadcasts had aired before the FCC's change in policy. The FCC ruled that these broadcasts were indecent, and Fox appealed. Ultimately, the case reached the United States Supreme Court, which determined that the FCC's order should be set aside. Because the FCC had not provided fair notice that fleeting expletives could constitute actionable indecency before the broadcasts in question, the standards were unconstitutionally vague.[4]

steinphoto/iStock Unreleased/Getty Images

Was the FCC legally allowed to fine Fox Television for "fleeting" swear words that occurred on broadcasts before an agency rule change?

---

4. *Federal Communications Commission v. Fox Television Stations, Inc.,* 567 U.S. 239, 132 S.Ct. 2307, 183 L.Ed.2d 234 (2012).

37–3 The Administrative Process

All federal agencies have three basic functions: rulemaking, enforcement, and adjudication. These three functions make up what is known as the **administrative process**. As mentioned, the APA imposes requirements that all federal agencies must follow in fulfilling their functions. Thus, the APA is an integral part of the administrative process.

Administrative Process The procedure used by administrative agencies in fulfilling their basic functions: rulemaking, enforcement, and adjudication.

37–3a Rulemaking

The major function of an administrative agency is **rulemaking**—the formulation of new regulations, or rules. The APA defines a rule as "an agency statement of general or particular applicability and future effect designed to implement, interpret, or prescribe law and policy."[5]

Rulemaking The process by which an administrative agency formally adopts a new regulation or amends or removes an old one.

Regulations are sometimes said to be *legislative* because, like statutes, they have a binding effect. Thus, violators of agency rules may be punished. Because agency rules have such significant legal force, the APA established procedures for agencies to follow in creating (amending, or removing) rules. If an agency fails to follow the required procedures, a court may find that the resulting rule is invalid.

Many rules must be adopted using the APA's **notice-and-comment rulemaking** procedure, which involves three basic steps:

1. Notice of the proposed rulemaking.
2. A comment period.
3. The final rule.

Notice-and-Comment Rulemaking An administrative rulemaking procedure that requires notice, opportunity for comment, and a published draft of the final rule.

Notice-and-comment is the most common rulemaking procedure. **Example 37.4** The Occupational Safety and Health Act authorized the Occupational Safety and Health Administration (OSHA) to develop and issue rules governing safety in the workplace. When OSHA wants to formulate rules regarding safety in the steel industry, it has to follow the specific notice-and-comment procedures outlined by the APA. If the agency fails to follow the APA's rulemaking procedures, the resulting rule may not be binding.

The impetus for rulemaking may come from various sources, including Congress or the agency itself. In addition, private parties may petition an agency to begin a rulemaking (or repeal a rule). For instance, environmental groups have petitioned for stricter air-pollution controls to combat climate change.

Notice of the Proposed Rulemaking When a federal agency decides to create a new rule, the agency publishes a notice of the proposed rulemaking proceedings in the *Federal Register*. The *Federal Register* is a daily publication of the executive branch that prints government orders, rules, and regulations. The notice states where and when the proceedings will be held, the agency's legal authority for making the rule (usually its enabling legislation), and the terms or subject matter of the proposed rule. The agency must also make available to the public certain other information, such as the key scientific data underlying the proposal.

Learning Objective 3
What sequence of events must normally occur before an agency rule becomes law?

Comment Period Following the publication of the notice of the proposed rulemaking proceedings, the agency must allow ample time for persons to comment on the proposed rule. The purpose of this comment period is to give interested parties the opportunity to express their views on the proposed rule in an effort to influence agency policy. The comments may be in writing or, if a hearing is held, may be given orally. All comments become a public record that others can examine.

Example 37.5 The owner of Brown Trucking learns that the U.S. Department of Transportation is considering a new regulation that will have a negative impact on the company's ability to do business and on its profits. A notice of the rulemaking is published in the *Federal*

---

5. 5 U.S.C. Section 551(4).

A trucking company will lose profits because of a newly proposed federal transportation rule. How do the APA's procedures allow the company to voice its concerns about the proposed rule's negative impact?

Register. Later, a public hearing is held so that proponents and opponents can offer evidence and question witnesses. At this hearing, Brown's owner testifies as to his opinion about the pending rule.

The agency need not respond to all comments, but it must respond to any significant comments that bear directly on the proposed rule. The agency responds by either modifying its final rule or explaining, in a statement accompanying the final rule, why it did not make any changes. In some circumstances, particularly when the procedure being used in a specific instance is less formal, an agency may accept comments after the comment period is closed.

The Final Rule After the agency reviews the comments, it drafts the final rule and publishes it in the *Federal Register*. A final rule must contain a "concise general statement of . . . basis and purpose" that describes the reasoning behind the rule.[6] The final rule can include modifications based on public comments. If substantial changes are made, however, a new proposal and a new opportunity for comment are required. The final rule is later compiled along with the rules and regulations of other federal administrative agencies in the *Code of Federal Regulations*.

Final rules have binding legal effect unless the courts later overturn them. If an agency fails to follow proper rulemaking procedures when it issues a final rule, however, the rule may not be binding.

Example 37.6 Members of the Hemp Industries Association (HIA) manufacture and sell food products made from hemp seed and oil. These products may contain trace amounts of THC, a component of marijuana. Without following formal rulemaking procedures, the Drug Enforcement Administration (DEA) publishes rules that effectively ban the possession and sale of HIA's food products, treating them as controlled substances. A court will most likely overturn the rules because of the DEA's failure to follow formal rulemaking procedures.

Informal Agency Actions Rather than take the time to conduct notice-and-comment rulemaking, agencies have increasingly used more informal methods of policymaking. These methods include issuing interpretive rules and guidance documents.

Interpretive Rule An administrative agency rule that explains how the agency interprets and intends to apply the statutes it enforces.

Unlike legislative rules, defined earlier, **interpretive rules** are not legally binding. They simply indicate how an agency plans to interpret and enforce its statutory authority. **Example 37.7** The Equal Employment Opportunity Commission periodically issues interpretive rules indicating how it plans to interpret the provisions of the Americans with Disabilities Act. Guidance documents advise the public on the agencies' legal and policy positions.

Informal agency actions are exempt from the APA's requirements because they do not establish legal rights. A party cannot be directly prosecuted for violating an interpretive rule or a guidance document. Nevertheless, an informal action can be important because it warns regulated entities that the agency may engage in formal rulemaking if they ignore its informal policymaking.

Ethical Issue

Do administrative agencies exercise too much authority? Administrative agencies, such as the Federal Trade Commission, combine in a single governmental entity functions normally divided among the three branches of government. They create rules, conduct investigations, and prosecute and pass judgment on violators. Yet administrative agencies' powers often go unchecked by the other branches. Some businesspersons have suggested that it is unethical for agencies—which are not even mentioned in the U.S. Constitution—to wield so many powers.

---

6. 5 U.S.C. Section 555(c).

Although agency rulemaking must comply with the requirements of the Administrative Procedure Act (APA), the act applies only to legislative, not interpretive, rulemaking. In addition, the APA is largely procedural and aimed at preventing arbitrariness. It does little to ensure that the rules passed by agencies are fair or correct—or even cost-effective. On those rare occasions when an agency's ruling is challenged and later reviewed by a court, the court cannot reverse the agency's decision unless the agency exceeded its authority or acted arbitrarily. Courts typically are reluctant to second-guess an agency's rules, interpretations, and decisions. Moreover, once an agency has final regulations in place, it is difficult to revoke or alter them.

37–3b Enforcement

Although rulemaking is the most prominent agency activity, rule enforcement is also critical. Often, an agency itself enforces its rules. After final rules are issued, agencies conduct investigations to monitor compliance with those rules or the terms of the enabling statute.

A typical agency investigation of this kind might begin when the agency receives a report of a possible violation. Many agency rules also require compliance reporting from regulated entities, and such a report may trigger an enforcement investigation.

Inspections and Tests In conducting investigations, many agencies gather information through on-site inspections. Sometimes, inspecting an office, a factory, or some other business facility is the only way to obtain the evidence needed to prove a regulatory violation. At other times, an inspection or test is used in place of a formal hearing to show the need to correct or prevent an undesirable condition.

Administrative inspections and tests cover a wide range of activities. Examples include safety inspections of underground coal mines, safety tests of commercial equipment and automobiles, and environmental monitoring of factory emissions. An agency may also ask a firm or individual to submit certain documents or records to the agency for examination.

Normally, business firms comply with agency requests to inspect facilities or business records because it is in any firm's interest to maintain a good relationship with regulatory bodies. In some instances, however, a firm may refuse to comply with such a request. That might happen, for instance, if the firm thinks the request is unreasonable and may be detrimental to the firm's interests. In such situations, an agency may resort to the use of a subpoena or a search warrant.

"It's from the government—we'll have to file an environmental-impact statement before we can evolve."

Bob Zahn/Condé Nast

Subpoenas There are two basic types of subpoenas. The subpoena *ad testificandum*[7] (to testify) is an ordinary subpoena. It is a writ, or order, compelling a witness to appear at an agency hearing. The subpoena *duces tecum*[8] (bring it with you) compels an individual or organization to hand over books, papers, records, or documents to the agency. An administrative agency may use either type of subpoena.

There are limits on what an agency can demand. To determine whether an agency is abusing its discretion in pursuing information as part of an investigation, a court may consider such factors as the following:

1. *The purpose of the investigation.* An investigation must have a legitimate purpose. Harassment is an example of an improper purpose. An agency may not issue an administrative subpoena to inspect business records if the motive is to harass or pressure the business into settling an unrelated matter.

---

7. Pronounced ad tes-tee-*fee*-can-dum.
8. Pronounced *doo*-suhs *tee*-kum.

2. *The relevance of the information being sought.* Information is relevant if it reveals that the law is being violated or if it assures the agency that the law is not being violated.

3. *The specificity of the demand for testimony or documents.* A subpoena must, for example, adequately describe the material being sought.

4. *The burden of the demand on the party from whom the information is sought.* For instance, the cost of copying requested documents or providing digital information may become burdensome. (Note that a business generally is protected from revealing information such as trade secrets.)

Adjudication A proceeding in which an administrative law judge hears and decides issues that arise when an administrative agency charges a person or a firm with an agency violation.

Exhibit 37–3 The Process of Formal Administrative Agency Adjudication

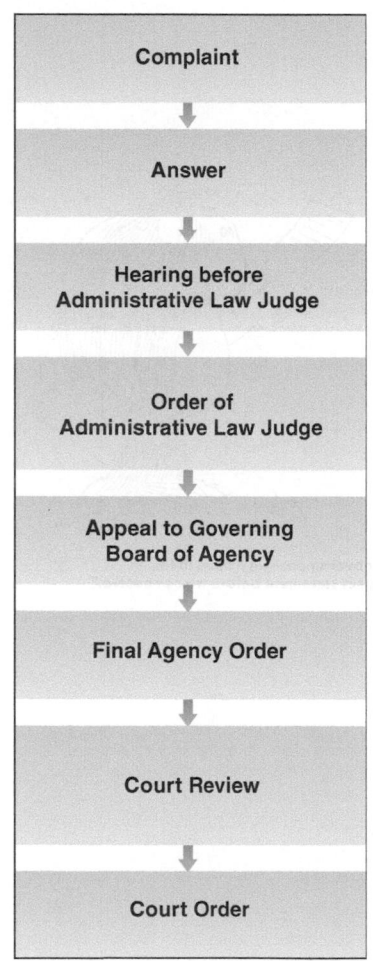

Complaint

↓

Answer

↓

Hearing before Administrative Law Judge

↓

Order of Administrative Law Judge

↓

Appeal to Governing Board of Agency

↓

Final Agency Order

↓

Court Review

↓

Court Order

Search Warrants The Fourth Amendment protects against unreasonable searches and seizures by requiring that in most instances a physical search for evidence must be conducted under the authority of a search warrant. An agency's search warrant is an order directing law enforcement officials to search a specific place for a specific item and seize it for the agency. It was once thought that administrative inspections were exempt from the warrant requirement, but the United States Supreme Court has held that the requirement does apply to the administrative process.[9]

Nevertheless, agencies can conduct warrantless searches in several situations. Warrants are not required to conduct searches in highly regulated industries. Firms that sell firearms or liquor, for instance, are automatically subject to inspections without warrants. Sometimes, a statute permits warrantless searches of certain types of hazardous operations, such as coal mines. Also, a warrantless inspection in an emergency situation is normally considered reasonable.

37–3c **Adjudication**

After conducting an investigation of a suspected rule violation, an agency may initiate an administrative action against an individual or organization. Most administrative actions are resolved through negotiated settlements at their initial stages. Sometimes, though, an action ends in formal **adjudication**—the resolution of the dispute through a hearing conducted by the agency.

Negotiated Settlements Depending on the agency, negotiations may take the form of a simple conversation or a series of informal conferences. Whatever form the negotiations take, their purpose is to rectify the problem to the agency's satisfaction and eliminate the need for additional proceedings.

Settlement is an appealing option to firms for two reasons: to avoid appearing uncooperative and to avoid the expense involved in formal adjudication proceedings and in possible later appeals. Settlement is also an attractive option for agencies. To conserve their own resources and avoid formal actions, administrative agencies devote a great deal of effort to giving advice and negotiating solutions to problems.

Formal Complaints If a settlement cannot be reached, the agency may issue a formal complaint against the suspected violator. **Example 37.8** The Environmental Protection Agency (EPA) finds that Acme Manufacturing, Inc., is polluting groundwater in violation of federal pollution laws. The EPA issues a complaint against the violator in an effort to bring the plant into compliance with federal regulations. ■ The basic steps of an administrative agency adjudication process are illustrated graphically in Exhibit 37–3.

The complaint is a public document, and a press release may accompany it. The party charged in the complaint responds by filing an answer to the allegations. If the charged party and the agency cannot agree on a settlement, the case will be adjudicated.

---

9. *Marshall v. Barlow's, Inc.,* 436 U.S. 307, 98 S.Ct. 1816, 56 L.Ed.2d 305 (1978).

Hearings Agency adjudication involves a hearing before an **administrative law judge (ALJ)**. Under the APA, before the hearing takes place, the agency must issue a notice that includes the facts and law on which the complaint is based, the legal authority for the hearing, and its time and place.

The Role of the Administrative Law Judge

The ALJ presides over the hearing and has the power to administer oaths, take testimony, rule on questions of evidence, and make determinations of fact. Technically, the ALJ, who works for the agency prosecuting the case, is not an independent judge. Nevertheless, the law requires the ALJ to be unbiased.

Certain safeguards prevent bias on the part of the ALJ and promote fairness in the proceedings. For instance, the APA requires that the ALJ be separate from the agency's investigative and prosecutorial staff. The APA also prohibits *ex parte* (private) communications between the ALJ and any party to an agency proceeding. Finally, provisions of the APA protect the ALJ from agency disciplinary actions unless the agency can show good cause for such an action.

Hearing Procedures

Hearing procedures vary widely from agency to agency. Administrative agencies generally exercise substantial discretion over the type of procedure that will be used.

Frequently, disputes are resolved through informal adjudication proceedings that resemble arbitration. **Example 37.9** The Federal Trade Commission (FTC) charges Good Foods, Inc., with deceptive advertising. Representatives of Good Foods and of the FTC, their counsel, and the ALJ meet in a conference room to resolve the dispute informally. ▪

A formal adjudicatory hearing, in contrast, resembles a trial in many respects. Prior to the hearing, the parties are permitted to undertake discovery—involving depositions, interrogatories, and requests for documents or other information. The discovery process usually is not quite as extensive as it would be in a court proceeding, however.

The hearing itself must comply with the procedural requirements of the APA and must also meet the constitutional standards of due process. The burden of proof in an enforcement proceeding is placed on the agency. During the hearing, the parties may give testimony, present other evidence, and cross-examine adverse witnesses.

Trials and agency hearings do differ in some respects. A significant difference is that normally much more information, including hearsay (secondhand information), can be introduced as evidence during an administrative hearing.

Agency Orders

Following a hearing, the ALJ renders an **initial order**, or decision, on the case. Either party can appeal the ALJ's decision to the board or commission that governs the agency and can subsequently appeal the agency decision to a federal court of appeals. **Example 37.10** The EPA issues a complaint against Acme Manufacturing, Inc., for polluting groundwater. The complaint results in a hearing before an ALJ, who rules in the agency's favor. If Acme is dissatisfied with the decision, it can appeal to the EPA. If it is dissatisfied with the EPA's decision, it can appeal to a federal appellate court. ▪

If no party appeals the case, the ALJ's decision becomes the **final order** of the agency. The ALJ's decision also becomes final if a party appeals and the commission and the court decline to review the case. If a party appeals and the case is reviewed, the final order comes from the commission's decision (or, if that decision is appealed, that of the reviewing court).

In the following case, a federal appellate court reviewed the Drug Enforcement Administration's denial of a university professor's application to register to cultivate marijuana.

Administrative Law Judge (ALJ) One who presides over an administrative agency hearing and has the power to administer oaths, take testimony, rule on questions of evidence, and make determinations of fact.

Initial Order An agency's disposition in a matter other than a rulemaking. An administrative law judge's initial order becomes final unless it is appealed.

Final Order The final decision of an administrative agency on an issue.

Case 37.2

Craker v. Drug Enforcement Administration

United States Court of Appeals, First Circuit, 714 F.3d 17 (2013).

Background and Facts Dr. Lyle Craker, a professor in the University of Massachusetts's Department of Plant, Soil and Insect Sciences, applied to the Drug Enforcement Administration (DEA) for permission to register to manufacture marijuana for clinical research. He stated that "a second source of plant material is needed to facilitate privately funded Food and Drug Administration (FDA)–approved research into medical uses of marijuana, ensuring a choice of sources and an adequate supply of quality, research-grade marijuana for medicinal applications."

Can the DEA restrict marijuana supplies to be used in research?

An administrative law judge recommended that Craker's application be granted, but a DEA deputy administrator issued an order denying his application. Under the DEA's interpretation, the Controlled Substances Act (CSA) requires an applicant to prove both that effective controls against diversion of the marijuana for unapproved purposes are in place and that its supply and the competition to supply it are inadequate. The administrator determined that the professor had not proved that effective controls against the marijuana's diversion were in place or that supply and competition were inadequate. Craker petitioned the U.S. Court of Appeals for the First Circuit to review the order.

In the Words of the Court
HOWARD, Circuit Judge.

* * * *

Since 1968, the National Center for Natural Products Research ("NCNPR") at the University of Mississippi has held the necessary registration and a government contract to grow marijuana for research purposes. The contract is administered by the National Institute on Drug Abuse ("NIDA"), a component of the National Institutes of Health ("NIH"), which, in turn, is a component of the [U.S.] Department of Health and Human Services ("HHS"). The contract is opened for competitive bidding every five years. The NCNPR is the only entity registered by the DEA to manufacture marijuana.

* * * *

Dr. Craker's argument with respect to competition is essentially that there cannot be "adequately competitive conditions" when there is only one manufacturer of marijuana.

The Administrator * * * observed that NIDA had provided marijuana manufactured by the University of Mississippi either at cost or free to researchers, and that Dr. Craker had made no showing of

how he could provide it for less * * *. Additionally, the Administrator noted that Dr. Craker is free to bid on the contract when it comes up for renewal.

We see nothing improper in the Administrator's approach. The [CSA's] term "adequately competitive conditions" is not necessarily as narrow as the petitioner suggests. * * * That the current regime may not be the most competitive situation possible does not render it "inadequate." [Emphasis added.]

* * * *

In finding that Dr. Craker failed to demonstrate that the current supply of marijuana was not adequate and uninterrupted, the Administrator observed that there were over 1,000 kilograms of marijuana in NIDA possession, an amount which far exceeds present research demands and "any foreseeable" future demand. Dr. Craker does not dispute this finding, or that the current amount is more than ninety times the amount he proposes to supply. Instead, he argues that the adequacy of supply must not be measured against NIDA-approved research, but by whether the supply is adequate to supply projects approved by the FDA. But even if we were to accept his premise—which we don't—Dr. Craker fails to demonstrate that the supply is inadequate for those needs, either. He merely states that certain projects were rejected as "not bona-fide" by NIDA, a claim which does not address the adequacy of supply. The fact that Dr. Craker disagrees with the method by which marijuana research is approved does not undermine the substantial evidence that supports the Administrator's conclusion.

Decision and Remedy The U.S. Court of Appeals for the First Circuit denied Craker's petition to review the agency's order "because the Administrator's interpretation of the CSA is permissible and her findings are reasonable and supported by the evidence."

Critical Thinking

• **Economic** *Why should a court wait to review an agency's order until the order has gone through the entire procedural process and can be considered final?*

• **Legal Environment** *Did the court in this case appear to agree with the DEA's interpretation of the Controlled Substances Act? Why or why not?*

37–4 Judicial Deference to Agency Decisions

When asked to review agency decisions, courts historically granted some deference to the agency's judgment. In other words, the courts tended to accept the agency's decision, often citing the agency's expertise in the subject area of the regulation. This deference seems especially appropriate when applied to an agency's analysis of factual questions, but should it also extend to an agency's interpretation of its own legal authority? In *Chevron U.S.A., Inc. v. Natural Resources Defense Council, Inc.*,[10] the United States Supreme Court held that it should. By so ruling, the Court created a standard of broadened deference to agencies on questions of legal interpretation.

37–4a The Holding of the *Chevron* Case

At issue in the *Chevron* case was whether the courts should defer to an agency's interpretation of the statute giving it authority to act. The Environmental Protection Agency (EPA) had interpreted the phrase "stationary source" in the Clean Air Act as referring to an entire manufacturing plant, and not to each facility within a plant. The agency's interpretation enabled it to adopt the so-called bubble policy, which allowed companies to offset increases in emissions in part of a plant with decreases elsewhere in the plant—an interpretation that reduced the pollution-control compliance costs faced by manufacturers. An environmental group challenged the legality of the EPA's interpretation.

The United States Supreme Court held that the courts should defer to an agency's interpretation of *law* as well as fact. The Court found that the agency's interpretation of the statute was reasonable and upheld the bubble policy. The Court's decision in the *Chevron* case created a new standard for courts to use when reviewing agency interpretations of law. The standard involves the following two questions:

1. Did Congress directly address the issue in dispute in the statute? If so, the statutory language prevails.

2. If the statute is silent or ambiguous, is the agency's interpretation "reasonable"? If it is, a court should uphold the agency's interpretation even if the court would have interpreted the law differently.

37–4b When Courts Will Give *Chevron* Deference to Agency Interpretation

Learning Objective 4

What is the importance of the *Chevron* case?

The notion that courts should defer to agencies on matters of law has been controversial. Under the holding of the *Chevron* case, when the meaning of a particular statute's language is unclear and an agency interprets it, the court must follow the agency's interpretation as long as it is reasonable. This has led to considerable discussion and litigation to test the boundaries of the *Chevron* holding.

For instance, are courts required to give deference to all agency interpretations or only to those that result from adjudication or formal rulemaking procedures? The United States Supreme Court has held that in order for agency interpretations to be assured *Chevron* deference, they must meet the formal legal standards for notice-and-comment rulemaking. Nevertheless, there are still gray areas, and many agency interpretations are challenged in court.

The following case concerns a federal agency's role in determining whether foreign pilots can be certified to operate large U.S.-registered aircraft.

---

10. 467 U.S. 837, 104 S.Ct. 2778, 81 L.Ed.2d 694 (1984).

Case 37.3

Olivares v. Transportation Security Administration

United States Court of Appeals, District of Columbia Circuit, 819 F.3d 454 (2016).

Background and Facts Citizens of foreign countries who seek training and certification from the Federal Aviation Administration (FAA) to operate U.S.-registered aircraft must first secure clearance by the Transportation Security Administration (TSA). Alberto Olivares, a citizen of Venezuela, applied to an FAA-certified flight school to learn how to pilot such an aircraft. After conducting a background check, the TSA determined that Olivares was a risk to aviation and national security and denied his application for training. The TSA did not offer any explanation of its action to Olivares. Olivares filed a petition in a federal appellate court seeking review of the TSA's decision.

In the Words of the Court

EDWARDS, Senior Circuit Judge:

* * * *

* * * Andrea Vara executed a sworn declaration explaining TSA's grounds for denying Petitioner's application for training. Ms. Vara is employed by [TSA] as the Alien Flight Student Program Manager. She has been responsible for managing TSA's Alien Flight Student Program, which conducts security threat assessments on individuals who are not U.S. citizens or nationals who seek flight instruction or recurrent training from FAA-certified flight training providers.

The Vara Declaration makes it clear that Ms. Vara was the Government official who made the determination that Petitioner's application should be denied * * * . The Vara Declaration states:

> * * * In 2007, Petitioner pled guilty to conspiracy to possess with intent to distribute controlled substances and the U.S. District Court for the Northern District of Illinois sentenced him to eighty (80) months imprisonment. Petitioner's conviction made him inadmissible to the United States and led to the revocation of his FAA Airman's Certificate. Petitioner was deported to his home country of Venezuela in March 2010.
>
> A public news article published after Petitioner was deported provided a U.S. address for Petitioner. Further, records indicated that Petitioner was a suspected international trafficker in firearms. There was evidence that Petitioner had previously been involved in the export of weapons and U.S. currency to Venezuela by private aircraft, was the second pilot of an aircraft from which several weapons and $500,000 was seized by local authorities in Aruba, and that one of his associates was arrested in Aruba for smuggling firearms.

This information, viewed as a whole, demonstrated Petitioner's willingness to consistently disregard the law and to use an aircraft for criminal activity, in opposition to U.S. security interests. The information also raised concerns that Petitioner may use his flight training to advance the interests of a criminal enterprise, which could include an enterprise that seeks to do harm to the United States.

* * * *

What is important here is that, because Congress has entrusted TSA with broad authority over civil aviation security, it is TSA's job—not * * * ours—to strike a balance between convenience and security. Therefore, *in cases of this sort, we must defer to TSA actions that reasonably interpret and enforce the safety and security obligations of the agency. * * * Courts do not second-guess expert agency judgments on potential risks to national security. Rather, we defer to the informed judgment of agency officials whose obligation it is to assess risks to national security.* [Emphasis added.]

Given TSA's broad authority to assess potential risks to aviation and national security, the agency's clear and reasonable explanation offered in the Vara Declaration, and the limited standard of review [under the holding in the *Chevron* case], we are in no position to second-guess TSA's judgment in denying Petitioner's application.

It is self-evident that TSA's action against Petitioner was related to the agency's goals of improving the safety of air travel. TSA was not required to show that Petitioner would engage in activities designed to compromise aviation or national security. Rather, the agency was merely required to give a reasonable explanation as to why it believed that Petitioner presented a risk to aviation or national security. The Vara Declaration satisfies this legal obligation. [Emphasis added.]

Decision and Remedy The federal appellate court denied Olivares's petition and upheld the TSA's ruling. The court concluded that the TSA had presented sufficient evidence to support its decision not to allow Olivares to attend the flight school. Therefore, even though the court found that the TSA had not notified Olivares of those reasons (as required under the Administrative Procedures Act), it upheld the agency's decision.

Critical Thinking

• **Legal Environment** *What impact did the Vara Declaration have on the court's ruling in this case?*

37–5 Public Accountability

As a result of growing public concern over the powers exercised by administrative agencies, Congress passed several laws to make agencies more accountable through public scrutiny. Here, we discuss the most significant of these laws.

37–5a Freedom of Information Act

The Freedom of Information Act (FOIA)[11] requires the federal government to disclose certain records to any person on request, even if no reason is given for the request. Federal government agencies must make their records available electronically on the Internet and in other electronic formats.

The FOIA exempts certain types of records, such as those involving national security, and those containing information that is personal or confidential. **Example 37.11** Quinn, a reporter from an online health magazine, makes an FOIA request to the Centers for Disease Control and Prevention for a list of people who have contracted a highly contagious virus. The Centers for Disease Control and Prevention will not have to comply, because the requested information is confidential and personal. ▇

For other records, a request that complies with the FOIA procedures need only contain a reasonable description of the information sought. An agency's failure to comply with an FOIA request can be challenged in a federal district court. The media, industry trade associations, public-interest groups, and even companies seeking information about competitors rely on these FOIA provisions to obtain information from government agencies.

When can the Centers for Disease Control and Prevention refuse a Freedom of Information Act request?

37–5b Government in the Sunshine Act

The Government in the Sunshine Act,[12] or open meeting law, requires that "every portion of every meeting of an agency" be open to "public observation." The act also requires procedures to ensure that the public is provided with adequate advance notice of the agency's scheduled meeting and agenda.

Like the FOIA, the Sunshine Act contains certain exceptions. Closed meetings are permitted in the following situations:

1. The subject of the meeting concerns accusing any person of a crime.

2. Open meetings would frustrate implementation of future agency actions.

3. The subject of the meeting involves matters relating to future litigation or rulemaking.

Courts interpret these exceptions to allow open access whenever possible.

Learning Objective 5

In what ways has federal legislation made agencies more accountable to the public?

37–5c Regulatory Flexibility Act

Concern over the effects of regulation on the efficiency of businesses, particularly smaller ones, led Congress to pass the Regulatory Flexibility Act.[13] Under this act, whenever a new regulation will have a "significant impact upon a substantial number of small entities," the agency must conduct a regulatory flexibility analysis. The analysis must measure the cost that the rule would impose on small businesses and must consider less burdensome alternatives. The act also contains provisions to alert small businesses about forthcoming regulations. The act relieved small businesses of some record-keeping burdens, especially with regard to hazardous waste management.

"Law . . . is a human institution, created by human agents to serve human ends."

Harlan F. Stone
1872–1946
(Chief justice of the United States Supreme Court, 1941–1946)

---

11. 5 U.S.C. Section 552.
12. 5 U.S.C. Section 552b.
13. 5 U.S.C. Sections 601–612.

37–5d Small Business Regulatory Enforcement Fairness Act

The Small Business Regulatory Enforcement Fairness Act (SBREFA)[14] includes various provisions intended to ease the regulatory burden on small businesses:

1. Federal agencies must prepare guides that explain in plain English how small businesses can comply with federal regulations.

2. Congress may review new federal regulations for at least sixty days before they take effect, giving opponents of the rules time to present their arguments.

3. The courts may enforce the Regulatory Flexibility Act. This provision helps to ensure that federal agencies will consider ways to reduce the economic impact of new regulations on small businesses.

4. The Office of the National Ombudsman at the Small Business Administration was established to receive comments from small businesses about their dealings with federal agencies. Based on these comments, Regional Small Business Fairness Boards rate the agencies and publicize their findings.

---

14. 5 U.S.C. Sections 801 *et seq.*

Practice and Review

Assume that the Securities and Exchange Commission (SEC) has a rule under which it enforces statutory provisions prohibiting insider trading only when the insiders make monetary profits for themselves. Then the SEC makes a new rule, declaring that it has the statutory authority to bring enforcement actions against individuals even if they did not personally profit from the insider trading. The SEC simply announces the new rule without conducting a rulemaking proceeding. A stockbrokerage firm objects and says that the new rule was unlawfully developed without opportunity for public comment. The brokerage firm challenges the rule in an action that ultimately is reviewed by a federal appellate court. Using the information presented in the chapter, answer the following questions.

1. Is the SEC an executive agency or an independent regulatory agency? Does it matter to the outcome of this dispute? Explain.

2. Suppose that the SEC asserts that it has always had the statutory authority to pursue persons for insider trading regardless of whether they personally profited from the transaction. This is the only argument the SEC makes to justify changing its enforcement rules. Would a court be likely to find that the SEC's action was arbitrary and capricious under the Administrative Procedure Act (APA)? Why or why not?

3. Would a court be likely to give *Chevron* deference to the SEC's interpretation of the law on insider trading? Why or why not?

4. Now assume that a court finds that the new rule is merely "interpretive." What effect would this determination have on whether the SEC had to follow the APA's rulemaking procedures?

Debate This
Because an administrative law judge (ALJ) acts as both judge and jury, there should always be at least three ALJs in each administrative hearing.

Key Terms

adjudication 882

administrative agency 873

administrative law 872

administrative law judge (ALJ) 883

administrative process 879

bureaucracy 876

delegation doctrine 876

enabling legislation 875

exhaustion doctrine 876

final order 883

initial order 883

interpretive rule 880

legislative rule 876

notice-and-comment rulemaking 879

rulemaking 879

Chapter Summary: Administrative Law

Agency Creation and Powers	1. Under the U.S. Constitution, Congress can delegate the implementation of its laws to government agencies. Congress can thus indirectly monitor an area in which it has passed laws without becoming bogged down in details relating to enforcement.
	2. Administrative agencies are created by enabling legislation, which usually specifies the name, composition, and powers of the agency.
	3. Agencies can create legislative rules, which are as binding as formal acts of Congress.
	4. The three branches of government exercise controls over agency powers and functions.
	a. Executive controls—The president can control agencies through appointments of federal officers and through vetoes of bills affecting agency powers.
	b. Legislative controls—Congress can give power to an agency, take it away, increase or decrease the agency's funding, or abolish the agency.
	c. Judicial controls—Administrative agencies are subject to the judicial review of the courts.
	5. The Administrative Procedure Act also limits agencies.
The Administrative Process	1. The administrative process consists of rulemaking, enforcement, and adjudication.
	2. Agencies are authorized to create new regulations—their rulemaking function. This power is conferred on an agency in the enabling legislation.
	3. Notice-and-comment rulemaking is the most common rulemaking procedure. It involves the publication of the proposed regulation in the *Federal Register*, followed by a comment period to allow private parties to comment on the proposed rule.
	4. As part of their enforcement function, administrative agencies investigate the entities that they regulate, both during the rulemaking process to obtain data and after rules are issued to monitor compliance.
	5. Some important investigative tools available to an agency are the following:
	a. Inspections and tests—Used to gather information and to correct or prevent undesirable conditions.
	b. Subpoenas—Orders that direct individuals to appear at a hearing or to hand over specified documents. The information must be sought for a legitimate purpose. It must also be relevant, and the demands on the company must be specific and not unreasonably burdensome.
	c. Search warrants—Orders directing law enforcement officials to search specific places for specific items and seize them for the agency.
	6. After a preliminary investigation, an agency may initiate an administrative action against an individual or organization by filing a complaint. Most such actions are resolved at this stage.
	7. If there is no settlement, the case is presented to an administrative law judge (ALJ) in a proceeding similar to a trial.
	8. After a case is concluded, the ALJ renders an initial order, which can be appealed by either party to the board or commission that governs the agency and ultimately to a federal appeals court. If no appeal is taken or the case is not reviewed, then the order becomes the final order of the agency.
Judicial Deference to Agency Decisions	1. When reviewing agency decisions, courts typically grant deference to an agency's findings of fact and interpretations of law.
	2. If Congress directly addressed the issue in dispute when enacting the statute, courts must follow the statutory language.

(*Continues*)

> 3. If the statute is silent or ambiguous, a court will uphold an agency's decision if the agency's interpretation of the statute was reasonable, even if the court would have interpreted the law differently. (This is known as *Chevron* deference.)
>
> 4. An agency must follow notice-and-comment rulemaking procedures to be entitled to judicial deference in its interpretation of the law.

Public Accountability   Congress has passed several laws to make agencies more accountable through public scrutiny. These laws include the Freedom of Information Act, the Government in the Sunshine Act, the Regulatory Flexibility Act, and the Small Business Regulatory Enforcement Fairness Act.

Issue Spotters

1. The U.S. Department of Transportation (DOT) sometimes hears an appeal from a party whose contract with the DOT has been canceled. An administrative law judge (ALJ) who works for the DOT hears this appeal. What safeguards promote the ALJ's fairness? (See *The Administrative Process*.)

2. Techplate Corporation learns that a federal administrative agency is considering a rule that will have a negative impact on the firm's ability to do business. Does the firm have any opportunity to express its opinion about the pending rule? Explain. (See *The Administrative Process*.)

   —**Check your answers to the *Issue Spotters* against the answers provided in Appendix C at the end of this text.**

Business Scenarios and Case Problems

37–1. Rulemaking. For decades, the Federal Trade Commission (FTC) resolved fair trade and advertising disputes through individual adjudications. In the 1960s, the FTC began setting forth rules that defined *unfair trade practices*. In cases involving violations of these rules, the due process rights of participants were more limited and did not include cross-examination. This was because, although anyone found violating a rule would receive a full adjudication, the legitimacy of the rule itself could not be challenged in the adjudication. Any party charged with violating a rule was almost certain to lose the adjudication. Affected parties complained to a court, arguing that their rights before the FTC were unduly limited by the new rules. What will the court examine to determine whether to uphold the new rules? (See *The Administrative Process*.)

37–2. Informal Rulemaking. Assume that the Food and Drug Administration (FDA), using proper procedures, adopts a rule describing its future investigations. This new rule covers all future circumstances in which the FDA wants to regulate food additives. Under the new rule, the FDA is not to regulate food additives without giving food companies an opportunity to cross-examine witnesses. Some time later, the FDA wants to regulate methylisocyanate, a food additive. After conducting an informal rulemaking procedure, without cross-examination, the FDA regulates methylisocyanate. Producers protest, saying that the FDA promised them the opportunity for cross-examination. The FDA responds that the Administrative Procedure Act does not require such cross-examination and that it is free to withdraw the promise made in its new rule. If the producers challenge the FDA in court, on what basis would the court rule in their favor? (See *The Administrative Process*.)

37–3. Spotlight on the Environmental Protection Agency—Powers of the Agency. A well-documented rise in global temperatures has coincided with a significant increase in the concentration of carbon dioxide in the atmosphere. Many scientists believe that the two trends are related, because when carbon dioxide is released into the atmosphere, it produces a greenhouse effect, trapping solar heat. Under the Clean Air Act (CAA), the Environmental Protection Agency (EPA) is authorized to regulate "any" air pollutants "emitted into . . . the ambient air" that in its "judgment cause, or contribute to, air pollution." A group of private organizations asked the EPA to regulate carbon dioxide and other "greenhouse gas" emissions from new motor vehicles. The EPA refused, stating that Congress last amended the CAA in 1990 without authorizing new, binding limits on auto emissions. Nineteen states, including Massachusetts, asked a district court to review the EPA's denial. Did the EPA have the authority to regulate greenhouse gas emissions from new motor vehicles? If so, was its stated reason for refusing to do so consistent with that authority? Discuss. [*Massachusetts v. Environmental Protection Agency*, 549 U.S. 497, 127 S.Ct. 1438, 167 L.Ed.2d 248 (2007)] (See *Agency Creation and Powers*.)

37–4. Judicial Deference. After Dave Conley died of lung cancer, his widow filed for benefits under the Black Lung Benefits Act. To qualify for benefits under the act, she had to show that exposure to coal dust was a substantial contributing factor to her husband's death. Conley had been a coal miner, but he had also been a longtime smoker. At the benefits hearing, a physician testified that coal dust was a substantial factor in Conley's death. No evidence was presented to support this conclusion, however. The administrative law judge awarded benefits. On appeal, should a court defer to this decision? Discuss. [*Conley v. National Mines Corp.*, 595 F.3d 297 (6th Cir. 2010)] (See *Judicial Deference to Agency Decisions*.)

37–5. Business Case Problem with Sample Answer— Arbitrary and Capricious Test. Michael Manin, an airline pilot, was twice convicted of disorderly conduct, a minor misdemeanor. To renew his flight certification with the National Transportation Safety Board (NTSB), Manin filed an application that asked him about his criminal history. He did not disclose his two convictions. When these came to light more than ten years later, Manin argued that he had not known that he was required to report convictions for minor misdemeanors. The NTSB's policy was to consider an applicant's understanding of what information a question sought before determining whether an answer was false. But without explanation, the agency departed from this policy, refused to consider Manin's argument, and revoked his certification. Was this action arbitrary or capricious? Explain. [*Manin v. National Transportation Safety Board*, 627 F.3d 1239 (D.C.Cir. 2011)] (See *Agency Creation and Powers*.)

—**For a sample answer to Problem 37–5, go to Appendix D at the end of this text.**

37–6. Adjudication. Mechanics replaced a brake assembly on the landing gear of a CRJ–700 plane operated by GoJet Airlines, LLC. The mechanics installed gear pins to lock the assembly in place during the repair, but failed to remove one of the pins after they had finished. On the plane's next flight, a warning light alerted the pilots that the landing gear would not retract after takeoff. There was a potential for danger, but the pilots flew the plane safely back to the departure airport. No one was injured, and no property was damaged. The Federal Aviation Administration (FAA) cited GoJet for violating FAA regulations by "carelessly or recklessly operating an unairworthy airplane." GoJet objected to the citation. To which court can GoJet appeal for review? On what ground might that court decline to review the case? [*GoJet Airlines, LLC v. F.A.A.*, 743 F.3d 1168 (8th Cir. 2014)] (See *The Administrative Process*.)

37–7. Judicial Deference to Agency Decisions. Knox Creek Coal Corporation operates coal mines in West Virginia. The U.S. Department of Labor charged Knox's Tiller No. 1 Mine with "significant and substantial" (S&S) violations of the Federal Mine Safety and Health Act. According to the charges, inadequately sealed enclosures of electrical equipment in the mine created the potential for an explosion. The Mine Act designates a violation as S&S when it "*could* significantly and substantially contribute to the cause and effect of a coal or other mine safety or health hazard." Challenging the S&S determination, Knox filed a suit against the secretary of labor. The secretary argued that "could" means "merely possible"—if there is a violation, the existence of a hazard is assumed. This position was consistent with agency and judicial precedent and the Mine Act's history and purpose. Knox argued that "could" requires proof of the likelihood of a hazard. When does a court defer to an agency's interpretation of law? Do those circumstances exist in this case? Discuss. [*Knox Creek Coal Corp. v. Secretary of Labor*, 811 F.3d 148 (4th Cir. 2016)] (See *Judicial Deference to Agency Decisions*.)

37–8. The Arbitrary and Capricious Test. The Sikh Cultural Society, Inc. (SCS), petitioned the United States Citizenship and Immigration Services (USCIS) for a special immigrant religious worker visa for Birender Singh. The USCIS denied the request for several reasons. Despite certain statutory requirements, there were discrepancies or inadequate evidence as to Singh's compensation, housing, and employment history. The SCS did not provide all of the requested information. In addition, the SCS did not show that Singh had worked continuously for the previous two years. The SCS filed a suit in a federal district court against the USCIS, arguing that the denial was arbitrary and capricious. In applying the arbitrary and capricious standard, what agency actions or omissions does a court typically consider? Does the denial of Singh's visa pass the test? Explain. [*Sikh Cultural Society, Inc. v. United States Citizenship and Immigration Services*, 720 Fed.Appx. 649 (2018)] (See *Agency Creation and Powers*.)

37–9. A Question of Ethics—The IDDR Approach and the Arbitrary and Capricious Test. *The Delaware River Port Authority (DRPA) solicited bids to repaint the Commodore Barry Bridge, a mile-long structure spanning the Delaware River between New Jersey and Pennsylvania. Alpha Painting & Construction Company, an experienced contractor that had previously worked for the DRPA, submitted the lowest bid. Under DRPA guidelines, a "responsible" contractor has the "capacity" and "capability" to do a certain job. A "responsive" contractor includes all required documents with its bid. Alpha's bid did not include certain required accident and insurance data. For this reason, and without checking further, the DRPA declared that Alpha was "not responsible" and awarded the contract to the second-lowest bidder. [Alpha Painting & Construction Co. v. Delaware River Port Authority, 853 F.3d 671 (3d Cir. 2017)] (See Agency Creation and Powers.)*

1. Using the *Inquiry* step of the IDDR approach, identify the ethical issue the DRPA faced when deciding whether to accept or reject Alpha's bid.

2. Using the *Discussion* step of the IDDR approach, consider whether the DRPA's rejection of Alpha was ethical.

Critical Thinking and Writing Assignments

37–10. Time-Limited Group Assignment—Investigation.

Maureen Droge was a flight attendant for United Air Lines, Inc. (UAL). After being assigned to work in Paris, France, she became pregnant. Because UAL does not allow its flight attendants to fly during their third trimester of pregnancy, Droge was placed on involuntary leave. She applied for temporary disability benefits through the French social security system. Her request was denied because UAL does not contribute to the French system on behalf of its U.S.-based flight attendants. Droge filed a charge of discrimination with the U.S. Equal Employment Opportunity Commission (EEOC), alleging that UAL had discriminated against her and other Americans. The EEOC issued a subpoena, asking UAL to detail all benefits received by all UAL employees living outside the United States.

UAL refused to provide the information on the ground that it was irrelevant and that compliance would be unduly burdensome. The EEOC filed a suit in a federal district court against UAL. (See *The Administrative Process*.)

1. The first group will decide whether the court should enforce the subpoena and explain why.

2. The second group will discuss whether the EEOC should be able to force a U.S. company operating overseas to provide the same disability benefits to employees located there as it does to employees in the United States.

3. The third group should determine whether UAL should be required to contribute to the French social security system for employees who reside in France and explain why or why not.

Antitrust Law and Promoting Competition

38

> "Competition is not only the basis of protection to the consumer but is the incentive to progress."

Herbert Hoover
1874–1964
(Thirty-first president of the United States, 1929–1933)

The laws regulating economic competition in the United States are referred to as *antitrust laws*. They include the Sherman Antitrust Act of 1890,[1] the Clayton Act,[2] and the Federal Trade Commission Act.[3] Congress later amended these acts to broaden and strengthen their coverage.

The basis of antitrust legislation is our society's desire to foster competition. As President Herbert Hoover said in the chapter-opening quotation, competition not only protects the consumer, but also provides "the incentive to progress." Consumers and society as a whole benefit when producers strive to develop better products that they can sell at lower prices to beat the competition.

How do antitrust laws promote competition? Suppose that Select Seafood Company is one of five major producers of prepackaged seafood in the United States. Casey Bowman, Select's chief executive officer, has been meeting with leaders of the other four producers for the last several years. They discuss market developments, supply issues, and other matters of common interest. But what if they were to agree eventually to work together to control the price of packaged seafood in the United States? Such a price-fixing agreement would be illegal because it would harm competition.

1. 15 U.S.C. Sections 1–7.
2. 15 U.S.C. Sections 12–27.
3. 15 U.S.C. Sections 41–58.

Learning Objectives

The six Learning Objectives *below are designed to help improve your understanding. After reading this chapter, you should be able to answer the following questions:*

1. What is a monopoly? What is market power? How do these concepts relate to each other?

2. What rule do courts apply to price-fixing agreements, and why?

3. What two types of activities are prohibited by Section 2 of the Sherman Act?

4. What are the four major provisions of the Clayton Act, and what types of activities do these provisions prohibit?

5. What agencies of the federal government enforce the federal antitrust laws?

6. When will a U.S. court apply the Sherman Act to foreign persons or entities?

If the government found out about it, the firms could be prosecuted under the laws discussed in this chapter. (See this chapter's *Business Web Log* feature for a discussion of European antitrust actions targeting two U.S.-based companies.)

38–1 The Sherman Antitrust Act

Antitrust Law Laws protecting commerce from unlawful restraints and anticompetitive practices.

Today's **antitrust laws** are the direct descendants of common law actions intended to limit *restraints of trade* (agreements between or among firms that have the effect of reducing competition in the marketplace). Such actions date to the fifteenth century in England.

After the U.S. Civil War (1861–1865), the American public became increasingly concerned about declining competition in the marketplace. Large corporate enterprises were attempting to reduce or eliminate competition by legally tying themselves together in contracts to create *business trusts* (unincorporated organizations with limited liability). The most powerful of these organizations was the Standard Oil trust.

Facebook and Google in a World of Antitrust Law

Like the United States, the European Union (EU) has laws to foster competition. One factor all such laws take into account is how much a particular company dominates the market for its product or service. Google clearly dominates the online search market and Facebook dominates the social media market. The EU and countries within it have been looking carefully at these two companies' market-leading positions.

Recently, the EU fined Google $2.7 billion for anticompetitive behavior.[a] (Read more about that case in the *Adapting the Law to the Online Environment* feature near the end of this chapter.) Germany is currently examining Facebook's terms and conditions. In order to use the social media site, Facebook's 2 billion users had to agree to those terms and conditions, which allow Facebook to collect personal information about the users from their posts. Having this information makes it possible for Facebook to sell targeted ads at high prices.

Each year, between $75 and $85 billion is spent on digital advertising. Google and Facebook account for more than 70 percent of that amount. Eighty percent of all online referral traffic comes from Facebook and Google. The result: Google's parent company, Alphabet, earns about $20 billion a year, and Facebook about $10 billion.

Both companies achieved their dominant positions in part through acquisitions that were not contested by the Federal Trade Commission (FTC) or the Justice Department (DOJ), which enforce U.S. antitrust laws. Google took over the online advertising industry by buying Admeld, AdMob, DoubleClick, and the mapping competitor Waze. Facebook, for its part, was allowed to acquire two direct competitors, Instagram and WhatsApp, without any antitrust interference.

Key Point

Google's and Facebook's market power comes, at least in part, from their access to users' data. In their current investigation,

German prosecutors claim that Facebook's data collection amounts to an antitrust violation. Users must agree to Facebook's terms and conditions if they wish to use the site, allowing Facebook to accumulate ever more information and thereby maintain its market dominance.

If Germany's antitrust investigation into Facebook is successful, it is possible that the FTC or the DOJ will reexamine Facebook in a different light. To prove an antitrust violation in the United States, however, may not be so easy. For example, U.S. antitrust authorities would have to show that Facebook is misusing its market position. In other words, antitrust authorities would have to prove that users accept Facebook's terms and conditions only because of Facebook's market dominance.

---

a. European Commission, Press Release, Brussels, Belgium, 27 June 2017.

In 1890, Congress passed "An Act to Protect Trade and Commerce against Unlawful Restraints and Monopolies"— commonly known as the Sherman Antitrust Act or, more simply, as the Sherman Act. The Sherman Act became (and still is) one of the gov-

Library of Congress Prints and Photographs Division

One of Standard Oil's refineries in Richmond, California, around 1900.

ernment's most powerful weapons in the effort to maintain a competitive economy. The act and the role of the Standard Oil trust in its passage are examined in this chapter's *Landmark in the Law* feature.

38–1a Major Provisions of the Sherman Act

Sections 1 and 2 contain the main provisions of the Sherman Act:

1. Every contract, combination in the form of trust or otherwise, or conspiracy, in restraint of trade or commerce among the several States, or with foreign nations, is hereby declared to be illegal [and is a felony punishable by a fine and/or imprisonment].

The Sherman Antitrust Act

Landmark in the Law

The author of the Sherman Antitrust Act, Senator John Sherman, was the brother of the famous Civil War general William Tecumseh Sherman and a recognized financial authority. Sherman had been concerned for years about diminishing competition in U.S. industry and the emergence of monopolies, such as the Standard Oil trust.

The Standard Oil Trust By 1890, the Standard Oil trust had become the foremost petroleum refining and marketing combination in the United States. Streamlined, integrated, and centrally controlled, Standard Oil maintained an indisputable monopoly over the industry. The trust controlled 90 percent of the U.S. market for refined petroleum products, making it impossible for small producers to compete.

The increasing consolidation in U.S. industry, and particularly the Standard Oil trust, came to the attention of the public in March 1881. Henry Demarest Lloyd, a young journalist from Chicago, published

an article in the *Atlantic Monthly* entitled "The Story of a Great Monopoly." The article argued that the U.S. petroleum industry was dominated by one firm—Standard Oil. Lloyd's article was so popular that the issue was reprinted six times. It marked the beginning of the U.S. public's growing concern over monopolies.

The Passage of the Sherman Antitrust Act The common law regarding trade regulation was not always consistent. Certainly, it was not very familiar to the members of Congress. The public concern over large business trusts was familiar, however. In 1888, 1889, and again in 1890, Senator Sherman introduced in Congress bills designed to destroy the large combinations of capital that, he felt, were creating imbalance within the nation's economy.

In 1890, the Fifty-First Congress finally enacted the bill into law. Generally, the act prohibits business combinations and

conspiracies that restrain trade and commerce, as well as certain monopolistic practices. According to its author, the Sherman Act "does not announce a new principle of law, but applies old and well-recognized principles of the common law."[a]

Application to Today's World *The Sherman Antitrust Act remains very relevant to today's world. The U.S. Department of Justice and state attorneys general investigate many complaints and prosecute a number of corporations for Sherman Act violations each year.*

_____

a. 21 *Congressional Record* 2456 (1890).

Learning Objective 1

What is a monopoly? What is market power? How do these concepts relate to each other?

2. Every person who shall monopolize, or attempt to monopolize, or combine or conspire with any other person or persons, to monopolize any part of the trade or commerce among the several States, or with foreign nations, shall be deemed guilty of a felony [and is similarly punishable].

38–1b Differences between Section 1 and Section 2

The two sections of the Sherman Act are quite different. Violation of Section 1 requires two or more persons, as a person cannot contract or combine or conspire alone. Thus, the essence of the illegal activity is *the act of joining together.* Section 2, though, can apply either to one person or to two or more persons because it refers to "every person." Thus, unilateral conduct can result in a violation of Section 2.

It follows that the cases brought under Section 1 of the Sherman Act differ from those brought under Section 2. Section 1 cases are often concerned with finding an agreement (written or oral) that leads to a restraint of trade. Section 2 cases deal with the structure of a monopoly that already exists in the marketplace.

Monopoly A market in which there is a single seller or a very limited number of sellers.

Monopoly Power The ability of a monopoly to dictate what takes place in a given market.

Market Power The power of a firm to control the market price of its product. A monopoly has the greatest degree of market power.

The term **monopoly** generally is used to describe a market in which there is a single seller or a very limited number of sellers. Whereas Section 1 focuses on agreements that are restrictive—that is, agreements that have a wrongful purpose—Section 2 addresses the misuse of **monopoly power** in the marketplace. Monopoly power exists when a firm has an extreme amount of **market power**—the power to affect the market price of its product.

Both Section 1 and Section 2 seek to curtail market practices that result in undesired monopoly pricing and output behavior. For a case to be brought under Section 2, however, the "threshold" or "necessary" amount of monopoly power must already exist. We illustrate the different requirements for violating these two sections of the Sherman Act in Exhibit 38–1.

38–1c Jurisdictional Requirements

The Sherman Act applies only to restraints that have a substantial impact on interstate commerce. Generally, any activity that substantially affects interstate commerce falls within the scope of the Sherman Act. The Sherman Act also extends to U.S. nationals abroad who are engaged in activities that have an effect on U.S. foreign commerce.

Federal courts have exclusive jurisdiction over antitrust cases brought under the Sherman Act. State laws regulate local restraints on competition, and state courts decide claims brought under those laws.

Exhibit 38–1 Required Elements of a Sherman Act Violation

SECTION 1 VIOLATION REQUIREMENTS	SECTION 2 VIOLATION REQUIREMENTS
1. An agreement between two or more parties that 2. unreasonably restrains competition and 3. affects interstate commerce.	1. The possession of monopoly power in the relevant market, and 2. the willful acquisition or maintenance of that power as distinguished from its growth or development as a consequence of a superior product, business acumen, or historic accident.

38–2 Section 1 of the Sherman Act

The underlying assumption of Section 1 of the Sherman Act is that society's welfare is harmed if rival firms are permitted to join in an agreement that consolidates their market power or otherwise restrains competition. The types of trade restraints that Section 1 of the Sherman Act prohibits generally fall into two broad categories: *horizontal restraints* and *vertical restraints,* both of which will be explained shortly. First, though, we look at the rules that the courts may apply when assessing the anticompetitive impact of alleged restraints on trade.

38–2a *Per Se* Violations versus the Rule of Reason

Some restraints are so blatantly and substantially anticompetitive that they are deemed *per se* **violations**—illegal *per se* (on their face, or inherently)—under Section 1. Other agreements, however, even though they result in enhanced market power, do not *unreasonably* restrain trade. Using what is called the **rule of reason**, the courts analyze anticompetitive agreements that allegedly violate Section 1 of the Sherman Act to determine whether they actually constitute reasonable restraints on trade.

Why the Rule of Reason Was Developed The need for a rule-of-reason analysis of some agreements in restraint of trade is obvious—if the rule of reason had not been developed, almost any business agreement could conceivably be held to violate the Sherman Act. Justice Louis Brandeis effectively phrased this sentiment in *Chicago Board of Trade v. United States,* a case decided in 1918:

> Every agreement concerning trade, every regulation of trade, restrains. To bind, to restrain, is of their very essence. The true test of legality is whether the restraint imposed is such as merely regulates and perhaps thereby promotes competition or whether it is such as may suppress or even destroy competition.[4]

Factors Courts Consider under the Rule of Reason When analyzing an alleged Section 1 violation under the rule of reason, a court will consider the following factors:

1. The purpose of the agreement.
2. The parties' ability to implement the agreement to achieve that purpose.
3. The effect or potential effect of the agreement on competition.
4. Whether the parties could have relied on less restrictive means to achieve their purpose.

⭐ **Spotlight Case Example 38.1** A group of consumers sued NBC Universal, the Walt Disney Company, and other broadcasters, as well as cable and satellite distributors, for antitrust violations. The consumers claimed that the bundling together of high-demand and low-demand television channels in cable and satellite programming packages violates the Sherman Act. Bundling forces consumers to pay for channels they do not watch to have access to channels they watch regularly.

The consumers argued that the defendants, through their control of high-demand programming, exercised market power that made it impossible for any distributor to offer unbundled programs. A federal appellate court ruled in favor of the defendants and dismissed the case. The court reasoned that the bundling of channels does not injure competition and thus does not violate the Sherman Act.[5]

> "I don't know what a monopoly is until somebody tells me."
>
> **Steve Ballmer**
> 1956–present
> (Chief executive officer of Microsoft Corporation, 2000–2014)

Per Se **Violation** A restraint of trade that is so anticompetitive that it is deemed inherently (*per se*) illegal.

Rule of Reason A test used to determine whether an anticompetitive agreement constitutes a reasonable restraint on trade. Courts consider such factors as the purpose of the agreement, its effect on competition, and whether less restrictive means could have been used.

Does forcing consumers to buy bundles of cable and satellite channels constitute an antitrust violation?

---

4. 246 U.S. 231, 38 S.Ct. 242, 62 L.Ed. 683 (1918).
5. *Brantley v. NBC Universal, Inc.,* 675 F.3d 1192 (9th Cir. 2012).

38–2b **Horizontal Restraints**

Horizontal Restraint Any agreement that restrains competition between rival firms competing in the same market.

The term **horizontal restraint** is encountered frequently in antitrust law. A horizontal restraint is any agreement that in some way restrains competition between rival firms competing in the same market. Horizontal restraints may include price fixing, group boycotts, market divisions, and trade associations.

Price-Fixing Agreement An agreement between competitors to fix the prices of products or services at a certain level.

Price Fixing
Any **price-fixing agreement**—an agreement among competitors to fix prices—constitutes a *per se* violation of Section 1. The agreement on price need not be explicit. As long as it restricts output or artificially fixes price, it violates the law.

Learning Objective 2

What rule do courts apply to price-fixing agreements, and why?

Classic Case Example 38.2 Independent oil producers in Texas and Louisiana were caught between falling demand due to the Great Depression of the 1930s and increasing supply from newly discovered oil fields in the region. In response to these conditions, a group of major refining companies agreed to buy "distress" gasoline (excess supplies) from the independents so as to dispose of it in an "orderly manner." Although there was no explicit agreement as to price, it was clear that the purpose of the agreement was to limit the supply of gasoline on the market and thereby raise prices.

There may have been good reasons for the agreement. Nonetheless, the United States Supreme Court recognized the potentially adverse effects that such an agreement could have on open and free competition. The Court held that the reasonableness of a price-fixing agreement is never a defense. Any agreement that restricts output or artificially fixes price is a *per se* violation of Section 1.[6]

Price-fixing cartels (groups) are commonplace in today's business world, particularly among global companies. International price-fixing cartels have been alleged in numerous industries, including air freight, auto parts, computer monitors, digital commerce, and pharmaceuticals. The U.S. government actively pursues companies that it suspects of being involved in price-fixing cartels.

Case Example 38.3 After Amazon released the Kindle e-book reader, it began selling e-book downloads at $9.99 (lower than the actual cost) and made up the difference by selling more Kindles. When the iPad entered the e-book scene, Apple and some book publishers agreed to use Apple's "agency" model, which Apple was already using for games and apps. The agency model allowed the book publishers to set their own prices, while Apple kept 30 percent as a commission.

The U.S. government sued Apple and the publishers for price fixing. Because the publishers involved in the arrangement chose prices that were relatively similar, the government argued that price fixing was evident and "would not have occurred without the conspiracy among the defendants." Ultimately, a federal appellate court held that Apple's agreement with publishers was a *per se* illegal price-fixing conspiracy. As a result, Apple was ordered to pay $400 million to consumers and $50 million in attorneys' fees.[7]

Group Boycott An agreement by two or more sellers to refuse to deal with a particular person or firm.

Group Boycotts
A **group boycott** is an agreement by two or more sellers to refuse to deal with (that is, to boycott) a particular person or firm. Because they involve concerted action, group boycotts have been held to constitute *per se* violations of Section 1 of the Sherman Act.

To prove a violation of Section 1, the plaintiff must demonstrate that the boycott or joint refusal to deal was undertaken with the intention of eliminating competition or preventing entry into a given market. Most boycotts are illegal. A few types of boycotts, such as group

---

6. *United States v. Socony-Vacuum Oil Co.*, 310 U.S. 150, 60 S.Ct. 811, 84 L.Ed. 1129 (1940).
7. *United States v. Apple, Inc.*, 791 F.3d 290 (2d Cir. 2015). Apple had previously agreed to settle the case for these amounts if its appeal was unsuccessful.

boycotts against a supplier for political reasons, may be protected under the First Amendment right to freedom of expression, however.

Market Divisions It is a *per se* violation of Section 1 of the Sherman Act for competitors to divide up territories or customers. **Example 38.4** Bell TV Basics, Hall Servo Supplies, and Prime Electronics compete against each other in the states of Kansas, Nebraska, and Oklahoma. The three firms agree that Bell will sell products only in Kansas, Hall will sell only in Nebraska, and Prime will sell only in Oklahoma. This concerted action violates Section 1 of the Sherman Act. It reduces marketing costs and allows all three firms (assuming there is no other competition) to raise the price of the goods they sell in their respective states.

The same violation would take place if the three firms divided up their customers by class rather than region. They might agree that Bell would sell only to institutional purchasers (such as governments and schools) in all three states, Hall only to wholesalers, and Prime only to retailers. The result would be the same. ■

Is it legal for three separate manufacturers of smart televisions to agree to divide up their sales into distinct geographical areas?

Trade Associations Businesses in the same general industry or profession frequently organize trade associations to pursue common interests. A trade association may engage in various joint activities, such as exchanging information, representing the members' business interests before governmental bodies, conducting advertising campaigns, and setting regulatory standards to govern the industry or profession.

Generally, the rule of reason is applied to many of these horizontal actions. If a court finds that a trade association practice or agreement that restrains trade is sufficiently beneficial both to the association and to the public, it may deem the restraint reasonable.

In concentrated industries, however, trade associations can be, and have been, used as a means to facilitate anticompetitive actions, such as fixing prices or allocating markets. A **concentrated industry** is one in which either a single firm or a small number of firms control a large percentage of market sales. When trade association agreements have substantially anticompetitive effects, a court will consider them to be in violation of Section 1 of the Sherman Act.

Concentrated Industry An industry in which a single firm or a small number of firms control a large percentage of market sales.

38–2c **Vertical Restraints**

A **vertical restraint** of trade results from an agreement between firms at different levels in the manufacturing and distribution process. In contrast to horizontal relationships, which occur at the same level of operation, vertical relationships encompass the entire chain of production. The chain of production normally includes the purchase of inventory, basic manufacturing, distribution to wholesalers, and eventual sale of a product at the retail level. When a single firm carries out two or more of the separate functional phases, it is considered to be a **vertically integrated firm.**

Even though firms operating at different functional levels are not in direct competition with one another, they are in competition with other firms. Thus, agreements between firms standing in a vertical relationship may affect competition. Some vertical restraints are *per se* violations of Section 1. Others are judged under the rule of reason.

Vertical Restraint A restraint of trade created by an agreement between firms at different levels in the manufacturing and distribution process.

Vertically Integrated Firm A firm that carries out two or more functional phases (manufacturing, distribution, and retailing, for instance) of the chain of production.

Territorial or Customer Restrictions In arranging for the distribution of its products, a manufacturing firm often wishes to insulate dealers from direct competition with other dealers selling the product. To do so, it may institute territorial restrictions or attempt to prohibit wholesalers or retailers from reselling the product to certain classes of buyers, such as competing retailers.

May Have Legitimate Purpose. A firm may have legitimate reasons for imposing such territorial or customer restrictions. For instance, an electronics manufacturer may wish to prevent a dealer from reducing costs and undercutting rivals by offering the manufacturer's products without promotion or customer service. In this situation, the cost-cutting dealer reaps the benefits (sales of the product) paid for by other dealers who undertake promotion and arrange for customer service. By not providing customer service (and relying on a nearby dealer to provide these services), the cost-cutting dealer may also harm the manufacturer's reputation.

Judged under the Rule of Reason. Territorial and customer restrictions were once considered *per se* violations of Section 1. In 1977, however the United States Supreme Court held that they should be judged under the rule of reason. **Classic Case Example 38.5** The Supreme Court case involved GTE Sylvania, Inc., a manufacturer of television sets. Sylvania limited the number of retail franchises that it granted in any given geographic area. It also required each franchise to sell only Sylvania products from that location.

Sylvania retained sole discretion to increase the number of retailers in an area. When the company decided to open a new franchise, it terminated the franchise of Continental T.V., Inc. Continental sued, claiming that Sylvania's vertically restrictive franchise system violated Section 1. The Supreme Court found that "vertical restrictions promote interbrand competition by allowing the manufacturer to achieve certain efficiencies in the distribution of his products." Therefore, Sylvania's vertical system, which was not price restrictive, did not constitute a *per se* violation of Section 1 of the Sherman Act.[8]

The decision in the *Continental* case marked a definite shift from rigid characterization of these kinds of vertical restraints to a more flexible, economic analysis under the rule of reason. A firm may have legitimate reasons for imposing territorial or customer restrictions, and not all such restrictions harm competition.

Resale Price Maintenance Agreements

An agreement between a manufacturer and a distributor or retailer in which the manufacturer specifies what the retail prices of its products must be is referred to as a **resale price maintenance agreement**. Such agreements were also once considered to be *per se* violations of the Sherman Act.

Today, however, both *maximum* resale price maintenance agreements and *minimum* resale price maintenance agreements are judged under the rule of reason.[9] The setting of a maximum—or a minimum—price that retailers and distributors can charge for a manufacturer's products may sometimes increase competition and benefit consumers.

Resale Price Maintenance Agreement An agreement between a manufacturer and a retailer in which the manufacturer specifies what the retail prices of its products must be.

Learning Objective 3

What two types of activities are prohibited by Section 2 of the Sherman Act?

Predatory Pricing The pricing of a product below cost with the intent to drive competitors out of the market.

38–3 Section 2 of the Sherman Act

Section 1 of the Sherman Act prohibits certain concerted activities that restrain trade. In contrast, Section 2 condemns "every person who shall monopolize, or attempt to monopolize." Thus, two distinct types of behavior are subject to sanction under Section 2: *monopolization* and *attempts to monopolize*.

One tactic that may be involved in either offense is **predatory pricing**. Predatory pricing involves an attempt by one firm to drive its competitors from the market by selling its product at prices substantially *below* the normal costs of production. Once the competitors are eliminated, the firm will presumably attempt to recapture its losses and go on to earn higher profits by driving prices up far above their competitive levels.

---

8. *Continental T.V., Inc. v. GTE Sylvania, Inc.*, 433 U.S. 36, 97 S.Ct. 2549, 53 L.Ed.2d 568 (1977).
9. The United States Supreme Court ruled that maximum resale price agreements should be judged under the rule of reason in *State Oil Co. v. Khan*, 522 U.S. 3, 118 S.Ct. 275, 139 L.Ed.2d 199 (1997). In *Leegin Creative Leather Products, Inc. v. PSKS, Inc.*, 551 U.S. 877, 127 S.Ct. 2705, 168 L.Ed.2d 623 (2007), the Supreme Court found that the rule of reason also applies to minimum resale price agreements.

38–3a **Monopolization**

The United States Supreme Court has defined the offense of **monopolization** as involving two elements:

1. The possession of monopoly power in the relevant market.
2. "The willful acquisition or maintenance of [that] power as distinguished from growth or development as a consequence of a superior product, business acumen, or historic accident."[10]

To establish a violation of Section 2, a plaintiff must prove both of these elements—monopoly power and an intent to monopolize.

Defining Monopoly Power The Sherman Act does not define *monopoly*. In economic theory, monopoly refers to control of a single market by a single entity. It is well established in antitrust law, however, that a firm may be deemed a monopolist even though it is not the sole seller in a market.

Additionally, size alone does not determine whether a firm is a monopoly. For instance, a "mom and pop" grocery located in an isolated town is a monopolist if it is the only grocery serving that particular market. Size in relation to the market is what matters, because monopoly involves the power to affect prices.

Proving Monopoly Power Monopoly power may be proved by direct evidence that the firm used its power to control prices and restrict output. Usually, though, there is not enough evidence to show that the firm was intentionally controlling prices, so the plaintiff has to offer indirect, or circumstantial, evidence of monopoly power.

To prove monopoly power indirectly, the plaintiff must show that the firm has a dominant share of the relevant market and that there are significant barriers for new competitors entering that market. **Case Example 38.6** DuPont manufactures and sells para-aramid fiber, a synthetic fiber used to make body armor, fiber-optic cables, and tires, among other things. Although several companies around the world manufacture this fiber, only three sell in the U.S. market—DuPont (based in the United States), Teijin (based in the Netherlands), and Kolon Industries, Inc. (based in Korea). DuPont is the industry leader and at times has produced 60 percent of all para-aramid fibers purchased in the United States.

After DuPont brought suit against Kolon for theft and misappropriation of trade secrets, Kolon counterclaimed that DuPont had illegally monopolized and attempted to monopolize the U.S. para-aramid market in violation of Section 2. Kolon claimed that, to deter competition, DuPont had illegally used multiyear supply agreements for all of its high-volume para-aramid customers. A federal appellate court, however, found that there was insufficient proof that DuPont possessed monopoly power in the U.S. market during the relevant time period (between 2006 and 2009). Additionally, the court concluded that Kolon had not showed that the supply agreements foreclosed competition. Therefore, the court held in favor of DuPont on the antitrust claims.[11]

Relevant Market Before a court can determine whether a firm has a dominant market share, it must define the relevant market. The relevant market consists of two elements: a relevant product market and a relevant geographic market.

Relevant Product Market. The relevant product market includes all products that, although produced by different firms, have identical attributes—for example, tea. It also includes reasonably interchangeable products. Products are considered reasonably interchangeable if consumers treat them as acceptable substitutes (coffee may be substituted for tea, for instance).

Monopolization The possession of monopoly power in the relevant market and the willful acquisition or maintenance of that power, as distinguished from growth or development as a consequence of a superior product, business acumen, or historic accident.

Do multi-year supply agreements necessarily deter competition in violation of the Sherman Act?

---

10. *United States v. Grinnell Corp.*, 384 U.S. 563, 86 S.Ct. 1698, 16 L.Ed.2d 778 (1966).
11. *Kolon Industries, Inc. v. E.I. DuPont de Nemours & Co.*, 748 F.3d 160 (4th Cir. 2014).

Know This

Section 5 of the Federal Trade Commission Act is broader than the other antitrust laws. It covers nearly all anticompetitive behavior, including conduct that does not violate either the Sherman Act or the Clayton Act.

Establishing the relevant product market is often a key issue in monopolization cases because the way the market is defined may determine whether a firm has monopoly power. When the product market is defined narrowly, the degree of a firm's market power appears greater. **Example 38.7** White Whale Apps acquires Springleaf Apps, its main competitor in nationwide Android-based mobile phone apps. White Whale maintains that the relevant product market consists of all online retailers of mobile phone apps. The Federal Trade Commission (FTC), however, argues that the relevant product market consists of retailers that sell only apps for Android mobile phones. Under the FTC's narrower definition, White Whale can be seen to have a dominant share of the relevant product market. Thus, the FTC can take appropriate actions against White Whale. ■

In the following case, the FTC alleged that the leading producer of domestic ductile iron pipefittings sought to maintain its alleged monopoly power in violation of antitrust law. The FTC filed this action under Section 5 of the Federal Trade Commission Act. Like Section 2 of the Sherman Act, Section 5 requires proof of both the possession of monopoly power in the relevant market and the willful acquisition or maintenance of that power.

■ Case 38.1

McWane, Inc. v. Federal Trade Commission

United States Court of Appeals, Eleventh Circuit, 783 F.3d 814 (2015).

Background and Facts Pipefittings join together pipes and help direct the flow of pressurized water in pipeline systems. Certain municipal, state, and federal laws require waterworks projects to use fittings made in the United States, so specifications for such projects may require the use of "domestic fittings." As a result, buyers sometimes issue "domestic-only specifications" for their projects.

McWane, Inc., is the dominant producer of domestic ductile iron fittings. When Star Pipe Products entered the market, McWane instituted a new policy. Unless McWane's distributors bought all of their domestic fittings from McWane, they would lose any rebates they had earned previously and would be cut off from purchases for twelve weeks. The Federal Trade Commission (FTC) brought an action against McWane alleging that McWane's policy was an unlawful attempt to maintain monopoly power by keeping competitors out of the market. The FTC ultimately ordered McWane to stop requiring exclusivity from distributors. McWane appealed the FTC decision to a federal court.

In the Words of the Court
MARCUS, Circuit Judge:
* * * *

uriy2007/iStock/Getty Images

If an iron pipefitting company forces all customers to buy all fittings from that company, what antitrust law is violated?

* * * The [Federal Trade] Commission * * * found that the relevant market was one for the supply of domestically-manufactured fittings for use in * * * projects with domestic-only specifications. It noted that various laws and end-user preferences requiring projects to use domestic fittings precluded imported fittings from being reasonable substitutes for those projects, even though the fittings themselves are functionally identical. The Commission also noted that McWane charged higher prices for (and reaped greater profits from) domestic fittings in domestic-only projects: * * * McWane charged approximately 20 percent–95 percent more for its domestic fittings for domestic-only projects than for open-specification projects. This price differentiation reflected McWane's ability to target customers with domestic-only project specifications who could not avoid the higher prices by substituting imported fittings.

* * * *

* * * Given the identification of persistent price differences between domestic fittings and imported fittings, the distinct customers, and the lack of reasonable substitutes in this case, there was sufficient evidence to support the Commission's market definition.

* * * *

In determining that McWane had monopoly power, the Commission found that McWane's market share of the domestic fittings market had been 100% * * * until Star's entry into the market * * *. Although Star was able to enter the market, * * * its share remained below 10 percent * * *, and, notably, its entry had no effect on McWane's prices. * * * *McWane's ability to control prices in the market provided direct evidence of its monopoly power.* [Emphasis added.]

* * * *

* * * The Commission [also found] that * * * substantial barriers to entry existed in * * * the domestic fittings market. * * * A significant capital investment is required to enter the * * * market, as new entrants must overcome existing relationships between existing manufacturers, and the distributors, and end users, in addition to developing hundreds of patterns and moldings. * * * Moreover, the Commission found that [McWane's exclusivity policy] posed a barrier to entry by shrinking the number of available distributors.

* * * *

* * * The evidence of McWane's overwhelming market share * * *, the large capital outlays required to enter the domestic fittings market, and McWane's undeniable continued power over domestic fittings prices * * * support the Commission's conclusion.

Decision and Remedy The U.S. Court of Appeals for the Eleventh Circuit affirmed the FTC's order. The federal appellate court's conclusion was supported by McWane's market share and its exclusivity policy for distributors. McWane's actions constituted an illegal attempt to maintain monopoly power.

Critical Thinking

• **Economic** *How did McWane's exclusivity policy harm competition? Explain.*

Relevant Geographic Market. The second component of the relevant market is the market's geographic extent. For products that are sold nationwide, the geographic market encompasses the entire United States. If transportation costs are significant or a producer and its competitors sell in only a limited area (one in which customers have no access to other sources of the product), the geographic market is limited to that area. A national firm may thus compete in several distinct areas and have monopoly power in one area but not in another.

Generally, the geographic market is that section of the country within which a firm can increase its price a bit without attracting new sellers or losing many customers to alternative suppliers outside that area. Of course, the Internet and e-commerce are changing the notion of the size and limits of a geographic market. It may become difficult to perceive any geographic market as local, except for products that are not easily transported, such as concrete.

The Intent Requirement Monopoly power, in and of itself, does not constitute the offense of monopolization under Section 2 of the Sherman Act. The offense also requires an *intent* to monopolize.

A dominant market share may be the result of business acumen or the development of a superior product. It may simply be the result of a historic accident. In these situations, the acquisition of monopoly power is not an antitrust violation. Indeed, it would be contrary to society's interest to condemn every firm that acquired a position of power because it was well managed and efficient, and marketed a product desired by consumers.

In contrast, if a firm possesses market power as a result of carrying out some purposeful act to acquire or maintain that power through anticompetitive means, then it is in violation of Section 2. In most monopolization cases, intent may be inferred from evidence that the firm had monopoly power and engaged in anticompetitive behavior.

Unilateral Refusals to Deal As discussed previously, joint refusals to deal (group boycotts) are subject to close scrutiny under Section 1 of the Sherman Act. A single manufacturer acting unilaterally, though, normally is free to deal, or not to deal, with whomever it wishes.

Know This
Section 2 of the Sherman Act essentially condemns the act of monopolizing, not the possession of monopoly power.

Attempted Monopolization An action by a firm that involves anticompetitive conduct, the intent to gain monopoly power, and a "dangerous probability" of success in achieving monopoly power.

If the dominant owner of downhill ski facilities refuses to include its smallest competitor in an inclusive all-area lift ticket, why is that a violation of antitrust laws?

Nevertheless, in some instances, a unilateral refusal to deal will violate Section 2 of the Sherman Act. These instances occur only if (1) the firm refusing to deal has—or is likely to acquire—monopoly power and (2) the refusal is likely to have an anticompetitive effect on a particular market.

Example 38.8 Clark Industries, the owner of three of the four major downhill ski areas in Blue Hills, Idaho, refuses to continue participating in a jointly offered six-day "all Blue Hills" lift ticket. Clark's refusal to cooperate with its smaller competitor is a violation of Section 2 of the Sherman Act. Because Clark owns three-fourths of the local ski areas, it has monopoly power. Thus, its unilateral refusal to deal has an anticompetitive effect on the market. ■

38–3b Attempts to Monopolize

Section 2 also prohibits **attempted monopolization** of a market, which requires proof of the following three elements:

1. Anticompetitive conduct.
2. The specific intent to exclude competitors and garner monopoly power.
3. A "dangerous" probability of success in achieving monopoly power. The probability cannot be dangerous unless the alleged offender possesses some degree of market power. Only *serious* threats of monopolization are condemned as violations.

38–4 The Clayton Act

Learning Objective 4

What are the four major provisions of the Clayton Act, and what types of activities do these provisions prohibit?

In 1914, Congress attempted to strengthen federal antitrust laws by enacting the Clayton Act. The act was aimed at specific anticompetitive or monopolistic practices that the Sherman Act did not cover. The substantive provisions of the act deal with four distinct forms of business behavior, which are declared illegal but not criminal. In each instance, the act states that the behavior is illegal only if it tends to substantially lessen competition or to create monopoly power.

The major offenses under the Clayton Act are set out in Sections 2, 3, 7, and 8 of the act.

38–4a Section 2—Price Discrimination

Price Discrimination A seller's act of charging competing buyers different prices for identical products or services.

Section 2 of the Clayton Act prohibits **price discrimination**, which occurs when a seller charges different prices to competing buyers for identical goods or services. Congress strengthened this section by amending it in 1936 with the passage of the Robinson-Patman Act. As amended, Section 2 prohibits price discrimination that cannot be justified by differences in production costs, transportation costs, or cost differences due to other reasons.

Requirements To violate Section 2, the seller must be engaged in interstate commerce, the goods must be of like grade and quality, and the goods must have been sold to two or more purchasers. In addition, the effect of the price discrimination must be to substantially lessen competition, tend to create a monopoly, or otherwise injure competition. Without proof of an actual injury resulting from the price discrimination, the plaintiff cannot recover damages.

Price discrimination claims can arise from discounts, offsets, rebates, or allowances given to one buyer over another. Giving favorable credit terms, delivery, or freight charges to only some buyers can also lead to allegations of price discrimination. For instance, in some circumstances, offering goods to different customers at the same price but including free delivery only for some of the customers may violate Section 2.

"Becoming number one is easier than remaining number one."

Bill Bradley
1943–present
(American politician and athlete)

Defenses There are several statutory defenses to liability for price discrimination.

1. *Cost justification.* If the seller can justify the price reduction by demonstrating that a particular buyer's purchases saved the seller costs in producing and selling the goods, the seller will not be liable for price discrimination.

2. *Meeting competitor's prices.* If the seller charged the lower price in a good-faith attempt to meet an equally low price of a competitor, the seller will not be liable for price discrimination. **Example 38.9** Rogue, Inc., is a retail dealer of Mercury Marine outboard motors in Shady Cove, Oregon. Mercury Marine also sells its motors to other dealers in the Shady Cove area. When Rogue discovers that Mercury is selling its outboard motors at a substantial discount to Rogue's largest competitor, it files a price discrimination lawsuit. Mercury Marine can defend itself by showing that the discounts given to Rogue's competitor were made in good faith to meet the low price charged by another manufacturer of marine motors. ■

3. *Changing market conditions.* A seller may lower its price on an item in response to changing conditions affecting the market for or the marketability of the goods concerned. Sellers are allowed to readjust their prices to meet the realities of the market without liability for price discrimination. Thus, if an advance in technology makes a particular product less marketable than it was previously, a seller can lower the product's price.

If an outboard motor manufacturer gives discounts to one dealer but not another, is it violating antitrust laws?

State Laws Concerning Price Discrimination Some states have enacted statutes to prohibit price discrimination, which can apply in addition to the Clayton Act. For instance, a state statute may apply when a business sells goods or services at different prices to buyers in different locations within the state. Some of these laws protect specific businesses, such as auto dealerships, from discriminatory wholesale or incentive pricing.

Other state laws protect businesses and consumers from economic injuries caused by wrongful business practices. These include unfair competition statutes. In the following case, a state court considered whether an allegation of age-based price discrimination in violation of the state's civil rights statute could support a claim for a violation of the state's unfair competition statute.

■ Case 38.2

Candelore v. Tinder, Inc.

California Court of Appeal, Second District, Division 3, 19 Cal.App.5th 1138, 228 Cal.Rptr.3d 336 (2018).

Background and Facts Tinder, Inc., owns and operates the dating app Tinder. The free version of Tinder presents users with photos of potential dates. When a photo appears on the device's screen, the user can swipe right to express approval, or swipe left to express disapproval. The premium service, Tinder Plus, allows users to access additional features of the app for a monthly fee. Tinder charges consumers who are age thirty and older $19.99 per month for Tinder Plus, while it charges consumers under the age of thirty only $9.99 or $14.99 per month for the Tinder Plus features.

On behalf of consumers who were over age thirty when they subscribed to Tinder Plus, Allan Candelore filed a suit in a California state court against Tinder, Inc. Candelore alleged age-based price discrimination in violation of California's civil rights statute, which prohibits arbitrary discrimination by businesses on the basis of personal characteristics, and the state's unfair competition law (UCL). The court concluded that the company's age-based pricing model was justified by public policies that promote "profit maximization by the vendor, a legitimate goal in our capitalistic economy." Candelore appealed.

(Continues)

In the Words of the Court

CURREY, J. [Judge]

* * * *

* * * Whatever interest society may have—if any—in increasing patronage among those under the age of thirty who may be interested in the premium features of an online dating app, that interest is not sufficiently compelling to justify discriminatory age-based pricing that may well exclude less economically advantaged individuals over the age of thirty from enjoying the same premium features.

As for profit maximization, we have no quarrel with the trial court's conclusion that it can be an acceptable business objective and can be advanced by price discrimination. As anyone who has attended an auction can attest, individuals may and often do value goods and services differently. Some are willing and able to pay a higher price than others for the same product. And, as any student of elementary microeconomics knows, sellers of goods and services could (at least theoretically) maximize profits if they could engage in price discrimination by charging higher prices to those consumers willing to pay them, and lower prices to the rest. For example, a seller might offer several versions of its product, with different features, trim, branding, etc., each at a different price, in an effort to increase overall profits. Or a seller might seek to attract bargain hunters by offering temporary price reductions during a sale or other promotion. *But the quest for profit maximization can never serve as an excuse for prohibited discrimination among potential customers.* [Emphasis added.]

* * * *

As alleged, Tinder's pricing model discriminates against users age thirty and over * * *. While we make no judgment about the true character of Tinder's pricing model, or whether evidence exists to establish a sufficient justification for charging older users more than younger users, we conclude the complaint's allegations are sufficient to state a claim for age discrimination in violation of the [state's civil rights statute].

* * * *

The UCL prohibits, and provides civil remedies for, unfair competition, which includes any unlawful, unfair or fraudulent business act or practice. Its purpose is to protect both consumers and competitors by promoting fair competition in commercial markets for goods and services.

* * * *Any law or regulation—federal or state, statutory or common law—can serve as a predicate [ground] for a * * * violation.* Because we conclude the complaint adequately states a claim for violation of the [civil rights statute], we also conclude the allegations are sufficient to state a claim under * * * the UCL. [Emphasis added.]

Decision and Remedy A state intermediate appellate court reversed the judgment of the lower court. "Tinder's alleged discriminatory pricing model violates the public policy embodied in the [civil rights statute, and] the UCL . . . provides an independent basis for relief on the facts alleged."

Critical Thinking

• **Legal Environment** *A California statute provides for the waiver of fees at state university campuses for senior citizens. What distinguishes this differential treatment from the discriminatory practice at issue in the* Candelore *case?*

• **Economic** *Instead of personal characteristics such as age, could a business like Tinder use economic distinctions to broaden its user base and increase profits? Discuss.*

38–4b Section 3—Exclusionary Practices

Under Section 3 of the Clayton Act, sellers or lessors cannot condition the sale or lease of goods on the buyer's or lessee's promise not to use or deal in the goods of the seller's competitor. In effect, this section prohibits two types of vertical agreements involving exclusionary practices—*exclusive-dealing contracts* and *tying arrangements*.

Exclusive-Dealing Contract An agreement under which a seller forbids a buyer to purchase products from the seller's competitors.

Exclusive-Dealing Contracts A contract under which a seller forbids a buyer to purchase products from the seller's competitors is called an **exclusive-dealing contract**. A seller is prohibited from making an exclusive-dealing contract under Section 3 if the effect of the contract is "to substantially lessen competition or tend to create a monopoly."

📖 **Classic Case Example 38.10** In a case decided by the United States Supreme Court in 1949, Standard Oil Company, the largest gasoline seller in the nation at that time, made exclusive-dealing contracts with independent stations in seven western states. The contracts involved 16 percent of all retail outlets, with sales amounting to approximately 7 percent of all retail sales in that market. The market was substantially concentrated because the seven largest gasoline suppliers all used exclusive-dealing contracts with their independent retailers. Together, these suppliers controlled 65 percent of the market.

The Court looked at market conditions after the arrangements were instituted and found that market shares were extremely stable and entry into the market was apparently restricted. Because competition was "foreclosed in a substantial share" of the relevant market, the Court held that Section 3 of the Clayton Act had been violated.[12] Note that since the Supreme Court's 1949 decision, a number of subsequent decisions have called the holding in this case into doubt.[13]

Today, it is clear that to violate antitrust law, an exclusive-dealing agreement (or a tying arrangement, discussed next) must qualitatively and substantially harm competition. To prevail, a plaintiff must present affirmative evidence that the performance of the agreement will foreclose competition and harm consumers.

Tying Arrangements When a seller conditions the sale of a product (the tying product) on the buyer's agreement to purchase another product (the tied product) produced or distributed by the same seller, a **tying arrangement** results. The legality of a tying arrangement (or *tie-in sales agreement*) depends on many factors, particularly the purpose of the agreement and its likely effect on competition in the relevant markets (the market for the tying product and the market for the tied product).

Section 3 of the Clayton Act has been held to apply only to commodities, not to services. Some tying arrangements, however, can also be considered agreements that restrain trade in violation of Section 1 of the Sherman Act. Thus, cases involving tying arrangements of services have been brought under Section 1 of the Sherman Act. Although earlier cases condemned tying arrangements as illegal *per se,* courts now evaluate tying agreements under the rule of reason.

Case Example 38.11 James Batson bought a nonrefundable ticket from Live Nation Entertainment, Inc., to attend a rock concert at the Charter One Pavilion in Chicago. The front of the ticket noted that the price included a $9 parking fee. Batson did not have a car to park, however. In fact, he had walked to the concert venue and bought the ticket just before the performance.

Frustrated at being charged for parking that he did not need, Batson filed a suit in a federal district court against Live Nation. He argued that the bundled parking fee was a tying arrangement in violation of Section 1 of the Sherman Act. The court dismissed the suit, and a federal appellate court affirmed. The court was unable to identify a product market in which Live Nation had sufficient power to force consumers who wanted to attend a concert (the tying product) to buy "useless parking rights" (the tied product). While such bundles may be annoying, there was no evidence that Live Nation's parking tie-in restrained competition for live concerts in Chicago.[14]

Tying Arrangement A seller's act of conditioning the sale of a product or service on the buyer's agreement to purchase another product or service from the seller.

Why can Live Nation "tie in" a parking fee with all of its concert tickets in Chicago?

38–4c Section 7—Mergers

Under Section 7 of the Clayton Act, a person or business organization cannot hold stock or assets in another entity "where the effect ... may be to substantially lessen competition." Section 7 is the statutory authority for preventing mergers or acquisitions that could result in monopoly power or a substantial lessening of competition in the marketplace.

---

12. *Standard Oil Co. of California v. United States*, 337 U.S. 293, 69 S.Ct. 1051, 93 L.Ed. 1371 (1949).

13. See, for instance, *Illinois Tool Works, Inc. v. Independent Ink, Inc.*, 547 U.S. 28, 126 S.Ct. 1281, 164 L.Ed.2d 26 (2006); and *Stop & Shop Supermarket Co. v. Blue Cross & Blue Shield of Rhode Island*, 373 F.3d 57 (1st Cir. 2004).

14. *Batson v. Live Nation Entertainment, Inc.*, 746 F.3d 827 (7th Cir. 2014).

Market Concentration The degree to which a small number of firms control a large percentage of a relevant market.

Market Concentration A crucial consideration in most merger cases is the **market concentration** of a product or business. Determining market concentration involves allocating percentage market shares among the various companies in the relevant market. When a small number of companies control a large share of the market, the market is concentrated.

Example 38.12 If the four largest grocery stores in Chicago account for 80 percent of all retail food sales, the market is concentrated in those four firms. If one of these stores absorbs the assets and liabilities of another, so that the other ceases to exist, the result is a merger that further concentrates the market and possibly diminishes competition. ▪

Competition is not necessarily diminished solely as a result of market concentration, and courts will consider other factors in determining whether a merger will violate Section 7. One factor of particular importance in evaluating the effects of a merger is whether the merger will make it more difficult for *potential* competitors to enter the relevant market.

Horizontal Merger A merger between two firms that are competing in the same market.

Horizontal Mergers Mergers between firms that compete with each other in the same market are called **horizontal mergers.** If a horizontal merger creates an entity with a significant market share, the merger will be presumed illegal because it increases market concentration. The Federal Trade Commission (FTC) and the U.S. Department of Justice (DOJ) have established guidelines for determining which mergers will actually be challenged. The guidelines focus on whether a merger will substantially lessen competition.

When analyzing the legality of a horizontal merger, the courts also consider three other factors: the overall concentration of the relevant product market, the relevant market's history of tending toward concentration, and whether the merger is apparently designed to establish market power or to restrict competition.

Vertical Merger The acquisition by a company at one stage of production of a company at a higher or lower stage of production (such as a company merging with one of its suppliers or retailers).

Vertical Mergers A **vertical merger** occurs when a company at one stage of production acquires a company at a higher or lower stage of production. An example of a vertical merger is a company merging with one of its suppliers or retailers.

Whether a vertical merger is illegal generally depends on several factors, such as whether the merger would produce a firm controlling an undue proportion of the relevant market. The courts also analyze the concentration of firms in the market, barriers to entry into the market, and the apparent intent of the merging parties. A vertical merger is unlawful if it prevents competitors of either merging firm from competing in a segment of the market that otherwise would be open to them, resulting in a substantial lessening of competition.

38–4d Section 8—Interlocking Directorates

Section 8 of the Clayton Act deals with *interlocking directorates*—that is, the practice whereby individuals serve as directors on the boards of two or more competing companies simultaneously. Specifically, no person may be a director in two or more competing corporations at the same time if either of the corporations has capital, surplus, or undivided profits aggregating more than $34,395,000 or competitive sales of $3,439,500 or more. (The FTC adjusts the threshold amounts each year. The amounts given here are those announced by the FTC in 2018.)

The reasoning behind the FTC's prohibition of interlocking directorates is that if two competing businesses share the same officers and directors, the firms are unlikely to compete with one another, or to compete aggressively. If directors or officers do not comply with this prohibition, they may be liable under the Clayton Act.

38–5 Enforcement and Exemptions

The federal agencies that enforce the federal antitrust laws are the U.S. Department of Justice (DOJ) and the Federal Trade Commission (FTC). The FTC was established in 1914 by the Federal Trade Commission Act. Section 5 of that act condemns all forms of anticompetitive behavior that are not covered under other federal antitrust laws.

Learning Objective 5

What agencies of the federal government enforce the federal antitrust laws?

38–5a Enforcement by Federal Agencies

Only the DOJ can prosecute violations of the Sherman Act, which may be either criminal or civil offenses. Violations of the Clayton Act are not crimes, but the act can be enforced by either the DOJ or the FTC through civil proceedings.

The DOJ or the FTC may ask the courts to impose various remedies, including **divestiture** (making a company give up one or more of its operating functions) and dissolution. A meat-packing firm, for instance, might be forced to divest itself of control or ownership of butcher shops.

Divestiture A company's sale of one or more of its divisions' operating functions under court order as part of the enforcement of the antitrust laws.

The FTC has sole authority to enforce violations of Section 5 of the Federal Trade Commission Act. FTC actions are effected through administrative orders, but if a firm violates an FTC order, the FTC can seek court sanctions for the violation.

38–5b Actions by Private Parties

A private party who has been injured as a result of a violation of the Sherman Act or the Clayton Act can sue for **treble damages** (three times the actual damages suffered) and attorneys' fees. In some instances, private parties may also seek injunctive relief to prevent antitrust violations. A party wishing to sue under the Sherman Act must prove the following:

Treble Damages Damages that, by statute, are three times the amount of actual damages suffered.

1. The antitrust violation either caused or was a substantial factor in causing the injury that was suffered.

2. The unlawful actions of the accused party affected business activities of the plaintiff that were protected by the antitrust laws.

Additionally, the United States Supreme Court has held that to pursue antitrust lawsuits, private parties must present some evidence suggesting that an illegal agreement was made.[15]

A private party can bring an action under Section 2 of the Sherman Act based on the attempted enforcement of a fraudulently obtained patent. Such an action is called a *Walker Process* claim.[16] To prevail, the plaintiff must first show that the defendant obtained the patent by committing fraud against the U.S. Patent and Trademark Office and enforced the patent with knowledge of the fraud. The plaintiff must then establish all the other elements of a Sherman Act monopolization claim—anticompetitive conduct, an intent to monopolize, and a dangerous probability of achieving monopoly power.

In the following case, a respiratory filter maker was accused of patent infringement. The maker sought a declaratory judgment of noninfringement, asserting a *Walker Process* claim. One of the primary issues was whether attorneys' fees were an appropriate basis for damages.

---

15. *Bell Atlantic Corp. v. Twombly*, 550 U.S. 544, 127 S.Ct. 1955, 167 L.Ed.2d 929 (2007).

16. The name of the claim comes from the title of the case in which the claim originated—*Walker Process Equipment v. Food Machine and Chemical Corp.*, 382 U.S. 172, 86 S.Ct. 347, 15 L.Ed.2d 247 (1965).

Case 38.3

TransWeb, LLC v. 3M Innovative Properties Co.

United States Court of Appeals, Federal Circuit, 812 F.3d 1295 (2016).

Background and Facts TransWeb, LLC, manufactures respirator filters made of nonwoven fibrous material to be worn by workers at contaminated work sites. At a filtration industry exposition, TransWeb's founder, Kumar Ogale, handed out samples of TransWeb's filter material. At the time, 3M Innovative Products Company was experimenting with filter materials. At the expo, 3M employees obtained the TransWeb samples.

More than a year later, 3M obtained patents for its filter products and filed a suit against TransWeb, claiming infringement. 3M asserted that it had not received the TransWeb samples until after its patent application had been filed. The suit was dismissed.

TransWeb then filed a suit in a federal district court, seeking a declaratory judgment of noninfringement and asserting a *Walker Process* claim. A jury found that 3M had obtained its patents through fraud, that its assertion of the patents against TransWeb violated antitrust law, and that TransWeb was entitled to attorneys' fees as damages. TransWeb had incurred $7.7 million in fees defending against 3M's infringement suit. The court trebled this to $23 million. 3M appealed.

In the Words of the Court
HUGHES, Circuit Judge.
* * * *

3M argues that the district court erred in awarding the $23 million of attorney-fees damages, because TransWeb failed to show any link between those attorney fees and an impact on competition. 3M argues that those attorney fees had no effect on competition because they did not force TransWeb out of the market or otherwise affect prices in the market.
* * * *

3M's argument focuses on the fact that the harmful effect on competition proven by TransWeb at trial never actually came about. TransWeb proved at trial that increased prices for fluorinated filter * * * respirators would have resulted had 3M succeeded in its suit.
* * * *

* * * 3M's unlawful act was * * * aimed at reducing competition and would have done so had the suit been successful. 3M's unlawful act was the bringing of suit based on a patent known to be fraudulently obtained. What made this act unlawful under the antitrust laws was its attempt to gain a monopoly based on

this fraudulently obtained patent. TransWeb's attorney fees flow directly from this unlawful aspect of 3M's act. * * * The attorney fees are precisely the type of loss that the claimed violations would be likely to cause.
* * * *

* * * *It is the abuse of the legal process by the antitrust-defendant that makes the attorney fees incurred by the antitrust-plaintiff during that legal process a relevant antitrust injury.* [Emphasis added.]

No assertion of a patent known to be fraudulently obtained can be a proper use of legal process. No successful outcome of that litigation, regardless of how much the patentee subjectively desires it, would save that suit from being improper due to its tainted origin. * * * The antitrust laws exist to protect competition. If we were to hold that TransWeb can seek antitrust damages only [by] forfeiture of competition, but not [by] defending the anticompetitive suit, then we would be incentivizing the former over the latter.

* * * This is not in accord with the purpose of those very same antitrust laws. Furthermore, it furthers the purpose of the antitrust laws to encourage TransWeb to bring its antitrust suit * * * instead of waiting to be excluded from the market * * *. If TransWeb proceeds only after being excluded from the market * * *, then the [injury] will no longer be borne by TransWeb alone, but rather would be shared by all consumers in the relevant markets.

Decision and Remedy The U.S. Court of Appeals for the Federal Circuit affirmed the lower court's judgment and award of trebled attorneys' fees. "TransWeb's attorney fees appropriately flow from the unlawful aspect of 3M's antitrust violation and thus are an antitrust injury that can properly serve as the basis for antitrust damages."

Critical Thinking

• **Legal Environment** *How would TransWeb's injury have been "shared by all consumers in the relevant markets" if TransWeb had not sued until after it had been driven out of those markets by 3M's actions?*

• **Ethical** *What does 3M's conduct suggest about its corporate ethics?*

38–5c Exemptions from Antitrust Laws

There are many legislative and constitutional limitations on antitrust enforcement. Most are statutory or judicially created exemptions applying to the areas listed in Exhibit 38–2. One of the most significant exemptions covers joint efforts by businesspersons to obtain legislative, judicial, or executive action. Under this exemption, for instance, Blu-ray producers can jointly lobby Congress to change the copyright laws without being held liable for attempting to restrain trade.

38–6 U.S. Antitrust Laws in the Global Context

U.S. antitrust laws have a broad application. Not only may persons in foreign nations be subject to their provisions, but the laws may also be applied to protect foreign consumers and competitors from violations committed by U.S. business firms. Consequently, *foreign persons*—a term that by definition includes foreign governments—may sue under U.S. antitrust laws in U.S. courts.

Exhibit 38–2 Exemptions to Antitrust Enforcement

EXEMPTION	SOURCE AND SCOPE
Labor	Clayton Act—Permits unions to organize and bargain without violating antitrust laws and specifies that strikes and other labor activities normally do not violate any federal law.
Agricultural associations	Clayton Act and Capper-Volstead Act—Allow agricultural cooperatives to set prices.
Fisheries	Fishery Cooperative Marketing Act—Allows the fishing industry to set prices.
Insurance companies	McCarran-Ferguson Act—Exempts the insurance business in states in which the industry is regulated.
Exporters	Webb-Pomerene Act—Allows U.S. exporters to engage in cooperative activity to compete with similar foreign associations. Export Trading Company Act—Permits the U.S. Department of Justice to exempt certain exporters.
Professional baseball	The United States Supreme Court has held that professional baseball is exempt because it is not "interstate commerce."[a]
Oil marketing	Interstate Oil Compact—Allows states to set quotas on oil to be marketed in interstate commerce.
Defense activities	Defense Production Act—Allows the president to approve, and thereby exempt, certain activities to further the military defense of the United States.
Small businesses' cooperative research	Small Business Administration Act—Allows small firms to undertake cooperative research.
State actions	The United States Supreme Court has held that actions by a state are exempt if the state clearly articulates and actively supervises the policy behind its action.[b]
Regulated industries	Industries (such as airlines) are exempt when a federal administrative agency (such as the Federal Aviation Administration) has primary regulatory authority.
Businesspersons' joint efforts to seek government action	Cooperative efforts by businesspersons to obtain legislative, judicial, or executive action are exempt unless it is clear that an effort is "objectively baseless" and is an attempt to make anticompetitive use of government processes.[c]

a. *Federal Baseball Club of Baltimore, Inc. v. National League of Professional Baseball Clubs,* 259 U.S. 200, 42 S.Ct. 465, 66 L.Ed. 898 (1922). See also *City of San Jose v. Office of the Commissioner of Baseball,* 776 F.3d 686 (9th Cir. 2015).

b. See *Parker v. Brown,* 317 U.S. 341, 63 S.Ct. 307, 87 L.Ed. 315 (1943).

c. *Eastern Railroad Presidents Conference v. Noerr Motor Freight, Inc.,* 365 U.S. 127, 81 S.Ct. 523, 5 L.Ed.2d 464 (1961); and *United Mine Workers of America v. Pennington,* 381 U.S. 657, 89 S.Ct. 1585, 14 L.Ed.2d 626 (1965). These two cases established the exception often referred to as the *Noerr-Pennington doctrine.*

Learning Objective 6

When will a U.S. court apply the Sherman Act to foreign persons or entities?

38–6a The Extraterritorial Application of U.S. Antitrust Laws

The United States is a major proponent of free competition in the global economy. Accordingly, Section 1 of the Sherman Act provides for the extraterritorial effect of the U.S. antitrust laws. Any conspiracy that has a *substantial effect* on U.S. commerce is within the reach of the Sherman Act. The violation may even occur outside the United States, and foreign persons, including governments, can be sued for violation of U.S. antitrust laws.

Before U.S. courts will exercise jurisdiction and apply antitrust laws, it must be shown that the alleged violation had a substantial effect on U.S. commerce. U.S. jurisdiction is automatically invoked, however, when a *per se* violation occurs. If a domestic firm, for instance, joins a foreign cartel to control the production, price, or distribution of goods, and this cartel has a *substantial effect* on U.S. commerce, a *per se* violation may arise. Hence, both the domestic firm and the foreign cartel could be sued for violation of the U.S. antitrust laws.

Likewise, if a foreign firm doing business in the United States enters into a price-fixing or other anticompetitive agreement to control a portion of U.S. markets, a *per se* violation may exist. **Case Example 38.13** Carrier Corporation is a U.S. firm that manufactures air-conditioning and refrigeration (ACR) equipment. To make these products, Carrier uses ACR copper tubing that it buys from Outokumpu Oyj, a Finnish company. Carrier is one of the world's largest purchasers of ACR copper tubing.

After the Commission of the European Communities (EC) found that Outokumpu had conspired with other companies to fix ACR tubing prices in Europe, Carrier filed a suit in a U.S. court. Carrier alleged that the cartel had also conspired to fix prices in the United States by agreeing that only Outokumpu would sell ACR tubing in the U.S. market. The district court dismissed the case for lack of jurisdiction, but a federal appellate court reversed. The appellate court found that the alleged anticompetitive conspiracy had a substantial effect on U.S. commerce. Therefore, the U.S. courts had jurisdiction over the Finnish defendant.[17]

38–6b The Application of Foreign Antitrust Laws

Large U.S. companies increasingly must be concerned about the application of foreign antitrust laws as well. The European Union (EU), in particular, has stepped up its enforcement actions against antitrust violators.

European Union Enforcement The EU's laws promoting competition are stricter in many respects than those of the United States and define more conduct as anticompetitive. The EU actively pursues antitrust violators, especially individual companies and cartels that allegedly engage in monopolistic conduct. EU investigations of possible antitrust violations often take years. See this chapter's *Adapting the Law to the Online Environment* feature for a discussion of how the EU is pursuing Google, Inc., for antitrust violations.

Increased Enforcement in Asia and Latin America Many other nations also have laws that promote competition and prohibit trade restraints. Japanese antitrust laws forbid unfair trade practices, monopolization, and restrictions that unreasonably restrain trade. China's antitrust rules restrict monopolization and price fixing (except that the Chinese government can set prices on exported goods). Indonesia, Malaysia, South Korea, and Vietnam all have statutes protecting competition. Argentina, Brazil, Chile, Peru, and several other Latin American countries have adopted modern antitrust laws as well.

Why did a U.S. court allow Carrier Corporation to sue a Finnish company for anti-competitive conduct that allegedly took place in Europe?

galinast/iStock/Getty Images

---

17. *Carrier Corp. v. Outokumpu Oyj*, 673 F.3d 430 (6th Cir. 2012).

The European Union Issues Record Fine against Google in Antitrust Case

Adapting the Law to the Online Environment

"Just google it." Google's search engine is so dominant that the company name has become a verb synonymous with conducting an Internet search. According to the European Commissioner for Competition, Margrethe Vestager, Google has become too dominant, at least with respect to comparison shopping and product searches. For that reason, the European Union (EU) spent seven years investigating Google's trade practices. The investigation culminated in 2017 with with a record fine of $2.7 billion and a ruling that Google had breached EU antitrust regulations by abusing its dominant position in the search engine market.

Google Put Its Shopping Results above Other Search Results

The EU claimed that for nearly ten years, Google had promoted its own comparison shopping service at the expense of competitors. It did this by "positioning and prominently displaying its comparison shopping service in its general search result pages, irrespective of its merits." As a result, "users [did] not necessarily see the most relevant results in response to queries—to the detriment of consumers and rival comparison shopping services."

Google has contended that it cannot change its core software and that the results in its search algorithms are based on relevance. In addition, Google has argued that it has actually boosted traffic to its Web competitors. Indeed, search engines have proliferated on the Web, suggesting that Google's success has not eliminated competition.

Nevertheless, the EU's decision ordered Google to change the way it displays search results in the EU—or face more fines. When Google shows comparison-shopping services in response to a user's query, the search results should show the most relevant services first.

Google has appealed the EU's order. Experts predict that the dispute could continue for years.

The Compartmentalization of a Search on the Web

More and more frequently, Internet users do not engage in general searches. Instead, they know exactly where to go to obtain product information. When they want information on movies, for instance, they go to the Internet Movie Data Base (IMDB) rather than to Google. When they want information on music, they go to iTunes. When they want to search for the cheapest airfares, they go to Kayak or similar sites. When they want to find the best rates on hotels, they go to sites such as hotels.com, tripadvisor.com, and trivago.com. And when they are interested in buying a product, they frequently go to Amazon or eBay. Amazon, in particular, has fine-tuned its ability to generate advertising revenues through its Amazon-sponsored links.

And, of course, social media must be considered. More people are on social media sites than ever before, particularly on their mobile devices. Users spend four times more time on Facebook than they do on Google. These users often "crowdsource"—that is, look for answers from Facebook friends rather than search on Google. Facebook is also becoming increasingly competitive with Google in the services it offers, including mobile payments and the Facebook Messenger instant-messaging service.

Critical Thinking

How does the increasing popularity of specialized search engines weaken the EU's argument that Google has harmed consumers?

Most of these antitrust laws apply extraterritorially, as U.S. antitrust laws do. This means that a U.S. company may be subject to another nation's antitrust laws if the company's conduct has a substantial effect on that nation's commerce. China, for instance, has recently stepped up its enforcement of laws against anticompetitive practices. It fined the U.S. chipmaker Qualcomm, Inc., $975 million for violating antitrust laws in 2015. China has also targeted Microsoft, Inc., in its antitrust investigations, and has searched Microsoft's company servers in China for evidence of violations. In 2018, China announced that it was consolidating its three existing antitrust enforcement agencies into one, signaling its intent to aggressively pursue violators.

Practice and Review

The Internet Corporation for Assigned Names and Numbers (ICANN) is a nonprofit entity that organizes Internet domain names. It is governed by a board of directors elected by various groups with commercial interests in the Internet. One of ICANN's functions is to authorize an entity to serve as a registrar for certain top-level domains (TLDs). ICANN entered into an agreement with VeriSign to provide registry services for the ".com" TLD in accordance with ICANN's specifications. VeriSign complained that ICANN was restricting the services that it could make available as a registrar, blocking new services, imposing unnecessary conditions on those services, and setting the prices at which the services were offered. VeriSign claimed that ICANN's control of the registry services for domain names violated Section 1 of the Sherman Act. Using the information presented in the chapter, answer the following questions.

1. Should ICANN's actions be judged under the rule of reason or be deemed a *per se* violation of Section 1 of the Sherman Act? Explain.
2. Should ICANN's actions be viewed as a horizontal or a vertical restraint of trade? Explain.
3. Does it matter that ICANN's directors are chosen by groups with a commercial interest in the Internet? Why or why not?
4. If the dispute is judged under the rule of reason, what might be ICANN's defense for having a standardized set of registry services that must be used?

Debate This

The Internet and the rise of e-commerce have rendered our antitrust concepts and laws obsolete.

Key Terms

Chapter Summary: Antitrust Law and Promoting Competition

The Sherman Antitrust Act (1890)	1. *Major provisions*—
	  a. Section 1—Prohibits contracts, combinations, and conspiracies in restraint of trade.
	    (1) Horizontal restraints subject to Section 1 include price-fixing agreements, group boycotts (joint refusals to deal), horizontal market divisions, and certain trade association agreements.
	    (2) Vertical restraints subject to Section 1 include territorial or customer restrictions and resale price maintenance agreements.
	  b. Section 2—Prohibits monopolies and attempts to monopolize.
	2. *Jurisdictional requirements*—The Sherman Act applies only to activities that have a significant impact on interstate commerce and those that affect U.S. foreign commerce.
	3. *Interpretive rules*—
	  a. *Per se* rule—Applied to restraints on trade that are so inherently anticompetitive that they cannot be justified and are deemed illegal as a matter of law.
	  b. Rule of reason—Applied when an anticompetitive agreement may be justified by legitimate benefits. Under the rule of reason, the lawfulness of a trade restraint will be determined by the purpose and effects of the restraint.

The Clayton Act (1914)	Aimed at specific anticompetitive or monopolistic acts not covered by the Sherman Act. The major provisions are as follows:
	1. *Section 2*—As amended in 1936 by the Robinson-Patman Act, prohibits a seller engaged in interstate commerce from price discrimination that substantially lessens competition.
	2. *Section 3*—Prohibits exclusionary practices, such as exclusive-dealing contracts and tying arrangements, when the effect may be to substantially lessen competition.
	3. *Section 7*—Prohibits mergers when the effect may be to substantially lessen competition or to tend to create a monopoly.
	  a. A horizontal merger will be presumed unlawful if the entity created by the merger will have a significant market share.
	  b. A vertical merger will be unlawful if the merger prevents competitors of either merging firm from competing in a segment of the market that otherwise would be open to them, resulting in a substantial lessening of competition.
	4. *Section 8*—Prohibits interlocking directorates.

Enforcement and Exemptions	1. *Enforcement by federal agencies*—The U.S. Department of Justice and the Federal Trade Commission enforce the federal antitrust laws. 2. *Actions by private parties*—Private parties who have been injured as a result of violations of the Sherman Act or Clayton Act may bring civil suits, and, if successful, they may be awarded treble damages and attorneys' fees. 3. *Exemptions from antitrust laws*—See Exhibit 38–2 for a list of significant exemptions.
U.S. Antitrust Laws in the Global Context	1. *Extraterritorial application of U.S. laws*—U.S. antitrust laws can be applied in foreign nations to protect foreign consumers and competitors. Foreign governments and persons can also bring actions under U.S. antitrust laws. Section 1 of the Sherman Act applies to any conspiracy that has a substantial effect on U.S. commerce. 2. *Application of foreign laws*—Many other nations also have laws that promote competition and prohibit trade restraints, and some are more restrictive than U.S. laws. These foreign antitrust laws are increasingly being applied to U.S. firms.

Issue Spotters

1. Under what circumstances would Pop's Market, a small store in a small, isolated town, be considered a monopolist? If Pop's is a monopolist, is it in violation of Section 2 of the Sherman Act? Why or why not? (See *Section 2 of the Sherman Act*.)

2. Maple Corporation conditions the sale of its syrup on buyers' agreement to buy Maple's pancake mix. What factors would a court consider to decide whether this arrangement violates the Clayton Act? (See *The Clayton Act*.)

   —**Check your answers to the *Issue Spotters* against the answers provided in Appendix D at the end of this text.**

Business Scenarios and Case Problems

38–1. Sherman Act. An agreement that is blatantly and substantially anticompetitive is deemed a *per se* violation of Section 1 of the Sherman Act. Under what rule is an agreement analyzed if it appears to be anticompetitive but is not a *per se* violation? In making this analysis, what factors will a court consider? (See *Section 1 of the Sherman Act.*)

38–2. Tying Arrangement. John Sheridan owned a Marathon gas station franchise. He sued Marathon Petroleum Co. under Section 1 of the Sherman Act and Section 3 of the Clayton Act, charging it with illegally tying the processing of credit-card sales to the gas station. As a condition of obtaining a Marathon dealership, dealers had to agree to let the franchisor process credit cards. They could not shop around to see if credit-card processing could be obtained at a lower price from another source. The district court dismissed the case for failure to state a claim. Sheridan appealed. Is there a tying arrangement? If so, does it violate the law? (See *The Clayton Act.*)

38–3. Spotlight on Digital Music—Price Fixing. Together, EMI, Sony BMG Music Entertainment, Universal Music Group Recordings, Inc., and Warner Music Group Corp. produced, licensed, and distributed 80 percent of the digital music sold in the United States. The companies formed MusicNet to sell music to online services that sold the songs to consumers. MusicNet required all of the services to sell the songs at the same price and subject to the same restrictions. Digitization of music became cheaper, but MusicNet did not change its prices. Did MusicNet violate the antitrust laws? Explain. [*Starr v. Sony BMG Music Entertainment*, 592 F.3d 314 (2d Cir. 2010)] (See *Section 1 of the Sherman Act.*)

38–4. Business Case Problem with Sample Answer— Price Discrimination. Dayton Superior Corp. sells its products in interstate commerce to several companies, including Spa Steel Products, Inc. The purchasers often compete directly with each other for customers. From 2005 to 2007, one of Spa Steel's customers purchased Dayton Superior's products from two of Spa Steel's competitors. According to the customer, Spa Steel's prices were always 10 to 15 percent higher for the same products. As a result, Spa Steel lost sales to at least that customer and perhaps others. Spa Steel wants to sue Dayton Superior for price discrimination. Which requirements for such a claim under Section 2 of the Clayton Act does Spa Steel satisfy? What additional facts will it need to prove? [*Dayton Superior Corp. v. Spa Steel Products, Inc.*, 2012 WL 113663 (N.D.N.Y. 2012)] (See *The Clayton Act.*)

—For a sample answer to Problem 38–4, go to Appendix E at the end of this text.

38–5. Section 1 of the Sherman Act. The National Collegiate Athletic Association (NCAA) and the National Federation of State High School Associations (NFHS), in an effort to enhance player safety and reduce technology-driven home runs and other big hits, set a standard for nonwood baseball bats to ensure that aluminum and composite bats performed like wood bats. Marucci Sports, LLC, makes nonwood bats. Under the new standard, four of Marucci's eleven products were decertified for use in high school and collegiate games. Marucci filed suit against the NCAA and the NFHS under Section 1 of the Sherman Act. At trial, Marucci's evidence focused on injury to its own business. Did the NCAA and NFHS's standard restrain trade in violation of the Sherman Act? Explain. [*Marucci Sports, LLC v. National Collegiate Athletic Association*, 751 F.3d 368 (5th Cir. 2014)] (See *Section 1 of the Sherman Act.*)

38–6. Mergers. St. Luke's Health Systems, Ltd., operated an emergency clinic in Nampa, Idaho. Saltzer Medical Group, P.A., had thirty-four physicians practicing at its offices in Nampa. Saint Alphonsus Health System, Inc., operated the only hospital in Nampa. St. Luke's acquired Saltzer's assets and entered into a five-year professional service agreement with the Saltzer physicians. This affiliation resulted in a combined share of two-thirds of the Nampa adult primary care provider market. Together, the two entities could impose a significant increase in the prices charged patients and insurers, and correspondence between the parties indicated that they would. Saint Alphonsus filed a suit against St. Luke's to block the merger. Did this affiliation violate antitrust law? Explain. [*Saint Alphonsus Medical Center-Nampa Inc. v. St. Luke's Health System, Ltd.*, 778 F.3d 775 (9th Cir. 2015)] (See *The Clayton Act.*)

38–7. Section 1 of the Sherman Act. Manitou North America, Inc., makes and distributes telehandlers (forklifts with extendable telescopic booms) to dealers throughout the United States. Manitou agreed to make McCormick International, LLC, its exclusive dealer in the state of Michigan. Later, Manitou entered into an agreement with Gehl Company, which also makes and sells telehandlers. The companies agreed to allocate territories within Michigan among certain dealers for each manufacturer, limiting the dealers' selection of competitive products to certain models. Under this agreement, McCormick was precluded from buying or selling Gehl telehandlers. What type of trade restraint did the agreement between Manitou and Gehl represent? Is this a violation of antitrust law? If so, who was injured, and how were they injured? Explain. [*Manitou North America, Inc. v. McCormick International, LLC*, 2016 WL 439354 (2016)] (See *Section 1 of the Sherman Act.*)

38–8. Tying Arrangements. PRC-Desoto International, Inc., makes and distributes more than 90 percent of the aerospace sealant used in military and commercial aircraft. Packaging Systems, Inc., buys the sealant in wholesale quantities, repackages it into special injection kits, and sells the kits on the retail market to aircraft maintenance companies. PRC-Desoto bought one of the two main manufacturing companies of injection kits and announced a new policy to prohibit the repackaging of its sealant for resale. Packaging Systems was forced to buy both the sealant and the kits from PRC-Desoto. Due to the anti-repackaging constraint, the reseller could no longer meet its buyers' needs for pre-filled injection kits. Does this policy represent an unlawful tying arrangement? Explain. [*Packaging Systems, Inc. v. PRC-Desoto International, Inc.*, ___ F.Supp.3d ___, 2018 WL 735978 (C.D.Cal. 2018)] (See *The Clayton Act.*)

38–9. A Question of Ethics—The IDDR Approach and Section 2 of the Sherman Act.

 Apple, Inc., controls which apps—such as ringtones, instant messaging, and video—can run on iPhone software. Apple's App Store is a website where iPhone users can find, buy, and download the apps. Apple prohibits third-party developers from selling iPhone apps through channels other than the App Store, threatening to cut off sales by any developer who violates this prohibition. Apple also discourages iPhone owners from downloading unapproved apps, threatening to void iPhone warranties if they do. Seven iPhone app buyers filed a complaint in a federal district court against Apple. The plaintiffs alleged that the firm monopolized the market for iPhone apps. [In re Apple iPhone Antitrust Litigation, 846 F.3d 313 (9th Cir. 2017)] (See Section 2 of the Sherman Act.)

1. Using the *Decision* step of the IDDR approach, provide reasons why Apple might attempt to protect iPhone software by setting narrow boundaries on the sales of related apps and aggressively enforcing them.

2. Explain why Apple's actions in this case might be considered unethical.

Critical Thinking and Writing Assignments

38–10. Business Law Writing.
Write two paragraphs explaining some ways in which antitrust laws might place too great a burden on commerce in the global marketplace. (See *Section 2 of the Sherman Act.*)

38–11. Time-Limited Group Assignment—Antitrust Violations.
Residents of the city of Madison, Wisconsin, became concerned about overconsumption of liquor near the campus of the University of Wisconsin (UW). The city took action by imposing conditions on area bars to discourage reduced-price "specials" that were believed to encourage high-volume and dangerous drinking. Later, the city began to draft an ordinance to ban all drink specials. Bar owners responded by announcing that they had "voluntarily" agreed to discontinue drink specials on Friday and Saturday nights after 8:00 P.M. The city put its ordinance on hold. Several UW students filed a lawsuit against the local bar owners' association alleging violations of antitrust law. (See *Section 1 of the Sherman Act.*)

1. The first group will identify the grounds on which the plaintiffs might base their claim for relief and formulate an argument on behalf of the plaintiffs.

2. The second group will determine whether the defendants are exempt from the antitrust laws.

3. The third group will decide how the court should rule in this dispute and provide reasons for its answer.

39 | Consumer and Environmental Law

Learning Objectives

The six Learning Objectives *below are designed to help improve your understanding. After reading this chapter, you should be able to answer the following questions:*

1. When will advertising be deemed deceptive?

2. What law protects consumers against contaminated and misbranded foods and drugs?

3. What does Regulation Z require, and how does it relate to the Truth in Lending Act?

4. What does an environmental impact statement contain, and who must file one?

5. What are three main goals of the Clean Water Act?

6. What is Superfund? What categories of people are liable under Superfund?

> "The good of the people is the greatest law."
>
> **Marcus Tullius Cicero**
> 106–43 B.C.E.
> (Roman politician and orator)

Congress has enacted a substantial amount of legislation to protect "the good of the people," to borrow Cicero's phrase from the chapter-opening quotation. All statutes, agency rules, and common law judicial decisions that attempt to protect the interests of consumers are classified as *consumer law*. Similarly, all laws and regulations designed to protect and preserve the environment are categorized as environmental law.

Sources of consumer protection exist at all levels of government. Numerous federal laws have been passed to define the duties of sellers and the rights of consumers. Exhibit 39–1 indicates some of the areas of consumer law that are regulated by statutes.

The Federal Trade Commission (FTC) is one of many federal agencies that work to protect consumers. One recent FTC action, for instance, involved Luminosity, a popular "brain-training" app made by Lumos Labs, Inc. Lumos advertised that playing the app's games led to better performance in school, sports, and work—in addition to helping prevent Alzheimer's disease and other forms of dementia. According to the ads, people who played ten minutes a day three times a week would realize their full potential in every aspect of life.

Lumos could not provide scientific evidence to support these claims, however. As a result, the FTC concluded that the advertising was deceptive in violation of consumer protection laws and filed an action against the company. Ultimately, Lumos was ordered to pay a $2 million fine and to stop running the deceptive ads.

39–1 Advertising, Marketing, Sales, and Labeling

Nearly every agency and department of the federal government has an office of consumer affairs. Most states have one or more such offices, including the offices of state attorneys general, to assist consumers. Many of the complaints received by these offices involve consumers who say they were misled by sellers' advertising, marketing, sales, and labeling tactics.

39–1a Deceptive Advertising

One of the most important federal consumer protection laws is the Federal Trade Commission Act.[1] The act created the Federal Trade Commission (FTC) to carry out the broadly stated goal of preventing unfair and deceptive trade practices, including deceptive advertising.

Generally, **deceptive advertising** involves a claim that would mislead a reasonable consumer. Vague generalities and obvious exaggerations (that a reasonable person would not believe to be true) are permissible. These claims are known as *puffery*.
Case Example 39.1 Sheila Cruz and others sued Anheuser-Busch Companies, LLC, for falsely advertising its "Bud Light Lime-A-Rita" beverages as "light." She argued that the word "light" was misleading because the drinks contained more calories than light beer (Bud Light). The court dismissed Cruz's case, and a federal appellate court affirmed. The Lime-A-Rita beverages were described and advertised as "Margaritas with a Twist," so no reasonable consumer would believe they were the same as light beer. They also contained fewer calories than traditional tequila margaritas. Thus, the court concluded the label was not misleading.[2] ▮ When a claim has the appearance of authenticity, however, it may create problems.

---

1. 15 U.S.C. Sections 41–58
2. *Cruz v. Anheuser-Busch Companies, LLC*, 682 Fed.Appx. 583 (9th Cir. 2017).

Learning Objective 1

When will advertising be deemed deceptive?

Deceptive Advertising Advertising that misleads consumers, either by making unjustified claims about a product or by omitting a material fact concerning the product.

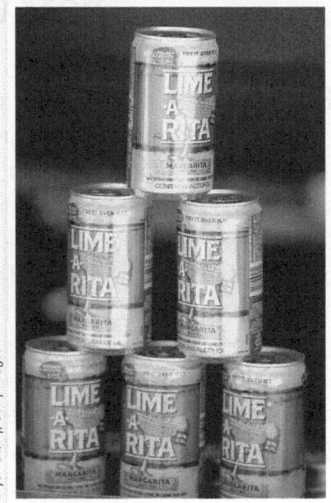

Was Anheuser-Busch's advertisement for a "light" alcoholic beverage deceptive?

Exhibit 39–1 Selected Areas of Consumer Law Regulated by Statutes

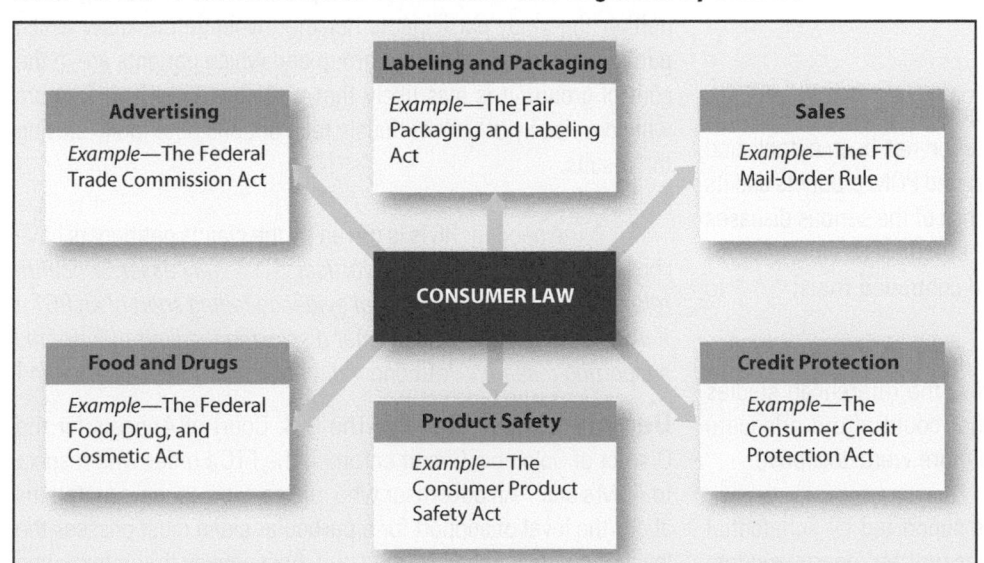

Labeling and Packaging
Example—The Fair Packaging and Labeling Act

Advertising
Example—The Federal Trade Commission Act

Sales
Example—The FTC Mail-Order Rule

CONSUMER LAW

Food and Drugs
Example—The Federal Food, Drug, and Cosmetic Act

Product Safety
Example—The Consumer Product Safety Act

Credit Protection
Example—The Consumer Credit Protection Act

Claims That Appear to Be Based on Factual Evidence Advertising that *appears* to be based on factual evidence but that in fact cannot be scientifically supported will be deemed deceptive. For instance, advertising that uses a phrase such as "scientifically proven" or "clinical studies show" may appear to be factual. But if no actual data support the claims, then the advertising is deceptive.

The following case involved an advertising claim based on limited scientific evidence.

Case 39.1

POM Wonderful, LLC v. Federal Trade Commission

United States Court of Appeals, District of Columbia Circuit, 777 F.3d 478 (2015).

Background and Facts POM Wonderful, LLC, makes and sells pomegranate-based products. In ads, POM touted medical studies claiming to show that daily consumption of its products could treat, prevent, or reduce the risk of heart disease, prostate cancer, and erectile dysfunction. These ads mischaracterized the scientific evidence.

The Federal Trade Commission (FTC) charged POM with, and held POM liable for, making false, misleading, and unsubstantiated representations in violation of the FTC act. POM was barred from running future ads asserting that its products treat or prevent any disease unless "randomized, controlled, human clinical trials" (RCTs) demonstrated statistically significant results. POM petitioned the U.S. Court of Appeals for the District of Columbia Circuit to review this injunctive order.

What kinds of health claims about pomegranate juice can its producer make?

In the Words of the Court

SRINIVASAN, Circuit Judge:

* * * *

* * * POM's ads * * * convey the net impression that clinical studies or trials show that a causal relation has been established between the consumption of the challenged POM products and its efficacy to treat, prevent or reduce the risk of the serious diseases in question. The Commission found that experts in the relevant fields would require RCTs [randomized controlled trials] * * * to establish such a causal relationship.

The Commission examined each of the studies invoked by petitioners in their ads, concluding that the referenced studies fail to qualify as RCTs of the kind that could afford adequate substantiation. Petitioners' claims therefore were deceptive.

* * * *

* * * The Commission's finding is supported by substantial record evidence. That evidence includes written reports and testimony from medical researchers stating that experts in the fields

of cardiology and urology require randomized, double-blinded, placebo-controlled clinical trials to substantiate any claim that a product treats, prevents, or reduces the risk of disease.

The Commission drew on that expert testimony to explain why the attributes of well-designed RCTs are necessary to substantiate petitioners' claims. A control group, for example, allows investigators to distinguish between real effects from the intervention, and other changes, including those due to the mere act of being treated (placebo effect) and the passage of time. Random assignment of a study's subjects to treatment and control groups increases the likelihood that the treatment and control groups are similar in relevant characteristics, so that any difference in the outcome between the two groups can be attributed to the treatment. And when a study is double-blinded ([that is,] when neither the study participants nor the investigators know which patients are in the treatment group and which patients are in the control group), it is less likely that participants or investigators will consciously or unconsciously take actions potentially biasing the results.

* * * *

* * * The need for RCTs is driven by the claims petitioners have chosen to make. * * * *An advertiser * * * may assert a health-related claim backed by medical evidence falling short of an RCT if it includes an effective disclaimer disclosing the limitations of the supporting research.* Petitioners did not do so. [Emphasis added.]

Decision and Remedy The U.S. Court of Appeals for the District of Columbia Circuit enforced the FTC's order with respect to POM's ads. "An advertiser who makes express representations about the level of support for a particular claim must possess the level of proof claimed in the ad and must convey that information to consumers in a non-misleading way."

• **Ethical** *POM claimed that, for ethical reasons, RCTs should not be required to substantiate disease-related claims about food products. It argued that, for instance, "doctors cannot … ethically deprive a control group of patients of all Vitamin C for a decade to determine whether Vitamin C helps prevent cancer." Is this a valid argument? Why or why not?*

Claims Based on Half-Truths Some advertisements contain "half-truths," meaning that the information is true but incomplete and, therefore, leads consumers to a false conclusion. **Example 39.2** The maker of Campbell's soups advertised that "most" Campbell's soups were low in fat and cholesterol and thus were helpful in fighting heart disease. What the ad did not say was that Campbell's soups were also high in sodium and that high-sodium diets may increase the risk of heart disease. Hence, the FTC ruled that the company's claims were deceptive. ■ In addition, advertising featuring an endorsement by a celebrity may be deemed deceptive if the celebrity does not actually use the product.

Bait-and-Switch Advertising The FTC has issued rules that govern specific advertising techniques.[3] Some retailers systematically advertise merchandise at low prices to get customers into their stores, and then fail to have that merchandise and encourage customers to purchase a more expensive item instead. This practice, known as **bait-and-switch advertising,** is a form of deceptive advertising.

The low price is the "bait" to lure the consumer into the store. The salesperson is instructed to "switch" the consumer to a different, more expensive item. According to the FTC, bait-and-switch advertising occurs if the seller refuses to show the advertised item or fails to have reasonable quantities of it available. It also occurs if the seller fails to promise to deliver the advertised item within a reasonable time or discourages employees from selling the item.

Example 39.3 Signs on the front of Shockoe Tire Store advertise tires for sale for $30 each. When consumers come in looking for the $30 tires, salespeople tell them the tires are sold out and try to convince them to buy more expensive tires instead. Under FTC guidelines, Shockoe's bait-and-switch sales tactics are deceptive advertising. ■

Online Deceptive Advertising Deceptive advertising occurs in the online environment as well. The FTC actively monitors online advertising and has identified numerous websites that have made false or deceptive claims for products and services.

The FTC issues guidelines to help online businesses comply with the laws prohibiting deceptive advertising. Current guidelines include the following basic requirements:

1. All advertisements—both online and offline—must be truthful and not misleading.

2. The claims made in an ad must be substantiated—that is, advertisers must have evidence to back up their claims.

3. Ads cannot be unfair, which the FTC defines as "likely to cause substantial consumer injury that consumers could not reasonably avoid and that is not outweighed by the benefit to consumers or competition."

4. Ads must disclose relevant limitations and qualifying information underlying the claims.

5. Required disclosures must be "clear and conspicuous." Because consumers may not read an entire Web page, an online disclosure should be placed as close as possible to the claim being qualified. Generally, hyperlinks to a disclosure are recommended only for lengthy disclosures. If hyperlinks are used, they should be obvious and should be placed as close as possible to the information they qualify.

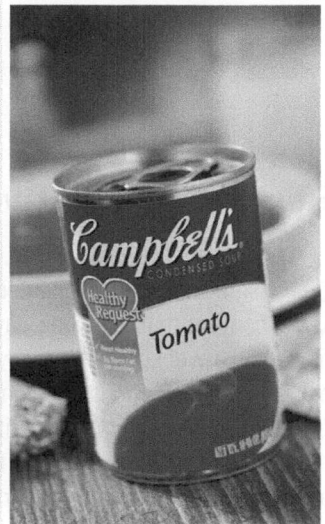

Can Campbell's advertise that its soups help fight heart disease even if they are high in sodium?

Bait-and-Switch Advertising Advertising a product at an attractive price and then telling the consumer that the advertised product is not available or is of poor quality and encouraging her or him to purchase a more expensive item.

Know This
Changes in technology often require changes in the law.

---

3. 16 C.F.R. Section 288.

The FTC creates additional guidelines as needed to respond to new issues that arise with online advertising. One new issue involves so-called native ads, which are discussed in this chapter's *Adapting the Law to the Online Environment* feature.

Federal Trade Commission Actions The FTC receives complaints from many sources, including competitors of alleged violators, consumers, trade associations, Better Business Bureaus, and government organizations and officials. When the agency receives numerous and widespread complaints about a particular problem, it will investigate.

Formal Complaint. If the FTC concludes that a given advertisement is unfair or deceptive, it sends a formal complaint to the alleged offender. The company may agree to settle the complaint without further proceedings. If not, the FTC can conduct a hearing before an administrative law judge in which the company can present its defense.

Regulating "Native" Ads on the Internet

Adapting the Law to the Online Environment

Sponsored content on the Internet—that is, content that someone pays to have placed on a website—is everywhere. One particular type of sponsored content is the "native ad." Here, *native* describes advertisements that follow the natural form and function of the user experience into which they are placed. Thus, such an ad matches the rest of a Web page's content, including the visual design, as if it were "native" to the page.

Native Ad Integration on Web Pages

Perhaps the most obvious native ads are in search engine results. When you type "native ads" in a Google search box, you will find that the first several "hits" listed in the search results are actually sponsored ads. Yet they have the look and feel of the rest of the search results.

Additionally, native ads are often placed within stories in online publications. Suppose, for instance, that you are reading a story about new clothing trends on your smartphone. You will likely see native ads that look as if they are part of the story. Those ads, though, are actually sponsored and perhaps written by clothing retailers.

The Federal Trade Commission Takes Action

In response to the growth in native advertising, the Federal Trade Commission (FTC) has issued guidelines.[a] The FTC starts out with the basic question: As native advertising evolves, are consumers able to differentiate advertising from other content? In its guidance document, the FTC suggests the following:

- Disclosures should be placed where consumers will notice them.
- Disclosures should be placed not after the native ad, but before or above it.
- Disclosures should remain with native ads if the ads are republished.
- On the click-through page where the complete native ad appears, disclosures should be placed as close as possible to where consumers will look first.
- Disclosures should stand out and should be understandable.[b]

---

a. Federal Trade Commission, *Native Advertising: A Guide to Business*, December 2015.
b. Federal Trade Commission, *.com Disclosures: How to Make Effective Disclosures in Digital Advertising*, March 2013, Web.

More Than 33 Percent of Native Ads Are Not Compliant

In spite of the FTC's guidelines for native advertising, more than one-third of publishers of such ads are not compliant. On average, a native advertising campaign runs for two months or longer. Consequently, millions of consumers view noncompliant native ads on the Internet on a regular basis.

The FTC has stepped up its compliance campaign and has brought actions against some retailers. For instance, Lord & Taylor was charged with deceiving consumers after running an extensive native advertising campaign. The campaign included an article in an online fashion publication and numerous Instagram posts—but none of this material was identified as sponsored content. Ultimately, the FTC settled its case against the retailer.

Critical Thinking

What is the equivalent of native advertising in commercially released movies?

FTC Orders and Remedies. If the FTC succeeds in proving that an advertisement is unfair or deceptive, it usually issues a **cease-and-desist order** requiring the company to stop the challenged advertising. In some circumstances, the FTC may also require **counteradvertising**, in which the company advertises anew—in print, on the Internet, on radio, or on television— to inform the public about the earlier misinformation. The FTC sometimes institutes a **multiple product order**, which requires a firm to cease and desist from false advertising in regard to all of its products, not just the product that was the subject of the action.

Damages When Consumers Are Injured. When a company's deceptive ad involves wrongful charges to consumers, the FTC may seek other remedies, including restitution. **Case Example 39.4** The FTC sued Bronson Partners, LLC, for deceptively advertising two products—Chinese Diet Tea and Bio-Slim Patch. Bronson's ads claimed that the diet tea "eliminates 91 percent of absorbed sugars," "prevents 83 percent of fat absorption," and "doubles your metabolic rate to burn calories fast." The Bio-Slim Patch ads promised consumers that "ugly fatty tissue will disappear at a spectacular rate" when they wore the patch and carried on their normal lifestyle.

Eventually, Bronson conceded that it had engaged in deceptive advertising, and the FTC sought damages. The court awarded the FTC $1,942,325, which was the amount of Bronson's unjust gains and consumer losses from the two products.[4] ■

39–1b False Advertising Claims under the Lanham Act

The Lanham Act protects trademarks, as discussed earlier in this text. The act also covers false advertising claims. To state a successful claim for false advertising under this act, a business must establish each of the following elements:

1. An injury to a commercial interest in reputation or sales.

2. Direct causation of the injury by false or deceptive advertising.

3. A loss of business from buyers who were deceived by the advertising.

39–1c State Laws Concerning False Advertising

State consumer-fraud statutes also prohibit false, misleading, and deceptive advertising. Recovery under a state law typically requires proof of the following elements:

1. The defendant committed a deceptive or unfair act.

2. The act was committed in the course of trade or commerce.

3. The defendant intended that others rely on the deception.

4. The plaintiff suffered actual damages proximately caused by the deception.

At issue in the following case was a plaintiff's claim under Illinois's consumer fraud statute.

---

4. *Federal Trade Commission v. Bronson Partners, LLC,* 654 F.3d 359 (2d Cir. 2011).

Cease-and-Desist Order An administrative or judicial order prohibiting a person or business firm from conducting activities that an agency or court has deemed illegal.

Counteradvertising New advertising that is undertaken to correct earlier false claims that were made about a product.

Multiple Product Order An order requiring a firm that has engaged in deceptive advertising to cease and desist from false advertising in regard to all the firm's products.

rezkrr/iStock/Getty Images

What remedies can the FTC seek when a company falsely advertises that its tea eliminates almost all absorbed sugars?

■ Case 39.2

Haywood v. Massage Envy Franchising, LLC

United States Court of Appeals, Seventh Circuit, 887 F.3d 329 (2018).

Background and Facts Massage Envy, LLC, is a franchisor based in Arizona that grants licenses to independently owned and operated entities for the use of its name, trademark, and standardized operations. Massage Envy's website advertises its services, including an "Introductory 1-hour Massage Session." At the bottom of the home page, a link to "pricing and promotional details" leads to a page with disclaimers. One disclaimer titled "Session" explains that a "session includes massage or facial and time for consultation and dressing."

(Continues)

Kathy Haywood, a resident of Illinois, scheduled an appointment through the website. At the session, for which Haywood paid with a gift card, she received a massage that lasted no more than fifty minutes. Citing Massage Envy's online ad, Haywood filed a suit in a federal district court against the company, alleging unfair and deceptive business practices in violation of the Illinois Consumer Fraud and Deceptive Business Practices Act (ICFA). The court dismissed the claim. Haywood appealed.

In the Words of the Court
BAUER, Circuit Judge.

* * * *

To state a claim under the ICFA * * * Haywood must plausibly allege: (1) a deceptive act or promise by Massage Envy; (2) Massage Envy's intent that she rely on the deceptive act; (3) the deceptive act occurred during a course of conduct involving trade or commerce; and (4) actual damage as a result of the deceptive act. *Actual damage in this context means that Haywood must have suffered actual pecuniary [financial] loss. Additionally, the deceptive act must have been the "but-for" cause of the damage.* [Emphasis added.]

* * * *

* * * [Haywood's] allegations fail to establish the requisite causation.

* * * Here, the only reasonable conclusion is that Massage Envy's representations regarding the one-hour massage session were not the but-for cause of any alleged injury. There is no allegation in the complaint that her belief about the length of the massage caused Haywood to make the appointment. To the contrary, the only reasonable and plausible inference is that only the receipt of a gift card caused her to book a massage; the alleged deceptive representations did not influence that decision. * * * She cannot, based on these allegations, establish that Massage Envy's alleged deception was the but-for cause of her injury, and her claims fail as a result.

Decision and Remedy The U.S. Court of Appeals for the Seventh Circuit affirmed the dismissal. The federal appellate court concluded that the "district court did not abuse its discretion in dismissing the complaint."

Critical Thinking

• **Economic** *A fraud injury can be measured in two ways. As a loss of the benefit of the bargain, damages consist of the difference between the value of what was promised and the value of what was received. Under the out-of-pocket rule, the measure is the difference between the price paid and the market value of what was received. If Haywood had established her claim, which of these methods would have applied? Why?*

• **What If the Facts Were Different?** *Suppose that reliance was not an element of a consumer fraud claim under the ICFA. Would the result in this case have been different? Explain.*

39–1d Marketing

In addition to regulating advertising practices, Congress has passed several laws to protect consumers against other marketing practices.

Telephone Solicitation The Telephone Consumer Protection Act (TCPA)[5] prohibits telephone solicitation using an automatic telephone dialing system or a prerecorded voice. In addition, most states have statutes regulating telephone solicitation. The TCPA also makes it illegal to transmit ads via fax without first obtaining the recipient's permission.

The Federal Communications Commission (FCC) enforces the TCPA. The FCC imposes substantial fines ($11,000 each day) on companies that violate the junk fax provisions of the act. The TCPA also gives consumers a right to sue and recover either $500 for each violation of the act or the actual monetary losses resulting from a violation, whichever is greater. If a court finds that a defendant willfully or knowingly violated the act, the court may treble (triple) the amount of damages awarded.

Fraudulent Telemarketing The FTC's Telemarketing Sales Rule (TSR)[6] requires a telemarketer to identify the seller's name, describe the product being sold, and disclose all material facts related to the sale (such as the total cost of the goods being sold). The TSR makes it illegal for

---

5. 47 U.S.C. Sections 227 *et seq.*
6. 16 C.F.R. Sections 310.1–310.8.

telemarketers to misrepresent information or facts about their goods or services. A telemarketer must also remove a consumer's name from its list of potential contacts if the customer so requests.

An amendment to the TSR established the national Do Not Call Registry. Telemarketers must refrain from calling consumers who have placed their names on the list. Significantly, the TSR applies to any offer made to consumers in the United States—even if the offer comes from a foreign firm. Thus, the TSR helps to protect consumers from illegal cross-border telemarketing operations.

Case Example 39.5 Jason Abraham formed Instant Response Systems, LLC (IRS), to sell medical alert monitoring systems to the elderly. IRS employed telemarketers to make sales calls to people sixty-four years old and older. Some of these consumers were on the Do Not Call Registry. The telemarketers, using company-supplied scripts, falsely told consumers that they were calling in response to a request for information about IRS's medical alert services. Consumers who did not order the IRS system were still billed for it, receiving follow-up letters and calls accusing them of nonpayment. When they objected, IRS employees resorted to threats.

The FTC sued IRS and Abraham for violating the Telemarketing Sales Rule and won. IRS's telemarketers had made false and misleading statements to consumers, and had used threats to force them to make payments. IRS had also called individuals on the Do Not Call Registry without permission. The court ordered Abraham to pay more than $3.4 million (the amount of revenues he had received through the company's unlawful scheme). The court also permanently enjoined (prohibited) Abraham from marketing medical alert systems in the future.[7]

Atstock Productions/Shutterstock.com

How did the Telemarketing Sales Rule affect a dispute between a medical-alert service and the Federal Trade Commission?

39–1e Sales

Various statutes protect consumers by requiring the disclosure of certain terms in sales transactions and providing rules governing such matters as unsolicited merchandise, door-to-door sales, and mail-order sales. The FTC has regulatory authority in this area, as do some other federal agencies.

Many states and the FTC have **"cooling-off" laws** that permit the buyers of goods sold in certain transactions to cancel certain sales contracts within three business days. The FTC rule also requires that consumers be notified in Spanish of this right if the oral negotiations for the sale were in that language.

The contracts that fall under these cancellation rules include trade show sales contracts, contracts for home equity loans, Internet purchase contracts, and home (door-to-door) sales contracts. In addition, certain states have passed laws allowing consumers to cancel contracts for things like dating services, gym memberships, and weight loss programs.

The FTC's Mail, Internet, or Telephone Order Merchandise Rule[8] protects consumers who purchase goods via mail, Internet, phone, or fax. Merchants must ship orders within the time promised in their advertisements and must notify consumers when orders cannot be shipped on time. If the seller does not give an estimated shipping time, it must ship within thirty days. Merchants must also issue a refund within a specified period of time when a consumer cancels an order.

39–1f Labeling

In general, labels must be accurate, and they must use words that are understood by the ordinary consumer. In some instances, labels must specify the raw materials used in the product, such as the percentage of cotton, nylon, or other fibers used in a garment.

"Cooling-Off" Laws Laws that allow buyers of goods sold in certain transactions to cancel their contracts within three business days.

---

7. *Federal Trade Commission v. Instant Response Systems, LLC,* 2015 WL 1650914 (E.D.N.Y. 2015).
8. 16 C.F.R. Sections 435.1–435.2.

In other instances, the product must carry a warning, such as those required on cigarette packages and advertising.[9]

Automobile Fuel Economy Labels

The Energy Policy and Conservation Act (EPCA)[10] requires automakers to attach an information label to every new car. This label must include the Environmental Protection Agency's fuel economy estimate for the vehicle.

★ Spotlight Case Example 39.6 Gaetano Paduano bought a new Honda Civic Hybrid in California. The information label on the car included the fuel economy estimate from the Environmental Protection Agency (EPA). Honda's sales brochure added, "Just drive the Hybrid like you would a conventional car and save on fuel bills."

When Paduano discovered that the car's fuel economy was less than half of the EPA's estimate, he sued Honda for deceptive advertising. The automaker claimed that the federal law (the EPCA) preempted the state's deceptive advertising law, but the court held in Paduano's favor, finding that the federal statute did not preempt a claim for deceptive advertising made under state law.[11]

Food Labeling

Because the quality and safety of food are so important to consumers, several statutes deal specifically with food labeling. The Fair Packaging and Labeling Act requires that food product labels identify (1) the product, (2) the net quantity of the contents, (3) the manufacturer, and (4) the packager or distributor.[12] The act includes additional requirements concerning descriptions on packages, savings claims, components of nonfood products, and standards for the partial filling of packages.

Nutritional Content. Food products must bear labels detailing the food's nutritional content, including the number of calories and the amounts of various nutrients. The Nutrition Labeling and Education Act requires food labels to provide standard nutrition facts and regulates the use of such terms as *fresh* and *low fat*.

The U.S. Food and Drug Administration (FDA) and the U.S. Department of Agriculture (USDA) are the primary agencies that issue regulations on food labeling. These rules are published in the *Federal Register* and updated annually. For instance, current rules require labels on fresh and frozen fruits and vegetables to indicate where the food originated so that consumers can know if their food was imported.

Which two federal agencies are primarily responsible for issuing regulations on food labeling?

Caloric Content of Restaurant Foods. The health-care reform bill enacted in 2010 (the Affordable Care Act, or "Obamacare") included provisions aimed at combating the problem of obesity in the United States. All restaurant chains with twenty or more locations are now required to post the caloric content of the foods on their menus so that customers will know how many calories the foods contain.[13] Foods offered through vending machines must also be labeled so that their caloric content is visible to would-be purchasers.

In addition, restaurants must post guidelines on the number of calories that an average person requires daily so that customers can determine what portion of a day's calories a particular food will provide. The hope is that consumers, armed with this information, will consider the number of calories when they make their food choices. The federal law on menu labeling supersedes all previous state and local laws.

---

9. 15 U.S.C. Sections 1331 *et seq.*
10. 49 U.S.C. Section 32908(b)(1).
11. *Paduano v. American Honda Motor Co.*, 169 Cal.App. 4th 1453, 88 Cal.Rptr.3d 90 (2009).
12. 15 U.S.C. Sections 4401–4408.
13. See Section 4205 of the Patient Protection and Affordable Care Act, Pub. L. No.111-148, March 23, 2010, 124 Stat. 119.

39–2 **Protection of Health and Safety**

Although labeling laws promote consumer health and safety, there is a significant distinction between regulating the information dispensed about a product and regulating the actual content of the product. The classic example is tobacco products. Producers of tobacco products are required to warn consumers about the hazards associated with the use of their products, but the sale of tobacco products has not been subjected to significant restrictions or banned outright despite the obvious dangers to health. We now examine various laws that regulate the actual products made available to consumers.

39–2a **Food and Drugs**

The most important legislation regulating food and drugs is the Federal Food, Drug, and Cosmetic Act (FDCA).[14] The act protects consumers against adulterated (contaminated) and misbranded foods and drugs.

The FDCA establishes food standards, specifies safe levels of potentially hazardous food additives, and provides guidelines for advertising and labeling food products. The FDCA also creates a reportable food registry, establishes record-keeping requirements, requires the registration of all food facilities, and provides for inspections. Most of these statutory requirements are monitored and enforced by the FDA.

Some foods considered safe by the FDCA in the United States are prohibited in Europe, however. For instance, products containing ingredients such as olestra (often in potato chips) and brominated vegetable oils (in certain sports drinks) are banned in the European Union. Many foreign nations also ban the use of certain chemicals and food colorings that are commonly found in U.S. food products.

Tainted Foods In the last several years, many people in the United States have contracted food poisoning from eating foods that were contaminated—often with salmonella or *E.coli* bacteria. **Example 39.7** Hundreds of people across the United States were sickened by eating contaminated food at the popular restaurant chain Chipotle Mexican Grill. Causes of illness in these outbreaks included *E.coli* and salmonella, as well as the highly contagious norovirus. ■ In response, Congress enacted the Food Safety Modernization Act (FSMA),[15] which provides greater government control over the U.S. food safety system.

The goal of the modernization act was to shift the focus of federal regulators from responding to incidents of contamination to preventing them. The act also gives the FDA authority to directly recall any food products that it suspects are tainted, rather than relying on the producers to recall items.

The FSMA requires any party that manufactures, processes, packs, distributes, receives, holds, or imports food products to pay a fee and register with the U.S. Department of Health and Human Services. (There are some exceptions for small farmers.) Owners and operators of such facilities are required to analyze and identify food safety hazards, implement preventive controls, monitor effectiveness, and take corrective actions. The act also places more restrictions on importers of food and requires them to verify that imported foods meet U.S. safety standards.

Drugs and Medical Devices The FDA is also responsible under the FDCA for ensuring that drugs are safe and effective before they are marketed to the public. It is the responsibility of the company seeking to market a drug to test it and submit evidence that it is safe and effective. The FDA has established extensive procedures that drug manufacturers must follow.

Know This

The U.S. Food and Drug Administration is authorized to obtain, among other things, orders for the recall and seizure of certain products.

Learning Objective 2

What law protects consumers against contaminated and misbranded foods and drugs?

---

14. 21 U.S.C. Section 301.
15. Pub. L. No. 111-353, 124 Stat. 3885 (January 4, 2011). This statute affected numerous parts of Title 21 of the U.S.C.

The FDA also has the authority to regulate medical devices, such as pacemakers, and to withdraw from the market any such device that is mislabeled.[16]

Because the FDA must ensure the safety of new medications, there is always a delay before drugs are available to the public, and this sometimes leads to controversy. **Case Example 39.8** A group of citizens petitioned the FDA to allow everyone access to "Plan B"—the morning-after birth control pill—without a prescription. The FDA denied the petition and continued to require women under the age of seventeen to obtain a prescription. The group appealed to a federal district court, claiming that the prescription requirement can delay access to the pill. The pill should be taken as soon as possible after sexual intercourse, preferably within twenty-four hours. The court ruled in favor of the plaintiffs and ordered the FDA to make the morning-after pill available to people of any age without a prescription.[17]

39–2b Consumer Product Safety

The Consumer Product Safety Act[18] created a comprehensive regulatory scheme over consumer safety matters and established the Consumer Product Safety Commission (CPSC).

The CPSC's Authority The CPSC conducts research on the safety of individual products and maintains a clearinghouse on the risks associated with various products. The Consumer Product Safety Act authorizes the CPSC to do the following:

1. Set safety standards for consumer products.

2. Ban the manufacture and sale of any product that the commission believes poses an "unreasonable risk" to consumers. (Products banned by the CPSC have included various types of fireworks, cribs, and toys, as well as many products containing asbestos or vinyl chloride.)

3. Remove from the market any products it believes to be imminently hazardous. The CPSC frequently works with manufacturers to voluntarily recall defective products from stores. **Example 39.9** In cooperation with the CPSC, the Scandinavian company IKEA recalled 3 million baby bed canopies and 30 million wall-mounted children's lamps because they posed a strangulation risk to children.

Why would IKEA want to cooperate with the Consumer Product Safety Commission?

buzbuzzer/iStock Unreleased/Getty Images

4. Require manufacturers to report any products already sold or intended for sale that have proved to be hazardous.

5. Administer other product-safety legislation, including the Child Protection and Toy Safety Act[19] and the Federal Hazardous Substances Act.[20]

Notification Requirements The Consumer Product Safety Act imposes notification requirements on distributors of consumer products. Distributors must immediately notify the CPSC when they receive information that a product "contains a defect which . . . creates a substantial risk to the public" or "an unreasonable risk of serious injury or death."

39–2c Health-Care Reforms

The health-care reforms (Obamacare) enacted in 2010 gave Americans new rights and benefits with regard to health care.[21] These laws prohibit certain insurance company practices, such as denial of coverage for preexisting conditions.

---

16. 21 U.S.C. Sections 352(o), 360(j), 360(k), and 360c–360k.

17. *Tummino v. Hamburg*, 936 F.Supp.2d 162 (E.D.N.Y. 2013).

18. 15 U.S.C. Section 2051.

19. 15 U.S.C. Section 1262(e).

20. 15 U.S.C. Sections 1261–1273.

21. Patient Protection and Affordable Health Care Act, Pub. L. No. 111-148, March 23, 2010, 124 Stat. 119; and Health Care and Education Reconciliation Act, Pub. L. No. 111-152, March 30, 2010, 124 Stat. 1029.

Expanded Coverage for Children and Seniors The reforms enabled more children to obtain health-insurance coverage and allowed young adults (under age twenty-six) to remain covered by their parents' health-insurance policies. The legislation also ended lifetime limits and most annual limits on care, and gave patients access to recommended preventive services (such as cancer screenings, vaccinations, and well-baby checks) without cost. Medicare recipients receive a 50 percent discount on name-brand drugs, and a gap that exists in Medicare's prescription drug coverage is supposed to be eliminated by 2020.

Controlling Costs of Health Insurance In an attempt to control the rising costs of health insurance, the Affordable Care Act placed restrictions on insurance companies. Insurance companies must spend at least 85 percent of all premium dollars collected from large employers (80 percent of premiums collected from individuals and small employers) on benefits and quality improvement. If insurance companies do not meet these goals, they must provide rebates to consumers. Additionally, states can require insurance companies to justify their premium increases to be eligible to participate in the health-insurance exchanges mandated by the law.

39–3 Credit Protection

Credit protection is one of the most important aspects of consumer protection legislation. A large percentage of U.S. consumers have credit cards, and many carry a balance on these cards, which amounts to over a trillion dollars of debt nationwide. The Consumer Financial Protection Bureau oversees the credit practices of banks, mortgage lenders, and credit-card companies.

39–3a Truth in Lending Act

A key statute regulating the credit and credit-card industries is the Truth in Lending Act (TILA), the name commonly given to Title 1 of the Consumer Credit Protection Act (CCPA), as amended.[22] The TILA is basically a *disclosure law.* It is administered by the Federal Reserve Board and requires sellers and lenders to disclose credit terms or loan terms (such as the annual percentage rate, or APR, and any finance charges) so that individuals can shop around for the best financing arrangements.

Application TILA requirements apply only to persons who, in the ordinary course of business, lend funds, sell on credit, or arrange for the extension of credit. Thus, sales or loans made between two consumers do not come under the act. Additionally, this law protects only debtors who are *natural* persons (as opposed to the artificial "person" of a corporation) and does not extend to other legal entities.

Disclosure The TILA's disclosure requirements are found in **Regulation Z,**[23] issued by the Federal Reserve Board of Governors. If the contracting parties are subject to the TILA, the requirements of Regulation Z apply to any transaction involving an installment sales contract that calls for payment to be made in more than four installments. Transactions subject to Regulation Z typically include installment loans, retail installment sales, car loans, home-improvement loans, and certain real estate loans, if the amount of financing is less than $25,000.

Regulation Z A set of rules issued by the Federal Reserve Board of Governors to implement the provisions of the Truth in Lending Act.

Learning Objective 3

What does Regulation Z require, and how does it relate to the Truth in Lending Act?

---

22. 15 U.S.C. Sections 1601–1693r. The TILA was amended in 1980 by the Truth-in-Lending Simplification and Reform Act and again in 2009 by the Credit Card Accountability Responsibility and Disclosure Act.
23. 12 C.F.R. Sections 226.1–226.30.

Equal Credit Opportunity The Equal Credit Opportunity Act (ECOA) amended the TILA. The ECOA prohibits the denial of credit solely on the basis of race, religion, national origin, color, gender, marital status, or age. The act also prohibits credit discrimination on the basis of whether an individual receives certain forms of income, such as public-assistance benefits.

A creditor may not require the signature of a co-signer on a credit instrument if the applicant qualifies under the creditor's standards of creditworthiness for the amount requested.
Case Example 39.10 T.R. Hughes, Inc., and Summit Pointe, LLC, obtained financing from Frontenac Bank to construct two real estate developments near St. Louis, Missouri. The bank also required the builder, Thomas R. Hughes, and his wife, Carolyn Hughes, to sign personal guaranty agreements for the loans.

When the borrowers failed to make the loan payments, the bank sued the two companies and Thomas and Carolyn Hughes personally, and foreclosed on the properties. Carolyn claimed that personal guaranty contracts that she signed were obtained in violation of the ECOA. The court held that because the applicant, Thomas R. Hughes, was creditworthy, the personal guarantees of Carolyn Hughes were obtained in violation of the ECOA and were therefore unenforceable.[24]

What are some basic TILA provisions that benefit credit-card holders?

Credit-Card Rules The TILA also contains provisions regarding credit cards. One provision limits the liability of a cardholder to $50 per card for unauthorized charges made before the creditor was notified that the card was lost. If a consumer received an *unsolicited* credit card in the mail that was later stolen, the company that issued the card cannot charge the consumer for any unauthorized charges.

Another provision requires credit-card companies to disclose the balance computation method that is used to determine the outstanding balance and to state when finance charges begin to accrue. Other provisions set forth procedures for resolving billing disputes with the credit-card company. These procedures may be used if, for instance, a cardholder wishes to withhold payment for a faulty product purchased with a credit card.

Amendments to Credit-Card Rules Amendments to TILA's credit-card rules added the following protections:

1. A company may not retroactively increase the interest rates on existing card balances unless the account is sixty days delinquent.

2. A company must provide forty-five days' advance notice to consumers before changing its credit-card terms.

3. Monthly bills must be sent to cardholders twenty-one days before the due date.

4. The interest rate charged on a customer's credit-card balance may not be increased except in specific situations, such as when a promotional rate ends.

5. A company may not charge fees for being over the credit card's limit except in specified situations.

6. When the customer has balances at different interest rates, payments in excess of the minimum amount due must be applied first to the balance with the highest rate (for instance, a higher interest rate is commonly charged for cash advances).

7. A company may not compute finance charges based on the previous billing cycle (a practice known as double-cycle billing, which hurts consumers because they are charged interest for the previous cycle even if they have paid the bill in full).

---

24. *Frontenac Bank v. T.R. Hughes, Inc.*, 404 S.W.3d 272 (Mo.App. 2012).

39–3b Fair Credit Reporting Act

The Fair Credit Reporting Act (FCRA)[25] protects consumers against inaccurate credit reporting and requires that lenders and other creditors report correct, relevant, and up-to-date information. The act provides that consumer credit reporting agencies may issue credit reports to users only for specified purposes. Legitimate purposes include the extension of credit, the issuance of insurance policies, and in response to the consumer's request.

Whether an Internet service provider had a legitimate purpose in obtaining a customer's credit report was at issue in the following case.

---

25. 15 U.S.C. Sections 1681 *et seq.*

■ Case 39.3

Santangelo v. Comcast Corp.

United States District Court, Northern District of Illinois, Eastern Division, 162 F.Supp.3d 691 (2016).

Background and Facts Keith Santangelo contacted Comcast Corporation through its online customer service "Chat" function in December 2014 and requested Internet service for his new apartment. During the chat session, a Comcast representative asked Santangelo for permission to run a credit inquiry. Santangelo asked if any option was available to avoid the credit inquiry. The Comcast representative told him that the company would forgo the inquiry if he paid a $50 deposit. The option to pay a $50 deposit in order to avoid a credit inquiry was an explicit part of Comcast's official Risk Management Policy. The policy also required a $50 deposit from any prospective customer who agreed to a credit inquiry but whose credit score proved to be unsatisfactory.

Santangelo opted to pay the $50 deposit in lieu of a credit inquiry. Nevertheless, Comcast, without Santangelo's permission, pulled his credit report. This unauthorized credit inquiry lowered Santangelo's credit score. Santangelo filed a complaint alleging that Comcast's actions violated the Fair Credit Reporting Act (FCRA) as well as Illinois state law. Comcast filed a motion to dismiss, arguing that Santangelo had not stated a claim under the FCRA.

In the Words of the Court

John Z. *LEE*, United States District Judge.

* * * *

FCRA prohibits the obtaining of a "consumer report," commonly known as a credit report, except for purposes authorized by that statute. *The statute lists specific permissible purposes, such as* * * * *any* * * * *"legitimate business need* * * * *in connection with a business transaction that is initiated by the consumer."* These limitations are intended to produce a balance between consumer privacy and the needs of a modern, credit-driven economy. [Emphasis added.]

Santangelo contends that Comcast did not have a permissible purpose for obtaining his credit report after he paid the $50 deposit in exchange for the company's promise not to check his credit. If he is correct and the company's violation was willful, he would be entitled to recover attorney's fees and either actual damages or statutory damages between $100 and $1,000. If the company's violation was merely negligent, Santangelo would be permitted to recover only attorney's fees and actual damages.

* * * *

Comcast * * * argues that Santangelo's allegations do not state an FCRA claim.

* * * *

In his * * * complaint, Santangelo * * * alleges that Comcast's deposit policies demonstrate its lack of a legitimate need to run credit checks with respect to consumers who paid a $50 deposit. According to the * * * complaint, Comcast's established policy is to forgo a credit check in exchange for a $50 deposit. The company also has a policy of accepting a $50 deposit from consumers who opt for a credit check but prove to have poor credit. Santangelo compares this situation to that of a car dealer who accepts a cash

(Continues)

payment for the full purchase price of a car. * * * The car dealer * * * does not have a legitimate need to obtain the purchaser's credit report. Similarly, a landlord does not have a legitimate need to obtain a tenant's credit report if the tenant is entitled to a lease renewal without regard to creditworthiness.

In response, Comcast * * * argues that it had a legitimate business need to establish Santangelo's creditworthiness despite his deposit because—unlike in the car dealer example—his $50 deposit would cover less than two months of service in a long-term contract. * * * [Santangelo] contends that, under company policy, his creditworthiness was irrelevant to Comcast's determination of his eligibility for service once the deposit was collected, much like the tenants in [the landlord example].

* * * *

* * * Comcast's mere violation of its alleged agreement not to pull Santangelo's credit report does not support an FCRA claim. But the possibility that the company itself believed that its customers' creditworthiness was irrelevant if they paid a deposit

is enough. * * * Although [Santangelo] does not use the word willful in his complaint, he alleges that the company obtained his credit report despite that it "knew that it did not have a legitimate business need." This allegation implies recklessness at the very least, and reckless conduct qualifies as willful conduct under the FCRA.

* * * *

Decision and Remedy The federal district court for the Northern District of Illinois held that Santangelo's complaint sufficiently alleged facts showing that Comcast obtained his credit report without a permissible purpose in violation of the FCRA. Therefore, the court denied Comcast's motion to dismiss.

Critical Thinking

• **Social** *Why might Comcast have immediately changed its official Risk Management Policy after this decision?*

• **Legal Environment** *What damages might Santangelo be able to prove based on the depletion of his credit score?*

Consumer Notification and Inaccurate Information Any time a consumer is denied credit or insurance on the basis of his or her credit report, the consumer must be notified of that fact. The same notice must be sent to consumers who are charged more than others ordinarily would be for credit or insurance because of their credit reports.

Under the FCRA, consumers can request the source of any information used by the credit agency, as well as the identity of anyone who has received an agency's report. Consumers are also permitted to have access to the information contained about them in a credit reporting agency's files.

If a consumer discovers that the agency's files contain inaccurate information, he or she should report the problem to the agency. On the consumer's written (or electronic) request, the agency must conduct a systematic examination of its records. Any unverifiable or erroneous information must be deleted within a reasonable period of time.

Remedies for Violations A credit reporting agency that fails to comply with the act is liable for actual damages, plus additional damages not to exceed $1,000 and attorneys' fees.[26] Creditors and other companies that use information from credit reporting agencies may also be liable for violations of the FCRA. Punitive damages may be awarded for *willful* violations. An insurance company's failure to notify new customers that they are paying higher insurance rates as a result of their credit scores is considered a willful violation of the FCRA.[27] Willful violations entitle a consumer to statutory and even punitive damages.

---

26. 15 U.S.C. Section 1681n.
27. This was the holding of the United States Supreme Court in *Safeco Insurance Co. of America v. Burr*, 551 U.S. 47, 127 S.Ct. 2201, 167 L.Ed.2d 1045 (2007).

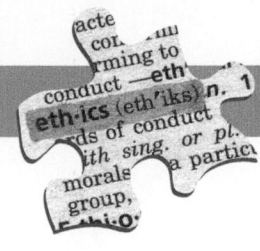

Can a company that provides background checks willfully violate the Fair Credit Reporting Act? After graduating from college with a bachelor's degree, Richard Williams applied for a job in his hometown with Rent-A-Center as an account representative. As part of the application process, he agreed to a drug test (which he passed) and a criminal-background check. Rent-A-Center contracted with First Advantage LNS Screening Solutions, Inc., a credit reporting agency that provides various background checks.

First Advantage reported to Rent-A-Center that a Richard Williams had a sale-of-cocaine record in another part of the state. Williams disputed the report. First Advantage admitted that Richard Williams is a common name and that it had not obtained three identifiers of that record. When First Advantage investigated, it determined that the criminal record was for a different person with the same name. It removed that criminal record from Williams's report. By then, however, it was too late, as Rent-A-Center had hired someone else.

Williams continued applying for a multitude of jobs. Eventually, another prospective employer ran a background check through First Advantage. This time, First Advantage reported to the employer that Williams had been convicted of aggravated battery on a pregnant woman. Again, it turned out to be a different Richard Williams, but by then, the employer had rejected Williams and hired someone else. Williams sued First Advantage in a federal district court for willfully violating the FCRA. After a jury trial, he was awarded $250,000 in compensatory damages and $3.3 million in punitive damages. First Advantage filed a motion for a new trial, which the court denied. Evidence supported the jury's finding that First Advantage willfully violated the FCRA and that the damages awarded were appropriate and not unconstitutionally excessive.[28]

Which law attempts to protect consumers against inaccurate credit information?

39–3c Fair and Accurate Credit Transactions Act

Congress passed the Fair and Accurate Credit Transactions (FACT) Act to combat identity theft.[29] The act established a national fraud alert system so that consumers who suspect that they have been or may be victimized by identity theft can place an alert in their credit files. The act also requires the major credit reporting agencies to provide consumers with a free copy of their credit reports every twelve months.

Another provision requires account numbers on credit-card receipts to be truncated (shortened) so that merchants, employees, and others who have access to the receipts cannot obtain a consumer's name and full credit-card number. The act also mandates that financial institutions work with the FTC to identify "red flag" indicators of identity theft and to develop rules for disposing of sensitive credit information.

39–3d Fair Debt Collection Practices Act

The Fair Debt Collection Practices Act (FDCPA)[30] attempts to curb abuses by collection agencies. The act applies only to specialized debt-collection agencies and attorneys who regularly attempt to collect debts on behalf of someone else, usually for a percentage of the amount owed. Creditors attempting to collect debts are not covered by the act unless, by misrepresenting themselves, they cause the debtors to believe that they are collection agencies.

> "Credit is a system whereby a person who can't pay gets another person who can't pay to guarantee that he can pay."
>
> **Charles Dickens**
> 1812–1870
> (English novelist)

---

28. *Williams v. First Advantage LSN Screening Solutions, Inc.*, 238 F.Supp.3d 1333 (N.D.Fla. 2017).
29. Pub. L. No. 108-159, 117 Stat. 1952 (December 4, 2003).
30. 15 U.S.C. Section 1692.

Requirements Under the FDCPA, a collection agency may not do any of the following:

1. Contact the debtor at the debtor's place of employment if the debtor's employer objects.

2. Contact the debtor at inconvenient or unusual times (such as three o'clock in the morning), or at any time if the debtor is being represented by an attorney.

3. Contact third parties other than the debtor's parents, spouse, or financial adviser about payment of a debt unless a court authorizes such action.

4. Harass or intimidate the debtor (by using abusive language or threatening violence, for instance) or make false or misleading statements (such as posing as a police officer).

5. Communicate with the debtor at any time after receiving notice that the debtor is refusing to pay the debt, except to advise the debtor of further action to be taken by the collection agency.

The FDCPA also requires a collection agency to include a *validation notice* whenever it initially contacts a debtor for payment of a debt or within five days of that initial contact. The notice must state that the debtor has thirty days in which to dispute the debt and to request a written verification of the debt from the collection agency. The debtor's request for debt validation must be in writing.

Enforcement The Federal Trade Commission is primarily responsible for enforcing the FDCPA. A debt collector who fails to comply with the act is liable for actual damages, plus additional damages not to exceed $1,000 and attorneys' fees.

Debt collectors who violate the act are exempt from liability if they can show that the violation was not intentional and resulted from a bona fide error. The "bona fide error" defense typically has been applied to mistakes of fact or clerical errors.

39–4 Protecting the Environment

We now turn to a discussion of the various ways in which businesses are regulated by the government in the interest of attempting to protect the environment. Environmental protection is not without a price. For many businesses, the costs of complying with environmental regulations are high, and for some, they may seem too high.

39–4a Federal Regulation

Congress has enacted a number of statutes to control the impact of human activities on the environment. Some of these laws have been passed in an attempt to improve the quality of air and water. Other laws specifically regulate toxic chemicals, including pesticides, herbicides, and hazardous wastes.

Environmental Regulatory Agencies The primary agency regulating environmental law is the Environmental Protection Agency (EPA). Other federal agencies with authority to regulate specific environmental matters include the Department of the Interior, the Department of Defense, the Department of Labor, the Food and Drug Administration, and the Nuclear Regulatory Commission.

State and local agencies also play an important role in enforcing federal environmental legislation. In addition, most federal environmental laws provide that private parties can sue to enforce environmental regulations if government agencies fail to do so. Typically, a threshold hurdle in such suits is meeting the requirements for standing to sue. (For an interesting variation on standing to sue, see this chapter's *Beyond Our Borders* feature.)

Environmental Impact Statements All agencies of the federal government must take environmental factors into consideration when making significant decisions. The National

Learning Objective 4

What does an environmental impact statement contain, and who must file one?

Can a River Be a Legal Person?

Years ago, a famous law journal article entitled, "Should Trees Have Standing?" addressed the issue of who has the legal right to bring a lawsuit when nature is involved.[a] The issue remains with us today. To have standing, a party wishing to sue must have a stake in the outcome. If the courts did not impose fairly strict requirements on who has standing, they would be flooded with many more lawsuits than are filed today.

New Zealand's Third-Longest River Is Now a Legal Person

So, can rivers have standing? In New Zealand, apparently so. A law that went into

effect in 2017 declares that the Whanganui River is a legal person, meaning that it can own property, incur debts, and petition the courts. Those in favor of this law point out that throughout the world certain organizations have legal rights and responsibilities that do not depend on the individuals who staff those entities. So why can't a river have legal rights as well?

"I Am the River, and the River Is Me"

New Zealand's new law is the outcome of a dispute between the indigenous Maori tribes and others who use the river. The Maori tribes contend that there is a deep spiritual connection between them and the river, stating "I am the river, and the river is me." The new law acknowledges that the river is a "living whole."

In principle, this law has put to rest an ownership dispute that dates back more than 140 years. Today, the river has two guardians: one from the government, and one from a group of Maori tribes.

Critical Thinking

Soon after passage of the New Zealand law, an Indian court ruled that two of the biggest rivers in India, the Yamuna and the Ganges, are legal persons. What is the purpose of such laws?

a. Stone, Christopher D., "Should Trees Have Standing? Toward Legal Rights for Natural Objects," *Southern California Law Review*, 45 (1972): pp. 450–501.

Environmental Policy Act (NEPA)[31] requires that an **environmental impact statement (EIS)** be prepared for every major federal action that significantly affects the quality of the environment (see Exhibit 39–2). An EIS must analyze the following:

1. The impact that the action will have on the environment.

2. Any adverse effects on the environment and alternative actions that might be taken.

3. Irreversible effects the action might generate.

Note that an EIS must be prepared for every major federal action. An action qualifies as "major" if it involves a substantial commitment of resources (monetary or otherwise). An action is "federal" if a federal agency has the power to control it. **Example 39.11** Development of a ski resort by a private developer on federal land may require an EIS. Construction or operation of a nuclear plant, which requires a federal permit, necessitates an EIS, as does creation of a dam as part of a federal project. ■

If an agency decides that an EIS is unnecessary, it must issue a statement supporting this conclusion. Private individuals, consumer interest groups, businesses, and others who believe that a federal agency's actions threaten the environment often use EISs as a means of challenging those actions.

The Whanganui River in New Zealand is sacred to the indigenous Maori tribes. Why pursue legislation to give the river "legal person" status?

Environmental Impact Statement (EIS) A formal analysis required for any major federal action that will significantly affect the quality of the environment to determine the action's impact and explore alternatives.

31. 42 U.S.C. Sections 4321–4370d.

Exhibit 39–2 Environmental Impact Statements

39–4b Common Law Actions

Even before there were statutes and regulations explicitly protecting the environment, the common law recognized that individuals have the right not to have their environment contaminated by others. Common law remedies against environmental pollution originated centuries ago in England. Those responsible for operations that created dirt, smoke, noxious odors, noise, or toxic substances were sometimes held liable under common law theories of nuisance or negligence. Today, individuals who have suffered harm from pollution continue to rely on the common law to obtain damages and injunctions against business polluters.

Nuisance Under the common law doctrine of **nuisance,** persons may be held liable if they use their property in a manner that unreasonably interferes with others' rights to use or enjoy their own property. In these situations, the courts commonly balance the harm caused by the pollution against the costs of stopping it.

Courts have often denied injunctive relief on the ground that the hardships that would be imposed on the polluter and on the community are relatively greater than the hardships suffered by the plaintiff. **Example 39.12** Hewitt's Factory causes neighboring landowners to suffer from smoke, soot, and vibrations. If the factory is the core of the local economy, a court may leave it in operation and award monetary damages to the injured parties. Damages may include compensation for any decline in the value of their property caused by Hewitt's operation.

To obtain relief from pollution under the nuisance doctrine, a property owner may have to identify a distinct harm (a "private" nuisance) separate from that affecting the general public. Under the common law—which is still followed in some states—individuals must establish a private nuisance to have standing to sue. A public authority (such as a state's attorney general), though, can sue to stop or reduce a "public" nuisance.

Negligence and Strict Liability An injured party may sue a business polluter under the negligence and strict liability theories discussed in the torts chapter. A negligence action is based on a business's alleged failure to use reasonable care toward a party whose injury was foreseeable and was caused by the lack of reasonable care. For instance, employees might sue an employer whose failure to use proper pollution controls contaminated the air and caused the employees to suffer respiratory illnesses.

Nuisance A common law doctrine under which persons may be held liable for using their property in a manner that unreasonably interferes with others' rights to use or enjoy their own property.

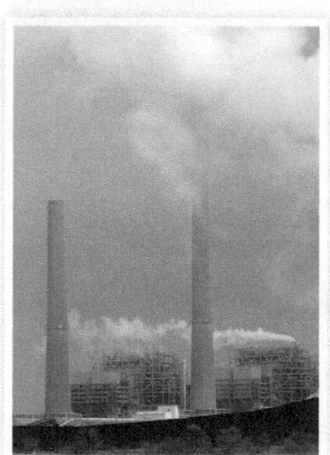

How can a local factory that is considered a "nuisance" by nearby property owners be held liable for noise or air pollution?

Businesses that engage in ultrahazardous activities—such as the transportation of radioactive materials—are strictly liable for any injuries the activities cause. In a strict liability action, the injured party does not need to prove that the business failed to exercise reasonable care.

Lawsuits for personal injuries caused by exposure to a toxic substance, such as asbestos, radiation, or hazardous waste, have given rise to a growing body of tort law known as **toxic torts**. These torts may be based on a theory of negligence or strict liability.

Toxic Tort A civil wrong arising from exposure to a toxic substance, such as asbestos, radiation, or hazardous waste.

39–5 Air and Water Pollution

The United States has long recognized the need to protect our natural resources. During the industrial revolution, factories began discharging substances into our air and water. Over time, it became clear that many of these substances were harmful to our environment, and the government began regulating.

39–5a Air Pollution

Federal involvement with air pollution goes back to the 1950s and 1960s, when Congress authorized funds for air-pollution research and enacted the Clean Air Act.[32] The Clean Air Act provides the basis for issuing regulations to control multistate air pollution. It covers both mobile sources of pollution (such as automobiles and other vehicles) and stationary sources of pollution (such as electric utilities and industrial plants).

Mobile Sources of Air Pollution Regulations governing air pollution from automobiles and other mobile sources specify pollution standards and establish time schedules for meeting the standards. The EPA periodically updates the pollution standards to reduce the amount of emissions allowed in light of new developments and data.

The Obama administration set a long-term goal of reducing emissions of certain pollutants, including those from automobiles, by 80 percent by 2050. The EPA then developed national standards regulating fuel economy and emissions for medium- and heavy-duty trucks (starting with 2014 models) and requiring most vehicles to average more than fifty miles per gallon by 2025. In 2017, the Trump administration announced that it will roll back some of the emissions standards set during the prior administration.

Stationary Sources of Air Pollution The Clean Air Act authorizes the EPA to establish air-quality standards for stationary sources, such as manufacturing plants. But the act recognizes that the primary responsibility for preventing and controlling air pollution rests with state and local governments. The standards are aimed at controlling hazardous air pollutants—those likely to cause death or a serious, irreversible, or incapacitating condition, such as cancer or neurological or reproductive damage.

The EPA sets primary and secondary levels of ambient standards—that is, the maximum permissible levels of certain pollutants—and the states formulate plans to achieve those standards. Different standards apply depending on whether the sources of pollution are located in clean areas or polluted areas and whether they are existing sources or major new sources.

Hazardous Air Pollutants. The Clean Air Act requires the EPA to list all regulated hazardous air pollutants on a prioritized schedule. In all, nearly two hundred substances, including asbestos, benzene, beryllium, cadmium, and vinyl chloride, have been classified as hazardous. They are emitted from stationary sources by a variety of business activities, including smelting (melting ore to produce metal), dry cleaning, house painting, and commercial baking.

"There's so much pollution in the air now that if it weren't for our lungs, there'd be no place to put it all."

Robert Orben
1927–present
(American comedian)

---

32. 42 U.S.C. Sections 7401 *et seq.*

Maximum Achievable Control Technology. The Clean Air Act does not establish specific emissions standards for each hazardous air pollutant. Instead, the act requires *major new sources* of pollutants to use pollution-control equipment that represents the *maximum achievable control technology,* or MACT, to reduce emissions. The EPA issues guidelines as to what equipment meets this standard.[33]

Greenhouse Gases

Although greenhouse gases, such as carbon dioxide (CO_2), are generally thought to contribute to global climate change, the Clean Air Act does not specifically mention CO_2 emissions. Therefore, the EPA did not regulate CO_2 emissions until 2009, after the Supreme Court ruled that it had the authority to do so.

Does the Environmental Protection Agency have the power to regulate CO_2 emissions from power plants?

Classic Case Example 39.13 Environmental groups and several states, including Massachusetts, sued the EPA in an effort to force the agency to regulate CO_2 emissions. When the case reached the United States Supreme Court, the EPA argued that the plaintiffs lacked standing. The agency claimed that because climate change has widespread effects, an individual plaintiff cannot show the particularized harm required for standing. The agency also maintained that it did not have authority under the Clean Air Act to address global climate change and regulate CO_2.

The Court, however, ruled that Massachusetts had standing because its coastline, including state-owned lands, faced a threat from the rising sea levels that may result from climate change. The Court also held that the Clean Air Act's broad definition of air pollution gives the EPA authority to regulate CO_2 and requires the EPA to regulate any air pollutants that might "endanger public health or welfare." Accordingly, the Court ordered the EPA to determine whether CO_2 was a pollutant that endangered the public health.[34] The EPA went on to conclude that greenhouse gases, including CO_2 emissions, do constitute a public danger and began regulating them in 2011.

Controlling Climate Change

In 2016, a federal court allowed an unprecedented lawsuit to go forward against the U.S. government for doing too little to control climate change. **Case Example 39.14** A group of young people (aged eight to nineteen) filed a suit against the federal government, as well as the fossil fuel industry. The plaintiffs argued that the government has known for years that CO_2 pollution causes climate change and threatens catastrophic environmental consequences. By failing to address the causes of this pollution, they claimed the government had violated their constitutional rights.

The court found that the plaintiffs had alleged particular, concrete harms to young people and future generations sufficient to give them standing to pursue their claims in court. Of course, this ruling means only that the plaintiffs have met their threshold burden of establishing standing. The court simply denied the government's motion to dismiss—it did not decide the merits of the case or grant relief to the plaintiffs. Those issues have yet to be resolved.[35]

Violations of the Clean Air Act

For violations of emission limits under the Clean Air Act, the EPA can assess civil penalties of up to $25,000 per day. Additional fines of up to $5,000 per day can be assessed for other violations, such as failing to maintain the required records. To penalize those who find it more cost-effective to violate the act than to comply with it, the EPA is authorized to obtain a penalty equal to the violator's economic benefits from noncompliance. Persons who provide information about violators may be paid up to $10,000. Private individuals can also sue violators.

---

33. The EPA has also issued rules to regulate hazardous air pollutants emitted by landfills. See 40 C.F.R. Sections 60.750–60.759.

34. *Massachusetts v. Environmental Protection Agency,* 549 U.S. 497, 127 S.Ct. 1438, 167 L.Ed.2d 248 (2007).

35. *Juliana v. United States,* 217 F.Supp.3d 1224 (D.Or. 2016). The government's request for an appellate court to issue an order dismissing the case was denied: *In re United States,* 884 F.3d 830 (9th Cir. 2018).

39–5b Water Pollution

Water pollution stems mostly from industrial, municipal, and agricultural sources. Pollutants entering streams, lakes, and oceans include organic wastes, heated water, sediments from soil runoff, nutrients (including fertilizers and human and animal wastes), and toxic chemicals and other hazardous substances.

Federal regulations governing the pollution of water can be traced back to the 1899 Rivers and Harbors Appropriation Act.[36] These regulations prohibited ships and manufacturers from discharging or depositing refuse in navigable waterways without a permit. In 1948, Congress passed the Federal Water Pollution Control Act (FWPCA),[37] but its regulatory system and enforcement powers proved to be inadequate.

The Clean Water Act   In 1972, amendments to the FWPCA—known as the Clean Water Act (CWA)—established the following goals: (1) make waters safe for swimming, (2) protect fish and wildlife, and (3) eliminate the discharge of pollutants into the water. The amendments set specific time schedules, which were extended by amendment and by the Water Quality Act.[38] Under these schedules, the EPA limits the discharge of various types of pollutants based on the technology available for controlling them.

> **Learning Objective 5**
> What are three main goals of the Clean Water Act?

Permit System for Point-Source Emissions. The CWA established a permit system, called the National Pollutant Discharge Elimination System (NPDES), for regulating discharges from "point sources" of pollution. Point sources include industrial facilities, municipal facilities (such as sewer pipes and sewage treatment plants), and agricultural facilities.[39] Under this system, industrial, municipal, and agricultural polluters must apply for permits before discharging wastes into surface waters.

NPDES permits can be issued by the EPA, authorized state agencies, and Indian tribes, but only if the discharge will not violate water-quality standards (either federal or state standards). Special requirements must be met to discharge toxic chemicals and residue from oil spills. NPDES permits must be renewed every five years.

Storm Water. Although the NPDES system initially focused mainly on industrial wastewater, it was later expanded to cover storm water discharge. **Case Example 39.15** The Maryland Department of the Environment (MDE) issued separate storm sewer system (MS4) discharge permits to various counties in Maryland. A number of environmental organizations, including Anacosta Riverkeeper, sued the MDE, claiming that its MS4 permits did not comply with federal law. They argued that the MS4 permits allowed permit holders to discharge chemicals and other substances into the Chesapeake Bay at levels exceeding the daily maximum load set by the EPA. A state trial court ruled in the MDE's favor, and the plaintiffs appealed.

A state appellate court reviewed the requirements of the state's MS4 permit system and determined that it complied with the Clean Water Act. Although Maryland's storm water management system was not perfect, the court concluded that it was a reasonable attempt to control and restore the state's water quality. The court reasoned that municipal storm water discharge is highly intermittent and includes relatively high flows that occur over short periods. The fact that the discharges sometimes exceeded the daily maximum load did not mean that the MS4 permits violated the Clean Water Act.[40]

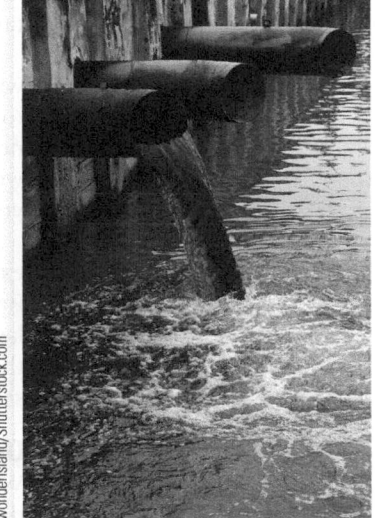

What law governs discharge of pollutants into water?

---

36. 33 U.S.C. Sections 401–418.
37. 33 U.S.C. Sections 1251–1387.
38. This act amended 33 U.S.C. Section 1251.
39. 33 U.S.C. Section 1342.
40. *Maryland Department of the Environment v. Anacosta Riverkeeper,* 447 Md. 88, 134 A.3d 892 (2016).

Standards for Equipment. Regulations generally specify that the *best available control technology*, or BACT, be installed. The EPA issues guidelines as to what equipment meets this standard. Essentially, the guidelines require the most effective pollution-control equipment available.

New sources must install BACT equipment before beginning operations. Existing sources are subject to timetables for the installation of BACT equipment and must immediately install equipment that utilizes the *best practical control technology*, or BPCT. The EPA also issues guidelines as to what equipment meets this standard.

Violations of the Clean Water Act

Because point-source water pollution control is based on a permit system, the permits are the key to enforcement. States have primary responsibility for enforcing the permit system, subject to EPA monitoring.

Discharging emissions into navigable waters without a permit, or in violation of pollution limits under a permit, violates the CWA. Violators are subject to a variety of civil and criminal penalties. Depending on the violation, civil penalties range from $10,000 to $25,000 per day, but not more than $25,000 per violation.

Criminal penalties, which apply only if a violation was intentional, range from a fine of $2,500 per day and imprisonment for up to one year to a fine of $1 million and fifteen years' imprisonment. Injunctive relief and damages can also be imposed. The polluting party can be required to clean up the pollution or pay for the cost of doing so.

Drinking Water

The Safe Drinking Water Act[41] requires the EPA to set maximum levels for pollutants in public water systems. Public water system operators must come as close as possible to meeting the EPA's standards by using the best available technology that is economically and technologically feasible.

Each supplier of drinking water must send an annual statement describing the source of its water to every household it supplies. The statement must disclose the level of any contaminants in the water and any possible health concerns associated with the contaminants.

Example 39.16 In 2014, the city of Flint, Michigan, changed its source of drinking water from the Detroit water system to the Flint River. Detroit's water had been treated to prevent lead from leaching from aging lead pipes into the water. Flint River water was not treated, which allowed lead to leach into the water from the pipes. Flint's drinking water became contaminated with lead—a serious public health hazard, especially for young children.

By the time Flint sent out the required EPA notices, thousands of children had been exposed to drinking water with high lead levels. A federal state of emergency was declared. Residents of Flint were instructed to use only bottled or filtered water. Numerous civil lawsuits—and nine criminal actions—were filed against government officials as a result of the incident. Inevitably, fixing the problem will cost the city millions of dollars and take several years. ■

Oil Pollution

When more than 10 million gallons of oil leaked into Alaska's Prince William Sound from the *Exxon Valdez* supertanker in 1989, Congress responded by passing the Oil Pollution Act.[42] (At that time, the *Exxon Valdez* disaster was the worst oil spill in U.S. history, but the British Petroleum *Deepwater Horizon* oil spill in the Gulf of Mexico in 2010 surpassed it.)

Under this act, any onshore or offshore oil facility, oil shipper, vessel owner, or vessel operator that discharges oil into navigable waters or onto an adjoining shore can be liable for clean-up costs and damages. In addition, the polluter can be ordered to pay for damage to natural resources, private property, and the local economy, including the increased cost of providing public services.

> "Among these treasures of our land is water— fast becoming our most valuable, most prized, most critical resource."
>
> **Dwight D. Eisenhower**
> 1890–1969
> (Thirty-fourth president of the United States, 1953–1961)

---

41. 42 U.S.C. Sections 300f to 300j-25.
42. 33 U.S.C. Sections 2701–2761.

39–6 Toxic Chemicals and Hazardous Waste

Today, the control of toxic chemicals used in agriculture and in industry has become increasingly important. If not properly disposed of, these toxic chemicals may present a substantial danger to human health and the environment—for instance, by contaminating public drinking water resources.

39–6a Pesticides and Herbicides

The Federal Insecticide, Fungicide, and Rodenticide Act (FIFRA)[43] regulates the use of pesticides and herbicides. These substances must be (1) registered before they can be sold, (2) certified and used only for approved applications, and (3) used in limited quantities when applied to food crops. The act gives the EPA authority to oversee the sale and use of these substances and to determine whether, and at what levels, a substance may be harmful.

It is a violation of FIFRA to sell a pesticide or herbicide that is unregistered or has had its registration canceled or suspended. It is also a violation to sell a pesticide or herbicide with a false or misleading label, or to destroy or deface any labeling required under the act.

Penalties for commercial dealers include imprisonment for up to one year and a fine of up to $25,000. Farmers and other private users of pesticides or herbicides who violate the act are subject to a $1,000 fine and incarceration for up to thirty days. Note that a state can also regulate the sale and use of federally registered pesticides.

39–6b Toxic Substances

The Toxic Substances Control Act[44] regulates chemicals and chemical compounds that are known to be toxic, such as asbestos and polychlorinated biphenyls (PCBs). The act also controls the introduction of new chemical compounds by requiring investigation of any possible harmful effects from these substances.

The act authorizes the EPA to require that manufacturers, processors, and other organizations planning to use chemicals first determine their effects on human health and the environment. The EPA can regulate substances that could pose an imminent hazard or an unreasonable risk of injury to health or the environment. The EPA may require special labeling, limit the use of a substance, set production quotas, or prohibit the use of a substance altogether.

39–6c Resource Conservation and Recovery Act

The Resource Conservation and Recovery Act (RCRA)[45] was passed in reaction to concern over the effects of hazardous waste materials on the environment. The RCRA required the EPA to determine which forms of solid waste should be considered hazardous and to establish regulations to monitor and control hazardous waste disposal.

The act authorized the EPA to issue technical requirements for facilities that store and treat hazardous waste. The act also required all producers of hazardous waste materials to label and package properly any hazardous waste to be transported. Amendments to the RCRA decreased the use of land containment in the disposal of hazardous waste and required smaller generators of hazardous waste to comply with the act.

Under the RCRA, a company may be assessed a civil penalty of up to $25,000 for each violation. Penalties are based on the seriousness of the violation, the probability of harm, and the extent to which the violation deviates from RCRA requirements. Criminal penalties include fines of up to $50,000 for each day of violation, imprisonment for up to two years

---

43. 7 U.S.C. Sections 135–136y.
44. 15 U.S.C. Sections 2601–2692.
45. 42 U.S.C. Sections 6901 *et seq.*

(in most instances), or both. Criminal fines and the period of imprisonment can be doubled for certain repeat offenders.

Learning Objective 6

What is Superfund? What categories of people are liable under Superfund?

39–6d Superfund

The Comprehensive Environmental Response, Compensation, and Liability Act (CERCLA),[46] commonly known as Superfund, regulates the clean-up of disposal sites in which hazardous waste is leaking into the environment. CERCLA, as amended, has four primary elements:

1. It established an information-gathering and analysis system that enables the government to identify chemical dump sites and determine the appropriate action.

2. It authorized the EPA to respond to hazardous substance emergencies and to arrange for the clean-up of a leaking site directly if the persons responsible for the problem fail to clean up the site.

3. It created a Hazardous Substance Response Trust Fund (also called Superfund) to pay for the clean-up of hazardous sites using funds obtained through taxes on certain businesses.

4. It allowed the government to recover the cost of clean-up from persons who were responsible (even remotely) for hazardous substance releases.

Potentially Responsible Parties Superfund provides that when a release or a potential release of hazardous chemicals from a site occurs, the following persons may be held responsible for cleaning up the site:

1. A person who generated the wastes disposed of at the site.

2. A person who transported the waste to the site.

3. The person who owned or operated the site at the time of the disposal.

4. The current owner or operator of the site.

Potentially Responsible Party (PRP) A party liable for the costs of cleaning up a hazardous waste disposal site under the Comprehensive Environmental Response, Compensation, and Liability Act.

A person falling within one of these categories is referred to as a **potentially responsible party (PRP)**. If the PRPs do not clean up the site, the EPA can clean up the site and recover the costs from the PRPs.

Strict Liability of PRPs Superfund imposes strict liability on PRPs, and that liability cannot be avoided through transfer of ownership. Thus, selling a site where hazardous wastes were disposed of does not relieve the seller of liability, and the buyer also becomes liable for the clean-up. Liability also extends to businesses that merge with or buy corporations that have violated CERCLA.

Joint and Several Liability Liability under Superfund is usually joint and several—that is, a person who generated *only a fraction of the hazardous waste* disposed of at the site may nevertheless be liable for *all* of the clean-up costs. CERCLA authorizes a party who has incurred clean-up costs to bring a "contribution action" against any other person who is liable or potentially liable for a percentage of the costs.

Minimizing Liability One way for a business to minimize its potential liability under Superfund is to conduct environmental compliance audits of its own operations regularly. That is, the business can investigate its own operations and property to determine whether any environmental hazards exist.

The EPA encourages companies to conduct self-audits and promptly detect, disclose, and correct wrongdoing. Companies that do so are subject to lighter penalties for violations of environmental laws. (Fines may be reduced by as much as 75 percent.)

---

46. 42 U.S.C. Sections 9601–9675.

In addition, under EPA guidelines, the EPA will waive all fines if a small company corrects environmental violations within 180 days after being notified of the violations (or 360 days if pollution-prevention techniques are involved). The policy does not apply to criminal violations of environmental laws, though, or to violations that pose a significant threat to public health, safety, or the environment.

Defenses There are a few defenses to liability under CERCLA. The most important is the *innocent landowner defense*. Under this defense, an innocent property owner may be able to avoid liability by showing that he or she had no contractual or employment relationship with the party who released the hazardous substance onto the land. If the party who disposed of the substances transferred the property *by contract* to the current owner, the defense normally will not be available.

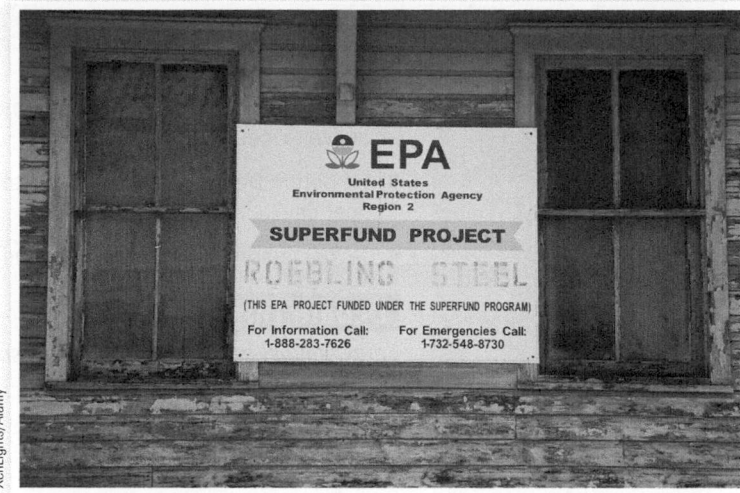

Who is liable for the clean-up of leaking hazardous waste?

The current owner may still be able to assert the defense, however, by showing that at the time the property was acquired, she or he had no reason to know that it had been used for hazardous waste disposal. The owner must show that at the time of the purchase, she or he undertook all appropriate investigation into the previous ownership and uses of the property to determine whether there was reason to be concerned about hazardous substances. In effect, this defense protects only property owners who took precautions and investigated the possibility of environmental hazards at the time they bought the property.

Practice and Review

Residents of Lake Caliopa, Minnesota, began noticing an unusually high number of lung ailments among the local population. Several concerned citizens pooled their resources and commissioned a study to compare the frequency of these health conditions in Lake Caliopa with national averages. The study concluded that residents of Lake Caliopa experienced four to seven times the rate of frequency of asthma, bronchitis, and emphysema as the population nationwide.

During the study period, citizens began expressing concerns about the large volume of smog emitted by the Cotton Design apparel manufacturing plant on the outskirts of town. The plant had a production facility two miles east of town beside the Tawakoni River and employed seventy workers. Just downstream on the Tawakoni River, the city of Lake Caliopa operated a public waterworks facility, which supplied all city residents with water.

After conducting its own investigation, the Minnesota Pollution Control Agency ordered Cotton Design to install new equipment to control air and water pollution. Later, citizens brought a lawsuit in a Minnesota state court against Cotton Design for various respiratory ailments allegedly caused or compounded by smog from Cotton Design's factory. Using the information presented in the chapter, answer the following questions.

1. Under the common law, what would each plaintiff be required to identify in order to be given relief by the court?

(Continues)

2. What standard for limiting emissions into the air does Cotton Design's pollution-control equipment have to meet?

3. If Cotton Design's emissions violated the Clean Air Act, how much can the EPA assess in fines per day?

4. What information must the city send to every household that it supplies with water?

Debate This

Laws against bait-and-switch advertising should be abolished because no consumer is ever forced to buy anything.

Key Terms

bait-and-switch advertising 921	**environmental impact statement**	**potentially responsible party**
cease-and-desist order 923	**(EIS)** 935	**(PRP)** 942
"cooling-off" laws 925	**multiple product order** 923	**Regulation Z** 929
counteradvertising 923	**nuisance** 936	**toxic tort** 937
deceptive advertising 919		

Chapter Summary: Consumer and Environmental Law

CONSUMER LAW

Advertising, Marketing, Sales, and Labeling	1. *Deceptive advertising*—Generally, an advertising claim will be deemed deceptive if it would mislead a reasonable consumer.
	   a. Bait-and-switch advertising—Advertising a lower-priced product (the bait) to lure consumers into the store and then telling them the product is unavailable and urging them to buy a higher-priced product (the switch) is prohibited by the FTC.
	   b. Online deceptive advertising—The FTC has issued guidelines to help online businesses comply with the laws prohibiting deceptive advertising.
	   c. FTC actions against deceptive advertising—(1) A formal complaint is sent to the alleged offender. (2) A cease and-desist order is generally issued, requiring the advertiser to stop the challenged advertising. (3) Counteradvertising may be required, so that the advertiser can correct the earlier misinformation. (4) Restitution may be sought.
	 2. *False advertising claims under the Lanham Act*—A successful claim for false advertising requires that a business establish (a) an injury to a commercial interest in reputation or sales, (b) direct causation of the injury by false or deceptive advertising, and (c) a loss of business from buyers who were deceived by the advertising.
	 3. *Marketing*—Telemarketers are prohibited from using automatic dialing systems and prerecorded voices and cannot fax ads without the recipient's permission. Telemarketers must identify the seller, describe the product being sold, and disclose all material facts related to the sale.
	 4. *Sales*—"Cooling-off" laws permit buyers of goods sold in certain sales transactions (such as trade shows and door-to-door sales) to cancel their contracts within three business days.
	 5. *Labeling*—Manufacturers must comply with the labeling requirements for their specific products. In general, all labels must be accurate and not misleading.

Protection of Health and Safety	1. *Food and drugs*—The federal Food, Drug, and Cosmetic Act protects consumers against adulterated and misbranded foods and drugs. The act establishes food standards, specifies safe levels of potentially hazardous food additives, and provides guidelines for advertising and labeling food products.
	2. *Consumer product safety*—The Consumer Product Safety Act seeks to protect consumers from injury from hazardous products. The Consumer Product Safety Commission has the power, among others, to set safety standards for consumer products, ban the manufacture and sale of products that pose unreasonable risk, and remove products that are deemed imminently hazardous from the market.
Credit Protection	1. *Truth in Lending Act, or TILA*—A disclosure law that requires sellers and lenders to disclose credit terms or loan terms in certain transactions, including retail installment sales and loans, car loans, home-improvement loans, and certain real estate loans. Additionally, the TILA provides for the following:
	a. Equal credit opportunity—Creditors are prohibited from discriminating on the basis of race, religion, marital status, gender, national origin, color, or age.
	b. Credit-card protection—Liability of cardholders for unauthorized charges is limited to $50, providing notice requirements are met. Consumers are not liable for unauthorized charges made on unsolicited credit cards. The act also sets out procedures to be used in settling disputes between credit-card companies and their cardholders.
	2. *Fair Credit Reporting Act*—Entitles consumers to request verification of the accuracy of a credit report and to have unverified or false information removed from their files.
	3. *Fair and Accurate Credit Transactions Act*—Combats identity theft by establishing a national fraud alert system. It requires account numbers to be truncated and credit reporting agencies to provide one free credit report per year to consumers.
	4. *Fair Debt Collection Practices Act*—Prohibits debt collectors from using unfair debt-collection practices, such as contacting the debtor at his or her place of employment if the employer objects or at unreasonable times, contacting third parties about the debt, and harassing the debtor.

ENVIRONMENTAL LAW

Protecting the Environment	1. *Federal regulation*—
	a. The Environmental Protection Agency (EPA) is the primary agency regulating environmental law and administers most federal environmental policies and statutes.
	b. An environmental impact statement (EIS) is required for every major federal action. An EIS must analyze the action's impact on the environment, its adverse effects and possible alternatives, and its irreversible effects on environmental quality.
	2. *Common law actions*—
	a. Nuisance—A common law doctrine under which persons may be held liable if their use of their property unreasonably interferes with others' rights to use their own property.
	b. Negligence and strict liability—Parties may recover damages for injuries sustained as a result of a firm's pollution-causing activities if they can demonstrate that the harm was a foreseeable result of the firm's failure to exercise reasonable care (negligence). Businesses engaging in ultrahazardous activities are liable for whatever injuries the activities cause, regardless of whether the firms exercise reasonable care.
Air and Water Pollution	1. *Air pollution*—Regulated under the authority of the Clean Air Act and its amendments.
	2. *Water pollution*—Regulated under the authority of the Rivers and Harbors Appropriation Act and the Federal Water Pollution Control Act, as amended by the Clean Water Act.
Toxic Chemicals and Hazardous Waste	Pesticides and herbicides, toxic substances, and hazardous waste are regulated under the authority of the Federal Insecticide, Fungicide, and Rodenticide Act; the Toxic Substances Control Act; and the Resource Conservation and Recovery Act, respectively. The Comprehensive Environmental Response, Compensation, and Liability Act (CERCLA), or Superfund, regulates clean-up of hazardous waste disposal sites.

Issue Spotters

1. United Pharmaceuticals, Inc., has developed a new drug that it believes will be effective in the treatment of patients with AIDS. The drug has had only limited testing, but United wants to make the drug widely available as soon as possible. To market the drug, what must United prove to the U.S. Food and Drug Administration? (See *Protection of Health and Safety*.)

2. ChemCorp generates hazardous wastes from its operations. Disposal Trucking Company transports those wastes to Eliminators, Inc., which owns a site for hazardous waste disposal. Eliminators sells the property on which the disposal site is located to Fluid Properties, Inc. If the Environmental Protection Agency cleans up the site, from whom can it recover the cost? (See *Toxic Chemicals and Hazardous Waste*.)

   —**Check your answers to the *Issue Spotters* against the answers provided in Appendix D at the end of this text.**

Business Scenarios and Case Problems

39–1. Environmental Laws. Fruitade, Inc., is a processor of a soft drink called Freshen Up. Fruitade uses returnable glass bottles, which it cleans with a special acid to allow for further beverage processing. The acid is diluted with water and then allowed to pass into a navigable stream. Fruitade crushes its broken bottles and throws the crushed glass into the stream. Discuss fully any environmental laws that Fruitade may have violated. (See *Air and Water Pollution*.)

39–2. Credit Protection. Maria Ochoa receives two new credit cards on May 1. She has solicited one of them from Midtown Department Store, and the other arrives unsolicited from High-Flying Airlines. During the month of May, Ochoa makes numerous credit-card purchases from Midtown Department Store, but she does not use the High-Flying Airlines card. On May 31, a burglar breaks into Ochoa's home and steals both credit cards, along with other items.

Ochoa notifies Midtown Department Store of the theft on June 2, but she fails to notify High-Flying Airlines. Using the Midtown credit card, the burglar makes a $500 purchase on June 1 and a $200 purchase on June 3. The burglar then charges a vacation flight on the High-Flying Airlines card for $1,000 on June 5. Ochoa receives the bills for these charges and refuses to pay them. Discuss Ochoa's liability in these situations. (See *Credit Protection*.)

39–3. Spotlight on McDonald's—Food Labeling. A McDonald's Happy Meal® consists of an entrée, a small order of French fries, a small drink, and a toy. In the early 1990s, McDonald's Corp. began to aim its Happy Meal marketing at children aged one to three. In 1995, McDonald's began making nutritional information for its food products available in documents known as "McDonald's Nutrition Facts." The documents list the food items that the restaurant serves and provide a nutritional breakdown, but the Happy Meal is not included.

Marc Cohen filed a suit in an Illinois state court against McDonald's. Cohen alleged, among other things, that McDonald's had violated a state law prohibiting consumer fraud and deceptive business practices by failing to follow the Nutrition Labeling and Education Act (NLEA). The NLEA generally requires that standard nutrition facts be listed on food labels. The act, however, sets out different, less detailed requirements for products specifically intended for children under the age of four. Does it make sense to have different requirements for children of this age? Why or why not? Should a state court impose regulations when the NLEA has not done so? Explain. [*Cohen v. McDonald's Corp.*, 347 Ill.App.3d 627, 808 N.E.2d 1, 283 Ill.Dec. 451 (1 Dist. 2004)] (See *Advertising, Marketing, Sales, and Labeling*.)

39–4. Environmental Impact Statements. The U.S. Forest Service (USFS) proposed a travel management plan (TMP) for the Beartooth Ranger District in the Pryor and Absaroka Mountains in the Custer National Forest of southern Montana. The TMP would convert unauthorized user-created routes within the wilderness to routes authorized for motor vehicle use. It would also permit off-road "dispersed vehicle camping" within 300 feet of the routes, with some seasonal restrictions. The TMP would ban cross-country motorized travel outside the designated routes. Is an environmental impact statement required before the USFS implements the TMP? If so, what aspects of the environment should the USFS consider in preparing it? Discuss. [*Pryors Coalition v. Weldon,* 551 Fed.Appx. 426 (9th Cir. 2014)] (See *Protecting the Environment*.)

39–5. Business Case Problem with Sample Answer—Deceptive Advertising. Innovative Marketing, Inc. (IMI), sold "scareware"—computer security software. IMI's Internet ads redirected consumers to sites where they were told that a scan of their computers had detected dangerous files—viruses, spyware, and "illegal" pornography. In fact, no scans were conducted. Kristy Ross, an IMI cofounder and vice president, reviewed and edited the ads. She was also aware of the many complaints that consumers had made about them. An individual can be held liable under the Federal Trade Commission Act's prohibition of deceptive acts or practices if the person (1) participated directly in the deceptive practices or had the authority to control them and (2) had or should have had knowledge of them. Were IMI's ads deceptive? If so, can Ross be held liable? Explain. [*Federal Trade Commission v. Ross*, 743 F.3d 886 (4th Cir. 2014)] (See *Advertising, Marketing, Sales, and Labeling*.)

—For a sample answer to Problem 39–5, go to Appendix E at the end of this text.

39–6. The Clean Water Act. ICG Hazard, LLC, operated the Thunder Ridge surface coal mine in Leslie County, Kentucky, under a National Pollutant Discharge Elimination System permit issued by the Kentucky Division of Water (KDOW). As part of the operation, ICG discharges selenium into the surrounding water. Selenium is a naturally occurring element that endangers aquatic life at a certain concentration. KDOW knew when it issued the permit that mines in the area may produce selenium but did not specify discharge limits for the element in ICG's permit. Instead, the agency imposed a one-time monitoring requirement, which ICG met. Does ICG's discharge of selenium violate the Clean Water Act? Explain. [*Sierra Club v. ICG Hazard, LLC*, 781 F.3d 281 (6th Cir. 2015)] (See *Air and Water Pollution*.)

39–7. Debt Collection. Zakia Mashiri owns a home in San Diego, California. She is a member of the Westwood Club Homeowners' Association (HOA), which charges each member an annual fee. When Mashiri failed to pay the fee, the law firm of Epsten Grinnell & Howell sent her a letter demanding payment. The letter read, "Failure to pay your . . . account in full within thirty-five days from the date of this letter will result in a lien . . . against your property." Mashiri asked for validation of the debt. Within two weeks of receiving it, she sent the HOA a check for the fee. Meanwhile, the law firm filed a lien against her property. Mashiri filed a lawsuit in a federal district court against the law firm, alleging a violation of the Fair Debt Collection Practices Act. On what provision of the act did Mashiri likely base her allegation? Will she succeed in her lawsuit against the law firm? Explain your answer. [*Mashiri v. Epsten Grinnell & Howell*, 845 F.3d 984 (9th Cir. 2017)] (See *Credit Protection*.)

39–8. False Advertising. Rainbow School, Inc., has run a child-care facility in Fayetteville, North Carolina, for over twenty years. In addition to using the word "rainbow" in its name, the school uses rainbow imagery on its logo. Rainbow Early Education

Holding, LLC, operates child-care facilities in several states. Early Education opened a branch in Fayetteville near the school under the name "Rainbow Child Care Center" that also used rainbow imagery on its logo. The school filed a suit in a federal district court against Early Education, alleging a violation of the Lanham Act. The parties entered into a settlement agreement that required Early Education to stop using the word "rainbow" in connection with its Fayetteville facility. The court issued an injunction to enforce the agreement. Early Education continued to use the word "rainbow" in domain names, links, and meta tags associated with its Fayetteville facility's website. Rainbow imagery was used in a mailer inviting residents to the "nearest Rainbow Child Care Center." Did Early Education violate the Lanham Act? Explain. [*Rainbow School, Inc. v. Rainbow Early Education Holding LLC*, 887 F.3d 610 (4th Cir. 2018)] (See *Advertising, Marketing, Sales, and Labeling*.)

39–9. A Question of Ethics—The IDDR Approach and Consumer Protection. *In Richland, Washington, Robert Ingersoll planned his wedding to include about a hundred guests, a photographer, a caterer, a wedding cake, and flowers. Ingersoll had been a customer of Arlene's Flowers and Gifts for more than nine years and had spent several thousand dollars at the shop. When he approached Arlene's owner, Baronelle Stutzman, to buy flowers for his wedding, she refused because Ingersoll and his fiancé, Curt Freed, were a same-sex couple. Deeply offended, Ingersoll and Freed dropped their wedding plans and married in a modest ceremony. [Arlene's Flowers, Inc., v. State of Washington, ___ U.S. ___, ___ S.Ct. ___, ___ L.Ed.2d ___, 2018 WL 3096308 (2018)] (See Advertising, Marketing, Sales, and Labeling.)*

1. Federal and state laws attempt to protect consumers from unfair trade practices, including discriminatory requirements, related to consumer transactions. Using the *Review* step of the IDDR approach, consider whether it would be ethically fair to hold Stutzman personally liable for a violation of these laws.

2. Using the *Discussion* step of the IDDR approach, consider actions that Ingersoll and Freed as consumers might take in response to Arlene's—Stutzman's—discriminatory rejection of their offer to do business.

Critical Thinking and Writing Assignments

39–10. Time-Limited Group Assignment—Consumer Protections. Many states have enacted laws that go even further than federal laws to protect consumers against deceptive and false advertising. These laws vary tremendously from state to state. (See *Advertising, Marketing, Sales, and Labeling*.)

1. The first group will decide whether having different laws is fair to sellers, who may be prohibited from engaging in a practice in one state that is legal in another.

2. The second group will consider how these different laws might affect a business.

3. A third group will determine whether it is fair that residents of one state have more protection than residents of another.

40 | Liability of Accountants and Other Professionals

Learning Objectives

The five Learning Objectives *below are designed to help improve your understanding. After reading this chapter, you should be able to answer the following questions:*

1. Under what common law theories may professionals be liable to clients?

2. What are the rules concerning an auditor's liability to third parties?

3. How might an accountant violate the Securities Act?

4. What crimes might an accountant commit under the Internal Revenue Code?

5. What is protected by the attorney-client privilege?

"A member should observe the profession's technical and ethical standards ... and discharge professional responsibility to the best of the member's ability."

Article V,
Code of Professional Conduct
American Institute of
Certified Public Accountants

Professionals, such as accountants, attorneys, physicians, and architects, are increasingly faced with the threat of liability. In part, this is because the public has become more aware that professionals are required to deliver competent services and adhere to certain standards of performance within their professions.

The standard of due care to which the members of the American Institute of Certified Public Accountants are expected to adhere is set out in the chapter-opening quotation. Investors rely heavily on the opinions of certified public accountants when making decisions about whether to invest in a company.

The failure of several major companies and leading public accounting firms in the past twenty years has focused attention on the importance of abiding by professional accounting standards. Numerous corporations—from American International Group (AIG, the world's largest insurance company), to HealthSouth, Goldman Sachs, Lehman Brothers, Tyco International, and India-based Mahindra Satyam—have been accused of engaging in accounting fraud. These companies may have reported fictitious revenues, concealed liabilities or debts, or artificially inflated their assets.

40–1 Potential Liability to Clients

Under the common law, professionals may be liable to clients for breach of contract, negligence, or fraud.

Learning Objective 1

Under what common law theories may professionals be liable to clients?

40–1a Liability for Breach of Contract

Accountants and other professionals face liability under the common law for any breach of contract. A professional owes a duty to his or her client to honor the terms of their contract and to perform the contract within the stated time period. If the professional fails to perform as agreed, then he or she has breached the contract, and the client has the right to pursue recovery of damages.

Possible damages include expenses incurred by the client in securing another professional to provide the contracted-for services and any other reasonable and foreseeable losses that arise from the professional's breach. For instance, if the client had to pay penalties for failing to meet deadlines, the court may order the professional to pay an equivalent amount in damages to the client.

40–1b Liability for Negligence

Accountants and other professionals may also be held liable under the common law for negligence in the performance of their services. Recall that the following elements must be proved to establish negligence:

1. A duty of care existed.
2. That duty of care was breached.
3. The plaintiff suffered an injury.
4. The injury was proximately caused by the defendant's breach of the duty of care.

Negligence cases against professionals often focus on the standard of care exercised by the professional. All professionals are subject to standards of conduct established by codes of professional ethics, by state statutes, and by judicial decisions. They are also governed by the contracts they enter into with their clients.

In performing their contracts, professionals must exercise the established standards of care, knowledge, and judgment generally accepted by members of their professional group. Here, we look at the duty of care owed by two groups of professionals that frequently perform services for business firms: accountants and attorneys.

Accountant's Duty of Care Accountants play a major role in a business's financial system. Accountants establish and maintain financial records, as well as design, control, and audit record-keeping systems. They also prepare statements that reflect an individual's or a business's financial status, give tax advice, and prepare tax returns.

Generally, an accountant must possess the skills that an ordinarily prudent accountant would have and must exercise the degree of care that an ordinarily prudent accountant would exercise. The level of skill expected of accountants and the degree of care that they should exercise in performing their services are reflected in the standards discussed next.

GAAP and GAAS. When performing their services, accountants must comply with **generally accepted accounting principles (GAAP)** and **generally accepted auditing standards (GAAS)**. The Financial Accounting Standards Board (FASB, usually pronounced "faz-bee") determines what accounting conventions, rules, and procedures constitute GAAP at a given point in time. GAAS, established by the American Institute of Certified Public Accountants, set forth the professional qualities and judgment that an auditor should exercise in performing an audit. Normally, if an accountant conforms to generally accepted standards and acts in good faith, he or she will not be held liable to the client for incorrect judgment.

Generally Accepted Accounting Principles (GAAP) The conventions, rules, and procedures developed by the Financial Accounting Standards Board to define accepted accounting practices at a particular time.

Generally Accepted Auditing Standards (GAAS) Standards established by the American Institute of Certified Public Accountants to define the professional qualities and judgment that should be exercised by an auditor in performing an audit.

A violation of GAAP or GAAS is considered *prima facie* evidence of negligence on the part of the accountant. Compliance with GAAP and GAAS, however, does not *necessarily* relieve an accountant from potential legal liability. An accountant may be held to a higher standard of conduct established by state statute or by judicial decisions.

For a discussion of how **International Financial Reporting Standards (IFRS)** are replacing GAAP, see this chapter's *Landmark in the Law* feature.

Discovering Improprieties. An accountant is not required to discover every impropriety, **defalcation**[1] (embezzlement), or fraud in her or his client's books. If, however, the impropriety, defalcation, or fraud has gone undiscovered because of the accountant's negligence or failure to perform an express or implied duty, the accountant will be liable for any resulting

International Financial Reporting Standards (IFRS) A set of global accounting standards that are being phased in by U.S. companies.

Defalcation Embezzlement or misappropriation of funds.

---

1. This term, pronounced deh-fal-*kay*-shun, is derived from the Latin *de* ("off") and *falx* ("sickle"—a tool used for cutting grain or tall grass). As used here, the term refers to the act of an embezzler.

The SEC Adopts Global Accounting Rules

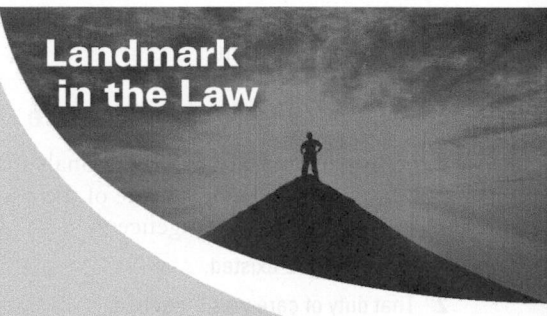

Landmark in the Law

At one time, investors and companies considered U.S. accounting rules, known as generally accepted accounting principles (GAAP), to be the gold standard—the best system for reporting earnings and other financial information. Then came the subprime mortgage meltdown and a global economic crisis, which caused many to question the effectiveness and superiority of GAAP.

In 2008, the Securities and Exchange Commission (SEC) unanimously approved a plan to require U.S. companies to use a set of global accounting rules known as the International Financial Reporting Standards (IFRS). These rules, which are established by the London-based International Accounting Standards Board, are being phased in and will be required for all financial reports filed with the SEC.

Why Shift to Global Accounting Standards? The SEC decided to replace the GAAP with the IFRS for several reasons. GAAP rules are detailed and fill nearly 25,000 pages. The IFRS are simpler and more straightforward, filling only 2,500 pages, and they focus more on general principles than on specific rules. Consequently, companies should eventually find it less difficult to comply with the

international rules, and this should lead to cost savings.

Another benefit is that investors will find it easier to make cross-country comparisons between, say, a technology company in Silicon Valley and one in Germany or Japan. Furthermore, having uniform accounting rules that apply to all nations makes sense in a global economy. The European Union and 113 other nations—including nearly all of the United States' trading partners—already use the IFRS.

The Downside to Adopting Global Rules Despite these benefits, the shift to the global rules has had some drawbacks. Making the change has proved to be both costly and time consuming. Companies have had to upgrade their communications and software systems, study and implement the new rules, and train their employees, accountants, and tax attorneys in the rules' use. Some smaller U.S. firms have found it difficult to absorb the costs of converting to the IFRS.

Another concern is that although IFRS rules are simpler than GAAP rules, they may not be better. Because the global rules are broader and less detailed, they give companies more leeway in

reporting, so less financial information may be disclosed. There are also indications that using the IFRS can lead to wide variances in profit reporting and may tend to boost earnings above what they would have been under GAAP. Finally, the role of the U.S. Financial Accounting Standards Board and the SEC in shaping and overseeing accounting standards will necessarily be reduced because the London-based International Accounting Standards Board sets the IFRS.

Application to Today's World *The shift to the IFRS received broad bipartisan political support even during the economic recession. Nevertheless, it will take years for the United States to completely implement global accounting rules. Business students should study and understand the IFRS so that they are prepared to use these rules in their future careers.*

losses suffered by the client. Therefore, an accountant who uncovers suspicious financial transactions and fails to investigate the matter fully or to inform the client of the discovery can be held liable to the client for the resulting loss.

Audits. One of the most important tasks that an accountant may perform for a business is an audit. An *audit* is a systematic inspection, by analyses and tests, of a business's financial records. An accountant qualified to perform audits is often called an **auditor.** After performing an audit, the auditor issues an opinion letter stating whether, in his or her opinion, the financial statements fairly present the business's financial position.

The purpose of an audit is to provide the auditor with evidence to support an opinion on the reliability of the business's financial statements. A normal audit is not intended to uncover fraud or other misconduct. Nevertheless, an accountant may be liable for failing to detect misconduct if a normal audit would have revealed it. Also, if the auditor agreed to examine the records for evidence of fraud or other obvious misconduct and then failed to detect it, he or she may be liable.

Qualified Opinions and Disclaimers. In issuing an opinion letter, an auditor may *qualify* the opinion or include a *disclaimer.* In a disclaimer, the auditor basically states that she or he does not have sufficient information to issue an opinion. A qualified opinion or a disclaimer must be specific and must identify the reason for the qualification or disclaimer.

Example 40.1 Richard Zehr performs an audit of Lacey Corporation. In the opinion letter, Zehr qualifies his opinion by stating that there is uncertainty about how a lawsuit against the firm will be resolved. In this situation, Zehr will not be liable if the outcome of the suit is unfavorable for the firm. Zehr could still be liable, however, for failing to discover other problems that an audit in compliance with IFRS or GAAS rules would have revealed. ■

Unaudited Financial Statements. Sometimes, accountants are called on to prepare unaudited financial statements. (A financial statement is considered unaudited if incomplete auditing procedures have been used in its preparation or if insufficient procedures have been used to justify an opinion.) Lesser standards of care are typically required in this situation.

Nevertheless, accountants may be liable for omissions from unaudited statements. Accountants may be subject to liability for failing, in accordance with standard accounting procedures, to designate a balance sheet as "unaudited." An accountant will also be held liable for failure to disclose to a client any facts or circumstances that give reason to believe that misstatements have been made or that a fraud has been committed.

Defenses to Negligence. If an accountant is found guilty of negligence, the client can collect damages for losses that arose from the accountant's negligence. An accountant facing a claim of negligence, however, has several possible defenses, including the following:

1. The accountant was not negligent.

2. If the accountant was negligent, this negligence was not the proximate cause of the client's losses.

3. The client was also negligent (depending on whether state law allows contributory negligence as a defense).

Example 40.2 Coopers & Peterson, LLP, provides accounting services for Bandon Steel Mills, Inc. (BSM). Coopers advises BSM to report a certain transaction as a $12.3 million gain on its financial statements. Later, BSM plans to make a public offering of its stock. The SEC reviews its financial statements and determines that the accounting treatment of the transaction has to be corrected before the sale.

Because of the delay, the public offering does not occur on May 2, when BSM's stock is selling for $16 per share. Instead, it takes place on June 13, when, due to unrelated factors, the price has fallen to $13.50. If BSM files a lawsuit against Coopers, claiming that the negligent accounting resulted in the stock's being sold at a lower price, BSM is unlikely to prevail. Although the accounting firm's negligence may have delayed the stock offering,

Auditor An accountant qualified to perform audits (systematic inspections) of a business's financial records.

"Never call an accountant a credit to his profession; a good accountant is a debit to his profession."

Attributed to Charles Lyell
1797–1875
(British lawyer)

the negligence was not the proximate cause of the decline in the stock price. Thus, Coopers would not be liable for damages based on the price decline.

Attorney's Duty of Care The conduct of attorneys is governed by rules established by each state and by the American Bar Association's Model Rules of Professional Conduct. All attorneys owe a duty to provide competent and diligent representation.

Attorneys are required to be familiar with well-settled principles of law applicable to a case and to find relevant law that can be discovered through a reasonable amount of research. They must also investigate and discover facts that could materially affect clients' legal rights.

Normally, an attorney's performance is expected to be that of a reasonably competent general practitioner of ordinary skill, experience, and capacity. An attorney who holds himself or herself out as having expertise in a particular area of law (such as intellectual property) is held to a higher standard of care in that area of the law than attorneys without such expertise.

Assume that the accounting firm for this steel manufacturer makes an error in a financial statement. If the initial public offering is delayed and the stock price falls in the meantime, is the accounting firm liable for the lower price?

braney/iStock/Getty Images

Ethical Issue

What are an attorney's responsibilities with respect to protecting data stored on the cloud? To achieve both cost savings and better security, more and more attorneys are storing their data, including confidential client information, on the cloud. Sometimes, professionals assume that once their data have migrated to the cloud, they no longer have to be concerned with keeping the information secure. But cloud computing is simply the virtualization of the computing process. In other words, the professional is still ultimately responsible for the information.

Attorneys' obligations for their clients' information are spelled out in the American Bar Association's Model Rules of Professional Conduct, which serve as the basis for the ethics rules for attorneys adopted by most states. Comment 17 to Model Rule 1.6 states, "The lawyer must take reasonable precautions to prevent the [client's] information from coming into the hands of unintended recipients." Thus, lawyers have an ethical duty to safeguard confidential client information, whether it is stored as documents in a filing cabinet or as electromagnetic impulses on a server that might be located anywhere. (Note that Rule 1.6 does not require an attorney to *guarantee* that a breach of confidentiality will never occur.)

Certainly, it is harder to maintain control over information stored on the cloud. Although the attorney "owns" the data, he or she probably does not even know the location of the computer where the information is stored. Furthermore, a provider of cloud computing services may move data from one server to another. Nevertheless, attorneys should be aware of jurisdictional issues and make sure that their cloud computing service provider is complying with data protection regulations and privacy notification requirements wherever the provider's servers are located.

Misconduct. Typically, a state's rules of professional conduct for attorneys provide that committing a criminal act that reflects adversely on the person's "honesty or trustworthiness, or fitness as a lawyer in other respects" is professional misconduct. The rules often further provide that a lawyer should not engage in conduct involving "dishonesty, fraud, deceit, or misrepresentation." Under these rules, state authorities can discipline attorneys for many types of misconduct.

Case Example 40.3 Daniel Johns, a Wisconsin attorney, was the driver in a one-vehicle drunk driving accident in which his brother was killed. He pleaded guilty to homicide by use of a vehicle while driving with a blood alcohol level over the legal limit. Johns served 120 days in jail and was released on five years' probation. The court terminated his probation early because of his good behavior, and he went back to practicing law.

The state's office of lawyer regulation (OLR) then initiated disciplinary proceedings seeking to suspend Johns's license to practice for sixty days for professional misconduct. The court, however, explained that the "commission of a criminal act by a Wisconsin licensed lawyer does not, *per se,* constitute professional misconduct." The OLR had not proved that Johns's crime reflected adversely on his honesty, trustworthiness, or fitness as a lawyer in other respects. In fact, except for this one tragic event, Johns had led an exemplary life without a hint of professional misconduct. The court therefore dismissed the disciplinary complaint.[2]

Liability for Malpractice. When an attorney fails to exercise reasonable care and professional judgment, she or he breaches the duty of care and can be held liable for **malpractice** (professional negligence). In malpractice cases—as in all cases involving allegations of negligence—the plaintiff must prove that the attorney's breach of the duty of care actually caused the plaintiff to suffer some injury.

Case Example 40.4 The law firm of Husch Blackwell Sanders, LLP, represented Brian Nail in a dispute with his former employer over stock options. When Nail left the company, he acquired options to purchase his former employer's stock within eighteen months. But then the former employer merged with another company, and the stock was "locked up" for twelve months after the merger. The value of the stock declined significantly during this period. Husch Blackwell eventually negotiated a settlement that extended Nail's option period. When Nail attempted to exercise his options under the settlement agreement, however, complications arose that prevented him from immediately obtaining the stock.

Nail sued Husch Blackwell in a Missouri state court for malpractice, alleging that the firm had negligently drafted the settlement agreement and negligently delayed advising him to exercise the options. Nail sought to recover damages equal to the difference between the highest value of the stock during the lock-up period and his cost to acquire the stock. The trial court granted a summary judgment in favor of the law firm, and the Missouri Supreme Court affirmed. Nail had failed to prove that Husch Blackwell's alleged negligence was the proximate cause of his damages. The decline in the stock price was unrelated to the law firm's alleged misconduct.[3]

40–1c Liability for Fraud

Recall that fraud, or fraudulent misrepresentation, involves the following elements:

1. A misrepresentation of a material fact.
2. An intent to deceive.
3. Justifiable reliance by the innocent party on the misrepresentation.

In addition, to obtain damages, the innocent party must have been injured. Both actual and constructive fraud are potential sources of legal liability for an accountant or other professional.

Actual Fraud A professional may be held liable for *actual fraud* when (1) he or she intentionally misstates a material fact to mislead a client, and (2) the client is injured as a result of justifiably relying on the misstated fact. A material fact is one that a reasonable person would consider important in deciding whether to act.

Malpractice Professional negligence, or failure to exercise reasonable care and professional judgment, that results in injury, loss, or damage to those relying on the professional.

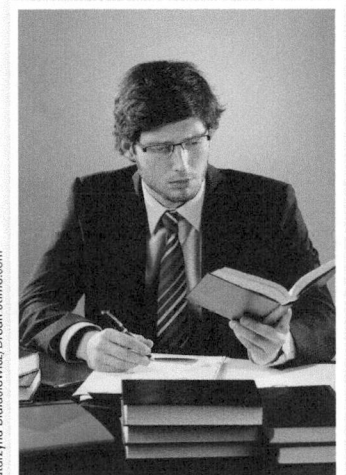

What must a plaintiff prove when when claiming that an attorney has committed malpractice?

2. *In re Disciplinary Proceedings against Johns,* 2014 WI 32, 353 Wis.2d 746, 847 N.W.2d 179 (2014).
3. *Nail v. Husch Blackwell Sanders, LLP,* 436 S.W.3d 556 (Mo. 2014).

Among other penalties, an accountant guilty of fraudulent conduct may suffer penalties imposed by a state board of accountancy. **Case Example 40.5** Michael Walsh, a certified public accountant (CPA), impersonated his brother-in-law, Stephen Teiper, on the phone to obtain financial information from Teiper's insurance company. Teiper wrote a letter reporting Walsh's conduct to the Nebraska Board of Public Accountancy. After a hearing, the board reprimanded Walsh, placed him on probation for three months, and ordered him to attend four hours of ethics training. He also had to pay the costs of the hearing. The Nebraska Supreme Court affirmed the board's decision on appeal.[4]

Constructive Fraud Conduct that is treated as fraud under the law even when there is no proof of intent to defraud, usually because of the existence of a special relationship or fiduciary duty.

Constructive Fraud

A professional may sometimes be held liable for **constructive fraud** whether or not he or she acted with fraudulent intent. Liability arises because the professional has a duty to the client and violates that duty by making a material misrepresentation. The client must be injured as a result of justifiably relying on the professional's misstatements to obtain damages.

Constructive fraud may be found when an accountant is grossly negligent in performing his or her duties. **Example 40.6** Paula, an accountant, is conducting an audit of ComCo, Inc. Paula accepts the explanations of Ron, a ComCo officer, regarding certain financial irregularities, despite evidence that contradicts those explanations and indicates that the irregularities may be illegal. Paula's conduct could be characterized as an intentional failure to perform a duty in reckless disregard of the consequences of such failure. This would constitute gross negligence and could be held to be constructive fraud. ■

40–2 Potential Liability to Third Parties

Traditionally, an accountant or other professional owed a duty only to those with whom she or he had a direct contractual relationship—that is, those with whom she or he was in *privity of contract*. A professional's duty was solely to her or his client. Violations of statutes, fraud, and other intentional or reckless acts of wrongdoing were the only exceptions to this general rule.

Today, numerous third parties—including investors, shareholders, creditors, corporate managers and directors, and regulatory agencies—rely on the opinions of auditors when making decisions. In view of this extensive reliance, many courts have all but abandoned the privity requirement in regard to accountants' liability to third parties.

In this section, we focus primarily on the potential liability of auditors to third parties. The majority of courts now hold that auditors can be held liable to third parties for negligence, but the standard for the imposition of this liability varies.

40–2a The *Ultramares* Rule

Learning Objective 2

What are the rules concerning an auditor's liability to third parties?

The traditional rule regarding an accountant's liability to third parties is based on privity of contract and was enunciated by Chief Judge Benjamin Cardozo (of the New York Court of Appeals) in 1931. **Classic Case Example 40.7** Fred Stern & Company hired the public accounting firm of Touche, Niven & Company to review Stern's financial records and prepare a balance sheet for the year ending December 31, 1923.[5] Touche prepared the balance sheet and supplied Stern with thirty-two certified copies. According to the certified balance sheet, Stern had a net worth (assets less liabilities) of $1,070,715.26.

---

4. *Walsh v. State of Nebraska*, 276 Neb. 1034, 759 N.W.2d 100 (2009).

5. Banks, creditors, stockholders, purchasers, and sellers often rely on a balance sheet as a basis for making decisions relating to a company's business.

In reality, however, Stern's liabilities exceeded its assets. The company's records had been falsified by insiders at Stern so that assets exceeded liabilities, resulting in a positive net worth. In reliance on the certified balance sheets, Ultramares Corporation loaned substantial amounts to Stern. After Stern was declared bankrupt, Ultramares brought an action against Touche for negligence in an attempt to recover damages.

The New York Court of Appeals (that state's highest court) refused to impose liability on Touche. The court concluded that Touche's accountants owed a duty of care only to those persons for whose "primary benefit" the statements were intended. In this case, the statements were intended only for the primary benefit of Stern. The court held that in the absence of privity or a relationship "so close as to approach that of privity," a party could not recover from an accountant.[6]

To what extent is an accounting firm liable for incorrect balance-sheet information that is distributed to the public?

The Requirement of Privity The requirement of privity has since been referred to as the *Ultramares* rule, or the New York rule. It continues to be used in some states. **Case Example 40.8** Toro Company supplied equipment and credit to Summit Power Equipment Distributors and required Summit to submit audited reports indicating its financial condition. Accountants at Krouse, Kern & Company prepared the reports, which allegedly contained mistakes and omissions regarding Summit's financial condition.

Toro extended large amounts of credit to Summit in reliance on the audited reports. When Summit was unable to repay the loans, Toro brought a negligence action against the accounting firm and proved that accountants at Krouse knew the reports would be used by Summit to induce Toro to extend credit. Nevertheless, under the *Ultramares* rule, the court refused to hold the accounting firm liable because the firm was not in privity with Toro.[7]

"Near Privity" Modification The *Ultramares* rule was modified somewhat in a 1985 New York case, *Credit Alliance Corp. v. Arthur Andersen & Co.*[8] In that case, the court held that if a third party has a sufficiently close relationship or *nexus* (link or connection) with an accountant, then the *Ultramares* privity requirement may be satisfied without the establishment of an accountant-client relationship. The rule enunciated in the *Credit Alliance* case is often referred to as the "near privity" rule. Only a minority of states has adopted this rule.

40–2b The *Restatement* Rule

The *Ultramares* rule has been severely criticized. Because much of the work performed by auditors is intended for use by persons who are not parties to the contract, many argue that auditors should owe a duty to these third parties. As support for this position has grown, there has been an erosion of the *Ultramares* rule to expose accountants to liability to third parties in some situations.

The majority of courts have adopted the position taken by the *Restatement (Third) of Torts,* which states that accountants are subject to liability for negligence not only to their clients but also to foreseen or *known* users—or classes of users—of their reports or financial statements. Under the *Restatement (Third) of Torts,* an accountant's liability extends to the following:

1. Persons for whose benefit and guidance the accountant "intends to supply the information or knows that the recipient intends to supply it."

2. Persons whom the accountant "intends the information to influence or knows that the recipient so intends."

---

6. *Ultramares Corp. v. Touche,* 255 N.Y. 170, 174 N.E. 441 (1931).

7. *Toro Co. v. Krouse, Kern & Co.,* 827 F.2d 155 (7th Cir. 1987).

8. 66 N.Y.2d 812, 489 N.E.2d 249, 498 N.Y.S.2d 362 (1985).

Example 40.9 Steve, an accountant, prepares a financial statement for Tech Software, Inc., a client, knowing that Tech Software will submit the statement when it applies for a loan from First National Bank. If Steve makes negligent misstatements or omissions in the statement, he may be held liable to the bank because he knew that the bank would rely on his work product when deciding whether to make the loan. ▮

40–2c The "Reasonably Foreseeable Users" Rule

A small minority of courts hold accountants liable to any users whose reliance on an accountant's statements or reports was *reasonably foreseeable*. This standard has been criticized as extending liability too far and exposing accountants to massive liability.

The majority of courts have concluded that the *Restatement*'s approach is more reasonable because it allows accountants to control their exposure to liability. Liability is "fixed by the accountants' particular knowledge at the moment the audit is published," not by the foreseeability of the harm that might occur to a third party after the report is released. Exhibit 40–1 summarizes the three different views of accountants' liability to third parties.

40–2d Liability of Attorneys to Third Parties

Like accountants, attorneys may be held liable under the common law to third parties who rely on legal opinions to their detriment. Generally, an attorney is not liable to a nonclient unless there is fraud (or malicious conduct) by the attorney. The liability principles stated in the *Restatement (Third) of Torts*, however, may apply to attorneys as well as to accountants.

40–3 Liability of Accountants under Other Federal Laws

Accountants also face potential liability under other federal statutes, several of which merit special discussion. These include the Sarbanes-Oxley Act, the Securities Act of 1933, the 1934 Securities Exchange Act, and the Private Securities Litigation Reform Act.

40–3a The Sarbanes-Oxley Act

The Sarbanes-Oxley Act imposes a number of strict requirements on both domestic and foreign public accounting firms. These requirements apply to firms that provide auditing services to companies ("issuers") whose securities are sold to public investors. The act

Exhibit 40–1 Three Basic Rules of Accountant's Liability to Third Parties

RULE	DESCRIPTION	APPLICATION
Ultramares rule	Liability is imposed only if the accountant is in privity, or near privity, with the third party.	A minority of courts apply this rule.
Restatement rule	Liability is imposed only if the third party's reliance is foreseen, or known, or if the third party is among a class of foreseen, or known, users.	The majority of courts have adopted this rule.
"Reasonably foreseeable users" rule	Liability is imposed if the third party's use was reasonably foreseeable.	A small minority of courts use this rule.

defines an *issuer* as a company that (1) has securities that are registered under Section 12 of the Securities Exchange Act of 1934, (2) is required to file reports under Section 15(d) of the 1934 act, or (3) files—or has filed—a registration statement that has not yet become effective under the Securities Act of 1933.

The Public Company Accounting Oversight Board The Sarbanes-Oxley Act increased government oversight of public accounting practices by creating the Public Company Accounting Oversight Board, which reports to the Securities and Exchange Commission. The board oversees the audit of public companies that are subject to securities laws. The goal is to protect public investors and to ensure that public accounting firms comply with the provisions of the act. The act defines *public accounting firms* as firms "engaged in the practice of public accounting or preparing or issuing audit reports." The key provisions relating to the duties of the oversight board and the requirements relating to public accounting firms are summarized in Exhibit 40–2.

As part of an audit, the board may compel persons to testify in an investigative interview. Under the board's rules, any person compelled to testify "may be accompanied, represented and advised by counsel." The board can limit attendance at the interview to the person being examined, his or her counsel, and other persons that the board determines are "appropriate."

Deloitte & Touche audits public companies. What law requires oversight of its procedures?

Exhibit 40–2 Key Provisions of the Sarbanes-Oxley Act Relating to Public Accounting Firms

AUDITOR INDEPENDENCE
To help ensure that auditors remain independent of the firms that they audit, Title II of the Sarbanes-Oxley Act does the following:
1. Makes it unlawful for Registered Public Accounting Firms (RPAFs) to perform both audit and nonaudit services for the same company at the same time. Nonaudit services include the following: • Bookkeeping or other services related to the accounting records or financial statements of the audit client. • Financial information systems design and implementation. • Appraisal or valuation services. • Fairness opinions. • Management functions. • Broker or dealer, investment adviser, or investment banking services.
2. Requires preapproval for most auditing services from the issuer's (the corporation's) audit committee.
3. Requires audit partner rotation by prohibiting RPAFs from providing audit services to an issuer if either the lead audit partner or the audit partner responsible for reviewing the audit has provided such services to that corporation in each of the prior five years.
4. Requires RPAFs to make timely reports to the audit committees of the corporations. The report must indicate all critical accounting policies and practices to be used; all alternative treatments of financial information within generally accepted accounting principles that have been discussed with the corporation's management officials, the ramifications of the use of such alternative treatments, and the treatment preferred by the auditor; and other material written communications between the auditor and the corporation's management.
5. Makes it unlawful for an RPAF to provide auditing services to an issuer if the corporation's chief executive officer, chief financial officer, chief accounting officer, or controller was previously employed by the auditor and participated in any capacity in the audit of the corporation during the one-year period preceding the date that the audit began.
DOCUMENT INTEGRITY AND RETENTION
1. The act provides that anyone who destroys, alters, or falsifies records with the intent to obstruct or influence a federal investigation or in relation to bankruptcy proceedings can be criminally prosecuted and sentenced to a fine, imprisonment for up to twenty years, or both.
2. The act requires accountants who audit or review publicly traded companies to retain all working papers related to the audit or review for a period of five years (amended to seven years). Violators can be sentenced to a fine, imprisonment for up to ten years, or both.

Whether the board infringed a witness's right to counsel under these rules was at issue in the following case.

Case 40.1

Laccetti v. Securities and Exchange Commission

United States Court of Appeals, District of Columbia Circuit, 885 F.3d 724 (2018).

Background and Facts The Public Company Accounting Oversight Board investigated an audit by the Ernst & Young accounting firm. The investigation focused on Mark Laccetti, who was the Ernst & Young partner in charge of the audit. As part of the investigation, the board interviewed Laccetti. During the interview, the board allowed him to be accompanied by an Ernst & Young attorney. But the board denied his request to also be accompanied by an accounting expert who would assist his counsel. Ultimately, the board found that Laccetti had violated the board's rules and auditing standards. The board suspended him from the accounting profession for two years and fined him $85,000. The Securities and Exchange Commission (SEC) upheld the sanctions. Laccetti appealed.

In the Words of the Court
KAVANAUGH, Circuit Judge:
* * * *

* * * The Board stated that it denied Laccetti's request because Laccetti's expert was employed at Ernst & Young. The Board did not want Ernst & Young personnel present for the testimony of the Ernst & Young witnesses because it apparently did not want Ernst & Young personnel to monitor the investigation.

The Board's rationale suffers from three independent flaws.

First, *the arbitrary and capricious standard requires that an agency's action be reasonable and reasonably explained.* Here, the Board's explanation for denying Laccetti's request was not reasonable. [Emphasis added.]

* * * Given the presence of the Ernst & Young attorney at the interview, the Board's rationale for excluding the Ernst & Young accounting expert * * * makes no sense here.
* * * *

Second, even if the Board wanted to bar an Ernst & Young-affiliated accounting expert, that explanation would not justify the Board's denying Laccetti *any* accounting expert. * * * The Board could have told Laccetti that he could bring to the interview an accounting expert who was not affiliated with Ernst & Young. The Board did not do so.
* * * *

Third, even putting those points aside, the Board's rules establish that the Board could not bar Laccetti from using an * * * expert to assist his counsel in these circumstances.

* * * Given the extraordinary complexity of matters raised in agency investigations * * *, counsel trained only in the law, no matter how skillful, may on occasion be less than fully equipped to serve the client in agency proceedings. Unless the lawyer can receive substantive guidance from an expert technician—in this case, an accountant—when he determines in his professional judgment that such assistance is essential, his client's absolute right to counsel during the proceedings would become substantially qualified. *In this context, an expert is an extension of counsel.* [Emphasis added.]
* * * *

Under the Board's rules, the Board therefore may not bar a witness from bringing an * * * expert who could assist the witness's counsel during an investigative interview. * * * The Board itself has long directed its staff to permit a technical consultant to be present during investigative testimony. * * * The problem is that the Board did not follow its rules in this particular case.

Decision and Remedy The U.S. Court of Appeals for the District of Columbia Circuit vacated the orders and sanctions against Laccetti, and remanded the case. "The Board acted unlawfully when it barred Laccetti from bringing an accounting expert to assist his [legal] counsel at the investigative interview."

Critical Thinking

• **Legal Environment** *If the board were to open a new disciplinary proceeding against Laccetti and re-interview him, what would it have to do to comply with the court's decision?*

• **What If the Facts Were Different?** *Suppose that the board's rules guaranteed a witness's right to counsel but expressly excluded "technical consultants and experts" during an investigative interview. Would the result have been different? Explain.*

Requirements for Maintaining Working Papers Performing an audit for a client involves an accumulation of **working papers**—the documents used and developed during the audit. These include notes, computations, memoranda, copies, and other papers that make up the work product of an accountant's services to a client.

Under the common law, which in this instance has been codified in a number of states, working papers remain the accountant's property. It is important for accountants to retain such records in the event that they need to defend against lawsuits for negligence or other actions in which their competence is challenged. The client also has a right to access an accountant's working papers because they reflect the client's financial situation. On a client's request, an accountant must return to the client any of the client's records or journals, and failure to do so may result in liability.

Section 802(a)(1) of the Sarbanes-Oxley Act required accountants to maintain working papers relating to an audit or review for five years from the end of the fiscal period in which the audit or review was concluded. The requirement was subsequently extended to seven years. A knowing violation of this requirement will subject the accountant to a fine, imprisonment for up to ten years, or both.

Working Papers The documents used and developed by an accountant during an audit, such as notes, computations, and memoranda.

40–3b The Securities Act of 1933

The Securities Act requires issuers to file registration statements with the Securities and Exchange Commission (SEC) prior to an offering of securities.[9] Accountants frequently prepare and certify the financial statements that are included in the issuer's registration statement.

Liability under Section 11 Section 11 of the 1933 Securities Act imposes civil liability on accountants for misstatements and omissions of material facts in registration statements. Accountants may be liable if a financial statement they prepared for inclusion "contained an untrue statement of a material fact or omitted to state a material fact required to be stated therein or necessary to make the statements therein not misleading."[10]

An accountant's liability for a misstatement or omission of a material fact in a registration statement extends to anyone who acquires a security covered by the registration statement. A purchaser of a security need only demonstrate that she or he has suffered a loss on the security. Proof of reliance on the materially false statement or misleading omission ordinarily is not required. Nor is there a requirement of privity between the accountant and the security purchaser.

The Due Diligence Standard. Section 11 imposes a duty on accountants to use **due diligence** in preparing the financial statements included in registration statements. Thus, after a purchaser has proved a loss on a security, the accountant has the burden of showing that he or she exercised due diligence in preparing the financial statements.

To prove due diligence, an accountant must demonstrate that she or he followed generally accepted standards and did not commit negligence or fraud. Specifically, to avoid liability, the accountant must show that he or she did the following:

1. Conducted a reasonable investigation.

2. Had reasonable grounds to believe and did believe, at the time the registration statement became effective, that the statements therein were true and that there was no omission of a material fact that would be misleading.[11]

"Destroy the old files, but make copies first."

Samuel Goldwyn
1879–1974
(American motion picture producer)

Learning Objective 3
How might an accountant violate the Securities Act?

Due Diligence A required standard of care that certain professionals, such as accountants, must meet to avoid liability for securities violations.

---

9. Many securities and transactions are expressly exempted from the 1933 Securities Act.
10. 15 U.S.C. Section 77k(a).
11. 15 U.S.C. Section 77k(b)(3).

In particular, the due diligence standard places a burden on accountants to verify information furnished by a corporation's officers and directors. Merely asking questions is not always sufficient to satisfy the requirement. Accountants may be held liable for failing to detect danger signals in documents furnished by corporate officers that required further investigation.

Other Defenses to Liability. Besides proving that he or she has acted with due diligence, an accountant can raise the following defenses to Section 11 liability:

1. There were no misstatements or omissions.
2. The misstatements or omissions were not of material facts.
3. The misstatements or omissions had no causal connection to the plaintiff's loss.
4. The plaintiff-purchaser invested in the securities knowing of the misstatements or omissions.

Liability under Section 12(2)

Section 12(2) of the 1933 Securities Act imposes civil liability for fraud in relation to offerings or sales of securities.[12] Liability arises when an oral statement to an investor or a written prospectus[13] includes an untrue statement or omits a material fact. Some courts have applied Section 12(2) to accountants who aided and abetted (assisted) the seller or the offeror of the securities in violating Section 12(2).

Those who purchase securities and suffer harm as a result of a false or omitted statement, or some other violation, may bring a suit in a federal court to recover their losses and other damages. The U.S. Department of Justice brings criminal actions against those who commit willful violations. The penalties include fines of up to $10,000, imprisonment for up to five years, or both. The SEC is authorized to seek an injunction against a willful violator to prevent further violations. The SEC can also ask a court to grant other relief, such as an order to a violator to refund profits derived from an illegal transaction.

Which federal agency can bring criminal actions against professionals who commit willful violations under Section 12(2) of the Securities Act of 1933?

Hero Images/Getty Images

40–3c The Securities Exchange Act of 1934

Under Sections 18 and 10(b) of the Securities Exchange Act and SEC Rule 10b-5, an accountant may be found liable for fraud. A plaintiff has a substantially heavier burden of proof under the 1934 act than under the 1933 act because an accountant does not have to prove due diligence to escape liability under the 1934 act.

Liability under Section 18

Section 18 of the 1934 act imposes civil liability on an accountant who makes or causes to be made in any application, report, or document a statement that at the time and in light of the circumstances was false or misleading with respect to any material fact.[14]

Section 18 liability is narrow in that it applies only to applications, reports, documents, and registration statements filed with the SEC. This remedy is further limited in that it applies only to sellers and purchasers. Under Section 18, a seller or purchaser must prove one of the following:

1. That the false or misleading statement affected the price of the security.
2. That the purchaser or seller relied on the false or misleading statement in making the purchase or sale and was not aware of the inaccuracy of the statement.

---

12. 15 U.S.C. Section 77l.
13. A *prospectus* contains financial disclosures about the corporation for the benefit of potential investors.
14. 15 U.S.C. Section 78r(a).

Good Faith Defense. An accountant will not be liable for violating Section 18 if he or she acted in good faith in preparing the financial statement. To demonstrate good faith, an accountant must show that he or she had no knowledge that the financial statement was false and misleading. In addition, the accountant must have had no intent to deceive, manipulate, defraud, or seek unfair advantage over another party.

Note that "mere" negligence in preparing a financial statement does not lead to liability under the 1934 act. This differs from the 1933 act, under which an accountant is liable for *all* negligent acts.

Other Defenses. In addition to the good faith defense, accountants can escape liability by proving that the buyer or seller of the security in question knew that the financial statement was false and misleading. Also, the statute of limitations may be asserted as a defense to liability under the 1934 act.

Liability under Section 10(b) and Rule 10b-5

Accountants additionally face potential legal liability under the antifraud provisions contained in the Securities Exchange Act and SEC Rule 10b-5. The scope of these antifraud provisions is very broad and allows private parties to bring civil actions against violators.

Prohibited Conduct. Section 10(b) makes it unlawful for any person, including accountants, to use, in connection with the purchase or sale of any security, any manipulative or deceptive device or contrivance in contravention of SEC rules and regulations.[15] Rule 10b-5 further makes it unlawful for any person, by use of any means or instrumentality of interstate commerce, to do the following:

1. Employ any device, scheme, or artifice (pretense) to defraud.

2. Make any untrue statement of a material fact or omit a material fact necessary to ensure that the statements made were not misleading, in light of the circumstances.

3. Engage in any act, practice, or course of business that operates or would operate as a fraud or deceit on any person, in connection with the purchase or sale of any security.[16]

Extent of Liability. Accountants may be held liable only to sellers or purchasers of securities under Section 10(b) and Rule 10b-5. Privity is not necessary for a recovery.

An accountant may be found liable not only for fraudulent misstatements of material facts in written material filed with the SEC, but also for any fraudulent oral statements or omissions made in connection with the purchase or sale of any security. In some situations, accountants may also have the duty to correct misstatements that they discover in previous financial statements. For a plaintiff to succeed in recovering damages under these antifraud provisions, he or she must prove intent (*scienter*) to commit the fraudulent or deceptive act. Ordinary negligence is not enough.

40–3d The Private Securities Litigation Reform Act

The Private Securities Litigation Reform Act made some changes to the potential liability of accountants and other professionals in securities fraud cases. Among other things, the act imposed a statutory obligation on accountants. An auditor must use adequate procedures in an audit to detect any illegal acts of the company being audited. If something illegal is detected, the auditor must disclose it to the company's board of directors, the audit committee, or the SEC, depending on the circumstances.[17]

---

15. 15 U.S.C. Section 78j(b)
16. 17 C.F.R. Section 240.10b-5.
17. 15 U.S.C. Section 78j-1.

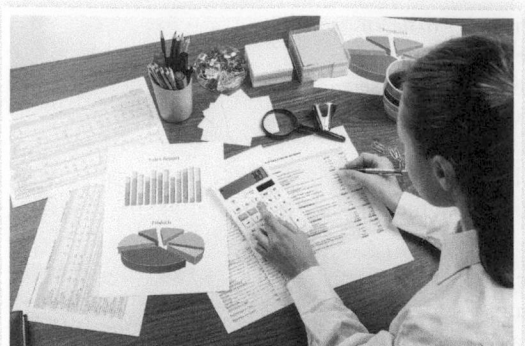

If an accountant is unaware of a company officer's fraud, will she still be held fully liable for any losses caused by the misstatements?

Proportionate Liability The act provides that, in most situations, a party is liable only for the proportion of damages for which he or she is responsible.[18] An accountant who participates in, but is unaware of, illegal conduct may not be liable for the entire loss caused by the illegality.

Example 40.10 Nina, an accountant, helps the president and owner of Midstate Trucking company draft financial statements. The statements misrepresent Midstate's financial condition, but Nina is not aware of the fraud. Nina might be held liable, but the amount of her liability could be proportionately less than the entire loss. ▪

Aiding and Abetting The act also made it a separate crime to aid and abet a violation of the Securities Exchange Act. Aiding and abetting might include knowingly participating in such an act, assisting in it, or keeping quiet about it. If an accountant knowingly aids and abets a primary violator, the SEC can seek an injunction or monetary damages.

Example 40.11 Smith & Jones, an accounting firm, performs an audit for ABC Sales Company that is so inadequate as to constitute gross negligence. ABC uses the materials provided by Smith & Jones as part of a scheme to defraud investors. When the scheme is uncovered, the SEC can bring an action against Smith & Jones for aiding and abetting on the ground that the firm knew or should have known of the material misrepresentations that were in its audit and on which investors were likely to rely. ▪

40–4 Potential Criminal Liability

An accountant may be found criminally liable for violations of securities laws and tax laws. In addition, most states make it a crime to (1) knowingly certify false reports, (2) falsify, alter, or destroy books of account, and (3) obtain property or credit through the use of false financial statements.

40–4a Criminal Violations of Securities Laws

Accountants may be subject to criminal penalties for *willful* violations of the 1933 Securities Act and the 1934 Securities Exchange Act. If convicted, they face imprisonment for up to five years and/or a fine of up to $10,000 under the 1933 act, and imprisonment for up to ten years and a fine of $100,000 under the 1934 act.

Under the Sarbanes-Oxley Act, if an accountant's false or misleading certified audit statement is used in a securities filing, the accountant may be held criminally liable. The accountant may be fined up to $5 million, imprisoned for up to twenty years, or both.

40–4b Criminal Violations of Tax Laws

Learning Objective 4

What crimes might an accountant commit under the Internal Revenue Code?

The Internal Revenue Code makes it a felony to willfully make false statements in a tax return or to willfully aid or assist others in preparing a false tax return. Felony violations are punishable by a fine of $100,000 ($500,000 in the case of a corporation) and imprisonment for up to three years.[19] This provision applies to anyone who prepares tax returns for others for compensation—not just to accountants.[20]

---

18. 15 U.S.C. Section 78u-4(g).
19. 26 U.S.C. Section 7206(2).
20. 26 U.S.C. Section 7701(a)(36).

A penalty of $250 per tax return is levied on tax preparers for negligent understatement of the client's tax liability. For willful understatement of tax liability or reckless or intentional disregard of rules or regulations, a penalty of $1,000 is imposed.[21] A tax preparer may also be subject to penalties for failing to furnish the taxpayer with a copy of the return, failing to sign the return, or failing to furnish the appropriate tax identification numbers.

In addition, a tax preparer may be fined $1,000 per document for aiding and abetting another's understatement of tax liability (the penalty is increased to $10,000 in corporate cases).[22] The tax preparer's liability is limited to one penalty per taxpayer per tax year.

40–5 Confidentiality and Privilege

Professionals are restrained by the ethical tenets of their professions to keep all communications with their clients confidential.

40–5a Attorney-Client Relationships

The confidentiality of attorney-client communications is protected by law, which confers a privilege on such communications. This privilege exists because of the client's need to fully disclose the facts of his or her case to the attorney.

To encourage frankness, confidential attorney-client communications relating to representation are normally held in strictest confidence and protected by law. The attorney and her or his employees may not discuss the client's case with anyone—even under court order—without the client's permission. The client holds the privilege, and only the client may waive it—by disclosing privileged information to someone outside the privilege, for instance.

Note, however, that the SEC has implemented rules requiring attorneys who become aware that a client has violated securities laws to report the violation to the SEC. Because reporting a client's misconduct can be a breach of the attorney-client privilege, these rules have created potential conflicts for some attorneys.

Once an attorney-client relationship arises, all communications between the parties are privileged. The question in the following case was whether communications between an attorney and an individual *before* that individual was informed that the attorney was *not* his counsel were privileged.

> **Learning Objective 5**
> What is protected by the attorney-client privilege?

---

21. 26 U.S.C. Section 6694.
22. 26 U.S.C. Section 6701.

■ **Case 40.2**

Commonwealth of Pennsylvania v. Schultz

Superior Court of Pennsylvania, 133 A.3d 294 (2016).

Background and Facts An investigation into allegations of sexual misconduct involving minors and Jerry Sandusky, a former defensive coordinator for the Pennsylvania State University football team, led a grand jury to subpoena Gary Schultz. Schultz, a retired vice president of the university, had overseen the campus police at the time of the alleged events.

Before testifying, Schultz met with Cynthia Baldwin, counsel for Penn State. He told her that he did not have any documents relating to the two incidents, believing this disclosure to be in the strictest confidence between attorney and client. Baldwin, however, saw her role as counsel only for Penn State, representing Schultz as an agent of the university, not personally.

(Continues)

She did not explain this to him, and she appeared with him during his testimony.

Later, a file was found in Schultz's office containing notes pertaining to the two incidents. When Baldwin was called to testify, she revealed what he had told her at their meeting. On the basis of this testimony, the grand jury charged Schultz with the crimes of perjury, obstruction of justice, and conspiracy. Before a trial was held on these charges, Schultz filed a motion to preclude Baldwin's testimony and quash (suppress) the charges, arguing that her testimony violated the attorney-client privilege. The court denied the motion. Schulz appealed.

In the Words of the Court
Opinion by *BOWES*, J. [Judge]
* * * *

Communications between a putative [assumed] client and corporate counsel are generally privileged prior to counsel informing the individual of the distinction between representing the individual as an agent of the corporation and representing the person in his or her personal capacity. [Emphasis added.]

When corporate counsel clarifies the potential inherent conflict of interest in representing the corporation and an individual and explains that the attorney may divulge the communications between that person and the attorney because they do not represent the individual, the individual may then make a knowing, intelligent, and voluntary decision whether to continue communicating with corporate counsel.
* * * *

* * * Where an attorney purports to offer only limited representation before and at a grand jury proceeding, * * * a putative client must be made expressly aware of that fact. As Schultz consulted with Ms. Baldwin for purposes of preparing for his grand jury testimony * * *, and reasonably believed she represented him, and Ms. Baldwin neglected to adequately explain the distinction between personal representation and agency representation * * *, we conclude that all the communications

between Schultz and Ms. Baldwin were protected by the attorney-client privilege.

* * * Accordingly, we preclude Ms. Baldwin from testifying in future proceedings regarding privileged communications between her and Schultz, absent a waiver by Schultz.
* * * *

* * * Schultz * * * was not aware that Ms. Baldwin was not appearing with him [during his grand jury testimony] in order to protect his interests and therefore unable to provide advice concerning whether he should answer potentially incriminating questions or invoke his right against self-incrimination. Since Schultz was constructively without counsel during his grand jury testimony, and he did not provide informed consent as to limited representation, * * * his right against self-incrimination was not protected by Ms. Baldwin's agency representation, and the appropriate remedy is to quash the perjury charge.
* * * *

[Finally,] since the obstruction of justice and related conspiracy charges in this matter relied extensively on a presentment from an investigating grand jury privy to impermissible privileged communications, we quash the counts of obstruction of justice and the related conspiracy charge.

Decision and Remedy
A state intermediate appellate court reversed the order of the lower court regarding Schultz's pretrial motion. Baldwin was precluded from testifying about Schultz's privileged communications with her, and the charges of perjury, obstruction of justice, and conspiracy against Schultz were quashed.

Critical Thinking

• **What If the Facts Were Different?** *Suppose that a hearing had been held on the question of the attorney-client privilege before Baldwin testified. Would the result have been different?*

40–5b Accountant-Client Relationships

In a few states, accountant-client communications are privileged by state statute. In these states, accountant-client communications may not be revealed even in court or in court-sanctioned proceedings without the client's permission.

The majority of states, however, abide by the common law, which provides that, if a court so orders, an accountant must disclose information about his or her client to the court. Physicians and other professionals may similarly be compelled to disclose in court information given to them in confidence by patients or clients.

Communications between professionals and their clients—other than those between an attorney and her or his client—are not privileged under federal law. In cases involving federal law, state-provided rights to confidentiality of accountant-client communications are not recognized. Thus, in those cases, an accountant must provide all information requested in a court order.

Practice and Review

Superior Wholesale Corporation planned to purchase Regal Furniture, Inc., and wished to determine Regal's net worth. Superior hired Lynette Shuebke, of the accounting firm Shuebke Delgado, to review an audit that had been prepared by Norman Chase, the accountant for Regal. Shuebke advised Superior that Chase had performed a high-quality audit and that Regal's inventory on the audit dates was stated accurately on the general ledger. As a result of these representations, Superior went forward with its purchase of Regal.

After the purchase, Superior discovered that the audit by Chase had been materially inaccurate and misleading, primarily because the inventory had been grossly overstated on the balance sheet. Later, a former Regal employee who had begun working for Superior exposed an e-mail exchange between Chase and former Regal chief executive officer Buddy Gantry. The exchange revealed that Chase had cooperated in overstating the inventory and understating Regal's tax liability. Using the information presented in the chapter, answer the following questions.

1. If Shuebke's review was conducted in good faith and conformed to generally accepted accounting principles, could Superior hold Shuebke Delgado liable for negligently failing to detect material omissions in Chase's audit? Why or why not?

2. According to the rule adopted by the majority of courts to determine accountants' liability to third parties, could Chase be liable to Superior? Explain.

3. Generally, what requirements must be met before Superior can recover damages under Section 10(b) of the Securities Exchange Act of 1934 and SEC Rule 10b-5? Can Superior meet these requirements?

4. Suppose that a court determined that Chase had aided Regal in willfully understating its tax liability. What is the maximum penalty that could be imposed on Chase?

Debate This

Only the largest publicly held companies should be subject to the Sarbanes-Oxley Act.

Key Terms

auditor 951
constructive fraud 954
defalcation 950
due diligence 959

generally accepted accounting
   principles (GAAP) 949
generally accepted auditing
   standards (GAAS) 949

International Financial Reporting
   Standards (IFRS) 950
malpractice 953
working papers 959

Chapter Summary: Liability of Accountants and Other Professionals

Potential Liability to Clients	1. *Breach of contract*—A professional who fails to fulfill contractual obligations can be held liable for breach of contract and resulting damages. 2. *Negligence*—An accountant, attorney, or other professional, in performing her or his duties, must use the care, knowledge, and judgment generally used by professionals in the same or similar circumstances. Failure to do so is negligence. An accountant's violation of generally accepted accounting principles or generally accepted auditing standards is *prima facie* evidence of negligence. 3. *Fraud*—Intentionally misrepresenting a material fact to a client, when the client relies on the misrepresentation, is fraud. Gross negligence in performance of duties is constructive fraud.
Potential Liability to Third Parties	An accountant may be liable for negligence to any third person the accountant knows or should have known will benefit from the accountant's work. The standard for imposing this liability varies, but generally courts follow one of the following rules (see Exhibit 40–1): 1. *Ultramares rule*—Liability will be imposed only if the accountant is in privity, or near privity, with the third party. 2. *Restatement rule*—Liability will be imposed only if the third party's reliance is foreseen or known, or if the third party is among a class of foreseen or known users. The majority of courts have adopted this rule. 3. *"Reasonably foreseeable users" rule*—Liability will be imposed if the third party's reliance was reasonably foreseeable.

Liability of Accountants under Other Federal Laws	1. *The Sarbanes-Oxley Act*—The act imposes requirements on public accounting firms that provide auditing services to companies whose securities are sold to public investors. It created the Public Company Accounting Oversight Board, which oversees the audit of public companies that are subject to securities laws. The act requires accountants to maintain working papers relating to an audit or review for seven years from the end of the fiscal period in which the audit or review was concluded.
	
	2. *The Securities Act of 1933*—
	  a. Section 11—An accountant who makes a false statement or omits a material fact in audited financial statements required for registration of securities under the act may be liable to anyone who acquires securities covered by the registration statement. The accountant's defense is basically the use of due diligence and the reasonable belief that the work was complete and correct. The burden of proof is on the accountant. Willful violations of this act may be subject to criminal penalties.
	  b. Section 12(2)—An accountant may be liable when a prospectus or other communication presented to an investor contained an untrue statement or omitted a material fact.
	
	3. *The Securities Exchange Act of 1934*—
	  a. Section 18—Accountants may be held liable for false and misleading applications, reports, and documents filed with the SEC. The burden is on the plaintiff, and the accountant has numerous defenses, including good faith and lack of knowledge that what was submitted was false. Mere negligence is not enough.
	  b. Section 10(b) and Rule 10b-5—Provisions allow private parties to bring civil actions against violators. Accountants may be held liable only to sellers or purchasers of securities. Privity is not necessary for recovery.
	
	4. *The Private Securities Litigation Reform Act*—An auditor must use adequate procedures to detect any illegal acts of the company being audited and disclose any illegalities detected. Parties are liable only for the proportion of damages for which they are responsible.

Potential Criminal Liability	1. Willful violations of the Securities Act of 1933 and the Securities Exchange Act of 1934 may be subject to criminal penalties.
	2. Willfully making false statements in a tax return or willfully aiding or assisting in the preparation of a false tax return is a felony. Aiding and abetting an individual's understatement of tax liability is a separate crime.
Confidentiality and Privilege	Communications other than those between attorneys and clients are not privileged under federal law.
	1. *Attorney-client relationships*—Communications relating to representation are normally held in the strictest confidence and protected by law. Only the client may waive the privilege. The SEC, however, has implemented rules requiring attorneys who learn that a client has violated securities laws to report the violation to the SEC.
	2. *Accountant-client relationships*—The majority of states follow the common law. If a court so orders, an accountant must disclose information about his or her client to the court.

Issue Spotters

1. Dave, an accountant, prepares a financial statement for Excel Company, a client, knowing that Excel will use the statement to obtain a loan from First National Bank. Dave makes negligent omissions in the statement that result in a loss to the bank. Can the bank successfully sue Dave? Why or why not? (See *Potential Liability to Third Parties.*)

2. Nora, an accountant, prepares a financial statement as part of a registration statement that Omega, Inc., files with the Securities and Exchange Commission before making a public offering of securities. The statement contains a misstatement of material fact that is not attributable to Nora's fraud or negligence. Pat relies on the misstatement, buys some of the securities, and suffers a loss. Can Nora be held liable to Pat? Explain. (See *Liability of Accountants under Other Federal Laws.*)

—**Check your answers to the *Issue Spotters* against the answers provided in Appendix D at the end of this text.**

Business Scenarios and Case Problems

40–1. The *Ultramares* Rule. Larkin, Inc., retains Howard Perkins to manage its books and prepare its financial statements. Perkins, a certified public accountant, lives in Indiana and practices there. After twenty years, Perkins has become a bit bored with generally accepted accounting principles (GAAP) and has adopted more creative accounting methods. Now, though, Perkins has a problem. He is being sued by Molly Tucker, one of Larkin's creditors. Tucker alleges that Perkins either knew or should have known that Larkin's financial statements would be distributed to various individuals. Furthermore, she asserts that these financial statements were negligently prepared and seriously inaccurate. What are the consequences of Perkins's failure to follow GAAP? Under the traditional *Ultramares* rule, can Tucker recover damages from Perkins? Explain. (See *Potential Liability to Third Parties.*)

40–2. The *Restatement* Rule. The accounting firm of Goldman, Walters, Johnson & Co. prepared financial statements for Lucy's Fashions, Inc. After reviewing the financial statements, Happydays State Bank agreed to loan Lucy's Fashions $35,000 for expansion. When Lucy's Fashions declared bankruptcy under Chapter 11 six months later, Happydays State Bank filed an action against Goldman, Walters, Johnson & Co., alleging negligent preparation of financial statements. Assuming that

the court has abandoned the *Ultramares* approach, what is the result? What are the policy reasons for holding accountants liable to third parties with whom they are not in privity? (See *Potential Liability to Third Parties.*)

40–3. Accountant's Liability under Rule 10b-5. In early 2018, Bennett, Inc., offered a substantial number of new common shares to the public. Harvey Helms had a long-standing interest in Bennett because his grandfather had once been president of the company. On receiving Bennett's prospectus, Helms was dismayed by the pessimism it embodied, so he decided to delay purchasing stock in the company. Later, Helms asserted that the prospectus prepared by the accountants had been overly pessimistic and had contained materially misleading statements. Discuss fully how successful Helms would be in bringing a suit under Rule 10b-5 against Bennett's accountants. (See *Liability of Accountants under Other Federal Laws.*)

40–4. Professional's Liability. Soon after Teresa DeYoung's husband died, her mother-in-law also died, leaving an inheritance of more than $400,000 for DeYoung's children. DeYoung hired John Ruggiero, an attorney, to ensure that her children would receive it. Ruggiero advised her to invest the funds in his real estate business. She declined. A few months later,

$300,000 of the inheritance was sent to Ruggiero. Without telling DeYoung, he deposited the $300,000 in his account and began to use the funds in his real estate business. Nine months later, $109,000 of the inheritance was sent to Ruggiero. He paid this to DeYoung. She asked about the remaining amount. Ruggiero lied to hide his theft. Unable to access these funds, DeYoung's children changed their college plans to attend less expensive institutions. Nearly three years later, DeYoung learned the truth. Can she bring a suit against Ruggiero? If so, on what ground? If not, why not? Did Ruggiero violate any standard of professional ethics? Discuss. [*DeYoung v. Ruggiero,* 2009 VT 9, 971 A.2d 627 (2009)] (See *Potential Liability to Clients.*)

40–5. Professional Malpractice. Jeffery Guerrero hired James McDonald, a certified public accountant, to represent him and his business in an appeal to the Internal Revenue Service. The appeal concerned audits that showed Guerrero owed more taxes. When the appeal failed, McDonald assisted in preparing materials for an appeal to the Tax Court, which was not successful. Guerrero then sued McDonald for professional negligence in the preparation of his evidence for the court. Specifically, Guerrero claimed that he would have won the case if McDonald had adequately prepared witnesses and had presented all the arguments that could have been made on his behalf. Guerrero contended that McDonald was liable for all of the additional taxes he was required to pay. Is Guerrero's claim likely to result in liability on McDonald's part? What factors would the court consider? [*Guerrero v. McDonald,* 302 Ga.App. 164, 690 S.E.2d 486 (2010)] (See *Potential Liability to Clients.*)

40–6. Business Case Problem with Sample Answer—Potential Liability to Third Parties. In 2006, twenty-seven parties became limited partners in two hedge funds that had invested with Bernard Madoff and his investment firm. The partners' investment adviser gave them various investment information, including a memorandum indicating that an independent certified public accountant, KPMG, LLP, had audited the hedge funds' annual reports. Since 2004, KPMG had also prepared annual reports addressed to the funds' "partners." Each report stated that KPMG had investigated the funds' financial statements, had followed generally accepted auditing principles, and had concluded that the statements fairly summarized the funds' financial conditions. Moreover, KPMG used the information from its audits to prepare individual tax statements for each fund partner.

In 2008, Madoff was charged with securities fraud for running a massive Ponzi scheme. In a 2009 report, the Securities and Exchange Commission identified numerous "red flags" that should have been discovered by investment advisers and auditors. Unfortunately, they were not, and the hedge funds' partners lost millions of dollars. Is KPMG potentially liable to the funds' partners under the *Restatement (Third) of Torts?* Why or why not? [*Askenazy v. Tremont Group Holdings, Inc.,* 2012 WL 440675 (Mass.Super. 2012)] (See *Potential Liability to Third Parties.*)

—For a sample answer to Problem 40–6, go to Appendix E at the end of this text.

40–7. Attorney's Duty of Care. Luis and Maria Rojas contracted to buy a house in Westchester County, New York, from Andrew and Karen Paine. The house was on property designated as "Lot No. 8" on a subdivision map filed in the county clerk's office. The Paines had acquired the property in two parts by the transfer of two separate deeds. At the closing, they delivered a deed stating that it covered "the same property." In fact, however, the legal description attached to the deed covered only the portion of Lot No. 8 described in one of the two previous deeds. Attorney Paul Herrick represented the Rojases in the deal with the Paines. When the Rojases sought to sell the property two years later, the title search revealed that they owned only part of Lot No. 8, and the buyer refused to go through with the sale. Is Herrick liable for malpractice? Explain. [*Rojas v. Paine,* 125 A.D.3d 745, 4 N.Y.S.3d 223 (2 Dept. 2015)] (See *Potential Liability to Clients.*)

40–8. Attorney Misconduct. Solomons One, LLC, was formed to develop waterfront property in Maryland. Vernon Donnelly was a member of the LLC and served as the company's counsel. The state denied Solomons's request for a permit to build a pier. Donnelly appealed the denial. Meanwhile, he assigned Solomons's potential right to build a pier to a trust, appointed himself trustee, and changed his fee arrangement with the company. These steps were taken without Solomons's authorization, but there was no financial harm to the LLC and no additional evidence that Donnelly engaged in dishonesty or deceit. On learning of Donnelly's actions, however, a majority of the LLC members voted to terminate his representation. Despite the vote, he pursued the pier case until the LLC ultimately gained the right to build a pier. Donnelly had not previously been disciplined for misconduct. Should he be disciplined in this case? Why or why not? [*Attorney Grievance Commission of Maryland v. Donnelly,* 458 Md. 237, 182 A.3d 743 (2018)] (See *Potential Liability to Clients.*)

40–9. A Question of Ethics—The IDDR Approach and Attorney Misconduct. *Brandy Sutton was the sole owner of the law firm Pendleton & Sutton in Lawrence, Kansas. Sutton offered a retirement plan as a benefit to the members of her staff. Each employee could contribute up to 3 percent of his or her salary. Sutton withheld the contributions from the employees' paychecks, which indicated that the amounts were deposited into the plan. For a period of years, however, she failed to make the deposits, using the funds to cover her professional expenses instead.*

An associate attorney with the firm discovered the discrepancy and filed a complaint with the state disciplinary office. In response, Sutton argued that the misconduct was caused by financial difficulties, including "several items" involving the associate who filed the complaint. Sutton expressed remorse, and within sixteen months properly funded all of the employees' accounts. [In the Matter of Sutton, 307 Kan. 95, 405 P.3d 1205 (2017)] (See Potential Liability to Clients.)

Critical Thinking and Writing Assignments

40–10. Time-Limited Group Assignment—Attorney-Client Privilege. Napster, Inc., offered a service that allowed its users to browse digital music files on other users' computers and download selections for free. Music industry principals sued Napster for copyright infringement, and the court ordered Napster to remove files that were identified as infringing from its service. When Napster failed to comply, it was shut down.

A few months later, Bertelsmann, a German corporation, loaned Napster $85 million to fund its anticipated transition to a licensed digital music distribution system. The terms allowed Napster to spend the loan on "general, administrative and overhead expenses." In an e-mail, Napster's chief executive officer referred to a "side deal" under which Napster could use up to $10 million of the loan to pay litigation expenses. Napster failed to launch the new system before declaring bankruptcy. The plaintiffs filed a suit against Bertelsmann, alleging that its loan had prolonged Napster's infringement. The plaintiffs asked the court to order the disclosure of all attorney-client communications related to the loan. (See *Confidentiality and Privilege.*)

1. When a business experiences financial difficulties, can it withhold amounts owed to its employees to pay more immediate obligations? Consider this question from an ethical perspective, using the IDDR approach.

2. Should a sanction be imposed on Sutton in this case? If so, what should it be? Possibilities include suspension from the practice of law for a limited time or an indefinite period, and probation. Explain.

1. The first group will identify the principle that Bertelsmann could assert to protect these communications and outline the purpose of this protection.

2. The second group will decide whether this principle should protect a client who consults an attorney for advice that will help the client commit fraud.

3. A third group will determine whether the court should grant the plaintiffs' request.

Unit Six—Task-Based Simulation

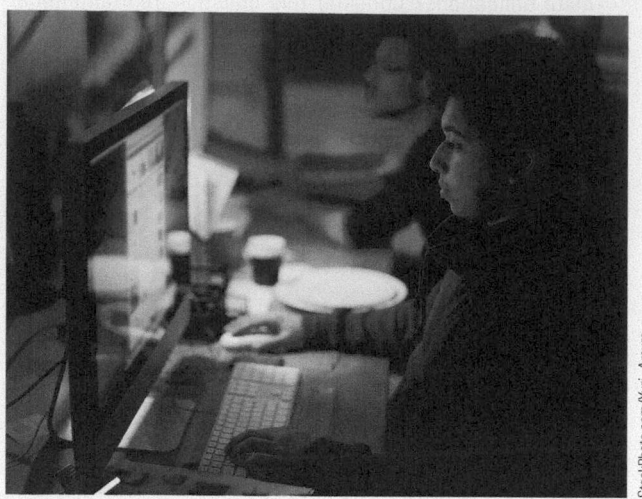

StockPhoto.com/Yuri_Arcurs

Alpha Software, Inc., and Beta Products Corporation—both small firms—are competitors in the business of software research, development, and production.

1. **Antitrust Law.** Alpha and Beta form a joint venture to research, develop, and produce new software for a particular line of computers. Does this business combination violate the antitrust laws? If so, is it a *per se* violation, or is it subject to the rule of reason? Alpha and Beta decide to merge. After the merger, Beta is the surviving firm. What aspect of this firm's presence in the market will be assessed to decide whether this merger is in violation of any antitrust laws?

2. **Consumer Law.** To market its products profitably, Beta considers a number of advertising and labeling proposals. One proposal is that Beta suggest in its advertising that one of its software products has a certain function, even though the product does not actually have that capability. Another suggestion is that Beta sell half of a certain program in packaging that misleads the buyer into believing the entire program is included. To obtain the entire program, customers would need to buy a second product. Can Beta implement these suggestions or otherwise market its products in any way it likes? If not, why not?

3. **Environmental Law.** The production part of Beta's operations generates hazardous waste. Gamma Transport Company transports the waste to Omega Waste Corporation, which owns and operates a hazardous waste disposal site. At the site, some containers leak hazardous waste, and the Environmental Protection Agency (EPA) cleans it up. From whom can the EPA recover the cost of the cleanup?

4. **Liability of Accountants.** Beta hires a certified public accountant, Aaron Schleger, to prepare its financial reports and issue opinion letters based on those reports. One year, Beta falls into serious financial trouble, but this is not reflected in Schleger's reports and opinion letters. Relying on Schleger's portrayal of the company's fiscal health, Beta borrows substantial amounts to develop a new product. The bank, in lending funds to Beta, relies on an opinion letter from Schleger, and Schleger is aware of the bank's reliance. Assuming that Schleger was negligent but did not engage in intentional fraud, what is his potential liability in this situation? Discuss fully.

Unit 7
Property and Its Protection

Michal Kalasek/Shutterstock.com

41

Personal Property and Bailments

Learning Objectives

The four Learning Objectives *below are designed to help improve your understanding. After reading this chapter, you should be able to answer the following questions:*

1. What is real property? What is personal property?

2. What are the three necessary elements for an effective gift?

3. How does lost property differ from mislaid property? Does a finder of such property acquire title to it?

4. What are the three elements of a bailment?

"The great ... end ... of men's uniting into commonwealths, and putting themselves under government, is the preservation of their property."

John Locke
1632–1704
(English political philosopher)

Property consists of the legally protected rights and interests a person has in anything with an ascertainable value that is subject to ownership. For instance, digital property has become quite valuable in today's world. When a couple divorces, they might dispute who owns the virtual world assets they have acquired, their Internet accounts, or the data stored on their devices. Property would have little value, however, if the law did not define owners' rights to use their property, to sell or dispose of it, and to prevent trespass on it. Indeed, John Locke, as indicated in the chapter-opening quotation, considered the preservation of property to be the primary reason for the establishment of government.

In this chapter, we first examine the differences between personal and real property. We then look at the methods of acquiring ownership of personal property and consider issues relating to mislaid, lost, and abandoned personal property. In the remainder of the chapter, we discuss bailment relationships. A *bailment* is created when personal property is temporarily delivered into the care of another without a transfer of title, such as when a person takes an item of clothing to the dry cleaners.

41–1 Personal Property versus Real Property

Property is divided into real property and personal property. **Real property** (sometimes called *realty* or *real estate*) consists of land and everything permanently attached to it, including structures and anything permanently attached to the structures. Everything else

Real Property Land and everything permanently attached to it, such as trees and buildings.

is **personal property,** or *personalty*. Attorneys sometimes refer to personal property as **chattel,** a term used under the common law to denote all forms of personal property.

Personal property can be tangible or intangible. *Tangible* personal property, such as a 4K UHD TV, heavy construction equipment, or a car, has physical substance. *Intangible* personal property represents some set of rights and interests but has no physical substance. Stocks and bonds, patents, trademarks, and copyrights—as well as digital property—are examples of intangible personal property.

Both personal property and real property can be owned by an individual person or by some other entity, such as an organization. When two or more persons own real or personal property together, concurrent ownership exists. (The different types of concurrent ownership will be discussed in the real property chapter.)

41-1a **Why Is the Distinction Important?**

The distinction between real and personal property is important for several reasons. How property is taxed and what is required to transfer or acquire the property is determined by whether the property is classified as real or personal.

Taxation The two types of property are usually subject to different types of taxes. Generally, each state assesses property taxes on real property. Typically, the tax rate is based on the market value of the real property and the various services provided by the city, state, and county in which the property is located. For instance, higher taxes may be imposed on real property located within the city limits to pay for schools, roads, and libraries.

Businesses often also pay taxes on the personal property they own, use, or lease, including office or farm equipment and supplies. Individuals may pay sales tax when purchasing personal property, but generally they are not required to pay annual taxes on personal property that is not used for business.

Acquisition Another reason for distinguishing between real and personal property has to do with the way the property is acquired or transferred. Personal property can be transferred with a minimum of formality—such as by selling goods on Craigslist or at a garage sale. In contrast, real property transfers generally involve a written sales contract and a *deed* that is recorded with the state.

Similarly, establishing ownership rights is simpler for personal property than for real property. **Example 41.1** If Mia gives Shawn an iPad as a gift, Shawn does not need to have any paperwork evidencing title, as he would if she had given him real property. ▮ The ways to acquire ownership of personal property will be discussed shortly.

41-1b **Conversion of Real Property to Personal Property**

Sometimes, real property can be turned into personal property by detaching it from the land. For instance, the trees, bushes, and plants growing on land are considered part of the real property (with the exception of crops that must be planted every year, such as wheat). If the property is sold, all the vegetation growing on the land normally is transferred to the new owner of the real property.

Once the items are severed (removed) from the land, however, they become personal property. If the trees are cut from the land, the timber is personal property. If apples, grapes, or raspberries are picked from trees or vines growing on real property, they become personal property. Similarly, if land contains minerals (including oil) or other natural resources (such as marble), the resources are part of the real property. But once removed, they become personal property.

Conversely, personal property may be converted into real property by permanently attaching it to the real property. Personal property that is affixed to real property in a permanent way, such as tile installed in a house, is known as a *fixture*.

Personal Property Property that is movable. Any property that is not real property.

Chattel Personal property.

Learning Objective 1
What is real property? What is personal property?

41–2 Acquiring Ownership of Personal Property

The most common way of acquiring personal property is by purchasing it. (Today, even virtual property is often purchased—see this chapter's *Adapting the Law to the Online Environment* feature for a discussion.)

We reviewed the purchase and sale of goods (which are personal property) in earlier chapters. Often, property is acquired by will or inheritance, as we will discuss in a later chapter. Here, we look at additional ways in which ownership of personal property can be acquired, including acquisition by possession, production, gifts, accession, and confusion.

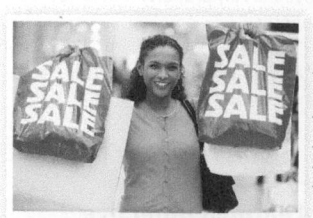

What is the most common way to acquire ownership rights in personal property?

41–2a Possession

Sometimes, a person can become the owner of personal property merely by possessing it. An example of acquiring ownership by possession is the capture of wild animals. Wild animals belong to no one in their natural state, and the first person to take possession of a wild animal normally owns it. A hunter who kills a deer, for instance, has assumed ownership of it (unless he or she acted in violation of the law). Those who find lost or abandoned property can also acquire ownership rights through mere possession of the property, as will be discussed later in this chapter.

41–2b Production

Production—the fruits of labor—is another means of acquiring ownership of personal property. For instance, writers, inventors, and manufacturers produce personal property and thereby acquire title to it. (In some situations, as when a researcher is hired to develop a new product, the researcher-producer may not own what is produced.)

Adapting the Law to the Online Environment

The Exploding World of Digital Property

Jon Jacobs took out a real mortgage on his real house so that he could pay $100,000 in real dollars for a virtual asteroid near the virtual Planet Calypso in the virtual-world Entropia Universe. A few years later, he sold Club Neverdie, the virtual space resort he had constructed on the virtual asteroid, for more than $600,000. At the time, Jacobs was making $200,000 per year from players' purchases of virtual goods at the resort.

If the prospect of paying real funds for virtual property seems disconcerting, remember that property does not have to be tangible. Property consists of a bundle of rights in anything that has an ascertainable value and is subject to ownership. This definition encompasses virtual property, including all the intangible objects used in virtual worlds like Entropia Universe and Second Life.

Digital Goods Have Value, Too

Digital goods include virtual goods. More importantly, they include digital books, music libraries, and movie downloads, as well as domain names and expensively created websites. This digital property has real value. Some digital music libraries, for example, cost thousands of dollars.

Who Keeps the Digital Goods?

The growing value of digital goods raises some legal questions. For instance, what are the respective rights of the creator/owner of a virtual-world website and the players at that site? What happens when a husband and wife decide to divorce after they have purchased virtual real estate or digital goods with real-world dollars? The couple—or a court—will have to figure out a way to divide the goods. Property and divorce laws will have to adapt to take this emerging world of digital property into account.

Critical Thinking

How might a couple who enjoy purchasing digital goods together avoid property division issues in the event of a divorce?

41–2c Gifts

A **gift** is another fairly common means of acquiring and transferring ownership of real and personal property. A gift is essentially a *voluntary* transfer of property ownership for which no consideration is given. The absence of consideration is what distinguishes a gift from a contractual obligation to transfer ownership of property.

For a gift to be effective, the following three elements are required:

1. Donative intent on the part of the *donor* (the one giving the gift).

2. Delivery.

3. Acceptance by the *donee* (the one receiving the gift).

Until these three requirements are met, no effective gift has been made. **Example 41.2** Your aunt tells you that she *intends* to give you a new Mercedes-Benz for your next birthday. This is simply a promise to make a gift. It is not considered a gift until the Mercedes-Benz is delivered and accepted. ▮

Gift A voluntary transfer of property made without consideration, past or present.

Learning Objective 2

What are the three necessary elements for an effective gift?

Ethical Issue

Who owns the engagement ring? Often, when two people decide to marry, one party (traditionally the man in an opposite-sex relationship) gives the other an engagement ring. What if the engagement is called off? Etiquette authorities routinely counsel that if the woman breaks the engagement, she should return the ring, but if the man calls the wedding off, the woman is entitled to keep the ring. When the party who gave the ring (the donor) sues for its return after a breakup, the courts are split.

Courts in a majority of states, including Kansas, Michigan, New York, and Ohio, hold that an engagement ring is not a real gift. Rather, it is a "conditional gift" that becomes final only if the marriage occurs. If the marriage does not take place, the ring is returned to the donor regardless of who broke the engagement. This position is similar to the law of ancient Rome, which mandated that when an engagement was broken, the woman had to return the ring, as a penalty, regardless of who was at fault. Some judges, however, disagree with the conditional-gift theory and contend that an engagement ring is a gift and, as such, belongs to the donee, even if the engagement is broken.

Donative Intent When a gift is challenged in court, the court will determine whether donative intent exists by looking at the language of the donor and the surrounding circumstances. A court may look at the relationship between the parties and the size of the gift in relation to the donor's other assets. When a person has given away a large portion of her or his assets, the court will scrutinize the transaction closely to determine the donor's mental capacity and to look for indications of fraud or duress.

✳ **Spotlight Case Example 41.3** Over a period of three months, Jean Knowles Goodman, who was eighty-five years old, gave Steven Atwood several checks that totaled $56,100. Atwood was a veterinarian who had cared for Goodman's dogs for nearly twenty years, and he and Goodman had become friends. Shortly after writing the last check, Goodman was hospitalized and diagnosed with dementia (loss of brain function) and alcohol dependency.

The guardian who was appointed to represent Goodman filed a lawsuit to invalidate the gifts, claiming that Goodman had lacked mental capacity and

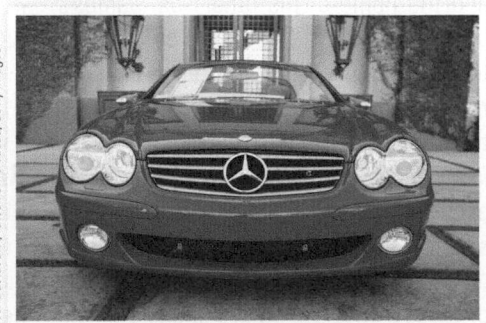

If a close relative tells you that she intends to give you a Mercedes-Benz convertible, has she gifted you the car? Why or why not?

donative intent. At trial, a psychiatrist who had examined Goodman testified on behalf of Atwood that while Goodman lacked the capacity to care for herself, she would have understood that she was giving away her funds. Therefore, the court concluded that Goodman had donative intent to make the gifts to Atwood.[1]

Delivery   The gift must be delivered to the donee. Delivery may be accomplished by means of a third person who is the agent of either the donor or the donee. Naturally, no delivery is necessary if the gift is already in the hands of the donee. Delivery is obvious in most cases, but some objects cannot be relinquished physically. Then the question of delivery depends on the surrounding circumstances.

Constructive Delivery A symbolic delivery of property that cannot be physically delivered.

Constructive Delivery. When the object itself cannot be physically delivered, a symbolic, or constructive, delivery will be sufficient. **Constructive delivery** confers the right to take possession of the object in question. **Example 41.4** Angela wants to make a gift of various rare coins that she has stored in a safe-deposit box. She obviously cannot deliver the box itself to the donee, and she does not want to take the coins out of the bank. Angela can simply deliver the key to the box to the donee and authorize the donee's access to the box and its contents. This action constitutes a constructive delivery of the contents of the box. ▪

Constructive delivery is always necessary for gifts of intangible property, such as stocks, bonds, insurance policies, and contracts. What will be delivered are documents that represent rights and are not, in themselves, the true property. (See this chapter's *Business Law Analysis* feature for an illustration.)

---

1. *Goodman v. Atwood*, 78 Mass.App.Ct. 655, 940 N.E.2d 514 (2011).

Effective Gift of a Brokerage Account

Business Law Analysis

John Weider opened a brokerage account with Quick and Reilly, Inc., in the name of his son James. Twelve years later, when the balance was $52,085, John closed the account and transferred the funds to a joint account in his own name and the name of his other son, James's brother. James did not learn of the existence of the account in his name until the transfer, when he received a tax form for the account's final year. James filed a suit in a Connecticut state court against Quick and Reilly, alleging breach of contract and seeking to recover the account's principal and interest. What are the elements of a valid gift? Did John's opening of the account in James's name with Quick and Reilly constitute a gift to James?

Analysis: A gift is a transfer of property without consideration. To make a valid gift, the donor must have "donative intent" (an intent that title to the property will pass to the donee). The donor must also hand over control of the property to the recipient of the gift. The three requirements for an effective gift are (1) the donor's donative intent, (2) delivery of the property, and (3) the donee's acceptance.

Result and Reasoning: John's use of James's name to open the account may indicate donative intent. But the most significant element in this situation is delivery, which requires the donor to part with possession of the property and relinquish control. Delivery may be actual or constructive. In this scenario, James never received actual delivery of the funds in the account. Notice to James of the account's existence might have been sufficient to constitute constructive delivery, but James was not aware of the existence of the account (or his right to any of the funds) until after the funds were withdrawn and the account was closed. Without actual or constructive delivery, there is no way for James to prove that the account constituted a valid gift.

Relinquishing Dominion and Control. An effective delivery also requires giving up complete control and **dominion** (ownership rights) over the subject matter of the gift. The outcome of disputes often turns on whether control has actually been relinquished. The Internal Revenue Service carefully examines transactions between relatives, especially when one claims to have given income-producing property to another who is in a lower marginal tax bracket. Unless complete control over the property has been relinquished, the "donor"—not the family member who received the "gift"—will have to pay taxes on the income from that property.

In the following *Classic Case*, the court focused on the requirement that a donor must relinquish complete control and dominion over property given to the donee before a gift can be effectively delivered.

Dominion Ownership rights in property, including the right to possess and control the property.

🏛 Classic Case 41.1

In re Estate of Piper
Missouri Court of Appeals, 676 S.W.2d 897 (1984).

Background and Facts Gladys Piper died intestate (without a will) in 1982. At her death, she owned miscellaneous personal property worth $5,000 and had in her purse $200 in cash and two diamond rings. Wanda Brown, Piper's niece, took the contents of the purse, allegedly to preserve the items for the estate. Clara Kauffman, a friend of Piper's, filed a claim against the estate for $4,800. From October 1974 until Piper's death, Kauffman had taken Piper to the doctor, beauty shop, and grocery store. Kauffman had also written Piper's checks to pay her bills and had helped her care for her home.

Kauffman maintained that Piper had promised to pay her for these services and had given her the diamond rings as a gift. A Missouri state trial court denied her request for payment. The court found that her services had been voluntary. Kauffman then filed a petition for delivery of personal property—the rings— which was granted by the trial court. Brown, other heirs, and the administrator of Piper's estate appealed.

How can two diamond rings have been gifted if they remained in the owner's purse after her death?

doram/iStock/Getty Images

In the Words of the Court
GREENE, Judge.
* * * *

While no particular form is necessary to effect a delivery, and while the delivery may be actual, constructive, or symbolical, there must be some evidence to support a delivery theory. What we have here, at best, * * * was an intention on the part of Gladys, at some future time, to make a gift of the rings to Clara. Such an intention, no matter how clearly expressed, which has not been

carried into effect, confers no ownership rights in the property in the intended donee. *Language written or spoken, expressing an intention to give, does not constitute a gift, unless the intention is executed by a complete and unconditional delivery of the subject matter, or delivery of a proper written instrument evidencing the gift.* There is no evidence in this case to prove delivery, and, for such reason, the trial court's judgment is erroneous. [Emphasis added.]

Decision and Remedy The state appellate court reversed the judgment of the trial court. No effective gift of the rings had been made, because Piper had never delivered the rings to Kauffman.

Critical Thinking

• **What If the Facts Were Different?** *Suppose that Gladys Piper had told Clara Kauffman that she was giving the rings to Clara but wished to keep them in her possession for a few more days. Would this have affected the court's decision in this case? Explain.*

• **Impact of This Case on Today's Law** *This case clearly illustrates the delivery requirement when making a gift. Assuming that Piper did, indeed, intend for Kauffman to have the rings, it was unfortunate that Kauffman had no right to receive them after Piper's death. Yet the alternative could lead to perhaps even more unfairness. The policy behind the delivery requirement is to protect property owners and their heirs from fraudulent claims based solely on parol evidence. If not for this policy, a person could easily claim that a gift had been made when, in fact, it had not.*

Acceptance The final requirement of a valid gift is acceptance by the donee. This rarely presents any problem, as most donees readily accept their gifts. The courts generally assume acceptance unless the circumstances indicate otherwise.

Gifts *Inter Vivos* and Gifts *Causa Mortis* A gift made during one's lifetime is termed a **gift *inter vivos***. A **gift *causa mortis*** (a so-called *deathbed gift*) is made in contemplation of imminent death. To be effective, a gift *causa mortis* must meet not only the three requirements discussed earlier—donative intent, delivery, and acceptance—but also some additional rules.

> **Gift *Inter Vivos*** A gift made during one's lifetime and not in contemplation of imminent death, in contrast to a gift *causa mortis*.

> **Gift *Causa Mortis*** A gift made in contemplation of imminent death. The gift is revoked if the donor does not die as contemplated.

Automatically Revoked if Donor Recovers. A gift *causa mortis* does not become absolute until the donor dies from the contemplated event, and it is automatically revoked if the donor survives. **Example 41.5** Yang, who is about to undergo surgery to remove a cancerous tumor, delivers an envelope to Chao, a close business associate. The envelope contains a letter saying, "I want to give you this check for $1 million in the event of my death from this operation." Chao cashes the check. The surgeon performs the operation and removes the tumor. Yang recovers fully. Several months later, Yang dies from a heart attack that is totally unrelated to the operation.

If the administrator of Yang's estate tries to recover the $1 million, she will normally succeed. The gift *causa mortis* to Chao is automatically revoked if Yang recovers. The *specific event* that was contemplated in making the gift was death from a particular operation. Because Yang's death was not the result of this event, the gift is revoked, and the $1 million passes to Yang's estate.

Automatically Revoked if Donee Dies. A gift *causa mortis* is also revoked if the prospective donee dies before the donor. Therefore, even if Yang in *Example 41.5* had died during the operation, the gift would have been revoked if Chao had died a few minutes earlier. In that event, the $1 million would have passed to Yang's estate, and not to Chao's heirs.

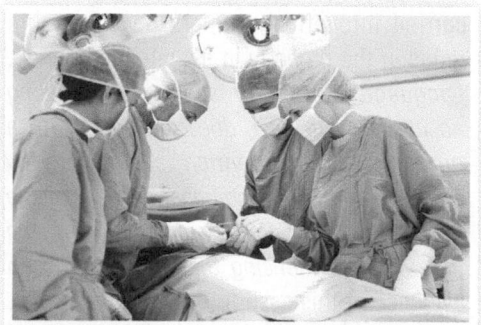

What effect does a patient's survival have on a gift of $1 million given in the event of the patient's death to a close friend just before the surgery?

Squaredpixels/E+/Getty Images

41–2d Accession

> **Accession** The addition of value to personal property by the use of labor or materials.

Accession means "something added." Accession occurs when someone adds value to an item of personal property by the use of either labor or materials.

Generally, there is no dispute about who owns the property after an accession occurs, especially when the accession is accomplished with the owner's consent. **Example 41.6** Harvey buys all the materials necessary to customize his Corvette. He hires Zach, a customizing specialist, to come to his house to perform the work. Harvey pays Zach for the value of the labor, obviously retaining title to the property.

If an improvement is made wrongfully—without the permission of the owner—the owner retains title to the property and normally does not have to pay for the improvement. This is true even if the accession increases the value of the property substantially. **Example 41.7** Colton steals a truck and puts expensive new tires on it. If the rightful owner later recovers the truck, the owner obviously will not be required to compensate Colton, a thief, for the value of the new tires.

41–2e Confusion

> **Confusion** The mixing together of goods belonging to two or more owners to such an extent that the separately owned goods cannot be identified.

Confusion is the commingling (mixing together) of goods to such an extent that one person's personal property cannot be distinguished from another's. Confusion frequently occurs with *fungible goods,* such as grain or oil, which consist of identical units.

If confusion occurs as a result of agreement, an honest mistake, or the act of some third party, the owners share ownership and will share any loss in proportion to their ownership interests in the property. **Example 41.8** Five farmers in a small Iowa community enter into a cooperative arrangement. Each fall, the farmers harvest the same amount of number 2–grade yellow corn and store it in silos that are held by the cooperative. Each farmer thus owns one-fifth of the total corn in the silos. If a fire burns down one of the silos, each farmer will bear one-fifth of the loss. ■ If goods are confused due to an intentional wrongful act, then the innocent party ordinarily acquires title to the whole.

41–3 Mislaid, Lost, and Abandoned Property

As already mentioned, one of the methods of acquiring ownership of property is to possess it. Simply finding something and holding on to it, however, does not necessarily give the finder any legal rights in the property. Different rules apply, depending on whether the property was mislaid, lost, or abandoned. Exhibit 41–1 illustrates the distinctions among these types of property, which are discussed in the following subsections.

41–3a Mislaid Property

Property that has been *voluntarily* placed somewhere by the owner and then inadvertently forgotten is **mislaid property.** A person who finds mislaid property does not obtain title to it. Instead, the owner of the place where the property was mislaid becomes the caretaker of the property because it is highly likely that the true owner will return.[2] **Example 41.9** Maya goes to a movie theater. While paying for popcorn at the concessions stand, she sets her iPhone on the counter and then leaves it there. The phone is mislaid property, and the theater owner is entrusted with the duty of reasonably caring for it. ■

Mislaid Property Property that the owner has voluntarily parted with and then has inadvertently forgotten.

Lost Property Property that the owner has involuntarily parted with and then cannot find or recover.

41–3b Lost Property

Property that is *involuntarily* left is **lost property.** A finder of the property can claim title to the property against the whole world—*except the true owner.*[3] If the true owner is identified and demands that the lost property be returned, the finder must return it. In contrast, if a third party attempts to take possession of the lost property, the finder will have a better title than the third party.

Example 41.10 Kayla works in a large library at night. As she crosses the courtyard on her way home, she finds a gold bracelet set with what seem to be precious stones. She takes the bracelet to a jeweler to have it appraised.

When a person leaves a smartphone at a movie theatre, is it mislaid, lost, or abandoned property?

---

2. For a classic English case establishing this principle, see *Armory v. Delamirie,* 93 Eng.Rep. 664 (K.B. [King's Bench] 1722).
3. The finder of mislaid property is an involuntary bailee.

Exhibit 41–1 Mislaid, Lost, and Abandoned Property

Mislaid Property	Property that is placed somewhere voluntarily by the owner and then inadvertently forgotten. A finder of mislaid property will not acquire title to the goods, and the owner of the place where the property was mislaid becomes a caretaker of the mislaid property.
Lost Property	Property that is involuntarily left by the owner. A finder of lost property can claim title to the property against the whole world except the true owner.
Abandoned Property	Property that has been discarded by the true owner, who has no intention of reclaiming title to the property in the future. A finder of abandoned property can claim title to it against the whole world, including the original owner.

While pretending to weigh the bracelet, the jeweler's employee removes several of the stones. If Kayla brings an action to recover the stones from the jeweler, she normally will win, because she found lost property and holds title against everyone *except the true owner.*

Conversion of Lost Property When a finder of lost property knows the true owner and fails to return the property to that person, the finder has committed the tort of *conversion* (the wrongful taking of another's property). **Example 41.11** Mike finds a bicycle lying on the sidewalk in front of his house. He knows that the bicycle belongs to Geneva. If Mike does not return the bicycle, he can be held liable for conversion. ■ Many states require the finder to make a reasonably diligent search to locate the true owner of lost property.

Estray Statute A statute defining finders' rights in property when the true owners are unknown.

Estray Statutes Many states have **estray statutes,** which encourage and facilitate the return of property to its true owner and reward the finder for honesty if the property remains unclaimed. These laws provide an incentive for finders to report their discoveries by making it possible for them, after a specified period of time, to acquire legal title to the property they have found.

Generally, the item must be lost property, not merely mislaid property, for estray statutes to apply. Estray statutes usually require the finder or the county clerk to advertise the property in an attempt to help the owner recover it.

✦ **Spotlight Case Example 41.12** Drug smugglers often enter the United States illegally from Canada via a frozen river that flows through Van Buren, Maine. When two railroad employees walking near the railroad tracks in Van Buren found a duffel bag that contained $165,580 in cash, they reported their find to U.S. Customs agents, who took custody of the bag and cash. A drug-sniffing dog gave a positive alert on the bag for the scent of drugs. The federal government filed a lawsuit claiming title to the property under criminal forfeiture laws (because the property was involved in illegal drug transactions).

The two employees argued that they were entitled to the $165,580 under Maine's estray statute. That statute required finders to (1) provide written notice to the town clerk within seven days after finding the property, (2) post a public notice in the town, and (3) advertise in the town's newspaper for one month. Because the employees had not fulfilled these requirements, the court ruled that they had not acquired title to the property. Thus, the federal government had a right to seize the cash.[4] ■

Abandoned Property Property that has been discarded by the owner, who has no intention of reclaiming it.

41–3c **Abandoned Property**

Property that has been *discarded* by the true owner, who has *no intention* of reclaiming title to it, is **abandoned property.** Someone who finds abandoned property acquires title to it that is good against the whole world, *including the original owner.* If a person finds abandoned property while trespassing on the property of another, however, the owner of the land, not the finder, will acquire title to the property.

An owner of lost property who eventually gives up any further attempt to find it is frequently held to have abandoned the property. **Example 41.13** As Alekis is hiking in the redwoods, her expensive watch falls off her wrist. She retraces her route and searches for the watch but cannot find it. She finally gives up her search and returns home some five hundred miles away. When Frye later finds the watch, he acquires title to it that is good even against Alekis. By completely giving up her search, Alekis abandoned the watch just as effectively as if she had intentionally discarded it. ■

If a hiker loses an expensive watch, when is it considered abandoned property?

barang/Shutterstock.com

4.   *United States v. One Hundred Sixty-Five Thousand Five Hundred Eighty Dollars ($165,580) in U.S. Currency,* 502 F.Supp.2d 114 (D.Me. 2007).

Is it reasonable to believe that a diamond ring found on the floor of a store is abandoned property? That was the finder's contention in the following case.

■ Case 41.2

State of Washington v. Preston

Court of Appeals of Washington, Division 2, 3 Wash.App.2d 1036 (2018).

Background and Facts Michael Preston found a diamond ring on the floor of a Walmart store in Tumwater, Washington. He kept the ring and later pawned it. The ring belonged to Nicole Amacker who had removed it to assist a fellow shopper and then had forgotten to put it back on. Amacker posted an ad on Craigslist offering a reward for the ring. Preston responded, telling her that he had found the ring and pawned it. Amacker said that Preston had to be present to retrieve the ring from the pawnshop. She would then pay him the reward minus the cost to redeem the ring.

Preston refused to cooperate. Amacker contacted the police. Walmart's surveillance video showed that Amacker had been in the area where Preston had found the ring. In a Washington state court, Preston was charged with theft and convicted. He appealed.

In the Words of the Court
MAXA, C.J. [Chief Judge]

[Under the Revised Code of Washington,] the statutory definition of *theft* includes appropriating another's property when the actor knows the property has been lost.

* * * *

The common law distinguishes between property that has been "lost" and property that had been "abandoned." Property is lost when the owner has parted with possession unwittingly and no longer knows its location. Property is abandoned when the owner intentionally relinquishes possession and rights in the property. *A person who loses property retains ownership, but a person who abandons property loses any ownership interest.* As a result, appropriation of abandoned property generally does not constitute theft. [Emphasis added.]

* * * *

Preston argues that the State [of Washington] failed to present evidence that he knew the ring he found was lost rather than abandoned. He claims that the State proved only that he picked up a ring that he knew nothing about. But the evidence created at least a reasonable inference that Preston knew that the ring was lost when he appropriated it.

First, the mere fact that Preston picked up a diamond ring from the floor of a Walmart store gives rise to an inference that he knew the ring was lost rather than abandoned. It is unlikely that the owner of a diamond ring would choose to abandon it on the floor of a store.

Second, when Preston pawned the ring he concealed the fact that he had found it, claiming that it belonged to his girlfriend in Texas. A reasonable juror could infer from Preston lying about ownership of the ring that he was aware that he had appropriated a ring belonging to someone else and that he was trying to hide his appropriation of it.

Third, Preston's own testimony provides evidence that he knew the ring was lost. When asked * * * if he had found something somebody had lost, Preston stated, "I'm believing that, yes, at that point initially." He also testified that when he found the ring he wanted "to try to find the owner" because "if it was real it's obviously missing." And Preston testified that he pawned the ring because "I was going to be needing money trying to find the owner."

Viewing the evidence in the light most favorable to the State, a reasonable jury could have found that Preston knew the ring was lost when he took possession of and pawned it.

Decision and Remedy A state intermediate appellate court affirmed Preston's conviction for theft because there was "sufficient evidence to prove that Preston knew the ring was lost property."

Critical Thinking

• **Legal Environment** *On what legal theory could Preston be held civilly liable to Amacker for failing to return the ring? Explain.*

• **What If the Facts Were Different?** *Suppose that Amacker had not posted an ad on Craigslist offering a reward for the ring and had not contacted the police. Would the result have been different? Discuss.*

Bailment A situation in which the personal property of one person (a bailor) is entrusted to another (a bailee), who is obligated to return the bailed property to the bailor or dispose of it as directed.

Bailor One who entrusts goods to a bailee.

Bailee One to whom goods are entrusted by a bailor.

A friend loaned this bike as a favor. Has a bailment been created?

Learning Objective 4

What are the three elements of a bailment?

41–4 Bailments

Many routine personal and business transactions involve bailments. A **bailment** is formed by the delivery of personal property without transfer of title by one person, called a **bailor**, to another, called a **bailee**. Usually, a bailment is formed for a particular purpose—for instance, to loan, lease, store, repair, or transport the property. What distinguishes a bailment from a sale or a gift is that there is no passage of title and no intent to transfer title. On completion of the purpose, the bailee is obligated to return the bailed property in the same or better condition to the bailor or a third person or to dispose of it as directed.

Bailments typically arise by contract. Many commercial bailments, such as the delivery of clothing to the cleaners for dry cleaning, are based on contract, for instance. Not all of the elements of a contract must necessarily be present for a bailment to be created. **Example 41.14** If Amy lends her bicycle to a friend, a bailment is created, but not by contract, because there is no consideration. ■

41–4a Elements of a Bailment

Not all transactions involving the delivery of property from one person to another create a bailment. For such a transfer to become a bailment, the following three elements must be present:

1. Personal property.
2. Delivery of possession without title.
3. Agreement that the property will be returned to the bailor or otherwise disposed of according to its owner's directions.

Personal Property Requirement Only personal property, not real property or persons, can be the subject of a bailment. **Example 41.15** When Jai checks her bags at the airport, a bailment of Jai's luggage is created because the luggage is personal property. When Jai boards the plane as a passenger, no bailment is created. ■ Although bailments commonly involve *tangible* items—jewelry, cattle, automobiles, and the like—*intangible* personal property, such as promissory notes and shares of stock, may also be bailed.

Delivery of Possession *Delivery of possession* means the transfer of possession of the property to the bailee. For delivery to occur, the bailee must be given exclusive possession and control over the property, and the bailee must *knowingly* accept the personal property.[5] In other words, the bailee must *intend* to exercise control over it.

If either delivery of possession or knowing acceptance is lacking, there is no bailment relationship. **Example 41.16** Sophia goes to a five-star restaurant and checks her coat at the door. She forgets that there is a $20,000 diamond necklace in the coat pocket. In accepting the coat, the bailee does not *knowingly* also accept the necklace. Thus, a bailment of the coat exists—because the restaurant has exclusive possession and control over the coat and has knowingly accepted it—but not a bailment of the necklace. ■

Physical versus Constructive Delivery. Either *physical* or *constructive* delivery will result in the bailee's exclusive possession of and control over the property. As discussed earlier, in the context of gifts, constructive delivery is a substitute, or symbolic, delivery. What is delivered to the bailee is not the actual property bailed (such as a car) but something so related to the property (such as the car keys) that the requirement of delivery is satisfied.

Involuntary Bailments. In certain situations, a bailment is found despite the apparent lack of the requisite elements of control and knowledge. One instance occurs when the bailee acquires the property accidentally or by mistake—as in finding someone else's lost or mislaid property. A bailment is created even though the bailor did not voluntarily deliver the property to the bailee. Such bailments are called *constructive* or *involuntary* bailments.

---

5. The requirements outlined in this sentence apply to *voluntary bailments*, not to *involuntary bailments*.

Example 41.17 Several corporate managers attend a meeting at the law office of Jacobs & Matheson. One of the corporate officers, Kyle Gustafson, inadvertently leaves his briefcase at the office at the conclusion of the meeting. In this situation, a court may find that an involuntary bailment has been created, even though Gustafson has not voluntarily delivered the briefcase and the law firm has not intentionally accepted it. If an involuntary bailment exists, the firm is responsible for taking care of the briefcase and returning it to Gustafson. ▮

Bailment Agreement A bailment agreement can be express or implied. Although a written contract is not required for bailments of less than one year (that is, the Statute of Frauds does not apply), it is a good idea to have one, especially when valuable property is involved.

The bailment agreement expressly or impliedly provides for the return of the bailed property to the bailor or to a third person, or for the disposal of the property by the bailee. It is assumed that the bailee will return the identical goods originally given by the bailor. In certain types of bailments, such as bailments of fungible goods, however, the property returned need only be equivalent property.

Example 41.18 A bailment is created when Holman stores his grain (fungible goods) in Joe's Warehouse. At the end of the storage period, however, the warehouse is not obligated to return to Holman exactly the same grain that he stored. As long as the warehouse returns grain of the same *type, grade*, and *quantity*, the warehouse—the bailee—has performed its obligation. ▮

41–4b Ordinary Bailments

Bailments are either *ordinary* or *special (extraordinary)*. There are three types of ordinary bailments. They are distinguished according to *which party receives a benefit from the bailment*. This factor will dictate the rights and liabilities of the parties, and the courts use it to determine the standard of care required of the bailee in possession of the personal property.

The three types of ordinary bailments are as follows:

1. *Bailment for the sole benefit of the bailor.* This is a gratuitous bailment (a bailment that involves no consideration) for the convenience and benefit of the bailor. Basically, the bailee is caring for the bailor's property as a favor. Therefore, the bailee owes only a slight duty of care and will be liable only if she or he is grossly negligent in caring for the property.

   Example 41.19 Allen asks his friend Sumi to store his car in her garage while he is away. If Sumi agrees to do so, a gratuitous bailment will be created, because the bailment will be for the sole benefit of the bailor (Allen). If the car is damaged while in Sumi's garage, Sumi will not be responsible for the damage unless it is caused by her gross negligence. ▮

2. *Bailment for the sole benefit of the bailee.* This type of bailment typically occurs when one person lends an item to another person (the bailee) solely for the bailee's convenience and benefit. Because the bailee is borrowing the item for her or his own benefit, the bailee owes a duty to exercise the utmost care and will be liable for even slight negligence.

   Example 41.20 Allen asks to borrow Sumi's boat so that he can go sailing over the weekend. The bailment of the boat is for Allen's (the bailee's) sole benefit. If Allen fails to pay attention and runs the boat aground, damaging its hull, he is liable for the costs of repairing the boat. ▮

What type of bailment is created if a garage owner agrees to store a friend's car?

3. *Bailment for the mutual benefit of the bailee and the bailor.* This is the most common kind of bailment and involves some form of compensation for storing property or holding property while it is being serviced. It is a contractual bailment and may be referred to as a *bailment for hire* or a *commercial bailment*. In this type of bailment, the bailee owes a duty to exercise a reasonable degree of care.

   Example 41.21 Allen leaves his car at Quick Lube for an oil change. Because Quick Lube will be paid to change Allen's oil, this is a mutual-benefit bailment. If Quick Lube fails to put the correct amount of oil back into Allen's car and the engine is damaged as a result, Quick Lube will be liable for failure to exercise reasonable care. ▮

Rights of the Bailee Certain rights are implicit in the bailment agreement. Generally, the bailee has the right to take possession of the property, to use it to accomplish the purpose of the bailment. The bailee also has a right to receive compensation (unless otherwise agreed), and to limit her or his liability for the bailed goods. These rights of the bailee are present (with some limitations) in varying degrees in all bailment transactions.

Right of Possession. A hallmark of the bailment agreement is that the bailee acquires the *right to control and possess the property temporarily.* The bailee's right of possession permits the bailee to recover damages from any third person for damage or loss of the property. **Example 41.22** No-Spot Dry Cleaners sends all suede leather garments to Cleanall Company for special processing. If Cleanall loses or damages any leather goods, No-Spot has the right to recover against Cleanall. ■ In addition, if the bailed property is stolen, the bailee has a legal right to regain possession of it.

Right to Use Bailed Property. The extent to which bailees can use the property entrusted to them depends in part on the terms of the bailment contract. When no provision is made, the extent of use depends on how necessary it is for the goods to be at the bailee's disposal for the ordinary purpose of the bailment to be carried out.

Example 41.23 If Lauren borrows a car to drive Devin to the airport, she, as the bailee, will obviously be expected to use the car. In contrast, if Devin drives his own car to the airport and places it in long-term storage nearby, the storage company, as the bailee, will not be expected to use the car. The ordinary purpose of a storage bailment does not include use of the property. The bailee will, however, be expected to use or move the car if necessary in an emergency (such as a hurricane or flood) to protect it from harm. ■

Right of Compensation. Except in a gratuitous bailment, a bailee has a right to be compensated as provided for in the bailment agreement. The bailee also has a right to be reimbursed for services rendered and costs incurred in keeping the bailed property (even in a gratuitous bailment).

To enforce the right of compensation, the bailee has a right to place a *possessory lien* on the bailed property until he or she has been fully compensated. A lien on bailed property is referred to as a **bailee's lien**, or an *artisan's lien.* If the bailor refuses to pay or cannot pay, in most states the bailee is entitled to foreclose on the lien and sell the property to recover the amount owed.

Example 41.24 Liam leaves his car at Jack's Automotive for repairs. Jack's informs Liam that the car needs a new transmission, and Liam authorizes Jack's to perform the work. When Liam returns to pick up the car, he refuses to pay the amount due for the transmission work. Jack's has a right to keep the car and place a lien on it until Liam pays for the repairs. If Liam continues to refuse to pay, Jack's can follow the state statutory process for foreclosing on the lien and selling the car to recover what is owed. ■

Right to Limit Liability. In ordinary bailments, bailees have the right to limit their liability, provided that both of the following are true:

1. *The limitations are called to the attention of the bailor.* It is essential that the bailor be informed of the limitation in some way. **Example 41.25** A sign in Nikolai's garage states that Nikolai will not be responsible "for loss due to theft, fire, or vandalism." Whether the sign will constitute notice will depend on the size of the sign, its location, and any other circumstances affecting the likelihood that customers will see it. ■

2. *The limitations are not against public policy.* Even when the bailor knows of the limitation, courts consider certain types of disclaimers of liability to be against public policy and therefore illegal. The courts carefully scrutinize *exculpatory clauses,* which limit a party's liability for the party's own wrongful acts. In bailments, especially mutual-benefit bailments, exculpatory clauses are often held to be illegal. **Example 41.26** A receipt from Al's Parking Garage expressly disclaims liability for any damage to parked cars, regardless of the cause. Because the bailee (the garage) has attempted to exclude liability for the bailee's own negligence, the clause will likely be deemed unenforceable because it is against public policy. ■

Bailee's Lien A possessory (artisan's) lien that a bailee entitled to compensation can place on the bailed property to ensure that he or she will be paid for the services provided.

Duties of the Bailee The bailee's duties are based on a mixture of tort law and contract law and include two basic responsibilities:

1. To take appropriate care of the property.
2. To surrender the property to the bailor or dispose of it in accordance with the bailor's instructions at the end of the bailment.

The Duty of Care. The bailee must exercise reasonable care in preserving the bailed property. What constitutes reasonable care in a bailment situation normally depends on the nature and specific circumstances of the bailment.

The courts determine the appropriate standard of care on the basis of the type of bailment involved. As mentioned earlier, in a bailment for the sole benefit of the bailor, the bailee need exercise only a slight degree of care. In a mutual-benefit bailment, courts normally impose a reasonable standard of care. In a bailment for the sole benefit of the bailee, the bailee must exercise great care. Exhibit 41–2 illustrates these concepts.

Determining whether a bailee exercised an appropriate degree of care is usually a question of fact for the jury or (in a nonjury trial) the judge. A bailee's failure to exercise appropriate care in handling the bailor's property results in tort liability.

Case Example 41.27 Bridge Tower Dental contracted with Meridian Computer Center to develop a computer system for its dental practice. Bridge Tower paid a computer consultant, Al Colson, to install the system and to provide maintenance and support. When Colson noticed that one of the server's two hard drives had stopped working, he informed Bridge Tower and took the server to Meridian Computer to be repaired. Meridian's owner, Jason Patten, agreed to replace the failing hard drive under the warranty. In attempting to copy data from the mirrored hard drive, however, Patten accidentally erased all the data, which he had not backed up. As a result, Bridge Tower lost all of its patients' records and contact information.

Bridge Tower sued Meridian for negligence. The Supreme Court of Idaho ruled in favor of Bridge Tower. Colson had entrusted Meridian with a server containing a failing hard drive (which was to be replaced) and a fully functional mirrored hard drive containing data. Meridian had a duty to protect and safeguard this bailed property in order to return it in the same condition that it was in when delivered. Patten mistakenly erased the data on the mirrored hard drive, which constituted negligence.[6]

What duty of care is required from a bailee that repairs computer hard drives?

Duty to Return Bailed Property. At the end of the bailment, the bailee normally must hand over the bailed property to the bailor or to someone the bailor designates, or must otherwise dispose of it as directed. Failure to give up possession at the time the bailment ends is a breach of contract and can result in a tort lawsuit for conversion or negligence.

Case Example 41.28 SANY America, Inc., loaned a crane to Turner Brothers, LLC, a construction contractor, for demonstration purposes. SANY wanted to sell the crane to Turner and continued to allow Turner to use it during their negotiations, but the parties never came to an agreement on a price. After the negotiations ended, SANY asked Turner for the crane's

---

6. *Bridge Tower Dental, P.A. v. Meridian Computer Center, Inc.*, 272 P.3d 541 (Idaho Sup.Ct. 2012).

Exhibit 41–2 Degree of Care Required of a Bailee

Bailment for the Sole Benefit of the Bailor	Mutual-Benefit Bailment	Bailment for the Sole Benefit of the Bailee
Degree of Care →		
Slight	Reasonable	Great

location to arrange retrieval. Before SANY retrieved the crane from Turner, however, it was severely damaged while being operated at Turner's construction site.

Turner removed the inoperable crane from the site at its own expense and then notified SANY that it expected compensation for the transportation expenses. In addition, Turner refused to return the crane to SANY and began billing SANY for daily storage costs. SANY sued for conversion, and Turner counterclaimed. A federal district court held that the parties' transaction was a bailment. Because Turner had wrongfully retained the crane after SANY demanded its return, SANY was entitled to summary judgment for conversion.[7]

A bailee may also be liable for conversion if the goods being held are delivered to the wrong person. Hence, the bailee should verify that the person (other than the bailor) to whom the goods are given is authorized to take possession.

Lost or Damaged Property. If the bailed property has been lost or is returned damaged, a court will presume that the bailee was negligent. The bailee's obligation is excused, however, if the property was destroyed, lost, or stolen through no fault of the bailee (or claimed by a third party with a superior claim). In other words, the bailee can rebut the presumption of negligence by showing that he or she exercised due care.

Case Example 41.29 Hornbeck Offshore Service engaged R&R Marine, Inc., to repair the ship *Erie Service* at R&R's shipyard on Lake Sabine in Port Arthur, Texas. While repairs were being made, a tropical storm warning was issued for Port Arthur. R&R's personnel left the shipyard without securing the *Erie Service* or preparing it for the storm. During the night, rain and water from Lake Sabine swamped the vessel. R&R's insurer, National Liability & Fire Insurance Company, asked a federal district court to declare that it was not required to pay the salvage cost. Hornbeck filed a counterclaim with the court alleging that R&R had been negligent. The lower court issued a decision in Hornbeck's favor, and R&R appealed.

A federal appellate court affirmed the lower court's ruling. The ship was delivered to R&R afloat, R&R had full custody of the vessel, and it sank while in R&R's care. This gave rise to a presumption of negligence. The severity of the weather conditions in Port Arthur had been foreseeable, and R&R showed no evidence that it had exercised ordinary care. The court held that R&R—not the insurer—was liable for the salvage cost because R&R had been negligent in failing to protect the ship from damage from the storm.[8]

In the following case, the court had to determine whether a constructive bailment existed with respect to the personal property of tenants who were evicted. If so, was the landlord-bailor negligent for removing the tenants' personal property and leaving it outside?

A bailee did not secure a ship to the dock when the ship was in the bailee's care. If the ship is damaged during a storm as a result, will the bailee be liable? Why or why not?

Photomarine/Shutterstock.com

---

7. *SANY America, Inc. v. Turner Brothers, LLC*, 2016 WL 1452341 (D.Mass. 2016).
8. *National Liability & Fire Insurance Co. v. R&R Marine, Inc.*, 756 F.3d 825 (5th Cir. 2014).

■ Case 41.3

Zissu v. IH2 Property Illinois, L.P.
United States District Court, Northern District of Illinois, Eastern Division, 157 F.Supp.3d 797 (2016).

Background and Facts Pavel and Aise Zissu lived in an apartment in Chicago, Illinois, owned by IH2 Property Illinois, LP. IH2 obtained an order from an Illinois state court allowing it to evict the Zissus. IH2 entered the apartment and moved the Zissus' personal property outside, placing it on the curb. The property, which included jewelry, furniture, and personal documents, was then either stolen or damaged. The Zissus filed a suit in a federal district court against IH2. The tenants alleged that IH2's taking possession of their property had constituted a bailment and that the company had been negligent in its care of the bailed property. IH2 filed a motion to dismiss the suit.

In the Words of the Court

John Z. *LEE,* United States District Judge

* * * *

A complaint * * * must * * * allege sufficient factual matter, accepted as true, to state a claim to relief that is plausible on its face. For a claim to have facial plausibility, a plaintiff must plead factual content that allows the court to draw the reasonable inference that the defendant is liable for the misconduct alleged. [Emphasis added.]

* * * *

The Zissus allege that IH2 negligently removed their personal property from the premises following the eviction, causing much of it to be damaged or stolen. * * * In its motion to dismiss, IH2 argues that the Zissus cannot state a claim for negligence because IH2, as the landlord, did not owe a duty to protect personal property left on the premises following the eviction.

* * * *

* * * [A]lthough a landlord does not have a general duty under common law to care for the personal property of a former tenant after a proper and legal eviction, a duty of care does arise when a landlord acts as an actual or constructive bailee with respect to the tenant's property. [If] the complaint states a claim for bailment * * *, the Court finds that Plaintiffs have sufficiently alleged the existence of a duty and a breach of that duty to survive a motion to dismiss as to their negligence claim.

* * * *

A bailment occurs when goods, or other personal property, are delivered to another, who under contract either express or implied has agreed to accept delivery and deal with the property in a particular way. To recover under a bailment theory, the plaintiff must allege: (1) an express or implied agreement to create a bailment, (2) delivery of the property, (3) the bailee's acceptance of the property, and (4) the bailee's failure to return the property or the bailee's delivery of the property in a damaged condition. [Emphasis added.]

An implied bailment—also called a constructive bailment—may be found where the property of one person is voluntarily received by another for some purpose other than that of obtaining ownership. The implied bailment may be deduced from the circumstances surrounding the transaction, including the benefits received by the parties, their intentions, the kind of property involved, and the opportunities of each to exercise control over the property.

The Zissus contend that, by actively removing the property from the premises and putting it on the street, IH2 assumed control over the property.

* * * *

* * * It was IH2's alleged actions after the sheriff had turned over possession of the premises to IH2 that gave rise to the bailment relationship. * * * The allegations are sufficient [to establish this claim] at the pleading stage.

Decision and Remedy The U.S. District Court held that IH2 could be held liable and denied IH2's motion to dismiss.

Critical Thinking

• **What If the Facts Were Different?** *Suppose that instead of putting the Zissus' personal property outside, IH2 had taken it to a storage facility. Would the result have been different? Why or why not?*

Duties of the Bailor The duties of a bailor are essentially the same as the rights of a bailee. A bailor has a duty to compensate the bailee as agreed and to reimburse the bailee for costs incurred by the bailee in keeping the bailed property. A bailor also has an all-encompassing duty to provide the bailee with goods or chattels that are free from known defects that could cause injury to the bailee.

Bailor's Duty to Reveal Defects. The bailor's duty to reveal defects to the bailee translates into two rules:

1. In a mutual-benefit bailment, the bailor must notify the bailee of all known defects and any hidden defects that the bailor knows of or could have discovered with reasonable diligence and proper inspection.

2. In a bailment for the sole benefit of the bailee, the bailor must notify the bailee of any known defects.

The bailor's duty to reveal defects is based on a negligence theory of tort law. A bailor who fails to give the appropriate notice is liable to the bailee and to any other person who might reasonably be expected to come into contact with the defective article.

Example 41.30 Rentco (the bailor) rents a tractor to Hal Iverson. Unknown to Rentco, the brake mechanism on the tractor is defective at the time the bailment is made. Rentco could have discovered the defect on reasonable inspection. Iverson uses the defective tractor without knowledge of the brake problem and is injured, along with two other field workers, when the tractor rolls downhill out of control after failing to stop. In this situation, Rentco is liable for the injuries sustained by Iverson and the other workers because it negligently failed to discover the defect and notify Iverson.

Warranty Liability for Defective Goods. A bailor can also incur *warranty liability* (discussed in an earlier chapter) based on contract law for injuries resulting from the bailment of defective articles. Property that is leased from a bailor must be *fit for the intended purpose of the bailment.* Warranties of fitness arise by law in sales contracts and leases, and courts have held that these warranties apply to bailments "for hire." Article 2A of the Uniform Commercial Code (UCC) extends the implied warranties of merchantability and fitness for a particular purpose to bailments that include rights to use the bailed goods.[9]

41–4c Special Types of Bailments

A business is likely to engage in some special types of bailment transactions in which the bailee's duty of care is *extraordinary* and the bailee's liability for loss or damage to the property is absolute. These situations usually involve common carriers and hotel operators. Warehouse companies have a higher duty of care than ordinary bailees but are not subject to strict liability. Like carriers, warehouse companies are subject to extensive regulation under federal and state laws, including Article 7 of the UCC.

Common Carriers *Common carriers* are publicly licensed to transport goods or passengers on regular routes at set rates. They are legally bound to carry all passengers or freight as long as there is enough space, the fee is paid, and there are no reasonable grounds to refuse service. Common carriers differ from private carriers, which operate transportation facilities for only a select clientele. A private carrier is not required to provide service to every person or company making a request.

Strict Liability Applies. The delivery of goods to a common carrier creates a bailment relationship between the shipper (bailor) and the common carrier (bailee). Unlike ordinary bailees, the common carrier is held to a standard of care based on *strict liability,* rather than reasonable care, in protecting the bailed personal property. This means that the common carrier is absolutely liable, regardless of due care, for all loss or damage to goods except when damage was caused by a natural disaster or war.

Limitations on Liability. Common carriers cannot contract away their liability for damaged goods. Subject to government regulations, however, they are permitted to limit their dollar liability to an amount stated on the shipment contract or rate filing.

Example 41.31 A jewelry store (Martinez Daughters) uses UPS to ship a diamond ring worth $200,000. The owner of the jewelry store, Julie Martinez, arranges for the shipment on UPS's website, which requires her to click on two on-screen boxes to agree to "My UPS Terms and Conditions." In these terms, UPS and its insurer limit their liability and the amount of insurance coverage on packages to $50,000 and refuse to ship items worth more than $50,000. Both UPS and its insurer disclaim liability *entirely* for such items. Nevertheless, Martinez purchases $50,000 in insurance for the package.

---

9. UCC 2A–212, 2A–213.

If the ring is subsequently lost in shipping, the jewelry store cannot recover any amount from UPS under the insurance policy. UPS's disclaimer of liability is enforceable, and the jewelry store breached the contract by indicating that the shipment was worth less than $50,000. ▪

Warehouse Companies *Warehousing* is the business of storing property for compensation. Like ordinary bailees, warehouse companies are liable for loss or damage to property resulting from negligence. But because a warehouse company is a professional bailee, it is expected to exercise a high degree of care to protect and preserve the goods.

Limitations on Liability. A warehouse company can limit the dollar amount of its liability. Under the UCC, however, it must give the bailor the option of paying a higher storage rate for an increase in the liability limit.[10]

A jewelry storeowner ships a $200,000 diamond ring knowing that the shipper's maximum shipment value is only $50,000. What happens if the ring never arrives at its destination?

Warehouse Receipts. Warehouse companies often issue *documents of title*—in particular, *warehouse receipts*.[11] A warehouse receipt describes the bailed property and the terms of the bailment contract. It can be negotiable or nonnegotiable, depending on how it is written. It is negotiable if its terms provide that the warehouse company will deliver the goods "to the bearer" of the receipt or "to the order of" a person named on the receipt.[12]

The warehouse receipt represents the goods (that is, it indicates title) and hence has value and utility in financing commercial transactions. **Example 41.32** Ossip delivers 6,500 cases of canned corn to Chaney, the owner of a warehouse. Chaney issues a negotiable warehouse receipt payable "to bearer" and gives it to Ossip. Ossip sells and delivers the warehouse receipt to Better Foods, Inc. Better Foods is now the owner of the corn and has the right to obtain the cases by simply presenting the warehouse receipt to Chaney. ▪

Hotel Operators At common law, hotel owners were strictly liable for the loss of any cash or property that guests brought into their rooms. Today, state statutes continue to apply strict liability to hotel operators for any loss or damage to their guests' personal property. In many states, however, hotel operators can avoid strict liability by providing a safe in which to keep guests' valuables and notifying guests that a safe is available.

In addition, state statutes often limit the liability of hotels with regard to articles that are not kept in the safe and may limit the availability of damages in the absence of negligence. Most statutes require that the hotel post these limitations on the doors of the rooms or otherwise notify guests. The failure of the hotel to follow the state statutory requirements can lead to liability.

Example 41.33 A guest at Crown Place hotel is traveling with jewelry valued at $1 million. She puts the jewelry in the safe in her room, but someone comes into the room and removes the jewelry from the safe without the use of force. The woman sues the hotel, which claims that it is not liable under the state statute. If Crown Place did not comply with statutory requirements that it post the legal limitations in the guest rooms, however, it will not be protected from liability. Crown Place will be strictly liable for the loss of the woman's jewelry. ▪

---

10. UCC 7–204(1), (2).
11. A *document of title* is defined in UCC 1–201(15) as any "document which in the regular course of business or financing is treated as adequately evidencing that the person in possession of it is entitled to receive, hold, and dispose of the document and the goods it covers." A *warehouse receipt* is a document of title issued by a person engaged for hire in the business of storing goods for hire.
12. UCC 7–104.

Practice and Review

Vanessa Denai owned forty acres of land in rural Louisiana. On the property were a 1,600-square-foot house and a metal barn. Denai met Lance Finney, who had been seeking a small plot of rural property to rent. After several meetings, Denai invited Finney to live on a corner of her land in exchange for Finney's assistance in cutting wood and tending her property. Denai agreed to store Finney's sailboat in her barn.

With Denai's consent, Finney constructed a concrete and oak foundation on Denai's property and purchased a 190-square-foot dome from Dome Baja for $3,395. The dome was shipped by Doty Express, a transportation company licensed to serve the public. When it arrived, Finney installed the dome frame and fabric exterior so that the dome was detachable from the foundation. A year after Finney installed the dome, Denai wrote Finney a note stating, "I've decided to give you four acres of land surrounding your dome as drawn on this map." This gift violated no local land-use restrictions. Using the information presented in the chapter, answer the following questions.

1. Is the dome real property or personal property? Explain.

2. Is Denai's gift of land to Finney a gift *causa mortis* or a gift *inter vivos*?

3. What type of bailment relationship was created when Denai agreed to store Finney's boat? What degree of care was Denai required to exercise in storing the boat?

4. What standard of care applied to the shipment of the dome by Doty Express?

Debate This

Common carriers should not be able to limit their liability.

Key Terms

abandoned property 980	chattel 973	gift *causa mortis* 978
accession 978	confusion 978	gift *inter vivos* 978
bailee 982	constructive delivery 976	lost property 979
bailee's lien 984	dominion 977	mislaid property 979
bailment 982	estray statute 980	personal property 973
bailor 982	gift 975	real property 972

Chapter Summary: Personal Property and Bailments

PERSONAL PROPERTY	
Personal Property versus Real Property	Personal property (personalty or chattel) includes all property not classified as real property (realty). Personal property can be tangible (such as a car) or intangible (such as stocks or bonds). The two types of property are usually subject to different types of taxes. In addition, acquiring or transferring real property requires a greater degree of formality than acquiring or transferring personal property.
Acquiring Ownership of Personal Property	The most common way of acquiring ownership in personal property is by purchasing it. The following are additional methods of acquiring personal property: 1. *Possession*—Property may be acquired by possession if no other person has title to the property (for instance, capturing wild animals). 2. *Production*—Any item produced by an individual (with minor exceptions) becomes the property of that individual.

	3. *Gifts*—A gift is effective under the following conditions:
	a. There is evidence of *intent* to make a gift of the property in question.
	b. The gift is *delivered* (physically or constructively) to the donee or the donee's agent.
	c. The gift is *accepted* by the donee.
	4. *Accession*—When value is added to personal property by the use of labor or materials, the owner of the original property generally retains title to the property and benefits from the added value.
	5. *Confusion*—If confusion of fungible goods occurs as a result of agreement, an honest mistake, or the act of some third party, the owners share ownership as tenants in common. If goods are confused due to an intentional wrongful act, the innocent party ordinarily acquires title to the whole.
Mislaid, Lost, and Abandoned Property	The finder of property acquires different rights depending on whether the property was mislaid, lost, or abandoned.
	1. *Mislaid property*—Property that is placed somewhere voluntarily by the owner and then inadvertently forgotten. The finder does not acquire title.
	2. *Lost property*—Property that the owner has involuntarily parted with and then cannot find or recover. The finder can claim title to the property against the whole world except the true owner.
	3. *Abandoned property*—Property that is discarded by the owner, who has no intention of reclaiming it in the future. The finder can claim title to the property against the whole world, including the original owner.

BAILMENTS	

Elements of a Bailment	1. *Personal property*—Bailments involve only personal property.
	2. *Delivery of possession without title*—For an effective bailment to exist, the bailee (the one receiving the property) must be given exclusive possession and control over the property. In a voluntary bailment, the bailee must knowingly accept the personal property.
	3. *The bailment agreement*—The agreement expressly or impliedly provides for the return of the bailed property to the bailor or a third party, or for the disposal of the bailed property by the bailee.
Ordinary Bailments	1. *Types of bailments*—
	a. Bailment for the sole benefit of the bailor—A gratuitous bailment undertaken for the sole benefit of the bailor (for example, as a favor to the bailor).
	b. Bailment for the sole benefit of the bailee—A gratuitous loan of an article to a person (the bailee) solely for the bailee's benefit.
	c. Mutual-benefit (contractual) bailment—This is the most common kind of bailment and involves compensation between the bailee and bailor for the service provided.
	2. *Rights of a bailee (duties of a bailor)*—
	a. The right of possession—Allows a bailee to sue any third persons for damage or loss of the bailed property.
	b. The right to use the property—Allowed to the extent it is necessary to carry out the purpose of the bailment.
	c. The right to be compensated and reimbursed for expenses—In the event of nonpayment, the bailee has the right to place a possessory (bailee's) lien on the bailed property until fully compensated.
	d. The right to limit liability—An ordinary bailee can limit his or her liability for loss or damage, provided proper notice is given and the limitation is not against public policy. In special bailments, limitations on liability for negligence or on types of losses usually are not allowed, but limitations on the monetary amount of liability are permitted.
	e. Duty to reveal defects—A bailor must notify the bailee of any known defects and, in mutual-benefit bailments, hidden defects as well.
	f. Warranty liability—A bailor can incur warranty liability for injuries resulting from the bailment of defective articles.
	3. *Duties of a bailee (rights of a bailor)*—
	a. A bailee must exercise appropriate care over property entrusted to her or him. What constitutes appropriate care normally depends on the nature and circumstances of the bailment. See Exhibit 41–2.
	b. Bailed goods in a bailee's possession must be either returned to the bailor or disposed of according to the bailor's directions. A bailee's failure to return the bailed property creates a presumption of negligence and constitutes a breach of contract or the tort of conversion.

(Continues)

Special Types of Bailments	1. *Common carriers*—Carriers that are publicly licensed to provide transportation services to the general public are held to a standard of care based on strict liability.
	2. *Warehouse companies*—Because a warehouse company is a professional bailee, it is expected to exercise a high degree of care to protect and preserve the bailed goods. Warehouse companies often issue documents of title (warehouse receipts) for goods, which may be negotiable or nonnegotiable.
	3. *Hotel operators*—Operators of hotels are subject to strict liability for any loss or damage to their guests' personal property. State statutes may limit liability if the hotel provides a safe and properly notifies its guests.

Issue Spotters

1. While walking to work, Bill finds an expensive ring lying on the curb. Bill gives the ring to his son, Hunter. Two weeks later, Martin Avery, the true owner of the ring, discovers that Bill found the ring and demands that Hunter return it. Who is entitled to the ring, and why? (See *Mislaid, Lost, and Abandoned Property*.)

2. Rosa de la Mar Corporation ships a load of goods via Southeast Delivery Company. The load of goods is lost in a hurricane in Florida. Who suffers the loss? Explain your answer. (See *Bailments*.)

   —**Check your answers to the *Issue Spotters* against the answers provided in Appendix D at the end of this text.**

Business Scenarios and Case Problems

41–1. Duties of the Bailee. Discuss the standard of care traditionally required of the bailee for the bailed property in each of the following situations, and determine whether the bailee breached that duty. (See *Bailments*.)

1. Ricardo borrows Steve's lawn mower because his own lawn mower needs repair. Ricardo mows his front yard. To mow the backyard, he needs to move some hoses and lawn furniture. He leaves the mower in front of his house while doing so. When he returns to the front yard, he discovers that the mower has been stolen.

2. Alicia owns a valuable speedboat. She is going on vacation and asks her neighbor, Maureen, to store the boat in one stall of Maureen's double garage. Maureen consents, and the boat is moved into the garage. Maureen needs some grocery items for dinner and drives to the store. She leaves the garage door open while she is gone, as is her custom, and the speedboat is stolen during that time.

41–2. Gifts. Jaspal has a severe heart attack and is taken to the hospital. He is aware that he is not expected to live. Because he is a bachelor with no close relatives nearby, Jaspal gives his car keys to his close friend Friedrich, telling Friedrich that he is expected to die and that the car is Friedrich's. Jaspal survives the heart attack, but two months later he dies from pneumonia. Sam, Jaspal's uncle and the executor of his estate, wants Friedrich to return the car. Friedrich refuses, claiming that the car was a gift from Jaspal. Discuss whether Friedrich will be required to return the car to Jaspal's estate. (See *Acquiring Ownership of Personal Property*.)

41–3. Lost Property. Sara Simon misplaced her Galaxy cell phone in Manhattan, Kansas. Days later, Shawn Vargo contacted her, claiming to have bought the phone from someone else. He promised to mail it to Simon if she would wire $100 to

him through a third party, Mark Lawrence. When Simon spoke to Lawrence about the wire transfer, she referred to the phone as hers and asked, "Are you going to send my phone to me?" Simon paid, but she did not get the phone. Instead, Lawrence took it to a Best Buy store and traded it in for credit. Charged with the theft of lost property, Lawrence claimed that he did not know Simon was the owner of the phone. Was Simon's phone lost, mislaid, or abandoned? What is the finder's responsibility with respect to this type of property? Can Lawrence successfully argue that he did not know the phone was Simon's? Explain. [*State of Kansas v. Lawrence*, 347 P.3d 240 (Kan.Ct.App. 2015)] (See *Mislaid, Lost, and Abandoned Property*.)

41–4. Bailments. Christie's Fine Art Storage Services, Inc. (CFASS), is in the business of storing fine works of art at its warehouse in Brooklyn, New York. The warehouse is next to the East River in a flood zone. Boyd Sullivan owns works of art by Alberto Vargas, including *Beauty and the Beast* and *Miss Universe*. Sullivan contracted to store the works at CFASS's facility under an agreement that limited the warehouser's liability for damage to the goods to $200,000. A few months later, as Hurricane Sandy approached, CFASS was warned, along with the other businesses in the flood zone, of the potential for damage from the storm. CFASS e-mailed its clients that extra precautions were being taken. Despite this assurance, Sullivan's works were left exposed on a ground floor and sustained severe damage in the storm. Who is most likely to suffer the loss? Why? [*Sullivan v. Christie's Fine Art Storage Services, Inc.*, 2016 WL 427615 (Sup. N.Y. County 2016)] (See *Bailments*.)

41–5. Duties of the Bailee. James Heal owned a vehicle salvage yard in Homestead, Iowa. Brian Anderson contracted with Heal to run the business. Anderson cleaned up the property, removed trash, installed heat and fixed the plumbing in the buildings, and brought in tools and equipment. He used his own resources to rebuild the aging inventory. Anderson reinvested all of the profits in the business. When Anderson sold a 2004 Ford F-150 that he had bought with his own money for his own use, however, Heal pocketed the proceeds and locked Anderson out of the business. Heal filed a suit in an Iowa state court against Anderson, alleging breach of contract, and obtained an injunction to keep him off the property. Do these circumstances create a bailment? What is the appropriate standard of care if there is a bailment? Discuss. [*Heal v. Anderson,* 900 N.W.2d 617 (Iowa App. 2017)] (See *Bailments.*)

41–6. The Nature of Personal Property. American Multi-Cinema, Inc. (AMC), owns movie theaters. To determine the amount of taxes it owed to Texas, AMC subtracted its cost of goods sold (COGS) from its total revenue. AMC included the cost of showing movies in its COGS. In other words, it treated showing movies as a "good." Texas, however, refused to allow AMC to claim this cost. AMC protested, arguing it was in the business of showing movies. Specifically, AMC sold its "product"—the right to watch films in its theaters—to moviegoers. The state countered that this right is intangible "non-property," arguing that an AMC customer exits a theater with memories but not a copy of the film. Thus, AMC's product is not considered a "good" for the purpose of COGS. Does the right to watch a film in a movie theater constitute property? Discuss. [*American Multi-Cinema, Inc. v. Hegar,* 2017 WL 74416 (Tex.App.— Austin 2017)] (See *Personal Property versus Real Property.*)

41–7. Business Case Problem with Sample Answer— Duties of the Bailee. KZY Logistics, LLC, transported a load of Mrs. Ressler's Food Products from New Jersey to California. When KZY's driver delivered the cargo, the customer rejected it—its temperature was higher than expected, making it unsafe. Mrs. Ressler's filed a suit against KZY in a federal district court. KZY contended that the temperature in its refrigerated trailer was proper and that Mrs. Ressler's had delivered a "hot" product for transport. KZY supplemented its allegations with temperature readings from the unit during the time in question. In transporting the cargo, what level of care did KZY owe Mrs. Ressler's? Did KZY meet this standard? Explain. [*Mrs. Ressler's Food Products v. KZY Logistics, LLC,* 675 Fed.Appx. 136 (3d Cir. 2017)] (See *Bailments.*)

—**For a sample answer to Problem 41–7, go to Appendix E at the end of this text.**

41–8. Bailor's Duty to Reveal Defects. Anastasio Guerra agreed to loan his pick-up truck to Gina Mandujano so that she could go grocery shopping in exchange for her making him lunch. When Mandujano drove out of the store's parking lot, the truck's power steering failed. Her wrist was caught in the spokes of the steering wheel, and she was severely injured. Guerra knew that there was a problem with his truck's steering, but he thought he had fixed the problem by replenishing the steering fluid. He did not believe that the issue was dangerous and had not told Mandujano. What type of bailment existed between Guerra and Mandujano? What standard of care did the bailor owe the bailee? Was the duty breached? Who is liable for the cost of Mandujano's injury? Explain. [*Mandujano v. Guerra,* 2018 WL 1611458 (Mich.Ct.App. 2018)] (See *Bailments.*)

41–9. A Question of Ethics—The IDDR Approach and Abandoned Property. *Mansoor Akhtar lived rent-free in the basement of Anila Dairkee's duplex in Minneapolis, Minnesota, for more than a year. When Dairkee asked Akhtar to move out, he refused. She changed the locks and advised him to remove his property from the duplex. But he did not. About a year later, while Dairkee was staying in New York, her father had the basement cleaned out. When Dairkee returned four months later, she learned that her father had disposed of Akhtar's property. Akhtar filed a suit in a Minnesota state court against Dairkee, alleging that she had wrongfully disposed of his property. [Akhtar v Dairkee, 2017 WL 1210140 (Minn.App. 2017)] (See* Mislaid, Lost, and Abandoned Property.*)*

1. Dairkee contended that Akhtar had abandoned his property. Is she correct? Explain.

2. Using the *Review* step of the IDDR approach, consider whether Dairkee's handling of Akhtar's property was ethical.

Critical Thinking and Writing Assignments

41–10. Time-Limited Group Assignment—Bailments. On learning that Sébastien planned to travel abroad, Roslyn asked him to deliver $25,000 in cash to her family in Mexico. During a customs inspection at the border, Sébastien told the customs inspector that he carried less than $10,000. The officer discovered the actual amount of cash that Sébastien was carrying, seized it, and arrested Sébastien. Roslyn asked the government to return what she claimed were her funds, arguing that the arrangement with Sébastien was a bailment and that she still held title to the cash. (See *Bailments.*)

1. The first group will argue that Roslyn is entitled to the cash.

2. The second group will take the position of the government and develop an argument that Roslyn's agreement with Sébastien does not qualify as a bailment.

3. The third group will assume that a bailment was created, identify what type of bailment it was, and explain the degree of care required of the bailee.

42 Real Property and Landlord-Tenant Law

Learning Objectives

The four Learning Objectives *below are designed to help improve your understanding. After reading this chapter, you should be able to answer the following questions:*

1. What is a fixture, and how does it relate to real property rights?

2. What is the difference between a joint tenancy and a tenancy in common?

3. What are the requirements for acquiring property by adverse possession?

4. What are the duties of the landlord and the tenant with respect to the use and maintenance of leased property?

"The right of property is the most sacred of all the rights of citizenship."

Jean-Jacques Rousseau
1712–1778
(French writer and philosopher)

From earliest times, property has provided a means for survival. Primitive peoples lived off the fruits of the land, eating the vegetation and wildlife. Later, as the vegetation was cultivated and the wildlife domesticated, property provided farmland and pasture.

Throughout history, property has continued to be an indicator of family wealth and social position. Indeed, an individual's right to his or her property has become, in the words of Jean-Jacques Rousseau, one of the "most sacred of all the rights of citizenship."

In this chapter, we examine the nature of real property and the ways in which it can be owned and transferred. We even consider whether the buyer of a haunted house can rescind the sale in this chapter's *Spotlight Case.* We also discuss leased property and landlord-tenant relationships.

42–1 The Nature of Real Property

Real property consists of land and the buildings, plants, and trees that are on it. Real property also includes subsurface and airspace rights, as well as personal property that has become permanently attached to the real property. Whereas personal property is movable, real property—also called *real estate* or *realty*—is immovable.

42–1a Land and Structures

Land includes the soil on the surface of the earth and the natural or artificial structures that are attached to it. It further includes all the waters contained on or under the surface and much, but not necessarily all, of the airspace above it. The exterior boundaries of land extend down to the center of the earth and up to the farthest reaches of the atmosphere (subject to certain qualifications).

42–1b Airspace and Subsurface Rights

The owner of real property has rights to the airspace above the land, as well as to the soil and minerals underneath it. Limitations on either airspace rights or subsurface rights normally must be indicated on the document that transfers title at the time of purchase. When no such limitations, or *encumbrances,* are noted, a purchaser generally can expect to have an unlimited right to possession of the property.

Airspace Rights Disputes concerning airspace rights may involve the right of commercial and private planes to fly over property and the right of individuals and governments to seed clouds and produce rain artificially. Flights over private land normally do not violate property rights unless the flights are so low and so frequent that they directly interfere with the owner's enjoyment and use of the land. Leaning walls or buildings and projecting eave spouts or roofs may also violate the airspace rights of an adjoining property owner.

Subsurface Rights In many states, land ownership may be separated, in that the surface of a piece of land and the subsurface may have different owners. Subsurface rights can be extremely valuable, as these rights include the ownership of minerals, oil, and natural gas. Subsurface rights would be of little value, however, if the owner could not use the surface to exercise those rights. Hence, a subsurface owner has a right (called a *profit,* to be discussed later in this chapter) to go onto the surface of the land to, for instance, discover and mine minerals.

When ownership is separated into surface and subsurface rights, each owner can pass title to what she or he owns without the consent of the other owner. Of course, conflicts can arise between the surface owner's use of the property and the subsurface owner's need to extract minerals, oil, or natural gas. In that situation, one party's interest may become subservient (secondary) to the other party's interest either by statute or by case law.

If the owners of the subsurface rights excavate (dig), they are absolutely liable if their excavation causes the surface to collapse. Many states have statutes that also make the excavators liable for any damage to structures on the land. Typically, these statutes provide precise requirements for excavations of various depths.

42–1c Plant Life and Vegetation

Plant life, both natural and cultivated, is also considered to be real property. In many instances, natural vegetation, such as trees, adds greatly to the value of the realty. When a parcel of land is sold and the land has growing crops on it, the sale includes the crops, unless otherwise specified in the sales contract. When crops are sold by themselves, however, they are considered to be personal property, or goods. Consequently, the sale of crops is a sale of goods and thus is governed by the Uniform Commercial Code (UCC) rather than by real property law.[1]

42–1d Fixtures

Certain personal property can become so closely associated with the real property to which it is attached that the law views it as real property. Such property is known as a **fixture**—an item *affixed* to realty, meaning that it is attached to the real property in a permanent way.

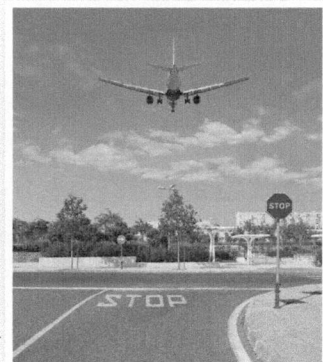

Who owns airspace above residential land?

"The meek shall inherit the earth, but not its mineral rights."

J. Paul Getty
1892–1976
(American entrepreneur and industrialist)

Fixture An item of personal property that has become so closely associated with real property that it is legally regarded as part of that real property.

---

1. See UCC 2–107(2).

The item may be embedded in the land, or permanently attached to the property or to another fixture on the property by means of cement, mortar, bolts, nails, roots, or screws. An item, such as a statue, may even sit on the land without being attached, as long as the owner intends the property to be a fixture.

Fixtures are included in the sale of land if the sales contract does not provide otherwise.[2] The sale of a house includes the land and the house and any detached garage on the land, as well as the cabinets, plumbing, and windows. Because these are permanently affixed to the property, they are considered to be a part of it. Certain items, such as drapes and window-unit air conditioners, are difficult to classify. Thus, a contract for the sale of a house or commercial realty should indicate which items of this sort are included in the sale.

Example 42.1 Rosemary & Sage Farm has an eight-tower center-pivot irrigation system that is bolted to a cement slab and connected to an underground well. The bank holds a mortgage note on the farm secured by "all buildings, improvements, and fixtures." Later, when Rosemary & Sage files for bankruptcy, a dispute arises between the bank and another creditor over the irrigation system. In this situation, a court is likely to find that the irrigation system is a fixture because it is firmly attached to the land and integral to the operation of the farm. Therefore, the bank's security interest will have priority over the other creditor's interest.

42–2 Ownership Interests and Leases

Ownership of real property is abstract and differs from ownership of personal property. No one can actually possess or *hold* a piece of land, the airspace above it, the earth below it, and all the water contained on it. The legal system therefore recognizes certain rights and duties that constitute ownership interests in real property.

Traditionally, ownership interests in real property were referred to as *estates in land,* which include fee simple estates, life estates, and leasehold estates. We examine estates in land, forms of concurrent ownership, and certain other interests in real property in the following subsections.

As you will see, ownership of real property (as well as personal property) can be viewed as a bundle of rights, including the right to possess the property and to dispose of it by sale, gift, lease, or other means. A person can own either the whole bundle of rights (a fee simple) or only a part of the rights. When only some of the rights are transferred, the effect is to limit the ownership rights of both the transferor of the rights and the recipient.

42–2a Ownership in Fee Simple

One who possesses the entire bundle of rights is said to hold the property in **fee simple** (usually referring to *fee simple absolute*), which is the most complete form of ownership. An owner in fee simple is entitled to use, possess, or dispose of the property as he or she chooses during his or her lifetime. The owner has the rights of *exclusive* possession and use of the property. The owner can give the property away, sell it, or lease it.

Duration On the fee simple owner's death, the interests in the property descend (pass down) to his or her heirs, even if the owner has not executed a will. Thus, a fee simple is potentially infinite in duration and is assigned forever to a person and her or his heirs without limitation or condition.

Limitations on Use The rights that accompany a fee simple include the right to use the land for whatever purpose the owner sees fit. Of course, other laws, including applicable zoning regulations, noise regulations, and environmental laws, may limit the owner's ability to use the property in certain ways. A fee simple owner cannot build a manufacturing plant on the property if doing so would violate applicable city or county rules and regulations, for

---

Learning Objective 1
What is a fixture, and how does it relate to real property rights?

Songbird839/iStock/Getty Images

Under what circumstances is an industrial-quality irrigation system considered a fixture?

Fee Simple An ownership interest in land in which the owner has the greatest possible aggregation of rights, privileges, and power.

"Few ... men own their property. The property owns them."

Robert G. Ingersoll
1833–1899
(American politician and lecturer)

---

2. Trade fixtures, which are items installed by a tenant for a commercial purpose (such as a walk-in cooler for a restaurant), are an exception and do not become part of the landowner's real property.

instance. Also, a person who uses his or her property in a manner that unreasonably interferes with others' right to use or enjoy their own property can be liable for the tort of *nuisance*.

■ **Spotlight Case Example 42.2** Nancy and James Biglane owned and lived in a building in Natchez, Mississippi. Next door to the couple's property was the Under the Hill Saloon, a popular bar that featured live music. During the summer, the Saloon, which had no air-conditioning, opened its windows and doors, and live music echoed up and down the street.

Although the Biglanes installed extra insulation, thicker windows, and air-conditioning units in their building, the noise from the Saloon kept them awake at night. Eventually, the Biglanes sued the owners of the Saloon for nuisance. The court held that the noise from the bar unreasonably interfered with the Biglanes' right to enjoy their property and prohibited the Saloon from opening its windows and doors while playing music.[3] ■

42–2b Life Estates

A **life estate** is an estate that lasts for the life of some specified individual. A **conveyance,** or transfer of real property, "to Alex Munson for his life" creates a life estate. In a life estate, the life tenant's ownership rights cease to exist on the life tenant's death.

The life tenant has the right to use the land provided that he or she commits no **waste** (injury to the land). In other words, the life tenant cannot use the land in a manner that would adversely affect its value. **Example 42.3** Julian, a life tenant on Blazin Acres, can use the land to harvest crops. If mines and oil wells are already on the land, Julian can extract minerals and oil from it, but he cannot drill new oil wells or excavate mines on the property. ■

The life tenant also has the right to create liens, *easements* (discussed shortly), and leases, but none can extend beyond the life of the tenant. In addition, with a few exceptions, the owner of a life estate has an exclusive right to possession during her or his lifetime.

Along with these rights, the life tenant also has some duties. He or she must keep the property in repair and pay property taxes. In short, the owner of a life estate has the same rights as a fee simple owner, with a few exceptions. The life tenant must maintain the value of the property during her or his tenancy and he or she cannot sell the property or leave it to his or her heirs.

The distinction between a life estate and a fee simple determined the result in the following case.

Life Estate An interest in land that exists only for the duration of the life of a specified individual, usually the holder of the estate.

Conveyance The transfer of title to real property from one person to another by deed or other document.

Waste The use of real property in a manner that damages or destroys its value.

---

3. *Biglane v. Under the Hill Corp.*, 949 So.2d 9 (Miss.Sup.Ct. 2007).

■ **Case 42.1**

In the Matter of the Estate of Nelson

North Dakota Supreme Court, 2018 ND 118, 910 N.W.2d 856 (2018).

Background and Facts When Sidney Solberg died, 100 mineral acres—that is, the right to all of the minerals under a certain 100 acres—and other real property in his estate were distributed to his widow, Lillian, for her life. The remainder interest (the right of ownership after Lillian's interest ended) was conveyed to their four children, including Glenn Solberg.

Later, Lillian married Lyle Nelson. When Lillian passed away, a codicil (addition) to her will allegedly gave the 100 mineral acres to Glenn. The codicil also purported to create for Glenn an option to buy the other real property she had inherited from Sidney. When Lyle Nelson died, Glenn filed a claim in a North Dakota state court against Nelson's estate. Glenn claimed that under the terms of the codicil to Lillian's will, he was entitled to the ownership of the 100 mineral acres and the right to buy the other property. The court dismissed Glenn's claim. He appealed to the state supreme court.

In the Words of the Court
JENSEN, Justice.
* * * *

(Continues)

Our law regarding the rights of someone who holds a life interest in property is * * * well established. It is well-settled [that] a life estate holder is entitled to both the possession and the use of the property, * * * including the right to rents, issues, and profits generated by the parcel * * *. *A life tenant is entitled to possession and enjoyment of the property as long as the estate endures; he or she may convey or lease his or her interest, but may not disregard the rights of those who take when the life estate ends.* * * * No future interest can be defeated or barred by any alienation [voluntary transfer of real property] or other act of the owner of the [life] interest. [Emphasis added.]

In this case, Lillian Nelson obtained a life estate interest in the 100 mineral acres and in the option property * * * from Sidney Solberg's estate. The codicil relied upon by Glenn Solberg itself identifies Lillian Nelson's interest as being limited to a life estate. As a life tenant she was limited to conveying an interest in her property only to the extent of her life and she could not make any transfers that would disregard the rights of those who would take the property when her life ended. As such, Lillian Nelson's attempt to provide an interest in the 100 mineral acres to Glenn Solberg in her * * * will is invalid because it disregards the rights of those who would take the property when her life ended. Similarly, her

attempt to convey a right of first refusal to the option property * * * is also invalid because it disregards the rights of those who would take the property when her life ended.

Upon Lillian Nelson's death * * * her life interest ended and the 100 mineral acres and the option property became the property of her four children as the holders of the remainder interest. * * * The Lyle Nelson Estate did not hold, and Lyle Nelson never held, an interest in the 100 mineral acres or the option property. * * * Glenn Solberg could not recover property from the Lyle Nelson Estate if Lyle Nelson never held an interest in the property.

Decision and Remedy The North Dakota Supreme Court affirmed the dismissal of Glenn's claim. "The [lower] court properly concluded that, with certainty, it would be impossible for Glenn Solberg to obtain the relief he requested from the Lyle Nelson Estate."

Critical Thinking

• **What If the Facts Were Different?** *Suppose that Sidney Solberg had disposed of his entire estate in fee simple before his death. Would the result have been different? Discuss.*

42–2c Concurrent Ownership

Concurrent Ownership Joint ownership.

Persons who share ownership rights simultaneously in particular property (including real property and personal property) are said to have **concurrent ownership**. There are two principal types of concurrent ownership: *tenancy in common* and *joint tenancy*. Concurrent ownership rights can also be held in a *tenancy by the entirety* or as *community property*, but these types of concurrent ownership are less common.

Tenancy in Common Joint ownership of property in which each party owns an undivided interest that passes to his or her heirs at death.

Tenancy in Common The term **tenancy in common** refers to a form of co-ownership in which each of two or more persons owns an undivided interest in the property. The interest is undivided because each tenant shares rights in the whole property. On the death of a tenant in common, that tenant's interest in the property passes to her or his heirs.

Example 42.4 Four friends purchase a condominium unit in Hawaii together as tenants in common. This means that each of them has a one-fourth ownership interest in the whole. If one of the four owners dies a year after the purchase, his ownership interest passes to his heirs (his wife and children, for instance) rather than to the other tenants in common.

Unless the co-tenants have agreed otherwise, a tenant in common can transfer her or his interest in the property to anyone without the consent of the remaining co-owners. In most states, it is presumed that a co-tenancy is a tenancy in common unless there is specific language indicating the intent to establish a joint tenancy (discussed next).

Joint Tenancy Joint ownership of property in which each co-owner owns an undivided portion of the property. On the death of one of the joint tenants, his or her interest automatically passes to the surviving joint tenant(s).

Joint Tenancy In a **joint tenancy**, each of two or more persons owns an undivided interest in the property, but a deceased joint tenant's interest passes to the surviving joint tenant or tenants.

Right of Survivorship. The right of a surviving joint tenant to inherit a deceased joint tenant's ownership interest—referred to as a *right of survivorship*—distinguishes a joint tenancy from a tenancy in common. **Example 42.5** Jerrold and Eva are married and purchase a house as joint tenants. The title to the house clearly expresses the intent to create a joint tenancy because it says "to Jerrold and Eva as joint tenants with right of survivorship." Jerrold has three children from a prior marriage. If Jerrold dies, his interest in the house automatically passes to Eva rather than to his children from the prior marriage. ▉

Termination of a Joint Tenancy. A joint tenant can transfer her or his rights by sale or gift to another without the consent of the other joint tenants. Doing so terminates the joint tenancy. The person who purchases the property or receives it as a gift becomes a tenant in common, not a joint tenant. **Example 42.6** Three brothers, Brody, Saul, and Jacob, own land as joint tenants. Brody is experiencing financial difficulties and sells his interest in the property to Beth. The sale terminates the joint tenancy, and now Beth, Saul, and Jacob hold the property as tenants in common. ▉

A joint tenant's interest can also be levied against (seized by court order) to satisfy the tenant's judgment creditors. If this occurs, the joint tenancy terminates, and the remaining owners hold the property as tenants in common. (Judgment creditors can also seize the interests of tenants in a tenancy in common.)

Tenancy by the Entirety

A less common form of shared ownership of real property by married persons is a **tenancy by the entirety**. It differs from a joint tenancy in that neither spouse may separately transfer his or her interest during his or her lifetime unless the other spouse consents. In some states in which statutes give the wife the right to convey her property, this form of concurrent ownership has effectively been abolished. A divorce, either spouse's death, or mutual agreement will terminate a tenancy by the entirety.

Community Property

A limited number of states[4] allow married couples to own property as **community property**. If property is held as community property, each spouse technically owns an undivided one-half interest in the property. This type of ownership applies to most property acquired by either spouse during the course of the marriage. It generally does *not* apply to property acquired prior to the marriage or to property acquired by gift or inheritance as separate property during the marriage. After a divorce, community property is divided equally in some states and according to the discretion of the court in other states.

42–2d Leasehold Estates

A **leasehold estate** is created when a real property owner or lessor (landlord) agrees to convey the right to possess and use the property to a lessee (tenant) for a certain period of time. The tenant has a *qualified* right to exclusive possession. It is qualified because the landlord has a right to enter onto the premises to ensure that no waste (damage or destruction) is being committed.

The *temporary* nature of possession under a lease is what distinguishes a tenant from a purchaser, who acquires title to the property. The tenant can use the land—for instance, by harvesting crops—but cannot injure it by such activities as cutting down timber for sale or extracting oil.

Fixed-Term Tenancy

A **fixed-term tenancy**, also called a *tenancy for years*, is created by an express contract by which property is leased for a specified period of time. Signing a one-year lease to occupy an apartment, for instance, creates a fixed-term tenancy. The term need not be specified by date and can be conditioned on the occurrence of an event, such as leasing a cabin for the summer or an apartment in New Orleans during Mardi Gras.

At the end of the period specified in the lease, the lease ends (without notice), and possession of the property returns to the lessor. If the tenant dies during the period of the lease, the lease interest passes to the tenant's heirs as personal property. Often, leases include renewal or extension provisions.

Learning Objective 2
What is the difference between a joint tenancy and a tenancy in common?

Tenancy by the Entirety Joint ownership of property by a married couple in which neither spouse can transfer his or her interest in the property without the consent of the other.

Community Property A form of concurrent property ownership in which each spouse owns an undivided one-half interest in property acquired during the marriage.

Leasehold Estate An interest in real property that gives a tenant a qualified right to possess and/or use the property for a limited time under a lease.

Fixed-Term Tenancy A type of tenancy under which property is leased for a specified period of time, such as a month, a year, or a period of years. It is also called a *tenancy for years*.

---

4. These states include Alaska, Arizona, California, Idaho, Louisiana, Nevada, New Mexico, Texas, Washington, and Wisconsin. Puerto Rico allows property to be owned as community property as well.

Periodic Tenancy A lease interest for an indefinite period involving payment of rent at fixed intervals, such as week to week, month to month, or year to year.

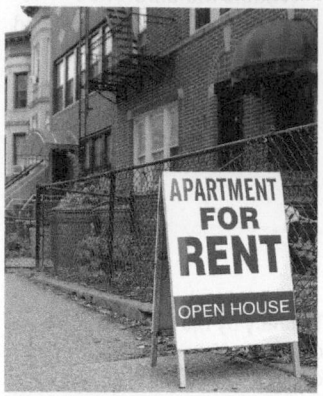

The lease agreement for the apartment in this building states that rent is due on the first of each month. What type of tenancy is created?

Tenancy at Will A type of tenancy that either the landlord or the tenant can terminate without notice.

Tenancy at Sufferance A tenancy that arises when a tenant wrongfully continues to occupy leased property after the lease has terminated.

Nonpossessory Interest In the context of real property, an interest that involves the right to use land but not the right to possess it.

Easement A nonpossessory right, established by express or implied agreement, to make limited use of another's property without removing anything from the property.

Profit In real property law, the right to enter onto another's property and remove something of value from that property.

Periodic Tenancy

A **periodic tenancy** is created by a lease that does not specify how long it is to last but does specify that rent is to be paid at certain intervals. This type of tenancy is automatically renewed for another rental period unless properly terminated. **Example 42.7** Kayla enters into a lease with Capital Properties. The lease states, "Rent is due on the tenth day of every month." This provision creates a periodic tenancy from month to month. ▪ This type of tenancy can also extend from week to week or from year to year.

Under the common law, to terminate a periodic tenancy, the landlord or tenant must give at least one period's notice to the other party. If the tenancy extends from month to month, for instance, one month's notice must be given prior to the last month's rent payment. Today, however, many states' statutes require a different period for notice of termination in a periodic tenancy.

Tenancy at Will

With a **tenancy at will,** either party can terminate the tenancy without notice. This type of tenancy can arise if a landlord allows a person to live on the premises without paying rent or rents property to a tenant "for as long as both agree." Tenancies at will are rare today because most state statutes require a landlord to provide some period of notice to terminate a tenancy. States may also require a landowner to have sufficient cause to end a residential tenancy.

Tenancy at Sufferance

The mere possession of land without right is called a **tenancy at sufferance.** A tenancy at sufferance is not a true tenancy because it is created when a tenant *wrongfully* retains possession of property. Whenever a tenancy for years or a periodic tenancy ends and the tenant continues to retain possession of the premises without the owner's permission, a tenancy at sufferance is created.

42–2e Nonpossessory Interests—Easements, Profits, and Licenses

In contrast to the types of property interests just described, some interests in land do not include any rights to possess the property. These interests are known as **nonpossessory interests** and include easements, profits, and licenses.

An **easement** is the right of a person to make limited use of another person's real property without taking anything from the property. An easement, for instance, can be the right to walk or drive across another's property. In contrast, a **profit**[5] is the right to go onto land owned by another and take away some part of the land itself or some product of the land. **Example 42.8** Shawn owns The Dunes. Shawn gives Carmen the right to go there to remove all the sand and gravel that she needs for her cement business. Carmen has a profit. ▪

Easements and profits can be classified as either *appurtenant* or *in gross.* Because easements and profits are similar and the same rules apply to both, we discuss them together.

Easement or Profit Appurtenant

An easement or profit *appurtenant* arises when the owner of one piece of land has a right to go onto (or remove something from) an adjacent piece of land owned by another. The land that is benefited by the easement is called the *dominant estate,* and the land that is burdened is called the *servient estate.*

Because easements appurtenant are intended to *benefit the land,* they run (are conveyed) with the land when it is transferred. **Example 42.9** Taylor has a right to drive his car across Green's land, which is adjacent to Taylor's land. This right-of-way over Green's property is an easement appurtenant to Taylor's property and can be used only by Taylor. If Taylor sells his land, the easement runs with the land to benefit the new owner. ▪

Easement or Profit in Gross

In an easement or profit *in gross,* the right to use or take things from another's land is given to one who does not own an adjacent tract of land. These easements are intended to *benefit a particular person or business,* not a particular piece of land, and cannot be transferred.

---

5. As used here, the term *profit* does not refer to the profits made by a business firm. Rather, it means a gain or an advantage.

Example 42.10 Avery owns a parcel of land with a marble quarry. Avery conveys (transfers) to Classic Stone Corporation the right to come onto her land and remove up to five hundred pounds of marble per day. Classic Stone owns a profit in gross and cannot transfer this right to another. ▪ Similarly, when a utility company is granted an easement to run its power lines across another's property, it obtains an easement in gross.

Creation of an Easement or Profit
Most easements and profits are created by an express grant in a contract, a deed, or a will. This allows the parties to include terms defining the extent and length of time of use. In some situations, an easement or profit can also be created without an express agreement.

An easement or profit may arise by *implication* when the circumstances surrounding the division of a parcel of property imply its existence. **Example 42.11** Mathews divides a parcel of land that has only one well for drinking water. If Mathews conveys the half without a well to Dean, a profit by implication arises because Dean needs drinking water. ▪

An easement or profit may also be created by *necessity*. An easement by necessity does not require a division of property for its existence. A person who rents an apartment, for instance, has an easement by necessity in the private road leading up to the apartment building.

An easement or profit may arise by *prescription* when one person uses another person's land without the landowner's consent. The use must be apparent and continue for the length of time required by the applicable statute of limitations. (In much the same way, title to property may be obtained by *adverse possession,* discussed later in this chapter.)

Case Example 42.12 Junior and Wilma Thompson sold twenty-one of their fifty acres of land in Missouri to Walnut Bowls, Inc. The deed expressly reserved an easement to the Thompsons' remaining twenty-nine acres, but it did not fix a precise location for the easement. James and Linda Baker subsequently bought the remaining acreage of the Thompsons' land. Many years later—on learning of the easement to the Bakers' property—a potential buyer of Walnut Bowls' property refused to go through with the sale.

Walnut Bowls then put steel cables across its driveway entrances, installed a lock and chain on an access gate, and bolted a "No Trespassing" sign facing the Bakers' property. The Bakers sued. Ultimately, a state intermediate appellate court found that an easement existed and instructed the trial court to determine its location. An easement can be created by deed even though its specific location is not identified. If the easement is not identified by agreement between the parties or inferred from use, then a court must determine its location.[6] ▪

Termination of an Easement or Profit
An easement or profit can be terminated in several ways. The simplest way is to deed it back to the owner of the land that is burdened by it. Similarly, if the owner of an easement or profit becomes the owner of the property burdened by it, then it is merged into the property.

Another way to terminate an easement or profit is to abandon it and create evidence of intent to relinquish the right to use it. Mere nonuse will not extinguish an easement or profit *unless the nonuse is accompanied by an overt act showing the intent to abandon.*

License
In the context of real property, a **license** is the revocable right to enter onto another person's land. It is a personal privilege that arises from the consent of the owner of the land and can be revoked by the owner. A ticket to attend a movie at a theater or a concert is an example of a license.

In essence, a license grants a person the authority to enter the land of another and perform a specified act or series of acts without obtaining any permanent interest in the land. When a person with a license exceeds the authority granted and undertakes an action that is not permitted, the property owner can sue that person in tort law for trespass.

---

6. *Baker v. Walnut Bowls, Inc.,* 423 S.W.3d 293 (Mo.App. 2014).

Know This
An easement appurtenant requires two adjacent pieces of land owned by two different persons, but an easement in gross needs only one piece of land owned by someone other than the owner of the easement.

If an easement's location is not precisely fixed, is the easement still valid?

License In the context of real property, a revocable right or privilege to enter onto another person's land.

Case Example 42.13 Richard and Mary Orman purchased real property owned at one time by Sandra Curtis. Part of the garage extended nine feet onto Curtis's neighboring property. In an agreement on file with the deed, Curtis had given the Ormans permission to use the garage as long as it continued to be used as a garage. After the Ormans moved in, they converted the garage's workshop into guest quarters but continued to use the garage as a garage.

A dispute arose over the driveway shared by Curtis and the Ormans, which straddled the property line. The Ormans filed a suit claiming that Curtis left "junk objects" near the driveway that impeded their access. Curtis countered that the permission she had given the buyers to use the garage was a license. She claimed that the Ormans, by converting the workshop into living quarters, had exceeded their authority under the license, which she could therefore revoke. The court looked at the agreement's wording, which clearly gave the Ormans the right to use the garage but did not mention the workshop. The court concluded that because the Ormans were continuing to use the garage as a garage, Curtis could not revoke their right to do so.[7]

Exhibit 42–1 illustrates the various interests in property discussed in this chapter.

42–3 Transfer of Ownership

Ownership interests in real property are frequently transferred (conveyed) by sale, and the terms of the transfer are specified in a real estate sales contract.

Real property ownership can also be transferred by gift, by will or inheritance, by adverse possession, or by eminent domain. When ownership rights in real property are transferred, the type of interest being transferred and the conditions of the transfer normally are set forth in a *deed* executed by the person who is conveying the property.

42–3a Real Estate Sales Contracts

In some ways, a sale of real estate is similar to a sale of goods, because it involves a transfer of ownership, often with specific warranties. A sale of real estate, however, is a more complicated transaction that involves certain formalities that are not required in a sale of goods. In part because of these complications, real estate brokers or agents who are licensed by the state generally assist the buyers and sellers during a real estate sales transaction.

Usually, the parties to a sale of real estate enter into a detailed contract setting forth their agreement. The contract includes such terms as the purchase price, the type of deed the buyer will receive, the condition of the premises, and any items that will be included.

---

7. *Orman v. Curtis,* 54 Misc.3d 1206(A), 50 N.Y.S.3d 27 (2017).

Exhibit 42–1 Interests in Real Property

Ownership Interests	1. *Fee simple*—The most complete form of ownership.
	2. *Life estate*—An estate that lasts for the life of a specified individual.
	3. *Concurrent ownership*—Ownership by two or more persons who hold title to property together. Types of concurrent ownership are as follows:
	a. Tenancy in common
	b. Joint tenancy
	c. Tenancy by the entirety
	d. Community property
Leasehold Estates	1. Fixed-term tenancy (tenancy for years)
	2. Periodic tenancy
	3. Tenancy at will
	4. Tenancy at sufferance
Nonpossessory Interests	1. Easements
	2. Profits
	3. Licenses

Unless the buyer pays cash for the property, he or she must obtain financing through a mortgage loan. Real estate sales contracts can be made contingent on the buyer's ability to obtain financing at or below a specified rate of interest. The contract may also be contingent on certain events, such as the completion of a land survey or the property's passing one or more inspections. Normally, the buyer is responsible for having the premises inspected for physical or mechanical defects and for insect infestation.

Implied Warranties in the Sale of New Homes Most states recognize a warranty—the **implied warranty of habitability**—in the sale of new homes. Because the warranty is implied, it need not be included in the contract of sale or the deed to be effective.

Under this warranty, the seller of a new home essentially warrants that it is in reasonable working order and is of reasonably sound construction. Thus, the seller is in effect a guarantor of the home's fitness. In some states, the warranty protects not only the first purchaser but any subsequent purchaser as well.

Implied Warranty of Habitability
An implied promise by a seller of a new house that the house is fit for human habitation. Also, the implied promise by a landlord that rented residential premises are habitable.

Seller's Duty to Disclose Hidden Defects In most jurisdictions, courts impose on sellers a duty to disclose any known defect that materially affects the value of the property and that the buyer could not reasonably discover. Failure to disclose such a material defect gives the buyer the right to rescind the contract and to sue for damages based on fraud or misrepresentation. The buyer generally must bring such a suit within a specified time.

Example 42.14 Matthew Newson partially renovates a house in Louisiana and sells it to Terry and Tabitha Moreland for $68,000. Two months after the Morelands move in, they discover rotten wood behind the tile in the bathroom and experience problems with the plumbing. The state statute specifies that the Morelands have one year from the date of the sale or the discovery of the defect to file a lawsuit. Therefore, the Morelands must file suit within twelve months of discovering the defects (which would be fourteen months from the date of the sale).

In the following *Spotlight Case*, the court had to decide whether the buyer of a "haunted" house had the right to rescind the sales contract.

If this homeowner discovers numerous defects in her recently purchased house, can she wait years to attempt to rescind the contract?

✸ Spotlight on Sales of Haunted Houses: Case 42.2

Stambovsky v. Ackley

Supreme Court, Appellate Division, New York, 572 N.Y.S.2d 672, 169 A.D.2d 254 (1991).

Background and Facts Jeffrey Stambovsky signed a contract to buy Helen Ackley's house in Nyack, New York. After the contract was signed, Stambovsky discovered that the house was widely reputed to be haunted. The Ackley family claimed to have seen poltergeists on numerous occasions over the previous nine years. The Ackleys had been interviewed about the house in both a national publication (*Reader's Digest*) and the local newspaper. The house was included on a walking tour of Nyack, New York, as "a riverfront Victorian (with ghost)."

When will a buyer of a house that is allegedly haunted have the right to rescind the deal?

When Stambovsky learned of the house's reputation, he sued to rescind the contract, alleging that Ackley and her real estate agent had made material misrepresentations when they failed to disclose Ackley's belief that the house was haunted. Ackley argued that she was under no duty to disclose to the buyer the home's haunted reputation. The trial court dismissed Stambovsky's case, and Stambovsky appealed.

In the Words of the Court
Justice *RUBIN* delivered the opinion of the Court.
* * * *

(Continues)

While I agree with [the trial court] that the real estate broker, as agent for the seller, is under no duty to disclose to a potential buyer the phantasmal reputation of the premises and that, in his pursuit of a legal remedy for fraudulent misrepresentation against the seller, plaintiff hasn't a ghost of a chance, I am nevertheless moved by the spirit of equity to allow the buyer to seek rescission of the contract of sale and recovery of his down payment. New York law fails to recognize any remedy for damages incurred as a result of the seller's mere silence, applying instead the strict rule of *caveat emptor* [Latin for "let the buyer beware"]. Therefore, the theoretical basis for granting relief, even under the extraordinary facts of this case, is elusive if not ephemeral [short-lived].

* * * *

The doctrine of caveat emptor *requires that a buyer act prudently to assess the fitness and value of his purchase and operates to bar the purchaser who fails to exercise due care from seeking the equitable remedy of rescission.* * * * Applying the strict rule of *caveat emptor* to a contract involving a house possessed by poltergeists conjures up visions of a psychic or medium routinely accompanying the structural engineer and Terminix man on an inspection of every home subject to a contract of sale. It portends that the prudent attorney will establish an escrow account lest the subject of the transaction come back to haunt him and his client—or pray that his malpractice insurance coverage extends to supernatural disasters. In the interest of avoiding such untenable consequences, the notion that a haunting is a condition which can and should be ascertained upon reasonable inspection of the premises is a hobgoblin which should be exorcised from the body of legal precedent and laid quietly to rest. [Emphasis added.]

* * * *

In the case at bar [under consideration], defendant seller deliberately fostered the public belief that her home was possessed. Having undertaken to inform the public at large, to whom she has no legal relationship, about the supernatural occurrences on her property, she may be said to owe no less a duty to her contract vendee. It has been remarked that the occasional modern cases which permit a seller to take unfair advantage of a buyer's ignorance so long as he is not actively misled are "singularly unappetizing." Where, as here, the seller not only takes unfair advantage of the buyer's ignorance but has created and perpetuated a condition about which he is unlikely to even inquire, enforcement of the contract (in whole or in part) is offensive to the court's sense of equity. Application of the remedy of rescission, within the bounds of the narrow exception to the doctrine of *caveat emptor* set forth herein, is entirely appropriate to relieve the unwitting purchaser from the consequences of a most unnatural bargain.

Decision and Remedy The New York appellate court found that the doctrine of *caveat emptor* did not apply in this case. The court reinstated Stambovsky's claim for rescission of the purchase contract and the down payment.

Critical Thinking

• **Ethical** *Assuming that Ackley's behavior was unethical, was it unethical because she failed to tell Stambovsky something about the house that he did not know, or was it unethical because of the nature of the information she omitted? What if Ackley had failed to mention that the roof leaked or that the well was dry—conditions that a buyer would normally investigate? Explain your answer.*

42–3b Deeds

Deed A document by which title to real property is passed.

Possession and title to land are passed from person to person by means of a **deed**—the instrument of conveyance of real property. Unlike a contract, a deed does not have to be supported by legally sufficient consideration. To be valid, a deed must include the following elements:

1. The names of the grantor (the giver or seller) and the grantee (the donee or buyer).

2. Words evidencing the intent to convey the property (such as, "I hereby bargain, sell, grant, or give"). No specific words are necessary. If the deed does not specify the type of estate being transferred, it is presumed to transfer the property in fee simple absolute.

3. A legally sufficient description of the land. The description must include enough detail to distinguish the property being conveyed from every other parcel of land. The property can be identified by reference to an official survey or recorded plat map, or each boundary can be described by metes and bounds. *Metes and bounds* is a system of measuring boundary lines by the distance between two points, often using physical features of the local geography—for instance, "beginning at the southwesterly intersection of Court and Main Streets, then West 40 feet to the fence, then South 100 feet, then Northeast approximately 120 feet back to the beginning."

Know This

Gifts of real property are common, and they require deeds even though there is no consideration for the gift.

4. The grantor's (and often her or his spouse's) signature.

5. Delivery of the deed.

Different types of deeds provide different degrees of protection against defects of title. A defect of title exists, for instance, if an undisclosed third person has an ownership interest in the property.

Warranty Deeds A **warranty deed** contains the greatest number of *covenants,* or promises, of title and thus provides the greatest protection against defects of title. In most states, special language is required to create a general warranty deed. Warranty deeds commonly include the following covenants:

1. A covenant that the grantor has the title to, and the power to convey, the property.

2. A covenant of quiet enjoyment (a warranty that the buyer will not be disturbed in her or his possession of the land).

3. A covenant that transfer of the property is made without knowledge of adverse claims of third parties.

Generally, the warranty deed makes the grantor liable for all defects of title during the time that the property was held by the grantor and previous titleholders. **Example 42.15** Mandal sells a two-acre lot and office building by warranty deed to Flash Technologies, LLC. Subsequently, Perkins shows that he has better title to the property than Mandal had and evicts Flash Technologies. Here, Flash Technologies can sue Mandal for breaching the covenant of quiet enjoyment. Flash Technologies can recover the purchase price of the land, plus any other damages incurred as a result. ■

Special Warranty Deeds A **special warranty deed,** or *limited warranty deed,* in contrast, warrants only that the grantor or seller held good title during his or her ownership of the property. In other words, the grantor does not warrant that there were no defects of title when the property was held by previous owners.

If the special warranty deed discloses all liens and other encumbrances, the seller will not be liable to the buyer if a third person subsequently interferes with the buyer's ownership. If the third person's claim arises out of, or is related to, some act of the seller, though, the seller will be liable to the buyer for damages.

Quitclaim Deeds A **quitclaim deed** offers the least amount of protection against defects of title. Basically, a quitclaim deed conveys to the grantee whatever interest the grantor had. Therefore, if the grantor had no interest, then the grantee receives no interest.

Quitclaim deeds are often used when the seller, or grantor, is uncertain as to the extent of his or her rights in the property. They may also be used to release a party's interest in a particular parcel of property, such as in divorce settlements or business dissolutions when the grantors are dividing up their interests in real property.

Recording Statutes Every state has a **recording statute,** which allows a deed to be recorded for a fee. Deeds are recorded in the county where the property is located. Recording a deed gives notice to the public that a certain person is now the owner of a particular parcel of real estate. By putting everyone on notice as to the true owner, recording a deed prevents the previous owners from fraudulently conveying the land to other purchasers. Thus, prospective buyers can check the public records to see whether there have been earlier transactions creating interests or rights in specific parcels of real property.

42–3c **Will or Inheritance**

Property that is transferred on an owner's death is passed either by will or by state inheritance laws. If the owner of land dies with a will, the land passes in accordance with the terms of the will. If the owner dies without a will, state inheritance statutes prescribe how and to whom the property will pass.

Warranty Deed A deed that provides the greatest amount of protection for the grantee. The grantor promises that she or he has title to the property conveyed in the deed, that there are no undisclosed encumbrances on the property, and that the grantee will enjoy quiet possession of the property.

Special Warranty Deed A deed that warrants only that the grantor held good title during his or her ownership of the property and does not warrant that there were no defects of title when the property was held by previous owners.

Quitclaim Deed A deed that conveys only whatever interest the grantor had in the property and therefore offers the least amount of protection against defects of title.

Recording Statute A statute that allow deeds, mortgages, and other real property transactions to be recorded so as to provide notice to future purchasers or creditors of an existing claim on the property.

42–3d Adverse Possession

A person who wrongfully possesses the real property of another (by occupying or using it) may eventually acquire title to it through adverse possession. **Adverse possession** is a means of obtaining title to land without delivery of a deed and without the consent of—or payment to—the true owner. Thus, adverse possession is a method of *involuntarily* transferring title to the property from the true owner to the adverse possessor.

Essentially, when one person possesses the property of another for a certain statutory period, that person acquires title to the land. The statutory period varies from three to thirty years, depending on the state, with ten years being the most common.

Requirements for Adverse Possession For property to be held adversely, four elements must be satisfied:

1. *Possession must be actual and exclusive.* The possessor must physically occupy the property. This requirement is clearly met if the possessor lives on the property, but it may also be met if the possessor builds fences, erects structures, plants crops, or even grazes animals on the land.

2. *Possession must be open, visible, and notorious,* not secret or clandestine. The possessor must occupy the land for all the world to see. The obviousness requirement ensures that the true owner is on notice that someone is possessing the owner's property wrongfully.

3. *Possession must be continuous and peaceable for the required period of time.* This requirement means that the possessor must not be interrupted in the occupancy by the true owner or by the courts. *Continuous* does not mean constant. It simply means that the possessor has continuously occupied the property in some fashion for the statutory time. *Peaceable* means that no force was used to possess the land.

4. *Possession must be hostile and adverse.* In other words, the possessor cannot be living on the property with the owner's permission and must claim the property as against the whole world. (See this chapter's *Business Law Analysis* feature for an illustration.)

Adverse Possession The acquisition of title to real property through open occupation, without the consent of the owner, for a period of time specified by a state statute. The occupation must be actual, exclusive, open, continuous, and in opposition to all others, including the owner.

Learning Objective 3

What are the requirements for acquiring property by adverse possession?

When Possession of Property Is Not "Adverse"

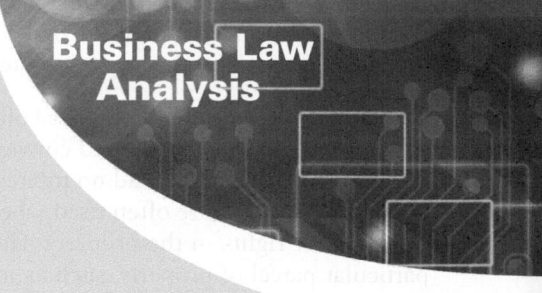

Business Law Analysis

The McKeag family operated a marina on their lakefront property in Bolton, New York. For more than forty years, the McKeags used a section of property belonging to their neighbors, the Finleys, as a beach for the marina's customers. The McKeags also stored a large float on the beach during the winter months, built their own retaining wall, and planted bushes and flowers there.

The McKeags prevented others from using the property, including the Finleys. Nevertheless, the families always had a friendly relationship, and one of the Finleys gave the McKeags permission to continue using the beach. He also reminded them of his ownership several times, to which they said nothing. The McKeags also asked for permission to mow grass on the property and once apologized for leaving a jet ski there. Can the McKeags establish adverse possession over the statutory period of ten years?

Analysis: There are four requirements to acquire title to property through adverse possession. The possession must be (1) actual and exclusive, (2) open and obvious, (3) continuous for the required period of time, and (4) hostile and adverse.

Result and Reasoning: The McKeags satisfied the first three requirements for adverse possession:

1. Their possession was actual and exclusive because they used the beach and prevented others from doing so, including the Finleys.

2. Their possession was open and visible because they made improvements to the beach and regularly kept their belongings there.

3. Their possession was continuous and peaceable for the required ten years. They possessed the property for more than four decades, and they even kept a large float there during the winter months.

Nevertheless, the McKeags' possession was *not* hostile and adverse, which is the fourth requirement. The Finleys provided substantial evidence that they had given the McKeags permission to use the beach.

Rather than reject the Finleys' permission as unnecessary, the McKeags sometimes said nothing and other times seemingly affirmed that the property belonged to the Finleys (by asking permission to mow grass,

for instance). Thus, because the McKeags did not satisfy all four requirements, they cannot establish adverse possession.

Case Example 42.16 Leslie and Ethel Cline owned a 141-acre property to the south of State Route 316 in Ohio. Rogers Farm Enterprises, LLC, owned 399 acres to the north of State Route 316. When the Clines bought their farm in 1987, they believed that State Route 316 was the dividing line between their property and Rogers Farm. Later, a survey showed that a 3.95-acre strip of land on the Clines' side of the road, which the Clines had been farming, actually belonged to Rogers Farm.

In 2013, the Clines filed a suit claiming that they had acquired title to the property through adverse possession. The court granted title to the Clines. Rogers Farm appealed. An Ohio state appellate court affirmed. The Clines had been openly and continuously farming on the disputed strip of land for the requisite period of time under Ohio's statute (twenty-one years) and legally owned it.[8]

The following case raised the question of whether the owner of land next to a railroad line could acquire a portion of the right-of-way by adverse possession.

---

8. *Cline v. Rogers Farm Enterprises, LLC,* 2017 -Ohio- 1379, 87 N.E.3d 637 (Ohio App. 2017).

■ Case 42.3

Montgomery County v. Bhatt
Court of Appeals of Maryland, 446 Md. 79, 130 A.3d 424 (2016).

Background and Facts The Capital Crescent Trail is a well-known hiking and biking route that runs between the District of Columbia and Silver Spring, Maryland. The path was formerly used as a railroad line and was later sold to Montgomery County, Maryland, for $10 million. The county planned to use the Maryland portion of the property for the proposed Purple Line, a commuter light rail project.

Ajay Bhatt owns a residence backing on the county-owned property. He purchased the residence in 2006 from his aunt, who had owned it since the 1970s. Montgomery County issued a civil citation to Bhatt for having a shed and a fence on his property that was within the former railroad line's right-of-way. The county had obtained the right-of-way from the railroad company pursuant to the federal Rails-to-Trails Act. A state district court found Bhatt guilty and ordered him to remove the fence and shed.

Bhatt appealed, claiming that he owned the encroached-upon land by adverse possession. Because a fence had been standing in its current location (beyond the property line) since 1963, Bhatt argued that

he had met the state's twenty-year period for adverse possession. A circuit court vacated the district court's decision and held that Bhatt had a credible claim for adverse possession. The county appealed.

In the Words of the Court
Glenn T. *HARRELL*, Jr., J. [Judge]

> Driving that train, high on cocaine,
> Casey Jones, you better watch your speed.
> Trouble ahead, trouble behind,
> And you know that notion just crossed my mind.
>
> — The Grateful Dead, *Casey Jones*, on *Workingman's Dead* (Warner Bros. Records 1970).

Although the record of the present case does not reflect a comparable level of drama as captured by the refrain of "Casey Jones," it hints at plenty of potential trouble, both ahead and behind, for a pair of public works projects (one in place and the other incipient [in development]) cherished by the government and some citizens of Montgomery County.

(Continues)

* * * *

* * * The County contends * * * that, because this Court has considered previously a railroad line to be analogous to a public highway for most purposes, the land in question is not subject to an adverse possession claim.

* * * Bhatt rejects the public highway–railroad line analogy because the land was in private, not public, use during its operation as a rail line.

* * * *

A railroad is in many essential respects a public highway, and the rules of law applicable to one are generally applicable to the other. Railroads are owned frequently by private corporations, but this has never been considered a matter of any importance * * * because the function performed is that of the State. Railroad companies operate as a public use and are not viewed strictly as private corporations since they are publicly regulated common carriers. *Essentially, a railroad is a highway dedicated to the public use.* [Emphasis added.]

* * * *Nothing is more solidly established than the rule that title to property held by a municipal corporation in its governmental capacity, for a public use, cannot be acquired by adverse possession.* [Emphasis added.]

* * * *

* * * Because time does not run against the state, or the public, * * * public highways are not subject to a claim for adverse possession, except in the limited circumstances of a clear abandonment by the State. By parity [equivalence] of reasoning applied to the present case, railway lines [are] also not * * * subject to a claim for adverse possession, without evidence of clear abandonment or a clear shift away from public use.

* * * *

Because no evidence was presented by Bhatt to show that * * * the Railroad or the County abandoned the right-of-way, no claim for adverse possession will lie.

Decision and Remedy A state intermediate appellate court reversed the lower court. Railroad companies operate as a public use. Land that is held by government for public use cannot be acquired by adverse possession unless the government has clearly abandoned its right to the land.

Critical Thinking

• **Legal Environment** *Bhatt claimed to have met all of the requirements to acquire land through adverse possession. Based on the facts provided, which element would a court likely find was lacking?*

Purpose of the Doctrine There are a number of public-policy reasons for the adverse possession doctrine. These include society's interest in resolving boundary disputes, determining title when title to property is in question, and ensuring that real property remains in the stream of commerce. More fundamentally, the doctrine punishes owners who do not take action when they see adverse possession and rewards possessors for putting land to productive use.

42–3e Eminent Domain

No ownership rights in real property can ever really be absolute. Even ownership in fee simple absolute is limited by a superior ownership. In the United States, the government has an ultimate ownership right in all land. This right, known as **eminent domain,** is sometimes referred to as the *condemnation power* of government to take land for public use. It gives the government the right to acquire possession of real property in the manner directed by the U.S. Constitution and the laws of the state whenever the public interest requires it. Property normally may be taken only for public use, not for private benefit.

The power of eminent domain generally is invoked through **condemnation proceedings** that occur before a judge. For instance, when a new public highway is to be built, the government must decide where to build it and how much land it needs. After the government determines that a particular parcel of land is necessary for public use, it will first offer to buy the property. If the owner refuses the offer, the government brings a judicial (*condemnation*) proceeding to obtain title to the land. Condemnation proceedings usually involve two distinct phases—the first to establish the government's right to take the property, and the second to determine the fair value of the property.

Eminent Domain The power of a government to take land from private citizens for public use on the payment of just compensation.

Condemnation Proceedings The judicial procedure by which the government exercises its power of eminent domain. It generally involves two phases: a taking and a determination of fair value.

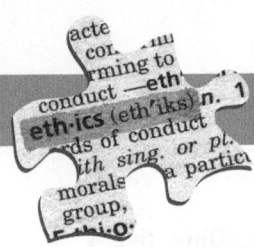

Should eminent domain be used to promote private development? Issues of fairness often arise when the government takes private property for public use. One issue is whether it is fair for a government to take property by eminent domain and then convey it to private developers. For instance, suppose a city government decides that it is in the public interest to have a larger parking lot for a local, privately owned sports stadium or to have a manufacturing plant locate in the city to create more jobs. The government may condemn certain tracts of existing housing or business property and then convey the land to the privately owned stadium or manufacturing plant. Such actions may bring in private developers and businesses that provide jobs and increase tax revenues, thus revitalizing communities. But is the land really being taken for "public use," as required by the Fifth Amendment to the U.S. Constitution?

In 2005, the United States Supreme Court ruled that the power of eminent domain may be used to further economic development.[9] At the same time, the Court recognized that individual states have the right to pass laws that prohibit takings for economic development. Since then, the vast majority of the states have passed laws to curb the government's ability to take private property and subsequently give it to private developers. Nevertheless, loopholes in some state legislation would still allow takings for redevelopment of slum areas. Thus, the debate over whether (and when) it is fair for the government to take citizens' property for economic development continues.

Ethical Issue

The Taking   When the government takes land owned by a private party for public use, it is referred to as a **taking.** Under the *takings clause* of the Fifth Amendment to the U.S. Constitution, the government may take private property for public use with just compensation to the property owner. State constitutions contain similar provisions. In the first phase of condemnation proceedings, the government must prove that it needs to acquire privately owned property for a public use.

Example 42.17 Franklin County, Iowa, engages Bosque Systems to build a liquefied natural gas pipeline across the property of more than two hundred landowners. Some property owners consent to this use and accept Bosque's offer of compensation. Others refuse the firm's offer. A court will likely deem Bosque's pipeline to be a public use. Therefore, the government can exert its eminent domain power to "take" the land, provided that it pays just compensation to the property owners. ■

The Compensation   The U.S. Constitution and state constitutions require that the government pay just compensation to the landowner when invoking its condemnation power. Just compensation means fair value. In the second phase of the condemnation proceeding, the court determines the fair value of the land, which usually is approximately equal to its market value.

Taking The taking of private property by the government for public use through the power of eminent domain.

Why does the U.S. Constitution require that a government taking, such as the acquisition of private land for a gas pipeline, be for "public use"?

42–4 Landlord-Tenant Relationships

A landlord-tenant relationship is established by a lease contract. In most states, statutes require leases for terms exceeding one year to be in writing. The lease should describe the property and indicate the length of the term, the amount of the rent, and how and when it is to be paid.

State or local law often dictates permissible lease terms, particularly in residential leases. For instance, a statute or ordinance might prohibit the leasing of a structure that is not in compliance with local building codes. As in other areas of law, the National Conference of Commissioners on Uniform State Laws has issued a model act to create more uniformity in the laws governing landlord-tenant relationships. The Uniform Residential Landlord

Know This

Sound business practice dictates that a lease for commercial property should be written carefully and should clearly define the parties' rights and obligations.

---

9. See *Kelo v. City of New London, Connecticut*, 545 U.S. 469, 125 S.Ct. 2655, 162 L.Ed.2d 439 (2005).

and Tenant Act (URLTA), which was issued in 1972, has been adopted in some form by twenty-one states. A revised version of the act was issued in 2015, but no states had adopted it prior to the publication of this text.

42–4a Rights and Duties

The rights and duties of landlords and tenants generally pertain to four broad areas of concern—the possession, use, and maintenance of the leased property and, of course, rent.

Possession A landlord is obligated to give a tenant possession of the property that the tenant has agreed to lease. After obtaining possession, the tenant retains the property exclusively until the lease expires, unless the lease states otherwise.

Quiet Enjoyment. The covenant of quiet enjoyment mentioned previously also applies to leased premises. Under this covenant, the landlord promises that during the lease term, neither the landlord nor anyone having a superior title to the property will disturb the tenant's use and enjoyment of the property. This covenant forms the essence of the landlord-tenant relationship, and if it is breached, the tenant can terminate the lease and sue for damages.

Eviction. If the landlord deprives the tenant of possession of the leased property or interferes with the tenant's use or enjoyment of it, an **eviction** occurs. A **constructive eviction** occurs when the landlord wrongfully performs or fails to perform any of the duties the lease requires, thereby making the tenant's further use and enjoyment of the property exceedingly difficult or impossible. Examples of constructive eviction include a landlord's failure to provide heat in the winter, electricity, or other essential utilities.

Use of the Premises The tenant normally may make any use of the leased property, provided the use is legal and does not injure the landlord's interest. The parties are free to limit by agreement the uses to which the property may be put.

Maintenance of the Premises The tenant is responsible for any damage to the premises that he or she causes, intentionally or negligently, and may be held liable for the cost of returning the property to the physical condition it was in when the lease began. Unless the parties have agreed otherwise, the tenant is not responsible for ordinary wear and tear and the property's consequent depreciation in value.

Landlords must, of course, comply with any applicable state statutes and city ordinances regarding maintenance and repair of buildings. In some jurisdictions, landlords of residential property are also required by statute to maintain the premises in good repair.

In addition, the implied warranty of habitability discussed earlier may apply to residential leases. The warranty requires the landlord to ensure that the premises are habitable— that is, a safe and suitable place for people to live. Also, the landlord must make repairs to maintain the premises in that condition for the lease's duration.

Generally, this warranty applies to major, or *substantial,* physical defects that the landlord knows or should know about and has had a reasonable time to repair—such as a large hole in the roof or a broken heating system. **Example 42.18** Carol and Ken Galprin own a house within the city limits of Redmond. A city regulation states that a residence must be connected to the city sewer system before anyone, including tenants, can live in the residence. The Galprins' house is not connected to the city system. Thus, it is not legally habitable, and they cannot lease it to tenants. ■

Rent *Rent* is the tenant's payment to the landlord for the tenant's occupancy or use of the landlord's real property. Usually, the tenant must pay the rent even if she or he refuses to occupy the property or moves out, as long as the refusal or the move is unjustified and the lease is in force. **Example 42.19** Lifetime Insurance Agency enters into a lease with Mallory for a suite of offices in Mallory's building. Lifetime's revenue is less than managers had projected, however, and the rent is now more than the company wants to pay. Lifetime vacates the offices before

Learning Objective 4
What are the duties of the landlord and the tenant with respect to the use and maintenance of leased property?

Eviction A landlord's act of depriving a tenant of possession of the leased premises.

Constructive Eviction A form of eviction that occurs when a landlord fails to perform adequately any of the duties required by the lease, thereby making the tenant's further use and enjoyment of the property exceedingly difficult or impossible.

Know This
Options that may be available to a tenant on a landlord's breach of the implied warranty of habitability include repairing the defect and deducting the cost from the rent, canceling the lease, and suing for damages.

the end of the lease. In terms of the landlord-tenant relationship, the move is unjustified, and the lease remains in force. Lifetime must continue to pay the rent.

Under the common law, if leased premises were destroyed by fire or flood, the tenant still had to pay rent. Today, however, if an apartment building is destroyed, most states' laws do not require tenants to continue to pay rent.

In some situations, such as when a landlord breaches the implied warranty of habitability, a tenant may be allowed to withhold rent as a remedy. When rent withholding is authorized under a statute, the tenant must usually put the amount withheld into an *escrow account*. The funds are held in the name of the tenant and are returned to the tenant if the landlord fails to make the premises habitable.

Commercial Lease Terms State statutes often allow tenants and landlords more flexibility in negotiating the terms of a commercial lease. **Case Example 42.20** Lynwood Place, LLC, owned an office building in Newtown, Connecticut. Sandy Hook Hydro, LLC, agreed to lease a part of the building containing a hydroelectric turbine. The lease required Sandy Hook to pay a base annual rent, plus an additional amount of rent equal to 6 percent of any increase in operating expenses incurred by the landlord. "Operating expenses" included all costs of maintenance and repair related to the premises.

When Sandy Hook did not pay the additional rent due under this provision, Lynwood Place filed a suit in a Connecticut state court to take immediate possession of the property. The court issued a judgment in the landlord's favor. The tenant appealed, but the reviewing court affirmed. The court concluded that Sandy Hook had signed the lease, which clearly indicated that the rent was subject to a 6 percent increase for operating expenses. Therefore, even though Sandy Hook occupied only part of the building, the lease gave the landlord the right to increase its rent by that amount.[10]

If a lessee agrees to rent a part of a building that houses a turbine, what happens when the lessee doesn't pay the agreed-upon annual increase in lease payments?

42–4b Transferring Rights to Leased Property

Either the landlord or the tenant may wish to transfer her or his rights to the leased property during the term of the lease. If a landlord transfers complete title to the leased property to another, the tenant becomes the tenant of the new owner. The new owner may collect subsequent rent but must abide by the terms of the existing lease. A tenant's transfer of rights in the leased property may result in an assignment or a sublease.

Assignment The tenant's transfer of his or her entire interest in the leased property to a third person is an *assignment* of the lease. Many leases require the landlord's written consent for an assignment to be valid. The landlord can nullify (avoid) an assignment made without the required consent and evict the assignee. State statutes may specify that the landlord may not unreasonably withhold consent, however. Also, a landlord who knowingly accepts rent from the assignee may be held to have waived the consent requirement.

When an assignment is valid, the assignee acquires all of the tenant's rights under the lease. Nevertheless, an assignment does not release the original tenant (the assignor) from the obligation to pay rent should the assignee default. In addition, if the assignee exercises an option under the original lease to extend the term, the assignor remains liable for the rent during the extension, unless the landlord agrees otherwise.

Subleases The tenant's transfer of all or part of the premises for a period shorter than the lease term is a **sublease**. Many leases also require the landlord's written consent for a sublease. If the landlord's consent is required, a sublease without such permission is ineffective. Also, like an assignment, a sublease does not release the tenant from her or his obligations under the lease.

Example 42.21 Derek, a student, leases an apartment for a two-year period. Although Derek had planned on attending summer school, he decides to accept a job offer in Europe

Sublease A tenant's transfer of all or part of the leased premises to a third person for a period shorter than the lease term.

10. *Lynwood Place, LLC v. Sandy Hook Hydro, LLC,* 150 Conn.App. 682, 92 A.3d 996 (2014).

for the summer months instead. Derek therefore obtains his landlord's consent to sublease the apartment to Ava. Ava is bound by the same terms of the lease as Derek, and the landlord can hold Derek liable if Ava violates the lease terms.

42–4c Termination of the Lease

Usually, a lease terminates when its term ends. The tenant surrenders the property to the landlord, who retakes possession. If the lease states the time it will end, the landlord is not required to give the tenant notice. The lease terminates automatically.

A lease can also be terminated in several other ways. If the tenant purchases the leased property from the landlord during the term of the lease, for instance, the lease will be terminated. The parties may also agree to end a tenancy before it would otherwise terminate. In addition, the tenant may *abandon* the premises—move out completely with no intention of returning before the lease term expires.

At common law, a tenant who abandoned leased property was still obligated to pay the rent for the full term of the lease. The landlord could let the property stand vacant and charge the tenant for the remainder of the term. This is still the rule in some states. In most states today, however, the landlord has a duty to *mitigate* his or her damages—that is, to make a reasonable attempt to lease the property to another party. Consequently, the tenant's liability for unpaid rent is restricted to the period of time that the landlord would reasonably need to lease the property to another tenant. Damages may also be allowed for the landlord's costs in leasing the property again.

Practice and Review

Vern Shoepke bought a two-story home in Roche, Maine. The warranty deed did not specify what covenants would be included in the conveyance. The property was adjacent to a public park that included a popular Frisbee golf course. (Frisbee golf is a sport similar to golf but using Frisbees.) Wayakichi Creek ran along the north end of the park and along Shoepke's property. The deed allowed Roche citizens the right to walk across a five-foot-wide section of the lot beside Wayakichi Creek as part of a two-mile public trail system. Teenagers regularly threw Frisbee golf discs from the walking path behind Shoepke's property over his yard to the adjacent park. Shoepke habitually shouted and cursed at the teenagers, demanding that they not throw the discs over his yard.

Two months after moving into his Roche home, Shoepke leased the second floor to Lauren Slater for nine months. The lease agreement did not specify that Shoepke's consent would be required to sublease the second floor. After three months of tenancy, Slater sublet the second floor to a local artist, Javier Indalecio. Over the remaining six months, Indalecio's use of oil paints damaged the carpeting in Shoepke's home. Using the information presented in the chapter, answer the following questions.

1. What is the term for the right of Roche citizens to walk across Shoepke's land on the trail?

2. What covenants would most courts infer were included in the warranty deed that Shoepke received when he bought his house?

3. Can Shoepke hold Slater financially responsible for the damage to the carpeting caused by Indalecio? Explain.

4. Could the fact that teenagers continually throw Frisbees over Shoepke's yard outside the second-floor windows arguably be a breach of the covenant of quiet enjoyment? Why or why not?

Debate This

Under no circumstances should a local government be able to condemn property in order to sell it later to real estate developers for private use.

Key Terms

Chapter Summary: Real Property and Landlord-Tenant Law

The Nature of Real Property	Real property (also called real estate or realty) includes land and structures, subsurface and airspace rights, plant life and vegetation, and fixtures.
Ownership Interests and Leases	1. *Fee simple*—The most complete form of ownership. Owners can use, possess, or dispose of the property as they choose during their lifetimes and pass on the property to their heirs at death.

1. *Fee simple*—The most complete form of ownership. Owners can use, possess, or dispose of the property as they choose during their lifetimes and pass on the property to their heirs at death.
2. *Life estate*—An estate that lasts for the life of a specified individual, during which time the individual is entitled to possess, use, and benefit from the estate. The life tenant cannot use the land in a manner that would adversely affect its value. The life tenant's ownership rights cease to exist on her or his death.
3. *Concurrent ownership*—When two or more persons hold title to property together, concurrent ownership exists.
   a. A tenancy in common exists when two or more persons own an undivided interest in property. On a tenant's death, that tenant's property interest passes to his or her heirs.
   b. A joint tenancy exists when two or more persons own an undivided interest in property, with a right of survivorship. On the death of a joint tenant, that tenant's property interest transfers to the remaining tenant(s), not to the heirs of the deceased.
   c. A tenancy by the entirety is a form of co-ownership between married persons that is similar to a joint tenancy, except that a spouse cannot separately transfer her or his interest during her or his lifetime unless the other spouse consents.
   d. Community property is a form of co-ownership between married persons in which each spouse technically owns an undivided one-half interest in property acquired during the marriage. This type of ownership exists in only a few states.
4. *Leasehold estates*—A leasehold estate is an interest in real property that is held for only a limited period of time, as specified in the lease agreement. Types of tenancies relating to leased property include the following:
   a. Fixed-term tenancy (tenancy for years)—Tenancy for a period of time stated by express contract.
   b. Periodic tenancy—Tenancy for a period determined by the frequency of rent payments. It is automatically renewed unless proper notice is given.
   c. Tenancy at will—Tenancy for as long as both parties agree. No notice of termination is required.
   d. Tenancy at sufferance—Possession of land without legal right.
5. *Nonpossessory interest*—An interest that involves the right to use real property but not to possess it. Easements, profits, and licenses are nonpossessory interests.

(Continues)

Transfer of Ownership	1. *By sales contract*—A contract for the sale of land includes the purchase price, the type of deed the buyer will receive, the condition of the premises, and any items that will be included. It is often contingent on the buyer's ability to obtain financing and on certain events, such as satisfactory inspections.
	2. *By deed*—When real property is sold or transferred as a gift, title to the property is conveyed by means of a deed. A deed must meet specific legal requirements. A *warranty deed* provides the most extensive protection against defects of title. A *quitclaim deed* conveys to the grantee only whatever interest the grantor had in the property. A deed may be recorded in the manner prescribed by *recording statutes* in the appropriate jurisdiction to give third parties notice of the owner's interest.
	3. *By will or inheritance*—If the owner dies after having made a valid will, the land passes as specified in the will. If the owner dies without having made a will, the heirs inherit according to state inheritance statutes.
	4. *By adverse possession*—When a person possesses the property of another for a statutory period of time (ten years is the most common), that person acquires title to the property, provided the possession is actual and exclusive, open and visible, continuous and peaceable, and hostile and adverse (without the permission of the owner).
	5. *By eminent domain*—The government can take land for public use, with just compensation, when the public interest requires the taking.
Landlord-Tenant Relationships	The landlord-tenant relationship is created by a lease agreement. State or local laws may dictate whether the lease must be in writing and what lease terms are permissible.
	1. *Rights and duties*—The rights and duties of landlords and tenants that arise under a lease agreement generally pertain to the following areas:
	a. Possession—The tenant has an exclusive right to possess the leased premises. Under the covenant of quiet enjoyment, the landlord promises that during the lease term, neither the landlord nor anyone having superior title to the property will disturb the tenant's use and enjoyment of the property.
	b. Use of the premises—Unless the parties agree otherwise, the tenant may make any legal use of the property.
	c. Maintenance of the premises—The tenant is responsible for any damage that he or she causes. The landlord must comply with laws that set specific standards for the maintenance of real property and must maintain residential premises in a habitable condition (safe and suitable for human life).
	d. Rent—The tenant must pay the rent as long as the lease is in force, unless the tenant justifiably refuses to occupy the property or withholds the rent because of the landlord's failure to maintain the premises properly.
	2. *Transferring rights to leased property*—
	a. If the landlord transfers complete title to the leased property, the tenant becomes the tenant of the new owner. The new owner may collect the rent but must abide by the existing lease.
	b. Generally, in the absence of an agreement to the contrary, tenants may assign their rights (but not their duties) under a lease contract to a third person. Tenants may also sublease leased property to a third person, but the original tenant is not relieved of any obligations to the landlord under the lease. In either situation, the landlord's consent may be required, but statutes may prohibit the landlord from unreasonably withholding consent.

Issue Spotters

1. Bernie sells his house to Consuela under a warranty deed. Later, Delmira appears, holding a better title to the house than Consuela has. Delmira wants Consuela off the property. What can Consuela do? (See *Transfer of Ownership*.)

2. Grey owns a commercial building in fee simple. Grey transfers temporary possession of the building to Haven Corporation. Can Haven transfer possession for even less time to Idyll Company? Explain. (See *Landlord-Tenant Relationships*.)

   —Check your answers to the *Issue Spotters* against the answers provided in Appendix D at the end of this text.

Business Scenarios and Case Problems

42–1. Property Ownership. Twenty-two years ago, Lorenz was a wanderer. At that time, he decided to settle down on an unoccupied, three-acre parcel of land that he did not own. People in the area told him that they had no idea who owned the property. Lorenz built a house on the land, got married, and raised three children while living there. He fenced in the land, installed a gate with a sign above it that read "Lorenz's Homestead," and removed trespassers. Lorenz is now confronted by Joe Reese, who has a deed in his name as owner of the property. Reese, claiming ownership of the land, orders Lorenz and his family off the property. Discuss who has the better "title" to the property. (See *Transfer of Ownership.*)

42–2. Deeds. Wiley and Gemma are neighbors. Wiley's lot is extremely large, and his present and future use of it will not involve the entire area. Gemma wants to build a single-car garage and driveway along the present lot boundary. Because the placement of her existing structures makes it impossible for her to comply with an ordinance requiring buildings to be set back fifteen feet from an adjoining property line, Gemma cannot build the garage. Gemma contracts to purchase ten feet of Wiley's property along their boundary line for $3,000. Wiley is willing to sell but will give Gemma only a quitclaim deed, whereas Gemma wants a warranty deed. Discuss the differences between these deeds as they would affect the rights of the parties if the title to this ten feet of land later proves to be defective. (See *Transfer of Ownership.*)

42–3. Implied Warranty of Habitability. Sarah has rented a house from Frank. The house is only two years old, but the roof leaks every time it rains. The water that has accumulated in the attic has caused stucco to fall off ceilings in the upstairs bedrooms, and one ceiling has started to sag. Sarah has complained to Frank and asked him to have the roof repaired. Frank says that he has caulked the roof, but the roof still leaks. Frank claims that because Sarah has sole control of the leased premises, she has the duty to repair the roof. Sarah insists that repairing the roof is Frank's responsibility. Discuss fully who is responsible for repairing the roof and, if the responsibility belongs to Frank, what remedies are available to Sarah. (See *Landlord-Tenant Relationships.*)

42–4. Rent. Flawlace, LLC, leased unfinished commercial real estate in Las Vegas, Nevada, from Francis Lin to operate a beauty salon. The lease required Flawlace to obtain a "certificate of occupancy" from the city to commence business. This required the installation of a fire protection system. The lease did not allocate responsibility for the installation to either party. Lin voluntarily undertook to install the system. After a month of delays, Flawlace moved out. Three months later, the installation was complete, and Lin leased the premises to a new tenant. Did Flawlace owe rent for the three months between the time that it moved out and the time that the new tenant moved in? Explain. [*Tri-Lin Holdings, LLC v. Flawlace, LLC,* 2014 WL 1101577 (Nev. Sup.Ct. 2014)] (See *Landlord-Tenant Relationships.*)

42–5. Landlord-Tenant Relationships. Bhanmattie Kumar was walking on a sidewalk in Flushing, New York, when she tripped over a chipped portion of the sidewalk and fell. The defective sidewalk was in front of a Pretty Girl store—one of a chain of apparel stores headquartered in Brooklyn—on premises leased from PI Associates, LLC. Kumar filed a claim in a New York state court against PI, seeking to recover damages for her injuries. PI filed a cross-claim against Pretty Girl. On what basis would the court impose liability on PI? In what situation would Pretty Girl be the liable party? Is there any circumstance in which Kumar could be at least partially responsible for her injury? Discuss. [*Bhanmattie Rajkumar Kumar v. PI Associates, LLC,* 125 A.D.3d 609, 3 N.Y.S.3d 372 (2 Dept. 2015)] (See *Landlord-Tenant Relationships.*)

42–6. Business Case Problem with Sample Answer— Joint Tenancies. Arthur and Diana Ebanks owned three properties in the Cayman Islands in joint tenancy. With respect to joint tenancies, Cayman law is the same as U.S. law. When the Ebanks divorced, the decree did not change the tenancy in which the properties were held. On the same day as the divorce filing, Arthur executed a will providing that "any property in my name and that of another as joint tenants . . . will pass to the survivor, and I instruct my Personal Representative to make no claim thereto." Four years later, Arthur died. His brother Curtis, the personal representative of his estate, asserted that Arthur's interest in the Cayman properties was part of the estate. Diana said that the sole interest in the properties was hers. To whom do the Cayman properties belong? Why? [*Ebanks v. Ebanks,* 41 Fla. L. Weekly D291, 198 So.3d 716 (2 Dist. 2016)] (See *Ownership Interests and Leases.*)

—For a sample answer to Problem 42–6, go to Appendix E at the end of this text.

42–7. Eminent Domain. In Tarrytown, New York, Citibank operated a branch that included a building and a parking lot with thirty-six spaces. Tarrytown leased twenty-one of the spaces from Citibank for use as public parking. When Citibank closed the branch and decided to sell the building, the public was denied access to the parking lot. After a public hearing, the city concluded that it should exercise its power of eminent domain to acquire the twenty-one spaces to provide public parking. Is this an appropriate use of the power of eminent domain? Suppose that Citibank opposes the plan and alternative sites are available. Should Tarrytown be required to acquire those sites instead of Citibank's property? In any event, what is Tarrytown's next step? Explain. [*Citibank, N.A. v. Village of Tarrytown*, 149 A.D.3d 931, 52 N.Y.S.3d 398 (2 Dept. 2017)] (See *Transfer of Ownership*.)

42–8. Transfer of Ownership. Craig and Sue Shaffer divided their real property into two lots. They enclosed one lot with a fence and sold it to the Murdocks. The other lot was sold to the Cromwells. All of the parties orally agreed that the fence marked the property line. Over the next three decades, each lot was sold three more times. Houses were built, and the lots were landscaped, including lilac bushes planted against the fence. Later, one of the owners removed the fence, and another built a shed next to where it had been. On the lot with the shed, the Talbots erected a carport abutting the lilac bushes. The Nielsons bought the adjacent lot from the Parkers and measured it according to the legal description in the deed. They discovered that the Talbots' carport encroached on the Nielsons' property by about thirteen feet. Are the Nielsons entitled to damages for their "lost" property from any party? Explain. [*Nielson v. Talbot,* 163 Idaho 480, 415 P.3d 348 (2018)] (See *Transfer of Ownership*.)

42–9. A Question of Ethics—The IDDR Approach and Easements. Two organizations, *Class A Investors Post Oak, LP,* and *Cosmopolitan Condominium VP, LP,* owned adjacent pieces of property in Houston, Texas. Each owner organization planned to build a high-rise tower on its lot. The organizations signed an agreement that granted each of them an easement in the other's property to "facilitate the development." Cosmopolitan built its residential high-rise first. Later, Class A began moving forward with its plan for a mixed-use high-rise. Cosmopolitan objected that the proposed tower would "be vastly oversized for its proposed location; situated perilously close to [Cosmopolitan's] building; create extraordinary traffic hazards; impede fire protection and other emergency vehicles in the area; and substantially interfere with the use and enjoyment of [Cosmopolitan's] property." [Cosmopolitan Condominium Owners Association v. Class A Investors Post Oak, LP, *2017 WL 1520448 (Tex.App.—Houston 2017)] (See* Ownership Interests.*)*

1. On what basis can Class A proceed with its plan? Explain, using the IDDR approach.

2. On what ethical ground might Cosmopolitan continue to oppose its neighbor's project? Discuss.

Critical Thinking and Writing Assignments

42–10. Time-Limited Group Assignment—Adverse Possession. The Wallen family owned a cabin on Lummi Island in the state of Washington. A driveway ran from the cabin across their property to South Nugent Road. Floyd Massey bought the adjacent lot and built a cabin on it in 1985. To gain access to his property, Massey used a bulldozer to extend the driveway, without the Wallens' permission but also without their objection. In 2010, the Wallens sold their property to Wright Fish Company. Massey continued to use and maintain the driveway without permission or objection. In 2016, Massey sold his property to Robert Drake. Drake and his employees continued to use and maintain the driveway without permission or objection, although Drake knew it was located largely on Wright's property. In 2018, Wright sold its lot to Robert Smersh. The next year, Smersh told Drake to stop using the driveway. Drake filed a suit against Smersh, claiming an easement by prescription (which is created by meeting the same requirements as adverse possession). (See *Transfer of Ownership*.)

1. The first group will decide whether Drake's use of the driveway meets all of the requirements for adverse possession (easement by prescription).

2. The second group will determine how the court should rule in this case and why. Does it matter that Drake knew the driveway was located largely on Wright's (and then Smersh's) property? Should it matter?

3. The third group will evaluate the underlying policy and fairness of adverse possession laws. Should the law reward persons who take possession of someone else's land for their own use? Does it make sense to punish owners who allow someone else to use their land without complaint?

4. The fourth group will consider how the laws governing adverse possession (easement by prescription) vary from state to state. To acquire title through adverse possession, a person might be required to possess the property for five years in one state, for instance, and for twenty years in another. Are there any legitimate reasons for such regional differences? Would it be better if all states had the same requirements? Explain your answers.

Insurance, Wills, and Trusts

43

"Insurance is part charity and part business, but all common sense."

Calvin Coolidge
1872–1933
(Thirtieth president of the United States, 1923–1929)

Most individuals insure their real and personal property (as well as their lives). As Calvin Coolidge asserted in the chapter-opening quotation, insurance is "all common sense"—by insuring our property, we protect ourselves against damage and loss. In the first part of this chapter, we focus on insurance, which is a foremost concern of all property owners.

In the remainder of the chapter, we examine how property is transferred on the death of its owner. Certainly, the laws governing such transfers are a necessary corollary to the concept of private ownership of property. Our laws require that on death, title to the property of the decedent (the one who has died) must be delivered in full somewhere. This can be done through wills, trusts, or state laws prescribing distribution of property among heirs or next of kin.

In today's world, a person's property may include social media. We discuss social media estate planning later in the chapter.

Learning Objectives

The four Learning Objectives *below are designed to help improve your understanding. After reading this chapter, you should be able to answer the following questions:*

1. What is an insurable interest? When must an insurable interest exist?

2. What are the basic requirements for executing a will?

3. What is the difference between a *per stirpes* distribution and a *per capita* distribution of an estate to the grandchildren of the deceased?

4. What are the four essential elements of a trust?

43–1 Insurance

Many precautions may be taken to protect against the hazards of life. For instance, an individual may wear a seat belt to protect against injuries from automobile accidents and install smoke detectors to guard against injury from fire. Of course, no one can predict whether an accident or a fire will ever occur, but individuals and businesses must establish plans to protect their personal and financial interests should some event threaten to undermine their security.

Insurance A contract by which the insurer promises to reimburse the insured or a beneficiary in the event that the insured is injured, dies, or sustains damage to property as a result of particular, stated contingencies.

Risk Management In the context of insurance, the transfer of certain risks from the insured to the insurance company by contractual agreement.

Risk A prediction concerning potential loss based on known and unknown factors.

Insurance is a contract by which the insurance company (the insurer) promises to pay an amount or to give something of value to another (either the insured or the beneficiary) in the event that the insured is injured, dies, or sustains damage to her or his property as a result of particular, stated contingencies. Basically, insurance is an arrangement for *transferring and allocating risk*—that is, for **risk management**. In many instances, **risk** can be described as a prediction concerning potential loss based on known and unknown factors.

Risk management normally involves the transfer of certain risks from the individual to the insurance company by a contractual agreement. The insurance contract and its provisions will be examined shortly. First, however, we look at the different types of insurance that can be obtained, insurance terminology, and the concept of insurable interest.

43–1a Classifications of Insurance

Insurance is classified according to the nature of the risk involved. For instance, fire insurance, casualty insurance, life insurance, and title insurance apply to different types of risk and protect different interests. This is reasonable because the types of losses that are expected and that are foreseeable or unforeseeable vary with the nature of the activity. Exhibit 43–1 presents a list of selected insurance classifications.

Exhibit 43–1 Selected Insurance Classifications

TYPE OF INSURANCE	COVERAGE
Accident	Covers expenses, losses, and suffering incurred by the insured because of accidents causing physical injury and any consequent disability; sometimes includes a specified payment to heirs of the insured if death results from an accident.
All-risk	Covers all losses that the insured may incur except those that are specifically excluded. Typical exclusions are war, pollution, earthquakes, and floods.
Automobile	May cover damage to automobiles resulting from specified hazards or occurrences (such as fire, vandalism, theft, or collision); normally provides protection against liability for personal injuries and property damage resulting from the operation of the vehicle.
Casualty	Protects against losses incurred by the insured as a result of being held liable for personal injuries or property damage sustained by others.
Disability	Replaces a portion of the insured's monthly income from employment in the event that illness or injury causes a short- or long-term disability. Benefits typically last a set period of time, such as six months or five years.
Fire	Covers losses incurred by the insured as a result of fire.
Floater	Covers movable property, as long as the property is within the territorial boundaries specified in the contract.
Homeowners'	Protects homeowners against some or all risks of loss to their residences and the residences' contents or liability arising from the use of the property.
Key-person	Protects a business in the event of the death or disability of a key employee.
Liability	Protects against liability imposed on the insured as a result of injuries to the person or property of another.
Life	Covers the death of the policyholder. On the death of the insured, the insurer pays the amount specified in the policy to the insured's beneficiary.
Major medical	Protects the insured against major hospital, medical, or surgical expenses.
Malpractice	Protects professionals (physicians, lawyers, and others) against malpractice claims brought against them by their patients or clients; a form of liability insurance.
Term life	Provides life insurance for a specified period of time (term) with no cash surrender value; usually renewable.

43–1b Insurance Terminology

An insurance contract is called a **policy,** the consideration paid to the insurer is called a **premium,** and the insurance company is sometimes called an **underwriter.** The parties to an insurance policy are the *insurer* (the insurance company) and the *insured* (the person covered by its provisions or the holder of the policy).

Insurance contracts are usually obtained through an *agent,* who typically works for the insurance company, or through a *broker,* who is ordinarily an *independent contractor.* When a broker deals with an applicant for insurance, the broker is, in effect, the applicant's agent and not an agent of the insurance company. In contrast, an insurance agent is an agent of the insurance company, not of the applicant. Thus, the agent owes fiduciary duties to the insurance company, but not to the person who is applying for insurance. As a general rule, the insurance company is bound by the acts of its agents when they act within the scope of the agency relationship.

43–1c Insurable Interest

A person can insure anything in which she or he has an **insurable interest.** Without an insurable interest, there is no enforceable insurance contract, and a transaction to purchase insurance coverage would have to be treated as a wager.

Life Insurance In regard to life insurance, a person must have a reasonable expectation of benefit from the continued life of another in order to have an insurable interest in that person's life. The insurable interest must exist *at the time the policy is obtained.* The benefit may be pecuniary (monetary), or it may be founded on the relationship between the parties (by blood or affinity).

Key-person insurance is a type of life insurance obtained by an organization on the life of a person (such as a talented executive) who is important to that organization. Because the organization expects to experience some financial gain from the continuation of the key person's life or some financial loss from the key person's death, the organization has an insurable interest.

Property Insurance In regard to real and personal property, an insurable interest exists when the insured derives a pecuniary (monetary) benefit from the preservation and continued existence of the property. Put another way, a person has an insurable interest in property when she or he would sustain a financial loss from its destruction. For property insurance, the insurable interest must exist at the time the loss occurs but need not exist when the policy is purchased.

The existence of an insurable interest is a primary concern in determining liability under an insurance policy. ✖ **Spotlight Case Example 43.1** ABM Industries, Inc., leased office and storage space in the World Trade Center (WTC) in New York City in 2001. ABM also ran the building's heating, ventilation, and air-conditioning systems, and maintained all of the WTC's common areas. At the time, ABM employed more than eight hundred workers at the WTC. Zurich American Insurance Company insured ABM against losses resulting from "business interruption" caused by direct physical loss or damage "to property owned, controlled, used, leased or intended for use" by ABM.

After the terrorist attacks on September 11, 2001, ABM filed a claim with Zurich to recover for the loss of all income derived from ABM's WTC operations. Zurich argued that ABM's recovery should be limited to the income lost as a result of the destruction of ABM's office and storage space and supplies. A court, however, ruled that ABM was entitled

Policy In insurance law, the contract between the insurer and the insured.

Premium In insurance law, the price paid by the insured for insurance protection for a specified period of time.

Underwriter In insurance law, the insurer, or the one assuming a risk in return for the payment of a premium.

Insurable Interest An interest that exists when a person benefits from the preservation of the health or life of the insured or the property to be insured.

Learning Objective **1**

What is an insurable interest? When must an insurable interest exist?

After the World Trade Center was destroyed on September 11, 2001, should the company providing maintenance have been reimbursed by its insurance company for all of its income losses?

to compensation for the loss of all of its WTC operations. The court reasoned that the "policy's scope expressly includes real or personal property that the insured 'used,' 'controlled,' or 'intended for use.'" Because ABM's income depended on "the common areas and leased premises in the WTC complex," it had an insurable interest in that property at the time of the loss.[1]

In the following case, the plaintiff sought to retain his insurable interest in a home he no longer owned.

1. *Zurich American Insurance Co. v. ABM Industries, Inc.*, 397 F.3d 158 (2d Cir. 2005).

■ Case 43.1

Breeden v. Buchanan
Court of Appeals of Mississippi, 164 So.3d 1057 (2015).

Background and Facts Donald Breeden and Willie Buchanan were married in Marion County, Mississippi. They lived in a home in Sandy Hook. Nationwide Property & Casualty Insurance Company insured the home under a policy bought by Breeden that named him as the insured. The policy provided that the spouse of the named insured was covered as an insured. After eight years of marriage, Breeden and Buchanan divorced. Breeden transferred his interest in the home to Buchanan as part of the couple's property settlement.

Less than a year later, a fire completely destroyed the home. A claim was filed with Nationwide. Nationwide paid Buchanan. Breeden filed a suit in a Mississippi state court against Buchanan and Nationwide, asserting claims for breach of contract and bad faith, and seeking to recover the proceeds under the policy. The court dismissed the suit. Breeden appealed.

A year after a couple divorces, fire destroys their house. Who should obtain the insurance proceeds?

satori13/iStock/Getty Images

In the Words of the Court
GRIFFIS, P.J. [Presiding Judge], for the Court:
* * * *

Breeden's claims for breach of contract [and] bad-faith denial of insurance benefits * * * are based on the insurance policy. The [lower] court ruled that Breeden had no "insurable interest" in the Nationwide policy and had no right to the proceeds of the policy. Specifically, the * * * court ruled:

The court finds that the pleadings reflect no insurable interest in Breeden in and to the policy or to the proceeds, as Breeden transferred and conveyed his right, title, and interest in and to the insured property to his former spouse, Buchanan, as part and

parcel of their divorce proceeding and property settlement agreement, this transfer and conveyance having transpired several months before the occurrence of the loss, which is the subject matter of Breeden's complaint.

Finding that Breeden had no insurable interest in and to the property—and thus no entitlement to any of the insurance proceeds—it follows that Nationwide did not breach the insurance contract by failing to pay Breeden any insurance proceeds from the loss, nor did it act in bad faith.

* * * *

Breeden argues that the [lower] court was in error to determine that he had no insurable interest in the home. The home, which was Breeden's and Buchanan's marital residence, was insured under a Nationwide homeowners' insurance policy. The policy was effective from May 27, 2010, to May 27, 2011. The policy insured the home and its contents. At the beginning of the policy period, May 27, 2010, both Breeden and Buchanan had an insurable interest in the home because they were married and lived together in the home. The policy provided that the spouse of the named insured who resides at the same premises is covered as an insured. Based on the allegations of the complaint, the documents attached to the complaint, and Nationwide's motion [to dismiss], the * * * judge determined that Breeden did not have an insurable interest in the home at the time of the fire loss.

The fire loss occurred in April 2011. *At that time, Breeden did not have an insurable interest in the home. * * * The factual allegations of the complaint indicated that he did not have any ownership interest in the home at the time of the loss.* [Emphasis added.]

* * * *

Based on the complaint and the accompanying documents, there was simply nothing further that Nationwide owed under the insurance policy.

Decision and Remedy A state intermediate appellate court affirmed the lower court's dismissal of Breeden's suit. Buchanan, not Breeden, was entitled to the proceeds of the insurance claim filed with Nationwide. At the time of the fire, the insurable interest in the property existed solely with Buchanan.

Critical Thinking

• **Economic** *Why is an insurable interest required for the enforcement of an insurance contract?*

43–1d The Insurance Contract

An insurance contract is governed by the general principles of contract law, although the insurance industry is heavily regulated by the states.[2] Customarily, a party offers to purchase insurance by submitting an application to the insurance company. The company can either accept or reject the offer. For the contract to be binding, consideration (in the form of a premium) must be given, and the parties forming the contract must have the required contractual capacity to do so.

Application The filled-in application form for insurance is usually attached to the policy and made a part of the insurance contract. The person applying for insurance normally is bound by any false statements that appear in the application (subject to certain exceptions). Because the insurance company evaluates the risk factors based on the information included in the insurance application, misstatements or misrepresentations can void a policy. This is particularly true if the insurance company can show that it would not have extended insurance if it had known the true facts.

Effective Date The effective date of an insurance contract—the date on which the insurance coverage begins—is important. In some situations, the insurance applicant is not protected until a formal written policy is issued. In other situations, the applicant is protected between the time the application is received and the time the insurance company either accepts or rejects it. Four facts should be kept in mind:

1. As stated earlier, a broker is an agent of the applicant, not an agent of the insurance company. Therefore, if a person hires a broker to obtain insurance, and the broker fails to procure a policy, the applicant normally is not insured.

2. A person who seeks insurance from an insurance company's agent is usually protected from the moment the application is made, provided—for life insurance—that some form of premium has been paid. Usually, the agent will write a memorandum, or **binder,** indicating that a policy is pending and stating its essential terms.

3. If the parties agree that the policy will be issued and delivered at a later time, the contract is not effective until the policy is issued and delivered. Thus, any loss sustained between the time of application and the delivery of the policy is not covered.

4. Parties may agree that a life insurance policy will be binding at the time the insured pays the first premium, or the policy may be expressly contingent on the applicant's passing a physical examination. If the applicant pays the premium and passes the examination, then the policy coverage is continuously in effect. If the applicant pays the premium but dies before having the physical examination, the policy may still be effective. Then, in order to collect, the applicant's estate normally must show that the applicant *would have passed* the examination had he or she not died.

KNOW THIS

The federal government has the power to regulate the insurance industry under the commerce clause of the U.S. Constitution. Instead of exercising this power itself, Congress allows the states to regulate insurance.

Binder A written, temporary insurance policy.

---

2. The states were given authority to regulate the insurance industry by the McCarran-Ferguson Act of 1945, 15 U.S.C. Sections 1011–1015.

Coinsurance Clauses Often, when taking out fire insurance policies, property owners insure their property for less than full value because most fires do not result in a total loss. To encourage owners to insure their property for an amount as close to full value as possible, fire insurance policies commonly include a coinsurance clause.

Typically, a *coinsurance clause* provides that if the owner insures the property up to a specified percentage—usually 80 percent—of its value, she or he will recover any loss up to the face amount of the policy. If the insurance is for less than the specified percentage, the owner is responsible for a proportionate share of the loss.

Coinsurance applies only in instances of partial loss. The amount of the recovery is calculated by using the following formula:

$$\text{Loss} \times \left(\frac{\text{Amount of Insurance Coverage}}{\text{Coinsurance Percentage} \times \text{Property Value}} \right) = \text{Amount of Recovery}$$

Example 43.2 Madison, who owns property valued at $200,000, takes out a policy in the amount of $100,000. If Madison then suffers a loss of $80,000, her recovery will be $50,000. Madison will be responsible for (coinsure) the balance of the loss, or $30,000, which is the amount of loss ($80,000) minus the amount of recovery ($50,000).

$$\$80,000 \times \left(\frac{\$100,000}{0.8 \times \$200,000} \right) = \$50,000$$

If Madison had taken out a policy in the amount of 80 percent of the value of the property, or $160,000, then according to the same formula, she would have recovered the full amount of the loss (the face amount of the policy).

Incontestability Clauses Statutes commonly require that a policy for life or health insurance include an **incontestability clause.** Under this clause, after the policy has been in force for a specified length of time—often two or three years—the insurer cannot contest statements made in the application. Once a policy becomes incontestable, the insurer cannot later avoid a claim on the basis of, for instance, fraud on the part of the insured, unless the clause provides an exception for that circumstance.

Some important provisions and clauses that are frequently included in insurance contracts are described in Exhibit 43–2.

Incontestability Clause A clause in a policy for life or health insurance stating that after the policy has been in force for a specified length of time (usually two or three years), the insurer cannot contest statements made in the policyholder's application.

Interpreting the Insurance Contract The courts recognize that most people do not have the special training necessary to understand the intricate terminology used in insurance policies. Therefore, when disputes arise, the courts will interpret the words used in an insurance contract according to their ordinary meanings in light of the nature of the coverage involved.

When there is an ambiguity in the policy, the provision generally is interpreted *against the insurance company.* Also, when it is unclear whether an insurance contract actually exists because the written policy has not been delivered, the uncertainty normally is resolved against the insurance company. The court presumes that the policy is in effect unless the company can show otherwise. Similarly, an insurer must make sure that the insured is adequately notified of any change in coverage under an existing policy.

Disputes over insurance often focus on the application of exclusions in the policy. **Case Example 43.3** Alberto and Karelli Mila were insured under a liability policy that contained a list of twelve exclusions. "Exclusion k" stated that coverage did not apply to "bodily injury arising out of sexual molestation, corporal punishment or physical or mental abuse." Verushka Valero, on behalf of her child, filed a suit against the Milas, charging them with negligent supervision of a perpetrator who sexually molested Valero's child.

Exhibit 43–2 Insurance Contract Provisions and Clauses

TYPE OF CLAUSE	DESCRIPTION
Antilapse clause	An antilapse clause provides that the policy will not automatically lapse if no payment is made on the date due. Ordinarily, under such a provision, the insured has a *grace period* of thirty or thirty-one days within which to pay an overdue premium before the policy is canceled.
Appraisal clause	Insurance policies frequently provide that if the parties cannot agree on the amount of a loss covered under the policy or the value of the property lost, an appraisal, or estimate, by an impartial and qualified third party can be demanded.
Arbitration clause	Many insurance policies include clauses that call for arbitration of any disputes that arise between the insurer and the insured concerning the settlement of claims.
Incontestability clause	An incontestability clause provides that after a policy has been in force for a specified length of time—usually two or three years—the insurer cannot contest statements made in the application.
Multiple insurance policies clause	Many insurance policies include a clause providing that if the insured has multiple insurance policies that cover the same property and the amount of coverage exceeds the loss, the loss will be shared proportionately by the insurance companies.

The Milas filed a claim with their insurer to provide a defense against the charges. The insurer refused and sought a court order declaring that it had no obligation under the policy to provide such a defense. The court ruled in favor of the insurer, and the decision was affirmed on appeal. The language in the Milas' policy excluding coverage for "bodily injury arising out of sexual molestation" was clear and unambiguous. The exclusion applied, and the insurer was not required to defend the Milas.[3]

Cancellation The insured can cancel a policy at any time, and the insurer can cancel under certain circumstances. When an insurance company can cancel its insurance contract, the policy or a state statute usually requires that the insurer give advance written notice of the cancellation to the insured. The same requirement applies when only part of a policy is canceled. Any premium paid in advance may be refundable on the policy's cancellation. The insured may also be entitled to a life insurance policy's cash surrender value.

What exclusions might be in a homeowner's liability policy?

The insurer may cancel an insurance policy for various reasons, depending on the type of insurance. Following are some examples:

1. Automobile insurance can be canceled for nonpayment of premiums or suspension of the insured's driver's license.

2. Property insurance can be canceled for nonpayment of premiums or for other reasons, including the insured's fraud or misrepresentation, gross negligence, or conviction for a crime that increases the risk assumed by the insurer.

3. Life and health policies can be canceled because of false statements made by the insured in the application, but the cancellation must take place before the effective date of an incontestability clause.

An insurer cannot cancel—or refuse to renew—a policy for discriminatory reasons or other reasons that violate public policy. Also, an insurer cannot cancel a policy because the insured has appeared as a witness in a case brought against the company.

Duties and Obligations of the Parties Both parties to an insurance contract are responsible for the obligations they assume under the contract. In addition, both the insured and the insurer have an implied duty to act in good faith.

---

3. *Valero v. Florida Insurance Guaranty Association, Inc.*, 59 So.3d 1166 (Fla.App. 2011). See also, *Dueno v. Modern USA Ins. Co.*, 152 So.3d 60 (Fla.App. 2014).

Duties of the Insured. Good faith requires the party who is applying for insurance to reveal everything necessary for the insurer to evaluate the risk. The applicant must disclose all material facts, including all facts that an insurer would consider in determining whether to charge a higher premium or to refuse to issue a policy altogether. Many insurance companies today require that an applicant give the company permission to access other information, such as private medical records and credit ratings, for the purpose of evaluating the risk.

Once the insurance policy is issued, the insured has three basic duties under the contract:

1. To pay the premiums as stated in the contract.

2. To notify the insurer within a reasonable time if an event occurs that gives rise to a claim.

3. To cooperate with the insurer during any investigation or litigation.

Duties of the Insurer. Once the insurer has accepted the risk, and some event occurs that gives rise to a claim, the insurer has a *duty to investigate* to determine the facts. When a policy provides insurance against third party claims, the insurer is obligated to make reasonable efforts to settle such a claim.

If a settlement cannot be reached, then regardless of the claim's merit, the insurer has a *duty to defend* any suit against the insured. Usually, a policy provides that in this situation the insured must cooperate in the defense and attend hearings and trials if necessary. An insurer has a duty to provide or pay an attorney to defend its insured when a complaint alleges facts that could, if proved, impose liability on the insured within the policy's coverage.

✳ **Spotlight Case Example 43.4** Dentist Robert Woo installed implants for one of his employees, Tina Alberts, whose family raised potbellied pigs. As a joke, while Alberts was anesthetized, Woo installed a set of "flippers" (temporary partial bridges) shaped like boar tusks and took photos. A month later, Woo's staff showed the photos to Alberts at a party. Alberts refused to return to work. She filed a suit against Woo for battery.

Woo's insurance company refused to defend him in the suit, and he ended up paying Alberts $250,000 to settle her claim. Woo then sued the insurance company and won. The court held that the insurance company had a duty to defend Woo under the professional liability provision of his policy because Woo's practical joke took place during a routine dental procedure.[4]

Bad-Faith Actions. Although insurance law generally follows contract law, most states now recognize a "bad-faith" tort action against insurers. Thus, if an insurer in bad faith denies coverage of a claim, the insured may recover in tort in an amount exceeding the policy's coverage limits and may also recover punitive damages. Some courts have held insurers liable for bad-faith refusals to settle claims for reasonable amounts within the policy limits.

Defenses against Payment
An insurance company can raise any of the defenses that would be valid in an ordinary action on a contract, as well as some defenses that do not apply in ordinary contract actions.

1. *Fraud or misrepresentation.* If the insurance company can show that the policy was procured by fraud or misrepresentation, it may have a valid defense for not paying on a claim. (The insurance company may also have the right to disaffirm or rescind the insurance contract.)

2. *Lack of an insurable interest.* An absolute defense exists if the insurer can show that the insured lacked an insurable interest—thus rendering the policy void from the beginning.

3. *Illegal actions of the insured.* Improper actions, such as those that are against public policy or that are otherwise illegal, can also give the insurance company a defense against the payment of a claim or allow it to rescind the contract.

---

4. *Woo v. Fireman's Fund Insurance Co.*, 161 Wash.2d 43, 164 P.3d 454 (2007).

Case Example 43.5 Charles Pendleton, an antique vehicle collector, bought a 1956 Mercedes-Benz and insured it with Foremost Insurance Company. Two weeks later, Pendleton filed a claim saying that the car had been destroyed in a collision with a Ford truck on an icy road. Foremost refused to pay the claim because it believed that Pendleton was lying about how the car was destroyed. Foremost sued, seeking a court declaration releasing it from liability.

At trial, Foremost provided enough evidence to show that Pendleton had towed the antique, inoperative Mercedes onto an icy road and then pushed it into a tree using the truck. A jury found that Pendleton had intentionally destroyed the Mercedes and issued a verdict in favor of Foremost. Pendleton appealed, but the reviewing court affirmed the jury's verdict. The insurance company did not have to pay for the damage to the Mercedes.[5] ■

An insurance company can be prevented, or estopped, from asserting some defenses that are usually available. For instance, an insurance company normally cannot escape payment on the death of an insured on the ground that the person's age was stated incorrectly on the application. Also, incontestability clauses prevent the insurer from asserting certain defenses.

Is an insurer of an antique car liable for damages when the insured lies about how the damage occurred? Why or why not?

43–2 Wills

Not only do the owners of property want to protect it during their lifetime through insurance coverage, but they typically also wish to transfer it to their loved ones at the time of their death. A **will** is the final declaration of how a person desires to have her or his property disposed of after death. It is a formal instrument that must follow exactly the requirements of state law to be effective. A will is referred to as a *testamentary disposition* of property, and one who dies after having made a valid will is said to have died **testate.**

A will can serve other purposes besides the distribution of property. It can appoint a guardian for minor children or incapacitated adults. It can also appoint a personal representative to settle the affairs of the deceased. Exhibit 43–3 presents excerpts from the will of Michael Jackson, the "King of Pop," who died from cardiac arrest at the age of fifty. Jackson held a substantial amount of tangible and intangible property, including the publishing rights to most of the Beatles' music catalogue. The will is a "pour-over" will, meaning that it transfers all of Jackson's property (that is not already held in the name of the trust) into the Michael Jackson Family Trust (trusts are discussed later in this chapter). Jackson's will also appoints his mother, Katherine Jackson, as the guardian of his three minor children.

Will An instrument made by a testator directing what is to be done with her or his property after death.

Testate Having left a will at death.

43–2a Terminology of Wills

A person who makes out a will is known as a **testator** (from the Latin *testari,* "to make a will"). The court responsible for administering any legal problems surrounding a will is called a *probate court.*

When a person dies, a personal representative administers the estate and settles all of the decedent's affairs. An **executor** is a personal representative named in the will, whereas an **administrator** is a personal representative appointed by the court for a decedent who dies without a will. The court will also appoint an administrator if the will does not name an executor or if the named person lacks the capacity to serve as an executor.

Testator One who makes and executes a will.

Executor A person appointed by a testator in a will to administer her or his estate.

Administrator One who is appointed by a court to administer a person's estate if the decedent died without a valid will or if the executor named in the will cannot serve.

---

5. *Foremost Insurance Co. v. Charles Pendleton,* 675 Fed.Appx. 457 (5th Cir. 2017).

Exhibit 43–3 Excerpts from Michael Jackson's Will

LAST WILL OF MICHAEL JOSEPH JACKSON

I, MICHAEL JOSEPH JACKSON, a resident of the State of California, declare this to be my last Will, and do hereby revoke all former wills and codicils made by me.

I   I declare that I am not married. My marriage to DEBORAH JEAN ROWE JACKSON has been dissolved. I have three children now living, PRINCE MICHAEL JACKSON, JR., PARIS MICHAEL KATHERINE JACKSON and PRINCE MICHAEL JOSEPH JACKSON, II. I have no other children, living or deceased.

II   It is my intention by this Will to dispose of all property which I am entitled to dispose of by will. I specifically refrain from exercising all powers of appointment that I may possess at the time of my death.

III   I give my entire estate to the Trustee or Trustees then acting under that certain Amended and Restated Declaration of Trust executed on March 22, 2002 by me as Trustee and Trustor which is called the MICHAEL JACKSON FAMILY TRUST, giving effect to any amendments thereto made prior to my death. All such assets shall be held, managed and distributed as a part of said Trust according to its terms and not as a separate testamentary trust.

   If for any reason this gift is not operative or is invalid, or if the aforesaid Trust fails or has been revoked, I give my residuary estate to the Trustee or Trustees named to act in the MICHAEL JACKSON FAMILY TRUST, as Amended and Restated on March 22, 2002, and I direct said Trustee or Trustees to divide, administer, hold and distribute the trust estate pursuant to the provisions of said Trust * * *.
      * * * *

IV   I direct that all federal estate taxes and state inheritance or succession taxes payable upon or resulting from or by reason of my death (herein "Death Taxes") attributable to property which is part of the trust estate of the MICHAEL JACKSON FAMILY TRUST, including property which passes to said trust from my probate estate shall be paid by the Trustee of said trust in accordance with its terms. Death Taxes attributable to property passing outside this Will, other than property constituting the trust estate of the trust mentioned in the preceding sentence, shall be charged against the taker of said property.

V   * * * *

VI   * * * *

VIII   If any of my children are minors at the time of my death, I nominate my mother, KATHERINE JACKSON as guardian of the persons and estates of such minor children. If KATHERINE JACKSON fails to survive me, or is unable or unwilling to act as guardian, I nominate DIANA ROSS as guardian of the persons and estates of such minor children.

Intestate As a noun, one who has died without having created a valid will. As an adjective, the state of having died without a will.

Intestacy Laws State statutes that specify how property will be distributed when a person dies intestate (without a valid will).

Devise A gift of real property by will, or the act of giving real property by will.

Bequest A gift of personal property by will (from the verb *to bequeath*).

Legacy A gift of personal property under a will.

Devisee One designated in a will to receive a gift of real property.

Legatee One designated in a will to receive a gift of personal property.

A person who dies without having created a valid will is said to have died **intestate**. In this situation, state **intestacy laws** (sometimes referred to as *laws of descent*) prescribe the distribution of the property among heirs or next of kin (relatives). If no heirs or kin can be found, title to the property will be transferred to the state.

A gift of real estate by will is generally called a **devise**, and a gift of personal property by will is called a **bequest**, or **legacy**. The recipient of a gift by will is a **devisee** or a **legatee**, depending on whether the gift was a devise or a legacy.

43–2b Types of Gifts

Gifts by will can be specific, general, or residuary. If a decedent's assets are not sufficient to cover all the gifts identified in the will, an abatement is necessary.

Specific and General Devises A *specific* devise or bequest (legacy) describes particular property (such as "Eastwood Estate" or "my gold pocket watch") that can be distinguished from all the rest of the testator's property.

A *general* devise or bequest (legacy) does not single out any particular item of property to be transferred by will. For instance, "I devise all my lands" is a general devise.

A general bequest may specify the property's value in monetary terms (such as "two diamonds worth $10,000") or simply state a dollar amount (such as "$30,000 to my nephew, Carleton").

Residuary Clause Sometimes, a will provides that any assets remaining after the estate's debts have been paid and specific gifts have been made are to be distributed in a specific way through a *residuary clause*. Residuary clauses are often used when the exact amount to be distributed cannot be determined until all of the other gifts and payouts have been made. If the testator has not indicated what party or parties should receive the residuary of the estate, the residuary passes according to state laws of intestacy.

Abatement If the assets of an estate are insufficient to pay in full all general bequests provided for in the will, an *abatement* takes place. In an abatement, the legatees receive reduced benefits. **Example 43.6** Julie's will leaves $15,000 each to her children, Tamara and Stan. On Julie's death, only $10,000 is available to honor these bequests. By abatement, each child will receive $5,000. ■ If bequests are more complicated, abatement may be more complex. The testator's intent, as expressed in the will, controls.

43–2c Requirements for a Valid Will

A will must comply with statutory formalities designed to ensure that the testator understood his or her actions at the time the will was made. These formalities are intended to help prevent fraud. Unless they are followed, the will is declared void, and the decedent's property is distributed according to the laws of intestacy of that state, as discussed later in this chapter.

Although the required formalities vary among jurisdictions, most states have certain basic requirements for executing a will. The National Conference of Commissioners on Uniform State Laws has issued the Uniform Probate Code (UPC) to govern various aspects of wills, inheritance, and estates. Almost half of the states have enacted some part of the UPC and incorporated it into their own probate codes.

For a valid will, most states require proof of (1) the testator's capacity, (2) testamentary intent, (3) a written document, (4) the testator's signature, and (5) the signatures of persons who witnessed the testator's signing of the will.

Testamentary Capacity and Intent To have testamentary capacity, a testator must be of legal age and sound mind *at the time the will is made*. The minimum legal age for executing a will in most states and under the UPC is eighteen years [UPC 2–501]. Thus, the will of a twenty-one-year-old decedent written when the person was sixteen is invalid if, under state law, the legal age for executing a will is eighteen.

The concept of "being of sound mind" refers to the testator's ability to formulate and to comprehend a personal plan for the disposition of property. Persons who have been declared incompetent in a legal proceeding do not meet the sound mind requirement.

Related to the requirement of capacity is the concept of intent. A valid will is one that represents the maker's intention to transfer and distribute her or his property. Generally, a testator must:

1. Know the nature of the act (of making a will).

2. Comprehend and remember the "natural objects of his or her bounty"—that is, the people to whom the testator would naturally leave his or her estate (such as family members and friends).

If this couple leaves a sum of money to each of their children, but there are not enough assets to pay the amount specified in the will, what happens?

monkeybusinessimages/iStock/Getty Images

Learning Objective 2

What are the basic requirements for executing a will?

"If you want to see a man's true character, watch him divide an estate."

Benjamin Franklin
1706–1790
(American diplomat, author, and scientist)

3. Know the nature and extent of her or his property.

4. Understand the distribution of assets called for by the will.

Undue Influence. When it can be shown that the decedent's plan of distribution was the result of fraud or of undue influence, the will is declared invalid. A court may sometimes infer undue influence when the named beneficiary was in a position to influence the making of the will. If the testator ignored blood relatives and named as a beneficiary a nonrelative who was in constant close contact with the testator, for instance, a court might infer undue influence.

Case Example 43.7 Laura and Marvin Farmer had four children—Gary, Rita, Roger, and Sharon. The year that Marvin died, Laura underwent triple bypass surgery and moved in with Sharon, who lived nearby.

Sharon took control of most of Laura's daily life. She refused to allow her brothers and sister to visit their mother. She convinced Laura that they stole from her and wanted to put her in a nursing home. Neither of these beliefs was true, but they affected Laura's decision making. Laura revoked her will—which named all four of her children as beneficiaries—and executed a new will leaving most of her estate to Sharon. After Laura died, Sharon offered the new will for probate. Her siblings contested the will. Sharon argued that it was the product of Laura's "free and independent judgment." The court dismissed the siblings' claim and affirmed the will. Gary, Rita, and Roger appealed.

A state intermediate appellate court vacated the lower court's decision and remanded the case. Sharon had not presented "clear and convincing evidence" that Laura had exercised "free and independent judgment" in making the second will. Thus, the will was not valid, because Laura's intent was in doubt. It was possible that Sharon had exercised undue influence over Laura.[6]

Disinheritance. Although a testator must be able to remember the persons who would naturally be heirs to the estate, there is no requirement that testators give their estates to the natural heirs. A testator may decide to disinherit, or leave nothing to, an individual for various reasons. Most states have laws that attempt to prevent accidental disinheritance, however. There are also laws that protect minor children from loss of the family residence. Therefore, the testator's intent to disinherit needs to be clear.

Case Example 43.8 In 1975, William Melton executed a will that, among other things, stated that his daughter, Vicki Palm, was to receive nothing. In 1979, he added a handwritten note to the will, saying that his friend Alberta Kelleher was to receive a small portion of his estate.

In 1995, Melton sent a signed, handwritten letter to Kelleher. The letter said that Melton wanted to put "something in writing" leaving Kelleher his "entire estate." Melton also said, "I *do not* want my brother Larry J. Melton or Vicki Palm or any of my other relatives to have one penny of my estate."

When Melton died in 2008, Kelleher had already passed away, and Melton's daughter, Vicki Palm, was his only natural heir. The state of Nevada argued that it should receive everything because Palm had been disinherited. Nevertheless, the trial court applied the state's intestacy laws and distributed the entire estate to Palm. The state appealed. The Nevada Supreme Court reversed the judgment of the lower court. It held that the disinheritance clause was clear and enforceable and that Melton's estate should therefore go to the state of Nevada.[7]

The following case involved an heir's petition to change the distribution under a will by disinheriting some of the legatees.

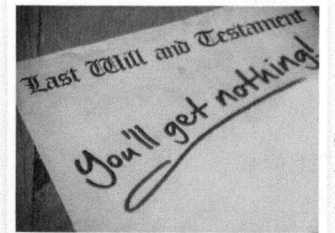

Can a parent disinherit his or her daughter?

---

6. *In re Estate of Farmer,* 2017 WL 1830096 (Tenn.Ct.App. 2017).
7. *In re Estate of Melton,* 272 P.3d 668 (Nev.Sup.Ct. 2012).

■ Case 43.2

In re Navarra

Pennsylvania Superior Court, 2018 PA Super 84, 185 A.3d 342 (2018).

Background and Facts Fred and Sandra Navarra were married and lived in New Wilmington, Pennsylvania. Each of their wills provided that 70 percent of the residuary estate would pass to Fred's legatees—his children from a previous marriage, Richard Navarra, Linda D'Augostine, Charlene Shelledy, and Joanne Navarra, and Richard's ex-wife, Chris Navarra. The other 30 percent of the residuary estate would pass to Sandra's children from her previous marriage, Chrystie Clarke and Brent Young. After the wills were executed, Fred was seriously injured in an automobile accident and needed a full-time caregiver. Sandra developed dementia and also needed continuous care.

When friction developed between her children and his legatees, his children transferred assets jointly owned by Fred and Sandra to themselves. Further, his children mistreated Sandra by denying caregiver visits and isolating her from Fred. Suspecting abuse, Clarke moved Sandra to a nursing home. Fred executed a revised will disinheriting Sandra and her children and leaving his entire residuary estate to his children. Sandra lacked the capacity to amend her will due to dementia. After Fred died, Clarke filed a petition in a Pennsylvania state court, asking the court to substitute its judgment for Sandra's and amend her will to disinherit Fred's legatees. Fred's legatees opposed the petition. The court granted Clarke's request. Fred's legatees appealed.

In the Words of the Court

Opinion by *STABILE*, J. [Judge]:

* * * *

[Pennsylvania Consolidated Statutes] Section 5536, entitled "Distributions of Income and Principal During Incapacity," * * * is part of Chapter 55 of the Probate, Estates and Fiduciaries Code (PEF Code), whose purpose is to protect the rights of incapacitated persons * * * . Chapter 55 defines an "incapacitated person" as "an adult whose ability to receive and evaluate information effectively and communicate decisions in any way is impaired to such a significant extent that he is partially or totally unable to manage his financial resources or to meet essential requirements for his physical health and safety."

Section 5536(b) provides:

* * * The court * * * shall have the power to substitute its judgment for that of the incapacitated person with respect to the estate and affairs of the incapacitated person for the benefit of the incapacitated person [and her] family * * * . The court in exercising its judgment shall consider the testamentary and *inter vivos* [among the living] intentions of the incapacitated person insofar as they can be ascertained.

* * * *

* * * The power in question here—modification of Wife's [Sandra's] will to disinherit several residuary legatees—fits easily within Section 5536(b)'s broad scope, for it concerns an incapacitated person's estate, and its exercise will benefit family members of the incapacitated person by augmenting their residuary shares. [Emphasis added.]

* * * *

* * * It could be safely concluded that the reason Clarke was removed by Husband [Fred] is because Husband simply did not like her based largely on his perception that she had Wife taken from the home Husband and Wife shared without consultation with Husband or his approval. Moreover, the record reflects that Husband was very upset at Clarke. [Also,] Wife's natural children were removed by Husband from his Will at least in part for the purposes of benefiting Husband's children in that they were left the entirety of his estate. * * * Since Husband's legatees have already received an inheritance to the exclusion of Wife's natural children, Wife could logically disinherit Husband's legatees from her will as a response, thereby leaving the entirety of her estate to her two biological children.

Decision and Remedy A state intermediate appellate court affirmed the lower court's decision to substitute its judgment and disinherit the legatees. The court had the power under Section 5536, and using it in this case was "permissible because a reasonable person would conclude that [Sandra] would have disinherited [Fred's] legatees."

Critical Thinking

• **Legal Environment** *What facts support the conclusion that the court had good cause to substitute its judgment and remove Fred's legatees as heirs from Sandra's will?*

• **Economic** *Can the act of disinheriting an institutionalized spouse be used as an estate-planning tool? Explain.*

Writing Requirements Generally, a will must be in writing. The writing itself can be informal as long as it substantially complies with the statutory requirements. In some states, a will can be handwritten in crayon or ink. It can be written on a sheet or scrap of paper, on a paper bag, or on a piece of cloth. A will that is completely in the handwriting of the testator is called a **holographic will** (sometimes referred to as an *olographic will*).

A **nuncupative will** is an oral will made before witnesses. Oral wills are not permitted in most states. Where authorized by statute, such wills are generally valid only if made during the last illness of the testator and are therefore sometimes referred to as *deathbed wills*. Normally, only personal property can be transferred by a nuncupative will. Statutes may also permit members of the military to make nuncupative wills when on active duty.

Signature Requirements A fundamental requirement is that the testator's signature must appear on the will, generally at the end. Each jurisdiction dictates by statute and court decision what constitutes a signature. Initials, an X or other mark, and words such as "Mom" have all been upheld as valid when it was shown that the testators *intended* them to be signatures.

Witness Requirements A will usually must be attested (sworn to) by two, and sometimes three, witnesses. The number of witnesses, their qualifications, and the manner in which the witnessing must be done are generally set out in a statute. A witness can be required to be disinterested—that is, not a beneficiary under the will. The UPC, however, allows even interested witnesses to attest to a will [UPC 2–505]. There are no age requirements for witnesses, but they must be mentally competent.

The purpose of the witnesses is to verify that the testator actually executed (signed) the will and had the requisite intent and capacity at the time. A witness does not have to read the contents of the will. Usually, the testator and all witnesses sign in the sight or the presence of one another. The UPC does not require all parties to sign in the presence of one another, however, and deems it sufficient if the testator acknowledges her or his signature to the witnesses [UPC 2–502]. The UPC also provides an alternative to traditional witnesses—the signature may be acknowledged by the testator before a notary public.

43–2d Revocation of Wills

A testator can revoke a will at any time during his or her life, either by a physical act or by a subsequent writing. Wills can also be revoked by operation of law. Revocation can be partial or complete, and must follow certain strict formalities.

Revocation by a Physical Act A testator can revoke a will by *intentionally* burning, tearing, canceling, obliterating, or otherwise destroying it.[8] A testator can also revoke a will by intentionally having someone else destroy it in the testator's presence and at the testator's direction.

In some states, a testator can partially revoke a will by the physical act of crossing out some provisions in the will. Then, those portions that are crossed out are dropped, and the remaining parts of the will are valid. In no circumstances, however, can a provision be crossed out and an additional or substitute provision written in its place. Such altered portions require reexecution (re-signing) and reattestation (rewitnessing).

To revoke a will by physical act, it is necessary to follow the mandates of a state statute exactly. When a state statute prescribes the specific methods for revoking a will by physical act, only those methods can be used to revoke the will.

Revocation by a Subsequent Writing A will may be wholly or partially revoked by a **codicil**, a written instrument separate from the will that amends or revokes provisions in the

---

Holographic Will A will written entirely in the testator's handwriting.

Nuncupative Will An oral will (often called a *deathbed will*) made before witnesses. Usually, such wills are limited to transfers of personal property.

When does tearing up a will legally revoke it?

Petr Malyshev/ShutterStock.com

Codicil A written supplement or modification to a will. A codicil must be executed with the same formalities as a will.

---

8. The destruction cannot be inadvertent. The testator must have the intent to revoke the will.

will. A codicil eliminates the necessity of redrafting an entire will merely to add to it or amend it. It can also be used to revoke an entire will. The codicil must be executed with the same formalities required for a will, and it must refer expressly to the will. In effect, it updates a will, because the will is "incorporated by reference" into the codicil.

A new will (second will) can be executed that may or may not revoke the first or a prior will, depending on the language used. To revoke a prior will, the second will must use language specifically revoking other wills, such as "This will hereby revokes all prior wills." If the express *declaration of revocation* is missing, then both wills are read together. If there are any discrepancies between the wills, the second will controls.

Revocation by Operation of Law Revocation by *operation of law* occurs when marriage, divorce or annulment, or the birth of a child takes place after a will has been executed.

Marriage and Divorce. In most states, when a testator marries after executing a will that does not include the new spouse, the spouse can still receive a share of the testator's estate. On the testator's death, the surviving spouse can receive the amount he or she would have taken had the testator died intestate (intestacy laws will be discussed shortly). The rest of the estate is passed under the will [UPC 2–301, 2–508].

If, however, the new spouse is otherwise provided for in the will (or by transfer of property outside the will), he or she will not be given an intestate amount. Also, if the parties had a valid *prenuptial agreement* (a contract made prior to marriage), its provisions dictate what the surviving spouse receives.

Divorce or annulment does not necessarily revoke the entire will. Rather, a divorce or an annulment occurring after a will has been executed revokes those dispositions of property made under the will to the former spouse [UPC 2–508].

Children. If a child is born after a will has been executed, that child may be entitled to a portion of the estate. Most state laws allow a child of the deceased to receive some portion of a parent's estate even if no provision is made in the parent's will. This is true *unless it is clear from the will's terms that the testator intended to disinherit the child* (see *Case Example 43.8*). Under the UPC, the rule is the same.

43–2e Probate Procedures and Estate Planning

To **probate** a will means to establish its validity and to carry the administration of the estate through a court process. Probate laws vary from state to state. Typically, the procedure depends on the size and complexity of the decedent's estate.

People commonly engage in estate planning in an attempt to avoid formal probate procedures and to maximize the value of their estate by reducing taxes and other expenses. Individuals should also consider formulating a social media estate plan, as discussed in this chapter's *Adapting the Law to the Online Environment* feature.

Probate The process of proving and validating a will and settling all matters pertaining to an estate.

Informal Probate For smaller estates, most state statutes provide for the distribution of assets without formal probate proceedings. Faster and less expensive methods are then used. Property can be transferred by *affidavit* (a written statement taken before a person who has authority to affirm it). Problems or questions can be handled during an administrative hearing. Some state statutes allow car titles, savings and checking accounts, and certain other property to be transferred simply by filling out forms.

A majority of states also provide for *family settlement agreements,* which are private agreements among the beneficiaries. Once a will is admitted to probate, the family members can agree among themselves on how to distribute the decedent's assets. Although a family settlement agreement speeds the settlement process, a court order is still needed to protect the estate from future creditors and to clear title to the assets involved.

Social Media Estate Planning

People are generally quite careful about choosing the personal representatives who will deal with their real estate, bank accounts, and investments after they are gone. Today, the same care should be taken in choosing an online executor to deal with a deceased's online identity, particularly in social media.

What an Online Executor Should Do

An online executor is responsible for dealing with a decedent's e-mail addresses, social media profiles, and blogs. E-mail accounts should be closed, but some people do not want their social media profiles to be erased after they die. They want the profiles to be maintained, at least for some specified time after death, so that family and friends can visit them. Some people ask that their online executors place a memorial profile in their social media accounts.

Why Social Media Estate Planning Is Important

Online estate planning is essential because the deceased can still be a victim of identity theft. Unscrupulous fraudsters often use dead people's online identities to defraud private companies, individuals, and federal and state governments. If all of a person's e-mail addresses and social media accounts are closed, it is harder for online fraudsters to use them for identity theft.

In addition, closing an e-mail account not only protects family members from being harassed with continuing spam after the person's death but also prevents spammers from hijacking the account. Spammers can use a dead person's e-mail account as the sender of billions of unwanted bulk e-mails.

Critical Thinking

Why might an online executor need a copy of the deceased's death certificate?

Formal Probate For larger estates, formal probate proceedings normally are undertaken, and the probate court supervises every aspect of the process. Additionally, in some situations—such as when a guardian for minor children must be appointed—more formal probate procedures cannot be avoided.

Formal probate proceedings may take several months or several years to complete, depending on the size and complexity of the estate and whether the will is contested. As a result, a sizable portion of the decedent's assets (as much as 10 percent) may go toward payment of court costs and fees charged by attorneys and personal representatives.

Property Transfers outside the Probate Process Often, people can avoid the cost of probate by employing various **will substitutes.** Examples include *living trusts* (discussed later in this chapter), life insurance policies, and individual retirement accounts (IRAs) with named beneficiaries.

Will Substitutes Various instruments, such as living trusts and life insurance plans, that may be used to avoid the formal probate process.

One way to transfer property outside the probate process is to make gifts to children or others while one is still living. Another way is to own property in a joint tenancy. As previously discussed, in a joint tenancy, when one joint tenant dies, the other joint tenant or tenants automatically inherit the deceased tenant's share of the property. This is true even if the deceased tenant has provided otherwise in her or his will. Not all alternatives to formal probate administration are suitable to every estate, however.

"You cannot live without lawyers, and certainly you cannot die without them."

Joseph H. Choate
1832–1917
(American lawyer and diplomat)

43–2f Intestacy Laws

As mentioned, each state regulates by statute how property will be distributed when a person dies intestate (without a valid will). Intestacy laws attempt to carry out the likely intent and wishes of the decedent. These laws assume that deceased persons would have intended that their natural heirs (spouses, children, grandchildren, or other family members) inherit their property. Therefore, intestacy statutes set out rules and priorities under which these heirs inherit the property. If no heirs exist, the state will assume ownership of the property. The rules of descent vary widely from state to state.

Surviving Spouse and Children Usually, state statutes provide that the estate must be used to satisfy first the debts of the decedent. Then, the remaining assets pass to the surviving spouse and to the children. A surviving spouse usually receives only a share of the estate—one-half if there is also a surviving child and one-third if there are two or more children. Only if no children or grandchildren survive the decedent will a surviving spouse be entitled to the entire estate.

Example 43.9 Allen dies intestate and is survived by his wife, Beth, and his children, Duane and Tara. Allen's property passes according to intestacy laws. After his outstanding debts are paid, Beth will receive the family home (either in fee simple or as a life estate) and ordinarily a one-third interest in all other property. The remaining real and personal property will pass to Duane and Tara in equal portions. ▪

Under most state intestacy laws and under the UPC, in-laws do not share in an estate. Thus, if a child dies before his or her parents, the child's spouse will not receive an inheritance on the parents' death. For instance, if Duane died before his father (Allen) in *Example 43.9*, Duane's spouse would not inherit Duane's share of Allen's estate.

When a person dies without a will (intestate), how do states normally distribute the property of the deceased person?

When There Is No Surviving Spouse or Child When there is no surviving spouse or child, the order of inheritance is grandchildren, then brothers and sisters, and, in some states, parents of the decedent. These relatives are usually called *lineal descendants*.

If there are no lineal descendants, then *collateral heirs*—nieces, nephews, aunts, and uncles of the decedent—make up the next group to share. If there are no survivors in any of these groups, most statutes provide for the property to be distributed among the next of kin of the collateral heirs.

Stepchildren, Adopted Children, and Illegitimate Children Under intestacy laws, stepchildren are not considered kin. Legally adopted children, however, are recognized as lawful heirs of their adoptive parents (as are children who are in the process of being adopted at the time of the parents' death).

Statutes vary from state to state in regard to the inheritance rights of illegitimate children (children born out of wedlock). In some states, an illegitimate child has the right to inherit only from the mother and her relatives, unless the father's paternity has been established by a legal proceeding. In the majority of states, however, a child born of any union that has the characteristics of a formal marriage relationship (such as unmarried parents who cohabit) is considered to be legitimate.

Under the revised UPC, a child is the child of his or her natural (biological) parents, regardless of their marital status, as long as the natural parent has openly treated the child as her or his child [UPC 2–114]. Although illegitimate children may have inheritance rights in most states, their rights are not necessarily identical to those of legitimate children.

Learning Objective 3
What is the difference between a *per stirpes* distribution and a *per capita* distribution of an estate to the grandchildren of the deceased?

Grandchildren Usually, a decedent's will provides for how the estate will be distributed to descendants of deceased children—that is, to the decedent's grandchildren. If a will does not include such a provision—or if a person dies intestate—the question arises as to what share the grandchildren of the decedent will receive. Each state uses one of two methods of distributing the assets of intestate decedents—*per stirpes* or *per capita*.

Per Stirpes Distribution. Under the **per stirpes**[9] method, within a class or group of distributees (such as grandchildren), the children of a descendant take the share that their deceased

Per Stirpes A method of distributing an intestate's estate so that each heir in a certain class (such as grandchildren) takes the share to which her or his deceased ancestor (such as a mother or father) would have been entitled.

---

9. *Per stirpes* is a Latin term meaning "by the roots" or "by stock." When used in estate law, it means proportionally divided among beneficiaries according to their deceased ancestor's share.

parent *would have been* entitled to inherit. Thus, a grandchild with no siblings inherits all of his or her parent's share, while grandchildren with siblings divide their parent's share.

Example 43.10 Michael, a widower, has two children, Scott and Jonathan. Scott has two children (Becky and Holly), and Jonathan has one child (Paul). Scott and Jonathan die before their father, and then Michael dies. If Michael's estate is distributed *per stirpes,* Becky and Holly each receive one-fourth of the estate (dividing Scott's one-half share). Paul receives one-half of the estate (taking Jonathan's one-half share). ■ Exhibit 43–4 illustrates the *per stirpes* method of distribution.

Per Capita *Distribution.* An estate may also be distributed on a **per capita**[10] basis, which means that each person in a class or group takes an equal share of the estate. In *Example 43.10,* if Michael's estate is distributed *per capita,* Becky, Holly, and Paul each receive a one-third share. Exhibit 43–5 illustrates the *per capita* method of distribution.

Per Capita A method of distributing an intestate's estate so that each heir in a certain class (such as grandchildren) receives an equal share.

---

10. *Per capita* is a Latin term meaning "per person" or "for each head." When used in estate law, it means equally divided among beneficiaries.

Exhibit 43–4 *Per Stirpes* Distribution

Under this method of distribution, an heir takes the share that his or her deceased parent would have been entitled to inherit had the parent lived. This may mean that a class of distributees—the grandchildren in this example—will not inherit in equal portions. Note that Becky and Holly receive only one-fourth of Michael's estate while Paul inherits one-half.

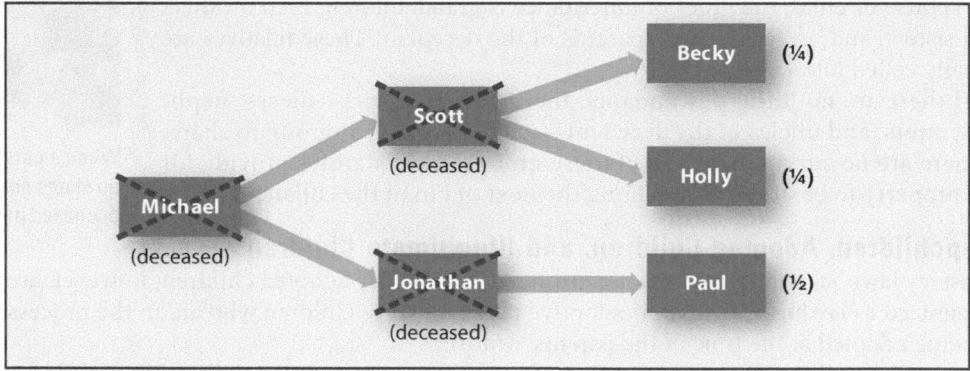

Exhibit 43–5 *Per Capita* Distribution

Under this method of distribution, all heirs in a certain class—in this example, the grandchildren—inherit equally. Note that Becky and Holly in this situation each inherit one-third, as does Paul.

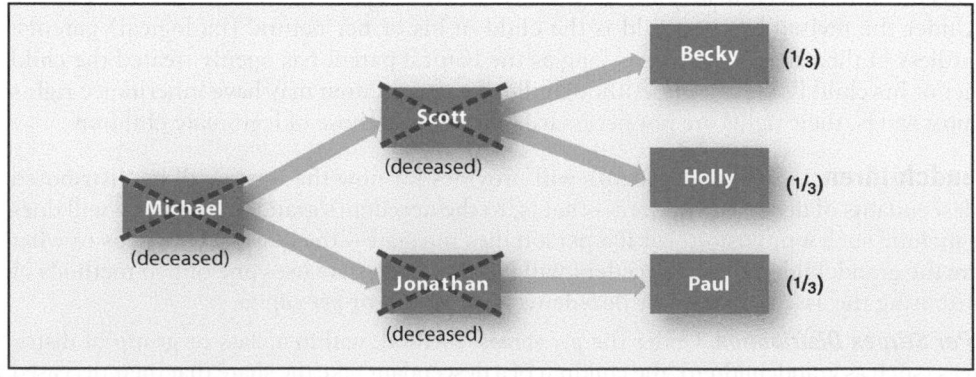

43–3 Trusts

A **trust** is any arrangement through which property is transferred from one person to a trustee to be administered for the transferor's or another party's benefit. It can also be defined as a right of property held by one party for the benefit of another. A trust can be created for any purpose that is not illegal or against public policy, and it can be express or implied.

The essential elements of a trust are as follows:

1. A designated beneficiary.

2. A designated trustee.

3. A fund sufficiently identified to enable title to pass to the trustee.

4. Actual delivery by the *grantor* (or *settlor,* the person creating the trust) to the trustee with the intention of passing title.

Trust An arrangement in which title to property is held by one person (a trustee) for the benefit of another (a beneficiary).

Learning Objective 4
What are the four essential elements of a trust?

43–3a Express Trusts

An express trust is created or declared in explicit terms, usually in writing. There are many types of express trusts, each with its own special characteristics.

Living Trusts A **living (*inter vivos*) trust**—*inter vivos* is Latin for "between or among the living"—is a trust created by a grantor during her or his lifetime. Living trusts have become a popular estate-planning option because at the grantor's death, assets held in a living trust can pass to the heirs without going through probate.

Note, however, that living trusts do not shelter assets from estate taxes. Furthermore, the grantor may have to pay income taxes on trust earnings, depending on whether the trust is revocable or irrevocable.

Revocable Living Trusts. Living trusts can be revocable or irrevocable. In a *revocable* living trust, which is the most common type, the grantor retains control over the trust property. The grantor deeds the property to the trust but retains the power to amend, alter, or revoke the trust during her or his lifetime.

The grantor may also serve as a trustee or co-trustee and can arrange to receive income earned by the trust assets during her or his lifetime. Because the grantor is in control of the funds, she or he is required to pay income taxes on the trust earnings. Unless the trust is revoked, the principal of the trust is transferred to the trust beneficiary or beneficiaries on the grantor's death.

Example 43.11 James Cortez owns and operates a large farm. After his wife dies, James contacts his attorney to create a living trust for the benefit of his three children, Alicia, Emma, and Jayden. The attorney prepares the documents creating the trust. James then executes a deed conveying the farm to the trust and transfers the farm's bank accounts into the name of the trust.

The trust designates James as the trustee and names his son, Jayden, as the *successor trustee,* who will take over the management of the trust when James dies or becomes incapacitated. Each of the children and James (as *income beneficiaries*) will receive income from the trust while James is alive. When James dies, the farm will pass to them without having to go through probate. By holding the property in a revocable living trust, James retains control over the farm during his life (and can make changes to the trust at any time). This trust arrangement is illustrated in Exhibit 43–6. ▪

Living (*Inter Vivos*) Trust A trust created by the grantor (settlor) and effective during his or her lifetime.

Exhibit 43–6 A Revocable Living Trust Arrangement

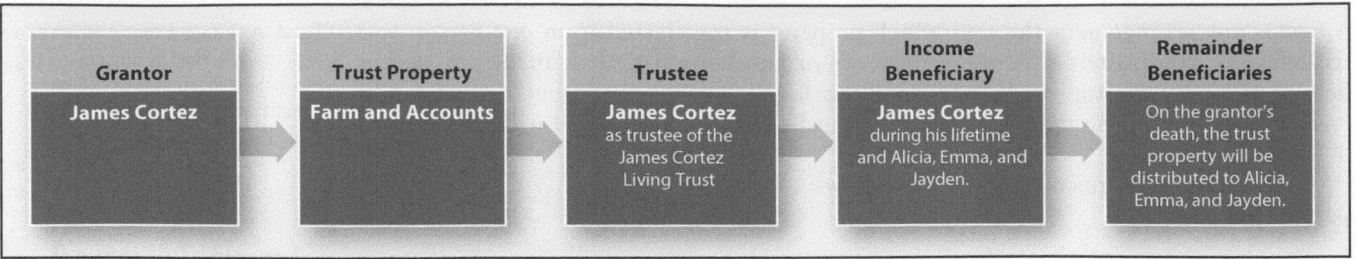

Grantor	Trust Property	Trustee	Income Beneficiary	Remainder Beneficiaries
James Cortez	**Farm and Accounts**	**James Cortez** as trustee of the James Cortez Living Trust	**James Cortez** during his lifetime and Alicia, Emma, and Jayden.	On the grantor's death, the trust property will be distributed to Alicia, Emma, and Jayden.

The following case involved a revocable living trust that included the phrase, "death of each." The resolution of the dispute turned on whether, in the context, "each" meant "either" or "both."

Case 43.3

Dowdy v. Dowdy

District Court of Appeal of Florida, Second District, 41 Fla.L.Weekly D85, 182 So.3d 807 (2016).

Background and Facts Betty and Dennis Dowdy created the Dowdy Family Trust. The property of the trust comprised two parcels of real estate. The trust document identified Betty and Dennis as the settlors, the initial trustees, and the initial beneficiaries. The trust document provided for the revocation or amendment of the trust and for distributions to the settlors. It also appointed one of each settlor's children as co-successor trustees and, following the settlors' deaths, provided for liquidation and distribution to all of their children.

Dennis had three children, and Betty had two—they did not have any children in common. After Dennis died, Betty amended the trust to remove Dennis's children as successor trustees and as beneficiaries. Betty also sold the trust's property.

Dennis's son, Michael, who was named as a co-successor trustee in the trust document along with Betty's daughter, Deborah, learned of the sale and filed a petition in a Florida state court against Betty. Michael maintained that Betty's amendment was invalid because it had been executed after

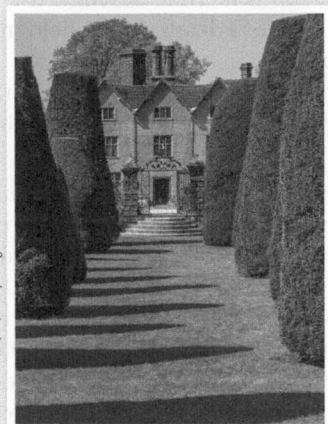

If a married couple holds this house in a revocable family trust, can one spouse sell the property after the other spouse dies?

kodachrome25/E+/Getty Images

Dennis's death. He argued that when Dennis died, the trust became irrevocable and he succeeded Dennis as co-trustee. The court ordered Betty to deposit the proceeds of the sale with the court pending its construction of the trust. Betty appealed.

In the Words of the Court
NORTHCUTT, Judge.

* * * *

* * * Article IV of the original trust document provided as follows:

> During the Settlors' lifetime, the Trustees, in the Trustees' sole discretion, may pay, invade, or apply the income or corpus [trust property], or so much as they may choose, to or for the benefit, support and maintenance of the initial primary beneficiaries * * * .

Thus, if Betty was the only trustee following the death of her husband, she had sole and unfettered authority to sell the trust property for her own benefit.

Michael claims to be a successor co-trustee under Article III of the original trust:

* * * In the event of the death of each of the Initial Trustees, * * * the Settlors nominate and appoint Settlors' son and stepson, Michael R. Dowdy * * * , and Settlors' daughter and stepdaughter, Deborah Ann Andrews [Betty's daughter], as Co-Successor Trustees.

In Michael's view, the phrase "death of each" meant the death of *either* initial trustee. Therefore, he asserts that he became a co-trustee with Betty upon his father's death.

* * * Our view [is] that the succession of trustees occurred only upon the death of *both* initial trustees. This view is confirmed by the use of the same phraseology elsewhere in the original trust document. Article V provides:

After the death of each of the Settlors, the Co-Successor Trustees are directed to liquidate the Trust Estate and immediately pay and distribute the Trust Estate to the children and stepchildren of the Settlors * * * .

Clearly, in this instance the phrase "death of each" must mean the death of both. Otherwise, the article's direction to liquidate the trust estate and immediately distribute it to the settlors' children would nullify Article IV's grant of authority to invade the income or corpus of the trust for the benefit of the initial primary beneficiaries "or the survivor." Indeed, upon the death of one settlor it would altogether nullify the survivor's status as beneficiary.

This, of course, would be an absurd interpretation in complete contravention [contradiction] of a central purpose of the trust. [Emphasis added.]

There is nothing in the original trust document to suggest that the phrase "death of each" has a different meaning in Article III. To the contrary, that article is otherwise consistent with this interpretation. We conclude, then, that Michael did not succeed Dennis as a trustee when Dennis died.

Decision and Remedy The state intermediate appellate court reversed the order of the lower court. Under the appellate court's interpretation of the terms of the trust, "at all times . . . , Betty has been the sole trustee and beneficiary of the trust . . . . As such, she had sole authority and discretion to sell the remaining trust property for her own benefit." The court concluded that Michael's petition had no likelihood of success.

Critical Thinking

• **What If the Facts Were Different?** *Suppose that the Dowdy Family Trust had provided for a specific child to become co-trustee on the death of his or her parent—Deborah to succeed Betty, for example. How would the result have been different?*

Irrevocable Living Trusts. In an *irrevocable* living trust, the grantor permanently gives up control over the property to the trustee. The grantor executes a trust deed, and legal title to the trust property passes to the named trustee. The trustee has a duty to administer the property as directed by the grantor for the benefit and in the interest of the beneficiaries.

The trustee must preserve the trust property and make it productive. If required by the terms of the trust agreement, the trustee must pay income to the beneficiaries in accordance with the terms of the trust. Because the grantor has, in effect, given over the property for the benefit of the beneficiaries, he or she is no longer responsible for paying income taxes on the trust earnings.

Testamentary Trusts A **testamentary trust** is created by will and comes into existence on the grantor's death. Although a testamentary trust has a trustee who maintains legal title to the trust property, the trustee's actions are subject to judicial approval. This trustee can be named in the will or be appointed by the court (if not named in the will). The legal responsibilities of the trustee are the same as in a living trust.

If a court finds that the will setting up a testamentary trust is invalid, then the trust will also be invalid. The property that was supposed to be in the trust will then pass according to intestacy laws, not according to the terms of the trust.

Testamentary Trust A trust that is created by will and therefore does not take effect until the death of the testator.

Charitable Trust A trust in which the property held by the trustee must be used for a charitable purpose, such as the advancement of health, education, or religion.

Charitable Trusts A **charitable trust** is an express trust designed for the benefit of a segment of the public or the public in general. It differs from other types of trusts in that the identities of the beneficiaries are uncertain and it can be established to last indefinitely. Usually, to be deemed a charitable trust, a trust must be created for charitable, educational, religious, or scientific purposes.

Spendthrift Trust A trust created to protect the beneficiary from spending all the funds to which she or he is entitled. Only a certain portion of the total amount is given to the beneficiary at any one time, and most states prohibit creditors from attaching assets of the trust.

Spendthrift Trusts A **spendthrift trust** is created to provide for the maintenance of a beneficiary by preventing him or her from being careless with the bestowed funds. Unlike the beneficiaries of other trusts, the beneficiary in a spendthrift trust is not permitted to transfer or assign his or her right to the trust's principal or future payments from the trust. Essentially, the beneficiary can withdraw only a certain portion of the total amount to which he or she is entitled at any one time. The majority of states allow spendthrift trust provisions that prohibit creditors from attaching such trusts.

Totten Trust A trust created when a person deposits funds in his or her own name for a specific beneficiary, who will receive the funds on the depositor's death. The trust is revocable at will until the depositor dies or completes the gift.

Totten Trusts A **Totten trust**[11] is created when a grantor deposits funds in her or his own name with instructions that on the grantor's death, whatever is in that account should go to a specific beneficiary. This type of trust is revocable at will until the depositor dies or completes the gift during her or his lifetime (by delivering the funds to the intended beneficiary, for instance). The beneficiary has no access to the funds until the depositor's death, when the beneficiary obtains property rights to the balance on hand.

43–3b Implied Trusts

Sometimes, a trust will be imposed (implied) by law, even in the absence of an express trust. Implied trusts include constructive trusts and resulting trusts.

Constructive Trust An equitable trust that is imposed in the interests of fairness and justice when someone wrongfully holds legal title to property.

Constructive Trusts A **constructive trust** is an equitable trust imposed by a court in the interests of fairness and justice. In a constructive trust, the owner of the property is declared to be a trustee for the parties who are, in fairness, actually entitled to the benefits that flow from the property.

Courts often impose constructive trusts when someone who is in a confidential or fiduciary relationship with another person, such as a guardian to a ward, has breached a duty to that person. A court may also impose a constructive trust when someone wrongfully holds legal title to property—because the property was obtained through fraud or in breach of a legal duty, for instance.

Case Example 43.12 Stella Jankowski added her niece Genevieve Viarengo as a joint owner on bank accounts and other financial assets valued at $500,000. Jankowski also executed a will that divided her estate equally among her ten nieces, nephews, and cousins, and named Viarengo and Richard Golebiewski as coexecutors. She did not tell the attorney who drafted the will about the jointly held accounts.

When Jankowski died, Viarengo emptied her safe, removed her financial records, and claimed that the funds in the accounts were hers. Jankowski's other relatives filed a suit and asked the court to impose a constructive trust. The court found that Viarengo had committed fraud in obtaining the assets that she had held jointly with Jankowski and would be unjustly enriched if she were allowed to retain them. Therefore, the court imposed a constructive trust.[12]

Resulting Trust An implied trust that arises when one party holds the legal title to another's property only for that other's benefit.

Resulting Trusts A **resulting trust** arises from the conduct of the parties. When circumstances raise an inference that one party holds legal title to the property for the benefit of another, a court may infer a resulting trust.

---

11. This type of trust derives its unusual name from the case *In re Totten*, 179 N.Y. 112, 71 N.E. 748 (1904).
12. *Garrigus v. Viarengo*, 112 Conn.App. 655, 963 A.2d 1065 (2009).

Example 43.13 Gabriela Fuentes wants to put one acre of land she owns on the market for sale. Because she is going out of the country for two years and will not be able to deed the property to a buyer during that period, Fuentes conveys (transfers) the property to her good friend Oswald. Oswald can then attempt to sell the property while Fuentes is gone.

The transaction in which Fuentes conveyed the property to Oswald was intended to be neither a sale nor a gift. Consequently, Oswald will hold the property in a resulting trust for the benefit of Fuentes. When Fuentes returns, Oswald will be required either to deed the property back to her or, if the property has been sold, to turn over the proceeds (held in trust) to her. ▪

43–3c The Trustee

The *trustee* is the person holding the trust property. Anyone legally capable of holding title to, and dealing in, property can be a trustee. If a trust fails to name a trustee, or if a named trustee cannot or will not serve, the trust does not fail—an appropriate court can appoint a trustee.

Trustee's Duties A trustee must act with honesty, good faith, and prudence in administering the trust and must exercise a high degree of loyalty toward the trust beneficiary. The general standard of care is the degree of care a prudent person would exercise in his or her personal affairs.[13] The duty of loyalty requires that the trustee act in the exclusive interest of the beneficiary.

A trustee's specific duties include the following:

1. Maintain clear and accurate accounts of the trust's administration.
2. Furnish complete and correct information to the beneficiary.
3. Keep trust assets separate from her or his own assets.
4. Pay to an income beneficiary the net income of the trust assets at reasonable intervals.
5. Limit the risk of loss from investments by reasonable diversification, and dispose of assets that do not represent prudent investments. (Prudent investment choices might include federal, state, or municipal bonds and some corporate bonds and stocks.)

What are some specific duties of a trustee?

Trustee's Powers When a grantor creates a trust, he or she may set forth the trustee's powers and performance. State law governs in the absence of specific terms in the trust, and the states often restrict the trustee's investment of trust funds.

Typically, statutes confine trustees to investments in conservative debt securities such as government, utility, and railroad bonds. Frequently, though, a grantor gives a trustee discretionary investment power. In that circumstance, any statute may be considered only advisory, with the trustee's decisions subject in most states to the prudent person rule.

Of course, a trustee is responsible for carrying out the purposes of the trust. If the trustee fails to comply with the terms of the trust or the controlling statute, he or she is personally liable for any loss.

Allocations between Principal and Income Often, a grantor will provide one beneficiary with a life estate and another beneficiary with the remainder interest in a trust. A farmer, for instance, may create a testamentary trust providing that the farm's income be paid to the surviving spouse and that on the surviving spouse's death, the farm be given to their children. In this situation, the surviving spouse has a *life estate* in the farm's income, and the children have a *remainder interest* in the farm (the principal).

When a trust is set up in this manner, questions may arise as to how the receipts and expenses for the farm's management and the trust's administration should be allocated

> "Put not your trust in money, but put your money in trust."
>
> **Oliver Wendell Holmes, Jr.**
> 1841–1935
> (Associate justice of the United States Supreme Court, 1902–1932)

---

13. Revised Uniform Principal and Income Act, Section 2(a)(3); *Restatement (Third) of Trusts (Prudent Investor Rule)*, Section 227. This rule is in force in the majority of states by statute and in a small number of states under the common law.

between income and principal. When a trust instrument does not provide instructions, a trustee must refer to applicable state law.

The general rule is that ordinary receipts and expenses are chargeable to the income beneficiary, whereas extraordinary receipts and expenses are allocated to the principal beneficiaries.[14] The receipt of rent from trust realty would be ordinary, as would the expense of paying the property's taxes. The cost of long-term improvements and proceeds from the property's sale, however, would be extraordinary.

43–3d Trust Termination

The terms of a trust should expressly state the event on which the grantor wishes it to terminate—for instance, the beneficiary's or the trustee's death. If the trust instrument does not provide for termination on the beneficiary's death, the beneficiary's death will not end the trust. Similarly, without an express provision, a trust will not terminate on the trustee's death.

Typically, a trust instrument specifies a termination date. For instance, a trust created to educate the grantor's child may provide that the trust ends when the beneficiary reaches the age of twenty-five. If the trust's purpose is fulfilled before that date, a court may order the trust's termination. If no date is specified, a trust will terminate when its purpose has been fulfilled. Of course, if a trust's purpose becomes impossible or illegal, the trust will terminate.

---

14. Revised Uniform Principal and Income Act, Sections 3, 6, 8, and 13; *Restatement (Second) of Trusts*, Section 233.

Practice and Review

In June 2018, Bernard Ramish set up a $48,000 trust fund through West Plains Credit Union to provide tuition for his nephew, Nathan Covacek, to attend Tri-State Polytechnic Institute. The trust was established under Ramish's control and went into effect that August. In December, Ramish suffered a brain aneurysm that caused frequent, severe headaches but no other symptoms. In August 2019, Ramish developed heat stroke and collapsed on the golf course at La Prima Country Club.

After recuperating at the clubhouse, Ramish quickly wrote his will on the back of a wine list. It stated, "My last will and testament: Upon my death, I give all of my personal property to my friend Bernard Eshom and my home to Lizzie Johansen." He signed the will at the bottom in the presence of five men in the La Prima clubhouse, and all five men signed as witnesses.

A week later, Ramish suffered a second aneurysm and died in his sleep. He was survived by his mother (Dorris Ramish), his nephew (Nathan Covacek), his son-in-law (Bruce Lupin), and his granddaughter (Tori Lupin). Using the information presented in the chapter, answer the following questions.

1. Does Ramish's testament on the back of the wine list meet the requirements for a valid will?

2. Suppose that after Ramish's first aneurysm in 2018, Covacek contacted an insurance company to obtain a life insurance policy on Ramish's life. Would Covacek have had an insurable interest in his uncle's life? Why or why not?

3. What would the order of inheritance have been if Ramish had died intestate?

4. What will most likely happen to the trust fund established for Covacek on Ramish's death?

Debate This

Any changes to existing, fully witnessed wills should also have to be witnessed.

Key Terms

administrator 1025	insurance 1018	resulting trust 1038
bequest 1026	intestacy laws 1026	risk 1018
binder 1021	intestate 1026	risk management 1018
charitable trust 1038	legacy 1026	spendthrift trust 1038
codicil 1030	legatee 1026	testamentary trust 1037
constructive trust 1038	living (*inter vivos*) trust 1035	testate 1025
devise 1026	nuncupative will 1030	testator 1025
devisee 1026	*per capita* 1034	Totten trust 1038
executor 1025	*per stirpes* 1033	trust 1035
holographic will 1030	policy 1019	underwriter 1019
incontestability clause 1022	premium 1019	will 1025
insurable interest 1019	probate 1031	will substitutes 1032

Chapter Summary: Insurance, Wills, and Trusts

	INSURANCE
Classifications	See Exhibit 43–1 for a list of types of insurance.
Terminology	1. *Policy*—The insurance contract. 2. *Premium*—The consideration paid to the insurer for a policy. 3. *Underwriter*—The insurance company. 4. *Parties*—Include the insurer (the insurance company), the insured (the person covered by insurance), and an agent (a representative of the insurance company) or a broker (ordinarily an independent contractor). Certain types of insurance also include a beneficiary (a person to receive proceeds under the policy) other than the insured.
Insurable Interest	An insurable interest exists whenever an individual or entity benefits from the preservation of the health or life of the insured or the property to be insured. For life insurance, an insurable interest must exist at the time the policy is issued. For property insurance, an insurable interest must exist at the time of the loss.
The Insurance Contract	1. *Laws governing*—The general principles of contract law are applied. The insurance industry is also heavily regulated by the states. 2. *Application*—An insurance applicant is bound by any false statements that appear in the application (subject to certain exceptions), which is part of the insurance contract. Misstatements or misrepresentations may be grounds for voiding the policy. 3. *Effective date*—Coverage on an insurance policy can begin when a *binder* (a written memorandum indicating that a formal policy is pending and stating its essential terms) is written; when the policy is issued and delivered; depending on the terms of the contract, when certain conditions are met (such as payment of the premium). 4. *Provisions and clauses*—See Exhibit 43–2 for specific provisions. Words will be given their ordinary meanings, and any ambiguity in the policy will be interpreted against the insurance company. When the written policy has not been delivered and it is unclear whether an insurance contract actually exists, the uncertainty will be resolved against the insurance company. The court will presume that the policy is in effect unless the company can show otherwise. 5. *Cancellation*—The insured can cancel a policy at any time, and the insurer can cancel under certain circumstances.

6. *Duties and obligations of the parties*—
   a. Duties of the insured—Once the policy has been issued, the insured must pay the premiums, notify the insurer within a reasonable time if an event gives rise to a claim, and cooperate with the insurer during any investigation or litigation.
   b. Duties of the insurer—The insurer has a duty to investigate any event that gives rise to a claim and is obligated to make reasonable efforts to settle any third-party claims. The insurer also has a duty to defend any suit against the insured.
7. *Defenses against payment to the insured*—Defenses include misrepresentation or fraud by the applicant, lack of an insurable interest, and the illegal actions of the insured.

WILLS	
Terminology	1. *Testator*—A person who makes out a will. 2. *Executor*—A person named in a will to settle the affairs of a decedent. 3. *Administrator*—A personal representative appointed by the court to settle the affairs of an intestate decedent. 4. *Intestate*—One who dies without a valid will. 5. *Devise*—A gift of real estate by will; may be general or specific. The recipient of a devise is a *devisee*. 6. *Bequest, or legacy*—A gift of personal property by will; may be general or specific. The recipient of a bequest (legacy) is a *legatee*.
Requirements for a Valid Will	1. The testator must have testamentary capacity (be of legal age and sound mind at the time the will is made). 2. The testator must have the necessary intent to transfer and distribute his or her property. 3. A will must be in writing (except for nuncupative wills). A holographic will is completely in the handwriting of the testator. 4. A will must be signed by the testator. What constitutes a signature varies from jurisdiction to jurisdiction. 5. A nonholographic will (an attested will) must be witnessed in the manner prescribed by state statute.

Revocation of Wills	1. *By physical act of the maker*—Intentionally burning, tearing up, canceling, obliterating, or otherwise destroying a will.
	 2. *By subsequent writing*—
	   a. Codicil—A formal, separate document to amend or revoke an existing will.
	   b. Second will or new will—A new, properly executed will expressly revoking the existing will.
	 3. *By operation of law*—
	   a. Marriage—Generally revokes part of a will written before the marriage.
	   b. Divorce or annulment—Revokes dispositions of property made under a will to a former spouse.
	   c. Subsequently born child—Most states allow the child to receive a portion of the estate.

Probate Procedures and Estate Planning	To probate a will means to establish its validity and to carry the administration of the estate through a state court process. Probate procedures may be informal or formal, depending on the size of the estate and other factors, such as whether a guardian for minor children must be appointed.
Intestacy Laws	1. Intestacy laws vary widely from state to state. Usually, the law provides that the surviving spouse and children inherit the property of the decedent (after the decedent's debts are paid). The spouse usually inherits the entire estate if there are no children, one-half of the estate if there is one child, and one-third of the estate if there are two or more children. 2. If there is no surviving spouse or child, then, in order, lineal descendants (grandchildren, brothers and sisters, and—in some states—parents of the decedent) inherit. If there are no lineal descendants, then collateral heirs (nieces, nephews, aunts, and uncles of the decedent) inherit. 3. Each state uses one of two methods to distribute assets of the decedent. Under the *per stirpes* method, within a class or group of distributees (such as grandchildren), the children of a descendant take the share that their deceased parent *would have been* entitled to inherit (see Exhibit 43–4). Under the *per capita* method, each person in a class or group takes an equal share of the estate (see Exhibit 43–5).

TRUSTS	
Definition and Elements	A trust is any arrangement through which property is transferred from one person to a trustee to be administered for the transferor's or another party's benefit. The essential elements of a trust are (1) a designated beneficiary, (2) a designated trustee, (3) a fund sufficiently identified to enable title to pass to the trustee, and (4) actual delivery by the grantor to the trustee with the intention of passing title.
Express Trusts	Express trusts are created by explicit terms, usually in writing, and include the following: 1. *Living* (inter vivos) *trust*—A trust created by a grantor during her or his lifetime. 2. *Testamentary trust*—A trust that is created by will and comes into existence on the death of the grantor. 3. *Charitable trust*—A trust designed for the benefit of a public group or the public in general. 4. *Spendthrift trust*—A trust created to provide for a beneficiary by allowing the beneficiary to withdraw only a certain amount at any one time. 5. *Totten trust*—A trust created when one person deposits funds in his or her own name as a trustee for a specific beneficiary.
Implied Trusts	Implied trusts, which are imposed by law in the interests of fairness and justice, include the following: 1. *Constructive trust*—Arises by operation of law when a person wrongfully takes title to property. A court may require the owner to hold the property in trust for those who, in equity, are entitled to enjoy the benefits from the trust. 2. *Resulting trust*—Arises from the conduct of the parties when an apparent intention to create a trust is present.
Trustee	A trustee must act with honesty, good faith, and prudence in administering the trust, and must exercise a high degree of loyalty toward the trust beneficiary.
Termination	Typically, a trust instrument specifies a termination date. If no date is specified, a trust will terminate when its purpose has been fulfilled.

Issue Spotters

1. Sheila makes out a will, leaving her property in equal thirds to Toby and Uma, her children, and Velda, her niece. Two years later, Sheila is adjudged mentally incompetent, and that same year, she dies. Can Toby and Uma have Sheila's will revoked on the ground that she did not have the capacity to make a will? Why or why not? (See *Wills.*)

2. When Ralph dies, he has not made a will and is survived by many relatives—a spouse, children, adopted children, sisters, brothers, uncles, aunts, cousins, nephews, and nieces. What determines who inherits what? (See *Wills.*)

—**Check your answers to the *Issue Spotters* against the answers provided in Appendix D at the end of this text.**

Business Scenarios and Case Problems

43–1. Timing of Insurance Coverage. On October 10, Joleen Vora applied for a $50,000 life insurance policy with Magnum Life Insurance Co. She named her husband, Jay, as the beneficiary. Joleen paid the insurance company the first year's premium on making the application. Two days later, before she had a chance to take the physical examination required by the insurance company and before the policy was issued, Joleen was killed in an automobile accident. Jay submitted a claim to the insurance company for $50,000. Can Jay collect? Explain. (See *Insurance.*)

43–2. Wills and Intestacy Laws. Benjamin is a widower who has two married children, Edward and Patricia. Patricia has two children, Perry and Paul. Edward has no children. Benjamin makes a will leaving all his property equally to Edward and

Patricia. The will provides that should a child predecease him, the grandchildren are to take *per stirpes*. The will is witnessed by Patricia and by Benjamin's lawyer and is signed by Benjamin in their presence. Benjamin dies, and Patricia has predeceased him. Edward claims the will is invalid. (See *Wills.*)

1. Discuss whether the will is valid.
2. Discuss the distribution of Benjamin's estate if the will is invalid.
3. Discuss the distribution of Benjamin's estate if the will is valid.

43–3. Undue Influence. Louise Kane executed a will that left her entire estate to her grandson. When her grandson died, Louise executed a new will that named her great-grandson as her sole beneficiary and specifically disinherited her son, Tommy. At the time, Tommy's ex-wife was living with Louise.

After Louise died, Tommy filed a suit, claiming that her will was the product of undue influence on the part of his ex-wife. Several witnesses testified that Louise had been mentally competent when she executed her will. Does undue influence appear likely based on these facts? Why or why not? (See *Wills*.)

43–4. Insurance Provisions and Clauses. Darling's Rent-a-Car carried property insurance on its cars under a policy issued by Philadelphia Indemnity Insurance Co. The policy listed Darling's as the "insured." Darling's rented a car to Joshuah Farrington. In the rental contract, Farrington agreed to be responsible for any damage to the car and declined the optional insurance. Later, Farrington collided with a moose. Philadelphia paid Darling's for the damage to the car and sought to collect this amount from Farrington. Farrington argued that he was an "insured" under Darling's policy. How should "insured" be interpreted in this case? Why? [*Philadelphia Indemnity Insurance Co. v. Farrington,* 37 A.3d 305 (Me. 2012)] (See *Insurance*.)

43–5. Requirements of a Will. Sherman Hemsley was a well-known actor from the 1970s. Most notably, he played George Jefferson on the television shows *All in the Family* and *The Jeffersons*. He was born to Arsena Chisolm and William Thornton. Thornton was married to another woman, and Hemsley never had a relationship with his father or that side of the family. Hemsley never married and had no children. He lived with Flora Bernal, his business manager. Diagnosed with cancer, Hemsley executed a will naming Bernal the sole beneficiary of his estate. At the signing, Hemsley indicated that he knew he was executing his will and that he had deliberately chosen Bernal, but did not discuss his relatives or the nature of his property with his attorney or the witnesses. After his death, the Thorntons challenged the will. Was Hemsley of sound mind? Discuss. [*In re Estate of Hemsley,* 460 S.W.3d 629 (Tex.App.—El Paso 2014)] (See *Wills*.)

43–6. Business Case Problem with Sample Answer— Wills. Andrew Walker executed a will giving a certain parcel of real estate in fee simple to his three children from a previous marriage—Mark Walker, Michelle Peters, and Andrea Knox—with a "life use" in the property granted to his current spouse, Nora Walker. A year later, Andrew, who suffered from asbestosis, was discharged from a hospital to spend his last days at home. He told Nora that he wished to execute a new will to change the disposition of the property to devise half of it to her. Nora recorded his wish and took her notes to the office of attorney Frederick Meagher to have the document drafted. Meagher did not see Nora's notes, he did not talk to Walker, no one from his office was present at the signing of the document, and, when Walker signed it, he did not declare that it was his will, as required by state law. Is the document a valid will? Explain. [*In re Estate of Walker,* 124 A.D.3d 970, 2 N.Y.S.3d 628 (3 Dept. 2015)] (See *Wills*.)

—For a sample answer to Problem 43–6, go to Appendix E at the end of this text.

43–7. Defenses against Insurance Payment. American National Property and Casualty Co. issued an insurance policy to Robert Houston, insuring certain residential property and its contents against fire and other hazards. Twenty months later, Houston issued a quitclaim deed to the property to John and Judy Sykes, reserving a life estate for himself. Houston died two years after that, but John continued to renew the American policy in Houston's name. When a fire substantially damaged the property, John filed a claim with the insurer on behalf of Houston, whom John said was out of town and unavailable. On learning that Houston had died seven years earlier, American refused to pay, claiming that it had no liability. Who will suffer the loss under these circumstances? Why? How might this loss have been avoided? Explain. [*American National Property and Casualty Co. v. Sykes,* 2016 WL 390069 (S.D.Miss. E.Div. 2016)] (See *Insurance*.)

43–8. Testamentary Intent. When Larry Neal died, Gary, his brother and his estate's executor, applied to a Texas state court to probate Larry's will. The will provided, "I do give and bequeath to my niece, Valorie Jean (Neal) White, all my personal effects and all my tangible personal property, including automobiles, hangars, aircraft, fly-drive vehicles, patents, companies, and all other things owned by me at the time of my death," including bank accounts, securities, and other "intangibles." Gary interpreted this provision to entitle Valorie to all of Larry's personal and real property. Larry's daughter, Lori, objected, arguing that under the terms of the will, Larry's personal property passed to Valorie and his real property passed by intestacy to her and Larry's sons. Did Larry's will devise his real property to Valorie? Discuss. [*Estate of Neal,* 2018 WL 283780 (Tex.App.—Fort Worth 2018)] (See *Wills*.)

43–9. A Question of Ethics—The IDDR Approach and Bad Faith. *Bernd Moving Systems owned a warehouse in Yakima, Washington. American Guarantee & Liability Insurance Co. insured Bernd under a policy that included coverage of "Personal property of others in your care, custody and control." Before storing property in the warehouse, William and Colleen Merriman were told that their goods would be fully insured. Later, a fire destroyed the warehouse and the Merrimans' property. American Guarantee did not inform them of Bernd's coverage, however. Instead, they were advised to file a claim under their homeowner's insurance because there would most likely be no coverage under Bernd's policy. [Merriman v. American Guarantee & Liability Insurance Co., 198 Wash.App. 594, 396 P.3d 351 (Div. 3 2017)] (See Insurance.)*

1. On what grounds might the Merrimans base a legal action against American Guarantee?

2. Are there sufficient grounds to argue that the insurer acted unethically? Discuss.

Critical Thinking and Writing Assignments

43–10. Time-Limited Group Assignment—Intestacy Laws. Three and a half years after Lauren and Warren Woodward were married, they were informed that Warren had leukemia. At the time, the couple had no children, and physicians told the Woodwards that the leukemia treatment might leave Warren sterile. The couple arranged for Warren's sperm to be collected and placed in a sperm bank for later use.

Two years after Warren died, Lauren gave birth to twin girls who had been conceived through artificial insemination using his sperm. The following year, Lauren applied for Social Security survivor benefits for the two children. Her application was rejected on the ground that she had not established that the twins were the husband's children within the meaning of the Social Security Act. Woodward then filed a paternity action in Massachusetts, and the probate court determined that Warren Woodward was the twins' father. She then filed an action in court to determine the inheritance rights of the twins. (See *Wills*.)

1. The first group will outline how a court should decide the inheritance rights of children conceived from the sperm of a deceased individual and his surviving spouse.

2. The second group will decide if children conceived after a parent's death (by means of artificial insemination or *in vitro* fertilization) still inherit under intestate succession laws, and will explain why or why not.

3. The third group will consider the inheritance rights of a child who was conceived by means of artificial insemination, *in vitro* fertilization, or a surrogate. Should they be different from the rights of a child conceived in the traditional manner? Assuming the biological parent is not part of the child's life, should the child still be able to inherit from the biological parent? Why or why not?

Unit Seven—Task-Based Simulation

StockPhoto.com/proxyminder

Dave graduates from State University with an engineering degree and goes into business as a self-employed computer programmer.

1. Ownership of Personal Property. To advertise his services on the Internet, Dave creates and produces a short digital video. Venture Films, Inc., sees the video and hires Dave to program the special effects for a short sequence in a Venture Films movie. Their contract states that all rights to the sequence belong to Venture Films. What belongs to Dave: the digital video, the movie sequence, both, or neither? Explain.

2. **Landlord-Tenant Law.** Dave leases an office in Carl's Riverside Plaza office building for a two-year term. What is Dave's obligation for the rent if he moves out before the end of the term? If Dave dies during the term, who is entitled to possession of the office? What is Dave's obligation for the rent if Carl sells the building to Commercial Investments, Inc., before Dave's lease is up?

3. **Real Property Deeds.** At the end of the lease term, Dave buys the office building from Carl, who gives Dave a warranty deed. Commercial Investments later challenges Dave's ownership of the building and presents its own allegedly valid deed. What will it mean if a court rules that Dave owns the building in fee simple? If Commercial Investments is successful, can Dave recover anything from Carl? Explain.

4. **Insurance.** Dave's programming business expands, and he hires Mary as an employee. Mary becomes invaluable to the business, and Dave obtains a key-person insurance policy on her life. She dies six years later. If the insurance company discovers that Dave understated Mary's age when applying for the policy (which includes an incontestability clause), can the insurer legitimately refuse payment? If Mary had resigned to start her own programming firm one year before she died, could Dave have collected payment under the policy? Why or why not?

5. **Wills and Trusts.** Over time, Dave acquires other commercial property, which eventually becomes the most lucrative part of his business. Dave wants his adult children, Frank and Terry, to get the benefit of this property when he dies. Dave does not think that Frank and Terry can manage the property, however, because they have their own careers and live in other states. How can Dave provide for them to get the benefit of the property under someone else's management? In his will, Dave designates Hal, his attorney, as executor. What does an executor do?

How to Brief Cases and Analyze Case Problems

How to Brief Cases

To fully understand the law with respect to business, you need to be able to read and understand court decisions. To make this task easier, you can use a method of case analysis that is called *briefing*. There is a fairly standard procedure that you can follow when you "brief" any court case. You must first read the case opinion carefully. When you feel you understand the case, you can prepare a brief of it.

Although the format of the brief may vary, typically it will present the essentials of the case under headings such as those listed below.

1. **Citation.** Give the full citation for the case, including the name of the case, the date it was decided, and the court that decided it.

2. **Facts.** Briefly indicate (a) the reasons for the lawsuit; (b) the identity and arguments of the plaintiff(s) and defendant(s), respectively; and (c) the lower court's decision—if appropriate.

3. **Issue.** Concisely phrase, in the form of a question, the essential issue before the court. (If more than one issue is involved, you may have two—or even more—questions here.)

4. **Decision.** Indicate here—with a "yes" or "no," if possible—the court's answer to the question (or questions) in the Issue section above.

5. **Reason.** Summarize as briefly as possible the reasons given by the court for its decision (or decisions) and the case or statutory law relied on by the court in arriving at its decision.

For a case-specific example of what should be included under each of the above headings when briefing a case, see the review of the sample court case presented in the appendix to Chapter 1 of this text.

Analyzing Case Problems

In addition to learning how to brief cases, students of business law and the legal environment also find it helpful to know how to analyze case problems. Part of the study of business law and the legal environment usually involves analyzing case problems, such as those included in this text at the end of each chapter.

For each case problem in this book, we provide the relevant background and facts of the lawsuit and the issue before the court. When you are assigned one of these problems, your job will be to determine how the court should decide the issue, and why. In other words, you will need to engage in legal analysis and reasoning. Here, we offer some suggestions on how to make this task less daunting. We begin by presenting a sample case problem:

> While Janet Lawson, a famous pianist, was shopping in Quality Market, she slipped and fell on a wet floor in one of the aisles. The floor had recently been mopped by one of the store's employees, but there were no signs warning customers that the floor in that area was wet. As a result of the fall, Lawson injured her right arm and was unable to perform piano concerts for the next six months. Had she been able to perform the scheduled concerts, she would have earned approximately $60,000 over that period of time. Lawson sued Quality Market for this amount, plus another $10,000 in medical expenses. She claimed that the store's failure to warn customers of the wet floor constituted negligence and therefore the market was liable for her injuries. Will the court agree with Lawson? Discuss.

Understand the Facts

This may sound obvious, but before you can analyze or apply the relevant law to a specific set of facts, you must clearly understand those facts. In other words, you should read through the case problem carefully—more than once, if necessary—to make sure you understand the identity of the plaintiff(s) and defendant(s) in the case and the progression of events that led to the lawsuit.

In the sample case problem just given, the identity of the parties is fairly obvious. Janet Lawson is the one bringing the suit; therefore, she is the plaintiff. Lawson is bringing the suit against Quality Market, so it is the defendant. Some of the case problems you work on may have multiple plaintiffs or defendants. Often, it is helpful to use abbreviations for the parties. To indicate a reference to a plaintiff, for example, the *pi* symbol—π—is often used, and a defendant is denoted by a *delta*—Δ—a triangle.

The events leading to the lawsuit are also fairly straightforward. Lawson slipped and fell on a wet floor, and she contends that Quality Market should be liable for her injuries because it was negligent in not posting a sign warning customers of the wet floor.

When you are working on case problems, realize that the facts should be accepted as they are given. For instance, in our sample problem, it should be accepted that the floor was wet and that there was no sign. In other words, avoid making conjectures, such as "Maybe the floor wasn't too wet," or "Maybe an employee was getting a sign to put up," or "Maybe someone stole the sign." Questioning the facts as they are presented only adds confusion to your analysis.

Legal Analysis and Reasoning

Once you understand the facts given in the case problem, you can begin to analyze the case. The **IRAC method** is a helpful tool to use in the legal analysis and reasoning process. IRAC is an acronym for **I**ssue, **R**ule, **A**pplication, **C**onclusion. Applying this method to our sample problem would involve the following steps:

1. First, you need to decide what legal **issue** is involved in the case. In our sample case, the basic issue is whether Quality Market's failure to warn customers of the wet floor constituted negligence. Negligence is a *tort*—a civil wrong. In a tort lawsuit, the plaintiff seeks to be compensated for another's wrongful act. A defendant will be deemed negligent if he or she breached a duty of care owed to the plaintiff and the breach of that duty caused the plaintiff to suffer harm.

2. Once you have identified the issue, the next step is to determine what **rule of law** applies to the issue. To make this determination, you will want to carefully review the text discussion relating to the issue involved in the problem. Our sample case problem involves the tort of negligence. The applicable rule of law is the tort law principle that business owners owe a duty to exercise reasonable care to protect their customers (*business invitees*). Reasonable care, in this context, includes either removing—or warning customers of—*foreseeable* risks about which the owner *knew* or *should have known.* Business owners need not warn customers of "open and obvious" risks, however. If a business owner breaches this duty of care (fails to exercise the appropriate degree of care toward customers), and the breach of duty causes a customer to be injured, the business owner will be liable to the customer for the customer's injuries.

3. The next—and usually the most difficult—step in analyzing case problems is the **application** of the relevant rule of law to the specific facts of the case you are studying. In our sample problem, applying the tort law principle just discussed presents few difficulties. An employee of the store had mopped the floor in the aisle where Lawson slipped and fell, but no sign was present indicating that the floor was wet. That a customer might fall on a wet floor is clearly a foreseeable risk. Therefore, the failure to warn customers about the wet floor was a breach of the duty of care owed by the business owner to the store's customers.

4. Once you have completed Step 3 in the IRAC method, you should be ready to draw your **conclusion.** In our sample problem, Quality Market is liable to Lawson for her injuries because the market's breach of its duty of care caused Lawson's injuries.

The fact patterns in the case problems presented in this text are not always as simple as those presented in our sample problem. Often, a case has more than one plaintiff or defendant. A case may also involve more than one issue and have more than one applicable rule of law. Furthermore, in some case problems the facts may indicate that the general rule of law should not apply. Suppose that a store employee told Lawson about the wet floor and advised her not to walk in that aisle, but Lawson decided to walk there anyway. This fact could alter the outcome of the case because the store could then raise the defense of *assumption of risk.* Nonetheless, a careful review of the chapter should always provide you with the knowledge you need to analyze the problem thoroughly and arrive at accurate conclusions.

Appendix B

The Constitution of the United States

One of the primary sources of American law is the U.S. Constitution, which is the supreme law of the land. As such, it is the basis of all law in the United States. A law in violation of the U.S. Constitution, if challenged, will be declared unconstitutional and will not be enforced, no matter what its source.

The U.S. Constitution is available on many websites, including https://www.usa.gov/history.

Appendix C

The Uniform Commercial Code

One of the most important uniform acts is the Uniform Commercial Code (UCC), which was created through the joint efforts of the National Conference of Commissioners on Uniform State Laws (NCCUSL) and the American Law Institute. The UCC was first issued in 1952 and has been adopted in all fifty states (at least in part), the District of Columbia, and the Virgin Islands. The UCC facilitates commerce among the states by providing a uniform, yet flexible, set of rules governing commercial transactions. Because of its importance in the area of commercial law, we cite the UCC frequently in this text.

To view sections of the UCC, see the American Law Institute website at https://www.ali.org/ or the Uniform Law Commission website at http://www.uniformlaws.org/. Articles 1, 2, and 2A are the most pertinent to students of *Business Law Today*.

Appendix D

Chapter 1

1. No. The U.S. Constitution is the supreme law of the land and applies to all jurisdictions. A law in violation of the Constitution (in this question, the First Amendment to the Constitution) will be declared unconstitutional.

2. Case law includes courts' interpretations of statutes, as well as constitutional provisions and administrative rules. Statutes often codify common law rules. For these reasons, a judge might rely on the common law as a guide to the intent and purpose of a statute.

Chapter 2

1. Even if commercial speech is neither related to illegal activities nor misleading, it may be restricted if a state has a substantial interest that cannot be achieved by less restrictive means. In this situation, the state's interest in energy conservation is substantial, but it could be achieved by less restrictive means. That would be the utilities' defense against the enforcement of this state law.

2. Yes. The tax would limit the liberty of some persons, such as out-of-state businesses, so it is subject to a review under the equal protection clause. Protecting local businesses from out-of-state competition is not a legitimate government objective. Thus, such a tax would violate the equal protection clause.

Chapter 3

1. When a corporation decides to respond to what it sees as a moral obligation to correct for past discrimination by adjusting pay differences among its employees, an ethical conflict is raised between the firm and its employees and between the firm and its shareholders. This dilemma arises directly out of the effect such a decision has on the firm's profits. If satisfying this obligation increases profitability, then the dilemma is easily resolved in favor of "doing the right thing."

2. Maybe. On the one hand, it is not the company's "fault" when a product is misused. Also, keeping the product on the market is not a violation of the law, and stopping sales would hurt profits. On the other hand, suspending sales could reduce suffering and could prevent negative publicity that might occur if sales continued.

Chapter 4

1. Tom could file a motion for a directed verdict. This motion asks the judge to direct a verdict for Tom on the ground that Sue presented no evidence that would justify granting her relief. The judge grants the motion if there is insufficient evidence to raise an issue of fact.

2. Yes. Submission of the dispute to mediation or non-binding arbitration is mandatory, but compliance with the decision of the mediator or arbitrator is voluntary.

Chapter 5

1. Probably. To recover on the basis of negligence, the injured party as a plaintiff must show that the truck's owner owed the plaintiff a duty of care, that the owner breached that duty, that the plaintiff was injured, and that the breach caused the injury. In this problem, the owner's actions breached the duty of reasonable care. The billboard falling on the plaintiff was the direct cause of the injury, not the plaintiff's own negligence. Thus, liability turns on whether the plaintiff can connect the breach of duty to the injury. This involves the test of proximate cause—the question of foreseeability. The consequences to the injured party must have been a foreseeable result of the owner's carelessness.

2. The company might defend against this electrician's claim by asserting that the electrician should have known of the risk and, therefore, the company had no duty to warn. According to the problem, the danger is common knowledge in the electrician's field and should have been apparent to this electrician, given his years of training and experience. In other words, the company most likely had no need to warn the electrician of the risk.

The firm could also raise comparative negligence. Both parties' negligence, if any, could be weighed and the liability distributed proportionally. The defendant could furthermore assert assumption of risk, claiming that the electrician voluntarily entered into a dangerous situation, knowing the risk involved.

Chapter 6

1. Yes. Those who make, sell, or lease goods are liable for the harm or damages caused by those goods to a consumer, user, or bystander. The maker of component parts may also be liable. In this situation, Rim Corporation makes tires that Superior installs on its vehicles before selling them to dealers. Thus, Superior is the manufacturer, and Rim is the maker of component parts. A manufacturer is liable for its failure to exercise due care to any person who sustains an injury proximately caused by a negligently made (defective) product. Superior's failure to inspect and test the tires it installs is a failure to use due care. Thus, Superior is liable to the injured buyer, Uri. Rim Corporation may also be liable.

2. Bensing can assert the defense of preemption. An injured party may not be able to sue the manufacturer of defective products that are subject to comprehensive federal regulatory schemes (such as medical devices and vaccinations). In this situation, it is likely that a court would conclude that the federal regulations pertaining to drug labeling preempt Ohio's common law rules. Therefore, Bensing would not be liable to Rothfus for defective labeling if it complied with federal law.

Chapter 7

1. Yes, Roslyn has committed theft of trade secrets. Lists of suppliers and customers cannot be patented, copyrighted, or trademarked, but the information they contain is protected against appropriation by others as trade secrets. Most likely, Roslyn signed a contract agreeing not to use this information outside her employment by Organic. But even without this contract, Organic could make a convincing case against its ex-employee for a theft of trade secrets.

2. This is patent infringement. A software maker in this situation might best protect its product, save litigation costs, and profit from its patent by the use of a license. In the context of this problem, a license would grant permission to sell a patented item. (A license can be limited to certain purposes and to the licensee only.)

Chapter 8

1. Karl may have committed trademark infringement. Search engines compile their results by looking through websites' key-word fields. A site that appropriates the key words of other sites with more frequent hits will appear in the same search engine results as the more popular sites. But using another's trademark as a key word without the owner's permission normally constitutes trademark infringement. Of course, some uses of another's trademark as a meta tag may be permissible if the use is reasonably necessary and does not suggest that the owner authorized or sponsored the use.

2. Yes. This may be an instance of trademark dilution. Dilution occurs when a trademark is used, without permission, in a way that diminishes the distinctive quality of the mark. Dilution does not require proof that consumers are likely to be confused by the use of the unauthorized mark. The products involved do not have to be similar. Dilution does require, however, that a mark be famous when the dilution occurs.

Chapter 9

1. Yes. With respect to the gas station, Dana has obtained goods by false pretenses. She might also be charged with the crimes of larceny and forgery, and most states have special statutes covering illegal use of credit cards.

2. Yes. The Counterfeit Access Device and Computer Fraud and Abuse Act provides that a person who accesses a computer online, without permission, to obtain classified data—such as consumer credit files in a credit agency's database—is subject to criminal

prosecution. The crime has two elements: accessing the computer without permission and taking data. It is a felony if done for private financial gain. Penalties include fines and imprisonment for up to twenty years. The victim of the theft can also bring a civil suit against the criminal to obtain damages and other relief.

Chapter 10

1. Under the objective theory of contracts, if a reasonable person would have thought that Joli had accepted Kerin's offer when she signed and returned the letter, then a contract was made, and Joli is obligated to buy the book. This depends, in part, on what was said in the letter and what was said in response. For instance, did the letter contain a valid offer, and did the response constitute a valid acceptance? Under any circumstances, the issue is not whether either party subjectively believed that a contract had been made.

2. No. This contract, although not fully executed, is for an illegal purpose and therefore is void. A void contract gives rise to no legal obligation on the part of any party. A contract that is void is no contract. There is nothing to enforce.

Chapter 11

1. No. Revocation of an offer may be implied by conduct inconsistent with the offer. When Fidelity Corporation rehired Monica, and Ron learned of the hiring, the offer was revoked. His acceptance was too late.

2. First, it might be noted that the Uniform Electronic Transactions Act (UETA) does not apply unless the parties to a contract agree to use e-commerce in their transaction. In this deal, of course, the parties used e-commerce. The UETA removes barriers to e-commerce by giving the same legal effect to e-records and e-signatures as to paper documents and signatures. The UETA itself does not include rules for e-commerce transactions, however.

Chapter 12

1. Yes. The original contract was executory. The parties rescinded it and agreed to a new contract. If Sharyn had broken the contract to accept a contract with

another employer, she might have been held liable for damages for the breach.

2. Yes. Under the doctrine of promissory estoppel, the promisee is entitled to payment of $5,000 from the promisor on graduation. There was a promise on which the promisee relied, the reliance was substantial and definite (the promisee went to college for the full term, incurring considerable expense, and will likely graduate), and it would only be fair to enforce the promise.

Chapter 13

1. A minor may effectively ratify a contract after he or she reaches the age of majority either expressly or impliedly. Failing to disaffirm an otherwise enforceable contract within a reasonable time after reaching the age of majority would also effectively ratify it. Nothing a minor does before attaining majority, however, will ratify a contract.

2. No. Generally, an exculpatory clause—a clause attempting to absolve parties of negligence or other wrongs—is not enforced if the party seeking its enforcement is involved in a business that is important to the public as a matter of practical necessity, such as an airline. Because of the essential nature of such services, the parties have an advantage in bargaining strength and could insist that anyone contracting for its services agree not to hold it liable.

Chapter 14

1. Yes. Rescission may be granted on the basis of fraudulent misrepresentation. The elements of fraudulent misrepresentation include intent to deceive, or *scienter*. *Scienter* exists if a party makes a statement recklessly, without regard to whether it is true or false, or if a party says or implies that a statement is made on some basis such as personal knowledge or personal investigation when it is not.

2. No. Brad exerted economic duress on Dina. The threat to break a contract on the eve of the deadline in this scenario was sufficiently coercive to constitute duress. Duress involves coercive conduct—forcing a party to enter into a contract by threatening the party with a wrongful act.

Chapter 15

1. No. Under the Uniform Commercial Code, a contract for a sale of goods priced at $500 or more must be in writing to be enforceable. In this scenario, the contract is not enforceable beyond the quantity already delivered and paid for.

2. The court might conclude that under the doctrine of promissory estoppel, the employer is estopped from claiming the lack of a written contract as a defense. The oral contract may be enforced because the employer made a promise on which the employee justifiably relied in moving to New York, the reliance was foreseeable, and injustice can be avoided only by enforcing the promise. If the court strictly enforces the Statute of Frauds, however, the employee may be without a remedy.

Chapter 16

1. Contracts that are *executory* on both sides—that is, contracts on which neither party has performed—can be rescinded solely by agreement. Contracts that are *executed* on one side—that is, contracts on which one party has performed—can be rescinded only if the party who has performed receives consideration for the promise to call off the deal. Thus, in this situation, if neither party starts to perform, the deal can be rescinded solely by agreement. If Stealth already shipped the pizzas, however, the contract can be rescinded only if Stealth receives consideration to call off the deal.

2. This is a novation. Novation substitutes a new party for an original party by agreement of all the parties. The requirements are a previous valid obligation, an agreement of all the parties to a new contract, extinguishment of the old obligation, and a new, valid contract. Novation revokes and discharges the previous obligation. Here, C&D delegated its duties under its contract with Ace to Dean, with Ace's consent. Ace's obligation to pay C&D for the execution of those duties is discharged, but its obligation under the new contract to pay Dean for those services will not be discharged until Dean is paid. The novation did, however, discharge C&D's obligation under the contract.

Chapter 17

1. A nonbreaching party is entitled to the benefit of the bargain under the contract. Here, the innocent party is entitled to be put in the position she would have been in if the contract had been fully performed. The measure of the benefit is the cost to complete the work ($500). These are compensatory damages.

2. No. To recover damages that flow from the consequences of a breach but that are caused by circumstances beyond the contract (consequential damages), the breaching party must know, or have reason to know, that special circumstances will cause the non-breaching party to suffer the additional loss. That was not the situation in this problem.

Chapter 18

1. Yes. Generally, if a contract clearly states that a right is not assignable, no assignment will be effective, but there are exceptions. Assignment of the right to receive monetary payment cannot be prohibited.

2. Yes. When one person makes a promise with the intention of benefiting a third person, the third person can sue to enforce it. This is a third party beneficiary contract. The third party in this problem (Jeff) is an intended beneficiary.

Chapter 19

1. A shipment of nonconforming goods constitutes an acceptance and a breach, unless the seller seasonably notifies the buyer that the nonconforming shipment does not constitute an acceptance and is offered only as an accommodation. Thus, since there was no notification in this problem, the shipment was both an acceptance and a breach.

2. Yes. In a transaction between merchants, the requirement of a writing is satisfied if one of them sends to the other a signed written confirmation that indicates the terms of the agreement, and the merchant receiving it has reason to know of its contents. If the merchant who receives the confirmation does not object in writing within ten days after receipt, the writing will be enforceable against him or her even though he or she has not signed anything.

Chapter 20

1. The result would be the same as if the contract stated, "F.O.B. New York." For the risk of loss to remain with the seller, a seller must specifically agree to deliver

goods to a particular destination. Remember, all contracts are assumed to be shipment contracts unless they state otherwise.

2. No. A seller has voidable title if the goods that he or she is selling were paid for with a bad check (a check that is later dishonored). Normally, a buyer acquires only the title that the seller had, or had the power to transfer, but a seller with voidable title can transfer good title to a good faith purchaser (one who buys in good faith without knowledge that the seller did not have the right to sell the goods). Under those circumstances, an original owner cannot recover goods from a good faith purchaser. Here, the ultimate buyer is a good faith purchaser.

Chapter 21

1. Yes. A seller is obligated to deliver goods in conformity with a contract in every detail. This is the perfect tender rule. The exception of the seller's right to cure does not apply here because the seller delivered too little too late to take advantage of this exception.

2. Yes. When anticipatory repudiation occurs, a buyer (or lessee) can resort to any remedy for breach even if the buyer tells the seller (the repudiating party in this problem) that the buyer will wait for the seller's performance.

Chapter 22

1. A statement that "I.O.U." money (or anything else) or an instruction to a bank stating, "I wish you would pay," would render any instrument nonnegotiable. To be negotiable, an instrument must contain an express promise to pay. An I.O.U. is only an acknowledgment of indebtedness. An order stating, "I wish you would pay," is not sufficiently precise.

2. No. When a drawer's employee provides the drawer with the name of a fictitious payee (a payee whom the drawer does not actually intend to have any interest in an instrument), a forgery of the payee's name is effective to pass good title to subsequent transferees.

Chapter 23

1. Under the principle of comity, a U.S court would defer and give effect to foreign laws and judicial decrees that are consistent with U.S. law and public policy.

2. The practice described in this problem is known as dumping, which is regarded as an unfair international trade practice. Dumping is the sale of imported goods at "less than fair value." Based on the price of those goods in the exporting country, an extra tariff—known as an antidumping duty—can be imposed on the imports.

Chapter 24

1. Yes, to both questions. In a civil suit, a drawer (Lyn) is liable to a payee (Jan) or to a holder of a check that is not honored. If intent to defraud can be proved, the drawer (Lyn) can also be subject to criminal prosecution for writing a bad check.

2. The general rule is that the bank must recredit a customer's account when it pays on a forged signature. The bank has no right to recover from a holder who, without knowledge, cashes a check bearing a forged drawer's signature. Thus, the bank in this problem can collect from neither its customer nor the party who cashed the check. The bank's only recourse is to look for the thief.

Chapter 25

1. When collateral consists of consumer goods, and the debtor has paid less than 60 percent of the debt or the purchase price, the creditor has the option of disposing of the collateral in a commercially reasonable manner. This generally requires notice to the debtor of the place, time, and manner of sale. A debtor can waive the right to notice, but only after default. Before the disposal, a debtor can redeem the collateral by tendering performance of all of the obligations secured by the collateral and by paying the creditor's reasonable expenses in retaking and maintaining the collateral.

2. The creditor (Midwest) can place a mechanic's lien on the debtor's property. If the debtor does not pay what is owed, the property can be sold to satisfy the debt. The only requirements are that the lien be filed within a specific time from the time of the work, depending on the state statute, and that notice of the foreclosure and sale be given to the debtor in advance.

Chapter 26

1. No. Besides the claims listed in this problem, the debts that cannot be discharged in bankruptcy include amounts borrowed to pay back taxes, goods obtained

by fraud, debts that were not listed in the petition, domestic support obligations, certain cash advances, and others.

2. Yes. A debtor's payment to a creditor made for a preexisting debt, within ninety days (one year in the case of an insider or fraud) of a bankruptcy filing, can be recovered if it gives a creditor more than he or she would have received in the bankruptcy proceedings. A trustee can recover this preference using his or her specific avoidance powers.

Chapter 27

1. No. Nadine, as an agent, is prohibited from taking advantage of the agency relationship to obtain property that the principal (Dimka Corporation) wants to purchase. This is the duty of loyalty that arises with every agency relationship.

2. Yes. A principal has a duty to indemnify (reimburse) an agent for liabilities incurred because of authorized and lawful acts and transactions and for losses suffered because of the principal's failure to perform his or her duties.

Chapter 28

1. No, to the first question. Yes, to the second question. Workers' compensation laws establish a procedure for compensating workers who are injured on the job. Instead of suing to collect benefits, an injured worker notifies the employer of the injury and files a claim with the appropriate state agency. The right to recover is normally determined without regard to negligence or fault, but intentionally inflicted injuries are not covered. Unlike the potential for recovery in a lawsuit based on negligence or fault, recovery under a workers' compensation statute is limited to the specific amount designated in the statute for the employee's injury.

2. A closed shop—a company that requires union membership as a condition of employment—is illegal. A union shop—a company that does not require union membership as a condition of employment but requires workers to join the union after a certain time on the job—is illegal in a state with a right-to-work law, which makes it illegal in that state to require union membership for continued employment.

Chapter 29

1. Yes. One type of sexual harassment occurs when a request for sexual favors is a condition of employment and the person making the request is a supervisor or acts with the authority of the employer. A tangible employment action, such as a promise of continued employment, may also lead to the employer's liability for the supervisor's conduct. That the injured employee is a male and the supervisor a female, instead of the other way around, would not affect the outcome. Same-gender harassment is also actionable.

2. Yes, Koko can succeed in a discrimination suit if she can show that she was not hired solely because of her disability. The other elements for a discrimination suit based on a disability are that the plaintiff (1) has a disability and (2) is otherwise qualified for the job. Both of these elements appear to be satisfied in this scenario.

Chapter 30

1. Yes. When a business is relatively small and is not diversified, employs relatively few people, has modest profits, and is not likely to expand significantly or require extensive financing in the immediate future, the most appropriate form for doing business may be a sole proprietorship.

2. Yes. Failing to meet a specified sales quota can constitute a breach of a franchise agreement. If the franchisor is acting in good faith, "cause" may also include the death or disability of the franchisee, the insolvency of the franchisee, and a breach of another term of the franchise agreement.

Chapter 31

1. No. A widow (or widower) has no right to take a dead partner's place. A partner's death causes dissociation, after which the partnership must purchase the dissociated partner's partnership interest. Therefore, the surviving partners must pay the decedent's estate (for his widow) the value of the deceased partner's interest in the partnership.

2. No. Under the partners' fiduciary duty, a partner must account to the partnership for any personal profits or benefits derived without the consent of all the partners

in connection with the use of any partnership property. Here, Finian, the leasing partner, may not keep the funds.

Chapter 32

1. The members of a limited liability company (LLC) may designate a group to run their firm. In that situation, the firm would be a manager-managed LLC. The group may include only members, only nonmembers, or members and nonmembers. If, instead, all members participate in management, the firm would be a member-managed LLC. In fact, unless the members agree otherwise, all members are considered to participate in the management of the firm.

2. Although there are differences, all of these forms of business organization resemble corporations. A joint stock company, for example, is owned by shareholders, is managed by directors and officers, and has perpetual existence. A business trust, like a corporation, distributes profits to persons who are not personally responsible for the debts of the organization, and management of the business is in the hands of trustees, just as the management of a corporation is in the hands of directors and officers. An incorporated cooperative, which is subject to state laws covering nonprofit corporations, distributes profits to its owners.

Chapter 33

1. Small businesses that meet certain requirements can qualify as S corporations, created specifically to permit small businesses to avoid double taxation. The six requirements of an S corporation are (1) the firm must be a domestic corporation; (2) the firm must not be a member of an affiliated group of corporations; (3) the shareholders must be individuals, estates, or qualified trusts (or corporations in some cases); (4) the firm must have no more than one hundred shareholders; (5) there can be only one class of stock; and (6) no shareholder can be a nonresident alien.

2. Broad authority to conduct business can be granted in a corporation's articles of incorporation. For example, the term "any lawful purpose" is often used. This can be important because acts of a corporation that are beyond the authority given to it in its articles or charter (or state statutes) are considered illegal, *ultra vires* acts.

Chapter 34

1. Yes. A shareholder can bring a derivative suit on behalf of a corporation if some wrong is done to the corporation. Normally, any damages recovered go into the corporate treasury.

2. Yes. A single shareholder—or a few shareholders acting together—who owns enough stock to exercise *de facto* control over a corporation owes the corporation and minority shareholders a fiduciary duty when transferring those shares.

Chapter 35

1. This combination is a consolidation (a new entity takes the place of the consolidating disappearing firms). In a merger, in contrast, one of the merging entities continues to exist. In this consolidation, the new corporation, MM, Inc., inherits all of Micro's assets, property, and liabilities.

2. Maybe. If a corporation organizes another corporation with practically the same shareholders and directors, and transfers all the assets but does not pay all the first corporation's debts, a court can hold the new corporation liable. Here, the new corporation continued to carry on the same business as Peppertree with all of Peppertree's assets so it would be fair for a court to hold the new corporation liable for Peppertree's debts.

Chapter 36

1. The average investor is concerned not with minor inaccuracies but with facts that if disclosed would tend to deter him or her from buying the securities. These include material facts that have an important bearing on the condition of the issuer and its business—such as liabilities, loans to officers and directors, customer delinquencies, and pending lawsuits.

2. No. The Securities Exchange Act of 1934 extends liability to officers and directors in their personal transactions for taking advantage of inside information when they know it is unavailable to the persons with whom they are dealing.

Chapter 37

1. Under the Administrative Procedure Act (APA), the administrative law judge (ALJ) must be separate from the agency's investigative and prosecutorial staff. *Ex parte* communications between the ALJ and a party to a proceeding are prohibited. Under the APA, an ALJ is exempt from agency discipline except on a showing of good cause.

2. Yes. Administrative rulemaking starts with the publication of a notice of the rulemaking in the *Federal Register.* A public hearing is then held at which proponents and opponents can offer evidence and question witnesses. After the hearing, the agency considers what was presented at the hearing and drafts the final rule.

Chapter 38

1. Size alone does not determine whether a firm is a monopoly—size in relation to the market is what matters. A small store in a small, isolated town is a monopolist if it is the only store serving that market. Monopoly involves the power to affect prices and output. If a firm has sufficient market power to control prices and exclude competition, that firm has monopoly power. Monopoly power in itself is not a violation of Section 2 of the Sherman Act. The offense also requires an intent to acquire or maintain that power through anticompetitive means.

2. This agreement is a tying arrangement. The legality of a tying arrangement depends on the purpose of the agreement, the agreement's likely effect on competition in the relevant markets (the market for the tying product and the market for the tied product), and other factors. Tying arrangements for commodities are subject to Section 3 of the Clayton Act. Tying arrangements for services can be agreements in restraint of trade in violation of Section 1 of the Sherman Act.

Chapter 39

1. Under an extensive set of procedures established by the U.S. Food and Drug Administration, which administers the Federal Food, Drug, and Cosmetic Act, drugs must be shown to be effective as well as safe before they may be marketed to the public. In general, manufacturers are responsible for ensuring that the drugs they offer for sale are free of any substances that could injure consumers.

2. The Comprehensive Environmental Response, Compensation, and Liability Act (CERCLA) regulates the cleanup of hazardous waste disposal sites. Any potentially responsible party can be charged with the entire cost of cleaning up a site. Potentially responsible parties include the party that generated the waste (ChemCorp), the party that transported the waste to the site (Disposal), the party that owned or operated the site at the time of the disposal (Eliminators), and the current owner or operator of the site (Fluid). A party held responsible for the entire cost may be able to recoup some of it in a lawsuit against other potentially responsible parties.

Chapter 40

1. Yes. In these circumstances, when the accountant knows that the bank will use the statement, the bank is a foreseeable user. A foreseeable user is a third party within the class of parties to whom an accountant may be liable for negligence.

2. No. In the circumstances described, the accountant will not be held liable to a purchaser of the securities. Although an accountant may be liable under securities laws for including untrue statements in or omitting material facts from financial statements, due diligence is a defense to liability. Due diligence requires an accountant to conduct a reasonable investigation and to reasonably believe that the financial statements are accurate. The problem scenario specifies that the misstatement of material fact in Omega's financial statement was not attributable to any fraud or negligence on Nora's part. Therefore, Nora can show that she used due diligence and will not be held liable to Pat.

Chapter 41

1. The ring is classified as lost property because it was discovered under circumstances indicating that the owner had not voluntarily placed it where it was found. The general rule is that the finder of the lost property has the right to possession (and eventual title) over all others *except* the true owner of the lost property. Therefore, Martin, as the true owner of the ring, is entitled to repossess the ring from Hunter.

2. Rosa de la Mar Corporation, the shipper, suffers the loss. A common carrier is liable for damage caused by the willful acts of third persons or by an accident. Other losses must be borne by the shipper (or the recipient, depending on the terms of their contract). In this situation, this shipment was lost due to an act of God.

Chapter 42

1. This is a breach of the warranty deed's covenant of quiet enjoyment. Consuela can sue Bernie and recover the purchase price of the house, plus any damages.

2. Yes. An owner of a fee simple has the most rights possible—he or she can give the property away, sell it, transfer it by will, use it for almost any purpose, possess it to the exclusion of all the world, or, as in this case, transfer possession for any period of time. The party to whom possession is transferred can also transfer her or his interest (usually only with the owner's permission) for any lesser period of time.

Chapter 43

1. No. To have testamentary capacity, a testator must be of legal age and sound mind *at the time the will is made.* Generally, the testator must (1) know the nature of the act, (2) comprehend and remember the "natural objects of his or her bounty," (3) know the nature and extent of her or his property, and (4) understand the distribution of assets called for by the will. In this situation, Sheila had testamentary capacity at the time she made the will. The fact that she was ruled mentally incompetent two years after making the will does not provide sufficient grounds to revoke it.

2. The estate will pass according to the state's intestacy laws. Intestacy laws set out how property is distributed when a person dies without a will. Their purpose is to carry out the likely intent of the decedent. The laws determine which of the deceased's natural heirs (including, in this order, the surviving spouse, lineal descendants, parents, and collateral heirs) inherit his or her property.

Sample Answers for *Business Case Problems with Sample Answer*

1–6. Sample Answer—Reading Citations.

The court's opinion in this case—*Worldwide TechServices, LLC v. Commissioner of Revenue*, 479 Mass. 20, 91 N.E.3d 650 (2018)—can be found in Volume 479 of the *Massachusetts Reports* on page 20, and in Volume 91 of *North Eastern Reporter*, Third Series, on page 650. The Supreme Judicial Court of Massachusetts issued the opinion in 2018.

2–3. Sample Answer—Freedom of Speech.

No. Wooden's conviction was not unconstitutional. Certain speech is not protected under the First Amendment. Speech that violates criminal laws—threatening speech, for example—is not constitutionally protected. Other unprotected speech includes fighting words, or words that are likely to incite others to respond violently. And speech that harms the good reputation of another, or defamatory speech, is not protected under the First Amendment.

In his e-mail and audio notes to the alderwoman, Wooden referred to a sawed-off shotgun, domestic terrorism, and the assassination and murder of various politicians. He compared the alderwoman to the biblical character Jezebel, referring to her as a "bitch in the Sixth Ward." These references caused the alderwoman to feel threatened. The First Amendment does not protect such threats, which in this case violated a state criminal statute. There was nothing unconstitutional about punishing Wooden for this unprotected speech.

In the actual case on which this problem is based, Wooden appealed his conviction, arguing that it violated his right to freedom of speech. Under the principles set out above, the Missouri Supreme Court affirmed the conviction.

3–6. Sample Answer—Business Ethics.

It seems obvious from the facts stated in this problem that Hratch Ilanjian behaved unethically. Ethics, of course, involves questions relating to the fairness, justness, rightness, or wrongness of an action. Business ethics focuses on how businesspersons apply moral and ethical principles in making their decisions and whether those decisions are right or wrong.

In this problem, Ilanjian misrepresented himself to Vicken Setrakian, the president of Kenset Corporation, leading Setrakian to believe that Ilanjian was an international businessman who could help turn around Kenset's business in the Middle East. Ilanjian insisted that Setrakian provide him with confidential business documents. Then, claiming that they had an agreement, Ilanjian demanded full and immediate payment. He threatened to disclose the confidential information to a Kenset supplier if payment was not forthcoming. Kenset denied that they had a contract. In the ensuing litigation, during discovery, Ilanjian was uncooperative. Each of these acts was unethical.

In the actual case on which this problem is based, a trial court concluded that there was no contract, ordered the return of the confidential documents, and enjoined Ilanjian from using the information. The U.S. Court of Appeals for the Third Circuit affirmed.

4–6. Sample Answer—Corporate Contacts.

No. The defendants' motion to dismiss the suit for lack of personal jurisdiction should not be granted. A corporation normally is subject to jurisdiction in a state in which it is doing business. A court applies the minimum-contacts test to determine whether it can exercise jurisdiction over an out-of-state corporation. This requirement is met if the corporation sells its products within the state or places them in the "stream of commerce" with the intention of selling them in the state.

In this problem, the state of Washington filed a suit in a Washington state court against LG Electronics, Inc., and nineteen other foreign companies that participated in the global market for cathode ray tube (CRT) products. The state alleged a conspiracy to raise prices and set production levels in the market for CRTs in violation of a state consumer protection statute. The defendants filed a motion to dismiss the suit for lack of personal jurisdiction. For many years, however, these companies had sold CRTs in high volume in the United States, including the state of Washington. In other words, the corporations had purposefully established minimum contacts in the state of Washington. This is a sufficient basis for a Washington state court to assert personal jurisdiction over the defendants.

In the actual case on which this problem is based, the trial court dismissed the suit for lack of personal jurisdiction. On appeal, a state intermediate appellate court reversed based on the reasoning stated above.

5–4. Sample Answer—Negligence.

Negligence requires proof that (a) the defendant owed a duty of care to the plaintiff, (b) the defendant breached that duty, (c) the defendant's breach caused the plaintiff's injury, and (d) the plaintiff suffered a legally recognizable injury. With respect to the duty of care, a business owner has a duty to use reasonable care to protect business invitees. This duty includes an obligation to discover and correct or warn of unreasonably dangerous conditions that the owner of the premises should reasonably foresee might endanger an invitee. Some risks are so obvious that an owner need not warn of them. But even if a risk is obvious, a business owner may not be excused from the duty to protect the business's customers from foreseeable harm.

Because Lucario was the Weatherford's business invitee, the hotel owed her a duty of reasonable care to make its premises safe for her use. The balcony ran nearly the entire width of the window in Lucario's room. She could have reasonably believed that the window was a means of access to the balcony. The window/balcony configuration was dangerous, however, because the window opened wide enough for an adult to climb out, but the twelve-inch gap between one side of the window and the balcony was unprotected. This unprotected gap opened to a drop of more than three stories to a concrete surface below.

Should the hotel have anticipated the potential harm to a guest who opened the window in Room 59 and attempted to access the balcony? The hotel encouraged guests to "step out onto the balcony" to smoke. The dangerous window/balcony configuration could have been remedied at a minimal cost. These circumstances could be perceived as creating an "unreasonably dangerous" condition. And it could be concluded that the hotel created or knew of the condition and failed to take reasonable steps to warn of it or correct it. Of course, the Weatherford might argue that

the window/balcony configuration was so obvious that the hotel was not liable for Lucario's fall.

In the actual case on which this problem is based, the court concluded that the Weatherford did not breach its duty of care to Lucario. On McMurtry's appeal, a state intermediate appellate court held that this conclusion was in error, vacated the lower court's judgment in favor of the hotel on this issue, and remanded the case.

6–4. Sample Answer—Product Liability.

The accident in this case was caused by Jett's inattention, not by the texting device in the cab of his truck. In a product-liability case based on a design defect, the plaintiff has to prove that the product was defective at the time it left the hands of the seller or lessor. The plaintiff must also show that this defective condition made it "unreasonably dangerous" to the user or consumer. If the product was delivered in a safe condition and subsequent mishandling made it harmful to the user, the seller or lessor normally is not liable. To successfully assert a design defect, a plaintiff has to show that a reasonable alternative design was available and that the defendant failed to use it.

The plaintiffs could argue that the defendant manufacturer of the texting device owed them a duty of care because injuries to vehicle drivers, passengers, and others on the roads were reasonably foreseeable. They could claim that the product's design (1) required the driver to divert his eyes from the road to view an incoming text, and (2) permitted the receipt of texts while the vehicle was moving.

But manufacturers are not required to design a product incapable of distracting a driver. The duty owed by a manufacturer to the user or consumer of a product does not require guarding against hazards that are commonly known or obvious. Nor does a manufacturer's duty extend to protecting against injuries that result from a user's careless conduct, such as Jett's carelessness in this situation.

7–5. Sample Answer—Patents.

One ground on which the denial of Raymond Gianelli's patent application in this problem could be reversed on appeal is that the design of his "Rowing Machine" is *not obvious* in light of the design of the "Chest Press Apparatus for Exercising Regions of the Upper Body."

To obtain a patent, an applicant must demonstrate to the satisfaction of the U.S. Patent and Trademark Office (PTO) that the invention, discovery, process, or design is novel, useful, and not obvious in light of current technology.

In this problem, the PTO denied Gianelli's application for a patent for his "Rowing Machine"—an exercise machine on which a user *pulls* on handles to perform a rowing motion against a selected resistance to strengthen the back muscles. The PTO considered the device obvious in light of a patented "Chest Press Apparatus for Exercising Regions of the Upper Body"—a chest press exercise machine on which a user *pushes* on handles to overcome a selected resistance. But it can be easily argued that it is *not* obvious to modify a machine with handles designed to be *pushed* into one with handles designed to be *pulled*. In fact, anyone who has used exercise machines knows that a way to cause injury is to use a machine in a manner not intended by the manufacturer.

In the actual case on which this problem is based, the U.S. Court of Appeals for the Federal Circuit reversed the PTO's denial of Gianelli's application for a patent based on the reasoning stated above.

8–5. Sample Answer—Social Media.

Law enforcement can use social media to detect and prosecute suspected criminals. But there must be an authenticated connection between the suspects and the posts. To make this connection, law enforcement officials can present the testimony or certification of authoritative representatives of the social media site or other experts. The posts can be traced from the pages on which they are displayed and the accounts of the "owners" of the pages to the posters through Internet Protocol (IP) addresses. An IP address can reveal the e-mail address, and even the mailing address, of an otherwise anonymous poster.

The custodians of Facebook, for example, can verify Facebook pages and posts because they maintain those items as business records in the course of regularly conducted business activities. From those sources, the prosecution in Hassan's case could have tracked the IP address to discover his identity.

In the actual case on which this problem is based, on Hassan's appeal of his conviction, the U.S. Court of Appeals for the Fourth Circuit affirmed.

9–3. Sample Answer—White-Collar Crime.

Yes. The acts committed by Matthew Simpson and the others constituted wire and mail fraud. Federal law makes it a crime to devise any scheme that uses the U.S. mail, commercial carriers (such as FedEx or UPS), or wire (such as telegraph, telephone, television, the Internet, or e-mail) with the intent to defraud the public.

Here, as stated in the facts, Simpson and his cohorts created and operated a series of corporate entities to defraud telecommunications companies, creditors, credit reporting agencies, and others. Through these entities, Simpson and the others used routing codes and spoofing services to make long distance calls appear to be local. They stole other firms' network capacity and diverted payments to themselves. They leased goods and services without paying for them. And they assumed false identities, addresses, and credit histories, and issued false bills, invoices, financial statements, and credit references, in order to hide their association with their entities and with each other. Through the use of this "scheme," the perpetrators defrauded telecommunications companies and other members of the public in order to gain goods and services for themselves. They used wire services—the Internet and, presumably, phones and other qualifying services—to further the scheme.

In the actual case on which this problem is based, a federal district court convicted Simpson of participating in a wire and mail fraud conspiracy (and other crimes). On appeal, the U.S. Court of Appeals for the Fifth Circuit affirmed the conviction.

10–5. Sample Answer—Implied Contracts.

Yes. Allstate was liable under the homeowner's policy under an implied contract theory. An implied contract differs from an express contract in that the conduct of the parties, rather than their words, creates and defines the terms of the contract. An implied contract arises when a party furnishes a service or property (which includes money), the party expects to receive something in return for that property or service, and the other party knows or should know of that expectation and has a chance to reject the property or service but does not.

A contract may be a mix of express and implied terms. That was the case with the homeowner's policy in this problem. As to the elements showing the existence of the implied terms, the payments for the premiums on the policy continued after Ralph's death, but the amounts were paid from Douglas's account. Undoubtedly, Douglas expected to receive coverage under the policy in return for his payments. Allstate must have known that Douglas expected the coverage—insurance has long been Allstate's business, and the company obviously understands the relationship between the payments of premiums and the expectation of insurance coverage. And Allstate had the opportunity to cancel the homeowner's policy—as it canceled Ralph's auto insurance—but did not do so.

In the actual case on which this problem is based, the court issued a judgment in Allstate's favor on the implied contract issue. The U.S. Court of Appeals for the Sixth Circuit reversed this judgment—"A reasonable fact-finder could determine that [Allstate's] continuation of the premium payments constituted a contract implied in fact with Douglas."

11–6. Sample Answer—Requirement of the Offer.

No. TCP is not correct—the bonus plan was not too indefinite to be an offer. One of the requirements for an effective offer is that its terms must be reasonably definite. This enables a court to determine whether a breach has occurred and award an appropriate remedy. Generally, the offer's terms include an identification of the parties and the object or subject of the contract, the consideration to be paid, and the time of performance.

In this problem, TCP provided its employees, including Bahr, with the details of a bonus plan. A district sales manager such as Bahr who achieved 100 percent year-over-year sales growth and a 42 percent gross margin would earn 200 percent of his or her base salary. TCP added that it retained absolute discretion to modify the plan. Bahr exceeded the goal and expected a bonus commensurate with her performance. TCP paid her less than half what its plan promised, however. In the ensuing litigation, TCP claimed that the bonus plan was too indefinite to constitute an offer, but this was not, in fact, the case. The plan provided clear criteria to determine an employee's eligibility for a certain amount within a specific time. A court asked to apply the plan would have little or no doubt as to the amount an employee would be entitled to. The term that reserved discretion to TCP to modify the plan did not sufficiently undercut the clarity of the offer to prevent the formation of a contract.

In the actual case on which this problem is based, the trial court concluded that the reservation of discretion to revoke a plan makes an offer too indefinite and issued a judgment in TCP's favor. A state intermediate appellate court reversed this judgment, holding that TCP's plan was a sufficiently definite offer.

12–6. Sample Answer—Agreements That Lack Consideration.

Yes. There was consideration to support the Telephone Deal. Consideration can consist of a promise, a performance, or a forbearance (refraining from an action that one has a legal right to undertake).

In this problem, Mark Garnett, an owner of Arkansas-Missouri Forest Products, LLC (Ark-Mo), and Stuart Lerner, an owner of Blue Chip Manufacturing (BCM), agreed to engage in wood-pallet enterprises together, with Ark-Mo to have a 30 percent ownership interest in their future projects. When Lerner formed Blue Chip Recycling, LLC (BCR), to manage a pallet repair facility in California, however, he allocated only a 5 percent interest to Ark-Mo. Garnett objected. In a "Telephone Deal," Lerner promised that Ark-Mo would receive a 30 percent interest in their future projects in the Midwest. Garnett then agreed to forego an ownership interest in BCR.

Acting on Ark-Mo's behalf, Garnett could have accepted the 5 percent allocation in BCR, but he refrained from doing so. Instead, he accepted Lerner's promise of a 30 percent share in their future projects in the Midwest and made no more demands regarding BCR. In other words, Garnett gave up the opportunity to have an ownership interest in BCR in exchange for Lerner's agreement that Ark-Mo would have a 30 percent ownership interest in certain future projects.

In the actual case on which this problem is based, Ark-Mo filed a suit in a Missouri state court against Lerner, alleging breach of contract. The court issued a judgment in Lerner's favor. A state intermediate appellate court reversed, in part on the reasoning stated here. "Valid legal consideration supported the Telephone Deal."

13–4. Sample Answer—Minors.

No. A minor does not so lack the capacity to contract that he or she cannot enter into a binding settlement without court approval. The general rule is that a minor can enter into any contract an adult can, unless the contract is prohibited by law for minors (for example, the sale of tobacco or alcoholic beverages). A contract entered into by a minor, however, is voidable at the option of that minor. An adult who enters into a contract with a minor cannot avoid his or her contractual duties on the ground that the minor can. Unless the minor exercises the option to disaffirm the contract, the adult party normally is bound by it.

In this problem, it is clear that a contract existed at the time of D.V.G.'s death. As a minor, she did not lack the capacity to enter into a binding settlement of her potential claims. She would not have been liable on the contract, however, if she had chosen to avoid the deal. But she was the only party to the settlement that had this option. At the time that the settlement was agreed to, the contract was binding on Nationwide, notwithstanding that it was voidable at D.V.G.'s option.

In the actual case on which this problem is based, Nationwide asked a federal district court to declare that there was no settlement. The question was certified to the Alabama Supreme Court, which held that Nationwide was bound to the agreement.

14–6. Sample Answer—Fraudulent Misrepresentation.

Yes. The facts in this problem evidence fraud. There are three elements to fraud: (1) the misrepresentation of a material fact, (2) an intent to deceive, and (3) an innocent party's justifiable reliance on the misrepresentation. To collect damages, the innocent party must suffer an injury.

Here, Pervis represented to Pauley that no further commission would be paid by Osbrink. This representation was false—despite Pervis's statement to the contrary, Osbrink continued to send payments to Pervis. Pervis knew the representation was false, as shown by the fact that she made it more than once during the time that she was continuing to receive payments from Osbrink. Each time Pauley asked about commissions, Pervis replied that she was not receiving any. Pauley's reliance on her business associate's statements was justified and reasonable. And for the purpose of recovering damages, Pauley suffered an injury in the amount of her share of the commissions that Pervis received as a result of the fraud.

In the actual case on which this problem is based, Pauley filed a suit in a Georgia state court against Pervis, who filed for bankruptcy in a federal bankruptcy court to stay the state action. The federal court held Pervis liable on the ground of fraud for the amount of the commissions that were not paid to Pauley and denied Pervis a discharge of the debt.

15–5. Sample Answer—The Parol Evidence Rule.

Vaks and Mangano may not recover for breach of an oral contract. Under the parol evidence rule, if there is a written contract representing the complete and final statement of the parties' agreement, a party may not introduce any evidence of past agreements. Here, the written agreement was an integrated contract because the parties intended it to be a complete and final statement of the terms of their agreement. Vaks and Mangano therefore may not introduce evidence of any inconsistent oral representations made before the contract was executed.

16–6. Sample Answer—Conditions of Performance.

The requirement that the contractor obtain an engineer's certificate of final completion before the final payment will be made is a condition precedent. In most contracts, promises of performance are not expressly conditioned—they are absolute and must be performed to avoid a breach of the contract. In some situations, however, performance is contingent on the occurrence of a certain event. If the condition is not satisfied, the obligations of the parties are discharged. A condition that must be fulfilled before a party's performance can be required is a condition precedent.

In this problem, H&J Ditching was hired to excavate and grade land for a residential construction project. Cornerstone Community Bank financed the project. As the work progressed, H&J received payments totaling 90 percent of the price on its contract. But the last payment was not forthcoming when H&J believed it was due. The contractor filed a suit in a Tennessee state court against the bank to recover the final payment. The bank responded that H&J did not receive the payment because it had failed to obtain an engineer's certificate of final completion, a condition under its contract. H&J argued that it had completed all the work it contracted to do.

H&J is not entitled to the final payment on the contract because it did not comply with the condition to obtain the engineer's certificate. This condition preceded the bank's obligation under the contract to make the final payment. Even assuming that H&J "completed all the work it contracted to do," the final payment need not be made without the certificate.

In the actual case on which this problem is based, the trial court issued a judgment in the bank's favor. A state intermediate appellate court affirmed. "No certificate of substantial completion was ever issued, a condition precedent to final payment."

17–5. Sample Answer—Limitation-of-Liability Clauses.

Yes, the limitation-of-liability agreement that Eriksson signed is likely to be enforced in her parents' suit against Nunnink, their daughter's riding coach. And this would likely result in a judgment against them unless they can establish "direct, willful and wanton negligence" on Nunnink's part. A limitation-of-liability clause affects the availability of certain remedies. Under basic contract principles, to be enforceable, these clauses must be clear and unambiguous.

In this problem, Eriksson, a young horseback-riding competitor, signed an agreement that released Nunnink from all liability except for damages caused by Nunnink's "direct, willful and wanton negligence." During an event, Eriksson's horse struck a hurdle, causing her to fall from the horse. The horse fell on her, resulting in her death. Her parents filed a suit against Nunnink for wrongful death. The limitation-of-liability clause signed by Eriksson, however, was straightforward, clear, and unambiguous, and therefore enforceable. Nunnink would be liable only if Eriksson's death was caused by Nunnink's gross negligence. The facts do not state that Eriksson's parents proved that Nunnink was grossly negligent.

In the actual case on which this problem is based, the trial court issued a judgment in Nunnink's favor. A state intermediate appellate court affirmed the judgment on the basis explained here.

18–4. Sample Answer—Third Party Beneficiary.

Yes. The Kincaids can bring an action against the Desses for breach of their contract with Sirva. A third person becomes an intended third party beneficiary of a contract when the original parties to the contract expressly agree that the performance should be rendered to or directly benefit a third person. As the intended beneficiary of a contract, a third party has legal rights and can sue the promisor directly for breach of the contract.

Here, the Desses agreed in their contract with Sirva to disclose all information about their property. They further agreed that Sirva and "other prospective buyers" could rely on the Desses' disclosure in deciding "whether and on what terms to purchase the Property." The Kincaids were not direct parties to the contract between Sirva and the Desses, but the Kincaids were "other prospective buyers." Thus, the language of the contract indicated that the Kincaids were intended by Sirva and the Desses to be third party beneficiaries of it. As intended beneficiaries of the contract, the Kincaids could sue the Desses directly for its breach.

In the actual case on which this problem is based, the Kincaids filed a suit in a Kansas state court against the Desses. From a judgment in the Desses' favor (for lack of privity), the Kincaids appealed. A state intermediate appellate court reversed on the basis of the reasoning stated above and remanded the case for trial.

19–6. Sample Answer—Goods and Services Combined.

A court will apply common law principles to a dispute over a contract that involves both goods and services when the court finds the services to be the dominant feature of the agreement. In contrast, a court will rule that the UCC should be applied when it finds the goods to be the dominant

aspect of the deal. In either situation, the applicable law covers both the goods and services parts of the contract.

In this problem, because the trial court applied common law contract principles to rule in National's favor on both parties' claims, the court must have concluded that the services part of the contract was the dominant aspect.

In the actual case on which this problem is based, a state intermediate appellate court affirmed the lower court's ruling in National's favor. The appellate court recognized that the contract was a hybrid involving goods and services and reasoned that the lower court must have found the services portion of the agreement to be the dominant factor. But the parties did not provide a trial transcript or a copy of the contract, so the appellate court could only affirm the lower court's order.

20–4. Sample Answer—Passage of Title.

Altieri held title to the car that she was driving at the time of the accident in which Godfrey was injured. Once goods exist and are identified, title can be determined. Under the Uniform Commercial Code (UCC), any explicit understanding between the buyer and the seller determines when title passes. If there is no such agreement, title passes to the buyer at the time and place that the seller physically delivers the goods.

In lease contracts, title to the goods is retained by the lessor-owner of the goods. The UCC's provisions relating to passage to title do not apply to leased goods. Here, Altieri originally leased the car from G.E. Capital Auto Lease, Inc., but by the time of the accident she had bought it. Even though she had not fully paid for the car or completed the transfer-of-title paperwork, she owned it. Title to the car passed to Altieri when she bought it and took delivery of it. Thus, Altieri, not G.E., was the owner of the car at the time of the accident.

In the actual case on which this problem is based, the court concluded that G.E. was not the owner of the vehicle when Godfrey was injured.

21–6. Sample Answer—Remedies of the Buyer or Lessee.

No. At this point the Morrises are not entitled to revoke their acceptance of the cabinets that IO delivered. Under the UCC, acceptance of a lot or a commercial unit can be revoked if a nonconformity substantially impairs the value of the lot or unit and acceptance was based on the reasonable assumption that the nonconformity would be cured, and it has not been cured within a reasonable period of time. One of the corollaries to this rule is, of course, that the seller must be given a reasonable time within which to effect a cure.

Here, the Morrises contracted with IO to rebuild the kitchen in their home on the Gulf coast of Mississippi after it was extensively damaged in a hurricane. As part of the deal, IO delivered new cabinets. Some defects were apparent, and as installation progressed, others emerged. IO ordered replacement parts to cure the defects and later offered to remove the cabinets and refund the price. The Morrises asked to be reimbursed for the installation fee as well. IO refused this request, but at all times, the seller emphasized that it was willing to fulfill its contractual obligations. The buyers then attempted to revoke their acceptance of the cabinets—before the replacement parts arrived and without attempting to negotiate any other accommodation.

In the actual case on which this problem is based, the Morrises filed a suit in a Mississippi state court against IO. The court dismissed the complaint and entered a judgment in the defendant's favor. A state intermediate appellate court affirmed. "The Morrises were not entitled to recovery because they revoked acceptance of the cabinets before giving IO a reasonable opportunity to cure the defects."

22–6. Sample Answer—Indorsements.

Yes. The evidence offered by Nationstar Mortgage, LLC, established that the attachment was sufficiently affixed to the note to prove Nationstar's status as the holder with the right to enforce the note. When an indorsement accompanies the transfer of a negotiable instrument, it is most often written on the back of the instrument. If there is no room, the indorsement can be written on a separate piece of paper—an attachment—that is affixed to the instrument and, under the UCC, thereby made part of it. A blank indorsement does not specify a particular indorsee and can consist of a mere signature.

In this problem, the Purificatos signed a note secured by their interest in certain real property. The note was transferred through several parties to Aurora Loan Services. The Purificatos defaulted, and Aurora sought to enforce the note and foreclose on the property. While the suit was pending, Nationstar Mortgage succeeded Aurora and became the plaintiff. To establish standing, Nationstar offered a screen shot of the note and an attachment. The items had been imaged simultaneously as a single document before Aurora filed the complaint. Nationstar also provided the original note and attachment. The attachment, which ended in a blank indorsement, stated that it was "affixed and a permanent part of said note." This evidence showed that the attachment was sufficiently affixed to the note to become part of it. The blank indorsement made the note a bearer instrument, supporting Nationstar's right, as the party in possession, to enforce it.

In the actual case on which this problem is based, the trial court entered a judgment in Nationstar's favor. A state intermediate appellate court affirmed. The Purificatos argued that the attachment was invalid because it was not *firmly* affixed to the note. This had been a requirement under previous versions of the UCC, but the provision applicable in this case "simply requires the paper to be affixed to the instrument." The court held that affixment can be proved by "clear intent" that the documents "were to be physically attached." The note, attachment, and testimony established that intent.

23–5. Sample Answer—Import Controls.

Yes. An antidumping duty can be assessed retrospectively (retroactively). But it does not seem likely that such a duty should be assessed here.

In this problem, the Wind Tower Trade Coalition (an association of domestic manufacturers of utility-scale wind towers) filed a suit in the U.S. Court of International Trade against the U.S. Department of Commerce. Wind Tower challenged the Commerce Department's decision to impose only *prospective* antidumping duties on imports of utility-scale wind towers from China and Vietnam. The Commerce Department had found that the domestic industry had not suffered any "material injury" or "threat of material injury" and that it would be protected by a prospective assessment. Because the domestic industry had not suffered discernible injury, any retrospective duties collected would not be payable to members of the industry. Thus, it does not seem likely that retroactive duties should be imposed.

In the actual case on which this problem is based, the court denied the plaintiff's request for an injunction. On appeal, the U.S. Court of Appeals for the Federal Circuit affirmed the denial, holding that the lower court acted within its discretion in determining that retrospective duties were not appropriate.

24–4. Sample Answer—Consumer Fund Transfers.

Yes. The bank's refusal to reimburse Patterson more than $677.46 was justified. Under the Electronic Fund Transfer

Act (EFTA), if a customer's debit card is lost or stolen and used without her or his permission, the customer does not have to pay more than $50. But for this limit to apply, the customer must notify the bank of the loss or theft within two days of learning about it. Otherwise, the liability increases to $500. The customer may be liable for more than $500 if the unauthorized use is not reported within sixty days after it appears on the customer's statement.

In this problem, Stephen Patterson held an account with SunTrust Bank. He was briefly involved in a romantic relationship with Juanita Wehrman, who stole his debit card and used it for sixteen months (well beyond the length of their relationship), spending more than $30,000. When Patterson learned what was happening, he closed his account. But, of course, sixteen months is much more than sixty days, and the bank refused to reimburse him more than $677.46. This was the amount of unauthorized transactions that occurred within sixty days of the transmittal of the bank statement that revealed the first unauthorized transaction.

In the actual case on which this problem is based, Patterson filed suit in a Tennessee state court against the bank to recover the rest of the spent funds. The court upheld the bank's refusal, and a state intermediate appellate court affirmed.

25–5. Sample Answer—Perfection of a Security Interest.

Yes. The description in PHI's financing statement was sufficient to perfect the creditor's security interest in the SURE payment. A financing statement must describe the collateral in which a secured party has a security interest in order to provide public notice of the fact that certain property of the debtor is subject to a security interest. The UCC permits broad, general descriptions in a financing statement, such as "all assets."

In this problem, G&K Farms was insured under the federal Supplemental Revenue Assistance Payments Program (SURE), which provides financial assistance for crop losses caused by natural disasters. PHI loaned G&K $6.6 million and filed a financing statement that described the collateral as G&K's interest in "Government Payments." The statement did not refer specifically to the farm's crops. G&K defaulted on the loan. When G&K received a SURE payment for crop losses and transferred some of the funds to its law firm, Johnston Law Office, PHI sought to recover the funds as a partial payment on its loan. Johnston argued

that PHI did not have a perfected security interest in the SURE payment because PHI's financing statement did not identify the farm's crops.

Johnston's argument is faulty because the debtor's crops were not the collateral at issue. The government's SURE payment was the disputed collateral, and PHI's financing statement sufficiently described it with the general reference to "Government Payments." PHI's security interest was perfected.

In the actual case on which this problem is based, PHI filed its suit against Johnston in a North Dakota state court, which entered a judgment in the creditor's favor. The North Dakota Supreme Court affirmed on the issue highlighted in this problem based on the reasoning stated here.

26–4. Sample Answer—Discharge.

No. Michael is not entitled to a discharge of the debt to Dianne. The debt, comprising unpaid alimony, child support, and investment funds, qualifies as an exception to discharge. As far as a debtor is concerned, the primary purpose of a liquidation proceeding is to obtain a fresh start through a discharge of debts. But certain debts are not dischargeable in bankruptcy. These debts include domestic-support obligations and property settlements provided for in a divorce decree and claims based on willful or malicious conduct by the debtor toward another.

In this problem, on Michael and Dianne's divorce, a court ordered Michael to pay Dianne alimony and child support, as well as half of the $184,000 in their investment accounts. Instead of complying with the order, Michael withdrew half of the investment funds and spent them on himself. Meanwhile, the court repeatedly held him in contempt for failing to pay Dianne alimony, child support, and half of the investment funds. These items are nondischargeable because they are domestic-support obligations and part of the property settlement provided for in the parties' divorce decree. The unpaid investment funds also constitute a claim based on willful and malicious conduct. Michael deliberately defied multiple contempt orders, leaving Dianne uncompensated and thereby inflicting harm on her.

In the actual case on which this problem is based, the court concluded that Michael's conduct was willful and malicious and that the debt to Dianne listed in the petition's schedule was therefore nondischargeable. On Michael's appeal, the U.S. Court of Appeals for the Fifth Circuit affirmed.

27–5. Sample Answer—Determining Employee Status.

No. Cox is not liable to Cayer for the injuries or damages that she sustained in the accident with Ovalles. Generally, an employer is not liable for physical harm caused to a third person by the negligent act of an independent contractor in the performance of a contract. This is because the employer does not have the right to control the details of the performance. In determining whether a worker has the status of an independent contractor, how much control the employer can exercise over the details of the work is the most important factor weighed by the courts.

In this problem, Ovalles worked as a cable installer for Cox under an agreement with M&M. The agreement disavowed any employer-employee relationship between Cox and M&M's installers. Ovalles was required to designate his affiliation with Cox on his van, clothing, and an I.D. badge. But Cox had minimal contact with Ovalles and limited power to control the manner in which he performed his work. Cox supplied cable wire and other equipment, but these items were delivered to M&M, not Ovalles. These facts indicate that Ovalles was an independent contractor, not an employee. Thus, Cox was not liable to Cayer for the harm caused to her by Ovalles when his van rear-ended her car.

In the actual case on which this problem is based, the court issued a judgment in Cox's favor. The Rhode Island Supreme Court affirmed, applying the principles stated above to arrive at the same conclusion.

28–5. Sample Answer—Unemployment Compensation.

Yes. Ramirez qualifies for unemployment compensation. Generally, to be eligible for unemployment compensation, a worker must be willing and able to work. Workers who have been fired for misconduct or who have voluntarily left their jobs are not eligible for benefits. In the facts of this problem, the applicable state statute disqualifies an employee from receiving benefits if he or she voluntarily leaves work without "good cause."

The issue is whether Ramirez left her job for "good cause." When her father in the Dominican Republic had a stroke, she asked her employer for time off to be with him. Her employer refused the request. But Ramirez left to be with her father and called to inform her employer. It seems likely that this family emergency would constitute "good cause," and Ramirez's call and return to work after

her father's death indicated that she did not disregard her employer's interests.

In the actual case on which this problem is based, the state of Florida denied Ramirez unemployment compensation. On Ramirez's appeal, a state intermediate appellate court reversed based on the reasoning stated above.

29–6. Sample Answer—Sexual Harassment.

Newton's best defense to Blanton's assertion of liability is the "*Ellerth/Faragher* affirmative defense." To establish this defense, an employer must show that it has taken reasonable care to prevent and promptly correct any sexually harassing behavior and that the plaintiff unreasonably failed to take advantage of any opportunity provided by the employer to avoid the harm.

In this problem, Blanton was subjected to sexual harassment by the general manager at their place of employment, a Pizza Hut restaurant operated by Newton. Blanton alerted low-level supervisors about the harassment, but they, like Blanton, were subordinate to the general manager and had no authority over her. Newton had a clear, straightforward antidiscrimination policy and complaint procedure, which provided that an employee should complain to the harasser's supervisor in such a situation. Once Blanton finally complained to a manager with authority over the general manager, Newton promptly and effectively responded to Blanton's complaint. His delay in reporting the harassment to the appropriate authority can be construed as an unreasonable failure to take advantage of the opportunity provided by the employer to avoid the harm.

In the actual case on which this problem is based, Blanton filed suit against Newton seeking to hold it liable for the general manager's actions. A jury found that the plaintiff had been harassed as he claimed, but it also found that the defendant had proved the *Ellerth/Faragher* affirmative defense. The court issued a judgment in the employer's favor, and the U.S. Court of Appeals for the Fifth Circuit affirmed.

30–4. Sample Answer—Quality Control.

Yes. Liberty can be held liable for the statements in its franchisees' ads. The validity of a provision permitting the franchisor to establish and enforce certain quality standards is unquestioned. The franchisor has a legitimate interest in maintaining the quality of the product or service to protect its name and reputation. If a franchisor exercises too much control over the operations of its franchisees, however, the franchisor risks potential liability. A franchisor may occasionally be held liable under the doctrine of *respondeat superior* for the tortious acts of a franchisee or the franchisees' employees.

In this problem, Liberty's agreement with its franchisees reserved the right to control their ads. In operations manuals, Liberty provided its franchisees with step-by-step instructions, directions, and limitations regarding their ads and retained the right to unilaterally modify the steps at any time. This seems to give the franchisor a great deal of control over its franchisees' marketing, which under the principles stated above, points to the franchisor's liability for the franchisees' misleading or deceptive ads.

In the actual case on which this problem is based, the trial court issued a judgment in California's favor. Liberty appealed. A state intermediate appellate court affirmed. "Liberty retained the right to control, and in fact did seek to control, its franchisees' advertising and other marketing activities beyond that necessary to protect its marks and goodwill."

31–4. Sample Answer—Partnerships.

Yes. Sacco is entitled to 50 percent of the profits of Pierce Paxton Collections. The requirements for establishing a partnership are (1) a sharing of profits and losses, (2) a joint ownership of the business, and (3) an equal right to be involved in the management of the business.

The effort and time that Sacco expended in the business constituted a sharing of losses. His proprietary interest in the assets of the partnership consisted of his share of the profits, which he expressly left in the business to "grow the company" and "build sweat equity" for the future. He was involved in every aspect of the business. Although he was not paid a salary, he was reimbursed for business expenses charged to his personal credit card, which Paxton also used. These facts arguably meet the requirements for establishing a partnership.

In the actual case on which this problem is based, Sacco filed a suit in a Louisiana state court against Paxton, and the court awarded Sacco 50 percent of the profits. A state intermediate appellate court affirmed based generally on the reasoning stated above.

32–4. Sample Answer—LLC Operation.

Smith, Mosser, and Floyd violated Bluewater's operating agreement by attempting to "fire" Williford, the fourth member, without providing a reason. Part of the attractiveness of an LLC as a form of business enterprise is its flexibility. The members can decide how to operate the business through an operating agreement. For example, the agreement can set forth procedures for choosing or removing members or managers.

Here, the Bluewater operating agreement provided for a "supermajority" vote to remove a member under circumstances that would jeopardize the firm's contractor status. The members comprising the supermajority could not, however, terminate the other's interest in the firm without providing a reason. Moreover, the only acceptable reason would be a circumstance that undercut the firm's status as a contractor.

The flexibility of the LLC business form relates to its framework, not to its members' capacity to violate its operating agreement. In the actual case on which this problem is based, three Bluewater members—Smith, Mosser, and Floyd—attempted to "fire" Williford, the fourth member, without providing a reason. In Williford's suit, the court issued a judgment in his favor.

33–4. Sample Answer—Piercing the Corporate Veil.

Yes. there are sufficient grounds in the facts of this problem to support piercing the corporate veil and holding Kappeler personally liable to Snapp. First, in a case in which a plaintiff seeks to pierce a corporate veil, fraud or some other injustice must have taken place. In that situation, a court will consider whether the following factors were present: (1) a party was tricked or misled into dealing with the corporation rather than the individual; (2) the corporation had insufficient capital to meet its prospective debts or other potential liabilities; (3) corporate formalities, such as holding required corporate meetings, were not followed; and (4) personal and corporate interests were commingled.

In this problem, the amount that Snapp ultimately paid the builder exceeded the original estimate by nearly $1 million—and the project was still unfinished. Kappeler could not provide an accounting for the Snapp project—he could not explain double and triple charges nor whether the amount that Snapp paid had actually been spent on the project. These facts support a conclusion of fraud, and they also suggest that Kappeler may have tricked or misled Snapp into dealing with Castlebrook, the corporation, rather than with Kappeler as an individual. Castlebrook had issued no shares of stock, which points to insufficient capitalization. The minutes of the corporate meetings "all looked exactly the same," indicating that, in fact, the required corporate meetings had not been held. Finally, Kappeler had commingled personal and corporate funds.

In the actual case on which this problem is based, Snapp filed suit against the builder seeking to pierce the corporate veil. The court did so and held Kappeler personally liable. A state intermediate appellate court affirmed.

34–5. Sample Answer—Business Judgment Rule.

No. The Songers are not personally liable for Country's failure to complete its contract with A Westside Storage. A hallmark of the corporate form of business organization is that shareholders are not personally liable for the debts of the corporation. If the corporation fails, the shareholders can lose their investments, but that is generally the limit of their liability. A court may pierce the corporate veil to hold the shareholders personally liable in certain instances of fraud, undercapitalization, or a failure to observe corporate formalities. But these situations are exceptions.

In this problem, the facts state that the Songers had not misused the corporate form to engage in misconduct, the firm had not been undercapitalized, personal and corporate funds had not been commingled, and Country had kept accounting records and minutes of its annual board meetings. These circumstances fall under none of the exceptions to the limit on shareholders' liability for corporate obligations. Thus, as shareholders, the Songers are not personally liable for the failure of their company to complete its job.

In the actual case on which this problem is based, A Westside Storage filed a suit in an Indiana state court against the Songers for breach of contract. The court held the defendants liable. On the Songers' appeal, a state intermediate appellate court reversed. There was no evidence to support piercing the corporate veil.

35–6. Sample Answer—Purchase of Assets.

No. Alcoa does not have to indemnify Glencore for costs related to Lockheed's suit. Generally, a corporation that purchases the assets of another corporation is not automatically responsible for the liabilities of the selling corporation. Exceptions to this rule are made in certain circumstances, including when the purchasing corporation expressly assumes the seller's liabilities. Thus, as Glencore's successor, Alcoa would not have to indemnify Glencore in Lockheed's suit unless Alcoa had expressly assumed liability for Glencore's contract with Lockheed.

In this problem, Lockheed owned an aluminum refinery in the Virgin Islands that produced hazardous waste. Lockheed sold the refinery to Glencore under a contract that provided the buyer would indemnify the seller for "pre-closing" environmental conditions. Alcoa bought the refinery from Glencore. When the government of the Virgin Islands brought actions against the refinery's current and former owners to recover for environmental damage, Lockheed agreed in a settlement to pay for some of the clean up, and filed a suit against Glencore to recover costs related to this settlement. Glencore is likely liable to Lockheed under its purchase agreement for the refinery, in which it agreed to indemnify the seller for "pre-closing" environmental conditions.

But Alcoa is not liable to indemnify Glencore for its costs in Lockheed's action. Alcoa's contract to buy the refinery from Glencore did not contain an express undertaking to assume Glencore's liability under its contract with Lockheed. Alcoa's contract did state that the buyer assumed certain liabilities, including those relating to two specific contracts. But Glencore's liability under its contract with Lockheed was not part of this list.

In the actual case on which this problem is based, Alcoa filed an action in a Delaware state court, asking for a declaratory judgment that Alcoa did not have to defend Glencore in the Lockheed suit or indemnify Glencore for costs related to it. According to the reasoning stated here, the court entered a judgment in Alcoa's favor.

36–4. Sample Answer—Disclosure under SEC Rule 10b-5.

Even if Goldman did not affirmatively misrepresent any facts about the collateralized debt obligations (CDOs), Dodona can recover if Goldman failed to disclose material facts. An omission is regarded as material if it is significant enough that it would have affected an investor's decision concerning the securities. Here, Dodona might recover by showing that Goldman did not fully disclose the risks of investing in the CDOs. Goldman may have misled Dodona by providing only boilerplate statements about investments that it knew were particularly risky.

37–5. Sample Answer—Arbitrary and Capricious Test.

Yes. The agency's decision to revoke Manin's certification was arbitrary and capricious. When reviewing an agency decision, a court considers whether the agency's actions were arbitrary, capricious, or an abuse of discretion. An action is arbitrary or capricious if, for example, the agency changed its prior policy without justification or entirely failed to consider a relevant factor. When an agency's action is arbitrary or capricious, a court can hold it to be unlawful and set it aside.

In this problem, the agency departed from its prior policy without explanation. That policy was to consider an applicant's understanding of what information a question was asking for before determining whether the applicant's answer was false. Manin argued that he had not known he was required to report convictions for minor misdemeanors. For policy reasons, the agency should have allowed him to present evidence that he did not know the statements he made on his application were false. But the agency refused to consider this argument and revoked his certification.

In the actual case on which this problem is based, the court held that the agency's action had been arbitrary and capricious.

38–4. Sample Answer—Price Discrimination.

Spa Steel satisfies most of the requirements for a price discrimination claim under Section 2 of the Clayton Act. Dayton Superior is engaged in interstate commerce, and it sells goods of like grade and quality to at least three purchasers. Moreover, Spa Steel can show that, because it sells Dayton Superior's products at a higher price, it lost business and thus suffered an injury. To recover, however, Spa Steel will also need to prove that Dayton Superior charged Spa Steel's competitors a lower price for the same product. Spa Steel cannot recover if its prices were higher for reasons related to its own business, such as having higher overhead or seeking a larger profit.

39–5. Sample Answer—Deceptive Advertising.

Yes. Ross can be held personally liable for a violation of the Federal Trade Commission Act's prohibition of deceptive acts or practices. Generally, deceptive advertising occurs if a reasonable consumer would be misled by the advertising claim. Advertising that appears to be based on factual evidence but that in fact cannot be supported will be deemed deceptive. An individual can be held personally liable under the act if the person (1) participated directly in the deceptive practices or had the authority to control them and (2) had or should have had knowledge of them.

In this problem, the facts indicate that IMI's ads were deceptive. Consumers were misled by the ads, which appeared to be based on factual evidence but were not supportable—the ads claimed that a scan of the consumers' computers had detected dangerous files, such as viruses, when in fact no scans were conducted. The issue is whether Ross can be held individually liable for these violations. She was an IMI co-founder and vice president, reviewed and edited the ads, and was aware of the many complaints

about them. Thus, under the Federal Trade Commission Act, Ross met the standard for personal liability—she knew of the deceptive practices, she had the authority to control them, and she directly participated in them.

In the actual case on which this problem is based, the Federal Trade Commission filed a suit against Ross, and a federal district court held her jointly and severally liable. On appeal, the U.S. Court of Appeals for the Fourth Circuit affirmed.

40–6. Sample Answer—Potential Liability to Third Parties.

KPMG is potentially liable to the hedge funds' partners under the *Restatement (Third) of Torts*. Under Section 552 of the *Restatement,* an auditor owes a duty to "persons for whose benefit and guidance the accountant intends to supply . . . information."

In this case, KPMG prepared annual reports on the hedge funds and addressed them to the funds' "Partners." Additionally, KPMG knew who the partners were because it prepared individual tax forms for them each year. Thus, KPMG's annual reports were for the partners' benefit and guidance. The partners relied on the reports, including representations that they complied with generally accepted accounting principles. As a result, they lost millions of dollars, which exposes KPMG to possible liability under Section 552.

41–7. Sample Answer—Duties of the Bailee.

KZY owed Mrs. Ressler's a duty to exercise reasonable care. A bailee must exercise reasonable care in preserving bailed property. What constitutes reasonable care depends on the nature and circumstances of the bailment. A bailment for the mutual benefit of the bailee and the bailor involves compensation. Here, the bailee must exercise ordinary care—the care that a reasonably careful person would use under the circumstances. If the bailee fails to exercise reasonable care, he or she will be liable for ordinary negligence. If bailed property is returned damaged, a bailee will be presumed to have been negligent. The bailee is excused, however, if the property was damaged through no fault of the bailee.

In this problem, KZY transported a load of Mrs. Ressler's Food Products. When it delivered the cargo, the customer rejected it because its temperature was higher than expected, making it unsafe. In Mrs. Ressler's suit against KZY, the defendant asserted that the temperature in its refrigerated trailer was proper and that Mrs. Ressler's had delivered a "hot" product for transport. KZY provided temperature readings from the refrigerated unit during the time in question. This would be a complete defense to a claim that the bailee was negligent in failing to maintain a proper temperature during the transport.

In the actual case on which this problem is based, KZY failed to file a timely response to Mrs. Ressler's suit, and the trial court entered a default judgment against the defendant. The U.S. Court of Appeals for the Third Circuit reversed the lower court's decision. "KZY alleged a *prima facie* meritorious defense to the action" and "there was no direct evidence that KZY acted in bad faith."

42–6. Sample Answer—Joint Tenancies.

Under the law of the Cayman Islands, and according to Arthur's will, the three disputed Cayman properties became Diana's sole property when Arthur died. In a joint tenancy, each of two or more persons owns an undivided interest in the property. A deceased joint tenant's interest passes to the surviving joint tenant or tenants. The right of a surviving joint tenant to inherit a deceased joint tenant's ownership interest is referred to as a right of survivorship.

In this problem, Arthur and Diana owned three properties in the Cayman Islands in joint tenancy. (For this purpose, Cayman law is the same as U.S. law.) When the couple divorced, the decree did not change the tenancy. Later, Arthur died. His will provided that any property he held in joint tenancy "will pass to the survivor, and I instruct my Personal Representative to make no claim thereto." Despite this provision, his brother Curtis, personal representative of his estate, asserted that Arthur's interest in the properties was part of the estate. Diana said that the properties were entirely hers. Clearly, Diana was correct. Under the applicable principles of ownership of property by joint tenancy, as well as under the terms of Arthur's will, his interest passed to her.

In the actual case on which this problem is based, Curtis asked the Florida state court that issued the couple's divorce decree to declare that Arthur's interest in the Cayman properties was part of his estate. The court ruled in the estate's favor and ordered Diana to sell the properties or buy Arthur's interest in them. A state intermediate appellate court reversed the order.

43–6. Sample Answer—Wills.

No. The document that Walker signed was not a valid will. A will is a person's final declaration of how his or her property is to be disposed of after death. It is a formal instrument that must follow exactly the requirements of state law. These formalities are intended to help prevent fraud. Unless they are followed, the will is void. Generally, a will must be attested to by two or three witnesses in a specified manner. The testator typically must either sign the will in the witnesses' presence or acknowledge that the signature on the document is his or hers. In some states, at the signing, the testator must declare that the document is his or her will.

Here, Andrew told Nora that he wished to change the disposition of his property provided for in a prior will by devising half of it to her in a new will. She noted his wish and took her notes to the office of attorney Meagher to have the document drafted. Meagher did not see Nora's notes, he did not talk to Walker, no one from his office was present at the signing of the document, and, when Walker signed it, he did not declare that it was his will, as required by state law. These facts indicate that formalities required by state law for the execution of a will were not followed strictly, undercutting the validity of the document as a will.

In the actual case on which this problem is based, Nora submitted this document to a New York state court as Walker's will. His children objected. The court denied the admission of the will to probate. "In light of the uncertainty surrounding the [will's] drafting and execution," a state intermediate appellate court affirmed.

A

Abandoned Property Property that has been discarded by the owner, who has no intention of reclaiming it.

Acceleration Clause A clause that allows a payee or other holder of a time instrument to demand payment of the entire amount due, with interest, if a certain event occurs, such as a default in the payment of an installment when due.

Acceptance The act of voluntarily agreeing, through words or conduct, to the terms of an offer, thereby creating a contract. In negotiable instruments law, a drawee's signed agreement to pay a draft when it is presented.

Acceptor A drawee that accepts, or promises to pay, an instrument when it is presented later for payment.

Accession The addition of value to personal property by the use of labor or materials.

Accord and Satisfaction A common means of settling a disputed claim, whereby a debtor offers to pay a lesser amount than the creditor purports to be owed.

Accredited Investor In the context of securities offerings, sophisticated investors, such as banks, insurance companies, investment companies, the issuer's executive officers and directors, and persons whose income or net worth exceeds certain limits.

Actionable Capable of serving as the basis of a lawsuit. An actionable claim can be pursued in a lawsuit or other court action.

Act of State Doctrine A doctrine providing that the judicial branch of one country will not examine the validity of public acts committed by a recognized foreign government within its own territory.

Actual Malice The deliberate intent to cause harm that exists when a person makes a statement with either knowledge of its falsity or reckless disregard of the truth. It is required to establish defamation against public figures.

Actus Reus A guilty (prohibited) act. It is one of the two essential elements required to establish criminal liability.

Adequate Protection Doctrine A doctrine that protects secured creditors from losing the value of their security (because the collateral depreciates, for instance) as a result of an automatic stay in a bankruptcy proceeding.

Adhesion Contract A standard-form contract in which the stronger party dictates the terms.

Adjudication A proceeding in which an administrative law judge hears and decides issues that arise when an administrative agency charges a person or a firm with an agency violation.

Administrative Agency A federal or state government agency established to perform a specific function.

Administrative Law The body of law created by administrative agencies in order to carry out their duties and responsibilities.

Administrative Law Judge (ALJ) One who presides over an administrative agency hearing and has the power to administer oaths, take testimony, rule on questions of evidence, and make determinations of fact.

Administrative Process The procedure used by administrative agencies in fulfilling their basic functions: rulemaking, enforcement, and adjudication.

Administrator One who is appointed by a court to administer a person's estate if the decedent died without a valid will or if the executor named in the will cannot serve.

Adverse Possession The acquisition of title to real property through open occupation, without the consent of the owner, for a period of time specified by a state statute. The occupation must be actual, exclusive, open, continuous, and in opposition to all others, including the owner.

Affirmative Action Job-hiring policies that give special consideration to members of protected classes in an effort to overcome present effects of past discrimination.

After-Acquired Property Property that is acquired by the debtor after the execution of a security agreement.

Agency A relationship between two parties in which one party (the agent) agrees to represent or act for the other (the principal).

Agency Coupled with an Interest An agency, created for the benefit of the agent, in which the agent has some legal right (interest) in the property that is the subject of the agency

Age of Majority The age (eighteen years, in most states) at which a person, formerly a minor, is recognized by law as an adult and is legally responsible for his or her actions.

Agreement A mutual understanding or meeting of the minds between two or more individuals regarding the terms of a contract.

Alien Corporation A corporation formed in another country but doing business in the United States.

Alienation The transfer of title to real property (which "alienates" the real property from the former owner).

Allege To state, recite, assert, or charge.

Alternative Dispute Resolution (ADR) The resolution of disputes in ways other than those involved in the traditional judicial process, such as negotiation, mediation, and arbitration.

Answer Procedurally, a defendant's response to the plaintiff's complaint.

Anticipatory Repudiation An assertion or action by a party indicating that he or she will not perform a contractual obligation.

Antitrust Law Laws protecting commerce from unlawful restraints and anticompetitive practices.

Apparent Authority Authority that is only apparent, not real. An agent's apparent authority arises when the principal causes a third party to believe that the agent has authority, even though she or he does not.

Appraisal Right The right of a dissenting shareholder, who objects to a merger or consolidation of the corporation, to have his or her shares appraised and to be paid the fair value of those shares by the corporation.

Appropriation In tort law, the use by one person of another person's name, likeness, or other identifying characteristic without permission and for the benefit of the user.

Arbitration Clause A clause in a contract that provides that, in the event of a dispute, the parties will submit the dispute to arbitration rather than litigate the dispute in court.

Arbitration The settling of a dispute by submitting it to a disinterested third party (other than a court), who renders a decision.

Arson The intentional burning of a building.

Articles of Incorporation The document that is filed with the appropriate state official, usually the secretary of state, when a business is incorporated and that contains basic information about the corporation.

Articles of Organization The document filed with a designated state official by which a limited liability company is formed.

Articles of Partnership A written agreement that sets forth each partner's rights and obligations with respect to the partnership.

Artisan's Lien A possessory lien held by a party who has made improvements and added value to the personal property of another party as security for payment for services performed.

Assault Any word or action intended to make another person fearful of immediate physical harm—a reasonably believable threat.

Assignee A party to whom the rights under a contract are transferred, or assigned.

Assignment The transfer to another of all or part of one's rights arising under a contract.

Assignor A party who transfers (assigns) his or her rights under a contract to another party (the *assignee*).

Assumption of Risk A defense to negligence that bars a plaintiff from recovering for injuries or damage suffered as a result of risks he or she knew of and voluntarily assumed.

Attachment In a secured transaction, the process by which a secured creditor's interest "attaches" to the collateral and the creditor's security interest becomes enforceable.

Attempted Monopolization An action by a firm that involves anticompetitive conduct, the intent to gain monopoly power, and a "dangerous probability" of success in achieving monopoly power.

Auditor An accountant qualified to perform audits (systematic inspections) of a business's financial records.

Authenticate To sign, execute, or adopt any symbol on an electronic record that verifies the intent to adopt or accept the record.

Authorization Card A card signed by an employee that gives a union permission to act on his or her behalf in negotiations with management.

Automatic Stay In bankruptcy proceedings, the suspension of almost all litigation and other actions by creditors against the debtor or the debtor's property. The stay is effective the moment the debtor files a petition in bankruptcy.

Award The monetary compensation given to a party at the end of a trial or other proceeding.

B

Bailee One to whom goods are entrusted by a bailor.

Bailee's Lien A possessory (artisan's) lien that a bailee entitled to compensation can place on the bailed property to ensure that he or she will be paid for the services provided.

Bailment A situation in which the personal property of one person (a bailor) is entrusted to another (a bailee), who is obligated to return the bailed property to the bailor or dispose of it as directed.

Bailor One who entrusts goods to a bailee.

Bait-and-Switch Advertising Advertising a product at an attractive price and then telling the consumer that the advertised product is not available or is of poor quality and encouraging her or him to purchase a more expensive item.

Bankruptcy Court A federal court of limited jurisdiction that handles only bankruptcy proceedings, which are governed by federal bankruptcy law.

Bankruptcy Trustee A person appointed by the court to manage the debtor's funds.

Battery Physical contact with another that is unexcused, harmful or offensive, and intentionally performed.

Bearer A person in possession of an instrument payable to bearer or indorsed in blank.

Bearer Instrument Any instrument that is not payable to a specific person, including instruments payable to bearer or to cash.

Benefit Corporation A for-profit corporation that seeks to have a material positive impact on society and the environment. It is available by statute in a number of states.

Bequest A gift of personal property by will (from the verb *to bequeath*).

Beyond a Reasonable Doubt The standard of proof used in criminal cases.

Bilateral Contract A type of contract that arises when a promise is given in exchange for a return promise.

Bilateral Mistake A mistake that occurs when both parties to a contract are mistaken about the same material fact.

Bill of Rights The first ten amendments to the U.S. Constitution.

Binder A written, temporary insurance policy.

Binding Authority Any source of law that a court *must* follow when deciding a case.

Blank Indorsement An indorsement on an instrument that specifies no indorsee. An order instrument that is indorsed in blank becomes a bearer instrument.

Bona Fide Occupational Qualification (BFOQ) An identifiable characteristic reasonably necessary to the normal operation of a particular business. Such characteristics can include gender, national origin, and religion, but not race.

Bond A security that evidences a corporate (or government) debt.

Botnet A network of compromised computers connected to the Internet that can be used to generate spam, relay viruses, or cause servers to fail.

Breach of Contract The failure, without legal excuse, of a promisor to perform the obligations of a contract.

Brief A written summary or statement prepared by one side in a lawsuit to explain its case to the judge.

Browse-Wrap Term A term or condition of use that is presented when an online buyer downloads a product but to which the buyer does not have to agree before installing or using the product.

Bureaucracy The organizational structure, consisting of government bureaus and agencies, through which the government implements and enforces the laws.

Burglary The unlawful entry or breaking into a building with the intent to commit a felony.

Business Ethics The application of moral principles and values in a business context.

Business Invitee A person, such as a customer or a client, who is invited onto business premises by the owner of those premises for business purposes.

Business Judgment Rule A rule under which courts will not hold corporate officers and directors liable for honest mistakes of judgment and bad business decisions that were made in good faith.

Business Necessity A defense to an allegation of employment discrimination in which the employer demonstrates that an employment practice that discriminates against members of a protected class is related to job performance.

Business Tort Wrongful interference with another's business rights and relationships.

Business Trust A form of business organization, created by a written trust agreement, that resembles a corporation. Legal ownership and management of the trust's property stay with the trustees, and the profits are distributed to the beneficiaries, who have limited liability.

Buyer in the Ordinary Course of Business A buyer who, in good faith and without knowledge that the sale violates the ownership rights or security interest of a third party in the goods, purchases goods in the ordinary course of business from a person in the business of selling goods of that kind.

Buyout Price The amount payable to a partner on his or her dissociation from a partnership, based on the amount distributable to that partner if the partnership had been wound up on that date and offset by any damages for wrongful dissociation.

Buy-Sell Agreement An agreement made at the time of partnership formation providing for one or more of the partners to buy out the other or others, in the event the firm is dissolved. It is also called a *buyout agreement.*

Bylaws The internal rules of management adopted by a corporation at its first organizational meeting.

C

Case Law The rules of law announced in court decisions. Case law interprets statutes, regulations, and constitutional provisions, and governs all areas not covered by statutory or administrative law.

Case on Point A previous case involving factual circumstances and issues that are similar to those in the case before the court.

Cashier's Check A check drawn by a bank on itself.

Categorical Imperative An ethical guideline developed by Immanuel Kant under which an action is evaluated in terms of what would happen if everybody else in the same situation, or category, acted the same way.

Causation in Fact An act or omission without which an event would not have occurred.

Cease-and-Desist Order An administrative or judicial order prohibiting a person or business firm from conducting activities that an agency or court has deemed illegal.

Certificate of Deposit (CD) A note issued by a bank in which the bank acknowledges the receipt of funds from a party and promises to repay that amount, with interest, to the party on a certain date.

Certificate of Limited Partnership The document that must be filed with a designated state official to form a limited partnership.

Certification Mark A mark used by one or more persons, other than the owner, to certify the region, materials, mode of manufacture, quality, or other characteristic of specific goods or services.

Certified Check A check that has been accepted in writing by the bank on which it is drawn. By certifying (accepting) the check, the bank promises to pay the check at the time it is presented.

Charging Order In partnership law, an order granted by a court to a judgment creditor that entitles the creditor to attach a partner's interest in the partnership.

Charitable Trust A trust in which the property held by the trustee must be used for a charitable purpose, such as the advancement of health, education, or religion.

Chattel Personal property.

Check A draft drawn by a drawer ordering the drawee bank or financial institution to pay a certain amount of funds to the payee on demand.

Checks and Balances The system under which the powers of the national government are divided among three separate branches—the executive, legislative, and judicial branches—each of which exercises a check on the actions of the others.

Choice-of-Law Clause A clause in a contract designating the law (such as the law of a particular state or nation) that will govern the contract.

Citation A reference to a publication in which a legal authority—such as a statute or a court decision—or other source can be found.

Civil Law The branch of law dealing with the definition and enforcement of all private or public rights, as opposed to criminal matters.

Civil Law System A system of law derived from Roman law that is based on codified laws (rather than on case precedents).

Clearinghouse A system or place where banks exchange checks and drafts drawn on each other and settle daily balances.

Click-On Agreement An agreement that arises when an online buyer clicks on "I agree" or otherwise indicates her or his assent to be bound by the terms of an offer.

Close Corporation A corporation whose shareholders are limited to a small group of persons, often family members.

Closed Shop A firm that requires union membership as a condition of employment.

Cloud Computing The delivery to users of on-demand services from third-party servers over a network.

Codicil A written supplement or modification to a will. A codicil must be executed with the same formalities as a will.

Collateral Under Article 9 of the UCC, the property subject to a security interest.

Collateral Promise A secondary promise to a primary transaction, such as a promise made by one person to pay the debts of another if the latter fails to perform. A collateral promise normally must be in writing to be enforceable.

Collecting Bank Any bank handling an item for collection, except the payor bank.

Collective Bargaining The process by which labor and management negotiate the terms and conditions of employment, including working hours and workplace conditions.

Collective Mark A mark used by members of a cooperative, association, union, or other organization to certify the region, materials, mode of manufacture, quality, or other characteristic of specific goods or services.

Comity The principle by which one nation defers to and gives effect to the laws and judicial decrees of another nation. This recognition is based primarily on respect.

Commerce Clause The provision in Article I, Section 8, of the U.S. Constitution that gives Congress the power to regulate interstate commerce.

Commercial Impracticability A doctrine that may excuse the duty to perform a contract when performance becomes much more difficult or costly due to forces that neither party could control or foresee at the time the contract was formed.

Commingle To mix funds or goods together to such a degree that they no longer have separate identities.

Common Law The body of law developed from custom or judicial decisions in English and U.S. courts, not attributable to a legislature.

Common Stock Shares of ownership in a corporation that give the owner a proportionate interest in the corporation with regard to control, earnings, and net assets. Common stock is lowest in priority with respect to payment of dividends and distribution of the corporation's assets on dissolution.

Community Property A form of concurrent property ownership in which each spouse owns an undivided one-half interest in property acquired during the marriage.

Comparative Negligence A rule in tort law, used in the majority of states, that reduces the plaintiff's recovery in proportion to the plaintiff's degree of fault, rather than barring recovery completely.

Compelling Government Interest A test of constitutionality that requires the government to have convincing reasons for passing any law that restricts fundamental rights, such as free speech, or distinguishes between people based on a suspect trait.

Compensatory Damages A monetary award equivalent to the actual value of injuries or damage sustained by the aggrieved party.

Complaint The pleading made by a plaintiff alleging wrongdoing on the part of the defendant. When filed with a court, the complaint initiates a lawsuit.

Computer Crime Any violation of criminal law that involves knowledge of computer technology for its perpetration, investigation, or prosecution.

Concentrated Industry An industry in which a single firm or a small number of firms control a large percentage of market sales.

Concurrent Conditions Conditions that must occur or be performed at the same time—they are mutually dependent. No obligations arise until these conditions are simultaneously performed.

Concurrent Jurisdiction Jurisdiction that exists when two different courts have the power to hear a case.

Concurrent Ownership Joint ownership.

Concurring Opinion A court opinion by one or more judges or justices who agree with the majority but want to make or emphasize a point that was not made or emphasized in the majority's opinion.

Condemnation Proceedings The judicial procedure by which the government exercises its power of eminent domain. It generally involves two phases: a taking and a determination of fair value.

Condition A qualification, provision, or clause in a contractual agreement, the occurrence or nonoccurrence of which creates, suspends, or terminates the obligations of the contracting parties.

Condition Precedent A condition in a contract that must be met before a party's promise becomes absolute.

Condition Subsequent A condition in a contract that, if it occurs, operates to terminate a party's absolute promise to perform.

Confiscation A government's taking of a privately owned business or personal property without a proper public purpose or an award of just compensation.

Conforming Goods Goods that conform to contract specifications.

Confusion The mixing together of goods belonging to two or more owners to such an extent that the separately owned goods cannot be identified.

Consequential Damages Foreseeable damages that result from a party's breach of contract but are caused by special circumstances beyond the contract itself.

Consideration The value given in return for a promise or performance in a contractual agreement.

Consolidation The legal combination of two or more corporations in such a way that the original corporations cease to exist, and a new corporation emerges with all their assets and liabilities.

Constitutional Law The body of law derived from the U.S. Constitution and the constitutions of the various states.

Constructive Delivery A symbolic delivery of property that cannot be physically delivered.

Constructive Discharge A termination of employment brought about by making the employee's working conditions so intolerable that the employee reasonably feels compelled to leave.

Constructive Eviction A form of eviction that occurs when a landlord fails to perform adequately any of the duties required by the lease, thereby making the tenant's further use and enjoyment of the property exceedingly difficult or impossible.

Constructive Fraud Conduct that is treated as fraud under the law even when there is no proof of intent to defraud, usually because of the existence of a special relationship or fiduciary duty.

Constructive Trust An equitable trust that is imposed in the interests of fairness and justice when someone wrongfully holds legal title to property.

Consumer-Debtor One whose debts result primarily from the purchase of goods for personal, family, or household use.

Continuation Statement A statement that, if filed within six months prior to the expiration date of the original financing statement, continues the perfection of the security interest for another five years.

Contract A set of promises constituting an agreement between parties, giving each a legal duty to the other and the right to seek a remedy for the breach of the promises or duties.

Contractual Capacity The capacity required by the law for a party who enters into a contract to be bound by that contract.

Contributory Negligence A rule in tort law, used in only a few states, that completely bars the plaintiff from recovering any damages if the harm suffered is partly the plaintiff's own fault.

Conversion Wrongfully taking or retaining possession of an individual's personal property and placing it in the service of another.

Conveyance The transfer of title to real property from one person to another by deed or other document.

Cookie A small file sent from a website and stored in a user's Web browser to track the user's Web browsing activities.

"Cooling-Off" Laws Laws that allow buyers of goods sold in certain transactions to cancel their contracts within three business days.

Cooperative An association, which may or may not be incorporated, that is organized to provide an economic service to its members. Unincorporated cooperatives are often treated like partnerships for tax and other legal purposes.

Copyright The exclusive right of an author or originator of a literary or artistic production to publish, print, sell, or otherwise use that production for a statutory period of time.

Corporate Governance A set of policies specifying the rights and responsibilities of the various participants in a corporation and spelling out the rules and procedures for making corporate decisions.

Corporate Social Responsibility (CSR) The idea that corporations can and should act ethically and be accountable to society for their actions.

Corporation A legal entity formed in compliance with statutory requirements that is distinct from its shareholder-owners.

Cost-Benefit Analysis A decision-making technique that involves weighing the costs of a given action against the benefits of that action.

Co-Surety A party who assumes liability jointly with another surety for the payment of a debtor's obligation under a suretyship arrangement.

Counteradvertising New advertising that is undertaken to correct earlier false claims that were made about a product.

Counterclaim A claim made by a defendant in a civil lawsuit against the plaintiff. In effect, the defendant is suing the plaintiff.

Counteroffer An offeree's response to an offer in which the offeree rejects the original offer and at the same time makes a new offer.

Course of Dealing Prior conduct between the parties to a contract that establishes a common basis for their understanding.

Course of Performance The conduct that occurs under the terms of a particular agreement, which indicates what the parties to that agreement intended the agreement to mean.

Covenant Not to Compete A contractual promise of one party to refrain from conducting business similar to that of another party for a certain period of time and within a specified geographical area.

Covenant Not to Sue An agreement to substitute a contractual obligation for another legal action based on a valid claim.

Cover A remedy that allows the buyer or lessee, on the seller's or lessor's breach, to obtain substitute goods from another seller or lessor.

Cram-Down Provision A provision of the Bankruptcy Code that allows a court to confirm a debtor's Chapter 11 reorganization plan even though only one class of creditors has accepted it.

Creditors' Composition Agreement A contract between a debtor and his or her creditors in which the creditors agree to discharge the debts on the debtor's payment of a sum less than the amount actually owed.

Crime A wrong against society proclaimed in a statute and, if committed, punishable by society through fines, imprisonment, or death.

Criminal Law The branch of law that defines and punishes wrongful actions committed against the public.

Cross-Collateralization The use of an asset that is not the subject of a loan to collateralize that loan.

Crowdfunding A cooperative activity in which people network and pool funds and other resources via the Internet to assist a cause (such as disaster relief) or invest in a venture (business).

Cure The right of a party who tenders nonconforming performance to correct his or her performance within the contract period.

Cyber Crime A crime that occurs in the online environment.

Cyber Fraud Any misrepresentation knowingly made over the Internet with the intention of deceiving another for the purpose of obtaining property or funds.

Cyberlaw An informal term used to refer to all laws governing electronic communications and transactions, particularly those conducted via the Internet.

Cybersquatting The act of registering a domain name that is the same as, or confusingly similar to, the trademark of another and then offering to sell that domain name back to the trademark owner.

Cyberterrorist Criminals who use technology and the Internet to cause fear, violence, and extreme financial harm.

Cyber Tort A tort committed via the Internet.

D

Damages A monetary award sought as a remedy for a breach of contract or a tortious action.

Debtor in Possession (DIP) In Chapter 11 bankruptcy proceedings, a debtor who is allowed to continue in possession of the business and to continue business operations.

Debtor Under Article 9 of the UCC, any party who owes payment or performance of a secured obligation.

Deceptive Advertising Advertising that misleads consumers, either by making unjustified claims about a product or by omitting a material fact concerning the product.

Deed A document by which title to real property is passed.

Defalcation Embezzlement or misappropriation of funds.

Defamation Anything published or publicly spoken that causes injury to another's good name, reputation, or character.

Default Failure to pay a debt when it is due.

Default Judgment A judgment entered by a court against a defendant who has failed to appear in court to answer or defend against the plaintiff's claim.

Defendant One against whom a lawsuit is brought or the accused person in a criminal proceeding.

Defense A reason offered by a defendant in an action or lawsuit as to why the plaintiff should not recover or establish what she or he seeks.

Deficiency Judgment A judgment against a debtor for the amount of a debt remaining unpaid after the collateral has been repossessed and sold.

Delegatee A party to whom contractual obligations are transferred, or delegated.

Delegation Doctrine A doctrine, based on the U.S. Constitution, which has been construed to allow Congress to delegate some of its power to make and implement laws to administrative agencies.

Delegation of Duties The transfer to another of a contractual duty.

Delegator A party who transfers (delegates) her or his obligations under a contract to another party (the *delegatee*).

Depositary Bank The first bank to receive a check for payment.

Deposition The testimony of a party to a lawsuit or a witness taken under oath before a trial.

Destination Contract A contract for the sale of goods in which the seller is required or authorized to ship the goods by carrier and tender delivery of the goods at a particular destination. The seller assumes liability for any losses or damage to the goods until they are tendered at the destination specified in the contract.

Devise A gift of real property by will, or the act of giving real property by will.

Devisee One designated in a will to receive a gift of real property.

Disaffirmance The legal avoidance, or setting aside, of a contractual obligation.

Discharge The termination of an obligation, such as occurs when the parties to a contract have fully performed their contractual obligations. In bankruptcy proceedings, the termination of a debtor's obligation to pay debts.

Disclosed Principal A principal whose identity is known to a third party at the time the agent makes a contract with the third party.

Discovery A method by which the opposing parties obtain information from each other to prepare for trial.

Dishonor To refuse to pay or to accept a negotiable instrument that has been presented in a timely and proper manner.

Disparagement of Property An economically injurious falsehood about another's product or property.

Disparate-Impact Discrimination Discrimination that results from certain employer practices or procedures that, although not discriminatory on their face, have a discriminatory effect.

Disparate-Treatment Discrimination A form of employment discrimination that results when an employer intentionally discriminates against employees who are members of protected classes.

Dissenting Opinion A court opinion that presents the views of one or more judges or justices who disagree with the majority's decision.

Dissociation The severance of the relationship between a partner and a partnership.

Dissolution The formal disbanding of a corporation.

Dissolution The formal disbanding of a partnership or a corporation. Partnerships can be dissolved by acts of the partners, by operation of law, or by judicial decree.

Distributed Network A network that can be used by persons located (distributed) around the country or the globe to share computer files.

Distribution Agreement A contract between a seller and a distributor of the seller's products setting out the terms and conditions of the distributorship.

Diversity of Citizenship A basis for federal court jurisdiction over a lawsuit between citizens of different states or a lawsuit involving a U.S. citizen and a citizen of a different country.

Divestiture A company's sale of one or more of its divisions' operating functions under court order as part of the enforcement of the antitrust laws.

Dividend A distribution of corporate profits to the corporation's shareholders in proportion to the number of shares held.

Docket The list of cases entered on a court's calendar and thus scheduled to be heard by the court.

Document of Title A paper exchanged in the regular course of business that evidences the right to possession of goods (for example, a bill of lading or a warehouse receipt).

Domain Name The series of letters and symbols used to identify a site operator on the Internet (an Internet address).

Domestic Corporation In a given state, a corporation that is organized under the law of that state.

Dominion Ownership rights in property, including the right to possess and control the property.

Double Jeopardy The Fifth Amendment requirement that prohibits a person from being tried twice for the same criminal offense.

Draft Any instrument drawn on a drawee that orders the drawee to pay a certain amount of funds, usually to a third party (the payee), on demand or at a definite future time.

Dram Shop Act A state statute that imposes liability on bar owners, as well as bartenders and social hosts who serve alcohol, for injuries resulting from accidents caused by intoxicated persons when the sellers or servers of alcoholic drinks contributed to the intoxication.

Drawee The party that is ordered to pay a draft or check. With a check, a bank or a financial institution is always the drawee.

Drawer The party that initiates a draft (such as a check), thereby ordering the drawee to pay.

Due Diligence A required standard of care that certain professionals, such as accountants, must meet to avoid liability for securities violations.

Due Process Clause The provisions in the Fifth and Fourteenth Amendments that guarantee that no person shall be deprived of life, liberty, or property without due process of law. State constitutions often include similar clauses.

Dumping The sale of goods in a foreign country at a price below the price charged for the same goods in the domestic market.

Duress Unlawful pressure brought to bear on a person, causing the person to perform an act that she or he would not otherwise perform.

Duty-Based Ethics An ethical philosophy rooted in the idea that every person (and every business) has certain duties to others, including both humans and the planet.

Duty of Care The duty of all persons, as established by tort law, to exercise a reasonable amount of care in their dealings with others. Failure to exercise due care, which is normally determined by the reasonable person standard, constitutes the tort of negligence.

E

Easement A nonpossessory right, established by express or implied agreement, to make limited use of another's property without removing anything from the property.

E-Contract A contract that is formed electronically.

E-Evidence A type of evidence that consists of computer-generated or electronically recorded information.

Electronic Fund Transfer (EFT) A transfer of funds through the use of an electronic terminal, smartphone, tablet, telephone, or computer.

Emancipation In regard to minors, the act of being freed from parental control.

Embezzlement The fraudulent appropriation of funds or other property by a person who was entrusted with the funds or property.

Eminent Domain The power of a government to take land from private citizens for public use on the payment of just compensation.

E-Money Prepaid funds stored on microchips in laptops, smartphones, tablets, and other devices.

Employment at Will A common law doctrine under which either party may terminate an employment relationship at any time for any reason, unless it would violate a contract or statute.

Employment Contract A contract between an employer and an employee in which the terms and conditions of employment are stated.

Enabling Legislation A statute enacted by Congress that authorizes the creation of an administrative agency and specifies the name, composition, and powers of the agency.

Entrapment A defense in which a defendant claims that he or she was induced by a public official to commit a crime that he or she would otherwise not have committed.

Entrepreneur One who initiates and assumes the financial risk of a new business enterprise and undertakes to provide or control its management.

Entrustment Rule The rule that entrusting goods to a merchant who deals in goods of that kind gives that merchant the power to transfer those goods and all rights to them to a buyer in the ordinary course of business.

Environmental Impact Statement (EIS) A formal analysis required for any major federal action that will significantly affect the quality of the environment to determine the action's impact and explore alternatives.

Equal Dignity Rule A rule requiring that an agent's authority be in writing if the contract to be made on behalf of the principal must be in writing.

Equal Protection Clause The provision in the Fourteenth Amendment that requires state governments to treat similarly situated individuals in a similar manner.

Equitable Maxims General propositions or principles of law that have to do with fairness (equity).

E-Signature An electronic sound, symbol, or process attached to or logically associated with a record and adopted by a person with the intent to sign the record.

Establishment Clause The provision in the First Amendment that prohibits the government from establishing any state-sponsored religion or enacting any law that promotes religion or favors one religion over another.

Estate in Bankruptcy All of the property owned by a person, including real estate and personal property.

Estopped Barred, impeded, or precluded.

Estray Statute A statute defining finders' rights in property when the true owners are unknown.

Ethical Reasoning A reasoning process in which an individual links his or her moral convictions or ethical standards to the situation at hand.

Ethics Moral principles and values applied to social behavior.

Eviction A landlord's act of depriving a tenant of possession of the leased premises.

Exclusionary Rule A rule that prevents evidence that is obtained illegally or without a proper search warrant from being admissible in court.

Exclusive-Dealing Contract An agreement under which a seller forbids a buyer to purchase products from the seller's competitors.

Exclusive Jurisdiction Jurisdiction that exists when a case can be heard only in a particular court or type of court.

Exculpatory Clause A clause that releases a contractual party from liability in the event of monetary or physical injury, no matter who is at fault.

Executed Contract A contract that has been fully performed by both parties.

Execution The implementation of a court's decree or judgment.

Executor A person appointed by a testator in a will to administer her or his estate.

Executory Contract A contract that has not yet been fully performed.

Exhaustion Doctrine In administrative law, the principle that a complaining party normally must have exhausted all available administrative remedies before seeking judicial review.

Export The sale of goods and services by domestic firms to buyers located in other countries.

Express Contract A contract in which the terms of the agreement are stated in words, oral or written.

Express Warranty A seller's or lessor's promise as to the quality, condition, description, or performance of the goods being sold or leased.

Expropriation A government's seizure of a privately owned business or personal property for a proper public purpose and with just compensation.

Extension Clause A clause in a time instrument that allows the instrument's date of maturity to be extended into the future.

Extrinsic Evidence Any evidence not contained in the contract itself, which may include the testimony of the parties, additional agreements or communications, or other information relevant to determining the parties' intent.

F

Federal Form of Government A system of government in which the states form a union and the sovereign power is divided between the central government and the member states.

Federal Question A question that pertains to the U.S. Constitution, an act of Congress, or a treaty and provides a basis for federal jurisdiction in a case.

Federal Reserve System A network of twelve district banks and related branches located around the country and headed by the Federal Reserve Board of Governors. Most banks in the United States have Federal Reserve accounts.

Fee Simple An ownership interest in land in which the owner has the greatest possible aggregation of rights, privileges, and power.

Felony A serious crime—such as arson, murder, rape, or robbery—that carries the most severe sanctions, ranging from more than one year in a state or federal prison to the death penalty.

Fictitious Payee A payee on a negotiable instrument whom the maker or drawer did not intend to have an interest in the instrument. Indorsements by fictitious payees are treated as authorized indorsements under UCC Article 3.

Fiduciary As a noun, a person having a duty created by his or her undertaking to act primarily for another's benefit in matters connected with the undertaking. As an adjective, a relationship founded on trust and confidence.

Filtering Software A computer program that is designed to block access to certain websites, based on their content. The software blocks the retrieval of a site whose URL or key words are on a list within the program.

Final Order The final decision of an administrative agency on an issue.

Financing Statement A document filed by a secured creditor with the appropriate official to give notice to the public of the creditor's security interest in collateral belonging to the debtor named in the statement.

Firm Offer An offer (by a merchant) that is irrevocable without the necessity of consideration for a stated period of time or, if no definite period is stated, for a reasonable time (neither period to exceed three months).

Fixed-Term Tenancy A type of tenancy under which property is leased for a specified period of time, such as a month, a year, or a period of years. It is also called a *tenancy for years.*

Fixture An item of personal property that has become so closely associated with real property that it is legally regarded as part of that real property.

Floating Lien A security interest in proceeds, after-acquired property, or collateral subject to future advances by the secured party (or all three). The security interest is retained even when the collateral changes in character, classification, or location.

Forbearance The act of refraining from an action that one has a legal right to undertake.

Foreign Corporation In a given state, a corporation that does business in that state but is not incorporated there.

Forgery The fraudulent making or altering of any writing in a way that changes the legal rights and liabilities of another.

Formal Contract An agreement that by law requires a specific form for its validity.

Forum-Selection Clause A provision in a contract designating the court, jurisdiction, or tribunal that will decide any disputes arising under the contract.

Franchise Any arrangement in which the owner of a trademark, trade name, or copyright licenses another to use that trademark, trade name, or copyright in the selling of goods or services.

Franchisee One receiving a license to use another's (the franchisor's) trademark, trade name, or copyright in the sale of goods and services.

Franchisor One licensing another (the franchisee) to use the owner's trademark, trade name, or copyright in the selling of goods or services.

Fraudulent Misrepresentation Any misrepresentation, either by misstatement or by omission of a material fact, knowingly made with the intention of deceiving another and on which a reasonable person would and does rely to his or her detriment.

Free Exercise Clause The provision in the First Amendment that prohibits the government from interfering with people's religious practices or forms of worship.

Free-Writing Prospectus A written, electronic, or graphic communication associated with the offer to sell a security and used during the waiting period to supplement other information about the security.

Frustration of Purpose A court-created doctrine under which a party to a contract will be relieved of her or his duty to perform when the objective purpose for performance no longer exists due to reasons beyond that party's control.

Full Faith and Credit Clause A provision in Article IV, Section 1, of the U.S. Constitution that ensures that rights established under deeds, wills, contracts, and similar instruments in one state will be honored by other states and that judicial decisions will be honored and enforced in all states.

Fungible Goods Goods that are alike by physical nature, agreement, or trade usage.

G

Garnishment A legal process whereby a creditor collects a debt by seizing property of the debtor that is in the hands of a third party.

General Damages In a tort case, an amount awarded to compensate individuals for the nonmonetary aspects of the harm suffered, such as pain and suffering. Not available to companies.

Generally Accepted Accounting Principles (GAAP) The conventions, rules, and procedures developed by the Financial Accounting Standards Board to define accepted accounting practices at a particular time.

Generally Accepted Auditing Standards (GAAS) Standards established by the American Institute of Certified Public Accountants to define the professional qualities and judgment that should be exercised by an auditor in performing an audit.

General Partner In a limited partnership, a partner who assumes responsibility for the management of the partnership and has full liability for all partnership debts.

Gift A voluntary transfer of property made without consideration, past or present.

Gift *Causa Mortis* A gift made in contemplation of imminent death. The gift is revoked if the donor does not die as contemplated.

Gift *Inter Vivos* A gift made during one's lifetime and not in contemplation of imminent death.

Good Faith Purchaser A purchaser who buys without notice of any circumstance that would cause a person of ordinary prudence to inquire as to whether the seller has valid title to the goods being sold.

Good Samaritan Statute A state statute stipulating that persons who provide emergency services to, or rescue, someone in peril cannot be sued for negligence unless they act recklessly and cause further harm.

Goodwill In the business context, the valuable reputation of a business viewed as an intangible asset.

Grand Jury A group of citizens who decide, after hearing the state's evidence, whether a reasonable basis (probable cause) exists for believing that a crime has been committed and that a trial ought to be held.

Group Boycott An agreement by two or more sellers to refuse to deal with a particular person or firm.

Guarantor A third party who agrees to be secondarily liable for the debt of another (the debtor) only after the principal debtor defaults.

H

Hacker A person who uses computers to gain unauthorized access to data.

Historical School A school of legal thought that looks to the past to determine what the principles of contemporary law should be.

Holder Any person in possession of an instrument drawn, issued, or indorsed to him or her, to his or her order, to bearer, or in blank.

Holder in Due Course (HDC) A holder who acquires a negotiable instrument for value, in good faith, and without notice that the instrument is defective.

Holographic Will A will written entirely in the testator's handwriting.

Homestead Exemption A law permitting a debtor to retain the family home, either in its entirety or up to a specified dollar amount, free from the claims of unsecured creditors or trustees in bankruptcy.

Horizontal Merger A merger between two firms that are competing in the same market.

Horizontal Restraint Any agreement that restrains competition between rival firms competing in the same market.

Hot-Cargo Agreement An illegal agreement in which employers voluntarily agree with unions not to handle, use, or deal in the nonunion-produced goods of other employers.

I

I-9 Verification The process of verifying the employment eligibility and identity of a new worker. It must be completed within three days after the worker commences employment.

I-551 Permanent Resident Card A document, known as a "green card," that shows that a foreign-born individual can legally work in the United States.

Identification In a sale of goods, the express designation of the goods provided for in the contract.

Identity Theft The illegal use of someone else's personal information to access the victim's financial resources.

Implied Contract A contract formed in whole or in part from the conduct of the parties.

Implied Warranty A warranty that arises by law because of the circumstances of a sale and not from the seller's express promise.

Implied Warranty of Fitness for a Particular Purpose A warranty that goods sold or leased are fit for the particular purpose for which the buyer or lessee will use the goods.

Implied Warranty of Habitability An implied promise by a seller of a new house that the house is fit for human habitation. Also, the implied promise by a landlord that rented residential premises are habitable.

Implied Warranty of Merchantability A warranty that goods being sold or leased are reasonably fit for the general purpose for which they are sold or leased, are properly packaged and labeled, and are of proper quality.

Impossibility of Performance A doctrine under which a party to a contract is relieved of his or her duty to perform when performance becomes objectively impossible or totally impracticable.

Imposter One who induces a maker or drawer to issue a negotiable instrument in the name of an impersonated payee. Indorsements by imposters are treated as authorized indorsements under UCC Article 3.

Incidental Beneficiary A third party who benefits from a contract even though the contract was not formed for that purpose. An incidental beneficiary has no rights in the contract and cannot sue to have it enforced.

Incidental Damages Damages that compensate for expenses directly incurred because of a breach of contract, such as those incurred to obtain performance from another source.

Incontestability Clause A clause in a policy for life or health insurance stating that after the policy has been in force for a specified length of time (usually two or three years), the insurer cannot contest statements made in the policyholder's application.

Independent Contractor One who works for, and receives payment from, an employer but whose working conditions and methods are not controlled by the employer. An independent contractor is not an employee but may be an agent.

Indictment A charge by a grand jury that a reasonable basis (probable cause) exists for believing that a crime has been committed and that a trial should be held.

Indorsement A signature placed on an instrument for the purpose of transferring ownership rights in the instrument.

Informal Contract A contract that does not require a specific form or method of creation to be valid.

Information A formal accusation or complaint (without an indictment) issued in certain types of actions (usually criminal actions involving lesser crimes) by a government prosecutor.

Information Return A tax return submitted by a partnership that reports the business's income and losses. The partnership itself does not pay taxes on the income received by the partnership.

Initial Order An agency's disposition in a matter other than a rulemaking. An administrative law judge's initial order becomes final unless it is appealed.

Innocent Misrepresentation A misrepresentation that occurs when a person makes a false statement of fact that he or she believes is true.

Inside Director A person on the board of directors who is also an officer of the corporation.

Insider In bankruptcy proceedings, any individual, partnership, or corporation with a close personal or business relation with the debtor.

Insider Trading The purchase or sale of securities on the basis of information that has not been made available to the public.

Insolvent A condition in which a person cannot pay his or her debts as they become due or ceases to pay debts in the ordinary course of business.

Installment Contract A contract that requires or authorizes delivery in two or more separate lots to be accepted and paid for separately.

Insurable Interest A property interest in goods being sold or leased that is sufficiently substantial to permit a party to insure against damage to the goods. An insurable interest exists when a person benefits from the preservation of the health or life of the insured or the property to be insured.

Insurance A contract by which the insurer promises to reimburse the insured or a beneficiary in the event that the insured is injured, dies, or sustains damage to property as a result of particular, stated contingencies.

Intangible Property Property that cannot be seen or touched but exists only conceptually, such as corporate stocks. Such property is not governed by Article 2 of the UCC.

Integrated Contract A written contract that constitutes the final expression of the parties' agreement. Evidence extraneous to the contract that contradicts or alters the meaning of the contract in any way is inadmissible.

Intellectual Property Property resulting from intellectual and creative processes.

Intended Beneficiary A third party for whose benefit a contract is formed. An intended beneficiary can sue the promisor if the contract is breached.

Intentional Tort A wrongful act knowingly committed.

Intermediary Bank Any bank to which an item is transferred in the course of collection, except the depositary or payor bank.

International Financial Reporting Standards (IFRS) A set of global accounting standards that are being phased in by U.S. companies.

International Law Law—based on international customs, organizations, and treaties—that governs relations among nations.

International Organization An organization composed mainly of member nations and usually established by treaty—for instance, the United Nations. More broadly, the term also includes nongovernmental organizations (NGOs), such as the Red Cross.

Internet Service Provider (ISP) A business or organization that offers users access to the Internet and related services.

Interpretive Rule An administrative agency rule that explains how the agency interprets and intends to apply the statutes it enforces.

Interrogatories A series of written questions for which written answers are prepared by a party to a lawsuit, usually with the assistance of the party's attorney, and then signed under oath.

Intestacy Laws State statutes that specify how property will be distributed when a person dies intestate (without a valid will).

Intestate As a noun, one who has died without having created a valid will. As an adjective, the state of having died without a will.

Investment Company A company that acts on the behalf of many smaller shareholders-owners by buying a large portfolio of securities and professionally managing that portfolio.

Investment Contract In securities law, a transaction in which a person invests in a common enterprise reasonably expecting profits that are derived primarily from the efforts of others.

J

Joint and Several Liability In partnership law, a doctrine under which a plaintiff may sue, and collect a judgment from, all of the partners together (jointly) or one or more of the partners separately (severally, or individually). A partner can be held liable even if she or he did not participate in, ratify, or know about the conduct that gave rise to the lawsuit.

Joint Liability In partnership law, the partners' shared liability for partnership obligations and debts. A third party must sue all of the partners as a group, but each partner can be held liable for the full amount.

Joint Stock Company A hybrid form of business organization that combines characteristics of a corporation and a partnership. Usually, a joint stock company is regarded as a partnership for tax and other legal purposes.

Joint Tenancy Joint ownership of property in which each co-owner owns an undivided portion of the property. On the death of one of the joint tenants, his or her interest automatically passes to the surviving joint tenant(s).

Joint Venture A joint undertaking by two or more persons or business entities to combine their efforts or their property for a single transaction or project or for a related series of transactions or projects. A joint venture is generally treated like a partnership for tax and other legal purposes.

Judicial Review The process by which a court decides on the constitutionality of legislative enactments and actions of the executive branch.

Jurisdiction The authority of a court to hear and decide a specific case.

Jurisprudence The science or philosophy of law.

Justiciable Controversy A controversy that is not hypothetical or academic but real and substantial. It is a requirement that must be satisfied before a court will hear a case.

L

Larceny The wrongful taking and carrying away of another person's personal property with the intent to permanently deprive the owner of the property.

Latent Defect A defect that is not obvious or cannot readily be ascertained.

Law A body of enforceable rules governing relationships among individuals and between individuals and their society.

Lease Under Article 2A of the UCC, a transfer of the right to possess and use goods for a period of time in exchange for payment.

Lease Agreement An agreement in which one person (the lessor) agrees to transfer the right to the possession and use of property to another person (the lessee) in exchange for rental payments.

Leasehold Estate An interest in real property that gives a tenant a qualified right to possess and/or use the property for a limited time under a lease.

Legacy A gift of personal property under a will.

Legal Positivism A school of legal thought centered on the assumption that there is no law higher than the laws created by a national government. Laws must be obeyed, even if they are unjust, to prevent anarchy.

Legal Realism A school of legal thought that holds that the law is only one factor to be considered when deciding cases, and that social and economic circumstances should also be taken into account.

Legal Reasoning The process of reasoning by which a judge harmonizes his or her opinion with the judicial decisions in previous cases.

Legatee One designated in a will to receive a gift of personal property.

Legislative Rule An administrative agency rule that carries the same weight as a congressionally enacted statute.

Lessee A person who acquires the right to the possession and use of another's goods in exchange for rental payments.

Lessor A person who transfers the right to the possession and use of goods to another in exchange for rental payments.

Levy The legal process of obtaining funds through the seizure and sale of nonexempt property, usually done after a writ of execution has been issued.

Liability The state of being legally responsible (liable) for something, such as a debt or obligation.

Libel Defamation in writing or another permanent form (such as a digital recording).

License An agreement by the owner of intellectual property to permit another to use a trademark, copyright, patent, or trade secret for certain limited purposes. In the context of real property, a revocable right or privilege to enter onto another person's land.

Lien An encumbrance on a property to satisfy a debt or protect a claim for payment of a debt.

Life Estate An interest in land that exists only for the duration of the life of a specified individual, usually the holder of the estate.

Limited Liability Company (LLC) A hybrid form of business enterprise that offers the limited liability of a corporation and the tax advantages of a partnership.

Limited Liability Partnership (LLP) A hybrid form of business organization that is used mainly by professionals who normally do business in a partnership. An LLP is a pass-through entity for tax purposes, but a partner's personal liability for the malpractice of other partners is limited.

Limited Partner In a limited partnership, a partner who contributes capital to the partnership but has no right to participate in its management and has no liability for partnership debts beyond the amount of her or his investment.

Limited Partnership (LP) A partnership consisting of one or more general partners and one or more limited partners.

Liquidated Damages An amount, stipulated in a contract, that the parties to the contract believe to be a reasonable estimation of the damages that will occur in the event of a breach.

Liquidated Debt A debt whose amount has been ascertained, fixed, agreed on, settled, or exactly determined.

Liquidation The sale of the nonexempt assets of a debtor and the distribution of the funds received to creditors.

Litigation The process of resolving a dispute through the court system.

Living (*Inter Vivos*) Trust A trust created by the grantor (settlor) and effective during his or her lifetime.

Long Arm Statute A state statute that permits a state to exercise jurisdiction over nonresident defendants.

Lost Property Property that the owner has involuntarily parted with and then cannot find or recover.

M

Mailbox Rule A common law rule that acceptance takes effect, and thus completes formation of the contract, at the time the offeree sends or delivers the acceptance via the communication mode expressly or impliedly authorized by the offeror.

Majority Opinion A court opinion that represents the views of the majority (more than half) of the judges or justices deciding the case.

Maker One who promises to pay a fixed amount of funds to the holder of a promissory note or a certificate of deposit (CD).

Malpractice Professional negligence, or failure to exercise reasonable care and professional judgment, that results in injury, loss, or damage to those relying on the professional.

Malware Malicious software programs, such as viruses and worms, that are designed to cause harm to a computer, network, or other device.

Market Concentration The degree to which a small number of firms control a large percentage of a relevant market.

Market Power The power of a firm to control the market price of its product. A monopoly has the greatest degree of market power.

Market-Share Liability A theory under which liability is shared among all firms that manufactured and distributed a particular product during a certain period of time. This form of liability sharing is used only when the specific source of the harmful product is unidentifiable.

Mechanic's Lien A nonpossessory, filed lien on an owner's real estate for labor, services, or materials furnished for making improvements on the realty.

Mediation A method of settling disputes outside the courts by using the services of a neutral third party, who acts as a communicating agent between the parties and assists them in negotiating a settlement.

Member A person who has an ownership interest in a limited liability company.

Mens Rea A wrongful mental state ("guilty mind"), or intent. It is one of the two essential elements required to establish criminal liability.

Merchant Under the UCC, a person who deals in goods of the kind involved in the sales contract or who holds herself or himself out as having skill or knowledge peculiar to the practices or goods being purchased or sold.

Merger The legal combination of two or more corporations in such a way that only one corporation (the surviving corporation) continues to exist.

Metadata Data that are automatically recorded by electronic devices and provide information about who created a file and when, and who accessed, modified, or transmitted the file. It can be described as data about data.

Meta Tag A key word in a document that can serve as an index reference to the document. On the Web, search engines return results based, in part, on the tags in Web documents.

Minimum Wage The lowest wage, either by government regulation or by union contract, that an employer may pay an hourly worker.

Mirror Image Rule A common law rule that requires that the terms of the offeree's acceptance adhere exactly to the terms of the offeror's offer for a valid contract to be formed.

Misdemeanor A lesser crime than a felony, punishable by a fine or incarceration in jail for up to one year.

Mislaid Property Property that the owner has voluntarily parted with and then has inadvertently forgotten.

Mitigation of Damages The requirement that a plaintiff do whatever is reasonable to minimize the damages caused by the defendant's breach of contract.

Money Laundering Engaging in financial transactions to conceal the identity, source, or destination of illegally gained funds.

Monopolization The possession of monopoly power in the relevant market and the willful acquisition or maintenance of that power, as distinguished from growth or development as a consequence of a superior product, business acumen, or historic accident.

Monopoly A market in which there is a single seller or a very limited number of sellers.

Monopoly Power The ability of a monopoly to dictate what takes place in a given market.

Moral Minimum The minimum level of ethical behavior expected by society, which is usually defined as compliance with the law.

Motion for a Directed Verdict A motion for the judge to take the decision out of the hands of the jury and to direct a verdict for the party making the motion on the ground that the other party has not produced sufficient evidence to support her or his claim.

Motion for a New Trial A motion asserting that the trial was so fundamentally flawed (because of error, newly discovered evidence, prejudice, or another reason) that a new trial is necessary to prevent a miscarriage of justice.

Motion for Judgment *n.o.v.* A motion requesting the court to grant judgment in favor of the party making the motion on the ground that the jury's verdict against him or her was unreasonable and erroneous.

Motion for Judgment on the Pleadings A motion by either party to a lawsuit at the close of the pleadings requesting the court to decide the issue solely on the pleadings without proceeding to trial. The motion will be granted only if no facts are in dispute.

Motion for Summary Judgment A motion requesting the court to enter a judgment without proceeding to trial. The motion can be based on evidence outside the pleadings and will be granted only if no facts are in dispute.

Motion to Dismiss A pleading in which a defendant admits the facts as alleged by the plaintiff but asserts that the plaintiff's claim to state a cause of action has no basis in law.

Multiple Product Order An order requiring a firm that has engaged in deceptive advertising to cease and desist from false advertising in regard to all the firm's products.

Mutual Fund A specific type of investment company that continually buys or sells to investors shares of ownership in a portfolio.

N

National Law Law that pertains to a particular nation.

Natural Law The oldest school of legal thought, based on the belief that the legal system should reflect universal ("higher") moral and ethical principles that are inherent in human nature.

Necessaries Necessities required to maintain a standard of living, such as food, shelter, clothing, and medical attention.

Negligence The failure to exercise the standard of care that a reasonable person would exercise in similar circumstances.

Negligent Misrepresentation A misrepresentation that occurs when a person makes a false statement of fact because he or she did not exercise reasonable care or use the skill and competence required by her or his business or profession.

Negotiable Instrument A signed writing (record) that contains an unconditional promise or order to pay an exact sum on demand or at a specified future time to a specific person or order, or to bearer.

Negotiation A process in which parties attempt to settle their dispute informally, with or without attorneys to represent them. In negotiable instruments law, the transfer of an instrument in such form that the transferee (the person to whom the instrument is transferred) becomes a holder.

Nominal Damages A small monetary award (often one dollar) granted to a plaintiff when no actual damage was suffered.

Nonpossessory Interest In the context of real property, an interest that involves the right to use land but not the right to possess it.

Normal Trade Relations (NTR) Status A legal trade status granted to member countries of the World Trade Organization.

Notary Public A public official authorized to attest to the authenticity of signatures.

Notice-and-Comment Rulemaking An administrative rulemaking procedure that requires notice, opportunity for comment, and a published draft of the final rule.

Novation The substitution, by agreement, of a new contract for an old one, with the rights under the old one being terminated.

Nuisance A common law doctrine under which persons may be held liable for using their property in a manner that unreasonably interferes with others' rights to use or enjoy their own property.

Nuncupative Will An oral will (often called a *deathbed will*) made before witnesses. Usually, such wills are limited to transfers of personal property.

O

Objective Theory of Contracts The view that contracting parties shall be bound only by terms that can be objectively inferred from promises made.

Obligee One to whom an obligation is owed.

Obligor One who owes an obligation to another.

Offer A promise or commitment to perform or refrain from performing some specified act in the future.

Offeree A person to whom an offer is made.

Offeror A person who makes an offer.

Online Dispute Resolution (ODR) The resolution of disputes with the assistance of organizations that offer dispute-resolution services via the Internet.

Operating Agreement An agreement in which the members of a limited liability company set forth the details of how the business will be managed and operated.

Option Contract A contract under which the offeror cannot revoke the offer for a stipulated time period (because the offeree has given consideration for the offer to remain open).

Order for Relief A court's grant of assistance to a debtor in bankruptcy that relieves the debtor of the immediate obligation to pay debts.

Order Instrument A negotiable instrument that is payable "to the order of an identified person" or "to an identified person or order."

Ordinance A regulation enacted by a city or county legislative body that becomes part of that state's statutory law.

Outcome-Based Ethics An ethical philosophy that focuses on the consequences of any given action in order to maximize benefits and minimize harms.

Output Contract An agreement in which a seller agrees to sell and a buyer agrees to buy all or up to a stated amount of what the seller produces.

Outside Director A person on the board of directors who does not hold a management position at the corporation.

Outsourcing The practice by which a company hires an outside firm or individual to perform work rather than hiring employees to do it.

Overdraft A check that is paid by a bank when the checking account on which the check is written contains insufficient funds to cover the check.

P

Parol Evidence Rule A rule of contracts under which a court will not receive into evidence prior or contemporaneous external agreements that contradict the terms of the parties' written contract.

Partially Disclosed Principal A principal whose identity is unknown by a third party, but the third party knows that the agent is or may be acting for a principal at the time the agent and the third party form a contract.

Partnering Agreement An agreement between a seller and a buyer who frequently do business with each other concerning the terms and conditions that will apply to all subsequently formed electronic contracts.

Partnership An agreement by two or more persons to carry on, as co-owners, a business for profit.

Partnership by Estoppel A partnership imposed by a court when nonpartners have held themselves out to be partners, or have allowed themselves to be held out as partners, and others have detrimentally relied on their misrepresentations.

Pass-Through Entity A business entity that has no tax liability. The entity's income is passed through to the owners, and they pay taxes on the income.

Past Consideration Something given or some act done in the past, which cannot ordinarily be consideration for a later bargain.

Patent A property right granted by the federal government that gives an inventor an exclusive right to make, use, and sell an invention for a limited time.

Payee A person to whom an instrument is made payable.

Payor Bank The bank on which a check is drawn (the drawee bank).

Peer-to-Peer (P2P) Networking The sharing of resources among multiple computers without the requirement of a central network server.

Penalty A sum specified in a contract not as a measure of compensation for its breach but rather as a punishment for a default. The agreement as to the amount will not be enforced, and recovery will be limited to the actual damages.

Per Capita A method of distributing an intestate's estate so that each heir in a certain class (such as grandchildren) receives an equal share.

Per Curiam **Opinion** A court opinion that does not indicate which judge or justice authored the opinion.

Perfect Tender Rule The legal right of a buyer or lessee of goods to insist on perfect tender by the seller or lessor. If the goods fail to conform to the contract, the buyer may accept the goods, reject the goods, or accept part and reject part of the goods tendered.

Perfection The legal process by which secured parties protect themselves against the claims of third parties who may wish to have their debts satisfied out of the same collateral. It is usually accomplished by filing a financing statement with the appropriate government official.

Performance The fulfillment of one's duties under a contract—the normal way of discharging one's contractual obligations.

Periodic Tenancy A lease interest for an indefinite period involving payment of rent at fixed intervals, such as week to week, month to month, or year to year.

Per Se Violation A restraint of trade that is so anticompetitive that it is deemed inherently (*per se*) illegal.

Personal Defense A defense that can be used to avoid payment to an ordinary holder of a negotiable instrument but not a holder in due course (HDC) or a holder with the rights of an HDC. It is also called a *limited defense*.

Personal Property Property that is movable. Any property that is not real property.

Per Stirpes A method of distributing an intestate's estate so that each heir in a certain class (such as grandchildren) takes the share to which her or his deceased ancestor (such as a mother or father) would have been entitled.

Persuasive Authority Any legal authority or source of law that a court may look to for guidance but need not follow when making its decision.

Petition in Bankruptcy The document that is filed with a bankruptcy court to initiate bankruptcy proceedings.

Petty Offense The least serious kind of criminal offense, such as a traffic or building-code violation.

Phishing A form of identity theft in which the perpetrator sends e-mails purporting to be from legitimate businesses to induce recipients to reveal their personal financial data, passwords, or other information.

Piercing the Corporate Veil The action of a court to disregard the corporate entity and hold the shareholders personally liable for corporate debts and obligations.

Plaintiff One who initiates a lawsuit.

Plea Bargaining The process by which a criminal defendant and the prosecutor work out an agreement to dispose of the criminal case, subject to court approval.

Pleadings Statements by the plaintiff and the defendant that detail the facts, charges, and defenses of a case.

Pledge A security device in which personal property is transferred into the possession of the creditor as security for the payment of a debt and retained by the creditor until the debt is paid.

Plurality Opinion A court opinion that is joined by the largest number of the judges or justices hearing the case, but less than half of the total number.

Police Powers Powers possessed by the states as part of their inherent sovereignty. These powers may be exercised to protect or promote the public order, health, safety, morals, and general welfare.

Policy In insurance law, the contract between the insurer and the insured.

Potentially Responsible Party (PRP) A party liable for the costs of cleaning up a hazardous waste disposal site under the Comprehensive Environmental Response, Compensation, and Liability Act.

Power of Attorney Authorization for another to act as one's agent or attorney either in specified circumstances (special) or in all situations (general).

Precedent A court decision that furnishes an example or authority for deciding subsequent cases involving identical or similar facts.

Predatory Pricing The pricing of a product below cost with the intent to drive competitors out of the market.

Predominant-Factor Test A test courts use to determine whether a contract is primarily for the sale of goods or for the sale of services.

Preemption A doctrine under which certain federal laws preempt, or take precedence over, conflicting state or local laws.

Preemptive Right The right of a shareholder in a corporation to have the first opportunity to purchase a new issue of that corporation's stock in proportion to the amount of stock already owned by the shareholder.

Preference In bankruptcy proceedings, a property transfer or payment made by the debtor that favors one creditor over others.

Preferred Creditor In the context of bankruptcy, a creditor who has received a preferential transfer from a debtor.

Preferred Stock Stock that has priority over common stock as to payment of dividends and distribution of assets on the corporation's dissolution.

Premium In insurance law, the price paid by the insured for insurance protection for a specified period of time.

Prenuptial Agreement An agreement made before marriage that defines each partner's ownership rights in the other partner's property. Prenuptial agreements must be in writing to be enforceable.

Presentment The act of presenting an instrument to the party liable on the instrument in order to collect payment. Presentment also occurs when a person presents an instrument to a drawee for a required acceptance.

Presentment Warranty An implied warranty made by any person who presents an instrument for payment or acceptance that he or she is entitled to enforce the instrument, that the instrument has not been altered, and that he or she is unaware of any unauthorized signatures.

Price Discrimination A seller's act of charging competing buyers different prices for identical products or services.

Price-Fixing Agreement An agreement between competitors to fix the prices of products or services at a certain level.

Prima Facie Case A case in which the plaintiff has produced sufficient evidence of his or her claim that the case will be decided for the plaintiff unless the defendant produces evidence to rebut the claim.

Primary Source of Law A document that establishes the law on a particular issue, such as a constitution, a statute, an administrative rule, or a court decision.

Principle of Rights The belief that human beings have certain fundamental rights.

Private Equity Capital Funds invested in an existing corporation by a private equity firm, usually to purchase and reorganize it.

Privilege A special right, advantage, or immunity that enables a person or a class of persons to avoid liability for defamation.

Privileges and Immunities Clause Article IV, Section 2, of the U.S. Constitution requires states not to discriminate against one another's citizens. A resident of one state, when in another state, cannot be denied the privileges and immunities of that state.

Privity of Contract The relationship that exists between the promisor and the promisee of a contract.

Probable Cause Reasonable grounds for believing that a search or seizure should be conducted.

Probate The process of proving and validating a will and settling all matters pertaining to an estate.

Probate Court A state court of limited jurisdiction that conducts proceedings relating to the settlement of a deceased person's estate.

Procedural Law Law that establishes the methods of enforcing the rights established by substantive law.

Proceeds Under Article 9 of the UCC, whatever is received when collateral is sold or disposed of in some other way.

Product Liability The legal liability of manufacturers, sellers, and lessors of goods for injuries or damage caused by the goods to consumers, users, or bystanders.

Profit In real property law, the right to enter onto another's property and remove something of value from that property.

Promise A declaration that binds a person who makes the promisor do or not do a certain act.

Promisee A person to whom a promise is made.

Promisor A person who makes a promise.

Promissory Estoppel A doctrine that can be used to enforce a promise when the promisee has justifiably relied on the promise and when justice will be better served by enforcing the promise.

Promissory Note A written promise made by one person (the maker) to pay a fixed amount of funds to another person (the payee or a subsequent holder) on demand or on a specified date.

Prospectus A written document required by securities laws when a security is being sold. The prospectus describes the security, the financial operations of the issuing corporation, and the risk attaching to the security.

Protected Class A group of persons protected by specific laws because of the group's defining characteristics, including race, color, religion, national origin, gender, age, disability, and military status.

Proximate Cause Legal cause. It exists when the connection between an act and an injury is strong enough to justify imposing liability.

Proxy In corporate law, formal authorization to serve as a corporate shareholder's agent and vote his or her shares in a certain manner.

Public Corporation A corporation owned by a federal, state, or municipal government to meet a political or governmental purpose.

Publicly Held Corporation A corporation whose shares are publicly traded in securities markets, such as the New York Stock Exchange or the NASDAQ.

Puffery A salesperson's exaggerated claims concerning the quality of property offered for sale. Such claims involve opinions rather than facts and are not legally binding promises or warranties.

Punitive Damages Monetary damages that may be awarded to a plaintiff to punish the defendant and deter similar conduct in the future.

Purchase-Money Security Interest (PMSI) A security interest that arises when a seller or lender extends credit for part or all of the price of goods purchased by a buyer.

Q

Qualified Indorsement An indorsement on a negotiable instrument in which the indorser disclaims any contract liability on the instrument. The notation "without recourse" is commonly used to create a qualified indorsement.

Quantum Meruit A Latin phrase meaning "as much as he or she deserves." The expression describes the extent of compensation owed under a quasi contract.

Quasi Contract An obligation or contract imposed by law (a court), in the absence of an agreement, to prevent the unjust enrichment of one party.

Question of Fact In a lawsuit, an issue that involves only disputed facts, and not what the law is on a given point.

Question of Law In a lawsuit, an issue involving the application or interpretation of a law.

Quitclaim Deed A deed that conveys only whatever interest the grantor had in the property and therefore offers the least amount of protection against defects of title.

Quorum The number of members of a decision-making body that must be present before business may be transacted.

Quota A set limit on the amount of goods that can be imported.

R

Ratification A party's act of accepting or giving legal force to a contract or other obligation entered into on his or her behalf by another that previously was not enforceable.

Reaffirmation Agreement An agreement between a debtor and a creditor in which the debtor voluntarily agrees to pay a debt dischargeable in bankruptcy.

Real Property Land and everything permanently attached to it, such as trees and buildings.

Reasonable Person Standard The standard of behavior expected of a hypothetical "reasonable person." It is the standard against which negligence is measured and that must be observed to avoid liability for negligence.

Receiver In a corporate dissolution, a court-appointed person who winds up corporate affairs and liquidates corporate assets.

Record Information that is either inscribed on a tangible medium or stored in an electronic or other medium and is retrievable in visual form.

Recording Statute A statute that allow deeds, mortgages, and other real property transactions to be recorded so as to provide notice to future purchasers or creditors of an existing claim on the property.

Reformation A court-ordered correction of a written contract so that it reflects the true intentions of the parties.

Regulation E A set of rules issued by the Federal Reserve System's Board of Governors to protect users of electronic fund transfer systems.

Regulation Z A set of rules issued by the Federal Reserve Board of Governors to implement the provisions of the Truth in Lending Act.

Release An agreement in which one party gives up the right to pursue a legal claim against another party.

Remedy The relief given to an innocent party to enforce a right or compensate for the violation of a right.

Replevin An action that can be used by a buyer or lessee to recover identified goods from a third party, such as a bailee, who is wrongfully withholding them.

Reply Procedurally, a plaintiff's response to a defendant's answer.

Requirements Contract An agreement in which a buyer agrees to purchase and a seller agrees to sell all or up to a stated amount of what the buyer needs or requires.

Resale Price Maintenance Agreement An agreement between a manufacturer and a retailer in which the manufacturer specifies what the retail prices of its products must be.

Rescission A remedy whereby a contract is canceled and the parties are returned to the positions they occupied before the contract was made.

Respondeat Superior A doctrine under which a principal or an employer is held liable for the wrongful acts committed by agents or employees while acting within the course and scope of their agency or employment.

Restitution An equitable remedy under which a person is restored to his or her original position prior to loss or injury, or placed in the position he or she would have been in had the breach not occurred.

Restrictive Indorsement An indorsement on a negotiable instrument that requires the indorsee to comply with certain instructions regarding the funds involved.

Resulting Trust An implied trust that arises when one party holds the legal title to another's property only for that other's benefit.

Retained Earnings The portion of a corporation's profits that has not been paid out as dividends to shareholders.

Revocation The withdrawal of a contract offer by the offeror. Unless an offer is irrevocable, it can be revoked at any time prior to acceptance without liability.

Right of Contribution The right of a co-surety who pays more than his or her proportionate share on a debtor's default to recover the excess paid from other co-sureties.

Right of Reimbursement The right of a party to be repaid for costs, expenses, or losses incurred on behalf of another.

Right of Subrogation The right of a party to stand in the place of another, giving the substituted party the same legal rights that the original party had.

Right-to-Work Law A state law providing that employees may not be required to join a union as a condition of retaining employment.

Risk A prediction concerning potential loss based on known and unknown factors.

Risk Management In the context of insurance, the transfer of certain risks from the insured to the insurance company by contractual agreement.

Robbery The act of forcefully and unlawfully taking personal property of any value from another.

Rulemaking The process by which an administrative agency formally adopts a new regulation or amends or removes an old one.

Rule of Four A rule of the United States Supreme Court under which the Court will not issue a writ of *certiorari* unless at least four justices approve of the decision to issue the writ.

Rule of Reason A test used to determine whether an anticompetitive agreement constitutes a reasonable restraint on trade. Courts consider such factors as the purpose of the agreement, its effect on competition, and whether less restrictive means could have been used.

S

Sale The passing of title to property from the seller to the buyer for a price.

Sales Contract A contract for the sale of goods.

Scienter Knowledge on the part of a misrepresenting party that material facts have been falsely represented or omitted with an intent to deceive.

S Corporation A close business corporation that has most corporate attributes, including limited liability, but qualifies under the Internal Revenue Code to be taxed as a partnership.

Search Warrant An order granted by a public authority, such as a judge, that authorizes law enforcement personnel to search particular premises or property.

Seasonably Within a specified time period or, if no period is specified, within a reasonable time.

Secondary Source of Law A publication that summarizes or interprets the law, such as a legal encyclopedia, a legal treatise, or an article in a law review.

SEC Rule 10b-5 A rule of the Securities and Exchange Commission that prohibits the commission of fraud in connection with the purchase or sale of any security.

Secured Party A creditor who has a security interest in the debtor's collateral, including a seller, lender, cosigner, or buyer of accounts or chattel paper.

Secured Transaction Any transaction in which the payment of a debt is guaranteed, or secured, by personal property owned by the debtor or in which the debtor has a legal interest.

Securities Generally, stocks, bonds, or other items that represent an ownership interest in a corporation or a promise of repayment of debt by a corporation.

Security Agreement An agreement that creates or provides for a security interest between the debtor and a secured party.

Security Interest Any interest in personal property or fixtures that secures payment or performance of an obligation.

Self-Defense The legally recognized privilege to do what is reasonably necessary to protect oneself, one's property, or someone else against injury by another.

Self-Incrimination Giving testimony in a trial or other legal proceeding that could expose the person testifying to criminal prosecution.

Seniority System A system in which those who have worked longest for an employer are first in line for promotions, salary increases, and other benefits, and are last to be laid off if the workforce must be reduced.

Service Mark A trademark that is used to distinguish the services (rather than the products) of one person or company from those of another.

Service of Process The delivery of the complaint and summons to a defendant.

Sexual Harassment The demanding of sexual favors in return for job promotions or other benefits, or language or conduct that is so sexually offensive that it creates a hostile working environment.

Share Exchange A transaction in which some or all of the shares of one corporation are exchanged for some or all of the shares of another corporation, but both corporations continue to exist.

Shareholder's Derivative Suit A suit brought by a shareholder to enforce a corporate cause of action against a third person.

Shelter Principle The principle that the holder of a negotiable instrument who cannot qualify as a holder in due course (HDC), but who derives his or her title through an HDC, acquires the rights of an HDC.

Shipment Contract A contract for the sale of goods in which the seller is required or authorized to ship the goods by carrier.

The seller assumes liability for any losses or damage to the goods until they are delivered to the carrier.

Short-Form Merger A merger that can be accomplished without the approval of the shareholders of either corporation because one company (the parent corporation) owns at least 90 percent of the outstanding shares of each class of stock of the other corporation (the subsidiary corporation).

Short-Swing Profits Profits earned by a purchase and sale, or sale and purchase, of the same security within a six-month period.

Shrink-Wrap Agreement An agreement whose terms are expressed in a document located inside a box in which goods (usually software) are packaged.

Slander Defamation in oral form.

Slander of Quality (Trade Libel) The publication of false information about another's product, alleging that it is not what its seller claims.

Slander of Title The publication of a statement that denies or casts doubt on another's legal ownership of property, causing financial loss to that property's owner.

Small Claims Court A special court in which parties can litigate small claims without an attorney.

Smart Card A card containing a microprocessor with security programming that is typically used for financial transactions, personal identification, and other purposes.

Social Media Forms of communication through which users create and share information, ideas, messages, and other content via the Internet.

Sole Proprietorship The simplest form of business organization, in which the owner is the business. The owner reports business income on his or her personal income tax return and is legally responsible for all debts and obligations incurred by the business.

Sovereign Immunity A doctrine that immunizes foreign nations from the jurisdiction of U.S. courts when certain conditions are satisfied.

Sovereignty The power of a state to do what is necessary to govern itself. Individual state sovereignty is determined by the U.S. Constitution.

Space Law Law consisting of the international and national laws that govern activities in outer space.

Spam Bulk, unsolicited (junk) e-mail.

Special Damages In a tort case, an amount awarded to compensate the plaintiff for quantifiable monetary losses, such as medical expenses, property damage, and lost wages and benefits (now and in the future).

Special Indorsement An indorsement on an instrument that identifies the specific person to whom the indorser intends to make the instrument payable.

Special Warranty Deed A deed that warrants only that the grantor held good title during his or her ownership of the property and does not warrant that there were no defects of title when the property was held by previous owners.

Specific Performance An equitable remedy in which a court orders the parties to perform as promised in the contract. This remedy normally is granted only when the legal remedy (monetary damages) is inadequate.

Spendthrift Trust A trust created to protect the beneficiary from spending all the funds to which she or he is entitled. Only a certain portion of the total amount is given to the beneficiary at any one time, and most states prohibit creditors from attaching assets of the trust.

Stakeholders Groups that are affected by corporate decisions. Stakeholders include employees, customers, creditors, suppliers, and the community in which the corporation operates.

Stale Check A check, other than a certified check, that is presented for payment more than six months after its date.

Standing to Sue The legal requirement that an individual must have a sufficient stake in a controversy before he or she can bring a lawsuit.

Stare Decisis A common law doctrine under which judges are obligated to follow the precedents established in prior decisions.

Statute of Frauds A state statute that requires certain types of contracts to be in writing to be enforceable.

Statute of Repose A statute that places outer time limits on product liability actions. Such statutes cut off absolutely the right to bring an action after a specified period of time following some event (often the product's manufacture or purchase) other than the occurrence of an injury.

Statutory Law The body of law enacted by legislative bodies (as opposed to constitutional law, administrative law, or case law).

Stock An ownership (equity) interest in a corporation, measured in units of shares.

Stock Certificate A certificate issued by a corporation evidencing the ownership of a specified number of shares in the corporation.

Stock Option A right to buy a given number of shares of stock at a set price, usually within a specified time period.

Stop-Payment Order An order by a bank customer to his or her bank not to pay or certify a certain check.

Stored-Value Card A card bearing a magnetic strip that holds magnetically encoded data providing access to stored funds.

Strict Liability Liability regardless of fault, which is imposed on those engaged in abnormally dangerous activities, on persons who keep dangerous animals, and on manufacturers or sellers that introduce into commerce defective and unreasonably dangerous goods.

Strike An action undertaken by unionized workers when collective bargaining fails. The workers leave their jobs, refuse to work, and (typically) picket the employer's workplace.

Sublease A tenant's transfer of all or part of the leased premises to a third person for a period shorter than the lease term.

Substantive Law Law that defines, describes, regulates, and creates legal rights and obligations.

Summary Jury Trial (SJT) A method of settling disputes by holding a trial in which the jury's verdict is not binding but instead guides the parties toward reaching an agreement during the mandatory negotiations that immediately follow.

Summons A document informing a defendant that a legal action has been commenced against her or him and that the defendant must appear in court on a certain date to answer the plaintiff's complaint.

Supremacy Clause The provision in Article VI of the U.S. Constitution that the Constitution, laws, and treaties of the United States are "the supreme Law of the Land."

Surety A third party who agrees to be primarily responsible for the debt of another.

Suretyship A promise made by a third party to be responsible for a debtor's obligation.

Symbolic Speech Nonverbal expressions of beliefs. Symbolic speech, which includes gestures, movements, and articles of clothing, is given substantial protection by the courts.

Syndicate A group of individuals or firms that join together to finance a project. A syndicate is also called an *investment group*.

T

Takeover The acquisition of control over a corporation through the purchase of a substantial number of the voting shares of the corporation.

Taking The taking of private property by the government for public use through the power of eminent domain.

Tangible Employment Action A significant change in employment status or benefits, such as occurs when an employee is fired, refused a promotion, or reassigned to a lesser position.

Tangible Property Property that has physical existence and can be distinguished by the senses of touch and sight.

Tariff A tax on imported goods.

Tenancy at Sufferance A tenancy that arises when a tenant wrongfully continues to occupy leased property after the lease has terminated.

Tenancy at Will A type of tenancy that either the landlord or the tenant can terminate without notice.

Tenancy by the Entirety Joint ownership of property by a married couple in which neither spouse can transfer his or her interest in the property without the consent of the other.

Tenancy in Common Joint ownership of property in which each party owns an undivided interest that passes to his or her heirs at death.

Tender An unconditional offer to perform an obligation by a person who is ready, willing, and able to do so.

Tender of Delivery A seller's or lessor's act of placing conforming goods at the disposal of the buyer or lessee and providing whatever notification is reasonably necessary to enable the buyer or lessee to take delivery.

Tender Offer An offer made by one company directly to the shareholders of another (target) company to purchase their shares of stock.

Testamentary Trust A trust that is created by will and therefore does not take effect until the death of the testator.

Testate Having left a will at death.

Testator One who makes and executes a will.

Third Party Beneficiary One who is not a party to the contract but who stands to benefit from the contract's performance.

Tippee A person who receives inside information.

Toll To temporarily suspend the running of a prescribed time period, such as a statute of limitations.

Tort A wrongful act (other than a breach of contract) that results in harm or injury to another and leads to civil liability.

Tortfeasor One who commits a tort.

Totten Trust A trust created when a person deposits funds in his or her own name for a specific beneficiary, who will receive the funds on the depositor's death. The trust is revocable at will until the depositor dies or completes the gift.

Toxic Tort A civil wrong arising from exposure to a toxic substance, such as asbestos, radiation, or hazardous waste.

Trade Dress The image and overall appearance of a product.

Trade Name A name that a business uses to identify itself and its brand. A trade name is directly related to a business's reputation and goodwill, and is protected under trademark law.

Trade Secret A formula, device, idea, process, or other information used in a business that gives the owner a competitive advantage in the marketplace.

Trademark A distinctive word, symbol, sound, or design that identifies the manufacturer as the source of particular goods and distinguishes its products from those made or sold by others.

Trademark Dilution The unauthorized use of a distinctive and famous mark in a way that impairs the mark's distinctiveness or harms its reputation.

Transfer Warranty An implied warranty made by any person who transfers an instrument for consideration that the person is entitled to enforce the instrument, the signatures are authentic, it has not been altered, there are no defenses, and the transferor is unaware of any bankruptcy proceedings of parties to the instrument.

Transferred Intent A legal principle under which a person who intends to harm one individual, but unintentionally harms a different individual, can be liable to the second victim for an intentional tort.

Traveler's Check A check that is payable on demand, drawn on or payable through a financial institution, and designated as a traveler's check.

Treaty A formal international agreement negotiated between two nations or among several nations.

Treble Damages Damages that, by statute, are three times the amount of actual damages suffered.

Trespass to Land Entry onto, above, or below the surface of land owned by another without the owner's permission or legal authorization.

Trespass to Personal Property Wrongfully taking or harming the personal property of another or otherwise interfering with the lawful owner's possession of personal property.

Triple Bottom Line A measure that includes a corporation's profits, its impact on people, and its impact on the planet.

Trust An arrangement in which title to property is held by one person (a trustee) for the benefit of another (a beneficiary).

Trust Indorsements An indorsement to a person who is to hold or use funds for the benefit of the indorser or a third person. It is also known as an *agency indorsement*.

Tying Arrangement A seller's act of conditioning the sale of a product or service on the buyer's agreement to purchase another product or service from the seller.

Typosquatting A form of cybersquatting that relies on mistakes, such as typographical errors, made by Internet users when entering information into a Web browser.

U

Ultra Vires Acts Acts of a corporation that are beyond its express and implied powers to undertake (the Latin phrase means "beyond the powers").

Unconscionable A contract or clause that is void on the basis of public policy because one party was forced to accept terms that are unfairly burdensome and that unfairly benefit the other party.

Underwriter In insurance law, the insurer, or the one assuming a risk in return for the payment of a premium.

Undisclosed Principal A principal whose identity is unknown by a third party, and the third party has no knowledge that the agent is acting for a principal at the time the agent and the third party form a contract.

Undue Influence Persuasion that is less than actual force but more than advice and that induces a person to act according to the will or purposes of the dominating party.

Unenforceable Contract A valid contract rendered unenforceable by some statute or law.

Uniform Law A model law developed by the National Conference of Commissioners on Uniform State Laws for the states to consider enacting into statute.

Unilateral Contract A type of contract that results when an offer can be accepted only by the offeree's performance.

Unilateral Mistake A mistake that occurs when one party to a contract is mistaken as to a material fact.

Union Shop A firm that requires all workers, once employed, to become union members within a specified period of time as a condition of their continued employment.

Universal Defense A defense that can be used to avoid payment to all holders of a negotiable instrument, including a holder in due course (HDC) or a holder with the rights of an HDC. It is also called a real defense.

Unliquidated Debt A debt that is uncertain in amount.

Unreasonably Dangerous Product A product that is so defective that it is dangerous beyond the expectation of an ordinary consumer, or a product for which a less dangerous alternative was feasible but the manufacturer failed to produce it.

Usage of Trade Any practice or method of dealing that is so regularly observed in a place, vocation, or trade that parties justifiably expect it will be observed in their transaction.

U.S. Trustee A government official who performs administrative tasks that a bankruptcy judge would otherwise have to perform.

Usury Charging an illegal rate of interest.

Utilitarianism An approach to ethical reasoning in which an action is evaluated in terms of its consequences for those whom it will affect. A "good" action is one that results in the greatest good for the greatest number of people.

V

Valid Contract A contract that results when the elements necessary for contract formation (agreement, consideration, capacity, and legality) are present.

Venture Capital Financing provided by professional, outside investors (venture capitalists) to new business ventures.

Venue The geographic district in which a legal action is tried and from which the jury is selected.

Vertical Merger The acquisition by a company at one stage of production of a company at a higher or lower stage of production (such as a company merging with one of its suppliers or retailers).

Vertical Restraint A restraint of trade created by an agreement between firms at different levels in the manufacturing and distribution process.

Vertically Integrated Firm A firm that carries out two or more functional phases (manufacturing, distribution, and retailing, for instance) of the chain of production.

Vesting The creation of an absolute or unconditional right or power.

Vicarious Liability Indirect liability imposed on a supervisory party (such as an employer) for the actions of a subordinate (such as an employee) because of the relationship between the two parties.

Virus A software program that can replicate itself over a network and spread from one device to another, altering files and interfering with normal operations.

Void Contract A contract having no legal force or binding effect.

Voidable Contract A contract that may be legally avoided at the option of one or both of the parties.

Voir Dire An important part of the jury selection process in which the attorneys question prospective jurors about their backgrounds, attitudes, and biases to ascertain whether they can be impartial jurors.

Voluntary Consent Knowledge of and genuine assent to the terms of a contract.

W

Warranty Deed A deed that provides the greatest amount of protection for the grantee. The grantor promises that she or he has title to the property conveyed in the deed, that there are no undisclosed encumbrances on the property, and that the grantee will enjoy quiet possession of the property.

Waste The use of real property in a manner that damages or destroys its value.

Whistleblowing An employee's disclosure to government authorities, upper-level managers, or the media that the employer is engaged in unsafe or illegal activities.

White-Collar Crime Nonviolent crime committed by individuals or business entities to obtain a personal or business advantage.

Will An instrument made by a testator directing what is to be done with her or his property after death.

Will Substitutes Various instruments, such as living trusts and life insurance plans, that may be used to avoid the formal probate process.

Winding Up The second of two stages in the termination of a partnership or corporation, in which the firm's assets are collected, liquidated, and distributed, and liabilities are discharged.

Workers' Compensation Laws State statutes that establish an administrative process for compensating workers for injuries that arise in the course of their employment, regardless of fault.

Working Papers The documents used and developed by an accountant during an audit, such as notes, computations, and memoranda.

Workout An agreement outlining the respective rights and responsibilities of a borrower and a lender as they try to resolve the borrower's default.

Worm A software program that automatically replicates itself over a network but does not alter files and is usually invisible to the user until it has consumed system resources.

Writ of Attachment A court order to seize a debtor's nonexempt property prior to a court's final determination of a creditor's rights to the property.

Writ of *Certiorari* A writ from a higher court asking a lower court for the record of a case.

Writ of Execution A court order directing the sheriff to seize (levy) and sell a debtor's nonexempt real or personal property to satisfy a court's judgment in the creditor's favor.

Wrongful Discharge An employer's termination of an employee's employment in violation of the law or an employment contract.

Table of Cases

For your convenience and reference, here is a list of all the cases mentioned in this text, including those within the footnotes, features, and case problems. Any case that was an excerpted case for a chapter is given special emphasis by having its title **boldfaced**.

O

P

Q

R

S

Index